MW00769834

Presented to:

_____

by: _____

_____

occasion & date: _____

_____

Those who are wise will shine like the brightness of the heavens, and those who lead many to righteousness, like the stars for ever and ever.

DANIEL 12:3

my
grandchildren

GRANDCHILD'S NAME

DATE OF BIRTH

PARENTS' NAMES

MILESTONES TO REMEMBER

GRANDCHILD'S SIGNATURE

GRANDCHILD'S NAME

DATE OF BIRTH

PARENTS' NAMES

MILESTONES TO REMEMBER

GRANDCHILD'S SIGNATURE

GRANDCHILD'S NAME

DATE OF BIRTH

PARENTS' NAMES

MILESTONES TO REMEMBER

GRANDCHILD'S SIGNATURE

GRANDCHILD'S NAME

DATE OF BIRTH

PARENTS' NAMES

MILESTONES TO REMEMBER

GRANDCHILD'S SIGNATURE

"MAY THE LORD BLESS YOU . . .
ALL THE DAYS OF YOUR LIFE;
AND MAY YOU LIVE TO SEE YOUR
CHILDREN'S CHILDREN,"

PSALM 128:5–6

GRANDCHILD'S NAME   DATE OF BIRTH

PARENTS' NAMES

MILESTONES TO REMEMBER

GRANDCHILD'S SIGNATURE

GRANDCHILD'S NAME   DATE OF BIRTH

PARENTS' NAMES

MILESTONES TO REMEMBER

GRANDCHILD'S SIGNATURE

GRANDCHILD'S NAME   DATE OF BIRTH

PARENTS' NAMES

MILESTONES TO REMEMBER

GRANDCHILD'S SIGNATURE

GRANDCHILD'S NAME   DATE OF BIRTH

PARENTS' NAMES

MILESTONES TO REMEMBER

GRANDCHILD'S SIGNATURE

my
grandchildren

GRANDCHILD'S NAME   DATE OF BIRTH

PARENTS' NAMES

MILESTONES TO REMEMBER

GRANDCHILD'S SIGNATURE

GRANDCHILD'S NAME   DATE OF BIRTH

PARENTS' NAMES

MILESTONES TO REMEMBER

GRANDCHILD'S SIGNATURE

GRANDCHILD'S NAME   DATE OF BIRTH

PARENTS' NAMES

MILESTONES TO REMEMBER

GRANDCHILD'S SIGNATURE

GRANDCHILD'S NAME   DATE OF BIRTH

PARENTS' NAMES

MILESTONES TO REMEMBER

GRANDCHILD'S SIGNATURE

"MAY THE LORD BLESS YOU . . .
ALL THE DAYS OF YOUR LIFE;
AND MAY YOU LIVE TO SEE YOUR
CHILDREN'S CHILDREN."

PSALM 128:5–6

GRANDCHILD'S NAME | DATE OF BIRTH

PARENTS' NAMES

MILESTONES TO REMEMBER

GRANDCHILD'S SIGNATURE

GRANDCHILD'S NAME | DATE OF BIRTH

PARENTS' NAMES

MILESTONES TO REMEMBER

GRANDCHILD'S SIGNATURE

GRANDCHILD'S NAME | DATE OF BIRTH

PARENTS' NAMES

MILESTONES TO REMEMBER

GRANDCHILD'S SIGNATURE

GRANDCHILD'S NAME | DATE OF BIRTH

PARENTS' NAMES

MILESTONES TO REMEMBER

GRANDCHILD'S SIGNATURE

the power of
prayer

MY PRAYER

_____

_____

HOW GOD ANSWERED

_____

_____

MY PRAYER

_____

_____

HOW GOD ANSWERED

_____

_____

MY PRAYER

_____

_____

HOW GOD ANSWERED

_____

_____

MY PRAYER

_____

_____

HOW GOD ANSWERED

_____

_____

"Do not be anxious about anything,
but in everything, by prayer and
petition, with thanksgiving,
present your requests to God."

PHILIPPIANS 4:6

MY PRAYER

HOW GOD ANSWERED

MY PRAYER

HOW GOD ANSWERED

MY PRAYER

HOW GOD ANSWERED

MY PRAYER

HOW GOD ANSWERED

God is
faithful

"LET THIS BE WRITTEN FOR
A FUTURE GENERATION, THAT
A PEOPLE NOT YET CREATED
MAY PRAISE THE LORD."

PSALM 102:18

WHAT GOD HAS DONE IN MY LIFE

_____
_____
_____
_____
_____
_____
_____
_____
_____
_____
_____
_____
_____
_____
_____
_____
_____
_____
_____
_____
_____
_____
_____

the grandmother's *Bible*

NEW
INTERNATIONAL
VERSION

the grandmother's *Bible*

ZONDERVAN®

Table of Contents

THE OLD TESTAMENT

THE NEW TESTAMENT

Abbreviations

Genesis	Ge	Nahum	Na
Exodus	Ex	Habakkuk	Hab
Leviticus	Lev	Zephaniah	Zep
Numbers	Nu	Haggai	Hag
Deuteronomy	Dt	Zechariah	Zec
Joshua	Jos	Malachi	Mal
Judges	Jdg	Matthew	Mt
Ruth	Ru	Mark	Mk
1 Samuel	1Sa	Luke	Lk
2 Samuel	2Sa	John	Jn
1 Kings	1Ki	Acts	Ac
2 Kings	2Ki	Romans	Ro
1 Chronicles	1Ch	1 Corinthians	1Co
2 Chronicles	2Ch	2 Corinthians	2Co
Ezra	Ezr	Galatians	Gal
Nehemiah	Neh	Ephesians	Eph
Esther	Est	Philippians	Php
Job	Job	Colossians	Col
Psalms	Ps	1 Thessalonians	1Th
Proverbs	Pr	2 Thessalonians	2Th
Ecclesiastes	Ecc	1 Timothy	1Ti
Song of Songs	SS	2 Timothy	2Ti
Isaiah	Isa	Titus	Tit
Jeremiah	Jer	Philemon	Phm
Lamentations	La	Hebrews	Heb
Ezekiel	Eze	James	Jas
Daniel	Da	1 Peter	1Pe
Hosea	Hos	2 Peter	2Pe
Joel	Joel	1 John	1Jn
Amos	Am	2 John	2Jn
Obadiah	Ob	3 John	3Jn
Jonah	Jnh	Jude	Jude
Micah	Mic	Revelation	Rev

An Invitation

The Grandmother's Bible has been a labor of love for the past several years. We've prayed about it, dreamed about it, developed it and refined it to meet your needs. Over 100 grandmothers have joined us to design, write and launch this Bible. Their enthusiasm and prayers have sustained and inspired us through the entire process.

With great pleasure we invite you to use this Bible faithfully, to focus on your grandchildren and pray for them daily, to study God's Word and feed your heart through the devotions and articles. May this Bible nourish your soul and equip you to nurture the souls of your grandchildren.

We pray that the words of Daniel 12:3 become the reality of your life:

Those who are wise will shine like the brightness of the heavens, and those who lead many to righteousness, like the stars for ever and ever.

Doris Wynbeek Rikkers, Executive Editor
Jeannette Taylor, Development Editor

Acknowledgments and Authors

Through the ten years of dreaming, development and writing that have transpired in the creation of *The Grandmother's Bible*, we have had the joy of sharing this idea with many individuals. We would like to thank our families, friends, business associates and even complete strangers who sat next to us in airports for listening to our constant chatter about this idea as it grew and changed and formed itself into the Bible you hold in your hands.

A special thanks goes to those who volunteered to serve on *The Grandmother's Bible* Advisory Board. Your enthusiasm, vision and expert advice were immensely helpful.

Linda Beaumont
Marty Begeman
Elaine Beyer
Jill Bolinder
Diane Boyd
Jerri Brooks
Georgia Bulthouse
Mary Bulthuis
Margaret Clark
Cindy Corbin
Bettie Davis
Ann Eberhard
Sara Eberhard
Pat Errick
Karen Folkerts
Pat Gaines
Barbara Gates

Cheryl Geister
Carol Holquist
Rhonda Jones
Pamela Kite
Ruth Koppenaal
Betty Lankheet
Cindy Lambert
Reba Ledbetter
Flo McKeever
Beth Moore
Lucille Nagelkirk
Joyce Roossien
Carol Schaaf
Judy Schutte
Pat Taylor
Jan Vriesenga
Sandee Word

To all the authors who contributed their personal stories we owe a great deal of thanks. Your kind words, encouragement and overwhelming enthusiasm kept us motivated throughout the editing process. Reading your contributions was a great source of delight for us, bringing tears and laughter and an overall sense of well-being, knowing that wonderful, wise women like you are nurturing the next generations. We pray that your words will induce the same emotions from our readers. It has been a blessing and a privilege to work with all of you.

Claudia Arp
Cheryl Baker
Emilie Barnes
Terri Blackstock
Natalie J. Block
Dee Brestin
Sue Buchanan
Ruth Harms Calkin
Patsy Clairmont
Lori Copeland
Carol Cymbala
Joy Morgan Davis
Ruth A. DeJager
Margaret Fishback Powers
Ruthanne Garlock
Elizabeth George
Ruth Graham
Helen Haidle
Robin Lee Hatcher
Cynthia Heald
Martha Whitmore Hickman
Linda H. Hollies
Helen Kooiman Hosier
Mary Ruth Howes
Donna Huisjen
Gladys Hunt
Neta Jackson
Barbara Johnson
Dawn Scott Jones
Jan Karon
Carol Kent
Karen Kingsbury
Diane Komp
Carol Kuykendall
Susan Lenzkes
Florence Littauer

Rebecca Lutzer
Karen Mains
Marilyn Meberg
Elisa Morgan
Fern Nichols
Karen O'Connor
Anne Ortlund
Barbara Owen
Marjorie Parker
Leslie Parrott
Rebecca Manley Pippert
Margaret Fishback Powers
Dottie Rambo
Debby Kerner Rettino
Gayle Roper
Jane Schlenvogt
Mari Serebrov
Jean Shaw
Luci Shaw
Quin Sherrer
Dorothy E. Sickal
Jan Silvious
Patricia Sprinkle
Millie Stamm
Charlotte Stemple
Leslie Strobel
Jean E. Syswerda
Joni Eareckson Tada
Gigi Graham Tchividjian
Corrie ten Boom
Phyllis Ten Elshof
Phyllis Tickle
Sheila Walsh
Thelma Wells
Bobbie Wolgemuth

It has taken many people in various capacities to make this dream become reality. We thank everyone who has been a part of this project. We hope and continue to pray that this Bible will richly bless the grandmothers who read and use it and their grandchildren who will benefit from having a godly grandmother.

Doris Wynbeek Rikkers
Jeannette Taylor
July 2007

About the Features in this Bible

All the features of *The Grandmother's Bible* have been designed with you and your grandchildren in mind. Some features will nourish you as an individual and help you grow spiritually in your relationship with God. Other features will help you nurture your grandchildren and build them up spiritually.

Presentation Pages

We allocated the majority of the custom-designed presentation pages for you to record events about your grandchildren. Since the number of grandchildren varies greatly (some of you have 2, some 22!), we left some open lines for you to use as you see fit. The page entitled "God Is Faithful" may also be used to record grandchild information.

Devotions

This Bible features 365 devotions. They are written to nurture you in your Christian walk and help you grow in your relationship with the Lord. Every Monday through Friday you will be reading a devotion that will inspire you, delight you or instruct you as you seek to be a godly grandmother. We encourage you to read at least the recommended portion of Scripture for the day to continue building your knowledge of the Word of God.

On Saturday and Sunday, you'll find a slight change of pace. Saturday will be the time to focus on activities with your grandchildren. You'll discover helpful suggestions to pass on your faith, to put your faith in action or to just have some fun. Sunday will be a day to focus on God through praise, thanksgiving and worship.

The devotions are linked together; a note at the bottom of each one tells you where to locate the next devotion. They are deliberately not dated so that you can start using this Bible at any point in the year.

Perspectives

Twenty articles on essential topics relating to grandparenting and growing as a Christian are located throughout the Bible. These articles will provide you with wise counsel and guidance based on Biblical principles that will increase your joy and strengthen you in your role as a grandmother.

Book Introductions

Each book of the Bible is introduced with general information and themes that are of interest to you as a grandmother. Sidebar notes provide an overview of the book's author, intended audience, approximate date of writing and key purpose.

Prayers

A significant feature of this Bible is the use of prayer. Prayer is something you can do for yourself and your grandchildren, any time, any place, no matter the closeness of your relationship or how far apart you and your grandchildren live.

Daily Prayers

Each weekday devotion ends with a short prayer that relates to the subject matter of the devotion. The Saturday prayers let you pray about a variety of subjects relating to fun, enjoyment and grandchildren. On Sunday, your prayer will focus on praise and thanksgiving to God.

Grandchild in Focus Prayer

A special feature located at the end of each devotion is a prayer you can pray for your "Grandchild in Focus." If you have more than one grandchild, we suggest you select one of them to be your focus grandchild. You will cover 14 different themes as you pray for your focus grandchild for 14 days. After two weeks, select another grandchild to be the focus of your prayers. The prayers will repeat every 14 days.

Week One:

1. Salvation
2. Physical Well-Being
3. Emotional Development
4. Spiritual Growth
5. Relationships at Home
6. Friends
7. Self-Image

Week Two:

8. Protection from Worldliness
9. Respect for Authority
10. Courage
11. Future Spouse
12. School/Career
13. Character
14. Talents

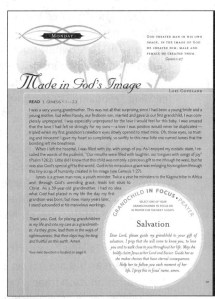

Written prayers are included to help you know what to pray. Of course, you may alter or expand the prayer any way you like. To personalize the prayers, substitute your grandchild's name for any reference of "grandchild" and then use the appropriate pronoun (he/she, him/her, etc.) throughout the prayer.

Let your grandchildren know that they are your focus in prayer. Place their picture in the photo sleeve located in the front of the Bible, point the picture out to them, and show them the prayers you are praying.

Praying the Scriptures for Your Grandchild

Praying Bible verses is a powerful and effective way to communicate with God. This Bible includes prayer tracks on different topics to help you pray key Scriptures based on the specific needs of your grandchildren. Once again, to personalize the prayer, substitute your grandchild's name for the word "grandchild" and adjust the pronouns.

The Topical and Feature Index includes only the *first* scripture reference of each track under the appropriate topic.

Talking Points

As a godly grandmother, you know that God's Word is the best source of advice and encouragement to share when your grandchildren come seeking your counsel. The Bible reminds us that Scripture is useful for "instruction, teaching, rebuking, correcting and training" (2 Timothy 3:16). The Talking Points feature will track you through a short series of Bible verses that reveal what the Bible has to say about a certain topic. Equipped with examples, you will be ready to discuss these important issues with your grandchild. Brief comments at each verse will direct you on how best to use that Scripture verse.

Note: The Talking Points tracks provide you with key verses but are not an exhaustive list of scriptures on each topic. A more complete list of references by topic is listed in the Topical and Feature Index.

Stories to Share

Reading Bible stories to your grandchildren is a special way to interact with them. Having your grandchild see you read and use the Bible is not just a good idea, it's a God idea (see Psalm 119:9–11). "Stories to Share" enables you to easily find and discuss your favorite Bible stories.

Over 150 Bible stories are highlighted in this feature. At the end of each story, a Life Lesson gives you the story's overall theme. You can use this aspect of the feature to help teach a Biblical truth or value to your grandchild. In addition, two levels of questions are listed. The first two questions are factual and are appropriate for younger children. The answers to these questions come from the story itself. The other two questions are more appropriate for older children who can handle abstract concepts and participate in a discussion about the story. Use your judgment in selecting the stories and questions that are most appropriate for the age and/or ability of your grandchildren.

In the gospels, we selected a story only once even if it is told in multiple books. The Parallel Passage references (listed under the section headings in the text) will help you locate the passage in the other Gospel books.

Topical and Feature Index

This index is a combination of a concordance, a topical index and an index to the features in this Bible. Many topics contain a list of Scripture references and a brief explanation of the content of the text to help you find exactly what you are looking for. Topics included in the Talking Points feature are indicated with an asterisk. An asterisk also marks the first verse reference in the Talking Points track.

The features of this Bible (Devotions, Perspectives, Praying the Scriptures and Stories to Share) are listed individually under their topic to make it easier for you to find exactly what you are looking for.

Preface to the New International Version

THE NEW INTERNATIONAL VERSION is a completely new translation of the Holy Bible made by over a hundred scholars working directly from the best available Hebrew, Aramaic and Greek texts. It had its beginning in 1965 when, after several years of exploratory study by committees from the Christian Reformed Church and the National Association of Evangelicals, a group of scholars met at Palos Heights, Illinois, and concurred in the need for a new translation of the Bible in contemporary English. This group, though not made up of official church representatives, was transdenominational. Its conclusion was endorsed by a large number of leaders from many denominations who met in Chicago in 1966.

Responsibility for the new version was delegated by the Palos Heights group to a self-governing body of fifteen, the Committee on Bible Translation, composed for the most part of biblical scholars from colleges, universities and seminaries. In 1967 the New York Bible Society (now the International Bible Society) generously undertook the financial sponsorship of the project — a sponsorship that made it possible to enlist the help of many distinguished scholars. The fact that participants from the United States, Great Britain, Canada, Australia and New Zealand worked together gave the project its international scope. That they were from many denominations — including Anglican, Assemblies of God, Baptist, Brethren, Christian Reformed, Church of Christ, Evangelical Free, Lutheran, Mennonite, Methodist, Nazarene, Presbyterian, Wesleyan and other churches — helped to safeguard the translation from sectarian bias.

How it was made helps to give the New International Version its distinctiveness. The translation of each book was assigned to a team of scholars. Next, one of the Intermediate Editorial Committees revised the initial translation, with constant reference to the Hebrew, Aramaic or Greek. Their work then went to one of the General Editorial Committees, which checked it in detail and made another thorough revision. This revision in turn was carefully reviewed by the Committee on Bible Translation, which made further changes and then released the final version for publication. In this way the entire Bible underwent three revisions, during each of which the translation was examined for its faithfulness to the original languages and for its English style.

All this involved many thousands of hours of research and discussion regarding the meaning of the texts and the precise way of putting them into English. It may well be that no other translation has been made by a more thorough process of review and revision from committee to committee than this one.

From the beginning of the project, the Committee on Bible Translation held to certain goals for the New International Version: that it would be an accurate translation and one that would have clarity and literary quality and so prove suitable for public and private reading, teaching, preaching, memorizing and liturgical use. The Committee also sought to preserve some measure of continuity with the long tradition of translating the Scriptures into English.

In working toward these goals, the translators were united in their commitment to the authority and infallibility of the Bible as God's Word in written form. They believe that it contains the divine answer to the deepest needs of humanity, that it sheds unique light on our path in a dark world, and that it sets forth the way to our eternal well-being.

The first concern of the translators has been the accuracy of the translation and its fidelity to the thought of the biblical writers. They have weighed the significance of the lexical and grammatical details of the Hebrew, Aramaic and Greek texts. At the same time, they have striven for more than a word-for-word translation. Because thought patterns and syntax differ from language to language, faithful communication of the meaning of the writers of the Bible demands frequent modifications in sentence structure and constant regard for the contextual meanings of words.

A sensitive feeling for style does not always accompany scholarship. Accordingly the Committee on Bible Translation submitted the developing version to a number of stylistic consultants. Two of them read every book of both Old and New Testaments twice — once before and once after the last major revision — and made invaluable suggestions. Samples of the translation were tested for clarity and ease of reading by various kinds of people — young and old, highly educated and less well educated, ministers and laymen.

Concern for clear and natural English — that the New International Version should be idiomatic but not idiosyncratic, contemporary but not dated — motivated the translators and consultants. At the same time, they tried to reflect the differing styles of the biblical writers. In view of the international use of English, the translators sought to avoid obvious Americanisms on the one hand and obvious Anglicisms on the other. A British edition reflects the comparatively few differences of significant idiom and of spelling.

As for the traditional pronouns "thou," "thee" and "thine" in reference to the Deity, the translators judged that to use these archaisms (along with the old verb forms such as "doest," "wouldest" and "hadst") would violate accuracy in translation. Neither Hebrew, Aramaic nor Greek uses special pronouns for the persons of the Godhead. A present-day translation is not enhanced by forms that in the time of the King James Version were used in everyday speech, whether referring to God or man.

For the Old Testament the standard Hebrew text, the Masoretic Text as published in the latest editions of *Biblia Hebraica,* was used throughout. The Dead Sea Scrolls contain material bearing on an earlier stage of the Hebrew text. They were consulted, as were the Samaritan Pentateuch and the ancient scribal traditions relating to textual changes. Sometimes a variant Hebrew reading in the margin of the Masoretic Text was followed instead of the text itself. Such instances, being variants within the Masoretic tradition, are not specified by footnotes. In rare cases, words in the consonantal text were divided differently from the way they appear in the Masoretic Text. Footnotes indicate this. The translators also consulted the more important early versions — the Septuagint; Aquila, Symmachus and Theodotion; the Vulgate; the Syriac Peshitta; the Targums; and for the Psalms the *Juxta Hebraica* of Jerome. Readings from these versions were occasionally followed where the Masoretic Text seemed doubtful and where accepted principles of textual criticism showed that one or more of these textual witnesses appeared to provide the correct reading. Such instances are footnoted. Sometimes vowel letters and vowel signs did not, in the judgment of the translators, represent the correct vowels for the original consonantal text. Accordingly some words were read with a different set of vowels. These instances are usually not indicated by footnotes.

The Greek text used in translating the New Testament was an eclectic one. No other piece of ancient literature has such an abundance of manuscript witnesses as does the New Testament. Where existing manuscripts differ, the translators made their choice of readings according to accepted principles of New Testament textual criticism. Footnotes call attention to places where there was uncertainty about what the original text was. The best current printed texts of the Greek New Testament were used.

There is a sense in which the work of translation is never wholly finished. This applies to all great literature and uniquely so to the Bible. In 1973 the New Testament in the New International Version was published. Since then, suggestions for corrections and revisions have been received from various sources. The Committee on Bible Translation carefully considered the suggestions and adopted a number of them. These were incorporated in the first printing of the entire Bible in 1978. Additional revisions were made by the Committee on Bible Translation in 1983 and appear in printings after that date.

As in other ancient documents, the precise meaning of the biblical texts is sometimes uncertain. This is more often the case with the Hebrew and Aramaic texts than with the Greek text. Although archaeological and linguistic discoveries in this century aid in understanding difficult passages, some uncertainties remain. The more significant of these have been called to the reader's attention in the footnotes.

In regard to the divine name *YHWH*, commonly referred to as the *Tetragrammaton*, the translators adopted the device used in most English versions of rendering that name as "Lord" in capital letters to distinguish it from *Adonai*, another Hebrew word rendered "Lord," for which small letters are used. Wherever the two names stand together in the Old Testament as a compound name of God, they are rendered "Sovereign Lord."

Because for most readers today the phrases "the Lord of hosts" and "God of hosts" have little meaning, this version renders them "the LORD Almighty" and "God Almighty." These renderings convey the sense of the Hebrew, namely, "he who is sovereign over all the 'hosts' (powers) in heaven and on earth, especially over the 'hosts' (armies) of Israel." For readers unacquainted with Hebrew this does not make clear the distinction between *Sabaoth* ("hosts" or "Almighty") and *Shaddai* (which can also be translated "Almighty"), but the latter occurs infrequently and is always footnoted. When *Adonai* and *YHWH Sabaoth* occur together, they are rendered "the Lord, the LORD Almighty."

As for other proper nouns, the familiar spellings of the King James Version are generally retained. Names traditionally spelled with "ch," except where it is final, are usually spelled in this translation with "k" or "c," since the biblical languages do not have the sound that "ch" frequently indicates in English — for example, in *chant*. For well-known names such as Zechariah, however, the traditional spelling has been retained. Variation in the spelling of names in the original languages has usually not been indicated. Where a person or place has two or more different names in the Hebrew, Aramaic or Greek texts, the more familiar one has generally been used, with footnotes where needed.

To achieve clarity the translators sometimes supplied words not in the original texts but required by the context. If there was uncertainty about such material, it is enclosed in brackets. Also for the sake of clarity or style, nouns, including some proper nouns, are sometimes substituted for pronouns, and vice versa. And though the Hebrew writers often shifted back and forth between first, second and third personal pronouns without change of antecedent, this translation often makes them uniform, in accordance with English style and without the use of footnotes.

Poetical passages are printed as poetry, that is, with indentation of lines and with separate stanzas. These are generally designed to reflect the structure of Hebrew poetry. This poetry is normally characterized by parallelism in balanced lines. Most of the poetry in the Bible is in the Old Testament, and scholars differ regarding the scansion of Hebrew lines. The translators determined the stanza divisions for the most part by analysis of the subject matter. The stanzas therefore serve as poetic paragraphs.

As an aid to the reader, italicized sectional headings are inserted in most of the books. They are not to be regarded as part of the NIV text, are not for oral reading, and are not intended to dictate the interpretation of the sections they head.

The footnotes in this version are of several kinds, most of which need no explanation. Those giving alternative translations begin with "Or" and generally introduce the alternative with the last word preceding it in the text, except when it is a single-word alternative; in poetry quoted in a footnote a slant mark indicates a line division. Footnotes introduced by "Or" do not have uniform significance. In some cases two possible translations were considered to have about equal validity. In other cases, though the translators were convinced that the translation in the text was correct, they judged that another interpretation was possible and of sufficient importance to be represented in a footnote.

In the New Testament, footnotes that refer to uncertainty regarding the original text are introduced by "Some manuscripts" or similar expressions. In the Old Testament, evidence for the reading chosen is given first and evidence for the alternative is added after a semicolon (for example: Septuagint; Hebrew *father*). In such notes the term "Hebrew" refers to the Masoretic Text.

It should be noted that minerals, flora and fauna, architectural details, articles of clothing and jewelry, musical instruments and other articles cannot always be identified with precision. Also measures of capacity in the biblical period are particularly uncertain (see the table of weights and measures).

Like all translations of the Bible, made as they are by imperfect man, this one undoubtedly falls short of its goals. Yet we are grateful to God for the extent to which he has enabled us to realize these goals and for the strength he has given us and our colleagues to complete our task. We offer this version of the Bible to him in whose name and for whose glory it has been made. We pray that it will lead many into a better understanding of the Holy Scriptures and a fuller knowledge of Jesus Christ the incarnate Word, of whom the Scriptures so faithfully testify.

The Committee on Bible Translation

June 1978
(Revised August 1983)

Names of the translators and editors may be secured from the
International Bible Society, translation sponsors of the New International Version,
1820 Jet Stream Drive, Colorado Springs, Colorado 80921-3696 U.S.A.

Table of
Weights and Measures

	Biblical Unit	Approximate American Equivalent	Approximate Metric Equivalent
Weights	talent (60 minas)	75 pounds	34 kilograms
	mina (50 shekels)	1 1/4 pounds	0.6 kilogram
	shekel (2 bekas)	2/5 ounce	11.5 grams
	pim (2/3 shekel)	1/3 ounce	7.6 grams
	beka (10 gerahs)	1/5 ounce	5.5 grams
	gerah	1/50 ounce	0.6 gram
Length	cubit	18 inches	0.5 meter
	span	9 inches	23 centimeters
	handbreadth	3 inches	8 centimeters
Capacity			
Dry Measure	cor [homer] (10 ephahs)	6 bushels	220 liters
	lethek (5 ephahs)	3 bushels	110 liters
	ephah (10 omers)	3/5 bushel	22 liters
	seah (1/3 ephah)	7 quarts	7.3 liters
	omer (1/10 ephah)	2 quarts	2 liters
	cab (1/18 ephah)	1 quart	1 liter
Liquid Measure	bath (1 ephah)	6 gallons	22 liters
	hin (1/6 bath)	4 quarts	4 liters
	log (1/72 bath)	1/3 quart	0.3 liter

The figures of the table are calculated on the basis of a shekel equaling 11.5 grams, a cubit equaling 18 inches and an ephah equaling 22 liters. The quart referred to is either a dry quart (slightly larger than a liter) or a liquid quart (slightly smaller than a liter), whichever is applicable. The ton referred to in the footnotes is the American ton of 2,000 pounds.

This table is based upon the best available information, but it is not intended to be mathematically precise; like the measurement equivalents in the footnotes, it merely gives approximate amounts and distances. Weights and measures differed somewhat at various times and places in the ancient world. There is uncertainty particularly about the ephah and the bath; further discoveries may shed more light on these units of capacity.

THE Old Testament

A Book
OF FIRSTS

The first book of the Bible is a book that explodes with firsts: the first day, the first humans, the first family, the first grandchild (Enoch, see Genesis 4:17). Perhaps most important for our situation today, in Genesis we read the story of the first sin and see the beginnings of God's plan for our redemption. The delight that God expressed in the creation of Adam and Eve turned to disappointment when they chose to pull away from him. But God didn't turn away from his creation: he put into motion his plan to save the world from sin through the death and resurrection of his Son, Jesus!

The book of Genesis, through its many well-known stories, also teaches us about God's plan for human relationships and emotions, especially within the family. Although the words "grandmother" or "grandfather" do not appear in Genesis, they easily could. These stories tell about individuals who lived for hundreds of years, living to see many generations. We can learn from their successes and from their failures.

So Genesis is indeed a book of firsts. These stories point out the humanness and sinfulness of all of us, but they also loudly declare God's love, faithfulness and promise to redeem us.

VERSE *to* REMEMBER | GENESIS 17:7

"I will establish my covenant as an everlasting covenant between me and you and your descendants after you for the generations to come, to be your God and the God of your descendants after you."

ABOUT GENESIS

WRITTEN BY:
Moses

WRITTEN FOR:
God's chosen people,
the Israelites

DATE WRITTEN:
Between 1446 and
1406 B.C.

WHY WRITTEN:
To help us come to
know God as our Creator
and to demonstrate
his covenant love for
his people

The Beginning

1 In the beginning God created the heavens and the earth. ²Now the earth was *ᵃ* formless and empty, darkness was over the surface of the deep, and the Spirit of God was hovering over the waters.

³And God said, "Let there be light," and there was light. ⁴God saw that the light was good, and he separated the light from the darkness. ⁵God called the light "day," and the darkness he called "night." And there was evening, and there was morning—the first day.

⁶And God said, "Let there be an expanse between the waters to separate water from water." ⁷So God made the expanse and separated the water under the expanse from the water above it. And it was so. ⁸God called the expanse "sky." And there was evening, and there was morning—the second day.

⁹And God said, "Let the water under the sky be gathered to one place, and let dry ground appear." And it was so. ¹⁰God called the dry ground "land," and the gathered waters he called "seas." And God saw that it was good.

¹¹Then God said, "Let the land produce vegetation: seed-bearing plants and trees on the land that bear fruit with seed in it, according to their various kinds." And it was so. ¹²The land produced vegetation: plants bearing seed according to their kinds and trees bearing fruit with seed in it according to their kinds. And God saw that it was good. ¹³And there was evening, and there was morning—the third day.

¹⁴And God said, "Let there be lights in the expanse of the sky to separate the day from the night, and let them serve as signs to mark seasons and days and years, ¹⁵and let them be lights in the expanse of the sky to give light on the earth." And it was so. ¹⁶God made two great lights—the greater light to govern the day and the lesser light to govern the night. He also made the stars. ¹⁷God set them in the expanse of the sky to give light on the earth, ¹⁸to govern the day and the night, and to separate light from darkness. And God saw that it was good. ¹⁹And there was evening, and there was morning—the fourth day.

²⁰And God said, "Let the water teem with living creatures, and let birds fly above the earth across the expanse of the sky." ²¹So God created the great creatures of the sea and every living and moving thing with which the water teems, according to their kinds, and every winged bird according to its kind. And God saw that it was good. ²²God blessed them and said, "Be fruitful and increase in number and fill the water in the seas, and let the birds increase on the earth." ²³And there was evening, and there was morning—the fifth day.

ᵃ 2 Or possibly became

---

stories to share

GENESIS 1:1–26

The Beginning

LIFE LESSON: Our world belongs to God.

TO TALK ABOUT

✦ How many days did it take God to create the world?

✦ What did God do on the next day?

✦ What did God say about his creation?

✦ Is God's creation still good? Explain.

GOD CREATED MAN IN HIS OWN
IMAGE, IN THE IMAGE OF GOD
HE CREATED HIM; MALE AND
FEMALE HE CREATED THEM.

Genesis 1:27

Made in God's Image

LORI COPELAND

READ | GENESIS 1:1 — 2:3

I was a very young grandmother. This was not all that surprising since I had been a young bride and a young mother, but when Randy, our firstborn son, married and gave us our first grandchild, I was completely unprepared. I was especially unprepared for the love I would feel for this baby. I was amazed that the love I had felt so strongly for my sons—a love I was positive would never be duplicated—tripled when my first grandson's newborn eyes slowly opened to meet mine. Oh, those eyes, so trusting and innocent! I gave my heart so completely, so swiftly to this new little one named James that the bonding left me breathless.

When I left the hospital, I was filled with joy, with songs of joy. As I enjoyed my ecstatic state, I recalled the words of the psalmist, "Our mouths were filled with laughter, our tongues with songs of joy" (Psalm 126:2). Little did I know that this child was not only a precious gift to me (though he was), but he was also God's special gift to the world. God in his miraculous grace was enlarging his kingdom through this tiny scrap of humanity created in his image (see Genesis 1:27).

James is a grown man now, a youth minister. Twice a year he ministers to the Kagora tribe in Africa and, through God's unending grace, leads lost souls to Christ. As a 39-year-old grandmother, I had no idea what God had placed in my life the day my first grandson was born; but now, many years later, I stand astounded at his marvelous workings.

Thank you, God, for placing grandchildren in my life and into my care as a grandmother. As they grow, lead them in the ways of righteousness, that their days may be long and fruitful on this earth. Amen.

Your next devotion is located on page 6.

GRANDCHILD IN FOCUS · PRAYER

SELECT ONE OF YOUR
GRANDCHILDREN TO FOCUS ON
IN PRAYER FOR THE NEXT 14 DAYS.

Salvation

Dear Lord, please guide my grandchild to your gift of salvation. I pray that she will come to know you, to love you and to walk close to you throughout her life. May she boldly claim Jesus as her Lord and Savior. Guide her as she makes choices that have eternal consequences. Help her to follow you each moment of her life. I pray this in Jesus' name, amen.

24 And God said, "Let the land produce living creatures according to their kinds: livestock, creatures that move along the ground, and wild animals, each according to its kind." And it was so. 25 God made the wild animals according to their kinds, the livestock according to their kinds, and all the creatures that move along the ground according to their kinds. And God saw that it was good.

26 Then God said, "Let us make man in our image, in our likeness, and let them rule over the fish of the sea and the birds of the air, over the livestock, over all the earth,ᵃ and over all the creatures that move along the ground."

27 So God created man in his own image,
　　in the image of God he created him;
　　male and female he created them.

TALKING POINTS

Self-Esteem

We were created in God's image.

GENESIS 1:26–27

For more on self-esteem, go to Psalm 139:13–18.

---

28 God blessed them and said to them, "Be fruitful and increase in number; fill the earth and subdue it. Rule over the fish of the sea and the birds of the air and over every living creature that moves on the ground."

29 Then God said, "I give you every seed-bearing plant on the face of the whole earth and every tree that has fruit with seed in it. They will be yours for food. 30 And to all the beasts of the earth and all the birds of the air and all the creatures that move on the ground—everything that has the breath of

stories to share

GENESIS 1:27—2:24

Adam and Eve

LIFE LESSON: God created human beings, male and female, in his image.

TO TALK ABOUT

✦ How did God make the first man, Adam?

✦ How did God create Eve?

✦ How are we created in God's image?

✦ In what ways are you like God? How are you different?

life in it—I give every green plant for food." And it was so.

31 God saw all that he had made, and it was very good. And there was evening, and there was morning—the sixth day.

2 Thus the heavens and the earth were completed in all their vast array.

2 By the seventh day God had finished the work he had been doing; so on the seventh day he restedᵇ from all his work. 3 And God blessed the seventh day and made it holy, because on it he rested from all the work of creating that he had done.

Adam and Eve

4 This is the account of the heavens and the earth when they were created.

ᵃ 26 Hebrew; Syriac *all the wild animals*　　ᵇ 2 Or *ceased*; also in verse 3

When the Lord God made the earth and the heavens— [5]and no shrub of the field had yet appeared on the earth[a] and no plant of the field had yet sprung up, for the Lord God had not sent rain on the earth[a] and there was no man to work the ground, [6]but streams[b] came up from the earth and watered the whole surface of the ground— [7]the Lord God formed the man[c] from the dust of the ground and breathed into his nostrils the breath of life, and the man became a living being.

[8]Now the Lord God had planted a garden in the east, in Eden; and there he put the man he had formed. [9]And the Lord God made all kinds of trees grow out of the ground—trees that were pleasing to the eye and good for food. In the middle of the garden were the tree of life and the tree of the knowledge of good and evil.

[10]A river watering the garden flowed from Eden; from there it was separated into four headwaters. [11]The name of the first is the Pishon; it winds through the entire land of Havilah, where there is gold. [12](The gold of that land is good; aromatic resin[d] and onyx are also there.) [13]The name of the second river is the Gihon; it winds through the entire land of Cush.[e] [14]The name of the third river is the Tigris; it runs along the east side of Asshur. And the fourth river is the Euphrates.

[15]The Lord God took the man and put him in the Garden of Eden to work it and take care of it. [16]And the Lord God commanded the man, "You are free to eat from any tree in the garden; [17]but you must not eat from the tree of the knowledge of good and evil, for when you eat of it you will surely die."

[18]The Lord God said, "It is not good for the man to be alone. I will make a helper suitable for him."

[19]Now the Lord God had formed out of the ground all the beasts of the field and all the birds of the air. He brought them to the man to see what he would name them; and whatever the man called each living creature, that was its name. [20]So the man gave names to all the livestock, the birds of the air and all the beasts of the field.

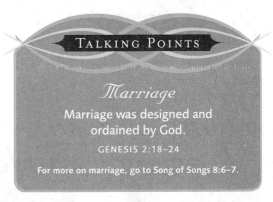

TALKING POINTS

Marriage

Marriage was designed and ordained by God.

GENESIS 2:18–24

For more on marriage, go to Song of Songs 8:6–7.

But for Adam[f] no suitable helper was found. [21]So the Lord God caused the man to fall into a deep sleep; and while he was sleeping, he took one of the man's ribs[g] and closed up the place with flesh. [22]Then the Lord God made a woman from the rib[h] he had taken out of the man, and he brought her to the man.

[23]The man said,

"This is now bone of my bones
    and flesh of my flesh;
she shall be called 'woman,[i]'
    for she was taken out of man."

[24]For this reason a man will leave his father and mother and be united to his wife, and they will become one flesh.

[25]The man and his wife were both naked, and they felt no shame.

The Fall of Man

3 Now the serpent was more crafty than any of the wild animals the Lord God had made. He said to the woman, "Did God really say, 'You must not eat from any tree in the garden'?"

[2]The woman said to the serpent, "We may eat fruit from the trees in the garden, [3]but God did say, 'You must not eat fruit from the tree that is

---

[a] 5 Or *land*; also in verse 6   [b] 6 Or *mist*   [c] 7 The Hebrew for *man* (*adam*) sounds like and may be related to the Hebrew for *ground* (*adamah*); it is also the name *Adam* (see Gen. 2:20).
[d] 12 Or *good; pearls*   [e] 13 Possibly southeast Mesopotamia
[f] 20 Or *the man*   [g] 21 Or *took part of the man's side*
[h] 22 Or *part*   [i] 23 The Hebrew for *woman* sounds like the Hebrew for *man*.

> FOR THIS REASON A MAN
> WILL LEAVE HIS FATHER AND
> MOTHER AND BE UNITED TO HIS
> WIFE, AND THEY WILL BECOME
> ONE FLESH.
>
> *Genesis 2:24*

Being a Positive Marriage Model

CLAUDIA ARP

READ | GENESIS 2:4–25

In the beginning God created marriage, and it—along with all God had made—was "very good" (Genesis 1:31). Intended as the closest and most satisfying of all human relationships, the marriage bond remains strong when we follow the three principles in this passage: leaving, "cleaving" and becoming one. It doesn't matter if we have been married for five months or 50 years, these three principles are foundational for building a strong, healthy and loving Christian marriage. It's this model of marriage that I pray we will pass on to future generations. Grandchildren are blessed when they are able to observe a "very good" marriage.

Look at your marriage and see if you are living out these three principles. "Leaving" our parents many years ago was the easy part, but that's not all we need to leave. Over the years, leaving involves realigning our priorities from what I want for *me* to what I want for *us*. It includes staying in the relationship through hard times, being faithful and putting our marriage first. "Being united" (some translations say "cleaving") involves being best friends and soul mates, making choices that pull us together rather than those that put distance between us. Becoming "one flesh" means that we are lovers for life. God created the sexual relationship, and he is the one who placed the passion deep within our hearts to love each other physically.

Think about your own marriage as a model for your children and grandchildren. What might you need to "leave" to make your relationship a higher priority? What steps do you need to take to become better friends and soul mates? And how's your love life? Do your grandchildren see you display a tender, playful and loving attitude? Do your grandchildren look at you and say, "I want to have a marriage like my grandparents'"? They will if you live out Genesis 2:24.

Dear Father, thank you that in the beginning you created marriage and that you can empower me to leave behind a me-centered attitude and unite with my husband to be one with him. Thank you that my husband and I can be a positive marriage model for our grandchildren. Amen.

GRANDCHILD IN FOCUS • PRAYER

Physical Well-Being

Almighty God, Creator of us all, I pray that you will watch over my grandchild's physical development. May he grow in strength through the stages of his life. As he grows in awareness of his body, help him to understand that each body develops uniquely, yet is within your plan and your control. Please guard his health so that his diseases are few, his injuries are minor and his infirmities are brief. Amen.

Your next devotion is located on page 19.

in the middle of the garden, and you must not touch it, or you will die.'"

⁴"You will not surely die," the serpent said to the woman. ⁵"For God knows that when you eat of it your eyes will be opened, and you will be like God, knowing good and evil."

⁶When the woman saw that the fruit of the tree was good for food and pleasing to the eye, and also desirable for gaining wisdom, she took some and ate it. She also gave some to her husband, who was with her, and he ate it. ⁷Then the eyes of both of them were opened, and they realized they were naked; so they sewed fig leaves together and made coverings for themselves.

⁸Then the man and his wife heard the sound of the LORD God as he was walking in the garden in the cool of the day, and they hid from the LORD God among the trees of the garden. ⁹But the LORD God called to the man, "Where are you?"

¹⁰He answered, "I heard you in the garden, and I was afraid because I was naked; so I hid."

¹¹And he said, "Who told you that you were naked? Have you eaten from the tree that I commanded you not to eat from?"

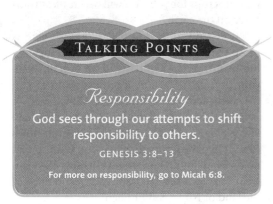

TALKING POINTS

Responsibility

God sees through our attempts to shift responsibility to others.

GENESIS 3:8–13

For more on responsibility, go to Micah 6:8.

¹²The man said, "The woman you put here with me—she gave me some fruit from the tree, and I ate it."

¹³Then the LORD God said to the woman, "What is this you have done?"

The woman said, "The serpent deceived me, and I ate."

¹⁴So the LORD God said to the serpent, "Because you have done this,

"Cursed are you above all the livestock
and all the wild animals!
You will crawl on your belly
and you will eat dust
all the days of your life.
¹⁵And I will put enmity
between you and the woman,
and between your offspring ᵃ and hers;
he will crush ᵇ your head,
and you will strike his heel."

¹⁶To the woman he said,

"I will greatly increase your pains in
childbearing;
with pain you will give birth to children.
Your desire will be for your husband,
and he will rule over you."

¹⁷To Adam he said, "Because you listened to your wife and ate from the tree about which I commanded you, 'You must not eat of it,'

"Cursed is the ground because of you;
through painful toil you will eat of it
all the days of your life.
¹⁸It will produce thorns and thistles for you,
and you will eat the plants of the field.
¹⁹By the sweat of your brow
you will eat your food
until you return to the ground,
since from it you were taken;
for dust you are
and to dust you will return."

²⁰Adam ᶜ named his wife Eve, ᵈ because she would become the mother of all the living.

²¹The LORD God made garments of skin for Adam and his wife and clothed them. ²²And the LORD God said, "The man has now become like one of us, knowing good and evil. He must not

ᵃ 15 Or seed   ᵇ 15 Or strike   ᶜ 20 Or The man   ᵈ 20 Eve probably means living.

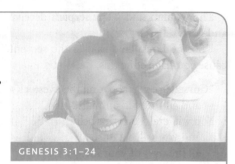

GENESIS 3:1–24

Sin Enters the World

LIFE LESSON: Choices have consequences.

TO TALK ABOUT

✦ What rule did Adam and Eve break? (Hint: Read Genesis 2:16–17.)

✦ Why did Eve eat the fruit? Why did Adam?

✦ What happened to Adam and Eve because they disobeyed God?

✦ Does God want us to hide from him when we sin? What should we do instead?

be allowed to reach out his hand and take also from the tree of life and eat, and live forever." ²³So the LORD God banished him from the Garden of Eden to work the ground from which he had been taken. ²⁴After he drove the man out, he placed on the east side *a* of the Garden of Eden cherubim and a flaming sword flashing back and forth to guard the way to the tree of life.

Cain and Abel

4 Adam *b* lay with his wife Eve, and she became pregnant and gave birth to Cain. *c* She said, "With the help of the LORD I have brought forth *d* a man." ²Later she gave birth to his brother Abel.

Now Abel kept flocks, and Cain worked the soil. ³In the course of time Cain brought some of the fruits of the soil as an offering to the LORD.

⁴But Abel brought fat portions from some of the firstborn of his flock. The LORD looked with favor on Abel and his offering, ⁵but on Cain and his offering he did not look with favor. So Cain was very angry, and his face was downcast.

⁶Then the LORD said to Cain, "Why are you angry? Why is your face downcast? ⁷If you do what is right, will you not be accepted? But if you do not do what is right, sin is crouching at your door; it desires to have you, but you must master it."

⁸Now Cain said to his brother Abel, "Let's go out to the field." *e* And while they were in the field, Cain attacked his brother Abel and killed him.

⁹Then the LORD said to Cain, "Where is your brother Abel?"

"I don't know," he replied. "Am I my brother's keeper?"

¹⁰The LORD said, "What have you done? Listen! Your brother's blood cries out to me from the ground. ¹¹Now you are under a curse and driven from the ground, which opened its mouth to receive your brother's blood from your hand. ¹²When you work the ground, it will no longer yield its crops for you. You will be a restless wanderer on the earth."

¹³Cain said to the LORD, "My punishment is more than I can bear. ¹⁴Today you are driving me from the land, and I will be hidden from your presence; I will be a restless wanderer on the earth, and whoever finds me will kill me."

¹⁵But the LORD said to him, "Not so *f*; if anyone kills Cain, he will suffer vengeance seven times over." Then the LORD put a mark on Cain so that no one who found him would kill him. ¹⁶So Cain went out from the LORD's presence and lived in the land of Nod, *g* east of Eden.

¹⁷Cain lay with his wife, and she became pregnant and gave birth to Enoch. Cain was then

a 24 Or *placed in front*   *b 1* Or *The man*   *c 1 Cain* sounds like the Hebrew for *brought forth* or *acquired.*   *d 1* Or *have acquired*   *e 8* Samaritan Pentateuch, Septuagint, Vulgate and Syriac; Masoretic Text does not have *"Let's go out to the field."*   *f 15* Septuagint, Vulgate and Syriac; Hebrew *Very well*   *g 16 Nod* means *wandering* (see verses 12 and 14).

building a city, and he named it after his son Enoch. ¹⁸To Enoch was born Irad, and Irad was the father of Mehujael, and Mehujael was the father of Methushael, and Methushael was the father of Lamech.

¹⁹Lamech married two women, one named Adah and the other Zillah. ²⁰Adah gave birth to Jabal; he was the father of those who live in tents and raise livestock. ²¹His brother's name was Jubal; he was the father of all who play the harp and flute. ²²Zillah also had a son, Tubal-Cain, who forged all kinds of tools out of ª bronze and iron. Tubal-Cain's sister was Naamah.

²³Lamech said to his wives,

"Adah and Zillah, listen to me;
 wives of Lamech, hear my words.

I have killed ᵇ a man for wounding me,
 a young man for injuring me.
²⁴If Cain is avenged seven times,
 then Lamech seventy-seven times."

²⁵Adam lay with his wife again, and she gave birth to a son and named him Seth, ᶜ saying, "God has granted me another child in place of Abel, since Cain killed him." ²⁶Seth also had a son, and he named him Enosh.

At that time men began to call on ᵈ the name of the LORD.

From Adam to Noah

5 This is the written account of Adam's line.

When God created man, he made him in the likeness of God. ²He created them male and female and blessed them. And when they were created, he called them "man. ᵉ"

³When Adam had lived 130 years, he had a son in his own likeness, in his own image; and he named him Seth. ⁴After Seth was born, Adam lived 800 years and had other sons and daughters. ⁵Altogether, Adam lived 930 years, and then he died.

⁶When Seth had lived 105 years, he became the father ᶠ of Enosh. ⁷And after he became the father of Enosh, Seth lived 807 years and had other sons and daughters. ⁸Altogether, Seth lived 912 years, and then he died.

⁹When Enosh had lived 90 years, he became the father of Kenan. ¹⁰And after he became the father of Kenan, Enosh lived 815 years and had other sons and daughters. ¹¹Altogether, Enosh lived 905 years, and then he died.

¹²When Kenan had lived 70 years, he became the father of Mahalalel. ¹³And after he became the father of Mahalalel, Kenan lived 840 years and had other sons and daughters. ¹⁴Altogether, Kenan lived 910 years, and then he died.

¹⁵When Mahalalel had lived 65 years, he became the father of Jared. ¹⁶And after he became

stories to share

GENESIS 4:1–16

Cain and Abel

LIFE LESSON: Uncontrolled anger leads to sin.

TO TALK ABOUT

✦ What happened to Cain after he attacked his brother, Abel?

✦ How could Cain have better handled his jealous anger?

✦ Did Cain's question to God, "Am I my brother's keeper?" sound like he was sorry?

✦ In what ways are we responsible for one another?

ª 22 Or who instructed all who work in ᵇ 23 Or I will kill
ᶜ 25 Seth probably means granted. ᵈ 26 Or to proclaim
ᵉ 2 Hebrew adam ᶠ 6 Father may mean ancestor; also in verses 7-26.

the father of Jared, Mahalalel lived 830 years and had other sons and daughters. ¹⁷Altogether, Mahalalel lived 895 years, and then he died.

¹⁸When Jared had lived 162 years, he became the father of Enoch. ¹⁹And after he became the father of Enoch, Jared lived 800 years and had other sons and daughters. ²⁰Altogether, Jared lived 962 years, and then he died.

²¹When Enoch had lived 65 years, he became the father of Methuselah. ²²And after he became the father of Methuselah, Enoch walked with God 300 years and had other sons and daughters. ²³Altogether, Enoch lived 365 years. ²⁴Enoch walked with God; then he was no more, because God took him away.

²⁵When Methuselah had lived 187 years, he became the father of Lamech. ²⁶And after he became the father of Lamech, Methuselah lived 782 years and had other sons and daughters. ²⁷Altogether, Methuselah lived 969 years, and then he died.

²⁸When Lamech had lived 182 years, he had a son. ²⁹He named him Noah ᵃ and said, "He will comfort us in the labor and painful toil of our hands caused by the ground the LORD has cursed." ³⁰After Noah was born, Lamech lived 595 years and had other sons and daughters. ³¹Altogether, Lamech lived 777 years, and then he died.

³²After Noah was 500 years old, he became the father of Shem, Ham and Japheth.

The Flood

6 When men began to increase in number on the earth and daughters were born to them, ²the sons of God saw that the daughters of men were beautiful, and they married any of them they chose. ³Then the LORD said, "My Spirit will not contend with ᵇ man forever, for he is mortal ᶜ; his days will be a hundred and twenty years."

⁴The Nephilim were on the earth in those days — and also afterward — when the sons of God went to the daughters of men and had children by them. They were the heroes of old, men of renown.

⁵The LORD saw how great man's wickedness on the earth had become, and that every inclination of the thoughts of his heart was only evil all the time. ⁶The LORD was grieved that he had made man on the earth, and his heart was filled with pain. ⁷So the LORD said, "I will wipe mankind, whom I have created, from the face of the earth — men and animals, and creatures that move along the ground, and birds of the air — for I am grieved that I have made them." ⁸But Noah found favor in the eyes of the LORD.

TALKING POINTS

Worldliness

Noah resisted sin and stayed faithful to God.

GENESIS 6:5–22

For more on worldliness, go to Romans 12:1–2.

⁹This is the account of Noah.

Noah was a righteous man, blameless among the people of his time, and he walked with God. ¹⁰Noah had three sons: Shem, Ham and Japheth.

¹¹Now the earth was corrupt in God's sight and was full of violence. ¹²God saw how corrupt the earth had become, for all the people on earth had corrupted their ways. ¹³So God said to Noah, "I am going to put an end to all people, for the earth is filled with violence because of them. I am surely going to destroy both them and the earth. ¹⁴So make yourself an ark of cypress ᵈ wood; make rooms in it and coat it with pitch inside and out. ¹⁵This is how you are to build it: The ark is to be 450 feet long, 75 feet wide and

---

ᵃ 29 *Noah* sounds like the Hebrew for *comfort.*   ᵇ 3 Or *My spirit will not remain in*   ᶜ 3 Or *corrupt*   ᵈ 14 The meaning of the Hebrew for this word is uncertain.

45 feet high.*a* ¹⁶Make a roof for it and finish *b* the ark to within 18 inches*c* of the top. Put a door in the side of the ark and make lower, middle and upper decks. ¹⁷I am going to bring floodwaters on the earth to destroy all life under the heavens, every creature that has the breath of life in it. Everything on earth will perish. ¹⁸But I will establish my covenant with you, and you will enter the ark—you and your sons and your wife and your sons' wives with you. ¹⁹You are to bring into the ark two of all living creatures, male and female, to keep them alive with you. ²⁰Two of every kind of bird, of every kind of animal and of every kind of creature that moves along the ground will come to you to be kept alive. ²¹You are to take every kind of food that is to be eaten and store it away as food for you and for them."

²²Noah did everything just as God commanded him.

7 The Lord then said to Noah, "Go into the ark, you and your whole family, because I have found you righteous in this generation. ²Take with you seven*d* of every kind of clean animal, a male and its mate, and two of every kind of unclean animal, a male and its mate, ³and also seven of every kind of bird, male and female, to keep their various kinds alive throughout the earth. ⁴Seven days from now I will send rain on the earth for forty days and forty nights, and I will wipe from the face of the earth every living creature I have made."

⁵And Noah did all that the Lord commanded him.

⁶Noah was six hundred years old when the floodwaters came on the earth. ⁷And Noah and his sons and his wife and his sons' wives entered the ark to escape the waters of the flood. ⁸Pairs of clean and unclean animals, of birds and of all creatures that move along the ground, ⁹male and female, came to Noah and entered the ark, as God had commanded Noah. ¹⁰And after the seven days the floodwaters came on the earth.

¹¹In the six hundredth year of Noah's life, on the seventeenth day of the second month—on that day all the springs of the great deep burst

stories to share

GENESIS 6:9—7:10

Noah Builds an Ark

LIFE LESSON: God values our obedience.

TO TALK ABOUT

✦ What did God ask Noah to do? Why?

✦ How do you think Noah felt about obeying instructions from God that didn't seem to make sense, like building a huge boat on dry ground?

✦ What would you have done if you had been Noah and God had told you to do this?

✦ We can imagine that people made fun of Noah for building the ark. Have you ever been teased for obeying God? How did you handle the situation?

forth, and the floodgates of the heavens were opened. ¹²And rain fell on the earth forty days and forty nights.

¹³On that very day Noah and his sons, Shem, Ham and Japheth, together with his wife and the wives of his three sons, entered the ark. ¹⁴They had with them every wild animal according to its

a 15 Hebrew *300 cubits long, 50 cubits wide and 30 cubits high* (about 140 meters long, 23 meters wide and 13.5 meters high) *b* 16 Or *Make an opening for light by finishing*   *c* 16 Hebrew *a cubit* (about 0.5 meter)   *d* 2 Or *seven pairs*; also in verse 3 kind, all livestock according to their kinds, every creature that moves along the ground according to its kind and every bird according to its kind, everything with wings. ¹⁵Pairs of all creatures that have the breath of life in them came to Noah and entered the ark. ¹⁶The animals going in were male and female of every living thing, as God had commanded Noah. Then the LORD shut him in.

¹⁷For forty days the flood kept coming on the earth, and as the waters increased they lifted the ark high above the earth. ¹⁸The waters rose and increased greatly on the earth, and the ark floated on the surface of the water. ¹⁹They rose greatly on the earth, and all the high mountains under the entire heavens were covered. ²⁰The waters rose and covered the mountains to a depth of more than twenty feet. *a, b* ²¹Every living thing that moved on the earth perished—birds, livestock, wild animals, all the creatures that swarm over the earth, and all mankind. ²²Everything on dry land that had the breath of life in its nostrils died. ²³Every living thing on the face of the earth was wiped out; men and animals and the creatures that move along the ground and the birds of the air were wiped from the earth. Only Noah was left, and those with him in the ark.

²⁴The waters flooded the earth for a hundred and fifty days.

8 But God remembered Noah and all the wild animals and the livestock that were with him in the ark, and he sent a wind over the earth, and the waters receded. ²Now the springs of the deep and the floodgates of the heavens had been closed, and the rain had stopped falling from the sky. ³The water receded steadily from the earth. At the end of the hundred and fifty days the water had gone down, ⁴and on the seventeenth day of the seventh month the ark came to rest on the mountains of Ararat. ⁵The waters continued to recede until the tenth month, and on the first day of the tenth month the tops of the mountains became visible.

⁶After forty days Noah opened the window he had made in the ark ⁷and sent out a raven, and it kept flying back and forth until the water had dried up from the earth. ⁸Then he sent out a dove to see if the water had receded from the surface of the ground. ⁹But the dove could find no place to set its feet because there was water over all the surface of the earth; so it returned to Noah in the ark. He reached out his hand and took the dove and brought it back to himself in the ark. ¹⁰He waited seven more days and again sent out the dove from the ark. ¹¹When the dove returned to him in the evening, there in its beak was a freshly plucked olive leaf! Then Noah knew that the water had receded from the earth. ¹²He waited seven more days and sent the dove out again, but this time it did not return to him.

¹³By the first day of the first month of Noah's six hundred and first year, the water had dried up from the earth. Noah then removed the covering from the ark and saw that the surface of the

a 20 Hebrew *fifteen cubits* (about 6.9 meters)   *b 20* Or *rose more than twenty feet, and the mountains were covered*

stories to share

GENESIS 7:11—9:17

The Great Flood

LIFE LESSON: God keeps his promises.

TO TALK ABOUT

✦ Who shut the door of the ark when everyone was inside?

✦ How did Noah know it was safe to leave the ark?

✦ What promise from God does a rainbow remind us of?

✦ Do you trust God's promises? Why?

ground was dry. ¹⁴By the twenty-seventh day of the second month the earth was completely dry.

¹⁵Then God said to Noah, ¹⁶"Come out of the ark, you and your wife and your sons and their wives. ¹⁷Bring out every kind of living creature that is with you—the birds, the animals, and all the creatures that move along the ground—so they can multiply on the earth and be fruitful and increase in number upon it."

¹⁸So Noah came out, together with his sons and his wife and his sons' wives. ¹⁹All the animals and all the creatures that move along the ground and all the birds—everything that moves on the earth—came out of the ark, one kind after another.

²⁰Then Noah built an altar to the LORD and, taking some of all the clean animals and clean birds, he sacrificed burnt offerings on it. ²¹The LORD smelled the pleasing aroma and said in his heart: "Never again will I curse the ground because of man, even though *a* every inclination of his heart is evil from childhood. And never again will I destroy all living creatures, as I have done.

²²"As long as the earth endures,
seedtime and harvest,
cold and heat,
summer and winter,
day and night
will never cease."

God's Covenant With Noah

9 Then God blessed Noah and his sons, saying to them, "Be fruitful and increase in number and fill the earth. ²The fear and dread of you will fall upon all the beasts of the earth and all the birds of the air, upon every creature that moves along the ground, and upon all the fish of the sea; they are given into your hands. ³Everything that lives and moves will be food for you. Just as I gave you the green plants, I now give you everything.

⁴"But you must not eat meat that has its lifeblood still in it. ⁵And for your lifeblood I will surely demand an accounting. I will demand an accounting from every animal. And from each man, too, I will demand an accounting for the life of his fellow man.

⁶"Whoever sheds the blood of man,
by man shall his blood be shed;
for in the image of God
has God made man.

⁷As for you, be fruitful and increase in number; multiply on the earth and increase upon it."

⁸Then God said to Noah and to his sons with him: ⁹"I now establish my covenant with you and with your descendants after you ¹⁰and with every living creature that was with you—the birds, the livestock and all the wild animals, all those that came out of the ark with you—every living creature on earth. ¹¹I establish my covenant with you: Never again will all life be cut off by the waters of a flood; never again will there be a flood to destroy the earth."

¹²And God said, "This is the sign of the covenant I am making between me and you and every living creature with you, a covenant for all generations to come: ¹³I have set my rainbow in the clouds, and it will be the sign of the covenant between me and the earth. ¹⁴Whenever I bring clouds over the earth and the rainbow appears in the clouds, ¹⁵I will remember my covenant between me and you and all living creatures of every kind. Never again will the waters become a flood to destroy all life. ¹⁶Whenever the rainbow appears in the clouds, I will see it and remember the everlasting covenant between God and all living creatures of every kind on the earth."

¹⁷So God said to Noah, "This is the sign of the covenant I have established between me and all life on the earth."

The Sons of Noah

¹⁸The sons of Noah who came out of the ark were Shem, Ham and Japheth. (Ham was the father of Canaan.) ¹⁹These were the three sons of Noah, and from them came the people who were scattered over the earth.

a 21 Or man, for

²⁰Noah, a man of the soil, proceeded *ᵃ* to plant a vineyard. ²¹When he drank some of its wine, he became drunk and lay uncovered inside his tent.

²²Ham, the father of Canaan, saw his father's nakedness and told his two brothers outside. ²³But Shem and Japheth took a garment and laid it across their shoulders; then they walked in backward and covered their father's nakedness. Their faces were turned the other way so that they would not see their father's nakedness.

²⁴When Noah awoke from his wine and found out what his youngest son had done to him, ²⁵he said,

"Cursed be Canaan!
    The lowest of slaves
    will he be to his brothers."

²⁶He also said,

"Blessed be the Lord, the God of Shem!
    May Canaan be the slave of Shem. *ᵇ*
²⁷May God extend the territory of Japheth *ᶜ*;
    may Japheth live in the tents of Shem,
    and may Canaan be his *ᵈ* slave."

²⁸After the flood Noah lived 350 years. ²⁹Altogether, Noah lived 950 years, and then he died.

The Table of Nations

10 This is the account of Shem, Ham and Japheth, Noah's sons, who themselves had sons after the flood.

The Japhethites
10:2–5pp — 1Ch 1:5–7

²The sons *ᵉ* of Japheth:
    Gomer, Magog, Madai, Javan, Tubal, Meshech and Tiras.
³The sons of Gomer:
    Ashkenaz, Riphath and Togarmah.
⁴The sons of Javan:
    Elishah, Tarshish, the Kittim and the Rodanim. *ᶠ* ⁵(From these the maritime peoples spread out into their territories by their clans within their nations, each with its own language.)

The Hamites
10:6–20pp — 1Ch 1:8–16

⁶The sons of Ham:
    Cush, Mizraim, *ᵍ* Put and Canaan.
⁷The sons of Cush:
    Seba, Havilah, Sabtah, Raamah and Sabteca.
The sons of Raamah:
    Sheba and Dedan.

⁸Cush was the father *ʰ* of Nimrod, who grew to be a mighty warrior on the earth. ⁹He was a mighty hunter before the Lord; that is why it is said, "Like Nimrod, a mighty hunter before the Lord." ¹⁰The first centers of his kingdom were Babylon, Erech, Akkad and Calneh, in *ⁱ* Shinar. *ʲ* ¹¹From that land he went to Assyria, where he built Nineveh, Rehoboth Ir, *ᵏ* Calah ¹²and Resen, which is between Nineveh and Calah; that is the great city.

¹³Mizraim was the father of
    the Ludites, Anamites, Lehabites, Naphtuhites, ¹⁴Pathrusites, Casluhites (from whom the Philistines came) and Caphtorites.

ᵃ 20 Or *soil, was the first*   *ᵇ 26* Or *be his slave*   *ᶜ 27 Japheth* sounds like the Hebrew for *extend.*   *ᵈ 27* Or *their*   *ᵉ 2 Sons* may mean *descendants* or *successors* or *nations*; also in verses 3, 4, 6, 7, 20-23, 29 and 31.   *ᶠ 4* Some manuscripts of the Masoretic Text and Samaritan Pentateuch (see also Septuagint and 1 Chron. 1:7); most manuscripts of the Masoretic Text *Dodanim*   *ᵍ 6* That is, Egypt; also in verse 13   *ʰ 8 Father* may mean *ancestor* or *predecessor* or *founder*; also in verses 13, 15, 24 and 26.   *ⁱ 10* Or *Erech and Akkad—all of them in*   *ʲ 10* That is, Babylonia   *ᵏ 11* Or *Nineveh with its city squares*

15 Canaan was the father of
Sidon his firstborn,ᵃ and of the Hittites,
16 Jebusites, Amorites, Girgashites, 17 Hivites, Arkites, Sinites, 18 Arvadites, Zemarites and Hamathites.

Later the Canaanite clans scattered 19 and the borders of Canaan reached from Sidon toward Gerar as far as Gaza, and then toward Sodom, Gomorrah, Admah and Zeboiim, as far as Lasha.

20 These are the sons of Ham by their clans and languages, in their territories and nations.

The Semites

10:21–31pp — Ge 11:10–27; 1Ch 1:17–27

21 Sons were also born to Shem, whose older brother wasᵇ Japheth; Shem was the ancestor of all the sons of Eber.

22 The sons of Shem:
Elam, Asshur, Arphaxad, Lud and Aram.
23 The sons of Aram:
Uz, Hul, Gether and Meshech.ᶜ
24 Arphaxad was the father ofᵈ Shelah,
and Shelah the father of Eber.
25 Two sons were born to Eber:
One was named Peleg,ᵉ because in his time the earth was divided; his brother was named Joktan.
26 Joktan was the father of
Almodad, Sheleph, Hazarmaveth, Jerah, 27 Hadoram, Uzal, Diklah, 28 Obal, Abimael, Sheba, 29 Ophir, Havilah and Jobab. All these were sons of Joktan.

30 The region where they lived stretched from Mesha toward Sephar, in the eastern hill country.

31 These are the sons of Shem by their clans and languages, in their territories and nations.

32 These are the clans of Noah's sons, according to their lines of descent, within their nations. From these the nations spread out over the earth after the flood.

The Tower of Babel

11 Now the whole world had one language and a common speech. 2 As men moved eastward,ᶠ they found a plain in Shinarᵍ and settled there.

3 They said to each other, "Come, let's make bricks and bake them thoroughly." They used brick instead of stone, and tar for mortar. 4 Then they said, "Come, let us build ourselves a city, with a tower that reaches to the heavens, so that we may make a name for ourselves and not be scattered over the face of the whole earth."

5 But the LORD came down to see the city and the tower that the men were building. 6 The LORD said, "If as one people speaking the same language they have begun to do this, then nothing they

---

ᵃ 15 Or of the Sidonians, the foremost ᵇ 21 Or Shem, the older brother of ᶜ 23 See Septuagint and 1 Chron. 1:17; Hebrew Mash ᵈ 24 Hebrew; Septuagint father of Cainan, and Cainan was the father of ᵉ 25 Peleg means division. ᶠ 2 Or from the east; or in the east ᵍ 2 That is, Babylonia

stories to share

GENESIS 11:1–9

The Tower of Babel

LIFE LESSON: No human being can ever be as great as God.

TO TALK ABOUT

✦ Why did the people want to build a tower reaching into the sky?

✦ Why did God give the people various languages?

✦ What did the people do when they realized they were speaking different languages?

✦ Can a person ever be as great as God? Why or why not?

SUE BUCHANAN

The Family Reunion...
AND THE GENEALOGY

Am I the only person who has ever wondered why Moses, when he was on such a roll writing Genesis, decided to stop in midstream and work on his lineage up until Abraham?

"What's that all about?" I would ask myself each time I encountered those long lists of the sons of so-and-so in Genesis 10 and the record of how old so-and-so was when he became the father of so-and-so in Genesis 11. Then one autumn-colored weekend in the rolling hills of southern Ohio at a family reunion, I felt the magic of connecting as a family. Reuniting with loved ones was a satisfying experience! Some of us picked up right where we'd left off. Others of us picked up where our mothers and fathers had left off years before.

At the tiny motel where we met, we pulled out our frayed photo albums and shared stories. Some compared computer programs that told us who was married to whom, who died when and where they were buried. Others knew where property lines were drawn and what military honors had been conferred.

The next morning after breakfast, we headed out to the countryside.

The railroad, the very lifeblood of our family long ago, was still making its way along the winding creek, through fields of lush yellow, between green copse and rolling hills. I thought perhaps I'd imagined it, but it was exactly as I had remembered it for more than 50 years.

Leading Creek

Leading Creek! We swam there and fished there. Nancy, my cousin, told us about a time when the older kids were swimming and my Grandpa (her Uncle Lew) surreptitiously went beyond the spot where they were playing and came floating toward them on his back — fully clothed, hat intact and smoking his pipe. It was one of those forever memories for a bunch of kids.

The Old Home Place was gone, but there were gentle reminders of what once was: the barn, the stone steps up from the road, and the white lattice structure that housed the well from which we drew our drinking water even long after the addition of indoor plumbing.

We remembered telling ghost stories in the dark attic and playing paper dolls on the winding stairs. There were picnics on the lawn with fried chicken, deviled eggs and butter (churned by loving hands) dripping from Aunt Maggie's fresh, warm bread. Mouth-watering pies for dessert. Sometimes homemade ice cream. And watermelon! Always watermelon.

We wallowed for a moment in memories of slicky-slides of freshly mowed hay, hide-and-seek in the barn, and the thought occurred to me: perhaps what's tucked away in the corners of our minds is far better than the real thing.

He Leadeth Me

At the Langsville Church on Sunday morning there were more of "us" than there were of "them," but we were welcomed with open arms. Such a hospitable bunch. Smiling generously, shaking our hands and hugging us. Greeting us with "Praise the Lord."

We sang unfamiliar songs, but from a far-off place I could hear ghosts singing a countermelody, and the sound crescendoed in my head until it drowned out the other: "He leadeth me, Oh, blessed thought ..." and "In the sweet bye and bye, we shall meet on that beautiful shore." From that pulpit a country preacher, who visited only once a month, promised redemption and heaven to those who believed. And I did. I believed. (Still do!)

I'll Treasure Their Memory

I'm back home. Photographs are scattered about on my kitchen cabinet. Some old and faded, some spewed from a Kodak machine only hours ago. One of five-year-old Grant captures my heart as he sits innocently atop the tallest of our family tombstones, and it strikes me ... he looks for all the world like those red-haired Entsmingers of days gone by.

Suddenly I become aware of other faces, other resemblances. I shuffle tattered images and line them up side by side with more modern ones and find it remarkable. We are them! And as I finger their sepia-colored pictures, I promise them, and me, that I'll treasure their memory and tell their stories. This is my genealogy.

Let history come alive for you, dear friend ... and for your precious children and grandchildren. Teach them to love the word *family*. Encourage them to understand their history — the good and the bad. Pray with them that they'll examine their own lives in light of generations to come and in light of eternity.

plan to do will be impossible for them. ⁷Come, let us go down and confuse their language so they will not understand each other."

⁸So the LORD scattered them from there over all the earth, and they stopped building the city. ⁹That is why it was called Babel^a—because there the LORD confused the language of the whole world. From there the LORD scattered them over the face of the whole earth.

From Shem to Abram

11:10–27pp — Ge 10:21–31; 1Ch 1:17–27

¹⁰This is the account of Shem.

Two years after the flood, when Shem was 100 years old, he became the father^b of Arphaxad. ¹¹And after he became the father of Arphaxad, Shem lived 500 years and had other sons and daughters.

¹²When Arphaxad had lived 35 years, he became the father of Shelah. ¹³And after he became the father of Shelah, Arphaxad lived 403 years and had other sons and daughters.^c

¹⁴When Shelah had lived 30 years, he became the father of Eber. ¹⁵And after he became the father of Eber, Shelah lived 403 years and had other sons and daughters.

¹⁶When Eber had lived 34 years, he became the father of Peleg. ¹⁷And after he became the father of Peleg, Eber lived 430 years and had other sons and daughters.

¹⁸When Peleg had lived 30 years, he became the father of Reu. ¹⁹And after he became the father of Reu, Peleg lived 209 years and had other sons and daughters.

²⁰When Reu had lived 32 years, he became the father of Serug. ²¹And after he became the father of Serug, Reu lived 207 years and had other sons and daughters.

²²When Serug had lived 30 years, he became the father of Nahor. ²³And after he became the father of Nahor, Serug lived 200 years and had other sons and daughters.

²⁴When Nahor had lived 29 years, he became the father of Terah. ²⁵And after he became the

father of Terah, Nahor lived 119 years and had other sons and daughters.

²⁶After Terah had lived 70 years, he became the father of Abram, Nahor and Haran.

²⁷This is the account of Terah.

Terah became the father of Abram, Nahor and Haran. And Haran became the father of Lot. ²⁸While his father Terah was still alive, Haran died in Ur of the Chaldeans, in the land of his birth. ²⁹Abram and Nahor both married. The name of Abram's wife was Sarai, and the name of Nahor's wife was Milcah; she was the daughter of Haran, the father of both Milcah and Iscah. ³⁰Now Sarai was barren; she had no children.

³¹Terah took his son Abram, his grandson Lot son of Haran, and his daughter-in-law Sarai, the wife of his son Abram, and together they set out from Ur of the Chaldeans to go to Canaan. But when they came to Haran, they settled there.

³²Terah lived 205 years, and he died in Haran.

The Call of Abram

12 The LORD had said to Abram, "Leave your country, your people and your father's household and go to the land I will show you.

²"I will make you into a great nation
 and I will bless you;
I will make your name great,
 and you will be a blessing.
³I will bless those who bless you,
 and whoever curses you I will curse;
and all peoples on earth
 will be blessed through you."

⁴So Abram left, as the LORD had told him; and Lot went with him. Abram was seventy-five years old when he set out from Haran. ⁵He took his wife Sarai, his nephew Lot, all the possessions

---

^a *9* That is, Babylon; *Babel* sounds like the Hebrew for *confused.* ^b *10 Father* may mean *ancestor;* also in verses 11-25. ^c *12,13* Hebrew; Septuagint (see also Luke 3:35, 36 and note at Gen. 10:24) *35 years, he became the father of Cainan.* ¹³*And after he became the father of Cainan, Arphaxad lived 430 years and had other sons and daughters, and then he died. When Cainan had lived 130 years, he became the father of Shelah. And after he became the father of Shelah, Cainan lived 330 years and had other sons and daughters*

THE LORD HAD SAID TO ABRAM,
"LEAVE YOUR COUNTRY, YOUR
PEOPLE AND YOUR FATHER'S
HOUSEHOLD AND GO TO THE
LAND I WILL SHOW YOU."

Genesis 12:1

New Directions

PATRICIA SPRINKLE

READ | GENESIS 12:1 – 9

I never imagined how much becoming a grandmother would alter my life. Both my budget and my joints creaked at some of the changes required. I needed to rearrange furniture to create spaces where the baby could sleep, eat and play. I had to get a crib, a swing, a high chair, pacifiers, diapers, wipes, books and toys. When I priced car seats, I demanded, "Why doesn't somebody give *me* a baby shower?"

I found myself driving miles for a brief glimpse of the child and changing my important schedule so I could spend an afternoon with him. I would have sworn I was too old to climb jungle gyms, run races up and down the hall, chase bubbles full of rainbows, crawl around the floor playing cars, or bury my toes in a sandbox. I learned I am not too old. Being a grandmother constantly extends my horizon of what I am capable of. Could grandchildren be God's way of reminding us we are never too old to change?

Abraham was 75 when he responded to God's call to leave home, make an arduous journey and begin a new life in a new land. Moses was 80 when God appeared to him in a burning bush and sent him to lead the Israelites out of Egypt. God has never accepted age as an excuse to refuse to change or take on new assignments. Neither does a grandchild!

Lord, thank you that just when I am getting set in comfortable ways, you send grandchildren to remind me that I'm not as old as I think I am and that change is your way of giving new meaning and direction to my life. Amen.

Your next devotion is located on page 21.

GRANDCHILD IN FOCUS • PRAYER

Emotional Development

O God, Creator of mind and body, I pray that you will give my grandchild emotional health and strength. Where there is anger, bring peace. Where there is confusion, bring clarity and focus. Where there are dark shadows, cast a ray of hope. Fill her with the sunshine of your Spirit. Warm her with the presence of your peace. Amen.

they had accumulated and the people they had acquired in Haran, and they set out for the land of Canaan, and they arrived there.

[6] Abram traveled through the land as far as the site of the great tree of Moreh at Shechem. At that time the Canaanites were in the land. [7] The LORD appeared to Abram and said, "To your offspring[a] I will give this land." So he built an altar there to the LORD, who had appeared to him.

[8] From there he went on toward the hills east of Bethel and pitched his tent, with Bethel on the west and Ai on the east. There he built an altar to the LORD and called on the name of the LORD. [9] Then Abram set out and continued toward the Negev.

Abram in Egypt

12:10–20Ref — Ge 20:1–18; 26:1–11

[10] Now there was a famine in the land, and Abram went down to Egypt to live there for a while because the famine was severe. [11] As he was about to enter Egypt, he said to his wife Sarai, "I know what a beautiful woman you are. [12] When the Egyptians see you, they will say, 'This is his wife.' Then they will kill me but will let you live. [13] Say you are my sister, so that I will be treated well for your sake and my life will be spared because of you."

[14] When Abram came to Egypt, the Egyptians saw that she was a very beautiful woman. [15] And when Pharaoh's officials saw her, they praised her to Pharaoh, and she was taken into his palace. [16] He treated Abram well for her sake, and Abram acquired sheep and cattle, male and female donkeys, menservants and maidservants, and camels.

[17] But the LORD inflicted serious diseases on Pharaoh and his household because of Abram's wife Sarai. [18] So Pharaoh summoned Abram. "What have you done to me?" he said. "Why didn't you tell me she was your wife? [19] Why did you say, 'She is my sister,' so that I took her to be my wife? Now then, here is your wife. Take her and go!" [20] Then Pharaoh gave orders about Abram to his men, and they sent him on his way, with his wife and everything he had.

GENESIS 12:1–9; 17:1–8

God's Covenant With Abraham

LIFE LESSON: Faith requires action.

TO TALK ABOUT

✦ What did God ask Abraham to do?

✦ Who went with Abraham to the land of Canaan?

✦ Why is God's covenant (or promise) with Abraham important to us today?

✦ In what way are we Abraham's descendants?

Abram and Lot Separate

13 So Abram went up from Egypt to the Negev, with his wife and everything he had, and Lot went with him. [2] Abram had become very wealthy in livestock and in silver and gold.

[3] From the Negev he went from place to place until he came to Bethel, to the place between Bethel and Ai where his tent had been earlier [4] and where he had first built an altar. There Abram called on the name of the LORD.

[5] Now Lot, who was moving about with Abram, also had flocks and herds and tents. [6] But the land could not support them while they stayed together, for their possessions were so great that they were not able to stay together. [7] And quarreling arose between Abram's herdsmen and the herds-

[a] 7 Or seed

> "GO, WALK THROUGH THE
> LENGTH AND BREADTH OF
> THE LAND, FOR I AM GIVING
> IT TO YOU."
>
> *Genesis 13:17*

Claim Your Territory

ANNE ORTLUND

READ | GENESIS 13:1 – 18

Ray and I used to love to sit under the sparkling preaching of Dr. Donald Grey Barnhouse. Here's one thing we remember he said:

Picture your Bible in the way Abraham must have pictured the land of Canaan. Remember God had said to him, "Go, walk through the length and breadth of the land, for I am giving it to you" (Genesis 13:17).

That evening Abraham took a walk, and he walked about an acre, and that night he owned an acre. During the next month he grazed his sheep over the neighboring hills, and he owned them all. "I am giving it to you." In the course of years he came to own everything from Dan to Beersheba, just by putting his foot down.

Lots of Christians have very "small" Bibles (said Dr. Barnhouse). They have Psalm 23 and John 3:16 and a few other places, and they keep going back and forth from one to the other, grazing them down to bare rock — and that's all they have. But God says, "Go, walk through the length and breadth of the land."

I challenge you to extend your holdings in God's Word! Start now with the New Testament and read three chapters a day. In about three months you'll have walked through it. Or begin with Genesis and read through the Bible in a year!

Start claiming new territory today.

. . . .

Thank you, Lord, for the freedom to openly read the Bible. Instill in me the desire to read your Word and claim new territory for my life. Amen.

Your next devotion is located on page 24.

GRANDCHILD IN FOCUS · PRAYER

Spiritual Growth

Dear Lord, today I pray for my grandchild's spiritual growth. I ask that you instill in him the desire to read and memorize your Word. Give him a passion to be in conversation with you. May loving and serving you be part of his daily life. I ask that you stay close to him and lead him to be transformed to your likeness, to reflect your grace and to radiate your love. I pray this in Jesus' name, amen.

men of Lot. The Canaanites and Perizzites were also living in the land at that time.

⁸So Abram said to Lot, "Let's not have any quarreling between you and me, or between your herdsmen and mine, for we are brothers. ⁹Is not the whole land before you? Let's part company. If you go to the left, I'll go to the right; if you go to the right, I'll go to the left."

¹⁰Lot looked up and saw that the whole plain of the Jordan was well watered, like the garden of the LORD, like the land of Egypt, toward Zoar. (This was before the LORD destroyed Sodom and Gomorrah.) ¹¹So Lot chose for himself the whole plain of the Jordan and set out toward the east. The two men parted company: ¹²Abram lived in the land of Canaan, while Lot lived among the cities of the plain and pitched his tents near Sodom. ¹³Now the men of Sodom were wicked and were sinning greatly against the LORD.

¹⁴The LORD said to Abram after Lot had parted from him, "Lift up your eyes from where you are and look north and south, east and west. ¹⁵All the land that you see I will give to you and your offspring[a] forever. ¹⁶I will make your offspring like the dust of the earth, so that if anyone could count the dust, then your offspring could be counted. ¹⁷Go, walk through the length and breadth of the land, for I am giving it to you."

¹⁸So Abram moved his tents and went to live near the great trees of Mamre at Hebron, where he built an altar to the LORD.

Abram Rescues Lot

14 At this time Amraphel king of Shinar,[b] Arioch king of Ellasar, Kedorlaomer king of Elam and Tidal king of Goiim ²went to war against Bera king of Sodom, Birsha king of Gomorrah, Shinab king of Admah, Shemeber king of Zeboiim, and the king of Bela (that is, Zoar). ³All these latter kings joined forces in the Valley of Siddim (the Salt Sea[c]). ⁴For twelve years they had been subject to Kedorlaomer, but in the thirteenth year they rebelled.

⁵In the fourteenth year, Kedorlaomer and the kings allied with him went out and defeated the Rephaites in Ashteroth Karnaim, the Zuzites in Ham, the Emites in Shaveh Kiriathaim ⁶and the Horites in the hill country of Seir, as far as El Paran near the desert. ⁷Then they turned back and went to En Mishpat (that is, Kadesh), and they conquered the whole territory of the Amalekites, as well as the Amorites who were living in Hazazon Tamar.

⁸Then the king of Sodom, the king of Gomorrah, the king of Admah, the king of Zeboiim and the king of Bela (that is, Zoar) marched out and drew up their battle lines in the Valley of Siddim ⁹against Kedorlaomer king of Elam, Tidal king of Goiim, Amraphel king of Shinar and Arioch king of Ellasar—four kings against five. ¹⁰Now the Valley of Siddim was full of tar pits, and when the kings of Sodom and Gomorrah fled, some of the men fell into them and the rest fled to the hills. ¹¹The four kings seized all the goods of Sodom and Gomorrah and all their food; then they went away. ¹²They also carried off Abram's nephew Lot and his possessions, since he was living in Sodom.

¹³One who had escaped came and reported this to Abram the Hebrew. Now Abram was living near the great trees of Mamre the Amorite, a brother[d] of Eshcol and Aner, all of whom were allied with Abram. ¹⁴When Abram heard that his relative had been taken captive, he called out the 318 trained men born in his household and went in pursuit as far as Dan. ¹⁵During the night Abram divided his men to attack them and he routed them, pursuing them as far as Hobah, north of Damascus. ¹⁶He recovered all the goods and brought back his relative Lot and his possessions, together with the women and the other people.

¹⁷After Abram returned from defeating Kedorlaomer and the kings allied with him, the king of Sodom came out to meet him in the Valley of Shaveh (that is, the King's Valley).

¹⁸Then Melchizedek king of Salem[e] brought out bread and wine. He was priest of God Most High, ¹⁹and he blessed Abram, saying,

---

[a] 15 Or *seed*; also in verse 16   [b] 1 That is, Babylonia; also in verse 9   [c] 3 That is, the Dead Sea   [d] 13 Or *a relative*; or *an ally*   [e] 18 That is, Jerusalem

"Blessed be Abram by God Most High,
  Creator *a* of heaven and earth.
²⁰And blessed be *b* God Most High,
  who delivered your enemies into your
    hand."

Then Abram gave him a tenth of everything.

²¹The king of Sodom said to Abram, "Give me the people and keep the goods for yourself."

²²But Abram said to the king of Sodom, "I have raised my hand to the LORD, God Most High, Creator of heaven and earth, and have taken an oath ²³that I will accept nothing belonging to you, not even a thread or the thong of a sandal, so that you will never be able to say, 'I made Abram rich.' ²⁴I will accept nothing but what my men have eaten and the share that belongs to the men who went with me—to Aner, Eshcol and Mamre. Let them have their share."

God's Covenant With Abram

15 After this, the word of the LORD came to Abram in a vision:

"Do not be afraid, Abram.
  I am your shield, *c*
  your very great reward. *d*"

²But Abram said, "O Sovereign LORD, what can you give me since I remain childless and the one who will inherit *e* my estate is Eliezer of Damascus?" ³And Abram said, "You have given me no children; so a servant in my household will be my heir."

⁴Then the word of the LORD came to him: "This man will not be your heir, but a son coming from your own body will be your heir." ⁵He took him outside and said, "Look up at the heavens and count the stars—if indeed you can count them." Then he said to him, "So shall your offspring be."

⁶Abram believed the LORD, and he credited it to him as righteousness.

⁷He also said to him, "I am the LORD, who brought you out of Ur of the Chaldeans to give you this land to take possession of it."

⁸But Abram said, "O Sovereign LORD, how can I know that I will gain possession of it?"

⁹So the LORD said to him, "Bring me a heifer, a goat and a ram, each three years old, along with a dove and a young pigeon."

¹⁰Abram brought all these to him, cut them in two and arranged the halves opposite each other; the birds, however, he did not cut in half. ¹¹Then birds of prey came down on the carcasses, but Abram drove them away.

¹²As the sun was setting, Abram fell into a deep sleep, and a thick and dreadful darkness came over him. ¹³Then the LORD said to him, "Know for certain that your descendants will be strangers in a country not their own, and they will be enslaved and mistreated four hundred years. ¹⁴But I will punish the nation they serve as slaves, and afterward they will come out with great possessions. ¹⁵You, however, will go to your fathers in peace and be buried at a good old age. ¹⁶In the fourth generation your descendants will come back here, for the sin of the Amorites has not yet reached its full measure."

¹⁷When the sun had set and darkness had fallen, a smoking firepot with a blazing torch appeared and passed between the pieces. ¹⁸On that day the LORD made a covenant with Abram and said, "To your descendants I give this land, from the river *f* of Egypt to the great river, the Euphrates— ¹⁹the land of the Kenites, Kenizzites, Kadmonites, ²⁰Hittites, Perizzites, Rephaites, ²¹Amorites, Canaanites, Girgashites and Jebusites."

Hagar and Ishmael

16 Now Sarai, Abram's wife, had borne him no children. But she had an Egyptian maidservant named Hagar; ²so she said to Abram, "The LORD has kept me from having children. Go, sleep with my maidservant; perhaps I can build a family through her."

Abram agreed to what Sarai said. ³So after

---

a 19 Or *Possessor;* also in verse 22   *b* 20 Or *And praise be to*
c 1 Or *sovereign*   *d* 1 Or *shield; / your reward will be very great*
e 2 The meaning of the Hebrew for this phrase is uncertain.
f 18 Or *Wadi*

ABRAM BELIEVED THE LORD,
AND HE CREDITED IT TO HIM
AS RIGHTEOUSNESS.

Genesis 15:6

He Knows Our Needs

RUTHANNE GARLOCK

READ | GENESIS 15:1–21

My tenth-grade granddaughter, Amanda, received a partial scholarship from the private school she wanted to attend, but distance was a problem. Though her mom, Linda, had put their house on the market and was searching for a rented house near the school, sales were weak and rentals scarce.

Toward summer's end, I flew to California to help them pack, even though their housing problem remained unsolved. The next day we looked at rentals, all of them disappointing, then drove to one last house before heading home.

"It's perfect!" we all agreed. Only one problem: thirty other families had already submitted applications to rent the place. Mr. Smith, the owner, showed us around and gave Linda an application form, asking her to leave it in the mailbox by 8:00 P.M. He and his family would then review the applicants and make their choice.

Back at home, Linda filled out the form, gathered backup documents and wrote a letter detailing their dilemma — even offering to pay a higher security deposit because of Amanda's dog. While they rushed to return the application, I unloaded the china cupboard and began packing dishes, praying as I worked.

"What are you doing?" Linda asked in shock when they returned.

"I'm packing boxes, and you gals are moving!" I said. "I believe God is going to help you sell this house and rent that one."

Two days later we shouted for joy when the owner called to say the house was theirs. Soon after, Linda had a buyer. Mr. Smith never checked Linda's references and refused her offer to pay a higher security deposit. He simply "had a feeling" she should have the house.

Lord, I want to have faith like Abraham — faith that isn't tethered to circumstances. Help me to remember that you know the needs of my family even before I pray about them. May I acknowledge your provision and faithfulness, and give you thanks. Amen.

GRANDCHILD IN FOCUS • PRAYER

Relationships at Home

O Lord, I pray that you will bless the home and family of my grandchild. May the relationships she has with her parents and siblings enhance her well-being, support her self-confidence and increase her faith. May her home life reflect your love, your grace, your compassion and your peace. Guide her parents to direct her in love and truth, so she will grow into a strong and compassionate individual. Amen.

Your next devotion is located on page 26.

Abram had been living in Canaan ten years, Sarai his wife took her Egyptian maidservant Hagar and gave her to her husband to be his wife. ⁴He slept with Hagar, and she conceived.

When she knew she was pregnant, she began to despise her mistress. ⁵Then Sarai said to Abram, "You are responsible for the wrong I am suffering. I put my servant in your arms, and now that she knows she is pregnant, she despises me. May the LORD judge between you and me."

⁶"Your servant is in your hands," Abram said. "Do with her whatever you think best." Then Sarai mistreated Hagar; so she fled from her.

⁷The angel of the LORD found Hagar near a spring in the desert; it was the spring that is beside the road to Shur. ⁸And he said, "Hagar, servant of Sarai, where have you come from, and where are you going?"

"I'm running away from my mistress Sarai," she answered.

⁹Then the angel of the LORD told her, "Go back to your mistress and submit to her." ¹⁰The angel added, "I will so increase your descendants that they will be too numerous to count."

¹¹The angel of the LORD also said to her:

"You are now with child
    and you will have a son.
You shall name him Ishmael,ᵃ
    for the LORD has heard of your misery.
¹²He will be a wild donkey of a man;
    his hand will be against everyone
    and everyone's hand against him,
and he will live in hostility
    towardᵇ all his brothers."

¹³She gave this name to the LORD who spoke to her: "You are the God who sees me," for she said, "I have now seenᶜ the One who sees me." ¹⁴That is why the well was called Beer Lahai Roiᵈ; it is still there, between Kadesh and Bered.

¹⁵So Hagar bore Abram a son, and Abram gave the name Ishmael to the son she had borne. ¹⁶Abram was eighty-six years old when Hagar bore him Ishmael.

The Covenant of Circumcision

17 When Abram was ninety-nine years old, the LORD appeared to him and said, "I am God Almightyᵉ; walk before me and be blameless. ²I will confirm my covenant between me and you and will greatly increase your numbers."

³Abram fell facedown, and God said to him, ⁴"As for me, this is my covenant with you: You will be the father of many nations. ⁵No longer will you be called Abramᶠ; your name will be Abraham,ᵍ for I have made you a father of many nations. ⁶I will make you very fruitful; I will make nations of you, and kings will come from you. ⁷I will establish my covenant as an everlasting covenant between me and you and your descendants after you for the generations to come, to be your God and the God of your descendants after you. ⁸The whole land of Canaan, where you are now an alien, I will give as an everlasting possession to you and your descendants after you; and I will be their God."

⁹Then God said to Abraham, "As for you, you must keep my covenant, you and your descendants after you for the generations to come. ¹⁰This is my covenant with you and your descendants after you, the covenant you are to keep: Every male among you shall be circumcised. ¹¹You are to undergo circumcision, and it will be the sign of the covenant between me and you. ¹²For the generations to come every male among you who is eight days old must be circumcised, including those born in your household or bought with money from a foreigner—those who are not your offspring. ¹³Whether born in your household or bought with your money, they must be circumcised. My covenant in your flesh is to be an everlasting covenant. ¹⁴Any uncircumcised male, who has not been circumcised in the flesh, will be cut off from his people; he has broken my covenant."

¹⁵God also said to Abraham, "As for Sarai your wife, you are no longer to call her Sarai; her name

ᵃ 11 Ishmael means God hears.   ᵇ 12 Or live to the east / of
ᶜ 13 Or seen the back of   ᵈ 14 Beer Lahai Roi means well of the
Living One who sees me.   ᵉ 1 Hebrew El-Shaddai   ᶠ 5 Abram
means exalted father.   ᵍ 5 Abraham means father of many.

Blessing Breakfast

Take some time with your grandkids over a special breakfast (either at a restaurant or at your home) to talk about how and why some people have been a blessing to you. Ask them to identify people who have been a blessing to them. Distribute postcards or blank greeting cards, and invite (or help) them to write brief notes to these special people in their lives; include drawings or a poem if they desire. Talk about how important it is to let people know that you care about them (see 1 Thessalonians 5:11; Philemon 4).

Go on to express how each of your grandchildren is a blessing to you. Distribute your own handwritten cards telling them how important they are to you and what you love about them. Pick a favorite Bible verse for them or write out one of the blessings from the Bible (see the index entry "Blessing" in the back of this Bible). Give it to them along with a small gift that says something about each of them.

Long-Distance Variation: Send postcards and blank greeting cards to the out-of-towners as well, suggesting that they follow through with the same activity. Include in the package your notes of blessing and a small gift.

You have showered me with blessings, Father, more than I can begin to count. Thank you for your continuing faithfulness to me and to my family. Show me how to bless my grandchildren in your name and to be a blessing in their lives. Amen.

Your next devotion is located on page 27.

GRANDCHILD IN FOCUS • PRAYER

Friends

Dear Lord and Father, I pray for my grandchild's social life and his friends. Bring diverse friends into his life who will love and encourage him, who will bring joy and laughter to the good times and comfort and support through difficulties and disappointments. Grant him wisdom and discernment as he selects his friends; help him to avoid cliques that restrict, activities that endanger, and foolish and dangerous behaviors that harm. I ask that you fill his life with close and caring relationships. Amen.

Worship the Lord

Shout for joy to the LORD, all the earth.
>   Worship the LORD with gladness;
>   come before him with joyful songs.
Know that the LORD is God.
>   It is he who made us, and we are his;
>   we are his people, the sheep of his pasture.

Enter his gates with thanksgiving
>   and his courts with praise;
>   give thanks to him and praise his name.
For the LORD is good and his love endures forever;
>   his faithfulness continues through all
>   generations.

Psalm 100

Thank you, Father, for building into the week a day set aside for rest for me and all your people. I rejoice in your faithfulness and thank you for the goodness and love that you have shown — and will continue to show — through the generations. Amen.

Your next devotion is located on page 29.

GRANDCHILD IN FOCUS • PRAYER

Self-Image

O loving God, I praise you for creating my grandchild as a unique individual. Now I ask you to help her appreciate her uniqueness. Build up her self-image so she can enjoy her individuality. Help her to stand firm for who she is, where she has come from and what she believes in. Encourage her not only to have hopes and dreams but to also enjoy each day as it comes. In Jesus' name, amen.

will be Sarah. ¹⁶I will bless her and will surely give you a son by her. I will bless her so that she will be the mother of nations; kings of peoples will come from her."

¹⁷Abraham fell facedown; he laughed and said to himself, "Will a son be born to a man a hundred years old? Will Sarah bear a child at the age of ninety?" ¹⁸And Abraham said to God, "If only Ishmael might live under your blessing!"

¹⁹Then God said, "Yes, but your wife Sarah will bear you a son, and you will call him Isaac.ᵃ I will establish my covenant with him as an everlasting covenant for his descendants after him. ²⁰And as for Ishmael, I have heard you: I will surely bless him; I will make him fruitful and will greatly increase his numbers. He will be the father of twelve rulers, and I will make him into a great nation. ²¹But my covenant I will establish with Isaac, whom Sarah will bear to you by this time next year." ²²When he had finished speaking with Abraham, God went up from him.

²³On that very day Abraham took his son Ishmael and all those born in his household or bought with his money, every male in his household, and circumcised them, as God told him. ²⁴Abraham was ninety-nine years old when he was circumcised, ²⁵and his son Ishmael was thirteen; ²⁶Abraham and his son Ishmael were both circumcised on that same day. ²⁷And every male in Abraham's household, including those born in his household or bought from a foreigner, was circumcised with him.

The Three Visitors

18 The LORD appeared to Abraham near the great trees of Mamre while he was sitting at the entrance to his tent in the heat of the day. ²Abraham looked up and saw three men standing nearby. When he saw them, he hurried from the entrance of his tent to meet them and bowed low to the ground.

³He said, "If I have found favor in your eyes, my lord,ᵇ do not pass your servant by. ⁴Let a little water be brought, and then you may all wash your feet and rest under this tree. ⁵Let me get you

something to eat, so you can be refreshed and then go on your way—now that you have come to your servant."

"Very well," they answered, "do as you say."

⁶So Abraham hurried into the tent to Sarah. "Quick," he said, "get three seahsᶜ of fine flour and knead it and bake some bread."

TALKING POINTS

Doubt

Sarah doubted God's ability to do the "impossible."

GENESIS 18:1–15

For more on doubt, go to Mark 11:23.

⁷Then he ran to the herd and selected a choice, tender calf and gave it to a servant, who hurried to prepare it. ⁸He then brought some curds and milk and the calf that had been prepared, and set these before them. While they ate, he stood near them under a tree.

⁹"Where is your wife Sarah?" they asked him.

"There, in the tent," he said.

¹⁰Then the LORDᵈ said, "I will surely return to you about this time next year, and Sarah your wife will have a son."

Now Sarah was listening at the entrance to the tent, which was behind him. ¹¹Abraham and Sarah were already old and well advanced in years, and Sarah was past the age of childbearing. ¹²So Sarah laughed to herself as she thought, "After I am worn out and my masterᵉ is old, will I now have this pleasure?"

¹³Then the LORD said to Abraham, "Why did Sarah laugh and say, 'Will I really have a child, now that I am old?' ¹⁴Is anything too hard for the

ᵃ 19 Isaac means he laughs.   ᵇ 3 Or O Lord   ᶜ 6 That is, probably about 20 quarts (about 22 liters)   ᵈ 10 Hebrew Then he
ᵉ 12 Or husband

> "I WILL ESTABLISH MY COVENANT AS
> AN EVERLASTING COVENANT BETWEEN
> ME AND YOU AND YOUR DESCENDANTS
> AFTER YOU FOR THE GENERATIONS TO
> COME, TO BE YOUR GOD AND THE GOD
> OF YOUR DESCENDANTS AFTER YOU."
>
> *Genesis 17:7*

Generations of Faith

KAREN KINGSBURY

READ | GENESIS 17:1–27

I never met my grandmother on my mom's side of the family. Doris Parsons died at age 45, a young victim of breast cancer. She left behind five kids; her youngest was only eight years old at the time. My mom was the oldest, just 22 and newly married to my father. And so my mom is the one who has filled me in on the details of my grandma's life.

Doris was a dynamic woman, a woman with a passion for God, for family and for something very dear to my heart: books. You see, Doris was a librarian, and it is in that one detail that I see Genesis 17:7 come to life. God made promises to his people, a covenant that would last for generations to come. That covenant involved life — ultimately eternal life through our Savior Jesus Christ. But it was also a covenant of connectivity, a covenant of faith.

Not long ago, my mom and I took a trip to Canada to visit the grave where Grandma Doris is buried. Since she died just three months before I was born, I wanted to feel that connectivity, to know that I was standing in the same spot where my grandfather once stood, grieving the loss of his vibrant wife.

Sometimes I can picture Grandma Doris smiling down from heaven, seeing the covenant of faith passed on from her to my mom and then passed down again to me. How thrilled she would have been to know that her granddaughter became an author and that, in writing books, God would use the power of story to change lives for his kingdom. How gracious our God is to demonstrate the strength of connection through generations of faith.

Dear Lord, I pray that I would see great value in the lives of those who lived before me, in the connectivity of generations and in the lessons of faith learned. Let me also be a shining example of your grace and power to my children and grandchildren. In Christ's name, amen.

Your next devotion is located on page 35.

GRANDCHILD IN FOCUS • PRAYER

Protection From Worldliness

O Sovereign Lord, the world surrounds my grandchild, pressing in and tempting him in so many ways. Help him set appropriate limits. Give him sound judgment to choose wisely. Guard him from temptation; protect him from physical and mental predators; lead him into paths of righteousness and light. And reassure me with your promise that you are holding him in your hands. Amen.

LORD? I will return to you at the appointed time next year and Sarah will have a son."

¹⁵Sarah was afraid, so she lied and said, "I did not laugh."

But he said, "Yes, you did laugh."

GENESIS 18:1–15; 21:1–7

Sarah Has a Baby

LIFE LESSON: Nothing is too hard for God.

TO TALK ABOUT

✦ Who came to visit Abraham? (Hint: Read Genesis 18:2,13; 19:1.)

✦ Why did Sarah laugh about having a baby?

✦ How was Sarah's laughter in Genesis 18 different from her laughter in Genesis 21?

✦ Do you ever doubt God's ability to accomplish something? Why?

Abraham Pleads for Sodom

¹⁶When the men got up to leave, they looked down toward Sodom, and Abraham walked along with them to see them on their way. ¹⁷Then the LORD said, "Shall I hide from Abraham what I am about to do? ¹⁸Abraham will surely become a great and powerful nation, and all nations on earth will be blessed through him. ¹⁹For I have chosen him, so that he will direct his children and his household after him to keep the way of the LORD by doing what is right and just, so that

the LORD will bring about for Abraham what he has promised him."

²⁰Then the LORD said, "The outcry against Sodom and Gomorrah is so great and their sin so grievous ²¹that I will go down and see if what they have done is as bad as the outcry that has reached me. If not, I will know."

²²The men turned away and went toward Sodom, but Abraham remained standing before the LORD.ᵃ ²³Then Abraham approached him and said: "Will you sweep away the righteous with the wicked? ²⁴What if there are fifty righteous people in the city? Will you really sweep it away and not spareᵇ the place for the sake of the fifty righteous people in it? ²⁵Far be it from you to do such a thing—to kill the righteous with the wicked, treating the righteous and the wicked alike. Far be it from you! Will not the Judgeᶜ of all the earth do right?"

²⁶The LORD said, "If I find fifty righteous people in the city of Sodom, I will spare the whole place for their sake."

²⁷Then Abraham spoke up again: "Now that I have been so bold as to speak to the Lord, though I am nothing but dust and ashes, ²⁸what if the number of the righteous is five less than fifty? Will you destroy the whole city because of five people?"

"If I find forty-five there," he said, "I will not destroy it."

²⁹Once again he spoke to him, "What if only forty are found there?"

He said, "For the sake of forty, I will not do it."

³⁰Then he said, "May the Lord not be angry, but let me speak. What if only thirty can be found there?"

He answered, "I will not do it if I find thirty there."

³¹Abraham said, "Now that I have been so bold as to speak to the Lord, what if only twenty can be found there?"

ᵃ 22 Masoretic Text; an ancient Hebrew scribal tradition *but the LORD remained standing before Abraham* ᵇ 24 Or *forgive*; also in verse 26 ᶜ 25 Or *Ruler*

He said, "For the sake of twenty, I will not destroy it."

³²Then he said, "May the Lord not be angry, but let me speak just once more. What if only ten can be found there?"

He answered, "For the sake of ten, I will not destroy it."

³³When the Lord had finished speaking with Abraham, he left, and Abraham returned home.

Sodom and Gomorrah Destroyed

19 The two angels arrived at Sodom in the evening, and Lot was sitting in the gateway of the city. When he saw them, he got up to meet them and bowed down with his face to the ground. ²"My lords," he said, "please turn aside to your servant's house. You can wash your feet and spend the night and then go on your way early in the morning."

"No," they answered, "we will spend the night in the square."

³But he insisted so strongly that they did go with him and entered his house. He prepared a meal for them, baking bread without yeast, and they ate. ⁴Before they had gone to bed, all the men from every part of the city of Sodom—both young and old—surrounded the house. ⁵They called to Lot, "Where are the men who came to you tonight? Bring them out to us so that we can have sex with them."

⁶Lot went outside to meet them and shut the door behind him ⁷and said, "No, my friends. Don't do this wicked thing. ⁸Look, I have two daughters who have never slept with a man. Let me bring them out to you, and you can do what you like with them. But don't do anything to these men, for they have come under the protection of my roof."

⁹"Get out of our way," they replied. And they said, "This fellow came here as an alien, and now he wants to play the judge! We'll treat you worse than them." They kept bringing pressure on Lot and moved forward to break down the door.

¹⁰But the men inside reached out and pulled Lot back into the house and shut the door. ¹¹Then they struck the men who were at the door of the house, young and old, with blindness so that they could not find the door.

¹²The two men said to Lot, "Do you have anyone else here—sons-in-law, sons or daughters, or anyone else in the city who belongs to you? Get them out of here, ¹³because we are going to destroy this place. The outcry to the Lord against its people is so great that he has sent us to destroy it."

¹⁴So Lot went out and spoke to his sons-in-law, who were pledged to marry[a] his daughters. He said, "Hurry and get out of this place, because the Lord is about to destroy the city!" But his sons-in-law thought he was joking.

¹⁵With the coming of dawn, the angels urged Lot, saying, "Hurry! Take your wife and your two daughters who are here, or you will be swept away when the city is punished."

¹⁶When he hesitated, the men grasped his hand and the hands of his wife and of his two daughters and led them safely out of the city, for the Lord was merciful to them. ¹⁷As soon as they had brought them out, one of them said, "Flee for your lives! Don't look back, and don't stop anywhere in the plain! Flee to the mountains or you will be swept away!"

¹⁸But Lot said to them, "No, my lords,[b] please! ¹⁹Your[c] servant has found favor in your[c] eyes, and you[c] have shown great kindness to me in sparing my life. But I can't flee to the mountains; this disaster will overtake me, and I'll die. ²⁰Look, here is a town near enough to run to, and it is small. Let me flee to it—it is very small, isn't it? Then my life will be spared."

²¹He said to him, "Very well, I will grant this request too; I will not overthrow the town you speak of. ²²But flee there quickly, because I cannot do anything until you reach it." (That is why the town was called Zoar.[d])

²³By the time Lot reached Zoar, the sun had risen over the land. ²⁴Then the Lord rained down burning sulfur on Sodom and Gomorrah—from

---

[a] 14 Or were married to   [b] 18 Or No, Lord; or No, my lord
[c] 19 The Hebrew is singular.   [d] 22 Zoar means small.

the LORD out of the heavens. ²⁵Thus he overthrew those cities and the entire plain, including all those living in the cities—and also the vegetation in the land. ²⁶But Lot's wife looked back, and she became a pillar of salt.

²⁷Early the next morning Abraham got up and returned to the place where he had stood before the LORD. ²⁸He looked down toward Sodom and Gomorrah, toward all the land of the plain, and he saw dense smoke rising from the land, like smoke from a furnace.

²⁹So when God destroyed the cities of the plain, he remembered Abraham, and he brought Lot out of the catastrophe that overthrew the cities where Lot had lived.

Lot and His Daughters

³⁰Lot and his two daughters left Zoar and settled in the mountains, for he was afraid to stay in Zoar. He and his two daughters lived in a cave. ³¹One day the older daughter said to the younger, "Our father is old, and there is no man around here to lie with us, as is the custom all over the earth. ³²Let's get our father to drink wine and then lie with him and preserve our family line through our father."

³³That night they got their father to drink wine, and the older daughter went in and lay with him. He was not aware of it when she lay down or when she got up.

³⁴The next day the older daughter said to the younger, "Last night I lay with my father. Let's get him to drink wine again tonight, and you go in and lie with him so we can preserve our family line through our father." ³⁵So they got their father to drink wine that night also, and the younger daughter went and lay with him. Again he was not aware of it when she lay down or when she got up.

³⁶So both of Lot's daughters became pregnant by their father. ³⁷The older daughter had a son, and she named him Moab[a]; he is the father of the Moabites of today. ³⁸The younger daughter also had a son, and she named him Ben-Ammi[b]; he is the father of the Ammonites of today.

Abraham and Abimelech

20:1–18Ref — Ge 12:10–20; 26:1–11

20 Now Abraham moved on from there into the region of the Negev and lived between Kadesh and Shur. For a while he stayed in Gerar, ²and there Abraham said of his wife Sarah, "She is my sister." Then Abimelech king of Gerar sent for Sarah and took her.

³But God came to Abimelech in a dream one night and said to him, "You are as good as dead because of the woman you have taken; she is a married woman."

⁴Now Abimelech had not gone near her, so he said, "Lord, will you destroy an innocent nation? ⁵Did he not say to me, 'She is my sister,' and didn't she also say, 'He is my brother'? I have done this with a clear conscience and clean hands."

⁶Then God said to him in the dream, "Yes, I know you did this with a clear conscience, and so I have kept you from sinning against me. That is why I did not let you touch her. ⁷Now return the man's wife, for he is a prophet, and he will pray for you and you will live. But if you do not return her, you may be sure that you and all yours will die."

⁸Early the next morning Abimelech summoned all his officials, and when he told them all that had happened, they were very much afraid. ⁹Then Abimelech called Abraham in and said, "What have you done to us? How have I wronged you that you have brought such great guilt upon me and my kingdom? You have done things to me that should not be done." ¹⁰And Abimelech asked Abraham, "What was your reason for doing this?"

¹¹Abraham replied, "I said to myself, 'There is surely no fear of God in this place, and they will kill me because of my wife.' ¹²Besides, she really is my sister, the daughter of my father though not of my mother; and she became my wife. ¹³And when God had me wander from my father's household, I said to her, 'This is how you can show your love to me: Everywhere we go, say of me, "He is my brother." ' "

---

^a 37 Moab sounds like the Hebrew for from father.   ^b 38 Ben-Ammi means son of my people.

[14] Then Abimelech brought sheep and cattle and male and female slaves and gave them to Abraham, and he returned Sarah his wife to him. [15] And Abimelech said, "My land is before you; live wherever you like."

[16] To Sarah he said, "I am giving your brother a thousand shekels[a] of silver. This is to cover the offense against you before all who are with you; you are completely vindicated."

[17] Then Abraham prayed to God, and God healed Abimelech, his wife and his slave girls so they could have children again, [18] for the LORD had closed up every womb in Abimelech's household because of Abraham's wife Sarah.

The Birth of Isaac

21 Now the LORD was gracious to Sarah as he had said, and the LORD did for Sarah what he had promised. [2] Sarah became pregnant and bore a son to Abraham in his old age, at the very time God had promised him. [3] Abraham gave the name Isaac[b] to the son Sarah bore him. [4] When his son Isaac was eight days old, Abraham circumcised him, as God commanded him. [5] Abraham was a hundred years old when his son Isaac was born to him.

[6] Sarah said, "God has brought me laughter, and everyone who hears about this will laugh with me." [7] And she added, "Who would have said to Abraham that Sarah would nurse children? Yet I have borne him a son in his old age."

Hagar and Ishmael Sent Away

[8] The child grew and was weaned, and on the day Isaac was weaned Abraham held a great feast. [9] But Sarah saw that the son whom Hagar the Egyptian had borne to Abraham was mocking, [10] and she said to Abraham, "Get rid of that slave woman and her son, for that slave woman's son will never share in the inheritance with my son Isaac."

[11] The matter distressed Abraham greatly because it concerned his son. [12] But God said to him, "Do not be so distressed about the boy and your maidservant. Listen to whatever Sarah tells you, because it is through Isaac that your offspring[c] will be reckoned. [13] I will make the son of the maidservant into a nation also, because he is your offspring."

TALKING POINTS

Blended Family

Abraham and Sarah struggled with their blended family.

GENESIS 21:8–11

For more on blended family, go to Joshua 24:14–15.

[14] Early the next morning Abraham took some food and a skin of water and gave them to Hagar. He set them on her shoulders and then sent her off with the boy. She went on her way and wandered in the desert of Beersheba.

[15] When the water in the skin was gone, she put the boy under one of the bushes. [16] Then she went off and sat down nearby, about a bowshot away, for she thought, "I cannot watch the boy die." And as she sat there nearby, she[d] began to sob.

[17] God heard the boy crying, and the angel of God called to Hagar from heaven and said to her, "What is the matter, Hagar? Do not be afraid; God has heard the boy crying as he lies there. [18] Lift the boy up and take him by the hand, for I will make him into a great nation."

[19] Then God opened her eyes and she saw a well of water. So she went and filled the skin with water and gave the boy a drink.

[20] God was with the boy as he grew up. He lived in the desert and became an archer. [21] While he was living in the Desert of Paran, his mother got a wife for him from Egypt.

---

[a] 16 That is, about 25 pounds (about 11.5 kilograms)   [b] 3 *Isaac* means *he laughs*.   [c] 12 Or *seed*   [d] 16 Hebrew; Septuagint *the child*

The Treaty at Beersheba

22 At that time Abimelech and Phicol the commander of his forces said to Abraham, "God is with you in everything you do. 23 Now swear to me here before God that you will not deal falsely with me or my children or my descendants. Show to me and the country where you are living as an alien the same kindness I have shown to you."

24 Abraham said, "I swear it."

25 Then Abraham complained to Abimelech about a well of water that Abimelech's servants had seized. 26 But Abimelech said, "I don't know who has done this. You did not tell me, and I heard about it only today."

27 So Abraham brought sheep and cattle and gave them to Abimelech, and the two men made a treaty. 28 Abraham set apart seven ewe lambs from the flock, 29 and Abimelech asked Abraham, "What is the meaning of these seven ewe lambs you have set apart by themselves?"

30 He replied, "Accept these seven lambs from my hand as a witness that I dug this well."

31 So that place was called Beersheba,[a] because the two men swore an oath there.

32 After the treaty had been made at Beersheba, Abimelech and Phicol the commander of his forces returned to the land of the Philistines. 33 Abraham planted a tamarisk tree in Beersheba, and there he called upon the name of the LORD, the Eternal God. 34 And Abraham stayed in the land of the Philistines for a long time.

Abraham Tested

22 Some time later God tested Abraham. He said to him, "Abraham!"

"Here I am," he replied.

2 Then God said, "Take your son, your only son, Isaac, whom you love, and go to the region of Moriah. Sacrifice him there as a burnt offering on one of the mountains I will tell you about."

3 Early the next morning Abraham got up and saddled his donkey. He took with him two of his servants and his son Isaac. When he had cut enough wood for the burnt offering, he set out for the place God had told him about. 4 On the third day Abraham looked up and saw the place in the distance. 5 He said to his servants, "Stay here with the donkey while I and the boy go over there. We will worship and then we will come back to you."

6 Abraham took the wood for the burnt offering and placed it on his son Isaac, and he himself carried the fire and the knife. As the two of them went on together, 7 Isaac spoke up and said to his father Abraham, "Father?"

"Yes, my son?" Abraham replied.

"The fire and wood are here," Isaac said, "but where is the lamb for the burnt offering?"

8 Abraham answered, "God himself will provide the lamb for the burnt offering, my son." And the two of them went on together.

9 When they reached the place God had told him about, Abraham built an altar there and arranged the wood on it. He bound his son Isaac and laid him on the altar, on top of the wood. 10 Then he reached out his hand and took the knife to slay his son. 11 But the angel of the LORD called out to him from heaven, "Abraham! Abraham!"

"Here I am," he replied.

12 "Do not lay a hand on the boy," he said. "Do not do anything to him. Now I know that you fear God, because you have not withheld from me your son, your only son."

13 Abraham looked up and there in a thicket he saw a ram[b] caught by its horns. He went over and took the ram and sacrificed it as a burnt offering instead of his son. 14 So Abraham called that place The LORD Will Provide. And to this day it is said, "On the mountain of the LORD it will be provided."

15 The angel of the LORD called to Abraham from heaven a second time 16 and said, "I swear by myself, declares the LORD, that because you have done this and have not withheld your son, your only son, 17 I will surely bless you and make

---

a 31 Beersheba can mean well of seven or well of the oath.
b 13 Many manuscripts of the Masoretic Text, Samaritan Pentateuch, Septuagint and Syriac; most manuscripts of the Masoretic Text a ram behind ⸢him⸣

> "I WILL SURELY BLESS YOU AND
> MAKE YOUR DESCENDANTS AS
> NUMEROUS AS THE STARS IN THE
> SKY AND AS THE SAND ON THE
> SEASHORE."
>
> *Genesis 22:17*

The Sands of Time

CLAUDIA ARP

READ | GENESIS 22:1–19

Hand in hand, my husband and I walk along the beach. We relax. Beaches do that to us. It's like our eyes and ears are opened—and our hearts. We pause to appreciate the rolling waves, the seagulls flying above, the birds standing on one leg. At times like this, life slows down. We look at each other through the filter of so many years of being best friends and soul mates.

But then Dave and I are joined by our son, daughter-in-law and Lily, our 12-month-old granddaughter, and an amazing thing happens. Lily sees the beach for the very first time. The glee. The delight. Her parents revel in the wonder of it all. It's a magical moment. As we reflect on our son and daughter-in-law, we realize that they are much better prepared to be parents, better prepared to build a marriage, than we were at their age. And then, we realize that life goes forward, not backward, and just as constant as the sands of time, our heavenly Father goes forward with us. Just as constant as the waves of the ocean, his love will always encompass us.

We think of our other sons, their wives, our grandchildren, including precious Lily, who was named after her great-grandmother Lillian—Dave's mother, who several years ago passed on from this life to a better one. Yet, even now Dave can remember his parents, in years gone by, walking on the beach, hand in hand. Then he was the child. Today he's the husband, the dad, the granddad. Now is the time to invest in future generations. We wonder, will Lily one day walk on this beach with her granddaughter?

Lord, may I realize that with the passing of time, I can pass on a godly heritage to my children and grandchildren. Please help me be a positive model, and may I leave a positive path for them to follow in the sands of time.

Your next devotion is located on page 42.

GRANDCHILD IN FOCUS • PRAYER

Respect for Authority

Dear Lord, I pray that my grandchild will continually grow to respect those in authority. May she learn to be cooperative and fair in work and play. Instill in her a high regard for officials who govern our land and enforce the laws. May her relationships with parents, teachers, coaches, mentors and bosses be respectful, admirable, constructive and caring. Amen.

your descendants as numerous as the stars in the sky and as the sand on the seashore. Your descendants will take possession of the cities of their enemies, [18]and through your offspring[a] all nations on earth will be blessed, because you have obeyed me."

[19]Then Abraham returned to his servants, and they set off together for Beersheba. And Abraham stayed in Beersheba.

GENESIS 22:1–18

God Tests Abraham's Faith

LIFE LESSON: God wants us to trust and obey him, no matter what.

TO TALK ABOUT

- ✦ What did God ask Abraham to do?

- ✦ Why was Abraham willing to obey God's difficult instructions?

- ✦ Do you think Abraham would have obeyed if he hadn't believed God could raise Isaac from the dead (see Hebrews 11:19)?

- ✦ What would it be like to face a test like this from God?

Nahor's Sons

[20]Some time later Abraham was told, "Milcah is also a mother; she has borne sons to your brother Nahor: [21]Uz the firstborn, Buz his brother, Kemuel (the father of Aram), [22]Kesed, Hazo, Pildash, Jidlaph and Bethuel." [23]Bethuel became

the father of Rebekah. Milcah bore these eight sons to Abraham's brother Nahor. [24]His concubine, whose name was Reumah, also had sons: Tebah, Gaham, Tahash and Maacah.

The Death of Sarah

23 Sarah lived to be a hundred and twenty-seven years old. [2]She died at Kiriath Arba (that is, Hebron) in the land of Canaan, and Abraham went to mourn for Sarah and to weep over her.

[3]Then Abraham rose from beside his dead wife and spoke to the Hittites.[b] He said, [4]"I am an alien and a stranger among you. Sell me some property for a burial site here so I can bury my dead."

[5]The Hittites replied to Abraham, [6]"Sir, listen to us. You are a mighty prince among us. Bury your dead in the choicest of our tombs. None of us will refuse you his tomb for burying your dead."

[7]Then Abraham rose and bowed down before the people of the land, the Hittites. [8]He said to them, "If you are willing to let me bury my dead, then listen to me and intercede with Ephron son of Zohar on my behalf [9]so he will sell me the cave of Machpelah, which belongs to him and is at the end of his field. Ask him to sell it to me for the full price as a burial site among you."

[10]Ephron the Hittite was sitting among his people and he replied to Abraham in the hearing of all the Hittites who had come to the gate of his city. [11]"No, my lord," he said. "Listen to me; I give[c] you the field, and I give[c] you the cave that is in it. I give[c] it to you in the presence of my people. Bury your dead."

[12]Again Abraham bowed down before the people of the land [13]and he said to Ephron in their hearing, "Listen to me, if you will. I will pay the price of the field. Accept it from me so I can bury my dead there."

[14]Ephron answered Abraham, [15]"Listen to me, my lord; the land is worth four hundred shekels[d]

[a] 18 Or seed   [b] 3 Or the sons of Heth; also in verses 5, 7, 10, 16, 18 and 20   [c] 11 Or sell   [d] 15 That is, about 10 pounds (about 4.5 kilograms)

of silver, but what is that between me and you? Bury your dead."

¹⁶Abraham agreed to Ephron's terms and weighed out for him the price he had named in the hearing of the Hittites: four hundred shekels of silver, according to the weight current among the merchants.

¹⁷So Ephron's field in Machpelah near Mamre—both the field and the cave in it, and all the trees within the borders of the field—was deeded ¹⁸to Abraham as his property in the presence of all the Hittites who had come to the gate of the city. ¹⁹Afterward Abraham buried his wife Sarah in the cave in the field of Machpelah near Mamre (which is at Hebron) in the land of Canaan. ²⁰So the field and the cave in it were deeded to Abraham by the Hittites as a burial site.

Isaac and Rebekah

24 Abraham was now old and well advanced in years, and the Lord had blessed him in every way. ²He said to the chief ᵃ servant in his household, the one in charge of all that he had, "Put your hand under my thigh. ³I want you to swear by the Lord, the God of heaven and the God of earth, that you will not get a wife for my son from the daughters of the Canaanites, among whom I am living, ⁴but will go to my country and my own relatives and get a wife for my son Isaac."

⁵The servant asked him, "What if the woman is unwilling to come back with me to this land? Shall I then take your son back to the country you came from?"

⁶"Make sure that you do not take my son back there," Abraham said. ⁷"The Lord, the God of heaven, who brought me out of my father's household and my native land and who spoke to me and promised me on oath, saying, 'To your offspring ᵇ I will give this land'—he will send his angel before you so that you can get a wife for my son from there. ⁸If the woman is unwilling to come back with you, then you will be released from this oath of mine. Only do not take my son back there." ⁹So the servant put his hand under the thigh of his master Abraham and swore an oath to him concerning this matter.

¹⁰Then the servant took ten of his master's camels and left, taking with him all kinds of good things from his master. He set out for Aram Naharaim ᶜ and made his way to the town of Nahor. ¹¹He had the camels kneel down near the well outside the town; it was toward evening, the time the women go out to draw water.

¹²Then he prayed, "O Lord, God of my master Abraham, give me success today, and show kindness to my master Abraham. ¹³See, I am standing beside this spring, and the daughters of the townspeople are coming out to draw water. ¹⁴May it be that when I say to a girl, 'Please let down your jar that I may have a drink,' and she says, 'Drink, and I'll water your camels too'—let her be the one you have chosen for your servant Isaac. By this I will know that you have shown kindness to my master."

¹⁵Before he had finished praying, Rebekah came out with her jar on her shoulder. She was the daughter of Bethuel son of Milcah, who was the wife of Abraham's brother Nahor. ¹⁶The girl was very beautiful, a virgin; no man had ever lain with her. She went down to the spring, filled her jar and came up again.

¹⁷The servant hurried to meet her and said, "Please give me a little water from your jar."

¹⁸"Drink, my lord," she said, and quickly lowered the jar to her hands and gave him a drink.

¹⁹After she had given him a drink, she said, "I'll draw water for your camels too, until they have finished drinking." ²⁰So she quickly emptied her jar into the trough, ran back to the well to draw more water, and drew enough for all his camels. ²¹Without saying a word, the man watched her closely to learn whether or not the Lord had made his journey successful.

²²When the camels had finished drinking, the man took out a gold nose ring weighing a beka ᵈ and two gold bracelets weighing ten shekels. ᵉ

ᵃ 2 Or oldest   ᵇ 7 Or seed   ᶜ 10 That is, Northwest Mesopotamia   ᵈ 22 That is, about 1/5 ounce (about 5.5 grams)   ᵉ 22 That is, about 4 ounces (about 110 grams)

²³Then he asked, "Whose daughter are you? Please tell me, is there room in your father's house for us to spend the night?"

²⁴She answered him, "I am the daughter of Bethuel, the son that Milcah bore to Nahor." ²⁵And she added, "We have plenty of straw and fodder, as well as room for you to spend the night."

²⁶Then the man bowed down and worshiped the LORD, ²⁷saying, "Praise be to the LORD, the God of my master Abraham, who has not abandoned his kindness and faithfulness to my master. As for me, the LORD has led me on the journey to the house of my master's relatives."

²⁸The girl ran and told her mother's household about these things. ²⁹Now Rebekah had a brother named Laban, and he hurried out to the man at the spring. ³⁰As soon as he had seen the nose ring, and the bracelets on his sister's arms, and had heard Rebekah tell what the man said to her, he went out to the man and found him standing by the camels near the spring. ³¹"Come, you who are blessed by the LORD," he said. "Why are you standing out here? I have prepared the house and a place for the camels."

³²So the man went to the house, and the camels were unloaded. Straw and fodder were brought for the camels, and water for him and his men to wash their feet. ³³Then food was set before him, but he said, "I will not eat until I have told you what I have to say."

"Then tell us," Laban said.

³⁴So he said, "I am Abraham's servant. ³⁵The LORD has blessed my master abundantly, and he has become wealthy. He has given him sheep and cattle, silver and gold, menservants and maidservants, and camels and donkeys. ³⁶My master's wife Sarah has borne him a son in her[a] old age, and he has given him everything he owns. ³⁷And my master made me swear an oath, and said, 'You must not get a wife for my son from the daughters of the Canaanites, in whose land I live, ³⁸but go to my father's family and to my own clan, and get a wife for my son.'

³⁹"Then I asked my master, 'What if the woman will not come back with me?'

stories to share

GENESIS 24:1–67

Isaac and Rebekah Get Married

LIFE LESSON: God hears our prayers.

TO TALK ABOUT

✦ What did Abraham's servant pray for?

✦ How did Abraham's servant know that Rebekah was the right wife for Isaac?

✦ What do you know about Rebekah just from reading about her behavior toward the servant?

✦ Have you ever done something kind without hoping for any sort of reward?

⁴⁰"He replied, 'The LORD, before whom I have walked, will send his angel with you and make your journey a success, so that you can get a wife for my son from my own clan and from my father's family. ⁴¹Then, when you go to my clan, you will be released from my oath even if they refuse to give her to you—you will be released from my oath.'

⁴²"When I came to the spring today, I said, 'O LORD, God of my master Abraham, if you will, please grant success to the journey on which I have come. ⁴³See, I am standing beside this spring; if a maiden comes out to draw water and I

a 36 Or his

say to her, "Please let me drink a little water from your jar," ⁴⁴and if she says to me, "Drink, and I'll draw water for your camels too," let her be the one the LORD has chosen for my master's son.'

⁴⁵"Before I finished praying in my heart, Rebekah came out, with her jar on her shoulder. She went down to the spring and drew water, and I said to her, 'Please give me a drink.'

⁴⁶"She quickly lowered her jar from her shoulder and said, 'Drink, and I'll water your camels too.' So I drank, and she watered the camels also.

⁴⁷"I asked her, 'Whose daughter are you?'

"She said, 'The daughter of Bethuel son of Nahor, whom Milcah bore to him.'

"Then I put the ring in her nose and the bracelets on her arms, ⁴⁸and I bowed down and worshiped the LORD. I praised the LORD, the God of my master Abraham, who had led me on the right road to get the granddaughter of my master's brother for his son. ⁴⁹Now if you will show kindness and faithfulness to my master, tell me; and if not, tell me, so I may know which way to turn."

⁵⁰Laban and Bethuel answered, "This is from the LORD; we can say nothing to you one way or the other. ⁵¹Here is Rebekah; take her and go, and let her become the wife of your master's son, as the LORD has directed."

⁵²When Abraham's servant heard what they said, he bowed down to the ground before the LORD. ⁵³Then the servant brought out gold and silver jewelry and articles of clothing and gave them to Rebekah; he also gave costly gifts to her brother and to her mother. ⁵⁴Then he and the men who were with him ate and drank and spent the night there.

When they got up the next morning, he said, "Send me on my way to my master."

⁵⁵But her brother and her mother replied, "Let the girl remain with us ten days or so; then you ᵃ may go."

⁵⁶But he said to them, "Do not detain me, now that the LORD has granted success to my journey. Send me on my way so I may go to my master."

⁵⁷Then they said, "Let's call the girl and ask her about it." ⁵⁸So they called Rebekah and asked her, "Will you go with this man?"

"I will go," she said.

⁵⁹So they sent their sister Rebekah on her way, along with her nurse and Abraham's servant and his men. ⁶⁰And they blessed Rebekah and said to her,

"Our sister, may you increase
    to thousands upon thousands;
may your offspring possess
    the gates of their enemies."

⁶¹Then Rebekah and her maids got ready and mounted their camels and went back with the man. So the servant took Rebekah and left.

⁶²Now Isaac had come from Beer Lahai Roi, for he was living in the Negev. ⁶³He went out to the field one evening to meditate,ᵇ and as he looked up, he saw camels approaching. ⁶⁴Rebekah also looked up and saw Isaac. She got down from her camel ⁶⁵and asked the servant, "Who is that man in the field coming to meet us?"

"He is my master," the servant answered. So she took her veil and covered herself.

⁶⁶Then the servant told Isaac all he had done. ⁶⁷Isaac brought her into the tent of his mother Sarah, and he married Rebekah. So she became his wife, and he loved her; and Isaac was comforted after his mother's death.

The Death of Abraham
25:1–4pp — 1Ch 1:32–33

25 Abraham tookᶜ another wife, whose name was Keturah. ²She bore him Zimran, Jokshan, Medan, Midian, Ishbak and Shuah. ³Jokshan was the father of Sheba and Dedan; the descendants of Dedan were the Asshurites, the Letushites and the Leummites. ⁴The sons of Midian were Ephah, Epher, Hanoch, Abida and Eldaah. All these were descendants of Keturah.

⁵Abraham left everything he owned to Isaac. ⁶But while he was still living, he gave gifts to the

---

ᵃ 55 Or she   ᵇ 63 The meaning of the Hebrew for this word is uncertain.   ᶜ 1 Or had taken sons of his concubines and sent them away from his son Isaac to the land of the east.

⁷Altogether, Abraham lived a hundred and seventy-five years. ⁸Then Abraham breathed his last and died at a good old age, an old man and full of years; and he was gathered to his people. ⁹His sons Isaac and Ishmael buried him in the cave of Machpelah near Mamre, in the field of Ephron son of Zohar the Hittite, ¹⁰the field Abraham had bought from the Hittites.ᵃ There Abraham was buried with his wife Sarah. ¹¹After Abraham's death, God blessed his son Isaac, who then lived near Beer Lahai Roi.

Ishmael's Sons

25:12–16pp — 1Ch 1:29–31

¹²This is the account of Abraham's son Ishmael, whom Sarah's maidservant, Hagar the Egyptian, bore to Abraham.

¹³These are the names of the sons of Ishmael, listed in the order of their birth: Nebaioth the firstborn of Ishmael, Kedar, Adbeel, Mibsam, ¹⁴Mishma, Dumah, Massa, ¹⁵Hadad, Tema, Jetur, Naphish and Kedemah. ¹⁶These were the sons of Ishmael, and these are the names of the twelve tribal rulers according to their settlements and camps. ¹⁷Altogether, Ishmael lived a hundred and thirty-seven years. He breathed his last and died, and he was gathered to his people. ¹⁸His descendants settled in the area from Havilah to Shur, near the border of Egypt, as you go toward Asshur. And they lived in hostility towardᵇ all their brothers.

Jacob and Esau

¹⁹This is the account of Abraham's son Isaac.

Abraham became the father of Isaac, ²⁰and Isaac was forty years old when he married Rebekah daughter of Bethuel the Aramean from Paddan Aramᶜ and sister of Laban the Aramean.

²¹Isaac prayed to the LORD on behalf of his wife, because she was barren. The LORD answered his prayer, and his wife Rebekah became pregnant. ²²The babies jostled each other within

her, and she said, "Why is this happening to me?" So she went to inquire of the LORD.

²³The LORD said to her,

"Two nations are in your womb,
    and two peoples from within you will be
        separated;
one people will be stronger than the other,
    and the older will serve the younger."

stories to share

GENESIS 25:19–34

Jacob and Esau

LIFE LESSON: God is pleased when we value what he values.

TO TALK ABOUT

✦ What did Esau like to do? What did Jacob like to do?

✦ Why was Esau so hungry?

✦ God gave Rebekah a riddle before her sons were born (see verse 23). How did it come true?

✦ What does it mean that Esau "despised his birthright" (verse 34)?

²⁴When the time came for her to give birth, there were twin boys in her womb. ²⁵The first to come out was red, and his whole body was like a hairy garment; so they named him Esau.ᵈ ²⁶After this, his brother came out, with his hand grasping

---

ᵃ *10* Or *the sons of Heth*   ᵇ *18* Or *lived to the east of*   ᶜ *20* That is, Northwest Mesopotamia   ᵈ *25 Esau* may mean *hairy*; he was also called Edom, which means *red*.

Esau's heel; so he was named Jacob.[a] Isaac was sixty years old when Rebekah gave birth to them.

²⁷The boys grew up, and Esau became a skillful hunter, a man of the open country, while Jacob was a quiet man, staying among the tents. ²⁸Isaac, who had a taste for wild game, loved Esau, but Rebekah loved Jacob.

²⁹Once when Jacob was cooking some stew, Esau came in from the open country, famished. ³⁰He said to Jacob, "Quick, let me have some of that red stew! I'm famished!" (That is why he was also called Edom.[b])

³¹Jacob replied, "First sell me your birthright."

³²"Look, I am about to die," Esau said. "What good is the birthright to me?"

³³But Jacob said, "Swear to me first." So he swore an oath to him, selling his birthright to Jacob.

³⁴Then Jacob gave Esau some bread and some lentil stew. He ate and drank, and then got up and left.

So Esau despised his birthright.

Isaac and Abimelech

26:1–11Ref — Ge 12:10–20; 20:1–18

26 Now there was a famine in the land — besides the earlier famine of Abraham's time — and Isaac went to Abimelech king of the Philistines in Gerar. ²The LORD appeared to Isaac and said, "Do not go down to Egypt; live in the land where I tell you to live. ³Stay in this land for a while, and I will be with you and will bless you. For to you and your descendants I will give all these lands and will confirm the oath I swore to your father Abraham. ⁴I will make your descendants as numerous as the stars in the sky and will give them all these lands, and through your offspring[c] all nations on earth will be blessed, ⁵because Abraham obeyed me and kept my requirements, my commands, my decrees and my laws."

⁶So Isaac stayed in Gerar.

⁷When the men of that place asked him about his wife, he said, "She is my sister," because he was afraid to say, "She is my wife." He thought,

"The men of this place might kill me on account of Rebekah, because she is beautiful."

⁸When Isaac had been there a long time, Abimelech king of the Philistines looked down from a window and saw Isaac caressing his wife Rebekah. ⁹So Abimelech summoned Isaac and said, "She is really your wife! Why did you say, 'She is my sister'?"

Isaac answered him, "Because I thought I might lose my life on account of her."

¹⁰Then Abimelech said, "What is this you have done to us? One of the men might well have slept with your wife, and you would have brought guilt upon us."

¹¹So Abimelech gave orders to all the people: "Anyone who molests this man or his wife shall surely be put to death."

¹²Isaac planted crops in that land and the same year reaped a hundredfold, because the LORD blessed him. ¹³The man became rich, and his wealth continued to grow until he became very wealthy. ¹⁴He had so many flocks and herds and servants that the Philistines envied him. ¹⁵So all the wells that his father's servants had dug in the time of his father Abraham, the Philistines stopped up, filling them with earth.

¹⁶Then Abimelech said to Isaac, "Move away from us; you have become too powerful for us."

¹⁷So Isaac moved away from there and encamped in the Valley of Gerar and settled there. ¹⁸Isaac reopened the wells that had been dug in the time of his father Abraham, which the Philistines had stopped up after Abraham died, and he gave them the same names his father had given them.

¹⁹Isaac's servants dug in the valley and discovered a well of fresh water there. ²⁰But the herdsmen of Gerar quarreled with Isaac's herdsmen and said, "The water is ours!" So he named the well Esek,[d] because they disputed with him. ²¹Then they dug another well, but they quarreled over that one also; so he named it Sitnah.[e]

---

[a] 26 Jacob means he grasps the heel (figuratively, he deceives).
[b] 30 Edom means red.   [c] 4 Or seed   [d] 20 Esek means dispute.
[e] 21 Sitnah means opposition.

> THAT NIGHT THE LORD APPEARED TO HIM AND SAID, "I AM THE GOD OF YOUR FATHER ABRAHAM. DO NOT BE AFRAID, FOR I AM WITH YOU; I WILL BLESS YOU AND WILL INCREASE THE NUMBER OF YOUR DESCENDANTS FOR THE SAKE OF MY SERVANT ABRAHAM."
>
> *Genesis 26:24*

God Is Not Done Yet

DEBBY KERNER RETTINO

READ | GENESIS 26:1–35

My kids were almost perfect at birth. However, I was shocked the first time they lay prostrate on the ground and pounded their tiny fists, refusing to do what I asked. Surprise! They had minds of their own.

I am not quite as shocked as I watch my grandkids grow up. Their perceptions of the world around them can be very different than mine and their choices are not always the ones I wish they would make. At one point, my daughter had a propensity for dressing gothic style and dyed my grandson's hair green. I didn't know whether to laugh, cry or stomp my foot!

We watch our adult (or becoming adult) kids grow and change, and sometimes it's hard. We long for them to have a close relationship with God, one in which their lives are guided by the Holy Spirit. As our children and grandchildren mature, they sometimes challenge our faith and standards, and it scares us to death!

The reality is that my kids make choices over which I have no control. I realize that is exactly what I am trying to do: take control. I am trying to be God in their lives. I stay up nights, thinking I can change the course of their histories, and anxious thoughts tear up my insides. Failing to see God's perspective, I focus on what's in front of me. I see their lives as chapters in a book, and I am trying to write the ending. But I must not be afraid; the Holy Spirit is faithful to whisper in my ear, "Trust me to do my work in their lives. I'm not done yet." That's right; I agree with the Holy Spirit. God is working to bless me through my children and grandchildren. Their stories are still being written. They are building their testimonies. I must trust in God.

Thank you, Lord, that you are not done with us yet. Help me not to be discouraged by looking at slices of life out of context; instead, help me to know that you have eternal perspective in mind. You are Almighty God, and I trust you. I pray in the powerful name of Jesus.

Your next devotion is located on page 58.

GRANDCHILD IN FOCUS • PRAYER

Courage

O Father, builder of character and courage, may my grandchild grow strong in the light of your love. Grant him courage to stand for what is right, to guard the truth and to ensure justice in every aspect of life. May he boldly grow in grace, revere your name and proudly proclaim you as the Lord of lords and King of kings. Amen.

²²He moved on from there and dug another well, and no one quarreled over it. He named it Rehoboth,ᵃ saying, "Now the Lᴏʀᴅ has given us room and we will flourish in the land,"

²³From there he went up to Beersheba. ²⁴That night the Lᴏʀᴅ appeared to him and said, "I am the God of your father Abraham. Do not be afraid, for I am with you; I will bless you and will increase the number of your descendants for the sake of my servant Abraham."

²⁵Isaac built an altar there and called on the name of the Lᴏʀᴅ. There he pitched his tent, and there his servants dug a well.

²⁶Meanwhile, Abimelech had come to him from Gerar, with Ahuzzath his personal adviser and Phicol the commander of his forces. ²⁷Isaac asked them, "Why have you come to me, since you were hostile to me and sent me away?"

²⁸They answered, "We saw clearly that the Lᴏʀᴅ was with you; so we said, 'There ought to be a sworn agreement between us'—between us and you. Let us make a treaty with you ²⁹that you will do us no harm, just as we did not molest you but always treated you well and sent you away in peace. And now you are blessed by the Lᴏʀᴅ."

³⁰Isaac then made a feast for them, and they ate and drank. ³¹Early the next morning the men swore an oath to each other. Then Isaac sent them on their way, and they left him in peace.

³²That day Isaac's servants came and told him about the well they had dug. They said, "We've found water!" ³³He called it Shibah,ᵇ and to this day the name of the town has been Beersheba.ᶜ

³⁴When Esau was forty years old, he married Judith daughter of Beeri the Hittite, and also Basemath daughter of Elon the Hittite. ³⁵They were a source of grief to Isaac and Rebekah.

Jacob Gets Isaac's Blessing

27 When Isaac was old and his eyes were so weak that he could no longer see, he called for Esau his older son and said to him, "My son."

"Here I am," he answered.

²Isaac said, "I am now an old man and don't know the day of my death. ³Now then, get your weapons—your quiver and bow—and go out to the open country to hunt some wild game for me. ⁴Prepare me the kind of tasty food I like and bring it to me to eat, so that I may give you my blessing before I die."

⁵Now Rebekah was listening as Isaac spoke to his son Esau. When Esau left for the open country to hunt game and bring it back, ⁶Rebekah said to her son Jacob, "Look, I overheard your father say to your brother Esau, ⁷'Bring me some game and prepare me some tasty food to eat, so that I may give you my blessing in the presence of the Lᴏʀᴅ before I die.' ⁸Now, my son, listen carefully and do what I tell you: ⁹Go out to the flock and bring me two choice young goats, so I can prepare some tasty food for your father, just the way he likes it. ¹⁰Then take it to your father to eat, so that he may give you his blessing before he dies."

¹¹Jacob said to Rebekah his mother, "But my brother Esau is a hairy man, and I'm a man with smooth skin. ¹²What if my father touches me? I would appear to be tricking him and would bring down a curse on myself rather than a blessing."

¹³His mother said to him, "My son, let the curse fall on me. Just do what I say; go and get them for me."

¹⁴So he went and got them and brought them to his mother, and she prepared some tasty food, just the way his father liked it. ¹⁵Then Rebekah took the best clothes of Esau her older son, which she had in the house, and put them on her younger son Jacob. ¹⁶She also covered his hands and the smooth part of his neck with the goatskins. ¹⁷Then she handed to her son Jacob the tasty food and the bread she had made.

¹⁸He went to his father and said, "My father."

"Yes, my son," he answered. "Who is it?"

¹⁹Jacob said to his father, "I am Esau your firstborn. I have done as you told me. Please sit up and eat some of my game so that you may give me your blessing."

ᵃ 22 *Rehoboth* means *room.*   ᵇ 33 *Shibah* can mean *oath* or *seven.*
ᶜ 33 *Beersheba* can mean *well of the oath* or *well of seven.*

²⁰Isaac asked his son, "How did you find it so quickly, my son?"

"The LORD your God gave me success," he replied.

²¹Then Isaac said to Jacob, "Come near so I can touch you, my son, to know whether you really are my son Esau or not."

²²Jacob went close to his father Isaac, who touched him and said, "The voice is the voice of Jacob, but the hands are the hands of Esau." ²³He did not recognize him, for his hands were hairy like those of his brother Esau; so he blessed him. ²⁴"Are you really my son Esau?" he asked.

"I am," he replied.

²⁵Then he said, "My son, bring me some of your game to eat, so that I may give you my blessing."

Jacob brought it to him and he ate; and he brought some wine and he drank. ²⁶Then his father Isaac said to him, "Come here, my son, and kiss me."

²⁷So he went to him and kissed him. When Isaac caught the smell of his clothes, he blessed him and said,

"Ah, the smell of my son
    is like the smell of a field
    that the LORD has blessed.
²⁸May God give you of heaven's dew
    and of earth's richness—
    an abundance of grain and new wine.
²⁹May nations serve you
    and peoples bow down to you.
Be lord over your brothers,
    and may the sons of your mother bow
        down to you.
May those who curse you be cursed
    and those who bless you be blessed."

³⁰After Isaac finished blessing him and Jacob had scarcely left his father's presence, his brother Esau came in from hunting. ³¹He too prepared some tasty food and brought it to his father. Then he said to him, "My father, sit up and eat some of my game, so that you may give me your blessing."

³²His father Isaac asked him, "Who are you?"

"I am your son," he answered, "your firstborn, Esau."

³³Isaac trembled violently and said, "Who was it, then, that hunted game and brought it to me? I ate it just before you came and I blessed him—and indeed he will be blessed!"

³⁴When Esau heard his father's words, he burst out with a loud and bitter cry and said to his father, "Bless me—me too, my father!"

³⁵But he said, "Your brother came deceitfully and took your blessing."

stories to share

GENESIS 27:1–40

Jacob Receives Isaac's Blessing

LIFE LESSON: Don't take matters into your own hands.

TO TALK ABOUT

✦ Whom did Isaac want to get the blessing—Jacob or Esau?

✦ How was Rebekah able to make Isaac think that Jacob was Esau?

✦ Why did Rebekah want to trick Isaac, even though God had already told her that Jacob would be more blessed than Esau (see Genesis 25:23)?

✦ What would you do if a grown-up you loved encouraged you to do something wrong?

³⁶Esau said, "Isn't he rightly named Jacob*a*? He has deceived me these two times: He took my birthright, and now he's taken my blessing!" Then he asked, "Haven't you reserved any blessing for me?"

³⁷Isaac answered Esau, "I have made him lord over you and have made all his relatives his servants, and I have sustained him with grain and new wine. So what can I possibly do for you, my son?"

³⁸Esau said to his father, "Do you have only one blessing, my father? Bless me too, my father!" Then Esau wept aloud.

³⁹His father Isaac answered him,

"Your dwelling will be
   away from the earth's richness,
   away from the dew of heaven above.
⁴⁰You will live by the sword
   and you will serve your brother.
But when you grow restless,
   you will throw his yoke
   from off your neck."

Jacob Flees to Laban

⁴¹Esau held a grudge against Jacob because of the blessing his father had given him. He said to himself, "The days of mourning for my father are near; then I will kill my brother Jacob."

⁴²When Rebekah was told what her older son Esau had said, she sent for her younger son Jacob and said to him, "Your brother Esau is consoling himself with the thought of killing you. ⁴³Now then, my son, do what I say: Flee at once to my brother Laban in Haran. ⁴⁴Stay with him for a while until your brother's fury subsides. ⁴⁵When your brother is no longer angry with you and forgets what you did to him, I'll send word for you to come back from there. Why should I lose both of you in one day?"

⁴⁶Then Rebekah said to Isaac, "I'm disgusted with living because of these Hittite women. If Jacob takes a wife from among the women of this land, from Hittite women like these, my life will not be worth living."

28 So Isaac called for Jacob and blessed*b* him and commanded him: "Do not marry a Canaanite woman. ²Go at once to Paddan Aram,*c* to the house of your mother's father Bethuel. Take a wife for yourself there, from among the daughters of Laban, your mother's brother. ³May God Almighty*d* bless you and make you fruitful and increase your numbers until you become a community of peoples. ⁴May he give you and your descendants the blessing given to Abraham, so that you may take possession of the land where you now live as an alien, the land God gave to Abraham." ⁵Then Isaac sent Jacob on his way, and he went to Paddan Aram, to Laban son of Bethuel the Aramean, the brother of Rebekah, who was the mother of Jacob and Esau.

⁶Now Esau learned that Isaac had blessed Jacob and had sent him to Paddan Aram to take a wife from there, and that when he blessed him he commanded him, "Do not marry a Canaanite woman," ⁷and that Jacob had obeyed his father and mother and had gone to Paddan Aram. ⁸Esau then realized how displeasing the Canaanite women were to his father Isaac; ⁹so he went to Ishmael and married Mahalath, the sister of Nebaioth and daughter of Ishmael son of Abraham, in addition to the wives he already had.

Jacob's Dream at Bethel

¹⁰Jacob left Beersheba and set out for Haran. ¹¹When he reached a certain place, he stopped for the night because the sun had set. Taking one of the stones there, he put it under his head and lay down to sleep. ¹²He had a dream in which he saw a stairway*e* resting on the earth, with its top reaching to heaven, and the angels of God were ascending and descending on it. ¹³There above it*f* stood the LORD, and he said: "I am the LORD, the God of your father Abraham and the God of Isaac. I will give you and your descendants the land on which you are lying. ¹⁴Your descendants will be like the dust of the earth, and you will spread out to the

---

a 36 Jacob means he grasps the heel (figuratively, he deceives).
b 1 Or greeted   *c 2* That is, Northwest Mesopotamia; also in verses 5, 6 and 7   *d 3* Hebrew El-Shaddai   *e 12* Or ladder
f 13 Or There beside him

west and to the east, to the north and to the south. All peoples on earth will be blessed through you and your offspring. ¹⁵I am with you and will watch over you wherever you go, and I will bring you back to this land. I will not leave you until I have done what I have promised you."

¹⁶When Jacob awoke from his sleep, he thought, "Surely the LORD is in this place, and I was not aware of it." ¹⁷He was afraid and said, "How awesome is this place! This is none other than the house of God; this is the gate of heaven."

¹⁸Early the next morning Jacob took the stone he had placed under his head and set it up as a pillar and poured oil on top of it. ¹⁹He called that place Bethel,ᵃ though the city used to be called Luz.

GENESIS 28:10–22

Jacob's Dream

LIFE LESSON: God encourages his children.

TO TALK ABOUT

✦ What did Jacob use for a pillow that night?

✦ What did God say to Jacob in his dream?

✦ How would this make Jacob feel, since he was fleeing far from home because of his brother's anger?

✦ Has there ever been a time when you really needed God's encouragement?

Stories to share (side margin)

PRAYING THE SCRIPTURES

Guidance

GENESIS 28:15

O God, be with my grandchild and watch over him wherever he goes. Thank you for working out your promised plan for his life.

Next prayer in Guidance Prayer Track:
Deuteronomy 6:13,18

²⁰Then Jacob made a vow, saying, "If God will be with me and will watch over me on this journey I am taking and will give me food to eat and clothes to wear ²¹so that I return safely to my father's house, then the LORD ᵇ will be my God ²²and ᶜ this stone that I have set up as a pillar will be God's house, and of all that you give me I will give you a tenth."

Jacob Arrives in Paddan Aram

29 Then Jacob continued on his journey and came to the land of the eastern peoples. ²There he saw a well in the field, with three flocks of sheep lying near it because the flocks were watered from that well. The stone over the mouth of the well was large. ³When all the flocks were gathered there, the shepherds would roll the stone away from the well's mouth and water the sheep. Then they would return the stone to its place over the mouth of the well.

⁴Jacob asked the shepherds, "My brothers, where are you from?"

"We're from Haran," they replied.

⁵He said to them, "Do you know Laban, Nahor's grandson?"

"Yes, we know him," they answered.

⁶Then Jacob asked them, "Is he well?"

"Yes, he is," they said, "and here comes his daughter Rachel with the sheep."

ᵃ 19 Bethel means house of God.   ᵇ 20,21 Or Since God . . . father's house, the LORD   ᶜ 21,22 Or house, and the LORD will be my God, ²²then

⁷"Look," he said, "the sun is still high; it is not time for the flocks to be gathered. Water the sheep and take them back to pasture."

⁸"We can't," they replied, "until all the flocks are gathered and the stone has been rolled away from the mouth of the well. Then we will water the sheep."

⁹While he was still talking with them, Rachel came with her father's sheep, for she was a shepherdess. ¹⁰When Jacob saw Rachel daughter of Laban, his mother's brother, and Laban's sheep, he went over and rolled the stone away from the mouth of the well and watered his uncle's sheep. ¹¹Then Jacob kissed Rachel and began to weep aloud. ¹²He had told Rachel that he was a relative of her father and a son of Rebekah. So she ran and told her father.

¹³As soon as Laban heard the news about Jacob, his sister's son, he hurried to meet him. He embraced him and kissed him and brought him to his home, and there Jacob told him all these things. ¹⁴Then Laban said to him, "You are my own flesh and blood."

Jacob Marries Leah and Rachel

After Jacob had stayed with him for a whole month, ¹⁵Laban said to him, "Just because you are a relative of mine, should you work for me for nothing? Tell me what your wages should be."

¹⁶Now Laban had two daughters; the name of the older was Leah, and the name of the younger was Rachel. ¹⁷Leah had weak ᵃ eyes, but Rachel was lovely in form, and beautiful. ¹⁸Jacob was in love with Rachel and said, "I'll work for you seven years in return for your younger daughter Rachel."

¹⁹Laban said, "It's better that I give her to you than to some other man. Stay here with me." ²⁰So Jacob served seven years to get Rachel, but they seemed like only a few days to him because of his love for her.

²¹Then Jacob said to Laban, "Give me my wife. My time is completed, and I want to lie with her."

²²So Laban brought together all the people of the place and gave a feast. ²³But when evening came, he took his daughter Leah and gave her to Jacob, and Jacob lay with her. ²⁴And Laban gave his servant girl Zilpah to his daughter as her maidservant.

²⁵When morning came, there was Leah! So Jacob said to Laban, "What is this you have done to me? I served you for Rachel, didn't I? Why have you deceived me?"

GENESIS 29:1–30

Jacob Is Tricked

LIFE LESSON: God wants us to treat one another with honesty and integrity.

TO TALK ABOUT

✦ How many extra years did Jacob have to work for Laban after he married Rachel?

✦ Why did Laban want Jacob to marry Leah, not Rachel? Why did he trick Jacob?

✦ Do you remember when Jacob tricked someone?

✦ Is honesty important, no matter what the circumstances?

²⁶Laban replied, "It is not our custom here to give the younger daughter in marriage before the older one. ²⁷Finish this daughter's bridal week; then we will give you the younger one also, in return for another seven years of work."

ᵃ 17 Or delicate

stories to share

28 And Jacob did so. He finished the week with Leah, and then Laban gave him his daughter Rachel to be his wife. 29 Laban gave his servant girl Bilhah to his daughter Rachel as her maidservant. 30 Jacob lay with Rachel also, and he loved Rachel more than Leah. And he worked for Laban another seven years.

Jacob's Children

31 When the LORD saw that Leah was not loved, he opened her womb, but Rachel was barren. 32 Leah became pregnant and gave birth to a son. She named him Reuben,[a] for she said, "It is because the LORD has seen my misery. Surely my husband will love me now."

33 She conceived again, and when she gave birth to a son she said, "Because the LORD heard that I am not loved, he gave me this one too." So she named him Simeon.[b]

34 Again she conceived, and when she gave birth to a son she said, "Now at last my husband will become attached to me, because I have borne him three sons." So he was named Levi.[c]

35 She conceived again, and when she gave birth to a son she said, "This time I will praise the LORD." So she named him Judah.[d] Then she stopped having children.

30 When Rachel saw that she was not bearing Jacob any children, she became jealous of her sister. So she said to Jacob, "Give me children, or I'll die!"

2 Jacob became angry with her and said, "Am I in the place of God, who has kept you from having children?"

3 Then she said, "Here is Bilhah, my maidservant. Sleep with her so that she can bear children for me and that through her I too can build a family."

4 So she gave him her servant Bilhah as a wife. Jacob slept with her, 5 and she became pregnant and bore him a son. 6 Then Rachel said, "God has vindicated me; he has listened to my plea and given me a son." Because of this she named him Dan.[e]

7 Rachel's servant Bilhah conceived again and bore Jacob a second son. 8 Then Rachel said, "I have had a great struggle with my sister, and I have won." So she named him Naphtali.[f]

9 When Leah saw that she had stopped having children, she took her maidservant Zilpah and gave her to Jacob as a wife. 10 Leah's servant Zilpah bore Jacob a son. 11 Then Leah said, "What good fortune!"[g] So she named him Gad.[h]

12 Leah's servant Zilpah bore Jacob a second son. 13 Then Leah said, "How happy I am! The women will call me happy." So she named him Asher.[i]

14 During wheat harvest, Reuben went out into the fields and found some mandrake plants, which he brought to his mother Leah. Rachel said to Leah, "Please give me some of your son's mandrakes."

15 But she said to her, "Wasn't it enough that you took away my husband? Will you take my son's mandrakes too?"

"Very well," Rachel said, "he can sleep with you tonight in return for your son's mandrakes."

16 So when Jacob came in from the fields that evening, Leah went out to meet him. "You must sleep with me," she said. "I have hired you with my son's mandrakes." So he slept with her that night.

17 God listened to Leah, and she became pregnant and bore Jacob a fifth son. 18 Then Leah said, "God has rewarded me for giving my maidservant to my husband." So she named him Issachar.[j]

19 Leah conceived again and bore Jacob a sixth son. 20 Then Leah said, "God has presented me with a precious gift. This time my husband will treat me with honor, because I have borne him six sons." So she named him Zebulun.[k]

21 Some time later she gave birth to a daughter and named her Dinah.

---

a 32 Reuben sounds like the Hebrew for he has seen my misery; the name means see, a son.   b 33 Simeon probably means one who hears.   c 34 Levi sounds like and may be derived from the Hebrew for attached.   d 35 Judah sounds like and may be derived from the Hebrew for praise.   e 6 Dan here means he has vindicated.   f 8 Naphtali means my struggle.   g 11 Or "A troop is coming!"   h 11 Gad can mean good fortune or a troop.   i 13 Asher means happy.   j 18 Issachar sounds like the Hebrew for reward.   k 20 Zebulun probably means honor.

²²Then God remembered Rachel; he listened to her and opened her womb. ²³She became pregnant and gave birth to a son and said, "God has taken away my disgrace," ²⁴She named him Joseph,ª and said, "May the LORD add to me another son."

Jacob's Flocks Increase

²⁵After Rachel gave birth to Joseph, Jacob said to Laban, "Send me on my way so I can go back to my own homeland. ²⁶Give me my wives and children, for whom I have served you, and I will be on my way. You know how much work I've done for you."

²⁷But Laban said to him, "If I have found favor in your eyes, please stay. I have learned by divination thatᵇ the LORD has blessed me because of you." ²⁸He added, "Name your wages, and I will pay them."

²⁹Jacob said to him, "You know how I have worked for you and how your livestock has fared under my care. ³⁰The little you had before I came has increased greatly, and the LORD has blessed you wherever I have been. But now, when may I do something for my own household?"

³¹"What shall I give you?" he asked.

"Don't give me anything," Jacob replied. "But if you will do this one thing for me, I will go on tending your flocks and watching over them: ³²Let me go through all your flocks today and remove from them every speckled or spotted sheep, every dark-colored lamb and every spotted or speckled goat. They will be my wages. ³³And my honesty will testify for me in the future, whenever you check on the wages you have paid me. Any goat in my possession that is not speckled or spotted, or any lamb that is not dark-colored, will be considered stolen."

³⁴"Agreed," said Laban. "Let it be as you have said." ³⁵That same day he removed all the male goats that were streaked or spotted, and all the speckled or spotted female goats (all that had white on them) and all the dark-colored lambs, and he placed them in the care of his sons. ³⁶Then he put a three-day journey between himself and Jacob, while Jacob continued to tend the rest of Laban's flocks.

³⁷Jacob, however, took fresh-cut branches from poplar, almond and plane trees and made white stripes on them by peeling the bark and exposing the white inner wood of the branches. ³⁸Then he placed the peeled branches in all the watering troughs, so that they would be directly in front of the flocks when they came to drink. When the flocks were in heat and came to drink, ³⁹they mated in front of the branches. And they bore young that were streaked or speckled or spotted. ⁴⁰Jacob set apart the young of the flock by themselves, but made the rest face the streaked and dark-colored animals that belonged to Laban. Thus he made separate flocks for himself and did not put them with Laban's animals. ⁴¹Whenever the stronger females were in heat, Jacob would place the branches in the troughs in front of the animals so they would mate near the branches, ⁴²but if the animals were weak, he would not place them there. So the weak animals went to Laban and the strong ones to Jacob. ⁴³In this way the man grew exceedingly prosperous and came to own large flocks, and maidservants and menservants, and camels and donkeys.

Jacob Flees From Laban

31 Jacob heard that Laban's sons were saying, "Jacob has taken everything our father owned and has gained all this wealth from what belonged to our father." ²And Jacob noticed that Laban's attitude toward him was not what it had been.

³Then the LORD said to Jacob, "Go back to the land of your fathers and to your relatives, and I will be with you."

⁴So Jacob sent word to Rachel and Leah to come out to the fields where his flocks were. ⁵He said to them, "I see that your father's attitude toward me is not what it was before, but the God of my father has been with me. ⁶You know that I've worked for your father with all my strength,

---

ª 24 *Joseph* means *may he add.*   ᵇ 27 Or possibly *have become rich and*

[7] yet your father has cheated me by changing my wages ten times. However, God has not allowed him to harm me. [8] If he said, 'The speckled ones will be your wages,' then all the flocks gave birth to speckled young; and if he said, 'The streaked ones will be your wages,' then all the flocks bore streaked young. [9] So God has taken away your father's livestock and has given them to me.

[10] "In breeding season I once had a dream in which I looked up and saw that the male goats mating with the flock were streaked, speckled or spotted. [11] The angel of God said to me in the dream, 'Jacob.' I answered, 'Here I am.' [12] And he said, 'Look up and see that all the male goats mating with the flock are streaked, speckled or spotted, for I have seen all that Laban has been doing to you. [13] I am the God of Bethel, where you anointed a pillar and where you made a vow to me. Now leave this land at once and go back to your native land.' "

[14] Then Rachel and Leah replied, "Do we still have any share in the inheritance of our father's estate? [15] Does he not regard us as foreigners? Not only has he sold us, but he has used up what was paid for us. [16] Surely all the wealth that God took away from our father belongs to us and our children. So do whatever God has told you."

[17] Then Jacob put his children and his wives on camels, [18] and he drove all his livestock ahead of him, along with all the goods he had accumulated in Paddan Aram,[a] to go to his father Isaac in the land of Canaan.

[19] When Laban had gone to shear his sheep, Rachel stole her father's household gods. [20] Moreover, Jacob deceived Laban the Aramean by not telling him he was running away. [21] So he fled with all he had, and crossing the River,[b] he headed for the hill country of Gilead.

Laban Pursues Jacob

[22] On the third day Laban was told that Jacob had fled. [23] Taking his relatives with him, he pursued Jacob for seven days and caught up with him in the hill country of Gilead. [24] Then God came to Laban the Aramean in a dream at night and said to him, "Be careful not to say anything to Jacob, either good or bad."

[25] Jacob had pitched his tent in the hill country of Gilead when Laban overtook him, and Laban and his relatives camped there too. [26] Then Laban said to Jacob, "What have you done? You've deceived me, and you've carried off my daughters like captives in war. [27] Why did you run off secretly and deceive me? Why didn't you tell me, so I could send you away with joy and singing to the music of tambourines and harps? [28] You didn't even let me kiss my grandchildren and my daughters good-by. You have done a foolish thing. [29] I have the power to harm you; but last night the God of your father said to me, 'Be careful not to say anything to Jacob, either good or bad.' [30] Now you have gone off because you longed to return to your father's house. But why did you steal my gods?"

[31] Jacob answered Laban, "I was afraid, because I thought you would take your daughters away from me by force. [32] But if you find anyone who has your gods, he shall not live. In the presence of our relatives, see for yourself whether there is anything of yours here with me; and if so, take it." Now Jacob did not know that Rachel had stolen the gods.

[33] So Laban went into Jacob's tent and into Leah's tent and into the tent of the two maidservants, but he found nothing. After he came out of Leah's tent, he entered Rachel's tent. [34] Now Rachel had taken the household gods and put them inside her camel's saddle and was sitting on them. Laban searched through everything in the tent but found nothing.

[35] Rachel said to her father, "Don't be angry, my lord, that I cannot stand up in your presence; I'm having my period." So he searched but could not find the household gods.

[36] Jacob was angry and took Laban to task. "What is my crime?" he asked Laban. "What sin have I committed that you hunt me down? [37] Now that you have searched through all my goods,

---

[a] 18 That is, Northwest Mesopotamia   [b] 21 That is, the Euphrates

what have you found that belongs to your household? Put it here in front of your relatives and mine, and let them judge between the two of us.

³⁸"I have been with you for twenty years now. Your sheep and goats have not miscarried, nor have I eaten rams from your flocks. ³⁹I did not bring you animals torn by wild beasts; I bore the loss myself. And you demanded payment from me for whatever was stolen by day or night. ⁴⁰This was my situation: The heat consumed me in the daytime and the cold at night, and sleep fled from my eyes. ⁴¹It was like this for the twenty years I was in your household. I worked for you fourteen years for your two daughters and six years for your flocks, and you changed my wages ten times. ⁴²If the God of my father, the God of Abraham and the Fear of Isaac, had not been with me, you would surely have sent me away empty-handed. But God has seen my hardship and the toil of my hands, and last night he rebuked you."

⁴³Laban answered Jacob, "The women are my daughters, the children are my children, and the flocks are my flocks. All you see is mine. Yet what can I do today about these daughters of mine, or about the children they have borne? ⁴⁴Come now, let's make a covenant, you and I, and let it serve as a witness between us."

⁴⁵So Jacob took a stone and set it up as a pillar. ⁴⁶He said to his relatives, "Gather some stones." So they took stones and piled them in a heap, and they ate there by the heap. ⁴⁷Laban called it Jegar Sahadutha,ᵃ and Jacob called it Galeed.ᵇ

⁴⁸Laban said, "This heap is a witness between you and me today." That is why it was called Galeed. ⁴⁹It was also called Mizpah,ᶜ because he said, "May the LORD keep watch between you and me when we are away from each other. ⁵⁰If you mistreat my daughters or if you take any wives besides my daughters, even though no one is with us, remember that God is a witness between you and me."

⁵¹Laban also said to Jacob, "Here is this heap, and here is this pillar I have set up between you and me. ⁵²This heap is a witness, and this pillar is a witness, that I will not go past this heap to your side to harm you and that you will not go past this heap and pillar to my side to harm me. ⁵³May the God of Abraham and the God of Nahor, the God of their father, judge between us."

So Jacob took an oath in the name of the Fear of his father Isaac. ⁵⁴He offered a sacrifice there in the hill country and invited his relatives to a meal. After they had eaten, they spent the night there.

⁵⁵Early the next morning Laban kissed his grandchildren and his daughters and blessed them. Then he left and returned home.

Jacob Prepares to Meet Esau

32 Jacob also went on his way, and the angels of God met him. ²When Jacob saw them, he said, "This is the camp of God!" So he named that place Mahanaim.ᵈ

³Jacob sent messengers ahead of him to his brother Esau in the land of Seir, the country of Edom. ⁴He instructed them: "This is what you are to say to my master Esau: 'Your servant Jacob says, I have been staying with Laban and have remained there till now. ⁵I have cattle and donkeys, sheep and goats, menservants and maidservants. Now I am sending this message to my lord, that I may find favor in your eyes.'"

⁶When the messengers returned to Jacob, they said, "We went to your brother Esau, and now he is coming to meet you, and four hundred men are with him."

⁷In great fear and distress Jacob divided the people who were with him into two groups,ᵉ and the flocks and herds and camels as well. ⁸He thought, "If Esau comes and attacks one group,ᶠ the groupᶠ that is left may escape."

⁹Then Jacob prayed, "O God of my father Abraham, God of my father Isaac, O LORD, who said to me, 'Go back to your country and your relatives, and I will make you prosper,' ¹⁰I am unworthy of

---

ᵃ 47 The Aramaic *Jegar Sahadutha* means *witness heap.*
ᵇ 47 The Hebrew *Galeed* means *witness heap.* ᶜ 49 *Mizpah* means *watchtower.* ᵈ 2 *Mahanaim* means *two camps.* ᵉ 7 Or *camps;* also in verse 10 ᶠ 8 Or *camp*

all the kindness and faithfulness you have shown your servant. I had only my staff when I crossed this Jordan, but now I have become two groups. ¹¹ Save me, I pray, from the hand of my brother Esau, for I am afraid he will come and attack me, and also the mothers with their children. ¹² But you have said, 'I will surely make you prosper and will make your descendants like the sand of the sea, which cannot be counted.'"

¹³ He spent the night there, and from what he had with him he selected a gift for his brother Esau: ¹⁴ two hundred female goats and twenty male goats, two hundred ewes and twenty rams, ¹⁵ thirty female camels with their young, forty cows and ten bulls, and twenty female donkeys and ten male donkeys. ¹⁶ He put them in the care of his servants, each herd by itself, and said to his servants, "Go ahead of me, and keep some space between the herds."

¹⁷ He instructed the one in the lead: "When my brother Esau meets you and asks, 'To whom do you belong, and where are you going, and who owns all these animals in front of you?' ¹⁸ then you are to say, 'They belong to your servant Jacob. They are a gift sent to my lord Esau, and he is coming behind us.'"

¹⁹ He also instructed the second, the third and all the others who followed the herds: "You are to say the same thing to Esau when you meet him. ²⁰ And be sure to say, 'Your servant Jacob is coming behind us.'" For he thought, "I will pacify him with these gifts I am sending on ahead; later, when I see him, perhaps he will receive me." ²¹ So Jacob's gifts went on ahead of him, but he himself spent the night in the camp.

Jacob Wrestles With God

²² That night Jacob got up and took his two wives, his two maidservants and his eleven sons and crossed the ford of the Jabbok. ²³ After he had sent them across the stream, he sent over all his possessions. ²⁴ So Jacob was left alone, and a man wrestled with him till daybreak. ²⁵ When the man saw that he could not overpower him, he touched the socket of Jacob's hip so that his hip was wrenched as he wrestled with the man. ²⁶ Then the man said, "Let me go, for it is daybreak."

But Jacob replied, "I will not let you go unless you bless me."

²⁷ The man asked him, "What is your name?"

"Jacob," he answered.

²⁸ Then the man said, "Your name will no longer be Jacob, but Israel,ᵃ because you have struggled with God and with men and have overcome."

²⁹ Jacob said, "Please tell me your name."

But he replied, "Why do you ask my name?" Then he blessed him there.

³⁰ So Jacob called the place Peniel,ᵇ saying, "It is because I saw God face to face, and yet my life was spared."

³¹ The sun rose above him as he passed Peniel,ᶜ and he was limping because of his hip. ³² Therefore to this day the Israelites do not eat the tendon attached to the socket of the hip, because the socket of Jacob's hip was touched near the tendon.

Jacob Meets Esau

33 Jacob looked up and there was Esau, coming with his four hundred men; so he divided the children among Leah, Rachel and the two maidservants. ² He put the maidservants and their children in front, Leah and her children next, and Rachel and Joseph in the rear. ³ He himself went on ahead and bowed down to the ground seven times as he approached his brother.

⁴ But Esau ran to meet Jacob and embraced him; he threw his arms around his neck and kissed him. And they wept. ⁵ Then Esau looked up and saw the women and children. "Who are these with you?" he asked.

Jacob answered, "They are the children God has graciously given your servant."

⁶ Then the maidservants and their children approached and bowed down. ⁷ Next, Leah and her children came and bowed down. Last of all came Joseph and Rachel, and they too bowed down.

ᵃ 28 Israel means he struggles with God.   ᵇ 30 Peniel means face of God.   ᶜ 31 Hebrew Penuel, a variant of Peniel

[8] Esau asked, "What do you mean by all these droves I met?"

"To find favor in your eyes, my lord," he said.

[9] But Esau said, "I already have plenty, my brother. Keep what you have for yourself."

[10] "No, please!" said Jacob. "If I have found favor in your eyes, accept this gift from me. For to see your face is like seeing the face of God, now that you have received me favorably. [11] Please accept the present that was brought to you, for God has been gracious to me and I have all I need." And because Jacob insisted, Esau accepted it.

[12] Then Esau said, "Let us be on our way; I'll accompany you."

[13] But Jacob said to him, "My lord knows that the children are tender and that I must care for the ewes and cows that are nursing their young. If they are driven hard just one day, all the animals will die. [14] So let my lord go on ahead of his servant, while I move along slowly at the pace of the droves before me and that of the children, until I come to my lord in Seir."

[15] Esau said, "Then let me leave some of my men with you."

"But why do that?" Jacob asked. "Just let me find favor in the eyes of my lord."

[16] So that day Esau started on his way back to Seir. [17] Jacob, however, went to Succoth, where he built a place for himself and made shelters for his livestock. That is why the place is called Succoth. [a]

[18] After Jacob came from Paddan Aram, [b] he arrived safely at the [c] city of Shechem in Canaan and camped within sight of the city. [19] For a hundred pieces of silver, [d] he bought from the sons of Hamor, the father of Shechem, the plot of ground where he pitched his tent. [20] There he set up an altar and called it El Elohe Israel. [e]

Dinah and the Shechemites

34 Now Dinah, the daughter Leah had borne to Jacob, went out to visit the women of the land. [2] When Shechem son of Hamor the Hivite, the ruler of that area, saw her, he took her and violated her. [3] His heart was drawn to Dinah daughter of Jacob, and he loved the girl and spoke tenderly to her. [4] And Shechem said to his father Hamor, "Get me this girl as my wife."

[5] When Jacob heard that his daughter Dinah had been defiled, his sons were in the fields with his livestock; so he kept quiet about it until they came home.

[6] Then Shechem's father Hamor went out to talk with Jacob. [7] Now Jacob's sons had come in from the fields as soon as they heard what had happened. They were filled with grief and fury, because Shechem had done a disgraceful thing in [f] Israel by lying with Jacob's daughter — a thing that should not be done.

[8] But Hamor said to them, "My son Shechem has his heart set on your daughter. Please give her to him as his wife. [9] Intermarry with us; give us your daughters and take our daughters for yourselves. [10] You can settle among us; the land is open to you. Live in it, trade [g] in it, and acquire property in it."

[11] Then Shechem said to Dinah's father and brothers, "Let me find favor in your eyes, and I will give you whatever you ask. [12] Make the price for the bride and the gift I am to bring as great as you like, and I'll pay whatever you ask me. Only give me the girl as my wife."

[13] Because their sister Dinah had been defiled, Jacob's sons replied deceitfully as they spoke to Shechem and his father Hamor. [14] They said to them, "We can't do such a thing; we can't give our sister to a man who is not circumcised. That would be a disgrace to us. [15] We will give our consent to you on one condition only: that you become like us by circumcising all your males. [16] Then we will give you our daughters and take your daughters for ourselves. We'll settle among you and become one people with you. [17] But if you will not agree to be circumcised, we'll take our sister [h] and go."

[18] Their proposal seemed good to Hamor and his son Shechem. [19] The young man, who was the

---

[a] 17 *Succoth* means *shelters.*   [b] 18 That is, Northwest Mesopotamia   [c] 18 Or *arrived at Shalem, a*   [d] 19 Hebrew *hundred kesitahs;* a kesitah was a unit of money of unknown weight and value.   [e] 20 *El Elohe Israel* can mean *God, the God of Israel* or *mighty is the God of Israel.*   [f] 7 Or *against*   [g] 10 Or *move about freely;* also in verse 21   [h] 17 Hebrew *daughter*

most honored of all his father's household, lost no time in doing what they said, because he was delighted with Jacob's daughter. ²⁰So Hamor and his son Shechem went to the gate of their city to speak to their fellow townsmen. ²¹"These men are friendly toward us," they said. "Let them live in our land and trade in it; the land has plenty of room for them. We can marry their daughters and they can marry ours. ²²But the men will consent to live with us as one people only on the condition that our males be circumcised, as they themselves are. ²³Won't their livestock, their property and all their other animals become ours? So let us give our consent to them, and they will settle among us."

²⁴All the men who went out of the city gate agreed with Hamor and his son Shechem, and every male in the city was circumcised.

²⁵Three days later, while all of them were still in pain, two of Jacob's sons, Simeon and Levi, Dinah's brothers, took their swords and attacked the unsuspecting city, killing every male. ²⁶They put Hamor and his son Shechem to the sword and took Dinah from Shechem's house and left. ²⁷The sons of Jacob came upon the dead bodies and looted the city where[a] their sister had been defiled. ²⁸They seized their flocks and herds and donkeys and everything else of theirs in the city and out in the fields. ²⁹They carried off all their wealth and all their women and children, taking as plunder everything in the houses.

³⁰Then Jacob said to Simeon and Levi, "You have brought trouble on me by making me a stench to the Canaanites and Perizzites, the people living in this land. We are few in number, and if they join forces against me and attack me, I and my household will be destroyed."

³¹But they replied, "Should he have treated our sister like a prostitute?"

Jacob Returns to Bethel

35 Then God said to Jacob, "Go up to Bethel and settle there, and build an altar there to God, who appeared to you when you were fleeing from your brother Esau."

²So Jacob said to his household and to all who were with him, "Get rid of the foreign gods you have with you, and purify yourselves and change your clothes. ³Then come, let us go up to Bethel, where I will build an altar to God, who answered me in the day of my distress and who has been with me wherever I have gone." ⁴So they gave Jacob all the foreign gods they had and the rings in their ears, and Jacob buried them under the oak at Shechem. ⁵Then they set out, and the terror of God fell upon the towns all around them so that no one pursued them.

⁶Jacob and all the people with him came to Luz (that is, Bethel) in the land of Canaan. ⁷There he built an altar, and he called the place El Bethel,[b] because it was there that God revealed himself to him when he was fleeing from his brother.

⁸Now Deborah, Rebekah's nurse, died and was buried under the oak below Bethel. So it was named Allon Bacuth.[c]

⁹After Jacob returned from Paddan Aram,[d] God appeared to him again and blessed him. ¹⁰God said to him, "Your name is Jacob,[e] but you will no longer be called Jacob; your name will be Israel.[f]" So he named him Israel.

¹¹And God said to him, "I am God Almighty[g]; be fruitful and increase in number. A nation and a community of nations will come from you, and kings will come from your body. ¹²The land I gave to Abraham and Isaac I also give to you, and I will give this land to your descendants after you." ¹³Then God went up from him at the place where he had talked with him.

¹⁴Jacob set up a stone pillar at the place where God had talked with him, and he poured out a drink offering on it; he also poured oil on it. ¹⁵Jacob called the place where God had talked with him Bethel.[h]

The Deaths of Rachel and Isaac
35:23–26pp — 1Ch 2:1–2

¹⁶Then they moved on from Bethel. While they were still some distance from Ephrath, Rachel be-

[a] 27 Or because   [b] 7 El Bethel means God of Bethel.   [c] 8 Allon Bacuth means oak of weeping.   [d] 9 That is, Northwest Mesopotamia; also in verse 26   [e] 10 Jacob means he grasps the heel (figuratively, he deceives).   [f] 10 Israel means he struggles with God.   [g] 11 Hebrew El-Shaddai   [h] 15 Bethel means house of God.

gan to give birth and had great difficulty. ¹⁷And as she was having great difficulty in childbirth, the midwife said to her, "Don't be afraid, for you have another son." ¹⁸As she breathed her last—for she was dying—she named her son Ben-Oni.ᵃ But his father named him Benjamin.ᵇ

¹⁹So Rachel died and was buried on the way to Ephrath (that is, Bethlehem). ²⁰Over her tomb Jacob set up a pillar, and to this day that pillar marks Rachel's tomb.

²¹Israel moved on again and pitched his tent beyond Migdal Eder. ²²While Israel was living in that region, Reuben went in and slept with his father's concubine Bilhah, and Israel heard of it.

Jacob had twelve sons:
²³The sons of Leah:
> Reuben the firstborn of Jacob,
> Simeon, Levi, Judah, Issachar and Zebulun.
²⁴The sons of Rachel:
> Joseph and Benjamin.
²⁵The sons of Rachel's maidservant Bilhah:
> Dan and Naphtali.
²⁶The sons of Leah's maidservant Zilpah:
> Gad and Asher.

These were the sons of Jacob, who were born to him in Paddan Aram.

²⁷Jacob came home to his father Isaac in Mamre, near Kiriath Arba (that is, Hebron), where Abraham and Isaac had stayed. ²⁸Isaac lived a hundred and eighty years. ²⁹Then he breathed his last and died and was gathered to his people, old and full of years. And his sons Esau and Jacob buried him.

Esau's Descendants

36:10–14pp — 1Ch 1:35–37
36:20–28pp — 1Ch 1:38–42

36 This is the account of Esau (that is, Edom).

²Esau took his wives from the women of Canaan: Adah daughter of Elon the Hittite, and Oholibamah daughter of Anah and granddaughter of Zibeon the Hivite— ³also Basemath daughter of Ishmael and sister of Nebaioth.

⁴Adah bore Eliphaz to Esau, Basemath bore Reuel, ⁵and Oholibamah bore Jeush, Jalam and Korah. These were the sons of Esau, who were born to him in Canaan.

⁶Esau took his wives and sons and daughters and all the members of his household, as well as his livestock and all his other animals and all the goods he had acquired in Canaan, and moved to a land some distance from his brother Jacob. ⁷Their possessions were too great for them to remain together; the land where they were staying could not support them both because of their livestock. ⁸So Esau (that is, Edom) settled in the hill country of Seir.

⁹This is the account of Esau the father of the Edomites in the hill country of Seir.

¹⁰These are the names of Esau's sons:
> Eliphaz, the son of Esau's wife Adah, and Reuel, the son of Esau's wife Basemath.
¹¹The sons of Eliphaz:
> Teman, Omar, Zepho, Gatam and Kenaz.
> ¹²Esau's son Eliphaz also had a concubine named Timna, who bore him Amalek. These were grandsons of Esau's wife Adah.
¹³The sons of Reuel:
> Nahath, Zerah, Shammah and Mizzah. These were grandsons of Esau's wife Basemath.
¹⁴The sons of Esau's wife Oholibamah daughter of Anah and granddaughter of Zibeon, whom she bore to Esau:
> Jeush, Jalam and Korah.

¹⁵These were the chiefs among Esau's descendants:

The sons of Eliphaz the firstborn of Esau:
> Chiefs Teman, Omar, Zepho, Kenaz, ¹⁶Korah,ᶜ Gatam and Amalek. These were the

---

ᵃ 18 *Ben-Oni* means *son of my trouble.* ᵇ 18 *Benjamin* means *son of my right hand.* ᶜ 16 Masoretic Text; Samaritan Pentateuch (see also Gen. 36:11 and 1 Chron. 1:36) does not have *Korah.*

chiefs descended from Eliphaz in Edom; they were grandsons of Adah.

17 The sons of Esau's son Reuel:

Chiefs Nahath, Zerah, Shammah and Mizzah. These were the chiefs descended from Reuel in Edom; they were grandsons of Esau's wife Basemath.

18 The sons of Esau's wife Oholibamah:

Chiefs Jeush, Jalam and Korah. These were the chiefs descended from Esau's wife Oholibamah daughter of Anah.

19 These were the sons of Esau (that is, Edom), and these were their chiefs.

20 These were the sons of Seir the Horite, who were living in the region:

Lotan, Shobal, Zibeon, Anah, 21 Dishon, Ezer and Dishan. These sons of Seir in Edom were Horite chiefs.

22 The sons of Lotan:

Hori and Homam.*a* Timna was Lotan's sister.

23 The sons of Shobal:

Alvan, Manahath, Ebal, Shepho and Onam.

24 The sons of Zibeon:

Aiah and Anah. This is the Anah who discovered the hot springs*b* in the desert while he was grazing the donkeys of his father Zibeon.

25 The children of Anah:

Dishon and Oholibamah daughter of Anah.

26 The sons of Dishon*c*:

Hemdan, Eshban, Ithran and Keran.

27 The sons of Ezer:

Bilhan, Zaavan and Akan.

28 The sons of Dishan:

Uz and Aran.

29 These were the Horite chiefs:

Lotan, Shobal, Zibeon, Anah, 30 Dishon, Ezer and Dishan. These were the Horite chiefs, according to their divisions, in the land of Seir.

The Rulers of Edom

36:31–43pp — 1Ch 1:43–54

31 These were the kings who reigned in Edom before any Israelite king reigned*d*:

32 Bela son of Beor became king of Edom. His city was named Dinhabah.

33 When Bela died, Jobab son of Zerah from Bozrah succeeded him as king.

34 When Jobab died, Husham from the land of the Temanites succeeded him as king.

35 When Husham died, Hadad son of Bedad, who defeated Midian in the country of Moab, succeeded him as king. His city was named Avith.

36 When Hadad died, Samlah from Masrekah succeeded him as king.

37 When Samlah died, Shaul from Rehoboth on the river*e* succeeded him as king.

38 When Shaul died, Baal-Hanan son of Acbor succeeded him as king.

39 When Baal-Hanan son of Acbor died, Hadad*f* succeeded him as king. His city was named Pau, and his wife's name was Mehetabel daughter of Matred, the daughter of Me-Zahab.

40 These were the chiefs descended from Esau, by name, according to their clans and regions:

Timna, Alvah, Jetheth, 41 Oholibamah, Elah, Pinon, 42 Kenaz, Teman, Mibzar, 43 Magdiel and Iram. These were the chiefs of Edom, according to their settlements in the land they occupied.

This was Esau the father of the Edomites.

Joseph's Dreams

37 Jacob lived in the land where his father had stayed, the land of Canaan.

2 This is the account of Jacob.

a 22 Hebrew *Hemam,* a variant of *Homam* (see 1 Chron. 1:39)
b 24 Vulgate; Syriac *discovered water;* the meaning of the Hebrew for this word is uncertain.   *c 26* Hebrew *Dishan,* a variant of *Dishon*
d 31 Or *before an Israelite king reigned over them*   *e 37* Possibly the Euphrates   *f 39* Many manuscripts of the Masoretic Text, Samaritan Pentateuch and Syriac (see also 1 Chron. 1:50); most manuscripts of the Masoretic Text *Hadar*

Joseph, a young man of seventeen, was tending the flocks with his brothers, the sons of Bilhah and the sons of Zilpah, his father's wives, and he brought their father a bad report about them.

³Now Israel loved Joseph more than any of his other sons, because he had been born to him in his old age; and he made a richly ornamented[a] robe for him. ⁴When his brothers saw that their father loved him more than any of them, they hated him and could not speak a kind word to him.

⁵Joseph had a dream, and when he told it to his brothers, they hated him all the more. ⁶He said to them, "Listen to this dream I had: ⁷We were binding sheaves of grain out in the field when suddenly my sheaf rose and stood upright, while your sheaves gathered around mine and bowed down to it."

⁸His brothers said to him, "Do you intend to reign over us? Will you actually rule us?" And they hated him all the more because of his dream and what he had said.

⁹Then he had another dream, and he told it to his brothers. "Listen," he said, "I had another dream, and this time the sun and moon and eleven stars were bowing down to me."

¹⁰When he told his father as well as his brothers, his father rebuked him and said, "What is this dream you had? Will your mother and I and your brothers actually come and bow down to the ground before you?" ¹¹His brothers were jealous of him, but his father kept the matter in mind.

Joseph Sold by His Brothers

¹²Now his brothers had gone to graze their father's flocks near Shechem, ¹³and Israel said to Joseph, "As you know, your brothers are grazing the flocks near Shechem. Come, I am going to send you to them."

"Very well," he replied.

¹⁴So he said to him, "Go and see if all is well with your brothers and with the flocks, and bring word back to me." Then he sent him off from the Valley of Hebron.

When Joseph arrived at Shechem, ¹⁵a man found him wandering around in the fields and asked him, "What are you looking for?"

¹⁶He replied, "I'm looking for my brothers. Can you tell me where they are grazing their flocks?"

¹⁷"They have moved on from here," the man answered. "I heard them say, 'Let's go to Dothan.'"

So Joseph went after his brothers and found them near Dothan. ¹⁸But they saw him in the distance, and before he reached them, they plotted to kill him.

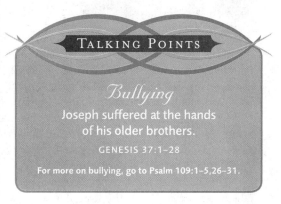

TALKING POINTS

Bullying

Joseph suffered at the hands of his older brothers.

GENESIS 37:1–28

For more on bullying, go to Psalm 109:1–5,26–31.

¹⁹"Here comes that dreamer!" they said to each other. ²⁰"Come now, let's kill him and throw him into one of these cisterns and say that a ferocious animal devoured him. Then we'll see what comes of his dreams."

²¹When Reuben heard this, he tried to rescue him from their hands. "Let's not take his life," he said. ²²"Don't shed any blood. Throw him into this cistern here in the desert, but don't lay a hand on him." Reuben said this to rescue him from them and take him back to his father.

²³So when Joseph came to his brothers, they stripped him of his robe—the richly ornamented robe he was wearing— ²⁴and they took him and threw him into the cistern. Now the cistern was empty; there was no water in it.

²⁵As they sat down to eat their meal, they looked up and saw a caravan of Ishmaelites com-

---

ᵃ 3 The meaning of the Hebrew for *richly ornamented* is uncertain; also in verses 23 and 32.

> NOW ISRAEL [JACOB] LOVED JOSEPH MORE
> THAN ANY OF HIS OTHER SONS, BECAUSE HE
> HAD BEEN BORN TO HIM IN HIS OLD AGE;
> AND HE MADE A RICHLY ORNAMENTED ROBE
> FOR HIM. WHEN HIS BROTHERS SAW THAT
> THEIR FATHER LOVED HIM MORE THAN ANY
> OF THEM, THEY HATED HIM AND COULD
> NOT SPEAK A KIND WORD TO HIM.
>
> *Genesis 37:3–4*

Playing Favorites

GLADYS HUNT

READ | GENESIS 37:1–36

Playing favorites in families always leads to trouble. You can read the story in Genesis 27 of how Rebekah helped Jacob trick his father into believing that he was Esau so that Jacob could get the firstborn's blessing. "I am Esau," he said (Genesis 27:19). This subterfuge led to so much hate that Jacob fled and became an exile in another land. The family's unity was destroyed.

Years later Jacob repeated his parents' mistake. He showed inordinate favoritism to his son Joseph — born to him in his old age by his favorite wife, Rachel — symbolized by the ornamental robe Joseph wore. For that indulgence and others, Joseph's half brothers grew to hate him. They sent Joseph into involuntary exile by selling him as a slave to traveling Midianite merchants. The history of what followed their dastardly deed takes up the remainder of the book of Genesis.

The Old Testament does not provide us with many models for happy family life. Instead it exposes the consequences of jealousy and self-absorption. Cain was jealous of Abel, and killed him (see Genesis 4:8). David's favorite son, whom he failed to discipline, became a sorrow to him (see 2 Samuel 15). It's a familiar story line that continues in families today.

People who "play favorites" usually do so to meet their own needs. Their actions are basically self-centered. (Remember Isaac and his love of the wild game Esau provided.) Favoritism brings no good to the "favored," who suffers resentment and hatred from the "un-favored." "Favorites" learn how to manipulate a situation to their advantage, sometimes with a kind of ruthlessness. Favoritism encourages people to say "I am Esau" when they are Jacob. It produces a no-win situation that often leads to tragedy.

Don't play favorites. Instead, spread God's love and acceptance within your family.

Father, meet my needs with such fullness that I will not be tempted to meet them by playing favorites in my family. Give me a heart overflowing with understanding and love, so that I see my family members as you see them. Amen.

Your next devotion is located on page 70.

GRANDCHILD IN FOCUS · PRAYER

Future Spouse

Dear Lord, if it is your will, I pray my grandchild will be united in a loving and Christian marriage. Keep her sexually pure so that she will honor you with her body and mind. As she seeks a spouse who will honor and care for her, give her patience and discernment. May her choice for a life partner be your choice for her, so that she and her husband will together glorify you in a lasting love. I pray this in Jesus' name, amen.

stories to share

GENESIS 37:1–36

Joseph and His Brothers

LIFE LESSON: Jealousy can ruin relationships.

TO TALK ABOUT

✦ How did Joseph's special coat and his dreams make his brothers feel?

✦ What did Joseph's brothers do because of those feelings?

✦ Have you ever been jealous of someone?

✦ What do you think God wants you to do when you're jealous?

ing from Gilead. Their camels were loaded with spices, balm and myrrh, and they were on their way to take them down to Egypt.

²⁶ Judah said to his brothers, "What will we gain if we kill our brother and cover up his blood? ²⁷ Come, let's sell him to the Ishmaelites and not lay our hands on him; after all, he is our brother, our own flesh and blood." His brothers agreed.

²⁸ So when the Midianite merchants came by, his brothers pulled Joseph up out of the cistern and sold him for twenty shekels *ᵃ* of silver to the Ishmaelites, who took him to Egypt.

²⁹ When Reuben returned to the cistern and saw that Joseph was not there, he tore his clothes. ³⁰ He went back to his brothers and said, "The boy isn't there! Where can I turn now?"

³¹ Then they got Joseph's robe, slaughtered a goat and dipped the robe in the blood. ³² They took the ornamented robe back to their father and said, "We found this. Examine it to see whether it is your son's robe."

³³ He recognized it and said, "It is my son's robe! Some ferocious animal has devoured him. Joseph has surely been torn to pieces."

³⁴ Then Jacob tore his clothes, put on sackcloth and mourned for his son many days. ³⁵ All his sons and daughters came to comfort him, but he refused to be comforted. "No," he said, "in mourning will I go down to the grave *ᵇ* to my son." So his father wept for him.

³⁶ Meanwhile, the Midianites *ᶜ* sold Joseph in Egypt to Potiphar, one of Pharaoh's officials, the captain of the guard.

Judah and Tamar

38 At that time, Judah left his brothers and went down to stay with a man of Adullam named Hirah. ²There Judah met the daughter of a Canaanite man named Shua. He married her and lay with her; ³she became pregnant and gave birth to a son, who was named Er. ⁴She conceived again and gave birth to a son and named him Onan. ⁵She gave birth to still another son and named him Shelah. It was at Kezib that she gave birth to him.

⁶Judah got a wife for Er, his firstborn, and her name was Tamar. ⁷But Er, Judah's firstborn, was wicked in the Lord's sight; so the Lord put him to death.

⁸Then Judah said to Onan, "Lie with your brother's wife and fulfill your duty to her as a brother-in-law to produce offspring for your brother." ⁹But Onan knew that the offspring would not be his; so whenever he lay with his brother's wife, he spilled his semen on the ground to keep from producing offspring for his brother. ¹⁰What he did was wicked in the Lord's sight; so he put him to death also.

ᵃ 28 That is, about 8 ounces (about 0.2 kilogram)   *ᵇ 35* Hebrew *Sheol*   *ᶜ 36* Samaritan Pentateuch, Septuagint, Vulgate and Syriac (see also verse 28); Masoretic Text *Medanites*

DONNA HUISJEN

Access Denied:
A SEVERED CONNECTION WITH GRANDCHILDREN

Life has gotten more complicated, and so has being a grandmother. When I was a child, families were stable. The family package was rather simple: one set of parents, two sets of grandparents; everyone stayed in touch. Difficult relationships were evidenced only when families got together on holidays.

Things are different now. Families are more complex: parents divorce and remarry (sometimes more than once); there are stepchildren and half brothers and sisters; there are multiple sets of grandparents. There are custody battles and restraining orders, complex visitation schedules and estrangements in relationships. After a divorce, a once close relationship with a grandchild or with grandchildren can be destroyed, leaving the grandparents and grandchildren victims of the situation.

At such times, the grandchildren are hurt and confused by the shuffling of households and guardians. If one parent chooses to refuse access to a grandparent, then the children may feel abandoned. And to make matters worse, in many states grandparents have no legal right to information about their grandchildren, and there are few options besides court battles.

I May Never See or Hear From My Grandchildren Again

I've "lost" two grandchildren in this manner several times. Each time my grieving process has been full-blown, my ordinarily optimistic outlook shattered by the possibility that I may never see or hear from my grandchildren again. In my situation, my daughter gave up custody of her children to her ex-husband, who now has full custody of my grandchildren. He only sporadically allows me to have contact with them.

Periodically, my former son-in-law and the children have returned from their out-of-state wandering, but with each return, the children are older, more cynical, more wary, less inclined toward unreserved confidence in their grandmother.

God's Strength Allows Me to Love Them

In whatever the situation, God's strength allows me to love them, care for them, pray for them, accept the phone calls when they come, gladly receive any bit of news or information, and welcome my grandchildren with open arms when they are allowed to visit.

One summer, during a rare visit, my grandson made a proposition: He wanted to live with me. His four-year-old brother, less articulate but fully as desirous of finalizing an arrangement while he could, pleaded simply, "Grandma, please keep me!" I have no idea what message my empathetic but negative response gave them; I can only hope that they were secure enough in my love to know how badly I wanted them. The email came the following day: their father thought it best, once again, to cut off all contact. And so another round of grief slammed in anew—for myself, for the children's aunts and uncle, and most poignantly, for the children themselves.

Months later I was back in full communication with the family, and the children seemed fine. The oldest was settling into kindergarten, while the younger was pining for the beginning of life beyond the confines of home the next year. All's well . . . for now.

No One Will Take Away Your Joy

Jacob was consumed by grief when he "lost" his beloved son Joseph (see Genesis 37:34–35). After many years of separation and not knowing what had truly become of Joseph, Jacob saw him again (see Genesis 45:25–28; 46:28–30)—an absolutely unexpected blessing for this bereaved and disillusioned old man.

When we suffer the loss of contact with our grandchildren—whether through divorce or separation or because our grandchildren live far from us—Jesus reminds us that sorrow for the believer is never a permanent state: "Now is your time of grief, but I will see you again and you will rejoice, and no one will take away your joy" (John 16:22). In the meantime, we can thank the Lord for our grandchildren and pray for their salvation and continuing welfare.

¹¹Judah then said to his daughter-in-law Tamar, "Live as a widow in your father's house until my son Shelah grows up." For he thought, "He may die too, just like his brothers." So Tamar went to live in her father's house.

¹²After a long time Judah's wife, the daughter of Shua, died. When Judah had recovered from his grief, he went up to Timnah, to the men who were shearing his sheep, and his friend Hirah the Adullamite went with him.

¹³When Tamar was told, "Your father-in-law is on his way to Timnah to shear his sheep," ¹⁴she took off her widow's clothes, covered herself with a veil to disguise herself, and then sat down at the entrance to Enaim, which is on the road to Timnah. For she saw that, though Shelah had now grown up, she had not been given to him as his wife.

¹⁵When Judah saw her, he thought she was a prostitute, for she had covered her face. ¹⁶Not realizing that she was his daughter-in-law, he went over to her by the roadside and said, "Come now, let me sleep with you."

"And what will you give me to sleep with you?" she asked.

¹⁷"I'll send you a young goat from my flock," he said.

"Will you give me something as a pledge until you send it?" she asked.

¹⁸He said, "What pledge should I give you?"

"Your seal and its cord, and the staff in your hand," she answered. So he gave them to her and slept with her, and she became pregnant by him. ¹⁹After she left, she took off her veil and put on her widow's clothes again.

²⁰Meanwhile Judah sent the young goat by his friend the Adullamite in order to get his pledge back from the woman, but he did not find her. ²¹He asked the men who lived there, "Where is the shrine prostitute who was beside the road at Enaim?"

"There hasn't been any shrine prostitute here," they said.

²²So he went back to Judah and said, "I didn't find her. Besides, the men who lived there said, 'There hasn't been any shrine prostitute here.'"

²³Then Judah said, "Let her keep what she has, or we will become a laughingstock. After all, I did send her this young goat, but you didn't find her."

²⁴About three months later Judah was told, "Your daughter-in-law Tamar is guilty of prostitution, and as a result she is now pregnant."

Judah said, "Bring her out and have her burned to death!"

²⁵As she was being brought out, she sent a message to her father-in-law. "I am pregnant by the man who owns these," she said. And she added, "See if you recognize whose seal and cord and staff these are."

²⁶Judah recognized them and said, "She is more righteous than I, since I wouldn't give her to my son Shelah." And he did not sleep with her again.

²⁷When the time came for her to give birth, there were twin boys in her womb. ²⁸As she was giving birth, one of them put out his hand; so the midwife took a scarlet thread and tied it on his wrist and said, "This one came out first." ²⁹But when he drew back his hand, his brother came out, and she said, "So this is how you have broken out!" And he was named Perez. ᵃ ³⁰Then his brother, who had the scarlet thread on his wrist, came out and he was given the name Zerah. ᵇ

Joseph and Potiphar's Wife

39 Now Joseph had been taken down to Egypt. Potiphar, an Egyptian who was one of Pharaoh's officials, the captain of the guard, bought him from the Ishmaelites who had taken him there.

²The Lord was with Joseph and he prospered, and he lived in the house of his Egyptian master. ³When his master saw that the Lord was with him and that the Lord gave him success in everything he did, ⁴Joseph found favor in his eyes and became his attendant. Potiphar put him in charge of his household, and he entrusted to his care everything he owned. ⁵From the time he put

---

ᵃ 29 Perez means breaking out.   ᵇ 30 Zerah can mean scarlet or brightness.

him in charge of his household and of all that he owned, the LORD blessed the household of the Egyptian because of Joseph. The blessing of the LORD was on everything Potiphar had, both in the house and in the field. ⁶So he left in Joseph's care everything he had; with Joseph in charge, he did not concern himself with anything except the food he ate.

Now Joseph was well-built and handsome, ⁷and after a while his master's wife took notice of Joseph and said, "Come to bed with me!"

⁸But he refused. "With me in charge," he told her, "my master does not concern himself with anything in the house; everything he owns he has entrusted to my care. ⁹No one is greater in this house than I am. My master has withheld nothing from me except you, because you are his wife. How then could I do such a wicked thing and sin against God?" ¹⁰And though she spoke to Joseph day after day, he refused to go to bed with her or even be with her.

¹¹One day he went into the house to attend to his duties, and none of the household servants was inside. ¹²She caught him by his cloak and said, "Come to bed with me!" But he left his cloak in her hand and ran out of the house.

¹³When she saw that he had left his cloak in her hand and had run out of the house, ¹⁴she called her household servants. "Look," she said to them, "this Hebrew has been brought to us to make sport of us! He came in here to sleep with me, but I screamed. ¹⁵When he heard me scream for help, he left his cloak beside me and ran out of the house."

¹⁶She kept his cloak beside her until his master came home. ¹⁷Then she told him this story: "That Hebrew slave you brought us came to me to make sport of me. ¹⁸But as soon as I screamed for help, he left his cloak beside me and ran out of the house."

¹⁹When his master heard the story his wife told him, saying, "This is how your slave treated me," he burned with anger. ²⁰Joseph's master took him and put him in prison, the place where the king's prisoners were confined.

But while Joseph was there in the prison, ²¹the LORD was with him; he showed him kindness and granted him favor in the eyes of the prison warden. ²²So the warden put Joseph in charge of all those held in the prison, and he was made responsible for all that was done there. ²³The warden paid no attention to anything under Joseph's care, because the LORD was with Joseph and gave him success in whatever he did.

The Cupbearer and the Baker

40 Some time later, the cupbearer and the baker of the king of Egypt offended their master, the king of Egypt. ²Pharaoh was angry with his two officials, the chief cupbearer and the chief baker, ³and put them in custody in the house of the captain of the guard, in the same prison where Joseph was confined. ⁴The captain of the guard assigned them to Joseph, and he attended them.

After they had been in custody for some time, ⁵each of the two men—the cupbearer and the baker of the king of Egypt, who were being held in prison—had a dream the same night, and each dream had a meaning of its own.

⁶When Joseph came to them the next morning, he saw that they were dejected. ⁷So he asked Pharaoh's officials who were in custody with him in his master's house, "Why are your faces so sad today?"

⁸"We both had dreams," they answered, "but there is no one to interpret them."

Then Joseph said to them, "Do not interpretations belong to God? Tell me your dreams."

⁹So the chief cupbearer told Joseph his dream. He said to him, "In my dream I saw a vine in front of me, ¹⁰and on the vine were three branches. As soon as it budded, it blossomed, and its clusters ripened into grapes. ¹¹Pharaoh's cup was in my hand, and I took the grapes, squeezed them into Pharaoh's cup and put the cup in his hand."

¹²"This is what it means," Joseph said to him. "The three branches are three days. ¹³Within three days Pharaoh will lift up your head and restore you to your position, and you will put Pharaoh's

cup in his hand, just as you used to do when you were his cupbearer. ¹⁴But when all goes well with you, remember me and show me kindness; mention me to Pharaoh and get me out of this prison. ¹⁵For I was forcibly carried off from the land of the Hebrews, and even here I have done nothing to deserve being put in a dungeon."

¹⁶When the chief baker saw that Joseph had given a favorable interpretation, he said to Joseph, "I too had a dream: On my head were three baskets of bread.ᵃ ¹⁷In the top basket were all kinds of baked goods for Pharaoh, but the birds were eating them out of the basket on my head."

¹⁸"This is what it means," Joseph said. "The three baskets are three days. ¹⁹Within three days Pharaoh will lift off your head and hang you on a tree.ᵇ And the birds will eat away your flesh."

²⁰Now the third day was Pharaoh's birthday, and he gave a feast for all his officials. He lifted up the heads of the chief cupbearer and the chief baker in the presence of his officials: ²¹He restored the chief cupbearer to his position, so that he once again put the cup into Pharaoh's hand, ²²but he hangedᶜ the chief baker, just as Joseph had said to them in his interpretation.

²³The chief cupbearer, however, did not remember Joseph; he forgot him.

Pharaoh's Dreams

41 When two full years had passed, Pharaoh had a dream: He was standing by the Nile, ²when out of the river there came up seven cows, sleek and fat, and they grazed among the reeds. ³After them, seven other cows, ugly and gaunt, came up out of the Nile and stood beside those on the riverbank. ⁴And the cows that were ugly and gaunt ate up the seven sleek, fat cows. Then Pharaoh woke up.

⁵He fell asleep again and had a second dream: Seven heads of grain, healthy and good, were growing on a single stalk. ⁶After them, seven other heads of grain sprouted—thin and scorched by the east wind. ⁷The thin heads of grain swallowed up the seven healthy, full heads. Then Pharaoh woke up; it had been a dream.

⁸In the morning his mind was troubled, so he sent for all the magicians and wise men of Egypt. Pharaoh told them his dreams, but no one could interpret them for him.

⁹Then the chief cupbearer said to Pharaoh, "Today I am reminded of my shortcomings. ¹⁰Pharaoh was once angry with his servants, and he imprisoned me and the chief baker in the house of the captain of the guard. ¹¹Each of us had a dream the same night, and each dream had a meaning of its own. ¹²Now a young Hebrew was there with us, a servant of the captain of the guard. We told him our dreams, and he interpreted them for us, giving each man the interpretation of his dream. ¹³And things turned out exactly as he interpreted them to us: I was restored to my position, and the other man was hanged.ᶜ"

¹⁴So Pharaoh sent for Joseph, and he was quickly brought from the dungeon. When he had shaved and changed his clothes, he came before Pharaoh.

¹⁵Pharaoh said to Joseph, "I had a dream, and no one can interpret it. But I have heard it said of you that when you hear a dream you can interpret it."

¹⁶"I cannot do it," Joseph replied to Pharaoh, "but God will give Pharaoh the answer he desires."

¹⁷Then Pharaoh said to Joseph, "In my dream I was standing on the bank of the Nile, ¹⁸when out of the river there came up seven cows, fat and sleek, and they grazed among the reeds. ¹⁹After them, seven other cows came up—scrawny and very ugly and lean. I had never seen such ugly cows in all the land of Egypt. ²⁰The lean, ugly cows ate up the seven fat cows that came up first. ²¹But even after they ate them, no one could tell that they had done so; they looked just as ugly as before. Then I woke up.

²²"In my dreams I also saw seven heads of grain, full and good, growing on a single stalk. ²³After them, seven other heads sprouted—withered and thin and scorched by the east wind.

ᵃ 16 Or *three wicker baskets*   ᵇ 19 Or *and impale you on a pole*
ᶜ 22,13 Or *impaled*

24 The thin heads of grain swallowed up the seven good heads. I told this to the magicians, but none could explain it to me."

25 Then Joseph said to Pharaoh, "The dreams of Pharaoh are one and the same. God has revealed to Pharaoh what he is about to do. 26 The seven good cows are seven years, and the seven good heads of grain are seven years; it is one and the same dream. 27 The seven lean, ugly cows that came up afterward are seven years, and so are the seven worthless heads of grain scorched by the east wind: They are seven years of famine.

28 "It is just as I said to Pharaoh: God has shown Pharaoh what he is about to do. 29 Seven years of great abundance are coming throughout the land of Egypt, 30 but seven years of famine will follow them. Then all the abundance in Egypt will be forgotten, and the famine will ravage the land. 31 The abundance in the land will not be remembered, because the famine that follows it will be so severe. 32 The reason the dream was given to Pharaoh in two forms is that the matter has been firmly decided by God, and God will do it soon.

33 "And now let Pharaoh look for a discerning and wise man and put him in charge of the land of Egypt. 34 Let Pharaoh appoint commissioners over the land to take a fifth of the harvest of Egypt during the seven years of abundance. 35 They should collect all the food of these good years that are coming and store up the grain under the authority of Pharaoh, to be kept in the cities for food. 36 This food should be held in reserve for the country, to be used during the seven years of famine that will come upon Egypt, so that the country may not be ruined by the famine."

37 The plan seemed good to Pharaoh and to all his officials. 38 So Pharaoh asked them, "Can we find anyone like this man, one in whom is the spirit of God *a* ?"

39 Then Pharaoh said to Joseph, "Since God has made all this known to you, there is no one so discerning and wise as you. 40 You shall be in charge of my palace, and all my people are to submit to your orders. Only with respect to the throne will I be greater than you."

stories to share

GENESIS 41:1–40

Pharaoh's Dreams

LIFE LESSON: God can bring good out of evil.

TO TALK ABOUT

✦ What did Pharaoh dream?

✦ How did Joseph know what Pharaoh's dreams meant?

✦ How did God make good come out of evil in Joseph's life?

✦ Were the brothers still wrong for what they did to Joseph? Why or why not?

Joseph in Charge of Egypt

41 So Pharaoh said to Joseph, "I hereby put you in charge of the whole land of Egypt." 42 Then Pharaoh took his signet ring from his finger and put it on Joseph's finger. He dressed him in robes of fine linen and put a gold chain around his neck. 43 He had him ride in a chariot as his second-in-command, *b* and men shouted before him, "Make way *c* !" Thus he put him in charge of the whole land of Egypt.

44 Then Pharaoh said to Joseph, "I am Pharaoh, but without your word no one will lift hand or foot in all Egypt." 45 Pharaoh gave Joseph the name Zaphenath-Paneah and gave him Asenath daughter of Potiphera, priest of On, *d* to be his

a 38 Or of the gods   *b 43 Or in the chariot of his second-in-command; or in his second chariot*   *c 43 Or Bow down*
d 45 That is, Heliopolis; also in verse 50

wife. And Joseph went throughout the land of Egypt.

⁴⁶Joseph was thirty years old when he entered the service of Pharaoh king of Egypt. And Joseph went out from Pharaoh's presence and traveled throughout Egypt. ⁴⁷During the seven years of abundance the land produced plentifully. ⁴⁸Joseph collected all the food produced in those seven years of abundance in Egypt and stored it in the cities. In each city he put the food grown in the fields surrounding it. ⁴⁹Joseph stored up huge quantities of grain, like the sand of the sea; it was so much that he stopped keeping records because it was beyond measure.

⁵⁰Before the years of famine came, two sons were born to Joseph by Asenath daughter of Potiphera, priest of On. ⁵¹Joseph named his firstborn Manasseh ᵃ and said, "It is because God has made me forget all my trouble and all my father's household." ⁵²The second son he named Ephraim ᵇ and said, "It is because God has made me fruitful in the land of my suffering."

⁵³The seven years of abundance in Egypt came to an end, ⁵⁴and the seven years of famine began, just as Joseph had said. There was famine in all the other lands, but in the whole land of Egypt there was food. ⁵⁵When all Egypt began to feel the famine, the people cried to Pharaoh for food. Then Pharaoh told all the Egyptians, "Go to Joseph and do what he tells you."

⁵⁶When the famine had spread over the whole country, Joseph opened the storehouses and sold grain to the Egyptians, for the famine was severe throughout Egypt. ⁵⁷And all the countries came to Egypt to buy grain from Joseph, because the famine was severe in all the world.

Joseph's Brothers Go to Egypt

42 When Jacob learned that there was grain in Egypt, he said to his sons, "Why do you just keep looking at each other?" ²He continued, "I have heard that there is grain in Egypt. Go down there and buy some for us, so that we may live and not die."

³Then ten of Joseph's brothers went down to buy grain from Egypt. ⁴But Jacob did not send Benjamin, Joseph's brother, with the others, because he was afraid that harm might come to him. ⁵So Israel's sons were among those who went to buy grain, for the famine was in the land of Canaan also.

⁶Now Joseph was the governor of the land, the one who sold grain to all its people. So when Joseph's brothers arrived, they bowed down to him with their faces to the ground. ⁷As soon as Joseph saw his brothers, he recognized them, but he pretended to be a stranger and spoke harshly to them. "Where do you come from?" he asked.

"From the land of Canaan," they replied, "to buy food."

⁸Although Joseph recognized his brothers, they did not recognize him. ⁹Then he remembered his dreams about them and said to them, "You are spies! You have come to see where our land is unprotected."

¹⁰"No, my lord," they answered. "Your servants have come to buy food. ¹¹We are all the sons of one man. Your servants are honest men, not spies."

¹²"No!" he said to them. "You have come to see where our land is unprotected."

¹³But they replied, "Your servants were twelve brothers, the sons of one man, who lives in the land of Canaan. The youngest is now with our father, and one is no more."

¹⁴Joseph said to them, "It is just as I told you: You are spies! ¹⁵And this is how you will be tested: As surely as Pharaoh lives, you will not leave this place unless your youngest brother comes here. ¹⁶Send one of your number to get your brother; the rest of you will be kept in prison, so that your words may be tested to see if you are telling the truth. If you are not, then as surely as Pharaoh lives, you are spies!" ¹⁷And he put them all in custody for three days.

¹⁸On the third day, Joseph said to them, "Do this and you will live, for I fear God: ¹⁹If you are honest men, let one of your brothers stay here in

---

ᵃ 51 *Manasseh* sounds like and may be derived from the Hebrew for *forget.* ᵇ 52 *Ephraim* sounds like the Hebrew for *twice fruitful.*

prison, while the rest of you go and take grain back for your starving households. ²⁰But you must bring your youngest brother to me, so that your words may be verified and that you may not die." This they proceeded to do.

GENESIS 42:1–20; 43:1–2,15–17,24–34; 45:1–11

Joseph's Brothers Go to Egypt

LIFE LESSON: God is in control of everything that happens.

TO TALK ABOUT

✦ Why did Joseph's brothers go to Egypt?

✦ What special part did Benjamin, Joseph's only full brother, play in this story?

✦ Why do you think Joseph waited so long to make himself known to his brothers?

✦ What did Joseph mean when he told his brothers, "It was not you who sent me here, but God" (Genesis 45:8)?

²¹They said to one another, "Surely we are being punished because of our brother. We saw how distressed he was when he pleaded with us for his life, but we would not listen; that's why this distress has come upon us."

²²Reuben replied, "Didn't I tell you not to sin

against the boy? But you wouldn't listen! Now we must give an accounting for his blood." ²³They did not realize that Joseph could understand them, since he was using an interpreter.

²⁴He turned away from them and began to weep, but then turned back and spoke to them again. He had Simeon taken from them and bound before their eyes.

²⁵Joseph gave orders to fill their bags with grain, to put each man's silver back in his sack, and to give them provisions for their journey. After this was done for them, ²⁶they loaded their grain on their donkeys and left.

²⁷At the place where they stopped for the night one of them opened his sack to get feed for his donkey, and he saw his silver in the mouth of his sack. ²⁸"My silver has been returned," he said to his brothers. "Here it is in my sack."

Their hearts sank and they turned to each other trembling and said, "What is this that God has done to us?"

²⁹When they came to their father Jacob in the land of Canaan, they told him all that had happened to them. They said, ³⁰"The man who is lord over the land spoke harshly to us and treated us as though we were spying on the land. ³¹But we said to him, 'We are honest men; we are not spies. ³²We were twelve brothers, sons of one father. One is no more, and the youngest is now with our father in Canaan.'

³³"Then the man who is lord over the land said to us, 'This is how I will know whether you are honest men: Leave one of your brothers here with me, and take food for your starving households and go. ³⁴But bring your youngest brother to me so I will know that you are not spies but honest men. Then I will give your brother back to you, and you can trade*ᵃ* in the land.'"

³⁵As they were emptying their sacks, there in each man's sack was his pouch of silver! When they and their father saw the money pouches, they were frightened. ³⁶Their father Jacob said to them, "You have deprived me of my children. Joseph is no more and Simeon is no more, and

---

ᵃ 34 Or move about freely

now you want to take Benjamin. Everything is against me!"

37 Then Reuben said to his father, "You may put both of my sons to death if I do not bring him back to you. Entrust him to my care, and I will bring him back."

38 But Jacob said, "My son will not go down there with you; his brother is dead and he is the only one left. If harm comes to him on the journey you are taking, you will bring my gray head down to the grave[a] in sorrow."

The Second Journey to Egypt

43 Now the famine was still severe in the land. 2 So when they had eaten all the grain they had brought from Egypt, their father said to them, "Go back and buy us a little more food."

3 But Judah said to him, "The man warned us solemnly, 'You will not see my face again unless your brother is with you.' 4 If you will send our brother along with us, we will go down and buy food for you. 5 But if you will not send him, we will not go down, because the man said to us, 'You will not see my face again unless your brother is with you.'"

6 Israel asked, "Why did you bring this trouble on me by telling the man you had another brother?"

7 They replied, "The man questioned us closely about ourselves and our family. 'Is your father still living?' he asked us. 'Do you have another brother?' We simply answered his questions. How were we to know he would say, 'Bring your brother down here'?"

8 Then Judah said to Israel his father, "Send the boy along with me and we will go at once, so that we and you and our children may live and not die. 9 I myself will guarantee his safety; you can hold me personally responsible for him. If I do not bring him back to you and set him here before you, I will bear the blame before you all my life. 10 As it is, if we had not delayed, we could have gone and returned twice."

11 Then their father Israel said to them, "If it must be, then do this: Put some of the best products of the land in your bags and take them down to the man as a gift — a little balm and a little honey, some spices and myrrh, some pistachio nuts and almonds. 12 Take double the amount of silver with you, for you must return the silver that was put back into the mouths of your sacks. Perhaps it was a mistake. 13 Take your brother also and go back to the man at once. 14 And may God Almighty[b] grant you mercy before the man so that he will let your other brother and Benjamin come back with you. As for me, if I am bereaved, I am bereaved."

15 So the men took the gifts and double the amount of silver, and Benjamin also. They hurried down to Egypt and presented themselves to Joseph. 16 When Joseph saw Benjamin with them, he said to the steward of his house, "Take these men to my house, slaughter an animal and prepare dinner; they are to eat with me at noon."

17 The man did as Joseph told him and took the men to Joseph's house. 18 Now the men were frightened when they were taken to his house. They thought, "We were brought here because of the silver that was put back into our sacks the first time. He wants to attack us and overpower us and seize us as slaves and take our donkeys."

19 So they went up to Joseph's steward and spoke to him at the entrance to the house. 20 "Please, sir," they said, "we came down here the first time to buy food. 21 But at the place where we stopped for the night we opened our sacks and each of us found his silver — the exact weight — in the mouth of his sack. So we have brought it back with us. 22 We have also brought additional silver with us to buy food. We don't know who put our silver in our sacks."

23 "It's all right," he said. "Don't be afraid. Your God, the God of your father, has given you treasure in your sacks; I received your silver." Then he brought Simeon out to them.

24 The steward took the men into Joseph's house, gave them water to wash their feet and provided fodder for their donkeys. 25 They prepared

a 38 Hebrew Sheol   b 14 Hebrew El-Shaddai

their gifts for Joseph's arrival at noon, because they had heard that they were to eat there.

²⁶ When Joseph came home, they presented to him the gifts they had brought into the house, and they bowed down before him to the ground. ²⁷ He asked them how they were, and then he said, "How is your aged father you told me about? Is he still living?"

²⁸ They replied, "Your servant our father is still alive and well." And they bowed low to pay him honor.

²⁹ As he looked about and saw his brother Benjamin, his own mother's son, he asked, "Is this your youngest brother, the one you told me about?" And he said, "God be gracious to you, my son." ³⁰ Deeply moved at the sight of his brother, Joseph hurried out and looked for a place to weep. He went into his private room and wept there.

³¹ After he had washed his face, he came out and, controlling himself, said, "Serve the food."

³² They served him by himself, the brothers by themselves, and the Egyptians who ate with him by themselves, because Egyptians could not eat with Hebrews, for that is detestable to Egyptians. ³³ The men had been seated before him in the order of their ages, from the firstborn to the youngest; and they looked at each other in astonishment. ³⁴ When portions were served to them from Joseph's table, Benjamin's portion was five times as much as anyone else's. So they feasted and drank freely with him.

A Silver Cup in a Sack

44 Now Joseph gave these instructions to the steward of his house: "Fill the men's sacks with as much food as they can carry, and put each man's silver in the mouth of his sack. ² Then put my cup, the silver one, in the mouth of the youngest one's sack, along with the silver for his grain." And he did as Joseph said.

³ As morning dawned, the men were sent on their way with their donkeys. ⁴ They had not gone far from the city when Joseph said to his steward, "Go after those men at once, and when you catch up with them, say to them, 'Why have you repaid good with evil? ⁵ Isn't this the cup my master drinks from and also uses for divination? This is a wicked thing you have done.'"

⁶ When he caught up with them, he repeated these words to them. ⁷ But they said to him, "Why does my lord say such things? Far be it from your servants to do anything like that! ⁸ We even brought back to you from the land of Canaan the silver we found inside the mouths of our sacks. So why would we steal silver or gold from your master's house? ⁹ If any of your servants is found to have it, he will die; and the rest of us will become my lord's slaves."

¹⁰ "Very well, then," he said, "let it be as you say. Whoever is found to have it will become my slave; the rest of you will be free from blame."

¹¹ Each of them quickly lowered his sack to the ground and opened it. ¹² Then the steward proceeded to search, beginning with the oldest and ending with the youngest. And the cup was found in Benjamin's sack. ¹³ At this, they tore their clothes. Then they all loaded their donkeys and returned to the city.

¹⁴ Joseph was still in the house when Judah and his brothers came in, and they threw themselves to the ground before him. ¹⁵ Joseph said to them, "What is this you have done? Don't you know that a man like me can find things out by divination?"

¹⁶ "What can we say to my lord?" Judah replied. "What can we say? How can we prove our innocence? God has uncovered your servants' guilt. We are now my lord's slaves—we ourselves and the one who was found to have the cup."

¹⁷ But Joseph said, "Far be it from me to do such a thing! Only the man who was found to have the cup will become my slave. The rest of you, go back to your father in peace."

¹⁸ Then Judah went up to him and said: "Please, my lord, let your servant speak a word to my lord. Do not be angry with your servant, though you are equal to Pharaoh himself. ¹⁹ My lord asked his servants, 'Do you have a father or a brother?' ²⁰ And we answered, 'We have an aged father, and

> "WHAT CAN WE SAY TO MY LORD?"
> JUDAH REPLIED. "WHAT CAN WE SAY?
> HOW CAN WE PROVE OUR INNOCENCE?
> GOD HAS UNCOVERED YOUR SERVANTS'
> GUILT. WE ARE NOW MY LORD'S
> SLAVES — WE OURSELVES AND THE ONE
> WHO WAS FOUND TO HAVE THE CUP."
>
> *Genesis 44:16*

A Heavy Load

RUTH A. DeJAGER

READ | GENESIS 44:1 – 34

Guilt can tear a family apart, as it did in Jacob's family. The load of guilt on the backs of Joseph's brothers likely felt as heavy as the sacks of grain they had set out to lug to Canaan and as hot as the "stolen" silver cup that rested in the mouth of Benjamin's sack. How they must have squirmed with anxiety as they traveled back to the city. The buckets of tears shed by their father Jacob over the years probably made their guilt seem even heavier, even as those same tears softened their hearts toward their father and their "dead" brother (see Genesis 44:20,30 – 31).

But their years-old guilt was not to stay hidden forever. With a twist of timely irony, God prodded them toward recognizing their culpability. Brought face-to-face with Joseph once again, Judah had no choice but to spill out the history of their family's dysfunction and their father's grief. In a sweep of grace, Joseph made himself known, and the brothers were forgiven and restored (see Genesis 45).

Guilt buried is guilt carried. If you or your family is weighed down by guilt, what can you do to clear it away? You might ask God for the courage to become a facilitator for bringing past wrongs out into the open; then wait for his wisdom and timing. Or you could take the lead in asking for forgiveness for any part you may have had in the conflict, and then encourage your loved ones to forgive and ask for forgiveness in kind. Be assured — God can turn guilt into gladness for your family, as he did for Jacob's.

God of grace and mercy, be with my family as we seek peace and forgiveness with one another. Help us to forgive as you forgave us. In the name of Jesus, amen.

Your next devotion is located on page 73.

GRANDCHILD IN FOCUS • PRAYER

School/Career

Dear God, may learning be a joy rather than a chore for my grandchild. May exploration of new ideas bring a sense of wonder, awe and excitement. Grant him clarity of mind, the ability to concentrate on the task at hand and recollection of what has been learned. Help him to appreciate the tasks that come easily and to persevere through those that challenge. Amen.

there is a young son born to him in his old age. His brother is dead, and he is the only one of his mother's sons left, and his father loves him.'

²¹"Then you said to your servants, 'Bring him down to me so I can see him for myself.' ²²And we said to my lord, 'The boy cannot leave his father; if he leaves him, his father will die.' ²³But you told your servants, 'Unless your youngest brother comes down with you, you will not see my face again.' ²⁴When we went back to your servant my father, we told him what my lord had said.

²⁵"Then our father said, 'Go back and buy a little more food.' ²⁶But we said, 'We cannot go down. Only if our youngest brother is with us will we go. We cannot see the man's face unless our youngest brother is with us.'

²⁷"Your servant my father said to us, 'You know that my wife bore me two sons. ²⁸One of them went away from me, and I said, "He has surely been torn to pieces." And I have not seen him since. ²⁹If you take this one from me too and harm comes to him, you will bring my gray head down to the grave[a] in misery.'

³⁰"So now, if the boy is not with us when I go back to your servant my father and if my father, whose life is closely bound up with the boy's life, ³¹sees that the boy isn't there, he will die. Your servants will bring the gray head of our father down to the grave in sorrow. ³²Your servant guaranteed the boy's safety to my father. I said, 'If I do not bring him back to you, I will bear the blame before you, my father, all my life!'

³³"Now then, please let your servant remain here as my lord's slave in place of the boy, and let the boy return with his brothers. ³⁴How can I go back to my father if the boy is not with me? No! Do not let me see the misery that would come upon my father."

Joseph Makes Himself Known

45 Then Joseph could no longer control himself before all his attendants, and he cried out, "Have everyone leave my presence!" So there was no one with Joseph when he made himself known to his brothers. ²And he wept so loudly that the Egyptians heard him, and Pharaoh's household heard about it.

³Joseph said to his brothers, "I am Joseph! Is my father still living?" But his brothers were not able to answer him, because they were terrified at his presence.

⁴Then Joseph said to his brothers, "Come close to me." When they had done so, he said, "I am your brother Joseph, the one you sold into Egypt! ⁵And now, do not be distressed and do not be angry with yourselves for selling me here, because it was to save lives that God sent me ahead of you. ⁶For two years now there has been famine in the land, and for the next five years there will not be plowing and reaping. ⁷But God sent me ahead of you to preserve for you a remnant on earth and to save your lives by a great deliverance.[b]

⁸"So then, it was not you who sent me here, but God. He made me father to Pharaoh, lord of his entire household and ruler of all Egypt. ⁹Now hurry back to my father and say to him, 'This is what your son Joseph says: God has made me lord of all Egypt. Come down to me; don't delay. ¹⁰You shall live in the region of Goshen and be near me—you, your children and grandchildren, your flocks and herds, and all you have. ¹¹I will provide for you there, because five years of famine are still to come. Otherwise you and your household and all who belong to you will become destitute.'

¹²"You can see for yourselves, and so can my brother Benjamin, that it is really I who am speaking to you. ¹³Tell my father about all the honor accorded me in Egypt and about everything you have seen. And bring my father down here quickly."

¹⁴Then he threw his arms around his brother Benjamin and wept, and Benjamin embraced him, weeping. ¹⁵And he kissed all his brothers and wept over them. Afterward his brothers talked with him.

¹⁶When the news reached Pharaoh's palace

---

[a] 29 Hebrew *Sheol*; also in verse 31   [b] 7 Or *save you as a great band of survivors*

that Joseph's brothers had come, Pharaoh and all his officials were pleased. [17]Pharaoh said to Joseph, "Tell your brothers, 'Do this: Load your animals and return to the land of Canaan, [18]and bring your father and your families back to me. I will give you the best of the land of Egypt and you can enjoy the fat of the land.'

[19]"You are also directed to tell them, 'Do this: Take some carts from Egypt for your children and your wives, and get your father and come. [20]Never mind about your belongings, because the best of all Egypt will be yours.'"

[21]So the sons of Israel did this. Joseph gave them carts, as Pharaoh had commanded, and he also gave them provisions for their journey. [22]To each of them he gave new clothing, but to Benjamin he gave three hundred shekels[a] of silver and five sets of clothes. [23]And this is what he sent to his father: ten donkeys loaded with the best things of Egypt, and ten female donkeys loaded with grain and bread and other provisions for his journey. [24]Then he sent his brothers away, and as they were leaving he said to them, "Don't quarrel on the way!"

[25]So they went up out of Egypt and came to their father Jacob in the land of Canaan. [26]They told him, "Joseph is still alive! In fact, he is ruler of all Egypt." Jacob was stunned; he did not believe them. [27]But when they told him everything Joseph had said to them, and when he saw the carts Joseph had sent to carry him back, the spirit of their father Jacob revived. [28]And Israel said, "I'm convinced! My son Joseph is still alive. I will go and see him before I die."

Jacob Goes to Egypt

46 So Israel set out with all that was his, and when he reached Beersheba, he offered sacrifices to the God of his father Isaac.

[2]And God spoke to Israel in a vision at night and said, "Jacob! Jacob!"

"Here I am," he replied.

[3]"I am God, the God of your father," he said. "Do not be afraid to go down to Egypt, for I will make you into a great nation there. [4]I will go down to Egypt with you, and I will surely bring you back again. And Joseph's own hand will close your eyes."

[5]Then Jacob left Beersheba, and Israel's sons took their father Jacob and their children and their wives in the carts that Pharaoh had sent to transport him. [6]They also took with them their livestock and the possessions they had acquired in Canaan, and Jacob and all his offspring went to Egypt. [7]He took with him to Egypt his sons and grandsons and his daughters and granddaughters—all his offspring.

[8]These are the names of the sons of Israel (Jacob and his descendants) who went to Egypt:

Reuben the firstborn of Jacob.
[9]The sons of Reuben:
Hanoch, Pallu, Hezron and Carmi.
[10]The sons of Simeon:
Jemuel, Jamin, Ohad, Jakin, Zohar and Shaul the son of a Canaanite woman.
[11]The sons of Levi:
Gershon, Kohath and Merari.
[12]The sons of Judah:
Er, Onan, Shelah, Perez and Zerah (but Er and Onan had died in the land of Canaan).
The sons of Perez:
Hezron and Hamul.
[13]The sons of Issachar:
Tola, Puah,[b] Jashub[c] and Shimron.
[14]The sons of Zebulun:
Sered, Elon and Jahleel.
[15]These were the sons Leah bore to Jacob in Paddan Aram,[d] besides his daughter Dinah. These sons and daughters of his were thirty-three in all.

[16]The sons of Gad:
Zephon,[e] Haggi, Shuni, Ezbon, Eri, Arodi and Areli.

[a] 22 That is, about 7 1/2 pounds (about 3.5 kilograms)
[b] 13 Samaritan Pentateuch and Syriac (see also 1 Chron. 7:1); Masoretic Text *Puvah*   [c] 13 Samaritan Pentateuch and some Septuagint manuscripts (see also Num. 26:24 and 1 Chron. 7:1); Masoretic Text *Iob*   [d] 15 That is, Northwest Mesopotamia
[e] 16 Samaritan Pentateuch and Septuagint (see also Num. 26:15); Masoretic Text *Ziphion*

Slumber Party

There's something about a sleepover that inspires — and energizes — kids. So go ahead and plan an overnight visit for one or more of your grandchildren. If Grandpa's around, invite him to join the fun.

Create a space indoors or out for a campout, complete with s'mores and sleeping bags. Or let the kids have the guest room or line up their sleeping bags on your bedroom floor. Be flexible; they may have some other sleeping arrangement they prefer.

If you all enjoy thrills and chills, rent a scary movie and hug during the tense parts. If nostalgia's your thing, leaf through albums or explore memorabilia. If you're competitive, challenge each other to a game tournament.

Older-Grandkids Variation: An invitation to stay overnight with plenty of time to talk (and lots of food) may be all that's needed for teens. They'll love the attention.

Long-Distance Variation: Plan a similar experience during your next visit to see your grandchildren. If you're staying in a hotel, invite them over for the night. If you're staying at their house, offer to handle everything and let their parents get away overnight.

Thank you, Lord, for the opportunity to have time with my grandchildren to laugh and to make memories together. Help us to appreciate one another and to deeply love each other. Amen.

Your next devotion is located on page 74.

GRANDCHILD IN FOCUS • PRAYER

Character

Dear Lord and Father, I ask that you fill my grandchild with your Spirit so her character reflects your goodness and love. Give her kindness and love for others. Bring joy to her life so she will be a joy to others. Grant her patience and self-control through difficult and trying times. May she show mercy and generosity to those who are less fortunate. Grant her integrity and a sense of justice, and surround her with your peace. Amen.

Worship the Lord

The LORD is my strength and my song;
    he has become my salvation.
He is my God, and I will praise him,
    my father's God, and I will exalt him.
The LORD is a warrior;
    the LORD is his name.
Pharaoh's chariots and his army
    he has hurled into the sea.
The best of Pharaoh's officers
    are drowned in the Red Sea.
The deep waters have covered them;
    they sank to the depths like a stone.

Who among the gods is like you, O LORD?
    Who is like you—
        majestic in holiness,
        awesome in glory,
        working wonders?

Exodus 15:2—5,11

Lord, you are my God and I praise you. I pray that you will be the God of my children and grandchildren—and their children after them. I pray that you will pour your blessings upon them and be their strength and their song. To you be all honor and glory. Amen.

Your next devotion is located on page 77.

GRANDCHILD IN FOCUS • PRAYER

Talents

Dear Lord, the giver of gifts, bless my grandchild as he develops his talents. Help him identify his talents and be proud and confident of the gifts you have given him. Give him patience and understanding, Lord, so he will not grow weary of striving and searching to reach the goals you have set for him. May each milestone bring satisfaction and a healthy desire for greater achievement and success to bring glory to you. Amen.

¹⁷The sons of Asher:

Imnah, Ishvah, Ishvi and Beriah.

Their sister was Serah.

The sons of Beriah:

Heber and Malkiel.

¹⁸These were the children born to Jacob by Zilpah, whom Laban had given to his daughter Leah — sixteen in all.

¹⁹The sons of Jacob's wife Rachel:

Joseph and Benjamin. ²⁰In Egypt, Manasseh and Ephraim were born to Joseph by Asenath daughter of Potiphera, priest of On.ᵃ

²¹The sons of Benjamin:

Bela, Beker, Ashbel, Gera, Naaman, Ehi, Rosh, Muppim, Huppim and Ard.

²²These were the sons of Rachel who were born to Jacob — fourteen in all.

²³The son of Dan:

Hushim.

²⁴The sons of Naphtali:

Jahziel, Guni, Jezer and Shillem.

²⁵These were the sons born to Jacob by Bilhah, whom Laban had given to his daughter Rachel — seven in all.

²⁶All those who went to Egypt with Jacob — those who were his direct descendants, not counting his sons' wives — numbered sixty-six persons. ²⁷With the two sonsᵇ who had been born to Joseph in Egypt, the members of Jacob's family, which went to Egypt, were seventyᶜ in all.

²⁸Now Jacob sent Judah ahead of him to Joseph to get directions to Goshen. When they arrived in the region of Goshen, ²⁹Joseph had his chariot made ready and went to Goshen to meet his father Israel. As soon as Joseph appeared before him, he threw his arms around his fatherᵈ and wept for a long time.

³⁰Israel said to Joseph, "Now I am ready to die, since I have seen for myself that you are still alive."

³¹Then Joseph said to his brothers and to his father's household, "I will go up and speak to Pharaoh and will say to him, 'My brothers and my father's household, who were living in the land of Canaan, have come to me. ³²The men are shepherds; they tend livestock, and they have brought along their flocks and herds and everything they own.' ³³When Pharaoh calls you in and asks, 'What is your occupation?' ³⁴you should answer, 'Your servants have tended livestock from our boyhood on, just as our fathers did.' Then you will be allowed to settle in the region of Goshen, for all shepherds are detestable to the Egyptians."

47 Joseph went and told Pharaoh, "My father and brothers, with their flocks and herds and everything they own, have come from the land of Canaan and are now in Goshen." ²He chose five of his brothers and presented them before Pharaoh.

³Pharaoh asked the brothers, "What is your occupation?"

"Your servants are shepherds," they replied to Pharaoh, "just as our fathers were." ⁴They also said to him, "We have come to live here awhile, because the famine is severe in Canaan and your servants' flocks have no pasture. So now, please let your servants settle in Goshen."

⁵Pharaoh said to Joseph, "Your father and your brothers have come to you, ⁶and the land of Egypt is before you; settle your father and your brothers in the best part of the land. Let them live in Goshen. And if you know of any among them with special ability, put them in charge of my own livestock."

⁷Then Joseph brought his father Jacob in and presented him before Pharaoh. After Jacob blessedᵉ Pharaoh, ⁸Pharaoh asked him, "How old are you?"

⁹And Jacob said to Pharaoh, "The years of my pilgrimage are a hundred and thirty. My years have been few and difficult, and they do not equal the years of the pilgrimage of my fathers." ¹⁰Then Jacob blessedᶠ Pharaoh and went out from his presence.

ᵃ 20 That is, Heliopolis   ᵇ 27 Hebrew; Septuagint the nine children   ᶜ 27 Hebrew (see also Exodus 1:5 and footnote); Septuagint (see also Acts 7:14) seventy-five   ᵈ 29 Hebrew around him   ᵉ 7 Or greeted   ᶠ 10 Or said farewell to

¹¹So Joseph settled his father and his brothers in Egypt and gave them property in the best part of the land, the district of Rameses, as Pharaoh directed. ¹²Joseph also provided his father and his brothers and all his father's household with food, according to the number of their children.

Joseph and the Famine

¹³There was no food, however, in the whole region because the famine was severe; both Egypt and Canaan wasted away because of the famine. ¹⁴Joseph collected all the money that was to be found in Egypt and Canaan in payment for the grain they were buying, and he brought it to Pharaoh's palace. ¹⁵When the money of the people of Egypt and Canaan was gone, all Egypt came to Joseph and said, "Give us food. Why should we die before your eyes? Our money is used up."

¹⁶"Then bring your livestock," said Joseph. "I will sell you food in exchange for your livestock, since your money is gone." ¹⁷So they brought their livestock to Joseph, and he gave them food in exchange for their horses, their sheep and goats, their cattle and donkeys. And he brought them through that year with food in exchange for all their livestock.

¹⁸When that year was over, they came to him the following year and said, "We cannot hide from our lord the fact that since our money is gone and our livestock belongs to you, there is nothing left for our lord except our bodies and our land. ¹⁹Why should we perish before your eyes—we and our land as well? Buy us and our land in exchange for food, and we with our land will be in bondage to Pharaoh. Give us seed so that we may live and not die, and that the land may not become desolate."

²⁰So Joseph bought all the land in Egypt for Pharaoh. The Egyptians, one and all, sold their fields, because the famine was too severe for them. The land became Pharaoh's, ²¹and Joseph reduced the people to servitude,ᵃ from one end of Egypt to the other. ²²However, he did not buy the land of the priests, because they received a regular allotment from Pharaoh and had food enough from the allotment Pharaoh gave them. That is why they did not sell their land.

²³Joseph said to the people, "Now that I have bought you and your land today for Pharaoh, here is seed for you so you can plant the ground. ²⁴But when the crop comes in, give a fifth of it to Pharaoh. The other four-fifths you may keep as seed for the fields and as food for yourselves and your households and your children."

²⁵"You have saved our lives," they said. "May we find favor in the eyes of our lord; we will be in bondage to Pharaoh."

²⁶So Joseph established it as a law concerning land in Egypt—still in force today—that a fifth of the produce belongs to Pharaoh. It was only the land of the priests that did not become Pharaoh's.

²⁷Now the Israelites settled in Egypt in the region of Goshen. They acquired property there and were fruitful and increased greatly in number.

²⁸Jacob lived in Egypt seventeen years, and the years of his life were a hundred and forty-seven. ²⁹When the time drew near for Israel to die, he called for his son Joseph and said to him, "If I have found favor in your eyes, put your hand under my thigh and promise that you will show me kindness and faithfulness. Do not bury me in Egypt, ³⁰but when I rest with my fathers, carry me out of Egypt and bury me where they are buried."

"I will do as you say," he said.

³¹"Swear to me," he said. Then Joseph swore to him, and Israel worshiped as he leaned on the top of his staff.ᵇ

Manasseh and Ephraim

48 Some time later Joseph was told, "Your father is ill." So he took his two sons Manasseh and Ephraim along with him. ²When Jacob was told, "Your son Joseph has come to you," Israel rallied his strength and sat up on the bed.

³Jacob said to Joseph, "God Almightyᶜ ap-

ᵃ 21 Samaritan Pentateuch and Septuagint (see also Vulgate); Masoretic Text *and he moved the people into the cities*   ᵇ 31 Or *Israel bowed down at the head of his bed*   ᶜ 3 Hebrew *El-Shaddai*

> ISRAEL SAID TO JOSEPH, "I NEVER EXPECTED TO SEE YOUR FACE AGAIN, AND NOW GOD HAS ALLOWED ME TO SEE YOUR CHILDREN TOO."
>
> *Genesis 48:11*

"I Really Miss the Children"

JAN SILVIOUS

READ | GENESIS 48:1 – 22

My friend Carolyn and I raised our children together. Recently, we reminisced as we drove together on a short trip. We laughed about the things our boys had done together and mused over the steely will of her daughter, who carved out her place as the boss among three brothers. Having enjoyed our memories, we both fell silent as we rode in the sunlight. Suddenly, she turned to me and poignantly said, "I really do miss the children." That thought touched a tender place deep within me as I thought, "I really miss the children too." Our grown children are alive and well, living close by, but they are all adults now, people with their own families, jobs and lives. They are not children anymore, and we miss the children they were.

That is why the gift of grandchildren is so amazing. When Israel (Jacob) and his son Joseph finally had an emotional reunion after so many years of separation, he stated, "Now I am ready to die" (Genesis 46:30). But there remained the additional gift of seeing his grandchildren.

Grandchildren have a way of taking us back to the wonder of having children in the house. Everything that was good about having little ones is suddenly reawakened when that first grandchild is born. Suddenly, a love you never dreamed you could feel for another human being overwhelms you.

When you have grandchildren, everything changes. You take on a new persona. You are given a fresh start. You receive another chance to do it better. The longing you feel for the children who have grown up and left your arms is filled with a little baby who doesn't even know who you are. That's the wonder of being a grandparent. You'll always "miss the children," but somehow when he gives you "grands," God makes it all okay.

Father, may I never take the gift of grandchildren for granted. I pray that I will always think to remind them that you love them and that I adore the fact that you made them my grandchildren. Thank you, Lord, for this blessing. Amen.

Your next devotion is located on page 79.

GRANDCHILD IN FOCUS • PRAYER

SELECT ONE OF YOUR GRANDCHILDREN TO FOCUS ON IN PRAYER FOR THE NEXT 14 DAYS.

Salvation

Dear Lord, please guide my grandchild to your gift of salvation. I pray that she will come to know you, to love you and to walk close to you throughout her life. May she boldly claim Jesus as her Lord and Savior. Guide her as she makes choices that have eternal consequences. Help her to follow you each moment of her life. I pray this in Jesus' name, amen.

peared to me at Luz in the land of Canaan, and there he blessed me [4]and said to me, 'I am going to make you fruitful and will increase your numbers. I will make you a community of peoples, and I will give this land as an everlasting possession to your descendants after you.'

[5]"Now then, your two sons born to you in Egypt before I came to you here will be reckoned as mine; Ephraim and Manasseh will be mine, just as Reuben and Simeon are mine. [6]Any children born to you after them will be yours; in the territory they inherit they will be reckoned under the names of their brothers. [7]As I was returning from Paddan,[a] to my sorrow Rachel died in the land of Canaan while we were still on the way, a little distance from Ephrath. So I buried her there beside the road to Ephrath" (that is, Bethlehem).

[8]When Israel saw the sons of Joseph, he asked, "Who are these?"

[9]"They are the sons God has given me here," Joseph said to his father.

Then Israel said, "Bring them to me so I may bless them."

[10]Now Israel's eyes were failing because of old age, and he could hardly see. So Joseph brought his sons close to him, and his father kissed them and embraced them.

[11]Israel said to Joseph, "I never expected to see your face again, and now God has allowed me to see your children too."

[12]Then Joseph removed them from Israel's knees and bowed down with his face to the ground. [13]And Joseph took both of them, Ephraim on his right toward Israel's left hand and Manasseh on his left toward Israel's right hand, and brought them close to him. [14]But Israel reached out his right hand and put it on Ephraim's head, though he was the younger, and crossing his arms, he put his left hand on Manasseh's head, even though Manasseh was the firstborn.

[15]Then he blessed Joseph and said,

"May the God before whom my fathers
    Abraham and Isaac walked,

the God who has been my shepherd
    all my life to this day,
[16]the Angel who has delivered me from all harm
    —may he bless these boys.
May they be called by my name
    and the names of my fathers Abraham and
        Isaac,
and may they increase greatly
    upon the earth."

[17]When Joseph saw his father placing his right hand on Ephraim's head he was displeased; so he took hold of his father's hand to move it from Ephraim's head to Manasseh's head. [18]Joseph said to him, "No, my father, this one is the firstborn; put your right hand on his head."

[19]But his father refused and said, "I know, my son, I know. He too will become a people, and he too will become great. Nevertheless, his younger brother will be greater than he, and his descendants will become a group of nations." [20]He blessed them that day and said,

"In your[b] name will Israel pronounce this
        blessing:
    'May God make you like Ephraim and
        Manasseh.'"

So he put Ephraim ahead of Manasseh.

[21]Then Israel said to Joseph, "I am about to die, but God will be with you[c] and take you[c] back to the land of your[c] fathers. [22]And to you, as one who is over your brothers, I give the ridge of land[d] I took from the Amorites with my sword and my bow."

Jacob Blesses His Sons
49:1–28Ref — Dt 33:1–29

49 Then Jacob called for his sons and said: "Gather around so I can tell you what will happen to you in days to come.

[2]"Assemble and listen, sons of Jacob;
    listen to your father Israel.

---

[a] 7 That is, Northwest Mesopotamia   [b] 20 The Hebrew is singular.   [c] 21 The Hebrew is plural.   [d] 22 Or *And to you I give one portion more than to your brothers—the portion*

"ASSEMBLE AND LISTEN, SONS
OF JACOB; LISTEN TO YOUR
FATHER ISRAEL."
Genesis 49:2

Blessings and Prayers

HELEN HAIDLE

READ | GENESIS 49:1 – 27

"I've decided to give a blessing to all my children and grandchildren," announced Oma when she came to visit. "I don't want to wait 'til I'm on my deathbed."

She opened her Bible to Genesis 49 and pulled her granddaughter close. "Jacob blessed his 12 sons before he died," she said. "Now I have asked God to give me a Scripture blessing for each person in our family."

Gently, Oma laid her hand on Beth's head. "For you I have a special Scripture blessing." She smiled, remembering the times she had rescued her adventuresome granddaughter who had climbed too high and couldn't get back down safely. Once she had even rescued Beth from a swarm of bees.

Closing her eyes, Beth solemnly folded her hands.

"He will command his angels concerning you to guard you in all your ways; they will lift you up in their hands, so you will not strike your foot against a stone" (Psalm 91:11 – 12).

Then Oma held up a piece of paper cut in an oval shape. "I've also written a special prayer for you on this paper seed. I pray it for you often. I've planted it like a seed in my Bible. God will answer my prayer. Someday I hope you'll put this 'seed' in your Bible. Every time you read it, remember my blessing and prayers."

Oma shared her idea with other grandmothers. "Blessings and prayers deposit in our grandchildren a sense of being loved—by us and by God," she said. "If our grandchildren know we value them, it gives them a sense of stability. I pray it will also help them trust our faithful God. Remember God's promise: the seeds of his Word always grow and bear fruit (see Isaiah 55:10 – 11).

O Lord, you have blessed me with many blessings. Thank you for letting me bless my family like Jacob blessed his sons. Draw my loved ones close to you. Help me know how to pray for each child and grandchild. Please grow the seeds I plant. For Jesus' sake, amen.

Your next devotion is located on page 82.

GRANDCHILD IN FOCUS • PRAYER

Physical Well-Being

Almighty God, Creator of us all, I pray that you will watch over my grandchild's physical development. May he grow in strength through the stages of his life. As he grows in awareness of his body, help him to understand that each body develops uniquely, yet is within your plan and your control. Please guard his health so that his diseases are few, his injuries are minor and his infirmities are brief. Amen.

3 "Reuben, you are my firstborn,
  my might, the first sign of my strength,
  excelling in honor, excelling in power.
4 Turbulent as the waters, you will no longer
    excel,
  for you went up onto your father's bed,
  onto my couch and defiled it.

5 "Simeon and Levi are brothers—
  their swords[a] are weapons of violence.
6 Let me not enter their council,
  let me not join their assembly,
for they have killed men in their anger
  and hamstrung oxen as they pleased.
7 Cursed be their anger, so fierce,
  and their fury, so cruel!
I will scatter them in Jacob
  and disperse them in Israel.

8 "Judah,[b] your brothers will praise you;
  your hand will be on the neck of your
      enemies;
  your father's sons will bow down to you.
9 You are a lion's cub, O Judah;
  you return from the prey, my son.
Like a lion he crouches and lies down,
  like a lioness—who dares to rouse him?
10 The scepter will not depart from Judah,
  nor the ruler's staff from between his
      feet,
until he comes to whom it belongs[c]
  and the obedience of the nations is his.
11 He will tether his donkey to a vine,
  his colt to the choicest branch;
he will wash his garments in wine,
  his robes in the blood of grapes.
12 His eyes will be darker than wine,
  his teeth whiter than milk.[d]

13 "Zebulun will live by the seashore
  and become a haven for ships;
  his border will extend toward Sidon.

14 "Issachar is a rawboned[e] donkey
  lying down between two saddlebags.[f]
15 When he sees how good is his resting place
  and how pleasant is his land,

he will bend his shoulder to the burden
  and submit to forced labor.

16 "Dan[g] will provide justice for his people
  as one of the tribes of Israel.
17 Dan will be a serpent by the roadside,
  a viper along the path,
that bites the horse's heels
  so that its rider tumbles backward.

18 "I look for your deliverance, O LORD.

19 "Gad[h] will be attacked by a band of raiders,
  but he will attack them at their heels.

20 "Asher's food will be rich;
  he will provide delicacies fit for a king.

21 "Naphtali is a doe set free
  that bears beautiful fawns.[i]

22 "Joseph is a fruitful vine,
  a fruitful vine near a spring,
  whose branches climb over a wall.[j]
23 With bitterness archers attacked him;
  they shot at him with hostility.
24 But his bow remained steady,
  his strong arms stayed[k] limber,
because of the hand of the Mighty One of
      Jacob,
  because of the Shepherd, the Rock of Israel,
25 because of your father's God, who helps you,
  because of the Almighty,[l] who blesses you
with blessings of the heavens above,
  blessings of the deep that lies below,
  blessings of the breast and womb.
26 Your father's blessings are greater
  than the blessings of the ancient
      mountains,
  than[m] the bounty of the age-old hills.

---

[a] 5 The meaning of the Hebrew for this word is uncertain.
[b] 8 Judah sounds like and may be derived from the Hebrew for
praise.   [c] 10 Or until Shiloh comes; or until he comes to whom
tribute belongs   [d] 12 Or will be dull from wine, / his teeth white
from milk   [e] 14 Or strong   [f] 14 Or campfires   [g] 16 Dan here
means he provides justice.   [h] 19 Gad can mean attack and band of
raiders.   [i] 21 Or free; / he utters beautiful words   [j] 22 Or Joseph
is a wild colt, / a wild colt near a spring, / a wild donkey on a terraced
hill   [k] 23,24 Or archers will attack . . . will shoot . . . will remain . . .
will stay   [l] 25 Hebrew Shaddai   [m] 26 Or of my progenitors, /
as great as

Let all these rest on the head of Joseph,
on the brow of the prince among[a] his
brothers.

[27]"Benjamin is a ravenous wolf;
in the morning he devours the prey,
in the evening he divides the plunder."

[28]All these are the twelve tribes of Israel, and this is what their father said to them when he blessed them, giving each the blessing appropriate to him.

The Death of Jacob

[29]Then he gave them these instructions: "I am about to be gathered to my people. Bury me with my fathers in the cave in the field of Ephron the Hittite, [30]the cave in the field of Machpelah, near Mamre in Canaan, which Abraham bought as a burial place from Ephron the Hittite, along with the field. [31]There Abraham and his wife Sarah were buried, there Isaac and his wife Rebekah were buried, and there I buried Leah. [32]The field and the cave in it were bought from the Hittites.[b]"

[33]When Jacob had finished giving instructions to his sons, he drew his feet up into the bed, breathed his last and was gathered to his people.

50 Joseph threw himself upon his father and wept over him and kissed him. [2]Then Joseph directed the physicians in his service to embalm his father Israel. So the physicians embalmed him, [3]taking a full forty days, for that was the time required for embalming. And the Egyptians mourned for him seventy days.

[4]When the days of mourning had passed, Joseph said to Pharaoh's court, "If I have found favor in your eyes, speak to Pharaoh for me. Tell him, [5]'My father made me swear an oath and said, "I am about to die; bury me in the tomb I dug for myself in the land of Canaan." Now let me go up and bury my father; then I will return.'"

[6]Pharaoh said, "Go up and bury your father, as he made you swear to do."

[7]So Joseph went up to bury his father. All

stories to share

GENESIS 49:33; 50:15–21

Joseph Forgives His Brothers

LIFE LESSON: God wants us to forgive others.

TO TALK ABOUT

✦ What did Joseph's brothers do to him that was wrong? (Hint: Read Genesis 37:12–36.)

✦ Why were Joseph's brothers afraid after their father died?

✦ What did Joseph mean when he asked his brothers, "Am I in the place of God" (Genesis 50:19)?

✦ How do you react when someone hurts you? What can you learn from the story of Joseph?

Pharaoh's officials accompanied him—the dignitaries of his court and all the dignitaries of Egypt— [8]besides all the members of Joseph's household and his brothers and those belonging to his father's household. Only their children and their flocks and herds were left in Goshen. [9]Chariots and horsemen[c] also went up with him. It was a very large company.

[10]When they reached the threshing floor of Atad, near the Jordan, they lamented loudly and bitterly; and there Joseph observed a seven-day period of mourning for his father. [11]When the

---

[a] 26 Or the one separated from   [b] 32 Or the sons of Heth
[c] 9 Or charioteers

ALL THESE ARE THE TWELVE TRIBES
OF ISRAEL, AND THIS IS WHAT THEIR
FATHER SAID TO THEM WHEN HE
BLESSED THEM, GIVING EACH THE
BLESSING APPROPRIATE TO HIM.
Genesis 49:28

Affirming Grown Children

JAN SILVIOUS

READ | GENESIS 49:28

One of the wisest women I ever met was a very unassuming secretary. I don't remember her name, but I'll never forget the lesson she taught me. I was a young mother in the throes of seeing my children grow into young adults, and I was all ears for advice that could make that transition easier. Somehow, in our brief woman-to-woman conversation, the question came up about how she let her children go. She quietly smiled and said, "I gave them apron strings." She continued with her explanation. "I raised my children alone. Their father was gone, and as each child grew, I knew there would be a time when they would have to become responsible for themselves. I wanted them to view that step as an honor, a rite of passage, not just something they had to do because I had limited resources and they didn't have a daddy to help them launch."

"So when my first child turned 18, I cut the strings off my apron, wrapped them in a box with a beautiful bow and wrote her a note declaring that 'the apron strings were now officially cut.' I told her I admired who she had become and would support her in prayer as she found her way into adulthood. There were other small gifts that day, but the apron strings were her most treasured one. She was thrilled with the newfound respect and status that little ceremony gave her. I repeated that celebration four more times, until my nest was empty. All five of my children cherished the apron strings, and I believe the affirmation that gave them as they became young adults was critical to who they eventually became."

Father, give me the grace to support my grown children with affirming words and meaningful blessings. Help me to remember that what I say (or don't say) will be with them always. Amen.

Your next devotion is located on page 86.

GRANDCHILD IN FOCUS · PRAYER

Emotional Development

O God, Creator of mind and body, I pray that you will give my grandchild emotional health and strength. Where there is anger, bring peace. Where there is confusion, bring clarity and focus. Where there are dark shadows, cast a ray of hope. Fill her with the sunshine of your Spirit. Warm her with the presence of your peace. Amen.

Canaanites who lived there saw the mourning at the threshing floor of Atad, they said, "The Egyptians are holding a solemn ceremony of mourning." That is why that place near the Jordan is called Abel Mizraim. *a*

¹²So Jacob's sons did as he had commanded them: ¹³They carried him to the land of Canaan and buried him in the cave in the field of Machpelah, near Mamre, which Abraham had bought as a burial place from Ephron the Hittite, along with the field. ¹⁴After burying his father, Joseph returned to Egypt, together with his brothers and all the others who had gone with him to bury his father.

Joseph Reassures His Brothers

¹⁵When Joseph's brothers saw that their father was dead, they said, "What if Joseph holds a grudge against us and pays us back for all the wrongs we did to him?" ¹⁶So they sent word to Joseph, saying, "Your father left these instructions before he died: ¹⁷'This is what you are to say to Joseph: I ask you to forgive your brothers the sins and the wrongs they committed in treating you so badly.' Now please forgive the sins of the servants of the God of your father." When their message came to him, Joseph wept.

¹⁸His brothers then came and threw themselves down before him. "We are your slaves," they said.

¹⁹But Joseph said to them, "Don't be afraid. Am I in the place of God? ²⁰You intended to harm me, but God intended it for good to accomplish what is now being done, the saving of many lives. ²¹So then, don't be afraid. I will provide for you and your children." And he reassured them and spoke kindly to them.

The Death of Joseph

²²Joseph stayed in Egypt, along with all his father's family. He lived a hundred and ten years ²³and saw the third generation of Ephraim's children. Also the children of Makir son of Manasseh were placed at birth on Joseph's knees. *b*

²⁴Then Joseph said to his brothers, "I am about to die. But God will surely come to your aid and take you up out of this land to the land he promised on oath to Abraham, Isaac and Jacob." ²⁵And Joseph made the sons of Israel swear an oath and said, "God will surely come to your aid, and then you must carry my bones up from this place."

²⁶So Joseph died at the age of a hundred and ten. And after they embalmed him, he was placed in a coffin in Egypt.

a 11 *Abel Mizraim* means *mourning of the Egyptians.*   *b* 23 That is, were counted as his

Knowing GOD

Exodus is a book about knowing God. Although the Israelites had not become completely godless while living in Egypt (see Exodus 1:17), they did not enjoy a full relationship with the Lord. But God was still with them, even in their slavery, and the book of Exodus demonstrates how God revealed himself to his people.

With compassion God heard the cries of the enslaved Israelites (see Exodus 2:23 – 25). He provided a deliverer in Moses and, through a series of dramatic miracles, freed them from their oppression in Egypt and from Pharaoh's army. God's faithful provision and protection would continue through 40 years of wilderness wandering and stay strong as he led them to conquer the land God had promised to them.

God moved to restore and protect the nation of Israel, and he expected commitment from them in return. Exodus records the event of the first Passover, along with its establishment as an ongoing celebration, as well as the details of the construction of the tabernacle. The book also introduces the laws, the offerings, and the feasts and festivals that would draw God's people closer to him.

Exodus also shows us God's clear standards of right and wrong, and records the giving of the Ten Commandments (see Exodus 20) as a guide to provide God's people with a long and happy life — a guide as reliable and true today as it was thousands of years ago.

VERSE *to* **REMEMBER** | EXODUS 2:24 – 25

God heard their groaning and he remembered his covenant with Abraham, with Isaac and with Jacob. So God looked on the Israelites and was concerned about them.

ABOUT EXODUS

WRITTEN BY:
Moses

WRITTEN FOR:
God's chosen people, the Israelites

DATE WRITTEN:
Between 1446 and 1406 B.C.

WHY WRITTEN:
To show how God revealed himself to his people and how he used his power to rescue the Israelites from slavery

The Israelites Oppressed

1 These are the names of the sons of Israel who went to Egypt with Jacob, each with his family: ²Reuben, Simeon, Levi and Judah; ³Issachar, Zebulun and Benjamin; ⁴Dan and Naphtali; Gad and Asher. ⁵The descendants of Jacob numbered seventy ᵃ in all; Joseph was already in Egypt.

⁶Now Joseph and all his brothers and all that generation died, ⁷but the Israelites were fruitful and multiplied greatly and became exceedingly numerous, so that the land was filled with them.

⁸Then a new king, who did not know about Joseph, came to power in Egypt. ⁹"Look," he said to his people, "the Israelites have become much too numerous for us. ¹⁰Come, we must deal shrewdly with them or they will become even more numerous and, if war breaks out, will join our enemies, fight against us and leave the country."

¹¹So they put slave masters over them to oppress them with forced labor, and they built Pithom and Rameses as store cities for Pharaoh. ¹²But the more they were oppressed, the more they multiplied and spread; so the Egyptians came to dread the Israelites ¹³and worked them ruthlessly. ¹⁴They made their lives bitter with hard labor in brick and mortar and with all kinds of work in the fields; in all their hard labor the Egyptians used them ruthlessly.

¹⁵The king of Egypt said to the Hebrew midwives, whose names were Shiphrah and Puah, ¹⁶"When you help the Hebrew women in childbirth and observe them on the delivery stool, if it is a boy, kill him; but if it is a girl, let her live." ¹⁷The midwives, however, feared God and did not do what the king of Egypt had told them to do; they let the boys live. ¹⁸Then the king of Egypt summoned the midwives and asked them, "Why have you done this? Why have you let the boys live?"

¹⁹The midwives answered Pharaoh, "Hebrew women are not like Egyptian women; they are vigorous and give birth before the midwives arrive."

²⁰So God was kind to the midwives and the people increased and became even more numerous.

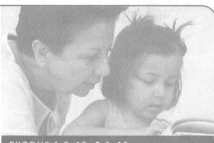

EXODUS 1:8–19; 2:1–10

The Birth of Moses

LIFE LESSON: Even great kings can't stop God's plan.

TO TALK ABOUT

✦ Why was Pharaoh afraid of the Israelites?

✦ What did Moses' mom and sister do to save him?

✦ Why do you think Pharaoh let his daughter adopt an Israelite baby boy?

✦ What do you see God doing to help his people in this story?

²¹And because the midwives feared God, he gave them families of their own.

²²Then Pharaoh gave this order to all his people: "Every boy that is born ᵇ you must throw into the Nile, but let every girl live."

The Birth of Moses

2 Now a man of the house of Levi married a Levite woman, ²and she became pregnant and gave birth to a son. When she saw that he was a fine child, she hid him for three months. ³But when she could hide him no longer, she got a papyrus basket for him and coated it with tar and pitch. Then she placed the child in it and put

ᵃ 5 Masoretic Text (see also Gen. 46:27); Dead Sea Scrolls and Septuagint (see also Acts 7:14 and note at Gen. 46:27) *seventy-five*
ᵇ 22 Masoretic Text; Samaritan Pentateuch, Septuagint and Targums *born to the Hebrews*

> THE MIDWIVES, HOWEVER,
> FEARED GOD AND DID NOT DO
> WHAT THE KING OF EGYPT HAD
> TOLD THEM TO DO; THEY LET
> THE BOYS LIVE.
>
> *Exodus 1:17*

Women Bringing Life

LINDA H. HOLLIES

READ | EXODUS 1:1 – 22

Pharaoh's plan brings us to Exodus 1:15, when two women, Shiphrah and Puah, are called before Pharaoh. You know these sisters are important because they are named. (The name *Shiphrah* means "joy of parent." The name *Puah* means "one who will procreate.")

Now, Pharaoh believed that he was almighty, all-powerful and in-charge. Pharaoh felt that women were insignificant, of little importance, yet he called for these midwives to carry out his decree. Boyfriend didn't have a clue. This ignorant man ordered these women to commit murder, but they were committed to God's plan of life. When Pharaoh desired death, these women were determined in their hearts to provide unauthorized leadership through their silent acts of intervention. Not daring to talk back and having better sense than to be outright with their defiance, they were wise enough not to be openly rebellious. These sisters show us how those who are accorded secondary status and excluded from the circles of power were the very ones that the God of Glory utilized to be the unproclaimed heroes and giants in the land. Of course, God's call to the midwives brought them great personal chaos. But God paid great benefits by giving them both land and families.

It's women who continue to pull male leadership out of murky waters. It's godly women who stand, watching, waiting and actively looking for ways to connect resources with needy people. God is still calling women to lend their hands and help erect and shape deliverance in the village.

Father, I ask that you give me your strength so that I can make an impact on my family, community and world — an impact and impression that speaks eloquently of your power, love and deliverance.

Your next devotion is located on page 100.

GRANDCHILD IN FOCUS • PRAYER

Spiritual Growth

Dear Lord, today I pray for my grandchild's spiritual growth. I ask that you instill in him the desire to read and memorize your Word. Give him a passion to be in conversation with you. May loving and serving you be part of his daily life. I ask that you stay close to him and lead him to be transformed to your likeness, to reflect your grace and to radiate your love. I pray this in Jesus' name, amen.

it among the reeds along the bank of the Nile. ⁴His sister stood at a distance to see what would happen to him.

⁵Then Pharaoh's daughter went down to the Nile to bathe, and her attendants were walking along the river bank. She saw the basket among the reeds and sent her slave girl to get it. ⁶She opened it and saw the baby. He was crying, and she felt sorry for him. "This is one of the Hebrew babies," she said.

⁷Then his sister asked Pharaoh's daughter, "Shall I go and get one of the Hebrew women to nurse the baby for you?"

⁸"Yes, go," she answered. And the girl went and got the baby's mother. ⁹Pharaoh's daughter said to her, "Take this baby and nurse him for me, and I will pay you." So the woman took the baby and nursed him. ¹⁰When the child grew older, she took him to Pharaoh's daughter and he became her son. She named him Moses,ᵃ saying, "I drew him out of the water."

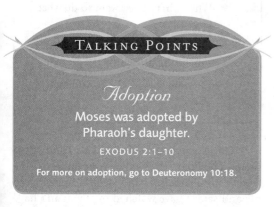

TALKING POINTS

Adoption

Moses was adopted by Pharaoh's daughter.

EXODUS 2:1–10

For more on adoption, go to Deuteronomy 10:18.

Moses Flees to Midian

¹¹One day, after Moses had grown up, he went out to where his own people were and watched them at their hard labor. He saw an Egyptian beating a Hebrew, one of his own people. ¹²Glancing this way and that and seeing no one, he killed the Egyptian and hid him in the sand. ¹³The next day he went out and saw two Hebrews fighting. He asked the one in the wrong, "Why are you hitting your fellow Hebrew?"

¹⁴The man said, "Who made you ruler and judge over us? Are you thinking of killing me as you killed the Egyptian?" Then Moses was afraid and thought, "What I did must have become known."

¹⁵When Pharaoh heard of this, he tried to kill Moses, but Moses fled from Pharaoh and went to live in Midian, where he sat down by a well. ¹⁶Now a priest of Midian had seven daughters, and they came to draw water and fill the troughs to water their father's flock. ¹⁷Some shepherds came along and drove them away, but Moses got up and came to their rescue and watered their flock.

¹⁸When the girls returned to Reuel their father, he asked them, "Why have you returned so early today?"

¹⁹They answered, "An Egyptian rescued us from the shepherds. He even drew water for us and watered the flock."

²⁰"And where is he?" he asked his daughters. "Why did you leave him? Invite him to have something to eat."

²¹Moses agreed to stay with the man, who gave his daughter Zipporah to Moses in marriage. ²²Zipporah gave birth to a son, and Moses named him Gershom,ᵇ saying, "I have become an alien in a foreign land."

²³During that long period, the king of Egypt died. The Israelites groaned in their slavery and cried out, and their cry for help because of their slavery went up to God. ²⁴God heard their groaning and he remembered his covenant with Abraham, with Isaac and with Jacob. ²⁵So God looked on the Israelites and was concerned about them.

Moses and the Burning Bush

3 Now Moses was tending the flock of Jethro his father-in-law, the priest of Midian, and he led the flock to the far side of the desert and came to Horeb, the mountain of God. ²There the angel of the LORD appeared to him in flames of fire from within a bush. Moses saw that though

---

ᵃ 10 Moses sounds like the Hebrew for draw out.　ᵇ 22 Gershom sounds like the Hebrew for an alien there.

the bush was on fire it did not burn up. ³ So Moses thought, "I will go over and see this strange sight — why the bush does not burn up."

⁴ When the Lord saw that he had gone over to look, God called to him from within the bush, "Moses! Moses!"

And Moses said, "Here I am."

⁵ "Do not come any closer," God said. "Take off your sandals, for the place where you are standing is holy ground." ⁶ Then he said, "I am the God of your father, the God of Abraham, the God of Isaac and the God of Jacob." At this, Moses hid his face, because he was afraid to look at God.

⁷ The Lord said, "I have indeed seen the misery of my people in Egypt. I have heard them crying out because of their slave drivers, and I am concerned about their suffering. ⁸ So I have come down to rescue them from the hand of the Egyptians and to bring them up out of that land into a good and spacious land, a land flowing with milk and honey — the home of the Canaanites, Hittites, Amorites, Perizzites, Hivites and Jebusites. ⁹ And now the cry of the Israelites has reached me, and I have seen the way the Egyptians are oppressing them. ¹⁰ So now, go. I am sending you to Pharaoh to bring my people the Israelites out of Egypt."

¹¹ But Moses said to God, "Who am I, that I should go to Pharaoh and bring the Israelites out of Egypt?"

¹² And God said, "I will be with you. And this will be the sign to you that it is I who have sent you: When you have brought the people out of Egypt, you*ᵃ* will worship God on this mountain."

¹³ Moses said to God, "Suppose I go to the Israelites and say to them, 'The God of your fathers has sent me to you,' and they ask me, 'What is his name?' Then what shall I tell them?"

¹⁴ God said to Moses, "I AM WHO I AM.*ᵇ* This is what you are to say to the Israelites: 'I AM has sent me to you.'"

¹⁵ God also said to Moses, "Say to the Israelites, 'The Lord,*ᶜ* the God of your fathers — the God of Abraham, the God of Isaac and the God of Jacob — has sent me to you.' This is my name for-

ever, the name by which I am to be remembered from generation to generation.

stories to share

EXODUS 3:1–15; 4:1–17

Moses and the Burning Bush

LIFE LESSON: God's opinion of us is what really matters.

TO TALK ABOUT

✦ What did God want Moses to do?

✦ Why didn't Moses want to do what God asked?

✦ When has God chosen you to do something difficult?

✦ How did you get the confidence to obey?

¹⁶ "Go, assemble the elders of Israel and say to them, 'The Lord, the God of your fathers — the God of Abraham, Isaac and Jacob — appeared to me and said: I have watched over you and have seen what has been done to you in Egypt. ¹⁷ And I have promised to bring you up out of your misery in Egypt into the land of the Canaanites, Hittites, Amorites, Perizzites, Hivites and Jebusites — a land flowing with milk and honey.'

¹⁸ "The elders of Israel will listen to you. Then you and the elders are to go to the king of Egypt and say to him, 'The Lord, the God of the Hebrews,

---

ᵃ 12 The Hebrew is plural.   *ᵇ 14* Or *I WILL BE WHAT I WILL BE*
ᶜ 15 The Hebrew for Lord sounds like and may be derived from the Hebrew for *I AM* in verse 14.

has met with us. Let us take a three-day journey into the desert to offer sacrifices to the LORD our God.' ¹⁹But I know that the king of Egypt will not let you go unless a mighty hand compels him. ²⁰So I will stretch out my hand and strike the Egyptians with all the wonders that I will perform among them. After that, he will let you go.

²¹"And I will make the Egyptians favorably disposed toward this people, so that when you leave you will not go empty-handed. ²²Every woman is to ask her neighbor and any woman living in her house for articles of silver and gold and for clothing, which you will put on your sons and daughters. And so you will plunder the Egyptians."

Signs for Moses

4 Moses answered, "What if they do not believe me or listen to me and say, 'The LORD did not appear to you'?"

²Then the LORD said to him, "What is that in your hand?"

"A staff," he replied.

³The LORD said, "Throw it on the ground."

Moses threw it on the ground and it became a snake, and he ran from it. ⁴Then the LORD said to him, "Reach out your hand and take it by the tail." So Moses reached out and took hold of the snake and it turned back into a staff in his hand. ⁵"This," said the LORD, "is so that they may believe that the LORD, the God of their fathers — the God of Abraham, the God of Isaac and the God of Jacob — has appeared to you."

⁶Then the LORD said, "Put your hand inside your cloak." So Moses put his hand into his cloak, and when he took it out, it was leprous,ᵃ like snow.

⁷"Now put it back into your cloak," he said. So Moses put his hand back into his cloak, and when he took it out, it was restored, like the rest of his flesh.

⁸Then the LORD said, "If they do not believe you or pay attention to the first miraculous sign, they may believe the second. ⁹But if they do not believe these two signs or listen to you, take some water from the Nile and pour it on the dry ground. The water you take from the river will become blood on the ground."

¹⁰Moses said to the LORD, "O Lord, I have never been eloquent, neither in the past nor since you have spoken to your servant. I am slow of speech and tongue."

¹¹The LORD said to him, "Who gave man his mouth? Who makes him deaf or mute? Who gives him sight or makes him blind? Is it not I, the LORD? ¹²Now go; I will help you speak and will teach you what to say."

¹³But Moses said, "O Lord, please send someone else to do it."

¹⁴Then the LORD's anger burned against Moses and he said, "What about your brother, Aaron the Levite? I know he can speak well. He is already on his way to meet you, and his heart will be glad when he sees you. ¹⁵You shall speak to him and put words in his mouth; I will help both of you speak and will teach you what to do. ¹⁶He will speak to the people for you, and it will be as if he were your mouth and as if you were God to him. ¹⁷But take this staff in your hand so you can perform miraculous signs with it."

Moses Returns to Egypt

¹⁸Then Moses went back to Jethro his father-in-law and said to him, "Let me go back to my own people in Egypt to see if any of them are still alive."

Jethro said, "Go, and I wish you well."

¹⁹Now the LORD had said to Moses in Midian, "Go back to Egypt, for all the men who wanted to kill you are dead." ²⁰So Moses took his wife and sons, put them on a donkey and started back to Egypt. And he took the staff of God in his hand.

²¹The LORD said to Moses, "When you return to Egypt, see that you perform before Pharaoh all the wonders I have given you the power to do. But I will harden his heart so that he will not let the people go. ²²Then say to Pharaoh, 'This is what the LORD says: Israel is my firstborn son, ²³and I told you, "Let my son go, so he may worship me."

ᵃ 6 The Hebrew word was used for various diseases affecting the skin — not necessarily leprosy.

GLADYS HUNT

Staying ON THE CUTTING EDGE

When I was a university student, one of my mentors warned, "Avoid the most dreadful words in the English language: settling down." He urged us to keep our lives on the cutting edge of what God is doing in the world rather than have our highest goal be a cozy home, a couple of children and a comfortable, safe life. I have since often thought of what an exciting, useful life came from following his advice.

Growing older has its hazards, and one of the deadliest of these, it seems to me, is having life be all about me and my comforts and my family. Having grandchildren and maybe great-grandchildren indicates that life has already known some stresses. Financial worries, unexpected crises, raising a family, getting children educated — all of these can lead us to think we deserve some days of leisure without worry.

I Don't Want to Take My Blessings for Granted

I like creature comforts as much as the next person. In fact, I thank God for running hot water every time I shower. While doing the laundry, I think of women in many parts of the world who are washing clothes on stones in a river. When rocking a sick grandchild, I give thanks for the pediatrician that cares for this family — and I also pray for an Afghan woman who has 13 children in graves, all having died before age four. I don't want to take my blessings for granted.

The Scriptures remind me again and again that God cares about the poor and needy, and he wants me to care too. When I read Isaiah, I hear God tell his people to seek justice, to care about the oppressed, to rescue those who suffer. I hear God urging me to do something about the desperate condition of the world.

None of us can take on suffering and injustice on a global scale. It's too much, and that makes it easy to deceive ourselves into thinking that since we can't do everything, we can't do anything. It's an easy cop-out that allows us to shut out what we know is all around us. It lets us sleep at night. What can *I* do? My prime years are past.

Give What You Have

Moses liked his slow-paced life in the desert and had all sorts of excuses about why he couldn't do anything to rescue his people stuck in Egypt. After all, he was 80 years old! Unimpressed by his objections, God asked Moses, "What is that in your hand?" (Exodus 4:2). He told Moses to take what he had and expect God to use it. Give what you have.

Years ago we brought flowers from our church to an elderly woman who was bedridden and without many resources. Pain kept her from sleeping much at night. She refused our sympathy, looking downright happy and contented as she told us how she spent those hours each night. She traveled the world, she said, and pointed to a stand by her bedside with pictures of missionaries and clippings of items that interested her. She and God talked together about a world in need.

I Can Pray and Take Risks

Give what you have! What do I have, and what does the world need? I can start in my neighborhood. People who don't know they are loved by God also suffer a kind of oppression. I notice a shortage of justice. I can be informed and make my voice heard. Indignation over injustices, linked with compassion, is a great motivator. I can pray. Praying is the beginning of caring. In situations that I can do something about, I give, I protest, I write letters. When someone is needy, I can do something. Loving needy people can sometimes be messy and time-consuming and unsafe. It takes courage and love to care about the immigrants who are in my own community or help at the shelter for battered women.

But God wants us to know that we are so safe in his love that we can take some risks. His promise to those who reach out is pretty impressive. In Isaiah 58:10–11 he says that if we spend ourselves on behalf of others, we "will be like a well-watered garden, like a spring whose waters never fail." I would like my grandchildren to have the example of that kind of fruitful life as part of their inheritance from me.

You and I are God's plan for making God's love believable. This calling will look different for each of us. We simply need to find out where God wants us to show a bit of bravery for this season of life and then go do something.

But you refused to let him go; so I will kill your firstborn son.'"

²⁴At a lodging place on the way, the LORD met ⌐Moses¬ᵃ and was about to kill him. ²⁵But Zipporah took a flint knife, cut off her son's foreskin and touched ⌐Moses'¬ feet with it.ᵇ "Surely you are a bridegroom of blood to me," she said. ²⁶So the LORD let him alone. (At that time she said "bridegroom of blood," referring to circumcision.)

²⁷The LORD said to Aaron, "Go into the desert to meet Moses." So he met Moses at the mountain of God and kissed him. ²⁸Then Moses told Aaron everything the LORD had sent him to say, and also about all the miraculous signs he had commanded him to perform.

²⁹Moses and Aaron brought together all the elders of the Israelites, ³⁰and Aaron told them everything the LORD had said to Moses. He also performed the signs before the people, ³¹and they believed. And when they heard that the LORD was concerned about them and had seen their misery, they bowed down and worshiped.

Bricks Without Straw

5 Afterward Moses and Aaron went to Pharaoh and said, "This is what the LORD, the God of Israel, says: 'Let my people go, so that they may hold a festival to me in the desert.'"

²Pharaoh said, "Who is the LORD, that I should obey him and let Israel go? I do not know the LORD and I will not let Israel go." ³Then they said, "The God of the Hebrews has met with us. Now let us take a three-day journey into the desert to offer sacrifices to the LORD our God, or he may strike us with plagues or with the sword."

⁴But the king of Egypt said, "Moses and Aaron, why are you taking the people away from their labor? Get back to your work!" ⁵Then Pharaoh said, "Look, the people of the land are now numerous, and you are stopping them from working."

⁶That same day Pharaoh gave this order to the slave drivers and foremen in charge of the people: ⁷"You are no longer to supply the people with straw for making bricks; let them go and gather their own straw. ⁸But require them to make the same number of bricks as before; don't reduce the quota. They are lazy; that is why they are crying out, 'Let us go and sacrifice to our God.' ⁹Make the work harder for the men so that they keep working and pay no attention to lies."

¹⁰Then the slave drivers and the foremen went out and said to the people, "This is what Pharaoh says: 'I will not give you any more straw. ¹¹Go and get your own straw wherever you can find it, but your work will not be reduced at all.'" ¹²So the people scattered all over Egypt to gather stubble to use for straw. ¹³The slave drivers kept pressing them, saying, "Complete the work required of you for each day, just as when you had straw." ¹⁴The Israelite foremen appointed by Pharaoh's slave drivers were beaten and were asked, "Why didn't you meet your quota of bricks yesterday or today, as before?"

¹⁵Then the Israelite foremen went and appealed to Pharaoh: "Why have you treated your servants this way? ¹⁶Your servants are given no straw, yet we are told, 'Make bricks!' Your servants are being beaten, but the fault is with your own people."

¹⁷Pharaoh said, "Lazy, that's what you are—lazy! That is why you keep saying, 'Let us go and sacrifice to the LORD.' ¹⁸Now get to work. You will not be given any straw, yet you must produce your full quota of bricks."

¹⁹The Israelite foremen realized they were in trouble when they were told, "You are not to reduce the number of bricks required of you for each day." ²⁰When they left Pharaoh, they found Moses and Aaron waiting to meet them, ²¹and they said, "May the LORD look upon you and judge you! You have made us a stench to Pharaoh and his officials and have put a sword in their hand to kill us."

God Promises Deliverance

²²Moses returned to the LORD and said, "O Lord, why have you brought trouble upon

ᵃ 24 Or ⌐Moses' son¬; Hebrew him   ᵇ 25 Or and drew near ⌐Moses'¬ feet this people? Is this why you sent me? ²³Ever since I went to Pharaoh to speak in your name, he has brought trouble upon this people, and you have not rescued your people at all."

6 Then the LORD said to Moses, "Now you will see what I will do to Pharaoh: Because of my mighty hand he will let them go; because of my mighty hand he will drive them out of his country."

²God also said to Moses, "I am the LORD. ³I appeared to Abraham, to Isaac and to Jacob as God Almighty,ᵃ but by my name the LORD ᵇ I did not make myself known to them.ᶜ ⁴I also established my covenant with them to give them the land of Canaan, where they lived as aliens. ⁵Moreover, I have heard the groaning of the Israelites, whom the Egyptians are enslaving, and I have remembered my covenant.

⁶"Therefore, say to the Israelites: 'I am the LORD, and I will bring you out from under the yoke of the Egyptians. I will free you from being slaves to them, and I will redeem you with an outstretched arm and with mighty acts of judgment. ⁷I will take you as my own people, and I will be your God. Then you will know that I am the LORD your God, who brought you out from under the yoke of the Egyptians. ⁸And I will bring you to the land I swore with uplifted hand to give to Abraham, to Isaac and to Jacob. I will give it to you as a possession. I am the LORD.'"

⁹Moses reported this to the Israelites, but they did not listen to him because of their discouragement and cruel bondage.

¹⁰Then the LORD said to Moses, ¹¹"Go, tell Pharaoh king of Egypt to let the Israelites go out of his country."

¹²But Moses said to the LORD, "If the Israelites will not listen to me, why would Pharaoh listen to me, since I speak with faltering lips ᵈ?"

Family Record of Moses and Aaron

¹³Now the LORD spoke to Moses and Aaron about the Israelites and Pharaoh king of Egypt, and he commanded them to bring the Israelites out of Egypt.

¹⁴These were the heads of their families ᵉ:

The sons of Reuben the firstborn son of Israel were Hanoch and Pallu, Hezron and Carmi. These were the clans of Reuben.

¹⁵The sons of Simeon were Jemuel, Jamin, Ohad, Jakin, Zohar and Shaul the son of a Canaanite woman. These were the clans of Simeon.

¹⁶These were the names of the sons of Levi according to their records: Gershon, Kohath and Merari. Levi lived 137 years.

¹⁷The sons of Gershon, by clans, were Libni and Shimei.

¹⁸The sons of Kohath were Amram, Izhar, Hebron and Uzziel. Kohath lived 133 years.

¹⁹The sons of Merari were Mahli and Mushi.

These were the clans of Levi according to their records.

²⁰Amram married his father's sister Jochebed, who bore him Aaron and Moses. Amram lived 137 years.

²¹The sons of Izhar were Korah, Nepheg and Zicri.

²²The sons of Uzziel were Mishael, Elzaphan and Sithri.

²³Aaron married Elisheba, daughter of Amminadab and sister of Nahshon, and she bore him Nadab and Abihu, Eleazar and Ithamar.

²⁴The sons of Korah were Assir, Elkanah and Abiasaph. These were the Korahite clans.

²⁵Eleazar son of Aaron married one of the daughters of Putiel, and she bore him Phinehas.

These were the heads of the Levite families, clan by clan.

²⁶It was this same Aaron and Moses to whom the LORD said, "Bring the Israelites out of Egypt

---

ᵃ 3 Hebrew *El-Shaddai*   ᵇ 3 See note at Exodus 3:15.
ᶜ 3 Or *Almighty, and by my name the LORD did I not let myself be known to them?*   ᵈ 12 Hebrew *I am uncircumcised of lips;* also in verse 30   ᵉ 14 The Hebrew for *families* here and in verse 25 refers to units larger than clans.

by their divisions." ²⁷They were the ones who spoke to Pharaoh king of Egypt about bringing the Israelites out of Egypt. It was the same Moses and Aaron.

Aaron to Speak for Moses

²⁸Now when the LORD spoke to Moses in Egypt, ²⁹he said to him, "I am the LORD. Tell Pharaoh king of Egypt everything I tell you."

³⁰But Moses said to the LORD, "Since I speak with faltering lips, why would Pharaoh listen to me?"

7 Then the LORD said to Moses, "See, I have made you like God to Pharaoh, and your brother Aaron will be your prophet. ²You are to say everything I command you, and your brother Aaron is to tell Pharaoh to let the Israelites go out of his country. ³But I will harden Pharaoh's heart, and though I multiply my miraculous signs and wonders in Egypt, ⁴he will not listen to you. Then I will lay my hand on Egypt and with mighty acts of judgment I will bring out my divisions, my people the Israelites. ⁵And the Egyptians will know that I am the LORD when I stretch out my hand against Egypt and bring the Israelites out of it."

⁶Moses and Aaron did just as the LORD commanded them. ⁷Moses was eighty years old and Aaron eighty-three when they spoke to Pharaoh.

Aaron's Staff Becomes a Snake

⁸The LORD said to Moses and Aaron, ⁹"When Pharaoh says to you, 'Perform a miracle,' then say to Aaron, 'Take your staff and throw it down before Pharaoh,' and it will become a snake."

¹⁰So Moses and Aaron went to Pharaoh and did just as the LORD commanded. Aaron threw his staff down in front of Pharaoh and his officials, and it became a snake. ¹¹Pharaoh then summoned wise men and sorcerers, and the Egyptian magicians also did the same things by their secret arts: ¹²Each one threw down his staff and it became a snake. But Aaron's staff swallowed up their staffs. ¹³Yet Pharaoh's heart became hard and he would not listen to them, just as the LORD had said.

The Plague of Blood

¹⁴Then the LORD said to Moses, "Pharaoh's heart is unyielding; he refuses to let the people go. ¹⁵Go to Pharaoh in the morning as he goes out to the water. Wait on the bank of the Nile to meet him, and take in your hand the staff that was changed into a snake. ¹⁶Then say to him, 'The LORD, the God of the Hebrews, has sent me to say to you: Let my people go, so that they may worship me in the desert. But until now you have not listened. ¹⁷This is what the LORD says: By this you will know that I am the LORD: With the staff that is in my hand I will strike the water of the Nile, and it will be changed into blood. ¹⁸The fish in the Nile will die, and the river will stink; the Egyptians will not be able to drink its water.' "

¹⁹The LORD said to Moses, "Tell Aaron, 'Take your staff and stretch out your hand over the waters of Egypt—over the streams and canals, over the ponds and all the reservoirs'—and they will turn to blood. Blood will be everywhere in Egypt, even in the wooden buckets and stone jars."

²⁰Moses and Aaron did just as the LORD had commanded. He raised his staff in the presence of Pharaoh and his officials and struck the water of the Nile, and all the water was changed into blood. ²¹The fish in the Nile died, and the river smelled so bad that the Egyptians could not drink its water. Blood was everywhere in Egypt.

²²But the Egyptian magicians did the same things by their secret arts, and Pharaoh's heart became hard; he would not listen to Moses and Aaron, just as the LORD had said. ²³Instead, he turned and went into his palace, and did not take even this to heart. ²⁴And all the Egyptians dug along the Nile to get drinking water, because they could not drink the water of the river.

The Plague of Frogs

²⁵Seven days passed after the LORD struck the Nile. ¹Then the LORD said to Moses, "Go to 8 Pharaoh and say to him, 'This is what the LORD says: Let my people go, so that they may worship me. ²If you refuse to let them go, I will plague your whole country with frogs. ³The Nile

will teem with frogs. They will come up into your palace and your bedroom and onto your bed, into the houses of your officials and on your people, and into your ovens and kneading troughs. ⁴The frogs will go up on you and your people and all your officials.'"

EXODUS 7:6–22; 8:1–15; 11:1,9–10

stories to share

Pharaoh Will Not Let the People Go

LIFE LESSON: God will work out his plans no matter what.

TO TALK ABOUT

✦ Why didn't Pharaoh let the Israelites leave Egypt?

✦ What is a hard heart?

✦ At first Pharaoh hardened his own heart. What does it mean that later *God* hardened Pharaoh's heart?

✦ How does God accomplish his plans today?

⁵Then the LORD said to Moses, "Tell Aaron, 'Stretch out your hand with your staff over the streams and canals and ponds, and make frogs come up on the land of Egypt.'"

⁶So Aaron stretched out his hand over the waters of Egypt, and the frogs came up and covered the land. ⁷But the magicians did the same things by their secret arts; they also made frogs come up on the land of Egypt.

⁸Pharaoh summoned Moses and Aaron and said, "Pray to the LORD to take the frogs away from me and my people, and I will let your people go to offer sacrifices to the LORD."

⁹Moses said to Pharaoh, "I leave to you the honor of setting the time for me to pray for you and your officials and your people that you and your houses may be rid of the frogs, except for those that remain in the Nile."

¹⁰"Tomorrow," Pharaoh said.

Moses replied, "It will be as you say, so that you may know there is no one like the LORD our God. ¹¹The frogs will leave you and your houses, your officials and your people; they will remain only in the Nile."

¹²After Moses and Aaron left Pharaoh, Moses cried out to the LORD about the frogs he had brought on Pharaoh. ¹³And the LORD did what Moses asked. The frogs died in the houses, in the courtyards and in the fields. ¹⁴They were piled into heaps, and the land reeked of them. ¹⁵But when Pharaoh saw that there was relief, he hardened his heart and would not listen to Moses and Aaron, just as the LORD had said.

The Plague of Gnats

¹⁶Then the LORD said to Moses, "Tell Aaron, 'Stretch out your staff and strike the dust of the ground,' and throughout the land of Egypt the dust will become gnats." ¹⁷They did this, and when Aaron stretched out his hand with the staff and struck the dust of the ground, gnats came upon men and animals. All the dust throughout the land of Egypt became gnats. ¹⁸But when the magicians tried to produce gnats by their secret arts, they could not. And the gnats were on men and animals.

¹⁹The magicians said to Pharaoh, "This is the finger of God." But Pharaoh's heart was hard and he would not listen, just as the LORD had said.

The Plague of Flies

²⁰Then the LORD said to Moses, "Get up early in the morning and confront Pharaoh as he goes to the water and say to him, 'This is what the LORD says: Let my people go, so that they may

worship me. ²¹If you do not let my people go, I will send swarms of flies on you and your officials, on your people and into your houses. The houses of the Egyptians will be full of flies, and even the ground where they are.

²²" 'But on that day I will deal differently with the land of Goshen, where my people live; no swarms of flies will be there, so that you will know that I, the LORD, am in this land. ²³I will make a distinction ᵃ between my people and your people. This miraculous sign will occur tomorrow.' "

²⁴And the LORD did this. Dense swarms of flies poured into Pharaoh's palace and into the houses of his officials, and throughout Egypt the land was ruined by the flies.

²⁵Then Pharaoh summoned Moses and Aaron and said, "Go, sacrifice to your God here in the land."

²⁶But Moses said, "That would not be right. The sacrifices we offer the LORD our God would be detestable to the Egyptians. And if we offer sacrifices that are detestable in their eyes, will they not stone us? ²⁷We must take a three-day journey into the desert to offer sacrifices to the LORD our God, as he commands us."

²⁸Pharaoh said, "I will let you go to offer sacrifices to the LORD your God in the desert, but you must not go very far. Now pray for me."

²⁹Moses answered, "As soon as I leave you, I will pray to the LORD, and tomorrow the flies will leave Pharaoh and his officials and his people. Only be sure that Pharaoh does not act deceitfully again by not letting the people go to offer sacrifices to the LORD."

³⁰Then Moses left Pharaoh and prayed to the LORD, ³¹and the LORD did what Moses asked: The flies left Pharaoh and his officials and his people; not a fly remained. ³²But this time also Pharaoh hardened his heart and would not let the people go.

The Plague on Livestock

9 Then the LORD said to Moses, "Go to Pharaoh and say to him, 'This is what the LORD, the God of the Hebrews, says: "Let my people go, so that they may worship me." ²If you refuse to let them go and continue to hold them back, ³the hand of the LORD will bring a terrible plague on your livestock in the field—on your horses and donkeys and camels and on your cattle and sheep and goats. ⁴But the LORD will make a distinction between the livestock of Israel and that of Egypt, so that no animal belonging to the Israelites will die.' "

⁵The LORD set a time and said, "Tomorrow the LORD will do this in the land." ⁶And the next day the LORD did it: All the livestock of the Egyptians died, but not one animal belonging to the Israelites died. ⁷Pharaoh sent men to investigate and found that not even one of the animals of the Israelites had died. Yet his heart was unyielding and he would not let the people go.

The Plague of Boils

⁸Then the LORD said to Moses and Aaron, "Take handfuls of soot from a furnace and have Moses toss it into the air in the presence of Pharaoh. ⁹It will become fine dust over the whole land of Egypt, and festering boils will break out on men and animals throughout the land."

¹⁰So they took soot from a furnace and stood before Pharaoh. Moses tossed it into the air, and festering boils broke out on men and animals. ¹¹The magicians could not stand before Moses because of the boils that were on them and on all the Egyptians. ¹²But the LORD hardened Pharaoh's heart and he would not listen to Moses and Aaron, just as the LORD had said to Moses.

The Plague of Hail

¹³Then the LORD said to Moses, "Get up early in the morning, confront Pharaoh and say to him, 'This is what the LORD, the God of the Hebrews, says: Let my people go, so that they may worship me, ¹⁴or this time I will send the full force of my plagues against you and against your officials and your people, so you may know that there is no one like me in all the earth. ¹⁵For

ᵃ 23 Septuagint and Vulgate; Hebrew will put a deliverance

by now I could have stretched out my hand and struck you and your people with a plague that would have wiped you off the earth. [16]But I have raised you up[a] for this very purpose, that I might show you my power and that my name might be proclaimed in all the earth. [17]You still set yourself against my people and will not let them go. [18]Therefore, at this time tomorrow I will send the worst hailstorm that has ever fallen on Egypt, from the day it was founded till now. [19]Give an order now to bring your livestock and everything you have in the field to a place of shelter, because the hail will fall on every man and animal that has not been brought in and is still out in the field, and they will die.' "

[20]Those officials of Pharaoh who feared the word of the LORD hurried to bring their slaves and their livestock inside. [21]But those who ignored the word of the LORD left their slaves and livestock in the field.

[22]Then the LORD said to Moses, "Stretch out your hand toward the sky so that hail will fall all over Egypt—on men and animals and on everything growing in the fields of Egypt." [23]When Moses stretched out his staff toward the sky, the LORD sent thunder and hail, and lightning flashed down to the ground. So the LORD rained hail on the land of Egypt; [24]hail fell and lightning flashed back and forth. It was the worst storm in all the land of Egypt since it had become a nation. [25]Throughout Egypt hail struck everything in the fields—both men and animals; it beat down everything growing in the fields and stripped every tree. [26]The only place it did not hail was the land of Goshen, where the Israelites were.

[27]Then Pharaoh summoned Moses and Aaron. "This time I have sinned," he said to them. "The LORD is in the right, and I and my people are in the wrong. [28]Pray to the LORD, for we have had enough thunder and hail. I will let you go; you don't have to stay any longer."

[29]Moses replied, "When I have gone out of the city, I will spread out my hands in prayer to the LORD. The thunder will stop and there will be no more hail, so you may know that the earth is the LORD's. [30]But I know that you and your officials still do not fear the LORD God."

[31](The flax and barley were destroyed, since the barley had headed and the flax was in bloom. [32]The wheat and spelt, however, were not destroyed, because they ripen later.)

[33]Then Moses left Pharaoh and went out of the city. He spread out his hands toward the LORD; the thunder and hail stopped, and the rain no longer poured down on the land. [34]When Pharaoh saw that the rain and hail and thunder had stopped, he sinned again: He and his officials hardened their hearts. [35]So Pharaoh's heart was hard and he would not let the Israelites go, just as the LORD had said through Moses.

The Plague of Locusts

10 Then the LORD said to Moses, "Go to Pharaoh, for I have hardened his heart and the hearts of his officials so that I may perform these miraculous signs of mine among them [2]that you may tell your children and grandchildren how I dealt harshly with the Egyptians and how I performed my signs among them, and that you may know that I am the LORD."

[3]So Moses and Aaron went to Pharaoh and said to him, "This is what the LORD, the God of the Hebrews, says: 'How long will you refuse to humble yourself before me? Let my people go, so that they may worship me. [4]If you refuse to let them go, I will bring locusts into your country tomorrow. [5]They will cover the face of the ground so that it cannot be seen. They will devour what little you have left after the hail, including every tree that is growing in your fields. [6]They will fill your houses and those of all your officials and all the Egyptians—something neither your fathers nor your forefathers have ever seen from the day they settled in this land till now.' " Then Moses turned and left Pharaoh.

[7]Pharaoh's officials said to him, "How long will this man be a snare to us? Let the people go, so that they may worship the LORD their God. Do you not yet realize that Egypt is ruined?"

[a] 16 Or have spared you

⁸Then Moses and Aaron were brought back to Pharaoh. "Go, worship the Lord your God," he said. "But just who will be going?"

⁹Moses answered, "We will go with our young and old, with our sons and daughters, and with our flocks and herds, because we are to celebrate a festival to the Lord."

¹⁰Pharaoh said, "The Lord be with you—if I let you go, along with your women and children! Clearly you are bent on evil.ᵃ ¹¹No! Have only the men go; and worship the Lord, since that's what you have been asking for." Then Moses and Aaron were driven out of Pharaoh's presence.

¹²And the Lord said to Moses, "Stretch out your hand over Egypt so that locusts will swarm over the land and devour everything growing in the fields, everything left by the hail."

¹³So Moses stretched out his staff over Egypt, and the Lord made an east wind blow across the land all that day and all that night. By morning the wind had brought the locusts; ¹⁴they invaded all Egypt and settled down in every area of the country in great numbers. Never before had there been such a plague of locusts, nor will there ever be again. ¹⁵They covered all the ground until it was black. They devoured all that was left after the hail—everything growing in the fields and the fruit on the trees. Nothing green remained on tree or plant in all the land of Egypt.

¹⁶Pharaoh quickly summoned Moses and Aaron and said, "I have sinned against the Lord your God and against you. ¹⁷Now forgive my sin once more and pray to the Lord your God to take this deadly plague away from me."

¹⁸Moses then left Pharaoh and prayed to the Lord. ¹⁹And the Lord changed the wind to a very strong west wind, which caught up the locusts and carried them into the Red Sea.ᵇ Not a locust was left anywhere in Egypt. ²⁰But the Lord hardened Pharaoh's heart, and he would not let the Israelites go.

The Plague of Darkness

²¹Then the Lord said to Moses, "Stretch out your hand toward the sky so that darkness will spread over Egypt—darkness that can be felt." ²²So Moses stretched out his hand toward the sky, and total darkness covered all Egypt for three days. ²³No one could see anyone else or leave his place for three days. Yet all the Israelites had light in the places where they lived.

²⁴Then Pharaoh summoned Moses and said, "Go, worship the Lord. Even your women and children may go with you; only leave your flocks and herds behind."

²⁵But Moses said, "You must allow us to have sacrifices and burnt offerings to present to the Lord our God. ²⁶Our livestock too must go with us; not a hoof is to be left behind. We have to use some of them in worshiping the Lord our God, and until we get there we will not know what we are to use to worship the Lord."

²⁷But the Lord hardened Pharaoh's heart, and he was not willing to let them go. ²⁸Pharaoh said to Moses, "Get out of my sight! Make sure you do not appear before me again! The day you see my face you will die."

²⁹"Just as you say," Moses replied, "I will never appear before you again."

The Plague on the Firstborn

11 Now the Lord had said to Moses, "I will bring one more plague on Pharaoh and on Egypt. After that, he will let you go from here, and when he does, he will drive you out completely. ²Tell the people that men and women alike are to ask their neighbors for articles of silver and gold." ³(The Lord made the Egyptians favorably disposed toward the people, and Moses himself was highly regarded in Egypt by Pharaoh's officials and by the people.)

⁴So Moses said, "This is what the Lord says: 'About midnight I will go throughout Egypt. ⁵Every firstborn son in Egypt will die, from the firstborn son of Pharaoh, who sits on the throne, to the firstborn son of the slave girl, who is at her hand mill, and all the firstborn of the cattle as well. ⁶There will be loud wailing throughout

---

ᵃ 10 Or *Be careful, trouble is in store for you!* ᵇ 19 Hebrew *Yam Suph*; that is, Sea of Reeds

Egypt—worse than there has ever been or ever will be again. [7]But among the Israelites not a dog will bark at any man or animal.' Then you will know that the LORD makes a distinction between Egypt and Israel. [8]All these officials of yours will come to me, bowing down before me and saying, 'Go, you and all the people who follow you!' After that I will leave." Then Moses, hot with anger, left Pharaoh.

[9]The LORD had said to Moses, "Pharaoh will refuse to listen to you—so that my wonders may be multiplied in Egypt." [10]Moses and Aaron performed all these wonders before Pharaoh, but the LORD hardened Pharaoh's heart, and he would not let the Israelites go out of his country.

The Passover

12:14–20pp — Lev 23:4–8; Nu 28:16–25; Dt 16:1–8

12 The LORD said to Moses and Aaron in Egypt, [2]"This month is to be for you the first month, the first month of your year. [3]Tell the whole community of Israel that on the tenth day of this month each man is to take a lamb[a] for his family, one for each household. [4]If any household is too small for a whole lamb, they must share one with their nearest neighbor, having taken into account the number of people there are. You are to determine the amount of lamb needed in accordance with what each person will eat. [5]The animals you choose must be year-old males without defect, and you may take them from the sheep or the goats. [6]Take care of them until the fourteenth day of the month, when all the people of the community of Israel must slaughter them at twilight. [7]Then they are to take some of the blood and put it on the sides and tops of the doorframes of the houses where they eat the lambs. [8]That same night they are to eat the meat roasted over the fire, along with bitter herbs, and bread made without yeast. [9]Do not eat the meat raw or cooked in water, but roast it over the fire—head, legs and inner parts. [10]Do not leave any of it till morning; if some is left till morning, you must burn it. [11]This is how you are to eat it: with your cloak tucked into your belt, your sandals on your feet and your staff in your hand. Eat it in haste; it is the LORD's Passover.

[12]"On that same night I will pass through Egypt and strike down every firstborn   both men and animals—and I will bring judgment on all the gods of Egypt. I am the LORD. [13]The blood will be a sign for you on the houses where you are; and when I see the blood, I will pass over you. No destructive plague will touch you when I strike Egypt.

[14]"This is a day you are to commemorate; for the generations to come you shall celebrate it as a festival to the LORD—a lasting ordinance. [15]For seven days you are to eat bread made without yeast. On the first day remove the yeast from your houses, for whoever eats anything with yeast in it from the first day through the seventh must be cut off from Israel. [16]On the first day hold a sacred assembly, and another one on the seventh day. Do no work at all on these days, except to prepare food for everyone to eat—that is all you may do.

[17]"Celebrate the Feast of Unleavened Bread, because it was on this very day that I brought your divisions out of Egypt. Celebrate this day as a lasting ordinance for the generations to come. [18]In the first month you are to eat bread made without yeast, from the evening of the fourteenth day until the evening of the twenty-first day. [19]For seven days no yeast is to be found in your houses. And whoever eats anything with yeast in it must be cut off from the community of Israel, whether he is an alien or native-born. [20]Eat nothing made with yeast. Wherever you live, you must eat unleavened bread."

[21]Then Moses summoned all the elders of Israel and said to them, "Go at once and select the animals for your families and slaughter the Passover lamb. [22]Take a bunch of hyssop, dip it into the blood in the basin and put some of the blood on the top and on both sides of the doorframe. Not one of you shall go out the door of his house until morning. [23]When the LORD goes through

---

a 3 The Hebrew word can mean lamb or kid; also in verse 4.

"THIS IS A DAY YOU ARE TO COMMEMORATE; FOR THE GENERATIONS TO COME YOU SHALL CELEBRATE IT AS A FESTIVAL TO THE LORD — A LASTING ORDINANCE."

Exodus 12:14

Commemoration

KAREN KINGSBURY

READ | EXODUS 12:1–30

My grandmother on my mom's side died at age 45. But Grandma Doris spent her last months in joyful celebration, working with my mom to plan her wedding. Grandma Doris had five children, and my mother was the oldest. The two were very close. When it became clear that cancer would win the battle for Grandma Doris's life, she refused to stay in a hospital bed.

Instead she spent her time looking through magazines for bridal dresses and dreaming with my mom about flowers and color schemes and, ultimately, my mother's wedding dress. With frail fingers, my Grandma Doris helped my mom button up her wedding gown as she tried it on for the first time. She marveled at the beautiful woman my mother had become, and she prayed at night for God's blessings on my mother's marriage.

My parents' wedding was beautiful, and though Grandma Doris was very ill, she can be seen in the grainy video clips greeting guests and smiling with her whole heart. My parents returned from their honeymoon and helped care for Grandma Doris until she died, six months later. But Doris's prayers have been answered in a dramatic way. My parents' marriage is still going strong — nearly 50 years now. When we celebrate their wedding anniversary, it is always with a special thought for Grandma Doris and the lasting value of her love shown on that special wedding date.

In addition, I included a picture of my Grandma Doris and my mother through my novel *Reunion*. The fictitious story of Elizabeth Baxter and her daughter Ashley is a tribute, in many ways, to the love my Grandma Doris had for her children, especially the love she showed my mother in the days before her wedding.

Dear Lord, there is something special about a grandmother's love, something that brings generations together. Thank you for this time with the people we love. Thank you that we can commemorate those we love during special celebrations and times of remembrance. Amen.

Your next devotion is located on page 103.

GRANDCHILD IN FOCUS • PRAYER

Relationships at Home

O Lord, I pray that you will bless the home and family of my grandchild. May the relationships she has with her parents and siblings enhance her well-being, support her self-confidence and increase her faith. May her home life reflect your love, your grace, your compassion and your peace. Guide her parents to direct her in love and truth, so she will grow into a strong and compassionate individual. Amen.

the land to strike down the Egyptians, he will see the blood on the top and sides of the doorframe and will pass over that doorway, and he will not permit the destroyer to enter your houses and strike you down.

²⁴"Obey these instructions as a lasting ordinance for you and your descendants. ²⁵When you enter the land that the LORD will give you as he promised, observe this ceremony. ²⁶And when your children ask you, 'What does this ceremony mean to you?' ²⁷then tell them, 'It is the Passover sacrifice to the LORD, who passed over the houses of the Israelites in Egypt and spared our homes when he struck down the Egyptians.'" Then the people bowed down and worshiped. ²⁸The Israelites did just what the LORD commanded Moses and Aaron.

²⁹At midnight the LORD struck down all the firstborn in Egypt, from the firstborn of Pharaoh, who sat on the throne, to the firstborn of the prisoner, who was in the dungeon, and the firstborn of all the livestock as well. ³⁰Pharaoh and all his officials and all the Egyptians got up during the night, and there was loud wailing in Egypt, for there was not a house without someone dead.

The Exodus

³¹During the night Pharaoh summoned Moses and Aaron and said, "Up! Leave my people, you and the Israelites! Go, worship the LORD as you have requested. ³²Take your flocks and herds, as you have said, and go. And also bless me."

³³The Egyptians urged the people to hurry and leave the country. "For otherwise," they said, "we will all die!" ³⁴So the people took their dough before the yeast was added, and carried it on their shoulders in kneading troughs wrapped in clothing. ³⁵The Israelites did as Moses instructed and asked the Egyptians for articles of silver and gold and for clothing. ³⁶The LORD had made the Egyptians favorably disposed toward the people, and they gave them what they asked for; so they plundered the Egyptians.

³⁷The Israelites journeyed from Rameses to Succoth. There were about six hundred thousand men on foot, besides women and children. ³⁸Many other people went up with them, as well as large droves of livestock, both flocks and herds. ³⁹With the dough they had brought from Egypt, they baked cakes of unleavened bread. The dough was without yeast because they had been driven out of Egypt and did not have time to prepare food for themselves.

⁴⁰Now the length of time the Israelite people lived in Egypt ᵃ was 430 years. ⁴¹At the end of the 430 years, to the very day, all the LORD's divisions left Egypt. ⁴²Because the LORD kept vigil that night to bring them out of Egypt, on this night all the Israelites are to keep vigil to honor the LORD for the generations to come.

Passover Restrictions

⁴³The LORD said to Moses and Aaron, "These are the regulations for the Passover:

"No foreigner is to eat of it. ⁴⁴Any slave you have bought may eat of it after you have circumcised him, ⁴⁵but a temporary resident and a hired worker may not eat of it.

⁴⁶"It must be eaten inside one house; take none of the meat outside the house. Do not break any of the bones. ⁴⁷The whole community of Israel must celebrate it.

⁴⁸"An alien living among you who wants to celebrate the LORD's Passover must have all the males in his household circumcised; then he may take part like one born in the land. No uncircumcised male may eat of it. ⁴⁹The same law applies to the native-born and to the alien living among you."

⁵⁰All the Israelites did just what the LORD had commanded Moses and Aaron. ⁵¹And on that very day the LORD brought the Israelites out of Egypt by their divisions.

Consecration of the Firstborn

13 The LORD said to Moses, ²"Consecrate to me every firstborn male. The first offspring of every womb among the Israelites belongs to me, whether man or animal."

ᵃ 40 Masoretic Text; Samaritan Pentateuch and Septuagint *Egypt and Canaan*

³Then Moses said to the people, "Commemorate this day, the day you came out of Egypt, out of the land of slavery, because the LORD brought you out of it with a mighty hand. Eat nothing containing yeast. ⁴Today, in the month of Abib, you are leaving. ⁵When the LORD brings you into the land of the Canaanites, Hittites, Amorites, Hivites and Jebusites—the land he swore to your forefathers to give you, a land flowing with milk and honey—you are to observe this ceremony in this month: ⁶For seven days eat bread made without yeast and on the seventh day hold a festival to the LORD. ⁷Eat unleavened bread during those seven days; nothing with yeast in it is to be seen among you, nor shall any yeast be seen anywhere within your borders. ⁸On that day tell your son, 'I do this because of what the LORD did for me when I came out of Egypt.' ⁹This observance will be for you like a sign on your hand and a reminder on your forehead that the law of the LORD is to be on your lips. For the LORD brought you out of Egypt with his mighty hand. ¹⁰You must keep this ordinance at the appointed time year after year.

¹¹"After the LORD brings you into the land of the Canaanites and gives it to you, as he promised on oath to you and your forefathers, ¹²you are to give over to the LORD the first offspring of every womb. All the firstborn males of your livestock belong to the LORD. ¹³Redeem with a lamb every firstborn donkey, but if you do not redeem it, break its neck. Redeem every firstborn among your sons.

¹⁴"In days to come, when your son asks you, 'What does this mean?' say to him, 'With a mighty hand the LORD brought us out of Egypt, out of the land of slavery. ¹⁵When Pharaoh stubbornly refused to let us go, the LORD killed every firstborn in Egypt, both man and animal. This is why I sacrifice to the LORD the first male offspring of every womb and redeem each of my firstborn sons.' ¹⁶And it will be like a sign on your hand and a symbol on your forehead that the LORD brought us out of Egypt with his mighty hand."

Crossing the Sea

¹⁷When Pharaoh let the people go, God did not lead them on the road through the Philistine country, though that was shorter. For God said, "If they face war, they might change their minds and return to Egypt." ¹⁸So God led the people around by the desert road toward the Red Sea.[a] The Israelites went up out of Egypt armed for battle.

¹⁹Moses took the bones of Joseph with him because Joseph had made the sons of Israel swear an oath. He had said, "God will surely come to your aid, and then you must carry my bones up with you from this place."[b]

²⁰After leaving Succoth they camped at Etham on the edge of the desert. ²¹By day the LORD went ahead of them in a pillar of cloud to guide them on their way and by night in a pillar of fire to give them light, so that they could travel by day or night. ²²Neither the pillar of cloud by day nor the pillar of fire by night left its place in front of the people.

14 Then the LORD said to Moses, ²"Tell the Israelites to turn back and encamp near Pi Hahiroth, between Migdol and the sea. They are to encamp by the sea, directly opposite Baal Zephon. ³Pharaoh will think, 'The Israelites are wandering around the land in confusion, hemmed in by the desert.' ⁴And I will harden Pharaoh's heart, and he will pursue them. But I will gain glory for myself through Pharaoh and all his army, and the Egyptians will know that I am the LORD." So the Israelites did this.

⁵When the king of Egypt was told that the people had fled, Pharaoh and his officials changed their minds about them and said, "What have we done? We have let the Israelites go and have lost their services!" ⁶So he had his chariot made ready and took his army with him. ⁷He took six hundred of the best chariots, along with all the other chariots of Egypt, with officers over all of them. ⁸The LORD hardened the heart of Pharaoh king of Egypt, so that he pursued the Israelites, who

[a] 18 Hebrew *Yam Suph*; that is, Sea of Reeds   [b] 19 See Gen. 50:25.

Movie Matinee

A worthwhile family movie can be a great Saturday afternoon treat for all of you. Why not forego the popcorn and find a quiet booth at a restaurant to talk after the movie? Here are some possible questions to get the conversation started: Which character did you enjoy the most? What did you think was the funniest part? Did any scenes make you sad? Does anything in the movie remind you of an experience you've had, a book you've read, etc.? Name one important thing you learned from the movie.

If you prefer, rent a movie instead and view it together at your house. Then have your discussion together afterward.

Long-Distance Variation: Suggest that the long-distance grandkids watch the same movie and answer the same questions in writing. Then call them and have your discussion.

Thank you, God, for the gift of stories and the imagination they inspire. Thank you for the wealth of unforgettable stories in your Word and for preserving them through generations. I praise and thank you for the uniqueness of each of my grandchildren. Let our time together be a joy-filled experience for everyone. Amen.

Your next devotion is located on page 104.

GRANDCHILD IN FOCUS • PRAYER

Friends

Dear Lord and Father, I pray for my grandchild's social life and his friends. Bring diverse friends into his life who will love and encourage him, who will bring joy and laughter to the good times and comfort and support through difficulties and disappointments. Grant him wisdom and discernment as he selects his friends; help him to avoid cliques that restrict, activities that endanger, and foolish and dangerous behaviors that harm. I ask that you fill his life with close and caring relationships. Amen.

Worship the Lord

He who dwells in the shelter of the Most High
  will rest in the shadow of the Almighty.
I will say of the LORD, "He is my refuge and my fortress,
  my God, in whom I trust."

Surely he will save you from the fowler's snare
  and from the deadly pestilence.
He will cover you with his feathers,
  and under his wings you will find refuge;
  his faithfulness will be your shield and rampart.
You will not fear the terror of night,
  nor the arrow that flies by day,
nor the pestilence that stalks in the darkness,
  nor the plague that destroys at midday.
A thousand may fall at your side,
  ten thousand at your right hand,
  but it will not come near you.

Psalm 91:1 – 7

*What blessed shelter, Lord, to be pro-
tected by your shadow and beneath your
wings. Thank you for reassuring me that I
have nothing to fear, that neither my imagination during the night nor my anxiety during the day is beyond the scope of your power.
Amen.*

Your next devotion is located on page 107.

GRANDCHILD IN FOCUS • PRAYER

Self-Image

*O loving God, I praise you for creating my
grandchild as a unique individual. Now I ask you
to help her appreciate her uniqueness. Build up her
self-image so she can enjoy her individuality. Help
her to stand firm for who she is, where she has
come from and what she believes in. Encourage
her not only to have hopes and dreams but
to also enjoy each day as it comes.
In Jesus' name, amen.*

EXODUS 13:17—14:31

Crossing the Red Sea

LIFE LESSON: God can do what seems impossible to us.

TO TALK ABOUT

✦ How did God show his people the right way to go?

✦ Why did Pharaoh change his mind about letting the Israelites go?

✦ Why did the Israelites have so much trouble trusting in God?

✦ When have trusting and obeying God been hard for you? Why?

were marching out boldly. [9] The Egyptians—all Pharaoh's horses and chariots, horsemen[a] and troops—pursued the Israelites and overtook them as they camped by the sea near Pi Hahiroth, opposite Baal Zephon.

[10] As Pharaoh approached, the Israelites looked up, and there were the Egyptians, marching after them. They were terrified and cried out to the LORD. [11] They said to Moses, "Was it because there were no graves in Egypt that you brought us to the desert to die? What have you done to us by bringing us out of Egypt? [12] Didn't we say to you in Egypt, 'Leave us alone; let us serve the Egyptians'? It would have been better for us to serve the Egyptians than to die in the desert!"

[13] Moses answered the people, "Do not be afraid. Stand firm and you will see the deliverance the LORD will bring you today. The Egyptians you see today you will never see again. [14] The LORD will fight for you; you need only to be still."

[15] Then the LORD said to Moses, "Why are you crying out to me? Tell the Israelites to move on. [16] Raise your staff and stretch out your hand over the sea to divide the water so that the Israelites can go through the sea on dry ground. [17] I will harden the hearts of the Egyptians so that they will go in after them. And I will gain glory through Pharaoh and all his army, through his chariots and his horsemen. [18] The Egyptians will know that I am the LORD when I gain glory through Pharaoh, his chariots and his horsemen."

[19] Then the angel of God, who had been traveling in front of Israel's army, withdrew and went behind them. The pillar of cloud also moved from in front and stood behind them, [20] coming between the armies of Egypt and Israel. Throughout the night the cloud brought darkness to the one side and light to the other side; so neither went near the other all night long.

[21] Then Moses stretched out his hand over the sea, and all that night the LORD drove the sea back with a strong east wind and turned it into dry land. The waters were divided, [22] and the Israelites went through the sea on dry ground, with a wall of water on their right and on their left.

[23] The Egyptians pursued them, and all Pharaoh's horses and chariots and horsemen followed them into the sea. [24] During the last watch of the night the LORD looked down from the pillar of fire and cloud at the Egyptian army and threw it into confusion. [25] He made the wheels of their chariots come off[b] so that they had difficulty driving. And the Egyptians said, "Let's get away from the Israelites! The LORD is fighting for them against Egypt."

[26] Then the LORD said to Moses, "Stretch out your hand over the sea so that the waters may flow back over the Egyptians and their chariots and horsemen." [27] Moses stretched out his hand over the sea, and at daybreak the sea went back to its place. The Egyptians were fleeing toward[c]

---

[a] 9 Or *charioteers*; also in verses 17, 18, 23, 26 and 28   [b] 25 Or *He jammed the wheels of their chariots* (see Samaritan Pentateuch, Septuagint and Syriac)   [c] 27 Or *from*

it, and the LORD swept them into the sea. ²⁸The water flowed back and covered the chariots and horsemen—the entire army of Pharaoh that had followed the Israelites into the sea. Not one of them survived.

²⁹But the Israelites went through the sea on dry ground, with a wall of water on their right and on their left. ³⁰That day the LORD saved Israel from the hands of the Egyptians, and Israel saw the Egyptians lying dead on the shore. ³¹And when the Israelites saw the great power the LORD displayed against the Egyptians, the people feared the LORD and put their trust in him and in Moses his servant.

The Song of Moses and Miriam

15 Then Moses and the Israelites sang this song to the LORD:

"I will sing to the LORD,
for he is highly exalted.
The horse and its rider
he has hurled into the sea.
²The LORD is my strength and my song;
he has become my salvation.
He is my God, and I will praise him,
my father's God, and I will exalt him.
³The LORD is a warrior;
the LORD is his name.
⁴Pharaoh's chariots and his army
he has hurled into the sea.
The best of Pharaoh's officers
are drowned in the Red Sea.ᵃ
⁵The deep waters have covered them;
they sank to the depths like a stone.

⁶"Your right hand, O LORD,
was majestic in power.
Your right hand, O LORD,
shattered the enemy.
⁷In the greatness of your majesty
you threw down those who opposed you.
You unleashed your burning anger;
it consumed them like stubble.
⁸By the blast of your nostrils
the waters piled up.

The surging waters stood firm like a wall;
the deep waters congealed in the heart
of the sea.
⁹"The enemy boasted,
'I will pursue, I will overtake them.
I will divide the spoils;
I will gorge myself on them.
I will draw my sword
and my hand will destroy them.'
¹⁰But you blew with your breath,
and the sea covered them.
They sank like lead
in the mighty waters.

¹¹"Who among the gods is like you, O LORD?
Who is like you—
majestic in holiness,
awesome in glory,
working wonders?
¹²You stretched out your right hand
and the earth swallowed them.

¹³"In your unfailing love you will lead
the people you have redeemed.
In your strength you will guide them
to your holy dwelling.
¹⁴The nations will hear and tremble;
anguish will grip the people of Philistia.
¹⁵The chiefs of Edom will be terrified,
the leaders of Moab will be seized with
trembling,
the people ᵇ of Canaan will melt away;
¹⁶   terror and dread will fall upon them.
By the power of your arm
they will be as still as a stone—
until your people pass by, O LORD,
until the people you bought ᶜ pass by.
¹⁷You will bring them in and plant them
on the mountain of your inheritance—
the place, O LORD, you made for your dwelling,
the sanctuary, O Lord, your hands
established.
¹⁸The LORD will reign
for ever and ever."

ᵃ 4 Hebrew *Yam Suph*; that is, Sea of Reeds; also in verse 22
ᵇ 15 Or *rulers*   ᶜ 16 Or *created*

MIRIAM SANG TO THEM: "SING
TO THE LORD, FOR HE IS
HIGHLY EXALTED. THE HORSE
AND ITS RIDER HE HAS HURLED
INTO THE SEA."

Exodus 15:21

Singing All the Time

DEBBY KERNER RETTINO

READ | EXODUS 15:1 – 21

I sing almost all the time. My family is musical, and my husband and I record albums for kids and lead worship at our church. Songs bubble out of me as I come through the doors at work, drive in the car or pick out melons at the market. My neighbors know I am in the store from the next aisle over. Praise songs, old hymns or my latest composition — it is quite unconscious. I sing almost constantly, and it drives my grandson crazy. At 13 years of age, it is soooo embarrassing to be out with Grandma. I try to curb my spontaneous melodies when I am in public with him. (Something about not provoking your children to wrath comes to mind.)

When he was little, I would sing into his ear, "Who loves you more than I do?" He would answer in his tiny, toddler voice, "God does." That's the best wisdom I could give him. Over and over and over I sang about God's love for him in his ear. I wanted it to stick. I wanted it to stick so that when he faced temptation, the songs I sang in his ear would come back to him. I wanted it to stick so that when he smacked into the realities of life, not only would he remember how much I loved him, but more important, God's love for him would be engraved on his heart. I wanted it to stick so that when he faced hard things in his future, he would remember that his grandma loved him like crazy — but God loved him more. So I sing. Almost all the time.

Father in heaven, thank you for the song you have put in my heart. I praise you for the Word of God that lives in me and bubbles over in music. Thank you that no matter how much I love my grandkids, you love them more than I do.

Your next devotion is located on page 128.

GRANDCHILD IN FOCUS • PRAYER

Protection From Worldliness

O Sovereign Lord, the world surrounds my grandchild, pressing in and tempting him in so many ways. Help him set appropriate limits. Give him sound judgment to choose wisely. Guard him from temptation; protect him from physical and mental predators; lead him into paths of righteousness and light. And reassure me with your promise that you are holding him in your hands. Amen.

¹⁹When Pharaoh's horses, chariots and horsemen *a* went into the sea, the LORD brought the waters of the sea back over them, but the Israelites walked through the sea on dry ground. ²⁰Then Miriam the prophetess, Aaron's sister, took a tambourine in her hand, and all the women followed her, with tambourines and dancing. ²¹Miriam sang to them:

"Sing to the LORD,
    for he is highly exalted.
The horse and its rider
    he has hurled into the sea."

The Waters of Marah and Elim

²²Then Moses led Israel from the Red Sea and they went into the Desert of Shur. For three days they traveled in the desert without finding water. ²³When they came to Marah, they could not drink its water because it was bitter. (That is why the place is called Marah. *b*) ²⁴So the people grumbled against Moses, saying, "What are we to drink?"

²⁵Then Moses cried out to the LORD, and the LORD showed him a piece of wood. He threw it into the water, and the water became sweet.

There the LORD made a decree and a law for them, and there he tested them. ²⁶He said, "If you listen carefully to the voice of the LORD your God and do what is right in his eyes, if you pay attention to his commands and keep all his decrees, I will not bring on you any of the diseases I brought on the Egyptians, for I am the LORD, who heals you."

stories to share

EXODUS 15:22–27

Water in the Wilderness

LIFE LESSON: God takes care of his people.

TO TALK ABOUT

✦ What was wrong with the water?

✦ How did God tell Moses to fix it?

✦ What promise did God make to the people if they would obey?

✦ How does God take care of his people today?

²⁷Then they came to Elim, where there were twelve springs and seventy palm trees, and they camped there near the water.

Manna and Quail

16 The whole Israelite community set out from Elim and came to the Desert of Sin, which is between Elim and Sinai, on the fifteenth day of the second month after they had come out of Egypt. ²In the desert the whole community grumbled against Moses and Aaron. ³The Israelites said to them, "If only we had died by the LORD's hand in Egypt! There we sat around pots of meat and ate all the food we wanted, but you have brought us out into this desert to starve this entire assembly to death."

⁴Then the LORD said to Moses, "I will rain down bread from heaven for you. The people are to go out each day and gather enough for that

---

TALKING POINTS

Illness

God is our healer.

EXODUS 15:26

For more on illness, go to 2 Kings 20:1–11.

---

a 19 Or charioteers   *b 23 Marah means bitter.*

day. In this way I will test them and see whether they will follow my instructions. ⁵On the sixth day they are to prepare what they bring in, and that is to be twice as much as they gather on the other days."

⁶So Moses and Aaron said to all the Israelites, "In the evening you will know that it was the Lord who brought you out of Egypt, ⁷and in the morning you will see the glory of the Lord, because he has heard your grumbling against him. Who are we, that you should grumble against us?" ⁸Moses also said, "You will know that it was the Lord when he gives you meat to eat in the evening and all the bread you want in the morning, because he has heard your grumbling against him. Who are we? You are not grumbling against us, but against the Lord."

⁹Then Moses told Aaron, "Say to the entire Israelite community, 'Come before the Lord, for he has heard your grumbling.'"

¹⁰While Aaron was speaking to the whole Israelite community, they looked toward the desert, and there was the glory of the Lord appearing in the cloud.

¹¹The Lord said to Moses, ¹²"I have heard the grumbling of the Israelites. Tell them, 'At twilight you will eat meat, and in the morning you will be filled with bread. Then you will know that I am the Lord your God.'"

¹³That evening quail came and covered the camp, and in the morning there was a layer of dew around the camp. ¹⁴When the dew was gone, thin flakes like frost on the ground appeared on the desert floor. ¹⁵When the Israelites saw it, they said to each other, "What is it?" For they did not know what it was.

Moses said to them, "It is the bread the Lord has given you to eat. ¹⁶This is what the Lord has commanded: 'Each one is to gather as much as he needs. Take an omer ᵃ for each person you have in your tent.'"

¹⁷The Israelites did as they were told; some gathered much, some little. ¹⁸And when they measured it by the omer, he who gathered much did not have too much, and he who gathered little did not have too little. Each one gathered as much as he needed.

¹⁹Then Moses said to them, "No one is to keep any of it until morning."

²⁰However, some of them paid no attention to Moses; they kept part of it until morning, but it was full of maggots and began to smell. So Moses was angry with them.

²¹Each morning everyone gathered as much as he needed, and when the sun grew hot, it melted away. ²²On the sixth day, they gathered twice as much—two omers ᵇ for each person—and the leaders of the community came and reported this to Moses. ²³He said to them, "This is what the Lord commanded: 'Tomorrow is to be a day of rest, a holy Sabbath to the Lord. So bake what you want to bake and boil what you want to boil. Save whatever is left and keep it until morning.'"

²⁴So they saved it until morning, as Moses commanded, and it did not stink or get maggots in it. ²⁵"Eat it today," Moses said, "because today is a Sabbath to the Lord. You will not find any of it on the ground today. ²⁶Six days you are to gather it, but on the seventh day, the Sabbath, there will not be any."

²⁷Nevertheless, some of the people went out on the seventh day to gather it, but they found none. ²⁸Then the Lord said to Moses, "How long will you ᶜ refuse to keep my commands and my instructions? ²⁹Bear in mind that the Lord has given you the Sabbath; that is why on the sixth day he gives you bread for two days. Everyone is to stay where he is on the seventh day; no one is to go out." ³⁰So the people rested on the seventh day.

³¹The people of Israel called the bread manna. ᵈ It was white like coriander seed and tasted like wafers made with honey. ³²Moses said, "This is what the Lord has commanded: 'Take an omer of manna and keep it for the generations to come, so they can see the bread I gave you to eat in the desert when I brought you out of Egypt.'"

ᵃ 16 That is, probably about 2 quarts (about 2 liters); also in verses 18, 32, 33 and 36   ᵇ 22 That is, probably about 4 quarts (about 4.5 liters)   ᶜ 28 The Hebrew is plural.   ᵈ 31 Manna means What is it? (see verse 15).

33 So Moses said to Aaron, "Take a jar and put an omer of manna in it. Then place it before the LORD to be kept for the generations to come."

34 As the LORD commanded Moses, Aaron put the manna in front of the Testimony, that it might be kept. 35 The Israelites ate manna forty years, until they came to a land that was settled; they ate manna until they reached the border of Canaan.

36 (An omer is one tenth of an ephah.)

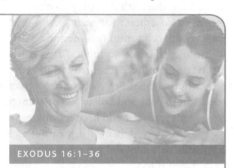

EXODUS 16:1–36

God Provides Food From Heaven

LIFE LESSON: God supplies our daily needs.

TO TALK ABOUT

✦ Why was it hard to find food for so many people in the desert?

✦ How did God feed the hungry Israelites?

✦ Why did God make rules about manna?

✦ What lessons can we learn from this story about trusting God in our lives?

Water From the Rock

17 The whole Israelite community set out from the Desert of Sin, traveling from place to place as the LORD commanded. They camped at Rephidim, but there was no water for the people to drink. 2 So they quarreled with Moses and said, "Give us water to drink."

Moses replied, "Why do you quarrel with me? Why do you put the LORD to the test?"

3 But the people were thirsty for water there, and they grumbled against Moses. They said, "Why did you bring us up out of Egypt to make us and our children and livestock die of thirst?"

4 Then Moses cried out to the LORD, "What am I to do with these people? They are almost ready to stone me."

5 The LORD answered Moses, "Walk on ahead of the people. Take with you some of the elders of Israel and take in your hand the staff with which you struck the Nile, and go. 6 I will stand there before you by the rock at Horeb. Strike the rock, and water will come out of it for the people to drink." So Moses did this in the sight of the elders of Israel. 7 And he called the place Massah^a and Meribah^b because the Israelites quarreled and because they tested the LORD saying, "Is the LORD among us or not?"

The Amalekites Defeated

8 The Amalekites came and attacked the Israelites at Rephidim. 9 Moses said to Joshua, "Choose some of our men and go out to fight the Amalekites. Tomorrow I will stand on top of the hill with the staff of God in my hands."

10 So Joshua fought the Amalekites as Moses had ordered, and Moses, Aaron and Hur went to the top of the hill. 11 As long as Moses held up his hands, the Israelites were winning, but whenever he lowered his hands, the Amalekites were winning. 12 When Moses' hands grew tired, they took a stone and put it under him and he sat on it. Aaron and Hur held his hands up — one on one side, one on the other — so that his hands remained steady till sunset. 13 So Joshua overcame the Amalekite army with the sword.

14 Then the LORD said to Moses, "Write this on a scroll as something to be remembered and make sure that Joshua hears it, because I will com-

^a 7 Massah means testing. ^b 7 Meribah means quarreling.

pletely blot out the memory of Amalek from under heaven."

15 Moses built an altar and called it The LORD is my Banner. 16 He said, "For hands were lifted up to the throne of the LORD. The *a* LORD will be at war against the Amalekites from generation to generation."

Jethro Visits Moses

18 Now Jethro, the priest of Midian and father-in-law of Moses, heard of everything God had done for Moses and for his people Israel, and how the LORD had brought Israel out of Egypt.

2 After Moses had sent away his wife Zipporah, his father-in-law Jethro received her 3 and her two sons. One son was named Gershom,*b* for Moses said, "I have become an alien in a foreign land"; 4 and the other was named Eliezer,*c* for he said, "My father's God was my helper; he saved me from the sword of Pharaoh."

5 Jethro, Moses' father-in-law, together with Moses' sons and wife, came to him in the desert, where he was camped near the mountain of God. 6 Jethro had sent word to him, "I, your father-in-law Jethro, am coming to you with your wife and her two sons."

7 So Moses went out to meet his father-in-law and bowed down and kissed him. They greeted each other and then went into the tent. 8 Moses told his father-in-law about everything the LORD had done to Pharaoh and the Egyptians for Israel's sake and about all the hardships they had met along the way and how the LORD had saved them.

9 Jethro was delighted to hear about all the good things the LORD had done for Israel in rescuing them from the hand of the Egyptians. 10 He said, "Praise be to the LORD, who rescued you from the hand of the Egyptians and of Pharaoh, and who rescued the people from the hand of the Egyptians. 11 Now I know that the LORD is greater than all other gods, for he did this to those who had treated them arrogantly." 12 Then Jethro, Moses' father-in-law, brought a burnt offering and other sacrifices to God, and Aaron came with all the elders of Israel to eat bread with Moses' father-in-law in the presence of God.

13 The next day Moses took his seat to serve as judge for the people, and they stood around him from morning till evening. 14 When his father-in-law saw all that Moses was doing for the people, he said, "What is this you are doing for the people? Why do you alone sit as judge, while all these people stand around you from morning till evening?"

15 Moses answered him, "Because the people come to me to seek God's will. 16 Whenever they have a dispute, it is brought to me, and I decide between the parties and inform them of God's decrees and laws."

17 Moses' father-in-law replied, "What you are doing is not good. 18 You and these people who come to you will only wear yourselves out. The work is too heavy for you; you cannot handle it alone. 19 Listen now to me and I will give you some advice, and may God be with you. You must be the people's representative before God and bring their disputes to him. 20 Teach them the decrees and laws, and show them the way to live and the duties they are to perform. 21 But select capable men from all the people—men who fear God, trustworthy men who hate dishonest gain—and appoint them as officials over thousands, hundreds, fifties and tens. 22 Have them serve as judges for the people at all times, but have them bring every difficult case to you; the simple cases they can decide themselves. That will make your load lighter, because they will share it with you. 23 If you do this and God so commands, you will be able to stand the strain, and all these people will go home satisfied."

24 Moses listened to his father-in-law and did everything he said. 25 He chose capable men from all Israel and made them leaders of the people, officials over thousands, hundreds, fifties and tens. 26 They served as judges for the people at all

---

a 16 Or "Because a hand was against the throne of the LORD, the
b 3 Gershom sounds like the Hebrew for an alien there.   *c* 4 Eliezer means my God is helper.

times. The difficult cases they brought to Moses, but the simple ones they decided themselves.

²⁷Then Moses sent his father-in-law on his way, and Jethro returned to his own country.

At Mount Sinai

19 In the third month after the Israelites left Egypt—on the very day—they came to the Desert of Sinai. ²After they set out from Rephidim, they entered the Desert of Sinai, and Israel camped there in the desert in front of the mountain.

³Then Moses went up to God, and the Lord called to him from the mountain and said, "This is what you are to say to the house of Jacob and what you are to tell the people of Israel: ⁴'You yourselves have seen what I did to Egypt, and how I carried you on eagles' wings and brought you to myself. ⁵Now if you obey me fully and keep my covenant, then out of all nations you will be my treasured possession. Although the whole earth is mine, ⁶you ᵃ will be for me a kingdom of priests and a holy nation.' These are the words you are to speak to the Israelites."

⁷So Moses went back and summoned the elders of the people and set before them all the words the Lord had commanded him to speak. ⁸The people all responded together, "We will do everything the Lord has said." So Moses brought their answer back to the Lord.

⁹The Lord said to Moses, "I am going to come to you in a dense cloud, so that the people will hear me speaking with you and will always put their trust in you." Then Moses told the Lord what the people had said.

¹⁰And the Lord said to Moses, "Go to the people and consecrate them today and tomorrow. Have them wash their clothes ¹¹and be ready by the third day, because on that day the Lord will come down on Mount Sinai in the sight of all the people. ¹²Put limits for the people around the mountain and tell them, 'Be careful that you do not go up the mountain or touch the foot of it. Whoever touches the mountain shall surely be put to death. ¹³He shall surely be stoned or

stories to share

EXODUS 19:1–9; 20:1–21

God Gives Moses the Ten Commandments

LIFE LESSON: God is holy, and he deserves our respect.

TO TALK ABOUT

✦ What were some of God's ten rules for his people?

✦ If everyone obeyed these rules, what would the world be like?

✦ God is holy, and he wants us to "fear" him. How is reverent fear different from feeling afraid?

✦ Do you think of God as awesome or as scary? Why?

shot with arrows; not a hand is to be laid on him. Whether man or animal, he shall not be permitted to live.' Only when the ram's horn sounds a long blast may they go up to the mountain."

¹⁴After Moses had gone down the mountain to the people, he consecrated them, and they washed their clothes. ¹⁵Then he said to the people, "Prepare yourselves for the third day. Abstain from sexual relations."

¹⁶On the morning of the third day there was thunder and lightning, with a thick cloud over the mountain, and a very loud trumpet blast. Everyone in the camp trembled. ¹⁷Then Moses led the people out of the camp to meet with God, and

ᵃ 5,6 Or possession, for the whole earth is mine. ⁶You

they stood at the foot of the mountain. ¹⁸Mount Sinai was covered with smoke, because the LORD descended on it in fire. The smoke billowed up from it like smoke from a furnace, the whole mountain ᵃ trembled violently, ¹⁹and the sound of the trumpet grew louder and louder. Then Moses spoke and the voice of God answered him. ᵇ

²⁰The LORD descended to the top of Mount Sinai and called Moses to the top of the mountain. So Moses went up ²¹and the LORD said to him, "Go down and warn the people so they do not force their way through to see the LORD and many of them perish. ²²Even the priests, who approach the LORD, must consecrate themselves, or the LORD will break out against them."

²³Moses said to the LORD, "The people cannot come up Mount Sinai, because you yourself warned us, 'Put limits around the mountain and set it apart as holy.'"

²⁴The LORD replied, "Go down and bring Aaron up with you. But the priests and the people must not force their way through to come up to the LORD, or he will break out against them."

²⁵So Moses went down to the people and told them.

The Ten Commandments

20:1–17pp — Dt 5:6–21

20 And God spoke all these words:

²"I am the LORD your God, who brought you out of Egypt, out of the land of slavery.

³"You shall have no other gods before ᶜ me.

⁴"You shall not make for yourself an idol in the form of anything in heaven above or on the earth beneath or in the waters below. ⁵You shall not bow down to them or worship them; for I, the LORD your God, am a jealous God, punishing the children for the sin of the fathers to the third and fourth generation of those who hate me, ⁶but showing love to a thousand ⌞generations⌟ of those who love me and keep my commandments.

⁷"You shall not misuse the name of the LORD your God, for the LORD will not hold anyone guiltless who misuses his name.

⁸"Remember the Sabbath day by keeping it holy. ⁹Six days you shall labor and do all your work, ¹⁰but the seventh day is a Sabbath to the LORD your God. On it you shall not do any work, neither you, nor your son or daughter, nor your manservant or maidservant, nor your animals, nor the alien within your gates. ¹¹For in six days the LORD made the heavens and the earth, the sea, and all that is in them, but he rested on the seventh day. Therefore the LORD blessed the Sabbath day and made it holy.

¹²"Honor your father and your mother, so that you may live long in the land the LORD your God is giving you.

TALKING POINTS

Parents

One of God's ten commandments tells us to honor our parents.

EXODUS 20:12

For more on parents, go to Levticus 19:3.

¹³"You shall not murder.

¹⁴"You shall not commit adultery.

¹⁵"You shall not steal.

¹⁶"You shall not give false testimony against your neighbor.

¹⁷"You shall not covet your neighbor's house. You shall not covet your neighbor's

---

ᵃ 18 Most Hebrew manuscripts; a few Hebrew manuscripts and Septuagint *all the people*   ᵇ 19 Or *and God answered him with thunder*   ᶜ 3 Or *besides* wife, or his manservant or maidservant, his ox or donkey, or anything that belongs to your neighbor."

TALKING POINTS

Lying

False testimony about another is wrong.

EXODUS 20:16

For more on lying, go to Psalm 34:13.

¹⁸When the people saw the thunder and lightning and heard the trumpet and saw the mountain in smoke, they trembled with fear. They stayed at a distance ¹⁹and said to Moses, "Speak to us yourself and we will listen. But do not have God speak to us or we will die."

²⁰Moses said to the people, "Do not be afraid. God has come to test you, so that the fear of God will be with you to keep you from sinning."

²¹The people remained at a distance, while Moses approached the thick darkness where God was.

Idols and Altars

²²Then the LORD said to Moses, "Tell the Israelites this: 'You have seen for yourselves that I have spoken to you from heaven: ²³Do not make any gods to be alongside me; do not make for yourselves gods of silver or gods of gold.

²⁴" 'Make an altar of earth for me and sacrifice on it your burnt offerings and fellowship offerings,[a] your sheep and goats and your cattle. Wherever I cause my name to be honored, I will come to you and bless you. ²⁵If you make an altar of stones for me, do not build it with dressed stones, for you will defile it if you use a tool on it. ²⁶And do not go up to my altar on steps, lest your nakedness be exposed on it.'

21 "These are the laws you are to set before them:

Hebrew Servants

21:2–6pp — Dt 15:12–18
21:2–11Ref — Lev 25:39–55

²"If you buy a Hebrew servant, he is to serve you for six years. But in the seventh year, he shall go free, without paying anything. ³If he comes alone, he is to go free alone; but if he has a wife when he comes, she is to go with him. ⁴If his master gives him a wife and she bears him sons or daughters, the woman and her children shall belong to her master, and only the man shall go free.

⁵"But if the servant declares, 'I love my master and my wife and children and do not want to go free,' ⁶then his master must take him before the judges.[b] He shall take him to the door or the doorpost and pierce his ear with an awl. Then he will be his servant for life.

⁷"If a man sells his daughter as a servant, she is not to go free as menservants do. ⁸If she does not please the master who has selected her for himself,[c] he must let her be redeemed. He has no right to sell her to foreigners, because he has broken faith with her. ⁹If he selects her for his son, he must grant her the rights of a daughter. ¹⁰If he marries another woman, he must not deprive the first one of her food, clothing and marital rights. ¹¹If he does not provide her with these three things, she is to go free, without any payment of money.

Personal Injuries

¹²"Anyone who strikes a man and kills him shall surely be put to death. ¹³However, if he does not do it intentionally, but God lets it happen, he is to flee to a place I will designate. ¹⁴But if a man schemes and kills another man deliberately, take him away from my altar and put him to death.

¹⁵"Anyone who attacks[d] his father or his mother must be put to death.

---

[a] 24 Traditionally *peace offerings*   [b] 6 Or *before God*
[c] 8 Or *master so that he does not choose her*   [d] 15 Or *kills*

¹⁶"Anyone who kidnaps another and either sells him or still has him when he is caught must be put to death.

¹⁷"Anyone who curses his father or mother must be put to death.

¹⁸"If men quarrel and one hits the other with a stone or with his fist ᵃ and he does not die but is confined to bed, ¹⁹the one who struck the blow will not be held responsible if the other gets up and walks around outside with his staff; however, he must pay the injured man for the loss of his time and see that he is completely healed.

²⁰"If a man beats his male or female slave with a rod and the slave dies as a direct result, he must be punished, ²¹but he is not to be punished if the slave gets up after a day or two, since the slave is his property.

²²"If men who are fighting hit a pregnant woman and she gives birth prematurely ᵇ but there is no serious injury, the offender must be fined whatever the woman's husband demands and the court allows. ²³But if there is serious injury, you are to take life for life, ²⁴eye for eye, tooth for tooth, hand for hand, foot for foot, ²⁵burn for burn, wound for wound, bruise for bruise.

²⁶"If a man hits a manservant or maidservant in the eye and destroys it, he must let the servant go free to compensate for the eye. ²⁷And if he knocks out the tooth of a manservant or maidservant, he must let the servant go free to compensate for the tooth.

²⁸"If a bull gores a man or a woman to death, the bull must be stoned to death, and its meat must not be eaten. But the owner of the bull will not be held responsible. ²⁹If, however, the bull has had the habit of goring and the owner has been warned but has not kept it penned up and it kills a man or woman, the bull must be stoned and the owner also must be put to death. ³⁰However, if payment is demanded of him, he may redeem his life by paying whatever is demanded. ³¹This law also applies if the bull gores a son or daughter. ³²If the bull gores a male or female slave, the owner must pay thirty shekels ᶜ of silver to the master of the slave, and the bull must be stoned.

³³"If a man uncovers a pit or digs one and fails to cover it and an ox or a donkey falls into it, ³⁴the owner of the pit must pay for the loss; he must pay its owner, and the dead animal will be his.

³⁵"If a man's bull injures the bull of another and it dies, they are to sell the live one and divide both the money and the dead animal equally. ³⁶However, if it was known that the bull had the habit of goring, yet the owner did not keep it penned up, the owner must pay, animal for animal, and the dead animal will be his.

Protection of Property

22 "If a man steals an ox or a sheep and slaughters it or sells it, he must pay back five head of cattle for the ox and four sheep for the sheep.

²"If a thief is caught breaking in and is struck so that he dies, the defender is not guilty of bloodshed; ³but if it happens ᵈ after sunrise, he is guilty of bloodshed.

"A thief must certainly make restitution, but if he has nothing, he must be sold to pay for his theft.

⁴"If the stolen animal is found alive in his possession—whether ox or donkey or sheep—he must pay back double.

⁵"If a man grazes his livestock in a field or vineyard and lets them stray and they graze in another man's field, he must make restitution from the best of his own field or vineyard.

⁶"If a fire breaks out and spreads into thornbushes so that it burns shocks of grain or standing grain or the whole field, the one who started the fire must make restitution.

⁷"If a man gives his neighbor silver or goods for safekeeping and they are stolen from the neighbor's house, the thief, if he is caught, must pay back double. ⁸But if the thief is not found, the owner of the house must appear before the judges ᵉ to determine whether he has laid his hands on the other man's property. ⁹In all cases of illegal possession of an ox, a donkey, a sheep, a

---

ᵃ 18 Or *with a tool*   ᵇ 22 Or *she has a miscarriage*   ᶜ 32 That is, about 12 ounces (about 0.3 kilogram)   ᵈ 3 Or *if he strikes him*   ᵉ 8 Or *before God*; also in verse 9

RUTH GRAHAM

No Substitutes

Not long ago I had just gotten back from a weeklong trip. My desk was stacked high with mail. My computer told me I had many emails that needed prompt responses. And the phone was ringing. On top of that it was the holiday season. I was feeling frantic and overwhelmed. It just didn't seem like I could ever catch up or was even making a dent. Frustrated and frazzled would be a good description of how I was feeling.

My oldest daughter, Noelle, called me to ask if I could keep my two-year-old granddaughter for part of the afternoon. She assured me that it would be Virginia Ruth's naptime. Always glad to spend time with her and assured that she would nap, I quickly agreed. I'd put her in bed and then continue to dig through the pile on my desk.

When Noelle and Virginia Ruth arrived, Noelle informed me that she had left "bear" and "blanket" at home. It was naptime, and Virginia Ruth was ready. But not without bear and blanket. I tried to show her the monkey that was a leftover from my son Graham's childhood, but she looked horrified when she saw it. Then I tried to comfort her with a baby blanket that belonged to her mother as a baby. Her big blue eyes filled with tears and she moaned, "Nooo." I reached for an old doll, hoping that would comfort her. Her wails grew louder. There was no substitute for the real blanket and bear!

I felt helpless. I scooped her up and held her close. I sat down in my favorite chair as she snuggled up close and nested her little blond head on my shoulder. Soon she was breathing heavily and sleeping sweetly.

Virginia Ruth would take no substitute for bear and blanket. She looked at each thing offered and knew it would not satisfy her need for comfort. Only in my arms did she find the rest and peace she needed.

How many times am I offered a "substitute" for the comfort only God can provide? God reminds us in his Word that he is the only God; all other substitutes are idols before him (see Exodus 20:3–6).

When I am faced with choosing the true God or something else, do I react like little

Virginia Ruth and long only for the real thing? Or do I take the offered substitute only to be left feeling more empty than before? Do I rest in the strong arms of Jesus or grow restless because things aren't as I want them to be?

I have a choice.

You have a choice.

Make the Choice

Today make the choice to refuse any substitute for the Lord Jesus. If you do not know him personally, let me invite you to do so right now! You can open your heart and tell God you want him and him alone. Tell him you need him and are sorry for your sins — for those substitutes you've accepted. Tell him you believe that Jesus died on the cross and rose again from the dead for you. Ask Jesus to take up residence in your heart and life as Lord and Savior. The moment you ask, God is there.

If you like, you can say this prayer — the words aren't as important as the sincerity of your heart: "God, I recognize that I have been filling my life with substitutes for you. I am sorry. I want to change, but I need your help. I believe that Jesus died and rose again for me. Please forgive my sins and come into my heart and life. I give it to you. I refuse all substitutes. I receive you as Lord and Savior and turn my life over to you. Help me to trust you more and more. I rest in your arms. Thank you. In Jesus' name, amen."

God Has Done It

If you prayed that prayer, then God has done it — he has come into your heart and life! You are his. You will no longer be satisfied with substitutes. In him you will find comfort and rest for your spirit.

As you start this new relationship with God, I encourage you to set aside time to be with him each day. It doesn't have to be a great amount of time. Begin today to daily read the Scriptures and pray to the Lord. You can start with the Bible you hold in your hands right now. Read until a verse or maybe just a phrase speaks to you. Then talk to Jesus — prayer is just like talking to your best friend — about what it says to you, what is on your heart. It is that simple.

Refuse all substitutes.

garment, or any other lost property about which somebody says, 'This is mine,' both parties are to bring their cases before the judges. The one whom the judges declare^a guilty must pay back double to his neighbor.

¹⁰"If a man gives a donkey, an ox, a sheep or any other animal to his neighbor for safekeeping and it dies or is injured or is taken away while no one is looking, ¹¹the issue between them will be settled by the taking of an oath before the LORD that the neighbor did not lay hands on the other person's property. The owner is to accept this, and no restitution is required. ¹²But if the animal was stolen from the neighbor, he must make restitution to the owner. ¹³If it was torn to pieces by a wild animal, he shall bring in the remains as evidence and he will not be required to pay for the torn animal.

¹⁴"If a man borrows an animal from his neighbor and it is injured or dies while the owner is not present, he must make restitution. ¹⁵But if the owner is with the animal, the borrower will not have to pay. If the animal was hired, the money paid for the hire covers the loss.

Social Responsibility

¹⁶"If a man seduces a virgin who is not pledged to be married and sleeps with her, he must pay the bride-price, and she shall be his wife. ¹⁷If her father absolutely refuses to give her to him, he must still pay the bride-price for virgins.

¹⁸"Do not allow a sorceress to live.

¹⁹"Anyone who has sexual relations with an animal must be put to death.

²⁰"Whoever sacrifices to any god other than the LORD must be destroyed.^b

²¹"Do not mistreat an alien or oppress him, for you were aliens in Egypt.

²²"Do not take advantage of a widow or an orphan. ²³If you do and they cry out to me, I will certainly hear their cry. ²⁴My anger will be aroused, and I will kill you with the sword; your wives will become widows and your children fatherless.

²⁵"If you lend money to one of my people among you who is needy, do not be like a mon-

eylender; charge him no interest.^c ²⁶If you take your neighbor's cloak as a pledge, return it to him by sunset, ²⁷because his cloak is the only covering he has for his body. What else will he sleep in? When he cries out to me, I will hear, for I am compassionate.

²⁸"Do not blaspheme God^d or curse the ruler of your people.

²⁹"Do not hold back offerings from your granaries or your vats.^e

"You must give me the firstborn of your sons. ³⁰Do the same with your cattle and your sheep. Let them stay with their mothers for seven days, but give them to me on the eighth day.

³¹"You are to be my holy people. So do not eat the meat of an animal torn by wild beasts; throw it to the dogs.

Laws of Justice and Mercy

23 "Do not spread false reports. Do not help a wicked man by being a malicious witness.

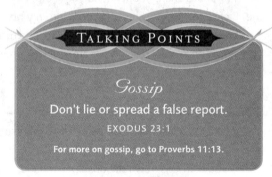

TALKING POINTS

Gossip

Don't lie or spread a false report.

EXODUS 23:1

For more on gossip, go to Proverbs 11:13.

²"Do not follow the crowd in doing wrong. When you give testimony in a lawsuit, do not pervert justice by siding with the crowd, ³and do not show favoritism to a poor man in his lawsuit.

⁴"If you come across your enemy's ox or donkey wandering off, be sure to take it back to him. ⁵If you see the donkey of someone who hates you

---

^a 9 Or *whom God declares*   ^b 20 The Hebrew term refers to the irrevocable giving over of things or persons to the LORD, often by totally destroying them.   ^c 25 Or *excessive interest*   ^d 28 Or *Do not revile the judges*   ^e 29 The meaning of the Hebrew for this phrase is uncertain.

fallen down under its load, do not leave it there; be sure you help him with it.

⁶"Do not deny justice to your poor people in their lawsuits. ⁷Have nothing to do with a false charge and do not put an innocent or honest person to death, for I will not acquit the guilty.

⁸"Do not accept a bribe, for a bribe blinds those who see and twists the words of the righteous.

⁹"Do not oppress an alien; you yourselves know how it feels to be aliens, because you were aliens in Egypt.

TALKING POINTS

Social Justice
God calls us to a life of justice and mercy.
EXODUS 23:1–9

For more on social justice, go to Isaiah 58:6–9.

Sabbath Laws

¹⁰"For six years you are to sow your fields and harvest the crops, ¹¹but during the seventh year let the land lie unplowed and unused. Then the poor among your people may get food from it, and the wild animals may eat what they leave. Do the same with your vineyard and your olive grove.

¹²"Six days do your work, but on the seventh day do not work, so that your ox and your donkey may rest and the slave born in your household, and the alien as well, may be refreshed.

¹³"Be careful to do everything I have said to you. Do not invoke the names of other gods; do not let them be heard on your lips.

The Three Annual Festivals

¹⁴"Three times a year you are to celebrate a festival to me.

¹⁵"Celebrate the Feast of Unleavened Bread; for seven days eat bread made without yeast,

as I commanded you. Do this at the appointed time in the month of Abib, for in that month you came out of Egypt.

"No one is to appear before me empty-handed.

¹⁶"Celebrate the Feast of Harvest with the firstfruits of the crops you sow in your field.

"Celebrate the Feast of Ingathering at the end of the year, when you gather in your crops from the field.

¹⁷"Three times a year all the men are to appear before the Sovereign LORD.

¹⁸"Do not offer the blood of a sacrifice to me along with anything containing yeast.

"The fat of my festival offerings must not be kept until morning.

¹⁹"Bring the best of the firstfruits of your soil to the house of the LORD your God.

"Do not cook a young goat in its mother's milk.

God's Angel to Prepare the Way

²⁰"See, I am sending an angel ahead of you to guard you along the way and to bring you to the place I have prepared. ²¹Pay attention to him and listen to what he says. Do not rebel against him; he will not forgive your rebellion, since my Name is in him. ²²If you listen carefully to what he says and do all that I say, I will be an enemy to your enemies and will oppose those who oppose you. ²³My angel will go ahead of you and bring you into the land of the Amorites, Hittites, Perizzites, Canaanites, Hivites and Jebusites, and I will wipe them out. ²⁴Do not bow down before their gods or worship them or follow their practices. You must demolish them and break their sacred stones to pieces. ²⁵Worship the LORD your God, and his blessing will be on your food and water. I will take away sickness from among you, ²⁶and none will miscarry or be barren in your land. I will give you a full life span.

²⁷"I will send my terror ahead of you and throw into confusion every nation you encounter. I will make all your enemies turn their backs and run. ²⁸I will send the hornet ahead of you to drive the Hivites, Canaanites and Hittites out

of your way. ²⁹But I will not drive them out in a single year, because the land would become desolate and the wild animals too numerous for you. ³⁰Little by little I will drive them out before you, until you have increased enough to take possession of the land.

³¹"I will establish your borders from the Red Sea^a to the Sea of the Philistines,^b and from the desert to the River.^c I will hand over to you the people who live in the land and you will drive them out before you. ³²Do not make a covenant with them or with their gods. ³³Do not let them live in your land, or they will cause you to sin against me, because the worship of their gods will certainly be a snare to you."

The Covenant Confirmed

24 Then he said to Moses, "Come up to the LORD, you and Aaron, Nadab and Abihu, and seventy of the elders of Israel. You are to worship at a distance, ²but Moses alone is to approach the LORD; the others must not come near. And the people may not come up with him."

³When Moses went and told the people all the LORD's words and laws, they responded with one voice, "Everything the LORD has said we will do." ⁴Moses then wrote down everything the LORD had said.

He got up early the next morning and built an altar at the foot of the mountain and set up twelve stone pillars representing the twelve tribes of Israel. ⁵Then he sent young Israelite men, and they offered burnt offerings and sacrificed young bulls as fellowship offerings^d to the LORD. ⁶Moses took half of the blood and put it in bowls, and the other half he sprinkled on the altar. ⁷Then he took the Book of the Covenant and read it to the people. They responded, "We will do everything the LORD has said; we will obey."

⁸Moses then took the blood, sprinkled it on the people and said, "This is the blood of the covenant that the LORD has made with you in accordance with all these words."

⁹Moses and Aaron, Nadab and Abihu, and seventy elders of Israel went up ¹⁰and saw the God of Israel. Under his feet was something like a pavement made of sapphire,^e clear as the sky itself. ¹¹But God did not raise his hand against these leaders of the Israelites; they saw God, and they ate and drank.

¹²The LORD said to Moses, "Come up to me on the mountain and stay here, and I will give you the tablets of stone, with the law and commands I have written for their instruction."

¹³Then Moses set out with Joshua his aide, and Moses went up on the mountain of God. ¹⁴He said to the elders, "Wait here for us until we come back to you. Aaron and Hur are with you, and anyone involved in a dispute can go to them."

¹⁵When Moses went up on the mountain, the cloud covered it, ¹⁶and the glory of the LORD settled on Mount Sinai. For six days the cloud covered the mountain, and on the seventh day the LORD called to Moses from within the cloud. ¹⁷To the Israelites the glory of the LORD looked like a consuming fire on top of the mountain. ¹⁸Then Moses entered the cloud as he went on up the mountain. And he stayed on the mountain forty days and forty nights.

Offerings for the Tabernacle
25:1–7pp — Ex 35:4–9

25 The LORD said to Moses, ²"Tell the Israelites to bring me an offering. You are to receive the offering for me from each man whose heart prompts him to give. ³These are the offerings you are to receive from them: gold, silver and bronze; ⁴blue, purple and scarlet yarn and fine linen; goat hair; ⁵ram skins dyed red and hides of sea cows^f; acacia wood; ⁶olive oil for the light; spices for the anointing oil and for the fragrant incense; ⁷and onyx stones and other gems to be mounted on the ephod and breastpiece.

⁸"Then have them make a sanctuary for me, and I will dwell among them. ⁹Make this tabernacle and all its furnishings exactly like the pattern I will show you.

---

^a 31 Hebrew *Yam Suph*; that is, Sea of Reeds   ^b 31 That is, the Mediterranean   ^c 31 That is, the Euphrates   ^d 5 Traditionally *peace offerings*   ^e 10 Or *lapis lazuli*   ^f 5 That is, dugongs

The Ark

25:10–20pp — Ex 37:1–9

¹⁰"Have them make a chest of acacia wood—two and a half cubits long, a cubit and a half wide, and a cubit and a half high.[a] ¹¹Overlay it with pure gold, both inside and out, and make a gold molding around it. ¹²Cast four gold rings for it and fasten them to its four feet, with two rings on one side and two rings on the other. ¹³Then make poles of acacia wood and overlay them with gold. ¹⁴Insert the poles into the rings on the sides of the chest to carry it. ¹⁵The poles are to remain in the rings of this ark; they are not to be removed. ¹⁶Then put in the ark the Testimony, which I will give you.

¹⁷"Make an atonement cover[b] of pure gold—two and a half cubits long and a cubit and a half wide.[c] ¹⁸And make two cherubim out of hammered gold at the ends of the cover. ¹⁹Make one cherub on one end and the second cherub on the other; make the cherubim of one piece with the cover, at the two ends. ²⁰The cherubim are to have their wings spread upward, overshadowing the cover with them. The cherubim are to face each other, looking toward the cover. ²¹Place the cover on top of the ark and put in the ark the Testimony, which I will give you. ²²There, above the cover between the two cherubim that are over the ark of the Testimony, I will meet with you and give you all my commands for the Israelites.

The Table

25:23–29pp — Ex 37:10–16

²³"Make a table of acacia wood—two cubits long, a cubit wide and a cubit and a half high.[d] ²⁴Overlay it with pure gold and make a gold molding around it. ²⁵Also make around it a rim a handbreadth[e] wide and put a gold molding on the rim. ²⁶Make four gold rings for the table and fasten them to the four corners, where the four legs are. ²⁷The rings are to be close to the rim to hold the poles used in carrying the table. ²⁸Make the poles of acacia wood, overlay them with gold and carry the table with them. ²⁹And make its plates and dishes of pure gold, as well as its pitchers and bowls for the pouring out of offerings. ³⁰Put the bread of the Presence on this table to be before me at all times.

The Lampstand

25:31–39pp — Ex 37:17–24

³¹"Make a lampstand of pure gold and hammer it out, base and shaft; its flowerlike cups, buds and blossoms shall be of one piece with it. ³²Six branches are to extend from the sides of the lampstand—three on one side and three on the other. ³³Three cups shaped like almond flowers with buds and blossoms are to be on one branch, three on the next branch, and the same for all six branches extending from the lampstand. ³⁴And on the lampstand there are to be four cups shaped like almond flowers with buds and blossoms. ³⁵One bud shall be under the first pair of branches extending from the lampstand, a second bud under the second pair, and a third bud under the third pair—six branches in all. ³⁶The buds and branches shall all be of one piece with the lampstand, hammered out of pure gold.

³⁷"Then make its seven lamps and set them up on it so that they light the space in front of it. ³⁸Its wick trimmers and trays are to be of pure gold. ³⁹A talent[f] of pure gold is to be used for the lampstand and all these accessories. ⁴⁰See that you make them according to the pattern shown you on the mountain.

The Tabernacle

26:1–37pp — Ex 36:8–38

26 "Make the tabernacle with ten curtains of finely twisted linen and blue, purple and scarlet yarn, with cherubim worked into them by a skilled craftsman. ²All the curtains are to be the same size—twenty-eight cubits long and four cubits wide.[g] ³Join five of the curtains

---

a 10 That is, about 3 3/4 feet (about 1.1 meters) long and 2 1/4 feet (about 0.7 meter) wide and high   *b 17* Traditionally *a mercy seat*   *c 17* That is, about 3 3/4 feet (about 1.1 meters) long and 2 1/4 feet (about 0.7 meter) wide   *d 23* That is, about 3 feet (about 0.9 meter) long and 1 1/2 feet (about 0.5 meter) wide and 2 1/4 feet (about 0.7 meter) high   *e 25* That is, about 3 inches (about 8 centimeters)   *f 39* That is, about 75 pounds (about 34 kilograms)   *g 2* That is, about 42 feet (about 12.5 meters) long and 6 feet (about 1.8 meters) wide together, and do the same with the other five. [4] Make loops of blue material along the edge of the end curtain in one set, and do the same with the end curtain in the other set. [5] Make fifty loops on one curtain and fifty loops on the end curtain of the other set, with the loops opposite each other. [6] Then make fifty gold clasps and use them to fasten the curtains together so that the tabernacle is a unit.

[7] "Make curtains of goat hair for the tent over the tabernacle—eleven altogether. [8] All eleven curtains are to be the same size—thirty cubits long and four cubits wide.[a] [9] Join five of the curtains together into one set and the other six into another set. Fold the sixth curtain double at the front of the tent. [10] Make fifty loops along the edge of the end curtain in one set and also along the edge of the end curtain in the other set. [11] Then make fifty bronze clasps and put them in the loops to fasten the tent together as a unit. [12] As for the additional length of the tent curtains, the half curtain that is left over is to hang down at the rear of the tabernacle. [13] The tent curtains will be a cubit[b] longer on both sides; what is left will hang over the sides of the tabernacle so as to cover it. [14] Make for the tent a covering of ram skins dyed red, and over that a covering of hides of sea cows.[c]

[15] "Make upright frames of acacia wood for the tabernacle. [16] Each frame is to be ten cubits long and a cubit and a half wide,[d] [17] with two projections set parallel to each other. Make all the frames of the tabernacle in this way. [18] Make twenty frames for the south side of the tabernacle [19] and make forty silver bases to go under them—two bases for each frame, one under each projection. [20] For the other side, the north side of the tabernacle, make twenty frames [21] and forty silver bases—two under each frame. [22] Make six frames for the far end, that is, the west end of the tabernacle, [23] and make two frames for the corners at the far end. [24] At these two corners they must be double from the bottom all the way to the top, and fitted into a single ring; both shall be like that. [25] So there will be eight frames and sixteen silver bases—two under each frame.

[26] "Also make crossbars of acacia wood: five for the frames on one side of the tabernacle, [27] five for those on the other side, and five for the frames on the west, at the far end of the tabernacle. [28] The center crossbar is to extend from end to end at the middle of the frames. [29] Overlay the frames with gold and make gold rings to hold the crossbars. Also overlay the crossbars with gold.

[30] "Set up the tabernacle according to the plan shown you on the mountain.

[31] "Make a curtain of blue, purple and scarlet yarn and finely twisted linen, with cherubim worked into it by a skilled craftsman. [32] Hang it with gold hooks on four posts of acacia wood overlaid with gold and standing on four silver bases. [33] Hang the curtain from the clasps and place the ark of the Testimony behind the curtain. The curtain will separate the Holy Place from the Most Holy Place. [34] Put the atonement cover on the ark of the Testimony in the Most Holy Place. [35] Place the table outside the curtain on the north side of the tabernacle and put the lampstand opposite it on the south side.

[36] "For the entrance to the tent make a curtain of blue, purple and scarlet yarn and finely twisted linen—the work of an embroiderer. [37] Make gold hooks for this curtain and five posts of acacia wood overlaid with gold. And cast five bronze bases for them.

The Altar of Burnt Offering
27:1–8pp — Ex 38:1–7

27 "Build an altar of acacia wood, three cubits[e] high; it is to be square, five cubits long and five cubits wide.[f] [2] Make a horn at each of the four corners, so that the horns and the altar are of one piece, and overlay the altar with bronze. [3] Make all its utensils of bronze—its pots

[a] 8 That is, about 45 feet (about 13.5 meters) long and 6 feet (about 1.8 meters) wide   [b] 13 That is, about 1 1/2 feet (about 0.5 meter)   [c] 14 That is, dugongs   [d] 16 That is, about 15 feet (about 4.5 meters) long and 2 1/4 feet (about 0.7 meter) wide   [e] 1 That is, about 4 1/2 feet (about 1.3 meters)   [f] 1 That is, about 7 1/2 feet (about 2.3 meters) long and wide

to remove the ashes, and its shovels, sprinkling bowls, meat forks and firepans. ⁴Make a grating for it, a bronze network, and make a bronze ring at each of the four corners of the network. ⁵Put it under the ledge of the altar so that it is halfway up the altar. ⁶Make poles of acacia wood for the altar and overlay them with bronze. ⁷The poles are to be inserted into the rings so they will be on two sides of the altar when it is carried. ⁸Make the altar hollow, out of boards. It is to be made just as you were shown on the mountain.

The Courtyard
27:9–19pp — Ex 38:9–20

⁹"Make a courtyard for the tabernacle. The south side shall be a hundred cubits *a* long and is to have curtains of finely twisted linen, ¹⁰with twenty posts and twenty bronze bases and with silver hooks and bands on the posts. ¹¹The north side shall also be a hundred cubits long and is to have curtains, with twenty posts and twenty bronze bases and with silver hooks and bands on the posts.

¹²"The west end of the courtyard shall be fifty cubits *b* wide and have curtains, with ten posts and ten bases. ¹³On the east end, toward the sunrise, the courtyard shall also be fifty cubits wide. ¹⁴Curtains fifteen cubits *c* long are to be on one side of the entrance, with three posts and three bases, ¹⁵and curtains fifteen cubits long are to be on the other side, with three posts and three bases.

¹⁶"For the entrance to the courtyard, provide a curtain twenty cubits *d* long, of blue, purple and scarlet yarn and finely twisted linen — the work of an embroiderer — with four posts and four bases. ¹⁷All the posts around the courtyard are to have silver bands and hooks, and bronze bases. ¹⁸The courtyard shall be a hundred cubits long and fifty cubits wide, *e* with curtains of finely twisted linen five cubits *f* high, and with bronze bases. ¹⁹All the other articles used in the service of the tabernacle, whatever their function, including all the tent pegs for it and those for the courtyard, are to be of bronze.

Oil for the Lampstand
27:20–21pp — Lev 24:1–3

²⁰"Command the Israelites to bring you clear oil of pressed olives for the light so that the lamps may be kept burning. ²¹In the Tent of Meeting, outside the curtain that is in front of the Testimony, Aaron and his sons are to keep the lamps burning before the LORD from evening till morning. This is to be a lasting ordinance among the Israelites for the generations to come.

The Priestly Garments

28 "Have Aaron your brother brought to you from among the Israelites, along with his sons Nadab and Abihu, Eleazar and Ithamar, so they may serve me as priests. ²Make sacred garments for your brother Aaron, to give him dignity and honor. ³Tell all the skilled men to whom I have given wisdom in such matters that they are to make garments for Aaron, for his consecration, so he may serve me as priest. ⁴These are the garments they are to make: a breastpiece, an ephod, a robe, a woven tunic, a turban and a sash. They are to make these sacred garments for your brother Aaron and his sons, so they may serve me as priests. ⁵Have them use gold, and blue, purple and scarlet yarn, and fine linen.

The Ephod
28:6–14pp — Ex 39:2–7

⁶"Make the ephod of gold, and of blue, purple and scarlet yarn, and of finely twisted linen — the work of a skilled craftsman. ⁷It is to have two shoulder pieces attached to two of its corners, so it can be fastened. ⁸Its skillfully woven waistband is to be like it — of one piece with the ephod and made with gold, and with blue, purple and scarlet yarn, and with finely twisted linen.

⁹"Take two onyx stones and engrave on them the names of the sons of Israel ¹⁰in the order of

---

a 9 That is, about 150 feet (about 46 meters); also in verse 11
b 12 That is, about 75 feet (about 23 meters); also in verse 13
c 14 That is, about 22 1/2 feet (about 6.9 meters); also in verse 15
d 16 That is, about 30 feet (about 9 meters)   *e 18* That is, about 150 feet (about 46 meters) long and 75 feet (about 23 meters) wide
f 18 That is, about 7 1/2 feet (about 2.3 meters)

their birth — six names on one stone and the remaining six on the other. ¹¹Engrave the names of the sons of Israel on the two stones the way a gem cutter engraves a seal. Then mount the stones in gold filigree settings ¹²and fasten them on the shoulder pieces of the ephod as memorial stones for the sons of Israel. Aaron is to bear the names on his shoulders as a memorial before the Lord. ¹³Make gold filigree settings ¹⁴and two braided chains of pure gold, like a rope, and attach the chains to the settings.

The Breastpiece
28:15–28pp — Ex 39:8–21

¹⁵"Fashion a breastpiece for making decisions — the work of a skilled craftsman. Make it like the ephod: of gold, and of blue, purple and scarlet yarn, and of finely twisted linen. ¹⁶It is to be square — a span *a* long and a span wide — and folded double. ¹⁷Then mount four rows of precious stones on it. In the first row there shall be a ruby, a topaz and a beryl; ¹⁸in the second row a turquoise, a sapphire *b* and an emerald; ¹⁹in the third row a jacinth, an agate and an amethyst; ²⁰in the fourth row a chrysolite, an onyx and a jasper. *c* Mount them in gold filigree settings. ²¹There are to be twelve stones, one for each of the names of the sons of Israel, each engraved like a seal with the name of one of the twelve tribes.

²²"For the breastpiece make braided chains of pure gold, like a rope. ²³Make two gold rings for it and fasten them to two corners of the breastpiece. ²⁴Fasten the two gold chains to the rings at the corners of the breastpiece, ²⁵and the other ends of the chains to the two settings, attaching them to the shoulder pieces of the ephod at the front. ²⁶Make two gold rings and attach them to the other two corners of the breastpiece on the inside edge next to the ephod. ²⁷Make two more gold rings and attach them to the bottom of the shoulder pieces on the front of the ephod, close to the seam just above the waistband of the ephod. ²⁸The rings of the breastpiece are to be tied to the rings of the ephod with blue cord,

connecting it to the waistband, so that the breastpiece will not swing out from the ephod.

²⁹"Whenever Aaron enters the Holy Place, he will bear the names of the sons of Israel over his heart on the breastpiece of decision as a continuing memorial before the Lord. ³⁰Also put the Urim and the Thummim in the breastpiece, so they may be over Aaron's heart whenever he enters the presence of the Lord. Thus Aaron will always bear the means of making decisions for the Israelites over his heart before the Lord.

Other Priestly Garments
28:31–43pp — Ex 39:22–31

³¹"Make the robe of the ephod entirely of blue cloth, ³²with an opening for the head in its center. There shall be a woven edge like a collar *d* around this opening, so that it will not tear. ³³Make pomegranates of blue, purple and scarlet yarn around the hem of the robe, with gold bells between them. ³⁴The gold bells and the pomegranates are to alternate around the hem of the robe. ³⁵Aaron must wear it when he ministers. The sound of the bells will be heard when he enters the Holy Place before the Lord and when he comes out, so that he will not die.

³⁶"Make a plate of pure gold and engrave on it as on a seal: HOLY TO THE LORD. ³⁷Fasten a blue cord to it to attach it to the turban; it is to be on the front of the turban. ³⁸It will be on Aaron's forehead, and he will bear the guilt involved in the sacred gifts the Israelites consecrate, whatever their gifts may be. It will be on Aaron's forehead continually so that they will be acceptable to the Lord.

³⁹"Weave the tunic of fine linen and make the turban of fine linen. The sash is to be the work of an embroiderer. ⁴⁰Make tunics, sashes and headbands for Aaron's sons, to give them dignity and honor. ⁴¹After you put these clothes on your brother Aaron and his sons, anoint and ordain them. Consecrate them so they may serve me as priests.

---

a 16 That is, about 9 inches (about 22 centimeters)   *b 18* Or *lapis lazuli*   *c 20* The precise identification of some of these precious stones is uncertain.   *d 32* The meaning of the Hebrew for this word is uncertain.

⁴²"Make linen undergarments as a covering for the body, reaching from the waist to the thigh. ⁴³Aaron and his sons must wear them whenever they enter the Tent of Meeting or approach the altar to minister in the Holy Place, so that they will not incur guilt and die.

"This is to be a lasting ordinance for Aaron and his descendants.

Consecration of the Priests

29:1–37pp — Lev 8:1–36

29 "This is what you are to do to consecrate them, so they may serve me as priests: Take a young bull and two rams without defect. ²And from fine wheat flour, without yeast, make bread, and cakes mixed with oil, and wafers spread with oil. ³Put them in a basket and present them in it—along with the bull and the two rams. ⁴Then bring Aaron and his sons to the entrance to the Tent of Meeting and wash them with water. ⁵Take the garments and dress Aaron with the tunic, the robe of the ephod, the ephod itself and the breastpiece. Fasten the ephod on him by its skillfully woven waistband. ⁶Put the turban on his head and attach the sacred diadem to the turban. ⁷Take the anointing oil and anoint him by pouring it on his head. ⁸Bring his sons and dress them in tunics ⁹and put headbands on them. Then tie sashes on Aaron and his sons.ᵃ The priesthood is theirs by a lasting ordinance. In this way you shall ordain Aaron and his sons.

¹⁰"Bring the bull to the front of the Tent of Meeting, and Aaron and his sons shall lay their hands on its head. ¹¹Slaughter it in the Lord's presence at the entrance to the Tent of Meeting. ¹²Take some of the bull's blood and put it on the horns of the altar with your finger, and pour out the rest of it at the base of the altar. ¹³Then take all the fat around the inner parts, the covering of the liver, and both kidneys with the fat on them, and burn them on the altar. ¹⁴But burn the bull's flesh and its hide and its offal outside the camp. It is a sin offering.

¹⁵"Take one of the rams, and Aaron and his sons shall lay their hands on its head. ¹⁶Slaughter it and take the blood and sprinkle it against the altar on all sides. ¹⁷Cut the ram into pieces and wash the inner parts and the legs, putting them with the head and the other pieces. ¹⁸Then burn the entire ram on the altar. It is a burnt offering to the Lord, a pleasing aroma, an offering made to the Lord by fire.

¹⁹"Take the other ram, and Aaron and his sons shall lay their hands on its head. ²⁰Slaughter it, take some of its blood and put it on the lobes of the right ears of Aaron and his sons, on the thumbs of their right hands, and on the big toes of their right feet. Then sprinkle blood against the altar on all sides. ²¹And take some of the blood on the altar and some of the anointing oil and sprinkle it on Aaron and his garments and on his sons and their garments. Then he and his sons and their garments will be consecrated.

²²"Take from this ram the fat, the fat tail, the fat around the inner parts, the covering of the liver, both kidneys with the fat on them, and the right thigh. (This is the ram for the ordination.) ²³From the basket of bread made without yeast, which is before the Lord, take a loaf, and a cake made with oil, and a wafer. ²⁴Put all these in the hands of Aaron and his sons and wave them before the Lord as a wave offering. ²⁵Then take them from their hands and burn them on the altar along with the burnt offering for a pleasing aroma to the Lord, an offering made to the Lord by fire. ²⁶After you take the breast of the ram for Aaron's ordination, wave it before the Lord as a wave offering, and it will be your share.

²⁷"Consecrate those parts of the ordination ram that belong to Aaron and his sons: the breast that was waved and the thigh that was presented. ²⁸This is always to be the regular share from the Israelites for Aaron and his sons. It is the contribution the Israelites are to make to the Lord from their fellowship offerings.ᵇ

²⁹"Aaron's sacred garments will belong to his descendants so that they can be anointed and ordained in them. ³⁰The son who succeeds him

---

ᵃ 9 Hebrew; Septuagint *on them*   ᵇ 28 Traditionally *peace offerings* as priest and comes to the Tent of Meeting to minister in the Holy Place is to wear them seven days.

31 "Take the ram for the ordination and cook the meat in a sacred place. 32 At the entrance to the Tent of Meeting, Aaron and his sons are to eat the meat of the ram and the bread that is in the basket. 33 They are to eat these offerings by which atonement was made for their ordination and consecration. But no one else may eat them, because they are sacred. 34 And if any of the meat of the ordination ram or any bread is left over till morning, burn it up. It must not be eaten, because it is sacred.

35 "Do for Aaron and his sons everything I have commanded you, taking seven days to ordain them. 36 Sacrifice a bull each day as a sin offering to make atonement. Purify the altar by making atonement for it, and anoint it to consecrate it. 37 For seven days make atonement for the altar and consecrate it. Then the altar will be most holy, and whatever touches it will be holy.

38 "This is what you are to offer on the altar regularly each day: two lambs a year old. 39 Offer one in the morning and the other at twilight. 40 With the first lamb offer a tenth of an ephah[a] of fine flour mixed with a quarter of a hin[b] of oil from pressed olives, and a quarter of a hin of wine as a drink offering. 41 Sacrifice the other lamb at twilight with the same grain offering and its drink offering as in the morning—a pleasing aroma, an offering made to the LORD by fire.

42 "For the generations to come this burnt offering is to be made regularly at the entrance to the Tent of Meeting before the LORD. There I will meet you and speak to you; 43 there also I will meet with the Israelites, and the place will be consecrated by my glory.

44 "So I will consecrate the Tent of Meeting and the altar and will consecrate Aaron and his sons to serve me as priests. 45 Then I will dwell among the Israelites and be their God. 46 They will know that I am the LORD their God, who brought them out of Egypt so that I might dwell among them. I am the LORD their God.

The Altar of Incense

30:1–5pp — Ex 37:25–28

30 "Make an altar of acacia wood for burning incense. 2 It is to be square, a cubit long and a cubit wide, and two cubits high[c]—its horns of one piece with it. 3 Overlay the top and all the sides and the horns with pure gold, and make a gold molding around it. 4 Make two gold rings for the altar below the molding—two on opposite sides—to hold the poles used to carry it. 5 Make the poles of acacia wood and overlay them with gold. 6 Put the altar in front of the curtain that is before the ark of the Testimony—before the atonement cover that is over the Testimony—where I will meet with you.

7 "Aaron must burn fragrant incense on the altar every morning when he tends the lamps. 8 He must burn incense again when he lights the lamps at twilight so incense will burn regularly before the LORD for the generations to come. 9 Do not offer on this altar any other incense or any burnt offering or grain offering, and do not pour a drink offering on it. 10 Once a year Aaron shall make atonement on its horns. This annual atonement must be made with the blood of the atoning sin offering for the generations to come. It is most holy to the LORD."

Atonement Money

11 Then the LORD said to Moses, 12 "When you take a census of the Israelites to count them, each one must pay the LORD a ransom for his life at the time he is counted. Then no plague will come on them when you number them. 13 Each one who crosses over to those already counted is to give a half shekel,[d] according to the sanctuary shekel, which weighs twenty gerahs. This half shekel is an offering to the LORD. 14 All who cross over, those twenty years old or more, are to give an offering to the LORD. 15 The rich are not to give more than a half shekel and the poor are not to

---

[a] 40 That is, probably about 2 quarts (about 2 liters) [b] 40 That is, probably about 1 quart (about 1 liter) [c] 2 That is, about 1 1/2 feet (about 0.5 meter) long and wide and about 3 feet (about 0.9 meter) high [d] 13 That is, about 1/5 ounce (about 6 grams); also in verse 15

give less when you make the offering to the Lord to atone for your lives. [16]Receive the atonement money from the Israelites and use it for the service of the Tent of Meeting. It will be a memorial for the Israelites before the Lord, making atonement for your lives."

Basin for Washing

[17]Then the Lord said to Moses, [18]"Make a bronze basin, with its bronze stand, for washing. Place it between the Tent of Meeting and the altar, and put water in it. [19]Aaron and his sons are to wash their hands and feet with water from it. [20]Whenever they enter the Tent of Meeting, they shall wash with water so that they will not die. Also, when they approach the altar to minister by presenting an offering made to the Lord by fire, [21]they shall wash their hands and feet so that they will not die. This is to be a lasting ordinance for Aaron and his descendants for the generations to come."

Anointing Oil

[22]Then the Lord said to Moses, [23]"Take the following fine spices: 500 shekels[a] of liquid myrrh, half as much (that is, 250 shekels) of fragrant cinnamon, 250 shekels of fragrant cane, [24]500 shekels of cassia—all according to the sanctuary shekel—and a hin[b] of olive oil. [25]Make these into a sacred anointing oil, a fragrant blend, the work of a perfumer. It will be the sacred anointing oil. [26]Then use it to anoint the Tent of Meeting, the ark of the Testimony, [27]the table and all its articles, the lampstand and its accessories, the altar of incense, [28]the altar of burnt offering and all its utensils, and the basin with its stand. [29]You shall consecrate them so they will be most holy, and whatever touches them will be holy.

[30]"Anoint Aaron and his sons and consecrate them so they may serve me as priests. [31]Say to the Israelites, 'This is to be my sacred anointing oil for the generations to come. [32]Do not pour it on men's bodies and do not make any oil with the same formula. It is sacred, and you are to consider it sacred. [33]Whoever makes perfume like it and whoever puts it on anyone other than a priest must be cut off from his people.' "

Incense

[34]Then the Lord said to Moses, "Take fragrant spices—gum resin, onycha and galbanum—and pure frankincense, all in equal amounts, [35]and make a fragrant blend of incense, the work of a perfumer. It is to be salted and pure and sacred. [36]Grind some of it to powder and place it in front of the Testimony in the Tent of Meeting, where I will meet with you. It shall be most holy to you. [37]Do not make any incense with this formula for yourselves; consider it holy to the Lord. [38]Whoever makes any like it to enjoy its fragrance must be cut off from his people."

Bezalel and Oholiab

31:2–6pp — Ex 35:30–35

31 Then the Lord said to Moses, [2]"See, I have chosen Bezalel son of Uri, the son of Hur, of the tribe of Judah, [3]and I have filled him with the Spirit of God, with skill, ability and knowledge in all kinds of crafts— [4]to make artistic designs for work in gold, silver and bronze, [5]to cut and set stones, to work in wood, and to engage in all kinds of craftsmanship. [6]Moreover, I have appointed Oholiab son of Ahisamach, of the tribe of Dan, to help him. Also I have given skill to all the craftsmen to make everything I have commanded you: [7]the Tent of Meeting, the ark of the Testimony with the atonement cover on it, and all the other furnishings of the tent— [8]the table and its articles, the pure gold lampstand and all its accessories, the altar of incense, [9]the altar of burnt offering and all its utensils, the basin with its stand— [10]and also the woven garments, both the sacred garments for Aaron the priest and the garments for his sons when they serve as priests, [11]and the anointing oil and fragrant incense for the Holy Place. They are to make them just as I commanded you."

---

[a] 23 That is, about 12 1/2 pounds (about 6 kilograms)   [b] 24 That is, probably about 4 quarts (about 4 liters)

> "I HAVE FILLED HIM WITH THE
> SPIRIT OF GOD, WITH SKILL,
> ABILITY AND KNOWLEDGE IN ALL
> KINDS OF CRAFTS."
>
> *Exodus 31:3*

Creative Spirit

RUTH A. DEJAGER

READ | EXODUS 31:1–11

I love this passage. It inspires me. I love the idea that the Spirit of God infused these guys with the skills, abilities and knowledge to build God's tabernacle, the epoch of all artwork until the later construction of Solomon's temple. And the materials they were given! It gives a crafty person like me shivers of joy to think of it.

The Scriptures don't talk about human creativity much, but perhaps that's because it's a "given." After all, we are made in the image of our Creator, who crafted the beautiful and intriguing things of our world: sunsets, stars, trees, beaches, oceans, flamingos, armadillos, strawberries, honeybees, our exquisitely complex bodies and, of course, life itself. And he has instilled in men and women throughout time the urge to create—from the cave paintings of ancient people to the psalms of David to the building of cathedrals to the invention of the printing press and beyond.

We tend to think of creativity as having to do with art, but one can be creative in almost any area of life. Creativity is a useful and necessary tool in business, medicine, housekeeping and even in the nurturing of a grandchild. And to do all these things creatively, inspired by the Spirit of God, is to use our gifts in his service.

It's easy to lose sight of our God-given creativity in the blur of routine and the drudgery of daily life. Sometimes we need to get away on what Julia Cameron calls an "artist date." That may involve taking a class or a vacation, going for a hike in the woods or sipping a mocha at the bookstore. Use the time to tune in to your creativity, to re-create your openness to new ways of thinking, feeling and doing. Listen to the Spirit of God telling you how to be creative in your own unique way.

Creator of all things, thank you for the creative gifts you have given me. Help me to discover the creative gifts still hidden within me. And grant me the wisdom to nurture the creative gifts within my grandchildren as well. Amen.

Your next devotion is located on page 134.

GRANDCHILD IN FOCUS • PRAYER

Respect for Authority

Dear Lord, I pray that my grandchild will continually grow to respect those in authority. May she learn to be cooperative and fair in work and play. Instill in her a high regard for officials who govern our land and enforce the laws. May her relationships with parents, teachers, coaches, mentors and bosses be respectful, admirable, constructive and caring. Amen.

The Sabbath

[12] Then the LORD said to Moses, [13] "Say to the Israelites, 'You must observe my Sabbaths. This will be a sign between me and you for the generations to come, so you may know that I am the LORD, who makes you holy.[a]

[14] "'Observe the Sabbath, because it is holy to you. Anyone who desecrates it must be put to death; whoever does any work on that day must be cut off from his people. [15] For six days, work is to be done, but the seventh day is a Sabbath of rest, holy to the LORD. Whoever does any work on the Sabbath day must be put to death. [16] The Israelites are to observe the Sabbath, celebrating it for the generations to come as a lasting covenant. [17] It will be a sign between me and the Israelites forever, for in six days the LORD made the heavens and the earth, and on the seventh day he abstained from work and rested.'"

[18] When the LORD finished speaking to Moses on Mount Sinai, he gave him the two tablets of the Testimony, the tablets of stone inscribed by the finger of God.

The Golden Calf

32 When the people saw that Moses was so long in coming down from the mountain, they gathered around Aaron and said, "Come, make us gods[b] who will go before us. As for this fellow Moses who brought us up out of Egypt, we don't know what has happened to him."

[2] Aaron answered them, "Take off the gold earrings that your wives, your sons and your daughters are wearing, and bring them to me." [3] So all the people took off their earrings and brought them to Aaron. [4] He took what they handed him and made it into an idol cast in the shape of a calf, fashioning it with a tool. Then they said, "These are your gods,[c] O Israel, who brought you up out of Egypt."

[5] When Aaron saw this, he built an altar in front of the calf and announced, "Tomorrow there will be a festival to the LORD." [6] So the next day the people rose early and sacrificed burnt offerings and presented fellowship offerings.[d] Afterward they sat down to eat and drink and got up to indulge in revelry.

[7] Then the LORD said to Moses, "Go down, because your people, whom you brought up out of Egypt, have become corrupt. [8] They have been quick to turn away from what I commanded them and have made themselves an idol cast in the shape of a calf. They have bowed down to it and sacrificed to it and have said, 'These are your gods, O Israel, who brought you up out of Egypt.'

[9] "I have seen these people," the LORD said to Moses, "and they are a stiff-necked people. [10] Now leave me alone so that my anger may burn against them and that I may destroy them. Then I will make you into a great nation."

[11] But Moses sought the favor of the LORD his God. "O LORD," he said, "why should your anger burn against your people, whom you brought out of Egypt with great power and a mighty hand? [12] Why should the Egyptians say, 'It was with evil intent that he brought them out, to kill them in the mountains and to wipe them off the face of the earth'? Turn from your fierce anger; relent and do not bring disaster on your people. [13] Remember your servants Abraham, Isaac and Israel, to whom you swore by your own self: 'I will make your descendants as numerous as the stars in the sky and I will give your descendants all this land I promised them, and it will be their inheritance forever.'" [14] Then the LORD relented and did not bring on his people the disaster he had threatened.

[15] Moses turned and went down the mountain with the two tablets of the Testimony in his hands. They were inscribed on both sides, front and back. [16] The tablets were the work of God; the writing was the writing of God, engraved on the tablets.

[17] When Joshua heard the noise of the people shouting, he said to Moses, "There is the sound of war in the camp."

---

[a] 13 Or *who sanctifies you; or who sets you apart as holy*   [b] 1 Or *a god*; also in verses 23 and 31   [c] 4 Or *This is your god*; also in verse 8   [d] 6 Traditionally *peace offerings*

¹⁸ Moses replied:

"It is not the sound of victory,
 it is not the sound of defeat;
 it is the sound of singing that I hear."

¹⁹ When Moses approached the camp and saw the calf and the dancing, his anger burned and he threw the tablets out of his hands, breaking them to pieces at the foot of the mountain. ²⁰ And he took the calf they had made and burned it in the fire; then he ground it to powder, scattered it on the water and made the Israelites drink it.

²¹ He said to Aaron, "What did these people do to you, that you led them into such great sin?"

²² "Do not be angry, my lord," Aaron answered. "You know how prone these people are to evil.

²³ They said to me, 'Make us gods who will go before us. As for this fellow Moses who brought us up out of Egypt, we don't know what has happened to him.' ²⁴ So I told them, 'Whoever has any gold jewelry, take it off.' Then they gave me the gold, and I threw it into the fire, and out came this calf!"

²⁵ Moses saw that the people were running wild and that Aaron had let them get out of control and so become a laughingstock to their enemies. ²⁶ So he stood at the entrance to the camp and said, "Whoever is for the LORD, come to me." And all the Levites rallied to him.

²⁷ Then he said to them, "This is what the LORD, the God of Israel, says: 'Each man strap a sword to his side. Go back and forth through the camp from one end to the other, each killing his brother and friend and neighbor.' " ²⁸ The Levites did as Moses commanded, and that day about three thousand of the people died. ²⁹ Then Moses said, "You have been set apart to the LORD today, for you were against your own sons and brothers, and he has blessed you this day."

³⁰ The next day Moses said to the people, "You have committed a great sin. But now I will go up to the LORD; perhaps I can make atonement for your sin."

³¹ So Moses went back to the LORD and said, "Oh, what a great sin these people have committed! They have made themselves gods of gold. ³² But now, please forgive their sin — but if not, then blot me out of the book you have written."

³³ The LORD replied to Moses, "Whoever has sinned against me I will blot out of my book. ³⁴ Now go, lead the people to the place I spoke of, and my angel will go before you. However, when the time comes for me to punish, I will punish them for their sin."

³⁵ And the LORD struck the people with a plague because of what they did with the calf Aaron had made.

33 Then the LORD said to Moses, "Leave this place, you and the people you brought up out of Egypt, and go up to the land I promised on oath to Abraham, Isaac and Jacob, saying,

EXODUS 32:1–20

The Golden Calf

LIFE LESSON: God punishes disobedience.

TO TALK ABOUT

✦ How did the people disobey God? Why did they do this?

✦ What did Moses do when he returned to the camp and saw what was happening?

✦ What was the result of Moses' prayers for the people?

✦ Do you think our prayers can have that kind of effect? Why or why not?

stories to share

'I will give it to your descendants.' ²I will send an angel before you and drive out the Canaanites, Amorites, Hittites, Perizzites, Hivites and Jebusites. ³Go up to the land flowing with milk and honey. But I will not go with you, because you are a stiff-necked people and I might destroy you on the way."

⁴When the people heard these distressing words, they began to mourn and no one put on any ornaments. ⁵For the LORD had said to Moses, "Tell the Israelites, 'You are a stiff-necked people. If I were to go with you even for a moment, I might destroy you. Now take off your ornaments and I will decide what to do with you.'" ⁶So the Israelites stripped off their ornaments at Mount Horeb.

The Tent of Meeting

⁷Now Moses used to take a tent and pitch it outside the camp some distance away, calling it the "tent of meeting." Anyone inquiring of the LORD would go to the tent of meeting outside the camp. ⁸And whenever Moses went out to the tent, all the people rose and stood at the entrances to their tents, watching Moses until he entered the tent. ⁹As Moses went into the tent, the pillar of cloud would come down and stay at the entrance, while the LORD spoke with Moses. ¹⁰Whenever the people saw the pillar of cloud standing at the entrance to the tent, they all stood and worshiped, each at the entrance to his tent. ¹¹The LORD would speak to Moses face to face, as a man speaks with his friend. Then Moses would return to the camp, but his young aide Joshua son of Nun did not leave the tent.

Moses and the Glory of the LORD

¹²Moses said to the LORD, "You have been telling me, 'Lead these people,' but you have not let me know whom you will send with me. You have said, 'I know you by name and you have found favor with me.' ¹³If you are pleased with me, teach me your ways so I may know you and continue to find favor with you. Remember that this nation is your people."

¹⁴The LORD replied, "My Presence will go with you, and I will give you rest."

TALKING POINTS

Anxiety

God's presence will bring us peace and rest.

EXODUS 33:14

For more on anxiety, go to Psalm 73:26.

¹⁵Then Moses said to him, "If your Presence does not go with us, do not send us up from here. ¹⁶How will anyone know that you are pleased with me and with your people unless you go with us? What else will distinguish me and your people from all the other people on the face of the earth?"

¹⁷And the LORD said to Moses, "I will do the very thing you have asked, because I am pleased with you and I know you by name."

¹⁸Then Moses said, "Now show me your glory."

¹⁹And the LORD said, "I will cause all my goodness to pass in front of you, and I will proclaim my name, the LORD, in your presence. I will have mercy on whom I will have mercy, and I will have compassion on whom I will have compassion. ²⁰But," he said, "you cannot see my face, for no one may see me and live."

²¹Then the LORD said, "There is a place near me where you may stand on a rock. ²²When my glory passes by, I will put you in a cleft in the rock and cover you with my hand until I have passed by. ²³Then I will remove my hand and you will see my back; but my face must not be seen."

The New Stone Tablets

34 The LORD said to Moses, "Chisel out two stone tablets like the first ones, and I will write on them the words that were on the first

tablets, which you broke. ²Be ready in the morning, and then come up on Mount Sinai. Present yourself to me there on top of the mountain. ³No one is to come with you or be seen anywhere on the mountain; not even the flocks and herds may graze in front of the mountain."

⁴So Moses chiseled out two stone tablets like the first ones and went up Mount Sinai early in the morning, as the LORD had commanded him; and he carried the two stone tablets in his hands. ⁵Then the LORD came down in the cloud and stood there with him and proclaimed his name, the LORD. ⁶And he passed in front of Moses, proclaiming, "The LORD, the LORD, the compassionate and gracious God, slow to anger, abounding in love and faithfulness, ⁷maintaining love to thousands, and forgiving wickedness, rebellion and sin. Yet he does not leave the guilty unpunished; he punishes the children and their children for the sin of the fathers to the third and fourth generation."

⁸Moses bowed to the ground at once and worshiped. ⁹"O Lord, if I have found favor in your eyes," he said, "then let the Lord go with us. Although this is a stiff-necked people, forgive our wickedness and our sin, and take us as your inheritance."

¹⁰Then the LORD said: "I am making a covenant with you. Before all your people I will do wonders never before done in any nation in all the world. The people you live among will see how awesome is the work that I, the LORD, will do for you. ¹¹Obey what I command you today. I will drive out before you the Amorites, Canaanites, Hittites, Perizzites, Hivites and Jebusites. ¹²Be careful not to make a treaty with those who live in the land where you are going, or they will be a snare among you. ¹³Break down their altars, smash their sacred stones and cut down their Asherah poles.ᵃ ¹⁴Do not worship any other god, for the LORD, whose name is Jealous, is a jealous God.

¹⁵"Be careful not to make a treaty with those who live in the land; for when they prostitute themselves to their gods and sacrifice to them, they will invite you and you will eat their sacrifices. ¹⁶And when you choose some of their daughters as wives for your sons and those daughters prostitute themselves to their gods, they will lead your sons to do the same.

¹⁷"Do not make cast idols.

¹⁸"Celebrate the Feast of Unleavened Bread. For seven days eat bread made without yeast, as I commanded you. Do this at the appointed time in the month of Abib, for in that month you came out of Egypt.

¹⁹"The first offspring of every womb belongs to me, including all the firstborn males of your livestock, whether from herd or flock. ²⁰Redeem the firstborn donkey with a lamb, but if you do not redeem it, break its neck. Redeem all your firstborn sons.

"No one is to appear before me empty-handed.

²¹"Six days you shall labor, but on the seventh day you shall rest; even during the plowing season and harvest you must rest.

²²"Celebrate the Feast of Weeks with the firstfruits of the wheat harvest, and the Feast of Ingathering at the turn of the year.ᵇ ²³Three times a year all your men are to appear before the Sovereign LORD, the God of Israel. ²⁴I will drive out nations before you and enlarge your territory, and no one will covet your land when you go up three times each year to appear before the LORD your God.

²⁵"Do not offer the blood of a sacrifice to me along with anything containing yeast, and do not let any of the sacrifice from the Passover Feast remain until morning.

²⁶"Bring the best of the firstfruits of your soil to the house of the LORD your God.

"Do not cook a young goat in its mother's milk."

²⁷Then the LORD said to Moses, "Write down these words, for in accordance with these words I have made a covenant with you and with Israel." ²⁸Moses was there with the LORD forty days and forty nights without eating bread or drinking

---

ᵃ 13 That is, symbols of the goddess Asherah   ᵇ 22 That is, in the fall water. And he wrote on the tablets the words of the covenant—the Ten Commandments.

The Radiant Face of Moses

29 When Moses came down from Mount Sinai with the two tablets of the Testimony in his hands, he was not aware that his face was radiant because he had spoken with the LORD. 30 When Aaron and all the Israelites saw Moses, his face was radiant, and they were afraid to come near him. 31 But Moses called to them; so Aaron and all the leaders of the community came back to him, and he spoke to them. 32 Afterward all the Israelites came near him, and he gave them all the commands the LORD had given him on Mount Sinai.

33 When Moses finished speaking to them, he put a veil over his face. 34 But whenever he entered the LORD's presence to speak with him, he removed the veil until he came out. And when he came out and told the Israelites what he had been commanded, 35 they saw that his face was radiant. Then Moses would put the veil back over his face until he went in to speak with the LORD.

Sabbath Regulations

35 Moses assembled the whole Israelite community and said to them, "These are the things the LORD has commanded you to do: 2 For six days, work is to be done, but the seventh day shall be your holy day, a Sabbath of rest to the LORD. Whoever does any work on it must be put to death. 3 Do not light a fire in any of your dwellings on the Sabbath day."

Materials for the Tabernacle

35:4–9pp — Ex 25:1–7
35:10–19pp — Ex 39:32–41

4 Moses said to the whole Israelite community, "This is what the LORD has commanded: 5 From what you have, take an offering for the LORD. Everyone who is willing is to bring to the LORD an offering of gold, silver and bronze; 6 blue, purple and scarlet yarn and fine linen; goat hair; 7 ram skins dyed red and hides of sea cows a; acacia wood; 8 olive oil for the light; spices for the anointing oil and for the fragrant incense; 9 and onyx stones and other gems to be mounted on the ephod and breastpiece.

10 "All who are skilled among you are to come and make everything the LORD has commanded: 11 the tabernacle with its tent and its covering, clasps, frames, crossbars, posts and bases; 12 the ark with its poles and the atonement cover and the curtain that shields it; 13 the table with its poles and all its articles and the bread of the Presence; 14 the lampstand that is for light with its accessories, lamps and oil for the light; 15 the altar of incense with its poles, the anointing oil and the fragrant incense; the curtain for the doorway at the entrance to the tabernacle; 16 the altar of burnt offering with its bronze grating, its poles and all its utensils; the bronze basin with its stand; 17 the curtains of the courtyard with its posts and bases, and the curtain for the entrance to the courtyard; 18 the tent pegs for the tabernacle and for the courtyard, and their ropes; 19 the woven garments worn for ministering in the sanctuary—both the sacred garments for Aaron the priest and the garments for his sons when they serve as priests."

20 Then the whole Israelite community withdrew from Moses' presence, 21 and everyone who was willing and whose heart moved him came and brought an offering to the LORD for the work on the Tent of Meeting, for all its service, and for the sacred garments. 22 All who were willing, men and women alike, came and brought gold jewelry of all kinds: brooches, earrings, rings and ornaments. They all presented their gold as a wave offering to the LORD. 23 Everyone who had blue, purple or scarlet yarn or fine linen, or goat hair, ram skins dyed red or hides of sea cows brought them. 24 Those presenting an offering of silver or bronze brought it as an offering to the LORD, and everyone who had acacia wood for any part of the work brought it. 25 Every skilled woman spun with her hands and brought what she had

a 7 That is, dugongs; also in verse 23

WHEN MOSES CAME DOWN FROM
MOUNT SINAI WITH THE TWO
TABLETS OF THE TESTIMONY IN HIS
HANDS, HE WAS NOT AWARE THAT
HIS FACE WAS RADIANT BECAUSE
HE HAD SPOKEN WITH THE LORD.

Exodus 34:29

Radiant Light

DORIS WYNBEEK RIKKERS

READ | EXODUS 34:29 – 35

Sylvia had a special something about her — her look was radiant, her attitude was upbeat, she was happy and content. I was puzzled. I had known her for years; in fact, she was one of my closest friends. I could testify that she had experienced her quota of trials and joy, just like the rest of us who were on the plus side of 40. What was going on?

Over the next few weeks, I watched her closely. Perhaps she's fallen in love again, I thought. Perhaps she has another grandchild on the way. Finally I asked her.

"It's all a matter of perspective," she replied. "I am *alive* in Christ and that's how I intend to live — as fully ALIVE as I can. I want to live every minute to the fullest in gratitude and joy to the Lord." I couldn't have agreed with her more. What a wonderful perspective for living.

Moses' face radiated light after he had the unique privilege of speaking face-to-face with God on Mount Sinai. As Christians, we have the same privilege of living in God's presence. Our lives reflect the contents of our hearts. If we are filled with God's Spirit, we are truly alive (see Ephesians 2:4 – 5). God's love will then shine through our hearts and into our lives. Oh, there may still be dark moments and shadowy valleys, but God's love and presence will shine through even then.

God's blessings abound. We are renewed every morning to be alive in Christ. Every day is a new day — a glorious day to rejoice and be glad (see Psalm 118:24). So let's live our lives so that we are fully alive. Shine in God's love. Live in God's peace. Surround yourself in the knowledge of his mercy and grace, and LIVE.

O God, I thank you for the privilege of living in your presence. May your light and love shine through me in all I do and say. Amen.

GRANDCHILD IN FOCUS · PRAYER

Courage

O Father, builder of character and courage, may my grandchild grow strong in the light of your love. Grant him courage to stand for what is right, to guard the truth and to ensure justice in every aspect of life. May he boldly grow in grace, revere your name and proudly proclaim you as the Lord of lords and King of kings. Amen.

Your next devotion is located on page 136.

spun—blue, purple or scarlet yarn or fine linen. ²⁶ And all the women who were willing and had the skill spun the goat hair. ²⁷ The leaders brought onyx stones and other gems to be mounted on the ephod and breastpiece. ²⁸ They also brought spices and olive oil for the light and for the anointing oil and for the fragrant incense. ²⁹ All the Israelite men and women who were willing brought to the LORD freewill offerings for all the work the LORD through Moses had commanded them to do.

Bezalel and Oholiab

35:30–35pp — Ex 31:2–6

³⁰ Then Moses said to the Israelites, "See, the LORD has chosen Bezalel son of Uri, the son of Hur, of the tribe of Judah, ³¹ and he has filled him with the Spirit of God, with skill, ability and knowledge in all kinds of crafts— ³² to make artistic designs for work in gold, silver and bronze, ³³ to cut and set stones, to work in wood and to engage in all kinds of artistic craftsmanship. ³⁴ And he has given both him and Oholiab son of Ahisamach, of the tribe of Dan, the ability to teach others. ³⁵ He has filled them with skill to do all kinds of work as craftsmen, designers, embroiderers in blue, purple and scarlet yarn and fine linen, and weavers—all of them master craftsmen and

36 designers. ¹ So Bezalel, Oholiab and every skilled person to whom the LORD has given skill and ability to know how to carry out all the work of constructing the sanctuary are to do the work just as the LORD has commanded."

² Then Moses summoned Bezalel and Oholiab and every skilled person to whom the LORD had given ability and who was willing to come and do the work. ³ They received from Moses all the offerings the Israelites had brought to carry out the work of constructing the sanctuary. And the people continued to bring freewill offerings morning after morning. ⁴ So all the skilled craftsmen who were doing all the work on the sanctuary left their work ⁵ and said to Moses, "The people are bringing more than enough for doing the work the LORD commanded to be done."

⁶ Then Moses gave an order and they sent this word throughout the camp: "No man or woman is to make anything else as an offering for the sanctuary." And so the people were restrained from bringing more, ⁷ because what they already had was more than enough to do all the work.

The Tabernacle

36:8–38pp — Ex 26:1–37

⁸ All the skilled men among the workmen made the tabernacle with ten curtains of finely twisted linen and blue, purple and scarlet yarn, with cherubim worked into them by a skilled craftsman. ⁹ All the curtains were the same size—twenty-eight cubits long and four cubits wide. ^a ¹⁰ They joined five of the curtains together and did the same with the other five. ¹¹ Then they made loops of blue material along the edge of the end curtain in one set, and the same was done with the end curtain in the other set. ¹² They also made fifty loops on one curtain and fifty loops on the end curtain of the other set, with the loops opposite each other. ¹³ Then they made fifty gold clasps and used them to fasten the two sets of curtains together so that the tabernacle was a unit.

¹⁴ They made curtains of goat hair for the tent over the tabernacle—eleven altogether. ¹⁵ All eleven curtains were the same size—thirty cubits long and four cubits wide. ^b ¹⁶ They joined five of the curtains into one set and the other six into another set. ¹⁷ Then they made fifty loops along the edge of the end curtain in one set and also along the edge of the end curtain in the other set. ¹⁸ They made fifty bronze clasps to fasten the tent together as a unit. ¹⁹ Then they made for the tent a covering of ram skins dyed red, and over that a covering of hides of sea cows. ^c

²⁰ They made upright frames of acacia wood for the tabernacle. ²¹ Each frame was ten cubits long and a cubit and a half wide, ^d ²² with two

---

^a 9 That is, about 42 feet (about 12.5 meters) long and 6 feet (about 1.8 meters) wide   ^b 15 That is, about 45 feet (about 13.5 meters) long and 6 feet (about 1.8 meters) wide   ^c 19 That is, dugongs   ^d 21 That is, about 15 feet (about 4.5 meters) long and 2 1/4 feet (about 0.7 meter) wide

> EVERY SKILLED WOMAN SPUN WITH HER HANDS AND BROUGHT WHAT SHE HAD SPUN—BLUE, PURPLE OR SCARLET YARN OR FINE LINEN. AND ALL THE WOMEN WHO WERE WILLING AND HAD THE SKILL SPUN THE GOAT HAIR.
>
> *Exodus 35:25–26*

Beauty in Busy Hands

BOBBIE WOLGEMUTH

READ | EXODUS 35:4–29

Have you recently noticed the creative art of God? Color, texture, arrangement, unique design and images of beauty are everywhere.

Made in God's image, women have been gifted with a capacity to generate and display beauty. Any expression that brings loveliness into the world exposes the artist's soul and is a visible reminder that God is the master designer.

A vase with a single flower on the table, a pretty scarf around the neck, vegetables and fruit arranged on a plate, a burst of color planted in the garden, a watercolor painting, or some pretty yarn knit into a shawl . . . there's no limit to the variety of creative expressions that can stir our souls.

Recently my granddaughter asked me to teach her how to crochet. It's one of the old crafts coming back into fashion for young people. After visiting a craft store and selecting hooks and brightly colored yarn, I asked the clerk to give me a refresher course. It had been years since I had crocheted, but her kindness and simple instructions were all I needed.

My granddaughter and I sat on the sofa together. Busy hands worked the yarn as good conversation wove our hearts together.

God has gifted us with good ideas. And when we share our skills and art with our family, our lives can be woven together. Maybe it's time for you to listen to the creative stirring in your soul. Busy hands can arrange beauty and blend hearts. What artistic project can you try—or try again—today?

Father in heaven, thank you for beauty. Thank you for the inspiration to try new projects. Help me to enjoy what you have provided. Give me wisdom to share art and loveliness with my grandchildren. Amen.

Your next devotion is located on page 158.

GRANDCHILD IN FOCUS • PRAYER

Future Spouse

Dear Lord, if it is your will, I pray my grandchild will be united in a loving and Christian marriage. Keep her sexually pure so that she will honor you with her body and mind. As she seeks a spouse who will honor and care for her, give her patience and discernment. May her choice for a life partner be your choice for her, so that she and her husband will together glorify you in a lasting love. I pray this in Jesus' name, amen.

projections set parallel to each other. They made all the frames of the tabernacle in this way. ²³They made twenty frames for the south side of the tabernacle ²⁴and made forty silver bases to go under them—two bases for each frame, one under each projection. ²⁵For the other side, the north side of the tabernacle, they made twenty frames ²⁶and forty silver bases—two under each frame. ²⁷They made six frames for the far end, that is, the west end of the tabernacle, ²⁸and two frames were made for the corners of the tabernacle at the far end. ²⁹At these two corners the frames were double from the bottom all the way to the top and fitted into a single ring; both were made alike. ³⁰So there were eight frames and sixteen silver bases—two under each frame.

³¹They also made crossbars of acacia wood: five for the frames on one side of the tabernacle, ³²five for those on the other side, and five for the frames on the west, at the far end of the tabernacle. ³³They made the center crossbar so that it extended from end to end at the middle of the frames. ³⁴They overlaid the frames with gold and made gold rings to hold the crossbars. They also overlaid the crossbars with gold.

³⁵They made the curtain of blue, purple and scarlet yarn and finely twisted linen, with cherubim worked into it by a skilled craftsman. ³⁶They made four posts of acacia wood for it and overlaid them with gold. They made gold hooks for them and cast their four silver bases. ³⁷For the entrance to the tent they made a curtain of blue, purple and scarlet yarn and finely twisted linen—the work of an embroiderer; ³⁸and they made five posts with hooks for them. They overlaid the tops of the posts and their bands with gold and made their five bases of bronze.

The Ark

37:1–9pp — Ex 25:10–20

37 Bezalel made the ark of acacia wood— two and a half cubits long, a cubit and a half wide, and a cubit and a half high. ^a ²He overlaid it with pure gold, both inside and out, and made a gold molding around it. ³He cast four

gold rings for it and fastened them to its four feet, with two rings on one side and two rings on the other. ⁴Then he made poles of acacia wood and overlaid them with gold. ⁵And he inserted the poles into the rings on the sides of the ark to carry it.

⁶He made the atonement cover of pure gold— two and a half cubits long and a cubit and a half wide. ^b ⁷Then he made two cherubim out of hammered gold at the ends of the cover. ⁸He made one cherub on one end and the second cherub on the other; at the two ends he made them of one piece with the cover. ⁹The cherubim had their wings spread upward, overshadowing the cover with them. The cherubim faced each other, looking toward the cover.

The Table

37:10–16pp — Ex 25:23–29

¹⁰They^c made the table of acacia wood—two cubits long, a cubit wide, and a cubit and a half high. ^d ¹¹Then they overlaid it with pure gold and made a gold molding around it. ¹²They also made around it a rim a handbreadth^e wide and put a gold molding on the rim. ¹³They cast four gold rings for the table and fastened them to the four corners, where the four legs were. ¹⁴The rings were put close to the rim to hold the poles used in carrying the table. ¹⁵The poles for carrying the table were made of acacia wood and were overlaid with gold. ¹⁶And they made from pure gold the articles for the table—its plates and dishes and bowls and its pitchers for the pouring out of drink offerings.

The Lampstand

37:17–24pp — Ex 25:31–39

¹⁷They made the lampstand of pure gold and hammered it out, base and shaft; its flowerlike cups, buds and blossoms were of one piece with it.

^a *1* That is, about 3 3/4 feet (about 1.1 meters) long and 2 1/4 feet (about 0.7 meter) wide and high   ^b *6* That is, about 3 3/4 feet (about 1.1 meters) long and 2 1/4 feet (about 0.7 meter) wide   ^c *10* Or *He*; also in verses 11-29   ^d *10* That is, about 3 feet (about 0.9 meter) long, 1 1/2 feet (about 0.5 meter) wide, and 2 1/4 feet (about 0.7 meter) high   ^e *12* That is, about 3 inches (about 8 centimeters)

¹⁸Six branches extended from the sides of the lampstand—three on one side and three on the other. ¹⁹Three cups shaped like almond flowers with buds and blossoms were on one branch, three on the next branch and the same for all six branches extending from the lampstand. ²⁰And on the lampstand were four cups shaped like almond flowers with buds and blossoms. ²¹One bud was under the first pair of branches extending from the lampstand, a second bud under the second pair, and a third bud under the third pair—six branches in all. ²²The buds and the branches were all of one piece with the lampstand, hammered out of pure gold.

²³They made its seven lamps, as well as its wick trimmers and trays, of pure gold. ²⁴They made the lampstand and all its accessories from one talent[a] of pure gold.

The Altar of Incense
37:25–28pp — Ex 30:1–5

²⁵They made the altar of incense out of acacia wood. It was square, a cubit long and a cubit wide, and two cubits high[b]—its horns of one piece with it. ²⁶They overlaid the top and all the sides and the horns with pure gold, and made a gold molding around it. ²⁷They made two gold rings below the molding—two on opposite sides—to hold the poles used to carry it. ²⁸They made the poles of acacia wood and overlaid them with gold.

²⁹They also made the sacred anointing oil and the pure, fragrant incense—the work of a perfumer.

The Altar of Burnt Offering
38:1–7pp — Ex 27:1–8

38 They[c] built the altar of burnt offering of acacia wood, three cubits[d] high; it was square, five cubits long and five cubits wide.[e] ²They made a horn at each of the four corners, so that the horns and the altar were of one piece, and they overlaid the altar with bronze. ³They made all its utensils of bronze—its pots, shovels, sprinkling bowls, meat forks and firepans. ⁴They

made a grating for the altar, a bronze network, to be under its ledge, halfway up the altar. ⁵They cast bronze rings to hold the poles for the four corners of the bronze grating. ⁶They made the poles of acacia wood and overlaid them with bronze. ⁷They inserted the poles into the rings so they would be on the sides of the altar for carrying it. They made it hollow, out of boards.

Basin for Washing

⁸They made the bronze basin and its bronze stand from the mirrors of the women who served at the entrance to the Tent of Meeting.

The Courtyard
38:9–20pp — Ex 27:9–19

⁹Next they made the courtyard. The south side was a hundred cubits[f] long and had curtains of finely twisted linen, ¹⁰with twenty posts and twenty bronze bases, and with silver hooks and bands on the posts. ¹¹The north side was also a hundred cubits long and had twenty posts and twenty bronze bases, with silver hooks and bands on the posts.

¹²The west end was fifty cubits[g] wide and had curtains, with ten posts and ten bases, with silver hooks and bands on the posts. ¹³The east end, toward the sunrise, was also fifty cubits wide. ¹⁴Curtains fifteen cubits[h] long were on one side of the entrance, with three posts and three bases, ¹⁵and curtains fifteen cubits long were on the other side of the entrance to the courtyard, with three posts and three bases. ¹⁶All the curtains around the courtyard were of finely twisted linen. ¹⁷The bases for the posts were bronze. The hooks and bands on the posts were silver, and their tops were overlaid with silver; so all the posts of the courtyard had silver bands.

¹⁸The curtain for the entrance to the courtyard

---

[a] 24 That is, about 75 pounds (about 34 kilograms)   [b] 25 That is, about 1 1/2 feet (about 0.5 meter) long and wide, and about 3 feet (about 0.9 meter) high   [c] 1 Or He; also in verses 2-9   [d] 1 That is, about 4 1/2 feet (about 1.3 meters)   [e] 1 That is, about 7 1/2 feet (about 2.3 meters) long and wide   [f] 9 That is, about 150 feet (about 46 meters)   [g] 12 That is, about 75 feet (about 23 meters)   [h] 14 That is, about 22 1/2 feet (about 6.9 meters)

was of blue, purple and scarlet yarn and finely twisted linen—the work of an embroiderer. It was twenty cubits[a] long and, like the curtains of the courtyard, five cubits[h] high, ¹⁹with four posts and four bronze bases. Their hooks and bands were silver, and their tops were overlaid with silver. ²⁰All the tent pegs of the tabernacle and of the surrounding courtyard were bronze.

The Materials Used

²¹These are the amounts of the materials used for the tabernacle, the tabernacle of the Testimony, which were recorded at Moses' command by the Levites under the direction of Ithamar son of Aaron, the priest. ²²(Bezalel son of Uri, the son of Hur, of the tribe of Judah, made everything the LORD commanded Moses; ²³with him was Oholiab son of Ahisamach, of the tribe of Dan—a craftsman and designer, and an embroiderer in blue, purple and scarlet yarn and fine linen.) ²⁴The total amount of the gold from the wave offering used for all the work on the sanctuary was 29 talents and 730 shekels,[c] according to the sanctuary shekel.

²⁵The silver obtained from those of the community who were counted in the census was 100 talents and 1,775 shekels,[d] according to the sanctuary shekel— ²⁶one beka per person, that is, half a shekel,[e] according to the sanctuary shekel, from everyone who had crossed over to those counted, twenty years old or more, a total of 603,550 men. ²⁷The 100 talents[f] of silver were used to cast the bases for the sanctuary and for the curtain—100 bases from the 100 talents, one talent for each base. ²⁸They used the 1,775 shekels[g] to make the hooks for the posts, to overlay the tops of the posts, and to make their bands.

²⁹The bronze from the wave offering was 70 talents and 2,400 shekels.[h] ³⁰They used it to make the bases for the entrance to the Tent of Meeting, the bronze altar with its bronze grating and all its utensils, ³¹the bases for the surrounding courtyard and those for its entrance and all the tent pegs for the tabernacle and those for the surrounding courtyard.

The Priestly Garments

39 From the blue, purple and scarlet yarn they made woven garments for ministering in the sanctuary. They also made sacred garments for Aaron, as the LORD commanded Moses.

The Ephod

39:2–7pp — Ex 28:6–14

²They[i] made the ephod of gold, and of blue, purple and scarlet yarn, and of finely twisted linen. ³They hammered out thin sheets of gold and cut strands to be worked into the blue, purple and scarlet yarn and fine linen—the work of a skilled craftsman. ⁴They made shoulder pieces for the ephod, which were attached to two of its corners, so it could be fastened. ⁵Its skillfully woven waistband was like it—of one piece with the ephod and made with gold, and with blue, purple and scarlet yarn, and with finely twisted linen, as the LORD commanded Moses.

⁶They mounted the onyx stones in gold filigree settings and engraved them like a seal with the names of the sons of Israel. ⁷Then they fastened them on the shoulder pieces of the ephod as memorial stones for the sons of Israel, as the LORD commanded Moses.

The Breastpiece

39:8–21pp — Ex 28:15–28

⁸They fashioned the breastpiece—the work of a skilled craftsman. They made it like the ephod: of gold, and of blue, purple and scarlet yarn, and of finely twisted linen. ⁹It was square—a span[j] long and a span wide—and folded double. ¹⁰Then they mounted four rows of precious stones on it. In the first row there was a ruby,

---

a 18 That is, about 30 feet (about 9 meters)   *b 18* That is, about 7 1/2 feet (about 2.3 meters)   *c 24* The weight of the gold was a little over one ton (about 1 metric ton).   *d 25* The weight of the silver was a little over 3 3/4 tons (about 3.4 metric tons).   *e 26* That is, about 1/5 ounce (about 5.5 grams)   *f 27* That is, about 3 3/4 tons (about 3.4 metric tons)   *g 28* That is, about 45 pounds (about 20 kilograms)   *h 29* The weight of the bronze was about 2 1/2 tons (about 2.4 metric tons).   *i 2* Or *He;* also in verses 7, 8 and 22   *j 9* That is, about 9 inches (about 22 centimeters) a topaz and a beryl; ¹¹ in the second row a turquoise, a sapphire^a and an emerald; ¹² in the third row a jacinth, an agate and an amethyst; ¹³ in the fourth row a chrysolite, an onyx and a jasper.^b They were mounted in gold filigree settings. ¹⁴ There were twelve stones, one for each of the names of the sons of Israel, each engraved like a seal with the name of one of the twelve tribes.

¹⁵ For the breastpiece they made braided chains of pure gold, like a rope. ¹⁶ They made two gold filigree settings and two gold rings, and fastened the rings to two of the corners of the breastpiece. ¹⁷ They fastened the two gold chains to the rings at the corners of the breastpiece, ¹⁸ and the other ends of the chains to the two settings, attaching them to the shoulder pieces of the ephod at the front. ¹⁹ They made two gold rings and attached them to the other two corners of the breastpiece on the inside edge next to the ephod. ²⁰ Then they made two more gold rings and attached them to the bottom of the shoulder pieces on the front of the ephod, close to the seam just above the waistband of the ephod. ²¹ They tied the rings of the breastpiece to the rings of the ephod with blue cord, connecting it to the waistband so that the breastpiece would not swing out from the ephod — as the LORD commanded Moses.

Other Priestly Garments
39:22–31pp — Ex 28:31–43

²² They made the robe of the ephod entirely of blue cloth — the work of a weaver — ²³ with an opening in the center of the robe like the opening of a collar,^c and a band around this opening, so that it would not tear. ²⁴ They made pomegranates of blue, purple and scarlet yarn and finely twisted linen around the hem of the robe. ²⁵ And they made bells of pure gold and attached them around the hem between the pomegranates. ²⁶ The bells and pomegranates alternated around the hem of the robe to be worn for ministering, as the LORD commanded Moses.

²⁷ For Aaron and his sons, they made tunics of fine linen — the work of a weaver — ²⁸ and the turban of fine linen, the linen headbands and the undergarments of finely twisted linen. ²⁹ The sash was of finely twisted linen and blue, purple and scarlet yarn — the work of an embroiderer — as the LORD commanded Moses.

³⁰ They made the plate, the sacred diadem, out of pure gold and engraved on it, like an inscription on a seal: HOLY TO THE LORD. ³¹ Then they fastened a blue cord to it to attach it to the turban, as the LORD commanded Moses.

Moses Inspects the Tabernacle
39:32–41pp — Ex 35:10–19

³² So all the work on the tabernacle, the Tent of Meeting, was completed. The Israelites did everything just as the LORD commanded Moses. ³³ Then they brought the tabernacle to Moses: the tent and all its furnishings, its clasps, frames, crossbars, posts and bases; ³⁴ the covering of ram skins dyed red, the covering of hides of sea cows^d and the shielding curtain; ³⁵ the ark of the Testimony with its poles and the atonement cover; ³⁶ the table with all its articles and the bread of the Presence; ³⁷ the pure gold lampstand with its row of lamps and all its accessories, and the oil for the light; ³⁸ the gold altar, the anointing oil, the fragrant incense, and the curtain for the entrance to the tent; ³⁹ the bronze altar with its bronze grating, its poles and all its utensils; the basin with its stand; ⁴⁰ the curtains of the courtyard with its posts and bases, and the curtain for the entrance to the courtyard; the ropes and tent pegs for the courtyard; all the furnishings for the tabernacle, the Tent of Meeting; ⁴¹ and the woven garments worn for ministering in the sanctuary, both the sacred garments for Aaron the priest and the garments for his sons when serving as priests.

⁴² The Israelites had done all the work just as the LORD had commanded Moses. ⁴³ Moses inspected the work and saw that they had done it just as the LORD had commanded. So Moses blessed them.

---

^a 11 Or *lapis lazuli*   ^b 13 The precise identification of some of these precious stones is uncertain.   ^c 23 The meaning of the Hebrew for this word is uncertain.   ^d 34 That is, dugongs

Setting Up the Tabernacle

40 Then the LORD said to Moses: [2]"Set up the tabernacle, the Tent of Meeting, on the first day of the first month. [3]Place the ark of the Testimony in it and shield the ark with the curtain. [4]Bring in the table and set out what belongs on it. Then bring in the lampstand and set up its lamps. [5]Place the gold altar of incense in front of the ark of the Testimony and put the curtain at the entrance to the tabernacle.

[6]"Place the altar of burnt offering in front of the entrance to the tabernacle, the Tent of Meeting; [7]place the basin between the Tent of Meeting and the altar and put water in it. [8]Set up the courtyard around it and put the curtain at the entrance to the courtyard.

[9]"Take the anointing oil and anoint the tabernacle and everything in it; consecrate it and all its furnishings, and it will be holy. [10]Then anoint the altar of burnt offering and all its utensils; consecrate the altar, and it will be most holy. [11]Anoint the basin and its stand and consecrate them.

[12]"Bring Aaron and his sons to the entrance to the Tent of Meeting and wash them with water. [13]Then dress Aaron in the sacred garments, anoint him and consecrate him so he may serve me as priest. [14]Bring his sons and dress them in tunics. [15]Anoint them just as you anointed their father, so they may serve me as priests. Their anointing will be to a priesthood that will continue for all generations to come." [16]Moses did everything just as the LORD commanded him.

[17]So the tabernacle was set up on the first day of the first month in the second year. [18]When Moses set up the tabernacle, he put the bases in place, erected the frames, inserted the crossbars and set up the posts. [19]Then he spread the tent over the tabernacle and put the covering over the tent, as the LORD commanded him.

[20]He took the Testimony and placed it in the ark, attached the poles to the ark and put the atonement cover over it. [21]Then he brought the ark into the tabernacle and hung the shielding curtain and shielded the ark of the Testimony, as the LORD commanded him.

[22]Moses placed the table in the Tent of Meeting on the north side of the tabernacle outside the curtain [23]and set out the bread on it before the LORD, as the LORD commanded him.

[24]He placed the lampstand in the Tent of Meeting opposite the table on the south side of the tabernacle [25]and set up the lamps before the LORD, as the LORD commanded him.

[26]Moses placed the gold altar in the Tent of Meeting in front of the curtain [27]and burned fragrant incense on it, as the LORD commanded him. [28]Then he put up the curtain at the entrance to the tabernacle.

[29]He set the altar of burnt offering near the entrance to the tabernacle, the Tent of Meeting, and offered on it burnt offerings and grain offerings, as the LORD commanded him.

[30]He placed the basin between the Tent of Meeting and the altar and put water in it for washing, [31]and Moses and Aaron and his sons used it to wash their hands and feet. [32]They washed whenever they entered the Tent of Meeting or approached the altar, as the LORD commanded Moses.

[33]Then Moses set up the courtyard around the tabernacle and altar and put up the curtain at the entrance to the courtyard. And so Moses finished the work.

The Glory of the LORD

[34]Then the cloud covered the Tent of Meeting, and the glory of the LORD filled the tabernacle. [35]Moses could not enter the Tent of Meeting because the cloud had settled upon it, and the glory of the LORD filled the tabernacle.

[36]In all the travels of the Israelites, whenever the cloud lifted from above the tabernacle, they would set out; [37]but if the cloud did not lift, they did not set out—until the day it lifted. [38]So the cloud of the LORD was over the tabernacle by day, and fire was in the cloud by night, in the sight of all the house of Israel during all their travels.

Building RELATIONSHIPS

The book of Leviticus records the regulations God instituted as a means of separating his people from the pagan practices that surrounded them in the promised land. The Almighty God who had saved his people from Egyptian slavery was now eager to solidify his relationship with them; having saved them, he didn't want to lose them to the superstitions and sins of the surrounding peoples.

So Leviticus is God's handbook to his people for living in relationship with him. Although it may superficially appear to be a book of endless offerings, purification rights, dietary laws, cleanliness laws and myriad other regulations, the underlying themes demonstrate God's holiness and reveal how he wanted his people to live holy (consecrated, set apart) lives before him and with each other.

These laws and rituals would establish the Israelites as a people dedicated to God's ways and purposes. As you read through this book, notice that many of these regulations helped to keep the people healthy, both physically and relationally. Others helped to keep them holy and pure to enhance their relationship with God.

The message that comes through clearly in all this is that every single detail of the Israelites' life mattered to God. No detail was too small for him to acknowledge and be concerned about. This is the truth that you can communicate to your grandchildren still today.

VERSE *to* REMEMBER | LEVITICUS 20:7 – 8

"Consecrate yourselves and be holy, because I am the LORD your God. Keep my decrees and follow them. I am the LORD, who makes you holy."

ABOUT LEVITICUS

WRITTEN BY:
Moses

WRITTEN FOR:
God's chosen people, the Israelites

DATE WRITTEN:
Between 1446 and 1406 B.C.

WHY WRITTEN:
To show the Israelites how to worship God and live a holy life

The Burnt Offering

1 The Lord called to Moses and spoke to him from the Tent of Meeting. He said, ²"Speak to the Israelites and say to them: 'When any of you brings an offering to the Lord, bring as your offering an animal from either the herd or the flock.

³" 'If the offering is a burnt offering from the herd, he is to offer a male without defect. He must present it at the entrance to the Tent of Meeting so that it*a* will be acceptable to the Lord. ⁴He is to lay his hand on the head of the burnt offering, and it will be accepted on his behalf to make atonement for him. ⁵He is to slaughter the young bull before the Lord, and then Aaron's sons the priests shall bring the blood and sprinkle it against the altar on all sides at the entrance to the Tent of Meeting. ⁶He is to skin the burnt offering and cut it into pieces. ⁷The sons of Aaron the priest are to put fire on the altar and arrange wood on the fire. ⁸Then Aaron's sons the priests shall arrange the pieces, including the head and the fat, on the burning wood that is on the altar. ⁹He is to wash the inner parts and the legs with water, and the priest is to burn all of it on the altar. It is a burnt offering, an offering made by fire, an aroma pleasing to the Lord.

¹⁰" 'If the offering is a burnt offering from the flock, from either the sheep or the goats, he is to offer a male without defect. ¹¹He is to slaughter it at the north side of the altar before the Lord, and Aaron's sons the priests shall sprinkle its blood against the altar on all sides. ¹²He is to cut it into pieces, and the priest shall arrange them, including the head and the fat, on the burning wood that is on the altar. ¹³He is to wash the inner parts and the legs with water, and the priest is to bring all of it and burn it on the altar. It is a burnt offering, an offering made by fire, an aroma pleasing to the Lord.

¹⁴" 'If the offering to the Lord is a burnt offering of birds, he is to offer a dove or a young pigeon. ¹⁵The priest shall bring it to the altar, wring off the head and burn it on the altar; its blood shall be drained out on the side of the altar. ¹⁶He is to remove the crop with its contents*b*

and throw it to the east side of the altar, where the ashes are. ¹⁷He shall tear it open by the wings, not severing it completely, and then the priest shall burn it on the wood that is on the fire on the altar. It is a burnt offering, an offering made by fire, an aroma pleasing to the Lord.

The Grain Offering

2 " 'When someone brings a grain offering to the Lord, his offering is to be of fine flour. He is to pour oil on it, put incense on it ²and take it to Aaron's sons the priests. The priest shall take a handful of the fine flour and oil, together with all the incense, and burn this as a memorial portion on the altar, an offering made by fire, an aroma pleasing to the Lord. ³The rest of the grain offering belongs to Aaron and his sons; it is a most holy part of the offerings made to the Lord by fire.

⁴" 'If you bring a grain offering baked in an oven, it is to consist of fine flour: cakes made without yeast and mixed with oil, or*c* wafers made without yeast and spread with oil. ⁵If your grain offering is prepared on a griddle, it is to be made of fine flour mixed with oil, and without yeast. ⁶Crumble it and pour oil on it; it is a grain offering. ⁷If your grain offering is cooked in a pan, it is to be made of fine flour and oil. ⁸Bring the grain offering made of these things to the Lord; present it to the priest, who shall take it to the altar. ⁹He shall take out the memorial portion from the grain offering and burn it on the altar as an offering made by fire, an aroma pleasing to the Lord. ¹⁰The rest of the grain offering belongs to Aaron and his sons; it is a most holy part of the offerings made to the Lord by fire.

¹¹" 'Every grain offering you bring to the Lord must be made without yeast, for you are not to burn any yeast or honey in an offering made to the Lord by fire. ¹²You may bring them to the Lord as an offering of the firstfruits, but they are not to be offered on the altar as a pleasing aroma. ¹³Season all your grain offerings with salt.

---

a 3 Or *he*   *b* 16 Or *crop and the feathers*; the meaning of the Hebrew for this word is uncertain.   *c* 4 Or *and*

Do not leave the salt of the covenant of your God out of your grain offerings; add salt to all your offerings.

[14] " 'If you bring a grain offering of firstfruits to the LORD, offer crushed heads of new grain roasted in the fire. [15] Put oil and incense on it; it is a grain offering. [16] The priest shall burn the memorial portion of the crushed grain and the oil, together with all the incense, as an offering made to the LORD by fire.

The Fellowship Offering

3 " 'If someone's offering is a fellowship offering,[a] and he offers an animal from the herd, whether male or female, he is to present before the LORD an animal without defect. [2] He is to lay his hand on the head of his offering and slaughter it at the entrance to the Tent of Meeting. Then Aaron's sons the priests shall sprinkle the blood against the altar on all sides. [3] From the fellowship offering he is to bring a sacrifice made to the LORD by fire: all the fat that covers the inner parts or is connected to them, [4] both kidneys with the fat on them near the loins, and the covering of the liver, which he will remove with the kidneys. [5] Then Aaron's sons are to burn it on the altar on top of the burnt offering that is on the burning wood, as an offering made by fire, an aroma pleasing to the LORD.

[6] " 'If he offers an animal from the flock as a fellowship offering to the LORD, he is to offer a male or female without defect. [7] If he offers a lamb, he is to present it before the LORD. [8] He is to lay his hand on the head of his offering and slaughter it in front of the Tent of Meeting. Then Aaron's sons shall sprinkle its blood against the altar on all sides. [9] From the fellowship offering he is to bring a sacrifice made to the LORD by fire: its fat, the entire fat tail cut off close to the backbone, all the fat that covers the inner parts or is connected to them, [10] both kidneys with the fat on them near the loins, and the covering of the liver, which he will remove with the kidneys. [11] The priest shall burn them on the altar as food, an offering made to the LORD by fire.

[12] " 'If his offering is a goat, he is to present it before the LORD. [13] He is to lay his hand on its head and slaughter it in front of the Tent of Meeting. Then Aaron's sons shall sprinkle its blood against the altar on all sides. [14] From what he offers he is to make this offering to the LORD by fire: all the fat that covers the inner parts or is connected to them, [15] both kidneys with the fat on them near the loins, and the covering of the liver, which he will remove with the kidneys. [16] The priest shall burn them on the altar as food, an offering made by fire, a pleasing aroma. All the fat is the LORD's.

[17] " 'This is a lasting ordinance for the generations to come, wherever you live: You must not eat any fat or any blood.' "

The Sin Offering

4 The LORD said to Moses, [2] "Say to the Israelites: 'When anyone sins unintentionally and does what is forbidden in any of the LORD's commands—

[3] " 'If the anointed priest sins, bringing guilt on the people, he must bring to the LORD a young bull without defect as a sin offering for the sin he has committed. [4] He is to present the bull at the entrance to the Tent of Meeting before the LORD. He is to lay his hand on its head and slaughter it before the LORD. [5] Then the anointed priest shall take some of the bull's blood and carry it into the Tent of Meeting. [6] He is to dip his finger into the blood and sprinkle some of it seven times before the LORD, in front of the curtain of the sanctuary. [7] The priest shall then put some of the blood on the horns of the altar of fragrant incense that is before the LORD in the Tent of Meeting. The rest of the bull's blood he shall pour out at the base of the altar of burnt offering at the entrance to the Tent of Meeting. [8] He shall remove all the fat from the bull of the sin offering—the fat that covers the inner parts or is connected to them, [9] both kidneys with the fat on them near the loins, and the covering of the liver, which he will remove

---

[a] 1 Traditionally *peace offering*; also in verses 3, 6 and 9

with the kidneys— ¹⁰just as the fat is removed from the ox*a* sacrificed as a fellowship offering.*b* Then the priest shall burn them on the altar of burnt offering. ¹¹But the hide of the bull and all its flesh, as well as the head and legs, the inner parts and offal— ¹²that is, all the rest of the bull—he must take outside the camp to a place ceremonially clean, where the ashes are thrown, and burn it in a wood fire on the ash heap.

¹³ "'If the whole Israelite community sins unintentionally and does what is forbidden in any of the Lord's commands, even though the community is unaware of the matter, they are guilty. ¹⁴When they become aware of the sin they committed, the assembly must bring a young bull as a sin offering and present it before the Tent of Meeting. ¹⁵The elders of the community are to lay their hands on the bull's head before the Lord, and the bull shall be slaughtered before the Lord. ¹⁶Then the anointed priest is to take some of the bull's blood into the Tent of Meeting. ¹⁷He shall dip his finger into the blood and sprinkle it before the Lord seven times in front of the curtain. ¹⁸He is to put some of the blood on the horns of the altar that is before the Lord in the Tent of Meeting. The rest of the blood he shall pour out at the base of the altar of burnt offering at the entrance to the Tent of Meeting. ¹⁹He shall remove all the fat from it and burn it on the altar, ²⁰and do with this bull just as he did with the bull for the sin offering. In this way the priest will make atonement for them, and they will be forgiven. ²¹Then he shall take the bull outside the camp and burn it as he burned the first bull. This is the sin offering for the community.

²² "'When a leader sins unintentionally and does what is forbidden in any of the commands of the Lord his God, he is guilty. ²³When he is made aware of the sin he committed, he must bring as his offering a male goat without defect. ²⁴He is to lay his hand on the goat's head and slaughter it at the place where the burnt offering is slaughtered before the Lord. It is a sin offering. ²⁵Then the priest shall take some of the blood of the sin offering with his finger and put it on the horns of the altar of burnt offering and pour out the rest of the blood at the base of the altar. ²⁶He shall burn all the fat on the altar as he burned the fat of the fellowship offering. In this way the priest will make atonement for the man's sin, and he will be forgiven.

²⁷ "'If a member of the community sins unintentionally and does what is forbidden in any of the Lord's commands, he is guilty. ²⁸When he is made aware of the sin he committed, he must bring as his offering for the sin he committed a female goat without defect. ²⁹He is to lay his hand on the head of the sin offering and slaughter it at the place of the burnt offering. ³⁰Then the priest is to take some of the blood with his finger and put it on the horns of the altar of burnt offering and pour out the rest of the blood at the base of the altar. ³¹He shall remove all the fat, just as the fat is removed from the fellowship offering, and the priest shall burn it on the altar as an aroma pleasing to the Lord. In this way the priest will make atonement for him, and he will be forgiven.

³² "'If he brings a lamb as his sin offering, he is to bring a female without defect. ³³He is to lay his hand on its head and slaughter it for a sin offering at the place where the burnt offering is slaughtered. ³⁴Then the priest shall take some of the blood of the sin offering with his finger and put it on the horns of the altar of burnt offering and pour out the rest of the blood at the base of the altar. ³⁵He shall remove all the fat, just as the fat is removed from the lamb of the fellowship offering, and the priest shall burn it on the altar on top of the offerings made to the Lord by fire. In this way the priest will make atonement for him for the sin he has committed, and he will be forgiven.

5 "'If a person sins because he does not speak up when he hears a public charge to testify regarding something he has seen or learned about, he will be held responsible.

---

a 10 The Hebrew word can include both male and female.
b 10 Traditionally *peace offering*; also in verses 26, 31 and 35

2 " 'Or if a person touches anything ceremonially unclean—whether the carcasses of unclean wild animals or of unclean livestock or of unclean creatures that move along the ground—even though he is unaware of it, he has become unclean and is guilty.

3 " 'Or if he touches human uncleanness—anything that would make him unclean—even though he is unaware of it, when he learns of it he will be guilty.

4 " 'Or if a person thoughtlessly takes an oath to do anything, whether good or evil—in any matter one might carelessly swear about—even though he is unaware of it, in any case when he learns of it it will be guilty.

5 " 'When anyone is guilty in any of these ways, he must confess in what way he has sinned 6 and, as a penalty for the sin he has committed, he must bring to the LORD a female lamb or goat from the flock as a sin offering; and the priest shall make atonement for him for his sin.

7 " 'If he cannot afford a lamb, he is to bring two doves or two young pigeons to the LORD as a penalty for his sin—one for a sin offering and the other for a burnt offering. 8 He is to bring them to the priest, who shall first offer the one for the sin offering. He is to wring its head from its neck, not severing it completely, 9 and is to sprinkle some of the blood of the sin offering against the side of the altar; the rest of the blood must be drained out at the base of the altar. It is a sin offering. 10 The priest shall then offer the other as a burnt offering in the prescribed way and make atonement for him for the sin he has committed, and he will be forgiven.

11 " 'If, however, he cannot afford two doves or two young pigeons, he is to bring as an offering for his sin a tenth of an ephah[a] of fine flour for a sin offering. He must not put oil or incense on it, because it is a sin offering. 12 He is to bring it to the priest, who shall take a handful of it as a memorial portion and burn it on the altar on top of the offerings made to the LORD by fire. It is a sin offering. 13 In this way the priest will make atonement for him for any of these sins he has

committed, and he will be forgiven. The rest of the offering will belong to the priest, as in the case of the grain offering.' "

The Guilt Offering

14 The LORD said to Moses: 15 "When a person commits a violation and sins unintentionally in regard to any of the LORD's holy things, he is to bring to the LORD as a penalty a ram from the flock, one without defect and of the proper value in silver, according to the sanctuary shekel.[b] It is a guilt offering. 16 He must make restitution for what he has failed to do in regard to the holy things, add a fifth of the value to that and give it all to the priest, who will make atonement for him with the ram as a guilt offering, and he will be forgiven.

17 "If a person sins and does what is forbidden in any of the LORD's commands, even though he does not know it, he is guilty and will be held responsible. 18 He is to bring to the priest as a guilt offering a ram from the flock, one without defect and of the proper value. In this way the priest will make atonement for him for the wrong he has committed unintentionally, and he will be forgiven. 19 It is a guilt offering; he has been guilty of[c] wrongdoing against the LORD."

6 The LORD said to Moses: 2 "If anyone sins and is unfaithful to the LORD by deceiving his neighbor about something entrusted to him or left in his care or stolen, or if he cheats him, 3 or if he finds lost property and lies about it, or if he swears falsely, or if he commits any such sin that people may do— 4 when he thus sins and becomes guilty, he must return what he has stolen or taken by extortion, or what was entrusted to him, or the lost property he found, 5 or whatever it was he swore falsely about. He must make restitution in full, add a fifth of the value to it and give it all to the owner on the day he presents his guilt offering. 6 And as a penalty he must bring to the priest, that is, to the LORD, his guilt offering,

---

a 11 That is, probably about 2 quarts (about 2 liters)   *b 15* That is, about 2/5 ounce (about 11.5 grams)   *c 19* Or *has made full expiation for his* a ram from the flock, one without defect and of the proper value. [7]In this way the priest will make atonement for him before the Lord, and he will be forgiven for any of these things he did that made him guilty."

The Burnt Offering

[8]The Lord said to Moses: [9]"Give Aaron and his sons this command: 'These are the regulations for the burnt offering: The burnt offering is to remain on the altar hearth throughout the night, till morning, and the fire must be kept burning on the altar. [10]The priest shall then put on his linen clothes, with linen undergarments next to his body, and shall remove the ashes of the burnt offering that the fire has consumed on the altar and place them beside the altar. [11]Then he is to take off these clothes and put on others, and carry the ashes outside the camp to a place that is ceremonially clean. [12]The fire on the altar must be kept burning; it must not go out. Every morning the priest is to add firewood and arrange the burnt offering on the fire and burn the fat of the fellowship offerings[a] on it. [13]The fire must be kept burning on the altar continuously; it must not go out.

The Grain Offering

[14]" 'These are the regulations for the grain offering: Aaron's sons are to bring it before the Lord, in front of the altar. [15]The priest is to take a handful of fine flour and oil, together with all the incense on the grain offering, and burn the memorial portion on the altar as an aroma pleasing to the Lord. [16]Aaron and his sons shall eat the rest of it, but it is to be eaten without yeast in a holy place; they are to eat it in the courtyard of the Tent of Meeting. [17]It must not be baked with yeast; I have given it as their share of the offerings made to me by fire. Like the sin offering and the guilt offering, it is most holy. [18]Any male descendant of Aaron may eat it. It is his regular share of the offerings made to the Lord by fire for the generations to come. Whatever touches them will become holy.[b]' "

[19]The Lord also said to Moses, [20]"This is the offering Aaron and his sons are to bring to the Lord on the day he[c] is anointed: a tenth of an ephah[d] of fine flour as a regular grain offering, half of it in the morning and half in the evening. [21]Prepare it with oil on a griddle; bring it well-mixed and present the grain offering broken[e] in pieces as an aroma pleasing to the Lord. [22]The son who is to succeed him as anointed priest shall prepare it. It is the Lord's regular share and is to be burned completely. [23]Every grain offering of a priest shall be burned completely; it must not be eaten."

The Sin Offering

[24]The Lord said to Moses, [25]"Say to Aaron and his sons: 'These are the regulations for the sin offering: The sin offering is to be slaughtered before the Lord in the place the burnt offering is slaughtered; it is most holy. [26]The priest who offers it shall eat it; it is to be eaten in a holy place, in the courtyard of the Tent of Meeting. [27]Whatever touches any of the flesh will become holy, and if any of the blood is spattered on a garment, you must wash it in a holy place. [28]The clay pot the meat is cooked in must be broken; but if it is cooked in a bronze pot, the pot is to be scoured and rinsed with water. [29]Any male in a priest's family may eat it; it is most holy. [30]But any sin offering whose blood is brought into the Tent of Meeting to make atonement in the Holy Place must not be eaten; it must be burned.

The Guilt Offering

7 " 'These are the regulations for the guilt offering, which is most holy: [2]The guilt offering is to be slaughtered in the place where the burnt offering is slaughtered, and its blood is to be sprinkled against the altar on all sides. [3]All its fat shall be offered: the fat tail and the fat that covers the inner parts, [4]both kidneys with the fat on them near the loins, and the covering of the liver,

---

[a] 12 Traditionally *peace offerings*   [b] 18 Or *Whoever touches them must be holy*; similarly in verse 27   [c] 20 Or *each*   [d] 20 That is, probably about 2 quarts (about 2 liters)   [e] 21 The meaning of the Hebrew for this word is uncertain.

which is to be removed with the kidneys. ⁵The priest shall burn them on the altar as an offering made to the LORD by fire. It is a guilt offering. ⁶Any male in a priest's family may eat it, but it must be eaten in a holy place; it is most holy.

⁷" 'The same law applies to both the sin offering and the guilt offering: They belong to the priest who makes atonement with them. ⁸The priest who offers a burnt offering for anyone may keep its hide for himself. ⁹Every grain offering baked in an oven or cooked in a pan or on a griddle belongs to the priest who offers it, ¹⁰and every grain offering, whether mixed with oil or dry, belongs equally to all the sons of Aaron.

The Fellowship Offering

¹¹" 'These are the regulations for the fellowship offering ᵃ a person may present to the LORD:

¹²" 'If he offers it as an expression of thankfulness, then along with this thank offering he is to offer cakes of bread made without yeast and mixed with oil, wafers made without yeast and spread with oil, and cakes of fine flour well-kneaded and mixed with oil. ¹³Along with his fellowship offering of thanksgiving he is to present an offering with cakes of bread made with yeast. ¹⁴He is to bring one of each kind as an offering, a contribution to the LORD; it belongs to the priest who sprinkles the blood of the fellowship offerings. ¹⁵The meat of his fellowship offering of thanksgiving must be eaten on the day it is offered; he must leave none of it till morning.

¹⁶" 'If, however, his offering is the result of a vow or is a freewill offering, the sacrifice shall be eaten on the day he offers it, but anything left over may be eaten on the next day. ¹⁷Any meat of the sacrifice left over till the third day must be burned up. ¹⁸If any meat of the fellowship offering is eaten on the third day, it will not be accepted. It will not be credited to the one who offered it, for it is impure; the person who eats any of it will be held responsible.

¹⁹" 'Meat that touches anything ceremonially unclean must not be eaten; it must be burned up. As for other meat, anyone ceremonially clean may eat it. ²⁰But if anyone who is unclean eats any meat of the fellowship offering belonging to the LORD, that person must be cut off from his people. ²¹If anyone touches something unclean—whether human uncleanness or an unclean animal or any unclean, detestable thing—and then eats any of the meat of the fellowship offering belonging to the LORD, that person must be cut off from his people.' "

Eating Fat and Blood Forbidden

²²The LORD said to Moses, ²³"Say to the Israelites: 'Do not eat any of the fat of cattle, sheep or goats. ²⁴The fat of an animal found dead or torn by wild animals may be used for any other purpose, but you must not eat it. ²⁵Anyone who eats the fat of an animal from which an offering by fire may be ᵇ made to the LORD must be cut off from his people. ²⁶And wherever you live, you must not eat the blood of any bird or animal. ²⁷If anyone eats blood, that person must be cut off from his people.' "

The Priests' Share

²⁸The LORD said to Moses, ²⁹"Say to the Israelites: 'Anyone who brings a fellowship offering to the LORD is to bring part of it as his sacrifice to the LORD. ³⁰With his own hands he is to bring the offering made to the LORD by fire; he is to bring the fat, together with the breast, and wave the breast before the LORD as a wave offering. ³¹The priest shall burn the fat on the altar, but the breast belongs to Aaron and his sons. ³²You are to give the right thigh of your fellowship offerings to the priest as a contribution. ³³The son of Aaron who offers the blood and the fat of the fellowship offering shall have the right thigh as his share. ³⁴From the fellowship offerings of the Israelites, I have taken the breast that is waved and the thigh that is presented and have given them to Aaron the priest and his sons as their regular share from the Israelites.' "

³⁵This is the portion of the offerings made to the LORD by fire that were allotted to Aaron

---

ᵃ 11 Traditionally *peace offering*; also in verses 13-37   ᵇ 25 Or *fire is* and his sons on the day they were presented to serve the Lord as priests. ³⁶On the day they were anointed, the Lord commanded that the Israelites give this to them as their regular share for the generations to come.

³⁷These, then, are the regulations for the burnt offering, the grain offering, the sin offering, the guilt offering, the ordination offering and the fellowship offering, ³⁸which the Lord gave Moses on Mount Sinai on the day he commanded the Israelites to bring their offerings to the Lord, in the Desert of Sinai.

The Ordination of Aaron and His Sons

8:1–36pp — Ex 29:1–37

8 The Lord said to Moses, ²"Bring Aaron and his sons, their garments, the anointing oil, the bull for the sin offering, the two rams and the basket containing bread made without yeast, ³and gather the entire assembly at the entrance to the Tent of Meeting." ⁴Moses did as the Lord commanded him, and the assembly gathered at the entrance to the Tent of Meeting.

⁵Moses said to the assembly, "This is what the Lord has commanded to be done." ⁶Then Moses brought Aaron and his sons forward and washed them with water. ⁷He put the tunic on Aaron, tied the sash around him, clothed him with the robe and put the ephod on him. He also tied the ephod to him by its skillfully woven waistband; so it was fastened on him. ⁸He placed the breastpiece on him and put the Urim and Thummim in the breastpiece. ⁹Then he placed the turban on Aaron's head and set the gold plate, the sacred diadem, on the front of it, as the Lord commanded Moses.

¹⁰Then Moses took the anointing oil and anointed the tabernacle and everything in it, and so consecrated them. ¹¹He sprinkled some of the oil on the altar seven times, anointing the altar and all its utensils and the basin with its stand, to consecrate them. ¹²He poured some of the anointing oil on Aaron's head and anointed him to consecrate him. ¹³Then he brought Aaron's

sons forward, put tunics on them, tied sashes around them and put headbands on them, as the Lord commanded Moses.

¹⁴He then presented the bull for the sin offering, and Aaron and his sons laid their hands on its head. ¹⁵Moses slaughtered the bull and took some of the blood, and with his finger he put it on all the horns of the altar to purify the altar. He poured out the rest of the blood at the base of the altar. So he consecrated it to make atonement for it. ¹⁶Moses also took all the fat around the inner parts, the covering of the liver, and both kidneys and their fat, and burned it on the altar. ¹⁷But the bull with its hide and its flesh and its offal he burned up outside the camp, as the Lord commanded Moses.

¹⁸He then presented the ram for the burnt offering, and Aaron and his sons laid their hands on its head. ¹⁹Then Moses slaughtered the ram and sprinkled the blood against the altar on all sides. ²⁰He cut the ram into pieces and burned the head, the pieces and the fat. ²¹He washed the inner parts and the legs with water and burned the whole ram on the altar as a burnt offering, a pleasing aroma, an offering made to the Lord by fire, as the Lord commanded Moses.

²²He then presented the other ram, the ram for the ordination, and Aaron and his sons laid their hands on its head. ²³Moses slaughtered the ram and took some of its blood and put it on the lobe of Aaron's right ear, on the thumb of his right hand and on the big toe of his right foot. ²⁴Moses also brought Aaron's sons forward and put some of the blood on the lobes of their right ears, on the thumbs of their right hands and on the big toes of their right feet. Then he sprinkled blood against the altar on all sides. ²⁵He took the fat, the fat tail, all the fat around the inner parts, the covering of the liver, both kidneys and their fat and the right thigh. ²⁶Then from the basket of bread made without yeast, which was before the Lord, he took a cake of bread, and one made with oil, and a wafer; he put these on the fat portions and on the right thigh. ²⁷He put all these in the hands of Aaron and his sons and waved

them before the LORD as a wave offering. ²⁸Then Moses took them from their hands and burned them on the altar on top of the burnt offering as an ordination offering, a pleasing aroma, an offering made to the LORD by fire. ²⁹He also took the breast—Moses' share of the ordination ram—and waved it before the LORD as a wave offering, as the LORD commanded Moses.

³⁰Then Moses took some of the anointing oil and some of the blood from the altar and sprinkled them on Aaron and his garments and on his sons and their garments. So he consecrated Aaron and his garments and his sons and their garments.

³¹Moses then said to Aaron and his sons, "Cook the meat at the entrance to the Tent of Meeting and eat it there with the bread from the basket of ordination offerings, as I commanded, saying,ᵃ 'Aaron and his sons are to eat it.' ³²Then burn up the rest of the meat and the bread. ³³Do not leave the entrance to the Tent of Meeting for seven days, until the days of your ordination are completed, for your ordination will last seven days. ³⁴What has been done today was commanded by the LORD to make atonement for you. ³⁵You must stay at the entrance to the Tent of Meeting day and night for seven days and do what the LORD requires, so you will not die; for that is what I have been commanded." ³⁶So Aaron and his sons did everything the LORD commanded through Moses.

The Priests Begin Their Ministry

9 On the eighth day Moses summoned Aaron and his sons and the elders of Israel. ²He said to Aaron, "Take a bull calf for your sin offering and a ram for your burnt offering, both without defect, and present them before the LORD. ³Then say to the Israelites: 'Take a male goat for a sin offering, a calf and a lamb—both a year old and without defect—for a burnt offering, ⁴and an oxᵇ and a ram for a fellowship offeringᶜ to sacrifice before the LORD, together with a grain offering mixed with oil. For today the LORD will appear to you.'"

⁵They took the things Moses commanded to the front of the Tent of Meeting, and the entire assembly came near and stood before the LORD. ⁶Then Moses said, "This is what the LORD has commanded you to do, so that the glory of the LORD may appear to you."

⁷Moses said to Aaron, "Come to the altar and sacrifice your sin offering and your burnt offering and make atonement for yourself and the people; sacrifice the offering that is for the people and make atonement for them, as the LORD has commanded."

⁸So Aaron came to the altar and slaughtered the calf as a sin offering for himself. ⁹His sons brought the blood to him, and he dipped his finger into the blood and put it on the horns of the altar; the rest of the blood he poured out at the base of the altar. ¹⁰On the altar he burned the fat, the kidneys and the covering of the liver from the sin offering, as the LORD commanded Moses; ¹¹the flesh and the hide he burned up outside the camp.

¹²Then he slaughtered the burnt offering. His sons handed him the blood, and he sprinkled it against the altar on all sides. ¹³They handed him the burnt offering piece by piece, including the head, and he burned them on the altar. ¹⁴He washed the inner parts and the legs and burned them on top of the burnt offering on the altar.

¹⁵Aaron then brought the offering that was for the people. He took the goat for the people's sin offering and slaughtered it and offered it for a sin offering as he did with the first one.

¹⁶He brought the burnt offering and offered it in the prescribed way. ¹⁷He also brought the grain offering, took a handful of it and burned it on the altar in addition to the morning's burnt offering.

¹⁸He slaughtered the ox and the ram as the fellowship offering for the people. His sons handed him the blood, and he sprinkled it against the altar on all sides. ¹⁹But the fat portions of the ox

ᵃ 31 Or I was commanded: ᵇ 4 The Hebrew word can include both male and female; also in verses 18 and 19.   ᶜ 4 Traditionally peace offering; also in verses 18 and 22 and the ram—the fat tail, the layer of fat, the kidneys and the covering of the liver— ²⁰these they laid on the breasts, and then Aaron burned the fat on the altar. ²¹Aaron waved the breasts and the right thigh before the LORD as a wave offering, as Moses commanded.

²²Then Aaron lifted his hands toward the people and blessed them. And having sacrificed the sin offering, the burnt offering and the fellowship offering, he stepped down.

²³Moses and Aaron then went into the Tent of Meeting. When they came out, they blessed the people; and the glory of the LORD appeared to all the people. ²⁴Fire came out from the presence of the LORD and consumed the burnt offering and the fat portions on the altar. And when all the people saw it, they shouted for joy and fell facedown.

The Death of Nadab and Abihu

10 Aaron's sons Nadab and Abihu took their censers, put fire in them and added incense; and they offered unauthorized fire before the LORD, contrary to his command. ²So fire came out from the presence of the LORD and consumed them, and they died before the LORD. ³Moses then said to Aaron, "This is what the LORD spoke of when he said:

" 'Among those who approach me
I will show myself holy;
in the sight of all the people
I will be honored.' "

Aaron remained silent.

⁴Moses summoned Mishael and Elzaphan, sons of Aaron's uncle Uzziel, and said to them, "Come here; carry your cousins outside the camp, away from the front of the sanctuary." ⁵So they came and carried them, still in their tunics, outside the camp, as Moses ordered.

⁶Then Moses said to Aaron and his sons Eleazar and Ithamar, "Do not let your hair become unkempt,^a and do not tear your clothes, or you will die and the LORD will be angry with the whole community. But your relatives, all the house of Israel, may mourn for those the LORD has destroyed by fire. ⁷Do not leave the entrance to the Tent of Meeting or you will die, because the LORD's anointing oil is on you." So they did as Moses said.

⁸Then the LORD said to Aaron, ⁹"You and your sons are not to drink wine or other fermented drink whenever you go into the Tent of Meeting, or you will die. This is a lasting ordinance for the generations to come. ¹⁰You must distinguish between the holy and the common, between the unclean and the clean, ¹¹and you must teach the Israelites all the decrees the LORD has given them through Moses."

¹²Moses said to Aaron and his remaining sons, Eleazar and Ithamar, "Take the grain offering left over from the offerings made to the LORD by fire and eat it prepared without yeast beside the altar, for it is most holy. ¹³Eat it in a holy place, because it is your share and your sons' share of the offerings made to the LORD by fire; for so I have been commanded. ¹⁴But you and your sons and your daughters may eat the breast that was waved and the thigh that was presented. Eat them in a ceremonially clean place; they have been given to you and your children as your share of the Israelites' fellowship offerings.^b ¹⁵The thigh that was presented and the breast that was waved must be brought with the fat portions of the offerings made by fire, to be waved before the LORD as a wave offering. This will be the regular share for you and your children, as the LORD has commanded."

¹⁶When Moses inquired about the goat of the sin offering and found that it had been burned up, he was angry with Eleazar and Ithamar, Aaron's remaining sons, and asked, ¹⁷"Why didn't you eat the sin offering in the sanctuary area? It is most holy; it was given to you to take away the guilt of the community by making atonement for them before the LORD. ¹⁸Since its blood was not taken into the Holy Place, you should have eaten the goat in the sanctuary area, as I commanded."

^a 6 Or Do not uncover your heads   ^b 14 Traditionally peace offerings

[19] Aaron replied to Moses, "Today they sacrificed their sin offering and their burnt offering before the LORD, but such things as this have happened to me. Would the LORD have been pleased if I had eaten the sin offering today?" [20] When Moses heard this, he was satisfied.

Clean and Unclean Food
11:1–23pp — Dt 14:3–20

[11] The LORD said to Moses and Aaron, [2] "Say to the Israelites: 'Of all the animals that live on land, these are the ones you may eat: [3] You may eat any animal that has a split hoof completely divided and that chews the cud.

[4] "'There are some that only chew the cud or only have a split hoof, but you must not eat them. The camel, though it chews the cud, does not have a split hoof; it is ceremonially unclean for you. [5] The coney,[a] though it chews the cud, does not have a split hoof; it is unclean for you. [6] The rabbit, though it chews the cud, does not have a split hoof; it is unclean for you. [7] And the pig, though it has a split hoof completely divided, does not chew the cud; it is unclean for you. [8] You must not eat their meat or touch their carcasses; they are unclean for you.

[9] "'Of all the creatures living in the water of the seas and the streams, you may eat any that have fins and scales. [10] But all creatures in the seas or streams that do not have fins and scales — whether among all the swarming things or among all the other living creatures in the water — you are to detest. [11] And since you are to detest them, you must not eat their meat and you must detest their carcasses. [12] Anything living in the water that does not have fins and scales is to be detestable to you.

[13] "'These are the birds you are to detest and not eat because they are detestable: the eagle, the vulture, the black vulture, [14] the red kite, any kind of black kite, [15] any kind of raven, [16] the horned owl, the screech owl, the gull, any kind of hawk, [17] the little owl, the cormorant, the great owl, [18] the white owl, the desert owl, the osprey, [19] the stork, any kind of heron, the hoopoe and the bat.[b]

[20] "'All flying insects that walk on all fours are to be detestable to you. [21] There are, however, some winged creatures that walk on all fours that you may eat: those that have jointed legs for hopping on the ground. [22] Of these you may eat any kind of locust, katydid, cricket or grasshopper. [23] But all other winged creatures that have four legs you are to detest.

[24] "'You will make yourselves unclean by these; whoever touches their carcasses will be unclean till evening. [25] Whoever picks up one of their carcasses must wash his clothes, and he will be unclean till evening.

[26] "'Every animal that has a split hoof not completely divided or that does not chew the cud is unclean for you; whoever touches ⌊the carcass of⌋ any of them will be unclean. [27] Of all the animals that walk on all fours, those that walk on their paws are unclean for you; whoever touches their carcasses will be unclean till evening. [28] Anyone who picks up their carcasses must wash his clothes, and he will be unclean till evening. They are unclean for you.

[29] "'Of the animals that move about on the ground, these are unclean for you: the weasel, the rat, any kind of great lizard, [30] the gecko, the monitor lizard, the wall lizard, the skink and the chameleon. [31] Of all those that move along the ground, these are unclean for you. Whoever touches them when they are dead will be unclean till evening. [32] When one of them dies and falls on something, that article, whatever its use, will be unclean, whether it is made of wood, cloth, hide or sackcloth. Put it in water; it will be unclean till evening, and then it will be clean. [33] If one of them falls into a clay pot, everything in it will be unclean, and you must break the pot. [34] Any food that could be eaten but has water on it from such a pot is unclean, and any liquid that could be drunk from it is unclean. [35] Anything that one of their carcasses falls on becomes unclean; an oven or cooking pot must be broken up. They are

---

[a] 5 That is, the hyrax or rock badger   [b] 19 The precise identification of some of the birds, insects and animals in this chapter is uncertain.

unclean, and you are to regard them as unclean. ³⁶A spring, however, or a cistern for collecting water remains clean, but anyone who touches one of these carcasses is unclean. ³⁷If a carcass falls on any seeds that are to be planted, they remain clean. ³⁸But if water has been put on the seed and a carcass falls on it, it is unclean for you.

³⁹" 'If an animal that you are allowed to eat dies, anyone who touches the carcass will be unclean till evening. ⁴⁰Anyone who eats some of the carcass must wash his clothes, and he will be unclean till evening. Anyone who picks up the carcass must wash his clothes, and he will be unclean till evening.

⁴¹" 'Every creature that moves about on the ground is detestable; it is not to be eaten. ⁴²You are not to eat any creature that moves about on the ground, whether it moves on its belly or walks on all fours or on many feet; it is detestable. ⁴³Do not defile yourselves by any of these creatures. Do not make yourselves unclean by means of them or be made unclean by them. ⁴⁴I am the LORD your God; consecrate yourselves and be holy, because I am holy. Do not make yourselves unclean by any creature that moves about on the ground. ⁴⁵I am the LORD who brought you up out of Egypt to be your God; therefore be holy, because I am holy.

⁴⁶" 'These are the regulations concerning animals, birds, every living thing that moves in the water and every creature that moves about on the ground. ⁴⁷You must distinguish between the unclean and the clean, between living creatures that may be eaten and those that may not be eaten.' "

Purification After Childbirth

12 The LORD said to Moses, ²"Say to the Israelites: 'A woman who becomes pregnant and gives birth to a son will be ceremonially unclean for seven days, just as she is unclean during her monthly period. ³On the eighth day the boy is to be circumcised. ⁴Then the woman must wait thirty-three days to be purified from her bleeding. She must not touch anything sacred or go to the sanctuary until the days of her purification

are over. ⁵If she gives birth to a daughter, for two weeks the woman will be unclean, as during her period. Then she must wait sixty-six days to be purified from her bleeding.

⁶" 'When the days of her purification for a son or daughter are over, she is to bring to the priest at the entrance to the Tent of Meeting a year-old lamb for a burnt offering and a young pigeon or a dove for a sin offering. ⁷He shall offer them before the LORD to make atonement for her, and then she will be ceremonially clean from her flow of blood.

" 'These are the regulations for the woman who gives birth to a boy or a girl. ⁸If she cannot afford a lamb, she is to bring two doves or two young pigeons, one for a burnt offering and the other for a sin offering. In this way the priest will make atonement for her, and she will be clean.' "

Regulations About Infectious Skin Diseases

13 The LORD said to Moses and Aaron, ²"When anyone has a swelling or a rash or a bright spot on his skin that may become an infectious skin disease,ᵃ he must be brought to Aaron the priest or to one of his sonsᵇ who is a priest. ³The priest is to examine the sore on his skin, and if the hair in the sore has turned white and the sore appears to be more than skin deep,ᶜ it is an infectious skin disease. When the priest examines him, he shall pronounce him ceremonially unclean. ⁴If the spot on his skin is white but does not appear to be more than skin deep and the hair in it has not turned white, the priest is to put the infected person in isolation for seven days. ⁵On the seventh day the priest is to examine him, and if he sees that the sore is unchanged and has not spread in the skin, he is to keep him in isolation another seven days. ⁶On the seventh day the priest is to examine him again, and if the sore has faded and has not spread in the skin, the priest shall pronounce him clean; it is only a

---

ᵃ 2 Traditionally *leprosy*; the Hebrew word was used for various diseases affecting the skin — not necessarily leprosy; also elsewhere in this chapter.   ᵇ 2 Or *descendants*   ᶜ 3 Or *be lower than the rest of the skin*; also elsewhere in this chapter rash. The man must wash his clothes, and he will be clean. 7But if the rash does spread in his skin after he has shown himself to the priest to be pronounced clean, he must appear before the priest again. 8The priest is to examine him, and if the rash has spread in the skin, he shall pronounce him unclean; it is an infectious disease.

9"When anyone has an infectious skin disease, he must be brought to the priest. 10The priest is to examine him, and if there is a white swelling in the skin that has turned the hair white and if there is raw flesh in the swelling, 11it is a chronic skin disease and the priest shall pronounce him unclean. He is not to put him in isolation, because he is already unclean.

12"If the disease breaks out all over his skin and, so far as the priest can see, it covers all the skin of the infected person from head to foot, 13the priest is to examine him, and if the disease has covered his whole body, he shall pronounce that person clean. Since it has all turned white, he is clean. 14But whenever raw flesh appears on him, he will be unclean. 15When the priest sees the raw flesh, he shall pronounce him unclean. The raw flesh is unclean; he has an infectious disease. 16Should the raw flesh change and turn white, he must go to the priest. 17The priest is to examine him, and if the sores have turned white, the priest shall pronounce the infected person clean; then he will be clean.

18"When someone has a boil on his skin and it heals, 19and in the place where the boil was, a white swelling or reddish-white spot appears, he must present himself to the priest. 20The priest is to examine it, and if it appears to be more than skin deep and the hair in it has turned white, the priest shall pronounce him unclean. It is an infectious skin disease that has broken out where the boil was. 21But if, when the priest examines it, there is no white hair in it and it is not more than skin deep and has faded, then the priest is to put him in isolation for seven days. 22If it is spreading in the skin, the priest shall pronounce him unclean; it is infectious. 23But if the spot is unchanged and has not spread, it is only a scar from the boil, and the priest shall pronounce him clean.

24"When someone has a burn on his skin and a reddish-white or white spot appears in the raw flesh of the burn, 25the priest is to examine the spot, and if the hair in it has turned white, and it appears to be more than skin deep, it is an infectious disease that has broken out in the burn. The priest shall pronounce him unclean; it is an infectious skin disease. 26But if the priest examines it and there is no white hair in the spot and if it is not more than skin deep and has faded, then the priest is to put him in isolation for seven days. 27On the seventh day the priest is to examine him, and if it is spreading in the skin, the priest shall pronounce him unclean; it is an infectious skin disease. 28If, however, the spot is unchanged and has not spread in the skin but has faded, it is a swelling from the burn, and the priest shall pronounce him clean; it is only a scar from the burn.

29"If a man or woman has a sore on the head or on the chin, 30the priest is to examine the sore, and if it appears to be more than skin deep and the hair in it is yellow and thin, the priest shall pronounce that person unclean; it is an itch, an infectious disease of the head or chin. 31But if, when the priest examines this kind of sore, it does not seem to be more than skin deep and there is no black hair in it, then the priest is to put the infected person in isolation for seven days. 32On the seventh day the priest is to examine the sore, and if the itch has not spread and there is no yellow hair in it and it does not appear to be more than skin deep, 33he must be shaved except for the diseased area, and the priest is to keep him in isolation another seven days. 34On the seventh day the priest is to examine the itch, and if it has not spread in the skin and appears to be no more than skin deep, the priest shall pronounce him clean. He must wash his clothes, and he will be clean. 35But if the itch does spread in the skin after he is pronounced clean, 36the priest is to examine him, and if the itch has spread in the skin, the priest does not need to look for yellow hair;

the person is unclean. [37] If, however, in his judgment it is unchanged and black hair has grown in it, the itch is healed. He is clean, and the priest shall pronounce him clean.

[38] "When a man or woman has white spots on the skin, [39] the priest is to examine them, and if the spots are dull white, it is a harmless rash that has broken out on the skin; that person is clean.

[40] "When a man has lost his hair and is bald, he is clean. [41] If he has lost his hair from the front of his scalp and has a bald forehead, he is clean. [42] But if he has a reddish-white sore on his bald head or forehead, it is an infectious disease breaking out on his head or forehead. [43] The priest is to examine him, and if the swollen sore on his head or forehead is reddish-white like an infectious skin disease, [44] the man is diseased and is unclean. The priest shall pronounce him unclean because of the sore on his head.

[45] "The person with such an infectious disease must wear torn clothes, let his hair be unkempt,[a] cover the lower part of his face and cry out, 'Unclean! Unclean!' [46] As long as he has the infection he remains unclean. He must live alone; he must live outside the camp.

Regulations About Mildew

[47] "If any clothing is contaminated with mildew—any woolen or linen clothing, [48] any woven or knitted material of linen or wool, any leather or anything made of leather— [49] and if the contamination in the clothing, or leather, or woven or knitted material, or any leather article, is greenish or reddish, it is a spreading mildew and must be shown to the priest. [50] The priest is to examine the mildew and isolate the affected article for seven days. [51] On the seventh day he is to examine it, and if the mildew has spread in the clothing, or the woven or knitted material, or the leather, whatever its use, it is a destructive mildew; the article is unclean. [52] He must burn up the clothing, or the woven or knitted material of wool or linen, or any leather article that has the contamination in it, because the mildew is destructive; the article must be burned up.

[53] "But if, when the priest examines it, the mildew has not spread in the clothing, or the woven or knitted material, or the leather article, [54] he shall order that the contaminated article be washed. Then he is to isolate it for another seven days. [55] After the affected article has been washed, the priest is to examine it, and if the mildew has not changed its appearance, even though it has not spread, it is unclean. Burn it with fire, whether the mildew has affected one side or the other. [56] If, when the priest examines it, the mildew has faded after the article has been washed, he is to tear the contaminated part out of the clothing, or the leather, or the woven or knitted material. [57] But if it reappears in the clothing, or in the woven or knitted material, or in the leather article, it is spreading, and whatever has the mildew must be burned with fire. [58] The clothing, or the woven or knitted material, or any leather article that has been washed and is rid of the mildew, must be washed again, and it will be clean."

[59] These are the regulations concerning contamination by mildew in woolen or linen clothing, woven or knitted material, or any leather article, for pronouncing them clean or unclean.

Cleansing From Infectious Skin Diseases

14 The LORD said to Moses, [2] "These are the regulations for the diseased person at the time of his ceremonial cleansing, when he is brought to the priest: [3] The priest is to go outside the camp and examine him. If the person has been healed of his infectious skin disease,[b] [4] the priest shall order that two live clean birds and some cedar wood, scarlet yarn and hyssop be brought for the one to be cleansed. [5] Then the priest shall order that one of the birds be killed over fresh water in a clay pot. [6] He is then to take the live bird and dip it, together with the cedar wood, the scarlet yarn and the hyssop, into the blood of the bird that was killed over the fresh water. [7] Seven times he shall sprinkle the one to be

---

[a] 45 Or clothes, uncover his head   [b] 3 Traditionally leprosy; the Hebrew word was used for various diseases affecting the skin—not necessarily leprosy; also elsewhere in this chapter.

cleansed of the infectious disease and pronounce him clean. Then he is to release the live bird in the open fields.

⁸"The person to be cleansed must wash his clothes, shave off all his hair and bathe with water; then he will be ceremonially clean. After this he may come into the camp, but he must stay outside his tent for seven days. ⁹On the seventh day he must shave off all his hair; he must shave his head, his beard, his eyebrows and the rest of his hair. He must wash his clothes and bathe himself with water, and he will be clean.

¹⁰"On the eighth day he must bring two male lambs and one ewe lamb a year old, each without defect, along with three-tenths of an ephah ᵃ of fine flour mixed with oil for a grain offering, and one log ᵇ of oil. ¹¹The priest who pronounces him clean shall present both the one to be cleansed and his offerings before the LORD at the entrance to the Tent of Meeting.

¹²"Then the priest is to take one of the male lambs and offer it as a guilt offering, along with the log of oil; he shall wave them before the LORD as a wave offering. ¹³He is to slaughter the lamb in the holy place where the sin offering and the burnt offering are slaughtered. Like the sin offering, the guilt offering belongs to the priest; it is most holy. ¹⁴The priest is to take some of the blood of the guilt offering and put it on the lobe of the right ear of the one to be cleansed, on the thumb of his right hand and on the big toe of his right foot. ¹⁵The priest shall then take some of the log of oil, pour it in the palm of his own left hand, ¹⁶dip his right forefinger into the oil in his palm, and with his finger sprinkle some of it before the LORD seven times. ¹⁷The priest is to put some of the oil remaining in his palm on the lobe of the right ear of the one to be cleansed, on the thumb of his right hand and on the big toe of his right foot, on top of the blood of the guilt offering. ¹⁸The rest of the oil in his palm the priest shall put on the head of the one to be cleansed and make atonement for him before the LORD.

¹⁹"Then the priest is to sacrifice the sin offering and make atonement for the one to be cleansed

from his uncleanness. After that, the priest shall slaughter the burnt offering ²⁰and offer it on the altar, together with the grain offering, and make atonement for him, and he will be clean.

²¹"If, however, he is poor and cannot afford these, he must take one male lamb as a guilt offering to be waved to make atonement for him, together with a tenth of an ephah ᶜ of fine flour mixed with oil for a grain offering, a log of oil, ²²and two doves or two young pigeons, which he can afford, one for a sin offering and the other for a burnt offering.

²³"On the eighth day he must bring them for his cleansing to the priest at the entrance to the Tent of Meeting, before the LORD. ²⁴The priest is to take the lamb for the guilt offering, together with the log of oil, and wave them before the LORD as a wave offering. ²⁵He shall slaughter the lamb for the guilt offering and take some of its blood and put it on the lobe of the right ear of the one to be cleansed, on the thumb of his right hand and on the big toe of his right foot. ²⁶The priest is to pour some of the oil into the palm of his own left hand, ²⁷and with his right forefinger sprinkle some of the oil from his palm seven times before the LORD. ²⁸Some of the oil in his palm he is to put on the same places he put the blood of the guilt offering—on the lobe of the right ear of the one to be cleansed, on the thumb of his right hand and on the big toe of his right foot. ²⁹The rest of the oil in his palm the priest shall put on the head of the one to be cleansed, to make atonement for him before the LORD. ³⁰Then he shall sacrifice the doves or the young pigeons, which the person can afford, ³¹one ᵈ as a sin offering and the other as a burnt offering, together with the grain offering. In this way the priest will make atonement before the LORD on behalf of the one to be cleansed."

³²These are the regulations for anyone who has an infectious skin disease and who cannot afford the regular offerings for his cleansing.

ᵃ 10 That is, probably about 6 quarts (about 6.5 liters)   ᵇ 10 That is, probably about 2/3 pint (about 0.3 liter); also in verses 12, 15, 21 and 24   ᶜ 21 That is, probably about 2 quarts (about 2 liters)   ᵈ 31 Septuagint and Syriac; Hebrew ³¹such as the person can afford, one

Cleansing From Mildew

33 The Lord said to Moses and Aaron, 34 "When you enter the land of Canaan, which I am giving you as your possession, and I put a spreading mildew in a house in that land, 35 the owner of the house must go and tell the priest, 'I have seen something that looks like mildew in my house.' 36 The priest is to order the house to be emptied before he goes in to examine the mildew, so that nothing in the house will be pronounced unclean. After this the priest is to go in and inspect the house. 37 He is to examine the mildew on the walls, and if it has greenish or reddish depressions that appear to be deeper than the surface of the wall, 38 the priest shall go out the doorway of the house and close it up for seven days. 39 On the seventh day the priest shall return to inspect the house. If the mildew has spread on the walls, 40 he is to order that the contaminated stones be torn out and thrown into an unclean place outside the town. 41 He must have all the inside walls of the house scraped and the material that is scraped off dumped into an unclean place outside the town. 42 Then they are to take other stones to replace these and take new clay and plaster the house.

43 "If the mildew reappears in the house after the stones have been torn out and the house scraped and plastered, 44 the priest is to go and examine it and, if the mildew has spread in the house, it is a destructive mildew; the house is unclean. 45 It must be torn down — its stones, timbers and all the plaster — and taken out of the town to an unclean place.

46 "Anyone who goes into the house while it is closed up will be unclean till evening. 47 Anyone who sleeps or eats in the house must wash his clothes.

48 "But if the priest comes to examine it and the mildew has not spread after the house has been plastered, he shall pronounce the house clean, because the mildew is gone. 49 To purify the house he is to take two birds and some cedar wood, scarlet yarn and hyssop. 50 He shall kill one of the birds over fresh water in a clay pot. 51 Then he is to take the cedar wood, the hyssop, the scarlet yarn and the live bird, dip them into the blood of the dead bird and the fresh water, and sprinkle the house seven times. 52 He shall purify the house with the bird's blood, the fresh water, the live bird, the cedar wood, the hyssop and the scarlet yarn. 53 Then he is to release the live bird in the open fields outside the town. In this way he will make atonement for the house, and it will be clean."

54 These are the regulations for any infectious skin disease, for an itch, 55 for mildew in clothing or in a house, 56 and for a swelling, a rash or a bright spot, 57 to determine when something is clean or unclean.

These are the regulations for infectious skin diseases and mildew.

Discharges Causing Uncleanness

15 The Lord said to Moses and Aaron, 2 "Speak to the Israelites and say to them: 'When any man has a bodily discharge, the discharge is unclean. 3 Whether it continues flowing from his body or is blocked, it will make him unclean. This is how his discharge will bring about uncleanness:

4 " 'Any bed the man with a discharge lies on will be unclean, and anything he sits on will be unclean. 5 Anyone who touches his bed must wash his clothes and bathe with water, and he will be unclean till evening. 6 Whoever sits on anything that the man with a discharge sat on must wash his clothes and bathe with water, and he will be unclean till evening.

7 " 'Whoever touches the man who has a discharge must wash his clothes and bathe with water, and he will be unclean till evening.

8 " 'If the man with the discharge spits on someone who is clean, that person must wash his clothes and bathe with water, and he will be unclean till evening.

9 " 'Everything the man sits on when riding will be unclean, 10 and whoever touches any of the things that were under him will be unclean

ON THE SEVENTH DAY THE PRIEST
SHALL RETURN TO INSPECT THE
HOUSE. IF THE MILDEW HAS SPREAD
ON THE WALLS, HE IS TO ORDER
THAT THE CONTAMINATED STONES
BE TORN OUT AND THROWN INTO AN
UNCLEAN PLACE OUTSIDE THE TOWN.

Leviticus 14:39−40

The Best Rules Endure

DORIS WYNBEEK RIKKERS

READ | LEVITICUS 14:33 – 57

Ask anyone who returned home to New Orleans after Hurricane Katrina ravaged the area and they'll tell you about mildew. Thousands of homes were condemned, stripped to the studs or bulldozed because of mildew that coated surfaces and penetrated deep into walls. Local health officials knew how great a hazard mildew was and refused the owners re-entry into beloved homes.

God established similar health and sanitation rules with his people centuries ago to protect them from everyday hazards like mildew. Not only that, but he also gave them regulations for every aspect of life: food, family, politics, education, economics, worship. When obeyed, the laws of Leviticus allowed the Israelites to maintain a relationship with God and the world around them. He repeatedly told his people: "Be holy, because I am holy" (Leviticus 11:45). God wanted his people to be different and set apart from the peoples around them. The laws and regulations described in Leviticus ensured that the Israelites would live and worship in relationship to their holy God.

Times change, rules loosen; however, the best regulations endure to ensure safety, health and well-being. Many of the rules and regulations that maintain a civil society are rooted in the basics found in the book of Leviticus (see especially chapter 19). The basic principle of Christian conduct is located there: "Love your neighbor as yourself" (Leviticus 19:18).

God's rules for living in a civilized, compassionate and just society were established centuries ago; many of them have endured, many of them are now classified as common sense. And although we have been freed through Christ from many of the offerings and sacrificial rituals described in Leviticus, many regulations remain foundational to our civilization today.

Dear God, thank you for loving and caring for my everyday needs. Help me to recognize that even the rules and regulations made for the Israelites so many centuries ago still hold timeless truth for me today. Allow opportunities for me to pass these principles along to my children and grandchildren. Amen.

Your next devotion is located on page 163.

GRANDCHILD IN FOCUS • PRAYER

School/Career

Dear God, may learning be a joy rather than a chore for my grandchild. May exploration of new ideas bring a sense of wonder, awe and excitement. Grant him clarity of mind, the ability to concentrate on the task at hand and recollection of what has been learned. Help him to appreciate the tasks that come easily and to persevere through those that challenge. Amen.

till evening; whoever picks up those things must wash his clothes and bathe with water, and he will be unclean till evening.

¹¹ " 'Anyone the man with a discharge touches without rinsing his hands with water must wash his clothes and bathe with water, and he will be unclean till evening.

¹² " 'A clay pot that the man touches must be broken, and any wooden article is to be rinsed with water.

¹³ " 'When a man is cleansed from his discharge, he is to count off seven days for his ceremonial cleansing; he must wash his clothes and bathe himself with fresh water, and he will be clean. ¹⁴On the eighth day he must take two doves or two young pigeons and come before the LORD to the entrance to the Tent of Meeting and give them to the priest. ¹⁵The priest is to sacrifice them, the one for a sin offering and the other for a burnt offering. In this way he will make atonement before the LORD for the man because of his discharge.

¹⁶ " 'When a man has an emission of semen, he must bathe his whole body with water, and he will be unclean till evening. ¹⁷Any clothing or leather that has semen on it must be washed with water, and it will be unclean till evening. ¹⁸When a man lies with a woman and there is an emission of semen, both must bathe with water, and they will be unclean till evening.

¹⁹ " 'When a woman has her regular flow of blood, the impurity of her monthly period will last seven days, and anyone who touches her will be unclean till evening.

²⁰ " 'Anything she lies on during her period will be unclean, and anything she sits on will be unclean. ²¹Whoever touches her bed must wash his clothes and bathe with water, and he will be unclean till evening. ²²Whoever touches anything she sits on must wash his clothes and bathe with water, and he will be unclean till evening. ²³Whether it is the bed or anything she was sitting on, when anyone touches it, he will be unclean till evening.

²⁴ " 'If a man lies with her and her monthly flow touches him, he will be unclean for seven days; any bed he lies on will be unclean.

²⁵ " 'When a woman has a discharge of blood for many days at a time other than her monthly period or has a discharge that continues beyond her period, she will be unclean as long as she has the discharge, just as in the days of her period. ²⁶Any bed she lies on while her discharge continues will be unclean, as is her bed during her monthly period, and anything she sits on will be unclean, as during her period. ²⁷Whoever touches them will be unclean; he must wash his clothes and bathe with water, and he will be unclean till evening.

²⁸ " 'When she is cleansed from her discharge, she must count off seven days, and after that she will be ceremonially clean. ²⁹On the eighth day she must take two doves or two young pigeons and bring them to the priest at the entrance to the Tent of Meeting. ³⁰The priest is to sacrifice one for a sin offering and the other for a burnt offering. In this way he will make atonement for her before the LORD for the uncleanness of her discharge.

³¹ " 'You must keep the Israelites separate from things that make them unclean, so they will not die in their uncleanness for defiling my dwelling place,ᵃ which is among them.' "

³²These are the regulations for a man with a discharge, for anyone made unclean by an emission of semen, ³³for a woman in her monthly period, for a man or a woman with a discharge, and for a man who lies with a woman who is ceremonially unclean.

The Day of Atonement
16:2–34pp — Lev 23:26–32; Nu 29:7–11

16 The LORD spoke to Moses after the death of the two sons of Aaron who died when they approached the LORD. ²The LORD said to Moses: "Tell your brother Aaron not to come whenever he chooses into the Most Holy Place behind the curtain in front of the atonement cover

---

ᵃ *31 Or my tabernacle*

on the ark, or else he will die, because I appear in the cloud over the atonement cover.

³"This is how Aaron is to enter the sanctuary area: with a young bull for a sin offering and a ram for a burnt offering. ⁴He is to put on the sacred linen tunic, with linen undergarments next to his body; he is to tie the linen sash around him and put on the linen turban. These are sacred garments; so he must bathe himself with water before he puts them on. ⁵From the Israelite community he is to take two male goats for a sin offering and a ram for a burnt offering.

⁶"Aaron is to offer the bull for his own sin offering to make atonement for himself and his household. ⁷Then he is to take the two goats and present them before the LORD at the entrance to the Tent of Meeting. ⁸He is to cast lots for the two goats—one lot for the LORD and the other for the scapegoat.ᵃ ⁹Aaron shall bring the goat whose lot falls to the LORD and sacrifice it for a sin offering. ¹⁰But the goat chosen by lot as the scapegoat shall be presented alive before the LORD to be used for making atonement by sending it into the desert as a scapegoat.

¹¹"Aaron shall bring the bull for his own sin offering to make atonement for himself and his household, and he is to slaughter the bull for his own sin offering. ¹²He is to take a censer full of burning coals from the altar before the LORD and two handfuls of finely ground fragrant incense and take them behind the curtain. ¹³He is to put the incense on the fire before the LORD, and the smoke of the incense will conceal the atonement cover above the Testimony, so that he will not die. ¹⁴He is to take some of the bull's blood and with his finger sprinkle it on the front of the atonement cover; then he shall sprinkle some of it with his finger seven times before the atonement cover.

¹⁵"He shall then slaughter the goat for the sin offering for the people and take its blood behind the curtain and do with it as he did with the bull's blood: He shall sprinkle it on the atonement cover and in front of it. ¹⁶In this way he will make atonement for the Most Holy Place

because of the uncleanness and rebellion of the Israelites, whatever their sins have been. He is to do the same for the Tent of Meeting, which is among them in the midst of their uncleanness. ¹⁷No one is to be in the Tent of Meeting from the time Aaron goes in to make atonement in the Most Holy Place until he comes out, having made atonement for himself, his household and the whole community of Israel.

¹⁸"Then he shall come out to the altar that is before the LORD and make atonement for it. He shall take some of the bull's blood and some of the goat's blood and put it on all the horns of the altar. ¹⁹He shall sprinkle some of the blood on it with his finger seven times to cleanse it and to consecrate it from the uncleanness of the Israelites.

²⁰"When Aaron has finished making atonement for the Most Holy Place, the Tent of Meeting and the altar, he shall bring forward the live goat. ²¹He is to lay both hands on the head of the live goat and confess over it all the wickedness and rebellion of the Israelites—all their sins—and put them on the goat's head. He shall send the goat away into the desert in the care of a man appointed for the task. ²²The goat will carry on itself all their sins to a solitary place; and the man shall release it in the desert.

²³"Then Aaron is to go into the Tent of Meeting and take off the linen garments he put on before he entered the Most Holy Place, and he is to leave them there. ²⁴He shall bathe himself with water in a holy place and put on his regular garments. Then he shall come out and sacrifice the burnt offering for himself and the burnt offering for the people, to make atonement for himself and for the people. ²⁵He shall also burn the fat of the sin offering on the altar.

²⁶"The man who releases the goat as a scapegoat must wash his clothes and bathe himself with water; afterward he may come into the camp. ²⁷The bull and the goat for the sin offerings, whose blood was brought into the Most

---

ᵃ 8 That is, the goat of removal; Hebrew *azazel*; also in verses 10 and 26

Holy Place to make atonement, must be taken outside the camp; their hides, flesh and offal are to be burned up. ²⁸The man who burns them must wash his clothes and bathe himself with water; afterward he may come into the camp.

²⁹"This is to be a lasting ordinance for you: On the tenth day of the seventh month you must deny yourselves*a* and not do any work—whether native-born or an alien living among you—³⁰because on this day atonement will be made for you, to cleanse you. Then, before the Lord, you will be clean from all your sins. ³¹It is a sabbath of rest, and you must deny yourselves; it is a lasting ordinance. ³²The priest who is anointed and ordained to succeed his father as high priest is to make atonement. He is to put on the sacred linen garments ³³and make atonement for the Most Holy Place, for the Tent of Meeting and the altar, and for the priests and all the people of the community.

³⁴"This is to be a lasting ordinance for you: Atonement is to be made once a year for all the sins of the Israelites."

And it was done, as the Lord commanded Moses.

Eating Blood Forbidden

17 The Lord said to Moses, ²"Speak to Aaron and his sons and to all the Israelites and say to them: 'This is what the Lord has commanded: ³Any Israelite who sacrifices an ox,*b* a lamb or a goat in the camp or outside of it ⁴instead of bringing it to the entrance to the Tent of Meeting to present it as an offering to the Lord in front of the tabernacle of the Lord—that man shall be considered guilty of bloodshed; he has shed blood and must be cut off from his people. ⁵This is so the Israelites will bring to the Lord the sacrifices they are now making in the open fields. They must bring them to the priest, that is, to the Lord, at the entrance to the Tent of Meeting and sacrifice them as fellowship offerings.*c* ⁶The priest is to sprinkle the blood against the altar of the Lord at the entrance to the Tent of Meeting and burn the fat as an aroma pleasing to the Lord. ⁷They must no longer offer any of their sacrifices to the goat idols*d* to whom they prostitute themselves. This is to be a lasting ordinance for them and for the generations to come.'

⁸"Say to them: 'Any Israelite or any alien living among them who offers a burnt offering or sacrifice ⁹and does not bring it to the entrance to the Tent of Meeting to sacrifice it to the Lord—that man must be cut off from his people.

¹⁰"'Any Israelite or any alien living among them who eats any blood—I will set my face against that person who eats blood and will cut him off from his people. ¹¹For the life of a creature is in the blood, and I have given it to you to make atonement for yourselves on the altar; it is the blood that makes atonement for one's life. ¹²Therefore I say to the Israelites, "None of you may eat blood, nor may an alien living among you eat blood."

¹³"'Any Israelite or any alien living among you who hunts any animal or bird that may be eaten must drain out the blood and cover it with earth, ¹⁴because the life of every creature is its blood. That is why I have said to the Israelites, "You must not eat the blood of any creature, because the life of every creature is its blood; anyone who eats it must be cut off."

¹⁵"'Anyone, whether native-born or alien, who eats anything found dead or torn by wild animals must wash his clothes and bathe with water, and he will be ceremonially unclean till evening; then he will be clean. ¹⁶But if he does not wash his clothes and bathe himself, he will be held responsible.'"

Unlawful Sexual Relations

18 The Lord said to Moses, ²"Speak to the Israelites and say to them: 'I am the Lord your God. ³You must not do as they do in Egypt, where you used to live, and you must not do as they do in the land of Canaan, where I am bringing you. Do not follow their practices. ⁴You must

---

a 29 Or must fast; also in verse 31   *b 3 The Hebrew word can include both male and female.   c 5 Traditionally peace offerings   d 7 Or demons* obey my laws and be careful to follow my decrees. I am the LORD your God. 5 Keep my decrees and laws, for the man who obeys them will live by them. I am the LORD.

6 " 'No one is to approach any close relative to have sexual relations. I am the LORD.

7 " 'Do not dishonor your father by having sexual relations with your mother. She is your mother; do not have relations with her.

8 " 'Do not have sexual relations with your father's wife; that would dishonor your father.

9 " 'Do not have sexual relations with your sister, either your father's daughter or your mother's daughter, whether she was born in the same home or elsewhere.

10 " 'Do not have sexual relations with your son's daughter or your daughter's daughter; that would dishonor you.

11 " 'Do not have sexual relations with the daughter of your father's wife, born to your father; she is your sister.

12 " 'Do not have sexual relations with your father's sister; she is your father's close relative.

13 " 'Do not have sexual relations with your mother's sister, because she is your mother's close relative.

14 " 'Do not dishonor your father's brother by approaching his wife to have sexual relations; she is your aunt.

15 " 'Do not have sexual relations with your daughter-in-law. She is your son's wife; do not have relations with her.

16 " 'Do not have sexual relations with your brother's wife; that would dishonor your brother.

17 " 'Do not have sexual relations with both a woman and her daughter. Do not have sexual relations with either her son's daughter or her daughter's daughter; they are her close relatives. That is wickedness.

18 " 'Do not take your wife's sister as a rival wife and have sexual relations with her while your wife is living.

19 " 'Do not approach a woman to have sexual relations during the uncleanness of her monthly period.

20 " 'Do not have sexual relations with your neighbor's wife and defile yourself with her.

21 " 'Do not give any of your children to be sacrificed *a* to Molech, for you must not profane the name of your God. I am the LORD.

22 " 'Do not lie with a man as one lies with a woman; that is detestable.

23 " 'Do not have sexual relations with an animal and defile yourself with it. A woman must not present herself to an animal to have sexual relations with it; that is a perversion.

24 " 'Do not defile yourselves in any of these ways, because this is how the nations that I am going to drive out before you became defiled. 25 Even the land was defiled; so I punished it for its sin, and the land vomited out its inhabitants. 26 But you must keep my decrees and my laws. The native-born and the aliens living among you must not do any of these detestable things, 27 for all these things were done by the people who lived in the land before you, and the land became defiled. 28 And if you defile the land, it will vomit you out as it vomited out the nations that were before you.

29 " 'Everyone who does any of these detestable things — such persons must be cut off from their people. 30 Keep my requirements and do not follow any of the detestable customs that were practiced before you came and do not defile yourselves with them. I am the LORD your God.' "

Various Laws

19 The LORD said to Moses, 2 "Speak to the entire assembly of Israel and say to them: 'Be holy because I, the LORD your God, am holy.

3 " 'Each of you must respect his mother and father, and you must observe my Sabbaths. I am the LORD your God.

4 " 'Do not turn to idols or make gods of cast metal for yourselves. I am the LORD your God.

5 " 'When you sacrifice a fellowship offering *b* to the LORD, sacrifice it in such a way that it will be

---

a 21 Or to be passed through ˌthe fireˌ   *b* 5 Traditionally *peace offering*

TOGETHER
TIME

Sharing Books and Stories

Chances are your cherished childhood memories include listening to a parent read stories aloud. Your pleas of "Read it again!" or "Just one more chapter!" before bedtime may or may not have gotten results.

Relive the time-honored pleasure of reading by spending an evening reading aloud with your grandchildren. You'll need several sessions if you select a longer book to read, but that's a good thing. Let the kids bring their favorite books, or get a selection of "the best" from the library. Ask the librarian for recommendations if you need ideas. Whether you read for a short time or for hours, you'll have spent precious time together sharing.

Older-Grandkids Variation: Find out what they're reading for school or pleasure. Read the same book and discuss it with them. If you dare, ask for the quiz or test questions they have to answer and see if you can answer them!

Long-Distance Variation: Record a story in your own voice and send it to your grandchildren along with a copy of the book so they can follow along. It will make their bedtime a special treat.

Thank you, Lord, for the magic of books — and for the opportunity to snuggle and read together. Let this time together expand my grandkids' horizons, exercise their imaginations and bring us closer together as we share the joy of reading. Amen.

Your next devotion is located on page 166.

GRANDCHILD **IN FOCUS** • PRAYER

Character

Dear Lord and Father, I ask that you fill my grandchild with your Spirit so her character reflects your goodness and love. Give her kindness and love for others. Bring joy to her life so she will be a joy to others. Grant her patience and self-control through difficult and trying times. May she show mercy and generosity to those who are less fortunate. Grant her integrity and a sense of justice, and surround her with your peace. Amen.

TALKING POINTS

Parents

God tells us to respect our parents.

LEVITICUS 19:3

For more on parents, go to Proverb 1:8–9.

accepted on your behalf. ⁶It shall be eaten on the day you sacrifice it or on the next day; anything left over until the third day must be burned up. ⁷If any of it is eaten on the third day, it is impure and will not be accepted. ⁸Whoever eats it will be held responsible because he has desecrated what is holy to the LORD; that person must be cut off from his people.

⁹" 'When you reap the harvest of your land, do not reap to the very edges of your field or gather the gleanings of your harvest. ¹⁰Do not go over your vineyard a second time or pick up the grapes that have fallen. Leave them for the poor and the alien. I am the LORD your God.

¹¹" 'Do not steal.

" 'Do not lie.

" 'Do not deceive one another.

¹²" 'Do not swear falsely by my name and so profane the name of your God. I am the LORD.

¹³" 'Do not defraud your neighbor or rob him.

" 'Do not hold back the wages of a hired man overnight.

¹⁴" 'Do not curse the deaf or put a stumbling block in front of the blind, but fear your God. I am the LORD.

¹⁵" 'Do not pervert justice; do not show partiality to the poor or favoritism to the great, but judge your neighbor fairly.

¹⁶" 'Do not go about spreading slander among your people.

" 'Do not do anything that endangers your neighbor's life. I am the LORD.

¹⁷" 'Do not hate your brother in your heart. Rebuke your neighbor frankly so you will not share in his guilt.

¹⁸" 'Do not seek revenge or bear a grudge against one of your people, but love your neighbor as yourself. I am the LORD.

¹⁹" 'Keep my decrees.

" 'Do not mate different kinds of animals.

" 'Do not plant your field with two kinds of seed.

" 'Do not wear clothing woven of two kinds of material.

²⁰" 'If a man sleeps with a woman who is a slave girl promised to another man but who has not been ransomed or given her freedom, there must be due punishment. Yet they are not to be put

stories to share

LEVITICUS 19:1–3, 9–10, 32–37

God's Holiness

LIFE LESSON: God wants us to be holy and fair, like he is.

TO TALK ABOUT

✦ What does it mean that God is holy?

✦ Can people be perfect? Can they be holy?

✦ How does God want us to treat people who are old, poor or foreign?

✦ What do these laws say about who God is? What do they say about who God wants us to be?

to death, because she had not been freed. ²¹The man, however, must bring a ram to the entrance to the Tent of Meeting for a guilt offering to the LORD. ²²With the ram of the guilt offering the priest is to make atonement for him before the LORD for the sin he has committed, and his sin will be forgiven.

²³ "When you enter the land and plant any kind of fruit tree, regard its fruit as forbidden.^a For three years you are to consider it forbidden^a; it must not be eaten. ²⁴In the fourth year all its fruit will be holy, an offering of praise to the LORD. ²⁵But in the fifth year you may eat its fruit. In this way your harvest will be increased. I am the LORD your God.

²⁶ "Do not eat any meat with the blood still in it.

" 'Do not practice divination or sorcery.

²⁷ "Do not cut the hair at the sides of your head or clip off the edges of your beard.

²⁸ "Do not cut your bodies for the dead or put tattoo marks on yourselves. I am the LORD.

²⁹ "Do not degrade your daughter by making her a prostitute, or the land will turn to prostitution and be filled with wickedness.

³⁰ "Observe my Sabbaths and have reverence for my sanctuary. I am the LORD.

³¹ "Do not turn to mediums or seek out spiritists, for you will be defiled by them. I am the LORD your God.

³² "Rise in the presence of the aged, show respect for the elderly and revere your God. I am the LORD.

³³ "When an alien lives with you in your land, do not mistreat him. ³⁴The alien living with you must be treated as one of your native-born. Love him as yourself, for you were aliens in Egypt. I am the LORD your God.

³⁵ "Do not use dishonest standards when measuring length, weight or quantity. ³⁶Use honest scales and honest weights, an honest ephah^b and an honest hin.^c I am the LORD your God, who brought you out of Egypt.

³⁷ "Keep all my decrees and all my laws and follow them. I am the LORD.' "

Punishments for Sin

20 The LORD said to Moses, ² "Say to the Israelites: 'Any Israelite or any alien living in Israel who gives^d any of his children to Molech must be put to death. The people of the community are to stone him. ³I will set my face against that man and I will cut him off from his people; for by giving his children to Molech, he has defiled my sanctuary and profaned my holy name. ⁴If the people of the community close their eyes when that man gives one of his children to Molech and they fail to put him to death, ⁵I will set my face against that man and his family and will cut off from their people both him and all who follow him in prostituting themselves to Molech.

⁶ "I will set my face against the person who turns to mediums and spiritists to prostitute himself by following them, and I will cut him off from his people.

⁷ "Consecrate yourselves and be holy, because I am the LORD your God. ⁸Keep my decrees and follow them. I am the LORD, who makes you holy.^e

⁹ "If anyone curses his father or mother, he must be put to death. He has cursed his father or his mother, and his blood will be on his own head.

¹⁰ "If a man commits adultery with another man's wife—with the wife of his neighbor—both the adulterer and the adulteress must be put to death.

¹¹ "If a man sleeps with his father's wife, he has dishonored his father. Both the man and the woman must be put to death; their blood will be on their own heads.

¹² "If a man sleeps with his daughter-in-law, both of them must be put to death. What they have done is a perversion; their blood will be on their own heads.

¹³ "If a man lies with a man as one lies with a woman, both of them have done what is detestable. They must be put to death; their blood will be on their own heads.

^a 23 Hebrew uncircumcised   ^b 36 An ephah was a dry measure.
^c 36 A hin was a liquid measure.   ^d 2 Or sacrifices; also in verses 3 and 4   ^e 8 Or who sanctifies you; or who sets you apart as holy

Worship the Lord

All the ends of the earth
    will remember and turn to the LORD,
and all the families of the nations
    will bow down before him,
for dominion belongs to the LORD
    and he rules over the nations.

All the rich of the earth will feast and worship;
    all who go down to the dust will kneel before him —
    those who cannot keep themselves alive.
Posterity will serve him;
    future generations will be told about the Lord.
They will proclaim his righteousness
    to a people yet unborn —
    for he has done it.

Psalm 22:27 – 31

Lord of the universe and ruler of all nations, I praise and thank you for all your
blessings. I pray that my children and
my grandchildren will come to know and
serve you. Lord, as you have done so faithfully in the past, hear my prayer. Amen.

Your next devotion is located on page 188.

GRANDCHILD IN FOCUS • PRAYER

Talents

*Dear Lord, the giver of gifts, bless my
grandchild as he develops his talents. Help him
identify his talents and be proud and confident of
the gifts you have given him. Give him patience and
understanding, Lord, so he will not grow weary of
striving and searching to reach the goals you have
set for him. May each milestone bring satisfaction and a healthy desire for greater
achievement and success to bring
glory to you. Amen.*

14 " 'If a man marries both a woman and her mother, it is wicked. Both he and they must be burned in the fire, so that no wickedness will be among you.

15 " 'If a man has sexual relations with an animal, he must be put to death, and you must kill the animal.

16 " 'If a woman approaches an animal to have sexual relations with it, kill both the woman and the animal. They must be put to death; their blood will be on their own heads.

17 " 'If a man marries his sister, the daughter of either his father or his mother, and they have sexual relations, it is a disgrace. They must be cut off before the eyes of their people. He has dishonored his sister and will be held responsible.

18 " 'If a man lies with a woman during her monthly period and has sexual relations with her, he has exposed the source of her flow, and she has also uncovered it. Both of them must be cut off from their people.

19 " 'Do not have sexual relations with the sister of either your mother or your father, for that would dishonor a close relative; both of you would be held responsible.

20 " 'If a man sleeps with his aunt, he has dishonored his uncle. They will be held responsible; they will die childless.

21 " 'If a man marries his brother's wife, it is an act of impurity; he has dishonored his brother. They will be childless.

22 " 'Keep all my decrees and laws and follow them, so that the land where I am bringing you to live may not vomit you out. 23 You must not live according to the customs of the nations I am going to drive out before you. Because they did all these things, I abhorred them. 24 But I said to you, "You will possess their land; I will give it to you as an inheritance, a land flowing with milk and honey." I am the LORD your God, who has set you apart from the nations.

25 " 'You must therefore make a distinction between clean and unclean animals and between unclean and clean birds. Do not defile yourselves by any animal or bird or anything that moves along the ground—those which I have set apart as unclean for you. 26 You are to be holy to me [a] because I, the LORD, am holy, and I have set you apart from the nations to be my own.

27 " 'A man or woman who is a medium or spiritist among you must be put to death. You are to stone them; their blood will be on their own heads.' "

Rules for Priests

21 The LORD said to Moses, "Speak to the priests, the sons of Aaron, and say to them: 'A priest must not make himself ceremonially unclean for any of his people who die, 2 except for a close relative, such as his mother or father, his son or daughter, his brother, 3 or an unmarried sister who is dependent on him since she has no husband—for her he may make himself unclean. 4 He must not make himself unclean for people related to him by marriage, [b] and so defile himself.

5 " 'Priests must not shave their heads or shave off the edges of their beards or cut their bodies. 6 They must be holy to their God and must not profane the name of their God. Because they present the offerings made to the LORD by fire, the food of their God, they are to be holy.

7 " 'They must not marry women defiled by prostitution or divorced from their husbands, because priests are holy to their God. 8 Regard them as holy, because they offer up the food of your God. Consider them holy, because I the LORD am holy—I who make you holy. [c]

9 " 'If a priest's daughter defiles herself by becoming a prostitute, she disgraces her father; she must be burned in the fire.

10 " 'The high priest, the one among his brothers who has had the anointing oil poured on his head and who has been ordained to wear the priestly garments, must not let his hair become unkempt [d] or tear his clothes. 11 He must not enter a place where there is a dead body. He must not make himself unclean, even for his father or mother, 12 nor leave the sanctuary of his God or

---

[a] 26 Or be my holy ones [b] 4 Or unclean as a leader among his people [c] 8 Or who sanctify you; or who set you apart as holy [d] 10 Or not uncover his head

desecrate it, because he has been dedicated by the anointing oil of his God. I am the LORD.

13 " 'The woman he marries must be a virgin. 14 He must not marry a widow, a divorced woman, or a woman defiled by prostitution, but only a virgin from his own people, 15 so he will not defile his offspring among his people. I am the LORD, who makes him holy.*a*' "

16 The LORD said to Moses, 17 "Say to Aaron: 'For the generations to come none of your descendants who has a defect may come near to offer the food of his God. 18 No man who has any defect may come near: no man who is blind or lame, disfigured or deformed; 19 no man with a crippled foot or hand, 20 or who is hunchbacked or dwarfed, or who has any eye defect, or who has festering or running sores or damaged testicles. 21 No descendant of Aaron the priest who has any defect is to come near to present the offerings made to the LORD by fire. He has a defect; he must not come near to offer the food of his God. 22 He may eat the most holy food of his God, as well as the holy food; 23 yet because of his defect, he must not go near the curtain or approach the altar, and so desecrate my sanctuary. I am the LORD, who makes them holy.*b*' "

24 So Moses told this to Aaron and his sons and to all the Israelites.

22 The LORD said to Moses, 2 "Tell Aaron and his sons to treat with respect the sacred offerings the Israelites consecrate to me, so they will not profane my holy name. I am the LORD.

3 "Say to them: 'For the generations to come, if any of your descendants is ceremonially unclean and yet comes near the sacred offerings that the Israelites consecrate to the LORD, that person must be cut off from my presence. I am the LORD.

4 " 'If a descendant of Aaron has an infectious skin disease*c* or a bodily discharge, he may not eat the sacred offerings until he is cleansed. He will also be unclean if he touches something defiled by a corpse or by anyone who has an emission of semen, 5 or if he touches any crawling thing that makes him unclean, or any person who makes him unclean, whatever the uncleanness may be.

6 The one who touches any such thing will be unclean till evening. He must not eat any of the sacred offerings unless he has bathed himself with water. 7 When the sun goes down, he will be clean, and after that he may eat the sacred offerings, for they are his food. 8 He must not eat anything found dead or torn by wild animals, and so become unclean through it. I am the LORD.

9 " 'The priests are to keep my requirements so that they do not become guilty and die for treating them with contempt. I am the LORD, who makes them holy.*d*

10 " 'No one outside a priest's family may eat the sacred offering, nor may the guest of a priest or his hired worker eat it. 11 But if a priest buys a slave with money, or if a slave is born in his household, that slave may eat his food. 12 If a priest's daughter marries anyone other than a priest, she may not eat any of the sacred contributions. 13 But if a priest's daughter becomes a widow or is divorced, yet has no children, and she returns to live in her father's house as in her youth, she may eat of her father's food. No unauthorized person, however, may eat any of it.

14 " 'If anyone eats a sacred offering by mistake, he must make restitution to the priest for the offering and add a fifth of the value to it. 15 The priests must not desecrate the sacred offerings the Israelites present to the LORD 16 by allowing them to eat the sacred offerings and so bring upon them guilt requiring payment. I am the LORD, who makes them holy.' "

Unacceptable Sacrifices

17 The LORD said to Moses, 18 "Speak to Aaron and his sons and to all the Israelites and say to them: 'If any of you—either an Israelite or an alien living in Israel—presents a gift for a burnt offering to the LORD, either to fulfill a vow or as a freewill offering, 19 you must present a male without defect from the cattle, sheep or goats

---

a 15 Or *who sanctifies him*; or *who sets him apart as holy*
b 23 Or *who sanctifies them*; or *who sets them apart as holy*
c 4 Traditionally *leprosy*; the Hebrew word was used for various diseases affecting the skin—not necessarily leprosy.   *d* 9 Or *who sanctifies them*; or *who sets them apart as holy*; also in verse 16

in order that it may be accepted on your behalf. [20]Do not bring anything with a defect, because it will not be accepted on your behalf. [21]When anyone brings from the herd or flock a fellowship offering[a] to the LORD to fulfill a special vow or as a freewill offering, it must be without defect or blemish to be acceptable. [22]Do not offer to the LORD the blind, the injured or the maimed, or anything with warts or festering or running sores. Do not place any of these on the altar as an offering made to the LORD by fire. [23]You may, however, present as a freewill offering an ox[b] or a sheep that is deformed or stunted, but it will not be accepted in fulfillment of a vow. [24]You must not offer to the LORD an animal whose testicles are bruised, crushed, torn or cut. You must not do this in your own land, [25]and you must not accept such animals from the hand of a foreigner and offer them as the food of your God. They will not be accepted on your behalf, because they are deformed and have defects.' "

[26]The LORD said to Moses, [27]"When a calf, a lamb or a goat is born, it is to remain with its mother for seven days. From the eighth day on, it will be acceptable as an offering made to the LORD by fire. [28]Do not slaughter a cow or a sheep and its young on the same day.

[29]"When you sacrifice a thank offering to the LORD, sacrifice it in such a way that it will be accepted on your behalf. [30]It must be eaten that same day; leave none of it till morning. I am the LORD.

[31]"Keep my commands and follow them. I am the LORD. [32]Do not profane my holy name. I must be acknowledged as holy by the Israelites. I am the LORD, who makes[c] you holy[d] [33]and who brought you out of Egypt to be your God. I am the LORD."

23

The LORD said to Moses, [2]"Speak to the Israelites and say to them: 'These are my appointed feasts, the appointed feasts of the LORD, which you are to proclaim as sacred assemblies.

The Sabbath

[3]" 'There are six days when you may work, but the seventh day is a Sabbath of rest, a day of sacred assembly. You are not to do any work; wherever you live, it is a Sabbath to the LORD.

The Passover and Unleavened Bread
23:4–8pp — Ex 12:14–20; Nu 28:16–25; Dt 16:1–8

[4]" 'These are the LORD's appointed feasts, the sacred assemblies you are to proclaim at their appointed times: [5]The LORD's Passover begins at twilight on the fourteenth day of the first month. [6]On the fifteenth day of that month the LORD's Feast of Unleavened Bread begins; for seven days you must eat bread made without yeast. [7]On the first day hold a sacred assembly and do no regular work. [8]For seven days present an offering made to the LORD by fire. And on the seventh day hold a sacred assembly and do no regular work.' "

Firstfruits

[9]The LORD said to Moses, [10]"Speak to the Israelites and say to them: 'When you enter the land I am going to give you and you reap its harvest, bring to the priest a sheaf of the first grain you harvest. [11]He is to wave the sheaf before the LORD so it will be accepted on your behalf; the priest is to wave it on the day after the Sabbath. [12]On the day you wave the sheaf, you must sacrifice as a burnt offering to the LORD a lamb a year old without defect, [13]together with its grain offering of two-tenths of an ephah[e] of fine flour mixed with oil—an offering made to the LORD by fire,

[a] 21 Traditionally *peace offering*   [b] 23 The Hebrew word can include both male and female.   [c] 32 Or *made*   [d] 32 Or *who sanctifies you*; or *who sets you apart as holy*   [e] 13 That is, probably about 4 quarts (about 4.5 liters); also in verse 17

a pleasing aroma—and its drink offering of a quarter of a hin^a of wine. [14] You must not eat any bread, or roasted or new grain, until the very day you bring this offering to your God. This is to be a lasting ordinance for the generations to come, wherever you live.

Feast of Weeks

23:15–22pp — Nu 28:26–31; Dt 16:9–12

[15] "From the day after the Sabbath, the day you brought the sheaf of the wave offering, count off seven full weeks. [16] Count off fifty days up to the day after the seventh Sabbath, and then present an offering of new grain to the LORD. [17] From wherever you live, bring two loaves made of two-tenths of an ephah of fine flour, baked with yeast, as a wave offering of firstfruits to the LORD. [18] Present with this bread seven male lambs, each a year old and without defect, one young bull and two rams. They will be a burnt offering to the LORD, together with their grain offerings and drink offerings—an offering made by fire, an aroma pleasing to the LORD. [19] Then sacrifice one male goat for a sin offering and two lambs, each a year old, for a fellowship offering.^b [20] The priest is to wave the two lambs before the LORD as a wave offering, together with the bread of the firstfruits. They are a sacred offering to the LORD for the priest. [21] On that same day you are to proclaim a sacred assembly and do no regular work. This is to be a lasting ordinance for the generations to come, wherever you live.

[22] "When you reap the harvest of your land, do not reap to the very edges of your field or gather the gleanings of your harvest. Leave them for the poor and the alien. I am the LORD your God.'"

Feast of Trumpets

23:23–25pp — Nu 29:1–6

[23] The LORD said to Moses, [24] "Say to the Israelites: 'On the first day of the seventh month you are to have a day of rest, a sacred assembly commemorated with trumpet blasts. [25] Do no regular work, but present an offering made to the LORD by fire.'"

Day of Atonement

23:26–32pp — Lev 16:2–34; Nu 29:7–11

[26] The LORD said to Moses, [27] "The tenth day of this seventh month is the Day of Atonement. Hold a sacred assembly and deny yourselves,^c and present an offering made to the LORD by fire. [28] Do no work on that day, because it is the Day of Atonement, when atonement is made for you before the LORD your God. [29] Anyone who does not deny himself on that day must be cut off from his people. [30] I will destroy from among his people anyone who does any work on that day. [31] You shall do no work at all. This is to be a lasting ordinance for the generations to come, wherever you live. [32] It is a sabbath of rest for you, and you must deny yourselves. From the evening of the ninth day of the month until the following evening you are to observe your sabbath."

Feast of Tabernacles

23:33–43pp — Nu 29:12–39; Dt 16:13–17

[33] The LORD said to Moses, [34] "Say to the Israelites: 'On the fifteenth day of the seventh month the LORD's Feast of Tabernacles begins, and it lasts for seven days. [35] The first day is a sacred assembly; do no regular work. [36] For seven days present offerings made to the LORD by fire, and on the eighth day hold a sacred assembly and present an offering made to the LORD by fire. It is the closing assembly; do no regular work.

[37] ("'These are the LORD's appointed feasts, which you are to proclaim as sacred assemblies for bringing offerings made to the LORD by fire—the burnt offerings and grain offerings, sacrifices and drink offerings required for each day. [38] These offerings are in addition to those for the LORD's Sabbaths and^d in addition to your gifts and whatever you have vowed and all the freewill offerings you give to the LORD.)

[39] "'So beginning with the fifteenth day of the seventh month, after you have gathered the crops of the land, celebrate the festival to the LORD for

---

^a 13 That is, probably about 1 quart (about 1 liter)
^b 19 Traditionally *peace offering*   ^c 27 Or *and fast*; also in verses 29 and 32   ^d 38 Or *These feasts are in addition to the LORD's Sabbaths, and these offerings are*

seven days; the first day is a day of rest, and the eighth day also is a day of rest. **40** On the first day you are to take choice fruit from the trees, and palm fronds, leafy branches and poplars, and rejoice before the LORD your God for seven days. **41** Celebrate this as a festival to the LORD for seven days each year. This is to be a lasting ordinance for the generations to come; celebrate it in the seventh month. **42** Live in booths for seven days: All native-born Israelites are to live in booths **43** so your descendants will know that I had the Israelites live in booths when I brought them out of Egypt. I am the LORD your God.'"

44 So Moses announced to the Israelites the appointed feasts of the LORD.

Oil and Bread Set Before the LORD
24:1–3pp — Ex 27:20–21

24 The LORD said to Moses, **2** "Command the Israelites to bring you clear oil of pressed olives for the light so that the lamps may be kept burning continually. **3** Outside the curtain of the Testimony in the Tent of Meeting, Aaron is to tend the lamps before the LORD from evening till morning, continually. This is to be a lasting ordinance for the generations to come. **4** The lamps on the pure gold lampstand before the LORD must be tended continually.

5 "Take fine flour and bake twelve loaves of bread, using two-tenths of an ephah *a* for each loaf. **6** Set them in two rows, six in each row, on the table of pure gold before the LORD. **7** Along each row put some pure incense as a memorial portion to represent the bread and to be an offering made to the LORD by fire. **8** This bread is to be set out before the LORD regularly, Sabbath after Sabbath, on behalf of the Israelites, as a lasting covenant. **9** It belongs to Aaron and his sons, who are to eat it in a holy place, because it is a most holy part of their regular share of the offerings made to the LORD by fire."

A Blasphemer Stoned

10 Now the son of an Israelite mother and an Egyptian father went out among the Israelites, and a fight broke out in the camp between him and an Israelite. **11** The son of the Israelite woman blasphemed the Name with a curse; so they brought him to Moses. (His mother's name was Shelomith, the daughter of Dibri the Danite.) **12** They put him in custody until the will of the LORD should be made clear to them.

13 Then the LORD said to Moses: **14** "Take the blasphemer outside the camp. All those who heard him are to lay their hands on his head, and the entire assembly is to stone him. **15** Say to the Israelites: 'If anyone curses his God, he will be held responsible; **16** anyone who blasphemes the name of the LORD must be put to death. The entire assembly must stone him. Whether an alien or native-born, when he blasphemes the Name, he must be put to death.

17 "'If anyone takes the life of a human being, he must be put to death. **18** Anyone who takes the life of someone's animal must make restitution—life for life. **19** If anyone injures his neighbor, whatever he has done must be done to him: **20** fracture for fracture, eye for eye, tooth for tooth. As he has injured the other, so he is to be injured. **21** Whoever kills an animal must make restitution, but whoever kills a man must be put to death. **22** You are to have the same law for the alien and the native-born. I am the LORD your God.'"

23 Then Moses spoke to the Israelites, and they took the blasphemer outside the camp and stoned him. The Israelites did as the LORD commanded Moses.

The Sabbath Year

25 The LORD said to Moses on Mount Sinai, **2** "Speak to the Israelites and say to them: 'When you enter the land I am going to give you, the land itself must observe a sabbath to the LORD. **3** For six years sow your fields, and for six years prune your vineyards and gather their crops. **4** But in the seventh year the land is to have a sabbath of rest, a sabbath to the LORD. Do not sow your fields or prune your vineyards. **5** Do not reap what grows of itself or harvest the grapes of

a 5 That is, probably about 4 quarts (about 4.5 liters)

your untended vines. The land is to have a year of rest. ⁶Whatever the land yields during the sabbath year will be food for you—for yourself, your manservant and maidservant, and the hired worker and temporary resident who live among you, ⁷as well as for your livestock and the wild animals in your land. Whatever the land produces may be eaten.

The Year of Jubilee
25:8–38Ref — Dt 15:1–11
25:39–55Ref — Ex 21:2–11; Dt 15:12–18

⁸" 'Count off seven sabbaths of years—seven times seven years—so that the seven sabbaths of years amount to a period of forty-nine years. ⁹Then have the trumpet sounded everywhere on the tenth day of the seventh month; on the Day of Atonement sound the trumpet throughout your land. ¹⁰Consecrate the fiftieth year and proclaim liberty throughout the land to all its inhabitants. It shall be a jubilee for you; each one of you is to return to his family property and each to his own clan. ¹¹The fiftieth year shall be a jubilee for you; do not sow and do not reap what grows of itself or harvest the untended vines. ¹²For it is a jubilee and is to be holy for you; eat only what is taken directly from the fields.

¹³" 'In this Year of Jubilee everyone is to return to his own property.

¹⁴" 'If you sell land to one of your countrymen or buy any from him, do not take advantage of each other. ¹⁵You are to buy from your countryman on the basis of the number of years since the Jubilee. And he is to sell to you on the basis of the number of years left for harvesting crops. ¹⁶When the years are many, you are to increase the price, and when the years are few, you are to decrease the price, because what he is really selling you is the number of crops. ¹⁷Do not take advantage of each other, but fear your God. I am the Lord your God.

¹⁸" 'Follow my decrees and be careful to obey my laws, and you will live safely in the land. ¹⁹Then the land will yield its fruit, and you will eat your fill and live there in safety. ²⁰You may ask, "What will we eat in the seventh year if we do not plant or harvest our crops?" ²¹I will send you such a blessing in the sixth year that the land will yield enough for three years. ²²While you plant during the eighth year, you will eat from the old crop and will continue to eat from it until the harvest of the ninth year comes in.

²³" 'The land must not be sold permanently, because the land is mine and you are but aliens and my tenants. ²⁴Throughout the country that you hold as a possession, you must provide for the redemption of the land.

²⁵" 'If one of your countrymen becomes poor and sells some of his property, his nearest relative is to come and redeem what his countryman has sold. ²⁶If, however, a man has no one to redeem it for him but he himself prospers and acquires sufficient means to redeem it, ²⁷he is to determine the value for the years since he sold it and refund the balance to the man to whom he sold it; he can then go back to his own property. ²⁸But if he does not acquire the means to repay him, what he sold will remain in the possession of the buyer until the Year of Jubilee. It will be returned in the Jubilee, and he can then go back to his property.

²⁹" 'If a man sells a house in a walled city, he retains the right of redemption a full year after its sale. During that time he may redeem it. ³⁰If it is not redeemed before a full year has passed, the house in the walled city shall belong permanently to the buyer and his descendants. It is not to be returned in the Jubilee. ³¹But houses in villages without walls around them are to be considered as open country. They can be redeemed, and they are to be returned in the Jubilee.

³²" 'The Levites always have the right to redeem their houses in the Levitical towns, which they possess. ³³So the property of the Levites is redeemable—that is, a house sold in any town they hold—and is to be returned in the Jubilee, because the houses in the towns of the Levites are their property among the Israelites. ³⁴But the pastureland belonging to their towns must not be sold; it is their permanent possession.

³⁵" 'If one of your countrymen becomes poor

and is unable to support himself among you, help him as you would an alien or a temporary resident, so he can continue to live among you. ³⁶Do not take interest of any kind^a from him, but fear your God, so that your countryman may continue to live among you. ³⁷You must not lend him money at interest or sell him food at a profit. ³⁸I am the LORD your God, who brought you out of Egypt to give you the land of Canaan and to be your God.

³⁹" 'If one of your countrymen becomes poor among you and sells himself to you, do not make him work as a slave. ⁴⁰He is to be treated as a hired worker or a temporary resident among you; he is to work for you until the Year of Jubilee. ⁴¹Then he and his children are to be released, and he will go back to his own clan and to the property of his forefathers. ⁴²Because the Israelites are my servants, whom I brought out of Egypt, they must not be sold as slaves. ⁴³Do not rule over them ruthlessly, but fear your God.

⁴⁴" 'Your male and female slaves are to come from the nations around you; from them you may buy slaves. ⁴⁵You may also buy some of the temporary residents living among you and members of their clans born in your country, and they will become your property. ⁴⁶You can will them to your children as inherited property and can make them slaves for life, but you must not rule over your fellow Israelites ruthlessly.

⁴⁷" 'If an alien or a temporary resident among you becomes rich and one of your countrymen becomes poor and sells himself to the alien living among you or to a member of the alien's clan, ⁴⁸he retains the right of redemption after he has sold himself. One of his relatives may redeem him: ⁴⁹An uncle or a cousin or any blood relative in his clan may redeem him. Or if he prospers, he may redeem himself. ⁵⁰He and his buyer are to count the time from the year he sold himself up to the Year of Jubilee. The price for his release is to be based on the rate paid to a hired man for that number of years. ⁵¹If many years remain, he must pay for his redemption a larger share of the price paid for him. ⁵²If only a few years remain until the Year of Jubilee, he is to compute that and pay for his redemption accordingly. ⁵³He is to be treated as a man hired from year to year; you must see to it that his owner does not rule over him ruthlessly.

⁵⁴" 'Even if he is not redeemed in any of these ways, he and his children are to be released in the Year of Jubilee, ⁵⁵for the Israelites belong to me as servants. They are my servants, whom I brought out of Egypt. I am the LORD your God.

Reward for Obedience

26 " 'Do not make idols or set up an image or a sacred stone for yourselves, and do not place a carved stone in your land to bow down before it. I am the LORD your God.

²" 'Observe my Sabbaths and have reverence for my sanctuary. I am the LORD.

³" 'If you follow my decrees and are careful to obey my commands, ⁴I will send you rain in its season, and the ground will yield its crops and the trees of the field their fruit. ⁵Your threshing will continue until grape harvest and the grape harvest will continue until planting, and you will eat all the food you want and live in safety in your land.

⁶" 'I will grant peace in the land, and you will lie down and no one will make you afraid. I will remove savage beasts from the land, and the sword will not pass through your country. ⁷You will pursue your enemies, and they will fall by the sword before you. ⁸Five of you will chase a hundred, and a hundred of you will chase ten thousand, and your enemies will fall by the sword before you.

⁹" 'I will look on you with favor and make you fruitful and increase your numbers, and I will keep my covenant with you. ¹⁰You will still be eating last year's harvest when you will have to move it out to make room for the new. ¹¹I will put my dwelling place^b among you, and I will not abhor you. ¹²I will walk among you and be your God, and you will be my people. ¹³I am the LORD

---

^a 36 Or take excessive interest; similarly in verse 37   ^b 11 Or my tabernacle

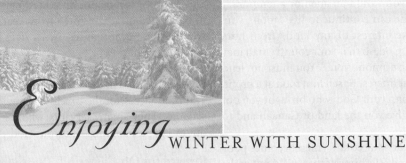

EMILIE BARNES

Enjoying WINTER WITH SUNSHINE

Much of what happens in the first three seasons (spring, summer and fall) determines what life will be like in the final season of the year (winter). The *Farmers' Almanac* gives detailed descriptions about preparing the soil, planting, reaping and harvesting—when to plant and when to rest. The fruits of sowing our seeds are based not only on what we do but also on the elements of nature. We must be prepared to do all we can and then be willing to let God do the rest.

Spring

In the springtime of life, we plant our seeds. We are so excited about the newness of life: courtship, a wedding, a new job, children, a new home. We are full of hope and anticipation of what life has to offer. Many times we are naive about what we are doing and, unless we really have it together as a couple, we give little thought or reason to why we do what we do.

A tried-and-true farmer isn't quite as nonchalant about this season of life. He realizes that in order to have a good harvest, he must have a good spring. He must know what crop he is planting, make proper seed selection, plant after the last frost and pray that rain or irrigation comes at the proper time. Spring is crucial in life because what happens in these months greatly affects what the remaining three seasons of the year will be like.

One of my mottoes is "Success is progressive realization of worthwhile goals." Spring is the time of life when we begin to establish these goals.

Summer

Many times the drudgery of summer makes us lose sight of what life is all about. During these long, hot days we press on, remembering that it isn't by accident that we are here on earth. And occasionally we have a thunderstorm to break the monotony of this period of life.

Spring brings the freshness of newness, but summer tests us to see if we really have the discipline and godly character to see life through the difficult periods. Many would-be farmers and would-be marriages never get through this phase of life. Only those with dedicated and serious purpose survive. Life often gets boring during this season, but to get to the harvest season, we have to get through the summer.

Fall

Now fall is here — all that we have worked so long and so hard for is ready for harvest — if we have done a good job in spring and summer. This is the season of life during which we receive our blessings. But in order to have abundance, we must have sown with abundance. "Whoever sows sparingly will also reap sparingly, and whoever sows generously will also reap generously" (2 Corinthians 9:6).

In Leviticus 26:3 – 5, God promises his people that when they follow him he will provide a bounteous harvest. For the Israelites the harvest was crops and wine, but for us, the harvest is our children, our grandchildren, friends, good health, emotional and psychological stability, and, above all, our love for the Lord — all the things we hoped for when we were in the springtime of life!

One of the warnings to heed during this season is to not use up all of our harvest. We must save some seed and fruit to plant again in spring. There will be more springs, and we certainly want to be prepared when they come. As grandparents we certainly see the importance of saving for the next spring — not only for our own springs, but also for the many springs of the generations to come.

Winter

When winter arrives, we have a more relaxed and easy pace around the farm. The days are cold, the land is frozen and an icy wind blows from the plains of the north. We can spend rich times conversing with our spouses, looking back over life with smiles and frowns, but generally we are pleased about our accomplishments. It's cozy with just the two of us around the fireplace. A good book, soft music, a nap in the afternoon, an early dinner and off to a good night's sleep — these make the winter enjoyable. We can look each other in the eyes and say, "God bless and good night. You are truly my best friend!"

Enjoy each season of life as it comes.

your God, who brought you out of Egypt so that you would no longer be slaves to the Egyptians; I broke the bars of your yoke and enabled you to walk with heads held high.

LEVITICUS 26:1–13

Promises for Obedience

LIFE LESSON: God rewards obedience.

TO TALK ABOUT

✦ What is one thing God asked his people to do?

✦ What rewards did God promise to his people for obeying his rules?

✦ Do bad things ever happen to obedient people? What does it mean when that happens?

✦ What kind of "idol" might we "bow down" to today?

Punishment for Disobedience

14 " 'But if you will not listen to me and carry out all these commands, 15 and if you reject my decrees and abhor my laws and fail to carry out all my commands and so violate my covenant, 16 then I will do this to you: I will bring upon you sudden terror, wasting diseases and fever that will destroy your sight and drain away your life. You will plant seed in vain, because your enemies will eat it. 17 I will set my face against you so that you will be defeated by your enemies; those who hate you will rule over you, and you will flee even when no one is pursuing you.

18 " 'If after all this you will not listen to me, I will punish you for your sins seven times over. 19 I will break down your stubborn pride and make the sky above you like iron and the ground beneath you like bronze. 20 Your strength will be spent in vain, because your soil will not yield its crops, nor will the trees of the land yield their fruit.

21 " 'If you remain hostile toward me and refuse to listen to me, I will multiply your afflictions seven times over, as your sins deserve. 22 I will send wild animals against you, and they will rob you of your children, destroy your cattle and make you so few in number that your roads will be deserted.

23 " 'If in spite of these things you do not accept my correction but continue to be hostile toward me, 24 I myself will be hostile toward you and will afflict you for your sins seven times over. 25 And I will bring the sword upon you to avenge the breaking of the covenant. When you withdraw into your cities, I will send a plague among you, and you will be given into enemy hands. 26 When I cut off your supply of bread, ten women will be able to bake your bread in one oven, and they will dole out the bread by weight. You will eat, but you will not be satisfied.

27 " 'If in spite of this you still do not listen to me but continue to be hostile toward me, 28 then in my anger I will be hostile toward you, and I myself will punish you for your sins seven times over. 29 You will eat the flesh of your sons and the flesh of your daughters. 30 I will destroy your high places, cut down your incense altars and pile your dead bodies on the lifeless forms of your idols, and I will abhor you. 31 I will turn your cities into ruins and lay waste your sanctuaries, and I will take no delight in the pleasing aroma of your offerings. 32 I will lay waste the land, so that your enemies who live there will be appalled. 33 I will scatter you among the nations and will draw out my sword and pursue you. Your land will be laid waste, and your cities will lie in ruins. 34 Then the land will enjoy its sabbath years all the time that it lies desolate and you are in the country of your enemies; then the land will rest and enjoy its sabbaths. 35 All the time that it lies desolate, the

land will have the rest it did not have during the sabbaths you lived in it.

[36] " 'As for those of you who are left, I will make their hearts so fearful in the lands of their enemies that the sound of a windblown leaf will put them to flight. They will run as though fleeing from the sword, and they will fall, even though no one is pursuing them. [37] They will stumble over one another as though fleeing from the sword, even though no one is pursuing them. So you will not be able to stand before your enemies. [38] You will perish among the nations; the land of your enemies will devour you. [39] Those of you who are left will waste away in the lands of their enemies because of their sins; also because of their fathers' sins they will waste away.

[40] " 'But if they will confess their sins and the sins of their fathers—their treachery against me and their hostility toward me, [41] which made me hostile toward them so that I sent them into the land of their enemies—then when their uncircumcised hearts are humbled and they pay for their sin, [42] I will remember my covenant with Jacob and my covenant with Isaac and my covenant with Abraham, and I will remember the land. [43] For the land will be deserted by them and will enjoy its sabbaths while it lies desolate without them. They will pay for their sins because they rejected my laws and abhorred my decrees. [44] Yet in spite of this, when they are in the land of their enemies, I will not reject them or abhor them so as to destroy them completely, breaking my covenant with them. I am the LORD their God. [45] But for their sake I will remember the covenant with their ancestors whom I brought out of Egypt in the sight of the nations to be their God. I am the LORD.' "

[46] These are the decrees, the laws and the regulations that the LORD established on Mount Sinai between himself and the Israelites through Moses.

Redeeming What Is the LORD's

27 The LORD said to Moses, [2] "Speak to the Israelites and say to them: 'If anyone makes a special vow to dedicate persons to the LORD by giving equivalent values, [3] set the value of a male between the ages of twenty and sixty at fifty shekels[a] of silver, according to the sanctuary shekel[b]; [4] and if it is a female, set her value at thirty shekels.[c] [5] If it is a person between the ages of five and twenty, set the value of a male at twenty shekels[d] and of a female at ten shekels.[e] [6] If it is a person between one month and five years, set the value of a male at five shekels[f] of silver and that of a female at three shekels[g] of silver. [7] If it is a person sixty years old or more, set the value of a male at fifteen shekels[h] and of a female at ten shekels. [8] If anyone making the vow is too poor to pay the specified amount, he is to present the person to the priest, who will set the value for him according to what the man making the vow can afford.

[9] " 'If what he vowed is an animal that is acceptable as an offering to the LORD, such an animal given to the LORD becomes holy. [10] He must not exchange it or substitute a good one for a bad one, or a bad one for a good one; if he should substitute one animal for another, both it and the substitute become holy. [11] If what he vowed is a ceremonially unclean animal—one that is not acceptable as an offering to the LORD—the animal must be presented to the priest, [12] who will judge its quality as good or bad. Whatever value the priest then sets, that is what it will be. [13] If the owner wishes to redeem the animal, he must add a fifth to its value.

[14] " 'If a man dedicates his house as something holy to the LORD, the priest will judge its quality as good or bad. Whatever value the priest then sets, so it will remain. [15] If the man who dedicates his house redeems it, he must add a fifth to its value, and the house will again become his.

[16] " 'If a man dedicates to the LORD part of his family land, its value is to be set according to the amount of seed required for it—fifty shekels of

---

[a] 3 That is, about 1 1/4 pounds (about 0.6 kilogram); also in verse 16   [b] 3 That is, about 2/5 ounce (about 11.5 grams); also in verse 25   [c] 4 That is, about 12 ounces (about 0.3 kilogram)   [d] 5 That is, about 8 ounces (about 0.2 kilogram)   [e] 5 That is, about 4 ounces (about 110 grams); also in verse 7   [f] 6 That is, about 2 ounces (about 55 grams)   [g] 6 That is, about 1 1/4 ounces (about 35 grams)   [h] 7 That is, about 6 ounces (about 170 grams)

silver to a homer *a* of barley seed. ¹⁷ If he dedicates his field during the Year of Jubilee, the value that has been set remains. ¹⁸ But if he dedicates his field after the Jubilee, the priest will determine the value according to the number of years that remain until the next Year of Jubilee, and its set value will be reduced. ¹⁹ If the man who dedicates the field wishes to redeem it, he must add a fifth to its value, and the field will again become his. ²⁰ If, however, he does not redeem the field, or if he has sold it to someone else, it can never be redeemed. ²¹ When the field is released in the Jubilee, it will become holy, like a field devoted to the LORD; it will become the property of the priests. *b*

²² "If a man dedicates to the LORD a field he has bought, which is not part of his family land, ²³ the priest will determine its value up to the Year of Jubilee, and the man must pay its value on that day as something holy to the LORD. ²⁴ In the Year of Jubilee the field will revert to the person from whom he bought it, the one whose land it was. ²⁵ Every value is to be set according to the sanctuary shekel, twenty gerahs to the shekel.

²⁶ "'No one, however, may dedicate the firstborn of an animal, since the firstborn already belongs to the LORD; whether an ox *c* or a sheep, it is the LORD's. ²⁷ If it is one of the unclean animals, he may buy it back at its set value, adding a fifth of the value to it. If he does not redeem it, it is to be sold at its set value.

²⁸ "'But nothing that a man owns and devotes *d* to the LORD—whether man or animal or family land—may be sold or redeemed; everything so devoted is most holy to the LORD.

²⁹ "'No person devoted to destruction *e* may be ransomed; he must be put to death.

³⁰ "'A tithe of everything from the land, whether grain from the soil or fruit from the trees, belongs to the LORD; it is holy to the LORD. ³¹ If a man redeems any of his tithe, he must add a fifth of the value to it. ³² The entire tithe of the herd and flock—every tenth animal that passes under the shepherd's rod—will be holy to the LORD. ³³ He must not pick out the good from the bad or make any substitution. If he does make a substitution, both the animal and its substitute become holy and cannot be redeemed.'"

³⁴ These are the commands the LORD gave Moses on Mount Sinai for the Israelites.

---

a 16 That is, probably about 6 bushels (about 220 liters)   *b 21* Or priest   *c 26* The Hebrew word can include both male and female. *d 28* The Hebrew term refers to the irrevocable giving over of things or persons to the LORD.   *e 29* The Hebrew term refers to the irrevocable giving over of things or persons to the LORD, often by totally destroying them.

Counting ON GOD

Numbers

As its name states, this book is partially about numbers. It recounts the wilderness trek of the Israelites and in so doing keeps a neat accounting of the different tribes, or families, of Israel. It also outlines many of the rituals the Israelites were to observe, and it confirms the priesthood of Aaron and his descendants to represent and regulate Israelite religious observance.

But the book of Numbers also reveals how God holds his people accountable to their relationship with him. And in this book we see how the people of Israel fell short. God had promised the people a land where they would settle and devote themselves to him and his ways. However, when the people came to the brink of the land, they listened to their own fears and insecurities. They refused to move ahead in faith and conquer the land God had promised to give them (see Numbers 14).

Despite the people's rebellion, Numbers is a case study in the constancy of God's love. Despite his people's unresponsiveness and stubbornness, God's love remained firm and consistent. He followed the rules he had established and kept his promises to his people, blessing when there was obedience and disciplining when there was disobedience.

Even today God confronts our disobedience with love, our stubbornness with mercy, our rebellion with grace. He still longs for his people to be known as his followers, to stand out in a world that has ignored and rejected him.

VERSE *to* REMEMBER | NUMBERS 6:24 – 26

"The LORD bless you and keep you; the LORD make his face shine upon you and be gracious to you; the LORD turn his face toward you and give you peace."

ABOUT NUMBERS

WRITTEN BY:
Moses

WRITTEN FOR:
God's chosen people, the Israelites

DATE WRITTEN:
Between 1446 and 1406 B.C.

WHY WRITTEN:
To explain how the Israelites' disobedience kept them from entering the promised land

The Census

1 The Lord spoke to Moses in the Tent of Meeting in the Desert of Sinai on the first day of the second month of the second year after the Israelites came out of Egypt. He said: ²"Take a census of the whole Israelite community by their clans and families, listing every man by name, one by one. ³You and Aaron are to number by their divisions all the men in Israel twenty years old or more who are able to serve in the army. ⁴One man from each tribe, each the head of his family, is to help you. ⁵These are the names of the men who are to assist you:

from Reuben, Elizur son of Shedeur;
⁶from Simeon, Shelumiel son of Zurishaddai;
⁷from Judah, Nahshon son of Amminadab;
⁸from Issachar, Nethanel son of Zuar;
⁹from Zebulun, Eliab son of Helon;
¹⁰from the sons of Joseph:
from Ephraim, Elishama son of Ammihud;
from Manasseh, Gamaliel son of Pedahzur;
¹¹from Benjamin, Abidan son of Gideoni;
¹²from Dan, Ahiezer son of Ammishaddai;
¹³from Asher, Pagiel son of Ocran;
¹⁴from Gad, Eliasaph son of Deuel;
¹⁵from Naphtali, Ahira son of Enan."

¹⁶These were the men appointed from the community, the leaders of their ancestral tribes. They were the heads of the clans of Israel.

¹⁷Moses and Aaron took these men whose names had been given, ¹⁸and they called the whole community together on the first day of the second month. The people indicated their ancestry by their clans and families, and the men twenty years old or more were listed by name, one by one, ¹⁹as the Lord commanded Moses. And so he counted them in the Desert of Sinai:

²⁰From the descendants of Reuben the firstborn son of Israel:

All the men twenty years old or more who were able to serve in the army were listed by name, one by one, according to the records of their clans and families. ²¹The number from the tribe of Reuben was 46,500.

²²From the descendants of Simeon:

All the men twenty years old or more who were able to serve in the army were counted and listed by name, one by one, according to the records of their clans and families. ²³The number from the tribe of Simeon was 59,300.

²⁴From the descendants of Gad:

All the men twenty years old or more who were able to serve in the army were listed by name, according to the records of their clans and families. ²⁵The number from the tribe of Gad was 45,650.

²⁶From the descendants of Judah:

All the men twenty years old or more who were able to serve in the army were listed by name, according to the records of their clans and families. ²⁷The number from the tribe of Judah was 74,600.

²⁸From the descendants of Issachar:

All the men twenty years old or more who were able to serve in the army were listed by name, according to the records of their clans and families. ²⁹The number from the tribe of Issachar was 54,400.

³⁰From the descendants of Zebulun:

All the men twenty years old or more who were able to serve in the army were listed by name, according to the records of their clans and families. ³¹The number from the tribe of Zebulun was 57,400.

³²From the sons of Joseph:

From the descendants of Ephraim:

All the men twenty years old or more who were able to serve in the army were listed by name, according to the records of their clans and families. ³³The number from the tribe of Ephraim was 40,500.

³⁴From the descendants of Manasseh:

All the men twenty years old or more who were able to serve in the army were listed by name, according to the records of their clans and families. ³⁵The number from the tribe of Manasseh was 32,200.

³⁶From the descendants of Benjamin:

All the men twenty years old or more who were able to serve in the army were listed by name, according to the records of their clans and families. ³⁷The number from the tribe of Benjamin was 35,400.

³⁸From the descendants of Dan:

All the men twenty years old or more who were able to serve in the army were listed by name, according to the records of their clans and families. ³⁹The number from the tribe of Dan was 62,700.

⁴⁰From the descendants of Asher:

All the men twenty years old or more who were able to serve in the army were listed by name, according to the records of their clans and families. ⁴¹The number from the tribe of Asher was 41,500.

⁴²From the descendants of Naphtali:

All the men twenty years old or more who were able to serve in the army were listed by name, according to the records of their clans and families. ⁴³The number from the tribe of Naphtali was 53,400.

⁴⁴These were the men counted by Moses and Aaron and the twelve leaders of Israel, each one representing his family. ⁴⁵All the Israelites twenty years old or more who were able to serve in Israel's army were counted according to their families. ⁴⁶The total number was 603,550.

⁴⁷The families of the tribe of Levi, however, were not counted along with the others. ⁴⁸The LORD had said to Moses: ⁴⁹"You must not count the tribe of Levi or include them in the census of the other Israelites. ⁵⁰Instead, appoint the Levites to be in charge of the tabernacle of the Tes-timony—over all its furnishings and everything belonging to it. They are to carry the tabernacle and all its furnishings; they are to take care of it and encamp around it. ⁵¹Whenever the tabernacle is to move, the Levites are to take it down, and whenever the tabernacle is to be set up, the Levites shall do it. Anyone else who goes near it shall be put to death. ⁵²The Israelites are to set up their tents by divisions, each man in his own camp under his own standard. ⁵³The Levites, however, are to set up their tents around the tabernacle of the Testimony so that wrath will not fall on the Israelite community. The Levites are to be responsible for the care of the tabernacle of the Testimony."

⁵⁴The Israelites did all this just as the LORD commanded Moses.

The Arrangement of the Tribal Camps

2 The LORD said to Moses and Aaron: ²"The Israelites are to camp around the Tent of Meeting some distance from it, each man under his standard with the banners of his family."

³On the east, toward the sunrise, the divisions of the camp of Judah are to encamp under their standard. The leader of the people of Judah is Nahshon son of Amminadab. ⁴His division numbers 74,600.

⁵The tribe of Issachar will camp next to them. The leader of the people of Issachar is Nethanel son of Zuar. ⁶His division numbers 54,400.

⁷The tribe of Zebulun will be next. The leader of the people of Zebulun is Eliab son of Helon. ⁸His division numbers 57,400.

⁹All the men assigned to the camp of Judah, according to their divisions, number 186,400. They will set out first.

¹⁰On the south will be the divisions of the camp of Reuben under their standard. The leader of the people of Reuben is Elizur son of Shedeur. ¹¹His division numbers 46,500.

¹²The tribe of Simeon will camp next to them. The leader of the people of Simeon

is Shelumiel son of Zurishaddai. [13] His division numbers 59,300.

[14] The tribe of Gad will be next. The leader of the people of Gad is Eliasaph son of Deuel.[a] [15] His division numbers 45,650.

[16] All the men assigned to the camp of Reuben, according to their divisions, number 151,450. They will set out second.

[17] Then the Tent of Meeting and the camp of the Levites will set out in the middle of the camps. They will set out in the same order as they encamp, each in his own place under his standard.

[18] On the west will be the divisions of the camp of Ephraim under their standard. The leader of the people of Ephraim is Elishama son of Ammihud. [19] His division numbers 40,500.

[20] The tribe of Manasseh will be next to them. The leader of the people of Manasseh is Gamaliel son of Pedahzur. [21] His division numbers 32,200.

[22] The tribe of Benjamin will be next. The leader of the people of Benjamin is Abidan son of Gideoni. [23] His division numbers 35,400.

[24] All the men assigned to the camp of Ephraim, according to their divisions, number 108,100. They will set out third.

[25] On the north will be the divisions of the camp of Dan, under their standard. The leader of the people of Dan is Ahiezer son of Ammishaddai. [26] His division numbers 62,700.

[27] The tribe of Asher will camp next to them. The leader of the people of Asher is Pagiel son of Ocran. [28] His division numbers 41,500.

[29] The tribe of Naphtali will be next. The leader of the people of Naphtali is Ahira son of Enan. [30] His division numbers 53,400.

[31] All the men assigned to the camp of Dan number 157,600. They will set out last, under their standards.

[32] These are the Israelites, counted according to their families. All those in the camps, by their divisions, number 603,550. [33] The Levites, however, were not counted along with the other Israelites, as the LORD commanded Moses.

[34] So the Israelites did everything the LORD commanded Moses; that is the way they encamped under their standards, and that is the way they set out, each with his clan and family.

The Levites

3 This is the account of the family of Aaron and Moses at the time the LORD talked with Moses on Mount Sinai.

[2] The names of the sons of Aaron were Nadab the firstborn and Abihu, Eleazar and Ithamar. [3] Those were the names of Aaron's sons, the anointed priests, who were ordained to serve as priests. [4] Nadab and Abihu, however, fell dead before the LORD when they made an offering with unauthorized fire before him in the Desert of Sinai. They had no sons; so only Eleazar and Ithamar served as priests during the lifetime of their father Aaron.

[5] The LORD said to Moses, [6] "Bring the tribe of Levi and present them to Aaron the priest to assist him. [7] They are to perform duties for him and for the whole community at the Tent of Meeting by doing the work of the tabernacle. [8] They are to take care of all the furnishings of the Tent of Meeting, fulfilling the obligations of the Israelites by doing the work of the tabernacle. [9] Give the Levites to Aaron and his sons; they are the Israelites who are to be given wholly to him.[b] [10] Appoint Aaron and his sons to serve as priests; anyone else who approaches the sanctuary must be put to death."

[11] The LORD also said to Moses, [12] "I have taken the Levites from among the Israelites in place of

a 14 Many manuscripts of the Masoretic Text, Samaritan Pentateuch and Vulgate (see also Num. 1:14); most manuscripts of the Masoretic Text *Reuel*   b 9 Most manuscripts of the Masoretic Text; some manuscripts of the Masoretic Text, Samaritan Pentateuch and Septuagint (see also Num. 8:16) *to me* the first male offspring of every Israelite woman. The Levites are mine, ¹³for all the firstborn are mine. When I struck down all the firstborn in Egypt, I set apart for myself every firstborn in Israel, whether man or animal. They are to be mine. I am the LORD."

¹⁴The LORD said to Moses in the Desert of Sinai, ¹⁵"Count the Levites by their families and clans. Count every male a month old or more." ¹⁶So Moses counted them, as he was commanded by the word of the LORD.

¹⁷These were the names of the sons of Levi:
Gershon, Kohath and Merari.
¹⁸These were the names of the Gershonite clans:
Libni and Shimei.
¹⁹The Kohathite clans:
Amram, Izhar, Hebron and Uzziel.
²⁰The Merarite clans:
Mahli and Mushi.
These were the Levite clans, according to their families.

²¹To Gershon belonged the clans of the Libnites and Shimeites; these were the Gershonite clans. ²²The number of all the males a month old or more who were counted was 7,500. ²³The Gershonite clans were to camp on the west, behind the tabernacle. ²⁴The leader of the families of the Gershonites was Eliasaph son of Lael. ²⁵At the Tent of Meeting the Gershonites were responsible for the care of the tabernacle and tent, its coverings, the curtain at the entrance to the Tent of Meeting, ²⁶the curtains of the courtyard, the curtain at the entrance to the courtyard surrounding the tabernacle and altar, and the ropes—and everything related to their use.

²⁷To Kohath belonged the clans of the Amramites, Izharites, Hebronites and Uzzielites; these were the Kohathite clans. ²⁸The number of all the males a month old or more was 8,600.ᵃ The Kohathites were responsible for the care of the sanctuary. ²⁹The Kohathite clans were to camp on the south side of the tabernacle. ³⁰The lead-

er of the families of the Kohathite clans was Elizaphan son of Uzziel. ³¹They were responsible for the care of the ark, the table, the lampstand, the altars, the articles of the sanctuary used in ministering, the curtain, and everything related to their use. ³²The chief leader of the Levites was Eleazar son of Aaron, the priest. He was appointed over those who were responsible for the care of the sanctuary.

³³To Merari belonged the clans of the Mahlites and the Mushites; these were the Merarite clans. ³⁴The number of all the males a month old or more who were counted was 6,200. ³⁵The leader of the families of the Merarite clans was Zuriel son of Abihail; they were to camp on the north side of the tabernacle. ³⁶The Merarites were appointed to take care of the frames of the tabernacle, its crossbars, posts, bases, all its equipment, and everything related to their use, ³⁷as well as the posts of the surrounding courtyard with their bases, tent pegs and ropes.

³⁸Moses and Aaron and his sons were to camp to the east of the tabernacle, toward the sunrise, in front of the Tent of Meeting. They were responsible for the care of the sanctuary on behalf of the Israelites. Anyone else who approached the sanctuary was to be put to death.

³⁹The total number of Levites counted at the LORD's command by Moses and Aaron according to their clans, including every male a month old or more, was 22,000.

⁴⁰The LORD said to Moses, "Count all the firstborn Israelite males who are a month old or more and make a list of their names. ⁴¹Take the Levites for me in place of all the firstborn of the Israelites, and the livestock of the Levites in place of all the firstborn of the livestock of the Israelites. I am the LORD."

⁴²So Moses counted all the firstborn of the Israelites, as the LORD commanded him. ⁴³The total

ᵃ 28 Hebrew; some Septuagint manuscripts 8,300

number of firstborn males a month old or more, listed by name, was 22,273.

⁴⁴The Lord also said to Moses, ⁴⁵"Take the Levites in place of all the firstborn of Israel, and the livestock of the Levites in place of their livestock. The Levites are to be mine. I am the Lord. ⁴⁶To redeem the 273 firstborn Israelites who exceed the number of the Levites, ⁴⁷collect five shekels[a] for each one, according to the sanctuary shekel, which weighs twenty gerahs. ⁴⁸Give the money for the redemption of the additional Israelites to Aaron and his sons."

⁴⁹So Moses collected the redemption money from those who exceeded the number redeemed by the Levites. ⁵⁰From the firstborn of the Israelites he collected silver weighing 1,365 shekels,[b] according to the sanctuary shekel. ⁵¹Moses gave the redemption money to Aaron and his sons, as he was commanded by the word of the Lord.

The Kohathites

4 The Lord said to Moses and Aaron: ²"Take a census of the Kohathite branch of the Levites by their clans and families. ³Count all the men from thirty to fifty years of age who come to serve in the work in the Tent of Meeting.

⁴"This is the work of the Kohathites in the Tent of Meeting: the care of the most holy things. ⁵When the camp is to move, Aaron and his sons are to go in and take down the shielding curtain and cover the ark of the Testimony with it. ⁶Then they are to cover this with hides of sea cows,[c] spread a cloth of solid blue over that and put the poles in place.

⁷"Over the table of the Presence they are to spread a blue cloth and put on it the plates, dishes and bowls, and the jars for drink offerings; the bread that is continually there is to remain on it. ⁸Over these they are to spread a scarlet cloth, cover that with hides of sea cows and put its poles in place.

⁹"They are to take a blue cloth and cover the lampstand that is for light, together with its lamps, its wick trimmers and trays, and all its jars for the oil used to supply it. ¹⁰Then they are to wrap it and all its accessories in a covering of hides of sea cows and put it on a carrying frame.

¹¹"Over the gold altar they are to spread a blue cloth and cover that with hides of sea cows and put its poles in place.

¹²"They are to take all the articles used for ministering in the sanctuary, wrap them in a blue cloth, cover that with hides of sea cows and put them on a carrying frame.

¹³"They are to remove the ashes from the bronze altar and spread a purple cloth over it. ¹⁴Then they are to place on it all the utensils used for ministering at the altar, including the firepans, meat forks, shovels and sprinkling bowls. Over it they are to spread a covering of hides of sea cows and put its poles in place.

¹⁵"After Aaron and his sons have finished covering the holy furnishings and all the holy articles, and when the camp is ready to move, the Kohathites are to come to do the carrying. But they must not touch the holy things or they will die. The Kohathites are to carry those things that are in the Tent of Meeting.

¹⁶"Eleazar son of Aaron, the priest, is to have charge of the oil for the light, the fragrant incense, the regular grain offering and the anointing oil. He is to be in charge of the entire tabernacle and everything in it, including its holy furnishings and articles."

¹⁷The Lord said to Moses and Aaron, ¹⁸"See that the Kohathite tribal clans are not cut off from the Levites. ¹⁹So that they may live and not die when they come near the most holy things, do this for them: Aaron and his sons are to go into the sanctuary and assign to each man his work and what he is to carry. ²⁰But the Kohathites must not go in to look at the holy things, even for a moment, or they will die."

The Gershonites

²¹The Lord said to Moses, ²²"Take a census also of the Gershonites by their families and clans. ²³Count all the men from thirty to fifty

ᵃ 47 That is, about 2 ounces (about 55 grams) ᵇ 50 That is, about 35 pounds (about 15.5 kilograms) ᶜ 6 That is, dugongs; also in verses 8, 10, 11, 12, 14 and 25

years of age who come to serve in the work at the Tent of Meeting.

24 "This is the service of the Gershonite clans as they work and carry burdens: 25 They are to carry the curtains of the tabernacle, the Tent of Meeting, its covering and the outer covering of hides of sea cows, the curtains for the entrance to the Tent of Meeting, 26 the curtains of the courtyard surrounding the tabernacle and altar, the curtain for the entrance, the ropes and all the equipment used in its service. The Gershonites are to do all that needs to be done with these things. 27 All their service, whether carrying or doing other work, is to be done under the direction of Aaron and his sons. You shall assign to them as their responsibility all they are to carry. 28 This is the service of the Gershonite clans at the Tent of Meeting. Their duties are to be under the direction of Ithamar son of Aaron, the priest.

The Merarites

29 "Count the Merarites by their clans and families. 30 Count all the men from thirty to fifty years of age who come to serve in the work at the Tent of Meeting. 31 This is their duty as they perform service at the Tent of Meeting: to carry the frames of the tabernacle, its crossbars, posts and bases, 32 as well as the posts of the surrounding courtyard with their bases, tent pegs, ropes, all their equipment and everything related to their use. Assign to each man the specific things he is to carry. 33 This is the service of the Merarite clans as they work at the Tent of Meeting under the direction of Ithamar son of Aaron, the priest."

The Numbering of the Levite Clans

34 Moses, Aaron and the leaders of the community counted the Kohathites by their clans and families. 35 All the men from thirty to fifty years of age who came to serve in the work in the Tent of Meeting, 36 counted by clans, were 2,750. 37 This was the total of all those in the Kohathite clans who served in the Tent of Meeting. Moses and Aaron counted them according to the LORD's command through Moses.

38 The Gershonites were counted by their clans and families. 39 All the men from thirty to fifty years of age who came to serve in the work at the Tent of Meeting, 40 counted by their clans and families, were 2,630. 41 This was the total of those in the Gershonite clans who served at the Tent of Meeting. Moses and Aaron counted them according to the LORD's command.

42 The Merarites were counted by their clans and families. 43 All the men from thirty to fifty years of age who came to serve in the work at the Tent of Meeting, 44 counted by their clans, were 3,200. 45 This was the total of those in the Merarite clans. Moses and Aaron counted them according to the LORD's command through Moses.

46 So Moses, Aaron and the leaders of Israel counted all the Levites by their clans and families. 47 All the men from thirty to fifty years of age who came to do the work of serving and carrying the Tent of Meeting 48 numbered 8,580. 49 At the LORD's command through Moses, each was assigned his work and told what to carry.

Thus they were counted, as the LORD commanded Moses.

The Purity of the Camp

5 The LORD said to Moses, 2 "Command the Israelites to send away from the camp anyone who has an infectious skin disease *a* or a discharge of any kind, or who is ceremonially unclean because of a dead body. 3 Send away male and female alike; send them outside the camp so they will not defile their camp, where I dwell among them." 4 The Israelites did this; they sent them outside the camp. They did just as the LORD had instructed Moses.

Restitution for Wrongs

5 The LORD said to Moses, 6 "Say to the Israelites: 'When a man or woman wrongs another in any way *b* and so is unfaithful to the LORD, that person is guilty 7 and must confess the sin he has

---

a 2 Traditionally *leprosy*; the Hebrew word was used for various diseases affecting the skin — not necessarily leprosy.
b 6 Or *woman commits any wrong common to mankind*

committed. He must make full restitution for his wrong, add one fifth to it and give it all to the person he has wronged. [8]But if that person has no close relative to whom restitution can be made for the wrong, the restitution belongs to the LORD and must be given to the priest, along with the ram with which atonement is made for him. [9]All the sacred contributions the Israelites bring to a priest will belong to him. [10]Each man's sacred gifts are his own, but what he gives to the priest will belong to the priest.' "

The Test for an Unfaithful Wife

[11]Then the LORD said to Moses, [12]"Speak to the Israelites and say to them: 'If a man's wife goes astray and is unfaithful to him [13]by sleeping with another man, and this is hidden from her husband and her impurity is undetected (since there is no witness against her and she has not been caught in the act), [14]and if feelings of jealousy come over her husband and he suspects his wife and she is impure—or if he is jealous and suspects her even though she is not impure— [15]then he is to take his wife to the priest. He must also take an offering of a tenth of an ephah [a] of barley flour on her behalf. He must not pour oil on it or put incense on it, because it is a grain offering for jealousy, a reminder offering to draw attention to guilt.

[16]" 'The priest shall bring her and have her stand before the LORD. [17]Then he shall take some holy water in a clay jar and put some dust from the tabernacle floor into the water. [18]After the priest has had the woman stand before the LORD, he shall loosen her hair and place in her hands the reminder offering, the grain offering for jealousy, while he himself holds the bitter water that brings a curse. [19]Then the priest shall put the woman under oath and say to her, "If no other man has slept with you and you have not gone astray and become impure while married to your husband, may this bitter water that brings a curse not harm you. [20]But if you have gone astray while married to your husband and you have defiled yourself by sleeping with a man other than your husband"— [21]here the priest is to put the woman under this curse of the oath—"may the LORD cause your people to curse and denounce you when he causes your thigh to waste away and your abdomen to swell. [b] [22]May this water that brings a curse enter your body so that your abdomen swells and your thigh wastes away. [c]"

" 'Then the woman is to say, "Amen. So be it."

[23]" 'The priest is to write these curses on a scroll and then wash them off into the bitter water. [24]He shall have the woman drink the bitter water that brings a curse, and this water will enter her and cause bitter suffering. [25]The priest is to take from her hands the grain offering for jealousy, wave it before the LORD and bring it to the altar. [26]The priest is then to take a handful of the grain offering as a memorial offering and burn it on the altar; after that, he is to have the woman drink the water. [27]If she has defiled herself and been unfaithful to her husband, then when she is made to drink the water that brings a curse, it will go into her and cause bitter suffering; her abdomen will swell and her thigh waste away, [d] and she will become accursed among her people. [28]If, however, the woman has not defiled herself and is free from impurity, she will be cleared of guilt and will be able to have children.

[29]" 'This, then, is the law of jealousy when a woman goes astray and defiles herself while married to her husband, [30]or when feelings of jealousy come over a man because he suspects his wife. The priest is to have her stand before the LORD and is to apply this entire law to her. [31]The husband will be innocent of any wrongdoing, but the woman will bear the consequences of her sin.' "

The Nazirite

6 The LORD said to Moses, [2]"Speak to the Israelites and say to them: 'If a man or woman wants to make a special vow, a vow of separation to the LORD as a Nazirite, [3]he must abstain from wine and other fermented drink and must not

---

[a] 15 That is, probably about 2 quarts (about 2 liters)
[b] 21 Or causes you to have a miscarrying womb and barrenness
[c] 22 Or body and cause you to be barren and have a miscarrying womb   [d] 27 Or suffering; she will have barrenness and a miscarrying womb

drink vinegar made from wine or from other fermented drink. He must not drink grape juice or eat grapes or raisins. ⁴As long as he is a Nazirite, he must not eat anything that comes from the grapevine, not even the seeds or skins.

⁵" 'During the entire period of his vow of separation no razor may be used on his head. He must be holy until the period of his separation to the LORD is over; he must let the hair of his head grow long. ⁶Throughout the period of his separation to the LORD he must not go near a dead body. ⁷Even if his own father or mother or brother or sister dies, he must not make himself ceremonially unclean on account of them, because the symbol of his separation to God is on his head. ⁸Throughout the period of his separation he is consecrated to the LORD.

⁹" 'If someone dies suddenly in his presence, thus defiling the hair he has dedicated, he must shave his head on the day of his cleansing—the seventh day. ¹⁰Then on the eighth day he must bring two doves or two young pigeons to the priest at the entrance to the Tent of Meeting. ¹¹The priest is to offer one as a sin offering and the other as a burnt offering to make atonement for him because he sinned by being in the presence of the dead body. That same day he is to consecrate his head. ¹²He must dedicate himself to the LORD for the period of his separation and must bring a year-old male lamb as a guilt offering. The previous days do not count, because he became defiled during his separation.

¹³" 'Now this is the law for the Nazirite when the period of his separation is over. He is to be brought to the entrance to the Tent of Meeting. ¹⁴There he is to present his offerings to the LORD: a year-old male lamb without defect for a burnt offering, a year-old ewe lamb without defect for a sin offering, a ram without defect for a fellowship offering,^a ¹⁵together with their grain offerings and drink offerings, and a basket of bread made without yeast—cakes made of fine flour mixed with oil, and wafers spread with oil.

¹⁶" 'The priest is to present them before the LORD and make the sin offering and the burnt offering. ¹⁷He is to present the basket of unleavened bread and is to sacrifice the ram as a fellowship offering to the LORD, together with its grain offering and drink offering.

¹⁸" 'Then at the entrance to the Tent of Meeting, the Nazirite must shave off the hair that he dedicated. He is to take the hair and put it in the fire that is under the sacrifice of the fellowship offering.

¹⁹" 'After the Nazirite has shaved off the hair of his dedication, the priest is to place in his hands a boiled shoulder of the ram, and a cake and a wafer from the basket, both made without yeast. ²⁰The priest shall then wave them before the LORD as a wave offering; they are holy and belong to the priest, together with the breast that was waved and the thigh that was presented. After that, the Nazirite may drink wine.

²¹" 'This is the law of the Nazirite who vows his offering to the LORD in accordance with his separation, in addition to whatever else he can afford. He must fulfill the vow he has made, according to the law of the Nazirite.' "

The Priestly Blessing

²²The LORD said to Moses, ²³"Tell Aaron and his sons, 'This is how you are to bless the Israelites. Say to them:

²⁴" ' "The LORD bless you
    and keep you;

^a 14 Traditionally *peace offering*; also in verses 17 and 18

PRAYING THE SCRIPTURES

Blessing

NUMBERS 6:24–26

O Lord, bless and keep my grandchild. Make your face shine upon him and be gracious to him; turn your face toward him and give him peace.

Next prayer in Blessing Prayer Track: Ruth 2:12

> "THE LORD BLESS YOU AND
> KEEP YOU; THE LORD MAKE HIS
> FACE SHINE UPON YOU AND BE
> GRACIOUS TO YOU; THE LORD
> TURN HIS FACE TOWARD YOU AND
> GIVE YOU PEACE."
>
> *Numbers 6:24 – 26*

The Priestly Blessing

HELEN HAIDLE

READ | NUMBERS 6:22 – 27

Even as a child, I loved the closing benediction of the Sunday worship service. I would stand still with my eyes closed as the pastor's words poured down deep into my spirit.

At that time I was not aware of God's instruction to Aaron the priest and his descendants. When I discovered God's promise that accompanies this blessing (see verse 27), I realized why something special seemed to happen in me when someone spoke these words. I, as a member of the "priesthood" of believers (see 1 Peter 2:5,9), wanted to pray this blessing over every person I loved.

On the day I held my first granddaughter in my arms, I blessed her with this blessing. And I blessed her every day of my two-week stay in our son's home.

One afternoon my son, Paul, and his wife drove downtown while I had the joy of feeding baby Ava from her first bottle. Ava's little tongue kept pushing the strange nipple away until she finally recognized the familiar breast milk. Then she began to drink.

This seemed a good time to say another blessing out loud. So I spoke slowly and deliberately, "The Lord bless you and keep you, Ava."

Suddenly she stopped drinking. Raising her eyebrows, her big brown eyes stared directly into mine.

While I spoke the remainder of Aaron's blessing, Ava never once blinked or turned her eyes away from me. Only when I finished did she focus her full attention back on the bottle of milk.

I'm thankful the words of my spoken blessings aren't just "words." Since God uses people to bless others, my blessings take on eternal consequences. After all, what better gift could I give anyone than the blessing of our Almighty God?

Thank you, God, for your blessing on my life. Help me speak words of blessing wherever I go. Thank you for blessing those whom I bless. It's an awesome privilege to affect the lives of others in this simple yet powerful way. Amen.

GRANDCHILD IN FOCUS • PRAYER

SELECT ONE OF YOUR
GRANDCHILDREN TO FOCUS ON
IN PRAYER FOR THE NEXT 14 DAYS.

Salvation

Dear Lord, please guide my grandchild to your gift of salvation. I pray that she will come to know you, to love you and to walk close to you throughout her life. May she boldly claim Jesus as her Lord and Savior. Guide her as she makes choices that have eternal consequences. Help her to follow you each moment of her life. I pray this in Jesus' name, amen.

Your next devotion is located on page 194.

²⁵the LORD make his face shine upon you
    and be gracious to you;
²⁶the LORD turn his face toward you
    and give you peace."'

²⁷"So they will put my name on the Israelites, and I will bless them."

Offerings at the Dedication of the Tabernacle

7 When Moses finished setting up the tabernacle, he anointed it and consecrated it and all its furnishings. He also anointed and consecrated the altar and all its utensils. ²Then the leaders of Israel, the heads of families who were the tribal leaders in charge of those who were counted, made offerings. ³They brought as their gifts before the LORD six covered carts and twelve oxen—an ox from each leader and a cart from every two. These they presented before the tabernacle.

⁴The LORD said to Moses, ⁵"Accept these from them, that they may be used in the work at the Tent of Meeting. Give them to the Levites as each man's work requires."

⁶So Moses took the carts and oxen and gave them to the Levites. ⁷He gave two carts and four oxen to the Gershonites, as their work required, ⁸and he gave four carts and eight oxen to the Merarites, as their work required. They were all under the direction of Ithamar son of Aaron, the priest. ⁹But Moses did not give any to the Kohathites, because they were to carry on their shoulders the holy things, for which they were responsible.

¹⁰When the altar was anointed, the leaders brought their offerings for its dedication and presented them before the altar. ¹¹For the LORD had said to Moses, "Each day one leader is to bring his offering for the dedication of the altar."

¹²The one who brought his offering on the first day was Nahshon son of Amminadab of the tribe of Judah.

¹³His offering was one silver plate weighing a hundred and thirty shekels,ᵃ and one silver sprinkling bowl weighing seventy shekels,ᵇ both according to the sanctuary shekel, each filled with fine flour mixed with oil as a grain offering; ¹⁴one gold dish weighing ten shekels,ᶜ filled with incense; ¹⁵one young bull, one ram and one male lamb a year old, for a burnt offering; ¹⁶one male goat for a sin offering; ¹⁷and two oxen, five rams, five male goats and five male lambs a year old, to be sacrificed as a fellowship offering.ᵈ This was the offering of Nahshon son of Amminadab.

¹⁸On the second day Nethanel son of Zuar, the leader of Issachar, brought his offering.

¹⁹The offering he brought was one silver plate weighing a hundred and thirty shekels, and one silver sprinkling bowl weighing seventy shekels, both according to the sanctuary shekel, each filled with fine flour mixed with oil as a grain offering; ²⁰one gold dish weighing ten shekels, filled with incense; ²¹one young bull, one ram and one male lamb a year old, for a burnt offering; ²²one male goat for a sin offering; ²³and two oxen, five rams, five male goats and five male lambs a year old, to be sacrificed as a fellowship offering. This was the offering of Nethanel son of Zuar.

²⁴On the third day, Eliab son of Helon, the leader of the people of Zebulun, brought his offering.

²⁵His offering was one silver plate weighing a hundred and thirty shekels, and one silver sprinkling bowl weighing seventy shekels, both according to the sanctuary shekel, each filled with fine flour mixed with oil as a grain offering; ²⁶one gold dish weighing ten shekels, filled with incense; ²⁷one young bull, one ram and one male lamb a year old, for a burnt offering; ²⁸one male goat for a sin offering; ²⁹and two oxen, five rams, five male goats and five male lambs a year old, to be sacrificed as a fellowship offering. This was the offering of Eliab son of Helon.

ᵃ 13 That is, about 3 1/4 pounds (about 1.5 kilograms); also elsewhere in this chapter   ᵇ 13 That is, about 1 3/4 pounds (about 0.8 kilogram); also elsewhere in this chapter   ᶜ 14 That is, about 4 ounces (about 110 grams); also elsewhere in this chapter   ᵈ 17 Traditionally peace offering; also elsewhere in this chapter

30 On the fourth day Elizur son of Shedeur, the leader of the people of Reuben, brought his offering.

31 His offering was one silver plate weighing a hundred and thirty shekels, and one silver sprinkling bowl weighing seventy shekels, both according to the sanctuary shekel, each filled with fine flour mixed with oil as a grain offering; 32 one gold dish weighing ten shekels, filled with incense; 33 one young bull, one ram and one male lamb a year old, for a burnt offering; 34 one male goat for a sin offering; 35 and two oxen, five rams, five male goats and five male lambs a year old, to be sacrificed as a fellowship offering. This was the offering of Elizur son of Shedeur.

36 On the fifth day Shelumiel son of Zurishaddai, the leader of the people of Simeon, brought his offering.

37 His offering was one silver plate weighing a hundred and thirty shekels, and one silver sprinkling bowl weighing seventy shekels, both according to the sanctuary shekel, each filled with fine flour mixed with oil as a grain offering; 38 one gold dish weighing ten shekels, filled with incense; 39 one young bull, one ram and one male lamb a year old, for a burnt offering; 40 one male goat for a sin offering; 41 and two oxen, five rams, five male goats and five male lambs a year old, to be sacrificed as a fellowship offering. This was the offering of Shelumiel son of Zurishaddai.

42 On the sixth day Eliasaph son of Deuel, the leader of the people of Gad, brought his offering.

43 His offering was one silver plate weighing a hundred and thirty shekels, and one silver sprinkling bowl weighing seventy shekels, both according to the sanctuary shekel, each filled with fine flour mixed with oil as a grain offering; 44 one gold dish weighing ten shekels, filled with incense; 45 one young bull, one ram and one male lamb a year old, for a burnt offering; 46 one male goat for a

sin offering; 47 and two oxen, five rams, five male goats and five male lambs a year old, to be sacrificed as a fellowship offering. This was the offering of Eliasaph son of Deuel.

48 On the seventh day Elishama son of Ammihud, the leader of the people of Ephraim, brought his offering.

49 His offering was one silver plate weighing a hundred and thirty shekels, and one silver sprinkling bowl weighing seventy shekels, both according to the sanctuary shekel, each filled with fine flour mixed with oil as a grain offering; 50 one gold dish weighing ten shekels, filled with incense; 51 one young bull, one ram and one male lamb a year old, for a burnt offering; 52 one male goat for a sin offering; 53 and two oxen, five rams, five male goats and five male lambs a year old, to be sacrificed as a fellowship offering. This was the offering of Elishama son of Ammihud.

54 On the eighth day Gamaliel son of Pedahzur, the leader of the people of Manasseh, brought his offering.

55 His offering was one silver plate weighing a hundred and thirty shekels, and one silver sprinkling bowl weighing seventy shekels, both according to the sanctuary shekel, each filled with fine flour mixed with oil as a grain offering; 56 one gold dish weighing ten shekels, filled with incense; 57 one young bull, one ram and one male lamb a year old, for a burnt offering; 58 one male goat for a sin offering; 59 and two oxen, five rams, five male goats and five male lambs a year old, to be sacrificed as a fellowship offering. This was the offering of Gamaliel son of Pedahzur.

60 On the ninth day Abidan son of Gideoni, the leader of the people of Benjamin, brought his offering.

61 His offering was one silver plate weighing a hundred and thirty shekels, and one silver

sprinkling bowl weighing seventy shekels, both according to the sanctuary shekel, each filled with fine flour mixed with oil as a grain offering; [62] one gold dish weighing ten shekels, filled with incense; [63] one young bull, one ram and one male lamb a year old, for a burnt offering; [64] one male goat for a sin offering; [65] and two oxen, five rams, five male goats and five male lambs a year old, to be sacrificed as a fellowship offering. This was the offering of Abidan son of Gideoni.

[66] On the tenth day Ahiezer son of Ammishaddai, the leader of the people of Dan, brought his offering.

[67] His offering was one silver plate weighing a hundred and thirty shekels, and one silver sprinkling bowl weighing seventy shekels, both according to the sanctuary shekel, each filled with fine flour mixed with oil as a grain offering; [68] one gold dish weighing ten shekels, filled with incense; [69] one young bull, one ram and one male lamb a year old, for a burnt offering; [70] one male goat for a sin offering; [71] and two oxen, five rams, five male goats and five male lambs a year old, to be sacrificed as a fellowship offering. This was the offering of Ahiezer son of Ammishaddai.

[72] On the eleventh day Pagiel son of Ocran, the leader of the people of Asher, brought his offering.

[73] His offering was one silver plate weighing a hundred and thirty shekels, and one silver sprinkling bowl weighing seventy shekels, both according to the sanctuary shekel, each filled with fine flour mixed with oil as a grain offering; [74] one gold dish weighing ten shekels, filled with incense; [75] one young bull, one ram and one male lamb a year old, for a burnt offering; [76] one male goat for a sin offering; [77] and two oxen, five rams, five male goats and five male lambs a year old, to be sacrificed as a fellowship offering. This was the offering of Pagiel son of Ocran.

[78] On the twelfth day Ahira son of Enan, the leader of the people of Naphtali, brought his offering.

[79] His offering was one silver plate weighing a hundred and thirty shekels, and one silver sprinkling bowl weighing seventy shekels, both according to the sanctuary shekel, each filled with fine flour mixed with oil as a grain offering; [80] one gold dish weighing ten shekels, filled with incense; [81] one young bull, one ram and one male lamb a year old, for a burnt offering; [82] one male goat for a sin offering; [83] and two oxen, five rams, five male goats and five male lambs a year old, to be sacrificed as a fellowship offering. This was the offering of Ahira son of Enan.

[84] These were the offerings of the Israelite leaders for the dedication of the altar when it was anointed: twelve silver plates, twelve silver sprinkling bowls and twelve gold dishes. [85] Each silver plate weighed a hundred and thirty shekels, and each sprinkling bowl seventy shekels. Altogether, the silver dishes weighed two thousand four hundred shekels, [a] according to the sanctuary shekel. [86] The twelve gold dishes filled with incense weighed ten shekels each, according to the sanctuary shekel. Altogether, the gold dishes weighed a hundred and twenty shekels. [b] [87] The total number of animals for the burnt offering came to twelve young bulls, twelve rams and twelve male lambs a year old, together with their grain offering. Twelve male goats were used for the sin offering. [88] The total number of animals for the sacrifice of the fellowship offering came to twenty-four oxen, sixty rams, sixty male goats and sixty male lambs a year old. These were the offerings for the dedication of the altar after it was anointed.

[89] When Moses entered the Tent of Meeting to speak with the LORD, he heard the voice speaking to him from between the two cherubim above the atonement cover on the ark of the Testimony. And he spoke with him.

---

[a] 85 That is, about 60 pounds (about 28 kilograms) [b] 86 That is, about 3 pounds (about 1.4 kilograms)

Setting Up the Lamps

8 The LORD said to Moses, [2]"Speak to Aaron and say to him, 'When you set up the seven lamps, they are to light the area in front of the lampstand.'"

[3]Aaron did so; he set up the lamps so that they faced forward on the lampstand, just as the LORD commanded Moses. [4]This is how the lampstand was made: It was made of hammered gold—from its base to its blossoms. The lampstand was made exactly like the pattern the LORD had shown Moses.

The Setting Apart of the Levites

[5]The LORD said to Moses: [6]"Take the Levites from among the other Israelites and make them ceremonially clean. [7]To purify them, do this: Sprinkle the water of cleansing on them; then have them shave their whole bodies and wash their clothes, and so purify themselves. [8]Have them take a young bull with its grain offering of fine flour mixed with oil; then you are to take a second young bull for a sin offering. [9]Bring the Levites to the front of the Tent of Meeting and assemble the whole Israelite community. [10]You are to bring the Levites before the LORD, and the Israelites are to lay their hands on them. [11]Aaron is to present the Levites before the LORD as a wave offering from the Israelites, so that they may be ready to do the work of the LORD.

[12]"After the Levites lay their hands on the heads of the bulls, use the one for a sin offering to the LORD and the other for a burnt offering, to make atonement for the Levites. [13]Have the Levites stand in front of Aaron and his sons and then present them as a wave offering to the LORD. [14]In this way you are to set the Levites apart from the other Israelites, and the Levites will be mine.

[15]"After you have purified the Levites and presented them as a wave offering, they are to come to do their work at the Tent of Meeting. [16]They are the Israelites who are to be given wholly to me. I have taken them as my own in place of the firstborn, the first male offspring from every Israelite woman. [17]Every firstborn male in Israel, whether man or animal, is mine. When I struck down all the firstborn in Egypt, I set them apart for myself. [18]And I have taken the Levites in place of all the firstborn sons in Israel. [19]Of all the Israelites, I have given the Levites as gifts to Aaron and his sons to do the work at the Tent of Meeting on behalf of the Israelites and to make atonement for them so that no plague will strike the Israelites when they go near the sanctuary."

[20]Moses, Aaron and the whole Israelite community did with the Levites just as the LORD commanded Moses. [21]The Levites purified themselves and washed their clothes. Then Aaron presented them as a wave offering before the LORD and made atonement for them to purify them. [22]After that, the Levites came to do their work at the Tent of Meeting under the supervision of Aaron and his sons. They did with the Levites just as the LORD commanded Moses.

[23]The LORD said to Moses, [24]"This applies to the Levites: Men twenty-five years old or more shall come to take part in the work at the Tent of Meeting, [25]but at the age of fifty, they must retire from their regular service and work no longer. [26]They may assist their brothers in performing their duties at the Tent of Meeting, but they themselves must not do the work. This, then, is how you are to assign the responsibilities of the Levites."

The Passover

9 The LORD spoke to Moses in the Desert of Sinai in the first month of the second year after they came out of Egypt. He said, [2]"Have the Israelites celebrate the Passover at the appointed time. [3]Celebrate it at the appointed time, at twilight on the fourteenth day of this month, in accordance with all its rules and regulations."

[4]So Moses told the Israelites to celebrate the Passover, [5]and they did so in the Desert of Sinai at twilight on the fourteenth day of the first month. The Israelites did everything just as the LORD commanded Moses.

[6]But some of them could not celebrate the

Passover on that day because they were ceremonially unclean on account of a dead body. So they came to Moses and Aaron that same day ⁷and said to Moses, "We have become unclean because of a dead body, but why should we be kept from presenting the Lord's offering with the other Israelites at the appointed time?"

⁸Moses answered them, "Wait until I find out what the Lord commands concerning you."

⁹Then the Lord said to Moses, ¹⁰"Tell the Israelites: 'When any of you or your descendants are unclean because of a dead body or are away on a journey, they may still celebrate the Lord's Passover. ¹¹They are to celebrate it on the fourteenth day of the second month at twilight. They are to eat the lamb, together with unleavened bread and bitter herbs. ¹²They must not leave any of it till morning or break any of its bones. When they celebrate the Passover, they must follow all the regulations. ¹³But if a man who is ceremonially clean and not on a journey fails to celebrate the Passover, that person must be cut off from his people because he did not present the Lord's offering at the appointed time. That man will bear the consequences of his sin.

¹⁴"'An alien living among you who wants to celebrate the Lord's Passover must do so in accordance with its rules and regulations. You must have the same regulations for the alien and the native-born.'"

The Cloud Above the Tabernacle

¹⁵On the day the tabernacle, the Tent of the Testimony, was set up, the cloud covered it. From evening till morning the cloud above the tabernacle looked like fire. ¹⁶That is how it continued to be; the cloud covered it, and at night it looked like fire. ¹⁷Whenever the cloud lifted from above the Tent, the Israelites set out; wherever the cloud settled, the Israelites encamped. ¹⁸At the Lord's command the Israelites set out, and at his command they encamped. As long as the cloud stayed over the tabernacle, they remained in camp. ¹⁹When the cloud remained over the tabernacle a long time, the Israelites obeyed the Lord's or-der and did not set out. ²⁰Sometimes the cloud was over the tabernacle only a few days; at the Lord's command they would encamp, and then at his command they would set out. ²¹Sometimes the cloud stayed only from evening till morning, and when it lifted in the morning, they set out. Whether by day or by night, whenever the cloud lifted, they set out. ²²Whether the cloud stayed over the tabernacle for two days or a month or a year, the Israelites would remain in camp and not set out; but when it lifted, they would set out. ²³At the Lord's command they encamped, and at the Lord's command they set out. They obeyed the Lord's order, in accordance with his command through Moses.

stories to share

NUMBERS 9:15–23

God's Presence With His People

LIFE LESSON: God is present with his people.

TO TALK ABOUT

✦ How did the Israelites know God was with them?

✦ How do you know God is with you?

✦ When God led the people, they obeyed. How do you know when God is asking you to do something?

✦ How do you respond when you think God wants you to do something?

WHEN THE CLOUD REMAINED
OVER THE TABERNACLE A LONG
TIME, THE ISRAELITES OBEYED
THE LORD'S ORDER AND DID NOT
SET OUT.

Numbers 9:19

When the Cloud Says Wait

MILLIE STAMM

READ | NUMBERS 9:15–23

The children of Israel had been told to watch the cloud for guidance. With great expectancy they moved forward as it directed. But there were also times when the cloud indicated that they were to wait.

The wilderness was not the most delightful place in which to wait. The barrenness of the desert was not inviting. Waiting in itself is not easy. Regardless of their strength and eagerness to start out again, regardless of their impatience to be on the way, the Israelites did not move until God, by means of the cloud, directed them to do so. It may not have been difficult to wait a short time. But [sometimes they had to wait "a long time."] This was no doubt difficult. It was a test of their obedience.

Sometimes we are kept waiting too. We may be in the midst of heartaches, of problems, of trials, of temptation when we see the cloud stop and tarry. If we want what is best for us, we must stop and wait. Sometimes our waiting is for a short period. We may, on the other hand, be kept waiting for a long time. But we dare not move until He moves us.

There are times when we seem settled in a comfortable place. We are happy and contented. Suddenly the cloud begins to move. "If the LORD delights in a man's way, he makes his steps firm" (Psalm 37:23). Both the steps and the stops of our lives are ordered by the Lord. The important thing is for us to follow where He leads.

Father, I confess that waiting and watching for your guidance is sometimes difficult. I ask for the gift of patience as I wait for your sure direction.

Your next devotion is located on page 201.

GRANDCHILD IN FOCUS • PRAYER

Physical Well-Being

Almighty God, Creator of us all, I pray that you will watch over my grandchild's physical development. May he grow in strength through the stages of his life. As he grows in awareness of his body, help him to understand that each body develops uniquely, yet is within your plan and your control. Please guard his health so that his diseases are few, his injuries are minor and his infirmities are brief. Amen.

The Silver Trumpets

10 The LORD said to Moses: [2]"Make two trumpets of hammered silver, and use them for calling the community together and for having the camps set out. [3]When both are sounded, the whole community is to assemble before you at the entrance to the Tent of Meeting. [4]If only one is sounded, the leaders—the heads of the clans of Israel—are to assemble before you. [5]When a trumpet blast is sounded, the tribes camping on the east are to set out. [6]At the sounding of a second blast, the camps on the south are to set out. The blast will be the signal for setting out. [7]To gather the assembly, blow the trumpets, but not with the same signal.

[8]"The sons of Aaron, the priests, are to blow the trumpets. This is to be a lasting ordinance for you and the generations to come. [9]When you go into battle in your own land against an enemy who is oppressing you, sound a blast on the trumpets. Then you will be remembered by the LORD your God and rescued from your enemies. [10]Also at your times of rejoicing—your appointed feasts and New Moon festivals—you are to sound the trumpets over your burnt offerings and fellowship offerings,[a] and they will be a memorial for you before your God. I am the LORD your God."

The Israelites Leave Sinai

[11]On the twentieth day of the second month of the second year, the cloud lifted from above the tabernacle of the Testimony. [12]Then the Israelites set out from the Desert of Sinai and traveled from place to place until the cloud came to rest in the Desert of Paran. [13]They set out, this first time, at the LORD's command through Moses.

[14]The divisions of the camp of Judah went first, under their standard. Nahshon son of Amminadab was in command. [15]Nethanel son of Zuar was over the division of the tribe of Issachar, [16]and Eliab son of Helon was over the division of the tribe of Zebulun. [17]Then the tabernacle was taken down, and the Gershonites and Merarites, who carried it, set out.

[18]The divisions of the camp of Reuben went next, under their standard. Elizur son of Shedeur was in command. [19]Shelumiel son of Zurishaddai was over the division of the tribe of Simeon, [20]and Eliasaph son of Deuel was over the division of the tribe of Gad. [21]Then the Kohathites set out, carrying the holy things. The tabernacle was to be set up before they arrived.

[22]The divisions of the camp of Ephraim went next, under their standard. Elishama son of Ammihud was in command. [23]Gamaliel son of Pedahzur was over the division of the tribe of Manasseh, [24]and Abidan son of Gideoni was over the division of the tribe of Benjamin.

[25]Finally, as the rear guard for all the units, the divisions of the camp of Dan set out, under their standard. Ahiezer son of Ammishaddai was in command. [26]Pagiel son of Ocran was over the division of the tribe of Asher, [27]and Ahira son of Enan was over the division of the tribe of Naphtali. [28]This was the order of march for the Israelite divisions as they set out.

[29]Now Moses said to Hobab son of Reuel the Midianite, Moses' father-in-law, "We are setting out for the place about which the LORD said, 'I will give it to you.' Come with us and we will treat you well, for the LORD has promised good things to Israel."

[30]He answered, "No, I will not go; I am going back to my own land and my own people."

[31]But Moses said, "Please do not leave us. You know where we should camp in the desert, and you can be our eyes. [32]If you come with us, we will share with you whatever good things the LORD gives us."

[33]So they set out from the mountain of the LORD and traveled for three days. The ark of the covenant of the LORD went before them during those three days to find them a place to rest. [34]The cloud of the LORD was over them by day when they set out from the camp.

[35]Whenever the ark set out, Moses said,

"Rise up, O LORD!
May your enemies be scattered;
may your foes flee before you."

[a] 10 Traditionally *peace offerings*

³⁶Whenever it came to rest, he said,

"Return, O Lord,
　to the countless thousands of Israel."

Fire From the Lord

11 Now the people complained about their hardships in the hearing of the Lord, and when he heard them his anger was aroused. Then fire from the Lord burned among them and consumed some of the outskirts of the camp. ²When the people cried out to Moses, he prayed to the Lord and the fire died down. ³So that place was called Taberah,ᵃ because fire from the Lord had burned among them.

Quail From the Lord

⁴The rabble with them began to crave other food, and again the Israelites started wailing and said, "If only we had meat to eat! ⁵We remember the fish we ate in Egypt at no cost—also the cucumbers, melons, leeks, onions and garlic. ⁶But now we have lost our appetite; we never see anything but this manna!"

⁷The manna was like coriander seed and looked like resin. ⁸The people went around gathering it, and then ground it in a handmill or crushed it in a mortar. They cooked it in a pot or made it into cakes. And it tasted like something made with olive oil. ⁹When the dew settled on the camp at night, the manna also came down.

¹⁰Moses heard the people of every family wailing, each at the entrance to his tent. The Lord became exceedingly angry, and Moses was troubled. ¹¹He asked the Lord, "Why have you brought this trouble on your servant? What have I done to displease you that you put the burden of all these people on me? ¹²Did I conceive all these people? Did I give them birth? Why do you tell me to carry them in my arms, as a nurse carries an infant, to the land you promised on oath to their forefathers? ¹³Where can I get meat for all these people? They keep wailing to me, 'Give us meat to eat!' ¹⁴I cannot carry all these people by myself; the burden is too heavy for me. ¹⁵If this is how you are going to treat me, put me to death right now—if I have found favor in your eyes—and do not let me face my own ruin."

¹⁶The Lord said to Moses: "Bring me seventy of Israel's elders who are known to you as leaders and officials among the people. Have them come to the Tent of Meeting, that they may stand there with you. ¹⁷I will come down and speak with you there, and I will take of the Spirit that is on you and put the Spirit on them. They will help you carry the burden of the people so that you will not have to carry it alone.

¹⁸"Tell the people: 'Consecrate yourselves in preparation for tomorrow, when you will eat meat. The Lord heard you when you wailed, "If only we had meat to eat! We were better off in Egypt!" Now the Lord will give you meat, and you will eat it. ¹⁹You will not eat it for just one day, or two days, or five, ten or twenty days, ²⁰but for a whole month—until it comes out of your nostrils and you loathe it—because you have rejected the Lord, who is among you, and have wailed before him, saying, "Why did we ever leave Egypt?" ' "

²¹But Moses said, "Here I am among six hundred thousand men on foot, and you say, 'I will give them meat to eat for a whole month!' ²²Would they have enough if flocks and herds were slaughtered for them? Would they have enough if all the fish in the sea were caught for them?"

²³The Lord answered Moses, "Is the Lord's arm too short? You will now see whether or not what I say will come true for you."

²⁴So Moses went out and told the people what the Lord had said. He brought together seventy of their elders and had them stand around the Tent. ²⁵Then the Lord came down in the cloud and spoke with him, and he took of the Spirit that was on him and put the Spirit on the seventy elders. When the Spirit rested on them, they prophesied, but they did not do so again.ᵇ

ᵃ 3 *Taberah* means *burning.*　　ᵇ 25 Or *prophesied and continued to do so*

²⁶However, two men, whose names were Eldad and Medad, had remained in the camp. They were listed among the elders, but did not go out to the Tent. Yet the Spirit also rested on them, and they prophesied in the camp. ²⁷A young man ran and told Moses, "Eldad and Medad are prophesying in the camp."

²⁸Joshua son of Nun, who had been Moses' aide since youth, spoke up and said, "Moses, my lord, stop them!"

²⁹But Moses replied, "Are you jealous for my sake? I wish that all the LORD's people were prophets and that the LORD would put his Spirit on them!" ³⁰Then Moses and the elders of Israel returned to the camp.

³¹Now a wind went out from the LORD and drove quail in from the sea. It brought them^a down all around the camp to about three feet^b above the ground, as far as a day's walk in any direction. ³²All that day and night and all the next day the people went out and gathered quail. No one gathered less than ten homers.^c Then they spread them out all around the camp. ³³But while the meat was still between their teeth and before it could be consumed, the anger of the LORD burned against the people, and he struck them with a severe plague. ³⁴Therefore the place was named Kibroth Hattaavah,^d because there they buried the people who had craved other food.

³⁵From Kibroth Hattaavah the people traveled to Hazeroth and stayed there.

Miriam and Aaron Oppose Moses

12 Miriam and Aaron began to talk against Moses because of his Cushite wife, for he had married a Cushite. ²"Has the LORD spoken only through Moses?" they asked. "Hasn't he also spoken through us?" And the LORD heard this.

³(Now Moses was a very humble man, more humble than anyone else on the face of the earth.)

⁴At once the LORD said to Moses, Aaron and Miriam, "Come out to the Tent of Meeting, all three of you." So the three of them came out. ⁵Then the LORD came down in a pillar of cloud;

he stood at the entrance to the Tent and summoned Aaron and Miriam. When both of them stepped forward, ⁶he said, "Listen to my words:

"When a prophet of the LORD is among you,
I reveal myself to him in visions,
I speak to him in dreams.
⁷But this is not true of my servant Moses;
he is faithful in all my house.
⁸With him I speak face to face,
clearly and not in riddles;
he sees the form of the LORD.
Why then were you not afraid
to speak against my servant Moses?"

⁹The anger of the LORD burned against them, and he left them.

¹⁰When the cloud lifted from above the Tent, there stood Miriam—leprous,^e like snow. Aaron turned toward her and saw that she had leprosy; ¹¹and he said to Moses, "Please, my lord, do not hold against us the sin we have so foolishly committed. ¹²Do not let her be like a stillborn infant coming from its mother's womb with its flesh half eaten away."

¹³So Moses cried out to the LORD, "O God, please heal her!"

¹⁴The LORD replied to Moses, "If her father had spit in her face, would she not have been in disgrace for seven days? Confine her outside the camp for seven days; after that she can be brought back." ¹⁵So Miriam was confined outside the camp for seven days, and the people did not move on till she was brought back.

¹⁶After that, the people left Hazeroth and encamped in the Desert of Paran.

Exploring Canaan

13 The LORD said to Moses, ²"Send some men to explore the land of Canaan, which I am giving to the Israelites. From each ancestral tribe send one of its leaders."

<hr/>

^a 31 Or *They flew*   ^b 31 Hebrew *two cubits* (about 1 meter)
^c 32 That is, probably about 60 bushels (about 2.2 kiloliters)
^d 34 *Kibroth Hattaavah* means *graves of craving.*
^e 10 The Hebrew word was used for various diseases affecting the skin—not necessarily leprosy.

³So at the LORD's command Moses sent them out from the Desert of Paran. All of them were leaders of the Israelites. ⁴These are their names:

from the tribe of Reuben, Shammua son of Zaccur;

⁵from the tribe of Simeon, Shaphat son of Hori;

⁶from the tribe of Judah, Caleb son of Jephunneh;

⁷from the tribe of Issachar, Igal son of Joseph;

⁸from the tribe of Ephraim, Hoshea son of Nun;

⁹from the tribe of Benjamin, Palti son of Raphu;

¹⁰from the tribe of Zebulun, Gaddiel son of Sodi;

¹¹from the tribe of Manasseh (a tribe of Joseph), Gaddi son of Susi;

¹²from the tribe of Dan, Ammiel son of Gemalli;

¹³from the tribe of Asher, Sethur son of Michael;

¹⁴from the tribe of Naphtali, Nahbi son of Vophsi;

¹⁵from the tribe of Gad, Geuel son of Maki.

¹⁶These are the names of the men Moses sent to explore the land. (Moses gave Hoshea son of Nun the name Joshua.)

¹⁷When Moses sent them to explore Canaan, he said, "Go up through the Negev and on into the hill country. ¹⁸See what the land is like and whether the people who live there are strong or weak, few or many. ¹⁹What kind of land do they live in? Is it good or bad? What kind of towns do they live in? Are they unwalled or fortified? ²⁰How is the soil? Is it fertile or poor? Are there trees on it or not? Do your best to bring back some of the fruit of the land." (It was the season for the first ripe grapes.)

²¹So they went up and explored the land from the Desert of Zin as far as Rehob, toward Lebo ᵃ Hamath. ²²They went up through the Negev and came to Hebron, where Ahiman, Sheshai and Talmai, the descendants of Anak, lived. (Hebron had been built seven years before Zoan in Egypt.) ²³When they reached the Valley of Eshcol, ᵇ they cut off a branch bearing a single cluster of grapes. Two of them carried it on a pole between them, along with some pomegranates and figs. ²⁴That place was called the Valley of Eshcol because of the cluster of grapes the Israelites cut off there. ²⁵At the end of forty days they returned from exploring the land.

Report on the Exploration

²⁶They came back to Moses and Aaron and the whole Israelite community at Kadesh in the Des-

---

stories to share

NUMBERS 13:1-3; 13:26—14:23

Exploring the Promised Land

LIFE LESSON: It takes courage to do what's right.

TO TALK ABOUT

✦ Even though they discovered that the land was good, why did ten of the twelve spies say the Israelites shouldn't go in?

✦ What did Joshua and Caleb say? Why weren't they afraid?

✦ Why was God so angry with the Israelites?

✦ Was there ever a situation when you were afraid to do the right thing? What happened?

ᵃ 21 Or toward the entrance to   ᵇ 23 Eshcol means cluster; also in verse 24.

ert of Paran. There they reported to them and to the whole assembly and showed them the fruit of the land. ²⁷They gave Moses this account: "We went into the land to which you sent us, and it does flow with milk and honey! Here is its fruit. ²⁸But the people who live there are powerful, and the cities are fortified and very large. We even saw descendants of Anak there. ²⁹The Amalekites live in the Negev; the Hittites, Jebusites and Amorites live in the hill country; and the Canaanites live near the sea and along the Jordan."

³⁰Then Caleb silenced the people before Moses and said, "We should go up and take possession of the land, for we can certainly do it."

³¹But the men who had gone up with him said, "We can't attack those people; they are stronger than we are." ³²And they spread among the Israelites a bad report about the land they had explored. They said, "The land we explored devours those living in it. All the people we saw there are of great size. ³³We saw the Nephilim there (the descendants of Anak come from the Nephilim). We seemed like grasshoppers in our own eyes, and we looked the same to them."

The People Rebel

14 That night all the people of the community raised their voices and wept aloud. ²All the Israelites grumbled against Moses and Aaron, and the whole assembly said to them, "If only we had died in Egypt! Or in this desert! ³Why is the LORD bringing us to this land only to let us fall by the sword? Our wives and children will be taken as plunder. Wouldn't it be better for us to go back to Egypt?" ⁴And they said to each other, "We should choose a leader and go back to Egypt."

⁵Then Moses and Aaron fell facedown in front of the whole Israelite assembly gathered there. ⁶Joshua son of Nun and Caleb son of Jephunneh, who were among those who had explored the land, tore their clothes ⁷and said to the entire Israelite assembly, "The land we passed through and explored is exceedingly good. ⁸If the LORD is pleased with us, he will lead us into that land, a land flowing with milk and honey, and will give

it to us. ⁹Only do not rebel against the LORD. And do not be afraid of the people of the land, because we will swallow them up. Their protection is gone, but the LORD is with us. Do not be afraid of them."

¹⁰But the whole assembly talked about stoning them. Then the glory of the LORD appeared at the Tent of Meeting to all the Israelites. ¹¹The LORD said to Moses, "How long will these people treat me with contempt? How long will they refuse to believe in me, in spite of all the miraculous signs I have performed among them? ¹²I will strike them down with a plague and destroy them, but I will make you into a nation greater and stronger than they."

¹³Moses said to the LORD, "Then the Egyptians will hear about it! By your power you brought these people up from among them. ¹⁴And they will tell the inhabitants of this land about it. They have already heard that you, O LORD, are with these people and that you, O LORD, have been seen face to face, that your cloud stays over them, and that you go before them in a pillar of cloud by day and a pillar of fire by night. ¹⁵If you put these people to death all at one time, the nations who have heard this report about you will say, ¹⁶'The LORD was not able to bring these people into the land he promised them on oath; so he slaughtered them in the desert.'

¹⁷"Now may the Lord's strength be displayed, just as you have declared: ¹⁸'The LORD is slow to anger, abounding in love and forgiving sin and rebellion. Yet he does not leave the guilty unpunished; he punishes the children for the sin of the fathers to the third and fourth generation.' ¹⁹In accordance with your great love, forgive the sin of these people, just as you have pardoned them from the time they left Egypt until now."

²⁰The LORD replied, "I have forgiven them, as you asked. ²¹Nevertheless, as surely as I live and as surely as the glory of the LORD fills the whole earth, ²²not one of the men who saw my glory and the miraculous signs I performed in Egypt and in the desert but who disobeyed me and tested me ten times— ²³not one of them will ever

see the land I promised on oath to their forefathers. No one who has treated me with contempt will ever see it. ²⁴But because my servant Caleb has a different spirit and follows me wholeheartedly, I will bring him into the land he went to, and his descendants will inherit it. ²⁵Since the Amalekites and Canaanites are living in the valleys, turn back tomorrow and set out toward the desert along the route to the Red Sea. ^a"

²⁶The LORD said to Moses and Aaron: ²⁷"How long will this wicked community grumble against me? I have heard the complaints of these grumbling Israelites. ²⁸So tell them, 'As surely as I live, declares the LORD, I will do to you the very things I heard you say: ²⁹In this desert your bodies will fall — every one of you twenty years old or more who was counted in the census and who has grumbled against me. ³⁰Not one of you will enter the land I swore with uplifted hand to make your home, except Caleb son of Jephunneh and Joshua son of Nun. ³¹As for your children that you said would be taken as plunder, I will bring them in to enjoy the land you have rejected. ³²But you — your bodies will fall in this desert. ³³Your children will be shepherds here for forty years, suffering for your unfaithfulness, until the last of your bodies lies in the desert. ³⁴For forty years — one year for each of the forty days you explored the land — you will suffer for your sins and know what it is like to have me against you.' ³⁵I, the LORD, have spoken, and I will surely do these things to this whole wicked community, which has banded together against me. They will meet their end in this desert; here they will die."

³⁶So the men Moses had sent to explore the land, who returned and made the whole community grumble against him by spreading a bad report about it — ³⁷these men responsible for spreading the bad report about the land were struck down and died of a plague before the LORD. ³⁸Of the men who went to explore the land, only Joshua son of Nun and Caleb son of Jephunneh survived.

³⁹When Moses reported this to all the Israelites, they mourned bitterly. ⁴⁰Early the next morning they went up toward the high hill country. "We have sinned," they said. "We will go up to the place the LORD promised."

⁴¹But Moses said, "Why are you disobeying the LORD's command? This will not succeed! ⁴²Do not go up, because the LORD is not with you. You will be defeated by your enemies, ⁴³for the Amalekites and Canaanites will face you there. Because you have turned away from the LORD, he will not be with you and you will fall by the sword."

⁴⁴Nevertheless, in their presumption they went up toward the high hill country, though neither Moses nor the ark of the LORD's covenant moved from the camp. ⁴⁵Then the Amalekites and Canaanites who lived in that hill country came down and attacked them and beat them down all the way to Hormah.

Supplementary Offerings

15 The LORD said to Moses, ²"Speak to the Israelites and say to them: 'After you enter the land I am giving you as a home ³and you present to the LORD offerings made by fire, from the herd or the flock, as an aroma pleasing to the LORD — whether burnt offerings or sacrifices, for special vows or freewill offerings or festival offerings — ⁴then the one who brings his offering shall present to the LORD a grain offering of a tenth of an ephah ^b of fine flour mixed with a quarter of a hin ^c of oil. ⁵With each lamb for the burnt offering or the sacrifice, prepare a quarter of a hin of wine as a drink offering.

⁶"'With a ram prepare a grain offering of two-tenths of an ephah ^d of fine flour mixed with a third of a hin ^e of oil, ⁷and a third of a hin of wine as a drink offering. Offer it as an aroma pleasing to the LORD.

⁸"'When you prepare a young bull as a burnt offering or sacrifice, for a special vow or a fellowship offering ^f to the LORD, ⁹bring with the bull

^a 25 Hebrew *Yam Suph*; that is, Sea of Reeds   ^b 4 That is, probably about 2 quarts (about 2 liters)   ^c 4 That is, probably about 1 quart (about 1 liter); also in verse 5   ^d 6 That is, probably about 4 quarts (about 4.5 liters)   ^e 6 That is, probably about 1 1/4 quarts (about 1.2 liters); also in verse 7   ^f 8 Traditionally *peace offering*

TURN BACK TOMORROW AND SET
OUT TOWARD THE DESERT ALONG
THE ROUTE TO THE RED SEA.
Numbers 14:25

Lessons in the Desert

LUCI SHAW

READ | NUMBERS 14:1 – 35

[The desert] has been defined as territory that is uncivilized, unmanaged, "nature in the raw." In Scripture, [the desert] is never seen as an easy place; it is often the arena of trial and hardship, of wandering (forty years of it) for the Hebrews after they left Egypt, of solitary testing (forty days of it) for Jesus before his public ministry began. In Bible descriptions, nearly always with Middle Eastern settings, [it] is consistently barren, dry, desolate.

But there were always special lessons to be learned in the wild, unique challenges that developed the spiritual muscles and endurance that make up the character that pleases God. By hindsight I have often found these times and places of human wilderness to be the times and places where God was at work within me, showing me where I am most dry and unproductive. But he is also showing me his resources, the things I need most — manna, springs of water, guidance by cloud (the shadowed years) and fire (the furnace of testing) along an untrodden path, challenges to action that seem beyond my human possibility but are possible with God as my leader.

This was especially true during the years I mothered five children and tried to keep my own vocation as a writer alive. And even more so later, after the death of my husband, Harold, when for the first time I had to make major decisions on my own at the ripe age of fifty-nine. I'd had a protected life with my family, at college, and with a godly husband, and suddenly I had no one to protect and guide me but God. It was, perhaps, another example of his severe mercy, to lead me into this new [desert] journey.

It is in the [desert] that we are forced to leave our human resources behind and where we learn total dependence upon God.

O God, help me to have patience through the times I wander in the desert of life. Let me trust you as my guide and leader. Amen.

Your next devotion is located on page 210.

GRANDCHILD IN FOCUS • PRAYER

Emotional Development

O God, Creator of mind and body, I pray that you will give my grandchild emotional health and strength. Where there is anger, bring peace. Where there is confusion, bring clarity and focus. Where there are dark shadows, cast a ray of hope. Fill her with the sunshine of your Spirit. Warm her with the presence of your peace. Amen.

a grain offering of three-tenths of an ephah ^{a} of fine flour mixed with half a hin ^{b} of oil. ^{10}Also bring half a hin of wine as a drink offering. It will be an offering made by fire, an aroma pleasing to the Lord. ^{11}Each bull or ram, each lamb or young goat, is to be prepared in this manner. ^{12}Do this for each one, for as many as you prepare.

^{13}" 'Everyone who is native-born must do these things in this way when he brings an offering made by fire as an aroma pleasing to the Lord. ^{14}For the generations to come, whenever an alien or anyone else living among you presents an offering made by fire as an aroma pleasing to the Lord, he must do exactly as you do. ^{15}The community is to have the same rules for you and for the alien living among you; this is a lasting ordinance for the generations to come. You and the alien shall be the same before the Lord: ^{16}The same laws and regulations will apply both to you and to the alien living among you.' "

^{17}The Lord said to Moses, ^{18}"Speak to the Israelites and say to them: 'When you enter the land to which I am taking you ^{19}and you eat the food of the land, present a portion as an offering to the Lord. ^{20}Present a cake from the first of your ground meal and present it as an offering from the threshing floor. ^{21}Throughout the generations to come you are to give this offering to the Lord from the first of your ground meal.

Offerings for Unintentional Sins

^{22}" 'Now if you unintentionally fail to keep any of these commands the Lord gave Moses — ^{23}any of the Lord's commands to you through him, from the day the Lord gave them and continuing through the generations to come — ^{24}and if this is done unintentionally without the community being aware of it, then the whole community is to offer a young bull for a burnt offering as an aroma pleasing to the Lord, along with its prescribed grain offering and drink offering, and a male goat for a sin offering. ^{25}The priest is to make atonement for the whole Israelite community, and they will be forgiven, for it was not intentional and they have brought to the Lord for

their wrong an offering made by fire and a sin offering. ^{26}The whole Israelite community and the aliens living among them will be forgiven, because all the people were involved in the unintentional wrong.

^{27}" 'But if just one person sins unintentionally, he must bring a year-old female goat for a sin offering. ^{28}The priest is to make atonement before the Lord for the one who erred by sinning unintentionally, and when atonement has been made for him, he will be forgiven. ^{29}One and the same law applies to everyone who sins unintentionally, whether he is a native-born Israelite or an alien.

^{30}" 'But anyone who sins defiantly, whether native-born or alien, blasphemes the Lord, and that person must be cut off from his people. ^{31}Because he has despised the Lord's word and broken his commands, that person must surely be cut off; his guilt remains on him.' "

The Sabbath-Breaker Put to Death

^{32}While the Israelites were in the desert, a man was found gathering wood on the Sabbath day. ^{33}Those who found him gathering wood brought him to Moses and Aaron and the whole assembly, ^{34}and they kept him in custody, because it was not clear what should be done to him. ^{35}Then the Lord said to Moses, "The man must die. The whole assembly must stone him outside the camp." ^{36}So the assembly took him outside the camp and stoned him to death, as the Lord commanded Moses.

Tassels on Garments

^{37}The Lord said to Moses, ^{38}"Speak to the Israelites and say to them: 'Throughout the generations to come you are to make tassels on the corners of your garments, with a blue cord on each tassel. ^{39}You will have these tassels to look at and so you will remember all the commands of the Lord, that you may obey them and not prostitute yourselves by going after the lusts of your own hearts and eyes. ^{40}Then you will remember

^{a} 9 That is, probably about 6 quarts (about 6.5 liters) ^{b} 9 That is, probably about 2 quarts (about 2 liters); also in verse 10 to obey all my commands and will be consecrated to your God. **41**I am the LORD your God, who brought you out of Egypt to be your God. I am the LORD your God.' "

Korah, Dathan and Abiram

16 Korah son of Izhar, the son of Kohath, the son of Levi, and certain Reubenites—Dathan and Abiram, sons of Eliab, and On son of Peleth—became insolent[a] **2**and rose up against Moses. With them were 250 Israelite men, well-known community leaders who had been appointed members of the council. **3**They came as a group to oppose Moses and Aaron and said to them, "You have gone too far! The whole community is holy, every one of them, and the LORD is with them. Why then do you set yourselves above the LORD's assembly?"

4When Moses heard this, he fell facedown. **5**Then he said to Korah and all his followers: "In the morning the LORD will show who belongs to him and who is holy, and he will have that person come near him. The man he chooses he will cause to come near him. **6**You, Korah, and all your followers are to do this: Take censers **7**and tomorrow put fire and incense in them before the LORD. The man the LORD chooses will be the one who is holy. You Levites have gone too far!"

8Moses also said to Korah, "Now listen, you Levites! **9**Isn't it enough for you that the God of Israel has separated you from the rest of the Israelite community and brought you near himself to do the work at the LORD's tabernacle and to stand before the community and minister to them? **10**He has brought you and all your fellow Levites near himself, but now you are trying to get the priesthood too. **11**It is against the LORD that you and all your followers have banded together. Who is Aaron that you should grumble against him?"

12Then Moses summoned Dathan and Abiram, the sons of Eliab. But they said, "We will not come! **13**Isn't it enough that you have brought us up out of a land flowing with milk and honey to kill us in the desert? And now you also want to lord it over us? **14**Moreover, you haven't brought

us into a land flowing with milk and honey or given us an inheritance of fields and vineyards. Will you gouge out the eyes of[b] these men? No, we will not come!"

15Then Moses became very angry and said to the LORD, "Do not accept their offering. I have not taken so much as a donkey from them, nor have I wronged any of them."

16Moses said to Korah, "You and all your followers are to appear before the LORD tomorrow—you and they and Aaron. **17**Each man is to take his censer and put incense in it—250 censers in all—and present it before the LORD. You and Aaron are to present your censers also." **18**So each man took his censer, put fire and incense in it, and stood with Moses and Aaron at the entrance to the Tent of Meeting. **19**When Korah had gathered all his followers in opposition to them at the entrance to the Tent of Meeting, the glory of the LORD appeared to the entire assembly. **20**The LORD said to Moses and Aaron, **21**"Separate yourselves from this assembly so I can put an end to them at once."

22But Moses and Aaron fell facedown and cried out, "O God, God of the spirits of all mankind, will you be angry with the entire assembly when only one man sins?"

23Then the LORD said to Moses, **24**"Say to the assembly, 'Move away from the tents of Korah, Dathan and Abiram.' "

25Moses got up and went to Dathan and Abiram, and the elders of Israel followed him. **26**He warned the assembly, "Move back from the tents of these wicked men! Do not touch anything belonging to them, or you will be swept away because of all their sins." **27**So they moved away from the tents of Korah, Dathan and Abiram. Dathan and Abiram had come out and were standing with their wives, children and little ones at the entrances to their tents.

28Then Moses said, "This is how you will know that the LORD has sent me to do all these things and that it was not my idea: **29**If these men die a

---

a 1 Or Peleth—took men   *b 14 Or you make slaves of; or you deceive* natural death and experience only what usually happens to men, then the LORD has not sent me. ³⁰But if the LORD brings about something totally new, and the earth opens its mouth and swallows them, with everything that belongs to them, and they go down alive into the grave,ᵃ then you will know that these men have treated the LORD with contempt."

³¹As soon as he finished saying all this, the ground under them split apart ³²and the earth opened its mouth and swallowed them, with their households and all Korah's men and all their possessions. ³³They went down alive into the grave, with everything they owned; the earth closed over them, and they perished and were gone from the community. ³⁴At their cries, all the Israelites around them fled, shouting, "The earth is going to swallow us too!"

³⁵And fire came out from the LORD and consumed the 250 men who were offering the incense.

³⁶The LORD said to Moses, ³⁷"Tell Eleazar son of Aaron, the priest, to take the censers out of the smoldering remains and scatter the coals some distance away, for the censers are holy— ³⁸the censers of the men who sinned at the cost of their lives. Hammer the censers into sheets to overlay the altar, for they were presented before the LORD and have become holy. Let them be a sign to the Israelites."

³⁹So Eleazar the priest collected the bronze censers brought by those who had been burned up, and he had them hammered out to overlay the altar, ⁴⁰as the LORD directed him through Moses. This was to remind the Israelites that no one except a descendant of Aaron should come to burn incense before the LORD, or he would become like Korah and his followers.

⁴¹The next day the whole Israelite community grumbled against Moses and Aaron. "You have killed the LORD's people," they said.

⁴²But when the assembly gathered in opposition to Moses and Aaron and turned toward the Tent of Meeting, suddenly the cloud covered it and the glory of the LORD appeared. ⁴³Then Mo-

ses and Aaron went to the front of the Tent of Meeting, ⁴⁴and the LORD said to Moses, ⁴⁵"Get away from this assembly so I can put an end to them at once." And they fell facedown.

⁴⁶Then Moses said to Aaron, "Take your censer and put incense in it, along with fire from the altar, and hurry to the assembly to make atonement for them. Wrath has come out from the LORD; the plague has started." ⁴⁷So Aaron did as Moses said, and ran into the midst of the assembly. The plague had already started among the people, but Aaron offered the incense and made atonement for them. ⁴⁸He stood between the living and the dead, and the plague stopped. ⁴⁹But 14,700 people died from the plague, in addition to those who had died because of Korah. ⁵⁰Then Aaron returned to Moses at the entrance to the Tent of Meeting, for the plague had stopped.

The Budding of Aaron's Staff

17 The LORD said to Moses, ²"Speak to the Israelites and get twelve staffs from them, one from the leader of each of their ancestral tribes. Write the name of each man on his staff. ³On the staff of Levi write Aaron's name, for there must be one staff for the head of each ancestral tribe. ⁴Place them in the Tent of Meeting in front of the Testimony, where I meet with you. ⁵The staff belonging to the man I choose will sprout, and I will rid myself of this constant grumbling against you by the Israelites."

⁶So Moses spoke to the Israelites, and their leaders gave him twelve staffs, one for the leader of each of their ancestral tribes, and Aaron's staff was among them. ⁷Moses placed the staffs before the LORD in the Tent of the Testimony.

⁸The next day Moses entered the Tent of the Testimony and saw that Aaron's staff, which represented the house of Levi, had not only sprouted but had budded, blossomed and produced almonds. ⁹Then Moses brought out all the staffs from the LORD's presence to all the Israelites. They looked at them, and each man took his own staff.

ᵃ 30 Hebrew Sheol; also in verse 33

[10] The LORD said to Moses, "Put back Aaron's staff in front of the Testimony, to be kept as a sign to the rebellious. This will put an end to their grumbling against me, so that they will not die." [11] Moses did just as the LORD commanded him.

[12] The Israelites said to Moses, "We will die! We are lost, we are all lost! [13] Anyone who even comes near the tabernacle of the LORD will die. Are we all going to die?"

Duties of Priests and Levites

18 The LORD said to Aaron, "You, your sons and your father's family are to bear the responsibility for offenses against the sanctuary, and you and your sons alone are to bear the responsibility for offenses against the priesthood. [2] Bring your fellow Levites from your ancestral tribe to join you and assist you when you and your sons minister before the Tent of the Testimony. [3] They are to be responsible to you and are to perform all the duties of the Tent, but they must not go near the furnishings of the sanctuary or the altar, or both they and you will die. [4] They are to join you and be responsible for the care of the Tent of Meeting—all the work at the Tent—and no one else may come near where you are.

[5] "You are to be responsible for the care of the sanctuary and the altar, so that wrath will not fall on the Israelites again. [6] I myself have selected your fellow Levites from among the Israelites as a gift to you, dedicated to the LORD to do the work at the Tent of Meeting. [7] But only you and your sons may serve as priests in connection with everything at the altar and inside the curtain. I am giving you the service of the priesthood as a gift. Anyone else who comes near the sanctuary must be put to death."

Offerings for Priests and Levites

[8] Then the LORD said to Aaron, "I myself have put you in charge of the offerings presented to me; all the holy offerings the Israelites give me I give to you and your sons as your portion and regular share. [9] You are to have the part of the most holy offerings that is kept from the fire. From all the gifts they bring me as most holy offerings, whether grain or sin or guilt offerings, that part belongs to you and your sons. [10] Eat it as something most holy; every male shall eat it. You must regard it as holy.

[11] "This also is yours: whatever is set aside from the gifts of all the wave offerings of the Israelites. I give this to you and your sons and daughters as your regular share. Everyone in your household who is ceremonially clean may eat it.

[12] "I give you all the finest olive oil and all the finest new wine and grain they give the LORD as the firstfruits of their harvest. [13] All the land's firstfruits that they bring to the LORD will be yours. Everyone in your household who is ceremonially clean may eat it.

[14] "Everything in Israel that is devoted[a] to the LORD is yours. [15] The first offspring of every womb, both man and animal, that is offered to the LORD is yours. But you must redeem every firstborn son and every firstborn male of unclean animals. [16] When they are a month old, you must redeem them at the redemption price set at five shekels[b] of silver, according to the sanctuary shekel, which weighs twenty gerahs.

[17] "But you must not redeem the firstborn of an ox, a sheep or a goat; they are holy. Sprinkle their blood on the altar and burn their fat as an offering made by fire, an aroma pleasing to the LORD. [18] Their meat is to be yours, just as the breast of the wave offering and the right thigh are yours. [19] Whatever is set aside from the holy offerings the Israelites present to the LORD I give to you and your sons and daughters as your regular share. It is an everlasting covenant of salt before the LORD for both you and your offspring."

[20] The LORD said to Aaron, "You will have no inheritance in their land, nor will you have any share among them; I am your share and your inheritance among the Israelites.

[21] "I give to the Levites all the tithes in Israel

---

[a] 14 The Hebrew term refers to the irrevocable giving over of things or persons to the LORD.   [b] 16 That is, about 2 ounces (about 55 grams)

as their inheritance in return for the work they do while serving at the Tent of Meeting. [22]From now on the Israelites must not go near the Tent of Meeting, or they will bear the consequences of their sin and will die. [23]It is the Levites who are to do the work at the Tent of Meeting and bear the responsibility for offenses against it. This is a lasting ordinance for the generations to come. They will receive no inheritance among the Israelites. [24]Instead, I give to the Levites as their inheritance the tithes that the Israelites present as an offering to the LORD. That is why I said concerning them: 'They will have no inheritance among the Israelites.'"

[25]The LORD said to Moses, [26]"Speak to the Levites and say to them: 'When you receive from the Israelites the tithe I give you as your inheritance, you must present a tenth of that tithe as the LORD's offering. [27]Your offering will be reckoned to you as grain from the threshing floor or juice from the winepress. [28]In this way you also will present an offering to the LORD from all the tithes you receive from the Israelites. From these tithes you must give the LORD's portion to Aaron the priest. [29]You must present as the LORD's portion the best and holiest part of everything given to you.'

[30]"Say to the Levites: 'When you present the best part, it will be reckoned to you as the product of the threshing floor or the winepress. [31]You and your households may eat the rest of it anywhere, for it is your wages for your work at the Tent of Meeting. [32]By presenting the best part of it you will not be guilty in this matter; then you will not defile the holy offerings of the Israelites, and you will not die.'"

The Water of Cleansing

19 The LORD said to Moses and Aaron: [2]"This is a requirement of the law that the LORD has commanded: Tell the Israelites to bring you a red heifer without defect or blemish and that has never been under a yoke. [3]Give it to Eleazar the priest; it is to be taken outside the camp and slaughtered in his presence. [4]Then El-

eazar the priest is to take some of its blood on his finger and sprinkle it seven times toward the front of the Tent of Meeting. [5]While he watches, the heifer is to be burned—its hide, flesh, blood and offal. [6]The priest is to take some cedar wood, hyssop and scarlet wool and throw them onto the burning heifer. [7]After that, the priest must wash his clothes and bathe himself with water. He may then come into the camp, but he will be ceremonially unclean till evening. [8]The man who burns it must also wash his clothes and bathe with water, and he too will be unclean till evening.

[9]"A man who is clean shall gather up the ashes of the heifer and put them in a ceremonially clean place outside the camp. They shall be kept by the Israelite community for use in the water of cleansing; it is for purification from sin. [10]The man who gathers up the ashes of the heifer must also wash his clothes, and he too will be unclean till evening. This will be a lasting ordinance both for the Israelites and for the aliens living among them.

[11]"Whoever touches the dead body of anyone will be unclean for seven days. [12]He must purify himself with the water on the third day and on the seventh day; then he will be clean. But if he does not purify himself on the third and seventh days, he will not be clean. [13]Whoever touches the dead body of anyone and fails to purify himself defiles the LORD's tabernacle. That person must be cut off from Israel. Because the water of cleansing has not been sprinkled on him, he is unclean; his uncleanness remains on him.

[14]"This is the law that applies when a person dies in a tent: Anyone who enters the tent and anyone who is in it will be unclean for seven days, [15]and every open container without a lid fastened on it will be unclean.

[16]"Anyone out in the open who touches someone who has been killed with a sword or someone who has died a natural death, or anyone who touches a human bone or a grave, will be unclean for seven days.

[17]"For the unclean person, put some ashes from the burned purification offering into a jar

and pour fresh water over them. ¹⁸Then a man who is ceremonially clean is to take some hyssop, dip it in the water and sprinkle the tent and all the furnishings and the people who were there. He must also sprinkle anyone who has touched a human bone or a grave or someone who has been killed or someone who has died a natural death. ¹⁹The man who is clean is to sprinkle the unclean person on the third and seventh days, and on the seventh day he is to purify him. The person being cleansed must wash his clothes and bathe with water, and that evening he will be clean. ²⁰But if a person who is unclean does not purify himself, he must be cut off from the community, because he has defiled the sanctuary of the Lord. The water of cleansing has not been sprinkled on him, and he is unclean. ²¹This is a lasting ordinance for them.

"The man who sprinkles the water of cleansing must also wash his clothes, and anyone who touches the water of cleansing will be unclean till evening. ²²Anything that an unclean person touches becomes unclean, and anyone who touches it becomes unclean till evening."

Water From the Rock

20 In the first month the whole Israelite community arrived at the Desert of Zin, and they stayed at Kadesh. There Miriam died and was buried.

²Now there was no water for the community, and the people gathered in opposition to Moses and Aaron. ³They quarreled with Moses and said, "If only we had died when our brothers fell dead before the Lord! ⁴Why did you bring the Lord's community into this desert, that we and our livestock should die here? ⁵Why did you bring us up out of Egypt to this terrible place? It has no grain or figs, grapevines or pomegranates. And there is no water to drink!"

⁶Moses and Aaron went from the assembly to the entrance to the Tent of Meeting and fell facedown, and the glory of the Lord appeared to them. ⁷The Lord said to Moses, ⁸"Take the staff, and you and your brother Aaron gather the assembly together. Speak to that rock before their eyes and it will pour out its water. You will bring water out of the rock for the community so they and their livestock can drink."

⁹So Moses took the staff from the Lord's presence, just as he commanded him. ¹⁰He and Aaron gathered the assembly together in front of the rock and Moses said to them, "Listen, you rebels, must we bring you water out of this rock?" ¹¹Then Moses raised his arm and struck the rock twice with his staff. Water gushed out, and the community and their livestock drank.

¹²But the Lord said to Moses and Aaron, "Because you did not trust in me enough to honor me as holy in the sight of the Israelites, you will not bring this community into the land I give them."

¹³These were the waters of Meribah,ᵃ where the Israelites quarreled with the Lord and where he showed himself holy among them.

TALKING POINTS

Anger

Because Moses responded in anger and disobeyed God's command, God did not permit him to enter the promised land.

NUMBERS 20:1–13

For more on anger, go to Psalm 4:4.

Edom Denies Israel Passage

¹⁴Moses sent messengers from Kadesh to the king of Edom, saying:

"This is what your brother Israel says: You know about all the hardships that have come upon us. ¹⁵Our forefathers went down into Egypt, and we lived there many

ᵃ 13 Meribah means quarreling.

NUMBERS 20:1-13

Water From the Rock

LIFE LESSON: God wants us to trust and obey him.

TO TALK ABOUT

✦ Why did the Israelites start complaining again?

✦ What did God tell Moses to do about the situation? What did Moses do instead?

✦ Why do you think God punished Moses so severely?

✦ What does this story teach us about our attitude?

years. The Egyptians mistreated us and our fathers, [16] but when we cried out to the LORD, he heard our cry and sent an angel and brought us out of Egypt.

"Now we are here at Kadesh, a town on the edge of your territory. [17] Please let us pass through your country. We will not go through any field or vineyard, or drink water from any well. We will travel along the king's highway and not turn to the right or to the left until we have passed through your territory."

[18] But Edom answered:

"You may not pass through here; if you try, we will march out and attack you with the sword."

[19] The Israelites replied:

"We will go along the main road, and if we or our livestock drink any of your water, we will pay for it. We only want to pass through on foot—nothing else."

[20] Again they answered:

"You may not pass through."

Then Edom came out against them with a large and powerful army. [21] Since Edom refused to let them go through their territory, Israel turned away from them.

The Death of Aaron

[22] The whole Israelite community set out from Kadesh and came to Mount Hor. [23] At Mount Hor, near the border of Edom, the LORD said to Moses and Aaron, [24] "Aaron will be gathered to his people. He will not enter the land I give the Israelites, because both of you rebelled against my command at the waters of Meribah. [25] Get Aaron and his son Eleazar and take them up Mount Hor. [26] Remove Aaron's garments and put them on his son Eleazar, for Aaron will be gathered to his people; he will die there."

[27] Moses did as the LORD commanded: They went up Mount Hor in the sight of the whole community. [28] Moses removed Aaron's garments and put them on his son Eleazar. And Aaron died there on top of the mountain. Then Moses and Eleazar came down from the mountain, [29] and when the whole community learned that Aaron had died, the entire house of Israel mourned for him thirty days.

Arad Destroyed

21 When the Canaanite king of Arad, who lived in the Negev, heard that Israel was coming along the road to Atharim, he attacked the Israelites and captured some of them. [2] Then Israel made this vow to the LORD: "If you will deliver these people into our hands, we will totally destroy[a] their cities." [3] The LORD listened

[a] 2 The Hebrew term refers to the irrevocable giving over of things or persons to the LORD, often by totally destroying them; also in verse 3.

to Israel's plea and gave the Canaanites over to them. They completely destroyed them and their towns; so the place was named Hormah.ᵃ

The Bronze Snake

⁴They traveled from Mount Hor along the route to the Red Sea,ᵇ to go around Edom. But the people grew impatient on the way; ⁵they spoke against God and against Moses, and said, "Why have you brought us up out of Egypt to die in the desert? There is no bread! There is no water! And we detest this miserable food!"

⁶Then the LORD sent venomous snakes among them; they bit the people and many Israelites died.

⁷The people came to Moses and said, "We sinned when we spoke against the LORD and against you. Pray that the LORD will take the snakes away from us." So Moses prayed for the people.

⁸The LORD said to Moses, "Make a snake and put it up on a pole; anyone who is bitten can look at it and live." ⁹So Moses made a bronze snake and put it up on a pole. Then when anyone was bitten by a snake and looked at the bronze snake, he lived.

The Journey to Moab

¹⁰The Israelites moved on and camped at Oboth. ¹¹Then they set out from Oboth and camped in Iye Abarim, in the desert that faces Moab toward the sunrise. ¹²From there they moved on and camped in the Zered Valley. ¹³They set out from there and camped alongside the Arnon, which is in the desert extending into Amorite territory. The Arnon is the border of Moab, between Moab and the Amorites. ¹⁴That is why the Book of the Wars of the LORD says:

> ". . . Waheb in Suphah ᶜ and the ravines,
>   the Arnon ¹⁵and ᵈ the slopes of the ravines
> that lead to the site of Ar
>   and lie along the border of Moab."

¹⁶From there they continued on to Beer, the well where the LORD said to Moses, "Gather the people together and I will give them water."

¹⁷Then Israel sang this song:

> "Spring up, O well!
>   Sing about it,
> ¹⁸about the well that the princes dug,
>   that the nobles of the people sank—
>   the nobles with scepters and staffs."

Then they went from the desert to Mattanah, ¹⁹from Mattanah to Nahaliel, from Nahaliel to Bamoth, ²⁰and from Bamoth to the valley in Moab where the top of Pisgah overlooks the wasteland.

stories to share

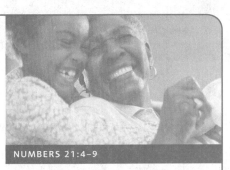

NUMBERS 21:4–9

The Bronze Snake

LIFE LESSON: God provides a way out of trouble when we sin.

TO TALK ABOUT

✦ Why do you think the Israelites grew to hate the manna God gave them, calling it "this miserable food" (verse 5)?

✦ Why is it sometimes hard not to grumble?

✦ What remedy did God provide for people who got bit by a snake?

✦ How does the pole with the bronze snake remind you of a story about Jesus? (Hint: John 3:14–15 might help you.)

ᵃ 3 *Hormah* means *destruction.*   ᵇ 4 Hebrew *Yam Suph*; that is, Sea of Reeds   ᶜ 14 The meaning of the Hebrew for this phrase is uncertain.   ᵈ 14,15 Or *"I have been given from Suphah and the ravines / of the Arnon ¹⁵to*

THEN ISRAEL SANG THIS SONG:
"SPRING UP, O WELL! SING
ABOUT IT, ABOUT THE WELL
THAT THE PRINCES DUG."

Numbers 21:17—18

Sing About It!

JOY MORGAN DAVIS

READ | NUMBERS 21:10 – 20

Dear Lord . . .
Little Anna lay in my arms,
One week old and wonderful,
And suddenly I wanted
To sing!
No matter that I
Can't carry a tune
Or hold a note
Or harmonize . . .
There was music
In me . . .
Music!
This must be what it means
To have a
Song in my heart!

O, let's don't stop with
A song, Lord . . .
Let's do a
Symphony!

Lord, thank you for your provision. Let me sing when you bless me with what I need and when you bless me with gracious gifts. Amen.

Your next devotion is located on page 214.

GRANDCHILD **IN FOCUS** • PRAYER

Spiritual Growth

Dear Lord, today I pray for my grandchild's spiritual growth. I ask that you instill in him the desire to read and memorize your Word. Give him a passion to be in conversation with you. May loving and serving you be part of his daily life. I ask that you stay close to him and lead him to be transformed to your likeness, to reflect your grace and to radiate your love. I pray this in Jesus' name, amen.

Defeat of Sihon and Og

²¹Israel sent messengers to say to Sihon king of the Amorites:

²²"Let us pass through your country. We will not turn aside into any field or vineyard, or drink water from any well. We will travel along the king's highway until we have passed through your territory."

²³But Sihon would not let Israel pass through his territory. He mustered his entire army and marched out into the desert against Israel. When he reached Jahaz, he fought with Israel. ²⁴Israel, however, put him to the sword and took over his land from the Arnon to the Jabbok, but only as far as the Ammonites, because their border was fortified. ²⁵Israel captured all the cities of the Amorites and occupied them, including Heshbon and all its surrounding settlements. ²⁶Heshbon was the city of Sihon king of the Amorites, who had fought against the former king of Moab and had taken from him all his land as far as the Arnon.

²⁷That is why the poets say:

"Come to Heshbon and let it be rebuilt;
    let Sihon's city be restored.

²⁸"Fire went out from Heshbon,
    a blaze from the city of Sihon.
It consumed Ar of Moab,
    the citizens of Arnon's heights.
²⁹Woe to you, O Moab!
    You are destroyed, O people of Chemosh!
He has given up his sons as fugitives
    and his daughters as captives
    to Sihon king of the Amorites.

³⁰"But we have overthrown them;
    Heshbon is destroyed all the way to Dibon.
We have demolished them as far as Nophah,
    which extends to Medeba."

³¹So Israel settled in the land of the Amorites.
³²After Moses had sent spies to Jazer, the Israelites captured its surrounding settlements and drove out the Amorites who were there. ³³Then they turned and went up along the road toward Bashan, and Og king of Bashan and his whole army marched out to meet them in battle at Edrei.

³⁴The LORD said to Moses, "Do not be afraid of him, for I have handed him over to you, with his whole army and his land. Do to him what you did to Sihon king of the Amorites, who reigned in Heshbon."

³⁵So they struck him down, together with his sons and his whole army, leaving them no survivors. And they took possession of his land.

Balak Summons Balaam

22 Then the Israelites traveled to the plains of Moab and camped along the Jordan across from Jericho.ᵃ

²Now Balak son of Zippor saw all that Israel had done to the Amorites, ³and Moab was terrified because there were so many people. Indeed, Moab was filled with dread because of the Israelites.

⁴The Moabites said to the elders of Midian, "This horde is going to lick up everything around us, as an ox licks up the grass of the field."

So Balak son of Zippor, who was king of Moab at that time, ⁵sent messengers to summon Balaam son of Beor, who was at Pethor, near the River,ᵇ in his native land. Balak said:

"A people has come out of Egypt; they cover the face of the land and have settled next to me. ⁶Now come and put a curse on these people, because they are too powerful for me. Perhaps then I will be able to defeat them and drive them out of the country. For I know that those you bless are blessed, and those you curse are cursed."

⁷The elders of Moab and Midian left, taking with them the fee for divination. When they came to Balaam, they told him what Balak had said.

ᵃ 1 Hebrew *Jordan of Jericho*; possibly an ancient name for the Jordan River   ᵇ 5 That is, the Euphrates

⁸"Spend the night here," Balaam said to them, "and I will bring you back the answer the LORD gives me." So the Moabite princes stayed with him.

⁹God came to Balaam and asked, "Who are these men with you?"

¹⁰Balaam said to God, "Balak son of Zippor, king of Moab, sent me this message: ¹¹'A people that has come out of Egypt covers the face of the land. Now come and put a curse on them for me. Perhaps then I will be able to fight them and drive them away.'"

¹²But God said to Balaam, "Do not go with them. You must not put a curse on those people, because they are blessed."

¹³The next morning Balaam got up and said to Balak's princes, "Go back to your own country, for the LORD has refused to let me go with you."

¹⁴So the Moabite princes returned to Balak and said, "Balaam refused to come with us."

¹⁵Then Balak sent other princes, more numerous and more distinguished than the first. ¹⁶They came to Balaam and said:

"This is what Balak son of Zippor says: Do not let anything keep you from coming to me, ¹⁷because I will reward you handsomely and do whatever you say. Come and put a curse on these people for me."

¹⁸But Balaam answered them, "Even if Balak gave me his palace filled with silver and gold, I could not do anything great or small to go beyond the command of the LORD my God. ¹⁹Now stay here tonight as the others did, and I will find out what else the LORD will tell me."

²⁰That night God came to Balaam and said, "Since these men have come to summon you, go with them, but do only what I tell you."

Balaam's Donkey

²¹Balaam got up in the morning, saddled his donkey and went with the princes of Moab. ²²But God was very angry when he went, and the angel of the LORD stood in the road to oppose him. Balaam was riding on his donkey, and his two servants were with him. ²³When the donkey saw the angel of the LORD standing in the road with a drawn sword in his hand, she turned off the road into a field. Balaam beat her to get her back on the road.

²⁴Then the angel of the LORD stood in a narrow path between two vineyards, with walls on both sides. ²⁵When the donkey saw the angel of the LORD, she pressed close to the wall, crushing Balaam's foot against it. So he beat her again.

²⁶Then the angel of the LORD moved on ahead and stood in a narrow place where there was no room to turn, either to the right or to the left. ²⁷When the donkey saw the angel of the LORD, she lay down under Balaam, and he was angry and beat her with his staff. ²⁸Then the LORD opened the donkey's mouth, and she said to Balaam, "What have I done to you to make you beat me these three times?"

²⁹Balaam answered the donkey, "You have made a fool of me! If I had a sword in my hand, I would kill you right now."

³⁰The donkey said to Balaam, "Am I not your own donkey, which you have always ridden, to this day? Have I been in the habit of doing this to you?"

"No," he said.

³¹Then the LORD opened Balaam's eyes, and he saw the angel of the LORD standing in the road with his sword drawn. So he bowed low and fell facedown.

³²The angel of the LORD asked him, "Why have you beaten your donkey these three times? I have come here to oppose you because your path is a reckless one before me.ᵃ ³³The donkey saw me and turned away from me these three times. If she had not turned away, I would certainly have killed you by now, but I would have spared her."

³⁴Balaam said to the angel of the LORD, "I have sinned. I did not realize you were standing in the road to oppose me. Now if you are displeased, I will go back."

³⁵The angel of the LORD said to Balaam, "Go

ᵃ 32 The meaning of the Hebrew for this clause is uncertain.

with the men, but speak only what I tell you." So Balaam went with the princes of Balak.

³⁶ When Balak heard that Balaam was coming, he went out to meet him at the Moabite town on the Arnon border, at the edge of his territory. ³⁷ Balak said to Balaam, "Did I not send you an urgent summons? Why didn't you come to me? Am I really not able to reward you?"

³⁸ "Well, I have come to you now," Balaam replied. "But can I say just anything? I must speak only what God puts in my mouth."

³⁹ Then Balaam went with Balak to Kiriath Huzoth. ⁴⁰ Balak sacrificed cattle and sheep, and gave some to Balaam and the princes who were with him. ⁴¹ The next morning Balak took Balaam up to Bamoth Baal, and from there he saw part of the people.

Balaam's First Oracle

23 Balaam said, "Build me seven altars here, and prepare seven bulls and seven rams for me." ² Balak did as Balaam said, and the two of them offered a bull and a ram on each altar.

³ Then Balaam said to Balak, "Stay here beside your offering while I go aside. Perhaps the LORD will come to meet with me. Whatever he reveals to me I will tell you." Then he went off to a barren height.

⁴ God met with him, and Balaam said, "I have prepared seven altars, and on each altar I have offered a bull and a ram."

⁵ The LORD put a message in Balaam's mouth and said, "Go back to Balak and give him this message."

⁶ So he went back to him and found him standing beside his offering, with all the princes of Moab. ⁷ Then Balaam uttered his oracle:

"Balak brought me from Aram,
　the king of Moab from the eastern
　　mountains.
'Come,' he said, 'curse Jacob for me;
　come, denounce Israel.'
⁸ How can I curse
　those whom God has not cursed?

How can I denounce
　those whom the LORD has not denounced?
⁹ From the rocky peaks I see them,
　from the heights I view them.
I see a people who live apart
　and do not consider themselves one of the
　　nations.
¹⁰ Who can count the dust of Jacob
　or number the fourth part of Israel?
Let me die the death of the righteous,
　and may my end be like theirs!"

¹¹ Balak said to Balaam, "What have you done to me? I brought you to curse my enemies, but you have done nothing but bless them!"

¹² He answered, "Must I not speak what the LORD puts in my mouth?"

Balaam's Second Oracle

¹³ Then Balak said to him, "Come with me to another place where you can see them; you will see only a part but not all of them. And from there, curse them for me." ¹⁴ So he took him to the field of Zophim on the top of Pisgah, and there he built seven altars and offered a bull and a ram on each altar.

¹⁵ Balaam said to Balak, "Stay here beside your offering while I meet with him over there."

¹⁶ The LORD met with Balaam and put a message in his mouth and said, "Go back to Balak and give him this message."

¹⁷ So he went to him and found him standing beside his offering, with the princes of Moab. Balak asked him, "What did the LORD say?"

¹⁸ Then he uttered his oracle:

"Arise, Balak, and listen;
　hear me, son of Zippor.
¹⁹ God is not a man, that he should lie,
　nor a son of man, that he should change
　　his mind.
Does he speak and then not act?
　Does he promise and not fulfill?
²⁰ I have received a command to bless;
　he has blessed, and I cannot change it.

> "GOD IS NOT A MAN, THAT HE
> SHOULD LIE, NOR A SON OF
> MAN, THAT HE SHOULD CHANGE
> HIS MIND. DOES HE SPEAK
> AND THEN NOT ACT? DOES HE
> PROMISE AND NOT FULFILL?"
>
> *Numbers 23:19*

God Is Faithful to Bring Me Through

DAWN SCOTT JONES

READ | NUMBERS 23:13 – 26

I took a deep breath and composed myself. The hospital door rolled open, and I saw my daughter, Lisa, inside. Our eyes met and locked. I hoped she wouldn't notice my legs shaking beneath my coat.

"The doctor thinks Alexia has a tumor in her leg." Her words seemed surreal; fear clutched my throat.

"When will we know?" I tried to sound calm, but the tears in my eyes betrayed me.

"Not soon enough," she whispered.

When faced with difficulties, I have always clung to the promise that God walks with me through every trial. In each circumstance, God has proven that he can be trusted and that he is faithful to bring me though every storm.

But would God's grace be enough this time? In spite of his continual faithfulness, I wavered.

It can happen in a moment. That unexpected call, a tragedy or sudden storm that rocks our world and shakes us to the core. God allows a test to come into our life, and we wonder if we can endure it. But God's Word is true. His grace is sufficient! His love is enough! His arm is strong enough to sustain us and lift us up. When we reach for him, we will find his grace reaching back. God promises that his strong arm will uphold us, and he always fulfills his promises.

We hugged with tears of joy as the doctor informed us that my granddaughter was perfect—no tumors.

I finally exhaled, "Thank you, Jesus."

Heavenly Father, you are strong and mighty to save. I trust your ability to sustain me in all of life's circumstances. I turn my eyes upon you and believe that you will enable me to endure and that you will be with me through every storm. Amen.

Your next devotion is located on page 221.

GRANDCHILD IN FOCUS · PRAYER

Relationships at Home

O Lord, I pray that you will bless the home and family of my grandchild. May the relationships she has with her parents and siblings enhance her well-being, support her self-confidence and increase her faith. May her home life reflect your love, your grace, your compassion and your peace. Guide her parents to direct her in love and truth, so she will grow into a strong and compassionate individual. Amen.

21 "No misfortune is seen in Jacob,
  no misery observed in Israel.*
The LORD their God is with them;
  the shout of the King is among them.
22 God brought them out of Egypt;
  they have the strength of a wild ox.
23 There is no sorcery against Jacob,
  no divination against Israel.
It will now be said of Jacob
  and of Israel, 'See what God has done!'
24 The people rise like a lioness;
  they rouse themselves like a lion
that does not rest till he devours his prey
  and drinks the blood of his victims."

25 Then Balak said to Balaam, "Neither curse them at all nor bless them at all!"

26 Balaam answered, "Did I not tell you I must do whatever the LORD says?"

Balaam's Third Oracle

27 Then Balak said to Balaam, "Come, let me take you to another place. Perhaps it will please God to let you curse them for me from there." 28 And Balak took Balaam to the top of Peor, overlooking the wasteland.

29 Balaam said, "Build me seven altars here, and prepare seven bulls and seven rams for me." 30 Balak did as Balaam had said, and offered a bull and a ram on each altar.

24 Now when Balaam saw that it pleased the LORD to bless Israel, he did not resort to sorcery as at other times, but turned his face toward the desert. 2 When Balaam looked out and saw Israel encamped tribe by tribe, the Spirit of God came upon him 3 and he uttered his oracle:

"The oracle of Balaam son of Beor,
  the oracle of one whose eye sees clearly,
4 the oracle of one who hears the words of God,
  who sees a vision from the Almighty,*
  who falls prostrate, and whose eyes are
    opened:

5 "How beautiful are your tents, O Jacob,
  your dwelling places, O Israel!

6 "Like valleys they spread out,
  like gardens beside a river,
like aloes planted by the LORD,
  like cedars beside the waters.
7 Water will flow from their buckets;
  their seed will have abundant water.

"Their king will be greater than Agag;
  their kingdom will be exalted.

8 "God brought them out of Egypt;
  they have the strength of a wild ox.
They devour hostile nations
  and break their bones in pieces;
  with their arrows they pierce them.
9 Like a lion they crouch and lie down,
  like a lioness—who dares to rouse them?

"May those who bless you be blessed
  and those who curse you be cursed!"

10 Then Balak's anger burned against Balaam. He struck his hands together and said to him, "I summoned you to curse my enemies, but you have blessed them these three times. 11 Now leave at once and go home! I said I would reward you handsomely, but the LORD has kept you from being rewarded."

12 Balaam answered Balak, "Did I not tell the messengers you sent me, 13 'Even if Balak gave me his palace filled with silver and gold, I could not do anything of my own accord, good or bad, to go beyond the command of the LORD—and I must say only what the LORD says'? 14 Now I am going back to my people, but come, let me warn you of what this people will do to your people in days to come."

Balaam's Fourth Oracle

15 Then he uttered his oracle:

"The oracle of Balaam son of Beor,
  the oracle of one whose eye sees clearly,
16 the oracle of one who hears the words of
    God,
  who has knowledge from the Most High,

---

a 21 Or He has not looked on Jacob's offenses / or on the wrongs found in Israel. b 4 Hebrew Shaddai; also in verse 16

who sees a vision from the Almighty,
who falls prostrate, and whose eyes are
opened:

¹⁷"I see him, but not now;
I behold him, but not near.
A star will come out of Jacob;
a scepter will rise out of Israel.
He will crush the foreheads of Moab,
the skulls [a] of [b] all the sons of Sheth. [c]
¹⁸Edom will be conquered;
Seir, his enemy, will be conquered,
but Israel will grow strong.
¹⁹A ruler will come out of Jacob
and destroy the survivors of the city."

Balaam's Final Oracles

²⁰Then Balaam saw Amalek and uttered his oracle:

"Amalek was first among the nations,
but he will come to ruin at last."

²¹Then he saw the Kenites and uttered his oracle:

"Your dwelling place is secure,
your nest is set in a rock;
²²yet you Kenites will be destroyed
when Asshur takes you captive."

²³Then he uttered his oracle:

"Ah, who can live when God does this? [d]
²⁴   Ships will come from the shores of Kittim;
they will subdue Asshur and Eber,
but they too will come to ruin."

²⁵Then Balaam got up and returned home and Balak went his own way.

Moab Seduces Israel

25 While Israel was staying in Shittim, the men began to indulge in sexual immorality with Moabite women, ²who invited them to the sacrifices to their gods. The people ate and bowed down before these gods. ³So Israel joined in worshiping the Baal of Peor. And the LORD's anger burned against them.

⁴The LORD said to Moses, "Take all the leaders of these people, kill them and expose them in broad daylight before the LORD, so that the LORD's fierce anger may turn away from Israel."

⁵So Moses said to Israel's judges, "Each of you must put to death those of your men who have joined in worshiping the Baal of Peor."

⁶Then an Israelite man brought to his family a Midianite woman right before the eyes of Moses and the whole assembly of Israel while they were weeping at the entrance to the Tent of Meeting. ⁷When Phinehas son of Eleazar, the son of Aaron, the priest, saw this, he left the assembly, took a spear in his hand ⁸and followed the Israelite into the tent. He drove the spear through both of them—through the Israelite and into the woman's body. Then the plague against the Israelites was stopped; ⁹but those who died in the plague numbered 24,000.

¹⁰The LORD said to Moses, ¹¹"Phinehas son of Eleazar, the son of Aaron, the priest, has turned my anger away from the Israelites; for he was as zealous as I am for my honor among them, so that in my zeal I did not put an end to them. ¹²Therefore tell him I am making my covenant of peace with him. ¹³He and his descendants will have a covenant of a lasting priesthood, because he was zealous for the honor of his God and made atonement for the Israelites."

¹⁴The name of the Israelite who was killed with the Midianite woman was Zimri son of Salu, the leader of a Simeonite family. ¹⁵And the name of the Midianite woman who was put to death was Cozbi daughter of Zur, a tribal chief of a Midianite family.

¹⁶The LORD said to Moses, ¹⁷"Treat the Midianites as enemies and kill them, ¹⁸because they treated you as enemies when they deceived you in the affair of Peor and their sister Cozbi, the daughter of a Midianite leader, the woman who was killed when the plague came as a result of Peor."

---

[a] 17 Samaritan Pentateuch (see also Jer. 48:45); the meaning of the word in the Masoretic Text is uncertain.   [b] 17 Or possibly Moab, / batter   [c] 17 Or all the noisy boasters   [d] 23 Masoretic Text; with a different word division of the Hebrew A people will gather from the north.

The Second Census

26 After the plague the LORD said to Moses and Eleazar son of Aaron, the priest, ²"Take a census of the whole Israelite community by families—all those twenty years old or more who are able to serve in the army of Israel." ³So on the plains of Moab by the Jordan across from Jericho,ᵃ Moses and Eleazar the priest spoke with them and said, ⁴"Take a census of the men twenty years old or more, as the LORD commanded Moses."

These were the Israelites who came out of Egypt:

⁵The descendants of Reuben, the firstborn son of Israel, were:

through Hanoch, the Hanochite clan;

through Pallu, the Palluite clan;

⁶through Hezron, the Hezronite clan;

through Carmi, the Carmite clan.

⁷These were the clans of Reuben; those numbered were 43,730.

⁸The son of Pallu was Eliab, ⁹and the sons of Eliab were Nemuel, Dathan and Abiram. The same Dathan and Abiram were the community officials who rebelled against Moses and Aaron and were among Korah's followers when they rebelled against the LORD. ¹⁰The earth opened its mouth and swallowed them along with Korah, whose followers died when the fire devoured the 250 men. And they served as a warning sign. ¹¹The line of Korah, however, did not die out.

¹²The descendants of Simeon by their clans were:

through Nemuel, the Nemuelite clan;

through Jamin, the Jaminite clan;

through Jakin, the Jakinite clan;

¹³through Zerah, the Zerahite clan;

through Shaul, the Shaulite clan.

¹⁴These were the clans of Simeon; there were 22,200 men.

¹⁵The descendants of Gad by their clans were:

through Zephon, the Zephonite clan;

through Haggi, the Haggite clan;

through Shuni, the Shunite clan;

¹⁶through Ozni, the Oznite clan;

through Eri, the Erite clan;

¹⁷through Arodi,ᵇ the Arodite clan;

through Areli, the Arelite clan.

¹⁸These were the clans of Gad; those numbered were 40,500.

¹⁹Er and Onan were sons of Judah, but they died in Canaan.

²⁰The descendants of Judah by their clans were:

through Shelah, the Shelanite clan;

through Perez, the Perezite clan;

through Zerah, the Zerahite clan.

²¹The descendants of Perez were:

through Hezron, the Hezronite clan;

through Hamul, the Hamulite clan.

²²These were the clans of Judah; those numbered were 76,500.

²³The descendants of Issachar by their clans were:

through Tola, the Tolaite clan;

through Puah, the Puiteᶜ clan;

²⁴through Jashub, the Jashubite clan;

through Shimron, the Shimronite clan.

²⁵These were the clans of Issachar; those numbered were 64,300.

²⁶The descendants of Zebulun by their clans were:

through Sered, the Seredite clan;

through Elon, the Elonite clan;

through Jahleel, the Jahleelite clan.

²⁷These were the clans of Zebulun; those numbered were 60,500.

²⁸The descendants of Joseph by their clans through Manasseh and Ephraim were:

²⁹The descendants of Manasseh:

through Makir, the Makirite clan (Makir was the father of Gilead);

through Gilead, the Gileadite clan.

ᵃ 3 Hebrew *Jordan of Jericho*; possibly an ancient name for the Jordan River; also in verse 63   ᵇ 17 Samaritan Pentateuch and Syriac (see also Gen. 46:16); Masoretic Text *Arod*   ᶜ 23 Samaritan Pentateuch, Septuagint, Vulgate and Syriac (see also 1 Chron. 7:1); Masoretic Text *through Puvah, the Punite*

30 These were the descendants of Gilead:

through Iezer, the Iezerite clan;

through Helek, the Helekite clan;

31 through Asriel, the Asrielite clan;

through Shechem, the Shechemite clan;

32 through Shemida, the Shemidaite clan;

through Hepher, the Hepherite clan.

33 (Zelophehad son of Hepher had no sons; he had only daughters, whose names were Mahlah, Noah, Hoglah, Milcah and Tirzah.)

34 These were the clans of Manasseh; those numbered were 52,700.

35 These were the descendants of Ephraim by their clans:

through Shuthelah, the Shuthelahite clan;

through Beker, the Bekerite clan;

through Tahan, the Tahanite clan.

36 These were the descendants of Shuthelah:

through Eran, the Eranite clan.

37 These were the clans of Ephraim; those numbered were 32,500.

These were the descendants of Joseph by their clans.

38 The descendants of Benjamin by their clans were:

through Bela, the Belaite clan;

through Ashbel, the Ashbelite clan;

through Ahiram, the Ahiramite clan;

39 through Shupham,[a] the Shuphamite clan;

through Hupham, the Huphamite clan.

40 The descendants of Bela through Ard and Naaman were:

through Ard,[b] the Ardite clan;

through Naaman, the Naamite clan.

41 These were the clans of Benjamin; those numbered were 45,600.

42 These were the descendants of Dan by their clans:

through Shuham, the Shuhamite clan.

These were the clans of Dan: 43 All of them were Shuhamite clans; and those numbered were 64,400.

44 The descendants of Asher by their clans were:

through Imnah, the Imnite clan;

through Ishvi, the Ishvite clan;

through Beriah, the Beriite clan;

45 and through the descendants of Beriah:

through Heber, the Heberite clan;

through Malkiel, the Malkielite clan.

46 (Asher had a daughter named Serah.)

47 These were the clans of Asher; those numbered were 53,400.

48 The descendants of Naphtali by their clans were:

through Jahzeel, the Jahzeelite clan;

through Guni, the Gunite clan;

49 through Jezer, the Jezerite clan;

through Shillem, the Shillemite clan.

50 These were the clans of Naphtali; those numbered were 45,400.

51 The total number of the men of Israel was 601,730.

52 The LORD said to Moses, 53 "The land is to be allotted to them as an inheritance based on the number of names. 54 To a larger group give a larger inheritance, and to a smaller group a smaller one; each is to receive its inheritance according to the number of those listed. 55 Be sure that the land is distributed by lot. What each group inherits will be according to the names for its ancestral tribe. 56 Each inheritance is to be distributed by lot among the larger and smaller groups."

57 These were the Levites who were counted by their clans:

through Gershon, the Gershonite clan;

through Kohath, the Kohathite clan;

through Merari, the Merarite clan.

58 These also were Levite clans:

the Libnite clan,

the Hebronite clan,

the Mahlite clan,

---

a 39 A few manuscripts of the Masoretic Text, Samaritan Pentateuch, Vulgate and Syriac (see also Septuagint); most manuscripts of the Masoretic Text *Shephupham*   b 40 Samaritan Pentateuch and Vulgate (see also Septuagint); Masoretic Text does not have *through Ard*.

the Mushite clan,
the Korahite clan.

(Kohath was the forefather of Amram; [59] the name of Amram's wife was Jochebed, a descendant of Levi, who was born to the Levites[a] in Egypt. To Amram she bore Aaron, Moses and their sister Miriam. [60] Aaron was the father of Nadab and Abihu, Eleazar and Ithamar. [61] But Nadab and Abihu died when they made an offering before the LORD with unauthorized fire.)

[62] All the male Levites a month old or more numbered 23,000. They were not counted along with the other Israelites because they received no inheritance among them.

[63] These are the ones counted by Moses and Eleazar the priest when they counted the Israelites on the plains of Moab by the Jordan across from Jericho. [64] Not one of them was among those counted by Moses and Aaron the priest when they counted the Israelites in the Desert of Sinai. [65] For the LORD had told those Israelites they would surely die in the desert, and not one of them was left except Caleb son of Jephunneh and Joshua son of Nun.

Zelophehad's Daughters

27:1–11pp — Nu 36:1–12

27 The daughters of Zelophehad son of Hepher, the son of Gilead, the son of Makir, the son of Manasseh, belonged to the clans of Manasseh son of Joseph. The names of the daughters were Mahlah, Noah, Hoglah, Milcah and Tirzah. They approached [2] the entrance to the Tent of Meeting and stood before Moses, Eleazar the priest, the leaders and the whole assembly, and said, [3] "Our father died in the desert. He was not among Korah's followers, who banded together against the LORD, but he died for his own sin and left no sons. [4] Why should our father's name disappear from his clan because he had no son? Give us property among our father's relatives."

[5] So Moses brought their case before the LORD [6] and the LORD said to him, [7] "What Zelophehad's daughters are saying is right. You must certainly give them property as an inheritance among their father's relatives and turn their father's inheritance over to them.

[8] "Say to the Israelites, 'If a man dies and leaves no son, turn his inheritance over to his daughter. [9] If he has no daughter, give his inheritance to his brothers. [10] If he has no brothers, give his inheritance to his father's brothers. [11] If his father had no brothers, give his inheritance to the nearest relative in his clan, that he may possess it. This is to be a legal requirement for the Israelites, as the LORD commanded Moses.'"

Joshua to Succeed Moses

[12] Then the LORD said to Moses, "Go up this mountain in the Abarim range and see the land I have given the Israelites. [13] After you have seen it, you too will be gathered to your people, as your brother Aaron was, [14] for when the community rebelled at the waters in the Desert of Zin, both of you disobeyed my command to honor me as holy before their eyes." (These were the waters of Meribah Kadesh, in the Desert of Zin.)

[15] Moses said to the LORD, [16] "May the LORD, the God of the spirits of all mankind, appoint a man over this community [17] to go out and come in before them, one who will lead them out and bring them in, so the LORD's people will not be like sheep without a shepherd."

[18] So the LORD said to Moses, "Take Joshua son of Nun, a man in whom is the spirit,[b] and lay your hand on him. [19] Have him stand before Eleazar the priest and the entire assembly and commission him in their presence. [20] Give him some of your authority so the whole Israelite community will obey him. [21] He is to stand before Eleazar the priest, who will obtain decisions for him by inquiring of the Urim before the LORD. At his command he and the entire community of the Israelites will go out, and at his command they will come in."

[22] Moses did as the LORD commanded him. He took Joshua and had him stand before Eleazar

---

[a] 59 Or *Jochebed, a daughter of Levi, who was born to Levi*
[b] 18 Or *Spirit*

the priest and the whole assembly. 23 Then he laid his hands on him and commissioned him, as the LORD instructed through Moses.

Daily Offerings

28 The LORD said to Moses, 2 "Give this command to the Israelites and say to them: 'See that you present to me at the appointed time the food for my offerings made by fire, as an aroma pleasing to me.' 3 Say to them: 'This is the offering made by fire that you are to present to the LORD: two lambs a year old without defect, as a regular burnt offering each day. 4 Prepare one lamb in the morning and the other at twilight, 5 together with a grain offering of a tenth of an ephah *a* of fine flour mixed with a quarter of a hin *b* of oil from pressed olives. 6 This is the regular burnt offering instituted at Mount Sinai as a pleasing aroma, an offering made to the LORD by fire. 7 The accompanying drink offering is to be a quarter of a hin of fermented drink with each lamb. Pour out the drink offering to the LORD at the sanctuary. 8 Prepare the second lamb at twilight, along with the same kind of grain offering and drink offering that you prepare in the morning. This is an offering made by fire, an aroma pleasing to the LORD.

Sabbath Offerings

9 " 'On the Sabbath day, make an offering of two lambs a year old without defect, together with its drink offering and a grain offering of two-tenths of an ephah *c* of fine flour mixed with oil. 10 This is the burnt offering for every Sabbath, in addition to the regular burnt offering and its drink offering.

Monthly Offerings

11 " 'On the first of every month, present to the LORD a burnt offering of two young bulls, one ram and seven male lambs a year old, all without defect. 12 With each bull there is to be a grain offering of three-tenths of an ephah *d* of fine flour mixed with oil; with the ram, a grain offering of two-tenths of an ephah of fine flour mixed with oil; 13 and with each lamb, a grain offering of a tenth of an ephah of fine flour mixed with oil. This is for a burnt offering, a pleasing aroma, an offering made to the LORD by fire. 14 With each bull there is to be a drink offering of half a hin *e* of wine; with the ram, a third of a hin *f*; and with each lamb, a quarter of a hin. This is the monthly burnt offering to be made at each new moon during the year. 15 Besides the regular burnt offering with its drink offering, one male goat is to be presented to the LORD as a sin offering.

The Passover

28:16–25pp — Ex 12:14–20; Lev 23:4–8; Dt 16:1–8

16 " 'On the fourteenth day of the first month the LORD's Passover is to be held. 17 On the fifteenth day of this month there is to be a festival; for seven days eat bread made without yeast. 18 On the first day hold a sacred assembly and do no regular work. 19 Present to the LORD an offering made by fire, a burnt offering of two young bulls, one ram and seven male lambs a year old, all without defect. 20 With each bull prepare a grain offering of three-tenths of an ephah of fine flour mixed with oil; with the ram, two-tenths; 21 and with each of the seven lambs, one-tenth. 22 Include one male goat as a sin offering to make atonement for you. 23 Prepare these in addition to the regular morning burnt offering. 24 In this way prepare the food for the offering made by fire every day for seven days as an aroma pleasing to the LORD; it is to be prepared in addition to the regular burnt offering and its drink offering. 25 On the seventh day hold a sacred assembly and do no regular work.

Feast of Weeks

28:26–31pp — Lev 23:15–22; Dt 16:9–12

26 " 'On the day of firstfruits, when you present to the LORD an offering of new grain during the Feast of Weeks, hold a sacred assembly and do

a 5 That is, probably about 2 quarts (about 2 liters); also in verses 13, 21 and 29   *b 5* That is, probably about 1 quart (about 1 liter); also in verses 7 and 14   *c 9* That is, probably about 4 quarts (about 4.5 liters); also in verses 12, 20 and 28   *d 12* That is, probably about 6 quarts (about 6.5 liters); also in verses 20 and 28   *e 14* That is, probably about 2 quarts (about 2 liters)   *f 14* That is, probably about 1 1/4 quarts (about 1.2 liters)

FAITH IN
ACTION

Celebrate Diversity

Help your grandkids understand the Biblical teaching that we are "all one in Christ Jesus" (Galatians 3:28) by hosting an "international" gathering. Have two or more grandchildren invite a friend over for a casual get-together or dinner. Ask each guest to bring a dish representing their country or their family history, or if you think it would be too much for them, cook or buy ethnic food yourself.

Ask if anyone would like to dress in clothing that represents their heritage. Display any artwork or other special items important to the heritage of each child. Select some music from your guests' various traditions. Make sure that you participate and that your guests are made to feel special.

You might also want to ask people from your church or community to join you. Use your imagination to celebrate diversity. Discuss how people can be different yet all one in Christ. You may find this experience so enriching that you make it a family tradition.

Long-Distance Variation: Ask your grandchildren to interview friends from different cultural/ethnic backgrounds and report their discoveries about how their friends live or fascinating facts about their background.

Creator God, help me and my grandkids to value the variety of life all around us. Help us to have an appreciation for the unique perspective of friends and neighbors who are culturally different from us. We praise you for the variety of cultures and traditions around us. Amen.

Your next devotion is located on page 228.

GRANDCHILD IN FOCUS • PRAYER

Friends

Dear Lord and Father, I pray for my grandchild's social life and his friends. Bring diverse friends into his life who will love and encourage him, who will bring joy and laughter to the good times and comfort and support through difficulties and disappointments. Grant him wisdom and discernment as he selects his friends; help him to avoid cliques that restrict, activities that endanger, and foolish and dangerous behaviors that harm. I ask that you fill his life with close and caring relationships. Amen.

no regular work. [27] Present a burnt offering of two young bulls, one ram and seven male lambs a year old as an aroma pleasing to the LORD. [28] With each bull there is to be a grain offering of three-tenths of an ephah of fine flour mixed with oil; with the ram, two-tenths; [29] and with each of the seven lambs, one-tenth. [30] Include one male goat to make atonement for you. [31] Prepare these together with their drink offerings, in addition to the regular burnt offering and its grain offering. Be sure the animals are without defect.

Feast of Trumpets

29:1–6pp — Lev 23:23–25

29 " 'On the first day of the seventh month hold a sacred assembly and do no regular work. It is a day for you to sound the trumpets. [2] As an aroma pleasing to the LORD, prepare a burnt offering of one young bull, one ram and seven male lambs a year old, all without defect. [3] With the bull prepare a grain offering of three-tenths of an ephah [a] of fine flour mixed with oil; with the ram, two-tenths [b]; [4] and with each of the seven lambs, one-tenth. [c] [5] Include one male goat as a sin offering to make atonement for you. [6] These are in addition to the monthly and daily burnt offerings with their grain offerings and drink offerings as specified. They are offerings made to the LORD by fire — a pleasing aroma.

Day of Atonement

29:7–11pp — Lev 16:2–34: 23:26–32

[7] " 'On the tenth day of this seventh month hold a sacred assembly. You must deny yourselves [d] and do no work. [8] Present as an aroma pleasing to the LORD a burnt offering of one young bull, one ram and seven male lambs a year old, all without defect. [9] With the bull prepare a grain offering of three-tenths of an ephah of fine flour mixed with oil; with the ram, two-tenths; [10] and with each of the seven lambs, one-tenth. [11] Include one male goat as a sin offering, in addition to the sin offering for atonement and the regular burnt offering with its grain offering, and their drink offerings.

Feast of Tabernacles

29:12–39pp — Lev 23:33–43; Dt 16:13–17

[12] " 'On the fifteenth day of the seventh month, hold a sacred assembly and do no regular work. Celebrate a festival to the LORD for seven days. [13] Present an offering made by fire as an aroma pleasing to the LORD, a burnt offering of thirteen young bulls, two rams and fourteen male lambs a year old, all without defect. [14] With each of the thirteen bulls prepare a grain offering of three-tenths of an ephah of fine flour mixed with oil; with each of the two rams, two-tenths; [15] and with each of the fourteen lambs, one-tenth. [16] Include one male goat as a sin offering, in addition to the regular burnt offering with its grain offering and drink offering.

[17] " 'On the second day prepare twelve young bulls, two rams and fourteen male lambs a year old, all without defect. [18] With the bulls, rams and lambs, prepare their grain offerings and drink offerings according to the number specified. [19] Include one male goat as a sin offering, in addition to the regular burnt offering with its grain offering, and their drink offerings.

[20] " 'On the third day prepare eleven bulls, two rams and fourteen male lambs a year old, all without defect. [21] With the bulls, rams and lambs, prepare their grain offerings and drink offerings according to the number specified. [22] Include one male goat as a sin offering, in addition to the regular burnt offering with its grain offering and drink offering.

[23] " 'On the fourth day prepare ten bulls, two rams and fourteen male lambs a year old, all without defect. [24] With the bulls, rams and lambs, prepare their grain offerings and drink offerings according to the number specified. [25] Include one male goat as a sin offering, in addition to the regular burnt offering with its grain offering and drink offering.

[26] " 'On the fifth day prepare nine bulls, two

---

[a] 3 That is, probably about 6 quarts (about 6.5 liters); also in verses 9 and 14   [b] 3 That is, probably about 4 quarts (about 4.5 liters); also in verses 9 and 14   [c] 4 That is, probably about 2 quarts (about 2 liters); also in verses 10 and 15   [d] 7 Or *must fast*

rams and fourteen male lambs a year old, all without defect. ²⁷ With the bulls, rams and lambs, prepare their grain offerings and drink offerings according to the number specified. ²⁸ Include one male goat as a sin offering, in addition to the regular burnt offering with its grain offering and drink offering.

²⁹ " 'On the sixth day prepare eight bulls, two rams and fourteen male lambs a year old, all without defect. ³⁰ With the bulls, rams and lambs, prepare their grain offerings and drink offerings according to the number specified. ³¹ Include one male goat as a sin offering, in addition to the regular burnt offering with its grain offering and drink offering.

³² " 'On the seventh day prepare seven bulls, two rams and fourteen male lambs a year old, all without defect. ³³ With the bulls, rams and lambs, prepare their grain offerings and drink offerings according to the number specified. ³⁴ Include one male goat as a sin offering, in addition to the regular burnt offering with its grain offering and drink offering.

³⁵ " 'On the eighth day hold an assembly and do no regular work. ³⁶ Present an offering made by fire as an aroma pleasing to the LORD, a burnt offering of one bull, one ram and seven male lambs a year old, all without defect. ³⁷ With the bull, the ram and the lambs, prepare their grain offerings and drink offerings according to the number specified. ³⁸ Include one male goat as a sin offering, in addition to the regular burnt offering with its grain offering and drink offering.

³⁹ " 'In addition to what you vow and your freewill offerings, prepare these for the LORD at your appointed feasts: your burnt offerings, grain offerings, drink offerings and fellowship offerings.*' "

⁴⁰ Moses told the Israelites all that the LORD commanded him.

Vows

30 Moses said to the heads of the tribes of Israel: "This is what the LORD commands: ²When a man makes a vow to the LORD or takes an oath to obligate himself by a pledge, he must not break his word but must do everything he said.

³ "When a young woman still living in her father's house makes a vow to the LORD or obligates herself by a pledge ⁴ and her father hears about her vow or pledge but says nothing to her, then all her vows and every pledge by which she obligated herself will stand. ⁵ But if her father forbids her when he hears about it, none of her vows or the pledges by which she obligated herself will stand; the LORD will release her because her father has forbidden her.

⁶ "If she marries after she makes a vow or after her lips utter a rash promise by which she obligates herself ⁷ and her husband hears about it but says nothing to her, then her vows or the pledges by which she obligated herself will stand. ⁸ But if her husband forbids her when he hears about it, he nullifies the vow that obligates her or the rash promise by which she obligates herself, and the LORD will release her.

⁹ "Any vow or obligation taken by a widow or divorced woman will be binding on her.

¹⁰ "If a woman living with her husband makes a vow or obligates herself by a pledge under oath ¹¹ and her husband hears about it but says nothing to her and does not forbid her, then all her vows or the pledges by which she obligated herself will stand. ¹² But if her husband nullifies them when he hears about them, then none of the vows or pledges that came from her lips will stand. Her husband has nullified them, and the LORD will release her. ¹³ Her husband may confirm or nullify any vow she makes or any sworn pledge to deny herself. ¹⁴ But if her husband says nothing to her about it from day to day, then he confirms all her vows or the pledges binding on her. He confirms them by saying nothing to her when he hears about them. ¹⁵ If, however, he nullifies them some time after he hears about them, then he is responsible for her guilt."

¹⁶ These are the regulations the LORD gave Moses concerning relationships between a man

ᵃ 39 Traditionally peace offerings

and his wife, and between a father and his young daughter still living in his house.

Vengeance on the Midianites

31 The LORD said to Moses, ² "Take vengeance on the Midianites for the Israelites. After that, you will be gathered to your people."

³ So Moses said to the people, "Arm some of your men to go to war against the Midianites and to carry out the LORD's vengeance on them. ⁴ Send into battle a thousand men from each of the tribes of Israel." ⁵ So twelve thousand men armed for battle, a thousand from each tribe, were supplied from the clans of Israel. ⁶ Moses sent them into battle, a thousand from each tribe, along with Phinehas son of Eleazar, the priest, who took with him articles from the sanctuary and the trumpets for signaling.

⁷ They fought against Midian, as the LORD commanded Moses, and killed every man. ⁸ Among their victims were Evi, Rekem, Zur, Hur and Reba — the five kings of Midian. They also killed Balaam son of Beor with the sword. ⁹ The Israelites captured the Midianite women and children and took all the Midianite herds, flocks and goods as plunder. ¹⁰ They burned all the towns where the Midianites had settled, as well as all their camps. ¹¹ They took all the plunder and spoils, including the people and animals, ¹² and brought the captives, spoils and plunder to Moses and Eleazar the priest and the Israelite assembly at their camp on the plains of Moab, by the Jordan across from Jericho.ᵃ

¹³ Moses, Eleazar the priest and all the leaders of the community went to meet them outside the camp. ¹⁴ Moses was angry with the officers of the army — the commanders of thousands and commanders of hundreds — who returned from the battle.

¹⁵ "Have you allowed all the women to live?" he asked them. ¹⁶ "They were the ones who followed Balaam's advice and were the means of turning the Israelites away from the LORD in what happened at Peor, so that a plague struck the LORD's people. ¹⁷ Now kill all the boys. And kill every woman who has slept with a man, ¹⁸ but save for yourselves every girl who has never slept with a man.

¹⁹ "All of you who have killed anyone or touched anyone who was killed must stay outside the camp seven days. On the third and seventh days you must purify yourselves and your captives. ²⁰ Purify every garment as well as everything made of leather, goat hair or wood."

²¹ Then Eleazar the priest said to the soldiers who had gone into battle, "This is the requirement of the law that the LORD gave Moses: ²² Gold, silver, bronze, iron, tin, lead ²³ and anything else that can withstand fire must be put through the fire, and then it will be clean. But it must also be purified with the water of cleansing. And whatever cannot withstand fire must be put through that water. ²⁴ On the seventh day wash your clothes and you will be clean. Then you may come into the camp."

Dividing the Spoils

²⁵ The LORD said to Moses, ²⁶ "You and Eleazar the priest and the family heads of the community are to count all the people and animals that were captured. ²⁷ Divide the spoils between the soldiers who took part in the battle and the rest of the community. ²⁸ From the soldiers who fought in the battle, set apart as tribute for the LORD one out of every five hundred, whether persons, cattle, donkeys, sheep or goats. ²⁹ Take this tribute from their half share and give it to Eleazar the priest as the LORD's part. ³⁰ From the Israelites' half, select one out of every fifty, whether persons, cattle, donkeys, sheep, goats or other animals. Give them to the Levites, who are responsible for the care of the LORD's tabernacle." ³¹ So Moses and Eleazar the priest did as the LORD commanded Moses.

³² The plunder remaining from the spoils that the soldiers took was 675,000 sheep, ³³ 72,000 cattle, ³⁴ 61,000 donkeys ³⁵ and 32,000 women who had never slept with a man.

ᵃ 12 Hebrew *Jordan of Jericho*; possibly an ancient name for the Jordan River

³⁶The half share of those who fought in the battle was:

> 337,500 sheep, ³⁷of which the tribute for the Lord was 675;
> ³⁸36,000 cattle, of which the tribute for the Lord was 72;
> ³⁹30,500 donkeys, of which the tribute for the Lord was 61;
> ⁴⁰16,000 people, of which the tribute for the Lord was 32.

⁴¹Moses gave the tribute to Eleazar the priest as the Lord's part, as the Lord commanded Moses.

⁴²The half belonging to the Israelites, which Moses set apart from that of the fighting men— ⁴³the community's half—was 337,500 sheep, ⁴⁴36,000 cattle, ⁴⁵30,500 donkeys ⁴⁶and 16,000 people. ⁴⁷From the Israelites' half, Moses selected one out of every fifty persons and animals, as the Lord commanded him, and gave them to the Levites, who were responsible for the care of the Lord's tabernacle.

⁴⁸Then the officers who were over the units of the army—the commanders of thousands and commanders of hundreds—went to Moses ⁴⁹and said to him, "Your servants have counted the soldiers under our command, and not one is missing. ⁵⁰So we have brought as an offering to the Lord the gold articles each of us acquired— armlets, bracelets, signet rings, earrings and necklaces—to make atonement for ourselves before the Lord."

⁵¹Moses and Eleazar the priest accepted from them the gold—all the crafted articles. ⁵²All the gold from the commanders of thousands and commanders of hundreds that Moses and Eleazar presented as a gift to the Lord weighed 16,750 shekels.ᵃ ⁵³Each soldier had taken plunder for himself. ⁵⁴Moses and Eleazar the priest accepted the gold from the commanders of thousands and commanders of hundreds and brought it into the Tent of Meeting as a memorial for the Israelites before the Lord.

The Transjordan Tribes

32 The Reubenites and Gadites, who had very large herds and flocks, saw that the lands of Jazer and Gilead were suitable for livestock. ²So they came to Moses and Eleazar the priest and to the leaders of the community, and said, ³"Ataroth, Dibon, Jazer, Nimrah, Heshbon, Elealeh, Sebam, Nebo and Beon— ⁴the land the Lord subdued before the people of Israel—are suitable for livestock, and your servants have livestock. ⁵If we have found favor in your eyes," they said, "let this land be given to your servants as our possession. Do not make us cross the Jordan."

⁶Moses said to the Gadites and Reubenites, "Shall your countrymen go to war while you sit here? ⁷Why do you discourage the Israelites from going over into the land the Lord has given them? ⁸This is what your fathers did when I sent them from Kadesh Barnea to look over the land. ⁹After they went up to the Valley of Eshcol and viewed the land, they discouraged the Israelites from entering the land the Lord had given them. ¹⁰The Lord's anger was aroused that day and he swore this oath: ¹¹'Because they have not followed me wholeheartedly, not one of the men twenty years old or more who came up out of Egypt will see the land I promised on oath to Abraham, Isaac and Jacob— ¹²not one except Caleb son of Jephunneh the Kenizzite and Joshua son of Nun, for they followed the Lord wholeheartedly.' ¹³The Lord's anger burned against Israel and he made them wander in the desert forty years, until the whole generation of those who had done evil in his sight was gone.

¹⁴"And here you are, a brood of sinners, standing in the place of your fathers and making the Lord even more angry with Israel. ¹⁵If you turn away from following him, he will again leave all this people in the desert, and you will be the cause of their destruction."

¹⁶Then they came up to him and said, "We would like to build pens here for our livestock

ᵃ 52 That is, about 420 pounds (about 190 kilograms)

and cities for our women and children. ¹⁷But we are ready to arm ourselves and go ahead of the Israelites until we have brought them to their place. Meanwhile our women and children will live in fortified cities, for protection from the inhabitants of the land. ¹⁸We will not return to our homes until every Israelite has received his inheritance. ¹⁹We will not receive any inheritance with them on the other side of the Jordan, because our inheritance has come to us on the east side of the Jordan."

²⁰Then Moses said to them, "If you will do this—if you will arm yourselves before the LORD for battle, ²¹and if all of you will go armed over the Jordan before the LORD until he has driven his enemies out before him— ²²then when the land is subdued before the LORD, you may return and be free from your obligation to the LORD and to Israel. And this land will be your possession before the LORD.

²³"But if you fail to do this, you will be sinning against the LORD; and you may be sure that your sin will find you out. ²⁴Build cities for your women and children, and pens for your flocks, but do what you have promised."

²⁵The Gadites and Reubenites said to Moses, "We your servants will do as our lord commands. ²⁶Our children and wives, our flocks and herds will remain here in the cities of Gilead. ²⁷But your servants, every man armed for battle, will cross over to fight before the LORD, just as our lord says."

²⁸Then Moses gave orders about them to Eleazar the priest and Joshua son of Nun and to the family heads of the Israelite tribes. ²⁹He said to them, "If the Gadites and Reubenites, every man armed for battle, cross over the Jordan with you before the LORD, then when the land is subdued before you, give them the land of Gilead as their possession. ³⁰But if they do not cross over with you armed, they must accept their possession with you in Canaan."

³¹The Gadites and Reubenites answered, "Your servants will do what the LORD has said. ³²We will cross over before the LORD into Canaan armed, but the property we inherit will be on this side of the Jordan."

³³Then Moses gave to the Gadites, the Reubenites and the half-tribe of Manasseh son of Joseph the kingdom of Sihon king of the Amorites and the kingdom of Og king of Bashan—the whole land with its cities and the territory around them.

³⁴The Gadites built up Dibon, Ataroth, Aroer, ³⁵Atroth Shophan, Jazer, Jogbehah, ³⁶Beth Nimrah and Beth Haran as fortified cities, and built pens for their flocks. ³⁷And the Reubenites rebuilt Heshbon, Elealeh and Kiriathaim, ³⁸as well as Nebo and Baal Meon (these names were changed) and Sibmah. They gave names to the cities they rebuilt.

³⁹The descendants of Makir son of Manasseh went to Gilead, captured it and drove out the Amorites who were there. ⁴⁰So Moses gave Gilead to the Makirites, the descendants of Manasseh, and they settled there. ⁴¹Jair, a descendant of Manasseh, captured their settlements and called them Havvoth Jair.^a ⁴²And Nobah captured Kenath and its surrounding settlements and called it Nobah after himself.

Stages in Israel's Journey

33 Here are the stages in the journey of the Israelites when they came out of Egypt by divisions under the leadership of Moses and Aaron. ²At the LORD's command Moses recorded the stages in their journey. This is their journey by stages:

³The Israelites set out from Rameses on the fifteenth day of the first month, the day after the Passover. They marched out boldly in full view of all the Egyptians, ⁴who were burying all their firstborn, whom the LORD had struck down among them; for the LORD had brought judgment on their gods.

⁵The Israelites left Rameses and camped at Succoth.

⁶They left Succoth and camped at Etham, on the edge of the desert.

^a 41 Or them the settlements of Jair

⁷They left Etham, turned back to Pi Hahiroth, to the east of Baal Zephon, and camped near Migdol.

⁸They left Pi Hahiroth [a] and passed through the sea into the desert, and when they had traveled for three days in the Desert of Etham, they camped at Marah.

⁹They left Marah and went to Elim, where there were twelve springs and seventy palm trees, and they camped there.

¹⁰They left Elim and camped by the Red Sea. [b]

¹¹They left the Red Sea and camped in the Desert of Sin.

¹²They left the Desert of Sin and camped at Dophkah.

¹³They left Dophkah and camped at Alush.

¹⁴They left Alush and camped at Rephidim, where there was no water for the people to drink.

¹⁵They left Rephidim and camped in the Desert of Sinai.

¹⁶They left the Desert of Sinai and camped at Kibroth Hattaavah.

¹⁷They left Kibroth Hattaavah and camped at Hazeroth.

¹⁸They left Hazeroth and camped at Rithmah.

¹⁹They left Rithmah and camped at Rimmon Perez.

²⁰They left Rimmon Perez and camped at Libnah.

²¹They left Libnah and camped at Rissah.

²²They left Rissah and camped at Kehelathah.

²³They left Kehelathah and camped at Mount Shepher.

²⁴They left Mount Shepher and camped at Haradah.

²⁵They left Haradah and camped at Makheloth.

²⁶They left Makheloth and camped at Tahath.

²⁷They left Tahath and camped at Terah.

²⁸They left Terah and camped at Mithcah.

²⁹They left Mithcah and camped at Hashmonah.

³⁰They left Hashmonah and camped at Moseroth.

³¹They left Moseroth and camped at Bene Jaakan.

³²They left Bene Jaakan and camped at Hor Haggidgad.

³³They left Hor Haggidgad and camped at Jotbathah.

³⁴They left Jotbathah and camped at Abronah.

³⁵They left Abronah and camped at Ezion Geber.

³⁶They left Ezion Geber and camped at Kadesh, in the Desert of Zin.

³⁷They left Kadesh and camped at Mount Hor, on the border of Edom. ³⁸At the LORD's command Aaron the priest went up Mount Hor, where he died on the first day of the fifth month of the fortieth year after the Israelites came out of Egypt. ³⁹Aaron was a hundred and twenty-three years old when he died on Mount Hor.

⁴⁰The Canaanite king of Arad, who lived in the Negev of Canaan, heard that the Israelites were coming.

⁴¹They left Mount Hor and camped at Zalmonah.

⁴²They left Zalmonah and camped at Punon.

⁴³They left Punon and camped at Oboth.

⁴⁴They left Oboth and camped at Iye Abarim, on the border of Moab.

⁴⁵They left Iyim [c] and camped at Dibon Gad.

⁴⁶They left Dibon Gad and camped at Almon Diblathaim.

⁴⁷They left Almon Diblathaim and camped in the mountains of Abarim, near Nebo.

---

[a] 8 Many manuscripts of the Masoretic Text, Samaritan Pentateuch and Vulgate; most manuscripts of the Masoretic Text *left from before Hahiroth*   [b] 10 Hebrew *Yam Suph*; that is, Sea of Reeds; also in verse 11   [c] 45 That is, Iye Abarim

Worship the Lord

Praise the LORD.
Praise the LORD, O my soul.
>I will praise the LORD all my life;
>I will sing praise to my God as long as I live.

Do not put your trust in princes,
>in mortal men, who cannot save.
When their spirit departs, they return to the ground;
>on that very day their plans come to nothing.

Blessed is he whose help is the God of Jacob,
>whose hope is in the LORD his God,
the Maker of heaven and earth,
>the sea, and everything in them —
>the LORD, who remains faithful
>>forever.

Psalm 146:1 – 6

Almighty and wonderful God, I praise you for all that I am. I put my trust and my life in your hands. Thank you for a life full of wonder and joy and grace. May everything I do bring honor and glory to your name. Amen.

Your next devotion is located on page 238.

GRANDCHILD IN FOCUS • PRAYER

Self-Image

O loving God, I praise you for creating my grandchild as a unique individual. Now I ask you to help her appreciate her uniqueness. Build up her self-image so she can enjoy her individuality. Help her to stand firm for who she is, where she has come from and what she believes in. Encourage her not only to have hopes and dreams but to also enjoy each day as it comes. In Jesus' name, amen.

48 They left the mountains of Abarim and camped on the plains of Moab by the Jordan across from Jericho,[a] 49 There on the plains of Moab they camped along the Jordan from Beth Jeshimoth to Abel Shittim.

50 On the plains of Moab by the Jordan across from Jericho the LORD said to Moses, 51 "Speak to the Israelites and say to them: 'When you cross the Jordan into Canaan, 52 drive out all the inhabitants of the land before you. Destroy all their carved images and their cast idols, and demolish all their high places. 53 Take possession of the land and settle in it, for I have given you the land to possess. 54 Distribute the land by lot, according to your clans. To a larger group give a larger inheritance, and to a smaller group a smaller one. Whatever falls to them by lot will be theirs. Distribute it according to your ancestral tribes.

55 " 'But if you do not drive out the inhabitants of the land, those you allow to remain will become barbs in your eyes and thorns in your sides. They will give you trouble in the land where you will live. 56 And then I will do to you what I plan to do to them.' "

Boundaries of Canaan

34 The LORD said to Moses, 2 "Command the Israelites and say to them: 'When you enter Canaan, the land that will be allotted to you as an inheritance will have these boundaries:

3 " 'Your southern side will include some of the Desert of Zin along the border of Edom. On the east, your southern boundary will start from the end of the Salt Sea,[b] 4 cross south of Scorpion[c] Pass, continue on to Zin and go south of Kadesh Barnea. Then it will go to Hazar Addar and over to Azmon, 5 where it will turn, join the Wadi of Egypt and end at the Sea.[d]

6 " 'Your western boundary will be the coast of the Great Sea. This will be your boundary on the west.

7 " 'For your northern boundary, run a line from the Great Sea to Mount Hor 8 and from Mount Hor to Lebo[e] Hamath. Then the bound-

ary will go to Zedad, 9 continue to Ziphron and end at Hazar Enan. This will be your boundary on the north.

10 " 'For your eastern boundary, run a line from Hazar Enan to Shepham. 11 The boundary will go down from Shepham to Riblah on the east side of Ain and continue along the slopes east of the Sea of Kinnereth.[f] 12 Then the boundary will go down along the Jordan and end at the Salt Sea.

" 'This will be your land, with its boundaries on every side.' "

13 Moses commanded the Israelites: "Assign this land by lot as an inheritance. The LORD has ordered that it be given to the nine and a half tribes, 14 because the families of the tribe of Reuben, the tribe of Gad and the half-tribe of Manasseh have received their inheritance. 15 These two and a half tribes have received their inheritance on the east side of the Jordan of Jericho,[g] toward the sunrise."

16 The LORD said to Moses, 17 "These are the names of the men who are to assign the land for you as an inheritance: Eleazar the priest and Joshua son of Nun. 18 And appoint one leader from each tribe to help assign the land. 19 These are their names:

Caleb son of Jephunneh,
 from the tribe of Judah;
20 Shemuel son of Ammihud,
 from the tribe of Simeon;
21 Elidad son of Kislon,
 from the tribe of Benjamin;
22 Bukki son of Jogli,
 the leader from the tribe of Dan;
23 Hanniel son of Ephod,
 the leader from the tribe of Manasseh son
 of Joseph;
24 Kemuel son of Shiphtan,
 the leader from the tribe of Ephraim son
 of Joseph;

---

a 48 Hebrew *Jordan of Jericho*; possibly an ancient name for the Jordan River; also in verse 50   b 3 That is, the Dead Sea; also in verse 12   c 4 Hebrew *Akrabbim*   d 5 That is, the Mediterranean; also in verses 6 and 7   e 8 Or *to the entrance to*   f 11 That is, Galilee   g 15 *Jordan of Jericho* was possibly an ancient name for the Jordan River.

²⁵ Elizaphan son of Parnach,
    the leader from the tribe of Zebulun;
²⁶ Paltiel son of Azzan,
    the leader from the tribe of Issachar;
²⁷ Ahihud son of Shelomi,
    the leader from the tribe of Asher;
²⁸ Pedahel son of Ammihud,
    the leader from the tribe of Naphtali."

²⁹ These are the men the LORD commanded to assign the inheritance to the Israelites in the land of Canaan.

Towns for the Levites

35 On the plains of Moab by the Jordan across from Jericho,ᵃ the LORD said to Moses, ²"Command the Israelites to give the Levites towns to live in from the inheritance the Israelites will possess. And give them pasturelands around the towns. ³Then they will have towns to live in and pasturelands for their cattle, flocks and all their other livestock.

⁴"The pasturelands around the towns that you give the Levites will extend out fifteen hundred feetᵇ from the town wall. ⁵Outside the town, measure three thousand feetᶜ on the east side, three thousand on the south side, three thousand on the west and three thousand on the north, with the town in the center. They will have this area as pastureland for the towns.

Cities of Refuge

35:6–34Ref — Dt 4:41–43; 19:1–14; Jos 20:1–9

⁶"Six of the towns you give the Levites will be cities of refuge, to which a person who has killed someone may flee. In addition, give them forty-two other towns. ⁷In all you must give the Levites forty-eight towns, together with their pasturelands. ⁸The towns you give the Levites from the land the Israelites possess are to be given in proportion to the inheritance of each tribe: Take many towns from a tribe that has many, but few from one that has few."

⁹Then the LORD said to Moses: ¹⁰"Speak to the Israelites and say to them: 'When you cross the Jordan into Canaan, ¹¹select some towns to be your cities of refuge, to which a person who killed someone accidentally may flee. ¹²They will be places of refuge from the avenger, so that a person accused of murder may not die before he stands trial before the assembly. ¹³These six towns you give will be your cities of refuge. ¹⁴Give three on this side of the Jordan and three in Canaan as cities of refuge. ¹⁵These six towns will be a place of refuge for Israelites, aliens and any other people living among them, so that anyone who has killed another accidentally can flee there.

¹⁶"'If a man strikes someone with an iron object so that he dies, he is a murderer; the murderer shall be put to death. ¹⁷Or if anyone has a stone in his hand that could kill, and he strikes someone so that he dies, he is a murderer; the murderer shall be put to death. ¹⁸Or if anyone has a wooden object in his hand that could kill, and he hits someone so that he dies, he is a murderer; the murderer shall be put to death. ¹⁹The avenger of blood shall put the murderer to death; when he meets him, he shall put him to death. ²⁰If anyone with malice aforethought shoves another or throws something at him intentionally so that he dies ²¹or if in hostility he hits him with his fist so that he dies, that person shall be put to death; he is a murderer. The avenger of blood shall put the murderer to death when he meets him.

²²"'But if without hostility someone suddenly shoves another or throws something at him unintentionally ²³or, without seeing him, drops a stone on him that could kill him, and he dies, then since he was not his enemy and he did not intend to harm him, ²⁴the assembly must judge between him and the avenger of blood according to these regulations. ²⁵The assembly must protect the one accused of murder from the avenger of blood and send him back to the city of refuge to which he fled. He must stay there until the death of the high priest, who was anointed with the holy oil.

ᵃ 1 Hebrew *Jordan of Jericho*; possibly an ancient name for the Jordan River   ᵇ 4 Hebrew *a thousand cubits* (about 450 meters)   ᶜ 5 Hebrew *two thousand cubits* (about 900 meters)

26 " 'But if the accused ever goes outside the limits of the city of refuge to which he has fled and the avenger of blood finds him outside the city, the avenger of blood may kill the accused without being guilty of murder. 28 The accused must stay in his city of refuge until the death of the high priest; only after the death of the high priest may he return to his own property.

29 " 'These are to be legal requirements for you throughout the generations to come, wherever you live.

30 " 'Anyone who kills a person is to be put to death as a murderer only on the testimony of witnesses. But no one is to be put to death on the testimony of only one witness.

31 " 'Do not accept a ransom for the life of a murderer, who deserves to die. He must surely be put to death.

32 " 'Do not accept a ransom for anyone who has fled to a city of refuge and so allow him to go back and live on his own land before the death of the high priest.

33 " 'Do not pollute the land where you are. Bloodshed pollutes the land, and atonement cannot be made for the land on which blood has been shed, except by the blood of the one who shed it. 34 Do not defile the land where you live and where I dwell, for I, the LORD, dwell among the Israelites.' "

Inheritance of Zelophehad's Daughters
36:1 – 12pp — Nu 27:1 – 11

36 The family heads of the clan of Gilead son of Makir, the son of Manasseh, who were from the clans of the descendants of Joseph, came and spoke before Moses and the leaders, the heads of the Israelite families. 2 They said, "When the LORD commanded my lord to give the land as an inheritance to the Israelites by lot, he ordered you to give the inheritance of our brother Zelophehad to his daughters. 3 Now suppose they marry men from other Israelite tribes; then their inheritance will be taken from our ancestral inheritance and added to that of the tribe they marry into. And so part of the inheritance allotted to us will be taken away. 4 When the Year of Jubilee for the Israelites comes, their inheritance will be added to that of the tribe into which they marry, and their property will be taken from the tribal inheritance of our forefathers."

5 Then at the LORD's command Moses gave this order to the Israelites: "What the tribe of the descendants of Joseph is saying is right. 6 This is what the LORD commands for Zelophehad's daughters: They may marry anyone they please as long as they marry within the tribal clan of their father. 7 No inheritance in Israel is to pass from tribe to tribe, for every Israelite shall keep the tribal land inherited from his forefathers. 8 Every daughter who inherits land in any Israelite tribe must marry someone in her father's tribal clan, so that every Israelite will possess the inheritance of his fathers. 9 No inheritance may pass from tribe to tribe, for each Israelite tribe is to keep the land it inherits."

10 So Zelophehad's daughters did as the LORD commanded Moses. 11 Zelophehad's daughters — Mahlah, Tirzah, Hoglah, Milcah and Noah — married their cousins on their father's side. 12 They married within the clans of the descendants of Manasseh son of Joseph, and their inheritance remained in their father's clan and tribe.

13 These are the commands and regulations the LORD gave through Moses to the Israelites on the plains of Moab by the Jordan across from Jericho.*a*

a 13 Hebrew *Jordan of Jericho*; possibly an ancient name for the Jordan River

The Importance
OF REMEMBERING

The book of Deuteronomy is Moses' reminder to the people of Israel: Remember what God has done. Remember his goodness. Remember his faithfulness. Remember his promises. Remember his warnings. In this book God calls his people to know him, to remember him, to follow him.

In the book of Deuteronomy (which literally means "repetition of the law"), Moses retells the entire historical saga of the nation of Israel. We can only imagine that this group of ex-slaves, then living in the desert, must have been awed once again by the story of their amazing history. As they prepared to move into the promised land, Moses wanted to be absolutely sure that the people understood God's laws and regulations, his promises and blessings, his warnings about the consequences for disobedience. It was critically important that each generation of Israelites remember all that God had done for his chosen people.

As a grandmother, you have the special role of sharing with your grandchildren your lifetime of experiences. Retelling the stories of God's blessings, his goodness and his faithfulness to the next generation is a critical calling and responsibility. Reminding your children and grandchildren to hear and obey God's commands is as awesome a responsibility as the one Moses had.

VERSE to REMEMBER | DEUTERONOMY 6:6 – 7

"These commandments that I give you today are to be upon your hearts. Impress them on your children. Talk about them when you sit at home and when you walk along the road, when you lie down and when you get up."

ABOUT DEUTERONOMY

WRITTEN BY:
Moses

WRITTEN FOR:
God's chosen people,
the Israelites

DATE WRITTEN:
Just before the Israelites
entered the promised land,
about 1406 B.C.

WHY WRITTEN:
To help a new generation
of Israelites understand
how God wanted
them to know, love and
interact with him

The Command to Leave Horeb

1 These are the words Moses spoke to all Israel in the desert east of the Jordan— that is, in the Arabah—opposite Suph, between Paran and Tophel, Laban, Hazeroth and Dizahab. ²(It takes eleven days to go from Horeb to Kadesh Barnea by the Mount Seir road.)

³In the fortieth year, on the first day of the eleventh month, Moses proclaimed to the Israelites all that the LORD had commanded him concerning them. ⁴This was after he had defeated Sihon king of the Amorites, who reigned in Heshbon, and at Edrei had defeated Og king of Bashan, who reigned in Ashtaroth.

⁵East of the Jordan in the territory of Moab, Moses began to expound this law, saying:

⁶The LORD our God said to us at Horeb, "You have stayed long enough at this mountain. ⁷Break camp and advance into the hill country of the Amorites; go to all the neighboring peoples in the Arabah, in the mountains, in the western foothills, in the Negev and along the coast, to the land of the Canaanites and to Lebanon, as far as the great river, the Euphrates. ⁸See, I have given you this land. Go in and take possession of the land that the LORD swore he would give to your fathers—to Abraham, Isaac and Jacob—and to their descendants after them."

The Appointment of Leaders

⁹At that time I said to you, "You are too heavy a burden for me to carry alone. ¹⁰The LORD your God has increased your numbers so that today you are as many as the stars in the sky. ¹¹May the LORD, the God of your fathers, increase you a thousand times and bless you as he has promised! ¹²But how can I bear your problems and your burdens and your disputes all by myself? ¹³Choose some wise, understanding and respected men from each of your tribes, and I will set them over you."

¹⁴You answered me, "What you propose to do is good."

¹⁵So I took the leading men of your tribes, wise and respected men, and appointed them to have authority over you—as commanders of thousands, of hundreds, of fifties and of tens and as tribal officials. ¹⁶And I charged your judges at that time: Hear the disputes between your brothers and judge fairly, whether the case is between brother Israelites or between one of them and an alien. ¹⁷Do not show partiality in judging; hear both small and great alike. Do not be afraid of any man, for judgment belongs to God. Bring me any case too hard for you, and I will hear it. ¹⁸And at that time I told you everything you were to do.

Spies Sent Out

¹⁹Then, as the LORD our God commanded us, we set out from Horeb and went toward the hill country of the Amorites through all that vast and dreadful desert that you have seen, and so we reached Kadesh Barnea. ²⁰Then I said to you, "You have reached the hill country of the Amorites, which the LORD our God is giving us. ²¹See, the LORD your God has given you the land. Go up and take possession of it as the LORD, the God of your fathers, told you. Do not be afraid; do not be discouraged."

²²Then all of you came to me and said, "Let us send men ahead to spy out the land for us and bring back a report about the route we are to take and the towns we will come to."

²³The idea seemed good to me; so I selected twelve of you, one man from each tribe. ²⁴They left and went up into the hill country, and came to the Valley of Eshcol and explored it. ²⁵Taking with them some of the fruit of the land, they brought it down to us and reported, "It is a good land that the LORD our God is giving us."

Rebellion Against the LORD

²⁶But you were unwilling to go up; you rebelled against the command of the LORD your God. ²⁷You grumbled in your tents and said, "The LORD hates us; so he brought us out of Egypt to deliver us into the hands of the Amorites to destroy us. ²⁸Where can we go? Our brothers

have made us lose heart. They say, 'The people are stronger and taller than we are; the cities are large, with walls up to the sky. We even saw the Anakites there.'"

²⁹Then I said to you, "Do not be terrified; do not be afraid of them. ³⁰The LORD your God, who is going before you, will fight for you, as he did for you in Egypt, before your very eyes, ³¹and in the desert. There you saw how the LORD your God carried you, as a father carries his son, all the way you went until you reached this place."

³²In spite of this, you did not trust in the LORD your God, ³³who went ahead of you on your journey, in fire by night and in a cloud by day, to search out places for you to camp and to show you the way you should go.

³⁴When the LORD heard what you said, he was angry and solemnly swore: ³⁵"Not a man of this evil generation shall see the good land I swore to give your forefathers, ³⁶except Caleb son of Jephunneh. He will see it, and I will give him and his descendants the land he set his feet on, because he followed the LORD wholeheartedly."

³⁷Because of you the LORD became angry with me also and said, "You shall not enter it, either. ³⁸But your assistant, Joshua son of Nun, will enter it. Encourage him, because he will lead Israel to inherit it. ³⁹And the little ones that you said would be taken captive, your children who do not yet know good from bad—they will enter the land. I will give it to them and they will take possession of it. ⁴⁰But as for you, turn around and set out toward the desert along the route to the Red Sea.ᵃ"

⁴¹Then you replied, "We have sinned against the LORD. We will go up and fight, as the LORD our God commanded us." So every one of you put on his weapons, thinking it easy to go up into the hill country.

⁴²But the LORD said to me, "Tell them, 'Do not go up and fight, because I will not be with you. You will be defeated by your enemies.'"

⁴³So I told you, but you would not listen. You rebelled against the LORD's command and in your arrogance you marched up into the hill country. ⁴⁴The Amorites who lived in those hills came out against you; they chased you like a swarm of bees and beat you down from Seir all the way to Hormah. ⁴⁵You came back and wept before the LORD, but he paid no attention to your weeping and turned a deaf ear to you. ⁴⁶And so you stayed in Kadesh many days—all the time you spent there.

Wanderings in the Desert

2 Then we turned back and set out toward the desert along the route to the Red Sea,ᵃ as the LORD had directed me. For a long time we made our way around the hill country of Seir.

²Then the LORD said to me, ³"You have made your way around this hill country long enough; now turn north. ⁴Give the people these orders: 'You are about to pass through the territory of your brothers the descendants of Esau, who live in Seir. They will be afraid of you, but be very careful. ⁵Do not provoke them to war, for I will not give you any of their land, not even enough to put your foot on. I have given Esau the hill country of Seir as his own. ⁶You are to pay them in silver for the food you eat and the water you drink.'"

⁷The LORD your God has blessed you in all the work of your hands. He has watched over your journey through this vast desert. These forty years the LORD your God has been with you, and you have not lacked anything.

⁸So we went on past our brothers the descendants of Esau, who live in Seir. We turned from the Arabah road, which comes up from Elath and Ezion Geber, and traveled along the desert road of Moab.

⁹Then the LORD said to me, "Do not harass the Moabites or provoke them to war, for I will not give you any part of their land. I have given Ar to the descendants of Lot as a possession."

¹⁰(The Emites used to live there—a people strong and numerous, and as tall as the Anakites. ¹¹Like the Anakites, they too were considered

ᵃ 40,1 Hebrew Yam Suph; that is, Sea of Reeds

Rephaites, but the Moabites called them Emites. [12] Horites used to live in Seir, but the descendants of Esau drove them out. They destroyed the Horites from before them and settled in their place, just as Israel did in the land the LORD gave them as their possession.)

[13] And the LORD said, "Now get up and cross the Zered Valley." So we crossed the valley.

[14] Thirty-eight years passed from the time we left Kadesh Barnea until we crossed the Zered Valley. By then, that entire generation of fighting men had perished from the camp, as the LORD had sworn to them. [15] The LORD's hand was against them until he had completely eliminated them from the camp.

[16] Now when the last of these fighting men among the people had died, [17] the LORD said to me, [18] "Today you are to pass by the region of Moab at Ar. [19] When you come to the Ammonites, do not harass them or provoke them to war, for I will not give you possession of any land belonging to the Ammonites. I have given it as a possession to the descendants of Lot."

[20] (That too was considered a land of the Rephaites, who used to live there; but the Ammonites called them Zamzummites. [21] They were a people strong and numerous, and as tall as the Anakites. The LORD destroyed them from before the Ammonites, who drove them out and settled in their place. [22] The LORD had done the same for the descendants of Esau, who lived in Seir, when he destroyed the Horites from before them. They drove them out and have lived in their place to this day. [23] And as for the Avvites who lived in villages as far as Gaza, the Caphtorites coming out from Caphtor[a] destroyed them and settled in their place.)

Defeat of Sihon King of Heshbon

[24] "Set out now and cross the Arnon Gorge. See, I have given into your hand Sihon the Amorite, king of Heshbon, and his country. Begin to take possession of it and engage him in battle. [25] This very day I will begin to put the terror and fear of you on all the nations under heaven. They will hear reports of you and will tremble and be in anguish because of you."

[26] From the desert of Kedemoth I sent messengers to Sihon king of Heshbon offering peace and saying, [27] "Let us pass through your country. We will stay on the main road; we will not turn aside to the right or to the left. [28] Sell us food to eat and water to drink for their price in silver. Only let us pass through on foot— [29] as the descendants of Esau, who live in Seir, and the Moabites, who live in Ar, did for us—until we cross the Jordan into the land the LORD our God is giving us." [30] But Sihon king of Heshbon refused to let us pass through. For the LORD your God had made his spirit stubborn and his heart obstinate in order to give him into your hands, as he has now done.

[31] The LORD said to me, "See, I have begun to deliver Sihon and his country over to you. Now begin to conquer and possess his land."

[32] When Sihon and all his army came out to meet us in battle at Jahaz, [33] the LORD our God delivered him over to us and we struck him down, together with his sons and his whole army. [34] At that time we took all his towns and completely destroyed[b] them—men, women and children. We left no survivors. [35] But the livestock and the plunder from the towns we had captured we carried off for ourselves. [36] From Aroer on the rim of the Arnon Gorge, and from the town in the gorge, even as far as Gilead, not one town was too strong for us. The LORD our God gave us all of them. [37] But in accordance with the command of the LORD our God, you did not encroach on any of the land of the Ammonites, neither the land along the course of the Jabbok nor that around the towns in the hills.

Defeat of Og King of Bashan

3 Next we turned and went up along the road toward Bashan, and Og king of Bashan with his whole army marched out to meet us in battle

---

[a] 23 That is, Crete   [b] 34 The Hebrew term refers to the irrevocable giving over of things or persons to the LORD, often by totally destroying them.

at Edrei. [2] The LORD said to me, "Do not be afraid of him, for I have handed him over to you with his whole army and his land. Do to him what you did to Sihon king of the Amorites, who reigned in Heshbon."

[3] So the LORD our God also gave into our hands Og king of Bashan and all his army. We struck them down, leaving no survivors. [4] At that time we took all his cities. There was not one of the sixty cities that we did not take from them—the whole region of Argob, Og's kingdom in Bashan. [5] All these cities were fortified with high walls and with gates and bars, and there were also a great many unwalled villages. [6] We completely destroyed[a] them, as we had done with Sihon king of Heshbon, destroying[a] every city—men, women and children. [7] But all the livestock and the plunder from their cities we carried off for ourselves.

[8] So at that time we took from these two kings of the Amorites the territory east of the Jordan, from the Arnon Gorge as far as Mount Hermon. [9] (Hermon is called Sirion by the Sidonians; the Amorites call it Senir.) [10] We took all the towns on the plateau, and all Gilead, and all Bashan as far as Salecah and Edrei, towns of Og's kingdom in Bashan. [11] (Only Og king of Bashan was left of the remnant of the Rephaites. His bed[b] was made of iron and was more than thirteen feet long and six feet wide.[c] It is still in Rabbah of the Ammonites.)

Division of the Land

[12] Of the land that we took over at that time, I gave the Reubenites and the Gadites the territory north of Aroer by the Arnon Gorge, including half the hill country of Gilead, together with its towns. [13] The rest of Gilead and also all of Bashan, the kingdom of Og, I gave to the half-tribe of Manasseh. (The whole region of Argob in Bashan used to be known as a land of the Rephaites. [14] Jair, a descendant of Manasseh, took the whole region of Argob as far as the border of the Geshurites and the Maacathites; it was named after him, so that to this day Bashan is called Havvoth

Jair.[d]) [15] And I gave Gilead to Makir. [16] But to the Reubenites and the Gadites I gave the territory extending from Gilead down to the Arnon Gorge (the middle of the gorge being the border) and out to the Jabbok River, which is the border of the Ammonites. [17] Its western border was the Jordan in the Arabah, from Kinnereth to the Sea of the Arabah (the Salt Sea[e]), below the slopes of Pisgah.

[18] I commanded you at that time: "The LORD your God has given you this land to take possession of it. But all your able-bodied men, armed for battle, must cross over ahead of your brother Israelites. [19] However, your wives, your children and your livestock (I know you have much livestock) may stay in the towns I have given you, [20] until the LORD gives rest to your brothers as he has to you, and they too have taken over the land that the LORD your God is giving them, across the Jordan. After that, each of you may go back to the possession I have given you."

Moses Forbidden to Cross the Jordan

[21] At that time I commanded Joshua: "You have seen with your own eyes all that the LORD your God has done to these two kings. The LORD will do the same to all the kingdoms over there where you are going. [22] Do not be afraid of them; the LORD your God himself will fight for you."

[23] At that time I pleaded with the LORD: [24] "O Sovereign LORD, you have begun to show to your servant your greatness and your strong hand. For what god is there in heaven or on earth who can do the deeds and mighty works you do? [25] Let me go over and see the good land beyond the Jordan—that fine hill country and Lebanon."

[26] But because of you the LORD was angry with me and would not listen to me. "That is enough," the LORD said. "Do not speak to me anymore about this matter. [27] Go up to the top of Pisgah and look west and north and south and east.

---

[a] 6 The Hebrew term refers to the irrevocable giving over of things or persons to the LORD, often by totally destroying them.
[b] 11 Or *sarcophagus*   [c] 11 Hebrew *nine cubits long and four cubits wide* (about 4 meters long and 1.8 meters wide)   [d] 14 Or *called the settlements of Jair*   [e] 17 That is, the Dead Sea

Look at the land with your own eyes, since you are not going to cross this Jordan. ²⁸But commission Joshua, and encourage and strengthen him, for he will lead this people across and will cause them to inherit the land that you will see." ²⁹So we stayed in the valley near Beth Peor.

Obedience Commanded

4 Hear now, O Israel, the decrees and laws I am about to teach you. Follow them so that you may live and may go in and take possession of the land that the LORD, the God of your fathers, is giving you. ²Do not add to what I command you and do not subtract from it, but keep the commands of the LORD your God that I give you.

³You saw with your own eyes what the LORD did at Baal Peor. The LORD your God destroyed from among you everyone who followed the Baal of Peor, ⁴but all of you who held fast to the LORD your God are still alive today.

⁵See, I have taught you decrees and laws as the LORD my God commanded me, so that you may follow them in the land you are entering to take possession of it. ⁶Observe them carefully, for this will show your wisdom and understanding to the nations, who will hear about all these decrees and say, "Surely this great nation is a wise and understanding people." ⁷What other nation is so great as to have their gods near them the way the LORD our God is near us whenever we pray to him? ⁸And what other nation is so great as to have such righteous decrees and laws as this body of laws I am setting before you today?

⁹Only be careful, and watch yourselves closely so that you do not forget the things your eyes have seen or let them slip from your heart as long as you live. Teach them to your children and to their children after them. ¹⁰Remember the day you stood before the LORD your God at Horeb, when he said to me, "Assemble the people before me to hear my words so that they may learn to revere me as long as they live in the land and may teach them to their children." ¹¹You came near and stood at the foot of the mountain while it blazed with fire to the very heavens, with black clouds and deep darkness. ¹²Then the LORD spoke to you out of the fire. You heard the sound of words but saw no form; there was only a voice. ¹³He declared to you his covenant, the Ten Commandments, which he commanded you to follow and then wrote them on two stone tablets. ¹⁴And the LORD directed me at that time to teach you the decrees and laws you are to follow in the land that you are crossing the Jordan to possess.

Idolatry Forbidden

¹⁵You saw no form of any kind the day the LORD spoke to you at Horeb out of the fire. Therefore watch yourselves very carefully, ¹⁶so that you do not become corrupt and make for yourselves an idol, an image of any shape, whether formed like a man or a woman, ¹⁷or like any animal on earth or any bird that flies in the air, ¹⁸or like any creature that moves along the ground or any fish in the waters below. ¹⁹And when you look up to the sky and see the sun, the moon and the stars — all the heavenly array — do not be enticed into bowing down to them and worshiping things the LORD your God has apportioned to all the nations under heaven. ²⁰But as for you, the LORD took you and brought you out of the iron-smelting furnace, out of Egypt, to be the people of his inheritance, as you now are.

²¹The LORD was angry with me because of you, and he solemnly swore that I would not cross the Jordan and enter the good land the LORD your God is giving you as your inheritance. ²²I will die in this land; I will not cross the Jordan; but you are about to cross over and take possession of that good land. ²³Be careful not to forget the covenant of the LORD your God that he made with you; do not make for yourselves an idol in the form of anything the LORD your God has forbidden. ²⁴For the LORD your God is a consuming fire, a jealous God.

²⁵After you have had children and grandchildren and have lived in the land a long time — if you then become corrupt and make any kind of idol, doing evil in the eyes of the LORD your God

ONLY BE CAREFUL, AND WATCH YOURSELVES
CLOSELY SO THAT YOU DO NOT FORGET
THE THINGS YOUR EYES HAVE SEEN OR LET
THEM SLIP FROM YOUR HEART AS LONG AS
YOU LIVE. TEACH THEM TO YOUR CHILDREN
AND TO THEIR CHILDREN AFTER THEM.

Deuteronomy 4:9

Nothing Like Home to Me

DOTTIE RAMBO

READ | DEUTERONOMY 4:1 – 14

The other day I thought of my Grandma Luttrell while I was tightening my belt. It looked just like what she used to do! Instantly I recalled her little Kentucky home that smelled of beans and cornbread, and her sweet voice singing.

Grandma was not conventional. She dared to be different. Not in a bad way; she simply refused to follow the path that her family and friends trod. She felt she should live life to its fullest. She didn't use the word *excellence*, but it was in everything she did. And it had an impact on me, even though I didn't know it then. "God wants you to tend to every part of your life. It doesn't matter if it's your home, your garden or yourself. You have to keep it as if you're preparing for him to stop by." For me it was great training being in her shadow.

Everywhere I've gone I've taken the teachings of Grandma Luttrell with me. It's in how I treat people, how I cook, how I've planted gardens, how I dress, how I put on makeup and how I've trained my daughter and all my grandbabies. They all know how serious I am when it comes to doing things the best I can. And I know that's planted in them.

So as the baton is passed to yet another generation, I'm comforted in seeing my grandbabies hold their heads high because they care enough to look, live and love with all their hearts. The same love of Jesus that Grandma Luttrell planted in my heart I see in them. They are not inhibited in their worship. They are not ashamed of their testimony. Regardless of what others may think, they do everything with passionate excellence. And they are now living it out all around the world.

Not bad seed having come from a little lady from Kentucky.

Heavenly Father, let me wait upon your voice to guide and refresh me. And as I live out my life in my daily tasks, may I do them without compromise and with passion. I want to be an example to my children and grandchildren in all I say and do. In Jesus' precious name, amen.

GRANDCHILD IN FOCUS • PRAYER

Protection From Worldliness

O Sovereign Lord, the world surrounds my grandchild, pressing in and tempting him in so many ways. Help him set appropriate limits. Give him sound judgment to choose wisely. Guard him from temptation; protect him from physical and mental predators; lead him into paths of righteousness and light. And reassure me with your promise that you are holding him in your hands. Amen.

Your next devotion is located on page 242.

and provoking him to anger, ²⁶I call heaven and earth as witnesses against you this day that you will quickly perish from the land that you are crossing the Jordan to possess. You will not live there long but will certainly be destroyed. ²⁷The LORD will scatter you among the peoples, and only a few of you will survive among the nations to which the LORD will drive you. ²⁸There you will worship man-made gods of wood and stone, which cannot see or hear or eat or smell. ²⁹But if from there you seek the LORD your God, you will find him if you look for him with all your heart and with all your soul. ³⁰When you are in distress and all these things have happened to you, then in later days you will return to the LORD your God and obey him. ³¹For the LORD your God is a merciful God; he will not abandon or destroy you or forget the covenant with your forefathers, which he confirmed to them by oath.

PRAYING THE SCRIPTURES

Salvation

DEUTERONOMY 4:29

O God, help my grandchild to seek you with all her heart and soul — and in her seeking, to find you, the Lord her God.

Next prayer in Salvation Prayer Track: Psalm 51:5,7,10–12

The LORD Is God

³²Ask now about the former days, long before your time, from the day God created man on the earth; ask from one end of the heavens to the other. Has anything so great as this ever happened, or has anything like it ever been heard of? ³³Has any other people heard the voice of God^a speaking out of fire, as you have, and lived? ³⁴Has any god ever tried to take for himself one nation out of another nation, by testings, by miraculous signs and wonders, by war, by a mighty hand and

an outstretched arm, or by great and awesome deeds, like all the things the LORD your God did for you in Egypt before your very eyes?

³⁵You were shown these things so that you might know that the LORD is God; besides him there is no other. ³⁶From heaven he made you hear his voice to discipline you. On earth he showed you his great fire, and you heard his words from out of the fire. ³⁷Because he loved your forefathers and chose their descendants after them, he brought you out of Egypt by his Presence and his great strength, ³⁸to drive out before you nations greater and stronger than you and to bring you into their land to give it to you for your inheritance, as it is today.

³⁹Acknowledge and take to heart this day that the LORD is God in heaven above and on the earth below. There is no other. ⁴⁰Keep his decrees and commands, which I am giving you today, so that it may go well with you and your children after you and that you may live long in the land the LORD your God gives you for all time.

Cities of Refuge

4:41–43Ref — Nu 35:6–34; Dt 19:1–14; Jos 20:1–9

⁴¹Then Moses set aside three cities east of the Jordan, ⁴²to which anyone who had killed a person could flee if he had unintentionally killed his neighbor without malice aforethought. He could flee into one of these cities and save his life. ⁴³The cities were these: Bezer in the desert plateau, for the Reubenites; Ramoth in Gilead, for the Gadites; and Golan in Bashan, for the Manassites.

Introduction to the Law

⁴⁴This is the law Moses set before the Israelites. ⁴⁵These are the stipulations, decrees and laws Moses gave them when they came out of Egypt ⁴⁶and were in the valley near Beth Peor east of the Jordan, in the land of Sihon king of the Amorites, who reigned in Heshbon and was defeated by Moses and the Israelites as they came out of Egypt. ⁴⁷They took possession of his land and the land

^a 33 Or of a god

of Og king of Bashan, the two Amorite kings east of the Jordan. ⁴⁸This land extended from Aroer on the rim of the Arnon Gorge to Mount Siyon *a* (that is, Hermon), ⁴⁹and included all the Arabah east of the Jordan, as far as the Sea of the Arabah, *b* below the slopes of Pisgah.

The Ten Commandments
5:6 – 21pp — Ex 20:1 – 17

5 Moses summoned all Israel and said:
Hear, O Israel, the decrees and laws I declare in your hearing today. Learn them and be sure to follow them. ²The LORD our God made a covenant with us at Horeb. ³It was not with our fathers that the LORD made this covenant, but with us, with all of us who are alive here today. ⁴The LORD spoke to you face to face out of the fire on the mountain. ⁵(At that time I stood between the LORD and you to declare to you the word of the LORD, because you were afraid of the fire and did not go up the mountain.) And he said:

⁶ "I am the LORD your God, who brought you out of Egypt, out of the land of slavery.
⁷ "You shall have no other gods before *c* me.
⁸ "You shall not make for yourself an idol in the form of anything in heaven above or on the earth beneath or in the waters below. ⁹You shall not bow down to them or worship them; for I, the LORD your God, am a jealous God, punishing the children for the sin of the fathers to the third and fourth generation of those who hate me, ¹⁰but showing love to a thousand ⌐generations⌐ of those who love me and keep my commandments.
¹¹ "You shall not misuse the name of the LORD your God, for the LORD will not hold anyone guiltless who misuses his name.
¹² "Observe the Sabbath day by keeping it holy, as the LORD your God has commanded you. ¹³Six days you shall labor and do all your work, ¹⁴but the seventh day is a Sabbath to the LORD your God. On it you shall not do any work, neither you, nor your son or daughter, nor your manservant or maidservant, nor your ox, your donkey or any of your animals, nor the alien within your gates, so that your manservant and maidservant may rest, as you do. ¹⁵Remember that you were slaves in Egypt and that the LORD your God brought you out of there with a mighty hand and an outstretched arm. Therefore the LORD your God has commanded you to observe the Sabbath day.
¹⁶ "Honor your father and your mother, as the LORD your God has commanded you, so that you may live long and that it may go well with you in the land the LORD your God is giving you.
¹⁷ "You shall not murder.
¹⁸ "You shall not commit adultery.
¹⁹ "You shall not steal.
²⁰ "You shall not give false testimony against your neighbor.
²¹ "You shall not covet your neighbor's wife. You shall not set your desire on your neighbor's house or land, his manservant or maidservant, his ox or donkey, or anything that belongs to your neighbor."

²²These are the commandments the LORD proclaimed in a loud voice to your whole assembly there on the mountain from out of the fire, the cloud and the deep darkness; and he added nothing more. Then he wrote them on two stone tablets and gave them to me.

²³When you heard the voice out of the darkness, while the mountain was ablaze with fire, all the leading men of your tribes and your elders came to me. ²⁴And you said, "The LORD our God has shown us his glory and his majesty, and we have heard his voice from the fire. Today we have

a 48 Hebrew; Syriac (see also Deut. 3:9) *Sirion*   *b* 49 That is, the Dead Sea   *c* 7 Or *besides* seen that a man can live even if God speaks with him. ²⁵But now, why should we die? This great fire will consume us, and we will die if we hear the voice of the LORD our God any longer. ²⁶For what mortal man has ever heard the voice of the living God speaking out of fire, as we have, and survived? ²⁷Go near and listen to all that the LORD our God says. Then tell us whatever the LORD our God tells you. We will listen and obey."

²⁸The LORD heard you when you spoke to me and the LORD said to me, "I have heard what this people said to you. Everything they said was good. ²⁹Oh, that their hearts would be inclined to fear me and keep all my commands always, so that it might go well with them and their children forever!

³⁰"Go, tell them to return to their tents. ³¹But you stay here with me so that I may give you all the commands, decrees and laws you are to teach them to follow in the land I am giving them to possess."

³²So be careful to do what the LORD your God has commanded you; do not turn aside to the right or to the left. ³³Walk in all the way that the LORD your God has commanded you, so that you may live and prosper and prolong your days in the land that you will possess.

Love the LORD Your God

6 These are the commands, decrees and laws the LORD your God directed me to teach you to observe in the land that you are crossing the Jordan to possess, ²so that you, your children and their children after them may fear the LORD your God as long as you live by keeping all his decrees and commands that I give you, and so that you may enjoy long life. ³Hear, O Israel, and be careful to obey so that it may go well with you and that you may increase greatly in a land flowing with milk and honey, just as the LORD, the God of your fathers, promised you.

⁴Hear, O Israel: The LORD our God, the LORD is one.ᵃ ⁵Love the LORD your God with all your heart and with all your soul and with all your strength. ⁶These commandments that I give you

today are to be upon your hearts. ⁷Impress them on your children. Talk about them when you sit at home and when you walk along the road, when you lie down and when you get up. ⁸Tie them as symbols on your hands and bind them on your foreheads. ⁹Write them on the doorframes of your houses and on your gates.

TALKING POINTS

Love

We are to love God completely and unreservedly.

DEUTERONOMY 6:4–9

For more on love, go to John 15:9–17.

¹⁰When the LORD your God brings you into the land he swore to your fathers, to Abraham, Isaac and Jacob, to give you—a land with large, flourishing cities you did not build, ¹¹houses filled with all kinds of good things you did not provide, wells you did not dig, and vineyards and olive groves you did not plant—then when you eat and are satisfied, ¹²be careful that you do not forget the LORD, who brought you out of Egypt, out of the land of slavery.

¹³Fear the LORD your God, serve him only and take your oaths in his name. ¹⁴Do not follow other gods, the gods of the peoples around you; ¹⁵for the LORD your God, who is among you, is a jealous God and his anger will burn against you, and he will destroy you from the face of the land. ¹⁶Do not test the LORD your God as you did at Massah. ¹⁷Be sure to keep the commands of the LORD your God and the stipulations and decrees he has given you. ¹⁸Do what is right and good in the LORD's sight, so that it may go well with you and you may go in and take over the good land

---

ᵃ 4 Or *The LORD our God is one LORD*; or *The LORD is our God, the LORD is one*; or *The LORD is our God, the LORD alone*

THESE COMMANDMENTS THAT I GIVE
YOU TODAY ARE TO BE UPON YOUR
HEARTS. IMPRESS THEM ON YOUR
CHILDREN. TALK ABOUT THEM WHEN
YOU SIT AT HOME AND WHEN YOU
WALK ALONG THE ROAD, WHEN YOU
LIE DOWN AND WHEN YOU GET UP.

Deuteronomy 6:6 – 7

Teach the Children

FERN NICHOLS

READ | DEUTERONOMY 6:1 – 9

One evening when my grandchildren, Joshua and Mimi (Jessica) came over, God gave me an idea of how to teach them the story of blind Bartimaeus receiving his sight (see Mark 10:46 – 52; Luke 18:35 – 43). I decided to turn it into a little play. I shared the story from the Bible and had them practice their lines.

The drama went something like this: I was the friend that led Mimi (Bartimaeus) to Jesus. Joshua was Jesus, sitting on the couch. I led Mimi around the house with her little eyes squinted. I brought her to Jesus.

Joshua: "What do you want me to do for you?"

Mimi: "I want to see."

Joshua touched her eyes and said, "See."

Mimi opened her eyes very wide and shouted and jumped up and down saying, "I can see. I can see." That night the Word came alive to them. Jesus came alive.

I try to live out Deuteronomy 6:6 – 7 by being observant in everyday happenings and relating them to God. One time we saw a lizard scamper across the sidewalk. We talked about who made the lizard and how awesome God, the creator, is.

Yes, sometimes I get tired, but the joy of influencing my grandchildren for Jesus when we sit at home, when we walk along the road, when we lie down and when we get up is a great gift from the Lord. I desire to impress upon their hearts that there is a God who loves them and desires a relationship with them. There is no greater gift than to love my children's children to Jesus.

Sovereign Lord of heaven and earth, I pray that by your grace you would place on my heart an excitement to live out this passage from Deuteronomy. Give me wisdom in how to do it in my daily activities and in special times together with my grandchildren. Help me to be especially creative with the grandchildren I don't see often. May I know that my godly influence can change the lives of my grandchildren. In Jesus' name, amen.

GRANDCHILD IN FOCUS • PRAYER

Respect for Authority

Dear Lord, I pray that my grandchild will continually grow to respect those in authority. May she learn to be cooperative and fair in work and play. Instill in her a high regard for officials who govern our land and enforce the laws. May her relationships with parents, teachers, coaches, mentors and bosses be respectful, admirable, constructive and caring. Amen.

Your next devotion is located on page 243.

> WRITE THEM ON THE
> DOORFRAMES OF YOUR HOUSES
> AND ON YOUR GATES.
>
> *Deuteronomy 6:9*

Writing on the Walls Is Permitted in This House!

SUE BUCHANAN

READ | DEUTERONOMY 6:4 – 12

A poem from my childhood has been spinning around in my head most of my life. I can't get rid of it. Why? Because my mother "wrote it on the doorframes" of our house. It goes:

> Goops! They lick their fingers.
> Goops! They lick their knives.
> Goops spill things on tablecloths.
> My! They lead dreadful lives!

She repeated it often. Once, as a second grader, I came home to find cute little handwritten notes taped everywhere. "Goops," one note said, "don't make their beds or hang up their clothes." Another was prominent on the bathroom mirror: "Goops leave a dirty sink and tub, and never put the cap back on the toothpaste. They never wipe the splashes off the mirror."

The little "goops" notes apparently worked! I'm proud to say that all these years later, I don't lick my fingers or my knife. I'm quick to make the bed in the morning. I hang up my clothes and spiff up the bathroom when I'm finished. Heaven forbid I be called a goop!

My friend Joy MacKenzie, an educator and author of many educational books, has an even better idea for writing on the walls. When her children were growing up, her walls . . . and cabinets . . . and refrigerator . . . and door jams were covered with Scripture verses.

Joy is quick to explain that there are three parts to teaching a child: "One is to teach God's Word outright or disguise it," she says. "Make it fun. Two is to apply it. You have to show children how to translate what they've learned into real life. Show them they need it. The third part is to model it." Self-explanatory! Right?

Dear God, help me use any means available to teach your Word, your principles and your very lifestyle to our little ones. Thank you. Amen.

Your next devotion is located on page 245.

GRANDCHILD IN FOCUS • PRAYER

Courage

O Father, builder of character and courage, may my grandchild grow strong in the light of your love. Grant him courage to stand for what is right, to guard the truth and to ensure justice in every aspect of life. May he boldly grow in grace, revere your name and proudly proclaim you as the Lord of lords and King of kings. Amen.

243

that the LORD promised on oath to your forefathers, ¹⁹thrusting out all your enemies before you, as the LORD said.

PRAYING THE SCRIPTURES

Guidance

DEUTERONOMY 6:13,18

I pray, O Lord, that my grandchild will fear you and serve you only. Let her do what is right and good in your sight, so that all may go well with her.

Next prayer in Guidance Prayer Track: Deuteronomy 7:9

²⁰In the future, when your son asks you, "What is the meaning of the stipulations, decrees and laws the LORD our God has commanded you?" ²¹tell him: "We were slaves of Pharaoh in Egypt, but the LORD brought us out of Egypt with a mighty hand. ²²Before our eyes the LORD sent miraculous signs and wonders—great and terrible—upon Egypt and Pharaoh and his whole household. ²³But he brought us out from there to bring us in and give us the land that he promised on oath to our forefathers. ²⁴The LORD commanded us to obey all these decrees and to fear the LORD our God, so that we might always prosper and be kept alive, as is the case today. ²⁵And if we are careful to obey all this law before the LORD our God, as he has commanded us, that will be our righteousness."

Driving Out the Nations

7 When the LORD your God brings you into the land you are entering to possess and drives out before you many nations—the Hittites, Girgashites, Amorites, Canaanites, Perizzites, Hivites and Jebusites, seven nations larger and stronger than you— ²and when the LORD your God has delivered them over to you and you have defeated them, then you must destroy them totally.^a

Make no treaty with them, and show them no mercy. ³Do not intermarry with them. Do not give your daughters to their sons or take their daughters for your sons, ⁴for they will turn your sons away from following me to serve other gods, and the LORD's anger will burn against you and will quickly destroy you. ⁵This is what you are to do to them: Break down their altars, smash their sacred stones, cut down their Asherah poles^b and burn their idols in the fire. ⁶For you are a people holy to the LORD your God. The LORD your God has chosen you out of all the peoples on the face of the earth to be his people, his treasured possession.

⁷The LORD did not set his affection on you and choose you because you were more numerous than other peoples, for you were the fewest of all peoples. ⁸But it was because the LORD loved you and kept the oath he swore to your forefathers that he brought you out with a mighty hand and redeemed you from the land of slavery, from the power of Pharaoh king of Egypt. ⁹Know therefore that the LORD your God is God; he is the faithful God, keeping his covenant of love to a thousand generations of those who love him and keep his commands. ¹⁰But

^a 2 The Hebrew term refers to the irrevocable giving over of things or persons to the LORD, often by totally destroying them; also in verse 26. ^b 5 That is, symbols of the goddess Asherah; here and elsewhere in Deuteronomy

PRAYING THE SCRIPTURES

Guidance

DEUTERONOMY 7:9

Dear Lord, I pray that my grandchild will know you are God, the faithful God who keeps your covenant of love to a thousand generations of those who love you and keep your commands.

Next prayer in Guidance Prayer Track:
Deuteronomy 30:19–20

I Trust in the Faithfulness of God

KNOW THEREFORE THAT THE LORD YOUR GOD IS GOD; HE IS THE FAITHFUL GOD, KEEPING HIS COVENANT OF LOVE TO A THOUSAND GENERATIONS OF THOSE WHO LOVE HIM AND KEEP HIS COMMANDS.

Deuteronomy 7:9

JAN SILVIOUS

READ | DEUTERONOMY 7:1–11

One of the wonderful treasures of growing older is the memories we carry of the faithfulness of God. When I was a young mother, I harbored many fears. My husband was a helicopter pilot in the Vietnam War, and I was afraid that he wouldn't come home.

As each of our sons was born, I became more and more afraid I would not live until they were grown. My worst fear was that they would be motherless. It seemed that everywhere I turned there was something to be afraid of, and I felt helpless to do anything about it.

More than 40 years down the road, I have come to understand that I am helpless to do anything about the issues of life (and death), but my God is faithful. He has done his part without fail through every fearful situation I have experienced. His record is amazingly consistent. This is good news I confidently pass on to my children and grandchildren. It is the desire of my heart that they would know that all that we are, all that we have and all that has been part of our lives together has been given by the good hand of God.

I keep this quote on a wall in our home to remind us all.

Do not look forward to what might happen tomorrow. The same everlasting Father, who cares for you today, will take care of you tomorrow and every day. Either He will shield you from suffering or He will give you unfailing strength to bear it. Be at peace then and put aside all anxious thoughts and imaginations.

St. Francis de Sales

Father, you have been my "help in ages past," and you continue to extend your outstretched hand to me today. May I forever recognize that it is you who has brought me through, and it is you who will take me safely home.

Your next devotion is located on page 258.

GRANDCHILD IN FOCUS • PRAYER

Future Spouse

Dear Lord, if it is your will, I pray my grandchild will be united in a loving and Christian marriage. Keep her sexually pure so that she will honor you with her body and mind. As she seeks a spouse who will honor and care for her, give her patience and discernment. May her choice for a life partner be your choice for her, so that she and her husband will together glorify you in a lasting love. I pray this in Jesus' name, amen.

245

those who hate him he will repay to their face
    by destruction;
he will not be slow to repay to their face
    those who hate him.

[11] Therefore, take care to follow the commands,
decrees and laws I give you today.

[12] If you pay attention to these laws and are
careful to follow them, then the LORD your God
will keep his covenant of love with you, as he
swore to your forefathers. [13] He will love you and
bless you and increase your numbers. He will
bless the fruit of your womb, the crops of your
land — your grain, new wine and oil — the calves
of your herds and the lambs of your flocks in the
land that he swore to your forefathers to give you.
[14] You will be blessed more than any other people;
none of your men or women will be childless,
nor any of your livestock without young. [15] The
LORD will keep you free from every disease. He
will not inflict on you the horrible diseases you
knew in Egypt, but he will inflict them on all who
hate you. [16] You must destroy all the peoples the
LORD your God gives over to you. Do not look on
them with pity and do not serve their gods, for
that will be a snare to you.

[17] You may say to yourselves, "These nations
are stronger than we are. How can we drive them
out?" [18] But do not be afraid of them; remember
well what the LORD your God did to Pharaoh and
to all Egypt. [19] You saw with your own eyes the
great trials, the miraculous signs and wonders,
the mighty hand and outstretched arm, with
which the LORD your God brought you out. The
LORD your God will do the same to all the peoples you now fear. [20] Moreover, the LORD your
God will send the hornet among them until even
the survivors who hide from you have perished.
[21] Do not be terrified by them, for the LORD your
God, who is among you, is a great and awesome
God. [22] The LORD your God will drive out those
nations before you, little by little. You will not
be allowed to eliminate them all at once, or the
wild animals will multiply around you. [23] But the
LORD your God will deliver them over to you,
throwing them into great confusion until they
are destroyed. [24] He will give their kings into your
hand, and you will wipe out their names from
under heaven. No one will be able to stand up
against you; you will destroy them. [25] The images of their gods you are to burn in the fire. Do
not covet the silver and gold on them, and do
not take it for yourselves, or you will be ensnared
by it, for it is detestable to the LORD your God.
[26] Do not bring a detestable thing into your house
or you, like it, will be set apart for destruction.
Utterly abhor and detest it, for it is set apart for
destruction.

Do Not Forget the LORD

8 Be careful to follow every command I am
giving you today, so that you may live and
increase and may enter and possess the land that
the LORD promised on oath to your forefathers.
[2] Remember how the LORD your God led you all
the way in the desert these forty years, to humble
you and to test you in order to know what was
in your heart, whether or not you would keep
his commands. [3] He humbled you, causing you to
hunger and then feeding you with manna, which
neither you nor your fathers had known, to teach
you that man does not live on bread alone but
on every word that comes from the mouth of the
LORD. [4] Your clothes did not wear out and your
feet did not swell during these forty years. [5] Know
then in your heart that as a man disciplines his
son, so the LORD your God disciplines you.

⁶Observe the commands of the Lord your God, walking in his ways and revering him. ⁷For the Lord your God is bringing you into a good land—a land with streams and pools of water, with springs flowing in the valleys and hills; ⁸a land with wheat and barley, vines and fig trees, pomegranates, olive oil and honey; ⁹a land where bread will not be scarce and you will lack nothing; a land where the rocks are iron and you can dig copper out of the hills.

¹⁰When you have eaten and are satisfied, praise the Lord your God for the good land he has given you. ¹¹Be careful that you do not forget the Lord your God, failing to observe his commands, his laws and his decrees that I am giving you this day. ¹²Otherwise, when you eat and are satisfied, when you build fine houses and settle down, ¹³and when your herds and flocks grow large and your silver and gold increase and all you have is multiplied, ¹⁴then your heart will become proud and you will forget the Lord your God, who brought you out of Egypt, out of the land of slavery. ¹⁵He led you through the vast and dreadful desert, that thirsty and waterless land, with its venomous snakes and scorpions. He brought you water out of hard rock. ¹⁶He gave you manna to eat in the desert, something your fathers had never known, to humble and to test you so that in the end it might go well with you. ¹⁷You may say to yourself, "My power and the strength of my hands have produced this wealth for me." ¹⁸But remember the Lord your God, for it is he who gives you the ability to produce wealth, and so confirms his covenant, which he swore to your forefathers, as it is today.

¹⁹If you ever forget the Lord your God and follow other gods and worship and bow down to them, I testify against you today that you will surely be destroyed. ²⁰Like the nations the Lord destroyed before you, so you will be destroyed for not obeying the Lord your God.

Not Because of Israel's Righteousness

9 Hear, O Israel. You are now about to cross the Jordan to go in and dispossess nations greater and stronger than you, with large cities that have walls up to the sky. ²The people are strong and tall—Anakites! You know about them and have heard it said: "Who can stand up against the Anakites?" ³But be assured today that the Lord your God is the one who goes across ahead of you like a devouring fire. He will destroy them; he will subdue them before you. And you will drive them out and annihilate them quickly, as the Lord has promised you.

⁴After the Lord your God has driven them out before you, do not say to yourself, "The Lord has brought me here to take possession of this land because of my righteousness." No, it is on account of the wickedness of these nations that the Lord is going to drive them out before you. ⁵It is not because of your righteousness or your integrity that you are going in to take possession of their land; but on account of the wickedness of these nations, the Lord your God will drive them out before you, to accomplish what he swore to your fathers, to Abraham, Isaac and Jacob. ⁶Understand, then, that it is not because of your righteousness that the Lord your God is giving you this good land to possess, for you are a stiff-necked people.

The Golden Calf

⁷Remember this and never forget how you provoked the Lord your God to anger in the desert. From the day you left Egypt until you arrived here, you have been rebellious against the Lord. ⁸At Horeb you aroused the Lord's wrath so that

TALKING POINTS

Money

God gives us the ability to make money.

DEUTERONOMY 8:17–18

For more on money, go to 1 Chronicles 29:12–14.

247

he was angry enough to destroy you. ⁹When I went up on the mountain to receive the tablets of stone, the tablets of the covenant that the LORD had made with you, I stayed on the mountain forty days and forty nights; I ate no bread and drank no water. ¹⁰The LORD gave me two stone tablets inscribed by the finger of God. On them were all the commandments the LORD proclaimed to you on the mountain out of the fire, on the day of the assembly.

¹¹At the end of the forty days and forty nights, the LORD gave me the two stone tablets, the tablets of the covenant. ¹²Then the LORD told me, "Go down from here at once, because your people whom you brought out of Egypt have become corrupt. They have turned away quickly from what I commanded them and have made a cast idol for themselves."

¹³And the LORD said to me, "I have seen this people, and they are a stiff-necked people indeed! ¹⁴Let me alone, so that I may destroy them and blot out their name from under heaven. And I will make you into a nation stronger and more numerous than they."

¹⁵So I turned and went down from the mountain while it was ablaze with fire. And the two tablets of the covenant were in my hands.ᵃ ¹⁶When I looked, I saw that you had sinned against the LORD your God; you had made for yourselves an idol cast in the shape of a calf. You had turned aside quickly from the way that the LORD had commanded you. ¹⁷So I took the two tablets and threw them out of my hands, breaking them to pieces before your eyes.

¹⁸Then once again I fell prostrate before the LORD for forty days and forty nights; I ate no bread and drank no water, because of all the sin you had committed, doing what was evil in the LORD's sight and so provoking him to anger. ¹⁹I feared the anger and wrath of the LORD, for he was angry enough with you to destroy you. But again the LORD listened to me. ²⁰And the LORD was angry enough with Aaron to destroy him, but at that time I prayed for Aaron too. ²¹Also I took that sinful thing of yours, the calf you had made, and burned it in the fire. Then I crushed it and ground it to powder as fine as dust and threw the dust into a stream that flowed down the mountain.

²²You also made the LORD angry at Taberah, at Massah and at Kibroth Hattaavah.

²³And when the LORD sent you out from Kadesh Barnea, he said, "Go up and take possession of the land I have given you." But you rebelled against the command of the LORD your God. You did not trust him or obey him. ²⁴You have been rebellious against the LORD ever since I have known you.

²⁵I lay prostrate before the LORD those forty days and forty nights because the LORD had said he would destroy you. ²⁶I prayed to the LORD and said, "O Sovereign LORD, do not destroy your people, your own inheritance that you redeemed by your great power and brought out of Egypt with a mighty hand. ²⁷Remember your servants Abraham, Isaac and Jacob. Overlook the stubbornness of this people, their wickedness and their sin. ²⁸Otherwise, the country from which you brought us will say, 'Because the LORD was not able to take them into the land he had promised them, and because he hated them, he brought them out to put them to death in the desert.' ²⁹But they are your people, your inheritance that you brought out by your great power and your outstretched arm."

Tablets Like the First Ones

10 At that time the LORD said to me, "Chisel out two stone tablets like the first ones and come up to me on the mountain. Also make a wooden chest.ᵇ ²I will write on the tablets the words that were on the first tablets, which you broke. Then you are to put them in the chest."

³So I made the ark out of acacia wood and chiseled out two stone tablets like the first ones, and I went up on the mountain with the two tablets in my hands. ⁴The LORD wrote on these tablets what he had written before, the Ten Commandments

---

ᵃ 15 Or *And I had the two tablets of the covenant with me, one in each hand*   ᵇ 1 That is, an ark he had proclaimed to you on the mountain, out of the fire, on the day of the assembly. And the LORD gave them to me. ⁵Then I came back down the mountain and put the tablets in the ark I had made, as the LORD commanded me, and they are there now.

⁶(The Israelites traveled from the wells of the Jaakanites to Moserah. There Aaron died and was buried, and Eleazar his son succeeded him as priest. ⁷From there they traveled to Gudgodah and on to Jotbathah, a land with streams of water. ⁸At that time the LORD set apart the tribe of Levi to carry the ark of the covenant of the LORD, to stand before the LORD to minister and to pronounce blessings in his name, as they still do today. ⁹That is why the Levites have no share or inheritance among their brothers; the LORD is their inheritance, as the LORD your God told them.)

¹⁰Now I had stayed on the mountain forty days and nights, as I did the first time, and the LORD listened to me at this time also. It was not his will to destroy you. ¹¹"Go," the LORD said to me, "and lead the people on their way, so that they may enter and possess the land that I swore to their fathers to give them."

Fear the LORD

¹²And now, O Israel, what does the LORD your God ask of you but to fear the LORD your God, to walk in all his ways, to love him, to serve the LORD your God with all your heart and with all your soul, ¹³and to observe the LORD's commands and decrees that I am giving you today for your own good?

¹⁴To the LORD your God belong the heavens, even the highest heavens, the earth and everything in it. ¹⁵Yet the LORD set his affection on your forefathers and loved them, and he chose you, their descendants, above all the nations, as it is today. ¹⁶Circumcise your hearts, therefore, and do not be stiff-necked any longer. ¹⁷For the LORD your God is God of gods and Lord of lords, the great God, mighty and awesome, who shows no partiality and accepts no bribes. ¹⁸He defends the cause of the fatherless and the widow, and loves the alien, giving him food and clothing. ¹⁹And you are to love those who are aliens, for you yourselves were aliens in Egypt. ²⁰Fear the LORD your God and serve him. Hold fast to him and take your oaths in his name. ²¹He is your praise; he is your God, who performed for you those great and awesome wonders you saw with your own eyes. ²²Your forefathers who went down into Egypt were seventy in all, and now the LORD your God has made you as numerous as the stars in the sky.

TALKING POINTS

Adoption

God defends the fatherless.

DEUTERONOMY 10:18

For more on adoption, go to Psalm 10:14.

Love and Obey the LORD

11 Love the LORD your God and keep his requirements, his decrees, his laws and his commands always. ²Remember today that your children were not the ones who saw and experienced the discipline of the LORD your God: his majesty, his mighty hand, his outstretched arm; ³the signs he performed and the things he did in the heart of Egypt, both to Pharaoh king of Egypt and to his whole country; ⁴what he did to the Egyptian army, to its horses and chariots, how he overwhelmed them with the waters of the Red Sea ᵃ as they were pursuing you, and how the LORD brought lasting ruin on them. ⁵It was not your children who saw what he did for you in the desert until you arrived at this place, ⁶and what he did to Dathan and Abiram, sons of Eliab the Reubenite, when the earth opened its mouth

---

ᵃ 4 Hebrew *Yam Suph*; that is, Sea of Reeds

CYNTHIA HEALD

Leaving A LEGACY LETTER

Over the years I have written notes of spiritual encouragement for young women who were celebrating notable occasions in their lives. As my own granddaughter was approaching her 16th birthday, I wanted to present her with a special gift that she would treasure for years. I purchased a lovely leather journal that included Scripture and had a pretty ribbon for a bookmark. I wrote a foreword and filled the first page with my favorite verses and my prayer for her as she made her entrance into adulthood.

It is good for us as grandmothers to share our spiritual journey and insights with our grandchildren in written form. We're reminded in Deuteronomy 11:19 that we are to teach our children and grandchildren about our God, and sharing our thoughts with them in such a way is a permanent reminder of our love for God and for them.

Hopefully, the thoughts I wrote then, which I have copied below, will serve to prompt you in gifting your grandchildren in your own unique way.

Frances,

As you turn 16, I wanted to give you a journal to record special insights, helpful quotations, prayers and memorable events in your life.

I also would encourage you to ask any older women you respect to write in your journal. Ask them to give you a favorite verse of Scripture or any counsel they might have about becoming a godly woman.

I have taken the first page! And it is with joy that I wish you a very Happy Birthday as you begin your journey into adulthood and into deeper intimacy with God.

My dear Frances,

There are two verses from Scripture that have been the basis of my life. The first one is Psalm 73:25 – 26 and the other one is John 15:5.

The verses in the Psalms have taught me that God is enough. He is all I need. His grace is sufficient. No matter what happens to me, God will always be the strength of my heart. He will do this for me when all I desire on earth is to be intimate with him. Jesus said, "Seek first the kingdom of God." When God knows that he is first in our lives, he delights in giving us his strength and the fruit of his Spirit in order for us to live for his glory. When our eyes are on him and not ourselves or the world, then we experience the blessing of his presence and the joy of living for the eternal.

I love the verse in John because Jesus is so clear about what we need to do. We need to remain in him. He gives the illustration of a branch remaining in the trunk of the vine. Essentially all Jesus asks us to do is to stay connected to him — to live in him, to remain in him, to walk with him. A branch cannot bear fruit unless it is connected to the trunk of a tree, and so it is with our walk with him. We cannot bear the fruit of his character, we cannot become like him, unless we stay connected. Jesus sums it by saying, "Apart from me you can do nothing." Years ago I told the Lord that I did not want to go through life doing nothing, and if it took my remaining in him in order to do something, then for the rest of my life I wanted to remain in him.

I like to illustrate the idea of *remaining* as "keeping your hand in his." If I am holding on to Jesus' hand, I am connected; he is leading, we are talking and I am secure. My definition of remaining is consistently sitting at the feet of Jesus, listening to his words with an obedient heart. So every day I look forward to sitting at his feet by reading his Word and listening to what he has to say. For the last 40 years that is what I have been doing, and I am so thankful that I have, for he is more than enough. His grace is more than sufficient, and he continually strengthens my heart.

Charles Spurgeon said, "God gives the very best to those who leave the choice to him." We can only leave the choice to him as we remain and seek him first. As you turn 16, my prayer for you is that you will continue to love the Lord with all of your heart, that you will have precious times of remaining in him, and that you will experience the very best that God has for you.

You will always be in my heart, and I will always love you,

— Mimi

right in the middle of all Israel and swallowed them up with their households, their tents and every living thing that belonged to them. [7]But it was your own eyes that saw all these great things the LORD has done.

[8]Observe therefore all the commands I am giving you today, so that you may have the strength to go in and take over the land that you are crossing the Jordan to possess, [9]and so that you may live long in the land that the LORD swore to your forefathers to give to them and their descendants, a land flowing with milk and honey. [10]The land you are entering to take over is not like the land of Egypt, from which you have come, where you planted your seed and irrigated it by foot as in a vegetable garden. [11]But the land you are crossing the Jordan to take possession of is a land of mountains and valleys that drinks rain from heaven. [12]It is a land the LORD your God cares for; the eyes of the LORD your God are continually on it from the beginning of the year to its end.

[13]So if you faithfully obey the commands I am giving you today—to love the LORD your God and to serve him with all your heart and with all your soul— [14]then I will send rain on your land in its season, both autumn and spring rains, so that you may gather in your grain, new wine and oil. [15]I will provide grass in the fields for your cattle, and you will eat and be satisfied.

[16]Be careful, or you will be enticed to turn away and worship other gods and bow down to them. [17]Then the LORD's anger will burn against you, and he will shut the heavens so that it will not rain and the ground will yield no produce, and you will soon perish from the good land the LORD is giving you. [18]Fix these words of mine in your hearts and minds; tie them as symbols on your hands and bind them on your foreheads. [19]Teach them to your children, talking about them when you sit at home and when you walk along the road, when you lie down and when you get up. [20]Write them on the doorframes of your houses and on your gates, [21]so that your days and the days of your children may be many in the land that the LORD swore to give your forefathers,

as many as the days that the heavens are above the earth.

[22]If you carefully observe all these commands I am giving you to follow—to love the LORD your God, to walk in all his ways and to hold fast to him— [23]then the LORD will drive out all these nations before you, and you will dispossess nations larger and stronger than you. [24]Every place where you set your foot will be yours: Your territory will extend from the desert to Lebanon, and from the Euphrates River to the western sea.[a] [25]No man will be able to stand against you. The LORD your God, as he promised you, will put the terror and fear of you on the whole land, wherever you go.

[26]See, I am setting before you today a blessing and a curse— [27]the blessing if you obey the commands of the LORD your God that I am giving you today; [28]the curse if you disobey the commands of the LORD your God and turn from the way that I command you today by following other gods, which you have not known. [29]When the LORD your God has brought you into the land you are entering to possess, you are to proclaim on Mount Gerizim the blessings, and on Mount Ebal the curses. [30]As you know, these mountains are across the Jordan, west of the road,[b] toward the setting sun, near the great trees of Moreh, in the territory of those Canaanites living in the Arabah in the vicinity of Gilgal. [31]You are about to cross the Jordan to enter and take possession of the land the LORD your God is giving you. When you have taken it over and are living there, [32]be sure that you obey all the decrees and laws I am setting before you today.

The One Place of Worship

12 These are the decrees and laws you must be careful to follow in the land that the LORD, the God of your fathers, has given you to possess—as long as you live in the land. [2]Destroy completely all the places on the high mountains and on the hills and under every spreading tree where the nations you are dispossessing worship their gods. [3]Break down their altars, smash their

---

[a] 24 That is, the Mediterranean   [b] 30 Or *Jordan, westward*

sacred stones and burn their Asherah poles in the fire; cut down the idols of their gods and wipe out their names from those places.

4You must not worship the LORD your God in their way. 5But you are to seek the place the LORD your God will choose from among all your tribes to put his Name there for his dwelling. To that place you must go; 6there bring your burnt offerings and sacrifices, your tithes and special gifts, what you have vowed to give and your freewill offerings, and the firstborn of your herds and flocks. 7There, in the presence of the LORD your God, you and your families shall eat and shall rejoice in everything you have put your hand to, because the LORD your God has blessed you.

8You are not to do as we do here today, everyone as he sees fit, 9since you have not yet reached the resting place and the inheritance the LORD your God is giving you. 10But you will cross the Jordan and settle in the land the LORD your God is giving you as an inheritance, and he will give you rest from all your enemies around you so that you will live in safety. 11Then to the place the LORD your God will choose as a dwelling for his Name—there you are to bring everything I command you: your burnt offerings and sacrifices, your tithes and special gifts, and all the choice possessions you have vowed to the LORD. 12And there rejoice before the LORD your God, you, your sons and daughters, your menservants and maidservants, and the Levites from your towns, who have no allotment or inheritance of their own. 13Be careful not to sacrifice your burnt offerings anywhere you please. 14Offer them only at the place the LORD will choose in one of your tribes, and there observe everything I command you.

15Nevertheless, you may slaughter your animals in any of your towns and eat as much of the meat as you want, as if it were gazelle or deer, according to the blessing the LORD your God gives you. Both the ceremonially unclean and the clean may eat it. 16But you must not eat the blood; pour it out on the ground like water. 17You must not eat in your own towns the tithe of your grain and new wine and oil, or the firstborn of your herds and flocks, or whatever you have vowed to give, or your freewill offerings or special gifts. 18Instead, you are to eat them in the presence of the LORD your God at the place the LORD your God will choose—you, your sons and daughters, your menservants and maidservants, and the Levites from your towns—and you are to rejoice before the LORD your God in everything you put your hand to. 19Be careful not to neglect the Levites as long as you live in your land.

20When the LORD your God has enlarged your territory as he promised you, and you crave meat and say, "I would like some meat," then you may eat as much of it as you want. 21If the place where the LORD your God chooses to put his Name is too far away from you, you may slaughter animals from the herds and flocks the LORD has given you, as I have commanded you, and in your own towns you may eat as much of them as you want. 22Eat them as you would gazelle or deer. Both the ceremonially unclean and the clean may eat. 23But be sure you do not eat the blood, because the blood is the life, and you must not eat the life with the meat. 24You must not eat the blood; pour it out on the ground like water. 25Do not eat it, so that it may go well with you and your children after you, because you will be doing what is right in the eyes of the LORD.

26But take your consecrated things and whatever you have vowed to give, and go to the place the LORD will choose. 27Present your burnt offerings on the altar of the LORD your God, both the meat and the blood. The blood of your sacrifices must be poured beside the altar of the LORD your God, but you may eat the meat. 28Be careful to obey all these regulations I am giving you, so that it may always go well with you and your children after you, because you will be doing what is good and right in the eyes of the LORD your God.

29The LORD your God will cut off before you the nations you are about to invade and dispossess. But when you have driven them out and settled in their land, 30and after they have been destroyed before you, be careful not to be ensnared by inquiring about their gods, saying, "How do these nations serve their gods? We will do the same." ³¹ You must not worship the LORD your God in their way, because in worshiping their gods, they do all kinds of detestable things the LORD hates. They even burn their sons and daughters in the fire as sacrifices to their gods.

³² See that you do all I command you; do not add to it or take away from it.

Worshiping Other Gods

13 If a prophet, or one who foretells by dreams, appears among you and announces to you a miraculous sign or wonder, ² and if the sign or wonder of which he has spoken takes place, and he says, "Let us follow other gods" (gods you have not known) "and let us worship them," ³ you must not listen to the words of that prophet or dreamer. The LORD your God is testing you to find out whether you love him with all your heart and with all your soul. ⁴ It is the LORD your God you must follow, and him you must revere. Keep his commands and obey him; serve him and hold fast to him. ⁵ That prophet or dreamer must be put to death, because he preached rebellion against the LORD your God, who brought you out of Egypt and redeemed you from the land of slavery; he has tried to turn you from the way the LORD your God commanded you to follow. You must purge the evil from among you.

⁶ If your very own brother, or your son or daughter, or the wife you love, or your closest friend secretly entices you, saying, "Let us go and worship other gods" (gods that neither you nor your fathers have known, ⁷ gods of the peoples around you, whether near or far, from one end of the land to the other), ⁸ do not yield to him or listen to him. Show him no pity. Do not spare him or shield him. ⁹ You must certainly put him to death. Your hand must be the first in putting him to death, and then the hands of all the people. ¹⁰ Stone him to death, because he tried to turn you away from the LORD your God, who brought you out of Egypt, out of the land of slavery. ¹¹ Then all Israel will hear and be afraid, and no one among you will do such an evil thing again.

¹² If you hear it said about one of the towns the LORD your God is giving you to live in ¹³ that wicked men have arisen among you and have led the people of their town astray, saying, "Let us go and worship other gods" (gods you have not known), ¹⁴ then you must inquire, probe and investigate it thoroughly. And if it is true and it has been proved that this detestable thing has been done among you, ¹⁵ you must certainly put to the sword all who live in that town. Destroy it completely,^a both its people and its livestock. ¹⁶ Gather all the plunder of the town into the middle of the public square and completely burn the town and all its plunder as a whole burnt offering to the LORD your God. It is to remain a ruin forever, never to be rebuilt. ¹⁷ None of those condemned things^a shall be found in your hands, so that the LORD will turn from his fierce anger; he will show you mercy, have compassion on you, and increase your numbers, as he promised on oath to your forefathers, ¹⁸ because you obey the LORD your God, keeping all his commands that I am giving you today and doing what is right in his eyes.

Clean and Unclean Food

14:3–20pp — Lev 11:1–23

14 You are the children of the LORD your God. Do not cut yourselves or shave the front of your heads for the dead, ² for you are a people holy to the LORD your God. Out of all the peoples on the face of the earth, the LORD has chosen you to be his treasured possession.

³ Do not eat any detestable thing. ⁴ These are the animals you may eat: the ox, the sheep, the goat, ⁵ the deer, the gazelle, the roe deer, the wild goat, the ibex, the antelope and the mountain sheep.^b ⁶ You may eat any animal that has a split hoof divided in two and that chews the cud. ⁷ However, of those that chew the cud or that

---

^a 15,17 The Hebrew term refers to the irrevocable giving over of things or persons to the LORD, often by totally destroying them. ^b 5 The precise identification of some of the birds and animals in this chapter is uncertain.

have a split hoof completely divided you may not eat the camel, the rabbit or the coney. [a] Although they chew the cud, they do not have a split hoof; they are ceremonially unclean for you. [8] The pig is also unclean; although it has a split hoof, it does not chew the cud. You are not to eat their meat or touch their carcasses.

[9] Of all the creatures living in the water, you may eat any that has fins and scales. [10] But anything that does not have fins and scales you may not eat; for you it is unclean.

[11] You may eat any clean bird. [12] But these you may not eat: the eagle, the vulture, the black vulture, [13] the red kite, the black kite, any kind of falcon, [14] any kind of raven, [15] the horned owl, the screech owl, the gull, any kind of hawk, [16] the little owl, the great owl, the white owl, [17] the desert owl, the osprey, the cormorant, [18] the stork, any kind of heron, the hoopoe and the bat.

[19] All flying insects that swarm are unclean to you; do not eat them. [20] But any winged creature that is clean you may eat.

[21] Do not eat anything you find already dead. You may give it to an alien living in any of your towns, and he may eat it, or you may sell it to a foreigner. But you are a people holy to the LORD your God.

Do not cook a young goat in its mother's milk.

Tithes

[22] Be sure to set aside a tenth of all that your fields produce each year. [23] Eat the tithe of your grain, new wine and oil, and the firstborn of your herds and flocks in the presence of the LORD your God at the place he will choose as a dwelling for his Name, so that you may learn to revere the LORD your God always. [24] But if that place is too distant and you have been blessed by the LORD your God and cannot carry your tithe (because the place where the LORD will choose to put his Name is so far away), [25] then exchange your tithe for silver, and take the silver with you and go to the place the LORD your God will choose. [26] Use the silver to buy whatever you like: cattle, sheep, wine or other fermented drink, or anything you

wish. Then you and your household shall eat there in the presence of the LORD your God and rejoice. [27] And do not neglect the Levites living in your towns, for they have no allotment or inheritance of their own.

[28] At the end of every three years, bring all the tithes of that year's produce and store it in your towns, [29] so that the Levites (who have no allotment or inheritance of their own) and the aliens, the fatherless and the widows who live in your towns may come and eat and be satisfied, and so that the LORD your God may bless you in all the work of your hands.

The Year for Canceling Debts

15:1–11Ref — Lev 25:8–38

15 At the end of every seven years you must cancel debts. [2] This is how it is to be done: Every creditor shall cancel the loan he has made to his fellow Israelite. He shall not require payment from his fellow Israelite or brother, because the LORD's time for canceling debts has been proclaimed. [3] You may require payment from a foreigner, but you must cancel any debt your brother owes you. [4] However, there should be no poor among you, for in the land the LORD your God is giving you to possess as your inheritance, he will richly bless you, [5] if only you fully obey the LORD your God and are careful to follow all these commands I am giving you today. [6] For the LORD your God will bless you as he has promised, and you will lend to many nations but will borrow from none. You will rule over many nations but none will rule over you.

[7] If there is a poor man among your brothers in any of the towns of the land that the LORD your God is giving you, do not be hardhearted or tightfisted toward your poor brother. [8] Rather be openhanded and freely lend him whatever he needs. [9] Be careful not to harbor this wicked thought: "The seventh year, the year for canceling debts, is near," so that you do not show ill will toward your needy brother and give him nothing. He

---

[a] 7 That is, the hyrax or rock badger

may then appeal to the LORD against you, and you will be found guilty of sin. ¹⁰Give generously to him and do so without a grudging heart; then because of this the LORD your God will bless you in all your work and in everything you put your hand to. ¹¹There will always be poor people in the land. Therefore I command you to be open-handed toward your brothers and toward the poor and needy in your land.

Freeing Servants

15:12–18pp — Ex 21:2–6
15:12–18Ref — Lev 25:38–55

¹²If a fellow Hebrew, a man or a woman, sells himself to you and serves you six years, in the seventh year you must let him go free. ¹³And when you release him, do not send him away empty-handed. ¹⁴Supply him liberally from your flock, your threshing floor and your winepress. Give to him as the LORD your God has blessed you. ¹⁵Remember that you were slaves in Egypt and the LORD your God redeemed you. That is why I give you this command today.

¹⁶But if your servant says to you, "I do not want to leave you," because he loves you and your family and is well off with you, ¹⁷then take an awl and push it through his ear lobe into the door, and he will become your servant for life. Do the same for your maidservant.

¹⁸Do not consider it a hardship to set your servant free, because his service to you these six years has been worth twice as much as that of a hired hand. And the LORD your God will bless you in everything you do.

The Firstborn Animals

¹⁹Set apart for the LORD your God every first-born male of your herds and flocks. Do not put the firstborn of your oxen to work, and do not shear the firstborn of your sheep. ²⁰Each year you and your family are to eat them in the presence of the LORD your God at the place he will choose. ²¹If an animal has a defect, is lame or blind, or has any serious flaw, you must not sacrifice it to the LORD your God. ²²You are to eat it in your own towns. Both the ceremonially unclean and the clean may eat it, as if it were gazelle or deer. ²³But you must not eat the blood; pour it out on the ground like water.

Passover

16:1–8pp — Ex 12:14–20; Lev 23:4–8; Nu 28:16–25

16 Observe the month of Abib and celebrate the Passover of the LORD your God, because in the month of Abib he brought you out of Egypt by night. ²Sacrifice as the Passover to the LORD your God an animal from your flock or herd at the place the LORD will choose as a dwelling for his Name. ³Do not eat it with bread made with yeast, but for seven days eat unleavened bread, the bread of affliction, because you left Egypt in haste — so that all the days of your life you may remember the time of your departure from Egypt. ⁴Let no yeast be found in your possession in all your land for seven days. Do not let any of the meat you sacrifice on the evening of the first day remain until morning.

⁵You must not sacrifice the Passover in any town the LORD your God gives you ⁶except in the place he will choose as a dwelling for his Name. There you must sacrifice the Passover in the evening, when the sun goes down, on the anniversary*ᵃ* of your departure from Egypt. ⁷Roast it and eat it at the place the LORD your God will choose. Then in the morning return to your tents. ⁸For six days eat unleavened bread and on the seventh day hold an assembly to the LORD your God and do no work.

Feast of Weeks

16:9–12pp — Lev 23:15–22; Nu 28:26–31

⁹Count off seven weeks from the time you begin to put the sickle to the standing grain. ¹⁰Then celebrate the Feast of Weeks to the LORD your God by giving a freewill offering in proportion to the blessings the LORD your God has given you. ¹¹And rejoice before the LORD your God at the place he will choose as a dwelling for his Name —

ᵃ 6 Or down, at the time of day

you, your sons and daughters, your menservants and maidservants, the Levites in your towns, and the aliens, the fatherless and the widows living among you. ¹²Remember that you were slaves in Egypt, and follow carefully these decrees.

Feast of Tabernacles

16:13–17pp — Lev 23:33–43; Nu 29:12–39

¹³Celebrate the Feast of Tabernacles for seven days after you have gathered the produce of your threshing floor and your winepress. ¹⁴Be joyful at your Feast—you, your sons and daughters, your menservants and maidservants, and the Levites, the aliens, the fatherless and the widows who live in your towns. ¹⁵For seven days celebrate the Feast to the Lord your God at the place the Lord will choose. For the Lord your God will bless you in all your harvest and in all the work of your hands, and your joy will be complete.

PRAYING THE SCRIPTURES

Joy

DEUTERONOMY 16:15

O Lord my God, bless my grandchild in all the work of his hands, that his joy may be complete.

Next prayer in Joy Prayer Track: Nehemiah 8:10

¹⁶Three times a year all your men must appear before the Lord your God at the place he will choose: at the Feast of Unleavened Bread, the Feast of Weeks and the Feast of Tabernacles. No man should appear before the Lord empty-handed: ¹⁷Each of you must bring a gift in proportion to the way the Lord your God has blessed you.

Judges

¹⁸Appoint judges and officials for each of your tribes in every town the Lord your God is giving you, and they shall judge the people fairly. ¹⁹Do not pervert justice or show partiality. Do not accept a bribe, for a bribe blinds the eyes of the wise and twists the words of the righteous. ²⁰Follow justice and justice alone, so that you may live and possess the land the Lord your God is giving you.

Worshiping Other Gods

²¹Do not set up any wooden Asherah pole [a] beside the altar you build to the Lord your God, ²²and do not erect a sacred stone, for these the Lord your God hates.

17 Do not sacrifice to the Lord your God an ox or a sheep that has any defect or flaw in it, for that would be detestable to him.

²If a man or woman living among you in one of the towns the Lord gives you is found doing evil in the eyes of the Lord your God in violation of his covenant, ³and contrary to my command has worshiped other gods, bowing down to them or to the sun or the moon or the stars of the sky, ⁴and this has been brought to your attention, then you must investigate it thoroughly. If it is true and it has been proved that this detestable thing has been done in Israel, ⁵take the man or woman who has done this evil deed to your city gate and stone that person to death. ⁶On the testimony of two or three witnesses a man shall be put to death, but no one shall be put to death on the testimony of only one witness. ⁷The hands of the witnesses must be the first in putting him to death, and then the hands of all the people. You must purge the evil from among you.

Law Courts

⁸If cases come before your courts that are too difficult for you to judge—whether bloodshed, lawsuits or assaults—take them to the place the Lord your God will choose. ⁹Go to the priests, who are Levites, and to the judge who is in office at that time. Inquire of them and they will give you the verdict. ¹⁰You must act according to the decisions they give you at the place the Lord will choose. Be careful to do everything they direct

---

a 21 Or Do not plant any tree dedicated to Asherah

> FOR SEVEN DAYS CELEBRATE THE FEAST TO THE LORD YOUR GOD AT THE PLACE THE LORD WILL CHOOSE. FOR THE LORD YOUR GOD WILL BLESS YOU IN ALL YOUR HARVEST AND IN ALL THE WORK OF YOUR HANDS, AND YOUR JOY WILL BE COMPLETE.
>
> *Deuteronomy 16:15*

Shout for Joy

RUTH HARMS CALKIN

READ | DEUTERONOMY 16:13 – 17

When I think of Your lavish goodness
The longings You've satisfied
The forgiveness You've granted
The promises You've kept
When I think of Your irresistible love
Your ceaseless care
Your unfailing protection . . .

O Lord God
I want to raise flags
And fly banners
And sound bugles.
I want to run with lighted torches
And praise You
From the mountaintop.
I want to write symphonies
And shout for joy.
I want to throw a festive party
For ten thousand guests.
I want to celebrate with streamers
And bright lights
And an elaborate banquet.

Fine, dear child.
I'm ready.

GRANDCHILD IN FOCUS • PRAYER

School/Career

Dear God, may learning be a joy rather than a chore for my grandchild. May exploration of new ideas bring a sense of wonder, awe and excitement. Grant him clarity of mind, the ability to concentrate on the task at hand and recollection of what has been learned. Help him to appreciate the tasks that come easily and to persevere through those that challenge. Amen.

O Lord God, I shout for joy and praise your name for all the blessings you have given me. Help me to see and appreciate your gifts of all shapes and sizes that fill my life with wonder. Amen.

Your next devotion is located on page 265.

you to do. ¹¹Act according to the law they teach you and the decisions they give you. Do not turn aside from what they tell you, to the right or to the left. ¹²The man who shows contempt for the judge or for the priest who stands ministering there to the LORD your God must be put to death. You must purge the evil from Israel. ¹³All the people will hear and be afraid, and will not be contemptuous again.

The King

¹⁴When you enter the land the LORD your God is giving you and have taken possession of it and settled in it, and you say, "Let us set a king over us like all the nations around us," ¹⁵be sure to appoint over you the king the LORD your God chooses. He must be from among your own brothers. Do not place a foreigner over you, one who is not a brother Israelite. ¹⁶The king, moreover, must not acquire great numbers of horses for himself or make the people return to Egypt to get more of them, for the LORD has told you, "You are not to go back that way again." ¹⁷He must not take many wives, or his heart will be led astray. He must not accumulate large amounts of silver and gold.

¹⁸When he takes the throne of his kingdom, he is to write for himself on a scroll a copy of this law, taken from that of the priests, who are Levites. ¹⁹It is to be with him, and he is to read it all the days of his life so that he may learn to revere the LORD his God and follow carefully all the words of this law and these decrees ²⁰and not consider himself better than his brothers and turn from the law to the right or to the left. Then he and his descendants will reign a long time over his kingdom in Israel.

Offerings for Priests and Levites

18 The priests, who are Levites — indeed the whole tribe of Levi — are to have no allotment or inheritance with Israel. They shall live on the offerings made to the LORD by fire, for that is their inheritance. ²They shall have no inheritance among their brothers; the LORD is their inheritance, as he promised them.

³This is the share due the priests from the people who sacrifice a bull or a sheep: the shoulder, the jowls and the inner parts. ⁴You are to give them the firstfruits of your grain, new wine and oil, and the first wool from the shearing of your sheep, ⁵for the LORD your God has chosen them and their descendants out of all your tribes to stand and minister in the LORD's name always.

⁶If a Levite moves from one of your towns anywhere in Israel where he is living, and comes in all earnestness to the place the LORD will choose, ⁷he may minister in the name of the LORD his God like all his fellow Levites who serve there in the presence of the LORD. ⁸He is to share equally in their benefits, even though he has received money from the sale of family possessions.

Detestable Practices

⁹When you enter the land the LORD your God is giving you, do not learn to imitate the detestable ways of the nations there. ¹⁰Let no one be found among you who sacrifices his son or daughter in ᵃ the fire, who practices divination or sorcery, interprets omens, engages in witchcraft, ¹¹or casts spells, or who is a medium or spiritist or who consults the dead. ¹²Anyone who does these things is detestable to the LORD, and because of these detestable practices the LORD your God will drive out those nations before you. ¹³You must be blameless before the LORD your God.

The Prophet

¹⁴The nations you will dispossess listen to those who practice sorcery or divination. But as for you, the LORD your God has not permitted you to do so. ¹⁵The LORD your God will raise up for you a prophet like me from among your own brothers. You must listen to him. ¹⁶For this is what you asked of the LORD your God at Horeb on the day of the assembly when you said, "Let us not hear the voice of the LORD our God nor see this great fire anymore, or we will die."

¹⁷The LORD said to me: "What they say is good. ¹⁸I will raise up for them a prophet like you

ᵃ 10 Or who makes his son or daughter pass through

from among their brothers; I will put my words in his mouth, and he will tell them everything I command him. ¹⁹If anyone does not listen to my words that the prophet speaks in my name, I myself will call him to account. ²⁰But a prophet who presumes to speak in my name anything I have not commanded him to say, or a prophet who speaks in the name of other gods, must be put to death."

²¹You may say to yourselves, "How can we know when a message has not been spoken by the LORD?" ²²If what a prophet proclaims in the name of the LORD does not take place or come true, that is a message the LORD has not spoken. That prophet has spoken presumptuously. Do not be afraid of him.

Cities of Refuge

19:1–14Ref — Nu 35:6–34; Dt 4:41–43; Jos 20:1–9

19 When the LORD your God has destroyed the nations whose land he is giving you, and when you have driven them out and settled in their towns and houses, ²then set aside for yourselves three cities centrally located in the land the LORD your God is giving you to possess. ³Build roads to them and divide into three parts the land the LORD your God is giving you as an inheritance, so that anyone who kills a man may flee there.

⁴This is the rule concerning the man who kills another and flees there to save his life — one who kills his neighbor unintentionally, without malice aforethought. ⁵For instance, a man may go into the forest with his neighbor to cut wood, and as he swings his ax to fell a tree, the head may fly off and hit his neighbor and kill him. That man may flee to one of these cities and save his life. ⁶Otherwise, the avenger of blood might pursue him in a rage, overtake him if the distance is too great, and kill him even though he is not deserving of death, since he did it to his neighbor without malice aforethought. ⁷This is why I command you to set aside for yourselves three cities.

⁸If the LORD your God enlarges your territory, as he promised on oath to your forefathers, and gives you the whole land he promised them,

⁹because you carefully follow all these laws I command you today — to love the LORD your God and to walk always in his ways — then you are to set aside three more cities. ¹⁰Do this so that innocent blood will not be shed in your land, which the LORD your God is giving you as your inheritance, and so that you will not be guilty of bloodshed.

¹¹But if a man hates his neighbor and lies in wait for him, assaults and kills him, and then flees to one of these cities, ¹²the elders of his town shall send for him, bring him back from the city, and hand him over to the avenger of blood to die. ¹³Show him no pity. You must purge from Israel the guilt of shedding innocent blood, so that it may go well with you.

¹⁴Do not move your neighbor's boundary stone set up by your predecessors in the inheritance you receive in the land the LORD your God is giving you to possess.

Witnesses

¹⁵One witness is not enough to convict a man accused of any crime or offense he may have committed. A matter must be established by the testimony of two or three witnesses.

¹⁶If a malicious witness takes the stand to accuse a man of a crime, ¹⁷the two men involved in the dispute must stand in the presence of the LORD before the priests and the judges who are in office at the time. ¹⁸The judges must make a thorough investigation, and if the witness proves to be a liar, giving false testimony against his brother, ¹⁹then do to him as he intended to do to his brother. You must purge the evil from among you. ²⁰The rest of the people will hear of this and be afraid, and never again will such an evil thing be done among you. ²¹Show no pity: life for life, eye for eye, tooth for tooth, hand for hand, foot for foot.

Going to War

20 When you go to war against your enemies and see horses and chariots and an army greater than yours, do not be afraid of them, because the Lord your God, who brought you up out of Egypt, will be with you. ²When you are about to go into battle, the priest shall come forward and address the army. ³He shall say: "Hear, O Israel, today you are going into battle against your enemies. Do not be fainthearted or afraid; do not be terrified or give way to panic before them. ⁴For the Lord your God is the one who goes with you to fight for you against your enemies to give you victory."

⁵The officers shall say to the army: "Has anyone built a new house and not dedicated it? Let him go home, or he may die in battle and someone else may dedicate it. ⁶Has anyone planted a vineyard and not begun to enjoy it? Let him go home, or he may die in battle and someone else enjoy it. ⁷Has anyone become pledged to a woman and not married her? Let him go home, or he may die in battle and someone else marry her." ⁸Then the officers shall add, "Is any man afraid or fainthearted? Let him go home so that his brothers will not become disheartened too." ⁹When the officers have finished speaking to the army, they shall appoint commanders over it.

¹⁰When you march up to attack a city, make its people an offer of peace. ¹¹If they accept and open their gates, all the people in it shall be subject to forced labor and shall work for you. ¹²If they refuse to make peace and they engage you in battle, lay siege to that city. ¹³When the Lord your God delivers it into your hand, put to the sword all the men in it. ¹⁴As for the women, the children, the livestock and everything else in the city, you may take these as plunder for yourselves. And you may use the plunder the Lord your God gives you from your enemies. ¹⁵This is how you are to treat all the cities that are at a distance from you and do not belong to the nations nearby.

¹⁶However, in the cities of the nations the Lord your God is giving you as an inheritance, do not leave alive anything that breathes. ¹⁷Completely destroy*a* them — the Hittites, Amorites, Canaanites, Perizzites, Hivites and Jebusites — as the Lord your God has commanded you. ¹⁸Oth-

erwise, they will teach you to follow all the detestable things they do in worshiping their gods, and you will sin against the Lord your God.

¹⁹When you lay siege to a city for a long time, fighting against it to capture it, do not destroy its trees by putting an ax to them, because you can eat their fruit. Do not cut them down. Are the trees of the field people, that you should besiege them?*b* ²⁰However, you may cut down trees that you know are not fruit trees and use them to build siege works until the city at war with you falls.

Atonement for an Unsolved Murder

21 If a man is found slain, lying in a field in the land the Lord your God is giving you to possess, and it is not known who killed him, ²your elders and judges shall go out and measure the distance from the body to the neighboring towns. ³Then the elders of the town nearest the body shall take a heifer that has never been worked and has never worn a yoke ⁴and lead her down to a valley that has not been plowed or planted and where there is a flowing stream. There in the valley they are to break the heifer's neck. ⁵The priests, the sons of Levi, shall step forward, for the Lord your God has chosen them to minister and to pronounce blessings in the name of the Lord and to decide all cases of dispute and assault. ⁶Then all the elders of the town nearest the body shall wash their hands over the heifer whose neck was broken in the valley, ⁷and they shall declare: "Our hands did not shed this blood, nor did our eyes see it done. ⁸Accept this atonement for your people Israel, whom you have redeemed, O Lord, and do not hold your people guilty of the blood of an innocent man." And the bloodshed will be atoned for. ⁹So you will purge from yourselves the guilt of shedding innocent blood, since you have done what is right in the eyes of the Lord.

a 17 The Hebrew term refers to the irrevocable giving over of things or persons to the Lord, often by totally destroying them.
b 19 Or *down to use in the siege, for the fruit trees are for the benefit of man.*

Marrying a Captive Woman

[10] When you go to war against your enemies and the LORD your God delivers them into your hands and you take captives, [11] if you notice among the captives a beautiful woman and are attracted to her, you may take her as your wife. [12] Bring her into your home and have her shave her head, trim her nails [13] and put aside the clothes she was wearing when captured. After she has lived in your house and mourned her father and mother for a full month, then you may go to her and be her husband and she shall be your wife. [14] If you are not pleased with her, let her go wherever she wishes. You must not sell her or treat her as a slave, since you have dishonored her.

The Right of the Firstborn

[15] If a man has two wives, and he loves one but not the other, and both bear him sons but the firstborn is the son of the wife he does not love, [16] when he wills his property to his sons, he must not give the rights of the firstborn to the son of the wife he loves in preference to his actual firstborn, the son of the wife he does not love. [17] He must acknowledge the son of his unloved wife as the firstborn by giving him a double share of all he has. That son is the first sign of his father's strength. The right of the firstborn belongs to him.

A Rebellious Son

[18] If a man has a stubborn and rebellious son who does not obey his father and mother and will not listen to them when they discipline him, [19] his father and mother shall take hold of him and bring him to the elders at the gate of his town. [20] They shall say to the elders, "This son of ours is stubborn and rebellious. He will not obey us. He is a profligate and a drunkard." [21] Then all the men of his town shall stone him to death. You must purge the evil from among you. All Israel will hear of it and be afraid.

Various Laws

[22] If a man guilty of a capital offense is put to death and his body is hung on a tree, [23] you must not leave his body on the tree overnight. Be sure to bury him that same day, because anyone who is hung on a tree is under God's curse. You must not desecrate the land the LORD your God is giving you as an inheritance.

22 If you see your brother's ox or sheep straying, do not ignore it but be sure to take it back to him. [2] If the brother does not live near you or if you do not know who he is, take it home with you and keep it until he comes looking for it. Then give it back to him. [3] Do the same if you find your brother's donkey or his cloak or anything he loses. Do not ignore it.

[4] If you see your brother's donkey or his ox fallen on the road, do not ignore it. Help him get it to its feet.

[5] A woman must not wear men's clothing, nor a man wear women's clothing, for the LORD your God detests anyone who does this.

[6] If you come across a bird's nest beside the road, either in a tree or on the ground, and the mother is sitting on the young or on the eggs, do not take the mother with the young. [7] You may take the young, but be sure to let the mother go, so that it may go well with you and you may have a long life.

[8] When you build a new house, make a parapet around your roof so that you may not bring the guilt of bloodshed on your house if someone falls from the roof.

[9] Do not plant two kinds of seed in your vineyard; if you do, not only the crops you plant but also the fruit of the vineyard will be defiled. [a]

[10] Do not plow with an ox and a donkey yoked together.

[11] Do not wear clothes of wool and linen woven together.

[12] Make tassels on the four corners of the cloak you wear.

Marriage Violations

[13] If a man takes a wife and, after lying with her, dislikes her [14] and slanders her and gives her a bad name, saying, "I married this woman, but

---

[a] 9 Or be forfeited to the sanctuary

when I approached her, I did not find proof of her virginity," ¹⁵then the girl's father and mother shall bring proof that she was a virgin to the town elders at the gate. ¹⁶The girl's father will say to the elders, "I gave my daughter in marriage to this man, but he dislikes her. ¹⁷Now he has slandered her and said, 'I did not find your daughter to be a virgin.' But here is the proof of my daughter's virginity." Then her parents shall display the cloth before the elders of the town, ¹⁸and the elders shall take the man and punish him. ¹⁹They shall fine him a hundred shekels of silver[a] and give them to the girl's father, because this man has given an Israelite virgin a bad name. She shall continue to be his wife; he must not divorce her as long as he lives.

²⁰If, however, the charge is true and no proof of the girl's virginity can be found, ²¹she shall be brought to the door of her father's house and there the men of her town shall stone her to death. She has done a disgraceful thing in Israel by being promiscuous while still in her father's house. You must purge the evil from among you.

²²If a man is found sleeping with another man's wife, both the man who slept with her and the woman must die. You must purge the evil from Israel.

²³If a man happens to meet in a town a virgin pledged to be married and he sleeps with her, ²⁴you shall take both of them to the gate of that town and stone them to death — the girl because she was in a town and did not scream for help, and the man because he violated another man's wife. You must purge the evil from among you.

²⁵But if out in the country a man happens to meet a girl pledged to be married and rapes her, only the man who has done this shall die. ²⁶Do nothing to the girl; she has committed no sin deserving death. This case is like that of someone who attacks and murders his neighbor, ²⁷for the man found the girl out in the country, and though the betrothed girl screamed, there was no one to rescue her.

²⁸If a man happens to meet a virgin who is not pledged to be married and rapes her and they are discovered, ²⁹he shall pay the girl's father fifty shekels of silver.[b] He must marry the girl, for he has violated her. He can never divorce her as long as he lives.

³⁰A man is not to marry his father's wife; he must not dishonor his father's bed.

Exclusion From the Assembly

23 No one who has been emasculated by crushing or cutting may enter the assembly of the LORD.

²No one born of a forbidden marriage[c] nor any of his descendants may enter the assembly of the LORD, even down to the tenth generation.

³No Ammonite or Moabite or any of his descendants may enter the assembly of the LORD, even down to the tenth generation. ⁴For they did not come to meet you with bread and water on your way when you came out of Egypt, and they hired Balaam son of Beor from Pethor in Aram Naharaim[d] to pronounce a curse on you. ⁵However, the LORD your God would not listen to Balaam but turned the curse into a blessing for you, because the LORD your God loves you. ⁶Do not seek a treaty of friendship with them as long as you live.

⁷Do not abhor an Edomite, for he is your brother. Do not abhor an Egyptian, because you lived as an alien in his country. ⁸The third generation of children born to them may enter the assembly of the LORD.

Uncleanness in the Camp

⁹When you are encamped against your enemies, keep away from everything impure. ¹⁰If one of your men is unclean because of a nocturnal emission, he is to go outside the camp and stay there. ¹¹But as evening approaches he is to wash himself, and at sunset he may return to the camp.

¹²Designate a place outside the camp where you can go to relieve yourself. ¹³As part of your equipment have something to dig with, and when you relieve yourself, dig a hole and cover

a 19 That is, about 2 1/2 pounds (about 1 kilogram)   b 29 That is, about 1 1/4 pounds (about 0.6 kilogram)   c 2 Or one of illegitimate birth   d 4 That is, Northwest Mesopotamia up your excrement. [14]For the LORD your God moves about in your camp to protect you and to deliver your enemies to you. Your camp must be holy, so that he will not see among you anything indecent and turn away from you.

Miscellaneous Laws

[15]If a slave has taken refuge with you, do not hand him over to his master. [16]Let him live among you wherever he likes and in whatever town he chooses. Do not oppress him.

[17]No Israelite man or woman is to become a shrine prostitute. [18]You must not bring the earnings of a female prostitute or of a male prostitute[a] into the house of the LORD your God to pay any vow, because the LORD your God detests them both.

[19]Do not charge your brother interest, whether on money or food or anything else that may earn interest. [20]You may charge a foreigner interest, but not a brother Israelite, so that the LORD your God may bless you in everything you put your hand to in the land you are entering to possess.

[21]If you make a vow to the LORD your God, do not be slow to pay it, for the LORD your God will certainly demand it of you and you will be guilty of sin. [22]But if you refrain from making a vow, you will not be guilty. [23]Whatever your lips utter you must be sure to do, because you made your vow freely to the LORD your God with your own mouth.

[24]If you enter your neighbor's vineyard, you may eat all the grapes you want, but do not put any in your basket. [25]If you enter your neighbor's grainfield, you may pick kernels with your hands, but you must not put a sickle to his standing grain.

24 If a man marries a woman who becomes displeasing to him because he finds something indecent about her, and he writes her a certificate of divorce, gives it to her and sends her from his house, [2]and if after she leaves his house she becomes the wife of another man, [3]and her second husband dislikes her and writes her a certificate of divorce, gives it to her and sends her from his house, or if he dies, [4]then her first husband, who divorced her, is not allowed to marry her again after she has been defiled. That would be detestable in the eyes of the LORD. Do not bring sin upon the land the LORD your God is giving you as an inheritance.

[5]If a man has recently married, he must not be sent to war or have any other duty laid on him. For one year he is to be free to stay at home and bring happiness to the wife he has married.

[6]Do not take a pair of millstones—not even the upper one—as security for a debt, because that would be taking a man's livelihood as security.

[7]If a man is caught kidnapping one of his brother Israelites and treats him as a slave or sells him, the kidnapper must die. You must purge the evil from among you.

[8]In cases of leprous[b] diseases be very careful to do exactly as the priests, who are Levites, instruct you. You must follow carefully what I have commanded them. [9]Remember what the LORD your God did to Miriam along the way after you came out of Egypt.

[10]When you make a loan of any kind to your neighbor, do not go into his house to get what he is offering as a pledge. [11]Stay outside and let the man to whom you are making the loan bring the pledge out to you. [12]If the man is poor, do not go to sleep with his pledge in your possession. [13]Return his cloak to him by sunset so that he may sleep in it. Then he will thank you, and it will be regarded as a righteous act in the sight of the LORD your God.

[14]Do not take advantage of a hired man who is poor and needy, whether he is a brother Israelite or an alien living in one of your towns. [15]Pay him his wages each day before sunset, because he is poor and is counting on it. Otherwise he may cry to the LORD against you, and you will be guilty of sin.

[16]Fathers shall not be put to death for their children, nor children put to death for their fathers; each is to die for his own sin.

---

[a] 18 Hebrew *of a dog*   [b] 8 The Hebrew word was used for various diseases affecting the skin—not necessarily leprosy.

LET'S HAVE
FUN

Got Cookies?

Everyone loves cookies. And now it's easier than ever to be the grandma with home-made (or at least fresh-baked) cookies. If you love to go at it from scratch, that's great. Not so good at that? Then do it the easy way: Buy the cookie dough in a roll or even in the little break-apart cubes. The fun is in being together, smelling that fresh-baked smell, decorating and eating warm, gooey cookies.

Older-Grandkids Variation: Have a baking marathon before a sporting event, play rehearsal, slumber party, etc. so that lots of people can enjoy your cookies. Or together take batches of cookies to a retirement home, a Ronald McDonald House or the local fire station.

Long-Distance Variation: Bake some cookies and leave them undecorated. Mail them with a tube of icing, some sprinkles and a note expressing your love.

Dear God, thank you for grandchildren I can spend time with. Thank you for the good foods we can share. Help me to remember that doing simple things with my grandchildren will bring as much pleasure and joy as any elaborate event. Fill our hours together with joy and laughter. Amen.

Your next devotion is located on page 268.

GRANDCHILD **IN FOCUS** • PRAYER

Character

Dear Lord and Father, I ask that you fill my grandchild with your Spirit so her character reflects your goodness and love. Give her kindness and love for others. Bring joy to her life so she will be a joy to others. Grant her patience and self-control through difficult and trying times. May she show mercy and generosity to those who are less fortu-nate. Grant her integrity and a sense of justice, and surround her with your peace. Amen.

¹⁷Do not deprive the alien or the fatherless of justice, or take the cloak of the widow as a pledge. ¹⁸Remember that you were slaves in Egypt and the LORD your God redeemed you from there. That is why I command you to do this.

¹⁹When you are harvesting in your field and you overlook a sheaf, do not go back to get it. Leave it for the alien, the fatherless and the widow, so that the LORD your God may bless you in all the work of your hands. ²⁰When you beat the olives from your trees, do not go over the branches a second time. Leave what remains for the alien, the fatherless and the widow. ²¹When you harvest the grapes in your vineyard, do not go over the vines again. Leave what remains for the alien, the fatherless and the widow. ²²Remember that you were slaves in Egypt. That is why I command you to do this.

25 When men have a dispute, they are to take it to court and the judges will decide the case, acquitting the innocent and condemning the guilty. ²If the guilty man deserves to be beaten, the judge shall make him lie down and have him flogged in his presence with the number of lashes his crime deserves, ³but he must not give him more than forty lashes. If he is flogged more than that, your brother will be degraded in your eyes.

⁴Do not muzzle an ox while it is treading out the grain.

⁵If brothers are living together and one of them dies without a son, his widow must not marry outside the family. Her husband's brother shall take her and marry her and fulfill the duty of a brother-in-law to her. ⁶The first son she bears shall carry on the name of the dead brother so that his name will not be blotted out from Israel.

⁷However, if a man does not want to marry his brother's wife, she shall go to the elders at the town gate and say, "My husband's brother refuses to carry on his brother's name in Israel. He will not fulfill the duty of a brother-in-law to me." ⁸Then the elders of his town shall summon him and talk to him. If he persists in saying, "I do not want to marry her," ⁹his brother's widow shall go up to him in the presence of the elders, take off one of his sandals, spit in his face and say, "This is what is done to the man who will not build up his brother's family line." ¹⁰That man's line shall be known in Israel as The Family of the Unsandaled.

¹¹If two men are fighting and the wife of one of them comes to rescue her husband from his assailant, and she reaches out and seizes him by his private parts, ¹²you shall cut off her hand. Show her no pity.

¹³Do not have two differing weights in your bag—one heavy, one light. ¹⁴Do not have two differing measures in your house—one large, one small. ¹⁵You must have accurate and honest weights and measures, so that you may live long in the land the LORD your God is giving you. ¹⁶For the LORD your God detests anyone who does these things, anyone who deals dishonestly.

¹⁷Remember what the Amalekites did to you along the way when you came out of Egypt. ¹⁸When you were weary and worn out, they met you on your journey and cut off all who were lagging behind; they had no fear of God. ¹⁹When the LORD your God gives you rest from all the enemies around you in the land he is giving you to possess as an inheritance, you shall blot out the memory of Amalek from under heaven. Do not forget!

Firstfruits and Tithes

26 When you have entered the land the LORD your God is giving you as an inheritance and have taken possession of it and settled in it, ²take some of the firstfruits of all that you produce from the soil of the land the LORD your God is giving you and put them in a basket. Then go to the place the LORD your God will choose as a dwelling for his Name ³and say to the priest in office at the time, "I declare today to the LORD your God that I have come to the land the LORD swore to our forefathers to give us." ⁴The priest shall take the basket from your hands and set it down in front of the altar of the LORD your God.

5Then you shall declare before the LORD your God: "My father was a wandering Aramean, and he went down into Egypt with a few people and lived there and became a great nation, powerful and numerous. 6But the Egyptians mistreated us and made us suffer, putting us to hard labor. 7Then we cried out to the LORD, the God of our fathers, and the LORD heard our voice and saw our misery, toil and oppression. 8So the LORD brought us out of Egypt with a mighty hand and an outstretched arm, with great terror and with miraculous signs and wonders. 9He brought us to this place and gave us this land, a land flowing with milk and honey; 10and now I bring the firstfruits of the soil that you, O LORD, have given me." Place the basket before the LORD your God and bow down before him. 11And you and the Levites and the aliens among you shall rejoice in all the good things the LORD your God has given to you and your household.

12When you have finished setting aside a tenth of all your produce in the third year, the year of the tithe, you shall give it to the Levite, the alien, the fatherless and the widow, so that they may eat in your towns and be satisfied. 13Then say to the LORD your God: "I have removed from my house the sacred portion and have given it to the Levite, the alien, the fatherless and the widow, according to all you commanded. I have not turned aside from your commands nor have I forgotten any of them. 14I have not eaten any of the sacred portion while I was in mourning, nor have I removed any of it while I was unclean, nor have I offered any of it to the dead. I have obeyed the LORD my God; I have done everything you commanded me. 15Look down from heaven, your holy dwelling place, and bless your people Israel and the land you have given us as you promised on oath to our forefathers, a land flowing with milk and honey."

Follow the LORD's Commands

16The LORD your God commands you this day to follow these decrees and laws; carefully observe them with all your heart and with all your soul. 17You have declared this day that the LORD is your God and that you will walk in his ways, that you will keep his decrees, commands and laws, and that you will obey him. 18And the LORD has declared this day that you are his people, his treasured possession as he promised, and that you are to keep all his commands. 19He has declared that he will set you in praise, fame and honor high above all the nations he has made and that you will be a people holy to the LORD your God, as he promised.

The Altar on Mount Ebal

27 Moses and the elders of Israel commanded the people: "Keep all these commands that I give you today. 2When you have crossed the Jordan into the land the LORD your God is giving you, set up some large stones and coat them with plaster. 3Write on them all the words of this law when you have crossed over to enter the land the LORD your God is giving you, a land flowing with milk and honey, just as the LORD, the God of your fathers, promised you. 4And when you have crossed the Jordan, set up these stones on Mount Ebal, as I command you today, and coat them with plaster. 5Build there an altar to the LORD your God, an altar of stones. Do not use any iron tool upon them. 6Build the altar of the LORD your God with fieldstones and offer burnt offerings on it to the LORD your God. 7Sacrifice fellowship offerings[a] there, eating them and rejoicing in the presence of the LORD your God. 8And you shall write very clearly all the words of this law on these stones you have set up."

Curses From Mount Ebal

9Then Moses and the priests, who are Levites, said to all Israel, "Be silent, O Israel, and listen! You have now become the people of the LORD your God. 10Obey the LORD your God and follow his commands and decrees that I give you today."

11On the same day Moses commanded the people:

---

[a] 7 Traditionally peace offerings

Worship the Lord

Listen, O heavens, and I will speak;
    hear, O earth, the words of my mouth.
Let my teaching fall like rain
    and my words descend like dew,
like showers on new grass,
    like abundant rain on tender plants.

I will proclaim the name of the LORD.
    Oh, praise the greatness of our God!
He is the Rock, his works are perfect,
    and all his ways are just.
A faithful God who does no wrong,
    upright and just is he.

Deuteronomy 32:1 – 4

Thank you, Lord, for the opportunities I have to hear your Word proclaimed. Let your words descend on me like refreshing rain. You are great, you are perfect, you are faithful and you are just. Amen.

Your next devotion is located on page 275.

GRANDCHILD IN FOCUS • PRAYER

Talents

Dear Lord, the giver of gifts, bless my grandchild as he develops his talents. Help him identify his talents and be proud and confident of the gifts you have given him. Give him patience and understanding, Lord, so he will not grow weary of striving and searching to reach the goals you have set for him. May each milestone bring satisfaction and a healthy desire for greater achievement and success to bring glory to you. Amen.

¹²When you have crossed the Jordan, these tribes shall stand on Mount Gerizim to bless the people: Simeon, Levi, Judah, Issachar, Joseph and Benjamin. ¹³And these tribes shall stand on Mount Ebal to pronounce curses: Reuben, Gad, Asher, Zebulun, Dan and Naphtali.

¹⁴The Levites shall recite to all the people of Israel in a loud voice:

¹⁵"Cursed is the man who carves an image or casts an idol—a thing detestable to the LORD, the work of the craftsman's hands—and sets it up in secret."

Then all the people shall say, "Amen!"

¹⁶"Cursed is the man who dishonors his father or his mother."

Then all the people shall say, "Amen!"

¹⁷"Cursed is the man who moves his neighbor's boundary stone."

Then all the people shall say, "Amen!"

¹⁸"Cursed is the man who leads the blind astray on the road."

Then all the people shall say, "Amen!"

¹⁹"Cursed is the man who withholds justice from the alien, the fatherless or the widow."

Then all the people shall say, "Amen!"

²⁰"Cursed is the man who sleeps with his father's wife, for he dishonors his father's bed."

Then all the people shall say, "Amen!"

²¹"Cursed is the man who has sexual relations with any animal."

Then all the people shall say, "Amen!"

²²"Cursed is the man who sleeps with his sister, the daughter of his father or the daughter of his mother."

Then all the people shall say, "Amen!"

²³"Cursed is the man who sleeps with his mother-in-law."

Then all the people shall say, "Amen!"

²⁴"Cursed is the man who kills his neighbor secretly."

Then all the people shall say, "Amen!"

²⁵"Cursed is the man who accepts a bribe to kill an innocent person."

Then all the people shall say, "Amen!"

²⁶"Cursed is the man who does not uphold the words of this law by carrying them out."

Then all the people shall say, "Amen!"

Blessings for Obedience

28 If you fully obey the LORD your God and carefully follow all his commands I give you today, the LORD your God will set you high above all the nations on earth. ²All these blessings will come upon you and accompany you if you obey the LORD your God:

³You will be blessed in the city and blessed in the country.

⁴The fruit of your womb will be blessed, and the crops of your land and the young of your livestock—the calves of your herds and the lambs of your flocks.

⁵Your basket and your kneading trough will be blessed.

⁶You will be blessed when you come in and blessed when you go out.

⁷The LORD will grant that the enemies who rise up against you will be defeated before you. They will come at you from one direction but flee from you in seven.

⁸The LORD will send a blessing on your barns and on everything you put your hand to. The LORD your God will bless you in the land he is giving you.

⁹The LORD will establish you as his holy people, as he promised you on oath, if you keep the commands of the LORD your God and walk in his ways. ¹⁰Then all the peoples on earth will see that you are called by the name of the LORD, and they will fear you. ¹¹The LORD will grant you abundant prosperity—in the fruit of your womb, the young of your livestock and the crops of your ground—in the land he swore to your forefathers to give you.

¹²The LORD will open the heavens, the storehouse of his bounty, to send rain on your land in season and to bless all the work of your hands.

You will lend to many nations but will borrow from none. ¹³The Lord will make you the head, not the tail. If you pay attention to the commands of the Lord your God that I give you this day and carefully follow them, you will always be at the top, never at the bottom. ¹⁴Do not turn aside from any of the commands I give you today, to the right or to the left, following other gods and serving them.

Curses for Disobedience

¹⁵However, if you do not obey the Lord your God and do not carefully follow all his commands and decrees I am giving you today, all these curses will come upon you and overtake you:

¹⁶You will be cursed in the city and cursed in the country.

¹⁷Your basket and your kneading trough will be cursed.

¹⁸The fruit of your womb will be cursed, and the crops of your land, and the calves of your herds and the lambs of your flocks.

¹⁹You will be cursed when you come in and cursed when you go out.

²⁰The Lord will send on you curses, confusion and rebuke in everything you put your hand to, until you are destroyed and come to sudden ruin because of the evil you have done in forsaking him.ᵃ ²¹The Lord will plague you with diseases until he has destroyed you from the land you are entering to possess. ²²The Lord will strike you with wasting disease, with fever and inflammation, with scorching heat and drought, with blight and mildew, which will plague you until you perish. ²³The sky over your head will be bronze, the ground beneath you iron. ²⁴The Lord will turn the rain of your country into dust and powder; it will come down from the skies until you are destroyed.

²⁵The Lord will cause you to be defeated before your enemies. You will come at them from one direction but flee from them in seven, and you will become a thing of horror to all the kingdoms on earth. ²⁶Your carcasses will be food for all the birds of the air and the beasts of the earth, and there will be no one to frighten them away. ²⁷The Lord will afflict you with the boils of Egypt and with tumors, festering sores and the itch, from which you cannot be cured. ²⁸The Lord will afflict you with madness, blindness and confusion of mind. ²⁹At midday you will grope about like a blind man in the dark. You will be unsuccessful in everything you do; day after day you will be oppressed and robbed, with no one to rescue you.

³⁰You will be pledged to be married to a woman, but another will take her and ravish her. You will build a house, but you will not live in it. You will plant a vineyard, but you will not even begin to enjoy its fruit. ³¹Your ox will be slaughtered before your eyes, but you will eat none of it. Your donkey will be forcibly taken from you and will not be returned. Your sheep will be given to your enemies, and no one will rescue them. ³²Your sons and daughters will be given to another nation, and you will wear out your eyes watching for them day after day, powerless to lift a hand. ³³A people that you do not know will eat what your land and labor produce, and you will have nothing but cruel oppression all your days. ³⁴The sights you see will drive you mad. ³⁵The Lord will afflict your knees and legs with painful boils that cannot be cured, spreading from the soles of your feet to the top of your head.

³⁶The Lord will drive you and the king you set over you to a nation unknown to you or your fathers. There you will worship other gods, gods of wood and stone. ³⁷You will become a thing of horror and an object of scorn and ridicule to all the nations where the Lord will drive you.

³⁸You will sow much seed in the field but you will harvest little, because locusts will devour it. ³⁹You will plant vineyards and cultivate them but you will not drink the wine or gather the grapes, because worms will eat them. ⁴⁰You will have olive trees throughout your country but you will not use the oil, because the olives will drop off. ⁴¹You will have sons and daughters but you will

ᵃ 20 Hebrew me

not keep them, because they will go into captivity. ⁴²Swarms of locusts will take over all your trees and the crops of your land.

⁴³The alien who lives among you will rise above you higher and higher, but you will sink lower and lower. ⁴⁴He will lend to you, but you will not lend to him. He will be the head, but you will be the tail.

⁴⁵All these curses will come upon you. They will pursue you and overtake you until you are destroyed, because you did not obey the LORD your God and observe the commands and decrees he gave you. ⁴⁶They will be a sign and a wonder to you and your descendants forever. ⁴⁷Because you did not serve the LORD your God joyfully and gladly in the time of prosperity, ⁴⁸therefore in hunger and thirst, in nakedness and dire poverty, you will serve the enemies the LORD sends against you. He will put an iron yoke on your neck until he has destroyed you.

⁴⁹The LORD will bring a nation against you from far away, from the ends of the earth, like an eagle swooping down, a nation whose language you will not understand, ⁵⁰a fierce-looking nation without respect for the old or pity for the young. ⁵¹They will devour the young of your livestock and the crops of your land until you are destroyed. They will leave you no grain, new wine or oil, nor any calves of your herds or lambs of your flocks until you are ruined. ⁵²They will lay siege to all the cities throughout your land until the high fortified walls in which you trust fall down. They will besiege all the cities throughout the land the LORD your God is giving you.

⁵³Because of the suffering that your enemy will inflict on you during the siege, you will eat the fruit of the womb, the flesh of the sons and daughters the LORD your God has given you. ⁵⁴Even the most gentle and sensitive man among you will have no compassion on his own brother or the wife he loves or his surviving children, ⁵⁵and he will not give to one of them any of the flesh of his children that he is eating. It will be all he has left because of the suffering your enemy will inflict on you during the siege of all your cities. ⁵⁶The

most gentle and sensitive woman among you—so sensitive and gentle that she would not venture to touch the ground with the sole of her foot—will begrudge the husband she loves and her own son or daughter ⁵⁷the afterbirth from her womb and the children she bears. For she intends to eat them secretly during the siege and in the distress that your enemy will inflict on you in your cities.

⁵⁸If you do not carefully follow all the words of this law, which are written in this book, and do not revere this glorious and awesome name—the LORD your God—⁵⁹the LORD will send fearful plagues on you and your descendants, harsh and prolonged disasters, and severe and lingering illnesses. ⁶⁰He will bring upon you all the diseases of Egypt that you dreaded, and they will cling to you. ⁶¹The LORD will also bring on you every kind of sickness and disaster not recorded in this Book of the Law, until you are destroyed. ⁶²You who were as numerous as the stars in the sky will be left but few in number, because you did not obey the LORD your God. ⁶³Just as it pleased the LORD to make you prosper and increase in number, so it will please him to ruin and destroy you. You will be uprooted from the land you are entering to possess.

⁶⁴Then the LORD will scatter you among all nations, from one end of the earth to the other. There you will worship other gods—gods of wood and stone, which neither you nor your fathers have known. ⁶⁵Among those nations you will find no repose, no resting place for the sole of your foot. There the LORD will give you an anxious mind, eyes weary with longing, and a despairing heart. ⁶⁶You will live in constant suspense, filled with dread both night and day, never sure of your life. ⁶⁷In the morning you will say, "If only it were evening!" and in the evening, "If only it were morning!"—because of the terror that will fill your hearts and the sights that your eyes will see. ⁶⁸The LORD will send you back in ships to Egypt on a journey I said you should never make again. There you will offer yourselves for sale to your enemies as male and female slaves, but no one will buy you.

Renewal of the Covenant

29 These are the terms of the covenant the LORD commanded Moses to make with the Israelites in Moab, in addition to the covenant he had made with them at Horeb.

²Moses summoned all the Israelites and said to them:

Your eyes have seen all that the LORD did in Egypt to Pharaoh, to all his officials and to all his land. ³With your own eyes you saw those great trials, those miraculous signs and great wonders. ⁴But to this day the LORD has not given you a mind that understands or eyes that see or ears that hear. ⁵During the forty years that I led you through the desert, your clothes did not wear out, nor did the sandals on your feet. ⁶You ate no bread and drank no wine or other fermented drink. I did this so that you might know that I am the LORD your God.

⁷When you reached this place, Sihon king of Heshbon and Og king of Bashan came out to fight against us, but we defeated them. ⁸We took their land and gave it as an inheritance to the Reubenites, the Gadites and the half-tribe of Manasseh.

⁹Carefully follow the terms of this covenant, so that you may prosper in everything you do. ¹⁰All of you are standing today in the presence of the LORD your God—your leaders and chief men, your elders and officials, and all the other men of Israel, ¹¹together with your children and your wives, and the aliens living in your camps who chop your wood and carry your water. ¹²You are standing here in order to enter into a covenant with the LORD your God, a covenant the LORD is making with you this day and sealing with an oath, ¹³to confirm you this day as his people, that he may be your God as he promised you and as he swore to your fathers, Abraham, Isaac and Jacob. ¹⁴I am making this covenant, with its oath, not only with you ¹⁵who are standing here with us today in the presence of the LORD our God but also with those who are not here today.

¹⁶You yourselves know how we lived in Egypt and how we passed through the countries on the way here. ¹⁷You saw among them their detestable images and idols of wood and stone, of silver and gold. ¹⁸Make sure there is no man or woman, clan or tribe among you today whose heart turns away from the LORD our God to go and worship the gods of those nations; make sure there is no root among you that produces such bitter poison.

¹⁹When such a person hears the words of this oath, he invokes a blessing on himself and therefore thinks, "I will be safe, even though I persist in going my own way." This will bring disaster on the watered land as well as the dry. *ᵃ* ²⁰The LORD will never be willing to forgive him; his wrath and zeal will burn against that man. All the curses written in this book will fall upon him, and the LORD will blot out his name from under heaven. ²¹The LORD will single him out from all the tribes of Israel for disaster, according to all the curses of the covenant written in this Book of the Law.

²²Your children who follow you in later generations and foreigners who come from distant lands will see the calamities that have fallen on the land and the diseases with which the LORD has afflicted it. ²³The whole land will be a burning waste of salt and sulfur—nothing planted, nothing sprouting, no vegetation growing on it. It will be like the destruction of Sodom and Gomorrah, Admah and Zeboiim, which the LORD overthrew in fierce anger. ²⁴All the nations will ask: "Why has the LORD done this to this land? Why this fierce, burning anger?"

²⁵And the answer will be: "It is because this people abandoned the covenant of the LORD, the God of their fathers, the covenant he made with them when he brought them out of Egypt. ²⁶They went off and worshiped other gods and bowed down to them, gods they did not know, gods he had not given them. ²⁷Therefore the LORD's anger burned against this land, so that he brought on it all the curses written in this book. ²⁸In furious anger and in great wrath the LORD uprooted them from their land and thrust them into another land, as it is now."

ᵃ 19 Or way, in order to add drunkenness to thirst."

²⁹The secret things belong to the Lord our God, but the things revealed belong to us and to our children forever, that we may follow all the words of this law.

Prosperity After Turning to the Lord

30 When all these blessings and curses I have set before you come upon you and you take them to heart wherever the Lord your God disperses you among the nations, ²and when you and your children return to the Lord your God and obey him with all your heart and with all your soul according to everything I command you today, ³then the Lord your God will restore your fortunes [a] and have compassion on you and gather you again from all the nations where he scattered you. ⁴Even if you have been banished to the most distant land under the heavens, from there the Lord your God will gather you and bring you back. ⁵He will bring you to the land that belonged to your fathers, and you will take possession of it. He will make you more prosperous and numerous than your fathers. ⁶The Lord your God will circumcise your hearts and the hearts of your descendants, so that you may love him with all your heart and with all your soul, and live. ⁷The Lord your God will put all these curses on your enemies who hate and persecute you. ⁸You will again obey the Lord and follow all his commands I am giving you today. ⁹Then the Lord your God will make you most prosperous in all the work of your hands and in the fruit of your womb, the young of your livestock and the crops of your land. The Lord will again delight in you and make you prosperous, just as he delighted in your fathers, ¹⁰if you obey the Lord your God and keep his commands and decrees that are written in this Book of the Law and turn to the Lord your God with all your heart and with all your soul.

The Offer of Life or Death

¹¹Now what I am commanding you today is not too difficult for you or beyond your reach. ¹²It is not up in heaven, so that you have to ask, "Who will ascend into heaven to get it and proclaim it to us so we may obey it?" ¹³Nor is it beyond the sea, so that you have to ask, "Who will cross the sea to get it and proclaim it to us so we may obey it?" ¹⁴No, the word is very near you; it is in your mouth and in your heart so you may obey it.

¹⁵See, I set before you today life and prosperity, death and destruction. ¹⁶For I command you today to love the Lord your God, to walk in his ways, and to keep his commands, decrees and laws; then you will live and increase, and the Lord your God will bless you in the land you are entering to possess.

¹⁷But if your heart turns away and you are not obedient, and if you are drawn away to bow down to other gods and worship them, ¹⁸I declare to you this day that you will certainly be destroyed. You will not live long in the land you are crossing the Jordan to enter and possess.

¹⁹This day I call heaven and earth as witnesses against you that I have set before you life and death, blessings and curses. Now choose life, so that you and your children may live ²⁰and that you may love the Lord your God, listen to his voice, and hold fast to him. For the Lord is your life, and he will give you many years in the land he swore to give to your fathers, Abraham, Isaac and Jacob.

[a] 3 Or *will bring you back from captivity*

PRAYING THE SCRIPTURES

Guidance

DEUTERONOMY 30:19–20

This day, O Lord, I pray that my grandchild will choose life, so that he and his children may live, and that he may love you, the Lord his God, that he will listen to your voice and hold fast to you — for you are his life.

Next prayer in Guidance Prayer Track: Psalm 119:33–36

Joshua to Succeed Moses

31 Then Moses went out and spoke these words to all Israel: ²"I am now a hundred and twenty years old and I am no longer able to lead you. The LORD has said to me, 'You shall not cross the Jordan.' ³The LORD your God himself will cross over ahead of you. He will destroy these nations before you, and you will take possession of their land. Joshua also will cross over ahead of you, as the LORD said. ⁴And the LORD will do to them what he did to Sihon and Og, the kings of the Amorites, whom he destroyed along with their land. ⁵The LORD will deliver them to you, and you must do to them all that I have commanded you. ⁶Be strong and courageous. Do not be afraid or terrified because of them, for the LORD your God goes with you; he will never leave you nor forsake you."

⁷Then Moses summoned Joshua and said to him in the presence of all Israel, "Be strong and courageous, for you must go with this people into the land that the LORD swore to their forefathers to give them, and you must divide it among them as their inheritance. ⁸The LORD himself goes before you and will be with you; he will never leave you nor forsake you. Do not be afraid; do not be discouraged."

TALKING POINTS

Military

God is with us wherever we go.

DEUTERONOMY 31:8

For more on military, go to Psalm 138:7–8.

The Reading of the Law

⁹So Moses wrote down this law and gave it to the priests, the sons of Levi, who carried the ark of the covenant of the LORD, and to all the elders of Israel. ¹⁰Then Moses commanded them:

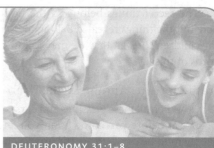

stories to share

DEUTERONOMY 31:1–8

Joshua Becomes the Next Leader of Israel

LIFE LESSON: We can trust God's promises.

TO TALK ABOUT

✦ What did God promise the Israelites?

✦ What did God promise Joshua?

✦ What are some other promises in the Bible?

✦ How do you know you can trust God's promises?

"At the end of every seven years, in the year for canceling debts, during the Feast of Tabernacles, ¹¹when all Israel comes to appear before the LORD your God at the place he will choose, you shall read this law before them in their hearing. ¹²Assemble the people—men, women and children, and the aliens living in your towns—so they can listen and learn to fear the LORD your God and follow carefully all the words of this law. ¹³Their children, who do not know this law, must hear it and learn to fear the LORD your God as long as you live in the land you are crossing the Jordan to possess."

Israel's Rebellion Predicted

¹⁴The LORD said to Moses, "Now the day of your death is near. Call Joshua and present yourselves at the Tent of Meeting, where I will com-

MONDAY

"THE LORD HIMSELF GOES
BEFORE YOU AND WILL BE WITH
YOU; HE WILL NEVER LEAVE
YOU NOR FORSAKE YOU. DO
NOT BE AFRAID; DO NOT BE
DISCOURAGED."

Deuteronomy 31:8

God Is Already There

BARBARA JOHNSON

READ | DEUTERONOMY 31:1–8

Don't you think we should delight in seeing ourselves the way God does? Then we can go out and share our best with the world. Our future is glorious in him because he has already said, "Have a good day and a fabulous forever!" He is growing us into saints. Though it may take a lifetime, shouldn't we rejoice along the way? Shouldn't we be grateful for how God is using us, even when the people around us might not appreciate it at the time?

My friend, remember to take this life one day at a time. When several days attack you, don't give up. A successful woman takes the bricks the Devil throws at her and uses them to lay a firm foundation. We all need enough trials to challenge us, enough challenges to strengthen us, and enough strength to do our part in making this a better place to live and love. Grace is receiving the gift of God in exactly who we are and bearing its fruit in the world. Just think how it changed the world because Noah didn't say, "I don't do arks." Moses didn't say, "I don't do seas." Paul didn't say, "I don't do letters." Michelangelo didn't say, "I don't do ceilings." Martin Luther didn't say, "I don't do doors." And of course, Jesus didn't say, "I don't do crosses."

Some people can't afford the tuition of the school of hard knocks. But that's where grace comes in. When God believes in you, your situation is never hopeless. When he walks with you, you are never alone. When God is on your side, you can never ever lose. So don't be afraid of tomorrow; God is already there!

Dear Lord, thank you for being in my today, my yesterday and my tomorrows. Let me feel your presence and your strength as I face each new challenge, each opportunity to make the world a better and more loving place. Amen.

GRANDCHILD IN FOCUS • PRAYER

SELECT ONE OF YOUR
GRANDCHILDREN TO FOCUS ON
IN PRAYER FOR THE NEXT 14 DAYS.

Salvation

Dear Lord, please guide my grandchild to your gift of salvation. I pray that she will come to know you, to love you and to walk close to you throughout her life. May she boldly claim Jesus as her Lord and Savior. Guide her as she makes choices that have eternal consequences. Help her to follow you each moment of her life. I pray this in Jesus' name, amen.

mission him." So Moses and Joshua came and presented themselves at the Tent of Meeting.

[15] Then the LORD appeared at the Tent in a pillar of cloud, and the cloud stood over the entrance to the Tent. [16] And the LORD said to Moses: "You are going to rest with your fathers, and these people will soon prostitute themselves to the foreign gods of the land they are entering. They will forsake me and break the covenant I made with them. [17] On that day I will become angry with them and forsake them; I will hide my face from them, and they will be destroyed. Many disasters and difficulties will come upon them, and on that day they will ask, 'Have not these disasters come upon us because our God is not with us?' [18] And I will certainly hide my face on that day because of all their wickedness in turning to other gods.

[19] "Now write down for yourselves this song and teach it to the Israelites and have them sing it, so that it may be a witness for me against them. [20] When I have brought them into the land flowing with milk and honey, the land I promised on oath to their forefathers, and when they eat their fill and thrive, they will turn to other gods and worship them, rejecting me and breaking my covenant. [21] And when many disasters and difficulties come upon them, this song will testify against them, because it will not be forgotten by their descendants. I know what they are disposed to do, even before I bring them into the land I promised them on oath." [22] So Moses wrote down this song that day and taught it to the Israelites.

[23] The LORD gave this command to Joshua son of Nun: "Be strong and courageous, for you will bring the Israelites into the land I promised them on oath, and I myself will be with you."

[24] After Moses finished writing in a book the words of this law from beginning to end, [25] he gave this command to the Levites who carried the ark of the covenant of the LORD: [26] "Take this Book of the Law and place it beside the ark of the covenant of the LORD your God. There it will remain as a witness against you. [27] For I know how rebellious and stiff-necked you are. If you have been rebellious against the LORD while I am still alive and with you, how much more will you rebel after I die! [28] Assemble before me all the elders of your tribes and all your officials, so that I can speak these words in their hearing and call heaven and earth to testify against them. [29] For I know that after my death you are sure to become utterly corrupt and to turn from the way I have commanded you. In days to come, disaster will fall upon you because you will do evil in the sight of the LORD and provoke him to anger by what your hands have made."

The Song of Moses

[30] And Moses recited the words of this song from beginning to end in the hearing of the whole assembly of Israel:

32 Listen, O heavens, and I will speak;
hear, O earth, the words of my mouth.
[2] Let my teaching fall like rain
and my words descend like dew,
like showers on new grass,
like abundant rain on tender plants.

[3] I will proclaim the name of the LORD.
Oh, praise the greatness of our God!
[4] He is the Rock, his works are perfect,
and all his ways are just.
A faithful God who does no wrong,
upright and just is he.

[5] They have acted corruptly toward him;
to their shame they are no longer his
children,
but a warped and crooked generation. [a]
[6] Is this the way you repay the LORD,
O foolish and unwise people?
Is he not your Father, your Creator, [b]
who made you and formed you?

[7] Remember the days of old;
consider the generations long past.
Ask your father and he will tell you,
your elders, and they will explain to you.

---

[a] 5 Or Corrupt are they and not his children, / a generation warped and twisted to their shame   [b] 6 Or Father, who bought you

⁸When the Most High gave the nations their
inheritance,
when he divided all mankind,
he set up boundaries for the peoples
according to the number of the sons of
Israel.ᵃ
⁹For the LORD's portion is his people,
Jacob his allotted inheritance.

¹⁰In a desert land he found him,
in a barren and howling waste.
He shielded him and cared for him;
he guarded him as the apple of his eye,
¹¹like an eagle that stirs up its nest
and hovers over its young,
that spreads its wings to catch them
and carries them on its pinions.
¹²The LORD alone led him;
no foreign god was with him.

¹³He made him ride on the heights of the land
and fed him with the fruit of the fields.
He nourished him with honey from the rock,
and with oil from the flinty crag,
¹⁴with curds and milk from herd and flock
and with fattened lambs and goats,
with choice rams of Bashan
and the finest kernels of wheat.
You drank the foaming blood of the grape.

¹⁵Jeshurunᵇ grew fat and kicked;
filled with food, he became heavy and
sleek.
He abandoned the God who made him
and rejected the Rock his Savior.
¹⁶They made him jealous with their foreign
gods
and angered him with their detestable
idols.
¹⁷They sacrificed to demons, which are not
God—
gods they had not known,
gods that recently appeared,
gods your fathers did not fear.
¹⁸You deserted the Rock, who fathered you;
you forgot the God who gave you birth.

¹⁹The LORD saw this and rejected them
because he was angered by his sons and
daughters.
²⁰"I will hide my face from them," he said,
"and see what their end will be;
for they are a perverse generation,
children who are unfaithful.
²¹They made me jealous by what is no god
and angered me with their worthless idols.
I will make them envious by those who are
not a people;
I will make them angry by a nation that
has no understanding.
²²For a fire has been kindled by my wrath,
one that burns to the realm of deathᶜ
below.
It will devour the earth and its harvests
and set afire the foundations of the
mountains.

²³"I will heap calamities upon them
and spend my arrows against them.
²⁴I will send wasting famine against them,
consuming pestilence and deadly plague;
I will send against them the fangs of wild
beasts,
the venom of vipers that glide in the dust.
²⁵In the street the sword will make them
childless;
in their homes terror will reign.
Young men and young women will perish,
infants and gray-haired men.
²⁶I said I would scatter them
and blot out their memory from mankind,
²⁷but I dreaded the taunt of the enemy,
lest the adversary misunderstand
and say, 'Our hand has triumphed;
the LORD has not done all this.'"

²⁸They are a nation without sense,
there is no discernment in them.
²⁹If only they were wise and would understand
this
and discern what their end will be!

ᵃ 8 Masoretic Text; Dead Sea Scrolls (see also Septuagint) sons
of God   ᵇ 15 Jeshurun means the upright one, that is, Israel.
ᶜ 22 Hebrew to Sheol

³⁰How could one man chase a thousand,
  or two put ten thousand to flight,
unless their Rock had sold them,
  unless the LORD had given them up?
³¹For their rock is not like our Rock,
  as even our enemies concede.
³²Their vine comes from the vine of Sodom
  and from the fields of Gomorrah.
Their grapes are filled with poison,
  and their clusters with bitterness.
³³Their wine is the venom of serpents,
  the deadly poison of cobras.

³⁴"Have I not kept this in reserve
  and sealed it in my vaults?
³⁵It is mine to avenge; I will repay.
  In due time their foot will slip;
their day of disaster is near
  and their doom rushes upon them."

³⁶The LORD will judge his people
  and have compassion on his servants
when he sees their strength is gone
  and no one is left, slave or free.
³⁷He will say: "Now where are their gods,
  the rock they took refuge in,
³⁸the gods who ate the fat of their sacrifices
  and drank the wine of their drink
    offerings?
Let them rise up to help you!
  Let them give you shelter!

³⁹"See now that I myself am He!
  There is no god besides me.
I put to death and I bring to life,
  I have wounded and I will heal,
  and no one can deliver out of my hand.
⁴⁰I lift my hand to heaven and declare:
  As surely as I live forever,
⁴¹when I sharpen my flashing sword
  and my hand grasps it in judgment,
I will take vengeance on my adversaries
  and repay those who hate me.
⁴²I will make my arrows drunk with blood,
  while my sword devours flesh:
the blood of the slain and the captives,
  the heads of the enemy leaders."

⁴³Rejoice, O nations, with his people,^{a, b}
  for he will avenge the blood of his servants;
he will take vengeance on his enemies
  and make atonement for his land and
    people.

⁴⁴Moses came with Joshua^c son of Nun and spoke all the words of this song in the hearing of the people. ⁴⁵When Moses finished reciting all these words to all Israel, ⁴⁶he said to them, "Take to heart all the words I have solemnly declared to you this day, so that you may command your children to obey carefully all the words of this law. ⁴⁷They are not just idle words for you—they are your life. By them you will live long in the land you are crossing the Jordan to possess."

Moses to Die on Mount Nebo

⁴⁸On that same day the LORD told Moses, ⁴⁹"Go up into the Abarim Range to Mount Nebo in Moab, across from Jericho, and view Canaan, the land I am giving the Israelites as their own possession. ⁵⁰There on the mountain that you have climbed you will die and be gathered to your people, just as your brother Aaron died on Mount Hor and was gathered to his people. ⁵¹This is because both of you broke faith with me in the presence of the Israelites at the waters of Meribah Kadesh in the Desert of Zin and because you did not uphold my holiness among the Israelites. ⁵²Therefore, you will see the land only from a distance; you will not enter the land I am giving to the people of Israel."

Moses Blesses the Tribes

33:1–29Ref — Ge 49:1–28

33 This is the blessing that Moses the man of God pronounced on the Israelites before his death. ²He said:

  "The LORD came from Sinai
    and dawned over them from Seir;
  he shone forth from Mount Paran.

^a 43 Or *Make his people rejoice, O nations* ^b 43 Masoretic Text; Dead Sea Scrolls (see also Septuagint) *people, / and let all the angels worship him /* ^c 44 Hebrew *Hoshea,* a variant of *Joshua*

He came with [a] myriads of holy ones
  from the south, from his mountain slopes. [b]
³ Surely it is you who love the people;
  all the holy ones are in your hand.
At your feet they all bow down,
  and from you receive instruction,
⁴ the law that Moses gave us,
  the possession of the assembly of Jacob.
⁵ He was king over Jeshurun [c]
  when the leaders of the people assembled,
  along with the tribes of Israel.

⁶ "Let Reuben live and not die,
  nor [d] his men be few."

⁷ And this he said about Judah:

"Hear, O Lᴏʀᴅ, the cry of Judah;
  bring him to his people.
With his own hands he defends his cause.
  Oh, be his help against his foes!"

⁸ About Levi he said:

"Your Thummim and Urim belong
  to the man you favored.
You tested him at Massah;
  you contended with him at the waters of
  Meribah.
⁹ He said of his father and mother,
  'I have no regard for them.'
He did not recognize his brothers
  or acknowledge his own children,
but he watched over your word
  and guarded your covenant.
¹⁰ He teaches your precepts to Jacob
  and your law to Israel.
He offers incense before you
  and whole burnt offerings on your altar.
¹¹ Bless all his skills, O Lᴏʀᴅ,
  and be pleased with the work of his hands.
Smite the loins of those who rise up against
  him;
  strike his foes till they rise no more."

¹² About Benjamin he said:

"Let the beloved of the Lᴏʀᴅ rest secure in
  him,

for he shields him all day long,
  and the one the Lᴏʀᴅ loves rests between
  his shoulders."

¹³ About Joseph he said:

"May the Lᴏʀᴅ bless his land
  with the precious dew from heaven above
  and with the deep waters that lie below;
¹⁴ with the best the sun brings forth
  and the finest the moon can yield;
¹⁵ with the choicest gifts of the ancient
  mountains
  and the fruitfulness of the everlasting hills;
¹⁶ with the best gifts of the earth and its fullness
  and the favor of him who dwelt in the
  burning bush.
Let all these rest on the head of Joseph,
  on the brow of the prince among [e] his
  brothers.
¹⁷ In majesty he is like a firstborn bull;
  his horns are the horns of a wild ox.
With them he will gore the nations,
  even those at the ends of the earth.
Such are the ten thousands of Ephraim;
  such are the thousands of Manasseh."

¹⁸ About Zebulun he said:

"Rejoice, Zebulun, in your going out,
  and you, Issachar, in your tents.
¹⁹ They will summon peoples to the mountain
  and there offer sacrifices of righteousness;
they will feast on the abundance of the seas,
  on the treasures hidden in the sand."

²⁰ About Gad he said:

"Blessed is he who enlarges Gad's domain!
  Gad lives there like a lion,
  tearing at arm or head.
²¹ He chose the best land for himself;
  the leader's portion was kept for him.
When the heads of the people assembled,
  he carried out the Lᴏʀᴅ's righteous will,
  and his judgments concerning Israel."

---

[a] 2 Or *from*   [b] 2 The meaning of the Hebrew for this phrase is
uncertain.   [c] 5 *Jeshurun* means *the upright one,* that is, Israel; also
in verse 26.   [d] 6 Or *but let*   [e] 16 Or *of the one separated from*

"SURELY IT IS YOU WHO LOVE
THE PEOPLE; ALL THE HOLY
ONES ARE IN YOUR HAND.
AT YOUR FEET THEY ALL BOW
DOWN, AND FROM YOU RECEIVE
INSTRUCTION."

Deuteronomy 33:3

Places of Rest

MILLIE STAMM

READ | DEUTERONOMY 33:1–5

Do you have a particular spot where you like to go to escape the strain of daily living — a place that is peaceful and quiet? There the cares of life slip away and you forget everything but the joy of solitude. At least you may wish for such a place. The above verse suggests three resting places for God's children — in His heart; in His hand; at His feet.

First, we have a resting place in His great heart of love: "I have loved you with an everlasting love" (Jeremiah 31:3). Second, there is a resting place in His hand. This is a place of security. "So do not fear, for I am with you; do not be dismayed, for I am your God. I will strengthen you and help you; I will uphold you with my righteous right hand" (Isaiah 41:10). Third, we have a resting place at His feet (see Luke 10:39). Mary found this resting place. This is a place of fellowship with Him, a place to hear His voice, a place of instruction. Sitting at His feet, listening to Him, loving Him we find peace and refreshment. What blessed resting places God has provided for us — in His heart; in His hand; at His feet!

One night a preacher was using as his text, "Come to me, all you who are weary and burdened, and I will give you rest" (Matthew 11:28). He asked, "What does this verse mean?" A little girl answered, "It means He wants me." Both the preacher and the people felt that no more need be said.

Father, thank you for inviting me to sit at your feet. Thank you for inviting me into your great heart of love, where I find rest for my soul. Thank you for accepting me as your own dear child and upholding me in your loving hand.

Your next devotion is located on page 284.

GRANDCHILD IN FOCUS • PRAYER

Physical Well-Being

Almighty God, Creator of us all, I pray that you will watch over my grandchild's physical development. May he grow in strength through the stages of his life. As he grows in awareness of his body, help him to understand that each body develops uniquely, yet is within your plan and your control. Please guard his health so that his diseases are few, his injuries are minor and his infirmities are brief. Amen.

²² About Dan he said:

"Dan is a lion's cub,
　　springing out of Bashan."

²³ About Naphtali he said:

"Naphtali is abounding with the favor of
　　the LORD
　　and is full of his blessing;
　　he will inherit southward to the lake."

²⁴ About Asher he said:

"Most blessed of sons is Asher;
　　let him be favored by his brothers,
　　and let him bathe his feet in oil.
²⁵ The bolts of your gates will be iron and
　　bronze,
　　and your strength will equal your days.

²⁶ "There is no one like the God of
　　Jeshurun,
　　who rides on the heavens to help you
　　and on the clouds in his majesty.
²⁷ The eternal God is your refuge,
　　and underneath are the everlasting
　　arms.
He will drive out your enemy before you,
　　saying, 'Destroy him!'
²⁸ So Israel will live in safety alone;
　　Jacob's spring is secure
in a land of grain and new wine,
　　where the heavens drop dew.

²⁹ Blessed are you, O Israel!
　　Who is like you,
　　a people saved by the LORD?
He is your shield and helper
　　and your glorious sword.
Your enemies will cower before you,
　　and you will trample down their high
　　　　places. ^a"

The Death of Moses

34 Then Moses climbed Mount Nebo from the plains of Moab to the top of Pisgah, across from Jericho. There the LORD showed him the whole land—from Gilead to Dan, ² all of Naphtali, the territory of Ephraim and Manasseh, all the land of Judah as far as the western sea, ^b ³ the Negev and the whole region from the Valley of Jericho, the City of Palms, as far as Zoar. ⁴ Then the LORD said to him, "This is the land I promised on oath to Abraham, Isaac and Jacob when I said, 'I will give it to your descendants.' I have let you see it with your eyes, but you will not cross over into it."

⁵ And Moses the servant of the LORD died there in Moab, as the LORD had said. ⁶ He buried him ^c in Moab, in the valley opposite Beth Peor, but to this day no one knows where his grave is. ⁷ Moses was a hundred and twenty years old when he died, yet his eyes were not weak nor his strength gone. ⁸ The Israelites grieved for Moses in the plains of Moab thirty days, until the time of weeping and mourning was over.

⁹ Now Joshua son of Nun was filled with the spirit ^d of wisdom because Moses had laid his hands on him. So the Israelites listened to him and did what the LORD had commanded Moses.

¹⁰ Since then, no prophet has risen in Israel like Moses, whom the LORD knew face to face, ¹¹ who did all those miraculous signs and wonders the LORD sent him to do in Egypt—to Pharaoh and to all his officials and to his whole land. ¹² For no one has ever shown the mighty power or performed the awesome deeds that Moses did in the sight of all Israel.

TALKING POINTS

Disability

God, our refuge, holds us securely
in his everlasting arms.

DEUTERONOMY 33:26–27

For more on disability, go to 2 Samuel 9:1–13.

---

^a 29 Or *will tread upon their bodies*　　^b 2 That is, the Mediterranean　　^c 6 Or *He was buried*　　^d 9 Or *Spirit*

A Time TO TRUST

After 40 years in the wilderness, the time had come for the Israelites to see the execution of God's plan to give them the promised land. In fulfillment of God's decree in Numbers 14:26–35, the generation of adults who had witnessed the wonders of the ten plagues and had miraculously crossed the Red Sea—only to rebel against the Lord and refuse to enter the promised land—was gone. In their place was a new generation, one that had to believe that God would help them replace fear with courage, weakness with strength, doubt with faith. In short, they had to believe that God could make the impossible possible.

Still today, each new generation must be told of God's love and power. The members of each generation must choose God as their God and believe that they can be strong and courageous when they have him on their side.

As grandmothers we have been called, like Joshua, to lead the next generation into God's land of promise. Our calling is to teach our grandchildren about God's faithfulness, about his love, about his power. As we do this, we'll realize one of the most important lessons of this book: God uses the younger generation of faithful people to carry on his work in the world.

VERSE *to* REMEMBER | JOSHUA 10:25

Joshua said to them, "Do not be afraid; do not be discouraged. Be strong and courageous. This is what the LORD will do to all the enemies you are going to fight."

ABOUT JOSHUA

WRITTEN BY:
Unknown; probably Joshua in its earliest form

WRITTEN FOR:
God's chosen people, the Israelites

DATE WRITTEN:
Probably around 1390 B.C.

WHY WRITTEN:
To recount how God helped the Israelites enter and possess the promised land

Joshua

The Lord Commands Joshua

1 After the death of Moses the servant of the Lord, the Lord said to Joshua son of Nun, Moses' aide: ²"Moses my servant is dead. Now then, you and all these people, get ready to cross the Jordan River into the land I am about to give to them—to the Israelites. ³I will give you every place where you set your foot, as I promised Moses. ⁴Your territory will extend from the desert to Lebanon, and from the great river, the Euphrates—all the Hittite country—to the Great Sea *a* on the west. ⁵No one will be able to stand up against you all the days of your life. As I was with Moses, so I will be with you; I will never leave you nor forsake you.

⁶"Be strong and courageous, because you will lead these people to inherit the land I swore to their forefathers to give them. ⁷Be strong and very courageous. Be careful to obey all the law my servant Moses gave you; do not turn from it to the right or to the left, that you may be successful wherever you go. ⁸Do not let this Book of the Law depart from your mouth; meditate on it day and night, so that you may be careful to do everything written in it. Then you will be prosperous and successful. ⁹Have I not commanded you? Be strong and courageous. Do not be terrified; do not be discouraged, for the Lord your God will be with you wherever you go."

TALKING POINTS

Fear

God is always with us, eliminating any need to fear.

JOSHUA 1:9

For more on fear, go to Psalm 46:1–11.

¹⁰So Joshua ordered the officers of the people: ¹¹"Go through the camp and tell the people, 'Get your supplies ready. Three days from now you will cross the Jordan here to go in and take possession of the land the Lord your God is giving you for your own.'"

¹²But to the Reubenites, the Gadites and the half-tribe of Manasseh, Joshua said, ¹³"Remember the command that Moses the servant of the Lord gave you: 'The Lord your God is giving you rest and has granted you this land.' ¹⁴Your wives, your children and your livestock may stay in the land that Moses gave you east of the Jordan, but all your fighting men, fully armed, must cross over ahead of your brothers. You are to help your brothers ¹⁵until the Lord gives them rest, as he has done for you, and until they too have taken possession of the land that the Lord your God is giving them. After that, you may go back and occupy your own land, which Moses the servant of the Lord gave you east of the Jordan toward the sunrise."

¹⁶Then they answered Joshua, "Whatever you have commanded us we will do, and wherever you send us we will go. ¹⁷Just as we fully obeyed Moses, so we will obey you. Only may the Lord your God be with you as he was with Moses. ¹⁸Whoever rebels against your word and does not obey your words, whatever you may command them, will be put to death. Only be strong and courageous!"

PRAYING THE SCRIPTURES

Reassurance

JOSHUA 1:9

Lord, help my grandchild to be strong and courageous. Help her not to be terrified or discouraged, but to remember that you, the Lord her God, will be with her wherever she goes.

Next prayer in Reassurance Prayer Track: Judges 2:18

a 4 That is, the Mediterranean

> "HAVE I NOT COMMANDED YOU?
> BE STRONG AND COURAGEOUS.
> DO NOT BE TERRIFIED; DO NOT
> BE DISCOURAGED, FOR THE LORD
> YOUR GOD WILL BE WITH YOU
> WHEREVER YOU GO."
>
> *Joshua 1:9*

That First Jump

GAYLE ROPER

READ | JOSHUA 1:1 – 18

"Okay, kids, who wants to go tubing?" Chuck asked.

"Me! Me!" Clad in their life preservers, they surged into the four-man inflated tube. Devan claimed the deep front pocket. PJ and Abbie took the two side pockets, and Brianne, at ten the oldest of the group, sat in the back. Only shoulders and heads were visible. Chuck made big circles with the motorboat, with Cindy, PJ's mom, acting as spotter. Whenever they whooshed by the dock, Audrey, the girls' mom, and I cheered.

On one pass, Brianne yelled, "Now!" She and Abbie stood in their pockets and bailed out of the tube, something they had done before. PJ stood and jumped too, his first try. He made the mistake of jumping out the front instead of the back or side, and the tube went right over him. Given the speed of the boat, the tube was gone in no time, but when PJ bobbed to the surface, tears were clearly a blink away.

Audrey and I began clapping and cheering. "Yeah, PJ! Way to go, PJ! Good for you, PJ!" Suddenly PJ's face cleared, and he began to smile. Soon he was strutting around, bragging about his great jump and his plans to do it again.

I thought about the phenomenal power of encouragement, of knowing you have cheerleaders, of knowing there are people who are proud of you. We are capable of surviving much with the courage we get from others. How much more are we strengthened and made courageous by the knowledge that our God is with us wherever we go, under tubes or into life's storms?

Lord, give PJ and grandchildren everywhere both the encouragers and the courage they need in life. And please give me the same. Amen.

Your next devotion is located on page 288.

GRANDCHILD IN FOCUS • PRAYER

Emotional Development

O God, Creator of mind and body, I pray that you will give my grandchild emotional health and strength. Where there is anger, bring peace. Where there is confusion, bring clarity and focus. Where there are dark shadows, cast a ray of hope. Fill her with the sunshine of your Spirit. Warm her with the presence of your peace. Amen.

Rahab and the Spies

2 Then Joshua son of Nun secretly sent two spies from Shittim. "Go, look over the land," he said, "especially Jericho." So they went and entered the house of a prostitute *a* named Rahab and stayed there.

²The king of Jericho was told, "Look! Some of the Israelites have come here tonight to spy out the land." ³So the king of Jericho sent this message to Rahab: "Bring out the men who came to you and entered your house, because they have come to spy out the whole land."

⁴But the woman had taken the two men and hidden them. She said, "Yes, the men came to me, but I did not know where they had come from. ⁵At dusk, when it was time to close the city gate, the men left. I don't know which way they went. Go after them quickly. You may catch up with them." ⁶(But she had taken them up to the roof and hidden them under the stalks of flax she had laid out on the roof.) ⁷So the men set out in pursuit of the spies on the road that leads to the fords of the Jordan, and as soon as the pursuers had gone out, the gate was shut.

⁸Before the spies lay down for the night, she went up on the roof ⁹and said to them, "I know that the LORD has given this land to you and that a great fear of you has fallen on us, so that all who live in this country are melting in fear because of you. ¹⁰We have heard how the LORD dried up the water of the Red Sea *b* for you when you came out of Egypt, and what you did to Sihon and Og, the two kings of the Amorites east of the Jordan, whom you completely destroyed. *c* ¹¹When we heard of it, our hearts melted and everyone's courage failed because of you, for the LORD your God is God in heaven above and on the earth below. ¹²Now then, please swear to me by the LORD that you will show kindness to my family, because I have shown kindness to you. Give me a sure sign ¹³that you will spare the lives of my father and mother, my brothers and sisters, and all who belong to them, and that you will save us from death."

¹⁴"Our lives for your lives!" the men assured her. "If you don't tell what we are doing, we will treat you kindly and faithfully when the LORD gives us the land."

JOSHUA 2:1–24

Rahab and the Spies

LIFE LESSON: God can use anyone to accomplish his plans.

TO TALK ABOUT

✦ How did the spies escape from the city?

✦ Why did Rahab help the Israelite spies?

✦ Do you think it was okay for Rahab to lie about the spies in her house? Explain.

✦ Why do you think God used Rahab to help the Israelites?

¹⁵So she let them down by a rope through the window, for the house she lived in was part of the city wall. ¹⁶Now she had said to them, "Go to the hills so the pursuers will not find you. Hide yourselves there three days until they return, and then go on your way."

¹⁷The men said to her, "This oath you made us swear will not be binding on us ¹⁸unless, when we enter the land, you have tied this scarlet cord

---

a 1 Or possibly *an innkeeper*   *b 10* Hebrew *Yam Suph*; that is, Sea of Reeds   *c 10* The Hebrew term refers to the irrevocable giving over of things or persons to the LORD, often by totally destroying them.

stories to share

in the window through which you let us down, and unless you have brought your father and mother, your brothers and all your family into your house. ¹⁹ If anyone goes outside your house into the street, his blood will be on his own head; we will not be responsible. As for anyone who is in the house with you, his blood will be on our head if a hand is laid on him. ²⁰ But if you tell what we are doing, we will be released from the oath you made us swear."

²¹ "Agreed," she replied. "Let it be as you say." So she sent them away and they departed. And she tied the scarlet cord in the window.

²² When they left, they went into the hills and stayed there three days, until the pursuers had searched all along the road and returned without finding them. ²³ Then the two men started back. They went down out of the hills, forded the river and came to Joshua son of Nun and told him everything that had happened to them. ²⁴ They said to Joshua, "The LORD has surely given the whole land into our hands; all the people are melting in fear because of us."

Crossing the Jordan

3 Early in the morning Joshua and all the Israelites set out from Shittim and went to the Jordan, where they camped before crossing over. ² After three days the officers went throughout the camp, ³ giving orders to the people: "When you see the ark of the covenant of the LORD your God, and the priests, who are Levites, carrying it, you are to move out from your positions and follow it. ⁴ Then you will know which way to go, since you have never been this way before. But keep a distance of about a thousand yards ᵃ between you and the ark; do not go near it."

⁵ Joshua told the people, "Consecrate yourselves, for tomorrow the LORD will do amazing things among you."

⁶ Joshua said to the priests, "Take up the ark of the covenant and pass on ahead of the people." So they took it up and went ahead of them.

⁷ And the LORD said to Joshua, "Today I will begin to exalt you in the eyes of all Israel, so they may know that I am with you as I was with Moses. ⁸ Tell the priests who carry the ark of the covenant: 'When you reach the edge of the Jordan's waters, go and stand in the river.' "

⁹ Joshua said to the Israelites, "Come here and listen to the words of the LORD your God. ¹⁰ This is how you will know that the living God is among you and that he will certainly drive out before you the Canaanites, Hittites, Hivites, Perizzites, Girgashites, Amorites and Jebusites. ¹¹ See, the ark of the covenant of the Lord of all the earth will go into the Jordan ahead of you. ¹² Now then, choose twelve men from the tribes

ᵃ 4 Hebrew *about two thousand cubits* (about 900 meters)

stories to share

JOSHUA 3:1–17

Crossing the Jordan River

LIFE LESSON: God sometimes uses miracles to accomplish his purposes.

TO TALK ABOUT

✦ What did the priests need to do so that the Israelites could cross the flooded river?

✦ What other story does this remind you of? (Hint: Read Exodus 14.)

✦ Why do you think God sometimes uses miracles?

✦ Why does God often wait until we "step out" in faith to provide a solution to our problems?

of Israel, one from each tribe. ¹³And as soon as the priests who carry the ark of the LORD — the Lord of all the earth — set foot in the Jordan, its waters flowing downstream will be cut off and stand up in a heap."

¹⁴So when the people broke camp to cross the Jordan, the priests carrying the ark of the covenant went ahead of them. ¹⁵Now the Jordan is at flood stage all during harvest. Yet as soon as the priests who carried the ark reached the Jordan and their feet touched the water's edge, ¹⁶the water from upstream stopped flowing. It piled up in a heap a great distance away, at a town called Adam in the vicinity of Zarethan, while the water flowing down to the Sea of the Arabah (the Salt Sea ᵃ) was completely cut off. So the people crossed over opposite Jericho. ¹⁷The priests who carried the ark of the covenant of the LORD stood firm on dry ground in the middle of the Jordan, while all Israel passed by until the whole nation had completed the crossing on dry ground.

4 When the whole nation had finished crossing the Jordan, the LORD said to Joshua, ²"Choose twelve men from among the people, one from each tribe, ³and tell them to take up twelve stones from the middle of the Jordan from right where the priests stood and to carry them over with you and put them down at the place where you stay tonight."

⁴So Joshua called together the twelve men he had appointed from the Israelites, one from each tribe, ⁵and said to them, "Go over before the ark of the LORD your God into the middle of the Jordan. Each of you is to take up a stone on his shoulder, according to the number of the tribes of the Israelites, ⁶to serve as a sign among you. In the future, when your children ask you, 'What do these stones mean?' ⁷tell them that the flow of the Jordan was cut off before the ark of the covenant of the LORD. When it crossed the Jordan, the waters of the Jordan were cut off. These stones are to be a memorial to the people of Israel forever."

⁸So the Israelites did as Joshua commanded them. They took twelve stones from the middle of the Jordan, according to the number of the

tribes of the Israelites, as the LORD had told Joshua; and they carried them over with them to their camp, where they put them down. ⁹Joshua set up the twelve stones that had been ᵇ in the middle of the Jordan at the spot where the priests who carried the ark of the covenant had stood. And they are there to this day.

¹⁰Now the priests who carried the ark remained standing in the middle of the Jordan until everything the LORD had commanded Joshua was done by the people, just as Moses had directed Joshua. The people hurried over, ¹¹and as soon as all of them had crossed, the ark of the LORD and the priests came to the other side while the people watched. ¹²The men of Reuben, Gad and the half-tribe of Manasseh crossed over, armed, in front of the Israelites, as Moses had directed them. ¹³About forty thousand armed for battle crossed over before the LORD to the plains of Jericho for war.

¹⁴That day the LORD exalted Joshua in the sight of all Israel; and they revered him all the days of his life, just as they had revered Moses.

¹⁵Then the LORD said to Joshua, ¹⁶"Command the priests carrying the ark of the Testimony to come up out of the Jordan."

¹⁷So Joshua commanded the priests, "Come up out of the Jordan."

¹⁸And the priests came up out of the river carrying the ark of the covenant of the LORD. No sooner had they set their feet on the dry ground than the waters of the Jordan returned to their place and ran at flood stage as before.

¹⁹On the tenth day of the first month the people went up from the Jordan and camped at Gilgal on the eastern border of Jericho. ²⁰And Joshua set up at Gilgal the twelve stones they had taken out of the Jordan. ²¹He said to the Israelites, "In the future when your descendants ask their fathers, 'What do these stones mean?' ²²tell them, 'Israel crossed the Jordan on dry ground.' ²³For the LORD your God dried up the Jordan before you until you had crossed over. The LORD your

ᵃ 16 That is, the Dead Sea   ᵇ 9 Or Joshua also set up twelve stones

JOSHUA SET UP AT GILGAL
THE TWELVE STONES THEY HAD
TAKEN OUT OF THE JORDAN.
Joshua 4:20

Visual Aids

CAROL KUYKENDALL

READ | JOSHUA 4:1 – 24

When our children were growing up, our refrigerator door looked like a wonderful, messy collage of scribbled artwork, photographs, various school schedules, cartoons, quotes, Scripture verses and personal messages. Then in our early empty-nest years, we totally cleared off the clutter. Our refrigerator door looked refreshingly clean — and boring.

Thankfully, our refrigerator door has taken on a meaningful personality once again. Along with photographs of our grandchildren, we have brightly crayoned pieces of priceless art, mostly of stick figure families and pointy-edged suns. I love our refrigerator door once again because it is filled with visual aids that remind us of the importance of our grandchildren in our lives. I hope these visual aids give our grandchildren the same message.

I believe that God created us as visual learners who respond well to visual aids. The Bible is filled with such examples, like the monument of 12 stones piled up at Gilgal to remind the people of God's great faithfulness in miraculously enabling them to cross the Jordan River at flood stage. Visual aids are powerful reminders of an important message.

Children are dependent upon outside sources to meet their need for love, which gives them a foundation of security and confidence. That was true for my own children, and it is still true for my grandchildren. When they come into our house and see their artwork and photos on our refrigerator and scattered throughout our house, I hope they are reminded that they are loved and matter greatly to us.

That's an important message.

Lord, you teach us that visual aids are powerful reminders. May we use them to remind our grandchildren of your love for us and our love for them.

Your next devotion is located on page 315.

GRANDCHILD IN FOCUS • PRAYER

Spiritual Growth

Dear Lord, today I pray for my grandchild's spiritual growth. I ask that you instill in him the desire to read and memorize your Word. Give him a passion to be in conversation with you. May loving and serving you be part of his daily life. I ask that you stay close to him and lead him to be transformed to your likeness, to reflect your grace and to radiate your love. I pray this in Jesus' name, amen.

God did to the Jordan just what he had done to the Red Sea[a] when he dried it up before us until we had crossed over. ²⁴He did this so that all the peoples of the earth might know that the hand of the LORD is powerful and so that you might always fear the LORD your God."

Circumcision at Gilgal

5 Now when all the Amorite kings west of the Jordan and all the Canaanite kings along the coast heard how the LORD had dried up the Jordan before the Israelites until we had crossed over, their hearts melted and they no longer had the courage to face the Israelites.

²At that time the LORD said to Joshua, "Make flint knives and circumcise the Israelites again." ³So Joshua made flint knives and circumcised the Israelites at Gibeath Haaraloth.[b]

⁴Now this is why he did so: All those who came out of Egypt—all the men of military age—died in the desert on the way after leaving Egypt. ⁵All the people that came out had been circumcised, but all the people born in the desert during the journey from Egypt had not. ⁶The Israelites had moved about in the desert forty years until all the men who were of military age when they left Egypt had died, since they had not obeyed the LORD. For the LORD had sworn to them that they would not see the land that he had solemnly promised their fathers to give us, a land flowing with milk and honey. ⁷So he raised up their sons in their place, and these were the ones Joshua circumcised. They were still uncircumcised because they had not been circumcised on the way. ⁸And after the whole nation had been circumcised, they remained where they were in camp until they were healed.

⁹Then the LORD said to Joshua, "Today I have rolled away the reproach of Egypt from you." So the place has been called Gilgal[c] to this day.

¹⁰On the evening of the fourteenth day of the month, while camped at Gilgal on the plains of Jericho, the Israelites celebrated the Passover. ¹¹The day after the Passover, that very day, they ate some of the produce of the land: unleavened bread and roasted grain. ¹²The manna stopped the day after[d] they ate this food from the land; there was no longer any manna for the Israelites, but that year they ate of the produce of Canaan.

The Fall of Jericho

¹³Now when Joshua was near Jericho, he looked up and saw a man standing in front of him with a drawn sword in his hand. Joshua went up to him and asked, "Are you for us or for our enemies?"

¹⁴"Neither," he replied, "but as commander of the army of the LORD I have now come." Then Joshua fell facedown to the ground in reverence, and asked him, "What message does my Lord[e] have for his servant?"

¹⁵The commander of the LORD's army replied, "Take off your sandals, for the place where you are standing is holy." And Joshua did so.

6 Now Jericho was tightly shut up because of the Israelites. No one went out and no one came in.

²Then the LORD said to Joshua, "See, I have delivered Jericho into your hands, along with its king and its fighting men. ³March around the city once with all the armed men. Do this for six days. ⁴Have seven priests carry trumpets of rams' horns in front of the ark. On the seventh day, march around the city seven times, with the priests blowing the trumpets. ⁵When you hear them sound a long blast on the trumpets, have all the people give a loud shout; then the wall of the city will collapse and the people will go up, every man straight in."

⁶So Joshua son of Nun called the priests and said to them, "Take up the ark of the covenant of the LORD and have seven priests carry trumpets in front of it." ⁷And he ordered the people, "Advance! March around the city, with the armed guard going ahead of the ark of the LORD."

⁸When Joshua had spoken to the people, the seven priests carrying the seven trumpets before

---

a 23 Hebrew *Yam Suph*; that is, Sea of Reeds   *b 3* Gibeath Haaraloth means *hill of foreskins.*   *c 9* Gilgal sounds like the Hebrew for *roll.*   *d 12* Or *the day*   *e 14* Or *lord*

JOSHUA 5:13—6:20,25

Israel Captures Jericho

LIFE LESSON: God gives us victories.

TO TALK ABOUT

+ How many days did the people have to march around the city?

+ What do you think the Israelites thought about God's strange instructions?

+ What happened to Rahab and her family after the walls collapsed?

+ Did the people's shouts make the walls of Jericho collapse? Who or what did?

the LORD went forward, blowing their trumpets, and the ark of the LORD's covenant followed them. ⁹The armed guard marched ahead of the priests who blew the trumpets, and the rear guard followed the ark. All this time the trumpets were sounding. ¹⁰But Joshua had commanded the people, "Do not give a war cry, do not raise your voices, do not say a word until the day I tell you to shout. Then shout!" ¹¹So he had the ark of the LORD carried around the city, circling it once. Then the people returned to camp and spent the night there.

¹²Joshua got up early the next morning and the priests took up the ark of the LORD. ¹³The seven priests carrying the seven trumpets went

forward, marching before the ark of the LORD and blowing the trumpets. The armed men went ahead of them and the rear guard followed the ark of the LORD, while the trumpets kept sounding. ¹⁴So on the second day they marched around the city once and returned to the camp. They did this for six days.

¹⁵On the seventh day, they got up at daybreak and marched around the city seven times in the same manner, except that on that day they circled the city seven times. ¹⁶The seventh time around, when the priests sounded the trumpet blast, Joshua commanded the people, "Shout! For the LORD has given you the city! ¹⁷The city and all that is in it are to be devoted *ᵃ* to the LORD. Only Rahab the prostitute *ᵇ* and all who are with her in her house shall be spared, because she hid the spies we sent. ¹⁸But keep away from the devoted things, so that you will not bring about your own destruction by taking any of them. Otherwise you will make the camp of Israel liable to destruction and bring trouble on it. ¹⁹All the silver and gold and the articles of bronze and iron are sacred to the LORD and must go into his treasury."

²⁰When the trumpets sounded, the people shouted, and at the sound of the trumpet, when the people gave a loud shout, the wall collapsed; so every man charged straight in, and they took the city. ²¹They devoted the city to the LORD and destroyed with the sword every living thing in it—men and women, young and old, cattle, sheep and donkeys.

²²Joshua said to the two men who had spied out the land, "Go into the prostitute's house and bring her out and all who belong to her, in accordance with your oath to her." ²³So the young men who had done the spying went in and brought out Rahab, her father and mother and brothers and all who belonged to her. They brought out her entire family and put them in a place outside the camp of Israel.

ᵃ 17 The Hebrew term refers to the irrevocable giving over of things or persons to the LORD, often by totally destroying them; also in verses 18 and 21.   *ᵇ* 17 Or possibly *innkeeper*; also in verses 22 and 25

²⁴Then they burned the whole city and everything in it, but they put the silver and gold and the articles of bronze and iron into the treasury of the LORD's house. ²⁵But Joshua spared Rahab the prostitute, with her family and all who belonged to her, because she hid the men Joshua had sent as spies to Jericho—and she lives among the Israelites to this day.

²⁶At that time Joshua pronounced this solemn oath: "Cursed before the LORD is the man who undertakes to rebuild this city, Jericho:

"At the cost of his firstborn son
    will he lay its foundations;
at the cost of his youngest
    will he set up its gates."

²⁷So the LORD was with Joshua, and his fame spread throughout the land.

Achan's Sin

7 But the Israelites acted unfaithfully in regard to the devoted things ᵃ; Achan son of Carmi, the son of Zimri, ᵇ the son of Zerah, of the tribe of Judah, took some of them. So the LORD's anger burned against Israel.

²Now Joshua sent men from Jericho to Ai, which is near Beth Aven to the east of Bethel, and told them, "Go up and spy out the region." So the men went up and spied out Ai.

³When they returned to Joshua, they said, "Not all the people will have to go up against Ai. Send two or three thousand men to take it and do not weary all the people, for only a few men are there." ⁴So about three thousand men went up; but they were routed by the men of Ai, ⁵who killed about thirty-six of them. They chased the Israelites from the city gate as far as the stone quarries ᶜ and struck them down on the slopes. At this the hearts of the people melted and became like water.

⁶Then Joshua tore his clothes and fell facedown to the ground before the ark of the LORD, remaining there till evening. The elders of Israel did the same, and sprinkled dust on their heads. ⁷And Joshua said, "Ah, Sovereign LORD, why did you ever bring this people across the Jordan to deliver us into the hands of the Amorites to destroy us? If only we had been content to stay on the other side of the Jordan! ⁸O Lord, what can I say, now that Israel has been routed by its enemies? ⁹The Canaanites and the other people of the country will hear about this and they will surround us and wipe out our name from the earth. What then will you do for your own great name?"

¹⁰The LORD said to Joshua, "Stand up! What are you doing down on your face? ¹¹Israel has sinned; they have violated my covenant, which I commanded them to keep. They have taken some of the devoted things; they have stolen, they have lied, they have put them with their own possessions. ¹²That is why the Israelites cannot stand against their enemies; they turn their backs and run because they have been made liable to destruction. I will not be with you anymore unless you destroy whatever among you is devoted to destruction.

¹³"Go, consecrate the people. Tell them, 'Consecrate yourselves in preparation for tomorrow; for this is what the LORD, the God of Israel, says: That which is devoted is among you, O Israel. You cannot stand against your enemies until you remove it.

¹⁴"'In the morning, present yourselves tribe by tribe. The tribe that the LORD takes shall come forward clan by clan; the clan that the LORD takes shall come forward family by family; and the family that the LORD takes shall come forward man by man. ¹⁵He who is caught with the devoted things shall be destroyed by fire, along with all that belongs to him. He has violated the covenant of the LORD and has done a disgraceful thing in Israel!'"

¹⁶Early the next morning Joshua had Israel come forward by tribes, and Judah was taken. ¹⁷The clans of Judah came forward, and he took the Zerahites. He had the clan of the Zerahites

---

ᵃ 1 The Hebrew term refers to the irrevocable giving over of things or persons to the LORD, often by totally destroying them; also in verses 11, 12, 13 and 15.   ᵇ 1 See Septuagint and 1 Chron. 2:6; Hebrew *Zabdi*; also in verses 17 and 18.   ᶜ 5 Or *as far as Shebarim* come forward by families, and Zimri was taken. [18]Joshua had his family come forward man by man, and Achan son of Carmi, the son of Zimri, the son of Zerah, of the tribe of Judah, was taken.

[19]Then Joshua said to Achan, "My son, give glory to the LORD,[a] the God of Israel, and give him the praise.[b] Tell me what you have done; do not hide it from me."

[20]Achan replied, "It is true! I have sinned against the LORD, the God of Israel. This is what I have done: [21]When I saw in the plunder a beautiful robe from Babylonia,[c] two hundred shekels[d] of silver and a wedge of gold weighing fifty shekels,[e] I coveted them and took them. They are hidden in the ground inside my tent, with the silver underneath."

[22]So Joshua sent messengers, and they ran to the tent, and there it was, hidden in his tent, with the silver underneath. [23]They took the things from the tent, brought them to Joshua and all the Israelites and spread them out before the LORD.

[24]Then Joshua, together with all Israel, took Achan son of Zerah, the silver, the robe, the gold wedge, his sons and daughters, his cattle, donkeys and sheep, his tent and all that he had, to the Valley of Achor. [25]Joshua said, "Why have you brought this trouble on us? The LORD will bring trouble on you today."

Then all Israel stoned him, and after they had stoned the rest, they burned them. [26]Over Achan they heaped up a large pile of rocks, which remains to this day. Then the LORD turned from his fierce anger. Therefore that place has been called the Valley of Achor[f] ever since.

Ai Destroyed

8 Then the LORD said to Joshua, "Do not be afraid; do not be discouraged. Take the whole army with you, and go up and attack Ai. For I have delivered into your hands the king of Ai, his people, his city and his land. [2]You shall do to Ai and its king as you did to Jericho and its king, except that you may carry off their plunder and livestock for yourselves. Set an ambush behind the city."

[3]So Joshua and the whole army moved out to attack Ai. He chose thirty thousand of his best fighting men and sent them out at night [4]with these orders: "Listen carefully. You are to set an ambush behind the city. Don't go very far from it. All of you be on the alert. [5]I and all those with me will advance on the city, and when the men come out against us, as they did before, we will flee from them. [6]They will pursue us until we have lured them away from the city, for they will say, 'They are running away from us as they did before.' So when we flee from them, [7]you are to rise up from ambush and take the city. The LORD your God will give it into your hand. [8]When you have taken the city, set it on fire. Do what the LORD has commanded. See to it; you have my orders."

[9]Then Joshua sent them off, and they went to the place of ambush and lay in wait between Bethel and Ai, to the west of Ai—but Joshua spent that night with the people.

[10]Early the next morning Joshua mustered his men, and he and the leaders of Israel marched before them to Ai. [11]The entire force that was with him marched up and approached the city and arrived in front of it. They set up camp north of Ai, with the valley between them and the city. [12]Joshua had taken about five thousand men and set them in ambush between Bethel and Ai, to the west of the city. [13]They had the soldiers take up their positions—all those in the camp to the north of the city and the ambush to the west of it. That night Joshua went into the valley.

[14]When the king of Ai saw this, he and all the men of the city hurried out early in the morning to meet Israel in battle at a certain place overlooking the Arabah. But he did not know that an ambush had been set against him behind the city. [15]Joshua and all Israel let themselves be driven back before them, and they fled toward the desert. [16]All the men of Ai were called to pursue them, and they pursued Joshua and were lured

---

[a] 19 A solemn charge to tell the truth   [b] 19 Or *and confess to him*   [c] 21 Hebrew *Shinar*   [d] 21 That is, about 5 pounds (about 2.3 kilograms)   [e] 21 That is, about 1 1/4 pounds (about 0.6 kilogram)   [f] 26 *Achor* means *trouble*.

away from the city. ¹⁷Not a man remained in Ai or Bethel who did not go after Israel. They left the city open and went in pursuit of Israel.

¹⁸Then the LORD said to Joshua, "Hold out toward Ai the javelin that is in your hand, for into your hand I will deliver the city." So Joshua held out his javelin toward Ai. ¹⁹As soon as he did this, the men in the ambush rose quickly from their position and rushed forward. They entered the city and captured it and quickly set it on fire.

²⁰The men of Ai looked back and saw the smoke of the city rising against the sky, but they had no chance to escape in any direction, for the Israelites who had been fleeing toward the desert had turned back against their pursuers. ²¹For when Joshua and all Israel saw that the ambush had taken the city and that smoke was going up from the city, they turned around and attacked the men of Ai. ²²The men of the ambush also came out of the city against them, so that they were caught in the middle, with Israelites on both sides. Israel cut them down, leaving them neither survivors nor fugitives. ²³But they took the king of Ai alive and brought him to Joshua.

²⁴When Israel had finished killing all the men of Ai in the fields and in the desert where they had chased them, and when every one of them had been put to the sword, all the Israelites returned to Ai and killed those who were in it. ²⁵Twelve thousand men and women fell that day—all the people of Ai. ²⁶For Joshua did not draw back the hand that held out his javelin until he had destroyed[a] all who lived in Ai. ²⁷But Israel did carry off for themselves the livestock and plunder of this city, as the LORD had instructed Joshua.

²⁸So Joshua burned Ai and made it a permanent heap of ruins, a desolate place to this day. ²⁹He hung the king of Ai on a tree and left him there until evening. At sunset, Joshua ordered them to take his body from the tree and throw it down at the entrance of the city gate. And they raised a large pile of rocks over it, which remains to this day.

The Covenant Renewed at Mount Ebal

³⁰Then Joshua built on Mount Ebal an altar to the LORD, the God of Israel, ³¹as Moses the servant of the LORD had commanded the Israelites. He built it according to what is written in the Book of the Law of Moses—an altar of uncut stones, on which no iron tool had been used. On it they offered to the LORD burnt offerings and sacrificed fellowship offerings.[b] ³²There, in the presence of the Israelites, Joshua copied on stones the law of Moses, which he had written. ³³All Israel, aliens and citizens alike, with their elders, officials and judges, were standing on both sides of the ark of the covenant of the LORD, facing those who carried it—the priests, who were Levites. Half of the people stood in front of Mount Gerizim and half of them in front of Mount Ebal, as Moses the servant of the LORD had formerly commanded when he gave instructions to bless the people of Israel.

³⁴Afterward, Joshua read all the words of the law—the blessings and the curses—just as it is written in the Book of the Law. ³⁵There was not a word of all that Moses had commanded that Joshua did not read to the whole assembly of Israel, including the women and children, and the aliens who lived among them.

The Gibeonite Deception

9 Now when all the kings west of the Jordan heard about these things—those in the hill country, in the western foothills, and along the entire coast of the Great Sea[c] as far as Lebanon (the kings of the Hittites, Amorites, Canaanites, Perizzites, Hivites and Jebusites)— ²they came together to make war against Joshua and Israel.

³However, when the people of Gibeon heard what Joshua had done to Jericho and Ai, ⁴they resorted to a ruse: They went as a delegation whose donkeys were loaded[d] with worn-out sacks and

---

[a] 26 The Hebrew term refers to the irrevocable giving over of things or persons to the LORD, often by totally destroying them.
[b] 31 Traditionally *peace offerings* [c] 1 That is, the Mediterranean
[d] 4 Most Hebrew manuscripts; some Hebrew manuscripts, Vulgate and Syriac (see also Septuagint) *They prepared provisions and loaded their donkeys*

old wineskins, cracked and mended. ⁵The men put worn and patched sandals on their feet and wore old clothes. All the bread of their food supply was dry and moldy. ⁶Then they went to Joshua in the camp at Gilgal and said to him and the men of Israel, "We have come from a distant country; make a treaty with us."

⁷The men of Israel said to the Hivites, "But perhaps you live near us. How then can we make a treaty with you?"

⁸"We are your servants," they said to Joshua.

But Joshua asked, "Who are you and where do you come from?"

⁹They answered: "Your servants have come from a very distant country because of the fame of the LORD your God. For we have heard reports of him: all that he did in Egypt, ¹⁰and all that he did to the two kings of the Amorites east of the Jordan—Sihon king of Heshbon, and Og king of Bashan, who reigned in Ashtaroth. ¹¹And our elders and all those living in our country said to us, 'Take provisions for your journey; go and meet them and say to them, "We are your servants; make a treaty with us." ' ¹²This bread of ours was warm when we packed it at home on the day we left to come to you. But now see how dry and moldy it is. ¹³And these wineskins that we filled were new, but see how cracked they are. And our clothes and sandals are worn out by the very long journey."

¹⁴The men of Israel sampled their provisions but did not inquire of the LORD. ¹⁵Then Joshua made a treaty of peace with them to let them live, and the leaders of the assembly ratified it by oath.

¹⁶Three days after they made the treaty with the Gibeonites, the Israelites heard that they were neighbors, living near them. ¹⁷So the Israelites set out and on the third day came to their cities: Gibeon, Kephirah, Beeroth and Kiriath Jearim. ¹⁸But the Israelites did not attack them, because the leaders of the assembly had sworn an oath to them by the LORD, the God of Israel.

The whole assembly grumbled against the leaders, ¹⁹but all the leaders answered, "We have given them our oath by the LORD, the God of Israel, and we cannot touch them now. ²⁰This is what we will do to them: We will let them live, so that wrath will not fall on us for breaking the oath we swore to them." ²¹They continued, "Let them live, but let them be woodcutters and water carriers for the entire community." So the leaders' promise to them was kept.

²²Then Joshua summoned the Gibeonites and said, "Why did you deceive us by saying, 'We live a long way from you,' while actually you live near us? ²³You are now under a curse: You will never cease to serve as woodcutters and water carriers for the house of my God."

²⁴They answered Joshua, "Your servants were clearly told how the LORD your God had commanded his servant Moses to give you the whole land and to wipe out all its inhabitants from before you. So we feared for our lives because of you, and that is why we did this. ²⁵We are now in your hands. Do to us whatever seems good and right to you."

²⁶So Joshua saved them from the Israelites, and they did not kill them. ²⁷That day he made the Gibeonites woodcutters and water carriers for the community and for the altar of the LORD at the place the LORD would choose. And that is what they are to this day.

The Sun Stands Still

10 Now Adoni-Zedek king of Jerusalem heard that Joshua had taken Ai and totally destroyed[a] it, doing to Ai and its king as he had done to Jericho and its king, and that the people of Gibeon had made a treaty of peace with Israel and were living near them. ²He and his people were very much alarmed at this, because Gibeon was an important city, like one of the royal cities; it was larger than Ai, and all its men were good fighters. ³So Adoni-Zedek king of Jerusalem appealed to Hoham king of Hebron, Piram king of Jarmuth, Japhia king of Lachish and Debir king

---

[a] 1 The Hebrew term refers to the irrevocable giving over of things or persons to the LORD, often by totally destroying them; also in verses 28, 35, 37, 39 and 40.

of Eglon. ⁴"Come up and help me attack Gibeon," he said, "because it has made peace with Joshua and the Israelites."

⁵Then the five kings of the Amorites—the kings of Jerusalem, Hebron, Jarmuth, Lachish and Eglon—joined forces. They moved up with all their troops and took up positions against Gibeon and attacked it.

⁶The Gibeonites then sent word to Joshua in the camp at Gilgal: "Do not abandon your servants. Come up to us quickly and save us! Help us, because all the Amorite kings from the hill country have joined forces against us."

⁷So Joshua marched up from Gilgal with his entire army, including all the best fighting men. ⁸The LORD said to Joshua, "Do not be afraid of them; I have given them into your hand. Not one of them will be able to withstand you."

⁹After an all-night march from Gilgal, Joshua took them by surprise. ¹⁰The LORD threw them into confusion before Israel, who defeated them in a great victory at Gibeon. Israel pursued them along the road going up to Beth Horon and cut them down all the way to Azekah and Makkedah. ¹¹As they fled before Israel on the road down from Beth Horon to Azekah, the LORD hurled large hailstones down on them from the sky, and more of them died from the hailstones than were killed by the swords of the Israelites.

¹²On the day the LORD gave the Amorites over to Israel, Joshua said to the LORD in the presence of Israel:

"O sun, stand still over Gibeon,
 O moon, over the Valley of Aijalon."
¹³So the sun stood still,
 and the moon stopped,
 till the nation avenged itself on ᵃ its
  enemies,

as it is written in the Book of Jashar.

The sun stopped in the middle of the sky and delayed going down about a full day. ¹⁴There has never been a day like it before or since, a day when the LORD listened to a man. Surely the LORD was fighting for Israel!

stories to share

JOSHUA 10:1-15

The Sun Stands Still

LIFE LESSON: Our prayers matter to God.

TO TALK ABOUT

✦ What force of nature did God use to kill more soldiers than the Israelites' swords?

✦ What miracle did God perform because Joshua asked him to?

✦ Do you think God sometimes does things because we ask, or would he have done the same thing anyway?

✦ What prayer has God answered for you?

¹⁵Then Joshua returned with all Israel to the camp at Gilgal.

Five Amorite Kings Killed

¹⁶Now the five kings had fled and hidden in the cave at Makkedah. ¹⁷When Joshua was told that the five kings had been found hiding in the cave at Makkedah, ¹⁸he said, "Roll large rocks up to the mouth of the cave, and post some men there to guard it. ¹⁹But don't stop! Pursue your enemies, attack them from the rear and don't let them reach their cities, for the LORD your God has given them into your hand."

²⁰So Joshua and the Israelites destroyed them completely—almost to a man—but the few

ᵃ 13 Or nation triumphed over

who were left reached their fortified cities. ²¹The whole army then returned safely to Joshua in the camp at Makkedah, and no one uttered a word against the Israelites.

²²Joshua said, "Open the mouth of the cave and bring those five kings out to me." ²³So they brought the five kings out of the cave—the kings of Jerusalem, Hebron, Jarmuth, Lachish and Eglon. ²⁴When they had brought these kings to Joshua, he summoned all the men of Israel and said to the army commanders who had come with him, "Come here and put your feet on the necks of these kings." So they came forward and placed their feet on their necks.

²⁵Joshua said to them, "Do not be afraid; do not be discouraged. Be strong and courageous. This is what the Lord will do to all the enemies you are going to fight." ²⁶Then Joshua struck and killed the kings and hung them on five trees, and they were left hanging on the trees until evening.

²⁷At sunset Joshua gave the order and they took them down from the trees and threw them into the cave where they had been hiding. At the mouth of the cave they placed large rocks, which are there to this day.

²⁸That day Joshua took Makkedah. He put the city and its king to the sword and totally destroyed everyone in it. He left no survivors. And he did to the king of Makkedah as he had done to the king of Jericho.

Southern Cities Conquered

²⁹Then Joshua and all Israel with him moved on from Makkedah to Libnah and attacked it. ³⁰The Lord also gave that city and its king into Israel's hand. The city and everyone in it Joshua put to the sword. He left no survivors there. And he did to its king as he had done to the king of Jericho.

³¹Then Joshua and all Israel with him moved on from Libnah to Lachish; he took up positions against it and attacked it. ³²The Lord handed Lachish over to Israel, and Joshua took it on the second day. The city and everyone in it he put to the sword, just as he had done to Libnah. ³³Mean-while, Horam king of Gezer had come up to help Lachish, but Joshua defeated him and his army—until no survivors were left.

³⁴Then Joshua and all Israel with him moved on from Lachish to Eglon; they took up positions against it and attacked it. ³⁵They captured it that same day and put it to the sword and totally destroyed everyone in it, just as they had done to Lachish.

³⁶Then Joshua and all Israel with him went up from Eglon to Hebron and attacked it. ³⁷They took the city and put it to the sword, together with its king, its villages and everyone in it. They left no survivors. Just as at Eglon, they totally destroyed it and everyone in it.

³⁸Then Joshua and all Israel with him turned around and attacked Debir. ³⁹They took the city, its king and its villages, and put them to the sword. Everyone in it they totally destroyed. They left no survivors. They did to Debir and its king as they had done to Libnah and its king and to Hebron.

⁴⁰So Joshua subdued the whole region, including the hill country, the Negev, the western foothills and the mountain slopes, together with all their kings. He left no survivors. He totally destroyed all who breathed, just as the Lord, the God of Israel, had commanded. ⁴¹Joshua subdued them from Kadesh Barnea to Gaza and from the whole region of Goshen to Gibeon. ⁴²All these kings and their lands Joshua conquered in one campaign, because the Lord, the God of Israel, fought for Israel.

⁴³Then Joshua returned with all Israel to the camp at Gilgal.

Northern Kings Defeated

11 When Jabin king of Hazor heard of this, he sent word to Jobab king of Madon, to the kings of Shimron and Acshaph, ²and to the northern kings who were in the mountains, in the Arabah south of Kinnereth, in the western foothills and in Naphoth Dor *a* on the west; ³to

a 2 Or in the heights of Dor

the Canaanites in the east and west; to the Amorites, Hittites, Perizzites and Jebusites in the hill country; and to the Hivites below Hermon in the region of Mizpah. ⁴They came out with all their troops and a large number of horses and chariots—a huge army, as numerous as the sand on the seashore. ⁵All these kings joined forces and made camp together at the Waters of Merom, to fight against Israel.

⁶The LORD said to Joshua, "Do not be afraid of them, because by this time tomorrow I will hand all of them over to Israel, slain. You are to hamstring their horses and burn their chariots."

⁷So Joshua and his whole army came against them suddenly at the Waters of Merom and attacked them, ⁸and the LORD gave them into the hand of Israel. They defeated them and pursued them all the way to Greater Sidon, to Misrephoth Maim, and to the Valley of Mizpah on the east, until no survivors were left. ⁹Joshua did to them as the LORD had directed: He hamstrung their horses and burned their chariots.

¹⁰At that time Joshua turned back and captured Hazor and put its king to the sword. (Hazor had been the head of all these kingdoms.) ¹¹Everyone in it they put to the sword. They totally destroyed *a* them, not sparing anything that breathed, and he burned up Hazor itself.

¹²Joshua took all these royal cities and their kings and put them to the sword. He totally destroyed them, as Moses the servant of the LORD had commanded. ¹³Yet Israel did not burn any of the cities built on their mounds—except Hazor, which Joshua burned. ¹⁴The Israelites carried off for themselves all the plunder and livestock of these cities, but all the people they put to the sword until they completely destroyed them, not sparing anyone that breathed. ¹⁵As the LORD commanded his servant Moses, so Moses commanded Joshua, and Joshua did it; he left nothing undone of all that the LORD commanded Moses.

¹⁶So Joshua took this entire land: the hill country, all the Negev, the whole region of Goshen, the western foothills, the Arabah and the moun-

tains of Israel with their foothills, ¹⁷from Mount Halak, which rises toward Seir, to Baal Gad in the Valley of Lebanon below Mount Hermon. He captured all their kings and struck them down, putting them to death. ¹⁸Joshua waged war against all these kings for a long time. ¹⁹Except for the Hivites living in Gibeon, not one city made a treaty of peace with the Israelites, who took them all in battle. ²⁰For it was the LORD himself who hardened their hearts to wage war against Israel, so that he might destroy them totally, exterminating them without mercy, as the LORD had commanded Moses.

²¹At that time Joshua went and destroyed the Anakites from the hill country: from Hebron, Debir and Anab, from all the hill country of Judah, and from all the hill country of Israel. Joshua totally destroyed them and their towns. ²²No Anakites were left in Israelite territory; only in Gaza, Gath and Ashdod did any survive. ²³So Joshua took the entire land, just as the LORD had directed Moses, and he gave it as an inheritance to Israel according to their tribal divisions.

Then the land had rest from war.

List of Defeated Kings

12 These are the kings of the land whom the Israelites had defeated and whose territory they took over east of the Jordan, from the Arnon Gorge to Mount Hermon, including all the eastern side of the Arabah:

²Sihon king of the Amorites,
who reigned in Heshbon. He ruled from Aroer on the rim of the Arnon Gorge—from the middle of the gorge—to the Jabbok River, which is the border of the Ammonites. This included half of Gilead. ³He also ruled over the eastern Arabah from the Sea of Kinnereth *b* to the Sea of the Arabah (the Salt Sea *c*), to Beth Jeshimoth, and then southward below the slopes of Pisgah.

---

a 11 The Hebrew term refers to the irrevocable giving over of things or persons to the LORD, often by totally destroying them; also in verses 12, 20 and 21.   *b* 3 That is, Galilee   *c* 3 That is, the Dead Sea

⁴And the territory of Og king of Bashan, one of the last of the Rephaites, who reigned in Ashtaroth and Edrei. ⁵He ruled over Mount Hermon, Salecah, all of Bashan to the border of the people of Geshur and Maacah, and half of Gilead to the border of Sihon king of Heshbon.

⁶Moses, the servant of the LORD, and the Israelites conquered them. And Moses the servant of the LORD gave their land to the Reubenites, the Gadites and the half-tribe of Manasseh to be their possession.

⁷These are the kings of the land that Joshua and the Israelites conquered on the west side of the Jordan, from Baal Gad in the Valley of Lebanon to Mount Halak, which rises toward Seir (their lands Joshua gave as an inheritance to the tribes of Israel according to their tribal divisions— ⁸the hill country, the western foothills, the Arabah, the mountain slopes, the desert and the Negev—the lands of the Hittites, Amorites, Canaanites, Perizzites, Hivites and Jebusites):

⁹the king of Jericho	one
the king of Ai (near Bethel)	one
¹⁰the king of Jerusalem	one
the king of Hebron	one
¹¹the king of Jarmuth	one
the king of Lachish	one
¹²the king of Eglon	one
the king of Gezer	one
¹³the king of Debir	one
the king of Geder	one
¹⁴the king of Hormah	one
the king of Arad	one
¹⁵the king of Libnah	one
the king of Adullam	one
¹⁶the king of Makkedah	one
the king of Bethel	one
¹⁷the king of Tappuah	one
the king of Hepher	one
¹⁸the king of Aphek	one
the king of Lasharon	one
¹⁹the king of Madon	one
the king of Hazor	one
²⁰the king of Shimron Meron	one
the king of Acshaph	one
²¹the king of Taanach	one
the king of Megiddo	one
²²the king of Kedesh	one
the king of Jokneam in Carmel	one
²³the king of Dor (in Naphoth Dor ᵃ)	one
the king of Goyim in Gilgal	one
²⁴the king of Tirzah	one

thirty-one kings in all.

Land Still to Be Taken

13 When Joshua was old and well advanced in years, the LORD said to him, "You are very old, and there are still very large areas of land to be taken over.

²"This is the land that remains: all the regions of the Philistines and Geshurites: ³from the Shihor River on the east of Egypt to the territory of Ekron on the north, all of it counted as Canaanite (the territory of the five Philistine rulers in Gaza, Ashdod, Ashkelon, Gath and Ekron—that of the Avvites); ⁴from the south, all the land of the Canaanites, from Arah of the Sidonians as far as Aphek, the region of the Amorites, ⁵the area of the Gebalites ᵇ; and all Lebanon to the east, from Baal Gad below Mount Hermon to Lebo ᶜ Hamath.

⁶"As for all the inhabitants of the mountain regions from Lebanon to Misrephoth Maim, that is, all the Sidonians, I myself will drive them out before the Israelites. Be sure to allocate this land to Israel for an inheritance, as I have instructed you, ⁷and divide it as an inheritance among the nine tribes and half of the tribe of Manasseh."

Division of the Land East of the Jordan

⁸The other half of Manasseh, ᵈ the Reubenites and the Gadites had received the inheritance that Moses had given them east of the Jordan, as he, the servant of the LORD, had assigned it to them.

ᵃ 23 Or *in the heights of Dor*   ᵇ 5 That is, the area of Byblos
ᶜ 5 Or *to the entrance to*   ᵈ 8 Hebrew *With it* (that is, with the other half of Manasseh)

⁹It extended from Aroer on the rim of the Arnon Gorge, and from the town in the middle of the gorge, and included the whole plateau of Medeba as far as Dibon, ¹⁰and all the towns of Sihon king of the Amorites, who ruled in Heshbon, out to the border of the Ammonites. ¹¹It also included Gilead, the territory of the people of Geshur and Maacah, all of Mount Hermon and all Bashan as far as Salecah— ¹²that is, the whole kingdom of Og in Bashan, who had reigned in Ashtaroth and Edrei and had survived as one of the last of the Rephaites. Moses had defeated them and taken over their land. ¹³But the Israelites did not drive out the people of Geshur and Maacah, so they continue to live among the Israelites to this day.

¹⁴But to the tribe of Levi he gave no inheritance, since the offerings made by fire to the Lord, the God of Israel, are their inheritance, as he promised them.

¹⁵This is what Moses had given to the tribe of Reuben, clan by clan:

¹⁶The territory from Aroer on the rim of the Arnon Gorge, and from the town in the middle of the gorge, and the whole plateau past Medeba ¹⁷to Heshbon and all its towns on the plateau, including Dibon, Bamoth Baal, Beth Baal Meon, ¹⁸Jahaz, Kedemoth, Mephaath, ¹⁹Kiriathaim, Sibmah, Zereth Shahar on the hill in the valley, ²⁰Beth Peor, the slopes of Pisgah, and Beth Jeshimoth— ²¹all the towns on the plateau and the entire realm of Sihon king of the Amorites, who ruled at Heshbon. Moses had defeated him and the Midianite chiefs, Evi, Rekem, Zur, Hur and Reba—princes allied with Sihon—who lived in that country. ²²In addition to those slain in battle, the Israelites had put to the sword Balaam son of Beor, who practiced divination. ²³The boundary of the Reubenites was the bank of the Jordan. These towns and their villages were the inheritance of the Reubenites, clan by clan.

²⁴This is what Moses had given to the tribe of Gad, clan by clan:

²⁵The territory of Jazer, all the towns of Gilead and half the Ammonite country as far as Aroer, near Rabbah; ²⁶and from Heshbon to Ramath Mizpah and Betonim, and from Mahanaim to the territory of Debir; ²⁷and in the valley, Beth Haram, Beth Nimrah, Succoth and Zaphon with the rest of the realm of Sihon king of Heshbon (the east side of the Jordan, the territory up to the end of the Sea of Kinnereth ᵃ). ²⁸These towns and their villages were the inheritance of the Gadites, clan by clan.

²⁹This is what Moses had given to the half-tribe of Manasseh, that is, to half the family of the descendants of Manasseh, clan by clan:

³⁰The territory extending from Mahanaim and including all of Bashan, the entire realm of Og king of Bashan—all the settlements of Jair in Bashan, sixty towns, ³¹half of Gilead, and Ashtaroth and Edrei (the royal cities of Og in Bashan). This was for the descendants of Makir son of Manasseh—for half of the sons of Makir, clan by clan.

³²This is the inheritance Moses had given when he was in the plains of Moab across the Jordan east of Jericho. ³³But to the tribe of Levi, Moses had given no inheritance; the Lord, the God of Israel, is their inheritance, as he promised them.

Division of the Land West of the Jordan

14 Now these are the areas the Israelites received as an inheritance in the land of Canaan, which Eleazar the priest, Joshua son of Nun and the heads of the tribal clans of Israel allotted to them. ²Their inheritances were assigned by lot to the nine-and-a-half tribes, as the Lord had commanded through Moses. ³Moses had granted the two-and-a-half tribes their inheritance east of the Jordan but had not granted the Levites

---

ᵃ 27 That is, Galilee

an inheritance among the rest, [4]for the sons of Joseph had become two tribes—Manasseh and Ephraim. The Levites received no share of the land but only towns to live in, with pasturelands for their flocks and herds. [5]So the Israelites divided the land, just as the LORD had commanded Moses.

Hebron Given to Caleb

[6]Now the men of Judah approached Joshua at Gilgal, and Caleb son of Jephunneh the Kenizzite said to him, "You know what the LORD said to Moses the man of God at Kadesh Barnea about you and me. [7]I was forty years old when Moses the servant of the LORD sent me from Kadesh Barnea to explore the land. And I brought him back a report according to my convictions, [8]but my brothers who went up with me made the hearts of the people melt with fear. I, however, followed the LORD my God wholeheartedly. [9]So on that day Moses swore to me, 'The land on which your feet have walked will be your inheritance and that of your children forever, because you have followed the LORD my God wholeheartedly.'[a]

[10]"Now then, just as the LORD promised, he has kept me alive for forty-five years since the time he said this to Moses, while Israel moved about in the desert. So here I am today, eighty-five years old! [11]I am still as strong today as the day Moses sent me out; I'm just as vigorous to go out to battle now as I was then. [12]Now give me this hill country that the LORD promised me that day. You yourself heard then that the Anakites were there and their cities were large and fortified, but, the LORD helping me, I will drive them out just as he said."

[13]Then Joshua blessed Caleb son of Jephunneh and gave him Hebron as his inheritance. [14]So Hebron has belonged to Caleb son of Jephunneh the Kenizzite ever since, because he followed the LORD, the God of Israel, wholeheartedly. [15](Hebron used to be called Kiriath Arba after Arba, who was the greatest man among the Anakites.)

Then the land had rest from war.

Allotment for Judah

15:15–19pp — Jdg 1:11–15

15 The allotment for the tribe of Judah, clan by clan, extended down to the territory of Edom, to the Desert of Zin in the extreme south.

[2]Their southern boundary started from the bay at the southern end of the Salt Sea,[b] [3]crossed south of Scorpion[c] Pass, continued on to Zin and went over to the south of Kadesh Barnea. Then it ran past Hezron up to Addar and curved around to Karka. [4]It then passed along to Azmon and joined the Wadi of Egypt, ending at the sea. This is their[d] southern boundary.

[5]The eastern boundary is the Salt Sea as far as the mouth of the Jordan.

The northern boundary started from the bay of the sea at the mouth of the Jordan, [6]went up to Beth Hoglah and continued north of Beth Arabah to the Stone of Bohan son of Reuben. [7]The boundary then went up to Debir from the Valley of Achor and turned north to Gilgal, which faces the Pass of Adummim south of the gorge. It continued along to the waters of En Shemesh and came out at En Rogel. [8]Then it ran up the Valley of Ben Hinnom along the southern slope of the Jebusite city (that is, Jerusalem). From there it climbed to the top of the hill west of the Hinnom Valley at the northern end of the Valley of Rephaim. [9]From the hilltop the boundary headed toward the spring of the waters of Nephtoah, came out at the towns of Mount Ephron and went down toward Baalah (that is, Kiriath Jearim). [10]Then it curved westward from Baalah to Mount Seir, ran along the northern slope of Mount Jearim (that is, Kesalon), continued down to Beth Shemesh and crossed to Timnah. [11]It went to the northern slope of Ekron, turned toward Shikkeron, passed along to Mount Baalah and reached Jabneel. The boundary ended at the sea.

---

*[a] 9 Deut. 1:36   [b] 2 That is, the Dead Sea; also in verse 5
[c] 3 Hebrew Akrabbim   [d] 4 Hebrew your*

¹²The western boundary is the coastline of the Great Sea. *ᵃ*

These are the boundaries around the people of Judah by their clans

¹³In accordance with the LORD's command to him, Joshua gave to Caleb son of Jephunneh a portion in Judah — Kiriath Arba, that is, Hebron. (Arba was the forefather of Anak.) ¹⁴From Hebron Caleb drove out the three Anakites — Sheshai, Ahiman and Talmai — descendants of Anak. ¹⁵From there he marched against the people living in Debir (formerly called Kiriath Sepher). ¹⁶And Caleb said, "I will give my daughter Acsah in marriage to the man who attacks and captures Kiriath Sepher." ¹⁷Othniel son of Kenaz, Caleb's brother, took it; so Caleb gave his daughter Acsah to him in marriage.

¹⁸One day when she came to Othniel, she urged him *ᵇ* to ask her father for a field. When she got off her donkey, Caleb asked her, "What can I do for you?"

¹⁹She replied, "Do me a special favor. Since you have given me land in the Negev, give me also springs of water." So Caleb gave her the upper and lower springs.

²⁰This is the inheritance of the tribe of Judah, clan by clan:

²¹The southernmost towns of the tribe of Judah in the Negev toward the boundary of Edom were:

Kabzeel, Eder, Jagur, ²²Kinah, Dimonah, Adadah, ²³Kedesh, Hazor, Ithnan, ²⁴Ziph, Telem, Bealoth, ²⁵Hazor Hadattah, Kerioth Hezron (that is, Hazor), ²⁶Amam, Shema, Moladah, ²⁷Hazar Gaddah, Heshmon, Beth Pelet, ²⁸Hazar Shual, Beersheba, Biziothiah, ²⁹Baalah, Iim, Ezem, ³⁰Eltolad, Kesil, Hormah, ³¹Ziklag, Madmannah, Sansannah, ³²Lebaoth, Shilhim, Ain and Rimmon — a total of twenty-nine towns and their villages.

³³In the western foothills:

Eshtaol, Zorah, Ashnah, ³⁴Zanoah, En Gannim, Tappuah, Enam, ³⁵Jarmuth, Adullam, Socoh, Azekah, ³⁶Shaaraim, Adithaim

and Gederah (or Gederothaim) *ᶜ* — fourteen towns and their villages.

³⁷Zenan, Hadashah, Migdal Gad, ³⁸Dilean, Mizpah, Joktheel, ³⁹Lachish, Bozkath, Eglon, ⁴⁰Cabbon, Lahmas, Kitlish, ⁴¹Gederoth, Beth Dagon, Naamah and Makkedah — sixteen towns and their villages.

⁴²Libnah, Ether, Ashan, ⁴³Iphtah, Ashnah, Nezib, ⁴⁴Keilah, Aczib and Mareshah — nine towns and their villages.

⁴⁵Ekron, with its surrounding settlements and villages; ⁴⁶west of Ekron, all that were in the vicinity of Ashdod, together with their villages; ⁴⁷Ashdod, its surrounding settlements and villages; and Gaza, its settlements and villages, as far as the Wadi of Egypt and the coastline of the Great Sea.

⁴⁸In the hill country:

Shamir, Jattir, Socoh, ⁴⁹Dannah, Kiriath Sannah (that is, Debir), ⁵⁰Anab, Eshtemoh, Anim, ⁵¹Goshen, Holon and Giloh — eleven towns and their villages.

⁵²Arab, Dumah, Eshan, ⁵³Janim, Beth Tappuah, Aphekah, ⁵⁴Humtah, Kiriath Arba (that is, Hebron) and Zior — nine towns and their villages.

⁵⁵Maon, Carmel, Ziph, Juttah, ⁵⁶Jezreel, Jokdeam, Zanoah, ⁵⁷Kain, Gibeah and Timnah — ten towns and their villages.

⁵⁸Halhul, Beth Zur, Gedor, ⁵⁹Maarath, Beth Anoth and Eltekon — six towns and their villages.

⁶⁰Kiriath Baal (that is, Kiriath Jearim) and Rabbah — two towns and their villages.

⁶¹In the desert:

Beth Arabah, Middin, Secacah, ⁶²Nibshan, the City of Salt and En Gedi — six towns and their villages.

⁶³Judah could not dislodge the Jebusites, who were living in Jerusalem; to this day the Jebusites live there with the people of Judah.

ᵃ 12 That is, the Mediterranean; also in verse 47   *ᵇ 18* Hebrew and some Septuagint manuscripts; other Septuagint manuscripts (see also note at Judges 1:14) *Othniel, he urged her*   *ᶜ 36* Or *Gederah and Gederothaim*

Allotment for Ephraim and Manasseh

16 The allotment for Joseph began at the Jordan of Jericho,[a] east of the waters of Jericho, and went up from there through the desert into the hill country of Bethel. ²It went on from Bethel (that is, Luz),[b] crossed over to the territory of the Arkites in Ataroth, ³descended westward to the territory of the Japhletites as far as the region of Lower Beth Horon and on to Gezer, ending at the sea.

⁴So Manasseh and Ephraim, the descendants of Joseph, received their inheritance.

⁵This was the territory of Ephraim, clan by clan:

The boundary of their inheritance went from Ataroth Addar in the east to Upper Beth Horon ⁶and continued to the sea. From Micmethath on the north it curved eastward to Taanath Shiloh, passing by it to Janoah on the east. ⁷Then it went down from Janoah to Ataroth and Naarah, touched Jericho and came out at the Jordan. ⁸From Tappuah the border went west to the Kanah Ravine and ended at the sea. This was the inheritance of the tribe of the Ephraimites, clan by clan. ⁹It also included all the towns and their villages that were set aside for the Ephraimites within the inheritance of the Manassites.

¹⁰They did not dislodge the Canaanites living in Gezer; to this day the Canaanites live among the people of Ephraim but are required to do forced labor.

17 This was the allotment for the tribe of Manasseh as Joseph's firstborn, that is, for Makir, Manasseh's firstborn. Makir was the ancestor of the Gileadites, who had received Gilead and Bashan because the Makirites were great soldiers. ²So this allotment was for the rest of the people of Manasseh—the clans of Abiezer, Helek, Asriel, Shechem, Hepher and Shemida. These are the other male descendants of Manasseh son of Joseph by their clans.

³Now Zelophehad son of Hepher, the son of Gilead, the son of Makir, the son of Manasseh, had no sons but only daughters, whose names were Mahlah, Noah, Hoglah, Milcah and Tirzah. ⁴They went to Eleazar the priest, Joshua son of Nun, and the leaders and said, "The LORD commanded Moses to give us an inheritance among our brothers." So Joshua gave them an inheritance along with the brothers of their father, according to the LORD's command. ⁵Manasseh's share consisted of ten tracts of land besides Gilead and Bashan east of the Jordan, ⁶because the daughters of the tribe of Manasseh received an inheritance among the sons. The land of Gilead belonged to the rest of the descendants of Manasseh.

⁷The territory of Manasseh extended from Asher to Micmethath east of Shechem. The boundary ran southward from there to include the people living at En Tappuah. ⁸(Manasseh had the land of Tappuah, but Tappuah itself, on the boundary of Manasseh, belonged to the Ephraimites.) ⁹Then the boundary continued south to the Kanah Ravine. There were towns belonging to Ephraim lying among the towns of Manasseh, but the boundary of Manasseh was the northern side of the ravine and ended at the sea. ¹⁰On the south the land belonged to Ephraim, on the north to Manasseh. The territory of Manasseh reached the sea and bordered Asher on the north and Issachar on the east. ¹¹Within Issachar and Asher, Manasseh also had Beth Shan, Ibleam and the people of Dor, Endor, Taanach and Megiddo, together with their surrounding settlements (the third in the list is Naphoth[c]).

¹²Yet the Manassites were not able to occupy these towns, for the Canaanites were determined to live in that region. ¹³However, when the Israelites grew stronger, they subjected the Canaanites to forced labor but did not drive them out completely.

---

[a] 1 *Jordan of Jericho* was possibly an ancient name for the Jordan River.   [b] 2 Septuagint; Hebrew *Bethel to Luz*   [c] 11 That is, Naphoth Dor

¹⁴The people of Joseph said to Joshua, "Why have you given us only one allotment and one portion for an inheritance? We are a numerous people and the LORD has blessed us abundantly."

¹⁵"If you are so numerous," Joshua answered, "and if the hill country of Ephraim is too small for you, go up into the forest and clear land for yourselves there in the land of the Perizzites and Rephaites."

¹⁶The people of Joseph replied, "The hill country is not enough for us, and all the Canaanites who live in the plain have iron chariots, both those in Beth Shan and its settlements and those in the Valley of Jezreel."

¹⁷But Joshua said to the house of Joseph—to Ephraim and Manasseh—"You are numerous and very powerful. You will have not only one allotment ¹⁸but the forested hill country as well. Clear it, and its farthest limits will be yours; though the Canaanites have iron chariots and though they are strong, you can drive them out."

Division of the Rest of the Land

18 The whole assembly of the Israelites gathered at Shiloh and set up the Tent of Meeting there. The country was brought under their control, ²but there were still seven Israelite tribes who had not yet received their inheritance.

³So Joshua said to the Israelites: "How long will you wait before you begin to take possession of the land that the LORD, the God of your fathers, has given you? ⁴Appoint three men from each tribe. I will send them out to make a survey of the land and to write a description of it, according to the inheritance of each. Then they will return to me. ⁵You are to divide the land into seven parts. Judah is to remain in its territory on the south and the house of Joseph in its territory on the north. ⁶After you have written descriptions of the seven parts of the land, bring them here to me and I will cast lots for you in the presence of the LORD our God. ⁷The Levites, however, do not get a portion among you, because the priestly service of the LORD is their inheritance. And Gad, Reuben and the half-tribe of Manasseh have already received their inheritance on the east side of the Jordan. Moses the servant of the LORD gave it to them."

⁸As the men started on their way to map out the land, Joshua instructed them, "Go and make a survey of the land and write a description of it. Then return to me, and I will cast lots for you here at Shiloh in the presence of the LORD." ⁹So the men left and went through the land. They wrote its description on a scroll, town by town, in seven parts, and returned to Joshua in the camp at Shiloh. ¹⁰Joshua then cast lots for them in Shiloh in the presence of the LORD, and there he distributed the land to the Israelites according to their tribal divisions.

Allotment for Benjamin

¹¹The lot came up for the tribe of Benjamin, clan by clan. Their allotted territory lay between the tribes of Judah and Joseph:

¹²On the north side their boundary began at the Jordan, passed the northern slope of Jericho and headed west into the hill country, coming out at the desert of Beth Aven. ¹³From there it crossed to the south slope of Luz (that is, Bethel) and went down to Ataroth Addar on the hill south of Lower Beth Horon.

¹⁴From the hill facing Beth Horon on the south the boundary turned south along the western side and came out at Kiriath Baal (that is, Kiriath Jearim), a town of the people of Judah. This was the western side.

¹⁵The southern side began at the outskirts of Kiriath Jearim on the west, and the boundary came out at the spring of the waters of Nephtoah. ¹⁶The boundary went down to the foot of the hill facing the Valley of Ben Hinnom, north of the Valley of Rephaim. It continued down the Hinnom Valley along the southern slope of the Jebusite city and so to En Rogel. ¹⁷It then curved north, went to En Shemesh, continued to Geliloth, which faces the Pass of Adummim, and ran

down to the Stone of Bohan son of Reuben. [18]It continued to the northern slope of Beth Arabah[a] and on down into the Arabah. [19]It then went to the northern slope of Beth Hoglah and came out at the northern bay of the Salt Sea,[b] at the mouth of the Jordan in the south. This was the southern boundary.

[20]The Jordan formed the boundary on the eastern side.

These were the boundaries that marked out the inheritance of the clans of Benjamin on all sides.

[21]The tribe of Benjamin, clan by clan, had the following cities:

Jericho, Beth Hoglah, Emek Keziz, [22]Beth Arabah, Zemaraim, Bethel, [23]Avvim, Parah, Ophrah, [24]Kephar Ammoni, Ophni and Geba—twelve towns and their villages.

[25]Gibeon, Ramah, Beeroth, [26]Mizpah, Kephirah, Mozah, [27]Rekem, Irpeel, Taralah, [28]Zelah, Haeleph, the Jebusite city (that is, Jerusalem), Gibeah and Kiriath—fourteen towns and their villages.

This was the inheritance of Benjamin for its clans.

Allotment for Simeon

19:2–10pp — 1Ch 4:28–33

19 The second lot came out for the tribe of Simeon, clan by clan. Their inheritance lay within the territory of Judah. [2]It included:

Beersheba (or Sheba),[c] Moladah, [3]Hazar Shual, Balah, Ezem, [4]Eltolad, Bethul, Hormah, [5]Ziklag, Beth Marcaboth, Hazar Susah, [6]Beth Lebaoth and Sharuhen—thirteen towns and their villages;

[7]Ain, Rimmon, Ether and Ashan—four towns and their villages— [8]and all the villages around these towns as far as Baalath Beer (Ramah in the Negev).

This was the inheritance of the tribe of the Simeonites, clan by clan. [9]The inheritance of the Simeonites was taken from the share of Judah, because Judah's portion was more than they needed. So the Simeonites received their inheritance within the territory of Judah.

Allotment for Zebulun

[10]The third lot came up for Zebulun, clan by clan:

The boundary of their inheritance went as far as Sarid. [11]Going west it ran to Maralah, touched Dabbesheth, and extended to the ravine near Jokneam. [12]It turned east from Sarid toward the sunrise to the territory of Kisloth Tabor and went on to Daberath and up to Japhia. [13]Then it continued eastward to Gath Hepher and Eth Kazin; it came out at Rimmon and turned toward Neah. [14]There the boundary went around on the north to Hannathon and ended at the Valley of Iphtah El. [15]Included were Kattath, Nahalal, Shimron, Idalah and Bethlehem. There were twelve towns and their villages.

[16]These towns and their villages were the inheritance of Zebulun, clan by clan.

Allotment for Issachar

[17]The fourth lot came out for Issachar, clan by clan. [18]Their territory included:

Jezreel, Kesulloth, Shunem, [19]Hapharaim, Shion, Anaharath, [20]Rabbith, Kishion, Ebez, [21]Remeth, En Gannim, En Haddah and Beth Pazzez. [22]The boundary touched Tabor, Shahazumah and Beth Shemesh, and ended at the Jordan. There were sixteen towns and their villages.

[23]These towns and their villages were the inheritance of the tribe of Issachar, clan by clan.

Allotment for Asher

[24]The fifth lot came out for the tribe of Asher, clan by clan. [25]Their territory included:

Helkath, Hali, Beten, Acshaph, [26]Allammelech, Amad and Mishal. On the west the

---

[a] 18 Septuagint; Hebrew *slope facing the Arabah*   [b] 19 That is, the Dead Sea   [c] 2 Or *Beersheba, Sheba*; 1 Chron. 4:28 does not have *Sheba*.

boundary touched Carmel and Shihor Libnath. ²⁷It then turned east toward Beth Dagon, touched Zebulun and the Valley of Iphtah El, and went north to Beth Emek and Neiel, passing Cabul on the left. ²⁸It went to Abdon,ᵃ Rehob, Hammon and Kanah, as far as Greater Sidon. ²⁹The boundary then turned back toward Ramah and went to the fortified city of Tyre, turned toward Hosah and came out at the sea in the region of Aczib, ³⁰Ummah, Aphek and Rehob. There were twenty-two towns and their villages.

³¹These towns and their villages were the inheritance of the tribe of Asher, clan by clan.

Allotment for Naphtali

³²The sixth lot came out for Naphtali, clan by clan:

³³Their boundary went from Heleph and the large tree in Zaanannim, passing Adami Nekeb and Jabneel to Lakkum and ending at the Jordan. ³⁴The boundary ran west through Aznoth Tabor and came out at Hukkok. It touched Zebulun on the south, Asher on the west and the Jordanᵇ on the east. ³⁵The fortified cities were Ziddim, Zer, Hammath, Rakkath, Kinnereth, ³⁶Adamah, Ramah, Hazor, ³⁷Kedesh, Edrei, En Hazor, ³⁸Iron, Migdal El, Horem, Beth Anath and Beth Shemesh. There were nineteen towns and their villages.

³⁹These towns and their villages were the inheritance of the tribe of Naphtali, clan by clan.

Allotment for Dan

⁴⁰The seventh lot came out for the tribe of Dan, clan by clan. ⁴¹The territory of their inheritance included:

Zorah, Eshtaol, Ir Shemesh, ⁴²Shaalabbin, Aijalon, Ithlah, ⁴³Elon, Timnah, Ekron, ⁴⁴Eltekeh, Gibbethon, Baalath, ⁴⁵Jehud, Bene Berak, Gath Rimmon, ⁴⁶Me Jarkon and Rakkon, with the area facing Joppa.

⁴⁷(But the Danites had difficulty taking possession of their territory, so they went up and attacked Leshem, took it, put it to the sword and occupied it. They settled in Leshem and named it Dan after their forefather.)

⁴⁸These towns and their villages were the inheritance of the tribe of Dan, clan by clan.

Allotment for Joshua

⁴⁹When they had finished dividing the land into its allotted portions, the Israelites gave Joshua son of Nun an inheritance among them, ⁵⁰as the LORD had commanded. They gave him the town he asked for—Timnath Serahᶜ in the hill country of Ephraim. And he built up the town and settled there.

⁵¹These are the territories that Eleazar the priest, Joshua son of Nun and the heads of the tribal clans of Israel assigned by lot at Shiloh in the presence of the LORD at the entrance to the Tent of Meeting. And so they finished dividing the land.

Cities of Refuge

20:1–9Ref — Nu 35:9–34; Dt 4:41–43; 19:1–14

20 Then the LORD said to Joshua: ²"Tell the Israelites to designate the cities of refuge, as I instructed you through Moses, ³so that anyone who kills a person accidentally and unintentionally may flee there and find protection from the avenger of blood.

⁴"When he flees to one of these cities, he is to stand in the entrance of the city gate and state his case before the elders of that city. Then they are to admit him into their city and give him a place to live with them. ⁵If the avenger of blood pursues him, they must not surrender the one accused, because he killed his neighbor unintentionally and without malice aforethought. ⁶He is to stay in that city until he has stood trial before the assembly and until the death of the high priest who is serving at that time. Then he may go back to his own home in the town from which he fled."

ᵃ 28 Some Hebrew manuscripts (see also Joshua 21:30); most Hebrew manuscripts *Ebron*   ᵇ 34 Septuagint; Hebrew *west, and Judah, the Jordan,*   ᶜ 50 Also known as *Timnath Heres* (see Judges 2:9)

⁷So they set apart Kedesh in Galilee in the hill country of Naphtali, Shechem in the hill country of Ephraim, and Kiriath Arba (that is, Hebron) in the hill country of Judah. ⁸On the east side of the Jordan of Jericho*ᵃ* they designated Bezer in the desert on the plateau in the tribe of Reuben, Ramoth in Gilead in the tribe of Gad, and Golan in Bashan in the tribe of Manasseh. ⁹Any of the Israelites or any alien living among them who killed someone accidentally could flee to these designated cities and not be killed by the avenger of blood prior to standing trial before the assembly.

Towns for the Levites

21:4–39pp — 1Ch 6:54–80

21 Now the family heads of the Levites approached Eleazar the priest, Joshua son of Nun, and the heads of the other tribal families of Israel ²at Shiloh in Canaan and said to them, "The Lord commanded through Moses that you give us towns to live in, with pasturelands for our livestock." ³So, as the Lord had commanded, the Israelites gave the Levites the following towns and pasturelands out of their own inheritance:

⁴The first lot came out for the Kohathites, clan by clan. The Levites who were descendants of Aaron the priest were allotted thirteen towns from the tribes of Judah, Simeon and Benjamin. ⁵The rest of Kohath's descendants were allotted ten towns from the clans of the tribes of Ephraim, Dan and half of Manasseh.

⁶The descendants of Gershon were allotted thirteen towns from the clans of the tribes of Issachar, Asher, Naphtali and the half-tribe of Manasseh in Bashan.

⁷The descendants of Merari, clan by clan, received twelve towns from the tribes of Reuben, Gad and Zebulun.

⁸So the Israelites allotted to the Levites these towns and their pasturelands, as the Lord had commanded through Moses.

⁹From the tribes of Judah and Simeon they allotted the following towns by name ¹⁰(these towns were assigned to the descendants of Aaron who were from the Kohathite clans of the Levites, because the first lot fell to them):

¹¹They gave them Kiriath Arba (that is, Hebron), with its surrounding pastureland, in the hill country of Judah. (Arba was the forefather of Anak.) ¹²But the fields and villages around the city they had given to Caleb son of Jephunneh as his possession.

¹³So to the descendants of Aaron the priest they gave Hebron (a city of refuge for one accused of murder), Libnah, ¹⁴Jattir, Eshtemoa, ¹⁵Holon, Debir, ¹⁶Ain, Juttah and Beth Shemesh, together with their pasturelands—nine towns from these two tribes.

¹⁷And from the tribe of Benjamin they gave them Gibeon, Geba, ¹⁸Anathoth and Almon, together with their pasturelands—four towns.

¹⁹All the towns for the priests, the descendants of Aaron, were thirteen, together with their pasturelands.

²⁰The rest of the Kohathite clans of the Levites were allotted towns from the tribe of Ephraim:

²¹In the hill country of Ephraim they were given Shechem (a city of refuge for one accused of murder) and Gezer, ²²Kibzaim and Beth Horon, together with their pasturelands—four towns.

²³Also from the tribe of Dan they received Eltekeh, Gibbethon, ²⁴Aijalon and Gath Rimmon, together with their pasturelands—four towns.

²⁵From half the tribe of Manasseh they received Taanach and Gath Rimmon, together with their pasturelands—two towns.

²⁶All these ten towns and their pasturelands were given to the rest of the Kohathite clans.

²⁷The Levite clans of the Gershonites were given:
from the half-tribe of Manasseh,
Golan in Bashan (a city of refuge for one accused of murder) and Be Eshtarah, together with their pasturelands—two towns;

ᵃ 8 Jordan of Jericho was possibly an ancient name for the Jordan River.

28 from the tribe of Issachar,
    Kishion, Daberath, 29 Jarmuth and En Gannim, together with their pasturelands—four towns;
30 from the tribe of Asher,
    Mishal, Abdon, 31 Helkath and Rehob, together with their pasturelands—four towns;
32 from the tribe of Naphtali,
    Kedesh in Galilee (a city of refuge for one accused of murder), Hammoth Dor and Kartan, together with their pasturelands—three towns.

33 All the towns of the Gershonite clans were thirteen, together with their pasturelands.

34 The Merarite clans (the rest of the Levites) were given:
    from the tribe of Zebulun,
    Jokneam, Kartah, 35 Dimnah and Nahalal, together with their pasturelands—four towns;
36 from the tribe of Reuben,
    Bezer, Jahaz, 37 Kedemoth and Mephaath, together with their pasturelands—four towns;
38 from the tribe of Gad,
    Ramoth in Gilead (a city of refuge for one accused of murder), Mahanaim, 39 Heshbon and Jazer, together with their pasturelands—four towns in all.

40 All the towns allotted to the Merarite clans, who were the rest of the Levites, were twelve.

41 The towns of the Levites in the territory held by the Israelites were forty-eight in all, together with their pasturelands. 42 Each of these towns had pasturelands surrounding it; this was true for all these towns.

43 So the LORD gave Israel all the land he had sworn to give their forefathers, and they took possession of it and settled there. 44 The LORD gave them rest on every side, just as he had sworn to their forefathers. Not one of their enemies withstood them; the LORD handed all their enemies over to them. 45 Not one of all the LORD's good promises to the house of Israel failed; every one was fulfilled.

Eastern Tribes Return Home

22 Then Joshua summoned the Reubenites, the Gadites and the half-tribe of Manasseh 2 and said to them, "You have done all that Moses the servant of the LORD commanded, and you have obeyed me in everything I commanded. 3 For a long time now—to this very day—you have not deserted your brothers but have carried out the mission the LORD your God gave you. 4 Now that the LORD your God has given your brothers rest as he promised, return to your homes in the land that Moses the servant of the LORD gave you on the other side of the Jordan. 5 But be very careful to keep the commandment and the law that Moses the servant of the LORD gave you: to love the LORD your God, to walk in all his ways, to obey his commands, to hold fast to him and to serve him with all your heart and all your soul."

6 Then Joshua blessed them and sent them away, and they went to their homes. 7 (To the half-tribe of Manasseh Moses had given land in Bashan, and to the other half of the tribe Joshua gave land on the west side of the Jordan with their brothers.) When Joshua sent them home, he blessed them, 8 saying, "Return to your homes with your great wealth—with large herds of livestock, with silver, gold, bronze and iron, and a great quantity of clothing—and divide with your brothers the plunder from your enemies."

9 So the Reubenites, the Gadites and the half-tribe of Manasseh left the Israelites at Shiloh in Canaan to return to Gilead, their own land, which they had acquired in accordance with the command of the LORD through Moses.

10 When they came to Geliloth near the Jordan in the land of Canaan, the Reubenites, the Gadites and the half-tribe of Manasseh built an imposing altar there by the Jordan. 11 And when the Israelites heard that they had built the altar on the border of Canaan at Geliloth near the Jordan on the Israelite side, 12 the whole assembly of Israel gathered at Shiloh to go to war against them.

13 So the Israelites sent Phinehas son of Eleazar, the priest, to the land of Gilead—to Reuben,

Gad and the half-tribe of Manasseh. [14]With him they sent ten of the chief men, one for each of the tribes of Israel, each the head of a family division among the Israelite clans.

[15]When they went to Gilead — to Reuben, Gad and the half-tribe of Manasseh — they said to them: [16]"The whole assembly of the Lord says: 'How could you break faith with the God of Israel like this? How could you turn away from the Lord and build yourselves an altar in rebellion against him now? [17]Was not the sin of Peor enough for us? Up to this very day we have not cleansed ourselves from that sin, even though a plague fell on the community of the Lord! [18]And are you now turning away from the Lord?

" 'If you rebel against the Lord today, tomorrow he will be angry with the whole community of Israel. [19]If the land you possess is defiled, come over to the Lord's land, where the Lord's tabernacle stands, and share the land with us. But do not rebel against the Lord or against us by building an altar for yourselves, other than the altar of the Lord our God. [20]When Achan son of Zerah acted unfaithfully regarding the devoted things,[a] did not wrath come upon the whole community of Israel? He was not the only one who died for his sin.' "

[21]Then Reuben, Gad and the half-tribe of Manasseh replied to the heads of the clans of Israel: [22]"The Mighty One, God, the Lord! The Mighty One, God, the Lord! He knows! And let Israel know! If this has been in rebellion or disobedience to the Lord, do not spare us this day. [23]If we have built our own altar to turn away from the Lord and to offer burnt offerings and grain offerings, or to sacrifice fellowship offerings[b] on it, may the Lord himself call us to account.

[24]"No! We did it for fear that some day your descendants might say to ours, 'What do you have to do with the Lord, the God of Israel? [25]The Lord has made the Jordan a boundary between us and you — you Reubenites and Gadites! You have no share in the Lord.' So your descendants might cause ours to stop fearing the Lord.

[26]"That is why we said, 'Let us get ready and build an altar — but not for burnt offerings or sacrifices.' [27]On the contrary, it is to be a witness between us and you and the generations that follow, that we will worship the Lord at his sanctuary with our burnt offerings, sacrifices and fellowship offerings. Then in the future your descendants will not be able to say to ours, 'You have no share in the Lord.'

[28]"And we said, 'If they ever say this to us, or to our descendants, we will answer: Look at the replica of the Lord's altar, which our fathers built, not for burnt offerings and sacrifices, but as a witness between us and you.'

[29]"Far be it from us to rebel against the Lord and turn away from him today by building an altar for burnt offerings, grain offerings and sacrifices, other than the altar of the Lord our God that stands before his tabernacle."

[30]When Phinehas the priest and the leaders of the community — the heads of the clans of the Israelites — heard what Reuben, Gad and Manasseh had to say, they were pleased. [31]And Phinehas son of Eleazar, the priest, said to Reuben, Gad and Manasseh, "Today we know that the Lord is with us, because you have not acted unfaithfully toward the Lord in this matter. Now you have rescued the Israelites from the Lord's hand."

[32]Then Phinehas son of Eleazar, the priest, and the leaders returned to Canaan from their meeting with the Reubenites and Gadites in Gilead and reported to the Israelites. [33]They were glad to hear the report and praised God. And they talked no more about going to war against them to devastate the country where the Reubenites and the Gadites lived.

[34]And the Reubenites and the Gadites gave the altar this name: A Witness Between Us that the Lord is God.

Joshua's Farewell to the Leaders

23 After a long time had passed and the Lord had given Israel rest from all their enemies around them, Joshua, by then old and

---

[a] 20 The Hebrew term refers to the irrevocable giving over of things or persons to the Lord, often by totally destroying them.
[b] 23 Traditionally *peace offerings*; also in verse 27

well advanced in years, ²summoned all Israel—their elders, leaders, judges and officials—and said to them: "I am old and well advanced in years. ³You yourselves have seen everything the LORD your God has done to all these nations for your sake; it was the LORD your God who fought for you. ⁴Remember how I have allotted as an inheritance for your tribes all the land of the nations that remain—the nations I conquered—between the Jordan and the Great Sea ᵃ in the west. ⁵The LORD your God himself will drive them out of your way. He will push them out before you, and you will take possession of their land, as the LORD your God promised you.

⁶"Be very strong; be careful to obey all that is written in the Book of the Law of Moses, without turning aside to the right or to the left. ⁷Do not associate with these nations that remain among you; do not invoke the names of their gods or swear by them. You must not serve them or bow down to them. ⁸But you are to hold fast to the LORD your God, as you have until now.

⁹"The LORD has driven out before you great and powerful nations; to this day no one has been able to withstand you. ¹⁰One of you routs a thousand, because the LORD your God fights for you, just as he promised. ¹¹So be very careful to love the LORD your God.

¹²"But if you turn away and ally yourselves with the survivors of these nations that remain among you and if you intermarry with them and associate with them, ¹³then you may be sure that the LORD your God will no longer drive out these nations before you. Instead, they will become snares and traps for you, whips on your backs and thorns in your eyes, until you perish from this good land, which the LORD your God has given you.

¹⁴"Now I am about to go the way of all the earth. You know with all your heart and soul that not one of all the good promises the LORD your God gave you has failed. Every promise has been fulfilled; not one has failed. ¹⁵But just as every good promise of the LORD your God has come true, so the LORD will bring on you all the evil he has threatened, until he has destroyed you from this good land he has given you. ¹⁶If you violate the covenant of the LORD your God, which he commanded you, and go and serve other gods and bow down to them, the LORD's anger will burn against you, and you will quickly perish from the good land he has given you."

The Covenant Renewed at Shechem

24 Then Joshua assembled all the tribes of Israel at Shechem. He summoned the elders, leaders, judges and officials of Israel, and they presented themselves before God.

²Joshua said to all the people, "This is what the LORD, the God of Israel, says: 'Long ago your forefathers, including Terah the father of Abraham and Nahor, lived beyond the River ᵇ and worshiped other gods. ³But I took your father Abraham from the land beyond the River and led him throughout Canaan and gave him many descendants. I gave him Isaac, ⁴and to Isaac I gave Jacob and Esau. I assigned the hill country of Seir to Esau, but Jacob and his sons went down to Egypt.

⁵"'Then I sent Moses and Aaron, and I afflicted the Egyptians by what I did there, and I brought you out. ⁶When I brought your fathers out of Egypt, you came to the sea, and the Egyptians pursued them with chariots and horsemen ᶜ as far as the Red Sea. ᵈ ⁷But they cried to the LORD for help, and he put darkness between you and the Egyptians; he brought the sea over them and covered them. You saw with your own eyes what I did to the Egyptians. Then you lived in the desert for a long time.

⁸"'I brought you to the land of the Amorites who lived east of the Jordan. They fought against you, but I gave them into your hands. I destroyed them from before you, and you took possession of their land. ⁹When Balak son of Zippor, the king of Moab, prepared to fight against Israel, he sent for Balaam son of Beor to put a curse on

---

ᵃ 4 That is, the Mediterranean   ᵇ 2 That is, the Euphrates; also in verses 3, 14 and 15   ᶜ 6 Or *charioteers*   ᵈ 6 Hebrew *Yam Suph*; that is, Sea of Reeds you. ¹⁰But I would not listen to Balaam, so he blessed you again and again, and I delivered you out of his hand.

¹¹" 'Then you crossed the Jordan and came to Jericho. The citizens of Jericho fought against you, as did also the Amorites, Perizzites, Canaanites, Hittites, Girgashites, Hivites and Jebusites, but I gave them into your hands. ¹²I sent the hornet ahead of you, which drove them out before you—also the two Amorite kings. You did not do it with your own sword and bow. ¹³So I gave you a land on which you did not toil and cities you did not build; and you live in them and eat from vineyards and olive groves that you did not plant.'

¹⁴"Now fear the LORD and serve him with all faithfulness. Throw away the gods your forefathers worshiped beyond the River and in Egypt, and serve the LORD. ¹⁵But if serving the LORD seems undesirable to you, then choose for yourselves this day whom you will serve, whether the gods your forefathers served beyond the River, or the gods of the Amorites, in whose land you are living. But as for me and my household, we will serve the LORD."

TALKING POINTS

Blended Family

Every family can choose to serve the Lord.

JOSHUA 24:14–15

For more on blended family, go to Esther 2:5-7.

¹⁶Then the people answered, "Far be it from us to forsake the LORD to serve other gods! ¹⁷It was the LORD our God himself who brought us and our fathers up out of Egypt, from that land of slavery, and performed those great signs before our eyes. He protected us on our entire journey and among all the nations through which we traveled. ¹⁸And the LORD drove out before us all the nations, including the Amorites, who lived in the land. We too will serve the LORD, because he is our God."

¹⁹Joshua said to the people, "You are not able to serve the LORD. He is a holy God; he is a jealous God. He will not forgive your rebellion and your sins. ²⁰If you forsake the LORD and serve foreign gods, he will turn and bring disaster on you and make an end of you, after he has been good to you."

²¹But the people said to Joshua, "No! We will serve the LORD."

²²Then Joshua said, "You are witnesses against yourselves that you have chosen to serve the LORD."

"Yes, we are witnesses," they replied.

²³"Now then," said Joshua, "throw away the foreign gods that are among you and yield your hearts to the LORD, the God of Israel."

²⁴And the people said to Joshua, "We will serve the LORD our God and obey him."

²⁵On that day Joshua made a covenant for the people, and there at Shechem he drew up for them decrees and laws. ²⁶And Joshua recorded these things in the Book of the Law of God. Then he took a large stone and set it up there under the oak near the holy place of the LORD.

²⁷"See!" he said to all the people. "This stone will be a witness against us. It has heard all the words the LORD has said to us. It will be a witness against you if you are untrue to your God."

Buried in the Promised Land
24:29–31pp — Jdg 2:6–9

²⁸Then Joshua sent the people away, each to his own inheritance.

²⁹After these things, Joshua son of Nun, the servant of the LORD, died at the age of a hundred and ten. ³⁰And they buried him in the land of his inheritance, at Timnath Serah ᵃ in the hill country of Ephraim, north of Mount Gaash.

³¹Israel served the LORD throughout the life-

ᵃ 30 Also known as *Timnath Heres* (see Judges 2:9)

time of Joshua and of the elders who outlived him and who had experienced everything the LORD had done for Israel.

³²And Joseph's bones, which the Israelites had brought up from Egypt, were buried at Shechem in the tract of land that Jacob bought for a hundred pieces of silver *a* from the sons of Hamor, the father of Shechem. This became the inheritance of Joseph's descendants.

³³And Eleazar son of Aaron died and was buried at Gibeah, which had been allotted to his son Phinehas in the hill country of Ephraim.

a 32 Hebrew *hundred kesitahs*; a kesitah was a unit of money of unknown weight and value.

The Vicious CYCLE

A clear pattern emerges throughout the narratives in the book of Judges: The people of Israel turned from God; they were oppressed by foreign invaders; they cried out to God for help; and God sent a deliverer in the form of a leader, or "judge," from among them. After that a period of peace prevailed, but in time the cycle was repeated. The book of Judges records six of these cycles and ends with a story of total moral decay.

Only God's vast patience and gracious love for his people explains the way he repeatedly rescued generation after generation during this time period. He was faithful — both to discipline when Israel erred and to forgive when they returned to him.

At times, grandmothers see their grandchildren moving away from the right path. Misguided choices and outright sin can put young people in desperate situations that they can't get out of on their own. As God was faithful to his people during this time period, so we also need to be faithful to our children and grandchildren, never withdrawing our love but never carelessly ignoring sin.

Like our Father in heaven, we too must listen and be moved with compassion when our children and grandchildren cry out for our forgiveness and help. And, like God, we need to show compassion and mercy when we see true repentance.

VERSE *to* REMEMBER | JUDGES 10:15 – 16

But the Israelites said to the LORD, "We have sinned. Do with us whatever you think best, but please rescue us now." Then they got rid of the foreign gods among them and served the LORD. And he could bear Israel's misery no longer.

ABOUT JUDGES

WRITTEN BY:
Possibly Samuel

WRITTEN FOR:
God's chosen people, the Israelites

DATE WRITTEN:
Around 1000 B.C.

WHY WRITTEN:
To show what happened when the Israelites abandoned the Lord to worship false gods

Israel Fights the Remaining Canaanites

1:11–15pp — Jos 15:15–19

1 After the death of Joshua, the Israelites asked the LORD, "Who will be the first to go up and fight for us against the Canaanites?"

[2] The LORD answered, "Judah is to go; I have given the land into their hands."

[3] Then the men of Judah said to the Simeonites their brothers, "Come up with us into the territory allotted to us, to fight against the Canaanites. We in turn will go with you into yours." So the Simeonites went with them.

[4] When Judah attacked, the LORD gave the Canaanites and Perizzites into their hands and they struck down ten thousand men at Bezek. [5] It was there that they found Adoni-Bezek and fought against him, putting to rout the Canaanites and Perizzites. [6] Adoni-Bezek fled, but they chased him and caught him, and cut off his thumbs and big toes.

[7] Then Adoni-Bezek said, "Seventy kings with their thumbs and big toes cut off have picked up scraps under my table. Now God has paid me back for what I did to them." They brought him to Jerusalem, and he died there.

[8] The men of Judah attacked Jerusalem also and took it. They put the city to the sword and set it on fire.

[9] After that, the men of Judah went down to fight against the Canaanites living in the hill country, the Negev and the western foothills. [10] They advanced against the Canaanites living in Hebron (formerly called Kiriath Arba) and defeated Sheshai, Ahiman and Talmai.

[11] From there they advanced against the people living in Debir (formerly called Kiriath Sepher). [12] And Caleb said, "I will give my daughter Acsah in marriage to the man who attacks and captures Kiriath Sepher." [13] Othniel son of Kenaz, Caleb's younger brother, took it; so Caleb gave his daughter Acsah to him in marriage.

[14] One day when she came to Othniel, she urged him[a] to ask her father for a field. When she got off her donkey, Caleb asked her, "What can I do for you?"

[15] She replied, "Do me a special favor. Since you have given me land in the Negev, give me also springs of water." Then Caleb gave her the upper and lower springs.

[16] The descendants of Moses' father-in-law, the Kenite, went up from the City of Palms[b] with the men of Judah to live among the people of the Desert of Judah in the Negev near Arad.

[17] Then the men of Judah went with the Simeonites their brothers and attacked the Canaanites living in Zephath, and they totally destroyed[c] the city. Therefore it was called Hormah.[d] [18] The men of Judah also took[e] Gaza, Ashkelon and Ekron—each city with its territory.

[19] The LORD was with the men of Judah. They took possession of the hill country, but they were unable to drive the people from the plains, because they had iron chariots. [20] As Moses had promised, Hebron was given to Caleb, who drove from it the three sons of Anak. [21] The Benjamites, however, failed to dislodge the Jebusites, who were living in Jerusalem; to this day the Jebusites live there with the Benjamites.

[22] Now the house of Joseph attacked Bethel, and the LORD was with them. [23] When they sent men to spy out Bethel (formerly called Luz), [24] the spies saw a man coming out of the city and they said to him, "Show us how to get into the city and we will see that you are treated well." [25] So he showed them, and they put the city to the sword but spared the man and his whole family. [26] He then went to the land of the Hittites, where he built a city and called it Luz, which is its name to this day.

[27] But Manasseh did not drive out the people of Beth Shan or Taanach or Dor or Ibleam or Megiddo and their surrounding settlements, for the Canaanites were determined to live in that land. [28] When Israel became strong, they pressed the Canaanites into forced labor but never drove them out completely. [29] Nor did Ephraim drive out the

---

[a] 14 Hebrew; Septuagint and Vulgate *Othniel, he urged her*   [b] 16 That is, Jericho   [c] 17 The Hebrew term refers to the irrevocable giving over of things or persons to the LORD, often by totally destroying them.   [d] 17 *Hormah* means *destruction*.   [e] 18 Hebrew; Septuagint *Judah did not take*

Canaanites living in Gezer, but the Canaanites continued to live there among them. [30]Neither did Zebulun drive out the Canaanites living in Kitron or Nahalol, who remained among them; but they did subject them to forced labor. [31]Nor did Asher drive out those living in Acco or Sidon or Ahlab or Aczib or Helbah or Aphek or Rehob, [32]and because of this the people of Asher lived among the Canaanite inhabitants of the land. [33]Neither did Naphtali drive out those living in Beth Shemesh or Beth Anath; but the Naphtalites too lived among the Canaanite inhabitants of the land, and those living in Beth Shemesh and Beth Anath became forced laborers for them. [34]The Amorites confined the Danites to the hill country, not allowing them to come down into the plain. [35]And the Amorites were determined also to hold out in Mount Heres, Aijalon and Shaalbim, but when the power of the house of Joseph increased, they too were pressed into forced labor. [36]The boundary of the Amorites was from Scorpion[a] Pass to Sela and beyond.

The Angel of the LORD at Bokim

2 The angel of the LORD went up from Gilgal to Bokim and said, "I brought you up out of Egypt and led you into the land that I swore to give to your forefathers. I said, 'I will never break my covenant with you, [2]and you shall not make a covenant with the people of this land, but you shall break down their altars.' Yet you have disobeyed me. Why have you done this? [3]Now therefore I tell you that I will not drive them out before you; they will be ⌞thorns⌟ in your sides and their gods will be a snare to you."

[4]When the angel of the LORD had spoken these things to all the Israelites, the people wept aloud, [5]and they called that place Bokim.[b] There they offered sacrifices to the LORD.

Disobedience and Defeat

2:6–9pp — Jos 24:29–31

[6]After Joshua had dismissed the Israelites, they went to take possession of the land, each to his own inheritance. [7]The people served the LORD throughout the lifetime of Joshua and of the elders who outlived him and who had seen all the great things the LORD had done for Israel.

[8]Joshua son of Nun, the servant of the LORD, died at the age of a hundred and ten. [9]And they buried him in the land of his inheritance, at Timnath Heres[c] in the hill country of Ephraim, north of Mount Gaash.

[10]After that whole generation had been gathered to their fathers, another generation grew up, who knew neither the LORD nor what he had done for Israel. [11]Then the Israelites did evil in the eyes of the LORD and served the Baals. [12]They forsook the LORD, the God of their fathers, who had brought them out of Egypt. They followed and worshiped various gods of the peoples around them. They provoked the LORD to anger [13]because they forsook him and served Baal and the Ashtoreths. [14]In his anger against Israel the LORD handed them over to raiders who plundered them. He sold them to their enemies all around, whom they were no longer able to resist. [15]Whenever Israel went out to fight, the hand of the LORD was against them to defeat them, just as he had sworn to them. They were in great distress.

[16]Then the LORD raised up judges,[d] who saved them out of the hands of these raiders. [17]Yet they would not listen to their judges but prostituted themselves to other gods and worshiped them. Unlike their fathers, they quickly turned from the way in which their fathers had walked, the way of obedience to the LORD's commands. [18]Whenever the LORD raised up a judge for them, he was with the judge and saved them out of the hands of their enemies as long as the judge lived; for the LORD had compassion on them as they groaned under those who oppressed and afflicted them. [19]But when the judge died, the people returned to ways even more corrupt than those of their fathers, following other gods and serving and worshiping them. They refused to give up their evil practices and stubborn ways.

---

[a] 36 Hebrew *Akrabbim*   [b] 5 *Bokim* means *weepers.*   [c] 9 Also known as *Timnath Serah* (see Joshua 19:50 and 24:30)   [d] 16 Or *leaders*; similarly in verses 17-19

> AFTER THAT WHOLE GENERATION
> HAD BEEN GATHERED TO THEIR
> FATHERS, ANOTHER GENERATION
> GREW UP, WHO KNEW NEITHER
> THE LORD NOR WHAT HE HAD
> DONE FOR ISRAEL.
>
> *Judges 2:10*

Leaving a Legacy

JEAN E. SYSWERDA

READ | JUDGES 2:6 — 3:6

What an incredible denunciation! The mothers and fathers and grandmothers and grandfathers in Israel had been completely lax in their responsibility to teach their children (see God's command in Deuteronomy 6:4 – 7). If children of any generation grow up in an atmosphere void of instruction about God and his actions, the only ones to blame are the parents and grandparents. I take this verse very seriously. I hope we all do! I want to leave something more than my china or silver or a car to my grandchildren. I want to leave a legacy of a grandmother who was a woman of faith.

A legacy can be many things. It can be the product of wise spending and investment . . . money left behind for children and grandchildren. It can be the genetic predisposition to a disease or to athletic ability. It can be an aptitude for certain skills. It can be a sunny disposition or a grumpy temperament. It can be a house brimming with laughter or a house filled with harsh words. It can be the heritage of faithful living that you build around your children and grandchildren.

As grandmothers we have an opportunity to do again what we might think we didn't do so well the first time around. Our grandchildren present us with an amazing second chance. Let's not take that opportunity lightly. We have the chance to ensure that their generation doesn't grow up knowing nothing of God or his deeds. We can let all that the years have taught us about God spill over in abundance into their lives, building a legacy of faith and trust, an inheritance of knowing all about God's goodness and depending on him.

Dear Lord, as I spend time with my grandchildren, help me to live a life in front of them that teaches them about you. May my words and actions reveal my love for you. May I take every teachable moment and use it fully to share with my grandchildren the truth of your love for them. Thank you, Lord, for loving all of us with an amazing and a saving love. Amen.

Your next devotion is located on page 317.

GRANDCHILD IN FOCUS • PRAYER

Relationships at Home

O Lord, I pray that you will bless the home and family of my grandchild. May the relationships she has with her parents and siblings enhance her well-being, support her self-confidence and increase her faith. May her home life reflect your love, your grace, your compassion and your peace. Guide her parents to direct her in love and truth, so she will grow into a strong and compassionate individual. Amen.

PRAYING THE SCRIPTURES

Reassurance

JUDGES 2:18

Dear Lord of mercy, have compassion on my grandchild and save him from those who oppress and afflict him.

Next prayer in Reassurance Prayer Track: Psalm 34:18

²⁰Therefore the LORD was very angry with Israel and said, "Because this nation has violated the covenant that I laid down for their forefathers and has not listened to me, ²¹I will no longer drive out before them any of the nations Joshua left when he died. ²²I will use them to test Israel and see whether they will keep the way of the LORD and walk in it as their forefathers did." ²³The LORD had allowed those nations to remain; he did not drive them out at once by giving them into the hands of Joshua.

3 These are the nations the LORD left to test all those Israelites who had not experienced any of the wars in Canaan ²(he did this only to teach warfare to the descendants of the Israelites who had not had previous battle experience): ³the five rulers of the Philistines, all the Canaanites, the Sidonians, and the Hivites living in the Lebanon mountains from Mount Baal Hermon to Lebo *ᵃ* Hamath. ⁴They were left to test the Israelites to see whether they would obey the LORD's commands, which he had given their forefathers through Moses.

⁵The Israelites lived among the Canaanites, Hittites, Amorites, Perizzites, Hivites and Jebusites. ⁶They took their daughters in marriage and gave their own daughters to their sons, and served their gods.

Othniel

⁷The Israelites did evil in the eyes of the LORD; they forgot the LORD their God and served the Baals and the Asherahs. ⁸The anger of the LORD burned against Israel so that he sold them into the hands of Cushan-Rishathaim king of Aram Naharaim,*ᵇ* to whom the Israelites were subject for eight years. ⁹But when they cried out to the LORD, he raised up for them a deliverer, Othniel son of Kenaz, Caleb's younger brother, who saved them. ¹⁰The Spirit of the LORD came upon him, so that he became Israel's judge *ᶜ* and went to war. The LORD gave Cushan-Rishathaim king of Aram into the hands of Othniel, who overpowered him. ¹¹So the land had peace for forty years, until Othniel son of Kenaz died.

Ehud

¹²Once again the Israelites did evil in the eyes of the LORD, and because they did this evil the LORD gave Eglon king of Moab power over Israel. ¹³Getting the Ammonites and Amalekites to join him, Eglon came and attacked Israel, and they took possession of the City of Palms. *ᵈ* ¹⁴The Israelites were subject to Eglon king of Moab for eighteen years.

¹⁵Again the Israelites cried out to the LORD, and he gave them a deliverer—Ehud, a left-handed man, the son of Gera the Benjamite. The Israelites sent him with tribute to Eglon king of Moab. ¹⁶Now Ehud had made a double-edged sword about a foot and a half *ᵉ* long, which he strapped to his right thigh under his clothing. ¹⁷He presented the tribute to Eglon king of Moab, who was a very fat man. ¹⁸After Ehud had presented the tribute, he sent on their way the men who had carried it. ¹⁹At the idols *ᶠ* near Gilgal he himself turned back and said, "I have a secret message for you, O king."

The king said, "Quiet!" And all his attendants left him.

²⁰Ehud then approached him while he was sitting alone in the upper room of his summer palace *ᵍ* and said, "I have a message from God

---

ᵃ 3 Or *to the entrance to*   *ᵇ 8* That is, Northwest Mesopotamia   *ᶜ 10* Or *leader*   *ᵈ 13* That is, Jericho   *ᵉ 16* Hebrew *a cubit* (about 0.5 meter)   *ᶠ 19* Or *the stone quarries*; also in verse 26   *ᵍ 20* The meaning of the Hebrew for this phrase is uncertain.

LET'S TALK

Character Counts

Invite a couple of your grandkids over. Ask them to write down five things about themselves that make them special. (Assure them that, in this case, it's okay to brag.) Then, on another sheet of paper, ask them to write the name of the person sitting beside them and record five special qualities of that person. Take the time for each child to share both lists (this is sure to lead to lots of interaction). Then have them pass along the list to the person they were writing about.

Making sure each child has a Bible, read the story of David's anointing in 1 Samuel 16:1–13. What verses stand out? Point out the end of verse 7: "Man looks at the outward appearance, but the LORD looks at the heart." Discuss what this means.

Ask the kids to make new lists for themselves that focus only on character traits they think are important to God. Then ask them to record five traits they would like develop.

Long-Distance Variation: Send a form and a letter asking the kids to fill in the blanks for these categories. Invite them to send the form back to you if they'd like to. Remind them of 1 Samuel 16:1–13 and of how special they are to God.

Dear God, thank you for the uniqueness of each of my grandchildren. Help me to value each of them for who they are. Guard my tongue and mind from making comparisons among these precious children. Above all, help me to model for them a character that's worth imitating. Amen.

Your next devotion is located on page 318.

GRANDCHILD IN FOCUS • PRAYER

Friends

Dear Lord and Father, I pray for my grandchild's social life and his friends. Bring diverse friends into his life who will love and encourage him, who will bring joy and laughter to the good times and comfort and support through difficulties and disappointments. Grant him wisdom and discernment as he selects his friends; help him to avoid cliques that restrict, activities that endanger, and foolish and dangerous behaviors that harm. I ask that you fill his life with close and caring relationships. Amen.

Worship the Lord

As a father has compassion on his children,
    so the LORD has compassion on those who fear him;
for he knows how we are formed,
    he remembers that we are dust.
As for man, his days are like grass,
    he flourishes like a flower of the field;
the wind blows over it and it is gone,
    and its place remembers it no more.
But from everlasting to everlasting
    the LORD's love is with those who fear him,
    and his righteousness with their children's
        children—
with those who keep his covenant
    and remember to obey his precepts.

Psalm 103:13–18

Thank you, Lord, for your fatherly love
and compassion that last for eternity. In
you are life and breath and hope. Thank
you for your promise to remain with my
children's children. I pray that they will
love and keep your covenant. Help them
to obey you. Amen.

Your next devotion is located on page 320.

GRANDCHILD IN FOCUS • PRAYER

Self-Image

*O loving God, I praise you for creating my
grandchild as a unique individual. Now I ask you
to help her appreciate her uniqueness. Build up her
self-image so she can enjoy her individuality. Help
her to stand firm for who she is, where she has
come from and what she believes in. Encourage
her not only to have hopes and dreams but
to also enjoy each day as it comes.
In Jesus' name, amen.*

for you." As the king rose from his seat, ²¹Ehud reached with his left hand, drew the sword from his right thigh and plunged it into the king's belly. ²²Even the handle sank in after the blade, which came out his back. Ehud did not pull the sword out, and the fat closed in over it. ²³Then Ehud went out to the porch ᵃ; he shut the doors of the upper room behind him and locked them.

²⁴After he had gone, the servants came and found the doors of the upper room locked. They said, "He must be relieving himself in the inner room of the house." ²⁵They waited to the point of embarrassment, but when he did not open the doors of the room, they took a key and unlocked them. There they saw their lord fallen to the floor, dead.

²⁶While they waited, Ehud got away. He passed by the idols and escaped to Seirah. ²⁷When he arrived there, he blew a trumpet in the hill country of Ephraim, and the Israelites went down with him from the hills, with him leading them.

²⁸"Follow me," he ordered, "for the LORD has given Moab, your enemy, into your hands." So they followed him down and, taking possession of the fords of the Jordan that led to Moab, they allowed no one to cross over. ²⁹At that time they struck down about ten thousand Moabites, all vigorous and strong; not a man escaped. ³⁰That day Moab was made subject to Israel, and the land had peace for eighty years.

Shamgar

³¹After Ehud came Shamgar son of Anath, who struck down six hundred Philistines with an oxgoad. He too saved Israel.

Deborah

4 After Ehud died, the Israelites once again did evil in the eyes of the LORD. ²So the LORD sold them into the hands of Jabin, a king of Canaan, who reigned in Hazor. The commander of his army was Sisera, who lived in Harosheth Haggoyim. ³Because he had nine hundred iron chariots and had cruelly oppressed the Israelites for twenty years, they cried to the LORD for help.

⁴Deborah, a prophetess, the wife of Lappidoth, was leading ᵇ Israel at that time. ⁵She held court under the Palm of Deborah between Ramah and Bethel in the hill country of Ephraim, and the Israelites came to her to have their disputes decided. ⁶She sent for Barak son of Abinoam from Kedesh in Naphtali and said to him, "The LORD, the God of Israel, commands you: 'Go, take with you ten thousand men of Naphtali and Zebulun and lead the way to Mount Tabor. ⁷I will lure Sisera, the commander of Jabin's army, with his chariots and his troops to the Kishon River and give him into your hands.'"

⁸Barak said to her, "If you go with me, I will go; but if you don't go with me, I won't go."

ᵃ 23 The meaning of the Hebrew for this word is uncertain.
ᵇ 4 Traditionally *judging*

stories to share

JUDES 4:1–16

Deborah the Judge

LIFE LESSON: God gives us leaders to help us.

TO TALK ABOUT

✦ What was Deborah's job in Israel?

✦ What did Deborah tell Barak would happen if she went along with him to battle?

✦ Why do you think Barak was so afraid to go to battle without Deborah?

✦ When has God brought someone into your life to help you?

> "MOST BLESSED OF WOMEN
> BE JAEL, THE WIFE OF HEBER
> THE KENITE, MOST BLESSED OF
> TENT-DWELLING WOMEN."
>
> *Judges 5:24*

Jael's Story

DORIS WYNBEEK RIKKERS

READ | JUDGES 4:1 — 5:31

Everyone has family stories. Imagine the stories Jael's children recounted about *their* mother. Her legendary actions were heralded in song by another renowned woman: Deborah (see Judges 5:24–27). Jael was a heroine among the Israelites, and the people applauded her bravery.

Jael's story is often overlooked when we recount Bible stories. Perhaps the story is just too gory. We don't like the thought of a woman plotting an assassination. The imagery is disconcerting: a hammer, a tent peg, a sleeping man — yikes! Let's not tell this one to the grandkids.

Yet Jael's children and grandchildren must have loved retelling the story of their mom and grandma to others. Though Jael's husband, Heber the Kenite, apparently had allied himself with Israel's enemies (see Judges 4:11,17), Jael remained true to the Kenites' longstanding alliance with Israel. When the Israelites were threatened, Jael did not stand idly by. When she had the opportunity to act, she took it. The results of that fateful day, culminated by Jael's bravery, were significant: "Then the land had peace forty years" (Judges 5:31).

Nevertheless, it is difficult in our culture and within our peace-loving minds to praise the bloody acts recounted in the Bible. We are horrified by the wars and bloodshed. But these are the kinds of stories that the Israelites were commanded to retell to their children. It was their duty to pass on the history of their nation and to applaud the brave acts of those who kept their nation intact.

Few of us will become legends or be heralded in song like Jael was, but all of us have stories. All of us will be remembered in family stories (or legends) or family histories for some characteristic or special act or event. What stories will your children and grandchildren tell about you?

Dear Lord and Father, thank you for using ordinary men and women to further your plans and establish your kingdom. Help me to be brave and discerning, like Jael, and to know your will and act upon it. Amen.

GRANDCHILD IN FOCUS · PRAYER

Protection From Worldliness

O Sovereign Lord, the world surrounds my grandchild, pressing in and tempting him in so many ways. Help him set appropriate limits. Give him sound judgment to choose wisely. Guard him from temptation; protect him from physical and mental predators; lead him into paths of righteousness and light. And reassure me with your promise that you are holding him in your hands. Amen.

Your next devotion is located on page 324.

⁹"Very well," Deborah said, "I will go with you. But because of the way you are going about this,ᵃ the honor will not be yours, for the LORD will hand Sisera over to a woman." So Deborah went with Barak to Kedesh, ¹⁰where he summoned Zebulun and Naphtali. Ten thousand men followed him, and Deborah also went with him.

¹¹Now Heber the Kenite had left the other Kenites, the descendants of Hobab, Moses' brother-in-law,ᵇ and pitched his tent by the great tree in Zaanannim near Kedesh.

¹²When they told Sisera that Barak son of Abinoam had gone up to Mount Tabor, ¹³Sisera gathered together his nine hundred iron chariots and all the men with him, from Harosheth Haggoyim to the Kishon River.

¹⁴Then Deborah said to Barak, "Go! This is the day the LORD has given Sisera into your hands. Has not the LORD gone ahead of you?" So Barak went down Mount Tabor, followed by ten thousand men. ¹⁵At Barak's advance, the LORD routed Sisera and all his chariots and army by the sword, and Sisera abandoned his chariot and fled on foot. ¹⁶But Barak pursued the chariots and army as far as Harosheth Haggoyim. All the troops of Sisera fell by the sword; not a man was left.

¹⁷Sisera, however, fled on foot to the tent of Jael, the wife of Heber the Kenite, because there were friendly relations between Jabin king of Hazor and the clan of Heber the Kenite.

¹⁸Jael went out to meet Sisera and said to him, "Come, my lord, come right in. Don't be afraid." So he entered her tent, and she put a covering over him.

¹⁹"I'm thirsty," he said. "Please give me some water." She opened a skin of milk, gave him a drink, and covered him up.

²⁰"Stand in the doorway of the tent," he told her. "If someone comes by and asks you, 'Is anyone here?' say 'No.'"

²¹But Jael, Heber's wife, picked up a tent peg and a hammer and went quietly to him while he lay fast asleep, exhausted. She drove the peg through his temple into the ground, and he died.

²²Barak came by in pursuit of Sisera, and Jael went out to meet him. "Come," she said, "I will show you the man you're looking for." So he went in with her, and there lay Sisera with the tent peg through his temple — dead.

²³On that day God subdued Jabin, the Canaanite king, before the Israelites. ²⁴And the hand of the Israelites grew stronger and stronger against Jabin, the Canaanite king, until they destroyed him.

The Song of Deborah

5 On that day Deborah and Barak son of Abinoam sang this song:

² "When the princes in Israel take the lead,
  when the people willingly offer
    themselves —
  praise the LORD!

³ "Hear this, you kings! Listen, you rulers!
  I will sing toᶜ the LORD, I will sing;
  I will make music toᵈ the LORD, the God
    of Israel.

⁴ "O LORD, when you went out from Seir,
  when you marched from the land of
    Edom,
 the earth shook, the heavens poured,
  the clouds poured down water.
⁵ The mountains quaked before the LORD, the
    One of Sinai,
  before the LORD, the God of Israel.

⁶ "In the days of Shamgar son of Anath,
  in the days of Jael, the roads were
    abandoned;
  travelers took to winding paths.
⁷ Village lifeᵉ in Israel ceased,
  ceased until I,ᶠ Deborah, arose,
  arose a mother in Israel.
⁸ When they chose new gods,
  war came to the city gates,
 and not a shield or spear was seen
  among forty thousand in Israel.

ᵃ 9 Or But on the expedition you are undertaking   ᵇ 11 Or father-in-law   ᶜ 3 Or of   ᵈ 3 Or / with song I will praise   ᵉ 7 Or Warriors   ᶠ 7 Or you

9 My heart is with Israel's princes,
    with the willing volunteers among the
      people.
  Praise the LORD!

10 "You who ride on white donkeys,
    sitting on your saddle blankets,
    and you who walk along the road,
  consider 11 the voice of the singers a at the
      watering places.
  They recite the righteous acts of the LORD,
    the righteous acts of his warriors b in Israel.

"Then the people of the LORD
    went down to the city gates.
12 'Wake up, wake up, Deborah!
    Wake up, wake up, break out in song!
  Arise, O Barak!
    Take captive your captives, O son of
      Abinoam.'

13 "Then the men who were left
    came down to the nobles;
  the people of the LORD
    came to me with the mighty.
14 Some came from Ephraim, whose roots were
    in Amalek;
    Benjamin was with the people who
      followed you.
  From Makir captains came down,
    from Zebulun those who bear a
      commander's staff.
15 The princes of Issachar were with Deborah;
    yes, Issachar was with Barak,
    rushing after him into the valley.
  In the districts of Reuben
    there was much searching of heart.
16 Why did you stay among the campfires c
    to hear the whistling for the flocks?
  In the districts of Reuben
    there was much searching of heart.
17 Gilead stayed beyond the Jordan.
    And Dan, why did he linger by the ships?
  Asher remained on the coast
    and stayed in his coves.
18 The people of Zebulun risked their very lives;
    so did Naphtali on the heights of the field.

19 "Kings came, they fought;
    the kings of Canaan fought
  at Taanach by the waters of Megiddo,
    but they carried off no silver, no plunder.
20 From the heavens the stars fought,
    from their courses they fought against
      Sisera.
21 The river Kishon swept them away,
    the age-old river, the river Kishon.
  March on, my soul; be strong!
22 Then thundered the horses' hoofs—
    galloping, galloping go his mighty
      steeds.
23 'Curse Meroz,' said the angel of the LORD.
    'Curse its people bitterly,
  because they did not come to help the
      LORD,
    to help the LORD against the mighty.'

24 "Most blessed of women be Jael,
    the wife of Heber the Kenite,
    most blessed of tent-dwelling women.
25 He asked for water, and she gave him milk;
    in a bowl fit for nobles she brought him
      curdled milk.
26 Her hand reached for the tent peg,
    her right hand for the workman's
      hammer.
  She struck Sisera, she crushed his head,
    she shattered and pierced his temple.
27 At her feet he sank,
    he fell; there he lay.
  At her feet he sank, he fell;
    where he sank, there he fell—dead.

28 "Through the window peered Sisera's
    mother;
    behind the lattice she cried out,
  'Why is his chariot so long in coming?
    Why is the clatter of his chariots
      delayed?'
29 The wisest of her ladies answer her;
    indeed, she keeps saying to herself,

a 11 Or *archers*; the meaning of the Hebrew for this word is
uncertain.   b 11 Or *villagers*   c 16 Or *saddlebags*

³⁰ 'Are they not finding and dividing the spoils:
    a girl or two for each man,
    colorful garments as plunder for Sisera,
    colorful garments embroidered,
    highly embroidered garments for my
        neck—
all this as plunder?'

³¹ "So may all your enemies perish, O LORD!
    But may they who love you be like the sun
    when it rises in its strength."

Then the land had peace forty years.

Gideon

6 Again the Israelites did evil in the eyes of the LORD, and for seven years he gave them into the hands of the Midianites. ²Because the power of Midian was so oppressive, the Israelites prepared shelters for themselves in mountain clefts, caves and strongholds. ³Whenever the Israelites planted their crops, the Midianites, Amalekites and other eastern peoples invaded the country. ⁴They camped on the land and ruined the crops all the way to Gaza and did not spare a living thing for Israel, neither sheep nor cattle nor donkeys. ⁵They came up with their livestock and their tents like swarms of locusts. It was impossible to count the men and their camels; they invaded the land to ravage it. ⁶Midian so impoverished the Israelites that they cried out to the LORD for help.

⁷When the Israelites cried to the LORD because of Midian, ⁸he sent them a prophet, who said, "This is what the LORD, the God of Israel, says: I brought you up out of Egypt, out of the land of slavery. ⁹I snatched you from the power of Egypt and from the hand of all your oppressors. I drove them from before you and gave you their land. ¹⁰I said to you, 'I am the LORD your God; do not worship the gods of the Amorites, in whose land you live.' But you have not listened to me."

¹¹The angel of the LORD came and sat down under the oak in Ophrah that belonged to Joash the Abiezrite, where his son Gideon was threshing wheat in a winepress to keep it from the Midianites. ¹²When the angel of the LORD appeared to Gideon, he said, "The LORD is with you, mighty warrior."

¹³"But sir," Gideon replied, "if the LORD is with us, why has all this happened to us? Where are all his wonders that our fathers told us about when they said, 'Did not the LORD bring us up out of Egypt?' But now the LORD has abandoned us and put us into the hand of Midian."

¹⁴The LORD turned to him and said, "Go in the strength you have and save Israel out of Midian's hand. Am I not sending you?"

¹⁵"But Lord,ᵃ" Gideon asked, "how can I save Israel? My clan is the weakest in Manasseh, and I am the least in my family."

¹⁶The LORD answered, "I will be with you, and you will strike down all the Midianites together."

¹⁷Gideon replied, "If now I have found favor in your eyes, give me a sign that it is really you talking to me. ¹⁸Please do not go away until I come back and bring my offering and set it before you."

And the LORD said, "I will wait until you return."

¹⁹Gideon went in, prepared a young goat, and from an ephahᵇ of flour he made bread without yeast. Putting the meat in a basket and its broth in a pot, he brought them out and offered them to him under the oak.

²⁰The angel of God said to him, "Take the meat and the unleavened bread, place them on this rock, and pour out the broth." And Gideon did so. ²¹With the tip of the staff that was in his hand, the angel of the LORD touched the meat and the unleavened bread. Fire flared from the rock, consuming the meat and the bread. And the angel of the LORD disappeared. ²²When Gideon realized that it was the angel of the LORD, he exclaimed, "Ah, Sovereign LORD! I have seen the angel of the LORD face to face!"

ᵃ 15 Or *sir*   ᵇ 19 That is, probably about 3/5 bushel (about 22 liters)

WHEN THE ANGEL OF THE LORD
APPEARED TO GIDEON, HE
SAID, "THE LORD IS WITH YOU,
MIGHTY WARRIOR."

Judges 6:12

You're a Sparkler

BOBBIE WOLGEMUTH

READ | JUDGES 6:1–24

We can learn a lot about the power of spoken words from the angel who spoke to a frightened man named Gideon. The angel set a wonderful example for us to follow with our grandchildren.

Showing up is the first thing to do. The angel appeared at the place where Gideon was hiding. Where do you go to meet your grandchild? His soccer game, her gymnastics meet, the kitchen table, the hallway of your church, the phone? Find a place to applaud a child with your presence.

Next, look at what the angel said about God. "The LORD is with you." One of our family's favorite goodbye lines to say over the phone or when we part company with each other is, "The Lord be with you." It is a simple way to assure someone that God is always a companion close at hand.

Then, the angel called Gideon a mighty warrior. A seed was planted in his heart . . . a thought of potential identity. Until then Gideon most likely hadn't thought of himself as a soldier — especially not a mighty one.

I learned how a simple phrase has the potential to foster identity when my grandson, Luke, was coloring at the kitchen table one day. He surprised me with a creative picture, and I exclaimed, "Luke, you're an artist!" I didn't think anything else about the comment until two days later when Luke was on the floor with art paper and markers around him. When I came to look at his newest project, Luke said, "You're right, Nanny, I *am* an artist!"

To bless your grandchildren, it's easy to follow this pattern. Show up where they are, tell them that the Lord is with them and give them a strong word of identity. Speaking something as simple as, "You're a sparkler," may cause a child to shine brighter than ever.

Lord, thank you for showing up with words of hope and identity every day. I want to bless my grandchildren with my presence and by speaking simple words of encouragement to them. Amen.

Your next devotion is located on page 335.

GRANDCHILD IN FOCUS • PRAYER

Respect for Authority

Dear Lord, I pray that my grandchild will continually grow to respect those in authority. May she learn to be cooperative and fair in work and play. Instill in her a high regard for officials who govern our land and enforce the laws. May her relationships with parents, teachers, coaches, mentors and bosses be respectful, admirable, constructive and caring. Amen.

JUDGES 6:7–40

Stories to share

Gideon Tests God

LIFE LESSON: God can be trusted.

TO TALK ABOUT

✦ How did Gideon know he was talking to the angel of the Lord?

✦ What two things did Gideon later ask God to do before he would believe God's words to him?

✦ Why do you think Gideon didn't believe God right away?

✦ Do you ever want proof from God? Explain.

²³ But the LORD said to him, "Peace! Do not be afraid. You are not going to die."

²⁴ So Gideon built an altar to the LORD there and called it The LORD is Peace. To this day it stands in Ophrah of the Abiezrites.

²⁵ That same night the LORD said to him, "Take the second bull from your father's herd, the one seven years old.ᵃ Tear down your father's altar to Baal and cut down the Asherah poleᵇ beside it. ²⁶ Then build a proper kind ofᶜ altar to the LORD your God on the top of this height. Using the wood of the Asherah pole that you cut down, offer the secondᵈ bull as a burnt offering."

²⁷ So Gideon took ten of his servants and did as the LORD told him. But because he was afraid of his family and the men of the town, he did it at night rather than in the daytime.

²⁸ In the morning when the men of the town got up, there was Baal's altar, demolished, with the Asherah pole beside it cut down and the second bull sacrificed on the newly built altar!

²⁹ They asked each other, "Who did this?"

When they carefully investigated, they were told, "Gideon son of Joash did it."

³⁰ The men of the town demanded of Joash, "Bring out your son. He must die, because he has broken down Baal's altar and cut down the Asherah pole beside it."

³¹ But Joash replied to the hostile crowd around him, "Are you going to plead Baal's cause? Are you trying to save him? Whoever fights for him shall be put to death by morning! If Baal really is a god, he can defend himself when someone breaks down his altar." ³² So that day they called Gideon "Jerub-Baal,ᵉ" saying, "Let Baal contend with him," because he broke down Baal's altar.

³³ Now all the Midianites, Amalekites and other eastern peoples joined forces and crossed over the Jordan and camped in the Valley of Jezreel. ³⁴ Then the Spirit of the LORD came upon Gideon, and he blew a trumpet, summoning the Abiezrites to follow him. ³⁵ He sent messengers throughout Manasseh, calling them to arms, and also into Asher, Zebulun and Naphtali, so that they too went up to meet them.

³⁶ Gideon said to God, "If you will save Israel by my hand as you have promised— ³⁷ look, I will place a wool fleece on the threshing floor. If there is dew only on the fleece and all the ground is dry, then I will know that you will save Israel by my hand, as you said." ³⁸ And that is what happened. Gideon rose early the next day; he squeezed the fleece and wrung out the dew—a bowlful of water.

³⁹ Then Gideon said to God, "Do not be angry with me. Let me make just one more request. Allow me one more test with the fleece. This time make the fleece dry and the ground covered with dew." ⁴⁰ That night God did so. Only the fleece was dry; all the ground was covered with dew.

ᵃ *25 Or Take a full-grown, mature bull from your father's herd*
ᵇ *25 That is, a symbol of the goddess Asherah; here and elsewhere in Judges* ᶜ *26 Or build with layers of stone an* ᵈ *26 Or full-grown; also in verse 28* ᵉ *32 Jerub-Baal means let Baal contend.*

Gideon Defeats the Midianites

7 Early in the morning, Jerub-Baal (that is, Gideon) and all his men camped at the spring of Harod. The camp of Midian was north of them in the valley near the hill of Moreh. ²The LORD said to Gideon, "You have too many men for me to deliver Midian into their hands. In order that Israel may not boast against me that her own strength has saved her, ³announce now to the people, 'Anyone who trembles with fear may turn back and leave Mount Gilead.'" So twenty-two thousand men left, while ten thousand remained.

⁴But the LORD said to Gideon, "There are still too many men. Take them down to the water, and I will sift them for you there. If I say, 'This one shall go with you,' he shall go; but if I say, 'This one shall not go with you,' he shall not go."

⁵So Gideon took the men down to the water. There the LORD told him, "Separate those who lap the water with their tongues like a dog from those who kneel down to drink." ⁶Three hundred men lapped with their hands to their mouths. All the rest got down on their knees to drink.

⁷The LORD said to Gideon, "With the three hundred men that lapped I will save you and give the Midianites into your hands. Let all the other men go, each to his own place." ⁸So Gideon sent the rest of the Israelites to their tents but kept the three hundred, who took over the provisions and trumpets of the others.

Now the camp of Midian lay below him in the valley. ⁹During that night the LORD said to Gideon, "Get up, go down against the camp, because I am going to give it into your hands. ¹⁰If you are afraid to attack, go down to the camp with your servant Purah ¹¹and listen to what they are saying. Afterward, you will be encouraged to attack the camp." So he and Purah his servant went down to the outposts of the camp. ¹²The Midianites, the Amalekites and all the other eastern peoples had settled in the valley, thick as locusts. Their camels could no more be counted than the sand on the seashore.

¹³Gideon arrived just as a man was telling a friend his dream. "I had a dream," he was saying.

"A round loaf of barley bread came tumbling into the Midianite camp. It struck the tent with such force that the tent overturned and collapsed."

¹⁴His friend responded, "This can be nothing other than the sword of Gideon son of Joash, the Israelite. God has given the Midianites and the whole camp into his hands."

JUDGES 7:1–21

Gideon Defeats the Midianites

LIFE LESSON: God is the source of our strength.

TO TALK ABOUT

✦ How did God reduce Gideon's army from 32,000 to 300?

✦ What reason did God give for this troop reduction?

✦ Who really won the victory over the Midianites?

✦ Are you ever tempted to think you can handle all your problems on your own?

¹⁵When Gideon heard the dream and its interpretation, he worshiped God. He returned to the camp of Israel and called out, "Get up! The LORD has given the Midianite camp into your hands." ¹⁶Dividing the three hundred men into three companies, he placed trumpets and empty jars in the hands of all of them, with torches inside. ¹⁷"Watch me," he told them. "Follow my lead.

When I get to the edge of the camp, do exactly as I do. ¹⁸When I and all who are with me blow our trumpets, then from all around the camp blow yours and shout, 'For the LORD and for Gideon.'"

¹⁹Gideon and the hundred men with him reached the edge of the camp at the beginning of the middle watch, just after they had changed the guard. They blew their trumpets and broke the jars that were in their hands. ²⁰The three companies blew the trumpets and smashed the jars. Grasping the torches in their left hands and holding in their right hands the trumpets they were to blow, they shouted, "A sword for the LORD and for Gideon!" ²¹While each man held his position around the camp, all the Midianites ran, crying out as they fled.

²²When the three hundred trumpets sounded, the LORD caused the men throughout the camp to turn on each other with their swords. The army fled to Beth Shittah toward Zererah as far as the border of Abel Meholah near Tabbath. ²³Israelites from Naphtali, Asher and all Manasseh were called out, and they pursued the Midianites. ²⁴Gideon sent messengers throughout the hill country of Ephraim, saying, "Come down against the Midianites and seize the waters of the Jordan ahead of them as far as Beth Barah."

So all the men of Ephraim were called out and they took the waters of the Jordan as far as Beth Barah. ²⁵They also captured two of the Midianite leaders, Oreb and Zeeb. They killed Oreb at the rock of Oreb, and Zeeb at the winepress of Zeeb. They pursued the Midianites and brought the heads of Oreb and Zeeb to Gideon, who was by the Jordan.

Zebah and Zalmunna

8 Now the Ephraimites asked Gideon, "Why have you treated us like this? Why didn't you call us when you went to fight Midian?" And they criticized him sharply.

²But he answered them, "What have I accomplished compared to you? Aren't the gleanings of Ephraim's grapes better than the full grape harvest of Abiezer? ³God gave Oreb and Zeeb, the

Midianite leaders, into your hands. What was I able to do compared to you?" At this, their resentment against him subsided.

⁴Gideon and his three hundred men, exhausted yet keeping up the pursuit, came to the Jordan and crossed it. ⁵He said to the men of Succoth, "Give my troops some bread; they are worn out, and I am still pursuing Zebah and Zalmunna, the kings of Midian."

⁶But the officials of Succoth said, "Do you already have the hands of Zebah and Zalmunna in your possession? Why should we give bread to your troops?"

⁷Then Gideon replied, "Just for that, when the LORD has given Zebah and Zalmunna into my hand, I will tear your flesh with desert thorns and briers."

⁸From there he went up to Peniel[a] and made the same request of them, but they answered as the men of Succoth had. ⁹So he said to the men of Peniel, "When I return in triumph, I will tear down this tower."

¹⁰Now Zebah and Zalmunna were in Karkor with a force of about fifteen thousand men, all that were left of the armies of the eastern peoples; a hundred and twenty thousand swordsmen had fallen. ¹¹Gideon went up by the route of the nomads east of Nobah and Jogbehah and fell upon the unsuspecting army. ¹²Zebah and Zalmunna, the two kings of Midian, fled, but he pursued them and captured them, routing their entire army.

¹³Gideon son of Joash then returned from the battle by the Pass of Heres. ¹⁴He caught a young man of Succoth and questioned him, and the young man wrote down for him the names of the seventy-seven officials of Succoth, the elders of the town. ¹⁵Then Gideon came and said to the men of Succoth, "Here are Zebah and Zalmunna, about whom you taunted me by saying, 'Do you already have the hands of Zebah and Zalmunna in your possession? Why should we give bread to your exhausted men?'" ¹⁶He took the elders of the town and taught the men of Succoth a lesson

---

a 8 Hebrew Penuel, a variant of Peniel; also in verses 9 and 17 by punishing them with desert thorns and briers. ¹⁷He also pulled down the tower of Peniel and killed the men of the town.

¹⁸Then he asked Zebah and Zalmunna, "What kind of men did you kill at Tabor?"

"Men like you," they answered, "each one with the bearing of a prince."

¹⁹Gideon replied, "Those were my brothers, the sons of my own mother. As surely as the LORD lives, if you had spared their lives, I would not kill you." ²⁰Turning to Jether, his oldest son, he said, "Kill them!" But Jether did not draw his sword, because he was only a boy and was afraid.

²¹Zebah and Zalmunna said, "Come, do it yourself. 'As is the man, so is his strength.' " So Gideon stepped forward and killed them, and took the ornaments off their camels' necks.

Gideon's Ephod

²²The Israelites said to Gideon, "Rule over us—you, your son and your grandson—because you have saved us out of the hand of Midian."

²³But Gideon told them, "I will not rule over you, nor will my son rule over you. The LORD will rule over you." ²⁴And he said, "I do have one request, that each of you give me an earring from your share of the plunder." (It was the custom of the Ishmaelites to wear gold earrings.)

²⁵They answered, "We'll be glad to give them." So they spread out a garment, and each man threw a ring from his plunder onto it. ²⁶The weight of the gold rings he asked for came to seventeen hundred shekels,ᵃ not counting the ornaments, the pendants and the purple garments worn by the kings of Midian or the chains that were on their camels' necks. ²⁷Gideon made the gold into an ephod, which he placed in Ophrah, his town. All Israel prostituted themselves by worshiping it there, and it became a snare to Gideon and his family.

Gideon's Death

²⁸Thus Midian was subdued before the Israelites and did not raise its head again. During Gideon's lifetime, the land enjoyed peace forty years.

²⁹Jerub-Baal son of Joash went back home to live. ³⁰He had seventy sons of his own, for he had many wives. ³¹His concubine, who lived in Shechem, also bore him a son, whom he named Abimelech. ³²Gideon son of Joash died at a good old age and was buried in the tomb of his father Joash in Ophrah of the Abiezrites.

³³No sooner had Gideon died than the Israelites again prostituted themselves to the Baals. They set up Baal-Berith as their god ³⁴and did not remember the LORD their God, who had rescued them from the hands of all their enemies on every side. ³⁵They also failed to show kindness to the family of Jerub-Baal (that is, Gideon) for all the good things he had done for them.

Abimelech

9 Abimelech son of Jerub-Baal went to his mother's brothers in Shechem and said to them and to all his mother's clan, ²"Ask all the citizens of Shechem, 'Which is better for you: to have all seventy of Jerub-Baal's sons rule over you, or just one man?' Remember, I am your flesh and blood."

³When the brothers repeated all this to the citizens of Shechem, they were inclined to follow Abimelech, for they said, "He is our brother." ⁴They gave him seventy shekelsᵇ of silver from the temple of Baal-Berith, and Abimelech used it to hire reckless adventurers, who became his followers. ⁵He went to his father's home in Ophrah and on one stone murdered his seventy brothers, the sons of Jerub-Baal. But Jotham, the youngest son of Jerub-Baal, escaped by hiding. ⁶Then all the citizens of Shechem and Beth Millo gathered beside the great tree at the pillar in Shechem to crown Abimelech king.

⁷When Jotham was told about this, he climbed up on the top of Mount Gerizim and shouted to them, "Listen to me, citizens of Shechem, so that God may listen to you. ⁸One day the trees went out to anoint a king for themselves. They said to the olive tree, 'Be our king.'

ᵃ 26 That is, about 43 pounds (about 19.5 kilograms)   ᵇ 4 That is, about 1 3/4 pounds (about 0.8 kilogram)

⁹"But the olive tree answered, 'Should I give up my oil, by which both gods and men are honored, to hold sway over the trees?'

¹⁰"Next, the trees said to the fig tree, 'Come and be our king.'

¹¹"But the fig tree replied, 'Should I give up my fruit, so good and sweet, to hold sway over the trees?'

¹²"Then the trees said to the vine, 'Come and be our king.'

¹³"But the vine answered, 'Should I give up my wine, which cheers both gods and men, to hold sway over the trees?'

¹⁴"Finally all the trees said to the thornbush, 'Come and be our king.'

¹⁵"The thornbush said to the trees, 'If you really want to anoint me king over you, come and take refuge in my shade; but if not, then let fire come out of the thornbush and consume the cedars of Lebanon!'

¹⁶"Now if you have acted honorably and in good faith when you made Abimelech king, and if you have been fair to Jerub-Baal and his family, and if you have treated him as he deserves— ¹⁷and to think that my father fought for you, risked his life to rescue you from the hand of Midian ¹⁸(but today you have revolted against my father's family, murdered his seventy sons on a single stone, and made Abimelech, the son of his slave girl, king over the citizens of Shechem because he is your brother)— ¹⁹if then you have acted honorably and in good faith toward Jerub-Baal and his family today, may Abimelech be your joy, and may you be his, too! ²⁰But if you have not, let fire come out from Abimelech and consume you, citizens of Shechem and Beth Millo, and let fire come out from you, citizens of Shechem and Beth Millo, and consume Abimelech!"

²¹Then Jotham fled, escaping to Beer, and he lived there because he was afraid of his brother Abimelech.

²²After Abimelech had governed Israel three years, ²³God sent an evil spirit between Abimelech and the citizens of Shechem, who acted treacherously against Abimelech. ²⁴God did this in order that the crime against Jerub-Baal's seventy sons, the shedding of their blood, might be avenged on their brother Abimelech and on the citizens of Shechem, who had helped him murder his brothers. ²⁵In opposition to him these citizens of Shechem set men on the hilltops to ambush and rob everyone who passed by, and this was reported to Abimelech.

²⁶Now Gaal son of Ebed moved with his brothers into Shechem, and its citizens put their confidence in him. ²⁷After they had gone out into the fields and gathered the grapes and trodden them, they held a festival in the temple of their god. While they were eating and drinking, they cursed Abimelech. ²⁸Then Gaal son of Ebed said, "Who is Abimelech, and who is Shechem, that we should be subject to him? Isn't he Jerub-Baal's son, and isn't Zebul his deputy? Serve the men of Hamor, Shechem's father! Why should we serve Abimelech? ²⁹If only this people were under my command! Then I would get rid of him. I would say to Abimelech, 'Call out your whole army!'"ᵃ

³⁰When Zebul the governor of the city heard what Gaal son of Ebed said, he was very angry. ³¹Under cover he sent messengers to Abimelech, saying, "Gaal son of Ebed and his brothers have come to Shechem and are stirring up the city against you. ³²Now then, during the night you and your men should come and lie in wait in the fields. ³³In the morning at sunrise, advance against the city. When Gaal and his men come out against you, do whatever your hand finds to do."

³⁴So Abimelech and all his troops set out by night and took up concealed positions near Shechem in four companies. ³⁵Now Gaal son of Ebed had gone out and was standing at the entrance to the city gate just as Abimelech and his soldiers came out from their hiding place.

³⁶When Gaal saw them, he said to Zebul, "Look, people are coming down from the tops of the mountains!"

ᵃ 29 Septuagint; Hebrew *him." Then he said to Abimelech, "Call out your whole army!"*

Zebul replied, "You mistake the shadows of the mountains for men."

³⁷But Gaal spoke up again: "Look, people are coming down from the center of the land, and a company is coming from the direction of the soothsayers' tree."

³⁸Then Zebul said to him, "Where is your big talk now, you who said, 'Who is Abimelech that we should be subject to him?' Aren't these the men you ridiculed? Go out and fight them!"

³⁹So Gaal led out ᵃ the citizens of Shechem and fought Abimelech. ⁴⁰Abimelech chased him, and many fell wounded in the flight—all the way to the entrance to the gate. ⁴¹Abimelech stayed in Arumah, and Zebul drove Gaal and his brothers out of Shechem.

⁴²The next day the people of Shechem went out to the fields, and this was reported to Abimelech. ⁴³So he took his men, divided them into three companies and set an ambush in the fields. When he saw the people coming out of the city, he rose to attack them. ⁴⁴Abimelech and the companies with him rushed forward to a position at the entrance to the city gate. Then two companies rushed upon those in the fields and struck them down. ⁴⁵All that day Abimelech pressed his attack against the city until he had captured it and killed its people. Then he destroyed the city and scattered salt over it.

⁴⁶On hearing this, the citizens in the tower of Shechem went into the stronghold of the temple of El-Berith. ⁴⁷When Abimelech heard that they had assembled there, ⁴⁸he and all his men went up Mount Zalmon. He took an ax and cut off some branches, which he lifted to his shoulders. He ordered the men with him, "Quick! Do what you have seen me do!" ⁴⁹So all the men cut branches and followed Abimelech. They piled them against the stronghold and set it on fire over the people inside. So all the people in the tower of Shechem, about a thousand men and women, also died.

⁵⁰Next Abimelech went to Thebez and besieged it and captured it. ⁵¹Inside the city, however, was a strong tower, to which all the men and women—all the people of the city—fled. They locked themselves in and climbed up on the tower roof. ⁵²Abimelech went to the tower and stormed it. But as he approached the entrance to the tower to set it on fire, ⁵³a woman dropped an upper millstone on his head and cracked his skull.

⁵⁴Hurriedly he called to his armor-bearer, "Draw your sword and kill me, so that they can't say, 'A woman killed him.' " So his servant ran him through, and he died. ⁵⁵When the Israelites saw that Abimelech was dead, they went home.

⁵⁶Thus God repaid the wickedness that Abimelech had done to his father by murdering his seventy brothers. ⁵⁷God also made the men of Shechem pay for all their wickedness. The curse of Jotham son of Jerub-Baal came on them.

Tola

10 After the time of Abimelech a man of Issachar, Tola son of Puah, the son of Dodo, rose to save Israel. He lived in Shamir, in the hill country of Ephraim. ²He led ᵇ Israel twenty-three years; then he died, and was buried in Shamir.

Jair

³He was followed by Jair of Gilead, who led Israel twenty-two years. ⁴He had thirty sons, who rode thirty donkeys. They controlled thirty towns in Gilead, which to this day are called Havvoth Jair.ᶜ ⁵When Jair died, he was buried in Kamon.

Jephthah

⁶Again the Israelites did evil in the eyes of the LORD. They served the Baals and the Ashtoreths, and the gods of Aram, the gods of Sidon, the gods of Moab, the gods of the Ammonites and the gods of the Philistines. And because the Israelites forsook the LORD and no longer served him, ⁷he became angry with them. He sold them into the hands of the Philistines and the Ammonites, ⁸who that year shattered and crushed them. For

---

ᵃ 39 Or *Gaal went out in the sight of*   ᵇ 2 Traditionally *judged;* also in verse 3   ᶜ 4 Or *called the settlements of Jair* eighteen years they oppressed all the Israelites on the east side of the Jordan in Gilead, the land of the Amorites. ⁹The Ammonites also crossed the Jordan to fight against Judah, Benjamin and the house of Ephraim; and Israel was in great distress. ¹⁰Then the Israelites cried out to the LORD, "We have sinned against you, forsaking our God and serving the Baals."

¹¹The LORD replied, "When the Egyptians, the Amorites, the Ammonites, the Philistines, ¹²the Sidonians, the Amalekites and the Maonites*a* oppressed you and you cried to me for help, did I not save you from their hands? ¹³But you have forsaken me and served other gods, so I will no longer save you. ¹⁴Go and cry out to the gods you have chosen. Let them save you when you are in trouble!"

¹⁵But the Israelites said to the LORD, "We have sinned. Do with us whatever you think best, but please rescue us now." ¹⁶Then they got rid of the foreign gods among them and served the LORD. And he could bear Israel's misery no longer.

¹⁷When the Ammonites were called to arms and camped in Gilead, the Israelites assembled and camped at Mizpah. ¹⁸The leaders of the people of Gilead said to each other, "Whoever will launch the attack against the Ammonites will be the head of all those living in Gilead."

11 Jephthah the Gileadite was a mighty warrior. His father was Gilead; his mother was a prostitute. ²Gilead's wife also bore him sons, and when they were grown up, they drove Jephthah away. "You are not going to get any inheritance in our family," they said, "because you are the son of another woman." ³So Jephthah fled from his brothers and settled in the land of Tob, where a group of adventurers gathered around him and followed him.

⁴Some time later, when the Ammonites made war on Israel, ⁵the elders of Gilead went to get Jephthah from the land of Tob. ⁶"Come," they said, "be our commander, so we can fight the Ammonites."

⁷Jephthah said to them, "Didn't you hate me

and drive me from my father's house? Why do you come to me now, when you're in trouble?"

⁸The elders of Gilead said to him, "Nevertheless, we are turning to you now; come with us to fight the Ammonites, and you will be our head over all who live in Gilead."

⁹Jephthah answered, "Suppose you take me back to fight the Ammonites and the LORD gives them to me — will I really be your head?"

¹⁰The elders of Gilead replied, "The LORD is our witness; we will certainly do as you say." ¹¹So Jephthah went with the elders of Gilead, and the people made him head and commander over them. And he repeated all his words before the LORD in Mizpah.

¹²Then Jephthah sent messengers to the Ammonite king with the question: "What do you have against us that you have attacked our country?"

¹³The king of the Ammonites answered Jephthah's messengers, "When Israel came up out of Egypt, they took away my land from the Arnon to the Jabbok, all the way to the Jordan. Now give it back peaceably."

¹⁴Jephthah sent back messengers to the Ammonite king, ¹⁵saying:

"This is what Jephthah says: Israel did not take the land of Moab or the land of the Ammonites. ¹⁶But when they came up out of Egypt, Israel went through the desert to the Red Sea*b* and on to Kadesh. ¹⁷Then Israel sent messengers to the king of Edom, saying, 'Give us permission to go through your country,' but the king of Edom would not listen. They sent also to the king of Moab, and he refused. So Israel stayed at Kadesh.

¹⁸"Next they traveled through the desert, skirted the lands of Edom and Moab, passed along the eastern side of the country of Moab, and camped on the other side of the Arnon. They did not enter the territory of Moab, for the Arnon was its border.

---

a 12 Hebrew; some Septuagint manuscripts *Midianites*
b 16 Hebrew *Yam Suph*; that is, Sea of Reeds

¹⁹"Then Israel sent messengers to Sihon king of the Amorites, who ruled in Heshbon, and said to him, 'Let us pass through your country to our own place.' ²⁰Sihon, however, did not trust Israel[a] to pass through his territory. He mustered all his men and encamped at Jahaz and fought with Israel.

²¹"Then the LORD, the God of Israel, gave Sihon and all his men into Israel's hands, and they defeated them. Israel took over all the land of the Amorites who lived in that country, ²²capturing all of it from the Arnon to the Jabbok and from the desert to the Jordan.

²³"Now since the LORD, the God of Israel, has driven the Amorites out before his people Israel, what right have you to take it over? ²⁴Will you not take what your god Chemosh gives you? Likewise, whatever the LORD our God has given us, we will possess. ²⁵Are you better than Balak son of Zippor, king of Moab? Did he ever quarrel with Israel or fight with them? ²⁶For three hundred years Israel occupied Heshbon, Aroer, the surrounding settlements and all the towns along the Arnon. Why didn't you retake them during that time? ²⁷I have not wronged you, but you are doing me wrong by waging war against me. Let the LORD, the Judge,[b] decide the dispute this day between the Israelites and the Ammonites."

²⁸The king of Ammon, however, paid no attention to the message Jephthah sent him.

²⁹Then the Spirit of the LORD came upon Jephthah. He crossed Gilead and Manasseh, passed through Mizpah of Gilead, and from there he advanced against the Ammonites. ³⁰And Jephthah made a vow to the LORD: "If you give the Ammonites into my hands, ³¹whatever comes out of the door of my house to meet me when I return in triumph from the Ammonites will be the LORD's, and I will sacrifice it as a burnt offering."

³²Then Jephthah went over to fight the Ammonites, and the LORD gave them into his hands.

³³He devastated twenty towns from Aroer to the vicinity of Minnith, as far as Abel Keramim. Thus Israel subdued Ammon.

³⁴When Jephthah returned to his home in Mizpah, who should come out to meet him but his daughter, dancing to the sound of tambourines! She was an only child. Except for her he had neither son nor daughter. ³⁵When he saw her, he tore his clothes and cried, "Oh! My daughter! You have made me miserable and wretched, because I have made a vow to the LORD that I cannot break."

³⁶"My father," she replied, "you have given your word to the LORD. Do to me just as you promised, now that the LORD has avenged you of your enemies, the Ammonites. ³⁷But grant me this one request," she said. "Give me two months to roam the hills and weep with my friends, because I will never marry."

³⁸"You may go," he said. And he let her go for two months. She and the girls went into the hills and wept because she would never marry. ³⁹After the two months, she returned to her father and he did to her as he had vowed. And she was a virgin.

From this comes the Israelite custom ⁴⁰that each year the young women of Israel go out for four days to commemorate the daughter of Jephthah the Gileadite.

Jephthah and Ephraim

12 The men of Ephraim called out their forces, crossed over to Zaphon and said to Jephthah, "Why did you go to fight the Ammonites without calling us to go with you? We're going to burn down your house over your head."

²Jephthah answered, "I and my people were engaged in a great struggle with the Ammonites, and although I called, you didn't save me out of their hands. ³When I saw that you wouldn't help, I took my life in my hands and crossed over to fight the Ammonites, and the LORD gave me the victory over them. Now why have you come up today to fight me?"

[a] 20 Or however, would not make an agreement for Israel
[b] 27 Or Ruler

[4] Jephthah then called together the men of Gilead and fought against Ephraim. The Gileadites struck them down because the Ephraimites had said, "You Gileadites are renegades from Ephraim and Manasseh." [5] The Gileadites captured the fords of the Jordan leading to Ephraim, and whenever a survivor of Ephraim said, "Let me cross over," the men of Gilead asked him, "Are you an Ephraimite?" If he replied, "No," [6] they said, "All right, say 'Shibboleth.' " If he said, "Sibboleth," because he could not pronounce the word correctly, they seized him and killed him at the fords of the Jordan. Forty-two thousand Ephraimites were killed at that time.

[7] Jephthah led[a] Israel six years. Then Jephthah the Gileadite died, and was buried in a town in Gilead.

Ibzan, Elon and Abdon

[8] After him, Ibzan of Bethlehem led Israel. [9] He had thirty sons and thirty daughters. He gave his daughters away in marriage to those outside his clan, and for his sons he brought in thirty young women as wives from outside his clan. Ibzan led Israel seven years. [10] Then Ibzan died, and was buried in Bethlehem.

[11] After him, Elon the Zebulunite led Israel ten years. [12] Then Elon died, and was buried in Aijalon in the land of Zebulun.

[13] After him, Abdon son of Hillel, from Pirathon, led Israel. [14] He had forty sons and thirty grandsons, who rode on seventy donkeys. He led Israel eight years. [15] Then Abdon son of Hillel died, and was buried at Pirathon in Ephraim, in the hill country of the Amalekites.

The Birth of Samson

13 Again the Israelites did evil in the eyes of the LORD, so the LORD delivered them into the hands of the Philistines for forty years.

[2] A certain man of Zorah, named Manoah, from the clan of the Danites, had a wife who was sterile and remained childless. [3] The angel of the LORD appeared to her and said, "You are sterile and childless, but you are going to conceive and have a son. [4] Now see to it that you drink no wine or other fermented drink and that you do not eat anything unclean, [5] because you will conceive and give birth to a son. No razor may be used on his head, because the boy is to be a Nazirite, set apart to God from birth, and he will begin the deliverance of Israel from the hands of the Philistines."

[6] Then the woman went to her husband and told him, "A man of God came to me. He looked like an angel of God, very awesome. I didn't ask him where he came from, and he didn't tell me his name. [7] But he said to me, 'You will conceive and give birth to a son. Now then, drink no wine or other fermented drink and do not eat anything unclean, because the boy will be a Nazirite of God from birth until the day of his death.' "

[8] Then Manoah prayed to the LORD: "O Lord, I beg you, let the man of God you sent to us come again to teach us how to bring up the boy who is to be born."

[9] God heard Manoah, and the angel of God came again to the woman while she was out in the field; but her husband Manoah was not with her. [10] The woman hurried to tell her husband, "He's here! The man who appeared to me the other day!"

[11] Manoah got up and followed his wife. When he came to the man, he said, "Are you the one who talked to my wife?"

"I am," he said.

[12] So Manoah asked him, "When your words are fulfilled, what is to be the rule for the boy's life and work?"

[13] The angel of the LORD answered, "Your wife must do all that I have told her. [14] She must not eat anything that comes from the grapevine, nor drink any wine or other fermented drink nor eat anything unclean. She must do everything I have commanded her."

[15] Manoah said to the angel of the LORD, "We would like you to stay until we prepare a young goat for you."

[16] The angel of the LORD replied, "Even though

---

[a] 7 Traditionally judged; also in verses 8-14

you detain me, I will not eat any of your food. But if you prepare a burnt offering, offer it to the LORD." (Manoah did not realize that it was the angel of the LORD.)

[17] Then Manoah inquired of the angel of the LORD, "What is your name, so that we may honor you when your word comes true?"

[18] He replied, "Why do you ask my name? It is beyond understanding. [a]" [19] Then Manoah took a young goat, together with the grain offering, and sacrificed it on a rock to the LORD. And the LORD did an amazing thing while Manoah and his wife watched: [20] As the flame blazed up from the altar toward heaven, the angel of the LORD ascended in the flame. Seeing this, Manoah and his wife fell with their faces to the ground. [21] When the angel of the LORD did not show himself again to Manoah and his wife, Manoah realized that it was the angel of the LORD.

[22] "We are doomed to die!" he said to his wife. "We have seen God!"

[23] But his wife answered, "If the LORD had meant to kill us, he would not have accepted a burnt offering and grain offering from our hands, nor shown us all these things or now told us this."

[24] The woman gave birth to a boy and named him Samson. He grew and the LORD blessed him, [25] and the Spirit of the LORD began to stir him while he was in Mahaneh Dan, between Zorah and Eshtaol.

Samson's Marriage

14 Samson went down to Timnah and saw there a young Philistine woman. [2] When he returned, he said to his father and mother, "I have seen a Philistine woman in Timnah; now get her for me as my wife."

[3] His father and mother replied, "Isn't there an acceptable woman among your relatives or among all our people? Must you go to the uncircumcised Philistines to get a wife?"

But Samson said to his father, "Get her for me. She's the right one for me." [4] (His parents did not know that this was from the LORD, who was seeking an occasion to confront the Philistines; for at that time they were ruling over Israel.) [5] Samson went down to Timnah together with his father and mother. As they approached the vineyards of Timnah, suddenly a young lion came roaring toward him. [6] The Spirit of the LORD came upon him in power so that he tore the lion apart with his bare hands as he might have torn a young goat. But he told neither his father nor his mother what he had done. [7] Then he went down and talked with the woman, and he liked her.

[8] Some time later, when he went back to marry her, he turned aside to look at the lion's carcass. In it was a swarm of bees and some honey, [9] which he scooped out with his hands and ate as he went along. When he rejoined his parents, he gave them some, and they too ate it. But he did not tell them that he had taken the honey from the lion's carcass.

[10] Now his father went down to see the woman. And Samson made a feast there, as was customary for bridegrooms. [11] When he appeared, he was given thirty companions.

[12] "Let me tell you a riddle," Samson said to them. "If you can give me the answer within the seven days of the feast, I will give you thirty linen garments and thirty sets of clothes. [13] If you can't tell me the answer, you must give me thirty linen garments and thirty sets of clothes."

"Tell us your riddle," they said. "Let's hear it." [14] He replied,

"Out of the eater, something to eat;
    out of the strong, something sweet."

For three days they could not give the answer.

[15] On the fourth [b] day, they said to Samson's wife, "Coax your husband into explaining the riddle for us, or we will burn you and your father's household to death. Did you invite us here to rob us?"

[16] Then Samson's wife threw herself on him, sobbing, "You hate me! You don't really love me. You've given my people a riddle, but you haven't told me the answer."

---

[a] 18 Or is wonderful   [b] 15 Some Septuagint manuscripts and Syriac; Hebrew seventh

HIS PARENTS DID NOT KNOW
THAT THIS WAS FROM THE LORD,
WHO WAS SEEKING AN OCCASION
TO CONFRONT THE PHILISTINES;
FOR AT THAT TIME THEY WERE
RULING OVER ISRAEL.

Judges 14:4

This Is From the Lord?

DORIS WYNBEEK RIKKERS

READ | JUDGES 14:1 – 20

It looked all wrong. This was not the woman they wanted their son to marry. She was a Philistine! One of the enemy. How could Samson have even thought of falling in love with her? Samson's parents truly were enraged at the thought of a heathen woman being related to them. There was no way they wanted this for their son.

Samson's parents had waited a long time for a child. At first they thought they would remain childless; then the angel of the Lord gave them the astonishing news that they would have a special son — a Nazirite, one set apart from the others of Israel, consecrated to God (see Judges 13; see also Numbers 6:1 – 21). His life had been blessed (see Judges 13:24), but now Samson was making a terrible choice. How could this be?

We all hope that our children will marry well. We pray for God to provide the perfect spouse for them — at least what *we* think is perfect: someone who is a Christian, is loving, kind and smart. None of us would ever wish for or pray for the complete opposite: an outsider, an unbeliever. Samson's parents were no different. But look at the verse again; *this was from the Lord*. No, God didn't *cause* Samson to break his command against marrying non-Israelites (see Exodus 34:15 – 16; Deuteronomy 7:1 – 4). But God does use even our sinful human weaknesses to accomplish his purposes and bring praise to his name (see Genesis 50:20; Romans 8:28).

So when things aren't as we think they should be (the spouse of our child's choosing isn't up to our standards), we need to keep praying. We need to pray that God will change our attitude. We need to pray that God will show us his will and his plan for their marriage. All things are in God's plan. We need to trust him to work out every situation for good.

O God, I commit the lives of my children and grandchildren into your hands. Help me to trust that you have everything in your hands, no matter how things may appear on the surface. Amen.

Your next devotion is located on page 347.

GRANDCHILD IN FOCUS • PRAYER

Courage

O Father, builder of character and courage, may my grandchild grow strong in the light of your love. Grant him courage to stand for what is right, to guard the truth and to ensure justice in every aspect of life. May he boldly grow in grace, revere your name and proudly proclaim you as the Lord of lords and King of kings. Amen.

"I haven't even explained it to my father or mother," he replied, "so why should I explain it to you?" [17]She cried the whole seven days of the feast. So on the seventh day he finally told her, because she continued to press him. She in turn explained the riddle to her people.

[18]Before sunset on the seventh day the men of the town said to him,

"What is sweeter than honey?
 What is stronger than a lion?"

Samson said to them,

"If you had not plowed with my heifer,
 you would not have solved my riddle."

[19]Then the Spirit of the LORD came upon him in power. He went down to Ashkelon, struck down thirty of their men, stripped them of their belongings and gave their clothes to those who had explained the riddle. Burning with anger, he went up to his father's house. [20]And Samson's wife was given to the friend who had attended him at his wedding.

Samson's Vengeance on the Philistines

15 Later on, at the time of wheat harvest, Samson took a young goat and went to visit his wife. He said, "I'm going to my wife's room." But her father would not let him go in.

[2]"I was so sure you thoroughly hated her," he said, "that I gave her to your friend. Isn't her younger sister more attractive? Take her instead."

[3]Samson said to them, "This time I have a right to get even with the Philistines; I will really harm them." [4]So he went out and caught three hundred foxes and tied them tail to tail in pairs. He then fastened a torch to every pair of tails, [5]lit the torches and let the foxes loose in the standing grain of the Philistines. He burned up the shocks and standing grain, together with the vineyards and olive groves.

[6]When the Philistines asked, "Who did this?" they were told, "Samson, the Timnite's son-in-law, because his wife was given to his friend."

So the Philistines went up and burned her and her father to death. [7]Samson said to them, "Since you've acted like this, I won't stop until I get my revenge on you." [8]He attacked them viciously and slaughtered many of them. Then he went down and stayed in a cave in the rock of Etam.

[9]The Philistines went up and camped in Judah, spreading out near Lehi. [10]The men of Judah asked, "Why have you come to fight us?"

"We have come to take Samson prisoner," they answered, "to do to him as he did to us."

[11]Then three thousand men from Judah went down to the cave in the rock of Etam and said to Samson, "Don't you realize that the Philistines are rulers over us? What have you done to us?"

He answered, "I merely did to them what they did to me."

[12]They said to him, "We've come to tie you up and hand you over to the Philistines."

Samson said, "Swear to me that you won't kill me yourselves."

[13]"Agreed," they answered. "We will only tie you up and hand you over to them. We will not kill you." So they bound him with two new ropes and led him up from the rock. [14]As he approached Lehi, the Philistines came toward him shouting. The Spirit of the LORD came upon him in power. The ropes on his arms became like charred flax, and the bindings dropped from his hands. [15]Finding a fresh jawbone of a donkey, he grabbed it and struck down a thousand men.

[16]Then Samson said,

"With a donkey's jawbone
 I have made donkeys of them. [a]
With a donkey's jawbone
 I have killed a thousand men."

[17]When he finished speaking, he threw away the jawbone; and the place was called Ramath Lehi. [b]

[18]Because he was very thirsty, he cried out to the LORD, "You have given your servant this great victory. Must I now die of thirst and fall into the hands of the uncircumcised?" [19]Then God opened up the hollow place in Lehi, and water

---

[a] 16 Or *made a heap or two*; the Hebrew for *donkey* sounds like the Hebrew for *heap*. [b] 17 *Ramath Lehi* means *jawbone hill*.

came out of it. When Samson drank, his strength returned and he revived. So the spring was called En Hakkore,[a] and it is still there in Lehi.

20 Samson led[b] Israel for twenty years in the days of the Philistines.

Samson and Delilah

16 One day Samson went to Gaza, where he saw a prostitute. He went in to spend the night with her. 2 The people of Gaza were told, "Samson is here!" So they surrounded the place and lay in wait for him all night at the city gate. They made no move during the night, saying, "At dawn we'll kill him."

3 But Samson lay there only until the middle of the night. Then he got up and took hold of the doors of the city gate, together with the two posts, and tore them loose, bar and all. He lifted them to his shoulders and carried them to the top of the hill that faces Hebron.

4 Some time later, he fell in love with a woman in the Valley of Sorek whose name was Delilah. 5 The rulers of the Philistines went to her and said, "See if you can lure him into showing you the secret of his great strength and how we can overpower him so we may tie him up and subdue him. Each one of us will give you eleven hundred shekels[c] of silver."

6 So Delilah said to Samson, "Tell me the secret of your great strength and how you can be tied up and subdued."

7 Samson answered her, "If anyone ties me with seven fresh thongs[d] that have not been dried, I'll become as weak as any other man."

8 Then the rulers of the Philistines brought her seven fresh thongs that had not been dried, and she tied him with them. 9 With men hidden in the room, she called to him, "Samson, the Philistines are upon you!" But he snapped the thongs as easily as a piece of string snaps when it comes close to a flame. So the secret of his strength was not discovered.

10 Then Delilah said to Samson, "You have made a fool of me; you lied to me. Come now, tell me how you can be tied."

stories to share

JUDGES 15:20; 16:4–31

Samson and Delilah

LIFE LESSON: God can use anyone to accomplish his plans.

TO TALK ABOUT

+ Why did Delilah want to find out the secret to Samson's strength?

+ Why did Samson finally tell Delilah his secret?

+ Why do you think Samson was included in a group of people who were praised in Hebrews 11:32–38?

+ Was Samson a hero? Why or why not?

11 He said, "If anyone ties me securely with new ropes that have never been used, I'll become as weak as any other man."

12 So Delilah took new ropes and tied him with them. Then, with men hidden in the room, she called to him, "Samson, the Philistines are upon you!" But he snapped the ropes off his arms as if they were threads.

13 Delilah then said to Samson, "Until now, you have been making a fool of me and lying to me. Tell me how you can be tied."

He replied, "If you weave the seven braids of my head into the fabric ⌐on the loom⌐ and tighten it with the pin, I'll become as weak as any other

---

[a] 19 *En Hakkore* means *caller's spring.*   [b] 20 Traditionally *judged*   [c] 5 That is, about 28 pounds (about 13 kilograms)   [d] 7 Or *bowstrings*; also in verses 8 and 9

man." So while he was sleeping, Delilah took the seven braids of his head, wove them into the fabric [14]and[a] tightened it with the pin.

Again she called to him, "Samson, the Philistines are upon you!" He awoke from his sleep and pulled up the pin and the loom, with the fabric.

[15]Then she said to him, "How can you say, 'I love you,' when you won't confide in me? This is the third time you have made a fool of me and haven't told me the secret of your great strength." [16]With such nagging she prodded him day after day until he was tired to death.

[17]So he told her everything. "No razor has ever been used on my head," he said, "because I have been a Nazirite set apart to God since birth. If my head were shaved, my strength would leave me, and I would become as weak as any other man."

[18]When Delilah saw that he had told her everything, she sent word to the rulers of the Philistines, "Come back once more; he has told me everything." So the rulers of the Philistines returned with the silver in their hands. [19]Having put him to sleep on her lap, she called a man to shave off the seven braids of his hair, and so began to subdue him.[b] And his strength left him.

[20]Then she called, "Samson, the Philistines are upon you!"

He awoke from his sleep and thought, "I'll go out as before and shake myself free." But he did not know that the LORD had left him.

[21]Then the Philistines seized him, gouged out his eyes and took him down to Gaza. Binding him with bronze shackles, they set him to grinding in the prison. [22]But the hair on his head began to grow again after it had been shaved.

The Death of Samson

[23]Now the rulers of the Philistines assembled to offer a great sacrifice to Dagon their god and to celebrate, saying, "Our god has delivered Samson, our enemy, into our hands."

[24]When the people saw him, they praised their god, saying,

> "Our god has delivered our enemy
> into our hands,

> the one who laid waste our land
> and multiplied our slain."

[25]While they were in high spirits, they shouted, "Bring out Samson to entertain us." So they called Samson out of the prison, and he performed for them.

When they stood him among the pillars, [26]Samson said to the servant who held his hand, "Put me where I can feel the pillars that support the temple, so that I may lean against them." [27]Now the temple was crowded with men and women; all the rulers of the Philistines were there, and on the roof were about three thousand men and women watching Samson perform. [28]Then Samson prayed to the LORD, "O Sovereign LORD, remember me. O God, please strengthen me just once more, and let me with one blow get revenge on the Philistines for my two eyes." [29]Then Samson reached toward the two central pillars on which the temple stood. Bracing himself against them, his right hand on the one and his left hand on the other, [30]Samson said, "Let me die with the Philistines!" Then he pushed with all his might, and down came the temple on the rulers and all the people in it. Thus he killed many more when he died than while he lived.

[31]Then his brothers and his father's whole family went down to get him. They brought him back and buried him between Zorah and Eshtaol in the tomb of Manoah his father. He had led[c] Israel twenty years.

Micah's Idols

17 Now a man named Micah from the hill country of Ephraim [2]said to his mother, "The eleven hundred shekels[d] of silver that were taken from you and about which I heard you utter a curse—I have that silver with me; I took it."

Then his mother said, "The LORD bless you, my son!"

---

[a] 13,14 Some Septuagint manuscripts; Hebrew "I can, if you weave the seven braids of my head into the fabric on the loom." [14]So she
[b] 19 Hebrew; some Septuagint manuscripts and he began to weaken
[c] 31 Traditionally judged   [d] 2 That is, about 28 pounds (about 13 kilograms)

³When he returned the eleven hundred shekels of silver to his mother, she said, "I solemnly consecrate my silver to the LORD for my son to make a carved image and a cast idol. I will give it back to you."

⁴So he returned the silver to his mother, and she took two hundred shekels *ᵃ* of silver and gave them to a silversmith, who made them into the image and the idol. And they were put in Micah's house.

⁵Now this man Micah had a shrine, and he made an ephod and some idols and installed one of his sons as his priest. ⁶In those days Israel had no king; everyone did as he saw fit.

⁷A young Levite from Bethlehem in Judah, who had been living within the clan of Judah, ⁸left that town in search of some other place to stay. On his way *ᵇ* he came to Micah's house in the hill country of Ephraim.

⁹Micah asked him, "Where are you from?"

"I'm a Levite from Bethlehem in Judah," he said, "and I'm looking for a place to stay."

¹⁰Then Micah said to him, "Live with me and be my father and priest, and I'll give you ten shekels *ᶜ* of silver a year, your clothes and your food." ¹¹So the Levite agreed to live with him, and the young man was to him like one of his sons. ¹²Then Micah installed the Levite, and the young man became his priest and lived in his house. ¹³And Micah said, "Now I know that the LORD will be good to me, since this Levite has become my priest."

Danites Settle in Laish

18 In those days Israel had no king.

And in those days the tribe of the Danites was seeking a place of their own where they might settle, because they had not yet come into an inheritance among the tribes of Israel. ²So the Danites sent five warriors from Zorah and Eshtaol to spy out the land and explore it. These men represented all their clans. They told them, "Go, explore the land."

The men entered the hill country of Ephraim and came to the house of Micah, where they spent the night. ³When they were near Micah's house, they recognized the voice of the young Levite; so they turned in there and asked him, "Who brought you here? What are you doing in this place? Why are you here?"

⁴He told them what Micah had done for him, and said, "He has hired me and I am his priest."

⁵Then they said to him, "Please inquire of God to learn whether our journey will be successful."

⁶The priest answered them, "Go in peace. Your journey has the LORD's approval."

⁷So the five men left and came to Laish, where they saw that the people were living in safety, like the Sidonians, unsuspecting and secure. And since their land lacked nothing, they were prosperous. *ᵈ* Also, they lived a long way from the Sidonians and had no relationship with anyone else. *ᵉ*

⁸When they returned to Zorah and Eshtaol, their brothers asked them, "How did you find things?"

⁹They answered, "Come on, let's attack them! We have seen that the land is very good. Aren't you going to do something? Don't hesitate to go there and take it over. ¹⁰When you get there, you will find an unsuspecting people and a spacious land that God has put into your hands, a land that lacks nothing whatever."

¹¹Then six hundred men from the clan of the Danites, armed for battle, set out from Zorah and Eshtaol. ¹²On their way they set up camp near Kiriath Jearim in Judah. This is why the place west of Kiriath Jearim is called Mahaneh Dan *ᶠ* to this day. ¹³From there they went on to the hill country of Ephraim and came to Micah's house.

¹⁴Then the five men who had spied out the land of Laish said to their brothers, "Do you know that one of these houses has an ephod, other household gods, a carved image and a cast idol? Now you know what to do." ¹⁵So they turned in there and went to the house of the young Levite at

---

ᵃ 4 That is, about 5 pounds (about 2.3 kilograms)   *ᵇ 8* Or *To carry on his profession*   *ᶜ 10* That is, about 4 ounces (about 110 grams)   *ᵈ 7* The meaning of the Hebrew for this clause is uncertain.   *ᵉ 7* Hebrew; some Septuagint manuscripts *with the Arameans*   *ᶠ 12* *Mahaneh Dan* means *Dan's camp.*

Micah's place and greeted him. [16] The six hundred Danites, armed for battle, stood at the entrance to the gate. [17] The five men who had spied out the land went inside and took the carved image, the ephod, the other household gods and the cast idol while the priest and the six hundred armed men stood at the entrance to the gate.

[18] When these men went into Micah's house and took the carved image, the ephod, the other household gods and the cast idol, the priest said to them, "What are you doing?"

[19] They answered him, "Be quiet! Don't say a word. Come with us, and be our father and priest. Isn't it better that you serve a tribe and clan in Israel as priest rather than just one man's household?" [20] Then the priest was glad. He took the ephod, the other household gods and the carved image and went along with the people. [21] Putting their little children, their livestock and their possessions in front of them, they turned away and left.

[22] When they had gone some distance from Micah's house, the men who lived near Micah were called together and overtook the Danites. [23] As they shouted after them, the Danites turned and said to Micah, "What's the matter with you that you called out your men to fight?"

[24] He replied, "You took the gods I made, and my priest, and went away. What else do I have? How can you ask, 'What's the matter with you?'"

[25] The Danites answered, "Don't argue with us, or some hot-tempered men will attack you, and you and your family will lose your lives." [26] So the Danites went their way, and Micah, seeing that they were too strong for him, turned around and went back home.

[27] Then they took what Micah had made, and his priest, and went on to Laish, against a peaceful and unsuspecting people. They attacked them with the sword and burned down their city. [28] There was no one to rescue them because they lived a long way from Sidon and had no relationship with anyone else. The city was in a valley near Beth Rehob.

The Danites rebuilt the city and settled there. [29] They named it Dan after their forefather Dan, who was born to Israel—though the city used to be called Laish. [30] There the Danites set up for themselves the idols, and Jonathan son of Gershom, the son of Moses,[a] and his sons were priests for the tribe of Dan until the time of the captivity of the land. [31] They continued to use the idols Micah had made, all the time the house of God was in Shiloh.

A Levite and His Concubine

19 In those days Israel had no king.
Now a Levite who lived in a remote area in the hill country of Ephraim took a concubine from Bethlehem in Judah. [2] But she was unfaithful to him. She left him and went back to her father's house in Bethlehem, Judah. After she had been there four months, [3] her husband went to her to persuade her to return. He had with him his servant and two donkeys. She took him into her father's house, and when her father saw him, he gladly welcomed him. [4] His father-in-law, the girl's father, prevailed upon him to stay; so he remained with him three days, eating and drinking, and sleeping there.

[5] On the fourth day they got up early and he prepared to leave, but the girl's father said to his son-in-law, "Refresh yourself with something to eat; then you can go." [6] So the two of them sat down to eat and drink together. Afterward the girl's father said, "Please stay tonight and enjoy yourself." [7] And when the man got up to go, his father-in-law persuaded him, so he stayed there that night. [8] On the morning of the fifth day, when he rose to go, the girl's father said, "Refresh yourself. Wait till afternoon!" So the two of them ate together.

[9] Then when the man, with his concubine and his servant, got up to leave, his father-in-law, the girl's father, said, "Now look, it's almost evening. Spend the night here; the day is nearly over. Stay and enjoy yourself. Early tomorrow morning you

---

[a] 30 An ancient Hebrew scribal tradition, some Septuagint manuscripts and Vulgate; Masoretic Text *Manasseh*

can get up and be on your way home." ¹⁰But, unwilling to stay another night, the man left and went toward Jebus (that is, Jerusalem), with his two saddled donkeys and his concubine.

¹¹When they were near Jebus and the day was almost gone, the servant said to his master, "Come, let's stop at this city of the Jebusites and spend the night."

¹²His master replied, "No. We won't go into an alien city, whose people are not Israelites. We will go on to Gibeah." ¹³He added, "Come, let's try to reach Gibeah or Ramah and spend the night in one of those places." ¹⁴So they went on, and the sun set as they neared Gibeah in Benjamin. ¹⁵There they stopped to spend the night. They went and sat in the city square, but no one took them into his home for the night.

¹⁶That evening an old man from the hill country of Ephraim, who was living in Gibeah (the men of the place were Benjamites), came in from his work in the fields. ¹⁷When he looked and saw the traveler in the city square, the old man asked, "Where are you going? Where did you come from?"

¹⁸He answered, "We are on our way from Bethlehem in Judah to a remote area in the hill country of Ephraim where I live. I have been to Bethlehem in Judah and now I am going to the house of the LORD. No one has taken me into his house. ¹⁹We have both straw and fodder for our donkeys and bread and wine for ourselves your servants — me, your maidservant, and the young man with us. We don't need anything."

²⁰"You are welcome at my house," the old man said. "Let me supply whatever you need. Only don't spend the night in the square." ²¹So he took him into his house and fed his donkeys. After they had washed their feet, they had something to eat and drink.

²²While they were enjoying themselves, some of the wicked men of the city surrounded the house. Pounding on the door, they shouted to the old man who owned the house, "Bring out the man who came to your house so we can have sex with him."

²³The owner of the house went outside and said to them, "No, my friends, don't be so vile. Since this man is my guest, don't do this disgraceful thing. ²⁴Look, here is my virgin daughter, and his concubine. I will bring them out to you now, and you can use them and do to them whatever you wish. But to this man, don't do such a disgraceful thing."

²⁵But the men would not listen to him. So the man took his concubine and sent her outside to them, and they raped her and abused her throughout the night, and at dawn they let her go. ²⁶At daybreak the woman went back to the house where her master was staying, fell down at the door and lay there until daylight.

²⁷When her master got up in the morning and opened the door of the house and stepped out to continue on his way, there lay his concubine, fallen in the doorway of the house, with her hands on the threshold. ²⁸He said to her, "Get up; let's go." But there was no answer. Then the man put her on his donkey and set out for home.

²⁹When he reached home, he took a knife and cut up his concubine, limb by limb, into twelve parts and sent them into all the areas of Israel. ³⁰Everyone who saw it said, "Such a thing has never been seen or done, not since the day the Israelites came up out of Egypt. Think about it! Consider it! Tell us what to do!"

Israelites Fight the Benjamites

20 Then all the Israelites from Dan to Beersheba and from the land of Gilead came out as one man and assembled before the LORD in Mizpah. ²The leaders of all the people of the tribes of Israel took their places in the assembly of the people of God, four hundred thousand soldiers armed with swords. ³(The Benjamites heard that the Israelites had gone up to Mizpah.) Then the Israelites said, "Tell us how this awful thing happened."

⁴So the Levite, the husband of the murdered woman, said, "I and my concubine came to Gibeah in Benjamin to spend the night. ⁵During the night the men of Gibeah came after me and

surrounded the house, intending to kill me. They raped my concubine, and she died. ⁶I took my concubine, cut her into pieces and sent one piece to each region of Israel's inheritance, because they committed this lewd and disgraceful act in Israel. ⁷Now, all you Israelites, speak up and give your verdict."

⁸All the people rose as one man, saying, "None of us will go home. No, not one of us will return to his house. ⁹But now this is what we'll do to Gibeah: We'll go up against it as the lot directs. ¹⁰We'll take ten men out of every hundred from all the tribes of Israel, and a hundred from a thousand, and a thousand from ten thousand, to get provisions for the army. Then, when the army arrives at Gibeah*ᵃ* in Benjamin, it can give them what they deserve for all this vileness done in Israel." ¹¹So all the men of Israel got together and united as one man against the city.

¹²The tribes of Israel sent men throughout the tribe of Benjamin, saying, "What about this awful crime that was committed among you? ¹³Now surrender those wicked men of Gibeah so that we may put them to death and purge the evil from Israel."

But the Benjamites would not listen to their fellow Israelites. ¹⁴From their towns they came together at Gibeah to fight against the Israelites. ¹⁵At once the Benjamites mobilized twenty-six thousand swordsmen from their towns, in addition to seven hundred chosen men from those living in Gibeah. ¹⁶Among all these soldiers there were seven hundred chosen men who were left-handed, each of whom could sling a stone at a hair and not miss.

¹⁷Israel, apart from Benjamin, mustered four hundred thousand swordsmen, all of them fighting men.

¹⁸The Israelites went up to Bethel*ᵇ* and inquired of God. They said, "Who of us shall go first to fight against the Benjamites?"

The LORD replied, "Judah shall go first."

¹⁹The next morning the Israelites got up and pitched camp near Gibeah. ²⁰The men of Israel went out to fight the Benjamites and took up

battle positions against them at Gibeah. ²¹The Benjamites came out of Gibeah and cut down twenty-two thousand Israelites on the battlefield that day. ²²But the men of Israel encouraged one another and again took up their positions where they had stationed themselves the first day. ²³The Israelites went up and wept before the LORD until evening, and they inquired of the LORD. They said, "Shall we go up again to battle against the Benjamites, our brothers?"

The LORD answered, "Go up against them."

²⁴Then the Israelites drew near to Benjamin the second day. ²⁵This time, when the Benjamites came out from Gibeah to oppose them, they cut down another eighteen thousand Israelites, all of them armed with swords.

²⁶Then the Israelites, all the people, went up to Bethel, and there they sat weeping before the LORD. They fasted that day until evening and presented burnt offerings and fellowship offerings*ᶜ* to the LORD. ²⁷And the Israelites inquired of the LORD. (In those days the ark of the covenant of God was there, ²⁸with Phinehas son of Eleazar, the son of Aaron, ministering before it.) They asked, "Shall we go up again to battle with Benjamin our brother, or not?"

The LORD responded, "Go, for tomorrow I will give them into your hands."

²⁹Then Israel set an ambush around Gibeah. ³⁰They went up against the Benjamites on the third day and took up positions against Gibeah as they had done before. ³¹The Benjamites came out to meet them and were drawn away from the city. They began to inflict casualties on the Israelites as before, so that about thirty men fell in the open field and on the roads — the one leading to Bethel and the other to Gibeah.

³²While the Benjamites were saying, "We are defeating them as before," the Israelites were saying, "Let's retreat and draw them away from the city to the roads."

³³All the men of Israel moved from their plac-

ᵃ 10 One Hebrew manuscript; most Hebrew manuscripts *Geba,* a variant of *Gibeah*   *ᵇ 18* Or *to the house of God;* also in verse 26   *ᶜ 26* Traditionally *peace offerings* es and took up positions at Baal Tamar, and the Israelite ambush charged out of its place on the west[a] of Gibeah.[b] ³⁴ Then ten thousand of Israel's finest men made a frontal attack on Gibeah. The fighting was so heavy that the Benjamites did not realize how near disaster was. ³⁵ The LORD defeated Benjamin before Israel, and on that day the Israelites struck down 25,100 Benjamites, all armed with swords. ³⁶ Then the Benjamites saw that they were beaten.

Now the men of Israel had given way before Benjamin, because they relied on the ambush they had set near Gibeah. ³⁷ The men who had been in ambush made a sudden dash into Gibeah, spread out and put the whole city to the sword. ³⁸ The men of Israel had arranged with the ambush that they should send up a great cloud of smoke from the city, ³⁹ and then the men of Israel would turn in the battle.

The Benjamites had begun to inflict casualties on the men of Israel (about thirty), and they said, "We are defeating them as in the first battle." ⁴⁰ But when the column of smoke began to rise from the city, the Benjamites turned and saw the smoke of the whole city going up into the sky. ⁴¹ Then the men of Israel turned on them, and the men of Benjamin were terrified, because they realized that disaster had come upon them. ⁴² So they fled before the Israelites in the direction of the desert, but they could not escape the battle. And the men of Israel who came out of the towns cut them down there. ⁴³ They surrounded the Benjamites, chased them and easily[c] overran them in the vicinity of Gibeah on the east. ⁴⁴ Eighteen thousand Benjamites fell, all of them valiant fighters. ⁴⁵ As they turned and fled toward the desert to the rock of Rimmon, the Israelites cut down five thousand men along the roads. They kept pressing after the Benjamites as far as Gidom and struck down two thousand more.

⁴⁶ On that day twenty-five thousand Benjamite swordsmen fell, all of them valiant fighters. ⁴⁷ But six hundred men turned and fled into the desert to the rock of Rimmon, where they stayed four months. ⁴⁸ The men of Israel went back to Benjamin and put all the towns to the sword, including the animals and everything else they found. All the towns they came across they set on fire.

Wives for the Benjamites

21 The men of Israel had taken an oath at Mizpah: "Not one of us will give his daughter in marriage to a Benjamite."

² The people went to Bethel,[d] where they sat before God until evening, raising their voices and weeping bitterly. ³ "O LORD, the God of Israel," they cried, "why has this happened to Israel? Why should one tribe be missing from Israel today?"

⁴ Early the next day the people built an altar and presented burnt offerings and fellowship offerings.[e]

⁵ Then the Israelites asked, "Who from all the tribes of Israel has failed to assemble before the LORD?" For they had taken a solemn oath that anyone who failed to assemble before the LORD at Mizpah should certainly be put to death.

⁶ Now the Israelites grieved for their brothers, the Benjamites. "Today one tribe is cut off from Israel," they said. ⁷ "How can we provide wives for those who are left, since we have taken an oath by the LORD not to give them any of our daughters in marriage?" ⁸ Then they asked, "Which one of the tribes of Israel failed to assemble before the LORD at Mizpah?" They discovered that no one from Jabesh Gilead had come to the camp for the assembly. ⁹ For when they counted the people, they found that none of the people of Jabesh Gilead were there.

¹⁰ So the assembly sent twelve thousand fighting men with instructions to go to Jabesh Gilead and put to the sword those living there, including the women and children. ¹¹ "This is what you are to do," they said. "Kill every male and every woman who is not a virgin." ¹² They found among the people living in Jabesh Gilead four hundred young women who had never slept

---

[a] 33 Some Septuagint manuscripts and Vulgate; the meaning of the Hebrew for this word is uncertain.   [b] 33 Hebrew *Geba*, a variant of *Gibeah*   [c] 43 The meaning of the Hebrew for this word is uncertain.   [d] 2 Or *to the house of God*   [e] 4 Traditionally *peace offerings*

with a man, and they took them to the camp at Shiloh in Canaan.

¹³ Then the whole assembly sent an offer of peace to the Benjamites at the rock of Rimmon. ¹⁴ So the Benjamites returned at that time and were given the women of Jabesh Gilead who had been spared. But there were not enough for all of them.

¹⁵ The people grieved for Benjamin, because the LORD had made a gap in the tribes of Israel. ¹⁶ And the elders of the assembly said, "With the women of Benjamin destroyed, how shall we provide wives for the men who are left? ¹⁷ The Benjamite survivors must have heirs," they said, "so that a tribe of Israel will not be wiped out. ¹⁸ We can't give them our daughters as wives, since we Israelites have taken this oath: 'Cursed be anyone who gives a wife to a Benjamite.' ¹⁹ But look, there is the annual festival of the LORD in Shiloh, to the north of Bethel, and east of the road that goes from Bethel to Shechem, and to the south of Lebonah."

²⁰ So they instructed the Benjamites, saying, "Go and hide in the vineyards ²¹ and watch. When the girls of Shiloh come out to join in the dancing, then rush from the vineyards and each of you seize a wife from the girls of Shiloh and go to the land of Benjamin. ²² When their fathers or brothers complain to us, we will say to them, 'Do us a kindness by helping them, because we did not get wives for them during the war, and you are innocent, since you did not give your daughters to them.'"

²³ So that is what the Benjamites did. While the girls were dancing, each man caught one and carried her off to be his wife. Then they returned to their inheritance and rebuilt the towns and settled in them.

²⁴ At that time the Israelites left that place and went home to their tribes and clans, each to his own inheritance.

²⁵ In those days Israel had no king; everyone did as he saw fit.

God HAS A PLAN

If the story of Ruth reveals anything about God, it shows us that even when circumstances are tragic and life is hard, God still has a plan. Even when life is chaotic, when we don't have the resources we need, and when we feel lost and alone, God provides. At such times we may think there is no option for happiness. But God breaks in, shakes things up, introduces new options and restores us.

The story of Ruth is about friendship, love, loyalty and family. Ruth and Naomi went from loss and desolation to restoration and hope. Through Ruth's faithful love and commitment to her mother-in-law, Naomi gained a precious daughter-in-law as a consolation for the loss of her husband and two sons. When Naomi, accompanied by Ruth, returned to Israel and Ruth met Boaz for the first time, Boaz stated how Ruth's devotion to Naomi had become the talk of the town (see 2:11 – 12).

Take a moment to read Ruth 4:16 – 17 for a beautiful word picture of a grandmother's joy at having a grandchild. And Naomi's joy has become our joy, for, in God's plan, the child born to Ruth and Boaz is in the lineage of kings — first King David (see 4:22) and eventually King Jesus, our Savior.

VERSE *to* REMEMBER | RUTH 1:16

But Ruth replied, "Don't urge me to leave you or to turn back from you. Where you go I will go, and where you stay I will stay. Your people will be my people and your God my God."

ABOUT RUTH

WRITTEN BY:
Unknown

WRITTEN FOR:
God's chosen people, the Israelites

DATE WRITTEN:
Sometime after David became king in 1010 B.C.

WHY WRITTEN:
To show that faith was not absent during the time of the judges and to establish the lineage of Israel's kings

Naomi and Ruth

1 In the days when the judges ruled,[a] there was a famine in the land, and a man from Bethlehem in Judah, together with his wife and two sons, went to live for a while in the country of Moab. ²The man's name was Elimelech, his wife's name Naomi, and the names of his two sons were Mahlon and Kilion. They were Ephrathites from Bethlehem, Judah. And they went to Moab and lived there.

³Now Elimelech, Naomi's husband, died, and she was left with her two sons. ⁴They married Moabite women, one named Orpah and the other Ruth. After they had lived there about ten years, ⁵both Mahlon and Kilion also died, and Naomi was left without her two sons and her husband.

⁶When she heard in Moab that the LORD had come to the aid of his people by providing food for them, Naomi and her daughters-in-law prepared to return home from there. ⁷With her two daughters-in-law she left the place where she had been living and set out on the road that would take them back to the land of Judah.

⁸Then Naomi said to her two daughters-in-law, "Go back, each of you, to your mother's home. May the LORD show kindness to you, as you have shown to your dead and to me. ⁹May the LORD grant that each of you will find rest in the home of another husband."

Then she kissed them and they wept aloud ¹⁰and said to her, "We will go back with you to your people."

¹¹But Naomi said, "Return home, my daughters.

TALKING POINTS

Friendship

Friends stick together.

RUTH 1:1-22

For more on friendship, go to 1 Samuel 20:1-42.

---

stories to share

RUTH 1:1–22

Naomi and Ruth

LIFE LESSON: The way we act and live can point others to God.

TO TALK ABOUT

✦ How did Naomi become related to Orpah and Ruth?

✦ Why did Naomi want Orpah and Ruth to go back to their homes?

✦ Why do you think Ruth made the hard choice to go to a foreign country with her mother-in-law?

✦ What would you have done if you had been Ruth?

Why would you come with me? Am I going to have any more sons, who could become your husbands? ¹²Return home, my daughters; I am too old to have another husband. Even if I thought there was still hope for me—even if I had a husband tonight and then gave birth to sons—¹³would you wait until they grew up? Would you remain unmarried for them? No, my daughters. It is more bitter for me than for you, because the LORD's hand has gone out against me!"

¹⁴At this they wept again. Then Orpah kissed her mother-in-law good-by, but Ruth clung to her.

¹⁵"Look," said Naomi, "your sister-in-law is going back to her people and her gods. Go back with her."

[a] 1 Traditionally *judged*

BUT RUTH REPLIED, "DON'T URGE ME TO LEAVE YOU OR TO TURN BACK FROM YOU. WHERE YOU GO I WILL GO, AND WHERE YOU STAY I WILL STAY. YOUR PEOPLE WILL BE MY PEOPLE AND YOUR GOD MY GOD."

Ruth 1:16

Covenant Relationships

LINDA H. HOLLIES

READ | RUTH 1:1 – 18

These sacred words emerge from the lips of a younger woman for an older woman. With these words, a woman who has been following the orders of her beloved mother-in-law begins to sing "Lean on Me."

Covenant relationships are not about equality. Covenant relationships are not about "what's in it for me?" Covenant relationships are about a serious competition in serving and meeting the needs of another. These women were not "blood kin." These women were not of the same racial or ethnic group. These women, after the death of the males that had brought them together, really had nothing more in common except seeking survival in a harsh world. This was enough for Ruth. She recognized the fear in Naomi. She understood the depression that had taken root within her. She knew the common exhaustion of trying to make a living without a male as provider or protector, yet she stepped up and took charge. She was willing to take the lead to ensure that Naomi was not alone . . .

Ruth didn't have a clue that God had used this strange and painful turn of events to make her an ancestor of Jesus Christ. There was not a thought in her mind that one day she would be in the genealogy of the One who will reign throughout eternity. She didn't know that love was waiting down the road and around the corner. But she did know determination. She did know that where there was a will to live, methods could be discovered for survival. She had ego strength enough for herself and for Naomi. Wisdom instructed her and encouraged her to prompt Naomi, "Come on, Girlfriend. Let's go make ourselves a home!"

Teach me your wisdom and give me your strength, Lord, as I support and help others even as I rely on you.

Your next devotion is located on page 349.

GRANDCHILD IN FOCUS • PRAYER

Future Spouse

Dear Lord, if it is your will, I pray my grandchild will be united in a loving and Christian marriage. Keep her sexually pure so that she will honor you with her body and mind. As she seeks a spouse who will honor and care for her, give her patience and discernment. May her choice for a life partner be your choice for her, so that she and her husband will together glorify you in a lasting love. I pray this in Jesus' name, amen.

¹⁶But Ruth replied, "Don't urge me to leave you or to turn back from you. Where you go I will go, and where you stay I will stay. Your people will be my people and your God my God. ¹⁷Where you die I will die, and there I will be buried. May the LORD deal with me, be it ever so severely, if anything but death separates you and me." ¹⁸When Naomi realized that Ruth was determined to go with her, she stopped urging her.

¹⁹So the two women went on until they came to Bethlehem. When they arrived in Bethlehem, the whole town was stirred because of them, and the women exclaimed, "Can this be Naomi?"

²⁰"Don't call me Naomi,ᵃ" she told them. "Call me Mara,ᵇ because the Almightyᶜ has made my life very bitter. ²¹I went away full, but the LORD has brought me back empty. Why call me Naomi? The LORD has afflictedᵈ me; the Almighty has brought misfortune upon me."

²²So Naomi returned from Moab accompanied by Ruth the Moabitess, her daughter-in-law, arriving in Bethlehem as the barley harvest was beginning.

Ruth Meets Boaz

2 Now Naomi had a relative on her husband's side, from the clan of Elimelech, a man of standing, whose name was Boaz.

²And Ruth the Moabitess said to Naomi, "Let me go to the fields and pick up the leftover grain behind anyone in whose eyes I find favor."

Naomi said to her, "Go ahead, my daughter." ³So she went out and began to glean in the fields behind the harvesters. As it turned out, she found herself working in a field belonging to Boaz, who was from the clan of Elimelech.

⁴Just then Boaz arrived from Bethlehem and greeted the harvesters, "The LORD be with you!"

"The LORD bless you!" they called back.

⁵Boaz asked the foreman of his harvesters, "Whose young woman is that?"

⁶The foreman replied, "She is the Moabitess who came back from Moab with Naomi. ⁷She said, 'Please let me glean and gather among the sheaves behind the harvesters.' She went into the field and has worked steadily from morning till now, except for a short rest in the shelter."

⁸So Boaz said to Ruth, "My daughter, listen to me. Don't go and glean in another field and don't go away from here. Stay here with my servant girls. ⁹Watch the field where the men are harvesting, and follow along after the girls. I have told the men not to touch you. And whenever you are thirsty, go and get a drink from the water jars the men have filled."

¹⁰At this, she bowed down with her face to the ground. She exclaimed, "Why have I found such favor in your eyes that you notice me—a foreigner?"

¹¹Boaz replied, "I've been told all about what you have done for your mother-in-law since the death of your husband—how you left your father and mother and your homeland and came to live with a people you did not know before. ¹²May the LORD repay you for what you have done. May you be richly rewarded by the LORD, the God of Israel, under whose wings you have come to take refuge."

PRAYING THE SCRIPTURES

Blessing
RUTH 2:12

O Lord, repay my grandchild for the good that she does. May she be richly rewarded by you, our God, as she comes to take refuge under your wings.

Next prayer in Blessing Prayer Track: Psalm 90:17

¹³"May I continue to find favor in your eyes, my lord," she said. "You have given me comfort and have spoken kindly to your servant—though I do not have the standing of one of your servant girls."

ᵃ 20 Naomi means pleasant; also in verse 21.   ᵇ 20 Mara means bitter.   ᶜ 20 Hebrew Shaddai; also in verse 21   ᵈ 21 Or has testified against

"I WENT AWAY FULL, BUT THE LORD
HAS BROUGHT ME BACK EMPTY."
Ruth 1:21

You're Not Alone

DEE BRESTIN

READ | RUTH 1:19 – 22

My 59-year-old husband, Steve, lost his valiant battle with colon cancer. Now, like many of you, I'm traveling the path I never wanted: the widow's walk. When I bought my first car alone, a silver Honda, my nine-year-old grandson, Simeon, said:

"Grandma, you should name this car the Silver Bullet."

I smiled. "I've already named it the Grey Goose."

"Why?"

"Because when the mate of a grey goose dies, the other flies on alone for the rest of her life."

Simeon looked at me tenderly. "You aren't alone, Grandma; you've got us."

Tears welled up in my eyes. It's true. And how thankful I am.

When Naomi lost her husband and sons, she came home to an empty house, haunted by their absence. She said, "I went away full, but the LORD has brought me back empty" (Ruth 1:21). After burying Steve, coming home was one of the hardest things I'd ever done. Each room I wandered through cried "Empty!" I felt *so* alone.

Yet, in truth, we aren't alone. Not only will the Lord never leave us, but we are blessed with family still. Naomi had her daughter-in-law Ruth, who committed her whole life to Naomi with her famous words, "Where you go I will go" (Ruth 1:16). At the close of the book, when Naomi was cradling her newborn grandson, the women of Bethlehem praised the Lord for not leaving Naomi alone. The Lord had given Naomi not only a daughter-in-law who was "better to [her] than seven sons" (Ruth 4:15), but also now a grandson who would grow up to love her and care for her.

As Simeon said to me, "You're not alone, Grandma; you've got us."

Father, help me to be thankful for my grandchildren. Help me not to dwell on what I've lost but to be thankful for what I still have.

GRANDCHILD IN FOCUS • PRAYER

School/Career

Dear God, may learning be a joy rather than a chore for my grandchild. May exploration of new ideas bring a sense of wonder, awe and excitement. Grant him clarity of mind, the ability to concentrate on the task at hand and recollection of what has been learned. Help him to appreciate the tasks that come easily and to persevere through those that challenge. Amen.

Your next devotion is located on page 351.

¹⁴At mealtime Boaz said to her, "Come over here. Have some bread and dip it in the wine vinegar."

When she sat down with the harvesters, he offered her some roasted grain. She ate all she wanted and had some left over. ¹⁵As she got up to glean, Boaz gave orders to his men, "Even if she gathers among the sheaves, don't embarrass her. ¹⁶Rather, pull out some stalks for her from the bundles and leave them for her to pick up, and don't rebuke her."

¹⁷So Ruth gleaned in the field until evening. Then she threshed the barley she had gathered, and it amounted to about an ephah.ᵃ ¹⁸She carried it back to town, and her mother-in-law saw how much she had gathered. Ruth also brought out and gave her what she had left over after she had eaten enough.

¹⁹Her mother-in-law asked her, "Where did you glean today? Where did you work? Blessed be the man who took notice of you!"

Then Ruth told her mother-in-law about the one at whose place she had been working. "The name of the man I worked with today is Boaz," she said.

²⁰"The LORD bless him!" Naomi said to her daughter-in-law. "He has not stopped showing his kindness to the living and the dead." She added, "That man is our close relative; he is one of our kinsman-redeemers."

²¹Then Ruth the Moabitess said, "He even said to me, 'Stay with my workers until they finish harvesting all my grain.'"

²²Naomi said to Ruth her daughter-in-law, "It will be good for you, my daughter, to go with his girls, because in someone else's field you might be harmed."

²³So Ruth stayed close to the servant girls of Boaz to glean until the barley and wheat harvests were finished. And she lived with her mother-in-law.

Ruth and Boaz at the Threshing Floor

3 One day Naomi her mother-in-law said to her, "My daughter, should I not try to find a home ᵇ for you, where you will be well provided for? ²Is not Boaz, with whose servant girls

you have been, a kinsman of ours? Tonight he will be winnowing barley on the threshing floor. ³Wash and perfume yourself, and put on your best clothes. Then go down to the threshing floor, but don't let him know you are there until he has finished eating and drinking. ⁴When he lies down, note the place where he is lying. Then go and uncover his feet and lie down. He will tell you what to do."

⁵"I will do whatever you say," Ruth answered. ⁶So she went down to the threshing floor and did everything her mother-in-law told her to do.

⁷When Boaz had finished eating and drinking and was in good spirits, he went over to lie down at the far end of the grain pile. Ruth approached quietly, uncovered his feet and lay down. ⁸In the middle of the night something startled the man, and he turned and discovered a woman lying at his feet.

⁹"Who are you?" he asked.

"I am your servant Ruth," she said. "Spread the corner of your garment over me, since you are a kinsman-redeemer."

¹⁰"The LORD bless you, my daughter," he replied. "This kindness is greater than that which you showed earlier: You have not run after the younger men, whether rich or poor. ¹¹And now, my daughter, don't be afraid. I will do for you all you ask. All my fellow townsmen know that you are a woman of noble character. ¹²Although it is true that I am near of kin, there is a kinsman-redeemer nearer than I. ¹³Stay here for the night, and in the morning if he wants to redeem, good; let him redeem. But if he is not willing, as surely as the LORD lives I will do it. Lie here until morning."

¹⁴So she lay at his feet until morning, but got up before anyone could be recognized; and he said, "Don't let it be known that a woman came to the threshing floor."

¹⁵He also said, "Bring me the shawl you are wearing and hold it out." When she did so, he poured into it six measures of barley and put it on her. Then heᶜ went back to town.

ᵃ 17 That is, probably about 3/5 bushel (about 22 liters)
ᵇ 1 Hebrew find rest (see Ruth 1:9)   ᶜ 15 Most Hebrew manuscripts; many Hebrew manuscripts, Vulgate and Syriac she

TOGETHER
TIME

Mail Call

Receiving mail is exciting for kids of all ages. Make a point of sending cards or postcards for special occasions, as well as to celebrate "minor" events — going back to school, losing a tooth, doing well on a test, etc.

The next time you get together with your grandchildren, why not host a card fest? Set up a table complete with the names and addresses of family and friends, stamps, envelopes, cards and postcards. Have each child send greetings to one or more people. Suggest that they invite a response by including a self-addressed, stamped envelope and a blank card. Your youngest grandchildren will enjoy coloring or placing stickers on cards that you write for them.

Long-Distance Variation: Send a large envelope containing blank cards; self-addressed, stamped envelopes; and names and addresses of cousins, aunts and uncles (and, of course, yourself). Invite them to send greetings to several people.

What fun it is, Lord, to send a hug through the mail. Bless my notes as they go from my hand to someone else's. May the recipients receive as much joy from the notes as I had in writing and sending them. Help my grandchildren to find joy in sending notes to one another. Amen.

Your next devotion is located on page 352.

GRANDCHILD IN FOCUS • PRAYER

Character

Dear Lord and Father, I ask that you fill my grandchild with your Spirit so her character reflects your goodness and love. Give her kindness and love for others. Bring joy to her life so she will be a joy to others. Grant her patience and self-control through difficult and trying times. May she show mercy and generosity to those who are less fortunate. Grant her integrity and a sense of justice, and surround her with your peace. Amen.

Worship the Lord

Give thanks to the LORD, call on his name;
>   make known among the nations what he has done.
Sing to him, sing praise to him;
>   tell of all his wonderful acts.
Glory in his holy name;
>   let the hearts of those who seek the LORD rejoice.
Look to the LORD and his strength;
>   seek his face always.
Remember the wonders he has done,
>   his miracles, and the judgments he pronounced,
O descendants of Israel his servant,
>   O sons of Jacob, his chosen ones.

He is the LORD our God;
>   his judgments are in all the earth.
He remembers his covenant forever,
>   the word he commanded, for a
>   thousand generations.

1 Chronicles 16:8 – 15

A thousand generations! What an amazing perspective on your faithfulness, Lord. Thank you for each opportunity I have to pass on your truth to my grandchildren. Amen.

Your next devotion is located on page 354.

GRANDCHILD IN FOCUS • PRAYER

Talents

Dear Lord, the giver of gifts, bless my grandchild as he develops his talents. Help him identify his talents and be proud and confident of the gifts you have given him. Give him patience and understanding, Lord, so he will not grow weary of striving and searching to reach the goals you have set for him. May each milestone bring satisfaction and a healthy desire for greater achievement and success to bring glory to you. Amen.

[16] When Ruth came to her mother-in-law, Naomi asked, "How did it go, my daughter?"

Then she told her everything Boaz had done for her [17] and added, "He gave me these six measures of barley, saying, 'Don't go back to your mother-in-law empty-handed.'"

[18] Then Naomi said, "Wait, my daughter, until you find out what happens. For the man will not rest until the matter is settled today."

Boaz Marries Ruth

4 Meanwhile Boaz went up to the town gate and sat there. When the kinsman-redeemer he had mentioned came along, Boaz said, "Come over here, my friend, and sit down." So he went over and sat down.

[2] Boaz took ten of the elders of the town and said, "Sit here," and they did so. [3] Then he said to the kinsman-redeemer, "Naomi, who has come back from Moab, is selling the piece of land that belonged to our brother Elimelech. [4] I thought I should bring the matter to your attention and suggest that you buy it in the presence of these seated here and in the presence of the elders of my people. If you will redeem it, do so. But if you[a] will not, tell me, so I will know. For no one has the right to do it except you, and I am next in line."

"I will redeem it," he said.

[5] Then Boaz said, "On the day you buy the land from Naomi and from Ruth the Moabitess, you acquire[b] the dead man's widow, in order to maintain the name of the dead with his property."

[6] At this, the kinsman-redeemer said, "Then I cannot redeem it because I might endanger my own estate. You redeem it yourself. I cannot do it."

[7] (Now in earlier times in Israel, for the redemption and transfer of property to become final, one party took off his sandal and gave it to the other. This was the method of legalizing transactions in Israel.)

[8] So the kinsman-redeemer said to Boaz, "Buy it yourself." And he removed his sandal.

[9] Then Boaz announced to the elders and all the people, "Today you are witnesses that I have bought from Naomi all the property of Elimelech, Kilion and Mahlon. [10] I have also acquired Ruth the Moabitess, Mahlon's widow, as my wife, in order to maintain the name of the dead with his property, so that his name will not disappear from among his family or from the town records. Today you are witnesses!"

[11] Then the elders and all those at the gate said, "We are witnesses. May the LORD make the woman who is coming into your home like Rachel and Leah, who together built up the house of Israel. May you have standing in Ephrathah and be famous in Bethlehem. [12] Through the offspring the LORD gives you by this young woman, may your family be like that of Perez, whom Tamar bore to Judah."

The Genealogy of David

4:18–22pp — 1Ch 2:5–15; Mt 1:3–6; Lk 3:31–33

[13] So Boaz took Ruth and she became his wife. Then he went to her, and the LORD enabled her to conceive, and she gave birth to a son. [14] The women said to Naomi: "Praise be to the LORD, who this day has not left you without a kinsman-redeemer. May he become famous throughout Israel! [15] He will renew your life and sustain you in your old age. For your daughter-in-law, who loves you and who is better to you than seven sons, has given him birth."

[16] Then Naomi took the child, laid him in her lap and cared for him. [17] The women living there said, "Naomi has a son." And they named him Obed. He was the father of Jesse, the father of David.

[18] This, then, is the family line of Perez:

Perez was the father of Hezron,
[19] Hezron the father of Ram,
Ram the father of Amminadab,
[20] Amminadab the father of Nahshon,
Nahshon the father of Salmon,[c]
[21] Salmon the father of Boaz,
Boaz the father of Obed,
[22] Obed the father of Jesse,
and Jesse the father of David.

[a] 4 Many Hebrew manuscripts, Septuagint, Vulgate and Syriac; most Hebrew manuscripts *he* [b] 5 Hebrew; Vulgate and Syriac *Naomi, you acquire Ruth the Moabitess,* [c] 20 A few Hebrew manuscripts, some Septuagint manuscripts and Vulgate (see also verse 21 and Septuagint of 1 Chron. 2:11); most Hebrew manuscripts *Salma*

> THEN NAOMI TOOK THE CHILD,
> LAID HIM IN HER LAP AND
> CARED FOR HIM. THE WOMEN
> LIVING THERE SAID, "NAOMI
> HAS A SON." AND THEY NAMED
> HIM OBED.
>
> *Ruth 4:16–17*

A Grandmother's Heart

ELIZABETH GEORGE

READ | RUTH 4:1–22

During her life Naomi traveled from a satisfied existence with a husband and two sons into a deep and dark valley of sorrow. When Naomi (the name means "pleasant") left Bethlehem, she "went away full"; but when she returned, she came back "empty" (Ruth 1:21). Death had claimed Naomi's cherished husband and two beloved sons. It was a bitter, empty day when Naomi walked the road into Bethlehem with only one daughter-in-law, Ruth, and announced, "Call me Mara," which means "bitter" (Ruth 1:20).

But blessed be the Lord! He did not leave Naomi in her valley of despair. God blessed Naomi with a grandson, and she knew happiness again. How she must have welcomed the warmth of fresh-flowing love and life as a grandmother.

Tiny Obed was Naomi's first grandchild. What did he signify to her?

- He was a continuation of the heritage of her dead husband.
- He was an heir to take the place of her dead oldest son; in fact, for inheritance purposes Obed was considered Naomi's "son" (Ruth 4:17).
- He was a child to love and care for and serve as a nursemaid.
- He was a person who could care for Naomi in her old age.
- He was a "renewer of life" and a hope for the future!

Being a grandmother is a great privilege which also includes new opportunities, challenges and responsibilities. As a grandmom, are you living out the "grand"?

- Exemplify godliness.
- Always love your grandchildren's parents — no matter what!
- Never show favoritism.
- Develop a personal relationship with each grandchild.

Lord, thank you for entrusting me with grandchildren. Help me to invest my time, my heart and prayers in them. Give me opportunities to express my love to them.

GRANDCHILD IN FOCUS • PRAYER

SELECT ONE OF YOUR
GRANDCHILDREN TO FOCUS ON
IN PRAYER FOR THE NEXT 14 DAYS.

Salvation

Dear Lord, please guide my grandchild to your gift of salvation. I pray that she will come to know you, to love you and to walk close to you throughout her life. May she boldly claim Jesus as her Lord and Savior. Guide her as she makes choices that have eternal consequences. Help her to follow you each moment of her life. I pray this in Jesus' name, amen.

Your next devotion is located on page 357.

Standards FOR JUDGING

First Samuel shows Israel as a nation in transition. In this book the nation moves from being led by judges and priests to being ruled by a king.

Samuel anointed Saul as the first king of Israel. He was tall, handsome and regal looking. And, for a time, he followed God's plans for his people. However, he lost his kingdom when he disobeyed God. When God told Samuel to anoint one of Jesse's sons to be the next king (see 1 Samuel 16:1–13), the prophet assumed Jesse's oldest son Eliab, with his appearance and height, must be the Lord's choice. But God surprised Samuel by outlining a far different criteria. Samuel was to anoint the youngest son — a shepherd named David, who was "a man after [God's] own heart" (1 Samuel 13:14).

For various reasons, physical stature and overall appearance are of great importance to humans. God, however, is not distracted by "packaging." He looks at what is inside a person.

How important is physical appearance to you? We often forget the story of David's anointing when a child or grandchild's appearance doesn't quite match up to our standards or expectations. Remember this story when your grandchildren grow, change and make decisions about their dress, makeup, hair, piercings or body art. No matter what your grandchildren's ages, remember to look past their packaging and examine their hearts.

VERSE *to* REMEMBER | 1 SAMUEL 16:7

"The LORD does not look at the things man looks at. Man looks at the outward appearance, but the LORD looks at the heart."

ABOUT 1 SAMUEL

WRITTEN BY:
Unknown

WRITTEN FOR:
God's chosen people,
the Israelites

DATE WRITTEN:
Sometime after Israel
divided into the northern
and southern kingdoms
in 930 B.C.

WHY WRITTEN:
To show how the
Israelites came to be
ruled by kings

The Birth of Samuel

1 There was a certain man from Ramathaim, a Zuphite*a* from the hill country of Ephraim, whose name was Elkanah son of Jeroham, the son of Elihu, the son of Tohu, the son of Zuph, an Ephraimite. ²He had two wives; one was called Hannah and the other Peninnah. Peninnah had children, but Hannah had none.

³Year after year this man went up from his town to worship and sacrifice to the Lord Almighty at Shiloh, where Hophni and Phinehas, the two sons of Eli, were priests of the Lord. ⁴Whenever the day came for Elkanah to sacrifice, he would give portions of the meat to his wife Peninnah and to all her sons and daughters. ⁵But to Hannah he gave a double portion because he loved her, and the Lord had closed her womb. ⁶And because the Lord had closed her womb, her rival kept provoking her in order to irritate her. ⁷This went on year after year. Whenever Hannah went up to the house of the Lord, her rival provoked her till she wept and would not eat. ⁸Elkanah her husband would say to her, "Hannah, why are you weeping? Why don't you eat? Why are you downhearted? Don't I mean more to you than ten sons?"

⁹Once when they had finished eating and drinking in Shiloh, Hannah stood up. Now Eli the priest was sitting on a chair by the doorpost of the Lord's temple.*b* ¹⁰In bitterness of soul Hannah wept much and prayed to the Lord. ¹¹And she made a vow, saying, "O Lord Almighty, if you will only look upon your servant's misery and remember me, and not forget your servant but give her a son, then I will give him to the Lord for all the days of his life, and no razor will ever be used on his head."

¹²As she kept on praying to the Lord, Eli observed her mouth. ¹³Hannah was praying in her heart, and her lips were moving but her voice was not heard. Eli thought she was drunk ¹⁴and said to her, "How long will you keep on getting drunk? Get rid of your wine."

¹⁵"Not so, my lord," Hannah replied, "I am a woman who is deeply troubled. I have not been drinking wine or beer; I was pouring out my soul to the Lord. ¹⁶Do not take your servant for a wicked woman; I have been praying here out of my great anguish and grief."

¹⁷Eli answered, "Go in peace, and may the God of Israel grant you what you have asked of him."

¹⁸She said, "May your servant find favor in your eyes." Then she went her way and ate something, and her face was no longer downcast.

¹⁹Early the next morning they arose and worshiped before the Lord and then went back to their home at Ramah. Elkanah lay with Hannah his wife, and the Lord remembered her. ²⁰So in the course of time Hannah conceived and gave birth to a son. She named him Samuel,*c* saying, "Because I asked the Lord for him."

a 1 Or *from Ramathaim Zuphim*   *b 9* That is, tabernacle
c 20 *Samuel* sounds like the Hebrew for *heard of God.*

stories to share

1 SAMUEL 1:1–28

Hannah Prays to God

LIFE LESSON: God hears our prayers.

TO TALK ABOUT

✦ Why was Hannah sad?

✦ What promise did Hannah make to God?

✦ Do you think it was hard for Hannah to keep her promise? Why?

✦ God always hears our prayers, but sometimes he doesn't answer them in the way we want him to. What should we do when that happens?

> "AS SURELY AS YOU LIVE, MY LORD, I AM THE WOMAN WHO STOOD HERE BESIDE YOU PRAYING TO THE LORD. I PRAYED FOR THIS CHILD, AND THE LORD HAS GRANTED ME WHAT I ASKED OF HIM. SO NOW I GIVE HIM TO THE LORD. FOR HIS WHOLE LIFE HE WILL BE GIVEN OVER TO THE LORD."
>
> *1 Samuel 1:26–28*

Who's the Boss?

CAROL KENT

READ | 1 SAMUEL 1:1–28

It was Thanksgiving weekend, and my husband and I were visiting our son and his family. After multiple meals of turkey, we were ready for a change of menu. Hannah, age eight, volunteered to accompany me on a run to Taco Bell.

Ah, I thought, this time alone with Hannah will give me an opportunity to let her know how precious she is to me, and I might get a chance to find out where she's coming from spiritually.

Waiting at a light, I queried, "Hannah, what do you want to be when you grow up?"

She quickly responded, "I want to be a movie star, so I can make a million bucks!"

"What would you do with that much money?" I asked.

She immediately responded, "I'd buy me a Hummer!"

"And what would you do with a Hummer?" I asked.

"Oh, Grammy, I'd pick up all of the lost and hurt dogs and take care of them."

I was struck by her compassion and wanted to know her thoughts about her destiny and her relationship with God. I went on, "Hannah, what do you want to do for God when you grow up?"

Crossing her arms, she stated emphatically, "I think I would like to be him, because then I could be the boss of me!"

Her reply took me by surprise. Later, I thought about Hannah's namesake in the Bible—a woman who had a strong desire for a son and believed God would grant her request. Hannah prayed. God answered. And the course of history was changed. I wondered how my strong-willed Hannah would change the course of history. My thoughts turned into a prayer as I pondered that important conversation.

Father, help me to listen carefully to my grandchildren's questions and to answer wisely. I pray that you will mold their will to yours and that they will find joy in submitting to you. Amen.

GRANDCHILD IN FOCUS · PRAYER

Physical Well-Being

Almighty God, Creator of us all, I pray that you will watch over my grandchild's physical development. May he grow in strength through the stages of his life. As he grows in awareness of his body, help him to understand that each body develops uniquely, yet is within your plan and your control. Please guard his health so that his diseases are few, his injuries are minor and his infirmities are brief. Amen.

Your next devotion is located on page 359.

Hannah Dedicates Samuel

²¹When the man Elkanah went up with all his family to offer the annual sacrifice to the Lord and to fulfill his vow, ²²Hannah did not go. She said to her husband, "After the boy is weaned, I will take him and present him before the Lord, and he will live there always."

²³"Do what seems best to you," Elkanah her husband told her. "Stay here until you have weaned him; only may the Lord make good his *a* word." So the woman stayed at home and nursed her son until she had weaned him.

²⁴After he was weaned, she took the boy with her, young as he was, along with a three-year-old bull,*b* an ephah*c* of flour and a skin of wine, and brought him to the house of the Lord at Shiloh. ²⁵When they had slaughtered the bull, they brought the boy to Eli, ²⁶and she said to him, "As surely as you live, my lord, I am the woman who stood here beside you praying to the Lord. ²⁷I prayed for this child, and the Lord has granted me what I asked of him. ²⁸So now I give him to the Lord. For his whole life he will be given over to the Lord." And he worshiped the Lord there.

Hannah's Prayer

2 Then Hannah prayed and said:

"My heart rejoices in the Lord;
　in the Lord my horn*d* is lifted high.
My mouth boasts over my enemies,
　for I delight in your deliverance.

²"There is no one holy*e* like the Lord;
　there is no one besides you;
　there is no Rock like our God.

³"Do not keep talking so proudly
　or let your mouth speak such arrogance,
for the Lord is a God who knows,
　and by him deeds are weighed.

⁴"The bows of the warriors are broken,
　but those who stumbled are armed with
　　strength.

⁵Those who were full hire themselves out for
　food,
　but those who were hungry hunger no
　　more.
She who was barren has borne seven
　children,
　but she who has had many sons pines
　　away.

⁶"The Lord brings death and makes alive;
　he brings down to the grave*f* and raises
　　up.
⁷The Lord sends poverty and wealth;
　he humbles and he exalts.
⁸He raises the poor from the dust
　and lifts the needy from the ash heap;
he seats them with princes
　and has them inherit a throne of honor.

"For the foundations of the earth are the
　Lord's;
　upon them he has set the world.
⁹He will guard the feet of his saints,
　but the wicked will be silenced in
　　darkness.

"It is not by strength that one prevails;
10　those who oppose the Lord will be
　　shattered.
He will thunder against them from heaven;
　the Lord will judge the ends of the
　　earth.

"He will give strength to his king
　and exalt the horn of his anointed."

¹¹Then Elkanah went home to Ramah, but the boy ministered before the Lord under Eli the priest.

Eli's Wicked Sons

¹²Eli's sons were wicked men; they had no regard for the Lord. ¹³Now it was the practice of

*a 23 Masoretic Text; Dead Sea Scrolls, Septuagint and Syriac
your   b 24 Dead Sea Scrolls, Septuagint and Syriac; Masoretic Text
with three bulls   c 24 That is, probably about 3/5 bushel (about
22 liters)   d 1 Horn here symbolizes strength; also in verse 10.
e 2 Or no Holy One   f 6 Hebrew Sheol*

THEN ELKANAH WENT HOME
TO RAMAH, BUT THE BOY
MINISTERED BEFORE THE LORD
UNDER ELI THE PRIEST.

1 Samuel 2:11

God: The Parent We Can Trust

REBECCA MANLEY PIPPERT

READ | 1 SAMUEL 2:1 – 11

What grandmother does not long to protect her children and grandchildren from the harsh realities of life? Consider Hannah, who not only sacrificed raising Samuel but also allowed him to be brought up in a temple that was fast becoming notorious for the sinful practices of the sons of Eli the high priest.

Imagine Hannah's feelings as she heard the gossip about temple life! No doubt her prayers deepened as her faith was tested. The worst form of evil is when the sacred and the obscene are united. Witnessing pagan debauchery is actually less damaging than seeing contemptuous religious hypocrisy. Objectively, one would think Samuel stood a much better chance being raised by his own loving, godly family than by Eli.

Samuel's upbringing could have produced a bitter man who felt abandoned by his parents; he could have become spiritually cynical. Instead, we find a thoroughly wholesome boy who was never corrupted by the ungodly behavior around him. Why? Above all, it is a testimony to the keeping power of God. God called Samuel to himself in response to Hannah's prayers, and God could be counted on to protect Samuel. God takes seriously the commitment of children to his service. We can entrust our children and grandchildren to God, who will parent them with the same skill and devotion with which he has parented us.

O Lord, as you protected Samuel so long ago, protect my children and grandchildren from the evils of this world. Surround them with your parental love and raise them to long for your will to be done. Amen.

Your next devotion is located on page 361.

GRANDCHILD IN FOCUS • PRAYER

Emotional Development

O God, Creator of mind and body, I pray that you will give my grandchild emotional health and strength. Where there is anger, bring peace. Where there is confusion, bring clarity and focus. Where there are dark shadows, cast a ray of hope. Fill her with the sunshine of your Spirit. Warm her with the presence of your peace. Amen.

the priests with the people that whenever anyone offered a sacrifice and while the meat was being boiled, the servant of the priest would come with a three-pronged fork in his hand. ¹⁴He would plunge it into the pan or kettle or caldron or pot, and the priest would take for himself whatever the fork brought up. This is how they treated all the Israelites who came to Shiloh. ¹⁵But even before the fat was burned, the servant of the priest would come and say to the man who was sacrificing, "Give the priest some meat to roast; he won't accept boiled meat from you, but only raw."

¹⁶If the man said to him, "Let the fat be burned up first, and then take whatever you want," the servant would then answer, "No, hand it over now; if you don't, I'll take it by force."

¹⁷This sin of the young men was very great in the LORD's sight, for they[a] were treating the LORD's offering with contempt.

¹⁸But Samuel was ministering before the LORD—a boy wearing a linen ephod. ¹⁹Each year his mother made him a little robe and took it to him when she went up with her husband to offer the annual sacrifice. ²⁰Eli would bless Elkanah and his wife, saying, "May the LORD give you children by this woman to take the place of the one she prayed for and gave to the LORD." Then they would go home. ²¹And the LORD was gracious to Hannah; she conceived and gave birth to three sons and two daughters. Meanwhile, the boy Samuel grew up in the presence of the LORD.

²²Now Eli, who was very old, heard about everything his sons were doing to all Israel and how they slept with the women who served at the entrance to the Tent of Meeting. ²³So he said to them, "Why do you do such things? I hear from all the people about these wicked deeds of yours. ²⁴No, my sons; it is not a good report that I hear spreading among the LORD's people. ²⁵If a man sins against another man, God[b] may mediate for him; but if a man sins against the LORD, who will intercede for him?" His sons, however, did not listen to their father's rebuke, for it was the LORD's will to put them to death.

²⁶And the boy Samuel continued to grow in stature and in favor with the LORD and with men.

Prophecy Against the House of Eli

²⁷Now a man of God came to Eli and said to him, "This is what the LORD says: 'Did I not clearly reveal myself to your father's house when they were in Egypt under Pharaoh? ²⁸I chose your father out of all the tribes of Israel to be my priest, to go up to my altar, to burn incense, and to wear an ephod in my presence. I also gave your father's house all the offerings made with fire by the Israelites. ²⁹Why do you[c] scorn my sacrifice and offering that I prescribed for my dwelling? Why do you honor your sons more than me by fattening yourselves on the choice parts of every offering made by my people Israel?'

³⁰"Therefore the LORD, the God of Israel, declares: 'I promised that your house and your father's house would minister before me forever.' But now the LORD declares: 'Far be it from me! Those who honor me I will honor, but those who despise me will be disdained. ³¹The time is coming when I will cut short your strength and the strength of your father's house, so that there will not be an old man in your family line ³²and you will see distress in my dwelling. Although good will be done to Israel, in your family line there will never be an old man. ³³Every one of you that I do not cut off from my altar will be spared only to blind your eyes with tears and to grieve your heart, and all your descendants will die in the prime of life.

³⁴" 'And what happens to your two sons, Hophni and Phinehas, will be a sign to you—they will both die on the same day. ³⁵I will raise up for myself a faithful priest, who will do according to what is in my heart and mind. I will firmly establish his house, and he will minister before my anointed one always. ³⁶Then everyone left in your family line will come and bow down before him for a piece of silver and a crust of bread and plead, "Appoint me to some priestly office so I can have food to eat." '"

---

[a] 17 Or men   [b] 25 Or the judges   [c] 29 The Hebrew is plural.

THIS SIN OF THE YOUNG MEN WAS
VERY GREAT IN THE LORD'S SIGHT,
FOR THEY WERE TREATING THE
LORD'S OFFERING WITH CONTEMPT.
BUT SAMUEL WAS MINISTERING
BEFORE THE LORD — A BOY
WEARING A LINEN EPHOD.

1 Samuel 2:17 — 18

Nothing Wasted

REBECCA MANLEY PIPPERT

READ | 1 SAMUEL 2:12 – 26

Children are shaped by the godly example of their parents and grandparents. Samuel saw, even if only once a year when Hannah visited the temple, his mother's unselfish devotion in contrast to the sinful self-indulgence of the priests (Eli's sons). And Samuel no doubt heard from Eli about the power of Hannah's prayers!

But we live on a fallen planet that is subject to evil. To think we can protect our loved ones from seeing this is folly. We worry about what our grandchildren will learn about sin while at college or fret about what will happen as they move away from our protective covering. But Samuel's training about sin was learned at the temple. That surely shows us that no place is free from sin's reach.

What gives us hope is that God can use even the examples of sin to train our children. Just as Samuel's family modeled the importance of obedience to God, so Eli's sons revealed the inevitable and disastrous consequences of sinful choices. Samuel saw what rebellion against God looks like at close range, which later enabled him to discern King Saul's rebellion almost from its inception.

Samuel had to learn to recognize God's ways and resist temptation in an evil world. So must our children and grandchildren. But our confidence is that God will waste nothing in building the kingdom of God into our children's lives. Even evil will not be wasted.

Dear God, I know my grandchildren cannot be completely sheltered from evil. When sin swirls around them and evil touches their lives, help me to entrust them to you. Let those encounters and experiences deepen their faith and build their character. Amen.

Your next devotion is located on page 371.

GRANDCHILD IN FOCUS • PRAYER

Spiritual Growth

Dear Lord, today I pray for my grandchild's spiritual growth. I ask that you instill in him the desire to read and memorize your Word. Give him a passion to be in conversation with you. May loving and serving you be part of his daily life. I ask that you stay close to him and lead him to be transformed to your likeness, to reflect your grace and to radiate your love. I pray this in Jesus' name, amen.

The LORD Calls Samuel

3 The boy Samuel ministered before the LORD under Eli. In those days the word of the LORD was rare; there were not many visions.

²One night Eli, whose eyes were becoming so weak that he could barely see, was lying down in his usual place. ³The lamp of God had not yet gone out, and Samuel was lying down in the temple*ᵃ* of the LORD, where the ark of God was. ⁴Then the LORD called Samuel.

Samuel answered, "Here I am." ⁵And he ran to Eli and said, "Here I am; you called me."

But Eli said, "I did not call; go back and lie down." So he went and lay down.

⁶Again the LORD called, "Samuel!" And Samuel got up and went to Eli and said, "Here I am; you called me."

"My son," Eli said, "I did not call; go back and lie down."

⁷Now Samuel did not yet know the LORD: The word of the LORD had not yet been revealed to him.

⁸The LORD called Samuel a third time, and Samuel got up and went to Eli and said, "Here I am; you called me."

Then Eli realized that the LORD was calling the boy. ⁹So Eli told Samuel, "Go and lie down, and if he calls you, say, 'Speak, LORD, for your servant is listening.' " So Samuel went and lay down in his place.

¹⁰The LORD came and stood there, calling as at the other times, "Samuel! Samuel!"

Then Samuel said, "Speak, for your servant is listening."

¹¹And the LORD said to Samuel: "See, I am about to do something in Israel that will make the ears of everyone who hears of it tingle. ¹²At that time I will carry out against Eli everything I spoke against his family—from beginning to end. ¹³For I told him that I would judge his family forever because of the sin he knew about; his sons made themselves contemptible,*ᵇ* and he failed to restrain them. ¹⁴Therefore, I swore to the house of Eli, 'The guilt of Eli's house will never be atoned for by sacrifice or offering.' "

1 SAMUEL 3:1–21

The Lord Calls Samuel

LIFE LESSON: God wants us to listen to his words.

TO TALK ABOUT

✦ Who did Samuel think was calling him?

✦ What did Eli finally tell him to do?

✦ How do you think Samuel felt when he realized God was speaking to him? How do you think he felt about what he heard?

✦ How does God speak to us today?

¹⁵Samuel lay down until morning and then opened the doors of the house of the LORD. He was afraid to tell Eli the vision, ¹⁶but Eli called him and said, "Samuel, my son."

Samuel answered, "Here I am."

¹⁷"What was it he said to you?" Eli asked. "Do not hide it from me. May God deal with you, be it ever so severely, if you hide from me anything he told you." ¹⁸So Samuel told him everything, hiding nothing from him. Then Eli said, "He is the LORD; let him do what is good in his eyes."

¹⁹The LORD was with Samuel as he grew up, and he let none of his words fall to the ground. ²⁰And all Israel from Dan to Beersheba recognized that Samuel was attested as a prophet of

ᵃ 3 That is, tabernacle   *ᵇ 13* Masoretic Text; an ancient Hebrew scribal tradition and Septuagint *sons blasphemed God* the LORD. [21] The LORD continued to appear at Shiloh, and there he revealed himself to Samuel through his word.

4 And Samuel's word came to all Israel.

The Philistines Capture the Ark

Now the Israelites went out to fight against the Philistines. The Israelites camped at Ebenezer, and the Philistines at Aphek. [2] The Philistines deployed their forces to meet Israel, and as the battle spread, Israel was defeated by the Philistines, who killed about four thousand of them on the battlefield. [3] When the soldiers returned to camp, the elders of Israel asked, "Why did the LORD bring defeat upon us today before the Philistines? Let us bring the ark of the LORD's covenant from Shiloh, so that it[a] may go with us and save us from the hand of our enemies."

[4] So the people sent men to Shiloh, and they brought back the ark of the covenant of the LORD Almighty, who is enthroned between the cherubim. And Eli's two sons, Hophni and Phinehas, were there with the ark of the covenant of God.

[5] When the ark of the LORD's covenant came into the camp, all Israel raised such a great shout that the ground shook. [6] Hearing the uproar, the Philistines asked, "What's all this shouting in the Hebrew camp?"

When they learned that the ark of the LORD had come into the camp, [7] the Philistines were afraid. "A god has come into the camp," they said. "We're in trouble! Nothing like this has happened before. [8] Woe to us! Who will deliver us from the hand of these mighty gods? They are the gods who struck the Egyptians with all kinds of plagues in the desert. [9] Be strong, Philistines! Be men, or you will be subject to the Hebrews, as they have been to you. Be men, and fight!"

[10] So the Philistines fought, and the Israelites were defeated and every man fled to his tent. The slaughter was very great; Israel lost thirty thousand foot soldiers. [11] The ark of God was captured, and Eli's two sons, Hophni and Phinehas, died.

Death of Eli

[12] That same day a Benjamite ran from the battle line and went to Shiloh, his clothes torn and dust on his head. [13] When he arrived, there was Eli sitting on his chair by the side of the road, watching, because his heart feared for the ark of God. When the man entered the town and told what had happened, the whole town sent up a cry.

[14] Eli heard the outcry and asked, "What is the meaning of this uproar?"

The man hurried over to Eli, [15] who was ninety-eight years old and whose eyes were set so that he could not see. [16] He told Eli, "I have just come from the battle line; I fled from it this very day."

Eli asked, "What happened, my son?"

[17] The man who brought the news replied, "Israel fled before the Philistines, and the army has suffered heavy losses. Also your two sons, Hophni and Phinehas, are dead, and the ark of God has been captured."

[18] When he mentioned the ark of God, Eli fell backward off his chair by the side of the gate. His neck was broken and he died, for he was an old man and heavy. He had led[b] Israel forty years.

[19] His daughter-in-law, the wife of Phinehas, was pregnant and near the time of delivery. When she heard the news that the ark of God had been captured and that her father-in-law and her husband were dead, she went into labor and gave birth, but was overcome by her labor pains. [20] As she was dying, the women attending her said, "Don't despair; you have given birth to a son." But she did not respond or pay any attention.

[21] She named the boy Ichabod,[c] saying, "The glory has departed from Israel"—because of the capture of the ark of God and the deaths of her father-in-law and her husband. [22] She said, "The glory has departed from Israel, for the ark of God has been captured."

The Ark in Ashdod and Ekron

5 After the Philistines had captured the ark of God, they took it from Ebenezer to Ashdod. [2] Then they carried the ark into Dagon's temple and

---

[a] 3 Or *he*   [b] 18 Traditionally *judged*   [c] 21 *Ichabod* means *no glory.*

set it beside Dagon. ³When the people of Ashdod rose early the next day, there was Dagon, fallen on his face on the ground before the ark of the LORD! They took Dagon and put him back in his place. ⁴But the following morning when they rose, there was Dagon, fallen on his face on the ground before the ark of the LORD! His head and hands had been broken off and were lying on the threshold; only his body remained. ⁵That is why to this day neither the priests of Dagon nor any others who enter Dagon's temple at Ashdod step on the threshold.

⁶The LORD's hand was heavy upon the people of Ashdod and its vicinity; he brought devastation upon them and afflicted them with tumors.ᵃ ⁷When the men of Ashdod saw what was happening, they said, "The ark of the god of Israel must not stay here with us, because his hand is heavy upon us and upon Dagon our god." ⁸So they called together all the rulers of the Philistines and asked them, "What shall we do with the ark of the god of Israel?"

They answered, "Have the ark of the god of Israel moved to Gath." So they moved the ark of the God of Israel.

⁹But after they had moved it, the LORD's hand was against that city, throwing it into a great panic. He afflicted the people of the city, both young and old, with an outbreak of tumors.ᵇ ¹⁰So they sent the ark of God to Ekron.

As the ark of God was entering Ekron, the people of Ekron cried out, "They have brought the ark of the god of Israel around to us to kill us and our people." ¹¹So they called together all the rulers of the Philistines and said, "Send the ark of the god of Israel away; let it go back to its own place, or itᶜ will kill us and our people." For death had filled the city with panic; God's hand was very heavy upon it. ¹²Those who did not die were afflicted with tumors, and the outcry of the city went up to heaven.

The Ark Returned to Israel

6 When the ark of the LORD had been in Philistine territory seven months, ²the Philistines called for the priests and the diviners and said,

"What shall we do with the ark of the LORD? Tell us how we should send it back to its place."

³They answered, "If you return the ark of the god of Israel, do not send it away empty, but by all means send a guilt offering to him. Then you will be healed, and you will know why his hand has not been lifted from you."

⁴The Philistines asked, "What guilt offering should we send to him?"

They replied, "Five gold tumors and five gold rats, according to the number of the Philistine rulers, because the same plague has struck both you and your rulers. ⁵Make models of the tumors and of the rats that are destroying the country, and pay honor to Israel's god. Perhaps he will lift his hand from you and your gods and your land. ⁶Why do you harden your hearts as the Egyptians and Pharaoh did? When heᵈ treated them harshly, did they not send the Israelites out so they could go on their way?

⁷"Now then, get a new cart ready, with two cows that have calved and have never been yoked. Hitch the cows to the cart, but take their calves away and pen them up. ⁸Take the ark of the LORD and put it on the cart, and in a chest beside it put the gold objects you are sending back to him as a guilt offering. Send it on its way, ⁹but keep watching it. If it goes up to its own territory, toward Beth Shemesh, then the LORD has brought this great disaster on us. But if it does not, then we will know that it was not his hand that struck us and that it happened to us by chance."

¹⁰So they did this. They took two such cows and hitched them to the cart and penned up their calves. ¹¹They placed the ark of the LORD on the cart and along with it the chest containing the gold rats and the models of the tumors. ¹²Then the cows went straight up toward Beth Shemesh, keeping on the road and lowing all the way; they did not turn to the right or to the left. The rulers of the Philistines followed them as far as the border of Beth Shemesh.

ᵃ 6 Hebrew; Septuagint and Vulgate *tumors. And rats appeared in their land, and death and destruction were throughout the city* ᵇ 9 Or *with tumors in the groin* (see Septuagint) ᶜ 11 Or *he* ᵈ 6 That is, God

¹³Now the people of Beth Shemesh were harvesting their wheat in the valley, and when they looked up and saw the ark, they rejoiced at the sight. ¹⁴The cart came to the field of Joshua of Beth Shemesh, and there it stopped beside a large rock. The people chopped up the wood of the cart and sacrificed the cows as a burnt offering to the LORD. ¹⁵The Levites took down the ark of the LORD, together with the chest containing the gold objects, and placed them on the large rock. On that day the people of Beth Shemesh offered burnt offerings and made sacrifices to the LORD. ¹⁶The five rulers of the Philistines saw all this and then returned that same day to Ekron.

¹⁷These are the gold tumors the Philistines sent as a guilt offering to the LORD—one each for Ashdod, Gaza, Ashkelon, Gath and Ekron. ¹⁸And the number of the gold rats was according to the number of Philistine towns belonging to the five rulers—the fortified towns with their country villages. The large rock, on which *a* they set the ark of the LORD, is a witness to this day in the field of Joshua of Beth Shemesh.

¹⁹But God struck down some of the men of Beth Shemesh, putting seventy *b* of them to death because they had looked into the ark of the LORD. The people mourned because of the heavy blow the LORD had dealt them, ²⁰and the men of Beth Shemesh asked, "Who can stand in the presence of the LORD, this holy God? To whom will the ark go up from here?"

²¹Then they sent messengers to the people of Kiriath Jearim, saying, "The Philistines have returned the ark of the LORD. Come down and take it up to your place." ¹So the men of Kiriath Jearim came and took up the ark of the LORD. They took it to Abinadab's house on the hill and consecrated Eleazar his son to guard the ark of the LORD.

Samuel Subdues the Philistines at Mizpah

²It was a long time, twenty years in all, that the ark remained at Kiriath Jearim, and all the people of Israel mourned and sought after the LORD. ³And Samuel said to the whole house of Israel, "If you are returning to the LORD with all your hearts, then rid yourselves of the foreign gods and the Ashtoreths and commit yourselves to the LORD and serve him only, and he will deliver you out of the hand of the Philistines." ⁴So the Israelites put away their Baals and Ashtoreths, and served the LORD only.

⁵Then Samuel said, "Assemble all Israel at Mizpah and I will intercede with the LORD for you." ⁶When they had assembled at Mizpah, they drew water and poured it out before the LORD. On that day they fasted and there they confessed, "We have sinned against the LORD." And Samuel was leader *c* of Israel at Mizpah.

⁷When the Philistines heard that Israel had assembled at Mizpah, the rulers of the Philistines came up to attack them. And when the Israelites heard of it, they were afraid because of the Philistines. ⁸They said to Samuel, "Do not stop crying out to the LORD our God for us, that he may rescue us from the hand of the Philistines." ⁹Then Samuel took a suckling lamb and offered it up as a whole burnt offering to the LORD. He cried out to the LORD on Israel's behalf, and the LORD answered him.

¹⁰While Samuel was sacrificing the burnt offering, the Philistines drew near to engage Israel in battle. But that day the LORD thundered with loud thunder against the Philistines and threw them into such a panic that they were routed before the Israelites. ¹¹The men of Israel rushed out of Mizpah and pursued the Philistines, slaughtering them along the way to a point below Beth Car.

¹²Then Samuel took a stone and set it up between Mizpah and Shen. He named it Ebenezer, *d* saying, "Thus far has the LORD helped us." ¹³So the Philistines were subdued and did not invade Israelite territory again.

Throughout Samuel's lifetime, the hand of the LORD was against the Philistines. ¹⁴The towns

---

a 18 A few Hebrew manuscripts (see also Septuagint); most Hebrew manuscripts *villages as far as Greater Abel, where*
b 19 A few Hebrew manuscripts; most Hebrew manuscripts and Septuagint *50,070*   *c* 6 Traditionally *judge*   *d* 12 Ebenezer means *stone of help.*

from Ekron to Gath that the Philistines had captured from Israel were restored to her, and Israel delivered the neighboring territory from the power of the Philistines. And there was peace between Israel and the Amorites.

¹⁵ Samuel continued as judge over Israel all the days of his life. ¹⁶ From year to year he went on a circuit from Bethel to Gilgal to Mizpah, judging Israel in all those places. ¹⁷ But he always went back to Ramah, where his home was, and there he also judged Israel. And he built an altar there to the LORD.

Israel Asks for a King

8 When Samuel grew old, he appointed his sons as judges for Israel. ² The name of his firstborn was Joel and the name of his second

1 SAMUEL 8:1-9; 10:17-25

Saul Becomes King

LIFE LESSON: We sometimes ask God for things that aren't good for us.

TO TALK ABOUT

✦ What did the Israelites want and why? Is this what God wanted for them?

✦ Who knows better what we need, us or God?

✦ Does God ever give us what we ask for, even if it isn't good for us?

✦ What might God want to teach us when he does this?

was Abijah, and they served at Beersheba. ³ But his sons did not walk in his ways. They turned aside after dishonest gain and accepted bribes and perverted justice.

⁴ So all the elders of Israel gathered together and came to Samuel at Ramah. ⁵ They said to him, "You are old, and your sons do not walk in your ways; now appoint a king to lead *ª* us, such as all the other nations have."

⁶ But when they said, "Give us a king to lead us," this displeased Samuel; so he prayed to the LORD. ⁷ And the LORD told him: "Listen to all that the people are saying to you; it is not you they have rejected, but they have rejected me as their king. ⁸ As they have done from the day I brought them up out of Egypt until this day, forsaking me and serving other gods, so they are doing to you. ⁹ Now listen to them; but warn them solemnly and let them know what the king who will reign over them will do."

¹⁰ Samuel told all the words of the LORD to the people who were asking him for a king. ¹¹ He said, "This is what the king who will reign over you will do: He will take your sons and make them serve with his chariots and horses, and they will run in front of his chariots. ¹² Some he will assign to be commanders of thousands and commanders of fifties, and others to plow his ground and reap his harvest, and still others to make weapons of war and equipment for his chariots. ¹³ He will take your daughters to be perfumers and cooks and bakers. ¹⁴ He will take the best of your fields and vineyards and olive groves and give them to his attendants. ¹⁵ He will take a tenth of your grain and of your vintage and give it to his officials and attendants. ¹⁶ Your menservants and maidservants and the best of your cattle *ᵇ* and donkeys he will take for his own use. ¹⁷ He will take a tenth of your flocks, and you yourselves will become his slaves. ¹⁸ When that day comes, you will cry out for relief from the king you have chosen, and the LORD will not answer you in that day."

¹⁹ But the people refused to listen to Samuel.

ª 5 Traditionally *judge*; also in verses 6 and 20   *ᵇ 16* Septuagint; Hebrew *young men*

"No!" they said. "We want a king over us. ²⁰Then we will be like all the other nations, with a king to lead us and to go out before us and fight our battles."

²¹When Samuel heard all that the people said, he repeated it before the LORD. ²²The LORD answered, "Listen to them and give them a king."

Then Samuel said to the men of Israel, "Everyone go back to his town."

Samuel Anoints Saul

9 There was a Benjamite, a man of standing, whose name was Kish son of Abiel, the son of Zeror, the son of Becorath, the son of Aphiah of Benjamin. ²He had a son named Saul, an impressive young man without equal among the Israelites—a head taller than any of the others.

³Now the donkeys belonging to Saul's father Kish were lost, and Kish said to his son Saul, "Take one of the servants with you and go and look for the donkeys." ⁴So he passed through the hill country of Ephraim and through the area around Shalisha, but they did not find them. They went on into the district of Shaalim, but the donkeys were not there. Then he passed through the territory of Benjamin, but they did not find them.

⁵When they reached the district of Zuph, Saul said to the servant who was with him, "Come, let's go back, or my father will stop thinking about the donkeys and start worrying about us."

⁶But the servant replied, "Look, in this town there is a man of God; he is highly respected, and everything he says comes true. Let's go there now. Perhaps he will tell us what way to take."

⁷Saul said to his servant, "If we go, what can we give the man? The food in our sacks is gone. We have no gift to take to the man of God. What do we have?"

⁸The servant answered him again. "Look," he said, "I have a quarter of a shekel *a* of silver. I will give it to the man of God so that he will tell us what way to take." ⁹(Formerly in Israel, if a man went to inquire of God, he would say, "Come, let us go to the seer," because the prophet of today used to be called a seer.)

¹⁰"Good," Saul said to his servant. "Come, let's go." So they set out for the town where the man of God was.

¹¹As they were going up the hill to the town, they met some girls coming out to draw water, and they asked them, "Is the seer here?"

¹²"He is," they answered. "He's ahead of you. Hurry now; he has just come to our town today, for the people have a sacrifice at the high place. ¹³As soon as you enter the town, you will find him before he goes up to the high place to eat. The people will not begin eating until he comes, because he must bless the sacrifice; afterward, those who are invited will eat. Go up now; you should find him about this time."

¹⁴They went up to the town, and as they were entering it, there was Samuel, coming toward them on his way up to the high place.

¹⁵Now the day before Saul came, the LORD had revealed this to Samuel: ¹⁶"About this time tomorrow I will send you a man from the land of Benjamin. Anoint him leader over my people Israel; he will deliver my people from the hand of the Philistines. I have looked upon my people, for their cry has reached me."

¹⁷When Samuel caught sight of Saul, the LORD said to him, "This is the man I spoke to you about; he will govern my people."

¹⁸Saul approached Samuel in the gateway and asked, "Would you please tell me where the seer's house is?"

¹⁹"I am the seer," Samuel replied. "Go up ahead of me to the high place, for today you are to eat with me, and in the morning I will let you go and will tell you all that is in your heart. ²⁰As for the donkeys you lost three days ago, do not worry about them; they have been found. And to whom is all the desire of Israel turned, if not to you and all your father's family?"

²¹Saul answered, "But am I not a Benjamite, from the smallest tribe of Israel, and is not my clan the least of all the clans of the tribe of Benjamin? Why do you say such a thing to me?"

a 8 That is, about 1/10 ounce (about 3 grams)

²²Then Samuel brought Saul and his servant into the hall and seated them at the head of those who were invited—about thirty in number. ²³Samuel said to the cook, "Bring the piece of meat I gave you, the one I told you to lay aside."

²⁴So the cook took up the leg with what was on it and set it in front of Saul. Samuel said, "Here is what has been kept for you. Eat, because it was set aside for you for this occasion, from the time I said, 'I have invited guests.' " And Saul dined with Samuel that day.

²⁵After they came down from the high place to the town, Samuel talked with Saul on the roof of his house. ²⁶They rose about daybreak and Samuel called to Saul on the roof, "Get ready, and I will send you on your way." When Saul got ready, he and Samuel went outside together. ²⁷As they were going down to the edge of the town, Samuel said to Saul, "Tell the servant to go on ahead of us"— and the servant did so—"but you stay here awhile, so that I may give you a message from God."

10 Then Samuel took a flask of oil and poured it on Saul's head and kissed him, saying, "Has not the Lord anointed you leader over his inheritance?[a] ²When you leave me today, you will meet two men near Rachel's tomb, at Zelzah on the border of Benjamin. They will say to you, 'The donkeys you set out to look for have been found. And now your father has stopped thinking about them and is worried about you. He is asking, "What shall I do about my son?" '

³"Then you will go on from there until you reach the great tree of Tabor. Three men going up to God at Bethel will meet you there. One will be carrying three young goats, another three loaves of bread, and another a skin of wine. ⁴They will greet you and offer you two loaves of bread, which you will accept from them.

⁵"After that you will go to Gibeah of God, where there is a Philistine outpost. As you approach the town, you will meet a procession of prophets coming down from the high place with lyres, tambourines, flutes and harps being played before them, and they will be prophesying. ⁶The Spirit of the Lord will come upon you in power,

and you will prophesy with them; and you will be changed into a different person. ⁷Once these signs are fulfilled, do whatever your hand finds to do, for God is with you.

⁸"Go down ahead of me to Gilgal. I will surely come down to you to sacrifice burnt offerings and fellowship offerings,[b] but you must wait seven days until I come to you and tell you what you are to do."

Saul Made King

⁹As Saul turned to leave Samuel, God changed Saul's heart, and all these signs were fulfilled that day. ¹⁰When they arrived at Gibeah, a procession of prophets met him; the Spirit of God came upon him in power, and he joined in their prophesying. ¹¹When all those who had formerly known him saw him prophesying with the prophets, they asked each other, "What is this that has happened to the son of Kish? Is Saul also among the prophets?"

¹²A man who lived there answered, "And who is their father?" So it became a saying: "Is Saul also among the prophets?" ¹³After Saul stopped prophesying, he went to the high place.

¹⁴Now Saul's uncle asked him and his servant, "Where have you been?"

"Looking for the donkeys," he said. "But when we saw they were not to be found, we went to Samuel."

¹⁵Saul's uncle said, "Tell me what Samuel said to you."

¹⁶Saul replied, "He assured us that the donkeys had been found." But he did not tell his uncle what Samuel had said about the kingship.

¹⁷Samuel summoned the people of Israel to the Lord at Mizpah ¹⁸and said to them, "This is what the Lord, the God of Israel, says: 'I brought Israel up out of Egypt, and I delivered you from the power of Egypt and all the kingdoms that oppressed you.' ¹⁹But you have now rejected your

---

a 1 Hebrew; Septuagint and Vulgate *over his people Israel? You will reign over the Lord's people and save them from the power of their enemies round about. And this will be a sign to you that the Lord has anointed you leader over his inheritance:*   *b 8* Traditionally *peace offerings*

God, who saves you out of all your calamities and distresses. And you have said, 'No, set a king over us.' So now present yourselves before the LORD by your tribes and clans."

²⁰When Samuel brought all the tribes of Israel near, the tribe of Benjamin was chosen. ²¹Then he brought forward the tribe of Benjamin, clan by clan, and Matri's clan was chosen. Finally Saul son of Kish was chosen. But when they looked for him, he was not to be found. ²²So they inquired further of the LORD, "Has the man come here yet?"

And the LORD said, "Yes, he has hidden himself among the baggage."

²³They ran and brought him out, and as he stood among the people he was a head taller than any of the others. ²⁴Samuel said to all the people, "Do you see the man the LORD has chosen? There is no one like him among all the people."

Then the people shouted, "Long live the king!"

²⁵Samuel explained to the people the regulations of the kingship. He wrote them down on a scroll and deposited it before the LORD. Then Samuel dismissed the people, each to his own home.

²⁶Saul also went to his home in Gibeah, accompanied by valiant men whose hearts God had touched. ²⁷But some troublemakers said, "How can this fellow save us?" They despised him and brought him no gifts. But Saul kept silent.

Saul Rescues the City of Jabesh

11 Nahash the Ammonite went up and besieged Jabesh Gilead. And all the men of Jabesh said to him, "Make a treaty with us, and we will be subject to you."

²But Nahash the Ammonite replied, "I will make a treaty with you only on the condition that I gouge out the right eye of every one of you and so bring disgrace on all Israel."

³The elders of Jabesh said to him, "Give us seven days so we can send messengers throughout Israel; if no one comes to rescue us, we will surrender to you."

⁴When the messengers came to Gibeah of Saul and reported these terms to the people, they all wept aloud. ⁵Just then Saul was returning from the fields, behind his oxen, and he asked, "What is wrong with the people? Why are they weeping?" Then they repeated to him what the men of Jabesh had said.

⁶When Saul heard their words, the Spirit of God came upon him in power, and he burned with anger. ⁷He took a pair of oxen, cut them into pieces, and sent the pieces by messengers throughout Israel, proclaiming, "This is what will be done to the oxen of anyone who does not follow Saul and Samuel." Then the terror of the LORD fell on the people, and they turned out as one man. ⁸When Saul mustered them at Bezek, the men of Israel numbered three hundred thousand and the men of Judah thirty thousand.

⁹They told the messengers who had come, "Say to the men of Jabesh Gilead, 'By the time the sun is hot tomorrow, you will be delivered.'" When the messengers went and reported this to the men of Jabesh, they were elated. ¹⁰They said to the Ammonites, "Tomorrow we will surrender to you, and you can do to us whatever seems good to you."

¹¹The next day Saul separated his men into three divisions; during the last watch of the night they broke into the camp of the Ammonites and slaughtered them until the heat of the day. Those who survived were scattered, so that no two of them were left together.

Saul Confirmed as King

¹²The people then said to Samuel, "Who was it that asked, 'Shall Saul reign over us?' Bring these men to us and we will put them to death."

¹³But Saul said, "No one shall be put to death today, for this day the LORD has rescued Israel."

¹⁴Then Samuel said to the people, "Come, let us go to Gilgal and there reaffirm the kingship." ¹⁵So all the people went to Gilgal and confirmed Saul as king in the presence of the LORD. There they sacrificed fellowship offerings ᵃ before the LORD, and Saul and all the Israelites held a great celebration.

ᵃ 15 Traditionally peace offerings

Samuel's Farewell Speech

12 Samuel said to all Israel, "I have listened to everything you said to me and have set a king over you. ²Now you have a king as your leader. As for me, I am old and gray, and my sons are here with you. I have been your leader from my youth until this day. ³Here I stand. Testify against me in the presence of the LORD and his anointed. Whose ox have I taken? Whose donkey have I taken? Whom have I cheated? Whom have I oppressed? From whose hand have I accepted a bribe to make me shut my eyes? If I have done any of these, I will make it right."

⁴"You have not cheated or oppressed us," they replied. "You have not taken anything from anyone's hand."

⁵Samuel said to them, "The LORD is witness against you, and also his anointed is witness this day, that you have not found anything in my hand."

"He is witness," they said.

⁶Then Samuel said to the people, "It is the LORD who appointed Moses and Aaron and brought your forefathers up out of Egypt. ⁷Now then, stand here, because I am going to confront you with evidence before the LORD as to all the righteous acts performed by the LORD for you and your fathers.

⁸"After Jacob entered Egypt, they cried to the LORD for help, and the LORD sent Moses and Aaron, who brought your forefathers out of Egypt and settled them in this place.

⁹"But they forgot the LORD their God; so he sold them into the hand of Sisera, the commander of the army of Hazor, and into the hands of the Philistines and the king of Moab, who fought against them. ¹⁰They cried out to the LORD and said, 'We have sinned; we have forsaken the LORD and served the Baals and the Ashtoreths. But now deliver us from the hands of our enemies, and we will serve you.' ¹¹Then the LORD sent Jerub-Baal,ᵃ Barak,ᵇ Jephthah and Samuel,ᶜ and he delivered you from the hands of your enemies on every side, so that you lived securely.

¹²"But when you saw that Nahash king of the Ammonites was moving against you, you said to me, 'No, we want a king to rule over us'— even though the LORD your God was your king. ¹³Now here is the king you have chosen, the one you asked for; see, the LORD has set a king over you. ¹⁴If you fear the LORD and serve and obey him and do not rebel against his commands, and if both you and the king who reigns over you follow the LORD your God—good! ¹⁵But if you do not obey the LORD, and if you rebel against his commands, his hand will be against you, as it was against your fathers.

¹⁶"Now then, stand still and see this great thing the LORD is about to do before your eyes! ¹⁷Is it not wheat harvest now? I will call upon the LORD to send thunder and rain. And you will realize what an evil thing you did in the eyes of the LORD when you asked for a king."

¹⁸Then Samuel called upon the LORD, and that same day the LORD sent thunder and rain. So all the people stood in awe of the LORD and of Samuel.

¹⁹The people all said to Samuel, "Pray to the LORD your God for your servants so that we will not die, for we have added to all our other sins the evil of asking for a king."

²⁰"Do not be afraid," Samuel replied. "You have done all this evil; yet do not turn away from the LORD, but serve the LORD with all your heart. ²¹Do not turn away after useless idols. They can do you no good, nor can they rescue you, because they are useless. ²²For the sake of his great name the LORD will not reject his people, because the LORD was pleased to make you his own. ²³As for me, far be it from me that I should sin against the LORD by failing to pray for you. And I will teach you the way that is good and right. ²⁴But be sure to fear the LORD and serve him faithfully with all your heart; consider what great things he has done for you. ²⁵Yet if you persist in doing evil, both you and your king will be swept away."

ᵃ 11 Also called *Gideon*   ᵇ 11 Some Septuagint manuscripts and Syriac; Hebrew *Bedan*   ᶜ 11 Hebrew; some Septuagint manuscripts and Syriac *Samson*

"AS FOR ME, FAR BE IT FROM ME
THAT I SHOULD SIN AGAINST THE
LORD BY FAILING TO PRAY FOR
YOU. AND I WILL TEACH YOU THE
WAY THAT IS GOOD AND RIGHT."
1 Samuel 12:23

God's Prayer Assignments

HELEN HAIDLE

READ | 1 SAMUEL 12:1 – 25

The nurse who monitored Oma's vital signs whispered to me, "She's very low." We had rushed our grandmother to the hospital that morning. Now she lay in a coma and was not expected to live. Suddenly Oma opened her eyes and looked upward.

"I see a tall door in front of me," she announced. "It must be my time to die." "Well, Lord, I'm ready," she said. "I know you have forgiven me. Nothing in my life matters except my Savior and what he has done for me."

After a moment of silence, she explained, "The door isn't opening . . . and God has called me by name, saying, 'Not yet, Ella. I have work for you to do.' So I'm not going to die."

Immediately Oma slipped back into a coma as the nurse exclaimed, "Her vital signs are improving! Blood pressure . . . heart rate. She's going to live!"

During her recovery, Oma reflected on her experience. God had called her by name. She pondered what work God wanted her to do. Then God showed her situations in need of prayer. An alert went out for a kidnapped boy. The newspaper showed photos of two children whose father died in a car accident. Her pastor sent several women to her for counsel and prayer regarding their marriages and families. Each need or crisis became Oma's prayer assignment. Many of the children Oma prayed for were not her own grandchildren, but she soon became their surrogate grandmother.

All of us desire to someday hear God's commendation: "Well done, good and faithful servant!" (Matthew 25:21). Prayer assignments remain a high calling from God for our lengthened days.

Dear God, I am your servant. As long as you give me life, help me faithfully fulfill my assignments. I know you will work behind the scenes when I pray. I entrust my prayers and all my days to you. Strengthen me to do your will. Amen.

Your next devotion is located on page 374.

GRANDCHILD **IN FOCUS** • PRAYER

Relationships at Home

O Lord, I pray that you will bless the home and family of my grandchild. May the relationships she has with her parents and siblings enhance her well-being, support her self-confidence and increase her faith. May her home life reflect your love, your grace, your compassion and your peace. Guide her parents to direct her in love and truth, so she will grow into a strong and compassionate individual. Amen.

Samuel Rebukes Saul

13 Saul was ˻thirty˼*ᵃ* years old when he became king, and he reigned over Israel ˻forty-˼*ᵇ* two years.

² Saul*ᶜ* chose three thousand men from Israel; two thousand were with him at Micmash and in the hill country of Bethel, and a thousand were with Jonathan at Gibeah in Benjamin. The rest of the men he sent back to their homes.

³ Jonathan attacked the Philistine outpost at Geba, and the Philistines heard about it. Then Saul had the trumpet blown throughout the land and said, "Let the Hebrews hear!" ⁴ So all Israel heard the news: "Saul has attacked the Philistine outpost, and now Israel has become a stench to the Philistines." And the people were summoned to join Saul at Gilgal.

⁵ The Philistines assembled to fight Israel, with three thousand*ᵈ* chariots, six thousand charioteers, and soldiers as numerous as the sand on the seashore. They went up and camped at Micmash, east of Beth Aven. ⁶ When the men of Israel saw that their situation was critical and that their army was hard pressed, they hid in caves and thickets, among the rocks, and in pits and cisterns. ⁷ Some Hebrews even crossed the Jordan to the land of Gad and Gilead.

Saul remained at Gilgal, and all the troops with him were quaking with fear. ⁸ He waited seven days, the time set by Samuel; but Samuel did not come to Gilgal, and Saul's men began to scatter. ⁹ So he said, "Bring me the burnt offering and the fellowship offerings.*ᵉ*" And Saul offered up the burnt offering. ¹⁰ Just as he finished making the offering, Samuel arrived, and Saul went out to greet him.

¹¹ "What have you done?" asked Samuel.

Saul replied, "When I saw that the men were scattering, and that you did not come at the set time, and that the Philistines were assembling at Micmash, ¹² I thought, 'Now the Philistines will come down against me at Gilgal, and I have not sought the LORD's favor.' So I felt compelled to offer the burnt offering."

¹³ "You acted foolishly," Samuel said. "You have not kept the command the LORD your God gave you; if you had, he would have established your kingdom over Israel for all time. ¹⁴ But now your kingdom will not endure; the LORD has sought out a man after his own heart and appointed him leader of his people, because you have not kept the LORD's command."

¹⁵ Then Samuel left Gilgal*ᶠ* and went up to Gibeah in Benjamin, and Saul counted the men who were with him. They numbered about six hundred.

Israel Without Weapons

¹⁶ Saul and his son Jonathan and the men with them were staying in Gibeah*ᵍ* in Benjamin, while the Philistines camped at Micmash. ¹⁷ Raiding parties went out from the Philistine camp in three detachments. One turned toward Ophrah in the vicinity of Shual, ¹⁸ another toward Beth Horon, and the third toward the borderland overlooking the Valley of Zeboim facing the desert.

¹⁹ Not a blacksmith could be found in the whole land of Israel, because the Philistines had said, "Otherwise the Hebrews will make swords or spears!" ²⁰ So all Israel went down to the Philistines to have their plowshares, mattocks, axes and sickles*ʰ* sharpened. ²¹ The price was two thirds of a shekel*ⁱ* for sharpening plowshares and mattocks, and a third of a shekel*ʲ* for sharpening forks and axes and for repointing goads.

²² So on the day of the battle not a soldier with Saul and Jonathan had a sword or spear in his hand; only Saul and his son Jonathan had them.

Jonathan Attacks the Philistines

²³ Now a detachment of Philistines had gone **14** out to the pass at Micmash. ¹ One day Jonathan son of Saul said to the young man bearing his armor, "Come, let's go over to

---

ᵃ 1 A few late manuscripts of the Septuagint; Hebrew does not have *thirty.* *ᵇ 1* See the round number in Acts 13:21; Hebrew does not have *forty-.* *ᶜ 1,2* Or *and when he had reigned over Israel two years,* ²*he* *ᵈ 5* Some Septuagint manuscripts and Syriac; Hebrew *thirty thousand* *ᵉ 9* Traditionally *peace offerings* *ᶠ 15* Hebrew; Septuagint *Gilgal and went his way; the rest of the people went after Saul to meet the army, and they went out of Gilgal* *ᵍ 16* Two Hebrew manuscripts; most Hebrew manuscripts *Geba,* a variant of *Gibeah* *ʰ 20* Septuagint; Hebrew *plowshares* *ⁱ 21* Hebrew *pim;* that is, about 1/4 ounce (about 8 grams) *ʲ 21* That is, about 1/8 ounce (about 4 grams) the Philistine outpost on the other side." But he did not tell his father.

²Saul was staying on the outskirts of Gibeah under a pomegranate tree in Migron. With him were about six hundred men, ³among whom was Ahijah, who was wearing an ephod. He was a son of Ichabod's brother Ahitub son of Phinehas, the son of Eli, the LORD's priest in Shiloh. No one was aware that Jonathan had left.

⁴On each side of the pass that Jonathan intended to cross to reach the Philistine outpost was a cliff; one was called Bozez, and the other Seneh. ⁵One cliff stood to the north toward Micmash, the other to the south toward Geba.

⁶Jonathan said to his young armor-bearer, "Come, let's go over to the outpost of those uncircumcised fellows. Perhaps the LORD will act in our behalf. Nothing can hinder the LORD from saving, whether by many or by few."

⁷"Do all that you have in mind," his armor-bearer said. "Go ahead; I am with you heart and soul."

⁸Jonathan said, "Come, then; we will cross over toward the men and let them see us. ⁹If they say to us, 'Wait there until we come to you,' we will stay where we are and not go up to them. ¹⁰But if they say, 'Come up to us,' we will climb up, because that will be our sign that the LORD has given them into our hands."

¹¹So both of them showed themselves to the Philistine outpost. "Look!" said the Philistines. "The Hebrews are crawling out of the holes they were hiding in." ¹²The men of the outpost shouted to Jonathan and his armor-bearer, "Come up to us and we'll teach you a lesson."

So Jonathan said to his armor-bearer, "Climb up after me; the LORD has given them into the hand of Israel."

¹³Jonathan climbed up, using his hands and feet, with his armor-bearer right behind him. The Philistines fell before Jonathan, and his armor-bearer followed and killed behind him. ¹⁴In that first attack Jonathan and his armor-bearer killed some twenty men in an area of about half an acre.ᵃ

Israel Routs the Philistines

¹⁵Then panic struck the whole army—those in the camp and field, and those in the outposts and raiding parties—and the ground shook. It was a panic sent by God.ᵇ

¹⁶Saul's lookouts at Gibeah in Benjamin saw the army melting away in all directions. ¹⁷Then Saul said to the men who were with him, "Muster the forces and see who has left us." When they did, it was Jonathan and his armor-bearer who were not there.

¹⁸Saul said to Ahijah, "Bring the ark of God." (At that time it was with the Israelites.)ᶜ ¹⁹While Saul was talking to the priest, the tumult in the Philistine camp increased more and more. So Saul said to the priest, "Withdraw your hand."

²⁰Then Saul and all his men assembled and went to the battle. They found the Philistines in total confusion, striking each other with their swords. ²¹Those Hebrews who had previously been with the Philistines and had gone up with them to their camp went over to the Israelites who were with Saul and Jonathan. ²²When all the Israelites who had hidden in the hill country of Ephraim heard that the Philistines were on the run, they joined the battle in hot pursuit. ²³So the LORD rescued Israel that day, and the battle moved on beyond Beth Aven.

Jonathan Eats Honey

²⁴Now the men of Israel were in distress that day, because Saul had bound the people under an oath, saying, "Cursed be any man who eats food before evening comes, before I have avenged myself on my enemies!" So none of the troops tasted food.

²⁵The entire armyᵈ entered the woods, and there was honey on the ground. ²⁶When they went into the woods, they saw the honey oozing out, yet no one put his hand to his mouth, because they feared the oath. ²⁷But Jonathan had

ᵃ 14 Hebrew half a yoke; a "yoke" was the land plowed by a yoke of oxen in one day.   ᵇ 15 Or a terrible panic   ᶜ 18 Hebrew; Septuagint "Bring the ephod." (At that time he wore the ephod before the Israelites.)   ᵈ 25 Or Now all the people of the land

FAITH IN
ACTION

Donating "Found" Money

Here's a way to help your grandchildren understand "It is more blessed to give than to receive" (Acts 20:35). Brainstorm with your grandchildren ways you could collect some extra money to give to someone in need. Perhaps the kids would be willing to donate their allowances or you could throw in the money you save by using coupons at the grocery store. Together you could gather change from random places: in junk drawers and penny pots, under car mats and couch cushions. (This is a great way to get some cleaning done, and your grandkids might see this as a treasure hunt!) The children could also earn money by helping you, their parents or others. Let your collective imaginations be your guide.

Decide how best to use your "found" money: Send it to a missionary your church sponsors, donate it to the church school, give it to a shelter for the homeless or a food bank, etc. Discuss with your grandchildren the purpose of giving in the Lord's name.

Long-Distance Variation: Include your out-of-town grandchildren in this collaborative effort by phoning them and telling them of your plans. Ask them to help think of ways to "find" money, and get their feedback on where to best donate it.

Lord, it's not only more blessed to give than to receive — it's also more fun! Help me to encourage the spirit of generosity in my grandkids through this activity. I pray that the experience will be impressed on their hearts and their minds. Amen.

Your next devotion is located on page 377.

GRANDCHILD IN FOCUS • PRAYER

Friends

Dear Lord and Father, I pray for my grandchild's social life and his friends. Bring diverse friends into his life who will love and encourage him, who will bring joy and laughter to the good times and comfort and support through difficulties and disappointments. Grant him wisdom and discernment as he selects his friends; help him to avoid cliques that restrict, activities that endanger, and foolish and dangerous behaviors that harm. I ask that you fill his life with close and caring relationships. Amen.

not heard that his father had bound the people with the oath, so he reached out the end of the staff that was in his hand and dipped it into the honeycomb. He raised his hand to his mouth, and his eyes brightened. [a] 28 Then one of the soldiers told him, "Your father bound the army under a strict oath, saying, 'Cursed be any man who eats food today!' That is why the men are faint."

29 Jonathan said, "My father has made trouble for the country. See how my eyes brightened [b] when I tasted a little of this honey. 30 How much better it would have been if the men had eaten today some of the plunder they took from their enemies. Would not the slaughter of the Philistines have been even greater?"

31 That day, after the Israelites had struck down the Philistines from Micmash to Aijalon, they were exhausted. 32 They pounced on the plunder and, taking sheep, cattle and calves, they butchered them on the ground and ate them, together with the blood. 33 Then someone said to Saul, "Look, the men are sinning against the LORD by eating meat that has blood in it."

"You have broken faith," he said. "Roll a large stone over here at once." 34 Then he said, "Go out among the men and tell them, 'Each of you bring me your cattle and sheep, and slaughter them here and eat them. Do not sin against the LORD by eating meat with blood still in it.'"

So everyone brought his ox that night and slaughtered it there. 35 Then Saul built an altar to the LORD; it was the first time he had done this.

36 Saul said, "Let us go down after the Philistines by night and plunder them till dawn, and let us not leave one of them alive."

"Do whatever seems best to you," they replied. But the priest said, "Let us inquire of God here."

37 So Saul asked God, "Shall I go down after the Philistines? Will you give them into Israel's hand?" But God did not answer him that day.

38 Saul therefore said, "Come here, all you who are leaders of the army, and let us find out what sin has been committed today. 39 As surely as the LORD who rescues Israel lives, even if it lies with my son Jonathan, he must die." But not one of the men said a word.

40 Saul then said to all the Israelites, "You stand over there; I and Jonathan my son will stand over here."

"Do what seems best to you," the men replied.

41 Then Saul prayed to the LORD, the God of Israel, "Give me the right answer." [c] And Jonathan and Saul were taken by lot, and the men were cleared. 42 Saul said, "Cast the lot between me and Jonathan my son." And Jonathan was taken.

43 Then Saul said to Jonathan, "Tell me what you have done."

So Jonathan told him, "I merely tasted a little honey with the end of my staff. And now must I die?"

44 Saul said, "May God deal with me, be it ever so severely, if you do not die, Jonathan."

45 But the men said to Saul, "Should Jonathan die — he who has brought about this great deliverance in Israel? Never! As surely as the LORD lives, not a hair of his head will fall to the ground, for he did this today with God's help." So the men rescued Jonathan, and he was not put to death.

46 Then Saul stopped pursuing the Philistines, and they withdrew to their own land.

47 After Saul had assumed rule over Israel, he fought against their enemies on every side: Moab, the Ammonites, Edom, the kings [d] of Zobah, and the Philistines. Wherever he turned, he inflicted punishment on them. [e] 48 He fought valiantly and defeated the Amalekites, delivering Israel from the hands of those who had plundered them.

Saul's Family

49 Saul's sons were Jonathan, Ishvi and Malki-Shua. The name of his older daughter was Merab, and that of the younger was Michal. 50 His wife's name was Ahinoam daughter of Ahimaaz. The name of the commander of Saul's army

---

[a] 27 Or his strength was renewed   [b] 29 Or my strength was renewed   [c] 41 Hebrew; Septuagint "Why have you not answered your servant today? If the fault is in me or my son Jonathan, respond with Urim, but if the men of Israel are at fault, respond with Thummim."   [d] 47 Masoretic Text; Dead Sea Scrolls and Septuagint king   [e] 47 Hebrew; Septuagint he was victorious

was Abner son of Ner, and Ner was Saul's uncle. [51] Saul's father Kish and Abner's father Ner were sons of Abiel.

[52] All the days of Saul there was bitter war with the Philistines, and whenever Saul saw a mighty or brave man, he took him into his service.

The LORD Rejects Saul as King

15 Samuel said to Saul, "I am the one the LORD sent to anoint you king over his people Israel; so listen now to the message from the LORD. [2] This is what the LORD Almighty says: 'I will punish the Amalekites for what they did to Israel when they waylaid them as they came up from Egypt. [3] Now go, attack the Amalekites and totally destroy[a] everything that belongs to them. Do not spare them; put to death men and women, children and infants, cattle and sheep, camels and donkeys.'"

[4] So Saul summoned the men and mustered them at Telaim—two hundred thousand foot soldiers and ten thousand men from Judah. [5] Saul went to the city of Amalek and set an ambush in the ravine. [6] Then he said to the Kenites, "Go away, leave the Amalekites so that I do not destroy you along with them; for you showed kindness to all the Israelites when they came up out of Egypt." So the Kenites moved away from the Amalekites.

[7] Then Saul attacked the Amalekites all the way from Havilah to Shur, to the east of Egypt. [8] He took Agag king of the Amalekites alive, and all his people he totally destroyed with the sword. [9] But Saul and the army spared Agag and the best of the sheep and cattle, the fat calves[b] and lambs—everything that was good. These they were unwilling to destroy completely, but everything that was despised and weak they totally destroyed.

[10] Then the word of the LORD came to Samuel: [11] "I am grieved that I have made Saul king, because he has turned away from me and has not carried out my instructions." Samuel was troubled, and he cried out to the LORD all that night.

[12] Early in the morning Samuel got up and went to meet Saul, but he was told, "Saul has gone to Carmel. There he has set up a monument in his own honor and has turned and gone on down to Gilgal."

[13] When Samuel reached him, Saul said, "The LORD bless you! I have carried out the LORD's instructions."

[14] But Samuel said, "What then is this bleating of sheep in my ears? What is this lowing of cattle that I hear?"

[15] Saul answered, "The soldiers brought them from the Amalekites; they spared the best of the sheep and cattle to sacrifice to the LORD your God, but we totally destroyed the rest."

[16] "Stop!" Samuel said to Saul. "Let me tell you what the LORD said to me last night."

"Tell me," Saul replied.

[17] Samuel said, "Although you were once small in your own eyes, did you not become the head of the tribes of Israel? The LORD anointed you king over Israel. [18] And he sent you on a mission, saying, 'Go and completely destroy those wicked people, the Amalekites; make war on them until you have wiped them out.' [19] Why did you not obey the LORD? Why did you pounce on the plunder and do evil in the eyes of the LORD?"

[20] "But I did obey the LORD," Saul said. "I went on the mission the LORD assigned me. I completely destroyed the Amalekites and brought back Agag their king. [21] The soldiers took sheep and cattle from the plunder, the best of what was devoted to God, in order to sacrifice them to the LORD your God at Gilgal."

[22] But Samuel replied:

"Does the LORD delight in burnt offerings
    and sacrifices
  as much as in obeying the voice of the
    LORD?
To obey is better than sacrifice,
    and to heed is better than the fat of rams.
[23] For rebellion is like the sin of divination,
    and arrogance like the evil of idolatry.

---

[a] 3 The Hebrew term refers to the irrevocable giving over of things or persons to the LORD, often by totally destroying them; also in verses 8, 9, 15, 18, 20 and 21.   [b] 9 Or the grown bulls; the meaning of the Hebrew for this phrase is uncertain.

Worship the Lord

Give thanks to the LORD, for he is good;
> his love endures forever.

Let Israel say:
> "His love endures forever."

Let the house of Aaron say:
> "His love endures forever."

Let those who fear the LORD say:
> "His love endures forever."

In my anguish I cried to the LORD,
> and he answered by setting me free.

The LORD is with me; I will not be afraid.
> What can man do to me?

The LORD is with me; he is my helper.
> I will look in triumph on my
> enemies.

Psalm 118:1 – 7

Like the psalmist, Lord, I've been afraid of people who might harm me. Comfort me with the assurance that my enemies hold no power if you are with me. Free me from fear and anxiety. Help me to praise you wholeheartedly, for your love endures forever! Amen.

Your next devotion is located on page 379.

GRANDCHILD IN FOCUS • PRAYER

Self-Image

O loving God, I praise you for creating my grandchild as a unique individual. Now I ask you to help her appreciate her uniqueness. Build up her self-image so she can enjoy her individuality. Help her to stand firm for who she is, where she has come from and what she believes in. Encourage her not only to have hopes and dreams but to also enjoy each day as it comes. In Jesus' name, amen.

Because you have rejected the word of the
    LORD,
  he has rejected you as king."

²⁴Then Saul said to Samuel, "I have sinned. I violated the LORD's command and your instructions. I was afraid of the people and so I gave in to them. ²⁵Now I beg you, forgive my sin and come back with me, so that I may worship the LORD."

²⁶But Samuel said to him, "I will not go back with you. You have rejected the word of the LORD, and the LORD has rejected you as king over Israel!"

²⁷As Samuel turned to leave, Saul caught hold of the hem of his robe, and it tore. ²⁸Samuel said to him, "The LORD has torn the kingdom of Israel from you today and has given it to one of your neighbors—to one better than you. ²⁹He who is the Glory of Israel does not lie or change his mind; for he is not a man, that he should change his mind."

³⁰Saul replied, "I have sinned. But please honor me before the elders of my people and before Israel; come back with me, so that I may worship the LORD your God." ³¹So Samuel went back with Saul, and Saul worshiped the LORD.

³²Then Samuel said, "Bring me Agag king of the Amalekites."

Agag came to him confidently,ᵃ thinking, "Surely the bitterness of death is past."

³³But Samuel said,

"As your sword has made women childless,
  so will your mother be childless among
    women."

And Samuel put Agag to death before the LORD at Gilgal.

³⁴Then Samuel left for Ramah, but Saul went up to his home in Gibeah of Saul. ³⁵Until the day Samuel died, he did not go to see Saul again, though Samuel mourned for him. And the LORD was grieved that he had made Saul king over Israel.

Samuel Anoints David

16 The LORD said to Samuel, "How long will you mourn for Saul, since I have rejected him as king over Israel? Fill your horn with oil and be on your way; I am sending you to Jesse of Bethlehem. I have chosen one of his sons to be king."

²But Samuel said, "How can I go? Saul will hear about it and kill me."

The LORD said, "Take a heifer with you and say, 'I have come to sacrifice to the LORD.' ³Invite Jesse to the sacrifice, and I will show you what to do. You are to anoint for me the one I indicate."

⁴Samuel did what the LORD said. When he arrived at Bethlehem, the elders of the town trembled when they met him. They asked, "Do you come in peace?"

⁵Samuel replied, "Yes, in peace; I have come to sacrifice to the LORD. Consecrate yourselves and come to the sacrifice with me." Then he consecrated Jesse and his sons and invited them to the sacrifice.

⁶When they arrived, Samuel saw Eliab and thought, "Surely the LORD's anointed stands here before the LORD."

⁷But the LORD said to Samuel, "Do not consider his appearance or his height, for I have rejected him. The LORD does not look at the things man looks at. Man looks at the outward appearance, but the LORD looks at the heart."

TALKING POINTS

Values

God values our character,
not how we look on the outside.

1 SAMUEL 16:1–7

For more on values, go to 1 Kings 2:2–3.

⁸Then Jesse called Abinadab and had him pass in front of Samuel. But Samuel said, "The LORD has not chosen this one either." ⁹Jesse then

ᵃ 32 Or *him trembling, yet*

> "THE LORD DOES NOT LOOK AT
> THE THINGS MAN LOOKS AT.
> MAN LOOKS AT THE OUTWARD
> APPEARANCE, BUT THE LORD
> LOOKS AT THE HEART."
>
> 1 Samuel 16:7

I Can Rise Above It All

DOTTIE RAMBO

READ | 1 SAMUEL 16:1 – 13

With a clank and a bang, here come my grandkids! They always show up with a friend or two and lots of joyful noise. These teenage years always surprise me. Their independence comes in the most unexpected ways. Hair color is one of them.

Two weeks ago their hair was their own natural brown. One week ago: pitch black. I bit my tongue. This week: pitch black with neon blue highlights. It was my grandmotherly duty to comment.

"Kids," I started, "I know you love the Lord." They shook their heads yes. "But I'm truly trying to understand your hair." They looked puzzled.

I explained how I look when I perform. "People expect GranDot to wear nice clothes when she ministers," I started. "As a matter of fact, they complain if I try to wear something casual. They like me to sparkle."

"But GranDot," Igs said. "We've got to reach *our* generation." He reached for the right words. "If we went out to our generation like you do yours, they wouldn't accept us. We want to do like the apostle Paul and become like them, but without sin."

At that moment, I knew the Lord was again teaching me. And through my own grandson! I quickly remembered all the places that had expected me this way or that. I'd had too much makeup or not enough.

"Kids, I understand." And that was enough. I could see their loving hearts once again and knew, like my song, that with the Lord I can "rise above it all."

Lord, help me to give godly counsel to my grandchildren and always be reminded to look at their hearts as I speak. In Jesus' precious name, amen.

Your next devotion is located on page 383.

GRANDCHILD IN FOCUS • PRAYER

Protection From Worldliness

O Sovereign Lord, the world surrounds my grandchild, pressing in and tempting him in so many ways. Help him set appropriate limits. Give him sound judgment to choose wisely. Guard him from temptation; protect him from physical and mental predators; lead him into paths of righteousness and light. And reassure me with your promise that you are holding him in your hands. Amen.

1 SAMUEL 16:1–13

Samuel Anoints David

LIFE LESSON: God values people whose hearts are right with him.

TO TALK ABOUT

✦ How did Samuel know whom to choose to anoint as the next king?

✦ How does God evaluate people?

✦ How do people often evaluate each other?

✦ How do you know God values you?

had Shammah pass by, but Samuel said, "Nor has the LORD chosen this one." [10]Jesse had seven of his sons pass before Samuel, but Samuel said to him, "The LORD has not chosen these." [11]So he asked Jesse, "Are these all the sons you have?"

"There is still the youngest," Jesse answered, "but he is tending the sheep."

Samuel said, "Send for him; we will not sit down[a] until he arrives."

[12]So he sent and had him brought in. He was ruddy, with a fine appearance and handsome features.

Then the LORD said, "Rise and anoint him; he is the one."

[13]So Samuel took the horn of oil and anointed him in the presence of his brothers, and from that day on the Spirit of the LORD came upon David in power. Samuel then went to Ramah.

David in Saul's Service

[14]Now the Spirit of the LORD had departed from Saul, and an evil[b] spirit from the LORD tormented him.

[15]Saul's attendants said to him, "See, an evil spirit from God is tormenting you. [16]Let our lord command his servants here to search for someone who can play the harp. He will play when the evil spirit from God comes upon you, and you will feel better."

[17]So Saul said to his attendants, "Find someone who plays well and bring him to me."

[18]One of the servants answered, "I have seen a son of Jesse of Bethlehem who knows how to play the harp. He is a brave man and a warrior. He speaks well and is a fine-looking man. And the LORD is with him."

[19]Then Saul sent messengers to Jesse and said, "Send me your son David, who is with the sheep." [20]So Jesse took a donkey loaded with bread, a skin of wine and a young goat and sent them with his son David to Saul.

[21]David came to Saul and entered his service. Saul liked him very much, and David became one of his armor-bearers. [22]Then Saul sent word to Jesse, saying, "Allow David to remain in my service, for I am pleased with him."

[23]Whenever the spirit from God came upon Saul, David would take his harp and play. Then relief would come to Saul; he would feel better, and the evil spirit would leave him.

David and Goliath

17 Now the Philistines gathered their forces for war and assembled at Socoh in Judah. They pitched camp at Ephes Dammim, between Socoh and Azekah. [2]Saul and the Israelites assembled and camped in the Valley of Elah and drew up their battle line to meet the Philistines. [3]The Philistines occupied one hill and the Israelites another, with the valley between them.

[4]A champion named Goliath, who was from Gath, came out of the Philistine camp. He was

[a] 11 Some Septuagint manuscripts; Hebrew *not gather around*
[b] 14 Or *injurious*; also in verses 15, 16 and 23

over nine feet^a tall. ⁵He had a bronze helmet on his head and wore a coat of scale armor of bronze weighing five thousand shekels^b; ⁶on his legs he wore bronze greaves, and a bronze javelin was slung on his back. ⁷His spear shaft was like a weaver's rod, and its iron point weighed six hundred shekels.^c His shield bearer went ahead of him.

⁸Goliath stood and shouted to the ranks of Israel, "Why do you come out and line up for battle? Am I not a Philistine, and are you not the servants of Saul? Choose a man and have him come down to me. ⁹If he is able to fight and kill me, we will become your subjects; but if I overcome him and kill him, you will become our subjects and serve us." ¹⁰Then the Philistine said, "This day I defy the ranks of Israel! Give me a man and let us fight each other." ¹¹On hearing the Philistine's words, Saul and all the Israelites were dismayed and terrified.

¹²Now David was the son of an Ephrathite named Jesse, who was from Bethlehem in Judah. Jesse had eight sons, and in Saul's time he was old and well advanced in years. ¹³Jesse's three oldest sons had followed Saul to the war: The firstborn was Eliab; the second, Abinadab; and the third, Shammah. ¹⁴David was the youngest. The three oldest followed Saul, ¹⁵but David went back and forth from Saul to tend his father's sheep at Bethlehem.

¹⁶For forty days the Philistine came forward every morning and evening and took his stand.

¹⁷Now Jesse said to his son David, "Take this ephah^d of roasted grain and these ten loaves of bread for your brothers and hurry to their camp. ¹⁸Take along these ten cheeses to the commander of their unit.^e See how your brothers are and bring back some assurance^f from them. ¹⁹They are with Saul and all the men of Israel in the Valley of Elah, fighting against the Philistines."

²⁰Early in the morning David left the flock with a shepherd, loaded up and set out, as Jesse had directed. He reached the camp as the army was going out to its battle positions, shouting the war cry. ²¹Israel and the Philistines were drawing up their lines facing each other. ²²David left his things

with the keeper of supplies, ran to the battle lines and greeted his brothers. ²³As he was talking with them, Goliath, the Philistine champion from Gath, stepped out from his lines and shouted his usual defiance, and David heard it. ²⁴When the Israelites saw the man, they all ran from him in great fear.

²⁵Now the Israelites had been saying, "Do you see how this man keeps coming out? He comes out to defy Israel. The king will give great wealth to the man who kills him. He will also give him his daughter in marriage and will exempt his father's family from taxes in Israel."

²⁶David asked the men standing near him, "What will be done for the man who kills this

^a 4 Hebrew *was six cubits and a span* (about 3 meters)   ^b 5 That is, about 125 pounds (about 57 kilograms)   ^c 7 That is, about 15 pounds (about 7 kilograms)   ^d 17 That is, probably about 3/5 bushel (about 22 liters)   ^e 18 Hebrew *thousand*   ^f 18 Or *some token; or some pledge of spoils*

stories to share

1 SAMUEL 17:1–58

David and Goliath

LIFE LESSON: God gives us courage to do difficult things.

TO TALK ABOUT

✦ Why were the Israelite soldiers scared of Goliath?

✦ Why wasn't David scared?

✦ Why do you think God chose a teenager without a sword or armor to accomplish his work?

✦ Can God use children today to do important things? Explain.

Philistine and removes this disgrace from Israel? Who is this uncircumcised Philistine that he should defy the armies of the living God?"

²⁷They repeated to him what they had been saying and told him, "This is what will be done for the man who kills him."

²⁸When Eliab, David's oldest brother, heard him speaking with the men, he burned with anger at him and asked, "Why have you come down here? And with whom did you leave those few sheep in the desert? I know how conceited you are and how wicked your heart is; you came down only to watch the battle."

²⁹"Now what have I done?" said David. "Can't I even speak?" ³⁰He then turned away to someone else and brought up the same matter, and the men answered him as before. ³¹What David said was overheard and reported to Saul, and Saul sent for him.

³²David said to Saul, "Let no one lose heart on account of this Philistine; your servant will go and fight him."

³³Saul replied, "You are not able to go out against this Philistine and fight him; you are only a boy, and he has been a fighting man from his youth."

³⁴But David said to Saul, "Your servant has been keeping his father's sheep. When a lion or a bear came and carried off a sheep from the flock, ³⁵I went after it, struck it and rescued the sheep from its mouth. When it turned on me, I seized it by its hair, struck it and killed it. ³⁶Your servant has killed both the lion and the bear; this uncircumcised Philistine will be like one of them, because he has defied the armies of the living God. ³⁷The LORD who delivered me from the paw of the lion and the paw of the bear will deliver me from the hand of this Philistine."

Saul said to David, "Go, and the LORD be with you."

³⁸Then Saul dressed David in his own tunic. He put a coat of armor on him and a bronze helmet on his head. ³⁹David fastened on his sword over the tunic and tried walking around, because he was not used to them.

"I cannot go in these," he said to Saul, "because I am not used to them." So he took them off. ⁴⁰Then he took his staff in his hand, chose five smooth stones from the stream, put them in the pouch of his shepherd's bag and, with his sling in his hand, approached the Philistine.

⁴¹Meanwhile, the Philistine, with his shield bearer in front of him, kept coming closer to David. ⁴²He looked David over and saw that he was only a boy, ruddy and handsome, and he despised him. ⁴³He said to David, "Am I a dog, that you come at me with sticks?" And the Philistine cursed David by his gods. ⁴⁴"Come here," he said, "and I'll give your flesh to the birds of the air and the beasts of the field!"

⁴⁵David said to the Philistine, "You come against me with sword and spear and javelin, but I come against you in the name of the LORD Almighty, the God of the armies of Israel, whom you have defied. ⁴⁶This day the LORD will hand you over to me, and I'll strike you down and cut off your head. Today I will give the carcasses of the Philistine army to the birds of the air and the beasts of the earth, and the whole world will know that there is a God in Israel. ⁴⁷All those gathered here will know that it is not by sword or spear that the LORD saves; for the battle is the LORD's, and he will give all of you into our hands."

⁴⁸As the Philistine moved closer to attack him, David ran quickly toward the battle line to meet him. ⁴⁹Reaching into his bag and taking out a stone, he slung it and struck the Philistine on the forehead. The stone sank into his forehead, and he fell facedown on the ground.

⁵⁰So David triumphed over the Philistine with a sling and a stone; without a sword in his hand he struck down the Philistine and killed him.

⁵¹David ran and stood over him. He took hold of the Philistine's sword and drew it from the scabbard. After he killed him, he cut off his head with the sword.

When the Philistines saw that their hero was dead, they turned and ran. ⁵²Then the men of Israel and Judah surged forward with a shout and pursued the Philistines to the entrance of

> "YOU COME AGAINST ME WITH
> SWORD AND SPEAR AND JAVELIN,
> BUT I COME AGAINST YOU IN THE
> NAME OF THE LORD ALMIGHTY, THE
> GOD OF THE ARMIES OF ISRAEL,
> WHOM YOU HAVE DEFIED."
>
> *1 Samuel 17:45*

Who Is Strong? Who Is Weak?

GLADYS HUNT

READ | 1 SAMUEL 17:1 – 58

We like the story of David and Goliath probably because the little guy wins. Five smooth stones and a slingshot are hardly the implements that win most battles. When you read 1 Samuel 17, you can feel the tension that was present on the day of this fight.

This is one of God's upside-down stories. It wasn't supposed to turn out as it did. It's an unlikely scene: a giant and a boy meeting in a valley. But this is often the way God's stories are.

The Philistines' hope of victory lay in a brutal giant of a man. The Israelites had no warrior to match him. Both sides were trusting in what could be seen. When David offered to fight, the Israelites encumbered this young shepherd with so much armor he had trouble walking. The hope of victory on both sides was tied to size and equipment and human strength.

David used what he had, but his faith was not in his slingshot (see verses 37, 45 – 47). Behind the arm that hurled the stone was the arm of the living God. When God is in on the story, it turns the obvious upside down. Who is the strong one? Who is the weak one?

This story tells us that things are not always as they seem. The problem we are facing may seem like our personal Goliath. What we *can't* do feels more real than what God *can* do. Fear and fussing become our first options.

David learned his lessons well, writing in one of his songs, "Some trust in chariots and some in horses, but we trust in the name of the LORD our God" (Psalm 20:7).

If you ever feel weak, remember this: If you let God in on your story, you will see what he can do.

Almighty God, thank you that your strength is made perfect in my weakness. Help me to prove this daily as I trust you. Amen.

Your next devotion is located on page 388.

GRANDCHILD IN FOCUS • PRAYER

Respect for Authority

Dear Lord, I pray that my grandchild will continually grow to respect those in authority. May she learn to be cooperative and fair in work and play. Instill in her a high regard for officials who govern our land and enforce the laws. May her relationships with parents, teachers, coaches, mentors and bosses be respectful, admirable, constructive and caring. Amen.

Maintaining
SPIRITUAL STABILITY

What do we do when life's trials stretch us beyond what we think our faith can handle?

How can we be strong when we feel weak?

How do we maintain our spiritual stability regardless of life's setbacks and disappointments?

The famous story of David and Goliath provides us with invaluable lessons (see 1 Samuel 17). Saul was clearly under real pressure when the powerful Philistines assembled to fight Israel. Yet he did not turn to God for strength. He allowed the Philistines and their champion, Goliath, to intimidate him and his troops. If he had turned to the Lord, he would have found relief for his anxiety, but instead he allowed people and circumstances to control him. No doubt Goliath was terribly intimidating, but Saul had to make a choice: Would he trust in appearances or in the unseen reality of God? His decision to trust in appearances rather than in the power of God caused him and his entire army to become immobilized.

David saw the crisis differently. David knew the danger he was up against, but he believed that beyond appearances was the deeper reality of God. To an outsider it sure looked like an unequal contest. But looks can be deceiving. David defeated Goliath before he ever made his first move. Why? Because there was an extraordinary power operating beyond David's own power — the power of the faithful, living God.

Risk Being Real With God

How do we obtain the faith that conquers our fears? Ironically, it's by refusing to pretend that we are *not* afraid. We must admit to God and to ourselves that we are frightened, that we aren't sure we have the faith necessary for the battle. God understands. He isn't mad at us for feeling uncertain and fearful. He will strengthen our faith if we ask. Saul was always too distant in his relationship with God; consequently, he ended up having no faith when he needed it most.

perspectives

Don't Fear Appearances

If there is an all-powerful, loving God who is accomplishing his purposes behind the scenes, then we must never look at present circumstances and conclude that this is all there is to reality. No matter what life looks like presently, no matter how much it appears that evil is winning, human beings don't have the last word. God does. And he gives words of hope, peace and victory to those who love him and walk in his ways.

Facing stress in life is unavoidable. So is being tested. But testing is for our good. It strengthens our character and our faith; it is allowed by God, who knows what he is doing and why he is doing it. In each new trial our temptation is to underestimate God and overestimate evil. We assume that because we don't always see what God is doing, he is therefore doing nothing. And because we see everything that evil is doing, we feel our fate is left dangling.

We need to face our problem realistically and squarely. But while we wait for God's answer, we need to remember to never trust in appearances alone.

Remember God's Character

When the odds truly are stacked against us and we feel overwhelmed, the single most important thing we can do is remember what is real: the character, power and rule of God. When the disciples were frightened by the Sanhedrin's threats in Acts 4:18–21, they prayed a prayer that reminded them of the nature and character of God (see Acts 4:24–30).

The Christian life is not easy. The Biblical writers described it as a long, hard race that we must run with patience and determination, deliberately getting rid of everything that hinders us from staying the course. No matter what struggles we face today, believers throughout history have gone through situations like ours. And they have discovered the truth that God doesn't leave us alone in our struggles. He gives us brothers and sisters in faith who encourage and comfort us, and in the grandstands of heaven are thousands upon thousands — a "great cloud" — of God's people from the past, cheering us on (see Hebrews 12:1). They ran the race and finished the course so that we might be encouraged by their example and press on to finish the race well.

David learned that, although following God was no passport to an easy life, he could find all the resources he needed for life's difficulties in God. He discovered that obstacles were God's opportunities to answer the prayers of his servant. And David learned, as we must, that God will use every difficulty, every tear shed, for his glory.

Gath^a and to the gates of Ekron. Their dead were strewn along the Shaaraim road to Gath and Ekron. ⁵³When the Israelites returned from chasing the Philistines, they plundered their camp. ⁵⁴David took the Philistine's head and brought it to Jerusalem, and he put the Philistine's weapons in his own tent.

⁵⁵As Saul watched David going out to meet the Philistine, he said to Abner, commander of the army, "Abner, whose son is that young man?"

Abner replied, "As surely as you live, O king, I don't know."

⁵⁶The king said, "Find out whose son this young man is."

⁵⁷As soon as David returned from killing the Philistine, Abner took him and brought him before Saul, with David still holding the Philistine's head.

⁵⁸"Whose son are you, young man?" Saul asked him.

David said, "I am the son of your servant Jesse of Bethlehem."

Saul's Jealousy of David

18 After David had finished talking with Saul, Jonathan became one in spirit with David, and he loved him as himself. ²From that day Saul kept David with him and did not let him return to his father's house. ³And Jonathan made a covenant with David because he loved him as himself. ⁴Jonathan took off the robe he was wearing and gave it to David, along with his tunic, and even his sword, his bow and his belt.

⁵Whatever Saul sent him to do, David did it so successfully^b that Saul gave him a high rank in the army. This pleased all the people, and Saul's officers as well.

⁶When the men were returning home after David had killed the Philistine, the women came out from all the towns of Israel to meet King Saul with singing and dancing, with joyful songs and with tambourines and lutes. ⁷As they danced, they sang:

"Saul has slain his thousands,
   and David his tens of thousands."

⁸Saul was very angry; this refrain galled him. "They have credited David with tens of thousands," he thought, "but me with only thousands. What more can he get but the kingdom?" ⁹And from that time on Saul kept a jealous eye on David.

¹⁰The next day an evil^c spirit from God came forcefully upon Saul. He was prophesying in his house, while David was playing the harp, as he usually did. Saul had a spear in his hand ¹¹and he hurled it, saying to himself, "I'll pin David to the wall." But David eluded him twice.

stories to share

1 SAMUEL 18:1–11; 20:1–42

David and Jonathan's Friendship

LIFE LESSON: Friends help each other.

TO TALK ABOUT

✦ What did Saul want to do to David?

✦ How did Jonathan know that his father wanted to hurt David?

✦ What did Jonathan know he would lose if David became the next king?

✦ Why do you think Jonathan and David were still such good friends?

¹²Saul was afraid of David, because the LORD was with David but had left Saul. ¹³So he sent David away from him and gave him command over a thousand men, and David led the troops in their campaigns. ¹⁴In everything he did he had

^a 52 Some Septuagint manuscripts; Hebrew *a valley*   ^b 5 Or *wisely*   ^c 10 Or *injurious*

great success,ᵃ because the LORD was with him. ¹⁵When Saul saw how successfulᵇ he was, he was afraid of him. ¹⁶But all Israel and Judah loved David, because he led them in their campaigns.

¹⁷Saul said to David, "Here is my older daughter Merab. I will give her to you in marriage; only serve me bravely and fight the battles of the LORD." For Saul said to himself, "I will not raise a hand against him. Let the Philistines do that!"

¹⁸But David said to Saul, "Who am I, and what is my family or my father's clan in Israel, that I should become the king's son-in-law?" ¹⁹Soᶜ when the time came for Merab, Saul's daughter, to be given to David, she was given in marriage to Adriel of Meholah.

²⁰Now Saul's daughter Michal was in love with David, and when they told Saul about it, he was pleased. ²¹"I will give her to him," he thought, "so that she may be a snare to him and so that the hand of the Philistines may be against him." So Saul said to David, "Now you have a second opportunity to become my son-in-law."

²²Then Saul ordered his attendants: "Speak to David privately and say, 'Look, the king is pleased with you, and his attendants all like you; now become his son-in-law.'"

²³They repeated these words to David. But David said, "Do you think it is a small matter to become the king's son-in-law? I'm only a poor man and little known."

²⁴When Saul's servants told him what David had said, ²⁵Saul replied, "Say to David, 'The king wants no other price for the bride than a hundred Philistine foreskins, to take revenge on his enemies.'" Saul's plan was to have David fall by the hands of the Philistines.

²⁶When the attendants told David these things, he was pleased to become the king's son-in-law. So before the allotted time elapsed, ²⁷David and his men went out and killed two hundred Philistines. He brought their foreskins and presented the full number to the king so that he might become the king's son-in-law. Then Saul gave him his daughter Michal in marriage.

²⁸When Saul realized that the LORD was with

David and that his daughter Michal loved David, ²⁹Saul became still more afraid of him, and he remained his enemy the rest of his days.

³⁰The Philistine commanders continued to go out to battle, and as often as they did, David met with more successᵈ than the rest of Saul's officers, and his name became well known.

Saul Tries to Kill David

19 Saul told his son Jonathan and all the attendants to kill David. But Jonathan was very fond of David ²and warned him, "My father Saul is looking for a chance to kill you. Be on your guard tomorrow morning; go into hiding and stay there. ³I will go out and stand with my father in the field where you are. I'll speak to him about you and will tell you what I find out."

⁴Jonathan spoke well of David to Saul his father and said to him, "Let not the king do wrong to his servant David; he has not wronged you, and what he has done has benefited you greatly. ⁵He took his life in his hands when he killed the Philistine. The LORD won a great victory for all Israel, and you saw it and were glad. Why then would you do wrong to an innocent man like David by killing him for no reason?"

⁶Saul listened to Jonathan and took this oath: "As surely as the LORD lives, David will not be put to death."

⁷So Jonathan called David and told him the whole conversation. He brought him to Saul, and David was with Saul as before.

⁸Once more war broke out, and David went out and fought the Philistines. He struck them with such force that they fled before him.

⁹But an evilᵉ spirit from the LORD came upon Saul as he was sitting in his house with his spear in his hand. While David was playing the harp, ¹⁰Saul tried to pin him to the wall with his spear, but David eluded him as Saul drove the spear into the wall. That night David made good his escape.

¹¹Saul sent men to David's house to watch it and to kill him in the morning. But Michal,

ᵃ 14 Or he was very wise   ᵇ 15 Or wise   ᶜ 19 Or However,
ᵈ 30 Or David acted more wisely   ᵉ 9 Or injurious

BUT AN EVIL SPIRIT FROM THE LORD CAME UPON SAUL AS HE WAS SITTING IN HIS HOUSE WITH HIS SPEAR IN HIS HAND. WHILE DAVID WAS PLAYING THE HARP, SAUL TRIED TO PIN HIM TO THE WALL WITH HIS SPEAR, BUT DAVID ELUDED HIM AS SAUL DROVE THE SPEAR INTO THE WALL. THAT NIGHT DAVID MADE GOOD HIS ESCAPE.

1 Samuel 19:9–10

Only God Is Constant

REBECCA MANLEY PIPPERT

READ | 1 SAMUEL 19:1–17

When we get a phone call from an adult child who has just been fired from a job or from a grandchild who has experienced a great injustice, what are we to say?

David had been victorious in battle after battle. He had the honor and respect of the people, he lived in the king's court, women sang his praises, the king's son was his devoted friend and Saul's daughter, Michal, fell in love with him and became his wife. Yet in one chapter he went from being the golden boy to an outlaw. All the favor was replaced by violent slander. He was forced to live off the land like a fugitive, and many previous admirers turned against him out of fear and confusion. In his early flush of glory, he could not have fathomed what would happen next.

What are we to learn from this?

We must help our adult children and our grandchildren understand that life is transitory. Circumstances can change overnight. Professional status, fame and popularity are shaky foundations upon which to put our trust. Human approval is unreliable. Rather, we must build our lives on the rock of God, who is the only one worthy of pleasing, and the only one who will not let us down. We need wisdom and a certain godly detachment to live life well. We need an attitude that recognizes, whether in times of blessing or suffering, that there is only one stable, reliable place of safety: trusting in the Lord Jesus, who promises that he will never leave us or forsake us.

Dear Lord and Father, help my children and grandchildren to realize that their strength and stability is in you, the God who never changes. Let them realize that the world is forever changing, that popularity and praise can fade in an instant, but you are their constant source of security and hope. Amen.

Your next devotion is located on page 391.

GRANDCHILD **IN FOCUS** • PRAYER

Courage

O Father, builder of character and courage, may my grandchild grow strong in the light of your love. Grant him courage to stand for what is right, to guard the truth and to ensure justice in every aspect of life. May he boldly grow in grace, revere your name and proudly proclaim you as the Lord of lords and King of kings. Amen.

David's wife, warned him, "If you don't run for your life tonight, tomorrow you'll be killed." ¹²So Michal let David down through a window, and he fled and escaped. ¹³Then Michal took an idol ᵃ and laid it on the bed, covering it with a garment and putting some goats' hair at the head.

¹⁴When Saul sent the men to capture David, Michal said, "He is ill."

¹⁵Then Saul sent the men back to see David and told them, "Bring him up to me in his bed so that I may kill him." ¹⁶But when the men entered, there was the idol in the bed, and at the head was some goats' hair.

¹⁷Saul said to Michal, "Why did you deceive me like this and send my enemy away so that he escaped?"

Michal told him, "He said to me, 'Let me get away. Why should I kill you?'"

¹⁸When David had fled and made his escape, he went to Samuel at Ramah and told him all that Saul had done to him. Then he and Samuel went to Naioth and stayed there. ¹⁹Word came to Saul: "David is in Naioth at Ramah"; ²⁰so he sent men to capture him. But when they saw a group of prophets prophesying, with Samuel standing there as their leader, the Spirit of God came upon Saul's men and they also prophesied. ²¹Saul was told about it, and he sent more men, and they prophesied too. Saul sent men a third time, and they also prophesied. ²²Finally, he himself left for Ramah and went to the great cistern at Secu. And he asked, "Where are Samuel and David?"

"Over in Naioth at Ramah," they said.

²³So Saul went to Naioth at Ramah. But the Spirit of God came even upon him, and he walked along prophesying until he came to Naioth. ²⁴He stripped off his robes and also prophesied in Samuel's presence. He lay that way all that day and night. This is why people say, "Is Saul also among the prophets?"

David and Jonathan

20 Then David fled from Naioth at Ramah and went to Jonathan and asked, "What have I done? What is my crime? How have I wronged your father, that he is trying to take my life?"

²"Never!" Jonathan replied. "You are not going to die! Look, my father doesn't do anything, great or small, without confiding in me. Why would he hide this from me? It's not so!"

³But David took an oath and said, "Your father knows very well that I have found favor in your eyes, and he has said to himself, 'Jonathan must not know this or he will be grieved.' Yet as surely as the LORD lives and as you live, there is only a step between me and death."

⁴Jonathan said to David, "Whatever you want me to do, I'll do for you."

⁵So David said, "Look, tomorrow is the New Moon festival, and I am supposed to dine with the king; but let me go and hide in the field until the evening of the day after tomorrow. ⁶If your father misses me at all, tell him, 'David earnestly asked my permission to hurry to Bethlehem, his hometown, because an annual sacrifice is being made there for his whole clan.' ⁷If he says, 'Very well,' then your servant is safe. But if he loses his temper, you can be sure that he is determined to harm me. ⁸As for you, show kindness to your servant, for you have brought him into a covenant with you before the LORD. If I am guilty, then kill me yourself! Why hand me over to your father?"

⁹"Never!" Jonathan said. "If I had the least inkling that my father was determined to harm you, wouldn't I tell you?"

¹⁰David asked, "Who will tell me if your father answers you harshly?"

¹¹"Come," Jonathan said, "let's go out into the field." So they went there together.

¹²Then Jonathan said to David: "By the LORD, the God of Israel, I will surely sound out my father by this time the day after tomorrow! If he is favorably disposed toward you, will I not send you word and let you know? ¹³But if my father is inclined to harm you, may the LORD deal with me, be it ever so severely, if I do not let you know and send you away safely. May the LORD be with

ᵃ 13 Hebrew teraphim; also in verse 16

TALKING POINTS

Friendship

Friends love each other and
stick up for each other.

1 SAMUEL 20:1–42

For more on friendship, go to Proverbs 17:17.

you as he has been with my father. ¹⁴But show me unfailing kindness like that of the LORD as long as I live, so that I may not be killed, ¹⁵and do not ever cut off your kindness from my family—not even when the LORD has cut off every one of David's enemies from the face of the earth."

¹⁶So Jonathan made a covenant with the house of David, saying, "May the LORD call David's enemies to account." ¹⁷And Jonathan had David reaffirm his oath out of love for him, because he loved him as he loved himself.

¹⁸Then Jonathan said to David: "Tomorrow is the New Moon festival. You will be missed, because your seat will be empty. ¹⁹The day after tomorrow, toward evening, go to the place where you hid when this trouble began, and wait by the stone Ezel. ²⁰I will shoot three arrows to the side of it, as though I were shooting at a target. ²¹Then I will send a boy and say, 'Go, find the arrows.' If I say to him, 'Look, the arrows are on this side of you; bring them here,' then come, because, as surely as the LORD lives, you are safe; there is no danger. ²²But if I say to the boy, 'Look, the arrows are beyond you,' then you must go, because the LORD has sent you away. ²³And about the matter you and I discussed—remember, the LORD is witness between you and me forever."

²⁴So David hid in the field, and when the New Moon festival came, the king sat down to eat. ²⁵He sat in his customary place by the wall, opposite Jonathan,ᵃ and Abner sat next to Saul, but David's place was empty. ²⁶Saul said nothing

that day, for he thought, "Something must have happened to David to make him ceremonially unclean—surely he is unclean." ²⁷But the next day, the second day of the month, David's place was empty again. Then Saul said to his son Jonathan, "Why hasn't the son of Jesse come to the meal, either yesterday or today?"

²⁸Jonathan answered, "David earnestly asked me for permission to go to Bethlehem. ²⁹He said, 'Let me go, because our family is observing a sacrifice in the town and my brother has ordered me to be there. If I have found favor in your eyes, let me get away to see my brothers.' That is why he has not come to the king's table."

³⁰Saul's anger flared up at Jonathan and he said to him, "You son of a perverse and rebellious woman! Don't I know that you have sided with the son of Jesse to your own shame and to the shame of the mother who bore you? ³¹As long as the son of Jesse lives on this earth, neither you nor your kingdom will be established. Now send and bring him to me, for he must die!"

³²"Why should he be put to death? What has he done?" Jonathan asked his father. ³³But Saul hurled his spear at him to kill him. Then Jonathan knew that his father intended to kill David.

³⁴Jonathan got up from the table in fierce anger; on that second day of the month he did not eat, because he was grieved at his father's shameful treatment of David.

³⁵In the morning Jonathan went out to the field for his meeting with David. He had a small boy with him, ³⁶and he said to the boy, "Run and find the arrows I shoot." As the boy ran, he shot an arrow beyond him. ³⁷When the boy came to the place where Jonathan's arrow had fallen, Jonathan called out after him, "Isn't the arrow beyond you?" ³⁸Then he shouted, "Hurry! Go quickly! Don't stop!" The boy picked up the arrow and returned to his master. ³⁹(The boy knew nothing of all this; only Jonathan and David knew.) ⁴⁰Then Jonathan gave his weapons to the boy and said, "Go, carry them back to town."

ᵃ 25 Septuagint; Hebrew *wall. Jonathan arose*

JONATHAN SAID TO DAVID, "GO
IN PEACE, FOR WE HAVE SWORN
FRIENDSHIP WITH EACH OTHER
IN THE NAME OF THE LORD."

1 Samuel 20:42

A Piece of Heaven

SHEILA WALSH

READ | 1 SAMUEL 20:1 – 42

I was searching through my box of photographs to find a picture of our dog's first birthday party to send to my mom. Before I unearthed Bentley's picture, I found three photographs that caught my attention. I made myself a cup of tea and sat outside in the shade to study them more closely. They captured three different occasions separated by some time. But many of the faces were the same.

I looked at these photographs and thought again of how rich I am. On each occasion after the larger crowd had left, a few of us lingered around the fire for several hours. I thought of the words of C. S. Lewis: "Is there any pleasure on earth as great as a circle of Christian friends by a fire?" Each of my close friends brings something different to me. We are richer together than we are apart. Because of what each person brings, our lives are deepened and our vision enlarged.

C. S. Lewis said that we picture lovers face to face but friends side by side; I think that is even more true when Christ is at the center of our lives — when we are all heading in the same direction with one heart and mind, to become more like Christ.

I can survive without a lot of things, but to live without friends would be to live in a cave and never see the sunrise again. We need the input, the challenge, the encouragement, even the "spur" that comes from others in community. We call on each other to celebrate, and we call on each other to weep. Surely this is a treasure above all others, a piece of heaven, a promise of what is to come.

The friends you have blessed me with, Lord Jesus, are so precious to me, for they encourage and challenge me with the love that comes from your heart. Thank you for the piece of heaven I experience when I am with them.

Your next devotion is located on page 397.

GRANDCHILD IN FOCUS • PRAYER

Future Spouse

Dear Lord, if it is your will, I pray my grandchild will be united in a loving and Christian marriage. Keep her sexually pure so that she will honor you with her body and mind. As she seeks a spouse who will honor and care for her, give her patience and discernment. May her choice for a life partner be your choice for her, so that she and her husband will together glorify you in a lasting love. I pray this in Jesus' name, amen.

41 After the boy had gone, David got up from the south side ⌊of the stone⌋ and bowed down before Jonathan three times, with his face to the ground. Then they kissed each other and wept together—but David wept the most.

42 Jonathan said to David, "Go in peace, for we have sworn friendship with each other in the name of the LORD, saying, 'The LORD is witness between you and me, and between your descendants and my descendants forever.'" Then David left, and Jonathan went back to the town.

David at Nob

21 David went to Nob, to Ahimelech the priest. Ahimelech trembled when he met him, and asked, "Why are you alone? Why is no one with you?"

2 David answered Ahimelech the priest, "The king charged me with a certain matter and said to me, 'No one is to know anything about your mission and your instructions.' As for my men, I have told them to meet me at a certain place. 3 Now then, what do you have on hand? Give me five loaves of bread, or whatever you can find."

4 But the priest answered David, "I don't have any ordinary bread on hand; however, there is some consecrated bread here—provided the men have kept themselves from women."

5 David replied, "Indeed women have been kept from us, as usual whenever *a* I set out. The men's things *b* are holy even on missions that are not holy. How much more so today!" 6 So the priest gave him the consecrated bread, since there was no bread there except the bread of the Presence that had been removed from before the LORD and replaced by hot bread on the day it was taken away.

7 Now one of Saul's servants was there that day, detained before the LORD; he was Doeg the Edomite, Saul's head shepherd.

8 David asked Ahimelech, "Don't you have a spear or a sword here? I haven't brought my sword or any other weapon, because the king's business was urgent."

9 The priest replied, "The sword of Goliath the Philistine, whom you killed in the Valley of Elah, is here; it is wrapped in a cloth behind the ephod. If you want it, take it; there is no sword here but that one."

David said, "There is none like it; give it to me."

David at Gath

10 That day David fled from Saul and went to Achish king of Gath. 11 But the servants of Achish said to him, "Isn't this David, the king of the land? Isn't he the one they sing about in their dances:

" 'Saul has slain his thousands,
    and David his tens of thousands'?"

12 David took these words to heart and was very much afraid of Achish king of Gath. 13 So he pretended to be insane in their presence; and while he was in their hands he acted like a madman, making marks on the doors of the gate and letting saliva run down his beard.

14 Achish said to his servants, "Look at the man! He is insane! Why bring him to me? 15 Am I so short of madmen that you have to bring this fellow here to carry on like this in front of me? Must this man come into my house?"

David at Adullam and Mizpah

22 David left Gath and escaped to the cave of Adullam. When his brothers and his father's household heard about it, they went down to him there. 2 All those who were in distress or in debt or discontented gathered around him, and he became their leader. About four hundred men were with him.

3 From there David went to Mizpah in Moab and said to the king of Moab, "Would you let my father and mother come and stay with you until I learn what God will do for me?" 4 So he left them with the king of Moab, and they stayed with him as long as David was in the stronghold.

5 But the prophet Gad said to David, "Do not stay in the stronghold. Go into the land of Judah." So David left and went to the forest of Hereth.

a 5 Or from us in the past few days since   *b 5 Or bodies*

Saul Kills the Priests of Nob

⁶Now Saul heard that David and his men had been discovered. And Saul, spear in hand, was seated under the tamarisk tree on the hill at Gibeah, with all his officials standing around him. ⁷Saul said to them, "Listen, men of Benjamin! Will the son of Jesse give all of you fields and vineyards? Will he make all of you commanders of thousands and commanders of hundreds? ⁸Is that why you have all conspired against me? No one tells me when my son makes a covenant with the son of Jesse. None of you is concerned about me or tells me that my son has incited my servant to lie in wait for me, as he does today."

⁹But Doeg the Edomite, who was standing with Saul's officials, said, "I saw the son of Jesse come to Ahimelech son of Ahitub at Nob. ¹⁰Ahimelech inquired of the LORD for him; he also gave him provisions and the sword of Goliath the Philistine."

¹¹Then the king sent for the priest Ahimelech son of Ahitub and his father's whole family, who were the priests at Nob, and they all came to the king. ¹²Saul said, "Listen now, son of Ahitub."

"Yes, my lord," he answered.

¹³Saul said to him, "Why have you conspired against me, you and the son of Jesse, giving him bread and a sword and inquiring of God for him, so that he has rebelled against me and lies in wait for me, as he does today?"

¹⁴Ahimelech answered the king, "Who of all your servants is as loyal as David, the king's son-in-law, captain of your bodyguard and highly respected in your household? ¹⁵Was that day the first time I inquired of God for him? Of course not! Let not the king accuse your servant or any of his father's family, for your servant knows nothing at all about this whole affair."

¹⁶But the king said, "You will surely die, Ahimelech, you and your father's whole family."

¹⁷Then the king ordered the guards at his side: "Turn and kill the priests of the LORD, because they too have sided with David. They knew he was fleeing, yet they did not tell me."

But the king's officials were not willing to raise a hand to strike the priests of the LORD.

¹⁸The king then ordered Doeg, "You turn and strike down the priests." So Doeg the Edomite turned and struck them down. That day he killed eighty-five men who wore the linen ephod. ¹⁹He also put to the sword Nob, the town of the priests, with its men and women, its children and infants, and its cattle, donkeys and sheep.

²⁰But Abiathar, a son of Ahimelech son of Ahitub, escaped and fled to join David. ²¹He told David that Saul had killed the priests of the LORD. ²²Then David said to Abiathar: "That day, when Doeg the Edomite was there, I knew he would be sure to tell Saul. I am responsible for the death of your father's whole family. ²³Stay with me; don't be afraid; the man who is seeking your life is seeking mine also. You will be safe with me."

David Saves Keilah

23 When David was told, "Look, the Philistines are fighting against Keilah and are looting the threshing floors," ²he inquired of the LORD, saying, "Shall I go and attack these Philistines?"

The LORD answered him, "Go, attack the Philistines and save Keilah."

³But David's men said to him, "Here in Judah we are afraid. How much more, then, if we go to Keilah against the Philistine forces!"

⁴Once again David inquired of the LORD, and the LORD answered him, "Go down to Keilah, for I am going to give the Philistines into your hand." ⁵So David and his men went to Keilah, fought the Philistines and carried off their livestock. He inflicted heavy losses on the Philistines and saved the people of Keilah. ⁶(Now Abiathar son of Ahimelech had brought the ephod down with him when he fled to David at Keilah.)

Saul Pursues David

⁷Saul was told that David had gone to Keilah, and he said, "God has handed him over to me, for David has imprisoned himself by entering a town with gates and bars." ⁸And Saul called up

all his forces for battle, to go down to Keilah to besiege David and his men.

⁹When David learned that Saul was plotting against him, he said to Abiathar the priest, "Bring the ephod." ¹⁰David said, "O LORD, God of Israel, your servant has heard definitely that Saul plans to come to Keilah and destroy the town on account of me. ¹¹Will the citizens of Keilah surrender me to him? Will Saul come down, as your servant has heard? O LORD, God of Israel, tell your servant."

And the LORD said, "He will."

¹²Again David asked, "Will the citizens of Keilah surrender me and my men to Saul?"

And the LORD said, "They will."

¹³So David and his men, about six hundred in number, left Keilah and kept moving from place to place. When Saul was told that David had escaped from Keilah, he did not go there.

¹⁴David stayed in the desert strongholds and in the hills of the Desert of Ziph. Day after day Saul searched for him, but God did not give David into his hands.

¹⁵While David was at Horesh in the Desert of Ziph, he learned that Saul had come out to take his life. ¹⁶And Saul's son Jonathan went to David at Horesh and helped him find strength in God. ¹⁷"Don't be afraid," he said. "My father Saul will not lay a hand on you. You will be king over Israel, and I will be second to you. Even my father Saul knows this." ¹⁸The two of them made a covenant before the LORD. Then Jonathan went home, but David remained at Horesh.

¹⁹The Ziphites went up to Saul at Gibeah and said, "Is not David hiding among us in the strongholds at Horesh, on the hill of Hakilah, south of Jeshimon? ²⁰Now, O king, come down whenever it pleases you to do so, and we will be responsible for handing him over to the king."

²¹Saul replied, "The LORD bless you for your concern for me. ²²Go and make further preparation. Find out where David usually goes and who has seen him there. They tell me he is very crafty. ²³Find out about all the hiding places he uses and come back to me with definite information.ᵃ

Then I will go with you; if he is in the area, I will track him down among all the clans of Judah."

²⁴So they set out and went to Ziph ahead of Saul. Now David and his men were in the Desert of Maon, in the Arabah south of Jeshimon. ²⁵Saul and his men began the search, and when David was told about it, he went down to the rock and stayed in the Desert of Maon. When Saul heard this, he went into the Desert of Maon in pursuit of David.

²⁶Saul was going along one side of the mountain, and David and his men were on the other side, hurrying to get away from Saul. As Saul and his forces were closing in on David and his men to capture them, ²⁷a messenger came to Saul, saying, "Come quickly! The Philistines are raiding the land." ²⁸Then Saul broke off his pursuit of David and went to meet the Philistines. That is why they call this place Sela Hammahlekoth.ᵇ ²⁹And David went up from there and lived in the strongholds of En Gedi.

David Spares Saul's Life

24 After Saul returned from pursuing the Philistines, he was told, "David is in the Desert of En Gedi." ²So Saul took three thousand chosen men from all Israel and set out to look for David and his men near the Crags of the Wild Goats.

³He came to the sheep pens along the way; a cave was there, and Saul went in to relieve himself. David and his men were far back in the cave. ⁴The men said, "This is the day the LORD spoke of when he saidᶜ to you, 'I will give your enemy into your hands for you to deal with as you wish.'" Then David crept up unnoticed and cut off a corner of Saul's robe.

⁵Afterward, David was conscience-stricken for having cut off a corner of his robe. ⁶He said to his men, "The LORD forbid that I should do such a thing to my master, the LORD's anointed, or lift my hand against him; for he is the anointed of the LORD." ⁷With these words David rebuked his

---

ᵃ 23 Or *me at Nacon*   ᵇ 28 *Sela Hammahlekoth* means *rock of parting.*   ᶜ 4 Or *"Today the LORD is saying* men and did not allow them to attack Saul. And Saul left the cave and went his way.

⁸ Then David went out of the cave and called out to Saul, "My lord the king!" When Saul looked behind him, David bowed down and prostrated himself with his face to the ground. ⁹ He said to Saul, "Why do you listen when men say, 'David is bent on harming you'? ¹⁰ This day you have seen with your own eyes how the LORD delivered you into my hands in the cave. Some urged me to kill you, but I spared you; I said, 'I will not lift my hand against my master, because he is the LORD's anointed.' ¹¹ See, my father, look at this piece of your robe in my hand! I cut off the corner of your robe but did not kill you. Now understand and recognize that I am not guilty of wrongdoing or rebellion. I have not wronged you, but you are hunting me down to take my life. ¹² May the LORD judge between you and me. And may the LORD avenge the wrongs you have done to me, but my hand will not touch you. ¹³ As the old saying goes, 'From evildoers come evil deeds,' so my hand will not touch you.

¹⁴ "Against whom has the king of Israel come out? Whom are you pursuing? A dead dog? A flea? ¹⁵ May the LORD be our judge and decide between us. May he consider my cause and uphold it; may he vindicate me by delivering me from your hand."

¹⁶ When David finished saying this, Saul asked, "Is that your voice, David my son?" And he wept aloud. ¹⁷ "You are more righteous than I," he said. "You have treated me well, but I have treated you badly. ¹⁸ You have just now told me of the good you did to me; the LORD delivered me into your hands, but you did not kill me. ¹⁹ When a man finds his enemy, does he let him get away unharmed? May the LORD reward you well for the way you treated me today. ²⁰ I know that you will surely be king and that the kingdom of Israel will be established in your hands. ²¹ Now swear to me by the LORD that you will not cut off my descendants or wipe out my name from my father's family."

²² So David gave his oath to Saul. Then Saul returned home, but David and his men went up to the stronghold.

David, Nabal and Abigail

25 Now Samuel died, and all Israel assembled and mourned for him; and they buried him at his home in Ramah.

Then David moved down into the Desert of Maon.ᵃ ²A certain man in Maon, who had property there at Carmel, was very wealthy. He had a thousand goats and three thousand sheep, which he was shearing in Carmel. ³ His name was Nabal and his wife's name was Abigail. She was an intelligent and beautiful woman, but her husband, a Calebite, was surly and mean in his dealings.

⁴ While David was in the desert, he heard that Nabal was shearing sheep. ⁵ So he sent ten young men and said to them, "Go up to Nabal at Carmel and greet him in my name. ⁶ Say to him: 'Long life to you! Good health to you and your household! And good health to all that is yours!

⁷ "'Now I hear that it is sheep-shearing time. When your shepherds were with us, we did not mistreat them, and the whole time they were at Carmel nothing of theirs was missing. ⁸ Ask your own servants and they will tell you. Therefore be favorable toward my young men, since we come at a festive time. Please give your servants and your son David whatever you can find for them.'"

⁹ When David's men arrived, they gave Nabal this message in David's name. Then they waited.

¹⁰ Nabal answered David's servants, "Who is this David? Who is this son of Jesse? Many servants are breaking away from their masters these days. ¹¹ Why should I take my bread and water, and the meat I have slaughtered for my shearers, and give it to men coming from who knows where?"

¹² David's men turned around and went back. When they arrived, they reported every word. ¹³ David said to his men, "Put on your swords!" So they put on their swords, and David put on his. About four hundred men went up with David, while two hundred stayed with the supplies.

¹⁴ One of the servants told Nabal's wife Abigail:

ᵃ 1 Some Septuagint manuscripts; Hebrew *Paran*

"David sent messengers from the desert to give our master his greetings, but he hurled insults at them. 15 Yet these men were very good to us. They did not mistreat us, and the whole time we were out in the fields near them nothing was missing. 16 Night and day they were a wall around us all the time we were herding our sheep near them. 17 Now think it over and see what you can do, because disaster is hanging over our master and his whole household. He is such a wicked man that no one can talk to him."

18 Abigail lost no time. She took two hundred loaves of bread, two skins of wine, five dressed sheep, five seahs *a* of roasted grain, a hundred cakes of raisins and two hundred cakes of pressed figs, and loaded them on donkeys. 19 Then she told her servants, "Go on ahead; I'll follow you." But she did not tell her husband Nabal.

20 As she came riding her donkey into a mountain ravine, there were David and his men descending toward her, and she met them. 21 David had just said, "It's been useless—all my watching over this fellow's property in the desert so that nothing of his was missing. He has paid me back evil for good. 22 May God deal with David, *b* be it ever so severely, if by morning I leave alive one male of all who belong to him!"

23 When Abigail saw David, she quickly got off her donkey and bowed down before David with her face to the ground. 24 She fell at his feet and said: "My lord, let the blame be on me alone. Please let your servant speak to you; hear what your servant has to say. 25 May my lord pay no attention to that wicked man Nabal. He is just like his name—his name is Fool, and folly goes with him. But as for me, your servant, I did not see the men my master sent.

26 "Now since the LORD has kept you, my master, from bloodshed and from avenging yourself with your own hands, as surely as the LORD lives and as you live, may your enemies and all who intend to harm my master be like Nabal. 27 And let this gift, which your servant has brought to my master, be given to the men who follow you. 28 Please forgive your servant's offense, for the LORD will certainly make a lasting dynasty for my master, because he fights the LORD's battles. Let no wrongdoing be found in you as long as you live. 29 Even though someone is pursuing you to take your life, the life of my master will be bound securely in the bundle of the living by the LORD your God. But the lives of your enemies he will hurl away as from the pocket of a sling. 30 When the LORD has done for my master every good thing he promised concerning him and has appointed him leader over Israel, 31 my master will not have on his conscience the staggering burden of needless bloodshed or of having avenged himself. And when the LORD has brought my master success, remember your servant."

32 David said to Abigail, "Praise be to the LORD, the God of Israel, who has sent you today to meet me. 33 May you be blessed for your good judgment and for keeping me from bloodshed this day and from avenging myself with my own hands. 34 Otherwise, as surely as the LORD, the God of Israel, lives, who has kept me from harming you, if you had not come quickly to meet me, not one male belonging to Nabal would have been left alive by daybreak."

35 Then David accepted from her hand what she had brought him and said, "Go home in peace. I have heard your words and granted your request."

36 When Abigail went to Nabal, he was in the house holding a banquet like that of a king. He was in high spirits and very drunk. So she told him nothing until daybreak. 37 Then in the morning, when Nabal was sober, his wife told him all these things, and his heart failed him and he became like a stone. 38 About ten days later, the LORD struck Nabal and he died.

39 When David heard that Nabal was dead, he said, "Praise be to the LORD, who has upheld my cause against Nabal for treating me with contempt. He has kept his servant from doing wrong and has brought Nabal's wrongdoing down on his own head."

a 18 That is, probably about a bushel (about 37 liters)   *b 22* Some Septuagint manuscripts; Hebrew *with David's enemies*

FRIDAY

NABAL ANSWERED DAVID'S SERVANTS, "WHO IS THIS DAVID? WHO IS THIS SON OF JESSE? MANY SERVANTS ARE BREAKING AWAY FROM THEIR MASTERS THESE DAYS. WHY SHOULD I TAKE MY BREAD AND WATER, AND THE MEAT I HAVE SLAUGHTERED FOR MY SHEARERS, AND GIVE IT TO MEN COMING FROM WHO KNOWS WHERE?"
1 Samuel 25:10–11

Divine Objectivity

REBECCA MANLEY PIPPERT

READ | 1 SAMUEL 25:1–44

Nothing causes us to rise up on our high horse faster than when someone criticizes us or our loved ones! How do we teach our children and grandchildren to gain discernment—especially when they have been criticized? Abigail shows us, by the way she responded to her husband's insults of David, that we gain discernment through having divine objectivity.

To gain divine objectivity, we first need to consider the source of the criticism. Is the person doing the criticizing someone whose opinion matters to us? It is foolish not to listen to the correction of someone we respect. But Abigail's argument to David was that he must not be offended by a man with a character like Nabal's (see 1 Samuel 25:25).

Second, our reputation is in God's hands. Let him bring judgment and promotion according to his timetable, not ours. Abigail recognized that God had great plans for David, plans for him to lead Israel. Once David's time of fleeing from Saul was over and he was made king, Abigail did not want him to have a marred record from having responded foolishly (see 1 Samuel 25:30–31).

Third, consider the style of the criticism. Remember that God convicts and Satan condemns. God never corrects us in ways that produce despair or self-loathing, rather he corrects in ways that bring hope and peace. And God will correct us in a way that we can "hear." Looking at the styles of Nabal and Abigail, it is not difficult to discern the different powers that were operating behind them. Never listen to the enemy's accusations. Always listen to God's correction.

Open my ears, Lord, so I can hear your coaching and correction. Make me wise so I can discern the judgment and criticism of others, accepting that which is valid and ignoring that which is false. Grant me the wisdom of divine objectivity. Amen.

Your next devotion is located on page 398.

GRANDCHILD IN FOCUS • PRAYER

School/Career

Dear God, may learning be a joy rather than a chore for my grandchild. May exploration of new ideas bring a sense of wonder, awe and excitement. Grant him clarity of mind, the ability to concentrate on the task at hand and recollection of what has been learned. Help him to appreciate the tasks that come easily and to persevere through those that challenge. Amen.

Staying in Motion

Grandmothers today are more physically active than ever before. Take advantage of your ability to participate in sports by inviting your grandchildren to join you. A day of skiing, a round of golf, a game of tennis — these are great activities to do together. If you run or walk, sign up with your grandchild to participate in a marathon, 10K, 5K or a fundraising walk; then train for it together. Biking or snowshoeing are other sports that adjust easily to different ages and abilities. You can share a great time getting outside and moving.

Even young children can take swimming lessons with you. Or you could visit a local fitness club or YMCA to find a class to take together. Participate in the activity, being mindful of your physical comfort level. Even if your grandchildren can go longer and play harder than you can, they will be thrilled to share time with you.

Long-Distance Variation: Share your favorite activity long-distance by doing the same activity on the same day. Then call and talk about the details. Or train separately and make a ski trip, golf outing or tennis match the highlight of your next visit.

Dear Lord, what a gift it is to have the ability and strength to participate with my grandchildren in physical activities. Thank you for letting me share these special times with them. Keep us safe from harm and injury while we play. Amen.

Your next devotion is located on page 401.

GRANDCHILD IN FOCUS • PRAYER

Character

Dear Lord and Father, I ask that you fill my grandchild with your Spirit so her character reflects your goodness and love. Give her kindness and love for others. Bring joy to her life so she will be a joy to others. Grant her patience and self-control through difficult and trying times. May she show mercy and generosity to those who are less fortunate. Grant her integrity and a sense of justice, and surround her with your peace. Amen.

Then David sent word to Abigail, asking her to become his wife. ⁴⁰His servants went to Carmel and said to Abigail, "David has sent us to you to take you to become his wife."

⁴¹She bowed down with her face to the ground and said, "Here is your maidservant, ready to serve you and wash the feet of my master's servants." ⁴²Abigail quickly got on a donkey and, attended by her five maids, went with David's messengers and became his wife. ⁴³David had also married Ahinoam of Jezreel, and they both were his wives. ⁴⁴But Saul had given his daughter Michal, David's wife, to Paltiel ⁿ son of Laish, who was from Gallim.

David Again Spares Saul's Life

26 The Ziphites went to Saul at Gibeah and said, "Is not David hiding on the hill of Hakilah, which faces Jeshimon?"

²So Saul went down to the Desert of Ziph, with his three thousand chosen men of Israel, to search there for David. ³Saul made his camp beside the road on the hill of Hakilah facing Jeshimon, but David stayed in the desert. When he saw that Saul had followed him there, ⁴he sent out scouts and learned that Saul had definitely arrived. ᵇ

⁵Then David set out and went to the place where Saul had camped. He saw where Saul and Abner son of Ner, the commander of the army, had lain down. Saul was lying inside the camp, with the army encamped around him.

⁶David then asked Ahimelech the Hittite and Abishai son of Zeruiah, Joab's brother, "Who will go down into the camp with me to Saul?"

"I'll go with you," said Abishai.

⁷So David and Abishai went to the army by night, and there was Saul, lying asleep inside the camp with his spear stuck in the ground near his head. Abner and the soldiers were lying around him.

⁸Abishai said to David, "Today God has delivered your enemy into your hands. Now let me pin him to the ground with one thrust of my spear; I won't strike him twice."

⁹But David said to Abishai, "Don't destroy him! Who can lay a hand on the LORD's anointed and be guiltless? ¹⁰As surely as the LORD lives," he said, "the LORD himself will strike him; either his time will come and he will die, or he will go into battle and perish. ¹¹But the LORD forbid that I should lay a hand on the LORD's anointed. Now get the spear and water jug that are near his head, and let's go."

¹²So David took the spear and water jug near Saul's head, and they left. No one saw or knew about it, nor did anyone wake up. They were all sleeping, because the LORD had put them into a deep sleep.

¹³Then David crossed over to the other side and stood on top of the hill some distance away; there was a wide space between them. ¹⁴He called out to the army and to Abner son of Ner, "Aren't you going to answer me, Abner?"

Abner replied, "Who are you who calls to the king?"

¹⁵David said, "You're a man, aren't you? And who is like you in Israel? Why didn't you guard your lord the king? Someone came to destroy your lord the king. ¹⁶What you have done is not good. As surely as the LORD lives, you and your men deserve to die, because you did not guard your master, the LORD's anointed. Look around you. Where are the king's spear and water jug that were near his head?"

¹⁷Saul recognized David's voice and said, "Is that your voice, David my son?"

David replied, "Yes it is, my lord the king." ¹⁸And he added, "Why is my lord pursuing his servant? What have I done, and what wrong am I guilty of? ¹⁹Now let my lord the king listen to his servant's words. If the LORD has incited you against me, then may he accept an offering. If, however, men have done it, may they be cursed before the LORD! They have now driven me from my share in the LORD's inheritance and have said, 'Go, serve other gods.' ²⁰Now do not let my blood fall to the ground far from the presence of the LORD. The

ⁿ 44 Hebrew *Palti*, a variant of *Paltiel*   ᵇ 4 Or *had come to Nacon* king of Israel has come out to look for a flea — as one hunts a partridge in the mountains."

²¹ Then Saul said, "I have sinned. Come back, David my son. Because you considered my life precious today, I will not try to harm you again. Surely I have acted like a fool and have erred greatly."

²² "Here is the king's spear," David answered. "Let one of your young men come over and get it. ²³ The LORD rewards every man for his righteousness and faithfulness. The LORD delivered you into my hands today, but I would not lay a hand on the LORD's anointed. ²⁴ As surely as I valued your life today, so may the LORD value my life and deliver me from all trouble."

²⁵ Then Saul said to David, "May you be blessed, my son David; you will do great things and surely triumph."

So David went on his way, and Saul returned home.

David Among the Philistines

27 But David thought to himself, "One of these days I will be destroyed by the hand of Saul. The best thing I can do is to escape to the land of the Philistines. Then Saul will give up searching for me anywhere in Israel, and I will slip out of his hand."

² So David and the six hundred men with him left and went over to Achish son of Maoch king of Gath. ³ David and his men settled in Gath with Achish. Each man had his family with him, and David had his two wives: Ahinoam of Jezreel and Abigail of Carmel, the widow of Nabal. ⁴ When Saul was told that David had fled to Gath, he no longer searched for him.

⁵ Then David said to Achish, "If I have found favor in your eyes, let a place be assigned to me in one of the country towns, that I may live there. Why should your servant live in the royal city with you?"

⁶ So on that day Achish gave him Ziklag, and it has belonged to the kings of Judah ever since. ⁷ David lived in Philistine territory a year and four months.

⁸ Now David and his men went up and raided the Geshurites, the Girzites and the Amalekites. (From ancient times these peoples had lived in the land extending to Shur and Egypt.) ⁹ Whenever David attacked an area, he did not leave a man or woman alive, but took sheep and cattle, donkeys and camels, and clothes. Then he returned to Achish.

¹⁰ When Achish asked, "Where did you go raiding today?" David would say, "Against the Negev of Judah" or "Against the Negev of Jerahmeel" or "Against the Negev of the Kenites." ¹¹ He did not leave a man or woman alive to be brought to Gath, for he thought, "They might inform on us and say, 'This is what David did.'" And such was his practice as long as he lived in Philistine territory. ¹² Achish trusted David and said to himself, "He has become so odious to his people, the Israelites, that he will be my servant forever."

Saul and the Witch of Endor

28 In those days the Philistines gathered their forces to fight against Israel. Achish said to David, "You must understand that you and your men will accompany me in the army."

² David said, "Then you will see for yourself what your servant can do."

Achish replied, "Very well, I will make you my bodyguard for life."

³ Now Samuel was dead, and all Israel had mourned for him and buried him in his own town of Ramah. Saul had expelled the mediums and spiritists from the land.

⁴ The Philistines assembled and came and set up camp at Shunem, while Saul gathered all the Israelites and set up camp at Gilboa. ⁵ When Saul saw the Philistine army, he was afraid; terror filled his heart. ⁶ He inquired of the LORD, but the LORD did not answer him by dreams or Urim or prophets. ⁷ Saul then said to his attendants, "Find me a woman who is a medium, so I may go and inquire of her."

"There is one in Endor," they said.

⁸ So Saul disguised himself, putting on other clothes, and at night he and two men went to the

Worship the Lord

I lift up my eyes to the hills —
    where does my help come from?
My help comes from the LORD,
    the Maker of heaven and earth.

He will not let your foot slip —
    he who watches over you will not slumber;
indeed, he who watches over Israel
    will neither slumber nor sleep.

The LORD watches over you —
    the LORD is your shade at your right hand;
the sun will not harm you by day,
    nor the moon by night.

The LORD will keep you from all harm —
    he will watch over your life;
the LORD will watch over your coming
        and going
    both now and forevermore.

Psalm 121

Thank you, Lord, that your sleepless eyes are on me and your protective hands are beside me. Remind me that no amount of worry can keep me or my loved ones safe. Soothe me with the knowledge that you will watch over us now and forever. Amen.

Your next devotion is located on page 404.

GRANDCHILD IN FOCUS • PRAYER

Talents

Dear Lord, the giver of gifts, bless my grandchild as he develops his talents. Help him identify his talents and be proud and confident of the gifts you have given him. Give him patience and understanding, Lord, so he will not grow weary of striving and searching to reach the goals you have set for him. May each milestone bring satisfaction and a healthy desire for greater achievement and success to bring glory to you. Amen.

woman. "Consult a spirit for me," he said, "and bring up for me the one I name."

⁹But the woman said to him, "Surely you know what Saul has done. He has cut off the mediums and spiritists from the land. Why have you set a trap for my life to bring about my death?"

¹⁰Saul swore to her by the Lord, "As surely as the Lord lives, you will not be punished for this."

¹¹Then the woman asked, "Whom shall I bring up for you?"

"Bring up Samuel," he said.

¹²When the woman saw Samuel, she cried out at the top of her voice and said to Saul, "Why have you deceived me? You are Saul!"

¹³The king said to her, "Don't be afraid. What do you see?"

The woman said, "I see a spirit *a* coming up out of the ground."

¹⁴"What does he look like?" he asked.

"An old man wearing a robe is coming up," she said.

Then Saul knew it was Samuel, and he bowed down and prostrated himself with his face to the ground.

¹⁵Samuel said to Saul, "Why have you disturbed me by bringing me up?"

"I am in great distress," Saul said. "The Philistines are fighting against me, and God has turned away from me. He no longer answers me, either by prophets or by dreams. So I have called on you to tell me what to do."

¹⁶Samuel said, "Why do you consult me, now that the Lord has turned away from you and become your enemy? ¹⁷The Lord has done what he predicted through me. The Lord has torn the kingdom out of your hands and given it to one of your neighbors—to David. ¹⁸Because you did not obey the Lord or carry out his fierce wrath against the Amalekites, the Lord has done this to you today. ¹⁹The Lord will hand over both Israel and you to the Philistines, and tomorrow you and your sons will be with me. The Lord will also hand over the army of Israel to the Philistines."

²⁰Immediately Saul fell full length on the ground, filled with fear because of Samuel's words. His strength was gone, for he had eaten nothing all that day and night.

²¹When the woman came to Saul and saw that he was greatly shaken, she said, "Look, your maidservant has obeyed you. I took my life in my hands and did what you told me to do. ²²Now please listen to your servant and let me give you some food so you may eat and have the strength to go on your way."

²³He refused and said, "I will not eat."

But his men joined the woman in urging him, and he listened to them. He got up from the ground and sat on the couch.

²⁴The woman had a fattened calf at the house, which she butchered at once. She took some flour, kneaded it and baked bread without yeast. ²⁵Then she set it before Saul and his men, and they ate. That same night they got up and left.

Achish Sends David Back to Ziklag

29 The Philistines gathered all their forces at Aphek, and Israel camped by the spring in Jezreel. ²As the Philistine rulers marched with their units of hundreds and thousands, David and his men were marching at the rear with Achish. ³The commanders of the Philistines asked, "What about these Hebrews?"

Achish replied, "Is this not David, who was an officer of Saul king of Israel? He has already been with me for over a year, and from the day he left Saul until now, I have found no fault in him."

⁴But the Philistine commanders were angry with him and said, "Send the man back, that he may return to the place you assigned him. He must not go with us into battle, or he will turn against us during the fighting. How better could he regain his master's favor than by taking the heads of our own men? ⁵Isn't this the David they sang about in their dances:

" 'Saul has slain his thousands,
and David his tens of thousands'?"

a 13 Or see spirits; or see gods

⁶So Achish called David and said to him, "As surely as the LORD lives, you have been reliable, and I would be pleased to have you serve with me in the army. From the day you came to me until now, I have found no fault in you, but the rulers don't approve of you. ⁷Turn back and go in peace; do nothing to displease the Philistine rulers."

⁸"But what have I done?" asked David. "What have you found against your servant from the day I came to you until now? Why can't I go and fight against the enemies of my lord the king?"

⁹Achish answered, "I know that you have been as pleasing in my eyes as an angel of God; nevertheless, the Philistine commanders have said, 'He must not go up with us into battle.' ¹⁰Now get up early, along with your master's servants who have come with you, and leave in the morning as soon as it is light."

¹¹So David and his men got up early in the morning to go back to the land of the Philistines, and the Philistines went up to Jezreel.

David Destroys the Amalekites

30 David and his men reached Ziklag on the third day. Now the Amalekites had raided the Negev and Ziklag. They had attacked Ziklag and burned it, ²and had taken captive the women and all who were in it, both young and old. They killed none of them, but carried them off as they went on their way.

³When David and his men came to Ziklag, they found it destroyed by fire and their wives and sons and daughters taken captive. ⁴So David and his men wept aloud until they had no strength left to weep. ⁵David's two wives had been captured—Ahinoam of Jezreel and Abigail, the widow of Nabal of Carmel. ⁶David was greatly distressed because the men were talking of stoning him; each one was bitter in spirit because of his sons and daughters. But David found strength in the LORD his God.

⁷Then David said to Abiathar the priest, the son of Ahimelech, "Bring me the ephod." Abiathar brought it to him, ⁸and David inquired of the LORD, "Shall I pursue this raiding party? Will I overtake them?"

"Pursue them," he answered. "You will certainly overtake them and succeed in the rescue."

⁹David and the six hundred men with him came to the Besor Ravine, where some stayed behind, ¹⁰for two hundred men were too exhausted to cross the ravine. But David and four hundred men continued the pursuit.

¹¹They found an Egyptian in a field and brought him to David. They gave him water to drink and food to eat— ¹²part of a cake of pressed figs and two cakes of raisins. He ate and was revived, for he had not eaten any food or drunk any water for three days and three nights.

¹³David asked him, "To whom do you belong, and where do you come from?"

He said, "I am an Egyptian, the slave of an Amalekite. My master abandoned me when I became ill three days ago. ¹⁴We raided the Negev of the Kerethites and the territory belonging to Judah and the Negev of Caleb. And we burned Ziklag."

¹⁵David asked him, "Can you lead me down to this raiding party?"

He answered, "Swear to me before God that you will not kill me or hand me over to my master, and I will take you down to them."

¹⁶He led David down, and there they were, scattered over the countryside, eating, drinking and reveling because of the great amount of plunder they had taken from the land of the Philistines and from Judah. ¹⁷David fought them from dusk until the evening of the next day, and none of them got away, except four hundred young men who rode off on camels and fled. ¹⁸David recovered everything the Amalekites had taken, including his two wives. ¹⁹Nothing was missing: young or old, boy or girl, plunder or anything else they had taken. David brought everything back. ²⁰He took all the flocks and herds, and his men drove them ahead of the other livestock, saying, "This is David's plunder."

²¹Then David came to the two hundred men who had been too exhausted to follow him and who were left behind at the Besor Ravine. They

DAVID WAS GREATLY DISTRESSED
BECAUSE THE MEN WERE TALKING OF
STONING HIM; EACH ONE WAS BITTER
IN SPIRIT BECAUSE OF HIS SONS
AND DAUGHTERS. BUT DAVID FOUND
STRENGTH IN THE LORD HIS GOD.

1 Samuel 30:6

Strength in Adversity

REBECCA MANLEY PIPPERT

READ | 1 SAMUEL 30:1 – 31

The measure of a person is seen in his or her response to adversity. There are many temptations in adversity: blaming God for the problem, denying responsibility, justifying or defending oneself to others, etc. Yet, when the pressure was the fiercest at Ziklag, we are told that David "found strength in the LORD his God."

David's life reminds us that being a believer, or even a future king, does not protect us from the ambiguities of life. God "sends rain on the righteous and the unrighteous" (Matthew 5:45). Our relationship with God does not protect us from the storm, but through knowing him, we are protected from the storm's power to destroy us. Indeed, God will use our suffering to forge our character and strengthen our faith.

But we must do our part. We need to be realistic about the fact that life is difficult. Instead of blaming God for our trials, we must turn to him, for he alone can give us the resources we need to overcome them. Let's follow David's example as we walk through life's difficulties and especially as we encourage our loved ones as they face trials. Let's teach them to pour out their honest feelings about their situation to the One who loves them, to the One who is there for them and longs to demonstrate that he will never let his children down. Not ever.

When trials come and people lash out at me, give me your strength, Lord. Close my mouth so I will not say words that I will regret. Open my heart to your love and to family and friends who understand and know my true character. Help me to remember that I live to please you; it is your opinion alone that matters eternally. Strengthen my faith through these trials. Amen.

Your next devotion is located on page 427.

GRANDCHILD IN FOCUS • PRAYER

SELECT ONE OF YOUR
GRANDCHILDREN TO FOCUS ON
IN PRAYER FOR THE NEXT 14 DAYS.

Salvation

Dear Lord, please guide my grandchild to your gift of salvation. I pray that she will come to know you, to love you and to walk close to you throughout her life. May she boldly claim Jesus as her Lord and Savior. Guide her as she makes choices that have eternal consequences. Help her to follow you each moment of her life. I pray this in Jesus' name, amen.

came out to meet David and the people with him. As David and his men approached, he greeted them. ²²But all the evil men and troublemakers among David's followers said, "Because they did not go out with us, we will not share with them the plunder we recovered. However, each man may take his wife and children and go."

²³David replied, "No, my brothers, you must not do that with what the Lord has given us. He has protected us and handed over to us the forces that came against us. ²⁴Who will listen to what you say? The share of the man who stayed with the supplies is to be the same as that of him who went down to the battle. All will share alike." ²⁵David made this a statute and ordinance for Israel from that day to this.

²⁶When David arrived in Ziklag, he sent some of the plunder to the elders of Judah, who were his friends, saying, "Here is a present for you from the plunder of the Lord's enemies."

²⁷He sent it to those who were in Bethel, Ramoth Negev and Jattir; ²⁸to those in Aroer, Siphmoth, Eshtemoa ²⁹and Racal; to those in the towns of the Jerahmeelites and the Kenites; ³⁰to those in Hormah, Bor Ashan, Athach ³¹and Hebron; and to those in all the other places where David and his men had roamed.

Saul Takes His Life

31:1–13pp — 2Sa 1:4–12; 1Ch 10:1–12

31 Now the Philistines fought against Israel; the Israelites fled before them, and many fell slain on Mount Gilboa. ²The Philistines pressed hard after Saul and his sons, and they killed his sons Jonathan, Abinadab and Malki-Shua. ³The fighting grew fierce around Saul, and when the archers overtook him, they wounded him critically.

⁴Saul said to his armor-bearer, "Draw your sword and run me through, or these uncircumcised fellows will come and run me through and abuse me."

But his armor-bearer was terrified and would not do it; so Saul took his own sword and fell on it. ⁵When the armor-bearer saw that Saul was dead, he too fell on his sword and died with him. ⁶So Saul and his three sons and his armor-bearer and all his men died together that same day.

⁷When the Israelites along the valley and those across the Jordan saw that the Israelite army had fled and that Saul and his sons had died, they abandoned their towns and fled. And the Philistines came and occupied them.

⁸The next day, when the Philistines came to strip the dead, they found Saul and his three sons fallen on Mount Gilboa. ⁹They cut off his head and stripped off his armor, and they sent messengers throughout the land of the Philistines to proclaim the news in the temple of their idols and among their people. ¹⁰They put his armor in the temple of the Ashtoreths and fastened his body to the wall of Beth Shan.

¹¹When the people of Jabesh Gilead heard of what the Philistines had done to Saul, ¹²all their valiant men journeyed through the night to Beth Shan. They took down the bodies of Saul and his sons from the wall of Beth Shan and went to Jabesh, where they burned them. ¹³Then they took their bones and buried them under a tamarisk tree at Jabesh, and they fasted seven days.

Problems
IN THE FAMILY

What we know as 1 and 2 Samuel were originally one book. Second Samuel details the accomplishments of King David, one of the greatest leaders of the nation of Israel. It also gives us a look into David's personal life. Although he was an exemplary leader, "a man after [God's] own heart" (1 Samuel 13:14), the author of 2 Samuel doesn't try to hide any of the issues that plagued David personally.

This book describes the infamous affair between David and Bathsheba. When David discovered that Bathsheba was pregnant with his child, he plotted to kill her husband, Uriah the Hittite (see 2 Samuel 11). The extensive consequences of his sin plagued him and his family both immediately, when his baby son died, and later, when some of his other children committed unspeakable horrors against each other (see 2 Samuel 12–13). Though David was good at governing and controlling his nation, he was unable to do either within his own family.

Unfortunately, we can often relate to David's family problems. We read about them in our daily newspapers and confront them at our own front doors. But hope is not lost. Even though those who walk with God are not sheltered from the consequences of their decisions, God never abandons his children. From David's story, we can be assured that our faithful God forgives and continues to love us and our families throughout our lives (see 2 Samuel 12:13; Psalm 51).

VERSE *to* REMEMBER | 2 SAMUEL 22:31

"As for God, his way is perfect; the word of the LORD is flawless. He is a shield for all who take refuge in him."

ABOUT 2 SAMUEL

WRITTEN BY:
Unknown

WRITTEN FOR:
God's chosen people, the Israelites

DATE WRITTEN:
Sometime after Israel divided into the northern and southern kingdoms in 930 B.C.

WHY WRITTEN:
To tell the story of David's 40-year reign as Israel's king

David Hears of Saul's Death

1:4–12pp — 1Sa 31:1–13; 1Ch 10:1–12

After the death of Saul, David returned from defeating the Amalekites and stayed in Ziklag two days. ²On the third day a man arrived from Saul's camp, with his clothes torn and with dust on his head. When he came to David, he fell to the ground to pay him honor.

³"Where have you come from?" David asked him.

He answered, "I have escaped from the Israelite camp."

⁴"What happened?" David asked. "Tell me."

He said, "The men fled from the battle. Many of them fell and died. And Saul and his son Jonathan are dead."

⁵Then David said to the young man who brought him the report, "How do you know that Saul and his son Jonathan are dead?"

⁶"I happened to be on Mount Gilboa," the young man said, "and there was Saul, leaning on his spear, with the chariots and riders almost upon him. ⁷When he turned around and saw me, he called out to me, and I said, 'What can I do?'

⁸"He asked me, 'Who are you?'

"'An Amalekite,' I answered.

⁹"Then he said to me, 'Stand over me and kill me! I am in the throes of death, but I'm still alive.'

¹⁰"So I stood over him and killed him, because I knew that after he had fallen he could not survive. And I took the crown that was on his head and the band on his arm and have brought them here to my lord."

¹¹Then David and all the men with him took hold of their clothes and tore them. ¹²They mourned and wept and fasted till evening for Saul and his son Jonathan, and for the army of the LORD and the house of Israel, because they had fallen by the sword.

¹³David said to the young man who brought him the report, "Where are you from?"

"I am the son of an alien, an Amalekite," he answered.

¹⁴David asked him, "Why were you not afraid to lift your hand to destroy the LORD's anointed?"

¹⁵Then David called one of his men and said, "Go, strike him down!" So he struck him down, and he died. ¹⁶For David had said to him, "Your blood be on your own head. Your own mouth testified against you when you said, 'I killed the LORD's anointed.'"

David's Lament for Saul and Jonathan

¹⁷David took up this lament concerning Saul and his son Jonathan, ¹⁸and ordered that the men of Judah be taught this lament of the bow (it is written in the Book of Jashar):

¹⁹"Your glory, O Israel, lies slain on your heights.
　　How the mighty have fallen!

²⁰"Tell it not in Gath,
　　proclaim it not in the streets of Ashkelon,
　lest the daughters of the Philistines be glad,
　　lest the daughters of the uncircumcised
　　　rejoice.

²¹"O mountains of Gilboa,
　　may you have neither dew nor rain,
　　nor fields that yield offerings ⌐of grain⌐.
　For there the shield of the mighty was defiled,
　　the shield of Saul—no longer rubbed with
　　　oil.

²²From the blood of the slain,
　　from the flesh of the mighty,
　the bow of Jonathan did not turn back,
　　the sword of Saul did not return
　　　unsatisfied.

²³"Saul and Jonathan—
　　in life they were loved and gracious,
　　and in death they were not parted.
　They were swifter than eagles,
　　they were stronger than lions.

²⁴"O daughters of Israel,
　　weep for Saul,
　who clothed you in scarlet and finery,
　　who adorned your garments with
　　　ornaments of gold.

25 "How the mighty have fallen in battle!
　　Jonathan lies slain on your heights.
26 I grieve for you, Jonathan my brother;
　　you were very dear to me.
　Your love for me was wonderful,
　　more wonderful than that of women.

27 "How the mighty have fallen!
　　The weapons of war have perished!"

David Anointed King Over Judah

2 In the course of time, David inquired of the
　LORD. "Shall I go up to one of the towns of
Judah?" he asked.

The LORD said, "Go up."

David asked, "Where shall I go?"

"To Hebron," the LORD answered.

2 So David went up there with his two wives,
Ahinoam of Jezreel and Abigail, the widow of
Nabal of Carmel. 3 David also took the men who
were with him, each with his family, and they set-
tled in Hebron and its towns. 4 Then the men of
Judah came to Hebron and there they anointed
David king over the house of Judah.

When David was told that it was the men of Jabesh Gilead who had buried Saul, 5 he sent messengers to the men of Jabesh Gilead to say to them,
"The LORD bless you for showing this kindness to
Saul your master by burying him. 6 May the LORD
now show you kindness and faithfulness, and I
too will show you the same favor because you
have done this. 7 Now then, be strong and brave,
for Saul your master is dead, and the house of Judah has anointed me king over them."

War Between the Houses of David and Saul

3:2–5pp — 1Ch 3:1–4

8 Meanwhile, Abner son of Ner, the commander of Saul's army, had taken Ish-Bosheth son of
Saul and brought him over to Mahanaim. 9 He
made him king over Gilead, Ashuri[a] and Jezreel,
and also over Ephraim, Benjamin and all Israel.

10 Ish-Bosheth son of Saul was forty years old
when he became king over Israel, and he reigned
two years. The house of Judah, however, followed
David. 11 The length of time David was king in
Hebron over the house of Judah was seven years
and six months.

12 Abner son of Ner, together with the men
of Ish-Bosheth son of Saul, left Mahanaim and
went to Gibeon. 13 Joab son of Zeruiah and David's men went out and met them at the pool of
Gibeon. One group sat down on one side of the
pool and one group on the other side.

14 Then Abner said to Joab, "Let's have some of
the young men get up and fight hand to hand in
front of us."

"All right, let them do it," Joab said.

15 So they stood up and were counted off —
twelve men for Benjamin and Ish-Bosheth son
of Saul, and twelve for David. 16 Then each man
grabbed his opponent by the head and thrust
his dagger into his opponent's side, and they
fell down together. So that place in Gibeon was
called Helkath Hazzurim.[b]

17 The battle that day was very fierce, and Abner and the men of Israel were defeated by David's men.

18 The three sons of Zeruiah were there: Joab,
Abishai and Asahel. Now Asahel was as fleet-footed as a wild gazelle. 19 He chased Abner, turning
neither to the right nor to the left as he pursued
him. 20 Abner looked behind him and asked, "Is
that you, Asahel?"

"It is," he answered.

21 Then Abner said to him, "Turn aside to the
right or to the left; take on one of the young men
and strip him of his weapons." But Asahel would
not stop chasing him.

22 Again Abner warned Asahel, "Stop chasing
me! Why should I strike you down? How could I
look your brother Joab in the face?"

23 But Asahel refused to give up the pursuit;
so Abner thrust the butt of his spear into Asahel's stomach, and the spear came out through
his back. He fell there and died on the spot. And
every man stopped when he came to the place
where Asahel had fallen and died.

---

a 9 Or *Asher*　b 16 *Helkath Hazzurim* means *field of daggers* or
field of hostilities.

24 But Joab and Abishai pursued Abner, and as the sun was setting, they came to the hill of Ammah, near Giah on the way to the wasteland of Gibeon. 25 Then the men of Benjamin rallied behind Abner. They formed themselves into a group and took their stand on top of a hill.

26 Abner called out to Joab, "Must the sword devour forever? Don't you realize that this will end in bitterness? How long before you order your men to stop pursuing their brothers?"

27 Joab answered, "As surely as God lives, if you had not spoken, the men would have continued the pursuit of their brothers until morning. *a*"

28 So Joab blew the trumpet, and all the men came to a halt; they no longer pursued Israel, nor did they fight anymore.

29 All that night Abner and his men marched through the Arabah. They crossed the Jordan, continued through the whole Bithron *b* and came to Mahanaim.

30 Then Joab returned from pursuing Abner and assembled all his men. Besides Asahel, nineteen of David's men were found missing. 31 But David's men had killed three hundred and sixty Benjamites who were with Abner. 32 They took Asahel and buried him in his father's tomb at Bethlehem. Then Joab and his men marched all night and arrived at Hebron by daybreak.

3 The war between the house of Saul and the house of David lasted a long time. David grew stronger and stronger, while the house of Saul grew weaker and weaker.

2 Sons were born to David in Hebron:

His firstborn was Amnon the son of Ahinoam of Jezreel;

3 his second, Kileab the son of Abigail the widow of Nabal of Carmel;

the third, Absalom the son of Maacah daughter of Talmai king of Geshur;

4 the fourth, Adonijah the son of Haggith;

the fifth, Shephatiah the son of Abital;

5 and the sixth, Ithream the son of David's wife Eglah.

These were born to David in Hebron.

Abner Goes Over to David

6 During the war between the house of Saul and the house of David, Abner had been strengthening his own position in the house of Saul. 7 Now Saul had had a concubine named Rizpah daughter of Aiah. And Ish-Bosheth said to Abner, "Why did you sleep with my father's concubine?"

8 Abner was very angry because of what Ish-Bosheth said and he answered, "Am I a dog's head—on Judah's side? This very day I am loyal to the house of your father Saul and to his family and friends. I haven't handed you over to David. Yet now you accuse me of an offense involving this woman! 9 May God deal with Abner, be it ever so severely, if I do not do for David what the LORD promised him on oath 10 and transfer the kingdom from the house of Saul and establish David's throne over Israel and Judah from Dan to Beersheba." 11 Ish-Bosheth did not dare to say another word to Abner, because he was afraid of him.

12 Then Abner sent messengers on his behalf to say to David, "Whose land is it? Make an agreement with me, and I will help you bring all Israel over to you."

13 "Good," said David. "I will make an agreement with you. But I demand one thing of you: Do not come into my presence unless you bring Michal daughter of Saul when you come to see me." 14 Then David sent messengers to Ish-Bosheth son of Saul, demanding, "Give me my wife Michal, whom I betrothed to myself for the price of a hundred Philistine foreskins."

15 So Ish-Bosheth gave orders and had her taken away from her husband Paltiel son of Laish. 16 Her husband, however, went with her, weeping behind her all the way to Bahurim. Then Abner said to him, "Go back home!" So he went back.

17 Abner conferred with the elders of Israel and said, "For some time you have wanted to make David your king. 18 Now do it! For the LORD promised

a 27 Or spoken this morning, the men would not have taken up the pursuit of their brothers; or spoken, the men would have given up the pursuit of their brothers by morning   b 29 Or morning; or ravine; the meaning of the Hebrew for this word is uncertain.

David, 'By my servant David I will rescue my people Israel from the hand of the Philistines and from the hand of all their enemies.'"

¹⁹Abner also spoke to the Benjamites in person. Then he went to Hebron to tell David everything that Israel and the whole house of Benjamin wanted to do. ²⁰When Abner, who had twenty men with him, came to David at Hebron, David prepared a feast for him and his men. ²¹Then Abner said to David, "Let me go at once and assemble all Israel for my lord the king, so that they may make a compact with you, and that you may rule over all that your heart desires." So David sent Abner away, and he went in peace.

Joab Murders Abner

²²Just then David's men and Joab returned from a raid and brought with them a great deal of plunder. But Abner was no longer with David in Hebron, because David had sent him away, and he had gone in peace. ²³When Joab and all the soldiers with him arrived, he was told that Abner son of Ner had come to the king and that the king had sent him away and that he had gone in peace.

²⁴So Joab went to the king and said, "What have you done? Look, Abner came to you. Why did you let him go? Now he is gone! ²⁵You know Abner son of Ner; he came to deceive you and observe your movements and find out everything you are doing."

²⁶Joab then left David and sent messengers after Abner, and they brought him back from the well of Sirah. But David did not know it. ²⁷Now when Abner returned to Hebron, Joab took him aside into the gateway, as though to speak with him privately. And there, to avenge the blood of his brother Asahel, Joab stabbed him in the stomach, and he died.

²⁸Later, when David heard about this, he said, "I and my kingdom are forever innocent before the LORD concerning the blood of Abner son of Ner. ²⁹May his blood fall upon the head of Joab and upon all his father's house! May Joab's house never be without someone who has a running sore or leprosy*ᵃ* or who leans on a crutch or who falls by the sword or who lacks food."

³⁰(Joab and his brother Abishai murdered Abner because he had killed their brother Asahel in the battle at Gibeon.)

³¹Then David said to Joab and all the people with him, "Tear your clothes and put on sackcloth and walk in mourning in front of Abner." King David himself walked behind the bier. ³²They buried Abner in Hebron, and the king wept aloud at Abner's tomb. All the people wept also.

³³The king sang this lament for Abner:

"Should Abner have died as the lawless die?
³⁴   Your hands were not bound,
    your feet were not fettered.
You fell as one falls before wicked men."

And all the people wept over him again.

³⁵Then they all came and urged David to eat something while it was still day; but David took an oath, saying, "May God deal with me, be it ever so severely, if I taste bread or anything else before the sun sets!"

³⁶All the people took note and were pleased; indeed, everything the king did pleased them. ³⁷So on that day all the people and all Israel knew that the king had no part in the murder of Abner son of Ner.

³⁸Then the king said to his men, "Do you not realize that a prince and a great man has fallen in Israel this day? ³⁹And today, though I am the anointed king, I am weak, and these sons of Zeruiah are too strong for me. May the LORD repay the evildoer according to his evil deeds!"

Ish-Bosheth Murdered

4 When Ish-Bosheth son of Saul heard that Abner had died in Hebron, he lost courage, and all Israel became alarmed. ²Now Saul's son had two men who were leaders of raiding bands. One was named Baanah and the other Recab; they were sons of Rimmon the Beerothite from the

---

ᵃ 29 The Hebrew word was used for various diseases affecting the skin—not necessarily leprosy.

tribe of Benjamin—Beeroth is considered part of Benjamin, ³because the people of Beeroth fled to Gittaim and have lived there as aliens to this day.

⁴(Jonathan son of Saul had a son who was lame in both feet. He was five years old when the news about Saul and Jonathan came from Jezreel. His nurse picked him up and fled, but as she hurried to leave, he fell and became crippled. His name was Mephibosheth.)

stories to share

2 SAMUEL 4:4; 9:1–13

David and Mephibosheth

LIFE LESSON: God expects us to keep our promises.

TO TALK ABOUT

✦ How did Mephibosheth get hurt?

✦ How old was he when this happened?

✦ Why might Mephibosheth have been afraid of David at first?

✦ Have you ever kept a promise you made to God or to someone else?

⁵Now Recab and Baanah, the sons of Rimmon the Beerothite, set out for the house of Ish-Bosheth, and they arrived there in the heat of the day while he was taking his noonday rest. ⁶They went into the inner part of the house as if to get some wheat, and they stabbed him in the stomach. Then Recab and his brother Baanah slipped away.

⁷They had gone into the house while he was lying on the bed in his bedroom. After they stabbed and killed him, they cut off his head. Taking it with them, they traveled all night by way of the Arabah. ⁸They brought the head of Ish-Bosheth to David at Hebron and said to the king, "Here is the head of Ish-Bosheth son of Saul, your enemy, who tried to take your life. This day the LORD has avenged my lord the king against Saul and his offspring."

⁹David answered Recab and his brother Baanah, the sons of Rimmon the Beerothite, "As surely as the LORD lives, who has delivered me out of all trouble, ¹⁰when a man told me, 'Saul is dead,' and thought he was bringing good news, I seized him and put him to death in Ziklag. That was the reward I gave him for his news! ¹¹How much more—when wicked men have killed an innocent man in his own house and on his own bed—should I not now demand his blood from your hand and rid the earth of you!"

¹²So David gave an order to his men, and they killed them. They cut off their hands and feet and hung the bodies by the pool in Hebron. But they took the head of Ish-Bosheth and buried it in Abner's tomb at Hebron.

David Becomes King Over Israel
5:1–3pp — 1Ch 11:1–3

5 All the tribes of Israel came to David at Hebron and said, "We are your own flesh and blood. ²In the past, while Saul was king over us, you were the one who led Israel on their military campaigns. And the LORD said to you, 'You will shepherd my people Israel, and you will become their ruler.'"

³When all the elders of Israel had come to King David at Hebron, the king made a compact with them at Hebron before the LORD, and they anointed David king over Israel.

⁴David was thirty years old when he became king, and he reigned forty years. ⁵In Hebron he reigned over Judah seven years and six months, and in Jerusalem he reigned over all Israel and Judah thirty-three years.

David Conquers Jerusalem

5:6–10pp — 1Ch 11:4–9
5:11–16pp — 1Ch 3:5–9; 14:1–7

⁶The king and his men marched to Jerusalem to attack the Jebusites, who lived there. The Jebusites said to David, "You will not get in here; even the blind and the lame can ward you off." They thought, "David cannot get in here." ⁷Nevertheless, David captured the fortress of Zion, the City of David.

⁸On that day, David said, "Anyone who conquers the Jebusites will have to use the water shaft ᵃ to reach those 'lame and blind' who are David's enemies. ᵇ" That is why they say, "The 'blind and lame' will not enter the palace."

⁹David then took up residence in the fortress and called it the City of David. He built up the area around it, from the supporting terraces ᶜ inward. ¹⁰And he became more and more powerful, because the Lord God Almighty was with him.

¹¹Now Hiram king of Tyre sent messengers to David, along with cedar logs and carpenters and stonemasons, and they built a palace for David. ¹²And David knew that the Lord had established him as king over Israel and had exalted his kingdom for the sake of his people Israel.

¹³After he left Hebron, David took more concubines and wives in Jerusalem, and more sons and daughters were born to him. ¹⁴These are the names of the children born to him there: Shammua, Shobab, Nathan, Solomon, ¹⁵Ibhar, Elishua, Nepheg, Japhia, ¹⁶Elishama, Eliada and Eliphelet.

David Defeats the Philistines

5:17–25pp — 1Ch 14:8–17

¹⁷When the Philistines heard that David had been anointed king over Israel, they went up in full force to search for him, but David heard about it and went down to the stronghold. ¹⁸Now the Philistines had come and spread out in the Valley of Rephaim; ¹⁹so David inquired of the Lord, "Shall I go and attack the Philistines? Will you hand them over to me?"

The Lord answered him, "Go, for I will surely hand the Philistines over to you."

stories to share

2 SAMUEL 5:1–5,17–25

David Becomes King of Israel

LIFE LESSON: When we trust in God, he helps us.

TO TALK ABOUT

✦ How old was David when he became king?

✦ What did David do when he heard that the Philistines were coming to attack him?

✦ How did God help David in the two battles?

✦ Why do you think God helped David?

²⁰So David went to Baal Perazim, and there he defeated them. He said, "As waters break out, the Lord has broken out against my enemies before me." So that place was called Baal Perazim. ᵈ ²¹The Philistines abandoned their idols there, and David and his men carried them off.

²²Once more the Philistines came up and spread out in the Valley of Rephaim; ²³so David inquired of the Lord, and he answered, "Do not go straight up, but circle around behind them and attack them in front of the balsam trees. ²⁴As soon as you hear the sound of marching in the tops of the balsam trees, move quickly, because that will mean the Lord has gone out in front of you to

ᵃ 8 Or *use scaling hooks*   ᵇ 8 Or *are hated by David*   ᶜ 9 *Or the Millo*   ᵈ 20 *Baal Perazim* means *the lord who breaks out*.

strike the Philistine army." [25] So David did as the LORD commanded him, and he struck down the Philistines all the way from Gibeon[a] to Gezer.

The Ark Brought to Jerusalem

6:1–11pp — 1Ch 13:1–14
6:12–19pp — 1Ch 15:25–16:3

6 David again brought together out of Israel chosen men, thirty thousand in all. [2] He and all his men set out from Baalah of Judah[b] to bring up from there the ark of God, which is called by the Name,[c] the name of the LORD Almighty, who is enthroned between the cherubim that are on the ark. [3] They set the ark of God on a new cart and brought it from the house of Abinadab, which was on the hill. Uzzah and Ahio, sons of Abinadab, were guiding the new cart [4] with the ark of God on it,[d] and Ahio was walking in front of it. [5] David and the whole house of Israel were celebrating with all their might before the LORD, with songs[e] and with harps, lyres, tambourines, sistrums and cymbals.

[6] When they came to the threshing floor of Nacon, Uzzah reached out and took hold of the ark of God, because the oxen stumbled. [7] The LORD's anger burned against Uzzah because of his irreverent act; therefore God struck him down and he died there beside the ark of God.

[8] Then David was angry because the LORD's wrath had broken out against Uzzah, and to this day that place is called Perez Uzzah.[f]

[9] David was afraid of the LORD that day and said, "How can the ark of the LORD ever come to me?" [10] He was not willing to take the ark of the LORD to be with him in the City of David. Instead, he took it aside to the house of Obed-Edom the Gittite. [11] The ark of the LORD remained in the house of Obed-Edom the Gittite for three months, and the LORD blessed him and his entire household.

[12] Now King David was told, "The LORD has blessed the household of Obed-Edom and everything he has, because of the ark of God." So David went down and brought up the ark of God from the house of Obed-Edom to the City of David

with rejoicing. [13] When those who were carrying the ark of the LORD had taken six steps, he sacrificed a bull and a fattened calf. [14] David, wearing a linen ephod, danced before the LORD with all his might, [15] while he and the entire house of Israel brought up the ark of the LORD with shouts and the sound of trumpets.

[16] As the ark of the LORD was entering the City of David, Michal daughter of Saul watched from a window. And when she saw King David leaping and dancing before the LORD, she despised him in her heart.

[17] They brought the ark of the LORD and set it in its place inside the tent that David had pitched for it, and David sacrificed burnt offerings and fellowship offerings[g] before the LORD. [18] After he had finished sacrificing the burnt offerings and fellowship offerings, he blessed the people in the name of the LORD Almighty. [19] Then he gave a loaf of bread, a cake of dates and a cake of raisins to each person in the whole crowd of Israelites, both men and women. And all the people went to their homes.

[20] When David returned home to bless his household, Michal daughter of Saul came out to meet him and said, "How the king of Israel has distinguished himself today, disrobing in the sight of the slave girls of his servants as any vulgar fellow would!"

[21] David said to Michal, "It was before the LORD, who chose me rather than your father or anyone from his house when he appointed me ruler over the LORD's people Israel — I will celebrate before the LORD. [22] I will become even more undignified than this, and I will be humiliated in my own eyes. But by these slave girls you spoke of, I will be held in honor."

---

[a] 25 Septuagint (see also 1 Chron. 14:16); Hebrew *Geba* [b] 2 That is, Kiriath Jearim; Hebrew *Baale Judah*, a variant of *Baalah of Judah* [c] 2 Hebrew; Septuagint and Vulgate do not have *the Name*. [d] 3,4 Dead Sea Scrolls and some Septuagint manuscripts; Masoretic Text *cart* [4] *and they brought it with the ark of God from the house of Abinadab, which was on the hill* [e] 5 See Dead Sea Scrolls, Septuagint and 1 Chronicles 13:8; Masoretic Text *celebrating before the LORD with all kinds of instruments made of pine.* [f] 8 *Perez Uzzah* means *outbreak against Uzzah.* [g] 17 Traditionally *peace offerings*; also in verse 18

²³ And Michal daughter of Saul had no children to the day of her death.

God's Promise to David

7:1–17pp — 1Ch 17:1–15

7 After the king was settled in his palace and the LORD had given him rest from all his enemies around him, ² he said to Nathan the prophet, "Here I am, living in a palace of cedar, while the ark of God remains in a tent."

³ Nathan replied to the king, "Whatever you have in mind, go ahead and do it, for the LORD is with you."

⁴ That night the word of the LORD came to Nathan, saying:

⁵ "Go and tell my servant David, 'This is what the LORD says: Are you the one to build me a house to dwell in? ⁶ I have not dwelt in a house from the day I brought the Israelites up out of Egypt to this day. I have been moving from place to place with a tent as my dwelling. ⁷ Wherever I have moved with all the Israelites, did I ever say to any of their rulers whom I commanded to shepherd my people Israel, "Why have you not built me a house of cedar?" '

⁸ "Now then, tell my servant David, 'This is what the LORD Almighty says: I took you from the pasture and from following the flock to be ruler over my people Israel. ⁹ I have been with you wherever you have gone, and I have cut off all your enemies from before you. Now I will make your name great, like the names of the greatest men of the earth. ¹⁰ And I will provide a place for my people Israel and will plant them so that they can have a home of their own and no longer be disturbed. Wicked people will not oppress them anymore, as they did at the beginning ¹¹ and have done ever since the time I appointed leaders[a] over my people Israel. I will also give you rest from all your enemies.

" 'The LORD declares to you that the LORD himself will establish a house for you:

¹² When your days are over and you rest with your fathers, I will raise up your offspring to succeed you, who will come from your own body, and I will establish his kingdom. ¹³ He is the one who will build a house for my Name, and I will establish the throne of his kingdom forever. ¹⁴ I will be his father, and he will be my son. When he does wrong, I will punish him with the rod of men, with floggings inflicted by men. ¹⁵ But my love will never be taken away from him, as I took it away from Saul, whom I removed from before you. ¹⁶ Your house and your kingdom will endure forever before me[b]; your throne will be established forever.' "

¹⁷ Nathan reported to David all the words of this entire revelation.

David's Prayer

7:18–29pp — 1Ch 17:16–27

¹⁸ Then King David went in and sat before the LORD, and he said:

"Who am I, O Sovereign LORD, and what is my family, that you have brought me this far? ¹⁹ And as if this were not enough in your sight, O Sovereign LORD, you have also spoken about the future of the house of your servant. Is this your usual way of dealing with man, O Sovereign LORD?

²⁰ "What more can David say to you? For you know your servant, O Sovereign LORD. ²¹ For the sake of your word and according to your will, you have done this great thing and made it known to your servant.

²² "How great you are, O Sovereign LORD! There is no one like you, and there is no God but you, as we have heard with our own ears. ²³ And who is like your people Israel—the one nation on earth that God went out to redeem as a people for himself, and to make a name for himself, and to perform great and awesome wonders by driving out

---

a 11 Traditionally *judges*   *b 16* Some Hebrew manuscripts and Septuagint; most Hebrew manuscripts *you* nations and their gods from before your people, whom you redeemed from Egypt?[a] [24]You have established your people Israel as your very own forever, and you, O Lord, have become their God.

[25]"And now, Lord God, keep forever the promise you have made concerning your servant and his house. Do as you promised, [26]so that your name will be great forever. Then men will say, 'The Lord Almighty is God over Israel!' And the house of your servant David will be established before you.

[27]"O Lord Almighty, God of Israel, you have revealed this to your servant, saying, 'I will build a house for you.' So your servant has found courage to offer you this prayer. [28]O Sovereign Lord, you are God! Your words are trustworthy, and you have promised these good things to your servant. [29]Now be pleased to bless the house of your servant, that it may continue forever in your sight; for you, O Sovereign Lord, have spoken, and with your blessing the house of your servant will be blessed forever."

David's Victories

8:1–14pp — 1Ch 18:1–13

8 In the course of time, David defeated the Philistines and subdued them, and he took Metheg Ammah from the control of the Philistines.

[2]David also defeated the Moabites. He made them lie down on the ground and measured them off with a length of cord. Every two lengths of them were put to death, and the third length was allowed to live. So the Moabites became subject to David and brought tribute.

[3]Moreover, David fought Hadadezer son of Rehob, king of Zobah, when he went to restore his control along the Euphrates River. [4]David captured a thousand of his chariots, seven thousand charioteers[b] and twenty thousand foot soldiers. He hamstrung all but a hundred of the chariot horses.

[5]When the Arameans of Damascus came to help Hadadezer king of Zobah, David struck down twenty-two thousand of them. [6]He put garrisons in the Aramean kingdom of Damascus, and the Arameans became subject to him and brought tribute. The Lord gave David victory wherever he went.

[7]David took the gold shields that belonged to the officers of Hadadezer and brought them to Jerusalem. [8]From Tebah[c] and Berothai, towns that belonged to Hadadezer, King David took a great quantity of bronze.

[9]When Tou[d] king of Hamath heard that David had defeated the entire army of Hadadezer, [10]he sent his son Joram[e] to King David to greet him and congratulate him on his victory in battle over Hadadezer, who had been at war with Tou. Joram brought with him articles of silver and gold and bronze.

[11]King David dedicated these articles to the Lord, as he had done with the silver and gold from all the nations he had subdued: [12]Edom[f] and Moab, the Ammonites and the Philistines, and Amalek. He also dedicated the plunder taken from Hadadezer son of Rehob, king of Zobah.

[13]And David became famous after he returned from striking down eighteen thousand Edomites[g] in the Valley of Salt.

[14]He put garrisons throughout Edom, and all the Edomites became subject to David. The Lord gave David victory wherever he went.

David's Officials

8:15–18pp — 1Ch 18:14–17

[15]David reigned over all Israel, doing what was just and right for all his people. [16]Joab son of Zeruiah was over the army; Jehoshaphat son of Ahilud was recorder; [17]Zadok son of Ahitub and Ahimelech son of Abiathar were priests; Seraiah

---

[a] *23* See Septuagint and 1 Chron. 17:21; Hebrew *wonders for your land and before your people, whom you redeemed from Egypt, from the nations and their gods.*   [b] *4* Septuagint (see also Dead Sea Scrolls and 1 Chron. 18:4); Masoretic Text *captured seventeen hundred of his charioteers*   [c] *8* See some Septuagint manuscripts (see also 1 Chron. 18:8); Hebrew *Betah.*   [d] *9* Hebrew *Toi,* a variant of *Tou;* also in verse 10   [e] *10* A variant of *Hadoram*   [f] *12* Some Hebrew manuscripts, Septuagint and Syriac (see also 1 Chron. 18:11); most Hebrew manuscripts *Aram*   [g] *13* A few Hebrew manuscripts, Septuagint and Syriac (see also 1 Chron. 18:12); most Hebrew manuscripts *Aram* (that is, Arameans)

was secretary; [18]Benaiah son of Jehoiada was over the Kerethites and Pelethites; and David's sons were royal advisers. [a]

David and Mephibosheth

9 David asked, "Is there anyone still left of the house of Saul to whom I can show kindness for Jonathan's sake?"

[2]Now there was a servant of Saul's household named Ziba. They called him to appear before David, and the king said to him, "Are you Ziba?"

"Your servant," he replied.

[3]The king asked, "Is there no one still left of the house of Saul to whom I can show God's kindness?"

Ziba answered the king, "There is still a son of Jonathan; he is crippled in both feet."

[4]"Where is he?" the king asked.

Ziba answered, "He is at the house of Makir son of Ammiel in Lo Debar."

[5]So King David had him brought from Lo Debar, from the house of Makir son of Ammiel.

[6]When Mephibosheth son of Jonathan, the son of Saul, came to David, he bowed down to pay him honor.

David said, "Mephibosheth!"

"Your servant," he replied.

[7]"Don't be afraid," David said to him, "for I will surely show you kindness for the sake of your father Jonathan. I will restore to you all the land that belonged to your grandfather Saul, and you will always eat at my table."

[8]Mephibosheth bowed down and said, "What is your servant, that you should notice a dead dog like me?"

[9]Then the king summoned Ziba, Saul's servant, and said to him, "I have given your master's grandson everything that belonged to Saul and his family. [10]You and your sons and your servants are to farm the land for him and bring in the crops, so that your master's grandson may be provided for. And Mephibosheth, grandson of your master, will always eat at my table." (Now Ziba had fifteen sons and twenty servants.)

[11]Then Ziba said to the king, "Your servant will do whatever my lord the king commands his servant to do." So Mephibosheth ate at David's [b] table like one of the king's sons.

[12]Mephibosheth had a young son named Mica, and all the members of Ziba's household were servants of Mephibosheth. [13]And Mephibosheth lived in Jerusalem, because he always ate at the king's table, and he was crippled in both feet.

David Defeats the Ammonites

10:1–19pp — 1Ch 19:1–19

10 In the course of time, the king of the Ammonites died, and his son Hanun succeeded him as king. [2]David thought, "I will show kindness to Hanun son of Nahash, just as his father showed kindness to me." So David sent a delegation to express his sympathy to Hanun concerning his father.

When David's men came to the land of the Ammonites, [3]the Ammonite nobles said to Hanun their lord, "Do you think David is honoring your father by sending men to you to express sympathy? Hasn't David sent them to you to explore the city and spy it out and overthrow it?" [4]So Hanun seized David's men, shaved off half of each man's beard, cut off their garments in the middle at the buttocks, and sent them away.

[5]When David was told about this, he sent messengers to meet the men, for they were greatly humiliated. The king said, "Stay at Jericho till your beards have grown, and then come back."

TALKING POINTS

Disability

David was kind to Jonathan's disabled son.

2 SAMUEL 9:1–13

For more on disability, go to Matthew 15:29–39.

---

[a] 18 Or were priests   [b] 11 Septuagint; Hebrew my

⁶When the Ammonites realized that they had become a stench in David's nostrils, they hired twenty thousand Aramean foot soldiers from Beth Rehob and Zobah, as well as the king of Maacah with a thousand men, and also twelve thousand men from Tob.

⁷On hearing this, David sent Joab out with the entire army of fighting men. ⁸The Ammonites came out and drew up in battle formation at the entrance to their city gate, while the Arameans of Zobah and Rehob and the men of Tob and Maacah were by themselves in the open country.

⁹Joab saw that there were battle lines in front of him and behind him; so he selected some of the best troops in Israel and deployed them against the Arameans. ¹⁰He put the rest of the men under the command of Abishai his brother and deployed them against the Ammonites. ¹¹Joab said, "If the Arameans are too strong for me, then you are to come to my rescue; but if the Ammonites are too strong for you, then I will come to rescue you. ¹²Be strong and let us fight bravely for our people and the cities of our God. The LORD will do what is good in his sight."

¹³Then Joab and the troops with him advanced to fight the Arameans, and they fled before him. ¹⁴When the Ammonites saw that the Arameans were fleeing, they fled before Abishai and went inside the city. So Joab returned from fighting the Ammonites and came to Jerusalem.

¹⁵After the Arameans saw that they had been routed by Israel, they regrouped. ¹⁶Hadadezer had Arameans brought from beyond the River[a]; they went to Helam, with Shobach the commander of Hadadezer's army leading them.

¹⁷When David was told of this, he gathered all Israel, crossed the Jordan and went to Helam. The Arameans formed their battle lines to meet David and fought against him. ¹⁸But they fled before Israel, and David killed seven hundred of their charioteers and forty thousand of their foot soldiers.[b] He also struck down Shobach the commander of their army, and he died there. ¹⁹When all the kings who were vassals of Hadadezer saw that they had been defeated by Israel, they made

peace with the Israelites and became subject to them.

So the Arameans were afraid to help the Ammonites anymore.

David and Bathsheba

11 In the spring, at the time when kings go off to war, David sent Joab out with the king's men and the whole Israelite army. They destroyed the Ammonites and besieged Rabbah. But David remained in Jerusalem.

²One evening David got up from his bed and walked around on the roof of the palace. From the roof he saw a woman bathing. The woman was very beautiful, ³and David sent someone to find out about her. The man said, "Isn't this Bathsheba, the daughter of Eliam and the wife of Uriah the Hittite?" ⁴Then David sent messengers to get her. She came to him, and he slept with her. (She had purified herself from her uncleanness.) Then[c] she went back home. ⁵The woman conceived and sent word to David, saying, "I am pregnant."

⁶So David sent this word to Joab: "Send me Uriah the Hittite." And Joab sent him to David. ⁷When Uriah came to him, David asked him how Joab was, how the soldiers were and how the war was going. ⁸Then David said to Uriah, "Go down to your house and wash your feet." So Uriah left the palace, and a gift from the king was sent after him. ⁹But Uriah slept at the entrance to the palace with all his master's servants and did not go down to his house.

¹⁰When David was told, "Uriah did not go home," he asked him, "Haven't you just come from a distance? Why didn't you go home?"

¹¹Uriah said to David, "The ark and Israel and Judah are staying in tents, and my master Joab and my lord's men are camped in the open fields. How could I go to my house to eat and drink and lie with my wife? As surely as you live, I will not do such a thing!"

---

[a] 16 That is, the Euphrates   [b] 18 Some Septuagint manuscripts (see also 1 Chron. 19:18); Hebrew *horsemen*   [c] 4 Or *with her. When she purified herself from her uncleanness,*

¹²Then David said to him, "Stay here one more day, and tomorrow I will send you back." So Uriah remained in Jerusalem that day and the next. ¹³At David's invitation, he ate and drank with him, and David made him drunk. But in the evening Uriah went out to sleep on his mat among his master's servants; he did not go home.

¹⁴In the morning David wrote a letter to Joab and sent it with Uriah. ¹⁵In it he wrote, "Put Uriah in the front line where the fighting is fiercest. Then withdraw from him so he will be struck down and die."

¹⁶So while Joab had the city under siege, he put Uriah at a place where he knew the strongest defenders were. ¹⁷When the men of the city came out and fought against Joab, some of the men in David's army fell; moreover, Uriah the Hittite died.

¹⁸Joab sent David a full account of the battle. ¹⁹He instructed the messenger: "When you have finished giving the king this account of the battle, ²⁰the king's anger may flare up, and he may ask you, 'Why did you get so close to the city to fight? Didn't you know they would shoot arrows from the wall? ²¹Who killed Abimelech son of Jerub-Besheth ª? Didn't a woman throw an upper millstone on him from the wall, so that he died in Thebez? Why did you get so close to the wall?' If he asks you this, then say to him, 'Also, your servant Uriah the Hittite is dead.'"

²²The messenger set out, and when he arrived he told David everything Joab had sent him to say. ²³The messenger said to David, "The men overpowered us and came out against us in the open, but we drove them back to the entrance to the city gate. ²⁴Then the archers shot arrows at your servants from the wall, and some of the king's men died. Moreover, your servant Uriah the Hittite is dead."

²⁵David told the messenger, "Say this to Joab: 'Don't let this upset you; the sword devours one as well as another. Press the attack against the city and destroy it.' Say this to encourage Joab."

²⁶When Uriah's wife heard that her husband was dead, she mourned for him. ²⁷After the time of mourning was over, David had her brought to his house, and she became his wife and bore him a son. But the thing David had done displeased the LORD.

Nathan Rebukes David

11:1; 12:29–31pp — 1Ch 20:1–3

12 The LORD sent Nathan to David. When he came to him, he said, "There were two men in a certain town, one rich and the other poor. ²The rich man had a very large number of sheep and cattle, ³but the poor man had nothing except one little ewe lamb he had bought. He raised it, and it grew up with him and his children. It shared his food, drank from his cup and even slept in his arms. It was like a daughter to him.

⁴"Now a traveler came to the rich man, but the rich man refrained from taking one of his own sheep or cattle to prepare a meal for the traveler who had come to him. Instead, he took the ewe lamb that belonged to the poor man and prepared it for the one who had come to him."

⁵David burned with anger against the man and said to Nathan, "As surely as the LORD lives, the man who did this deserves to die! ⁶He must pay for that lamb four times over, because he did such a thing and had no pity."

⁷Then Nathan said to David, "You are the man! This is what the LORD, the God of Israel, says: 'I anointed you king over Israel, and I delivered you from the hand of Saul. ⁸I gave your master's house to you, and your master's wives into your arms. I gave you the house of Israel and Judah. And if all this had been too little, I would have given you even more. ⁹Why did you despise the word of the LORD by doing what is evil in his eyes? You struck down Uriah the Hittite with the sword and took his wife to be your own. You killed him with the sword of the Ammonites. ¹⁰Now, therefore, the sword will never depart from your house, because you despised me and took the wife of Uriah the Hittite to be your own.'

ª 21 Also known as *Jerub-Baal* (that is, Gideon)

¹¹ "This is what the LORD says: 'Out of your own household I am going to bring calamity upon you. Before your very eyes I will take your wives and give them to one who is close to you, and he will lie with your wives in broad daylight. ¹² You did it in secret, but I will do this thing in broad daylight before all Israel.' "

¹³ Then David said to Nathan, "I have sinned against the LORD."

Nathan replied, "The LORD has taken away your sin. You are not going to die. ¹⁴ But because by doing this you have made the enemies of the LORD show utter contempt,ᵃ the son born to you will die."

¹⁵ After Nathan had gone home, the LORD struck the child that Uriah's wife had borne to David, and he became ill. ¹⁶ David pleaded with God for the child. He fasted and went into his house and spent the nights lying on the ground. ¹⁷ The elders of his household stood beside him to get him up from the ground, but he refused, and he would not eat any food with them.

¹⁸ On the seventh day the child died. David's servants were afraid to tell him that the child was dead, for they thought, "While the child was still living, we spoke to David but he would not listen to us. How can we tell him the child is dead? He may do something desperate."

¹⁹ David noticed that his servants were whispering among themselves and he realized the child was dead. "Is the child dead?" he asked.

"Yes," they replied, "he is dead."

²⁰ Then David got up from the ground. After he had washed, put on lotions and changed his clothes, he went into the house of the LORD and worshiped. Then he went to his own house, and at his request they served him food, and he ate.

²¹ His servants asked him, "Why are you acting this way? While the child was alive, you fasted and wept, but now that the child is dead, you get up and eat!"

²² He answered, "While the child was still alive, I fasted and wept. I thought, 'Who knows? The LORD may be gracious to me and let the child live.' ²³ But now that he is dead, why should I fast? Can I bring him back again? I will go to him, but he will not return to me."

²⁴ Then David comforted his wife Bathsheba, and he went to her and lay with her. She gave birth to a son, and they named him Solomon. The LORD loved him; ²⁵ and because the LORD loved him, he sent word through Nathan the prophet to name him Jedidiah.ᵇ

²⁶ Meanwhile Joab fought against Rabbah of the Ammonites and captured the royal citadel. ²⁷ Joab then sent messengers to David, saying, "I have fought against Rabbah and taken its water supply. ²⁸ Now muster the rest of the troops and besiege the city and capture it. Otherwise I will take the city, and it will be named after me."

²⁹ So David mustered the entire army and went to Rabbah, and attacked and captured it. ³⁰ He took the crown from the head of their kingᶜ— its weight was a talentᵈ of gold, and it was set with precious stones—and it was placed on David's head. He took a great quantity of plunder from the city ³¹ and brought out the people who were there, consigning them to labor with saws and with iron picks and axes, and he made them work at brickmaking.ᵉ He did this to all the Ammonite towns. Then David and his entire army returned to Jerusalem.

Amnon and Tamar

13 In the course of time, Amnon son of David fell in love with Tamar, the beautiful sister of Absalom son of David.

² Amnon became frustrated to the point of illness on account of his sister Tamar, for she was a virgin, and it seemed impossible for him to do anything to her.

³ Now Amnon had a friend named Jonadab son of Shimeah, David's brother. Jonadab was a very shrewd man. ⁴ He asked Amnon, "Why do you, the king's son, look so haggard morning after morning? Won't you tell me?"

ᵃ *14* Masoretic Text; an ancient Hebrew scribal tradition *this you have shown utter contempt for the LORD*   ᵇ *25 Jedidiah* means *loved by the LORD.*   ᶜ *30* Or *of Milcom* (that is, Molech)   ᵈ *30* That is, about 75 pounds (about 34 kilograms)   ᵉ *31* The meaning of the Hebrew for this clause is uncertain.

CLAUDIA ARP

You're Not Alone—
EVERYONE STRUGGLES

The favorite children's book *Alexander and the Terrible, Horrible, No Good, Very Bad Day* is a simple tale of a young boy who has a terrible day. Our young grandkids love this book — especially on days that don't go right. Amazingly, they seem to feel better knowing that even the fictional Alexander knew what it was like to have a bad day. But don't we all need someone to empathize with us from time to time?

Our own very bad days can lengthen into years of turmoil and sorrow when our families are in trouble: grandchildren who are involved in dangerous situations, children who are having marital problems, relatives who are arguing. Even though we would like a trouble-free family, all families have their own difficulties to accept and overcome.

Even the Saints Struggled

Know that you are not alone in your family struggles. Before you there lived many "saints" who struggled feebly through this life in the broad sweep of human history, and you are even now surrounded by "a great cloud of witnesses" (Hebrews 12:1). And guess what? They all had difficulties with their families too! If you don't believe me, just read about the families in the Old Testament.

Take the famous King David. Because he was a king and chosen by God, one would think that he would have had an easy life. But he suffered incredible loss and pain within his family — albeit as the result of his own poor choices (see 2 Samuel 12:7 – 14). They say that misery loves company, but I believe that when the going gets tough, we all need to know that others have experienced similar problems.

Regarding very complex problems, the painful truth is that in some situations very little can actually be done to solve the problem or make it go away — at least in the short term. That's why it's important to learn to accept the fact that none of us has control over every matter under heaven. We are not God. We are all finite, limited and sinful creatures — all of whom fall short of the glory of God.

Practice the Power of Prayer

When dealing with hard issues, the one thing that we can do is pray. Prayer helps a lot. Prayer is the best medicine that I know. Prayer even has an effect on the one who prays, and remember: we are praying to our heavenly Father, who is the author of every good and perfect gift and the creator of families.

Years ago, Reinhold Niebuhr penned a helpful prayer that has become popularly known as "The Serenity Prayer" and has been used by millions of folks who are in desperate circumstances. Read these words prayerfully and adopt them as your own: "God, give us grace to accept with serenity the things that cannot be changed, the courage to change the things that should be changed, and the wisdom to distinguish the one from the other. Amen."

Praying this particular prayer (or a similar one) can soothe your soul and give you strength to do only those things that matter or help. But don't be afraid to also pray for specific things, understanding that ultimately your goal is God's will. In Matthew 26 Jesus is our model. In the garden of Gethsemane he prayed, "May this cup be taken from me." But he concluded his prayer with, "Yet not as I will, but as you will" (Matthew 26:39). Ultimately our goal should not be to exert our own will but to see that God's will is done. God's ways are higher, more mysterious and more marvelous than our ways. So pray for your loved ones and trust them to his loving care.

Stay Connected

As you are praying, do what you can do to stay connected and in relationship with those who are mired in difficulty or those making life difficult for all. All too often when people are angry or disappointed with others, they shut off communication. Much better is to remain in contact with all the parties until an opportunity for reconciliation occurs. Yes, it may test your patience and your faith. You may need to "turn the other cheek" and "go the extra mile," as Jesus encouraged his disciples to do (see Matthew 5:39,41). But who knows when the light of God might shower down upon everyone and a new day might dawn. By staying in relationship, you might find yourself in a better position to be a positive witness and influence on others. Remember, nothing is impossible with God's help.

Do you need the capital of other women together with you in your life? It's a silly question, I know. What woman doesn't? And that's why I hope you have it. If not, I hope you'll pursue it through friendships and support groups, within your church, your family and your community.

Amnon said to him, "I'm in love with Tamar, my brother Absalom's sister."

⁵"Go to bed and pretend to be ill," Jonadab said. "When your father comes to see you, say to him, 'I would like my sister Tamar to come and give me something to eat. Let her prepare the food in my sight so I may watch her and then eat it from her hand.'"

⁶So Amnon lay down and pretended to be ill. When the king came to see him, Amnon said to him, "I would like my sister Tamar to come and make some special bread in my sight, so I may eat from her hand."

⁷David sent word to Tamar at the palace: "Go to the house of your brother Amnon and prepare some food for him." ⁸So Tamar went to the house of her brother Amnon, who was lying down. She took some dough, kneaded it, made the bread in his sight and baked it. ⁹Then she took the pan and served him the bread, but he refused to eat.

"Send everyone out of here," Amnon said. So everyone left him. ¹⁰Then Amnon said to Tamar, "Bring the food here into my bedroom so I may eat from your hand." And Tamar took the bread she had prepared and brought it to her brother Amnon in his bedroom. ¹¹But when she took it to him to eat, he grabbed her and said, "Come to bed with me, my sister."

¹²"Don't, my brother!" she said to him. "Don't force me. Such a thing should not be done in Israel! Don't do this wicked thing. ¹³What about me? Where could I get rid of my disgrace? And what about you? You would be like one of the wicked fools in Israel. Please speak to the king; he will not keep me from being married to you." ¹⁴But he refused to listen to her, and since he was stronger than she, he raped her.

¹⁵Then Amnon hated her with intense hatred. In fact, he hated her more than he had loved her. Amnon said to her, "Get up and get out!"

¹⁶"No!" she said to him. "Sending me away would be a greater wrong than what you have already done to me."

But he refused to listen to her. ¹⁷He called his personal servant and said, "Get this woman out of here and bolt the door after her." ¹⁸So his servant put her out and bolted the door after her. She was wearing a richly ornamented *ᵃ* robe, for this was the kind of garment the virgin daughters of the king wore. ¹⁹Tamar put ashes on her head and tore the ornamented *ᵇ* robe she was wearing. She put her hand on her head and went away, weeping aloud as she went.

²⁰Her brother Absalom said to her, "Has that Amnon, your brother, been with you? Be quiet now, my sister; he is your brother. Don't take this thing to heart." And Tamar lived in her brother Absalom's house, a desolate woman.

²¹When King David heard all this, he was furious. ²²Absalom never said a word to Amnon, either good or bad; he hated Amnon because he had disgraced his sister Tamar.

Absalom Kills Amnon

²³Two years later, when Absalom's sheepshearers were at Baal Hazor near the border of Ephraim, he invited all the king's sons to come there. ²⁴Absalom went to the king and said, "Your servant has had shearers come. Will the king and his officials please join me?"

²⁵"No, my son," the king replied. "All of us should not go; we would only be a burden to you." Although Absalom urged him, he still refused to go, but gave him his blessing.

²⁶Then Absalom said, "If not, please let my brother Amnon come with us."

The king asked him, "Why should he go with you?" ²⁷But Absalom urged him, so he sent with him Amnon and the rest of the king's sons.

²⁸Absalom ordered his men, "Listen! When Amnon is in high spirits from drinking wine and I say to you, 'Strike Amnon down,' then kill him. Don't be afraid. Have not I given you this order? Be strong and brave." ²⁹So Absalom's men did to Amnon what Absalom had ordered. Then all the king's sons got up, mounted their mules and fled.

³⁰While they were on their way, the report came to David: "Absalom has struck down all the

---

ᵃ 18 The meaning of the Hebrew for this phrase is uncertain.
ᵇ 19 The meaning of the Hebrew for this word is uncertain.

king's sons; not one of them is left." ³¹The king stood up, tore his clothes and lay down on the ground; and all his servants stood by with their clothes torn.

³²But Jonadab son of Shimeah, David's brother, said, "My lord should not think that they killed all the princes; only Amnon is dead. This has been Absalom's expressed intention ever since the day Amnon raped his sister Tamar. ³³My lord the king should not be concerned about the report that all the king's sons are dead. Only Amnon is dead."

³⁴Meanwhile, Absalom had fled.

Now the man standing watch looked up and saw many people on the road west of him, coming down the side of the hill. The watchman went and told the king, "I see men in the direction of Horonaim, on the side of the hill."ᵃ

³⁵Jonadab said to the king, "See, the king's sons are here; it has happened just as your servant said."

³⁶As he finished speaking, the king's sons came in, wailing loudly. The king, too, and all his servants wept very bitterly.

³⁷Absalom fled and went to Talmai son of Ammihud, the king of Geshur. But King David mourned for his son every day.

³⁸After Absalom fled and went to Geshur, he stayed there three years. ³⁹And the spirit of the kingᵇ longed to go to Absalom, for he was consoled concerning Amnon's death.

Absalom Returns to Jerusalem

14 Joab son of Zeruiah knew that the king's heart longed for Absalom. ²So Joab sent someone to Tekoa and had a wise woman brought from there. He said to her, "Pretend you are in mourning. Dress in mourning clothes, and don't use any cosmetic lotions. Act like a woman who has spent many days grieving for the dead. ³Then go to the king and speak these words to him." And Joab put the words in her mouth.

⁴When the woman from Tekoa wentᶜ to the king, she fell with her face to the ground to pay him honor, and she said, "Help me, O king!"

⁵The king asked her, "What is troubling you?"

She said, "I am indeed a widow; my husband is dead. ⁶I your servant had two sons. They got into a fight with each other in the field, and no one was there to separate them. One struck the other and killed him. ⁷Now the whole clan has risen up against your servant; they say, 'Hand over the one who struck his brother down, so that we may put him to death for the life of his brother whom he killed; then we will get rid of the heir as well.' They would put out the only burning coal I have left, leaving my husband neither name nor descendant on the face of the earth."

⁸The king said to the woman, "Go home, and I will issue an order in your behalf."

⁹But the woman from Tekoa said to him, "My lord the king, let the blame rest on me and on my father's family, and let the king and his throne be without guilt."

¹⁰The king replied, "If anyone says anything to you, bring him to me, and he will not bother you again."

¹¹She said, "Then let the king invoke the LORD his God to prevent the avenger of blood from adding to the destruction, so that my son will not be destroyed."

"As surely as the LORD lives," he said, "not one hair of your son's head will fall to the ground."

¹²Then the woman said, "Let your servant speak a word to my lord the king."

"Speak," he replied.

¹³The woman said, "Why then have you devised a thing like this against the people of God? When the king says this, does he not convict himself, for the king has not brought back his banished son? ¹⁴Like water spilled on the ground, which cannot be recovered, so we must die. But God does not take away life; instead, he devises ways so that a banished person may not remain estranged from him.

¹⁵"And now I have come to say this to my lord the king because the people have made me afraid.

ᵃ 34 Septuagint; Hebrew does not have this sentence.   ᵇ 39 Dead Sea Scrolls and some Septuagint manuscripts; Masoretic Text *But the spirit of, David the king*   ᶜ 4 Many Hebrew manuscripts, Septuagint, Vulgate and Syriac; most Hebrew manuscripts *spoke*

Your servant thought, 'I will speak to the king; perhaps he will do what his servant asks. [16]Perhaps the king will agree to deliver his servant from the hand of the man who is trying to cut off both me and my son from the inheritance God gave us.'

[17]"And now your servant says, 'May the word of my lord the king bring me rest, for my lord the king is like an angel of God in discerning good and evil. May the LORD your God be with you.'"

[18]Then the king said to the woman, "Do not keep from me the answer to what I am going to ask you."

"Let my lord the king speak," the woman said.

[19]The king asked, "Isn't the hand of Joab with you in all this?"

The woman answered, "As surely as you live, my lord the king, no one can turn to the right or to the left from anything my lord the king says. Yes, it was your servant Joab who instructed me to do this and who put all these words into the mouth of your servant. [20]Your servant Joab did this to change the present situation. My lord has wisdom like that of an angel of God — he knows everything that happens in the land."

[21]The king said to Joab, "Very well, I will do it. Go, bring back the young man Absalom."

[22]Joab fell with his face to the ground to pay him honor, and he blessed the king. Joab said, "Today your servant knows that he has found favor in your eyes, my lord the king, because the king has granted his servant's request."

[23]Then Joab went to Geshur and brought Absalom back to Jerusalem. [24]But the king said, "He must go to his own house; he must not see my face." So Absalom went to his own house and did not see the face of the king.

[25]In all Israel there was not a man so highly praised for his handsome appearance as Absalom. From the top of his head to the sole of his foot there was no blemish in him. [26]Whenever he cut the hair of his head — he used to cut his hair from time to time when it became too heavy for him — he would weigh it, and its weight was two hundred shekels[a] by the royal standard.

[27]Three sons and a daughter were born to Absalom. The daughter's name was Tamar, and she became a beautiful woman.

[28]Absalom lived two years in Jerusalem without seeing the king's face. [29]Then Absalom sent for Joab in order to send him to the king, but Joab refused to come to him. So he sent a second time, but he refused to come. [30]Then he said to his servants, "Look, Joab's field is next to mine, and he has barley there. Go and set it on fire." So Absalom's servants set the field on fire.

[31]Then Joab did go to Absalom's house and he said to him, "Why have your servants set my field on fire?"

[32]Absalom said to Joab, "Look, I sent word to you and said, 'Come here so I can send you to the king to ask, "Why have I come from Geshur? It would be better for me if I were still there!"' Now then, I want to see the king's face, and if I am guilty of anything, let him put me to death."

[33]So Joab went to the king and told him this. Then the king summoned Absalom, and he came in and bowed down with his face to the ground before the king. And the king kissed Absalom.

Absalom's Conspiracy

15 In the course of time, Absalom provided himself with a chariot and horses and with fifty men to run ahead of him. [2]He would get up early and stand by the side of the road leading to the city gate. Whenever anyone came with a complaint to be placed before the king for a decision, Absalom would call out to him, "What town are you from?" He would answer, "Your servant is from one of the tribes of Israel." [3]Then Absalom would say to him, "Look, your claims are valid and proper, but there is no representative of the king to hear you." [4]And Absalom would add, "If only I were appointed judge in the land! Then everyone who has a complaint or case could come to me and I would see that he gets justice."

[5]Also, whenever anyone approached him to bow down before him, Absalom would reach out

a 26 That is, about 5 pounds (about 2.3 kilograms)

his hand, take hold of him and kiss him. ⁶Absalom behaved in this way toward all the Israelites who came to the king asking for justice, and so he stole the hearts of the men of Israel.

⁷At the end of four *a* years, Absalom said to the king, "Let me go to Hebron and fulfill a vow I made to the LORD. ⁸While your servant was living at Geshur in Aram, I made this vow: 'If the LORD takes me back to Jerusalem, I will worship the LORD in Hebron. *b* '"

⁹The king said to him, "Go in peace." So he went to Hebron.

¹⁰Then Absalom sent secret messengers throughout the tribes of Israel to say, "As soon as you hear the sound of the trumpets, then say, 'Absalom is king in Hebron.'" ¹¹Two hundred men from Jerusalem had accompanied Absalom. They had been invited as guests and went quite innocently, knowing nothing about the matter. ¹²While Absalom was offering sacrifices, he also sent for Ahithophel the Gilonite, David's counselor, to come from Giloh, his hometown. And so the conspiracy gained strength, and Absalom's following kept on increasing.

David Flees

¹³A messenger came and told David, "The hearts of the men of Israel are with Absalom."

¹⁴Then David said to all his officials who were with him in Jerusalem, "Come! We must flee, or none of us will escape from Absalom. We must leave immediately, or he will move quickly to overtake us and bring ruin upon us and put the city to the sword."

¹⁵The king's officials answered him, "Your servants are ready to do whatever our lord the king chooses."

¹⁶The king set out, with his entire household following him; but he left ten concubines to take care of the palace. ¹⁷So the king set out, with all the people following him, and they halted at a place some distance away. ¹⁸All his men marched past him, along with all the Kerethites and Pelethites; and all the six hundred Gittites who had accompanied him from Gath marched before the king.

¹⁹The king said to Ittai the Gittite, "Why should you come along with us? Go back and stay with King Absalom. You are a foreigner, an exile from your homeland. ²⁰You came only yesterday. And today shall I make you wander about with us, when I do not know where I am going? Go back, and take your countrymen. May kindness and faithfulness be with you."

²¹But Ittai replied to the king, "As surely as the LORD lives, and as my lord the king lives, wherever my lord the king may be, whether it means life or death, there will your servant be."

²²David said to Ittai, "Go ahead, march on." So Ittai the Gittite marched on with all his men and the families that were with him.

²³The whole countryside wept aloud as all the people passed by. The king also crossed the Kidron Valley, and all the people moved on toward the desert.

²⁴Zadok was there, too, and all the Levites who were with him were carrying the ark of the covenant of God. They set down the ark of God, and Abiathar offered sacrifices *c* until all the people had finished leaving the city.

²⁵Then the king said to Zadok, "Take the ark of God back into the city. If I find favor in the LORD's eyes, he will bring me back and let me see it and his dwelling place again. ²⁶But if he says, 'I am not pleased with you,' then I am ready; let him do to me whatever seems good to him."

²⁷The king also said to Zadok the priest, "Aren't you a seer? Go back to the city in peace, with your son Ahimaaz and Jonathan son of Abiathar. You and Abiathar take your two sons with you. ²⁸I will wait at the fords in the desert until word comes from you to inform me." ²⁹So Zadok and Abiathar took the ark of God back to Jerusalem and stayed there.

³⁰But David continued up the Mount of Olives, weeping as he went; his head was covered and he was barefoot. All the people with him covered their heads too and were weeping as they

---

a 7 Some Septuagint manuscripts, Syriac and Josephus; Hebrew forty   *b 8 Some Septuagint manuscripts; Hebrew does not have in Hebron.*   *c 24 Or Abiathar went up* went up. [31] Now David had been told, "Ahithophel is among the conspirators with Absalom." So David prayed, "O LORD, turn Ahithophel's counsel into foolishness."

[32] When David arrived at the summit, where people used to worship God, Hushai the Arkite was there to meet him, his robe torn and dust on his head. [33] David said to him, "If you go with me, you will be a burden to me. [34] But if you return to the city and say to Absalom, 'I will be your servant, O king; I was your father's servant in the past, but now I will be your servant,' then you can help me by frustrating Ahithophel's advice. [35] Won't the priests Zadok and Abiathar be there with you? Tell them anything you hear in the king's palace. [36] Their two sons, Ahimaaz son of Zadok and Jonathan son of Abiathar, are there with them. Send them to me with anything you hear."

[37] So David's friend Hushai arrived at Jerusalem as Absalom was entering the city.

TALKING POINTS

Rebellion

Absalom's rebellion led to his death and to heartache for his family.

2 SAMUEL 15:1—18:33

For more on rebellion, go to Daniel 9:4–10.

David and Ziba

16 When David had gone a short distance beyond the summit, there was Ziba, the steward of Mephibosheth, waiting to meet him. He had a string of donkeys saddled and loaded with two hundred loaves of bread, a hundred cakes of raisins, a hundred cakes of figs and a skin of wine.

[2] The king asked Ziba, "Why have you brought these?"

Ziba answered, "The donkeys are for the king's household to ride on, the bread and fruit are for the men to eat, and the wine is to refresh those who become exhausted in the desert."

[3] The king then asked, "Where is your master's grandson?"

Ziba said to him, "He is staying in Jerusalem, because he thinks, 'Today the house of Israel will give me back my grandfather's kingdom.'"

[4] Then the king said to Ziba, "All that belonged to Mephibosheth is now yours."

"I humbly bow," Ziba said. "May I find favor in your eyes, my lord the king."

Shimei Curses David

[5] As King David approached Bahurim, a man from the same clan as Saul's family came out from there. His name was Shimei son of Gera, and he cursed as he came out. [6] He pelted David and all the king's officials with stones, though all the troops and the special guard were on David's right and left. [7] As he cursed, Shimei said, "Get out, get out, you man of blood, you scoundrel! [8] The LORD has repaid you for all the blood you shed in the household of Saul, in whose place you have reigned. The LORD has handed the kingdom over to your son Absalom. You have come to ruin because you are a man of blood!"

[9] Then Abishai son of Zeruiah said to the king, "Why should this dead dog curse my lord the king? Let me go over and cut off his head."

[10] But the king said, "What do you and I have in common, you sons of Zeruiah? If he is cursing because the LORD said to him, 'Curse David,' who can ask, 'Why do you do this?'"

[11] David then said to Abishai and all his officials, "My son, who is of my own flesh, is trying to take my life. How much more, then, this Benjamite! Leave him alone; let him curse, for the LORD has told him to. [12] It may be that the LORD will see my distress and repay me with good for the cursing I am receiving today."

[13] So David and his men continued along the road while Shimei was going along the hillside opposite him, cursing as he went and throwing

> "IT MAY BE THAT THE LORD WILL SEE MY DISTRESS AND REPAY ME WITH GOOD FOR THE CURSING I AM RECEIVING TODAY."
>
> 2 Samuel 16:12

The Art of Handling Rebuke

RUTH A. DEJAGER

READ | 2 SAMUEL 16:5 – 14

Because I had six brothers, I sometimes played pirates or other battle games in the neighborhood with all the guys. When one of us was "shot" by another or run through with their sword, we were supposed to fall down on the ground for an indefinite time, thus "taking our deads." Now this was a terrible blow to one's pride, not to mention it took you out of the game. And after all, one could argue (and I usually did) that the other person had missed, since it was all imaginary.

Our human tendency when God (or one of his messengers) calls us to account for sin is not to "take our deads"; instead we argue, justify ourselves, blame someone else or rationalize our sin away. Not David. He knew how to accept a rebuke from God. He knew he deserved Shimei's cursing because of the open rebellion in his family, the result of his sin. He recognized the possibility that the curses were from the Lord, and he proclaimed his confidence in God's mercy. That takes humility. Perhaps he had learned that kind of humility when Nathan rebuked him for the way in which he took Bathsheba as his wife (see 2 Samuel 12). David knew that admitting guilt, confessing it and asking for God's forgiveness was the best choice. He had already learned that God "disciplines those he loves" (Proverbs 3:12) — and what a blessing that is, even if it hurts.

As I settle into middle age, I wonder if, even now, I've learned the fine art of correctly handling a rebuke. And when I need to ask for God's forgiveness, I turn again to David, using his words from Psalm 51, a prayer expressing his acceptance of God's rebuke.

"Create in me a pure heart, O God, and renew a steadfast spirit within me. Do not cast me from your presence or take your Holy Spirit from me. Restore to me the joy of your salvation and grant me a willing spirit, to sustain me." Amen.

Your next devotion is located on page 437.

GRANDCHILD IN FOCUS • PRAYER

Physical Well-Being

Almighty God, Creator of us all, I pray that you will watch over my grandchild's physical development. May he grow in strength through the stages of his life. As he grows in awareness of his body, help him to understand that each body develops uniquely, yet is within your plan and your control. Please guard his health so that his diseases are few, his injuries are minor and his infirmities are brief. Amen.

stones at him and showering him with dirt. [14] The king and all the people with him arrived at their destination exhausted. And there he refreshed himself.

The Advice of Ahithophel and Hushai

[15] Meanwhile, Absalom and all the men of Israel came to Jerusalem, and Ahithophel was with him. [16] Then Hushai the Arkite, David's friend, went to Absalom and said to him, "Long live the king! Long live the king!"

[17] Absalom asked Hushai, "Is this the love you show your friend? Why didn't you go with your friend?"

[18] Hushai said to Absalom, "No, the one chosen by the LORD, by these people, and by all the men of Israel—his I will be, and I will remain with him. [19] Furthermore, whom should I serve? Should I not serve the son? Just as I served your father, so I will serve you."

[20] Absalom said to Ahithophel, "Give us your advice. What should we do?"

[21] Ahithophel answered, "Lie with your father's concubines whom he left to take care of the palace. Then all Israel will hear that you have made yourself a stench in your father's nostrils, and the hands of everyone with you will be strengthened." [22] So they pitched a tent for Absalom on the roof, and he lay with his father's concubines in the sight of all Israel.

[23] Now in those days the advice Ahithophel gave was like that of one who inquires of God. That was how both David and Absalom regarded all of Ahithophel's advice.

17 Ahithophel said to Absalom, "I would[a] choose twelve thousand men and set out tonight in pursuit of David. [2] I would[b] attack him while he is weary and weak. I would[b] strike him with terror, and then all the people with him will flee. I would[b] strike down only the king [3] and bring all the people back to you. The death of the man you seek will mean the return of all; all the people will be unharmed." [4] This plan seemed good to Absalom and to all the elders of Israel.

[5] But Absalom said, "Summon also Hushai the Arkite, so we can hear what he has to say." [6] When Hushai came to him, Absalom said, "Ahithophel has given this advice. Should we do what he says? If not, give us your opinion."

[7] Hushai replied to Absalom, "The advice Ahithophel has given is not good this time. [8] You know your father and his men; they are fighters, and as fierce as a wild bear robbed of her cubs. Besides, your father is an experienced fighter; he will not spend the night with the troops. [9] Even now, he is hidden in a cave or some other place. If he should attack your troops first,[c] whoever hears about it will say, 'There has been a slaughter among the troops who follow Absalom.' [10] Then even the bravest soldier, whose heart is like the heart of a lion, will melt with fear, for all Israel knows that your father is a fighter and that those with him are brave.

[11] "So I advise you: Let all Israel, from Dan to Beersheba—as numerous as the sand on the seashore—be gathered to you, with you yourself leading them into battle. [12] Then we will attack him wherever he may be found, and we will fall on him as dew settles on the ground. Neither he nor any of his men will be left alive. [13] If he withdraws into a city, then all Israel will bring ropes to that city, and we will drag it down to the valley until not even a piece of it can be found."

[14] Absalom and all the men of Israel said, "The advice of Hushai the Arkite is better than that of Ahithophel." For the LORD had determined to frustrate the good advice of Ahithophel in order to bring disaster on Absalom.

[15] Hushai told Zadok and Abiathar, the priests, "Ahithophel has advised Absalom and the elders of Israel to do such and such, but I have advised them to do so and so. [16] Now send a message immediately and tell David, 'Do not spend the night at the fords in the desert; cross over without fail, or the king and all the people with him will be swallowed up.'"

[17] Jonathan and Ahimaaz were staying at En Rogel. A servant girl was to go and inform them,

---

[a] 1 Or Let me   [b] 2 Or will   [c] 9 Or When some of the men fall at the first attack

and they were to go and tell King David, for they could not risk being seen entering the city. ¹⁸But a young man saw them and told Absalom. So the two of them left quickly and went to the house of a man in Bahurim. He had a well in his courtyard, and they climbed down into it. ¹⁹His wife took a covering and spread it out over the opening of the well and scattered grain over it. No one knew anything about it.

²⁰When Absalom's men came to the woman at the house, they asked, "Where are Ahimaaz and Jonathan?"

The woman answered them, "They crossed over the brook."ᵃ The men searched but found no one, so they returned to Jerusalem.

²¹After the men had gone, the two climbed out of the well and went to inform King David. They said to him, "Set out and cross the river at once; Ahithophel has advised such and such against you." ²²So David and all the people with him set out and crossed the Jordan. By daybreak, no one was left who had not crossed the Jordan.

²³When Ahithophel saw that his advice had not been followed, he saddled his donkey and set out for his house in his hometown. He put his house in order and then hanged himself. So he died and was buried in his father's tomb.

²⁴David went to Mahanaim, and Absalom crossed the Jordan with all the men of Israel. ²⁵Absalom had appointed Amasa over the army in place of Joab. Amasa was the son of a man named Jether,ᵇ an Israeliteᶜ who had married Abigail,ᵈ the daughter of Nahash and sister of Zeruiah the mother of Joab. ²⁶The Israelites and Absalom camped in the land of Gilead.

²⁷When David came to Mahanaim, Shobi son of Nahash from Rabbah of the Ammonites, and Makir son of Ammiel from Lo Debar, and Barzillai the Gileadite from Rogelim ²⁸brought bedding and bowls and articles of pottery. They also brought wheat and barley, flour and roasted grain, beans and lentils,ᵉ ²⁹honey and curds, sheep, and cheese from cows' milk for David and his people to eat. For they said, "The people have become hungry and tired and thirsty in the desert."

Absalom's Death

18 David mustered the men who were with him and appointed over them commanders of thousands and commanders of hundreds. ²David sent the troops out—a third under the command of Joab, a third under Joab's brother Abishai son of Zeruiah, and a third under Ittai the Gittite. The king told the troops, "I myself will surely march out with you."

³But the men said, "You must not go out; if we are forced to flee, they won't care about us. Even if half of us die, they won't care; but you are worth ten thousand of us.ᶠ It would be better now for you to give us support from the city."

⁴The king answered, "I will do whatever seems best to you."

So the king stood beside the gate while all the men marched out in units of hundreds and of thousands. ⁵The king commanded Joab, Abishai and Ittai, "Be gentle with the young man Absalom for my sake." And all the troops heard the king giving orders concerning Absalom to each of the commanders.

⁶The army marched into the field to fight Israel, and the battle took place in the forest of Ephraim. ⁷There the army of Israel was defeated by David's men, and the casualties that day were great—twenty thousand men. ⁸The battle spread out over the whole countryside, and the forest claimed more lives that day than the sword.

⁹Now Absalom happened to meet David's men. He was riding his mule, and as the mule went under the thick branches of a large oak, Absalom's head got caught in the tree. He was left hanging in midair, while the mule he was riding kept on going.

¹⁰When one of the men saw this, he told Joab, "I just saw Absalom hanging in an oak tree."

¹¹Joab said to the man who had told him this,

ᵃ 20 Or "They passed by the sheep pen toward the water."
ᵇ 25 Hebrew *Ithra*, a variant of *Jether*   ᶜ 25 Hebrew and some Septuagint manuscripts; other Septuagint manuscripts (see also 1 Chron. 2:17) *Ishmaelite* or *Jezreelite*   ᵈ 25 Hebrew *Abigal*, a variant of *Abigail*   ᵉ 28 Most Septuagint manuscripts and Syriac; Hebrew *lentils, and roasted grain*   ᶠ 3 Two Hebrew manuscripts, some Septuagint manuscripts and Vulgate; most Hebrew manuscripts *care; for now there are ten thousand like us*

"What! You saw him? Why didn't you strike him to the ground right there? Then I would have had to give you ten shekels^a of silver and a warrior's belt."

¹²But the man replied, "Even if a thousand shekels^b were weighed out into my hands, I would not lift my hand against the king's son. In our hearing the king commanded you and Abishai and Ittai, 'Protect the young man Absalom for my sake.'^c ¹³And if I had put my life in jeopardy^d—and nothing is hidden from the king— you would have kept your distance from me."

¹⁴Joab said, "I'm not going to wait like this for you." So he took three javelins in his hand and plunged them into Absalom's heart while Absalom was still alive in the oak tree. ¹⁵And ten of Joab's armor-bearers surrounded Absalom, struck him and killed him.

¹⁶Then Joab sounded the trumpet, and the troops stopped pursuing Israel, for Joab halted them. ¹⁷They took Absalom, threw him into a big pit in the forest and piled up a large heap of rocks over him. Meanwhile, all the Israelites fled to their homes.

¹⁸During his lifetime Absalom had taken a pillar and erected it in the King's Valley as a monument to himself, for he thought, "I have no son to carry on the memory of my name." He named the pillar after himself, and it is called Absalom's Monument to this day.

David Mourns

¹⁹Now Ahimaaz son of Zadok said, "Let me run and take the news to the king that the LORD has delivered him from the hand of his enemies."

²⁰"You are not the one to take the news today," Joab told him. "You may take the news another time, but you must not do so today, because the king's son is dead."

²¹Then Joab said to a Cushite, "Go, tell the king what you have seen." The Cushite bowed down before Joab and ran off.

²²Ahimaaz son of Zadok again said to Joab, "Come what may, please let me run behind the Cushite."

But Joab replied, "My son, why do you want to go? You don't have any news that will bring you a reward."

²³He said, "Come what may, I want to run."

So Joab said, "Run!" Then Ahimaaz ran by way of the plain^e and outran the Cushite.

²⁴While David was sitting between the inner and outer gates, the watchman went up to the roof of the gateway by the wall. As he looked out, he saw a man running alone. ²⁵The watchman called out to the king and reported it.

The king said, "If he is alone, he must have good news." And the man came closer and closer.

²⁶Then the watchman saw another man running, and he called down to the gatekeeper, "Look, another man running alone!"

The king said, "He must be bringing good news, too."

²⁷The watchman said, "It seems to me that the first one runs like Ahimaaz son of Zadok."

"He's a good man," the king said. "He comes with good news."

²⁸Then Ahimaaz called out to the king, "All is well!" He bowed down before the king with his face to the ground and said, "Praise be to the LORD your God! He has delivered up the men who lifted their hands against my lord the king."

²⁹The king asked, "Is the young man Absalom safe?"

Ahimaaz answered, "I saw great confusion just as Joab was about to send the king's servant and me, your servant, but I don't know what it was."

³⁰The king said, "Stand aside and wait here." So he stepped aside and stood there.

³¹Then the Cushite arrived and said, "My lord the king, hear the good news! The LORD has delivered you today from all who rose up against you."

³²The king asked the Cushite, "Is the young man Absalom safe?"

---

^a 11 That is, about 4 ounces (about 115 grams)   ^b 12 That is, about 25 pounds (about 11 kilograms)   ^c 12 A few Hebrew manuscripts, Septuagint, Vulgate and Syriac; most Hebrew manuscripts may be translated *Absalom, whoever you may be.*
^d 13 Or *Otherwise, if I had acted treacherously toward him*
^e 23 That is, the plain of the Jordan

The Cushite replied, "May the enemies of my lord the king and all who rise up to harm you be like that young man."

33 The king was shaken. He went up to the room over the gateway and wept. As he went, he said: "O my son Absalom! My son, my son Absalom! If only I had died instead of you—O Absalom, my son, my son!"

19 Joab was told, "The king is weeping and mourning for Absalom." 2 And for the whole army the victory that day was turned into mourning, because on that day the troops heard it said, "The king is grieving for his son." 3 The men stole into the city that day as men steal in who are ashamed when they flee from battle. 4 The king covered his face and cried aloud, "O my son Absalom! O Absalom, my son, my son!"

5 Then Joab went into the house to the king and said, "Today you have humiliated all your men, who have just saved your life and the lives of your sons and daughters and the lives of your wives and concubines. 6 You love those who hate you and hate those who love you. You have made it clear today that the commanders and their men mean nothing to you. I see that you would be pleased if Absalom were alive today and all of us were dead. 7 Now go out and encourage your men. I swear by the LORD that if you don't go out, not a man will be left with you by nightfall. This will be worse for you than all the calamities that have come upon you from your youth till now."

8 So the king got up and took his seat in the gateway. When the men were told, "The king is sitting in the gateway," they all came before him.

David Returns to Jerusalem

Meanwhile, the Israelites had fled to their homes. 9 Throughout the tribes of Israel, the people were all arguing with each other, saying, "The king delivered us from the hand of our enemies; he is the one who rescued us from the hand of the Philistines. But now he has fled the country because of Absalom; 10 and Absalom, whom we anointed to rule over us, has died in battle. So why do you say nothing about bringing the king back?"

11 King David sent this message to Zadok and Abiathar, the priests: "Ask the elders of Judah, 'Why should you be the last to bring the king back to his palace, since what is being said throughout Israel has reached the king at his quarters? 12 You are my brothers, my own flesh and blood. So why should you be the last to bring back the king?' 13 And say to Amasa, 'Are you not my own flesh and blood? May God deal with me, be it ever so severely, if from now on you are not the commander of my army in place of Joab.' "

14 He won over the hearts of all the men of Judah as though they were one man. They sent word to the king, "Return, you and all your men." 15 Then the king returned and went as far as the Jordan.

Now the men of Judah had come to Gilgal to go out and meet the king and bring him across the Jordan. 16 Shimei son of Gera, the Benjamite from Bahurim, hurried down with the men of Judah to meet King David. 17 With him were a thousand Benjamites, along with Ziba, the steward of Saul's household, and his fifteen sons and twenty servants. They rushed to the Jordan, where the king was. 18 They crossed at the ford to take the king's household over and to do whatever he wished.

When Shimei son of Gera crossed the Jordan, he fell prostrate before the king 19 and said to him, "May my lord not hold me guilty. Do not remember how your servant did wrong on the day my lord the king left Jerusalem. May the king put it out of his mind. 20 For I your servant know that I have sinned, but today I have come here as the first of the whole house of Joseph to come down and meet my lord the king."

21 Then Abishai son of Zeruiah said, "Shouldn't Shimei be put to death for this? He cursed the LORD's anointed."

22 David replied, "What do you and I have in common, you sons of Zeruiah? This day you have become my adversaries! Should anyone be put to death in Israel today? Do I not know that

today I am king over Israel?" ²³ So the king said to Shimei, "You shall not die." And the king promised him on oath.

²⁴ Mephibosheth, Saul's grandson, also went down to meet the king. He had not taken care of his feet or trimmed his mustache or washed his clothes from the day the king left until the day he returned safely. ²⁵ When he came from Jerusalem to meet the king, the king asked him, "Why didn't you go with me, Mephibosheth?"

²⁶ He said, "My lord the king, since I your servant am lame, I said, 'I will have my donkey saddled and will ride on it, so I can go with the king.' But Ziba my servant betrayed me. ²⁷ And he has slandered your servant to my lord the king. My lord the king is like an angel of God; so do whatever pleases you. ²⁸ All my grandfather's descendants deserved nothing but death from my lord the king, but you gave your servant a place among those who eat at your table. So what right do I have to make any more appeals to the king?"

²⁹ The king said to him, "Why say more? I order you and Ziba to divide the fields."

³⁰ Mephibosheth said to the king, "Let him take everything, now that my lord the king has arrived home safely."

³¹ Barzillai the Gileadite also came down from Rogelim to cross the Jordan with the king and to send him on his way from there. ³² Now Barzillai was a very old man, eighty years of age. He had provided for the king during his stay in Mahanaim, for he was a very wealthy man. ³³ The king said to Barzillai, "Cross over with me and stay with me in Jerusalem, and I will provide for you."

³⁴ But Barzillai answered the king, "How many more years will I live, that I should go up to Jerusalem with the king? ³⁵ I am now eighty years old. Can I tell the difference between what is good and what is not? Can your servant taste what he eats and drinks? Can I still hear the voices of men and women singers? Why should your servant be an added burden to my lord the king? ³⁶ Your servant will cross over the Jordan with the king for a short distance, but why should the king reward me in this way? ³⁷ Let your servant return, that I may die in my own town near the tomb of my father and mother. But here is your servant Kimham. Let him cross over with my lord the king. Do for him whatever pleases you."

³⁸ The king said, "Kimham shall cross over with me, and I will do for him whatever pleases you. And anything you desire from me I will do for you."

³⁹ So all the people crossed the Jordan, and then the king crossed over. The king kissed Barzillai and gave him his blessing, and Barzillai returned to his home.

⁴⁰ When the king crossed over to Gilgal, Kimham crossed with him. All the troops of Judah and half the troops of Israel had taken the king over.

⁴¹ Soon all the men of Israel were coming to the king and saying to him, "Why did our brothers, the men of Judah, steal the king away and bring him and his household across the Jordan, together with all his men?"

⁴² All the men of Judah answered the men of Israel, "We did this because the king is closely related to us. Why are you angry about it? Have we eaten any of the king's provisions? Have we taken anything for ourselves?"

⁴³ Then the men of Israel answered the men of Judah, "We have ten shares in the king; and besides, we have a greater claim on David than you have. So why do you treat us with contempt? Were we not the first to speak of bringing back our king?"

But the men of Judah responded even more harshly than the men of Israel.

Sheba Rebels Against David

20 Now a troublemaker named Sheba son of Bicri, a Benjamite, happened to be there. He sounded the trumpet and shouted,

"We have no share in David,
    no part in Jesse's son!
Every man to his tent, O Israel!"

²So all the men of Israel deserted David to follow Sheba son of Bicri. But the men of Judah stayed by their king all the way from the Jordan to Jerusalem.

³When David returned to his palace in Jerusalem, he took the ten concubines he had left to take care of the palace and put them in a house under guard. He provided for them, but did not lie with them. They were kept in confinement till the day of their death, living as widows.

⁴Then the king said to Amasa, "Summon the men of Judah to come to me within three days, and be here yourself." ⁵But when Amasa went to summon Judah, he took longer than the time the king had set for him.

⁶David said to Abishai, "Now Sheba son of Bicri will do us more harm than Absalom did. Take your master's men and pursue him, or he will find fortified cities and escape from us." ⁷So Joab's men and the Kerethites and Pelethites and all the mighty warriors went out under the command of Abishai. They marched out from Jerusalem to pursue Sheba son of Bicri.

⁸While they were at the great rock in Gibeon, Amasa came to meet them. Joab was wearing his military tunic, and strapped over it at his waist was a belt with a dagger in its sheath. As he stepped forward, it dropped out of its sheath.

⁹Joab said to Amasa, "How are you, my brother?" Then Joab took Amasa by the beard with his right hand to kiss him. ¹⁰Amasa was not on his guard against the dagger in Joab's hand, and Joab plunged it into his belly, and his intestines spilled out on the ground. Without being stabbed again, Amasa died. Then Joab and his brother Abishai pursued Sheba son of Bicri.

¹¹One of Joab's men stood beside Amasa and said, "Whoever favors Joab, and whoever is for David, let him follow Joab!" ¹²Amasa lay wallowing in his blood in the middle of the road, and the man saw that all the troops came to a halt there. When he realized that everyone who came up to Amasa stopped, he dragged him from the road into a field and threw a garment over him. ¹³After Amasa had been removed from the road,

all the men went on with Joab to pursue Sheba son of Bicri.

¹⁴Sheba passed through all the tribes of Israel to Abel Beth Maacah ᵃ and through the entire region of the Berites, who gathered together and followed him. ¹⁵All the troops with Joab came and besieged Sheba in Abel Beth Maacah. They built a siege ramp up to the city, and it stood against the outer fortifications. While they were battering the wall to bring it down, ¹⁶a wise woman called from the city, "Listen! Listen! Tell Joab to come here so I can speak to him." ¹⁷He went toward her, and she asked, "Are you Joab?"

"I am," he answered.

She said, "Listen to what your servant has to say."

"I'm listening," he said.

¹⁸She continued, "Long ago they used to say, 'Get your answer at Abel,' and that settled it. ¹⁹We are the peaceful and faithful in Israel. You are trying to destroy a city that is a mother in Israel. Why do you want to swallow up the LORD's inheritance?"

²⁰"Far be it from me!" Joab replied, "Far be it from me to swallow up or destroy! ²¹That is not the case. A man named Sheba son of Bicri, from the hill country of Ephraim, has lifted up his hand against the king, against David. Hand over this one man, and I'll withdraw from the city."

The woman said to Joab, "His head will be thrown to you from the wall."

²²Then the woman went to all the people with her wise advice, and they cut off the head of Sheba son of Bicri and threw it to Joab. So he sounded the trumpet, and his men dispersed from the city, each returning to his home. And Joab went back to the king in Jerusalem.

²³Joab was over Israel's entire army; Benaiah son of Jehoiada was over the Kerethites and Pelethites; ²⁴Adoniram ᵇ was in charge of forced labor; Jehoshaphat son of Ahilud was recorder; ²⁵Sheva was secretary; Zadok and Abiathar were priests; ²⁶and Ira the Jairite was David's priest.

ᵃ 14 Or *Abel, even Beth Maacah*; also in verse 15   ᵇ 24 Some Septuagint manuscripts (see also 1 Kings 4:6 and 5:14); Hebrew *Adoram*

The Gibeonites Avenged

21 During the reign of David, there was a famine for three successive years; so David sought the face of the LORD. The LORD said, "It is on account of Saul and his blood-stained house; it is because he put the Gibeonites to death."

²The king summoned the Gibeonites and spoke to them. (Now the Gibeonites were not a part of Israel but were survivors of the Amorites; the Israelites had sworn to ⸢spare⸣ them, but Saul in his zeal for Israel and Judah had tried to annihilate them.) ³David asked the Gibeonites, "What shall I do for you? How shall I make amends so that you will bless the LORD's inheritance?"

⁴The Gibeonites answered him, "We have no right to demand silver or gold from Saul or his family, nor do we have the right to put anyone in Israel to death."

"What do you want me to do for you?" David asked.

⁵They answered the king, "As for the man who destroyed us and plotted against us so that we have been decimated and have no place anywhere in Israel, ⁶let seven of his male descendants be given to us to be killed and exposed before the LORD at Gibeah of Saul—the LORD's chosen one."

So the king said, "I will give them to you."

⁷The king spared Mephibosheth son of Jonathan, the son of Saul, because of the oath before the LORD between David and Jonathan son of Saul. ⁸But the king took Armoni and Mephibosheth, the two sons of Aiah's daughter Rizpah, whom she had borne to Saul, together with the five sons of Saul's daughter Merab,ᵃ whom she had borne to Adriel son of Barzillai the Meholathite. ⁹He handed them over to the Gibeonites, who killed and exposed them on a hill before the LORD. All seven of them fell together; they were put to death during the first days of the harvest, just as the barley harvest was beginning.

¹⁰Rizpah daughter of Aiah took sackcloth and spread it out for herself on a rock. From the beginning of the harvest till the rain poured down from the heavens on the bodies, she did not let the birds of the air touch them by day or the wild animals by night. ¹¹When David was told what Aiah's daughter Rizpah, Saul's concubine, had done, ¹²he went and took the bones of Saul and his son Jonathan from the citizens of Jabesh Gilead. (They had taken them secretly from the public square at Beth Shan, where the Philistines had hung them after they struck Saul down on Gilboa.) ¹³David brought the bones of Saul and his son Jonathan from there, and the bones of those who had been killed and exposed were gathered up.

¹⁴They buried the bones of Saul and his son Jonathan in the tomb of Saul's father Kish, at Zela in Benjamin, and did everything the king commanded. After that, God answered prayer in behalf of the land.

Wars Against the Philistines
21:15–22pp — 1Ch 20:4–8

¹⁵Once again there was a battle between the Philistines and Israel. David went down with his men to fight against the Philistines, and he became exhausted. ¹⁶And Ishbi-Benob, one of the descendants of Rapha, whose bronze spearhead weighed three hundred shekelsᵇ and who was armed with a new ⸢sword⸣, said he would kill David. ¹⁷But Abishai son of Zeruiah came to David's rescue; he struck the Philistine down and killed him. Then David's men swore to him, saying, "Never again will you go out with us to battle, so that the lamp of Israel will not be extinguished."

¹⁸In the course of time, there was another battle with the Philistines, at Gob. At that time Sibbecai the Hushathite killed Saph, one of the descendants of Rapha.

¹⁹In another battle with the Philistines at Gob, Elhanan son of Jaare-Oregimᶜ the Bethlehemite killed Goliathᵈ the Gittite, who had a spear with a shaft like a weaver's rod.

ᵃ 8 Two Hebrew manuscripts, some Septuagint manuscripts and Syriac (see also 1 Samuel 18:19); most Hebrew and Septuagint manuscripts *Michal*   ᵇ 16 That is, about 7 1/2 pounds (about 3.5 kilograms)   ᶜ 19 Or *son of Jair the weaver*   ᵈ 19 Hebrew and Septuagint; 1 Chron. 20:5 *son of Jair killed Lahmi the brother of Goliath*

²⁰In still another battle, which took place at Gath, there was a huge man with six fingers on each hand and six toes on each foot—twenty-four in all. He also was descended from Rapha. ²¹When he taunted Israel, Jonathan son of Shimeah, David's brother, killed him.

²²These four were descendants of Rapha in Gath, and they fell at the hands of David and his men.

David's Song of Praise

22:1–51pp — Ps 18:1–50

22 David sang to the Lord the words of this song when the Lord delivered him from the hand of all his enemies and from the hand of Saul. ²He said:

"The Lord is my rock, my fortress and my
    deliverer;
³ my God is my rock, in whom I take refuge,
    my shield and the horn^a of my salvation.
He is my stronghold, my refuge and my
    savior—
    from violent men you save me.
⁴I call to the Lord, who is worthy of praise,
    and I am saved from my enemies.

⁵"The waves of death swirled about me;
    the torrents of destruction overwhelmed me.
⁶The cords of the grave^b coiled around me;
    the snares of death confronted me.

PRAYING THE SCRIPTURES

Protection

2 SAMUEL 22:2–3

O Lord, I pray that you will be a rock for my grandchild, the One in whom he may take refuge. Be for him a shield, stronghold, refuge and savior, and save him from violent people.

Next prayer in Protection Prayer Track: Psalm 4:6,8

⁷In my distress I called to the Lord;
    I called out to my God.
From his temple he heard my voice;
    my cry came to his ears.

⁸"The earth trembled and quaked,
    the foundations of the heavens^c shook;
    they trembled because he was angry.
⁹Smoke rose from his nostrils;
    consuming fire came from his mouth,
    burning coals blazed out of it.
¹⁰He parted the heavens and came down;
    dark clouds were under his feet.
¹¹He mounted the cherubim and flew;
    he soared^d on the wings of the wind.
¹²He made darkness his canopy around him—
    the dark^e rain clouds of the sky.
¹³Out of the brightness of his presence
    bolts of lightning blazed forth.
¹⁴The Lord thundered from heaven;
    the voice of the Most High resounded.
¹⁵He shot arrows and scattered ⸢the enemies⸥,
    bolts of lightning and routed them.
¹⁶The valleys of the sea were exposed
    and the foundations of the earth laid bare
at the rebuke of the Lord,
    at the blast of breath from his nostrils.

¹⁷"He reached down from on high and took
    hold of me;
    he drew me out of deep waters.
¹⁸He rescued me from my powerful enemy,
    from my foes, who were too strong for me.
¹⁹They confronted me in the day of my
    disaster,
    but the Lord was my support.
²⁰He brought me out into a spacious place;
    he rescued me because he delighted in me.

²¹"The Lord has dealt with me according to
    my righteousness;
    according to the cleanness of my hands he
    has rewarded me.

---

^a 3 *Horn* here symbolizes strength. ^b 6 Hebrew *Sheol*
^c 8 Hebrew; Vulgate and Syriac (see also Psalm 18:7) *mountains*
^d 11 Many Hebrew manuscripts (see also Psalm 18:10); most Hebrew manuscripts *appeared* ^e 12 Septuagint and Vulgate (see also Psalm 18:11); Hebrew *massed*

22 For I have kept the ways of the LORD;
   I have not done evil by turning from my
      God.
23 All his laws are before me;
   I have not turned away from his decrees.
24 I have been blameless before him
   and have kept myself from sin.
25 The LORD has rewarded me according to my
      righteousness,
   according to my cleanness *a* in his sight.

26 "To the faithful you show yourself faithful,
   to the blameless you show yourself
      blameless,
27 to the pure you show yourself pure,
   but to the crooked you show yourself
      shrewd.
28 You save the humble,
   but your eyes are on the haughty to bring
      them low.
29 You are my lamp, O LORD;
   the LORD turns my darkness into light.

TALKING POINTS

Depression

The Lord turns our darkness into light.

2 SAMUEL 22:29

For more on depression, go to Psalm 42:1–11.

30 With your help I can advance against a
      troop *b*;
   with my God I can scale a wall.

31 "As for God, his way is perfect;
   the word of the LORD is flawless.
   He is a shield
      for all who take refuge in him.
32 For who is God besides the LORD?
   And who is the Rock except our God?

33 It is God who arms me with strength *c*
   and makes my way perfect.
34 He makes my feet like the feet of a deer;
   he enables me to stand on the heights.
35 He trains my hands for battle;
   my arms can bend a bow of bronze.
36 You give me your shield of victory;
   you stoop down to make me great.
37 You broaden the path beneath me,
   so that my ankles do not turn.

38 "I pursued my enemies and crushed them;
   I did not turn back till they were
      destroyed.
39 I crushed them completely, and they could
      not rise;
   they fell beneath my feet.
40 You armed me with strength for battle;
   you made my adversaries bow at my feet.
41 You made my enemies turn their backs in
      flight,
   and I destroyed my foes.
42 They cried for help, but there was no one to
      save them—
   to the LORD, but he did not answer.
43 I beat them as fine as the dust of the earth;
   I pounded and trampled them like mud in
      the streets.

44 "You have delivered me from the attacks of
      my people;
   you have preserved me as the head of
      nations.
   People I did not know are subject to me,
45   and foreigners come cringing to me;
   as soon as they hear me, they obey me.
46 They all lose heart;
   they come trembling *d* from their
      strongholds.

47 "The LORD lives! Praise be to my Rock!
   Exalted be God, the Rock, my Savior!

a 25 Hebrew; Septuagint and Vulgate (see also Psalm 18:24) *to
the cleanness of my hands*   *b 30* Or *can run through a barricade*
c 33 Dead Sea Scrolls, some Septuagint manuscripts, Vulgate and
Syriac (see also Psalm 18:32); Masoretic Text *who is my strong refuge*
d 46 Some Septuagint manuscripts and Vulgate (see also Psalm
18:45); Masoretic Text *they arm themselves.*

"TO THE FAITHFUL YOU SHOW
YOURSELF FAITHFUL, TO THE
BLAMELESS YOU SHOW YOURSELF
BLAMELESS."

2 Samuel 22:26

Most Important of All

GIGI GRAHAM TCHIVIDJIAN

READ | 2 SAMUEL 22:1 – 51

We began class, as usual, with a brief devotional. I must admit I was distracted by the singing of the birds, the warm breezes and the sweet aromas. I found it hard to concentrate — until something my teacher said caught my attention.

"The only thing the Lord requires of us," she was saying in conclusion, "is faithfulness."

Both excitement and peace flooded me at those words. A huge weight was lifted from my shoulders. Because, you see, even at my tender age, I had been feeling an awesome responsibility to "measure up."

There was so much to live up to, so many big footsteps to walk in, so many examples to follow, that I just didn't see how I was going to do it!

But — if the Lord's only requirement of me was faithfulness, then He didn't expect me to be like anyone else! And if the importance was in the faithfulness and not in the "greatness" of the task, then with His help I could serve and please Him in my own unique way. What a comfort! From that day on, my prayer was that no matter what He gave me to do — whether great or small, public or private — I would be faithful.

Not everyone possesses boundless energy or a conspicuous talent. We are not equally blessed with great intellect or physical beauty or emotional strength. But we have all been given the same ability to be faithful. And as we are told in the parable of the talents, it is the faithfulness that receives the commendation of God: "Well done, good and faithful servant! You have been faithful with a few things; I will put you in charge of many things" (Matthew 25:21).

Lord, you have given me so much, and you ask so little of me but faithfulness. And yet, even the ability to be faithful comes from your heart. In whatever you give me to do, Lord, great or small, I will be faithful!

Your next devotion is located on page 440.

GRANDCHILD IN FOCUS • PRAYER

Emotional Development

O God, Creator of mind and body, I pray that you will give my grandchild emotional health and strength. Where there is anger, bring peace. Where there is confusion, bring clarity and focus. Where there are dark shadows, cast a ray of hope. Fill her with the sunshine of your Spirit. Warm her with the presence of your peace. Amen.

437

⁴⁸He is the God who avenges me,
  who puts the nations under me,
⁴⁹ who sets me free from my enemies.
You exalted me above my foes;
  from violent men you rescued me.
⁵⁰Therefore I will praise you, O LORD, among
    the nations;
  I will sing praises to your name.
⁵¹He gives his king great victories;
  he shows unfailing kindness to his
    anointed,
  to David and his descendants forever."

The Last Words of David

23 These are the last words of David:

"The oracle of David son of Jesse,
  the oracle of the man exalted by the Most
    High,
the man anointed by the God of Jacob,
  Israel's singer of songs*ᵃ*:

²"The Spirit of the LORD spoke through me;
  his word was on my tongue.
³The God of Israel spoke,
  the Rock of Israel said to me:
'When one rules over men in righteousness,
  when he rules in the fear of God,
⁴he is like the light of morning at sunrise
  on a cloudless morning,
like the brightness after rain
  that brings the grass from the earth.'

⁵"Is not my house right with God?
  Has he not made with me an everlasting
    covenant,
  arranged and secured in every part?
Will he not bring to fruition my salvation
  and grant me my every desire?
⁶But evil men are all to be cast aside like
    thorns,
  which are not gathered with the hand.
⁷Whoever touches thorns
  uses a tool of iron or the shaft of a
    spear;
  they are burned up where they lie."

David's Mighty Men

23:8–39pp — 1Ch 11:10–41

⁸These are the names of David's mighty men:
Josheb-Basshebeth,ᵇ a Tahkemonite,ᶜ was chief
of the Three; he raised his spear against eight hundred men, whom he killedᵈ in one encounter.

⁹Next to him was Eleazar son of Dodai the
Ahohite. As one of the three mighty men, he was
with David when they taunted the Philistines
gathered ˻at Pas Dammim˼ᵉ for battle. Then the
men of Israel retreated, ¹⁰but he stood his ground
and struck down the Philistines till his hand grew
tired and froze to the sword. The LORD brought
about a great victory that day. The troops returned to Eleazar, but only to strip the dead.

¹¹Next to him was Shammah son of Agee the
Hararite. When the Philistines banded together
at a place where there was a field full of lentils,
Israel's troops fled from them. ¹²But Shammah
took his stand in the middle of the field. He defended it and struck the Philistines down, and
the LORD brought about a great victory.

¹³During harvest time, three of the thirty chief
men came down to David at the cave of Adullam,
while a band of Philistines was encamped in the
Valley of Rephaim. ¹⁴At that time David was in
the stronghold, and the Philistine garrison was
at Bethlehem. ¹⁵David longed for water and said,
"Oh, that someone would get me a drink of water
from the well near the gate of Bethlehem!" ¹⁶So
the three mighty men broke through the Philistine lines, drew water from the well near the gate
of Bethlehem and carried it back to David. But
he refused to drink it; instead, he poured it out
before the LORD. ¹⁷"Far be it from me, O LORD,
to do this!" he said. "Is it not the blood of men
who went at the risk of their lives?" And David
would not drink it.

Such were the exploits of the three mighty
men.

ᵃ *1* Or *Israel's beloved singer*   ᵇ *8* Hebrew; some Septuagint
manuscripts suggest *Ish-Bosheth,* that is, *Esh-Baal* (see also 1 Chron.
11:11 *Jashobeam*).   ᶜ *8* Probably a variant of *Hacmonite* (see
1 Chron. 11:11)   ᵈ *8* Some Septuagint manuscripts (see also
1 Chron. 11:11); Hebrew and other Septuagint manuscripts
Three; it was Adino the Eznite who killed eight hundred men
ᵉ *9* See 1 Chron. 11:13; Hebrew *gathered there.*

¹⁸Abishai the brother of Joab son of Zeruiah was chief of the Three.[a] He raised his spear against three hundred men, whom he killed, and so he became as famous as the Three. ¹⁹Was he not held in greater honor than the Three? He became their commander, even though he was not included among them.

²⁰Benaiah son of Jehoiada was a valiant fighter from Kabzeel, who performed great exploits. He struck down two of Moab's best men. He also went down into a pit on a snowy day and killed a lion. ²¹And he struck down a huge Egyptian. Although the Egyptian had a spear in his hand, Benaiah went against him with a club. He snatched the spear from the Egyptian's hand and killed him with his own spear. ²²Such were the exploits of Benaiah son of Jehoiada; he too was as famous as the three mighty men. ²³He was held in greater honor than any of the Thirty, but he was not included among the Three. And David put him in charge of his bodyguard.

²⁴Among the Thirty were:
    Asahel the brother of Joab,
    Elhanan son of Dodo from Bethlehem,
²⁵Shammah the Harodite,
    Elika the Harodite,
²⁶Helez the Paltite,
    Ira son of Ikkesh from Tekoa,
²⁷Abiezer from Anathoth,
    Mebunnai[b] the Hushathite,
²⁸Zalmon the Ahohite,
    Maharai the Netophathite,
²⁹Heled[c] son of Baanah the Netophathite,
    Ithai son of Ribai from Gibeah in Benjamin,
³⁰Benaiah the Pirathonite,
    Hiddai[d] from the ravines of Gaash,
³¹Abi-Albon the Arbathite,
    Azmaveth the Barhumite,
³²Eliahba the Shaalbonite,
    the sons of Jashen,
    Jonathan ³³son of[e] Shammah the Hararite,
    Ahiam son of Sharar[f] the Hararite,

³⁴Eliphelet son of Ahasbai the Maacathite,
    Eliam son of Ahithophel the Gilonite,
³⁵Hezro the Carmelite,
    Paarai the Arbite,
³⁶Igal son of Nathan from Zobah,
    the son of Hagri,[g]
³⁷Zelek the Ammonite,
    Naharai the Beerothite, the armor-bearer of Joab son of Zeruiah,
³⁸Ira the Ithrite,
    Gareb the Ithrite
³⁹and Uriah the Hittite.
    There were thirty-seven in all.

David Counts the Fighting Men
24:1–17pp — 1Ch 21:1–17

24 Again the anger of the LORD burned against Israel, and he incited David against them, saying, "Go and take a census of Israel and Judah."

²So the king said to Joab and the army commanders[h] with him, "Go throughout the tribes of Israel from Dan to Beersheba and enroll the fighting men, so that I may know how many there are."

³But Joab replied to the king, "May the LORD your God multiply the troops a hundred times over, and may the eyes of my lord the king see it. But why does my lord the king want to do such a thing?"

⁴The king's word, however, overruled Joab and the army commanders; so they left the presence of the king to enroll the fighting men of Israel.

⁵After crossing the Jordan, they camped near Aroer, south of the town in the gorge, and then went through Gad and on to Jazer. ⁶They went

---

[a] 18 Most Hebrew manuscripts (see also 1 Chron. 11:20); two Hebrew manuscripts and Syriac *Thirty*   [b] 27 Hebrew; some Septuagint manuscripts (see also 1 Chron. 11:29) *Sibbecai*   [c] 29 Some Hebrew manuscripts and Vulgate (see also 1 Chron. 11:30); most Hebrew manuscripts *Heleb*   [d] 30 Hebrew; some Septuagint manuscripts (see also 1 Chron. 11:32) *Hurai*   [e] 33 Some Septuagint manuscripts (see also 1 Chron. 11:34); Hebrew does not have *son of*.   [f] 33 Hebrew; some Septuagint manuscripts (see also 1 Chron. 11:35) *Sacar*   [g] 36 Some Septuagint manuscripts (see also 1 Chron. 11:38); Hebrew *Haggadi*   [h] 2 Septuagint (see also verse 4 and 1 Chron. 21:2); Hebrew *Joab the army commander*

> BUT THE KING REPLIED TO ARAUNAH,
> "NO, I INSIST ON PAYING YOU FOR IT.
> I WILL NOT SACRIFICE TO THE LORD
> MY GOD BURNT OFFERINGS THAT COST
> ME NOTHING." SO DAVID BOUGHT THE
> THRESHING FLOOR AND THE OXEN AND
> PAID FIFTY SHEKELS OF SILVER FOR THEM.
>
> *2 Samuel 24:24*

The Cost of Giving

DOROTHY E. SICKAL

READ | 2 SAMUEL 24:1 – 25

David considered a sacrifice he didn't pay for no proper sacrifice at all.

Is it possible that we are not giving until it costs us something? Our cast-offs may be helpful to others in need, but is it possible that we may be giving them so we will not feel guilty for being so wasteful? We could be giving of our time to obliterate our own boredom.

The joy of giving comes when we deny self. Love thrives on self-denial — not in feeling holy about it, but in adding to someone's wholeness at the cost of self.

My mother always ate the bony pieces of chicken, giving the better parts to her children. I often wondered why she seemed to delight in nibbling around all those bones to get so little chicken. When I became a mother, I understood her better. She loved us so much that it was easy for her to give. Service because of love came natural for her.

The strange thing is that when she grew older, she was still "taking the bony pieces," not just in food but in life. Her life was a living sacrifice; her joy was a result of her way of life. Joy never comes from looking for it.

The witness of her giving service was all around her town and neighborhood. Only God knows what it cost her; only she knew the joy she gained. This is a discovery, not a pursuit.

Father, help me to rediscover the joy of sacrificial giving, just as you give me all good things. Whether to my grandchildren, their parents or to those in my community, help me be willing to deny self to add wholeness to the lives of others. Create in me a generous heart and make my life a living sacrifice of service to others and of praise to you.

Your next devotion is located on page 446.

GRANDCHILD IN FOCUS · PRAYER

Spiritual Growth

Dear Lord, today I pray for my grandchild's spiritual growth. I ask that you instill in him the desire to read and memorize your Word. Give him a passion to be in conversation with you. May loving and serving you be part of his daily life. I ask that you stay close to him and lead him to be transformed to your likeness, to reflect your grace and to radiate your love. I pray this in Jesus' name, amen.

to Gilead and the region of Tahtim Hodshi, and on to Dan Jaan and around toward Sidon. ⁷Then they went toward the fortress of Tyre and all the towns of the Hivites and Canaanites. Finally, they went on to Beersheba in the Negev of Judah.

⁸After they had gone through the entire land, they came back to Jerusalem at the end of nine months and twenty days.

⁹Joab reported the number of the fighting men to the king: In Israel there were eight hundred thousand able-bodied men who could handle a sword, and in Judah five hundred thousand.

¹⁰David was conscience-stricken after he had counted the fighting men, and he said to the LORD, "I have sinned greatly in what I have done. Now, O LORD, I beg you, take away the guilt of your servant. I have done a very foolish thing."

¹¹Before David got up the next morning, the word of the LORD had come to Gad the prophet, David's seer: ¹²"Go and tell David, 'This is what the LORD says: I am giving you three options. Choose one of them for me to carry out against you.'"

¹³So Gad went to David and said to him, "Shall there come upon you three ᵃ years of famine in your land? Or three months of fleeing from your enemies while they pursue you? Or three days of plague in your land? Now then, think it over and decide how I should answer the one who sent me."

¹⁴David said to Gad, "I am in deep distress. Let us fall into the hands of the LORD, for his mercy is great; but do not let me fall into the hands of men."

¹⁵So the LORD sent a plague on Israel from that morning until the end of the time designated, and seventy thousand of the people from Dan to Beersheba died. ¹⁶When the angel stretched out his hand to destroy Jerusalem, the LORD was grieved because of the calamity and said to the angel who was afflicting the people, "Enough! Withdraw your hand." The angel of the LORD

was then at the threshing floor of Araunah the Jebusite.

¹⁷When David saw the angel who was striking down the people, he said to the LORD, "I am the one who has sinned and done wrong. These are but sheep. What have they done? Let your hand fall upon me and my family."

David Builds an Altar
24:18–25pp — 1Ch 21:18–26

¹⁸On that day Gad went to David and said to him, "Go up and build an altar to the LORD on the threshing floor of Araunah the Jebusite." ¹⁹So David went up, as the LORD had commanded through Gad. ²⁰When Araunah looked and saw the king and his men coming toward him, he went out and bowed down before the king with his face to the ground.

²¹Araunah said, "Why has my lord the king come to his servant?"

"To buy your threshing floor," David answered, "so I can build an altar to the LORD, that the plague on the people may be stopped."

²²Araunah said to David, "Let my lord the king take whatever pleases him and offer it up. Here are oxen for the burnt offering, and here are threshing sledges and ox yokes for the wood. ²³O king, Araunah gives all this to the king." Araunah also said to him, "May the LORD your God accept you."

²⁴But the king replied to Araunah, "No, I insist on paying you for it. I will not sacrifice to the LORD my God burnt offerings that cost me nothing."

So David bought the threshing floor and the oxen and paid fifty shekels ᵇ of silver for them. ²⁵David built an altar to the LORD there and sacrificed burnt offerings and fellowship offerings. ᶜ Then the LORD answered prayer in behalf of the land, and the plague on Israel was stopped.

ᵃ 13 Septuagint (see also 1 Chron. 21:12); Hebrew *seven*
ᵇ 24 That is, about 1 1/4 pounds (about 0.6 kilogram)
ᶜ 25 Traditionally *peace offerings*

Imparting WORDS OF WISDOM

The beginning of this book reveals King David in his old age, ready to pass his kingship on to his successor. At first, David's son Solomon reigned wisely, building up the kingdom and constructing a temple for God. However, as Solomon aged, he unwisely allowed his foreign wives to introduce the worship of false gods into the kingdom.

The second half of this book recounts the division of the kingdom and records the kings of each nation. It describes the rise and fall of the various kings and each king's relationship with God. Often the writer labeled a king by saying that he "did what was right in the eyes of the LORD" or he "did evil in the eyes of the LORD." As the kings distanced themselves from God, God used the prophets to confront them and remind them of his will.

At the end of his life, King David imparted some essential words of wisdom to his son Solomon. He didn't just talk about building temples or monuments or ruling the kingdom. Instead, David stressed the importance of staying faithful to the Lord God (see 1 Kings 2:1 – 4). It was not enough that David was "a man after [God's] own heart" (1 Samuel 13:14). He understood that it was his responsibility to ensure that the generations after him would also love the Lord and follow his laws.

Once again the Scriptures remind us that we must pass on our faith, encouraging and instructing our children and grandchildren to love the Lord God and walk in his ways.

VERSE *to* REMEMBER | 1 KINGS 2:3

"Observe what the LORD your God requires: Walk in his ways, and keep his decrees and commands, his laws and requirements, as written in the Law of Moses, so that you may prosper in all you do and wherever you go."

ABOUT 1 KINGS

WRITTEN BY:
Unknown

WRITTEN FOR:
God's chosen people, the Israelites

DATE WRITTEN:
Probably around 550 B.C., during the Babylonian exile

WHY WRITTEN:
To show how the kings of Israel and Judah obeyed or disobeyed God

Adonijah Sets Himself Up as King

1 When King David was old and well advanced in years, he could not keep warm even when they put covers over him. ²So his servants said to him, "Let us look for a young virgin to attend the king and take care of him. She can lie beside him so that our lord the king may keep warm."

³Then they searched throughout Israel for a beautiful girl and found Abishag, a Shunammite, and brought her to the king. ⁴The girl was very beautiful; she took care of the king and waited on him, but the king had no intimate relations with her.

⁵Now Adonijah, whose mother was Haggith, put himself forward and said, "I will be king." So he got chariots and horses ᵃ ready, with fifty men to run ahead of him. ⁶(His father had never interfered with him by asking, "Why do you behave as you do?" He was also very handsome and was born next after Absalom.)

⁷Adonijah conferred with Joab son of Zeruiah and with Abiathar the priest, and they gave him their support. ⁸But Zadok the priest, Benaiah son of Jehoiada, Nathan the prophet, Shimei and Rei ᵇ and David's special guard did not join Adonijah.

⁹Adonijah then sacrificed sheep, cattle and fattened calves at the Stone of Zoheleth near En Rogel. He invited all his brothers, the king's sons, and all the men of Judah who were royal officials, ¹⁰but he did not invite Nathan the prophet or Benaiah or the special guard or his brother Solomon.

¹¹Then Nathan asked Bathsheba, Solomon's mother, "Have you not heard that Adonijah, the son of Haggith, has become king without our lord David's knowing it? ¹²Now then, let me advise you how you can save your own life and the life of your son Solomon. ¹³Go in to King David and say to him, 'My lord the king, did you not swear to me your servant: "Surely Solomon your son shall be king after me, and he will sit on my throne"? Why then has Adonijah become king?' ¹⁴While you are still there talking to the king, I will come in and confirm what you have said."

¹⁵So Bathsheba went to see the aged king in his room, where Abishag the Shunammite was attending him. ¹⁶Bathsheba bowed low and knelt before the king.

"What is it you want?" the king asked.

¹⁷She said to him, "My lord, you yourself swore to me your servant by the LORD your God: 'Solomon your son shall be king after me, and he will sit on my throne.' ¹⁸But now Adonijah has become king, and you, my lord the king, do not know about it. ¹⁹He has sacrificed great numbers of cattle, fattened calves, and sheep, and has invited all the king's sons, Abiathar the priest and Joab the commander of the army, but he has not invited Solomon your servant. ²⁰My lord the king, the eyes of all Israel are on you, to learn from you who will sit on the throne of my lord the king after him. ²¹Otherwise, as soon as my lord the king is laid to rest with his fathers, I and my son Solomon will be treated as criminals."

²²While she was still speaking with the king, Nathan the prophet arrived. ²³And they told the king, "Nathan the prophet is here." So he went before the king and bowed with his face to the ground.

²⁴Nathan said, "Have you, my lord the king, declared that Adonijah shall be king after you, and that he will sit on your throne? ²⁵Today he has gone down and sacrificed great numbers of cattle, fattened calves, and sheep. He has invited all the king's sons, the commanders of the army and Abiathar the priest. Right now they are eating and drinking with him and saying, 'Long live King Adonijah!' ²⁶But me your servant, and Zadok the priest, and Benaiah son of Jehoiada, and your servant Solomon he did not invite. ²⁷Is this something my lord the king has done without letting his servants know who should sit on the throne of my lord the king after him?"

David Makes Solomon King
1:28–53pp — 1Ch 29:21–25

²⁸Then King David said, "Call in Bathsheba." So she came into the king's presence and stood before him.

ᵃ 5 Or *charioteers*   ᵇ 8 Or *and his friends*

²⁹The king then took an oath: "As surely as the LORD lives, who has delivered me out of every trouble, ³⁰I will surely carry out today what I swore to you by the LORD, the God of Israel: Solomon your son shall be king after me, and he will sit on my throne in my place."

³¹Then Bathsheba bowed low with her face to the ground and, kneeling before the king, said, "May my lord King David live forever!"

³²King David said, "Call in Zadok the priest, Nathan the prophet and Benaiah son of Jehoiada." When they came before the king, ³³he said to them: "Take your lord's servants with you and set Solomon my son on my own mule and take him down to Gihon. ³⁴There have Zadok the priest and Nathan the prophet anoint him king over Israel. Blow the trumpet and shout, 'Long live King Solomon!' ³⁵Then you are to go up with him, and he is to come and sit on my throne and reign in my place. I have appointed him ruler over Israel and Judah."

³⁶Benaiah son of Jehoiada answered the king, "Amen! May the LORD, the God of my lord the king, so declare it. ³⁷As the LORD was with my lord the king, so may he be with Solomon to make his throne even greater than the throne of my lord King David!"

³⁸So Zadok the priest, Nathan the prophet, Benaiah son of Jehoiada, the Kerethites and the Pelethites went down and put Solomon on King David's mule and escorted him to Gihon. ³⁹Zadok the priest took the horn of oil from the sacred tent and anointed Solomon. Then they sounded the trumpet and all the people shouted, "Long live King Solomon!" ⁴⁰And all the people went up after him, playing flutes and rejoicing greatly, so that the ground shook with the sound.

⁴¹Adonijah and all the guests who were with him heard it as they were finishing their feast. On hearing the sound of the trumpet, Joab asked, "What's the meaning of all the noise in the city?"

⁴²Even as he was speaking, Jonathan son of Abiathar the priest arrived. Adonijah said, "Come in. A worthy man like you must be bringing good news."

⁴³"Not at all!" Jonathan answered. "Our lord King David has made Solomon king. ⁴⁴The king has sent with him Zadok the priest, Nathan the prophet, Benaiah son of Jehoiada, the Kerethites and the Pelethites, and they have put him on the king's mule, ⁴⁵and Zadok the priest and Nathan the prophet have anointed him king at Gihon. From there they have gone up cheering, and the city resounds with it. That's the noise you hear. ⁴⁶Moreover, Solomon has taken his seat on the royal throne. ⁴⁷Also, the royal officials have come to congratulate our lord King David, saying, 'May your God make Solomon's name more famous than yours and his throne greater than yours!' And the king bowed in worship on his bed ⁴⁸and said, 'Praise be to the LORD, the God of Israel, who has allowed my eyes to see a successor on my throne today.'"

⁴⁹At this, all Adonijah's guests rose in alarm and dispersed. ⁵⁰But Adonijah, in fear of Solomon, went and took hold of the horns of the altar. ⁵¹Then Solomon was told, "Adonijah is afraid of King Solomon and is clinging to the horns of the altar. He says, 'Let King Solomon swear to me today that he will not put his servant to death with the sword.'"

⁵²Solomon replied, "If he shows himself to be a worthy man, not a hair of his head will fall to the ground; but if evil is found in him, he will die." ⁵³Then King Solomon sent men, and they brought him down from the altar. And Adonijah came and bowed down to King Solomon, and Solomon said, "Go to your home."

David's Charge to Solomon

2:10–12pp — 1Ch 29:26–28

2 When the time drew near for David to die, he gave a charge to Solomon his son.

²"I am about to go the way of all the earth," he said. "So be strong, show yourself a man, ³and observe what the LORD your God requires: Walk in his ways, and keep his decrees and commands, his laws and requirements, as written in the Law of Moses, so that you may prosper in all you do and wherever you go, ⁴and that the LORD may

keep his promise to me: 'If your descendants watch how they live, and if they walk faithfully before me with all their heart and soul, you will never fail to have a man on the throne of Israel.'

⁵ "Now you yourself know what Joab son of Zeruiah did to me—what he did to the two commanders of Israel's armies, Abner son of Ner and Amasa son of Jether. He killed them, shedding their blood in peacetime as if in battle, and with that blood stained the belt around his waist and the sandals on his feet. ⁶ Deal with him according to your wisdom, but do not let his gray head go down to the grave *a* in peace.

⁷ "But show kindness to the sons of Barzillai of Gilead and let them be among those who eat at your table. They stood by me when I fled from your brother Absalom.

⁸ "And remember, you have with you Shimei son of Gera, the Benjamite from Bahurim, who called down bitter curses on me the day I went to Mahanaim. When he came down to meet me at the Jordan, I swore to him by the LORD: 'I will not put you to death by the sword.' ⁹ But now, do not consider him innocent. You are a man of wisdom; you will know what to do to him. Bring his gray head down to the grave in blood."

¹⁰ Then David rested with his fathers and was buried in the City of David. ¹¹ He had reigned forty years over Israel—seven years in Hebron and thirty-three in Jerusalem. ¹² So Solomon sat on the throne of his father David, and his rule was firmly established.

Solomon's Throne Established

¹³ Now Adonijah, the son of Haggith, went to Bathsheba, Solomon's mother. Bathsheba asked him, "Do you come peacefully?"

He answered, "Yes, peacefully." ¹⁴ Then he added, "I have something to say to you."

"You may say it," she replied.

¹⁵ "As you know," he said, "the kingdom was mine. All Israel looked to me as their king. But things changed, and the kingdom has gone to my brother; for it has come to him from the LORD. ¹⁶ Now I have one request to make of you. Do not refuse me."

"You may make it," she said.

¹⁷ So he continued, "Please ask King Solomon—he will not refuse you—to give me Abishag the Shunammite as my wife."

¹⁸ "Very well," Bathsheba replied, "I will speak to the king for you."

¹⁹ When Bathsheba went to King Solomon to speak to him for Adonijah, the king stood up to meet her, bowed down to her and sat down on his throne. He had a throne brought for the king's mother, and she sat down at his right hand.

²⁰ "I have one small request to make of you," she said. "Do not refuse me."

The king replied, "Make it, my mother; I will not refuse you."

²¹ So she said, "Let Abishag the Shunammite be given in marriage to your brother Adonijah."

²² King Solomon answered his mother, "Why do you request Abishag the Shunammite for Adonijah? You might as well request the kingdom for him—after all, he is my older brother—yes, for him and for Abiathar the priest and Joab son of Zeruiah!"

²³ Then King Solomon swore by the LORD: "May God deal with me, be it ever so severely, if Adonijah does not pay with his life for this request! ²⁴ And now, as surely as the LORD lives—he who has established me securely on the throne of my father David and has founded a dynasty for me as he promised—Adonijah shall be put to

a 6 Hebrew Sheol; also in verse 9

When the time drew near
for David to die, he gave a
charge to Solomon his son.

1 Kings 2:1

Passing the Torch

CLAUDIA ARP

READ | 1 KINGS 2:1–12

How great it would be to know and actually plan for the time we "pass the torch" to the next generation. However, few know the time of their death or are lucid enough beforehand to pass on a charge to their children. But if you did know you were dying, what would you say?

My husband and I have thought about what we would say to our children — especially concerning their marriages. We would encourage our sons to love their wives, to date them regularly, to laugh, to have some fun and to make their relationship a priority. We'd tell them to grab time for each other in the midst of parenting our grandchildren, to keep on leaving, cleaving and becoming one (see Genesis 2:24), and to grow closer to each other and to God.

We could even write a book and include a challenge for "passing the torch." But the cold facts are that our sons may or may not read our books. We can, however, be sure they will read our lives. Hopefully, they see our love for and dedication to each other. Over the years they have watched us work out our marriage in the laboratory of life. They've heard us argue — but also apologize and forgive each other. They have laughed and joined us in many of the fun times in our marriage. They've seen us on our knees in prayer. They've walked with us through the deaths of our parents. Each day we continue to live out our life book.

Now think about your own life. If the only charge you are able to leave is the book you write with your life, what legacy will you pass on?

As we consider our own lives, we see little areas we would like to change — such as our tendency to hurry through life and work too hard. What changes might you want to make? There is no time like the present to prepare for the future.

Dear Lord, let us live today so that in the future when our time comes to go to our heavenly home, we can pass on a godly heritage that will bless our children and grandchildren. Amen.

Your next devotion is located on page 451.

GRANDCHILD IN FOCUS • PRAYER

Relationships at Home

O Lord, I pray that you will bless the home and family of my grandchild. May the relationships she has with her parents and siblings enhance her well-being, support her self-confidence and increase her faith. May her home life reflect your love, your grace, your compassion and your peace. Guide her parents to direct her in love and truth, so she will grow into a strong and compassionate individual. Amen.

death today!" 25 So King Solomon gave orders to Benaiah son of Jehoiada, and he struck down Adonijah and he died.

26 To Abiathar the priest the king said, "Go back to your fields in Anathoth. You deserve to die, but I will not put you to death now, because you carried the ark of the Sovereign LORD before my father David and shared all my father's hardships." 27 So Solomon removed Abiathar from the priesthood of the LORD, fulfilling the word the LORD had spoken at Shiloh about the house of Eli.

28 When the news reached Joab, who had conspired with Adonijah though not with Absalom, he fled to the tent of the LORD and took hold of the horns of the altar. 29 King Solomon was told that Joab had fled to the tent of the LORD and was beside the altar. Then Solomon ordered Benaiah son of Jehoiada, "Go, strike him down!"

30 So Benaiah entered the tent of the LORD and said to Joab, "The king says, 'Come out!' "

But he answered, "No, I will die here."

Benaiah reported to the king, "This is how Joab answered me."

31 Then the king commanded Benaiah, "Do as he says. Strike him down and bury him, and so clear me and my father's house of the guilt of the innocent blood that Joab shed. 32 The LORD will repay him for the blood he shed, because without the knowledge of my father David he attacked two men and killed them with the sword. Both of them — Abner son of Ner, commander of Israel's army, and Amasa son of Jether, commander of Judah's army — were better men and more upright than he. 33 May the guilt of their blood rest on the head of Joab and his descendants forever. But on David and his descendants, his house and his throne, may there be the LORD's peace forever."

34 So Benaiah son of Jehoiada went up and struck down Joab and killed him, and he was buried on his own land [a] in the desert. 35 The king put Benaiah son of Jehoiada over the army in Joab's position and replaced Abiathar with Zadok the priest.

36 Then the king sent for Shimei and said to him, "Build yourself a house in Jerusalem and live there, but do not go anywhere else. 37 The day you leave and cross the Kidron Valley, you can be sure you will die; your blood will be on your own head."

38 Shimei answered the king, "What you say is good. Your servant will do as my lord the king has said." And Shimei stayed in Jerusalem for a long time.

39 But three years later, two of Shimei's slaves ran off to Achish son of Maacah, king of Gath, and Shimei was told, "Your slaves are in Gath." 40 At this, he saddled his donkey and went to Achish at Gath in search of his slaves. So Shimei went away and brought the slaves back from Gath.

41 When Solomon was told that Shimei had gone from Jerusalem to Gath and had returned, 42 the king summoned Shimei and said to him, "Did I not make you swear by the LORD and warn you, 'On the day you leave to go anywhere else, you can be sure you will die'? At that time you said to me, 'What you say is good. I will obey.' 43 Why then did you not keep your oath to the LORD and obey the command I gave you?"

44 The king also said to Shimei, "You know in your heart all the wrong you did to my father David. Now the LORD will repay you for your wrongdoing. 45 But King Solomon will be blessed, and David's throne will remain secure before the LORD forever."

46 Then the king gave the order to Benaiah son of Jehoiada, and he went out and struck Shimei down and killed him.

The kingdom was now firmly established in Solomon's hands.

Solomon Asks for Wisdom

3:4–15pp — 2Ch 1:2–13

3 Solomon made an alliance with Pharaoh king of Egypt and married his daughter. He brought her to the City of David until he finished building his palace and the temple of the LORD, and the wall around Jerusalem. 2 The people, however, were still sacrificing at the high places,

---

[a] 34 Or buried in his tomb

because a temple had not yet been built for the Name of the LORD. ³Solomon showed his love for the LORD by walking according to the statutes of his father David, except that he offered sacrifices and burned incense on the high places.

⁴The king went to Gibeon to offer sacrifices, for that was the most important high place, and Solomon offered a thousand burnt offerings on that altar. ⁵At Gibeon the LORD appeared to Solomon during the night in a dream, and God said, "Ask for whatever you want me to give you."

⁶Solomon answered, "You have shown great kindness to your servant, my father David, because he was faithful to you and righteous and upright in heart. You have continued this great kindness to him and have given him a son to sit on his throne this very day.

⁷"Now, O LORD my God, you have made your servant king in place of my father David. But I am only a little child and do not know how to carry out my duties. ⁸Your servant is here among the people you have chosen, a great people, too numerous to count or number. ⁹So give your servant a discerning heart to govern your people and to distinguish between right and wrong. For who is able to govern this great people of yours?"

¹⁰The Lord was pleased that Solomon had asked for this. ¹¹So God said to him, "Since you have asked for this and not for long life or wealth for yourself, nor have asked for the death of your enemies but for discernment in administering justice, ¹²I will do what you have asked. I will give you a wise and discerning heart, so that there will never have been anyone like you, nor will there ever be. ¹³Moreover, I will give you what you have not asked for—both riches and honor—so that in your lifetime you will have no equal among kings. ¹⁴And if you walk in my ways and obey my statutes and commands as David your father did, I will give you a long life." ¹⁵Then Solomon awoke—and he realized it had been a dream.

He returned to Jerusalem, stood before the ark of the Lord's covenant and sacrificed burnt offerings and fellowship offerings.ᵃ Then he gave a feast for all his court.

A Wise Ruling

¹⁶Now two prostitutes came to the king and stood before him. ¹⁷One of them said, "My lord, this woman and I live in the same house. I had a baby while she was there with me. ¹⁸The third day after my child was born, this woman also had a baby. We were alone; there was no one in the house but the two of us.

¹⁹"During the night this woman's son died because she lay on him. ²⁰So she got up in the middle of the night and took my son from my side while I your servant was asleep. She put him by her breast and put her dead son by my breast. ²¹The next morning, I got up to nurse my son—and he was dead! But when I looked at him close-

ᵃ 15 Traditionally *peace offerings*

stories to share

1 KINGS 3:4–28

Solomon's Wise Ruling

LIFE LESSON: God is pleased when we ask for wisdom.

TO TALK ABOUT

✦ When God told Solomon to ask for whatever he wanted, what did Solomon ask for?

✦ Why did two mothers want the same baby?

✦ How did Solomon's ruling demonstrate his wisdom?

✦ If God invited you to ask for whatever you wanted, what would you ask for?

ly in the morning light, I saw that it wasn't the son I had borne."

²²The other woman said, "No! The living one is my son; the dead one is yours."

But the first one insisted, "No! The dead one is yours; the living one is mine." And so they argued before the king.

²³The king said, "This one says, 'My son is alive and your son is dead,' while that one says, 'No! Your son is dead and mine is alive.'"

²⁴Then the king said, "Bring me a sword." So they brought a sword for the king. ²⁵He then gave an order: "Cut the living child in two and give half to one and half to the other."

²⁶The woman whose son was alive was filled with compassion for her son and said to the king, "Please, my lord, give her the living baby! Don't kill him!"

But the other said, "Neither I nor you shall have him. Cut him in two!"

²⁷Then the king gave his ruling: "Give the living baby to the first woman. Do not kill him; she is his mother."

²⁸When all Israel heard the verdict the king had given, they held the king in awe, because they saw that he had wisdom from God to administer justice.

Solomon's Officials and Governors

4 So King Solomon ruled over all Israel. ²And these were his chief officials:

Azariah son of Zadok—the priest;
³Elihoreph and Ahijah, sons of Shisha—secretaries;
Jehoshaphat son of Ahilud—recorder;
⁴Benaiah son of Jehoiada—commander in chief;
Zadok and Abiathar—priests;
⁵Azariah son of Nathan—in charge of the district officers;
Zabud son of Nathan—a priest and personal adviser to the king;
⁶Ahishar—in charge of the palace;
Adoniram son of Abda—in charge of forced labor.

⁷Solomon also had twelve district governors over all Israel, who supplied provisions for the king and the royal household. Each one had to provide supplies for one month in the year. ⁸These are their names:

Ben-Hur—in the hill country of Ephraim;
⁹Ben-Deker—in Makaz, Shaalbim, Beth Shemesh and Elon Bethhanan;
¹⁰Ben-Hesed—in Arubboth (Socoh and all the land of Hepher were his);
¹¹Ben-Abinadab—in Naphoth Dor*ᵃ* (he was married to Taphath daughter of Solomon);
¹²Baana son of Ahilud—in Taanach and Megiddo, and in all of Beth Shan next to Zarethan below Jezreel, from Beth Shan to Abel Meholah across to Jokmeam;
¹³Ben-Geber—in Ramoth Gilead (the settlements of Jair son of Manasseh in Gilead were his, as well as the district of Argob in Bashan and its sixty large walled cities with bronze gate bars);
¹⁴Ahinadab son of Iddo—in Mahanaim;
¹⁵Ahimaaz—in Naphtali (he had married Basemath daughter of Solomon);
¹⁶Baana son of Hushai—in Asher and in Aloth;
¹⁷Jehoshaphat son of Paruah—in Issachar;
¹⁸Shimei son of Ela—in Benjamin;
¹⁹Geber son of Uri—in Gilead (the country of Sihon king of the Amorites and the country of Og king of Bashan). He was the only governor over the district.

Solomon's Daily Provisions

²⁰The people of Judah and Israel were as numerous as the sand on the seashore; they ate, they drank and they were happy. ²¹And Solomon ruled over all the kingdoms from the River*ᵇ* to the land of the Philistines, as far as the border of Egypt. These countries brought tribute and were Solomon's subjects all his life.

ᵃ 11 Or *in the heights of Dor*   *ᵇ 21* That is, the Euphrates; also in verse 24

²²Solomon's daily provisions were thirty cors ᵃ of fine flour and sixty cors ᵇ of meal, ²³ten head of stall-fed cattle, twenty of pasture-fed cattle and a hundred sheep and goats, as well as deer, gazelles, roebucks and choice fowl. ²⁴For he ruled over all the kingdoms west of the River, from Tiphsah to Gaza, and had peace on all sides. ²⁵During Solomon's lifetime Judah and Israel, from Dan to Beersheba, lived in safety, each man under his own vine and fig tree.

²⁶Solomon had four ᶜ thousand stalls for chariot horses, and twelve thousand horses. ᵈ

²⁷The district officers, each in his month, supplied provisions for King Solomon and all who came to the king's table. They saw to it that nothing was lacking. ²⁸They also brought to the proper place their quotas of barley and straw for the chariot horses and the other horses.

Solomon's Wisdom

²⁹God gave Solomon wisdom and very great insight, and a breadth of understanding as measureless as the sand on the seashore. ³⁰Solomon's

PRAYING THE SCRIPTURES

Wisdom
1 KINGS 4:29

Lord, I pray that you will give my grandchild wisdom, insight and a breadth of understanding as measureless as the sand on the seashore.

Next prayer in Wisdom Prayer Track: Psalm 119:65–66

wisdom was greater than the wisdom of all the men of the East, and greater than all the wisdom of Egypt. ³¹He was wiser than any other man, including Ethan the Ezrahite—wiser than Heman, Calcol and Darda, the sons of Mahol. And his fame spread to all the surrounding nations. ³²He spoke three thousand proverbs and his songs

numbered a thousand and five. ³³He described plant life, from the cedar of Lebanon to the hyssop that grows out of walls. He also taught about animals and birds, reptiles and fish. ³⁴Men of all nations came to listen to Solomon's wisdom, sent by all the kings of the world, who had heard of his wisdom.

Preparations for Building the Temple
5:1–16pp — 2Ch 2:1–18

5 When Hiram king of Tyre heard that Solomon had been anointed king to succeed his father David, he sent his envoys to Solomon, because he had always been on friendly terms with David. ²Solomon sent back this message to Hiram:

³"You know that because of the wars waged against my father David from all sides, he could not build a temple for the Name of the LORD his God until the LORD put his enemies under his feet. ⁴But now the LORD my God has given me rest on every side, and there is no adversary or disaster. ⁵I intend, therefore, to build a temple for the Name of the LORD my God, as the LORD told my father David, when he said, 'Your son whom I will put on the throne in your place will build the temple for my Name.'

⁶"So give orders that cedars of Lebanon be cut for me. My men will work with yours, and I will pay you for your men whatever wages you set. You know that we have no one so skilled in felling timber as the Sidonians."

⁷When Hiram heard Solomon's message, he was greatly pleased and said, "Praise be to the LORD today, for he has given David a wise son to rule over this great nation."

⁸So Hiram sent word to Solomon:

"I have received the message you sent me and will do all you want in providing the cedar and pine logs. ⁹My men will haul them

ᵃ 22 That is, probably about 185 bushels (about 6.6 kiloliters)
ᵇ 22 That is, probably about 375 bushels (about 13.2 kiloliters)
ᶜ 26 Some Septuagint manuscripts (see also 2 Chron. 9:25); Hebrew *forty*   ᵈ 26 Or *charioteers*

Heritage Builder

All those names in 1 Chronicles 1–9 remind us of how important family heritage was to Israel. Take a moment to point out those chapters to your grandkids; then segue into your own family story. Younger children will enjoy a story about your childhood, and older kids will be eager to ask questions about your life. If Grandpa is available, have them do the same with him. The kids' parents will also have interesting input regarding their generation. Write out some of your memories and distribute them as a "living history" of your family.

If someone has been maintaining a family tree, include this in your packet. (While you're at it, fill out the information in the front of this Bible.) If you like, you can have photographs, stories and handwritten notes compiled, copied and bound into a book at your local copy center. Or a DVD with pictures showing the development of the family through the generations could be made as a special treasure.

Long-Distance Variation: Ask the children to send you questions about your life. Then write out the answers, compile a booklet and send a copy back to them.

Dear Lord and Father of all generations, thank you for my family and for my precious grandchildren. Guide me as I pass on my family heritage. Help me to openly share my values and my faith with my grandchildren. Let them see through my life how great and faithful you have been through the years. Amen.

Your next devotion is located on page 454.

GRANDCHILD IN FOCUS • PRAYER

Friends

Dear Lord and Father, I pray for my grandchild's social life and his friends. Bring diverse friends into his life who will love and encourage him, who will bring joy and laughter to the good times and comfort and support through difficulties and disappointments. Grant him wisdom and discernment as he selects his friends; help him to avoid cliques that restrict, activities that endanger, and foolish and dangerous behaviors that harm. I ask that you fill his life with close and caring relationships. Amen.

down from Lebanon to the sea, and I will float them in rafts by sea to the place you specify. There I will separate them and you can take them away. And you are to grant my wish by providing food for my royal household."

¹⁰In this way Hiram kept Solomon supplied with all the cedar and pine logs he wanted, ¹¹and Solomon gave Hiram twenty thousand cors ᵃ of wheat as food for his household, in addition to twenty thousand baths ᵇ,ᶜ of pressed olive oil. Solomon continued to do this for Hiram year after year. ¹²The LORD gave Solomon wisdom, just as he had promised him. There were peaceful relations between Hiram and Solomon, and the two of them made a treaty.

¹³King Solomon conscripted laborers from all Israel—thirty thousand men. ¹⁴He sent them off to Lebanon in shifts of ten thousand a month, so that they spent one month in Lebanon and two months at home. Adoniram was in charge of the forced labor. ¹⁵Solomon had seventy thousand carriers and eighty thousand stonecutters in the hills, ¹⁶as well as thirty-three hundred ᵈ foremen who supervised the project and directed the workmen. ¹⁷At the king's command they removed from the quarry large blocks of quality stone to provide a foundation of dressed stone for the temple. ¹⁸The craftsmen of Solomon and Hiram and the men of Gebal ᵉ cut and prepared the timber and stone for the building of the temple.

Solomon Builds the Temple

6:1–29pp — 2Ch 3:1–14

6 In the four hundred and eightieth ᶠ year after the Israelites had come out of Egypt, in the fourth year of Solomon's reign over Israel, in the month of Ziv, the second month, he began to build the temple of the LORD.

²The temple that King Solomon built for the LORD was sixty cubits long, twenty wide and thirty high. ᵍ ³The portico at the front of the main hall of the temple extended the width of the temple, that is twenty cubits, ʰ and projected ten cu-

bits ⁱ from the front of the temple. ⁴He made narrow clerestory windows in the temple. ⁵Against the walls of the main hall and inner sanctuary he built a structure around the building, in which there were side rooms. ⁶The lowest floor was five cubits ʲ wide, the middle floor six cubits ᵏ and the third floor seven. ˡ He made offset ledges around the outside of the temple so that nothing would be inserted into the temple walls.

⁷In building the temple, only blocks dressed at the quarry were used, and no hammer, chisel or any other iron tool was heard at the temple site while it was being built.

⁸The entrance to the lowest ᵐ floor was on the south side of the temple; a stairway led up to the middle level and from there to the third. ⁹So he built the temple and completed it, roofing it with beams and cedar planks. ¹⁰And he built the side rooms all along the temple. The height of each was five cubits, and they were attached to the temple by beams of cedar.

¹¹The word of the LORD came to Solomon: ¹²"As for this temple you are building, if you follow my decrees, carry out my regulations and keep all my commands and obey them, I will fulfill through you the promise I gave to David your father. ¹³And I will live among the Israelites and will not abandon my people Israel."

¹⁴So Solomon built the temple and completed it. ¹⁵He lined its interior walls with cedar boards, paneling them from the floor of the temple to the ceiling, and covered the floor of the temple with planks of pine. ¹⁶He partitioned off twenty cubits ʰ at the rear of the temple with cedar boards from floor to ceiling to form within the temple an inner sanctuary, the Most Holy Place.

ᵃ 11 That is, probably about 125,000 bushels (about 4,400 kiloliters)   ᵇ 11 Septuagint (see also 2 Chron. 2:10); Hebrew twenty cors   ᶜ 11 That is, about 115,000 gallons (about 440 kiloliters)   ᵈ 16 Hebrew; some Septuagint manuscripts (see also 2 Chron. 2:2,18) thirty-six hundred   ᵉ 18 That is, Byblos   ᶠ 1 Hebrew; Septuagint four hundred and fortieth   ᵍ 2 That is, about 90 feet (about 27 meters) long and 30 feet (about 9 meters) wide and 45 feet (about 13.5 meters) high   ʰ 3,16 That is, about 30 feet (about 9 meters)   ⁱ 3 That is, about 15 feet (about 4.5 meters)   ʲ 6 That is, about 7 1/2 feet (about 2.3 meters); also in verses 10 and 24   ᵏ 6 That is, about 9 feet (about 2.7 meters)   ˡ 6 That is, about 10 1/2 feet (about 3.1 meters)   ᵐ 8 Septuagint; Hebrew middle

¹⁷The main hall in front of this room was forty cubits ᵃ long. ¹⁸The inside of the temple was cedar, carved with gourds and open flowers. Everything was cedar; no stone was to be seen.

¹⁹He prepared the inner sanctuary within the temple to set the ark of the covenant of the LORD there. ²⁰The inner sanctuary was twenty cubits long, twenty wide and twenty high. ᵇ He overlaid the inside with pure gold, and he also overlaid the altar of cedar. ²¹Solomon covered the inside of the temple with pure gold, and he extended gold chains across the front of the inner sanctuary, which was overlaid with gold. ²²So he overlaid the whole interior with gold. He also overlaid with gold the altar that belonged to the inner sanctuary.

²³In the inner sanctuary he made a pair of cherubim of olive wood, each ten cubits ᶜ high. ²⁴One wing of the first cherub was five cubits long, and the other wing five cubits — ten cubits from wing tip to wing tip. ²⁵The second cherub also measured ten cubits, for the two cherubim were identical in size and shape. ²⁶The height of each cherub was ten cubits. ²⁷He placed the cherubim inside the innermost room of the temple, with their wings spread out. The wing of one cherub touched one wall, while the wing of the other touched the other wall, and their wings touched each other in the middle of the room. ²⁸He overlaid the cherubim with gold.

²⁹On the walls all around the temple, in both the inner and outer rooms, he carved cherubim, palm trees and open flowers. ³⁰He also covered the floors of both the inner and outer rooms of the temple with gold.

³¹For the entrance of the inner sanctuary he made doors of olive wood with five-sided jambs. ³²And on the two olive wood doors he carved cherubim, palm trees and open flowers, and overlaid the cherubim and palm trees with beaten gold. ³³In the same way he made four-sided jambs of olive wood for the entrance to the main hall. ³⁴He also made two pine doors, each having two leaves that turned in sockets. ³⁵He carved cherubim, palm trees and open flowers on them

and overlaid them with gold hammered evenly over the carvings.

³⁶And he built the inner courtyard of three courses of dressed stone and one course of trimmed cedar beams.

³⁷The foundation of the temple of the LORD was laid in the fourth year, in the month of Ziv. ³⁸In the eleventh year in the month of Bul, the eighth month, the temple was finished in all its details according to its specifications. He had spent seven years building it.

Solomon Builds His Palace

7 It took Solomon thirteen years, however, to complete the construction of his palace. ²He built the Palace of the Forest of Lebanon a hundred cubits long, fifty wide and thirty high, ᵈ with four rows of cedar columns supporting trimmed cedar beams. ³It was roofed with cedar above the beams that rested on the columns — forty-five beams, fifteen to a row. ⁴Its windows were placed high in sets of three, facing each other. ⁵All the doorways had rectangular frames; they were in the front part in sets of three, facing each other. ᵉ

⁶He made a colonnade fifty cubits long and thirty wide. ᶠ In front of it was a portico, and in front of that were pillars and an overhanging roof.

⁷He built the throne hall, the Hall of Justice, where he was to judge, and he covered it with cedar from floor to ceiling. ᵍ ⁸And the palace in which he was to live, set farther back, was similar in design. Solomon also made a palace like this hall for Pharaoh's daughter, whom he had married.

⁹All these structures, from the outside to the great courtyard and from foundation to eaves, were made of blocks of high-grade stone cut

---

ᵃ 17 That is, about 60 feet (about 18 meters)   ᵇ 20 That is, about 30 feet (about 9 meters) long, wide and high   ᶜ 23 That is, about 15 feet (about 4.5 meters)   ᵈ 2 That is, about 150 feet (about 46 meters) long, 75 feet (about 23 meters) wide and 45 feet (about 13.5 meters) high   ᵉ 5 The meaning of the Hebrew for this verse is uncertain.   ᶠ 6 That is, about 75 feet (about 23 meters) long and 45 feet (about 13.5 meters) wide   ᵍ 7 Vulgate and Syriac; Hebrew floor

Worship the Lord

Praise the LORD.

Praise the LORD from the heavens,
　　praise him in the heights above.
Praise him, all his angels,
　　praise him, all his heavenly hosts.
Praise him, sun and moon,
　　praise him, all you shining stars.
Praise him, you highest heavens
　　and you waters above the skies.
Let them praise the name of the LORD,
　　for he commanded and they were created.
He set them in place for ever and ever;
　　he gave a decree that will never pass
　　　　away.

Psalm 148:1 – 6

I praise you today, Lord, along with the angels and the whole creation. I join in worship with your faithful people around the world to praise your holy name. May everything that breathes praise your glorious name forever and ever. Amen.

Your next devotion is located on page 459.

GRANDCHILD IN FOCUS • PRAYER

Self-Image

O loving God, I praise you for creating my grandchild as a unique individual. Now I ask you to help her appreciate her uniqueness. Build up her self-image so she can enjoy her individuality. Help her to stand firm for who she is, where she has come from and what she believes in. Encourage her not only to have hopes and dreams but to also enjoy each day as it comes.
In Jesus' name, amen.

to size and trimmed with a saw on their inner and outer faces. [10]The foundations were laid with large stones of good quality, some measuring ten cubits[a] and some eight.[b] [11]Above were high-grade stones, cut to size, and cedar beams. [12]The great courtyard was surrounded by a wall of three courses of dressed stone and one course of trimmed cedar beams, as was the inner courtyard of the temple of the LORD with its portico.

The Temple's Furnishings
7:23–26pp — 2Ch 4:2–5
7:38–51pp — 2Ch 4:6,10–5:1

[13]King Solomon sent to Tyre and brought Huram,[c] [14]whose mother was a widow from the tribe of Naphtali and whose father was a man of Tyre and a craftsman in bronze. Huram was highly skilled and experienced in all kinds of bronze work. He came to King Solomon and did all the work assigned to him.

[15]He cast two bronze pillars, each eighteen cubits high and twelve cubits around,[d] by line. [16]He also made two capitals of cast bronze to set on the tops of the pillars; each capital was five cubits[e] high. [17]A network of interwoven chains festooned the capitals on top of the pillars, seven for each capital. [18]He made pomegranates in two rows[f] encircling each network to decorate the capitals on top of the pillars.[g] He did the same for each capital. [19]The capitals on top of the pillars in the portico were in the shape of lilies, four cubits[h] high. [20]On the capitals of both pillars, above the bowl-shaped part next to the network, were the two hundred pomegranates in rows all around. [21]He erected the pillars at the portico of the temple. The pillar to the south he named Jakin[i] and the one to the north Boaz.[j] [22]The capitals on top were in the shape of lilies. And so the work on the pillars was completed.

[23]He made the Sea of cast metal, circular in shape, measuring ten cubits[k] from rim to rim and five cubits high. It took a line of thirty cubits[l] to measure around it. [24]Below the rim, gourds encircled it — ten to a cubit. The gourds were cast in two rows in one piece with the Sea.

[25]The Sea stood on twelve bulls, three facing north, three facing west, three facing south and three facing east. The Sea rested on top of them, and their hindquarters were toward the center. [26]It was a handbreadth[m] in thickness, and its rim was like the rim of a cup, like a lily blossom. It held two thousand baths.[n]

[27]He also made ten movable stands of bronze; each was four cubits long, four wide and three high.[o] [28]This is how the stands were made: They had side panels attached to uprights. [29]On the panels between the uprights were lions, bulls and cherubim — and on the uprights as well. Above and below the lions and bulls were wreaths of hammered work. [30]Each stand had four bronze wheels with bronze axles, and each had a basin resting on four supports, cast with wreaths on each side. [31]On the inside of the stand there was an opening that had a circular frame one cubit[p] deep. This opening was round, and with its basework it measured a cubit and a half.[q] Around its opening there was engraving. The panels of the stands were square, not round. [32]The four wheels were under the panels, and the axles of the wheels were attached to the stand. The diameter of each wheel was a cubit and a half. [33]The wheels were made like chariot wheels; the axles, rims, spokes and hubs were all of cast metal.

[34]Each stand had four handles, one on each corner, projecting from the stand. [35]At the top of the stand there was a circular band half a cubit[r] deep. The supports and panels were attached to the top

---

[a] 10 That is, about 15 feet (about 4.5 meters)   [b] 10 That is, about 12 feet (about 3.6 meters)   [c] 13 Hebrew *Hiram*, a variant of *Huram*; also in verses 40 and 45   [d] 15 That is, about 27 feet (about 8.1 meters) high and 18 feet (about 5.4 meters) around   [e] 16 That is, about 7 1/2 feet (about 2.3 meters); also in verse 23   [f] 18 Two Hebrew manuscripts and Septuagint; most Hebrew manuscripts *made the pillars, and there were two rows*   [g] 18 Many Hebrew manuscripts and Syriac; most Hebrew manuscripts *pomegranates*   [h] 19 That is, about 6 feet (about 1.8 meters); also in verse 38   [i] 21 *Jakin* probably means *he establishes*.   [j] 21 *Boaz* probably means *in him is strength*.   [k] 23 That is, about 15 feet (about 4.5 meters)   [l] 23 That is, about 45 feet (about 13.5 meters)   [m] 26 That is, about 3 inches (about 8 centimeters)   [n] 26 That is, probably about 11,500 gallons (about 44 kiloliters); the Septuagint does not have this sentence.   [o] 27 That is, about 6 feet (about 1.8 meters) long and wide and about 4 1/2 feet (about 1.3 meters) high   [p] 31 That is, about 1 1/2 feet (about 0.5 meter)   [q] 31 That is, about 2 1/4 feet (about 0.7 meter); also in verse 32   [r] 35 That is, about 3/4 foot (about 0.2 meter)

of the stand. ³⁶He engraved cherubim, lions and palm trees on the surfaces of the supports and on the panels, in every available space, with wreaths all around. ³⁷This is the way he made the ten stands. They were all cast in the same molds and were identical in size and shape.

³⁸He then made ten bronze basins, each holding forty baths ᵃ and measuring four cubits across, one basin to go on each of the ten stands. ³⁹He placed five of the stands on the south side of the temple and five on the north. He placed the Sea on the south side, at the southeast corner of the temple. ⁴⁰He also made the basins and shovels and sprinkling bowls.

So Huram finished all the work he had undertaken for King Solomon in the temple of the LORD:

⁴¹the two pillars;

the two bowl-shaped capitals on top of the pillars;

the two sets of network decorating the two bowl-shaped capitals on top of the pillars;

⁴²the four hundred pomegranates for the two sets of network (two rows of pomegranates for each network, decorating the bowl-shaped capitals on top of the pillars);

⁴³the ten stands with their ten basins;

⁴⁴the Sea and the twelve bulls under it;

⁴⁵the pots, shovels and sprinkling bowls.

All these objects that Huram made for King Solomon for the temple of the LORD were of burnished bronze. ⁴⁶The king had them cast in clay molds in the plain of the Jordan between Succoth and Zarethan. ⁴⁷Solomon left all these things unweighed, because there were so many; the weight of the bronze was not determined.

⁴⁸Solomon also made all the furnishings that were in the LORD's temple:

the golden altar;

the golden table on which was the bread of the Presence;

⁴⁹the lampstands of pure gold (five on the right and five on the left, in front of the inner sanctuary);

the gold floral work and lamps and tongs;

⁵⁰the pure gold basins, wick trimmers, sprinkling bowls, dishes and censers;

and the gold sockets for the doors of the innermost room, the Most Holy Place, and also for the doors of the main hall of the temple.

⁵¹When all the work King Solomon had done for the temple of the LORD was finished, he brought in the things his father David had dedicated—the silver and gold and the furnishings—and he placed them in the treasuries of the LORD's temple.

The Ark Brought to the Temple

8:1–21pp — 2Ch 5:2–6:11

8 Then King Solomon summoned into his presence at Jerusalem the elders of Israel, all the heads of the tribes and the chiefs of the Israelite families, to bring up the ark of the LORD's covenant from Zion, the City of David. ²All the men of Israel came together to King Solomon at the time of the festival in the month of Ethanim, the seventh month.

³When all the elders of Israel had arrived, the priests took up the ark, ⁴and they brought up the ark of the LORD and the Tent of Meeting and all the sacred furnishings in it. The priests and Levites carried them up, ⁵and King Solomon and the entire assembly of Israel that had gathered about him were before the ark, sacrificing so many sheep and cattle that they could not be recorded or counted.

⁶The priests then brought the ark of the LORD's covenant to its place in the inner sanctuary of the temple, the Most Holy Place, and put it beneath the wings of the cherubim. ⁷The cherubim spread their wings over the place of the ark and overshadowed the ark and its carrying poles. ⁸These poles were so long that their ends could

---

ᵃ 38 That is, about 230 gallons (about 880 liters)

be seen from the Holy Place in front of the inner sanctuary, but not from outside the Holy Place; and they are still there today. ⁹There was nothing in the ark except the two stone tablets that Moses had placed in it at Horeb, where the LORD made a covenant with the Israelites after they came out of Egypt.

¹⁰When the priests withdrew from the Holy Place, the cloud filled the temple of the LORD. ¹¹And the priests could not perform their service because of the cloud, for the glory of the LORD filled his temple.

¹²Then Solomon said, "The LORD has said that he would dwell in a dark cloud; ¹³I have indeed built a magnificent temple for you, a place for you to dwell forever."

¹⁴While the whole assembly of Israel was standing there, the king turned around and blessed them. ¹⁵Then he said:

"Praise be to the LORD, the God of Israel, who with his own hand has fulfilled what he promised with his own mouth to my father David. For he said, ¹⁶'Since the day I brought my people Israel out of Egypt, I have not chosen a city in any tribe of Israel to have a temple built for my Name to be there, but I have chosen David to rule my people Israel.'

¹⁷"My father David had it in his heart to build a temple for the Name of the LORD, the God of Israel. ¹⁸But the LORD said to my father David, 'Because it was in your heart to build a temple for my Name, you did well to have this in your heart. ¹⁹Nevertheless, you are not the one to build the temple, but your son, who is your own flesh and blood—he is the one who will build the temple for my Name.'

²⁰"The LORD has kept the promise he made: I have succeeded David my father and now I sit on the throne of Israel, just as the LORD promised, and I have built the temple for the Name of the LORD, the God of Israel. ²¹I have provided a place there

for the ark, in which is the covenant of the LORD that he made with our fathers when he brought them out of Egypt."

Solomon's Prayer of Dedication
8:22–53pp — 2Ch 6:12–40

²²Then Solomon stood before the altar of the LORD in front of the whole assembly of Israel, spread out his hands toward heaven ²³and said:

"O LORD, God of Israel, there is no God like you in heaven above or on earth below—you who keep your covenant of love with your servants who continue wholeheartedly in your way. ²⁴You have kept your promise to your servant David my father; with your mouth you have promised and with your hand you have fulfilled it—as it is today.

²⁵"Now LORD, God of Israel, keep for your servant David my father the promises you made to him when you said, 'You shall never fail to have a man to sit before me on the throne of Israel, if only your sons are careful in all they do to walk before me as you have done.' ²⁶And now, O God of Israel, let your word that you promised your servant David my father come true.

²⁷"But will God really dwell on earth? The heavens, even the highest heaven, cannot contain you. How much less this temple I have built! ²⁸Yet give attention to your servant's prayer and his plea for mercy, O LORD my God. Hear the cry and the prayer that your servant is praying in your presence this day. ²⁹May your eyes be open toward this temple night and day, this place of which you said, 'My Name shall be there,' so that you will hear the prayer your servant prays toward this place. ³⁰Hear the supplication of your servant and of your people Israel when they pray toward this place. Hear from heaven, your dwelling place, and when you hear, forgive.

³¹"When a man wrongs his neighbor and

is required to take an oath and he comes and swears the oath before your altar in this temple, ³²then hear from heaven and act. Judge between your servants, condemning the guilty and bringing down on his own head what he has done. Declare the innocent not guilty, and so establish his innocence.

³³"When your people Israel have been defeated by an enemy because they have sinned against you, and when they turn back to you and confess your name, praying and making supplication to you in this temple, ³⁴then hear from heaven and forgive the sin of your people Israel and bring them back to the land you gave to their fathers.

³⁵"When the heavens are shut up and there is no rain because your people have sinned against you, and when they pray toward this place and confess your name and turn from their sin because you have afflicted them, ³⁶then hear from heaven and forgive the sin of your servants, your people Israel. Teach them the right way to live, and send rain on the land you gave your people for an inheritance.

³⁷"When famine or plague comes to the land, or blight or mildew, locusts or grasshoppers, or when an enemy besieges them in any of their cities, whatever disaster or disease may come, ³⁸and when a prayer or plea is made by any of your people Israel— each one aware of the afflictions of his own heart, and spreading out his hands toward this temple— ³⁹then hear from heaven, your dwelling place. Forgive and act; deal with each man according to all he does, since you know his heart (for you alone know the hearts of all men), ⁴⁰so that they will fear you all the time they live in the land you gave our fathers.

⁴¹"As for the foreigner who does not belong to your people Israel but has come from a distant land because of your name— ⁴²for men will hear of your great name and your mighty hand and your outstretched arm—

when he comes and prays toward this temple, ⁴³then hear from heaven, your dwelling place, and do whatever the foreigner asks of you, so that all the peoples of the earth may know your name and fear you, as do your own people Israel, and may know that this house I have built bears your Name.

⁴⁴"When your people go to war against their enemies, wherever you send them, and when they pray to the LORD toward the city you have chosen and the temple I have built for your Name, ⁴⁵then hear from heaven their prayer and their plea, and uphold their cause.

⁴⁶"When they sin against you—for there is no one who does not sin—and you become angry with them and give them over to the enemy, who takes them captive to his own land, far away or near; ⁴⁷and if they have a change of heart in the land where they are held captive, and repent and plead with you in the land of their conquerors and say, 'We have sinned, we have done wrong, we have acted wickedly'; ⁴⁸and if they turn back to you with all their heart and soul in the land of their enemies who took them captive, and pray to you toward the land you gave their fathers, toward the city you have chosen and the temple I have built for your Name; ⁴⁹then from heaven, your dwelling place, hear their prayer and their plea, and uphold their cause. ⁵⁰And forgive your people, who have sinned against you; forgive all the offenses they have committed against you, and cause their conquerors to show them mercy; ⁵¹for they are your people and your inheritance, whom you brought out of Egypt, out of that iron-smelting furnace.

⁵²"May your eyes be open to your servant's plea and to the plea of your people Israel, and may you listen to them whenever they cry out to you. ⁵³For you singled them out from all the nations of the world to be your own inheritance, just as you declared through your servant Moses when you,

"MAY YOUR EYES BE OPEN TOWARD THIS TEMPLE NIGHT AND DAY, THIS PLACE OF WHICH YOU SAID, 'MY NAME SHALL BE THERE,' SO THAT YOU WILL HEAR THE PRAYER YOUR SERVANT PRAYS TOWARD THIS PLACE. HEAR THE SUPPLICATION OF YOUR SERVANT AND OF YOUR PEOPLE ISRAEL WHEN THEY PRAY TOWARD THIS PLACE. HEAR FROM HEAVEN, YOUR DWELLING PLACE, AND WHEN YOU HEAR, FORGIVE."

1 Kings 8:29–30

Old Cathedrals

BARBARA OWEN

READ | 1 KINGS 8:22 – 53

What majesty we have seen in old cathedrals today! Art, sculpture, architecture of incredible grandeur and yet greater sensitivity. Some of us took pictures where allowed. Others bought postcards, all to remember what we've experienced here. But what I'll most remember is the feeling of being in those huge homes for God — the awe and wonder that envelops one, standing in the nave of a cathedral.

The feeling comes from more than the beauty or an appreciation of the craft of the builders. It also comes from the link with other Christians. They worshiped here, in some cathedrals for hundreds of years, in others for a thousand. It is that kinship that envelops one and gives an inkling of what the body of Christ really is — people gathering for centuries, praising and thanking God, asking him to "hear us and forgive us."

The forgiveness is experienced once again in the cathedral. Everywhere a cross mediates God's Word. These are buildings of love and hope, built by and for God's people, who rejoice in what God has done for them in Jesus Christ.

How can I take this home with me, this sense of awe and kinship? I will walk into my small, modern church building, bringing a link with the past to today's members of the body of Christ.

Father, I stand in awe at your power to bring together in kinship generations of those who have loved you and worshiped you. Thank you for inviting me to be part of your family called the church.

Your next devotion is located on page 461.

GRANDCHILD IN FOCUS • PRAYER

Protection From Worldliness

O Sovereign Lord, the world surrounds my grandchild, pressing in and tempting him in so many ways. Help him set appropriate limits. Give him sound judgment to choose wisely. Guard him from temptation; protect him from physical and mental predators; lead him into paths of righteousness and light. And reassure me with your promise that you are holding him in your hands. Amen.

O Sovereign LORD, brought our fathers out of Egypt."

⁵⁴When Solomon had finished all these prayers and supplications to the LORD, he rose from before the altar of the LORD, where he had been kneeling with his hands spread out toward heaven. ⁵⁵He stood and blessed the whole assembly of Israel in a loud voice, saying:

⁵⁶"Praise be to the LORD, who has given rest to his people Israel just as he promised. Not one word has failed of all the good promises he gave through his servant Moses. ⁵⁷May the LORD our God be with us as he was with our fathers; may he never leave us nor forsake us. ⁵⁸May he turn our hearts to him, to walk in all his ways and to keep the commands, decrees and regulations he gave our fathers. ⁵⁹And may these words of mine, which I have prayed before the LORD, be near to the LORD our God day and night, that he may uphold the cause of his servant and the cause of his people Israel according to each day's need, ⁶⁰so that all the peoples of the earth may know that the LORD is God and that there is no other. ⁶¹But your hearts must be fully committed to the LORD our God, to live by his decrees and obey his commands, as at this time."

The Dedication of the Temple
8:62–66pp — 2Ch 7:1–10

⁶²Then the king and all Israel with him offered sacrifices before the LORD. ⁶³Solomon offered a sacrifice of fellowship offerings[a] to the LORD: twenty-two thousand cattle and a hundred and twenty thousand sheep and goats. So the king and all the Israelites dedicated the temple of the LORD.

⁶⁴On that same day the king consecrated the middle part of the courtyard in front of the temple of the LORD, and there he offered burnt offerings, grain offerings and the fat of the fellowship offerings, because the bronze altar before the LORD was too small to hold the burnt offerings,

the grain offerings and the fat of the fellowship offerings.

⁶⁵So Solomon observed the festival at that time, and all Israel with him—a vast assembly, people from Lebo[b] Hamath to the Wadi of Egypt. They celebrated it before the LORD our God for seven days and seven days more, fourteen days in all. ⁶⁶On the following day he sent the people away. They blessed the king and then went home, joyful and glad in heart for all the good things the LORD had done for his servant David and his people Israel.

The LORD Appears to Solomon
9:1–9pp — 2Ch 7:11–22

9 When Solomon had finished building the temple of the LORD and the royal palace, and had achieved all he had desired to do, ²the LORD appeared to him a second time, as he had appeared to him at Gibeon. ³The LORD said to him:

"I have heard the prayer and plea you have made before me; I have consecrated this temple, which you have built, by putting my Name there forever. My eyes and my heart will always be there.

⁴"As for you, if you walk before me in integrity of heart and uprightness, as David your father did, and do all I command and observe my decrees and laws, ⁵I will establish your royal throne over Israel forever, as I promised David your father when I said, 'You shall never fail to have a man on the throne of Israel.'

⁶"But if you[c] or your sons turn away from me and do not observe the commands and decrees I have given you[c] and go off to serve other gods and worship them, ⁷then I will cut off Israel from the land I have given them and will reject this temple I have consecrated for my Name. Israel will then become a byword and an object of ridicule among all peoples. ⁸And though this temple

---

[a] 63 Traditionally *peace offerings*; also in verse 64   [b] 65 Or *from the entrance to*   [c] 6 The Hebrew is plural.

> "PRAISE BE TO THE LORD, WHO
> HAS GIVEN REST TO HIS PEOPLE
> ISRAEL JUST AS HE PROMISED. NOT
> ONE WORD HAS FAILED OF ALL THE
> GOOD PROMISES HE GAVE THROUGH
> HIS SERVANT MOSES."
>
> *1 Kings 8:56*

Homemade Memories

KAREN O'CONNOR

READ | 1 KINGS 8:54 – 61

Dear God:

Today I'm thinking about the beautiful quilt my mother-in-law made me when I was a young bride. She handed it to me and said tenderly, "I made it for you, but I hope you'll pass it on to one of your children one day. I'd like to think of it as a lovely link from one generation to the next."

At the time, I couldn't imagine getting to that point in my life, but here I am, a senior just like Momma Rose was when she gave me the quilt. When I die, it will go to my daughter and then to my granddaughter. Lord, Your Word is like that quilt. It covers me but never smothers me. And it is a living Word that I can pass on to future generations so they too will know of Your love for them and Your eternal plan for their lives.

You tell us, Lord, to pass on Your teachings to those who come after us. If we train up a child in Your ways, he or she will always return to them. I believe that to be true. It happened in my life.

Today, the quilt, our first Bible, and other treasured heirlooms (baby shoes, handmade doilies, a Shirley Temple cereal bowl, my first dictionary) are on display in a glass-front bookcase in the front hall of our home. This collection of treasures serves as an anchor to the past and a bridge to the future, where You have prepared a place for each of us.

I look forward to that day, O Lord, when I will be with You forever in person, rejoicing with the saints over the promises You have fulfilled.

Dear Lord, your Word and your teachings are so precious to me. Help me to pass on the power of your words and the comfort of your promises to my children and grandchildren, letting them feel the presence of your love. Amen.

Your next devotion is located on page 489.

GRANDCHILD **IN FOCUS** • PRAYER

Respect for Authority

Dear Lord, I pray that my grandchild will continually grow to respect those in authority. May she learn to be cooperative and fair in work and play. Instill in her a high regard for officials who govern our land and enforce the laws. May her relationships with parents, teachers, coaches, mentors and bosses be respectful, admirable, constructive and caring. Amen.

is now imposing, all who pass by will be appalled and will scoff and say, 'Why has the LORD done such a thing to this land and to this temple?' ⁹People will answer, 'Because they have forsaken the LORD their God, who brought their fathers out of Egypt, and have embraced other gods, worshiping and serving them—that is why the LORD brought all this disaster on them.' "

Solomon's Other Activities
9:10–28pp — 2Ch 8:1–18

¹⁰At the end of twenty years, during which Solomon built these two buildings—the temple of the LORD and the royal palace— ¹¹King Solomon gave twenty towns in Galilee to Hiram king of Tyre, because Hiram had supplied him with all the cedar and pine and gold he wanted. ¹²But when Hiram went from Tyre to see the towns that Solomon had given him, he was not pleased with them. ¹³"What kind of towns are these you have given me, my brother?" he asked. And he called them the Land of Cabul,ᵃ a name they have to this day. ¹⁴Now Hiram had sent to the king 120 talentsᵇ of gold.

¹⁵Here is the account of the forced labor King Solomon conscripted to build the LORD's temple, his own palace, the supporting terraces,ᶜ the wall of Jerusalem, and Hazor, Megiddo and Gezer. ¹⁶(Pharaoh king of Egypt had attacked and captured Gezer. He had set it on fire. He killed its Canaanite inhabitants and then gave it as a wedding gift to his daughter, Solomon's wife. ¹⁷And Solomon rebuilt Gezer.) He built up Lower Beth Horon, ¹⁸Baalath, and Tadmorᵈ in the desert, within his land, ¹⁹as well as all his store cities and the towns for his chariots and for his horsesᵉ—whatever he desired to build in Jerusalem, in Lebanon and throughout all the territory he ruled.

²⁰All the people left from the Amorites, Hittites, Perizzites, Hivites and Jebusites (these peoples were not Israelites), ²¹that is, their descendants remaining in the land, whom the Israelites could not exterminateᶠ—these Solomon conscripted for his slave labor force, as it is to this day. ²²But Solomon did not make slaves of any of the Israelites; they were his fighting men, his government officials, his officers, his captains, and the commanders of his chariots and charioteers. ²³They were also the chief officials in charge of Solomon's projects—550 officials supervising the men who did the work.

²⁴After Pharaoh's daughter had come up from the City of David to the palace Solomon had built for her, he constructed the supporting terraces.

²⁵Three times a year Solomon sacrificed burnt offerings and fellowship offeringsᵍ on the altar he had built for the LORD, burning incense before the LORD along with them, and so fulfilled the temple obligations.

²⁶King Solomon also built ships at Ezion Geber, which is near Elath in Edom, on the shore of the Red Sea.ʰ ²⁷And Hiram sent his men—sailors who knew the sea—to serve in the fleet with Solomon's men. ²⁸They sailed to Ophir and brought back 420 talentsⁱ of gold, which they delivered to King Solomon.

The Queen of Sheba Visits Solomon
10:1–13pp — 2Ch 9:1–12

10 When the queen of Sheba heard about the fame of Solomon and his relation to the name of the LORD, she came to test him with hard questions. ²Arriving at Jerusalem with a very great caravan—with camels carrying spices, large quantities of gold, and precious stones—she came to Solomon and talked with him about all that she had on her mind. ³Solomon answered all her questions; nothing was too hard for the king to explain to her. ⁴When the queen of Sheba saw all the wisdom of Solomon and the palace he had built, ⁵the food on his table, the seating of his officials, the attending servants in their robes, his cupbearers, and the

---

ᵃ 13 Cabul sounds like the Hebrew for good-for-nothing.
ᵇ 14 That is, about 4 1/2 tons (about 4 metric tons)   ᶜ 15 Or the Millo; also in verse 24   ᵈ 18 The Hebrew may also be read Tamar.   ᵉ 19 Or charioteers   ᶠ 21 The Hebrew term refers to the irrevocable giving over of things or persons to the LORD, often by totally destroying them.   ᵍ 25 Traditionally peace offerings   ʰ 26 Hebrew Yam Suph; that is, Sea of Reeds   ⁱ 28 That is, about 16 tons (about 14.5 metric tons)

stories to share

1 KINGS 10:1–13

The Queen of Sheba Visits Solomon

LIFE LESSON: Our friends and neighbors are watching our lives to see how we live.

TO TALK ABOUT

◆ What did the queen hear about Solomon?

◆ Was what she heard true?

◆ Where did Solomon get his wisdom and honor? (Hint: Read 1 Kings 3:1–15.)

◆ What do people learn about God when they look at your life?

burnt offerings he made at[a] the temple of the LORD, she was overwhelmed.

[6]She said to the king, "The report I heard in my own country about your achievements and your wisdom is true. [7]But I did not believe these things until I came and saw with my own eyes. Indeed, not even half was told me; in wisdom and wealth you have far exceeded the report I heard. [8]How happy your men must be! How happy your officials, who continually stand before you and hear your wisdom! [9]Praise be to the LORD your God, who has delighted in you and placed you on the throne of Israel. Because of the LORD's eternal love for Israel, he has made you king, to maintain justice and righteousness."

[10]And she gave the king 120 talents[b] of gold, large quantities of spices, and precious stones. Never again were so many spices brought in as those the queen of Sheba gave to King Solomon.

[11](Hiram's ships brought gold from Ophir; and from there they brought great cargoes of almugwood[c] and precious stones. [12]The king used the almugwood to make supports for the temple of the LORD and for the royal palace, and to make harps and lyres for the musicians. So much almugwood has never been imported or seen since that day.)

[13]King Solomon gave the queen of Sheba all she desired and asked for, besides what he had given her out of his royal bounty. Then she left and returned with her retinue to her own country.

Solomon's Splendor
10:14–29pp — 2Ch 1:14–17; 9:13–28

[14]The weight of the gold that Solomon received yearly was 666 talents,[d] [15]not including the revenues from merchants and traders and from all the Arabian kings and the governors of the land.

[16]King Solomon made two hundred large shields of hammered gold; six hundred bekas[e] of gold went into each shield. [17]He also made three hundred small shields of hammered gold, with three minas[f] of gold in each shield. The king put them in the Palace of the Forest of Lebanon.

[18]Then the king made a great throne inlaid with ivory and overlaid with fine gold. [19]The throne had six steps, and its back had a rounded top. On both sides of the seat were armrests, with a lion standing beside each of them. [20]Twelve lions stood on the six steps, one at either end of each step. Nothing like it had ever been made for any other kingdom. [21]All King Solomon's goblets were gold, and all the household articles in the Palace of the Forest of Lebanon were pure gold. Nothing was made of silver, because silver

---

[a] 5 Or *the ascent by which he went up to*   [b] 10 That is, about 4 1/2 tons (about 4 metric tons)   [c] 11 Probably a variant of *algumwood*; also in verse 12   [d] 14 That is, about 25 tons (about 23 metric tons)   [e] 16 That is, about 7 1/2 pounds (about 3.5 kilograms)   [f] 17 That is, about 3 3/4 pounds (about 1.7 kilograms)

was considered of little value in Solomon's days. [22] The king had a fleet of trading ships[a] at sea along with the ships of Hiram. Once every three years it returned, carrying gold, silver and ivory, and apes and baboons.

[23] King Solomon was greater in riches and wisdom than all the other kings of the earth. [24] The whole world sought audience with Solomon to hear the wisdom God had put in his heart. [25] Year after year, everyone who came brought a gift—articles of silver and gold, robes, weapons and spices, and horses and mules.

[26] Solomon accumulated chariots and horses; he had fourteen hundred chariots and twelve thousand horses,[b] which he kept in the chariot cities and also with him in Jerusalem. [27] The king made silver as common in Jerusalem as stones, and cedar as plentiful as sycamore-fig trees in the foothills. [28] Solomon's horses were imported from Egypt[c] and from Kue[d]—the royal merchants purchased them from Kue. [29] They imported a chariot from Egypt for six hundred shekels[e] of silver, and a horse for a hundred and fifty.[f] They also exported them to all the kings of the Hittites and of the Arameans.

Solomon's Wives

11 King Solomon, however, loved many foreign women besides Pharaoh's daughter—Moabites, Ammonites, Edomites, Sidonians and Hittites. [2] They were from nations about which the LORD had told the Israelites, "You must not intermarry with them, because they will surely turn your hearts after their gods." Nevertheless, Solomon held fast to them in love. [3] He had seven hundred wives of royal birth and three hundred concubines, and his wives led him astray. [4] As Solomon grew old, his wives turned his heart after other gods, and his heart was not fully devoted to the LORD his God, as the heart of David his father had been. [5] He followed Ashtoreth the goddess of the Sidonians, and Molech[g] the detestable god of the Ammonites. [6] So Solomon did evil in the eyes of the LORD; he did not follow the LORD completely, as David his father had done.

[7] On a hill east of Jerusalem, Solomon built a high place for Chemosh the detestable god of Moab, and for Molech the detestable god of the Ammonites. [8] He did the same for all his foreign wives, who burned incense and offered sacrifices to their gods.

[9] The LORD became angry with Solomon because his heart had turned away from the LORD, the God of Israel, who had appeared to him twice. [10] Although he had forbidden Solomon to follow other gods, Solomon did not keep the LORD's command. [11] So the LORD said to Solomon, "Since this is your attitude and you have not kept my covenant and my decrees, which I commanded you, I will most certainly tear the kingdom away from you and give it to one of your subordinates. [12] Nevertheless, for the sake of David your father, I will not do it during your lifetime. I will tear it out of the hand of your son. [13] Yet I will not tear the whole kingdom from him, but will give him one tribe for the sake of David my servant and for the sake of Jerusalem, which I have chosen."

Solomon's Adversaries

[14] Then the LORD raised up against Solomon an adversary, Hadad the Edomite, from the royal line of Edom. [15] Earlier when David was fighting with Edom, Joab the commander of the army, who had gone up to bury the dead, had struck down all the men in Edom. [16] Joab and all the Israelites stayed there for six months, until they had destroyed all the men in Edom. [17] But Hadad, still only a boy, fled to Egypt with some Edomite officials who had served his father. [18] They set out from Midian and went to Paran. Then taking men from Paran with them, they went to Egypt, to Pharaoh king of Egypt, who gave Hadad a house and land and provided him with food.

[19] Pharaoh was so pleased with Hadad that he

---

[a] 22 Hebrew *of ships of Tarshish*   [b] 26 Or *charioteers*
[c] 28 Or possibly *Muzur*, a region in Cilicia; also in verse 29
[d] 28 Probably *Cilicia*   [e] 29 That is, about 15 pounds (about 7 kilograms)   [f] 29 That is, about 3 3/4 pounds (about 1.7 kilograms)   [g] 5 Hebrew *Milcom*; also in verse 33

gave him a sister of his own wife, Queen Tahpenes, in marriage. [20] The sister of Tahpenes bore him a son named Genubath, whom Tahpenes brought up in the royal palace. There Genubath lived with Pharaoh's own children.

[21] While he was in Egypt, Hadad heard that David rested with his fathers and that Joab the commander of the army was also dead. Then Hadad said to Pharaoh, "Let me go, that I may return to my own country."

[22] "What have you lacked here that you want to go back to your own country?" Pharaoh asked.

"Nothing," Hadad replied, "but do let me go!"

[23] And God raised up against Solomon another adversary, Rezon son of Eliada, who had fled from his master, Hadadezer king of Zobah. [24] He gathered men around him and became the leader of a band of rebels when David destroyed the forces [a] of Zobah; the rebels went to Damascus, where they settled and took control. [25] Rezon was Israel's adversary as long as Solomon lived, adding to the trouble caused by Hadad. So Rezon ruled in Aram and was hostile toward Israel.

Jeroboam Rebels Against Solomon

[26] Also, Jeroboam son of Nebat rebelled against the king. He was one of Solomon's officials, an Ephraimite from Zeredah, and his mother was a widow named Zeruah.

[27] Here is the account of how he rebelled against the king: Solomon had built the supporting terraces [b] and had filled in the gap in the wall of the city of David his father. [28] Now Jeroboam was a man of standing, and when Solomon saw how well the young man did his work, he put him in charge of the whole labor force of the house of Joseph.

[29] About that time Jeroboam was going out of Jerusalem, and Ahijah the prophet of Shiloh met him on the way, wearing a new cloak. The two of them were alone out in the country, [30] and Ahijah took hold of the new cloak he was wearing and tore it into twelve pieces. [31] Then he said to Jeroboam, "Take ten pieces for yourself, for this is what the LORD, the God of Israel, says: 'See, I am going to tear the kingdom out of Solomon's hand and give you ten tribes. [32] But for the sake of my servant David and the city of Jerusalem, which I have chosen out of all the tribes of Israel, he will have one tribe. [33] I will do this because they have [c] forsaken me and worshiped Ashtoreth the goddess of the Sidonians, Chemosh the god of the Moabites, and Molech the god of the Ammonites, and have not walked in my ways, nor done what is right in my eyes, nor kept my statutes and laws as David, Solomon's father, did.

[34] " 'But I will not take the whole kingdom out of Solomon's hand; I have made him ruler all the days of his life for the sake of David my servant, whom I chose and who observed my commands and statutes. [35] I will take the kingdom from his son's hands and give you ten tribes. [36] I will give one tribe to his son so that David my servant may always have a lamp before me in Jerusalem, the city where I chose to put my Name. [37] However, as for you, I will take you, and you will rule over all that your heart desires; you will be king over Israel. [38] If you do whatever I command you and walk in my ways and do what is right in my eyes by keeping my statutes and commands, as David my servant did, I will be with you. I will build you a dynasty as enduring as the one I built for David and will give Israel to you. [39] I will humble David's descendants because of this, but not forever.' "

[40] Solomon tried to kill Jeroboam, but Jeroboam fled to Egypt, to Shishak the king, and stayed there until Solomon's death.

Solomon's Death

11:41–43pp — 2Ch 9:29–31

[41] As for the other events of Solomon's reign — all he did and the wisdom he displayed — are they not written in the book of the annals of Solomon? [42] Solomon reigned in Jerusalem over all Israel forty years. [43] Then he rested with his fathers and was buried in the city of David his father. And Rehoboam his son succeeded him as king.

---

[a] 24 Hebrew *destroyed them*   [b] 27 Or *the Millo*   [c] 33 Hebrew; Septuagint, Vulgate and Syriac *because he has*

Israel Rebels Against Rehoboam

12:1–24pp — 2Ch 10:1–11:4

12 Rehoboam went to Shechem, for all the Israelites had gone there to make him king. ²When Jeroboam son of Nebat heard this (he was still in Egypt, where he had fled from King Solomon), he returned from*ᵃ* Egypt. ³So they sent for Jeroboam, and he and the whole assembly of Israel went to Rehoboam and said to him: ⁴"Your father put a heavy yoke on us, but now lighten the harsh labor and the heavy yoke he put on us, and we will serve you."

⁵Rehoboam answered, "Go away for three days and then come back to me." So the people went away.

⁶Then King Rehoboam consulted the elders who had served his father Solomon during his lifetime. "How would you advise me to answer these people?" he asked.

⁷They replied, "If today you will be a servant to these people and serve them and give them a favorable answer, they will always be your servants."

⁸But Rehoboam rejected the advice the elders gave him and consulted the young men who had grown up with him and were serving him. ⁹He asked them, "What is your advice? How should we answer these people who say to me, 'Lighten the yoke your father put on us'?"

¹⁰The young men who had grown up with him replied, "Tell these people who have said to you, 'Your father put a heavy yoke on us, but make our yoke lighter'—tell them, 'My little finger is thicker than my father's waist. ¹¹My father laid on you a heavy yoke; I will make it even heavier. My father scourged you with whips; I will scourge you with scorpions.'"

¹²Three days later Jeroboam and all the people returned to Rehoboam, as the king had said, "Come back to me in three days." ¹³The king answered the people harshly. Rejecting the advice given him by the elders, ¹⁴he followed the advice of the young men and said, "My father made your yoke heavy; I will make it even heavier. My father scourged you with whips; I will scourge you with scorpions." ¹⁵So the king did not listen to the people, for this turn of events was from the LORD, to fulfill the word the LORD had spoken to Jeroboam son of Nebat through Ahijah the Shilonite.

¹⁶When all Israel saw that the king refused to listen to them, they answered the king:

"What share do we have in David,
   what part in Jesse's son?
To your tents, O Israel!
   Look after your own house, O David!"

So the Israelites went home. ¹⁷But as for the Israelites who were living in the towns of Judah, Rehoboam still ruled over them.

¹⁸King Rehoboam sent out Adoniram,*ᵇ* who was in charge of forced labor, but all Israel stoned him to death. King Rehoboam, however, managed to get into his chariot and escape to Jerusalem. ¹⁹So Israel has been in rebellion against the house of David to this day.

²⁰When all the Israelites heard that Jeroboam had returned, they sent and called him to the assembly and made him king over all Israel. Only the tribe of Judah remained loyal to the house of David.

²¹When Rehoboam arrived in Jerusalem, he mustered the whole house of Judah and the tribe of Benjamin—a hundred and eighty thousand fighting men—to make war against the house of Israel and to regain the kingdom for Rehoboam son of Solomon.

²²But this word of God came to Shemaiah the man of God: ²³"Say to Rehoboam son of Solomon king of Judah, to the whole house of Judah and Benjamin, and to the rest of the people, ²⁴'This is what the LORD says: Do not go up to fight against your brothers, the Israelites. Go home, every one of you, for this is my doing.'" So they obeyed the word of the LORD and went home again, as the LORD had ordered.

ᵃ 2 Or *he remained in*   *ᵇ* 18 Some Septuagint manuscripts and Syriac (see also 1 Kings 4:6 and 5:14); Hebrew *Adoram*

Golden Calves at Bethel and Dan

²⁵ Then Jeroboam fortified Shechem in the hill country of Ephraim and lived there. From there he went out and built up Peniel.[a]

²⁶ Jeroboam thought to himself, "The kingdom will now likely revert to the house of David. ²⁷ If these people go up to offer sacrifices at the temple of the Lord in Jerusalem, they will again give their allegiance to their lord, Rehoboam king of Judah. They will kill me and return to King Rehoboam."

²⁸ After seeking advice, the king made two golden calves. He said to the people, "It is too much for you to go up to Jerusalem. Here are your gods, O Israel, who brought you up out of Egypt." ²⁹ One he set up in Bethel, and the other in Dan. ³⁰ And this thing became a sin; the people went even as far as Dan to worship the one there.

³¹ Jeroboam built shrines on high places and appointed priests from all sorts of people, even though they were not Levites. ³² He instituted a festival on the fifteenth day of the eighth month, like the festival held in Judah, and offered sacrifices on the altar. This he did in Bethel, sacrificing to the calves he had made. And at Bethel he also installed priests at the high places he had made. ³³ On the fifteenth day of the eighth month, a month of his own choosing, he offered sacrifices on the altar he had built at Bethel. So he instituted the festival for the Israelites and went up to the altar to make offerings.

The Man of God From Judah

13 By the word of the Lord a man of God came from Judah to Bethel, as Jeroboam was standing by the altar to make an offering. ² He cried out against the altar by the word of the Lord: "O altar, altar! This is what the Lord says: 'A son named Josiah will be born to the house of David. On you he will sacrifice the priests of the high places who now make offerings here, and human bones will be burned on you.'" ³ That same day the man of God gave a sign: "This is the sign

the Lord has declared: The altar will be split apart and the ashes on it will be poured out."

⁴ When King Jeroboam heard what the man of God cried out against the altar at Bethel, he stretched out his hand from the altar and said, "Seize him!" But the hand he stretched out toward the man shriveled up, so that he could not pull it back. ⁵ Also, the altar was split apart and its ashes poured out according to the sign given by the man of God by the word of the Lord.

⁶ Then the king said to the man of God, "Intercede with the Lord your God and pray for me that my hand may be restored." So the man of God interceded with the Lord, and the king's hand was restored and became as it was before.

⁷ The king said to the man of God, "Come home with me and have something to eat, and I will give you a gift."

⁸ But the man of God answered the king, "Even if you were to give me half your possessions, I would not go with you, nor would I eat bread or drink water here. ⁹ For I was commanded by the word of the Lord: 'You must not eat bread or drink water or return by the way you came.'" ¹⁰ So he took another road and did not return by the way he had come to Bethel.

¹¹ Now there was a certain old prophet living in Bethel, whose sons came and told him all that the man of God had done there that day. They also told their father what he had said to the king. ¹² Their father asked them, "Which way did he go?" And his sons showed him which road the man of God from Judah had taken. ¹³ So he said to his sons, "Saddle the donkey for me." And when they had saddled the donkey for him, he mounted it ¹⁴ and rode after the man of God. He found him sitting under an oak tree and asked, "Are you the man of God who came from Judah?"

"I am," he replied.

¹⁵ So the prophet said to him, "Come home with me and eat."

¹⁶ The man of God said, "I cannot turn back and go with you, nor can I eat bread or drink water with

---

[a] 25 Hebrew *Penuel,* a variant of *Peniel*

you in this place. ¹⁷I have been told by the word of the LORD: 'You must not eat bread or drink water there or return by the way you came.' "

¹⁸The old prophet answered, "I too am a prophet, as you are. And an angel said to me by the word of the LORD: 'Bring him back with you to your house so that he may eat bread and drink water.' " (But he was lying to him.) ¹⁹So the man of God returned with him and ate and drank in his house.

²⁰While they were sitting at the table, the word of the LORD came to the old prophet who had brought him back. ²¹He cried out to the man of God who had come from Judah, "This is what the LORD says: 'You have defied the word of the LORD and have not kept the command the LORD your God gave you. ²²You came back and ate bread and drank water in the place where he told you not to eat or drink. Therefore your body will not be buried in the tomb of your fathers.' "

²³When the man of God had finished eating and drinking, the prophet who had brought him back saddled his donkey for him. ²⁴As he went on his way, a lion met him on the road and killed him, and his body was thrown down on the road, with both the donkey and the lion standing beside it. ²⁵Some people who passed by saw the body thrown down there, with the lion standing beside the body, and they went and reported it in the city where the old prophet lived.

²⁶When the prophet who had brought him back from his journey heard of it, he said, "It is the man of God who defied the word of the LORD. The LORD has given him over to the lion, which has mauled him and killed him, as the word of the LORD had warned him."

²⁷The prophet said to his sons, "Saddle the donkey for me," and they did so. ²⁸Then he went out and found the body thrown down on the road, with the donkey and the lion standing beside it. The lion had neither eaten the body nor mauled the donkey. ²⁹So the prophet picked up the body of the man of God, laid it on the donkey, and brought it back to his own city to mourn for him and bury him. ³⁰Then he laid the body in his own tomb, and they mourned over him and said, "Oh, my brother!"

³¹After burying him, he said to his sons, "When I die, bury me in the grave where the man of God is buried; lay my bones beside his bones. ³²For the message he declared by the word of the LORD against the altar in Bethel and against all the shrines on the high places in the towns of Samaria will certainly come true."

³³Even after this, Jeroboam did not change his evil ways, but once more appointed priests for the high places from all sorts of people. Anyone who wanted to become a priest he consecrated for the high places. ³⁴This was the sin of the house of Jeroboam that led to its downfall and to its destruction from the face of the earth.

Ahijah's Prophecy Against Jeroboam

14 At that time Abijah son of Jeroboam became ill, ²and Jeroboam said to his wife, "Go, disguise yourself, so you won't be recognized as the wife of Jeroboam. Then go to Shiloh. Ahijah the prophet is there—the one who told me I would be king over this people. ³Take ten loaves of bread with you, some cakes and a jar of honey, and go to him. He will tell you what will happen to the boy." ⁴So Jeroboam's wife did what he said and went to Ahijah's house in Shiloh.

Now Ahijah could not see; his sight was gone because of his age. ⁵But the LORD had told Ahijah, "Jeroboam's wife is coming to ask you about her son, for he is ill, and you are to give her such and such an answer. When she arrives, she will pretend to be someone else."

⁶So when Ahijah heard the sound of her footsteps at the door, he said, "Come in, wife of Jeroboam. Why this pretense? I have been sent to you with bad news. ⁷Go, tell Jeroboam that this is what the LORD, the God of Israel, says: 'I raised you up from among the people and made you a leader over my people Israel. ⁸I tore the kingdom away from the house of David and gave it to you, but you have not been like my servant David, who kept my commands and followed me with all his heart, doing only what was right in

my eyes. [9] You have done more evil than all who lived before you. You have made for yourself other gods, idols made of metal; you have provoked me to anger and thrust me behind your back.

[10] " 'Because of this, I am going to bring disaster on the house of Jeroboam. I will cut off from Jeroboam every last male in Israel—slave or free. I will burn up the house of Jeroboam as one burns dung, until it is all gone. [11] Dogs will eat those belonging to Jeroboam who die in the city, and the birds of the air will feed on those who die in the country. The LORD has spoken!'

[12] "As for you, go back home. When you set foot in your city, the boy will die. [13] All Israel will mourn for him and bury him. He is the only one belonging to Jeroboam who will be buried, because he is the only one in the house of Jeroboam in whom the LORD, the God of Israel, has found anything good.

[14] "The LORD will raise up for himself a king over Israel who will cut off the family of Jeroboam. This is the day! What? Yes, even now.[a] [15] And the LORD will strike Israel, so that it will be like a reed swaying in the water. He will uproot Israel from this good land that he gave to their forefathers and scatter them beyond the River,[b] because they provoked the LORD to anger by making Asherah poles.[c] [16] And he will give Israel up because of the sins Jeroboam has committed and has caused Israel to commit."

[17] Then Jeroboam's wife got up and left and went to Tirzah. As soon as she stepped over the threshold of the house, the boy died. [18] They buried him, and all Israel mourned for him, as the LORD had said through his servant the prophet Ahijah.

[19] The other events of Jeroboam's reign, his wars and how he ruled, are written in the book of the annals of the kings of Israel. [20] He reigned for twenty-two years and then rested with his fathers. And Nadab his son succeeded him as king.

Rehoboam King of Judah
14:21,25–31pp — 2Ch 12:9–16

[21] Rehoboam son of Solomon was king in Judah. He was forty-one years old when he became king, and he reigned seventeen years in Jerusalem, the city the LORD had chosen out of all the tribes of Israel in which to put his Name. His mother's name was Naamah; she was an Ammonite.

[22] Judah did evil in the eyes of the LORD. By the sins they committed they stirred up his jealous anger more than their fathers had done. [23] They also set up for themselves high places, sacred stones and Asherah poles on every high hill and under every spreading tree. [24] There were even male shrine prostitutes in the land; the people engaged in all the detestable practices of the nations the LORD had driven out before the Israelites.

[25] In the fifth year of King Rehoboam, Shishak king of Egypt attacked Jerusalem. [26] He carried off the treasures of the temple of the LORD and the treasures of the royal palace. He took everything, including all the gold shields Solomon had made. [27] So King Rehoboam made bronze shields to replace them and assigned these to the commanders of the guard on duty at the entrance to the royal palace. [28] Whenever the king went to the LORD's temple, the guards bore the shields, and afterward they returned them to the guardroom.

[29] As for the other events of Rehoboam's reign, and all he did, are they not written in the book of the annals of the kings of Judah? [30] There was continual warfare between Rehoboam and Jeroboam. [31] And Rehoboam rested with his fathers and was buried with them in the City of David. His mother's name was Naamah; she was an Ammonite. And Abijah[d] his son succeeded him as king.

Abijah King of Judah
15:1–2,6–8pp — 2Ch 13:1–2,22–14:1

15 In the eighteenth year of the reign of Jeroboam son of Nebat, Abijah[e] became king of Judah, [2] and he reigned in Jerusalem three

---

[a] 14 The meaning of the Hebrew for this sentence is uncertain. [b] 15 That is, the Euphrates   [c] 15 That is, symbols of the goddess Asherah; here and elsewhere in 1 Kings   [d] 31 Some Hebrew manuscripts and Septuagint (see also 2 Chron. 12:16); most Hebrew manuscripts *Abijam*   [e] 1 Some Hebrew manuscripts and Septuagint (see also 2 Chron. 12:16); most Hebrew manuscripts *Abijam*; also in verses 7 and 8

years. His mother's name was Maacah daughter of Abishalom. *a*

³He committed all the sins his father had done before him; his heart was not fully devoted to the LORD his God, as the heart of David his forefather had been. ⁴Nevertheless, for David's sake the LORD his God gave him a lamp in Jerusalem by raising up a son to succeed him and by making Jerusalem strong. ⁵For David had done what was right in the eyes of the LORD and had not failed to keep any of the LORD's commands all the days of his life—except in the case of Uriah the Hittite.

⁶There was war between Rehoboam *b* and Jeroboam throughout ⌊Abijah's⌋ lifetime. ⁷As for the other events of Abijah's reign, and all he did, are they not written in the book of the annals of the kings of Judah? There was war between Abijah and Jeroboam. ⁸And Abijah rested with his fathers and was buried in the City of David. And Asa his son succeeded him as king.

Asa King of Judah

15:9–22pp — 2Ch 14:2–3; 15:16–16:6
15:23–24pp — 2Ch 16:11–17:1

⁹In the twentieth year of Jeroboam king of Israel, Asa became king of Judah, ¹⁰and he reigned in Jerusalem forty-one years. His grandmother's name was Maacah daughter of Abishalom.

¹¹Asa did what was right in the eyes of the LORD, as his father David had done. ¹²He expelled the male shrine prostitutes from the land and got rid of all the idols his fathers had made. ¹³He even deposed his grandmother Maacah from her position as queen mother, because she had made a repulsive Asherah pole. Asa cut the pole down and burned it in the Kidron Valley. ¹⁴Although he did not remove the high places, Asa's heart was fully committed to the LORD all his life. ¹⁵He brought into the temple of the LORD the silver and gold and the articles that he and his father had dedicated.

¹⁶There was war between Asa and Baasha king of Israel throughout their reigns. ¹⁷Baasha king of Israel went up against Judah and fortified Ramah to prevent anyone from leaving or entering the territory of Asa king of Judah.

¹⁸Asa then took all the silver and gold that was left in the treasuries of the LORD's temple and of his own palace. He entrusted it to his officials and sent them to Ben-Hadad son of Tabrimmon, the son of Hezion, the king of Aram, who was ruling in Damascus. ¹⁹"Let there be a treaty between me and you," he said, "as there was between my father and your father. See, I am sending you a gift of silver and gold. Now break your treaty with Baasha king of Israel so he will withdraw from me."

²⁰Ben-Hadad agreed with King Asa and sent the commanders of his forces against the towns of Israel. He conquered Ijon, Dan, Abel Beth Maacah and all Kinnereth in addition to Naphtali. ²¹When Baasha heard this, he stopped building Ramah and withdrew to Tirzah. ²²Then King Asa issued an order to all Judah—no one was exempt—and they carried away from Ramah the stones and timber Baasha had been using there. With them King Asa built up Geba in Benjamin, and also Mizpah.

²³As for all the other events of Asa's reign, all his achievements, all he did and the cities he built, are they not written in the book of the annals of the kings of Judah? In his old age, however, his feet became diseased. ²⁴Then Asa rested with his fathers and was buried with them in the city of his father David. And Jehoshaphat his son succeeded him as king.

Nadab King of Israel

²⁵Nadab son of Jeroboam became king of Israel in the second year of Asa king of Judah, and he reigned over Israel two years. ²⁶He did evil in the eyes of the LORD, walking in the ways of his father and in his sin, which he had caused Israel to commit.

²⁷Baasha son of Ahijah of the house of Issachar plotted against him, and he struck him down at Gibbethon, a Philistine town, while Nadab and all Israel were besieging it. ²⁸Baasha killed Nadab

a 2 A variant of *Absalom*; also in verse 10   *b 6* Most Hebrew manuscripts; some Hebrew manuscripts and Syriac *Abijam* (that is, Abijah) in the third year of Asa king of Judah and succeeded him as king.

²⁹As soon as he began to reign, he killed Jeroboam's whole family. He did not leave Jeroboam anyone that breathed, but destroyed them all, according to the word of the LORD given through his servant Ahijah the Shilonite— ³⁰because of the sins Jeroboam had committed and had caused Israel to commit, and because he provoked the LORD, the God of Israel, to anger.

³¹As for the other events of Nadab's reign, and all he did, are they not written in the book of the annals of the kings of Israel? ³²There was war between Asa and Baasha king of Israel throughout their reigns.

Baasha King of Israel

³³In the third year of Asa king of Judah, Baasha son of Ahijah became king of all Israel in Tirzah, and he reigned twenty-four years. ³⁴He did evil in the eyes of the LORD, walking in the ways of Jeroboam and in his sin, which he had caused Israel to commit.

16 Then the word of the LORD came to Jehu son of Hanani against Baasha: ²"I lifted you up from the dust and made you leader of my people Israel, but you walked in the ways of Jeroboam and caused my people Israel to sin and to provoke me to anger by their sins. ³So I am about to consume Baasha and his house, and I will make your house like that of Jeroboam son of Nebat. ⁴Dogs will eat those belonging to Baasha who die in the city, and the birds of the air will feed on those who die in the country."

⁵As for the other events of Baasha's reign, what he did and his achievements, are they not written in the book of the annals of the kings of Israel? ⁶Baasha rested with his fathers and was buried in Tirzah. And Elah his son succeeded him as king.

⁷Moreover, the word of the LORD came through the prophet Jehu son of Hanani to Baasha and his house, because of all the evil he had done in the eyes of the LORD, provoking him to anger by the things he did, and becoming like the house of Jeroboam—and also because he destroyed it.

Elah King of Israel

⁸In the twenty-sixth year of Asa king of Judah, Elah son of Baasha became king of Israel, and he reigned in Tirzah two years.

⁹Zimri, one of his officials, who had command of half his chariots, plotted against him. Elah was in Tirzah at the time, getting drunk in the home of Arza, the man in charge of the palace at Tirzah. ¹⁰Zimri came in, struck him down and killed him in the twenty-seventh year of Asa king of Judah. Then he succeeded him as king.

¹¹As soon as he began to reign and was seated on the throne, he killed off Baasha's whole family. He did not spare a single male, whether relative or friend. ¹²So Zimri destroyed the whole family of Baasha, in accordance with the word of the LORD spoken against Baasha through the prophet Jehu— ¹³because of all the sins Baasha and his son Elah had committed and had caused Israel to commit, so that they provoked the LORD, the God of Israel, to anger by their worthless idols.

¹⁴As for the other events of Elah's reign, and all he did, are they not written in the book of the annals of the kings of Israel?

Zimri King of Israel

¹⁵In the twenty-seventh year of Asa king of Judah, Zimri reigned in Tirzah seven days. The army was encamped near Gibbethon, a Philistine town. ¹⁶When the Israelites in the camp heard that Zimri had plotted against the king and murdered him, they proclaimed Omri, the commander of the army, king over Israel that very day there in the camp. ¹⁷Then Omri and all the Israelites with him withdrew from Gibbethon and laid siege to Tirzah. ¹⁸When Zimri saw that the city was taken, he went into the citadel of the royal palace and set the palace on fire around him. So he died, ¹⁹because of the sins he had committed, doing evil in the eyes of the LORD and walking in the ways of Jeroboam and in the sin he had committed and had caused Israel to commit.

²⁰As for the other events of Zimri's reign, and the rebellion he carried out, are they not written in the book of the annals of the kings of Israel?

Omri King of Israel

²¹Then the people of Israel were split into two factions; half supported Tibni son of Ginath for king, and the other half supported Omri. ²²But Omri's followers proved stronger than those of Tibni son of Ginath. So Tibni died and Omri became king.

²³In the thirty-first year of Asa king of Judah, Omri became king of Israel, and he reigned twelve years, six of them in Tirzah. ²⁴He bought the hill of Samaria from Shemer for two talents^a of silver and built a city on the hill, calling it Samaria, after Shemer, the name of the former owner of the hill.

²⁵But Omri did evil in the eyes of the LORD and sinned more than all those before him. ²⁶He walked in all the ways of Jeroboam son of Nebat and in his sin, which he had caused Israel to commit, so that they provoked the LORD, the God of Israel, to anger by their worthless idols.

²⁷As for the other events of Omri's reign, what he did and the things he achieved, are they not written in the book of the annals of the kings of Israel? ²⁸Omri rested with his fathers and was buried in Samaria. And Ahab his son succeeded him as king.

Ahab Becomes King of Israel

²⁹In the thirty-eighth year of Asa king of Judah, Ahab son of Omri became king of Israel, and he reigned in Samaria over Israel twenty-two years. ³⁰Ahab son of Omri did more evil in the eyes of the LORD than any of those before him. ³¹He not only considered it trivial to commit the sins of Jeroboam son of Nebat, but he also married Jezebel daughter of Ethbaal king of the Sidonians, and began to serve Baal and worship him. ³²He set up an altar for Baal in the temple of Baal that he built in Samaria. ³³Ahab also made an Asherah pole and did more to provoke the LORD, the God of Israel, to anger than did all the kings of Israel before him.

³⁴In Ahab's time, Hiel of Bethel rebuilt Jericho. He laid its foundations at the cost of his firstborn son Abiram, and he set up its gates at the cost of his youngest son Segub, in accordance with the word of the LORD spoken by Joshua son of Nun.

Elijah Fed by Ravens

17 Now Elijah the Tishbite, from Tishbe^b in Gilead, said to Ahab, "As the LORD, the God of Israel, lives, whom I serve, there will be neither dew nor rain in the next few years except at my word."

²Then the word of the LORD came to Elijah: ³"Leave here, turn eastward and hide in the Kerith Ravine, east of the Jordan. ⁴You will drink from the brook, and I have ordered the ravens to feed you there."

⁵So he did what the LORD had told him. He went to the Kerith Ravine, east of the Jordan, and stayed there. ⁶The ravens brought him bread and meat in the morning and bread and meat in the evening, and he drank from the brook.

The Widow at Zarephath

⁷Some time later the brook dried up because there had been no rain in the land. ⁸Then the word of the LORD came to him: ⁹"Go at once to Zarephath of Sidon and stay there. I have commanded a widow in that place to supply you with food." ¹⁰So he went to Zarephath. When he came to the town gate, a widow was there gathering sticks. He called to her and asked, "Would you bring me a little water in a jar so I may have a drink?" ¹¹As she was going to get it, he called, "And bring me, please, a piece of bread."

¹²"As surely as the LORD your God lives," she replied, "I don't have any bread—only a handful of flour in a jar and a little oil in a jug. I am gathering a few sticks to take home and make a meal for myself and my son, that we may eat it—and die."

¹³Elijah said to her, "Don't be afraid. Go home and do as you have said. But first make a small

---

^a 24 That is, about 150 pounds (about 70 kilograms)
^b 1 Or Tishbite, of the settlers

cake of bread for me from what you have and bring it to me, and then make something for yourself and your son. ¹⁴For this is what the LORD, the God of Israel, says: 'The jar of flour will not be used up and the jug of oil will not run dry until the day the LORD gives rain on the land.' "

¹⁵She went away and did as Elijah had told her. So there was food every day for Elijah and for the woman and her family. ¹⁶For the jar of flour was not used up and the jug of oil did not run dry, in keeping with the word of the LORD spoken by Elijah.

¹⁷Some time later the son of the woman who owned the house became ill. He grew worse and worse, and finally stopped breathing. ¹⁸She said to Elijah, "What do you have against me, man of God? Did you come to remind me of my sin and kill my son?"

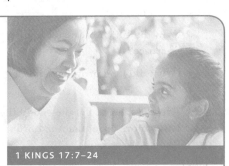

1 KINGS 17:7–24

Elijah Helps a Widow and Her Son

LIFE LESSON: God sometimes uses miracles to accomplish his purposes.

TO TALK ABOUT

✦ Why did God send Elijah to a widow in a foreign country?

✦ What happened to the widow's son?

✦ Could God have kept the boy from dying or made him get well again?

✦ What kind of miracles does God use to touch people's hearts today?

¹⁹"Give me your son," Elijah replied. He took him from her arms, carried him to the upper room where he was staying, and laid him on his bed. ²⁰Then he cried out to the LORD, "O LORD my God, have you brought tragedy also upon this widow I am staying with, by causing her son to die?" ²¹Then he stretched himself out on the boy three times and cried to the LORD, "O LORD my God, let this boy's life return to him!"

²²The LORD heard Elijah's cry, and the boy's life returned to him, and he lived. ²³Elijah picked up the child and carried him down from the room into the house. He gave him to his mother and said, "Look, your son is alive!"

²⁴Then the woman said to Elijah, "Now I know that you are a man of God and that the word of the LORD from your mouth is the truth."

Elijah and Obadiah

18 After a long time, in the third year, the word of the LORD came to Elijah: "Go and present yourself to Ahab, and I will send rain on the land." ²So Elijah went to present himself to Ahab.

Now the famine was severe in Samaria, ³and Ahab had summoned Obadiah, who was in charge of his palace. (Obadiah was a devout believer in the LORD. ⁴While Jezebel was killing off the LORD's prophets, Obadiah had taken a hundred prophets and hidden them in two caves, fifty in each, and had supplied them with food and water.) ⁵Ahab had said to Obadiah, "Go through the land to all the springs and valleys. Maybe we can find some grass to keep the horses and mules alive so we will not have to kill any of our animals." ⁶So they divided the land they were to cover, Ahab going in one direction and Obadiah in another.

⁷As Obadiah was walking along, Elijah met him. Obadiah recognized him, bowed down to the ground, and said, "Is it really you, my lord Elijah?"

⁸"Yes," he replied. "Go tell your master, 'Elijah is here.' "

⁹"What have I done wrong," asked Obadiah, "that you are handing your servant over to Ahab

to be put to death? ¹⁰As surely as the LORD your God lives, there is not a nation or kingdom where my master has not sent someone to look for you. And whenever a nation or kingdom claimed you were not there, he made them swear they could not find you. ¹¹But now you tell me to go to my master and say, 'Elijah is here.' ¹²I don't know where the Spirit of the LORD may carry you when I leave you. If I go and tell Ahab and he doesn't find you, he will kill me. Yet I your servant have worshiped the LORD since my youth. ¹³Haven't you heard, my lord, what I did while Jezebel was killing the prophets of the LORD? I hid a hundred of the LORD's prophets in two caves, fifty in each, and supplied them with food and water. ¹⁴And now you tell me to go to my master and say, 'Elijah is here.' He will kill me!"

¹⁵Elijah said, "As the LORD Almighty lives, whom I serve, I will surely present myself to Ahab today."

Elijah on Mount Carmel

¹⁶So Obadiah went to meet Ahab and told him, and Ahab went to meet Elijah. ¹⁷When he saw Elijah, he said to him, "Is that you, you troubler of Israel?"

¹⁸"I have not made trouble for Israel," Elijah replied. "But you and your father's family have. You have abandoned the LORD's commands and have followed the Baals. ¹⁹Now summon the people from all over Israel to meet me on Mount Carmel. And bring the four hundred and fifty prophets of Baal and the four hundred prophets of Asherah, who eat at Jezebel's table."

²⁰So Ahab sent word throughout all Israel and assembled the prophets on Mount Carmel. ²¹Elijah went before the people and said, "How long will you waver between two opinions? If the LORD is God, follow him; but if Baal is God, follow him."

But the people said nothing.

²²Then Elijah said to them, "I am the only one of the LORD's prophets left, but Baal has four hundred and fifty prophets. ²³Get two bulls for us. Let them choose one for themselves, and let them

stories to share

1 KINGS 18:16–46

Elijah and the Prophets of Baal

LIFE LESSON: God is the only true God.

TO TALK ABOUT

✦ What was the contest on Mount Carmel about?

✦ Why did Elijah add water to his sacrifice?

✦ What did God prove by sending fire?

✦ How was the rain at the end of the story more proof that the Lord is the only true God?

cut it into pieces and put it on the wood but not set fire to it. I will prepare the other bull and put it on the wood but not set fire to it. ²⁴Then you call on the name of your god, and I will call on the name of the LORD. The god who answers by fire—he is God."

Then all the people said, "What you say is good."

²⁵Elijah said to the prophets of Baal, "Choose one of the bulls and prepare it first, since there are so many of you. Call on the name of your god, but do not light the fire." ²⁶So they took the bull given them and prepared it.

Then they called on the name of Baal from morning till noon. "O Baal, answer us!" they shouted. But there was no response; no one answered. And they danced around the altar they had made.

²⁷At noon Elijah began to taunt them. "Shout louder!" he said. "Surely he is a god! Perhaps he is deep in thought, or busy, or traveling. Maybe he is sleeping and must be awakened." ²⁸So they shouted louder and slashed themselves with swords and spears, as was their custom, until their blood flowed. ²⁹Midday passed, and they continued their frantic prophesying until the time for the evening sacrifice. But there was no response, no one answered, no one paid attention.

³⁰Then Elijah said to all the people, "Come here to me." They came to him, and he repaired the altar of the Lord, which was in ruins. ³¹Elijah took twelve stones, one for each of the tribes descended from Jacob, to whom the word of the Lord had come, saying, "Your name shall be Israel." ³²With the stones he built an altar in the name of the Lord, and he dug a trench around it large enough to hold two seahs *a* of seed. ³³He arranged the wood, cut the bull into pieces and laid it on the wood. Then he said to them, "Fill four large jars with water and pour it on the offering and on the wood."

³⁴"Do it again," he said, and they did it again.

"Do it a third time," he ordered, and they did it the third time. ³⁵The water ran down around the altar and even filled the trench.

³⁶At the time of sacrifice, the prophet Elijah stepped forward and prayed: "O Lord, God of Abraham, Isaac and Israel, let it be known today that you are God in Israel and that I am your servant and have done all these things at your command. ³⁷Answer me, O Lord, answer me, so these people will know that you, O Lord, are God, and that you are turning their hearts back again."

³⁸Then the fire of the Lord fell and burned up the sacrifice, the wood, the stones and the soil, and also licked up the water in the trench.

³⁹When all the people saw this, they fell prostrate and cried, "The Lord—he is God! The Lord—he is God!"

⁴⁰Then Elijah commanded them, "Seize the prophets of Baal. Don't let anyone get away!" They seized them, and Elijah had them brought down to the Kishon Valley and slaughtered there.

⁴¹And Elijah said to Ahab, "Go, eat and drink, for there is the sound of a heavy rain." ⁴²So Ahab went off to eat and drink, but Elijah climbed to the top of Carmel, bent down to the ground and put his face between his knees.

⁴³"Go and look toward the sea," he told his servant. And he went up and looked.

"There is nothing there," he said.

Seven times Elijah said, "Go back."

⁴⁴The seventh time the servant reported, "A cloud as small as a man's hand is rising from the sea."

So Elijah said, "Go and tell Ahab, 'Hitch up your chariot and go down before the rain stops you.' "

⁴⁵Meanwhile, the sky grew black with clouds, the wind rose, a heavy rain came on and Ahab rode off to Jezreel. ⁴⁶The power of the Lord came upon Elijah and, tucking his cloak into his belt, he ran ahead of Ahab all the way to Jezreel.

Elijah Flees to Horeb

19 Now Ahab told Jezebel everything Elijah had done and how he had killed all the prophets with the sword. ²So Jezebel sent a messenger to Elijah to say, "May the gods deal with me, be it ever so severely, if by this time tomorrow I do not make your life like that of one of them."

³Elijah was afraid *b* and ran for his life. When he came to Beersheba in Judah, he left his servant there, ⁴while he himself went a day's journey into the desert. He came to a broom tree, sat down under it and prayed that he might die. "I have had enough, Lord," he said. "Take my life; I am no better than my ancestors." ⁵Then he lay down under the tree and fell asleep.

All at once an angel touched him and said, "Get up and eat." ⁶He looked around, and there

---

a 32 That is, probably about 13 quarts (about 15 liters)
b 3 Or *Elijah saw*

TALKING POINTS

Finding God

God demonstrated his presence to Elijah in a gentle whisper at a time when Elijah was afraid and discouraged.

1 KINGS 19:1–13

For more on finding God, go to 1 Chronicles 28:9.

by his head was a cake of bread baked over hot coals, and a jar of water. He ate and drank and then lay down again.

⁷The angel of the LORD came back a second time and touched him and said, "Get up and eat, for the journey is too much for you." ⁸So he got up and ate and drank. Strengthened by that food, he traveled forty days and forty nights until he reached Horeb, the mountain of God. ⁹There he went into a cave and spent the night.

The LORD Appears to Elijah

And the word of the LORD came to him: "What are you doing here, Elijah?"

¹⁰He replied, "I have been very zealous for the LORD God Almighty. The Israelites have rejected your covenant, broken down your altars, and put your prophets to death with the sword. I am the only one left, and now they are trying to kill me too."

¹¹The LORD said, "Go out and stand on the mountain in the presence of the LORD, for the LORD is about to pass by."

Then a great and powerful wind tore the mountains apart and shattered the rocks before the LORD, but the LORD was not in the wind. After the wind there was an earthquake, but the LORD was not in the earthquake. ¹²After the earthquake came a fire, but the LORD was not in the fire. And after the fire came a gentle whisper. ¹³When Elijah heard it, he pulled his cloak over his face and went out and stood at the mouth of the cave.

Then a voice said to him, "What are you doing here, Elijah?"

¹⁴He replied, "I have been very zealous for the LORD God Almighty. The Israelites have rejected your covenant, broken down your altars, and put your prophets to death with the sword. I am the only one left, and now they are trying to kill me too."

¹⁵The LORD said to him, "Go back the way you came, and go to the Desert of Damascus. When you get there, anoint Hazael king over Aram. ¹⁶Also, anoint Jehu son of Nimshi king over Israel, and anoint Elisha son of Shaphat from Abel Meholah to succeed you as prophet. ¹⁷Jehu will

stories to share

1 KINGS 19:1–18

The Lord Appears to Elijah

LIFE LESSON: God is there for us when we feel discouraged or overwhelmed.

TO TALK ABOUT

✦ Was Elijah really the only one left who served God? (Hint: See verse 18.)

✦ Why was Elijah feeling so discouraged after an important victory?

✦ When have you felt let down after an exciting time? Why do you think that was?

✦ Why did God appear to Elijah in a gentle whisper?

put to death any who escape the sword of Hazael, and Elisha will put to death any who escape the sword of Jehu. ¹⁸Yet I reserve seven thousand in Israel—all whose knees have not bowed down to Baal and all whose mouths have not kissed him."

The Call of Elisha

¹⁹So Elijah went from there and found Elisha son of Shaphat. He was plowing with twelve yoke of oxen, and he himself was driving the twelfth pair. Elijah went up to him and threw his cloak around him. ²⁰Elisha then left his oxen and ran after Elijah. "Let me kiss my father and mother good-by," he said, "and then I will come with you."

"Go back," Elijah replied. "What have I done to you?"

²¹So Elisha left him and went back. He took his yoke of oxen and slaughtered them. He burned the plowing equipment to cook the meat and gave it to the people, and they ate. Then he set out to follow Elijah and became his attendant.

Ben-Hadad Attacks Samaria

20 Now Ben-Hadad king of Aram mustered his entire army. Accompanied by thirty-two kings with their horses and chariots, he went up and besieged Samaria and attacked it. ²He sent messengers into the city to Ahab king of Israel, saying, "This is what Ben-Hadad says: ³'Your silver and gold are mine, and the best of your wives and children are mine.'"

⁴The king of Israel answered, "Just as you say, my lord the king. I and all I have are yours."

⁵The messengers came again and said, "This is what Ben-Hadad says: 'I sent to demand your silver and gold, your wives and your children. ⁶But about this time tomorrow I am going to send my officials to search your palace and the houses of your officials. They will seize everything you value and carry it away.'"

⁷The king of Israel summoned all the elders of the land and said to them, "See how this man is looking for trouble! When he sent for my wives and my children, my silver and my gold, I did not refuse him."

⁸The elders and the people all answered, "Don't listen to him or agree to his demands."

⁹So he replied to Ben-Hadad's messengers, "Tell my lord the king, 'Your servant will do all you demanded the first time, but this demand I cannot meet.'" They left and took the answer back to Ben-Hadad.

¹⁰Then Ben-Hadad sent another message to Ahab: "May the gods deal with me, be it ever so severely, if enough dust remains in Samaria to give each of my men a handful."

¹¹The king of Israel answered, "Tell him: 'One who puts on his armor should not boast like one who takes it off.'"

¹²Ben-Hadad heard this message while he and the kings were drinking in their tents,ᵃ and he ordered his men: "Prepare to attack." So they prepared to attack the city.

Ahab Defeats Ben-Hadad

¹³Meanwhile a prophet came to Ahab king of Israel and announced, "This is what the LORD says: 'Do you see this vast army? I will give it into your hand today, and then you will know that I am the LORD.'"

¹⁴"But who will do this?" asked Ahab.

The prophet replied, "This is what the LORD says: 'The young officers of the provincial commanders will do it.'"

"And who will start the battle?" he asked.

The prophet answered, "You will."

¹⁵So Ahab summoned the young officers of the provincial commanders, 232 men. Then he assembled the rest of the Israelites, 7,000 in all. ¹⁶They set out at noon while Ben-Hadad and the 32 kings allied with him were in their tents getting drunk. ¹⁷The young officers of the provincial commanders went out first.

Now Ben-Hadad had dispatched scouts, who reported, "Men are advancing from Samaria."

¹⁸He said, "If they have come out for peace,

ᵃ 12 Or *in Succoth*; also in verse 16

take them alive; if they have come out for war, take them alive."

¹⁹The young officers of the provincial commanders marched out of the city with the army behind them ²⁰and each one struck down his opponent. At that, the Arameans fled, with the Israelites in pursuit. But Ben-Hadad king of Aram escaped on horseback with some of his horsemen. ²¹The king of Israel advanced and overpowered the horses and chariots and inflicted heavy losses on the Arameans.

²²Afterward, the prophet came to the king of Israel and said, "Strengthen your position and see what must be done, because next spring the king of Aram will attack you again."

²³Meanwhile, the officials of the king of Aram advised him, "Their gods are gods of the hills. That is why they were too strong for us. But if we fight them on the plains, surely we will be stronger than they. ²⁴Do this: Remove all the kings from their commands and replace them with other officers. ²⁵You must also raise an army like the one you lost—horse for horse and chariot for chariot—so we can fight Israel on the plains. Then surely we will be stronger than they." He agreed with them and acted accordingly.

²⁶The next spring Ben-Hadad mustered the Arameans and went up to Aphek to fight against Israel. ²⁷When the Israelites were also mustered and given provisions, they marched out to meet them. The Israelites camped opposite them like two small flocks of goats, while the Arameans covered the countryside.

²⁸The man of God came up and told the king of Israel, "This is what the LORD says: 'Because the Arameans think the LORD is a god of the hills and not a god of the valleys, I will deliver this vast army into your hands, and you will know that I am the LORD.'"

²⁹For seven days they camped opposite each other, and on the seventh day the battle was joined. The Israelites inflicted a hundred thousand casualties on the Aramean foot soldiers in one day. ³⁰The rest of them escaped to the city of Aphek, where the wall collapsed on twenty-seven thousand of them. And Ben-Hadad fled to the city and hid in an inner room.

³¹His officials said to him, "Look, we have heard that the kings of the house of Israel are merciful. Let us go to the king of Israel with sackcloth around our waists and ropes around our heads. Perhaps he will spare your life."

³²Wearing sackcloth around their waists and ropes around their heads, they went to the king of Israel and said, "Your servant Ben-Hadad says: 'Please let me live.'"

The king answered, "Is he still alive? He is my brother."

³³The men took this as a good sign and were quick to pick up his word. "Yes, your brother Ben-Hadad!" they said.

"Go and get him," the king said. When Ben-Hadad came out, Ahab had him come up into his chariot.

³⁴"I will return the cities my father took from your father," Ben-Hadad offered. "You may set up your own market areas in Damascus, as my father did in Samaria."

⌊Ahab said,⌋ "On the basis of a treaty I will set you free." So he made a treaty with him, and let him go.

A Prophet Condemns Ahab

³⁵By the word of the LORD one of the sons of the prophets said to his companion, "Strike me with your weapon," but the man refused.

³⁶So the prophet said, "Because you have not obeyed the LORD, as soon as you leave me a lion will kill you." And after the man went away, a lion found him and killed him.

³⁷The prophet found another man and said, "Strike me, please." So the man struck him and wounded him. ³⁸Then the prophet went and stood by the road waiting for the king. He disguised himself with his headband down over his eyes. ³⁹As the king passed by, the prophet called out to him, "Your servant went into the thick of the battle, and someone came to me with a captive and said, 'Guard this man. If he is missing,

it will be your life for his life, or you must pay a talent *a* of silver.' ⁴⁰While your servant was busy here and there, the man disappeared."

"That is your sentence," the king of Israel said. "You have pronounced it yourself."

⁴¹Then the prophet quickly removed the headband from his eyes, and the king of Israel recognized him as one of the prophets. ⁴²He said to the king, "This is what the LORD says: 'You have set free a man I had determined should die. *b* Therefore it is your life for his life, your people for his people.'" ⁴³Sullen and angry, the king of Israel went to his palace in Samaria.

Naboth's Vineyard

21 Some time later there was an incident involving a vineyard belonging to Naboth the Jezreelite. The vineyard was in Jezreel, close to the palace of Ahab king of Samaria. ²Ahab said to Naboth, "Let me have your vineyard to use for a vegetable garden, since it is close to my palace. In exchange I will give you a better vineyard or, if you prefer, I will pay you whatever it is worth."

³But Naboth replied, "The LORD forbid that I should give you the inheritance of my fathers."

⁴So Ahab went home, sullen and angry because Naboth the Jezreelite had said, "I will not give you the inheritance of my fathers." He lay on his bed sulking and refused to eat.

⁵His wife Jezebel came in and asked him, "Why are you so sullen? Why won't you eat?"

⁶He answered her, "Because I said to Naboth the Jezreelite, 'Sell me your vineyard; or if you prefer, I will give you another vineyard in its place.' But he said, 'I will not give you my vineyard.'"

⁷Jezebel his wife said, "Is this how you act as king over Israel? Get up and eat! Cheer up. I'll get you the vineyard of Naboth the Jezreelite."

⁸So she wrote letters in Ahab's name, placed his seal on them, and sent them to the elders and nobles who lived in Naboth's city with him. ⁹In those letters she wrote:

"Proclaim a day of fasting and seat Naboth in a prominent place among the people. ¹⁰But seat two scoundrels opposite him and have them testify that he has cursed both God and the king. Then take him out and stone him to death."

¹¹So the elders and nobles who lived in Naboth's city did as Jezebel directed in the letters she had written to them. ¹²They proclaimed a fast and seated Naboth in a prominent place among the people. ¹³Then two scoundrels came and sat opposite him and brought charges against Naboth before the people, saying, "Naboth has cursed both God and the king." So they took him outside the city and stoned him to death. ¹⁴Then they sent word to Jezebel: "Naboth has been stoned and is dead."

¹⁵As soon as Jezebel heard that Naboth had been stoned to death, she said to Ahab, "Get up and take possession of the vineyard of Naboth the Jezreelite that he refused to sell you. He is no longer alive, but dead." ¹⁶When Ahab heard that Naboth was dead, he got up and went down to take possession of Naboth's vineyard.

¹⁷Then the word of the LORD came to Elijah the Tishbite: ¹⁸"Go down to meet Ahab king of Israel, who rules in Samaria. He is now in Naboth's vineyard, where he has gone to take possession of it. ¹⁹Say to him, 'This is what the LORD says: Have you not murdered a man and seized his property?' Then say to him, 'This is what the LORD says: In the place where dogs licked up Naboth's blood, dogs will lick up your blood—yes, yours!'"

²⁰Ahab said to Elijah, "So you have found me, my enemy!"

"I have found you," he answered, "because you have sold yourself to do evil in the eyes of the LORD. ²¹I am going to bring disaster on you. I will consume your descendants and cut off from Ahab every last male in Israel—slave or free. ²²I will make your house like that of Jeroboam son of Nebat and that of Baasha son of Ahijah, because you have provoked me to anger and have caused Israel to sin.'

---

a 39 That is, about 75 pounds (about 34 kilograms)
b 42 The Hebrew term refers to the irrevocable giving over of things or persons to the LORD, often by totally destroying them.

²³"And also concerning Jezebel the Lord says: 'Dogs will devour Jezebel by the wall of ᵃ Jezreel.'

²⁴"Dogs will eat those belonging to Ahab who die in the city, and the birds of the air will feed on those who die in the country."

²⁵(There was never a man like Ahab, who sold himself to do evil in the eyes of the Lord, urged on by Jezebel his wife. ²⁶He behaved in the vilest manner by going after idols, like the Amorites the Lord drove out before Israel.)

²⁷When Ahab heard these words, he tore his clothes, put on sackcloth and fasted. He lay in sackcloth and went around meekly.

²⁸Then the word of the Lord came to Elijah the Tishbite: ²⁹"Have you noticed how Ahab has humbled himself before me? Because he has humbled himself, I will not bring this disaster in his day, but I will bring it on his house in the days of his son."

Micaiah Prophesies Against Ahab
22:1–28pp — 2Ch 18:1–27

22 For three years there was no war between Aram and Israel. ²But in the third year Jehoshaphat king of Judah went down to see the king of Israel. ³The king of Israel had said to his officials, "Don't you know that Ramoth Gilead belongs to us and yet we are doing nothing to retake it from the king of Aram?"

⁴So he asked Jehoshaphat, "Will you go with me to fight against Ramoth Gilead?"

Jehoshaphat replied to the king of Israel, "I am as you are, my people as your people, my horses as your horses." ⁵But Jehoshaphat also said to the king of Israel, "First seek the counsel of the Lord."

⁶So the king of Israel brought together the prophets—about four hundred men—and asked them, "Shall I go to war against Ramoth Gilead, or shall I refrain?"

"Go," they answered, "for the Lord will give it into the king's hand."

⁷But Jehoshaphat asked, "Is there not a prophet of the Lord here whom we can inquire of?"

⁸The king of Israel answered Jehoshaphat, "There is still one man through whom we can inquire of the Lord, but I hate him because he never prophesies anything good about me, but always bad. He is Micaiah son of Imlah."

"The king should not say that," Jehoshaphat replied.

⁹So the king of Israel called one of his officials and said, "Bring Micaiah son of Imlah at once."

¹⁰Dressed in their royal robes, the king of Israel and Jehoshaphat king of Judah were sitting on their thrones at the threshing floor by the entrance of the gate of Samaria, with all the prophets prophesying before them. ¹¹Now Zedekiah son of Kenaanah had made iron horns and he declared, "This is what the Lord says: 'With these you will gore the Arameans until they are destroyed.'"

¹²All the other prophets were prophesying the same thing. "Attack Ramoth Gilead and be victorious," they said, "for the Lord will give it into the king's hand."

¹³The messenger who had gone to summon Micaiah said to him, "Look, as one man the other prophets are predicting success for the king. Let your word agree with theirs, and speak favorably."

¹⁴But Micaiah said, "As surely as the Lord lives, I can tell him only what the Lord tells me."

¹⁵When he arrived, the king asked him, "Micaiah, shall we go to war against Ramoth Gilead, or shall I refrain?"

"Attack and be victorious," he answered, "for the Lord will give it into the king's hand."

¹⁶The king said to him, "How many times must I make you swear to tell me nothing but the truth in the name of the Lord?"

¹⁷Then Micaiah answered, "I saw all Israel scattered on the hills like sheep without a shepherd, and the Lord said, 'These people have no master. Let each one go home in peace.'"

¹⁸The king of Israel said to Jehoshaphat, "Didn't I tell you that he never prophesies anything good about me, but only bad?"

ᵃ 23 Most Hebrew manuscripts; a few Hebrew manuscripts, Vulgate and Syriac (see also 2 Kings 9:26) *the plot of ground at*

¹⁹Micaiah continued, "Therefore hear the word of the LORD: I saw the LORD sitting on his throne with all the host of heaven standing around him on his right and on his left. ²⁰And the LORD said, 'Who will entice Ahab into attacking Ramoth Gilead and going to his death there?'

"One suggested this, and another that. ²¹Finally, a spirit came forward, stood before the LORD and said, 'I will entice him.'

²²"'By what means?' the LORD asked.

"'I will go out and be a lying spirit in the mouths of all his prophets,' he said.

"'You will succeed in enticing him,' said the LORD. 'Go and do it.'

²³"So now the LORD has put a lying spirit in the mouths of all these prophets of yours. The LORD has decreed disaster for you."

²⁴Then Zedekiah son of Kenaanah went up and slapped Micaiah in the face. "Which way did the spirit from ᵃ the LORD go when he went from me to speak to you?" he asked.

²⁵Micaiah replied, "You will find out on the day you go to hide in an inner room."

²⁶The king of Israel then ordered, "Take Micaiah and send him back to Amon the ruler of the city and to Joash the king's son ²⁷and say, 'This is what the king says: Put this fellow in prison and give him nothing but bread and water until I return safely.'"

²⁸Micaiah declared, "If you ever return safely, the LORD has not spoken through me." Then he added, "Mark my words, all you people!"

Ahab Killed at Ramoth Gilead

22:29–36pp — 2Ch 18:28–34

²⁹So the king of Israel and Jehoshaphat king of Judah went up to Ramoth Gilead. ³⁰The king of Israel said to Jehoshaphat, "I will enter the battle in disguise, but you wear your royal robes." So the king of Israel disguised himself and went into battle.

³¹Now the king of Aram had ordered his thirty-two chariot commanders, "Do not fight with anyone, small or great, except the king of Israel." ³²When the chariot commanders saw Jehoshaphat, they thought, "Surely this is the king of Israel." So they turned to attack him, but when Jehoshaphat cried out, ³³the chariot commanders saw that he was not the king of Israel and stopped pursuing him.

³⁴But someone drew his bow at random and hit the king of Israel between the sections of his armor. The king told his chariot driver, "Wheel around and get me out of the fighting. I've been wounded." ³⁵All day long the battle raged, and the king was propped up in his chariot facing the Arameans. The blood from his wound ran onto the floor of the chariot, and that evening he died. ³⁶As the sun was setting, a cry spread through the army: "Every man to his town; everyone to his land!"

³⁷So the king died and was brought to Samaria, and they buried him there. ³⁸They washed the chariot at a pool in Samaria (where the prostitutes bathed), ᵇ and the dogs licked up his blood, as the word of the LORD had declared.

³⁹As for the other events of Ahab's reign, including all he did, the palace he built and inlaid with ivory, and the cities he fortified, are they not written in the book of the annals of the kings of Israel? ⁴⁰Ahab rested with his fathers. And Ahaziah his son succeeded him as king.

Jehoshaphat King of Judah

22:41–50pp — 2Ch 20:31–21:1

⁴¹Jehoshaphat son of Asa became king of Judah in the fourth year of Ahab king of Israel. ⁴²Jehoshaphat was thirty-five years old when he became king, and he reigned in Jerusalem twenty-five years. His mother's name was Azubah daughter of Shilhi. ⁴³In everything he walked in the ways of his father Asa and did not stray from them; he did what was right in the eyes of the LORD. The high places, however, were not removed, and the people continued to offer sacrifices and burn incense there. ⁴⁴Jehoshaphat was also at peace with the king of Israel.

⁴⁵As for the other events of Jehoshaphat's

ᵃ 24 Or *Spirit of*   ᵇ 38 Or *Samaria and cleaned the weapons* reign, the things he achieved and his military exploits, are they not written in the book of the annals of the kings of Judah? ⁴⁶He rid the land of the rest of the male shrine prostitutes who remained there even after the reign of his father Asa. ⁴⁷There was then no king in Edom; a deputy ruled.

⁴⁸Now Jehoshaphat built a fleet of trading ships*a* to go to Ophir for gold, but they never set sail—they were wrecked at Ezion Geber. ⁴⁹At that time Ahaziah son of Ahab said to Jehoshaphat, "Let my men sail with your men," but Jehoshaphat refused.

⁵⁰Then Jehoshaphat rested with his fathers and was buried with them in the city of David his father. And Jehoram his son succeeded him.

Ahaziah King of Israel

⁵¹Ahaziah son of Ahab became king of Israel in Samaria in the seventeenth year of Jehoshaphat king of Judah, and he reigned over Israel two years. ⁵²He did evil in the eyes of the LORD, because he walked in the ways of his father and mother and in the ways of Jeroboam son of Nebat, who caused Israel to sin. ⁵³He served and worshiped Baal and provoked the LORD, the God of Israel, to anger, just as his father had done.

a 48 Hebrew *of ships of Tarshish*

God
BREAKS THROUGH

Second Kings, originally one book with 1 Kings, continues the record of decline of the kingdoms of Israel and Judah, which ultimately ends in their destruction and the people's captivity. The history of the northern kingdom (Israel) spanned approximately 210 years and included 20 rulers (virtually all of whom were evil). The history of the southern kingdom (Judah) spanned about 345 years and also included 20 kings, though at least a few of them were chronicled favorably.

Over and over again, God called his people to return to him. He sent them prophets to repeatedly warn them of the dangers of their unfaithfulness. As the people endured the reigns of evil king after evil king, God provided an occasional sign that he was breaking through their sins of idolatry, immorality and injustice. Obedience and hope shone through in the lives of prophets like Elijah and Elisha. Plans for the restoration and renewal of a God-fearing nation surfaced in the godly acts of kings like Joash, Hezekiah and Josiah.

In the end, the bright spots of revival became part of Israel's repetitive history of turning away from God and then turning back to God. Israel's history reminds us that, through both life's bright spots and its dark valleys, we need to remain faithful. Our grandchildren need to hear us tell the stories of our faith. As we keep planting seeds, we can be assured that, even if the seeds do not immediately sprout, they are always growing and will one day bloom.

VERSE *to* REMEMBER | 2 KINGS 17:38–39

"Do not forget the covenant I have made with you, and do not worship other gods. Rather, worship the LORD your God; it is he who will deliver you from the hand of all your enemies."

ABOUT 2 KINGS

WRITTEN BY:
Unknown

WRITTEN FOR:
God's chosen people, the Israelites

DATE WRITTEN:
Probably around 550 B.C., during the Babylonian exile

WHY WRITTEN:
To show why God finally exiled Israel and Judah from the promised land

The Lord's Judgment on Ahaziah

1 After Ahab's death, Moab rebelled against Israel. [2] Now Ahaziah had fallen through the lattice of his upper room in Samaria and injured himself. So he sent messengers, saying to them, "Go and consult Baal-Zebub, the god of Ekron, to see if I will recover from this injury."

[3] But the angel of the Lord said to Elijah the Tishbite, "Go up and meet the messengers of the king of Samaria and ask them, 'Is it because there is no God in Israel that you are going off to consult Baal-Zebub, the god of Ekron?' [4] Therefore this is what the Lord says: 'You will not leave the bed you are lying on. You will certainly die!'" So Elijah went.

[5] When the messengers returned to the king, he asked them, "Why have you come back?"

[6] "A man came to meet us," they replied. "And he said to us, 'Go back to the king who sent you and tell him, "This is what the Lord says: Is it because there is no God in Israel that you are sending men to consult Baal-Zebub, the god of Ekron? Therefore you will not leave the bed you are lying on. You will certainly die!"'"

[7] The king asked them, "What kind of man was it who came to meet you and told you this?"

[8] They replied, "He was a man with a garment of hair and with a leather belt around his waist."

The king said, "That was Elijah the Tishbite."

[9] Then he sent to Elijah a captain with his company of fifty men. The captain went up to Elijah, who was sitting on the top of a hill, and said to him, "Man of God, the king says, 'Come down!'"

[10] Elijah answered the captain, "If I am a man of God, may fire come down from heaven and consume you and your fifty men!" Then fire fell from heaven and consumed the captain and his men.

[11] At this the king sent to Elijah another captain with his fifty men. The captain said to him, "Man of God, this is what the king says, 'Come down at once!'"

[12] "If I am a man of God," Elijah replied, "may fire come down from heaven and consume you and your fifty men!" Then the fire of God fell from heaven and consumed him and his fifty men.

[13] So the king sent a third captain with his fifty men. This third captain went up and fell on his knees before Elijah. "Man of God," he begged, "please have respect for my life and the lives of these fifty men, your servants! [14] See, fire has fallen from heaven and consumed the first two captains and all their men. But now have respect for my life!"

[15] The angel of the Lord said to Elijah, "Go down with him; do not be afraid of him." So Elijah got up and went down with him to the king.

[16] He told the king, "This is what the Lord says: Is it because there is no God in Israel for you to consult that you have sent messengers to consult Baal-Zebub, the god of Ekron? Because you have done this, you will never leave the bed you are lying on. You will certainly die!" [17] So he died, according to the word of the Lord that Elijah had spoken.

Because Ahaziah had no son, Joram [a] succeeded him as king in the second year of Jehoram son of Jehoshaphat king of Judah. [18] As for all the other events of Ahaziah's reign, and what he did, are they not written in the book of the annals of the kings of Israel?

Elijah Taken Up to Heaven

2 When the Lord was about to take Elijah up to heaven in a whirlwind, Elijah and Elisha were on their way from Gilgal. [2] Elijah said to Elisha, "Stay here; the Lord has sent me to Bethel."

But Elisha said, "As surely as the Lord lives and as you live, I will not leave you." So they went down to Bethel.

[3] The company of the prophets at Bethel came out to Elisha and asked, "Do you know that the Lord is going to take your master from you today?"

"Yes, I know," Elisha replied, "but do not speak of it."

[4] Then Elijah said to him, "Stay here, Elisha; the Lord has sent me to Jericho."

---

[a] 17 Hebrew *Jehoram*, a variant of *Joram*

And he replied, "As surely as the LORD lives and as you live, I will not leave you." So they went to Jericho.

⁵The company of the prophets at Jericho went up to Elisha and asked him, "Do you know that the LORD is going to take your master from you today?"

"Yes, I know," he replied, "but do not speak of it."

⁶Then Elijah said to him, "Stay here; the LORD has sent me to the Jordan."

And he replied, "As surely as the LORD lives and as you live, I will not leave you." So the two of them walked on.

⁷Fifty men of the company of the prophets went and stood at a distance, facing the place where Elijah and Elisha had stopped at the Jordan. ⁸Elijah took his cloak, rolled it up and struck the water with it. The water divided to the right and to the left, and the two of them crossed over on dry ground.

⁹When they had crossed, Elijah said to Elisha, "Tell me, what can I do for you before I am taken from you?"

"Let me inherit a double portion of your spirit," Elisha replied.

¹⁰"You have asked a difficult thing," Elijah said, "yet if you see me when I am taken from you, it will be yours—otherwise not."

¹¹As they were walking along and talking together, suddenly a chariot of fire and horses of fire appeared and separated the two of them, and Elijah went up to heaven in a whirlwind. ¹²Elisha saw this and cried out, "My father! My father! The chariots and horsemen of Israel!" And Elisha saw him no more. Then he took hold of his own clothes and tore them apart.

¹³He picked up the cloak that had fallen from Elijah and went back and stood on the bank of the Jordan. ¹⁴Then he took the cloak that had fallen from him and struck the water with it. "Where now is the LORD, the God of Elijah?" he asked. When he struck the water, it divided to the right and to the left, and he crossed over.

¹⁵The company of the prophets from Jericho,

stories to share

2 KINGS 2:1–18

Elijah Is Taken Up to Heaven

LIFE LESSON: Our God is awesome.

TO TALK ABOUT

✦ How did Elijah go to heaven?

✦ After Elijah left for heaven, what happened to prove that God had chosen Elisha to take Elijah's place?

✦ God had supported Elijah's ministry from the start. Why was it important for Elisha to see the fiery chariot?

✦ Did God take anyone else to heaven without the person dying? (Hint: Read Genesis 5:18–24; Hebrews 11:5.) Why do you suppose God chose Enoch and Elijah for this honor?

who were watching, said, "The spirit of Elijah is resting on Elisha." And they went to meet him and bowed to the ground before him. ¹⁶"Look," they said, "we your servants have fifty able men. Let them go and look for your master. Perhaps the Spirit of the LORD has picked him up and set him down on some mountain or in some valley."

"No," Elisha replied, "do not send them."

¹⁷But they persisted until he was too ashamed to refuse. So he said, "Send them." And they sent fifty men, who searched for three days but did not find him. ¹⁸When they returned to Elisha,

who was staying in Jericho, he said to them, "Didn't I tell you not to go?"

Healing of the Water

¹⁹The men of the city said to Elisha, "Look, our lord, this town is well situated, as you can see, but the water is bad and the land is unproductive."

²⁰"Bring me a new bowl," he said, "and put salt in it." So they brought it to him.

²¹Then he went out to the spring and threw the salt into it, saying, "This is what the LORD says: 'I have healed this water. Never again will it cause death or make the land unproductive.'" ²²And the water has remained wholesome to this day, according to the word Elisha had spoken.

Elisha Is Jeered

²³From there Elisha went up to Bethel. As he was walking along the road, some youths came out of the town and jeered at him. "Go on up, you baldhead!" they said. "Go on up, you baldhead!" ²⁴He turned around, looked at them and called down a curse on them in the name of the LORD. Then two bears came out of the woods and mauled forty-two of the youths. ²⁵And he went on to Mount Carmel and from there returned to Samaria.

Moab Revolts

3 Joram*ᵃ* son of Ahab became king of Israel in Samaria in the eighteenth year of Jehoshaphat king of Judah, and he reigned twelve years. ²He did evil in the eyes of the LORD, but not as his father and mother had done. He got rid of the sacred stone of Baal that his father had made. ³Nevertheless he clung to the sins of Jeroboam son of Nebat, which he had caused Israel to commit; he did not turn away from them.

⁴Now Mesha king of Moab raised sheep, and he had to supply the king of Israel with a hundred thousand lambs and with the wool of a hundred thousand rams. ⁵But after Ahab died, the king of Moab rebelled against the king of Israel. ⁶So at that time King Joram set out from Samaria and mobilized all Israel. ⁷He also sent this message to Jehoshaphat king of Judah: "The king of Moab has rebelled against me. Will you go with me to fight against Moab?"

"I will go with you," he replied. "I am as you are, my people as your people, my horses as your horses."

⁸"By what route shall we attack?" he asked.

"Through the Desert of Edom," he answered.

⁹So the king of Israel set out with the king of Judah and the king of Edom. After a roundabout march of seven days, the army had no more water for themselves or for the animals with them.

¹⁰"What!" exclaimed the king of Israel. "Has the LORD called us three kings together only to hand us over to Moab?"

¹¹But Jehoshaphat asked, "Is there no prophet of the LORD here, that we may inquire of the LORD through him?"

An officer of the king of Israel answered, "Elisha son of Shaphat is here. He used to pour water on the hands of Elijah.*ᵇ*"

¹²Jehoshaphat said, "The word of the LORD is with him." So the king of Israel and Jehoshaphat and the king of Edom went down to him.

¹³Elisha said to the king of Israel, "What do we have to do with each other? Go to the prophets of your father and the prophets of your mother."

"No," the king of Israel answered, "because it was the LORD who called us three kings together to hand us over to Moab."

¹⁴Elisha said, "As surely as the LORD Almighty lives, whom I serve, if I did not have respect for the presence of Jehoshaphat king of Judah, I would not look at you or even notice you. ¹⁵But now bring me a harpist."

While the harpist was playing, the hand of the LORD came upon Elisha ¹⁶and he said, "This is what the LORD says: Make this valley full of ditches. ¹⁷For this is what the LORD says: You will see neither wind nor rain, yet this valley will be filled with water, and you, your cattle and your other animals will drink. ¹⁸This is an easy thing in the eyes of the LORD; he will also hand Moab over to

---

ᵃ 1 Hebrew *Jehoram*, a variant of *Joram*; also in verse 6   *ᵇ 11* That is, he was Elijah's personal servant.

you. [19] You will overthrow every fortified city and every major town. You will cut down every good tree, stop up all the springs, and ruin every good field with stones."

[20] The next morning, about the time for offering the sacrifice, there it was—water flowing from the direction of Edom! And the land was filled with water.

[21] Now all the Moabites had heard that the kings had come to fight against them; so every man, young and old, who could bear arms was called up and stationed on the border. [22] When they got up early in the morning, the sun was shining on the water. To the Moabites across the way, the water looked red—like blood. [23] "That's blood!" they said. "Those kings must have fought and slaughtered each other. Now to the plunder, Moab!"

[24] But when the Moabites came to the camp of Israel, the Israelites rose up and fought them until they fled. And the Israelites invaded the land and slaughtered the Moabites. [25] They destroyed the towns, and each man threw a stone on every good field until it was covered. They stopped up all the springs and cut down every good tree. Only Kir Hareseth was left with its stones in place, but men armed with slings surrounded it and attacked it as well.

[26] When the king of Moab saw that the battle had gone against him, he took with him seven hundred swordsmen to break through to the king of Edom, but they failed. [27] Then he took his firstborn son, who was to succeed him as king, and offered him as a sacrifice on the city wall. The fury against Israel was great; they withdrew and returned to their own land.

The Widow's Oil

4 The wife of a man from the company of the prophets cried out to Elisha, "Your servant my husband is dead, and you know that he revered the LORD. But now his creditor is coming to take my two boys as his slaves."

[2] Elisha replied to her, "How can I help you? Tell me, what do you have in your house?"

"Your servant has nothing there at all," she said, "except a little oil."

[3] Elisha said, "Go around and ask all your neighbors for empty jars. Don't ask for just a few. [4] Then go inside and shut the door behind you and your sons. Pour oil into all the jars, and as each is filled, put it to one side."

[5] She left him and afterward shut the door behind her and her sons. They brought the jars to her and she kept pouring. [6] When all the jars were full, she said to her son, "Bring me another one."

But he replied, "There is not a jar left." Then the oil stopped flowing.

[7] She went and told the man of God, and he said, "Go, sell the oil and pay your debts. You and your sons can live on what is left."

The Shunammite's Son Restored to Life

[8] One day Elisha went to Shunem. And a well-to-do woman was there, who urged him to stay for a meal. So whenever he came by, he stopped there to eat. [9] She said to her husband, "I know that this man who often comes our way is a holy man of God. [10] Let's make a small room on the roof and put in it a bed and a table, a chair and a lamp for him. Then he can stay there whenever he comes to us."

[11] One day when Elisha came, he went up to his room and lay down there. [12] He said to his servant Gehazi, "Call the Shunammite." So he called her, and she stood before him. [13] Elisha said to him, "Tell her, 'You have gone to all this trouble for us. Now what can be done for you? Can we speak on your behalf to the king or the commander of the army?'"

She replied, "I have a home among my own people."

[14] "What can be done for her?" Elisha asked.

Gehazi said, "Well, she has no son and her husband is old."

[15] Then Elisha said, "Call her." So he called her, and she stood in the doorway. [16] "About this time next year," Elisha said, "you will hold a son in your arms."

"No, my lord," she objected. "Don't mislead your servant, O man of God!"

[17] But the woman became pregnant, and the next year about that same time she gave birth to a son, just as Elisha had told her.

[18] The child grew, and one day he went out to his father, who was with the reapers. [19] "My head! My head!" he said to his father.

His father told a servant, "Carry him to his mother." [20] After the servant had lifted him up and carried him to his mother, the boy sat on her lap until noon, and then he died. [21] She went up and laid him on the bed of the man of God, then shut the door and went out.

[22] She called her husband and said, "Please send me one of the servants and a donkey so I can go to the man of God quickly and return."

[23] "Why go to him today?" he asked. "It's not the New Moon or the Sabbath."

"It's all right," she said.

[24] She saddled the donkey and said to her servant, "Lead on; don't slow down for me unless I tell you." [25] So she set out and came to the man of God at Mount Carmel.

When he saw her in the distance, the man of God said to his servant Gehazi, "Look! There's the Shunammite! [26] Run to meet her and ask her, 'Are you all right? Is your husband all right? Is your child all right?' "

"Everything is all right," she said.

[27] When she reached the man of God at the mountain, she took hold of his feet. Gehazi came over to push her away, but the man of God said, "Leave her alone! She is in bitter distress, but the LORD has hidden it from me and has not told me why."

[28] "Did I ask you for a son, my lord?" she said. "Didn't I tell you, 'Don't raise my hopes'?"

[29] Elisha said to Gehazi, "Tuck your cloak into your belt, take my staff in your hand and run. If you meet anyone, do not greet him, and if anyone greets you, do not answer. Lay my staff on the boy's face."

[30] But the child's mother said, "As surely as the LORD lives and as you live, I will not leave you." So he got up and followed her.

[31] Gehazi went on ahead and laid the staff on the boy's face, but there was no sound or response. So Gehazi went back to meet Elisha and told him, "The boy has not awakened."

[32] When Elisha reached the house, there was the boy lying dead on his couch. [33] He went in, shut the door on the two of them and prayed to the LORD. [34] Then he got on the bed and lay upon the boy, mouth to mouth, eyes to eyes, hands to hands. As he stretched himself out upon him, the boy's body grew warm. [35] Elisha turned away and walked back and forth in the room and then got on the bed and stretched out upon him once more. The boy sneezed seven times and opened his eyes.

[36] Elisha summoned Gehazi and said, "Call the Shunammite." And he did. When she came, he said, "Take your son." [37] She came in, fell at his

stories to share

2 KINGS 4:8–37

Elisha Brings a Boy Back to Life

LIFE LESSON: God rewards faith.

TO TALK ABOUT

✦ How was the woman from Shunem kind to Elisha?

✦ In what way was her son's birth a miracle?

✦ Whose faith did God reward by bringing the boy back to life?

✦ How does God reward our faith today?

"LET'S MAKE A SMALL ROOM
ON THE ROOF AND PUT IN IT
A BED AND A TABLE, A CHAIR
AND A LAMP FOR HIM. THEN HE
CAN STAY THERE WHENEVER HE
COMES TO US."

2 Kings 4:10

A Simple Welcome

BOBBIE WOLGEMUTH

READ | 2 KINGS 4:8 – 37

The woman in this Bible story provided the basics — a bed, a table, a chair and lamp — to show hospitality to God's prophet. Likewise, it doesn't take much to make a child feel welcomed.

I love having a grandchild — one at a time — stay overnight at our house. A grandmother's special nighttime ritual can make "just a bed" a very special place. Dim lights and quiet voices sometimes allow a child to talk about things they wouldn't give voice to anywhere else. My children remember their Grandma Grace Wolgemuth giving back rubs, telling stories and singing hymns.

Memories can also be made at a table. Our grandson loves building with Legos and has a little table-top all his own at our house to display his creations. Knowing he has a special place for his hobby gives Luke joy every time he comes for a visit.

The best place of all for making grandparent memories may be a chair. A creaky wooden rocker next to the kitchen window was where my grandmother held me when I was a little girl. Even now I can picture her sitting there with arms open wide to scoop me onto her lap for a story or a song.

And don't forget that even a little lamp — or a candle — can make a memory. My youngest grand-daughter, Ella, loves to take a bath by candlelight. An extra bonus is to dry off with a bath towel made toasty warm in the dryer.

It doesn't take much to give tender memories to your grandchild. It's the little things they will cherish: just a bed, table, chair, lamp. Little moments — one at a time — help to build a bond that will last forever.

Lord Jesus, thank you for using simple things to show your love to me. Help me to remember to show hospitality in little ways to others. Fill me with your love as I prepare a place to welcome my grandchildren and receive them with smiles, hugs and love. Amen.

GRANDCHILD **IN FOCUS** • PRAYER

Courage

O Father, builder of character and courage, may my grandchild grow strong in the light of your love. Grant him courage to stand for what is right, to guard the truth and to ensure justice in every aspect of life. May he boldly grow in grace, revere your name and proudly proclaim you as the Lord of lords and King of kings. Amen.

Your next devotion is located on page 492.

feet and bowed to the ground. Then she took her son and went out.

Death in the Pot

³⁸Elisha returned to Gilgal and there was a famine in that region. While the company of the prophets was meeting with him, he said to his servant, "Put on the large pot and cook some stew for these men."

³⁹One of them went out into the fields to gather herbs and found a wild vine. He gathered some of its gourds and filled the fold of his cloak. When he returned, he cut them up into the pot of stew, though no one knew what they were. ⁴⁰The stew was poured out for the men, but as they began to eat it, they cried out, "O man of God, there is death in the pot!" And they could not eat it.

⁴¹Elisha said, "Get some flour." He put it into the pot and said, "Serve it to the people to eat." And there was nothing harmful in the pot.

Feeding of a Hundred

⁴²A man came from Baal Shalishah, bringing the man of God twenty loaves of barley bread baked from the first ripe grain, along with some heads of new grain. "Give it to the people to eat," Elisha said.

⁴³"How can I set this before a hundred men?" his servant asked.

But Elisha answered, "Give it to the people to eat. For this is what the LORD says: 'They will eat and have some left over.'" ⁴⁴Then he set it before them, and they ate and had some left over, according to the word of the LORD.

Naaman Healed of Leprosy

5 Now Naaman was commander of the army of the king of Aram. He was a great man in the sight of his master and highly regarded, because through him the LORD had given victory to Aram. He was a valiant soldier, but he had leprosy.ᵃ

²Now bands from Aram had gone out and had taken captive a young girl from Israel, and she served Naaman's wife. ³She said to her mistress,

stories to share

2 KINGS 5:1–14

Naaman Is Healed of Leprosy

LIFE LESSON: Sometimes obedience in little things takes big faith.

TO TALK ABOUT

◆ Why did the Israelite slave girl help her master?

◆ What would you have done?

◆ Why didn't Elisha come out and cure Naaman in some grand and showy way?

◆ Have you ever found it easier to obey seemingly "big and important" rules rather than those that seem little and insignificant?

"If only my master would see the prophet who is in Samaria! He would cure him of his leprosy."

⁴Naaman went to his master and told him what the girl from Israel had said. ⁵"By all means, go," the king of Aram replied. "I will send a letter to the king of Israel." So Naaman left, taking with him ten talentsᵇ of silver, six thousand shekelsᶜ of gold and ten sets of clothing. ⁶The letter that he took to the king of Israel read: "With this letter I am sending my servant Naaman to you so that you may cure him of his leprosy."

ᵃ 1 The Hebrew word was used for various diseases affecting the skin—not necessarily leprosy; also in verses 3, 6, 7, 11 and 27.
ᵇ 5 That is, about 750 pounds (about 340 kilograms)   ᶜ 5 That is, about 150 pounds (about 70 kilograms)

7 As soon as the king of Israel read the letter, he tore his robes and said, "Am I God? Can I kill and bring back to life? Why does this fellow send someone to me to be cured of his leprosy? See how he is trying to pick a quarrel with me!"

8 When Elisha the man of God heard that the king of Israel had torn his robes, he sent him this message: "Why have you torn your robes? Have the man come to me and he will know that there is a prophet in Israel." 9 So Naaman went with his horses and chariots and stopped at the door of Elisha's house. 10 Elisha sent a messenger to say to him, "Go, wash yourself seven times in the Jordan, and your flesh will be restored and you will be cleansed."

11 But Naaman went away angry and said, "I thought that he would surely come out to me and stand and call on the name of the LORD his God, wave his hand over the spot and cure me of my leprosy. 12 Are not Abana and Pharpar, the rivers of Damascus, better than any of the waters of Israel? Couldn't I wash in them and be cleansed?" So he turned and went off in a rage.

13 Naaman's servants went to him and said, "My father, if the prophet had told you to do some great thing, would you not have done it? How much more, then, when he tells you, 'Wash and be cleansed'!" 14 So he went down and dipped himself in the Jordan seven times, as the man of God had told him, and his flesh was restored and became clean like that of a young boy.

15 Then Naaman and all his attendants went back to the man of God. He stood before him and said, "Now I know that there is no God in all the world except in Israel. Please accept now a gift from your servant."

16 The prophet answered, "As surely as the LORD lives, whom I serve, I will not accept a thing." And even though Naaman urged him, he refused.

17 "If you will not," said Naaman, "please let me, your servant, be given as much earth as a pair of mules can carry, for your servant will never again make burnt offerings and sacrifices to any other god but the LORD. 18 But may the LORD forgive your servant for this one thing: When my master enters the temple of Rimmon to bow down and he is leaning on my arm and I bow there also—when I bow down in the temple of Rimmon, may the LORD forgive your servant for this."

19 "Go in peace," Elisha said.

After Naaman had traveled some distance, 20 Gehazi, the servant of Elisha the man of God, said to himself, "My master was too easy on Naaman, this Aramean, by not accepting from him what he brought. As surely as the LORD lives, I will run after him and get something from him."

21 So Gehazi hurried after Naaman. When Naaman saw him running toward him, he got down from the chariot to meet him. "Is everything all right?" he asked.

22 "Everything is all right," Gehazi answered. "My master sent me to say, 'Two young men from the company of the prophets have just come to me from the hill country of Ephraim. Please give them a talent *a* of silver and two sets of clothing.'"

23 "By all means, take two talents," said Naaman. He urged Gehazi to accept them, and then tied up the two talents of silver in two bags, with two sets of clothing. He gave them to two of his servants, and they carried them ahead of Gehazi. 24 When Gehazi came to the hill, he took the things from the servants and put them away in the house. He sent the men away and they left. 25 Then he went in and stood before his master Elisha.

"Where have you been, Gehazi?" Elisha asked.

"Your servant didn't go anywhere," Gehazi answered.

26 But Elisha said to him, "Was not my spirit with you when the man got down from his chariot to meet you? Is this the time to take money, or to accept clothes, olive groves, vineyards, flocks, herds, or menservants and maidservants? 27 Naaman's leprosy will cling to you and to your descendants forever." Then Gehazi went from Elisha's presence and he was leprous, as white as snow.

a 22 That is, about 75 pounds (about 34 kilograms)

> SHE SAID TO HER MISTRESS,
> "IF ONLY MY MASTER WOULD
> SEE THE PROPHET WHO IS IN
> SAMARIA! HE WOULD CURE HIM
> OF HIS LEPROSY."
>
> 2 Kings 5:3

Changing a Life

DORIS WYNBEEK RIKKERS

READ | 2 KINGS 5:1 – 27

She didn't have formal training. She didn't have power or position. She didn't even have her name recorded in this Bible story. In fact, it was daring of her to open her mouth and say the simple thing she had to say. Although she was a slave girl in a foreign land, she was willing to share what she believed. And she believed Elisha, the man of God, could heal her master of leprosy. She was available and willing . . . and that's all that was needed to change a life.

This little girl is a perfect example of how God uses ordinary people to further the good of his kingdom. Through the simple words of a slave girl to her mistress, Naaman, a powerful and influential man, not only was healed of his disease but came to testify that "there is no God in all the world except in Israel" (2 Kings 5:15).

Too often we get hung up on our lack of ability, education or influence and think we can't do anything of significance to further God's kingdom. But the truth is that all of us, no matter who we are, can do something for God. His power is great when ours is not. He works in and through us. He does the extraordinary with the ordinary; and thus any small gesture is enough. The shortest speech is just the right amount of words to show God's love and to establish his kingdom in the heart of another person.

You don't have to be famous. You don't have to have a list of degrees and initials after your name. You don't have to be "somebody." God needs you as you are: simple or flamboyant, eloquent or plain-spoken, shy or outgoing. You just have to be willing to share what you believe. Every one of us can be a person of influence for God and for his kingdom.

O God of the extraordinary, fill my life with your love and your power. May I boldly share your love with others. May even my smallest actions and fewest words reflect your love and grace. Amen.

Your next devotion is located on page 528.

GRANDCHILD IN FOCUS • PRAYER

Future Spouse

Dear Lord, if it is your will, I pray my grandchild will be united in a loving and Christian marriage. Keep her sexually pure so that she will honor you with her body and mind. As she seeks a spouse who will honor and care for her, give her patience and discernment. May her choice for a life partner be your choice for her, so that she and her husband will together glorify you in a lasting love. I pray this in Jesus' name, amen.

An Axhead Floats

6 The company of the prophets said to Elisha, "Look, the place where we meet with you is too small for us. ²Let us go to the Jordan, where each of us can get a pole; and let us build a place there for us to live."

And he said, "Go."

³Then one of them said, "Won't you please come with your servants?"

"I will," Elisha replied. ⁴And he went with them.

They went to the Jordan and began to cut down trees. ⁵As one of them was cutting down a tree, the iron axhead fell into the water. "Oh, my lord," he cried out, "it was borrowed!"

⁶The man of God asked, "Where did it fall?" When he showed him the place, Elisha cut a stick and threw it there, and made the iron float. ⁷"Lift it out," he said. Then the man reached out his hand and took it.

Elisha Traps Blinded Arameans

⁸Now the king of Aram was at war with Israel. After conferring with his officers, he said, "I will set up my camp in such and such a place."

⁹The man of God sent word to the king of Israel: "Beware of passing that place, because the Arameans are going down there." ¹⁰So the king of Israel checked on the place indicated by the man of God. Time and again Elisha warned the king, so that he was on his guard in such places.

¹¹This enraged the king of Aram. He summoned his officers and demanded of them, "Will you not tell me which of us is on the side of the king of Israel?"

¹²"None of us, my lord the king," said one of his officers, "but Elisha, the prophet who is in Israel, tells the king of Israel the very words you speak in your bedroom."

¹³"Go, find out where he is," the king ordered, "so I can send men and capture him." The report came back: "He is in Dothan." ¹⁴Then he sent horses and chariots and a strong force there. They went by night and surrounded the city.

¹⁵When the servant of the man of God got up and went out early the next morning, an army with horses and chariots had surrounded the city. "Oh, my lord, what shall we do?" the servant asked.

¹⁶"Don't be afraid," the prophet answered. "Those who are with us are more than those who are with them."

¹⁷And Elisha prayed, "O LORD, open his eyes so he may see." Then the LORD opened the servant's eyes, and he looked and saw the hills full of horses and chariots of fire all around Elisha.

¹⁸As the enemy came down toward him, Elisha prayed to the LORD, "Strike these people with blindness." So he struck them with blindness, as Elisha had asked.

¹⁹Elisha told them, "This is not the road and this is not the city. Follow me, and I will lead you to the man you are looking for." And he led them to Samaria.

²⁰After they entered the city, Elisha said, "LORD, open the eyes of these men so they can see." Then the LORD opened their eyes and they looked, and there they were, inside Samaria.

²¹When the king of Israel saw them, he asked Elisha, "Shall I kill them, my father? Shall I kill them?"

²²"Do not kill them," he answered. "Would you kill men you have captured with your own sword or bow? Set food and water before them so that they may eat and drink and then go back to their master." ²³So he prepared a great feast for them, and after they had finished eating and drinking, he sent them away, and they returned to their master. So the bands from Aram stopped raiding Israel's territory.

Famine in Besieged Samaria

²⁴Some time later, Ben-Hadad king of Aram mobilized his entire army and marched up and laid siege to Samaria. ²⁵There was a great famine in the city; the siege lasted so long that a donkey's head sold for eighty shekels ᵃ of silver, and a quarter of a cab ᵇ of seed pods ᶜ for five shekels. ᵈ

ᵃ 25 That is, about 2 pounds (about 1 kilogram)   ᵇ 25 That is, probably about 1/2 pint (about 0.3 liter)   ᶜ 25 Or of doves' dung   ᵈ 25 That is, about 2 ounces (about 55 grams)

²⁶As the king of Israel was passing by on the wall, a woman cried to him, "Help me, my lord the king!"

²⁷The king replied, "If the LORD does not help you, where can I get help for you? From the threshing floor? From the winepress?" ²⁸Then he asked her, "What's the matter?"

She answered, "This woman said to me, 'Give up your son so we may eat him today, and tomorrow we'll eat my son.' ²⁹So we cooked my son and ate him. The next day I said to her, 'Give up your son so we may eat him,' but she had hidden him."

³⁰When the king heard the woman's words, he tore his robes. As he went along the wall, the people looked, and there, underneath, he had sackcloth on his body. ³¹He said, "May God deal with me, be it ever so severely, if the head of Elisha son of Shaphat remains on his shoulders today!"

³²Now Elisha was sitting in his house, and the elders were sitting with him. The king sent a messenger ahead, but before he arrived, Elisha said to the elders, "Don't you see how this murderer is sending someone to cut off my head? Look, when the messenger comes, shut the door and hold it shut against him. Is not the sound of his master's footsteps behind him?"

³³While he was still talking to them, the messenger came down to him. And ⌊the king⌋ said, "This disaster is from the LORD. Why should I wait for the LORD any longer?"

7 Elisha said, "Hear the word of the LORD. This is what the LORD says: About this time tomorrow, a seah ᵃ of flour will sell for a shekel ᵇ and two seahs ᶜ of barley for a shekel at the gate of Samaria."

²The officer on whose arm the king was leaning said to the man of God, "Look, even if the LORD should open the floodgates of the heavens, could this happen?"

"You will see it with your own eyes," answered Elisha, "but you will not eat any of it!"

The Siege Lifted

³Now there were four men with leprosy ᵈ at the entrance of the city gate. They said to each other,

"Why stay here until we die? ⁴If we say, 'We'll go into the city'—the famine is there, and we will die. And if we stay here, we will die. So let's go over to the camp of the Arameans and surrender. If they spare us, we live; if they kill us, then we die."

⁵At dusk they got up and went to the camp of the Arameans. When they reached the edge of the camp, not a man was there, ⁶for the Lord had caused the Arameans to hear the sound of chariots and horses and a great army, so that they said to one another, "Look, the king of Israel has hired the Hittite and Egyptian kings to attack us!" ⁷So they got up and fled in the dusk and abandoned their tents and their horses and donkeys. They left the camp as it was and ran for their lives.

⁸The men who had leprosy reached the edge of the camp and entered one of the tents. They ate and drank, and carried away silver, gold and clothes, and went off and hid them. They returned and entered another tent and took some things from it and hid them also.

⁹Then they said to each other, "We're not doing right. This is a day of good news and we are keeping it to ourselves. If we wait until daylight, punishment will overtake us. Let's go at once and report this to the royal palace."

¹⁰So they went and called out to the city gatekeepers and told them, "We went into the Aramean camp and not a man was there—not a sound of anyone—only tethered horses and donkeys, and the tents left just as they were." ¹¹The gatekeepers shouted the news, and it was reported within the palace.

¹²The king got up in the night and said to his officers, "I will tell you what the Arameans have done to us. They know we are starving; so they have left the camp to hide in the countryside, thinking, 'They will surely come out, and then we will take them alive and get into the city.'"

ᵃ *1* That is, probably about 7 quarts (about 7.3 liters); also in verses 16 and 18   ᵇ *1* That is, about 2/5 ounce (about 11 grams); also in verses 16 and 18   ᶜ *1* That is, probably about 13 quarts (about 15 liters); also in verses 16 and 18   ᵈ *3* The Hebrew word is used for various diseases affecting the skin—not necessarily leprosy; also in verse 8.

¹³ One of his officers answered, "Have some men take five of the horses that are left in the city. Their plight will be like that of all the Israelites left here — yes, they will only be like all these Israelites who are doomed. So let us send them to find out what happened."

¹⁴ So they selected two chariots with their horses, and the king sent them after the Aramean army. He commanded the drivers, "Go and find out what has happened." ¹⁵ They followed them as far as the Jordan, and they found the whole road strewn with the clothing and equipment the Arameans had thrown away in their headlong flight. So the messengers returned and reported to the king. ¹⁶ Then the people went out and plundered the camp of the Arameans. So a seah of flour sold for a shekel, and two seahs of barley sold for a shekel, as the LORD had said.

¹⁷ Now the king had put the officer on whose arm he leaned in charge of the gate, and the people trampled him in the gateway, and he died, just as the man of God had foretold when the king came down to his house. ¹⁸ It happened as the man of God had said to the king: "About this time tomorrow, a seah of flour will sell for a shekel and two seahs of barley for a shekel at the gate of Samaria."

¹⁹ The officer had said to the man of God, "Look, even if the LORD should open the floodgates of the heavens, could this happen?" The man of God had replied, "You will see it with your own eyes, but you will not eat any of it!" ²⁰ And that is exactly what happened to him, for the people trampled him in the gateway, and he died.

The Shunammite's Land Restored

8 Now Elisha had said to the woman whose son he had restored to life, "Go away with your family and stay for a while wherever you can, because the LORD has decreed a famine in the land that will last seven years." ² The woman proceeded to do as the man of God said. She and her family went away and stayed in the land of the Philistines seven years.

³ At the end of the seven years she came back from the land of the Philistines and went to the king to beg for her house and land. ⁴ The king was talking to Gehazi, the servant of the man of God, and had said, "Tell me about all the great things Elisha has done." ⁵ Just as Gehazi was telling the king how Elisha had restored the dead to life, the woman whose son Elisha had brought back to life came to beg the king for her house and land.

Gehazi said, "This is the woman, my lord the king, and this is her son whom Elisha restored to life." ⁶ The king asked the woman about it, and she told him.

Then he assigned an official to her case and said to him, "Give back everything that belonged to her, including all the income from her land from the day she left the country until now."

Hazael Murders Ben-Hadad

⁷ Elisha went to Damascus, and Ben-Hadad king of Aram was ill. When the king was told, "The man of God has come all the way up here," ⁸ he said to Hazael, "Take a gift with you and go to meet the man of God. Consult the LORD through him; ask him, 'Will I recover from this illness?'"

⁹ Hazael went to meet Elisha, taking with him as a gift forty camel-loads of all the finest wares of Damascus. He went in and stood before him, and said, "Your son Ben-Hadad king of Aram has sent me to ask, 'Will I recover from this illness?'"

¹⁰ Elisha answered, "Go and say to him, 'You will certainly recover'; but ᵃ the LORD has revealed to me that he will in fact die." ¹¹ He stared at him with a fixed gaze until Hazael felt ashamed. Then the man of God began to weep.

¹² "Why is my lord weeping?" asked Hazael.

"Because I know the harm you will do to the Israelites," he answered. "You will set fire to their fortified places, kill their young men with the sword, dash their little children to the ground, and rip open their pregnant women."

ᵃ 10 The Hebrew may also be read Go and say, 'You will certainly not recover,' for.

[13] Hazael said, "How could your servant, a mere dog, accomplish such a feat?"

"The LORD has shown me that you will become king of Aram," answered Elisha.

[14] Then Hazael left Elisha and returned to his master. When Ben-Hadad asked, "What did Elisha say to you?" Hazael replied, "He told me that you would certainly recover." [15] But the next day he took a thick cloth, soaked it in water and spread it over the king's face, so that he died. Then Hazael succeeded him as king.

Jehoram King of Judah
8:16–24pp — 2Ch 21:5–10,20

[16] In the fifth year of Joram son of Ahab king of Israel, when Jehoshaphat was king of Judah, Jehoram son of Jehoshaphat began his reign as king of Judah. [17] He was thirty-two years old when he became king, and he reigned in Jerusalem eight years. [18] He walked in the ways of the kings of Israel, as the house of Ahab had done, for he married a daughter of Ahab. He did evil in the eyes of the LORD. [19] Nevertheless, for the sake of his servant David, the LORD was not willing to destroy Judah. He had promised to maintain a lamp for David and his descendants forever.

[20] In the time of Jehoram, Edom rebelled against Judah and set up its own king. [21] So Jehoram [a] went to Zair with all his chariots. The Edomites surrounded him and his chariot commanders, but he rose up and broke through by night; his army, however, fled back home. [22] To this day Edom has been in rebellion against Judah. Libnah revolted at the same time.

[23] As for the other events of Jehoram's reign, and all he did, are they not written in the book of the annals of the kings of Judah? [24] Jehoram rested with his fathers and was buried with them in the City of David. And Ahaziah his son succeeded him as king.

Ahaziah King of Judah
8:25–29pp — 2Ch 22:1–6

[25] In the twelfth year of Joram son of Ahab king of Israel, Ahaziah son of Jehoram king of Judah began to reign. [26] Ahaziah was twenty-two years old when he became king, and he reigned in Jerusalem one year. His mother's name was Athaliah, a granddaughter of Omri king of Israel. [27] He walked in the ways of the house of Ahab and did evil in the eyes of the LORD, as the house of Ahab had done, for he was related by marriage to Ahab's family.

[28] Ahaziah went with Joram son of Ahab to war against Hazael king of Aram at Ramoth Gilead. The Arameans wounded Joram; [29] so King Joram returned to Jezreel to recover from the wounds the Arameans had inflicted on him at Ramoth [b] in his battle with Hazael king of Aram.

Then Ahaziah son of Jehoram king of Judah went down to Jezreel to see Joram son of Ahab, because he had been wounded.

Jehu Anointed King of Israel

9 The prophet Elisha summoned a man from the company of the prophets and said to him, "Tuck your cloak into your belt, take this flask of oil with you and go to Ramoth Gilead. [2] When you get there, look for Jehu son of Jehoshaphat, the son of Nimshi. Go to him, get him away from his companions and take him into an inner room. [3] Then take the flask and pour the oil on his head and declare, 'This is what the LORD says: I anoint you king over Israel.' Then open the door and run; don't delay!"

[4] So the young man, the prophet, went to Ramoth Gilead. [5] When he arrived, he found the army officers sitting together. "I have a message for you, commander," he said.

"For which of us?" asked Jehu.

"For you, commander," he replied.

[6] Jehu got up and went into the house. Then the prophet poured the oil on Jehu's head and declared, "This is what the LORD, the God of Israel, says: 'I anoint you king over the LORD's people Israel. [7] You are to destroy the house of Ahab your master, and I will avenge the blood of my servants the prophets and the blood of all the LORD's ser-

---

[a] 21 Hebrew *Joram*, a variant of *Jehoram*; also in verses 23 and 24
[b] 29 Hebrew *Ramah*, a variant of *Ramoth*

vants shed by Jezebel. ⁸The whole house of Ahab will perish. I will cut off from Ahab every last male in Israel—slave or free. ⁹I will make the house of Ahab like the house of Jeroboam son of Nebat and like the house of Baasha son of Ahijah. ¹⁰As for Jezebel, dogs will devour her on the plot of ground at Jezreel, and no one will bury her.'" Then he opened the door and ran.

¹¹When Jehu went out to his fellow officers, one of them asked him, "Is everything all right? Why did this madman come to you?"

"You know the man and the sort of things he says," Jehu replied.

¹²"That's not true!" they said. "Tell us."

Jehu said, "Here is what he told me: 'This is what the LORD says: I anoint you king over Israel.'"

¹³They hurried and took their cloaks and spread them under him on the bare steps. Then they blew the trumpet and shouted, "Jehu is king!"

Jehu Kills Joram and Ahaziah
9:21–29pp — 2Ch 22:7–9

¹⁴So Jehu son of Jehoshaphat, the son of Nimshi, conspired against Joram. (Now Joram and all Israel had been defending Ramoth Gilead against Hazael king of Aram, ¹⁵but King Joram ᵃ had returned to Jezreel to recover from the wounds the Arameans had inflicted on him in the battle with Hazael king of Aram.) Jehu said, "If this is the way you feel, don't let anyone slip out of the city to go and tell the news in Jezreel." ¹⁶Then he got into his chariot and rode to Jezreel, because Joram was resting there and Ahaziah king of Judah had gone down to see him.

¹⁷When the lookout standing on the tower in Jezreel saw Jehu's troops approaching, he called out, "I see some troops coming."

"Get a horseman," Joram ordered. "Send him to meet them and ask, 'Do you come in peace?'"

¹⁸The horseman rode off to meet Jehu and said, "This is what the king says: 'Do you come in peace?'"

"What do you have to do with peace?" Jehu replied. "Fall in behind me."

The lookout reported, "The messenger has reached them, but he isn't coming back."

¹⁹So the king sent out a second horseman. When he came to them he said, "This is what the king says: 'Do you come in peace?'"

Jehu replied, "What do you have to do with peace? Fall in behind me."

²⁰The lookout reported, "He has reached them, but he isn't coming back either. The driving is like that of Jehu son of Nimshi—he drives like a madman."

²¹"Hitch up my chariot," Joram ordered. And when it was hitched up, Joram king of Israel and Ahaziah king of Judah rode out, each in his own chariot, to meet Jehu. They met him at the plot of ground that had belonged to Naboth the Jezreelite. ²²When Joram saw Jehu he asked, "Have you come in peace, Jehu?"

"How can there be peace," Jehu replied, "as long as all the idolatry and witchcraft of your mother Jezebel abound?"

²³Joram turned about and fled, calling out to Ahaziah, "Treachery, Ahaziah!"

²⁴Then Jehu drew his bow and shot Joram between the shoulders. The arrow pierced his heart and he slumped down in his chariot. ²⁵Jehu said to Bidkar, his chariot officer, "Pick him up and throw him on the field that belonged to Naboth the Jezreelite. Remember how you and I were riding together in chariots behind Ahab his father when the LORD made this prophecy about him: ²⁶'Yesterday I saw the blood of Naboth and the blood of his sons, declares the LORD, and I will surely make you pay for it on this plot of ground, declares the LORD.' ᵇ Now then, pick him up and throw him on that plot, in accordance with the word of the LORD."

²⁷When Ahaziah king of Judah saw what had happened, he fled up the road to Beth Haggan. ᶜ Jehu chased him, shouting, "Kill him too!" They wounded him in his chariot on the way up to Gur near Ibleam, but he escaped to Megiddo and died there. ²⁸His servants took him by chariot to

---

ᵃ 15 Hebrew *Jehoram*, a variant of *Joram*; also in verses 17 and 21-24   ᵇ 26 See 1 Kings 21:19.   ᶜ 27 Or *fled by way of the garden house*

Jerusalem and buried him with his fathers in his tomb in the City of David. ²⁹(In the eleventh year of Joram son of Ahab, Ahaziah had become king of Judah.)

Jezebel Killed

³⁰Then Jehu went to Jezreel. When Jezebel heard about it, she painted her eyes, arranged her hair and looked out of a window. ³¹As Jehu entered the gate, she asked, "Have you come in peace, Zimri, you murderer of your master?"ᵃ

³²He looked up at the window and called out, "Who is on my side? Who?" Two or three eunuchs looked down at him. ³³"Throw her down!" Jehu said. So they threw her down, and some of her blood spattered the wall and the horses as they trampled her underfoot.

³⁴Jehu went in and ate and drank. "Take care of that cursed woman," he said, "and bury her, for she was a king's daughter." ³⁵But when they went out to bury her, they found nothing except her skull, her feet and her hands. ³⁶They went back and told Jehu, who said, "This is the word of the LORD that he spoke through his servant Elijah the Tishbite: On the plot of ground at Jezreel dogs will devour Jezebel's flesh.ᵇ ³⁷Jezebel's body will be like refuse on the ground in the plot at Jezreel, so that no one will be able to say, 'This is Jezebel.'"

Ahab's Family Killed

10 Now there were in Samaria seventy sons of the house of Ahab. So Jehu wrote letters and sent them to Samaria: to the officials of Jezreel,ᶜ to the elders and to the guardians of Ahab's children. He said, ²"As soon as this letter reaches you, since your master's sons are with you and you have chariots and horses, a fortified city and weapons, ³choose the best and most worthy of your master's sons and set him on his father's throne. Then fight for your master's house."

⁴But they were terrified and said, "If two kings could not resist him, how can we?"

⁵So the palace administrator, the city governor, the elders and the guardians sent this message to Jehu: "We are your servants and we will do anything you say. We will not appoint anyone as king; you do whatever you think best."

⁶Then Jehu wrote them a second letter, saying, "If you are on my side and will obey me, take the heads of your master's sons and come to me in Jezreel by this time tomorrow."

Now the royal princes, seventy of them, were with the leading men of the city, who were rearing them. ⁷When the letter arrived, these men took the princes and slaughtered all seventy of them. They put their heads in baskets and sent them to Jehu in Jezreel. ⁸When the messenger arrived, he told Jehu, "They have brought the heads of the princes."

Then Jehu ordered, "Put them in two piles at the entrance of the city gate until morning."

⁹The next morning Jehu went out. He stood before all the people and said, "You are innocent. It was I who conspired against my master and killed him, but who killed all these? ¹⁰Know then, that not a word the LORD has spoken against the house of Ahab will fail. The LORD has done what he promised through his servant Elijah." ¹¹So Jehu killed everyone in Jezreel who remained of the house of Ahab, as well as all his chief men, his close friends and his priests, leaving him no survivor.

¹²Jehu then set out and went toward Samaria. At Beth Eked of the Shepherds, ¹³he met some relatives of Ahaziah king of Judah and asked, "Who are you?"

They said, "We are relatives of Ahaziah, and we have come down to greet the families of the king and of the queen mother."

¹⁴"Take them alive!" he ordered. So they took them alive and slaughtered them by the well of Beth Eked—forty-two men. He left no survivor.

¹⁵After he left there, he came upon Jehonadab son of Recab, who was on his way to meet him. Jehu greeted him and said, "Are you in accord with me, as I am with you?"

ᵃ 31 Or "Did Zimri have peace, who murdered his master?"
ᵇ 36 See 1 Kings 21:23.   ᶜ 1 Hebrew; some Septuagint manuscripts and Vulgate of the city

"I am," Jehonadab answered.

"If so," said Jehu, "give me your hand." So he did, and Jehu helped him up into the chariot. ¹⁶Jehu said, "Come with me and see my zeal for the LORD." Then he had him ride along in his chariot.

¹⁷When Jehu came to Samaria, he killed all who were left there of Ahab's family; he destroyed them, according to the word of the LORD spoken to Elijah.

Ministers of Baal Killed

¹⁸Then Jehu brought all the people together and said to them, "Ahab served Baal a little; Jehu will serve him much. ¹⁹Now summon all the prophets of Baal, all his ministers and all his priests. See that no one is missing, because I am going to hold a great sacrifice for Baal. Anyone who fails to come will no longer live." But Jehu was acting deceptively in order to destroy the ministers of Baal.

²⁰Jehu said, "Call an assembly in honor of Baal." So they proclaimed it. ²¹Then he sent word throughout Israel, and all the ministers of Baal came; not one stayed away. They crowded into the temple of Baal until it was full from one end to the other. ²²And Jehu said to the keeper of the wardrobe, "Bring robes for all the ministers of Baal." So he brought out robes for them.

²³Then Jehu and Jehonadab son of Recab went into the temple of Baal. Jehu said to the ministers of Baal, "Look around and see that no servants of the LORD are here with you—only ministers of Baal." ²⁴So they went in to make sacrifices and burnt offerings. Now Jehu had posted eighty men outside with this warning: "If one of you lets any of the men I am placing in your hands escape, it will be your life for his life."

²⁵As soon as Jehu had finished making the burnt offering, he ordered the guards and officers: "Go in and kill them; let no one escape." So they cut them down with the sword. The guards and officers threw the bodies out and then entered the inner shrine of the temple of Baal. ²⁶They brought the sacred stone out of the temple of Baal and burned it. ²⁷They demolished the sacred stone of Baal and tore down the temple of Baal, and people have used it for a latrine to this day.

²⁸So Jehu destroyed Baal worship in Israel. ²⁹However, he did not turn away from the sins of Jeroboam son of Nebat, which he had caused Israel to commit—the worship of the golden calves at Bethel and Dan.

³⁰The LORD said to Jehu, "Because you have done well in accomplishing what is right in my eyes and have done to the house of Ahab all I had in mind to do, your descendants will sit on the throne of Israel to the fourth generation." ³¹Yet Jehu was not careful to keep the law of the LORD, the God of Israel, with all his heart. He did not turn away from the sins of Jeroboam, which he had caused Israel to commit.

³²In those days the LORD began to reduce the size of Israel. Hazael overpowered the Israelites throughout their territory ³³east of the Jordan in all the land of Gilead (the region of Gad, Reuben and Manasseh), from Aroer by the Arnon Gorge through Gilead to Bashan.

³⁴As for the other events of Jehu's reign, all he did, and all his achievements, are they not written in the book of the annals of the kings of Israel?

³⁵Jehu rested with his fathers and was buried in Samaria. And Jehoahaz his son succeeded him as king. ³⁶The time that Jehu reigned over Israel in Samaria was twenty-eight years.

Athaliah and Joash

11:1–21pp — 2Ch 22:10–23:21

11 When Athaliah the mother of Ahaziah saw that her son was dead, she proceeded to destroy the whole royal family. ²But Jehosheba, the daughter of King Jehoram[a] and sister of Ahaziah, took Joash son of Ahaziah and stole him away from among the royal princes, who were about to be murdered. She put him and his nurse in a bedroom to hide him from Athaliah; so he was not killed. ³He remained hidden with

---

[a] 2 Hebrew *Joram*, a variant of *Jehoram*

his nurse at the temple of the Lord for six years while Athaliah ruled the land.

⁴In the seventh year Jehoiada sent for the commanders of units of a hundred, the Carites and the guards and had them brought to him at the temple of the Lord. He made a covenant with them and put them under oath at the temple of the Lord. Then he showed them the king's son. ⁵He commanded them, saying, "This is what you are to do: You who are in the three companies that are going on duty on the Sabbath—a third of you guarding the royal palace, ⁶a third at the Sur Gate, and a third at the gate behind the guard, who take turns guarding the temple— ⁷and you who are in the other two companies that normally go off Sabbath duty are all to guard the temple for the king. ⁸Station yourselves around the king, each man with his weapon in his hand. Anyone who approaches your ranks ^a must be put to death. Stay close to the king wherever he goes."

⁹The commanders of units of a hundred did just as Jehoiada the priest ordered. Each one took his men—those who were going on duty on the Sabbath and those who were going off duty— and came to Jehoiada the priest. ¹⁰Then he gave the commanders the spears and shields that had belonged to King David and that were in the temple of the Lord. ¹¹The guards, each with his weapon in his hand, stationed themselves around the king—near the altar and the temple, from the south side to the north side of the temple.

¹²Jehoiada brought out the king's son and put the crown on him; he presented him with a copy of the covenant and proclaimed him king. They anointed him, and the people clapped their hands and shouted, "Long live the king!"

¹³When Athaliah heard the noise made by the guards and the people, she went to the people at the temple of the Lord. ¹⁴She looked and there was the king, standing by the pillar, as the custom was. The officers and the trumpeters were beside the king, and all the people of the land were rejoicing and blowing trumpets. Then Athaliah tore her robes and called out, "Treason! Treason!"

¹⁵Jehoiada the priest ordered the commanders of units of a hundred, who were in charge of the troops: "Bring her out between the ranks ^b and put to the sword anyone who follows her." For the priest had said, "She must not be put to death in the temple of the Lord." ¹⁶So they seized her as she reached the place where the horses enter the palace grounds, and there she was put to death.

¹⁷Jehoiada then made a covenant between the Lord and the king and people that they would be the Lord's people. He also made a covenant

^a 8 Or *approaches the precincts*   ^b 15 Or *out from the precincts*

2 KINGS 11:1–3, 12, 21

stories to share

Joash, the Boy King

LIFE LESSON: The Lord protects his children.

TO TALK ABOUT

- How did Joash's aunt protect him from his evil grandmother?

- Does it surprise you that Joash was safely hidden so close to Athaliah for six years? (Hint: Did Athaliah worship in the temple? Read 2 Chronicles 22:2–3.)

- Can you think of a time God protected you from harm?

- Joash was only seven years old when he became king. Is there something you think God would like you to do even though you're not an adult yet?

between the king and the people. ¹⁸All the people of the land went to the temple of Baal and tore it down. They smashed the altars and idols to pieces and killed Mattan the priest of Baal in front of the altars.

Then Jehoiada the priest posted guards at the temple of the LORD. ¹⁹He took with him the commanders of hundreds, the Carites, the guards and all the people of the land, and together they brought the king down from the temple of the LORD and went into the palace, entering by way of the gate of the guards. The king then took his place on the royal throne, ²⁰and all the people of the land rejoiced. And the city was quiet, because Athaliah had been slain with the sword at the palace.

²¹Joash[a] was seven years old when he began to reign.

Joash Repairs the Temple
12:1–21pp — 2Ch 24:1–14; 24:23–27

12 In the seventh year of Jehu, Joash[b] became king, and he reigned in Jerusalem forty years. His mother's name was Zibiah; she was from Beersheba. ²Joash did what was right in the eyes of the LORD all the years Jehoiada the priest instructed him. ³The high places, however, were not removed; the people continued to offer sacrifices and burn incense there.

⁴Joash said to the priests, "Collect all the money that is brought as sacred offerings to the temple of the LORD — the money collected in the census, the money received from personal vows and the money brought voluntarily to the temple. ⁵Let every priest receive the money from one of the treasurers, and let it be used to repair whatever damage is found in the temple."

⁶But by the twenty-third year of King Joash the priests still had not repaired the temple. ⁷Therefore King Joash summoned Jehoiada the priest and the other priests and asked them, "Why aren't you repairing the damage done to the temple? Take no more money from your treasurers, but hand it over for repairing the temple." ⁸The priests agreed that they would not collect any more money from the people and that they would not repair the temple themselves.

⁹Jehoiada the priest took a chest and bored a hole in its lid. He placed it beside the altar, on the right side as one enters the temple of the LORD. The priests who guarded the entrance put into the chest all the money that was brought to the temple of the LORD. ¹⁰Whenever they saw that there was a large amount of money in the chest, the royal secretary and the high priest came, counted the money that had been brought into the temple of the LORD and put it into bags. ¹¹When the amount had been determined, they gave the money to the men appointed to supervise the work on the temple. With it they paid those who worked on the temple of the LORD — the carpenters and builders, ¹²the masons and stonecutters. They purchased timber and dressed stone for the repair of the temple of the LORD, and met all the other expenses of restoring the temple.

¹³The money brought into the temple was not spent for making silver basins, wick trimmers, sprinkling bowls, trumpets or any other articles of gold or silver for the temple of the LORD; ¹⁴it was paid to the workmen, who used it to repair the temple. ¹⁵They did not require an accounting from those to whom they gave the money to pay the workers, because they acted with complete honesty. ¹⁶The money from the guilt offerings and sin offerings was not brought into the temple of the LORD; it belonged to the priests.

¹⁷About this time Hazael king of Aram went up and attacked Gath and captured it. Then he turned to attack Jerusalem. ¹⁸But Joash king of Judah took all the sacred objects dedicated by his fathers — Jehoshaphat, Jehoram and Ahaziah, the kings of Judah — and the gifts he himself had dedicated and all the gold found in the treasuries of the temple of the LORD and of the royal palace, and he sent them to Hazael king of Aram, who then withdrew from Jerusalem.

¹⁹As for the other events of the reign of Joash, and all he did, are they not written in the book

---

[a] 21 Hebrew *Jehoash*, a variant of *Joash*   [b] 1 Hebrew *Jehoash*, a variant of *Joash*; also in verses 2, 4, 6, 7 and 18

of the annals of the kings of Judah? ²⁰His officials conspired against him and assassinated him at Beth Millo, on the road down to Silla. ²¹The officials who murdered him were Jozabad son of Shimeath and Jehozabad son of Shomer. He died and was buried with his fathers in the City of David. And Amaziah his son succeeded him as king.

Jehoahaz King of Israel

13 In the twenty-third year of Joash son of Ahaziah king of Judah, Jehoahaz son of Jehu became king of Israel in Samaria, and he reigned seventeen years. ²He did evil in the eyes of the LORD by following the sins of Jeroboam son of Nebat, which he had caused Israel to commit, and he did not turn away from them. ³So the LORD's anger burned against Israel, and for a long time he kept them under the power of Hazael king of Aram and Ben-Hadad his son.

⁴Then Jehoahaz sought the LORD's favor, and the LORD listened to him, for he saw how severely the king of Aram was oppressing Israel. ⁵The LORD provided a deliverer for Israel, and they escaped from the power of Aram. So the Israelites lived in their own homes as they had before. ⁶But they did not turn away from the sins of the house of Jeroboam, which he had caused Israel to commit; they continued in them. Also, the Asherah pole[a] remained standing in Samaria.

⁷Nothing had been left of the army of Jehoahaz except fifty horsemen, ten chariots and ten thousand foot soldiers, for the king of Aram had destroyed the rest and made them like the dust at threshing time.

⁸As for the other events of the reign of Jehoahaz, all he did and his achievements, are they not written in the book of the annals of the kings of Israel? ⁹Jehoahaz rested with his fathers and was buried in Samaria. And Jehoash[b] his son succeeded him as king.

Jehoash King of Israel

¹⁰In the thirty-seventh year of Joash king of Judah, Jehoash son of Jehoahaz became king of Israel in Samaria, and he reigned sixteen years. ¹¹He did evil in the eyes of the LORD and did not turn away from any of the sins of Jeroboam son of Nebat, which he had caused Israel to commit; he continued in them.

¹²As for the other events of the reign of Jehoash, all he did and his achievements, including his war against Amaziah king of Judah, are they not written in the book of the annals of the kings of Israel? ¹³Jehoash rested with his fathers, and Jeroboam succeeded him on the throne. Jehoash was buried in Samaria with the kings of Israel.

¹⁴Now Elisha was suffering from the illness from which he died. Jehoash king of Israel went down to see him and wept over him. "My father! My father!" he cried. "The chariots and horsemen of Israel!"

¹⁵Elisha said, "Get a bow and some arrows," and he did so. ¹⁶"Take the bow in your hands," he said to the king of Israel. When he had taken it, Elisha put his hands on the king's hands.

¹⁷"Open the east window," he said, and he opened it. "Shoot!" Elisha said, and he shot. "The LORD's arrow of victory, the arrow of victory over Aram!" Elisha declared. "You will completely destroy the Arameans at Aphek."

¹⁸Then he said, "Take the arrows," and the king took them. Elisha told him, "Strike the ground." He struck it three times and stopped. ¹⁹The man of God was angry with him and said, "You should have struck the ground five or six times; then you would have defeated Aram and completely destroyed it. But now you will defeat it only three times."

²⁰Elisha died and was buried.

Now Moabite raiders used to enter the country every spring. ²¹Once while some Israelites were burying a man, suddenly they saw a band of raiders; so they threw the man's body into Elisha's tomb. When the body touched Elisha's bones, the man came to life and stood up on his feet.

²²Hazael king of Aram oppressed Israel

---

a 6 That is, a symbol of the goddess Asherah; here and elsewhere in 2 Kings   *b* 9 Hebrew *Joash*, a variant of *Jehoash*; also in verses 12-14 and 25 throughout the reign of Jehoahaz. ²³But the LORD was gracious to them and had compassion and showed concern for them because of his covenant with Abraham, Isaac and Jacob. To this day he has been unwilling to destroy them or banish them from his presence.

²⁴Hazael king of Aram died, and Ben-Hadad his son succeeded him as king. ²⁵Then Jehoash son of Jehoahaz recaptured from Ben-Hadad son of Hazael the towns he had taken in battle from his father Jehoahaz. Three times Jehoash defeated him, and so he recovered the Israelite towns.

Amaziah King of Judah

14:1–7pp — 2Ch 25:1–4,11–12
14:8–22pp — 2Ch 25:17–26:2

14 In the second year of Jehoash[a] son of Jehoahaz king of Israel, Amaziah son of Joash king of Judah began to reign. ²He was twenty-five years old when he became king, and he reigned in Jerusalem twenty-nine years. His mother's name was Jehoaddin; she was from Jerusalem. ³He did what was right in the eyes of the LORD, but not as his father David had done. In everything he followed the example of his father Joash. ⁴The high places, however, were not removed; the people continued to offer sacrifices and burn incense there.

⁵After the kingdom was firmly in his grasp, he executed the officials who had murdered his father the king. ⁶Yet he did not put the sons of the assassins to death, in accordance with what is written in the Book of the Law of Moses where the LORD commanded: "Fathers shall not be put to death for their children, nor children put to death for their fathers; each is to die for his own sins."[b]

⁷He was the one who defeated ten thousand Edomites in the Valley of Salt and captured Sela in battle, calling it Joktheel, the name it has to this day.

⁸Then Amaziah sent messengers to Jehoash son of Jehoahaz, the son of Jehu, king of Israel, with the challenge: "Come, meet me face to face."

⁹But Jehoash king of Israel replied to Amaziah king of Judah: "A thistle in Lebanon sent a message to a cedar in Lebanon, 'Give your daughter to my son in marriage.' Then a wild beast in Lebanon came along and trampled the thistle underfoot. ¹⁰You have indeed defeated Edom and now you are arrogant. Glory in your victory, but stay at home! Why ask for trouble and cause your own downfall and that of Judah also?"

¹¹Amaziah, however, would not listen, so Jehoash king of Israel attacked. He and Amaziah king of Judah faced each other at Beth Shemesh in Judah. ¹²Judah was routed by Israel, and every man fled to his home. ¹³Jehoash king of Israel captured Amaziah king of Judah, the son of Joash, the son of Ahaziah, at Beth Shemesh. Then Jehoash went to Jerusalem and broke down the wall of Jerusalem from the Ephraim Gate to the Corner Gate—a section about six hundred feet long.[c] ¹⁴He took all the gold and silver and all the articles found in the temple of the LORD and in the treasuries of the royal palace. He also took hostages and returned to Samaria.

¹⁵As for the other events of the reign of Jehoash, what he did and his achievements, including his war against Amaziah king of Judah, are they not written in the book of the annals of the kings of Israel? ¹⁶Jehoash rested with his fathers and was buried in Samaria with the kings of Israel. And Jeroboam his son succeeded him as king.

¹⁷Amaziah son of Joash king of Judah lived for fifteen years after the death of Jehoash son of Jehoahaz king of Israel. ¹⁸As for the other events of Amaziah's reign, are they not written in the book of the annals of the kings of Judah?

¹⁹They conspired against him in Jerusalem, and he fled to Lachish, but they sent men after him to Lachish and killed him there. ²⁰He was brought back by horse and was buried in Jerusalem with his fathers, in the City of David.

²¹Then all the people of Judah took Azariah,[d] who was sixteen years old, and made him king

---

[a] 1 Hebrew *Joash,* a variant of *Jehoash*; also in verses 13, 23 and 27   [b] 6 Deut. 24:16   [c] 13 Hebrew *four hundred cubits* (about 180 meters)   [d] 21 Also called *Uzziah*

in place of his father Amaziah. ²²He was the one who rebuilt Elath and restored it to Judah after Amaziah rested with his fathers.

Jeroboam II King of Israel

²³In the fifteenth year of Amaziah son of Joash king of Judah, Jeroboam son of Jehoash king of Israel became king in Samaria, and he reigned forty-one years. ²⁴He did evil in the eyes of the LORD and did not turn away from any of the sins of Jeroboam son of Nebat, which he had caused Israel to commit. ²⁵He was the one who restored the boundaries of Israel from Lebo ª Hamath to the Sea of the Arabah,ᵇ in accordance with the word of the LORD, the God of Israel, spoken through his servant Jonah son of Amittai, the prophet from Gath Hepher.

²⁶The LORD had seen how bitterly everyone in Israel, whether slave or free, was suffering; there was no one to help them. ²⁷And since the LORD had not said he would blot out the name of Israel from under heaven, he saved them by the hand of Jeroboam son of Jehoash.

²⁸As for the other events of Jeroboam's reign, all he did, and his military achievements, including how he recovered for Israel both Damascus and Hamath, which had belonged to Yaudi,ᶜ are they not written in the book of the annals of the kings of Israel? ²⁹Jeroboam rested with his fathers, the kings of Israel. And Zechariah his son succeeded him as king.

Azariah King of Judah

15:1–7pp — 2Ch 26:3–4,21–23

15 In the twenty-seventh year of Jeroboam king of Israel, Azariah son of Amaziah king of Judah began to reign. ²He was sixteen years old when he became king, and he reigned in Jerusalem fifty-two years. His mother's name was Jecoliah; she was from Jerusalem. ³He did what was right in the eyes of the LORD, just as his father Amaziah had done. ⁴The high places, however, were not removed; the people continued to offer sacrifices and burn incense there.

⁵The LORD afflicted the king with leprosyᵈ

until the day he died, and he lived in a separate house.ᵉ Jotham the king's son had charge of the palace and governed the people of the land.

⁶As for the other events of Azariah's reign, and all he did, are they not written in the book of the annals of the kings of Judah? ⁷Azariah rested with his fathers and was buried near them in the City of David. And Jotham his son succeeded him as king.

Zechariah King of Israel

⁸In the thirty-eighth year of Azariah king of Judah, Zechariah son of Jeroboam became king of Israel in Samaria, and he reigned six months. ⁹He did evil in the eyes of the LORD, as his fathers had done. He did not turn away from the sins of Jeroboam son of Nebat, which he had caused Israel to commit.

¹⁰Shallum son of Jabesh conspired against Zechariah. He attacked him in front of the people,ᶠ assassinated him and succeeded him as king. ¹¹The other events of Zechariah's reign are written in the book of the annals of the kings of Israel. ¹²So the word of the LORD spoken to Jehu was fulfilled: "Your descendants will sit on the throne of Israel to the fourth generation."ᵍ

Shallum King of Israel

¹³Shallum son of Jabesh became king in the thirty-ninth year of Uzziah king of Judah, and he reigned in Samaria one month. ¹⁴Then Menahem son of Gadi went from Tirzah up to Samaria. He attacked Shallum son of Jabesh in Samaria, assassinated him and succeeded him as king.

¹⁵The other events of Shallum's reign, and the conspiracy he led, are written in the book of the annals of the kings of Israel.

¹⁶At that time Menahem, starting out from Tirzah, attacked Tiphsah and everyone in the city and its vicinity, because they refused to open their gates. He sacked Tiphsah and ripped open all the pregnant women.

ª 25 Or *from the entrance to*   ᵇ 25 That is, the Dead Sea
ᶜ 28 Or *Judah*   ᵈ 5 The Hebrew word was used for various diseases affecting the skin — not necessarily leprosy.   ᵉ 5 Or *in a house where he was relieved of responsibility*   ᶠ 10 Hebrew; some Septuagint manuscripts *in Ibleam*   ᵍ 12 2 Kings 10:30

Menahem King of Israel

17 In the thirty-ninth year of Azariah king of Judah, Menahem son of Gadi became king of Israel, and he reigned in Samaria ten years. **18** He did evil in the eyes of the LORD. During his entire reign he did not turn away from the sins of Jeroboam son of Nebat, which he had caused Israel to commit.

19 Then Pul*a* king of Assyria invaded the land, and Menahem gave him a thousand talents*b* of silver to gain his support and strengthen his own hold on the kingdom. **20** Menahem exacted this money from Israel. Every wealthy man had to contribute fifty shekels*c* of silver to be given to the king of Assyria. So the king of Assyria withdrew and stayed in the land no longer.

21 As for the other events of Menahem's reign, and all he did, are they not written in the book of the annals of the kings of Israel? **22** Menahem rested with his fathers. And Pekahiah his son succeeded him as king.

Pekahiah King of Israel

23 In the fiftieth year of Azariah king of Judah, Pekahiah son of Menahem became king of Israel in Samaria, and he reigned two years. **24** Pekahiah did evil in the eyes of the LORD. He did not turn away from the sins of Jeroboam son of Nebat, which he had caused Israel to commit. **25** One of his chief officers, Pekah son of Remaliah, conspired against him. Taking fifty men of Gilead with him, he assassinated Pekahiah, along with Argob and Arieh, in the citadel of the royal palace at Samaria. So Pekah killed Pekahiah and succeeded him as king.

26 The other events of Pekahiah's reign, and all he did, are written in the book of the annals of the kings of Israel.

Pekah King of Israel

27 In the fifty-second year of Azariah king of Judah, Pekah son of Remaliah became king of Israel in Samaria, and he reigned twenty years. **28** He did evil in the eyes of the LORD. He did not turn away from the sins of Jeroboam son of Nebat, which he had caused Israel to commit.

29 In the time of Pekah king of Israel, Tiglath-Pileser king of Assyria came and took Ijon, Abel Beth Maacah, Janoah, Kedesh and Hazor. He took Gilead and Galilee, including all the land of Naphtali, and deported the people to Assyria. **30** Then Hoshea son of Elah conspired against Pekah son of Remaliah. He attacked and assassinated him, and then succeeded him as king in the twentieth year of Jotham son of Uzziah.

31 As for the other events of Pekah's reign, and all he did, are they not written in the book of the annals of the kings of Israel?

Jotham King of Judah
15:33–38pp — 2Ch 27:1–4,7–9

32 In the second year of Pekah son of Remaliah king of Israel, Jotham son of Uzziah king of Judah began to reign. **33** He was twenty-five years old when he became king, and he reigned in Jerusalem sixteen years. His mother's name was Jerusha daughter of Zadok. **34** He did what was right in the eyes of the LORD, just as his father Uzziah had done. **35** The high places, however, were not removed; the people continued to offer sacrifices and burn incense there. Jotham rebuilt the Upper Gate of the temple of the LORD.

36 As for the other events of Jotham's reign, and what he did, are they not written in the book of the annals of the kings of Judah? **37** (In those days the LORD began to send Rezin king of Aram and Pekah son of Remaliah against Judah.) **38** Jotham rested with his fathers and was buried with them in the City of David, the city of his father. And Ahaz his son succeeded him as king.

Ahaz King of Judah
16:1–20pp — 2Ch 28:1–27

16 In the seventeenth year of Pekah son of Remaliah, Ahaz son of Jotham king of Judah began to reign. **2** Ahaz was twenty years old when he became king, and he reigned in Jerusalem sixteen years. Unlike David his father, he did

---

a 19 Also called *Tiglath-Pileser*   *b 19* That is, about 37 tons (about 34 metric tons)   *c 20* That is, about 1 1/4 pounds (about 0.6 kilogram) not do what was right in the eyes of the Lord his God. [3] He walked in the ways of the kings of Israel and even sacrificed his son in [a] the fire, following the detestable ways of the nations the Lord had driven out before the Israelites. [4] He offered sacrifices and burned incense at the high places, on the hilltops and under every spreading tree.

[5] Then Rezin king of Aram and Pekah son of Remaliah king of Israel marched up to fight against Jerusalem and besieged Ahaz, but they could not overpower him. [6] At that time, Rezin king of Aram recovered Elath for Aram by driving out the men of Judah. Edomites then moved into Elath and have lived there to this day.

[7] Ahaz sent messengers to say to Tiglath-Pileser king of Assyria, "I am your servant and vassal. Come up and save me out of the hand of the king of Aram and of the king of Israel, who are attacking me." [8] And Ahaz took the silver and gold found in the temple of the Lord and in the treasuries of the royal palace and sent it as a gift to the king of Assyria. [9] The king of Assyria complied by attacking Damascus and capturing it. He deported its inhabitants to Kir and put Rezin to death.

[10] Then King Ahaz went to Damascus to meet Tiglath-Pileser king of Assyria. He saw an altar in Damascus and sent to Uriah the priest a sketch of the altar, with detailed plans for its construction. [11] So Uriah the priest built an altar in accordance with all the plans that King Ahaz had sent from Damascus and finished it before King Ahaz returned. [12] When the king came back from Damascus and saw the altar, he approached it and presented offerings [b] on it. [13] He offered up his burnt offering and grain offering, poured out his drink offering, and sprinkled the blood of his fellowship offerings [c] on the altar. [14] The bronze altar that stood before the Lord he brought from the front of the temple—from between the new altar and the temple of the Lord—and put it on the north side of the new altar.

[15] King Ahaz then gave these orders to Uriah the priest: "On the large new altar, offer the morning burnt offering and the evening grain offering, the king's burnt offering and his grain offering, and the burnt offering of all the people of the land, and their grain offering and their drink offering. Sprinkle on the altar all the blood of the burnt offerings and sacrifices. But I will use the bronze altar for seeking guidance." [16] And Uriah the priest did just as King Ahaz had ordered.

[17] King Ahaz took away the side panels and removed the basins from the movable stands. He removed the Sea from the bronze bulls that supported it and set it on a stone base. [18] He took away the Sabbath canopy [d] that had been built at the temple and removed the royal entryway outside the temple of the Lord, in deference to the king of Assyria.

[19] As for the other events of the reign of Ahaz, and what he did, are they not written in the book of the annals of the kings of Judah? [20] Ahaz rested with his fathers and was buried with them in the City of David. And Hezekiah his son succeeded him as king.

Hoshea Last King of Israel

17:3–7pp — 2Ki 18:9–12

17 In the twelfth year of Ahaz king of Judah, Hoshea son of Elah became king of Israel in Samaria, and he reigned nine years. [2] He did evil in the eyes of the Lord, but not like the kings of Israel who preceded him.

[3] Shalmaneser king of Assyria came up to attack Hoshea, who had been Shalmaneser's vassal and had paid him tribute. [4] But the king of Assyria discovered that Hoshea was a traitor, for he had sent envoys to So [e] king of Egypt, and he no longer paid tribute to the king of Assyria, as he had done year by year. Therefore Shalmaneser seized him and put him in prison. [5] The king of Assyria invaded the entire land, marched against Samaria and laid siege to it for three years. [6] In the ninth year of Hoshea, the king of Assyria captured Samaria and deported the Israelites to Assyria. He settled them in Halah, in Gozan on the Habor River and in the towns of the Medes.

[a] 3 Or even made his son pass through   [b] 12 Or and went up
[c] 13 Traditionally peace offerings   [d] 18 Or the dais of his throne
(see Septuagint)   [e] 4 Or to Sais, to the; So is possibly an abbreviation for Osorkon.

Israel Exiled Because of Sin

[7] All this took place because the Israelites had sinned against the LORD their God, who had brought them up out of Egypt from under the power of Pharaoh king of Egypt. They worshiped other gods [8] and followed the practices of the nations the LORD had driven out before them, as well as the practices that the kings of Israel had introduced. [9] The Israelites secretly did things against the LORD their God that were not right. From watchtower to fortified city they built themselves high places in all their towns. [10] They set up sacred stones and Asherah poles on every high hill and under every spreading tree. [11] At every high place they burned incense, as the nations whom the LORD had driven out before them had done. They did wicked things that provoked the LORD to anger. [12] They worshiped idols, though the LORD had said, "You shall not do this."[a] [13] The LORD warned Israel and Judah through all his prophets and seers: "Turn from your evil ways. Observe my commands and decrees, in accordance with the entire Law that I commanded your fathers to obey and that I delivered to you through my servants the prophets."

[14] But they would not listen and were as stiff-necked as their fathers, who did not trust in the LORD their God. [15] They rejected his decrees and the covenant he had made with their fathers and the warnings he had given them. They followed worthless idols and themselves became worthless. They imitated the nations around them although the LORD had ordered them, "Do not do as they do," and they did the things the LORD had forbidden them to do.

[16] They forsook all the commands of the LORD their God and made for themselves two idols cast in the shape of calves, and an Asherah pole. They bowed down to all the starry hosts, and they worshiped Baal. [17] They sacrificed their sons and daughters in[b] the fire. They practiced divination and sorcery and sold themselves to do evil in the eyes of the LORD, provoking him to anger.

[18] So the LORD was very angry with Israel and removed them from his presence. Only the tribe of Judah was left, [19] and even Judah did not keep the commands of the LORD their God. They followed the practices Israel had introduced. [20] Therefore the LORD rejected all the people of Israel; he afflicted them and gave them into the hands of plunderers, until he thrust them from his presence.

[21] When he tore Israel away from the house of David, they made Jeroboam son of Nebat their king. Jeroboam enticed Israel away from following the LORD and caused them to commit a great sin. [22] The Israelites persisted in all the sins of Jeroboam and did not turn away from them [23] until the LORD removed them from his presence, as he had warned through all his servants the prophets. So the people of Israel were taken from their homeland into exile in Assyria, and they are still there.

Samaria Resettled

[24] The king of Assyria brought people from Babylon, Cuthah, Avva, Hamath and Sepharvaim and settled them in the towns of Samaria to replace the Israelites. They took over Samaria and lived in its towns. [25] When they first lived there, they did not worship the LORD; so he sent lions among them and they killed some of the people. [26] It was reported to the king of Assyria: "The people you deported and resettled in the towns of Samaria do not know what the god of that country requires. He has sent lions among them, which are killing them off, because the people do not know what he requires."

[27] Then the king of Assyria gave this order: "Have one of the priests you took captive from Samaria go back to live there and teach the people what the god of the land requires." [28] So one of the priests who had been exiled from Samaria came to live in Bethel and taught them how to worship the LORD.

[29] Nevertheless, each national group made its own gods in the several towns where they settled, and set them up in the shrines the people of Samaria had made at the high places. [30] The men

---

[a] 12 Exodus 20:4,5   [b] 17 Or *They made their sons and daughters pass through*

DORIS WYNBEEK RIKKERS

perspectives

Witnessing TO YOUR GRANDCHILD

Sharing your faith with your grandchild can at first seem to be a daunting task. Where do I begin? What do I say? What if my words are not received warmly? Will my attempt create a problem? All these are good questions that can leave you overly cautious.

Witnessing to your grandchild can be done in subtle ways from the time your grandchildren are small. It is as much about what you do as it is about what you say. It appears in your countenance, your attitude, your acceptance of your grandchild. Your grandchildren can hear it in your voice, see it in your smile, feel it in your hug. Your actions will be copied, whether they are for good or evil. The author of 2 Kings observed how true this was in the mixed population of the former territory of the northern kingdom of Israel following its destruction: "To this day their children and grandchildren continue to do as their fathers did" (2 Kings 17:41). Unfortunately, it was evil that was duplicated generation after generation. We need to be sure that our witness is a good and godly one.

Ephesians 5:18b points out some very practical advice: "Be filled with the Spirit." God has promised to give each Christian the power and presence of the Holy Spirit. As a Christian, you are fully equipped to be a living witness to those around you, especially your precious grandchildren. The apostle Paul gave some practical tips in Ephesians 5:19–21 for making your life a witness.

"Speak to One Another With Psalms"

Paul meant this both literally and figuratively. If you've read the Psalms, you know that many of the psalms are overflowing with blessing, thanksgiving, gratitude, praise and encouragement. If your words are psalmlike, they will provide blessing, joy, praise and encouragement to your grandchildren. Quoting a psalm is also an excellent way of witnessing. Memorize verses that mean a lot to you and share them with your grandchild at appropriate times. Start with Psalm 23, Psalm 100, Psalm 56:3 and Psalm 46:1. Add other verses to your repertoire as you discover them.

"Speak ... [With] Hymns and Spiritual Songs"

Singing is a wonderful way to witness. I remember my mother singing while she did housework. She continued singing throughout her life. Her grandchildren remember her singing her favorite hymns and choruses to them at bedtime. Her pitch wasn't perfect, and yours doesn't have to be either. To God and to your grandchildren, you're singing it "just right." What is most important is that your grandchildren hear the joy of the Lord on your lips.

"Sing and Make Music in Your Heart to the Lord"

There's outward singing and there's inner singing. Both are necessary for Christian living. If our hearts are filled with music and joy, our lives will be too. "Whatever is true, whatever is noble, whatever is right, whatever is pure, whatever is lovely, whatever is admirable — if anything is excellent or praiseworthy — think about such things" (Philippians 4:8).

"Always [Give] Thanks to God the Father for Everything"

What a way to witness! In good times and bad, in joy and in sorrow, if we declare thanks to God for everything that comes our way, we will be a testimony to our grandchildren. We will be a true witness that we trust that our lives are in his hands and that "in all things God works for the good of those who love him" (Romans 8:28). What a blessing and a living testimony we can be to our grandchildren if we thank our Father for everything that comes our way.

"Submit to One Another Out of Reverence for Christ"

Constant arguing in any household creates disharmony. We need to strive for an agreeable atmosphere of mutual respect and love. Perhaps you will have to compromise with a daughter- or son-in-law and submit to their routines or discipline methods. Perhaps you will have to hold back a comment or relinquish control of household tasks in order to maintain peace. Christ was the ultimate peacemaker — the Prince of Peace. He brought peace to the world. We can do our part by ensuring peace in our hearts and our homes, thus showing Christ's likeness in our lives.

Witnessing to your grandchild can be your greatest calling and purpose. God will support you in your effort. He will provide you with the method and the words. To encourage yourself, use Psalm 19:14 as your prayer: "May the words of my mouth and the meditation of my heart be pleasing in your sight, O LORD, my Rock and my Redeemer."

from Babylon made Succoth Benoth, the men from Cuthah made Nergal, and the men from Hamath made Ashima; ³¹ the Avvites made Nibhaz and Tartak, and the Sepharvites burned their children in the fire as sacrifices to Adrammelech and Anammelech, the gods of Sepharvaim. ³² They worshiped the Lord, but they also appointed all sorts of their own people to officiate for them as priests in the shrines at the high places. ³³ They worshiped the Lord, but they also served their own gods in accordance with the customs of the nations from which they had been brought.

³⁴ To this day they persist in their former practices. They neither worship the Lord nor adhere to the decrees and ordinances, the laws and commands that the Lord gave the descendants of Jacob, whom he named Israel. ³⁵ When the Lord made a covenant with the Israelites, he commanded them: "Do not worship any other gods or bow down to them, serve them or sacrifice to them. ³⁶ But the Lord, who brought you up out of Egypt with mighty power and outstretched arm, is the one you must worship. To him you shall bow down and to him offer sacrifices. ³⁷ You must always be careful to keep the decrees and ordinances, the laws and commands he wrote for you. Do not worship other gods. ³⁸ Do not forget the covenant I have made with you, and do not worship other gods. ³⁹ Rather, worship the Lord your God; it is he who will deliver you from the hand of all your enemies."

⁴⁰ They would not listen, however, but persisted in their former practices. ⁴¹ Even while these people were worshiping the Lord, they were serving their idols. To this day their children and grandchildren continue to do as their fathers did.

Hezekiah King of Judah

18:2–4pp — 2Ch 29:1–2; 31:1
18:5–7pp — 2Ch 31:20–21
18:9–12pp — 2Ki 17:3–7

18 In the third year of Hoshea son of Elah king of Israel, Hezekiah son of Ahaz king of Judah began to reign. ² He was twenty-five years old when he became king, and he reigned

in Jerusalem twenty-nine years. His mother's name was Abijah ^a daughter of Zechariah. ³ He did what was right in the eyes of the Lord, just as his father David had done. ⁴ He removed the high places, smashed the sacred stones and cut down the Asherah poles. He broke into pieces the bronze snake Moses had made, for up to that time the Israelites had been burning incense to it. (It was called ^b Nehushtan. ^c)

⁵ Hezekiah trusted in the Lord, the God of Israel. There was no one like him among all the kings of Judah, either before him or after him. ⁶ He held fast to the Lord and did not cease to follow him; he kept the commands the Lord had given Moses. ⁷ And the Lord was with him; he was successful in whatever he undertook. He rebelled against the king of Assyria and did not serve him. ⁸ From watchtower to fortified city, he defeated the Philistines, as far as Gaza and its territory.

⁹ In King Hezekiah's fourth year, which was the seventh year of Hoshea son of Elah king of Israel, Shalmaneser king of Assyria marched against Samaria and laid siege to it. ¹⁰ At the end of three years the Assyrians took it. So Samaria was captured in Hezekiah's sixth year, which was the ninth year of Hoshea king of Israel. ¹¹ The king of Assyria deported Israel to Assyria and settled them in Halah, in Gozan on the Habor River and in towns of the Medes. ¹² This happened because they had not obeyed the Lord their God, but had violated his covenant—all that Moses the servant of the Lord commanded. They neither listened to the commands nor carried them out.

¹³ In the fourteenth year of King Hezekiah's reign, Sennacherib king of Assyria attacked all the fortified cities of Judah and captured them. ¹⁴ So Hezekiah king of Judah sent this message to the king of Assyria at Lachish: "I have done wrong. Withdraw from me, and I will pay whatever you demand of me." The king of Assyria exacted from Hezekiah king of Judah three hundred talents ^d of silver and thirty talents ^e of gold. ¹⁵ So

---

^a 2 Hebrew *Abi*, a variant of *Abijah*   ^b 4 Or *He called it*
^c 4 *Nehushtan* sounds like the Hebrew for *bronze* and *snake* and
unclean thing.   ^d 14 That is, about 11 tons (about 10 metric tons)
^e 14 That is, about 1 ton (about 1 metric ton)

Hezekiah gave him all the silver that was found in the temple of the LORD and in the treasuries of the royal palace.

[16] At this time Hezekiah king of Judah stripped off the gold with which he had covered the doors and doorposts of the temple of the LORD, and gave it to the king of Assyria.

Sennacherib Threatens Jerusalem

18:13,17–37pp — Isa 36:1–22
18:17–35pp — 2Ch 32:9–19

[17] The king of Assyria sent his supreme commander, his chief officer and his field commander with a large army, from Lachish to King Hezekiah at Jerusalem. They came up to Jerusalem and stopped at the aqueduct of the Upper Pool, on the road to the Washerman's Field. [18] They called for the king; and Eliakim son of Hilkiah the palace administrator, Shebna the secretary, and Joah son of Asaph the recorder went out to them.

[19] The field commander said to them, "Tell Hezekiah:

" 'This is what the great king, the king of Assyria, says: On what are you basing this confidence of yours? [20] You say you have strategy and military strength — but you speak only empty words. On whom are you depending, that you rebel against me? [21] Look now, you are depending on Egypt, that splintered reed of a staff, which pierces a man's hand and wounds him if he leans on it! Such is Pharaoh king of Egypt to all who depend on him. [22] And if you say to me, "We are depending on the LORD our God" — isn't he the one whose high places and altars Hezekiah removed, saying to Judah and Jerusalem, "You must worship before this altar in Jerusalem"?

[23] " 'Come now, make a bargain with my master, the king of Assyria: I will give you two thousand horses — if you can put riders on them! [24] How can you repulse one officer of the least of my master's officials, even though you are depending on Egypt for chariots and horsemen [a]? [25] Furthermore,

have I come to attack and destroy this place without word from the LORD? The LORD himself told me to march against this country and destroy it.' "

[26] Then Eliakim son of Hilkiah, and Shebna and Joah said to the field commander, "Please speak to your servants in Aramaic, since we understand it. Don't speak to us in Hebrew in the hearing of the people on the wall."

[27] But the commander replied, "Was it only to your master and you that my master sent me to say these things, and not to the men sitting on the wall — who, like you, will have to eat their own filth and drink their own urine?"

[28] Then the commander stood and called out in Hebrew: "Hear the word of the great king, the king of Assyria! [29] This is what the king says: Do not let Hezekiah deceive you. He cannot deliver you from my hand. [30] Do not let Hezekiah persuade you to trust in the LORD when he says, 'The LORD will surely deliver us; this city will not be given into the hand of the king of Assyria.'

[31] "Do not listen to Hezekiah. This is what the king of Assyria says: Make peace with me and come out to me. Then every one of you will eat from his own vine and fig tree and drink water from his own cistern, [32] until I come and take you to a land like your own, a land of grain and new wine, a land of bread and vineyards, a land of olive trees and honey. Choose life and not death!

"Do not listen to Hezekiah, for he is misleading you when he says, 'The LORD will deliver us.' [33] Has the god of any nation ever delivered his land from the hand of the king of Assyria? [34] Where are the gods of Hamath and Arpad? Where are the gods of Sepharvaim, Hena and Ivah? Have they rescued Samaria from my hand? [35] Who of all the gods of these countries has been able to save his land from me? How then can the LORD deliver Jerusalem from my hand?"

[36] But the people remained silent and said nothing in reply, because the king had commanded, "Do not answer him."

---

[a] *24 Or* charioteers

37 Then Eliakim son of Hilkiah the palace administrator, Shebna the secretary and Joah son of Asaph the recorder went to Hezekiah, with their clothes torn, and told him what the field commander had said.

Jerusalem's Deliverance Foretold
19:1–13pp — Isa 37:1–13

19 When King Hezekiah heard this, he tore his clothes and put on sackcloth and went into the temple of the LORD. **2** He sent Eliakim the palace administrator, Shebna the secretary and the leading priests, all wearing sackcloth, to the prophet Isaiah son of Amoz. **3** They told him, "This is what Hezekiah says: This day is a day of distress and rebuke and disgrace, as when children come to the point of birth and there is no strength to deliver them. **4** It may be that the LORD your God will hear all the words of the field commander, whom his master, the king of Assyria, has sent to ridicule the living God, and that he will rebuke him for the words the LORD your God has heard. Therefore pray for the remnant that still survives."

5 When King Hezekiah's officials came to Isaiah, **6** Isaiah said to them, "Tell your master, 'This is what the LORD says: Do not be afraid of what you have heard—those words with which the underlings of the king of Assyria have blasphemed me. **7** Listen! I am going to put such a spirit in him that when he hears a certain report, he will return to his own country, and there I will have him cut down with the sword.' "

8 When the field commander heard that the king of Assyria had left Lachish, he withdrew and found the king fighting against Libnah.

9 Now Sennacherib received a report that Tirhakah, the Cushite[a] king ⌞of Egypt⌟, was marching out to fight against him. So he again sent messengers to Hezekiah with this word: **10** "Say to Hezekiah king of Judah: Do not let the god you depend on deceive you when he says, 'Jerusalem will not be handed over to the king of Assyria.' **11** Surely you have heard what the kings of Assyria have done to all the countries, destroying them completely. And will you be delivered? **12** Did the gods of the nations that were destroyed by my forefathers deliver them: the gods of Gozan, Haran, Rezeph and the people of Eden who were in Tel Assar? **13** Where is the king of Hamath, the king of Arpad, the king of the city of Sepharvaim, or of Hena or Ivvah?"

Hezekiah's Prayer
19:14–19pp — Isa 37:14–20

14 Hezekiah received the letter from the messengers and read it. Then he went up to the temple of the LORD and spread it out before the LORD. **15** And Hezekiah prayed to the LORD: "O LORD, God of Israel, enthroned between the cherubim, you alone are God over all the kingdoms of the earth. You have made heaven and earth. **16** Give ear, O LORD, and hear; open your eyes, O LORD, and see; listen to the words Sennacherib has sent to insult the living God.

17 "It is true, O LORD, that the Assyrian kings have laid waste these nations and their lands. **18** They have thrown their gods into the fire and destroyed them, for they were not gods but only wood and stone, fashioned by men's hands. **19** Now, O LORD our God, deliver us from his hand, so that all kingdoms on earth may know that you alone, O LORD, are God."

Isaiah Prophesies Sennacherib's Fall
19:20–37pp — Isa 37:21–38
19:35–37pp — 2Ch 32:20–21

20 Then Isaiah son of Amoz sent a message to Hezekiah: "This is what the LORD, the God of Israel, says: I have heard your prayer concerning Sennacherib king of Assyria. **21** This is the word that the LORD has spoken against him:

" 'The Virgin Daughter of Zion
    despises you and mocks you.
The Daughter of Jerusalem
    tosses her head as you flee.
22 Who is it you have insulted and blasphemed?
    Against whom have you raised your voice

---

a 9 That is, from the upper Nile region

and lifted your eyes in pride?
  Against the Holy One of Israel!
23 By your messengers
  you have heaped insults on the Lord.
And you have said,
  "With my many chariots
I have ascended the heights of the mountains,
  the utmost heights of Lebanon.
I have cut down its tallest cedars,
  the choicest of its pines.
I have reached its remotest parts,
  the finest of its forests.
24 I have dug wells in foreign lands
  and drunk the water there.
With the soles of my feet
  I have dried up all the streams of Egypt."

25 " 'Have you not heard?
  Long ago I ordained it.
In days of old I planned it;
  now I have brought it to pass,
that you have turned fortified cities
  into piles of stone.
26 Their people, drained of power,
  are dismayed and put to shame.
They are like plants in the field,
  like tender green shoots,
like grass sprouting on the roof,
  scorched before it grows up.

27 " 'But I know where you stay
  and when you come and go
  and how you rage against me.
28 Because you rage against me
  and your insolence has reached my ears,
I will put my hook in your nose
  and my bit in your mouth,
and I will make you return
  by the way you came.'

29 "This will be the sign for you, O Hezekiah:

"This year you will eat what grows by itself,
  and the second year what springs from
    that.
But in the third year sow and reap,
  plant vineyards and eat their fruit.

30 Once more a remnant of the house of Judah
  will take root below and bear fruit above.
31 For out of Jerusalem will come a remnant,
  and out of Mount Zion a band of survivors.

The zeal of the LORD Almighty will accomplish this.

32 "Therefore this is what the LORD says concerning the king of Assyria:

"He will not enter this city
  or shoot an arrow here.
He will not come before it with shield
  or build a siege ramp against it.
33 By the way that he came he will return;
  he will not enter this city,
                    declares the LORD.
34 I will defend this city and save it,
  for my sake and for the sake of David my
    servant."

35 That night the angel of the LORD went out and put to death a hundred and eighty-five thousand men in the Assyrian camp. When the people got up the next morning—there were all the dead bodies! 36 So Sennacherib king of Assyria broke camp and withdrew. He returned to Nineveh and stayed there.

37 One day, while he was worshiping in the temple of his god Nisroch, his sons Adrammelech and Sharezer cut him down with the sword, and they escaped to the land of Ararat. And Esarhaddon his son succeeded him as king.

Hezekiah's Illness

20:1–11pp — 2Ch 32:24–26; Isa 38:1–8

20 In those days Hezekiah became ill and was at the point of death. The prophet Isaiah son of Amoz went to him and said, "This is what the LORD says: Put your house in order, because you are going to die; you will not recover." 2 Hezekiah turned his face to the wall and prayed to the LORD, 3 "Remember, O LORD, how I have walked before you faithfully and with wholehearted devotion and have done what is good in your eyes." And Hezekiah wept bitterly.

[4] Before Isaiah had left the middle court, the word of the LORD came to him: [5] "Go back and tell Hezekiah, the leader of my people, 'This is what the LORD, the God of your father David, says: I have heard your prayer and seen your tears; I will heal you. On the third day from now you will go up to the temple of the LORD. [6] I will

PRAYING THE SCRIPTURES

Comfort

2 KINGS 20:5

O God, my grandchild is grieving. I know you have heard her prayers and seen her tears. Comfort her heart, O Lord our healer.

Next prayer in Comfort Prayer Track: Psalm 119:49–50

add fifteen years to your life. And I will deliver you and this city from the hand of the king of Assyria. I will defend this city for my sake and for the sake of my servant David.'"

[7] Then Isaiah said, "Prepare a poultice of figs." They did so and applied it to the boil, and he recovered.

[8] Hezekiah had asked Isaiah, "What will be the sign that the LORD will heal me and that I will go up to the temple of the LORD on the third day from now?"

[9] Isaiah answered, "This is the LORD's sign to

TALKING POINTS

Illness

God answered Hezekiah's prayer.

2 KINGS 20:1–11

For more on illness, go to Psalm 63:6–8.

you that the LORD will do what he has promised: Shall the shadow go forward ten steps, or shall it go back ten steps?"

[10] "It is a simple matter for the shadow to go forward ten steps," said Hezekiah. "Rather, have it go back ten steps."

[11] Then the prophet Isaiah called upon the LORD, and the LORD made the shadow go back the ten steps it had gone down on the stairway of Ahaz.

Envoys From Babylon

20:12–19pp — Isa 39:1–8
20:20–21pp — 2Ch 32:32–33

[12] At that time Merodach-Baladan son of Baladan king of Babylon sent Hezekiah letters and a gift, because he had heard of Hezekiah's illness. [13] Hezekiah received the messengers and showed them all that was in his storehouses—the silver, the gold, the spices and the fine oil—his armory and everything found among his treasures. There was nothing in his palace or in all his kingdom that Hezekiah did not show them.

[14] Then Isaiah the prophet went to King Hezekiah and asked, "What did those men say, and where did they come from?"

"From a distant land," Hezekiah replied. "They came from Babylon."

[15] The prophet asked, "What did they see in your palace?"

"They saw everything in my palace," Hezekiah said. "There is nothing among my treasures that I did not show them."

[16] Then Isaiah said to Hezekiah, "Hear the word of the LORD: [17] The time will surely come when everything in your palace, and all that your fathers have stored up until this day, will be carried off to Babylon. Nothing will be left, says the LORD. [18] And some of your descendants, your own flesh and blood, that will be born to you, will be taken away, and they will become eunuchs in the palace of the king of Babylon."

[19] "The word of the LORD you have spoken is good," Hezekiah replied. For he thought, "Will there not be peace and security in my lifetime?"

[20] As for the other events of Hezekiah's reign, all

his achievements and how he made the pool and the tunnel by which he brought water into the city, are they not written in the book of the annals of the kings of Judah? [21] Hezekiah rested with his fathers. And Manasseh his son succeeded him as king.

Manasseh King of Judah
21:1–10pp — 2Ch 33:1–10
21:17–18pp — 2Ch 33:18–20

21 Manasseh was twelve years old when he became king, and he reigned in Jerusalem fifty-five years. His mother's name was Hephzibah. [2] He did evil in the eyes of the LORD, following the detestable practices of the nations the LORD had driven out before the Israelites. [3] He rebuilt the high places his father Hezekiah had destroyed; he also erected altars to Baal and made an Asherah pole, as Ahab king of Israel had done. He bowed down to all the starry hosts and worshiped them. [4] He built altars in the temple of the LORD, of which the LORD had said, "In Jerusalem I will put my Name." [5] In both courts of the temple of the LORD, he built altars to all the starry hosts. [6] He sacrificed his own son in[a] the fire, practiced sorcery and divination, and consulted mediums and spiritists. He did much evil in the eyes of the LORD, provoking him to anger.

[7] He took the carved Asherah pole he had made and put it in the temple, of which the LORD had said to David and to his son Solomon, "In this temple and in Jerusalem, which I have chosen out of all the tribes of Israel, I will put my Name forever. [8] I will not again make the feet of the Israelites wander from the land I gave their forefathers, if only they will be careful to do everything I commanded them and will keep the whole Law that my servant Moses gave them." [9] But the people did not listen. Manasseh led them astray, so that they did more evil than the nations the LORD had destroyed before the Israelites.

[10] The LORD said through his servants the prophets: [11] "Manasseh king of Judah has committed these detestable sins. He has done more evil than the Amorites who preceded him and has led Judah into sin with his idols. [12] Therefore

this is what the LORD, the God of Israel, says: I am going to bring such disaster on Jerusalem and Judah that the ears of everyone who hears of it will tingle. [13] I will stretch out over Jerusalem the measuring line used against Samaria and the plumb line used against the house of Ahab. I will wipe out Jerusalem as one wipes a dish, wiping it and turning it upside down. [14] I will forsake the remnant of my inheritance and hand them over to their enemies. They will be looted and plundered by all their foes, [15] because they have done evil in my eyes and have provoked me to anger from the day their forefathers came out of Egypt until this day."

[16] Moreover, Manasseh also shed so much innocent blood that he filled Jerusalem from end to end—besides the sin that he had caused Judah to commit, so that they did evil in the eyes of the LORD.

[17] As for the other events of Manasseh's reign, and all he did, including the sin he committed, are they not written in the book of the annals of the kings of Judah? [18] Manasseh rested with his fathers and was buried in his palace garden, the garden of Uzza. And Amon his son succeeded him as king.

Amon King of Judah
21:19–24pp — 2Ch 33:21–25

[19] Amon was twenty-two years old when he became king, and he reigned in Jerusalem two years. His mother's name was Meshullemeth daughter of Haruz; she was from Jotbah. [20] He did evil in the eyes of the LORD, as his father Manasseh had done. [21] He walked in all the ways of his father; he worshiped the idols his father had worshiped, and bowed down to them. [22] He forsook the LORD, the God of his fathers, and did not walk in the way of the LORD.

[23] Amon's officials conspired against him and assassinated the king in his palace. [24] Then the people of the land killed all who had plotted against King Amon, and they made Josiah his son king in his place.

---

a 6 Or He made his own son pass through

²⁵As for the other events of Amon's reign, and what he did, are they not written in the book of the annals of the kings of Judah? ²⁶He was buried in his grave in the garden of Uzza. And Josiah his son succeeded him as king.

The Book of the Law Found
22:1–20pp — 2Ch 34:1–2,8–28

22 Josiah was eight years old when he became king, and he reigned in Jerusalem thirty-one years. His mother's name was Jedidah daughter of Adaiah; she was from Bozkath. ²He did what was right in the eyes of the LORD and walked in all the ways of his father David, not turning aside to the right or to the left.

³In the eighteenth year of his reign, King Josiah sent the secretary, Shaphan son of Azaliah, the son of Meshullam, to the temple of the LORD. He said: ⁴"Go up to Hilkiah the high priest and have him get ready the money that has been brought into the temple of the LORD, which the doorkeepers have collected from the people. ⁵Have them entrust it to the men appointed to supervise the work on the temple. And have these men pay the workers who repair the temple of the LORD— ⁶the carpenters, the builders and the masons. Also have them purchase timber and dressed stone to repair the temple. ⁷But they need not account for the money entrusted to them, because they are acting faithfully."

⁸Hilkiah the high priest said to Shaphan the secretary, "I have found the Book of the Law in the temple of the LORD." He gave it to Shaphan, who read it. ⁹Then Shaphan the secretary went to the king and reported to him: "Your officials have paid out the money that was in the temple of the LORD and have entrusted it to the workers and supervisors at the temple." ¹⁰Then Shaphan the secretary informed the king, "Hilkiah the priest has given me a book." And Shaphan read from it in the presence of the king.

¹¹When the king heard the words of the Book of the Law, he tore his robes. ¹²He gave these orders to Hilkiah the priest, Ahikam son of Shaphan, Acbor son of Micaiah, Shaphan the secretary and Asaiah the king's attendant: ¹³"Go and inquire of the LORD for me and for the people and for all Judah about what is written in this book that has been found. Great is the LORD's anger that burns against us because our fathers have not obeyed the words of this book; they have not acted in accordance with all that is written there concerning us."

¹⁴Hilkiah the priest, Ahikam, Acbor, Shaphan and Asaiah went to speak to the prophetess Huldah, who was the wife of Shallum son of Tikvah, the son of Harhas, keeper of the wardrobe. She lived in Jerusalem, in the Second District.

¹⁵She said to them, "This is what the LORD, the God of Israel, says: Tell the man who sent you to me, ¹⁶'This is what the LORD says: I am going to bring disaster on this place and its people, according to everything written in the book the king of Judah has read. ¹⁷Because they have forsaken me and burned incense to other gods and provoked me to anger by all the idols their hands have made,ᵃ my anger will burn against this place and will not be quenched.' ¹⁸Tell the king of Judah, who sent you to inquire of the LORD, 'This is what the LORD, the God of Israel, says concerning the words you heard: ¹⁹Because your heart was responsive and you humbled yourself before the LORD when you heard what I have spoken against this place and its people, that they would become accursed and laid waste, and because you tore your robes and wept in my presence, I have heard you, declares the LORD. ²⁰Therefore I will gather you to your fathers, and you will be buried in peace. Your eyes will not see all the disaster I am going to bring on this place.'"

So they took her answer back to the king.

Josiah Renews the Covenant
23:1–3pp — 2Ch 34:29–32
23:4–20Ref — 2Ch 34:3–7,33
23:21–23pp — 2Ch 35:1,18–19
23:28–30pp — 2Ch 35:20–36:1

23 Then the king called together all the elders of Judah and Jerusalem. ²He went up to the temple of the LORD with the men of

---

ᵃ *17 Or by everything they have done*

Judah, the people of Jerusalem, the priests and the prophets — all the people from the least to the greatest. He read in their hearing all the words of the Book of the Covenant, which had been found in the temple of the LORD. ³The king stood by the pillar and renewed the covenant in the presence of the LORD — to follow the LORD and keep his commands, regulations and decrees with all his heart and all his soul, thus confirming the words of the covenant written in this book. Then all the people pledged themselves to the covenant.

⁴The king ordered Hilkiah the high priest, the priests next in rank and the doorkeepers to remove from the temple of the LORD all the articles made for Baal and Asherah and all the starry hosts. He burned them outside Jerusalem in the fields of the Kidron Valley and took the ashes to Bethel. ⁵He did away with the pagan priests appointed by the kings of Judah to burn incense on the high places of the towns of Judah and on those around Jerusalem — those who burned incense to Baal, to the sun and moon, to the constellations and to all the starry hosts. ⁶He took the Asherah pole from the temple of the LORD to the Kidron Valley outside Jerusalem and burned it there. He ground it to powder and scattered the dust over the graves of the common people. ⁷He also tore down the quarters of the male shrine prostitutes, which were in the temple of the LORD and where women did weaving for Asherah.

⁸Josiah brought all the priests from the towns of Judah and desecrated the high places, from Geba to Beersheba, where the priests had burned incense. He broke down the shrines *a* at the gates — at the entrance to the Gate of Joshua, the city governor, which is on the left of the city gate. ⁹Although the priests of the high places did not serve at the altar of the LORD in Jerusalem, they ate unleavened bread with their fellow priests.

¹⁰He desecrated Topheth, which was in the Valley of Ben Hinnom, so no one could use it to sacrifice his son or daughter in *b* the fire to Molech. ¹¹He removed from the entrance to the temple of the LORD the horses that the kings of Judah had dedicated to the sun. They were in the court near the room of an official named Nathan-Melech. Josiah then burned the chariots dedicated to the sun.

¹²He pulled down the altars the kings of Judah had erected on the roof near the upper room of Ahaz, and the altars Manasseh had built in the two courts of the temple of the LORD. He removed them from there, smashed them to pieces and threw the rubble into the Kidron Valley. ¹³The king also desecrated the high places that were east of Jerusalem on the south of the Hill of Corruption — the ones Solomon king of Israel had built for Ashtoreth the vile goddess of the Sidonians, for Chemosh the vile god of Moab, and for Molech *c* the detestable god of the people of Ammon. ¹⁴Josiah smashed the sacred stones and cut down the Asherah poles and covered the sites with human bones.

¹⁵Even the altar at Bethel, the high place made by Jeroboam son of Nebat, who had caused Israel to sin — even that altar and high place he demolished. He burned the high place and ground it to powder, and burned the Asherah pole also. ¹⁶Then Josiah looked around, and when he saw the tombs that were there on the hillside, he had the bones removed from them and burned on the altar to defile it, in accordance with the word of the LORD proclaimed by the man of God who foretold these things.

¹⁷The king asked, "What is that tombstone I see?"

The men of the city said, "It marks the tomb of the man of God who came from Judah and pronounced against the altar of Bethel the very things you have done to it."

¹⁸"Leave it alone," he said. "Don't let anyone disturb his bones." So they spared his bones and those of the prophet who had come from Samaria.

¹⁹Just as he had done at Bethel, Josiah removed and defiled all the shrines at the high places that

---

a 8 Or *high places*   *b 10* Or *to make his son or daughter pass through*   *c 13* Hebrew *Milcom* the kings of Israel had built in the towns of Samaria that had provoked the LORD to anger. [20] Josiah slaughtered all the priests of those high places on the altars and burned human bones on them. Then he went back to Jerusalem.

[21] The king gave this order to all the people: "Celebrate the Passover to the LORD your God, as it is written in this Book of the Covenant." [22] Not since the days of the judges who led Israel, nor throughout the days of the kings of Israel and the kings of Judah, had any such Passover been observed. [23] But in the eighteenth year of King Josiah, this Passover was celebrated to the LORD in Jerusalem.

[24] Furthermore, Josiah got rid of the mediums and spiritists, the household gods, the idols and all the other detestable things seen in Judah and Jerusalem. This he did to fulfill the requirements of the law written in the book that Hilkiah the priest had discovered in the temple of the LORD. [25] Neither before nor after Josiah was there a king like him who turned to the LORD as he did — with all his heart and with all his soul and with all his strength, in accordance with all the Law of Moses.

[26] Nevertheless, the LORD did not turn away from the heat of his fierce anger, which burned against Judah because of all that Manasseh had done to provoke him to anger. [27] So the LORD said, "I will remove Judah also from my presence as I removed Israel, and I will reject Jerusalem, the city I chose, and this temple, about which I said, 'There shall my Name be.'[a]"

[28] As for the other events of Josiah's reign, and all he did, are they not written in the book of the annals of the kings of Judah?

[29] While Josiah was king, Pharaoh Neco king of Egypt went up to the Euphrates River to help the king of Assyria. King Josiah marched out to meet him in battle, but Neco faced him and killed him at Megiddo. [30] Josiah's servants brought his body in a chariot from Megiddo to Jerusalem and buried him in his own tomb. And the people of the land took Jehoahaz son of Josiah and anointed him and made him king in place of his father.

Jehoahaz King of Judah
23:31–34pp — 2Ch 36:2–4

[31] Jehoahaz was twenty-three years old when he became king, and he reigned in Jerusalem three months. His mother's name was Hamutal daughter of Jeremiah; she was from Libnah. [32] He did evil in the eyes of the LORD, just as his fathers had done. [33] Pharaoh Neco put him in chains at Riblah in the land of Hamath[b] so that he might not reign in Jerusalem, and he imposed on Judah a levy of a hundred talents[c] of silver and a talent[d] of gold. [34] Pharaoh Neco made Eliakim son of Josiah king in place of his father Josiah and changed Eliakim's name to Jehoiakim. But he took Jehoahaz and carried him off to Egypt, and there he died. [35] Jehoiakim paid Pharaoh Neco the silver and gold he demanded. In order to do so, he taxed the land and exacted the silver and gold from the people of the land according to their assessments.

Jehoiakim King of Judah
23:36–24:6pp — 2Ch 36:5–8

[36] Jehoiakim was twenty-five years old when he became king, and he reigned in Jerusalem eleven years. His mother's name was Zebidah daughter of Pedaiah; she was from Rumah. [37] And he did evil in the eyes of the LORD, just as his fathers had done.

24 During Jehoiakim's reign, Nebuchadnezzar king of Babylon invaded the land, and Jehoiakim became his vassal for three years. But then he changed his mind and rebelled against Nebuchadnezzar. [2] The LORD sent Babylonian,[e] Aramean, Moabite and Ammonite raiders against him. He sent them to destroy Judah, in accordance with the word of the LORD proclaimed by his servants the prophets. [3] Surely these things happened to Judah according to the LORD's command, in order to remove them from his presence because of the sins of Manasseh and all he

[a] 27 1 Kings 8:29   [b] 33 Hebrew; Septuagint (see also 2 Chron. 36:3) *Neco at Riblah in Hamath removed him*   [c] 33 That is, about 3 3/4 tons (about 3.4 metric tons)   [d] 33 That is, about 75 pounds (about 34 kilograms)   [e] 2 Or *Chaldean*

had done, ⁴including the shedding of innocent blood. For he had filled Jerusalem with innocent blood, and the LORD was not willing to forgive.

⁵As for the other events of Jehoiakim's reign, and all he did, are they not written in the book of the annals of the kings of Judah? ⁶Jehoiakim rested with his fathers. And Jehoiachin his son succeeded him as king.

⁷The king of Egypt did not march out from his own country again, because the king of Babylon had taken all his territory, from the Wadi of Egypt to the Euphrates River.

Jehoiachin King of Judah

24:8–17pp — 2Ch 36:9–10

⁸Jehoiachin was eighteen years old when he became king, and he reigned in Jerusalem three months. His mother's name was Nehushta daughter of Elnathan; she was from Jerusalem. ⁹He did evil in the eyes of the LORD, just as his father had done.

¹⁰At that time the officers of Nebuchadnezzar king of Babylon advanced on Jerusalem and laid siege to it, ¹¹and Nebuchadnezzar himself came up to the city while his officers were besieging it. ¹²Jehoiachin king of Judah, his mother, his attendants, his nobles and his officials all surrendered to him.

In the eighth year of the reign of the king of Babylon, he took Jehoiachin prisoner. ¹³As the LORD had declared, Nebuchadnezzar removed all the treasures from the temple of the LORD and from the royal palace, and took away all the gold articles that Solomon king of Israel had made for the temple of the LORD. ¹⁴He carried into exile all Jerusalem: all the officers and fighting men, and all the craftsmen and artisans—a total of ten thousand. Only the poorest people of the land were left.

¹⁵Nebuchadnezzar took Jehoiachin captive to Babylon. He also took from Jerusalem to Babylon the king's mother, his wives, his officials and the leading men of the land. ¹⁶The king of Babylon also deported to Babylon the entire force of seven thousand fighting men, strong and fit for war, and a thousand craftsmen and artisans. ¹⁷He made Mattaniah, Jehoiachin's uncle, king in his place and changed his name to Zedekiah.

Zedekiah King of Judah

24:18–20pp — 2Ch 36:11–16; Jer 52:1–3

¹⁸Zedekiah was twenty-one years old when he became king, and he reigned in Jerusalem eleven years. His mother's name was Hamutal daughter of Jeremiah; she was from Libnah. ¹⁹He did evil in the eyes of the LORD, just as Jehoiakim had done. ²⁰It was because of the LORD's anger that all this happened to Jerusalem and Judah, and in the end he thrust them from his presence.

The Fall of Jerusalem

25:1–12pp — Jer 39:1–10
25:1–21pp — 2Ch 36:17–20; Jer 52:4–27
25:22–26pp — Jer 40:7–9; 41:1–3,16–18

Now Zedekiah rebelled against the king of Babylon.

25 So in the ninth year of Zedekiah's reign, on the tenth day of the tenth month, Nebuchadnezzar king of Babylon marched against Jerusalem with his whole army. He encamped outside the city and built siege works all around it. ²The city was kept under siege until the eleventh year of King Zedekiah. ³By the ninth day of the ⌊fourth⌋ᵃ month the famine in the city had become so severe that there was no food for the people to eat. ⁴Then the city wall was broken through, and the whole army fled at night through the gate between the two walls near the king's garden, though the Babyloniansᵇ were surrounding the city. They fled toward the Arabah,ᶜ ⁵but the Babylonianᵈ army pursued the king and overtook him in the plains of Jericho. All his soldiers were separated from him and scattered, ⁶and he was captured. He was taken to the king of Babylon at Riblah, where sentence was pronounced on him. ⁷They killed the sons of Zedekiah before his eyes. Then they put out his eyes, bound him with bronze shackles and took him to Babylon.

ᵃ 3 See Jer. 52:6.   ᵇ 4 Or *Chaldeans*; also in verses 13, 25 and 26
ᶜ 4 Or *the Jordan Valley*   ᵈ 5 Or *Chaldean*; also in verses 10 and 24

⁸On the seventh day of the fifth month, in the nineteenth year of Nebuchadnezzar king of Babylon, Nebuzaradan commander of the imperial guard, an official of the king of Babylon, came to Jerusalem. ⁹He set fire to the temple of the LORD, the royal palace and all the houses of Jerusalem. Every important building he burned down. ¹⁰The whole Babylonian army, under the commander of the imperial guard, broke down the walls around Jerusalem. ¹¹Nebuzaradan the commander of the guard carried into exile the people who remained in the city, along with the rest of the populace and those who had gone over to the king of Babylon. ¹²But the commander left behind some of the poorest people of the land to work the vineyards and fields.

¹³The Babylonians broke up the bronze pillars, the movable stands and the bronze Sea that were at the temple of the LORD and they carried the bronze to Babylon. ¹⁴They also took away the pots, shovels, wick trimmers, dishes and all the bronze articles used in the temple service. ¹⁵The commander of the imperial guard took away the censers and sprinkling bowls—all that were made of pure gold or silver.

¹⁶The bronze from the two pillars, the Sea and the movable stands, which Solomon had made for the temple of the LORD, was more than could be weighed. ¹⁷Each pillar was twenty-seven feet[a] high. The bronze capital on top of one pillar was four and a half feet[b] high and was decorated with a network and pomegranates of bronze all around. The other pillar, with its network, was similar.

¹⁸The commander of the guard took as prisoners Seraiah the chief priest, Zephaniah the priest next in rank and the three doorkeepers. ¹⁹Of those still in the city, he took the officer in charge of the fighting men and five royal advisers. He also took the secretary who was chief officer in charge of conscripting the people of the land and sixty of his men who were found in the city. ²⁰Nebuzaradan the commander took them all and brought them to the king of Babylon at Riblah. ²¹There at Riblah, in the land of Hamath, the king had them executed.

So Judah went into captivity, away from her land.

²²Nebuchadnezzar king of Babylon appointed Gedaliah son of Ahikam, the son of Shaphan, to be over the people he had left behind in Judah. ²³When all the army officers and their men heard that the king of Babylon had appointed Gedaliah as governor, they came to Gedaliah at Mizpah—Ishmael son of Nethaniah, Johanan son of Kareah, Seraiah son of Tanhumeth the Netophathite, Jaazaniah the son of the Maacathite, and their men. ²⁴Gedaliah took an oath to reassure them and their men. "Do not be afraid of the Babylonian officials," he said. "Settle down in the land and serve the king of Babylon, and it will go well with you."

²⁵In the seventh month, however, Ishmael son of Nethaniah, the son of Elishama, who was of royal blood, came with ten men and assassinated Gedaliah and also the men of Judah and the Babylonians who were with him at Mizpah. ²⁶At this, all the people from the least to the greatest, together with the army officers, fled to Egypt for fear of the Babylonians.

Jehoiachin Released

25:27–30pp — Jer 52:31–34

²⁷In the thirty-seventh year of the exile of Jehoiachin king of Judah, in the year Evil-Merodach[c] became king of Babylon, he released Jehoiachin from prison on the twenty-seventh day of the twelfth month. ²⁸He spoke kindly to him and gave him a seat of honor higher than those of the other kings who were with him in Babylon. ²⁹So Jehoiachin put aside his prison clothes and for the rest of his life ate regularly at the king's table. ³⁰Day by day the king gave Jehoiachin a regular allowance as long as he lived.

---

a 17 Hebrew *eighteen cubits* (about 8.1 meters)   *b 17* Hebrew *three cubits* (about 1.3 meters)   *c 27* Also called *Amel-Marduk*

Family TREE

The book of 1 Chronicles begins with Israel's genealogical record and then focuses on King David's reign, paralleling many of the events of 2 Samuel. The first nine chapters are a virtual "Who's who" of Israel's history, with a special emphasis on tracing David's family line. As you read through the chapters, notice some of the names: Adam, Noah, Abraham, Israel. You probably recognize quite a few, but then there are those who you've probably never heard of: Oholibamah, Shobal, Shephatiah. Why were the names of "unknown" people included in this book?

The point of the genealogies was first to remind the Israelites, who were in exile in Babylon at this time, of who they were historically and spiritually. Because the people were far from their homeland, living in a foreign land, the writer of the book wanted the people to remember where they had come from.

The book also reminds us today of our spiritual heritage and the importance of passing on a legacy of godliness to the next generation. As you read through the genealogies, think back to the thousands of faithful people who have gone before you in shaping your spiritual family tree. Imagine your place in the line, and then think of what kind of impact you'd like to have on those who follow you.

VERSE *to* REMEMBER | 1 CHRONICLES 16:13–15

O descendants of Israel his servant, O sons of Jacob, his chosen ones. He is the LORD our God; his judgments are in all the earth. He remembers his covenant forever, the word he commanded, for a thousand generations.

ABOUT 1 CHRONICLES

WRITTEN BY:
Unknown, possibly Ezra

WRITTEN FOR:
The people of Judah who had returned from exile in Babylon

DATE WRITTEN:
Between 450 and 400 B.C., much later than the events it records

WHY WRITTEN:
To remind the Jews of their history and godly heritage

Historical Records From Adam to Abraham

To Noah's Sons

1 Adam, Seth, Enosh, ²Kenan, Mahalalel, Jared, ³Enoch, Methuselah, Lamech, Noah.

⁴The sons of Noah:ᵃ
   Shem, Ham and Japheth.

The Japhethites

1:5–7pp — Ge 10:2–5

⁵The sonsᵇ of Japheth:
   Gomer, Magog, Madai, Javan, Tubal, Meshech and Tiras.
⁶The sons of Gomer:
   Ashkenaz, Riphathᶜ and Togarmah.
⁷The sons of Javan:
   Elishah, Tarshish, the Kittim and the Rodanim.

The Hamites

1:8–16pp — Ge 10:6–20

⁸The sons of Ham:
   Cush, Mizraim,ᵈ Put and Canaan.
⁹The sons of Cush:
   Seba, Havilah, Sabta, Raamah and Sabteca.
  The sons of Raamah:
   Sheba and Dedan.
¹⁰Cush was the fatherᵉ of
   Nimrod, who grew to be a mighty warrior on earth.
¹¹Mizraim was the father of
   the Ludites, Anamites, Lehabites, Naphtuhites, ¹²Pathrusites, Casluhites (from whom the Philistines came) and Caphtorites.
¹³Canaan was the father of
   Sidon his firstborn,ᶠ and of the Hittites, ¹⁴Jebusites, Amorites, Girgashites, ¹⁵Hivites, Arkites, Sinites, ¹⁶Arvadites, Zemarites and Hamathites.

The Semites

1:17–23pp — Ge 10:21–31; 11:10–27

¹⁷The sons of Shem:
   Elam, Asshur, Arphaxad, Lud and Aram.

The sons of Aram:ᵍ
   Uz, Hul, Gether and Meshech.
¹⁸Arphaxad was the father of Shelah,
   and Shelah the father of Eber.
¹⁹Two sons were born to Eber:
   One was named Peleg,ʰ because in his time the earth was divided; his brother was named Joktan.
²⁰Joktan was the father of
   Almodad, Sheleph, Hazarmaveth, Jerah, ²¹Hadoram, Uzal, Diklah, ²²Obal,ⁱ Abimael, Sheba, ²³Ophir, Havilah and Jobab. All these were sons of Joktan.

²⁴Shem, Arphaxad,ʲ Shelah,
²⁵Eber, Peleg, Reu,
²⁶Serug, Nahor, Terah
²⁷and Abram (that is, Abraham).

The Family of Abraham

²⁸The sons of Abraham:
   Isaac and Ishmael.

Descendants of Hagar

1:29–31pp — Ge 25:12–16

²⁹These were their descendants:
   Nebaioth the firstborn of Ishmael, Kedar, Adbeel, Mibsam, ³⁰Mishma, Dumah, Massa, Hadad, Tema, ³¹Jetur, Naphish and Kedemah. These were the sons of Ishmael.

Descendants of Keturah

1:32–33pp — Ge 25:1–4

³²The sons born to Keturah, Abraham's concubine:
   Zimran, Jokshan, Medan, Midian, Ishbak and Shuah.

ᵃ 4 Septuagint; Hebrew does not have this line.   ᵇ 5 *Sons* may mean *descendants* or *successors* or *nations*; also in verses 6-10, 17 and 20.   ᶜ 6 Many Hebrew manuscripts and Vulgate (see also Septuagint and Gen. 10:3); most Hebrew manuscripts *Diphath*   ᵈ 8 That is, Egypt; also in verse 11   ᵉ 10 *Father* may mean *ancestor* or *predecessor* or *founder*; also in verses 11, 13, 18 and 20.   ᶠ 13 Or *of the Sidonians, the foremost*   ᵍ 17 One Hebrew manuscript and some Septuagint manuscripts (see also Gen. 10:23); most Hebrew manuscripts do not have this line.   ʰ 19 *Peleg* means *division.*   ⁱ 22 Some Hebrew manuscripts and Syriac (see also Gen. 10:28); most Hebrew manuscripts *Ebal*   ʲ 24 Hebrew; some Septuagint manuscripts *Arphaxad, Cainan* (see also note at Gen. 11:10)

The sons of Jokshan:
Sheba and Dedan.
[33] The sons of Midian:
Ephah, Epher, Hanoch, Abida and Eldaah.
All these were descendants of Keturah.

Descendants of Sarah

1:35–37pp — Ge 36:10–14
[34] Abraham was the father of Isaac.
The sons of Isaac:
Esau and Israel.

Esau's Sons

[35] The sons of Esau:
Eliphaz, Reuel, Jeush, Jalam and Korah.
[36] The sons of Eliphaz:
Teman, Omar, Zepho,[a] Gatam and Kenaz;
by Timna: Amalek.[b]
[37] The sons of Reuel:
Nahath, Zerah, Shammah and Mizzah.

The People of Seir in Edom

1:38–42pp — Ge 36:20–28
[38] The sons of Seir:
Lotan, Shobal, Zibeon, Anah, Dishon,
Ezer and Dishan.
[39] The sons of Lotan:
Hori and Homam. Timna was Lotan's
sister.
[40] The sons of Shobal:
Alvan,[c] Manahath, Ebal, Shepho and
Onam.
The sons of Zibeon:
Aiah and Anah.
[41] The son of Anah:
Dishon.
The sons of Dishon:
Hemdan,[d] Eshban, Ithran and Keran.
[42] The sons of Ezer:
Bilhan, Zaavan and Akan.[e]
The sons of Dishan[f]:
Uz and Aran.

The Rulers of Edom

1:43–54pp — Ge 36:31–43
[43] These were the kings who reigned in Edom
before any Israelite king reigned[g]:
Bela son of Beor, whose city was named
Dinhabah.
[44] When Bela died, Jobab son of Zerah from
Bozrah succeeded him as king.
[45] When Jobab died, Husham from the land of
the Temanites succeeded him as king.
[46] When Husham died, Hadad son of Bedad,
who defeated Midian in the country of
Moab, succeeded him as king. His city
was named Avith.
[47] When Hadad died, Samlah from Masrekah
succeeded him as king.
[48] When Samlah died, Shaul from Rehoboth
on the river[h] succeeded him as king.
[49] When Shaul died, Baal-Hanan son of Acbor
succeeded him as king.
[50] When Baal-Hanan died, Hadad succeeded
him as king. His city was named Pau,[i]
and his wife's name was Mehetabel daughter of Matred, the daughter of Me-Zahab.
[51] Hadad also died.

The chiefs of Edom were:
Timna, Alvah, Jetheth, [52] Oholibamah,
Elah, Pinon, [53] Kenaz, Teman, Mibzar,
[54] Magdiel and Iram. These were the chiefs
of Edom.

Israel's Sons

2:1–2pp — Ge 35:23–26

2 These were the sons of Israel:
Reuben, Simeon, Levi, Judah, Issachar,
Zebulun, [2] Dan, Joseph, Benjamin, Naph-
tali, Gad and Asher.

---

[a] 36 Many Hebrew manuscripts, some Septuagint manuscripts
and Syriac (see also Gen. 36:11); most Hebrew manuscripts
Zephi [b] 36 Some Septuagint manuscripts (see also Gen. 36:12);
Hebrew *Gatam, Kenaz, Timna and Amalek* [c] 40 Many Hebrew
manuscripts and some Septuagint manuscripts (see also Gen. 36:23);
most Hebrew manuscripts *Alian* [d] 41 Many Hebrew manuscripts
and some Septuagint manuscripts (see also Gen. 36:26); most
Hebrew manuscripts *Hamran* [e] 42 Many Hebrew and Septuagint
manuscripts (see also Gen. 36:27); most Hebrew manuscripts
Zaavan, Jaakan [f] 42 Hebrew *Dishon,* a variant of *Dishan*
[g] 43 Or *before an Israelite king reigned over them* [h] 48 Possibly
the Euphrates [i] 50 Many Hebrew manuscripts, some Septuagint
manuscripts, Vulgate and Syriac (see also Gen. 36:39); most Hebrew
manuscripts *Pai*

DORIS WYNBEEK RIKKERS

Sharing YOUR FAMILY HISTORY

Edith Wynbeek Smith had shoeboxes full of scribbled notes, church bulletins marked with circles, and Bible verses written out and underlined. She wrote letters, poems, short essays and one-liners, vowing to herself and her family that someday she would write a book. Yet the dream was forgotten as Edith grew old and lost the ability to write or speak.

Later, Edith's granddaughter, Andrea, found the boxes and started reading. Pouring over the pieces consumed a weekend and then Andrea's life. She edited and created "the book" that captures her grandmother's family history. *Smith Can Be Anybody: a Life Walked by Faith* reveals deep feelings and family secrets with glimpses of humor and a constancy of faith in God. I'm thrilled that my Aunt Edith took the time to scribble notes and record her deepest thoughts, because Edith's story is her story and Andrea's story and *my* story as well.

Writing a family history and capturing family stories and traditions is a noble venture. Everyone would like to say they have written out, duplicated, bound at Kinkos and distributed to each family member a family treasure such as this. Nice thought, but it takes some effort to get there. Just like any project, handling it in small steps and pieces will get you to your final goal — even if it's collected in a shoebox. Here's how:

Just Start Writing

Recording genealogies and family histories were obviously important to the ancient Israelites, as evidenced in the opening chapters of 1 Chronicles. Our family histories and traditions are very special as well. At the end of a special or even an ordinary day that you want to remember, grab a piece of paper and write down your thoughts. Maybe it's something funny that your grandkids said or did. Maybe it's your feelings about your family.

Be Honest

Family history and heritage includes more than just the happy times. Life contains struggles, uncertainties, conflicts and difficult situations. Talk about them. Record how you handled the situation. When resolution, reconciliation or a turnaround occurs, be sure to focus on the positive outcome. Uncertainty and struggle go hand in hand with being strengthened by faith or consumed with doubt; share that too.

Talk About Your Faith

Tell your faith story. Whether it involves dramatic or steady growth, it's *your* story that your children and grandchildren will want to know. Write out the words to favorite hymns or Bible verses. You may want to add the date since over the years your favorites might change. A line or two explaining why it's a favorite will be cherished.

Hit the Highlights

You don't have to record every moment, especially if you just started doing this. Go for the milestones, the major events. If they are in the past, record your memories. Or talk about a topic: vacation, laughter, birthdays, family dos and don'ts, what makes life special.

Talk About the Past

Family trees just record dates and names. Family histories should describe personalities, occupations, what people loved, how they lived. Simple facts may become moments of revelation to future generations.

Talk About the Present

Simple descriptions of your home, the family cottage or a favorite vacation spot will be special years from now. Pictures will capture the visual, but your words will capture the emotion and heart of it all. Record the names, dates and relationships between the people there. Details that seem too obvious to record now will be important in the future.

Talk About the Future

Write down your hopes and dreams for the future. Record your concerns about what is yet to come. You may want to do this in the form of a letter.

Your collection of memories may not become a bound book like Edith's, but those memories that capture your family's history and heritage will later be cherished. Write down your thoughts, capture the moments in words, not just in pictures. Start today. A grandchild, a niece or someone unknown to you may be blessed by your family's story.

Judah

2:5–15pp — Ru 4:18–22; Mt 1:3–6

To Hezron's Sons

³ The sons of Judah:

Er, Onan and Shelah. These three were born to him by a Canaanite woman, the daughter of Shua. Er, Judah's firstborn, was wicked in the LORD's sight; so the LORD put him to death. ⁴ Tamar, Judah's daughter-in-law, bore him Perez and Zerah. Judah had five sons in all.

⁵ The sons of Perez:

Hezron and Hamul.

⁶ The sons of Zerah:

Zimri, Ethan, Heman, Calcol and Darda ᵃ — five in all.

⁷ The son of Carmi:

Achar, ᵇ who brought trouble on Israel by violating the ban on taking devoted things. ᶜ

⁸ The son of Ethan:

Azariah.

⁹ The sons born to Hezron were:

Jerahmeel, Ram and Caleb. ᵈ

From Ram Son of Hezron

¹⁰ Ram was the father of

Amminadab, and Amminadab the father of Nahshon, the leader of the people of Judah. ¹¹ Nahshon was the father of Salmon, ᵉ Salmon the father of Boaz, ¹² Boaz the father of Obed and Obed the father of Jesse.

¹³ Jesse was the father of

Eliab his firstborn; the second son was Abinadab, the third Shimea, ¹⁴ the fourth Nethanel, the fifth Raddai, ¹⁵ the sixth Ozem and the seventh David. ¹⁶ Their sisters were Zeruiah and Abigail. Zeruiah's three sons were Abishai, Joab and Asahel. ¹⁷ Abigail was the mother of Amasa, whose father was Jether the Ishmaelite.

Caleb Son of Hezron

¹⁸ Caleb son of Hezron had children by his wife Azubah (and by Jerioth). These were her sons: Jesher, Shobab and Ardon. ¹⁹ When Azubah died, Caleb married Ephrath, who bore him Hur. ²⁰ Hur was the father of Uri, and Uri the father of Bezalel.

²¹ Later, Hezron lay with the daughter of Makir the father of Gilead (he had married her when he was sixty years old), and she bore him Segub. ²² Segub was the father of Jair, who controlled twenty-three towns in Gilead. ²³ (But Geshur and Aram captured Havvoth Jair, ᶠ as well as Kenath with its surrounding settlements — sixty towns.) All these were descendants of Makir the father of Gilead.

²⁴ After Hezron died in Caleb Ephrathah, Abijah the wife of Hezron bore him Ashhur the father ᵍ of Tekoa.

Jerahmeel Son of Hezron

²⁵ The sons of Jerahmeel the firstborn of Hezron:

Ram his firstborn, Bunah, Oren, Ozem and ʰ Ahijah. ²⁶ Jerahmeel had another wife, whose name was Atarah; she was the mother of Onam.

²⁷ The sons of Ram the firstborn of Jerahmeel:

Maaz, Jamin and Eker.

²⁸ The sons of Onam:

Shammai and Jada.

The sons of Shammai:

Nadab and Abishur.

²⁹ Abishur's wife was named Abihail, who bore him Ahban and Molid.

ᵃ 6 Many Hebrew manuscripts, some Septuagint manuscripts and Syriac (see also 1 Kings 4:31); most Hebrew manuscripts *Dara*   ᵇ 7 *Achar* means *trouble*; *Achar* is called *Achan* in Joshua.   ᶜ 7 The Hebrew term refers to the irrevocable giving over of things or persons to the LORD, often by totally destroying them.   ᵈ 9 Hebrew *Kelubai*, a variant of *Caleb*   ᵉ 11 Septuagint (see also Ruth 4:21); Hebrew *Salma*   ᶠ 23 Or *captured the settlements of Jair*   ᵍ 24 *Father* may mean *civic leader* or *military leader*; also in verses 42, 45, 49-52 and possibly elsewhere.   ʰ 25 Or *Oren and Ozem, by*

³⁰The sons of Nadab:

Seled and Appaim. Seled died without children.

³¹The son of Appaim:

Ishi, who was the father of Sheshan. Sheshan was the father of Ahlai.

³²The sons of Jada, Shammai's brother:

Jether and Jonathan. Jether died without children.

³³The sons of Jonathan:

Peleth and Zaza.

These were the descendants of Jerahmeel.

³⁴Sheshan had no sons — only daughters.

He had an Egyptian servant named Jarha. ³⁵Sheshan gave his daughter in marriage to his servant Jarha, and she bore him Attai.

³⁶Attai was the father of Nathan,

Nathan the father of Zabad,

³⁷Zabad the father of Ephlal,

Ephlal the father of Obed,

³⁸Obed the father of Jehu,

Jehu the father of Azariah,

³⁹Azariah the father of Helez,

Helez the father of Eleasah,

⁴⁰Eleasah the father of Sismai,

Sismai the father of Shallum,

⁴¹Shallum the father of Jekamiah,

and Jekamiah the father of Elishama.

The Clans of Caleb

⁴²The sons of Caleb the brother of Jerahmeel:

Mesha his firstborn, who was the father of Ziph, and his son Mareshah,ᵃ who was the father of Hebron.

⁴³The sons of Hebron:

Korah, Tappuah, Rekem and Shema. ⁴⁴Shema was the father of Raham, and Raham the father of Jorkeam. Rekem was the father of Shammai. ⁴⁵The son of Shammai was Maon, and Maon was the father of Beth Zur.

⁴⁶Caleb's concubine Ephah was the mother of Haran, Moza and Gazez. Haran was the father of Gazez.

⁴⁷The sons of Jahdai:

Regem, Jotham, Geshan, Pelet, Ephah and Shaaph.

⁴⁸Caleb's concubine Maacah was the mother of Sheber and Tirhanah. ⁴⁹She also gave birth to Shaaph the father of Madmannah and to Sheva the father of Macbenah and Gibea. Caleb's daughter was Acsah. ⁵⁰These were the descendants of Caleb.

The sons of Hur the firstborn of Ephrathah:

Shobal the father of Kiriath Jearim, ⁵¹Salma the father of Bethlehem, and Hareph the father of Beth Gader.

⁵²The descendants of Shobal the father of Kiriath Jearim were:

Haroeh, half the Manahathites, ⁵³and the clans of Kiriath Jearim: the Ithrites, Puthites, Shumathites and Mishraites. From these descended the Zorathites and Eshtaolites.

⁵⁴The descendants of Salma:

Bethlehem, the Netophathites, Atroth Beth Joab, half the Manahathites, the Zorites, ⁵⁵and the clans of scribesᵇ who lived at Jabez: the Tirathites, Shimeathites and Sucathites. These are the Kenites who came from Hammath, the father of the house of Recab.ᶜ

The Sons of David

3:1–4pp — 2Sa 3:2–5
3:5–8pp — 2Sa 5:14–16; 1Ch 14:4–7

3 These were the sons of David born to him in Hebron:

The firstborn was Amnon the son of Ahinoam of Jezreel;

the second, Daniel the son of Abigail of Carmel;

²the third, Absalom the son of Maacah daughter of Talmai king of Geshur;

the fourth, Adonijah the son of Haggith;

ᵃ 42 The meaning of the Hebrew for this phrase is uncertain.
ᵇ 55 Or of the Sopherites   ᶜ 55 Or father of Beth Recab

SOLOMON'S SON WAS REHOBOAM, ABIJAH
HIS SON, ASA HIS SON, JEHOSHAPHAT HIS
SON, JEHORAM HIS SON, AHAZIAH HIS
SON, JOASH HIS SON, AMAZIAH HIS SON,
AZARIAH HIS SON, JOTHAM HIS SON, AHAZ
HIS SON, HEZEKIAH HIS SON, MANASSEH
HIS SON, AMON HIS SON, JOSIAH HIS SON.

1 Chronicles 3:10–14

The Komp-endium

DIANE KOMP

READ | 1 CHRONICLES 3:1–24

For years I've been researching my family tree. When I rummage through ancient graveyards, I feel like I'm a character in a grand mystery story. Something dynamic is happening in my family that has never died and never will.

One of my great-great-grandfathers, Samuel Pupplett Carr, came from Colchester, England. I found the Carr headstones in a churchyard near the eighteenth-century family home. The vicar of that church pointed to a framed silhouette on the wall of Samuel Pupplett Carr's uncle, one of his predecessors. The next day he introduced me to one of my living distant cousins who was also a vicar in Colchester.

Cousin Eric recited a fascinating saga of Flemish Huguenots exiled to Essex during the Reformation for the sake of "Gottes Worde." There were persecuted Quakers in the family bloodline as well. Years later, I found the last resting place of Heinrich and Elisabetha Komp. Reading through a mid-nineteenth-century German newspaper from the tiny Indiana farm town, I learned that one of the Komp sons became a circuit-riding preacher.

[Today] instead of listening to narratives that link our stories with the past, we focus inward as if our own stories eclipse all others. But I'm convinced that we can break the power of skeletons from the past if we dig for the blessings from generation to generation, name them, and remember.

Today not everyone in my family is a believer. For many years, neither was I. I've written down the heritage we share in what I call our "Komp-endium." When they are ready, all my relatives can read there of the mercies of the Lord.

In my family, mercy moves from generation to generation. I suspect it does in yours as well, even if you have to dig deep to find it.

Father, your mercy has been known to generation after generation. I praise you for your faithfulness to my family and to all my descendants now and in the future.

GRANDCHILD IN FOCUS • PRAYER

School/Career

Dear God, may learning be a joy rather than a chore for my grandchild. May exploration of new ideas bring a sense of wonder, awe and excitement. Grant him clarity of mind, the ability to concentrate on the task at hand and recollection of what has been learned. Help him to appreciate the tasks that come easily and to persevere through those that challenge. Amen.

Your next devotion is located on page 531.

³the fifth, Shephatiah the son of Abital;
and the sixth, Ithream, by his wife Eglah.
⁴These six were born to David in Hebron,
where he reigned seven years and six
months.

David reigned in Jerusalem thirty-three years,
⁵and these were the children born to him there:
Shammua,ᵃ Shobab, Nathan and Solo-
mon. These four were by Bathshebaᵇ
daughter of Ammiel. ⁶There were also
Ibhar, Elishua,ᶜ Eliphelet, ⁷Nogah, Nepheg, Japhia, ⁸Elishama, Eliada and Eliphelet—nine in all. ⁹All these were the sons
of David, besides his sons by his concubines. And Tamar was their sister.

The Kings of Judah

¹⁰Solomon's son was Rehoboam,
Abijah his son,
Asa his son,
Jehoshaphat his son,
¹¹Jehoramᵈ his son,
Ahaziah his son,
Joash his son,
¹²Amaziah his son,
Azariah his son,
Jotham his son,
¹³Ahaz his son,
Hezekiah his son,
Manasseh his son,
¹⁴Amon his son,
Josiah his son.
¹⁵The sons of Josiah:
Johanan the firstborn,
Jehoiakim the second son,
Zedekiah the third,
Shallum the fourth.
¹⁶The successors of Jehoiakim:
Jehoiachinᵉ his son,
and Zedekiah.

The Royal Line After the Exile

¹⁷The descendants of Jehoiachin the captive:
Shealtiel his son, ¹⁸Malkiram, Pedaiah,
Shenazzar, Jekamiah, Hoshama and Ned-
abiah.

¹⁹The sons of Pedaiah:
Zerubbabel and Shimei.
The sons of Zerubbabel:
Meshullam and Hananiah.
Shelomith was their sister.
²⁰There were also five others:
Hashubah, Ohel, Berekiah, Hasadiah and
Jushab-Hesed.
²¹The descendants of Hananiah:
Pelatiah and Jeshaiah, and the sons of
Rephaiah, of Arnan, of Obadiah and of
Shecaniah.
²²The descendants of Shecaniah:
Shemaiah and his sons:
Hattush, Igal, Bariah, Neariah and Sha-
phat—six in all.
²³The sons of Neariah:
Elioenai, Hizkiah and Azrikam—three
in all.
²⁴The sons of Elioenai:
Hodaviah, Eliashib, Pelaiah, Akkub, Joha-
nan, Delaiah and Anani—seven in all.

Other Clans of Judah

4 The descendants of Judah:
Perez, Hezron, Carmi, Hur and Shobal.
²Reaiah son of Shobal was the father of Jahath, and Jahath the father of Ahumai
and Lahad. These were the clans of the
Zorathites.
³These were the sonsᶠ of Etam:
Jezreel, Ishma and Idbash. Their sister
was named Hazzelelponi. ⁴Penuel was
the father of Gedor, and Ezer the father
of Hushah.
These were the descendants of Hur, the firstborn of Ephrathah and fatherᵍ of Bethlehem.

ᵃ 5 Hebrew *Shimea*, a variant of *Shammua*   ᵇ 5 One Hebrew
manuscript and Vulgate (see also Septuagint and 2 Samuel
11:3); most Hebrew manuscripts *Bathshua*   ᶜ 6 Two Hebrew
manuscripts (see also 2 Samuel 5:15 and 1 Chron. 14:5); most
Hebrew manuscripts *Elishama*   ᵈ 11 Hebrew *Joram*, a variant of
Jehoram   ᵉ 16 Hebrew *Jeconiah*, a variant of *Jehoiachin*; also in
verse 17   ᶠ 3 Some Septuagint manuscripts (see also Vulgate);
Hebrew *father*   ᵍ 4 *Father* may mean *civic leader* or *military
leader*; also in verses 12, 14, 17, 18 and possibly elsewhere.

5 Ashhur the father of Tekoa had two wives, Helah and Naarah.

6 Naarah bore him Ahuzzam, Hepher, Temeni and Haahashtari. These were the descendants of Naarah.

7 The sons of Helah:

Zereth, Zohar, Ethnan, 8 and Koz, who was the father of Anub and Hazzobebah and of the clans of Aharhel son of Harum.

9 Jabez was more honorable than his brothers. His mother had named him Jabez,[a] saying, "I gave birth to him in pain." 10 Jabez cried out to the God of Israel, "Oh, that you would bless me and enlarge my territory! Let your hand be with me, and keep me from harm so that I will be free from pain." And God granted his request.

11 Kelub, Shuhah's brother, was the father of Mehir, who was the father of Eshton. 12 Eshton was the father of Beth Rapha, Paseah and Tehinnah the father of Ir Nahash.[b] These were the men of Recah.

13 The sons of Kenaz:

Othniel and Seraiah.

The sons of Othniel:

Hathath and Meonothai.[c] 14 Meonothai was the father of Ophrah.

Seraiah was the father of Joab,

the father of Ge Harashim.[d] It was called this because its people were craftsmen.

15 The sons of Caleb son of Jephunneh:

Iru, Elah and Naam.

The son of Elah:

Kenaz.

16 The sons of Jehallelel:

Ziph, Ziphah, Tiria and Asarel.

17 The sons of Ezrah:

Jether, Mered, Epher and Jalon. One of Mered's wives gave birth to Miriam, Shammai and Ishbah the father of Eshtemoa. 18 (His Judean wife gave birth to Jered the father of Gedor, Heber the father of Soco, and Jekuthiel the father of Zanoah.) These were the children of Phar-

aoh's daughter Bithiah, whom Mered had married.

19 The sons of Hodiah's wife, the sister of Naham:

the father of Keilah the Garmite, and Eshtemoa the Maacathite.

20 The sons of Shimon:

Amnon, Rinnah, Ben-Hanan and Tilon.

The descendants of Ishi:

Zoheth and Ben-Zoheth.

21 The sons of Shelah son of Judah:

Er the father of Lecah, Laadah the father of Mareshah and the clans of the linen workers at Beth Ashbea, 22 Jokim, the men of Cozeba, and Joash and Saraph, who ruled in Moab and Jashubi Lehem. (These records are from ancient times.) 23 They were the potters who lived at Netaim and Gederah; they stayed there and worked for the king.

Simeon

4:28–33pp — Jos 19:2–10

24 The descendants of Simeon:

Nemuel, Jamin, Jarib, Zerah and Shaul;

25 Shallum was Shaul's son, Mibsam his son and Mishma his son.

26 The descendants of Mishma:

Hammuel his son, Zaccur his son and Shimei his son.

27 Shimei had sixteen sons and six daughters, but his brothers did not have many children; so their entire clan did not become as numerous as the people of Judah. 28 They lived in Beersheba, Moladah, Hazar Shual, 29 Bilhah, Ezem, Tolad, 30 Bethuel, Hormah, Ziklag, 31 Beth Marcaboth, Hazar Susim, Beth Biri and Shaaraim. These were their towns until the reign of David. 32 Their surrounding villages were Etam, Ain, Rimmon, Token and Ashan — five towns — 33 and all the villages around these towns as far as Baalath.[e]

---

[a] 9 Jabez sounds like the Hebrew for pain.   [b] 12 Or of the city of Nahash   [c] 13 Some Septuagint manuscripts and Vulgate; Hebrew does not have and Meonothai.   [d] 14 Ge Harashim means valley of craftsmen.   [e] 33 Some Septuagint manuscripts (see also Joshua 19:8); Hebrew Baal

Sewing Bee

Every child needs to learn the basics of handling a needle and thread, so they can at least hem a hem or sew on a button. If you have basic skills in sewing, invite your grandchildren to a sewing bee. Tell them to come over with an article of clothing in need of minor repair. Even fairly young children can learn to thread a needle, knot the thread and sew on a button. Older kids may enjoy threading the sewing machine, winding the bobbin, changing the "foot," and running the machine to fix a split seam. They might want to fix a hole in the pocket of their jeans or add some patches. To keep the youngest ones busy, give them sewing cards (you may have to do some hunting, but some toy stores do still sell them).

Long-Distance Variation: Cut out some fabric squares and send a variety of buttons for the kids to sew on. Or stamp the squares with embroidery patterns and send floss and instructions. Have them return the finished squares to you for your review.

Dear God, thank you for simple pleasures and skills like sewing on a button. Help my grandchildren to realize the importance of these tasks and to enjoy learning these skills. Give me patience and a sense of humor as we share this time together. Amen.

Your next devotion is located on page 536.

GRANDCHILD IN FOCUS • PRAYER

Character

Dear Lord and Father, I ask that you fill my grandchild with your Spirit so her character reflects your goodness and love. Give her kindness and love for others. Bring joy to her life so she will be a joy to others. Grant her patience and self-control through difficult and trying times. May she show mercy and generosity to those who are less fortunate. Grant her integrity and a sense of justice, and surround her with your peace. Amen.

These were their settlements. And they kept a genealogical record.

³⁴Meshobab, Jamlech, Joshah son of Amaziah, ³⁵Joel, Jehu son of Joshibiah, the son of Seraiah, the son of Asiel, ³⁶also Elioenai, Jaakobah, Jeshohaiah, Asaiah, Adiel, Jesimiel, Benaiah, ³⁷and Ziza son of Shiphi, the son of Allon, the son of Jedaiah, the son of Shimri, the son of Shemaiah.

³⁸The men listed above by name were leaders of their clans. Their families increased greatly, ³⁹and they went to the outskirts of Gedor to the east of the valley in search of pasture for their flocks. ⁴⁰They found rich, good pasture, and the land was spacious, peaceful and quiet. Some Hamites had lived there formerly.

⁴¹The men whose names were listed came in the days of Hezekiah king of Judah. They attacked the Hamites in their dwellings and also the Meunites who were there and completely destroyed[a] them, as is evident to this day. Then they settled in their place, because there was pasture for their flocks. ⁴²And five hundred of these Simeonites, led by Pelatiah, Neariah, Rephaiah and Uzziel, the sons of Ishi, invaded the hill country of Seir. ⁴³They killed the remaining Amalekites who had escaped, and they have lived there to this day.

Reuben

5 The sons of Reuben the firstborn of Israel (he was the firstborn, but when he defiled his father's marriage bed, his rights as firstborn were given to the sons of Joseph son of Israel; so he could not be listed in the genealogical record in accordance with his birthright, ²and though Judah was the strongest of his brothers and a ruler came from him, the rights of the firstborn belonged to Joseph)— ³the sons of Reuben the firstborn of Israel:

Hanoch, Pallu, Hezron and Carmi.

⁴The descendants of Joel:

Shemaiah his son, Gog his son,
Shimei his son, ⁵Micah his son,
Reaiah his son, Baal his son,

⁶and Beerah his son, whom Tiglath-Pileser[b] king of Assyria took into exile. Beerah was a leader of the Reubenites.

⁷Their relatives by clans, listed according to their genealogical records:

Jeiel the chief, Zechariah, ⁸and Bela son of Azaz, the son of Shema, the son of Joel. They settled in the area from Aroer to Nebo and Baal Meon. ⁹To the east they occupied the land up to the edge of the desert that extends to the Euphrates River, because their livestock had increased in Gilead.

¹⁰During Saul's reign they waged war against the Hagrites, who were defeated at their hands; they occupied the dwellings of the Hagrites throughout the entire region east of Gilead.

Gad

¹¹The Gadites lived next to them in Bashan, as far as Salecah:

¹²Joel was the chief, Shapham the second, then Janai and Shaphat, in Bashan.

¹³Their relatives, by families, were:

Michael, Meshullam, Sheba, Jorai, Jacan, Zia and Eber—seven in all.

¹⁴These were the sons of Abihail son of Huri, the son of Jaroah, the son of Gilead, the son of Michael, the son of Jeshishai, the son of Jahdo, the son of Buz.

¹⁵Ahi son of Abdiel, the son of Guni, was head of their family.

¹⁶The Gadites lived in Gilead, in Bashan and its outlying villages, and on all the pasturelands of Sharon as far as they extended.

¹⁷All these were entered in the genealogical records during the reigns of Jotham king of Judah and Jeroboam king of Israel.

¹⁸The Reubenites, the Gadites and the half-tribe of Manasseh had 44,760 men ready for military ser-

---

[a] 41 The Hebrew term refers to the irrevocable giving over of things or persons to the Lord, often by totally destroying them.
[b] 6 Hebrew Tilgath-Pilneser, a variant of Tiglath-Pileser; also in verse 26

vice—able-bodied men who could handle shield and sword, who could use a bow, and who were trained for battle. [19]They waged war against the Hagrites, Jetur, Naphish and Nodab. [20]They were helped in fighting them, and God handed the Hagrites and all their allies over to them, because they cried out to him during the battle. He answered their prayers, because they trusted in him. [21]They seized the livestock of the Hagrites—fifty thousand camels, two hundred fifty thousand sheep and two thousand donkeys. They also took one hundred thousand people captive, [22]and many others fell slain, because the battle was God's. And they occupied the land until the exile.

The Half-Tribe of Manasseh

[23]The people of the half-tribe of Manasseh were numerous; they settled in the land from Bashan to Baal Hermon, that is, to Senir (Mount Hermon).

[24]These were the heads of their families: Epher, Ishi, Eliel, Azriel, Jeremiah, Hodaviah and Jahdiel. They were brave warriors, famous men, and heads of their families. [25]But they were unfaithful to the God of their fathers and prostituted themselves to the gods of the peoples of the land, whom God had destroyed before them. [26]So the God of Israel stirred up the spirit of Pul king of Assyria (that is, Tiglath-Pileser king of Assyria), who took the Reubenites, the Gadites and the half-tribe of Manasseh into exile. He took them to Halah, Habor, Hara and the river of Gozan, where they are to this day.

Levi

6 The sons of Levi:
Gershon, Kohath and Merari.
[2]The sons of Kohath:
Amram, Izhar, Hebron and Uzziel.
[3]The children of Amram:
Aaron, Moses and Miriam.
The sons of Aaron:
Nadab, Abihu, Eleazar and Ithamar.
[4]Eleazar was the father of Phinehas,
Phinehas the father of Abishua,

[5]Abishua the father of Bukki,
Bukki the father of Uzzi,
[6]Uzzi the father of Zerahiah,
Zerahiah the father of Meraioth,
[7]Meraioth the father of Amariah,
Amariah the father of Ahitub,
[8]Ahitub the father of Zadok,
Zadok the father of Ahimaaz,
[9]Ahimaaz the father of Azariah,
Azariah the father of Johanan,
[10]Johanan the father of Azariah (it was he who served as priest in the temple Solomon built in Jerusalem),
[11]Azariah the father of Amariah,
Amariah the father of Ahitub,
[12]Ahitub the father of Zadok,
Zadok the father of Shallum,
[13]Shallum the father of Hilkiah,
Hilkiah the father of Azariah,
[14]Azariah the father of Seraiah,
and Seraiah the father of Jehozadak.
[15]Jehozadak was deported when the LORD sent Judah and Jerusalem into exile by the hand of Nebuchadnezzar.

[16]The sons of Levi:
Gershon,[a] Kohath and Merari.
[17]These are the names of the sons of Gershon:
Libni and Shimei.
[18]The sons of Kohath:
Amram, Izhar, Hebron and Uzziel.
[19]The sons of Merari:
Mahli and Mushi.
These are the clans of the Levites listed according to their fathers:
[20]Of Gershon:
Libni his son, Jehath his son,
Zimmah his son, [21]Joah his son,
Iddo his son, Zerah his son
and Jeatherai his son.
[22]The descendants of Kohath:
Amminadab his son, Korah his son,

[a] 16 Hebrew Gershom, a variant of Gershon; also in verses 17, 20, 43, 62 and 71

Assir his son, ²³ Elkanah his son,
Ebiasaph his son, Assir his son,
²⁴ Tahath his son, Uriel his son,
Uzziah his son and Shaul his son.
²⁵ The descendants of Elkanah:
Amasai, Ahimoth,
²⁶ Elkanah his son, [a] Zophai his son,
Nahath his son, ²⁷ Eliab his son,
Jeroham his son, Elkanah his son
and Samuel his son. [b]
²⁸ The sons of Samuel:
Joel [c] the firstborn
and Abijah the second son.
²⁹ The descendants of Merari:
Mahli, Libni his son,
Shimei his son, Uzzah his son,
³⁰ Shimea his son, Haggiah his son
and Asaiah his son.

The Temple Musicians

6:54–80pp — Jos 21:4–39

³¹ These are the men David put in charge of the music in the house of the LORD after the ark came to rest there. ³² They ministered with music before the tabernacle, the Tent of Meeting, until Solomon built the temple of the LORD in Jerusalem. They performed their duties according to the regulations laid down for them.

³³ Here are the men who served, together with their sons:

From the Kohathites:
Heman, the musician,
the son of Joel, the son of Samuel,
³⁴ the son of Elkanah, the son of Jeroham,
the son of Eliel, the son of Toah,
³⁵ the son of Zuph, the son of Elkanah,
the son of Mahath, the son of Amasai,
³⁶ the son of Elkanah, the son of Joel,
the son of Azariah, the son of Zephaniah,
³⁷ the son of Tahath, the son of Assir,
the son of Ebiasaph, the son of Korah,
³⁸ the son of Izhar, the son of Kohath,
the son of Levi, the son of Israel;

³⁹ and Heman's associate Asaph, who served at his right hand:
Asaph son of Berekiah, the son of Shimea,
⁴⁰ the son of Michael, the son of Baaseiah, [d]
the son of Malkijah, ⁴¹ the son of Ethni,
the son of Zerah, the son of Adaiah,
⁴² the son of Ethan, the son of Zimmah,
the son of Shimei, ⁴³ the son of Jahath,
the son of Gershon, the son of Levi;
⁴⁴ and from their associates, the Merarites, at his left hand:
Ethan son of Kishi, the son of Abdi,
the son of Malluch, ⁴⁵ the son of Hashabiah,
the son of Amaziah, the son of Hilkiah,
⁴⁶ the son of Amzi, the son of Bani,
the son of Shemer, ⁴⁷ the son of Mahli,
the son of Mushi, the son of Merari,
the son of Levi.

⁴⁸ Their fellow Levites were assigned to all the other duties of the tabernacle, the house of God. ⁴⁹ But Aaron and his descendants were the ones who presented offerings on the altar of burnt offering and on the altar of incense in connection with all that was done in the Most Holy Place, making atonement for Israel, in accordance with all that Moses the servant of God had commanded.

⁵⁰ These were the descendants of Aaron:
Eleazar his son, Phinehas his son,
Abishua his son, ⁵¹ Bukki his son,
Uzzi his son, Zerahiah his son,
⁵² Meraioth his son, Amariah his son,
Ahitub his son, ⁵³ Zadok his son
and Ahimaaz his son.

⁵⁴ These were the locations of their settlements allotted as their territory (they were assigned to

---

^a *26* Some Hebrew manuscripts, Septuagint and Syriac; most Hebrew manuscripts *Ahimoth* ²⁶ *and Elkanah. The sons of Elkanah:* ^b *27* Some Septuagint manuscripts (see also 1 Samuel 1:19,20 and 1 Chron. 6:33,34); Hebrew does not have *and Samuel his son.* ^c *28* Some Septuagint manuscripts and Syriac (see also 1 Samuel 8:2 and 1 Chron. 6:33); Hebrew does not have *Joel.* ^d *40* Most Hebrew manuscripts; some Hebrew manuscripts, one Septuagint manuscript and Syriac *Maaseiah*

the descendants of Aaron who were from the Kohathite clan, because the first lot was for them):

⁵⁵They were given Hebron in Judah with its surrounding pasturelands. ⁵⁶But the fields and villages around the city were given to Caleb son of Jephunneh.

⁵⁷So the descendants of Aaron were given Hebron (a city of refuge), and Libnah,ᵃ Jattir, Eshtemoa, ⁵⁸Hilen, Debir, ⁵⁹Ashan, Juttahᵇ and Beth Shemesh, together with their pasturelands. ⁶⁰And from the tribe of Benjamin they were given Gibeon,ᶜ Geba, Alemeth and Anathoth, together with their pasturelands.

These towns, which were distributed among the Kohathite clans, were thirteen in all.

⁶¹The rest of Kohath's descendants were allotted ten towns from the clans of half the tribe of Manasseh.

⁶²The descendants of Gershon, clan by clan, were allotted thirteen towns from the tribes of Issachar, Asher and Naphtali, and from the part of the tribe of Manasseh that is in Bashan.

⁶³The descendants of Merari, clan by clan, were allotted twelve towns from the tribes of Reuben, Gad and Zebulun.

⁶⁴So the Israelites gave the Levites these towns and their pasturelands. ⁶⁵From the tribes of Judah, Simeon and Benjamin they allotted the previously named towns.

⁶⁶Some of the Kohathite clans were given as their territory towns from the tribe of Ephraim.

⁶⁷In the hill country of Ephraim they were given Shechem (a city of refuge), and Gezer,ᵈ ⁶⁸Jokmeam, Beth Horon, ⁶⁹Aijalon and Gath Rimmon, together with their pasturelands.

⁷⁰And from half the tribe of Manasseh the Israelites gave Aner and Bileam, together with their pasturelands, to the rest of the Kohathite clans.

⁷¹The Gershonites received the following:
From the clan of the half-tribe of Manasseh they received Golan in Bashan and also Ashtaroth, together with their pasturelands;

⁷²from the tribe of Issachar
they received Kedesh, Daberath, ⁷³Ramoth and Anem, together with their pasturelands;

⁷⁴from the tribe of Asher
they received Mashal, Abdon, ⁷⁵Hukok and Rehob, together with their pasturelands;

⁷⁶and from the tribe of Naphtali
they received Kedesh in Galilee, Hammon and Kiriathaim, together with their pasturelands.

⁷⁷The Merarites (the rest of the Levites) received the following:
From the tribe of Zebulun
they received Jokneam, Kartah,ᵉ Rimmono and Tabor, together with their pasturelands;

⁷⁸from the tribe of Reuben across the Jordan east of Jericho
they received Bezer in the desert, Jahzah, ⁷⁹Kedemoth and Mephaath, together with their pasturelands;

⁸⁰and from the tribe of Gad
they received Ramoth in Gilead, Mahanaim, ⁸¹Heshbon and Jazer, together with their pasturelands.

Issachar

7 The sons of Issachar:
Tola, Puah, Jashub and Shimron—four in all.

²The sons of Tola:
Uzzi, Rephaiah, Jeriel, Jahmai, Ibsam and Samuel—heads of their families. During the reign of David, the descendants of Tola listed as fighting men in their genealogy numbered 22,600.

ᵃ 57 See Joshua 21:13; Hebrew *given the cities of refuge: Hebron, Libnah.*   ᵇ 59 Syriac (see also Septuagint and Joshua 21:16); Hebrew does not have *Juttah.*   ᶜ 60 See Joshua 21:17; Hebrew does not have *Gibeon.*   ᵈ 67 See Joshua 21:21; Hebrew *given the cities of refuge: Shechem, Gezer.*   ᵉ 77 See Septuagint and Joshua 21:34; Hebrew does not have *Jokneam, Kartah.*

Worship the Lord

I love the LORD, for he heard my voice;
    he heard my cry for mercy.
Because he turned his ear to me,
    I will call on him as long as I live.

The cords of death entangled me,
    the anguish of the grave came upon me;
    I was overcome by trouble and sorrow.
Then I called on the name of the LORD:
    "O LORD, save me!"

The LORD is gracious and righteous;
    our God is full of compassion.
The LORD protects the simplehearted;
    when I was in great need, he saved
    me.

Be at rest once more, O my soul,
    for the LORD has been good to
    you.

Psalm 116:1 – 7

Lord, you have been so good to me. Thank you for caring for my emotional and physical well-being. Thank you for loving me and giving me the promise of eternal life in Jesus. I love you, O Lord my God. Amen.

Your next devotion is located on page 541.

GRANDCHILD IN FOCUS • PRAYER

Talents

Dear Lord, the giver of gifts, bless my grandchild as he develops his talents. Help him identify his talents and be proud and confident of the gifts you have given him. Give him patience and understanding, Lord, so he will not grow weary of striving and searching to reach the goals you have set for him. May each milestone bring satisfaction and a healthy desire for greater achievement and success to bring glory to you. Amen.

536

[3] The son of Uzzi:

Izrahiah.

The sons of Izrahiah:

Michael, Obadiah, Joel and Isshiah. All five of them were chiefs. [4] According to their family genealogy, they had 36,000 men ready for battle, for they had many wives and children. [5] The relatives who were fighting men belonging to all the clans of Issachar, as listed in their genealogy, were 87,000 in all.

Benjamin

[6] Three sons of Benjamin:

Bela, Beker and Jediael.

[7] The sons of Bela:

Ezbon, Uzzi, Uzziel, Jerimoth and Iri, heads of families—five in all. Their genealogical record listed 22,034 fighting men.

[8] The sons of Beker:

Zemirah, Joash, Eliezer, Elioenai, Omri, Jeremoth, Abijah, Anathoth and Alemeth. All these were the sons of Beker. [9] Their genealogical record listed the heads of families and 20,200 fighting men.

[10] The son of Jediael:

Bilhan.

The sons of Bilhan:

Jeush, Benjamin, Ehud, Kenaanah, Zethan, Tarshish and Ahishahar. [11] All these sons of Jediael were heads of families. There were 17,200 fighting men ready to go out to war.

[12] The Shuppites and Huppites were the descendants of Ir, and the Hushites the descendants of Aher.

Naphtali

[13] The sons of Naphtali:

Jahziel, Guni, Jezer and Shillem[a]—the descendants of Bilhah.

Manasseh

[14] The descendants of Manasseh:

Asriel was his descendant through his Aramean concubine. She gave birth to Makir the father of Gilead. [15] Makir took a wife from among the Huppites and Shuppites. His sister's name was Maacah.

Another descendant was named Zelophehad, who had only daughters.

[16] Makir's wife Maacah gave birth to a son and named him Peresh. His brother was named Sheresh, and his sons were Ulam and Rakem.

[17] The son of Ulam:

Bedan.

These were the sons of Gilead son of Makir, the son of Manasseh. [18] His sister Hammoleketh gave birth to Ishhod, Abiezer and Mahlah.

[19] The sons of Shemida were:

Ahian, Shechem, Likhi and Aniam.

Ephraim

[20] The descendants of Ephraim:

Shuthelah, Bered his son,

Tahath his son, Eleadah his son,

Tahath his son, [21] Zabad his son

and Shuthelah his son.

Ezer and Elead were killed by the native-born men of Gath, when they went down to seize their livestock. [22] Their father Ephraim mourned for them many days, and his relatives came to comfort him. [23] Then he lay with his wife again, and she became pregnant and gave birth to a son. He named him Beriah,[b] because there had been misfortune in his family. [24] His daughter was Sheerah, who built Lower and Upper Beth Horon as well as Uzzen Sheerah.

[25] Rephah was his son, Resheph his son,[c]

Telah his son, Tahan his son,

[26] Ladan his son, Ammihud his son,

Elishama his son, [27] Nun his son

and Joshua his son.

---

[a] 13 Some Hebrew and Septuagint manuscripts (see also Gen. 46:24 and Num. 26:49); most Hebrew manuscripts *Shallum*
[b] 23 *Beriah* sounds like the Hebrew for *misfortune.*   [c] 25 Some Septuagint manuscripts; Hebrew does not have *his son.*

28 Their lands and settlements included Bethel and its surrounding villages, Naaran to the east, Gezer and its villages to the west, and Shechem and its villages all the way to Ayyah and its villages. 29 Along the borders of Manasseh were Beth Shan, Taanach, Megiddo and Dor, together with their villages. The descendants of Joseph son of Israel lived in these towns.

Asher

30 The sons of Asher:

Imnah, Ishvah, Ishvi and Beriah. Their sister was Serah.

31 The sons of Beriah:

Heber and Malkiel, who was the father of Birzaith.

32 Heber was the father of Japhlet, Shomer and Hotham and of their sister Shua.

33 The sons of Japhlet:

Pasach, Bimhal and Ashvath.

These were Japhlet's sons.

34 The sons of Shomer:

Ahi, Rohgah,[a] Hubbah and Aram.

35 The sons of his brother Helem:

Zophah, Imna, Shelesh and Amal.

36 The sons of Zophah:

Suah, Harnepher, Shual, Beri, Imrah, 37 Bezer, Hod, Shamma, Shilshah, Ithran[b] and Beera.

38 The sons of Jether:

Jephunneh, Pispah and Ara.

39 The sons of Ulla:

Arah, Hanniel and Rizia.

40 All these were descendants of Asher — heads of families, choice men, brave warriors and outstanding leaders. The number of men ready for battle, as listed in their genealogy, was 26,000.

The Genealogy of Saul the Benjamite

8:28–38pp — 1Ch 9:34–44

8 Benjamin was the father of Bela his firstborn,

Ashbel the second son, Aharah the third,

2 Nohah the fourth and Rapha the fifth.

3 The sons of Bela were:

Addar, Gera, Abihud,[c] 4 Abishua, Naaman, Ahoah, 5 Gera, Shephuphan and Huram.

6 These were the descendants of Ehud, who were heads of families of those living in Geba and were deported to Manahath:

7 Naaman, Ahijah, and Gera, who deported them and who was the father of Uzza and Ahihud.

8 Sons were born to Shaharaim in Moab after he had divorced his wives Hushim and Baara. 9 By his wife Hodesh he had Jobab, Zibia, Mesha, Malcam, 10 Jeuz, Sakia and Mirmah. These were his sons, heads of families. 11 By Hushim he had Abitub and Elpaal.

12 The sons of Elpaal:

Eber, Misham, Shemed (who built Ono and Lod with its surrounding villages), 13 and Beriah and Shema, who were heads of families of those living in Aijalon and who drove out the inhabitants of Gath.

14 Ahio, Shashak, Jeremoth, 15 Zebadiah, Arad, Eder, 16 Michael, Ishpah and Joha were the sons of Beriah.

17 Zebadiah, Meshullam, Hizki, Heber, 18 Ishmerai, Izliah and Jobab were the sons of Elpaal.

19 Jakim, Zicri, Zabdi, 20 Elienai, Zillethai, Eliel, 21 Adaiah, Beraiah and Shimrath were the sons of Shimei.

22 Ishpan, Eber, Eliel, 23 Abdon, Zicri, Hanan, 24 Hananiah, Elam, Anthothijah, 25 Iphdeiah and Penuel were the sons of Shashak.

26 Shamsherai, Shehariah, Athaliah, 27 Jaareshiah, Elijah and Zicri were the sons of Jeroham.

28 All these were heads of families, chiefs as listed in their genealogy, and they lived in Jerusalem.

29 Jeiel[d] the father[e] of Gibeon lived in Gibeon. His wife's name was Maacah, 30 and his firstborn son was Abdon, followed by

---

[a] 34 Or *of his brother Shomer: Rohgah*   [b] 37 Possibly a variant of *Jether*   [c] 3 Or *Gera the father of Ehud*   [d] 29 Some Septuagint manuscripts (see also 1 Chron. 9:35); Hebrew does not have *Jeiel.*
[e] 29 *Father* may mean *civic leader* or *military leader.*

Zur, Kish, Baal, Ner,[a] Nadab, [31]Gedor, Ahio, Zeker [32]and Mikloth, who was the father of Shimeah. They too lived near their relatives in Jerusalem.

[33]Ner was the father of Kish, Kish the father of Saul, and Saul the father of Jonathan, Malki-Shua, Abinadab and Esh-Baal.[b]

[34]The son of Jonathan:

Merib-Baal,[c] who was the father of Micah.

[35]The sons of Micah:

Pithon, Melech, Tarea and Ahaz.

[36]Ahaz was the father of Jehoaddah, Jehoaddah was the father of Alemeth, Azmaveth and Zimri, and Zimri was the father of Moza. [37]Moza was the father of Binea; Raphah was his son, Eleasah his son and Azel his son.

[38]Azel had six sons, and these were their names:

Azrikam, Bokeru, Ishmael, Sheariah, Obadiah and Hanan. All these were the sons of Azel.

[39]The sons of his brother Eshek:

Ulam his firstborn, Jeush the second son and Eliphelet the third. [40]The sons of Ulam were brave warriors who could handle the bow. They had many sons and grandsons — 150 in all.

All these were the descendants of Benjamin.

9 All Israel was listed in the genealogies recorded in the book of the kings of Israel.

The People in Jerusalem

9:1–17pp — Ne 11:3–19

The people of Judah were taken captive to Babylon because of their unfaithfulness. [2]Now the first to resettle on their own property in their own towns were some Israelites, priests, Levites and temple servants.

[3]Those from Judah, from Benjamin, and from Ephraim and Manasseh who lived in Jerusalem were:

[4]Uthai son of Ammihud, the son of Omri, the son of Imri, the son of Bani, a descendant of Perez son of Judah.

[5]Of the Shilonites:

Asaiah the firstborn and his sons.

[6]Of the Zerahites:

Jeuel.

The people from Judah numbered 690.

[7]Of the Benjamites:

Sallu son of Meshullam, the son of Hodaviah, the son of Hassenuah;

[8]Ibneiah son of Jeroham; Elah son of Uzzi, the son of Micri; and Meshullam son of Shephatiah, the son of Reuel, the son of Ibnijah.

[9]The people from Benjamin, as listed in their genealogy, numbered 956. All these men were heads of their families.

[10]Of the priests:

Jedaiah; Jehoiarib; Jakin;

[11]Azariah son of Hilkiah, the son of Meshullam, the son of Zadok, the son of Meraioth, the son of Ahitub, the official in charge of the house of God;

[12]Adaiah son of Jeroham, the son of Pashhur, the son of Malkijah; and Maasai son of Adiel, the son of Jahzerah, the son of Meshullam, the son of Meshillemith, the son of Immer.

[13]The priests, who were heads of families, numbered 1,760. They were able men, responsible for ministering in the house of God.

[14]Of the Levites:

Shemaiah son of Hasshub, the son of Azrikam, the son of Hashabiah, a Merarite; [15]Bakbakkar, Heresh, Galal and Mattaniah son of Mica, the son of Zicri, the son of Asaph; [16]Obadiah son of Shemaiah, the son of Galal, the son of Jeduthun; and Berekiah son of Asa, the son of Elkanah, who lived in the villages of the Netophathites.

---

[a] 30 Some Septuagint manuscripts (see also 1 Chron. 9:36); Hebrew does not have *Ner*.   [b] 33 Also known as *Ish-Bosheth*   [c] 34 Also known as *Mephibosheth*

¹⁷ The gatekeepers:

Shallum, Akkub, Talmon, Ahiman and their brothers, Shallum their chief ¹⁸ being stationed at the King's Gate on the east, up to the present time. These were the gatekeepers belonging to the camp of the Levites. ¹⁹ Shallum son of Kore, the son of Ebiasaph, the son of Korah, and his fellow gatekeepers from his family (the Korahites) were responsible for guarding the thresholds of the Tent*ᵃ* just as their fathers had been responsible for guarding the entrance to the dwelling of the LORD. ²⁰ In earlier times Phinehas son of Eleazar was in charge of the gatekeepers, and the LORD was with him. ²¹ Zechariah son of Meshelemiah was the gatekeeper at the entrance to the Tent of Meeting.

²² Altogether, those chosen to be gatekeepers at the thresholds numbered 212. They were registered by genealogy in their villages. The gatekeepers had been assigned to their positions of trust by David and Samuel the seer. ²³ They and their descendants were in charge of guarding the gates of the house of the LORD—the house called the Tent. ²⁴ The gatekeepers were on the four sides: east, west, north and south. ²⁵ Their brothers in their villages had to come from time to time and share their duties for seven-day periods. ²⁶ But the four principal gatekeepers, who were Levites, were entrusted with the responsibility for the rooms and treasuries in the house of God. ²⁷ They would spend the night stationed around the house of God, because they had to guard it; and they had charge of the key for opening it each morning.

²⁸ Some of them were in charge of the articles used in the temple service; they counted them when they were brought in and when they were taken out. ²⁹ Others were assigned to take care of the furnishings and all the other articles of the sanctuary, as well as the flour and wine, and the oil, incense and spices. ³⁰ But some of the priests took care of mixing the spices. ³¹ A Levite named Mattithiah, the firstborn son of Shallum the Ko-

rahite, was entrusted with the responsibility for baking the offering bread. ³² Some of their Kohathite brothers were in charge of preparing for every Sabbath the bread set out on the table.

³³ Those who were musicians, heads of Levite families, stayed in the rooms of the temple and were exempt from other duties because they were responsible for the work day and night.

³⁴ All these were heads of Levite families, chiefs as listed in their genealogy, and they lived in Jerusalem.

The Genealogy of Saul

9:34–44pp — 1Ch 8:28–38

³⁵ Jeiel the father*ᵇ* of Gibeon lived in Gibeon. His wife's name was Maacah, ³⁶ and his firstborn son was Abdon, followed by Zur, Kish, Baal, Ner, Nadab, ³⁷ Gedor, Ahio, Zechariah and Mikloth. ³⁸ Mikloth was the father of Shimeam. They too lived near their relatives in Jerusalem.

³⁹ Ner was the father of Kish, Kish the father of Saul, and Saul the father of Jonathan, Malki-Shua, Abinadab and Esh-Baal.*ᶜ*

⁴⁰ The son of Jonathan:

Merib-Baal,*ᵈ* who was the father of Micah.

⁴¹ The sons of Micah:

Pithon, Melech, Tahrea and Ahaz.*ᵉ*

⁴² Ahaz was the father of Jadah, Jadah*ᶠ* was the father of Alemeth, Azmaveth and Zimri, and Zimri was the father of Moza.

⁴³ Moza was the father of Binea; Rephaiah was his son, Eleasah his son and Azel his son.

⁴⁴ Azel had six sons, and these were their names:

Azrikam, Bokeru, Ishmael, Sheariah, Obadiah and Hanan. These were the sons of Azel.

ᵃ 19 That is, the temple; also in verses 21 and 23   *ᵇ 35* *Father* may mean *civic leader* or *military leader.*   *ᶜ 39* Also known as *Ish-Bosheth*   *ᵈ 40* Also known as *Mephibosheth*   *ᵉ 41* Vulgate and Syriac (see also Septuagint and 1 Chron. 8:35); Hebrew does not have *and Ahaz.*   *ᶠ 42* Some Hebrew manuscripts and Septuagint (see also 1 Chron. 8:36); most Hebrew manuscripts *Jarah, Jarah*

THOSE WHO WERE MUSICIANS, HEADS
OF LEVITE FAMILIES, STAYED IN THE
ROOMS OF THE TEMPLE AND WERE
EXEMPT FROM OTHER DUTIES BECAUSE
THEY WERE RESPONSIBLE FOR THE
WORK DAY AND NIGHT.

1 Chronicles 9:33

The Heart's Native Tongue

SUSAN LENZKES

READ | 1 CHRONICLES 9:22 – 34

Living can be a hard business. It can strip away our resources. We can lose confidence, patience, perspective and even our sense of humor. When this happens, we urgently need to find those gifts with the power to rejuvenate.

God hides these spirit-lifters everywhere — in his nature, in his Word, in prayer, in someone's arms, in a healthy cry or a hearty laugh. But for the unparalleled restorative power, music is hard to beat. It seems to be the heart's native tongue.

How often I have sat cross-legged between the speakers of my stereo, singing or just letting harmony wrap itself around my wounds and weariness. How often I have dragged myself to a rehearsal or performance and later skipped away restored. How often I have joined other voices in worship and praise and been lifted into the presence of God. Music has power to elevate, speak, soothe, teach, touch, energize and unify.

Melody adds wings to words and flies them over obstacles that stand in the way of understanding. Within its measures, music carries a large measure of comprehension. Somehow we can believe that love serenades us. Somehow we can hear hope that sings to us in the dark.

Yet even if music could do none of these things, it would still give soaring voice to our praise. And as we lift songs of worship, we too will be lifted. That's the promise of praise.

* * *

Thank you, Creator Spirit, for the gift of music to lift hearts, light ways and give hope. May all my songs bring you praise.

Your next devotion is located on page 549.

GRANDCHILD IN FOCUS • PRAYER

SELECT ONE OF YOUR
GRANDCHILDREN TO FOCUS ON
IN PRAYER FOR THE NEXT 14 DAYS.

Salvation

Dear Lord, please guide my grandchild to your gift of salvation. I pray that she will come to know you, to love you and to walk close to you throughout her life. May she boldly claim Jesus as her Lord and Savior. Guide her as she makes choices that have eternal consequences. Help her to follow you each moment of her life. I pray this in Jesus' name, amen.

Saul Takes His Life

10:1–12pp — 1Sa 31:1–13; 2Sa 1:4–12

10 Now the Philistines fought against Israel; the Israelites fled before them, and many fell slain on Mount Gilboa. ²The Philistines pressed hard after Saul and his sons, and they killed his sons Jonathan, Abinadab and Malki-Shua. ³The fighting grew fierce around Saul, and when the archers overtook him, they wounded him.

⁴Saul said to his armor-bearer, "Draw your sword and run me through, or these uncircumcised fellows will come and abuse me."

But his armor-bearer was terrified and would not do it; so Saul took his own sword and fell on it. ⁵When the armor-bearer saw that Saul was dead, he too fell on his sword and died. ⁶So Saul and his three sons died, and all his house died together.

⁷When all the Israelites in the valley saw that the army had fled and that Saul and his sons had died, they abandoned their towns and fled. And the Philistines came and occupied them.

⁸The next day, when the Philistines came to strip the dead, they found Saul and his sons fallen on Mount Gilboa. ⁹They stripped him and took his head and his armor, and sent messengers throughout the land of the Philistines to proclaim the news among their idols and their people. ¹⁰They put his armor in the temple of their gods and hung up his head in the temple of Dagon.

¹¹When all the inhabitants of Jabesh Gilead heard of everything the Philistines had done to Saul, ¹²all their valiant men went and took the bodies of Saul and his sons and brought them to Jabesh. Then they buried their bones under the great tree in Jabesh, and they fasted seven days.

¹³Saul died because he was unfaithful to the Lord; he did not keep the word of the Lord and even consulted a medium for guidance, ¹⁴and did not inquire of the Lord. So the Lord put him to death and turned the kingdom over to David son of Jesse.

David Becomes King Over Israel

11:1–3pp — 2Sa 5:1–3

11 All Israel came together to David at Hebron and said, "We are your own flesh and blood. ²In the past, even while Saul was king, you were the one who led Israel on their military campaigns. And the Lord your God said to you, 'You will shepherd my people Israel, and you will become their ruler.' "

³When all the elders of Israel had come to King David at Hebron, he made a compact with them at Hebron before the Lord, and they anointed David king over Israel, as the Lord had promised through Samuel.

David Conquers Jerusalem

11:4–9pp — 2Sa 5:6–10

⁴David and all the Israelites marched to Jerusalem (that is, Jebus). The Jebusites who lived there ⁵said to David, "You will not get in here." Nevertheless, David captured the fortress of Zion, the City of David.

⁶David had said, "Whoever leads the attack on the Jebusites will become commander-in-chief." Joab son of Zeruiah went up first, and so he received the command.

⁷David then took up residence in the fortress, and so it was called the City of David. ⁸He built up the city around it, from the supporting terraces ᵃ to the surrounding wall, while Joab restored the rest of the city. ⁹And David became more and more powerful, because the Lord Almighty was with him.

David's Mighty Men

11:10–41pp — 2Sa 23:8–39

¹⁰These were the chiefs of David's mighty men—they, together with all Israel, gave his kingship strong support to extend it over the whole land, as the Lord had promised— ¹¹this is the list of David's mighty men:

Jashobeam,ᵇ a Hacmonite, was chief of the officersᶜ; he raised his spear against three hundred men, whom he killed in one encounter.

ᵃ *8 Or the Millo*   ᵇ *11 Possibly a variant of Jashob-Baal*
ᶜ *11 Or Thirty; some Septuagint manuscripts Three (see also 2 Samuel 23:8)*

¹²Next to him was Eleazar son of Dodai the Ahohite, one of the three mighty men. ¹³He was with David at Pas Dammim when the Philistines gathered there for battle. At a place where there was a field full of barley, the troops fled from the Philistines. ¹⁴But they took their stand in the middle of the field. They defended it and struck the Philistines down, and the LORD brought about a great victory.

¹⁵Three of the thirty chiefs came down to David to the rock at the cave of Adullam, while a band of Philistines was encamped in the Valley of Rephaim. ¹⁶At that time David was in the stronghold, and the Philistine garrison was at Bethlehem. ¹⁷David longed for water and said, "Oh, that someone would get me a drink of water from the well near the gate of Bethlehem!" ¹⁸So the Three broke through the Philistine lines, drew water from the well near the gate of Bethlehem and carried it back to David. But he refused to drink it; instead, he poured it out before the LORD. ¹⁹"God forbid that I should do this!" he said. "Should I drink the blood of these men who went at the risk of their lives?" Because they risked their lives to bring it back, David would not drink it.

Such were the exploits of the three mighty men.

²⁰Abishai the brother of Joab was chief of the Three. He raised his spear against three hundred men, whom he killed, and so he became as famous as the Three. ²¹He was doubly honored above the Three and became their commander, even though he was not included among them.

²²Benaiah son of Jehoiada was a valiant fighter from Kabzeel, who performed great exploits. He struck down two of Moab's best men. He also went down into a pit on a snowy day and killed a lion. ²³And he struck down an Egyptian who was seven and a half feet ᵃ tall. Although the Egyptian had a spear like a weaver's rod in his hand, Benaiah went against him with a club. He snatched the spear from the Egyptian's hand and killed him with his own spear. ²⁴Such were the exploits of Benaiah son of Jehoiada; he too was as famous as the three mighty men. ²⁵He was held in greater honor than any of the Thirty, but he was not included among the Three. And David put him in charge of his bodyguard.

²⁶The mighty men were:
Asahel the brother of Joab,
Elhanan son of Dodo from Bethlehem,
²⁷Shammoth the Harorite,
Helez the Pelonite,
²⁸Ira son of Ikkesh from Tekoa,
Abiezer from Anathoth,
²⁹Sibbecai the Hushathite,
Ilai the Ahohite,
³⁰Maharai the Netophathite,
Heled son of Baanah the Netophathite,
³¹Ithai son of Ribai from Gibeah in Benjamin,
Benaiah the Pirathonite,
³²Hurai from the ravines of Gaash,
Abiel the Arbathite,
³³Azmaveth the Baharumite,
Eliahba the Shaalbonite,
³⁴the sons of Hashem the Gizonite,
Jonathan son of Shagee the Hararite,
³⁵Ahiam son of Sacar the Hararite,
Eliphal son of Ur,
³⁶Hepher the Mekerathite,
Ahijah the Pelonite,
³⁷Hezro the Carmelite,
Naarai son of Ezbai,
³⁸Joel the brother of Nathan,
Mibhar son of Hagri,
³⁹Zelek the Ammonite,
Naharai the Berothite, the armor-bearer of Joab son of Zeruiah,
⁴⁰Ira the Ithrite,
Gareb the Ithrite,
⁴¹Uriah the Hittite,
Zabad son of Ahlai,
⁴²Adina son of Shiza the Reubenite, who was chief of the Reubenites, and the thirty with him,
⁴³Hanan son of Maacah,
Joshaphat the Mithnite,

ᵃ 23 Hebrew *five cubits* (about 2.3 meters)

⁴⁴Uzzia the Ashterathite,
  Shama and Jeiel the sons of Hotham the
  Aroerite,
⁴⁵Jediael son of Shimri,
  his brother Joha the Tizite,
⁴⁶Eliel the Mahavite,
  Jeribai and Joshaviah the sons of Elnaam,
  Ithmah the Moabite,
⁴⁷Eliel, Obed and Jaasiel the Mezobaite.

Warriors Join David

12 These were the men who came to David at Ziklag, while he was banished from the presence of Saul son of Kish (they were among the warriors who helped him in battle; ²they were armed with bows and were able to shoot arrows or to sling stones right-handed or left-handed; they were kinsmen of Saul from the tribe of Benjamin):

³Ahiezer their chief and Joash the sons of Shemaah the Gibeathite; Jeziel and Pelet the sons of Azmaveth; Beracah, Jehu the Anathothite, ⁴and Ishmaiah the Gibeonite, a mighty man among the Thirty, who was a leader of the Thirty; Jeremiah, Jahaziel, Johanan, Jozabad the Gederathite, ⁵Eluzai, Jerimoth, Bealiah, Shemariah and Shephatiah the Haruphite; ⁶Elkanah, Isshiah, Azarel, Joezer and Jashobeam the Korahites; ⁷and Joelah and Zebadiah the sons of Jeroham from Gedor.

⁸Some Gadites defected to David at his stronghold in the desert. They were brave warriors, ready for battle and able to handle the shield and spear. Their faces were the faces of lions, and they were as swift as gazelles in the mountains.
⁹Ezer was the chief,
  Obadiah the second in command, Eliab the
    third,
¹⁰Mishmannah the fourth, Jeremiah the
    fifth,
¹¹Attai the sixth, Eliel the seventh,
¹²Johanan the eighth, Elzabad the ninth,
¹³Jeremiah the tenth and Macbannai the eleventh.

¹⁴These Gadites were army commanders; the least was a match for a hundred, and the greatest for a thousand. ¹⁵It was they who crossed the Jordan in the first month when it was overflowing all its banks, and they put to flight everyone living in the valleys, to the east and to the west.

¹⁶Other Benjamites and some men from Judah also came to David in his stronghold. ¹⁷David went out to meet them and said to them, "If you have come to me in peace, to help me, I am ready to have you unite with me. But if you have come to betray me to my enemies when my hands are free from violence, may the God of our fathers see it and judge you."

¹⁸Then the Spirit came upon Amasai, chief of the Thirty, and he said:

"We are yours, O David!
  We are with you, O son of Jesse!
Success, success to you,
    and success to those who help you,
    for your God will help you."

So David received them and made them leaders of his raiding bands.

¹⁹Some of the men of Manasseh defected to David when he went with the Philistines to fight against Saul. (He and his men did not help the Philistines because, after consultation, their rulers sent him away. They said, "It will cost us our heads if he deserts to his master Saul.") ²⁰When David went to Ziklag, these were the men of Manasseh who defected to him: Adnah, Jozabad, Jediael, Michael, Jozabad, Elihu and Zillethai, leaders of units of a thousand in Manasseh. ²¹They helped David against raiding bands, for all of them were brave warriors, and they were commanders in his army. ²²Day after day men came to help David, until he had a great army, like the army of God.[a]

Others Join David at Hebron

²³These are the numbers of the men armed for battle who came to David at Hebron to turn Saul's kingdom over to him, as the LORD had said:

---

[a] 22 Or a great and mighty army

24 men of Judah, carrying shield and spear—6,800 armed for battle;

25 men of Simeon, warriors ready for battle—7,100;

26 men of Levi—4,600, 27 including Jehoiada, leader of the family of Aaron, with 3,700 men, 28 and Zadok, a brave young warrior, with 22 officers from his family;

29 men of Benjamin, Saul's kinsmen—3,000, most of whom had remained loyal to Saul's house until then;

30 men of Ephraim, brave warriors, famous in their own clans—20,800;

31 men of half the tribe of Manasseh, designated by name to come and make David king—18,000;

32 men of Issachar, who understood the times and knew what Israel should do—200 chiefs, with all their relatives under their command;

33 men of Zebulun, experienced soldiers prepared for battle with every type of weapon, to help David with undivided loyalty—50,000;

34 men of Naphtali—1,000 officers, together with 37,000 men carrying shields and spears;

35 men of Dan, ready for battle—28,600;

36 men of Asher, experienced soldiers prepared for battle—40,000;

37 and from east of the Jordan, men of Reuben, Gad and the half-tribe of Manasseh, armed with every type of weapon—120,000.

38 All these were fighting men who volunteered to serve in the ranks. They came to Hebron fully determined to make David king over all Israel. All the rest of the Israelites were also of one mind to make David king. 39 The men spent three days there with David, eating and drinking, for their families had supplied provisions for them. 40 Also, their neighbors from as far away as Issachar, Zebulun and Naphtali came bringing food on donkeys, camels, mules and oxen. There were plentiful supplies of flour, fig cakes, raisin cakes, wine, oil, cattle and sheep, for there was joy in Israel.

Bringing Back the Ark
13:1–14pp — 2Sa 6:1–11

13 David conferred with each of his officers, the commanders of thousands and commanders of hundreds. 2 He then said to the whole assembly of Israel, "If it seems good to you and if it is the will of the LORD our God, let us send word far and wide to the rest of our brothers throughout the territories of Israel, and also to the priests and Levites who are with them in their towns and pasturelands, to come and join us. 3 Let us bring the ark of our God back to us, for we did not inquire of *a* it *b* during the reign of Saul." 4 The whole assembly agreed to do this, because it seemed right to all the people.

5 So David assembled all the Israelites, from the Shihor River in Egypt to Lebo *c* Hamath, to bring the ark of God from Kiriath Jearim. 6 David and all the Israelites with him went to Baalah of Judah (Kiriath Jearim) to bring up from there the ark of God the LORD, who is enthroned between the cherubim—the ark that is called by the Name.

7 They moved the ark of God from Abinadab's house on a new cart, with Uzzah and Ahio guiding it. 8 David and all the Israelites were celebrating with all their might before God, with songs and with harps, lyres, tambourines, cymbals and trumpets.

9 When they came to the threshing floor of Kidon, Uzzah reached out his hand to steady the ark, because the oxen stumbled. 10 The LORD's anger burned against Uzzah, and he struck him down because he had put his hand on the ark. So he died there before God.

11 Then David was angry because the LORD's wrath had broken out against Uzzah, and to this day that place is called Perez Uzzah. *d*

12 David was afraid of God that day and asked, "How can I ever bring the ark of God to me?"

a 3 Or *we neglected*   *b* 3 Or *him*   *c* 5 Or *to the entrance to*
d 11 *Perez Uzzah* means *outbreak against Uzzah.*

[13] He did not take the ark to be with him in the City of David. Instead, he took it aside to the house of Obed-Edom the Gittite. [14] The ark of God remained with the family of Obed-Edom in his house for three months, and the LORD blessed his household and everything he had.

David's House and Family

14:1–7pp — 2Sa 5:11–16; 1Ch 3:5–8

14 Now Hiram king of Tyre sent messengers to David, along with cedar logs, stonemasons and carpenters to build a palace for him. [2] And David knew that the LORD had established him as king over Israel and that his kingdom had been highly exalted for the sake of his people Israel.

[3] In Jerusalem David took more wives and became the father of more sons and daughters. [4] These are the names of the children born to him there: Shammua, Shobab, Nathan, Solomon, [5] Ibhar, Elishua, Elpelet, [6] Nogah, Nepheg, Japhia, [7] Elishama, Beeliada *a* and Eliphelet.

David Defeats the Philistines

14:8–17pp — 2Sa 5:17–25

[8] When the Philistines heard that David had been anointed king over all Israel, they went up in full force to search for him, but David heard about it and went out to meet them. [9] Now the Philistines had come and raided the Valley of Rephaim; [10] so David inquired of God: "Shall I go and attack the Philistines? Will you hand them over to me?"

The LORD answered him, "Go, I will hand them over to you."

[11] So David and his men went up to Baal Perazim, and there he defeated them. He said, "As waters break out, God has broken out against my enemies by my hand." So that place was called Baal Perazim. *b* [12] The Philistines had abandoned their gods there, and David gave orders to burn them in the fire.

[13] Once more the Philistines raided the valley; [14] so David inquired of God again, and God answered him, "Do not go straight up, but circle around them and attack them in front of the balsam trees. [15] As soon as you hear the sound of marching in the tops of the balsam trees, move out to battle, because that will mean God has gone out in front of you to strike the Philistine army." [16] So David did as God commanded him, and they struck down the Philistine army, all the way from Gibeon to Gezer.

[17] So David's fame spread throughout every land, and the LORD made all the nations fear him.

The Ark Brought to Jerusalem

15:25–16:3pp — 2Sa 6:12–19

15 After David had constructed buildings for himself in the City of David, he prepared a place for the ark of God and pitched a tent for it. [2] Then David said, "No one but the Levites may carry the ark of God, because the LORD chose them to carry the ark of the LORD and to minister before him forever."

[3] David assembled all Israel in Jerusalem to bring up the ark of the LORD to the place he had prepared for it. [4] He called together the descendants of Aaron and the Levites:

[5] From the descendants of Kohath,
  Uriel the leader and 120 relatives;
[6] from the descendants of Merari,
  Asaiah the leader and 220 relatives;
[7] from the descendants of Gershon, *c*
  Joel the leader and 130 relatives;
[8] from the descendants of Elizaphan,
  Shemaiah the leader and 200 relatives;
[9] from the descendants of Hebron,
  Eliel the leader and 80 relatives;
[10] from the descendants of Uzziel,
  Amminadab the leader and 112 relatives.
[11] Then David summoned Zadok and Abiathar the priests, and Uriel, Asaiah, Joel, Shemaiah, Eliel and Amminadab the Levites. [12] He said to them, "You are the heads of the Levitical families; you and your fellow Levites are to consecrate yourselves and bring up the ark of the LORD, the God

---

a 7 A variant of *Eliada*   *b 11 Baal Perazim* means *the lord who breaks out.*   *c 7* Hebrew *Gershom,* a variant of *Gershon* of Israel, to the place I have prepared for it. [13] It was because you, the Levites, did not bring it up the first time that the LORD our God broke out in anger against us. We did not inquire of him about how to do it in the prescribed way." [14] So the priests and Levites consecrated themselves in order to bring up the ark of the LORD, the God of Israel. [15] And the Levites carried the ark of God with the poles on their shoulders, as Moses had commanded in accordance with the word of the LORD.

[16] David told the leaders of the Levites to appoint their brothers as singers to sing joyful songs, accompanied by musical instruments: lyres, harps and cymbals.

[17] So the Levites appointed Heman son of Joel; from his brothers, Asaph son of Berekiah; and from their brothers the Merarites, Ethan son of Kushaiah; [18] and with them their brothers next in rank: Zechariah,[a] Jaaziel, Shemiramoth, Jehiel, Unni, Eliab, Benaiah, Maaseiah, Mattithiah, Eliphelehu, Mikneiah, Obed-Edom and Jeiel,[b] the gatekeepers.

[19] The musicians Heman, Asaph and Ethan were to sound the bronze cymbals; [20] Zechariah, Aziel, Shemiramoth, Jehiel, Unni, Eliab, Maaseiah and Benaiah were to play the lyres according to *alamoth*,[c] [21] and Mattithiah, Eliphelehu, Mikneiah, Obed-Edom, Jeiel and Azaziah were to play the harps, directing according to *sheminith*.[c] [22] Kenaniah the head Levite was in charge of the singing; that was his responsibility because he was skillful at it.

[23] Berekiah and Elkanah were to be doorkeepers for the ark. [24] Shebaniah, Joshaphat, Nethanel, Amasai, Zechariah, Benaiah and Eliezer the priests were to blow trumpets before the ark of God. Obed-Edom and Jehiah were also to be doorkeepers for the ark.

[25] So David and the elders of Israel and the commanders of units of a thousand went to bring up the ark of the covenant of the LORD from the house of Obed-Edom, with rejoicing. [26] Because God had helped the Levites who were carrying the ark of the covenant of the LORD, sev-

stories to share

1 CHRONICLES 15:1–16,25–28

The Ark Brought to Jerusalem

LIFE LESSON: Our God is holy.

TO TALK ABOUT

✦ Why was it important to bring the ark to Jerusalem?

✦ Who carried the ark, and how did they do so?

✦ What was so special about the ark?

✦ Do we still have God's ark? Where is God's holiness today?

en bulls and seven rams were sacrificed. [27] Now David was clothed in a robe of fine linen, as were all the Levites who were carrying the ark, and as were the singers, and Kenaniah, who was in charge of the singing of the choirs. David also wore a linen ephod. [28] So all Israel brought up the ark of the covenant of the LORD with shouts, with the sounding of rams' horns and trumpets, and of cymbals, and the playing of lyres and harps.

[29] As the ark of the covenant of the LORD was entering the City of David, Michal daughter of Saul watched from a window. And when she saw King David dancing and celebrating, she despised him in her heart.

---

a 18 Three Hebrew manuscripts and most Septuagint manuscripts (see also verse 20 and 1 Chron. 16:5); most Hebrew manuscripts *Zechariah son and* or *Zechariah, Ben and*   *b 18* Hebrew; Septuagint (see also verse 21) *Jeiel and Azaziah*   *c 20,21* Probably a musical term

16 They brought the ark of God and set it inside the tent that David had pitched for it, and they presented burnt offerings and fellowship offerings[a] before God. ²After David had finished sacrificing the burnt offerings and fellowship offerings, he blessed the people in the name of the LORD. ³Then he gave a loaf of bread, a cake of dates and a cake of raisins to each Israelite man and woman.

⁴He appointed some of the Levites to minister before the ark of the LORD, to make petition, to give thanks, and to praise the LORD, the God of Israel: ⁵Asaph was the chief, Zechariah second, then Jeiel, Shemiramoth, Jehiel, Mattithiah, Eliab, Benaiah, Obed-Edom and Jeiel. They were to play the lyres and harps, Asaph was to sound the cymbals, ⁶and Benaiah and Jahaziel the priests were to blow the trumpets regularly before the ark of the covenant of God.

David's Psalm of Thanks

16:8–22pp — Ps 105:1–15
16:23–33pp — Ps 96:1–13
16:34–36pp — Ps 106:1,47–48

⁷That day David first committed to Asaph and his associates this psalm of thanks to the LORD:

⁸Give thanks to the LORD, call on his
    name;
  make known among the nations what
    he has done.
⁹Sing to him, sing praise to him;
  tell of all his wonderful acts.
¹⁰Glory in his holy name;
  let the hearts of those who seek the LORD
    rejoice.
¹¹Look to the LORD and his strength;
  seek his face always.
¹²Remember the wonders he has done,
  his miracles, and the judgments he
    pronounced,
¹³O descendants of Israel his servant,
  O sons of Jacob, his chosen ones.

¹⁴He is the LORD our God;
  his judgments are in all the earth.

TALKING POINTS

Praise

Like David, we can praise and
thank God for all he has done.

1 CHRONICLES 16:7–13

For more on praise, go to Job 1:13–22.

---

¹⁵He remembers[b] his covenant forever,
  the word he commanded, for a thousand
    generations,
¹⁶the covenant he made with Abraham,
  the oath he swore to Isaac.
¹⁷He confirmed it to Jacob as a decree,
  to Israel as an everlasting covenant:
¹⁸"To you I will give the land of Canaan
  as the portion you will inherit."

¹⁹When they were but few in number,
  few indeed, and strangers in it,
²⁰they[c] wandered from nation to nation,
  from one kingdom to another.
²¹He allowed no man to oppress them;
  for their sake he rebuked kings:
²²"Do not touch my anointed ones;
  do my prophets no harm."

²³Sing to the LORD, all the earth;
  proclaim his salvation day after day.
²⁴Declare his glory among the nations,
  his marvelous deeds among all peoples.
²⁵For great is the LORD and most worthy of
    praise;
  he is to be feared above all gods.
²⁶For all the gods of the nations are idols,
  but the LORD made the heavens.
²⁷Splendor and majesty are before him;
  strength and joy in his dwelling place.

---

[a] 1 Traditionally *peace offerings*; also in verse 2   [b] 15 Some Septuagint manuscripts (see also Psalm 105:8); Hebrew *Remember*   [c] 18-20 One Hebrew manuscript, Septuagint and Vulgate (see also Psalm 105:12); most Hebrew manuscripts *inherit, / ¹⁹though you are but few in number, / few indeed, and strangers in it." / ²⁰They*

GIVE THANKS TO THE LORD,
FOR HE IS GOOD; HIS LOVE
ENDURES FOREVER.

1 Chronicles 16:34

Grandma Grace's Bible

JONI EARECKSON TADA

READ | 1 CHRONICLES 16:7–36

When I travel with my friends Bev and Francie, we always enjoy heading back to our hotel room after a busy day of appointments and speaking engagements. We put on our pajamas, pile into bed together and open up the Bible for devotions.

One evening it was Francie's turn to lead the hymns and Scripture reading. She rummaged through her suitcase and brought out an old, tattered Bible. "This is my Grandma Grace's," she smiled as she snuggled between Bev and me.

Francie cracked open the old Bible. The binding was torn, and she carefully turned each delicate page. Francie tilted the book so we could read Grandma Grace's faded scribbles in the margin. In old-fashioned script, we got an up-close look at this elderly woman's love for the Lord Jesus. Her words were nearly a century old, but the love of which she wrote was anything but obsolete.

As Francie read aloud her grandmother's personal notes, I felt as though this woman shared the rhythm of my heart. We were kindred spirits. We could have been best friends. And her notes weren't reminiscent of dusty days gone by, for each word was a powerful and poignant reminder that Jesus is the same yesterday, today and forever.

There's nothing old or worn out about the love of God. His love has not yellowed with age. It is neither fragile nor ragged at the edges. God's love is as current now as it was a century ago, as fresh today as it will be tomorrow. Today, praise the Lord that He is the same, always loving, always merciful, and that with Him there is no shadow of turning.

Lord God, I'm amazed that you never change. You are always faithful. Your promises are time-tested. Together with the saints of the ages, including Grandma Grace, I praise you!

Your next devotion is located on page 575.

GRANDCHILD IN FOCUS · PRAYER

Physical Well-Being

Almighty God, Creator of us all, I pray that you will watch over my grandchild's physical development. May he grow in strength through the stages of his life. As he grows in awareness of his body, help him to understand that each body develops uniquely, yet is within your plan and your control. Please guard his health so that his diseases are few, his injuries are minor and his infirmities are brief. Amen.

28 Ascribe to the LORD, O families of nations,
   ascribe to the LORD glory and strength,
29   ascribe to the LORD the glory due his
      name.
   Bring an offering and come before him;
      worship the LORD in the splendor of his *a*
      holiness.
30 Tremble before him, all the earth!
      The world is firmly established; it cannot
      be moved.
31 Let the heavens rejoice, let the earth be glad;
      let them say among the nations, "The
      LORD reigns!"
32 Let the sea resound, and all that is in it;
      let the fields be jubilant, and everything in
      them!
33 Then the trees of the forest will sing,
      they will sing for joy before the LORD,
      for he comes to judge the earth.

34 Give thanks to the LORD, for he is good;
      his love endures forever.
35 Cry out, "Save us, O God our Savior;
      gather us and deliver us from the nations,
      that we may give thanks to your holy name,
      that we may glory in your praise."
36 Praise be to the LORD, the God of Israel,
      from everlasting to everlasting.

Then all the people said "Amen" and "Praise the
LORD."

37 David left Asaph and his associates before the
ark of the covenant of the LORD to minister there
regularly, according to each day's requirements.
38 He also left Obed-Edom and his sixty-eight associates to minister with them. Obed-Edom son
of Jeduthun, and also Hosah, were gatekeepers.
39 David left Zadok the priest and his fellow
priests before the tabernacle of the LORD at the
high place in Gibeon 40 to present burnt offerings
to the LORD on the altar of burnt offering regularly, morning and evening, in accordance with
everything written in the Law of the LORD, which
he had given Israel. 41 With them were Heman
and Jeduthun and the rest of those chosen and

designated by name to give thanks to the LORD,
"for his love endures forever." 42 Heman and Jeduthun were responsible for the sounding of the
trumpets and cymbals and for the playing of the
other instruments for sacred song. The sons of
Jeduthun were stationed at the gate.

43 Then all the people left, each for his own home,
and David returned home to bless his family.

God's Promise to David
17:1–15pp — 2Sa 7:1–17

17 After David was settled in his palace, he
said to Nathan the prophet, "Here I am,
living in a palace of cedar, while the ark of the
covenant of the LORD is under a tent."

2 Nathan replied to David, "Whatever you have
in mind, do it, for God is with you."

3 That night the word of God came to Nathan,
saying:

4 "Go and tell my servant David, 'This is
what the LORD says: You are not the one to
build me a house to dwell in. 5 I have not
dwelt in a house from the day I brought Israel up out of Egypt to this day. I have moved
from one tent site to another, from one
dwelling place to another. 6 Wherever I have
moved with all the Israelites, did I ever say
to any of their leaders *b* whom I commanded to shepherd my people, "Why have you
not built me a house of cedar?" '

7 "Now then, tell my servant David, 'This
is what the LORD Almighty says: I took you
from the pasture and from following the
flock, to be ruler over my people Israel. 8 I
have been with you wherever you have gone,
and I have cut off all your enemies from before you. Now I will make your name like
the names of the greatest men of the earth.
9 And I will provide a place for my people
Israel and will plant them so that they can
have a home of their own and no longer be
disturbed. Wicked people will not oppress

---

a 29 Or LORD with the splendor of   *b* 6 Traditionally *judges*; also
in verse 10

them anymore, as they did at the beginning [10]and have done ever since the time I appointed leaders over my people Israel. I will also subdue all your enemies.

" 'I declare to you that the LORD will build a house for you: [11]When your days are over and you go to be with your fathers, I will raise up your offspring to succeed you, one of your own sons, and I will establish his kingdom. [12]He is the one who will build a house for me, and I will establish his throne forever. [13]I will be his father, and he will be my son. I will never take my love away from him, as I took it away from your predecessor. [14]I will set him over my house and my kingdom forever; his throne will be established forever.' "

[15]Nathan reported to David all the words of this entire revelation.

David's Prayer

17:16–27pp — 2Sa 7:18–29

[16]Then King David went in and sat before the LORD, and he said:

"Who am I, O LORD God, and what is my family, that you have brought me this far? [17]And as if this were not enough in your sight, O God, you have spoken about the future of the house of your servant. You have looked on me as though I were the most exalted of men, O LORD God.

[18]"What more can David say to you for honoring your servant? For you know your servant, [19]O LORD. For the sake of your servant and according to your will, you have done this great thing and made known all these great promises.

[20]"There is no one like you, O LORD, and there is no God but you, as we have heard with our own ears. [21]And who is like your people Israel—the one nation on earth whose God went out to redeem a people for himself, and to make a name for yourself, and to perform great and awesome wonders by driving out nations from before your peo-

ple, whom you redeemed from Egypt? [22]You made your people Israel your very own forever, and you, O LORD, have become their God.

[23]"And now, LORD, let the promise you have made concerning your servant and his house be established forever. Do as you promised, [24]so that it will be established and that your name will be great forever. Then men will say, 'The LORD Almighty, the God over Israel, is Israel's God!' And the house of your servant David will be established before you.

[25]"You, my God, have revealed to your servant that you will build a house for him. So your servant has found courage to pray to you. [26]O LORD, you are God! You have promised these good things to your servant. [27]Now you have been pleased to bless the house of your servant, that it may continue forever in your sight; for you, O LORD, have blessed it, and it will be blessed forever."

David's Victories

18:1–13pp — 2Sa 8:1–14

18 In the course of time, David defeated the Philistines and subdued them, and he took Gath and its surrounding villages from the control of the Philistines.

[2]David also defeated the Moabites, and they became subject to him and brought tribute.

[3]Moreover, David fought Hadadezer king of Zobah, as far as Hamath, when he went to establish his control along the Euphrates River. [4]David captured a thousand of his chariots, seven thousand charioteers and twenty thousand foot soldiers. He hamstrung all but a hundred of the chariot horses.

[5]When the Arameans of Damascus came to help Hadadezer king of Zobah, David struck down twenty-two thousand of them. [6]He put garrisons in the Aramean kingdom of Damascus, and the Arameans became subject to him and brought tribute. The LORD gave David victory everywhere he went.

⁷David took the gold shields carried by the officers of Hadadezer and brought them to Jerusalem. ⁸From Tebah *ᵃ* and Cun, towns that belonged to Hadadezer, David took a great quantity of bronze, which Solomon used to make the bronze Sea, the pillars and various bronze articles.

⁹When Tou king of Hamath heard that David had defeated the entire army of Hadadezer king of Zobah, ¹⁰he sent his son Hadoram to King David to greet him and congratulate him on his victory in battle over Hadadezer, who had been at war with Tou. Hadoram brought all kinds of articles of gold and silver and bronze.

¹¹King David dedicated these articles to the Lord, as he had done with the silver and gold he had taken from all these nations: Edom and Moab, the Ammonites and the Philistines, and Amalek.

¹²Abishai son of Zeruiah struck down eighteen thousand Edomites in the Valley of Salt. ¹³He put garrisons in Edom, and all the Edomites became subject to David. The Lord gave David victory everywhere he went.

David's Officials
18:14–17pp — 2Sa 8:15–18

¹⁴David reigned over all Israel, doing what was just and right for all his people. ¹⁵Joab son of Zeruiah was over the army; Jehoshaphat son of Ahilud was recorder; ¹⁶Zadok son of Ahitub and Ahimelech *ᵇ* son of Abiathar were priests; Shavsha was secretary; ¹⁷Benaiah son of Jehoiada was over the Kerethites and Pelethites; and David's sons were chief officials at the king's side.

The Battle Against the Ammonites
19:1–19pp — 2Sa 10:1–19

19 In the course of time, Nahash king of the Ammonites died, and his son succeeded him as king. ²David thought, "I will show kindness to Hanun son of Nahash, because his father showed kindness to me." So David sent a delegation to express his sympathy to Hanun concerning his father.

When David's men came to Hanun in the land of the Ammonites to express sympathy to him,

³the Ammonite nobles said to Hanun, "Do you think David is honoring your father by sending men to you to express sympathy? Haven't his men come to you to explore and spy out the country and overthrow it?" ⁴So Hanun seized David's men, shaved them, cut off their garments in the middle at the buttocks, and sent them away.

⁵When someone came and told David about the men, he sent messengers to meet them, for they were greatly humiliated. The king said, "Stay at Jericho till your beards have grown, and then come back."

⁶When the Ammonites realized that they had become a stench in David's nostrils, Hanun and the Ammonites sent a thousand talents *ᶜ* of silver to hire chariots and charioteers from Aram Naharaim, *ᵈ* Aram Maacah and Zobah. ⁷They hired thirty-two thousand chariots and charioteers, as well as the king of Maacah with his troops, who came and camped near Medeba, while the Ammonites were mustered from their towns and moved out for battle.

⁸On hearing this, David sent Joab out with the entire army of fighting men. ⁹The Ammonites came out and drew up in battle formation at the entrance to their city, while the kings who had come were by themselves in the open country.

¹⁰Joab saw that there were battle lines in front of him and behind him; so he selected some of the best troops in Israel and deployed them against the Arameans. ¹¹He put the rest of the men under the command of Abishai his brother, and they were deployed against the Ammonites. ¹²Joab said, "If the Arameans are too strong for me, then you are to rescue me; but if the Ammonites are too strong for you, then I will rescue you. ¹³Be strong and let us fight bravely for our people and the cities of our God. The Lord will do what is good in his sight."

¹⁴Then Joab and the troops with him advanced to fight the Arameans, and they fled before him. ¹⁵When the Ammonites saw that the Arameans

---

ᵃ 8 Hebrew *Tibhath,* a variant of *Tebah*   *ᵇ 16* Some Hebrew manuscripts, Vulgate and Syriac (see also 2 Samuel 8:17); most Hebrew manuscripts *Abimelech*   *ᶜ 6* That is, about 37 tons (about 34 metric tons)   *ᵈ 6* That is, Northwest Mesopotamia were fleeing, they too fled before his brother Abishai and went inside the city. So Joab went back to Jerusalem.

¹⁶ After the Arameans saw that they had been routed by Israel, they sent messengers and had Arameans brought from beyond the River,ᵃ with Shophach the commander of Hadadezer's army leading them.

¹⁷ When David was told of this, he gathered all Israel and crossed the Jordan; he advanced against them and formed his battle lines opposite them. David formed his lines to meet the Arameans in battle, and they fought against him. ¹⁸ But they fled before Israel, and David killed seven thousand of their charioteers and forty thousand of their foot soldiers. He also killed Shophach the commander of their army.

¹⁹ When the vassals of Hadadezer saw that they had been defeated by Israel, they made peace with David and became subject to him.

So the Arameans were not willing to help the Ammonites anymore.

The Capture of Rabbah
20:1–3pp — 2Sa 11:1; 12:29–31

20 In the spring, at the time when kings go off to war, Joab led out the armed forces. He laid waste the land of the Ammonites and went to Rabbah and besieged it, but David remained in Jerusalem. Joab attacked Rabbah and left it in ruins. ² David took the crown from the head of their kingᵇ — its weight was found to be a talentᶜ of gold, and it was set with precious stones — and it was placed on David's head. He took a great quantity of plunder from the city ³ and brought out the people who were there, consigning them to labor with saws and with iron picks and axes. David did this to all the Ammonite towns. Then David and his entire army returned to Jerusalem.

War With the Philistines
20:4–8pp — 2Sa 21:15–22

⁴ In the course of time, war broke out with the Philistines, at Gezer. At that time Sibbecai the Hushathite killed Sippai, one of the descendants of the Rephaites, and the Philistines were subjugated.

⁵ In another battle with the Philistines, Elhanan son of Jair killed Lahmi the brother of Goliath the Gittite, who had a spear with a shaft like a weaver's rod.

⁶ In still another battle, which took place at Gath, there was a huge man with six fingers on each hand and six toes on each foot — twenty-four in all. He also was descended from Rapha. ⁷ When he taunted Israel, Jonathan son of Shimea, David's brother, killed him.

⁸ These were descendants of Rapha in Gath, and they fell at the hands of David and his men.

David Numbers the Fighting Men
21:1–26pp — 2Sa 24:1–25

21 Satan rose up against Israel and incited David to take a census of Israel. ² So David said to Joab and the commanders of the troops, "Go and count the Israelites from Beersheba to Dan. Then report back to me so that I may know how many there are."

³ But Joab replied, "May the LORD multiply his troops a hundred times over. My lord the king, are they not all my lord's subjects? Why does my lord want to do this? Why should he bring guilt on Israel?"

⁴ The king's word, however, overruled Joab; so Joab left and went throughout Israel and then came back to Jerusalem. ⁵ Joab reported the number of the fighting men to David: In all Israel there were one million one hundred thousand men who could handle a sword, including four hundred and seventy thousand in Judah.

⁶ But Joab did not include Levi and Benjamin in the numbering, because the king's command was repulsive to him. ⁷ This command was also evil in the sight of God; so he punished Israel.

⁸ Then David said to God, "I have sinned greatly by doing this. Now, I beg you, take away the guilt of your servant. I have done a very foolish thing."

ᵃ 16 That is, the Euphrates   ᵇ 2 Or *of Milcom*, that is, Molech
ᶜ 2 That is, about 75 pounds (about 34 kilograms)

⁹The LORD said to Gad, David's seer, ¹⁰"Go and tell David, 'This is what the LORD says: I am giving you three options. Choose one of them for me to carry out against you.'"

¹¹So Gad went to David and said to him, "This is what the LORD says: 'Take your choice: ¹²three years of famine, three months of being swept away[a] before your enemies, with their swords overtaking you, or three days of the sword of the LORD — days of plague in the land, with the angel of the LORD ravaging every part of Israel.' Now then, decide how I should answer the one who sent me."

¹³David said to Gad, "I am in deep distress. Let me fall into the hands of the LORD, for his mercy is very great; but do not let me fall into the hands of men."

¹⁴So the LORD sent a plague on Israel, and seventy thousand men of Israel fell dead. ¹⁵And God sent an angel to destroy Jerusalem. But as the angel was doing so, the LORD saw it and was grieved because of the calamity and said to the angel who was destroying the people, "Enough! Withdraw your hand." The angel of the LORD was then standing at the threshing floor of Araunah[b] the Jebusite.

¹⁶David looked up and saw the angel of the LORD standing between heaven and earth, with a drawn sword in his hand extended over Jerusalem. Then David and the elders, clothed in sackcloth, fell facedown.

¹⁷David said to God, "Was it not I who ordered the fighting men to be counted? I am the one who has sinned and done wrong. These are but sheep. What have they done? O LORD my God, let your hand fall upon me and my family, but do not let this plague remain on your people."

¹⁸Then the angel of the LORD ordered Gad to tell David to go up and build an altar to the LORD on the threshing floor of Araunah the Jebusite. ¹⁹So David went up in obedience to the word that Gad had spoken in the name of the LORD.

²⁰While Araunah was threshing wheat, he turned and saw the angel; his four sons who were with him hid themselves. ²¹Then David ap-proached, and when Araunah looked and saw him, he left the threshing floor and bowed down before David with his face to the ground.

²²David said to him, "Let me have the site of your threshing floor so I can build an altar to the LORD, that the plague on the people may be stopped. Sell it to me at the full price."

²³Araunah said to David, "Take it! Let my lord the king do whatever pleases him. Look, I will give the oxen for the burnt offerings, the thresh-ing sledges for the wood, and the wheat for the grain offering. I will give all this."

²⁴But King David replied to Araunah, "No, I in-sist on paying the full price. I will not take for the LORD what is yours, or sacrifice a burnt offering that costs me nothing."

²⁵So David paid Araunah six hundred shekels[c] of gold for the site. ²⁶David built an altar to the LORD there and sacrificed burnt offerings and fel-lowship offerings.[d] He called on the LORD, and the LORD answered him with fire from heaven on the altar of burnt offering.

²⁷Then the LORD spoke to the angel, and he put his sword back into its sheath. ²⁸At that time, when David saw that the LORD had answered him on the threshing floor of Araunah the Jebu-site, he offered sacrifices there. ²⁹The tabernacle of the LORD, which Moses had made in the des-ert, and the altar of burnt offering were at that time on the high place at Gibeon. ³⁰But David could not go before it to inquire of God, because he was afraid of the sword of the angel of the LORD.

22 Then David said, "The house of the LORD God is to be here, and also the altar of burnt offering for Israel."

Preparations for the Temple

²So David gave orders to assemble the aliens living in Israel, and from among them he ap-pointed stonecutters to prepare dressed stone for building the house of God. ³He provided a large

---

a 12 Hebrew; Septuagint and Vulgate (see also 2 Samuel 24:13) *of fleeing*   *b 15* Hebrew *Ornan,* a variant of *Araunah*; also in verses 18-28   *c 25* That is, about 15 pounds (about 7 kilograms) *d 26* Traditionally *peace offerings* amount of iron to make nails for the doors of the gateways and for the fittings, and more bronze than could be weighed. ⁴He also provided more cedar logs than could be counted, for the Sidonians and Tyrians had brought large numbers of them to David.

⁵David said, "My son Solomon is young and inexperienced, and the house to be built for the LORD should be of great magnificence and fame and splendor in the sight of all the nations. Therefore I will make preparations for it." So David made extensive preparations before his death.

⁶Then he called for his son Solomon and charged him to build a house for the LORD, the God of Israel. ⁷David said to Solomon: "My son, I had it in my heart to build a house for the Name of the LORD my God. ⁸But this word of the LORD came to me: 'You have shed much blood and have fought many wars. You are not to build a house for my Name, because you have shed much blood on the earth in my sight. ⁹But you will have a son who will be a man of peace and rest, and I will give him rest from all his enemies on every side. His name will be Solomon,ᵃ and I will grant Israel peace and quiet during his reign. ¹⁰He is the one who will build a house for my Name. He will be my son, and I will be his father. And I will establish the throne of his kingdom over Israel forever.'

¹¹"Now, my son, the LORD be with you, and may you have success and build the house of the LORD your God, as he said you would. ¹²May the LORD give you discretion and understanding when he puts you in command over Israel, so that you may keep the law of the LORD your God. ¹³Then you will have success if you are careful to observe the decrees and laws that the LORD gave Moses for Israel. Be strong and courageous. Do not be afraid or discouraged.

¹⁴"I have taken great pains to provide for the temple of the LORD a hundred thousand talentsᵇ of gold, a million talentsᶜ of silver, quantities of bronze and iron too great to be weighed, and wood and stone. And you may add to them. ¹⁵You have many workmen: stonecutters, masons and carpenters, as well as men skilled in every kind of work ¹⁶in gold and silver, bronze and iron—craftsmen beyond number. Now begin the work, and the LORD be with you."

¹⁷Then David ordered all the leaders of Israel to help his son Solomon. ¹⁸He said to them, "Is not the LORD your God with you? And has he not granted you rest on every side? For he has handed the inhabitants of the land over to me, and the land is subject to the LORD and to his people. ¹⁹Now devote your heart and soul to seeking the LORD your God. Begin to build the sanctuary of the LORD God, so that you may bring the ark of the covenant of the LORD and the sacred articles belonging to God into the temple that will be built for the Name of the LORD."

The Levites

23 When David was old and full of years, he made his son Solomon king over Israel.

²He also gathered together all the leaders of Israel, as well as the priests and Levites. ³The Levites thirty years old or more were counted, and the total number of men was thirty-eight thousand. ⁴David said, "Of these, twenty-four thousand are to supervise the work of the temple of the LORD and six thousand are to be officials and judges. ⁵Four thousand are to be gatekeepers and four thousand are to praise the LORD with the musical instruments I have provided for that purpose."

⁶David divided the Levites into groups corresponding to the sons of Levi: Gershon, Kohath and Merari.

Gershonites

⁷Belonging to the Gershonites:
Ladan and Shimei.
⁸The sons of Ladan:
Jehiel the first, Zetham and Joel—three in all.
⁹The sons of Shimei:
Shelomoth, Haziel and Haran—three in all.

ᵃ 9 *Solomon* sounds like and may be derived from the Hebrew for *peace.*   ᵇ 14 That is, about 3,750 tons (about 3,450 metric tons)   ᶜ 14 That is, about 37,500 tons (about 34,500 metric tons)

These were the heads of the families of Ladan.

10 And the sons of Shimei:

Jahath, Ziza,[a] Jeush and Beriah.

These were the sons of Shimei—four in all.

11 Jahath was the first and Ziza the second, but Jeush and Beriah did not have many sons; so they were counted as one family with one assignment.

Kohathites

12 The sons of Kohath:

Amram, Izhar, Hebron and Uzziel—four in all.

13 The sons of Amram:

Aaron and Moses.

Aaron was set apart, he and his descendants forever, to consecrate the most holy things, to offer sacrifices before the LORD, to minister before him and to pronounce blessings in his name forever. 14 The sons of Moses the man of God were counted as part of the tribe of Levi.

15 The sons of Moses:

Gershom and Eliezer.

16 The descendants of Gershom:

Shubael was the first.

17 The descendants of Eliezer:

Rehabiah was the first.

Eliezer had no other sons, but the sons of Rehabiah were very numerous.

18 The sons of Izhar:

Shelomith was the first.

19 The sons of Hebron:

Jeriah the first, Amariah the second, Jahaziel the third and Jekameam the fourth.

20 The sons of Uzziel:

Micah the first and Isshiah the second.

Merarites

21 The sons of Merari:

Mahli and Mushi.

The sons of Mahli:

Eleazar and Kish.

22 Eleazar died without having sons: he had only daughters. Their cousins, the sons of Kish, married them.

23 The sons of Mushi:

Mahli, Eder and Jerimoth—three in all.

24 These were the descendants of Levi by their families—the heads of families as they were registered under their names and counted individually, that is, the workers twenty years old or more who served in the temple of the LORD. 25 For David had said, "Since the LORD, the God of Israel, has granted rest to his people and has come to dwell in Jerusalem forever, 26 the Levites no longer need to carry the tabernacle or any of the articles used in its service." 27 According to the last instructions of David, the Levites were counted from those twenty years old or more.

28 The duty of the Levites was to help Aaron's descendants in the service of the temple of the LORD: to be in charge of the courtyards, the side rooms, the purification of all sacred things and the performance of other duties at the house of God. 29 They were in charge of the bread set out on the table, the flour for the grain offerings, the unleavened wafers, the baking and the mixing, and all measurements of quantity and size. 30 They were also to stand every morning to thank and praise the LORD. They were to do the same in the evening 31 and whenever burnt offerings were presented to the LORD on Sabbaths and at New Moon festivals and at appointed feasts. They were to serve before the LORD regularly in the proper number and in the way prescribed for them.

32 And so the Levites carried out their responsibilities for the Tent of Meeting, for the Holy Place and, under their brothers the descendants of Aaron, for the service of the temple of the LORD.

The Divisions of Priests

24 These were the divisions of the sons of Aaron:

---

[a] 10 One Hebrew manuscript, Septuagint and Vulgate (see also verse 11); most Hebrew manuscripts *Zina*

The sons of Aaron were Nadab, Abihu, Eleazar and Ithamar. ²But Nadab and Abihu died before their father did, and they had no sons; so Eleazar and Ithamar served as the priests. ³With the help of Zadok a descendant of Eleazar and Ahimelech a descendant of Ithamar, David separated them into divisions for their appointed order of ministering. ⁴A larger number of leaders were found among Eleazar's descendants than among Ithamar's, and they were divided accordingly: sixteen heads of families from Eleazar's descendants and eight heads of families from Ithamar's descendants. ⁵They divided them impartially by drawing lots, for there were officials of the sanctuary and officials of God among the descendants of both Eleazar and Ithamar.

⁶The scribe Shemaiah son of Nethanel, a Levite, recorded their names in the presence of the king and of the officials: Zadok the priest, Ahimelech son of Abiathar and the heads of families of the priests and of the Levites — one family being taken from Eleazar and then one from Ithamar.

⁷The first lot fell to Jehoiarib,
  the second to Jedaiah,
⁸the third to Harim,
  the fourth to Seorim,
⁹the fifth to Malkijah,
  the sixth to Mijamin,
¹⁰the seventh to Hakkoz,
  the eighth to Abijah,
¹¹the ninth to Jeshua,
  the tenth to Shecaniah,
¹²the eleventh to Eliashib,
  the twelfth to Jakim,
¹³the thirteenth to Huppah,
  the fourteenth to Jeshebeab,
¹⁴the fifteenth to Bilgah,
  the sixteenth to Immer,
¹⁵the seventeenth to Hezir,
  the eighteenth to Happizzez,
¹⁶the nineteenth to Pethahiah,
  the twentieth to Jehezkel,
¹⁷the twenty-first to Jakin,
  the twenty-second to Gamul,
¹⁸the twenty-third to Delaiah
  and the twenty-fourth to Maaziah.

¹⁹This was their appointed order of ministering when they entered the temple of the Lord, according to the regulations prescribed for them by their forefather Aaron, as the Lord, the God of Israel, had commanded him.

The Rest of the Levites

²⁰As for the rest of the descendants of Levi:
  from the sons of Amram: Shubael;
    from the sons of Shubael: Jehdeiah.
  ²¹As for Rehabiah, from his sons:
    Isshiah was the first.
²²From the Izharites: Shelomoth;
  from the sons of Shelomoth: Jahath.
²³The sons of Hebron: Jeriah the first,ᵃ Amariah the second, Jahaziel the third and Jekameam the fourth.
²⁴The son of Uzziel: Micah;
  from the sons of Micah: Shamir.
  ²⁵The brother of Micah: Isshiah;
    from the sons of Isshiah: Zechariah.
²⁶The sons of Merari: Mahli and Mushi.
  The son of Jaaziah: Beno.
²⁷The sons of Merari:
  from Jaaziah: Beno, Shoham, Zaccur and Ibri.
²⁸From Mahli: Eleazar, who had no sons.
²⁹From Kish: the son of Kish:
  Jerahmeel.
³⁰And the sons of Mushi: Mahli, Eder and Jerimoth.

These were the Levites, according to their families. ³¹They also cast lots, just as their brothers the descendants of Aaron did, in the presence of King David and of Zadok, Ahimelech, and the heads of families of the priests and of the Levites. The families of the oldest brother were treated the same as those of the youngest.

ᵃ 23 Two Hebrew manuscripts and some Septuagint manuscripts (see also 1 Chron. 23:19); most Hebrew manuscripts *The sons of Jeriah:*

The Singers

25 David, together with the commanders of the army, set apart some of the sons of Asaph, Heman and Jeduthun for the ministry of prophesying, accompanied by harps, lyres and cymbals. Here is the list of the men who performed this service:

² From the sons of Asaph:

Zaccur, Joseph, Nethaniah and Asarelah. The sons of Asaph were under the supervision of Asaph, who prophesied under the king's supervision.

³ As for Jeduthun, from his sons:

Gedaliah, Zeri, Jeshaiah, Shimei,ᵃ Hashabiah and Mattithiah, six in all, under the supervision of their father Jeduthun, who prophesied, using the harp in thanking and praising the LORD.

⁴ As for Heman, from his sons:

Bukkiah, Mattaniah, Uzziel, Shubael and Jerimoth; Hananiah, Hanani, Eliathah, Giddalti and Romamti-Ezer; Joshbekashah, Mallothi, Hothir and Mahazioth. ⁵ All these were sons of Heman the king's seer. They were given him through the promises of God to exalt him.ᵇ God gave Heman fourteen sons and three daughters.

⁶ All these men were under the supervision of their fathers for the music of the temple of the LORD, with cymbals, lyres and harps, for the ministry at the house of God. Asaph, Jeduthun and Heman were under the supervision of the king. ⁷ Along with their relatives — all of them trained and skilled in music for the LORD — they numbered 288. ⁸ Young and old alike, teacher as well as student, cast lots for their duties.

⁹ The first lot, which was for Asaph,
  fell to Joseph,
    his sons and relatives,ᶜ   12ᵈ
  the second to Gedaliah,
    he and his relatives and sons,   12
¹⁰ the third to Zaccur,
    his sons and relatives,   12

¹¹ the fourth to Izri,ᵉ
    his sons and relatives,   12
¹² the fifth to Nethaniah,
    his sons and relatives,   12
¹³ the sixth to Bukkiah,
    his sons and relatives,   12
¹⁴ the seventh to Jesarelah,ᶠ
    his sons and relatives,   12
¹⁵ the eighth to Jeshaiah,
    his sons and relatives,   12
¹⁶ the ninth to Mattaniah,
    his sons and relatives,   12
¹⁷ the tenth to Shimei,
    his sons and relatives,   12
¹⁸ the eleventh to Azarel,ᵍ
    his sons and relatives,   12
¹⁹ the twelfth to Hashabiah,
    his sons and relatives,   12
²⁰ the thirteenth to Shubael,
    his sons and relatives,   12
²¹ the fourteenth to Mattithiah,
    his sons and relatives,   12
²² the fifteenth to Jerimoth,
    his sons and relatives,   12
²³ the sixteenth to Hananiah,
    his sons and relatives,   12
²⁴ the seventeenth to Joshbekashah,
    his sons and relatives,   12
²⁵ the eighteenth to Hanani,
    his sons and relatives,   12
²⁶ the nineteenth to Mallothi,
    his sons and relatives,   12
²⁷ the twentieth to Eliathah,
    his sons and relatives,   12
²⁸ the twenty-first to Hothir,
    his sons and relatives,   12
²⁹ the twenty-second to Giddalti,
    his sons and relatives,   12
³⁰ the twenty-third to Mahazioth,
    his sons and relatives,   12

ᵃ 3 One Hebrew manuscript and some Septuagint manuscripts (see also verse 17); most Hebrew manuscripts do not have *Shimei*.   ᵇ 5 Hebrew *exalt the horn*   ᶜ 9 See Septuagint; Hebrew does not have *his sons and relatives*.   ᵈ 9 See the total in verse 7; Hebrew does not have *twelve*.   ᵉ 11 A variant of *Zeri*   ᶠ 14 A variant of *Asarelah*   ᵍ 18 A variant of *Uzziel*

³¹ the twenty-fourth to Romamti-Ezer,
his sons and relatives,   12

The Gatekeepers

26

The divisions of the gatekeepers:

From the Korahites: Meshelemiah son of
Kore, one of the sons of Asaph.
² Meshelemiah had sons:
Zechariah the firstborn,
Jediael the second,
Zebadiah the third,
Jathniel the fourth,
³ Elam the fifth,
Jehohanan the sixth
and Eliehoenai the seventh.
⁴ Obed-Edom also had sons:
Shemaiah the firstborn,
Jehozabad the second,
Joah the third,
Sacar the fourth,
Nethanel the fifth,
⁵ Ammiel the sixth,
Issachar the seventh
and Peullethai the eighth.
(For God had blessed Obed-Edom.)

⁶ His son Shemaiah also had sons, who were
leaders in their father's family because
they were very capable men. ⁷ The sons
of Shemaiah: Othni, Rephael, Obed and
Elzabad; his relatives Elihu and Semaki-
ah were also able men. ⁸ All these were
descendants of Obed-Edom; they and
their sons and their relatives were capable
men with the strength to do the work —
descendants of Obed-Edom, 62 in all.
⁹ Meshelemiah had sons and relatives, who
were able men — 18 in all.

¹⁰ Hosah the Merarite had sons: Shimri the
first (although he was not the firstborn,
his father had appointed him the first),
¹¹ Hilkiah the second, Tabaliah the third
and Zechariah the fourth. The sons and
relatives of Hosah were 13 in all.

¹² These divisions of the gatekeepers, through
their chief men, had duties for ministering in the
temple of the LORD, just as their relatives had.
¹³ Lots were cast for each gate, according to their
families, young and old alike.
¹⁴ The lot for the East Gate fell to Shelemiah.ᵃ
Then lots were cast for his son Zechariah, a wise
counselor, and the lot for the North Gate fell to
him. ¹⁵ The lot for the South Gate fell to Obed-
Edom, and the lot for the storehouse fell to his
sons. ¹⁶ The lots for the West Gate and the Shal-
leketh Gate on the upper road fell to Shuppim
and Hosah.

Guard was alongside of guard: ¹⁷ There were six
Levites a day on the east, four a day on the north,
four a day on the south and two at a time at the
storehouse. ¹⁸ As for the court to the west, there
were four at the road and two at the court itself.
¹⁹ These were the divisions of the gatekeepers
who were descendants of Korah and Merari.

The Treasurers and Other Officials

²⁰ Their fellow Levites wereᵇ in charge of the
treasuries of the house of God and the treasuries
for the dedicated things.
²¹ The descendants of Ladan, who were Gershonites through Ladan and who were heads
of families belonging to Ladan the Gershonite,
were Jehieli, ²² the sons of Jehieli, Zetham and his
brother Joel. They were in charge of the treasuries of the temple of the LORD.
²³ From the Amramites, the Izharites, the Hebronites and the Uzzielites:

²⁴ Shubael, a descendant of Gershom son of
Moses, was the officer in charge of the
treasuries. ²⁵ His relatives through Eliezer:
Rehabiah his son, Jeshaiah his son, Joram
his son, Zicri his son and Shelomith his
son. ²⁶ Shelomith and his relatives were in
charge of all the treasuries for the things
dedicated by King David, by the heads
of families who were the commanders

ᵃ 14 A variant of *Meshelemiah*   ᵇ 20 Septuagint; Hebrew *As for
the Levites, Ahijah was*

of thousands and commanders of hundreds, and by the other army commanders. ²⁷Some of the plunder taken in battle they dedicated for the repair of the temple of the LORD. ²⁸And everything dedicated by Samuel the seer and by Saul son of Kish, Abner son of Ner and Joab son of Zeruiah, and all the other dedicated things were in the care of Shelomith and his relatives.

²⁹From the Izharites: Kenaniah and his sons were assigned duties away from the temple, as officials and judges over Israel.

³⁰From the Hebronites: Hashabiah and his relatives—seventeen hundred able men—were responsible in Israel west of the Jordan for all the work of the LORD and for the king's service. ³¹As for the Hebronites, Jeriah was their chief according to the genealogical records of their families. In the fortieth year of David's reign a search was made in the records, and capable men among the Hebronites were found at Jazer in Gilead. ³²Jeriah had twenty-seven hundred relatives, who were able men and heads of families, and King David put them in charge of the Reubenites, the Gadites and the half-tribe of Manasseh for every matter pertaining to God and for the affairs of the king.

Army Divisions

27 This is the list of the Israelites—heads of families, commanders of thousands and commanders of hundreds, and their officers, who served the king in all that concerned the army divisions that were on duty month by month throughout the year. Each division consisted of 24,000 men.

²In charge of the first division, for the first month, was Jashobeam son of Zabdiel. There were 24,000 men in his division. ³He was a descendant of Perez and chief of all the army officers for the first month.

⁴In charge of the division for the second month was Dodai the Ahohite; Mikloth was the leader of his division. There were 24,000 men in his division.

⁵The third army commander, for the third month, was Benaiah son of Jehoiada the priest. He was chief and there were 24,000 men in his division. ⁶This was the Benaiah who was a mighty man among the Thirty and was over the Thirty. His son Ammizabad was in charge of his division.

⁷The fourth, for the fourth month, was Asahel the brother of Joab; his son Zebadiah was his successor. There were 24,000 men in his division.

⁸The fifth, for the fifth month, was the commander Shamhuth the Izrahite. There were 24,000 men in his division.

⁹The sixth, for the sixth month, was Ira the son of Ikkesh the Tekoite. There were 24,000 men in his division.

¹⁰The seventh, for the seventh month, was Helez the Pelonite, an Ephraimite. There were 24,000 men in his division.

¹¹The eighth, for the eighth month, was Sibbecai the Hushathite, a Zerahite. There were 24,000 men in his division.

¹²The ninth, for the ninth month, was Abiezer the Anathothite, a Benjamite. There were 24,000 men in his division.

¹³The tenth, for the tenth month, was Maharai the Netophathite, a Zerahite. There were 24,000 men in his division.

¹⁴The eleventh, for the eleventh month, was Benaiah the Pirathonite, an Ephraimite. There were 24,000 men in his division.

¹⁵The twelfth, for the twelfth month, was Heldai the Netophathite, from the family of Othniel. There were 24,000 men in his division.

Officers of the Tribes

¹⁶The officers over the tribes of Israel:

over the Reubenites: Eliezer son of Zicri;
over the Simeonites: Shephatiah son of Maacah;

¹⁷over Levi: Hashabiah son of Kemuel;
    over Aaron: Zadok;
¹⁸over Judah: Elihu, a brother of David;
    over Issachar: Omri son of Michael;
¹⁹over Zebulun: Ishmaiah son of Obadiah;
    over Naphtali: Jerimoth son of Azriel;
²⁰over the Ephraimites: Hoshea son of Azaziah;
    over half the tribe of Manasseh: Joel son of Pedaiah;
²¹over the half-tribe of Manasseh in Gilead: Iddo son of Zechariah;
    over Benjamin: Jaasiel son of Abner;
²²over Dan: Azarel son of Jeroham.
These were the officers over the tribes of Israel.

²³David did not take the number of the men twenty years old or less, because the LORD had promised to make Israel as numerous as the stars in the sky. ²⁴Joab son of Zeruiah began to count the men but did not finish. Wrath came on Israel on account of this numbering, and the number was not entered in the book*a* of the annals of King David.

The King's Overseers

²⁵Azmaveth son of Adiel was in charge of the royal storehouses.

Jonathan son of Uzziah was in charge of the storehouses in the outlying districts, in the towns, the villages and the watchtowers.

²⁶Ezri son of Kelub was in charge of the field workers who farmed the land.

²⁷Shimei the Ramathite was in charge of the vineyards.

Zabdi the Shiphmite was in charge of the produce of the vineyards for the wine vats.

²⁸Baal-Hanan the Gederite was in charge of the olive and sycamore-fig trees in the western foothills.

Joash was in charge of the supplies of olive oil.

²⁹Shitrai the Sharonite was in charge of the herds grazing in Sharon.

Shaphat son of Adlai was in charge of the herds in the valleys.

³⁰Obil the Ishmaelite was in charge of the camels.

Jehdeiah the Meronothite was in charge of the donkeys.

³¹Jaziz the Hagrite was in charge of the flocks.

All these were the officials in charge of King David's property.

³²Jonathan, David's uncle, was a counselor, a man of insight and a scribe. Jehiel son of Hacmoni took care of the king's sons.

³³Ahithophel was the king's counselor.

Hushai the Arkite was the king's friend. ³⁴Ahithophel was succeeded by Jehoiada son of Benaiah and by Abiathar.

Joab was the commander of the royal army.

David's Plans for the Temple

28 David summoned all the officials of Israel to assemble at Jerusalem: the officers over the tribes, the commanders of the divisions in the service of the king, the commanders of thousands and commanders of hundreds, and the officials in charge of all the property and livestock belonging to the king and his sons, together with the palace officials, the mighty men and all the brave warriors.

²King David rose to his feet and said: "Listen to me, my brothers and my people. I had it in my heart to build a house as a place of rest for the ark of the covenant of the LORD, for the footstool of our God, and I made plans to build it. ³But God said to me, 'You are not to build a house for my Name, because you are a warrior and have shed blood.'

⁴"Yet the LORD, the God of Israel, chose me from my whole family to be king over Israel forever. He chose Judah as leader, and from the house of Judah he chose my family, and from my father's sons he was pleased to make me king over all Israel. ⁵Of all my sons—and the LORD has given me many—he has chosen my son Solomon to sit on the throne of the kingdom of the LORD over Israel. ⁶He said to me: 'Solomon your son is

a 24 Septuagint; Hebrew number

the one who will build my house and my courts, for I have chosen him to be my son, and I will be his father. [7] I will establish his kingdom forever if he is unswerving in carrying out my commands and laws, as is being done at this time.'

[8] "So now I charge you in the sight of all Israel and of the assembly of the LORD, and in the hearing of our God: Be careful to follow all the commands of the LORD your God, that you may possess this good land and pass it on as an inheritance to your descendants forever.

[9] "And you, my son Solomon, acknowledge the God of your father, and serve him with wholehearted devotion and with a willing mind, for the LORD searches every heart and understands every motive behind the thoughts. If you seek him, he will be found by you; but if you forsake him, he will reject you forever. [10] Consider now, for the LORD has chosen you to build a temple as a sanctuary. Be strong and do the work."

TALKING POINTS

Finding God

If we earnestly seek God,
we will find him.

1 CHRONICLES 28:9

For more on finding God, go to 2 Chronicles 15:1–4.

[11] Then David gave his son Solomon the plans for the portico of the temple, its buildings, its storerooms, its upper parts, its inner rooms and the place of atonement. [12] He gave him the plans of all that the Spirit had put in his mind for the courts of the temple of the LORD and all the surrounding rooms, for the treasuries of the temple of God and for the treasuries for the dedicated things. [13] He gave him instructions for the divisions of the priests and Levites, and for all the work of serving in the temple of the LORD, as well as for all the articles to be used in its service. [14] He designated the weight of gold for all the gold articles to be used in various kinds of service, and the weight of silver for all the silver articles to be used in various kinds of service: [15] the weight of gold for the gold lampstands and their lamps, with the weight for each lampstand and its lamps; and the weight of silver for each silver lampstand and its lamps, according to the use of each lampstand; [16] the weight of gold for each table for consecrated bread; the weight of silver for the silver tables; [17] the weight of pure gold for the forks, sprinkling bowls and pitchers; the weight of gold for each gold dish; the weight of silver for each silver dish; [18] and the weight of the refined gold for the altar of incense. He also gave him the plan for the chariot, that is, the cherubim of gold that spread their wings and shelter the ark of the covenant of the LORD.

[19] "All this," David said, "I have in writing from the hand of the LORD upon me, and he gave me understanding in all the details of the plan."

[20] David also said to Solomon his son, "Be strong and courageous, and do the work. Do not be afraid or discouraged, for the LORD God, my God, is with you. He will not fail you or forsake you until all the work for the service of the temple of the LORD is finished. [21] The divisions of the priests and Levites are ready for all the work on the temple of God, and every willing man skilled in any craft will help you in all the work. The officials and all the people will obey your every command."

Gifts for Building the Temple

29 Then King David said to the whole assembly: "My son Solomon, the one whom God has chosen, is young and inexperienced. The task is great, because this palatial structure is not for man but for the LORD God. [2] With all my resources I have provided for the temple of my God — gold for the gold work, silver for the silver, bronze for the bronze, iron for the iron and wood for the wood, as well as onyx for the settings, turquoise,[a] stones of various colors, and

---

[a] 2 The meaning of the Hebrew for this word is uncertain.

all kinds of fine stone and marble—all of these in large quantities. ³Besides, in my devotion to the temple of my God I now give my personal treasures of gold and silver for the temple of my God, over and above everything I have provided for this holy temple: ⁴three thousand talents *a* of gold (gold of Ophir) and seven thousand talents *b* of refined silver, for the overlaying of the walls of the buildings, ⁵for the gold work and the silver work, and for all the work to be done by the craftsmen. Now, who is willing to consecrate himself today to the LORD?"

⁶Then the leaders of families, the officers of the tribes of Israel, the commanders of thousands and commanders of hundreds, and the officials in charge of the king's work gave willingly. ⁷They gave toward the work on the temple of God five thousand talents *c* and ten thousand darics *d* of gold, ten thousand talents *e* of silver, eighteen thousand talents *f* of bronze and a hundred thousand talents *g* of iron. ⁸Any who had precious stones gave them to the treasury of the temple of the LORD in the custody of Jehiel the Gershonite. ⁹The people rejoiced at the willing response of their leaders, for they had given freely and wholeheartedly to the LORD. David the king also rejoiced greatly.

David's Prayer

¹⁰David praised the LORD in the presence of the whole assembly, saying,

"Praise be to you, O LORD,
    God of our father Israel,
    from everlasting to everlasting.
¹¹Yours, O LORD, is the greatness and the
        power
    and the glory and the majesty and the
        splendor,
    for everything in heaven and earth is
        yours.
Yours, O LORD, is the kingdom;
    you are exalted as head over all.
¹²Wealth and honor come from you;
    you are the ruler of all things.

In your hands are strength and power
    to exalt and give strength to all.
¹³Now, our God, we give you thanks,
    and praise your glorious name.

¹⁴"But who am I, and who are my people, that we should be able to give as generously as this? Everything comes from you, and we have given you only what comes from your hand. ¹⁵We are

TALKING POINTS

Money
God is the source of wealth.
1 CHRONICLES 29:12–14
For more on money, go to Ecclesiastes 5:19.

aliens and strangers in your sight, as were all our forefathers. Our days on earth are like a shadow, without hope. ¹⁶O LORD our God, as for all this abundance that we have provided for building you a temple for your Holy Name, it comes from your hand, and all of it belongs to you. ¹⁷I know, my God, that you test the heart and are pleased with integrity. All these things have I given willingly and with honest intent. And now I have seen with joy how willingly your people who are here have given to you. ¹⁸O LORD, God of our fathers Abraham, Isaac and Israel, keep this desire in the hearts of your people forever, and keep their hearts loyal to you. ¹⁹And give my son Solomon the wholehearted devotion to keep your commands, requirements and decrees and to do everything to build the palatial structure for which I have provided."

²⁰Then David said to the whole assembly,

---

a 4 That is, about 110 tons (about 100 metric tons)   *b 4* That is, about 260 tons (about 240 metric tons)   *c 7* That is, about 190 tons (about 170 metric tons)   *d 7* That is, about 185 pounds (about 84 kilograms)   *e 7* That is, about 375 tons (about 345 metric tons)   *f 7* That is, about 675 tons (about 610 metric tons)   *g 7* That is, about 3,750 tons (about 3,450 metric tons)

"Praise the LORD your God." So they all praised the LORD, the God of their fathers; they bowed low and fell prostrate before the LORD and the king.

Solomon Acknowledged as King

29:21–25pp — 1Ki 1:28–53

²¹The next day they made sacrifices to the LORD and presented burnt offerings to him: a thousand bulls, a thousand rams and a thousand male lambs, together with their drink offerings, and other sacrifices in abundance for all Israel. ²²They ate and drank with great joy in the presence of the LORD that day.

Then they acknowledged Solomon son of David as king a second time, anointing him before the LORD to be ruler and Zadok to be priest. ²³So Solomon sat on the throne of the LORD as king in place of his father David. He prospered and all Israel obeyed him. ²⁴All the officers and mighty men, as well as all of King David's sons, pledged their submission to King Solomon.

²⁵The LORD highly exalted Solomon in the sight of all Israel and bestowed on him royal splendor such as no king over Israel ever had before.

The Death of David

29:26–28pp — 1Ki 2:10–12

²⁶David son of Jesse was king over all Israel. ²⁷He ruled over Israel forty years—seven in Hebron and thirty-three in Jerusalem. ²⁸He died at a good old age, having enjoyed long life, wealth and honor. His son Solomon succeeded him as king.

²⁹As for the events of King David's reign, from beginning to end, they are written in the records of Samuel the seer, the records of Nathan the prophet and the records of Gad the seer, ³⁰together with the details of his reign and power, and the circumstances that surrounded him and Israel and the kingdoms of all the other lands.

God's LOVE ENDURES

When 1 and 2 Chronicles (originally one book) were written, a very dark period of history had finally ended for the Israelites. Some seeds of faith had remained through their long years in exile, and now the faithful had returned to their land. God had kept his promise. The promise he had made to Abraham and Isaac, to David, to Solomon and to his people — that they would possess the land promised to them — had been fulfilled. Though they had been separated from their country during the years of punishment, God's people were now restored.

Israel's history was integral to its future survival; it was critical to retell the stories of both prosperity and decline in order for the people to learn from the past, so they would not repeat the same mistakes. But it was also a time to begin again and to look to the future. After enduring 70 years of captivity, God's people were given a fresh start. Renewing a God-focus in their lives would not be easy, but they were determined to reestablish true worship and move forward.

From a broad perspective, 2 Chronicles is a book of hope. We are reassured that God's plans will come to pass. Even though wars rage and nations rise and fall, God's promises will prevail, and his love will always endure.

VERSE *to* REMEMBER | 2 CHRONICLES 6:14 – 15

[Solomon] said: "O LORD, God of Israel, there is no God like you in heaven or on earth — you who keep your covenant of love with your servants who continue wholeheartedly in your way. You have kept your promise to your servant David my father; with your mouth you have promised and with your hand you have fulfilled it — as it is today."

ABOUT 2 CHRONICLES

WRITTEN BY:
Unknown, possibly Ezra

WRITTEN FOR:
The people of Judah who had returned from exile in Babylon

DATE WRITTEN:
Between 450 and 400 B.C.

WHY WRITTEN:
To encourage the Jews to review the spiritual lessons of their history

Solomon Asks for Wisdom

1:2–13pp — 1Ki 3:4–15
1:14–17pp — 1Ki 10:26–29; 2Ch 9:25–28

1 Solomon son of David established himself firmly over his kingdom, for the Lord his God was with him and made him exceedingly great.

²Then Solomon spoke to all Israel—to the commanders of thousands and commanders of hundreds, to the judges and to all the leaders in Israel, the heads of families— ³and Solomon and the whole assembly went to the high place at Gibeon, for God's Tent of Meeting was there, which Moses the Lord's servant had made in the desert. ⁴Now David had brought up the ark of God from Kiriath Jearim to the place he had prepared for it, because he had pitched a tent for it in Jerusalem. ⁵But the bronze altar that Bezalel son of Uri, the son of Hur, had made was in Gibeon in front of the tabernacle of the Lord; so Solomon and the assembly inquired of him there. ⁶Solomon went up to the bronze altar before the Lord in the Tent of Meeting and offered a thousand burnt offerings on it.

⁷That night God appeared to Solomon and said to him, "Ask for whatever you want me to give you."

⁸Solomon answered God, "You have shown great kindness to David my father and have made me king in his place. ⁹Now, Lord God, let your promise to my father David be confirmed, for you have made me king over a people who are as numerous as the dust of the earth. ¹⁰Give me wisdom and knowledge, that I may lead this people, for who is able to govern this great people of yours?"

¹¹God said to Solomon, "Since this is your heart's desire and you have not asked for wealth, riches or honor, nor for the death of your enemies, and since you have not asked for a long life but for wisdom and knowledge to govern my people over whom I have made you king, ¹²therefore wisdom and knowledge will be given you. And I will also give you wealth, riches and honor, such as no king who was before you ever had and none after you will have."

¹³Then Solomon went to Jerusalem from the high place at Gibeon, from before the Tent of Meeting. And he reigned over Israel.

¹⁴Solomon accumulated chariots and horses; he had fourteen hundred chariots and twelve thousand horses,ᵃ which he kept in the chariot cities and also with him in Jerusalem. ¹⁵The king made silver and gold as common in Jerusalem as stones, and cedar as plentiful as sycamore-fig trees in the foothills. ¹⁶Solomon's horses were imported from Egyptᵇ and from Kueᶜ—the royal merchants purchased them from Kue. ¹⁷They imported a chariot from Egypt for six hundred shekelsᵈ of silver, and a horse for a hundred and fifty.ᵉ They also exported them to all the kings of the Hittites and of the Arameans.

Preparations for Building the Temple

2:1–18pp — 1Ki 5:1–16

2 Solomon gave orders to build a temple for the Name of the Lord and a royal palace for himself. ²He conscripted seventy thousand men as carriers and eighty thousand as stonecutters in the hills and thirty-six hundred as foremen over them.

³Solomon sent this message to Hiramᶠ king of Tyre:

"Send me cedar logs as you did for my father David when you sent him cedar to build a palace to live in. ⁴Now I am about to build a temple for the Name of the Lord my God and to dedicate it to him for burning fragrant incense before him, for setting out the consecrated bread regularly, and for making burnt offerings every morning and evening and on Sabbaths and New Moons and at the appointed feasts of the Lord our God. This is a lasting ordinance for Israel.

⁵"The temple I am going to build will be great, because our God is greater than all other gods. ⁶But who is able to build a

---

ᵃ 14 Or *charioteers*   ᵇ 16 Or possibly *Muzur*, a region in Cilicia; also in verse 17   ᶜ 16 Probably Cilicia   ᵈ 17 That is, about 15 pounds (about 7 kilograms)   ᵉ 17 That is, about 3 3/4 pounds (about 1.7 kilograms)   ᶠ 3 Hebrew *Huram*, a variant of *Hiram*; also in verses 11 and 12 temple for him, since the heavens, even the highest heavens, cannot contain him? Who then am I to build a temple for him, except as a place to burn sacrifices before him?

⁷"Send me, therefore, a man skilled to work in gold and silver, bronze and iron, and in purple, crimson and blue yarn, and experienced in the art of engraving, to work in Judah and Jerusalem with my skilled craftsmen, whom my father David provided.

⁸"Send me also cedar, pine and algum *a* logs from Lebanon, for I know that your men are skilled in cutting timber there. My men will work with yours ⁹to provide me with plenty of lumber, because the temple I build must be large and magnificent. ¹⁰I will give your servants, the woodsmen who cut the timber, twenty thousand cors *b* of ground wheat, twenty thousand cors of barley, twenty thousand baths *c* of wine and twenty thousand baths of olive oil."

¹¹Hiram king of Tyre replied by letter to Solomon:

"Because the LORD loves his people, he has made you their king."

¹²And Hiram added:

"Praise be to the LORD, the God of Israel, who made heaven and earth! He has given King David a wise son, endowed with intelligence and discernment, who will build a temple for the LORD and a palace for himself.

¹³"I am sending you Huram-Abi, a man of great skill, ¹⁴whose mother was from Dan and whose father was from Tyre. He is trained to work in gold and silver, bronze and iron, stone and wood, and with purple and blue and crimson yarn and fine linen. He is experienced in all kinds of engraving and can execute any design given to him. He will work with your craftsmen and with those of my lord, David your father.

¹⁵"Now let my lord send his servants the wheat and barley and the olive oil and wine he promised, ¹⁶and we will cut all the logs from Lebanon that you need and will float them in rafts by sea down to Joppa. You can then take them up to Jerusalem."

¹⁷Solomon took a census of all the aliens who were in Israel, after the census his father David had taken; and they were found to be 153,600. ¹⁸He assigned 70,000 of them to be carriers and 80,000 to be stonecutters in the hills, with 3,600 foremen over them to keep the people working.

Solomon Builds the Temple

3:1–14pp — 1Ki 6:1–29

3 Then Solomon began to build the temple of the LORD in Jerusalem on Mount Moriah, where the LORD had appeared to his father David. It was on the threshing floor of Araunah *d* the Jebusite, the place provided by David. ²He began building on the second day of the second month in the fourth year of his reign.

³The foundation Solomon laid for building the temple of God was sixty cubits long and twenty cubits wide *e* (using the cubit of the old standard). ⁴The portico at the front of the temple was twenty cubits *f* long across the width of the building and twenty cubits *g* high.

He overlaid the inside with pure gold. ⁵He paneled the main hall with pine and covered it with fine gold and decorated it with palm tree and chain designs. ⁶He adorned the temple with precious stones. And the gold he used was gold of Parvaim. ⁷He overlaid the ceiling beams, doorframes, walls and doors of the temple with gold, and he carved cherubim on the walls.

⁸He built the Most Holy Place, its length corresponding to the width of the temple—twenty cubits long and twenty cubits wide. He overlaid the inside with six hundred talents *h* of fine gold.

---

a 8 Probably a variant of *almug*; possibly juniper   *b 10* That is, probably about 125,000 bushels (about 4,400 kiloliters)   *c 10* That is, probably about 115,000 gallons (about 440 kiloliters)   *d 1* Hebrew *Ornan*, a variant of *Araunah*   *e 3* That is, about 90 feet (about 27 meters) long and 30 feet (about 9 meters) wide   *f 4* That is, about 30 feet (about 9 meters); also in verses 8, 11 and 13   *g 4* Some Septuagint and Syriac manuscripts; Hebrew *and a hundred and twenty*   *h 8* That is, about 23 tons (about 21 metric tons)

⁹The gold nails weighed fifty shekels.ᵃ He also overlaid the upper parts with gold.

¹⁰In the Most Holy Place he made a pair of sculptured cherubim and overlaid them with gold. ¹¹The total wingspan of the cherubim was twenty cubits. One wing of the first cherub was five cubitsᵇ long and touched the temple wall, while its other wing, also five cubits long, touched the wing of the other cherub. ¹²Similarly one wing of the second cherub was five cubits long and touched the other temple wall, and its other wing, also five cubits long, touched the wing of the first cherub. ¹³The wings of these cherubim extended twenty cubits. They stood on their feet, facing the main hall.ᶜ

¹⁴He made the curtain of blue, purple and crimson yarn and fine linen, with cherubim worked into it.

¹⁵In the front of the temple he made two pillars, which ⌊together⌋ were thirty-five cubitsᵈ long, each with a capital on top measuring five cubits. ¹⁶He made interwoven chainsᵉ and put them on top of the pillars. He also made a hundred pomegranates and attached them to the chains. ¹⁷He erected the pillars in the front of the temple, one to the south and one to the north. The one to the south he named Jakinᶠ and the one to the north Boaz.ᵍ

The Temple's Furnishings

4:2–6,10–5:1pp — 1Ki 7:23–26,38–51

4 He made a bronze altar twenty cubits long, twenty cubits wide and ten cubits high.ʰ ²He made the Sea of cast metal, circular in shape, measuring ten cubits from rim to rim and five cubitsⁱ high. It took a line of thirty cubitsʲ to measure around it. ³Below the rim, figures of bulls encircled it—ten to a cubit.ᵏ The bulls were cast in two rows in one piece with the Sea.

⁴The Sea stood on twelve bulls, three facing north, three facing west, three facing south and three facing east. The Sea rested on top of them, and their hindquarters were toward the center. ⁵It was a handbreadthˡ in thickness, and its rim was like the rim of a cup, like a lily blossom. It held three thousand baths.ᵐ

⁶He then made ten basins for washing and placed five on the south side and five on the north. In them the things to be used for the burnt offerings were rinsed, but the Sea was to be used by the priests for washing.

⁷He made ten gold lampstands according to the specifications for them and placed them in the temple, five on the south side and five on the north.

⁸He made ten tables and placed them in the temple, five on the south side and five on the north. He also made a hundred gold sprinkling bowls.

⁹He made the courtyard of the priests, and the large court and the doors for the court, and overlaid the doors with bronze. ¹⁰He placed the Sea on the south side, at the southeast corner.

¹¹He also made the pots and shovels and sprinkling bowls.

So Huram finished the work he had undertaken for King Solomon in the temple of God:

¹²the two pillars;

the two bowl-shaped capitals on top of the pillars;

the two sets of network decorating the two bowl-shaped capitals on top of the pillars;

¹³the four hundred pomegranates for the two sets of network (two rows of pomegranates for each network, decorating the bowl-shaped capitals on top of the pillars);

¹⁴the stands with their basins;

¹⁵the Sea and the twelve bulls under it;

¹⁶the pots, shovels, meat forks and all related articles.

ᵃ 9 That is, about 1 1/4 pounds (about 0.6 kilogram)   ᵇ 11 That is, about 7 1/2 feet (about 2.3 meters); also in verse 15   ᶜ 13 Or *facing inward*   ᵈ 15 That is, about 52 feet (about 16 meters)   ᵉ 16 Or possibly *made chains in the inner sanctuary*; the meaning of the Hebrew for this phrase is uncertain.   ᶠ 17 *Jakin* probably means *he establishes.*   ᵍ 17 *Boaz* probably means *in him is strength.*   ʰ 1 That is, about 30 feet (about 9 meters) long and wide, and about 15 feet (about 4.5 meters) high   ⁱ 2 That is, about 7 1/2 feet (about 2.3 meters)   ʲ 2 That is, about 45 feet (about 13.5 meters)   ᵏ 3 That is, about 1 1/2 feet (about 0.5 meter)   ˡ 5 That is, about 3 inches (about 8 centimeters)   ᵐ 5 That is, about 17,500 gallons (about 66 kiloliters)

All the objects that Huram-Abi made for King Solomon for the temple of the LORD were of polished bronze. [17] The king had them cast in clay molds in the plain of the Jordan between Succoth and Zarethan.[a] [18] All these things that Solomon made amounted to so much that the weight of the bronze was not determined.

[19] Solomon also made all the furnishings that were in God's temple:

the golden altar;
the tables on which was the bread of the Presence;
[20] the lampstands of pure gold with their lamps, to burn in front of the inner sanctuary as prescribed;
[21] the gold floral work and lamps and tongs (they were solid gold);
[22] the pure gold wick trimmers, sprinkling bowls, dishes and censers; and the gold doors of the temple: the inner doors to the Most Holy Place and the doors of the main hall.

5 When all the work Solomon had done for the temple of the LORD was finished, he brought in the things his father David had dedicated — the silver and gold and all the furnishings — and he placed them in the treasuries of God's temple.

The Ark Brought to the Temple
5:2–6:11pp — 1Ki 8:1–21

[2] Then Solomon summoned to Jerusalem the elders of Israel, all the heads of the tribes and the chiefs of the Israelite families, to bring up the ark of the LORD's covenant from Zion, the City of David. [3] And all the men of Israel came together to the king at the time of the festival in the seventh month.

[4] When all the elders of Israel had arrived, the Levites took up the ark, [5] and they brought up the ark and the Tent of Meeting and all the sacred furnishings in it. The priests, who were Levites, carried them up; [6] and King Solomon and the entire assembly of Israel that had gathered about him were before the ark, sacrificing so many sheep and cattle that they could not be recorded or counted.

[7] The priests then brought the ark of the LORD's covenant to its place in the inner sanctuary of the temple, the Most Holy Place, and put it beneath the wings of the cherubim. [8] The cherubim spread their wings over the place of the ark and covered the ark and its carrying poles. [9] These poles were so long that their ends, extending from the ark, could be seen from in front of the inner sanctuary, but not from outside the Holy Place; and they are still there today. [10] There was nothing in the ark except the two tablets that Moses had placed in it at Horeb, where the LORD made a covenant with the Israelites after they came out of Egypt.

[11] The priests then withdrew from the Holy Place. All the priests who were there had consecrated themselves, regardless of their divisions. [12] All the Levites who were musicians — Asaph, Heman, Jeduthun and their sons and relatives — stood on the east side of the altar, dressed in fine linen and playing cymbals, harps and lyres. They were accompanied by 120 priests sounding trumpets. [13] The trumpeters and singers joined in unison, as with one voice, to give praise and thanks to the LORD. Accompanied by trumpets, cymbals and other instruments, they raised their voices in praise to the LORD and sang:

"He is good;
his love endures forever."

Then the temple of the LORD was filled with a cloud, [14] and the priests could not perform their service because of the cloud, for the glory of the LORD filled the temple of God.

6 Then Solomon said, "The LORD has said that he would dwell in a dark cloud; [2] I have built a magnificent temple for you, a place for you to dwell forever."

[3] While the whole assembly of Israel was standing there, the king turned around and blessed them. [4] Then he said:

---

[a] 17 Hebrew *Zeredatha*, a variant of *Zarethan*

"Praise be to the LORD, the God of Israel, who with his hands has fulfilled what he promised with his mouth to my father David. For he said, [5]'Since the day I brought my people out of Egypt, I have not chosen a city in any tribe of Israel to have a temple built for my Name to be there, nor have I chosen anyone to be the leader over my people Israel. [6]But now I have chosen Jerusalem for my Name to be there, and I have chosen David to rule my people Israel.'

[7]"My father David had it in his heart to build a temple for the Name of the LORD, the God of Israel. [8]But the LORD said to my father David, 'Because it was in your heart to build a temple for my Name, you did well to have this in your heart. [9]Nevertheless, you are not the one to build the temple, but your son, who is your own flesh and blood—he is the one who will build the temple for my Name.'

[10]"The LORD has kept the promise he made. I have succeeded David my father and now I sit on the throne of Israel, just as the LORD promised, and I have built the temple for the Name of the LORD, the God of Israel. [11]There I have placed the ark, in which is the covenant of the LORD that he made with the people of Israel."

Solomon's Prayer of Dedication

6:12–40pp — 1Ki 8:22–53
6:41–42pp — Ps 132:8–10

[12]Then Solomon stood before the altar of the LORD in front of the whole assembly of Israel and spread out his hands. [13]Now he had made a bronze platform, five cubits[a] long, five cubits wide and three cubits[b] high, and had placed it in the center of the outer court. He stood on the platform and then knelt down before the whole assembly of Israel and spread out his hands toward heaven. [14]He said:

"O LORD, God of Israel, there is no God like you in heaven or on earth—you who keep your covenant of love with your servants who continue wholeheartedly in your way. [15]You have kept your promise to your servant David my father; with your mouth you have promised and with your hand you have fulfilled it—as it is today.

[16]"Now LORD, God of Israel, keep for your servant David my father the promises you made to him when you said, 'You shall never fail to have a man to sit before me on the throne of Israel, if only your sons are careful in all they do to walk before me according to my law, as you have done.' [17]And now, O LORD, God of Israel, let your word that you promised your servant David come true.

[18]"But will God really dwell on earth with men? The heavens, even the highest heavens, cannot contain you. How much less this temple I have built! [19]Yet give attention to your servant's prayer and his plea for mercy, O LORD my God. Hear the cry and the prayer that your servant is praying in your presence. [20]May your eyes be open toward this temple day and night, this place of which you said you would put your Name there. May you hear the prayer your servant prays toward this place. [21]Hear the supplications of your servant and of your people Israel when they pray toward this place. Hear from heaven, your dwelling place; and when you hear, forgive.

[22]"When a man wrongs his neighbor and is required to take an oath and he comes and swears the oath before your altar in this temple, [23]then hear from heaven and act. Judge between your servants, repaying the guilty by bringing down on his own head what he has done. Declare the innocent not guilty and so establish his innocence.

[24]"When your people Israel have been defeated by an enemy because they have sinned against you and when they turn back and confess your name, praying and making

---

[a] 13 That is, about 7 1/2 feet (about 2.3 meters)   [b] 13 That is, about 4 1/2 feet (about 1.3 meters)

supplication before you in this temple, [25] then hear from heaven and forgive the sin of your people Israel and bring them back to the land you gave to them and their fathers.

[26] "When the heavens are shut up and there is no rain because your people have sinned against you, and when they pray toward this place and confess your name and turn from their sin because you have afflicted them, [27] then hear from heaven and forgive the sin of your servants, your people Israel. Teach them the right way to live, and send rain on the land you gave your people for an inheritance.

[28] "When famine or plague comes to the land, or blight or mildew, locusts or grasshoppers, or when enemies besiege them in any of their cities, whatever disaster or disease may come, [29] and when a prayer or plea is made by any of your people Israel — each one aware of his afflictions and pains, and spreading out his hands toward this temple — [30] then hear from heaven, your dwelling place. Forgive, and deal with each man according to all he does, since you know his heart (for you alone know the hearts of men), [31] so that they will fear you and walk in your ways all the time they live in the land you gave our fathers.

[32] "As for the foreigner who does not belong to your people Israel but has come from a distant land because of your great name and your mighty hand and your outstretched arm — when he comes and prays toward this temple, [33] then hear from heaven, your dwelling place, and do whatever the foreigner asks of you, so that all the peoples of the earth may know your name and fear you, as do your own people Israel, and may know that this house I have built bears your Name.

[34] "When your people go to war against their enemies, wherever you send them, and when they pray to you toward this city you have chosen and the temple I have built for your Name, [35] then hear from heaven their prayer and their plea, and uphold their cause.

[36] "When they sin against you — for there is no one who does not sin — and you become angry with them and give them over to the enemy, who takes them captive to a land far away or near; [37] and if they have a change of heart in the land where they are held captive, and repent and plead with you in the land of their captivity and say, 'We have sinned, we have done wrong and acted wickedly'; [38] and if they turn back to you with all their heart and soul in the land of their captivity where they were taken, and pray toward the land you gave their fathers, toward the city you have chosen and toward the temple I have built for your Name; [39] then from heaven, your dwelling place, hear their prayer and their pleas, and uphold their cause. And forgive your people, who have sinned against you.

[40] "Now, my God, may your eyes be open and your ears attentive to the prayers offered in this place.

[41] "Now arise, O LORD God, and come to
　　your resting place,
　you and the ark of your might.
May your priests, O LORD God, be
　　clothed with salvation,
　may your saints rejoice in your
　　goodness.

⁴²O Lᴏʀᴅ God, do not reject your
    anointed one.
Remember the great love promised to
    David your servant."

The Dedication of the Temple
7:1–10pp — 1Ki 8:62–66

7 When Solomon finished praying, fire came down from heaven and consumed the burnt offering and the sacrifices, and the glory of the Lᴏʀᴅ filled the temple. ²The priests could not enter the temple of the Lᴏʀᴅ because the glory of the Lᴏʀᴅ filled it. ³When all the Israelites saw the fire coming down and the glory of the Lᴏʀᴅ above the temple, they knelt on the pavement with their faces to the ground, and they worshiped and gave thanks to the Lᴏʀᴅ, saying,

"He is good;
    his love endures forever."

⁴Then the king and all the people offered sacrifices before the Lᴏʀᴅ. ⁵And King Solomon offered a sacrifice of twenty-two thousand head of cattle and a hundred and twenty thousand sheep and goats. So the king and all the people dedicated the temple of God. ⁶The priests took their positions, as did the Levites with the Lᴏʀᴅ's musical instruments, which King David had made for praising the Lᴏʀᴅ and which were used when he gave thanks, saying, "His love endures forever." Opposite the Levites, the priests blew their trumpets, and all the Israelites were standing.

⁷Solomon consecrated the middle part of the courtyard in front of the temple of the Lᴏʀᴅ, and there he offered burnt offerings and the fat of the fellowship offerings,ᵃ because the bronze altar he had made could not hold the burnt offerings, the grain offerings and the fat portions.

⁸So Solomon observed the festival at that time for seven days, and all Israel with him—a vast assembly, people from Lebo ᵇ Hamath to the Wadi of Egypt. ⁹On the eighth day they held an assembly, for they had celebrated the dedication of the altar for seven days and the festival for seven days more. ¹⁰On the twenty-third day of the seventh month

he sent the people to their homes, joyful and glad in heart for the good things the Lᴏʀᴅ had done for David and Solomon and for his people Israel.

The Lᴏʀᴅ Appears to Solomon
7:11–22pp — 1Ki 9:1–9

¹¹When Solomon had finished the temple of the Lᴏʀᴅ and the royal palace, and had succeeded in carrying out all he had in mind to do in the temple of the Lᴏʀᴅ and in his own palace, ¹²the Lᴏʀᴅ appeared to him at night and said:

"I have heard your prayer and have chosen this place for myself as a temple for sacrifices.

¹³"When I shut up the heavens so that there is no rain, or command locusts to devour the land or send a plague among my people, ¹⁴if my people, who are called by my name, will humble themselves and pray and seek my face and turn from their wicked ways, then will I hear from heaven and will forgive their sin and will heal their land.

TALKING POINTS

Forgiveness
God longs to forgive and
heal his people.
2 CHRONICLES 7:13–14

For more on forgiveness, go to Psalm 130:3–4.

¹⁵Now my eyes will be open and my ears attentive to the prayers offered in this place. ¹⁶I have chosen and consecrated this temple so that my Name may be there forever. My eyes and my heart will always be there. ¹⁷"As for you, if you walk before me as David your father did, and do all I command,

ᵃ 7 Traditionally *peace offerings*   ᵇ 8 Or *from the entrance to* and observe my decrees and laws, [18] I will establish your royal throne, as I covenanted with David your father when I said, 'You shall never fail to have a man to rule over Israel.'

[19] "But if you[a] turn away and forsake the decrees and commands I have given you[a] and go off to serve other gods and worship them, [20] then I will uproot Israel from my land, which I have given them, and will reject this temple I have consecrated for my Name. I will make it a byword and an object of ridicule among all peoples. [21] And though this temple is now so imposing, all who pass by will be appalled and say, 'Why has the LORD done such a thing to this land and to this temple?' [22] People will answer, 'Because they have forsaken the LORD, the God of their fathers, who brought them out of Egypt, and have embraced other gods, worshiping and serving them — that is why he brought all this disaster on them.' "

Solomon's Other Activities

8:1–18pp — 1Ki 9:10–28

8 At the end of twenty years, during which Solomon built the temple of the LORD and his own palace, [2] Solomon rebuilt the villages that Hiram[b] had given him, and settled Israelites in them. [3] Solomon then went to Hamath Zobah and captured it. [4] He also built up Tadmor in the desert and all the store cities he had built in Hamath. [5] He rebuilt Upper Beth Horon and Lower Beth Horon as fortified cities, with walls and with gates and bars, [6] as well as Baalath and all his store cities, and all the cities for his chariots and for his horses[c] — whatever he desired to build in Jerusalem, in Lebanon and throughout all the territory he ruled.

[7] All the people left from the Hittites, Amorites, Perizzites, Hivites and Jebusites (these peoples were not Israelites), [8] that is, their descendants remaining in the land, whom the Israelites had not destroyed — these Solomon conscripted for his slave labor force, as it is to this day. [9] But Solomon did not make slaves of the Israelites for his work; they were his fighting men, commanders of his captains, and commanders of his chariots and charioteers. [10] They were also King Solomon's chief officials — two hundred and fifty officials supervising the men.

[11] Solomon brought Pharaoh's daughter up from the City of David to the palace he had built for her, for he said, "My wife must not live in the palace of David king of Israel, because the places the ark of the LORD has entered are holy."

[12] On the altar of the LORD that he had built

stories to share

2 CHRONICLES 7:1–22

The Dedication of the Temple

LIFE LESSON: God's glory is awesome.

TO TALK ABOUT

✦ Why couldn't the priests enter the temple? What was it full of?

✦ Today, God's temples are walking and breathing. Who are they? (Hint: Read 1 Corinthians 6:19.)

✦ How do people today see God's glory?

✦ How big a responsibility is it to be God's temple? What does God expect of his temples? (Hint: Read 1 Corinthians 6:20.)

---

[a] 19 The Hebrew is plural.   [b] 2 Hebrew *Huram*, a variant of *Hiram*; also in verse 18   [c] 6 Or *charioteers*

in front of the portico, Solomon sacrificed burnt offerings to the LORD, [13] according to the daily requirement for offerings commanded by Moses for Sabbaths, New Moons and the three annual feasts — the Feast of Unleavened Bread, the Feast of Weeks and the Feast of Tabernacles. [14] In keeping with the ordinance of his father David, he appointed the divisions of the priests for their duties, and the Levites to lead the praise and to assist the priests according to each day's requirement. He also appointed the gatekeepers by divisions for the various gates, because this was what David the man of God had ordered. [15] They did not deviate from the king's commands to the priests or to the Levites in any matter, including that of the treasuries.

[16] All Solomon's work was carried out, from the day the foundation of the temple of the LORD was laid until its completion. So the temple of the LORD was finished.

[17] Then Solomon went to Ezion Geber and Elath on the coast of Edom. [18] And Hiram sent him ships commanded by his own officers, men who knew the sea. These, with Solomon's men, sailed to Ophir and brought back four hundred and fifty talents[a] of gold, which they delivered to King Solomon.

The Queen of Sheba Visits Solomon
9:1–12pp — 1Ki 10:1–13

9 When the queen of Sheba heard of Solomon's fame, she came to Jerusalem to test him with hard questions. Arriving with a very great caravan — with camels carrying spices, large quantities of gold, and precious stones — she came to Solomon and talked with him about all she had on her mind. [2] Solomon answered all her questions; nothing was too hard for him to explain to her. [3] When the queen of Sheba saw the wisdom of Solomon, as well as the palace he had built, [4] the food on his table, the seating of his officials, the attending servants in their robes, the cupbearers in their robes and the burnt offerings he made at[b] the temple of the LORD, she was overwhelmed.

[5] She said to the king, "The report I heard in my own country about your achievements and your wisdom is true. [6] But I did not believe what they said until I came and saw with my own eyes. Indeed, not even half the greatness of your wisdom was told me; you have far exceeded the report I heard. [7] How happy your men must be! How happy your officials, who continually stand before you and hear your wisdom! [8] Praise be to the LORD your God, who has delighted in you and placed you on his throne as king to rule for the LORD your God. Because of the love of your God for Israel and his desire to uphold them forever, he has made you king over them, to maintain justice and righteousness."

[9] Then she gave the king 120 talents[c] of gold, large quantities of spices, and precious stones. There had never been such spices as those the queen of Sheba gave to King Solomon.

[10] (The men of Hiram and the men of Solomon brought gold from Ophir; they also brought algumwood[d] and precious stones. [11] The king used the algumwood to make steps for the temple of the LORD and for the royal palace, and to make harps and lyres for the musicians. Nothing like them had ever been seen in Judah.)

[12] King Solomon gave the queen of Sheba all she desired and asked for; he gave her more than she had brought to him. Then she left and returned with her retinue to her own country.

Solomon's Splendor
9:13–28pp — 1Ki 10:14–29; 2Ch 1:14–17

[13] The weight of the gold that Solomon received yearly was 666 talents,[e] [14] not including the revenues brought in by merchants and traders. Also all the kings of Arabia and the governors of the land brought gold and silver to Solomon.

[15] King Solomon made two hundred large shields of hammered gold; six hundred bekas[f] of hammered gold went into each shield. [16] He also made three hundred small shields of hammered

---

[a] 18 That is, about 17 tons (about 16 metric tons) [b] 4 Or *the ascent by which he went up to* [c] 9 That is, about 4 1/2 tons (about 4 metric tons) [d] 10 Probably a variant of *almugwood* [e] 13 That is, about 25 tons (about 23 metric tons) [f] 15 That is, about 7 1/2 pounds (about 3.5 kilograms)

THEN SHE GAVE THE KING 120
TALENTS OF GOLD, LARGE QUANTITIES
OF SPICES, AND PRECIOUS STONES.
THERE HAD NEVER BEEN SUCH SPICES
AS THOSE THE QUEEN OF SHEBA GAVE
TO KING SOLOMON.

2 Chronicles 9:9

Good Gifts

JEAN SHAW

READ | 2 CHRONICLES 9:1–12

People give gifts for many reasons. Jacob sent over 550 animals to pacify Esau, the brother he had deceived. When he was an old man, Jacob sent balm, honey, spices and nuts to the lord over the land, so that he would let Judah and Benjamin come back home. David took ten cheeses to the captain of the army to sustain him in his fight against the Philistines. David later received from Abigail enough food to feed his army, to dissuade him from slaying her entire household.

A true gift is given voluntarily, with no expectation of a favor in return. It must be distinguished from a bribe — difficult to do in these days when everything from ball-point pens to cruises in the Bahamas are used to buy special consideration.

Certain occasions, like Christmas, birthdays, anniversaries and bridal showers, require a gift. It is fun to open a present and decipher what the giver was thinking when she purchased it.

Best of all is the love gift that comes as a complete surprise. Last January I found a bag of white narcissus bulbs on my doorstep. Mary Anne had left them to "brighten up my winter days."

We will probably never have occasion to be ushered into the presence of a great person like a king or the president of the United States. Our gifts go to the relatively unknown. A loaf of bread to a new neighbor begins a rich friendship. A book to a child prepares her heart for the gospel. Giving an elderly friend a ride to the supermarket lessens her isolation and provides her with an opportunity to share all she knows about growing roses. When we proceed from a generous heart, we discover that great people are not found on thrones or in capitals, but right in our own block.

Dear Father, you know all about gifts, for you gave us your Son, Jesus, and you have given me many treasures in him. Lead me to someone today whom I can bless by whatever I have to give.

GRANDCHILD IN FOCUS • PRAYER

Emotional Development

O God, Creator of mind and body, I pray that you will give my grandchild emotional health and strength. Where there is anger, bring peace. Where there is confusion, bring clarity and focus. Where there are dark shadows, cast a ray of hope. Fill her with the sunshine of your Spirit. Warm her with the presence of your peace. Amen.

Your next devotion is located on page 587.

gold, with three hundred bekas^a of gold in each shield. The king put them in the Palace of the Forest of Lebanon.

¹⁷Then the king made a great throne inlaid with ivory and overlaid with pure gold. ¹⁸The throne had six steps, and a footstool of gold was attached to it. On both sides of the seat were armrests, with a lion standing beside each of them. ¹⁹Twelve lions stood on the six steps, one at either end of each step. Nothing like it had ever been made for any other kingdom. ²⁰All King Solomon's goblets were gold, and all the household articles in the Palace of the Forest of Lebanon were pure gold. Nothing was made of silver, because silver was considered of little value in Solomon's day. ²¹The king had a fleet of trading ships^b manned by Hiram's^c men. Once every three years it returned, carrying gold, silver and ivory, and apes and baboons.

²²King Solomon was greater in riches and wisdom than all the other kings of the earth. ²³All the kings of the earth sought audience with Solomon to hear the wisdom God had put in his heart. ²⁴Year after year, everyone who came brought a gift — articles of silver and gold, and robes, weapons and spices, and horses and mules.

²⁵Solomon had four thousand stalls for horses and chariots, and twelve thousand horses,^d which he kept in the chariot cities and also with him in Jerusalem. ²⁶He ruled over all the kings from the River^e to the land of the Philistines, as far as the border of Egypt. ²⁷The king made silver as common in Jerusalem as stones, and cedar as plentiful as sycamore-fig trees in the foothills. ²⁸Solomon's horses were imported from Egypt^f and from all other countries.

Solomon's Death
9:29–31pp — 1Ki 11:41–43

²⁹As for the other events of Solomon's reign, from beginning to end, are they not written in the records of Nathan the prophet, in the prophecy of Ahijah the Shilonite and in the visions of Iddo the seer concerning Jeroboam son of Nebat? ³⁰Solomon reigned in Jerusalem over all Israel

forty years. ³¹Then he rested with his fathers and was buried in the city of David his father. And Rehoboam his son succeeded him as king.

Israel Rebels Against Rehoboam
10:1–11:4pp — 1Ki 12:1–24

10 Rehoboam went to Shechem, for all the Israelites had gone there to make him king. ²When Jeroboam son of Nebat heard this (he was in Egypt, where he had fled from King Solomon), he returned from Egypt. ³So they sent for Jeroboam, and he and all Israel went to Rehoboam and said to him: ⁴"Your father put a heavy yoke on us, but now lighten the harsh labor and the heavy yoke he put on us, and we will serve you."

⁵Rehoboam answered, "Come back to me in three days." So the people went away.

⁶Then King Rehoboam consulted the elders who had served his father Solomon during his lifetime. "How would you advise me to answer these people?" he asked.

⁷They replied, "If you will be kind to these people and please them and give them a favorable answer, they will always be your servants."

⁸But Rehoboam rejected the advice the elders gave him and consulted the young men who had grown up with him and were serving him. ⁹He asked them, "What is your advice? How should we answer these people who say to me, 'Lighten the yoke your father put on us'?"

¹⁰The young men who had grown up with him replied, "Tell the people who have said to you, 'Your father put a heavy yoke on us, but make our yoke lighter'—tell them, 'My little finger is thicker than my father's waist. ¹¹My father laid on you a heavy yoke; I will make it even heavier. My father scourged you with whips; I will scourge you with scorpions.'"

¹²Three days later Jeroboam and all the people returned to Rehoboam, as the king had said, "Come back to me in three days." ¹³The king answered them harshly. Rejecting the advice of the

^a 16 That is, about 3 3/4 pounds (about 1.7 kilograms)
^b 21 Hebrew of ships that could go to Tarshish ^c 21 Hebrew Huram, a variant of Hiram ^d 25 Or charioteers ^e 26 That is, the Euphrates ^f 28 Or possibly Muzur, a region in Cilicia

elders, [14]he followed the advice of the young men and said, "My father made your yoke heavy; I will make it even heavier. My father scourged you with whips; I will scourge you with scorpions." [15]So the king did not listen to the people, for this turn of events was from God, to fulfill the word the LORD had spoken to Jeroboam son of Nebat through Ahijah the Shilonite.

[16]When all Israel saw that the king refused to listen to them, they answered the king:

"What share do we have in David,
what part in Jesse's son?
To your tents, O Israel!
Look after your own house, O David!"

So all the Israelites went home. [17]But as for the Israelites who were living in the towns of Judah, Rehoboam still ruled over them.

[18]King Rehoboam sent out Adoniram,[a] who was in charge of forced labor, but the Israelites stoned him to death. King Rehoboam, however, managed to get into his chariot and escape to Jerusalem. [19]So Israel has been in rebellion against the house of David to this day.

11

When Rehoboam arrived in Jerusalem, he mustered the house of Judah and Benjamin—a hundred and eighty thousand fighting men—to make war against Israel and to regain the kingdom for Rehoboam.

[2]But this word of the LORD came to Shemaiah the man of God: [3]"Say to Rehoboam son of Solomon king of Judah and to all the Israelites in Judah and Benjamin, [4]'This is what the LORD says: Do not go up to fight against your brothers. Go home, every one of you, for this is my doing.'" So they obeyed the words of the LORD and turned back from marching against Jeroboam.

Rehoboam Fortifies Judah

[5]Rehoboam lived in Jerusalem and built up towns for defense in Judah: [6]Bethlehem, Etam, Tekoa, [7]Beth Zur, Soco, Adullam, [8]Gath, Mareshah, Ziph, [9]Adoraim, Lachish, Azekah, [10]Zorah, Aijalon and Hebron. These were fortified cities in Judah and Benjamin. [11]He strengthened their defenses and put commanders in them, with supplies of food, olive oil and wine. [12]He put shields and spears in all the cities, and made them very strong. So Judah and Benjamin were his.

[13]The priests and Levites from all their districts throughout Israel sided with him. [14]The Levites even abandoned their pasturelands and property, and came to Judah and Jerusalem because Jeroboam and his sons had rejected them as priests of the LORD. [15]And he appointed his own priests for the high places and for the goat and calf idols he had made. [16]Those from every tribe of Israel who set their hearts on seeking the LORD, the God of Israel, followed the Levites to Jerusalem to offer sacrifices to the LORD, the God of their fathers. [17]They strengthened the kingdom of Judah and supported Rehoboam son of Solomon three years, walking in the ways of David and Solomon during this time.

Rehoboam's Family

[18]Rehoboam married Mahalath, who was the daughter of David's son Jerimoth and of Abihail, the daughter of Jesse's son Eliab. [19]She bore him sons: Jeush, Shemariah and Zaham. [20]Then he married Maacah daughter of Absalom, who bore him Abijah, Attai, Ziza and Shelomith. [21]Rehoboam loved Maacah daughter of Absalom more than any of his other wives and concubines. In all, he had eighteen wives and sixty concubines, twenty-eight sons and sixty daughters.

[22]Rehoboam appointed Abijah son of Maacah to be the chief prince among his brothers, in order to make him king. [23]He acted wisely, dispersing some of his sons throughout the districts of Judah and Benjamin, and to all the fortified cities. He gave them abundant provisions and took many wives for them.

Shishak Attacks Jerusalem

12:9–16pp — 1Ki 14:21,25–31

12

After Rehoboam's position as king was established and he had become strong, he

---

[a] 18 Hebrew Hadoram, a variant of Adoniram

and all Israel[a] with him abandoned the law of the LORD. [2]Because they had been unfaithful to the LORD, Shishak king of Egypt attacked Jerusalem in the fifth year of King Rehoboam. [3]With twelve hundred chariots and sixty thousand horsemen and the innumerable troops of Libyans, Sukkites and Cushites[b] that came with him from Egypt, [4]he captured the fortified cities of Judah and came as far as Jerusalem.

[5]Then the prophet Shemaiah came to Rehoboam and to the leaders of Judah who had assembled in Jerusalem for fear of Shishak, and he said to them, "This is what the LORD says, 'You have abandoned me; therefore, I now abandon you to Shishak.'"

[6]The leaders of Israel and the king humbled themselves and said, "The LORD is just."

[7]When the LORD saw that they humbled themselves, this word of the LORD came to Shemaiah: "Since they have humbled themselves, I will not destroy them but will soon give them deliverance. My wrath will not be poured out on Jerusalem through Shishak. [8]They will, however, become subject to him, so that they may learn the difference between serving me and serving the kings of other lands."

[9]When Shishak king of Egypt attacked Jerusalem, he carried off the treasures of the temple of the LORD and the treasures of the royal palace. He took everything, including the gold shields Solomon had made. [10]So King Rehoboam made bronze shields to replace them and assigned these to the commanders of the guard on duty at the entrance to the royal palace. [11]Whenever the king went to the LORD's temple, the guards went with him, bearing the shields, and afterward they returned them to the guardroom.

[12]Because Rehoboam humbled himself, the LORD's anger turned from him, and he was not totally destroyed. Indeed, there was some good in Judah.

[13]King Rehoboam established himself firmly in Jerusalem and continued as king. He was forty-one years old when he became king, and he reigned seventeen years in Jerusalem, the city the LORD had chosen out of all the tribes of Israel in which to put his Name. His mother's name was Naamah; she was an Ammonite. [14]He did evil because he had not set his heart on seeking the LORD.

[15]As for the events of Rehoboam's reign, from beginning to end, are they not written in the records of Shemaiah the prophet and of Iddo the seer that deal with genealogies? There was continual warfare between Rehoboam and Jeroboam. [16]Rehoboam rested with his fathers and was buried in the City of David. And Abijah his son succeeded him as king.

Abijah King of Judah

13:1–2,22–14:1pp — 1Ki 15:1–2,6–8

13 In the eighteenth year of the reign of Jeroboam, Abijah became king of Judah, [2]and he reigned in Jerusalem three years. His mother's name was Maacah,[c] a daughter[d] of Uriel of Gibeah.

There was war between Abijah and Jeroboam. [3]Abijah went into battle with a force of four hundred thousand able fighting men, and Jeroboam drew up a battle line against him with eight hundred thousand able troops.

[4]Abijah stood on Mount Zemaraim, in the hill country of Ephraim, and said, "Jeroboam and all Israel, listen to me! [5]Don't you know that the LORD, the God of Israel, has given the kingship of Israel to David and his descendants forever by a covenant of salt? [6]Yet Jeroboam son of Nebat, an official of Solomon son of David, rebelled against his master. [7]Some worthless scoundrels gathered around him and opposed Rehoboam son of Solomon when he was young and indecisive and not strong enough to resist them.

[8]"And now you plan to resist the kingdom of the LORD, which is in the hands of David's descendants. You are indeed a vast army and have with you the golden calves that Jeroboam made to be your gods. [9]But didn't you drive out the priests of the LORD, the sons of Aaron, and the Levites, and

---

[a] 1 That is, Judah, as frequently in 2 Chronicles   [b] 3 That is, people from the upper Nile region   [c] 2 Most Septuagint manuscripts and Syriac (see also 2 Chron. 11:20 and 1 Kings 15:2); Hebrew *Micaiah*   [d] 2 Or *granddaughter*

make priests of your own as the peoples of other lands do? Whoever comes to consecrate himself with a young bull and seven rams may become a priest of what are not gods.

10 "As for us, the LORD is our God, and we have not forsaken him. The priests who serve the LORD are sons of Aaron, and the Levites assist them. 11 Every morning and evening they present burnt offerings and fragrant incense to the LORD. They set out the bread on the ceremonially clean table and light the lamps on the gold lampstand every evening. We are observing the requirements of the LORD our God. But you have forsaken him. 12 God is with us; he is our leader. His priests with their trumpets will sound the battle cry against you. Men of Israel, do not fight against the LORD, the God of your fathers, for you will not succeed."

13 Now Jeroboam had sent troops around to the rear, so that while he was in front of Judah the ambush was behind them. 14 Judah turned and saw that they were being attacked at both front and rear. Then they cried out to the LORD. The priests blew their trumpets 15 and the men of Judah raised the battle cry. At the sound of their battle cry, God routed Jeroboam and all Israel before Abijah and Judah. 16 The Israelites fled before Judah, and God delivered them into their hands. 17 Abijah and his men inflicted heavy losses on them, so that there were five hundred thousand casualties among Israel's able men. 18 The men of Israel were subdued on that occasion, and the men of Judah were victorious because they relied on the LORD, the God of their fathers.

19 Abijah pursued Jeroboam and took from him the towns of Bethel, Jeshanah and Ephron, with their surrounding villages. 20 Jeroboam did not regain power during the time of Abijah. And the LORD struck him down and he died.

21 But Abijah grew in strength. He married fourteen wives and had twenty-two sons and sixteen daughters.

22 The other events of Abijah's reign, what he did and what he said, are written in the annotations of the prophet Iddo.

14

And Abijah rested with his fathers and was buried in the City of David. Asa his son succeeded him as king, and in his days the country was at peace for ten years.

Asa King of Judah
14:2–3pp — 1Ki 15:11–12

2 Asa did what was good and right in the eyes of the LORD his God. 3 He removed the foreign altars and the high places, smashed the sacred stones and cut down the Asherah poles.ᵃ 4 He commanded Judah to seek the LORD, the God of their fathers, and to obey his laws and commands. 5 He removed the high places and incense altars in every town in Judah, and the kingdom was at peace under him. 6 He built up the fortified cities of Judah, since the land was at peace. No one was at war with him during those years, for the LORD gave him rest.

7 "Let us build up these towns," he said to Judah, "and put walls around them, with towers, gates and bars. The land is still ours, because we have sought the LORD our God; we sought him and he has given us rest on every side." So they built and prospered.

8 Asa had an army of three hundred thousand men from Judah, equipped with large shields and with spears, and two hundred and eighty thousand from Benjamin, armed with small shields and with bows. All these were brave fighting men.

9 Zerah the Cushite marched out against them with a vast armyᵇ and three hundred chariots, and came as far as Mareshah. 10 Asa went out to meet him, and they took up battle positions in the Valley of Zephathah near Mareshah.

11 Then Asa called to the LORD his God and said, "LORD, there is no one like you to help the powerless against the mighty. Help us, O LORD our God, for we rely on you, and in your name we have come against this vast army. O LORD, you are our God; do not let man prevail against you."

ᵃ 3 That is, symbols of the goddess Asherah; here and elsewhere in 2 Chronicles   ᵇ 9 Hebrew with an army of a thousand thousands or with an army of thousands upon thousands

[12] The LORD struck down the Cushites before Asa and Judah. The Cushites fled, [13] and Asa and his army pursued them as far as Gerar. Such a great number of Cushites fell that they could not recover; they were crushed before the LORD and his forces. The men of Judah carried off a large amount of plunder. [14] They destroyed all the villages around Gerar, for the terror of the LORD had fallen upon them. They plundered all these villages, since there was much booty there. [15] They also attacked the camps of the herdsmen and carried off droves of sheep and goats and camels. Then they returned to Jerusalem.

Asa's Reform

15:16–19pp — 1Ki 15:13–16

15 The Spirit of God came upon Azariah son of Oded. [2] He went out to meet Asa and said to him, "Listen to me, Asa and all Judah and Benjamin. The LORD is with you when you are with him. If you seek him, he will be found by you, but if you forsake him, he will forsake you. [3] For a long time Israel was without the true God, without a priest to teach and without the law. [4] But in their distress they turned to the LORD, the God of Israel, and sought him, and he was found by them. [5] In those days it was not safe to travel

TALKING POINTS

Finding God

If we seek God, even in distress, we will find him.

2 CHRONICLES 15:1–4

For more on finding God, go to Isaiah 40:30–31.

about, for all the inhabitants of the lands were in great turmoil. [6] One nation was being crushed by another and one city by another, because God was troubling them with every kind of distress.

[7] But as for you, be strong and do not give up, for your work will be rewarded."

TALKING POINTS

Encouragement

Never give up; whatever you do for God will be rewarded.

2 CHRONICLES 15:7

For more on encouragement, go to Psalm 121:1–8.

[8] When Asa heard these words and the prophecy of Azariah son of [a] Oded the prophet, he took courage. He removed the detestable idols from the whole land of Judah and Benjamin and from the towns he had captured in the hills of Ephraim. He repaired the altar of the LORD that was in front of the portico of the LORD's temple.

[9] Then he assembled all Judah and Benjamin and the people from Ephraim, Manasseh and Simeon who had settled among them, for large numbers had come over to him from Israel when they saw that the LORD his God was with him.

[10] They assembled at Jerusalem in the third month of the fifteenth year of Asa's reign. [11] At that time they sacrificed to the LORD seven hundred head of cattle and seven thousand sheep and goats from the plunder they had brought back. [12] They entered into a covenant to seek the LORD, the God of their fathers, with all their heart and soul. [13] All who would not seek the LORD, the God of Israel, were to be put to death, whether small or great, man or woman. [14] They took an oath to the LORD with loud acclamation, with shouting and with trumpets and horns. [15] All Judah rejoiced about the oath because they had sworn it wholeheartedly. They sought God eagerly, and he was found by them. So the LORD gave them rest on every side.

---

[a] 8 Vulgate and Syriac (see also Septuagint and verse 1); Hebrew does not have *Azariah son of.*

¹⁶King Asa also deposed his grandmother Maacah from her position as queen mother, because she had made a repulsive Asherah pole. Asa cut the pole down, broke it up and burned it in the Kidron Valley. ¹⁷Although he did not remove the high places from Israel, Asa's heart was fully committed ⌐to the LORD⌐ all his life. ¹⁸He brought into the temple of God the silver and gold and the articles that he and his father had dedicated.

¹⁹There was no more war until the thirty-fifth year of Asa's reign.

Asa's Last Years

16:1–6pp — 1Ki 15:17–22
16:11–17:1pp — 1Ki 15:23–24

16 In the thirty-sixth year of Asa's reign Baasha king of Israel went up against Judah and fortified Ramah to prevent anyone from leaving or entering the territory of Asa king of Judah.

²Asa then took the silver and gold out of the treasuries of the LORD's temple and of his own palace and sent it to Ben-Hadad king of Aram, who was ruling in Damascus. ³"Let there be a treaty between me and you," he said, "as there was between my father and your father. See, I am sending you silver and gold. Now break your treaty with Baasha king of Israel so he will withdraw from me."

⁴Ben-Hadad agreed with King Asa and sent the commanders of his forces against the towns of Israel. They conquered Ijon, Dan, Abel Maim *a* and all the store cities of Naphtali. ⁵When Baasha heard this, he stopped building Ramah and abandoned his work. ⁶Then King Asa brought all the men of Judah, and they carried away from Ramah the stones and timber Baasha had been using. With them he built up Geba and Mizpah.

⁷At that time Hanani the seer came to Asa king of Judah and said to him: "Because you relied on the king of Aram and not on the LORD your God, the army of the king of Aram has escaped from your hand. ⁸Were not the Cushites *b* and Libyans a mighty army with great numbers of chariots and horsemen *c*? Yet when you relied on the LORD, he delivered them into your hand. ⁹For the eyes of the LORD range throughout the earth to strengthen those whose hearts are fully committed to him. You have done a foolish thing, and from now on you will be at war."

¹⁰Asa was angry with the seer because of this; he was so enraged that he put him in prison. At the same time Asa brutally oppressed some of the people.

¹¹The events of Asa's reign, from beginning to end, are written in the book of the kings of Judah and Israel. ¹²In the thirty-ninth year of his reign Asa was afflicted with a disease in his feet. Though his disease was severe, even in his illness he did not seek help from the LORD, but only from the physicians. ¹³Then in the forty-first year of his reign Asa died and rested with his fathers. ¹⁴They buried him in the tomb that he had cut out for himself in the City of David. They laid him on a bier covered with spices and various blended perfumes, and they made a huge fire in his honor.

Jehoshaphat King of Judah

17 Jehoshaphat his son succeeded him as king and strengthened himself against Israel. ²He stationed troops in all the fortified cities of Judah and put garrisons in Judah and in the towns of Ephraim that his father Asa had captured.

³The LORD was with Jehoshaphat because in his early years he walked in the ways his father David had followed. He did not consult the Baals ⁴but sought the God of his father and followed his commands rather than the practices of Israel. ⁵The LORD established the kingdom under his control; and all Judah brought gifts to Jehoshaphat, so that he had great wealth and honor. ⁶His heart was devoted to the ways of the LORD; furthermore, he removed the high places and the Asherah poles from Judah.

⁷In the third year of his reign he sent his officials Ben-Hail, Obadiah, Zechariah, Nethanel and

---

a 4 Also known as *Abel Beth Maacah*   *b 8* That is, people from the upper Nile region   *c 8* Or *charioteers*

Micaiah to teach in the towns of Judah. [8]With them were certain Levites—Shemaiah, Nethaniah, Zebadiah, Asahel, Shemiramoth, Jehonathan, Adonijah, Tobijah and Tob-Adonijah—and the priests Elishama and Jehoram. [9]They taught throughout Judah, taking with them the Book of the Law of the LORD; they went around to all the towns of Judah and taught the people.

[10]The fear of the LORD fell on all the kingdoms of the lands surrounding Judah, so that they did not make war with Jehoshaphat. [11]Some Philistines brought Jehoshaphat gifts and silver as tribute, and the Arabs brought him flocks: seven thousand seven hundred rams and seven thousand seven hundred goats.

[12]Jehoshaphat became more and more powerful; he built forts and store cities in Judah [13]and had large supplies in the towns of Judah. He also kept experienced fighting men in Jerusalem. [14]Their enrollment by families was as follows:

From Judah, commanders of units of 1,000:
    Adnah the commander, with 300,000 fighting men;
[15]next, Jehohanan the commander, with 280,000;
[16]next, Amasiah son of Zicri, who volunteered himself for the service of the LORD, with 200,000.
[17]From Benjamin:
    Eliada, a valiant soldier, with 200,000 men armed with bows and shields;
[18]next, Jehozabad, with 180,000 men armed for battle.

[19]These were the men who served the king, besides those he stationed in the fortified cities throughout Judah.

Micaiah Prophesies Against Ahab
18:1–27pp — 1Ki 22:1–28

18 Now Jehoshaphat had great wealth and honor, and he allied himself with Ahab by marriage. [2]Some years later he went down to visit Ahab in Samaria. Ahab slaughtered many sheep and cattle for him and the people with him and urged him to attack Ramoth Gilead. [3]Ahab king of Israel asked Jehoshaphat king of Judah, "Will you go with me against Ramoth Gilead?"

Jehoshaphat replied, "I am as you are, and my people as your people; we will join you in the war." [4]But Jehoshaphat also said to the king of Israel, "First seek the counsel of the LORD."

[5]So the king of Israel brought together the prophets—four hundred men—and asked them, "Shall we go to war against Ramoth Gilead, or shall I refrain?"

"Go," they answered, "for God will give it into the king's hand."

[6]But Jehoshaphat asked, "Is there not a prophet of the LORD here whom we can inquire of?"

[7]The king of Israel answered Jehoshaphat, "There is still one man through whom we can inquire of the LORD, but I hate him because he never prophesies anything good about me, but always bad. He is Micaiah son of Imlah."

"The king should not say that," Jehoshaphat replied.

[8]So the king of Israel called one of his officials and said, "Bring Micaiah son of Imlah at once."

[9]Dressed in their royal robes, the king of Israel and Jehoshaphat king of Judah were sitting on their thrones at the threshing floor by the entrance to the gate of Samaria, with all the prophets prophesying before them. [10]Now Zedekiah son of Kenaanah had made iron horns, and he declared, "This is what the LORD says: 'With these you will gore the Arameans until they are destroyed.'"

[11]All the other prophets were prophesying the same thing. "Attack Ramoth Gilead and be victorious," they said, "for the LORD will give it into the king's hand."

[12]The messenger who had gone to summon Micaiah said to him, "Look, as one man the other prophets are predicting success for the king. Let your word agree with theirs, and speak favorably."

[13]But Micaiah said, "As surely as the LORD lives, I can tell him only what my God says."

[14]When he arrived, the king asked him, "Mica-

iah, shall we go to war against Ramoth Gilead, or shall I refrain?"

"Attack and be victorious," he answered, "for they will be given into your hand."

¹⁵The king said to him, "How many times must I make you swear to tell me nothing but the truth in the name of the LORD?"

¹⁶Then Micaiah answered, "I saw all Israel scattered on the hills like sheep without a shepherd, and the LORD said, 'These people have no master. Let each one go home in peace.'"

¹⁷The king of Israel said to Jehoshaphat, "Didn't I tell you that he never prophesies anything good about me, but only bad?"

¹⁸Micaiah continued, "Therefore hear the word of the LORD: I saw the LORD sitting on his throne with all the host of heaven standing on his right and on his left. ¹⁹And the LORD said, 'Who will entice Ahab king of Israel into attacking Ramoth Gilead and going to his death there?'

"One suggested this, and another that. ²⁰Finally, a spirit came forward, stood before the LORD and said, 'I will entice him.'

"'By what means?' the LORD asked.

²¹"'I will go and be a lying spirit in the mouths of all his prophets,' he said.

"'You will succeed in enticing him,' said the LORD. 'Go and do it.'

²²"So now the LORD has put a lying spirit in the mouths of these prophets of yours. The LORD has decreed disaster for you."

²³Then Zedekiah son of Kenaanah went up and slapped Micaiah in the face. "Which way did the spirit from ᵃ the LORD go when he went from me to speak to you?" he asked.

²⁴Micaiah replied, "You will find out on the day you go to hide in an inner room."

²⁵The king of Israel then ordered, "Take Micaiah and send him back to Amon the ruler of the city and to Joash the king's son, ²⁶and say, 'This is what the king says: Put this fellow in prison and give him nothing but bread and water until I return safely.'"

²⁷Micaiah declared, "If you ever return safely, the LORD has not spoken through me." Then he added, "Mark my words, all you people!"

Ahab Killed at Ramoth Gilead
18:28–34pp — 1Ki 22:29–36

²⁸So the king of Israel and Jehoshaphat king of Judah went up to Ramoth Gilead. ²⁹The king of Israel said to Jehoshaphat, "I will enter the battle in disguise, but you wear your royal robes." So the king of Israel disguised himself and went into battle.

³⁰Now the king of Aram had ordered his chariot commanders, "Do not fight with anyone, small or great, except the king of Israel." ³¹When the chariot commanders saw Jehoshaphat, they thought, "This is the king of Israel." So they turned to attack him, but Jehoshaphat cried out, and the LORD helped him. God drew them away from him, ³²for when the chariot commanders saw that he was not the king of Israel, they stopped pursuing him.

³³But someone drew his bow at random and hit the king of Israel between the sections of his armor. The king told the chariot driver, "Wheel around and get me out of the fighting. I've been wounded." ³⁴All day long the battle raged, and the king of Israel propped himself up in his chariot facing the Arameans until evening. Then at sunset he died.

19 When Jehoshaphat king of Judah returned safely to his palace in Jerusalem, ²Jehu the seer, the son of Hanani, went out to meet him and said to the king, "Should you help the wicked and love ᵇ those who hate the LORD? Because of this, the wrath of the LORD is upon you. ³There is, however, some good in you, for you have rid the land of the Asherah poles and have set your heart on seeking God."

Jehoshaphat Appoints Judges

⁴Jehoshaphat lived in Jerusalem, and he went out again among the people from Beersheba to the hill country of Ephraim and turned them back to the LORD, the God of their fathers. ⁵He

ᵃ 23 Or *Spirit of*   ᵇ 2 Or *and make alliances with*

appointed judges in the land, in each of the fortified cities of Judah. ⁶He told them, "Consider carefully what you do, because you are not judging for man but for the LORD, who is with you whenever you give a verdict. ⁷Now let the fear of the LORD be upon you. Judge carefully, for with the LORD our God there is no injustice or partiality or bribery."

⁸In Jerusalem also, Jehoshaphat appointed some of the Levites, priests and heads of Israelite families to administer the law of the LORD and to settle disputes. And they lived in Jerusalem. ⁹He gave them these orders: "You must serve faithfully and wholeheartedly in the fear of the LORD. ¹⁰In every case that comes before you from your fellow countrymen who live in the cities—whether bloodshed or other concerns of the law, commands, decrees or ordinances—you are to warn them not to sin against the LORD; otherwise his wrath will come on you and your brothers. Do this, and you will not sin.

¹¹"Amariah the chief priest will be over you in any matter concerning the LORD, and Zebadiah son of Ishmael, the leader of the tribe of Judah, will be over you in any matter concerning the king, and the Levites will serve as officials before you. Act with courage, and may the LORD be with those who do well."

Jehoshaphat Defeats Moab and Ammon

20 After this, the Moabites and Ammonites with some of the Meunites ᵃ came to make war on Jehoshaphat.

²Some men came and told Jehoshaphat, "A vast army is coming against you from Edom, ᵇ from the other side of the Sea. ᶜ It is already in Hazazon Tamar" (that is, En Gedi). ³Alarmed, Jehoshaphat resolved to inquire of the LORD, and he proclaimed a fast for all Judah. ⁴The people of Judah came together to seek help from the LORD; indeed, they came from every town in Judah to seek him.

⁵Then Jehoshaphat stood up in the assembly of Judah and Jerusalem at the temple of the LORD in the front of the new courtyard ⁶and said:

"O LORD, God of our fathers, are you not the God who is in heaven? You rule over all the kingdoms of the nations. Power and might are in your hand, and no one can withstand you. ⁷O our God, did you not drive out the inhabitants of this land before your people Israel and give it forever to the descendants of Abraham your friend? ⁸They have lived in it and have built in it a sanctuary for your Name, saying, ⁹'If calamity comes upon us, whether the sword of judgment, or plague or famine, we will stand in your presence before this temple that bears your Name and will cry out to you in our distress, and you will hear us and save us.'

¹⁰"But now here are men from Ammon, Moab and Mount Seir, whose territory you would not allow Israel to invade when they came from Egypt; so they turned away from them and did not destroy them. ¹¹See how they are repaying us by coming to drive us out of the possession you gave us as an inheritance. ¹²O our God, will you not judge them? For we have no power to face this vast army that is attacking us. We do not know what to do, but our eyes are upon you."

¹³All the men of Judah, with their wives and children and little ones, stood there before the LORD.

¹⁴Then the Spirit of the LORD came upon Jahaziel son of Zechariah, the son of Benaiah, the son of Jeiel, the son of Mattaniah, a Levite and descendant of Asaph, as he stood in the assembly.

¹⁵He said: "Listen, King Jehoshaphat and all who live in Judah and Jerusalem! This is what the LORD says to you: 'Do not be afraid or discouraged because of this vast army. For the battle is not yours, but God's. ¹⁶Tomorrow march down against them. They will be climbing up by the Pass of Ziz, and you will find them at the end of the gorge in the Desert of Jeruel. ¹⁷You will not have to fight this battle. Take up your

---

ᵃ *1* Some Septuagint manuscripts; Hebrew *Ammonites*
ᵇ *2* One Hebrew manuscript; most Hebrew manuscripts, Septuagint and Vulgate *Aram*   ᶜ *2* That is, the Dead Sea

positions; stand firm and see the deliverance the LORD will give you, O Judah and Jerusalem. Do not be afraid; do not be discouraged. Go out to face them tomorrow, and the LORD will be with you.' "

¹⁸Jehoshaphat bowed with his face to the ground, and all the people of Judah and Jerusalem fell down in worship before the LORD. ¹⁹Then some Levites from the Kohathites and Korahites stood up and praised the LORD, the God of Israel, with a very loud voice.

²⁰Early in the morning they left for the Desert of Tekoa. As they set out, Jehoshaphat stood and said, "Listen to me, Judah and people of Jerusalem! Have faith in the LORD your God and you will be upheld; have faith in his prophets and you will be successful." ²¹After consulting the people, Jehoshaphat appointed men to sing to the LORD and to praise him for the splendor of his*a* holiness as they went out at the head of the army, saying:

"Give thanks to the LORD,
    for his love endures forever."

²²As they began to sing and praise, the LORD set ambushes against the men of Ammon and Moab and Mount Seir who were invading Judah, and they were defeated. ²³The men of Ammon and Moab rose up against the men from Mount Seir to destroy and annihilate them. After they finished slaughtering the men from Seir, they helped to destroy one another.

²⁴When the men of Judah came to the place that overlooks the desert and looked toward the vast army, they saw only dead bodies lying on the ground; no one had escaped. ²⁵So Jehoshaphat and his men went to carry off their plunder, and they found among them a great amount of equipment and clothing*b* and also articles of value — more than they could take away. There was so much plunder that it took three days to collect it. ²⁶On the fourth day they assembled in the Valley of Beracah, where they praised the LORD. This is why it is called the Valley of Beracah*c* to this day.

²⁷Then, led by Jehoshaphat, all the men of Judah and Jerusalem returned joyfully to Jerusalem, for the LORD had given them cause to rejoice over their enemies. ²⁸They entered Jerusalem and went to the temple of the LORD with harps and lutes and trumpets.

²⁹The fear of God came upon all the kingdoms of the countries when they heard how the LORD had fought against the enemies of Israel. ³⁰And the kingdom of Jehoshaphat was at peace, for his God had given him rest on every side.

The End of Jehoshaphat's Reign
20:31–21:1pp — 1Ki 22:41–50

³¹So Jehoshaphat reigned over Judah. He was thirty-five years old when he became king of Judah, and he reigned in Jerusalem twenty-five years. His mother's name was Azubah daughter of Shilhi. ³²He walked in the ways of his father Asa and did not stray from them; he did what was right in the eyes of the LORD. ³³The high places, however, were not removed, and the people still had not set their hearts on the God of their fathers.

³⁴The other events of Jehoshaphat's reign, from beginning to end, are written in the annals of Jehu son of Hanani, which are recorded in the book of the kings of Israel.

³⁵Later, Jehoshaphat king of Judah made an alliance with Ahaziah king of Israel, who was guilty of wickedness. ³⁶He agreed with him to construct a fleet of trading ships.*d* After these were built at Ezion Geber, ³⁷Eliezer son of Dodavahu of Mareshah prophesied against Jehoshaphat, saying, "Because you have made an alliance with Ahaziah, the LORD will destroy what you have made." The ships were wrecked and were not able to set sail to trade.*e*

21 Then Jehoshaphat rested with his fathers and was buried with them in the City of David. And Jehoram his son succeeded him as king. ²Jehoram's brothers, the sons of

---

a 21 Or *him with the splendor of*   *b 25* Some Hebrew manuscripts and Vulgate; most Hebrew manuscripts *corpses*   *c 26 Beracah* means *praise.*   *d 36* Hebrew *of ships that could go to Tarshish*   *e 37* Hebrew *sail for Tarshish*

Jehoshaphat, were Azariah, Jehiel, Zechariah, Azariahu, Michael and Shephatiah. All these were sons of Jehoshaphat king of Israel. *a* ³Their father had given them many gifts of silver and gold and articles of value, as well as fortified cities in Judah, but he had given the kingdom to Jehoram because he was his firstborn son.

Jehoram King of Judah
21:5–10,20pp — 2Ki 8:16–24

⁴When Jehoram established himself firmly over his father's kingdom, he put all his brothers to the sword along with some of the princes of Israel. ⁵Jehoram was thirty-two years old when he became king, and he reigned in Jerusalem eight years. ⁶He walked in the ways of the kings of Israel, as the house of Ahab had done, for he married a daughter of Ahab. He did evil in the eyes of the LORD. ⁷Nevertheless, because of the covenant the LORD had made with David, the LORD was not willing to destroy the house of David. He had promised to maintain a lamp for him and his descendants forever.

⁸In the time of Jehoram, Edom rebelled against Judah and set up its own king. ⁹So Jehoram went there with his officers and all his chariots. The Edomites surrounded him and his chariot commanders, but he rose up and broke through by night. ¹⁰To this day Edom has been in rebellion against Judah.

Libnah revolted at the same time, because Jehoram had forsaken the LORD, the God of his fathers. ¹¹He had also built high places on the hills of Judah and had caused the people of Jerusalem to prostitute themselves and had led Judah astray.

¹²Jehoram received a letter from Elijah the prophet, which said:

"This is what the LORD, the God of your father David, says: 'You have not walked in the ways of your father Jehoshaphat or of Asa king of Judah. ¹³But you have walked in the ways of the kings of Israel, and you have led Judah and the people of Jerusalem to prostitute themselves, just as the house of Ahab did. You have also murdered your own brothers, members of your father's house, men who were better than you. ¹⁴So now the LORD is about to strike your people, your sons, your wives and everything that is yours, with a heavy blow. ¹⁵You yourself will be very ill with a lingering disease of the bowels, until the disease causes your bowels to come out.'"

¹⁶The LORD aroused against Jehoram the hostility of the Philistines and of the Arabs who lived near the Cushites. ¹⁷They attacked Judah, invaded it and carried off all the goods found in the king's palace, together with his sons and wives. Not a son was left to him except Ahaziah, *b* the youngest.

¹⁸After all this, the LORD afflicted Jehoram with an incurable disease of the bowels. ¹⁹In the course of time, at the end of the second year, his bowels came out because of the disease, and he died in great pain. His people made no fire in his honor, as they had for his fathers.

²⁰Jehoram was thirty-two years old when he became king, and he reigned in Jerusalem eight years. He passed away, to no one's regret, and was buried in the City of David, but not in the tombs of the kings.

Ahaziah King of Judah
22:1–6pp — 2Ki 8:25–29
22:7–9pp — 2Ki 9:21–29

22 The people of Jerusalem made Ahaziah, Jehoram's youngest son, king in his place, since the raiders, who came with the Arabs into the camp, had killed all the older sons. So Ahaziah son of Jehoram king of Judah began to reign.

²Ahaziah was twenty-two *c* years old when he became king, and he reigned in Jerusalem one year. His mother's name was Athaliah, a granddaughter of Omri.

³He too walked in the ways of the house of

---

a 2 That is, Judah, as frequently in 2 Chronicles   *b* 17 Hebrew *Jehoahaz,* a variant of *Ahaziah*   *c* 2 Some Septuagint manuscripts and Syriac (see also 2 Kings 8:26); Hebrew *forty-two*

JEHORAM WAS THIRTY-TWO YEARS
OLD WHEN HE BECAME KING, AND HE
REIGNED IN JERUSALEM EIGHT YEARS.
HE PASSED AWAY, TO NO ONE'S REGRET,
AND WAS BURIED IN THE CITY OF DAVID,
BUT NOT IN THE TOMBS OF THE KINGS.

2 Chronicles 21:20

The Epitaph

NATALIE J. BLOCK

READ | 2 CHRONICLES 21:4 – 20

"He passed away, to no one's regret."

You've got to be kidding! At first read, this seems almost comical, but, after thinking about it for a few moments, it becomes clear that this is a short, sad commentary on someone's life. No one would want an epitaph on her grave marker that read: SHE DIED, TO NO ONE'S REGRET. It causes us to pause and think about the legacy each of us will leave behind.

So what did Jehoram do that was so terrible? Well, in short, he "did evil in the eyes of the LORD" (2 Chronicles 21:6) and led the people away from God (see 2 Chronicles 21:11). Jehoram was a powerful man who used his influence to leave a legacy of evil.

In contrast, Dorcas (aka Tabitha) was a woman who left a legacy of love. She was a kind woman who was "always doing good and helping the poor" (Acts 9:36). This woman was dearly loved. When she died, everyone was filled with regret. They had lost someone who had made an impact on their lives, and they wondered how they would go on without her. Their grief was so profound that it apparently moved not only Peter's heart but God's heart as well, and Dorcas was raised from the dead!

What we do with our lives is important. How we spend our time, the priorities we set, the attitudes we project, the goals we achieve — even the things we neglect — say something about us. As mothers and grandmothers, God has placed within us a desire to reach out to those in need — to mother not only our own sons, daughters and grandchildren but also others outside our immediate families. Be a mother or grandmother to someone today. Open your heart. Change a life. Change the world.

Dear Father, open my heart not only to my own children and grandchildren but also to those outside of my immediate family. Help me to live my life in a way that pleases you and brings joy to those around me. I want to be remembered with love. Amen.

Your next devotion is located on page 595.

GRANDCHILD IN FOCUS • PRAYER

Spiritual Growth

Dear Lord, today I pray for my grandchild's spiritual growth. I ask that you instill in him the desire to read and memorize your Word. Give him a passion to be in conversation with you. May loving and serving you be part of his daily life. I ask that you stay close to him and lead him to be transformed to your likeness, to reflect your grace and to radiate your love. I pray this in Jesus' name, amen.

Ahab, for his mother encouraged him in doing wrong. ⁴He did evil in the eyes of the LORD, as the house of Ahab had done, for after his father's death they became his advisers, to his undoing. ⁵He also followed their counsel when he went with Joram*a* son of Ahab king of Israel to war against Hazael king of Aram at Ramoth Gilead. The Arameans wounded Joram; ⁶so he returned to Jezreel to recover from the wounds they had inflicted on him at Ramoth*b* in his battle with Hazael king of Aram.

Then Ahaziah*c* son of Jehoram king of Judah went down to Jezreel to see Joram son of Ahab because he had been wounded.

⁷Through Ahaziah's visit to Joram, God brought about Ahaziah's downfall. When Ahaziah arrived, he went out with Joram to meet Jehu son of Nimshi, whom the LORD had anointed to destroy the house of Ahab. ⁸While Jehu was executing judgment on the house of Ahab, he found the princes of Judah and the sons of Ahaziah's relatives, who had been attending Ahaziah, and he killed them. ⁹He then went in search of Ahaziah, and his men captured him while he was hiding in Samaria. He was brought to Jehu and put to death. They buried him, for they said, "He was a son of Jehoshaphat, who sought the LORD with all his heart." So there was no one in the house of Ahaziah powerful enough to retain the kingdom.

Athaliah and Joash
22:10–23:21pp — 2Ki 11:1–21

¹⁰When Athaliah the mother of Ahaziah saw that her son was dead, she proceeded to destroy the whole royal family of the house of Judah. ¹¹But Jehosheba,*d* the daughter of King Jehoram, took Joash son of Ahaziah and stole him away from among the royal princes who were about to be murdered and put him and his nurse in a bedroom. Because Jehosheba,*d* the daughter of King Jehoram and wife of the priest Jehoiada, was Ahaziah's sister, she hid the child from Athaliah so she could not kill him. ¹²He remained hidden with them at the temple of God for six years while Athaliah ruled the land.

23 In the seventh year Jehoiada showed his strength. He made a covenant with the commanders of units of a hundred: Azariah son of Jeroham, Ishmael son of Jehohanan, Azariah son of Obed, Maaseiah son of Adaiah, and Elishaphat son of Zicri. ²They went throughout Judah and gathered the Levites and the heads of Israelite families from all the towns. When they came to Jerusalem, ³the whole assembly made a covenant with the king at the temple of God.

Jehoiada said to them, "The king's son shall reign, as the LORD promised concerning the descendants of David. ⁴Now this is what you are to do: A third of you priests and Levites who are going on duty on the Sabbath are to keep watch at the doors, ⁵a third of you at the royal palace and a third at the Foundation Gate, and all the other men are to be in the courtyards of the temple of the LORD. ⁶No one is to enter the temple of the LORD except the priests and Levites on duty; they may enter because they are consecrated, but all the other men are to guard what the LORD has assigned to them.*e* ⁷The Levites are to station themselves around the king, each man with his weapons in his hand. Anyone who enters the temple must be put to death. Stay close to the king wherever he goes."

⁸The Levites and all the men of Judah did just as Jehoiada the priest ordered. Each one took his men—those who were going on duty on the Sabbath and those who were going off duty—for Jehoiada the priest had not released any of the divisions. ⁹Then he gave the commanders of units of a hundred the spears and the large and small shields that had belonged to King David and that were in the temple of God. ¹⁰He stationed all the men, each with his weapon in his hand, around the king—near the altar and the temple, from the south side to the north side of the temple.

a 5 Hebrew *Jehoram,* a variant of *Joram*; also in verses 6 and 7   *b 6* Hebrew *Ramah,* a variant of *Ramoth*   *c 6* Some Hebrew manuscripts, Septuagint, Vulgate and Syriac (see also 2 Kings 8:29); most Hebrew manuscripts *Azariah*   *d 11* Hebrew *Jehoshabeath,* a variant of *Jehosheba*   *e 6* Or *to observe the LORD's command , not to enter ,*

¹¹Jehoiada and his sons brought out the king's son and put the crown on him; they presented him with a copy of the covenant and proclaimed him king. They anointed him and shouted, "Long live the king!"

¹²When Athaliah heard the noise of the people running and cheering the king, she went to them at the temple of the LORD. ¹³She looked, and there was the king, standing by his pillar at the entrance. The officers and the trumpeters were beside the king, and all the people of the land were rejoicing and blowing trumpets, and singers with musical instruments were leading the praises. Then Athaliah tore her robes and shouted, "Treason! Treason!"

¹⁴Jehoiada the priest sent out the commanders of units of a hundred, who were in charge of the troops, and said to them: "Bring her out between the ranks[a] and put to the sword anyone who follows her." For the priest had said, "Do not put her to death at the temple of the LORD." ¹⁵So they seized her as she reached the entrance of the Horse Gate on the palace grounds, and there they put her to death.

¹⁶Jehoiada then made a covenant that he and the people and the king[b] would be the LORD's people. ¹⁷All the people went to the temple of Baal and tore it down. They smashed the altars and idols and killed Mattan the priest of Baal in front of the altars.

¹⁸Then Jehoiada placed the oversight of the temple of the LORD in the hands of the priests, who were Levites, to whom David had made assignments in the temple, to present the burnt offerings of the LORD as written in the Law of Moses, with rejoicing and singing, as David had ordered. ¹⁹He also stationed doorkeepers at the gates of the LORD's temple so that no one who was in any way unclean might enter.

²⁰He took with him the commanders of hundreds, the nobles, the rulers of the people and all the people of the land and brought the king down from the temple of the LORD. They went into the palace through the Upper Gate and seated the king on the royal throne, ²¹and all the people of the land rejoiced. And the city was quiet, because Athaliah had been slain with the sword.

Joash Repairs the Temple

24:1–14pp — 2Ki 12:1–16
24:23–27pp — 2Ki 12:17–21

24 Joash was seven years old when he became king, and he reigned in Jerusalem forty years. His mother's name was Zibiah; she was from Beersheba. ²Joash did what was right in the eyes of the LORD all the years of Jehoiada the priest. ³Jehoiada chose two wives for him, and he had sons and daughters.

⁴Some time later Joash decided to restore the temple of the LORD. ⁵He called together the priests and Levites and said to them, "Go to the towns of Judah and collect the money due annually from all Israel, to repair the temple of your God. Do it now." But the Levites did not act at once.

⁶Therefore the king summoned Jehoiada the chief priest and said to him, "Why haven't you required the Levites to bring in from Judah and Jerusalem the tax imposed by Moses the servant of the LORD and by the assembly of Israel for the Tent of the Testimony?"

⁷Now the sons of that wicked woman Athaliah had broken into the temple of God and had used even its sacred objects for the Baals.

⁸At the king's command, a chest was made and placed outside, at the gate of the temple of the LORD. ⁹A proclamation was then issued in Judah and Jerusalem that they should bring to the LORD the tax that Moses the servant of God had required of Israel in the desert. ¹⁰All the officials and all the people brought their contributions gladly, dropping them into the chest until it was full. ¹¹Whenever the chest was brought in by the Levites to the king's officials and they saw that there was a large amount of money, the royal secretary and the officer of the chief priest would come and empty the chest and carry it back to its place. They did this regularly and collected a

---

[a] 14 Or *out from the precincts*   [b] 16 Or *covenant between ₊the LORD₋ and the people and the king that they* (see 2 Kings 11:17)

great amount of money. ¹²The king and Jehoiada gave it to the men who carried out the work required for the temple of the LORD. They hired masons and carpenters to restore the LORD's temple, and also workers in iron and bronze to repair the temple.

¹³The men in charge of the work were diligent, and the repairs progressed under them. They rebuilt the temple of God according to its original design and reinforced it. ¹⁴When they had finished, they brought the rest of the money to the king and Jehoiada, and with it were made articles for the LORD's temple: articles for the service and for the burnt offerings, and also dishes and other objects of gold and silver. As long as Jehoiada lived, burnt offerings were presented continually in the temple of the LORD.

¹⁵Now Jehoiada was old and full of years, and he died at the age of a hundred and thirty. ¹⁶He was buried with the kings in the City of David, because of the good he had done in Israel for God and his temple.

The Wickedness of Joash

¹⁷After the death of Jehoiada, the officials of Judah came and paid homage to the king, and he listened to them. ¹⁸They abandoned the temple of the LORD, the God of their fathers, and worshiped Asherah poles and idols. Because of their guilt, God's anger came upon Judah and Jerusalem. ¹⁹Although the LORD sent prophets to the people to bring them back to him, and though they testified against them, they would not listen.

²⁰Then the Spirit of God came upon Zechariah son of Jehoiada the priest. He stood before the people and said, "This is what God says: 'Why do you disobey the LORD's commands? You will not prosper. Because you have forsaken the LORD, he has forsaken you.'"

²¹But they plotted against him, and by order of the king they stoned him to death in the courtyard of the LORD's temple. ²²King Joash did not remember the kindness Zechariah's father Jehoiada had shown him but killed his son, who said

as he lay dying, "May the LORD see this and call you to account."

²³At the turn of the year,[a] the army of Aram marched against Joash; it invaded Judah and Jerusalem and killed all the leaders of the people. They sent all the plunder to their king in Damascus. ²⁴Although the Aramean army had come with only a few men, the LORD delivered into their hands a much larger army. Because Judah had forsaken the LORD, the God of their fathers, judgment was executed on Joash. ²⁵When the Arameans withdrew, they left Joash severely wounded. His officials conspired against him for murdering the son of Jehoiada the priest, and they killed him in his bed. So he died and was buried in the City of David, but not in the tombs of the kings.

²⁶Those who conspired against him were Zabad,[b] son of Shimeath an Ammonite woman, and Jehozabad, son of Shimrith[c] a Moabite woman. ²⁷The account of his sons, the many prophecies about him, and the record of the restoration of the temple of God are written in the annotations on the book of the kings. And Amaziah his son succeeded him as king.

Amaziah King of Judah

25:1–4pp — 2Ki 14:1–6
25:11–12pp — 2Ki 14:7
25:17–28pp — 2Ki 14:8–20

25 Amaziah was twenty-five years old when he became king, and he reigned in Jerusalem twenty-nine years. His mother's name was Jehoaddin[d]; she was from Jerusalem. ²He did what was right in the eyes of the LORD, but not wholeheartedly. ³After the kingdom was firmly in his control, he executed the officials who had murdered his father the king. ⁴Yet he did not put their sons to death, but acted in accordance with what is written in the Law, in the Book of Moses, where the LORD commanded: "Fathers shall not be put to death for their children, nor children put to death for their fathers; each is to die for his own sins."[e]

---

[a] 23 Probably in the spring   [b] 26 A variant of *Jozabad*   [c] 26 A variant of *Shomer*   [d] 1 Hebrew *Jehoaddan*, a variant of *Jehoaddin*   [e] 4 Deut. 24:16

⁵Amaziah called the people of Judah together and assigned them according to their families to commanders of thousands and commanders of hundreds for all Judah and Benjamin. He then mustered those twenty years old or more and found that there were three hundred thousand men ready for military service, able to handle the spear and shield. ⁶He also hired a hundred thousand fighting men from Israel for a hundred talents ᵃ of silver.

⁷But a man of God came to him and said, "O king, these troops from Israel must not march with you, for the Lᴏʀᴅ is not with Israel—not with any of the people of Ephraim. ⁸Even if you go and fight courageously in battle, God will overthrow you before the enemy, for God has the power to help or to overthrow."

⁹Amaziah asked the man of God, "But what about the hundred talents I paid for these Israelite troops?"

The man of God replied, "The Lᴏʀᴅ can give you much more than that."

¹⁰So Amaziah dismissed the troops who had come to him from Ephraim and sent them home. They were furious with Judah and left for home in a great rage.

¹¹Amaziah then marshaled his strength and led his army to the Valley of Salt, where he killed ten thousand men of Seir. ¹²The army of Judah also captured ten thousand men alive, took them to the top of a cliff and threw them down so that all were dashed to pieces.

¹³Meanwhile the troops that Amaziah had sent back and had not allowed to take part in the war raided Judean towns from Samaria to Beth Horon. They killed three thousand people and carried off great quantities of plunder.

¹⁴When Amaziah returned from slaughtering the Edomites, he brought back the gods of the people of Seir. He set them up as his own gods, bowed down to them and burned sacrifices to them. ¹⁵The anger of the Lᴏʀᴅ burned against Amaziah, and he sent a prophet to him, who said, "Why do you consult this people's gods, which could not save their own people from your hand?"

¹⁶While he was still speaking, the king said to him, "Have we appointed you an adviser to the king? Stop! Why be struck down?"

So the prophet stopped but said, "I know that God has determined to destroy you, because you have done this and have not listened to my counsel."

¹⁷After Amaziah king of Judah consulted his advisers, he sent this challenge to Jehoash ᵇ son of Jehoahaz, the son of Jehu, king of Israel: "Come, meet me face to face."

¹⁸But Jehoash king of Israel replied to Amaziah king of Judah: "A thistle in Lebanon sent a message to a cedar in Lebanon, 'Give your daughter to my son in marriage.' Then a wild beast in Lebanon came along and trampled the thistle underfoot. ¹⁹You say to yourself that you have defeated Edom, and now you are arrogant and proud. But stay at home! Why ask for trouble and cause your own downfall and that of Judah also?"

²⁰Amaziah, however, would not listen, for God so worked that he might hand them over to Jehoash, because they sought the gods of Edom. ²¹So Jehoash king of Israel attacked. He and Amaziah king of Judah faced each other at Beth Shemesh in Judah. ²²Judah was routed by Israel, and every man fled to his home. ²³Jehoash king of Israel captured Amaziah king of Judah, the son of Joash, the son of Ahaziah, ᶜ at Beth Shemesh. Then Jehoash brought him to Jerusalem and broke down the wall of Jerusalem from the Ephraim Gate to the Corner Gate—a section about six hundred feet ᵈ long. ²⁴He took all the gold and silver and all the articles found in the temple of God that had been in the care of Obed-Edom, together with the palace treasures and the hostages, and returned to Samaria.

²⁵Amaziah son of Joash king of Judah lived for fifteen years after the death of Jehoash son of Jehoahaz king of Israel. ²⁶As for the other events of Amaziah's reign, from beginning to end, are they not written in the book of the kings of Judah

---

ᵃ 6 That is, about 3 3/4 tons (about 3.4 metric tons); also in verse 9   ᵇ 17 Hebrew *Joash,* a variant of *Jehoash*; also in verses 18, 21, 23 and 25   ᶜ 23 Hebrew *Jehoahaz,* a variant of *Ahaziah*   ᵈ 23 Hebrew *four hundred cubits* (about 180 meters) and Israel? **27** From the time that Amaziah turned away from following the Lord, they conspired against him in Jerusalem and he fled to Lachish, but they sent men after him to Lachish and killed him there. **28** He was brought back by horse and was buried with his fathers in the City of Judah.

Uzziah King of Judah
26:1–4pp — 2Ki 14:21–22; 15:1–3
26:21–23pp — 2Ki 15:5–7

26 Then all the people of Judah took Uzziah,[a] who was sixteen years old, and made him king in place of his father Amaziah. **2** He was the one who rebuilt Elath and restored it to Judah after Amaziah rested with his fathers.

3 Uzziah was sixteen years old when he became king, and he reigned in Jerusalem fifty-two years. His mother's name was Jecoliah; she was from Jerusalem. **4** He did what was right in the eyes of the Lord, just as his father Amaziah had done. **5** He sought God during the days of Zechariah, who instructed him in the fear[b] of God. As long as he sought the Lord, God gave him success.

6 He went to war against the Philistines and broke down the walls of Gath, Jabneh and Ashdod. He then rebuilt towns near Ashdod and elsewhere among the Philistines. **7** God helped him against the Philistines and against the Arabs who lived in Gur Baal and against the Meunites. **8** The Ammonites brought tribute to Uzziah, and his fame spread as far as the border of Egypt, because he had become very powerful.

9 Uzziah built towers in Jerusalem at the Corner Gate, at the Valley Gate and at the angle of the wall, and he fortified them. **10** He also built towers in the desert and dug many cisterns, because he had much livestock in the foothills and in the plain. He had people working his fields and vineyards in the hills and in the fertile lands, for he loved the soil.

11 Uzziah had a well-trained army, ready to go out by divisions according to their numbers as mustered by Jeiel the secretary and Maaseiah the officer under the direction of Hananiah, one of the royal officials. **12** The total number of family leaders over the fighting men was 2,600. **13** Under their command was an army of 307,500 men trained for war, a powerful force to support the king against his enemies. **14** Uzziah provided shields, spears, helmets, coats of armor, bows and slingstones for the entire army. **15** In Jerusalem he made machines designed by skillful men for use on the towers and on the corner defenses to shoot arrows and hurl large stones. His fame spread far and wide, for he was greatly helped until he became powerful.

16 But after Uzziah became powerful, his pride led to his downfall. He was unfaithful to the Lord his God, and entered the temple of the Lord to burn incense on the altar of incense. **17** Azariah the priest with eighty other courageous priests of the Lord followed him in. **18** They confronted him and said, "It is not right for you, Uzziah, to burn incense to the Lord. That is for the priests, the descendants of Aaron, who have been consecrated to burn incense. Leave the sanctuary, for you have been unfaithful; and you will not be honored by the Lord God."

19 Uzziah, who had a censer in his hand ready to burn incense, became angry. While he was raging at the priests in their presence before the incense altar in the Lord's temple, leprosy[c] broke out on his forehead. **20** When Azariah the chief priest and all the other priests looked at him, they saw that he had leprosy on his forehead, so they hurried him out. Indeed, he himself was eager to leave, because the Lord had afflicted him.

21 King Uzziah had leprosy until the day he died. He lived in a separate house[d] —leprous, and excluded from the temple of the Lord. Jotham his son had charge of the palace and governed the people of the land.

22 The other events of Uzziah's reign, from beginning to end, are recorded by the prophet Isaiah son of Amoz. **23** Uzziah rested with his fathers and was buried near them in a field for burial that be-

---

a 1 Also called *Azariah*   *b 5* Many Hebrew manuscripts, Septuagint and Syriac; other Hebrew manuscripts *vision*
c 19 The Hebrew word was used for various diseases affecting the skin —not necessarily leprosy; also in verses 20, 21 and 23.
d 21 Or *in a house where he was relieved of responsibilities*

longed to the kings, for people said, "He had leprosy." And Jotham his son succeeded him as king.

Jotham King of Judah

27:1–4,7–9pp — 2Ki 15:33–38

27 Jotham was twenty-five years old when he became king, and he reigned in Jerusalem sixteen years. His mother's name was Jerusha daughter of Zadok. ²He did what was right in the eyes of the LORD, just as his father Uzziah had done, but unlike him he did not enter the temple of the LORD. The people, however, continued their corrupt practices. ³Jotham rebuilt the Upper Gate of the temple of the LORD and did extensive work on the wall at the hill of Ophel. ⁴He built towns in the Judean hills and forts and towers in the wooded areas.

⁵Jotham made war on the king of the Ammonites and conquered them. That year the Ammonites paid him a hundred talents[a] of silver, ten thousand cors[b] of wheat and ten thousand cors of barley. The Ammonites brought him the same amount also in the second and third years.

⁶Jotham grew powerful because he walked steadfastly before the LORD his God.

⁷The other events in Jotham's reign, including all his wars and the other things he did, are written in the book of the kings of Israel and Judah. ⁸He was twenty-five years old when he became king, and he reigned in Jerusalem sixteen years. ⁹Jotham rested with his fathers and was buried in the City of David. And Ahaz his son succeeded him as king.

Ahaz King of Judah

28:1–27pp — 2Ki 16:1–20

28 Ahaz was twenty years old when he became king, and he reigned in Jerusalem sixteen years. Unlike David his father, he did not do what was right in the eyes of the LORD. ²He walked in the ways of the kings of Israel and also made cast idols for worshiping the Baals. ³He burned sacrifices in the Valley of Ben Hinnom and sacrificed his sons in the fire, following the detestable ways of the nations the LORD had driven out before the Israelites. ⁴He offered sacrifices and burned incense at the high places, on the hilltops and under every spreading tree.

⁵Therefore the LORD his God handed him over to the king of Aram. The Arameans defeated him and took many of his people as prisoners and brought them to Damascus.

He was also given into the hands of the king of Israel, who inflicted heavy casualties on him. ⁶In one day Pekah son of Remaliah killed a hundred and twenty thousand soldiers in Judah—because Judah had forsaken the LORD, the God of their fathers. ⁷Zicri, an Ephraimite warrior, killed Maaseiah the king's son, Azrikam the officer in charge of the palace, and Elkanah, second to the king. ⁸The Israelites took captive from their kinsmen two hundred thousand wives, sons and daughters. They also took a great deal of plunder, which they carried back to Samaria.

⁹But a prophet of the LORD named Oded was there, and he went out to meet the army when it returned to Samaria. He said to them, "Because the LORD, the God of your fathers, was angry with Judah, he gave them into your hand. But you have slaughtered them in a rage that reaches to heaven. ¹⁰And now you intend to make the men and women of Judah and Jerusalem your slaves. But aren't you also guilty of sins against the LORD your God? ¹¹Now listen to me! Send back your fellow countrymen you have taken as prisoners, for the LORD's fierce anger rests on you."

¹²Then some of the leaders in Ephraim—Azariah son of Jehohanan, Berekiah son of Meshillemoth, Jehizkiah son of Shallum, and Amasa son of Hadlai—confronted those who were arriving from the war. ¹³"You must not bring those prisoners here," they said, "or we will be guilty before the LORD. Do you intend to add to our sin and guilt? For our guilt is already great, and his fierce anger rests on Israel."

¹⁴So the soldiers gave up the prisoners and plunder in the presence of the officials and all the assembly. ¹⁵The men designated by name took

---

[a] 5 That is, about 3 3/4 tons (about 3.4 metric tons) [b] 5 That is, probably about 62,000 bushels (about 2,200 kiloliters)

the prisoners, and from the plunder they clothed all who were naked. They provided them with clothes and sandals, food and drink, and healing balm. All those who were weak they put on donkeys. So they took them back to their fellow countrymen at Jericho, the City of Palms, and returned to Samaria.

¹⁶At that time King Ahaz sent to the king*a* of Assyria for help. ¹⁷The Edomites had again come and attacked Judah and carried away prisoners, ¹⁸while the Philistines had raided towns in the foothills and in the Negev of Judah. They captured and occupied Beth Shemesh, Aijalon and Gederoth, as well as Soco, Timnah and Gimzo, with their surrounding villages. ¹⁹The LORD had humbled Judah because of Ahaz king of Israel,*b* for he had promoted wickedness in Judah and had been most unfaithful to the LORD. ²⁰Tiglath-Pileser*c* king of Assyria came to him, but he gave him trouble instead of help. ²¹Ahaz took some of the things from the temple of the LORD and from the royal palace and from the princes and presented them to the king of Assyria, but that did not help him.

²²In his time of trouble King Ahaz became even more unfaithful to the LORD. ²³He offered sacrifices to the gods of Damascus, who had defeated him; for he thought, "Since the gods of the kings of Aram have helped them, I will sacrifice to them so they will help me." But they were his downfall and the downfall of all Israel.

²⁴Ahaz gathered together the furnishings from the temple of God and took them away.*d* He shut the doors of the LORD's temple and set up altars at every street corner in Jerusalem. ²⁵In every town in Judah he built high places to burn sacrifices to other gods and provoked the LORD, the God of his fathers, to anger.

²⁶The other events of his reign and all his ways, from beginning to end, are written in the book of the kings of Judah and Israel. ²⁷Ahaz rested with his fathers and was buried in the city of Jerusalem, but he was not placed in the tombs of the kings of Israel. And Hezekiah his son succeeded him as king.

Hezekiah Purifies the Temple

29:1–2pp — 2Ki 18:2–3

29 Hezekiah was twenty-five years old when he became king, and he reigned in Jerusalem twenty-nine years. His mother's name was Abijah daughter of Zechariah. ²He did what was right in the eyes of the LORD, just as his father David had done.

³In the first month of the first year of his reign, he opened the doors of the temple of the LORD and repaired them. ⁴He brought in the priests and the Levites, assembled them in the square on the east side ⁵and said: "Listen to me, Levites! Consecrate yourselves now and consecrate the temple of the LORD, the God of your fathers. Remove all defilement from the sanctuary. ⁶Our fathers were unfaithful; they did evil in the eyes of the LORD our God and forsook him. They turned their faces away from the LORD's dwelling place and turned their backs on him. ⁷They also shut the doors of the portico and put out the lamps. They did not burn incense or present any burnt offerings at the sanctuary to the God of Israel. ⁸Therefore, the anger of the LORD has fallen on Judah and Jerusalem; he has made them an object of dread and horror and scorn, as you can see with your own eyes. ⁹This is why our fathers have fallen by the sword and why our sons and daughters and our wives are in captivity. ¹⁰Now I intend to make a covenant with the LORD, the God of Israel, so that his fierce anger will turn away from us. ¹¹My sons, do not be negligent now, for the LORD has chosen you to stand before him and serve him, to minister before him and to burn incense."

¹²Then these Levites set to work:

from the Kohathites,

Mahath son of Amasai and Joel son of Azariah;

from the Merarites,

Kish son of Abdi and Azariah son of Jehallelel;

---

a 16 One Hebrew manuscript, Septuagint and Vulgate (see also 2 Kings 16:7); most Hebrew manuscripts *kings*   *b 19* That is, Judah, as frequently in 2 Chronicles   *c 20* Hebrew *Tilgath-Pilneser,* a variant of *Tiglath-Pileser*   *d 24* Or *and cut them up*

> "LISTEN TO ME, LEVITES!
> CONSECRATE YOURSELVES NOW AND
> CONSECRATE THE TEMPLE OF THE
> LORD, THE GOD OF YOUR FATHERS.
> REMOVE ALL DEFILEMENT FROM
> THE SANCTUARY."
>
> *2 Chronicles 29:5*

Cleaning House

RUTH A. DEJAGER

READ | 2 CHRONICLES 29:1–36

Perhaps you, like me, think it's satisfying to sit down and relax after doing a thorough housecleaning. Perhaps you found that once the kids grew up and moved out, there wasn't as much stuff to move and dust around. Now that you have grandchildren, the toy box, crayons, books and little shoes have returned. But it's a great problem to have, and you will have a clean house again all too soon, so you've learned not to get too stressed about it.

But God insisted on a clean house (the temple) in which to dwell. His holiness could settle for nothing less. King Ahaz had removed many precious items from the temple. It was closed up and dusty; the people had grown indifferent and negligent in worshiping the Lord. So the first thing young Hezekiah did when he became king was to reopen the temple doors, repair them and order the priests and Levites to do a thorough purification of the temple. He resolutely made sure that the house of God was restored to pristine condition. Then he led an assembly of Israelites as they offered sacrifices, worshiped and sang before the Lord once again. And afterward, all the people rejoiced!

This story makes me stop and think about our personal spiritual temples for God: our hearts. Is your heart clean enough to invite God in? Is there a lot of pride, indifference, lethargy and other spiritual junk laying around? Are the doors broken or jammed shut? If so, James says, "Come near to God and he will come near to you. Wash your hands, you sinners, and purify your hearts" (James 4:8). It's a housecleaning that Jesus is especially equipped to do, and it's great to sit down and chat with him in a clean house.

Lord God, I confess that I am often so busy with my own agenda that I neglect the temple where you want to dwell: my heart. Forgive me for the spiritual gunk I have let accumulate, and create in me a clean heart. Amen.

Your next devotion is located on page 598.

GRANDCHILD IN FOCUS • PRAYER

Relationships at Home

O Lord, I pray that you will bless the home and family of my grandchild. May the relationships she has with her parents and siblings enhance her well-being, support her self-confidence and increase her faith. May her home life reflect your love, your grace, your compassion and your peace. Guide her parents to direct her in love and truth, so she will grow into a strong and compassionate individual. Amen.

from the Gershonites,
> Joah son of Zimmah and Eden son of
> Joah;
¹³from the descendants of Elizaphan,
> Shimri and Jeiel;
from the descendants of Asaph,
> Zechariah and Mattaniah;
¹⁴from the descendants of Heman,
> Jehiel and Shimei;
from the descendants of Jeduthun,
> Shemaiah and Uzziel.

¹⁵When they had assembled their brothers and consecrated themselves, they went in to purify the temple of the Lord, as the king had ordered, following the word of the Lord. ¹⁶The priests went into the sanctuary of the Lord to purify it. They brought out to the courtyard of the Lord's temple everything unclean that they found in the temple of the Lord. The Levites took it and carried it out to the Kidron Valley. ¹⁷They began the consecration on the first day of the first month, and by the eighth day of the month they reached the portico of the Lord. For eight more days they consecrated the temple of the Lord itself, finishing on the sixteenth day of the first month.

¹⁸Then they went in to King Hezekiah and reported: "We have purified the entire temple of the Lord, the altar of burnt offering with all its utensils, and the table for setting out the consecrated bread, with all its articles. ¹⁹We have prepared and consecrated all the articles that King Ahaz removed in his unfaithfulness while he was king. They are now in front of the Lord's altar."

²⁰Early the next morning King Hezekiah gathered the city officials together and went up to the temple of the Lord. ²¹They brought seven bulls, seven rams, seven male lambs and seven male goats as a sin offering for the kingdom, for the sanctuary and for Judah. The king commanded the priests, the descendants of Aaron, to offer these on the altar of the Lord. ²²So they slaughtered the bulls, and the priests took the blood and sprinkled it on the altar; next they slaughtered the rams and sprinkled their blood on the altar; then they slaughtered the lambs and sprinkled

their blood on the altar. ²³The goats for the sin offering were brought before the king and the assembly, and they laid their hands on them. ²⁴The priests then slaughtered the goats and presented their blood on the altar for a sin offering to atone for all Israel, because the king had ordered the burnt offering and the sin offering for all Israel.

²⁵He stationed the Levites in the temple of the Lord with cymbals, harps and lyres in the way prescribed by David and Gad the king's seer and Nathan the prophet; this was commanded by the Lord through his prophets. ²⁶So the Levites stood ready with David's instruments, and the priests with their trumpets.

²⁷Hezekiah gave the order to sacrifice the burnt offering on the altar. As the offering began, singing to the Lord began also, accompanied by trumpets and the instruments of David king of Israel. ²⁸The whole assembly bowed in worship, while the singers sang and the trumpeters played. All this continued until the sacrifice of the burnt offering was completed.

²⁹When the offerings were finished, the king and everyone present with him knelt down and worshiped. ³⁰King Hezekiah and his officials ordered the Levites to praise the Lord with the words of David and of Asaph the seer. So they sang praises with gladness and bowed their heads and worshiped.

³¹Then Hezekiah said, "You have now dedicated yourselves to the Lord. Come and bring sacrifices and thank offerings to the temple of the Lord." So the assembly brought sacrifices and thank offerings, and all whose hearts were willing brought burnt offerings.

³²The number of burnt offerings the assembly brought was seventy bulls, a hundred rams and two hundred male lambs—all of them for burnt offerings to the Lord. ³³The animals consecrated as sacrifices amounted to six hundred bulls and three thousand sheep and goats. ³⁴The priests, however, were too few to skin all the burnt offerings; so their kinsmen the Levites helped them until the task was finished and until other priests had been consecrated, for the Levites had been

more conscientious in consecrating themselves than the priests had been. ³⁵There were burnt offerings in abundance, together with the fat of the fellowship offerings *a* and the drink offerings that accompanied the burnt offerings.

So the service of the temple of the LORD was reestablished. ³⁶Hezekiah and all the people rejoiced at what God had brought about for his people, because it was done so quickly.

Hezekiah Celebrates the Passover

30 Hezekiah sent word to all Israel and Judah and also wrote letters to Ephraim and Manasseh, inviting them to come to the temple of the LORD in Jerusalem and celebrate the Passover to the LORD, the God of Israel. ²The king and his officials and the whole assembly in Jerusalem decided to celebrate the Passover in the second month. ³They had not been able to celebrate it at the regular time because not enough priests had consecrated themselves and the people had not assembled in Jerusalem. ⁴The plan seemed right both to the king and to the whole assembly. ⁵They decided to send a proclamation throughout Israel, from Beersheba to Dan, calling the people to come to Jerusalem and celebrate the Passover to the LORD, the God of Israel. It had not been celebrated in large numbers according to what was written.

⁶At the king's command, couriers went throughout Israel and Judah with letters from the king and from his officials, which read:

"People of Israel, return to the LORD, the God of Abraham, Isaac and Israel, that he may return to you who are left, who have escaped from the hand of the kings of Assyria. ⁷Do not be like your fathers and brothers, who were unfaithful to the LORD, the God of their fathers, so that he made them an object of horror, as you see. ⁸Do not be stiff-necked, as your fathers were; submit to the LORD. Come to the sanctuary, which he has consecrated forever. Serve the LORD your God, so that his fierce anger will turn away from you. ⁹If you return to the LORD, then your brothers and your children will be shown compassion by their captors and will come back to this land, for the LORD your God is gracious and compassionate. He will not turn his face from you if you return to him."

¹⁰The couriers went from town to town in Ephraim and Manasseh, as far as Zebulun, but the people scorned and ridiculed them. ¹¹Nevertheless, some men of Asher, Manasseh and Zebulun humbled themselves and went to Jerusalem. ¹²Also in Judah the hand of God was on the people to give them unity of mind to carry out what the king and his officials had ordered, following the word of the LORD.

¹³A very large crowd of people assembled in Jerusalem to celebrate the Feast of Unleavened Bread in the second month. ¹⁴They removed the altars in Jerusalem and cleared away the incense altars and threw them into the Kidron Valley.

¹⁵They slaughtered the Passover lamb on the fourteenth day of the second month. The priests and the Levites were ashamed and consecrated themselves and brought burnt offerings to the temple of the LORD. ¹⁶Then they took up their regular positions as prescribed in the Law of Moses the man of God. The priests sprinkled the blood handed to them by the Levites. ¹⁷Since many in the crowd had not consecrated themselves, the Levites had to kill the Passover lambs for all those who were not ceremonially clean and could not consecrate ˎtheir lambsˎ to the LORD. ¹⁸Although most of the many people who came from Ephraim, Manasseh, Issachar and Zebulun had not purified themselves, yet they ate the Passover, contrary to what was written. But Hezekiah prayed for them, saying, "May the LORD, who is good, pardon everyone ¹⁹who sets his heart on seeking God—the LORD, the God of his fathers—even if he is not clean according to the rules of the sanctuary." ²⁰And the LORD heard Hezekiah and healed the people.

a 35 Traditionally *peace offerings*

Nursing Home Appreciation

Invite your grandkids to join you in a visit some afternoon to an elderly relative, family friend or church member who lives in a nursing home. This may be a new experience for your grandchild, so explain to them in advance what to expect. Many nursing home residents don't often see young people, so this will be a treat for them. Encourage the kids to tell about their school or their friends. Have them bring along a favorite toy or book to show and share. Be flexible in how long you stay.

When your visit is over, discuss the experience with the kids. Talk about why it was important to make this visit (even if it was unpleasant or uncomfortable — see Matthew 25:34 – 40). Encourage them to make another visit.

Long-Distance Variation: Invite your out-of-town grandkids to enter into a pen-pal relationship with a nursing home resident you know and visit.

God of generations, thank you for my relationship with my grandchildren. Help me to instill in them a new appreciation and compassion for those who find themselves confined. Help them to understand that what we do for others, we do for you. Amen.

Your next devotion is located on page 603.

GRANDCHILD IN FOCUS • PRAYER

Friends

Dear Lord and Father, I pray for my grandchild's social life and his friends. Bring diverse friends into his life who will love and encourage him, who will bring joy and laughter to the good times and comfort and support through difficulties and disappointments. Grant him wisdom and discernment as he selects his friends; help him to avoid cliques that restrict, activities that endanger, and foolish and dangerous behaviors that harm. I ask that you fill his life with close and caring relationships. Amen.

²¹ The Israelites who were present in Jerusalem celebrated the Feast of Unleavened Bread for seven days with great rejoicing, while the Levites and priests sang to the Lord every day, accompanied by the Lord's instruments of praise. *a*

²² Hezekiah spoke encouragingly to all the Levites, who showed good understanding of the service of the Lord. For the seven days they ate their assigned portion and offered fellowship offerings *b* and praised the Lord, the God of their fathers.

²³ The whole assembly then agreed to celebrate the festival seven more days; so for another seven days they celebrated joyfully. ²⁴ Hezekiah king of Judah provided a thousand bulls and seven thousand sheep and goats for the assembly, and the officials provided them with a thousand bulls and ten thousand sheep and goats. A great number of priests consecrated themselves. ²⁵ The entire assembly of Judah rejoiced, along with the priests and Levites and all who had assembled from Israel, including the aliens who had come from Israel and those who lived in Judah. ²⁶ There was great joy in Jerusalem, for since the days of Solomon son of David king of Israel there had been nothing like this in Jerusalem. ²⁷ The priests and the Levites stood to bless the people, and God heard them, for their prayer reached heaven, his holy dwelling place.

31 When all this had ended, the Israelites who were there went out to the towns of Judah, smashed the sacred stones and cut down the Asherah poles. They destroyed the high places and the altars throughout Judah and Benjamin and in Ephraim and Manasseh. After they had destroyed all of them, the Israelites returned to their own towns and to their own property.

Contributions for Worship

31:20–21pp — 2Ki 18:5–7

² Hezekiah assigned the priests and Levites to divisions—each of them according to their duties as priests or Levites—to offer burnt offerings and fellowship offerings, *b* to minister, to give thanks and to sing praises at the gates of the Lord's dwelling. ³ The king contributed from his own possessions for the morning and evening burnt offerings and for the burnt offerings on the Sabbaths, New Moons and appointed feasts as written in the Law of the Lord. ⁴ He ordered the people living in Jerusalem to give the portion due the priests and Levites so they could devote themselves to the Law of the Lord. ⁵ As soon as the order went out, the Israelites generously gave the firstfruits of their grain, new wine, oil and honey and all that the fields produced. They brought a great amount, a tithe of everything. ⁶ The men of Israel and Judah who lived in the towns of Judah also brought a tithe of their herds and flocks and a tithe of the holy things dedicated to the Lord their God, and they piled them in heaps. ⁷ They began doing this in the third month and finished in the seventh month. ⁸ When Hezekiah and his officials came and saw the heaps, they praised the Lord and blessed his people Israel.

⁹ Hezekiah asked the priests and Levites about the heaps; ¹⁰ and Azariah the chief priest, from the family of Zadok, answered, "Since the people began to bring their contributions to the temple of the Lord, we have had enough to eat and plenty to spare, because the Lord has blessed his people, and this great amount is left over."

¹¹ Hezekiah gave orders to prepare storerooms in the temple of the Lord, and this was done. ¹² Then they faithfully brought in the contributions, tithes and dedicated gifts. Conaniah, a Levite, was in charge of these things, and his brother Shimei was next in rank. ¹³ Jehiel, Azariah, Nahath, Asahel, Jerimoth, Jozabad, Eliel, Ismakiah, Mahath and Benaiah were supervisors under Conaniah and Shimei his brother, by appointment of King Hezekiah and Azariah the official in charge of the temple of God.

¹⁴ Kore son of Imnah the Levite, keeper of the East Gate, was in charge of the freewill offerings given to God, distributing the contributions made to the Lord and also the consecrated

---

a 21 Or *priests praised the Lord every day with resounding instruments belonging to the Lord* *b 22,2* Traditionally *peace offerings* gifts. ¹⁵Eden, Miniamin, Jeshua, Shemaiah, Amariah and Shecaniah assisted him faithfully in the towns of the priests, distributing to their fellow priests according to their divisions, old and young alike.

¹⁶In addition, they distributed to the males three years old or more whose names were in the genealogical records—all who would enter the temple of the LORD to perform the daily duties of their various tasks, according to their responsibilities and their divisions. ¹⁷And they distributed to the priests enrolled by their families in the genealogical records and likewise to the Levites twenty years old or more, according to their responsibilities and their divisions. ¹⁸They included all the little ones, the wives, and the sons and daughters of the whole community listed in these genealogical records. For they were faithful in consecrating themselves.

¹⁹As for the priests, the descendants of Aaron, who lived on the farm lands around their towns or in any other towns, men were designated by name to distribute portions to every male among them and to all who were recorded in the genealogies of the Levites.

²⁰This is what Hezekiah did throughout Judah, doing what was good and right and faithful before the LORD his God. ²¹In everything that he undertook in the service of God's temple and in obedience to the law and the commands, he sought his God and worked wholeheartedly. And so he prospered.

Sennacherib Threatens Jerusalem

32:9–19pp — 2Ki 18:17–35; Isa 36:2–20
32:20–21pp — 2Ki 19:35–37; Isa 37:36–38

32 After all that Hezekiah had so faithfully done, Sennacherib king of Assyria came and invaded Judah. He laid siege to the fortified cities, thinking to conquer them for himself. ²When Hezekiah saw that Sennacherib had come and that he intended to make war on Jerusalem, ³he consulted with his officials and military staff about blocking off the water from the springs outside the city, and they helped him. ⁴A large force of men assembled, and they blocked all the springs and the stream that flowed through the land. "Why should the kings *ᵃ* of Assyria come and find plenty of water?" they said. ⁵Then he worked hard repairing all the broken sections of the wall and building towers on it. He built another wall outside that one and reinforced the supporting terraces *ᵇ* of the City of David. He also made large numbers of weapons and shields.

⁶He appointed military officers over the people and assembled them before him in the square at the city gate and encouraged them with these words: ⁷"Be strong and courageous. Do not be afraid or discouraged because of the king of Assyria and the vast army with him, for there is a greater power with us than with him. ⁸With him is only the arm of flesh, but with us is the LORD our God to help us and to fight our battles." And the people gained confidence from what Hezekiah the king of Judah said.

⁹Later, when Sennacherib king of Assyria and all his forces were laying siege to Lachish, he sent his officers to Jerusalem with this message for Hezekiah king of Judah and for all the people of Judah who were there:

¹⁰"This is what Sennacherib king of Assyria says: On what are you basing your confidence, that you remain in Jerusalem under siege? ¹¹When Hezekiah says, 'The LORD our God will save us from the hand of the king of Assyria,' he is misleading you, to let

TALKING POINTS

Values

We should value seeking God
and honorable work.

2 CHRONICLES 31:20–21

For more on values, go to Jeremiah 9:23–24.

ᵃ 4 Hebrew; Septuagint and Syriac *king*   *ᵇ 5* Or *the Millo* you die of hunger and thirst. [12] Did not Hezekiah himself remove this god's high places and altars, saying to Judah and Jerusalem, 'You must worship before one altar and burn sacrifices on it'?

[13] "Do you not know what I and my fathers have done to all the peoples of the other lands? Were the gods of those nations ever able to deliver their land from my hand? [14] Who of all the gods of these nations that my fathers destroyed has been able to save his people from me? How then can your god deliver you from my hand? [15] Now do not let Hezekiah deceive you and mislead you like this. Do not believe him, for no god of any nation or kingdom has been able to deliver his people from my hand or the hand of my fathers. How much less will your god deliver you from my hand!"

[16] Sennacherib's officers spoke further against the LORD God and against his servant Hezekiah. [17] The king also wrote letters insulting the LORD, the God of Israel, and saying this against him: "Just as the gods of the peoples of the other lands did not rescue their people from my hand, so the god of Hezekiah will not rescue his people from my hand." [18] Then they called out in Hebrew to the people of Jerusalem who were on the wall, to terrify them and make them afraid in order to capture the city. [19] They spoke about the God of Jerusalem as they did about the gods of the other peoples of the world—the work of men's hands.

[20] King Hezekiah and the prophet Isaiah son of Amoz cried out in prayer to heaven about this. [21] And the LORD sent an angel, who annihilated all the fighting men and the leaders and officers in the camp of the Assyrian king. So he withdrew to his own land in disgrace. And when he went into the temple of his god, some of his sons cut him down with the sword.

[22] So the LORD saved Hezekiah and the people of Jerusalem from the hand of Sennacherib king of Assyria and from the hand of all others. He took care of them [a] on every side. [23] Many brought offerings to Jerusalem for the LORD and valuable gifts for Hezekiah king of Judah. From then on he was highly regarded by all the nations.

Hezekiah's Pride, Success and Death
32:24–33pp — 2Ki 20:1–21; Isa 37:21–38; 38:1–8

[24] In those days Hezekiah became ill and was at the point of death. He prayed to the LORD, who answered him and gave him a miraculous sign. [25] But Hezekiah's heart was proud and he did not respond to the kindness shown him; therefore the LORD's wrath was on him and on Judah and Jerusalem. [26] Then Hezekiah repented of the pride of his heart, as did the people of Jerusalem; therefore the LORD's wrath did not come upon them during the days of Hezekiah.

[27] Hezekiah had very great riches and honor, and he made treasuries for his silver and gold and for his precious stones, spices, shields and all kinds of valuables. [28] He also made buildings to store the harvest of grain, new wine and oil; and he made stalls for various kinds of cattle, and pens for the flocks. [29] He built villages and acquired great numbers of flocks and herds, for God had given him very great riches.

[30] It was Hezekiah who blocked the upper outlet of the Gihon spring and channeled the water down to the west side of the City of David. He succeeded in everything he undertook. [31] But when envoys were sent by the rulers of Babylon to ask him about the miraculous sign that had occurred in the land, God left him to test him and to know everything that was in his heart.

[32] The other events of Hezekiah's reign and his acts of devotion are written in the vision of the prophet Isaiah son of Amoz in the book of the kings of Judah and Israel. [33] Hezekiah rested with his fathers and was buried on the hill where the tombs of David's descendants are. All Judah and the people of Jerusalem honored him when he died. And Manasseh his son succeeded him as king.

[a] 22 Hebrew; Septuagint and Vulgate *He gave them rest*

Manasseh King of Judah

33:1–10pp — 2Ki 21:1–10
33:18–20pp — 2Ki 21:17–18

33 Manasseh was twelve years old when he became king, and he reigned in Jerusalem fifty-five years. [2]He did evil in the eyes of the LORD, following the detestable practices of the nations the LORD had driven out before the Israelites. [3]He rebuilt the high places his father Hezekiah had demolished; he also erected altars to the Baals and made Asherah poles. He bowed down to all the starry hosts and worshiped them. [4]He built altars in the temple of the LORD, of which the LORD had said, "My Name will remain in Jerusalem forever." [5]In both courts of the temple of the LORD, he built altars to all the starry hosts. [6]He sacrificed his sons in[a] the fire in the Valley of Ben Hinnom, practiced sorcery, divination and witchcraft, and consulted mediums and spiritists. He did much evil in the eyes of the LORD, provoking him to anger.

[7]He took the carved image he had made and put it in God's temple, of which God had said to David and to his son Solomon, "In this temple and in Jerusalem, which I have chosen out of all the tribes of Israel, I will put my Name forever. [8]I will not again make the feet of the Israelites leave the land I assigned to your forefathers, if only they will be careful to do everything I commanded them concerning all the laws, decrees and ordinances given through Moses." [9]But Manasseh led Judah and the people of Jerusalem astray, so that they did more evil than the nations the LORD had destroyed before the Israelites.

[10]The LORD spoke to Manasseh and his people, but they paid no attention. [11]So the LORD brought against them the army commanders of the king of Assyria, who took Manasseh prisoner, put a hook in his nose, bound him with bronze shackles and took him to Babylon. [12]In his distress he sought the favor of the LORD his God and humbled himself greatly before the God of his fathers. [13]And when he prayed to him, the LORD was moved by his entreaty and listened to his plea; so he brought him back to Jerusalem and to his kingdom. Then Manasseh knew that the LORD is God.

[14]Afterward he rebuilt the outer wall of the City of David, west of the Gihon spring in the valley, as far as the entrance of the Fish Gate and encircling the hill of Ophel; he also made it much higher. He stationed military commanders in all the fortified cities in Judah.

[15]He got rid of the foreign gods and removed the image from the temple of the LORD, as well as all the altars he had built on the temple hill and in Jerusalem; and he threw them out of the city. [16]Then he restored the altar of the LORD and sacrificed fellowship offerings[b] and thank offerings on it, and told Judah to serve the LORD, the God of Israel. [17]The people, however, continued to sacrifice at the high places, but only to the LORD their God.

[18]The other events of Manasseh's reign, including his prayer to his God and the words the seers spoke to him in the name of the LORD, the God of Israel, are written in the annals of the kings of Israel.[c] [19]His prayer and how God was moved by his entreaty, as well as all his sins and unfaithfulness, and the sites where he built high places and set up Asherah poles and idols before he humbled himself—all are written in the records of the seers.[d] [20]Manasseh rested with his fathers and was buried in his palace. And Amon his son succeeded him as king.

Amon King of Judah

33:21–25pp — 2Ki 21:19–24

[21]Amon was twenty-two years old when he became king, and he reigned in Jerusalem two years. [22]He did evil in the eyes of the LORD, as his father Manasseh had done. Amon worshiped and offered sacrifices to all the idols Manasseh had made. [23]But unlike his father Manasseh, he did not humble himself before the LORD; Amon increased his guilt.

---

[a] 6 Or *He made his sons pass through*   [b] 16 Traditionally *peace offerings*   [c] 18 That is, Judah, as frequently in 2 Chronicles   [d] 19 One Hebrew manuscript and Septuagint; most Hebrew manuscripts *of Hozai*

Worship the Lord

O LORD, our Lord,
>how majestic is your name in all the earth!

You have set your glory
>above the heavens.
From the lips of children and infants
>you have ordained praise
because of your enemies,
>to silence the foe and the avenger.

When I consider your heavens,
>the work of your fingers,
the moon and the stars,
>which you have set in place,
what is man that you are mindful of him,
>the son of man that you care for him?
You made him a little lower than the
>heavenly beings
and crowned him with glory and
>honor.

Psalm 8:1—5

My God and Creator, I pause to marvel at your glory. I stand in awe of your majesty and compassion. Thank you for keeping me in the forefront of your mind and holding me in such high regard. In this day of worship and praise, may the songs of little children tell the world of your love. Amen.

GRANDCHILD IN FOCUS • PRAYER

Self-Image

O loving God, I praise you for creating my grandchild as a unique individual. Now I ask you to help her appreciate her uniqueness. Build up her self-image so she can enjoy her individuality. Help her to stand firm for who she is, where she has come from and what she believes in. Encourage her not only to have hopes and dreams but to also enjoy each day as it comes.
In Jesus' name, amen.

Your next devotion is located on page 616.

²⁴Amon's officials conspired against him and assassinated him in his palace. ²⁵Then the people of the land killed all who had plotted against King Amon, and they made Josiah his son king in his place.

Josiah's Reforms

34:1–2pp — 2Ki 22:1–2
34:3–7Ref — 2Ki 23:4–20
34:8–13pp — 2Ki 22:3–7

34 Josiah was eight years old when he became king, and he reigned in Jerusalem thirty-one years. ²He did what was right in the eyes of the LORD and walked in the ways of his father David, not turning aside to the right or to the left.

³In the eighth year of his reign, while he was still young, he began to seek the God of his father David. In his twelfth year he began to purge Judah and Jerusalem of high places, Asherah poles, carved idols and cast images. ⁴Under his direction the altars of the Baals were torn down; he cut to pieces the incense altars that were above them, and smashed the Asherah poles, the idols and the images. These he broke to pieces and scattered over the graves of those who had sacrificed to them. ⁵He burned the bones of the priests on their altars, and so he purged Judah and Jerusalem. ⁶In the towns of Manasseh, Ephraim and Simeon, as far as Naphtali, and in the ruins around them, ⁷he tore down the altars and the Asherah poles and crushed the idols to powder and cut to pieces all the incense altars throughout Israel. Then he went back to Jerusalem.

⁸In the eighteenth year of Josiah's reign, to purify the land and the temple, he sent Shaphan son of Azaliah and Maaseiah the ruler of the city, with Joah son of Joahaz, the recorder, to repair the temple of the LORD his God.

⁹They went to Hilkiah the high priest and gave him the money that had been brought into the temple of God, which the Levites who were the doorkeepers had collected from the people of Manasseh, Ephraim and the entire remnant of Israel and from all the people of Judah and Ben-

stories to share

2 CHRONICLES 34:1–13

Josiah, the Boy King

LIFE LESSON: God values faithful service.

TO TALK ABOUT

✦ How would you like to be an eight-year-old king?

✦ Why is it important to serve God from the time we're young?

✦ In what ways have you been faithful to God?

✦ How can you remain faithful to God throughout your life?

jamin and the inhabitants of Jerusalem. ¹⁰Then they entrusted it to the men appointed to supervise the work on the LORD's temple. These men paid the workers who repaired and restored the temple. ¹¹They also gave money to the carpenters and builders to purchase dressed stone, and timber for joists and beams for the buildings that the kings of Judah had allowed to fall into ruin.

¹²The men did the work faithfully. Over them to direct them were Jahath and Obadiah, Levites descended from Merari, and Zechariah and Meshullam, descended from Kohath. The Levites—all who were skilled in playing musical instruments— ¹³had charge of the laborers and supervised all the workers from job to job. Some of the Levites were secretaries, scribes and doorkeepers.

The Book of the Law Found

34:14–28pp — 2Ki 22:8–20
34:29–32pp — 2Ki 23:1–3

¹⁴While they were bringing out the money that had been taken into the temple of the LORD, Hilkiah the priest found the Book of the Law of the LORD that had been given through Moses. ¹⁵Hilkiah said to Shaphan the secretary, "I have found the Book of the Law in the temple of the LORD." He gave it to Shaphan.

¹⁶Then Shaphan took the book to the king and reported to him: "Your officials are doing everything that has been committed to them. ¹⁷They have paid out the money that was in the temple of the LORD and have entrusted it to the supervisors and workers." ¹⁸Then Shaphan the secretary informed the king, "Hilkiah the priest has given me a book." And Shaphan read from it in the presence of the king.

¹⁹When the king heard the words of the Law, he tore his robes. ²⁰He gave these orders to Hilkiah, Ahikam son of Shaphan, Abdon son of Micah,[a] Shaphan the secretary and Asaiah the king's attendant: ²¹"Go and inquire of the LORD for me and for the remnant in Israel and Judah about what is written in this book that has been found. Great is the LORD's anger that is poured out on us because our fathers have not kept the word of the LORD; they have not acted in accordance with all that is written in this book."

²²Hilkiah and those the king had sent with him[b] went to speak to the prophetess Huldah, who was the wife of Shallum son of Tokhath,[c] the son of Hasrah,[d] keeper of the wardrobe. She lived in Jerusalem, in the Second District.

²³She said to them, "This is what the LORD, the God of Israel, says: Tell the man who sent you to me, ²⁴'This is what the LORD says: I am going to bring disaster on this place and its people—all the curses written in the book that has been read in the presence of the king of Judah. ²⁵Because they have forsaken me and burned incense to other gods and provoked me to anger by all that their hands have made,[e] my anger will be poured out on this place and will not be quenched.' ²⁶Tell the king of Judah, who sent you to inquire of the LORD, 'This is what the LORD, the God of Israel, says concerning the words you heard: ²⁷Because your heart was responsive and you humbled yourself before God when you heard what he spoke against this place and its people, and because you humbled yourself before me and tore your robes and wept in my presence, I have heard you, declares the LORD. ²⁸Now I will gather you to your fathers, and you will be buried in peace. Your eyes

---

[a] 20 Also called *Acbor son of Micaiah*   [b] 22 One Hebrew manuscript, Vulgate and Syriac; most Hebrew manuscripts do not have *had sent with him.*   [c] 22 Also called *Tikvah*   [d] 22 Also called *Harhas*   [e] 25 Or *by everything they have done*

stories to share

2 CHRONICLES 34:14–33

The Book of the Law Found

LIFE LESSON: God values faithful leaders.

TO TALK ABOUT

✦ What did Hilkiah find in the temple?

✦ How do you think it had gotten lost and forgotten?

✦ How would you have responded if God's Word had been forgotten and someone had found it?

✦ What difference can a faithful, committed leader make in the lives of those who follow him or her?

will not see all the disaster I am going to bring on this place and on those who live here.'"

So they took her answer back to the king.

²⁹ Then the king called together all the elders of Judah and Jerusalem. ³⁰ He went up to the temple of the LORD with the men of Judah, the people of Jerusalem, the priests and the Levites—all the people from the least to the greatest. He read in their hearing all the words of the Book of the Covenant, which had been found in the temple of the LORD. ³¹ The king stood by his pillar and renewed the covenant in the presence of the LORD—to follow the LORD and keep his commands, regulations and decrees with all his heart and all his soul, and to obey the words of the covenant written in this book.

³² Then he had everyone in Jerusalem and Benjamin pledge themselves to it; the people of Jerusalem did this in accordance with the covenant of God, the God of their fathers.

³³ Josiah removed all the detestable idols from all the territory belonging to the Israelites, and he had all who were present in Israel serve the LORD their God. As long as he lived, they did not fail to follow the LORD, the God of their fathers.

Josiah Celebrates the Passover
35:1,18–19pp — 2Ki 23:21–23

35 Josiah celebrated the Passover to the LORD in Jerusalem, and the Passover lamb was slaughtered on the fourteenth day of the first month. ² He appointed the priests to their duties and encouraged them in the service of the LORD's temple. ³ He said to the Levites, who instructed all Israel and who had been consecrated to the LORD: "Put the sacred ark in the temple that Solomon son of David king of Israel built. It is not to be carried about on your shoulders. Now serve the LORD your God and his people Israel. ⁴ Prepare yourselves by families in your divisions, according to the directions written by David king of Israel and by his son Solomon.

⁵ "Stand in the holy place with a group of Levites for each subdivision of the families of your fellow countrymen, the lay people. ⁶ Slaughter the Passover lambs, consecrate yourselves and prepare ⌊the lambs⌋ for your fellow countrymen, doing what the LORD commanded through Moses."

⁷ Josiah provided for all the lay people who were there a total of thirty thousand sheep and goats for the Passover offerings, and also three thousand cattle—all from the king's own possessions.

⁸ His officials also contributed voluntarily to the people and the priests and Levites. Hilkiah, Zechariah and Jehiel, the administrators of God's temple, gave the priests twenty-six hundred Passover offerings and three hundred cattle. ⁹ Also Conaniah along with Shemaiah and Nethanel, his brothers, and Hashabiah, Jeiel and Jozabad, the leaders of the Levites, provided five thousand Passover offerings and five hundred head of cattle for the Levites.

¹⁰ The service was arranged and the priests stood in their places with the Levites in their divisions as the king had ordered. ¹¹ The Passover lambs were slaughtered, and the priests sprinkled the blood handed to them, while the Levites skinned the animals. ¹² They set aside the burnt offerings to give them to the subdivisions of the families of the people to offer to the LORD, as is written in the Book of Moses. They did the same with the cattle. ¹³ They roasted the Passover animals over the fire as prescribed, and boiled the holy offerings in pots, caldrons and pans and served them quickly to all the people. ¹⁴ After this, they made preparations for themselves and for the priests, because the priests, the descendants of Aaron, were sacrificing the burnt offerings and the fat portions until nightfall. So the Levites made preparations for themselves and for the Aaronic priests.

¹⁵ The musicians, the descendants of Asaph, were in the places prescribed by David, Asaph, Heman and Jeduthun the king's seer. The gatekeepers at each gate did not need to leave their posts, because their fellow Levites made the preparations for them.

¹⁶ So at that time the entire service of the LORD was carried out for the celebration of the

Passover and the offering of burnt offerings on the altar of the LORD, as King Josiah had ordered. ¹⁷The Israelites who were present celebrated the Passover at that time and observed the Feast of Unleavened Bread for seven days. ¹⁸The Passover had not been observed like this in Israel since the days of the prophet Samuel; and none of the kings of Israel had ever celebrated such a Passover as did Josiah, with the priests, the Levites and all Judah and Israel who were there with the people of Jerusalem. ¹⁹This Passover was celebrated in the eighteenth year of Josiah's reign.

The Death of Josiah
35:20 – 36:1pp — 2Ki 23:28 – 30

²⁰After all this, when Josiah had set the temple in order, Neco king of Egypt went up to fight at Carchemish on the Euphrates, and Josiah marched out to meet him in battle. ²¹But Neco sent messengers to him, saying, "What quarrel is there between you and me, O king of Judah? It is not you I am attacking at this time, but the house with which I am at war. God has told me to hurry; so stop opposing God, who is with me, or he will destroy you."

²²Josiah, however, would not turn away from him, but disguised himself to engage him in battle. He would not listen to what Neco had said at God's command but went to fight him on the plain of Megiddo.

²³Archers shot King Josiah, and he told his officers, "Take me away; I am badly wounded." ²⁴So they took him out of his chariot, put him in the other chariot he had and brought him to Jerusalem, where he died. He was buried in the tombs of his fathers, and all Judah and Jerusalem mourned for him.

²⁵Jeremiah composed laments for Josiah, and to this day all the men and women singers commemorate Josiah in the laments. These became a tradition in Israel and are written in the Laments.

²⁶The other events of Josiah's reign and his acts of devotion, according to what is written in the Law of the LORD— ²⁷all the events, from beginning to end, are written in the book of the kings of Israel and Judah.

36

¹And the people of the land took Jehoahaz son of Josiah and made him king in Jerusalem in place of his father.

Jehoahaz King of Judah
36:2 – 4pp — 2Ki 23:31 – 34

²Jehoahaz[a] was twenty-three years old when he became king, and he reigned in Jerusalem three months. ³The king of Egypt dethroned him in Jerusalem and imposed on Judah a levy of a hundred talents[b] of silver and a talent[c] of gold. ⁴The king of Egypt made Eliakim, a brother of Jehoahaz, king over Judah and Jerusalem and changed Eliakim's name to Jehoiakim. But Neco took Eliakim's brother Jehoahaz and carried him off to Egypt.

Jehoiakim King of Judah
36:5 – 8pp — 2Ki 23:36 – 24:6

⁵Jehoiakim was twenty-five years old when he became king, and he reigned in Jerusalem eleven years. He did evil in the eyes of the LORD his God. ⁶Nebuchadnezzar king of Babylon attacked him and bound him with bronze shackles to take him to Babylon. ⁷Nebuchadnezzar also took to Babylon articles from the temple of the LORD and put them in his temple[d] there.

⁸The other events of Jehoiakim's reign, the detestable things he did and all that was found against him, are written in the book of the kings of Israel and Judah. And Jehoiachin his son succeeded him as king.

Jehoiachin King of Judah
36:9 – 10pp — 2Ki 24:8 – 17

⁹Jehoiachin was eighteen[e] years old when he became king, and he reigned in Jerusalem three months and ten days. He did evil in the eyes of

a 2 Hebrew Joahaz, a variant of Jehoahaz; also in verse 4   b 3 That is, about 3 3/4 tons (about 3.4 metric tons)   c 3 That is, about 75 pounds (about 34 kilograms)   d 7 Or palace   e 9 One Hebrew manuscript, some Septuagint manuscripts and Syriac (see also 2 Kings 24:8); most Hebrew manuscripts eight the Lord. [10]In the spring, King Nebuchadnezzar sent for him and brought him to Babylon, together with articles of value from the temple of the Lord, and he made Jehoiachin's uncle,[a] Zedekiah, king over Judah and Jerusalem.

Zedekiah King of Judah

36:11–16pp — 2Ki 24:18–20; Jer 52:1–3

[11]Zedekiah was twenty-one years old when he became king, and he reigned in Jerusalem eleven years. [12]He did evil in the eyes of the Lord his God and did not humble himself before Jeremiah the prophet, who spoke the word of the Lord. [13]He also rebelled against King Nebuchadnezzar, who had made him take an oath in God's name. He became stiff-necked and hardened his heart and would not turn to the Lord, the God of Israel. [14]Furthermore, all the leaders of the priests and the people became more and more unfaithful, following all the detestable practices of the nations and defiling the temple of the Lord, which he had consecrated in Jerusalem.

The Fall of Jerusalem

36:17–20pp — 2Ki 25:1–21; Jer 52:4–27
36:22–23pp — Ezr 1:1–3

[15]The Lord, the God of their fathers, sent word to them through his messengers again and again, because he had pity on his people and on his dwelling place. [16]But they mocked God's messengers, despised his words and scoffed at his prophets until the wrath of the Lord was aroused against his people and there was no remedy. [17]He brought up against them the king of the Babylonians,[b] who killed their young men with the sword in the sanctuary, and spared neither young man nor young woman, old man or aged. God handed all of them over to Nebuchadnezzar. [18]He carried to Babylon all the articles from the temple of God, both large and small, and the treasures of the Lord's temple and the treasures of the king and his officials. [19]They set fire to God's temple and broke down the wall of Jerusalem; they burned all the palaces and destroyed everything of value there.

[20]He carried into exile to Babylon the remnant, who escaped from the sword, and they became servants to him and his sons until the kingdom of Persia came to power. [21]The land enjoyed its sabbath rests; all the time of its desolation it rested, until the seventy years were completed in fulfillment of the word of the Lord spoken by Jeremiah.

[22]In the first year of Cyrus king of Persia, in order to fulfill the word of the Lord spoken by Jeremiah, the Lord moved the heart of Cyrus king of Persia to make a proclamation throughout his realm and to put it in writing:

[23]"This is what Cyrus king of Persia says:

"'The Lord, the God of heaven, has given me all the kingdoms of the earth and he has appointed me to build a temple for him at Jerusalem in Judah. Anyone of his people among you—may the Lord his God be with him, and let him go up.'"

[a] 10 Hebrew *brother,* that is, relative (see 2 Kings 24:17)
[b] 17 Or *Chaldeans*

Time
TO GO HOME

The book of Ezra records the story of God's people as they returned to Judah. The first part of the book records the Persian emperor's decree encouraging the Jews' return, which is followed by an account of the return of the first group of exiles, led by Sheshbazzar. Returning to their homeland was not easy for God's people. The trip was treacherous, and once they arrived, the enemies of Judah opposed them and delayed their work. In addition, the rebuilt temple (finally completed in 516 B.C.) was a joy to some but a disappointment to others who remembered the splendor of the original temple.

The second part of the book recounts the return of a second group of exiles, led by Ezra, a priest and an organized leader. Ezra's responsibilities included tracking the lineage of the returnees, ensuring Levites were in the group to help with worship, counting the temple treasures that rightfully belonged in God's temple, conducting the people in a confession of sin and praying for God's presence and guidance. Reconciling themselves to the laws of God was difficult, but the people had returned to their land and to their God, just as God had promised.

The story told in the book of Ezra is one that gives us all hope. God's people experienced some very difficult situations, but God never let them down. Like he did for his people during the time period chronicled in the book of Ezra, he will always keep his promises to us as well.

VERSE *to* REMEMBER | EZRA 1:3

"Anyone of his people among you — may his God be with him, and let him go up to Jerusalem in Judah and build the temple of the LORD, the God of Israel, the God who is in Jerusalem."

ABOUT EZRA

WRITTEN BY:
Unknown, possibly Ezra

WRITTEN FOR:
The people of Judah who had returned from exile in Babylon

DATE WRITTEN:
Sometime after 440 B.C.

WHY WRITTEN:
To show how God had kept his promise and brought the Jews back to their homeland

Cyrus Helps the Exiles to Return
1:1–3pp — 2Ch 36:22–23

1 In the first year of Cyrus king of Persia, in order to fulfill the word of the LORD spoken by Jeremiah, the LORD moved the heart of Cyrus king of Persia to make a proclamation throughout his realm and to put it in writing:

² "This is what Cyrus king of Persia says:

" 'The LORD, the God of heaven, has given me all the kingdoms of the earth and he has appointed me to build a temple for him at Jerusalem in Judah. ³ Anyone of his people among you — may his God be with him, and let him go up to Jerusalem in Judah and build the temple of the LORD, the God of Israel, the God who is in Jerusalem. ⁴ And the people of any place where survivors may now be living are to provide him with silver and gold, with goods and livestock, and with freewill offerings for the temple of God in Jerusalem.' "

⁵ Then the family heads of Judah and Benjamin, and the priests and Levites — everyone whose heart God had moved — prepared to go up and build the house of the LORD in Jerusalem. ⁶ All their neighbors assisted them with articles of silver and gold, with goods and livestock, and with valuable gifts, in addition to all the freewill offerings. ⁷ Moreover, King Cyrus brought out the articles belonging to the temple of the LORD, which Nebuchadnezzar had carried away from Jerusalem and had placed in the temple of his god.[a] ⁸ Cyrus king of Persia had them brought by Mithredath the treasurer, who counted them out to Sheshbazzar the prince of Judah.

⁹ This was the inventory:

gold dishes	30
silver dishes	1,000
silver pans[b]	29
¹⁰ gold bowls	30
matching silver bowls	410
other articles	1,000

¹¹ In all, there were 5,400 articles of gold and of silver. Sheshbazzar brought all these along when the exiles came up from Babylon to Jerusalem.

The List of the Exiles Who Returned
2:1–70pp — Ne 7:6–73

2 Now these are the people of the province who came up from the captivity of the exiles, whom Nebuchadnezzar king of Babylon had taken captive to Babylon (they returned to Jerusalem and Judah, each to his own town, ² in company with Zerubbabel, Jeshua, Nehemiah, Seraiah, Reelaiah, Mordecai, Bilshan, Mispar, Bigvai, Rehum and Baanah):

EZRA 1:1–8; 3:7–13

The Exiles Rebuild the Temple

LIFE LESSON: God guides his people.

TO TALK ABOUT

✦ What did many of the people do when the foundation of the new temple was laid?

✦ Why did some of the older people cry? (Hint: See the next question.)

✦ Do you think God was satisfied with a new, less luxurious temple? What really mattered to God?

✦ If you had been there when the foundation was laid, would you have cheered or cried? Explain.

stories to share (vertical text, left margin)

---

a 7 Or gods *b 9 The meaning of the Hebrew for this word is uncertain.*

The list of the men of the people of Israel:

³ the descendants of Parosh	2,172
⁴ of Shephatiah	372
⁵ of Arah	775
⁶ of Pahath-Moab (through the line of Jeshua and Joab)	2,812
⁷ of Elam	1,254
⁸ of Zattu	945
⁹ of Zaccai	760
¹⁰ of Bani	642
¹¹ of Bebai	623
¹² of Azgad	1,222
¹³ of Adonikam	666
¹⁴ of Bigvai	2,056
¹⁵ of Adin	454
¹⁶ of Ater (through Hezekiah)	98
¹⁷ of Bezai	323
¹⁸ of Jorah	112
¹⁹ of Hashum	223
²⁰ of Gibbar	95
²¹ the men of Bethlehem	123
²² of Netophah	56
²³ of Anathoth	128
²⁴ of Azmaveth	42
²⁵ of Kiriath Jearim,ᵃ Kephirah and Beeroth	743
²⁶ of Ramah and Geba	621
²⁷ of Micmash	122
²⁸ of Bethel and Ai	223
²⁹ of Nebo	52
³⁰ of Magbish	156
³¹ of the other Elam	1,254
³² of Harim	320
³³ of Lod, Hadid and Ono	725
³⁴ of Jericho	345
³⁵ of Senaah	3,630

³⁶ The priests:

the descendants of Jedaiah (through the family of Jeshua)	973
³⁷ of Immer	1,052
³⁸ of Pashhur	1,247
³⁹ of Harim	1,017

⁴⁰ The Levites:

the descendants of Jeshua and Kadmiel (through the line of Hodaviah)	74

⁴¹ The singers:

the descendants of Asaph	128

⁴² The gatekeepers of the temple:

the descendants of Shallum, Ater, Talmon, Akkub, Hatita and Shobai	139

⁴³ The temple servants:

the descendants of
Ziha, Hasupha, Tabbaoth,
⁴⁴ Keros, Siaha, Padon,
⁴⁵ Lebanah, Hagabah, Akkub,
⁴⁶ Hagab, Shalmai, Hanan,
⁴⁷ Giddel, Gahar, Reaiah,
⁴⁸ Rezin, Nekoda, Gazzam,
⁴⁹ Uzza, Paseah, Besai,
⁵⁰ Asnah, Meunim, Nephusim,
⁵¹ Bakbuk, Hakupha, Harhur,
⁵² Bazluth, Mehida, Harsha,
⁵³ Barkos, Sisera, Temah,
⁵⁴ Neziah and Hatipha

⁵⁵ The descendants of the servants of Solomon:

the descendants of
Sotai, Hassophereth, Peruda,
⁵⁶ Jaala, Darkon, Giddel,
⁵⁷ Shephatiah, Hattil,
Pokereth-Hazzebaim and Ami

⁵⁸ The temple servants and the descendants of the servants of Solomon	392

⁵⁹ The following came up from the towns of Tel Melah, Tel Harsha, Kerub, Addon and Immer, but they could not show that their families were descended from Israel:

ᵃ 25 See Septuagint (see also Neh. 7:29); Hebrew *Kiriath Arim.*

⁶⁰The descendants of

Delaiah, Tobiah and Nekoda   652

⁶¹And from among the priests:

The descendants of
Hobaiah, Hakkoz and Barzillai (a
man who had married a daughter of
Barzillai the Gileadite and was called
by that name).

⁶²These searched for their family records,
but they could not find them and so were excluded from the priesthood as unclean. ⁶³The
governor ordered them not to eat any of the
most sacred food until there was a priest ministering with the Urim and Thummim.

⁶⁴The whole company numbered 42,360,
⁶⁵besides their 7,337 menservants and maidservants; and they also had 200 men and
women singers. ⁶⁶They had 736 horses, 245
mules, ⁶⁷435 camels and 6,720 donkeys.

⁶⁸When they arrived at the house of the LORD
in Jerusalem, some of the heads of the families
gave freewill offerings toward the rebuilding of
the house of God on its site. ⁶⁹According to their
ability they gave to the treasury for this work
61,000 drachmas ᵃ of gold, 5,000 minas ᵇ of silver
and 100 priestly garments.

⁷⁰The priests, the Levites, the singers, the gatekeepers and the temple servants settled in their
own towns, along with some of the other people, and the rest of the Israelites settled in their
towns.

Rebuilding the Altar

3 When the seventh month came and the Israelites had settled in their towns, the people assembled as one man in Jerusalem. ²Then
Jeshua son of Jozadak and his fellow priests and
Zerubbabel son of Shealtiel and his associates
began to build the altar of the God of Israel to
sacrifice burnt offerings on it, in accordance with
what is written in the Law of Moses the man of
God. ³Despite their fear of the peoples around
them, they built the altar on its foundation and
sacrificed burnt offerings on it to the LORD, both
the morning and evening sacrifices. ⁴Then in accordance with what is written, they celebrated
the Feast of Tabernacles with the required number of burnt offerings prescribed for each day.
⁵After that, they presented the regular burnt offerings, the New Moon sacrifices and the sacrifices
for all the appointed sacred feasts of the LORD,
as well as those brought as freewill offerings to
the LORD. ⁶On the first day of the seventh month
they began to offer burnt offerings to the LORD,
though the foundation of the LORD's temple had
not yet been laid.

Rebuilding the Temple

⁷Then they gave money to the masons and
carpenters, and gave food and drink and oil to
the people of Sidon and Tyre, so that they would
bring cedar logs by sea from Lebanon to Joppa,
as authorized by Cyrus king of Persia.

⁸In the second month of the second year after
their arrival at the house of God in Jerusalem, Zerubbabel son of Shealtiel, Jeshua son of Jozadak
and the rest of their brothers (the priests and the
Levites and all who had returned from the captivity to Jerusalem) began the work, appointing
Levites twenty years of age and older to supervise
the building of the house of the LORD. ⁹Jeshua
and his sons and brothers and Kadmiel and his
sons (descendants of Hodaviah ᶜ) and the sons
of Henadad and their sons and brothers—all
Levites—joined together in supervising those
working on the house of God.

¹⁰When the builders laid the foundation of the
temple of the LORD, the priests in their vestments
and with trumpets, and the Levites (the sons of
Asaph) with cymbals, took their places to praise
the LORD, as prescribed by David king of Israel.
¹¹With praise and thanksgiving they sang to the
LORD:

"He is good;
his love to Israel endures forever."

ᵃ 69 That is, about 1,100 pounds (about 500 kilograms)
ᵇ 69 That is, about 3 tons (about 2.9 metric tons)   ᶜ 9 Hebrew
Yehudah, probably a variant of *Hodaviah*

And all the people gave a great shout of praise to the LORD, because the foundation of the house of the LORD was laid. ¹²But many of the older priests and Levites and family heads, who had seen the former temple, wept aloud when they saw the foundation of this temple being laid, while many others shouted for joy. ¹³No one could distinguish the sound of the shouts of joy from the sound of weeping, because the people made so much noise. And the sound was heard far away.

Opposition to the Rebuilding

4 When the enemies of Judah and Benjamin heard that the exiles were building a temple for the LORD, the God of Israel, ²they came to Zerubbabel and to the heads of the families and said, "Let us help you build because, like you, we seek your God and have been sacrificing to him since the time of Esarhaddon king of Assyria, who brought us here."

³But Zerubbabel, Jeshua and the rest of the heads of the families of Israel answered, "You have no part with us in building a temple to our God. We alone will build it for the LORD, the God of Israel, as King Cyrus, the king of Persia, commanded us."

⁴Then the peoples around them set out to discourage the people of Judah and make them afraid to go on building.ᵃ ⁵They hired counselors to work against them and frustrate their plans during the entire reign of Cyrus king of Persia and down to the reign of Darius king of Persia.

Later Opposition Under Xerxes and Artaxerxes

⁶At the beginning of the reign of Xerxes,ᵇ they lodged an accusation against the people of Judah and Jerusalem.

⁷And in the days of Artaxerxes king of Persia, Bishlam, Mithredath, Tabeel and the rest of his associates wrote a letter to Artaxerxes. The letter was written in Aramaic script and in the Aramaic language.ᶜ,ᵈ

⁸Rehum the commanding officer and Shimshai the secretary wrote a letter against Jerusalem to Artaxerxes the king as follows:

⁹Rehum the commanding officer and Shimshai the secretary, together with the rest of their associates—the judges and officials over the men from Tripolis, Persia,ᵉ Erech and Babylon, the Elamites of Susa, ¹⁰and the other people whom the great and honorable Ashurbanipalᶠ deported and settled in the city of Samaria and elsewhere in Trans-Euphrates.

¹¹(This is a copy of the letter they sent him.)

To King Artaxerxes,

From your servants, the men of Trans-Euphrates:

¹²The king should know that the Jews who came up to us from you have gone to Jerusalem and are rebuilding that rebellious and wicked city. They are restoring the walls and repairing the foundations.

¹³Furthermore, the king should know that if this city is built and its walls are restored, no more taxes, tribute or duty will be paid, and the royal revenues will suffer. ¹⁴Now since we are under obligation to the palace and it is not proper for us to see the king dishonored, we are sending this message to inform the king, ¹⁵so that a search may be made in the archives of your predecessors. In these records you will find that this city is a rebellious city, troublesome to kings and provinces, a place of rebellion from ancient times. That is why this city was destroyed. ¹⁶We inform the king that if this city is built and its walls are restored, you will be left with nothing in Trans-Euphrates.

¹⁷The king sent this reply:

To Rehum the commanding officer, Shimshai the secretary and the rest of their associates living in Samaria and elsewhere in Trans-Euphrates:

ᵃ 4 Or *and troubled them as they built*   ᵇ 6 Hebrew *Ahasuerus,* a variant of Xerxes' Persian name   ᶜ 7 Or *written in Aramaic and translated*   ᵈ 7 The text of Ezra 4:8–6:18 is in Aramaic.   ᵉ 9 Or *officials, magistrates and governors over the men from*   ᶠ 10 Aramaic *Osnappar,* a variant of *Ashurbanipal*

Greetings.

18 The letter you sent us has been read and translated in my presence. 19 I issued an order and a search was made, and it was found that this city has a long history of revolt against kings and has been a place of rebellion and sedition. 20 Jerusalem has had powerful kings ruling over the whole of Trans-Euphrates, and taxes, tribute and duty were paid to them. 21 Now issue an order to these men to stop work, so that this city will not be rebuilt until I so order. 22 Be careful not to neglect this matter. Why let this threat grow, to the detriment of the royal interests?

23 As soon as the copy of the letter of King Artaxerxes was read to Rehum and Shimshai the secretary and their associates, they went immediately to the Jews in Jerusalem and compelled them by force to stop.

24 Thus the work on the house of God in Jerusalem came to a standstill until the second year of the reign of Darius king of Persia.

Tattenai's Letter to Darius

5 Now Haggai the prophet and Zechariah the prophet, a descendant of Iddo, prophesied to the Jews in Judah and Jerusalem in the name of the God of Israel, who was over them. 2 Then Zerubbabel son of Shealtiel and Jeshua son of Jozadak set to work to rebuild the house of God in Jerusalem. And the prophets of God were with them, helping them.

3 At that time Tattenai, governor of Trans-Euphrates, and Shethar-Bozenai and their associates went to them and asked, "Who authorized you to rebuild this temple and restore this structure?" 4 They also asked, "What are the names of the men constructing this building?" a 5 But the eye of their God was watching over the elders of the Jews, and they were not stopped until a report could go to Darius and his written reply be received.

6 This is a copy of the letter that Tattenai, governor of Trans-Euphrates, and Shethar-Bozenai and their associates, the officials of Trans-Euphrates, sent to King Darius. 7 The report they sent him read as follows:

To King Darius:

Cordial greetings.

8 The king should know that we went to the district of Judah, to the temple of the great God. The people are building it with large stones and placing the timbers in the walls. The work is being carried on with diligence and is making rapid progress under their direction.

9 We questioned the elders and asked them, "Who authorized you to rebuild this temple and restore this structure?" 10 We also asked them their names, so that we could write down the names of their leaders for your information.

11 This is the answer they gave us:

"We are the servants of the God of heaven and earth, and we are rebuilding the temple that was built many years ago, one that a great king of Israel built and finished. 12 But because our fathers angered the God of heaven, he handed them over to Nebuchadnezzar the Chaldean, king of Babylon, who destroyed this temple and deported the people to Babylon.

13 "However, in the first year of Cyrus king of Babylon, King Cyrus issued a decree to rebuild this house of God. 14 He even removed from the temple b of Babylon the gold and silver articles of the house of God, which Nebuchadnezzar had taken from the temple in Jerusalem and brought to the temple b in Babylon.

"Then King Cyrus gave them to a man named Sheshbazzar, whom he had appointed governor, 15 and he told him, 'Take these

a 4 See Septuagint; Aramaic 4 We told them the names of the men constructing this building.   b 14 Or palace articles and go and deposit them in the temple in Jerusalem. And rebuild the house of God on its site.' [16]So this Sheshbazzar came and laid the foundations of the house of God in Jerusalem. From that day to the present it has been under construction but is not yet finished."

[17]Now if it pleases the king, let a search be made in the royal archives of Babylon to see if King Cyrus did in fact issue a decree to rebuild this house of God in Jerusalem. Then let the king send us his decision in this matter.

The Decree of Darius

6 King Darius then issued an order, and they searched in the archives stored in the treasury at Babylon. [2]A scroll was found in the citadel of Ecbatana in the province of Media, and this was written on it:

Memorandum:

[3]In the first year of King Cyrus, the king issued a decree concerning the temple of God in Jerusalem:

Let the temple be rebuilt as a place to present sacrifices, and let its foundations be laid. It is to be ninety feet[a] high and ninety feet wide, [4]with three courses of large stones and one of timbers. The costs are to be paid by the royal treasury. [5]Also, the gold and silver articles of the house of God, which Nebuchadnezzar took from the temple in Jerusalem and brought to Babylon, are to be returned to their places in the temple in Jerusalem; they are to be deposited in the house of God.

[6]Now then, Tattenai, governor of Trans-Euphrates, and Shethar-Bozenai and you, their fellow officials of that province, stay away from there. [7]Do not interfere with the work on this temple of God. Let the governor of the Jews and the Jewish elders rebuild this house of God on its site.

[8]Moreover, I hereby decree what you are to do for these elders of the Jews in the construction of this house of God:

The expenses of these men are to be fully paid out of the royal treasury, from the revenues of Trans-Euphrates, so that the work will not stop. [9]Whatever is needed—young bulls, rams, male lambs for burnt offerings to the God of heaven, and wheat, salt, wine and oil, as requested by the priests in Jerusalem—must be given them daily without fail, [10]so that they may offer sacrifices pleasing to the God of heaven and pray for the well-being of the king and his sons.

[11]Furthermore, I decree that if anyone changes this edict, a beam is to be pulled from his house and he is to be lifted up and impaled on it. And for this crime his house is to be made a pile of rubble. [12]May God, who has caused his Name to dwell there, overthrow any king or people who lifts a hand to change this decree or to destroy this temple in Jerusalem.

I Darius have decreed it. Let it be carried out with diligence.

Completion and Dedication of the Temple

[13]Then, because of the decree King Darius had sent, Tattenai, governor of Trans-Euphrates, and Shethar-Bozenai and their associates carried it out with diligence. [14]So the elders of the Jews continued to build and prosper under the preaching of Haggai the prophet and Zechariah, a descendant of Iddo. They finished building the temple according to the command of the God of Israel and the decrees of Cyrus, Darius and Artaxerxes, kings of Persia. [15]The temple was completed on the third day of the month Adar, in the sixth year of the reign of King Darius.

[16]Then the people of Israel—the priests, the Levites and the rest of the exiles—celebrated the dedication of the house of God with joy. [17]For the dedication of this house of God they offered

---

[a] 3 Aramaic *sixty cubits* (about 27 meters)

KING DARIUS THEN ISSUED AN ORDER,
AND THEY SEARCHED IN THE ARCHIVES
STORED IN THE TREASURY AT BABYLON.
A SCROLL WAS FOUND IN THE CITADEL OF
ECBATANA IN THE PROVINCE OF MEDIA,
AND THIS WAS WRITTEN ON IT:

MEMORANDUM:. . .

Ezra 6:1 – 2

Write a Memo Today

BOBBIE WOLGEMUTH

READ | EZRA 6:1 – 12

My friend Teddy Orr was facing a tough decision. Although her beloved grandmother had died years before, Teddy remembered thinking, "I wish I could talk to my grandmother about this."

Praying and wondering what next steps to take, Teddy waited for an answer. One day, soon after her prayer, she was rearranging the shelves in her office.

While moving a stack of books, something fell to the floor, practically in front of Teddy's feet. It was a piece of paper that had been tucked into her grandmother's Bible. Immediately recognizing her grandmother's handwriting, she began to weep as she read.

> My hope is built on nothing less
> Than Jesus' blood and righteousness.
> I dare not trust the sweetest frame,
> But wholly lean on Jesus' Name.[1]

Bathed in the strength of her grandmother's faith, Teddy was able to move ahead with certainty. God would surely enable her in the battle she faced.

A memorandum from King Cyrus discovered in the archives of ancient Persia had a great effect on the welfare of God's people, the Jewish remnant in Jerusalem. What can you write today to be stored in your family's treasury? The words to a hymn, a poem, a story of God's faithfulness — these may become the assurance your grandchildren or great-grandchildren need someday, long after you are gone.

"When all around my soul gives way, he then is all my hope and stay. On Christ the solid Rock I stand, all other ground is sinking sand."[2] Amen.

1. Edward Mote (1797 – 1874), "The Solid Rock."
2. Ibid.

Your next devotion is located on page 625.

GRANDCHILD IN FOCUS • PRAYER

Protection From Worldliness

O Sovereign Lord, the world surrounds my grandchild, pressing in and tempting him in so many ways. Help him set appropriate limits. Give him sound judgment to choose wisely. Guard him from temptation; protect him from physical and mental predators; lead him into paths of righteousness and light. And reassure me with your promise that you are holding him in your hands. Amen.

a hundred bulls, two hundred rams, four hundred male lambs and, as a sin offering for all Israel, twelve male goats, one for each of the tribes of Israel. [18]And they installed the priests in their divisions and the Levites in their groups for the service of God at Jerusalem, according to what is written in the Book of Moses.

The Passover

[19]On the fourteenth day of the first month, the exiles celebrated the Passover. [20]The priests and Levites had purified themselves and were all ceremonially clean. The Levites slaughtered the Passover lamb for all the exiles, for their brothers the priests and for themselves. [21]So the Israelites who had returned from the exile ate it, together with all who had separated themselves from the unclean practices of their Gentile neighbors in order to seek the LORD, the God of Israel. [22]For seven days they celebrated with joy the Feast of Unleavened Bread, because the LORD had filled them with joy by changing the attitude of the king of Assyria, so that he assisted them in the work on the house of God, the God of Israel.

Ezra Comes to Jerusalem

7 After these things, during the reign of Artaxerxes king of Persia, Ezra son of Seraiah, the son of Azariah, the son of Hilkiah, [2]the son of Shallum, the son of Zadok, the son of Ahitub, [3]the son of Amariah, the son of Azariah, the son of Meraioth, [4]the son of Zerahiah, the son of Uzzi, the son of Bukki, [5]the son of Abishua, the son of Phinehas, the son of Eleazar, the son of Aaron the chief priest— [6]this Ezra came up from Babylon. He was a teacher well versed in the Law of Moses, which the LORD, the God of Israel, had given. The king had granted him everything he asked, for the hand of the LORD his God was on him. [7]Some of the Israelites, including priests, Levites, singers, gatekeepers and temple servants, also came up to Jerusalem in the seventh year of King Artaxerxes.

[8]Ezra arrived in Jerusalem in the fifth month of the seventh year of the king. [9]He had begun his journey from Babylon on the first day of the first month, and he arrived in Jerusalem on the first day of the fifth month, for the gracious hand of his God was on him. [10]For Ezra had devoted himself to the study and observance of the Law of the LORD, and to teaching its decrees and laws in Israel.

King Artaxerxes' Letter to Ezra

[11]This is a copy of the letter King Artaxerxes had given to Ezra the priest and teacher, a man learned in matters concerning the commands and decrees of the LORD for Israel:

[12][a] Artaxerxes, king of kings,

To Ezra the priest, a teacher of the Law of the God of heaven:

Greetings.

[13]Now I decree that any of the Israelites in my kingdom, including priests and Levites, who wish to go to Jerusalem with you, may go. [14]You are sent by the king and his seven advisers to inquire about Judah and Jerusalem with regard to the Law of your God, which is in your hand. [15]Moreover, you are to take with you the silver and gold that the king and his advisers have freely given to the God of Israel, whose dwelling is in Jerusalem, [16]together with all the silver and gold you may obtain from the province of Babylon, as well as the freewill offerings of the people and priests for the temple of their God in Jerusalem. [17]With this money be sure to buy bulls, rams and male lambs, together with their grain offerings and drink offerings, and sacrifice them on the altar of the temple of your God in Jerusalem.

[18]You and your brother Jews may then do whatever seems best with the rest of the silver and gold, in accordance with the will of your God. [19]Deliver to the God of Jerusalem all the articles entrusted to you for worship in the temple of your God. [20]And anything

---

a 12 The text of Ezra 7:12-26 is in Aramaic.

else needed for the temple of your God that you may have occasion to supply, you may provide from the royal treasury.

²¹ Now I, King Artaxerxes, order all the treasurers of Trans-Euphrates to provide with diligence whatever Ezra the priest, a teacher of the Law of the God of heaven, may ask of you— ²² up to a hundred talents[a] of silver, a hundred cors[b] of wheat, a hundred baths[c] of wine, a hundred baths[c] of olive oil, and salt without limit. ²³ Whatever the God of heaven has prescribed, let it be done with diligence for the temple of the God of heaven. Why should there be wrath against the realm of the king and of his sons? ²⁴ You are also to know that you have no authority to impose taxes, tribute or duty on any of the priests, Levites, singers, gatekeepers, temple servants or other workers at this house of God.

²⁵ And you, Ezra, in accordance with the wisdom of your God, which you possess, appoint magistrates and judges to administer justice to all the people of Trans-Euphrates—all who know the laws of your God. And you are to teach any who do not know them. ²⁶ Whoever does not obey the law of your God and the law of the king must surely be punished by death, banishment, confiscation of property, or imprisonment.

²⁷ Praise be to the Lᴏʀᴅ, the God of our fathers, who has put it into the king's heart to bring honor to the house of the Lᴏʀᴅ in Jerusalem in this way ²⁸ and who has extended his good favor to me before the king and his advisers and all the king's powerful officials. Because the hand of the Lᴏʀᴅ my God was on me, I took courage and gathered leading men from Israel to go up with me.

List of the Family Heads Returning With Ezra

8 These are the family heads and those registered with them who came up with me from Babylon during the reign of King Artaxerxes:

² of the descendants of Phinehas, Gershom;

of the descendants of Ithamar, Daniel;

of the descendants of David, Hattush ³ of the descendants of Shecaniah;

of the descendants of Parosh, Zechariah, and with him were registered 150 men;

⁴ of the descendants of Pahath-Moab, Eliehoenai son of Zerahiah, and with him 200 men;

⁵ of the descendants of Zattu,[d] Shecaniah son of Jahaziel, and with him 300 men;

⁶ of the descendants of Adin, Ebed son of Jonathan, and with him 50 men;

⁷ of the descendants of Elam, Jeshaiah son of Athaliah, and with him 70 men;

⁸ of the descendants of Shephatiah, Zebadiah son of Michael, and with him 80 men;

⁹ of the descendants of Joab, Obadiah son of Jehiel, and with him 218 men;

¹⁰ of the descendants of Bani,[e] Shelomith son of Josiphiah, and with him 160 men;

¹¹ of the descendants of Bebai, Zechariah son of Bebai, and with him 28 men;

¹² of the descendants of Azgad, Johanan son of Hakkatan, and with him 110 men;

¹³ of the descendants of Adonikam, the last ones, whose names were Eliphelet, Jeuel and Shemaiah, and with them 60 men;

¹⁴ of the descendants of Bigvai, Uthai and Zaccur, and with them 70 men.

The Return to Jerusalem

¹⁵ I assembled them at the canal that flows toward Ahava, and we camped there three days. When I checked among the people and the priests, I found no Levites there. ¹⁶ So I summoned Eliezer, Ariel, Shemaiah, Elnathan, Jarib, Elnathan, Nathan, Zechariah and Meshullam, who were leaders, and Joiarib and Elnathan, who were men of learning, ¹⁷ and I sent them to

---

[a] 22 That is, about 3 3/4 tons (about 3.4 metric tons) [b] 22 That is, probably about 600 bushels (about 22 kiloliters) [c] 22 That is, probably about 600 gallons (about 2.2 kiloliters) [d] 5 Some Septuagint manuscripts (also 1 Esdras 8:32); Hebrew does not have Zattu. [e] 10 Some Septuagint manuscripts (also 1 Esdras 8:36); Hebrew does not have Bani.

Iddo, the leader in Casiphia. I told them what to say to Iddo and his kinsmen, the temple servants in Casiphia, so that they might bring attendants to us for the house of our God. **18**Because the gracious hand of our God was on us, they brought us Sherebiah, a capable man, from the descendants of Mahli son of Levi, the son of Israel, and Sherebiah's sons and brothers, 18 men; **19**and Hashabiah, together with Jeshaiah from the descendants of Merari, and his brothers and nephews, 20 men. **20**They also brought 220 of the temple servants—a body that David and the officials had established to assist the Levites. All were registered by name.

21There, by the Ahava Canal, I proclaimed a fast, so that we might humble ourselves before our God and ask him for a safe journey for us and our children, with all our possessions. **22**I was ashamed to ask the king for soldiers and horsemen to protect us from enemies on the road, because we had told the king, "The gracious hand of our God is on everyone who looks to him, but his great anger is against all who forsake him." **23**So we fasted and petitioned our God about this, and he answered our prayer.

24Then I set apart twelve of the leading priests, together with Sherebiah, Hashabiah and ten of their brothers, **25**and I weighed out to them the offering of silver and gold and the articles that the king, his advisers, his officials and all Israel present there had donated for the house of our God. **26**I weighed out to them 650 talents *a* of silver, silver articles weighing 100 talents, *b* 100 talents *b* of gold, **27**20 bowls of gold valued at 1,000 darics, *c* and two fine articles of polished bronze, as precious as gold.

28I said to them, "You as well as these articles are consecrated to the LORD. The silver and gold are a freewill offering to the LORD, the God of your fathers. **29**Guard them carefully until you weigh them out in the chambers of the house of the LORD in Jerusalem before the leading priests and the Levites and the family heads of Israel." **30**Then the priests and Levites received the silver and gold and sacred articles that had been weighed out to be taken to the house of our God in Jerusalem.

31On the twelfth day of the first month we set out from the Ahava Canal to go to Jerusalem. The hand of our God was on us, and he protected us from enemies and bandits along the way. **32**So we arrived in Jerusalem, where we rested three days.

33On the fourth day, in the house of our God, we weighed out the silver and gold and the sacred articles into the hands of Meremoth son of Uriah, the priest. Eleazar son of Phinehas was with him, and so were the Levites Jozabad son of Jeshua and Noadiah son of Binnui. **34**Everything was accounted for by number and weight, and the entire weight was recorded at that time.

35Then the exiles who had returned from captivity sacrificed burnt offerings to the God of Israel: twelve bulls for all Israel, ninety-six rams, seventy-seven male lambs and, as a sin offering, twelve male goats. All this was a burnt offering to the LORD. **36**They also delivered the king's orders to the royal satraps and to the governors of Trans-Euphrates, who then gave assistance to the people and to the house of God.

Ezra's Prayer About Intermarriage

9 After these things had been done, the leaders came to me and said, "The people of Israel, including the priests and the Levites, have not kept themselves separate from the neighboring peoples with their detestable practices, like those of the Canaanites, Hittites, Perizzites, Jebusites, Ammonites, Moabites, Egyptians and Amorites. **2**They have taken some of their daughters as wives for themselves and their sons, and have mingled the holy race with the peoples around them. And the leaders and officials have led the way in this unfaithfulness."

3When I heard this, I tore my tunic and cloak, pulled hair from my head and beard and sat down appalled. **4**Then everyone who trembled at the

---

a 26 That is, about 25 tons (about 22 metric tons)   *b 26* That is, about 3 3/4 tons (about 3.4 metric tons)   *c 27* That is, about 19 pounds (about 8.5 kilograms) words of the God of Israel gathered around me because of this unfaithfulness of the exiles. And I sat there appalled until the evening sacrifice.

⁵Then, at the evening sacrifice, I rose from my self-abasement, with my tunic and cloak torn, and fell on my knees with my hands spread out to the LORD my God ⁶and prayed:

"O my God, I am too ashamed and disgraced to lift up my face to you, my God, because our sins are higher than our heads and our guilt has reached to the heavens. ⁷From the days of our forefathers until now, our guilt has been great. Because of our sins, we and our kings and our priests have been subjected to the sword and captivity, to pillage and humiliation at the hand of foreign kings, as it is today.

⁸"But now, for a brief moment, the LORD our God has been gracious in leaving us a remnant and giving us a firm place in his sanctuary, and so our God gives light to our eyes and a little relief in our bondage. ⁹Though we are slaves, our God has not deserted us in our bondage. He has shown us kindness in the sight of the kings of Persia: He has granted us new life to rebuild the house of our God and repair its ruins, and he has given us a wall of protection in Judah and Jerusalem.

¹⁰"But now, O our God, what can we say after this? For we have disregarded the commands ¹¹you gave through your servants the prophets when you said: 'The land you are entering to possess is a land polluted by the corruption of its peoples. By their detestable practices they have filled it with their impurity from one end to the other. ¹²Therefore, do not give your daughters in marriage to their sons or take their daughters for your sons. Do not seek a treaty of friendship with them at any time, that you may be strong and eat the good things of the land and leave it to your children as an everlasting inheritance.'

¹³"What has happened to us is a result of our evil deeds and our great guilt, and yet, our God, you have punished us less than our sins have deserved and have given us a remnant like this. ¹⁴Shall we again break your commands and intermarry with the peoples who commit such detestable practices? Would you not be angry enough with us to destroy us, leaving us no remnant or survivor? ¹⁵O LORD, God of Israel, you are righteous! We are left this day as a remnant. Here we are before you in our guilt, though because of it not one of us can stand in your presence."

The People's Confession of Sin

10 While Ezra was praying and confessing, weeping and throwing himself down before the house of God, a large crowd of Israelites — men, women and children — gathered around him. They too wept bitterly. ²Then Shecaniah son of Jehiel, one of the descendants of Elam, said to Ezra, "We have been unfaithful to our God by marrying foreign women from the peoples around us. But in spite of this, there is still hope for Israel. ³Now let us make a covenant before our God to send away all these women and their children, in accordance with the counsel of my lord and of those who fear the commands of our God. Let it be done according to the Law. ⁴Rise up; this matter is in your hands. We will support you, so take courage and do it."

⁵So Ezra rose up and put the leading priests and Levites and all Israel under oath to do what had been suggested. And they took the oath. ⁶Then Ezra withdrew from before the house of God and went to the room of Jehohanan son of Eliashib. While he was there, he ate no food and drank no water, because he continued to mourn over the unfaithfulness of the exiles.

⁷A proclamation was then issued throughout Judah and Jerusalem for all the exiles to assemble in Jerusalem. ⁸Anyone who failed to appear within three days would forfeit all his property, in accordance with the decision of the officials

and elders, and would himself be expelled from the assembly of the exiles.

⁹Within the three days, all the men of Judah and Benjamin had gathered in Jerusalem. And on the twentieth day of the ninth month, all the people were sitting in the square before the house of God, greatly distressed by the occasion and because of the rain. ¹⁰Then Ezra the priest stood up and said to them, "You have been unfaithful; you have married foreign women, adding to Israel's guilt. ¹¹Now make confession to the LORD, the God of your fathers, and do his will. Separate yourselves from the peoples around you and from your foreign wives."

¹²The whole assembly responded with a loud voice: "You are right! We must do as you say. ¹³But there are many people here and it is the rainy season; so we cannot stand outside. Besides, this matter cannot be taken care of in a day or two, because we have sinned greatly in this thing. ¹⁴Let our officials act for the whole assembly. Then let everyone in our towns who has married a foreign woman come at a set time, along with the elders and judges of each town, until the fierce anger of our God in this matter is turned away from us." ¹⁵Only Jonathan son of Asahel and Jahzeiah son of Tikvah, supported by Meshullam and Shabbethai the Levite, opposed this.

¹⁶So the exiles did as was proposed. Ezra the priest selected men who were family heads, one from each family division, and all of them designated by name. On the first day of the tenth month they sat down to investigate the cases, ¹⁷and by the first day of the first month they finished dealing with all the men who had married foreign women.

Those Guilty of Intermarriage

¹⁸Among the descendants of the priests, the following had married foreign women:

From the descendants of Jeshua son of Jozadak, and his brothers: Maaseiah, Eliezer, Jarib and Gedaliah. ¹⁹(They all gave their hands in pledge to put away their wives, and for their guilt they each presented a ram from the flock as a guilt offering.)

²⁰From the descendants of Immer:
    Hanani and Zebadiah.
²¹From the descendants of Harim:
    Maaseiah, Elijah, Shemaiah, Jehiel and Uzziah.
²²From the descendants of Pashhur:
    Elioenai, Maaseiah, Ishmael, Nethanel, Jozabad and Elasah.

²³Among the Levites:

    Jozabad, Shimei, Kelaiah (that is, Kelita), Pethahiah, Judah and Eliezer.
²⁴From the singers:
    Eliashib.
    From the gatekeepers:
    Shallum, Telem and Uri.

²⁵And among the other Israelites:

    From the descendants of Parosh:
    Ramiah, Izziah, Malkijah, Mijamin, Eleazar, Malkijah and Benaiah.
²⁶From the descendants of Elam:
    Mattaniah, Zechariah, Jehiel, Abdi, Jeremoth and Elijah.
²⁷From the descendants of Zattu:
    Elioenai, Eliashib, Mattaniah, Jeremoth, Zabad and Aziza.
²⁸From the descendants of Bebai:
    Jehohanan, Hananiah, Zabbai and Athlai.
²⁹From the descendants of Bani:
    Meshullam, Malluch, Adaiah, Jashub, Sheal and Jeremoth.
³⁰From the descendants of Pahath-Moab:
    Adna, Kelal, Benaiah, Maaseiah, Mattaniah, Bezalel, Binnui and Manasseh.
³¹From the descendants of Harim:
    Eliezer, Ishijah, Malkijah, Shemaiah, Shimeon, ³²Benjamin, Malluch and Shemariah.
³³From the descendants of Hashum:
    Mattenai, Mattattah, Zabad, Eliphelet, Jeremai, Manasseh and Shimei.
³⁴From the descendants of Bani:
    Maadai, Amram, Uel, ³⁵Benaiah, Bedeiah,

Keluhi, ³⁶Vaniah, Meremoth, Eliashib, ³⁷Mattaniah, Mattenai and Jaasu.

³⁸From the descendants of Binnui:ᵃ

Shimei, ³⁹Shelemiah, Nathan, Adaiah, ⁴⁰Macnadebai, Shashai, Sharai, ⁴¹Azarel, Shelemiah, Shemariah, ⁴²Shallum, Amariah and Joseph.

⁴³From the descendants of Nebo:

Jeiel, Mattithiah, Zabad, Zebina, Jaddai, Joel and Benaiah.

⁴⁴All these had married foreign women, and some of them had children by these wives.ᵇ

ᵃ 37,38 See Septuagint (also 1 Esdras 9:34); Hebrew *Jaasu* ³⁸*and Bani and Binnui,* ᵇ 44 Or *and they sent them away with their children*

A Praying LEADER

The book of Nehemiah follows the continuing story of the returning exiles from Babylon and describes the call of their great leader Nehemiah, whose God-given wisdom and strength led them to rebuild the city walls of Jerusalem.

Nehemiah's faithfulness and commitment to God made him a powerful and courageous leader. He had a personal relationship with God and was known for his prayers. For example, when he heard that the Jewish exiles in Judah were "in great trouble and disgrace" (Nehemiah 1:3), he turned to God immediately (see Nehemiah 1:4). He also prayed before making his appeal to the king for help (see Nehemiah 2:4). And when the task of rebuilding the wall was disrupted by opposition, Nehemiah's first response was to pray (see Nehemiah 4:4–5). Prayer was central to Nehemiah's success as the leader of God's people.

As grandmothers we too are leaders, and we can learn much from Nehemiah and his style of leadership. He organized and coached God's people into action. He anticipated and developed a plan. He righted wrongs, cared for the poor and reformed worship. But above all, he did not rely on his own strength or ingenuity or talents; he relied on God through prayer. So should we.

VERSE *to* REMEMBER | NEHEMIAH 4:9

But we prayed to our God and posted a guard day and night to meet this threat.

ABOUT NEHEMIAH

WRITTEN BY:
Unknown, possibly Ezra or Nehemiah

WRITTEN FOR:
The people of Judah who had returned from exile in Babylon

DATE WRITTEN:
Sometime after 430 B.C.

WHY WRITTEN:
To demonstrate God's faithfulness to and through his people, such as in the rebuilding of the walls of Jerusalem

Nehemiah's Prayer

1 The words of Nehemiah son of Hacaliah:

In the month of Kislev in the twentieth year, while I was in the citadel of Susa, ²Hanani, one of my brothers, came from Judah with some other men, and I questioned them about the Jewish remnant that survived the exile, and also about Jerusalem.

³They said to me, "Those who survived the exile and are back in the province are in great trouble and disgrace. The wall of Jerusalem is broken down, and its gates have been burned with fire."

⁴When I heard these things, I sat down and wept. For some days I mourned and fasted and prayed before the God of heaven. ⁵Then I said:

"O Lord, God of heaven, the great and awesome God, who keeps his covenant of love with those who love him and obey his commands, ⁶let your ear be attentive and your eyes open to hear the prayer your servant is praying before you day and night for your servants, the people of Israel. I confess the sins we Israelites, including myself and my father's house, have committed against you. ⁷We have acted very wickedly toward you. We have not obeyed the commands, decrees and laws you gave your servant Moses.

⁸"Remember the instruction you gave your servant Moses, saying, 'If you are unfaithful, I will scatter you among the nations, ⁹but if you return to me and obey my commands, then even if your exiled people are at the farthest horizon, I will gather them from there and bring them to the place I have chosen as a dwelling for my Name.'

¹⁰"They are your servants and your people, whom you redeemed by your great strength and your mighty hand. ¹¹O Lord, let your ear be attentive to the prayer of this your servant and to the prayer of your servants who delight in revering your name. Give your servant success today by granting him favor in the presence of this man."

I was cupbearer to the king.

Artaxerxes Sends Nehemiah to Jerusalem

2 In the month of Nisan in the twentieth year of King Artaxerxes, when wine was brought for him, I took the wine and gave it to the king. I had not been sad in his presence before; ²so the king asked me, "Why does your face look so sad when you are not ill? This can be nothing but sadness of heart."

I was very much afraid, ³but I said to the king,

stories to share

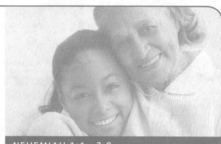

NEHEMIAH 1:1—2:9

A Call to Rebuild Jerusalem's Ruined Walls

LIFE LESSON: God wants us to pray when we need courage.

TO TALK ABOUT

✦ Why was Nehemiah sad?

✦ What did King Artaxerxes ask Nehemiah when he saw Nehemiah's face?

✦ Nehemiah was likely afraid because he wasn't supposed to be sad in the king's presence and because he was planning to ask the king to allow him to go to his home country. What gave Nehemiah the courage to make his request?

✦ When has serving God required bravery on your part? Did you pray and ask for God's help?

TUESDAY

> "O LORD, GOD OF HEAVEN, THE GREAT
> AND AWESOME GOD, WHO KEEPS HIS
> COVENANT OF LOVE WITH THOSE WHO
> LOVE HIM AND OBEY HIS COMMANDS
> ... I CONFESS THE SINS WE ISRAELITES,
> INCLUDING MYSELF AND MY FATHER'S
> HOUSE, HAVE COMMITTED AGAINST YOU."
> *Nehemiah 1:5 – 6*

Caring About God's Glory

GLADYS HUNT

READ | NEHEMIAH 1:1 – 11

Reading the book of Nehemiah is a soul-stretching and a world-stretching experience.

Nehemiah, cupbearer for the Persian king Artaxerxes, held a position of importance and honor. He was a Jewish exile, but he had become part of the royal court in a trusted position. Yet Nehemiah's concerns went beyond the security of the palace and his own comforts. When he heard that the wall of Jerusalem remained broken down and its residents were in great trouble and disgrace, he took the risk of caring. He prayed, asked for help and then did something about it.

Nehemiah first worshiped God by proclaiming who God is (see Nehemiah 1:5). This recital of God's character encouraged him to pray on. He then confessed sin—his sin, his family's sin and the sin of his people. He gave no complaints about "the way things are" because he knew that the people were responsible for their actions before God. He asked for forgiveness and grace.

It's hard to confess our own sins, let alone all the sins of our family and the sins of our nation. Nehemiah gives us a powerful example of taking responsibility and personally getting involved to right what has gone wrong. As you read his story, it becomes obvious that Nehemiah put his life on the line for the glory of God. He was not only courageous, but he also inspired others to courage and faith. He not only led in rebuilding the wall of Jerusalem, but he also put the people back in touch with God. He called them to repentance and worship (see Nehemiah 8 – 10).

Nehemiah's leadership skills and opportunities may outrank ours, but we can still care about the glory of God and take some risks. The Scriptures enlighten us about God's concerns for his world. The daily newspaper provides fodder that opens windows for prayer. We can begin by praying beyond ourselves and our own little world.

....

Lord, teach me to pray like Nehemiah. Show me how to care about what is on your heart. Give me a passion to see you glorified. Amen.

GRANDCHILD **IN FOCUS** · PRAYER

Respect for Authority

Dear Lord, I pray that my grandchild will continually grow to respect those in authority. May she learn to be cooperative and fair in work and play. Instill in her a high regard for officials who govern our land and enforce the laws. May her relationships with parents, teachers, coaches, mentors and bosses be respectful, admirable, constructive and caring. Amen.

Your next devotion is located on page 629.

"May the king live forever! Why should my face not look sad when the city where my fathers are buried lies in ruins, and its gates have been destroyed by fire?"

[4] The king said to me, "What is it you want?"

Then I prayed to the God of heaven, [5] and I answered the king, "If it pleases the king and if your servant has found favor in his sight, let him send me to the city in Judah where my fathers are buried so that I can rebuild it."

[6] Then the king, with the queen sitting beside him, asked me, "How long will your journey take, and when will you get back?" It pleased the king to send me; so I set a time.

[7] I also said to him, "If it pleases the king, may I have letters to the governors of Trans-Euphrates, so that they will provide me safe-conduct until I arrive in Judah? [8] And may I have a letter to Asaph, keeper of the king's forest, so he will give me timber to make beams for the gates of the citadel by the temple and for the city wall and for the residence I will occupy?" And because the gracious hand of my God was upon me, the king granted my requests. [9] So I went to the governors of Trans-Euphrates and gave them the king's letters. The king had also sent army officers and cavalry with me.

[10] When Sanballat the Horonite and Tobiah the Ammonite official heard about this, they were very much disturbed that someone had come to promote the welfare of the Israelites.

Nehemiah Inspects Jerusalem's Walls

[11] I went to Jerusalem, and after staying there three days [12] I set out during the night with a few men. I had not told anyone what my God had put in my heart to do for Jerusalem. There were no mounts with me except the one I was riding on.

[13] By night I went out through the Valley Gate toward the Jackal[a] Well and the Dung Gate, examining the walls of Jerusalem, which had been broken down, and its gates, which had been destroyed by fire. [14] Then I moved on toward the Fountain Gate and the King's Pool, but there was not enough room for my mount to get through; [15] so I went up the valley by night, examining the wall. Finally, I turned back and reentered through the Valley Gate. [16] The officials did not know where I had gone or what I was doing, because as yet I had said nothing to the Jews or the priests or nobles or officials or any others who would be doing the work.

[17] Then I said to them, "You see the trouble we are in: Jerusalem lies in ruins, and its gates have been burned with fire. Come, let us rebuild the wall of Jerusalem, and we will no longer be in disgrace." [18] I also told them about the gracious hand of my God upon me and what the king had said to me.

They replied, "Let us start rebuilding." So they began this good work.

[19] But when Sanballat the Horonite, Tobiah the Ammonite official and Geshem the Arab heard about it, they mocked and ridiculed us. "What is this you are doing?" they asked. "Are you rebelling against the king?"

[20] I answered them by saying, "The God of heaven will give us success. We his servants will start rebuilding, but as for you, you have no share in Jerusalem or any claim or historic right to it."

Builders of the Wall

3 Eliashib the high priest and his fellow priests went to work and rebuilt the Sheep Gate. They dedicated it and set its doors in place, building as far as the Tower of the Hundred, which they dedicated, and as far as the Tower of Hananel. [2] The men of Jericho built the adjoining section, and Zaccur son of Imri built next to them.

[3] The Fish Gate was rebuilt by the sons of Hassenaah. They laid its beams and put its doors and bolts and bars in place. [4] Meremoth son of Uriah, the son of Hakkoz, repaired the next section. Next to him Meshullam son of Berekiah, the son of Meshezabel, made repairs, and next to him Zadok son of Baana also made repairs. [5] The next section was repaired by the men of Tekoa, but their nobles would not put their shoulders to the work under their supervisors.[b]

---

[a] 13 Or Serpent or Fig   [b] 5 Or their Lord or the governor

⁶The Jeshanah *a* Gate was repaired by Joiada son of Paseah and Meshullam son of Besodeiah. They laid its beams and put its doors and bolts and bars in place. ⁷Next to them, repairs were made by men from Gibeon and Mizpah—Melatiah of Gibeon and Jadon of Meronoth—places under the authority of the governor of Trans-Euphrates. ⁸Uzziel son of Harhaiah, one of the goldsmiths, repaired the next section; and Hananiah, one of the perfume-makers, made repairs next to that. They restored *b* Jerusalem as far as the Broad Wall. ⁹Rephaiah son of Hur, ruler of a half-district of Jerusalem, repaired the next section. ¹⁰Adjoining this, Jedaiah son of Harumaph made repairs opposite his house, and Hattush son of Hashabneiah made repairs next to him. ¹¹Malkijah son of Harim and Hasshub son of Pahath-Moab repaired another section and the Tower of the Ovens. ¹²Shallum son of Hallohesh, ruler of a half-district of Jerusalem, repaired the next section with the help of his daughters.

¹³The Valley Gate was repaired by Hanun and the residents of Zanoah. They rebuilt it and put its doors and bolts and bars in place. They also repaired five hundred yards *c* of the wall as far as the Dung Gate.

¹⁴The Dung Gate was repaired by Malkijah son of Recab, ruler of the district of Beth Hakkerem. He rebuilt it and put its doors and bolts and bars in place.

¹⁵The Fountain Gate was repaired by Shallun son of Col-Hozeh, ruler of the district of Mizpah. He rebuilt it, roofing it over and putting its doors and bolts and bars in place. He also repaired the wall of the Pool of Siloam, *d* by the King's Garden, as far as the steps going down from the City of David. ¹⁶Beyond him, Nehemiah son of Azbuk, ruler of a half-district of Beth Zur, made repairs up to a point opposite the tombs *e* of David, as far as the artificial pool and the House of the Heroes.

¹⁷Next to him, the repairs were made by the Levites under Rehum son of Bani. Beside him, Hashabiah, ruler of half the district of Keilah, carried out repairs for his district. ¹⁸Next to him, the repairs were made by their countrymen under Binnui *f* son of Henadad, ruler of the other half-district of Keilah. ¹⁹Next to him, Ezer son of Jeshua, ruler of Mizpah, repaired another section, from a point facing the ascent to the armory as far as the angle. ²⁰Next to him, Baruch son of Zabbai zealously repaired another section, from the angle to the entrance of the house of Eliashib the high priest. ²¹Next to him, Meremoth son of Uriah, the son of Hakkoz, repaired another section, from the entrance of Eliashib's house to the end of it.

²²The repairs next to him were made by the priests from the surrounding region. ²³Beyond them, Benjamin and Hasshub made repairs in front of their house; and next to them, Azariah son of Maaseiah, the son of Ananiah, made repairs beside his house. ²⁴Next to him, Binnui son of Henadad repaired another section, from Azariah's house to the angle and the corner, ²⁵and Palal son of Uzai worked opposite the angle and the tower projecting from the upper palace near the court of the guard. Next to him, Pedaiah son of Parosh ²⁶and the temple servants living on the hill of Ophel made repairs up to a point opposite the Water Gate toward the east and the projecting tower. ²⁷Next to them, the men of Tekoa repaired another section, from the great projecting tower to the wall of Ophel.

²⁸Above the Horse Gate, the priests made repairs, each in front of his own house. ²⁹Next to them, Zadok son of Immer made repairs opposite his house. Next to him, Shemaiah son of Shecaniah, the guard at the East Gate, made repairs. ³⁰Next to him, Hananiah son of Shelemiah, and Hanun, the sixth son of Zalaph, repaired another section. Next to them, Meshullam son of Berekiah made repairs opposite his living quarters. ³¹Next to him, Malkijah, one of the goldsmiths,

a 6 Or *Old*   *b* 8 Or *They left out part of*   *c* 13 Hebrew *a thousand cubits* (about 450 meters)   *d* 15 Hebrew *Shelah,* a variant of *Shiloah,* that is, Siloam   *e* 16 Hebrew; Septuagint, some Vulgate manuscripts and Syriac *tomb*   *f* 18 Two Hebrew manuscripts and Syriac (see also Septuagint and verse 24); most Hebrew manuscripts *Bavvai* made repairs as far as the house of the temple servants and the merchants, opposite the Inspection Gate, and as far as the room above the corner; ³² and between the room above the corner and the Sheep Gate the goldsmiths and merchants made repairs.

Opposition to the Rebuilding

4 When Sanballat heard that we were rebuilding the wall, he became angry and was greatly incensed. He ridiculed the Jews, ²and in the presence of his associates and the army of Samaria, he said, "What are those feeble Jews doing? Will they restore their wall? Will they offer sacrifices? Will they finish in a day? Can they bring the stones back to life from those heaps of rubble—burned as they are?"

³Tobiah the Ammonite, who was at his side, said, "What they are building—if even a fox climbed up on it, he would break down their wall of stones!"

⁴Hear us, O our God, for we are despised. Turn their insults back on their own heads. Give them over as plunder in a land of captivity. ⁵Do not cover up their guilt or blot out their sins from your sight, for they have thrown insults in the face of^a the builders.

⁶So we rebuilt the wall till all of it reached half its height, for the people worked with all their heart.

⁷But when Sanballat, Tobiah, the Arabs, the Ammonites and the men of Ashdod heard that the repairs to Jerusalem's walls had gone ahead and that the gaps were being closed, they were very angry. ⁸They all plotted together to come and fight against Jerusalem and stir up trouble against it. ⁹But we prayed to our God and posted a guard day and night to meet this threat.

¹⁰Meanwhile, the people in Judah said, "The strength of the laborers is giving out, and there is so much rubble that we cannot rebuild the wall."

¹¹Also our enemies said, "Before they know it or see us, we will be right there among them and will kill them and put an end to the work."

TALKING POINTS

Prayer

Prayer and action work together.

NEHEMIAH 4:6–9

For more on prayer, go to Isaiah 65:24.

---

¹²Then the Jews who lived near them came and told us ten times over, "Wherever you turn, they will attack us."

¹³Therefore I stationed some of the people behind the lowest points of the wall at the exposed places, posting them by families, with their swords, spears and bows. ¹⁴After I looked things over, I stood up and said to the nobles, the officials and the rest of the people, "Don't be afraid of them. Remember the Lord, who is great and awesome, and fight for your brothers, your sons and your daughters, your wives and your homes."

¹⁵When our enemies heard that we were aware of their plot and that God had frustrated it, we all returned to the wall, each to his own work.

¹⁶From that day on, half of my men did the work, while the other half were equipped with spears, shields, bows and armor. The officers posted themselves behind all the people of Judah ¹⁷who were building the wall. Those who carried materials did their work with one hand and held a weapon in the other, ¹⁸and each of the builders wore his sword at his side as he worked. But the man who sounded the trumpet stayed with me.

¹⁹Then I said to the nobles, the officials and the rest of the people, "The work is extensive and spread out, and we are widely separated from each other along the wall. ²⁰Wherever you hear the sound of the trumpet, join us there. Our God will fight for us!"

^a 5 Or *have provoked you to anger before*

> ALSO OUR ENEMIES SAID, "BEFORE
> THEY KNOW IT OR SEE US, WE WILL
> BE RIGHT THERE AMONG THEM
> AND WILL KILL THEM AND PUT AN
> END TO THE WORK."
>
> *Nehemiah 4:11*

Opposition to a Dream

DORIS WYNBEEK RIKKERS

READ | NEHEMIAH 4:1 – 23

Everybody has dreams. We dream of a peaceful home, a successful career, grandchildren, retirement. We dream of taking on a new challenge, turning a hobby into a livelihood or sharing our years of experience in a classroom. If our dreams are reasonable, we get a lot of support. If our dreams are "way out there," we face opposition. There are always the naysayers, those who say, "You've got to be kidding." "You can't take that on now." "You don't have the energy to start something new." "Why do you want to work so hard?" "Oh, stop already. It's time to kick back and enjoy life."

Our friends may not be "our enemies," but they sometimes are certainly "right there" among us, ready to kill our dream and put an end to the work (see Nehemiah 4:11).

The Jewish remnant in Jerusalem faced stronger opposition than we ever will, but they handled it well. They did several things to protect themselves and their dream of restoring the city's wall of protection: They prayed (see Nehemiah 4:9). They guarded themselves (see Nehemiah 4:9,13). They believed God was on their side (see Nehemiah 4:14,20). The people of Judah had paid the price of unfaithfulness. They had endured years of captivity in a foreign land. Through it all they had dreamed of returning to the land God had promised them. They knew it would be hard to start over again, but they were determined to rebuild the wall of Jerusalem. But they never expected this kind of opposition—opposition so strong their lives were in danger.

There may come a time when we face opposition to our ideas, to our dreams, perhaps to our lives. Like Nehemiah, we must stand firm to guard our dreams and persevere through the opposition and firmly state, "The God of heaven will give us success" (Nehemiah 2:20).

O God of heaven, sustain me as I face opposition to my dreams. Guard and protect me from those who discourage me and drain me of energy, ambition and joy. Clearly reveal to me the plans and dreams you have for me, and give me success and joy in fulfilling them for you. Amen.

Your next devotion is located on page 641.

GRANDCHILD IN FOCUS • PRAYER

Courage

O Father, builder of character and courage, may my grandchild grow strong in the light of your love. Grant him courage to stand for what is right, to guard the truth and to ensure justice in every aspect of life. May he boldly grow in grace, revere your name and proudly proclaim you as the Lord of lords and King of kings. Amen.

²¹So we continued the work with half the men holding spears, from the first light of dawn till the stars came out. ²²At that time I also said to the people, "Have every man and his helper stay inside Jerusalem at night, so they can serve us as guards by night and workmen by day." ²³Neither I nor my brothers nor my men nor the guards with me took off our clothes; each had his weapon, even when he went for water. ᵃ

Nehemiah Helps the Poor

5 Now the men and their wives raised a great outcry against their Jewish brothers. ²Some were saying, "We and our sons and daughters are numerous; in order for us to eat and stay alive, we must get grain."

³Others were saying, "We are mortgaging our fields, our vineyards and our homes to get grain during the famine."

⁴Still others were saying, "We have had to borrow money to pay the king's tax on our fields and vineyards. ⁵Although we are of the same flesh and blood as our countrymen and though our sons are as good as theirs, yet we have to subject our sons and daughters to slavery. Some of our daughters have already been enslaved, but we are powerless, because our fields and our vineyards belong to others."

⁶When I heard their outcry and these charges, I was very angry. ⁷I pondered them in my mind and then accused the nobles and officials. I told them, "You are exacting usury from your own countrymen!" So I called together a large meeting to deal with them ⁸and said: "As far as possible, we have bought back our Jewish brothers who were sold to the Gentiles. Now you are selling your brothers, only for them to be sold back to us!" They kept quiet, because they could find nothing to say.

⁹So I continued, "What you are doing is not right. Shouldn't you walk in the fear of our God to avoid the reproach of our Gentile enemies? ¹⁰I and my brothers and my men are also lending the people money and grain. But let the exacting of usury stop! ¹¹Give back to them immediately their fields, vineyards, olive groves and houses, and also the usury you are charging them—the hundredth part of the money, grain, new wine and oil."

¹²"We will give it back," they said. "And we will not demand anything more from them. We will do as you say."

Then I summoned the priests and made the nobles and officials take an oath to do what they had promised. ¹³I also shook out the folds of my robe and said, "In this way may God shake out of his house and possessions every man who does not keep this promise. So may such a man be shaken out and emptied!"

At this the whole assembly said, "Amen," and praised the LORD. And the people did as they had promised.

¹⁴Moreover, from the twentieth year of King Artaxerxes, when I was appointed to be their governor in the land of Judah, until his thirty-second year—twelve years—neither I nor my brothers ate the food allotted to the governor. ¹⁵But the earlier governors—those preceding me—placed a heavy burden on the people and took forty shekels ᵇ of silver from them in addition to food and wine. Their assistants also lorded it over the people. But out of reverence for God I did not act like that. ¹⁶Instead, I devoted myself to the work on this wall. All my men were assembled there for the work; we ᶜ did not acquire any land.

¹⁷Furthermore, a hundred and fifty Jews and officials ate at my table, as well as those who came to us from the surrounding nations. ¹⁸Each day one ox, six choice sheep and some poultry were prepared for me, and every ten days an abundant supply of wine of all kinds. In spite of all this, I never demanded the food allotted to the governor, because the demands were heavy on these people.

¹⁹Remember me with favor, O my God, for all I have done for these people.

ᵃ 23 The meaning of the Hebrew for this clause is uncertain. ᵇ 15 That is, about 1 pound (about 0.5 kilogram)   ᶜ 16 Most Hebrew manuscripts; some Hebrew manuscripts, Septuagint, Vulgate and Syriac *I*

Further Opposition to the Rebuilding

6 When word came to Sanballat, Tobiah, Geshem the Arab and the rest of our enemies that I had rebuilt the wall and not a gap was left in it—though up to that time I had not set the doors in the gates— ²Sanballat and Geshem sent me this message: "Come, let us meet together in one of the villages[a] on the plain of Ono."

But they were scheming to harm me; ³so I sent messengers to them with this reply: "I am carrying on a great project and cannot go down. Why should the work stop while I leave it and go down to you?" ⁴Four times they sent me the same message, and each time I gave them the same answer.

⁵Then, the fifth time, Sanballat sent his aide to me with the same message, and in his hand was an unsealed letter ⁶in which was written:

> "It is reported among the nations—and Geshem[b] says it is true—that you and the Jews are plotting to revolt, and therefore you are building the wall. Moreover, according to these reports you are about to become their king ⁷and have even appointed prophets to make this proclamation about you in Jerusalem: 'There is a king in Judah!' Now this report will get back to the king; so come, let us confer together."

⁸I sent him this reply: "Nothing like what you are saying is happening; you are just making it up out of your head."

⁹They were all trying to frighten us, thinking, "Their hands will get too weak for the work, and it will not be completed."

⌐But I prayed,⌐ "Now strengthen my hands."

¹⁰One day I went to the house of Shemaiah son of Delaiah, the son of Mehetabel, who was shut in at his home. He said, "Let us meet in the house of God, inside the temple, and let us close the temple doors, because men are coming to kill you—by night they are coming to kill you."

¹¹But I said, "Should a man like me run away? Or should one like me go into the temple to save his life? I will not go!" ¹²I realized that God had not sent him, but that he had prophesied against me because Tobiah and Sanballat had hired him. ¹³He had been hired to intimidate me so that I would commit a sin by doing this, and then they would give me a bad name to discredit me.

¹⁴Remember Tobiah and Sanballat, O my God, because of what they have done; remember also the prophetess Noadiah and the rest of the prophets who have been trying to intimidate me.

The Completion of the Wall

¹⁵So the wall was completed on the twenty-fifth of Elul, in fifty-two days. ¹⁶When all our enemies heard about this, all the surrounding nations were afraid and lost their self-confidence, because they realized that this work had been done with the help of our God.

¹⁷Also, in those days the nobles of Judah were sending many letters to Tobiah, and replies from Tobiah kept coming to them. ¹⁸For many in Judah were under oath to him, since he was son-in-law to Shecaniah son of Arah, and his son Jehohanan had married the daughter of Meshullam son of Berekiah. ¹⁹Moreover, they kept reporting to me his good deeds and then telling him what I said. And Tobiah sent letters to intimidate me.

7 After the wall had been rebuilt and I had set the doors in place, the gatekeepers and the singers and the Levites were appointed. ²I put in charge of Jerusalem my brother Hanani, along with[c] Hananiah the commander of the citadel, because he was a man of integrity and feared God more than most men do. ³I said to them, "The gates of Jerusalem are not to be opened until the sun is hot. While the gatekeepers are still on duty, have them shut the doors and bar them. Also appoint residents of Jerusalem as guards, some at their posts and some near their own houses."

The List of the Exiles Who Returned
7:6–73pp — Ezr 2:1–70

⁴Now the city was large and spacious, but there were few people in it, and the houses had not yet been rebuilt. ⁵So my God put it into my heart

---

a 2 Or in Kephirim   *b 6 Hebrew Gashmu, a variant of Geshem*
c 2 Or Hanani, that is,

to assemble the nobles, the officials and the common people for registration by families. I found the genealogical record of those who had been the first to return. This is what I found written there:

⁶These are the people of the province who came up from the captivity of the exiles whom Nebuchadnezzar king of Babylon had taken captive (they returned to Jerusalem and Judah, each to his own town, ⁷in company with Zerubbabel, Jeshua, Nehemiah, Azariah, Raamiah, Nahamani, Mordecai, Bilshan, Mispereth, Bigvai, Nehum and Baanah):

The list of the men of Israel:

⁸the descendants of Parosh	2,172
⁹of Shephatiah	372
¹⁰of Arah	652
¹¹of Pahath-Moab (through the line of Jeshua and Joab)	2,818
¹²of Elam	1,254
¹³of Zattu	845
¹⁴of Zaccai	760
¹⁵of Binnui	648
¹⁶of Bebai	628
¹⁷of Azgad	2,322
¹⁸of Adonikam	667
¹⁹of Bigvai	2,067
²⁰of Adin	655
²¹of Ater (through Hezekiah)	98
²²of Hashum	328
²³of Bezai	324
²⁴of Hariph	112
²⁵of Gibeon	95
²⁶the men of Bethlehem and Netophah	188
²⁷of Anathoth	128
²⁸of Beth Azmaveth	42
²⁹of Kiriath Jearim, Kephirah and Beeroth	743
³⁰of Ramah and Geba	621
³¹of Micmash	122
³²of Bethel and Ai	123
³³of the other Nebo	52
³⁴of the other Elam	1,254
³⁵of Harim	320
³⁶of Jericho	345
³⁷of Lod, Hadid and Ono	721
³⁸of Senaah	3,930

³⁹The priests:

the descendants of Jedaiah (through the family of Jeshua)	973
⁴⁰of Immer	1,052
⁴¹of Pashhur	1,247
⁴²of Harim	1,017

⁴³The Levites:

the descendants of Jeshua (through Kadmiel through the line of Hodaviah)	74

⁴⁴The singers:

the descendants of Asaph	148

⁴⁵The gatekeepers:

the descendants of Shallum, Ater, Talmon, Akkub, Hatita and Shobai	138

⁴⁶The temple servants:

the descendants of
Ziha, Hasupha, Tabbaoth,
⁴⁷Keros, Sia, Padon,
⁴⁸Lebana, Hagaba, Shalmai,
⁴⁹Hanan, Giddel, Gahar,
⁵⁰Reaiah, Rezin, Nekoda,
⁵¹Gazzam, Uzza, Paseah,
⁵²Besai, Meunim, Nephusim,
⁵³Bakbuk, Hakupha, Harhur,
⁵⁴Bazluth, Mehida, Harsha,
⁵⁵Barkos, Sisera, Temah,
⁵⁶Neziah and Hatipha

⁵⁷The descendants of the servants of Solomon:

the descendants of
Sotai, Sophereth, Perida,

58 Jaala, Darkon, Giddel,
59 Shephatiah, Hattil,
    Pokereth-Hazzebaim and Amon

60 The temple servants and the
    descendants of the servants
    of Solomon   392

61 The following came up from the towns of Tel Melah, Tel Harsha, Kerub, Addon and Immer, but they could not show that their families were descended from Israel:

62 the descendants of
    Delaiah, Tobiah and Nekoda   642

63 And from among the priests:

the descendants of
    Hobaiah, Hakkoz and Barzillai (a
    man who had married a daughter of
    Barzillai the Gileadite and was called
    by that name).

64 These searched for their family records, but they could not find them and so were excluded from the priesthood as unclean. 65 The governor, therefore, ordered them not to eat any of the most sacred food until there should be a priest ministering with the Urim and Thummim.

66 The whole company numbered 42,360, 67 besides their 7,337 menservants and maidservants; and they also had 245 men and women singers. 68 There were 736 horses, 245 mules, *a* 69 435 camels and 6,720 donkeys.

70 Some of the heads of the families contributed to the work. The governor gave to the treasury 1,000 drachmas *b* of gold, 50 bowls and 530 garments for priests. 71 Some of the heads of the families gave to the treasury for the work 20,000 drachmas *c* of gold and 2,200 minas *d* of silver. 72 The total given by the rest of the people was 20,000 drachmas of gold, 2,000 minas *e* of silver and 67 garments for priests.

73 The priests, the Levites, the gatekeepers, the singers and the temple servants, along with certain of the people and the rest of the Israelites, settled in their own towns.

Ezra Reads the Law

8 When the seventh month came and the Israelites had settled in their towns, 1 all the people assembled as one man in the square before the Water Gate. They told Ezra the scribe to bring out the Book of the Law of Moses, which the LORD had commanded for Israel.

2 So on the first day of the seventh month Ezra the priest brought the Law before the assembly, which was made up of men and women and all who were able to understand. 3 He read it aloud from daybreak till noon as he faced the square before the Water Gate in the presence of the men, women and others who could understand. And all the people listened attentively to the Book of the Law.

4 Ezra the scribe stood on a high wooden platform built for the occasion. Beside him on his right stood Mattithiah, Shema, Anaiah, Uriah, Hilkiah and Maaseiah; and on his left were Pedaiah, Mishael, Malkijah, Hashum, Hashbaddanah, Zechariah and Meshullam.

5 Ezra opened the book. All the people could see him because he was standing above them; and as he opened it, the people all stood up. 6 Ezra praised the LORD, the great God; and all the people lifted their hands and responded, "Amen! Amen!" Then they bowed down and worshiped the LORD with their faces to the ground.

7 The Levites — Jeshua, Bani, Sherebiah, Jamin, Akkub, Shabbethai, Hodiah, Maaseiah, Kelita, Azariah, Jozabad, Hanan and Pelaiah — instructed the people in the Law while the people were standing there. 8 They read from the Book of the Law of God, making it clear *f* and giving the meaning

---

a 68 Some Hebrew manuscripts (see also Ezra 2:66); most Hebrew manuscripts do not have this verse.   *b 70* That is, about 19 pounds (about 8.5 kilograms)   *c 71* That is, about 375 pounds (about 170 kilograms); also in verse 72   *d 71* That is, about 1 1/3 tons (about 1.2 metric tons)   *e 72* That is, about 1 1/4 tons (about 1.1 metric tons)   *f 8* Or *God, translating it* so that the people could understand what was being read.

⁹Then Nehemiah the governor, Ezra the priest and scribe, and the Levites who were instructing the people said to them all, "This day is sacred to the Lord your God. Do not mourn or weep." For all the people had been weeping as they listened to the words of the Law.

¹⁰Nehemiah said, "Go and enjoy choice food and sweet drinks, and send some to those who have nothing prepared. This day is sacred to our Lord. Do not grieve, for the joy of the Lord is your strength."

¹¹The Levites calmed all the people, saying, "Be still, for this is a sacred day. Do not grieve."

¹²Then all the people went away to eat and drink, to send portions of food and to celebrate with great joy, because they now understood the words that had been made known to them.

PRAYING THE SCRIPTURES

Joy

NEHEMIAH 8:10

Dear God, I pray that my grandchild will experience firsthand that the joy of the Lord is her strength.

Next prayer in Joy Prayer Track: Job 8:21

¹³On the second day of the month, the heads of all the families, along with the priests and the Levites, gathered around Ezra the scribe to give attention to the words of the Law. ¹⁴They found written in the Law, which the Lord had commanded through Moses, that the Israelites were to live in booths during the feast of the seventh month ¹⁵and that they should proclaim this word and spread it throughout their towns and in Jerusalem: "Go out into the hill country and bring back branches from olive and wild olive

TALKING POINTS

Joy and Happiness

There are times when we are to celebrate God's goodness to us.

NEHEMIAH 8:10-12

For more on joy and happiness, go to Psalm 16:9-11.

trees, and from myrtles, palms and shade trees, to make booths"—as it is written. ᵃ

¹⁶So the people went out and brought back branches and built themselves booths on their own roofs, in their courtyards, in the courts of the house of God and in the square by the Water Gate and the one by the Gate of Ephraim. ¹⁷The whole company that had returned from exile built booths and lived in them. From the days of Joshua son of Nun until that day, the Israelites had not celebrated it like this. And their joy was very great.

¹⁸Day after day, from the first day to the last, Ezra read from the Book of the Law of God. They celebrated the feast for seven days, and on the eighth day, in accordance with the regulation, there was an assembly.

The Israelites Confess Their Sins

9 On the twenty-fourth day of the same month, the Israelites gathered together, fasting and wearing sackcloth and having dust on their heads. ²Those of Israelite descent had separated themselves from all foreigners. They stood in their places and confessed their sins and the wickedness of their fathers. ³They stood where they were and read from the Book of the Law of the Lord their God for a quarter of the day, and spent another quarter in confession and in worshiping the Lord their God. ⁴Standing on the stairs were the Levites—Jeshua, Bani, Kadmiel,

ᵃ 15 See Lev. 23:37-40.

Shebaniah, Bunni, Sherebiah, Bani and Kenani—who called with loud voices to the LORD their God. [5]And the Levites—Jeshua, Kadmiel, Bani, Hashabneiah, Sherebiah, Hodiah, Shebaniah and Pethahiah—said: "Stand up and praise the LORD your God, who is from everlasting to everlasting. [a]"

"Blessed be your glorious name, and may it be exalted above all blessing and praise. [6]You alone are the LORD. You made the heavens, even the highest heavens, and all their starry host, the earth and all that is on it, the seas and all that is in them. You give life to everything, and the multitudes of heaven worship you.

[7]"You are the LORD God, who chose Abram and brought him out of Ur of the Chaldeans and named him Abraham. [8]You found his heart faithful to you, and you made a covenant with him to give to his descendants the land of the Canaanites, Hittites, Amorites, Perizzites, Jebusites and Girgashites. You have kept your promise because you are righteous.

[9]"You saw the suffering of our forefathers in Egypt; you heard their cry at the Red Sea. [b] [10]You sent miraculous signs and wonders against Pharaoh, against all his officials and all the people of his land, for you knew how arrogantly the Egyptians treated them. You made a name for yourself, which remains to this day. [11]You divided the sea before them, so that they passed through it on dry ground, but you hurled their pursuers into the depths, like a stone into mighty waters. [12]By day you led them with a pillar of cloud, and by night with a pillar of fire to give them light on the way they were to take.

[13]"You came down on Mount Sinai; you spoke to them from heaven. You gave them regulations and laws that are just and right, and decrees and commands that are good. [14]You made known to them your holy Sabbath and gave them commands, decrees and laws through your servant Moses. [15]In their hunger you gave them bread from heaven and in their thirst you brought them water from the rock; you told them to go in and take possession of the land you had sworn with uplifted hand to give them.

[16]"But they, our forefathers, became arrogant and stiff-necked, and did not obey your commands. [17]They refused to listen and failed to remember the miracles you performed among them. They became stiff-necked and in their rebellion appointed a leader in order to return to their slavery. But you are a forgiving God, gracious and compassionate, slow to anger and abounding in love. Therefore you did not desert them, [18]even when they cast for themselves an image of a calf and said, 'This is your god, who brought you up out of Egypt,' or when they committed awful blasphemies.

[19]"Because of your great compassion you did not abandon them in the desert. By day the pillar of cloud did not cease to guide them on their path, nor the pillar of fire by night to shine on the way they were to take. [20]You gave your good Spirit to instruct them. You did not withhold your manna from their mouths, and you gave them water for their thirst. [21]For forty years you sustained them in the desert; they lacked nothing, their clothes did not wear out nor did their feet become swollen.

[22]"You gave them kingdoms and nations, allotting to them even the remotest frontiers. They took over the country of Sihon [c] king of Heshbon and the country of Og king of Bashan. [23]You made their sons as numerous as the stars in the sky, and you brought them into the land that you told their fathers to enter and possess. [24]Their sons went in and took possession of the land. You subdued

[a] 5 Or *God for ever and ever*   [b] 9 Hebrew *Yam Suph*; that is, Sea of Reeds   [c] 22 One Hebrew manuscript and Septuagint; most Hebrew manuscripts *Sihon, that is, the country of the*

before them the Canaanites, who lived in the land; you handed the Canaanites over to them, along with their kings and the peoples of the land, to deal with them as they pleased. 25 They captured fortified cities and fertile land; they took possession of houses filled with all kinds of good things, wells already dug, vineyards, olive groves and fruit trees in abundance. They ate to the full and were well-nourished; they reveled in your great goodness.

26 "But they were disobedient and rebelled against you; they put your law behind their backs. They killed your prophets, who had admonished them in order to turn them back to you; they committed awful blasphemies. 27 So you handed them over to their enemies, who oppressed them. But when they were oppressed they cried out to you. From heaven you heard them, and in your great compassion you gave them deliverers, who rescued them from the hand of their enemies.

28 "But as soon as they were at rest, they again did what was evil in your sight. Then you abandoned them to the hand of their enemies so that they ruled over them. And when they cried out to you again, you heard from heaven, and in your compassion you delivered them time after time.

29 "You warned them to return to your law, but they became arrogant and disobeyed your commands. They sinned against your ordinances, by which a man will live if he obeys them. Stubbornly they turned their backs on you, became stiff-necked and refused to listen. 30 For many years you were patient with them. By your Spirit you admonished them through your prophets. Yet they paid no attention, so you handed them over to the neighboring peoples. 31 But in your great mercy you did not put an end to them or abandon them, for you are a gracious and merciful God.

32 "Now therefore, O our God, the great, mighty and awesome God, who keeps his covenant of love, do not let all this hardship seem trifling in your eyes — the hardship that has come upon us, upon our kings and leaders, upon our priests and prophets, upon our fathers and all your people, from the days of the kings of Assyria until today. 33 In all that has happened to us, you have been just; you have acted faithfully, while we did wrong. 34 Our kings, our leaders, our priests and our fathers did not follow your law; they did not pay attention to your commands or the warnings you gave them. 35 Even while they were in their kingdom, enjoying your great goodness to them in the spacious and fertile land you gave them, they did not serve you or turn from their evil ways.

36 "But see, we are slaves today, slaves in the land you gave our forefathers so they could eat its fruit and the other good things it produces. 37 Because of our sins, its abundant harvest goes to the kings you have placed over us. They rule over our bodies and our cattle as they please. We are in great distress.

The Agreement of the People

38 "In view of all this, we are making a binding agreement, putting it in writing, and our leaders, our Levites and our priests are affixing their seals to it."

10 Those who sealed it were:

Nehemiah the governor, the son of Hacaliah.

Zedekiah, 2 Seraiah, Azariah, Jeremiah, 3 Pashhur, Amariah, Malkijah, 4 Hattush, Shebaniah, Malluch, 5 Harim, Meremoth, Obadiah, 6 Daniel, Ginnethon, Baruch, 7 Meshullam, Abijah, Mijamin, 8 Maaziah, Bilgai and Shemaiah.
These were the priests.

9 The Levites:

> Jeshua son of Azaniah, Binnui of the sons of Henadad, Kadmiel,
> 10 and their associates: Shebaniah, Hodiah, Kelita, Pelaiah, Hanan,
> 11 Mica, Rehob, Hashabiah,
> 12 Zaccur, Sherebiah, Shebaniah,
> 13 Hodiah, Bani and Beninu.

14 The leaders of the people:

> Parosh, Pahath-Moab, Elam, Zattu, Bani,
> 15 Bunni, Azgad, Bebai,
> 16 Adonijah, Bigvai, Adin,
> 17 Ater, Hezekiah, Azzur,
> 18 Hodiah, Hashum, Bezai,
> 19 Hariph, Anathoth, Nebai,
> 20 Magpiash, Meshullam, Hezir,
> 21 Meshezabel, Zadok, Jaddua,
> 22 Pelatiah, Hanan, Anaiah,
> 23 Hoshea, Hananiah, Hasshub,
> 24 Hallohesh, Pilha, Shobek,
> 25 Rehum, Hashabnah, Maaseiah,
> 26 Ahiah, Hanan, Anan,
> 27 Malluch, Harim and Baanah.

28 "The rest of the people—priests, Levites, gatekeepers, singers, temple servants and all who separated themselves from the neighboring peoples for the sake of the Law of God, together with their wives and all their sons and daughters who are able to understand— 29 all these now join their brothers the nobles, and bind themselves with a curse and an oath to follow the Law of God given through Moses the servant of God and to obey carefully all the commands, regulations and decrees of the LORD our Lord.

30 "We promise not to give our daughters in marriage to the peoples around us or take their daughters for our sons.

31 "When the neighboring peoples bring merchandise or grain to sell on the Sabbath, we will not buy from them on the Sabbath or on any holy day. Every seventh year we will forgo working the land and will cancel all debts.

32 "We assume the responsibility for carrying out the commands to give a third of a shekel[a] each year for the service of the house of our God: 33 for the bread set out on the table; for the regular grain offerings and burnt offerings; for the offerings on the Sabbaths, New Moon festivals and appointed feasts; for the holy offerings; for sin offerings to make atonement for Israel; and for all the duties of the house of our God.

34 "We—the priests, the Levites and the people—have cast lots to determine when each of our families is to bring to the house of our God at set times each year a contribution of wood to burn on the altar of the LORD our God, as it is written in the Law.

35 "We also assume responsibility for bringing to the house of the LORD each year the firstfruits of our crops and of every fruit tree.

36 "As it is also written in the Law, we will bring the firstborn of our sons and of our cattle, of our herds and of our flocks to the house of our God, to the priests ministering there.

37 "Moreover, we will bring to the storerooms of the house of our God, to the priests, the first of our ground meal, of our ⌞grain⌟ offerings, of the fruit of all our trees and of our new wine and oil. And we will bring a tithe of our crops to the Levites, for it is the Levites who collect the tithes in all the towns where we work. 38 A priest descended from Aaron is to accompany the Levites when they receive the tithes, and the Levites are to bring a tenth of the tithes up to the house of our God, to the storerooms of the treasury. 39 The people of Israel, including the Levites, are to bring their contributions of grain, new wine and oil to the storerooms where the articles for the sanctuary are kept

a 32 That is, about 1/8 ounce (about 4 grams)

and where the ministering priests, the gatekeepers and the singers stay.

"We will not neglect the house of our God."

The New Residents of Jerusalem

11:3–19pp — 1Ch 9:1–17

11 Now the leaders of the people settled in Jerusalem, and the rest of the people cast lots to bring one out of every ten to live in Jerusalem, the holy city, while the remaining nine were to stay in their own towns. [2] The people commended all the men who volunteered to live in Jerusalem.

[3] These are the provincial leaders who settled in Jerusalem (now some Israelites, priests, Levites, temple servants and descendants of Solomon's servants lived in the towns of Judah, each on his own property in the various towns, [4] while other people from both Judah and Benjamin lived in Jerusalem):

From the descendants of Judah:

Athaiah son of Uzziah, the son of Zechariah, the son of Amariah, the son of Shephatiah, the son of Mahalalel, a descendant of Perez; [5] and Maaseiah son of Baruch, the son of Col-Hozeh, the son of Hazaiah, the son of Adaiah, the son of Joiarib, the son of Zechariah, a descendant of Shelah. [6] The descendants of Perez who lived in Jerusalem totaled 468 able men.

[7] From the descendants of Benjamin:

Sallu son of Meshullam, the son of Joed, the son of Pedaiah, the son of Kolaiah, the son of Maaseiah, the son of Ithiel, the son of Jeshaiah, [8] and his followers, Gabbai and Sallai—928 men. [9] Joel son of Zicri was their chief officer, and Judah son of Hassenuah was over the Second District of the city.

[10] From the priests:

Jedaiah; the son of Joiarib; Jakin; [11] Seraiah son of Hilkiah, the son of Meshullam, the son of Zadok, the son of Meraioth, the son of Ahitub, supervisor in the house of God, [12] and their associates, who carried on work for the temple—822 men; Adaiah son of Jeroham, the son of Pelaliah, the son of Amzi, the son of Zechariah, the son of Pashhur, the son of Malkijah, [13] and his associates, who were heads of families—242 men; Amashsai son of Azarel, the son of Ahzai, the son of Meshillemoth, the son of Immer, [14] and his[a] associates, who were able men—128. Their chief officer was Zabdiel son of Haggedolim.

[15] From the Levites:

Shemaiah son of Hasshub, the son of Azrikam, the son of Hashabiah, the son of Bunni; [16] Shabbethai and Jozabad, two of the heads of the Levites, who had charge of the outside work of the house of God; [17] Mattaniah son of Mica, the son of Zabdi, the son of Asaph, the director who led in thanksgiving and prayer; Bakbukiah, second among his associates; and Abda son of Shammua, the son of Galal, the son of Jeduthun. [18] The Levites in the holy city totaled 284.

[19] The gatekeepers:

Akkub, Talmon and their associates, who kept watch at the gates—172 men.

[20] The rest of the Israelites, with the priests and Levites, were in all the towns of Judah, each on his ancestral property.

[21] The temple servants lived on the hill of Ophel, and Ziha and Gishpa were in charge of them.

[22] The chief officer of the Levites in Jerusalem was Uzzi son of Bani, the son of Hashabiah, the son of Mattaniah, the son of Mica. Uzzi was one of Asaph's descendants, who were the singers responsible for the service of the house of God. [23] The singers were under the king's orders, which regulated their daily activity.

---

[a] 14 Most Septuagint manuscripts; Hebrew their

24 Pethahiah son of Meshezabel, one of the descendants of Zerah son of Judah, was the king's agent in all affairs relating to the people.

25 As for the villages with their fields, some of the people of Judah lived in Kiriath Arba and its surrounding settlements, in Dibon and its settlements, in Jekabzeel and its villages, 26 in Jeshua, in Moladah, in Beth Pelet, 27 in Hazar Shual, in Beersheba and its settlements, 28 in Ziklag, in Meconah and its settlements, 29 in En Rimmon, in Zorah, in Jarmuth, 30 Zanoah, Adullam and their villages, in Lachish and its fields, and in Azekah and its settlements. So they were living all the way from Beersheba to the Valley of Hinnom.

31 The descendants of the Benjamites from Geba lived in Micmash, Aija, Bethel and its settlements, 32 in Anathoth, Nob and Ananiah, 33 in Hazor, Ramah and Gittaim, 34 in Hadid, Zeboim and Neballat, 35 in Lod and Ono, and in the Valley of the Craftsmen.

36 Some of the divisions of the Levites of Judah settled in Benjamin.

Priests and Levites

12 These were the priests and Levites who returned with Zerubbabel son of Shealtiel and with Jeshua:

Seraiah, Jeremiah, Ezra,
2 Amariah, Malluch, Hattush,
3 Shecaniah, Rehum, Meremoth,
4 Iddo, Ginnethon,[a] Abijah,
5 Mijamin,[b] Moadiah, Bilgah,
6 Shemaiah, Joiarib, Jedaiah,
7 Sallu, Amok, Hilkiah and Jedaiah.

These were the leaders of the priests and their associates in the days of Jeshua.

8 The Levites were Jeshua, Binnui, Kadmiel, Sherebiah, Judah, and also Mattaniah, who, together with his associates, was in charge of the songs of thanksgiving. 9 Bakbukiah and Unni, their associates, stood opposite them in the services.

10 Jeshua was the father of Joiakim, Joiakim the father of Eliashib, Eliashib the father of Joiada, 11 Joiada the father of Jonathan, and Jonathan the father of Jaddua.

12 In the days of Joiakim, these were the heads of the priestly families:

of Seraiah's family, Meraiah;
of Jeremiah's, Hananiah;
13 of Ezra's, Meshullam;
of Amariah's, Jehohanan;
14 of Malluch's, Jonathan;
of Shecaniah's,[c] Joseph;
15 of Harim's, Adna;
of Meremoth's,[d] Helkai;
16 of Iddo's, Zechariah;
of Ginnethon's, Meshullam;
17 of Abijah's, Zicri;
of Miniamin's and of Moadiah's, Piltai;
18 of Bilgah's, Shammua;
of Shemaiah's, Jehonathan;
19 of Joiarib's, Mattenai;
of Jedaiah's, Uzzi;
20 of Sallu's, Kallai;
of Amok's, Eber;
21 of Hilkiah's, Hashabiah;
of Jedaiah's, Nethanel.

22 The family heads of the Levites in the days of Eliashib, Joiada, Johanan and Jaddua, as well as those of the priests, were recorded in the reign of Darius the Persian. 23 The family heads among the descendants of Levi up to the time of Johanan son of Eliashib were recorded in the book of the annals. 24 And the leaders of the Levites were Hashabiah, Sherebiah, Jeshua son of Kadmiel, and their associates, who stood opposite them to give praise and thanksgiving, one section responding to the other, as prescribed by David the man of God.

25 Mattaniah, Bakbukiah, Obadiah, Meshullam, Talmon and Akkub were gatekeepers who guarded the storerooms at the gates. 26 They served in the days of Joiakim son of Jeshua, the son of Jozadak, and in the days of Nehemiah the governor and of Ezra the priest and scribe.

---

[a] 4 Many Hebrew manuscripts and Vulgate (see also Neh. 12:16); most Hebrew manuscripts Ginnethoi   [b] 5 A variant of Miniamin
[c] 14 Very many Hebrew manuscripts, some Septuagint and Syriac (see also Neh. 12:3); most Hebrew manuscripts Shebaniah's   [d] 15 Some Septuagint manuscripts (see also Neh. 12:3); Hebrew Meraioth's

Dedication of the Wall of Jerusalem

²⁷ At the dedication of the wall of Jerusalem, the Levites were sought out from where they lived and were brought to Jerusalem to celebrate joyfully the dedication with songs of thanksgiving and with the music of cymbals, harps and lyres. ²⁸ The singers also were brought together from the region around Jerusalem — from the villages of the Netophathites, ²⁹ from Beth Gilgal, and from the area of Geba and Azmaveth, for the singers had built villages for themselves around Jerusalem. ³⁰ When the priests and Levites had purified themselves ceremonially, they purified the people, the gates and the wall.

³¹ I had the leaders of Judah go up on top *a* of the wall. I also assigned two large choirs to give thanks. One was to proceed on top *b* of the wall to the right, toward the Dung Gate. ³² Hoshaiah and half the leaders of Judah followed them, ³³ along with Azariah, Ezra, Meshullam, ³⁴ Judah, Benjamin, Shemaiah, Jeremiah, ³⁵ as well as some priests with trumpets, and also Zechariah son of Jonathan, the son of Shemaiah, the son of Mattaniah, the son of Micaiah, the son of Zaccur, the son of Asaph, ³⁶ and his associates — Shemaiah, Azarel, Milalai, Gilalai, Maai, Nethanel, Judah and Hanani — with musical instruments ˌprescribed byˌ David the man of God. Ezra the scribe led the procession. ³⁷ At the Fountain Gate they continued directly up the steps of the City of David on the ascent to the wall and passed above the house of David to the Water Gate on the east.

³⁸ The second choir proceeded in the opposite direction. I followed them on top *c* of the wall, together with half the people — past the Tower of the Ovens to the Broad Wall, ³⁹ over the Gate of Ephraim, the Jeshanah *d* Gate, the Fish Gate, the Tower of Hananel and the Tower of the Hundred, as far as the Sheep Gate. At the Gate of the Guard they stopped.

⁴⁰ The two choirs that gave thanks then took their places in the house of God; so did I, together with half the officials, ⁴¹ as well as the priests — Eliakim, Maaseiah, Miniamin, Micaiah, Elioenai, Zechariah and Hananiah with their trumpets — ⁴² and also Maaseiah, Shemaiah, Eleazar, Uzzi, Jehohanan, Malkijah, Elam and Ezer. The choirs sang under the direction of Jezrahiah. ⁴³ And on that day they offered great sacrifices, rejoicing because God had given them great joy. The women and children also rejoiced. The sound of rejoicing in Jerusalem could be heard far away.

⁴⁴ At that time men were appointed to be in charge of the storerooms for the contributions, firstfruits and tithes. From the fields around the towns they were to bring into the storerooms the portions required by the Law for the priests and the Levites, for Judah was pleased with the ministering priests and Levites. ⁴⁵ They performed the service of their God and the service of purification, as did also the singers and gatekeepers, according to the commands of David and his son Solomon. ⁴⁶ For long ago, in the days of David and Asaph, there had been directors for the singers and for the songs of praise and thanksgiving to God. ⁴⁷ So in the days of Zerubbabel and of Nehemiah, all Israel contributed the daily portions for the singers and gatekeepers. They also set aside the portion for the other Levites, and the Levites set aside the portion for the descendants of Aaron.

Nehemiah's Final Reforms

13 On that day the Book of Moses was read aloud in the hearing of the people and there it was found written that no Ammonite or Moabite should ever be admitted into the assembly of God, ² because they had not met the Israelites with food and water but had hired Balaam to call a curse down on them. (Our God, however, turned the curse into a blessing.) ³ When the people heard this law, they excluded from Israel all who were of foreign descent.

⁴ Before this, Eliashib the priest had been put in charge of the storerooms of the house of our God. He was closely associated with Tobiah, ⁵ and he had provided him with a large room formerly

---

a 31 Or *go alongside*   *b 31* Or *proceed alongside*   *c 38* Or *them alongside*   *d 39* Or *Old*

I HAD THE LEADERS OF JUDAH
GO UP ON TOP OF THE WALL.
I ALSO ASSIGNED TWO LARGE
CHOIRS TO GIVE THANKS.

Nehemiah 12:31

Say Thank You for Little Things

SHEILA WALSH

READ | NEHEMIAH 12:27 – 47

I'm learning to stop for thankful moments. It's become a daily discipline of mine since I found that I was getting overwhelmed by all the daily stuff that "has to get done." Some of the feelings and fears I had before I was hospitalized for clinical depression were niggling at me again, buzzing around me like persistent house flies. I've learned enough about what makes me tick to pay attention when I feel myself sinking. So I'm learning to stop intentionally throughout every day and lift my heart and soul to heaven and say, "Thank you!"

Giving thanks does wonders for my soul. It refocuses me on what's really important so that instead of dwelling on the fact that my son just tried to flush my new pale blue suede pumps down the toilet, I can celebrate the gift of a child when so many arms are empty. Marcus Aurelius, a first-century Roman emperor, wrote that the most important things a man can choose is how he thinks. We can dwell every day on the things that are not working and let them drag us down, or we can thank God for the simple gifts of grace he gives us every day if we have a heart to see them.

Whether our "thank you's" are momentary, intentional pauses in the midst of a hectic day, thank-you notes to God for his many blessings, or lengthy discourses of his grace, cultivating an attitude of gratitude will remind us of the truth that undergirds our lives: "For the LORD is good and his love endures forever; his faithfulness continues through all generations" (Psalm 100:5).

Thank you, God, for all the many things you give me every day: morning sunshine, the smiles and hugs of children and grandchildren, a great cup of coffee, the laughter of a friend. May I always be grateful for the many blessings you shower upon me. Amen.

Your next devotion is located on page 649.

GRANDCHILD IN FOCUS • PRAYER

Future Spouse

Dear Lord, if it is your will, I pray my grandchild will be united in a loving and Christian marriage. Keep her sexually pure so that she will honor you with her body and mind. As she seeks a spouse who will honor and care for her, give her patience and discernment. May her choice for a life partner be your choice for her, so that she and her husband will together glorify you in a lasting love. I pray this in Jesus' name, amen.

used to store the grain offerings and incense and temple articles, and also the tithes of grain, new wine and oil prescribed for the Levites, singers and gatekeepers, as well as the contributions for the priests.

⁶But while all this was going on, I was not in Jerusalem, for in the thirty-second year of Artaxerxes king of Babylon I had returned to the king. Some time later I asked his permission ⁷and came back to Jerusalem. Here I learned about the evil thing Eliashib had done in providing Tobiah a room in the courts of the house of God. ⁸I was greatly displeased and threw all Tobiah's household goods out of the room. ⁹I gave orders to purify the rooms, and then I put back into them the equipment of the house of God, with the grain offerings and the incense.

¹⁰I also learned that the portions assigned to the Levites had not been given to them, and that all the Levites and singers responsible for the service had gone back to their own fields. ¹¹So I rebuked the officials and asked them, "Why is the house of God neglected?" Then I called them together and stationed them at their posts.

¹²All Judah brought the tithes of grain, new wine and oil into the storerooms. ¹³I put Shelemiah the priest, Zadok the scribe, and a Levite named Pedaiah in charge of the storerooms and made Hanan son of Zaccur, the son of Mattaniah, their assistant, because these men were considered trustworthy. They were made responsible for distributing the supplies to their brothers.

¹⁴Remember me for this, O my God, and do not blot out what I have so faithfully done for the house of my God and its services.

¹⁵In those days I saw men in Judah treading winepresses on the Sabbath and bringing in grain and loading it on donkeys, together with wine, grapes, figs and all other kinds of loads. And they were bringing all this into Jerusalem on the Sabbath. Therefore I warned them against selling food on that day. ¹⁶Men from Tyre who lived in Jerusalem were bringing in fish and all kinds of merchandise and selling them in Jerusalem on the Sabbath to the people of Judah. ¹⁷I rebuked the nobles of Judah and said to them, "What is this wicked thing you are doing—desecrating the Sabbath day? ¹⁸Didn't your forefathers do the same things, so that our God brought all this calamity upon us and upon this city? Now you are stirring up more wrath against Israel by desecrating the Sabbath."

¹⁹When evening shadows fell on the gates of Jerusalem before the Sabbath, I ordered the doors to be shut and not opened until the Sabbath was over. I stationed some of my own men at the gates so that no load could be brought in on the Sabbath day. ²⁰Once or twice the merchants and sellers of all kinds of goods spent the night outside Jerusalem. ²¹But I warned them and said, "Why do you spend the night by the wall? If you do this again, I will lay hands on you." From that time on they no longer came on the Sabbath. ²²Then I commanded the Levites to purify themselves and go and guard the gates in order to keep the Sabbath day holy.

Remember me for this also, O my God, and show mercy to me according to your great love.

²³Moreover, in those days I saw men of Judah who had married women from Ashdod, Ammon and Moab. ²⁴Half of their children spoke the language of Ashdod or the language of one of the other peoples, and did not know how to speak the language of Judah. ²⁵I rebuked them and called curses down on them. I beat some of the men and pulled out their hair. I made them take an oath in God's name and said: "You are not to give your daughters in marriage to their sons, nor are you to take their daughters in marriage for your sons or for yourselves. ²⁶Was it not because of marriages like these that Solomon king of Israel sinned? Among the many nations there was no king like him. He was loved by his God, and God made him king over all Israel, but even he was led into sin by foreign women. ²⁷Must we hear now that you too are doing all this terrible wickedness and are being unfaithful to our God by marrying foreign women?"

²⁸One of the sons of Joiada son of Eliashib the high priest was son-in-law to Sanballat the Horonite. And I drove him away from me.

²⁹Remember them, O my God, because they defiled the priestly office and the covenant of the priesthood and of the Levites.

³⁰So I purified the priests and the Levites of everything foreign, and assigned them duties, each to his own task. ³¹I also made provision for contributions of wood at designated times, and for the firstfruits.

Remember me with favor, O my God.

What A WOMAN!

Though some people may believe otherwise, Esther did not live a charmed life. A Jewish orphan, Esther was raised by her cousin Mordecai, and the two were living in Persia when the king chose the beautiful young exile first to be in his harem and then eventually to be queen. She had managed to keep her heritage a secret throughout her time in the king's palace, so when Haman hatched an evil plan to annihilate the Jews, Esther was forced into a dangerous and compromising situation (see Esther 4).

At its core, the book of Esther is a story about God's protection of his people. Although Esther's initial reaction was to fear for her life, she knew stepping back and letting Haman carry out his destructive plot was not the right thing to do. God sometimes puts us in uncomfortable situations, but no matter how dangerous or scary they might seem at the time, everything God does has a purpose.

You, your family, your children and your grandchildren are all in the right place at the right time. You're here in this moment of history, "for such a time as this" (Esther 4:14), to further God's kingdom and to fulfill his plan. Your actions might not be as grand and bold as Esther's — they may even appear to be small and insignificant — but who knows how they will affect the course of history. That outcome remains in God's hands.

VERSE *to* REMEMBER | ESTHER 4:14

"For if you remain silent at this time, relief and deliverance for the Jews will arise from another place, but you and your father's family will perish. And who knows but that you have come to royal position for such a time as this?"

ABOUT ESTHER

WRITTEN BY:
Unknown

WRITTEN FOR:
The Jewish people

DATE WRITTEN:
Sometime after
460 B.C.

WHY WRITTEN:
To reveal how God cares
for his people

Queen Vashti Deposed

1 This is what happened during the time of Xerxes,[a] the Xerxes who ruled over 127 provinces stretching from India to Cush[b]: ²At that time King Xerxes reigned from his royal throne in the citadel of Susa, ³and in the third year of his reign he gave a banquet for all his nobles and officials. The military leaders of Persia and Media, the princes, and the nobles of the provinces were present.

⁴For a full 180 days he displayed the vast wealth of his kingdom and the splendor and glory of his majesty. ⁵When these days were over, the king gave a banquet, lasting seven days, in the enclosed garden of the king's palace, for all the people from the least to the greatest, who were in the citadel of Susa. ⁶The garden had hangings of white and blue linen, fastened with cords of white linen and purple material to silver rings on marble pillars. There were couches of gold and silver on a mosaic pavement of porphyry, marble, mother-of-pearl and other costly stones. ⁷Wine was served in goblets of gold, each one different from the other, and the royal wine was abundant, in keeping with the king's liberality. ⁸By the king's command each guest was allowed to drink in his own way, for the king instructed all the wine stewards to serve each man what he wished.

⁹Queen Vashti also gave a banquet for the women in the royal palace of King Xerxes.

¹⁰On the seventh day, when King Xerxes was in high spirits from wine, he commanded the seven eunuchs who served him — Mehuman, Biztha, Harbona, Bigtha, Abagtha, Zethar and Carcas — ¹¹to bring before him Queen Vashti, wearing her royal crown, in order to display her beauty to the people and nobles, for she was lovely to look at. ¹²But when the attendants delivered the king's command, Queen Vashti refused to come. Then the king became furious and burned with anger.

¹³Since it was customary for the king to consult experts in matters of law and justice, he spoke with the wise men who understood the times ¹⁴and were closest to the king — Carshena, Shethar, Admatha, Tarshish, Meres, Marsena and Memucan, the seven nobles of Persia and Media who had special access to the king and were highest in the kingdom.

¹⁵"According to law, what must be done to Queen Vashti?" he asked. "She has not obeyed the command of King Xerxes that the eunuchs have taken to her."

¹⁶Then Memucan replied in the presence of the king and the nobles, "Queen Vashti has done wrong, not only against the king but also against all the nobles and the peoples of all the provinces of King Xerxes. ¹⁷For the queen's conduct will become known to all the women, and so they will despise their husbands and say, 'King Xerxes commanded Queen Vashti to be brought before him, but she would not come.' ¹⁸This very day the Persian and Median women of the nobility who have heard about the queen's conduct will respond to all the king's nobles in the same way. There will be no end of disrespect and discord.

¹⁹"Therefore, if it pleases the king, let him issue a royal decree and let it be written in the laws of Persia and Media, which cannot be repealed, that Vashti is never again to enter the presence of King Xerxes. Also let the king give her royal position to someone else who is better than she. ²⁰Then when the king's edict is proclaimed throughout all his vast realm, all the women will respect their husbands, from the least to the greatest."

²¹The king and his nobles were pleased with this advice, so the king did as Memucan proposed. ²²He sent dispatches to all parts of the kingdom, to each province in its own script and to each people in its own language, proclaiming in each people's tongue that every man should be ruler over his own household.

Esther Made Queen

2 Later when the anger of King Xerxes had subsided, he remembered Vashti and what she had done and what he had decreed about her. ²Then the king's personal attendants proposed, "Let a search be made for beautiful young virgins

---

[a] 1 Hebrew *Ahasuerus*, a variant of Xerxes' Persian name; here and throughout Esther   [b] 1 That is, the upper Nile region

for the king. ³Let the king appoint commissioners in every province of his realm to bring all these beautiful girls into the harem at the citadel of Susa. Let them be placed under the care of Hegai, the king's eunuch, who is in charge of the women; and let beauty treatments be given to them. ⁴Then let the girl who pleases the king be queen instead of Vashti." This advice appealed to the king, and he followed it.

⁵Now there was in the citadel of Susa a Jew of the tribe of Benjamin, named Mordecai son of Jair, the son of Shimei, the son of Kish, ⁶who had been carried into exile from Jerusalem by Nebuchadnezzar king of Babylon, among those taken captive with Jehoiachin ᵃ king of Judah. ⁷Mordecai had a cousin named Hadassah, whom he had brought up because she had neither father nor mother. This girl, who was also known as Esther, was lovely in form and features, and Mordecai had taken her as his own daughter when her father and mother died.

⁸When the king's order and edict had been proclaimed, many girls were brought to the citadel of Susa and put under the care of Hegai. Esther also was taken to the king's palace and entrusted to Hegai, who had charge of the harem. ⁹The girl pleased him and won his favor. Immediately he provided her with her beauty treatments and special food. He assigned to her seven maids selected from the king's palace and moved her and her maids into the best place in the harem.

¹⁰Esther had not revealed her nationality and

stories to share

ESTHER 2:1–18

Esther Becomes Queen

LIFE LESSON: A humble spirit pleases God.

TO TALK ABOUT

✦ Why was Esther taken to the king's palace?

✦ Do you like people just because they're good-looking?

✦ What was Esther like as a person (see verse 15)?

✦ What character traits draw people to you?

family background, because Mordecai had forbidden her to do so. ¹¹Every day he walked back and forth near the courtyard of the harem to find out how Esther was and what was happening to her.

¹²Before a girl's turn came to go in to King Xerxes, she had to complete twelve months of beauty treatments prescribed for the women, six months with oil of myrrh and six with perfumes and cosmetics. ¹³And this is how she would go to the king: Anything she wanted was given her to take with her from the harem to the king's palace. ¹⁴In the evening she would go there and in the morning return to another part of the harem to the care of Shaashgaz, the king's eunuch who was in charge of the concubines. She would not return to the king unless he was pleased with her and summoned her by name.

ᵃ 6 Hebrew *Jeconiah*, a variant of *Jehoiachin*

TALKING POINTS

Blended Family

Mordecai raised Esther as his own daughter.

ESTHER 2:5–7

For more on blended family, go to Psalm 68:6.

¹⁵When the turn came for Esther (the girl Mordecai had adopted, the daughter of his uncle Abihail) to go to the king, she asked for nothing other than what Hegai, the king's eunuch who was in charge of the harem, suggested. And Esther won the favor of everyone who saw her. ¹⁶She was taken to King Xerxes in the royal residence in the tenth month, the month of Tebeth, in the seventh year of his reign.

¹⁷Now the king was attracted to Esther more than to any of the other women, and she won his favor and approval more than any of the other virgins. So he set a royal crown on her head and made her queen instead of Vashti. ¹⁸And the king gave a great banquet, Esther's banquet, for all his nobles and officials. He proclaimed a holiday throughout the provinces and distributed gifts with royal liberality.

Mordecai Uncovers a Conspiracy

¹⁹When the virgins were assembled a second time, Mordecai was sitting at the king's gate. ²⁰But Esther had kept secret her family background and nationality just as Mordecai had told her to do, for she continued to follow Mordecai's instructions as she had done when he was bringing her up.

²¹During the time Mordecai was sitting at the king's gate, Bigthana^a and Teresh, two of the king's officers who guarded the doorway, became angry and conspired to assassinate King Xerxes. ²²But Mordecai found out about the plot and told Queen Esther, who in turn reported it to the king, giving credit to Mordecai. ²³And when the report was investigated and found to be true, the two officials were hanged on a gallows.^b All this was recorded in the book of the annals in the presence of the king.

Haman's Plot to Destroy the Jews

3 After these events, King Xerxes honored Haman son of Hammedatha, the Agagite, elevating him and giving him a seat of honor higher than that of all the other nobles. ²All the royal officials at the king's gate knelt down and paid honor to Haman, for the king had commanded this concerning him. But Mordecai would not kneel down or pay him honor.

³Then the royal officials at the king's gate asked Mordecai, "Why do you disobey the king's command?" ⁴Day after day they spoke to him but he refused to comply. Therefore they told Haman about it to see whether Mordecai's behavior would be tolerated, for he had told them he was a Jew.

⁵When Haman saw that Mordecai would not kneel down or pay him honor, he was enraged. ⁶Yet having learned who Mordecai's people were, he scorned the idea of killing only Mordecai. Instead Haman looked for a way to destroy all Mordecai's people, the Jews, throughout the whole kingdom of Xerxes.

⁷In the twelfth year of King Xerxes, in the first month, the month of Nisan, they cast the *pur* (that is, the lot) in the presence of Haman to select a day and month. And the lot fell on^c the twelfth month, the month of Adar.

⁸Then Haman said to King Xerxes, "There is a certain people dispersed and scattered among the peoples in all the provinces of your kingdom whose customs are different from those of all other people and who do not obey the king's laws; it is not in the king's best interest to tolerate them. ⁹If it pleases the king, let a decree be issued to destroy them, and I will put ten thousand talents^d of silver into the royal treasury for the men who carry out this business."

¹⁰So the king took his signet ring from his finger and gave it to Haman son of Hammedatha, the Agagite, the enemy of the Jews. ¹¹"Keep the money," the king said to Haman, "and do with the people as you please."

¹²Then on the thirteenth day of the first month the royal secretaries were summoned. They wrote out in the script of each province and in the language of each people all Haman's orders to the king's satraps, the governors of the various

^a 21 Hebrew *Bigthan*, a variant of *Bigthana*   ^b 23 Or *were hung* (or *impaled*) *on poles*; similarly elsewhere in Esther
^c 7 Septuagint; Hebrew does not have *And the lot fell on*.
^d 9 That is, about 375 tons (about 345 metric tons)

ESTHER 3:1–11; 4:1—5:8; 7:1–10; 8:3–13

Esther Saves Her People

LIFE LESSON: Sometimes it takes courage to do what God wants.

TO TALK ABOUT

✦ Why did Haman want to kill the Jews?

✦ Why did Mordecai ask Esther to help?

✦ The book of Esther never mentions God, but in what ways do you see his hand at work in these events?

✦ When have you been in just the right place to do something special for God? Did you do it?

provinces and the nobles of the various peoples. These were written in the name of King Xerxes himself and sealed with his own ring. [13]Dispatches were sent by couriers to all the king's provinces with the order to destroy, kill and annihilate all the Jews—young and old, women and little children—on a single day, the thirteenth day of the twelfth month, the month of Adar, and to plunder their goods. [14]A copy of the text of the edict was to be issued as law in every province and made known to the people of every nationality so they would be ready for that day.

[15]Spurred on by the king's command, the couriers went out, and the edict was issued in the citadel of Susa. The king and Haman sat down to drink, but the city of Susa was bewildered.

Mordecai Persuades Esther to Help

4 When Mordecai learned of all that had been done, he tore his clothes, put on sackcloth and ashes, and went out into the city, wailing loudly and bitterly. [2]But he went only as far as the king's gate, because no one clothed in sackcloth was allowed to enter it. [3]In every province to which the edict and order of the king came, there was great mourning among the Jews, with fasting, weeping and wailing. Many lay in sackcloth and ashes.

[4]When Esther's maids and eunuchs came and told her about Mordecai, she was in great distress. She sent clothes for him to put on instead of his sackcloth, but he would not accept them. [5]Then Esther summoned Hathach, one of the king's eunuchs assigned to attend her, and ordered him to find out what was troubling Mordecai and why.

[6]So Hathach went out to Mordecai in the open square of the city in front of the king's gate. [7]Mordecai told him everything that had happened to him, including the exact amount of money Haman had promised to pay into the royal treasury for the destruction of the Jews. [8]He also gave him a copy of the text of the edict for their annihilation, which had been published in Susa, to show to Esther and explain it to her, and he told him to urge her to go into the king's presence to beg for mercy and plead with him for her people.

[9]Hathach went back and reported to Esther what Mordecai had said. [10]Then she instructed him to say to Mordecai, [11]"All the king's officials and the people of the royal provinces know that for any man or woman who approaches the king in the inner court without being summoned the king has but one law: that he be put to death. The only exception to this is for the king to extend the gold scepter to him and spare his life. But thirty days have passed since I was called to go to the king."

[12]When Esther's words were reported to Mordecai, [13]he sent back this answer: "Do not think

> THEN ESTHER SENT THIS
> REPLY TO MORDECAI: "GO,
> GATHER TOGETHER ALL THE
> JEWS WHO ARE IN SUSA, AND
> FAST FOR ME."
>
> *Esther 4:15–16*

Howdy, Heartner

KAREN O'CONNOR

READ | ESTHER 4:1–17

My friend and writing colleague Lynni and I have decided to be "heartners" (our code word for "partners of the heart"). Can't you just see us strumming our gee-tars and tipping our Western hats to a crowd of onlookers? Not exactly! We both sing, but that's where the similarity to those wearing fringe jackets and pointy-toed boots ends.

So what does the term "heartner" mean to us? It means we support one another at work, at home and in our community with ongoing prayer, a listening ear or two, a heart of love, lots of e-mail chats. Advice when solicited and silence when it's not, and accountability — a fancy word for the freedom to say at times, "You did what?"

Sometimes being a heart partner can take you to the edge. One more step and the relationship will go over the cliff. You're sure of it. But still, you have to take the step — you have to be willing to risk — or you're no partner and certainly not a heartner. You're an accomplice!

You might want to find a heartner in your life — a friend who will support you in the workplace as well as at home, who will keep a mind and heart open to your needs and desires, and who will hold you fast to the high road with prayer and honest questions when you're about to stray. We all need individuals in our lives who care enough to be there in the trivial, in the trials, and in the triumphs, too.

Lord, I need a heartner. Will you point me in the right direction? Will you guide me to someone who needs me too?

Your next devotion is located on page 651.

GRANDCHILD IN FOCUS • PRAYER

School/Career

Dear God, may learning be a joy rather than a chore for my grandchild. May exploration of new ideas bring a sense of wonder, awe and excitement. Grant him clarity of mind, the ability to concentrate on the task at hand and recollection of what has been learned. Help him to appreciate the tasks that come easily and to persevere through those that challenge. Amen.

that because you are in the king's house you alone of all the Jews will escape. ¹⁴For if you remain silent at this time, relief and deliverance for the Jews will arise from another place, but you and your father's family will perish. And who knows but that you have come to royal position for such a time as this?"

¹⁵Then Esther sent this reply to Mordecai: ¹⁶"Go, gather together all the Jews who are in Susa, and fast for me. Do not eat or drink for three days, night or day. I and my maids will fast as you do. When this is done, I will go to the king, even though it is against the law. And if I perish, I perish."

¹⁷So Mordecai went away and carried out all of Esther's instructions.

Esther's Request to the King

5 On the third day Esther put on her royal robes and stood in the inner court of the palace, in front of the king's hall. The king was sitting on his royal throne in the hall, facing the entrance. ²When he saw Queen Esther standing in the court, he was pleased with her and held out to her the gold scepter that was in his hand. So Esther approached and touched the tip of the scepter.

³Then the king asked, "What is it, Queen Esther? What is your request? Even up to half the kingdom, it will be given you."

⁴"If it pleases the king," replied Esther, "let the king, together with Haman, come today to a banquet I have prepared for him."

⁵"Bring Haman at once," the king said, "so that we may do what Esther asks."

So the king and Haman went to the banquet Esther had prepared. ⁶As they were drinking wine, the king again asked Esther, "Now what is your petition? It will be given you. And what is your request? Even up to half the kingdom, it will be granted."

⁷Esther replied, "My petition and my request is this: ⁸If the king regards me with favor and if it pleases the king to grant my petition and fulfill my request, let the king and Haman come tomor-row to the banquet I will prepare for them. Then I will answer the king's question."

Haman's Rage Against Mordecai

⁹Haman went out that day happy and in high spirits. But when he saw Mordecai at the king's gate and observed that he neither rose nor showed fear in his presence, he was filled with rage against Mordecai. ¹⁰Nevertheless, Haman restrained himself and went home.

Calling together his friends and Zeresh, his wife, ¹¹Haman boasted to them about his vast wealth, his many sons, and all the ways the king had honored him and how he had elevated him above the other nobles and officials. ¹²"And that's not all," Haman added. "I'm the only person Queen Esther invited to accompany the king to the banquet she gave. And she has invited me along with the king tomorrow. ¹³But all this gives me no satisfaction as long as I see that Jew Mordecai sitting at the king's gate."

¹⁴His wife Zeresh and all his friends said to him, "Have a gallows built, seventy-five feet[a] high, and ask the king in the morning to have Mordecai hanged on it. Then go with the king to the dinner and be happy." This suggestion delighted Haman, and he had the gallows built.

Mordecai Honored

6 That night the king could not sleep; so he ordered the book of the chronicles, the record of his reign, to be brought in and read to him. ²It was found recorded there that Mordecai had exposed Bigthana and Teresh, two of the king's officers who guarded the doorway, who had conspired to assassinate King Xerxes.

³"What honor and recognition has Mordecai received for this?" the king asked.

"Nothing has been done for him," his attendants answered.

⁴The king said, "Who is in the court?" Now Haman had just entered the outer court of the palace to speak to the king about hanging Mordecai on the gallows he had erected for him.

a 14 Hebrew *fifty cubits* (about 23 meters)

Techno-Teaching

You have plenty of skills to teach your grandkids, but what about the other way around? How much do you know about iPods, mp3 players, video or computer games, burning CDs, downloading, surfing the Internet or uploading photos from a digital camera? Whether or not you're naturally tech-savvy, there are bound to be kid-oriented activities that have escaped your experience.

Ask your grandkids to spend time teaching you (or at least exposing you to) some new skills, new gadgets or new websites. They'll appreciate your open-mindedness and will love to be on the giving end of this teaching experience. At the very least, you'll come away impressed with your grandchild's ability, and you'll probably have a good time too. Remember, you can hear about it on the news, but you can learn about it from your grandkids.

Younger-Grandkids Variation: Little kids are accustomed to being learners but seldom get an opportunity to teach. Whatever their skill set, ask them to teach you something at which they're proficient. If you can get away with it, be a slow learner!

Changeless God, like many others I find myself challenged by ever-changing technology and new ways of doing things. Help me boldly face these changes and openly accept the knowledge my grandchildren have of these new technologies. Give us all patience as they teach me new skills. Amen.

Your next devotion is located on page 652.

GRANDCHILD IN FOCUS • PRAYER

Character

Dear Lord and Father, I ask that you fill my grandchild with your Spirit so her character reflects your goodness and love. Give her kindness and love for others. Bring joy to her life so she will be a joy to others. Grant her patience and self-control through difficult and trying times. May she show mercy and generosity to those who are less fortunate. Grant her integrity and a sense of justice, and surround her with your peace. Amen.

Worship the Lord

How lovely is your dwelling place,
        O Lord Almighty!
My soul yearns, even faints,
        for the courts of the Lord;
my heart and my flesh cry out
        for the living God.

Better is one day in your courts
        than a thousand elsewhere;
I would rather be a doorkeeper in the house of my God
        than dwell in the tents of the wicked.
For the Lord God is a sun and shield;
        the Lord bestows favor and honor;
no good thing does he withhold
        from those whose walk is blameless.

O Lord Almighty,
        blessed is the man who trusts in
            you.

Psalm 84:1 – 2, 10 – 12

*O God Almighty, I thank and praise you
for giving me the freedom to worship you.
Increase my faith and my desire to come into
your presence. Help me to share the passion
and the desire of the psalmist in praising your
name. Amen.*

Your next devotion is located on page 654.

GRANDCHILD IN FOCUS • PRAYER

Talents

*Dear Lord, the giver of gifts, bless my
grandchild as he develops his talents. Help him
identify his talents and be proud and confident of
the gifts you have given him. Give him patience and
understanding, Lord, so he will not grow weary of
striving and searching to reach the goals you have
set for him. May each milestone bring satisfaction and a healthy desire for greater
achievement and success to bring
glory to you. Amen.*

⁵His attendants answered, "Haman is standing in the court."

"Bring him in," the king ordered.

⁶When Haman entered, the king asked him, "What should be done for the man the king delights to honor?"

Now Haman thought to himself, "Who is there that the king would rather honor than me?" ⁷So he answered the king, "For the man the king delights to honor, ⁸have them bring a royal robe the king has worn and a horse the king has ridden, one with a royal crest placed on its head. ⁹Then let the robe and horse be entrusted to one of the king's most noble princes. Let them robe the man the king delights to honor, and lead him on the horse through the city streets, proclaiming before him, 'This is what is done for the man the king delights to honor!'"

¹⁰"Go at once," the king commanded Haman. "Get the robe and the horse and do just as you have suggested for Mordecai the Jew, who sits at the king's gate. Do not neglect anything you have recommended."

¹¹So Haman got the robe and the horse. He robed Mordecai, and led him on horseback through the city streets, proclaiming before him, "This is what is done for the man the king delights to honor!"

¹²Afterward Mordecai returned to the king's gate. But Haman rushed home, with his head covered in grief, ¹³and told Zeresh his wife and all his friends everything that had happened to him.

His advisers and his wife Zeresh said to him, "Since Mordecai, before whom your downfall has started, is of Jewish origin, you cannot stand against him—you will surely come to ruin!" ¹⁴While they were still talking with him, the king's eunuchs arrived and hurried Haman away to the banquet Esther had prepared.

Haman Hanged

7 So the king and Haman went to dine with Queen Esther, ²and as they were drinking wine on that second day, the king again asked, "Queen Esther, what is your petition? It will be given you. What is your request? Even up to half the kingdom, it will be granted."

³Then Queen Esther answered, "If I have found favor with you, O king, and if it pleases your majesty, grant me my life—this is my petition. And spare my people—this is my request. ⁴For I and my people have been sold for destruction and slaughter and annihilation. If we had merely been sold as male and female slaves, I would have kept quiet, because no such distress would justify disturbing the king.ᵃ"

⁵King Xerxes asked Queen Esther, "Who is he? Where is the man who has dared to do such a thing?"

⁶Esther said, "The adversary and enemy is this vile Haman."

Then Haman was terrified before the king and queen. ⁷The king got up in a rage, left his wine and went out into the palace garden. But Haman, realizing that the king had already decided his fate, stayed behind to beg Queen Esther for his life.

⁸Just as the king returned from the palace garden to the banquet hall, Haman was falling on the couch where Esther was reclining.

The king exclaimed, "Will he even molest the queen while she is with me in the house?"

As soon as the word left the king's mouth, they covered Haman's face. ⁹Then Harbona, one of the eunuchs attending the king, said, "A gallows seventy-five feetᵇ high stands by Haman's house. He had it made for Mordecai, who spoke up to help the king."

The king said, "Hang him on it!" ¹⁰So they hanged Haman on the gallows he had prepared for Mordecai. Then the king's fury subsided.

The King's Edict in Behalf of the Jews

8 That same day King Xerxes gave Queen Esther the estate of Haman, the enemy of the Jews. And Mordecai came into the presence of the king, for Esther had told how he was related

ᵃ 4 Or quiet, but the compensation our adversary offers cannot be compared with the loss the king would suffer   ᵇ 9 Hebrew fifty cubits (about 23 meters)

THEN QUEEN ESTHER ANSWERED,
"IF I HAVE FOUND FAVOR WITH YOU,
O KING, AND IF IT PLEASES YOUR
MAJESTY, GRANT ME MY LIFE—THIS
IS MY PETITION. AND SPARE MY
PEOPLE—THIS IS MY REQUEST."

Esther 7:3

What Grace Looks Like

PATSY CLAIRMONT

READ | ESTHER 7:1–10

Grace has a very different look from whining. Soft like down, gentle like a summer breeze. Its sound is a rippling brook, a sparrow's song, a hymn of praise. Grace wears well. It is chiffon, it is silk, it is gossamer. Others welcome grace, like a sister, a friend, a Savior. Grace moves with the ease of a monarch butterfly and the lilt of a leaf pirouetting toward the earth. Grace curtsies. Grace is polite, spacious, and richly endowed. Grace bows to serve and reigns with mercy.

Whiners neither enjoy nor give joy. But grace-filled people are reputable, sought after, and deeply loved. They stand heads above others even while on their knees. They are full of forgiveness and wisdom. You often find them nurturing children, caring for the ill, serving the underprivileged, applauding the successes of others, and celebrating God's generosity.

Grace is Ruth of the Bible, bent over in the scorching fields to feed herself and her mother-in-law. Grace is Naomi embracing Ruth's baby as if it were her own. Grace is Abigail, face down in the dirt before David as an advocate for her workers. It is Esther, kneeling before the king on behalf of a nation. It is Hagar, returning submissively to her angered employer. It is Hannah, turning her young son Samuel over to the priest Eli, as she promised. Grace is a young virgin who cried, "[May it be to me as you have said]" (Luke 1:38).

Yes, grace knows how to suffer well . . . and how to live well. Do we?

O Lord of grace, help me to graciously handle whatever I face in life. May my every word, every gesture, every sigh radiate with your love and grace. Amen.

Your next devotion is located on page 662.

GRANDCHILD IN FOCUS · PRAYER

SELECT ONE OF YOUR
GRANDCHILDREN TO FOCUS ON
IN PRAYER FOR THE NEXT 14 DAYS.

Salvation

Dear Lord, please guide my grandchild to your gift of salvation. I pray that she will come to know you, to love you and to walk close to you throughout her life. May she boldly claim Jesus as her Lord and Savior. Guide her as she makes choices that have eternal consequences. Help her to follow you each moment of her life. I pray this in Jesus' name, amen.

to her. [2] The king took off his signet ring, which he had reclaimed from Haman, and presented it to Mordecai. And Esther appointed him over Haman's estate.

[3] Esther again pleaded with the king, falling at his feet and weeping. She begged him to put an end to the evil plan of Haman the Agagite, which he had devised against the Jews. [4] Then the king extended the gold scepter to Esther and she arose and stood before him.

[5] "If it pleases the king," she said, "and if he regards me with favor and thinks it the right thing to do, and if he is pleased with me, let an order be written overruling the dispatches that Haman son of Hammedatha, the Agagite, devised and wrote to destroy the Jews in all the king's provinces. [6] For how can I bear to see disaster fall on my people? How can I bear to see the destruction of my family?"

[7] King Xerxes replied to Queen Esther and to Mordecai the Jew, "Because Haman attacked the Jews, I have given his estate to Esther, and they have hanged him on the gallows. [8] Now write another decree in the king's name in behalf of the Jews as seems best to you, and seal it with the king's signet ring — for no document written in the king's name and sealed with his ring can be revoked."

[9] At once the royal secretaries were summoned — on the twenty-third day of the third month, the month of Sivan. They wrote out all Mordecai's orders to the Jews, and to the satraps, governors and nobles of the 127 provinces stretching from India to Cush. [a] These orders were written in the script of each province and the language of each people and also to the Jews in their own script and language. [10] Mordecai wrote in the name of King Xerxes, sealed the dispatches with the king's signet ring, and sent them by mounted couriers, who rode fast horses especially bred for the king.

[11] The king's edict granted the Jews in every city the right to assemble and protect themselves; to destroy, kill and annihilate any armed force of any nationality or province that might attack them and their women and children; and to plunder the property of their enemies. [12] The day appointed for the Jews to do this in all the provinces of King Xerxes was the thirteenth day of the twelfth month, the month of Adar. [13] A copy of the text of the edict was to be issued as law in every province and made known to the people of every nationality so that the Jews would be ready on that day to avenge themselves on their enemies.

[14] The couriers, riding the royal horses, raced out, spurred on by the king's command. And the edict was also issued in the citadel of Susa.

[15] Mordecai left the king's presence wearing royal garments of blue and white, a large crown of gold and a purple robe of fine linen. And the city of Susa held a joyous celebration. [16] For the Jews it was a time of happiness and joy, gladness and honor. [17] In every province and in every city, wherever the edict of the king went, there was joy and gladness among the Jews, with feasting and celebrating. And many people of other nationalities became Jews because fear of the Jews had seized them.

Triumph of the Jews

9 On the thirteenth day of the twelfth month, the month of Adar, the edict commanded by the king was to be carried out. On this day the enemies of the Jews had hoped to overpower them, but now the tables were turned and the Jews got the upper hand over those who hated them. [2] The Jews assembled in their cities in all the provinces of King Xerxes to attack those seeking their destruction. No one could stand against them, because the people of all the other nationalities were afraid of them. [3] And all the nobles of the provinces, the satraps, the governors and the king's administrators helped the Jews, because fear of Mordecai had seized them. [4] Mordecai was prominent in the palace; his reputation spread throughout the provinces, and he became more and more powerful.

[5] The Jews struck down all their enemies with the sword, killing and destroying them, and they

[a] 9 That is, the upper Nile region

PHYLLIS TEN ELSHOF

Making
HOLY DAYS OF HOLIDAYS

The heap of trash at the foot of our neighbors' driveways a week after Christmas didn't consist of just boxes, torn wrapping paper and garbage. There were lots of new but broken toys in there too. It made me vow that holidays would be more than disposable toys or food or glitz for my kids. They would be holy days filled with Bible stories, songs, teaching and meaningful interactions.

Didn't happen, of course. As a young mom, I became as enmeshed in Thanksgiving turkeys, Easter baskets and Christmas gift exchanges as my kids — maybe more so since I had to do most of the prep. As a grandma, however, I have more time, money and sense than to let the holidays get by without giving my grandbabies more than what turns into driveway junk.

I can take a lesson from the Jewish people who, yet to this day, in the celebration of Purim observe the spiritual significance of their deliverance from destruction (see Esther 9:18–32). With this lesson in mind, I've developed some ways to gift my grandchildren with Christmas, Easter and Thanksgiving memories that can make each holy day brighter — both now and for eternity. See if some of these ideas will work for you.

Christmas Star

The first year we looked at Christmas lights was a whiner. There were lots of complaints from the back seat about how long it was taking to get from house to house. Solution? Tell the kids they're on a star hunt. Drive past each well-lit home, asking them to look for stars amid the decorations and lights. The one who spots the most stars gets to be the star in the Christmas story this year.

When you return home, spend a few moments looking at the stars and asking what they're there for. Which one, do you suppose, led the wise men to the baby Jesus in Bethlehem? Is it still there today? What does a star do besides look pretty? How do stars guide us today? How is Jesus like a star?

Have some salt-dough stars (put a hole in the top for an ornament hanger) ready when you get into the house, and let the grandkids decorate them with paint, glitter, macaroni letters, feathers and other sparkles. Put each child's name and the year on each one; then let them hang the stars on the tree.

Put a big star on the winner of the star hunt and let him or her tell the story of Christmas. Use a children's Bible or story Bible for help.

Easter Watch

If you have the entire weekend, take advantage of the time to really make this holiday a memorable one. Take the kids to a Good Friday service or else have your own service, telling the story of how Jesus suffered, died on the cross and was buried in a cave.

Give each child a flashlight and turn out all the lights in the house. Pray with the kids and tell them you are keeping watch while Jesus is in the tomb. How did Jesus' disciples and his mother and other women keep watch while Jesus was in the tomb? What did they do? How did they feel?

Continue the "watch" all of Saturday. During the day, go to a bookstore or library with the kids and get some books about Easter. At night, after supper, tell the story again of how Jesus suffered and died for us. Use cuddle time at bedtime to read the new books by flashlight.

On Easter morning, go to a sunrise service or let the older kids get up with you and go outside to watch the sun rise. (They can crawl back in bed afterward.) Turn the lights back on, turn up the music and say, "Jesus is risen. Hallelujah!" Serve favorite foods for breakfast, and give each child an Easter basket full of treats. Then go to church to worship and serve the risen Savior!

Thanksgiving Baskets

The day before Thanksgiving, get together with your grandkids and put together little baskets of goodies for their neighbors. Put in little packets of cranberries, nuts, candy corn, a mini-loaf of sweet bread, mini-pumpkins, apples, whatever—then write a note thanking each family for being such good neighbors. Each child should sign the note. So should Mom and Dad.

As you walk around the neighborhood, talk about how the Pilgrims made friends with the Indians, then feasted together, sharing what they had. Talk about what God has shared with you. What blessings has he put in each of your baskets? Then share those thoughts during prayer time at the Thanksgiving meal.

did what they pleased to those who hated them. [6]In the citadel of Susa, the Jews killed and destroyed five hundred men. [7]They also killed Parshandatha, Dalphon, Aspatha, [8]Poratha, Adalia, Aridatha, [9]Parmashta, Arisai, Aridai and Vaizatha, [10]the ten sons of Haman son of Hammedatha, the enemy of the Jews. But they did not lay their hands on the plunder.

[11]The number of those slain in the citadel of Susa was reported to the king that same day. [12]The king said to Queen Esther, "The Jews have killed and destroyed five hundred men and the ten sons of Haman in the citadel of Susa. What have they done in the rest of the king's provinces? Now what is your petition? It will be given you. What is your request? It will also be granted."

[13]"If it pleases the king," Esther answered, "give the Jews in Susa permission to carry out this day's edict tomorrow also, and let Haman's ten sons be hanged on gallows."

[14]So the king commanded that this be done. An edict was issued in Susa, and they hanged the ten sons of Haman. [15]The Jews in Susa came together on the fourteenth day of the month of Adar, and they put to death in Susa three hundred men, but they did not lay their hands on the plunder.

[16]Meanwhile, the remainder of the Jews who were in the king's provinces also assembled to protect themselves and get relief from their enemies. They killed seventy-five thousand of them but did not lay their hands on the plunder. [17]This happened on the thirteenth day of the month of Adar, and on the fourteenth they rested and made it a day of feasting and joy.

Purim Celebrated

[18]The Jews in Susa, however, had assembled on the thirteenth and fourteenth, and then on the fifteenth they rested and made it a day of feasting and joy.

[19]That is why rural Jews—those living in villages—observe the fourteenth of the month of Adar as a day of joy and feasting, a day for giving presents to each other.

[20]Mordecai recorded these events, and he sent letters to all the Jews throughout the provinces of King Xerxes, near and far, [21]to have them celebrate annually the fourteenth and fifteenth days of the month of Adar [22]as the time when the Jews got relief from their enemies, and as the month when their sorrow was turned into joy and their mourning into a day of celebration. He wrote them to observe the days as days of feasting and joy and giving presents of food to one another and gifts to the poor.

[23]So the Jews agreed to continue the celebration they had begun, doing what Mordecai had written to them. [24]For Haman son of Hammedatha, the Agagite, the enemy of all the Jews, had plotted against the Jews to destroy them and had cast the *pur* (that is, the lot) for their ruin and destruction. [25]But when the plot came to the king's attention,[a] he issued written orders that the evil scheme Haman had devised against the Jews should come back onto his own head, and that he and his sons should be hanged on the gallows. [26](Therefore these days were called Purim, from the word *pur*.) Because of everything written in this letter and because of what they had seen and what had happened to them, [27]the Jews took it upon themselves to establish the custom that they and their descendants and all who join them should without fail observe these two days every year, in the way prescribed and at the time appointed. [28]These days should be remembered and observed in every generation by every family, and in every province and in every city. And these days of Purim should never cease to be celebrated by the Jews, nor should the memory of them die out among their descendants.

[29]So Queen Esther, daughter of Abihail, along with Mordecai the Jew, wrote with full authority to confirm this second letter concerning Purim. [30]And Mordecai sent letters to all the Jews in the 127 provinces of the kingdom of Xerxes—words of goodwill and assurance— [31]to establish these days of Purim at their designated times, as Mordecai the Jew and Queen Esther had decreed for

---

[a] 25 Or *when Esther came before the king*

them, and as they had established for themselves and their descendants in regard to their times of fasting and lamentation. ³²Esther's decree confirmed these regulations about Purim, and it was written down in the records.

The Greatness of Mordecai

10 King Xerxes imposed tribute throughout the empire, to its distant shores. ²And all his acts of power and might, together with a full account of the greatness of Mordecai to which the king had raised him, are they not written in the book of the annals of the kings of Media and Persia? ³Mordecai the Jew was second in rank to King Xerxes, preeminent among the Jews, and held in high esteem by his many fellow Jews, because he worked for the good of his people and spoke up for the welfare of all the Jews.

Why ME?

Pain and suffering have always existed in the world, affecting even the most "blameless and upright" people like Job (Job 1:1). He was a good man in the eyes of the Lord, yet he suffered horrible loss, pain, misery and rejection. It seemed that Job endured all that could possibly go wrong in a person's life. The book of Job deals with the timeless and universal question of suffering people: "Why me?"

In the book of Job we see an entire lifetime of prosperity and goodness come crashing down in just hours. We read the long discussions between Job and his friends, who struggled in their own misguided ways to help Job and themselves understand why Job was experiencing such horrible circumstances. Then God spoke a litany of questions that challenged everyone's thinking and led Job to reaffirm his faith.

In reading Job's story we see God's hand working constantly in the life of one man, giving us hope for our lives and the lives of our children and grandchildren. No matter what transpires, God is in control, and nothing — not even Satan — can pull God's plan off course.

VERSE *to* REMEMBER | JOB 42:1 – 2

Then Job replied to the LORD: "I know that you can do all things; no plan of yours can be thwarted."

ABOUT JOB

WRITTEN BY:
Unknown

WRITTEN FOR:
God's people

DATE WRITTEN:
Unknown, though Job himself may have lived about the time of Abraham (around 2000 B.C.)

WHY WRITTEN:
To help people understand that bad things happen to good people and that suffering is not always punishment from God

Prologue

1 In the land of Uz there lived a man whose name was Job. This man was blameless and upright; he feared God and shunned evil. [2]He had seven sons and three daughters, [3]and he owned seven thousand sheep, three thousand camels, five hundred yoke of oxen and five hundred donkeys, and had a large number of servants. He was the greatest man among all the people of the East.

[4]His sons used to take turns holding feasts in their homes, and they would invite their three sisters to eat and drink with them. [5]When a period of feasting had run its course, Job would send and have them purified. Early in the morning he would sacrifice a burnt offering for each of them, thinking, "Perhaps my children have sinned and cursed God in their hearts." This was Job's regular custom.

Job's First Test

[6]One day the angels[a] came to present themselves before the LORD, and Satan[b] also came with them. [7]The LORD said to Satan, "Where have you come from?"

Satan answered the LORD, "From roaming through the earth and going back and forth in it."

[8]Then the LORD said to Satan, "Have you considered my servant Job? There is no one on earth like him; he is blameless and upright, a man who fears God and shuns evil."

[9]"Does Job fear God for nothing?" Satan replied. [10]"Have you not put a hedge around him and his household and everything he has? You have blessed the work of his hands, so that his flocks and herds are spread throughout the land. [11]But stretch out your hand and strike everything he has, and he will surely curse you to your face."

[12]The LORD said to Satan, "Very well, then, everything he has is in your hands, but on the man himself do not lay a finger."

Then Satan went out from the presence of the LORD.

[13]One day when Job's sons and daughters were feasting and drinking wine at the oldest brother's house, [14]a messenger came to Job and said, "The oxen were plowing and the donkeys were grazing nearby, [15]and the Sabeans attacked and carried them off. They put the servants to the sword, and I am the only one who has escaped to tell you!"

[16]While he was still speaking, another messenger came and said, "The fire of God fell from the sky and burned up the sheep and the servants, and I am the only one who has escaped to tell you!"

[17]While he was still speaking, another messenger came and said, "The Chaldeans formed three raiding parties and swept down on your camels and carried them off. They put the servants to the sword, and I am the only one who has escaped to tell you!"

TALKING POINTS

Praise

Even when things go wrong, God is worthy of our praise.

JOB 1:13–22

For more on praise, go to Psalm 150:1–6.

[18]While he was still speaking, yet another messenger came and said, "Your sons and daughters were feasting and drinking wine at the oldest brother's house, [19]when suddenly a mighty wind swept in from the desert and struck the four corners of the house. It collapsed on them and they are dead, and I am the only one who has escaped to tell you!"

[20]At this, Job got up and tore his robe and shaved his head. Then he fell to the ground in worship [21]and said:

---

[a] 6 Hebrew *the sons of God*   [b] 6 *Satan* means *accuser.*

> "THE LORD GAVE AND THE
> LORD HAS TAKEN AWAY;
> MAY THE NAME OF THE
> LORD BE PRAISED."
> *Job 1:21*

When We Don't Understand

REBECCA LUTZER

READ | JOB 1:1 – 22

Lori glowed with health as she entered the third trimester of pregnancy. I was already a doting grandmother, shopping for a pink layette and baby furniture.

One warm August morning my daughter called on her way to the doctor's office, worried that all was not normal. An hour passed and my phone rang again. With a sob in his voice, my son-in-law Bruce said, "Something has happened to the baby! Can you go to the hospital to be with Lori until I can get there?"

What must my precious daughter be going through? "Oh, God, please uphold and comfort her," I earnestly prayed.

The moment I saw her, weeping and in shock, I knew it was true. My first grandchild was dead. I gathered Lori in my arms, and we sobbed together. Our hopes and dreams for our precious bundle of joy were dashed. But I knew that God is faithful and would carry us through our sorrow.

The next day Lori delivered a stillborn baby girl — Sarah. I held her in my arms, desperately wanting to bring her back to life. As the nurse took her away from us, my heart ached for my children. Their loss was so great. It would take months, years, for them to adjust to empty arms and a silent nursery.

I wept for them, not for myself. Bowing my head, I worshiped God in that hospital room. "The LORD gave and the LORD has taken away; may the name of the LORD be praised" (Job 1:21).

Sovereign Lord, thank you for the grace to go on when my heart is broken. Help me to trust you even when I don't understand your ways and purposes. Please comfort my children and grandchildren when they go through trials and storms. Amen.

Your next devotion is located on page 664.

GRANDCHILD IN FOCUS · PRAYER

Physical Well-Being

Almighty God, Creator of us all, I pray that you will watch over my grandchild's physical development. May he grow in strength through the stages of his life. As he grows in awareness of his body, help him to understand that each body develops uniquely, yet is within your plan and your control. Please guard his health so that his diseases are few, his injuries are minor and his infirmities are brief. Amen.

"Naked I came from my mother's womb,
    and naked I will depart. *a*
The LORD gave and the LORD has taken away;
    may the name of the LORD be praised."

²²In all this, Job did not sin by charging God with wrongdoing.

Job's Second Test

2 On another day the angels *b* came to present themselves before the LORD, and Satan also came with them to present himself before him. ²And the LORD said to Satan, "Where have you come from?"

Satan answered the LORD, "From roaming through the earth and going back and forth in it."

³Then the LORD said to Satan, "Have you considered my servant Job? There is no one on earth like him; he is blameless and upright, a man who fears God and shuns evil. And he still maintains his integrity, though you incited me against him to ruin him without any reason."

⁴"Skin for skin!" Satan replied. "A man will give all he has for his own life. ⁵But stretch out your hand and strike his flesh and bones, and he will surely curse you to your face."

⁶The LORD said to Satan, "Very well, then, he is in your hands; but you must spare his life."

⁷So Satan went out from the presence of the LORD and afflicted Job with painful sores from the soles of his feet to the top of his head. ⁸Then Job took a piece of broken pottery and scraped himself with it as he sat among the ashes.

⁹His wife said to him, "Are you still holding on to your integrity? Curse God and die!"

¹⁰He replied, "You are talking like a foolish *c* woman. Shall we accept good from God, and not trouble?"

In all this, Job did not sin in what he said.

Job's Three Friends

¹¹When Job's three friends, Eliphaz the Temanite, Bildad the Shuhite and Zophar the Naamathite, heard about all the troubles that had come upon him, they set out from their homes and met together by agreement to go and sympathize with him and comfort him. ¹²When they saw him from a distance, they could hardly recognize him; they began to weep aloud, and they tore their robes and sprinkled dust on their heads. ¹³Then they sat on the ground with him for seven days and seven nights. No one said a word to him, because they saw how great his suffering was.

Job Speaks

3 After this, Job opened his mouth and cursed the day of his birth. ²He said:

³"May the day of my birth perish,
    and the night it was said, 'A boy is born!'
⁴That day—may it turn to darkness;
    may God above not care about it;
    may no light shine upon it.
⁵May darkness and deep shadow *d* claim it
        once more;
    may a cloud settle over it;
    may blackness overwhelm its light.
⁶That night—may thick darkness seize it;
    may it not be included among the days of
        the year
    nor be entered in any of the months.
⁷May that night be barren;
    may no shout of joy be heard in it.
⁸May those who curse days *e* curse that day,
    those who are ready to rouse Leviathan.
⁹May its morning stars become dark;
    may it wait for daylight in vain
    and not see the first rays of dawn,
¹⁰for it did not shut the doors of the womb
        on me
    to hide trouble from my eyes.

¹¹"Why did I not perish at birth,
    and die as I came from the womb?
¹²Why were there knees to receive me
    and breasts that I might be nursed?

---

a 21 Or *will return there*   *b 1* Hebrew *the sons of God*
c 10 The Hebrew word rendered *foolish* denotes moral deficiency.
d 5 Or *and the shadow of death*   *e 8* Or *the sea*

HIS WIFE SAID TO HIM, "ARE YOU STILL HOLDING ON TO YOUR INTEGRITY? CURSE GOD AND DIE!" HE REPLIED, "YOU ARE TALKING LIKE A FOOLISH WOMAN. SHALL WE ACCEPT GOOD FROM GOD, AND NOT TROUBLE?" IN ALL THIS, JOB DID NOT SIN IN WHAT HE SAID.

Job 2:9–10

Maligned

MARI SEREBROV

READ | JOB 2:1–10

The Bible is full of women who glorified God despite hardships. Then there's the one who didn't.

Throughout history, Job's wife has had bad press. She's been placed in league with all the bad mother-in-law jokes as the epitome of a nagging wife. As women we turn away from her, refusing to see our reflection in her grief, her weakness and her doubt.

Job's wife had everything wealth and love could bring. Her husband's prominent position made her the envy of many a woman. Her day revolved around her husband, her children and her home. She drew her strength from Job; he was her spiritual leader.

In one day, her world crumbled. [With] her children killed, her wealth destroyed and her position of pride turned to that of ridicule, Job's wife clung to him for support. That last crutch fell when Job was plagued with boils from head to foot.

It had been easy to serve God when everything was great. But why should she serve God when he treated her so shabbily?

Seeing her once-great husband sitting in the ashes, scraping at his open sores with a broken bit of pottery was more than this woman could endure. She turned on her husband, voicing her own human frustration: "Curse God and die."

Maybe that's why Job's wife has been maligned for these centuries. Maybe we see our own human short-comings portrayed — all too clearly — in her.

God, when I think of Job's wife, I see all too much of myself in her. When I'm facing hard times, comfort me in my grief, strengthen me in my weakness and banish my doubt. Forgive my human frailty. Amen.

Your next devotion is located on page 692.

GRANDCHILD IN FOCUS • PRAYER

Emotional Development

O God, Creator of mind and body, I pray that you will give my grandchild emotional health and strength. Where there is anger, bring peace. Where there is confusion, bring clarity and focus. Where there are dark shadows, cast a ray of hope. Fill her with the sunshine of your Spirit. Warm her with the presence of your peace. Amen.

13 For now I would be lying down in peace;
  I would be asleep and at rest
14 with kings and counselors of the earth,
    who built for themselves places now lying
      in ruins,
15 with rulers who had gold,
    who filled their houses with silver.
16 Or why was I not hidden in the ground like a
      stillborn child,
    like an infant who never saw the light of
      day?
17 There the wicked cease from turmoil,
    and there the weary are at rest.
18 Captives also enjoy their ease;
    they no longer hear the slave driver's
      shout.
19 The small and the great are there,
    and the slave is freed from his master.

20 "Why is light given to those in misery,
    and life to the bitter of soul,
21 to those who long for death that does not
      come,
    who search for it more than for hidden
      treasure,
22 who are filled with gladness
    and rejoice when they reach the grave?
23 Why is life given to a man
    whose way is hidden,
    whom God has hedged in?
24 For sighing comes to me instead of food;
    my groans pour out like water.

25 What I feared has come upon me;
    what I dreaded has happened to me.
26 I have no peace, no quietness;
    I have no rest, but only turmoil."

Eliphaz

4 Then Eliphaz the Temanite replied:

2 "If someone ventures a word with you, will
      you be impatient?
    But who can keep from speaking?
3 Think how you have instructed many,
    how you have strengthened feeble hands.
4 Your words have supported those who
      stumbled;
    you have strengthened faltering knees.
5 But now trouble comes to you, and you are
      discouraged;
    it strikes you, and you are dismayed.
6 Should not your piety be your confidence
    and your blameless ways your hope?

7 "Consider now: Who, being innocent, has
      ever perished?
    Where were the upright ever destroyed?
8 As I have observed, those who plow evil
    and those who sow trouble reap it.
9 At the breath of God they are destroyed;
    at the blast of his anger they perish.
10 The lions may roar and growl,
    yet the teeth of the great lions are broken.
11 The lion perishes for lack of prey,
    and the cubs of the lioness are scattered.

12 "A word was secretly brought to me,
    my ears caught a whisper of it.
13 Amid disquieting dreams in the night,
    when deep sleep falls on men,
14 fear and trembling seized me
    and made all my bones shake.
15 A spirit glided past my face,
    and the hair on my body stood on end.
16 It stopped,
    but I could not tell what it was.
  A form stood before my eyes,
    and I heard a hushed voice:

TALKING POINTS

Bitterness

Though it is a natural human trait,
bitterness can and should be worked
through and overcome.

JOB 3:20–26

For more on bitterness, go to Psalm 71:20.

¹⁷ 'Can a mortal be more righteous than God?
　　Can a man be more pure than his Maker?
¹⁸ If God places no trust in his servants,
　　if he charges his angels with error,
¹⁹ how much more those who live in houses of
　　clay,
　　whose foundations are in the dust,
　　who are crushed more readily than a moth!
²⁰ Between dawn and dusk they are broken to
　　pieces;
　　unnoticed, they perish forever.
²¹ Are not the cords of their tent pulled up,
　　so that they die without wisdom?'ᵃ

5 "Call if you will, but who will answer you?
　　To which of the holy ones will you turn?
² Resentment kills a fool,
　　and envy slays the simple.
³ I myself have seen a fool taking root,
　　but suddenly his house was cursed.
⁴ His children are far from safety,
　　crushed in court without a defender.
⁵ The hungry consume his harvest,
　　taking it even from among thorns,
　　and the thirsty pant after his wealth.
⁶ For hardship does not spring from the soil,
　　nor does trouble sprout from the ground.
⁷ Yet man is born to trouble
　　as surely as sparks fly upward.

⁸ "But if it were I, I would appeal to God;
　　I would lay my cause before him.
⁹ He performs wonders that cannot be
　　fathomed,
　　miracles that cannot be counted.
¹⁰ He bestows rain on the earth;
　　he sends water upon the countryside.
¹¹ The lowly he sets on high,
　　and those who mourn are lifted to safety.
¹² He thwarts the plans of the crafty,
　　so that their hands achieve no success.
¹³ He catches the wise in their craftiness,
　　and the schemes of the wily are swept
　　away.
¹⁴ Darkness comes upon them in the daytime;
　　at noon they grope as in the night.

¹⁵ He saves the needy from the sword in their
　　mouth;
　　he saves them from the clutches of the
　　powerful.
¹⁶ So the poor have hope,
　　and injustice shuts its mouth.

¹⁷ "Blessed is the man whom God corrects;
　　so do not despise the discipline of the
　　Almighty. ᵇ
¹⁸ For he wounds, but he also binds up;
　　he injures, but his hands also heal.
¹⁹ From six calamities he will rescue you;
　　in seven no harm will befall you.
²⁰ In famine he will ransom you from death,
　　and in battle from the stroke of the sword.
²¹ You will be protected from the lash of the
　　tongue,
　　and need not fear when destruction
　　comes.
²² You will laugh at destruction and famine,
　　and need not fear the beasts of the earth.
²³ For you will have a covenant with the stones
　　of the field,
　　and the wild animals will be at peace with
　　you.
²⁴ You will know that your tent is secure;
　　you will take stock of your property and
　　find nothing missing.
²⁵ You will know that your children will be
　　many,
　　and your descendants like the grass of the
　　earth.
²⁶ You will come to the grave in full vigor,
　　like sheaves gathered in season.

²⁷ "We have examined this, and it is true.
　　So hear it and apply it to yourself."

Job

6 Then Job replied:

² "If only my anguish could be weighed
　　and all my misery be placed on the scales!

ᵃ 21 Some interpreters end the quotation after verse 17.
ᵇ 17 Hebrew *Shaddai;* here and throughout Job

³ It would surely outweigh the sand of the
  seas —
  no wonder my words have been
  impetuous.
⁴ The arrows of the Almighty are in me,
  my spirit drinks in their poison;
  God's terrors are marshaled against me.
⁵ Does a wild donkey bray when it has grass,
  or an ox bellow when it has fodder?
⁶ Is tasteless food eaten without salt,
  or is there flavor in the white of an egg *a* ?
⁷ I refuse to touch it;
  such food makes me ill.

⁸ "Oh, that I might have my request,
  that God would grant what I hope for,
⁹ that God would be willing to crush me,
  to let loose his hand and cut me off!
¹⁰ Then I would still have this consolation —
  my joy in unrelenting pain —
  that I had not denied the words of the
  Holy One.

¹¹ "What strength do I have, that I should still
  hope?
  What prospects, that I should be patient?
¹² Do I have the strength of stone?
  Is my flesh bronze?
¹³ Do I have any power to help myself,
  now that success has been driven
  from me?

¹⁴ "A despairing man should have the devotion
  of his friends,
  even though he forsakes the fear of the
  Almighty.
¹⁵ But my brothers are as undependable as
  intermittent streams,
  as the streams that overflow
¹⁶ when darkened by thawing ice
  and swollen with melting snow,
¹⁷ but that cease to flow in the dry season,
  and in the heat vanish from their
  channels.
¹⁸ Caravans turn aside from their routes;
  they go up into the wasteland and perish.

¹⁹ The caravans of Tema look for water,
  the traveling merchants of Sheba look in
  hope.
²⁰ They are distressed, because they had been
  confident;
  they arrive there, only to be disappointed.
²¹ Now you too have proved to be of no help;
  you see something dreadful and are afraid.
²² Have I ever said, 'Give something on my
  behalf,
  pay a ransom for me from your wealth,
²³ deliver me from the hand of the enemy,
  ransom me from the clutches of the
  ruthless'?

²⁴ "Teach me, and I will be quiet;
  show me where I have been wrong.
²⁵ How painful are honest words!
  But what do your arguments prove?
²⁶ Do you mean to correct what I say,
  and treat the words of a despairing man as
  wind?
²⁷ You would even cast lots for the fatherless
  and barter away your friend.

²⁸ "But now be so kind as to look at me.
  Would I lie to your face?
²⁹ Relent, do not be unjust;
  reconsider, for my integrity is at stake. *b*
³⁰ Is there any wickedness on my lips?
  Can my mouth not discern malice?

7 "Does not man have hard service on earth?
  Are not his days like those of a hired man?
² Like a slave longing for the evening shadows,
  or a hired man waiting eagerly for his
  wages,
³ so I have been allotted months of futility,
  and nights of misery have been assigned
  to me.
⁴ When I lie down I think, 'How long before
  I get up?'
  The night drags on, and I toss till dawn.
⁵ My body is clothed with worms and scabs,
  my skin is broken and festering.

a 6 The meaning of the Hebrew for this phrase is uncertain.
b 29 Or my righteousness still stands

6 "My days are swifter than a weaver's shuttle,
   and they come to an end without hope.
7 Remember, O God, that my life is but a
      breath;
   my eyes will never see happiness again.
8 The eye that now sees me will see me no
      longer;
   you will look for me, but I will be no
      more.
9 As a cloud vanishes and is gone,
   so he who goes down to the grave *a* does
      not return.
10 He will never come to his house again;
   his place will know him no more.

11 "Therefore I will not keep silent;
   I will speak out in the anguish of my
      spirit,
   I will complain in the bitterness of my
      soul.
12 Am I the sea, or the monster of the deep,
   that you put me under guard?
13 When I think my bed will comfort me
   and my couch will ease my complaint,
14 even then you frighten me with dreams
   and terrify me with visions,
15 so that I prefer strangling and death,
   rather than this body of mine.
16 I despise my life; I would not live forever.
   Let me alone; my days have no meaning.

17 "What is man that you make so much of him,
   that you give him so much attention,
18 that you examine him every morning
   and test him every moment?
19 Will you never look away from me,
   or let me alone even for an instant?
20 If I have sinned, what have I done to you,
   O watcher of men?
   Why have you made me your target?
   Have I become a burden to you? *b*
21 Why do you not pardon my offenses
   and forgive my sins?
   For I will soon lie down in the dust;
   you will search for me, but I will be no
      more."

Bildad

8 Then Bildad the Shuhite replied:

2 "How long will you say such things?
   Your words are a blustering wind.
3 Does God pervert justice?
   Does the Almighty pervert what is
      right?
4 When your children sinned against him,
   he gave them over to the penalty of their
      sin.
5 But if you will look to God
   and plead with the Almighty,
6 if you are pure and upright,
   even now he will rouse himself on your
      behalf
   and restore you to your rightful place.
7 Your beginnings will seem humble,
   so prosperous will your future be.

8 "Ask the former generations
   and find out what their fathers learned,
9 for we were born only yesterday and know
      nothing,
   and our days on earth are but a shadow.
10 Will they not instruct you and tell you?
   Will they not bring forth words from their
      understanding?
11 Can papyrus grow tall where there is no
      marsh?
   Can reeds thrive without water?
12 While still growing and uncut,
   they wither more quickly than grass.
13 Such is the destiny of all who forget God;
   so perishes the hope of the godless.
14 What he trusts in is fragile *c*;
   what he relies on is a spider's web.
15 He leans on his web, but it gives way;
   he clings to it, but it does not hold.
16 He is like a well-watered plant in the
      sunshine,
   spreading its shoots over the garden;

---

a 9 Hebrew *Sheol*   *b* 20 A few manuscripts of the Masoretic
Text, an ancient Hebrew scribal tradition and Septuagint; most
manuscripts of the Masoretic Text *I have become a burden to myself.*
c 14 The meaning of the Hebrew for this word is uncertain.

¹⁷ it entwines its roots around a pile of rocks
    and looks for a place among the stones.
¹⁸ But when it is torn from its spot,
    that place disowns it and says, 'I never saw
        you.'
¹⁹ Surely its life withers away,
    and ᵃ from the soil other plants grow.

²⁰ "Surely God does not reject a blameless man
    or strengthen the hands of evildoers.
²¹ He will yet fill your mouth with laughter
    and your lips with shouts of joy.
²² Your enemies will be clothed in shame,
    and the tents of the wicked will be no
        more."

PRAYING THE SCRIPTURES

Joy

JOB 8:21

Dear God, as you promised, fill my grand-child's mouth with laughter and his lips with shouts of joy.

Next prayer in Joy Prayer Track: Psalm 90:14

Job

9 Then Job replied:

² "Indeed, I know that this is true.
    But how can a mortal be righteous before
        God?
³ Though one wished to dispute with him,
    he could not answer him one time out of a
        thousand.
⁴ His wisdom is profound, his power is vast.
    Who has resisted him and come out
        unscathed?
⁵ He moves mountains without their knowing it
    and overturns them in his anger.
⁶ He shakes the earth from its place
    and makes its pillars tremble.

⁷ He speaks to the sun and it does not shine;
    he seals off the light of the stars.
⁸ He alone stretches out the heavens
    and treads on the waves of the sea.
⁹ He is the Maker of the Bear and Orion,
    the Pleiades and the constellations of the
        south.
¹⁰ He performs wonders that cannot be
        fathomed,
    miracles that cannot be counted.
¹¹ When he passes me, I cannot see him;
    when he goes by, I cannot perceive him.
¹² If he snatches away, who can stop him?
    Who can say to him, 'What are you doing?'
¹³ God does not restrain his anger;
    even the cohorts of Rahab cowered at his
        feet.

¹⁴ "How then can I dispute with him?
    How can I find words to argue with him?
¹⁵ Though I were innocent, I could not answer
        him;
    I could only plead with my Judge for mercy.
¹⁶ Even if I summoned him and he responded,
    I do not believe he would give me a
        hearing.
¹⁷ He would crush me with a storm
    and multiply my wounds for no reason.
¹⁸ He would not let me regain my breath
    but would overwhelm me with misery.
¹⁹ If it is a matter of strength, he is mighty!
    And if it is a matter of justice, who will
        summon him ᵇ?
²⁰ Even if I were innocent, my mouth would
        condemn me;
    if I were blameless, it would pronounce me
        guilty.

²¹ "Although I am blameless,
    I have no concern for myself;
    I despise my own life.
²² It is all the same; that is why I say,
    'He destroys both the blameless and the
        wicked.'

ᵃ 19 Or *Surely all the joy it has / is that*   ᵇ 19 See Septuagint;
Hebrew *me.*

²³When a scourge brings sudden death,
  he mocks the despair of the innocent.
²⁴When a land falls into the hands of the
      wicked,
  he blindfolds its judges.
  If it is not he, then who is it?

²⁵"My days are swifter than a runner;
  they fly away without a glimpse of joy.
²⁶They skim past like boats of papyrus,
  like eagles swooping down on their prey.
²⁷If I say, 'I will forget my complaint,
  I will change my expression, and smile,'
²⁸I still dread all my sufferings,
  for I know you will not hold me innocent.
²⁹Since I am already found guilty,
  why should I struggle in vain?
³⁰Even if I washed myself with soap ᵃ
  and my hands with washing soda,
³¹you would plunge me into a slime pit
  so that even my clothes would detest me.

³²"He is not a man like me that I might answer
      him,
  that we might confront each other in
      court.
³³If only there were someone to arbitrate
      between us,
  to lay his hand upon us both,
³⁴someone to remove God's rod from me,
  so that his terror would frighten me no
      more.
³⁵Then I would speak up without fear of him,
  but as it now stands with me, I cannot.

10 "I loathe my very life;
  therefore I will give free rein to my
      complaint
    and speak out in the bitterness of my soul.
²I will say to God: Do not condemn me,
  but tell me what charges you have against
      me.
³Does it please you to oppress me,
  to spurn the work of your hands,
    while you smile on the schemes of the
      wicked?

⁴Do you have eyes of flesh?
  Do you see as a mortal sees?
⁵Are your days like those of a mortal
  or your years like those of a man,
⁶that you must search out my faults
  and probe after my sin—
⁷though you know that I am not guilty
  and that no one can rescue me from your
      hand?

⁸"Your hands shaped me and made me.
  Will you now turn and destroy me?
⁹Remember that you molded me like clay.
  Will you now turn me to dust again?
¹⁰Did you not pour me out like milk
  and curdle me like cheese,
¹¹clothe me with skin and flesh
  and knit me together with bones and
      sinews?
¹²You gave me life and showed me kindness,
  and in your providence watched over my
      spirit.

¹³"But this is what you concealed in your heart,
  and I know that this was in your mind:
¹⁴If I sinned, you would be watching me
  and would not let my offense go
      unpunished.
¹⁵If I am guilty—woe to me!
  Even if I am innocent, I cannot lift my
      head,
    for I am full of shame
    and drowned in ᵇ my affliction.
¹⁶If I hold my head high, you stalk me like a
      lion
  and again display your awesome power
      against me.
¹⁷You bring new witnesses against me
  and increase your anger toward me;
    your forces come against me wave upon
      wave.

¹⁸"Why then did you bring me out of the
      womb?
  I wish I had died before any eye saw me.

ᵃ 30 Or *snow*   ᵇ 15 Or *and aware of*

¹⁹ If only I had never come into being,
  or had been carried straight from the
    womb to the grave!
²⁰ Are not my few days almost over?
  Turn away from me so I can have a
    moment's joy
²¹ before I go to the place of no return,
  to the land of gloom and deep shadow,ᵃ
²² to the land of deepest night,
  of deep shadow and disorder,
    where even the light is like darkness."

Zophar

11 Then Zophar the Naamathite replied:

² "Are all these words to go unanswered?
  Is this talker to be vindicated?
³ Will your idle talk reduce men to silence?
  Will no one rebuke you when you mock?
⁴ You say to God, 'My beliefs are flawless
  and I am pure in your sight.'
⁵ Oh, how I wish that God would speak,
  that he would open his lips against you
⁶ and disclose to you the secrets of wisdom,
  for true wisdom has two sides.
  Know this: God has even forgotten some
    of your sin.

⁷ "Can you fathom the mysteries of God?
  Can you probe the limits of the Almighty?
⁸ They are higher than the heavens—what can
    you do?
  They are deeper than the depths of the
    graveᵇ—what can you know?
⁹ Their measure is longer than the earth
  and wider than the sea.

¹⁰ "If he comes along and confines you in
    prison
  and convenes a court, who can oppose him?
¹¹ Surely he recognizes deceitful men;
  and when he sees evil, does he not take
    note?
¹² But a witless man can no more become wise
  than a wild donkey's colt can be born a
    man.ᶜ

¹³ "Yet if you devote your heart to him
  and stretch out your hands to him,
¹⁴ if you put away the sin that is in your hand
  and allow no evil to dwell in your tent,
¹⁵ then you will lift up your face without shame;
  you will stand firm and without fear.
¹⁶ You will surely forget your trouble,
  recalling it only as waters gone by.
¹⁷ Life will be brighter than noonday,
  and darkness will become like morning.
¹⁸ You will be secure, because there is hope;
  you will look about you and take your rest
    in safety.
¹⁹ You will lie down, with no one to make you
    afraid,
  and many will court your favor.
²⁰ But the eyes of the wicked will fail,
  and escape will elude them;
    their hope will become a dying gasp."

Job

12 Then Job replied:

² "Doubtless you are the people,
  and wisdom will die with you!
³ But I have a mind as well as you;
  I am not inferior to you.
  Who does not know all these things?

⁴ "I have become a laughingstock to my
    friends,
  though I called upon God and he
    answered—
  a mere laughingstock, though righteous
    and blameless!
⁵ Men at ease have contempt for misfortune
  as the fate of those whose feet are slipping.
⁶ The tents of marauders are undisturbed,
  and those who provoke God are secure—
  those who carry their god in their hands.ᵈ

⁷ "But ask the animals, and they will teach you,
  or the birds of the air, and they will tell
    you;

ᵃ 21 Or and the shadow of death; also in verse 22   ᵇ 8 Hebrew
than Sheol   ᶜ 12 Or wild donkey can be born tame
ᵈ 6 Or secure / in what God's hand brings them

⁸or speak to the earth, and it will teach you,
or let the fish of the sea inform you.
⁹Which of all these does not know
that the hand of the Lord has done this?
¹⁰In his hand is the life of every creature
and the breath of all mankind.
¹¹Does not the ear test words
as the tongue tastes food?
¹²Is not wisdom found among the aged?
Does not long life bring understanding?

¹³"To God belong wisdom and power;
counsel and understanding are his.
¹⁴What he tears down cannot be rebuilt;
the man he imprisons cannot be released.
¹⁵If he holds back the waters, there is
drought;
if he lets them loose, they devastate the
land.
¹⁶To him belong strength and victory;
both deceived and deceiver are his.
¹⁷He leads counselors away stripped
and makes fools of judges.
¹⁸He takes off the shackles put on by kings
and ties a loincloth ᵃ around their waist.
¹⁹He leads priests away stripped
and overthrows men long established.
²⁰He silences the lips of trusted advisers
and takes away the discernment of elders.
²¹He pours contempt on nobles
and disarms the mighty.
²²He reveals the deep things of darkness
and brings deep shadows into the light.
²³He makes nations great, and destroys them;
he enlarges nations, and disperses them.
²⁴He deprives the leaders of the earth of their
reason;
he sends them wandering through a
trackless waste.
²⁵They grope in darkness with no light;
he makes them stagger like drunkards.

13 "My eyes have seen all this,
my ears have heard and understood it.
²What you know, I also know;
I am not inferior to you.

³But I desire to speak to the Almighty
and to argue my case with God.
⁴You, however, smear me with lies;
you are worthless physicians, all of you!
⁵If only you would be altogether silent!
For you, that would be wisdom.
⁶Hear now my argument;
listen to the plea of my lips.
⁷Will you speak wickedly on God's behalf?
Will you speak deceitfully for him?
⁸Will you show him partiality?
Will you argue the case for God?
⁹Would it turn out well if he examined you?
Could you deceive him as you might
deceive men?
¹⁰He would surely rebuke you
if you secretly showed partiality.
¹¹Would not his splendor terrify you?
Would not the dread of him fall on you?
¹²Your maxims are proverbs of ashes;
your defenses are defenses of clay.

¹³"Keep silent and let me speak;
then let come to me what may.
¹⁴Why do I put myself in jeopardy
and take my life in my hands?
¹⁵Though he slay me, yet will I hope in him;
I will surely ᵇ defend my ways to his face.
¹⁶Indeed, this will turn out for my deliverance,
for no godless man would dare come
before him!
¹⁷Listen carefully to my words;
let your ears take in what I say.
¹⁸Now that I have prepared my case,
I know I will be vindicated.
¹⁹Can anyone bring charges against me?
If so, I will be silent and die.

²⁰"Only grant me these two things, O God,
and then I will not hide from you:
²¹Withdraw your hand far from me,
and stop frightening me with your terrors.
²²Then summon me and I will answer,
or let me speak, and you reply.

ᵃ 18 Or shackles of kings / and ties a belt   ᵇ 15 Or He will surely
slay me; I have no hope — / yet I will

²³How many wrongs and sins have I committed?
  Show me my offense and my sin.
²⁴Why do you hide your face
  and consider me your enemy?
²⁵Will you torment a windblown leaf?
  Will you chase after dry chaff?
²⁶For you write down bitter things against me
  and make me inherit the sins of my youth.
²⁷You fasten my feet in shackles;
  you keep close watch on all my paths
  by putting marks on the soles of my feet.

²⁸"So man wastes away like something rotten,
  like a garment eaten by moths.

14 "Man born of woman
  is of few days and full of trouble.
²He springs up like a flower and withers away;
  like a fleeting shadow, he does not endure.
³Do you fix your eye on such a one?
  Will you bring him [a] before you for
    judgment?
⁴Who can bring what is pure from the impure?
  No one!
⁵Man's days are determined;
  you have decreed the number of his
    months
  and have set limits he cannot exceed.
⁶So look away from him and let him alone,
  till he has put in his time like a hired man.

⁷"At least there is hope for a tree:
  If it is cut down, it will sprout again,
  and its new shoots will not fail.
⁸Its roots may grow old in the ground
  and its stump die in the soil,
⁹yet at the scent of water it will bud
  and put forth shoots like a plant.
¹⁰But man dies and is laid low;
  he breathes his last and is no more.
¹¹As water disappears from the sea
  or a riverbed becomes parched and dry,
¹²so man lies down and does not rise;
  till the heavens are no more, men will not
    awake
  or be roused from their sleep.

¹³"If only you would hide me in the grave [b]
  and conceal me till your anger has passed!
  If only you would set me a time
  and then remember me!
¹⁴If a man dies, will he live again?
  All the days of my hard service
  I will wait for my renewal [c] to come.
¹⁵You will call and I will answer you;
  you will long for the creature your hands
    have made.
¹⁶Surely then you will count my steps
  but not keep track of my sin.
¹⁷My offenses will be sealed up in a bag;
  you will cover over my sin.

¹⁸"But as a mountain erodes and crumbles
  and as a rock is moved from its place,
¹⁹as water wears away stones
  and torrents wash away the soil,
  so you destroy man's hope.
²⁰You overpower him once for all, and he is
    gone;
  you change his countenance and send him
    away.
²¹If his sons are honored, he does not know it;
  if they are brought low, he does not see it.
²²He feels but the pain of his own body
  and mourns only for himself."

Eliphaz

15 Then Eliphaz the Temanite replied:

²"Would a wise man answer with empty
    notions
  or fill his belly with the hot east wind?
³Would he argue with useless words,
  with speeches that have no value?
⁴But you even undermine piety
  and hinder devotion to God.
⁵Your sin prompts your mouth;
  you adopt the tongue of the crafty.
⁶Your own mouth condemns you, not mine;
  your own lips testify against you.

JEAN E. SYSWERDA

Walking IN THE DARK

I've been walking in the dark for a number of years now.

I began this shadowed journey on August 1, 2005, when my youngest granddaughter, Ava, died in her bed at home. I was there when my daughter, Shelly, ran screaming down the stairs with her baby's lifeless body in her arms. I watched in shock as Shelly performed CPR with no results. I couldn't pray real words. I could only keep whispering, "O Jesus, O Jesus," in an effort to call on him during this time of horror. When the emergency personnel told us there was no hope, I held my daughter, sitting on her front lawn in the deep summer heat, as she cried for her baby.

Despair Was My Enemy

That day began a walk in darkness for me as a grandmother. I groped my way through those first days and months. My grief was two-pronged: I grieved for Ava as my precious, youngest grandchild, but I also grieved for my daughter and her husband and the sorrow that they faced at the loss of their little girl. Despair was my enemy, and he set up camp in the hole Ava's death had left in my heart.

Comfort in Scripture

In those early days I hung on to every word of comfort in Scripture as a lifeline. As I read, I began to realize how different my approach to life was from the men and women in the Bible. I took a good life as my due, as appropriate and suitable for me as a believer. I wouldn't have voiced it, but I lived as if I deserved ease and comfort. When something bad happened, I had to try to figure out why. Who caused this tragedy? God? Satan? Sinful forces in a broken world? The faithful in the Bible didn't seem to have that same outlook on life. They appeared to be more willing to take the good and the bad as natural parts of life on earth. David, especially as expressed in the Psalms, took life's difficulties, ranted and raved about them, and then turned to God for comfort and strength, leaving the questioning, the whys and the wherefores behind. He continued to trust God in the middle of life's problems.

As time went on, I began to realize that any answer I could find to my questions wouldn't satisfy. Even if I had some divine revelation of why Ava had died, I would still grieve, still think it wasn't fair, still go through life broken by my loss. So, like David, I began to turn to God for comfort and strength to face the day rather than search out all the answers. I prayed that God would do what I promised I would allow him to do. At Ava's funeral, standing near her tiny white casket on that windy August day, I spoke these words:

> Now that you are gone, nothing will ever be the same. We will never be the same. We are being changed, pruned, but still loved by our sovereign God. We offer up ourselves to God to accomplish his work in us.

I Hang on to God's Hand

I'm still walking in the dark. I cling desperately to God's hand in an effort to make my way in an Ava-less world, a world I no longer recognize. And as I hang on to God's hand, I ask him to redeem this terrible event by redeeming me. I ask him to use the grief and pain and fear to change me, to make me less like myself and more like him. The old me is slipping away more and more each day, being replaced by a new me that knows without a doubt that I can rely on God. And the darkness isn't quite so terrifying as I learn to trust that God is there, even when life doesn't make sense, even when the worst nightmare a grandmother could dream turns out to be reality.

So often when our lives spin out of control — at least from our viewpoint — we think that God is to blame and that we somehow should be spared such agony. But the one who gave his only Son up to an agony worse than we have ever known reaches his hand down to take ours and lead us through the darkness. He doesn't always give the answers we desire. He doesn't always change our circumstances as we may wish. He turns out the lights in order to teach us that gripping his hand on our journey, that trusting in him, is better than any light.

7 "Are you the first man ever born?
    Were you brought forth before the hills?
8 Do you listen in on God's council?
    Do you limit wisdom to yourself?
9 What do you know that we do not know?
    What insights do you have that we do not
        have?
10 The gray-haired and the aged are on our side,
    men even older than your father.
11 Are God's consolations not enough for you,
    words spoken gently to you?
12 Why has your heart carried you away,
    and why do your eyes flash,
13 so that you vent your rage against God
    and pour out such words from your mouth?

14 "What is man, that he could be pure,
    or one born of woman, that he could be
        righteous?
15 If God places no trust in his holy ones,
    if even the heavens are not pure in his eyes,
16 how much less man, who is vile and corrupt,
    who drinks up evil like water!

17 "Listen to me and I will explain to you;
    let me tell you what I have seen,
18 what wise men have declared,
    hiding nothing received from their fathers
19 (to whom alone the land was given
    when no alien passed among them):
20 All his days the wicked man suffers torment,
    the ruthless through all the years stored up
        for him.
21 Terrifying sounds fill his ears;
    when all seems well, marauders attack him.
22 He despairs of escaping the darkness;
    he is marked for the sword.
23 He wanders about—food for vultures[a];
    he knows the day of darkness is at hand.
24 Distress and anguish fill him with terror;
    they overwhelm him, like a king poised to
        attack,
25 because he shakes his fist at God
    and vaunts himself against the Almighty,
26 defiantly charging against him
    with a thick, strong shield.

27 "Though his face is covered with fat
    and his waist bulges with flesh,
28 he will inhabit ruined towns
    and houses where no one lives,
    houses crumbling to rubble.
29 He will no longer be rich and his wealth will
        not endure,
    nor will his possessions spread over the
        land.
30 He will not escape the darkness;
    a flame will wither his shoots,
    and the breath of God's mouth will carry
        him away.
31 Let him not deceive himself by trusting what
        is worthless,
    for he will get nothing in return.
32 Before his time he will be paid in full,
    and his branches will not flourish.
33 He will be like a vine stripped of its unripe
        grapes,
    like an olive tree shedding its blossoms.
34 For the company of the godless will be barren,
    and fire will consume the tents of those
        who love bribes.
35 They conceive trouble and give birth to evil;
    their womb fashions deceit."

Job

16 Then Job replied:

2 "I have heard many things like these;
    miserable comforters are you all!
3 Will your long-winded speeches never end?
    What ails you that you keep on arguing?
4 I also could speak like you,
    if you were in my place;
    I could make fine speeches against you
        and shake my head at you.
5 But my mouth would encourage you;
    comfort from my lips would bring you
        relief.

6 "Yet if I speak, my pain is not relieved;
    and if I refrain, it does not go away.

---

a 23 Or about, looking for food

7 Surely, O God, you have worn me out;
   you have devastated my entire household.
8 You have bound me—and it has become a
      witness;
   my gauntness rises up and testifies against
      me.
9 God assails me and tears me in his anger
   and gnashes his teeth at me;
   my opponent fastens on me his piercing
      eyes.
10 Men open their mouths to jeer at me;
   they strike my cheek in scorn
   and unite together against me.
11 God has turned me over to evil men
   and thrown me into the clutches of the
      wicked.
12 All was well with me, but he shattered me;
   he seized me by the neck and crushed me.
   He has made me his target;
13   his archers surround me.
   Without pity, he pierces my kidneys
   and spills my gall on the ground.
14 Again and again he bursts upon me;
   he rushes at me like a warrior.

15 "I have sewed sackcloth over my skin
   and buried my brow in the dust.
16 My face is red with weeping,
   deep shadows ring my eyes;
17 yet my hands have been free of violence
   and my prayer is pure.

18 "O earth, do not cover my blood;
   may my cry never be laid to rest!
19 Even now my witness is in heaven;
   my advocate is on high.
20 My intercessor is my friend*a*
   as my eyes pour out tears to God;
21 on behalf of a man he pleads with God
   as a man pleads for his friend.

22 "Only a few years will pass
   before I go on the journey of no return.

17 1 My spirit is broken,
   my days are cut short,
   the grave awaits me.

2 Surely mockers surround me;
   my eyes must dwell on their hostility.

3 "Give me, O God, the pledge you demand.
   Who else will put up security for me?
4 You have closed their minds to
      understanding;
   therefore you will not let them triumph.
5 If a man denounces his friends for reward,
   the eyes of his children will fail.

6 "God has made me a byword to everyone,
   a man in whose face people spit.
7 My eyes have grown dim with grief;
   my whole frame is but a shadow.
8 Upright men are appalled at this;
   the innocent are aroused against the
      ungodly.
9 Nevertheless, the righteous will hold to their
      ways,
   and those with clean hands will grow
      stronger.

10 "But come on, all of you, try again!
   I will not find a wise man among you.
11 My days have passed, my plans are shattered,
   and so are the desires of my heart.
12 These men turn night into day;
   in the face of darkness they say, 'Light is
      near.'
13 If the only home I hope for is the grave,*b*
   if I spread out my bed in darkness,
14 if I say to corruption, 'You are my father,'
   and to the worm, 'My mother' or 'My
      sister,'
15 where then is my hope?
   Who can see any hope for me?
16 Will it go down to the gates of death*b*?
   Will we descend together into the dust?"

Bildad

18 Then Bildad the Shuhite replied:

2 "When will you end these speeches?
   Be sensible, and then we can talk.

---

a 20 Or *My friends treat me with scorn*   *b 13,16* Hebrew *Sheol*

3 Why are we regarded as cattle
  and considered stupid in your sight?
4 You who tear yourself to pieces in your
    anger,
  is the earth to be abandoned for your sake?
  Or must the rocks be moved from their
    place?

5 "The lamp of the wicked is snuffed out;
  the flame of his fire stops burning.
6 The light in his tent becomes dark;
  the lamp beside him goes out.
7 The vigor of his step is weakened;
  his own schemes throw him down.
8 His feet thrust him into a net
  and he wanders into its mesh.
9 A trap seizes him by the heel;
  a snare holds him fast.
10 A noose is hidden for him on the ground;
  a trap lies in his path.
11 Terrors startle him on every side
  and dog his every step.
12 Calamity is hungry for him;
  disaster is ready for him when he falls.
13 It eats away parts of his skin;
  death's firstborn devours his limbs.
14 He is torn from the security of his tent
  and marched off to the king of terrors.
15 Fire resides a in his tent;
  burning sulfur is scattered over his
    dwelling.
16 His roots dry up below
  and his branches wither above.
17 The memory of him perishes from the earth;
  he has no name in the land.
18 He is driven from light into darkness
  and is banished from the world.
19 He has no offspring or descendants among
    his people,
  no survivor where once he lived.
20 Men of the west are appalled at his fate;
  men of the east are seized with horror.
21 Surely such is the dwelling of an evil man;
  such is the place of one who knows not
    God."

Job

19

Then Job replied:

2 "How long will you torment me
  and crush me with words?
3 Ten times now you have reproached me;
  shamelessly you attack me.
4 If it is true that I have gone astray,
  my error remains my concern alone.
5 If indeed you would exalt yourselves
    above me
  and use my humiliation against me,
6 then know that God has wronged me
  and drawn his net around me.

7 "Though I cry, 'I've been wronged!' I get no
    response;
  though I call for help, there is no justice.
8 He has blocked my way so I cannot pass;
  he has shrouded my paths in darkness.
9 He has stripped me of my honor
  and removed the crown from my head.
10 He tears me down on every side till I am
    gone;
  he uproots my hope like a tree.
11 His anger burns against me;
  he counts me among his enemies.
12 His troops advance in force;
  they build a siege ramp against me
  and encamp around my tent.

13 "He has alienated my brothers from me;
  my acquaintances are completely estranged
    from me.
14 My kinsmen have gone away;
  my friends have forgotten me.
15 My guests and my maidservants count me a
    stranger;
  they look upon me as an alien.
16 I summon my servant, but he does not
    answer,
  though I beg him with my own mouth.
17 My breath is offensive to my wife;
  I am loathsome to my own brothers.

a 15 Or Nothing he had remains

¹⁸ Even the little boys scorn me;
  when I appear, they ridicule me.
¹⁹ All my intimate friends detest me;
  those I love have turned against me.
²⁰ I am nothing but skin and bones;
  I have escaped with only the skin of my
    teeth. *a*

²¹ "Have pity on me, my friends, have pity,
  for the hand of God has struck me.
²² Why do you pursue me as God does?
  Will you never get enough of my flesh?

²³ "Oh, that my words were recorded,
  that they were written on a scroll,
²⁴ that they were inscribed with an iron tool
    on *b* lead,
  or engraved in rock forever!
²⁵ I know that my Redeemer *c* lives,
  and that in the end he will stand upon the
    earth. *d*
²⁶ And after my skin has been destroyed,
  yet *e* in *f* my flesh I will see God;
²⁷ I myself will see him
  with my own eyes — I, and not another.
  How my heart yearns within me!

²⁸ "If you say, 'How we will hound him,
  since the root of the trouble lies in him, *g*'
²⁹ you should fear the sword yourselves;
  for wrath will bring punishment by the
    sword,
  and then you will know that there is
    judgment. *h*"

Zophar

20 Then Zophar the Naamathite replied:

² "My troubled thoughts prompt me to answer
  because I am greatly disturbed.
³ I hear a rebuke that dishonors me,
  and my understanding inspires me to
    reply.

⁴ "Surely you know how it has been from of
    old,
  ever since man *i* was placed on the earth,

⁵ that the mirth of the wicked is brief,
  the joy of the godless lasts but a moment.
⁶ Though his pride reaches to the heavens
  and his head touches the clouds,
⁷ he will perish forever, like his own dung;
  those who have seen him will say, 'Where
    is he?'
⁸ Like a dream he flies away, no more to be
    found,
  banished like a vision of the night.
⁹ The eye that saw him will not see him again;
  his place will look on him no more.
¹⁰ His children must make amends to the poor;
  his own hands must give back his wealth.
¹¹ The youthful vigor that fills his bones
  will lie with him in the dust.

¹² "Though evil is sweet in his mouth
  and he hides it under his tongue,
¹³ though he cannot bear to let it go
  and keeps it in his mouth,
¹⁴ yet his food will turn sour in his stomach;
  it will become the venom of serpents
    within him.
¹⁵ He will spit out the riches he swallowed;
  God will make his stomach vomit them up.
¹⁶ He will suck the poison of serpents;
  the fangs of an adder will kill him.
¹⁷ He will not enjoy the streams,
  the rivers flowing with honey and cream.
¹⁸ What he toiled for he must give back
    uneaten;
  he will not enjoy the profit from his
    trading.
¹⁹ For he has oppressed the poor and left them
    destitute;
  he has seized houses he did not build.

²⁰ "Surely he will have no respite from his
    craving;
  he cannot save himself by his treasure.

a 20 Or only my gums   *b 24 Or and*   *c 25 Or defender*
d 25 Or upon my grave   *e 26 Or And after I awake, / though
this body has been destroyed, / then*   *f 26 Or / apart from*
*g 28 Many Hebrew manuscripts, Septuagint and Vulgate; most
Hebrew manuscripts me*   *h 29 Or / that you may come to know the
Almighty*   *i 4 Or Adam*

²¹ Nothing is left for him to devour;
　his prosperity will not endure.
²² In the midst of his plenty, distress will
　　overtake him;
　the full force of misery will come upon
　　him.
²³ When he has filled his belly,
　God will vent his burning anger against
　　him
　and rain down his blows upon him.
²⁴ Though he flees from an iron weapon,
　a bronze-tipped arrow pierces him.
²⁵ He pulls it out of his back,
　the gleaming point out of his liver.
　Terrors will come over him;
²⁶　total darkness lies in wait for his treasures.
　A fire unfanned will consume him
　and devour what is left in his tent.
²⁷ The heavens will expose his guilt;
　the earth will rise up against him.
²⁸ A flood will carry off his house,
　rushing waters ᵃ on the day of God's
　　wrath.
²⁹ Such is the fate God allots the wicked,
　the heritage appointed for them by God."

Job

21 Then Job replied:

² "Listen carefully to my words;
　let this be the consolation you give me.
³ Bear with me while I speak,
　and after I have spoken, mock on.

⁴ "Is my complaint directed to man?
　Why should I not be impatient?
⁵ Look at me and be astonished;
　clap your hand over your mouth.
⁶ When I think about this, I am terrified;
　trembling seizes my body.
⁷ Why do the wicked live on,
　growing old and increasing in power?
⁸ They see their children established around
　　them,
　their offspring before their eyes.

⁹ Their homes are safe and free from fear;
　the rod of God is not upon them.
¹⁰ Their bulls never fail to breed;
　their cows calve and do not miscarry.
¹¹ They send forth their children as a flock;
　their little ones dance about.
¹² They sing to the music of tambourine and
　　harp;
　they make merry to the sound of the flute.
¹³ They spend their years in prosperity
　and go down to the grave ᵇ in peace. ᶜ
¹⁴ Yet they say to God, 'Leave us alone!
　We have no desire to know your ways.
¹⁵ Who is the Almighty, that we should serve
　　him?
　What would we gain by praying to him?'
¹⁶ But their prosperity is not in their own
　　hands,
　so I stand aloof from the counsel of the
　　wicked.

¹⁷ "Yet how often is the lamp of the wicked
　　snuffed out?
　How often does calamity come upon them,
　the fate God allots in his anger?
¹⁸ How often are they like straw before the
　　wind,
　like chaff swept away by a gale?
¹⁹ It is said, 'God stores up a man's
　　punishment for his sons.'
　Let him repay the man himself, so that he
　　will know it!
²⁰ Let his own eyes see his destruction;
　let him drink of the wrath of the
　　Almighty. ᵈ
²¹ For what does he care about the family he
　　leaves behind
　when his allotted months come to an end?

²² "Can anyone teach knowledge to God,
　since he judges even the highest?
²³ One man dies in full vigor,
　completely secure and at ease,

ᵃ 28 Or *The possessions in his house will be carried off,* / *washed away*
ᵇ 13 Hebrew *Sheol*　　ᶜ 13 Or *in an instant*　　ᵈ 17-20 Verses 17
and 18 may be taken as exclamations and 19 and 20 as declarations.

²⁴his body ᵃ well nourished,
  his bones rich with marrow.
²⁵Another man dies in bitterness of soul,
  never having enjoyed anything good.
²⁶Side by side they lie in the dust,
  and worms cover them both.

²⁷"I know full well what you are thinking,
  the schemes by which you would wrong
    me.
²⁸You say, 'Where now is the great man's house,
  the tents where wicked men lived?'
²⁹Have you never questioned those who travel?
  Have you paid no regard to their
    accounts—
³⁰that the evil man is spared from the day of
    calamity,
  that he is delivered from ᵇ the day of
    wrath?
³¹Who denounces his conduct to his face?
  Who repays him for what he has done?
³²He is carried to the grave,
  and watch is kept over his tomb.
³³The soil in the valley is sweet to him;
  all men follow after him,
  and a countless throng goes ᶜ before him.

³⁴"So how can you console me with your
    nonsense?
  Nothing is left of your answers but
    falsehood!"

Eliphaz

22 Then Eliphaz the Temanite replied:

²"Can a man be of benefit to God?
  Can even a wise man benefit him?
³What pleasure would it give the Almighty if
    you were righteous?
  What would he gain if your ways were
    blameless?

⁴"Is it for your piety that he rebukes you
  and brings charges against you?
⁵Is not your wickedness great?
  Are not your sins endless?

⁶You demanded security from your brothers
    for no reason;
  you stripped men of their clothing, leaving
    them naked.
⁷You gave no water to the weary
  and you withheld food from the hungry,
⁸though you were a powerful man, owning
    land—
  an honored man, living on it.
⁹And you sent widows away empty-handed
  and broke the strength of the fatherless.
¹⁰That is why snares are all around you,
  why sudden peril terrifies you,
¹¹why it is so dark you cannot see,
  and why a flood of water covers you.

¹²"Is not God in the heights of heaven?
  And see how lofty are the highest stars!
¹³Yet you say, 'What does God know?
  Does he judge through such darkness?
¹⁴Thick clouds veil him, so he does not see us
  as he goes about in the vaulted heavens.'
¹⁵Will you keep to the old path
  that evil men have trod?
¹⁶They were carried off before their time,
  their foundations washed away by a
    flood.
¹⁷They said to God, 'Leave us alone!
  What can the Almighty do to us?'
¹⁸Yet it was he who filled their houses with
    good things,
  so I stand aloof from the counsel of the
    wicked.

¹⁹"The righteous see their ruin and rejoice;
  the innocent mock them, saying,
²⁰'Surely our foes are destroyed,
  and fire devours their wealth.'

²¹"Submit to God and be at peace with him;
  in this way prosperity will come to you.
²²Accept instruction from his mouth
  and lay up his words in your heart.

ᵃ 24 The meaning of the Hebrew for this word is uncertain.
ᵇ 30 Or man is reserved for the day of calamity, / that he is brought
forth to   ᶜ 33 Or / as a countless throng went

²³ If you return to the Almighty, you will be
restored:
If you remove wickedness far from your
tent
²⁴ and assign your nuggets to the dust,
your gold of Ophir to the rocks in the
ravines,
²⁵ then the Almighty will be your gold,
the choicest silver for you.
²⁶ Surely then you will find delight in the
Almighty
and will lift up your face to God.
²⁷ You will pray to him, and he will hear you,
and you will fulfill your vows.
²⁸ What you decide on will be done,
and light will shine on your ways.
²⁹ When men are brought low and you say,
'Lift them up!'
then he will save the downcast.
³⁰ He will deliver even one who is not innocent,
who will be delivered through the
cleanness of your hands."

Job

23

Then Job replied:

² "Even today my complaint is bitter;
his hand ᵃ is heavy in spite of ᵇ my
groaning.
³ If only I knew where to find him;
if only I could go to his dwelling!
⁴ I would state my case before him
and fill my mouth with arguments.
⁵ I would find out what he would answer me,
and consider what he would say.
⁶ Would he oppose me with great power?
No, he would not press charges against
me.
⁷ There an upright man could present his case
before him,
and I would be delivered forever from my
judge.

⁸ "But if I go to the east, he is not there;
if I go to the west, I do not find him.

⁹ When he is at work in the north, I do not see
him;
when he turns to the south, I catch no
glimpse of him.
¹⁰ But he knows the way that I take;
when he has tested me, I will come forth as
gold.
¹¹ My feet have closely followed his steps;
I have kept to his way without turning aside.
¹² I have not departed from the commands of
his lips;
I have treasured the words of his mouth
more than my daily bread.

¹³ "But he stands alone, and who can oppose
him?
He does whatever he pleases.
¹⁴ He carries out his decree against me,
and many such plans he still has in store.
¹⁵ That is why I am terrified before him;
when I think of all this, I fear him.
¹⁶ God has made my heart faint;
the Almighty has terrified me.
¹⁷ Yet I am not silenced by the darkness,
by the thick darkness that covers my face.

24

"Why does the Almighty not set times
for judgment?
Why must those who know him look in
vain for such days?
² Men move boundary stones;
they pasture flocks they have stolen.
³ They drive away the orphan's donkey
and take the widow's ox in pledge.
⁴ They thrust the needy from the path
and force all the poor of the land into
hiding.
⁵ Like wild donkeys in the desert,
the poor go about their labor of foraging
food;
the wasteland provides food for their
children.
⁶ They gather fodder in the fields
and glean in the vineyards of the wicked.

ᵃ 2 Septuagint and Syriac; Hebrew / the hand on me   ᵇ 2 Or heavy
on me in

⁷Lacking clothes, they spend the night naked;
  they have nothing to cover themselves in
    the cold.
⁸They are drenched by mountain rains
  and hug the rocks for lack of shelter.
⁹The fatherless child is snatched from the
    breast;
  the infant of the poor is seized for a debt.
¹⁰Lacking clothes, they go about naked;
  they carry the sheaves, but still go hungry.
¹¹They crush olives among the terraces ª;
  they tread the winepresses, yet suffer thirst.
¹²The groans of the dying rise from the city,
  and the souls of the wounded cry out for
    help.
  But God charges no one with wrongdoing.

¹³"There are those who rebel against the light,
  who do not know its ways
  or stay in its paths.
¹⁴When daylight is gone, the murderer rises up
  and kills the poor and needy;
  in the night he steals forth like a thief.
¹⁵The eye of the adulterer watches for dusk;
  he thinks, 'No eye will see me,'
  and he keeps his face concealed.
¹⁶In the dark, men break into houses,
  but by day they shut themselves in;
  they want nothing to do with the light.
¹⁷For all of them, deep darkness is their
    morning ᵇ;
  they make friends with the terrors of
    darkness. ᶜ

¹⁸"Yet they are foam on the surface of the
    water;
  their portion of the land is cursed,
  so that no one goes to the vineyards.
¹⁹As heat and drought snatch away the melted
    snow,
  so the grave ᵈ snatches away those who
    have sinned.
²⁰The womb forgets them,
  the worm feasts on them;
  evil men are no longer remembered
  but are broken like a tree.

²¹They prey on the barren and childless woman,
  and to the widow show no kindness.
²²But God drags away the mighty by his power;
  though they become established, they have
    no assurance of life.
²³He may let them rest in a feeling of security,
  but his eyes are on their ways.
²⁴For a little while they are exalted, and then
    they are gone;
  they are brought low and gathered up like
    all others;
  they are cut off like heads of grain.

²⁵"If this is not so, who can prove me false
  and reduce my words to nothing?"

Bildad

25 Then Bildad the Shuhite replied:

²"Dominion and awe belong to God;
  he establishes order in the heights of
    heaven.
³Can his forces be numbered?
  Upon whom does his light not rise?
⁴How then can a man be righteous before
    God?
  How can one born of woman be pure?
⁵If even the moon is not bright
  and the stars are not pure in his eyes,
⁶how much less man, who is but a maggot—
  a son of man, who is only a worm!"

Job

26 Then Job replied:

²"How you have helped the powerless!
  How you have saved the arm that is feeble!
³What advice you have offered to one without
    wisdom!
  And what great insight you have displayed!
⁴Who has helped you utter these words?
  And whose spirit spoke from your mouth?

ª 11 Or olives between the millstones; the meaning of the Hebrew
for this word is uncertain.   ᵇ 17 Or them, their morning is like the
shadow of death   ᶜ 17 Or of the shadow of death   ᵈ 19 Hebrew
Sheol

5 "The dead are in deep anguish,
   those beneath the waters and all that live in
      them.
6 Death *a* is naked before God;
   Destruction *b* lies uncovered.
7 He spreads out the northern ⌊skies⌋ over
      empty space;
   he suspends the earth over nothing.
8 He wraps up the waters in his clouds,
   yet the clouds do not burst under their
      weight.
9 He covers the face of the full moon,
   spreading his clouds over it.
10 He marks out the horizon on the face of the
      waters
   for a boundary between light and
      darkness.
11 The pillars of the heavens quake,
   aghast at his rebuke.
12 By his power he churned up the sea;
   by his wisdom he cut Rahab to pieces.
13 By his breath the skies became fair;
   his hand pierced the gliding serpent.
14 And these are but the outer fringe of his
      works;
   how faint the whisper we hear of him!
   Who then can understand the thunder of
      his power?"

27 And Job continued his discourse:

2 "As surely as God lives, who has denied me
      justice,
   the Almighty, who has made me taste
      bitterness of soul,
3 as long as I have life within me,
   the breath of God in my nostrils,
4 my lips will not speak wickedness,
   and my tongue will utter no deceit.
5 I will never admit you are in the right;
   till I die, I will not deny my integrity.
6 I will maintain my righteousness and never
      let go of it;
   my conscience will not reproach me as
      long as I live.

7 "May my enemies be like the wicked,
   my adversaries like the unjust!
8 For what hope has the godless when he is
      cut off,
   when God takes away his life?
9 Does God listen to his cry
   when distress comes upon him?
10 Will he find delight in the Almighty?
   Will he call upon God at all times?

11 "I will teach you about the power of God;
   the ways of the Almighty I will not
      conceal.
12 You have all seen this yourselves.
   Why then this meaningless talk?

13 "Here is the fate God allots to the wicked,
   the heritage a ruthless man receives from
      the Almighty:
14 However many his children, their fate is the
      sword;
   his offspring will never have enough to eat.
15 The plague will bury those who survive him,
   and their widows will not weep for them.
16 Though he heaps up silver like dust
   and clothes like piles of clay,
17 what he lays up the righteous will wear,
   and the innocent will divide his silver.
18 The house he builds is like a moth's cocoon,
   like a hut made by a watchman.
19 He lies down wealthy, but will do so no more;
   when he opens his eyes, all is gone.
20 Terrors overtake him like a flood;
   a tempest snatches him away in the night.
21 The east wind carries him off, and he is gone;
   it sweeps him out of his place.
22 It hurls itself against him without mercy
   as he flees headlong from its power.
23 It claps its hands in derision
   and hisses him out of his place.

28 "There is a mine for silver
   and a place where gold is refined.
2 Iron is taken from the earth,
   and copper is smelted from ore.

a 6 Hebrew Sheol   *b 6 Hebrew Abaddon*

³Man puts an end to the darkness;
  he searches the farthest recesses
  for ore in the blackest darkness.
⁴Far from where people dwell he cuts a shaft,
  in places forgotten by the foot of man;
  far from men he dangles and sways.
⁵The earth, from which food comes,
  is transformed below as by fire;
⁶sapphires ᵃ come from its rocks,
  and its dust contains nuggets of gold.
⁷No bird of prey knows that hidden path,
  no falcon's eye has seen it.
⁸Proud beasts do not set foot on it,
  and no lion prowls there.
⁹Man's hand assaults the flinty rock
  and lays bare the roots of the mountains.
¹⁰He tunnels through the rock;
  his eyes see all its treasures.
¹¹He searches ᵇ the sources of the rivers
  and brings hidden things to light.

¹²"But where can wisdom be found?
  Where does understanding dwell?
¹³Man does not comprehend its worth;
  it cannot be found in the land of the
    living.
¹⁴The deep says, 'It is not in me';
  the sea says, 'It is not with me.'
¹⁵It cannot be bought with the finest gold,
  nor can its price be weighed in silver.
¹⁶It cannot be bought with the gold of Ophir,
  with precious onyx or sapphires.
¹⁷Neither gold nor crystal can compare with it,
  nor can it be had for jewels of gold.
¹⁸Coral and jasper are not worthy of mention;
  the price of wisdom is beyond rubies.
¹⁹The topaz of Cush cannot compare with it;
  it cannot be bought with pure gold.

²⁰"Where then does wisdom come from?
  Where does understanding dwell?
²¹It is hidden from the eyes of every living
    thing,
  concealed even from the birds of the air.
²²Destruction ᶜ and Death say,
  'Only a rumor of it has reached our ears.'

²³God understands the way to it
  and he alone knows where it dwells,
²⁴for he views the ends of the earth
  and sees everything under the heavens.
²⁵When he established the force of the wind
  and measured out the waters,
²⁶when he made a decree for the rain
  and a path for the thunderstorm,
²⁷then he looked at wisdom and appraised it;
  he confirmed it and tested it.
²⁸And he said to man,
  'The fear of the Lord—that is wisdom,
  and to shun evil is understanding.'"

29 Job continued his discourse:

²"How I long for the months gone by,
  for the days when God watched over me,
³when his lamp shone upon my head
  and by his light I walked through darkness!
⁴Oh, for the days when I was in my prime,
  when God's intimate friendship blessed my
    house,
⁵when the Almighty was still with me
  and my children were around me,
⁶when my path was drenched with cream
  and the rock poured out for me streams of
    olive oil.

⁷"When I went to the gate of the city
  and took my seat in the public square,
⁸the young men saw me and stepped aside
  and the old men rose to their feet;
⁹the chief men refrained from speaking
  and covered their mouths with their hands;
¹⁰the voices of the nobles were hushed,
  and their tongues stuck to the roof of their
    mouths.
¹¹Whoever heard me spoke well of me,
  and those who saw me commended me,
¹²because I rescued the poor who cried for
    help,
  and the fatherless who had none to assist
    him.

ᵃ 6 Or lapis lazuli; also in verse 16   ᵇ 11 Septuagint, Aquila and
Vulgate; Hebrew He dams up   ᶜ 22 Hebrew Abaddon

¹³ The man who was dying blessed me;
    I made the widow's heart sing.
¹⁴ I put on righteousness as my clothing;
    justice was my robe and my turban.
¹⁵ I was eyes to the blind
    and feet to the lame.
¹⁶ I was a father to the needy;
    I took up the case of the stranger.
¹⁷ I broke the fangs of the wicked
    and snatched the victims from their teeth.

¹⁸ "I thought, 'I will die in my own house,
    my days as numerous as the grains of sand.
¹⁹ My roots will reach to the water,
    and the dew will lie all night on my
        branches.
²⁰ My glory will remain fresh in me,
    the bow ever new in my hand.'

²¹ "Men listened to me expectantly,
    waiting in silence for my counsel.
²² After I had spoken, they spoke no more;
    my words fell gently on their ears.
²³ They waited for me as for showers
    and drank in my words as the spring rain.
²⁴ When I smiled at them, they scarcely believed
    it;
    the light of my face was precious to them. ᵃ
²⁵ I chose the way for them and sat as their
    chief;
    I dwelt as a king among his troops;
    I was like one who comforts mourners.

30 "But now they mock me,
    men younger than I,
whose fathers I would have disdained
    to put with my sheep dogs.
² Of what use was the strength of their hands
    to me,
    since their vigor had gone from them?
³ Haggard from want and hunger,
    they roamed ᵇ the parched land
    in desolate wastelands at night.
⁴ In the brush they gathered salt herbs,
    and their food ᶜ was the root of the broom
        tree.

⁵ They were banished from their fellow men,
    shouted at as if they were thieves.
⁶ They were forced to live in the dry stream
        beds,
    among the rocks and in holes in the
        ground.
⁷ They brayed among the bushes
    and huddled in the undergrowth.
⁸ A base and nameless brood,
    they were driven out of the land.

⁹ "And now their sons mock me in song;
    I have become a byword among them.
¹⁰ They detest me and keep their distance;
    they do not hesitate to spit in my face.
¹¹ Now that God has unstrung my bow and
        afflicted me,
    they throw off restraint in my presence.
¹² On my right the tribe ᵈ attacks;
    they lay snares for my feet,
    they build their siege ramps against me.
¹³ They break up my road;
    they succeed in destroying me—
    without anyone's helping them. ᵉ
¹⁴ They advance as through a gaping breach;
    amid the ruins they come rolling in.
¹⁵ Terrors overwhelm me;
    my dignity is driven away as by the wind,
    my safety vanishes like a cloud.

¹⁶ "And now my life ebbs away;
    days of suffering grip me.
¹⁷ Night pierces my bones;
    my gnawing pains never rest.
¹⁸ In his great power ˎGodˎ becomes like
        clothing to me ᶠ;
    he binds me like the neck of my garment.
¹⁹ He throws me into the mud,
    and I am reduced to dust and ashes.

²⁰ "I cry out to you, O God, but you do not
        answer;
    I stand up, but you merely look at me.

ᵃ 24 The meaning of the Hebrew for this clause is uncertain.
ᵇ 3 Or gnawed   ᶜ 4 Or fuel   ᵈ 12 The meaning of the Hebrew
for this word is uncertain.   ᵉ 13 Or me. / 'No one can help him,'
ˎthey sayˎ.   ᶠ 18 Hebrew; Septuagint ˎGodˎ grasps my clothing

²¹ You turn on me ruthlessly;
  with the might of your hand you attack me.
²² You snatch me up and drive me before the
    wind;
  you toss me about in the storm.
²³ I know you will bring me down to death,
  to the place appointed for all the living.

²⁴ "Surely no one lays a hand on a broken man
  when he cries for help in his distress.
²⁵ Have I not wept for those in trouble?
  Has not my soul grieved for the poor?
²⁶ Yet when I hoped for good, evil came;
  when I looked for light, then came
    darkness.
²⁷ The churning inside me never stops;
  days of suffering confront me.
²⁸ I go about blackened, but not by the sun;
  I stand up in the assembly and cry for help.
²⁹ I have become a brother of jackals,
  a companion of owls.
³⁰ My skin grows black and peels;
  my body burns with fever.
³¹ My harp is tuned to mourning,
  and my flute to the sound of wailing.

31 "I made a covenant with my eyes
  not to look lustfully at a girl.
² For what is man's lot from God above,
  his heritage from the Almighty on high?
³ Is it not ruin for the wicked,
  disaster for those who do wrong?
⁴ Does he not see my ways
  and count my every step?

⁵ "If I have walked in falsehood
  or my foot has hurried after deceit—
⁶ let God weigh me in honest scales
  and he will know that I am blameless—
⁷ if my steps have turned from the path,
  if my heart has been led by my eyes,
  or if my hands have been defiled,
⁸ then may others eat what I have sown,
  and may my crops be uprooted.

⁹ "If my heart has been enticed by a woman,
  or if I have lurked at my neighbor's door,

¹⁰ then may my wife grind another man's grain,
  and may other men sleep with her.
¹¹ For that would have been shameful,
  a sin to be judged.
¹² It is a fire that burns to Destruction ᵃ;
  it would have uprooted my harvest.

¹³ "If I have denied justice to my menservants
    and maidservants
  when they had a grievance against me,
¹⁴ what will I do when God confronts me?
  What will I answer when called to account?
¹⁵ Did not he who made me in the womb make
    them?
  Did not the same one form us both within
    our mothers?

¹⁶ "If I have denied the desires of the poor
  or let the eyes of the widow grow weary,
¹⁷ if I have kept my bread to myself,
  not sharing it with the fatherless—
¹⁸ but from my youth I reared him as would a
    father,
  and from my birth I guided the widow—
¹⁹ if I have seen anyone perishing for lack of
    clothing,
  or a needy man without a garment,
²⁰ and his heart did not bless me
  for warming him with the fleece from my
    sheep,
²¹ if I have raised my hand against the fatherless,
  knowing that I had influence in court,

ᵃ 12 Hebrew *Abaddon*

²²then let my arm fall from the shoulder,
  let it be broken off at the joint.
²³For I dreaded destruction from God,
  and for fear of his splendor I could not do
    such things.

²⁴"If I have put my trust in gold
  or said to pure gold, 'You are my security,'
²⁵if I have rejoiced over my great wealth,
  the fortune my hands had gained,
²⁶if I have regarded the sun in its radiance
  or the moon moving in splendor,
²⁷so that my heart was secretly enticed
  and my hand offered them a kiss of
    homage,
²⁸then these also would be sins to be judged,
  for I would have been unfaithful to God on
    high.

²⁹"If I have rejoiced at my enemy's misfortune
  or gloated over the trouble that came to
    him—
³⁰I have not allowed my mouth to sin
  by invoking a curse against his life—
³¹if the men of my household have never said,
  'Who has not had his fill of Job's meat?'—
³²but no stranger had to spend the night in the
    street,
  for my door was always open to the
    traveler—
³³if I have concealed my sin as men do,ᵃ
  by hiding my guilt in my heart
³⁴because I so feared the crowd
  and so dreaded the contempt of the clans
    that I kept silent and would not go
      outside—

³⁵("Oh, that I had someone to hear me!
  I sign now my defense—let the Almighty
    answer me;
  let my accuser put his indictment in
    writing.
³⁶Surely I would wear it on my shoulder,
  I would put it on like a crown.
³⁷I would give you an account of my every
    step;
  like a prince I would approach him.)—

³⁸"if my land cries out against me
  and all its furrows are wet with tears,
³⁹if I have devoured its yield without payment
  or broken the spirit of its tenants,
⁴⁰then let briers come up instead of wheat
  and weeds instead of barley."

The words of Job are ended.

Elihu

32 So these three men stopped answering
Job, because he was righteous in his own
eyes. ²But Elihu son of Barakel the Buzite, of the
family of Ram, became very angry with Job for
justifying himself rather than God. ³He was also
angry with the three friends, because they had
found no way to refute Job, and yet had condemned him.ᵇ ⁴Now Elihu had waited before
speaking to Job because they were older than he.
⁵But when he saw that the three men had nothing more to say, his anger was aroused.

⁶So Elihu son of Barakel the Buzite said:

"I am young in years,
  and you are old;
that is why I was fearful,
  not daring to tell you what I know.
⁷I thought, 'Age should speak;
  advanced years should teach wisdom.'
⁸But it is the spiritᶜ in a man,
  the breath of the Almighty, that gives him
    understanding.
⁹It is not only the oldᵈ who are wise,
  not only the aged who understand what is
    right.

¹⁰"Therefore I say: Listen to me;
  I too will tell you what I know.
¹¹I waited while you spoke,
  I listened to your reasoning;
while you were searching for words,
¹² I gave you my full attention.
But not one of you has proved Job wrong;
  none of you has answered his arguments.

ᵃ 33 Or as Adam did   ᵇ 3 Masoretic Text; an ancient Hebrew
scribal tradition Job, and so had condemned God   ᶜ 8 Or Spirit;
also in verse 18   ᵈ 9 Or many; or great

¹³ Do not say, 'We have found wisdom;
     let God refute him, not man.'
¹⁴ But Job has not marshaled his words against
        me,
     and I will not answer him with your
        arguments.

¹⁵ "They are dismayed and have no more
        to say;
     words have failed them.
¹⁶ Must I wait, now that they are silent,
     now that they stand there with no reply?
¹⁷ I too will have my say;
     I too will tell what I know.
¹⁸ For I am full of words,
     and the spirit within me compels me;
¹⁹ inside I am like bottled-up wine,
     like new wineskins ready to burst.
²⁰ I must speak and find relief;
     I must open my lips and reply.
²¹ I will show partiality to no one,
     nor will I flatter any man;
²² for if I were skilled in flattery,
     my Maker would soon take me away.

33 "But now, Job, listen to my words;
     pay attention to everything I say.
² I am about to open my mouth;
     my words are on the tip of my tongue.
³ My words come from an upright heart;
     my lips sincerely speak what I know.
⁴ The Spirit of God has made me;
     the breath of the Almighty gives me life.
⁵ Answer me then, if you can;
     prepare yourself and confront me.
⁶ I am just like you before God;
     I too have been taken from clay.
⁷ No fear of me should alarm you,
     nor should my hand be heavy upon you.

⁸ "But you have said in my hearing—
     I heard the very words—
⁹ 'I am pure and without sin;
     I am clean and free from guilt.
¹⁰ Yet God has found fault with me;
     he considers me his enemy.

¹¹ He fastens my feet in shackles;
     he keeps close watch on all my paths.'

¹² "But I tell you, in this you are not right,
     for God is greater than man.
¹³ Why do you complain to him
     that he answers none of man's words *ᵃ*?
¹⁴ For God does speak—now one way, now
        another—
     though man may not perceive it.
¹⁵ In a dream, in a vision of the night,
     when deep sleep falls on men
     as they slumber in their beds,
¹⁶ he may speak in their ears
     and terrify them with warnings,
¹⁷ to turn man from wrongdoing
     and keep him from pride,
¹⁸ to preserve his soul from the pit, *ᵇ*
     his life from perishing by the sword. *ᶜ*
¹⁹ Or a man may be chastened on a bed of pain
     with constant distress in his bones,
²⁰ so that his very being finds food repulsive
     and his soul loathes the choicest meal.
²¹ His flesh wastes away to nothing,
     and his bones, once hidden, now stick out.
²² His soul draws near to the pit, *ᵈ*
     and his life to the messengers of death. *ᵉ*

²³ "Yet if there is an angel on his side
     as a mediator, one out of a thousand,
     to tell a man what is right for him,
²⁴ to be gracious to him and say,
     'Spare him from going down to the pit *ᶠ*;
     I have found a ransom for him'—
²⁵ then his flesh is renewed like a child's;
     it is restored as in the days of his youth.
²⁶ He prays to God and finds favor with him,
     he sees God's face and shouts for joy;
     he is restored by God to his righteous state.
²⁷ Then he comes to men and says,
     'I sinned, and perverted what was right,
     but I did not get what I deserved.

ᵃ 13 Or that he does not answer for any of his actions
ᵇ 18 Or preserve him from the grave   *ᶜ 18 Or from crossing the*
River   *ᵈ 22 Or He draws near to the grave*   *ᵉ 22 Or to the dead*
ᶠ 24 Or grave

28 He redeemed my soul from going down to
the pit, *a*
and I will live to enjoy the light.'

29 "God does all these things to a man—
twice, even three times—

30 to turn back his soul from the pit, *b*
that the light of life may shine on him.

31 "Pay attention, Job, and listen to me;
be silent, and I will speak.

32 If you have anything to say, answer me;
speak up, for I want you to be cleared.

33 But if not, then listen to me;
be silent, and I will teach you wisdom."

34

Then Elihu said:

2 "Hear my words, you wise men;
listen to me, you men of learning.

3 For the ear tests words
as the tongue tastes food.

4 Let us discern for ourselves what is right;
let us learn together what is good.

5 "Job says, 'I am innocent,
but God denies me justice.

6 Although I am right,
I am considered a liar;
although I am guiltless,
his arrow inflicts an incurable wound.'

7 What man is like Job,
who drinks scorn like water?

8 He keeps company with evildoers;
he associates with wicked men.

9 For he says, 'It profits a man nothing
when he tries to please God.'

10 "So listen to me, you men of understanding.
Far be it from God to do evil,
from the Almighty to do wrong.

11 He repays a man for what he has done;
he brings upon him what his conduct
deserves.

12 It is unthinkable that God would do wrong,
that the Almighty would pervert
justice.

13 Who appointed him over the earth?
Who put him in charge of the whole
world?

14 If it were his intention
and he withdrew his spirit *c* and breath,

15 all mankind would perish together
and man would return to the dust.

16 "If you have understanding, hear this;
listen to what I say.

17 Can he who hates justice govern?
Will you condemn the just and mighty
One?

18 Is he not the One who says to kings, 'You are
worthless,'
and to nobles, 'You are wicked,'

19 who shows no partiality to princes
and does not favor the rich over the poor,
for they are all the work of his hands?

20 They die in an instant, in the middle of the
night;
the people are shaken and they pass away;
the mighty are removed without human
hand.

21 "His eyes are on the ways of men;
he sees their every step.

22 There is no dark place, no deep shadow,
where evildoers can hide.

23 God has no need to examine men further,
that they should come before him for
judgment.

24 Without inquiry he shatters the mighty
and sets up others in their place.

25 Because he takes note of their deeds,
he overthrows them in the night and they
are crushed.

26 He punishes them for their wickedness
where everyone can see them,

27 because they turned from following him
and had no regard for any of his ways.

28 They caused the cry of the poor to come
before him,
so that he heard the cry of the needy.

a 28 Or redeemed me from going down to the grave   *b 30 Or turn
him back from the grave*   *c 14 Or Spirit*

²⁹ But if he remains silent, who can condemn
  him?
    If he hides his face, who can see him?
  Yet he is over man and nation alike,
³⁰   to keep a godless man from ruling,
    from laying snares for the people.

³¹ "Suppose a man says to God,
    'I am guilty but will offend no more.
³² Teach me what I cannot see;
    if I have done wrong, I will not do so again.'
³³ Should God then reward you on your terms,
    when you refuse to repent?
  You must decide, not I;
    so tell me what you know.

³⁴ "Men of understanding declare,
    wise men who hear me say to me,
³⁵ 'Job speaks without knowledge;
    his words lack insight.'
³⁶ Oh, that Job might be tested to the utmost
    for answering like a wicked man!
³⁷ To his sin he adds rebellion;
    scornfully he claps his hands among us
    and multiplies his words against God."

35 Then Elihu said:

² "Do you think this is just?
    You say, 'I will be cleared by God.'ᵃ
³ Yet you ask him, 'What profit is it to me,ᵇ
    and what do I gain by not sinning?'

⁴ "I would like to reply to you
    and to your friends with you.
⁵ Look up at the heavens and see;
    gaze at the clouds so high above you.
⁶ If you sin, how does that affect him?
    If your sins are many, what does that do to
      him?
⁷ If you are righteous, what do you give to him,
    or what does he receive from your hand?
⁸ Your wickedness affects only a man like
      yourself,
    and your righteousness only the sons of
      men.

⁹ "Men cry out under a load of oppression;
    they plead for relief from the arm of the
      powerful.
¹⁰ But no one says, 'Where is God my Maker,
    who gives songs in the night,
¹¹ who teaches more to us than toᶜ the beasts of
      the earth
    and makes us wiser thanᵈ the birds of the
      air?'
¹² He does not answer when men cry out
    because of the arrogance of the wicked.
¹³ Indeed, God does not listen to their empty
      plea;
    the Almighty pays no attention to it.
¹⁴ How much less, then, will he listen
    when you say that you do not see him,
  that your case is before him
    and you must wait for him,
¹⁵ and further, that his anger never punishes
    and he does not take the least notice of
      wickedness.ᵉ
¹⁶ So Job opens his mouth with empty talk;
    without knowledge he multiplies words."

36 Elihu continued:

² "Bear with me a little longer and I will show
      you
    that there is more to be said in God's
      behalf.
³ I get my knowledge from afar;
    I will ascribe justice to my Maker.
⁴ Be assured that my words are not false;
    one perfect in knowledge is with you.

⁵ "God is mighty, but does not despise men;
    he is mighty, and firm in his purpose.
⁶ He does not keep the wicked alive
    but gives the afflicted their rights.
⁷ He does not take his eyes off the righteous;
    he enthrones them with kings
    and exalts them forever.

ᵃ 2 Or My righteousness is more than God's   ᵇ 3 Or you
ᶜ 11 Or teaches us by   ᵈ 11 Or us wise by   ᵉ 15 Symmachus,
Theodotion and Vulgate; the meaning of the Hebrew for this word
is uncertain.

"MEN CRY OUT UNDER A LOAD OF OPPRESSION; THEY PLEAD FOR RELIEF FROM THE ARM OF THE POWERFUL. BUT NO ONE SAYS, 'WHERE IS GOD MY MAKER, WHO GIVES SONGS IN THE NIGHT?' "

Job 35:9–10

Songs in the Night

MILLIE STAMM

READ | JOB 35:1–16

Is there a song in your life today? Or has it ceased? It is easy to sing in the daytime when all is going well, but the test is the ability to sing when there is no ray of light. It is in the nighttime a special song is needed. It is then that God, the Composer of "songs in the night," gives a special song of faith and joy to encourage and comfort us. No night is too dark for His song.

Are you passing through a night experience that has stilled the song in your life? It may be sickness, depression, sorrow, discouragement or defeat. We spend the night hours tossing and turning, trying to solve our problem. It is then that God gives a special song to cheer us, one we can't compose, a gift from Him. As we wait before Him, He floods our whole being with His melodious song. It isn't a song for the future, or after the burden lifts, but for our present dark night.

The world's supply of attar of roses used to come from the Balkan mountains. The workers started picking the petals at 1:00 at night, stopping before dawn. Scientific tests had proven that forty percent of the fragrance of the roses disappears in the daylight.

"When the clouds of affliction have gathered, and hidden each star from my sight, I know if I turn to my Father, sweetest songs He will give in the night."

Father, I turn to you now. Teach me a new song, a song of joy and peace. Flood my being with your melodious voice.

Your next devotion is located on page 695.

GRANDCHILD **IN FOCUS** • PRAYER

Spiritual Growth

Dear Lord, today I pray for my grandchild's spiritual growth. I ask that you instill in him the desire to read and memorize your Word. Give him a passion to be in conversation with you. May loving and serving you be part of his daily life. I ask that you stay close to him and lead him to be transformed to your likeness, to reflect your grace and to radiate your love. I pray this in Jesus' name, amen.

8 But if men are bound in chains,
  held fast by cords of affliction,
9 he tells them what they have done—
  that they have sinned arrogantly.
10 He makes them listen to correction
  and commands them to repent of their
  evil.
11 If they obey and serve him,
  they will spend the rest of their days in
  prosperity
  and their years in contentment.
12 But if they do not listen,
  they will perish by the sword *a*
  and die without knowledge.

13 "The godless in heart harbor resentment;
  even when he fetters them, they do not cry
  for help.
14 They die in their youth,
  among male prostitutes of the shrines.
15 But those who suffer he delivers in their
  suffering;
  he speaks to them in their affliction.

16 "He is wooing you from the jaws of distress
  to a spacious place free from restriction,
  to the comfort of your table laden with
  choice food.
17 But now you are laden with the judgment
  due the wicked;
  judgment and justice have taken hold of
  you.
18 Be careful that no one entices you by
  riches;
  do not let a large bribe turn you aside.
19 Would your wealth
  or even all your mighty efforts
  sustain you so you would not be in
  distress?
20 Do not long for the night,
  to drag people away from their homes. *b*
21 Beware of turning to evil,
  which you seem to prefer to affliction.

22 "God is exalted in his power.
  Who is a teacher like him?
23 Who has prescribed his ways for him,
  or said to him, 'You have done wrong'?
24 Remember to extol his work,
  which men have praised in song.
25 All mankind has seen it;
  men gaze on it from afar.
26 How great is God—beyond our
  understanding!
  The number of his years is past finding
  out.

27 "He draws up the drops of water,
  which distill as rain to the streams *c*;
28 the clouds pour down their moisture
  and abundant showers fall on mankind.
29 Who can understand how he spreads out the
  clouds,
  how he thunders from his pavilion?
30 See how he scatters his lightning about him,
  bathing the depths of the sea.
31 This is the way he governs *d* the nations
  and provides food in abundance.
32 He fills his hands with lightning
  and commands it to strike its mark.
33 His thunder announces the coming storm;
  even the cattle make known its approach. *e*

37 "At this my heart pounds
  and leaps from its place.
2 Listen! Listen to the roar of his voice,
  to the rumbling that comes from his
  mouth.
3 He unleashes his lightning beneath the whole
  heaven
  and sends it to the ends of the earth.
4 After that comes the sound of his roar;
  he thunders with his majestic voice.
  When his voice resounds,
  he holds nothing back.
5 God's voice thunders in marvelous ways;
  he does great things beyond our
  understanding.

---

a 12 Or *will cross the River*   *b 20* The meaning of the Hebrew
for verses 18-20 is uncertain.   *c 27* Or *distill from the mist as rain*
d 31 Or *nourishes*   *e 33* Or *announces his coming— / the One
zealous against evil*

⁶He says to the snow, 'Fall on the earth,'
     and to the rain shower, 'Be a mighty
         downpour.'
⁷So that all men he has made may know his
     work,
     he stops every man from his labor. ᵃ
⁸The animals take cover;
     they remain in their dens.
⁹The tempest comes out from its chamber,
     the cold from the driving winds.
¹⁰The breath of God produces ice,
     and the broad waters become frozen.
¹¹He loads the clouds with moisture;
     he scatters his lightning through them.
¹²At his direction they swirl around
     over the face of the whole earth
     to do whatever he commands them.
¹³He brings the clouds to punish men,
     or to water his earth ᵇ and show his love.

¹⁴"Listen to this, Job;
     stop and consider God's wonders.
¹⁵Do you know how God controls the clouds
     and makes his lightning flash?
¹⁶Do you know how the clouds hang poised,
     those wonders of him who is perfect in
         knowledge?
¹⁷You who swelter in your clothes
     when the land lies hushed under the south
         wind,
¹⁸can you join him in spreading out the skies,
     hard as a mirror of cast bronze?

¹⁹"Tell us what we should say to him;
     we cannot draw up our case because of our
         darkness.
²⁰Should he be told that I want to speak?
     Would any man ask to be swallowed up?
²¹Now no one can look at the sun,
     bright as it is in the skies
     after the wind has swept them clean.
²²Out of the north he comes in golden
         splendor;
     God comes in awesome majesty.
²³The Almighty is beyond our reach and
         exalted in power;

in his justice and great righteousness, he
     does not oppress.
²⁴Therefore, men revere him,
     for does he not have regard for all the wise
         in heart? ᶜ"

The LORD Speaks

38 Then the LORD answered Job out of the
     storm. He said:

²"Who is this that darkens my counsel
     with words without knowledge?
³Brace yourself like a man;
     I will question you,
     and you shall answer me.

⁴"Where were you when I laid the earth's
         foundation?
     Tell me, if you understand.
⁵Who marked off its dimensions? Surely you
         know!
     Who stretched a measuring line across it?
⁶On what were its footings set,
     or who laid its cornerstone—
⁷while the morning stars sang together
     and all the angels ᵈ shouted for joy?

⁸"Who shut up the sea behind doors
     when it burst forth from the womb,
⁹when I made the clouds its garment
     and wrapped it in thick darkness,
¹⁰when I fixed limits for it
     and set its doors and bars in place,
¹¹when I said, 'This far you may come and no
         farther;
     here is where your proud waves halt'?

¹²"Have you ever given orders to the morning,
     or shown the dawn its place,
¹³that it might take the earth by the edges
     and shake the wicked out of it?
¹⁴The earth takes shape like clay under a seal;
     its features stand out like those of a
         garment.

ᵃ 7 Or / he fills all men with fear by his power   ᵇ 13 Or to favor
them   ᶜ 24 Or for he does not have regard for any who think they
are wise.   ᵈ 7 Hebrew the sons of God

THEN THE LORD ANSWERED JOB OUT OF THE STORM. HE SAID: "WHO IS THIS THAT DARKENS MY COUNSEL WITH WORDS WITHOUT KNOWLEDGE?"

Job 38:1 – 2

Words Without Knowledge

GLADYS HUNT

READ | JOB 38:1 – 41

Job's three friends, who thought they had life's mysteries — and even God himself — figured out, spoke long and eloquently in their attempt to comfort suffering Job. They might have gone on even longer, had God not interrupted and told them they didn't know what they were talking about (see Job 42:7).

When God finally addressed Job in chapters 38 – 41, he painted word pictures with such powerful metaphors that easy explanations sounded foolish. God asked, "Where were you when I laid the earth's foundation?" (Job 38:4). "Who shut up the sea behind doors . . . when I said, 'This far you may come and no farther; here is where your proud waves halt?' " (Job 38:8,11). It left Job absolutely speechless.

People still question God's actions. Some say, "My idea of God is . . ." or "I can't believe in a God who . . ." or ask, "Why did God allow that to happen?" Maybe you have said these words yourself. They most often come from people who don't pay much attention to God until something bad happens. Rarely does one ask, "Why does God allow me to be so happy?"

Life is full of mysteries. God welcomes inquiries from humble doubters, but he opposes arrogant people who try to put him in a box. We need God to tell us who he is. If we *could* comprehend God, we would be greater than he is. What we know about God is what he has chosen to reveal to us.

There is a mystery about evil in the world, but the apostle Paul also used the word "mystery" when speaking about our faith — the mystery of "Christ in you, the hope of glory" (Colossians 1:27). It is a mystery that God should love us as he does!

We need to place our "mysteries" in the hand of God and say with Job, "Surely I spoke of things I did not understand, things too wonderful for me to know" (Job 42:3).

. . . .

Great and wonderful God, help me to trust you in all circumstances, even when I can't understand them. Thank you for loving me. Help me to grow in my understanding of your great grace. Amen.

Your next devotion is located on page 697.

GRANDCHILD IN FOCUS • PRAYER

Relationships at Home

O Lord, I pray that you will bless the home and family of my grandchild. May the relationships she has with her parents and siblings enhance her well-being, support her self-confidence and increase her faith. May her home life reflect your love, your grace, your compassion and your peace. Guide her parents to direct her in love and truth, so she will grow into a strong and compassionate individual. Amen.

¹⁵ The wicked are denied their light,
  and their upraised arm is broken.

¹⁶ "Have you journeyed to the springs of the sea
  or walked in the recesses of the deep?
¹⁷ Have the gates of death been shown to you?
  Have you seen the gates of the shadow of
    death ᵃ?
¹⁸ Have you comprehended the vast expanses of
    the earth?
  Tell me, if you know all this.

¹⁹ "What is the way to the abode of light?
  And where does darkness reside?
²⁰ Can you take them to their places?
  Do you know the paths to their dwellings?
²¹ Surely you know, for you were already born!
  You have lived so many years!

²² "Have you entered the storehouses of the
    snow
  or seen the storehouses of the hail,
²³ which I reserve for times of trouble,
  for days of war and battle?
²⁴ What is the way to the place where the
    lightning is dispersed,
  or the place where the east winds are
    scattered over the earth?
²⁵ Who cuts a channel for the torrents of rain,
  and a path for the thunderstorm,
²⁶ to water a land where no man lives,
  a desert with no one in it,
²⁷ to satisfy a desolate wasteland
  and make it sprout with grass?
²⁸ Does the rain have a father?
  Who fathers the drops of dew?
²⁹ From whose womb comes the ice?
  Who gives birth to the frost from the
    heavens
³⁰ when the waters become hard as stone,
  when the surface of the deep is frozen?

³¹ "Can you bind the beautiful ᵇ Pleiades?
  Can you loose the cords of Orion?
³² Can you bring forth the constellations in
    their seasons ᶜ
  or lead out the Bear ᵈ with its cubs?

³³ Do you know the laws of the heavens?
  Can you set up ⌞God's ᵉ⌟ dominion over the
    earth?

³⁴ "Can you raise your voice to the clouds
  and cover yourself with a flood of water?
³⁵ Do you send the lightning bolts on their way?
  Do they report to you, 'Here we are'?
³⁶ Who endowed the heart ᶠ with wisdom
  or gave understanding to the mind ᶠ?
³⁷ Who has the wisdom to count the clouds?
  Who can tip over the water jars of the
    heavens
³⁸ when the dust becomes hard
  and the clods of earth stick together?

³⁹ "Do you hunt the prey for the lioness
  and satisfy the hunger of the lions
⁴⁰ when they crouch in their dens
  or lie in wait in a thicket?
⁴¹ Who provides food for the raven
  when its young cry out to God
  and wander about for lack of food?

39 "Do you know when the mountain
  goats give birth?
  Do you watch when the doe bears her
    fawn?
² Do you count the months till they bear?
  Do you know the time they give birth?
³ They crouch down and bring forth their
    young;
  their labor pains are ended.
⁴ Their young thrive and grow strong in the
    wilds;
  they leave and do not return.

⁵ "Who let the wild donkey go free?
  Who untied his ropes?
⁶ I gave him the wasteland as his home,
  the salt flats as his habitat.
⁷ He laughs at the commotion in the town;
  he does not hear a driver's shout.

ᵃ 17 Or *gates of deep shadows*   ᵇ 31 Or *the twinkling*; or *the chains
of the*   ᶜ 32 Or *the morning star in its season*   ᵈ 32 Or *out Leo*
ᵉ 33 Or *his*; or *their*   ᶠ 36 The meaning of the Hebrew for this
word is uncertain.

LET'S
TALK

Good or Bad?

Here's a fun way to get your grandkids talking about what they value. Start out with easy things to talk about and move on to more difficult concepts later.

Make a list of a lot of words. Write them in large letters on index cards (something like a set of flash cards). Pick words that are neutral (paper, apples, dogs, etc.) and words that are clearly either good or bad (crime, sunshine, the beach, hurricanes, etc.). Depending on the kids' ages, mix up abstract concepts with concrete ones. Throw in a few words that will get everyone talking (dating, divorce, adoption, fighting, etc.). You may or may not want to include some family issues or relevant hot topics.

When the word is announced, you can take turns or make it a free-for-all with everyone saying, "Good" or "Bad." Then take the time to let everyone explain their thoughts. Your older grandkids may find this a great way to discuss their values with you and to explore what you and they think about certain topics.

For the younger kids, use pictures instead of words and just have fun listening to what they have to say.

Dear Lord, thank you for the opportunity to share my ideas and values with my grandchildren. Bless this activity to create a comfortable setting in which I can share my faith in you with these precious children. Amen.

Your next devotion is located on page 698.

GRANDCHILD IN FOCUS • PRAYER

Friends

Dear Lord and Father, I pray for my grandchild's social life and his friends. Bring diverse friends into his life who will love and encourage him, who will bring joy and laughter to the good times and comfort and support through difficulties and disappointments. Grant him wisdom and discernment as he selects his friends; help him to avoid cliques that restrict, activities that endanger, and foolish and dangerous behaviors that harm. I ask that you fill his life with close and caring relationships. Amen.

Worship the Lord

God is our refuge and strength,
    an ever-present help in trouble.
Therefore we will not fear, though the earth give way
    and the mountains fall into the heart of the sea,
though its waters roar and foam
    and the mountains quake with their surging.   *Selah*

There is a river whose streams make glad the city of God,
    the holy place where the Most High dwells.
God is within her, she will not fall;
    God will help her at break of day.
Nations are in uproar, kingdoms fall;
    he lifts his voice, the earth melts.

The LORD Almighty is with us;
the God of Jacob is our fortress.
                                    Selah

Psalm 46:1 – 7

In the stillness, Lord, I praise you, marveling at your presence. Through tsunamis, earthquakes and hurricanes, whether they occur literally in nature or figuratively in my family or in my soul, I will praise you still, and count on you to be my refuge and strength. Amen.

Your next devotion is located on page 701.

GRANDCHILD IN FOCUS • PRAYER

Self-Image

O loving God, I praise you for creating my grandchild as a unique individual. Now I ask you to help her appreciate her uniqueness. Build up her self-image so she can enjoy her individuality. Help her to stand firm for who she is, where she has come from and what she believes in. Encourage her not only to have hopes and dreams but to also enjoy each day as it comes.
In Jesus' name, amen.

8 He ranges the hills for his pasture
  and searches for any green thing.

9 "Will the wild ox consent to serve you?
  Will he stay by your manger at night?
10 Can you hold him to the furrow with a
    harness?
  Will he till the valleys behind you?
11 Will you rely on him for his great strength?
  Will you leave your heavy work to him?
12 Can you trust him to bring in your grain
  and gather it to your threshing floor?

13 "The wings of the ostrich flap joyfully,
  but they cannot compare with the pinions
    and feathers of the stork.
14 She lays her eggs on the ground
  and lets them warm in the sand,
15 unmindful that a foot may crush them,
  that some wild animal may trample them.
16 She treats her young harshly, as if they were
    not hers;
  she cares not that her labor was in vain,
17 for God did not endow her with wisdom
  or give her a share of good sense.
18 Yet when she spreads her feathers to run,
  she laughs at horse and rider.

19 "Do you give the horse his strength
  or clothe his neck with a flowing mane?
20 Do you make him leap like a locust,
  striking terror with his proud snorting?
21 He paws fiercely, rejoicing in his strength,
  and charges into the fray.
22 He laughs at fear, afraid of nothing;
  he does not shy away from the sword.
23 The quiver rattles against his side,
  along with the flashing spear and lance.
24 In frenzied excitement he eats up the ground;
  he cannot stand still when the trumpet
    sounds.
25 At the blast of the trumpet he snorts, 'Aha!'
  He catches the scent of battle from afar,
  the shout of commanders and the battle cry.

26 "Does the hawk take flight by your wisdom
  and spread his wings toward the south?

27 Does the eagle soar at your command
  and build his nest on high?
28 He dwells on a cliff and stays there at night;
  a rocky crag is his stronghold.
29 From there he seeks out his food;
  his eyes detect it from afar.
30 His young ones feast on blood,
  and where the slain are, there is he."

40 The LORD said to Job:

2 "Will the one who contends with the
    Almighty correct him?
  Let him who accuses God answer him!"

3 Then Job answered the LORD:

4 "I am unworthy—how can I reply to you?
  I put my hand over my mouth.
5 I spoke once, but I have no answer—
  twice, but I will say no more."

6 Then the LORD spoke to Job out of the storm:

7 "Brace yourself like a man;
  I will question you,
  and you shall answer me.

8 "Would you discredit my justice?
  Would you condemn me to justify
    yourself?
9 Do you have an arm like God's,
  and can your voice thunder like his?
10 Then adorn yourself with glory and splendor,
  and clothe yourself in honor and majesty.
11 Unleash the fury of your wrath,
  look at every proud man and bring him low,
12 look at every proud man and humble him,
  crush the wicked where they stand.
13 Bury them all in the dust together;
  shroud their faces in the grave.
14 Then I myself will admit to you
  that your own right hand can save you.

15 "Look at the behemoth,[a]
  which I made along with you
  and which feeds on grass like an ox.

_____
a 15 Possibly the hippopotamus or the elephant

¹⁶What strength he has in his loins,
    what power in the muscles of his belly!
¹⁷His tail*ᵃ* sways like a cedar;
    the sinews of his thighs are close-knit.
¹⁸His bones are tubes of bronze,
    his limbs like rods of iron.
¹⁹He ranks first among the works of God,
    yet his Maker can approach him with his
        sword.
²⁰The hills bring him their produce,
    and all the wild animals play nearby.
²¹Under the lotus plants he lies,
    hidden among the reeds in the marsh.
²²The lotuses conceal him in their shadow;
    the poplars by the stream surround him.
²³When the river rages, he is not alarmed;
    he is secure, though the Jordan should
        surge against his mouth.
²⁴Can anyone capture him by the eyes,*ᵇ*
    or trap him and pierce his nose?

41 "Can you pull in the leviathan*ᶜ* with a
       fishhook
    or tie down his tongue with a rope?
²Can you put a cord through his nose
    or pierce his jaw with a hook?
³Will he keep begging you for mercy?
    Will he speak to you with gentle words?
⁴Will he make an agreement with you
    for you to take him as your slave for life?
⁵Can you make a pet of him like a bird
    or put him on a leash for your girls?
⁶Will traders barter for him?
    Will they divide him up among the
        merchants?
⁷Can you fill his hide with harpoons
    or his head with fishing spears?
⁸If you lay a hand on him,
    you will remember the struggle and never
        do it again!
⁹Any hope of subduing him is false;
    the mere sight of him is overpowering.
¹⁰No one is fierce enough to rouse him.
    Who then is able to stand against me?
¹¹Who has a claim against me that I must pay?
    Everything under heaven belongs to me.

¹²"I will not fail to speak of his limbs,
    his strength and his graceful form.
¹³Who can strip off his outer coat?
    Who would approach him with a bridle?
¹⁴Who dares open the doors of his mouth,
    ringed about with his fearsome teeth?
¹⁵His back has*ᵈ* rows of shields
    tightly sealed together;
¹⁶each is so close to the next
    that no air can pass between.
¹⁷They are joined fast to one another;
    they cling together and cannot be parted.
¹⁸His snorting throws out flashes of light;
    his eyes are like the rays of dawn.
¹⁹Firebrands stream from his mouth;
    sparks of fire shoot out.
²⁰Smoke pours from his nostrils
    as from a boiling pot over a fire of reeds.
²¹His breath sets coals ablaze,
    and flames dart from his mouth.
²²Strength resides in his neck;
    dismay goes before him.
²³The folds of his flesh are tightly joined;
    they are firm and immovable.
²⁴His chest is hard as rock,
    hard as a lower millstone.
²⁵When he rises up, the mighty are terrified;
    they retreat before his thrashing.
²⁶The sword that reaches him has no effect,
    nor does the spear or the dart or the
        javelin.
²⁷Iron he treats like straw
    and bronze like rotten wood.
²⁸Arrows do not make him flee;
    slingstones are like chaff to him.
²⁹A club seems to him but a piece of straw;
    he laughs at the rattling of the lance.
³⁰His undersides are jagged potsherds,
    leaving a trail in the mud like a threshing
        sledge.
³¹He makes the depths churn like a boiling
       caldron
    and stirs up the sea like a pot of ointment.

ᵃ 17 Possibly trunk   *ᵇ 24* Or *by a water hole*   *ᶜ 1* Possibly the crocodile   *ᵈ 15* Or *His pride is his*

THE LORD BLESSED THE
LATTER PART OF JOB'S LIFE
MORE THAN THE FIRST.

Job 42:12

New Beginnings

BARBARA JOHNSON

READ | JOB 42:7 – 17

Each one of us needs a new beginning at some point or other. But it needn't come with a bang of fireworks or a streaking comet. New beginnings often come slowly. They may even sneak up on you — like a tiny ray of sun slipping out from beneath a black cloud. You can be inspired by the smallest things, so keep your eyes open.

Consider these: A tea kettle singing on the stove inspired the steam engine. An apple falling from a tree inspired the discovery of gravity. A shirt waving on a clothesline inspired the balloon. A spider web strung across a garden path inspired the suspension bridge. God will use the simplest realities to inspire something bigger and better in your life.

NBC news anchor John Chancellor once quipped, "You want to make God laugh, tell him your plans." God has much greater ambitions for us than we have for ourselves. He laughs at our paltry plans, then plots to surprise us with the greatness of his grace. Author C. S. Lewis referred to God's extravagant nature when he said, "You thought you were being made into a decent little cottage? God wants to make of your life a palace!" Of course, we have to learn to live with the rain and the fog while we're waiting for our skies to clear up and God's glory to be revealed. But rest your hope upon the grace that will crown your life when Jesus' plan unfolds. With the touch of a button he will draw you under the protection of his umbrella where you can enjoy sunny skies forever.

O Lord of the future, give me hope in your promise that you have bigger and better things in mind for me than I can begin to imagine. Give me strength as I wait for your plans to unfold in my life. Amen.

Your next devotion is located on page 705.

GRANDCHILD IN FOCUS • PRAYER

Protection From Worldliness

O Sovereign Lord, the world surrounds my grandchild, pressing in and tempting him in so many ways. Help him set appropriate limits. Give him sound judgment to choose wisely. Guard him from temptation; protect him from physical and mental predators; lead him into paths of righteousness and light. And reassure me with your promise that you are holding him in your hands. Amen.

32 Behind him he leaves a glistening wake;
　　one would think the deep had white hair.
33 Nothing on earth is his equal —
　　a creature without fear.
34 He looks down on all that are haughty;
　　he is king over all that are proud.”

Job

42

Then Job replied to the LORD:

2 “I know that you can do all things;
　　no plan of yours can be thwarted.
3 ˌYou asked,ˌ ‘Who is this that obscures my
　　　　counsel without knowledge?’
　Surely I spoke of things I did not
　　　understand,
　　things too wonderful for me to know.

4 ˌ“You said,ˌ ‘Listen now, and I will speak;
　　I will question you,
　　and you shall answer me.’
5 My ears had heard of you
　　but now my eyes have seen you.
6 Therefore I despise myself
　　and repent in dust and ashes.”

Epilogue

7 After the LORD had said these things to Job, he said to Eliphaz the Temanite, “I am angry with you and your two friends, because you have not spoken of me what is right, as my servant Job has. 8 So now take seven bulls and seven rams and go to my servant Job and sacrifice a burnt offering for yourselves. My servant Job will pray for you, and I will accept his prayer and not deal with you according to your folly. You have not spoken of me what is right, as my servant Job has.” 9 So Eliphaz the Temanite, Bildad the Shuhite and Zophar the Naamathite did what the LORD told them; and the LORD accepted Job’s prayer.

10 After Job had prayed for his friends, the LORD made him prosperous again and gave him twice as much as he had before. 11 All his brothers and sisters and everyone who had known him before came and ate with him in his house. They comforted and consoled him over all the trouble the LORD had brought upon him, and each one gave him a piece of silver *a* and a gold ring.

12 The LORD blessed the latter part of Job’s life more than the first. He had fourteen thousand sheep, six thousand camels, a thousand yoke of oxen and a thousand donkeys. 13 And he also had seven sons and three daughters. 14 The first daughter he named Jemimah, the second Keziah and the third Keren-Happuch. 15 Nowhere in all the land were there found women as beautiful as Job’s daughters, and their father granted them an inheritance along with their brothers.

16 After this, Job lived a hundred and forty years; he saw his children and their children to the fourth generation. 17 And so he died, old and full of years.

a 11 Hebrew *him a kesitah*; a kesitah was a unit of money of unknown weight and value.

Poems
FOR EVERY EMOTION

The book of Psalms is perhaps one of the best-loved and most often used books of the Bible. It is a marvelous collection of poems and songs that can easily be read and shared. Some psalms are songs of praise, thanksgiving and adoration; others are laments, cries for help or petitions for mercy or justice.

What is outstanding about the psalms is that God encourages us to communicate with him through our wide range of human emotions. He wants us to interact with him and share our lives. He wants us to speak to him in praise and worship, to cry to him in despair, to question him, to share our hurts, our anger, our disappointments. Through all these emotions God is there. He will listen. We can approach him with confidence. We can use the psalms to communicate with him through every situation of life; it's all covered. But above all, the psalms help us to shout for joy and sing to God our creator, for his love endures forever!

VERSE *to* REMEMBER | PSALM 57:9 – 10

I will praise you, O Lord, among the nations; I will sing of you among the peoples. For great is your love, reaching to the heavens; your faithfulness reaches to the skies.

ABOUT PSALMS

WRITTEN BY:
Primarily David, but a number of other people as well

WRITTEN FOR:
God's people

DATE WRITTEN:
Between the time of Moses (around 1440 B.C.) and the time following the Babylonian captivity (after 538 B.C.)

WHY WRITTEN:
To instruct God's people in how to talk to him and worship him

BOOK I

Psalms 1–41

Psalm 1

¹Blessed is the man
who does not walk in the counsel of the
wicked
or stand in the way of sinners
or sit in the seat of mockers.
²But his delight is in the law of the LORD,
and on his law he meditates day and night.

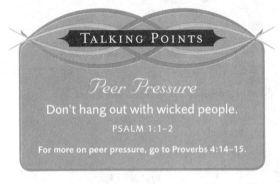

TALKING POINTS

Peer Pressure

Don't hang out with wicked people.

PSALM 1:1-2

For more on peer pressure, go to Proverbs 4:14–15.

³He is like a tree planted by streams of water,
which yields its fruit in season
and whose leaf does not wither.
Whatever he does prospers.

⁴Not so the wicked!
They are like chaff
that the wind blows away.
⁵Therefore the wicked will not stand in the
judgment,
nor sinners in the assembly of the
righteous.

⁶For the LORD watches over the way of the
righteous,
but the way of the wicked will perish.

Psalm 2

¹Why do the nations conspire[a]
and the peoples plot in vain?
²The kings of the earth take their stand
and the rulers gather together
against the LORD
and against his Anointed One.[b]
³"Let us break their chains," they say,
"and throw off their fetters."

⁴The One enthroned in heaven laughs;
the Lord scoffs at them.
⁵Then he rebukes them in his anger
and terrifies them in his wrath, saying,
⁶"I have installed my King[c]
on Zion, my holy hill."

⁷I will proclaim the decree of the LORD:

He said to me, "You are my Son[d];
today I have become your Father.[e]
⁸Ask of me,
and I will make the nations your
inheritance,
the ends of the earth your possession.
⁹You will rule them with an iron scepter[f];
you will dash them to pieces like
pottery."

¹⁰Therefore, you kings, be wise;
be warned, you rulers of the earth.
¹¹Serve the LORD with fear
and rejoice with trembling.
¹²Kiss the Son, lest he be angry
and you be destroyed in your way,
for his wrath can flare up in a moment.
Blessed are all who take refuge in him.

Psalm 3

*A psalm of David. When he fled
from his son Absalom.*

¹O LORD, how many are my foes!
How many rise up against me!
²Many are saying of me,
"God will not deliver him."   *Selah*[g]

---

[a] *1* Hebrew; Septuagint *rage*   [b] *2* Or *anointed one*   [c] *6* Or *king*
[d] *7* Or *son; also in verse 12*   [e] *7* Or *have begotten you*   [f] *9* Or
will break them with a rod of iron   [g] *2* A word of uncertain
meaning, occurring frequently in the Psalms; possibly a musical
term

> HE IS LIKE A TREE PLANTED
> BY STREAMS OF WATER, WHICH
> YIELDS ITS FRUIT IN SEASON AND
> WHOSE LEAF DOES NOT WITHER.
> WHATEVER HE DOES PROSPERS.
>
> *Psalm 1:3*

Growing Old Is Not for Wimps

DAWN SCOTT JONES

READ | PSALM 1:1 – 6

As I look in the mirror these days, I can't help but notice things are not as they used to be. My face has lines and creases that were not there before. (I refuse to call them wrinkles!) I have puckers and pouches that appear out of nowhere. However, while everything else is succumbing to gravity, I have been consoled by the fact that my eyelashes are thriving. They have been growing so well that they are sweeping the top of my eyelids. This was an exciting development until another discovery crushed my joy. "Dawn," I moaned to myself as I looked in the mirror, "your eyelashes aren't touching your brow because they're growing; your eyelids are sagging!"

What can I say? Growing old is not for wimps. God has promised, however, that in every season of life we can continue to be fruitful if we follow his antiaging prescription. Psalm 1 says if we delight ourselves in God and meditate on his Word, we will be like a tree planted by the water.

This word picture evokes a powerful image as we envision what that tree looks like. Age does not diminish it but instead increases its value. Its branches are strong and do not waver; its leaves are lush and offer shade; its fruit is plentiful and timely.

No matter our age, our lives — like this tree — will remain fruitful and meaningful when our roots stay planted in the Lord, the living water. We will bear fruit in every season of life, our leaf will not wither or fall away, and we will prosper in all our endeavors.

Ageless Father, you alone are the giver and sustainer of life. May my roots be firmly planted in you and your life-giving Word as I am daily renewed. I trust that as I remain planted in you, my life — body, soul and spirit — will be fruitful and prosperous. In Jesus' name, amen.

Your next devotion is located on page 709.

GRANDCHILD IN FOCUS • PRAYER

Respect for Authority

Dear Lord, I pray that my grandchild will continually grow to respect those in authority. May she learn to be cooperative and fair in work and play. Instill in her a high regard for officials who govern our land and enforce the laws. May her relationships with parents, teachers, coaches, mentors and bosses be respectful, admirable, constructive and caring. Amen.

³ But you are a shield around me, O LORD;
    you bestow glory on me and lift ᵃ up my
    head.
⁴ To the LORD I cry aloud,
    and he answers me from his holy hill. *Selah*

⁵ I lie down and sleep;
    I wake again, because the LORD sustains
    me.
⁶ I will not fear the tens of thousands
    drawn up against me on every side.

⁷ Arise, O LORD!
    Deliver me, O my God!
  Strike all my enemies on the jaw;
    break the teeth of the wicked.

⁸ From the LORD comes deliverance.
    May your blessing be on your people.
                    Selah

Psalm 4

*For the director of music. With stringed
instruments. A psalm of David.*

¹ Answer me when I call to you,
    O my righteous God.
  Give me relief from my distress;
    be merciful to me and hear my prayer.

² How long, O men, will you turn my glory
    into shame ᵇ?
  How long will you love delusions and
    seek false gods ᶜ?   *Selah*
³ Know that the LORD has set apart the godly
    for himself;
  the LORD will hear when I call to him.

⁴ In your anger do not sin;
    when you are on your beds,
    search your hearts and be silent.   *Selah*
⁵ Offer right sacrifices
    and trust in the LORD.

⁶ Many are asking, "Who can show us any
    good?"
  Let the light of your face shine upon us,
    O LORD.

TALKING POINTS

Anger

**Examine your heart when
you are angry.**

PSALM 4:4

For more on anger, go to Proverbs 29:11.

⁷ You have filled my heart with greater joy
    than when their grain and new wine
    abound.
⁸ I will lie down and sleep in peace,
    for you alone, O LORD,
    make me dwell in safety.

PRAYING THE SCRIPTURES

Protection

PSALM 4:6,8

Let the light of your face shine upon my
grandchild, O Lord. Let him lie down and
sleep in peace, for you alone make him dwell
in safety.

Next prayer in Protection Prayer Track: Psalm 5:11–12

Psalm 5

*For the director of music. For flutes.
A psalm of David.*

¹ Give ear to my words, O LORD,
    consider my sighing.
² Listen to my cry for help,
    my King and my God,
    for to you I pray.

ᵃ 3 Or LORD, / *my Glorious One, who lifts*   ᵇ 2 Or *you dishonor my*
Glorious One   ᶜ 2 Or *seek lies*

³In the morning, O Lᴏʀᴅ, you hear my voice;
in the morning I lay my requests before
you
and wait in expectation.

⁴You are not a God who takes pleasure in evil;
with you the wicked cannot dwell.
⁵The arrogant cannot stand in your presence;
you hate all who do wrong.
⁶You destroy those who tell lies;
bloodthirsty and deceitful men
the Lᴏʀᴅ abhors.

⁷But I, by your great mercy,
will come into your house;
in reverence will I bow down
toward your holy temple.
⁸Lead me, O Lᴏʀᴅ, in your righteousness
because of my enemies—
make straight your way before me.

⁹Not a word from their mouth can be
trusted;
their heart is filled with destruction.
Their throat is an open grave;
with their tongue they speak deceit.
¹⁰Declare them guilty, O God!
Let their intrigues be their downfall.
Banish them for their many sins,
for they have rebelled against you.

¹¹But let all who take refuge in you be glad;
let them ever sing for joy.
Spread your protection over them,
that those who love your name may rejoice
in you.
¹²For surely, O Lᴏʀᴅ, you bless the righteous;
you surround them with your favor as with
a shield.

Psalm 6

For the director of music. With stringed
instruments. According to *sheminith.* ᵃ
A psalm of David.

¹O Lᴏʀᴅ, do not rebuke me in your anger
or discipline me in your wrath.

PRAYING THE SCRIPTURES

Protection

PSALM 5:11–12

O God, let my grandchild, who takes refuge in you, be glad; let her ever sing for joy. Spread your protection over her, that she who loves your name may rejoice in you. For surely, O Lord, you bless the righteous; you surround them with your favor as with a shield.

**Next prayer in Protection Prayer Track:
Psalm 91:11–12,16**

²Be merciful to me, Lᴏʀᴅ, for I am faint;
O Lᴏʀᴅ, heal me, for my bones are in
agony.
³My soul is in anguish.
How long, O Lᴏʀᴅ, how long?

⁴Turn, O Lᴏʀᴅ, and deliver me;
save me because of your unfailing love.
⁵No one remembers you when he is dead.
Who praises you from the grave ᵇ?

⁶I am worn out from groaning;
all night long I flood my bed with weeping
and drench my couch with tears.

ᵃ Title: Probably a musical term   ᵇ 5 Hebrew *Sheol*

PRAYING THE SCRIPTURES

Well-Being

PSALM 6:2

Be merciful to my grandchild, Lord, for she is faint; O Lord, heal her, for her bones are in agony.

Next prayer in Well-being Prayer Track: Proverbs 3:7–8

⁷ My eyes grow weak with sorrow;
    they fail because of all my foes.

⁸ Away from me, all you who do evil,
    for the LORD has heard my weeping.
⁹ The LORD has heard my cry for mercy;
    the LORD accepts my prayer.
¹⁰ All my enemies will be ashamed and
      dismayed;
    they will turn back in sudden disgrace.

Psalm 7

*A shiggaion ᵃ of David, which he sang to the LORD
concerning Cush, a Benjamite.*

¹ O LORD my God, I take refuge in you;
    save and deliver me from all who pursue
      me,
² or they will tear me like a lion
    and rip me to pieces with no one to rescue
      me.

³ O LORD my God, if I have done this
    and there is guilt on my hands—
⁴ if I have done evil to him who is at peace
      with me
    or without cause have robbed my foe—
⁵ then let my enemy pursue and overtake me;
    let him trample my life to the ground
    and make me sleep in the dust.   *Selah*

⁶ Arise, O LORD, in your anger;
    rise up against the rage of my enemies.
    Awake, my God; decree justice.
⁷ Let the assembled peoples gather around you.
    Rule over them from on high;
⁸   let the LORD judge the peoples.
  Judge me, O LORD, according to my
      righteousness,
    according to my integrity, O Most High.
⁹ O righteous God,
    who searches minds and hearts,
  bring to an end the violence of the wicked
    and make the righteous secure.

¹⁰ My shield ᵇ is God Most High,
    who saves the upright in heart.

¹¹ God is a righteous judge,
    a God who expresses his wrath every day.
¹² If he does not relent,
    he ᶜ will sharpen his sword;
    he will bend and string his bow.
¹³ He has prepared his deadly weapons;
    he makes ready his flaming arrows.

¹⁴ He who is pregnant with evil
    and conceives trouble gives birth to
      disillusionment.
¹⁵ He who digs a hole and scoops it out
    falls into the pit he has made.
¹⁶ The trouble he causes recoils on himself;
    his violence comes down on his own head.

¹⁷ I will give thanks to the LORD because of his
      righteousness
    and will sing praise to the name of the
      LORD Most High.

Psalm 8

*For the director of music. According
to gittith. ᵈ A psalm of David.*

¹ O LORD, our Lord,
    how majestic is your name in all the earth!

  You have set your glory
    above the heavens.
² From the lips of children and infants
    you have ordained praise ᵉ
  because of your enemies,
    to silence the foe and the avenger.

³ When I consider your heavens,
    the work of your fingers,
  the moon and the stars,
    which you have set in place,
⁴ what is man that you are mindful of him,
    the son of man that you care for him?
⁵ You made him a little lower than the heavenly
      beings ᶠ
    and crowned him with glory and honor.

ᵃ Title: Probably a literary or musical term   ᵇ *10 Or sovereign*
ᶜ *12 Or If a man does not repent, / God*   ᵈ Title: Probably a musical
term   ᵉ *2 Or strength*   ᶠ *5 Or than God*

FROM THE LIPS OF CHILDREN AND INFANTS YOU HAVE ORDAINED PRAISE BECAUSE OF YOUR ENEMIES, TO SILENCE THE FOE AND THE AVENGER.

Psalm 8:2

Not Satan's Working Conditions

NETA JACKSON

READ | PSALM 8:1 – 9

Walking my grandson to preschool, which I do about once a week, is a far different experience than my "exercise walks." The first time we started out, I thought it would take us 15 minutes, even considering shorter legs. Uh-uh. Double that.

A five-year-old is delighted by all he sees. He carefully picks dandelion bouquets for his teacher, for his mom, for me. He examines the stem of one and wonders, "Why did God make that gooey white stuff inside?" (I'd never noticed dandelion stems had gooey white stuff inside. Imagine that.) We pause to admire purple tulips, knots in tree trunks, ants building anthills in sidewalk cracks.

The world is a wonder to a child, and he has no trouble at all assigning all the credit to God's handiwork.

So that's how I first read Psalm 8, praising God with childlike wonder for his awesome creation, especially the vast expanse of a nighttime sky, with its moon and stars and galaxies far, far away. But recently, verse two startled me: the praise of children silences the enemy. Wow! That's some pretty powerful praise! But if the praise of children and infants can silence the enemy, then my praise, too, is important spiritual warfare.

The more I meditate on this Scripture, the more it makes sense. Satan's work thrives in an atmosphere of doubt, worry, distraction, busyness and discouragement. But praise? Praise to the living God is not Satan's working condition. If I want to build a stronghold of protection against that old devil, I need to fill my heart, my thoughts and my home with praise!

Creator God, your wonderful works surround me — in nature, in my life, in the world at large — in spite of horrific world events that confirm Satan is bent on disruption and destruction. But, O God, let my praise to you be a shield and a defense. Amen.

Your next devotion is located on page 711.

GRANDCHILD IN FOCUS • PRAYER

Courage

O Father, builder of character and courage, may my grandchild grow strong in the light of your love. Grant him courage to stand for what is right, to guard the truth and to ensure justice in every aspect of life. May he boldly grow in grace, revere your name and proudly proclaim you as the Lord of lords and King of kings. Amen.

⁶You made him ruler over the works of your
hands;
you put everything under his feet:
⁷all flocks and herds,
and the beasts of the field,
⁸the birds of the air,
and the fish of the sea,
all that swim the paths of the seas.

⁹O Lᴏʀᴅ, our Lord,
how majestic is your name in all the earth!

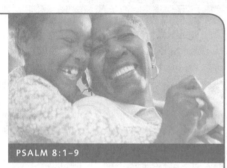

PSALM 8:1–9

The Majesty of God

LIFE LESSON: Our God is mighty and
majestic.

TO TALK ABOUT

✦ Who should praise God?

✦ What do people rule over?

✦ Why is our God so majestic?

✦ In what position has God placed
humans? Why?

Psalm 9 ᵃ

For the director of music. To the tune of
"The Death of the Son." A psalm
of David.

¹I will praise you, O Lᴏʀᴅ, with all my heart;
I will tell of all your wonders.
²I will be glad and rejoice in you;
I will sing praise to your name, O Most
High.

³My enemies turn back;
they stumble and perish before you.
⁴For you have upheld my right and my cause;
you have sat on your throne, judging
righteously.
⁵You have rebuked the nations and destroyed
the wicked;
you have blotted out their name for ever
and ever.
⁶Endless ruin has overtaken the enemy,
you have uprooted their cities;
even the memory of them has perished.

⁷The Lᴏʀᴅ reigns forever;
he has established his throne for judgment.
⁸He will judge the world in righteousness;
he will govern the peoples with justice.
⁹The Lᴏʀᴅ is a refuge for the oppressed,
a stronghold in times of trouble.
¹⁰Those who know your name will trust
in you,
for you, Lᴏʀᴅ, have never forsaken those
who seek you.

¹¹Sing praises to the Lᴏʀᴅ, enthroned in Zion;
proclaim among the nations what he has
done.
¹²For he who avenges blood remembers;
he does not ignore the cry of the afflicted.

¹³O Lᴏʀᴅ, see how my enemies persecute me!
Have mercy and lift me up from the gates
of death,
¹⁴that I may declare your praises
in the gates of the Daughter of Zion
and there rejoice in your salvation.
¹⁵The nations have fallen into the pit they have
dug;
their feet are caught in the net they have
hidden.
¹⁶The Lᴏʀᴅ is known by his justice;
the wicked are ensnared by the work
of their hands.   *Higgaion.* ᵇ *Selah*

ᵃ Psalms 9 and 10 may have been originally a single acrostic
poem, the stanzas of which begin with the successive letters of the
Hebrew alphabet. In the Septuagint they constitute one psalm.
ᵇ 16 Or *Meditation;* possibly a musical notation

I WILL PRAISE YOU, O LORD, WITH ALL MY HEART; I WILL TELL OF ALL YOUR WONDERS. I WILL BE GLAD AND REJOICE IN YOU; I WILL SING PRAISE TO YOUR NAME, O MOST HIGH.

Psalm 9:1 – 2

I Will... I Will...

BOBBIE WOLGEMUTH

READ | PSALM 9:1 – 20

Psalm 9 contains a great "I Will" activity list to remember when you spend time with your grandchild.

First, start with an attitude of praise. Tell the Lord what you are thankful for. Count your blessings; name them. It will be easy to have a heart full of thankfulness after you've named even a few. Your heart will be full and running over with the kind of attitude that pleases God and spills over on the young ones with the love of the Savior.

Second, tell the kids what God has done in the past. One of our greatest resources as grandmothers is the history we have lived. Tell your grandchild about the time his mother was a little girl and was sick or lost in the department store or scared to go to school and the way God provided a solution to the problem. Everyday miracles fill our memory banks. Pull a few past marvels out of your memory treasure chest and tell your grandchild of the Lord's wonders.

Third, be a happy grandmother. Open the door with a smile and a hug. Let your face show the gladness of the Lord. Your inside joy should envelop your grandchildren with every encounter, no matter where you are. They should want to be around you just because they feel your love. Remember to smile and laugh often with them.

The fourth "I will" is my favorite: sing. Sing with your grandchildren. Teach them the words of a hymn. They hear and remember rhyming lines so quickly that in no time they can memorize inspired verses. Leave a song in their hearts. It will bring them truth and comfort and peace for a lifetime.

Lord Jesus, I want to be the kind of grandmother who encourages others. Help me today to do your will by remembering the four "I Will" statements in Psalm 9. I want to praise, tell, rejoice and sing. Amen.

Your next devotion is located on page 722.

GRANDCHILD IN FOCUS • PRAYER

Future Spouse

Dear Lord, if it is your will, I pray my grandchild will be united in a loving and Christian marriage. Keep her sexually pure so that she will honor you with her body and mind. As she seeks a spouse who will honor and care for her, give her patience and discernment. May her choice for a life partner be your choice for her, so that she and her husband will together glorify you in a lasting love. I pray this in Jesus' name, amen.

¹⁷ The wicked return to the grave,ᵃ
  all the nations that forget God.
¹⁸ But the needy will not always be forgotten,
  nor the hope of the afflicted ever perish.

¹⁹ Arise, O Lᴏʀᴅ, let not man triumph;
  let the nations be judged in your presence.
²⁰ Strike them with terror, O Lᴏʀᴅ;
  let the nations know they are but men.

Selah

Psalm 10ᵇ

¹ Why, O Lᴏʀᴅ, do you stand far off?
  Why do you hide yourself in times of
    trouble?

² In his arrogance the wicked man hunts down
    the weak,
  who are caught in the schemes he devises.
³ He boasts of the cravings of his heart;
  he blesses the greedy and reviles the Lᴏʀᴅ.
⁴ In his pride the wicked does not seek him;
  in all his thoughts there is no room for
    God.
⁵ His ways are always prosperous;
  he is haughty and your laws are far from
    him;
  he sneers at all his enemies.
⁶ He says to himself, "Nothing will shake me;
  I'll always be happy and never have
    trouble."
⁷ His mouth is full of curses and lies and
    threats;
  trouble and evil are under his tongue.
⁸ He lies in wait near the villages;
  from ambush he murders the innocent,
  watching in secret for his victims.
⁹ He lies in wait like a lion in cover;
  he lies in wait to catch the helpless;
  he catches the helpless and drags them off
    in his net.
¹⁰ His victims are crushed, they collapse;
  they fall under his strength.
¹¹ He says to himself, "God has forgotten;
  he covers his face and never sees."

¹² Arise, Lᴏʀᴅ! Lift up your hand, O God.
  Do not forget the helpless.
¹³ Why does the wicked man revile God?
  Why does he say to himself,
  "He won't call me to account"?
¹⁴ But you, O God, do see trouble and grief;
  you consider it to take it in hand.
  The victim commits himself to you;
  you are the helper of the fatherless.

TALKING POINTS

Adoption

God helps the fatherless.

PSALM 10:14

For more on adoption, go to Psalm 27:10.

¹⁵ Break the arm of the wicked and evil man;
  call him to account for his wickedness
  that would not be found out.

¹⁶ The Lᴏʀᴅ is King for ever and ever;
  the nations will perish from his land.
¹⁷ You hear, O Lᴏʀᴅ, the desire of the afflicted;
  you encourage them, and you listen to
    their cry,
¹⁸ defending the fatherless and the oppressed,
  in order that man, who is of the earth, may
    terrify no more.

Psalm 11

For the director of music. Of David.

¹ In the Lᴏʀᴅ I take refuge.
  How then can you say to me:
  "Flee like a bird to your mountain.
² For look, the wicked bend their bows;
  they set their arrows against the strings

ᵃ 17 Hebrew *Sheol*   ᵇ Psalms 9 and 10 may have been originally a
single acrostic poem, the stanzas of which begin with the successive
letters of the Hebrew alphabet. In the Septuagint they constitute one
psalm.

to shoot from the shadows
　　at the upright in heart.
³When the foundations are being destroyed,
　　what can the righteous do *ª*?"

⁴The LORD is in his holy temple;
　　the LORD is on his heavenly throne.
He observes the sons of men;
　　his eyes examine them.
⁵The LORD examines the righteous,
　　but the wicked *ᵇ* and those who love
　　　　violence
　　his soul hates.
⁶On the wicked he will rain
　　fiery coals and burning sulfur;
　　a scorching wind will be their lot.

⁷For the LORD is righteous,
　　he loves justice;
　　upright men will see his face.

Psalm 12

For the director of music. According to
sheminith. *ᶜ* A psalm of David.

¹Help, LORD, for the godly are no more;
　　the faithful have vanished from among
　　　　men.
²Everyone lies to his neighbor;
　　their flattering lips speak with deception.

³May the LORD cut off all flattering lips
　　and every boastful tongue
⁴that says, "We will triumph with our tongues;
　　we own our lips *ᵈ*—who is our master?"

⁵"Because of the oppression of the weak
　　and the groaning of the needy,
I will now arise," says the LORD.
　　"I will protect them from those who
　　　　malign them."
⁶And the words of the LORD are flawless,
　　like silver refined in a furnace of clay,
　　purified seven times.

⁷O LORD, you will keep us safe
　　and protect us from such people forever.

⁸The wicked freely strut about
　　when what is vile is honored among men.

Psalm 13

For the director of music. A psalm of David.

¹How long, O LORD? Will you forget me
　　　　forever?
　　How long will you hide your face from
　　　　me?
²How long must I wrestle with my thoughts
　　and every day have sorrow in my heart?
　　How long will my enemy triumph over
　　　　me?

³Look on me and answer, O LORD my God.
　　Give light to my eyes, or I will sleep in
　　　　death;
⁴my enemy will say, "I have overcome him,"
　　and my foes will rejoice when I fall.

⁵But I trust in your unfailing love;
　　my heart rejoices in your salvation.
⁶I will sing to the LORD,
　　for he has been good to me.

Psalm 14

14:1–7pp — Ps 53:1–6
For the director of music. Of David.

¹The fool *ᵉ* says in his heart,
　　"There is no God."
They are corrupt, their deeds are vile;
　　there is no one who does good.

²The LORD looks down from heaven
　　on the sons of men
to see if there are any who understand,
　　any who seek God.
³All have turned aside,
　　they have together become corrupt;
there is no one who does good,
　　not even one.

ª 3 Or what is the Righteous One doing 　*ᵇ 5 Or The LORD, the
Righteous One, examines the wicked, / 　ᶜ Title: Probably a musical
term 　ᵈ 4 Or / our lips are our plowshares 　ᵉ 1 The Hebrew
words rendered fool in Psalms denote one who is morally deficient.*

⁴Will evildoers never learn —
  those who devour my people as men eat
    bread
  and who do not call on the LORD?
⁵There they are, overwhelmed with dread,
  for God is present in the company of the
    righteous.
⁶You evildoers frustrate the plans of the poor,
  but the LORD is their refuge.

⁷Oh, that salvation for Israel would come out
    of Zion!
  When the LORD restores the fortunes of his
    people,
  let Jacob rejoice and Israel be glad!

Psalm 15

A psalm of David.

¹LORD, who may dwell in your sanctuary?
  Who may live on your holy hill?

²He whose walk is blameless
  and who does what is righteous,
who speaks the truth from his heart
³   and has no slander on his tongue,
who does his neighbor no wrong
  and casts no slur on his fellowman,
⁴who despises a vile man
  but honors those who fear the LORD,
who keeps his oath
  even when it hurts,
⁵who lends his money without usury
  and does not accept a bribe against the
    innocent.

He who does these things
  will never be shaken.

Psalm 16

A *miktam*ᵃ of David.

¹Keep me safe, O God,
  for in you I take refuge.

²I said to the LORD, "You are my Lord;
  apart from you I have no good thing."

³As for the saints who are in the land,
  they are the glorious ones in whom is all
    my delight.ᵇ
⁴The sorrows of those will increase
  who run after other gods.
I will not pour out their libations of blood
  or take up their names on my lips.

⁵LORD, you have assigned me my portion and
    my cup;
  you have made my lot secure.
⁶The boundary lines have fallen for me in
    pleasant places;
  surely I have a delightful inheritance.

⁷I will praise the LORD, who counsels me;
  even at night my heart instructs me.
⁸I have set the LORD always before me.
  Because he is at my right hand,
  I will not be shaken.

⁹Therefore my heart is glad and my tongue
    rejoices;
  my body also will rest secure,
¹⁰because you will not abandon me to the
    grave,ᶜ
  nor will you let your Holy Oneᵈ see decay.
¹¹You have madeᵉ known to me the path of life;
  you will fill me with joy in your presence,
  with eternal pleasures at your right hand.

ᵃ Title: Probably a literary or musical term   ᵇ 3 Or As for the
pagan priests who are in the land / and the nobles in whom all
delight, I said: ᶜ 10 Hebrew Sheol   ᵈ 10 Or your faithful one
ᵉ 11 Or You will make

TALKING POINTS

Joy and Happiness
Our eternal life with God
fills us with joy.
PSALM 16:9–11

For more on joy and happiness, go to Psalm 32:11.

Psalm 17

A prayer of David.

¹ Hear, O Lord, my righteous plea;
  listen to my cry.
 Give ear to my prayer —
  it does not rise from deceitful lips.
² May my vindication come from you;
  may your eyes see what is right.

³ Though you probe my heart and examine me
   at night,
  though you test me, you will find nothing;
  I have resolved that my mouth will not sin.
⁴ As for the deeds of men —
  by the word of your lips
 I have kept myself
  from the ways of the violent.
⁵ My steps have held to your paths;
  my feet have not slipped.

⁶ I call on you, O God, for you will answer me;
  give ear to me and hear my prayer.
⁷ Show the wonder of your great love,
  you who save by your right hand
  those who take refuge in you from their
   foes.
⁸ Keep me as the apple of your eye;
  hide me in the shadow of your wings
⁹ from the wicked who assail me,
  from my mortal enemies who surround me.

¹⁰ They close up their callous hearts,
  and their mouths speak with arrogance.
¹¹ They have tracked me down, they now
   surround me,
  with eyes alert, to throw me to the ground.
¹² They are like a lion hungry for prey,
  like a great lion crouching in cover.

¹³ Rise up, O Lord, confront them, bring them
   down;
  rescue me from the wicked by your sword.
¹⁴ O Lord, by your hand save me from such
   men,
  from men of this world whose reward is in
   this life.

You still the hunger of those you cherish;
  their sons have plenty,
  and they store up wealth for their children.
¹⁵ And I — in righteousness I will see your face;
  when I awake, I will be satisfied with
   seeing your likeness.

Psalm 18

18:Title – 50pp — 2Sa 22:1 – 51

For the director of music. Of David the servant
 of the Lord. He sang to the Lord the words
 of this song when the Lord delivered him
 from the hand of all his enemies and
 from the hand of Saul. He said:

¹ I love you, O Lord, my strength.

² The Lord is my rock, my fortress and my
   deliverer;
  my God is my rock, in whom I take refuge.
 He is my shield and the horn *a* of my
   salvation, my stronghold.
³ I call to the Lord, who is worthy of praise,
  and I am saved from my enemies.

⁴ The cords of death entangled me;
  the torrents of destruction overwhelmed
   me.
⁵ The cords of the grave *b* coiled around me;
  the snares of death confronted me.
⁶ In my distress I called to the Lord;
  I cried to my God for help.
 From his temple he heard my voice;
  my cry came before him, into his ears.

⁷ The earth trembled and quaked,
  and the foundations of the mountains
   shook;
  they trembled because he was angry.
⁸ Smoke rose from his nostrils;
  consuming fire came from his mouth,
  burning coals blazed out of it.
⁹ He parted the heavens and came down;
  dark clouds were under his feet.
¹⁰ He mounted the cherubim and flew;
  he soared on the wings of the wind.

---

a 2 Horn here symbolizes strength.   *b 5* Hebrew *Sheol*

11 He made darkness his covering, his canopy
 around him—
 the dark rain clouds of the sky.
12 Out of the brightness of his presence clouds
 advanced,
 with hailstones and bolts of lightning.
13 The LORD thundered from heaven;
 the voice of the Most High resounded. *a*
14 He shot his arrows and scattered ⌊the
 enemies⌋,
 great bolts of lightning and routed them.
15 The valleys of the sea were exposed
 and the foundations of the earth laid bare
at your rebuke, O LORD,
 at the blast of breath from your nostrils.

16 He reached down from on high and took
 hold of me;
 he drew me out of deep waters.
17 He rescued me from my powerful enemy,
 from my foes, who were too strong for me.
18 They confronted me in the day of my
 disaster,
 but the LORD was my support.
19 He brought me out into a spacious place;
 he rescued me because he delighted in me.

20 The LORD has dealt with me according to my
 righteousness;
 according to the cleanness of my hands he
 has rewarded me.
21 For I have kept the ways of the LORD;
 I have not done evil by turning from my
 God.
22 All his laws are before me;
 I have not turned away from his decrees.
23 I have been blameless before him
 and have kept myself from sin.
24 The LORD has rewarded me according to my
 righteousness,
 according to the cleanness of my hands in
 his sight.

25 To the faithful you show yourself faithful,
 to the blameless you show yourself
 blameless,

26 to the pure you show yourself pure,
 but to the crooked you show yourself
 shrewd.
27 You save the humble
 but bring low those whose eyes are
 haughty.
28 You, O LORD, keep my lamp burning;
 my God turns my darkness into light.
29 With your help I can advance against a
 troop *b*;
 with my God I can scale a wall.

30 As for God, his way is perfect;
 the word of the LORD is flawless.
He is a shield
 for all who take refuge in him.
31 For who is God besides the LORD?
 And who is the Rock except our God?
32 It is God who arms me with strength
 and makes my way perfect.
33 He makes my feet like the feet of a deer;
 he enables me to stand on the heights.
34 He trains my hands for battle;
 my arms can bend a bow of bronze.
35 You give me your shield of victory,
 and your right hand sustains me;
 you stoop down to make me great.
36 You broaden the path beneath me,
 so that my ankles do not turn.

37 I pursued my enemies and overtook them;
 I did not turn back till they were
 destroyed.
38 I crushed them so that they could not rise;
 they fell beneath my feet.
39 You armed me with strength for battle;
 you made my adversaries bow at my feet.
40 You made my enemies turn their backs in
 flight,
 and I destroyed my foes.
41 They cried for help, but there was no one to
 save them—
 to the LORD, but he did not answer.

a 13 Some Hebrew manuscripts and Septuagint (see also 2 Samuel
22:14); most Hebrew manuscripts *resounded, / amid hailstones and
bolts of lightning* *b* 29 Or *can run through a barricade*

⁴²I beat them as fine as dust borne on the wind;
    I poured them out like mud in the streets.

⁴³You have delivered me from the attacks of the
      people;
    you have made me the head of nations;
    people I did not know are subject to me.
⁴⁴As soon as they hear me, they obey me;
    foreigners cringe before me.
⁴⁵They all lose heart;
    they come trembling from their
      strongholds.

⁴⁶The LORD lives! Praise be to my Rock!
    Exalted be God my Savior!
⁴⁷He is the God who avenges me,
    who subdues nations under me,
⁴⁸   who saves me from my enemies.
  You exalted me above my foes;
    from violent men you rescued me.
⁴⁹Therefore I will praise you among the
      nations, O LORD;
    I will sing praises to your name.
⁵⁰He gives his king great victories;
    he shows unfailing kindness to his
      anointed,
    to David and his descendants forever.

Psalm 19

For the director of music. A psalm of David.

¹The heavens declare the glory of God;
    the skies proclaim the work of his hands.
²Day after day they pour forth speech;
    night after night they display knowledge.
³There is no speech or language
    where their voice is not heard.ᵃ
⁴Their voiceᵇ goes out into all the earth,
    their words to the ends of the world.

In the heavens he has pitched a tent for the
      sun,
⁵   which is like a bridegroom coming forth
      from his pavilion,
    like a champion rejoicing to run his
      course.

⁶It rises at one end of the heavens
    and makes its circuit to the other;
    nothing is hidden from its heat.

⁷The law of the LORD is perfect,
    reviving the soul.
  The statutes of the LORD are trustworthy,
    making wise the simple.
⁸The precepts of the LORD are right,
    giving joy to the heart.
  The commands of the LORD are radiant,
    giving light to the eyes.
⁹The fear of the LORD is pure,
    enduring forever.
  The ordinances of the LORD are sure
    and altogether righteous.
¹⁰They are more precious than gold,
    than much pure gold;
  they are sweeter than honey,
    than honey from the comb.
¹¹By them is your servant warned;
    in keeping them there is great reward.

¹²Who can discern his errors?
    Forgive my hidden faults.
¹³Keep your servant also from willful sins;
    may they not rule over me.
  Then will I be blameless,
    innocent of great transgression.

¹⁴May the words of my mouth and the
      meditation of my heart
  be pleasing in your sight,
    O LORD, my Rock and my Redeemer.

Psalm 20

For the director of music. A psalm of David.

¹May the LORD answer you when you are in
      distress;
  may the name of the God of Jacob protect
      you.
²May he send you help from the sanctuary
    and grant you support from Zion.

ᵃ 3 Or *They have no speech, there are no words; / no sound is heard
from them*   ᵇ 4 Septuagint, Jerome and Syriac; Hebrew *line*

TALKING POINTS

Profanity
Everything we say should be
pleasing to God.
PSALM 19:14

For more on profanity, go to Matthew 12:36.

³May he remember all your sacrifices
and accept your burnt offerings.   *Selah*
⁴May he give you the desire of your heart
and make all your plans succeed.
⁵We will shout for joy when you are victorious
and will lift up our banners in the name of
our God.
May the LORD grant all your requests.

⁶Now I know that the LORD saves his
anointed;
he answers him from his holy heaven
with the saving power of his right hand.
⁷Some trust in chariots and some in horses,
but we trust in the name of the LORD our
God.
⁸They are brought to their knees and fall,
but we rise up and stand firm.

⁹O LORD, save the king!
Answer *ᵃ* us when we call!

Psalm 21

For the director of music. A psalm of David.

¹O LORD, the king rejoices in your strength.
How great is his joy in the victories you
give!
²You have granted him the desire of his heart
and have not withheld the request of his
lips.   *Selah*
³You welcomed him with rich blessings
and placed a crown of pure gold on his
head.

⁴He asked you for life, and you gave it to
him —
length of days, for ever and ever.
⁵Through the victories you gave, his glory is
great;
you have bestowed on him splendor and
majesty.
⁶Surely you have granted him eternal blessings
and made him glad with the joy of your
presence.
⁷For the king trusts in the LORD;
through the unfailing love of the Most
High
he will not be shaken.

⁸Your hand will lay hold on all your enemies;
your right hand will seize your foes.
⁹At the time of your appearing
you will make them like a fiery furnace.
In his wrath the LORD will swallow them up,
and his fire will consume them.
¹⁰You will destroy their descendants from the
earth,
their posterity from mankind.
¹¹Though they plot evil against you
and devise wicked schemes, they cannot
succeed;
¹²for you will make them turn their backs
when you aim at them with drawn bow.

¹³Be exalted, O LORD, in your strength;
we will sing and praise your might.

Psalm 22

For the director of music. To ⌞the tune of⌟
"The Doe of the Morning." A psalm
of David.

¹My God, my God, why have you forsaken
me?
Why are you so far from saving me,
so far from the words of my groaning?
²O my God, I cry out by day, but you do not
answer,
by night, and am not silent.

ᵃ 9 Or save! / O King, answer

³ Yet you are enthroned as the Holy One;
  you are the praise of Israel. *a*
⁴ In you our fathers put their trust;
  they trusted and you delivered them.
⁵ They cried to you and were saved;
  in you they trusted and were not
    disappointed.

⁶ But I am a worm and not a man,
  scorned by men and despised by the
    people.
⁷ All who see me mock me;
  they hurl insults, shaking their heads:
⁸ "He trusts in the LORD;
  let the LORD rescue him.
Let him deliver him,
  since he delights in him."

⁹ Yet you brought me out of the womb;
  you made me trust in you
    even at my mother's breast.
¹⁰ From birth I was cast upon you;
  from my mother's womb you have been
    my God.
¹¹ Do not be far from me,
  for trouble is near
    and there is no one to help.

¹² Many bulls surround me;
  strong bulls of Bashan encircle me.
¹³ Roaring lions tearing their prey
  open their mouths wide against me.
¹⁴ I am poured out like water,
  and all my bones are out of joint.
My heart has turned to wax;
  it has melted away within me.
¹⁵ My strength is dried up like a potsherd,
  and my tongue sticks to the roof of my
    mouth;
you lay me *b* in the dust of death.
¹⁶ Dogs have surrounded me;
  a band of evil men has encircled me,
  they have pierced *c* my hands and my feet.
¹⁷ I can count all my bones;
  people stare and gloat over me.
¹⁸ They divide my garments among them
  and cast lots for my clothing.

¹⁹ But you, O LORD, be not far off;
  O my Strength, come quickly to help me.
²⁰ Deliver my life from the sword,
  my precious life from the power of the
    dogs.
²¹ Rescue me from the mouth of the lions;
  save *d* me from the horns of the wild oxen.

²² I will declare your name to my brothers;
  in the congregation I will praise you.
²³ You who fear the LORD, praise him!
  All you descendants of Jacob, honor him!
  Revere him, all you descendants of Israel!
²⁴ For he has not despised or disdained
  the suffering of the afflicted one;
he has not hidden his face from him
  but has listened to his cry for help.

²⁵ From you comes the theme of my praise in
    the great assembly;
  before those who fear you *e* will I fulfill my
    vows.
²⁶ The poor will eat and be satisfied;
  they who seek the LORD will praise him—
  may your hearts live forever!
²⁷ All the ends of the earth
  will remember and turn to the LORD,
and all the families of the nations
  will bow down before him,
²⁸ for dominion belongs to the LORD
  and he rules over the nations.

²⁹ All the rich of the earth will feast and
    worship;
  all who go down to the dust will kneel
    before him—
  those who cannot keep themselves alive.
³⁰ Posterity will serve him;
  future generations will be told about the
    Lord.
³¹ They will proclaim his righteousness
  to a people yet unborn—
    for he has done it.

a 3 Or *Yet you are holy, / enthroned on the praises of Israel*
b 15 Or / *I am laid*   *c 16* Some Hebrew manuscripts, Septuagint
and Syriac; most Hebrew manuscripts / *like the lion,*   *d 21* Or /
you have heard   *e 25* Hebrew *him*

Psalm 23

A psalm of David.

[1] The LORD is my shepherd, I shall not be in want.
[2]   He makes me lie down in green pastures,
he leads me beside quiet waters,
[3]   he restores my soul.
He guides me in paths of righteousness
  for his name's sake.
[4] Even though I walk
  through the valley of the shadow of death,[a]
I will fear no evil,
  for you are with me;
your rod and your staff,
  they comfort me.

[5] You prepare a table before me
  in the presence of my enemies.
You anoint my head with oil;
  my cup overflows.
[6] Surely goodness and love will follow me
  all the days of my life,
and I will dwell in the house of the LORD
  forever.

Psalm 24

Of David. A psalm.

[1] The earth is the LORD's, and everything in it,
  the world, and all who live in it;
[2] for he founded it upon the seas
  and established it upon the waters.

[3] Who may ascend the hill of the LORD?
  Who may stand in his holy place?
[4] He who has clean hands and a pure heart,
  who does not lift up his soul to an idol
  or swear by what is false.[b]
[5] He will receive blessing from the LORD
  and vindication from God his Savior.
[6] Such is the generation of those who seek him,
  who seek your face, O God of Jacob.[c]

Selah

[7] Lift up your heads, O you gates;
  be lifted up, you ancient doors,
  that the King of glory may come in.

---

stories to share

PSALM 23:1-6

The Lord Is My Shepherd

LIFE LESSON: God cares for his people like a shepherd cares for sheep.

TO TALK ABOUT

✦ What do shepherds do?

✦ What are sheep like? Why do they need to be watched over so carefully?

✦ Why might David have thought of God as a shepherd?

✦ How has God been like a shepherd for you?

---

[a] 4 Or *through the darkest valley*   [b] 4 Or *swear falsely*
[c] 6 Two Hebrew manuscripts and Syriac (see also Septuagint); most
Hebrew manuscripts *face, Jacob*

8 Who is this King of glory?
  The LORD strong and mighty,
  the LORD mighty in battle.
9 Lift up your heads, O you gates;
  lift them up, you ancient doors,
  that the King of glory may come in.
10 Who is he, this King of glory?
  The LORD Almighty—
  he is the King of glory.   *Selah*

Psalm 25 *a*

Of David.

1 To you, O LORD, I lift up my soul;
2   in you I trust, O my God.
  Do not let me be put to shame,
    nor let my enemies triumph over me.
3 No one whose hope is in you
    will ever be put to shame,
  but they will be put to shame
    who are treacherous without excuse.

4 Show me your ways, O LORD,
    teach me your paths;
5 guide me in your truth and teach me,
    for you are God my Savior,
    and my hope is in you all day long.
6 Remember, O LORD, your great mercy and
    love,
    for they are from of old.
7 Remember not the sins of my youth
    and my rebellious ways;
  according to your love remember me,
    for you are good, O LORD.

8 Good and upright is the LORD;
    therefore he instructs sinners in his ways.
9 He guides the humble in what is right
    and teaches them his way.
10 All the ways of the LORD are loving and faithful
    for those who keep the demands of his
    covenant.
11 For the sake of your name, O LORD,
    forgive my iniquity, though it is great.
12 Who, then, is the man that fears the LORD?
    He will instruct him in the way chosen for
    him.

13 He will spend his days in prosperity,
    and his descendants will inherit the land.
14 The LORD confides in those who fear him;
    he makes his covenant known to them.
15 My eyes are ever on the LORD,
    for only he will release my feet from the
    snare.

16 Turn to me and be gracious to me,
    for I am lonely and afflicted.
17 The troubles of my heart have multiplied;
    free me from my anguish.
18 Look upon my affliction and my distress
    and take away all my sins.
19 See how my enemies have increased
    and how fiercely they hate me!

TALKING POINTS

Loneliness
Cry out to God in your loneliness.
PSALM 25:16–21

For more on loneliness, go to Mark 14:32–42.

20 Guard my life and rescue me;
    let me not be put to shame,
    for I take refuge in you.
21 May integrity and uprightness protect me,
    because my hope is in you.

22 Redeem Israel, O God,
    from all their troubles!

Psalm 26

Of David.

1 Vindicate me, O LORD,
    for I have led a blameless life;
  I have trusted in the LORD
    without wavering.

a This psalm is an acrostic poem, the verses of which begin with the
successive letters of the Hebrew alphabet.

TURN TO ME AND BE GRACIOUS
TO ME, FOR I AM LONELY AND
AFFLICTED.

Psalm 25:16

A Gracious Tradition

KAREN KINGSBURY

READ | PSALM 25:1–22

Each year at Christmastime my family has a number of special traditions. But no tradition is as long-lasting as the day each December when we bake plates of cookies and head to the local retirement home.

Each year, the residents — many of them well into their 80s — look forward with great anticipation to the day when we troop in, ready to entertain them. They come in their Sunday best, many sporting new hairdos and holiday earrings or sweaters. As for us, we bring a ragtag group of babies and teens and friends and family — all of us with red scarves and gloves and Santa hats. A few of the kids can sing well, but for the most part we're a strictly no-talent outfit. The point, we always tell our children, is not the quality of our song, but the quantity of our love.

When we sing, I'm always drawn to the women, the grandmothers, the ones who tear up the moment we launch into the first verse of our first song: "Silent Night." It occurs to me anew each time that the nights are all too silent for so many grandmothers. Done with their mothering and even their grand-mothering, these women are often lonely and afflicted, the people in their lives too busy for them. As we sing, I look to my own children, and I find myself silently praying that they will be the type of adults who will care about the generations that have come before them.

When we're finished singing, we do the thing we really came to do: We walk through the crowd and give out hugs. And for a brief hour before Christmas, the aging grandmothers in that retirement home no longer feel lonely and afflicted — because grandmothers desire not only to give love but also to receive it.

Dear Lord, help me to be mindful of the aging women in my life and community. Let me be part of the solution to their loneliness and affliction, and help me train up my children and grandchildren to love and care for the generations that have come before them. In Christ's name, amen.

Your next devotion is located on page 725.

GRANDCHILD IN FOCUS • PRAYER

School/Career

Dear God, may learning be a joy rather than a chore for my grandchild. May exploration of new ideas bring a sense of wonder, awe and excitement. Grant him clarity of mind, the ability to concentrate on the task at hand and recollection of what has been learned. Help him to appreciate the tasks that come easily and to persevere through those that challenge. Amen.

² Test me, O LORD, and try me,
　examine my heart and my mind;
³ for your love is ever before me,
　and I walk continually in your truth.
⁴ I do not sit with deceitful men,
　nor do I consort with hypocrites;
⁵ I abhor the assembly of evildoers
　and refuse to sit with the wicked.
⁶ I wash my hands in innocence,
　and go about your altar, O LORD,
⁷ proclaiming aloud your praise
　and telling of all your wonderful deeds.
⁸ I love the house where you live, O LORD,
　the place where your glory dwells.

⁹ Do not take away my soul along with sinners,
　my life with bloodthirsty men,
¹⁰ in whose hands are wicked schemes,
　whose right hands are full of bribes.
¹¹ But I lead a blameless life;
　redeem me and be merciful to me.

¹² My feet stand on level ground;
　in the great assembly I will praise the
　LORD.

Psalm 27

Of David.

¹ The LORD is my light and my salvation —
　whom shall I fear?
The LORD is the stronghold of my life —
　of whom shall I be afraid?
² When evil men advance against me
　to devour my flesh,ᵃ
when my enemies and my foes attack me,
　they will stumble and fall.
³ Though an army besiege me,
　my heart will not fear;
though war break out against me,
　even then will I be confident.

⁴ One thing I ask of the LORD,
　this is what I seek:
that I may dwell in the house of the LORD
　all the days of my life,

to gaze upon the beauty of the LORD
　and to seek him in his temple.
⁵ For in the day of trouble
　he will keep me safe in his dwelling;
he will hide me in the shelter of his
　tabernacle
　and set me high upon a rock.
⁶ Then my head will be exalted
　above the enemies who surround me;
at his tabernacle will I sacrifice with shouts
　of joy;
　I will sing and make music to the LORD.

⁷ Hear my voice when I call, O LORD;
　be merciful to me and answer me.
⁸ My heart says of you, "Seek his ᵇ face!"
　Your face, LORD, I will seek.
⁹ Do not hide your face from me,
　do not turn your servant away in anger;
　you have been my helper.
Do not reject me or forsake me,
　O God my Savior.
¹⁰ Though my father and mother forsake me,
　the LORD will receive me.

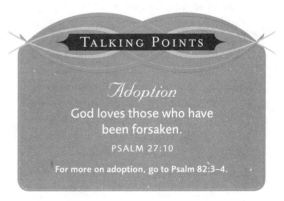

TALKING POINTS

Adoption
God loves those who have
been forsaken.
PSALM 27:10

For more on adoption, go to Psalm 82:3–4.

¹¹ Teach me your way, O LORD;
　lead me in a straight path
　because of my oppressors.
¹² Do not turn me over to the desire of my foes,
　for false witnesses rise up against me,
　breathing out violence.

ᵃ 2 Or to slander me　　ᵇ 8 Or To you, O my heart, he has said,
"Seek my

¹³ I am still confident of this:
　　I will see the goodness of the LORD
　　in the land of the living.
¹⁴ Wait for the LORD;
　　be strong and take heart
　　and wait for the LORD.

Psalm 28

Of David.

¹ To you I call, O LORD my Rock;
　　do not turn a deaf ear to me.
　For if you remain silent,
　　I will be like those who have gone down to
　　　the pit.
² Hear my cry for mercy
　　as I call to you for help,
　as I lift up my hands
　　toward your Most Holy Place.

³ Do not drag me away with the wicked,
　　with those who do evil,
　who speak cordially with their neighbors
　　but harbor malice in their hearts.
⁴ Repay them for their deeds
　　and for their evil work;
　repay them for what their hands have done
　　and bring back upon them what they
　　　deserve.
⁵ Since they show no regard for the works of
　　　the LORD
　　and what his hands have done,
　he will tear them down
　　and never build them up again.

⁶ Praise be to the LORD,
　　for he has heard my cry for mercy.
⁷ The LORD is my strength and my shield;
　　my heart trusts in him, and I am helped.
　My heart leaps for joy
　　and I will give thanks to him in song.

⁸ The LORD is the strength of his people,
　　a fortress of salvation for his anointed one.
⁹ Save your people and bless your inheritance;
　　be their shepherd and carry them forever.

TALKING POINTS

Eating Disorders

God hears our cry and
gives us his strength.

PSALM 28:6–7

For more on eating disorders, go to Jeremiah 32:17.

Psalm 29

A psalm of David.

¹ Ascribe to the LORD, O mighty ones,
　　ascribe to the LORD glory and strength.
² Ascribe to the LORD the glory due his name;
　　worship the LORD in the splendor of his ᵃ
　　　holiness.

³ The voice of the LORD is over the waters;
　　the God of glory thunders,
　　the LORD thunders over the mighty waters.
⁴ The voice of the LORD is powerful;
　　the voice of the LORD is majestic.
⁵ The voice of the LORD breaks the cedars;
　　the LORD breaks in pieces the cedars of
　　　Lebanon.
⁶ He makes Lebanon skip like a calf,
　　Sirion ᵇ like a young wild ox.
⁷ The voice of the LORD strikes
　　with flashes of lightning.
⁸ The voice of the LORD shakes the desert;
　　the LORD shakes the Desert of Kadesh.
⁹ The voice of the LORD twists the oaks ᶜ
　　and strips the forests bare.
　And in his temple all cry, "Glory!"

¹⁰ The LORD sits ᵈ enthroned over the flood;
　　the LORD is enthroned as King forever.
¹¹ The LORD gives strength to his people;
　　the LORD blesses his people with peace.

ᵃ 2 Or LORD with the splendor of　ᵇ 6 That is, Mount Hermon
ᶜ 9 Or LORD makes the deer give birth　ᵈ 10 Or sat

TOGETHER
TIME

Recipe Party

How about getting your grandchildren started on their own recipe boxes? It's as easy as locating your own recipe box, distributing index or recipe cards and working with them to copy recipes of their choice. Near the end of the activity, you could surprise them with hand-decorated recipe boxes or have them decorate their own. Be sure to send them home with a few extra cards so they can add to their collection of favorites at their own pace. From time to time throughout the year, you can continue to share the family favorites by tucking a recipe in with a birthday gift or greeting card.

If you prefer, you can create a notebook or a binder of recipes and family favorites rather than using a recipe box. This way they can include recipes they love from magazines or newspapers.

Long-Distance Variation: Start a recipe exchange (preferably via snail mail, so you can each benefit from receiving cards in each other's handwriting). Hopefully you'll receive the bonus each time of a short note, allowing you to keep up with your grandchild's interests and activities.

Thank you, God, for the abundance of food we have available. Help us to enjoy this activity and our time together. Let my grandchildren understand the importance of simple things, like family recipes, that need to be remembered and cherished. Amen.

Your next devotion is located on page 728.

GRANDCHILD IN FOCUS • PRAYER

Character

Dear Lord and Father, I ask that you fill my grandchild with your Spirit so her character reflects your goodness and love. Give her kindness and love for others. Bring joy to her life so she will be a joy to others. Grant her patience and self-control through difficult and trying times. May she show mercy and generosity to those who are less fortunate. Grant her integrity and a sense of justice, and surround her with your peace. Amen.

Psalm 30

A psalm. A song. For the dedication
of the temple.[a] Of David.

[1] I will exalt you, O LORD,
  for you lifted me out of the depths
  and did not let my enemies gloat over me.
[2] O LORD my God, I called to you for help
  and you healed me.
[3] O LORD, you brought me up from the grave[b];
  you spared me from going down into the
    pit.

[4] Sing to the LORD, you saints of his;
  praise his holy name.
[5] For his anger lasts only a moment,
  but his favor lasts a lifetime;
weeping may remain for a night,
  but rejoicing comes in the morning.

TALKING POINTS

Loss/Grief

Grief will give way to joy.
PSALM 30:5

For more on loss/grief, go to John 14:1–3.

[6] When I felt secure, I said,
  "I will never be shaken."
[7] O LORD, when you favored me,
  you made my mountain[c] stand firm;
but when you hid your face,
  I was dismayed.

[8] To you, O LORD, I called;
  to the Lord I cried for mercy:
[9] "What gain is there in my destruction,[d]
  in my going down into the pit?
Will the dust praise you?
  Will it proclaim your faithfulness?
[10] Hear, O LORD, and be merciful to me;
  O LORD, be my help."

[11] You turned my wailing into dancing;
  you removed my sackcloth and clothed me
    with joy,
[12] that my heart may sing to you and not be
    silent.
  O LORD my God, I will give you thanks
    forever.

Psalm 31

31:1–4pp — Ps 71:1–3

For the director of music.
A psalm of David.

[1] In you, O LORD, I have taken refuge;
  let me never be put to shame;
  deliver me in your righteousness.
[2] Turn your ear to me,
  come quickly to my rescue;
be my rock of refuge,
  a strong fortress to save me.
[3] Since you are my rock and my fortress,
  for the sake of your name lead and
    guide me.
[4] Free me from the trap that is set for me,
  for you are my refuge.
[5] Into your hands I commit my spirit;
  redeem me, O LORD, the God of truth.

[6] I hate those who cling to worthless idols;
  I trust in the LORD.
[7] I will be glad and rejoice in your love,
  for you saw my affliction
  and knew the anguish of my soul.
[8] You have not handed me over to the enemy
  but have set my feet in a spacious place.

[9] Be merciful to me, O LORD, for I am in
    distress;
  my eyes grow weak with sorrow,
  my soul and my body with grief.
[10] My life is consumed by anguish
  and my years by groaning;
  my strength fails because of my affliction,[e]
  and my bones grow weak.

---

[a] Title: Or *palace*   [b] 3 Hebrew *Sheol*   [c] 7 Or *hill country*
[d] 9 Or *there if I am silenced*   [e] 10 Or *guilt*

¹¹Because of all my enemies,
  I am the utter contempt of my neighbors;
I am a dread to my friends—
  those who see me on the street flee
    from me.
¹²I am forgotten by them as though I were
    dead;
  I have become like broken pottery.
¹³For I hear the slander of many;
  there is terror on every side;
they conspire against me
  and plot to take my life.

¹⁴But I trust in you, O Lord;
  I say, "You are my God."
¹⁵My times are in your hands;
  deliver me from my enemies
  and from those who pursue me.
¹⁶Let your face shine on your servant;
  save me in your unfailing love.
¹⁷Let me not be put to shame, O Lord,
  for I have cried out to you;
but let the wicked be put to shame
  and lie silent in the grave. ᵃ
¹⁸Let their lying lips be silenced,
  for with pride and contempt
  they speak arrogantly against the
    righteous.

¹⁹How great is your goodness,
  which you have stored up for those who
    fear you,
which you bestow in the sight of men
  on those who take refuge in you.
²⁰In the shelter of your presence you hide them
  from the intrigues of men;
in your dwelling you keep them safe
  from accusing tongues.

²¹Praise be to the Lord,
  for he showed his wonderful love to me
  when I was in a besieged city.
²²In my alarm I said,
  "I am cut off from your sight!"
Yet you heard my cry for mercy
  when I called to you for help.

²³Love the Lord, all his saints!
  The Lord preserves the faithful,
  but the proud he pays back in full.
²⁴Be strong and take heart,
  all you who hope in the Lord.

Psalm 32

Of David. A *maskil.* ᵇ

¹Blessed is he
  whose transgressions are forgiven,
  whose sins are covered.
²Blessed is the man
  whose sin the Lord does not count against
    him
  and in whose spirit is no deceit.

³When I kept silent,
  my bones wasted away
  through my groaning all day long.
⁴For day and night
  your hand was heavy upon me;
my strength was sapped
  as in the heat of summer.   *Selah*
⁵Then I acknowledged my sin to you
  and did not cover up my iniquity.
I said, "I will confess
  my transgressions to the Lord"—
and you forgave
  the guilt of my sin.   *Selah*

⁶Therefore let everyone who is godly pray to
    you
  while you may be found;
surely when the mighty waters rise,
  they will not reach him.
⁷You are my hiding place;
  you will protect me from trouble
  and surround me with songs of
    deliverance.   *Selah*

⁸I will instruct you and teach you in the way
    you should go;
  I will counsel you and watch over you.
⁹Do not be like the horse or the mule,
  which have no understanding

ᵃ *17* Hebrew *Sheol*   ᵇ Title: Probably a literary or musical term

Worship the Lord

"My soul glorifies the Lord
    and my spirit rejoices in God my Savior,
for he has been mindful
    of the humble state of his servant.
From now on all generations will call me blessed,
    for the Mighty One has done great things for me—
    holy is his name.
His mercy extends to those who fear him,
    from generation to generation.
He has performed mighty deeds with his arm;
    he has scattered those who are proud in their
        inmost thoughts.
He has brought down rulers from their thrones
    but has lifted up the humble.
He has filled the hungry with good things
    but has sent the rich away empty.
He has helped his servant Israel,
    remembering to be merciful
to Abraham and his descendants
        forever,
    even as he said to our fathers."

Luke 1:46–55

Father God, my soul echoes the praise that
flowed from Mary's lips so long ago. Accept,
Lord, my own song of praise for your mercy and
faithfulness. Amen.

Your next devotion is located on page 731.

GRANDCHILD IN FOCUS • PRAYER

Talents

*Dear Lord, the giver of gifts, bless my
grandchild as he develops his talents. Help him
identify his talents and be proud and confident of
the gifts you have given him. Give him patience and
understanding, Lord, so he will not grow weary of
striving and searching to reach the goals you have
set for him. May each milestone bring satisfaction and a healthy desire for greater
achievement and success to bring
glory to you. Amen.*

but must be controlled by bit and bridle
    or they will not come to you.
¹⁰ Many are the woes of the wicked,
    but the Lord's unfailing love
    surrounds the man who trusts in him.

¹¹ Rejoice in the Lord and be glad, you
    righteous;
    sing, all you who are upright in heart!

TALKING POINTS

Joy and Happiness

God calls us to be glad and
rejoice in him.

PSALM 32:11

For more on joy and happiness,
go to Habakkuk 3:17–18.

Psalm 33

¹ Sing joyfully to the Lord, you righteous;
    it is fitting for the upright to praise him.
² Praise the Lord with the harp;
    make music to him on the ten-stringed
    lyre.
³ Sing to him a new song;
    play skillfully, and shout for joy.

⁴ For the word of the Lord is right and true;
    he is faithful in all he does.
⁵ The Lord loves righteousness and justice;
    the earth is full of his unfailing love.

⁶ By the word of the Lord were the heavens
    made,
    their starry host by the breath of his
    mouth.
⁷ He gathers the waters of the sea into jars ᵃ;
    he puts the deep into storehouses.
⁸ Let all the earth fear the Lord;
    let all the people of the world revere him.

⁹ For he spoke, and it came to be;
    he commanded, and it stood firm.
¹⁰ The Lord foils the plans of the nations;
    he thwarts the purposes of the peoples.
¹¹ But the plans of the Lord stand firm forever,
    the purposes of his heart through all
    generations.

¹² Blessed is the nation whose God is the Lord,
    the people he chose for his inheritance.
¹³ From heaven the Lord looks down
    and sees all mankind;
¹⁴ from his dwelling place he watches
    all who live on earth—
¹⁵ he who forms the hearts of all,
    who considers everything they do.

¹⁶ No king is saved by the size of his army;
    no warrior escapes by his great strength.
¹⁷ A horse is a vain hope for deliverance;
    despite all its great strength it cannot save.
¹⁸ But the eyes of the Lord are on those who
    fear him,
    on those whose hope is in his unfailing
    love,
¹⁹ to deliver them from death
    and keep them alive in famine.

²⁰ We wait in hope for the Lord;
    he is our help and our shield.
²¹ In him our hearts rejoice,
    for we trust in his holy name.
²² May your unfailing love rest upon us,
    O Lord,
    even as we put our hope in you.

Psalm 34 ᵇ

Of David. When he pretended to be insane
before Abimelech, who drove him away,
and he left.

¹ I will extol the Lord at all times;
    his praise will always be on my lips.
² My soul will boast in the Lord;
    let the afflicted hear and rejoice.

ᵃ 7 Or *sea as into a heap*   ᵇ This psalm is an acrostic poem, the
verses of which begin with the successive letters of the Hebrew
alphabet.

³ Glorify the LORD with me;
    let us exalt his name together.

⁴ I sought the LORD, and he answered me;
    he delivered me from all my fears.
⁵ Those who look to him are radiant;
    their faces are never covered with
        shame.
⁶ This poor man called, and the LORD heard
        him;
    he saved him out of all his troubles.
⁷ The angel of the LORD encamps around
        those who fear him,
    and he delivers them.

⁸ Taste and see that the LORD is good;
    blessed is the man who takes refuge in
        him.
⁹ Fear the LORD, you his saints,
    for those who fear him lack nothing.
¹⁰ The lions may grow weak and hungry,
    but those who seek the LORD lack no good
        thing.

¹¹ Come, my children, listen to me;
    I will teach you the fear of the LORD.
¹² Whoever of you loves life
    and desires to see many good days,
¹³ keep your tongue from evil
    and your lips from speaking lies.
¹⁴ Turn from evil and do good;
    seek peace and pursue it.

¹⁵ The eyes of the LORD are on the righteous
    and his ears are attentive to their cry;

¹⁶ the face of the LORD is against those who do
        evil,
    to cut off the memory of them from the
        earth.

¹⁷ The righteous cry out, and the LORD hears
        them;
    he delivers them from all their troubles.
¹⁸ The LORD is close to the brokenhearted
    and saves those who are crushed in spirit.

PRAYING THE SCRIPTURES

Reassurance

PSALM 34:18

Dear God, be with my grandchild in her times of distress. Help her to realize that you, O Lord, are close to the brokenhearted and that you save those who are crushed in spirit.

Next prayer in Reassurance Prayer Track: Psalm 46:1

¹⁹ A righteous man may have many troubles,
    but the LORD delivers him from them all;
²⁰ he protects all his bones,
    not one of them will be broken.

²¹ Evil will slay the wicked;
    the foes of the righteous will be
        condemned.
²² The LORD redeems his servants;
    no one will be condemned who takes
        refuge in him.

Psalm 35

Of David.

¹ Contend, O LORD, with those who contend
        with me;
    fight against those who fight against me.
² Take up shield and buckler;
    arise and come to my aid.

TALKING POINTS

Lying

The command not to lie is clear.

PSALM 34:13

For more on lying, go to Proverbs 12:22.

I WILL EXTOL THE LORD AT ALL
TIMES; HIS PRAISE WILL ALWAYS
BE ON MY LIPS. MY SOUL WILL
BOAST IN THE LORD; LET THE
AFFLICTED HEAR AND REJOICE.
GLORIFY THE LORD WITH ME; LET
US EXALT HIS NAME TOGETHER.

Psalm 34:1 – 3

Praise Ribbons

NETA JACKSON

READ | PSALM 34:1 – 22

"Grandma, will you help me make a praise ribbon?"

"A praise ribbon?" Five-year-old Liam meant the colorful streamers I'd bought from a liturgical dance company. "Oh, honey, you can play with mine. I don't mind."

Liam shook his head. "I want one of my own to take to church on Sunday."

I knew exactly how he felt. From the moment I'd seen a group of dancers use the shimmering ribbons to lift banners of praise to God during a worship service, I wanted to worship like that. At my age, it wasn't likely I would become part of a "dance group," but I felt a deep longing to worship God with my whole being — body, soul and spirit. So I bought several ribbons, put on a gospel CD at home, and danced my praise to God.

It all started with reading the Psalms during my morning devotions. Psalm 34 begins, "I will extol the LORD at all times . . ." followed by a string of similar words: "praise" . . . "boast in the LORD" . . . "rejoice" . . . "glorify" . . . "exalt his name."

Wait a minute. Did all those words mean the same thing? I looked them up in the dictionary. Each word offered a slightly different meaning. But I was startled by the meaning of *exalt*: "to give lavish praise."

Lavish? As in "over the top," "extravagant," "excessive"? Had I ever given God *lavish* praise? I'd grown up with a lot of no-no's — and moving my body to music was one of them. Only it didn't square with the Bible: "Let them praise his name with dancing" (Psalm 149:3).

So Liam made his own praise ribbon. He took it to church. When the congregation sang their praises to God, he danced and waved his ribbon. Lavish praise.

O God, when I think about your faithfulness to me and my family, I want to dance! I want to shout! Because you are a lavish God, I want to give you lavish praise.

Your next devotion is located on page 734.

GRANDCHILD IN FOCUS · PRAYER

SELECT ONE OF YOUR
GRANDCHILDREN TO FOCUS ON
IN PRAYER FOR THE NEXT 14 DAYS.

Salvation

Dear Lord, please guide my grandchild to your gift of salvation. I pray that she will come to know you, to love you and to walk close to you throughout her life. May she boldly claim Jesus as her Lord and Savior. Guide her as she makes choices that have eternal consequences. Help her to follow you each moment of her life. I pray this in Jesus' name, amen.

731

3 Brandish spear and javelin [a]
  against those who pursue me.
Say to my soul,
  "I am your salvation."

4 May those who seek my life
  be disgraced and put to shame;
may those who plot my ruin
  be turned back in dismay.
5 May they be like chaff before the wind,
  with the angel of the LORD driving them
    away;
6 may their path be dark and slippery,
  with the angel of the LORD pursuing them.
7 Since they hid their net for me without cause
  and without cause dug a pit for me,
8 may ruin overtake them by surprise—
  may the net they hid entangle them,
  may they fall into the pit, to their ruin.
9 Then my soul will rejoice in the LORD
  and delight in his salvation.
10 My whole being will exclaim,
  "Who is like you, O LORD?
You rescue the poor from those too strong
    for them,
  the poor and needy from those who rob
    them."

11 Ruthless witnesses come forward;
  they question me on things I know
    nothing about.
12 They repay me evil for good
  and leave my soul forlorn.
13 Yet when they were ill, I put on sackcloth
  and humbled myself with fasting.
When my prayers returned to me unanswered,
14   I went about mourning
    as though for my friend or brother.
I bowed my head in grief
  as though weeping for my mother.
15 But when I stumbled, they gathered in glee;
  attackers gathered against me when I was
    unaware.
They slandered me without ceasing.
16 Like the ungodly they maliciously mocked [b];
  they gnashed their teeth at me.

17 O Lord, how long will you look on?
  Rescue my life from their ravages,
  my precious life from these lions.
18 I will give you thanks in the great assembly;
  among throngs of people I will praise you.

19 Let not those gloat over me
  who are my enemies without cause;
let not those who hate me without reason
  maliciously wink the eye.
20 They do not speak peaceably,
  but devise false accusations
  against those who live quietly in the land.
21 They gape at me and say, "Aha! Aha!
  With our own eyes we have seen it."

22 O LORD, you have seen this; be not silent.
  Do not be far from me, O Lord.
23 Awake, and rise to my defense!
  Contend for me, my God and Lord.
24 Vindicate me in your righteousness, O LORD
    my God;
  do not let them gloat over me.
25 Do not let them think, "Aha, just what we
    wanted!"
  or say, "We have swallowed him up."

26 May all who gloat over my distress
  be put to shame and confusion;
may all who exalt themselves over me
  be clothed with shame and disgrace.
27 May those who delight in my vindication
  shout for joy and gladness;
may they always say, "The LORD be exalted,
  who delights in the well-being of his
    servant."
28 My tongue will speak of your righteousness
  and of your praises all day long.

Psalm 36

For the director of music. Of David
the servant of the LORD.

1 An oracle is within my heart
  concerning the sinfulness of the wicked: [c]

---

a 3 Or and block the way   *b 16 Septuagint; Hebrew may mean*
ungodly circle of mockers.   *c 1 Or heart: / Sin proceeds from the*
wicked.

There is no fear of God
    before his eyes.
2 For in his own eyes he flatters himself
    too much to detect or hate his sin.
3 The words of his mouth are wicked and
        deceitful;
    he has ceased to be wise and to do good.
4 Even on his bed he plots evil;
    he commits himself to a sinful course
    and does not reject what is wrong.

5 Your love, O LORD, reaches to the heavens,
    your faithfulness to the skies.
6 Your righteousness is like the mighty
        mountains,
    your justice like the great deep.
    O LORD, you preserve both man and beast.
7   How priceless is your unfailing love!
    Both high and low among men
    find *a* refuge in the shadow of your wings.
8 They feast on the abundance of your house;
    you give them drink from your river of
        delights.
9 For with you is the fountain of life;
    in your light we see light.

10 Continue your love to those who know you,
    your righteousness to the upright in heart.
11 May the foot of the proud not come against
        me,
    nor the hand of the wicked drive me away.
12 See how the evildoers lie fallen —
    thrown down, not able to rise!

Psalm 37 *b*

Of David.

1 Do not fret because of evil men
    or be envious of those who do wrong;
2 for like the grass they will soon wither,
    like green plants they will soon die away.

3 Trust in the LORD and do good;
    dwell in the land and enjoy safe pasture.
4 Delight yourself in the LORD
    and he will give you the desires of your
        heart.

PSALM 37:1-7

Delight Yourself in the Lord

LIFE LESSON: God is trustworthy.

TO TALK ABOUT

✦ What will happen to evil people?

✦ What should we do instead of "fretting"?

✦ What does it mean to "delight yourself in the LORD" (verse 4)?

✦ Why should we trust in God?

5 Commit your way to the LORD;
    trust in him and he will do this:
6 He will make your righteousness shine like
        the dawn,
    the justice of your cause like the noonday
        sun.

a 7 Or love, O God! / Men find; or love! / Both heavenly beings and men / find   b This psalm is an acrostic poem, the stanzas of which begin with the successive letters of the Hebrew alphabet.

TALKING POINTS

Trust

Trusting God reaps great rewards.

PSALM 37:3-6

For more on trust, go to Isaiah 12:2.

BE STILL BEFORE THE LORD AND
WAIT PATIENTLY FOR HIM.
Psalm 37:7

Dawn

RUTH GRAHAM

READ | PSALM 37:1–11

I awakened early and got up to take a walk on the beach. But when I looked out, it was still dark. I sat down on the porch to wait for the sun to come up. I sat there for a bit with no hint of dawn. I poured myself a cup of coffee and returned to the porch to wait. It was quiet and still. Nothing seemed to be moving.

As I sat there, I saw the morning star . . . and the very faintest hint of light beginning in the horizon. Ever so slowly, the dawn crept up from the East. A lonely gull called and through the gentle light I began to see things the darkness had hidden: the railings of the walkway to the beach, the sea oats on the dunes, the distant horizon, and the gull swooping over the beach in search of food deposited by the waves. Soon, people walking their dogs emerged from darkened houses.

The sky slowly lightened. Gently. Night gave way to dawn — not to sunshine. I waited. The slowness had forced me to wait and to watch. I began to see color in the sky and grass and water. The day was revealing what the darkness had hidden. The beauty was still there — the dawn revealed it.

If the sun had appeared when I had wanted it to, its light and heat would have been too harsh. I would not have been ready. This way I was able to gently enter the day.

I began to reflect on God's grace, which brings us out of our darkness slowly and gently. How often I get impatient with the darkness. I get impatient with God's leisure. But his way is perfect. As I am still before him and wait for his timing, I see that it is his graciousness that grants me time to adjust to the new day dawning.

Dear Lord, grant me patience and understanding so I may appreciate the perfect timing of your grace that brings me from darkness into light. Amen.

Your next devotion is located on page 741.

GRANDCHILD IN FOCUS • PRAYER

Physical Well-Being

Almighty God, Creator of us all, I pray that you will watch over my grandchild's physical development. May he grow in strength through the stages of his life. As he grows in awareness of his body, help him to understand that each body develops uniquely, yet is within your plan and your control. Please guard his health so that his diseases are few, his injuries are minor and his infirmities are brief. Amen.

⁷Be still before the LORD and wait patiently for
him;
do not fret when men succeed in their
ways,
when they carry out their wicked schemes.

⁸Refrain from anger and turn from wrath;
do not fret—it leads only to evil.
⁹For evil men will be cut off,
but those who hope in the LORD will
inherit the land.

¹⁰A little while, and the wicked will be no
more;
though you look for them, they will not be
found.
¹¹But the meek will inherit the land
and enjoy great peace.

¹²The wicked plot against the righteous
and gnash their teeth at them;
¹³but the Lord laughs at the wicked,
for he knows their day is coming.

¹⁴The wicked draw the sword
and bend the bow
to bring down the poor and needy,
to slay those whose ways are upright.
¹⁵But their swords will pierce their own hearts,
and their bows will be broken.

¹⁶Better the little that the righteous have
than the wealth of many wicked;
¹⁷for the power of the wicked will be broken,
but the LORD upholds the righteous.

¹⁸The days of the blameless are known to the
LORD,
and their inheritance will endure forever.
¹⁹In times of disaster they will not wither;
in days of famine they will enjoy plenty.

²⁰But the wicked will perish:
The LORD's enemies will be like the beauty
of the fields,
they will vanish—vanish like smoke.

²¹The wicked borrow and do not repay,
but the righteous give generously;

²²those the LORD blesses will inherit the land,
but those he curses will be cut off.

²³If the LORD delights in a man's way,
he makes his steps firm;
²⁴though he stumble, he will not fall,
for the LORD upholds him with his hand.

²⁵I was young and now I am old,
yet I have never seen the righteous forsaken
or their children begging bread.
²⁶They are always generous and lend freely;
their children will be blessed.

²⁷Turn from evil and do good;
then you will dwell in the land forever.
²⁸For the LORD loves the just
and will not forsake his faithful ones.

They will be protected forever,
but the offspring of the wicked will be cut
off;
²⁹the righteous will inherit the land
and dwell in it forever.

³⁰The mouth of the righteous man utters
wisdom,
and his tongue speaks what is just.
³¹The law of his God is in his heart;
his feet do not slip.

³²The wicked lie in wait for the righteous,
seeking their very lives;
³³but the LORD will not leave them in their
power
or let them be condemned when brought
to trial.

³⁴Wait for the LORD
and keep his way.
He will exalt you to inherit the land;
when the wicked are cut off, you will see it.

³⁵I have seen a wicked and ruthless man
flourishing like a green tree in its native
soil,
³⁶but he soon passed away and was no more;
though I looked for him, he could not be
found.

37 Consider the blameless, observe the upright;
    there is a future[a] for the man of peace.
38 But all sinners will be destroyed;
    the future[b] of the wicked will be cut off.

39 The salvation of the righteous comes from
      the LORD;
    he is their stronghold in time of trouble.
40 The LORD helps them and delivers them;
    he delivers them from the wicked and saves
      them,
    because they take refuge in him.

Psalm 38

A psalm of David. A petition.

1 O LORD, do not rebuke me in your anger
    or discipline me in your wrath.
2 For your arrows have pierced me,
    and your hand has come down upon me.
3 Because of your wrath there is no health in
      my body;
    my bones have no soundness because of
      my sin.
4 My guilt has overwhelmed me
    like a burden too heavy to bear.

5 My wounds fester and are loathsome
    because of my sinful folly.
6 I am bowed down and brought very low;
    all day long I go about mourning.
7 My back is filled with searing pain;
    there is no health in my body.
8 I am feeble and utterly crushed;
    I groan in anguish of heart.

9 All my longings lie open before you, O Lord;
    my sighing is not hidden from you.
10 My heart pounds, my strength fails me;
    even the light has gone from my eyes.
11 My friends and companions avoid me
      because of my wounds;
    my neighbors stay far away.
12 Those who seek my life set their traps,
    those who would harm me talk of my ruin;
    all day long they plot deception.

13 I am like a deaf man, who cannot hear,
    like a mute, who cannot open his mouth;
14 I have become like a man who does not
      hear,
    whose mouth can offer no reply.
15 I wait for you, O LORD;
    you will answer, O Lord my God.
16 For I said, "Do not let them gloat
    or exalt themselves over me when my foot
      slips."

17 For I am about to fall,
    and my pain is ever with me.
18 I confess my iniquity;
    I am troubled by my sin.
19 Many are those who are my vigorous
      enemies;
    those who hate me without reason are
      numerous.
20 Those who repay my good with evil
    slander me when I pursue what is good.

21 O LORD, do not forsake me;
    be not far from me, O my God.
22 Come quickly to help me,
    O Lord my Savior.

Psalm 39

*For the director of music. For Jeduthun.
A psalm of David.*

1 I said, "I will watch my ways
    and keep my tongue from sin;
  I will put a muzzle on my mouth
    as long as the wicked are in my presence."
2 But when I was silent and still,
    not even saying anything good,
    my anguish increased.
3 My heart grew hot within me,
    and as I meditated, the fire burned;
    then I spoke with my tongue:

4 "Show me, O LORD, my life's end
    and the number of my days;
    let me know how fleeting is my life.

a 37 Or there will be posterity   b 38 Or posterity

5 You have made my days a mere handbreadth;
the span of my years is as nothing before
you.
Each man's life is but a breath. *Selah*
6 Man is a mere phantom as he goes to and fro:
He bustles about, but only in vain;
he heaps up wealth, not knowing who will
get it.

7 "But now, Lord, what do I look for?
My hope is in you.
8 Save me from all my transgressions;
do not make me the scorn of fools.
9 I was silent; I would not open my mouth,
for you are the one who has done this.
10 Remove your scourge from me;
I am overcome by the blow of your hand.
11 You rebuke and discipline men for their sin;
you consume their wealth like a moth —
each man is but a breath. *Selah*

12 "Hear my prayer, O LORD,
listen to my cry for help;
be not deaf to my weeping.
For I dwell with you as an alien,
a stranger, as all my fathers were.
13 Look away from me, that I may rejoice again
before I depart and am no more."

Psalm 40

40:13–17pp — Ps 70:1–5

For the director of music. Of David. A psalm.

1 I waited patiently for the LORD;
he turned to me and heard my cry.
2 He lifted me out of the slimy pit,
out of the mud and mire;
he set my feet on a rock
and gave me a firm place to stand.
3 He put a new song in my mouth,
a hymn of praise to our God.
Many will see and fear
and put their trust in the LORD.

4 Blessed is the man
who makes the LORD his trust,

TALKING POINTS

Patience
Wait patiently for God.
PSALM 40:1

For more on patience, go to Proverbs 14:29.

---

who does not look to the proud,
to those who turn aside to false gods. [a]
5 Many, O LORD my God,
are the wonders you have done.
The things you planned for us
no one can recount to you;
were I to speak and tell of them,
they would be too many to declare.

6 Sacrifice and offering you did not desire,
but my ears you have pierced [b, c];
burnt offerings and sin offerings
you did not require.
7 Then I said, "Here I am, I have come —
it is written about me in the scroll. [d]
8 I desire to do your will, O my God;
your law is within my heart."

9 I proclaim righteousness in the great
assembly;
I do not seal my lips,
as you know, O LORD.
10 I do not hide your righteousness in my
heart;
I speak of your faithfulness and salvation.
I do not conceal your love and your truth
from the great assembly.

11 Do not withhold your mercy from me,
O LORD;
may your love and your truth always
protect me.

---

*a 4 Or to falsehood   b 6 Hebrew; Septuagint but a body you
have prepared for me (see also Symmachus and Theodotion)
c 6 Or opened   d 7 Or come / with the scroll written for me*

¹²For troubles without number surround me;
  my sins have overtaken me, and I cannot
    see.
They are more than the hairs of my head,
  and my heart fails within me.

¹³Be pleased, O LORD, to save me;
  O LORD, come quickly to help me.
¹⁴May all who seek to take my life
  be put to shame and confusion;
may all who desire my ruin
  be turned back in disgrace.
¹⁵May those who say to me, "Aha! Aha!"
  be appalled at their own shame.
¹⁶But may all who seek you
  rejoice and be glad in you;
may those who love your salvation always say,
  "The LORD be exalted!"

¹⁷Yet I am poor and needy;
  may the Lord think of me.
You are my help and my deliverer;
  O my God, do not delay.

Psalm 41

For the director of music.
A psalm of David.

¹Blessed is he who has regard for the weak;
  the LORD delivers him in times of trouble.
²The LORD will protect him and preserve his
    life;
  he will bless him in the land
  and not surrender him to the desire of his
    foes.
³The LORD will sustain him on his sickbed
  and restore him from his bed of illness.

⁴I said, "O LORD, have mercy on me;
  heal me, for I have sinned against you."
⁵My enemies say of me in malice,
  "When will he die and his name perish?"
⁶Whenever one comes to see me,
  he speaks falsely, while his heart gathers
    slander;
  then he goes out and spreads it abroad.

⁷All my enemies whisper together against me;
  they imagine the worst for me, saying,
⁸"A vile disease has beset him;
  he will never get up from the place where
    he lies."
⁹Even my close friend, whom I trusted,
  he who shared my bread,
  has lifted up his heel against me.

¹⁰But you, O LORD, have mercy on me;
  raise me up, that I may repay them.
¹¹I know that you are pleased with me,
  for my enemy does not triumph over me.
¹²In my integrity you uphold me
  and set me in your presence forever.

¹³Praise be to the LORD, the God of Israel,
  from everlasting to everlasting.
    Amen and Amen.

BOOK II

Psalms 42–72

Psalm 42 ᵃ

For the director of music. A *maskil* ᵇ
of the Sons of Korah.

¹As the deer pants for streams of water,
  so my soul pants for you, O God.
²My soul thirsts for God, for the living God.
  When can I go and meet with God?
³My tears have been my food
  day and night,
while men say to me all day long,
  "Where is your God?"
⁴These things I remember
  as I pour out my soul:
how I used to go with the multitude,
  leading the procession to the house of
    God,
with shouts of joy and thanksgiving
  among the festive throng.

ᵃ In many Hebrew manuscripts Psalms 42 and 43 constitute one
psalm.   ᵇ Title: Probably a literary or musical term

⁵Why are you downcast, O my soul?
  Why so disturbed within me?
Put your hope in God,
  for I will yet praise him,
  my Savior and ⁶my God.

My *ᵃ* soul is downcast within me;
  therefore I will remember you
from the land of the Jordan,
  the heights of Hermon—from Mount
    Mizar.
⁷Deep calls to deep
  in the roar of your waterfalls;
all your waves and breakers
  have swept over me.

⁸By day the LORD directs his love,
  at night his song is with me—
a prayer to the God of my life.

⁹I say to God my Rock,
  "Why have you forgotten me?
Why must I go about mourning,
  oppressed by the enemy?"
¹⁰My bones suffer mortal agony
  as my foes taunt me,
saying to me all day long,
  "Where is your God?"

¹¹Why are you downcast, O my soul?
  Why so disturbed within me?
Put your hope in God,
  for I will yet praise him,
  my Savior and my God.

Psalm 43 *ᵇ*

¹Vindicate me, O God,
  and plead my cause against an ungodly
    nation;
  rescue me from deceitful and wicked men.
²You are God my stronghold.
  Why have you rejected me?
Why must I go about mourning,
  oppressed by the enemy?
³Send forth your light and your truth,
  let them guide me;
let them bring me to your holy mountain,
  to the place where you dwell.
⁴Then will I go to the altar of God,
  to God, my joy and my delight.
I will praise you with the harp,
  O God, my God.

⁵Why are you downcast, O my soul?
  Why so disturbed within me?
Put your hope in God,
  for I will yet praise him,
  my Savior and my God.

Psalm 44

For the director of music. Of the Sons
of Korah. A *maskil.* *ᶜ*

¹We have heard with our ears, O God;
  our fathers have told us
what you did in their days,
  in days long ago.
²With your hand you drove out the nations
  and planted our fathers;
you crushed the peoples
  and made our fathers flourish.
³It was not by their sword that they won the
    land,
  nor did their arm bring them victory;
it was your right hand, your arm,
  and the light of your face, for you loved
    them.

ᵃ 5,6 A few Hebrew manuscripts, Septuagint and Syriac; most
Hebrew manuscripts *praise him for his saving help.* / *⁶O my God, my*
ᵇ In many Hebrew manuscripts Psalms 42 and 43 constitute one
psalm. *ᶜ* Title: Probably a literary or musical term

⁴You are my King and my God,
  who decrees^a victories for Jacob.
⁵Through you we push back our enemies;
  through your name we trample our foes.
⁶I do not trust in my bow,
  my sword does not bring me victory;
⁷but you give us victory over our enemies,
  you put our adversaries to shame.
⁸In God we make our boast all day long,
  and we will praise your name forever.

Selah

⁹But now you have rejected and humbled us;
  you no longer go out with our armies.
¹⁰You made us retreat before the enemy,
  and our adversaries have plundered us.
¹¹You gave us up to be devoured like sheep
  and have scattered us among the nations.
¹²You sold your people for a pittance,
  gaining nothing from their sale.

¹³You have made us a reproach to our
    neighbors,
  the scorn and derision of those around us.
¹⁴You have made us a byword among the
    nations;
  the peoples shake their heads at us.
¹⁵My disgrace is before me all day long,
  and my face is covered with shame
¹⁶at the taunts of those who reproach and
    revile me,
  because of the enemy, who is bent on
    revenge.

¹⁷All this happened to us,
  though we had not forgotten you
  or been false to your covenant.
¹⁸Our hearts had not turned back;
  our feet had not strayed from your path.
¹⁹But you crushed us and made us a haunt for
    jackals
  and covered us over with deep darkness.

²⁰If we had forgotten the name of our God
  or spread out our hands to a foreign god,
²¹would not God have discovered it,
  since he knows the secrets of the heart?

²²Yet for your sake we face death all day long;
  we are considered as sheep to be
    slaughtered.

²³Awake, O Lord! Why do you sleep?
  Rouse yourself! Do not reject us forever.
²⁴Why do you hide your face
  and forget our misery and oppression?

²⁵We are brought down to the dust;
  our bodies cling to the ground.
²⁶Rise up and help us;
  redeem us because of your unfailing love.

Psalm 45

*For the director of music. To ⌊the tune of⌋
"Lilies." Of the Sons of Korah.
A* maskil.^b *A wedding song.*

¹My heart is stirred by a noble theme
  as I recite my verses for the king;
  my tongue is the pen of a skillful writer.

²You are the most excellent of men
  and your lips have been anointed with
    grace,
  since God has blessed you forever.
³Gird your sword upon your side, O mighty
    one;
  clothe yourself with splendor and majesty.
⁴In your majesty ride forth victoriously
  in behalf of truth, humility and
    righteousness;
  let your right hand display awesome deeds.
⁵Let your sharp arrows pierce the hearts of the
    king's enemies;
  let the nations fall beneath your feet.
⁶Your throne, O God, will last for ever and
    ever;
  a scepter of justice will be the scepter of
    your kingdom.
⁷You love righteousness and hate wickedness;
  therefore God, your God, has set you above
    your companions
  by anointing you with the oil of joy.

---

^a 4 Septuagint, Aquila and Syriac; Hebrew *King, O God; / command*
^b Title: Probably a literary or musical term

> I WILL PERPETUATE YOUR MEMORY THROUGH ALL GENERATIONS; THEREFORE THE NATIONS WILL PRAISE YOU FOR EVER AND EVER.
>
> *Psalm 45:17*

Perpetuating Memories

PATRICIA SPRINKLE

READ | PSALM 45:1 – 17

What will your grandchild remember? Mine will probably always remember that "Momo broke de door."

At 20 months old, my grandson locked himself in his father's study. He was too young to turn the knob, so after rejecting several alternatives, I found a wrench and commanded, "Go stand near the window. I have to break down the door."

He stood — frozen and wide-eyed — across the room, watching my disembodied hand coming through the jagged hole to turn the knob. For weeks afterwards, every time he passed that room, he'd announce, "Momo broke de door."

His parents and I decided to teach him an additional part of the story. When he'd say, "Momo broke de door," we'd ask, "Why did Momo break the door?" He'd beam as he repeated the answer we'd taught him: "To save me." He knows he's worth saving!

Psalm 45 is a song in praise of Israel's king on his wedding day. In verse 17 the psalmist pledged to perpetuate the king's memory throughout the generations and awaken the praise of the nations.

One of the privileges of being a grandparent is passing on faith-building stories to future generations. My father told us how his father assembled his nine children nightly for family devotions. Recently my son said, "It's such fun to see Joshua picking up on spiritual rhythms. He expects to pray before meals and bedtime. He knows to say 'Amen' after a prayer." Joshua has learned those rhythms through stories and memories from generations of believers. I suspect one of the earliest memories he'll pass down will be "When Momo Broke de Door — to Save Me."

Lord, thank you for those who believed in you in the past and passed that faith on to me. Help me to perpetuate both their faith and their memories of your faithfulness.

GRANDCHILD **IN FOCUS** • PRAYER

Emotional Development

O God, Creator of mind and body, I pray that you will give my grandchild emotional health and strength. Where there is anger, bring peace. Where there is confusion, bring clarity and focus. Where there are dark shadows, cast a ray of hope. Fill her with the sunshine of your Spirit. Warm her with the presence of your peace. Amen.

Your next devotion is located on page 743.

8 All your robes are fragrant with myrrh and
    aloes and cassia;
  from palaces adorned with ivory
    the music of the strings makes you glad.
9 Daughters of kings are among your honored
    women;
  at your right hand is the royal bride in gold
    of Ophir.

10 Listen, O daughter, consider and give ear:
  Forget your people and your father's
    house.
11 The king is enthralled by your beauty;
  honor him, for he is your lord.
12 The Daughter of Tyre will come with a gift, *a*
  men of wealth will seek your favor.

13 All glorious is the princess within ˌher
    chamberˌ;
  her gown is interwoven with gold.
14 In embroidered garments she is led to the
    king;
  her virgin companions follow her
  and are brought to you.
15 They are led in with joy and gladness;
  they enter the palace of the king.

16 Your sons will take the place of your fathers;
  you will make them princes throughout
    the land.
17 I will perpetuate your memory through all
    generations;
  therefore the nations will praise you for
    ever and ever.

Psalm 46

For the director of music. Of the Sons
of Korah. According to *alamoth.* *b*
A song.

1 God is our refuge and strength,
  an ever-present help in trouble.
2 Therefore we will not fear, though the earth
    give way
  and the mountains fall into the heart of
    the sea,

PRAYING THE SCRIPTURES

Reassurance

PSALM 46:1

O Lord, be a refuge and strength for my
grandchild, his ever-present help in this time
of trouble.

Next prayer in Reassurance Prayer Track: Psalm 57:1

3 though its waters roar and foam
  and the mountains quake with their
    surging.   *Selah*

4 There is a river whose streams make glad the
    city of God,
  the holy place where the Most High dwells.
5 God is within her, she will not fall;
  God will help her at break of day.
6 Nations are in uproar, kingdoms fall;
  he lifts his voice, the earth melts.

TALKING POINTS

Fear

God, our refuge and strength,
is always at our side to help us.

PSALM 46:1–11

For more on fear, go to Psalm 56:1–13.

7 The Lord Almighty is with us;
  the God of Jacob is our fortress.   *Selah*

8 Come and see the works of the Lord,
  the desolations he has brought on the
    earth.

a 12 Or A Tyrian robe is among the gifts   *b Title: Probably a musical term*

Be Still

EMILIE BARNES

READ | PSALM 46:1–11

"Be still, and know that I am God." Easier said than done, isn't it? It's hard to find a quiet moment in the day—a few minutes to relax and think and pray. Even as grandparents we're constantly on the move, pressured by demands of work and family, church and community activities, and recreation. Moments to be still with God don't just happen with full schedules.

So what's the solution? I make appointments with myself to rest, plan, regroup and draw closer to God.

My husband and I just returned from five days in San Diego, California. One afternoon we talked about family, ministry, goals, God's love, his Word and our writing. Now we're both quiet, and we're feeling that rare sense of stillness the psalmist talked about.

Our lives aren't usually like this. Often our lives aren't in balance. It's easy to be more outwardly focused than inwardly focused. But as we get older, it becomes a bit easier to concentrate on the inward things. I find I sincerely desire to glorify God more with my life now. I want to know him better. I want him to use me. And I want to better know his peace and stillness. You probably want those things for yourself as well.

The door of stillness is waiting for any of us to open it, but it won't open by itself. We have to choose to turn the knob, and then we have to choose to make time to enter and sit for awhile. All of us need to learn to balance the time we spend in quiet and calm with the time we spend in the fray of everyday existence. Ecclesiastes 3:1 says there is a time for everything—and that includes a time to be still despite our busy lives.

Father God, I struggle to take a time-out. I not only need quiet time to rejuvenate my body, but I also need times of peace and rest to be alone with you. Give me the desire to do both. I strive for a balanced life. Amen.

Your next devotion is located on page 752.

GRANDCHILD IN FOCUS • PRAYER

Spiritual Growth

Dear Lord, today I pray for my grandchild's spiritual growth. I ask that you instill in him the desire to read and memorize your Word. Give him a passion to be in conversation with you. May loving and serving you be part of his daily life. I ask that you stay close to him and lead him to be transformed to your likeness, to reflect your grace and to radiate your love. I pray this in Jesus' name, amen.

⁹He makes wars cease to the ends of the earth;
    he breaks the bow and shatters the spear,
    he burns the shields *a* with fire.
¹⁰"Be still, and know that I am God;
    I will be exalted among the nations,
    I will be exalted in the earth."

¹¹The Lord Almighty is with us;
    the God of Jacob is our fortress.   *Selah*

Psalm 47

For the director of music. Of the Sons
of Korah. A psalm.

¹Clap your hands, all you nations;
    shout to God with cries of joy.
²How awesome is the Lord Most High,
    the great King over all the earth!
³He subdued nations under us,
    peoples under our feet.
⁴He chose our inheritance for us,
    the pride of Jacob, whom he loved.   *Selah*

⁵God has ascended amid shouts of joy,
    the Lord amid the sounding of trumpets.
⁶Sing praises to God, sing praises;
    sing praises to our King, sing praises.

⁷For God is the King of all the earth;
    sing to him a psalm *b* of praise.
⁸God reigns over the nations;
    God is seated on his holy throne.
⁹The nobles of the nations assemble
    as the people of the God of Abraham,
for the kings *c* of the earth belong to God;
    he is greatly exalted.

Psalm 48

A song. A psalm of the Sons of Korah.

¹Great is the Lord, and most worthy of praise,
    in the city of our God, his holy mountain.
²It is beautiful in its loftiness,
    the joy of the whole earth.
Like the utmost heights of Zaphon *d* is Mount
    Zion,
    the *e* city of the Great King.

³God is in her citadels;
    he has shown himself to be her fortress.

⁴When the kings joined forces,
    when they advanced together,
⁵they saw ⌐her⌐ and were astounded;
    they fled in terror.
⁶Trembling seized them there,
    pain like that of a woman in labor.
⁷You destroyed them like ships of Tarshish
    shattered by an east wind.

⁸As we have heard,
    so have we seen
in the city of the Lord Almighty,
    in the city of our God:
    God makes her secure forever.   *Selah*

⁹Within your temple, O God,
    we meditate on your unfailing love.
¹⁰Like your name, O God,
    your praise reaches to the ends of the
        earth;
    your right hand is filled with
        righteousness.
¹¹Mount Zion rejoices,
    the villages of Judah are glad
    because of your judgments.

¹²Walk about Zion, go around her,
    count her towers,
¹³consider well her ramparts,
    view her citadels,
    that you may tell of them to the next
        generation.
¹⁴For this God is our God for ever and ever;
    he will be our guide even to the end.

Psalm 49

For the director of music. Of the Sons
of Korah. A psalm.

¹Hear this, all you peoples;
    listen, all who live in this world,

---

a 9 Or *chariots*   *b 7* Or *a maskil* (probably a literary or musical term)   *c 9* Or *shields*   *d 2 Zaphon* can refer to a sacred mountain or the direction north.   *e 2* Or *earth, / Mount Zion, on the northern side / of the*

²both low and high,
    rich and poor alike:
³My mouth will speak words of wisdom;
    the utterance from my heart will give
      understanding.
⁴I will turn my ear to a proverb;
    with the harp I will expound my riddle:

⁵Why should I fear when evil days come,
    when wicked deceivers surround me—
⁶those who trust in their wealth
    and boast of their great riches?
⁷No man can redeem the life of another
    or give to God a ransom for him—
⁸the ransom for a life is costly,
    no payment is ever enough—
⁹that he should live on forever
    and not see decay.

¹⁰For all can see that wise men die;
    the foolish and the senseless alike perish
    and leave their wealth to others.
¹¹Their tombs will remain their houses[a]
    forever,
    their dwellings for endless generations,
    though they had[b] named lands after
      themselves.

¹²But man, despite his riches, does not endure;
    he is[c] like the beasts that perish.

¹³This is the fate of those who trust in
    themselves,
    and of their followers, who approve their
      sayings.   *Selah*
¹⁴Like sheep they are destined for the grave,[d]
    and death will feed on them.
    The upright will rule over them in the
      morning;
    their forms will decay in the grave,[d]
    far from their princely mansions.
¹⁵But God will redeem my life[e] from the
    grave;
    he will surely take me to himself.   *Selah*

¹⁶Do not be overawed when a man grows rich,
    when the splendor of his house increases;

¹⁷for he will take nothing with him when he
    dies,
    his splendor will not descend with him.
¹⁸Though while he lived he counted himself
    blessed—
    and men praise you when you prosper—
¹⁹he will join the generation of his fathers,
    who will never see the light ⌊of life⌋.

²⁰A man who has riches without understanding
    is like the beasts that perish.

Psalm 50

A psalm of Asaph.

¹The Mighty One, God, the Lᴏʀᴅ,
    speaks and summons the earth
    from the rising of the sun to the place
      where it sets.
²From Zion, perfect in beauty,
    God shines forth.
³Our God comes and will not be silent;
    a fire devours before him,
    and around him a tempest rages.
⁴He summons the heavens above,
    and the earth, that he may judge his
      people:
⁵"Gather to me my consecrated ones,
    who made a covenant with me by
      sacrifice."
⁶And the heavens proclaim his righteousness,
    for God himself is judge.   *Selah*

⁷"Hear, O my people, and I will speak,
    O Israel, and I will testify against you:
    I am God, your God.
⁸I do not rebuke you for your sacrifices
    or your burnt offerings, which are ever
      before me.
⁹I have no need of a bull from your stall
    or of goats from your pens,
¹⁰for every animal of the forest is mine,
    and the cattle on a thousand hills.

---

[a] 11 Septuagint and Syriac; Hebrew *In their thoughts their houses will
remain*   [b] 11 Or */ for they have*   [c] 12 Hebrew; Septuagint and
Syriac read verse 12 the same as verse 20.   [d] 14 Hebrew *Sheol*; also
in verse 15   [e] 15 Or *soul*

11 I know every bird in the mountains,
   and the creatures of the field are mine.
12 If I were hungry I would not tell you,
   for the world is mine, and all that is in it.
13 Do I eat the flesh of bulls
   or drink the blood of goats?
14 Sacrifice thank offerings to God,
   fulfill your vows to the Most High,
15 and call upon me in the day of trouble;
   I will deliver you, and you will honor me."

16 But to the wicked, God says:

"What right have you to recite my laws
   or take my covenant on your lips?
17 You hate my instruction
   and cast my words behind you.
18 When you see a thief, you join with him;
   you throw in your lot with adulterers.
19 You use your mouth for evil
   and harness your tongue to deceit.
20 You speak continually against your brother
   and slander your own mother's son.
21 These things you have done and I kept
      silent;
   you thought I was altogether[a] like you.
But I will rebuke you
   and accuse you to your face.

22 "Consider this, you who forget God,
   or I will tear you to pieces, with none to
      rescue:
23 He who sacrifices thank offerings honors me,
   and he prepares the way
   so that I may show him[b] the salvation of
      God."

Psalm 51

For the director of music. A psalm of David.
When the prophet Nathan came to him
after David had committed adultery
with Bathsheba.

1 Have mercy on me, O God,
   according to your unfailing love;
   according to your great compassion
   blot out my transgressions.

PRAYING THE SCRIPTURES

Forgiveness

PSALM 51:1–2

Have mercy on my grandchild, O God, according to your unfailing love; according to your great compassion, blot out his transgressions. May he turn to you so that you can wash away his iniquity and cleanse him of his sin.

Next prayer in Forgiveness Prayer Track: Psalm 130:3–4

2 Wash away all my iniquity
   and cleanse me from my sin.

3 For I know my transgressions,
   and my sin is always before me.
4 Against you, you only, have I sinned
   and done what is evil in your sight,
so that you are proved right when you
      speak
   and justified when you judge.
5 Surely I was sinful at birth,
   sinful from the time my mother conceived
      me.
6 Surely you desire truth in the inner parts[c];
   you teach[d] me wisdom in the inmost
      place.

7 Cleanse me with hyssop, and I will be clean;
   wash me, and I will be whiter than snow.
8 Let me hear joy and gladness;
   let the bones you have crushed rejoice.
9 Hide your face from my sins
   and blot out all my iniquity.

10 Create in me a pure heart, O God,
   and renew a steadfast spirit within me.
11 Do not cast me from your presence
   or take your Holy Spirit from me.

---

[a] 21 Or thought the 'I AM' was   [b] 23 Or and to him who considers his way / I will show   [c] 6 The meaning of the Hebrew for this phrase is uncertain.   [d] 6 Or you desired . . . ; / you taught

¹²Restore to me the joy of your salvation
and grant me a willing spirit, to sustain
me.

¹³Then I will teach transgressors your ways,
and sinners will turn back to you.
¹⁴Save me from bloodguilt, O God,
the God who saves me,
and my tongue will sing of your
righteousness.
¹⁵O Lord, open my lips,
and my mouth will declare your praise.
¹⁶You do not delight in sacrifice, or I would
bring it;
you do not take pleasure in burnt
offerings.
¹⁷The sacrifices of God are[a] a broken spirit;
a broken and contrite heart,
O God, you will not despise.

¹⁸In your good pleasure make Zion prosper;
build up the walls of Jerusalem.
¹⁹Then there will be righteous sacrifices,
whole burnt offerings to delight you;
then bulls will be offered on your altar.

PRAYING THE SCRIPTURES

Salvation

PSALM 51:5,7,10–12

Lord, it is hard for me to comprehend that
my grandchild was sinful at birth, sinful from
the time his mother conceived him. So I pray
you will cleanse him that he may be clean
and wash him so that he will be whiter than
snow. Create in him a pure heart, O God,
and renew a steadfast spirit within him. Do
not cast him from your presence or take
your Holy Spirit from him. Restore to him
the joy of your salvation and grant him a willing spirit to sustain him.

Next prayer in Salvation Prayer Track: Isaiah 53:6

Psalm 52

For the director of music. A *maskil*[b]
of David. When Doeg the Edomite had gone
to Saul and told him: "David has gone to the
house of Ahimelech."

¹Why do you boast of evil, you mighty
man?
Why do you boast all day long,
you who are a disgrace in the eyes
of God?
²Your tongue plots destruction;
it is like a sharpened razor,
you who practice deceit.
³You love evil rather than good,
falsehood rather than speaking the
truth.   *Selah*
⁴You love every harmful word,
O you deceitful tongue!

⁵Surely God will bring you down to
everlasting ruin:
He will snatch you up and tear you from
your tent;
he will uproot you from the land of
the living.   *Selah*
⁶The righteous will see and fear;
they will laugh at him, saying,
⁷"Here now is the man
who did not make God his stronghold
but trusted in his great wealth
and grew strong by destroying others!"

⁸But I am like an olive tree
flourishing in the house of God;
I trust in God's unfailing love
for ever and ever.
⁹I will praise you forever for what you have
done;
in your name I will hope, for your name
is good.
I will praise you in the presence of your
saints.

[a] 17 Or *My sacrifice, O God, is*   [b] Title: Probably a literary or
musical term

Psalm 53

53:1–6pp — Ps 14:1–7

For the director of music. According to
mahalath.[a] A *maskil*[b] of David.

¹ The fool says in his heart,
  "There is no God."
They are corrupt, and their ways are vile;
  there is no one who does good.

² God looks down from heaven
    on the sons of men
to see if there are any who understand,
    any who seek God.
³ Everyone has turned away,
    they have together become corrupt;
there is no one who does good,
    not even one.

⁴ Will the evildoers never learn—
    those who devour my people as men eat
      bread
    and who do not call on God?
⁵ There they were, overwhelmed with dread,
    where there was nothing to dread.
God scattered the bones of those who
      attacked you;
    you put them to shame, for God despised
      them.

⁶ Oh, that salvation for Israel would come out
      of Zion!
    When God restores the fortunes of his
      people,
    let Jacob rejoice and Israel be glad!

Psalm 54

For the director of music. With stringed
instruments. A *maskil*[b] of David. When the
Ziphites had gone to Saul and said,
"Is not David hiding among us?"

¹ Save me, O God, by your name;
    vindicate me by your might.
² Hear my prayer, O God;
    listen to the words of my mouth.

³ Strangers are attacking me;
    ruthless men seek my life—
    men without regard for God.   *Selah*

⁴ Surely God is my help;
    the Lord is the one who sustains me.

⁵ Let evil recoil on those who slander me;
    in your faithfulness destroy them.

⁶ I will sacrifice a freewill offering to you;
    I will praise your name, O LORD,
    for it is good.
⁷ For he has delivered me from all my troubles,
    and my eyes have looked in triumph on
      my foes.

Psalm 55

For the director of music.
With stringed instruments.
A *maskil*[b] of David.

¹ Listen to my prayer, O God,
    do not ignore my plea;
²   hear me and answer me.
My thoughts trouble me and I am distraught
³   at the voice of the enemy,
    at the stares of the wicked;
for they bring down suffering upon me
    and revile me in their anger.

⁴ My heart is in anguish within me;
    the terrors of death assail me.
⁵ Fear and trembling have beset me;
    horror has overwhelmed me.
⁶ I said, "Oh, that I had the wings of a dove!
    I would fly away and be at rest—
⁷ I would flee far away
    and stay in the desert;   *Selah*
⁸ I would hurry to my place of shelter,
    far from the tempest and storm."

⁹ Confuse the wicked, O Lord, confound their
      speech,
    for I see violence and strife in the city.

---

[a] Title: Probably a musical term   [b] Title: Probably a literary or
musical term

¹⁰Day and night they prowl about on its walls;
   malice and abuse are within it.
¹¹Destructive forces are at work in the city;
   threats and lies never leave its streets.

¹²If an enemy were insulting me,
   I could endure it;
if a foe were raising himself against me,
   I could hide from him.
¹³But it is you, a man like myself,
   my companion, my close friend,
¹⁴with whom I once enjoyed sweet fellowship
   as we walked with the throng at the house
    of God.

¹⁵Let death take my enemies by surprise;
   let them go down alive to the grave,^a
   for evil finds lodging among them.

¹⁶But I call to God,
   and the Lord saves me.
¹⁷Evening, morning and noon
   I cry out in distress,
   and he hears my voice.
¹⁸He ransoms me unharmed
   from the battle waged against me,
   even though many oppose me.
¹⁹God, who is enthroned forever,
   will hear them and afflict them— *Selah*
men who never change their ways
   and have no fear of God.

²⁰My companion attacks his friends;
   he violates his covenant.
²¹His speech is smooth as butter,
   yet war is in his heart;
his words are more soothing than oil,
   yet they are drawn swords.

²²Cast your cares on the Lord
   and he will sustain you;
   he will never let the righteous fall.
²³But you, O God, will bring down the wicked
   into the pit of corruption;
bloodthirsty and deceitful men
   will not live out half their days.

But as for me, I trust in you.

Psalm 56

For the director of music. To ˌthe tune ofˌ
"A Dove on Distant Oaks." Of David. A *miktam.*^b
When the Philistines had seized him in Gath.

¹Be merciful to me, O God, for men hotly
   pursue me;
   all day long they press their attack.
²My slanderers pursue me all day long;
   many are attacking me in their pride.

³When I am afraid,
   I will trust in you.
⁴In God, whose word I praise,
   in God I trust; I will not be afraid.
   What can mortal man do to me?

⁵All day long they twist my words;
   they are always plotting to harm me.
⁶They conspire, they lurk,
   they watch my steps,
   eager to take my life.

⁷On no account let them escape;
   in your anger, O God, bring down the
    nations.
⁸Record my lament;
   list my tears on your scroll^c—
   are they not in your record?

⁹Then my enemies will turn back
   when I call for help.
   By this I will know that God is for me.

^a 15 Hebrew *Sheol*   ^b Title: Probably a literary or musical term
^c 8 Or / *put my tears in your wineskin*

TALKING POINTS

Fear

Trust in God; he is stronger
than any adversary.

PSALM 56:1–13

For more on fear, go to Isaiah 50:10.

¹⁰In God, whose word I praise,
in the Lᴏʀᴅ, whose word I praise—
¹¹in God I trust; I will not be afraid.
What can man do to me?

¹²I am under vows to you, O God;
I will present my thank offerings to you.
¹³For you have delivered me*ᵃ* from death
and my feet from stumbling,
that I may walk before God
in the light of life.*ᵇ*

Psalm 57

57:7–11pp — Ps 108:1–5

For the director of music. ⌊To the tune of⌋
"Do Not Destroy." Of David. A *miktam.*ᶜ When he
had fled from Saul into the cave.

¹Have mercy on me, O God, have mercy on
me,
for in you my soul takes refuge.
I will take refuge in the shadow of your wings
until the disaster has passed.

PRAYING THE SCRIPTURES

Reassurance

PSALM 57:1

Have mercy on my grandchild, O God; have
mercy on her, for in you her soul takes refuge. Let her take refuge in the shadow of
your wings until the disaster has passed.

Next prayer in Reassurance Prayer Track:
Psalm 86:6–7,10

²I cry out to God Most High,
to God, who fulfills ⌊his purpose⌋ for me.
³He sends from heaven and saves me,
rebuking those who hotly pursue me;
Selah
God sends his love and his faithfulness.

⁴I am in the midst of lions;
I lie among ravenous beasts—
men whose teeth are spears and arrows,
whose tongues are sharp swords.

⁵Be exalted, O God, above the heavens;
let your glory be over all the earth.

⁶They spread a net for my feet—
I was bowed down in distress.
They dug a pit in my path—
but they have fallen into it themselves.
Selah

⁷My heart is steadfast, O God,
my heart is steadfast;
I will sing and make music.
⁸Awake, my soul!
Awake, harp and lyre!
I will awaken the dawn.

⁹I will praise you, O Lord, among the nations;
I will sing of you among the peoples.
¹⁰For great is your love, reaching to the
heavens;
your faithfulness reaches to the skies.

¹¹Be exalted, O God, above the heavens;
let your glory be over all the earth.

Psalm 58

For the director of music. ⌊To the tune of⌋
"Do Not Destroy." Of David.
A *miktam.*ᶜ

¹Do you rulers indeed speak justly?
Do you judge uprightly among men?
²No, in your heart you devise injustice,
and your hands mete out violence on the
earth.
³Even from birth the wicked go astray;
from the womb they are wayward and
speak lies.
⁴Their venom is like the venom of a snake,
like that of a cobra that has stopped its
ears,

ᵃ 13 Or *my soul*   ᵇ 13 Or *the land of the living*   ᶜ Title: Probably
a literary or musical term

⁵that will not heed the tune of the charmer,
    however skillful the enchanter may be.

⁶Break the teeth in their mouths, O God;
    tear out, O Lord, the fangs of the
        lions!
⁷Let them vanish like water that flows
        away;
    when they draw the bow, let their arrows
        be blunted.
⁸Like a slug melting away as it moves along,
    like a stillborn child, may they not see the
        sun.

⁹Before your pots can feel ˌthe heat ofˌ the
        thorns—
    whether they be green or dry—the
        wicked will be swept away. ᵃ
¹⁰The righteous will be glad when they are
        avenged,
    when they bathe their feet in the blood
        of the wicked.
¹¹Then men will say,
    "Surely the righteous still are rewarded;
    surely there is a God who judges the
        earth."

Psalm 59

For the director of music. ˌTo the tune ofˌ
"Do Not Destroy." Of David. A *miktam.* ᵇ
When Saul had sent men to watch David's house
in order to kill him.

¹Deliver me from my enemies, O God;
    protect me from those who rise up against
        me.
²Deliver me from evildoers
    and save me from bloodthirsty men.

³See how they lie in wait for me!
    Fierce men conspire against me
    for no offense or sin of mine, O Lord.
⁴I have done no wrong, yet they are ready to
        attack me.
    Arise to help me; look on my plight!

⁵O Lord God Almighty, the God of Israel,
    rouse yourself to punish all the nations;
    show no mercy to wicked traitors.   *Selah*

⁶They return at evening,
    snarling like dogs,
    and prowl about the city.
⁷See what they spew from their mouths—
    they spew out swords from their lips,
    and they say, "Who can hear us?"
⁸But you, O Lord, laugh at them;
    you scoff at all those nations.

⁹O my Strength, I watch for you;
    you, O God, are my fortress, ¹⁰my loving
        God.

God will go before me
    and will let me gloat over those who
        slander me.
¹¹But do not kill them, O Lord our shield, ᶜ
    or my people will forget.
In your might make them wander about,
    and bring them down.
¹²For the sins of their mouths,
    for the words of their lips,
    let them be caught in their pride.
For the curses and lies they utter,
¹³   consume them in wrath,
    consume them till they are no more.
Then it will be known to the ends of the earth
    that God rules over Jacob.   *Selah*

¹⁴They return at evening,
    snarling like dogs,
    and prowl about the city.
¹⁵They wander about for food
    and howl if not satisfied.
¹⁶But I will sing of your strength,
    in the morning I will sing of your love;
for you are my fortress,
    my refuge in times of trouble.

¹⁷O my Strength, I sing praise to you;
    you, O God, are my fortress, my loving God.

ᵃ 9 The meaning of the Hebrew for this verse is uncertain.
ᵇ Title: Probably a literary or musical term   ᶜ 11 Or *sovereign*

751

But I will sing of your strength, in the morning I will sing of your love; for you are my fortress, my refuge in times of trouble.

Psalm 59:16

Day Glasses

KAREN MAINS

READ | PSALM 59:1 – 17

A funny thing happened last January on my 60th birthday. David bought me a card that was not one of those sing-song rhyming sentimental poems. Through the years, I have chosen not to measure my sweetheart's love by the poor literary quality of the birthday cards he buys.

So this January, my husband felt rather proud. He had purchased a funny card. On the front were two his-and-her towels pinned to a clothesline. The inside read: "It's been great hanging around with you all these years. Happy Anniversary!"

"David," I said gently, wondering if a little early dementia was showing up here, "this is an anniversary card, not a birthday card."

"Oh no!" he exclaimed. "I didn't have my glasses when I bought it! And I was so proud of finding a funny card."

For me, putting on the "right" glasses each morning is important if I'm going to give the day an appropriate greeting. One of my goals is to have my first thoughts fly to God.

So I have written a liturgy that I recite slowly each morning when I wake that lifts my soul and heart and mind to God first. Then, I step outside, no matter the weather, and look at the day, check out the morning star and the setting moon, watch the sunrise, smell the cup of coffee in my hand, and finally go back inside to write in my prayer journal.

These simple habits, these pauses in order to breathe thanks for one more day of life, are my "day glasses." Through these practices, my spiritual sight is focused. I can tell whether it is a happy birthday or an anniversary or simply a good day in ordinary time to live my life with God in my sight line.

O Lord, help me to want to see you in all of life. When I awake each morning, let my first thoughts be of you and your love. Help me to develop spiritual habits that will guide me in my morning worship and throughout my day. Amen.

GRANDCHILD IN FOCUS • PRAYER

Relationships at Home

O Lord, I pray that you will bless the home and family of my grandchild. May the relationships she has with her parents and siblings enhance her well-being, support her self-confidence and increase her faith. May her home life reflect your love, your grace, your compassion and your peace. Guide her parents to direct her in love and truth, so she will grow into a strong and compassionate individual. Amen.

Your next devotion is located on page 754.

Psalm 60

60:5–12pp — Ps 108:6–13

For the director of music. To ⌊the tune of⌋
"The Lily of the Covenant." A *miktam* [a]
of David. For teaching. When he fought
Aram Naharaim [b] and Aram Zobah, [c]
and when Joab returned and struck down
twelve thousand Edomites
in the Valley of Salt.

¹You have rejected us, O God, and burst forth
upon us;
you have been angry—now restore us!
²You have shaken the land and torn it
open;
mend its fractures, for it is quaking.
³You have shown your people desperate
times;
you have given us wine that makes us
stagger.

⁴But for those who fear you, you have raised
a banner
to be unfurled against the bow.   *Selah*

⁵Save us and help us with your right hand,
that those you love may be delivered.
⁶God has spoken from his sanctuary:
"In triumph I will parcel out Shechem
and measure off the Valley of Succoth.
⁷Gilead is mine, and Manasseh is mine;
Ephraim is my helmet,
Judah my scepter.
⁸Moab is my washbasin,
upon Edom I toss my sandal;
over Philistia I shout in triumph."

⁹Who will bring me to the fortified city?
Who will lead me to Edom?
¹⁰Is it not you, O God, you who have
rejected us
and no longer go out with our armies?
¹¹Give us aid against the enemy,
for the help of man is worthless.
¹²With God we will gain the victory,
and he will trample down our
enemies.

Psalm 61

For the director of music. With stringed
instruments. Of David.

¹Hear my cry, O God;
listen to my prayer.

²From the ends of the earth I call to you,
I call as my heart grows faint;
lead me to the rock that is higher than I.
³For you have been my refuge,
a strong tower against the foe.

⁴I long to dwell in your tent forever
and take refuge in the shelter of your
wings.   *Selah*
⁵For you have heard my vows, O God;
you have given me the heritage of those
who fear your name.

⁶Increase the days of the king's life,
his years for many generations.
⁷May he be enthroned in God's presence
forever;
appoint your love and faithfulness to
protect him.

⁸Then will I ever sing praise to your name
and fulfill my vows day after day.

Psalm 62

For the director of music. For Jeduthun.
A psalm of David.

¹My soul finds rest in God alone;
my salvation comes from him.
²He alone is my rock and my salvation;
he is my fortress, I will never be shaken.

³How long will you assault a man?
Would all of you throw him down—
this leaning wall, this tottering fence?
⁴They fully intend to topple him
from his lofty place;
they take delight in lies.

[a] Title: Probably a literary or musical term   [b] Title: That is,
Arameans of Northwest Mesopotamia   [c] Title: That is, Arameans
of central Syria

Environmental Cleanup

Together with your grandkids, select a small area within your community that could use sprucing up. Look for a field or stream strewn with unsightly litter. Grab some plastic trash bags and gloves and pitch in. Find a neighbor whose lawn needs to be cut, garden weeded or shrubs trimmed. Shovel snow for an elderly neighbor who can no longer handle the task. While you're at work, talk about the fact that God put humans in charge of his creation (see Genesis 1:28; 2:15; Psalm 8:6–8) and that it continues to be our responsibility to care for it.

A more ambitious project might involve joining a large community venture that you hear about. This more encompassing event will have appeal to older kids. A community service cleanup project is usually supervised, and the learning experience will be unforgettable.

Long-Distance Variation: Invite your out-of-town grandchildren to participate in a community or family activity of this nature and report back to you on their experience.

Creator God, thank you for the beauty of your creation that surrounds us. Forgive our carelessness and mistreatment of the environment. May this experience make my grandchildren realize how important it is for each of us to take care of your creation. Amen.

Your next devotion is located on page 755.

GRANDCHILD IN FOCUS • PRAYER

Friends

Dear Lord and Father, I pray for my grandchild's social life and his friends. Bring diverse friends into his life who will love and encourage him, who will bring joy and laughter to the good times and comfort and support through difficulties and disappointments. Grant him wisdom and discernment as he selects his friends; help him to avoid cliques that restrict, activities that endanger, and foolish and dangerous behaviors that harm. I ask that you fill his life with close and caring relationships. Amen.

Worship the Lord

Ascribe to the LORD, O mighty ones,
    ascribe to the LORD glory and strength.
Ascribe to the LORD the glory due his name;
    worship the LORD in the splendor of his holiness.

The voice of the LORD is over the waters;
    the God of glory thunders,
    the LORD thunders over the mighty waters.
The voice of the LORD is powerful;
    the voice of the LORD is majestic.
The voice of the LORD breaks the cedars;
    the LORD breaks in pieces the cedars of Lebanon.
He makes Lebanon skip like a calf,
    Sirion like a young wild ox.
The voice of the LORD strikes
    with flashes of lightning.

The LORD sits enthroned over the flood;
    the LORD is enthroned as King forever.
The LORD gives strength to his people;
    the Lord blesses his people with
      peace.

Psalm 29:1 – 7,10 – 11

....

Nature praises you, O Lord, from the pounding surf to the stars in the heavens to the wild animals in the field — all worship your name. I praise you for your majesty, your strength and your holiness. Amen.

Your next devotion is located on page 757.

GRANDCHILD **IN FOCUS** • PRAYER

Self-Image

O loving God, I praise you for creating my grandchild as a unique individual. Now I ask you to help her appreciate her uniqueness. Build up her self-image so she can enjoy her individuality. Help her to stand firm for who she is, where she has come from and what she believes in. Encourage her not only to have hopes and dreams but to also enjoy each day as it comes.
In Jesus' name, amen.

With their mouths they bless,
  but in their hearts they curse.   *Selah*

⁵Find rest, O my soul, in God alone;
  my hope comes from him.
⁶He alone is my rock and my salvation;
  he is my fortress, I will not be shaken.
⁷My salvation and my honor depend on
    God ᵃ;
  he is my mighty rock, my refuge.
⁸Trust in him at all times, O people;
  pour out your hearts to him,
  for God is our refuge.   *Selah*

⁹Lowborn men are but a breath,
  the highborn are but a lie;
  if weighed on a balance, they are nothing;
  together they are only a breath.
¹⁰Do not trust in extortion
  or take pride in stolen goods;
  though your riches increase,
  do not set your heart on them.

¹¹One thing God has spoken,
  two things have I heard:
  that you, O God, are strong,
¹² and that you, O Lord, are loving.
  Surely you will reward each person
  according to what he has done.

Psalm 63

A psalm of David. When he was in the
Desert of Judah.

¹O God, you are my God,
  earnestly I seek you;
  my soul thirsts for you,
  my body longs for you,
  in a dry and weary land
  where there is no water.

²I have seen you in the sanctuary
  and beheld your power and your glory.
³Because your love is better than life,
  my lips will glorify you.
⁴I will praise you as long as I live,
  and in your name I will lift up my hands.

⁵My soul will be satisfied as with the richest of
    foods;
  with singing lips my mouth will praise
    you.

TALKING POINTS

Contentment

Acknowledging God's love is the
key to contentment.
PSALM 63:3–5

For more on contentment, go to Proverbs 15:13,15–17.

⁶On my bed I remember you;
  I think of you through the watches of the
    night.
⁷Because you are my help,
  I sing in the shadow of your wings.
⁸My soul clings to you;
  your right hand upholds me.

TALKING POINTS

Illness

God, our helper, sustains and upholds us.
PSALM 63:6–8

For more on illness, go to Matthew 4:23–24.

⁹They who seek my life will be destroyed;
  they will go down to the depths of the
    earth.
¹⁰They will be given over to the sword
  and become food for jackals.

ᵃ 7 Or / God Most High is my salvation and my honor

My soul finds rest in God alone; my salvation comes from him. He alone is my rock and my salvation; he is my fortress, I will never be shaken.

Psalm 62:1–2

Building Something Worthy

JEAN E. SYSWERDA

READ | PSALM 62:1–12

I love houses. I could build a new one or redecorate the old one every year if it weren't for the mess and disruption of actual living. Oh, and the money, of course. So, instead of putting my money and my efforts into my house, I'm trying to put my money and efforts into my life, my family.

We're actually a pretty needy bunch, this family of mine. We've shared more difficulty and tragedy than most families; therefore, we've become more dependent on each other than most. We know from hard experience that with a breath it could all be gone. So the "house" I'm now building and decorating is one with a firm foundation for my family to live on, a foundation formed by faith in God and his Word.

This building takes many forms. Sometimes it's using the wakeful hours before dawn to pray for each grandchild individually. Sometimes it's teaching a new song to a couple of grandkids strapped into car seats. Sometimes it's emptying a grieving daughter's dishwasher or talking on the phone with an anxious daughter. Sometimes it's reassuring a son that lives thousands of miles away that, yes, we're all OK. At least for today.

Like the house in Jesus' parable that concluded the Sermon on the Mount (see Matthew 7:24–27), our house has known its share of storms. The rains have fallen, and the winds have blown and beaten against our house. But we built it on a firm foundation. "He alone is my rock and my salvation; he is my fortress, I will never be shaken" (Psalm 62:2). Life's events might shake us, but our foundation assures us that we will never fall.

O Lord, my Rock, you are the only foundation for my life. I need your strength, your firm footing, in order to make it through all that life throws my way, good and bad, easy and difficult, happy and sad. Help me, Lord, to keep my eyes on what's important: not the color of my kitchen but the foundation of my soul. In Jesus' name, amen.

Your next devotion is located on page 764.

GRANDCHILD IN FOCUS • PRAYER

Protection From Worldliness

O Sovereign Lord, the world surrounds my grandchild, pressing in and tempting him in so many ways. Help him set appropriate limits. Give him sound judgment to choose wisely. Guard him from temptation; protect him from physical and mental predators; lead him into paths of righteousness and light. And reassure me with your promise that you are holding him in your hands. Amen.

¹¹But the king will rejoice in God;
  all who swear by God's name will praise
    him,
  while the mouths of liars will be silenced.

Psalm 64

For the director of music. A psalm of David.

¹Hear me, O God, as I voice my complaint;
  protect my life from the threat of the
    enemy.
²Hide me from the conspiracy of the wicked,
  from that noisy crowd of evildoers.

³They sharpen their tongues like swords
  and aim their words like deadly arrows.
⁴They shoot from ambush at the innocent
    man;
  they shoot at him suddenly, without fear.

⁵They encourage each other in evil plans,
  they talk about hiding their snares;
  they say, "Who will see them ᵃ?"
⁶They plot injustice and say,
  "We have devised a perfect plan!"
  Surely the mind and heart of man are
    cunning.

⁷But God will shoot them with arrows;
  suddenly they will be struck down.
⁸He will turn their own tongues against them
  and bring them to ruin;
  all who see them will shake their heads in
    scorn.

⁹All mankind will fear;
  they will proclaim the works of God
  and ponder what he has done.
¹⁰Let the righteous rejoice in the Lord
  and take refuge in him;
  let all the upright in heart praise him!

Psalm 65

For the director of music.
A psalm of David. A song.

¹Praise awaits ᵇ you, O God, in Zion;
  to you our vows will be fulfilled.

²O you who hear prayer,
  to you all men will come.
³When we were overwhelmed by sins,
  you forgave ᶜ our transgressions.
⁴Blessed are those you choose
  and bring near to live in your courts!
We are filled with the good things of your
    house,
  of your holy temple.

⁵You answer us with awesome deeds of
    righteousness,
  O God our Savior,
the hope of all the ends of the earth
  and of the farthest seas,
⁶who formed the mountains by your
    power,
  having armed yourself with strength,
⁷who stilled the roaring of the seas,
  the roaring of their waves,
  and the turmoil of the nations.
⁸Those living far away fear your wonders;
  where morning dawns and evening
    fades
  you call forth songs of joy.

⁹You care for the land and water it;
  you enrich it abundantly.
The streams of God are filled with water
  to provide the people with grain,
  for so you have ordained it. ᵈ
¹⁰You drench its furrows
  and level its ridges;
  you soften it with showers
  and bless its crops.
¹¹You crown the year with your bounty,
  and your carts overflow with
    abundance.
¹²The grasslands of the desert overflow;
  the hills are clothed with gladness.
¹³The meadows are covered with flocks
  and the valleys are mantled with grain;
  they shout for joy and sing.

ᵃ 5 Or us   ᵇ 1 Or befits; the meaning of the Hebrew for this word
is uncertain.   ᶜ 3 Or made atonement for   ᵈ 9 Or for that is how
you prepare the land

Psalm 66

For the director of music. A song. A psalm.

¹ Shout with joy to God, all the earth!
²   Sing the glory of his name;
    make his praise glorious!
³ Say to God, "How awesome are your deeds!
    So great is your power
    that your enemies cringe before you.
⁴ All the earth bows down to you;
    they sing praise to you,
    they sing praise to your name."   *Selah*

⁵ Come and see what God has done,
    how awesome his works in man's behalf!
⁶ He turned the sea into dry land,
    they passed through the waters on foot—
    come, let us rejoice in him.
⁷ He rules forever by his power,
    his eyes watch the nations—
    let not the rebellious rise up against him.
                                    Selah

⁸ Praise our God, O peoples,
    let the sound of his praise be heard;
⁹ he has preserved our lives
    and kept our feet from slipping.
¹⁰ For you, O God, tested us;
    you refined us like silver.
¹¹ You brought us into prison
    and laid burdens on our backs.
¹² You let men ride over our heads;
    we went through fire and water,
    but you brought us to a place of
        abundance.

¹³ I will come to your temple with burnt
        offerings
    and fulfill my vows to you—
¹⁴ vows my lips promised and my mouth spoke
    when I was in trouble.
¹⁵ I will sacrifice fat animals to you
    and an offering of rams;
    I will offer bulls and goats.   *Selah*

¹⁶ Come and listen, all you who fear God;
    let me tell you what he has done for me.

¹⁷ I cried out to him with my mouth;
    his praise was on my tongue.
¹⁸ If I had cherished sin in my heart,
    the Lord would not have listened;
¹⁹ but God has surely listened
    and heard my voice in prayer.
²⁰ Praise be to God,
    who has not rejected my prayer
    or withheld his love from me!

Psalm 67

For the director of music. With stringed
instruments. A psalm. A song.

¹ May God be gracious to us and bless us
    and make his face shine upon us,   *Selah*
² that your ways may be known on earth,
    your salvation among all nations.

³ May the peoples praise you, O God;
    may all the peoples praise you.
⁴ May the nations be glad and sing for joy,
    for you rule the peoples justly
    and guide the nations of the earth.   *Selah*
⁵ May the peoples praise you, O God;
    may all the peoples praise you.

⁶ Then the land will yield its harvest,
    and God, our God, will bless us.
⁷ God will bless us,
    and all the ends of the earth will fear him.

Psalm 68

For the director of music. Of David.
A psalm. A song.

¹ May God arise, may his enemies be
        scattered;
    may his foes flee before him.
² As smoke is blown away by the wind,
    may you blow them away;
    as wax melts before the fire,
    may the wicked perish before God.
³ But may the righteous be glad
    and rejoice before God;
    may they be happy and joyful.

759

⁴Sing to God, sing praise to his name,
    extol him who rides on the clouds ^a—
his name is the LORD—
    and rejoice before him.
⁵A father to the fatherless, a defender of widows,
    is God in his holy dwelling.
⁶God sets the lonely in families, ^b
    he leads forth the prisoners with singing;
    but the rebellious live in a sun-scorched
        land.

TALKING POINTS

Blended Family

God brings people into our families.

PSALM 68:6

For more on blended family, go to Psalm 133:1–3.

⁷When you went out before your people,
    O God,
    when you marched through the
        wasteland,   *Selah*
⁸the earth shook,
    the heavens poured down rain,
before God, the One of Sinai,
    before God, the God of Israel.
⁹You gave abundant showers, O God;
    you refreshed your weary inheritance.
¹⁰Your people settled in it,
    and from your bounty, O God, you
        provided for the poor.

¹¹The Lord announced the word,
    and great was the company of those who
        proclaimed it:
¹²"Kings and armies flee in haste;
    in the camps men divide the plunder.
¹³Even while you sleep among the campfires, ^c
    the wings of ˻my˼ dove are sheathed with
        silver,
    its feathers with shining gold."

¹⁴When the Almighty ^d scattered the kings in
    the land,
    it was like snow fallen on Zalmon.

¹⁵The mountains of Bashan are majestic
    mountains;
    rugged are the mountains of Bashan.
¹⁶Why gaze in envy, O rugged mountains,
    at the mountain where God chooses to
        reign,
    where the LORD himself will dwell forever?
¹⁷The chariots of God are tens of thousands
    and thousands of thousands;
    the Lord ˻has come˼ from Sinai into his
        sanctuary.
¹⁸When you ascended on high,
    you led captives in your train;
    you received gifts from men,
even from ^e the rebellious—
    that you, ^f O LORD God, might dwell there.

¹⁹Praise be to the Lord, to God our Savior,
    who daily bears our burdens.   *Selah*
²⁰Our God is a God who saves;
    from the Sovereign LORD comes escape
        from death.
²¹Surely God will crush the heads of his
    enemies,
    the hairy crowns of those who go on in
        their sins.

^a 4 Or / *prepare the way for him who rides through the deserts*
^b 6 Or *the desolate in a homeland*   ^c 13 Or *saddlebags*
^d 14 Hebrew *Shaddai*   ^e 18 Or *gifts for men, / even*   ^f 18 Or *they*

PRAYING THE SCRIPTURES

Thankfulness

PSALM 68:19

Lord, I pray that my grandchild will give praise to you, her God and Savior, who daily bears her burdens.

Next prayer in Thankfulness Prayer Track: Psalm 145:3–5

²²The Lord says, "I will bring them from
        Bashan;
    I will bring them from the depths of the sea,
²³that you may plunge your feet in the blood of
        your foes,
    while the tongues of your dogs have their
        share."

²⁴Your procession has come into view, O God,
    the procession of my God and King into
        the sanctuary.
²⁵In front are the singers, after them the
        musicians;
    with them are the maidens playing
        tambourines.
²⁶Praise God in the great congregation;
    praise the LORD in the assembly of Israel.
²⁷There is the little tribe of Benjamin, leading
        them,
    there the great throng of Judah's princes,
    and there the princes of Zebulun and of
        Naphtali.

²⁸Summon your power, O God[a];
    show us your strength, O God, as you have
        done before.
²⁹Because of your temple at Jerusalem
    kings will bring you gifts.
³⁰Rebuke the beast among the reeds,
    the herd of bulls among the calves of the
        nations.
    Humbled, may it bring bars of silver.
    Scatter the nations who delight in war.
³¹Envoys will come from Egypt;
    Cush[b] will submit herself to God.

³²Sing to God, O kingdoms of the earth,
    sing praise to the Lord,   *Selah*
³³to him who rides the ancient skies above,
    who thunders with mighty voice.
³⁴Proclaim the power of God,
    whose majesty is over Israel,
    whose power is in the skies.
³⁵You are awesome, O God, in your sanctuary;
    the God of Israel gives power and strength
        to his people.

    Praise be to God!

Psalm 69

For the director of music. To ⌊the tune of⌋
"Lilies." Of David.

¹Save me, O God,
    for the waters have come up to my
        neck.
²I sink in the miry depths,
    where there is no foothold.
I have come into the deep waters;
    the floods engulf me.
³I am worn out calling for help;
    my throat is parched.
My eyes fail,
    looking for my God.
⁴Those who hate me without reason
    outnumber the hairs of my head;
many are my enemies without cause,
    those who seek to destroy me.
I am forced to restore
    what I did not steal.

⁵You know my folly, O God;
    my guilt is not hidden from you.

⁶May those who hope in you
    not be disgraced because of me,
    O Lord, the LORD Almighty;
may those who seek you
    not be put to shame because of me,
    O God of Israel.

[a] 28 Many Hebrew manuscripts, Septuagint and Syriac; most
Hebrew manuscripts *Your God has summoned power for you*
[b] 31 That is, the upper Nile region

TALKING POINTS

Guilt

We can't hide our guilt. It can affect
others as well as ourselves.

PSALM 69:5–6

For more on guilt, go to Psalm 103:12.

⁷For I endure scorn for your sake,
and shame covers my face.
⁸I am a stranger to my brothers,
an alien to my own mother's sons;
⁹for zeal for your house consumes me,
and the insults of those who insult you fall
on me.
¹⁰When I weep and fast,
I must endure scorn;
¹¹when I put on sackcloth,
people make sport of me.
¹²Those who sit at the gate mock me,
and I am the song of the drunkards.

¹³But I pray to you, O Lord,
in the time of your favor;
in your great love, O God,
answer me with your sure salvation.
¹⁴Rescue me from the mire,
do not let me sink;
deliver me from those who hate me,
from the deep waters.
¹⁵Do not let the floodwaters engulf me
or the depths swallow me up
or the pit close its mouth over me.
¹⁶Answer me, O Lord, out of the goodness of
your love;
in your great mercy turn to me.
¹⁷Do not hide your face from your servant;
answer me quickly, for I am in trouble.
¹⁸Come near and rescue me;
redeem me because of my foes.

¹⁹You know how I am scorned, disgraced and
shamed;
all my enemies are before you.
²⁰Scorn has broken my heart
and has left me helpless;
I looked for sympathy, but there was none,
for comforters, but I found none.
²¹They put gall in my food
and gave me vinegar for my thirst.

²²May the table set before them become a
snare;
may it become retribution and*ᵃ* a trap.

²³May their eyes be darkened so they cannot
see,
and their backs be bent forever.
²⁴Pour out your wrath on them;
let your fierce anger overtake them.
²⁵May their place be deserted;
let there be no one to dwell in their tents.
²⁶For they persecute those you wound
and talk about the pain of those you hurt.
²⁷Charge them with crime upon crime;
do not let them share in your salvation.
²⁸May they be blotted out of the book of life
and not be listed with the righteous.

²⁹I am in pain and distress;
may your salvation, O God, protect me.

³⁰I will praise God's name in song
and glorify him with thanksgiving.
³¹This will please the Lord more than an ox,
more than a bull with its horns and hoofs.
³²The poor will see and be glad—
you who seek God, may your hearts live!
³³The Lord hears the needy
and does not despise his captive people.

³⁴Let heaven and earth praise him,
the seas and all that move in them,
³⁵for God will save Zion
and rebuild the cities of Judah.
Then people will settle there and possess it;
³⁶ the children of his servants will inherit it,
and those who love his name will dwell
there.

Psalm 70

70:1–5pp — Ps 40:13–17

For the director of music. Of David. A petition.

¹Hasten, O God, to save me;
O Lord, come quickly to help me.
²May those who seek my life
be put to shame and confusion;
may all who desire my ruin
be turned back in disgrace.

ᵃ 22 Or snare / and their fellowship become

3 May those who say to me, "Aha! Aha!"
 turn back because of their shame.
4 But may all who seek you
 rejoice and be glad in you;
 may those who love your salvation always say,
 "Let God be exalted!"

5 Yet I am poor and needy;
 come quickly to me, O God.
 You are my help and my deliverer;
 O LORD, do not delay.

Psalm 71

71:1–3pp — Ps 31:1–4

1 In you, O LORD, I have taken refuge;
 let me never be put to shame.
2 Rescue me and deliver me in your
 righteousness;
 turn your ear to me and save me.
3 Be my rock of refuge,
 to which I can always go;
 give the command to save me,
 for you are my rock and my fortress.
4 Deliver me, O my God, from the hand of the
 wicked,
 from the grasp of evil and cruel men.

5 For you have been my hope, O Sovereign
 LORD,
 my confidence since my youth.
6 From birth I have relied on you;
 you brought me forth from my mother's
 womb.
 I will ever praise you.
7 I have become like a portent to many,
 but you are my strong refuge.
8 My mouth is filled with your praise,
 declaring your splendor all day long.

9 Do not cast me away when I am old;
 do not forsake me when my strength is
 gone.
10 For my enemies speak against me;
 those who wait to kill me conspire
 together.

11 They say, "God has forsaken him;
 pursue him and seize him,
 for no one will rescue him."
12 Be not far from me, O God;
 come quickly, O my God, to help me.
13 May my accusers perish in shame;
 may those who want to harm me
 be covered with scorn and disgrace.

14 But as for me, I will always have hope;
 I will praise you more and more.
15 My mouth will tell of your righteousness,
 of your salvation all day long,
 though I know not its measure.
16 I will come and proclaim your mighty acts,
 O Sovereign LORD;
 I will proclaim your righteousness, yours
 alone.
17 Since my youth, O God, you have taught me,
 and to this day I declare your marvelous
 deeds.
18 Even when I am old and gray,
 do not forsake me, O God,
 till I declare your power to the next
 generation,
 your might to all who are to come.

19 Your righteousness reaches to the skies,
 O God,
 you who have done great things.
 Who, O God, is like you?
20 Though you have made me see troubles,
 many and bitter,
 you will restore my life again;
 from the depths of the earth
 you will again bring me up.
21 You will increase my honor
 and comfort me once again.

22 I will praise you with the harp
 for your faithfulness, O my God;
 I will sing praise to you with the lyre,
 O Holy One of Israel.
23 My lips will shout for joy
 when I sing praise to you —
 I, whom you have redeemed.

FOR YOU HAVE BEEN MY HOPE, O
SOVEREIGN LORD, MY CONFIDENCE
SINCE MY YOUTH. FROM BIRTH I
HAVE RELIED ON YOU; YOU BROUGHT
ME FORTH FROM MY MOTHER'S
WOMB. I WILL EVER PRAISE YOU.
Psalm 71:5 – 6

From Womb to World

ELISA MORGAN

READ | PSALM 71:1 – 24

It's comforting to look back and see God's hand in my life. In so many ways he has indeed been "my confidence since my youth," as Psalm 71:5 describes: through the occasional nightmare in childhood; through the forking roads of middle school, when choices had to be made; then in high school, where those choices became values to be held; and eventually on into early adulthood and fresh, eager marriage, where so much "self" was revealed and redirected. Indeed, God has been my confidence since youth.

While my own children came to me from the womb of another — they were both adopted — I keenly felt God's presence in their safe delivery into my arms. Today, while I'm in the season of grandbabies, Psalm 71:6 comforts me with God's presence even in the manner in which a child comes into a family. "From birth I have relied on you; you brought me forth from my mother's womb."

As we hold our grandbabies in our arms, we see the journey of life yawning before them with its crossroads, bends and turns. With the perspective fashioned out of living life fully ourselves, we tense in expectation at both the joy and the tragedy surely ahead. Knowing for them what we could not know for ourselves, we trust that God's presence, so precious in our youth, will be the same abiding presence in their days.

Dear God, as you have brought little ones into your world, may they rely on you today and in all the days ahead. Just as you oversaw the birth of each child, may you oversee the steps and the choices ahead, and may each child welcome your presence as you guide him or her. Amen.

Your next devotion is located on page 769.

GRANDCHILD IN FOCUS • PRAYER

Respect for Authority

Dear Lord, I pray that my grandchild will continually grow to respect those in authority. May she learn to be cooperative and fair in work and play. Instill in her a high regard for officials who govern our land and enforce the laws. May her relationships with parents, teachers, coaches, mentors and bosses be respectful, admirable, constructive and caring. Amen.

TALKING POINTS

Bitterness

Troubles in life can be bitter,
but God will restore us.

PSALM 71:20

For more on bitterness, go to Hebrews 12:15.

²⁴ My tongue will tell of your righteous acts
all day long,
for those who wanted to harm me
have been put to shame and confusion.

Psalm 72

Of Solomon.

¹ Endow the king with your justice, O God,
the royal son with your righteousness.
² He will *ᵃ* judge your people in righteousness,
your afflicted ones with justice.
³ The mountains will bring prosperity to the
people,
the hills the fruit of righteousness.
⁴ He will defend the afflicted among the people
and save the children of the needy;
he will crush the oppressor.

⁵ He will endure *ᵇ* as long as the sun,
as long as the moon, through all generations.
⁶ He will be like rain falling on a mown field,
like showers watering the earth.
⁷ In his days the righteous will flourish;
prosperity will abound till the moon is no
more.

⁸ He will rule from sea to sea
and from the River *ᶜ* to the ends of the
earth. *ᵈ*
⁹ The desert tribes will bow before him
and his enemies will lick the dust.
¹⁰ The kings of Tarshish and of distant shores
will bring tribute to him;

the kings of Sheba and Seba
will present him gifts.
¹¹ All kings will bow down to him
and all nations will serve him.

¹² For he will deliver the needy who cry out,
the afflicted who have no one to help.
¹³ He will take pity on the weak and the needy
and save the needy from death.
¹⁴ He will rescue them from oppression and
violence,
for precious is their blood in his sight.

¹⁵ Long may he live!
May gold from Sheba be given him.
May people ever pray for him
and bless him all day long.
¹⁶ Let grain abound throughout the land;
on the tops of the hills may it sway.
Let its fruit flourish like Lebanon;
let it thrive like the grass of the field.
¹⁷ May his name endure forever;
may it continue as long as the sun.

All nations will be blessed through him,
and they will call him blessed.

¹⁸ Praise be to the LORD God, the God of Israel,
who alone does marvelous deeds.
¹⁹ Praise be to his glorious name forever;
may the whole earth be filled with his glory.
Amen and Amen.

²⁰ This concludes the prayers of David son of
Jesse.

BOOK III

Psalms 73–89

Psalm 73

A psalm of Asaph.

¹ Surely God is good to Israel,
to those who are pure in heart.

ᵃ 2 Or *May he*; similarly in verses 3–11 and 17   *ᵇ 5* Septuagint;
Hebrew *You will be feared*   *ᶜ 8* That is, the Euphrates
ᵈ 8 Or *the end of the land*

2 But as for me, my feet had almost slipped;
    I had nearly lost my foothold.
3 For I envied the arrogant
    when I saw the prosperity of the wicked.

4 They have no struggles;
    their bodies are healthy and strong. *a*
5 They are free from the burdens common to
    man;
    they are not plagued by human ills.
6 Therefore pride is their necklace;
    they clothe themselves with violence.
7 From their callous hearts comes iniquity *b*;
    the evil conceits of their minds know no
    limits.
8 They scoff, and speak with malice;
    in their arrogance they threaten oppression.
9 Their mouths lay claim to heaven,
    and their tongues take possession of the
    earth.
10 Therefore their people turn to them
    and drink up waters in abundance. *c*
11 They say, "How can God know?
    Does the Most High have knowledge?"

12 This is what the wicked are like—
    always carefree, they increase in wealth.

13 Surely in vain have I kept my heart pure;
    in vain have I washed my hands in
    innocence.
14 All day long I have been plagued;
    I have been punished every morning.

15 If I had said, "I will speak thus,"
    I would have betrayed your children.
16 When I tried to understand all this,
    it was oppressive to me
17 till I entered the sanctuary of God;
    then I understood their final destiny.

18 Surely you place them on slippery ground;
    you cast them down to ruin.
19 How suddenly are they destroyed,
    completely swept away by terrors!
20 As a dream when one awakes,
    so when you arise, O Lord,
    you will despise them as fantasies.

21 When my heart was grieved
    and my spirit embittered,
22 I was senseless and ignorant;
    I was a brute beast before you.

23 Yet I am always with you;
    you hold me by my right hand.
24 You guide me with your counsel,
    and afterward you will take me into glory.
25 Whom have I in heaven but you?
    And earth has nothing I desire besides you.
26 My flesh and my heart may fail,
    but God is the strength of my heart
    and my portion forever.

TALKING POINTS

Anxiety
God is our strength when we feel weak.
PSALM 73:26

For more on anxiety, go to Psalm 94:18–19.

27 Those who are far from you will perish;
    you destroy all who are unfaithful to you.
28 But as for me, it is good to be near God.
    I have made the Sovereign Lord my refuge;
    I will tell of all your deeds.

Psalm 74

A maskil d of Asaph.

1 Why have you rejected us forever, O God?
    Why does your anger smolder against the
    sheep of your pasture?
2 Remember the people you purchased of old,
    the tribe of your inheritance, whom you
    redeemed—
    Mount Zion, where you dwelt.

a 4 With a different word division of the Hebrew; Masoretic Text
struggles at their death; / their bodies are healthy   *b 7* Syriac
(see also Septuagint); Hebrew *Their eyes bulge with fat*
c 10 The meaning of the Hebrew for this verse is uncertain.
d Title: Probably a literary or musical term

³Turn your steps toward these everlasting
  ruins,
  all this destruction the enemy has brought
   on the sanctuary.

⁴Your foes roared in the place where you met
  with us;
  they set up their standards as signs.
⁵They behaved like men wielding axes
  to cut through a thicket of trees.
⁶They smashed all the carved paneling
  with their axes and hatchets.
⁷They burned your sanctuary to the ground;
  they defiled the dwelling place of your
   Name.
⁸They said in their hearts, "We will crush them
  completely!"
  They burned every place where God was
   worshiped in the land.
⁹We are given no miraculous signs;
  no prophets are left,
  and none of us knows how long this
   will be.

¹⁰How long will the enemy mock you, O God?
  Will the foe revile your name forever?
¹¹Why do you hold back your hand, your right
  hand?
  Take it from the folds of your garment and
   destroy them!

¹²But you, O God, are my king from of old;
  you bring salvation upon the earth.
¹³It was you who split open the sea by your
  power;
  you broke the heads of the monster in the
   waters.
¹⁴It was you who crushed the heads of
  Leviathan
  and gave him as food to the creatures of
   the desert.
¹⁵It was you who opened up springs and
  streams;
  you dried up the ever flowing rivers.
¹⁶The day is yours, and yours also the night;
  you established the sun and moon.

¹⁷It was you who set all the boundaries of the
  earth;
  you made both summer and winter.

¹⁸Remember how the enemy has mocked you,
  O LORD,
  how foolish people have reviled your
   name.
¹⁹Do not hand over the life of your dove to
  wild beasts;
  do not forget the lives of your afflicted
   people forever.
²⁰Have regard for your covenant,
  because haunts of violence fill the dark
   places of the land.
²¹Do not let the oppressed retreat in disgrace;
  may the poor and needy praise your name.

²²Rise up, O God, and defend your cause;
  remember how fools mock you all day
   long.
²³Do not ignore the clamor of your adversaries,
  the uproar of your enemies, which rises
   continually.

Psalm 75

For the director of music. ⌐To the tune of⌐
"Do Not Destroy." A psalm
of Asaph. A song.

¹We give thanks to you, O God,
  we give thanks, for your Name is near;
  men tell of your wonderful deeds.

²You say, "I choose the appointed time;
  it is I who judge uprightly.
³When the earth and all its people quake,
  it is I who hold its pillars firm.   *Selah*
⁴To the arrogant I say, 'Boast no more,'
  and to the wicked, 'Do not lift up your
   horns.
⁵Do not lift your horns against heaven;
  do not speak with outstretched neck.' "

⁶No one from the east or the west
  or from the desert can exalt a man.
⁷But it is God who judges:
  He brings one down, he exalts another.

8 In the hand of the Lord is a cup
      full of foaming wine mixed with
          spices;
    he pours it out, and all the wicked of the
        earth
      drink it down to its very dregs.

9 As for me, I will declare this forever;
      I will sing praise to the God of Jacob.
10 I will cut off the horns of all the wicked,
      but the horns of the righteous will be
          lifted up.

Psalm 76

For the director of music.
With stringed instruments.
A psalm of Asaph. A song.

1 In Judah God is known;
      his name is great in Israel.
2 His tent is in Salem,
      his dwelling place in Zion.
3 There he broke the flashing arrows,
      the shields and the swords, the weapons
          of war.   *Selah*

4 You are resplendent with light,
      more majestic than mountains rich with
          game.
5 Valiant men lie plundered,
      they sleep their last sleep;
    not one of the warriors
      can lift his hands.
6 At your rebuke, O God of Jacob,
      both horse and chariot lie still.
7 You alone are to be feared.
      Who can stand before you when you are
          angry?
8 From heaven you pronounced judgment,
      and the land feared and was quiet—
9 when you, O God, rose up to judge,
      to save all the afflicted of the land.   *Selah*
10 Surely your wrath against men brings you
        praise,
      and the survivors of your wrath are
          restrained. *a*

11 Make vows to the Lord your God and fulfill
        them;
      let all the neighboring lands
      bring gifts to the One to be feared.
12 He breaks the spirit of rulers;
      he is feared by the kings of the earth.

Psalm 77

For the director of music. For Jeduthun.
Of Asaph. A psalm.

1 I cried out to God for help;
      I cried out to God to hear me.
2 When I was in distress, I sought the Lord;
      at night I stretched out untiring hands
      and my soul refused to be comforted.

3 I remembered you, O God, and I groaned;
      I mused, and my spirit grew faint.   *Selah*
4 You kept my eyes from closing;
      I was too troubled to speak.
5 I thought about the former days,
      the years of long ago;
6 I remembered my songs in the night.
      My heart mused and my spirit inquired:

7 "Will the Lord reject forever?
      Will he never show his favor again?
8 Has his unfailing love vanished forever?
      Has his promise failed for all time?
9 Has God forgotten to be merciful?
      Has he in anger withheld his compassion?"
                                              Selah

10 Then I thought, "To this I will appeal:
      the years of the right hand of the Most
          High."
11 I will remember the deeds of the Lord;
      yes, I will remember your miracles of long
          ago.
12 I will meditate on all your works
      and consider all your mighty deeds.

13 Your ways, O God, are holy.
      What god is so great as our God?

*a 10 Or Surely the wrath of men brings you praise, / and with the
remainder of wrath you arm yourself*

I WILL REMEMBER THE DEEDS
OF THE LORD; YES, I WILL
REMEMBER YOUR MIRACLES
OF LONG AGO.

Psalm 77:11

Hats and Hearts

GAYLE ROPER

READ | PSALM 77:1 – 20

"Here are some hats you can play dress up with." I handed seven-year-old Ashley four hats I had been saving for the day hats became popular again, a trend I'd finally given up on. "This one was my favorite."

I put on the black felt, one side flipped up Australian style.

Ashley studied me for a moment. "Did people laugh at you when you wore it, Grandmom?"

So much for my sense of fashion.

Later I thought about Ashley's comment and knew it was more than generational tastes that made us view that black felt so differently. The hat held memories for me. I bought it to wear for the dedication of the new dining hall named after my grandfather at the college where he'd once been president.

To me the hat meant Granddad — who had married my then 20-year-old grandmother when he was 42, lived to celebrate their 50th wedding anniversary, and worked until he was 93. He had always given me silver dollars and was a whiz at croquet.

How will Ashley remember me? As the woman with weird hats? Undoubtedly. As a grandmother who dearly loved her and the rest of the grands? I pray so. ·

Memories are such permanent things. Am I giving the grandkids proud, positive ones like my grandfather gave me? Godly ones? Fun ones?

I also want Ashley and the other grandkids to remember God's past care for his people — and for them in particular — so that they will have the courage to face life's problems and the challenges that lie ahead.

Lord, help me give the grandkids happy and healthy memories, and may they always remember your deeds on their behalf. Amen.

Your next devotion is located on page 771.

GRANDCHILD IN FOCUS · PRAYER

Courage

O Father, builder of character and courage, may my grandchild grow strong in the light of your love. Grant him courage to stand for what is right, to guard the truth and to ensure justice in every aspect of life. May he boldly grow in grace, revere your name and proudly proclaim you as the Lord of lords and King of kings. Amen.

¹⁴You are the God who performs miracles;
you display your power among the peoples.
¹⁵With your mighty arm you redeemed your
people,
the descendants of Jacob and Joseph. *Selah*

¹⁶The waters saw you, O God,
the waters saw you and writhed;
the very depths were convulsed.
¹⁷The clouds poured down water,
the skies resounded with thunder;
your arrows flashed back and forth.
¹⁸Your thunder was heard in the whirlwind,
your lightning lit up the world;
the earth trembled and quaked.
¹⁹Your path led through the sea,
your way through the mighty waters,
though your footprints were not seen.

²⁰You led your people like a flock
by the hand of Moses and Aaron.

Psalm 78

A *maskil*^a of Asaph.

¹O my people, hear my teaching;
listen to the words of my mouth.
²I will open my mouth in parables,
I will utter hidden things, things from of
old—
³what we have heard and known,
what our fathers have told us.
⁴We will not hide them from their children;
we will tell the next generation
the praiseworthy deeds of the LORD,
his power, and the wonders he has done.
⁵He decreed statutes for Jacob
and established the law in Israel,
which he commanded our forefathers
to teach their children,
⁶so the next generation would know them,
even the children yet to be born,
and they in turn would tell their children.
⁷Then they would put their trust in God
and would not forget his deeds
but would keep his commands.

⁸They would not be like their forefathers—
a stubborn and rebellious generation,
whose hearts were not loyal to God,
whose spirits were not faithful to him.

⁹The men of Ephraim, though armed with
bows,
turned back on the day of battle;
¹⁰they did not keep God's covenant
and refused to live by his law.
¹¹They forgot what he had done,
the wonders he had shown them.
¹²He did miracles in the sight of their fathers
in the land of Egypt, in the region of
Zoan.
¹³He divided the sea and led them through;
he made the water stand firm like a wall.
¹⁴He guided them with the cloud by day
and with light from the fire all night.
¹⁵He split the rocks in the desert
and gave them water as abundant as the
seas;
¹⁶he brought streams out of a rocky crag
and made water flow down like rivers.

¹⁷But they continued to sin against him,
rebelling in the desert against the Most
High.
¹⁸They willfully put God to the test
by demanding the food they craved.
¹⁹They spoke against God, saying,
"Can God spread a table in the desert?
²⁰When he struck the rock, water gushed out,
and streams flowed abundantly.
But can he also give us food?
Can he supply meat for his people?"
²¹When the LORD heard them, he was very
angry;
his fire broke out against Jacob,
and his wrath rose against Israel,
²²for they did not believe in God
or trust in his deliverance.
²³Yet he gave a command to the skies above
and opened the doors of the heavens;

---

^a Title: Probably a literary or musical term

WE WILL TELL THE NEXT GENERATION THE
PRAISEWORTHY DEEDS OF THE LORD, HIS
POWER, AND THE WONDERS HE HAS DONE
. . . THEN THEY WOULD PUT THEIR TRUST
IN GOD AND WOULD NOT FORGET HIS
DEEDS BUT WOULD KEEP HIS COMMANDS.

Psalm 78:4,7

Being a Godly Influence

RUTHANNE GARLOCK

READ | PSALM 78:1–8

After years of having her grandchildren live in a distant state, Sandy was thrilled when a job transfer meant they would be close enough for more frequent visits. On one such visit, ten-year-old Julie asked for her help with a school assignment.

"We've been studying about different emotions at school," she said. "My teacher asked us to pick an emotion to write about, and give a report to the class. But I want to use Scripture verses with mine. Grandma, can you help me?"

The two searched the Bible together, exploring possibilities. Finally Julie decided. "Lots of kids in my class don't have peace and joy," she said. "If I share Scriptures about peace and joy, then they'll know God can give it to them." She chose two or three verses from the many that Grandma had helped her find and wrote her report.

A few days later Sandy called to ask how it went. "Some of the kids laughed at me when I talked about God," Julie said. "But that's OK — because I have peace and joy, and the ones who laughed don't. But now they know where they can get it!"

Sandy was thrilled that Julie wanted her friends to know the Lord and was brave enough to use this opportunity to share her faith. She decided early on that, besides praying for her grandchildren, she would try to be a positive spiritual influence in practical ways.

About three years after this experience, Sandy died suddenly from a heart attack. But she left her grandchildren a legacy of love for God that will remain with them always.

Lord, it's humbling to realize I have the opportunity to exert a godly influence on my grandchildren. Give me the wisdom and discretion to be a good example in both word and deed. Thank you for your help. Amen.

Your next devotion is located on page 774.

GRANDCHILD IN FOCUS • PRAYER

Future Spouse

Dear Lord, if it is your will, I pray my grandchild will be united in a loving and Christian marriage. Keep her sexually pure so that she will honor you with her body and mind. As she seeks a spouse who will honor and care for her, give her patience and discernment. May her choice for a life partner be your choice for her, so that she and her husband will together glorify you in a lasting love. I pray this in Jesus' name, amen.

²⁴he rained down manna for the people to eat,
    he gave them the grain of heaven.
²⁵Men ate the bread of angels;
    he sent them all the food they could eat.
²⁶He let loose the east wind from the heavens
    and led forth the south wind by his power.
²⁷He rained meat down on them like dust,
    flying birds like sand on the seashore.
²⁸He made them come down inside their
      camp,
    all around their tents.
²⁹They ate till they had more than enough,
    for he had given them what they craved.
³⁰But before they turned from the food they
      craved,
    even while it was still in their mouths,
³¹God's anger rose against them;
    he put to death the sturdiest among them,
    cutting down the young men of Israel.

³²In spite of all this, they kept on sinning;
    in spite of his wonders, they did not
      believe.
³³So he ended their days in futility
    and their years in terror.
³⁴Whenever God slew them, they would seek
      him;
    they eagerly turned to him again.
³⁵They remembered that God was their Rock,
    that God Most High was their Redeemer.
³⁶But then they would flatter him with their
      mouths,
    lying to him with their tongues;
³⁷their hearts were not loyal to him,
    they were not faithful to his covenant.
³⁸Yet he was merciful;
    he forgave their iniquities
    and did not destroy them.
    Time after time he restrained his anger
    and did not stir up his full wrath.
³⁹He remembered that they were but flesh,
    a passing breeze that does not return.

⁴⁰How often they rebelled against him in the
      desert
    and grieved him in the wasteland!

⁴¹Again and again they put God to the test;
    they vexed the Holy One of Israel.
⁴²They did not remember his power—
    the day he redeemed them from the
      oppressor,
⁴³the day he displayed his miraculous signs in
      Egypt,
    his wonders in the region of Zoan.
⁴⁴He turned their rivers to blood;
    they could not drink from their streams.
⁴⁵He sent swarms of flies that devoured them,
    and frogs that devastated them.
⁴⁶He gave their crops to the grasshopper,
    their produce to the locust.
⁴⁷He destroyed their vines with hail
    and their sycamore-figs with sleet.
⁴⁸He gave over their cattle to the hail,
    their livestock to bolts of lightning.
⁴⁹He unleashed against them his hot anger,
    his wrath, indignation and hostility—
    a band of destroying angels.
⁵⁰He prepared a path for his anger;
    he did not spare them from death
    but gave them over to the plague.
⁵¹He struck down all the firstborn of Egypt,
    the firstfruits of manhood in the tents of
      Ham.
⁵²But he brought his people out like a flock;
    he led them like sheep through the desert.
⁵³He guided them safely, so they were
      unafraid;
    but the sea engulfed their enemies.
⁵⁴Thus he brought them to the border of his
      holy land,
    to the hill country his right hand had
      taken.
⁵⁵He drove out nations before them
    and allotted their lands to them as an
      inheritance;
    he settled the tribes of Israel in their
      homes.

⁵⁶But they put God to the test
    and rebelled against the Most High;
    they did not keep his statutes.

⁵⁷Like their fathers they were disloyal and
faithless,
as unreliable as a faulty bow.
⁵⁸They angered him with their high places;
they aroused his jealousy with their idols.
⁵⁹When God heard them, he was very angry;
he rejected Israel completely.
⁶⁰He abandoned the tabernacle of Shiloh,
the tent he had set up among men.
⁶¹He sent ⌐the ark of⌐ his might into captivity,
his splendor into the hands of the enemy.
⁶²He gave his people over to the sword;
he was very angry with his inheritance.
⁶³Fire consumed their young men,
and their maidens had no wedding songs;
⁶⁴their priests were put to the sword,
and their widows could not weep.

⁶⁵Then the Lord awoke as from sleep,
as a man wakes from the stupor of wine.
⁶⁶He beat back his enemies;
he put them to everlasting shame.
⁶⁷Then he rejected the tents of Joseph,
he did not choose the tribe of Ephraim;
⁶⁸but he chose the tribe of Judah,
Mount Zion, which he loved.
⁶⁹He built his sanctuary like the heights,
like the earth that he established forever.
⁷⁰He chose David his servant
and took him from the sheep pens;
⁷¹from tending the sheep he brought him
to be the shepherd of his people Jacob,
of Israel his inheritance.
⁷²And David shepherded them with integrity
of heart;
with skillful hands he led them.

Psalm 79

A psalm of Asaph.

¹O God, the nations have invaded your
inheritance;
they have defiled your holy temple,
they have reduced Jerusalem to rubble.
²They have given the dead bodies of your
servants
as food to the birds of the air,
the flesh of your saints to the beasts of the
earth.
³They have poured out blood like water
all around Jerusalem,
and there is no one to bury the dead.
⁴We are objects of reproach to our neighbors,
of scorn and derision to those around us.

⁵How long, O LORD? Will you be angry
forever?
How long will your jealousy burn like fire?
⁶Pour out your wrath on the nations
that do not acknowledge you,
on the kingdoms
that do not call on your name;
⁷for they have devoured Jacob
and destroyed his homeland.
⁸Do not hold against us the sins of the fathers;
may your mercy come quickly to meet us,
for we are in desperate need.

⁹Help us, O God our Savior,
for the glory of your name;
deliver us and forgive our sins
for your name's sake.
¹⁰Why should the nations say,
"Where is their God?"
Before our eyes, make known among the
nations
that you avenge the outpoured blood of
your servants.
¹¹May the groans of the prisoners come before
you;
by the strength of your arm
preserve those condemned to die.

¹²Pay back into the laps of our neighbors seven
times
the reproach they have hurled at you,
O Lord.
¹³Then we your people, the sheep of your
pasture,
will praise you forever;
from generation to generation
we will recount your praise.

THEN WE YOUR PEOPLE, THE
SHEEP OF YOUR PASTURE, WILL
PRAISE YOU FOREVER; FROM
GENERATION TO GENERATION WE
WILL RECOUNT YOUR PRAISE.
Psalm 79:13

Establishing Traditions

QUIN SHERRER

READ | PSALM 79:1–13

In Biblical times families celebrated feasts, holy days and other special events in festive ways. Today's grandmothers initiate traditions of their own, some hopefully to be passed down to future generations.

For years my husband and I hosted a New Year's "blessing" party for our six grandchildren. Dressed in their Sunday best, they would stand in line waiting for their individual prayer and blessing from their grandparents for the coming year. Then they would eat the goodies I had cooked and laugh at jokes their cousins told. They loved it!

On the day before each grandchild enters first grade, my friend Rhonda lets him or her pick a restaurant where they can enjoy a scrumptious meal together. Afterward they go shopping for new school clothes. Now the younger ones can't wait until they are old enough to spend the day before they start school with their grandmother.

Twice a year Mary Jo arms her three granddaughters with cameras and tells them, "Go photograph what God is saying to you as you observe his world." They may hike a mountain, stroll the mall, walk through a park or even amble around their home. The photos are printed, put in an album and beside each picture a granddaughter writes what the Lord showed her when she snapped it. "Our photo-journey not only encourages them to hear God but also gives me, their grandmother, great insight into their hearts and lives," Mary Jo said.

Beth has a long-standing tradition that when her grandchildren turn 15 years old, they may go with her on a short-term mission trip to another country. Today two of them are grown and living overseas as missionaries. Grandmother Beth inspired them both.

The ideas for establishing traditions are endless, and it's never too late to start.

Thank you, Lord, for giving me fresh ideas for helping my grandchildren establish new traditions that they may eventually pass on to the next generation. Amen.

Your next devotion is located on page 779.

GRANDCHILD **IN FOCUS** • PRAYER

School/Career

Dear God, may learning be a joy rather than a chore for my grandchild. May exploration of new ideas bring a sense of wonder, awe and excitement. Grant him clarity of mind, the ability to concentrate on the task at hand and recollection of what has been learned. Help him to appreciate the tasks that come easily and to persevere through those that challenge. Amen.

Psalm 80

For the director of music. To ⌐the tune of⌐
"The Lilies of the Covenant."
Of Asaph. A psalm.

¹ Hear us, O Shepherd of Israel,
  you who lead Joseph like a flock;
you who sit enthroned between the cherubim,
  shine forth
² before Ephraim, Benjamin and Manasseh.
Awaken your might;
  come and save us.

³ Restore us, O God;
  make your face shine upon us,
  that we may be saved.

⁴ O LORD God Almighty,
  how long will your anger smolder
  against the prayers of your people?
⁵ You have fed them with the bread of tears;
  you have made them drink tears by the
    bowlful.
⁶ You have made us a source of contention to
    our neighbors,
  and our enemies mock us.

⁷ Restore us, O God Almighty;
  make your face shine upon us,
  that we may be saved.

⁸ You brought a vine out of Egypt;
  you drove out the nations and planted it.
⁹ You cleared the ground for it,
  and it took root and filled the land.
¹⁰ The mountains were covered with its
    shade,
  the mighty cedars with its branches.
¹¹ It sent out its boughs to the Sea,ᵃ
  its shoots as far as the River.ᵇ

¹² Why have you broken down its walls
  so that all who pass by pick its grapes?
¹³ Boars from the forest ravage it
  and the creatures of the field feed on it.
¹⁴ Return to us, O God Almighty!
  Look down from heaven and see!

Watch over this vine,
¹⁵ the root your right hand has planted,
  the sonᶜ you have raised up for yourself.

¹⁶ Your vine is cut down, it is burned with fire;
  at your rebuke your people perish.
¹⁷ Let your hand rest on the man at your right
    hand,
  the son of man you have raised up for
    yourself.
¹⁸ Then we will not turn away from you;
  revive us, and we will call on your name.

¹⁹ Restore us, O LORD God Almighty;
  make your face shine upon us,
  that we may be saved.

Psalm 81

For the director of music. According
to gittith.ᵈ Of Asaph.

¹ Sing for joy to God our strength;
  shout aloud to the God of Jacob!
² Begin the music, strike the tambourine,
  play the melodious harp and lyre.

³ Sound the ram's horn at the New Moon,
  and when the moon is full, on the day of
    our Feast;
⁴ this is a decree for Israel,
  an ordinance of the God of Jacob.
⁵ He established it as a statute for Joseph
  when he went out against Egypt,
  where we heard a language we did not
    understand.ᵉ

⁶ He says, "I removed the burden from their
    shoulders;
  their hands were set free from the basket.
⁷ In your distress you called and I rescued you,
  I answered you out of a thundercloud;
  I tested you at the waters of Meribah. Selah

⁸ "Hear, O my people, and I will warn you—
  if you would but listen to me, O Israel!

ᵃ 11 Probably the Mediterranean   ᵇ 11 That is, the Euphrates
ᶜ 15 Or branch   ᵈ Title: Probably a musical term   ᵉ 5 Or / and
we heard a voice we had not known

⁹You shall have no foreign god among you;
　you shall not bow down to an alien god.
¹⁰I am the LORD your God,
　who brought you up out of Egypt.
　Open wide your mouth and I will fill it.

¹¹"But my people would not listen to me;
　Israel would not submit to me.
¹²So I gave them over to their stubborn hearts
　to follow their own devices.

¹³"If my people would but listen to me,
　if Israel would follow my ways,
¹⁴how quickly would I subdue their enemies
　and turn my hand against their foes!
¹⁵Those who hate the LORD would cringe
　　before him,
　and their punishment would last forever.
¹⁶But you would be fed with the finest of
　　wheat;
　with honey from the rock I would satisfy
　　you."

Psalm 82

A psalm of Asaph.

¹God presides in the great assembly;
　he gives judgment among the "gods":

²"How long will you *a* defend the unjust
　and show partiality to the wicked?　*Selah*
³Defend the cause of the weak and fatherless;
　maintain the rights of the poor and
　　oppressed.

⁴Rescue the weak and needy;
　deliver them from the hand of the wicked.

⁵"They know nothing, they understand
　　nothing.
　They walk about in darkness;
　all the foundations of the earth are shaken.

⁶"I said, 'You are "gods";
　you are all sons of the Most High.'
⁷But you will die like mere men;
　you will fall like every other ruler."

⁸Rise up, O God, judge the earth,
　for all the nations are your inheritance.

Psalm 83

A song. A psalm of Asaph.

¹O God, do not keep silent;
　be not quiet, O God, be not still.
²See how your enemies are astir,
　how your foes rear their heads.
³With cunning they conspire against your
　　people;
　they plot against those you cherish.
⁴"Come," they say, "let us destroy them as a
　　nation,
　that the name of Israel be remembered no
　　more."

⁵With one mind they plot together;
　they form an alliance against you—
⁶the tents of Edom and the Ishmaelites,
　of Moab and the Hagrites,
⁷Gebal,*b* Ammon and Amalek,
　Philistia, with the people of Tyre.
⁸Even Assyria has joined them
　to lend strength to the descendants
　　of Lot.　*Selah*

⁹Do to them as you did to Midian,
　as you did to Sisera and Jabin at the river
　　Kishon,
¹⁰who perished at Endor
　and became like refuse on the ground.

a 2 The Hebrew is plural.　*b 7* That is, Byblos

¹¹ Make their nobles like Oreb and Zeeb,
    all their princes like Zebah and Zalmunna,
¹² who said, "Let us take possession
    of the pasturelands of God."

¹³ Make them like tumbleweed, O my God,
    like chaff before the wind.
¹⁴ As fire consumes the forest
    or a flame sets the mountains ablaze,
¹⁵ so pursue them with your tempest
    and terrify them with your storm.
¹⁶ Cover their faces with shame
    so that men will seek your name, O Lord.

¹⁷ May they ever be ashamed and dismayed;
    may they perish in disgrace.
¹⁸ Let them know that you, whose name is the
    Lord —
    that you alone are the Most High over all
    the earth.

Psalm 84

For the director of music. According
to *gittith.* ᵃ Of the Sons of Korah.
A psalm.

¹ How lovely is your dwelling place,
    O Lord Almighty!
² My soul yearns, even faints,
    for the courts of the Lord;
my heart and my flesh cry out
    for the living God.

³ Even the sparrow has found a home,
    and the swallow a nest for herself,
    where she may have her young —
a place near your altar,
    O Lord Almighty, my King and my God.
⁴ Blessed are those who dwell in your house;
    they are ever praising you.   *Selah*

⁵ Blessed are those whose strength is in you,
    who have set their hearts on pilgrimage.
⁶ As they pass through the Valley of Baca,
    they make it a place of springs;
    the autumn rains also cover it with
    pools. ᵇ

⁷ They go from strength to strength,
    till each appears before God in Zion.

⁸ Hear my prayer, O Lord God Almighty;
    listen to me, O God of Jacob.   *Selah*
⁹ Look upon our shield, ᶜ O God;
    look with favor on your anointed one.

¹⁰ Better is one day in your courts
    than a thousand elsewhere;
I would rather be a doorkeeper in the house
    of my God
    than dwell in the tents of the wicked.
¹¹ For the Lord God is a sun and shield;
    the Lord bestows favor and honor;
no good thing does he withhold
    from those whose walk is blameless.

¹² O Lord Almighty,
    blessed is the man who trusts in you.

Psalm 85

For the director of music. Of the Sons
of Korah. A psalm.

¹ You showed favor to your land, O Lord;
    you restored the fortunes of Jacob.
² You forgave the iniquity of your people
    and covered all their sins.   *Selah*
³ You set aside all your wrath
    and turned from your fierce anger.

⁴ Restore us again, O God our Savior,
    and put away your displeasure toward us.
⁵ Will you be angry with us forever?
    Will you prolong your anger through all
    generations?
⁶ Will you not revive us again,
    that your people may rejoice in you?
⁷ Show us your unfailing love, O Lord,
    and grant us your salvation.

⁸ I will listen to what God the Lord will say;
    he promises peace to his people, his
    saints —
    but let them not return to folly.

ᵃ Title: Probably a musical term   ᵇ 6 Or *blessings*
ᶜ 9 Or *sovereign*

⁹Surely his salvation is near those who fear him,
  that his glory may dwell in our land.

¹⁰Love and faithfulness meet together;
  righteousness and peace kiss each other.
¹¹Faithfulness springs forth from the earth,
  and righteousness looks down from
  heaven.
¹²The LORD will indeed give what is good,
  and our land will yield its harvest.
¹³Righteousness goes before him
  and prepares the way for his steps.

Psalm 86

A prayer of David.

¹Hear, O LORD, and answer me,
  for I am poor and needy.
²Guard my life, for I am devoted to you.
  You are my God; save your servant
  who trusts in you.
³Have mercy on me, O Lord,
  for I call to you all day long.
⁴Bring joy to your servant,
  for to you, O Lord,
  I lift up my soul.

⁵You are forgiving and good, O Lord,
  abounding in love to all who call to you.
⁶Hear my prayer, O LORD;
  listen to my cry for mercy.
⁷In the day of my trouble I will call to you,
  for you will answer me.

⁸Among the gods there is none like you,
    O Lord;
  no deeds can compare with yours.
⁹All the nations you have made
  will come and worship before you, O Lord;
  they will bring glory to your name.
¹⁰For you are great and do marvelous deeds;
  you alone are God.

¹¹Teach me your way, O LORD,
  and I will walk in your truth;
give me an undivided heart,
  that I may fear your name.

PRAYING THE SCRIPTURES

Reassurance

PSALM 86:6–7,10

Hear the prayers of my grandchild, O Lord; listen to his cry for mercy. In the day of his trouble may he call to you, knowing you will answer him. For you are great and do marvelous deeds; you alone are God.

Next prayer in Reassurance Prayer Track: Philippians 1:6

¹²I will praise you, O Lord my God, with all my
    heart;
  I will glorify your name forever.
¹³For great is your love toward me;
  you have delivered me from the depths of
    the grave.ᵃ

¹⁴The arrogant are attacking me, O God;
  a band of ruthless men seeks my life—
  men without regard for you.
¹⁵But you, O Lord, are a compassionate and
    gracious God,
  slow to anger, abounding in love and
    faithfulness.
¹⁶Turn to me and have mercy on me;
  grant your strength to your servant
  and save the son of your maidservant.ᵇ
¹⁷Give me a sign of your goodness,
  that my enemies may see it and be put to
    shame,
  for you, O LORD, have helped me and
    comforted me.

Psalm 87

Of the Sons of Korah. A psalm. A song.

¹He has set his foundation on the holy
    mountain;
² the LORD loves the gates of Zion
  more than all the dwellings of Jacob.

ᵃ 13 Hebrew *Sheol*   ᵇ 16 Or *save your faithful son*

LET'S HAVE
FUN

Let's Play Bible

For a new twist on reading a Bible story, turn your grandchildren's favorite Bible story into a play. This could become a family project as a surprise for their mom(s) and dad(s). Focus on each grandchild's talents for writing the script, making costumes, painting the backdrop or gathering the props. Make it as simple (write out the script yourself and have the kids read the various parts) or elaborate as their enthusiasm and attention allows.

You can also pick *your* favorite Bible story and seize the opportunity to share with them why it is your favorite.

Long-Distance Variation: If you think your grandchildren would like this, send them the script. Let them do the rest. Give them plenty of time before your next visit to get ready to stage the play for you as the honored guest. Or request that they send you a video of the event.

Dear Lord, thank you for the opportunity to share my faith creatively with my grandchildren. Let them enjoy this activity as much as I will. Help them to see that it takes teamwork to put this project together. Let laughter fill the room as we learn and grow and experience your love. Amen.

Your next devotion is located on page 781.

GRANDCHILD **IN FOCUS** • PRAYER

Character

Dear Lord and Father, I ask that you fill my grandchild with your Spirit so her character reflects your goodness and love. Give her kindness and love for others. Bring joy to her life so she will be a joy to others. Grant her patience and self-control through difficult and trying times. May she show mercy and generosity to those who are less fortunate. Grant her integrity and a sense of justice, and surround her with your peace. Amen.

³Glorious things are said of you,
  O city of God: Selah
⁴"I will record Rahab *a* and Babylon
  among those who acknowledge me—
Philistia too, and Tyre, along with Cush *b*—
  and will say, 'This *c* one was born in Zion.'"

⁵Indeed, of Zion it will be said,
  "This one and that one were born in her,
  and the Most High himself will establish
      her."
⁶The Lord will write in the register of the
      peoples:
  "This one was born in Zion."   Selah
⁷As they make music they will sing,
  "All my fountains are in you."

Psalm 88

A song. A psalm of the Sons of Korah.
For the director of music. According
to *mahalath leannoth.* *d* A *maskil* *e*
of Heman the Ezrahite.

¹O Lord, the God who saves me,
  day and night I cry out before you.
²May my prayer come before you;
  turn your ear to my cry.

³For my soul is full of trouble
  and my life draws near the grave. *f*
⁴I am counted among those who go down to
      the pit;
  I am like a man without strength.
⁵I am set apart with the dead,
  like the slain who lie in the grave,
whom you remember no more,
  who are cut off from your care.

⁶You have put me in the lowest pit,
  in the darkest depths.
⁷Your wrath lies heavily upon me;
  you have overwhelmed me with all your
      waves.   Selah
⁸You have taken from me my closest friends
  and have made me repulsive to them.
  I am confined and cannot escape;
⁹   my eyes are dim with grief.

I call to you, O Lord, every day;
  I spread out my hands to you.
¹⁰Do you show your wonders to the dead?
  Do those who are dead rise up and praise
      you?   Selah
¹¹Is your love declared in the grave,
  your faithfulness in Destruction *g*?
¹²Are your wonders known in the place of
      darkness,
  or your righteous deeds in the land of
      oblivion?

¹³But I cry to you for help, O Lord;
  in the morning my prayer comes before
      you.
¹⁴Why, O Lord, do you reject me
  and hide your face from me?

¹⁵From my youth I have been afflicted and
      close to death;
  I have suffered your terrors and am in
      despair.
¹⁶Your wrath has swept over me;
  your terrors have destroyed me.
¹⁷All day long they surround me like a flood;
  they have completely engulfed me.
¹⁸You have taken my companions and loved
      ones from me;
  the darkness is my closest friend.

Psalm 89

A *maskil* *e* of Ethan the Ezrahite.

¹I will sing of the Lord's great love forever;
  with my mouth I will make your
      faithfulness known through all
      generations.
²I will declare that your love stands firm
      forever,
  that you established your faithfulness in
      heaven itself.

---

a 4 A poetic name for Egypt   *b* 4 That is, the upper Nile region
c 4 Or "O Rahab and Babylon, / Philistia, Tyre and Cush, / I will
record concerning those who acknowledge me: / 'This   *d* Title:
Possibly a tune, "The Suffering of Affliction"   *e* Title: Probably
a literary or musical term   *f* 3 Hebrew *Sheol*   *g* 11 Hebrew
Abaddon

Worship the Lord

The people walking in darkness
 have seen a great light;
on those living in the land of the shadow of death
 a light has dawned.

For to us a child is born,
 to us a son is given,
 and the government will be on his shoulders.
And he will be called
 Wonderful Counselor, Mighty God,
 Everlasting Father, Prince of Peace.
Of the increase of his government and peace
 there will be no end.
He will reign on David's throne
 and over his kingdom,
establishing and upholding it
 with justice and righteousness
 from that time on and forever.
The zeal of the LORD Almighty
 will accomplish this.

Isaiah 9:2,6 – 7

*Dear Lord, I am amazed how you have ful-
filled your promises of so long ago. I praise
you for drawing me to the Light of the World.
Thank you that this child, the Prince of Peace,
has been born to save your people — the incredible accomplishment of your love and zeal. Amen.*

Your next devotion is located on page 784.

GRANDCHILD IN FOCUS • PRAYER

Talents

*Dear Lord, the giver of gifts, bless my
grandchild as he develops his talents. Help him
identify his talents and be proud and confident of
the gifts you have given him. Give him patience and
understanding, Lord, so he will not grow weary of
striving and searching to reach the goals you have
set for him. May each milestone bring satisfaction and a healthy desire for greater
achievement and success to bring
glory to you. Amen.*

³ You said, "I have made a covenant with my
    chosen one,
I have sworn to David my servant,
⁴ 'I will establish your line forever
    and make your throne firm through all
      generations.'"   *Selah*

⁵ The heavens praise your wonders, O LORD,
    your faithfulness too, in the assembly of
      the holy ones.
⁶ For who in the skies above can compare with
    the LORD?
Who is like the LORD among the heavenly
    beings?
⁷ In the council of the holy ones God is greatly
    feared;
he is more awesome than all who surround
    him.
⁸ O LORD God Almighty, who is like you?
    You are mighty, O LORD, and your
      faithfulness surrounds you.

⁹ You rule over the surging sea;
    when its waves mount up, you still them.
¹⁰ You crushed Rahab like one of the slain;
    with your strong arm you scattered your
      enemies.
¹¹ The heavens are yours, and yours also the
    earth;
you founded the world and all that is in it.
¹² You created the north and the south;
    Tabor and Hermon sing for joy at your
      name.
¹³ Your arm is endued with power;
    your hand is strong, your right hand
      exalted.

¹⁴ Righteousness and justice are the foundation
    of your throne;
love and faithfulness go before you.
¹⁵ Blessed are those who have learned to
    acclaim you,
who walk in the light of your presence,
    O LORD.
¹⁶ They rejoice in your name all day long;
    they exult in your righteousness.

¹⁷ For you are their glory and strength,
    and by your favor you exalt our horn.[a]
¹⁸ Indeed, our shield[b] belongs to the LORD,
    our king to the Holy One of Israel.

¹⁹ Once you spoke in a vision,
    to your faithful people you said:
"I have bestowed strength on a warrior;
    I have exalted a young man from among
      the people.
²⁰ I have found David my servant;
    with my sacred oil I have anointed him.
²¹ My hand will sustain him;
    surely my arm will strengthen him.
²² No enemy will subject him to tribute;
    no wicked man will oppress him.
²³ I will crush his foes before him
    and strike down his adversaries.
²⁴ My faithful love will be with him,
    and through my name his horn[c] will be
      exalted.
²⁵ I will set his hand over the sea,
    his right hand over the rivers.
²⁶ He will call out to me, 'You are my Father,
    my God, the Rock my Savior.'
²⁷ I will also appoint him my firstborn,
    the most exalted of the kings of the earth.
²⁸ I will maintain my love to him forever,
    and my covenant with him will never fail.
²⁹ I will establish his line forever,
    his throne as long as the heavens endure.

³⁰ "If his sons forsake my law
    and do not follow my statutes,
³¹ if they violate my decrees
    and fail to keep my commands,
³² I will punish their sin with the rod,
    their iniquity with flogging;
³³ but I will not take my love from him,
    nor will I ever betray my faithfulness.
³⁴ I will not violate my covenant
    or alter what my lips have uttered.
³⁵ Once for all, I have sworn by my holiness—
    and I will not lie to David—

---

a 17 Horn here symbolizes strong one.   *b 18* Or *sovereign*
c 24 Horn here symbolizes strength.

³⁶ that his line will continue forever
and his throne endure before me like the sun;
³⁷ it will be established forever like the moon,
the faithful witness in the sky." *Selah*

³⁸ But you have rejected, you have spurned,
you have been very angry with your
anointed one.
³⁹ You have renounced the covenant with your
servant
and have defiled his crown in the dust.
⁴⁰ You have broken through all his walls
and reduced his strongholds to ruins.
⁴¹ All who pass by have plundered him;
he has become the scorn of his neighbors.
⁴² You have exalted the right hand of his foes;
you have made all his enemies rejoice.
⁴³ You have turned back the edge of his sword
and have not supported him in battle.
⁴⁴ You have put an end to his splendor
and cast his throne to the ground.
⁴⁵ You have cut short the days of his youth;
you have covered him with a mantle
of shame. *Selah*

⁴⁶ How long, O Lord? Will you hide yourself
forever?
How long will your wrath burn like fire?
⁴⁷ Remember how fleeting is my life.
For what futility you have created all men!
⁴⁸ What man can live and not see death,
or save himself from the power of the
grave*[a]*? *Selah*
⁴⁹ O Lord, where is your former great love,
which in your faithfulness you swore to
David?
⁵⁰ Remember, Lord, how your servant has*[b]* been
mocked,
how I bear in my heart the taunts of all the
nations,
⁵¹ the taunts with which your enemies have
mocked, O Lord,
with which they have mocked every step of
your anointed one.

⁵² Praise be to the Lord forever!
Amen and Amen.

BOOK IV

Psalms 90 – 106

Psalm 90

A prayer of Moses the man of God.

¹ Lord, you have been our dwelling place
throughout all generations.
² Before the mountains were born
or you brought forth the earth and the
world,
from everlasting to everlasting you are
God.

³ You turn men back to dust,
saying, "Return to dust, O sons of men."
⁴ For a thousand years in your sight
are like a day that has just gone by,
or like a watch in the night.
⁵ You sweep men away in the sleep of death;
they are like the new grass of the
morning —
⁶ though in the morning it springs up new,
by evening it is dry and withered.

⁷ We are consumed by your anger
and terrified by your indignation.
⁸ You have set our iniquities before you,
our secret sins in the light of your
presence.
⁹ All our days pass away under your wrath;
we finish our years with a moan.
¹⁰ The length of our days is seventy years —
or eighty, if we have the strength;
yet their span*[c]* is but trouble and sorrow,
for they quickly pass, and we fly away.

¹¹ Who knows the power of your anger?
For your wrath is as great as the fear that is
due you.
¹² Teach us to number our days aright,
that we may gain a heart of wisdom.

¹³ Relent, O Lord! How long will it be?
Have compassion on your servants.

---

a 48 Hebrew *Sheol*   *b 50* Or *your servants have*   *c 10* Or *yet the best of them*

TEACH US TO NUMBER OUR DAYS
ARIGHT, THAT WE MAY GAIN A
HEART OF WISDOM.

Psalm 90:12

Do Something Big

KAREN MAINS

READ | PSALM 90:1 – 12

Prior to my 64th birthday, I sent emails to friends and family announcing, "My birthday is next week! What are we going to do about it?" I figured the life left to me was too precious not to celebrate, and if no one else wanted to mark it the way it needed to be marked, I'd give them a little push.

So one morning, most of my Covenant Group met for an early breakfast, and I opened a card that read, "I've heard that the one who has the most birthdays lives the longest." Perhaps an even more appropriate notice was the banner headline I tore from a *USA Today* ad: DO SOMETHING BIG (while there's still time to put it in your autobiography).

Shortly after that I watched *Hunt for Justice: The Louise Arbour Story*, a movie about Louise Arbour, the Canadian judge appointed in 1996 by NATO as the chief war crimes prosecutor at the International Criminal Tribunal in The Hague. This story tells how one woman inspired a team of investigators to keep searching for the elusive leads that would land the ultimate responsibility for the genocides in the Bosnian conflict at the foot of the highest official — in this case, the first serving head of state ever to be indicted for war crimes.

Despite the hard facts exposed in this docudrama, I finished the DVD thinking, "Thank God. Thank God there are people who dare to do something big! Now where are *you* going to take a stand, Mains?"

So the question I'm asking myself this year is: Behind what big cause am I going to throw my little weight — not so there's time to put it in my autobiography (what autobiography?), but so that I will not look back and regret wasted days?

O Lord, help me to live the rest of the life given to me in such a way that I can look back on it and say, "Yep, with your help I did one or two things that were pretty big!" Amen.

Your next devotion is located on page 786.

GRANDCHILD IN FOCUS • PRAYER

SELECT ONE OF YOUR
GRANDCHILDREN TO FOCUS ON
IN PRAYER FOR THE NEXT 14 DAYS.

Salvation

Dear Lord, please guide my grandchild to your gift of salvation. I pray that she will come to know you, to love you and to walk close to you throughout her life. May she boldly claim Jesus as her Lord and Savior. Guide her as she makes choices that have eternal consequences. Help her to follow you each moment of her life. I pray this in Jesus' name, amen.

PRAYING THE SCRIPTURES

Joy

PSALM 90:14

O Lord, satisfy my grandchild in the morning with your unfailing love, that she may sing for joy and be glad all her days.

Next prayer in Joy Prayer Track: Psalm 126:3

14 Satisfy us in the morning with your unfailing love,
   that we may sing for joy and be glad all our days.
15 Make us glad for as many days as you have afflicted us,
   for as many years as we have seen trouble.
16 May your deeds be shown to your servants,
   your splendor to their children.

17 May the favor *a* of the Lord our God rest upon us;
   establish the work of our hands for us—
   yes, establish the work of our hands.

PRAYING THE SCRIPTURES

Blessing

PSALM 90:17

May your favor, O Lord my God, rest upon my grandchild. O Lord, establish the work of his hands — yes, establish the work of his hands.

Next prayer in Blessing Prayer Track: Malachi 3:10

Psalm 91

1 He who dwells in the shelter of the Most High
   will rest in the shadow of the Almighty. *b*
2 I will say *c* of the LORD, "He is my refuge and my fortress,
   my God, in whom I trust."

3 Surely he will save you from the fowler's snare
   and from the deadly pestilence.
4 He will cover you with his feathers,
   and under his wings you will find refuge;
   his faithfulness will be your shield and rampart.

TALKING POINTS

Faithfulness

God's faithfulness will protect us.

PSALM 91:1–4

For more on faithfulness, go to Psalm 100:1–5.

5 You will not fear the terror of night,
   nor the arrow that flies by day,
6 nor the pestilence that stalks in the darkness,
   nor the plague that destroys at midday.
7 A thousand may fall at your side,
   ten thousand at your right hand,
   but it will not come near you.
8 You will only observe with your eyes
   and see the punishment of the wicked.

9 If you make the Most High your dwelling—
   even the LORD, who is my refuge—
10 then no harm will befall you,
   no disaster will come near your tent.
11 For he will command his angels concerning you
   to guard you in all your ways;

a 17 Or *beauty*   *b* 1 Hebrew *Shaddai*   *c* 2 Or *He says*

MAY YOUR DEEDS BE SHOWN TO
YOUR SERVANTS, YOUR SPLENDOR
TO THEIR CHILDREN.
Psalm 90:16

A Legacy of Love

CLAUDIA ARP

READ | PSALM 90:13 – 16

"Thank goodness, this day is almost over," Leah said to her daughter, Jill. Several weeks before, Leah's mother, after a lengthy illness, had passed on from this world to the next. This day's daunting task—clearing out her condo and going through her personal things—had left them both exhausted and emotionally drained.

Now one more load to the dumpster. Throughout the day, they had sorted through her stuff—boxes and boxes of letters, newspaper clippings, old magazines and pictures of so many unknown people. Memorabilia others didn't want or care about. Junk that may have been precious to Leah's mother. As Leah threw away the last garbage bags, she stared at the dumpster and thought, "My mom's life is in that dumpster."

Then it hit her: One day that may be my stuff! What heritage am I leaving to my daughter and to my grandchildren? A dumpster of stuff or a legacy of love and faith?

Leah suddenly realized the choice was hers.

We also have choices to make. The problem is that too often we invest in stuff and not people. We have, as Oz Guinness writes in *The Call*, "too much to live with and too little to live for." What are we doing today to build spiritual plenty instead of material plenty?

Are you so busy with things that you can't hear God's call in your life? What is God's calling for you? Do you need to invest in more stuff? Probably not. Perhaps what you really need to invest in is more time—time to declutter your life, time to invest in others. Consider this: Precious moments invested in your grandchildren today will never end up in a dumpster tomorrow.

Dear Father, thank you for the special people you have put into my life—especially my grandchildren. Please help me invest in their lives today so they will see your splendor and follow your call for their lives!

GRANDCHILD IN FOCUS • PRAYER

Physical Well-Being

Almighty God, Creator of us all, I pray that you will watch over my grandchild's physical development. May he grow in strength through the stages of his life. As he grows in awareness of his body, help him to understand that each body develops uniquely, yet is within your plan and your control. Please guard his health so that his diseases are few, his injuries are minor and his infirmities are brief. Amen.

Your next devotion is located on page 788.

12 they will lift you up in their hands,
    so that you will not strike your foot against
    a stone.
13 You will tread upon the lion and the cobra;
    you will trample the great lion and the
    serpent.

14 "Because he loves me," says the LORD, "I will
    rescue him;
    I will protect him, for he acknowledges my
    name.
15 He will call upon me, and I will answer him;
    I will be with him in trouble,
    I will deliver him and honor him.
16 With long life will I satisfy him
    and show him my salvation."

PRAYING THE SCRIPTURES

Protection

PSALM 91:11–12,16

O Lord, command your angels to guard my
grandchild in all his ways, to lift him up in
their hands so that he will not strike his foot
against a stone. Satisfy him with long life, I
pray, and show him your salvation.

Next prayer in Protection Prayer Track: Psalm 121:5–8

Psalm 92

A psalm. A song. For the Sabbath day.

1 It is good to praise the LORD
    and make music to your name, O Most
    High,
2 to proclaim your love in the morning
    and your faithfulness at night,
3 to the music of the ten-stringed lyre
    and the melody of the harp.

4 For you make me glad by your deeds,
    O LORD;
    I sing for joy at the works of your hands.

5 How great are your works, O LORD,
    how profound your thoughts!
6 The senseless man does not know,
    fools do not understand,
7 that though the wicked spring up like grass
    and all evildoers flourish,
they will be forever destroyed.

8 But you, O LORD, are exalted forever.

9 For surely your enemies, O LORD,
    surely your enemies will perish;
    all evildoers will be scattered.
10 You have exalted my horn [a] like that of a
    wild ox;
    fine oils have been poured upon me.
11 My eyes have seen the defeat of my
    adversaries;
    my ears have heard the rout of my wicked
    foes.

12 The righteous will flourish like a palm tree,
    they will grow like a cedar of Lebanon;
13 planted in the house of the LORD,
    they will flourish in the courts of our
    God.
14 They will still bear fruit in old age,
    they will stay fresh and green,
15 proclaiming, "The LORD is upright;
    he is my Rock, and there is no wickedness
    in him."

Psalm 93

1 The LORD reigns, he is robed in majesty;
    the LORD is robed in majesty
    and is armed with strength.
The world is firmly established;
    it cannot be moved.
2 Your throne was established long ago;
    you are from all eternity.

3 The seas have lifted up, O LORD,
    the seas have lifted up their voice;
    the seas have lifted up their pounding
    waves.

a 10 *Horn* here symbolizes strength.

THEY WILL STILL BEAR FRUIT IN
OLD AGE, THEY WILL STAY FRESH
AND GREEN, PROCLAIMING,
"THE LORD IS UPRIGHT; HE IS
MY ROCK."

Psalm 92:14–15

Staying Young

JEAN E. SYSWERDA

READ | PSALM 92:1–15

Some days I feel pretty old. Not that I truly am, you understand. I'm actually a pretty young grandmother. Still, my joints creak in the morning, I tend to run out of energy late in the afternoon, and evenings are sometimes reserved for slippers and books. But that's just my aging physical body. I don't want my mind and spirit to follow. For that reason, this verse in the Psalms is my new favorite. When I read it for the first time about a year ago, I laughed out loud. It so exactly states my goal to stay young in spirit and to bear fruit while doing it. I want to continue to engage my grandchildren in life-affirming activities. Even when I can no longer roll around on the floor with them, I want to connect with them, laugh with them, have fun with them and teach them by example to approach life with vigor and vitality.

Unfortunately, when our bodies age, our spirits often follow. We've all met women who have let their minds and spirits become as old as their bodies. It often shows itself in faces that no longer smile readily, in words that are negative and in attitudes that perceive the past as much better than the present or the future. Life for a woman like that is pretty much over. As her body ages, so her mind and spirit ages. And fruit is a thing of the past.

As believing grandmas, however, we have a remedy for aging spirits and emotions. His name is the Lord, our Rock. When he forms our foundation for living, no matter what happens to our aging bodies, we can find refreshment and strength in him. Our spirits will stay "fresh and green," and we will continue to bear the fruit of a life lived fully and enthusiastically.

Keep me young, Lord; keep me young. As my body continues the slow march to the grave, help me to keep my mind and spirit focused on you, energized by you and fruitful because of your touch on my life. Amen.

Your next devotion is located on page 794.

GRANDCHILD IN FOCUS · PRAYER

Emotional Development

O God, Creator of mind and body, I pray that you will give my grandchild emotional health and strength. Where there is anger, bring peace. Where there is confusion, bring clarity and focus. Where there are dark shadows, cast a ray of hope. Fill her with the sunshine of your Spirit. Warm her with the presence of your peace. Amen.

⁴Mightier than the thunder of the great
waters,
mightier than the breakers of the sea—
the LORD on high is mighty.

⁵Your statutes stand firm;
holiness adorns your house
for endless days, O LORD.

Psalm 94

¹O LORD, the God who avenges,
O God who avenges, shine forth.
²Rise up, O Judge of the earth;
pay back to the proud what they deserve.
³How long will the wicked, O LORD,
how long will the wicked be jubilant?

⁴They pour out arrogant words;
all the evildoers are full of boasting.
⁵They crush your people, O LORD;
they oppress your inheritance.
⁶They slay the widow and the alien;
they murder the fatherless.
⁷They say, "The LORD does not see;
the God of Jacob pays no heed."

⁸Take heed, you senseless ones among the
people;
you fools, when will you become wise?
⁹Does he who implanted the ear not hear?
Does he who formed the eye not see?
¹⁰Does he who disciplines nations not punish?
Does he who teaches man lack
knowledge?
¹¹The LORD knows the thoughts of man;
he knows that they are futile.

¹²Blessed is the man you discipline, O LORD,
the man you teach from your law;
¹³you grant him relief from days of trouble,
till a pit is dug for the wicked.
¹⁴For the LORD will not reject his people;
he will never forsake his inheritance.
¹⁵Judgment will again be founded on
righteousness,
and all the upright in heart will follow it.

¹⁶Who will rise up for me against the wicked?
Who will take a stand for me against
evildoers?
¹⁷Unless the LORD had given me help,
I would soon have dwelt in the silence of
death.
¹⁸When I said, "My foot is slipping,"
your love, O LORD, supported me.
¹⁹When anxiety was great within me,
your consolation brought joy to my soul.

TALKING POINTS

Anxiety
God will support and console us.
PSALM 94:18–19

For more on anxiety, go to Isaiah 45:5–7.

²⁰Can a corrupt throne be allied with you—
one that brings on misery by its decrees?
²¹They band together against the righteous
and condemn the innocent to death.
²²But the LORD has become my fortress,
and my God the rock in whom I take
refuge.
²³He will repay them for their sins
and destroy them for their wickedness;
the LORD our God will destroy them.

Psalm 95

¹Come, let us sing for joy to the LORD;
let us shout aloud to the Rock of our
salvation.
²Let us come before him with thanksgiving
and extol him with music and song.

³For the LORD is the great God,
the great King above all gods.
⁴In his hand are the depths of the earth,
and the mountain peaks belong to him.

⁵The sea is his, for he made it,
  and his hands formed the dry land.

⁶Come, let us bow down in worship,
  let us kneel before the LORD our Maker;
⁷for he is our God
  and we are the people of his pasture,
  the flock under his care.

Today, if you hear his voice,
⁸   do not harden your hearts as you did at
    Meribah,ᵃ
  as you did that day at Massahᵇ in the desert,
⁹where your fathers tested and tried me,
  though they had seen what I did.
¹⁰For forty years I was angry with that
    generation;
  I said, "They are a people whose hearts go
    astray,
  and they have not known my ways."
¹¹So I declared on oath in my anger,
  "They shall never enter my rest."

Psalm 96

96:1–13pp — 1Ch 16:23–33

¹Sing to the LORD a new song;
  sing to the LORD, all the earth.
²Sing to the LORD, praise his name;
  proclaim his salvation day after day.
³Declare his glory among the nations,
  his marvelous deeds among all peoples.

⁴For great is the LORD and most worthy of
    praise;
  he is to be feared above all gods.
⁵For all the gods of the nations are idols,
  but the LORD made the heavens.
⁶Splendor and majesty are before him;
  strength and glory are in his sanctuary.

⁷Ascribe to the LORD, O families of nations,
  ascribe to the LORD glory and strength.
⁸Ascribe to the LORD the glory due his name;
  bring an offering and come into his courts.
⁹Worship the LORD in the splendor of hisᶜ
    holiness;
  tremble before him, all the earth.

¹⁰Say among the nations, "The LORD reigns."
  The world is firmly established, it cannot
    be moved;
  he will judge the peoples with equity.
¹¹Let the heavens rejoice, let the earth be
    glad;
  let the sea resound, and all that is in it;
¹²   let the fields be jubilant, and everything in
    them.
  Then all the trees of the forest will sing for
    joy;
¹³   they will sing before the LORD, for he
    comes,
  he comes to judge the earth.
  He will judge the world in righteousness
    and the peoples in his truth.

Psalm 97

¹The LORD reigns, let the earth be glad;
  let the distant shores rejoice.

²Clouds and thick darkness surround him;
  righteousness and justice are the
    foundation of his throne.
³Fire goes before him
  and consumes his foes on every side.
⁴His lightning lights up the world;
  the earth sees and trembles.
⁵The mountains melt like wax before the
    LORD,
  before the Lord of all the earth.
⁶The heavens proclaim his righteousness,
  and all the peoples see his glory.

⁷All who worship images are put to shame,
  those who boast in idols—
  worship him, all you gods!

⁸Zion hears and rejoices
  and the villages of Judah are glad
  because of your judgments, O LORD.
⁹For you, O LORD, are the Most High over all
    the earth;
  you are exalted far above all gods.

ᵃ 8 *Meribah means quarreling.*   ᵇ 8 *Massah means testing.*
ᶜ 9 *Or* LORD *with the splendor of*

¹⁰ Let those who love the LORD hate evil,
  for he guards the lives of his faithful ones
  and delivers them from the hand of the
    wicked.
¹¹ Light is shed upon the righteous
  and joy on the upright in heart.
¹² Rejoice in the LORD, you who are righteous,
  and praise his holy name.

Psalm 98

A psalm.

¹ Sing to the LORD a new song,
  for he has done marvelous things;
his right hand and his holy arm
  have worked salvation for him.
² The LORD has made his salvation known
  and revealed his righteousness to the
    nations.
³ He has remembered his love
  and his faithfulness to the house of Israel;
all the ends of the earth have seen
  the salvation of our God.

⁴ Shout for joy to the LORD, all the earth,
  burst into jubilant song with music;
⁵ make music to the LORD with the harp,
  with the harp and the sound of singing,
⁶ with trumpets and the blast of the ram's
    horn—
  shout for joy before the LORD, the King.

⁷ Let the sea resound, and everything in it,
  the world, and all who live in it.
⁸ Let the rivers clap their hands,
  let the mountains sing together for joy;
⁹ let them sing before the LORD,
  for he comes to judge the earth.
He will judge the world in righteousness
  and the peoples with equity.

Psalm 99

¹ The LORD reigns,
  let the nations tremble;
he sits enthroned between the cherubim,
  let the earth shake.

² Great is the LORD in Zion;
  he is exalted over all the nations.
³ Let them praise your great and awesome
    name—
  he is holy.

⁴ The King is mighty, he loves justice—
  you have established equity;
in Jacob you have done
  what is just and right.
⁵ Exalt the LORD our God
  and worship at his footstool;
  he is holy.

⁶ Moses and Aaron were among his priests,
  Samuel was among those who called on
    his name;
they called on the LORD
  and he answered them.
⁷ He spoke to them from the pillar of cloud;
  they kept his statutes and the decrees he
    gave them.

⁸ O LORD our God,
  you answered them;
you were to Israel ᵃ a forgiving God,
  though you punished their misdeeds. ᵇ
⁹ Exalt the LORD our God
  and worship at his holy mountain,
  for the LORD our God is holy.

Psalm 100

A psalm. For giving thanks.

¹ Shout for joy to the LORD, all the earth.
²   Worship the LORD with gladness;
  come before him with joyful songs.
³ Know that the LORD is God.
  It is he who made us, and we are his ᶜ;
  we are his people, the sheep of his
    pasture.

⁴ Enter his gates with thanksgiving
  and his courts with praise;
  give thanks to him and praise his name.

ᵃ 8 Hebrew them   ᵇ 8 Or / an avenger of the wrongs done to them
ᶜ 3 Or and not we ourselves

TALKING POINTS

Faithfulness

God's faithfulness is never-ending.

PSALM 100:1–5

For more on faithfulness, go to Lamentations 3:19–24.

⁵ For the LORD is good and his love endures
    forever;
  his faithfulness continues through all
    generations.

stories to share

PSALM 100:1–5

*Give Thanks to
the Lord*

LIFE LESSON: God is faithful.

TO TALK ABOUT

✦ Why should we praise God? What
  has he done for us?

✦ How does the psalmist describe
  God?

✦ How has God shown his faithfulness
  to you and your family?

✦ What are some ways you can thank
  God today for what he has done for
  you?

Psalm 101

Of David. A psalm.

¹ I will sing of your love and justice;
    to you, O LORD, I will sing praise.
² I will be careful to lead a blameless life—
    when will you come to me?

  I will walk in my house
    with blameless heart.
³ I will set before my eyes
    no vile thing.

  The deeds of faithless men I hate;
    they will not cling to me.
⁴ Men of perverse heart shall be far from me;
    I will have nothing to do with evil.

⁵ Whoever slanders his neighbor in secret,
    him will I put to silence;
  whoever has haughty eyes and a proud heart,
    him will I not endure.

⁶ My eyes will be on the faithful in the land,
    that they may dwell with me;
  he whose walk is blameless
    will minister to me.

⁷ No one who practices deceit
    will dwell in my house;
  no one who speaks falsely
    will stand in my presence.

⁸ Every morning I will put to silence
    all the wicked in the land;
  I will cut off every evildoer
    from the city of the LORD.

Psalm 102

*A prayer of an afflicted man. When he is
faint and pours out his lament
before the LORD.*

¹ Hear my prayer, O LORD;
    let my cry for help come to you.
² Do not hide your face from me
    when I am in distress.
  Turn your ear to me;
    when I call, answer me quickly.

³For my days vanish like smoke;
    my bones burn like glowing embers.
⁴My heart is blighted and withered like grass;
    I forget to eat my food.
⁵Because of my loud groaning
    I am reduced to skin and bones.
⁶I am like a desert owl,
    like an owl among the ruins.
⁷I lie awake; I have become
    like a bird alone on a roof.
⁸All day long my enemies taunt me;
    those who rail against me use my name as
    a curse.
⁹For I eat ashes as my food
    and mingle my drink with tears
¹⁰because of your great wrath,
    for you have taken me up and thrown me
    aside.
¹¹My days are like the evening shadow;
    I wither away like grass.

¹²But you, O Lord, sit enthroned forever;
    your renown endures through all
    generations.
¹³You will arise and have compassion on
    Zion,
    for it is time to show favor to her;
    the appointed time has come.
¹⁴For her stones are dear to your servants;
    her very dust moves them to pity.
¹⁵The nations will fear the name of the Lord,
    all the kings of the earth will revere your
    glory.
¹⁶For the Lord will rebuild Zion
    and appear in his glory.
¹⁷He will respond to the prayer of the destitute;
    he will not despise their plea.

¹⁸Let this be written for a future generation,
    that a people not yet created may praise
    the Lord:
¹⁹"The Lord looked down from his sanctuary
    on high,
    from heaven he viewed the earth,
²⁰to hear the groans of the prisoners
    and release those condemned to death."

²¹So the name of the Lord will be declared in
    Zion
    and his praise in Jerusalem
²²when the peoples and the kingdoms
    assemble to worship the Lord.

²³In the course of my life ᵃ he broke my
    strength;
    he cut short my days.
²⁴So I said:
    "Do not take me away, O my God, in the
    midst of my days;
    your years go on through all generations.
²⁵In the beginning you laid the foundations of
    the earth,
    and the heavens are the work of your
    hands.
²⁶They will perish, but you remain;
    they will all wear out like a garment.
    Like clothing you will change them
    and they will be discarded.
²⁷But you remain the same,
    and your years will never end.
²⁸The children of your servants will live in your
    presence;
    their descendants will be established before
    you."

Psalm 103

Of David.

¹Praise the Lord, O my soul;
    all my inmost being, praise his holy name.
²Praise the Lord, O my soul,
    and forget not all his benefits—
³who forgives all your sins
    and heals all your diseases,
⁴who redeems your life from the pit
    and crowns you with love and compassion,
⁵who satisfies your desires with good things
    so that your youth is renewed like the
    eagle's.

⁶The Lord works righteousness
    and justice for all the oppressed.

ᵃ 23 Or By his power

LET THIS BE WRITTEN FOR A
FUTURE GENERATION, THAT A
PEOPLE NOT YET CREATED MAY
PRAISE THE LORD.

Psalm 102:18

Leaving a Legacy of Prayer

FERN NICHOLS

READ | PSALM 102:1 – 28

It's true that we as grandmothers desire to leave a godly imprint on future generations. Instead of working hard to leave stock portfolios, heirlooms, money or property, we can leave them something far more valuable that will last forever; we can leave them a legacy of answered prayer.

Pastor Ron Dunn states: "I can leave my children [grandchildren] an inheritance of answered prayer. I can be confident that long after I'm dead God will be answering the prayers in the lives of my children that I prayed while I was alive. What a privilege and opportunity to leave our children an inheritance like that. To wrap my children up in blankets of intercessory prayer."

I have purposed in my heart to leave that kind of legacy. I have six grandchildren and pray for each one. It takes time, but in light of eternity, it's worth it. I love praying the will and Word of God in regard to their lives. God's words are powerful and effective when we pray them.

For example, using God's Word I pray that they will

accept Jesus into their hearts (2 Timothy 3:15),
please God and desire his plans (Philippians 2:12 – 13),
love what God loves and hate what he hates (Psalm 97:10),
obey their parents (Colossians 3:20),
be a witness for Christ (Philippians 2:14 – 16),
be protected from the evil one (John 17:15), and
marry a Christian and remain pure until
   marriage (2 Corinthians 6:14).

Purpose in your heart to be a praying grandmother. We can do a lot of wonderful things for our grandchildren, but their lives are truly transformed when we pray.

Eternal God, I purpose in my heart to pray daily for my grandchildren. May I leave a legacy that will change the course of history. In Jesus' name, amen.

GRANDCHILD IN FOCUS • PRAYER

Spiritual Growth

Dear Lord, today I pray for my grandchild's spiritual growth. I ask that you instill in him the desire to read and memorize your Word. Give him a passion to be in conversation with you. May loving and serving you be part of his daily life. I ask that you stay close to him and lead him to be transformed to your likeness, to reflect your grace and to radiate your love. I pray this in Jesus' name, amen.

Your next devotion is located on page 796.

⁷He made known his ways to Moses,
his deeds to the people of Israel:
⁸The Lord is compassionate and gracious,
slow to anger, abounding in love.
⁹He will not always accuse,
nor will he harbor his anger forever;

TALKING POINTS

Compassion

The Lord has compassion
for those who fear him.

PSALM 103:8–18

For more on compassion, go to Acts 9:36–43.

¹⁰he does not treat us as our sins deserve
or repay us according to our iniquities.
¹¹For as high as the heavens are above the
earth,
so great is his love for those who fear him;
¹²as far as the east is from the west,
so far has he removed our transgressions
from us.

TALKING POINTS

Guilt

Our sins are long gone.

PSALM 103:12

For more on guilt, go to Isaiah 1:18.

¹³As a father has compassion on his children,
so the Lord has compassion on those who
fear him;
¹⁴for he knows how we are formed,
he remembers that we are dust.

¹⁵As for man, his days are like grass,
he flourishes like a flower of the field;
¹⁶the wind blows over it and it is gone,
and its place remembers it no more.
¹⁷But from everlasting to everlasting
the Lord's love is with those who fear him,
and his righteousness with their children's
children—
¹⁸with those who keep his covenant
and remember to obey his precepts.

¹⁹The Lord has established his throne in
heaven,
and his kingdom rules over all.

²⁰Praise the Lord, you his angels,
you mighty ones who do his bidding,
who obey his word.
²¹Praise the Lord, all his heavenly hosts,
you his servants who do his will.
²²Praise the Lord, all his works
everywhere in his dominion.

Praise the Lord, O my soul.

Psalm 104

¹Praise the Lord, O my soul.

O Lord my God, you are very great;
you are clothed with splendor and
majesty.
²He wraps himself in light as with a garment;
he stretches out the heavens like a tent
³ and lays the beams of his upper chambers
on their waters.
He makes the clouds his chariot
and rides on the wings of the wind.
⁴He makes winds his messengers,ᵃ
flames of fire his servants.

⁵He set the earth on its foundations;
it can never be moved.
⁶You covered it with the deep as with a
garment;
the waters stood above the mountains.

ᵃ 4 Or angels

PRAISE THE LORD ... WHO
SATISFIES YOUR DESIRES
WITH GOOD THINGS SO THAT
YOUR YOUTH IS RENEWED
LIKE THE EAGLE'S.

Psalm 103:2,5

Satisfied

ANNE ORTLUND

READ | PSALM 103:1 – 22

There's a need in my heart for more of You, Lord,
   A need in my heart for more of You,
So I turn, I turn away from this world's lesser things,
And I drink, drink so deep of everlasting springs,
And I find I am satisfied anew —
   I find I am satisfied with You!

There's a need in my heart for more of You, Lord,
   A need in my heart for more of You,
So I steal, I steal away to find a quiet nook,
And I read, read the pages of Your precious Book,
And I find I am satisfied anew —
   I find I am satisfied with You!

There's a need in my heart for more of You, Lord,
   A need in my heart for more of You,
So I kneel, I kneel again before Your throne in prayer,
And I thrill, thrill to find that You are waiting there!
And I find I am satisfied anew —
   I find I am satisfied with You!

*Dear Lord, fill me with desire for you and your
Word. Delight me with your love. Satisfy me
with your presence. Amen.*

Your next devotion is located on page 801.

GRANDCHILD IN FOCUS • PRAYER

Relationships at Home

*O Lord, I pray that you will bless the home and family
of my grandchild. May the relationships she has with her
parents and siblings enhance her well-being, support her
self-confidence and increase her faith. May her home
life reflect your love, your grace, your compassion and
your peace. Guide her parents to direct her in love
and truth, so she will grow into a strong and
compassionate individual. Amen.*

⁷ But at your rebuke the waters fled,
  at the sound of your thunder they took to
    flight;
⁸ they flowed over the mountains,
  they went down into the valleys,
  to the place you assigned for them.
⁹ You set a boundary they cannot cross;
  never again will they cover the earth.

¹⁰ He makes springs pour water into the
    ravines;
  it flows between the mountains.
¹¹ They give water to all the beasts of the field;
  the wild donkeys quench their thirst.
¹² The birds of the air nest by the waters;
  they sing among the branches.
¹³ He waters the mountains from his upper
    chambers;
  the earth is satisfied by the fruit of his
    work.
¹⁴ He makes grass grow for the cattle,
  and plants for man to cultivate —
  bringing forth food from the earth:
¹⁵ wine that gladdens the heart of man,
  oil to make his face shine,
  and bread that sustains his heart.
¹⁶ The trees of the LORD are well watered,
  the cedars of Lebanon that he planted.
¹⁷ There the birds make their nests;
  the stork has its home in the pine trees.
¹⁸ The high mountains belong to the wild goats;
  the crags are a refuge for the coneys. ᵃ

¹⁹ The moon marks off the seasons,
  and the sun knows when to go down.
²⁰ You bring darkness, it becomes night,
  and all the beasts of the forest prowl.
²¹ The lions roar for their prey
  and seek their food from God.
²² The sun rises, and they steal away;
  they return and lie down in their dens.
²³ Then man goes out to his work,
  to his labor until evening.

²⁴ How many are your works, O LORD!
  In wisdom you made them all;
  the earth is full of your creatures.

²⁵ There is the sea, vast and spacious,
  teeming with creatures beyond number —
  living things both large and small.
²⁶ There the ships go to and fro,
  and the leviathan, which you formed to
    frolic there.

²⁷ These all look to you
  to give them their food at the proper
    time.
²⁸ When you give it to them,
  they gather it up;
  when you open your hand,
  they are satisfied with good things.
²⁹ When you hide your face,
  they are terrified;
  when you take away their breath,
  they die and return to the dust.
³⁰ When you send your Spirit,
  they are created,
  and you renew the face of the earth.

³¹ May the glory of the LORD endure forever;
  may the LORD rejoice in his works —
³² he who looks at the earth, and it trembles,
  who touches the mountains, and they
    smoke.

³³ I will sing to the LORD all my life;
  I will sing praise to my God as long as
    I live.
³⁴ May my meditation be pleasing to him,
  as I rejoice in the LORD.
³⁵ But may sinners vanish from the earth
  and the wicked be no more.

  Praise the LORD, O my soul.

  Praise the LORD. ᵇ

Psalm 105

105:1–15pp — 1Ch 16:8–22

¹ Give thanks to the LORD, call on his name;
  make known among the nations what he
    has done.

ᵃ 18 That is, the hyrax or rock badger ᵇ 35 Hebrew *Hallelu Yah*;
in the Septuagint this line stands at the beginning of Psalm 105.

2 Sing to him, sing praise to him;
　　tell of all his wonderful acts.
3 Glory in his holy name;
　　let the hearts of those who seek the LORD
　　　rejoice.
4 Look to the LORD and his strength;
　　seek his face always.

5 Remember the wonders he has done,
　　his miracles, and the judgments he
　　　pronounced,
6 O descendants of Abraham his servant,
　　O sons of Jacob, his chosen ones.
7 He is the LORD our God;
　　his judgments are in all the earth.

8 He remembers his covenant forever,
　　the word he commanded, for a thousand
　　　generations,
9 the covenant he made with Abraham,
　　the oath he swore to Isaac.
10 He confirmed it to Jacob as a decree,
　　to Israel as an everlasting covenant:
11 "To you I will give the land of Canaan
　　as the portion you will inherit."

12 When they were but few in number,
　　few indeed, and strangers in it,
13 they wandered from nation to nation,
　　from one kingdom to another.
14 He allowed no one to oppress them;
　　for their sake he rebuked kings:
15 "Do not touch my anointed ones;
　　do my prophets no harm."

16 He called down famine on the land
　　and destroyed all their supplies of food;
17 and he sent a man before them—
　　Joseph, sold as a slave.
18 They bruised his feet with shackles,
　　his neck was put in irons,
19 till what he foretold came to pass,
　　till the word of the LORD proved him true.
20 The king sent and released him,
　　the ruler of peoples set him free.
21 He made him master of his household,
　　ruler over all he possessed,

22 to instruct his princes as he pleased
　　and teach his elders wisdom.

23 Then Israel entered Egypt;
　　Jacob lived as an alien in the land of Ham.
24 The LORD made his people very fruitful;
　　he made them too numerous for their foes,
25 whose hearts he turned to hate his people,
　　to conspire against his servants.
26 He sent Moses his servant,
　　and Aaron, whom he had chosen.
27 They performed his miraculous signs among
　　them,
　　his wonders in the land of Ham.
28 He sent darkness and made the land dark—
　　for had they not rebelled against his words?
29 He turned their waters into blood,
　　causing their fish to die.
30 Their land teemed with frogs,
　　which went up into the bedrooms of their
　　　rulers.
31 He spoke, and there came swarms of flies,
　　and gnats throughout their country.
32 He turned their rain into hail,
　　with lightning throughout their land;
33 he struck down their vines and fig trees
　　and shattered the trees of their country.
34 He spoke, and the locusts came,
　　grasshoppers without number;
35 they ate up every green thing in their land,
　　ate up the produce of their soil.
36 Then he struck down all the firstborn in their
　　land,
　　the firstfruits of all their manhood.

37 He brought out Israel, laden with silver and
　　gold,
　　and from among their tribes no one
　　　faltered.
38 Egypt was glad when they left,
　　because dread of Israel had fallen on them.
39 He spread out a cloud as a covering,
　　and a fire to give light at night.
40 They asked, and he brought them quail
　　and satisfied them with the bread of
　　　heaven.

41 He opened the rock, and water gushed out;
    like a river it flowed in the desert.

42 For he remembered his holy promise
    given to his servant Abraham.
43 He brought out his people with rejoicing,
    his chosen ones with shouts of joy;
44 he gave them the lands of the nations,
    and they fell heir to what others had toiled
        for—
45 that they might keep his precepts
    and observe his laws.

Praise the LORD. *a*

Psalm 106

106:1,47–48pp — 1Ch 16:34–36

1 Praise the LORD. *b*

Give thanks to the LORD, for he is good;
    his love endures forever.
2 Who can proclaim the mighty acts of the
        LORD
    or fully declare his praise?
3 Blessed are they who maintain justice,
    who constantly do what is right.
4 Remember me, O LORD, when you show
        favor to your people,
    come to my aid when you save them,
5 that I may enjoy the prosperity of your
        chosen ones,
    that I may share in the joy of your nation
    and join your inheritance in giving praise.

6 We have sinned, even as our fathers did;
    we have done wrong and acted wickedly.
7 When our fathers were in Egypt,
    they gave no thought to your miracles;
    they did not remember your many
        kindnesses,
    and they rebelled by the sea, the Red Sea. *c*
8 Yet he saved them for his name's sake,
    to make his mighty power known.
9 He rebuked the Red Sea, and it dried up;
    he led them through the depths as through
        a desert.

10 He saved them from the hand of the foe;
    from the hand of the enemy he redeemed
        them.
11 The waters covered their adversaries;
    not one of them survived.
12 Then they believed his promises
    and sang his praise.

13 But they soon forgot what he had done
    and did not wait for his counsel.
14 In the desert they gave in to their craving;
    in the wasteland they put God to the test.
15 So he gave them what they asked for,
    but sent a wasting disease upon them.

16 In the camp they grew envious of Moses
    and of Aaron, who was consecrated to the
        LORD.
17 The earth opened up and swallowed Dathan;
    it buried the company of Abiram.
18 Fire blazed among their followers;
    a flame consumed the wicked.

19 At Horeb they made a calf
    and worshiped an idol cast from metal.
20 They exchanged their Glory
    for an image of a bull, which eats grass.
21 They forgot the God who saved them,
    who had done great things in Egypt,
22 miracles in the land of Ham
    and awesome deeds by the Red Sea.
23 So he said he would destroy them—
    had not Moses, his chosen one,
    stood in the breach before him
    to keep his wrath from destroying them.

24 Then they despised the pleasant land;
    they did not believe his promise.
25 They grumbled in their tents
    and did not obey the LORD.
26 So he swore to them with uplifted hand
    that he would make them fall in the desert,
27 make their descendants fall among the
        nations
    and scatter them throughout the lands.

---

a 45 Hebrew *Hallelu Yah*   *b 1* Hebrew *Hallelu Yah*; also in verse 48
c 7 Hebrew *Yam Suph*; that is, Sea of Reeds; also in verses 9 and 22

28 They yoked themselves to the Baal of Peor
    and ate sacrifices offered to lifeless gods;
29 they provoked the LORD to anger by their
        wicked deeds,
    and a plague broke out among them.
30 But Phinehas stood up and intervened,
    and the plague was checked.
31 This was credited to him as righteousness
    for endless generations to come.

32 By the waters of Meribah they angered the
        LORD,
    and trouble came to Moses because of
        them;
33 for they rebelled against the Spirit of God,
    and rash words came from Moses' lips. *a*

34 They did not destroy the peoples
    as the LORD had commanded them,
35 but they mingled with the nations
    and adopted their customs.
36 They worshiped their idols,
    which became a snare to them.
37 They sacrificed their sons
    and their daughters to demons.
38 They shed innocent blood,
    the blood of their sons and daughters,
    whom they sacrificed to the idols of Canaan,
    and the land was desecrated by their blood.
39 They defiled themselves by what they did;
    by their deeds they prostituted themselves.

40 Therefore the LORD was angry with his
        people
    and abhorred his inheritance.
41 He handed them over to the nations,
    and their foes ruled over them.
42 Their enemies oppressed them
    and subjected them to their power.
43 Many times he delivered them,
    but they were bent on rebellion
    and they wasted away in their sin.

44 But he took note of their distress
    when he heard their cry;
45 for their sake he remembered his covenant
    and out of his great love he relented.

46 He caused them to be pitied
    by all who held them captive.

47 Save us, O LORD our God,
    and gather us from the nations,
    that we may give thanks to your holy name
    and glory in your praise.

48 Praise be to the LORD, the God of Israel,
    from everlasting to everlasting.
    Let all the people say, "Amen!"

    Praise the LORD.

BOOK V

Psalms 107–150

Psalm 107

1 Give thanks to the LORD, for he is good;
    his love endures forever.
2 Let the redeemed of the LORD say this—
    those he redeemed from the hand of the
        foe,
3 those he gathered from the lands,
    from east and west, from north and
        south. *b*

4 Some wandered in desert wastelands,
    finding no way to a city where they could
        settle.
5 They were hungry and thirsty,
    and their lives ebbed away.
6 Then they cried out to the LORD in their
        trouble,
    and he delivered them from their
        distress.
7 He led them by a straight way
    to a city where they could settle.
8 Let them give thanks to the LORD for his
        unfailing love
    and his wonderful deeds for men,
9 for he satisfies the thirsty
    and fills the hungry with good things.

a 33 Or against his spirit, / and rash words came from his lips
b 3 Hebrew north and the sea

LET'S TALK

The "In" Crowd

Even young children are aware of what it takes to be in the "in" crowd. At different ages they will have different perceptions of the meaning, but each of them will have some opinion that will get everyone talking and that might surprise you.

Guide the discussion (in person or over the phone) so they think about some of these questions:

- What are the benefits and drawbacks of being part of the "in" crowd?
- What do you expect will happen if you become part of it?
- What will the "in" crowd expect or require of you?
- What happens to those who aren't popular?
- Have you ever befriended someone who was lonely or made fun of?

Steer the discussion toward being part of God's "in" crowd: What does it take to be "in" with God? Are the criteria the same as or different than those for being popular at school or with other friends? Can you fit in with peers and with God at the same time, or do you have to make a choice? To help answer some of these questions, read Romans 12 together.

Thank you, Father, for letting me and my grandchildren be part of your crowd. Help me through this discussion to help them realize what it means to fit in with their peers and with their faith family. Amen.

Your next devotion is located on page 805.

GRANDCHILD IN FOCUS • PRAYER

Friends

Dear Lord and Father, I pray for my grandchild's so-cial life and his friends. Bring diverse friends into his life who will love and encourage him, who will bring joy and laughter to the good times and comfort and support through difficulties and disappointments. Grant him wisdom and discernment as he selects his friends; help him to avoid cliques that restrict, activities that endanger, and foolish and dangerous behaviors that harm. I ask that you fill his life with close and caring relationships. Amen.

¹⁰ Some sat in darkness and the deepest
        gloom,
    prisoners suffering in iron chains,
¹¹ for they had rebelled against the words of
        God
    and despised the counsel of the Most
        High.
¹² So he subjected them to bitter labor;
    they stumbled, and there was no one to
        help.
¹³ Then they cried to the LORD in their trouble,
    and he saved them from their distress.
¹⁴ He brought them out of darkness and the
        deepest gloom
    and broke away their chains.
¹⁵ Let them give thanks to the LORD for his
        unfailing love
    and his wonderful deeds for men,
¹⁶ for he breaks down gates of bronze
    and cuts through bars of iron.

¹⁷ Some became fools through their rebellious
        ways
    and suffered affliction because of their
        iniquities.
¹⁸ They loathed all food
    and drew near the gates of death.
¹⁹ Then they cried to the LORD in their trouble,
    and he saved them from their distress.
²⁰ He sent forth his word and healed them;
    he rescued them from the grave.
²¹ Let them give thanks to the LORD for his
        unfailing love
    and his wonderful deeds for men.
²² Let them sacrifice thank offerings
    and tell of his works with songs of joy.

²³ Others went out on the sea in ships;
    they were merchants on the mighty waters.
²⁴ They saw the works of the LORD,
    his wonderful deeds in the deep.
²⁵ For he spoke and stirred up a tempest
    that lifted high the waves.
²⁶ They mounted up to the heavens and went
        down to the depths;
    in their peril their courage melted away.

²⁷ They reeled and staggered like drunken men;
    they were at their wits' end.
²⁸ Then they cried out to the LORD in their
        trouble,
    and he brought them out of their distress.
²⁹ He stilled the storm to a whisper;
    the waves of the sea were hushed.
³⁰ They were glad when it grew calm,
    and he guided them to their desired
        haven.
³¹ Let them give thanks to the LORD for his
        unfailing love
    and his wonderful deeds for men.
³² Let them exalt him in the assembly of the
        people
    and praise him in the council of the elders.

³³ He turned rivers into a desert,
    flowing springs into thirsty ground,
³⁴ and fruitful land into a salt waste,
    because of the wickedness of those who
        lived there.
³⁵ He turned the desert into pools of water
    and the parched ground into flowing
        springs;
³⁶ there he brought the hungry to live,
    and they founded a city where they could
        settle.
³⁷ They sowed fields and planted vineyards
    that yielded a fruitful harvest;
³⁸ he blessed them, and their numbers greatly
        increased,
    and he did not let their herds diminish.

³⁹ Then their numbers decreased, and they were
        humbled
    by oppression, calamity and sorrow;
⁴⁰ he who pours contempt on nobles
    made them wander in a trackless waste.
⁴¹ But he lifted the needy out of their affliction
    and increased their families like flocks.
⁴² The upright see and rejoice,
    but all the wicked shut their mouths.

⁴³ Whoever is wise, let him heed these things
    and consider the great love of the LORD.

Psalm 108

108:1–5pp — Ps 57:7–11
108:6–13pp — Ps 60:5–12

A song. A psalm of David.

[1] My heart is steadfast, O God;
  I will sing and make music with all my
    soul.
[2] Awake, harp and lyre!
  I will awaken the dawn.
[3] I will praise you, O LORD, among the
    nations;
  I will sing of you among the peoples.
[4] For great is your love, higher than the
    heavens;
  your faithfulness reaches to the skies.
[5] Be exalted, O God, above the heavens,
  and let your glory be over all the earth.

[6] Save us and help us with your right hand,
  that those you love may be delivered.
[7] God has spoken from his sanctuary:
  "In triumph I will parcel out Shechem
  and measure off the Valley of Succoth.
[8] Gilead is mine, Manasseh is mine;
  Ephraim is my helmet,
  Judah my scepter.
[9] Moab is my washbasin,
  upon Edom I toss my sandal;
  over Philistia I shout in triumph."

[10] Who will bring me to the fortified city?
  Who will lead me to Edom?
[11] Is it not you, O God, you who have
    rejected us
  and no longer go out with our armies?
[12] Give us aid against the enemy,
  for the help of man is worthless.
[13] With God we will gain the victory,
  and he will trample down our enemies.

Psalm 109

For the director of music. Of David. A psalm.

[1] O God, whom I praise,
  do not remain silent,
[2] for wicked and deceitful men
  have opened their mouths against me;
  they have spoken against me with lying
    tongues.
[3] With words of hatred they surround me;
  they attack me without cause.
[4] In return for my friendship they accuse me,
  but I am a man of prayer.
[5] They repay me evil for good,
  and hatred for my friendship.

TALKING POINTS

Bullying

When people are cruel to us,
we can share our pain with God.

PSALM 109:1–5,26–31

For more on bullying, go to Luke 6:31.

[6] Appoint[a] an evil man[b] to oppose him;
  let an accuser[c] stand at his right hand.
[7] When he is tried, let him be found guilty,
  and may his prayers condemn him.
[8] May his days be few;
  may another take his place of leadership.
[9] May his children be fatherless
  and his wife a widow.
[10] May his children be wandering beggars;
  may they be driven[d] from their ruined
    homes.
[11] May a creditor seize all he has;
  may strangers plunder the fruits of his
    labor.
[12] May no one extend kindness to him
  or take pity on his fatherless children.
[13] May his descendants be cut off,
  their names blotted out from the next
    generation.

---

[a] 6 Or *They say:, "Appoint* (with quotation marks at the end of verse 19)   [b] 6 Or *the Evil One*   [c] 6 Or *let Satan*
[d] 10 Septuagint; Hebrew *sought*

14 May the iniquity of his fathers be
        remembered before the Lord;
    may the sin of his mother never be blotted
        out.
15 May their sins always remain before the Lord,
    that he may cut off the memory of them
        from the earth.

16 For he never thought of doing a kindness,
    but hounded to death the poor
    and the needy and the brokenhearted.
17 He loved to pronounce a curse—
    may it *a* come on him;
    he found no pleasure in blessing—
    may it be *b* far from him.
18 He wore cursing as his garment;
    it entered into his body like water,
    into his bones like oil.
19 May it be like a cloak wrapped about him,
    like a belt tied forever around him.
20 May this be the Lord's payment to my
        accusers,
    to those who speak evil of me.

21 But you, O Sovereign Lord,
    deal well with me for your name's sake;
    out of the goodness of your love,
        deliver me.
22 For I am poor and needy,
    and my heart is wounded within me.
23 I fade away like an evening shadow;
    I am shaken off like a locust.
24 My knees give way from fasting;
    my body is thin and gaunt.
25 I am an object of scorn to my accusers;
    when they see me, they shake their heads.

26 Help me, O Lord my God;
    save me in accordance with your love.
27 Let them know that it is your hand,
    that you, O Lord, have done it.
28 They may curse, but you will bless;
    when they attack they will be put to shame,
    but your servant will rejoice.
29 My accusers will be clothed with disgrace
    and wrapped in shame as in a cloak.

30 With my mouth I will greatly extol the Lord;
    in the great throng I will praise him.
31 For he stands at the right hand of the needy
        one,
    to save his life from those who condemn
        him.

Psalm 110

Of David. A psalm.

1 The Lord says to my Lord:
    "Sit at my right hand
until I make your enemies
    a footstool for your feet."

2 The Lord will extend your mighty scepter
        from Zion;
    you will rule in the midst of your enemies.
3 Your troops will be willing
    on your day of battle.
Arrayed in holy majesty,
    from the womb of the dawn
    you will receive the dew of your youth. *c*

4 The Lord has sworn
    and will not change his mind:
"You are a priest forever,
    in the order of Melchizedek."

5 The Lord is at your right hand;
    he will crush kings on the day of his wrath.
6 He will judge the nations, heaping up the
        dead
    and crushing the rulers of the whole earth.
7 He will drink from a brook beside the way *d*;
    therefore he will lift up his head.

Psalm 111 *e*

1 Praise the Lord. *f*

I will extol the Lord with all my heart
    in the council of the upright and in the
        assembly.

---

a 17 Or *curse, / and it has*   *b* 17 Or *blessing, / and it is*   *c* 3 Or /
your young men will come to you like the dew   *d* 7 Or / *The One
who grants succession will set him in authority*   *e* This psalm is an
acrostic poem, the lines of which begin with the successive letters of
the Hebrew alphabet.   *f* 1 Hebrew *Hallelu Yah*

Worship the Lord

Within your temple, O God,
  we meditate on your unfailing love.
Like your name, O God,
  your praise reaches to the ends of the earth;
  your right hand is filled with righteousness.
Mount Zion rejoices,
  the villages of Judah are glad
  because of your judgments.

Walk about Zion, go around her,
  count her towers,
consider well her ramparts,
  view her citadels,
  that you may tell of them to the
    next generation.
For this God is our God for ever and
    ever;
  he will be our guide even to the
    end.

Psalm 48:9–14

What a wonder, Lord, that you have transformed me into your walking, breathing temple. Help me to instill the wonder of your presence into the hearts of a new generation. How will
they know, Father, unless I tell them? Grant me courage
to declare that you are our God for ever and ever. Amen.

Your next devotion is located on page 808.

GRANDCHILD IN FOCUS • PRAYER

Self-Image

*O loving God, I praise you for creating my
grandchild as a unique individual. Now I ask you
to help her appreciate her uniqueness. Build up her
self-image so she can enjoy her individuality. Help
her to stand firm for who she is, where she has
come from and what she believes in. Encourage
her not only to have hopes and dreams but
to also enjoy each day as it comes.
In Jesus' name, amen.*

2 Great are the works of the LORD;
　　they are pondered by all who delight in
　　　them.
3 Glorious and majestic are his deeds,
　　and his righteousness endures forever.
4 He has caused his wonders to be
　　remembered;
　　the LORD is gracious and compassionate.
5 He provides food for those who fear him;
　　he remembers his covenant forever.
6 He has shown his people the power of his
　　works,
　　giving them the lands of other nations.
7 The works of his hands are faithful and
　　just;
　　all his precepts are trustworthy.
8 They are steadfast for ever and ever,
　　done in faithfulness and uprightness.
9 He provided redemption for his people;
　　he ordained his covenant forever —
　　holy and awesome is his name.

10 The fear of the LORD is the beginning of
　　wisdom;
　　all who follow his precepts have good
　　understanding.
　　To him belongs eternal praise.

Psalm 112 *a*

1 Praise the LORD. *b*

Blessed is the man who fears the LORD,
　　who finds great delight in his commands.

2 His children will be mighty in the land;
　　the generation of the upright will be
　　blessed.
3 Wealth and riches are in his house,
　　and his righteousness endures forever.
4 Even in darkness light dawns for the
　　upright,
　　for the gracious and compassionate and
　　righteous man. *c*
5 Good will come to him who is generous
　　and lends freely,
　　who conducts his affairs with justice.

6 Surely he will never be shaken;
　　a righteous man will be remembered
　　　forever.
7 He will have no fear of bad news;
　　his heart is steadfast, trusting in the LORD.
8 His heart is secure, he will have no fear;
　　in the end he will look in triumph on his
　　foes.
9 He has scattered abroad his gifts to the poor,
　　his righteousness endures forever;
　　his horn *d* will be lifted high in honor.

10 The wicked man will see and be vexed,
　　he will gnash his teeth and waste away;
　　the longings of the wicked will come to
　　nothing.

Psalm 113

1 Praise the LORD. *e*

Praise, O servants of the LORD,
　　praise the name of the LORD.
2 Let the name of the LORD be praised,
　　both now and forevermore.
3 From the rising of the sun to the place where
　　it sets,
　　the name of the LORD is to be praised.

4 The LORD is exalted over all the nations,
　　his glory above the heavens.
5 Who is like the LORD our God,
　　the One who sits enthroned on high,
6 who stoops down to look
　　on the heavens and the earth?

7 He raises the poor from the dust
　　and lifts the needy from the ash heap;
8 he seats them with princes,
　　with the princes of their people.
9 He settles the barren woman in her home
　　as a happy mother of children.

Praise the LORD.

Psalm 114

¹ When Israel came out of Egypt,
  the house of Jacob from a people of
    foreign tongue,
² Judah became God's sanctuary,
  Israel his dominion.

³ The sea looked and fled,
  the Jordan turned back;
⁴ the mountains skipped like rams,
  the hills like lambs.

⁵ Why was it, O sea, that you fled,
  O Jordan, that you turned back,
⁶ you mountains, that you skipped like rams,
  you hills, like lambs?

⁷ Tremble, O earth, at the presence of the
    Lord,
  at the presence of the God of Jacob,
⁸ who turned the rock into a pool,
  the hard rock into springs of water.

Psalm 115

115:4–11pp — Ps 135:15–20

¹ Not to us, O Lord, not to us
  but to your name be the glory,
  because of your love and faithfulness.

² Why do the nations say,
  "Where is their God?"
³ Our God is in heaven;
  he does whatever pleases him.
⁴ But their idols are silver and gold,
  made by the hands of men.
⁵ They have mouths, but cannot speak,
  eyes, but they cannot see;
⁶ they have ears, but cannot hear,
  noses, but they cannot smell;
⁷ they have hands, but cannot feel,
  feet, but they cannot walk;
  nor can they utter a sound with their
    throats.
⁸ Those who make them will be like them,
  and so will all who trust in them.

⁹ O house of Israel, trust in the Lord—
  he is their help and shield.
¹⁰ O house of Aaron, trust in the Lord—
  he is their help and shield.
¹¹ You who fear him, trust in the Lord—
  he is their help and shield.

¹² The Lord remembers us and will bless us:
  He will bless the house of Israel,
  he will bless the house of Aaron,
¹³ he will bless those who fear the Lord—
  small and great alike.

¹⁴ May the Lord make you increase,
  both you and your children.
¹⁵ May you be blessed by the Lord,
  the Maker of heaven and earth.

¹⁶ The highest heavens belong to the Lord,
  but the earth he has given to man.
¹⁷ It is not the dead who praise the Lord,
  those who go down to silence;
¹⁸ it is we who extol the Lord,
  both now and forevermore.

Praise the Lord. *ᵃ*

Psalm 116

¹ I love the Lord, for he heard my voice;
  he heard my cry for mercy.
² Because he turned his ear to me,
  I will call on him as long as I live.

³ The cords of death entangled me,
  the anguish of the grave *ᵇ* came upon me;
  I was overcome by trouble and sorrow.
⁴ Then I called on the name of the Lord:
  "O Lord, save me!"

⁵ The Lord is gracious and righteous;
  our God is full of compassion.
⁶ The Lord protects the simplehearted;
  when I was in great need, he saved me.

⁷ Be at rest once more, O my soul,
  for the Lord has been good to you.

ᵃ 18 Hebrew Hallelu Yah   *ᵇ 3 Hebrew Sheol*

BECAUSE HE TURNED HIS EAR
TO ME, I WILL CALL ON HIM AS
LONG AS I LIVE.

Psalm 116:2

Start Each Day With God

EMILIE BARNES

READ | PSALM 116:1–19

By the time we've reached this stage in our lives, we should have our priorities in line. One of the great things about the empty-nest years is that we have more time just for ourselves. But even though we have more free time, we must still select the important issues to follow—like starting each day with God. By spending time with God, we grow in the nine aspects of the "fruit of the Spirit": love, joy, peace, patience, kindness, goodness, faithfulness, gentleness and self-control (see Galatians 5:22–23). Which of us doesn't need a touch more of these in our lives?

I've designed part of my walk-in closet as a "prayer closet." It's my favorite spot to get away from everyone and all the distractions. In there, it's just me and the Lord. Beside my special Victorian chair I have a basket full of prayer tools: a Bible, a devotional book, Kleenex, my prayer journal, a packet of note cards, a pen. When I first started using my prayer closet, I allotted 15 minutes to spend with God, but now I often spend an hour with him. I pray, I listen, I respond to God. When I exit my closet, I feel refreshed, challenged, at peace and ready to meet the world.

As grandmothers we must ask ourselves, Are we doing what's important in our day—or only what is urgent? All of us make choices, and when we don't make time for the most important relationship in our lives, we are probably not making the best choices.

The times and places you meet God will vary, but the fact that you meet alone with him each day should be a constant in your life. Grandmothers need all the spiritual strength they can get. To keep up with the energy and movement of our kids and their kids, we need to possess the nine elements of the fruit of the Spirit.

Father God, may I never forget to call on you in every situation. I want to meet with you every day of my life and bring before you my adoration, confession, thanksgiving and supplications. Thank you for being willing to be within the sound of my voice and only a thought's distance away. Amen.

GRANDCHILD IN FOCUS • PRAYER

Protection From Worldliness

O Sovereign Lord, the world surrounds my grandchild, pressing in and tempting him in so many ways. Help him set appropriate limits. Give him sound judgment to choose wisely. Guard him from temptation; protect him from physical and mental predators; lead him into paths of righteousness and light. And reassure me with your promise that you are holding him in your hands. Amen.

Your next devotion is located on page 811.

⁸ For you, O LORD, have delivered my soul
    from death,
  my eyes from tears,
  my feet from stumbling,
⁹ that I may walk before the LORD
  in the land of the living.
¹⁰ I believed; therefore[a] I said,
  "I am greatly afflicted."
¹¹ And in my dismay I said,
  "All men are liars."

¹² How can I repay the LORD
  for all his goodness to me?
¹³ I will lift up the cup of salvation
  and call on the name of the LORD.
¹⁴ I will fulfill my vows to the LORD
  in the presence of all his people.

¹⁵ Precious in the sight of the LORD
  is the death of his saints.
¹⁶ O LORD, truly I am your servant;
  I am your servant, the son of your
    maidservant[b];
  you have freed me from my chains.

¹⁷ I will sacrifice a thank offering to you
  and call on the name of the LORD.
¹⁸ I will fulfill my vows to the LORD
  in the presence of all his people,
¹⁹ in the courts of the house of the LORD—
  in your midst, O Jerusalem.

Praise the LORD.[c]

Psalm 117

¹ Praise the LORD, all you nations;
  extol him, all you peoples.
² For great is his love toward us,
  and the faithfulness of the LORD endures
    forever.

Praise the LORD.[c]

Psalm 118

¹ Give thanks to the LORD, for he is good;
  his love endures forever.

² Let Israel say:
  "His love endures forever."
³ Let the house of Aaron say:
  "His love endures forever."
⁴ Let those who fear the LORD say:
  "His love endures forever."

⁵ In my anguish I cried to the LORD,
  and he answered by setting me free.
⁶ The LORD is with me; I will not be afraid.
  What can man do to me?
⁷ The LORD is with me; he is my helper.
  I will look in triumph on my enemies.

⁸ It is better to take refuge in the LORD
  than to trust in man.
⁹ It is better to take refuge in the LORD
  than to trust in princes.

¹⁰ All the nations surrounded me,
  but in the name of the LORD I cut them off.
¹¹ They surrounded me on every side,
  but in the name of the LORD I cut them off.
¹² They swarmed around me like bees,
  but they died out as quickly as burning
    thorns;
  in the name of the LORD I cut them off.

¹³ I was pushed back and about to fall,
  but the LORD helped me.
¹⁴ The LORD is my strength and my song;
  he has become my salvation.

¹⁵ Shouts of joy and victory
  resound in the tents of the righteous:
  "The LORD's right hand has done mighty
    things!
¹⁶   The LORD's right hand is lifted high;
  the LORD's right hand has done mighty
    things!"

¹⁷ I will not die but live,
  and will proclaim what the LORD has
    done.
¹⁸ The LORD has chastened me severely,
  but he has not given me over to death.

---

[a] 10 Or *believed even when*   [b] 16 Or *servant, your faithful son*
[c] 19,2 Hebrew *Hallelu Yah*

¹⁹ Open for me the gates of righteousness;
  I will enter and give thanks to the Lord.
²⁰ This is the gate of the Lord
  through which the righteous may enter.
²¹ I will give you thanks, for you answered me;
  you have become my salvation.

²² The stone the builders rejected
  has become the capstone;
²³ the Lord has done this,
  and it is marvelous in our eyes.
²⁴ This is the day the Lord has made;
  let us rejoice and be glad in it.

²⁵ O Lord, save us;
  O Lord, grant us success.
²⁶ Blessed is he who comes in the name of the
  Lord.
  From the house of the Lord we bless you. [a]
²⁷ The Lord is God,
  and he has made his light shine upon us.
  With boughs in hand, join in the festal
    procession
  up [b] to the horns of the altar.

²⁸ You are my God, and I will give you thanks;
  you are my God, and I will exalt you.

²⁹ Give thanks to the Lord, for he is good;
  his love endures forever.

Psalm 119 [c]

א Aleph

¹ Blessed are they whose ways are blameless,
  who walk according to the law of the
    Lord.
² Blessed are they who keep his statutes
  and seek him with all their heart.
³ They do nothing wrong;
  they walk in his ways.
⁴ You have laid down precepts
  that are to be fully obeyed.
⁵ Oh, that my ways were steadfast
  in obeying your decrees!
⁶ Then I would not be put to shame
  when I consider all your commands.

⁷ I will praise you with an upright heart
  as I learn your righteous laws.
⁸ I will obey your decrees;
  do not utterly forsake me.

ב Beth

⁹ How can a young man keep his way pure?
  By living according to your word.
¹⁰ I seek you with all my heart;
  do not let me stray from your commands.
¹¹ I have hidden your word in my heart
  that I might not sin against you.
¹² Praise be to you, O Lord;
  teach me your decrees.
¹³ With my lips I recount
  all the laws that come from your mouth.
¹⁴ I rejoice in following your statutes
  as one rejoices in great riches.
¹⁵ I meditate on your precepts
  and consider your ways.
¹⁶ I delight in your decrees;
  I will not neglect your word.

ג Gimel

¹⁷ Do good to your servant, and I will live;
  I will obey your word.
¹⁸ Open my eyes that I may see
  wonderful things in your law.
¹⁹ I am a stranger on earth;
  do not hide your commands from me.
²⁰ My soul is consumed with longing
  for your laws at all times.
²¹ You rebuke the arrogant, who are cursed
  and who stray from your commands.
²² Remove from me scorn and contempt,
  for I keep your statutes.
²³ Though rulers sit together and slander me,
  your servant will meditate on your
    decrees.
²⁴ Your statutes are my delight;
  they are my counselors.

---

[a] 26 The Hebrew is plural.   [b] 27 Or Bind the festal sacrifice with ropes / and take it   [c] This psalm is an acrostic poem; the verses of each stanza begin with the same letter of the Hebrew alphabet.

*I HAVE CHOSEN THE WAY OF
TRUTH; I HAVE SET MY HEART
ON YOUR LAWS.*

Psalm 119:30

My Grandson the Fabulist

KAREN MAINS

READ | PSALM 119:1–32

"Do you know what a fabulist is?" I asked the staff at our ministry office. They brainstormed possible answers. "Is a fabulist someone who is fabulous?" Well, not quite. You see, I know what a fabulist is; a fabulist is my grandson, age nine.

According to Merriam Webster's Collegiate Dictionary (Tenth Edition), a fabulist (pronounced fa-byə-list) is a creator or writer of fables. That is definition number 1; the other definition, number 2, is "Liar."

However, my grandson doesn't lie (most of the time); he strings together amazing stories so unbelievable in the complexity of their structure (for a nine-year-old) and totally conceived out of the wonder that is his imagination that I, a writer with not too shoddy an imaginative ability of my own, have been perfectly bamboozled by his capacities. I was flummoxed when, at the end of one ten-minute tale, I asked (finally suspicious), "Did this really happen or is this a wonderful story that you are creating?"

Posing this consideration is also the role of the Scriptures regarding our own personal stories. "Is it really true?" is one of the profound questions we need to learn to ask of ourselves. We go to the Word of God and compare what we are thinking and feeling against the standards so clearly explained in verses, chapters and books.

There are lies we know we are telling, and then there are lies we do not know we are telling. We need the invasive surgery of Scripture to discern what is really true about our own selves. That is the work of a lifetime. A fabulist at age nine is enchanting, endearing, frustrating, exasperating and wonder-provoking. A fabulist at age 39 (or 49 or 59 or 69) is scary.

O God, give me a love of truth. Help me to continually seek out your Word in order to be convicted of my own lies — the ones I know I am telling and the ones I don't. Amen.

Your next devotion is located on page 815.

GRANDCHILD IN FOCUS · PRAYER

Respect for Authority

Dear Lord, I pray that my grandchild will continually grow to respect those in authority. May she learn to be cooperative and fair in work and play. Instill in her a high regard for officials who govern our land and enforce the laws. May her relationships with parents, teachers, coaches, mentors and bosses be respectful, admirable, constructive and caring. Amen.

ד Daleth

²⁵ I am laid low in the dust;
   preserve my life according to your word.
²⁶ I recounted my ways and you answered me;
   teach me your decrees.
²⁷ Let me understand the teaching of your
      precepts;
   then I will meditate on your wonders.
²⁸ My soul is weary with sorrow;
   strengthen me according to your word.
²⁹ Keep me from deceitful ways;
   be gracious to me through your law.
³⁰ I have chosen the way of truth;
   I have set my heart on your laws.
³¹ I hold fast to your statutes, O LORD;
   do not let me be put to shame.
³² I run in the path of your commands,
   for you have set my heart free.

ה He

³³ Teach me, O LORD, to follow your decrees;
   then I will keep them to the end.
³⁴ Give me understanding, and I will keep your
      law
   and obey it with all my heart.
³⁵ Direct me in the path of your commands,
   for there I find delight.

PRAYING THE SCRIPTURES

Guidance

PSALM 119:33–36

Teach my grandchild, O Lord, to follow your
decrees and to keep them to the end. Give
her understanding, that she may keep your
law and obey it with all her heart. Direct her
in the path of your commands, for there she
will find delight. Turn her heart toward your
statutes and not toward selfish gain.

Next prayer in Guidance Prayer Track: Psalm 143:10

³⁶ Turn my heart toward your statutes
   and not toward selfish gain.
³⁷ Turn my eyes away from worthless things;
   preserve my life according to your word. ᵃ
³⁸ Fulfill your promise to your servant,
   so that you may be feared.
³⁹ Take away the disgrace I dread,
   for your laws are good.
⁴⁰ How I long for your precepts!
   Preserve my life in your righteousness.

ו Waw

⁴¹ May your unfailing love come to me,
      O LORD,
   your salvation according to your promise;
⁴² then I will answer the one who taunts me,
   for I trust in your word.
⁴³ Do not snatch the word of truth from my
      mouth,
   for I have put my hope in your laws.
⁴⁴ I will always obey your law,
   for ever and ever.
⁴⁵ I will walk about in freedom,
   for I have sought out your precepts.
⁴⁶ I will speak of your statutes before kings
   and will not be put to shame,
⁴⁷ for I delight in your commands
   because I love them.
⁴⁸ I lift up my hands to ᵇ your commands, which
      I love,
   and I meditate on your decrees.

ז Zayin

⁴⁹ Remember your word to your servant,
   for you have given me hope.
⁵⁰ My comfort in my suffering is this:
   Your promise preserves my life.
⁵¹ The arrogant mock me without restraint,
   but I do not turn from your law.
⁵² I remember your ancient laws, O LORD,
   and I find comfort in them.

ᵃ 37 Two manuscripts of the Masoretic Text and Dead Sea
Scrolls; most manuscripts of the Masoretic Text *life in your way*
ᵇ 48 Or *for*

PRAYING THE SCRIPTURES

Comfort
PSALM 119:49–50

Remember your word to my grandchild, O God, for you have given him hope. May his comfort in his suffering be this: Your promise preserves his life.

Next prayer in Comfort Prayer Track: Psalm 147:3

⁵³ Indignation grips me because of the wicked,
    who have forsaken your law.
⁵⁴ Your decrees are the theme of my song
    wherever I lodge.
⁵⁵ In the night I remember your name, O LORD,
    and I will keep your law.
⁵⁶ This has been my practice:
    I obey your precepts.

ח Heth

⁵⁷ You are my portion, O LORD;
    I have promised to obey your words.
⁵⁸ I have sought your face with all my heart;
    be gracious to me according to your
        promise.
⁵⁹ I have considered my ways
    and have turned my steps to your statutes.
⁶⁰ I will hasten and not delay
    to obey your commands.
⁶¹ Though the wicked bind me with ropes,
    I will not forget your law.
⁶² At midnight I rise to give you thanks
    for your righteous laws.
⁶³ I am a friend to all who fear you,
    to all who follow your precepts.
⁶⁴ The earth is filled with your love, O LORD;
    teach me your decrees.

ט Teth

⁶⁵ Do good to your servant
    according to your word, O LORD.

⁶⁶ Teach me knowledge and good judgment,
    for I believe in your commands.
⁶⁷ Before I was afflicted I went astray,
    but now I obey your word.
⁶⁸ You are good, and what you do is good;
    teach me your decrees.
⁶⁹ Though the arrogant have smeared me with
        lies,
    I keep your precepts with all my heart.
⁷⁰ Their hearts are callous and unfeeling,
    but I delight in your law.
⁷¹ It was good for me to be afflicted
    so that I might learn your decrees.
⁷² The law from your mouth is more precious
        to me
    than thousands of pieces of silver and gold.

PRAYING THE SCRIPTURES

Wisdom
PSALM 119:65–66

Do good to my grandchild according to your word, O Lord. Teach her knowledge and good judgment, for she believes in your commands.

Next prayer in Wisdom Prayer Track: Proverbs 4:5,7

י Yodh

⁷³ Your hands made me and formed me;
    give me understanding to learn your
        commands.
⁷⁴ May those who fear you rejoice when they
        see me,
    for I have put my hope in your word.
⁷⁵ I know, O LORD, that your laws are
        righteous,
    and in faithfulness you have afflicted me.
⁷⁶ May your unfailing love be my comfort,
    according to your promise to your
        servant.

⁷⁷ Let your compassion come to me that I
may live,
for your law is my delight.
⁷⁸ May the arrogant be put to shame for
wronging me without cause;
but I will meditate on your precepts.
⁷⁹ May those who fear you turn to me,
those who understand your statutes.
⁸⁰ May my heart be blameless toward your
decrees,
that I may not be put to shame.

⊃ Kaph

⁸¹ My soul faints with longing for your
salvation,
but I have put my hope in your word.
⁸² My eyes fail, looking for your promise;
I say, "When will you comfort me?"
⁸³ Though I am like a wineskin in the smoke,
I do not forget your decrees.
⁸⁴ How long must your servant wait?
When will you punish my persecutors?
⁸⁵ The arrogant dig pitfalls for me,
contrary to your law.
⁸⁶ All your commands are trustworthy;
help me, for men persecute me without
cause.
⁸⁷ They almost wiped me from the earth,
but I have not forsaken your precepts.
⁸⁸ Preserve my life according to your love,
and I will obey the statutes of your mouth.

ל Lamedh

⁸⁹ Your word, O Lᴏʀᴅ, is eternal;
it stands firm in the heavens.
⁹⁰ Your faithfulness continues through all
generations;
you established the earth, and it endures.
⁹¹ Your laws endure to this day,
for all things serve you.
⁹² If your law had not been my delight,
I would have perished in my affliction.
⁹³ I will never forget your precepts,
for by them you have preserved my life.

⁹⁴ Save me, for I am yours;
I have sought out your precepts.
⁹⁵ The wicked are waiting to destroy me,
but I will ponder your statutes.
⁹⁶ To all perfection I see a limit;
but your commands are boundless.

מ Mem

⁹⁷ Oh, how I love your law!
I meditate on it all day long.
⁹⁸ Your commands make me wiser than my
enemies,
for they are ever with me.
⁹⁹ I have more insight than all my teachers,
for I meditate on your statutes.
¹⁰⁰ I have more understanding than the elders,
for I obey your precepts.
¹⁰¹ I have kept my feet from every evil path
so that I might obey your word.
¹⁰² I have not departed from your laws,
for you yourself have taught me.
¹⁰³ How sweet are your words to my taste,
sweeter than honey to my mouth!
¹⁰⁴ I gain understanding from your precepts;
therefore I hate every wrong path.

נ Nun

¹⁰⁵ Your word is a lamp to my feet
and a light for my path.
¹⁰⁶ I have taken an oath and confirmed it,
that I will follow your righteous laws.
¹⁰⁷ I have suffered much;
preserve my life, O Lᴏʀᴅ, according to
your word.
¹⁰⁸ Accept, O Lᴏʀᴅ, the willing praise of my
mouth,
and teach me your laws.
¹⁰⁹ Though I constantly take my life in my hands,
I will not forget your law.
¹¹⁰ The wicked have set a snare for me,
but I have not strayed from your precepts.
¹¹¹ Your statutes are my heritage forever;
they are the joy of my heart.
¹¹² My heart is set on keeping your decrees
to the very end.

The Never-Failing Source

GIGI GRAHAM TCHIVIDJIAN

READ | PSALM 119:105 – 112

Memorized Scripture can comfort and strengthen. Two of our friends were on the other side of the world when they received word that their oldest son, his wife, and their infant grandchild had all been killed in an automobile accident. Later, those friends said that it was Scripture they had put to memory that kept them from going crazy those first few weeks.

One day we may not have the written Word, but it will be a lot more difficult to take away what we have hidden in our hearts and minds.

The Word of God is a living Word; it is the person of Jesus Christ Himself revealed to us. Psalm 119 says that the Word cleanses, strengthens, delights, teaches, saves, comforts, directs, and gives understanding. What a resource!

At the age of twelve I left home to go away to school. I can remember so well that awful, gnawing feeling in the pit of my stomach that comes from being lonely and homesick. But because I had been taught early to turn to the Lord and to His Word for strength and comfort, I now look back on those days as a spiritual experience for which I will be forever grateful. I learned many things during those weeks and months about the vast resource I had in my personal relationship with the Lord Jesus and in His Word. Since those days as a very young girl there have been many disappointments, heartaches, times of decision, times of discouragement; and each time I have gone to His Word. He has never once failed me.

For whatever life holds for you and your family in the coming days, weave the unfailing fabric of God's Word through your heart and mind.

It will hold strong, even if the rest of life unravels.

Lord Jesus, you are my strength and comfort. You have woven your Word through the fabric of my life, and I'm so grateful. It has brought me riches untold, and I thank you with all my heart!

Your next devotion is located on page 822.

GRANDCHILD IN FOCUS • PRAYER

Courage

O Father, builder of character and courage, may my grandchild grow strong in the light of your love. Grant him courage to stand for what is right, to guard the truth and to ensure justice in every aspect of life. May he boldly grow in grace, revere your name and proudly proclaim you as the Lord of lords and King of kings. Amen.

ס Samekh

[113]I hate double-minded men,
but I love your law.
[114]You are my refuge and my shield;
I have put my hope in your word.
[115]Away from me, you evildoers,
that I may keep the commands of my God!
[116]Sustain me according to your promise, and I will live;
do not let my hopes be dashed.
[117]Uphold me, and I will be delivered;
I will always have regard for your decrees.
[118]You reject all who stray from your decrees,
for their deceitfulness is in vain.
[119]All the wicked of the earth you discard like dross;
therefore I love your statutes.
[120]My flesh trembles in fear of you;
I stand in awe of your laws.

ע Ayin

[121]I have done what is righteous and just;
do not leave me to my oppressors.
[122]Ensure your servant's well-being;
let not the arrogant oppress me.
[123]My eyes fail, looking for your salvation,
looking for your righteous promise.
[124]Deal with your servant according to your love
and teach me your decrees.
[125]I am your servant; give me discernment
that I may understand your statutes.
[126]It is time for you to act, O LORD;
your law is being broken.
[127]Because I love your commands
more than gold, more than pure gold,
[128]and because I consider all your precepts right,
I hate every wrong path.

פ Pe

[129]Your statutes are wonderful;
therefore I obey them.
[130]The unfolding of your words gives light;
it gives understanding to the simple.

[131]I open my mouth and pant,
longing for your commands.
[132]Turn to me and have mercy on me,
as you always do to those who love your name.
[133]Direct my footsteps according to your word;
let no sin rule over me.
[134]Redeem me from the oppression of men,
that I may obey your precepts.
[135]Make your face shine upon your servant
and teach me your decrees.
[136]Streams of tears flow from my eyes,
for your law is not obeyed.

צ Tsadhe

[137]Righteous are you, O LORD,
and your laws are right.
[138]The statutes you have laid down are righteous;
they are fully trustworthy.
[139]My zeal wears me out,
for my enemies ignore your words.
[140]Your promises have been thoroughly tested,
and your servant loves them.
[141]Though I am lowly and despised,
I do not forget your precepts.
[142]Your righteousness is everlasting
and your law is true.
[143]Trouble and distress have come upon me,
but your commands are my delight.
[144]Your statutes are forever right;
give me understanding that I may live.

ק Qoph

[145]I call with all my heart; answer me, O LORD,
and I will obey your decrees.
[146]I call out to you; save me
and I will keep your statutes.
[147]I rise before dawn and cry for help;
I have put my hope in your word.
[148]My eyes stay open through the watches of the night,
that I may meditate on your promises.

¹⁴⁹Hear my voice in accordance with your
    love;
        preserve my life, O Lord, according to
            your laws.
¹⁵⁰Those who devise wicked schemes are near,
        but they are far from your law.
¹⁵¹Yet you are near, O Lord,
        and all your commands are true.
¹⁵²Long ago I learned from your statutes
        that you established them to last forever.

ר Resh

¹⁵³Look upon my suffering and deliver me,
        for I have not forgotten your law.
¹⁵⁴Defend my cause and redeem me;
        preserve my life according to your
            promise.
¹⁵⁵Salvation is far from the wicked,
        for they do not seek out your decrees.
¹⁵⁶Your compassion is great, O Lord;
        preserve my life according to your laws.
¹⁵⁷Many are the foes who persecute me,
        but I have not turned from your statutes.
¹⁵⁸I look on the faithless with loathing,
        for they do not obey your word.
¹⁵⁹See how I love your precepts;
        preserve my life, O Lord, according to
            your love.
¹⁶⁰All your words are true;
        all your righteous laws are eternal.

ש Sin and Shin

¹⁶¹Rulers persecute me without cause,
        but my heart trembles at your word.
¹⁶²I rejoice in your promise
        like one who finds great spoil.
¹⁶³I hate and abhor falsehood
        but I love your law.
¹⁶⁴Seven times a day I praise you
        for your righteous laws.
¹⁶⁵Great peace have they who love your law,
        and nothing can make them stumble.
¹⁶⁶I wait for your salvation, O Lord,
        and I follow your commands.

¹⁶⁷I obey your statutes,
        for I love them greatly.
¹⁶⁸I obey your precepts and your statutes,
        for all my ways are known to you.

ת Taw

¹⁶⁹May my cry come before you, O Lord;
        give me understanding according to your
            word.
¹⁷⁰May my supplication come before you;
        deliver me according to your promise.
¹⁷¹May my lips overflow with praise,
        for you teach me your decrees.
¹⁷²May my tongue sing of your word,
        for all your commands are righteous.
¹⁷³May your hand be ready to help me,
        for I have chosen your precepts.
¹⁷⁴I long for your salvation, O Lord,
        and your law is my delight.
¹⁷⁵Let me live that I may praise you,
        and may your laws sustain me.
¹⁷⁶I have strayed like a lost sheep.
        Seek your servant,
        for I have not forgotten your commands.

Psalm 120

A song of ascents.

¹I call on the Lord in my distress,
        and he answers me.
²Save me, O Lord, from lying lips
        and from deceitful tongues.

³What will he do to you,
        and what more besides, O deceitful
            tongue?
⁴He will punish you with a warrior's sharp
            arrows,
        with burning coals of the broom tree.

⁵Woe to me that I dwell in Meshech,
        that I live among the tents of Kedar!
⁶Too long have I lived
        among those who hate peace.
⁷I am a man of peace;
        but when I speak, they are for war.

LESLIE STROBEL

Teaching LITTLE ONES ABOUT GOD

I'm new to grandparenting. My granddaughter, Abigail, is 14 months old as of this writing, and all that I would love to accomplish as a grandmother is still in the early development stages in my mind. But it is my heart's desire to do all I can to help Abby, as well as all the other grandchildren to come, to have a personal relationship with Jesus. I also want them to know without question that they are loved not just by their parents and grandparents but by the one true God who made them.

Matthew 6:25–34 has always had a special place in my heart because it was one of the first passages that God used to reveal his love and care for me when I was a new believer. It tells us to "look at the birds of the air; they do not sow or reap or store away in barns, and yet your heavenly Father feeds them." And "See how the lilies of the field grow . . . God clothes the grass of the field . . . Will he not much more clothe you?"

How Does One Start the Process?

How does one start the process of teaching a one-year-old child the realities of the one true God of the universe? As I waited for Abby to be born, I often thought about how I'd go about it. But when she came for her first visit at four days old, a tradition was inadvertently started. She was fussy, and in an attempt to ease her, I took her for a walk in our garden. Living in Southern California allows me the joy of flowers year-round, and I set about to show them to her. She immediately stopped crying, and from that day on, every visit to Gigi and Grandpa's includes a stroll in the garden.

When we're in the garden together, Abby and I look at the flower petals, feel their softness and admire their color and perfume. We watch the hummingbirds dart from flower to flower getting their daily meal. We view life going on in my garden — God caring for its inhabitants.

Psalm 121:7–8 says, "The LORD will keep you from all harm — he will watch over your life; the LORD will watch over your coming and going both now and forevermore."

I want all my grandchildren to understand that the God of all creation has eyes that see and ears that hear each and every thought, word and deed. I want them to know that they can come to him with all their worries, needs and desires.

How could I start teaching Abby these precepts and how old would she need to be? The irony of being intent on teaching Abby about God's love and care for *her* is that, although I know in my head and through my history that God loves me, I am discovering once again the excitement and freshness of *my* relationship with him.

God's Provision

When I'm walking Abby in the garden to show her God's provision for the birds and flowers, I sense God's fatherly relationship to me. I feel like a child seeing these things in a way I haven't before. The birds are sweeter and more precious as creatures made by God. The flowers are more vibrant in color and delicate in their structure, clearly a work of the master gardener. As a child of 50-something, I have the knowledge of a world that often seems out of control. Yet in the garden I suddenly feel protected and sheltered, and I am reminded of all that I'm hoping for Abby to understand someday in new and more significant ways.

The concerns over the "how to" and "when" of starting to teach a child about God was forgotten during an obvious and natural activity that came about without planning or thought. You just do it! Could it be that, in the process, the real blessing of being a grand-mother isn't just once again having a child in your life, but rather becoming a child again in God's life?

Psalm 121

A song of ascents.

¹ I lift up my eyes to the hills—
    where does my help come from?
² My help comes from the LORD,
    the Maker of heaven and earth.

TALKING POINTS

Encouragement
God watches over us
to keep us from harm.
PSALM 121:1–8

For more on encouragement, go to Jeremiah 29:11–13.

³ He will not let your foot slip—
    he who watches over you will not slumber;
⁴ indeed, he who watches over Israel
    will neither slumber nor sleep.

⁵ The LORD watches over you—
    the LORD is your shade at your right hand;
⁶ the sun will not harm you by day,
    nor the moon by night.

PRAYING THE SCRIPTURES

Protection
PSALM 121:5–8
O Lord, watch over my grandchild. Be her shield, protecting her from harm both day and night. Keep her from all harm, I pray—watch over her life; watch over her coming and going both now and forevermore.

Next prayer in Protection Prayer Track: Matthew 28:20

⁷ The LORD will keep you from all harm—
    he will watch over your life;
⁸ the LORD will watch over your coming and
        going
    both now and forevermore.

Psalm 122

A song of ascents. Of David.

¹ I rejoiced with those who said to me,
    "Let us go to the house of the LORD."
² Our feet are standing
    in your gates, O Jerusalem.

³ Jerusalem is built like a city
    that is closely compacted together.
⁴ That is where the tribes go up,
    the tribes of the LORD,
  to praise the name of the LORD
    according to the statute given to Israel.
⁵ There the thrones for judgment stand,
    the thrones of the house of David.

⁶ Pray for the peace of Jerusalem:
    "May those who love you be secure.
⁷ May there be peace within your walls
    and security within your citadels."
⁸ For the sake of my brothers and friends,
    I will say, "Peace be within you."
⁹ For the sake of the house of the LORD our
        God,
    I will seek your prosperity.

Psalm 123

A song of ascents.

¹ I lift up my eyes to you,
    to you whose throne is in heaven.
² As the eyes of slaves look to the hand of their
        master,
    as the eyes of a maid look to the hand of
        her mistress,
  so our eyes look to the LORD our God,
    till he shows us his mercy.

³ Have mercy on us, O LORD, have mercy on us,
    for we have endured much contempt.

⁴We have endured much ridicule from the
proud,
much contempt from the arrogant.

Psalm 124

A song of ascents. Of David.

¹If the LORD had not been on our side—
let Israel say—
²if the LORD had not been on our side
when men attacked us,
³when their anger flared against us,
they would have swallowed us alive;
⁴the flood would have engulfed us,
the torrent would have swept over us,
⁵the raging waters
would have swept us away.

⁶Praise be to the LORD,
who has not let us be torn by their teeth.
⁷We have escaped like a bird
out of the fowler's snare;
the snare has been broken,
and we have escaped.
⁸Our help is in the name of the LORD,
the Maker of heaven and earth.

Psalm 125

A song of ascents.

¹Those who trust in the LORD are like Mount
Zion,
which cannot be shaken but endures forever.
²As the mountains surround Jerusalem,
so the LORD surrounds his people
both now and forevermore.

³The scepter of the wicked will not remain
over the land allotted to the righteous,
for then the righteous might use
their hands to do evil.

⁴Do good, O LORD, to those who are good,
to those who are upright in heart.
⁵But those who turn to crooked ways
the LORD will banish with the evildoers.

Peace be upon Israel.

Psalm 126

A song of ascents.

¹When the LORD brought back the captives
to ᵃ Zion,
we were like men who dreamed. ᵇ
²Our mouths were filled with laughter,
our tongues with songs of joy.
Then it was said among the nations,
"The LORD has done great things for
them."
³The LORD has done great things for us,
and we are filled with joy.

PRAYING THE SCRIPTURES

Joy
PSALM 126:3

O Lord, I praise and thank you, for you have
done great things for my grandchild, and we
are filled with joy.

Next prayer in Joy Prayer Track: Joel 2:21,23

⁴Restore our fortunes, ᶜ O LORD,
like streams in the Negev.
⁵Those who sow in tears
will reap with songs of joy.
⁶He who goes out weeping,
carrying seed to sow,
will return with songs of joy,
carrying sheaves with him.

Psalm 127

A song of ascents. Of Solomon.

¹Unless the LORD builds the house,
its builders labor in vain.
Unless the LORD watches over the city,
the watchmen stand guard in vain.

ᵃ 1 Or LORD restored the fortunes of   ᵇ 1 Or men restored to health
ᶜ 4 Or Bring back our captives

AS THE MOUNTAINS SURROUND
JERUSALEM, SO THE LORD
SURROUNDS HIS PEOPLE BOTH
NOW AND FOREVERMORE.

Psalm 125:2

Into His Light

CLAUDIA ARP

READ | PSALM 125:1 – 5

What should have been a lovely drive through the Austrian Alps with my husband, Dave, was not — all we could see were miles and miles of fog. Then the sky gradually became brighter and in one magical moment the fog at the very top of the Alps broke, revealing the peaks. But the next moment they disappeared — as if they were playing hide and seek with us.

How breathtaking it was when the fog lifted, and I could see the majesty of the mountains! Then how disappointing it was when the thick fog reappeared. But isn't this how life is sometimes? At times we see so clearly the beauty all around us — and at other times we only see the fog. Yet, like the Alps in the fog, the beauty is always there, whether we can see it or not. In my life there have been times I have felt close to God and other times when I have felt distant. But like the Alps, God is always present, and I need to trust him in the foggy times as well as in the sunny times.

As we drove along, after a few minutes of hide and seek, the sun suddenly broke through, and we were surrounded by God's majesty — 360 degrees of magnificent, stately mountains. What a wonderful word-picture reminder that in those times when fog reappears, in the midst of the darkness and dullness, God is still there — even when we don't feel his presence. His love and protection — more majestic than the Alps — surround us.

Dear Lord, thank you that you are with me in the foggy times as well as in the sunny times. Thank you for surrounding me with your love and protection. Help me to acknowledge your presence and trust you — whatever my stage in life.

Your next devotion is located on page 823.

GRANDCHILD IN FOCUS • PRAYER

Future Spouse

Dear Lord, if it is your will, I pray my grandchild will be united in a loving and Christian marriage. Keep her sexually pure so that she will honor you with her body and mind. As she seeks a spouse who will honor and care for her, give her patience and discernment. May her choice for a life partner be your choice for her, so that she and her husband will together glorify you in a lasting love. I pray this in Jesus' name, amen.

SONS ARE A HERITAGE
FROM THE LORD, CHILDREN
A REWARD FROM HIM.

Psalm 127:3

Abundant Blessings

LORI COPELAND

READ | PSALM 127:1–5

Seven males graced our family (three sons, four grandsons) when the coming of another grandchild was announced. Our thoughts of a baseball team vanished when our middle son, Rick, came through with a girl. Audrey Lauren Copeland made her entrance into the world on January 23, 2001. Wow! A baby girl! I just stared. Yep. She was a girl all right, with dark curly hair and blue eyes.

These days our greatest joy is having Wednesday evenings with Gage (age eight) and Audrey (age six). Wednesday nights are memory makers. We begin the evening with dinner at the cafeteria: chicken legs, mashed potatoes and white gravy (two servings for Gage), macaroni and cheese, and Jell-O. Then we go on to church to attend Mission Friends and Kid's Praise choir. Afterward, we ask Gage and Audrey what they learned that evening. Sometimes their observations are humorous and other times there are long, dramatic explanations about missionaries and their work.

I can't speak for my grandchildren, but these golden years of Wednesday nights will forever hold a place in my heart and my memory. My first three grandsons were born when I was a young, 39-year-old grandmother with a child still at home. The last two grandbabies came along when I was more mature, more grandmotherly. Age doesn't matter; it's a grandchild's youthful memories that linger and shape their adult lives.

Grandparenting is a responsibility and a blessing beyond comparison. Leading a child and shaping a child's life can be experienced whether you've been given your own grandchildren or you've been allowed access to other people's children. Memory making costs nothing but a dribble of time and a heaping cupful of love.

Dear God, thank you for my grandchildren. I couldn't have known or dreamed of how they would enrich my life and allow me to see the world through innocent eyes. I pray that you use each of these precious lives for your service. Amen.

Your next devotion is located on page 824.

GRANDCHILD IN FOCUS • PRAYER

School/Career

Dear God, may learning be a joy rather than a chore for my grandchild. May exploration of new ideas bring a sense of wonder, awe and excitement. Grant him clarity of mind, the ability to concentrate on the task at hand and recollection of what has been learned. Help him to appreciate the tasks that come easily and to persevere through those that challenge. Amen.

TOGETHER TIME

Day of Adventure

Establish a day of adventure with your grandkids. You might want to find a mutually adventurous activity for everyone: the museum, the zoo, an aquarium, the theater or a trip to the airport viewing area. Check out local attractions at different times of the year. There's usually something going on in your town or a large city nearby.

You could also explore another town, or just go someplace you have never been before. Don't tell the kids your final destination; make it a surprise. Try to pick something that will match their personalities and interests. Variety is always good. Be sure to include a food stop along the way or afterward — that's a stop that is guaranteed to please everyone.

Long-Distance Variation: Send tickets, gift certificates or a check for your grandkids to take an adventure with their parents. Then have them tell you about it via email, a letter or a phone call.

Add this day's adventures, Lord, as a treasure to our individual memories. Let our time together be filled with laughter and joy and happiness. Amen.

Your next devotion is located on page 825.

GRANDCHILD IN FOCUS • PRAYER

Character

Dear Lord and Father, I ask that you fill my grandchild with your Spirit so her character reflects your goodness and love. Give her kindness and love for others. Bring joy to her life so she will be a joy to others. Grant her patience and self-control through difficult and trying times. May she show mercy and generosity to those who are less fortunate. Grant her integrity and a sense of justice, and surround her with your peace. Amen.

Worship the Lord

The LORD is my shepherd, I shall not be in want.
　　He makes me lie down in green pastures,
he leads me beside quiet waters,
　　he restores my soul.
He guides me in paths of righteousness
　　for his name's sake.
Even though I walk
　　through the valley of the shadow of death,
I will fear no evil,
　　for you are with me;
your rod and your staff,
　　they comfort me.

You prepare a table before me
　　in the presence of my enemies.
You anoint my head with oil;
　　my cup overflows.
Surely goodness and love will follow me
　　all the days of my life,
and I will dwell in the house of the LORD
　　forever.

Psalm 23

Dear Lord and Father, what a comfort to know that no matter where I go, you will always be at my side. Strengthen me with your presence: to face my fears, to confront my enemies, to walk through dark valleys. May your goodness and love fill my life with joy. Amen.

GRANDCHILD IN FOCUS • PRAYER

Talents

Dear Lord, the giver of gifts, bless my grandchild as he develops his talents. Help him identify his talents and be proud and confident of the gifts you have given him. Give him patience and understanding, Lord, so he will not grow weary of striving and searching to reach the goals you have set for him. May each milestone bring satisfaction and a healthy desire for greater achievement and success to bring glory to you. Amen.

Your next devotion is located on page 827.

2 In vain you rise early
and stay up late,
toiling for food to eat—
for he grants sleep to [a] those he loves.

3 Sons are a heritage from the LORD,
children a reward from him.
4 Like arrows in the hands of a warrior
are sons born in one's youth.
5 Blessed is the man
whose quiver is full of them.
They will not be put to shame
when they contend with their enemies in
the gate.

Psalm 128

A song of ascents.

1 Blessed are all who fear the LORD,
who walk in his ways.
2 You will eat the fruit of your labor;
blessings and prosperity will be yours.
3 Your wife will be like a fruitful vine
within your house;
your sons will be like olive shoots
around your table.
4 Thus is the man blessed
who fears the LORD.

5 May the LORD bless you from Zion
all the days of your life;
may you see the prosperity of Jerusalem,
6 and may you live to see your children's
children.

Peace be upon Israel.

Psalm 129

A song of ascents.

1 They have greatly oppressed me from my
youth—
let Israel say—
2 they have greatly oppressed me from my
youth,
but they have not gained the victory
over me.

3 Plowmen have plowed my back
and made their furrows long.
4 But the LORD is righteous;
he has cut me free from the cords of the
wicked.

5 May all who hate Zion
be turned back in shame.
6 May they be like grass on the roof,
which withers before it can grow;
7 with it the reaper cannot fill his hands,
nor the one who gathers fill his arms.
8 May those who pass by not say,
"The blessing of the LORD be upon you;
we bless you in the name of the LORD."

Psalm 130

A song of ascents.

1 Out of the depths I cry to you, O LORD;
2 O Lord, hear my voice.
Let your ears be attentive
to my cry for mercy.

3 If you, O LORD, kept a record of sins,
O Lord, who could stand?
4 But with you there is forgiveness;
therefore you are feared.

5 I wait for the LORD, my soul waits,
and in his word I put my hope.

a 2 Or eat— / for while they sleep he provides for

PRAYING THE SCRIPTURES

Forgiveness

PSALM 130:3–4

If you, O Lord, kept a record of sins, who could stand? But with you there is forgiveness for my grandchild if she turns to you.

Next prayer in Forgiveness Prayer Track: Isaiah 43:25

MAY THE LORD BLESS YOU FROM ZION
ALL THE DAYS OF YOUR LIFE; MAY YOU
SEE THE PROSPERITY OF JERUSALEM,
AND MAY YOU LIVE TO SEE YOUR
CHILDREN'S CHILDREN.

Psalm 128:5–6

The Blessing of Being Close

FERN NICHOLS

READ | PSALM 128:1–6

I am blessed to have lived to see my children's children. I am blessed even more to have all six grand-children living within 50 minutes of my house. Five out of the six live within 10 minutes. Yes, I know, I am very blessed. Therefore I take very seriously the "touch" I can have on their lives. For those who have grandchildren living far away, I pray that, as I share how I am able to touch my grandchildren up close, God will spur creative thoughts in you of how to touch your grandchildren who do not live nearby.

Even though 50 minutes is not too far away, I was concerned about knowing this granddaughter like I would know the ones who live close by. So I asked God what I could do to see her more often. My daughter is a teacher, and I offered to take care of my granddaughter, Mikaila, every Friday. I scheduled my work hours so that I could take that day off and be with Mikaila all day. Now I have a whole day to play, sing and talk about Jesus, read Bible stories, take her to the park and pray over her when she takes her nap. Let me tell you, we are buds. When I am out of her sight, she yells, "NANA!!" And then when she sees me, she runs to me, with arms outstretched, as fast as her little legs can carry her. I sweep her up in my arms and hold her close.

The grandchildren that live nearby come to my house often. We have a little ritual when they come up the walkway and knock on my door. I say, "Who's at Nana's house?" and I swing open the door with glee, swoop them up in my arms, hug them tight and whisper in their ear my love and Jesus' love for them.

Dear Lord, thank you for blessing me with grandchildren who live so close to me. I pray for the grandmother who is unable to be near her grandchildren or is physically at a place where she cannot do a lot with them. I pray that you will comfort her heart and that she will know how very important her calls, letters and especially her prayers are to her precious grandchildren. In Jesus' name, amen.

Your next devotion is located on page 832.

GRANDCHILD IN FOCUS • PRAYER

SELECT ONE OF YOUR
GRANDCHILDREN TO FOCUS ON
IN PRAYER FOR THE NEXT 14 DAYS.

Salvation

Dear Lord, please guide my grandchild to your gift of salvation. I pray that she will come to know you, to love you and to walk close to you throughout her life. May she boldly claim Jesus as her Lord and Savior. Guide her as she makes choices that have eternal consequences. Help her to follow you each moment of her life. I pray this in Jesus' name, amen.

TALKING POINTS

Forgiveness

God doesn't keep a record of our sins.

PSALM 130:3–4

For more on forgiveness, go to Proverbs 24:17.

⁶My soul waits for the Lord
    more than watchmen wait for the
        morning,
    more than watchmen wait for the
        morning.

⁷O Israel, put your hope in the Lord,
    for with the Lord is unfailing love
    and with him is full redemption.
⁸He himself will redeem Israel
    from all their sins.

Psalm 131

A song of ascents. Of David.

¹My heart is not proud, O Lord,
    my eyes are not haughty;
 I do not concern myself with great matters
    or things too wonderful for me.
²But I have stilled and quieted my soul;
    like a weaned child with its mother,
    like a weaned child is my soul within me.

³O Israel, put your hope in the Lord
    both now and forevermore.

Psalm 132

132:8–10pp — 2Ch 6:41–42

A song of ascents.

¹O Lord, remember David
    and all the hardships he endured.

²He swore an oath to the Lord
    and made a vow to the Mighty One of
        Jacob:

³"I will not enter my house
    or go to my bed—
⁴I will allow no sleep to my eyes,
    no slumber to my eyelids,
⁵till I find a place for the Lord,
    a dwelling for the Mighty One of Jacob."

⁶We heard it in Ephrathah,
    we came upon it in the fields of Jaar[a: b]
⁷"Let us go to his dwelling place;
    let us worship at his footstool—
⁸arise, O Lord, and come to your resting
        place,
    you and the ark of your might.
⁹May your priests be clothed with
        righteousness;
    may your saints sing for joy."

¹⁰For the sake of David your servant,
    do not reject your anointed one.

¹¹The Lord swore an oath to David,
    a sure oath that he will not revoke:
"One of your own descendants
    I will place on your throne—
¹²if your sons keep my covenant
    and the statutes I teach them,
then their sons will sit
    on your throne for ever and ever."

¹³For the Lord has chosen Zion,
    he has desired it for his dwelling:
¹⁴"This is my resting place for ever and ever;
    here I will sit enthroned, for I have desired
        it—
¹⁵I will bless her with abundant provisions;
    her poor will I satisfy with food.
¹⁶I will clothe her priests with salvation,
    and her saints will ever sing for joy.

¹⁷"Here I will make a horn[c] grow for David
    and set up a lamp for my anointed one.
¹⁸I will clothe his enemies with shame,
    but the crown on his head will be
        resplendent."

---

*a 6 That is, Kiriath Jearim   b 6 Or heard of it in Ephrathah, /
we found it in the fields of Jaar. (And no quotes around verses 7-9)
c 17 Horn here symbolizes strong one, that is, king.*

Psalm 133

A song of ascents. Of David.

¹ How good and pleasant it is
    when brothers live together in unity!
² It is like precious oil poured on the head,
    running down on the beard,
    running down on Aaron's beard,
    down upon the collar of his robes.
³ It is as if the dew of Hermon
    were falling on Mount Zion.
For there the LORD bestows his blessing,
    even life forevermore.

TALKING POINTS

Blended Family

Unity within the family brings blessing.

PSALM 133:1–3

This is the last talking point on blended family.

Psalm 134

A song of ascents.

¹ Praise the LORD, all you servants of the LORD
    who minister by night in the house of the
        LORD.
² Lift up your hands in the sanctuary
    and praise the LORD.

³ May the LORD, the Maker of heaven and
        earth,
    bless you from Zion.

Psalm 135

135:15–20pp — Ps 115:4–11

¹ Praise the LORD. ᵃ

Praise the name of the LORD;
    praise him, you servants of the LORD,

² you who minister in the house of the LORD,
    in the courts of the house of our God.

³ Praise the LORD, for the LORD is good;
    sing praise to his name, for that is pleasant.
⁴ For the LORD has chosen Jacob to be his own,
    Israel to be his treasured possession.

⁵ I know that the LORD is great,
    that our Lord is greater than all gods.
⁶ The LORD does whatever pleases him,
    in the heavens and on the earth,
    in the seas and all their depths.
⁷ He makes clouds rise from the ends of the
        earth;
    he sends lightning with the rain
    and brings out the wind from his
        storehouses.

⁸ He struck down the firstborn of Egypt,
    the firstborn of men and animals.
⁹ He sent his signs and wonders into your
        midst, O Egypt,
    against Pharaoh and all his servants.
¹⁰ He struck down many nations
    and killed mighty kings—
¹¹ Sihon king of the Amorites,
    Og king of Bashan
    and all the kings of Canaan—
¹² and he gave their land as an inheritance,
    an inheritance to his people Israel.

¹³ Your name, O LORD, endures forever,
    your renown, O LORD, through all
        generations.
¹⁴ For the LORD will vindicate his people
    and have compassion on his servants.

¹⁵ The idols of the nations are silver and gold,
    made by the hands of men.
¹⁶ They have mouths, but cannot speak,
    eyes, but they cannot see;
¹⁷ they have ears, but cannot hear,
    nor is there breath in their mouths.
¹⁸ Those who make them will be like them,
    and so will all who trust in them.

ᵃ 1 Hebrew Hallelu Yah; also in verses 3 and 21

¹⁹O house of Israel, praise the LORD;
    O house of Aaron, praise the LORD;
²⁰O house of Levi, praise the LORD;
    you who fear him, praise the LORD.
²¹Praise be to the LORD from Zion,
    to him who dwells in Jerusalem.

Praise the LORD.

Psalm 136

¹Give thanks to the LORD, for he is good.
    His love endures forever.
²Give thanks to the God of gods.
    His love endures forever.
³Give thanks to the Lord of lords:
    His love endures forever.

⁴to him who alone does great wonders,
    His love endures forever.
⁵who by his understanding made the heavens,
    His love endures forever.
⁶who spread out the earth upon the waters,
    His love endures forever.
⁷who made the great lights—
    His love endures forever.
⁸the sun to govern the day,
    His love endures forever.
⁹the moon and stars to govern the night;
    His love endures forever.

¹⁰to him who struck down the firstborn of Egypt
    His love endures forever.
¹¹and brought Israel out from among them
    His love endures forever.

¹²with a mighty hand and outstretched arm;
    His love endures forever.
¹³to him who divided the Red Sea^{*a*} asunder
    His love endures forever.
¹⁴and brought Israel through the midst of it,
    His love endures forever.
¹⁵but swept Pharaoh and his army into the
    Red Sea;
    His love endures forever.

¹⁶to him who led his people through the desert,
    His love endures forever.
¹⁷who struck down great kings,
    His love endures forever.
¹⁸and killed mighty kings—
    His love endures forever.
¹⁹Sihon king of the Amorites
    His love endures forever.
²⁰and Og king of Bashan—
    His love endures forever.
²¹and gave their land as an inheritance,
    His love endures forever.
²²an inheritance to his servant Israel;
    His love endures forever.

²³to the One who remembered us in our low
    estate
    His love endures forever.
²⁴and freed us from our enemies,
    His love endures forever.
²⁵and who gives food to every creature.
    His love endures forever.

²⁶Give thanks to the God of heaven.
    His love endures forever.

Psalm 137

¹By the rivers of Babylon we sat and wept
    when we remembered Zion.
²There on the poplars
    we hung our harps,
³for there our captors asked us for songs,
    our tormentors demanded songs of joy;
    they said, "Sing us one of the songs of
    Zion!"

TALKING POINTS

Thankfulness

Give thanks to God for his goodness.

PSALM 136:1

For more on thankfulness, go to Psalm 147:7–9.

^{*a*} *13* Hebrew *Yam Suph*; that is, Sea of Reeds; also in verse 15

⁴How can we sing the songs of the LORD
    while in a foreign land?
⁵If I forget you, O Jerusalem,
    may my right hand forget ⌞its skill⌟.
⁶May my tongue cling to the roof of my
        mouth
    if I do not remember you,
    if I do not consider Jerusalem
        my highest joy.

⁷Remember, O LORD, what the Edomites did
        on the day Jerusalem fell.
    "Tear it down," they cried,
        "tear it down to its foundations!"

⁸O Daughter of Babylon, doomed to
        destruction,
    happy is he who repays you
        for what you have done to us—
⁹he who seizes your infants
    and dashes them against the rocks.

Psalm 138

Of David.

¹I will praise you, O LORD, with all my heart;
    before the "gods" I will sing your praise.
²I will bow down toward your holy temple
    and will praise your name
    for your love and your faithfulness,
    for you have exalted above all things
        your name and your word.
³When I called, you answered me;
    you made me bold and stouthearted.

⁴May all the kings of the earth praise you,
        O LORD,
    when they hear the words of your
        mouth.
⁵May they sing of the ways of the LORD,
    for the glory of the LORD is great.

⁶Though the LORD is on high, he looks upon
        the lowly,
    but the proud he knows from afar.
⁷Though I walk in the midst of trouble,
    you preserve my life;

you stretch out your hand against the anger
        of my foes,
    with your right hand you save me.
⁸The LORD will fulfill ⌞his purpose⌟ for me;
    your love, O LORD, endures forever—
    do not abandon the works of your hands.

TALKING POINTS

Military

God will protect us from our foes
so that he may fulfill his purposes.

PSALM 138:7–8

For more on military, go to Isaiah 2:2–4.

Psalm 139

For the director of music.
Of David. A psalm.

¹O LORD, you have searched me
    and you know me.
²You know when I sit and when I rise;
    you perceive my thoughts from afar.
³You discern my going out and my lying
        down;
    you are familiar with all my ways.
⁴Before a word is on my tongue
    you know it completely, O LORD.

⁵You hem me in—behind and before;
    you have laid your hand upon me.
⁶Such knowledge is too wonderful for me,
    too lofty for me to attain.

⁷Where can I go from your Spirit?
    Where can I flee from your presence?
⁸If I go up to the heavens, you are there;
    if I make my bed in the depths,ᵃ you are
        there.

ᵃ 8 Hebrew *Sheol*

O LORD, YOU HAVE SEARCHED ME
AND YOU KNOW ME. YOU KNOW
WHEN I SIT AND WHEN I RISE.
Psalm 139:1–2

God Delights in His Creation

JAN SILVIOUS

READ | PSALM 139:1–12

It's true that it's all about God, but in the long run, he is all about you. He created you, gave breath to your lungs and sustains your life. He wills you to bring him glory while you live and has determined the day of your death. He longs for you to be an accurate representation of who he is to the people who live on the earth he created.

His love for you is without bounds. His interest in you is intense. His provision for you is without measure. He created you with purpose and ability. He is sovereign over the events and circumstances of your life. He rules in the heavens above and in the earth below, but there is one place he will not claim his rights or establish his rule without invitation: He will not defy your free will.

God made you with the capacity to choose: to choose the way you live, the way you think, the way you react and, in the end, the way you will relate to him. He is a ruler, but he is not a dictator. He gives wisdom, but he does not force anyone to live wisely.

He is God. He created you, and he absolutely adores his creation. Pass that good news on to your grandchildren. They know you love them, but the greater news is that God, who created them, loves them without limit.

Father, I thank you that you are the Creator. You understand the works of your hands, and you love us all the same. I'll never fully understand your love, but I thank you for it nonetheless. I pray that you will show me how to make your role as Creator a living reality to those I love. Amen.

Your next devotion is located on page 834.

GRANDCHILD IN FOCUS • PRAYER

Physical Well-Being

Almighty God, Creator of us all, I pray that you will watch over my grandchild's physical development. May he grow in strength through the stages of his life. As he grows in awareness of his body, help him to understand that each body develops uniquely, yet is within your plan and your control. Please guard his health so that his diseases are few, his injuries are minor and his infirmities are brief. Amen.

⁹ If I rise on the wings of the dawn,
 if I settle on the far side of the sea,
¹⁰ even there your hand will guide me,
 your right hand will hold me fast.

¹¹ If I say, "Surely the darkness will hide me
 and the light become night around me,"
¹² even the darkness will not be dark to you;
 the night will shine like the day,
 for darkness is as light to you.

¹³ For you created my inmost being;
 you knit me together in my mother's
  womb.
¹⁴ I praise you because I am fearfully and
  wonderfully made;
 your works are wonderful,
 I know that full well.
¹⁵ My frame was not hidden from you
 when I was made in the secret place.
 When I was woven together in the depths of
  the earth,
¹⁶ your eyes saw my unformed body.
 All the days ordained for me
  were written in your book
  before one of them came to be.

¹⁷ How precious to ᵃ me are your thoughts,
 O God!
 How vast is the sum of them!
¹⁸ Were I to count them,
 they would outnumber the grains of sand.
 When I awake,
 I am still with you.

¹⁹ If only you would slay the wicked, O God!
 Away from me, you bloodthirsty men!
²⁰ They speak of you with evil intent;
 your adversaries misuse your name.
²¹ Do I not hate those who hate you, O LORD,
 and abhor those who rise up against you?
²² I have nothing but hatred for them;
 I count them my enemies.

²³ Search me, O God, and know my heart;
 test me and know my anxious thoughts.
²⁴ See if there is any offensive way in me,
 and lead me in the way everlasting.

Psalm 140

For the director of music. A psalm of David.

¹ Rescue me, O LORD, from evil men;
 protect me from men of violence,
² who devise evil plans in their hearts
 and stir up war every day.
³ They make their tongues as sharp as a
  serpent's;
 the poison of vipers is on their lips. *Selah*

⁴ Keep me, O LORD, from the hands of the
  wicked;
 protect me from men of violence
 who plan to trip my feet.
⁵ Proud men have hidden a snare for me;
 they have spread out the cords of their net
 and have set traps for me along my path.
          Selah

⁶ O LORD, I say to you, "You are my God."
 Hear, O LORD, my cry for mercy.
⁷ O Sovereign LORD, my strong deliverer,
 who shields my head in the day of battle—
⁸ do not grant the wicked their desires,
  O LORD;
 do not let their plans succeed,
 or they will become proud. *Selah*

⁹ Let the heads of those who surround me
 be covered with the trouble their lips have
  caused.

TALKING POINTS

Self-Esteem

God formed us and values us.

PSALM 139:13–18

For more on self-esteem, go to Jeremiah 1:5.

ᵃ 17 Or *concerning*

> YOU CREATED MY INMOST BEING; YOU KNIT ME TOGETHER IN MY MOTHER'S WOMB. I PRAISE YOU BECAUSE I AM FEARFULLY AND WONDERFULLY MADE; YOUR WORKS ARE WONDERFUL, I KNOW THAT FULL WELL.
>
> *Psalm 139:13 – 14*

Fearfully and Wonderfully Made

FERN NICHOLS

READ | PSALM 139:13 – 24

It was an intense, desperate prayer meeting as we grandmas cried out to the Lord in response to a friend's prayer request. Her pregnant daughter was carrying a son who had a fatal defect and would not live to full term. "O Lord," we prayed, "please grant your peace to this precious couple, peace that passes understanding. Help them to trust you. Let them know that you have a plan and that everything you do is to bring you glory."

Week after week we prayed. Later we received a letter the couple wrote to family and friends:

At the time we found out, the pain was insurmountable. Although we knew we would get through it, we did not know how. What we did know was that God had control of this little life.

God delivered Dominic on February 5th, two months shy of his due date. The moment he was born, the nurse gave him to me right away. I was overcome with intense sorrow. Then something unexplainable happened. After a couple minutes of weeping, I opened my eyes and saw how wonderful this child was. I saw his beautiful hands, his blue eyes and his little tongue. I had never seen anything so precious in all my life.

We do not think of our experience as the result of our fallen world, a mistake or even a regret. When we saw how much Dominic looked like his earthly father, we were reminded of how we are made in the image of our heavenly Father. Nothing God creates is bad or a mistake. Our son was and is perfect, and God's plan for his life was fulfilled.

God answered the prayers of a praying group of grandmothers — exceedingly, abundantly above and beyond what we could have even imagined!

Heavenly Father, I pray for the grandmothers who are carrying heavy burdens for their children and grandchildren. Help them know that the power of prayer is multiplied when we pray with others in the name of Jesus. Give them courage to start a prayer group or find an existing group with whom to pray for those they love. Amen.

Your next devotion is located on page 838.

GRANDCHILD IN FOCUS • PRAYER

Emotional Development

O God, Creator of mind and body, I pray that you will give my grandchild emotional health and strength. Where there is anger, bring peace. Where there is confusion, bring clarity and focus. Where there are dark shadows, cast a ray of hope. Fill her with the sunshine of your Spirit. Warm her with the presence of your peace. Amen.

10 Let burning coals fall upon them;
    may they be thrown into the fire,
    into miry pits, never to rise.
11 Let slanderers not be established in the land;
    may disaster hunt down men of violence.

12 I know that the LORD secures justice for the
    poor
    and upholds the cause of the needy.
13 Surely the righteous will praise your name
    and the upright will live before you.

Psalm 141

A psalm of David.

1 O LORD, I call to you; come quickly to me.
    Hear my voice when I call to you.
2 May my prayer be set before you like incense;
    may the lifting up of my hands be like the
      evening sacrifice.

3 Set a guard over my mouth, O LORD;
    keep watch over the door of my lips.
4 Let not my heart be drawn to what is evil,
    to take part in wicked deeds
with men who are evildoers;
    let me not eat of their delicacies.

5 Let a righteous man *a* strike me—it is a
    kindness;
    let him rebuke me—it is oil on my head.
    My head will not refuse it.

Yet my prayer is ever against the deeds of
    evildoers;
6   their rulers will be thrown down from the
    cliffs,
    and the wicked will learn that my words
    were well spoken.
7 ⌊They will say,⌋ "As one plows and breaks up
    the earth,
    so our bones have been scattered at the
    mouth of the grave. *b*"

8 But my eyes are fixed on you, O Sovereign
    LORD;
    in you I take refuge—do not give me over
    to death.

9 Keep me from the snares they have laid for me,
    from the traps set by evildoers.
10 Let the wicked fall into their own nets,
    while I pass by in safety.

Psalm 142

A *maskil* *c* of David. When he was
in the cave. A prayer.

1 I cry aloud to the LORD;
    I lift up my voice to the LORD for mercy.
2 I pour out my complaint before him;
    before him I tell my trouble.

3 When my spirit grows faint within me,
    it is you who know my way.
In the path where I walk
    men have hidden a snare for me.
4 Look to my right and see;
    no one is concerned for me.
I have no refuge;
    no one cares for my life.

5 I cry to you, O LORD;
    I say, "You are my refuge,
    my portion in the land of the living."
6 Listen to my cry,
    for I am in desperate need;
rescue me from those who pursue me,
    for they are too strong for me.
7 Set me free from my prison,
    that I may praise your name.

Then the righteous will gather about me
    because of your goodness to me.

Psalm 143

A psalm of David.

1 O LORD, hear my prayer,
    listen to my cry for mercy;
in your faithfulness and righteousness
    come to my relief.
2 Do not bring your servant into judgment,
    for no one living is righteous before you.

a 5 Or *Let the Righteous One*   *b* 7 Hebrew *Sheol*   *c* Title:
Probably a literary or musical term

³The enemy pursues me,
he crushes me to the ground;
he makes me dwell in darkness
like those long dead.
⁴So my spirit grows faint within me;
my heart within me is dismayed.

⁵I remember the days of long ago;
I meditate on all your works
and consider what your hands have done.
⁶I spread out my hands to you;
my soul thirsts for you like a parched land.
Selah

⁷Answer me quickly, O LORD;
my spirit fails.
Do not hide your face from me
or I will be like those who go down to the pit.
⁸Let the morning bring me word of your
unfailing love,
for I have put my trust in you.
Show me the way I should go,
for to you I lift up my soul.

TALKING POINTS

Depression

God will listen and respond to our cries.

PSALM 143:7–8

For more on depression, go to Isaiah 41:10.

⁹Rescue me from my enemies, O LORD,
for I hide myself in you.
¹⁰Teach me to do your will,
for you are my God;
may your good Spirit
lead me on level ground.

¹¹For your name's sake, O LORD, preserve my
life;
in your righteousness, bring me out of
trouble.

PRAYING THE SCRIPTURES

Guidance

PSALM 143:10

Dear Lord, teach my grandchild to do your will, for you are his God; may your good Spirit lead him on level ground.

Next prayer in Guidance Prayer Track: Proverbs 3:5–6

¹²In your unfailing love, silence my enemies;
destroy all my foes,
for I am your servant.

Psalm 144

Of David.

¹Praise be to the LORD my Rock,
who trains my hands for war,
my fingers for battle.
²He is my loving God and my fortress,
my stronghold and my deliverer,
my shield, in whom I take refuge,
who subdues peoples *ᵃ* under me.

³O LORD, what is man that you care for him,
the son of man that you think of him?
⁴Man is like a breath;
his days are like a fleeting shadow.

⁵Part your heavens, O LORD, and come down;
touch the mountains, so that they smoke.
⁶Send forth lightning and scatter ˌthe enemiesˌ;
shoot your arrows and rout them.
⁷Reach down your hand from on high;
deliver me and rescue me
from the mighty waters,
from the hands of foreigners
⁸whose mouths are full of lies,
whose right hands are deceitful.

ᵃ 2 Many manuscripts of the Masoretic Text, Dead Sea Scrolls, Aquila, Jerome and Syriac; most manuscripts of the Masoretic Text *subdues my people*

⁹ I will sing a new song to you, O God;
    on the ten-stringed lyre I will make music
        to you,
¹⁰ to the One who gives victory to kings,
    who delivers his servant David from the
        deadly sword.

¹¹ Deliver me and rescue me
    from the hands of foreigners
whose mouths are full of lies,
    whose right hands are deceitful.

¹² Then our sons in their youth
    will be like well-nurtured plants,
and our daughters will be like pillars
    carved to adorn a palace.
¹³ Our barns will be filled
    with every kind of provision.
Our sheep will increase by thousands,
    by tens of thousands in our fields;
¹⁴   our oxen will draw heavy loads. ᵃ
There will be no breaching of walls,
    no going into captivity,
    no cry of distress in our streets.

¹⁵ Blessed are the people of whom this is true;
    blessed are the people whose God is the
    Lord.

Psalm 145 ᵇ

A psalm of praise. Of David.

¹ I will exalt you, my God the King;
    I will praise your name for ever and ever.
² Every day I will praise you
    and extol your name for ever and ever.

³ Great is the Lord and most worthy of
        praise;
    his greatness no one can fathom.
⁴ One generation will commend your works
        to another;
    they will tell of your mighty acts.
⁵ They will speak of the glorious splendor of
        your majesty,
    and I will meditate on your wonderful
        works. ᶜ

PRAYING THE SCRIPTURES

Thankfulness

PSALM 145:3–5

Let my grandchild praise you, O Lord, for you are great and most worthy of praise; your greatness no one can fathom. May my grandchild commend your works to the next generation. May he speak of the glorious splendor of your majesty and meditate on your wonderful works.

Next prayer in Thankfulness Prayer Track: Isaiah 63:7

⁶ They will tell of the power of your awesome
        works,
    and I will proclaim your great deeds.
⁷ They will celebrate your abundant goodness
    and joyfully sing of your righteousness.

⁸ The Lord is gracious and compassionate,
    slow to anger and rich in love.
⁹ The Lord is good to all;
    he has compassion on all he has made.
¹⁰ All you have made will praise you, O Lord;
    your saints will extol you.
¹¹ They will tell of the glory of your kingdom
    and speak of your might,
¹² so that all men may know of your mighty acts
    and the glorious splendor of your
        kingdom.
¹³ Your kingdom is an everlasting kingdom,
    and your dominion endures through all
        generations.

The Lord is faithful to all his promises
    and loving toward all he has made. ᵈ

ᵃ 14 Or *our chieftains will be firmly established*   ᵇ This psalm is an acrostic poem, the verses of which (including verse 13b) begin with the successive letters of the Hebrew alphabet.   ᶜ 5 Dead Sea Scrolls and Syriac (see also Septuagint); Masoretic Text *On the glorious splendor of your majesty / and on your wonderful works I will meditate*   ᵈ 13 One manuscript of the Masoretic Text, Dead Sea Scrolls and Syriac (see also Septuagint); most manuscripts of the Masoretic Text do not have the last two lines of verse 13.

THE LORD IS NEAR TO ALL WHO
CALL ON HIM, TO ALL WHO CALL
ON HIM IN TRUTH.

Psalm 145:18

Please Call Home

JAN KARON

READ | PSALM 145:1 – 21

Imagine this:

Your children are grown and gone, and you miss them terribly. Much to your sorrow, they call home only once in a blue moon — or not at all.

This is loosely akin to the relationship that many of us have with God. There are some who check in with Him regularly, and some who never bother to call Home.

We know how we feel when our children don't call, and I believe it matters deeply to God when we fail to connect with Him in prayer.

As Father Tim says in *A New Song*, "God wishes to be as near to us as our very breath." There's simply no way to have a relationship with Him unless we talk to Him — and also listen.

St. James said, "[Come near to God and he will come near to you]."

King David said, "[The LORD is near to all who call on him, to all who call on him in truth]."

Oswald Chambers said this: "Prayer doesn't fit us for the greater work, prayer is the greater work."

I hope you'll call Home right now. And whether we tell Him everything or merely utter His name, God is longing to hear the prayer that's in our hearts.

Father God, too often I forget to call home to you. And when I do, I am amazed at how you always welcome me with open arms and embrace me with your love. Amen.

Your next devotion is located on page 841.

GRANDCHILD IN FOCUS • PRAYER

Spiritual Growth

Dear Lord, today I pray for my grandchild's spiritual growth. I ask that you instill in him the desire to read and memorize your Word. Give him a passion to be in conversation with you. May loving and serving you be part of his daily life. I ask that you stay close to him and lead him to be transformed to your likeness, to reflect your grace and to radiate your love. I pray this in Jesus' name, amen.

¹⁴ The Lord upholds all those who fall
  and lifts up all who are bowed down.
¹⁵ The eyes of all look to you,
  and you give them their food at the proper
    time.
¹⁶ You open your hand
  and satisfy the desires of every living thing.

¹⁷ The Lord is righteous in all his ways
  and loving toward all he has made.
¹⁸ The Lord is near to all who call on him,
  to all who call on him in truth.
¹⁹ He fulfills the desires of those who fear him;
  he hears their cry and saves them.
²⁰ The Lord watches over all who love him,
  but all the wicked he will destroy.

²¹ My mouth will speak in praise of the Lord.
  Let every creature praise his holy name
  for ever and ever.

Psalm 146

¹ Praise the Lord. *ᵃ*

Praise the Lord, O my soul.
² I will praise the Lord all my life;
  I will sing praise to my God as long as I
    live.

³ Do not put your trust in princes,
  in mortal men, who cannot save.
⁴ When their spirit departs, they return to the
    ground;
  on that very day their plans come to
    nothing.

⁵ Blessed is he whose help is the God of Jacob,
  whose hope is in the Lord his God,
⁶ the Maker of heaven and earth,
  the sea, and everything in them—
  the Lord, who remains faithful forever.
⁷ He upholds the cause of the oppressed
  and gives food to the hungry.
  The Lord sets prisoners free,
⁸ the Lord gives sight to the blind,
  the Lord lifts up those who are bowed down,
  the Lord loves the righteous.

⁹ The Lord watches over the alien
  and sustains the fatherless and the widow,
  but he frustrates the ways of the wicked.

¹⁰ The Lord reigns forever,
  your God, O Zion, for all generations.

Praise the Lord.

Psalm 147

¹ Praise the Lord. *ᵇ*

How good it is to sing praises to our God,
  how pleasant and fitting to praise him!

² The Lord builds up Jerusalem;
  he gathers the exiles of Israel.
³ He heals the brokenhearted
  and binds up their wounds.

PRAYING THE SCRIPTURES

Comfort
PSALM 147:3

Dear God, heal my grandchild's broken heart. Bind up her wounds and grant her your peace.

Next prayer in Comfort Prayer Track: Isaiah 66:12–13

⁴ He determines the number of the stars
  and calls them each by name.
⁵ Great is our Lord and mighty in power;
  his understanding has no limit.
⁶ The Lord sustains the humble
  but casts the wicked to the ground.

⁷ Sing to the Lord with thanksgiving;
  make music to our God on the harp.
⁸ He covers the sky with clouds;
  he supplies the earth with rain
  and makes grass grow on the hills.

ᵃ 1 Hebrew *Hallelu Yah;* also in verse 10   ᵇ 1 Hebrew *Hallelu Yah;*
also in verse 20

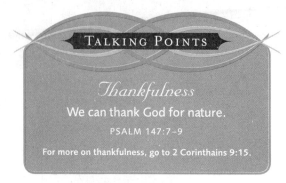

TALKING POINTS

Thankfulness

We can thank God for nature.

PSALM 147:7–9

For more on thankfulness, go to 2 Corinthains 9:15.

⁹ He provides food for the cattle
   and for the young ravens when they call.

¹⁰ His pleasure is not in the strength of the horse,
   nor his delight in the legs of a man;
¹¹ the LORD delights in those who fear him,
   who put their hope in his unfailing love.

¹² Extol the LORD, O Jerusalem;
   praise your God, O Zion,
¹³ for he strengthens the bars of your gates
   and blesses your people within you.
¹⁴ He grants peace to your borders
   and satisfies you with the finest of wheat.

¹⁵ He sends his command to the earth;
   his word runs swiftly.
¹⁶ He spreads the snow like wool
   and scatters the frost like ashes.
¹⁷ He hurls down his hail like pebbles.
   Who can withstand his icy blast?
¹⁸ He sends his word and melts them;
   he stirs up his breezes, and the waters flow.

¹⁹ He has revealed his word to Jacob,
   his laws and decrees to Israel.
²⁰ He has done this for no other nation;
   they do not know his laws.

   Praise the LORD.

Psalm 148

¹ Praise the LORD. ᵃ

   Praise the LORD from the heavens,
   praise him in the heights above.

² Praise him, all his angels,
   praise him, all his heavenly hosts.
³ Praise him, sun and moon,
   praise him, all you shining stars.
⁴ Praise him, you highest heavens
   and you waters above the skies.
⁵ Let them praise the name of the LORD,
   for he commanded and they were created.
⁶ He set them in place for ever and ever;
   he gave a decree that will never pass away.

⁷ Praise the LORD from the earth,
   you great sea creatures and all ocean
      depths,
⁸ lightning and hail, snow and clouds,
   stormy winds that do his bidding,
⁹ you mountains and all hills,
   fruit trees and all cedars,
¹⁰ wild animals and all cattle,
   small creatures and flying birds,
¹¹ kings of the earth and all nations,
   you princes and all rulers on earth,
¹² young men and maidens,
   old men and children.

¹³ Let them praise the name of the LORD,
   for his name alone is exalted;
   his splendor is above the earth and the
      heavens.
¹⁴ He has raised up for his people a horn,ᵇ
   the praise of all his saints,
   of Israel, the people close to his heart.

   Praise the LORD.

Psalm 149

¹ Praise the LORD. ᶜ

   Sing to the LORD a new song,
   his praise in the assembly of the saints.

² Let Israel rejoice in their Maker;
   let the people of Zion be glad in their
      King.

ᵃ 1 Hebrew *Hallelu Yah*; also in verse 14   ᵇ 14 *Horn* here
symbolizes strong one, that is, king.   ᶜ 1 Hebrew *Hallelu Yah*; also
in verse 9

LET THEM PRAISE HIS NAME WITH
DANCING AND MAKE MUSIC TO HIM
WITH TAMBOURINE AND HARP.

Psalm 149:3

I Hope You Dance—a Jig—Every Chance You Get!

SUE BUCHANAN

READ | PSALM 149:1–9

Dancing, or better said, *not* dancing, has always caused me problems. I grew up in a church where dancing was forbidden. Not that it hurt me one bit to miss the jitterbug contests or the slow dances. But in looking back, I think the rule was a means of control. It squelched our excitement for life. What was lost wasn't the chance to move around the dance floor, but rather the spirit of dance, a joy of heart that says, "I can't help myself; I just gotta *move!*"

Psalm 149 apparently wasn't in the Bible in the days of my youth. It seems to encourage dancing. The real question, I suppose, is whether or not you are dancing to praise God's name. Even in our church, every opportunity was taken to warn us about getting "carried away." They called it experiential Christianity—"feel-good religion"! It could lead to what? Saying "Praise God" right out loud? Rolling in the aisles? Pew leaping? Chandelier swinging? Snake handling? (That may seem like a stretch, but in West Virginia it's always a possibility.)

It seems to me, in retrospect, there were those who cared more about whether or not we danced than about whether or not we knew and loved God. The fact that I can still get my nose out of joint over something that happened so many years ago worries me. Scripture tells us, "Get rid of all bitterness . . ." (Eeek! Did you say bitterness?) " . . . rage and anger" (Ephesians 4:31).

Perhaps getting rid of the crud in my life and making things right with those around me—even forgiving them—would prepare my soul to tear loose and *really* go for it and freely praise his name with dancing!

Let's dance! In the kitchen, in the rain or under the sprinkler!

Dear God of joy! Don't let anything . . . anything or anyone . . . rob me of my joy!

Your next devotion is located on page 842.

GRANDCHILD IN FOCUS • PRAYER

Relationships at Home

O Lord, I pray that you will bless the home and family of my grandchild. May the relationships she has with her parents and siblings enhance her well-being, support her self-confidence and increase her faith. May her home life reflect your love, your grace, your compassion and your peace. Guide her parents to direct her in love and truth, so she will grow into a strong and compassionate individual. Amen.

FAITH IN ACTION

Honorary Grandma

Does one or more of your grandchildren have a friend who doesn't have a grandma nearby? Explain to your grandchildren that grandmas have an inexhaustible capacity for love and that you'd be happy to act as an honorary grandmother to one or more of their friends. If the children's parents know your grandchildren and feel comfortable with the situation, invite the children to join you for a particular activity.

Explain to your special guests that today you are their "honorary grandma" and that you would like to share some memorable events that day. The good time will create a bond between the children, as well as between the new children and you.

Older-Grandkids Variation: Teenagers and college-aged kids adapt naturally to this arrangement. In no time a friend or roommate of your grandchild may affectionately address you—and treat you—as "Grandma" whether you bake them some cookies, attend one of their games or let them know you can talk anytime.

Long-Distance Variation: Maybe some child would appreciate a pen-pal (or email) relationship with a letter-writing, "honorary" grandma. Check with parents to get their approval of the idea.

Father, the wonderful thing about love is that it can't be used up. Make me available for kids of all ages who may benefit from a relationship with a grandma. Let my example teach my grandchildren about being empathetic, sensitive and loving. Amen.

Your next devotion is located on page 846.

GRANDCHILD IN FOCUS · PRAYER

Friends

Dear Lord and Father, I pray for my grandchild's social life and his friends. Bring diverse friends into his life who will love and encourage him, who will bring joy and laughter to the good times and comfort and support through difficulties and disappointments. Grant him wisdom and discernment as he selects his friends; help him to avoid cliques that restrict, activities that endanger, and foolish and dangerous behaviors that harm. I ask that you fill his life with close and caring relationships. Amen.

³Let them praise his name with dancing
  and make music to him with tambourine
  and harp.
⁴For the LORD takes delight in his people;
  he crowns the humble with salvation.
⁵Let the saints rejoice in this honor
  and sing for joy on their beds.

⁶May the praise of God be in their mouths
  and a double-edged sword in their hands,
⁷to inflict vengeance on the nations
  and punishment on the peoples,
⁸to bind their kings with fetters,
  their nobles with shackles of iron,
⁹to carry out the sentence written against
    them.
  This is the glory of all his saints.

Praise the LORD.

Psalm 150

¹Praise the LORD.ᵃ

Praise God in his sanctuary;
  praise him in his mighty heavens.

²Praise him for his acts of power;
  praise him for his surpassing greatness.
³Praise him with the sounding of the trumpet,
  praise him with the harp and lyre,
⁴praise him with tambourine and dancing,
  praise him with the strings and flute,
⁵praise him with the clash of cymbals,
  praise him with resounding cymbals.

⁶Let everything that has breath praise the LORD.

Praise the LORD.

ᵃ 1 Hebrew *Hallelu Yah*; also in verse 6

stories to share

PSALM 150:1–6

Praise the Lord

LIFE LESSON: God is worthy of our praise and thanks.

TO TALK ABOUT

✦ Where should we praise God?

✦ What should we praise God for?

✦ How should we praise God?

✦ Who should praise God?

❮ TALKING POINTS ❯

Praise
Everyone should praise the Lord.
PSALM 150:1–6

For more on praise, go to Revelation 7:11–12.

The Advice-Giver's
HANDBOOK

Grandmothers are famous for giving advice. Sometimes our children, grandchildren and other family members come to us seeking it. Other times we feel obligated to speak out in love. Thankfully, with the help of the book of Proverbs, our advice can be sprinkled with truth from the Word of God, a truth that has endured for generations.

The book of Proverbs contains a collection of short, pithy instructions as well as timeless wisdom. At the heart of each proverb is God — the God who loves us and cares for us and wants the very best for our lives. Proverbs is his miniature book of directions for living happy, godly lives.

Take time to carefully read each of the proverbs. You will find that many of them are perfect for use in giving counsel to others. There are probably many more that you will come to treasure as your own. We all love to give advice. Here is the ultimate handbook for it. Use it often. Use it wisely. Use it with love.

VERSE *to* REMEMBER | PROVERBS 2:6

For the LORD gives wisdom, and from his mouth come knowledge and understanding.

ABOUT PROVERBS

WRITTEN BY:
Primarily King Solomon

WRITTEN FOR:
The people of Israel

DATE WRITTEN:
Primarily during Solomon's reign (970 – 930 B.C.)

WHY WRITTEN:
To help people make wise choices and to show that God is the true source of all wisdom

Prologue: Purpose and Theme

1 The proverbs of Solomon son of David, king of Israel:

² for attaining wisdom and discipline;
    for understanding words of insight;
³ for acquiring a disciplined and prudent life,
    doing what is right and just and fair;
⁴ for giving prudence to the simple,
    knowledge and discretion to the young—
⁵ let the wise listen and add to their learning,
    and let the discerning get guidance—
⁶ for understanding proverbs and parables,
    the sayings and riddles of the wise.

⁷ The fear of the Lord is the beginning of
        knowledge,
    but fools[a] despise wisdom and discipline.

Exhortations to Embrace Wisdom

Warning Against Enticement

⁸ Listen, my son, to your father's instruction
    and do not forsake your mother's teaching.
⁹ They will be a garland to grace your head
    and a chain to adorn your neck.

TALKING POINTS

Parents

We need to respect our
parents' advice.

PROVERBS 1:8–9

For more on parents, go to Proverbs 6:20–23.

¹⁰ My son, if sinners entice you,
    do not give in to them.
¹¹ If they say, "Come along with us;
    let's lie in wait for someone's blood,
    let's waylay some harmless soul;

¹² let's swallow them alive, like the grave,[b]
    and whole, like those who go down to the
        pit;
¹³ we will get all sorts of valuable things
    and fill our houses with plunder;
¹⁴ throw in your lot with us,
    and we will share a common purse"—
¹⁵ my son, do not go along with them,
    do not set foot on their paths;
¹⁶ for their feet rush into sin,
    they are swift to shed blood.
¹⁷ How useless to spread a net
    in full view of all the birds!
¹⁸ These men lie in wait for their own blood;
    they waylay only themselves!
¹⁹ Such is the end of all who go after ill-gotten
        gain;
    it takes away the lives of those who get it.

Warning Against Rejecting Wisdom

²⁰ Wisdom calls aloud in the street,
    she raises her voice in the public squares;
²¹ at the head of the noisy streets[c] she cries out,
    in the gateways of the city she makes her
        speech:

²² "How long will you simple ones[d] love your
        simple ways?
    How long will mockers delight in mockery
    and fools hate knowledge?
²³ If you had responded to my rebuke,
    I would have poured out my heart to you
    and made my thoughts known to you.
²⁴ But since you rejected me when I called
    and no one gave heed when I stretched out
        my hand,
²⁵ since you ignored all my advice
    and would not accept my rebuke,
²⁶ I in turn will laugh at your disaster;
    I will mock when calamity overtakes
        you—

ᵃ 7 The Hebrew words rendered *fool* in Proverbs, and often elsewhere in the Old Testament, denote one who is morally deficient. ᵇ 12 Hebrew *Sheol*   ᶜ 21 Hebrew; Septuagint / *on the tops of the walls*   ᵈ 22 The Hebrew word rendered *simple* in Proverbs generally denotes one without moral direction and inclined to evil.

Worship the Lord

I will exalt you, my God the King;
>I will praise your name for ever and ever.
Every day I will praise you
>and extol your name for ever and ever.

Great is the LORD and most worthy of praise;
>his greatness no one can fathom.
One generation will commend your works to another;
>they will tell of your mighty acts.
They will speak of the glorious splendor of your majesty,
>and I will meditate on your wonderful works.
They will tell of the power of your awesome works,
>and I will proclaim your great deeds.
They will celebrate your abundant goodness
>and joyfully sing of your
>>righteousness.

Psalm 145:1 – 7

....

*O God my King, may I praise your name,
not just on the Sabbath, but on every day
of the week, for you are worthy of contin-
uous praise. Make me bold to tell of your
faithfulness and speak of your wonderful
works to my children, my grandchildren and
everyone who enters my life. Let my life be a
joyful song to you. Amen.*

Your next devotion is located on page 848.

GRANDCHILD IN FOCUS • PRAYER

Self-Image

*O loving God, I praise you for creating my
grandchild as a unique individual. Now I ask you
to help her appreciate her uniqueness. Build up her
self-image so she can enjoy her individuality. Help
her to stand firm for who she is, where she has
come from and what she believes in. Encourage
her not only to have hopes and dreams but
to also enjoy each day as it comes.
In Jesus' name, amen.*

27 when calamity overtakes you like a storm,
    when disaster sweeps over you like a
        whirlwind,
    when distress and trouble overwhelm you.

28 "Then they will call to me but I will not
        answer;
    they will look for me but will not find me.
29 Since they hated knowledge
    and did not choose to fear the Lord,
30 since they would not accept my advice
    and spurned my rebuke,
31 they will eat the fruit of their ways
    and be filled with the fruit of their
        schemes.
32 For the waywardness of the simple will kill
        them,
    and the complacency of fools will destroy
        them;
33 but whoever listens to me will live in safety
    and be at ease, without fear of harm."

Moral Benefits of Wisdom

2 My son, if you accept my words
  and store up my commands within you,
2 turning your ear to wisdom
    and applying your heart to understanding,
3 and if you call out for insight
    and cry aloud for understanding,
4 and if you look for it as for silver
    and search for it as for hidden treasure,
5 then you will understand the fear of the
        Lord
    and find the knowledge of God.
6 For the Lord gives wisdom,
    and from his mouth come knowledge and
        understanding.
7 He holds victory in store for the upright,
    he is a shield to those whose walk is
        blameless,
8 for he guards the course of the just
    and protects the way of his faithful ones.

9 Then you will understand what is right and
        just
    and fair—every good path.

10 For wisdom will enter your heart,
    and knowledge will be pleasant to your
        soul.
11 Discretion will protect you,
    and understanding will guard you.

12 Wisdom will save you from the ways of
        wicked men,
    from men whose words are perverse,
13 who leave the straight paths
    to walk in dark ways,
14 who delight in doing wrong
    and rejoice in the perverseness of evil,
15 whose paths are crooked
    and who are devious in their ways.

16 It will save you also from the adulteress,
    from the wayward wife with her seductive
        words,
17 who has left the partner of her youth
    and ignored the covenant she made before
        God. *a*
18 For her house leads down to death
    and her paths to the spirits of the dead.
19 None who go to her return
    or attain the paths of life.

20 Thus you will walk in the ways of good men
    and keep to the paths of the righteous.
21 For the upright will live in the land,
    and the blameless will remain in it;
22 but the wicked will be cut off from the
        land,
    and the unfaithful will be torn from it.

Further Benefits of Wisdom

3 My son, do not forget my teaching,
  but keep my commands in your heart,
2 for they will prolong your life many years
    and bring you prosperity.

3 Let love and faithfulness never leave you;
    bind them around your neck,
    write them on the tablet of your heart.
4 Then you will win favor and a good name
    in the sight of God and man.

a 17 Or covenant of her God

IN ALL YOUR WAYS
ACKNOWLEDGE HIM, AND
HE WILL MAKE YOUR PATHS
STRAIGHT.

Proverbs 3:6

Staying on Top of Life

EMILIE BARNES

READ | PROVERBS 3:1–6

I now realize that the rhythm of a grandparent's life is much different than that of a parent's. I find that I run in spurts. There is more downtime between spurts, but if I don't consistently attend to details, they slide away, and it takes a bulldozer to get things back on track.

When I was 20 years old, my daughter was six months old. We then took in my brother's three children, and soon I became pregnant with our son. That gave us five children under five years old! My life was all work. I was always tired. I was fragmented, confused and stressed out. One day, I read Proverbs 3:6, in the King James Version: "In all thy ways acknowledge him, and he shall direct thy paths." I fell to my knees and prayed, "Please, God, direct my path. I'm on overload. I have no time for me or anyone else. Help me put it all together and make it work to glorify you. Amen."

God not only heard my prayer, he honored it. I began a program that changed my life. I committed 15 minutes each day to quiet time with the Lord. I read his Word and prayed. Next I committed 15 minutes each day to organizing our home, concentrating on things I never seemed to get done. After 30 days the pattern was set. God was directing my path.

Our home changed dramatically. Finally, I could truly understand the meaning of acknowledging God in all my ways. That meant looking to him for help and comfort in everything—family, home, finances, commitments and careers.

I still follow these principles each day: (1) Have a quiet time with my Lord. (2) Spend at least 15 minutes reorganizing part of my home. With these guidelines I stay on top of those things that want to get me disorganized and off track.

Father God, I sincerely want you to direct my paths. Over the many years you have done so, and I'm blessed by the results. Encourage me to keep on keeping on. Amen.

Your next devotion is located on page 850.

GRANDCHILD IN FOCUS • PRAYER

Protection From Worldliness

O Sovereign Lord, the world surrounds my grandchild, pressing in and tempting him in so many ways. Help him set appropriate limits. Give him sound judgment to choose wisely. Guard him from temptation; protect him from physical and mental predators; lead him into paths of righteousness and light. And reassure me with your promise that you are holding him in your hands. Amen.

⁵Trust in the Lord with all your heart
    and lean not on your own understanding;
⁶in all your ways acknowledge him,
    and he will make your paths straight. *ᵃ*

PRAYING THE SCRIPTURES

Guidance

PROVERBS 3:5–6

O Lord, I pray that my grandchild will trust in you with all her heart rather than lean on her own understanding. May she acknowledge you in all her ways, for you then promise to make her paths straight.

Next prayer in Guidance Prayer Track: Zechariah 7:9–10

⁷Do not be wise in your own eyes;
    fear the Lord and shun evil.
⁸This will bring health to your body
    and nourishment to your bones.

PRAYING THE SCRIPTURES

Well-Being

PROVERBS 3:7–8

O Lord, help my grandchild not to be wise in his own eyes but to fear you and shun evil. Thank you for your promise that this will bring health to his body and nourishment to his bones.

Next prayer in Well-being Prayer Track: Jeremiah 17:14

⁹Honor the Lord with your wealth,
    with the firstfruits of all your crops;
¹⁰then your barns will be filled to overflowing,
    and your vats will brim over with new
        wine.

¹¹My son, do not despise the Lord's discipline
    and do not resent his rebuke,
¹²because the Lord disciplines those he loves,
    as a father *ᵇ* the son he delights in.

¹³Blessed is the man who finds wisdom,
    the man who gains understanding,
¹⁴for she is more profitable than silver
    and yields better returns than gold.
¹⁵She is more precious than rubies;
    nothing you desire can compare with her.
¹⁶Long life is in her right hand;
    in her left hand are riches and honor.
¹⁷Her ways are pleasant ways,
    and all her paths are peace.
¹⁸She is a tree of life to those who embrace her;
    those who lay hold of her will be blessed.

¹⁹By wisdom the Lord laid the earth's
        foundations,
    by understanding he set the heavens in
        place;
²⁰by his knowledge the deeps were divided,
    and the clouds let drop the dew.

²¹My son, preserve sound judgment and
        discernment,
    do not let them out of your sight;
²²they will be life for you,
    an ornament to grace your neck.
²³Then you will go on your way in safety,
    and your foot will not stumble;
²⁴when you lie down, you will not be afraid;
    when you lie down, your sleep will be sweet.
²⁵Have no fear of sudden disaster
    or of the ruin that overtakes the wicked,
²⁶for the Lord will be your confidence
    and will keep your foot from being snared.

²⁷Do not withhold good from those who
        deserve it,
    when it is in your power to act.
²⁸Do not say to your neighbor,
    "Come back later; I'll give it tomorrow"—
    when you now have it with you.

ᵃ 6 Or *will direct your paths*   *ᵇ 12* Hebrew; Septuagint / *and he punishes*

WHEN YOU LIE DOWN, YOU WILL NOT BE AFRAID; WHEN YOU LIE DOWN, YOUR SLEEP WILL BE SWEET.

Proverbs 3:24

Make the Monsters Go Away!

QUIN SHERRER

READ | PROVERBS 3:21–26

One night I was babysitting our five-year-old grandson, Lyden, when he woke from a troubling dream.

"Mama Quin!" he screamed. "How do I get these monsters to go away?" he asked as he bolted upright in his bed.

"Just ask Jesus to make them go away," I answered. "He says he never leaves us. In fact, the Bible says God has angels watching over you. So you can go back to sleep."

"Oh, OK — is that all?" he asked. I prayed a short prayer, asking God to protect Lyden from nightmares and thanking him for his watchful care. Lyden repeated the prayer after me. Then he rolled over and fell asleep again.

When we grandmothers aren't bashful about praying aloud in front of our grandchildren, we are actually teaching them how to pray. As we intercede for them, we beseech God to work on their behalf. Other times, we find ourselves saying no to the adversary's tactics to harass and tempt them. The Scriptures are our arsenal, our prayer manual and our book of promises. As our grandchildren hear us pray, they can come to understand that even they can stand against the powers of darkness. They just need to call on the Lord, their deliverer.

Grandchildren just seem to trust their grandmas. And grandmas trust their God.

....

Heavenly Father, help me develop a lifestyle of praying with my grandchildren. May my example encourage and teach them to be intercessors. Thank you that we can trust you as our God of strength and deliverance. Amen.

Your next devotion is located on page 857.

GRANDCHILD IN FOCUS • PRAYER

Respect for Authority

Dear Lord, I pray that my grandchild will continually grow to respect those in authority. May she learn to be cooperative and fair in work and play. Instill in her a high regard for officials who govern our land and enforce the laws. May her relationships with parents, teachers, coaches, mentors and bosses be respectful, admirable, constructive and caring. Amen.

stories to share

PROVERBS 3:1–35

Wisdom Brings Rewards

LIFE LESSON: Wisdom helps us live lives that please God.

TO TALK ABOUT

✦ What does it mean to be wise?

✦ What are some promises God makes in this chapter? What does God ask us to do?

✦ Do the promises in this chapter always come true? Do they usually come true?

✦ Which of these promises have come true for you and your family?

Wisdom Is Supreme

4 Listen, my sons, to a father's instruction;
  pay attention and gain understanding.
²I give you sound learning,
  so do not forsake my teaching.
³When I was a boy in my father's house,
  still tender, and an only child of my
      mother,
⁴he taught me and said,
  "Lay hold of my words with all your heart;
  keep my commands and you will live.
⁵Get wisdom, get understanding;
  do not forget my words or swerve from
      them.
⁶Do not forsake wisdom, and she will protect
      you;
  love her, and she will watch over you.
⁷Wisdom is supreme; therefore get wisdom.
  Though it cost all you have,ᵃ get
      understanding.
⁸Esteem her, and she will exalt you;
  embrace her, and she will honor you.
⁹She will set a garland of grace on your head
  and present you with a crown of splendor."

¹⁰Listen, my son, accept what I say,
  and the years of your life will be many.

ᵃ 7 Or *Whatever else you get*

²⁹Do not plot harm against your neighbor,
  who lives trustfully near you.
³⁰Do not accuse a man for no reason—
  when he has done you no harm.

³¹Do not envy a violent man
  or choose any of his ways,
³²for the LORD detests a perverse man
  but takes the upright into his confidence.

³³The LORD's curse is on the house of the
      wicked,
  but he blesses the home of the righteous.
³⁴He mocks proud mockers
  but gives grace to the humble.
³⁵The wise inherit honor,
  but fools he holds up to shame.

PRAYING THE SCRIPTURES

Wisdom

PROVERBS 4:5,7

Dear Father, I ask that you help my grandchild to understand the importance of gaining wisdom and understanding, that he may not forget your words or swerve from them. Help him to understand that wisdom is supreme; though it cost all he has, nothing is more valuable than gaining understanding.

Next prayer in Wisdom Prayer Track: Ecclesiastes 2:26

¹¹I guide you in the way of wisdom
and lead you along straight paths.
¹²When you walk, your steps will not be
hampered;
when you run, you will not stumble.
¹³Hold on to instruction, do not let it go;
guard it well, for it is your life.
¹⁴Do not set foot on the path of the wicked
or walk in the way of evil men.
¹⁵Avoid it, do not travel on it;
turn from it and go on your way.

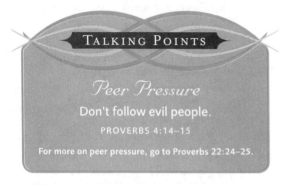

¹⁶For they cannot sleep till they do evil;
they are robbed of slumber till they make
someone fall.
¹⁷They eat the bread of wickedness
and drink the wine of violence.

¹⁸The path of the righteous is like the first
gleam of dawn,
shining ever brighter till the full light of
day.
¹⁹But the way of the wicked is like deep
darkness;
they do not know what makes them
stumble.

²⁰My son, pay attention to what I say;
listen closely to my words.
²¹Do not let them out of your sight,
keep them within your heart;
²²for they are life to those who find them
and health to a man's whole body.

²³Above all else, guard your heart,
for it is the wellspring of life.
²⁴Put away perversity from your mouth;
keep corrupt talk far from your lips.
²⁵Let your eyes look straight ahead,
fix your gaze directly before you.
²⁶Make level^a paths for your feet
and take only ways that are firm.
²⁷Do not swerve to the right or the left;
keep your foot from evil.

Warning Against Adultery

5 My son, pay attention to my wisdom,
listen well to my words of insight,
²that you may maintain discretion
and your lips may preserve knowledge.
³For the lips of an adulteress drip honey,
and her speech is smoother than oil;
⁴but in the end she is bitter as gall,
sharp as a double-edged sword.
⁵Her feet go down to death;
her steps lead straight to the grave.^b
⁶She gives no thought to the way of life;
her paths are crooked, but she knows it not.

⁷Now then, my sons, listen to me;
do not turn aside from what I say.
⁸Keep to a path far from her,
do not go near the door of her house,
⁹lest you give your best strength to others
and your years to one who is cruel,
¹⁰lest strangers feast on your wealth
and your toil enrich another man's house.
¹¹At the end of your life you will groan,
when your flesh and body are spent.
¹²You will say, "How I hated discipline!
How my heart spurned correction!
¹³I would not obey my teachers
or listen to my instructors.
¹⁴I have come to the brink of utter ruin
in the midst of the whole assembly."

¹⁵Drink water from your own cistern,
running water from your own well.

^a 26 Or Consider the   ^b 5 Hebrew Sheol

¹⁶Should your springs overflow in the streets,
    your streams of water in the public
      squares?
¹⁷Let them be yours alone,
    never to be shared with strangers.
¹⁸May your fountain be blessed,
    and may you rejoice in the wife of your
      youth.
¹⁹A loving doe, a graceful deer—
    may her breasts satisfy you always,
    may you ever be captivated by her love.
²⁰Why be captivated, my son, by an adulteress?
    Why embrace the bosom of another man's
      wife?

²¹For a man's ways are in full view of the LORD,
    and he examines all his paths.
²²The evil deeds of a wicked man ensnare him;
    the cords of his sin hold him fast.
²³He will die for lack of discipline,
    led astray by his own great folly.

Warnings Against Folly

6 My son, if you have put up security for
    your neighbor,
    if you have struck hands in pledge for
      another,
²if you have been trapped by what you said,
    ensnared by the words of your mouth,
³then do this, my son, to free yourself,
    since you have fallen into your neighbor's
      hands:
  Go and humble yourself;
    press your plea with your neighbor!
⁴Allow no sleep to your eyes,
    no slumber to your eyelids.
⁵Free yourself, like a gazelle from the hand of
    the hunter,
    like a bird from the snare of the fowler.

⁶Go to the ant, you sluggard;
    consider its ways and be wise!
⁷It has no commander,
    no overseer or ruler,
⁸yet it stores its provisions in summer
    and gathers its food at harvest.

⁹How long will you lie there, you sluggard?
    When will you get up from your sleep?
¹⁰A little sleep, a little slumber,
    a little folding of the hands to rest—
¹¹and poverty will come on you like a bandit
    and scarcity like an armed man.^{*a*}

¹²A scoundrel and villain,
    who goes about with a corrupt mouth,
¹³ who winks with his eye,
    signals with his feet
    and motions with his fingers,
¹⁴ who plots evil with deceit in his heart—
    he always stirs up dissension.
¹⁵Therefore disaster will overtake him in an
      instant;
    he will suddenly be destroyed—without
      remedy.

¹⁶There are six things the LORD hates,
    seven that are detestable to him:
¹⁷   haughty eyes,
    a lying tongue,
    hands that shed innocent blood,
¹⁸   a heart that devises wicked schemes,
    feet that are quick to rush into evil,
¹⁹   a false witness who pours out lies
    and a man who stirs up dissension
      among brothers.

Warning Against Adultery

²⁰My son, keep your father's commands
    and do not forsake your mother's teaching.
²¹Bind them upon your heart forever;
    fasten them around your neck.
²²When you walk, they will guide you;
    when you sleep, they will watch over you;
    when you awake, they will speak to you.
²³For these commands are a lamp,
    this teaching is a light,
  and the corrections of discipline
    are the way to life,
²⁴keeping you from the immoral woman,
    from the smooth tongue of the wayward
      wife.

a 11 Or like a vagrant / and scarcity like a beggar

25 Do not lust in your heart after her beauty
　　or let her captivate you with her eyes,
26 for the prostitute reduces you to a loaf of
　　bread,
　　and the adulteress preys upon your very
　　life.
27 Can a man scoop fire into his lap
　　without his clothes being burned?
28 Can a man walk on hot coals
　　without his feet being scorched?
29 So is he who sleeps with another man's wife;
　　no one who touches her will go
　　unpunished.

30 Men do not despise a thief if he steals
　　to satisfy his hunger when he is starving.
31 Yet if he is caught, he must pay sevenfold,
　　though it costs him all the wealth of his
　　house.
32 But a man who commits adultery lacks
　　judgment;
　　whoever does so destroys himself.
33 Blows and disgrace are his lot,
　　and his shame will never be wiped away;
34 for jealousy arouses a husband's fury,
　　and he will show no mercy when he takes
　　revenge.
35 He will not accept any compensation;
　　he will refuse the bribe, however great it is.

Warning Against the Adulteress

7 My son, keep my words
　　and store up my commands within you.

2 Keep my commands and you will live;
　　guard my teachings as the apple of your
　　eye.
3 Bind them on your fingers;
　　write them on the tablet of your heart.
4 Say to wisdom, "You are my sister,"
　　and call understanding your kinsman;
5 they will keep you from the adulteress,
　　from the wayward wife with her seductive
　　words.

6 At the window of my house
　　I looked out through the lattice.
7 I saw among the simple,
　　I noticed among the young men,
　　a youth who lacked judgment.
8 He was going down the street near her corner,
　　walking along in the direction of her house
9 at twilight, as the day was fading,
　　as the dark of night set in.

10 Then out came a woman to meet him,
　　dressed like a prostitute and with crafty
　　intent.
11 (She is loud and defiant,
　　her feet never stay at home;
12 now in the street, now in the squares,
　　at every corner she lurks.)
13 She took hold of him and kissed him
　　and with a brazen face she said:

14 "I have fellowship offerings *a* at home;
　　today I fulfilled my vows.
15 So I came out to meet you;
　　I looked for you and have found you!
16 I have covered my bed
　　with colored linens from Egypt.
17 I have perfumed my bed
　　with myrrh, aloes and cinnamon.
18 Come, let's drink deep of love till morning;
　　let's enjoy ourselves with love!
19 My husband is not at home;
　　he has gone on a long journey.
20 He took his purse filled with money
　　and will not be home till full moon."

a 14 Traditionally *peace offerings*

²¹With persuasive words she led him astray;
    she seduced him with her smooth talk.
²²All at once he followed her
    like an ox going to the slaughter,
    like a deer *a* stepping into a noose *b*
²³   till an arrow pierces his liver,
    like a bird darting into a snare,
      little knowing it will cost him his life.

²⁴Now then, my sons, listen to me;
    pay attention to what I say.
²⁵Do not let your heart turn to her ways
    or stray into her paths.
²⁶Many are the victims she has brought down;
    her slain are a mighty throng.
²⁷Her house is a highway to the grave, *c*
    leading down to the chambers of death.

Wisdom's Call

8 Does not wisdom call out?
    Does not understanding raise her voice?
²On the heights along the way,
    where the paths meet, she takes her stand;
³beside the gates leading into the city,
    at the entrances, she cries aloud:
⁴"To you, O men, I call out;
    I raise my voice to all mankind.
⁵You who are simple, gain prudence;
    you who are foolish, gain understanding.
⁶Listen, for I have worthy things to say;
    I open my lips to speak what is right.
⁷My mouth speaks what is true,
    for my lips detest wickedness.
⁸All the words of my mouth are just;
    none of them is crooked or perverse.
⁹To the discerning all of them are right;
    they are faultless to those who have
      knowledge.
¹⁰Choose my instruction instead of silver,
    knowledge rather than choice gold,
¹¹for wisdom is more precious than rubies,
    and nothing you desire can compare with
      her.

¹²"I, wisdom, dwell together with prudence;
    I possess knowledge and discretion.
¹³To fear the LORD is to hate evil;
    I hate pride and arrogance,
      evil behavior and perverse speech.
¹⁴Counsel and sound judgment are mine;
    I have understanding and power.
¹⁵By me kings reign
    and rulers make laws that are just;
¹⁶by me princes govern,
    and all nobles who rule on earth. *d*
¹⁷I love those who love me,
    and those who seek me find me.
¹⁸With me are riches and honor,
    enduring wealth and prosperity.
¹⁹My fruit is better than fine gold;
    what I yield surpasses choice silver.
²⁰I walk in the way of righteousness,
    along the paths of justice,
²¹bestowing wealth on those who love me
    and making their treasuries full.

²²"The LORD brought me forth as the first of
      his works, *e,f*
    before his deeds of old;
²³I was appointed *g* from eternity,
    from the beginning, before the world
      began.
²⁴When there were no oceans, I was given
      birth,
    when there were no springs abounding
      with water;
²⁵before the mountains were settled in place,
    before the hills, I was given birth,
²⁶before he made the earth or its fields
    or any of the dust of the world.
²⁷I was there when he set the heavens in place,
    when he marked out the horizon on the
      face of the deep,
²⁸when he established the clouds above
    and fixed securely the fountains of the
      deep,

---

a 22 Syriac (see also Septuagint); Hebrew *fool*   *b 22* The meaning
of the Hebrew for this line is uncertain.   *c 27* Hebrew *Sheol*
d 16 Many Hebrew manuscripts and Septuagint; most Hebrew
manuscripts *and nobles — all righteous rulers*   *e 22* Or *way*; or
dominion   *f 22* Or *The LORD possessed me at the beginning of
his work*; or *The LORD brought me forth at the beginning of his work*
g 23 Or *fashioned*

²⁹ when he gave the sea its boundary
    so the waters would not overstep his
        command,
    and when he marked out the foundations of
        the earth.
³⁰   Then I was the craftsman at his side.
    I was filled with delight day after day,
        rejoicing always in his presence,
³¹ rejoicing in his whole world
    and delighting in mankind.

³² "Now then, my sons, listen to me;
    blessed are those who keep my ways.
³³ Listen to my instruction and be wise;
    do not ignore it.
³⁴ Blessed is the man who listens to me,
    watching daily at my doors,
        waiting at my doorway.
³⁵ For whoever finds me finds life
    and receives favor from the LORD.
³⁶ But whoever fails to find me harms himself;
    all who hate me love death."

Invitations of Wisdom and of Folly

9 Wisdom has built her house;
    she has hewn out its seven pillars.
² She has prepared her meat and mixed her
        wine;
    she has also set her table.
³ She has sent out her maids, and she calls
    from the highest point of the city.
⁴ "Let all who are simple come in here!"
    she says to those who lack judgment.
⁵ "Come, eat my food
    and drink the wine I have mixed.
⁶ Leave your simple ways and you will live;
    walk in the way of understanding.

⁷ "Whoever corrects a mocker invites insult;
    whoever rebukes a wicked man incurs
        abuse.
⁸ Do not rebuke a mocker or he will hate you;
    rebuke a wise man and he will love you.
⁹ Instruct a wise man and he will be wiser still;
    teach a righteous man and he will add to
        his learning.

¹⁰ "The fear of the LORD is the beginning of
        wisdom,
    and knowledge of the Holy One is
        understanding.
¹¹ For through me your days will be many,
    and years will be added to your life.
¹² If you are wise, your wisdom will reward you;
    if you are a mocker, you alone will suffer."

¹³ The woman Folly is loud;
    she is undisciplined and without
        knowledge.
¹⁴ She sits at the door of her house,
    on a seat at the highest point of the city,
¹⁵ calling out to those who pass by,
    who go straight on their way.
¹⁶ "Let all who are simple come in here!"
    she says to those who lack judgment.
¹⁷ "Stolen water is sweet;
    food eaten in secret is delicious!"
¹⁸ But little do they know that the dead are
        there,
    that her guests are in the depths of the
        grave.ᵃ

Proverbs of Solomon

10 The proverbs of Solomon:

    A wise son brings joy to his father,
        but a foolish son grief to his mother.

² Ill-gotten treasures are of no value,
    but righteousness delivers from death.

³ The LORD does not let the righteous go
        hungry
    but he thwarts the craving of the wicked.

⁴ Lazy hands make a man poor,
    but diligent hands bring wealth.

⁵ He who gathers crops in summer is a wise
        son,
    but he who sleeps during harvest is a
        disgraceful son.

ᵃ 18 Hebrew Sheol

THE MEMORY OF THE RIGHTEOUS
WILL BE A BLESSING.
Proverbs 10:7

Making Memories

QUIN SHERRER

READ | PROVERBS 10:1 – 11

Remember when? The Hebrew people were told continually to remember certain events and people. Today we read those memories in the Bible.

Grandmothers can generate precious memories and give their grandchildren a priceless spiritual legacy too. Special moments may be spontaneous or come through planned activities. Remember memories of your grandmother?

"She was gentle and kind to me," a friend said, reflecting on her grandmother. "I learned much from her about the Christian faith. She was always swift to let me know right from wrong. I often walked, picked cherries or just sat with her, listening to the stories she told."

"My granny was a woman of character, faith and determination," another told me. "When her husband died, leaving her with two children, she put herself through college and taught second grade until her retirement. She possessed that same 'no quit' attitude with the Lord's work. She taught Sunday school even at the age of 80. After she lost her vision, she kept on crocheting afghans for all of her grandchildren and great-grandchildren. Her legacy speaks volumes to me and has helped mold me into a woman of faith with the same 'no quit' determination as my granny."

Like many grandmothers, my friend Gege loves to gather her three grandchildren in her kitchen and teach them to bake. She's been doing this since they were knee high. She took pictures of the first egg Grant cracked, the pie crust Bethanie rolled, the cookies Mackenzie deco-rated. As the years passed they graduated from desserts to sandwiches, soups and dinners. Each time they cooked, she snapped their photo. She later made each one a "Memory Cookbook" with the recipes written out and a picture of that grandchild on the day he or she made that special dish.

Memories are a keepsake forever in our hearts.

Thank you, Lord, for happy memories of our grandmothers. Give me creative ways to make sweet memories even now for my grandchildren. Amen.

Your next devotion is located on page 862.

GRANDCHILD IN FOCUS • PRAYER

Courage

O Father, builder of character and courage, may my grandchild grow strong in the light of your love. Grant him courage to stand for what is right, to guard the truth and to ensure justice in every aspect of life. May he boldly grow in grace, revere your name and proudly proclaim you as the Lord of lords and King of kings. Amen.

857

6 Blessings crown the head of the righteous,
   but violence overwhelms the mouth of the
     wicked. *a*

7 The memory of the righteous will be a
     blessing,
   but the name of the wicked will rot.

8 The wise in heart accept commands,
   but a chattering fool comes to ruin.

9 The man of integrity walks securely,
   but he who takes crooked paths will be
     found out.

10 He who winks maliciously causes grief,
   and a chattering fool comes to ruin.

11 The mouth of the righteous is a fountain of
     life,
   but violence overwhelms the mouth of the
     wicked.

12 Hatred stirs up dissension,
   but love covers over all wrongs.

13 Wisdom is found on the lips of the
     discerning,
   but a rod is for the back of him who lacks
     judgment.

14 Wise men store up knowledge,
   but the mouth of a fool invites ruin.

15 The wealth of the rich is their fortified city,
   but poverty is the ruin of the poor.

16 The wages of the righteous bring them life,
   but the income of the wicked brings them
     punishment.

17 He who heeds discipline shows the way to
     life,
   but whoever ignores correction leads
     others astray.

18 He who conceals his hatred has lying lips,
   and whoever spreads slander is a fool.

19 When words are many, sin is not absent,
   but he who holds his tongue is wise.

20 The tongue of the righteous is choice silver,
   but the heart of the wicked is of little value.

21 The lips of the righteous nourish many,
   but fools die for lack of judgment.

22 The blessing of the LORD brings wealth,
   and he adds no trouble to it.

23 A fool finds pleasure in evil conduct,
   but a man of understanding delights in
     wisdom.

24 What the wicked dreads will overtake him;
   what the righteous desire will be granted.

25 When the storm has swept by, the wicked are
     gone,
   but the righteous stand firm forever.

26 As vinegar to the teeth and smoke to the eyes,
   so is a sluggard to those who send him.

27 The fear of the LORD adds length to life,
   but the years of the wicked are cut short.

28 The prospect of the righteous is joy,
   but the hopes of the wicked come to
     nothing.

29 The way of the LORD is a refuge for the
     righteous,
   but it is the ruin of those who do evil.

30 The righteous will never be uprooted,
   but the wicked will not remain in the land.

31 The mouth of the righteous brings forth
     wisdom,
   but a perverse tongue will be cut out.

32 The lips of the righteous know what is fitting,
   but the mouth of the wicked only what is
     perverse.

11 The LORD abhors dishonest scales,
   but accurate weights are his delight.

2 When pride comes, then comes disgrace,
   but with humility comes wisdom.

---

a 6 Or *but the mouth of the wicked conceals violence*; also in verse 11

³ The integrity of the upright guides them,
but the unfaithful are destroyed by their
duplicity.

⁴ Wealth is worthless in the day of wrath,
but righteousness delivers from death.

⁵ The righteousness of the blameless makes a
straight way for them,
but the wicked are brought down by their
own wickedness.

⁶ The righteousness of the upright delivers
them,
but the unfaithful are trapped by evil desires.

⁷ When a wicked man dies, his hope perishes;
all he expected from his power comes to
nothing.

⁸ The righteous man is rescued from trouble,
and it comes on the wicked instead.

⁹ With his mouth the godless destroys his
neighbor,
but through knowledge the righteous
escape.

¹⁰ When the righteous prosper, the city rejoices;
when the wicked perish, there are shouts
of joy.

¹¹ Through the blessing of the upright a city is
exalted,
but by the mouth of the wicked it is
destroyed.

¹² A man who lacks judgment derides his
neighbor,
but a man of understanding holds his
tongue.

¹³ A gossip betrays a confidence,
but a trustworthy man keeps a secret.

¹⁴ For lack of guidance a nation falls,
but many advisers make victory sure.

¹⁵ He who puts up security for another will
surely suffer,
but whoever refuses to strike hands in
pledge is safe.

TALKING POINTS

Gossip

Don't betray a confidence or
reveal a secret.

PROVERBS 11:13

For more on gossip, go to Proverbs 16:23–24,28.

¹⁶ A kindhearted woman gains respect,
but ruthless men gain only wealth.

¹⁷ A kind man benefits himself,
but a cruel man brings trouble on
himself.

¹⁸ The wicked man earns deceptive wages,
but he who sows righteousness reaps a sure
reward.

¹⁹ The truly righteous man attains life,
but he who pursues evil goes to his death.

²⁰ The LORD detests men of perverse heart
but he delights in those whose ways are
blameless.

²¹ Be sure of this: The wicked will not go
unpunished,
but those who are righteous will go free.

²² Like a gold ring in a pig's snout
is a beautiful woman who shows no
discretion.

²³ The desire of the righteous ends only in
good,
but the hope of the wicked only in wrath.

²⁴ One man gives freely, yet gains even more;
another withholds unduly, but comes to
poverty.

²⁵ A generous man will prosper;
he who refreshes others will himself be
refreshed.

26 People curse the man who hoards grain,
but blessing crowns him who is willing to
sell.

27 He who seeks good finds goodwill,
but evil comes to him who searches for it.

28 Whoever trusts in his riches will fall,
but the righteous will thrive like a green
leaf.

29 He who brings trouble on his family will
inherit only wind,
and the fool will be servant to the wise.

30 The fruit of the righteous is a tree of life,
and he who wins souls is wise.

31 If the righteous receive their due on earth,
how much more the ungodly and the
sinner!

12 Whoever loves discipline loves
knowledge,
but he who hates correction is stupid.

2 A good man obtains favor from the LORD,
but the LORD condemns a crafty man.

3 A man cannot be established through
wickedness,
but the righteous cannot be uprooted.

4 A wife of noble character is her husband's
crown,
but a disgraceful wife is like decay in his
bones.

5 The plans of the righteous are just,
but the advice of the wicked is deceitful.

6 The words of the wicked lie in wait for blood,
but the speech of the upright rescues
them.

7 Wicked men are overthrown and are no
more,
but the house of the righteous stands firm.

8 A man is praised according to his wisdom,
but men with warped minds are despised.

9 Better to be a nobody and yet have a servant
than pretend to be somebody and have no
food.

10 A righteous man cares for the needs of his
animal,
but the kindest acts of the wicked are cruel.

11 He who works his land will have abundant
food,
but he who chases fantasies lacks
judgment.

12 The wicked desire the plunder of evil men,
but the root of the righteous flourishes.

13 An evil man is trapped by his sinful talk,
but a righteous man escapes trouble.

14 From the fruit of his lips a man is filled with
good things
as surely as the work of his hands rewards
him.

15 The way of a fool seems right to him,
but a wise man listens to advice.

16 A fool shows his annoyance at once,
but a prudent man overlooks an insult.

17 A truthful witness gives honest testimony,
but a false witness tells lies.

18 Reckless words pierce like a sword,
but the tongue of the wise brings healing.

19 Truthful lips endure forever,
but a lying tongue lasts only a moment.

20 There is deceit in the hearts of those who plot
evil,
but joy for those who promote peace.

21 No harm befalls the righteous,
but the wicked have their fill of trouble.

22 The LORD detests lying lips,
but he delights in men who are truthful.

23 A prudent man keeps his knowledge to
himself,
but the heart of fools blurts out folly.

²⁴ Diligent hands will rule,
    but laziness ends in slave labor.

²⁵ An anxious heart weighs a man down,
    but a kind word cheers him up.

²⁶ A righteous man is cautious in friendship,ᵃ
    but the way of the wicked leads them
     astray.

²⁷ The lazy man does not roastᵇ his game,
    but the diligent man prizes his possessions.

²⁸ In the way of righteousness there is life;
    along that path is immortality.

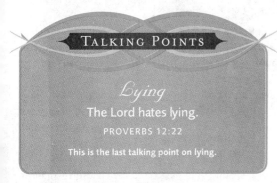

TALKING POINTS

Lying

The Lord hates lying.

PROVERBS 12:22

This is the last talking point on lying.

13 A wise son heeds his father's instruction,
    but a mocker does not listen to rebuke.

² From the fruit of his lips a man enjoys good
    things,
    but the unfaithful have a craving for
     violence.

³ He who guards his lips guards his life,
    but he who speaks rashly will come to
     ruin.

⁴ The sluggard craves and gets nothing,
    but the desires of the diligent are fully
     satisfied.

⁵ The righteous hate what is false,
    but the wicked bring shame and disgrace.

⁶ Righteousness guards the man of integrity,
    but wickedness overthrows the sinner.

⁷ One man pretends to be rich, yet has nothing;
    another pretends to be poor, yet has great
     wealth.

⁸ A man's riches may ransom his life,
    but a poor man hears no threat.

⁹ The light of the righteous shines brightly,
    but the lamp of the wicked is snuffed out.

¹⁰ Pride only breeds quarrels,
    but wisdom is found in those who take
     advice.

¹¹ Dishonest money dwindles away,
    but he who gathers money little by little
     makes it grow.

¹² Hope deferred makes the heart sick,
    but a longing fulfilled is a tree of life.

¹³ He who scorns instruction will pay for it,
    but he who respects a command is
     rewarded.

¹⁴ The teaching of the wise is a fountain of life,
    turning a man from the snares of death.

¹⁵ Good understanding wins favor,
    but the way of the unfaithful is hard.ᶜ

¹⁶ Every prudent man acts out of knowledge,
    but a fool exposes his folly.

¹⁷ A wicked messenger falls into trouble,
    but a trustworthy envoy brings healing.

¹⁸ He who ignores discipline comes to poverty
    and shame,
    but whoever heeds correction is honored.

¹⁹ A longing fulfilled is sweet to the soul,
    but fools detest turning from evil.

²⁰ He who walks with the wise grows wise,
    but a companion of fools suffers harm.

²¹ Misfortune pursues the sinner,
    but prosperity is the reward of the
     righteous.

ᵃ 26 Or *man is a guide to his neighbor*   ᵇ 27 The meaning of the
Hebrew for this word is uncertain.   ᶜ 15 Or *unfaithful does not
endure*

> A GOOD MAN LEAVES AN
> INHERITANCE FOR HIS
> CHILDREN'S CHILDREN.
>
> *Proverbs 13:22*

Who's Gonna Teach My Children's Children?

DOTTIE RAMBO

READ | PROVERBS 13:14 – 25

I've always loved to cook. It's something that touches people — a gift of hospitality that comes alive when friends and family pull up a chair and eat their fill.

My oldest grandbaby, Destiny, was always drawn to this gift. At my house she'd run in the kitchen and ask if she could help. "What does my grandbaby want to make?" I'd ask. "Cheese and noodles, GranDot!" she would sing in response. Cheese and noodles was her name for what we all know as macaroni and cheese. And she wouldn't hear it any other way.

So out came the cookware, spoons, noodles, cheeses and a dish to bake it in. (I would never have thought to make it from a box!) I'd talk little Des through preparing the pasta noodles and mixing our special cheeses, and make sure she didn't get burned on the oven. My beautiful granddaughter would clap and sing through each second. It was a special, special time for us. And it always came out just right.

I believe that our precious Lord opened these doors, so I could pass on to my children's children some of the talents he has given me.

Now that she's a young lady, I see the gifts I planted blossoming. She is not only an incredible performer and songwriter, but a fantastic hostess too. You barely have to lift a finger when visiting her house.

And if I'm coming over, she'll make sure there's extra "cheese and noodles."

Precious Lord, stir up the abilities you've given me so that I can pass them on to my children's children. I want your gifts to go on and on. In the holy name of Jesus, amen.

Your next devotion is located on page 867.

GRANDCHILD IN FOCUS • PRAYER

Future Spouse

Dear Lord, if it is your will, I pray my grandchild will be united in a loving and Christian marriage. Keep her sexually pure so that she will honor you with her body and mind. As she seeks a spouse who will honor and care for her, give her patience and discernment. May her choice for a life partner be your choice for her, so that she and her husband will together glorify you in a lasting love. I pray this in Jesus' name, amen.

²²A good man leaves an inheritance for his
  children's children,
  but a sinner's wealth is stored up for the
  righteous.

²³A poor man's field may produce abundant
  food,
  but injustice sweeps it away.

²⁴He who spares the rod hates his son,
  but he who loves him is careful to
  discipline him.

²⁵The righteous eat to their hearts' content,
  but the stomach of the wicked goes
  hungry.

14 The wise woman builds her house,
  but with her own hands the foolish one
  tears hers down.

²He whose walk is upright fears the LORD,
  but he whose ways are devious despises
  him.

³A fool's talk brings a rod to his back,
  but the lips of the wise protect them.

⁴Where there are no oxen, the manger is
  empty,
  but from the strength of an ox comes an
  abundant harvest.

⁵A truthful witness does not deceive,
  but a false witness pours out lies.

⁶The mocker seeks wisdom and finds none,
  but knowledge comes easily to the
  discerning.

⁷Stay away from a foolish man,
  for you will not find knowledge on his lips.

⁸The wisdom of the prudent is to give thought
  to their ways,
  but the folly of fools is deception.

⁹Fools mock at making amends for sin,
  but goodwill is found among the upright.

¹⁰Each heart knows its own bitterness,
  and no one else can share its joy.

¹¹The house of the wicked will be destroyed,
  but the tent of the upright will flourish.

¹²There is a way that seems right to a man,
  but in the end it leads to death.

¹³Even in laughter the heart may ache,
  and joy may end in grief.

¹⁴The faithless will be fully repaid for their
  ways,
  and the good man rewarded for his.

¹⁵A simple man believes anything,
  but a prudent man gives thought to his
  steps.

¹⁶A wise man fears the LORD and shuns evil,
  but a fool is hotheaded and reckless.

¹⁷A quick-tempered man does foolish things,
  and a crafty man is hated.

¹⁸The simple inherit folly,
  but the prudent are crowned with
  knowledge.

¹⁹Evil men will bow down in the presence of
  the good,
  and the wicked at the gates of the
  righteous.

²⁰The poor are shunned even by their
  neighbors,
  but the rich have many friends.

²¹He who despises his neighbor sins,
  but blessed is he who is kind to the needy.

²²Do not those who plot evil go astray?
  But those who plan what is good find ᵃ love
  and faithfulness.

²³All hard work brings a profit,
  but mere talk leads only to poverty.

²⁴The wealth of the wise is their crown,
  but the folly of fools yields folly.

²⁵A truthful witness saves lives,
  but a false witness is deceitful.

ᵃ 22 Or show

²⁶ He who fears the LORD has a secure fortress,
  and for his children it will be a refuge.

²⁷ The fear of the LORD is a fountain of life,
  turning a man from the snares of death.

²⁸ A large population is a king's glory,
  but without subjects a prince is ruined.

²⁹ A patient man has great understanding,
  but a quick-tempered man displays folly.

TALKING POINTS

Patience

To be patient is to be wise.

PROVERBS 14:29

For more on patience, go to Ecclesiastes 7:8.

---

³⁰ A heart at peace gives life to the body,
  but envy rots the bones.

³¹ He who oppresses the poor shows contempt
    for their Maker,
  but whoever is kind to the needy honors
    God.

³² When calamity comes, the wicked are
    brought down,
  but even in death the righteous have a
    refuge.

³³ Wisdom reposes in the heart of the discerning
  and even among fools she lets herself be
    known. ᵃ

³⁴ Righteousness exalts a nation,
  but sin is a disgrace to any people.

³⁵ A king delights in a wise servant,
  but a shameful servant incurs his wrath.

15 A gentle answer turns away wrath,
  but a harsh word stirs up anger.

² The tongue of the wise commends
    knowledge,
  but the mouth of the fool gushes folly.

³ The eyes of the LORD are everywhere,
  keeping watch on the wicked and the good.

⁴ The tongue that brings healing is a tree of
    life,
  but a deceitful tongue crushes the spirit.

⁵ A fool spurns his father's discipline,
  but whoever heeds correction shows
    prudence.

⁶ The house of the righteous contains great
    treasure,
  but the income of the wicked brings them
    trouble.

⁷ The lips of the wise spread knowledge;
  not so the hearts of fools.

⁸ The LORD detests the sacrifice of the wicked,
  but the prayer of the upright pleases him.

⁹ The LORD detests the way of the wicked
  but he loves those who pursue
    righteousness.

¹⁰ Stern discipline awaits him who leaves the
    path;
  he who hates correction will die.

¹¹ Death and Destruction ᵇ lie open before the
    LORD —
  how much more the hearts of men!

¹² A mocker resents correction;
  he will not consult the wise.

¹³ A happy heart makes the face cheerful,
  but heartache crushes the spirit.

¹⁴ The discerning heart seeks knowledge,
  but the mouth of a fool feeds on folly.

¹⁵ All the days of the oppressed are wretched,
  but the cheerful heart has a continual feast.

ᵃ 33 Hebrew; Septuagint and Syriac / but in the heart of fools she is
not known   ᵇ 11 Hebrew Sheol and Abaddon

¹⁶ Better a little with the fear of the LORD
  than great wealth with turmoil.

¹⁷ Better a meal of vegetables where there is love
  than a fattened calf with hatred.

TALKING POINTS

Contentment

Contentment brings perspective to life.

PROVERBS 15:13,15–17

For more on contentment, go to Proverbs 30:8–9.

---

¹⁸ A hot-tempered man stirs up dissension,
  but a patient man calms a quarrel.

¹⁹ The way of the sluggard is blocked with
    thorns,
  but the path of the upright is a highway.

²⁰ A wise son brings joy to his father,
  but a foolish man despises his mother.

²¹ Folly delights a man who lacks judgment,
  but a man of understanding keeps a
    straight course.

²² Plans fail for lack of counsel,
  but with many advisers they succeed.

²³ A man finds joy in giving an apt reply—
  and how good is a timely word!

²⁴ The path of life leads upward for the wise
  to keep him from going down to the grave.ᵃ

²⁵ The LORD tears down the proud man's house
  but he keeps the widow's boundaries
    intact.

²⁶ The LORD detests the thoughts of the wicked,
  but those of the pure are pleasing to him.

²⁷ A greedy man brings trouble to his family,
  but he who hates bribes will live.

²⁸ The heart of the righteous weighs its answers,
  but the mouth of the wicked gushes evil.

²⁹ The LORD is far from the wicked
  but he hears the prayer of the righteous.

³⁰ A cheerful look brings joy to the heart,
  and good news gives health to the bones.

³¹ He who listens to a life-giving rebuke
  will be at home among the wise.

³² He who ignores discipline despises himself,
  but whoever heeds correction gains
    understanding.

³³ The fear of the LORD teaches a man wisdom,ᵇ
  and humility comes before honor.

16 To man belong the plans of the heart,
  but from the LORD comes the reply of
    the tongue.

² All a man's ways seem innocent to him,
  but motives are weighed by the LORD.

³ Commit to the LORD whatever you do,
  and your plans will succeed.

⁴ The LORD works out everything for his own
    ends—
  even the wicked for a day of disaster.

⁵ The LORD detests all the proud of heart.
  Be sure of this: They will not go
    unpunished.

⁶ Through love and faithfulness sin is atoned
    for;
  through the fear of the LORD a man avoids
    evil.

⁷ When a man's ways are pleasing to the LORD,
  he makes even his enemies live at peace
    with him.

⁸ Better a little with righteousness
  than much gain with injustice.

⁹ In his heart a man plans his course,
  but the LORD determines his steps.

ᵃ 24 Hebrew *Sheol*   ᵇ 33 Or *Wisdom teaches the fear of the* LORD

¹⁰ The lips of a king speak as an oracle,
    and his mouth should not betray justice.

¹¹ Honest scales and balances are from the
        LORD;
    all the weights in the bag are of his
        making.

¹² Kings detest wrongdoing,
    for a throne is established through
        righteousness.

¹³ Kings take pleasure in honest lips;
    they value a man who speaks the truth.

¹⁴ A king's wrath is a messenger of death,
    but a wise man will appease it.

¹⁵ When a king's face brightens, it means life;
    his favor is like a rain cloud in spring.

¹⁶ How much better to get wisdom than gold,
    to choose understanding rather than silver!

¹⁷ The highway of the upright avoids evil;
    he who guards his way guards his life.

¹⁸ Pride goes before destruction,
    a haughty spirit before a fall.

¹⁹ Better to be lowly in spirit and among the
        oppressed
    than to share plunder with the proud.

²⁰ Whoever gives heed to instruction prospers,
    and blessed is he who trusts in the LORD.

²¹ The wise in heart are called discerning,
    and pleasant words promote instruction.ᵃ

²² Understanding is a fountain of life to those
        who have it,
    but folly brings punishment to fools.

²³ A wise man's heart guides his mouth,
    and his lips promote instruction.ᵇ

²⁴ Pleasant words are a honeycomb,
    sweet to the soul and healing to the bones.

²⁵ There is a way that seems right to a man,
    but in the end it leads to death.

²⁶ The laborer's appetite works for him;
    his hunger drives him on.

²⁷ A scoundrel plots evil,
    and his speech is like a scorching fire.

²⁸ A perverse man stirs up dissension,
    and a gossip separates close friends.

²⁹ A violent man entices his neighbor
    and leads him down a path that is not
        good.

³⁰ He who winks with his eye is plotting
        perversity;
    he who purses his lips is bent on evil.

³¹ Gray hair is a crown of splendor;
    it is attained by a righteous life.

³² Better a patient man than a warrior,
    a man who controls his temper than one
        who takes a city.

³³ The lot is cast into the lap,
    but its every decision is from the LORD.

TALKING POINTS

Gossip

We are wise to watch what we say.
Gossip destroys friendships.

PROVERBS 16:23–24,28

For more on gossip, go to Proverbs 20:19.

17 Better a dry crust with peace and quiet
    than a house full of feasting,ᶜ with strife.

² A wise servant will rule over a disgraceful
        son,
    and will share the inheritance as one of the
        brothers.

ᵃ 21 Or words make a man persuasive   ᵇ 23 Or mouth / and makes
his lips persuasive   ᶜ 1 Hebrew sacrifices

GRAY HAIR IS A CROWN OF
SPLENDOR; IT IS ATTAINED
BY A RIGHTEOUS LIFE.

Proverbs 16:31

Crowns of Splendor

JONI EARECKSON TADA

READ | PROVERBS 16:18–33

When Ken and I were in Russia, we befriended an old woman who cleaned the floors of our hotel lobby every day. Through an interpreter, we complimented her on doing an excellent job. Old and wrinkled, her round and red cheeks were framed with a tightly-knotted, colorful scarf. Her face sparkled with her blue eyes and golden-toothed smile. She had on layers of skirts and wore leggings and boots. With broom in hand, our elderly friend looked out of place in the hotel lobby; maybe that's why we were drawn to her.

We met many Russian "babushkas" like her. The praying grandmothers, they were called. These were the stalwart saints of whom Stalin had cruelly said, "If we can get rid of these old women, we will have the youth in our grasp."

Stalin failed. And thank God for praying grandmothers who served as a link, spanning a generation lost to atheism and connecting a new generation of young people who are asking open, honest questions about Jesus.

How grateful we can be to elderly saints who make prayer a life vocation. One day eternity shall reveal how far and wide Christ's gospel was advanced through the faithful prayers of old, faithful Christians.

If you have even one gray hair, you could almost qualify for Proverbs 16:31. But is your life a righteous one, hallmarked by the kind of intercessory prayer so many elderly saints offer to the Lord?

Praise God for that person over the age of sixty-five whom you know, a friend who still trusts the Lord despite arthritis, wrinkles and poor vision. These who wear a crown of splendor need our prayers too.

Father of all ages, as gray hairs abound, may righteousness abound. May I never resent the encroaching years but view them as an opportunity to deepen my life of praise and intercession.

Your next devotion is located on page 868.

GRANDCHILD IN FOCUS • PRAYER

School/Career

Dear God, may learning be a joy rather than a chore for my grandchild. May exploration of new ideas bring a sense of wonder, awe and excitement. Grant him clarity of mind, the ability to concentrate on the task at hand and recollection of what has been learned. Help him to appreciate the tasks that come easily and to persevere through those that challenge. Amen.

Playing Make-Believe

Younger children love nothing more than playing make-believe, especially if you're involved. Allow the kids to set up a scenario and assign roles, whether you'll be playing house, school or church — or acting out some known story (probably with liberal variations). If Grandpa is interested, invite him to join in as well.

Find a variety of items to use as props and costumes. You may want to keep a supply of old clothes and hats for costumes, and sheets or blankets to use in creating houses and tents. Perhaps your grandchildren would like to pretend they lived "way back when" you were a child. Tell them some stories ahead of time so they get some ideas of what your life was like. Videotape your "play" if you have the equipment.

Older-Grandkids Variation: Have your grandkids write down or reenact some of the stories that you've told them about your childhood. If they prefer, let them embellish the tale to make believe they were there with you.

Long-Distance Variation: Invite all the kids to write their version of the stories they have heard you tell about your childhood. Let them embellish as much as they like to give you a good laugh.

Dear God, thank you for our imaginations. Let us enjoy the time we have together to explore our ideas and to laugh. Bless my grandchildren in everything they do. Amen.

Your next devotion is located on page 869.

GRANDCHILD IN FOCUS • PRAYER

Character

Dear Lord and Father, I ask that you fill my grandchild with your Spirit so her character reflects your goodness and love. Give her kindness and love for others. Bring joy to her life so she will be a joy to others. Grant her patience and self-control through difficult and trying times. May she show mercy and generosity to those who are less fortunate. Grant her integrity and a sense of justice, and surround her with your peace. Amen.

Worship the Lord

The LORD is faithful to all his promises
    and loving toward all he has made.
The LORD upholds all those who fall
    and lifts up all who are bowed down.
The eyes of all look to you,
    and you give them their food at the proper time.
You open your hand
    and satisfy the desires of every living thing.

The LORD is righteous in all his ways
    and loving toward all he has made.
The LORD is near to all who call on him,
    to all who call on him in truth.

My mouth will speak in praise of the LORD.
    Let every creature praise his holy
        name
    for ever and ever.

Psalm 145:13b – 18, 21

Dear Lord and Father, your love surrounds me and fills my life through the food I eat, the home I live in and the work I do. Your generosity satisfies my deepest needs and my greatest desires. May my grateful heart proclaim how good you have been to me. Amen.

Your next devotion is located on page 871.

GRANDCHILD IN FOCUS • PRAYER

Talents

Dear Lord, the giver of gifts, bless my grandchild as he develops his talents. Help him identify his talents and be proud and confident of the gifts you have given him. Give him patience and understanding, Lord, so he will not grow weary of striving and searching to reach the goals you have set for him. May each milestone bring satisfaction and a healthy desire for greater achievement and success to bring glory to you. Amen.

³The crucible for silver and the furnace for
    gold,
  but the LORD tests the heart.

⁴A wicked man listens to evil lips;
  a liar pays attention to a malicious
    tongue.

⁵He who mocks the poor shows contempt
    for their Maker;
  whoever gloats over disaster will not go
    unpunished.

⁶Children's children are a crown to the aged,
  and parents are the pride of their
    children.

⁷Arrogant ᵃ lips are unsuited to a fool—
  how much worse lying lips to a ruler!

⁸A bribe is a charm to the one who gives it;
  wherever he turns, he succeeds.

⁹He who covers over an offense promotes love,
  but whoever repeats the matter separates
    close friends.

¹⁰A rebuke impresses a man of discernment
  more than a hundred lashes a fool.

¹¹An evil man is bent only on rebellion;
  a merciless official will be sent against him.

¹²Better to meet a bear robbed of her cubs
  than a fool in his folly.

¹³If a man pays back evil for good,
  evil will never leave his house.

¹⁴Starting a quarrel is like breaching a dam;
  so drop the matter before a dispute breaks
    out.

¹⁵Acquitting the guilty and condemning the
    innocent—
  the LORD detests them both.

¹⁶Of what use is money in the hand of a fool,
  since he has no desire to get wisdom?

¹⁷A friend loves at all times,
  and a brother is born for adversity.

TALKING POINTS

Friendship
Friends are faithful and reliable.
PROVERBS 17:17
For more on friendship, go to Proverbs 27:9.

¹⁸A man lacking in judgment strikes hands in
    pledge
  and puts up security for his neighbor.

¹⁹He who loves a quarrel loves sin;
  he who builds a high gate invites
    destruction.

²⁰A man of perverse heart does not prosper;
  he whose tongue is deceitful falls into
    trouble.

²¹To have a fool for a son brings grief;
  there is no joy for the father of a fool.

²²A cheerful heart is good medicine,
  but a crushed spirit dries up the bones.

²³A wicked man accepts a bribe in secret
  to pervert the course of justice.

²⁴A discerning man keeps wisdom in view,
  but a fool's eyes wander to the ends of the
    earth.

²⁵A foolish son brings grief to his father
  and bitterness to the one who bore him.

²⁶It is not good to punish an innocent man,
  or to flog officials for their integrity.

²⁷A man of knowledge uses words with restraint,
  and a man of understanding is even-
    tempered.

²⁸Even a fool is thought wise if he keeps silent,
  and discerning if he holds his tongue.

ᵃ 7 Or *Eloquent*

CHILDREN'S CHILDREN ARE
A CROWN TO THE AGED, AND
PARENTS ARE THE PRIDE OF
THEIR CHILDREN.

Proverbs 17:6

Overwhelming Love

LORI COPELAND

READ | PROVERBS 17:1–6

Our third grandson, Joshua Daniel Copeland, threw us a curve ball on February 6, 1990. The typical excited phone call came, alerting the family of the imminent birth. Both sets of grandparents bundled up tightly and headed for the hospital, where we sat for several hours until our son Randy came out and told everyone to go home, because the doctor said the birth wouldn't be until morning.

"Are you sure?" we questioned; we'd been there for James's and Joe's births, and we didn't want to miss this one.

"Morning," Randy verified. "Go home and get some rest."

The anxious grandparents left, braving the cold wind and frosted windshields. We climbed wearily into bed around 1:00 A.M., and at 1:30 the phone rang. You guessed it. Randy was calling from the delivery room, where our third grandson had just decided to make his entrance.

Josh, the little blonde-headed boy who would clomp around in cowboy boots and hat, and manage to shoot a fly's eye out at 30 feet, entered our lives on "a slider." We now had three sons and three grandsons. We began planning for a baseball team.

In my early years, I wondered why God would send his Son to die on a cross for me — for anyone. Then I became a mother — and then a grandmother, and I realized with each birth the overwhelming love and protection I felt for both my children and my grandchildren. The "why" suddenly became clear: There is no stronger love than that of a parent or grandparent. Did God love his Son any less? When you pause to reflect on his sacrifice, his gift to humanity, you fall to your knees in humble gratitude and praise.

Father, you have blessed me with children and grandchildren. I don't know why. I don't question the reason. This I do know: You've given me these precious souls not because I'm worthy but because you are worthy, Lord. Amen.

Your next devotion is located on page 874.

GRANDCHILD IN FOCUS • PRAYER

SELECT ONE OF YOUR
GRANDCHILDREN TO FOCUS ON
IN PRAYER FOR THE NEXT 14 DAYS.

Salvation

Dear Lord, please guide my grandchild to your gift of salvation. I pray that she will come to know you, to love you and to walk close to you throughout her life. May she boldly claim Jesus as her Lord and Savior. Guide her as she makes choices that have eternal consequences. Help her to follow you each moment of her life. I pray this in Jesus' name, amen.

871

18
An unfriendly man pursues selfish ends;
he defies all sound judgment.

2 A fool finds no pleasure in understanding
but delights in airing his own opinions.

3 When wickedness comes, so does contempt,
and with shame comes disgrace.

4 The words of a man's mouth are deep waters,
but the fountain of wisdom is a bubbling
brook.

5 It is not good to be partial to the wicked
or to deprive the innocent of justice.

6 A fool's lips bring him strife,
and his mouth invites a beating.

7 A fool's mouth is his undoing,
and his lips are a snare to his soul.

8 The words of a gossip are like choice morsels;
they go down to a man's inmost parts.

9 One who is slack in his work
is brother to one who destroys.

10 The name of the LORD is a strong tower;
the righteous run to it and are safe.

11 The wealth of the rich is their fortified city;
they imagine it an unscalable wall.

12 Before his downfall a man's heart is proud,
but humility comes before honor.

13 He who answers before listening—
that is his folly and his shame.

14 A man's spirit sustains him in sickness,
but a crushed spirit who can bear?

15 The heart of the discerning acquires
knowledge;
the ears of the wise seek it out.

16 A gift opens the way for the giver
and ushers him into the presence of the
great.

17 The first to present his case seems right,
till another comes forward and questions
him.

18 Casting the lot settles disputes
and keeps strong opponents apart.

19 An offended brother is more unyielding than
a fortified city,
and disputes are like the barred gates of a
citadel.

20 From the fruit of his mouth a man's stomach
is filled;
with the harvest from his lips he is
satisfied.

21 The tongue has the power of life and death,
and those who love it will eat its fruit.

22 He who finds a wife finds what is good
and receives favor from the LORD.

23 A poor man pleads for mercy,
but a rich man answers harshly.

24 A man of many companions may come to
ruin,
but there is a friend who sticks closer than
a brother.

19
Better a poor man whose walk is
blameless
than a fool whose lips are perverse.

2 It is not good to have zeal without
knowledge,
nor to be hasty and miss the way.

3 A man's own folly ruins his life,
yet his heart rages against the LORD.

4 Wealth brings many friends,
but a poor man's friend deserts him.

5 A false witness will not go unpunished,
and he who pours out lies will not go
free.

6 Many curry favor with a ruler,
and everyone is the friend of a man who
gives gifts.

7 A poor man is shunned by all his relatives—
how much more do his friends avoid him!

Though he pursues them with pleading,
  they are nowhere to be found.[a]

8 He who gets wisdom loves his own soul;
  he who cherishes understanding prospers.

9 A false witness will not go unpunished,
  and he who pours out lies will perish.

10 It is not fitting for a fool to live in luxury—
  how much worse for a slave to rule over
  princes!

11 A man's wisdom gives him patience;
  it is to his glory to overlook an offense.

12 A king's rage is like the roar of a lion,
  but his favor is like dew on the grass.

13 A foolish son is his father's ruin,
  and a quarrelsome wife is like a constant
  dripping.

14 Houses and wealth are inherited from
  parents,
  but a prudent wife is from the LORD.

15 Laziness brings on deep sleep,
  and the shiftless man goes hungry.

TALKING POINTS

Laziness

Laziness is destructive.

PROVERBS 19:15

For more on laziness, go to Galatians 6:9.

---

16 He who obeys instructions guards his life,
  but he who is contemptuous of his ways
  will die.

17 He who is kind to the poor lends to the
  LORD,
  and he will reward him for what he has
  done.

18 Discipline your son, for in that there is hope;
  do not be a willing party to his death.

19 A hot-tempered man must pay the penalty;
  if you rescue him, you will have to do it
  again.

20 Listen to advice and accept instruction,
  and in the end you will be wise.

21 Many are the plans in a man's heart,
  but it is the LORD's purpose that prevails.

22 What a man desires is unfailing love[b];
  better to be poor than a liar.

23 The fear of the LORD leads to life:
  Then one rests content, untouched by
  trouble.

24 The sluggard buries his hand in the dish;
  he will not even bring it back to his mouth!

25 Flog a mocker, and the simple will learn
  prudence;
  rebuke a discerning man, and he will gain
  knowledge.

26 He who robs his father and drives out his
  mother
  is a son who brings shame and disgrace.

27 Stop listening to instruction, my son,
  and you will stray from the words of
  knowledge.

28 A corrupt witness mocks at justice,
  and the mouth of the wicked gulps down
  evil.

29 Penalties are prepared for mockers,
  and beatings for the backs of fools.

20 Wine is a mocker and beer a brawler;
  whoever is led astray by them is not
  wise.

2 A king's wrath is like the roar of a lion;
  he who angers him forfeits his life.

---

[a] 7 The meaning of the Hebrew for this sentence is uncertain.
[b] 22 Or A man's greed is his shame

MANY ARE THE PLANS IN A
MAN'S HEART, BUT IT IS THE
LORD'S PURPOSE THAT PREVAILS.

Proverbs 19:21

Following God's Plan

CAROL CYMBALA

READ | PROVERBS 19:16 – 21

It is wonderful to know that in God's will there is safety, peace, joy and purpose. A heart that rejoices in God delights in doing his will. It's true that there are days in our lives when the sun shines brightly and others when clouds darken the skies. But no matter what life brings our way, God is still working on behalf of those who have put their trust in him.

A common mistake among Christians is to follow their own desires and plans, and then ask for God's blessings on the path they've chosen. However, deep spiritual peace and joy will never be discovered in pursuing our own will. Since God is our Creator, he is the only one who knows how we should live and why we are here.

True success in life is only measured by how closely we have followed God's plan for us. Those who live close to Jesus experience the reality of their Savior's words when he said, "My food . . . is to do the will of him who sent me and to finish his work" (John 4:34).

Lord, help me to see clearly your plan for my life. Give me the grace and wisdom to fulfill it each day that I live. Amen.

Your next devotion is located on page 879.

GRANDCHILD IN FOCUS • PRAYER

Physical Well-Being

Almighty God, Creator of us all, I pray that you will watch over my grandchild's physical development. May he grow in strength through the stages of his life. As he grows in awareness of his body, help him to understand that each body develops uniquely, yet is within your plan and your control. Please guard his health so that his diseases are few, his injuries are minor and his infirmities are brief. Amen.

³ It is to a man's honor to avoid strife,
but every fool is quick to quarrel.

⁴ A sluggard does not plow in season;
so at harvest time he looks but finds
nothing.

⁵ The purposes of a man's heart are deep
waters,
but a man of understanding draws them
out.

⁶ Many a man claims to have unfailing love,
but a faithful man who can find?

⁷ The righteous man leads a blameless life;
blessed are his children after him.

⁸ When a king sits on his throne to judge,
he winnows out all evil with his eyes.

⁹ Who can say, "I have kept my heart pure;
I am clean and without sin"?

¹⁰ Differing weights and differing measures—
the Lord detests them both.

¹¹ Even a child is known by his actions,
by whether his conduct is pure and right.

¹² Ears that hear and eyes that see—
the Lord has made them both.

¹³ Do not love sleep or you will grow poor;
stay awake and you will have food to
spare.

¹⁴ "It's no good, it's no good!" says the buyer;
then off he goes and boasts about his
purchase.

¹⁵ Gold there is, and rubies in abundance,
but lips that speak knowledge are a rare
jewel.

¹⁶ Take the garment of one who puts up
security for a stranger;
hold it in pledge if he does it for a wayward
woman.

¹⁷ Food gained by fraud tastes sweet to a man,
but he ends up with a mouth full of gravel.

¹⁸ Make plans by seeking advice;
if you wage war, obtain guidance.

¹⁹ A gossip betrays a confidence;
so avoid a man who talks too much.

TALKING POINTS

Gossip

Strive to be a trustworthy person.

PROVERBS 20:19

This is the last talking point on gossip.

²⁰ If a man curses his father or mother,
his lamp will be snuffed out in pitch
darkness.

²¹ An inheritance quickly gained at the beginning
will not be blessed at the end.

²² Do not say, "I'll pay you back for this wrong!"
Wait for the Lord, and he will deliver you.

²³ The Lord detests differing weights,
and dishonest scales do not please him.

²⁴ A man's steps are directed by the Lord.
How then can anyone understand his own
way?

²⁵ It is a trap for a man to dedicate something
rashly
and only later to consider his vows.

²⁶ A wise king winnows out the wicked;
he drives the threshing wheel over them.

²⁷ The lamp of the Lord searches the spirit of a
man [a];
it searches out his inmost being.

²⁸ Love and faithfulness keep a king safe;
through love his throne is made secure.

[a] 27 Or *The spirit of man is the Lord's lamp*

²⁹The glory of young men is their strength,
 gray hair the splendor of the old.

³⁰Blows and wounds cleanse away evil,
 and beatings purge the inmost being.

21

The king's heart is in the hand of the
 LORD;
he directs it like a watercourse wherever
 he pleases.

²All a man's ways seem right to him,
 but the LORD weighs the heart.

³To do what is right and just
 is more acceptable to the LORD than
  sacrifice.

⁴Haughty eyes and a proud heart,
 the lamp of the wicked, are sin!

⁵The plans of the diligent lead to profit
 as surely as haste leads to poverty.

⁶A fortune made by a lying tongue
 is a fleeting vapor and a deadly snare. ᵃ

⁷The violence of the wicked will drag them
 away,
 for they refuse to do what is right.

⁸The way of the guilty is devious,
 but the conduct of the innocent is upright.

⁹Better to live on a corner of the roof
 than share a house with a quarrelsome
  wife.

¹⁰The wicked man craves evil;
 his neighbor gets no mercy from him.

¹¹When a mocker is punished, the simple gain
 wisdom;
 when a wise man is instructed, he gets
  knowledge.

¹²The Righteous One ᵇ takes note of the house
 of the wicked
 and brings the wicked to ruin.

¹³If a man shuts his ears to the cry of the poor,
 he too will cry out and not be answered.

¹⁴A gift given in secret soothes anger,
 and a bribe concealed in the cloak pacifies
  great wrath.

¹⁵When justice is done, it brings joy to the
 righteous
 but terror to evildoers.

¹⁶A man who strays from the path of
 understanding
 comes to rest in the company of the dead.

¹⁷He who loves pleasure will become poor;
 whoever loves wine and oil will never be
  rich.

¹⁸The wicked become a ransom for the
 righteous,
 and the unfaithful for the upright.

¹⁹Better to live in a desert
 than with a quarrelsome and ill-tempered
  wife.

²⁰In the house of the wise are stores of choice
 food and oil,
 but a foolish man devours all he has.

²¹He who pursues righteousness and love
 finds life, prosperity ᶜ and honor.

²²A wise man attacks the city of the mighty
 and pulls down the stronghold in which
  they trust.

²³He who guards his mouth and his tongue
 keeps himself from calamity.

²⁴The proud and arrogant man—"Mocker" is
 his name;
 he behaves with overweening pride.

²⁵The sluggard's craving will be the death of
 him,
 because his hands refuse to work.

²⁶All day long he craves for more,
 but the righteous give without sparing.

ᵃ 6 Some Hebrew manuscripts, Septuagint and Vulgate; most
Hebrew manuscripts *vapor for those who seek death* ᵇ 12 Or *The
righteous man* ᶜ 21 Or *righteousness*

²⁷ The sacrifice of the wicked is detestable —
  how much more so when brought with
    evil intent!

²⁸ A false witness will perish,
  and whoever listens to him will be
    destroyed forever. ⁿ

²⁹ A wicked man puts up a bold front,
  but an upright man gives thought to his
    ways.

³⁰ There is no wisdom, no insight, no plan
  that can succeed against the LORD.

³¹ The horse is made ready for the day of
    battle,
  but victory rests with the LORD.

22 A good name is more desirable than
    great riches;
  to be esteemed is better than silver or gold.

² Rich and poor have this in common:
  The LORD is the Maker of them all.

³ A prudent man sees danger and takes refuge,
  but the simple keep going and suffer
    for it.

⁴ Humility and the fear of the LORD
  bring wealth and honor and life.

⁵ In the paths of the wicked lie thorns and
    snares,
  but he who guards his soul stays far from
    them.

⁶ Train ᵇ a child in the way he should go,
  and when he is old he will not turn from it.

⁷ The rich rule over the poor,
  and the borrower is servant to the lender.

⁸ He who sows wickedness reaps trouble,
  and the rod of his fury will be destroyed.

⁹ A generous man will himself be blessed,
  for he shares his food with the poor.

¹⁰ Drive out the mocker, and out goes strife;
  quarrels and insults are ended.

¹¹ He who loves a pure heart and whose speech
    is gracious
  will have the king for his friend.

¹² The eyes of the LORD keep watch over
    knowledge,
  but he frustrates the words of the
    unfaithful.

¹³ The sluggard says, "There is a lion outside!"
  or, "I will be murdered in the streets!"

¹⁴ The mouth of an adulteress is a deep pit;
  he who is under the LORD's wrath will fall
    into it.

¹⁵ Folly is bound up in the heart of a child,
  but the rod of discipline will drive it far
    from him.

¹⁶ He who oppresses the poor to increase his
    wealth
  and he who gives gifts to the rich — both
    come to poverty.

Sayings of the Wise

¹⁷ Pay attention and listen to the sayings of the
    wise;
  apply your heart to what I teach,
¹⁸ for it is pleasing when you keep them in your
    heart
  and have all of them ready on your lips.
¹⁹ So that your trust may be in the LORD,
  I teach you today, even you.
²⁰ Have I not written thirty ᶜ sayings for you,
  sayings of counsel and knowledge,
²¹ teaching you true and reliable words,
  so that you can give sound answers
    to him who sent you?

²² Do not exploit the poor because they are
      poor
  and do not crush the needy in court,
²³ for the LORD will take up their case
  and will plunder those who plunder them.

ᵃ 28 Or / but the words of an obedient man will live on
ᵇ 6 Or Start   ᶜ 20 Or not formerly written; or not written excellent

²⁴ Do not make friends with a hot-tempered man,
    do not associate with one easily angered,
²⁵ or you may learn his ways
    and get yourself ensnared.

TALKING POINTS

Peer Pressure

We need to choose our friends carefully.

PROVERBS 22:24–25

For more on peer pressure, go to Isaiah 51:7–8.

---

²⁶ Do not be a man who strikes hands in pledge
    or puts up security for debts;
²⁷ if you lack the means to pay,
    your very bed will be snatched from under
      you.

²⁸ Do not move an ancient boundary stone
    set up by your forefathers.

²⁹ Do you see a man skilled in his work?
    He will serve before kings;
    he will not serve before obscure men.

23 When you sit to dine with a ruler,
    note well what ᵃ is before you,
² and put a knife to your throat
    if you are given to gluttony.
³ Do not crave his delicacies,
    for that food is deceptive.

⁴ Do not wear yourself out to get rich;
    have the wisdom to show restraint.
⁵ Cast but a glance at riches, and they are gone,
    for they will surely sprout wings
    and fly off to the sky like an eagle.

⁶ Do not eat the food of a stingy man,
    do not crave his delicacies;
⁷ for he is the kind of man
    who is always thinking about the cost. ᵇ

"Eat and drink," he says to you,
    but his heart is not with you.
⁸ You will vomit up the little you have eaten
    and will have wasted your compliments.

⁹ Do not speak to a fool,
    for he will scorn the wisdom of your words.

¹⁰ Do not move an ancient boundary stone
    or encroach on the fields of the fatherless,
¹¹ for their Defender is strong;
    he will take up their case against you.

¹² Apply your heart to instruction
    and your ears to words of knowledge.

¹³ Do not withhold discipline from a child;
    if you punish him with the rod, he will not
      die.
¹⁴ Punish him with the rod
    and save his soul from death. ᶜ

¹⁵ My son, if your heart is wise,
    then my heart will be glad;
¹⁶ my inmost being will rejoice
    when your lips speak what is right.

¹⁷ Do not let your heart envy sinners,
    but always be zealous for the fear of the
      Lᴏʀᴅ.
¹⁸ There is surely a future hope for you,
    and your hope will not be cut off.

¹⁹ Listen, my son, and be wise,
    and keep your heart on the right path.
²⁰ Do not join those who drink too much wine
    or gorge themselves on meat,
²¹ for drunkards and gluttons become poor,
    and drowsiness clothes them in rags.

²² Listen to your father, who gave you life,
    and do not despise your mother when she
      is old.
²³ Buy the truth and do not sell it;
    get wisdom, discipline and understanding.
²⁴ The father of a righteous man has great joy;
    he who has a wise son delights in him.

ᵃ 1 Or who   ᵇ 7 Or for as he thinks within himself, / so he is; or for as he puts on a feast, / so he is   ᶜ 14 Hebrew Sheol

APPLY YOUR HEART TO
INSTRUCTION AND YOUR EARS
TO WORDS OF KNOWLEDGE.

Proverbs 23:12

Practicing Self-Discipline

FLORENCE LITTAUER

READ | PROVERBS 23:12–25

God's Word instructs us as parents and grandparents to train our little ones in the way they should go (see Proverbs 22:6). Through our example and guidance, they will learn to speak kindly to all and accept discipline from their elders.

My granddaughter Lianna went through a sarcastic phase during which she would correct simple statements that I made. Her mother, Kristy, would tell her to say she was sorry. Sometimes Lianna would apologize to me; other times she would stand defiantly, hands on her hips and lower lip curled under. "I'm not sorry," she would say. When she refused to apologize, her mother would say softly, "You need to take a time-out until you can come back and be pleasant."

Lianna learned quite quickly that her mother meant business, and so she would slink off to the dining room and climb up into an armchair. Sometimes she would sit there quietly for 15 minutes, hands folded and lower lip curled. Finally she would walk out to her mother, put her arms around her mother's knees and say, "I'm sorry." This discipline worked well, and she learned not to correct me or anyone else.

One day I was visiting, and I looked down the hall toward Lianna's room. She was standing against the wall with her face leaning into her folded hands. I beckoned to Kristy to take a look and whispered, "What is she doing?"

Kristy smiled and said, "She's done something wrong, and she's giving herself a time-out before I discover what she did."

What a great idea to punish yourself before someone catches you. If you can teach that to a child at four years old, you will save yourself and your little ones much trouble in the future. Discipline can work in both directions as we strive to please the Lord.

Dear Lord Jesus, thank you for this lesson from a little child. Let me see the error of my ways, accept the blame, confess to you and continue to improve my relationships with others. Forgive me for the mistakes I've made. In Jesus' name, amen.

Your next devotion is located on page 883.

GRANDCHILD IN FOCUS • PRAYER

Emotional Development

O God, Creator of mind and body, I pray that you will give my grandchild emotional health and strength. Where there is anger, bring peace. Where there is confusion, bring clarity and focus. Where there are dark shadows, cast a ray of hope. Fill her with the sunshine of your Spirit. Warm her with the presence of your peace. Amen.

²⁵ May your father and mother be glad;
  may she who gave you birth rejoice!

²⁶ My son, give me your heart
  and let your eyes keep to my ways,
²⁷ for a prostitute is a deep pit
  and a wayward wife is a narrow well.
²⁸ Like a bandit she lies in wait,
  and multiplies the unfaithful among men.

²⁹ Who has woe? Who has sorrow?
  Who has strife? Who has complaints?
  Who has needless bruises? Who has
    bloodshot eyes?
³⁰ Those who linger over wine,
  who go to sample bowls of mixed wine.
³¹ Do not gaze at wine when it is red,
  when it sparkles in the cup,
  when it goes down smoothly!
³² In the end it bites like a snake
  and poisons like a viper.
³³ Your eyes will see strange sights
  and your mind imagine confusing things.
³⁴ You will be like one sleeping on the high seas,
  lying on top of the rigging.
³⁵ "They hit me," you will say, "but I'm not
    hurt!
  They beat me, but I don't feel it!
When will I wake up
  so I can find another drink?"

24 Do not envy wicked men,
  do not desire their company;
² for their hearts plot violence,
  and their lips talk about making trouble.

³ By wisdom a house is built,
  and through understanding it is
    established;
⁴ through knowledge its rooms are filled
  with rare and beautiful treasures.

⁵ A wise man has great power,
  and a man of knowledge increases
    strength;
⁶ for waging war you need guidance,
  and for victory many advisers.

⁷ Wisdom is too high for a fool;
  in the assembly at the gate he has nothing
    to say.

⁸ He who plots evil
  will be known as a schemer.
⁹ The schemes of folly are sin,
  and men detest a mocker.

¹⁰ If you falter in times of trouble,
  how small is your strength!

¹¹ Rescue those being led away to death;
  hold back those staggering toward
    slaughter.
¹² If you say, "But we knew nothing about this,"
  does not he who weighs the heart perceive
    it?
  Does not he who guards your life know it?
  Will he not repay each person according to
    what he has done?

¹³ Eat honey, my son, for it is good;
  honey from the comb is sweet to your
    taste.
¹⁴ Know also that wisdom is sweet to your soul;
  if you find it, there is a future hope for you,
  and your hope will not be cut off.

¹⁵ Do not lie in wait like an outlaw against a
    righteous man's house,
  do not raid his dwelling place;
¹⁶ for though a righteous man falls seven times,
    he rises again,
  but the wicked are brought down by
    calamity.

¹⁷ Do not gloat when your enemy falls;
  when he stumbles, do not let your heart
    rejoice,
¹⁸ or the Lord will see and disapprove
  and turn his wrath away from him.

¹⁹ Do not fret because of evil men
  or be envious of the wicked,
²⁰ for the evil man has no future hope,
  and the lamp of the wicked will be snuffed
    out.

²¹ Fear the LORD and the king, my son,
  and do not join with the rebellious,
²² for those two will send sudden destruction
      upon them,
  and who knows what calamities they can
      bring?

TALKING POINTS

Forgiveness

Don't gloat over others' failures.

PROVERBS 24:17

For more on forgiveness, go to Matthew 18:21–22.

Further Sayings of the Wise

²³ These also are sayings of the wise:

To show partiality in judging is not good:
²⁴ Whoever says to the guilty, "You are
      innocent"—
  peoples will curse him and nations
      denounce him.
²⁵ But it will go well with those who convict the
      guilty,
  and rich blessing will come upon them.

²⁶ An honest answer
  is like a kiss on the lips.

²⁷ Finish your outdoor work
  and get your fields ready;
  after that, build your house.

²⁸ Do not testify against your neighbor without
      cause,
  or use your lips to deceive.
²⁹ Do not say, "I'll do to him as he has done
      to me;
  I'll pay that man back for what he did."

³⁰ I went past the field of the sluggard,
  past the vineyard of the man who lacks
      judgment;

³¹ thorns had come up everywhere,
  the ground was covered with weeds,
  and the stone wall was in ruins.
³² I applied my heart to what I observed
  and learned a lesson from what I saw:
³³ A little sleep, a little slumber,
  a little folding of the hands to rest—
³⁴ and poverty will come on you like a bandit
  and scarcity like an armed man.ᵃ

More Proverbs of Solomon

25 These are more proverbs of Solomon,
  copied by the men of Hezekiah king of
Judah:

² It is the glory of God to conceal a matter;
  to search out a matter is the glory of kings.

³ As the heavens are high and the earth is deep,
  so the hearts of kings are unsearchable.

⁴ Remove the dross from the silver,
  and out comes material forᵇ the
      silversmith;
⁵ remove the wicked from the king's presence,
  and his throne will be established through
      righteousness.

⁶ Do not exalt yourself in the king's presence,
  and do not claim a place among great men;
⁷ it is better for him to say to you, "Come up
      here,"
  than for him to humiliate you before a
      nobleman.

What you have seen with your eyes
⁸   do not bringᶜ hastily to court,
  for what will you do in the end
      if your neighbor puts you to shame?

⁹ If you argue your case with a neighbor,
  do not betray another man's confidence,
¹⁰ or he who hears it may shame you
  and you will never lose your bad
      reputation.

ᵃ 34 Or *like a vagrant / and scarcity like a beggar*   ᵇ 4 Or *comes a vessel from*   ᶜ 7,8 Or *nobleman / on whom you had set your eyes. / ⁸Do not go*

¹¹ A word aptly spoken
    is like apples of gold in settings of silver.

¹² Like an earring of gold or an ornament of
    fine gold
    is a wise man's rebuke to a listening ear.

¹³ Like the coolness of snow at harvest time
    is a trustworthy messenger to those who
    send him;
    he refreshes the spirit of his masters.

¹⁴ Like clouds and wind without rain
    is a man who boasts of gifts he does not
    give.

¹⁵ Through patience a ruler can be persuaded,
    and a gentle tongue can break a bone.

¹⁶ If you find honey, eat just enough—
    too much of it, and you will vomit.
¹⁷ Seldom set foot in your neighbor's house—
    too much of you, and he will hate you.

¹⁸ Like a club or a sword or a sharp arrow
    is the man who gives false testimony
    against his neighbor.

¹⁹ Like a bad tooth or a lame foot
    is reliance on the unfaithful in times of
    trouble.

²⁰ Like one who takes away a garment on a cold
    day,
    or like vinegar poured on soda,
    is one who sings songs to a heavy heart.

²¹ If your enemy is hungry, give him food
    to eat;
    if he is thirsty, give him water to drink.
²² In doing this, you will heap burning coals on
    his head,
    and the LORD will reward you.

²³ As a north wind brings rain,
    so a sly tongue brings angry looks.

²⁴ Better to live on a corner of the roof
    than share a house with a quarrelsome
    wife.

²⁵ Like cold water to a weary soul
    is good news from a distant land.

²⁶ Like a muddied spring or a polluted well
    is a righteous man who gives way to the
    wicked.

²⁷ It is not good to eat too much honey,
    nor is it honorable to seek one's own
    honor.

²⁸ Like a city whose walls are broken down
    is a man who lacks self-control.

26

Like snow in summer or rain in harvest,
    honor is not fitting for a fool.

² Like a fluttering sparrow or a darting
    swallow,
    an undeserved curse does not come to rest.

³ A whip for the horse, a halter for the donkey,
    and a rod for the backs of fools!

⁴ Do not answer a fool according to his folly,
    or you will be like him yourself.

⁵ Answer a fool according to his folly,
    or he will be wise in his own eyes.

⁶ Like cutting off one's feet or drinking
    violence
    is the sending of a message by the hand of
    a fool.

⁷ Like a lame man's legs that hang limp
    is a proverb in the mouth of a fool.

⁸ Like tying a stone in a sling
    is the giving of honor to a fool.

⁹ Like a thornbush in a drunkard's hand
    is a proverb in the mouth of a fool.

¹⁰ Like an archer who wounds at random
    is he who hires a fool or any passer-by.

¹¹ As a dog returns to its vomit,
    so a fool repeats his folly.

¹² Do you see a man wise in his own eyes?
    There is more hope for a fool than for him.

A WORD APTLY SPOKEN IS
LIKE APPLES OF GOLD IN
SETTINGS OF SILVER.

Proverbs 25:11

Affirming My Daughters

REBECCA LUTZER

READ | PROVERBS 25:11 – 15

Three daughters. Pink frills, dolls, jump rope, dress up, music, drama. What fun we had together as they grew up! Of course, there was sibling rivalry, hormones and many tears. There were discipline challenges that sent a weary mother to her knees in dependence upon God, praying for wisdom and strength.

Three college degrees. Three weddings. Six grandchildren! My daughters are good mothers and loving wives. Each is uniquely creative and talented. Each is different from me and has her own way of running her home and disciplining her children. I have had to accept that they do not want or need my advice about some things. Indeed, I have learned some painful lessons in this area.

However, they do need my love, encouragement, respect, affirmation and prayers — without criticism and judgment. "A word aptly spoken is like apples of gold in settings of silver" (Proverbs 25:11). When I disagree, I must speak in love and with carefully chosen words. I must respect their autonomy and pray over matters that concern me.

My daughters are experiencing the same joys and challenges I did, plus ones I didn't: husbands deployed to Afghanistan for 12 months or laid off for seven months or taking a new job in another state; children stillborn or hospitalized or traumatized by a father's long absence.

Whether a large or small trial, I tell them that God is always faithful to his Word. He loves them. His grace is sufficient.

"Trust him." "Obey him." "Don't give up." "Keep going." "I'm praying for you."

Often, these words are just what they need: "You're doing beautifully, and you will make it, just like I did!"

Dear loving heavenly Father, thank you for the precious gift of children. Please sustain, comfort and teach them by the Holy Spirit's power. Please give them grace, wisdom and patience to meet each day and each trial, that they may become godly women and men. Give me discernment and gracious words to uphold and encourage them. Amen.

Your next devotion is located on page 890.

GRANDCHILD IN FOCUS • PRAYER

Spiritual Growth

Dear Lord, today I pray for my grandchild's spiritual growth. I ask that you instill in him the desire to read and memorize your Word. Give him a passion to be in conversation with you. May loving and serving you be part of his daily life. I ask that you stay close to him and lead him to be transformed to your likeness, to reflect your grace and to radiate your love. I pray this in Jesus' name, amen.

13 The sluggard says, "There is a lion in the
    road,
    a fierce lion roaming the streets!"

14 As a door turns on its hinges,
    so a sluggard turns on his bed.

15 The sluggard buries his hand in the dish;
    he is too lazy to bring it back to his mouth.

16 The sluggard is wiser in his own eyes
    than seven men who answer discreetly.

17 Like one who seizes a dog by the ears
    is a passer-by who meddles in a quarrel
    not his own.

18 Like a madman shooting
    firebrands or deadly arrows
19 is a man who deceives his neighbor
    and says, "I was only joking!"

20 Without wood a fire goes out;
    without gossip a quarrel dies down.

21 As charcoal to embers and as wood to fire,
    so is a quarrelsome man for kindling
    strife.

22 The words of a gossip are like choice morsels;
    they go down to a man's inmost parts.

23 Like a coating of glaze ᵃ over earthenware
    are fervent lips with an evil heart.

24 A malicious man disguises himself with his
    lips,
    but in his heart he harbors deceit.
25 Though his speech is charming, do not
    believe him,
    for seven abominations fill his heart.
26 His malice may be concealed by deception,
    but his wickedness will be exposed in the
    assembly.

27 If a man digs a pit, he will fall into it;
    if a man rolls a stone, it will roll back on
    him.

28 A lying tongue hates those it hurts,
    and a flattering mouth works ruin.

27 Do not boast about tomorrow,
    for you do not know what a day may
    bring forth.

2 Let another praise you, and not your own
    mouth;
    someone else, and not your own lips.

3 Stone is heavy and sand a burden,
    but provocation by a fool is heavier than
    both.

4 Anger is cruel and fury overwhelming,
    but who can stand before jealousy?

5 Better is open rebuke
    than hidden love.

6 Wounds from a friend can be trusted,
    but an enemy multiplies kisses.

7 He who is full loathes honey,
    but to the hungry even what is bitter tastes
    sweet.

8 Like a bird that strays from its nest
    is a man who strays from his home.

9 Perfume and incense bring joy to the heart,
    and the pleasantness of one's friend
        springs from his earnest counsel.

10 Do not forsake your friend and the friend of
    your father,
    and do not go to your brother's house
        when disaster strikes you—
    better a neighbor nearby than a brother far
        away.

ᵃ 23 With a different word division of the Hebrew; Masoretic Text
of silver dross

TALKING POINTS

Friendship
True friends offer sincere advice.
PROVERBS 27:9

For more on friendship, go to John 11:1–44.

¹¹ Be wise, my son, and bring joy to my heart;
     then I can answer anyone who treats me
          with contempt.

¹² The prudent see danger and take refuge,
     but the simple keep going and suffer
          for it.

¹³ Take the garment of one who puts up
          security for a stranger;
     hold it in pledge if he does it for a wayward
          woman.

¹⁴ If a man loudly blesses his neighbor early in
          the morning,
     it will be taken as a curse.

¹⁵ A quarrelsome wife is like
     a constant dripping on a rainy day;
¹⁶ restraining her is like restraining the wind
     or grasping oil with the hand.

¹⁷ As iron sharpens iron,
     so one man sharpens another.

¹⁸ He who tends a fig tree will eat its fruit,
     and he who looks after his master will be
          honored.

¹⁹ As water reflects a face,
     so a man's heart reflects the man.

²⁰ Death and Destruction ᵃ are never satisfied,
     and neither are the eyes of man.

²¹ The crucible for silver and the furnace
          for gold,
     but man is tested by the praise he
          receives.

²² Though you grind a fool in a mortar,
     grinding him like grain with a pestle,
     you will not remove his folly from him.

²³ Be sure you know the condition of your
          flocks,
     give careful attention to your herds;
²⁴ for riches do not endure forever,
     and a crown is not secure for all
          generations.

²⁵ When the hay is removed and new growth
          appears
     and the grass from the hills is gathered in,
²⁶ the lambs will provide you with clothing,
     and the goats with the price of a field.
²⁷ You will have plenty of goats' milk
     to feed you and your family
     and to nourish your servant girls.

28 The wicked man flees though no one
          pursues,
     but the righteous are as bold as a lion.

² When a country is rebellious, it has many
          rulers,
     but a man of understanding and
          knowledge maintains order.

³ A ruler ᵇ who oppresses the poor
     is like a driving rain that leaves no crops.

⁴ Those who forsake the law praise the
          wicked,
     but those who keep the law resist them.

⁵ Evil men do not understand justice,
     but those who seek the LORD understand it
          fully.

⁶ Better a poor man whose walk is blameless
     than a rich man whose ways are perverse.

⁷ He who keeps the law is a discerning son,
     but a companion of gluttons disgraces his
          father.

⁸ He who increases his wealth by exorbitant
          interest
     amasses it for another, who will be kind to
          the poor.

⁹ If anyone turns a deaf ear to the law,
     even his prayers are detestable.

¹⁰ He who leads the upright along an evil path
     will fall into his own trap,
     but the blameless will receive a good
          inheritance.

ᵃ 20 Hebrew *Sheol and Abaddon*   ᵇ 3 Or *A poor man*

LESLIE PARROTT

Band
OF SISTERS

The Friday Friends

Some years ago, I took a risk. I asked six women — none of whom really knew any of the others — to join me in starting a small group. I didn't have the time, and neither did they, but I hoped they might share my desire. I wasn't suffering from a social deficit, and they weren't either, but I hoped they might recognize the value. All of these women were leading full and satisfying lives with very few empty spaces to fill. But I asked anyway.

That was four years ago, and we're still meeting.

We call ourselves "The Friday Friends," and every three weeks, on a Friday evening, the seven of us, living at all points of the compass in a 30-mile radius around the city of Seattle, jockey our schedules with husbands, children and jobs, and come together.

Each meeting centers around only one simple question, posed by the woman who's hosting us at her home for that session: What's been consuming your thoughts? What part of your life is weighing you down? Who contributed most to your character? How has your faith changed in the past year?

That's all it takes. One simple question, like any of these, and we're off and running. Each time we meet, I'm amazed that this is all it takes for us to have a lively discussion that usually goes until the wee hours of the morning.

What Difference Are You Making?

On one particular night recently, the question I brought to the group caught everyone a little off guard. Not that we weren't ready to discuss it, but it was apparent that we each needed a little time to let it sink in, to seriously consider our answers.

My question: As a woman, how do you make a difference in the world?

It was easy for each of us to see what a huge difference each of the other women was making. But our own difference-making sometimes seemed unclear and even hidden from ourselves. As we talked about it, as we began to see ourselves through the eyes of our band of sisters, the reality of our individual significance was impossible to miss. Sometimes it takes the social capital of other women together to help us recognize how the pieces of our lives, when collected and displayed, are more beautiful and meaningful than we might have ever imagined on our own.

It was this question — What difference are you making as a woman? — that prompted me to invite these women into a small group to begin with. I was needing more than girl friends. I was needing the collective female consciousness to help me better discern how to make a difference in my world. I needed a chorus of female voices to speak into my life with the kind of wisdom that comes from multiple perspectives.

Strengthening Each Other

Knowing that I couldn't always recognize it on my own — or even with the aid of a trusted girl friend — I realized that I needed the help of other women, together, to help me see how my life does, can and should be making a difference in my world. And I wanted to do the same for them. In short, I needed the social capital of other women together.

If I was to make a difference in my world, I knew that difference would be maximized, even multiplied, if it were considered, critiqued and supported by other women who were on the same path (see Proverbs 27:17). A band of sisters who carry deep values and watch over one another in love is stronger than any woman on her own.*

As anthropologist Margaret Mead has said, "Never doubt that a small group of thoughtful, committed citizens can change the world. Indeed, it is the only thing that ever has."

---

*In the movement associated with John Wesley, people met together in little communities to help clarify their deepest values and most important decisions. Wesley had a beautiful phrase for this; he called it watching over one another in love.

¹¹ A rich man may be wise in his own eyes,
    but a poor man who has discernment sees
        through him.

¹² When the righteous triumph, there is great
        elation;
    but when the wicked rise to power, men go
        into hiding.

¹³ He who conceals his sins does not prosper,
    but whoever confesses and renounces
        them finds mercy.

¹⁴ Blessed is the man who always fears the LORD,
    but he who hardens his heart falls into
        trouble.

¹⁵ Like a roaring lion or a charging bear
    is a wicked man ruling over a helpless
        people.

¹⁶ A tyrannical ruler lacks judgment,
    but he who hates ill-gotten gain will enjoy
        a long life.

¹⁷ A man tormented by the guilt of murder
    will be a fugitive till death;
    let no one support him.

¹⁸ He whose walk is blameless is kept safe,
    but he whose ways are perverse will
        suddenly fall.

¹⁹ He who works his land will have abundant
        food,
    but the one who chases fantasies will have
        his fill of poverty.

²⁰ A faithful man will be richly blessed,
    but one eager to get rich will not go
        unpunished.

²¹ To show partiality is not good—
    yet a man will do wrong for a piece of
        bread.

²² A stingy man is eager to get rich
    and is unaware that poverty awaits him.

²³ He who rebukes a man will in the end gain
        more favor
    than he who has a flattering tongue.

²⁴ He who robs his father or mother
    and says, "It's not wrong"—
    he is partner to him who destroys.

²⁵ A greedy man stirs up dissension,
    but he who trusts in the LORD will prosper.

²⁶ He who trusts in himself is a fool,
    but he who walks in wisdom is kept safe.

²⁷ He who gives to the poor will lack nothing,
    but he who closes his eyes to them receives
        many curses.

²⁸ When the wicked rise to power, people go
        into hiding;
    but when the wicked perish, the righteous
        thrive.

29 A man who remains stiff-necked after
        many rebukes
    will suddenly be destroyed—without
        remedy.

² When the righteous thrive, the people rejoice;
    when the wicked rule, the people groan.

³ A man who loves wisdom brings joy to his
        father,
    but a companion of prostitutes squanders
        his wealth.

⁴ By justice a king gives a country stability,
    but one who is greedy for bribes tears it
        down.

⁵ Whoever flatters his neighbor
    is spreading a net for his feet.

⁶ An evil man is snared by his own sin,
    but a righteous one can sing and be glad.

⁷ The righteous care about justice for the poor,
    but the wicked have no such concern.

⁸ Mockers stir up a city,
    but wise men turn away anger.

⁹ If a wise man goes to court with a fool,
    the fool rages and scoffs, and there is no
        peace.

¹⁰ Bloodthirsty men hate a man of integrity
   and seek to kill the upright.

¹¹ A fool gives full vent to his anger,
   but a wise man keeps himself under control.

TALKING POINTS

Anger

We are wise when we learn
to control our anger.

PROVERBS 29:11

For more on anger, go to Proverbs 29:22.

---

¹² If a ruler listens to lies,
   all his officials become wicked.

¹³ The poor man and the oppressor have this in
      common:
   The LORD gives sight to the eyes of both.

¹⁴ If a king judges the poor with fairness,
   his throne will always be secure.

¹⁵ The rod of correction imparts wisdom,
   but a child left to himself disgraces his
      mother.

¹⁶ When the wicked thrive, so does sin,
   but the righteous will see their downfall.

¹⁷ Discipline your son, and he will give you
      peace;
   he will bring delight to your soul.

¹⁸ Where there is no revelation, the people cast
      off restraint;
   but blessed is he who keeps the law.

¹⁹ A servant cannot be corrected by mere words;
   though he understands, he will not
      respond.

²⁰ Do you see a man who speaks in haste?
   There is more hope for a fool than for him.

²¹ If a man pampers his servant from youth,
   he will bring grief *ᵃ* in the end.

²² An angry man stirs up dissension,
   and a hot-tempered one commits many
      sins.

²³ A man's pride brings him low,
   but a man of lowly spirit gains honor.

²⁴ The accomplice of a thief is his own enemy;
   he is put under oath and dare not testify.

²⁵ Fear of man will prove to be a snare,
   but whoever trusts in the LORD is kept safe.

²⁶ Many seek an audience with a ruler,
   but it is from the LORD that man gets
      justice.

²⁷ The righteous detest the dishonest;
   the wicked detest the upright.

TALKING POINTS

Anger

Anger can lead to sin.

PROVERBS 29:22

For more on anger, go to Ephesians 4:26–27.

Sayings of Agur

30 The sayings of Agur son of Jakeh — an
   oracle *ᵇ*:

This man declared to Ithiel,
   to Ithiel and to Ucal: *ᶜ*

² "I am the most ignorant of men;
   I do not have a man's understanding.
³ I have not learned wisdom,
   nor have I knowledge of the Holy One.

ᵃ 21 The meaning of the Hebrew for this word is uncertain.
ᵇ 1 Or *Jakeh of Massa*   *ᶜ 1* Masoretic Text; with a different word
division of the Hebrew *declared, "I am weary, O God; / I am weary,
O God, and faint.*

"EVERY WORD OF GOD IS
FLAWLESS; HE IS A SHIELD
TO THOSE WHO TAKE
REFUGE IN HIM."

Proverbs 30:5

The Book

RUTH HARMS CALKIN

READ | PROVERBS 30:1–6

Lord, how deeply I cherish
My mother's Bible
With its worn leather cover—
Its frayed edges.
Slowly I turn the thin pages
And memories glisten
Between chapters and verses.
On every page, dear Lord
There are heart-prints of her:
Verses carefully underlined
Words neatly circled
Tiny arrows pointing to references
Secret desires written in margins.
How she loved Your Word, dear God.

I turn once more to the verse
She repeatedly quoted:
"And we know that all things
Work together for good
To them that love God . . ."
(Lord, the verse is tear-stained.
Her tears or mine?)
Gently now I touch the words
At the top of the page
Written so laboriously
Five days before she left us:
"Greater than the pain that pulls me down
Is the power that pulls me up."

GRANDCHILD IN FOCUS • PRAYER

Relationships at Home

O Lord, I pray that you will bless the home and family of my grandchild. May the relationships she has with her parents and siblings enhance her well-being, support her self-confidence and increase her faith. May her home life reflect your love, your grace, your compassion and your peace. Guide her parents to direct her in love and truth, so she will grow into a strong and compassionate individual. Amen.

God, thank you for your Word. Help me to cherish it and pass down my love for it to my children and grandchildren. Amen.

Your next devotion is located on page 892.

⁴ Who has gone up to heaven and come down?
　　Who has gathered up the wind in the
　　　hollow of his hands?
　Who has wrapped up the waters in his cloak?
　　Who has established all the ends of the
　　　earth?
　What is his name, and the name of his son?
　　Tell me if you know!

⁵ "Every word of God is flawless;
　　he is a shield to those who take refuge in
　　　him.
⁶ Do not add to his words,
　　or he will rebuke you and prove you a liar.

⁷ "Two things I ask of you, O Lord;
　　do not refuse me before I die:
⁸ Keep falsehood and lies far from me;
　　give me neither poverty nor riches,
　　but give me only my daily bread.
⁹ Otherwise, I may have too much and disown
　　　you
　　and say, 'Who is the Lord?'
　Or I may become poor and steal,
　　and so dishonor the name of my God.

TALKING POINTS

Contentment

Learn moderation and become content.

PROVERBS 30:8–9

For more on contentment, go to Matthew 6:19–21.

---

¹⁰ "Do not slander a servant to his master,
　　or he will curse you, and you will pay
　　　for it.

¹¹ "There are those who curse their fathers
　　and do not bless their mothers;
¹² those who are pure in their own eyes
　　and yet are not cleansed of their filth;

¹³ those whose eyes are ever so haughty,
　　whose glances are so disdainful;
¹⁴ those whose teeth are swords
　　and whose jaws are set with knives
　to devour the poor from the earth,
　　the needy from among mankind.

¹⁵ "The leech has two daughters.
　　'Give! Give!' they cry.

　"There are three things that are never satisfied,
　　four that never say, 'Enough!':
¹⁶ the grave,^a the barren womb,
　　land, which is never satisfied with water,
　　and fire, which never says, 'Enough!'

¹⁷ "The eye that mocks a father,
　　that scorns obedience to a mother,
　will be pecked out by the ravens of the valley,
　　will be eaten by the vultures.

¹⁸ "There are three things that are too amazing
　　　for me,
　　four that I do not understand:
¹⁹ the way of an eagle in the sky,
　　the way of a snake on a rock,
　the way of a ship on the high seas,
　　and the way of a man with a maiden.

²⁰ "This is the way of an adulteress:
　　She eats and wipes her mouth
　　and says, 'I've done nothing wrong.'

²¹ "Under three things the earth trembles,
　　under four it cannot bear up:
²² a servant who becomes king,
　　a fool who is full of food,
²³ an unloved woman who is married,
　　and a maidservant who displaces her
　　　mistress.

²⁴ "Four things on earth are small,
　　yet they are extremely wise:
²⁵ Ants are creatures of little strength,
　　yet they store up their food in the summer;
²⁶ coneys^b are creatures of little power,
　　yet they make their home in the crags;

---

^a 16 Hebrew Sheol　　^b 26 That is, the hyrax or rock badger

A Cemetery Stroll

Walking through a cemetery during the day can be an educational and interesting experience that will lead to some good conversation. Just by reading the etchings on gravestones, you and your grandchildren will learn a lot. You may want to check the layout of a cemetery ahead of time to find the oldest section or some very unusual tombstone epitaphs. If you choose, you could also locate and decorate the resting place of a veteran or use white copy paper and pencils to do rubbings that capture the information on a headstone.

Follow up at home with a discussion of what you learned. The conversation might go in several directions. Do the kids want to discuss war or patriotic themes? People they knew who are now deceased? Salvation and eternal life? Don't try to steer the dialogue in any given direction.

Younger-Grandkids Variation: Stroll through a cemetery, admiring the quiet atmosphere, pretty stones, flowers, grass and trees. Touch briefly on the meaning of death, resurrection and heaven.

Dear God, bless this activity. Help it to be interesting as well as a good opportunity for sharing with my grandchildren the promise of life after death. Let our conversation be meaningful, honest and hopeful. Amen.

Your next devotion is located on page 897.

GRANDCHILD IN FOCUS • PRAYER

Friends

Dear Lord and Father, I pray for my grandchild's social life and his friends. Bring diverse friends into his life who will love and encourage him, who will bring joy and laughter to the good times and comfort and support through difficulties and disappointments. Grant him wisdom and discernment as he selects his friends; help him to avoid cliques that restrict, activities that endanger, and foolish and dangerous behaviors that harm. I ask that you fill his life with close and caring relationships. Amen.

²⁷locusts have no king,
    yet they advance together in ranks;
²⁸a lizard can be caught with the hand,
    yet it is found in kings' palaces.

²⁹"There are three things that are stately in
        their stride,
    four that move with stately bearing:
³⁰a lion, mighty among beasts,
    who retreats before nothing;
³¹a strutting rooster, a he-goat,
    and a king with his army around him. ª

³²"If you have played the fool and exalted
        yourself,
    or if you have planned evil,
        clap your hand over your mouth!
³³For as churning the milk produces butter,
    and as twisting the nose produces blood,
    so stirring up anger produces strife."

Sayings of King Lemuel

31 The sayings of King Lemuel—an oracle ᵇ
    his mother taught him:

²"O my son, O son of my womb,
    O son of my vows, ᶜ
³do not spend your strength on women,
    your vigor on those who ruin kings.

⁴"It is not for kings, O Lemuel—
    not for kings to drink wine,
    not for rulers to crave beer,
⁵lest they drink and forget what the law
        decrees,
    and deprive all the oppressed of their
        rights.
⁶Give beer to those who are perishing,
    wine to those who are in anguish;
⁷let them drink and forget their poverty
    and remember their misery no more.

⁸"Speak up for those who cannot speak for
        themselves,
    for the rights of all who are destitute.
⁹Speak up and judge fairly;
    defend the rights of the poor and needy."

Epilogue: The Wife of Noble Character

¹⁰ ᵈA wife of noble character who can find?
    She is worth far more than rubies.
¹¹Her husband has full confidence in her
    and lacks nothing of value.
¹²She brings him good, not harm,
    all the days of her life.
¹³She selects wool and flax
    and works with eager hands.
¹⁴She is like the merchant ships,
    bringing her food from afar.

ª 31 Or *king secure against revolt*   ᵇ 1 Or *of Lemuel king of Massa,
which*   ᶜ 2 Or / *the answer to my prayers*   ᵈ 10 Verses 10-31
are an acrostic, each verse beginning with a successive letter of the
Hebrew alphabet.

stories to share

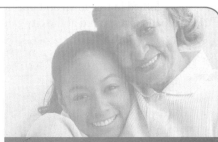

PROVERBS 31:10–31

The Wife of Noble Character

LIFE LESSON: Our character matters
to God.

TO TALK ABOUT

✦ What does it mean to have a "noble"
    character?

✦ What is a noble character worth?

✦ Who should follow this advice for
    living a life of noble character?

✦ Why do you think this passage was
    included in the book of Proverbs?

¹⁵ She gets up while it is still dark;
    she provides food for her family
    and portions for her servant girls.
¹⁶ She considers a field and buys it;
    out of her earnings she plants a
      vineyard.
¹⁷ She sets about her work vigorously;
    her arms are strong for her tasks.
¹⁸ She sees that her trading is profitable,
    and her lamp does not go out at night.
¹⁹ In her hand she holds the distaff
    and grasps the spindle with her fingers.
²⁰ She opens her arms to the poor
    and extends her hands to the needy.
²¹ When it snows, she has no fear for her
      household;
    for all of them are clothed in scarlet.
²² She makes coverings for her bed;
    she is clothed in fine linen and purple.
²³ Her husband is respected at the city gate,

where he takes his seat among the elders of
    the land.
²⁴ She makes linen garments and sells them,
    and supplies the merchants with sashes.
²⁵ She is clothed with strength and dignity;
    she can laugh at the days to come.
²⁶ She speaks with wisdom,
    and faithful instruction is on her tongue.
²⁷ She watches over the affairs of her household
    and does not eat the bread of idleness.
²⁸ Her children arise and call her blessed;
    her husband also, and he praises her:
²⁹ "Many women do noble things,
    but you surpass them all."
³⁰ Charm is deceptive, and beauty is fleeting;
    but a woman who fears the LORD is to be
      praised.
³¹ Give her the reward she has earned,
    and let her works bring her praise at the
      city gate.

The Meaning OF LIFE

People in every generation tend to rely on themselves and their own abilities. They chase after the things of the world that bring status, prestige, power and position. The Teacher (probably King Solomon) was a man who had all these things, yet he wisely took the time to think about such pursuits, and he discovered that none of them mattered.

In the book of Ecclesiastes, the Teacher addressed the question every generation asks: What is the meaning of life? He firmly concluded that many things in life are truly meaningless; they just don't make any sense or bring satisfaction. Although this attitude makes the book sound gloomy at times, the real point is that everything is meaningless without God. Only God brings richness and purpose to life.

The wisdom at the root of the book of Ecclesiastes is the wisdom we as grandmothers must convey to our grandchildren, who, at some point or another, are sure to question the meaning of life. Perhaps they will come to you with their questions. Perhaps you will seek them out and start the discussion. Either way, the book of Ecclesiastes will help you guide them through their uncertainty and provide the ultimate answer: Only a life centered on God has true meaning, purpose and joy.

VERSE *to* REMEMBER | ECCLESIASTES 2:24–25

A man can do nothing better than to eat and drink and find satisfaction in his work. This too, I see, is from the hand of God, for without him, who can eat or find enjoyment?

ABOUT ECCLESIASTES

WRITTEN BY:
The Teacher, probably King Solomon

WRITTEN FOR:
The people of Israel

DATE WRITTEN:
Probably near the end of Solomon's life in 930 B.C.

WHY WRITTEN:
To show that no one can experience true happiness and fulfillment without God

Everything Is Meaningless

1 The words of the Teacher,^{a} son of David, king in Jerusalem:

² "Meaningless! Meaningless!"
    says the Teacher.
  "Utterly meaningless!
    Everything is meaningless."

³ What does man gain from all his labor
    at which he toils under the sun?
⁴ Generations come and generations go,
    but the earth remains forever.
⁵ The sun rises and the sun sets,
    and hurries back to where it rises.
⁶ The wind blows to the south
    and turns to the north;
  round and round it goes,
    ever returning on its course.
⁷ All streams flow into the sea,
    yet the sea is never full.
  To the place the streams come from,
    there they return again.
⁸ All things are wearisome,
    more than one can say.
  The eye never has enough of seeing,
    nor the ear its fill of hearing.
⁹ What has been will be again,
    what has been done will be done again;
    there is nothing new under the sun.
¹⁰ Is there anything of which one can say,
    "Look! This is something new"?
  It was here already, long ago;
    it was here before our time.
¹¹ There is no remembrance of men of old,
    and even those who are yet to come
  will not be remembered
    by those who follow.

Wisdom Is Meaningless

¹² I, the Teacher, was king over Israel in Jerusalem. ¹³ I devoted myself to study and to explore by wisdom all that is done under heaven. What a heavy burden God has laid on men! ¹⁴ I have seen all the things that are done under the sun; all of them are meaningless, a chasing after the wind.

¹⁵ What is twisted cannot be straightened;
    what is lacking cannot be counted.

¹⁶ I thought to myself, "Look, I have grown and increased in wisdom more than anyone who has ruled over Jerusalem before me; I have experienced much of wisdom and knowledge." ¹⁷ Then I applied myself to the understanding of wisdom, and also of madness and folly, but I learned that this, too, is a chasing after the wind.

¹⁸ For with much wisdom comes much sorrow;
    the more knowledge, the more grief.

Pleasures Are Meaningless

2 I thought in my heart, "Come now, I will test you with pleasure to find out what is good." But that also proved to be meaningless. ² "Laughter," I said, "is foolish. And what does pleasure accomplish?" ³ I tried cheering myself with wine, and embracing folly—my mind still guiding me with wisdom. I wanted to see what was worthwhile for men to do under heaven during the few days of their lives.

⁴ I undertook great projects: I built houses for myself and planted vineyards. ⁵ I made gardens and parks and planted all kinds of fruit trees in them. ⁶ I made reservoirs to water groves of flourishing trees. ⁷ I bought male and female slaves and had other slaves who were born in my house. I also owned more herds and flocks than anyone in Jerusalem before me. ⁸ I amassed silver and gold for myself, and the treasure of kings and provinces. I acquired men and women singers, and a harem^b as well—the delights of the heart of man. ⁹ I became greater by far than anyone in Jerusalem before me. In all this my wisdom stayed with me.

¹⁰ I denied myself nothing my eyes desired;
    I refused my heart no pleasure.
  My heart took delight in all my work,
    and this was the reward for all my labor.

---

^{a} 1 Or leader of the assembly; also in verses 2 and 12
^{b} 8 The meaning of the Hebrew for this phrase is uncertain.

Worship the Lord

I will praise you, O Lord, with all my heart;
    I will tell of all your wonders.
I will be glad and rejoice in you;
    I will sing praise to your name, O Most High.

The Lord reigns forever;
    he has established his throne for judgment.
He will judge the world in righteousness;
    he will govern the peoples with justice.
The Lord is a refuge for the oppressed,
    a stronghold in times of trouble.
Those who know your name will trust in you,
    for you, Lord, have never forsaken those who
        seek you.

Sing praises to the Lord, enthroned in Zion;
    proclaim among the nations what
        he has done.

Psalm 9:1 – 2, 7 – 11

Dear God, my heart is filled with praise for
you as I remember how you have guided
me and as I think of all you have given me.
Thank you, Lord, that you see all that goes
on in this sad world and that you will ensure
that justice and righteousness have the last
word. Give me faith to trust you in times of
trouble. Amen.

Your next devotion is located on page 899.

GRANDCHILD IN FOCUS • PRAYER

Self-Image

*O loving God, I praise you for creating my
grandchild as a unique individual. Now I ask you
to help her appreciate her uniqueness. Build up her
self-image so she can enjoy her individuality. Help
her to stand firm for who she is, where she has
come from and what she believes in. Encourage
her not only to have hopes and dreams but
to also enjoy each day as it comes.
In Jesus' name, amen.*

¹¹ Yet when I surveyed all that my hands had
done
and what I had toiled to achieve,
everything was meaningless, a chasing after
the wind;
nothing was gained under the sun.

Wisdom and Folly Are Meaningless

¹² Then I turned my thoughts to consider
wisdom,
and also madness and folly.
What more can the king's successor do
than what has already been done?
¹³ I saw that wisdom is better than folly,
just as light is better than darkness.
¹⁴ The wise man has eyes in his head,
while the fool walks in the darkness;
but I came to realize
that the same fate overtakes them both.

¹⁵ Then I thought in my heart,

"The fate of the fool will overtake me also.
What then do I gain by being wise?"
I said in my heart,
"This too is meaningless."
¹⁶ For the wise man, like the fool, will not be
long remembered;
in days to come both will be forgotten.
Like the fool, the wise man too must die!

Toil Is Meaningless

¹⁷ So I hated life, because the work that is done
under the sun was grievous to me. All of it is
meaningless, a chasing after the wind. ¹⁸ I hated
all the things I had toiled for under the sun, because I must leave them to the one who comes
after me. ¹⁹ And who knows whether he will be a
wise man or a fool? Yet he will have control over
all the work into which I have poured my effort
and skill under the sun. This too is meaningless.
²⁰ So my heart began to despair over all my toilsome labor under the sun. ²¹ For a man may do
his work with wisdom, knowledge and skill, and
then he must leave all he owns to someone who
has not worked for it. This too is meaningless

and a great misfortune. ²² What does a man get
for all the toil and anxious striving with which
he labors under the sun? ²³ All his days his work
is pain and grief; even at night his mind does not
rest. This too is meaningless.

²⁴ A man can do nothing better than to eat
and drink and find satisfaction in his work. This
too, I see, is from the hand of God, ²⁵ for without
him, who can eat or find enjoyment? ²⁶ To the
man who pleases him, God gives wisdom, knowledge and happiness, but to the sinner he gives the
task of gathering and storing up wealth to hand
it over to the one who pleases God. This too is
meaningless, a chasing after the wind.

PRAYING THE SCRIPTURES

Wisdom

ECCLESIASTES 2:26

O Lord, let my grandchild be pleasing to
you; bless her, I pray, with wisdom, knowledge and happiness.

Next prayer in Wisdom Prayer Track: Isaiah 11:2–3

A Time for Everything

3 There is a time for everything,
and a season for every activity under heaven:

2   a time to be born and a time to die,
a time to plant and a time to uproot,
3   a time to kill and a time to heal,
a time to tear down and a time to build,
4   a time to weep and a time to laugh,
a time to mourn and a time to dance,
5   a time to scatter stones and a time to
gather them,
a time to embrace and a time to refrain,
6   a time to search and a time to give up,
a time to keep and a time to throw away,
7   a time to tear and a time to mend,
a time to be silent and a time to speak,

THERE IS A TIME FOR
EVERYTHING ... A TIME TO BE
SILENT AND A TIME TO SPEAK.
Ecclesiastes 3:1, 7

Let Me Tell You About My Grandchildren

JAN SILVIOUS

READ | ECCLESIASTES 3:1–8

"Let me tell you about my grandchildren" is not music to some people's ears. Despite the fact that baby pictures are adorable and sweet children's antics are amusing, not everyone wants to hear about your grandchildren! Can you imagine?

A grandmother's understanding of the appropriate moment to pull out the pictures or to tell the cute story is something we all need to keep in mind. Sensitivity is the key. Remember to whom you are speaking and remember what their level of interest might be. Those two factors determine what to tell and how much to tell.

If you are speaking to another grandmother who has lavished her stories on you, then go for it. Tell your stories and show your pictures to your heart's content. If, however, you are talking with someone who may not have grandchildren or someone who may have suffered a loss, remember to be sensitive and appropriate.

I have a sweet friend who has lost several unborn grandbabies through her daughter's miscarriages. To date, there is not a living grandchild in her life. Although she often asks about my grandchildren, out of deference to her, I reference them with general statements and change the subject. I would love to see the day when we could delight in one another's grandchildren and all the joy they bring, but until then, I want to love her with the gift of appropriate restraint. That is something we can do for one another as we live as friends. Being sensitive and being appropriate keeps relationships intact. Sometimes, our personal elation blinds us to the hurts in another's life.

Father, make me a sensitive friend. Tug on my spirit with a call for restraint if I ever step over the line of what is gracious and appropriate. Give me eyes to see beyond what I think and open my heart to hear what you would have me say and do. Amen.

Your next devotion is located on page 901.

GRANDCHILD IN FOCUS • PRAYER

Protection From Worldliness

O Sovereign Lord, the world surrounds my grandchild, pressing in and tempting him in so many ways. Help him set appropriate limits. Give him sound judgment to choose wisely. Guard him from temptation; protect him from physical and mental predators; lead him into paths of righteousness and light. And reassure me with your promise that you are holding him in your hands. Amen.

8 a time to love and a time to hate,
   a time for war and a time for peace.

⁹What does the worker gain from his toil? ¹⁰I have seen the burden God has laid on men. ¹¹He has made everything beautiful in its time. He has also set eternity in the hearts of men; yet they cannot fathom what God has done from beginning to end. ¹²I know that there is nothing better for men than to be happy and do good while they live. ¹³That everyone may eat and drink, and find satisfaction in all his toil—this is the gift of God. ¹⁴I know that everything God does will endure forever; nothing can be added to it and nothing taken from it. God does it so that men will revere him.

¹⁵Whatever is has already been,
   and what will be has been before;
   and God will call the past to account.ᵃ

ECCLESIASTES 3:1–14

stories to share

A Time for Everything

LIFE LESSON: God's timing is perfect.

TO TALK ABOUT

✦ What kinds of things are appropriate at certain times?

✦ When have you found it hard to accept God's timing? Why?

✦ Have you ever done something good but at the wrong time? Explain.

✦ In hard times, do you still believe that God knows best? How do you act on that belief?

TALKING POINTS

Accountability
God will judge the past.
ECCLESIASTES 3:15

For more on accountability, go to Matthew 12:36–37.

¹⁶And I saw something else under the sun:

In the place of judgment—wickedness was there,
   in the place of justice—wickedness was there.

¹⁷I thought in my heart,

"God will bring to judgment
   both the righteous and the wicked,
for there will be a time for every activity,
   a time for every deed."

¹⁸I also thought, "As for men, God tests them so that they may see that they are like the animals. ¹⁹Man's fate is like that of the animals; the same fate awaits them both: As one dies, so dies the other. All have the same breathᵇ; man has no advantage over the animal. Everything is meaningless. ²⁰All go to the same place; all come from dust, and to dust all return. ²¹Who knows if the spirit of man rises upward and if the spirit of the animalᶜ goes down into the earth?"

²²So I saw that there is nothing better for a man than to enjoy his work, because that is his lot. For who can bring him to see what will happen after him?

Oppression, Toil, Friendlessness

4 Again I looked and saw all the oppression that was taking place under the sun:

ᵃ 15 Or *God calls back the past* ᵇ 19 Or *spirit* ᶜ 21 Or *Who knows the spirit of man, which rises upward, or the spirit of the animal, which*

HE HAS MADE EVERYTHING
BEAUTIFUL IN ITS TIME. HE
HAS ALSO SET ETERNITY IN
THE HEARTS OF MEN; YET THEY
CANNOT FATHOM WHAT GOD HAS
DONE FROM BEGINNING TO END.
Ecclesiastes 3:11

Act Your Age

JOY MORGAN DAVIS

READ | ECCLESIASTES 3:9 – 15

It's easier to have faith
When you're fifty!
You look back on your life
And you see proof. . .
The promises He made
And kept,
The prayers He answered,
The children He protected,
The healing, the help,
His hands on your
Plans and purposes,
His timing, (which left you
Impatient and petulant), but which
Was always perfect. . .
Oh yes! It's easier to have faith
When you're fifty!

Then why do I so often
Act as if I'm
Twenty-five?!

Dear God, thank you for your faithfulness to me through every day, every month, every year of my life. I am grateful that through experience I know you keep your promises and answer my prayers. I praise you for all you have done for me. Amen.

Your next devotion is located on page 903.

GRANDCHILD IN FOCUS • PRAYER

Respect for Authority

Dear Lord, I pray that my grandchild will continually grow to respect those in authority. May she learn to be cooperative and fair in work and play. Instill in her a high regard for officials who govern our land and enforce the laws. May her relationships with parents, teachers, coaches, mentors and bosses be respectful, admirable, constructive and caring. Amen.

I saw the tears of the oppressed—
    and they have no comforter;
power was on the side of their oppressors—
    and they have no comforter.
2 And I declared that the dead,
    who had already died,
are happier than the living,
    who are still alive.
3 But better than both
    is he who has not yet been,
who has not seen the evil
    that is done under the sun.

4 And I saw that all labor and all achievement spring from man's envy of his neighbor. This too is meaningless, a chasing after the wind.

5 The fool folds his hands
    and ruins himself.
6 Better one handful with tranquillity
    than two handfuls with toil
    and chasing after the wind.

7 Again I saw something meaningless under the sun:

8 There was a man all alone;
    he had neither son nor brother.
There was no end to his toil,
    yet his eyes were not content with his
      wealth.
"For whom am I toiling," he asked,
    "and why am I depriving myself of
      enjoyment?"
This too is meaningless—
    a miserable business!

9 Two are better than one,
    because they have a good return for their
      work:
10 If one falls down,
    his friend can help him up.
But pity the man who falls
    and has no one to help him up!
11 Also, if two lie down together, they will keep
      warm.
    But how can one keep warm alone?

12 Though one may be overpowered,
    two can defend themselves.
A cord of three strands is not quickly broken.

Advancement Is Meaningless

13 Better a poor but wise youth than an old but foolish king who no longer knows how to take warning. 14 The youth may have come from prison to the kingship, or he may have been born in poverty within his kingdom. 15 I saw that all who lived and walked under the sun followed the youth, the king's successor. 16 There was no end to all the people who were before them. But those who came later were not pleased with the successor. This too is meaningless, a chasing after the wind.

Stand in Awe of God

5 Guard your steps when you go to the house of God. Go near to listen rather than to offer the sacrifice of fools, who do not know that they do wrong.

2 Do not be quick with your mouth,
    do not be hasty in your heart
    to utter anything before God.
God is in heaven
    and you are on earth,
    so let your words be few.
3 As a dream comes when there are many cares,
    so the speech of a fool when there are
      many words.

4 When you make a vow to God, do not delay in fulfilling it. He has no pleasure in fools; fulfill your vow. 5 It is better not to vow than to make a vow and not fulfill it. 6 Do not let your mouth lead you into sin. And do not protest to the ⌐temple⌐ messenger, "My vow was a mistake." Why should God be angry at what you say and destroy the work of your hands? 7 Much dreaming and many words are meaningless. Therefore stand in awe of God.

Riches Are Meaningless

8 If you see the poor oppressed in a district, and justice and rights denied, do not be surprised at

> AND I DECLARED THAT THE
> DEAD, WHO HAD ALREADY DIED,
> ARE HAPPIER THAN THE LIVING,
> WHO ARE STILL ALIVE.
> *Ecclesiastes 4:2*

Celebrate a Life Well Lived

BOBBIE WOLGEMUTH

READ | ECCLESIASTES 4:1–12

She told her friends to call her "Plain Jane," but Jane Denney was anything but plain. Jane was winsome, warm and wonderful.

One day Jane called me and asked if she could come by my home for a visit. In her late 70s, Jane had been fighting a long battle with breast cancer, and all of her prayer partners and friends, including me, had prayed hard and long for Jane's release from the disease.

After sipping a cup of tea, Jane announced, "I'm finally going to be cancer free." Her face was radiant when she added, "The doctor said I have about two months to finish my stay on this earth. I'm putting my funeral arrangements together and want you to sing a hymn at the service."

When Jane died, the funeral was just as she had planned. Friends, bright flowers, uplifting music and Scripture filled the hour-long service. On the program was a simple quote from "Plain Jane": "God is real; God is good."

A tearful young woman walked to the podium to deliver a eulogy for her grandmother. She began, "I remember when I was a little girl, sitting next to Mee-maw at a funeral for one of her friends. When I told her that I didn't like being in a place where everyone was crying, my grandmother held my hand and whispered, 'Oh, Darling, this isn't a sad day. We're celebrating a life well lived.'"

Everyone in the audience knew exactly what that granddaughter meant. With our tears we embraced the wisdom of "plain" Jane Denney.

A funeral is a great place to celebrate. It's a time for rededicating ourselves to living in the joy of the Lord Jesus.

Do you want to be like "Plain Jane"? Remember that God is real and God is good. And live every moment celebrating Jesus.

Lord, thank you for heaven and the promise of spending eternity with you. Help me to remember what's really important while I live here on earth so that my grandchildren will have a reason to celebrate when I'm gone. Amen.

Your next devotion is located on page 909.

GRANDCHILD IN FOCUS • PRAYER

Courage

O Father, builder of character and courage, may my grandchild grow strong in the light of your love. Grant him courage to stand for what is right, to guard the truth and to ensure justice in every aspect of life. May he boldly grow in grace, revere your name and proudly proclaim you as the Lord of lords and King of kings. Amen.

903

such things; for one official is eyed by a higher one, and over them both are others higher still. ⁹The increase from the land is taken by all; the king himself profits from the fields.

¹⁰Whoever loves money never has money
    enough;
  whoever loves wealth is never satisfied with
    his income.
This too is meaningless.

¹¹As goods increase,
  so do those who consume them.
And what benefit are they to the owner
  except to feast his eyes on them?

¹²The sleep of a laborer is sweet,
  whether he eats little or much,
but the abundance of a rich man
  permits him no sleep.

¹³I have seen a grievous evil under the sun:

wealth hoarded to the harm of its owner,
¹⁴ or wealth lost through some misfortune,
so that when he has a son
  there is nothing left for him.
¹⁵Naked a man comes from his mother's
    womb,
  and as he comes, so he departs.
He takes nothing from his labor
  that he can carry in his hand.

¹⁶This too is a grievous evil:

As a man comes, so he departs,
  and what does he gain,
    since he toils for the wind?
¹⁷All his days he eats in darkness,
  with great frustration, affliction and
    anger.

¹⁸Then I realized that it is good and proper for a man to eat and drink, and to find satisfaction in his toilsome labor under the sun during the few days of life God has given him—for this is his lot. ¹⁹Moreover, when God gives any man wealth and possessions, and enables him to enjoy them, to accept his lot and be happy in his work—this

TALKING POINTS

Money

The ability to enjoy our possessions
is a gift from God.

ECCLESIASTES 5:19

For more on money, go to Mark 12:41–44.

is a gift of God. ²⁰He seldom reflects on the days of his life, because God keeps him occupied with gladness of heart.

6 I have seen another evil under the sun, and it weighs heavily on men: ²God gives a man wealth, possessions and honor, so that he lacks nothing his heart desires, but God does not enable him to enjoy them, and a stranger enjoys them instead. This is meaningless, a grievous evil.

³A man may have a hundred children and live many years; yet no matter how long he lives, if he cannot enjoy his prosperity and does not receive proper burial, I say that a stillborn child is better off than he. ⁴It comes without meaning, it departs in darkness, and in darkness its name is shrouded. ⁵Though it never saw the sun or knew anything, it has more rest than does that man— ⁶even if he lives a thousand years twice over but fails to enjoy his prosperity. Do not all go to the same place?

⁷All man's efforts are for his mouth,
  yet his appetite is never satisfied.
⁸What advantage has a wise man
  over a fool?
What does a poor man gain
  by knowing how to conduct himself before
    others?
⁹Better what the eye sees
  than the roving of the appetite.
This too is meaningless,
  a chasing after the wind.

¹⁰Whatever exists has already been named,
and what man is has been known;
no man can contend
with one who is stronger than he.
¹¹The more the words,
the less the meaning,
and how does that profit anyone?

¹²For who knows what is good for a man in life, during the few and meaningless days he passes through like a shadow? Who can tell him what will happen under the sun after he is gone?

Wisdom

7 A good name is better than fine perfume,
and the day of death better than the day of birth.
²It is better to go to a house of mourning
than to go to a house of feasting,
for death is the destiny of every man;
the living should take this to heart.
³Sorrow is better than laughter,
because a sad face is good for the heart.
⁴The heart of the wise is in the house of mourning,
but the heart of fools is in the house of pleasure.
⁵It is better to heed a wise man's rebuke
than to listen to the song of fools.
⁶Like the crackling of thorns under the pot,
so is the laughter of fools.
This too is meaningless.
⁷Extortion turns a wise man into a fool,
and a bribe corrupts the heart.

⁸The end of a matter is better than its beginning,
and patience is better than pride.
⁹Do not be quickly provoked in your spirit,
for anger resides in the lap of fools.
¹⁰Do not say, "Why were the old days better than these?"
For it is not wise to ask such questions.
¹¹Wisdom, like an inheritance, is a good thing
and benefits those who see the sun.

¹²Wisdom is a shelter
as money is a shelter,
but the advantage of knowledge is this:
that wisdom preserves the life of its possessor.

¹³Consider what God has done:

Who can straighten
what he has made crooked?
¹⁴When times are good, be happy;
but when times are bad, consider:
God has made the one
as well as the other.
Therefore, a man cannot discover
anything about his future.

TALKING POINTS

Patience

Better to be patient than to be proud.
ECCLESIASTES 7:8

For more on patience, go to Romans 12:12.

¹⁵In this meaningless life of mine I have seen both of these:

a righteous man perishing in his righteousness,
and a wicked man living long in his wickedness.
¹⁶Do not be overrighteous,
neither be overwise—
why destroy yourself?
¹⁷Do not be overwicked,
and do not be a fool—
why die before your time?
¹⁸It is good to grasp the one
and not let go of the other.
The man who fears God will avoid all ⌐extremes⌐.ᵃ

ᵃ 18 Or will follow them both

¹⁹ Wisdom makes one wise man more powerful
than ten rulers in a city.

²⁰ There is not a righteous man on earth
who does what is right and never sins.

²¹ Do not pay attention to every word people say,
or you may hear your servant cursing
you—

²² for you know in your heart
that many times you yourself have cursed
others.

²³ All this I tested by wisdom and I said,

"I am determined to be wise"—
but this was beyond me.

²⁴ Whatever wisdom may be,
it is far off and most profound—
who can discover it?

²⁵ So I turned my mind to understand,
to investigate and to search out wisdom
and the scheme of things
and to understand the stupidity of
wickedness
and the madness of folly.

²⁶ I find more bitter than death
the woman who is a snare,
whose heart is a trap
and whose hands are chains.
The man who pleases God will escape her,
but the sinner she will ensnare.

²⁷ "Look," says the Teacher,[a] "this is what I have
discovered:

"Adding one thing to another to discover the
scheme of things—

²⁸   while I was still searching
but not finding—
I found one ⌊upright⌋ man among a
thousand,
but not one ⌊upright⌋ woman among them
all.

²⁹ This only have I found:
God made mankind upright,
but men have gone in search of many
schemes."

8 Who is like the wise man?
Who knows the explanation of things?
Wisdom brightens a man's face
and changes its hard appearance.

Obey the King

² Obey the king's command, I say, because you
took an oath before God. ³ Do not be in a hurry
to leave the king's presence. Do not stand up for
a bad cause, for he will do whatever he pleases.
⁴ Since a king's word is supreme, who can say to
him, "What are you doing?"

⁵ Whoever obeys his command will come to
no harm,
and the wise heart will know the proper
time and procedure.

⁶ For there is a proper time and procedure for
every matter,
though a man's misery weighs heavily
upon him.

⁷ Since no man knows the future,
who can tell him what is to come?

⁸ No man has power over the wind to contain
it[b];
so no one has power over the day of his
death.
As no one is discharged in time of war,
so wickedness will not release those who
practice it.

⁹ All this I saw, as I applied my mind to everything done under the sun. There is a time when a
man lords it over others to his own[c] hurt. ¹⁰ Then
too, I saw the wicked buried—those who used
to come and go from the holy place and receive
praise[d] in the city where they did this. This too
is meaningless.

¹¹ When the sentence for a crime is not quickly carried out, the hearts of the people are filled
with schemes to do wrong. ¹² Although a wicked
man commits a hundred crimes and still lives a
long time, I know that it will go better with God-

---

[a] 27 Or leader of the assembly   [b] 8 Or over his spirit to retain it
[c] 9 Or to their   [d] 10 Some Hebrew manuscripts and Septuagint
(Aquila); most Hebrew manuscripts and are forgotten

fearing men, who are reverent before God. [13] Yet because the wicked do not fear God, it will not go well with them, and their days will not lengthen like a shadow.

[14] There is something else meaningless that occurs on earth: righteous men who get what the wicked deserve, and wicked men who get what the righteous deserve. This too, I say, is meaningless. [15] So I commend the enjoyment of life, because nothing is better for a man under the sun than to eat and drink and be glad. Then joy will accompany him in his work all the days of the life God has given him under the sun.

[16] When I applied my mind to know wisdom and to observe man's labor on earth—his eyes not seeing sleep day or night— [17] then I saw all that God has done. No one can comprehend what goes on under the sun. Despite all his efforts to search it out, man cannot discover its meaning. Even if a wise man claims he knows, he cannot really comprehend it.

A Common Destiny for All

9 So I reflected on all this and concluded that the righteous and the wise and what they do are in God's hands, but no man knows whether love or hate awaits him. [2] All share a common destiny—the righteous and the wicked, the good and the bad,[a] the clean and the unclean, those who offer sacrifices and those who do not.

As it is with the good man,
    so with the sinner;
as it is with those who take oaths,
    so with those who are afraid to take them.

[3] This is the evil in everything that happens under the sun: The same destiny overtakes all. The hearts of men, moreover, are full of evil and there is madness in their hearts while they live, and afterward they join the dead. [4] Anyone who is among the living has hope[b]—even a live dog is better off than a dead lion!

[5] For the living know that they will die,
    but the dead know nothing;

they have no further reward,
    and even the memory of them is forgotten.
[6] Their love, their hate
    and their jealousy have long since
        vanished;
never again will they have a part
    in anything that happens under the sun.

[7] Go, eat your food with gladness, and drink your wine with a joyful heart, for it is now that God favors what you do. [8] Always be clothed in white, and always anoint your head with oil. [9] Enjoy life with your wife, whom you love, all the days of this meaningless life that God has given you under the sun—all your meaningless days. For this is your lot in life and in your toilsome labor under the sun. [10] Whatever your hand finds to do, do it with all your might, for in the grave,[c] where you are going, there is neither working nor planning nor knowledge nor wisdom.

[11] I have seen something else under the sun:

The race is not to the swift
    or the battle to the strong,
nor does food come to the wise
    or wealth to the brilliant
    or favor to the learned;
but time and chance happen to them all.

[12] Moreover, no man knows when his hour will come:

As fish are caught in a cruel net,
    or birds are taken in a snare,
so men are trapped by evil times
    that fall unexpectedly upon them.

Wisdom Better Than Folly

[13] I also saw under the sun this example of wisdom that greatly impressed me: [14] There was once a small city with only a few people in it. And a powerful king came against it, surrounded it and built huge siegeworks against it. [15] Now there lived in that city a man poor but wise, and he

---

[a] 2 Septuagint (Aquila), Vulgate and Syriac; Hebrew does not have *and the bad.*   [b] 4 Or *What then is to be chosen? With all who live, there is hope*   [c] 10 Hebrew *Sheol*

saved the city by his wisdom. But nobody remembered that poor man. ¹⁶So I said, "Wisdom is better than strength." But the poor man's wisdom is despised, and his words are no longer heeded.

¹⁷The quiet words of the wise are more to be heeded
>> than the shouts of a ruler of fools.
¹⁸Wisdom is better than weapons of war,
>> but one sinner destroys much good.

10 As dead flies give perfume a bad smell,
>> so a little folly outweighs wisdom and honor.
²The heart of the wise inclines to the right,
>> but the heart of the fool to the left.
³Even as he walks along the road,
>> the fool lacks sense
>> and shows everyone how stupid he is.
⁴If a ruler's anger rises against you,
>> do not leave your post;
>> calmness can lay great errors to rest.

⁵There is an evil I have seen under the sun,
>> the sort of error that arises from a ruler:
⁶Fools are put in many high positions,
>> while the rich occupy the low ones.
⁷I have seen slaves on horseback,
>> while princes go on foot like slaves.

⁸Whoever digs a pit may fall into it;
>> whoever breaks through a wall may be bitten by a snake.
⁹Whoever quarries stones may be injured by them;
>> whoever splits logs may be endangered by them.

¹⁰If the ax is dull
>> and its edge unsharpened,
>> more strength is needed
>> but skill will bring success.

¹¹If a snake bites before it is charmed,
>> there is no profit for the charmer.

¹²Words from a wise man's mouth are gracious,
>> but a fool is consumed by his own lips.

¹³At the beginning his words are folly;
>> at the end they are wicked madness—
¹⁴ and the fool multiplies words.

No one knows what is coming—
>> who can tell him what will happen after him?

¹⁵A fool's work wearies him;
>> he does not know the way to town.

¹⁶Woe to you, O land whose king was a servant ^a
>> and whose princes feast in the morning.
¹⁷Blessed are you, O land whose king is of noble birth
>> and whose princes eat at a proper time—
>> for strength and not for drunkenness.

¹⁸If a man is lazy, the rafters sag;
>> if his hands are idle, the house leaks.

¹⁹A feast is made for laughter,
>> and wine makes life merry,
>> but money is the answer for everything.

²⁰Do not revile the king even in your thoughts,
>> or curse the rich in your bedroom,
>> because a bird of the air may carry your words,
>> and a bird on the wing may report what you say.

Bread Upon the Waters

11 Cast your bread upon the waters,
>> for after many days you will find it again.
²Give portions to seven, yes to eight,
>> for you do not know what disaster may come upon the land.

³If clouds are full of water,
>> they pour rain upon the earth.
Whether a tree falls to the south or to the north,
>> in the place where it falls, there will it lie.
⁴Whoever watches the wind will not plant;
>> whoever looks at the clouds will not reap.

^a 16 Or king is a child

WORDS FROM A WISE MAN'S
MOUTH ARE GRACIOUS, BUT
A FOOL IS CONSUMED BY HIS
OWN LIPS.

Ecclesiastes 10:12

My Lips Are Sealed

JEAN SHAW

READ | ECCLESIASTES 10:12–14

The hardest thing about knowing a lot is keeping it to myself. If someone asks me a simple question in my chosen field of expertise, I want to give her two or three chapters of technical information. When my new daughter-in-law calls me on Sunday morning to find out how much water to put with the pot roast, she doesn't need a twenty-minute lesson on slow cooking.

People with much formal education have a way of intimidating those with less training. The graciousness to accept another person's limited knowledge, when you could spout off ten times as much, is a mark of Christian love because it requires doing whatever it takes to make the other person feel more valuable. This applies when a first grader makes you stop what you're doing while she triumphantly reads every page of her first primer. It has no less importance as your dinner guest offers you advice on how to raise African violets. You can accept her information without revealing all that you learned in your ten-week course at the botanical gardens.

Understanding how something or someone operates should bring with it a calm spirit. No need to flare up and kick the vacuum cleaner when it doesn't work if you know enough to see that the hose is clogged or the bag is full. No need to spank Martha for spilling her milk if you appreciate the limited motor-coordination of four-year-olds.

"Words from a wise man's mouth are gracious," says Ecclesiastes 10:12. We who claim Christ as Lord and Savior cannot separate facts in the head from love in the heart.

Loving Father, help me to be gracious every time I open my mouth to speak. Give me a discerning heart so that I will be sparing with my advice, judicious with my knowledge and calm when things go wrong. Amen.

Your next devotion is located on page 916.

GRANDCHILD IN FOCUS • PRAYER

Future Spouse

Dear Lord, if it is your will, I pray my grandchild will be united in a loving and Christian marriage. Keep her sexually pure so that she will honor you with her body and mind. As she seeks a spouse who will honor and care for her, give her patience and discernment. May her choice for a life partner be your choice for her, so that she and her husband will together glorify you in a lasting love. I pray this in Jesus' name, amen.

⁵ As you do not know the path of the wind,
　　or how the body is formed *a* in a mother's
　　　　womb,
　so you cannot understand the work of God,
　　the Maker of all things.

⁶ Sow your seed in the morning,
　　and at evening let not your hands be idle,
　for you do not know which will succeed,
　　whether this or that,
　　or whether both will do equally well.

Remember Your Creator While Young

⁷ Light is sweet,
　　and it pleases the eyes to see the sun.
⁸ However many years a man may live,
　　let him enjoy them all.
　But let him remember the days of darkness,
　　for they will be many.
　　Everything to come is meaningless.

⁹ Be happy, young man, while you are young,
　　and let your heart give you joy in the days
　　　　of your youth.
　Follow the ways of your heart
　　and whatever your eyes see,
　but know that for all these things
　　God will bring you to judgment.
¹⁰ So then, banish anxiety from your heart
　　and cast off the troubles of your body,
　　for youth and vigor are meaningless.

12 Remember your Creator
　　in the days of your youth,

stories to share

ECCLESIASTES 12:1–7

Remember Your Creator

LIFE LESSON: We're never too young to love and trust God.

TO TALK ABOUT

✦ Who is your Creator?

✦ Why is it important to remember your Creator while you're still young?

✦ Do you think children have less "trouble" in their lives than adults?

✦ This passage sounds like a riddle. What might some of the details mean?

before the days of trouble come
　　and the years approach when you
　　　　will say,
　　　"I find no pleasure in them"—
² before the sun and the light
　　and the moon and the stars grow dark,
　　and the clouds return after the rain;
³ when the keepers of the house tremble,
　　and the strong men stoop,
　when the grinders cease because they are
　　　　few,
　　and those looking through the windows
　　　　grow dim;
⁴ when the doors to the street are closed
　　and the sound of grinding fades;

TALKING POINTS

Dating
Follow God's will from an early age.
ECCLESIASTES 12:1

For more on dating, go to 2 Corinthians 6:14.

a 5 Or know how life (or the spirit) / enters the body being formed

when men rise up at the sound of birds,
    but all their songs grow faint;
5 when men are afraid of heights
    and of dangers in the streets;
when the almond tree blossoms
    and the grasshopper drags himself along
    and desire no longer is stirred.
Then man goes to his eternal home
    and mourners go about the streets.

6 Remember him — before the silver cord is
    severed,
    or the golden bowl is broken;
before the pitcher is shattered at the spring,
    or the wheel broken at the well,
7 and the dust returns to the ground it came
    from,
    and the spirit returns to God who gave it.

8 "Meaningless! Meaningless!" says the
    Teacher. *a*
    "Everything is meaningless!"

The Conclusion of the Matter

9 Not only was the Teacher wise, but also he imparted knowledge to the people. He pondered and searched out and set in order many proverbs. 10 The Teacher searched to find just the right words, and what he wrote was upright and true.

11 The words of the wise are like goads, their collected sayings like firmly embedded nails — given by one Shepherd. 12 Be warned, my son, of anything in addition to them.

Of making many books there is no end, and much study wearies the body.

13 Now all has been heard;
    here is the conclusion of the matter:
Fear God and keep his commandments,
    for this is the whole ⌐duty⌐ of man.
14 For God will bring every deed into judgment,
    including every hidden thing,
    whether it is good or evil.

a 8 Or the leader of the assembly; also in verses 9 and 10

A Standard
FOR SEXUALITY

In today's society in which sexuality is regarded by many as cheap and easy, treated lightly on prime-time TV and used to promote everything from shampoo to blue jeans, the book of Song of Songs sets a higher standard for the Christian view of sexuality. It exemplifies what sex and love should be: beautiful, intimate, desirable and reserved for two individuals who have committed to one another for life. More specifically, sex, with all its joys and pleasures, is something God created for enjoyment within a marriage relationship.

Although Song of Songs may not be appropriate reading for your young grandchildren, it's reassuring to know that this subject, considered taboo by some Christians, is clearly covered in God's Word. The relationship between a man and woman, introduced when God created Adam and Eve (see Genesis 2:24), is expounded on here in Song of Songs.

It is sometimes easier for us to acknowledge that God created sex than to acknowledge that God encourages us to enjoy the beautiful sensuality that exists between a man and a woman. But God created love and sex for our enjoyment. The world, unfortunately, has taken sex and God's intentions for it and twisted them into something else. A healthy and Biblical perspective on the subject is exactly what we and our grandchildren need.

VERSE *to* REMEMBER | SONG OF SONGS 2:10

My lover spoke and said to me, "Arise, my darling, my beautiful one, and come with me."

ABOUT SONG OF SONGS

WRITTEN BY:
Probably King Solomon

WRITTEN FOR:
The people of Israel

DATE WRITTEN:
Probably early in Solomon's reign, around 965 B.C.

WHY WRITTEN:
To help God's people better understand sex, love and marriage

1

Solomon's Song of Songs.

Beloved [a]

² Let him kiss me with the kisses of his
mouth—
for your love is more delightful than wine.
³ Pleasing is the fragrance of your perfumes;
your name is like perfume poured out.
No wonder the maidens love you!
⁴ Take me away with you—let us hurry!
Let the king bring me into his chambers.

Friends

We rejoice and delight in you [b];
we will praise your love more than wine.

Beloved

How right they are to adore you!

⁵ Dark am I, yet lovely,
O daughters of Jerusalem,
dark like the tents of Kedar,
like the tent curtains of Solomon. [c]
⁶ Do not stare at me because I am dark,
because I am darkened by the sun.
My mother's sons were angry with me
and made me take care of the vineyards;
my own vineyard I have neglected.
⁷ Tell me, you whom I love, where you graze
your flock
and where you rest your sheep at midday.
Why should I be like a veiled woman
beside the flocks of your friends?

Friends

⁸ If you do not know, most beautiful of
women,
follow the tracks of the sheep
and graze your young goats
by the tents of the shepherds.

Lover

⁹ I liken you, my darling, to a mare
harnessed to one of the chariots of
Pharaoh.

¹⁰ Your cheeks are beautiful with earrings,
your neck with strings of jewels.
¹¹ We will make you earrings of gold,
studded with silver.

Beloved

¹² While the king was at his table,
my perfume spread its fragrance.
¹³ My lover is to me a sachet of myrrh
resting between my breasts.
¹⁴ My lover is to me a cluster of henna blossoms
from the vineyards of En Gedi.

Lover

¹⁵ How beautiful you are, my darling!
Oh, how beautiful!
Your eyes are doves.

Beloved

¹⁶ How handsome you are, my lover!
Oh, how charming!
And our bed is verdant.

Lover

¹⁷ The beams of our house are cedars;
our rafters are firs.

Beloved [d]

2

I am a rose [e] of Sharon,
a lily of the valleys.

Lover

² Like a lily among thorns
is my darling among the maidens.

Beloved

³ Like an apple tree among the trees of the
forest
is my lover among the young men.

[a] Primarily on the basis of the gender of the Hebrew pronouns
used, male and female speakers are indicated in the margins by
the captions *Lover* and *Beloved* respectively. The words of others
are marked *Friends*. In some instances the divisions and their
captions are debatable.   [b] *4* The Hebrew is masculine singular.
[c] *5* Or *Salma*   [d] Or *Lover*   [e] *1* Possibly a member of the crocus
family

I delight to sit in his shade,
  and his fruit is sweet to my taste.
⁴He has taken me to the banquet hall,
  and his banner over me is love.
⁵Strengthen me with raisins,
  refresh me with apples,
    for I am faint with love.
⁶His left arm is under my head,
  and his right arm embraces me.
⁷Daughters of Jerusalem, I charge you
  by the gazelles and by the does of the field:
Do not arouse or awaken love
  until it so desires.

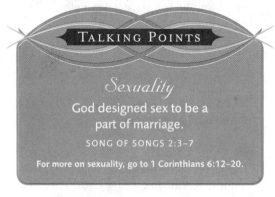

TALKING POINTS

Sexuality

God designed sex to be a
part of marriage.

SONG OF SONGS 2:3–7

For more on sexuality, go to 1 Corinthians 6:12–20.

⁸Listen! My lover!
  Look! Here he comes,
leaping across the mountains,
  bounding over the hills.
⁹My lover is like a gazelle or a young stag.
  Look! There he stands behind our wall,
gazing through the windows,
  peering through the lattice.
¹⁰My lover spoke and said to me,
  "Arise, my darling,
    my beautiful one, and come with me.
¹¹See! The winter is past;
  the rains are over and gone.
¹²Flowers appear on the earth;
  the season of singing has come,
the cooing of doves
  is heard in our land.

¹³The fig tree forms its early fruit;
  the blossoming vines spread their
    fragrance.
Arise, come, my darling;
  my beautiful one, come with me."

Lover

¹⁴My dove in the clefts of the rock,
  in the hiding places on the mountainside,
show me your face,
  let me hear your voice;
for your voice is sweet,
  and your face is lovely.
¹⁵Catch for us the foxes,
  the little foxes
that ruin the vineyards,
  our vineyards that are in bloom.

Beloved

¹⁶My lover is mine and I am his;
  he browses among the lilies.
¹⁷Until the day breaks
  and the shadows flee,
turn, my lover,
  and be like a gazelle
or like a young stag
  on the rugged hills.ᵃ

3 All night long on my bed
  I looked for the one my heart loves;
    I looked for him but did not find him.
²I will get up now and go about the city,
  through its streets and squares;
I will search for the one my heart loves.
  So I looked for him but did not find him.
³The watchmen found me
  as they made their rounds in the city.
    "Have you seen the one my heart loves?"
⁴Scarcely had I passed them
  when I found the one my heart loves.
I held him and would not let him go
  till I had brought him to my mother's
    house,
  to the room of the one who conceived me.

ᵃ 17 Or *the hills of Bether*

⁵ Daughters of Jerusalem, I charge you
  by the gazelles and by the does of the field:
Do not arouse or awaken love
  until it so desires.

⁶ Who is this coming up from the desert
  like a column of smoke,
perfumed with myrrh and incense
  made from all the spices of the merchant?
⁷ Look! It is Solomon's carriage,
  escorted by sixty warriors,
  the noblest of Israel,
⁸ all of them wearing the sword,
  all experienced in battle,
each with his sword at his side,
  prepared for the terrors of the night.
⁹ King Solomon made for himself the carriage;
  he made it of wood from Lebanon.
¹⁰ Its posts he made of silver,
  its base of gold.
Its seat was upholstered with purple,
  its interior lovingly inlaid
by ª the daughters of Jerusalem.
¹¹ Come out, you daughters of Zion,
  and look at King Solomon wearing the
    crown,
  the crown with which his mother crowned
    him
on the day of his wedding,
  the day his heart rejoiced.

Lover

4 How beautiful you are, my darling!
  Oh, how beautiful!
  Your eyes behind your veil are doves.
Your hair is like a flock of goats
  descending from Mount Gilead.
² Your teeth are like a flock of sheep just shorn,
  coming up from the washing.
Each has its twin;
  not one of them is alone.
³ Your lips are like a scarlet ribbon;
  your mouth is lovely.
Your temples behind your veil
  are like the halves of a pomegranate.

⁴ Your neck is like the tower of David,
  built with elegance ᵇ;
on it hang a thousand shields,
  all of them shields of warriors.
⁵ Your two breasts are like two fawns,
  like twin fawns of a gazelle
  that browse among the lilies.
⁶ Until the day breaks
  and the shadows flee,
I will go to the mountain of myrrh
  and to the hill of incense.
⁷ All beautiful you are, my darling;
  there is no flaw in you.

⁸ Come with me from Lebanon, my bride,
  come with me from Lebanon.
Descend from the crest of Amana,
  from the top of Senir, the summit of
    Hermon,
from the lions' dens
  and the mountain haunts of the leopards.
⁹ You have stolen my heart, my sister, my bride;
  you have stolen my heart
with one glance of your eyes,
  with one jewel of your necklace.
¹⁰ How delightful is your love, my sister, my
    bride!
  How much more pleasing is your love than
    wine,
  and the fragrance of your perfume than
    any spice!
¹¹ Your lips drop sweetness as the honeycomb,
    my bride;
  milk and honey are under your tongue.
  The fragrance of your garments is like that
    of Lebanon.
¹² You are a garden locked up, my sister, my
    bride;
  you are a spring enclosed, a sealed
    fountain.
¹³ Your plants are an orchard of pomegranates
  with choice fruits,
  with henna and nard,

ª *10 Or its inlaid interior a gift of love / from*   ᵇ *4 The meaning of*
the Hebrew for this word is uncertain.

YOUR LIPS ARE LIKE A
SCARLET RIBBON; YOUR
MOUTH IS LOVELY.

Song of Songs 4:3

Gracious Lips

BARBARA JOHNSON

READ | SONG OF SONGS 4:1 – 15

On the human face, there is plenty of exciting work for lips to do. They are given nearly the same prominence as eyes because they are capable of expressing a wide range of emotions. Lips can display everything from anger to ecstasy. They can quiver in fear, tremble with tears, open wide in laughter, bid welcome with a bright smile, or express contempt with rigid tension. That set of little muscles is capable of wide extremes of action and influence. Lips can criticize a child, then kiss him off to school. They might nag a spouse, then hope for the passionate press of his lips. Be careful how you use those lips, but be thankful you have them!

The process of smiling or forming speech begins elsewhere in the body, of course, in your mind and heart, where ideas and emotions are born. Thoughts and feelings rush to the voice box and tongue, then pass through the changing shapes of the lips. When God touches our lips with grace, those little organs can heal sadness with kind words or invite friendship with no words at all, just a smile.

Think twice before you use your lips for the wrong reasons! Use them to encourage, excite, enthuse, and inspire people. Use them to express true affection. A Swedish proverb exhorts: "Fear less, hope more; eat less, chew more; whine less, breathe more; talk less, say more; hate less, love more; and all good things are yours." Pray that each time you smile or speak, breathe or eat, pray or kiss someone, the power of your lips will be maximized by grace. Grace to you as you use those little organs of blessings!

O God of grace, thank you for lips that can be a blessing to others. Let my lips praise you and show your love to others in every word I speak and every smile I give away today. Amen.

Your next devotion is located on page 918.

GRANDCHILD IN FOCUS • PRAYER

School/Career

Dear God, may learning be a joy rather than a chore for my grandchild. May exploration of new ideas bring a sense of wonder, awe and excitement. Grant him clarity of mind, the ability to concentrate on the task at hand and recollection of what has been learned. Help him to appreciate the tasks that come easily and to persevere through those that challenge. Amen.

14 nard and saffron,
    calamus and cinnamon,
    with every kind of incense tree,
    with myrrh and aloes
    and all the finest spices.
15 You are *a* a garden fountain,
    a well of flowing water
    streaming down from Lebanon.

Beloved

16 Awake, north wind,
    and come, south wind!
    Blow on my garden,
      that its fragrance may spread abroad.
    Let my lover come into his garden
      and taste its choice fruits.

Lover

5 I have come into my garden, my sister, my
          bride;
    I have gathered my myrrh with my spice.
    I have eaten my honeycomb and my honey;
    I have drunk my wine and my milk.

Friends

    Eat, O friends, and drink;
      drink your fill, O lovers.

Beloved

2 I slept but my heart was awake.
    Listen! My lover is knocking:
  "Open to me, my sister, my darling,
    my dove, my flawless one.
  My head is drenched with dew,
    my hair with the dampness of the
          night."
3 I have taken off my robe —
    must I put it on again?
  I have washed my feet —
    must I soil them again?
4 My lover thrust his hand through the
          latch-opening;
    my heart began to pound for him.
5 I arose to open for my lover,
    and my hands dripped with myrrh,

my fingers with flowing myrrh,
    on the handles of the lock.
6 I opened for my lover,
    but my lover had left; he was gone.
    My heart sank at his departure. *b*
  I looked for him but did not find him.
    I called him but he did not answer.
7 The watchmen found me
    as they made their rounds in the city.
  They beat me, they bruised me;
    they took away my cloak,
    those watchmen of the walls!
8 O daughters of Jerusalem, I charge you —
    if you find my lover,
  what will you tell him?
    Tell him I am faint with love.

Friends

9 How is your beloved better than others,
    most beautiful of women?
  How is your beloved better than others,
    that you charge us so?

Beloved

10 My lover is radiant and ruddy,
    outstanding among ten thousand.
11 His head is purest gold;
    his hair is wavy
    and black as a raven.
12 His eyes are like doves
    by the water streams,
  washed in milk,
    mounted like jewels.
13 His cheeks are like beds of spice
    yielding perfume.
  His lips are like lilies
    dripping with myrrh.
14 His arms are rods of gold
    set with chrysolite.
  His body is like polished ivory
    decorated with sapphires. *c*
15 His legs are pillars of marble
    set on bases of pure gold.

*a 15 Or I am (spoken by the Beloved)   b 6 Or heart had gone out
to him when he spoke   c 14 Or lapis lazuli*

Vacation Time

Everyone loves to go on a trip. Invite one or two of your grandchildren (on a rotating basis) to join you (and grandpa) on a daylong adventure or a weeklong vacation. Present them in advance with the assignment of researching the history of the attraction or area, and then discuss what they've learned during the trip.

A scenic vacation provides an opportunity to give kids an appreciation of animals, plant life, and the unique climate and terrain of whatever area you have chosen to visit. If you're camping, fishing, swimming, canoeing, hiking or biking, make the most of these bonding experiences. It's surprising how much even younger children will remember years from now.

Long-Distance Variation: If your travels take you to your grandchildren's home, have them plan an activity and conduct some research. While you enjoy the outing, they can teach you something about their own special area of the country.

Creator God, thank you for the privilege of traveling to different places and of learning new things. Help this educational experience to be fun, beneficial and delightful for all of us. May the bond between me and my grandchild grow stronger through this activity. Amen.

Your next devotion is located on page 921.

GRANDCHILD IN FOCUS • PRAYER

Character

Dear Lord and Father, I ask that you fill my grandchild with your Spirit so her character reflects your goodness and love. Give her kindness and love for others. Bring joy to her life so she will be a joy to others. Grant her patience and self-control through difficult and trying times. May she show mercy and generosity to those who are less fortunate. Grant her integrity and a sense of justice, and surround her with your peace. Amen.

His appearance is like Lebanon,
  choice as its cedars.
[16]His mouth is sweetness itself;
  he is altogether lovely.
This is my lover, this my friend,
  O daughters of Jerusalem.

Friends

6 Where has your lover gone,
  most beautiful of women?
Which way did your lover turn,
  that we may look for him with you?

Beloved

[2]My lover has gone down to his garden,
  to the beds of spices,
to browse in the gardens
  and to gather lilies.
[3]I am my lover's and my lover is mine;
  he browses among the lilies.

Lover

[4]You are beautiful, my darling, as Tirzah,
  lovely as Jerusalem,
  majestic as troops with banners.
[5]Turn your eyes from me;
  they overwhelm me.
Your hair is like a flock of goats
  descending from Gilead.
[6]Your teeth are like a flock of sheep
  coming up from the washing.
Each has its twin,
  not one of them is alone.
[7]Your temples behind your veil
  are like the halves of a pomegranate.
[8]Sixty queens there may be,
  and eighty concubines,
  and virgins beyond number;
[9]but my dove, my perfect one, is unique,
  the only daughter of her mother,
  the favorite of the one who bore her.
The maidens saw her and called her
    blessed;
  the queens and concubines praised her.

Friends

[10]Who is this that appears like the dawn,
  fair as the moon, bright as the sun,
  majestic as the stars in procession?

Lover

[11]I went down to the grove of nut trees
  to look at the new growth in the valley,
to see if the vines had budded
  or the pomegranates were in bloom.
[12]Before I realized it,
  my desire set me among the royal chariots
    of my people.[a]

Friends

[13]Come back, come back, O Shulammite;
  come back, come back, that we may gaze
    on you!

Lover

Why would you gaze on the Shulammite
  as on the dance of Mahanaim?

7 How beautiful your sandaled feet,
  O prince's daughter!
Your graceful legs are like jewels,
  the work of a craftsman's hands.
[2]Your navel is a rounded goblet
  that never lacks blended wine.
Your waist is a mound of wheat
  encircled by lilies.
[3]Your breasts are like two fawns,
  twins of a gazelle.
[4]Your neck is like an ivory tower.
Your eyes are the pools of Heshbon
  by the gate of Bath Rabbim.
Your nose is like the tower of Lebanon
  looking toward Damascus.
[5]Your head crowns you like Mount Carmel.
  Your hair is like royal tapestry;
  the king is held captive by its tresses.
[6]How beautiful you are and how pleasing,
  O love, with your delights!

a 12 Or among the chariots of Amminadab; or among the chariots of the people of the prince

7 Your stature is like that of the palm,
   and your breasts like clusters of fruit.
8 I said, "I will climb the palm tree;
   I will take hold of its fruit."
May your breasts be like the clusters of the
      vine,
   the fragrance of your breath like apples,
9   and your mouth like the best wine.

Beloved

May the wine go straight to my lover,
   flowing gently over lips and teeth. *a*
10 I belong to my lover,
   and his desire is for me.
11 Come, my lover, let us go to the countryside,
   let us spend the night in the villages. *b*
12 Let us go early to the vineyards
   to see if the vines have budded,
if their blossoms have opened,
   and if the pomegranates are in bloom—
      there I will give you my love.
13 The mandrakes send out their fragrance,
   and at our door is every delicacy,
both new and old,
   that I have stored up for you, my lover.

8 If only you were to me like a brother,
   who was nursed at my mother's breasts!
Then, if I found you outside,
   I would kiss you,
      and no one would despise me.
2 I would lead you
   and bring you to my mother's house—
      she who has taught me.
I would give you spiced wine to drink,
   the nectar of my pomegranates.
3 His left arm is under my head
   and his right arm embraces me.
4 Daughters of Jerusalem, I charge you:
   Do not arouse or awaken love
      until it so desires.

Friends

5 Who is this coming up from the desert
   leaning on her lover?

Beloved

Under the apple tree I roused you;
   there your mother conceived you,
      there she who was in labor gave you birth.
6 Place me like a seal over your heart,
   like a seal on your arm;
for love is as strong as death,
   its jealousy *c* unyielding as the grave. *d*
It burns like blazing fire,
   like a mighty flame. *e*
7 Many waters cannot quench love;
   rivers cannot wash it away.
If one were to give
   all the wealth of his house for love,
      it *f* would be utterly scorned.

TALKING POINTS

Marriage

Love and sex in marriage are
ordained by God.

SONG OF SONGS 8:6–7

For more on marriage, go to 2 Corinthians 6:14.

Friends

8 We have a young sister,
   and her breasts are not yet grown.
What shall we do for our sister
   for the day she is spoken for?
9 If she is a wall,
   we will build towers of silver on her.
If she is a door,
   we will enclose her with panels of cedar.

Beloved

10 I am a wall,
   and my breasts are like towers.

a 9 Septuagint, Aquila, Vulgate and Syriac; Hebrew *lips of sleepers*
b 11 Or *henna bushes*   *c* 6 Or *ardor*   *d* 6 Hebrew *Sheol*
e 6 Or / *like the very flame of the* Lord   *f* 7 Or *he*

Worship the Lord

Praise the LORD from the earth,
    you great sea creatures and all ocean depths,
lightning and hail, snow and clouds,
    stormy winds that do his bidding,
you mountains and all hills,
    fruit trees and all cedars,
wild animals and all cattle,
    small creatures and flying birds,
kings of the earth and all nations,
    you princes and all rulers on earth,
young men and maidens,
    old men and children.

Let them praise the name of the LORD,
    for his name alone is exalted;
    his splendor is above the earth and the
        heavens.
He has raised up for his people a horn,
    the praise of all his saints,
    of Israel, the people close to his
        heart.
Praise the LORD.

Psalm 148:7—14

O Lord, everything I see is your handi-work—the birds, trees and flowers in my backyard. The face of my grandchild, Lord, is also your doing. And all of it, all your cre-ation, declares how good and splendid you are. For this I praise your holy name. Amen.

Your next devotion is located on page 928.

GRANDCHILD IN FOCUS • PRAYER

Talents

Dear Lord, the giver of gifts, bless my grandchild as he develops his talents. Help him identify his talents and be proud and confident of the gifts you have given him. Give him patience and understanding, Lord, so he will not grow weary of striving and searching to reach the goals you have set for him. May each milestone bring satis-faction and a healthy desire for greater achievement and success to bring glory to you. Amen.

Thus I have become in his eyes
  like one bringing contentment.
¹¹ Solomon had a vineyard in Baal
    Hamon;
  he let out his vineyard to tenants.
Each was to bring for its fruit
  a thousand shekels *a* of silver.
¹² But my own vineyard is mine to give;
  the thousand shekels are for you,
    O Solomon,
  and two hundred *b* are for those who tend
    its fruit.

Lover

¹³ You who dwell in the gardens
  with friends in attendance,
  let me hear your voice!

Beloved

¹⁴ Come away, my lover,
  and be like a gazelle
  or like a young stag
    on the spice-laden mountains.

a 11 That is, about 25 pounds (about 11.5 kilograms); also in
verse 12   *b 12* That is, about 5 pounds (about 2.3 kilograms)

Bright Promises
FOR THE FUTURE

Although Isaiah likely spent most of his life in Jerusalem, the capital of the southern kingdom of Judah, he proclaimed a message of judgment and salvation to both Judah and the northern kingdom of Israel. During Isaiah's lengthy ministry (from about 740 to 680 B.C.), the northern kingdom was destroyed by the Assyrians (722 B.C.). The prophet told the people of Judah that God would surely punish them for their sins as well. But Isaiah also prophesied that Judah would survive and a remnant of the population would someday return to the land. In the book that bears his name, he declared that God's love would endure through exile and alienation.

Through Isaiah God promised many things, including peace, a Messiah and a future glorious kingdom. One generation heard Isaiah's words of God's promises. Another generation many years later experienced the fruition of those promises in the coming of the Messiah, the Prince of Peace. And generations yet to come will witness the ultimate kingdom of peace. Though time passes and generations are born, live and then die, God's faithfulness and promises endure.

Isaiah's words are full of comfort and hope for a future that will be filled with God's love and peace. God assures us that he is faithful to his people and that he will call them back into his merciful arms. He will treat them justly and show them compassion and love.

VERSE *to* REMEMBER | ISAIAH 30:18

Yet the LORD longs to be gracious to you; he rises to show you compassion. For the LORD is a God of justice. Blessed are all who wait for him!

ABOUT ISAIAH

WRITTEN BY:
The prophet Isaiah

WRITTEN FOR:
The people of Judah and Israel

DATE WRITTEN:
Between 740 and 680 B.C.

WHY WRITTEN:
To warn the people of Judah and Israel that they would be punished if they continued their evil ways, and to assure God's people that he would also comfort them and bring hope and restoration through his future kingdom

1 The vision concerning Judah and Jerusalem that Isaiah son of Amoz saw during the reigns of Uzziah, Jotham, Ahaz and Hezekiah, kings of Judah.

A Rebellious Nation

2 Hear, O heavens! Listen, O earth!
    For the LORD has spoken:
"I reared children and brought them up,
    but they have rebelled against me.
3 The ox knows his master,
    the donkey his owner's manger,
but Israel does not know,
    my people do not understand."

4 Ah, sinful nation,
    a people loaded with guilt,
a brood of evildoers,
    children given to corruption!
They have forsaken the LORD;
    they have spurned the Holy One of Israel
    and turned their backs on him.

5 Why should you be beaten anymore?
    Why do you persist in rebellion?
Your whole head is injured,
    your whole heart afflicted.
6 From the sole of your foot to the top of your
        head
    there is no soundness—
only wounds and welts
    and open sores,
not cleansed or bandaged
    or soothed with oil.

7 Your country is desolate,
    your cities burned with fire;
your fields are being stripped by foreigners
    right before you,
    laid waste as when overthrown by strangers.
8 The Daughter of Zion is left
    like a shelter in a vineyard,
like a hut in a field of melons,
    like a city under siege.
9 Unless the LORD Almighty
    had left us some survivors,

we would have become like Sodom,
    we would have been like Gomorrah.

10 Hear the word of the LORD,
    you rulers of Sodom;
listen to the law of our God,
    you people of Gomorrah!
11 "The multitude of your sacrifices—
    what are they to me?" says the LORD.
"I have more than enough of burnt offerings,
    of rams and the fat of fattened animals;
I have no pleasure
    in the blood of bulls and lambs and goats.
12 When you come to appear before me,
    who has asked this of you,
    this trampling of my courts?
13 Stop bringing meaningless offerings!
    Your incense is detestable to me.
New Moons, Sabbaths and convocations—
    I cannot bear your evil assemblies.
14 Your New Moon festivals and your appointed
        feasts
    my soul hates.
They have become a burden to me;
    I am weary of bearing them.
15 When you spread out your hands in prayer,
    I will hide my eyes from you;
even if you offer many prayers,
    I will not listen.
Your hands are full of blood;
16   wash and make yourselves clean.
Take your evil deeds
    out of my sight!
Stop doing wrong,
17   learn to do right!
Seek justice,
    encourage the oppressed. [a]
Defend the cause of the fatherless,
    plead the case of the widow.

18 "Come now, let us reason together,"
    says the LORD.
"Though your sins are like scarlet,
    they shall be as white as snow;

---

[a] 17 Or / rebuke the oppressor

though they are red as crimson,
 they shall be like wool.
¹⁹ If you are willing and obedient,
 you will eat the best from the land;
²⁰ but if you resist and rebel,
 you will be devoured by the sword."
 For the mouth of the LORD
 has spoken.

TALKING POINTS

Guilt

God cleanses us from the guilt of our sin.

ISAIAH 1:18

For more on guilt, go to Isaiah 43:25.

²¹ See how the faithful city
 has become a harlot!
 She once was full of justice;
 righteousness used to dwell in her—
 but now murderers!
²² Your silver has become dross,
 your choice wine is diluted with water.
²³ Your rulers are rebels,
 companions of thieves;
 they all love bribes
 and chase after gifts.
 They do not defend the cause of the
 fatherless;
 the widow's case does not come before
 them.
²⁴ Therefore the Lord, the LORD Almighty,
 the Mighty One of Israel, declares:
 "Ah, I will get relief from my foes
 and avenge myself on my enemies.
²⁵ I will turn my hand against you;
 I will thoroughly purge away your dross
 and remove all your impurities.
²⁶ I will restore your judges as in days of old,
 your counselors as at the beginning.

Afterward you will be called
 the City of Righteousness,
 the Faithful City."

²⁷ Zion will be redeemed with justice,
 her penitent ones with righteousness.
²⁸ But rebels and sinners will both be broken,
 and those who forsake the LORD will
 perish.

²⁹ "You will be ashamed because of the sacred
 oaks
 in which you have delighted;
 you will be disgraced because of the gardens
 that you have chosen.
³⁰ You will be like an oak with fading leaves,
 like a garden without water.
³¹ The mighty man will become tinder
 and his work a spark;
 both will burn together,
 with no one to quench the fire."

The Mountain of the LORD

2:1–4pp — Mic 4:1–3

2 This is what Isaiah son of Amoz saw concerning Judah and Jerusalem:

²In the last days

the mountain of the LORD's temple will be
 established
 as chief among the mountains;
 it will be raised above the hills,
 and all nations will stream to it.

³Many peoples will come and say,

"Come, let us go up to the mountain of the
 LORD,
 to the house of the God of Jacob.
 He will teach us his ways,
 so that we may walk in his paths."
 The law will go out from Zion,
 the word of the LORD from Jerusalem.
⁴He will judge between the nations
 and will settle disputes for many peoples.
 They will beat their swords into plowshares
 and their spears into pruning hooks.

Nation will not take up sword against nation,
  nor will they train for war anymore.

⁵ Come, O house of Jacob,
  let us walk in the light of the LORD.

TALKING POINTS

Military

God promises a time of peace.

ISAIAH 2:2–4

For more on military, go to Isaiah 41:10.

The Day of the LORD

⁶ You have abandoned your people,
  the house of Jacob.
They are full of superstitions from the East;
  they practice divination like the Philistines
  and clasp hands with pagans.
⁷ Their land is full of silver and gold;
  there is no end to their treasures.
Their land is full of horses;
  there is no end to their chariots.
⁸ Their land is full of idols;
  they bow down to the work of their hands,
  to what their fingers have made.
⁹ So man will be brought low
  and mankind humbled—
  do not forgive them.ᵃ

¹⁰ Go into the rocks,
  hide in the ground
from dread of the LORD
  and the splendor of his majesty!
¹¹ The eyes of the arrogant man will be
    humbled
  and the pride of men brought low;
the LORD alone will be exalted in that day.

¹² The LORD Almighty has a day in store
  for all the proud and lofty,

for all that is exalted
  (and they will be humbled),
¹³ for all the cedars of Lebanon, tall and lofty,
  and all the oaks of Bashan,
¹⁴ for all the towering mountains
  and all the high hills,
¹⁵ for every lofty tower
  and every fortified wall,
¹⁶ for every trading ship ᵇ
  and every stately vessel.
¹⁷ The arrogance of man will be brought low
  and the pride of men humbled;
the LORD alone will be exalted in that day,
¹⁸ and the idols will totally disappear.

¹⁹ Men will flee to caves in the rocks
  and to holes in the ground
from dread of the LORD
  and the splendor of his majesty,
  when he rises to shake the earth.
²⁰ In that day men will throw away
  to the rodents and bats
their idols of silver and idols of gold,
  which they made to worship.
²¹ They will flee to caverns in the rocks
  and to the overhanging crags
from dread of the LORD
  and the splendor of his majesty,
  when he rises to shake the earth.

²² Stop trusting in man,
  who has but a breath in his nostrils.
Of what account is he?

Judgment on Jerusalem and Judah

3 See now, the Lord,
  the LORD Almighty,
is about to take from Jerusalem and Judah
  both supply and support:
all supplies of food and all supplies of
    water,
² the hero and warrior,
  the judge and prophet,
  the soothsayer and elder,

ᵃ 9 Or *not raise them up*   ᵇ 16 Hebrew *every ship of Tarshish*

³the captain of fifty and man of rank,
　　the counselor, skilled craftsman and clever
　　　enchanter.

⁴I will make boys their officials;
　　mere children will govern them.
⁵People will oppress each other—
　　man against man, neighbor against
　　　neighbor.
The young will rise up against the old,
　　the base against the honorable.

⁶A man will seize one of his brothers
　　at his father's home, and say,
"You have a cloak, you be our leader;
　　take charge of this heap of ruins!"
⁷But in that day he will cry out,
　　"I have no remedy.
I have no food or clothing in my house;
　　do not make me the leader of the people."

⁸Jerusalem staggers,
　　Judah is falling;
their words and deeds are against the LORD,
　　defying his glorious presence.
⁹The look on their faces testifies against
　　　them;
　　they parade their sin like Sodom;
　　they do not hide it.
Woe to them!
　　They have brought disaster upon
　　　themselves.

¹⁰Tell the righteous it will be well with them,
　　for they will enjoy the fruit of their deeds.
¹¹Woe to the wicked! Disaster is upon them!
　　They will be paid back for what their hands
　　　have done.

¹²Youths oppress my people,
　　women rule over them.
O my people, your guides lead you astray;
　　they turn you from the path.

¹³The LORD takes his place in court;
　　he rises to judge the people.
¹⁴The LORD enters into judgment
　　against the elders and leaders of his people:

"It is you who have ruined my vineyard;
　　the plunder from the poor is in your
　　　houses.
¹⁵What do you mean by crushing my people
　　and grinding the faces of the poor?"
　　　　　　　　declares the Lord,
　　　　　　　　the LORD Almighty.

¹⁶The LORD says,
"The women of Zion are haughty,
　　walking along with outstretched necks,
　　flirting with their eyes,
　　tripping along with mincing steps,
　　with ornaments jingling on their ankles.
¹⁷Therefore the Lord will bring sores on the
　　　heads of the women of Zion;
　　the LORD will make their scalps bald."

¹⁸In that day the Lord will snatch away their
finery: the bangles and headbands and crescent
necklaces, ¹⁹the earrings and bracelets and veils,
²⁰the headdresses and ankle chains and sashes,
the perfume bottles and charms, ²¹the signet
rings and nose rings, ²²the fine robes and the
capes and cloaks, the purses ²³and mirrors, and
the linen garments and tiaras and shawls.

²⁴Instead of fragrance there will be a stench;
　　instead of a sash, a rope;
instead of well-dressed hair, baldness;
　　instead of fine clothing, sackcloth;
　　instead of beauty, branding.
²⁵Your men will fall by the sword,
　　your warriors in battle.
²⁶The gates of Zion will lament and mourn;
　　destitute, she will sit on the ground.

4 ¹In that day seven women
　　will take hold of one man
and say, "We will eat our own food
　　and provide our own clothes;
only let us be called by your name.
　　Take away our disgrace!"

The Branch of the LORD

²In that day the Branch of the LORD will be
beautiful and glorious, and the fruit of the land

IN THAT DAY THE BRANCH OF
THE LORD WILL BE BEAUTIFUL
AND GLORIOUS, AND THE FRUIT
OF THE LAND WILL BE THE PRIDE
AND GLORY OF THE SURVIVORS
IN ISRAEL.

Isaiah 4:2

A Window of Hope

RUTH A. DEJAGER

READ | ISAIAH 4:2 – 6

The day you hold your grandchild for the first time is a moment of exquisite promise. Nothing on earth represents hope as a newborn baby does. A child is full of potential, a soft, fragrant bundle of dreams, representing a new start, a promise that family and community will continue as it should.

Judah, including the city of Jerusalem, had just about run out of dreams. In nearly all of his book up to this point, Isaiah had given the people a picture of their future that looked more like a nightmare than a dream. He had condemned them for turning away from God, offering empty sacrifices and exploiting the poor to pad their lifestyle. But then comes this passage about the Branch of the Lord — like a patch of blue sky in the midst of Isaiah's prophecies of doom. It speaks of the day God would restore to his "vineyard" its beauty and glory. It offers God's people a window of hope — hope of holiness, salvation and protection — a vision of when God would be present among them as their protection and shelter.

God always offers a window of hope for those who turn to him in faith and faithfulness. Our "picture window" of hope is Jesus, the Branch (see also Isaiah 11:1), who has rescued us from the cycle of sin and destruction. Born an infant of infinite potential and promise, he grew up and gave us a vision of protection and shelter in Revelation 22:3 – 5 that echoes Isaiah 4:5 – 6: "The throne of God and of the Lamb will be in the city, and his servants will serve him. They will see his face, and his name will be on their foreheads. There will be no more night. They will not need the light of a lamp or the light of the sun, for the Lord God will give them light. And they will reign for ever and ever."

Lord Jesus, thank you for becoming our window of hope — for eternal life, for a blessed future with you, for your redeeming love. Thank you for the promises you have fulfilled and the promises you will yet complete. I look forward to that day. Amen.

Your next devotion is located on page 931.

GRANDCHILD IN FOCUS • PRAYER

SELECT ONE OF YOUR
GRANDCHILDREN TO FOCUS ON
IN PRAYER FOR THE NEXT 14 DAYS.

Salvation

Dear Lord, please guide my grandchild to your gift of salvation. I pray that she will come to know you, to love you and to walk close to you throughout her life. May she boldly claim Jesus as her Lord and Savior. Guide her as she makes choices that have eternal consequences. Help her to follow you each moment of her life. I pray this in Jesus' name, amen.

will be the pride and glory of the survivors in Israel. ³Those who are left in Zion, who remain in Jerusalem, will be called holy, all who are recorded among the living in Jerusalem. ⁴The Lord will wash away the filth of the women of Zion; he will cleanse the bloodstains from Jerusalem by a spirit^a of judgment and a spirit^a of fire. ⁵Then the Lord will create over all of Mount Zion and over those who assemble there a cloud of smoke by day and a glow of flaming fire by night; over all the glory will be a canopy. ⁶It will be a shelter and shade from the heat of the day, and a refuge and hiding place from the storm and rain.

The Song of the Vineyard

5 I will sing for the one I love
  a song about his vineyard:
  My loved one had a vineyard
    on a fertile hillside.
²He dug it up and cleared it of stones
    and planted it with the choicest vines.
  He built a watchtower in it
    and cut out a winepress as well.
  Then he looked for a crop of good grapes,
    but it yielded only bad fruit.

³"Now you dwellers in Jerusalem and men of
      Judah,
  judge between me and my vineyard.
⁴What more could have been done for my
      vineyard
    than I have done for it?
  When I looked for good grapes,
    why did it yield only bad?
⁵Now I will tell you
    what I am going to do to my vineyard:
  I will take away its hedge,
    and it will be destroyed;
  I will break down its wall,
    and it will be trampled.
⁶I will make it a wasteland,
    neither pruned nor cultivated,
    and briers and thorns will grow there.
  I will command the clouds
    not to rain on it."

⁷The vineyard of the Lord Almighty
    is the house of Israel,
  and the men of Judah
    are the garden of his delight.
  And he looked for justice, but saw bloodshed;
    for righteousness, but heard cries of
      distress.

Woes and Judgments

⁸Woe to you who add house to house
    and join field to field
  till no space is left
    and you live alone in the land.

⁹The Lord Almighty has declared in my hearing:

  "Surely the great houses will become
      desolate,
    the fine mansions left without occupants.
¹⁰A ten-acre^b vineyard will produce only a
      bath^c of wine,
    a homer^d of seed only an ephah^e of grain."

¹¹Woe to those who rise early in the morning
    to run after their drinks,
  who stay up late at night
    till they are inflamed with wine.
¹²They have harps and lyres at their banquets,
    tambourines and flutes and wine,
  but they have no regard for the deeds of the
      Lord,
    no respect for the work of his hands.
¹³Therefore my people will go into exile
    for lack of understanding;
  their men of rank will die of hunger
    and their masses will be parched with
      thirst.
¹⁴Therefore the grave^f enlarges its appetite
    and opens its mouth without limit;
  into it will descend their nobles and masses
    with all their brawlers and revelers.

---

^a 4 Or the Spirit   ^b 10 Hebrew ten-yoke, that is, the land plowed by 10 yoke of oxen in one day   ^c 10 That is, probably about 6 gallons (about 22 liters)   ^d 10 That is, probably about 6 bushels (about 220 liters)   ^e 10 That is, probably about 3/5 bushel (about 22 liters)   ^f 14 Hebrew Sheol

¹⁵ So man will be brought low
  and mankind humbled,
  the eyes of the arrogant humbled.
¹⁶ But the LORD Almighty will be exalted by his
  justice,
  and the holy God will show himself holy
  by his righteousness.
¹⁷ Then sheep will graze as in their own pasture;
  lambs will feed ᵃ among the ruins of the
  rich.

¹⁸ Woe to those who draw sin along with cords
  of deceit,
  and wickedness as with cart ropes,
¹⁹ to those who say, "Let God hurry,
  let him hasten his work
  so we may see it.
Let it approach,
  let the plan of the Holy One of Israel come,
  so we may know it."

²⁰ Woe to those who call evil good
  and good evil,
who put darkness for light
  and light for darkness,
who put bitter for sweet
  and sweet for bitter.

²¹ Woe to those who are wise in their own eyes
  and clever in their own sight.

²² Woe to those who are heroes at drinking wine
  and champions at mixing drinks,
²³ who acquit the guilty for a bribe,
  but deny justice to the innocent.
²⁴ Therefore, as tongues of fire lick up straw
  and as dry grass sinks down in the flames,
  so their roots will decay
  and their flowers blow away like dust;
for they have rejected the law of the LORD
  Almighty
  and spurned the word of the Holy One of
  Israel.
²⁵ Therefore the LORD's anger burns against his
  people;
  his hand is raised and he strikes them
  down.

The mountains shake,
  and the dead bodies are like refuse in the
  streets.

Yet for all this, his anger is not turned away,
  his hand is still upraised.

²⁶ He lifts up a banner for the distant nations,
  he whistles for those at the ends of the
  earth.
Here they come,
  swiftly and speedily!
²⁷ Not one of them grows tired or stumbles,
  not one slumbers or sleeps;
not a belt is loosened at the waist,
  not a sandal thong is broken.
²⁸ Their arrows are sharp,
  all their bows are strung;
their horses' hoofs seem like flint,
  their chariot wheels like a whirlwind.
²⁹ Their roar is like that of the lion,
  they roar like young lions;
they growl as they seize their prey
  and carry it off with no one to rescue.
³⁰ In that day they will roar over it
  like the roaring of the sea.
And if one looks at the land,
  he will see darkness and distress;
  even the light will be darkened by the
  clouds.

Isaiah's Commission

6 In the year that King Uzziah died, I saw the
Lord seated on a throne, high and exalted,
and the train of his robe filled the temple. ² Above
him were seraphs, each with six wings: With two
wings they covered their faces, with two they covered their feet, and with two they were flying.
³ And they were calling to one another:

  "Holy, holy, holy is the LORD Almighty;
    the whole earth is full of his glory."

⁴ At the sound of their voices the doorposts and
thresholds shook and the temple was filled with
smoke.

ᵃ 17 Septuagint; Hebrew / strangers will eat

AND THEY WERE CALLING TO
ONE ANOTHER: "HOLY, HOLY,
HOLY IS THE LORD ALMIGHTY;
THE WHOLE EARTH IS FULL OF
HIS GLORY."

Isaiah 6:3

God Fills All

ANNE ORTLUND

READ | ISAIAH 6:1 – 13

Here's a ramification of the truth that God is "Immanuel" (see Isaiah 7:14; Matthew 1:23) — ever present, ever with you: suddenly sin looks definitely less appealing.

In secret we can be tempted to do things we'd never do if others were present. But Immanuel is present. His promise is, "I will never leave you nor forsake you" (Joshua 1:5). Jeremy Taylor once said, with tongue in cheek, "If you plan to sin, go do it somewhere where God isn't — so you won't feel so uncomfortable!"

This summer my husband and I were in a church service during which our elder son, Ray, Jr., was preaching on the words "filled" and "full" in Isaiah 6. He said, "Whenever God appears, he fills the whole scene; he is all there is. Psalm 139 says he is behind you, before you, over you, under you, in the east, in the west, in the dark, in the day. You can't outflank him; you can't do an end run around him. He fills all."

When you're tempted to sin, realize that giving in to temptation would mean you'd be sinning brazenly, right in front of him. How awkward. How embarrassing. You'd certainly disappoint him, but you'd also disappoint yourself. How cheap you'd feel, knowing that because of the cross he's already prepared to forgive you. What a low-down thing to do, to take advantage of such grace — of his suffering, his death, his love.

"What shall we say, then? Shall we go on sinning that grace may increase? By no means!" "Heavens, no! What a ghastly thought!" say different versions of Romans 6:1 – 2.

On the other hand, by deliberately practicing the presence of God, you'll not only hate sin, you'll actually love righteousness. In such company you'll stand taller; you'll live more nobly.

Sin will keep you from the felt presence of God; the felt presence of God will keep you from sin.

Help me to feel your presence, Lord. Guard me from sin so I may stand taller, live more nobly and glorify your name. Amen.

Your next devotion is located on page 935.

GRANDCHILD IN FOCUS · PRAYER

Physical Well-Being

Almighty God, Creator of us all, I pray that you will watch over my grandchild's physical development. May he grow in strength through the stages of his life. As he grows in awareness of his body, help him to understand that each body develops uniquely, yet is within your plan and your control. Please guard his health so that his diseases are few, his injuries are minor and his infirmities are brief. Amen.

931

5 "Woe to me!" I cried. "I am ruined! For I am a man of unclean lips, and I live among a people of unclean lips, and my eyes have seen the King, the LORD Almighty."

6 Then one of the seraphs flew to me with a live coal in his hand, which he had taken with tongs from the altar. 7 With it he touched my mouth and said, "See, this has touched your lips; your guilt is taken away and your sin atoned for."

8 Then I heard the voice of the Lord saying, "Whom shall I send? And who will go for us?"

And I said, "Here am I. Send me!"

9 He said, "Go and tell this people:

" 'Be ever hearing, but never understanding;
     be ever seeing, but never perceiving.'

10 Make the heart of this people calloused;
      make their ears dull
      and close their eyes.[a]
Otherwise they might see with their eyes,
      hear with their ears,
      understand with their hearts,
and turn and be healed."

11 Then I said, "For how long, O Lord?"
And he answered:

"Until the cities lie ruined
      and without inhabitant,
until the houses are left deserted
      and the fields ruined and ravaged,
12 until the LORD has sent everyone far away
      and the land is utterly forsaken.
13 And though a tenth remains in the land,
      it will again be laid waste.
But as the terebinth and oak
      leave stumps when they are cut down,
      so the holy seed will be the stump in the
            land."

The Sign of Immanuel

7 When Ahaz son of Jotham, the son of Uzziah, was king of Judah, King Rezin of Aram and Pekah son of Remaliah king of Israel marched up to fight against Jerusalem, but they could not overpower it.

2 Now the house of David was told, "Aram has allied itself with[b] Ephraim"; so the hearts of Ahaz and his people were shaken, as the trees of the forest are shaken by the wind.

3 Then the LORD said to Isaiah, "Go out, you and your son Shear-Jashub,[c] to meet Ahaz at the end of the aqueduct of the Upper Pool, on the road to the Washerman's Field. 4 Say to him, 'Be careful, keep calm and don't be afraid. Do not lose heart because of these two smoldering stubs of firewood — because of the fierce anger of Rezin and Aram and of the son of Remaliah.

---

stories to share

ISAIAH 6:1–13

God Calls Isaiah

LIFE LESSON: God wants us to answer when he calls us.

TO TALK ABOUT

◆ What did Isaiah see when he was called by God?

◆ Why did Isaiah say he was "ruined" (verse 5)? What did he mean?

◆ God spoke to Isaiah in a dramatic way. How do you know when God is talking to you?

◆ If God asked you to do something hard, would you be as willing as Isaiah was? Why or why not?

---

a 9,10 Hebrew; Septuagint 'You will be ever hearing, but never understanding; / you will be ever seeing, but never perceiving.' / 10This people's heart has become calloused; / they hardly hear with their ears, / and they have closed their eyes   b 2 Or has set up camp in   c 3 Shear-Jashub means a remnant will return.

5 Aram, Ephraim and Remaliah's son have plotted your ruin, saying, 6 "Let us invade Judah; let us tear it apart and divide it among ourselves, and make the son of Tabeel king over it." 7 Yet this is what the Sovereign Lord says:

" 'It will not take place,
    it will not happen,
8 for the head of Aram is Damascus,
    and the head of Damascus is only Rezin.
Within sixty-five years
    Ephraim will be too shattered to be a
        people.
9 The head of Ephraim is Samaria,
    and the head of Samaria is only Remaliah's
        son.
If you do not stand firm in your faith,
    you will not stand at all.' "

10 Again the Lord spoke to Ahaz, 11 "Ask the Lord your God for a sign, whether in the deepest depths or in the highest heights."

12 But Ahaz said, "I will not ask; I will not put the Lord to the test."

13 Then Isaiah said, "Hear now, you house of David! Is it not enough to try the patience of men? Will you try the patience of my God also? 14 Therefore the Lord himself will give you[a] a sign: The virgin will be with child and will give birth to a son, and[b] will call him Immanuel.[c] 15 He will eat curds and honey when he knows enough to reject the wrong and choose the right. 16 But before the boy knows enough to reject the wrong and choose the right, the land of the two kings you dread will be laid waste. 17 The Lord will bring on you and on your people and on the house of your father a time unlike any since Ephraim broke away from Judah—he will bring the king of Assyria."

18 In that day the Lord will whistle for flies from the distant streams of Egypt and for bees from the land of Assyria. 19 They will all come and settle in the steep ravines and in the crevices in the rocks, on all the thornbushes and at all the water holes. 20 In that day the Lord will use a razor hired from beyond the River[d]—the king of Assyria—to shave your head and the hair of your legs, and to take off your beards also. 21 In that day, a man will keep alive a young cow and two goats. 22 And because of the abundance of the milk they give, he will have curds to eat. All who remain in the land will eat curds and honey. 23 In that day, in every place where there were a thousand vines worth a thousand silver shekels,[e] there will be only briers and thorns. 24 Men will go there with bow and arrow, for the land will be covered with briers and thorns. 25 As for all the hills once cultivated by the hoe, you will no longer go there for fear of the briers and thorns; they will become places where cattle are turned loose and where sheep run.

Assyria, the Lord's Instrument

8 The Lord said to me, "Take a large scroll and write on it with an ordinary pen: Maher-Shalal-Hash-Baz.[f] 2 And I will call in Uriah the priest and Zechariah son of Jeberekiah as reliable witnesses for me."

3 Then I went to the prophetess, and she conceived and gave birth to a son. And the Lord said to me, "Name him Maher-Shalal-Hash-Baz. 4 Before the boy knows how to say 'My father' or 'My mother,' the wealth of Damascus and the plunder of Samaria will be carried off by the king of Assyria."

5 The Lord spoke to me again:

6 "Because this people has rejected
    the gently flowing waters of Shiloah
and rejoices over Rezin
    and the son of Remaliah,
7 therefore the Lord is about to bring against
        them
    the mighty floodwaters of the River[d]—
    the king of Assyria with all his pomp.
It will overflow all its channels,
    run over all its banks

---

[a] 14 The Hebrew is plural.   [b] 14 Masoretic Text; Dead Sea Scrolls and he or and they   [c] 14 Immanuel means God with us.   [d] 20,7 That is, the Euphrates   [e] 23 That is, about 25 pounds (about 11.5 kilograms)   [f] 1 Maher-Shalal-Hash-Baz means quick to the plunder, swift to the spoil; also in verse 3.

⁸and sweep on into Judah, swirling over it,
passing through it and reaching up to the
neck.
Its outspread wings will cover the breadth of
your land,
O Immanuel ᵃ!"

⁹Raise the war cry,ᵇ you nations, and be
shattered!
Listen, all you distant lands.
Prepare for battle, and be shattered!
Prepare for battle, and be shattered!
¹⁰Devise your strategy, but it will be thwarted;
propose your plan, but it will not stand,
for God is with us.ᶜ

Fear God

¹¹The LORD spoke to me with his strong hand
upon me, warning me not to follow the way of
this people. He said:

¹²"Do not call conspiracy
everything that these people call
conspiracyᵈ;
do not fear what they fear,
and do not dread it.
¹³The LORD Almighty is the one you are to
regard as holy,
he is the one you are to fear,
he is the one you are to dread,
¹⁴and he will be a sanctuary;
but for both houses of Israel he will be
a stone that causes men to stumble
and a rock that makes them fall.
And for the people of Jerusalem he will be
a trap and a snare.
¹⁵Many of them will stumble;
they will fall and be broken,
they will be snared and captured."

¹⁶Bind up the testimony
and seal up the law among my disciples.
¹⁷I will wait for the LORD,
who is hiding his face from the house of
Jacob.
I will put my trust in him.

¹⁸Here am I, and the children the LORD has giv-
en me. We are signs and symbols in Israel from
the LORD Almighty, who dwells on Mount Zion.
¹⁹When men tell you to consult mediums and
spiritists, who whisper and mutter, should not
a people inquire of their God? Why consult the
dead on behalf of the living? ²⁰To the law and
to the testimony! If they do not speak according
to this word, they have no light of dawn. ²¹Dis-
tressed and hungry, they will roam through the
land; when they are famished, they will become
enraged and, looking upward, will curse their
king and their God. ²²Then they will look toward
the earth and see only distress and darkness and
fearful gloom, and they will be thrust into utter
darkness.

To Us a Child Is Born

9 Nevertheless, there will be no more gloom
for those who were in distress. In the past
he humbled the land of Zebulun and the land of
Naphtali, but in the future he will honor Galilee
of the Gentiles, by the way of the sea, along the
Jordan —

²The people walking in darkness
have seen a great light;
on those living in the land of the shadow of
deathᵉ
a light has dawned.
³You have enlarged the nation
and increased their joy;
they rejoice before you
as people rejoice at the harvest,
as men rejoice
when dividing the plunder.
⁴For as in the day of Midian's defeat,
you have shattered
the yoke that burdens them,
the bar across their shoulders,
the rod of their oppressor.
⁵Every warrior's boot used in battle
and every garment rolled in blood

ᵃ 8 Immanuel means God with us.   ᵇ 9 Or Do your worst
ᶜ 10 Hebrew Immanuel   ᵈ 12 Or Do not call for a treaty / every
time these people call for a treaty   ᵉ 2 Or land of darkness

I WILL WAIT FOR THE LORD . . .
I WILL PUT MY TRUST IN HIM.

Isaiah 8:17

Broken Dreams

MARGARET FISHBACK POWERS

READ | ISAIAH 8:11–17

When our daughter turned four, she received a beautiful hand-carved wooden cradle for her large dolls. We carefully taught her that it was for dolls only. One day, however, she had a little boy over who would not listen to her concerning the cradle rule. He waited until she left the room to get another doll and then climbed right into the cradle!

Our daughter came to me, sobbing, and told me to come and see what had just happened. I stood in shock when I saw the boy on the floor, with all the carefully carved spokes shattered on his chest and head. He had fit perfectly inside the cradle, but it had not been built for a child!

The little boy was remorseful. He immediately asked forgiveness. I took that moment to forgive and comfort him, but I also stressed that he had been told the cradle was for dolls only. Although we tried to glue the cradle back together, we finally had to give up because the boy kept interfering; the cradle couldn't be salvaged.

That night I wrote a poem: "Broken Dreams." I hope that it will be passed on to my grandchildren.

As children bring their broken toys
With tears for me to mend,
I brought my broken dreams to God
Because He was my friend.

But then instead of leaving Him
In peace to work alone,
I hung around and tried to help
With ways that were my own.

At last I snatched them back and cried
"How can you be so slow?"
"My child," He said, "What could I do?
You never did let go."

Dear Father in heaven, teach us to leave our broken dreams at your feet. Help us to understand that through your power and in your perfect plans, you will mend and restore them for us. Amen.

GRANDCHILD IN FOCUS • PRAYER

Emotional Development

O God, Creator of mind and body, I pray that you will give my grandchild emotional health and strength. Where there is anger, bring peace. Where there is confusion, bring clarity and focus. Where there are dark shadows, cast a ray of hope. Fill her with the sunshine of your Spirit. Warm her with the presence of your peace. Amen.

Your next devotion is located on page 954.

will be destined for burning,
    will be fuel for the fire.
⁶For to us a child is born,
    to us a son is given,
    and the government will be on his
      shoulders.
And he will be called
    Wonderful Counselor,ᵃ Mighty God,
    Everlasting Father, Prince of Peace.
⁷Of the increase of his government and peace
    there will be no end.
He will reign on David's throne
    and over his kingdom,
establishing and upholding it
    with justice and righteousness
    from that time on and forever.
The zeal of the LORD Almighty
    will accomplish this.

The LORD's Anger Against Israel

⁸The Lord has sent a message against Jacob;
    it will fall on Israel.
⁹All the people will know it—
    Ephraim and the inhabitants of Samaria—
who say with pride
    and arrogance of heart,
¹⁰"The bricks have fallen down,
    but we will rebuild with dressed stone;
the fig trees have been felled,
    but we will replace them with cedars."
¹¹But the LORD has strengthened Rezin's foes
    against them
    and has spurred their enemies on.
¹²Arameans from the east and Philistines from
    the west
have devoured Israel with open mouth.

Yet for all this, his anger is not turned away,
    his hand is still upraised.

¹³But the people have not returned to him who
    struck them,
    nor have they sought the LORD Almighty.
¹⁴So the LORD will cut off from Israel both
    head and tail,
    both palm branch and reed in a single day;

¹⁵the elders and prominent men are the head,
    the prophets who teach lies are the tail.
¹⁶Those who guide this people mislead them,
    and those who are guided are led astray.
¹⁷Therefore the Lord will take no pleasure in
    the young men,
    nor will he pity the fatherless and
      widows,
for everyone is ungodly and wicked,
    every mouth speaks vileness.

Yet for all this, his anger is not turned away,
    his hand is still upraised.

¹⁸Surely wickedness burns like a fire;
    it consumes briers and thorns,
it sets the forest thickets ablaze,
    so that it rolls upward in a column of
      smoke.
¹⁹By the wrath of the LORD Almighty
    the land will be scorched
and the people will be fuel for the fire;
    no one will spare his brother.
²⁰On the right they will devour,
    but still be hungry;
on the left they will eat,
    but not be satisfied.
Each will feed on the flesh of his own
      offspringᵇ:
²¹   Manasseh will feed on Ephraim, and
      Ephraim on Manasseh;
    together they will turn against Judah.

Yet for all this, his anger is not turned away,
    his hand is still upraised.

10

Woe to those who make unjust laws,
    to those who issue oppressive decrees,
²to deprive the poor of their rights
    and withhold justice from the oppressed of
      my people,
making widows their prey
    and robbing the fatherless.
³What will you do on the day of reckoning,
    when disaster comes from afar?

ᵃ 6 Or Wonderful, Counselor   ᵇ 20 Or arm

To whom will you run for help?
  Where will you leave your riches?
⁴Nothing will remain but to cringe among the
    captives
  or fall among the slain.

Yet for all this, his anger is not turned away,
  his hand is still upraised.

God's Judgment on Assyria

⁵"Woe to the Assyrian, the rod of my anger,
  in whose hand is the club of my wrath!
⁶I send him against a godless nation,
  I dispatch him against a people who anger
    me,
to seize loot and snatch plunder,
  and to trample them down like mud in the
    streets.
⁷But this is not what he intends,
  this is not what he has in mind;
his purpose is to destroy,
  to put an end to many nations.
⁸'Are not my commanders all kings?' he says.
⁹   'Has not Calno fared like Carchemish?
  Is not Hamath like Arpad,
    and Samaria like Damascus?
¹⁰As my hand seized the kingdoms of the idols,
  kingdoms whose images excelled those of
    Jerusalem and Samaria—
¹¹shall I not deal with Jerusalem and her
    images
  as I dealt with Samaria and her idols?'"

¹²When the Lord has finished all his work
against Mount Zion and Jerusalem, he will say,
"I will punish the king of Assyria for the willful
pride of his heart and the haughty look in his
eyes. ¹³For he says:

" 'By the strength of my hand I have done
    this,
  and by my wisdom, because I have
    understanding.
I removed the boundaries of nations,
  I plundered their treasures;
like a mighty one I subdued[a] their kings.

¹⁴As one reaches into a nest,
  so my hand reached for the wealth of the
    nations;
as men gather abandoned eggs,
  so I gathered all the countries;
not one flapped a wing,
  or opened its mouth to chirp.' "

¹⁵Does the ax raise itself above him who
    swings it,
  or the saw boast against him who uses it?
As if a rod were to wield him who lifts it up,
  or a club brandish him who is not wood!
¹⁶Therefore, the Lord, the LORD Almighty,
  will send a wasting disease upon his sturdy
    warriors;
under his pomp a fire will be kindled
  like a blazing flame.
¹⁷The Light of Israel will become a fire,
  their Holy One a flame;
in a single day it will burn and consume
  his thorns and his briers.
¹⁸The splendor of his forests and fertile fields
  it will completely destroy,
  as when a sick man wastes away.
¹⁹And the remaining trees of his forests will be
    so few
  that a child could write them down.

The Remnant of Israel

²⁰In that day the remnant of Israel,
  the survivors of the house of Jacob,
will no longer rely on him
  who struck them down
but will truly rely on the LORD,
  the Holy One of Israel.
²¹A remnant will return,[b] a remnant of Jacob
  will return to the Mighty God.
²²Though your people, O Israel, be like the
    sand by the sea,
  only a remnant will return.
Destruction has been decreed,
  overwhelming and righteous.

---

[a] 13 Or / I subdued the mighty,   [b] 21 Hebrew shear-jashub; also
in verse 22

23 The Lord, the LORD Almighty, will carry out
    the destruction decreed upon the whole
    land.

24 Therefore, this is what the Lord, the LORD
Almighty, says:

"O my people who live in Zion,
    do not be afraid of the Assyrians,
who beat you with a rod
    and lift up a club against you, as Egypt did.
25 Very soon my anger against you will end
    and my wrath will be directed to their
        destruction."

26 The LORD Almighty will lash them with a
        whip,
    as when he struck down Midian at the
        rock of Oreb;
and he will raise his staff over the waters,
    as he did in Egypt.
27 In that day their burden will be lifted from
        your shoulders,
    their yoke from your neck;
the yoke will be broken
    because you have grown so fat.ᵃ

28 They enter Aiath;
    they pass through Migron;
    they store supplies at Micmash.
29 They go over the pass, and say,
    "We will camp overnight at Geba."
Ramah trembles;
    Gibeah of Saul flees.
30 Cry out, O Daughter of Gallim!
    Listen, O Laishah!
    Poor Anathoth!
31 Madmenah is in flight;
    the people of Gebim take cover.
32 This day they will halt at Nob;
    they will shake their fist
at the mount of the Daughter of Zion,
    at the hill of Jerusalem.

33 See, the Lord, the LORD Almighty,
    will lop off the boughs with great power.
The lofty trees will be felled,
    the tall ones will be brought low.

34 He will cut down the forest thickets with an ax;
    Lebanon will fall before the Mighty One.

The Branch From Jesse

11 A shoot will come up from the stump
        of Jesse;
    from his roots a Branch will bear fruit.
2 The Spirit of the LORD will rest on him—
    the Spirit of wisdom and of
        understanding,
    the Spirit of counsel and of power,
    the Spirit of knowledge and of the fear of
        the LORD—
3 and he will delight in the fear of the LORD.

He will not judge by what he sees with his
        eyes,
    or decide by what he hears with his ears;

PRAYING THE SCRIPTURES

Wisdom

ISAIAH 11:2-3

O Lord, as Isaiah prophesied concerning the
Messiah, Jesus Christ, may your Spirit rest
upon my grandchild. Give him the Spirit of
wisdom and of understanding, the Spirit of
counsel and of power, the Spirit of knowledge and of reverence of you, so that he
may delight in fearing you.

Next prayer in Wisdom Prayer Track: Daniel 2:21

4 but with righteousness he will judge the
        needy,
    with justice he will give decisions for the
        poor of the earth.
He will strike the earth with the rod of his
        mouth;
    with the breath of his lips he will slay the
        wicked.

ᵃ 27 Hebrew; Septuagint broken / from your shoulders

⁵Righteousness will be his belt
  and faithfulness the sash around his waist.

⁶The wolf will live with the lamb,
  the leopard will lie down with the goat,
the calf and the lion and the yearling *a*
    together;
  and a little child will lead them.
⁷The cow will feed with the bear,
  their young will lie down together,
  and the lion will eat straw like the ox.
⁸The infant will play near the hole of the
    cobra,
  and the young child put his hand into the
    viper's nest.
⁹They will neither harm nor destroy
  on all my holy mountain,
for the earth will be full of the knowledge of
    the LORD
  as the waters cover the sea.

¹⁰In that day the Root of Jesse will stand as a banner for the peoples; the nations will rally to him, and his place of rest will be glorious. ¹¹In that day the Lord will reach out his hand a second time to reclaim the remnant that is left of his people from Assyria, from Lower Egypt, from Upper Egypt, *b* from Cush, *c* from Elam, from Babylonia, *d* from Hamath and from the islands of the sea.

¹²He will raise a banner for the nations
  and gather the exiles of Israel;
he will assemble the scattered people of
    Judah
  from the four quarters of the earth.
¹³Ephraim's jealousy will vanish,
  and Judah's enemies *e* will be cut off;
Ephraim will not be jealous of Judah,
  nor Judah hostile toward Ephraim.
¹⁴They will swoop down on the slopes of
    Philistia to the west;
  together they will plunder the people to
    the east.
They will lay hands on Edom and Moab,
  and the Ammonites will be subject to
    them.

¹⁵The LORD will dry up
  the gulf of the Egyptian sea;
with a scorching wind he will sweep his hand
  over the Euphrates River. *f*
He will break it up into seven streams
  so that men can cross over in sandals.
¹⁶There will be a highway for the remnant of
    his people
  that is left from Assyria,
as there was for Israel
  when they came up from Egypt.

Songs of Praise

12 In that day you will say:

"I will praise you, O LORD.
  Although you were angry with me,
your anger has turned away
  and you have comforted me.
²Surely God is my salvation;
  I will trust and not be afraid.
The LORD, the LORD, is my strength and my
    song;
  he has become my salvation."
³With joy you will draw water
  from the wells of salvation.

⁴In that day you will say:

"Give thanks to the LORD, call on his name;
  make known among the nations what he
    has done,
  and proclaim that his name is exalted.

---

a 6 Hebrew; Septuagint *lion will feed*   *b* 11 Hebrew *from Pathros*
c 11 That is, the upper Nile region   *d* 11 Hebrew *Shinar*
e 13 Or *hostility*   *f* 15 Hebrew *the River*

TALKING POINTS

Trust

Trusting God leads to confidence.

ISAIAH 12:2

For more on trust, go to Isaiah 26:3–4.

QUIN SHERRER

Praying
SCRIPTURE PRAYERS

Grandmas are noted for giving gifts to their grandchildren, but the greatest and most lasting gift you can give is faithful prayer. But if you don't know where to begin, you might like to try praying Bible verses.

I learned to pray aloud when my friend Lib and I started praying together on the phone for just five minutes each morning at 8:00. We had a total of seven children, and they were our prayer focus. As young moms, we didn't know much about prayer. So I suggested we paraphrase Scripture by inserting the names of our children and praying verses for them that covered every aspect of their lives.

We prayed together faithfully each weekday for 17 years. We knew the Word was written by the Holy Spirit's inspiration and is full of power and hope. We also knew God said his Word would not return empty (see Isaiah 55:11). So our prayers were based on a solid foundation.

Today I pray for my six grandchildren, again paraphrasing Scriptures or inserting their names in certain verses, just as Lib and I prayed for our children.

For instance, in praying Isaiah 11:2, I ask that my grandchildren will have

> the Spirit of the Lord rest on them —
> the Spirit of wisdom and of understanding,
> the Spirit of counsel and of power,
> the Spirit of knowledge and of [reverential] fear of the Lord.

Here are some other topics to pray for:

Salvation

Thank you, heavenly Father, that you are not willing that any of my grandchildren should be lost. I trust that each one will become a believer in you. I thank you in advance that they will become believers. I pray that they will be taught by you and that great will be their peace (see Matthew 18:14; 2 Peter 3:9; Isaiah 54:13).

Learning

May my grandchildren show aptitude for every kind of learning, be well informed and quick to understand. May they have wisdom, very great insight and a breadth of understanding as measureless as the sand on the seashore (see Daniel 1:4; 1 Kings 4:29).

Maturity

May my grandchildren, like Jesus, grow in wisdom (mental) and stature (physical), and in favor with God (spiritual) and men (social). May they live lives worthy of you, Lord, and may they please you in every way: bearing fruit in every good work, growing in the knowledge of you (see Luke 2:52; Colossians 1:10).

Protection

Thank you, Lord, that you will command your angels concerning my grandchildren and guard them in all their ways (see Psalm 91:11).

Against Evil Influences

I pray, Lord, that you will deliver my grandchildren from wicked and evil people. May you strengthen and protect them from the evil one (see 2 Thessalonians 3:2–3).

Favor

May your favor, O Lord God, rest upon my grandchildren; establish the work of their hands for them (see Psalm 90:17).

Future

Lord, I thank you that you know the plans you have for my grandchildren — to prosper them and not to harm them, to give them hope and a future. I pray that my grandchildren will not walk in the counsel of the wicked or stand in the way of sinners or sit in the seat of mockers. But may their delight be in your law, and may they meditate on it day and night (see Jeremiah 29:11; Psalm 1:1–2).

Since the Word of God is "living and active" (Hebrews 4:12), when we form our prayers from it, we are speaking God's own words, aligned with his will. Our grandchildren need our persistent Bible-based prayers. Will we make a commitment to pray for them all their lives? It is the best gift we can give them.

⁵Sing to the Lord, for he has done glorious
things;
let this be known to all the world.
⁶Shout aloud and sing for joy, people of Zion,
for great is the Holy One of Israel among
you."

A Prophecy Against Babylon

13 An oracle concerning Babylon that Isaiah
son of Amoz saw:

²Raise a banner on a bare hilltop,
shout to them;
beckon to them
to enter the gates of the nobles.
³I have commanded my holy ones;
I have summoned my warriors to carry out
my wrath—
those who rejoice in my triumph.

⁴Listen, a noise on the mountains,
like that of a great multitude!
Listen, an uproar among the kingdoms,
like nations massing together!
The Lord Almighty is mustering
an army for war.
⁵They come from faraway lands,
from the ends of the heavens—
the Lord and the weapons of his wrath—
to destroy the whole country.

⁶Wail, for the day of the Lord is near;
it will come like destruction from the
Almighty.ᵃ
⁷Because of this, all hands will go limp,
every man's heart will melt.
⁸Terror will seize them,
pain and anguish will grip them;
they will writhe like a woman in labor.
They will look aghast at each other,
their faces aflame.

⁹See, the day of the Lord is coming
—a cruel day, with wrath and fierce
anger—
to make the land desolate
and destroy the sinners within it.

¹⁰The stars of heaven and their constellations
will not show their light.
The rising sun will be darkened
and the moon will not give its light.
¹¹I will punish the world for its evil,
the wicked for their sins.
I will put an end to the arrogance of the
haughty
and will humble the pride of the ruthless.
¹²I will make man scarcer than pure gold,
more rare than the gold of Ophir.
¹³Therefore I will make the heavens tremble;
and the earth will shake from its place
at the wrath of the Lord Almighty,
in the day of his burning anger.

¹⁴Like a hunted gazelle,
like sheep without a shepherd,
each will return to his own people,
each will flee to his native land.
¹⁵Whoever is captured will be thrust through;
all who are caught will fall by the sword.
¹⁶Their infants will be dashed to pieces before
their eyes;
their houses will be looted and their wives
ravished.

¹⁷See, I will stir up against them the Medes,
who do not care for silver
and have no delight in gold.
¹⁸Their bows will strike down the young men;
they will have no mercy on infants
nor will they look with compassion on
children.
¹⁹Babylon, the jewel of kingdoms,
the glory of the Babylonians'ᵇ pride,
will be overthrown by God
like Sodom and Gomorrah.
²⁰She will never be inhabited
or lived in through all generations;
no Arab will pitch his tent there,
no shepherd will rest his flocks there.
²¹But desert creatures will lie there,
jackals will fill her houses;

ᵃ 6 Hebrew Shaddai   ᵇ 19 Or Chaldeans'

there the owls will dwell,
and there the wild goats will leap about.
²² Hyenas will howl in her strongholds,
jackals in her luxurious palaces.
Her time is at hand,
and her days will not be prolonged.

14 The LORD will have compassion on
Jacob;
once again he will choose Israel
and will settle them in their own land.
Aliens will join them
and unite with the house of Jacob.
² Nations will take them
and bring them to their own place.
And the house of Israel will possess the
nations
as menservants and maidservants in the
LORD's land.
They will make captives of their captors
and rule over their oppressors.

³ On the day the LORD gives you relief from suffering and turmoil and cruel bondage, ⁴ you will take up this taunt against the king of Babylon:

How the oppressor has come to an end!
How his fury ᵃ has ended!
⁵ The LORD has broken the rod of the wicked,
the scepter of the rulers,
⁶ which in anger struck down peoples
with unceasing blows,
and in fury subdued nations
with relentless aggression.
⁷ All the lands are at rest and at peace;
they break into singing.
⁸ Even the pine trees and the cedars of Lebanon
exult over you and say,
"Now that you have been laid low,
no woodsman comes to cut us down."

⁹ The grave ᵇ below is all astir
to meet you at your coming;
it rouses the spirits of the departed to greet
you—
all those who were leaders in the world;

it makes them rise from their thrones—
all those who were kings over the nations.
¹⁰ They will all respond,
they will say to you,
"You also have become weak, as we are;
you have become like us."
¹¹ All your pomp has been brought down to the
grave,
along with the noise of your harps;
maggots are spread out beneath you
and worms cover you.

¹² How you have fallen from heaven,
O morning star, son of the dawn!
You have been cast down to the earth,
you who once laid low the nations!
¹³ You said in your heart,
"I will ascend to heaven;
I will raise my throne
above the stars of God;
I will sit enthroned on the mount of
assembly,
on the utmost heights of the sacred
mountain. ᶜ
¹⁴ I will ascend above the tops of the clouds;
I will make myself like the Most High."
¹⁵ But you are brought down to the grave,
to the depths of the pit.

¹⁶ Those who see you stare at you,
they ponder your fate:
"Is this the man who shook the earth
and made kingdoms tremble,
¹⁷ the man who made the world a desert,
who overthrew its cities
and would not let his captives go home?"

¹⁸ All the kings of the nations lie in state,
each in his own tomb.
¹⁹ But you are cast out of your tomb
like a rejected branch;
you are covered with the slain,
with those pierced by the sword,
those who descend to the stones of the pit.

ᵃ 4 Dead Sea Scrolls, Septuagint and Syriac; the meaning of the
word in the Masoretic Text is uncertain.   ᵇ 9 Hebrew *Sheol*; also
in verses 11 and 15   ᶜ 13 Or *the north;* Hebrew *Zaphon*

Like a corpse trampled underfoot,
20   you will not join them in burial,
for you have destroyed your land
and killed your people.

The offspring of the wicked
will never be mentioned again.
²¹ Prepare a place to slaughter his sons
for the sins of their forefathers;
they are not to rise to inherit the land
and cover the earth with their cities.

²² "I will rise up against them,"
declares the LORD Almighty.
"I will cut off from Babylon her name and
survivors,
her offspring and descendants,"
declares the LORD.
²³ "I will turn her into a place for owls
and into swampland;
I will sweep her with the broom of
destruction,"
declares the LORD Almighty.

A Prophecy Against Assyria
²⁴ The LORD Almighty has sworn,

"Surely, as I have planned, so it will be,
and as I have purposed, so it will stand.
²⁵ I will crush the Assyrian in my land;
on my mountains I will trample him down.
His yoke will be taken from my people,
and his burden removed from their
shoulders."

²⁶ This is the plan determined for the whole
world;
this is the hand stretched out over all
nations.
²⁷ For the LORD Almighty has purposed, and
who can thwart him?
His hand is stretched out, and who can
turn it back?

A Prophecy Against the Philistines
²⁸ This oracle came in the year King Ahaz
died:

²⁹ Do not rejoice, all you Philistines,
that the rod that struck you is broken;
from the root of that snake will spring up a
viper,
its fruit will be a darting, venomous
serpent.
³⁰ The poorest of the poor will find pasture,
and the needy will lie down in safety.
But your root I will destroy by famine;
it will slay your survivors.

³¹ Wail, O gate! Howl, O city!
Melt away, all you Philistines!
A cloud of smoke comes from the north,
and there is not a straggler in its ranks.
³² What answer shall be given
to the envoys of that nation?
"The LORD has established Zion,
and in her his afflicted people will find
refuge."

A Prophecy Against Moab
16:6–12pp — Jer 48:29–36

15 An oracle concerning Moab:

Ar in Moab is ruined,
destroyed in a night!
Kir in Moab is ruined,
destroyed in a night!
² Dibon goes up to its temple,
to its high places to weep;
Moab wails over Nebo and Medeba.
Every head is shaved
and every beard cut off.
³ In the streets they wear sackcloth;
on the roofs and in the public squares
they all wail,
prostrate with weeping.
⁴ Heshbon and Elealeh cry out,
their voices are heard all the way to Jahaz.
Therefore the armed men of Moab cry out,
and their hearts are faint.

⁵ My heart cries out over Moab;
her fugitives flee as far as Zoar,
as far as Eglath Shelishiyah.

They go up the way to Luhith,
　　weeping as they go;
on the road to Horonaim
　　they lament their destruction.
⁶The waters of Nimrim are dried up
　　and the grass is withered;
the vegetation is gone
　　and nothing green is left.
⁷So the wealth they have acquired and
　　　stored up
　　they carry away over the Ravine of the
　　　Poplars.
⁸Their outcry echoes along the border of
　　Moab;
　　their wailing reaches as far as Eglaim,
　　their lamentation as far as Beer Elim.
⁹Dimon's ᵃ waters are full of blood,
　　but I will bring still more upon
　　　Dimon ᵃ —
a lion upon the fugitives of Moab
　　and upon those who remain in the land.

16 Send lambs as tribute
　　to the ruler of the land,
from Sela, across the desert,
　　to the mount of the Daughter of Zion.
²Like fluttering birds
　　pushed from the nest,
so are the women of Moab
　　at the fords of the Arnon.

³"Give us counsel,
　　render a decision.
Make your shadow like night—
　　at high noon.
Hide the fugitives,
　　do not betray the refugees.
⁴Let the Moabite fugitives stay with you;
　　be their shelter from the destroyer."

The oppressor will come to an end,
　　and destruction will cease;
　　the aggressor will vanish from the land.
⁵In love a throne will be established;
　　in faithfulness a man will sit on it—
one from the house ᵇ of David—

one who in judging seeks justice
　　and speeds the cause of righteousness.

⁶We have heard of Moab's pride—
　　her overweening pride and conceit,
her pride and her insolence—
　　but her boasts are empty.
⁷Therefore the Moabites wail,
　　they wail together for Moab.
Lament and grieve
　　for the men ᶜ of Kir Hareseth.
⁸The fields of Heshbon wither,
　　the vines of Sibmah also.
The rulers of the nations
　　have trampled down the choicest vines,
which once reached Jazer
　　and spread toward the desert.
Their shoots spread out
　　and went as far as the sea.
⁹So I weep, as Jazer weeps,
　　for the vines of Sibmah.
O Heshbon, O Elealeh,
　　I drench you with tears!
The shouts of joy over your ripened fruit
　　and over your harvests have been stilled.
¹⁰Joy and gladness are taken away from the
　　　orchards;
　　no one sings or shouts in the vineyards;
no one treads out wine at the presses,
　　for I have put an end to the shouting.
¹¹My heart laments for Moab like a harp,
　　my inmost being for Kir Hareseth.
¹²When Moab appears at her high place,
　　she only wears herself out;
when she goes to her shrine to pray,
　　it is to no avail.

¹³This is the word the LORD has already spoken concerning Moab. ¹⁴But now the LORD says: "Within three years, as a servant bound by contract would count them, Moab's splendor and all her many people will be despised, and her survivors will be very few and feeble."

ᵃ 9 Masoretic Text; Dead Sea Scrolls, some Septuagint manuscripts and Vulgate *Dibon*　　ᵇ 5 Hebrew *tent*　　ᶜ 7 Or "*raisin cakes*," a wordplay

An Oracle Against Damascus

17 An oracle concerning Damascus:

"See, Damascus will no longer be a city
  but will become a heap of ruins.
² The cities of Aroer will be deserted
  and left to flocks, which will lie down,
  with no one to make them afraid.
³ The fortified city will disappear from
    Ephraim,
  and royal power from Damascus;
the remnant of Aram will be
  like the glory of the Israelites,"
            declares the Lord Almighty.

⁴ "In that day the glory of Jacob will fade;
  the fat of his body will waste away.
⁵ It will be as when a reaper gathers the
    standing grain
  and harvests the grain with his arm—
as when a man gleans heads of grain
  in the Valley of Rephaim.
⁶ Yet some gleanings will remain,
  as when an olive tree is beaten,
leaving two or three olives on the topmost
    branches,
  four or five on the fruitful boughs,"
            declares the Lord, the God of Israel.

⁷ In that day men will look to their Maker
  and turn their eyes to the Holy One of
    Israel.
⁸ They will not look to the altars,
  the work of their hands,
and they will have no regard for the Asherah
    poles ᵃ
  and the incense altars their fingers have
    made.

⁹ In that day their strong cities, which they left because of the Israelites, will be like places abandoned to thickets and undergrowth. And all will be desolation.

¹⁰ You have forgotten God your Savior;
  you have not remembered the Rock, your
    fortress.

Therefore, though you set out the finest plants
  and plant imported vines,
¹¹ though on the day you set them out, you
    make them grow,
  and on the morning when you plant them,
    you bring them to bud,
yet the harvest will be as nothing
  in the day of disease and incurable pain.

¹² Oh, the raging of many nations—
  they rage like the raging sea!
Oh, the uproar of the peoples—
  they roar like the roaring of great waters!
¹³ Although the peoples roar like the roar of
    surging waters,
  when he rebukes them they flee far away,
driven before the wind like chaff on the hills,
  like tumbleweed before a gale.
¹⁴ In the evening, sudden terror!
  Before the morning, they are gone!
This is the portion of those who loot us,
  the lot of those who plunder us.

A Prophecy Against Cush

18 Woe to the land of whirring wings ᵇ
    along the rivers of Cush, ᶜ
² which sends envoys by sea
  in papyrus boats over the water.

Go, swift messengers,
to a people tall and smooth-skinned,
  to a people feared far and wide,
an aggressive nation of strange speech,
  whose land is divided by rivers.

³ All you people of the world,
  you who live on the earth,
when a banner is raised on the mountains,
  you will see it,
and when a trumpet sounds,
  you will hear it.
⁴ This is what the Lord says to me:
  "I will remain quiet and will look on from
    my dwelling place,

ᵃ 8 That is, symbols of the goddess Asherah   ᵇ 1 Or of locusts
ᶜ 1 That is, the upper Nile region

like shimmering heat in the sunshine,
like a cloud of dew in the heat of harvest."
5 For, before the harvest, when the blossom is
gone
and the flower becomes a ripening grape,
he will cut off the shoots with pruning
knives,
and cut down and take away the spreading
branches.
6 They will all be left to the mountain birds of
prey
and to the wild animals;
the birds will feed on them all summer,
the wild animals all winter.

7 At that time gifts will be brought to the LORD
Almighty

from a people tall and smooth-skinned,
from a people feared far and wide,
an aggressive nation of strange speech,
whose land is divided by rivers—

the gifts will be brought to Mount Zion, the place
of the Name of the LORD Almighty.

A Prophecy About Egypt

19 An oracle concerning Egypt:

See, the LORD rides on a swift cloud
and is coming to Egypt.
The idols of Egypt tremble before him,
and the hearts of the Egyptians melt
within them.

2 "I will stir up Egyptian against Egyptian—
brother will fight against brother,
neighbor against neighbor,
city against city,
kingdom against kingdom.
3 The Egyptians will lose heart,
and I will bring their plans to nothing;
they will consult the idols and the spirits of
the dead,
the mediums and the spiritists.
4 I will hand the Egyptians over
to the power of a cruel master,

and a fierce king will rule over them,"
declares the Lord, the LORD Almighty.

5 The waters of the river will dry up,
and the riverbed will be parched and dry.
6 The canals will stink;
the streams of Egypt will dwindle and
dry up.
The reeds and rushes will wither,
7 also the plants along the Nile,
at the mouth of the river.
Every sown field along the Nile
will become parched, will blow away and
be no more.
8 The fishermen will groan and lament,
all who cast hooks into the Nile;
those who throw nets on the water
will pine away.
9 Those who work with combed flax will
despair,
the weavers of fine linen will lose hope.
10 The workers in cloth will be dejected,
and all the wage earners will be sick at heart.

11 The officials of Zoan are nothing but fools;
the wise counselors of Pharaoh give
senseless advice.
How can you say to Pharaoh,
"I am one of the wise men,
a disciple of the ancient kings"?

12 Where are your wise men now?
Let them show you and make known
what the LORD Almighty
has planned against Egypt.
13 The officials of Zoan have become fools,
the leaders of Memphis a are deceived;
the cornerstones of her peoples
have led Egypt astray.
14 The LORD has poured into them
a spirit of dizziness;
they make Egypt stagger in all that she does,
as a drunkard staggers around in his vomit.
15 There is nothing Egypt can do—
head or tail, palm branch or reed.

a 13 Hebrew Noph

¹⁶ In that day the Egyptians will be like women. They will shudder with fear at the uplifted hand that the Lord Almighty raises against them. ¹⁷ And the land of Judah will bring terror to the Egyptians; everyone to whom Judah is mentioned will be terrified, because of what the Lord Almighty is planning against them.

¹⁸ In that day five cities in Egypt will speak the language of Canaan and swear allegiance to the Lord Almighty. One of them will be called the City of Destruction.^a

¹⁹ In that day there will be an altar to the Lord in the heart of Egypt, and a monument to the Lord at its border. ²⁰ It will be a sign and witness to the Lord Almighty in the land of Egypt. When they cry out to the Lord because of their oppressors, he will send them a savior and defender, and he will rescue them. ²¹ So the Lord will make himself known to the Egyptians, and in that day they will acknowledge the Lord. They will worship with sacrifices and grain offerings; they will make vows to the Lord and keep them. ²² The Lord will strike Egypt with a plague; he will strike them and heal them. They will turn to the Lord, and he will respond to their pleas and heal them.

²³ In that day there will be a highway from Egypt to Assyria. The Assyrians will go to Egypt and the Egyptians to Assyria. The Egyptians and Assyrians will worship together. ²⁴ In that day Israel will be the third, along with Egypt and Assyria, a blessing on the earth. ²⁵ The Lord Almighty will bless them, saying, "Blessed be Egypt my people, Assyria my handiwork, and Israel my inheritance."

A Prophecy Against Egypt and Cush

20 In the year that the supreme commander, sent by Sargon king of Assyria, came to Ashdod and attacked and captured it— ² at that time the Lord spoke through Isaiah son of Amoz. He said to him, "Take off the sackcloth from your body and the sandals from your feet." And he did so, going around stripped and barefoot.

³ Then the Lord said, "Just as my servant Isaiah has gone stripped and barefoot for three years, as a sign and portent against Egypt and Cush,^b ⁴ so the king of Assyria will lead away stripped and barefoot the Egyptian captives and Cushite exiles, young and old, with buttocks bared—to Egypt's shame. ⁵ Those who trusted in Cush and boasted in Egypt will be afraid and put to shame. ⁶ In that day the people who live on this coast will say, 'See what has happened to those we relied on, those we fled to for help and deliverance from the king of Assyria! How then can we escape?' "

A Prophecy Against Babylon

21 An oracle concerning the Desert by the Sea:

Like whirlwinds sweeping through the
     southland,
  an invader comes from the desert,
  from a land of terror.

² A dire vision has been shown to me:
  The traitor betrays, the looter takes loot.
Elam, attack! Media, lay siege!
  I will bring to an end all the groaning she
     caused.

³ At this my body is racked with pain,
  pangs seize me, like those of a woman in
     labor;
I am staggered by what I hear,
  I am bewildered by what I see.
⁴ My heart falters,
  fear makes me tremble;
the twilight I longed for
  has become a horror to me.

⁵ They set the tables,
  they spread the rugs,
  they eat, they drink!
Get up, you officers,
  oil the shields!

⁶ This is what the Lord says to me:

"Go, post a lookout
  and have him report what he sees.

^a 18 Most manuscripts of the Masoretic Text; some manuscripts of the Masoretic Text, Dead Sea Scrolls and Vulgate *City of the Sun* (that is, Heliopolis)   ^b 3 That is, the upper Nile region; also in verse 5

⁷When he sees chariots
    with teams of horses,
riders on donkeys
    or riders on camels,
let him be alert,
    fully alert."

⁸And the lookout *a* shouted,

"Day after day, my lord, I stand on the
    watchtower;
    every night I stay at my post.
⁹Look, here comes a man in a chariot
    with a team of horses.
And he gives back the answer:
    'Babylon has fallen, has fallen!
All the images of its gods
    lie shattered on the ground!' "

¹⁰O my people, crushed on the threshing floor,
    I tell you what I have heard
from the Lord Almighty,
    from the God of Israel.

A Prophecy Against Edom

¹¹An oracle concerning Dumah *b*:

Someone calls to me from Seir,
    "Watchman, what is left of the night?
    Watchman, what is left of the night?"
¹²The watchman replies,
    "Morning is coming, but also the night.
If you would ask, then ask;
    and come back yet again."

A Prophecy Against Arabia

¹³An oracle concerning Arabia:

You caravans of Dedanites,
    who camp in the thickets of Arabia,
¹⁴   bring water for the thirsty;
you who live in Tema,
    bring food for the fugitives.
¹⁵They flee from the sword,
    from the drawn sword,
from the bent bow
    and from the heat of battle.

¹⁶This is what the Lord says to me: "Within
one year, as a servant bound by contract would
count it, all the pomp of Kedar will come to an
end. ¹⁷The survivors of the bowmen, the warriors of Kedar, will be few." The Lord, the God
of Israel, has spoken.

A Prophecy About Jerusalem

22 An oracle concerning the Valley of Vision:

What troubles you now,
    that you have all gone up on the roofs,
²O town full of commotion,
    O city of tumult and revelry?
Your slain were not killed by the sword,
    nor did they die in battle.
³All your leaders have fled together;
    they have been captured without using the
        bow.
All you who were caught were taken prisoner
    together,
    having fled while the enemy was still far
        away.
⁴Therefore I said, "Turn away from me;
    let me weep bitterly.
Do not try to console me
    over the destruction of my people."

⁵The Lord, the Lord Almighty, has a day
    of tumult and trampling and terror
    in the Valley of Vision,
a day of battering down walls
    and of crying out to the mountains.
⁶Elam takes up the quiver,
    with her charioteers and horses;
    Kir uncovers the shield.
⁷Your choicest valleys are full of chariots,
    and horsemen are posted at the city gates;
⁸   the defenses of Judah are stripped away.

And you looked in that day
    to the weapons in the Palace of the Forest;
⁹you saw that the City of David
    had many breaches in its defenses;

a 8 Dead Sea Scrolls and Syriac; Masoretic Text A lion
b 11 Dumah means silence or stillness, a wordplay on Edom.

you stored up water
in the Lower Pool.
¹⁰ You counted the buildings in Jerusalem
and tore down houses to strengthen the
wall.
¹¹ You built a reservoir between the two walls
for the water of the Old Pool,
but you did not look to the One who made it,
or have regard for the One who planned it
long ago.

¹² The Lord, the LORD Almighty,
called you on that day
to weep and to wail,
to tear out your hair and put on sackcloth.
¹³ But see, there is joy and revelry,
slaughtering of cattle and killing of sheep,
eating of meat and drinking of wine!
"Let us eat and drink," you say,
"for tomorrow we die!"

¹⁴ The LORD Almighty has revealed this in my
hearing: "Till your dying day this sin will not be
atoned for," says the Lord, the LORD Almighty.

¹⁵ This is what the Lord, the LORD Almighty,
says:

"Go, say to this steward,
to Shebna, who is in charge of the palace:
¹⁶ What are you doing here and who gave you
permission
to cut out a grave for yourself here,
hewing your grave on the height
and chiseling your resting place in the
rock?

¹⁷ "Beware, the LORD is about to take firm hold
of you
and hurl you away, O you mighty man.
¹⁸ He will roll you up tightly like a ball
and throw you into a large country.
There you will die
and there your splendid chariots will
remain—
you disgrace to your master's house!
¹⁹ I will depose you from your office,
and you will be ousted from your position.

²⁰ "In that day I will summon my servant, Eliakim son of Hilkiah. ²¹ I will clothe him with your
robe and fasten your sash around him and hand
your authority over to him. He will be a father
to those who live in Jerusalem and to the house
of Judah. ²² I will place on his shoulder the key to
the house of David; what he opens no one can
shut, and what he shuts no one can open. ²³ I will
drive him like a peg into a firm place; he will be
a seat ᵃ of honor for the house of his father. ²⁴ All
the glory of his family will hang on him: its offspring and offshoots—all its lesser vessels, from
the bowls to all the jars.

²⁵ "In that day," declares the LORD Almighty,
"the peg driven into the firm place will give way;
it will be sheared off and will fall, and the load
hanging on it will be cut down." The LORD has
spoken.

A Prophecy About Tyre

23 An oracle concerning Tyre:

Wail, O ships of Tarshish!
For Tyre is destroyed
and left without house or harbor.
From the land of Cyprus ᵇ
word has come to them.

² Be silent, you people of the island
and you merchants of Sidon,
whom the seafarers have enriched.
³ On the great waters
came the grain of the Shihor;
the harvest of the Nile ᶜ was the revenue of
Tyre,
and she became the marketplace of the
nations.

⁴ Be ashamed, O Sidon, and you, O fortress of
the sea,
for the sea has spoken:
"I have neither been in labor nor given birth;
I have neither reared sons nor brought up
daughters."

ᵃ 23 Or throne   ᵇ 1 Hebrew Kittim   ᶜ 2,3 Masoretic Text; one
Dead Sea Scroll Sidon, / who cross over the sea; / your envoys ³are on
the great waters. / The grain of the Shihor, / the harvest of the Nile,

⁵When word comes to Egypt,
  they will be in anguish at the report from
    Tyre.

⁶Cross over to Tarshish;
  wail, you people of the island.
⁷Is this your city of revelry,
  the old, old city,
whose feet have taken her
  to settle in far-off lands?
⁸Who planned this against Tyre,
  the bestower of crowns,
whose merchants are princes,
  whose traders are renowned in the earth?
⁹The LORD Almighty planned it,
  to bring low the pride of all glory
and to humble all who are renowned on
    the earth.

¹⁰Till*a* your land as along the Nile,
  O Daughter of Tarshish,
  for you no longer have a harbor.
¹¹The LORD has stretched out his hand over the
    sea
  and made its kingdoms tremble.
He has given an order concerning Phoenicia*b*
  that her fortresses be destroyed.
¹²He said, "No more of your reveling,
  O Virgin Daughter of Sidon, now crushed!

"Up, cross over to Cyprus*c*;
  even there you will find no rest."
¹³Look at the land of the Babylonians,*d*
  this people that is now of no account!
The Assyrians have made it
  a place for desert creatures;
they raised up their siege towers,
  they stripped its fortresses bare
  and turned it into a ruin.

¹⁴Wail, you ships of Tarshish;
  your fortress is destroyed!

¹⁵At that time Tyre will be forgotten for seventy years, the span of a king's life. But at the end
of these seventy years, it will happen to Tyre as in
the song of the prostitute:

¹⁶"Take up a harp, walk through the city,
  O prostitute forgotten;
play the harp well, sing many a song,
  so that you will be remembered."

¹⁷At the end of seventy years, the LORD will
deal with Tyre. She will return to her hire as a
prostitute and will ply her trade with all the kingdoms on the face of the earth. ¹⁸Yet her profit
and her earnings will be set apart for the LORD;
they will not be stored up or hoarded. Her profits will go to those who live before the LORD, for
abundant food and fine clothes.

The LORD's Devastation of the Earth

24 See, the LORD is going to lay waste the
    earth
  and devastate it;
he will ruin its face
  and scatter its inhabitants—
²it will be the same
  for priest as for people,
  for master as for servant,
  for mistress as for maid,
  for seller as for buyer,
  for borrower as for lender,
  for debtor as for creditor.
³The earth will be completely laid waste
  and totally plundered.
      The LORD has spoken this word.

⁴The earth dries up and withers,
  the world languishes and withers,
  the exalted of the earth languish.
⁵The earth is defiled by its people;
  they have disobeyed the laws,
  violated the statutes
  and broken the everlasting covenant.
⁶Therefore a curse consumes the earth;
  its people must bear their guilt.
Therefore earth's inhabitants are burned up,
  and very few are left.
⁷The new wine dries up and the vine withers;
  all the merrymakers groan.

a 10 Dead Sea Scrolls and some Septuagint manuscripts; Masoretic
Text *Go through*   *b 11* Hebrew *Canaan*   *c 12* Hebrew *Kittim*
d 13 Or *Chaldeans*

951

⁸ The gaiety of the tambourines is stilled,
the noise of the revelers has stopped,
the joyful harp is silent.
⁹ No longer do they drink wine with a song;
the beer is bitter to its drinkers.
¹⁰ The ruined city lies desolate;
the entrance to every house is barred.
¹¹ In the streets they cry out for wine;
all joy turns to gloom,
all gaiety is banished from the earth.
¹² The city is left in ruins,
its gate is battered to pieces.
¹³ So will it be on the earth
and among the nations,
as when an olive tree is beaten,
or as when gleanings are left after the
grape harvest.

¹⁴ They raise their voices, they shout for joy;
from the west they acclaim the LORD's
majesty.
¹⁵ Therefore in the east give glory to the LORD;
exalt the name of the LORD, the God of
Israel,
in the islands of the sea.
¹⁶ From the ends of the earth we hear singing:
"Glory to the Righteous One."

But I said, "I waste away, I waste away!
Woe to me!
The treacherous betray!
With treachery the treacherous betray!"
¹⁷ Terror and pit and snare await you,
O people of the earth.
¹⁸ Whoever flees at the sound of terror
will fall into a pit;
whoever climbs out of the pit
will be caught in a snare.

The floodgates of the heavens are opened,
the foundations of the earth shake.
¹⁹ The earth is broken up,
the earth is split asunder,
the earth is thoroughly shaken.
²⁰ The earth reels like a drunkard,
it sways like a hut in the wind;

so heavy upon it is the guilt of its rebellion
that it falls — never to rise again.

²¹ In that day the LORD will punish
the powers in the heavens above
and the kings on the earth below.
²² They will be herded together
like prisoners bound in a dungeon;
they will be shut up in prison
and be punished ᵃ after many days.
²³ The moon will be abashed, the sun
ashamed;
for the LORD Almighty will reign
on Mount Zion and in Jerusalem,
and before its elders, gloriously.

Praise to the LORD

25 O LORD, you are my God;
I will exalt you and praise your name,
for in perfect faithfulness
you have done marvelous things,
things planned long ago.

TALKING POINTS

Knowing God's Will

We can be confident of God's
faithfulness to fulfill his plan.

ISAIAH 25:1

For more on knowing God's will, go to Jeremiah 6:16.

² You have made the city a heap of rubble,
the fortified town a ruin,
the foreigners' stronghold a city no more;
it will never be rebuilt.
³ Therefore strong peoples will honor you;
cities of ruthless nations will revere you.
⁴ You have been a refuge for the poor,
a refuge for the needy in his distress,

ᵃ 22 Or *released*

a shelter from the storm
and a shade from the heat.
For the breath of the ruthless
is like a storm driving against a wall
5 and like the heat of the desert.
You silence the uproar of foreigners;
as heat is reduced by the shadow of a cloud,
so the song of the ruthless is stilled.

6 On this mountain the LORD Almighty will
prepare
a feast of rich food for all peoples,
a banquet of aged wine—
the best of meats and the finest of wines.
7 On this mountain he will destroy
the shroud that enfolds all peoples,
the sheet that covers all nations;
8 he will swallow up death forever.
The Sovereign LORD will wipe away the tears
from all faces;
he will remove the disgrace of his people
from all the earth.
The LORD has spoken.

9 In that day they will say,

"Surely this is our God;
we trusted in him, and he saved us.
This is the LORD, we trusted in him;
let us rejoice and be glad in his salvation."

10 The hand of the LORD will rest on this
mountain;
but Moab will be trampled under him
as straw is trampled down in the manure.
11 They will spread out their hands in it,
as a swimmer spreads out his hands to
swim.
God will bring down their pride
despite the cleverness[a] of their hands.
12 He will bring down your high fortified walls
and lay them low;
he will bring them down to the ground,
to the very dust.

A Song of Praise

26 In that day this song will be sung in the
land of Judah:

We have a strong city;
God makes salvation
its walls and ramparts.
2 Open the gates
that the righteous nation may enter,
the nation that keeps faith.
3 You will keep in perfect peace
him whose mind is steadfast,
because he trusts in you.
4 Trust in the LORD forever,
for the LORD, the LORD, is the Rock eternal.

TALKING POINTS

Trust

Trusting God brings peace.
ISAIAH 26:3–4

For more on trust, go to Daniel 3:1–30.

---

5 He humbles those who dwell on high,
he lays the lofty city low;
he levels it to the ground
and casts it down to the dust.
6 Feet trample it down—
the feet of the oppressed,
the footsteps of the poor.

7 The path of the righteous is level;
O upright One, you make the way of the
righteous smooth.
8 Yes, LORD, walking in the way of your laws,[b]
we wait for you;
your name and renown
are the desire of our hearts.
9 My soul yearns for you in the night;
in the morning my spirit longs for you.
When your judgments come upon the earth,
the people of the world learn
righteousness.

---

[a] 11 The meaning of the Hebrew for this word is uncertain.
[b] 8 Or *judgments*

MY SOUL YEARS FOR YOU IN
THE NIGHT; IN THE MORNING MY
SPIRIT LONGS FOR YOU. WHEN
YOUR JUDGMENTS COME UPON
THE EARTH, THE PEOPLE OF THE
WORLD LEARN RIGHTEOUSNESS.

Isaiah 26:9

Different Parts of the Day

MARTHA WHITMORE HICKMAN

READ | ISAIAH 26:1 – 15

I am impressed again with the different quality of different parts of the day. For me, mornings are the time for innovation, for creative work, for feelings of adventure and that anything can happen. It is, in some ways, harder to pray in the morning; there is such an urge to move on into the day's work that to stop for meditation, to listen and absorb a presence, seems like foot-dragging.

But if it goes right, if I find new freshness in some quiet moments, if a reading from the Bible or some other seminal work touches some creative nerve in my own consciousness, then it heightens that adventure of prayer too, and I find myself galloping along with some thought or awareness, some bubbling, holy delight. In prayer as in work, I have a sense that anything may happen. I'm prepared for a surprise!

In the afternoon or evening, when my own nature has quieted down and is beginning to grow tired, it's easier in some ways to pay attention to the Spirit. But my attention is thinner, less energetic. If there are surprises now, they will probably come from outside, not from within.

Maybe it's like going to school when I was a child: in the morning, the adventures all ahead, unknown; returning in the afternoon to security and rest, to the haven of home. So God can be the starter for the race or the quiet haven where, with encompassing love, the day is blest.

Jesus, I know you are always present with me. I know that I can pray anytime to you, and you hear me. Whether prayer is a holy delight in the morning or a haven at night, draw me ever nearer to you.

Your next devotion is located on page 960.

GRANDCHILD IN FOCUS • PRAYER

Spiritual Growth

Dear Lord, today I pray for my grandchild's spiritual growth. I ask that you instill in him the desire to read and memorize your Word. Give him a passion to be in conversation with you. May loving and serving you be part of his daily life. I ask that you stay close to him and lead him to be transformed to your likeness, to reflect your grace and to radiate your love. I pray this in Jesus' name, amen.

¹⁰ Though grace is shown to the wicked,
   they do not learn righteousness;
even in a land of uprightness they go on
         doing evil
   and regard not the majesty of the LORD.
¹¹ O LORD, your hand is lifted high,
   but they do not see it.
Let them see your zeal for your people and be
      put to shame;
   let the fire reserved for your enemies
      consume them.

¹² LORD, you establish peace for us;
   all that we have accomplished you have
      done for us.
¹³ O LORD, our God, other lords besides you
      have ruled over us,
   but your name alone do we honor.
¹⁴ They are now dead, they live no more;
   those departed spirits do not rise.
You punished them and brought them to
      ruin;
   you wiped out all memory of them.
¹⁵ You have enlarged the nation, O LORD;
   you have enlarged the nation.
You have gained glory for yourself;
   you have extended all the borders of the
      land.

¹⁶ LORD, they came to you in their distress;
   when you disciplined them,
   they could barely whisper a prayer. ª
¹⁷ As a woman with child and about to give
         birth
   writhes and cries out in her pain,
   so were we in your presence, O LORD.
¹⁸ We were with child, we writhed in pain,
   but we gave birth to wind.
We have not brought salvation to the earth;
   we have not given birth to people of the
      world.

¹⁹ But your dead will live;
   their bodies will rise.
You who dwell in the dust,
   wake up and shout for joy.

Your dew is like the dew of the morning;
   the earth will give birth to her dead.

²⁰ Go, my people, enter your rooms
   and shut the doors behind you;
hide yourselves for a little while
   until his wrath has passed by.
²¹ See, the LORD is coming out of his dwelling
   to punish the people of the earth for their
      sins.
The earth will disclose the blood shed upon
      her;
   she will conceal her slain no longer.

Deliverance of Israel

27 In that day,

the LORD will punish with his sword,
   his fierce, great and powerful sword,
Leviathan the gliding serpent,
   Leviathan the coiling serpent;
he will slay the monster of the sea.

² In that day —

"Sing about a fruitful vineyard:
³   I, the LORD, watch over it;
   I water it continually.
I guard it day and night
   so that no one may harm it.
⁴   I am not angry.
If only there were briers and thorns
         confronting me!
   I would march against them in battle;
   I would set them all on fire.
⁵ Or else let them come to me for refuge;
   let them make peace with me,
   yes, let them make peace with me."

⁶ In days to come Jacob will take root,
   Israel will bud and blossom
   and fill all the world with fruit.

⁷ Has ⌊the LORD⌋ struck her
   as he struck down those who struck her?
Has she been killed
   as those were killed who killed her?

ª 16 The meaning of the Hebrew for this clause is uncertain.

⁸By warfare*a* and exile you contend with
her—
with his fierce blast he drives her out,
as on a day the east wind blows.
⁹By this, then, will Jacob's guilt be atoned for,
and this will be the full fruitage of the
removal of his sin:
When he makes all the altar stones
to be like chalk stones crushed to pieces,
no Asherah poles*b* or incense altars
will be left standing.
¹⁰The fortified city stands desolate,
an abandoned settlement, forsaken like the
desert;
there the calves graze,
there they lie down;
they strip its branches bare.
¹¹When its twigs are dry, they are broken off
and women come and make fires with
them.
For this is a people without understanding;
so their Maker has no compassion on
them,
and their Creator shows them no favor.

¹²In that day the LORD will thresh from the
flowing Euphrates*c* to the Wadi of Egypt, and
you, O Israelites, will be gathered up one by one.
¹³And in that day a great trumpet will sound.
Those who were perishing in Assyria and those
who were exiled in Egypt will come and worship
the LORD on the holy mountain in Jerusalem.

Woe to Ephraim

28 Woe to that wreath, the pride of
Ephraim's drunkards,
to the fading flower, his glorious beauty,
set on the head of a fertile valley—
to that city, the pride of those laid low by
wine!
²See, the Lord has one who is powerful and
strong.
Like a hailstorm and a destructive wind,
like a driving rain and a flooding downpour,
he will throw it forcefully to the ground.

³That wreath, the pride of Ephraim's
drunkards,
will be trampled underfoot.
⁴That fading flower, his glorious beauty,
set on the head of a fertile valley,
will be like a fig ripe before harvest—
as soon as someone sees it and takes it in
his hand,
he swallows it.

⁵In that day the LORD Almighty
will be a glorious crown,
a beautiful wreath
for the remnant of his people.
⁶He will be a spirit of justice
to him who sits in judgment,
a source of strength
to those who turn back the battle at the gate.

⁷And these also stagger from wine
and reel from beer:
Priests and prophets stagger from beer
and are befuddled with wine;
they reel from beer,
they stagger when seeing visions,
they stumble when rendering decisions.
⁸All the tables are covered with vomit
and there is not a spot without filth.

⁹"Who is it he is trying to teach?
To whom is he explaining his message?
To children weaned from their milk,
to those just taken from the breast?
¹⁰For it is:
Do and do, do and do,
rule on rule, rule on rule*d*;
a little here, a little there."

¹¹Very well then, with foreign lips and strange
tongues
God will speak to this people,
¹²to whom he said,
"This is the resting place, let the weary
rest";

*a 8 See Septuagint; the meaning of the Hebrew for this word
is uncertain.   b 9 That is, symbols of the goddess Asherah
c 12 Hebrew River   d 10 Hebrew / sav lasav sav lasav / kav lakav
kav lakav (possibly meaningless sounds; perhaps a mimicking of the
prophet's words); also in verse 13*

and, "This is the place of repose"—
    but they would not listen.
¹³ So then, the word of the LORD to them will
    become:
    Do and do, do and do,
    rule on rule, rule on rule;
    a little here, a little there—
so that they will go and fall backward,
    be injured and snared and captured.

¹⁴ Therefore hear the word of the LORD, you
    scoffers
    who rule this people in Jerusalem.
¹⁵ You boast, "We have entered into a covenant
    with death,
    with the grave *a* we have made an
    agreement.
When an overwhelming scourge sweeps by,
    it cannot touch us,
for we have made a lie our refuge
    and falsehood *b* our hiding place."

¹⁶ So this is what the Sovereign LORD says:

"See, I lay a stone in Zion,
    a tested stone,
a precious cornerstone for a sure foundation;
    the one who trusts will never be dismayed.
¹⁷ I will make justice the measuring line
    and righteousness the plumb line;
hail will sweep away your refuge, the lie,
    and water will overflow your hiding place.
¹⁸ Your covenant with death will be annulled;
    your agreement with the grave will not
    stand.
When the overwhelming scourge sweeps by,
    you will be beaten down by it.
¹⁹ As often as it comes it will carry you away;
    morning after morning, by day and by
    night,
    it will sweep through."

The understanding of this message
    will bring sheer terror.
²⁰ The bed is too short to stretch out on,
    the blanket too narrow to wrap around
    you.

²¹ The LORD will rise up as he did at Mount
    Perazim,
    he will rouse himself as in the Valley of
    Gibeon—
to do his work, his strange work,
    and perform his task, his alien task.
²² Now stop your mocking,
    or your chains will become heavier;
the Lord, the LORD Almighty, has told me
    of the destruction decreed against the
    whole land.

²³ Listen and hear my voice;
    pay attention and hear what I say.
²⁴ When a farmer plows for planting, does he
    plow continually?
    Does he keep on breaking up and
    harrowing the soil?
²⁵ When he has leveled the surface,
    does he not sow caraway and scatter
    cummin?
Does he not plant wheat in its place, *c*
    barley in its plot, *c*
    and spelt in its field?
²⁶ His God instructs him
    and teaches him the right way.

²⁷ Caraway is not threshed with a sledge,
    nor is a cartwheel rolled over cummin;
caraway is beaten out with a rod,
    and cummin with a stick.
²⁸ Grain must be ground to make bread;
    so one does not go on threshing it forever.
Though he drives the wheels of his threshing
    cart over it,
    his horses do not grind it.
²⁹ All this also comes from the LORD Almighty,
    wonderful in counsel and magnificent in
    wisdom.

Woe to David's City

29 Woe to you, Ariel, Ariel,
    the city where David settled!
Add year to year
    and let your cycle of festivals go on.

---

a 15 Hebrew *Sheol*; also in verse 18   *b* 15 Or *false gods*
c 25 The meaning of the Hebrew for this word is uncertain.

² Yet I will besiege Ariel;
  she will mourn and lament,
  she will be to me like an altar hearth. ^a
³ I will encamp against you all around;
  I will encircle you with towers
  and set up my siege works against you.
⁴ Brought low, you will speak from the ground;
  your speech will mumble out of the dust.
Your voice will come ghostlike from the
   earth;
  out of the dust your speech will whisper.

⁵ But your many enemies will become like fine
   dust,
  the ruthless hordes like blown chaff.
Suddenly, in an instant,
⁶   the LORD Almighty will come
with thunder and earthquake and great noise,
  with windstorm and tempest and flames of
   a devouring fire.
⁷ Then the hordes of all the nations that fight
   against Ariel,
  that attack her and her fortress and besiege
   her,
will be as it is with a dream,
  with a vision in the night —
⁸ as when a hungry man dreams that he is
   eating,
  but he awakens, and his hunger remains;
as when a thirsty man dreams that he is
   drinking,
  but he awakens faint, with his thirst
   unquenched.
So will it be with the hordes of all the nations
  that fight against Mount Zion.

⁹ Be stunned and amazed,
  blind yourselves and be sightless;
be drunk, but not from wine,
  stagger, but not from beer.
¹⁰ The LORD has brought over you a deep sleep:
  He has sealed your eyes (the prophets);
  he has covered your heads (the seers).

¹¹ For you this whole vision is nothing but
words sealed in a scroll. And if you give the scroll
to someone who can read, and say to him, "Read
this, please," he will answer, "I can't; it is sealed."
¹² Or if you give the scroll to someone who can-
not read, and say, "Read this, please," he will answer, "I don't know how to read."

¹³ The Lord says:

"These people come near to me with their
   mouth
  and honor me with their lips,
  but their hearts are far from me.
Their worship of me
  is made up only of rules taught by men. ^b
¹⁴ Therefore once more I will astound these
   people
  with wonder upon wonder;
the wisdom of the wise will perish,
  the intelligence of the intelligent will
   vanish."
¹⁵ Woe to those who go to great depths
  to hide their plans from the LORD,
who do their work in darkness and think,
  "Who sees us? Who will know?"
¹⁶ You turn things upside down,
  as if the potter were thought to be like the
   clay!
Shall what is formed say to him who
   formed it,
  "He did not make me"?
Can the pot say of the potter,
  "He knows nothing"?

¹⁷ In a very short time, will not Lebanon be
   turned into a fertile field
  and the fertile field seem like a forest?
¹⁸ In that day the deaf will hear the words of the
   scroll,
  and out of gloom and darkness
  the eyes of the blind will see.
¹⁹ Once more the humble will rejoice in the
   LORD;
  the needy will rejoice in the Holy One of
   Israel.

---

^a 2 The Hebrew for *altar hearth* sounds like the Hebrew for *Ariel*.
^b 13 Hebrew; Septuagint *They worship me in vain; / their teachings
are but rules taught by men*

²⁰ The ruthless will vanish,
 the mockers will disappear,
 and all who have an eye for evil will be cut
  down—
²¹ those who with a word make a man out to be
  guilty,
 who ensnare the defender in court
 and with false testimony deprive the
  innocent of justice.

²² Therefore this is what the LORD, who redeemed Abraham, says to the house of Jacob:

"No longer will Jacob be ashamed;
 no longer will their faces grow pale.
²³ When they see among them their children,
 the work of my hands,
they will keep my name holy;
 they will acknowledge the holiness of the
  Holy One of Jacob,
 and will stand in awe of the God of Israel.
²⁴ Those who are wayward in spirit will gain
  understanding;
 those who complain will accept
  instruction."

Woe to the Obstinate Nation

30 "Woe to the obstinate children,"
 declares the LORD,
"to those who carry out plans that are not
  mine,
 forming an alliance, but not by my Spirit,
 heaping sin upon sin;
² who go down to Egypt
 without consulting me;
who look for help to Pharaoh's protection,
 to Egypt's shade for refuge.
³ But Pharaoh's protection will be to your
  shame,
 Egypt's shade will bring you disgrace.
⁴ Though they have officials in Zoan
 and their envoys have arrived in Hanes,
⁵ everyone will be put to shame
 because of a people useless to them,
who bring neither help nor advantage,
 but only shame and disgrace."

⁶ An oracle concerning the animals of the Negev:

Through a land of hardship and distress,
 of lions and lionesses,
 of adders and darting snakes,
the envoys carry their riches on donkeys'
  backs,
 their treasures on the humps of camels,
to that unprofitable nation,
⁷ to Egypt, whose help is utterly useless.
Therefore I call her
 Rahab the Do-Nothing.

⁸ Go now, write it on a tablet for them,
 inscribe it on a scroll,
that for the days to come
 it may be an everlasting witness.
⁹ These are rebellious people, deceitful children,
 children unwilling to listen to the LORD's
  instruction.
¹⁰ They say to the seers,
 "See no more visions!"
and to the prophets,
 "Give us no more visions of what is right!
Tell us pleasant things,
 prophesy illusions.
¹¹ Leave this way,
 get off this path,
and stop confronting us
 with the Holy One of Israel!"

¹² Therefore, this is what the Holy One of Israel
says:

"Because you have rejected this message,
 relied on oppression
 and depended on deceit,
¹³ this sin will become for you
 like a high wall, cracked and bulging,
 that collapses suddenly, in an instant.
¹⁴ It will break in pieces like pottery,
 shattered so mercilessly
that among its pieces not a fragment will be
  found
 for taking coals from a hearth
 or scooping water out of a cistern."

THIS IS WHAT THE SOVEREIGN LORD,
THE HOLY ONE OF ISRAEL, SAYS:
"IN REPENTANCE AND REST IS YOUR
SALVATION, IN QUIETNESS AND TRUST
IS YOUR STRENGTH, BUT YOU WOULD
HAVE NONE OF IT."

Isaiah 30:15

In Quietness

MILLIE STAMM

READ | ISAIAH 30:1 – 18

Does quietness describe your life today? Or is it filled with tension and turmoil? Such tension can bring depression of spirit, draining of energy and depleting of strength. Important, therefore, is an inner stability to carry us through the pressure times of life.

The children of Israel were in danger of an attack by the Assyrians. Instead of going to the Lord for help, they turned to Egypt. God warned them through the prophet Isaiah that only in returning to God and resting in Him could they find safety and security.

When problems arise in our lives, we begin to seek ways of solving them ourselves. We turn to those we think can give us assistance. We try plans and methods we think may handle our situation, but none of our self-seeking plans is adequate. This is not God's way.

Quiet tension is not trust, [either]. It is simply compressed anxiety. Only in returning to God and resting in Him will we have quietness in place of fear and a confidence in God that will be our strength.

In a partnership, each partner shares in the work. In our partnership with God, God does the work, but He uses our lives to accomplish it. Our part is to be available. God reminded the Israelites, "you would have none of it." We may have to learn the hard way. When we rebel against returning to the Lord for His help, He lets us experience the failure of going our own way.

Strength for meeting life each day becomes ours as we wait in His presence. It is there we learn of Him; we discover His direction for our lives and are empowered of Him to accomplish it. From there come His quietness and confidence that strengthens us, knowing that all is well in God's hands.

Father, I wait in your presence now. Help me to be quiet as I wait for your direction and power so that I may glorify you.

Your next devotion is located on page 963.

GRANDCHILD IN FOCUS • PRAYER

Relationships at Home

O Lord, I pray that you will bless the home and family of my grandchild. May the relationships she has with her parents and siblings enhance her well-being, support her self-confidence and increase her faith. May her home life reflect your love, your grace, your compassion and your peace. Guide her parents to direct her in love and truth, so she will grow into a strong and compassionate individual. Amen.

¹⁵This is what the Sovereign LORD, the Holy One of Israel, says:

"In repentance and rest is your salvation,
    in quietness and trust is your strength,
    but you would have none of it.
¹⁶You said, 'No, we will flee on horses.'
    Therefore you will flee!
You said, 'We will ride off on swift horses.'
    Therefore your pursuers will be swift!
¹⁷A thousand will flee
    at the threat of one;
at the threat of five
    you will all flee away,
till you are left
    like a flagstaff on a mountaintop,
    like a banner on a hill."

¹⁸Yet the LORD longs to be gracious to you;
    he rises to show you compassion.
For the LORD is a God of justice.
    Blessed are all who wait for him!

¹⁹O people of Zion, who live in Jerusalem, you will weep no more. How gracious he will be when you cry for help! As soon as he hears, he will answer you. ²⁰Although the Lord gives you the bread of adversity and the water of affliction, your teachers will be hidden no more; with your own eyes you will see them. ²¹Whether you turn to the right or to the left, your ears will hear a voice behind you, saying, "This is the way; walk in it." ²²Then you will defile your idols overlaid with silver and your images covered with gold; you will throw them away like a menstrual cloth and say to them, "Away with you!"

²³He will also send you rain for the seed you sow in the ground, and the food that comes from the land will be rich and plentiful. In that day your cattle will graze in broad meadows. ²⁴The oxen and donkeys that work the soil will eat fodder and mash, spread out with fork and shovel. ²⁵In the day of great slaughter, when the towers fall, streams of water will flow on every high mountain and every lofty hill. ²⁶The moon will shine like the sun, and the sunlight will be seven times brighter, like the light of seven full days, when the LORD binds up the bruises of his people and heals the wounds he inflicted.

²⁷See, the Name of the LORD comes from afar,
    with burning anger and dense clouds of
        smoke;
his lips are full of wrath,
    and his tongue is a consuming fire.
²⁸His breath is like a rushing torrent,
    rising up to the neck.
He shakes the nations in the sieve of
        destruction;
    he places in the jaws of the peoples
    a bit that leads them astray.
²⁹And you will sing
    as on the night you celebrate a holy
        festival;
your hearts will rejoice
    as when people go up with flutes
to the mountain of the LORD,
    to the Rock of Israel.
³⁰The LORD will cause men to hear his majestic
        voice
    and will make them see his arm coming
        down
with raging anger and consuming fire,
    with cloudburst, thunderstorm and hail.
³¹The voice of the LORD will shatter Assyria;
    with his scepter he will strike them down.
³²Every stroke the LORD lays on them
    with his punishing rod
will be to the music of tambourines and
        harps,
    as he fights them in battle with the blows
        of his arm.
³³Topheth has long been prepared;
    it has been made ready for the king.
Its fire pit has been made deep and wide,
    with an abundance of fire and wood;
the breath of the LORD,
    like a stream of burning sulfur,
    sets it ablaze.

Woe to Those Who Rely on Egypt

31 Woe to those who go down to Egypt for
help,
who rely on horses,
who trust in the multitude of their chariots
and in the great strength of their horsemen,
but do not look to the Holy One of Israel,
or seek help from the LORD.
² Yet he too is wise and can bring disaster;
he does not take back his words.
He will rise up against the house of the
wicked,
against those who help evildoers.
³ But the Egyptians are men and not God;
their horses are flesh and not spirit.
When the LORD stretches out his hand,
he who helps will stumble,
he who is helped will fall;
both will perish together.

⁴ This is what the LORD says to me:

"As a lion growls,
a great lion over his prey —
and though a whole band of shepherds
is called together against him,
he is not frightened by their shouts
or disturbed by their clamor —
so the LORD Almighty will come down
to do battle on Mount Zion and on its
heights.
⁵ Like birds hovering overhead,
the LORD Almighty will shield Jerusalem;
he will shield it and deliver it,
he will 'pass over' it and will rescue it."

⁶ Return to him you have so greatly revolted
against, O Israelites. ⁷ For in that day every one
of you will reject the idols of silver and gold your
sinful hands have made.

⁸ "Assyria will fall by a sword that is not of man;
a sword, not of mortals, will devour them.
They will flee before the sword
and their young men will be put to forced
labor.
⁹ Their stronghold will fall because of terror;
at sight of the battle standard their
commanders will panic,"
declares the LORD,
whose fire is in Zion,
whose furnace is in Jerusalem.

The Kingdom of Righteousness

32 See, a king will reign in righteousness
and rulers will rule with justice.
² Each man will be like a shelter from the wind
and a refuge from the storm,
like streams of water in the desert
and the shadow of a great rock in a thirsty
land.

³ Then the eyes of those who see will no longer
be closed,
and the ears of those who hear will listen.
⁴ The mind of the rash will know and
understand,
and the stammering tongue will be fluent
and clear.
⁵ No longer will the fool be called noble
nor the scoundrel be highly respected.
⁶ For the fool speaks folly,
his mind is busy with evil:
He practices ungodliness
and spreads error concerning the LORD;
the hungry he leaves empty
and from the thirsty he withholds water.
⁷ The scoundrel's methods are wicked,
he makes up evil schemes
to destroy the poor with lies,
even when the plea of the needy is just.
⁸ But the noble man makes noble plans,
and by noble deeds he stands.

The Women of Jerusalem

⁹ You women who are so complacent,
rise up and listen to me;
you daughters who feel secure,
hear what I have to say!
¹⁰ In little more than a year
you who feel secure will tremble;

Sharing Your Bible

Spend time with each grandchild individually to explain what the Bible is and why it is so important for us to read God's Word (see Psalm 119:11,105). Show them your Bible (this one and others you may use). Tell them your plan for using this Bible to pray and talk to God about them. Place their picture in the acetate sleeve in the front of this Bible, and let them know that for the next two weeks you will be praying specifically for them. Show them the prayers that you will be praying. Tell them you will be focusing on them every day.

Share with them one of your favorite Bible verses and explain why the verse means so much to you. Read from the Bible together—a psalm, a story or a favorite teaching. Let your grandchild know how important God's Word is to you.

Long-Distance Variation: On your next visit, be sure to carve out a little time for this activity. It will be very meaningful to both of you.

. . . .

Thank you, Lord, for giving me your Word. Let me openly and confidently share my faith with my grandchildren so that your promises and the gospel message will be accepted and cherished by another generation. Amen.

Your next devotion is located on page 966.

GRANDCHILD IN FOCUS · PRAYER

Friends

Dear Lord and Father, I pray for my grandchild's social life and his friends. Bring diverse friends into his life who will love and encourage him, who will bring joy and laughter to the good times and comfort and support through difficulties and disappointments. Grant him wisdom and discernment as he selects his friends; help him to avoid cliques that restrict, activities that endanger, and foolish and dangerous behaviors that harm. I ask that you fill his life with close and caring relationships. Amen.

the grape harvest will fail,
and the harvest of fruit will not come.
[11] Tremble, you complacent women;
shudder, you daughters who feel secure!
Strip off your clothes,
put sackcloth around your waists.
[12] Beat your breasts for the pleasant fields,
for the fruitful vines
[13] and for the land of my people,
a land overgrown with thorns and
briers—
yes, mourn for all houses of merriment
and for this city of revelry.
[14] The fortress will be abandoned,
the noisy city deserted;
citadel and watchtower will become a
wasteland forever,
the delight of donkeys, a pasture for flocks,
[15] till the Spirit is poured upon us from on
high,
and the desert becomes a fertile field,
and the fertile field seems like a forest.
[16] Justice will dwell in the desert
and righteousness live in the fertile field.
[17] The fruit of righteousness will be peace;
the effect of righteousness will be quietness
and confidence forever.
[18] My people will live in peaceful dwelling
places,
in secure homes,
in undisturbed places of rest.
[19] Though hail flattens the forest
and the city is leveled completely,
[20] how blessed you will be,
sowing your seed by every stream,
and letting your cattle and donkeys range
free.

Distress and Help

33 Woe to you, O destroyer,
you who have not been destroyed!
Woe to you, O traitor,
you who have not been betrayed!
When you stop destroying,
you will be destroyed;

when you stop betraying,
you will be betrayed.

[2] O LORD, be gracious to us;
we long for you.
Be our strength every morning,
our salvation in time of distress.
[3] At the thunder of your voice, the peoples flee;
when you rise up, the nations scatter.
[4] Your plunder, O nations, is harvested as by
young locusts;
like a swarm of locusts men pounce on it.

[5] The LORD is exalted, for he dwells on high;
he will fill Zion with justice and
righteousness.
[6] He will be the sure foundation for your
times,
a rich store of salvation and wisdom and
knowledge;
the fear of the LORD is the key to this
treasure.[a]

[7] Look, their brave men cry aloud in the
streets;
the envoys of peace weep bitterly.
[8] The highways are deserted,
no travelers are on the roads.
The treaty is broken,
its witnesses[b] are despised,
no one is respected.
[9] The land mourns[c] and wastes away,
Lebanon is ashamed and withers;
Sharon is like the Arabah,
and Bashan and Carmel drop their leaves.

[10] "Now will I arise," says the LORD.
"Now will I be exalted;
now will I be lifted up.
[11] You conceive chaff,
you give birth to straw;
your breath is a fire that consumes you.
[12] The peoples will be burned as if to lime;
like cut thornbushes they will be set
ablaze."

---

[a] 6 Or *is a treasure from him*   [b] 8 Dead Sea Scrolls; Masoretic Text
/ *the cities*   [c] 9 Or *dries up*

¹³ You who are far away, hear what I have done;
    you who are near, acknowledge my power!
¹⁴ The sinners in Zion are terrified;
    trembling grips the godless:
"Who of us can dwell with the consuming
      fire?
Who of us can dwell with everlasting
      burning?"
¹⁵ He who walks righteously
    and speaks what is right,
who rejects gain from extortion
    and keeps his hand from accepting bribes,
who stops his ears against plots of murder
    and shuts his eyes against contemplating
      evil—
¹⁶ this is the man who will dwell on the heights,
    whose refuge will be the mountain fortress.
His bread will be supplied,
    and water will not fail him.

¹⁷ Your eyes will see the king in his beauty
    and view a land that stretches afar.
¹⁸ In your thoughts you will ponder the former
      terror:
"Where is that chief officer?
Where is the one who took the revenue?
Where is the officer in charge of the
      towers?"
¹⁹ You will see those arrogant people no more,
    those people of an obscure speech,
    with their strange, incomprehensible
      tongue.

²⁰ Look upon Zion, the city of our festivals;
    your eyes will see Jerusalem,
    a peaceful abode, a tent that will not be
      moved;
its stakes will never be pulled up,
    nor any of its ropes broken.
²¹ There the Lord will be our Mighty One.
    It will be like a place of broad rivers and
      streams.
No galley with oars will ride them,
    no mighty ship will sail them.
²² For the Lord is our judge,
    the Lord is our lawgiver,

the Lord is our king;
    it is he who will save us.

²³ Your rigging hangs loose:
    The mast is not held secure,
    the sail is not spread.
Then an abundance of spoils will be divided
    and even the lame will carry off plunder.
²⁴ No one living in Zion will say, "I am ill";
    and the sins of those who dwell there will
      be forgiven.

Judgment Against the Nations

34 Come near, you nations, and listen;
    pay attention, you peoples!
Let the earth hear, and all that is in it,
    the world, and all that comes out of it!
² The Lord is angry with all nations;
    his wrath is upon all their armies.
He will totally destroy[a] them,
    he will give them over to slaughter.
³ Their slain will be thrown out,
    their dead bodies will send up a stench;
    the mountains will be soaked with their
      blood.
⁴ All the stars of the heavens will be dissolved
    and the sky rolled up like a scroll;
all the starry host will fall
    like withered leaves from the vine,
    like shriveled figs from the fig tree.

⁵ My sword has drunk its fill in the heavens;
    see, it descends in judgment on Edom,
    the people I have totally destroyed.
⁶ The sword of the Lord is bathed in blood,
    it is covered with fat—
the blood of lambs and goats,
    fat from the kidneys of rams.
For the Lord has a sacrifice in Bozrah
    and a great slaughter in Edom.
⁷ And the wild oxen will fall with them,
    the bull calves and the great bulls.
Their land will be drenched with blood,
    and the dust will be soaked with fat.

---

[a] 2 The Hebrew term refers to the irrevocable giving over of things or persons to the Lord, often by totally destroying them; also in verse 5.

Worship the Lord

Sing to God, sing praise to his name,
 extol him who rides on the clouds —
his name is the LORD —
 and rejoice before him.
A father to the fatherless, a defender of widows,
 is God in his holy dwelling.
God sets the lonely in families,
 he leads forth the prisoners with singing;
 but the rebellious live in a sun-scorched land.

When you went out before your people, O God,
 when you marched through the wasteland,   *Selah*
the earth shook,
 the heavens poured down rain,
before God, the One of Sinai,
 before God, the God of Israel.
You gave abundant showers, O God;
 you refreshed your weary inheritance.
Your people settled in it,
 and from your bounty, O God,
  you provided for the poor.

Psalm 68:4 – 10

*Thank you, Lord, for refreshing and renew-
ing my soul. I sing your praise and rejoice
before you today. You know how lonely I
would be, Father, without my family, and
you have provided them as companionship
for me. Help me to view each member of my
family as an incredible blessing from you. Amen.*

GRANDCHILD IN FOCUS • PRAYER

Self-Image

*O loving God, I praise you for creating my
grandchild as a unique individual. Now I ask you
to help her appreciate her uniqueness. Build up her
self-image so she can enjoy her individuality. Help
her to stand firm for who she is, where she has
come from and what she believes in. Encourage
her not only to have hopes and dreams but
to also enjoy each day as it comes.
In Jesus' name, amen.*

Your next devotion is located on page 968.

⁸For the LORD has a day of vengeance,
    a year of retribution, to uphold Zion's
      cause.
⁹Edom's streams will be turned into pitch,
    her dust into burning sulfur;
    her land will become blazing pitch!
¹⁰It will not be quenched night and day;
    its smoke will rise forever.
From generation to generation it will lie
      desolate;
    no one will ever pass through it again.
¹¹The desert owl[a] and screech owl[a] will
      possess it;
    the great owl[a] and the raven will nest there.
God will stretch out over Edom
    the measuring line of chaos
    and the plumb line of desolation.
¹²Her nobles will have nothing there to be
      called a kingdom,
    all her princes will vanish away.
¹³Thorns will overrun her citadels,
    nettles and brambles her strongholds.
She will become a haunt for jackals,
    a home for owls.
¹⁴Desert creatures will meet with hyenas,
    and wild goats will bleat to each other;
there the night creatures will also repose
    and find for themselves places of rest.
¹⁵The owl will nest there and lay eggs,
    she will hatch them, and care for her
      young under the shadow of her
      wings;
there also the falcons will gather,
    each with its mate.

¹⁶Look in the scroll of the LORD and read:

None of these will be missing,
    not one will lack her mate.
For it is his mouth that has given the order,
    and his Spirit will gather them together.
¹⁷He allots their portions;
    his hand distributes them by measure.
They will possess it forever
    and dwell there from generation to
      generation.

Joy of the Redeemed

35 The desert and the parched land will be
      glad;
    the wilderness will rejoice and blossom.
Like the crocus, ²it will burst into bloom;
    it will rejoice greatly and shout for joy.
The glory of Lebanon will be given to it,
    the splendor of Carmel and Sharon;
they will see the glory of the LORD,
    the splendor of our God.

³Strengthen the feeble hands,
    steady the knees that give way;
⁴say to those with fearful hearts,
    "Be strong, do not fear;
your God will come,
    he will come with vengeance;
with divine retribution
    he will come to save you."

⁵Then will the eyes of the blind be opened
    and the ears of the deaf unstopped.
⁶Then will the lame leap like a deer,
    and the mute tongue shout for joy.
Water will gush forth in the wilderness
    and streams in the desert.
⁷The burning sand will become a pool,
    the thirsty ground bubbling springs.
In the haunts where jackals once lay,
    grass and reeds and papyrus will grow.

⁸And a highway will be there;
    it will be called the Way of Holiness.
The unclean will not journey on it;
    it will be for those who walk in that Way;
    wicked fools will not go about on it.[b]
⁹No lion will be there,
    nor will any ferocious beast get up on it;
    they will not be found there.
But only the redeemed will walk there,
¹⁰   and the ransomed of the LORD will return.
They will enter Zion with singing;
    everlasting joy will crown their heads.
Gladness and joy will overtake them,
    and sorrow and sighing will flee away.

---

[a] 11 The precise identification of these birds is uncertain.
[b] 8 Or / the simple will not stray from it

THE DESERT AND THE PARCHED LAND
WILL BE GLAD; THE WILDERNESS
WILL REJOICE AND BLOSSOM. LIKE
THE CROCUS, IT WILL BURST INTO
BLOOM; IT WILL REJOICE GREATLY
AND SHOUT FOR JOY.

Isaiah 35:1 – 2

Come Spring

DOTTIE RAMBO

READ | ISAIAH 35:1 – 4

Grandma Lutrell had a green thumb. She could make anything grow — anywhere and for longer than seemed possible. I loved our walks among her roses. She taught me about the love of God through her gardening.

"Our heavenly Father was the original gardener," she would say. "He planted the first garden in Eden. But Adam didn't tend it too well."

I would giggle.

Oh, how her Biblical stories connected with her garden! Once she told me that Jesus was a gardener.

"He is?" I asked in awe.

"Why sure, little Dottie. After he rose again, Mary Magdalene looked at him and saw him as a gardener. I believe she saw him for who he is." She would wink and smile as I stood there, thinking of Jesus with a gardening tool instead of a staff.

During Grandma's last winter with us, she called me into her room. The snow fell softly outside her window. She reached for my hand, looked at me for a long time, sighed and whispered, "Before my roses bloom, I'll be gone to be with Jesus." My eyes filled with tears.
"But don't you fret none; I'll be in the best garden with the Gardener. And we'll meet again when he gathers his flowers, come spring."

Whenever I look through a snowy window, I hear the voice of my dear grandmother promising that we'll meet again. I echo her words to my own grandchildren as I tell of the promise of an eternal spring.

Lord, I hope in you for all I need to grow and bloom. Give me what I need so that I may tend to my grandchildren with the nurturing and watering needed for precious seed in fertile soil. In Jesus' marvelous name, amen.

GRANDCHILD IN FOCUS • PRAYER

Protection From Worldliness

O Sovereign Lord, the world surrounds my grandchild, pressing in and tempting him in so many ways. Help him set appropriate limits. Give him sound judgment to choose wisely. Guard him from temptation; protect him from physical and mental predators; lead him into paths of righteousness and light. And reassure me with your promise that you are holding him in your hands. Amen.

Your next devotion is located on page 969.

> AND THE RANSOMED OF THE LORD WILL RETURN. THEY WILL ENTER ZION WITH SINGING; EVERLASTING JOY WILL CROWN THEIR HEADS. GLADNESS AND JOY WILL OVERTAKE THEM, AND SORROW AND SIGHING WILL FLEE AWAY.
>
> *Isaiah 35:10*

A Harvest of Joy

SUSAN LENZKES

READ | ISAIAH 35:5 – 10

Through his great and precious promises, God generously sprinkles his seeds of joy in our heart. Yet too often we reap a harvest of misery. Joy's seed requires deep furrows of faith, sprouts in the rich soil of trust, is nourished by daily soaking in God's Word, blossoms in eager response to his love, grows strong through winds of adversity, and bears fruit only as we stay rooted in obedience to Christ's commands. And how true that the tender seedling of God's joy and the stubborn weed of self-pity cannot survive in the same garden!

Joy is not mere happiness. Nor does joy spring from a life of ease, comfort or peaceful circumstances. Joy is the soul's buoyant response to a God of promise, presence and power.

Joy lifts our spirit above earth's sorrow, dancing in jubilation at the hope set before us. Joy is faith feasting and celebrating the one in whom it trusts. Joy is the heart vibrating in grateful rhythm to the love of Almighty God who actually chooses to make his home within us. Joy is the child of God reclining in the luxury of a Father who is "able to do immeasurably more than all we ask or imagine, according to his power that is at work within us" (Ephesians 3:20).

Lord, joy is the vine-ripened fruit grown of your Spirit, who is at work within me as I trust and obey. It is sweet to you and to me. Amen.

Your next devotion is located on page 976.

GRANDCHILD IN FOCUS • PRAYER

Respect for Authority

Dear Lord, I pray that my grandchild will continually grow to respect those in authority. May she learn to be cooperative and fair in work and play. Instill in her a high regard for officials who govern our land and enforce the laws. May her relationships with parents, teachers, coaches, mentors and bosses be respectful, admirable, constructive and caring. Amen.

Sennacherib Threatens Jerusalem
36:1–22pp — 2Ki 18:13,17–37; 2Ch 32:9–19

36 In the fourteenth year of King Hezekiah's reign, Sennacherib king of Assyria attacked all the fortified cities of Judah and captured them. ²Then the king of Assyria sent his field commander with a large army from Lachish to King Hezekiah at Jerusalem. When the commander stopped at the aqueduct of the Upper Pool, on the road to the Washerman's Field, ³Eliakim son of Hilkiah the palace administrator, Shebna the secretary, and Joah son of Asaph the recorder went out to him.

⁴The field commander said to them, "Tell Hezekiah,

"'This is what the great king, the king of Assyria, says: On what are you basing this confidence of yours? ⁵You say you have strategy and military strength—but you speak only empty words. On whom are you depending, that you rebel against me? ⁶Look now, you are depending on Egypt, that splintered reed of a staff, which pierces a man's hand and wounds him if he leans on it! Such is Pharaoh king of Egypt to all who depend on him. ⁷And if you say to me, "We are depending on the Lord our God"—isn't he the one whose high places and altars Hezekiah removed, saying to Judah and Jerusalem, "You must worship before this altar"?

⁸"'Come now, make a bargain with my master, the king of Assyria: I will give you two thousand horses—if you can put riders on them! ⁹How then can you repulse one officer of the least of my master's officials, even though you are depending on Egypt for chariots and horsemen? ¹⁰Furthermore, have I come to attack and destroy this land without the Lord? The Lord himself told me to march against this country and destroy it.'"

¹¹Then Eliakim, Shebna and Joah said to the field commander, "Please speak to your servants in Aramaic, since we understand it. Don't speak to us in Hebrew in the hearing of the people on the wall."

¹²But the commander replied, "Was it only to your master and you that my master sent me to say these things, and not to the men sitting on the wall—who, like you, will have to eat their own filth and drink their own urine?"

¹³Then the commander stood and called out in Hebrew, "Hear the words of the great king, the king of Assyria! ¹⁴This is what the king says: Do not let Hezekiah deceive you. He cannot deliver you! ¹⁵Do not let Hezekiah persuade you to trust in the Lord when he says, 'The Lord will surely deliver us; this city will not be given into the hand of the king of Assyria.'

¹⁶"Do not listen to Hezekiah. This is what the king of Assyria says: Make peace with me and come out to me. Then every one of you will eat from his own vine and fig tree and drink water from his own cistern, ¹⁷until I come and take you to a land like your own—a land of grain and new wine, a land of bread and vineyards.

¹⁸"Do not let Hezekiah mislead you when he says, 'The Lord will deliver us.' Has the god of any nation ever delivered his land from the hand of the king of Assyria? ¹⁹Where are the gods of Hamath and Arpad? Where are the gods of Sepharvaim? Have they rescued Samaria from my hand? ²⁰Who of all the gods of these countries has been able to save his land from me? How then can the Lord deliver Jerusalem from my hand?"

²¹But the people remained silent and said nothing in reply, because the king had commanded, "Do not answer him."

²²Then Eliakim son of Hilkiah the palace administrator, Shebna the secretary, and Joah son of Asaph the recorder went to Hezekiah, with their clothes torn, and told him what the field commander had said.

Jerusalem's Deliverance Foretold
37:1–13pp — 2Ki 19:1–13

37 When King Hezekiah heard this, he tore his clothes and put on sackcloth and went into the temple of the Lord. ²He sent Eliakim the palace administrator, Shebna the secretary, and the leading priests, all wearing sackcloth, to the prophet Isaiah son of Amoz. ³They told him, "This is what Hezekiah says: This day is a day of distress and rebuke and disgrace, as when children come to the point of birth and there is no strength to deliver them. ⁴It may be that the LORD your God will hear the words of the field commander, whom his master, the king of Assyria, has sent to ridicule the living God, and that he will rebuke him for the words the LORD your God has heard. Therefore pray for the remnant that still survives."

⁵When King Hezekiah's officials came to Isaiah, ⁶Isaiah said to them, "Tell your master, 'This is what the LORD says: Do not be afraid of what you have heard—those words with which the underlings of the king of Assyria have blasphemed me. ⁷Listen! I am going to put a spirit in him so that when he hears a certain report, he will return to his own country, and there I will have him cut down with the sword.'"

⁸When the field commander heard that the king of Assyria had left Lachish, he withdrew and found the king fighting against Libnah.

⁹Now Sennacherib received a report that Tirhakah, the Cushite ᵃ king ⌐of Egypt⌐, was marching out to fight against him. When he heard it, he sent messengers to Hezekiah with this word: ¹⁰"Say to Hezekiah king of Judah: Do not let the god you depend on deceive you when he says, 'Jerusalem will not be handed over to the king of Assyria.' ¹¹Surely you have heard what the kings of Assyria have done to all the countries, destroying them completely. And will you be delivered? ¹²Did the gods of the nations that were destroyed by my forefathers deliver them—the gods of Gozan, Haran, Rezeph and the people of Eden who were in Tel Assar? ¹³Where is the king of Hamath, the king of Arpad, the king of the city of Sepharvaim, or of Hena or Ivvah?"

Hezekiah's Prayer
37:14–20pp — 2Ki 19:14–19

¹⁴Hezekiah received the letter from the messengers and read it. Then he went up to the temple of the LORD and spread it out before the LORD. ¹⁵And Hezekiah prayed to the LORD: ¹⁶"O LORD Almighty, God of Israel, enthroned between the cherubim, you alone are God over all the kingdoms of the earth. You have made heaven and earth. ¹⁷Give ear, O LORD, and hear; open your eyes, O LORD, and see; listen to all the words Sennacherib has sent to insult the living God.

¹⁸"It is true, O LORD, that the Assyrian kings have laid waste all these peoples and their lands. ¹⁹They have thrown their gods into the fire and destroyed them, for they were not gods but only wood and stone, fashioned by human hands. ²⁰Now, O LORD our God, deliver us from his hand, so that all kingdoms on earth may know that you alone, O LORD, are God. ᵇ"

Sennacherib's Fall
37:21–38pp — 2Ki 19:20–37; 2Ch 32:20–21

²¹Then Isaiah son of Amoz sent a message to Hezekiah: "This is what the LORD, the God of Israel, says: Because you have prayed to me concerning Sennacherib king of Assyria, ²²this is the word the LORD has spoken against him:

"The Virgin Daughter of Zion
    despises and mocks you.
The Daughter of Jerusalem
    tosses her head as you flee.
²³Who is it you have insulted and blasphemed?
    Against whom have you raised your voice
and lifted your eyes in pride?
    Against the Holy One of Israel!
²⁴By your messengers
    you have heaped insults on the Lord.
And you have said,
    'With my many chariots
I have ascended the heights of the mountains,
    the utmost heights of Lebanon.
I have cut down its tallest cedars,
    the choicest of its pines.
I have reached its remotest heights,
    the finest of its forests.

ᵃ 9 That is, from the upper Nile region   ᵇ 20 Dead Sea Scrolls (see also 2 Kings 19:19); Masoretic Text *alone are the LORD*

^{25}I have dug wells in foreign lands^a
and drunk the water there.
With the soles of my feet
I have dried up all the streams of Egypt.'

^{26}"Have you not heard?
Long ago I ordained it.
In days of old I planned it;
now I have brought it to pass,
that you have turned fortified cities
into piles of stone.
^{27}Their people, drained of power,
are dismayed and put to shame.
They are like plants in the field,
like tender green shoots,
like grass sprouting on the roof,
scorched^b before it grows up.

^{28}"But I know where you stay
and when you come and go
and how you rage against me.
^{29}Because you rage against me
and because your insolence has reached
my ears,
I will put my hook in your nose
and my bit in your mouth,
and I will make you return
by the way you came.

^{30}"This will be the sign for you, O Hezekiah:

"This year you will eat what grows by itself,
and the second year what springs from that.
But in the third year sow and reap,
plant vineyards and eat their fruit.
^{31}Once more a remnant of the house of Judah
will take root below and bear fruit above.
^{32}For out of Jerusalem will come a remnant,
and out of Mount Zion a band of
survivors.
The zeal of the LORD Almighty
will accomplish this.

^{33}"Therefore this is what the LORD says concerning the king of Assyria:

"He will not enter this city
or shoot an arrow here.
He will not come before it with shield
or build a siege ramp against it.
^{34}By the way that he came he will return;
he will not enter this city,"
declares the LORD.
^{35}"I will defend this city and save it,
for my sake and for the sake of David my
servant!"

^{36}Then the angel of the LORD went out and put to death a hundred and eighty-five thousand men in the Assyrian camp. When the people got up the next morning—there were all the dead bodies! ^{37}So Sennacherib king of Assyria broke camp and withdrew. He returned to Nineveh and stayed there.

^{38}One day, while he was worshiping in the temple of his god Nisroch, his sons Adrammelech and Sharezer cut him down with the sword, and they escaped to the land of Ararat. And Esarhaddon his son succeeded him as king.

Hezekiah's Illness

38:1–8pp — 2Ki 20:1–11; 2Ch 32:24–26

38 In those days Hezekiah became ill and was at the point of death. The prophet Isaiah son of Amoz went to him and said, "This is what the LORD says: Put your house in order, because you are going to die; you will not recover." ^{2}Hezekiah turned his face to the wall and prayed to the LORD, ^{3}"Remember, O LORD, how I have walked before you faithfully and with wholehearted devotion and have done what is good in your eyes." And Hezekiah wept bitterly.

^{4}Then the word of the LORD came to Isaiah: ^{5}"Go and tell Hezekiah, 'This is what the LORD, the God of your father David, says: I have heard your prayer and seen your tears; I will add fifteen years to your life. ^{6}And I will deliver you and this city from the hand of the king of Assyria. I will defend this city.

---

^{a} 25 Dead Sea Scrolls (see also 2 Kings 19:24); Masoretic Text does not have *in foreign lands.* ^{b} 27 Some manuscripts of the Masoretic Text, Dead Sea Scrolls and some Septuagint manuscripts (see also 2 Kings 19:26); most manuscripts of the Masoretic Text *roof / and terraced fields*

7 " 'This is the LORD's sign to you that the LORD will do what he has promised: 8 I will make the shadow cast by the sun go back the ten steps it has gone down on the stairway of Ahaz.' " So the sunlight went back the ten steps it had gone down.

9 A writing of Hezekiah king of Judah after his illness and recovery:

10 I said, "In the prime of my life
    must I go through the gates of death [a]
    and be robbed of the rest of my years?"
11 I said, "I will not again see the LORD,
    the LORD, in the land of the living;
no longer will I look on mankind,
    or be with those who now dwell in this
        world. [b]
12 Like a shepherd's tent my house
    has been pulled down and taken from me.
Like a weaver I have rolled up my life,
    and he has cut me off from the loom;
    day and night you made an end of me.
13 I waited patiently till dawn,
    but like a lion he broke all my bones;
    day and night you made an end of me.
14 I cried like a swift or thrush,
    I moaned like a mourning dove.
My eyes grew weak as I looked to the heavens.
    I am troubled; O Lord, come to my aid!"

15 But what can I say?
    He has spoken to me, and he himself has
        done this.
I will walk humbly all my years
    because of this anguish of my soul.
16 Lord, by such things men live;
    and my spirit finds life in them too.
You restored me to health
    and let me live.
17 Surely it was for my benefit
    that I suffered such anguish.
In your love you kept me
    from the pit of destruction;
you have put all my sins
    behind your back.

18 For the grave [a] cannot praise you,
    death cannot sing your praise;
those who go down to the pit
    cannot hope for your faithfulness.
19 The living, the living — they praise you,
    as I am doing today;
fathers tell their children
    about your faithfulness.

20 The LORD will save me,
    and we will sing with stringed instruments
all the days of our lives
    in the temple of the LORD.

21 Isaiah had said, "Prepare a poultice of figs and apply it to the boil, and he will recover."
22 Hezekiah had asked, "What will be the sign that I will go up to the temple of the LORD?"

Envoys From Babylon
39:1–8pp — 2Ki 20:12–19

39 At that time Merodach-Baladan son of Baladan king of Babylon sent Hezekiah letters and a gift, because he had heard of his illness and recovery. 2 Hezekiah received the envoys gladly and showed them what was in his storehouses — the silver, the gold, the spices, the fine oil, his entire armory and everything found among his treasures. There was nothing in his palace or in all his kingdom that Hezekiah did not show them.

3 Then Isaiah the prophet went to King Hezekiah and asked, "What did those men say, and where did they come from?"

"From a distant land," Hezekiah replied. "They came to me from Babylon."

4 The prophet asked, "What did they see in your palace?"

"They saw everything in my palace," Hezekiah said. "There is nothing among my treasures that I did not show them."

5 Then Isaiah said to Hezekiah, "Hear the word of the LORD Almighty: 6 The time will surely come when everything in your palace, and all that your

[a] 10,18 Hebrew Sheol   [b] 11 A few Hebrew manuscripts; most Hebrew manuscripts in the place of cessation

fathers have stored up until this day, will be carried off to Babylon. Nothing will be left, says the LORD. ⁷And some of your descendants, your own flesh and blood who will be born to you, will be taken away, and they will become eunuchs in the palace of the king of Babylon."

⁸"The word of the LORD you have spoken is good," Hezekiah replied. For he thought, "There will be peace and security in my lifetime."

Comfort for God's People

40 Comfort, comfort my people,
   says your God.
² Speak tenderly to Jerusalem,
   and proclaim to her
that her hard service has been completed,
   that her sin has been paid for,
that she has received from the LORD's hand
   double for all her sins.

³ A voice of one calling:
"In the desert prepare
   the way for the LORD ᵃ;
make straight in the wilderness
   a highway for our God. ᵇ
⁴ Every valley shall be raised up,
   every mountain and hill made low;
the rough ground shall become level,
   the rugged places a plain.
⁵ And the glory of the LORD will be revealed,
   and all mankind together will see it.
            For the mouth of the LORD
                     has spoken."

⁶ A voice says, "Cry out."
   And I said, "What shall I cry?"

"All men are like grass,
   and all their glory is like the flowers of the
      field.
⁷ The grass withers and the flowers fall,
   because the breath of the LORD blows on
      them.
   Surely the people are grass.
⁸ The grass withers and the flowers fall,
   but the word of our God stands forever."

⁹ You who bring good tidings to Zion,
   go up on a high mountain.
You who bring good tidings to Jerusalem, ᶜ
   lift up your voice with a shout,
lift it up, do not be afraid;
   say to the towns of Judah,
   "Here is your God!"
¹⁰ See, the Sovereign LORD comes with power,
   and his arm rules for him.
See, his reward is with him,
   and his recompense accompanies him.
¹¹ He tends his flock like a shepherd:
   He gathers the lambs in his arms
and carries them close to his heart;
   he gently leads those that have young.

¹² Who has measured the waters in the hollow
      of his hand,
   or with the breadth of his hand marked off
      the heavens?
Who has held the dust of the earth in a
      basket,
   or weighed the mountains on the scales
   and the hills in a balance?
¹³ Who has understood the mind ᵈ of the LORD,
   or instructed him as his counselor?
¹⁴ Whom did the LORD consult to enlighten him,
   and who taught him the right way?
Who was it that taught him knowledge
   or showed him the path of understanding?

¹⁵ Surely the nations are like a drop in a bucket;
   they are regarded as dust on the scales;
he weighs the islands as though they were
      fine dust.
¹⁶ Lebanon is not sufficient for altar fires,
   nor its animals enough for burnt offerings.
¹⁷ Before him all the nations are as nothing;
   they are regarded by him as worthless
   and less than nothing.

¹⁸ To whom, then, will you compare God?
   What image will you compare him to?

ᵃ 3 Or A voice of one calling in the desert: / "Prepare the way for the
LORD   ᵇ 3 Hebrew; Septuagint make straight the paths of our God
ᶜ 9 Or O Zion, bringer of good tidings, / go up on a high mountain. /
O Jerusalem, bringer of good tidings   ᵈ 13 Or Spirit; or spirit

¹⁹As for an idol, a craftsman casts it,
    and a goldsmith overlays it with gold
    and fashions silver chains for it.
²⁰A man too poor to present such an offering
    selects wood that will not rot.
He looks for a skilled craftsman
    to set up an idol that will not topple.

²¹Do you not know?
    Have you not heard?
Has it not been told you from the beginning?
    Have you not understood since the earth
        was founded?
²²He sits enthroned above the circle of the
        earth,
    and its people are like grasshoppers.
He stretches out the heavens like a canopy,
    and spreads them out like a tent to live in.
²³He brings princes to naught
    and reduces the rulers of this world to
        nothing.
²⁴No sooner are they planted,
    no sooner are they sown,
    no sooner do they take root in the ground,
than he blows on them and they wither,
    and a whirlwind sweeps them away like
        chaff.

²⁵"To whom will you compare me?
    Or who is my equal?" says the Holy One.
²⁶Lift your eyes and look to the heavens:
    Who created all these?
He who brings out the starry host one by
        one,
    and calls them each by name.
Because of his great power and mighty
        strength,
    not one of them is missing.

²⁷Why do you say, O Jacob,
    and complain, O Israel,
"My way is hidden from the LORD;
    my cause is disregarded by my God"?
²⁸Do you not know?
    Have you not heard?
The LORD is the everlasting God,
    the Creator of the ends of the earth.

He will not grow tired or weary,
    and his understanding no one can fathom.
²⁹He gives strength to the weary
    and increases the power of the weak.
³⁰Even youths grow tired and weary,
    and young men stumble and fall;
³¹but those who hope in the LORD
    will renew their strength.
They will soar on wings like eagles;
    they will run and not grow weary,
    they will walk and not be faint.

TALKING POINTS

Finding God

Those who hope and trust in the Lord
will renew their strength.

ISAIAH 40:30–31

For more on finding God, go to Isaiah 55:6–7.

The Helper of Israel

41 "Be silent before me, you islands!
    Let the nations renew their strength!
Let them come forward and speak;
    let us meet together at the place of
        judgment.

²"Who has stirred up one from the east,
    calling him in righteousness to his
        service^a?
He hands nations over to him
    and subdues kings before him.
He turns them to dust with his sword,
    to windblown chaff with his bow.
³He pursues them and moves on unscathed,
    by a path his feet have not traveled before.
⁴Who has done this and carried it through,
    calling forth the generations from the
        beginning?

^a 2 Or / whom victory meets at every step

But those who hope in the Lord will renew their strength. They will soar on wings like eagles; they will run and not grow weary, they will walk and not be faint.

Isaiah 40:31

Wing Power

MARGARET FISHBACK POWERS

READ | ISAIAH 40:27 – 31

My grandchildren are quite fascinated with the eagle pictures, sculptures and photos in their papa's office. They are intrigued as well with his heavy ring displaying two silver eagles on a wide gold band, inscribed with the verse from Isaiah 40:31.

I love to explain to my grandchildren the significance of this verse: It was given as a promise and encouragement by our pastor on the day we were married. As we faced burdens in life together, which often came down so heavily we could not carry them any longer, we would pray to God to remove them. However, over the years we discovered that God's plan was to use those burdens to develop "wing power" in our lives.

As we look at the eagles together, I tell my grandchildren about their nature. When the eagles know a storm is coming, they wait until it strikes. Then they face the storm, spread their wings and rise upward through it. We can be like the eagles, I explain to my grandchildren. When the pressures, burdens and obstacles of life come upon us, our "prayer power" takes us through the storm and lifts us above it. This prayer strength comes from learning to "wait upon the Lord," as the King James Version renders Isaiah 40:31. I tell them the waiting means complete and habitual trusting and "stick-to-it-ness" in spite of any problems and difficulties that arise.

A while ago I also shared this analogy with a young lad in Great Britain who was feeling very discouraged in his cross-country racing. He had been placing in the bottom section of the races he was in. After taking these words to heart, he is now "soaring and gliding" in the top five.

We must never give in or give up. We must keep trusting, and we will eventually soar.

O Lord, help me never to give in or give up. Sustain me with your presence. Uplift me with your strength. Let me see burdens and challenges as opportunities to develop "wing power" in my life, so I may soar above these earthly cares. Amen.

Your next devotion is located on page 978.

GRANDCHILD IN FOCUS • PRAYER

Courage

O Father, builder of character and courage, may my grandchild grow strong in the light of your love. Grant him courage to stand for what is right, to guard the truth and to ensure justice in every aspect of life. May he boldly grow in grace, revere your name and proudly proclaim you as the Lord of lords and King of kings. Amen.

I, the Lord—with the first of them
   and with the last—I am he."

⁵The islands have seen it and fear;
   the ends of the earth tremble.
 They approach and come forward;
⁶   each helps the other
   and says to his brother, "Be strong!"
⁷The craftsman encourages the goldsmith,
   and he who smooths with the hammer
   spurs on him who strikes the anvil.
 He says of the welding, "It is good."
   He nails down the idol so it will not topple.

⁸"But you, O Israel, my servant,
   Jacob, whom I have chosen,
   you descendants of Abraham my friend,
⁹I took you from the ends of the earth,
   from its farthest corners I called you.
 I said, 'You are my servant';
   I have chosen you and have not rejected
     you.
¹⁰So do not fear, for I am with you;
   do not be dismayed, for I am your God.
 I will strengthen you and help you;
   I will uphold you with my righteous right
     hand.

¹¹"All who rage against you
   will surely be ashamed and disgraced;
 those who oppose you
   will be as nothing and perish.
¹²Though you search for your enemies,
   you will not find them.

TALKING POINTS

Depression

God will strengthen, help and uphold us.

ISAIAH 41:10

For more on depression, go to Jonah 2:1–2.

TALKING POINTS

Military

God will strengthen and uphold us.

ISAIAH 41:10

This is the last talking point on military.

Those who wage war against you
   will be as nothing at all.
¹³For I am the Lord, your God,
   who takes hold of your right hand
 and says to you, Do not fear;
   I will help you.
¹⁴Do not be afraid, O worm Jacob,
   O little Israel,
 for I myself will help you," declares the Lord,
   your Redeemer, the Holy One of Israel.
¹⁵"See, I will make you into a threshing sledge,
   new and sharp, with many teeth.
 You will thresh the mountains and crush them,
   and reduce the hills to chaff.
¹⁶You will winnow them, the wind will pick
     them up,
   and a gale will blow them away.
 But you will rejoice in the Lord
   and glory in the Holy One of Israel.

¹⁷"The poor and needy search for water,
   but there is none;
   their tongues are parched with thirst.
 But I the Lord will answer them;
   I, the God of Israel, will not forsake them.
¹⁸I will make rivers flow on barren heights,
   and springs within the valleys.
 I will turn the desert into pools of water,
   and the parched ground into springs.
¹⁹I will put in the desert
   the cedar and the acacia, the myrtle and
     the olive.
 I will set pines in the wasteland,
   the fir and the cypress together,

> "SO DO NOT FEAR, FOR I AM
> WITH YOU; DO NOT BE DISMAYED,
> FOR I AM YOUR GOD. I WILL
> STRENGTHEN YOU AND HELP YOU;
> I WILL UPHOLD YOU WITH MY
> RIGHTEOUS RIGHT HAND."
>
> *Isaiah 41:10*

Blue Hair

CAROL KUYKENDALL

READ | ISAIAH 41:1 – 10

When I was diagnosed with stage 4 ovarian cancer and began chemotherapy a couple of years ago, one of my greatest fears was that my hair loss would frighten my grandchildren. Or maybe I just focused on that immediate fear to cover up lots of other fears that I had.

I don't know why hair loss feels so traumatic, but it seems like such a cruel and visible assault in the midst of the many other life changes that cancer brings. So in preparation, I bought a couple of look-just-like-me wigs and one absolutely ridiculous iridescent blue wig, for those times I wanted to lighten up and say, "Since we both know I don't have hair, let's have fun with the substitute."

To my surprise and delight, my daughter-in-law bought three-year-old Gabi a similar iridescent blue wig, so we could get used to the idea of wigs by playing dress up together. So there we sat one afternoon, in front of a mirror in my bathroom, putting on our wigs.

"Everyone will think we are so pretty, Oma," Gabi giggled.

"Do you know that Oma is going to wear a wig for a long time?"

"My mommy told me," she nodded. "Can we put on some lipstick too?" she asked, reaching for a tube.

"Good idea . . . Do you know Oma won't have any hair?"

"That's OK, Oma. Can we put on some of this too?" she asked, pointing to some sparkly eye shadow.

Obviously, no hair was no problem for Gabi.

Maybe, I thought as I dabbed on some eye shadow, I didn't have to fear those things I thought I feared the most.

Lord, children can put our fears into perspective. May I do the same as I keep trusting you with childlike faith.

Your next devotion is located on page 981.

GRANDCHILD IN FOCUS • PRAYER

Future Spouse

Dear Lord, if it is your will, I pray my grandchild will be united in a loving and Christian marriage. Keep her sexually pure so that she will honor you with her body and mind. As she seeks a spouse who will honor and care for her, give her patience and discernment. May her choice for a life partner be your choice for her, so that she and her husband will together glorify you in a lasting love. I pray this in Jesus' name, amen.

²⁰ so that people may see and know,
    may consider and understand,
that the hand of the LORD has done this,
    that the Holy One of Israel has created it.

²¹ "Present your case," says the LORD.
    "Set forth your arguments," says Jacob's
        King.
²² "Bring in ˻your idols˼ to tell us
    what is going to happen.
Tell us what the former things were,
    so that we may consider them
    and know their final outcome.
Or declare to us the things to come,
²³   tell us what the future holds,
    so we may know that you are gods.
Do something, whether good or bad,
    so that we will be dismayed and filled with
        fear.
²⁴ But you are less than nothing
    and your works are utterly worthless;
    he who chooses you is detestable.

²⁵ "I have stirred up one from the north, and he
        comes—
    one from the rising sun who calls on my
        name.
He treads on rulers as if they were mortar,
    as if he were a potter treading the clay.
²⁶ Who told of this from the beginning, so we
        could know,
    or beforehand, so we could say, 'He was
        right'?
No one told of this,
    no one foretold it,
    no one heard any words from you.
²⁷ I was the first to tell Zion, 'Look, here they
        are!'
    I gave to Jerusalem a messenger of good
        tidings.
²⁸ I look but there is no one—
    no one among them to give counsel,
    no one to give answer when I ask them.
²⁹ See, they are all false!
    Their deeds amount to nothing;
    their images are but wind and confusion.

The Servant of the LORD

42   "Here is my servant, whom I uphold,
    my chosen one in whom I delight;
I will put my Spirit on him
    and he will bring justice to the nations.
² He will not shout or cry out,
    or raise his voice in the streets.
³ A bruised reed he will not break,
    and a smoldering wick he will not snuff
        out.
In faithfulness he will bring forth justice;
⁴   he will not falter or be discouraged
till he establishes justice on earth.
    In his law the islands will put their hope."

⁵ This is what God the LORD says—
he who created the heavens and stretched
        them out,
    who spread out the earth and all that
        comes out of it,
who gives breath to its people,
    and life to those who walk on it:
⁶ "I, the LORD, have called you in righteousness;
    I will take hold of your hand.
I will keep you and will make you
    to be a covenant for the people
    and a light for the Gentiles,
⁷ to open eyes that are blind,
    to free captives from prison
    and to release from the dungeon those
        who sit in darkness.

⁸ "I am the LORD; that is my name!
    I will not give my glory to another
    or my praise to idols.
⁹ See, the former things have taken place,
    and new things I declare;
before they spring into being
    I announce them to you."

Song of Praise to the LORD

¹⁰ Sing to the LORD a new song,
    his praise from the ends of the earth,
you who go down to the sea, and all that is
        in it,
    you islands, and all who live in them.

11 Let the desert and its towns raise their voices;
  let the settlements where Kedar lives
    rejoice.
Let the people of Sela sing for joy;
  let them shout from the mountaintops.
12 Let them give glory to the LORD
  and proclaim his praise in the islands.
13 The LORD will march out like a mighty man,
  like a warrior he will stir up his zeal;
with a shout he will raise the battle cry
  and will triumph over his enemies.

14 "For a long time I have kept silent,
  I have been quiet and held myself back.
But now, like a woman in childbirth,
  I cry out, I gasp and pant.
15 I will lay waste the mountains and hills
  and dry up all their vegetation;
I will turn rivers into islands
  and dry up the pools.
16 I will lead the blind by ways they have not
    known,
  along unfamiliar paths I will guide them;
I will turn the darkness into light before
    them
  and make the rough places smooth.
These are the things I will do;
  I will not forsake them.
17 But those who trust in idols,
  who say to images, 'You are our gods,'
  will be turned back in utter shame.

Israel Blind and Deaf

18 "Hear, you deaf;
  look, you blind, and see!
19 Who is blind but my servant,
  and deaf like the messenger I send?
Who is blind like the one committed to me,
  blind like the servant of the LORD?
20 You have seen many things, but have paid no
    attention;
  your ears are open, but you hear nothing."
21 It pleased the LORD
  for the sake of his righteousness
  to make his law great and glorious.

22 But this is a people plundered and looted,
  all of them trapped in pits
  or hidden away in prisons.
They have become plunder,
  with no one to rescue them;
they have been made loot,
  with no one to say, "Send them back."

23 Which of you will listen to this
  or pay close attention in time to come?
24 Who handed Jacob over to become loot,
  and Israel to the plunderers?
Was it not the LORD,
  against whom we have sinned?
For they would not follow his ways;
  they did not obey his law.
25 So he poured out on them his burning anger,
  the violence of war.
It enveloped them in flames, yet they did not
    understand;
  it consumed them, but they did not take it
    to heart.

Israel's Only Savior

43 But now, this is what the LORD says—
  he who created you, O Jacob,
  he who formed you, O Israel:
"Fear not, for I have redeemed you;
  I have summoned you by name; you are
    mine.
2 When you pass through the waters,
  I will be with you;
and when you pass through the rivers,
  they will not sweep over you.
When you walk through the fire,
  you will not be burned;
  the flames will not set you ablaze.
3 For I am the LORD, your God,
  the Holy One of Israel, your Savior;
I give Egypt for your ransom,
  Cush a and Seba in your stead.
4 Since you are precious and honored in my
    sight,
  and because I love you,

---

a 3 That is, the upper Nile region

YOU ARE PRECIOUS AND
HONORED IN MY SIGHT,
AND ... I LOVE YOU.
Isaiah 43:4

Precious and Loved

LORI COPELAND

READ | ISAIAH 43:1–13

My second grandchild, Joseph, entered the world one cold December evening. By now I was a "seasoned" grandma. I was prepared for the moment of awe and wonder when our son would appear from the delivery room holding his newborn. No — wait. I wasn't prepared. There it was again. That thrill — the unexpected, unbelievable exhilaration when I looked upon our second grandson, and I couldn't get that silly grin off my face. I loved this one as much or more than my son and my first grandson? Impossible! Yet there it was, love so full and absolute all I could say was, "Oh my! Oh my!"

In this passage God speaks tenderly to Israel, the special people he has created, formed, redeemed and summoned by name. "You are mine," the Lord says (Isaiah 43:1). He tells those who are "precious and honored in [his] sight" of his love (Isaiah 43:4). Imperfect as we are, God has created us with the capacity, akin to his, of experiencing and expressing great love.

Today, I'm still saying, "Oh my!" about Joe. The little boy who teased me about my "awful" goulash is somewhere in Beijing, China, spreading the Good News, working with others his age to win souls for the Lord. Sometimes I feel so exhilarated by God's blessings it frightens me — because I'm wise enough to know that life is not all blessings, especially when children and grandchildren are involved. For now, I praise God and pray that whatever befalls Joe, his faith will sustain him, for he is precious in the Savior's sight.

Dear God, protect, strengthen and hearten all my grandchildren in their daily walk with you. Make them ever aware of your grace and love. Amen.

Your next devotion is located on page 985.

GRANDCHILD IN FOCUS • PRAYER

School/Career

Dear God, may learning be a joy rather than a chore for my grandchild. May exploration of new ideas bring a sense of wonder, awe and excitement. Grant him clarity of mind, the ability to concentrate on the task at hand and recollection of what has been learned. Help him to appreciate the tasks that come easily and to persevere through those that challenge. Amen.

I will give men in exchange for you,
and people in exchange for your life.
⁵ Do not be afraid, for I am with you;
I will bring your children from the east
and gather you from the west.
⁶ I will say to the north, 'Give them up!'
and to the south, 'Do not hold them back.'
Bring my sons from afar
and my daughters from the ends of the
earth —
⁷ everyone who is called by my name,
whom I created for my glory,
whom I formed and made."

⁸ Lead out those who have eyes but are blind,
who have ears but are deaf.
⁹ All the nations gather together
and the peoples assemble.
Which of them foretold this
and proclaimed to us the former things?
Let them bring in their witnesses to prove
they were right,
so that others may hear and say, "It is true."
¹⁰ "You are my witnesses," declares the LORD,
"and my servant whom I have chosen,
so that you may know and believe me
and understand that I am he.
Before me no god was formed,
nor will there be one after me.
¹¹ I, even I, am the LORD,
and apart from me there is no savior.
¹² I have revealed and saved and proclaimed —
I, and not some foreign god among you.
You are my witnesses," declares the LORD,
"that I am God.
¹³   Yes, and from ancient days I am he.
No one can deliver out of my hand.
When I act, who can reverse it?"

God's Mercy and Israel's Unfaithfulness

¹⁴ This is what the LORD says —
your Redeemer, the Holy One of Israel:
"For your sake I will send to Babylon
and bring down as fugitives all the
Babylonians,ᵃ

in the ships in which they took pride.
¹⁵ I am the LORD, your Holy One,
Israel's Creator, your King."

¹⁶ This is what the LORD says —
he who made a way through the sea,
a path through the mighty waters,
¹⁷ who drew out the chariots and horses,
the army and reinforcements together,
and they lay there, never to rise again,
extinguished, snuffed out like a wick:
¹⁸ "Forget the former things;
do not dwell on the past.
¹⁹ See, I am doing a new thing!
Now it springs up; do you not perceive it?
I am making a way in the desert
and streams in the wasteland.
²⁰ The wild animals honor me,
the jackals and the owls,
because I provide water in the desert
and streams in the wasteland,
to give drink to my people, my chosen,
²¹   the people I formed for myself
that they may proclaim my praise.

²² "Yet you have not called upon me, O Jacob,
you have not wearied yourselves for me,
O Israel.
²³ You have not brought me sheep for burnt
offerings,
nor honored me with your sacrifices.
I have not burdened you with grain offerings
nor wearied you with demands for incense.
²⁴ You have not bought any fragrant calamus
for me,
or lavished on me the fat of your sacrifices.
But you have burdened me with your sins
and wearied me with your offenses.

²⁵ "I, even I, am he who blots out
your transgressions, for my own sake,
and remembers your sins no more.
²⁶ Review the past for me,
let us argue the matter together;
state the case for your innocence.

ᵃ 14 Or Chaldeans

PRAYING THE SCRIPTURES

Forgiveness

ISAIAH 43:25

I praise you, O God, for your eagerness to blot out our transgressions, for your own sake, and remember our sins no more. Infuse this truth today into the heart and soul of my grandchild.

Next prayer in Forgiveness Prayer Track: Isaiah 55:6–7

²⁷ Your first father sinned;
  your spokesmen rebelled against me.
²⁸ So I will disgrace the dignitaries of your
    temple,
  and I will consign Jacob to destruction^{*a*}
  and Israel to scorn.

TALKING POINTS

Guilt

God forgives and forgets.

ISAIAH 43:25

For more on guilt, go to Nahum 1:3.

Israel the Chosen

44 "But now listen, O Jacob, my servant,
  Israel, whom I have chosen.
² This is what the LORD says—
  he who made you, who formed you in the
    womb,
  and who will help you:
  Do not be afraid, O Jacob, my servant,
  Jeshurun, whom I have chosen.
³ For I will pour water on the thirsty land,
  and streams on the dry ground;

I will pour out my Spirit on your offspring,
  and my blessing on your descendants.
⁴ They will spring up like grass in a meadow,
  like poplar trees by flowing streams.
⁵ One will say, 'I belong to the LORD';
  another will call himself by the name of
    Jacob;
still another will write on his hand, 'The
    LORD's,'
  and will take the name Israel.

The LORD, Not Idols

⁶ "This is what the LORD says—
  Israel's King and Redeemer, the LORD
    Almighty:
I am the first and I am the last;
  apart from me there is no God.
⁷ Who then is like me? Let him proclaim it.
  Let him declare and lay out before me
what has happened since I established my
    ancient people,
  and what is yet to come—
  yes, let him foretell what will come.
⁸ Do not tremble, do not be afraid.
  Did I not proclaim this and foretell it long
    ago?
You are my witnesses. Is there any God
    besides me?
  No, there is no other Rock; I know not
    one."

⁹ All who make idols are nothing,
  and the things they treasure are worthless.
Those who would speak up for them are
    blind;
  they are ignorant, to their own shame.
¹⁰ Who shapes a god and casts an idol,
  which can profit him nothing?
¹¹ He and his kind will be put to shame;
  craftsmen are nothing but men.
Let them all come together and take their
    stand;
  they will be brought down to terror and
    infamy.

---

^{*a*} *28* The Hebrew term refers to the irrevocable giving over of things or persons to the LORD, often by totally destroying them.

¹²The blacksmith takes a tool
　　and works with it in the coals;
he shapes an idol with hammers,
　　he forges it with the might of his arm.
He gets hungry and loses his strength;
　　he drinks no water and grows faint.
¹³The carpenter measures with a line
　　and makes an outline with a marker;
he roughs it out with chisels
　　and marks it with compasses.
He shapes it in the form of man,
　　of man in all his glory,
　　that it may dwell in a shrine.
¹⁴He cut down cedars,
　　or perhaps took a cypress or oak.
He let it grow among the trees of the
　　　forest,
　　or planted a pine, and the rain made it
　　　grow.
¹⁵It is man's fuel for burning;
　　some of it he takes and warms himself,
he kindles a fire and bakes bread.
But he also fashions a god and worships it;
　　he makes an idol and bows down to it.
¹⁶Half of the wood he burns in the fire;
　　over it he prepares his meal,
he roasts his meat and eats his fill.
He also warms himself and says,
　　"Ah! I am warm; I see the fire."
¹⁷From the rest he makes a god, his idol;
　　he bows down to it and worships.
He prays to it and says,
　　"Save me; you are my god."
¹⁸They know nothing, they understand
　　　nothing;
　　their eyes are plastered over so they
　　　cannot see,
　　and their minds closed so they cannot
　　　understand.
¹⁹No one stops to think,
　　no one has the knowledge or
　　　understanding to say,
"Half of it I used for fuel;
　　I even baked bread over its coals,
　　I roasted meat and I ate.

Shall I make a detestable thing from what is
　　　left?
　　Shall I bow down to a block of wood?"
²⁰He feeds on ashes, a deluded heart misleads
　　　him;
　　he cannot save himself, or say,
　　"Is not this thing in my right hand a lie?"

²¹"Remember these things, O Jacob,
　　for you are my servant, O Israel.
I have made you, you are my servant;
　　O Israel, I will not forget you.
²²I have swept away your offenses like a cloud,
　　your sins like the morning mist.
Return to me,
　　for I have redeemed you."

²³Sing for joy, O heavens, for the LORD has
　　　done this;
　　shout aloud, O earth beneath.
Burst into song, you mountains,
　　you forests and all your trees,
for the LORD has redeemed Jacob,
　　he displays his glory in Israel.

Jerusalem to Be Inhabited

²⁴"This is what the LORD says—
　　your Redeemer, who formed you in the
　　　womb:

I am the LORD,
　　who has made all things,
　　who alone stretched out the heavens,
　　who spread out the earth by myself,

²⁵who foils the signs of false prophets
　　and makes fools of diviners,
who overthrows the learning of the wise
　　and turns it into nonsense,
²⁶who carries out the words of his servants
　　and fulfills the predictions of his
　　　messengers,

who says of Jerusalem, 'It shall be inhabited,'
　　of the towns of Judah, 'They shall be
　　　built,'
　　and of their ruins, 'I will restore them,'

LET'S HAVE
FUN

Cliff-hanging Stories

Plan a special storytelling night with your grandchildren (various ages will work well). Sit in a circle. Beginning with yourself, start telling some outrageous tale that cuts off at a critical point. The next person in the circle picks up the narrative from there, adding detail, and so on around the circle. You can wind down the action with some happily-ever-after ending. If the exercise is a hit, repeat with the next person in the circle as the beginner.

Long-Distance Variation: Start writing a ridiculous story, leaving off the action at some critical point. Send the unfinished narrative to an out-of-town grandchild, asking him or her to write the next part (several paragraphs, a whole chapter or however much they want) and forward it on, either to a sibling or cousin or back to you. Keep the story going as long as interest holds out. The beauty of a written record is a "publishable" story.

Thank you, Lord, for the gifts of spontaneity and humor. Help me to embrace with my grand-kids the silly side of life. Through this experience, may we share and appreciate each other's ideas and creativity. Amen.

Your next devotion is located on page 989.

GRANDCHILD **IN FOCUS**•PRAYER

Character

Dear Lord and Father, I ask that you fill my grandchild with your Spirit so her character reflects your goodness and love. Give her kindness and love for others. Bring joy to her life so she will be a joy to others. Grant her patience and self-control through difficult and trying times. May she show mercy and generosity to those who are less fortu-nate. Grant her integrity and a sense of justice, and surround her with your peace. Amen.

27 who says to the watery deep, 'Be dry,
and I will dry up your streams,'
28 who says of Cyrus, 'He is my shepherd
and will accomplish all that I please;
he will say of Jerusalem, "Let it be rebuilt,"
and of the temple, "Let its foundations be
laid." '

45 "This is what the LORD says to his
anointed,
to Cyrus, whose right hand I take
hold of
to subdue nations before him
and to strip kings of their armor,
to open doors before him
so that gates will not be shut:
2 I will go before you
and will level the mountains*a*;
I will break down gates of bronze
and cut through bars of iron.
3 I will give you the treasures of darkness,
riches stored in secret places,
so that you may know that I am the LORD,
the God of Israel, who summons you
by name.
4 For the sake of Jacob my servant,
of Israel my chosen,
I summon you by name
and bestow on you a title of honor,
though you do not acknowledge me.
5 I am the LORD, and there is no other;
apart from me there is no God.

I will strengthen you,
though you have not acknowledged me,
6 so that from the rising of the sun
to the place of its setting
men may know there is none besides me.
I am the LORD, and there is no other.
7 I form the light and create darkness,
I bring prosperity and create disaster;
I, the LORD, do all these things.

8 "You heavens above, rain down
righteousness;
let the clouds shower it down.
Let the earth open wide,
let salvation spring up,
let righteousness grow with it;
I, the LORD, have created it.

9 "Woe to him who quarrels with his Maker,
to him who is but a potsherd among the
potsherds on the ground.
Does the clay say to the potter,
'What are you making?'
Does your work say,
'He has no hands'?
10 Woe to him who says to his father,
'What have you begotten?'
or to his mother,
'What have you brought to birth?'

11 "This is what the LORD says—
the Holy One of Israel, and its Maker:
Concerning things to come,
do you question me about my children,
or give me orders about the work of my
hands?
12 It is I who made the earth
and created mankind upon it.
My own hands stretched out the heavens;
I marshaled their starry hosts.
13 I will raise up Cyrus*b* in my righteousness:
I will make all his ways straight.
He will rebuild my city
and set my exiles free,

TALKING POINTS

Anxiety

God is sovereign.
Everything is under his control.

ISAIAH 45:5–7

For more on anxiety, go to Luke 12:22–26.

a 2 Dead Sea Scrolls and Septuagint; the meaning of the word in the
Masoretic Text is uncertain.   *b 13* Hebrew *him*

but not for a price or reward,
  says the LORD Almighty."

14 This is what the LORD says:

"The products of Egypt and the merchandise
    of Cush,^a
  and those tall Sabeans—
they will come over to you
  and will be yours;
they will trudge behind you,
  coming over to you in chains.
They will bow down before you
  and plead with you, saying,
'Surely God is with you, and there is no
    other;
  there is no other god.'"

15 Truly you are a God who hides himself,
  O God and Savior of Israel.
16 All the makers of idols will be put to shame
    and disgraced;
  they will go off into disgrace together.
17 But Israel will be saved by the LORD
  with an everlasting salvation;
you will never be put to shame or disgraced,
  to ages everlasting.

18 For this is what the LORD says—
he who created the heavens,
  he is God;
he who fashioned and made the earth,
  he founded it;
he did not create it to be empty,
  but formed it to be inhabited—
he says:
"I am the LORD,
  and there is no other.
19 I have not spoken in secret,
  from somewhere in a land of darkness;
I have not said to Jacob's descendants,
  'Seek me in vain.'
I, the LORD, speak the truth;
  I declare what is right.

20 "Gather together and come;
  assemble, you fugitives from the nations.

Ignorant are those who carry about idols of
    wood,
  who pray to gods that cannot save.
21 Declare what is to be, present it—
  let them take counsel together.
Who foretold this long ago,
  who declared it from the distant past?
Was it not I, the LORD?
  And there is no God apart from me,
a righteous God and a Savior;
  there is none but me.

22 "Turn to me and be saved,
  all you ends of the earth;
  for I am God, and there is no other.
23 By myself I have sworn,
  my mouth has uttered in all integrity
  a word that will not be revoked:
Before me every knee will bow;
  by me every tongue will swear.
24 They will say of me, 'In the LORD alone
  are righteousness and strength.'"
All who have raged against him
  will come to him and be put to shame.
25 But in the LORD all the descendants of Israel
  will be found righteous and will exult.

Gods of Babylon

46 Bel bows down, Nebo stoops low;
  their idols are borne by beasts of
    burden.^b
The images that are carried about are
    burdensome,
  a burden for the weary.
2 They stoop and bow down together;
  unable to rescue the burden,
  they themselves go off into captivity.

3 "Listen to me, O house of Jacob,
  all you who remain of the house of Israel,
you whom I have upheld since you were
    conceived,
  and have carried since your birth.
4 Even to your old age and gray hairs
  I am he, I am he who will sustain you.

---

^a 14 That is, the upper Nile region   ^b 1 Or are but beasts and
cattle

I have made you and I will carry you;
    I will sustain you and I will rescue you.

5 "To whom will you compare me or count me
      equal?
To whom will you liken me that we may be
      compared?
6 Some pour out gold from their bags
    and weigh out silver on the scales;
they hire a goldsmith to make it into a god,
    and they bow down and worship it.
7 They lift it to their shoulders and carry it;
    they set it up in its place, and there it stands.
    From that spot it cannot move.
Though one cries out to it, it does not
      answer;
    it cannot save him from his troubles.

8 "Remember this, fix it in mind,
    take it to heart, you rebels.
9 Remember the former things, those of long
      ago;
I am God, and there is no other;
    I am God, and there is none like me.
10 I make known the end from the beginning,
    from ancient times, what is still to come.
I say: My purpose will stand,
    and I will do all that I please.
11 From the east I summon a bird of prey;
    from a far-off land, a man to fulfill my
      purpose.
What I have said, that will I bring about;
    what I have planned, that will I do.
12 Listen to me, you stubborn-hearted,
    you who are far from righteousness.
13 I am bringing my righteousness near,
    it is not far away;
    and my salvation will not be delayed.
I will grant salvation to Zion,
    my splendor to Israel.

The Fall of Babylon

47 "Go down, sit in the dust,
    Virgin Daughter of Babylon;
sit on the ground without a throne,
    Daughter of the Babylonians. [a]

No more will you be called
    tender or delicate.
2 Take millstones and grind flour;
    take off your veil.
Lift up your skirts, bare your legs,
    and wade through the streams.
3 Your nakedness will be exposed
    and your shame uncovered.
I will take vengeance;
    I will spare no one."

4 Our Redeemer—the Lord Almighty is his
      name—
is the Holy One of Israel.

5 "Sit in silence, go into darkness,
    Daughter of the Babylonians;
no more will you be called
    queen of kingdoms.
6 I was angry with my people
    and desecrated my inheritance;
I gave them into your hand,
    and you showed them no mercy.
Even on the aged
    you laid a very heavy yoke.
7 You said, 'I will continue forever—
    the eternal queen!'
But you did not consider these things
    or reflect on what might happen.

8 "Now then, listen, you wanton creature,
    lounging in your security
and saying to yourself,
    'I am, and there is none besides me.
I will never be a widow
    or suffer the loss of children.'
9 Both of these will overtake you
    in a moment, on a single day:
    loss of children and widowhood.
They will come upon you in full
      measure,
    in spite of your many sorceries
    and all your potent spells.
10 You have trusted in your wickedness
    and have said, 'No one sees me.'

a 1 Or Chaldeans; also in verse 5

Worship the Lord

"Praise be to the Lord, the God of Israel,
     because he has come and has redeemed his people.
He has raised up a horn of salvation for us
     in the house of his servant David
(as he said through his holy prophets of long ago),
salvation from our enemies
     and from the hand of all who hate us —
to show mercy to our fathers
     and to remember his holy covenant,
     the oath he swore to our father Abraham:
to rescue us from the hand of our enemies,
     and to enable us to serve him without fear
     in holiness and righteousness before him
          all our days."

Luke 1:68 – 75

Dear Jesus, I praise you for sharing my humanity. I thank you for the sacrifice you made that I might live. Thank you for fulfilling every promise you have made, even those made generations ago. I ask for the will to faithfully and gratefully serve you through this day and all my days. Amen.

Your next devotion is located on page 992.

GRANDCHILD IN FOCUS • PRAYER

Talents

Dear Lord, the giver of gifts, bless my grandchild as he develops his talents. Help him identify his talents and be proud and confident of the gifts you have given him. Give him patience and understanding, Lord, so he will not grow weary of striving and searching to reach the goals you have set for him. May each milestone bring satisfaction and a healthy desire for greater achievement and success to bring glory to you. Amen.

Your wisdom and knowledge mislead you
    when you say to yourself,
    'I am, and there is none besides me.'
¹¹ Disaster will come upon you,
    and you will not know how to conjure it
        away.
A calamity will fall upon you
    that you cannot ward off with a ransom;
a catastrophe you cannot foresee
    will suddenly come upon you.

¹² "Keep on, then, with your magic spells
    and with your many sorceries,
    which you have labored at since childhood.
Perhaps you will succeed,
    perhaps you will cause terror.
¹³ All the counsel you have received has only
        worn you out!
Let your astrologers come forward,
those stargazers who make predictions
        month by month,
    let them save you from what is coming
        upon you.
¹⁴ Surely they are like stubble;
    the fire will burn them up.
They cannot even save themselves
    from the power of the flame.
Here are no coals to warm anyone;
    here is no fire to sit by.
¹⁵ That is all they can do for you—
    these you have labored with
    and trafficked with since childhood.
Each of them goes on in his error;
    there is not one that can save you.

Stubborn Israel

48 "Listen to this, O house of Jacob,
    you who are called by the name of Israel
    and come from the line of Judah,
you who take oaths in the name of the LORD
    and invoke the God of Israel—
    but not in truth or righteousness—
² you who call yourselves citizens of the holy
        city
    and rely on the God of Israel—
    the LORD Almighty is his name:

³ I foretold the former things long ago,
    my mouth announced them and I made
        them known;
    then suddenly I acted, and they came to
        pass.
⁴ For I knew how stubborn you were;
    the sinews of your neck were iron,
    your forehead was bronze.
⁵ Therefore I told you these things long ago;
    before they happened I announced them
        to you
    so that you could not say,
    'My idols did them;
    my wooden image and metal god ordained
        them.'
⁶ You have heard these things; look at them all.
    Will you not admit them?

"From now on I will tell you of new things,
    of hidden things unknown to you.
⁷ They are created now, and not long ago;
    you have not heard of them before today.
So you cannot say,
    'Yes, I knew of them.'
⁸ You have neither heard nor understood;
    from of old your ear has not been open.
Well do I know how treacherous you are;
    you were called a rebel from birth.
⁹ For my own name's sake I delay my wrath;
    for the sake of my praise I hold it back
        from you,
    so as not to cut you off.
¹⁰ See, I have refined you, though not as silver;
    I have tested you in the furnace of
        affliction.
¹¹ For my own sake, for my own sake, I do
        this.
    How can I let myself be defamed?
    I will not yield my glory to another.

Israel Freed

¹² "Listen to me, O Jacob,
    Israel, whom I have called:
I am he;
    I am the first and I am the last.

¹³ My own hand laid the foundations of the
earth,
and my right hand spread out the heavens;
when I summon them,
they all stand up together.

¹⁴ "Come together, all of you, and listen:
Which of ⌐the idols⌐ has foretold these
things?
The LORD's chosen ally
will carry out his purpose against Babylon;
his arm will be against the Babylonians. ᵃ
¹⁵ I, even I, have spoken;
yes, I have called him.
I will bring him,
and he will succeed in his mission.

¹⁶ "Come near me and listen to this:

"From the first announcement I have not
spoken in secret;
at the time it happens, I am there."

And now the Sovereign LORD has sent me,
with his Spirit.

¹⁷ This is what the LORD says—
your Redeemer, the Holy One of Israel:
"I am the LORD your God,
who teaches you what is best for you,
who directs you in the way you should go.
¹⁸ If only you had paid attention to my
commands,
your peace would have been like a river,
your righteousness like the waves of the
sea.
¹⁹ Your descendants would have been like the
sand,
your children like its numberless grains;
their name would never be cut off
nor destroyed from before me."

²⁰ Leave Babylon,
flee from the Babylonians!
Announce this with shouts of joy
and proclaim it.
Send it out to the ends of the earth;
say, "The LORD has redeemed his servant
Jacob."

²¹ They did not thirst when he led them
through the deserts;
he made water flow for them from the rock;
he split the rock
and water gushed out.

²² "There is no peace," says the LORD, "for the
wicked."

The Servant of the LORD

49 Listen to me, you islands;
hear this, you distant nations:
Before I was born the LORD called me;
from my birth he has made mention of my
name.
² He made my mouth like a sharpened sword,
in the shadow of his hand he hid me;
he made me into a polished arrow
and concealed me in his quiver.
³ He said to me, "You are my servant,
Israel, in whom I will display my splendor."
⁴ But I said, "I have labored to no purpose;
I have spent my strength in vain and for
nothing.
Yet what is due me is in the LORD's hand,
and my reward is with my God."

⁵ And now the LORD says—
he who formed me in the womb to be his
servant
to bring Jacob back to him
and gather Israel to himself,
for I am honored in the eyes of the LORD
and my God has been my strength—
⁶ he says:
"It is too small a thing for you to be my
servant
to restore the tribes of Jacob
and bring back those of Israel I have kept.
I will also make you a light for the Gentiles,
that you may bring my salvation to the
ends of the earth."

⁷ This is what the LORD says—
the Redeemer and Holy One of Israel—

ᵃ 14 Or *Chaldeans*; also in verse 20

BEFORE I WAS BORN THE
LORD CALLED ME; FROM
MY BIRTH HE HAS MADE
MENTION OF MY NAME.

Isaiah 49:1

Naming and Blessing

NETA JACKSON

READ | ISAIAH 49:1–7

"YOU ARE INVITED TO A BABY BLESSING SHOWER! Bring a blessing that can be put in a scrapbook. Baby gifts optional."

I had the joy of planning a shower for my grandson after he was born. I chose a Blessing Shower because of how important the naming and blessing of children were in the Bible times: The meaning of a name played a big role in the naming of a child, often indicative of the parents' hopes and dreams.

At times, God gave a new name to a man or woman when the direction of their spiritual life changed. For example, God changed Abram's name from Abram, meaning "exalted father," to Abraham, meaning "father of many." Jesus changed Simon's name ("one who hears") to Peter, which means "rock."

The blessing of children was also important. On his deathbed, Jacob blessed and prophesied over all his 12 sons (see Genesis 49). Jesus encouraged his disciples to "let the little children come to [him]," and he blessed them (see Mark 10:13–16). I like to think he called each child by name.

When someone calls me by my name, I feel acknowledged as an individual. It is the first step toward relationship. But if someone continually forgets my name, I assume they aren't interested in a relationship.

The amazing thing is that God knew my name before I was even born. He knows me that well — and my children and my grandchildren. We are each unique and precious in his sight. And he longs to bless us.

At the shower, we blessed little Liam Isaac ("helmet [of salvation]"; "he laughs") with words of hope, love and promise, and gathered the blessings into a scrapbook, which will be treasured long after the rattles and baby blankets are forgotten.

Father God, it makes me feel so loved that you call me to yourself by my name. Give me the sensitivity to address people respectfully, to learn and remember their names — especially children, who often feel ignored by adults.

GRANDCHILD IN FOCUS • PRAYER

SELECT ONE OF YOUR
GRANDCHILDREN TO FOCUS ON
IN PRAYER FOR THE NEXT 14 DAYS.

Salvation

Dear Lord, please guide my grandchild to your gift of salvation. I pray that she will come to know you, to love you and to walk close to you throughout her life. May she boldly claim Jesus as her Lord and Savior. Guide her as she makes choices that have eternal consequences. Help her to follow you each moment of her life. I pray this in Jesus' name, amen.

Your next devotion is located on page 994.

to him who was despised and abhorred by
the nation,
to the servant of rulers:
"Kings will see you and rise up,
princes will see and bow down,
because of the LORD, who is faithful,
the Holy One of Israel, who has chosen
you."

Restoration of Israel

8 This is what the LORD says:

"In the time of my favor I will answer you,
and in the day of salvation I will help you;
I will keep you and will make you
to be a covenant for the people,
to restore the land
and to reassign its desolate inheritances,
9 to say to the captives, 'Come out,'
and to those in darkness, 'Be free!'

"They will feed beside the roads
and find pasture on every barren hill.
10 They will neither hunger nor thirst,
nor will the desert heat or the sun beat
upon them.
He who has compassion on them will guide
them
and lead them beside springs of water.
11 I will turn all my mountains into roads,
and my highways will be raised up.
12 See, they will come from afar —
some from the north, some from the west,
some from the region of Aswan. *a*"

13 Shout for joy, O heavens;
rejoice, O earth;
burst into song, O mountains!
For the LORD comforts his people
and will have compassion on his afflicted
ones.

14 But Zion said, "The LORD has forsaken me,
the Lord has forgotten me."

15 "Can a mother forget the baby at her breast
and have no compassion on the child she
has borne?

Though she may forget,
I will not forget you!
16 See, I have engraved you on the palms of my
hands;
your walls are ever before me.
17 Your sons hasten back,
and those who laid you waste depart from
you.
18 Lift up your eyes and look around;
all your sons gather and come to you.
As surely as I live," declares the LORD,
"you will wear them all as ornaments;
you will put them on, like a bride.

19 "Though you were ruined and made desolate
and your land laid waste,
now you will be too small for your people,
and those who devoured you will be far
away.
20 The children born during your bereavement
will yet say in your hearing,
'This place is too small for us;
give us more space to live in.'
21 Then you will say in your heart,
'Who bore me these?
I was bereaved and barren;
I was exiled and rejected.
Who brought these up?
I was left all alone,
but these — where have they come from?'"

22 This is what the Sovereign LORD says:

"See, I will beckon to the Gentiles,
I will lift up my banner to the peoples;
they will bring your sons in their arms
and carry your daughters on their shoulders.
23 Kings will be your foster fathers,
and their queens your nursing mothers.
They will bow down before you with their
faces to the ground;
they will lick the dust at your feet.
Then you will know that I am the LORD;
those who hope in me will not be
disappointed."

a 12 Dead Sea Scrolls; Masoretic Text *Sinim*

"I HAVE ENGRAVED YOU ON THE PALMS OF MY HANDS."

Isaiah 49:16

Engraved on His Palms

LORI COPELAND

READ | ISAIAH 49:8 – 18

As years passed, our grandsons, James, Joe and Josh, were the apple of our eyes. Then Russ, the youngest of our three sons, married. A few years later, we were ecstatic when he and his wife announced a new baby was on the way! The hope of a granddaughter again loomed brightly. This time I wasn't naive. I knew, whatever the gender, I would love that child the instant I laid eyes on her *or* him.

Gage Russell Copeland took the world by storm on December 23, 1999, just in time to mess up his birthdays for the rest of his life. From December 23 to December 25 that child is buried in "blessings." With boy number seven in the family (three sons and four grandsons), we were now well on our way to forming the baseball team we always kidded about. And the fact that Gage was a he instead of a she didn't bother us a bit. Maybe we weren't "girl" material, my husband and I decided. Pink hair ribbons and frilly dresses were highly overrated. We had three sons and four grandsons, and we couldn't be happier.

We don't know what the Lord's plans are for Gage. We pray that he will feel the same calling as the older grandchildren, but every child has his own unique gift. We do know he loves the Lord, and we did discover one year that he could sing louder, and more off key, than any other four-year-old shepherd in the Ridgecrest children's Christmas choir. We were so proud of him and his passion that we wanted to crow! I believe (because I ask) God has singled Gage out for something special or maybe something very ordinary because his name is engraved on God's palms.

Heavenly Father, I pray a special blessing upon each of my grandchildren. Use their passion, enthusiasm and zest for your kingdom. Grant that each child will fulfill your unique and special purpose. Amen.

Your next devotion is located on page 996.

GRANDCHILD IN FOCUS · PRAYER

Physical Well-Being

Almighty God, Creator of us all, I pray that you will watch over my grandchild's physical development. May he grow in strength through the stages of his life. As he grows in awareness of his body, help him to understand that each body develops uniquely, yet is within your plan and your control. Please guard his health so that his diseases are few, his injuries are minor and his infirmities are brief. Amen.

24 Can plunder be taken from warriors,
    or captives rescued from the fierce [a]?

25 But this is what the LORD says:

"Yes, captives will be taken from warriors,
    and plunder retrieved from the fierce;
I will contend with those who contend with
        you,
    and your children I will save.
26 I will make your oppressors eat their own
        flesh;
    they will be drunk on their own blood, as
        with wine.
Then all mankind will know
    that I, the LORD, am your Savior,
    your Redeemer, the Mighty One of Jacob."

Israel's Sin and the Servant's Obedience

50 This is what the LORD says:

"Where is your mother's certificate of divorce
    with which I sent her away?
Or to which of my creditors
    did I sell you?
Because of your sins you were sold;
    because of your transgressions your
        mother was sent away.
2 When I came, why was there no one?
    When I called, why was there no one to
        answer?
Was my arm too short to ransom you?
    Do I lack the strength to rescue you?
By a mere rebuke I dry up the sea,
    I turn rivers into a desert;
their fish rot for lack of water
    and die of thirst.
3 I clothe the sky with darkness
    and make sackcloth its covering."

4 The Sovereign LORD has given me an
        instructed tongue,
    to know the word that sustains the weary.
He wakens me morning by morning,
    wakens my ear to listen like one being
        taught.

5 The Sovereign LORD has opened my ears,
    and I have not been rebellious;
    I have not drawn back.
6 I offered my back to those who beat me,
    my cheeks to those who pulled out my
        beard;
    I did not hide my face
        from mocking and spitting.
7 Because the Sovereign LORD helps me,
    I will not be disgraced.
Therefore have I set my face like flint,
    and I know I will not be put to shame.
8 He who vindicates me is near.
    Who then will bring charges against me?
    Let us face each other!
Who is my accuser?
    Let him confront me!
9 It is the Sovereign LORD who helps me.
    Who is he that will condemn me?
They will all wear out like a garment;
    the moths will eat them up.

10 Who among you fears the LORD
    and obeys the word of his servant?
Let him who walks in the dark,
    who has no light,
trust in the name of the LORD
    and rely on his God.
11 But now, all you who light fires
    and provide yourselves with flaming
        torches,

[a] 24 Dead Sea Scrolls, Vulgate and Syriac (see also Septuagint and
verse 25); Masoretic Text *righteous*

TALKING POINTS

Fear

When life seems dark,
trust in God and rely on him.
ISAIAH 50:10

For more on fear, go to Matthew 10:29–31.

BUT THIS IS WHAT THE LORD SAYS:
"YES, CAPTIVES WILL BE TAKEN FROM
WARRIORS, AND PLUNDER RETRIEVED
FROM THE FIERCE; I WILL CONTEND
WITH THOSE WHO CONTEND WITH YOU,
AND YOUR CHILDREN I WILL SAVE."

Isaiah 49:25

For the Mothers

TERRI BLACKSTOCK

READ | ISAIAH 49:19 – 26

She came to me with her heart broken. She had just learned that her adult daughter was badly addicted to pain killers, and it was ruining her life. Her daughter had almost hit bottom, and she feared that the bottom would be death itself.

She sat there weeping at the shock of it all, taking ferocious inventory of her life, trying to figure out where she had gone wrong as a mother. I suspected that it was not something she had done at all. I suspected that, somewhere in her daughter's life since she'd left home, enemies had attacked and plundered and taken her daughter captive.

Not knowing what to say or do, I opened my Bible and led her to Isaiah. I came to the passage that I knew God gave me for her: "But this is what the LORD says: 'Yes, captives will be taken from warriors, and plunder retrieved from the fierce; I will contend with those who contend with you, and your children I will save' " (Isaiah 49:25).

I knew that God was telling us that the warriors — the enemies — in her family's case were the drugs that had imprisoned her daughter. God was saying that he could deliver her from those enemies. He could take her daughter back. And he was giving her his word that he planned to do it.

I realized that we all have fierce warriors in our lives. Whether our enemies are pride, discouragement, sickness, despair, alcohol, drugs, physical abuse or financial crisis — God can overcome all of them. He can retrieve the plunder they've taken from us. He can contend with those who contend with us. He can save our children. And he can save us.

Lord of grace and hope, I offer up to you the most precious of all your gifts to me — my children and grandchildren. I realize the futility of thinking that I can keep them from harm in a world poised to destroy them. What comfort there is in knowing that you love them even more than I do. My arm is short, but yours is long. My understanding is small, but yours is great. I will trust in you. Amen.

Your next devotion is located on page 999.

GRANDCHILD IN FOCUS • PRAYER

Emotional Development

O God, Creator of mind and body, I pray that you will give my grandchild emotional health and strength. Where there is anger, bring peace. Where there is confusion, bring clarity and focus. Where there are dark shadows, cast a ray of hope. Fill her with the sunshine of your Spirit. Warm her with the presence of your peace. Amen.

go, walk in the light of your fires
and of the torches you have set ablaze.
This is what you shall receive from my hand:
You will lie down in torment.

Everlasting Salvation for Zion

51 "Listen to me, you who pursue
righteousness
and who seek the LORD:
Look to the rock from which you were cut
and to the quarry from which you were
hewn;
²look to Abraham, your father,
and to Sarah, who gave you birth.
When I called him he was but one,
and I blessed him and made him many.
³The LORD will surely comfort Zion
and will look with compassion on all her
ruins;
he will make her deserts like Eden,
her wastelands like the garden of the LORD.
Joy and gladness will be found in her,
thanksgiving and the sound of singing.

⁴"Listen to me, my people;
hear me, my nation:
The law will go out from me;
my justice will become a light to the
nations.
⁵My righteousness draws near speedily,
my salvation is on the way,
and my arm will bring justice to the
nations.
The islands will look to me
and wait in hope for my arm.
⁶Lift up your eyes to the heavens,
look at the earth beneath;
the heavens will vanish like smoke,
the earth will wear out like a garment
and its inhabitants die like flies.
But my salvation will last forever,
my righteousness will never fail.

⁷"Hear me, you who know what is right,
you people who have my law in your
hearts:

Do not fear the reproach of men
or be terrified by their insults.
⁸For the moth will eat them up like a
garment;
the worm will devour them like wool.
But my righteousness will last forever,
my salvation through all generations."

TALKING POINTS

Peer Pressure

Be strong in the face of criticism.

ISAIAH 51:7–8

For more on peer pressure, go to 1 Corinthians 10:13.

⁹Awake, awake! Clothe yourself with strength,
O arm of the LORD;
awake, as in days gone by,
as in generations of old.
Was it not you who cut Rahab to pieces,
who pierced that monster through?
¹⁰Was it not you who dried up the sea,
the waters of the great deep,
who made a road in the depths of the sea
so that the redeemed might cross over?
¹¹The ransomed of the LORD will return.
They will enter Zion with singing;
everlasting joy will crown their heads.
Gladness and joy will overtake them,
and sorrow and sighing will flee away.

¹²"I, even I, am he who comforts you.
Who are you that you fear mortal men,
the sons of men, who are but grass,
¹³that you forget the LORD your Maker,
who stretched out the heavens
and laid the foundations of the earth,
that you live in constant terror every day
because of the wrath of the oppressor,
who is bent on destruction?

For where is the wrath of the oppressor?
14 The cowering prisoners will soon be set free;
　　they will not die in their dungeon,
　　nor will they lack bread.
15 For I am the Lord your God,
　　who churns up the sea so that its waves
　　　　roar—
　　the Lord Almighty is his name.
16 I have put my words in your mouth
　　and covered you with the shadow of my
　　　　hand—
　　I who set the heavens in place,
　　who laid the foundations of the earth,
　　and who say to Zion, 'You are my people.' "

The Cup of the Lord's Wrath

17 Awake, awake!
　　Rise up, O Jerusalem,
　　you who have drunk from the hand of the
　　　　Lord
　　the cup of his wrath,
　　you who have drained to its dregs
　　　　the goblet that makes men stagger.
18 Of all the sons she bore
　　there was none to guide her;
　　of all the sons she reared
　　there was none to take her by the hand.
19 These double calamities have come upon
　　　　you—
　　who can comfort you?—
　　ruin and destruction, famine and sword—
　　who can *a* console you?
20 Your sons have fainted;
　　they lie at the head of every street,
　　like antelope caught in a net.
　　They are filled with the wrath of the Lord
　　and the rebuke of your God.

21 Therefore hear this, you afflicted one,
　　made drunk, but not with wine.
22 This is what your Sovereign Lord says,
　　your God, who defends his people:
　　"See, I have taken out of your hand
　　the cup that made you stagger;
　　from that cup, the goblet of my wrath,
　　you will never drink again.

23 I will put it into the hands of your
　　　　tormentors,
　　who said to you,
　　'Fall prostrate that we may walk over you.'
　　And you made your back like the ground,
　　like a street to be walked over."

52 Awake, awake, O Zion,
　　clothe yourself with strength.
　Put on your garments of splendor,
　　O Jerusalem, the holy city.
　The uncircumcised and defiled
　　will not enter you again.
2 Shake off your dust;
　　rise up, sit enthroned, O Jerusalem.
　Free yourself from the chains on your neck,
　　O captive Daughter of Zion.

3 For this is what the Lord says:

"You were sold for nothing,
　　and without money you will be redeemed."

4 For this is what the Sovereign Lord says:

"At first my people went down to Egypt to
　　　　live;
　　lately, Assyria has oppressed them.

5 "And now what do I have here?" declares the
Lord.

"For my people have been taken away for
　　　　nothing,
　　and those who rule them mock, *b* "
　　　　　　　　　　　　　　declares the Lord.
"And all day long
　　my name is constantly blasphemed.
6 Therefore my people will know my name;
　　therefore in that day they will know
　　that it is I who foretold it.
　　Yes, it is I."

7 How beautiful on the mountains
　　are the feet of those who bring good news,
　who proclaim peace,
　　who bring good tidings,
　　who proclaim salvation,

a 19 Dead Sea Scrolls, Septuagint, Vulgate and Syriac; Masoretic Text
/ how can I　　*b* 5 Dead Sea Scrolls and Vulgate; Masoretic Text wail

> "LISTEN TO ME, YOU WHO PURSUE RIGHTEOUS-
> NESS AND WHO SEEK THE LORD: LOOK TO THE
> ROCK FROM WHICH YOU WERE CUT AND TO THE
> QUARRY FROM WHICH YOU WERE HEWN; LOOK
> TO ABRAHAM, YOUR FATHER, AND TO SARAH,
> WHO GAVE YOU BIRTH."
>
> *Isaiah 51:1–2*

Yes, You Can Go Back

DOROTHY E. SICKAL

READ | ISAIAH 51:1–16

So often we hear people say, "You just can't go back." In some ways this is true. And it is a good thing we can't. Memory is a wonderful gift, but to try to retain the past by keeping our minds there is to shut off growth and miss today. We can cherish the good things in our past, learn by experience, and anticipate the future, but we only have the now.

However, some things we must go back to, such as the wisdom of our mothers. If yours was an unwise mother, you can pray for the wisdom your own children can go back to some day. Wisdom is partly inborn, partly learned. Wisdom is good sense; good sense is truth; truth is integrity. Yes, you can go back to all of them.

You can go back to simplicity — back to balance. You can go back to the Word. Go back to foundations, to the Chief Cornerstone. Go back to repentance. Go back to Calvary; go back to the beautiful Resurrection.

Yes, you can go back! Go back to go forward — to basics, to cardinal doctrines. Some things are eternal.

When things get so complicated you are dizzy, when right is called "square," when adultery is the expected thing, when license is called liberty, when selfishness is labeled "finding yourself," when convictions based on the Word of God are called opinions, and when sin abounds, it is time to go back.

Accepted clichés can lead you astray: Old dogs can't learn new tricks; you can't change a leopard's spots; you can't go back. These are not necessarily true. If you can't go back, you probably won't go forward. Go back to the solid rock. Yes, you can go back!

Lord, when our vision gets fuzzy because of warped psychology and misconceptions, give us the will to go back to your Word and your grace. Praise your name — we can go back.

Your next devotion is located on page 1012.

GRANDCHILD IN FOCUS · PRAYER

Spiritual Growth

Dear Lord, today I pray for my grandchild's spiritual growth. I ask that you instill in him the desire to read and memorize your Word. Give him a passion to be in conversation with you. May loving and serving you be part of his daily life. I ask that you stay close to him and lead him to be transformed to your likeness, to reflect your grace and to radiate your love. I pray this in Jesus' name, amen.

who say to Zion,
  "Your God reigns!"
⁸ Listen! Your watchmen lift up their voices;
  together they shout for joy.
When the Lᴏʀᴅ returns to Zion,
  they will see it with their own eyes.
⁹ Burst into songs of joy together,
  you ruins of Jerusalem,
for the Lᴏʀᴅ has comforted his people,
  he has redeemed Jerusalem.
¹⁰ The Lᴏʀᴅ will lay bare his holy arm
  in the sight of all the nations,
and all the ends of the earth will see
  the salvation of our God.

¹¹ Depart, depart, go out from there!
  Touch no unclean thing!
Come out from it and be pure,
  you who carry the vessels of the Lᴏʀᴅ.
¹² But you will not leave in haste
  or go in flight;
for the Lᴏʀᴅ will go before you,
  the God of Israel will be your rear guard.

The Suffering and Glory of the Servant

¹³ See, my servant will act wisely[a];
  he will be raised and lifted up and highly
    exalted.
¹⁴ Just as there were many who were appalled at
    him[b] —
  his appearance was so disfigured beyond
    that of any man
  and his form marred beyond human
    likeness —
¹⁵ so will he sprinkle many nations,[c]
  and kings will shut their mouths because
    of him.
For what they were not told, they will see,
  and what they have not heard, they will
    understand.

53 Who has believed our message
  and to whom has the arm of the Lᴏʀᴅ
    been revealed?
² He grew up before him like a tender shoot,
  and like a root out of dry ground.

He had no beauty or majesty to attract us to
    him,
  nothing in his appearance that we should
    desire him.
³ He was despised and rejected by men,
  a man of sorrows, and familiar with
    suffering.
Like one from whom men hide their faces
  he was despised, and we esteemed him not.

⁴ Surely he took up our infirmities
  and carried our sorrows,
yet we considered him stricken by God,
  smitten by him, and afflicted.
⁵ But he was pierced for our transgressions,
  he was crushed for our iniquities;
the punishment that brought us peace was
    upon him,
  and by his wounds we are healed.
⁶ We all, like sheep, have gone astray,
  each of us has turned to his own way;
and the Lᴏʀᴅ has laid on him
  the iniquity of us all.

PRAYING THE SCRIPTURES

Salvation

ISAIAH 53:6

My grandchild, Lord, has turned to her own way; help her to realize that Christ took upon himself the iniquities of us all.

Next prayer in Salvation Prayer Track: John 3:16

⁷ He was oppressed and afflicted,
  yet he did not open his mouth;
he was led like a lamb to the slaughter,
  and as a sheep before her shearers is silent,
  so he did not open his mouth.

[a] 13 Or *will prosper*   [b] 14 Hebrew *you*   [c] 15 Hebrew;
Septuagint *so will many nations marvel at him*

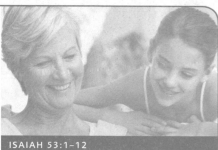

ISAIAH 53:1–12

Isaiah's Prophecy

LIFE LESSON: God planned our salvation.

TO TALK ABOUT

✦ Who was Isaiah talking about in this passage?

✦ Had Jesus already been born when Isaiah wrote this?

✦ Why was Jesus despised and rejected while he was on Earth?

✦ Why do some people still reject Jesus and his gift of salvation?

---

⁸ By oppression *a* and judgment he was taken away.
And who can speak of his descendants?
For he was cut off from the land of the living;
for the transgression of my people he was stricken. *b*
⁹ He was assigned a grave with the wicked,
and with the rich in his death,
though he had done no violence,
nor was any deceit in his mouth.
¹⁰ Yet it was the LORD's will to crush him and cause him to suffer,
and though the LORD makes *c* his life a guilt offering,
he will see his offspring and prolong his days,
and the will of the LORD will prosper in his hand.

¹¹ After the suffering of his soul,
he will see the light ⌐of life⌐ *d* and be satisfied *e*;
by his knowledge *f* my righteous servant will justify many,
and he will bear their iniquities.
¹² Therefore I will give him a portion among the great, *g*
and he will divide the spoils with the strong, *h*
because he poured out his life unto death,
and was numbered with the transgressors.
For he bore the sin of many,
and made intercession for the transgressors.

The Future Glory of Zion

54 "Sing, O barren woman,
you who never bore a child;
burst into song, shout for joy,
you who were never in labor;
because more are the children of the desolate woman
than of her who has a husband,"
says the LORD.
² "Enlarge the place of your tent,
stretch your tent curtains wide,
do not hold back;
lengthen your cords,
strengthen your stakes.
³ For you will spread out to the right and to the left;
your descendants will dispossess nations
and settle in their desolate cities.

⁴ "Do not be afraid; you will not suffer shame.
Do not fear disgrace; you will not be humiliated.
You will forget the shame of your youth
and remember no more the reproach of your widowhood.

---

a 8 Or *From arrest*   *b 8* Or *away. / Yet who of his generation considered / that he was cut off from the land of the living / for the transgression of my people, / to whom the blow was due?*
c 10 Hebrew *though you make*   *d 11* Dead Sea Scrolls (see also Septuagint); Masoretic Text does not have *the light ⌐of life⌐*
e 11 Or (with Masoretic Text) *11He will see the result of the suffering of his soul / and be satisfied*   *f 11* Or *by knowledge of him*
g 12 Or *many*   *h 12* Or *numerous*

RUTH GRAHAM

Leading YOUR GRANDCHILD TO CHRIST

I once heard that the only things we can take to heaven with us are people. And as grandmothers, we play an important role in being certain that the people closest to us — our own family members — will share the glory of eternity in God's presence. What a beautiful honor and privilege (see Isaiah 52:7)! I know that the task of ensuring our family's salvation may seem daunting, but it starts with just two responsibilities: First, we need to pray for our grandchildren. Second, we need to set the example of loving and living for Christ so our grandchildren will want to know Jesus for themselves.

My Own Grandmother

My own grandmother, Virginia Bell, was a wonderful example of a life lived for Christ. She spent her early married years as a medical missionary in China, living out her life in unselfish service to her husband (a busy medical doctor), her family and her church. She didn't preach or lecture; her spirituality wasn't forced or put on. I simply watched the way she approached life.

She was a practical, organized woman who was never too busy to be with me or include me in the countless things she did. Her vivid imagination made even mundane chores enjoyable; and when she read to me, she made the characters come alive with an assortment of accents. She instigated wonderful Bible games that taught me Biblical facts I probably would not have learned otherwise. She told bedtime stories with great flair and enthusiasm as she described her years in China with warlords and bandits, letting me share in her adventures.

My Role as "Mackie"

My role as grandmother looks quite different from hers. I am a working grandmother who travels a great deal, and when I am home, I have countless projects that demand my attention. But there is no greater joy than to hear my back doorbell ring and hear voices call out, "Mackie, where are you?" from the cherubic faces looking through the door. I love to be imaginative and silly with them.

All my grandchildren love hearing me read. The same stool my grandmother kept full of toys for her visiting grandchildren is now full of books in my family room. They open it, looking for just the right book for me to read.

Each summer my grandson comes to spend two weeks with me. Because he is here for an extended time, we have the opportunity to talk about things that are on his mind. He knows that he is loved unconditionally, that he holds a very special place in my heart and that I am pretty much unshockable.

Their Avenue to God

What does all this have to do with introducing your grandchild to Jesus? Everything. As grandmothers we build an avenue to share God's truths as we build nurturing relationships with the younger generation. If we are unavailable, critical, harsh, unpleasant, demanding or unbending, our grandchildren will not be interested in what we have to say. We want to be winsome for Christ.

Children have very open, tender hearts to spiritual truths. Their curiosity opens avenues of conversation that we can turn into opportunities for talking about God's love. And God has given us an endless resource in nature. As I walk along the beach with my grandchildren searching for shells, observing the shore birds, awaiting the hatching of turtle eggs, we talk about the creativity of God. As we watch the waves roll in, we talk about how the ocean reflects aspects of God's character: powerful, awesome, faithful, deep. Sunsets or the sun after a storm give rise to discussions about Jesus' return. In my yard as we look at the beautiful, fragrant lilies, we talk about how God has detailed them as an artist would paint his canvas. I explain to my grandchildren that God has given these things to us for his pleasure and ours.

I have openly made God part of my everyday life. My grandchildren know that God is a priority: They see me reading my Bible each day. They hear me pray with them and for them. They see me living out my faith.

Faith comes easily to a child. While our grandchildren are young, we need to take advantage of the opportunities to teach them about the reality of Christ in our own lives, so they will want to know him in a personal way too. Perhaps through our words and our living example, we will have the enormous privilege of leading them to the Savior! What an honor!

⁵For your Maker is your husband—
    the Lord Almighty is his name—
the Holy One of Israel is your Redeemer;
    he is called the God of all the earth.
⁶The Lord will call you back
    as if you were a wife deserted and
        distressed in spirit—
a wife who married young,
    only to be rejected," says your God.
⁷"For a brief moment I abandoned you,
    but with deep compassion I will bring you
        back.
⁸In a surge of anger
    I hid my face from you for a moment,
but with everlasting kindness
    I will have compassion on you,"
    says the Lord your Redeemer.

⁹"To me this is like the days of Noah,
    when I swore that the waters of Noah would
        never again cover the earth.
So now I have sworn not to be angry with
        you,
    never to rebuke you again.
¹⁰Though the mountains be shaken
    and the hills be removed,
yet my unfailing love for you will not be
        shaken
    nor my covenant of peace be removed,"
    says the Lord, who has compassion on
        you.

¹¹"O afflicted city, lashed by storms and not
        comforted,
    I will build you with stones of turquoise, [a]
    your foundations with sapphires. [b]
¹²I will make your battlements of rubies,
    your gates of sparkling jewels,
    and all your walls of precious stones.
¹³All your sons will be taught by the Lord,
    and great will be your children's peace.
¹⁴In righteousness you will be established:
    Tyranny will be far from you;
        you will have nothing to fear.
Terror will be far removed;
    it will not come near you.

¹⁵If anyone does attack you, it will not be my
        doing;
    whoever attacks you will surrender to you.

¹⁶"See, it is I who created the blacksmith
    who fans the coals into flame
    and forges a weapon fit for its work.
And it is I who have created the destroyer to
        work havoc;
¹⁷   no weapon forged against you will prevail,
    and you will refute every tongue that
        accuses you.
This is the heritage of the servants of the
    Lord,
    and this is their vindication from me,"
            declares the Lord.

Invitation to the Thirsty

55 "Come, all you who are thirsty,
    come to the waters;
and you who have no money,
    come, buy and eat!
Come, buy wine and milk
    without money and without cost.
²Why spend money on what is not bread,
    and your labor on what does not satisfy?
Listen, listen to me, and eat what is good,
    and your soul will delight in the richest of
        fare.
³Give ear and come to me;
    hear me, that your soul may live.
I will make an everlasting covenant with you,
    my faithful love promised to David.
⁴See, I have made him a witness to the
        peoples,
    a leader and commander of the peoples.
⁵Surely you will summon nations you know
        not,
    and nations that do not know you will
        hasten to you,
because of the Lord your God,
    the Holy One of Israel,
    for he has endowed you with splendor."

[a] 11 The meaning of the Hebrew for this word is uncertain.
[b] 11 Or *lapis lazuli*

⁶ Seek the LORD while he may be found;
 call on him while he is near.
⁷ Let the wicked forsake his way
 and the evil man his thoughts.
Let him turn to the LORD, and he will have
 mercy on him,
 and to our God, for he will freely pardon.

TALKING POINTS

Finding God

Seek the Lord.

ISAIAH 55:6–7

For more on finding God, go to Acts 17:27.

⁸ "For my thoughts are not your thoughts,
 neither are your ways my ways,"
 declares the LORD.
⁹ "As the heavens are higher than the earth,
 so are my ways higher than your ways
 and my thoughts than your thoughts.
¹⁰ As the rain and the snow
 come down from heaven,
 and do not return to it
 without watering the earth

PRAYING THE SCRIPTURES

Forgiveness

ISAIAH 55:6–7

O God, may my grandchild seek you while
you may be found and call on you while you
are near. Let her forsake any evil ways and
thoughts and turn to you, O Lord, for you
will have mercy on her and freely pardon.

Next prayer in Forgiveness Prayer Track: Daniel 9:9

and making it bud and flourish,
 so that it yields seed for the sower and
 bread for the eater,
¹¹ so is my word that goes out from my mouth:
 It will not return to me empty,
 but will accomplish what I desire
 and achieve the purpose for which I sent it.
¹² You will go out in joy
 and be led forth in peace;
 the mountains and hills
 will burst into song before you,
 and all the trees of the field
 will clap their hands.
¹³ Instead of the thornbush will grow the pine
 tree,
 and instead of briers the myrtle will grow.
This will be for the LORD's renown,
 for an everlasting sign,
 which will not be destroyed."

Salvation for Others

56 This is what the LORD says:

"Maintain justice
 and do what is right,
for my salvation is close at hand
 and my righteousness will soon be
 revealed.
² Blessed is the man who does this,
 the man who holds it fast,
who keeps the Sabbath without desecrating
 it,
 and keeps his hand from doing any evil."

³ Let no foreigner who has bound himself to
 the LORD say,
 "The LORD will surely exclude me from his
 people."
And let not any eunuch complain,
 "I am only a dry tree."

⁴ For this is what the LORD says:

"To the eunuchs who keep my Sabbaths,
 who choose what pleases me
 and hold fast to my covenant—

⁵to them I will give within my temple and
        its walls
    a memorial and a name
    better than sons and daughters;
    I will give them an everlasting name
        that will not be cut off.
⁶And foreigners who bind themselves to the
        Lord
    to serve him,
    to love the name of the Lord,
        and to worship him,
    all who keep the Sabbath without
        desecrating it
    and who hold fast to my covenant—
⁷these I will bring to my holy mountain
    and give them joy in my house of prayer.
    Their burnt offerings and sacrifices
        will be accepted on my altar;
    for my house will be called
        a house of prayer for all nations."
⁸The Sovereign Lord declares—
    he who gathers the exiles of Israel:
    "I will gather still others to them
        besides those already gathered."

God's Accusation Against the Wicked

⁹Come, all you beasts of the field,
        come and devour, all you beasts of the
        forest!
¹⁰Israel's watchmen are blind,
        they all lack knowledge;
    they are all mute dogs,
        they cannot bark;
    they lie around and dream,
        they love to sleep.
¹¹They are dogs with mighty appetites;
        they never have enough.
    They are shepherds who lack
        understanding;
    they all turn to their own way,
        each seeks his own gain.
¹²"Come," each one cries, "let me get wine!
    Let us drink our fill of beer!
    And tomorrow will be like today,
        or even far better."

57 The righteous perish,
        and no one ponders it in his heart;
    devout men are taken away,
        and no one understands
    that the righteous are taken away
        to be spared from evil.
²Those who walk uprightly
        enter into peace;
    they find rest as they lie in death.

³"But you—come here, you sons of a
        sorceress,
    you offspring of adulterers and prostitutes!
⁴Whom are you mocking?
    At whom do you sneer
        and stick out your tongue?
    Are you not a brood of rebels,
        the offspring of liars?
⁵You burn with lust among the oaks
        and under every spreading tree;
    you sacrifice your children in the ravines
        and under the overhanging crags.
⁶The idols among the smooth stones of the
        ravines are your portion;
    they, they are your lot.
    Yes, to them you have poured out drink
        offerings
    and offered grain offerings.
    In the light of these things, should I
        relent?
⁷You have made your bed on a high and lofty
        hill;
    there you went up to offer your sacrifices.
⁸Behind your doors and your doorposts
    you have put your pagan symbols.
    Forsaking me, you uncovered your bed,
        you climbed into it and opened it wide;
    you made a pact with those whose beds you
        love,
    and you looked on their nakedness.
⁹You went to Molech ᵃ with olive oil
        and increased your perfumes.
    You sent your ambassadors ᵇ far away;
        you descended to the grave ᶜ itself!

ᵃ 9 Or to the king   ᵇ 9 Or idols   ᶜ 9 Hebrew Sheol

¹⁰You were wearied by all your ways,
    but you would not say, 'It is hopeless.'
You found renewal of your strength,
    and so you did not faint.

¹¹"Whom have you so dreaded and feared
    that you have been false to me,
and have neither remembered me
    nor pondered this in your hearts?
Is it not because I have long been silent
    that you do not fear me?
¹²I will expose your righteousness and your
        works,
    and they will not benefit you.
¹³When you cry out for help,
    let your collection ⌊of idols⌋ save you!
The wind will carry all of them off,
    a mere breath will blow them away.
But the man who makes me his refuge
    will inherit the land
    and possess my holy mountain."

Comfort for the Contrite

¹⁴And it will be said:

"Build up, build up, prepare the road!
    Remove the obstacles out of the way of
        my people."
¹⁵For this is what the high and lofty One
        says—
    he who lives forever, whose name is holy:
"I live in a high and holy place,
    but also with him who is contrite and
        lowly in spirit,
to revive the spirit of the lowly
    and to revive the heart of the contrite.
¹⁶I will not accuse forever,
    nor will I always be angry,
for then the spirit of man would grow faint
        before me—
    the breath of man that I have created.
¹⁷I was enraged by his sinful greed;
    I punished him, and hid my face in
        anger,
    yet he kept on in his willful ways.

¹⁸I have seen his ways, but I will heal him;
    I will guide him and restore comfort to
        him,
¹⁹   creating praise on the lips of the mourners
        in Israel.
Peace, peace, to those far and near,"
    says the LORD. "And I will heal them."
²⁰But the wicked are like the tossing sea,
    which cannot rest,
    whose waves cast up mire and mud.
²¹"There is no peace," says my God, "for the
        wicked."

True Fasting

58 "Shout it aloud, do not hold back.
    Raise your voice like a trumpet.
Declare to my people their rebellion
    and to the house of Jacob their sins.
²For day after day they seek me out;
    they seem eager to know my ways,
as if they were a nation that does what is
        right
    and has not forsaken the commands of its
        God.
They ask me for just decisions
    and seem eager for God to come near them.
³'Why have we fasted,' they say,
    'and you have not seen it?
Why have we humbled ourselves,
    and you have not noticed?'

"Yet on the day of your fasting, you do as you
        please
    and exploit all your workers.
⁴Your fasting ends in quarreling and strife,
    and in striking each other with wicked
        fists.
You cannot fast as you do today
    and expect your voice to be heard on high.
⁵Is this the kind of fast I have chosen,
    only a day for a man to humble himself?
Is it only for bowing one's head like a reed
    and for lying on sackcloth and ashes?
Is that what you call a fast,
    a day acceptable to the LORD?

6 "Is not this the kind of fasting I have chosen:
    to loose the chains of injustice
        and untie the cords of the yoke,
    to set the oppressed free
        and break every yoke?
7 Is it not to share your food with the hungry
    and to provide the poor wanderer with
        shelter—
    when you see the naked, to clothe him,
        and not to turn away from your own flesh
        and blood?
8 Then your light will break forth like the dawn,
    and your healing will quickly appear;
    then your righteousness *a* will go before you,
        and the glory of the LORD will be your rear
        guard.
9 Then you will call, and the LORD will answer;
    you will cry for help, and he will say:
        Here am I.

"If you do away with the yoke of oppression,
    with the pointing finger and malicious
        talk,
10 and if you spend yourselves in behalf of the
        hungry
    and satisfy the needs of the oppressed,
    then your light will rise in the darkness,
        and your night will become like the
        noonday.
11 The LORD will guide you always;
    he will satisfy your needs in a sun-scorched
        land
    and will strengthen your frame.

You will be like a well-watered garden,
    like a spring whose waters never fail.
12 Your people will rebuild the ancient ruins
    and will raise up the age-old foundations;
    you will be called Repairer of Broken Walls,
        Restorer of Streets with Dwellings.

13 "If you keep your feet from breaking the
        Sabbath
    and from doing as you please on my holy
        day,
    if you call the Sabbath a delight
        and the LORD's holy day honorable,
    and if you honor it by not going your own
        way
        and not doing as you please or speaking
        idle words,
14 then you will find your joy in the LORD,
    and I will cause you to ride on the heights
        of the land
    and to feast on the inheritance of your
        father Jacob."
                    The mouth of the LORD
                        has spoken.

Sin, Confession and Redemption

59 Surely the arm of the LORD is not too
        short to save,
    nor his ear too dull to hear.
2 But your iniquities have separated
    you from your God;
    your sins have hidden his face from you,
        so that he will not hear.
3 For your hands are stained with blood,
    your fingers with guilt.
    Your lips have spoken lies,
        and your tongue mutters wicked things.
4 No one calls for justice;
    no one pleads his case with integrity.
    They rely on empty arguments and speak lies;
        they conceive trouble and give birth to
        evil.
5 They hatch the eggs of vipers
    and spin a spider's web.

TALKING POINTS

Social Justice

If we treat others with justice, then God
will answer when we call to him.

ISAIAH 58:6–9

For more on social justice, go to Amos 5:14–15.

---

a 8 Or your righteous One

Whoever eats their eggs will die,
and when one is broken, an adder is
hatched.
6 Their cobwebs are useless for clothing;
they cannot cover themselves with what
they make.
Their deeds are evil deeds,
and acts of violence are in their hands.
7 Their feet rush into sin;
they are swift to shed innocent blood.
Their thoughts are evil thoughts;
ruin and destruction mark their ways.
8 The way of peace they do not know;
there is no justice in their paths.
They have turned them into crooked roads;
no one who walks in them will know
peace.

9 So justice is far from us,
and righteousness does not reach us.
We look for light, but all is darkness;
for brightness, but we walk in deep
shadows.
10 Like the blind we grope along the wall,
feeling our way like men without eyes.
At midday we stumble as if it were twilight;
among the strong, we are like the dead.
11 We all growl like bears;
we moan mournfully like doves.
We look for justice, but find none;
for deliverance, but it is far away.

12 For our offenses are many in your sight,
and our sins testify against us.
Our offenses are ever with us,
and we acknowledge our iniquities:
13 rebellion and treachery against the LORD,
turning our backs on our God,
fomenting oppression and revolt,
uttering lies our hearts have conceived.
14 So justice is driven back,
and righteousness stands at a distance;
truth has stumbled in the streets,
honesty cannot enter.
15 Truth is nowhere to be found,
and whoever shuns evil becomes a prey.

The LORD looked and was displeased
that there was no justice.
16 He saw that there was no one,
he was appalled that there was no one to
intervene;
so his own arm worked salvation for him,
and his own righteousness sustained him.
17 He put on righteousness as his breastplate,
and the helmet of salvation on his head;
he put on the garments of vengeance
and wrapped himself in zeal as in a cloak.
18 According to what they have done,
so will he repay
wrath to his enemies
and retribution to his foes;
he will repay the islands their due.
19 From the west, men will fear the name of the
LORD,
and from the rising of the sun, they will
revere his glory.
For he will come like a pent-up flood
that the breath of the LORD drives along.[a]

20 "The Redeemer will come to Zion,
to those in Jacob who repent of their sins,"
declares the LORD.

21 "As for me, this is my covenant with them,"
says the LORD. "My Spirit, who is on you, and my
words that I have put in your mouth will not depart from your mouth, or from the mouths of your
children, or from the mouths of their descendants
from this time on and forever," says the LORD.

The Glory of Zion

60 "Arise, shine, for your light has come,
and the glory of the LORD rises upon
you.
2 See, darkness covers the earth
and thick darkness is over the peoples,
but the LORD rises upon you
and his glory appears over you.
3 Nations will come to your light,
and kings to the brightness of your dawn.

---

a 19 Or *When the enemy comes in like a flood, / the Spirit of the LORD
will put him to flight*

4 "Lift up your eyes and look about you:
  All assemble and come to you;
 your sons come from afar,
   and your daughters are carried on the
     arm.
5 Then you will look and be radiant,
   your heart will throb and swell with joy;
 the wealth on the seas will be brought to you,
   to you the riches of the nations will come.
6 Herds of camels will cover your land,
   young camels of Midian and Ephah.
 And all from Sheba will come,
   bearing gold and incense
   and proclaiming the praise of the LORD.
7 All Kedar's flocks will be gathered to you,
   the rams of Nebaioth will serve you;
 they will be accepted as offerings on my altar,
   and I will adorn my glorious temple.

8 "Who are these that fly along like clouds,
   like doves to their nests?
9 Surely the islands look to me;
   in the lead are the ships of Tarshish,ᵃ
 bringing your sons from afar,
   with their silver and gold,
 to the honor of the LORD your God,
   the Holy One of Israel,
   for he has endowed you with splendor.

10 "Foreigners will rebuild your walls,
   and their kings will serve you.
 Though in anger I struck you,
   in favor I will show you compassion.
11 Your gates will always stand open,
   they will never be shut, day or night,
 so that men may bring you the wealth of the
     nations—
   their kings led in triumphal procession.
12 For the nation or kingdom that will not serve
     you will perish;
   it will be utterly ruined.

13 "The glory of Lebanon will come to you,
   the pine, the fir and the cypress together,
 to adorn the place of my sanctuary;
   and I will glorify the place of my feet.

14 The sons of your oppressors will come
     bowing before you;
 all who despise you will bow down at your
     feet
 and will call you the City of the LORD,
   Zion of the Holy One of Israel.

15 "Although you have been forsaken and hated,
   with no one traveling through,
 I will make you the everlasting pride
   and the joy of all generations.
16 You will drink the milk of nations
   and be nursed at royal breasts.
 Then you will know that I, the LORD, am
     your Savior,
   your Redeemer, the Mighty One of Jacob.
17 Instead of bronze I will bring you gold,
   and silver in place of iron.
 Instead of wood I will bring you bronze,
   and iron in place of stones.
 I will make peace your governor
   and righteousness your ruler.
18 No longer will violence be heard in your land,
   nor ruin or destruction within your borders,
 but you will call your walls Salvation
   and your gates Praise.
19 The sun will no more be your light by day,
   nor will the brightness of the moon shine
     on you,
 for the LORD will be your everlasting light,
   and your God will be your glory.
20 Your sun will never set again,
   and your moon will wane no more;
 the LORD will be your everlasting light,
   and your days of sorrow will end.
21 Then will all your people be righteous
   and they will possess the land forever.
 They are the shoot I have planted,
   the work of my hands,
   for the display of my splendor.
22 The least of you will become a thousand,
   the smallest a mighty nation.
 I am the LORD;
   in its time I will do this swiftly."

ᵃ 9 Or the trading ships

The Year of the Lord's Favor

61 The Spirit of the Sovereign Lord is on me,
   because the Lord has anointed me
to preach good news to the poor.
He has sent me to bind up the brokenhearted,
   to proclaim freedom for the captives
   and release from darkness for the
      prisoners,[a]
² to proclaim the year of the Lord's favor
   and the day of vengeance of our God,
to comfort all who mourn,
³   and provide for those who grieve in
      Zion—
to bestow on them a crown of beauty
   instead of ashes,
the oil of gladness
   instead of mourning,
and a garment of praise
   instead of a spirit of despair.
They will be called oaks of righteousness,
   a planting of the Lord
   for the display of his splendor.

⁴ They will rebuild the ancient ruins
   and restore the places long devastated;
they will renew the ruined cities
   that have been devastated for generations.
⁵ Aliens will shepherd your flocks;
   foreigners will work your fields and
      vineyards.
⁶ And you will be called priests of the Lord,
   you will be named ministers of our God.
You will feed on the wealth of nations,
   and in their riches you will boast.

⁷ Instead of their shame
   my people will receive a double portion,
and instead of disgrace
   they will rejoice in their inheritance;
and so they will inherit a double portion in
      their land,
   and everlasting joy will be theirs.

⁸ "For I, the Lord, love justice;
   I hate robbery and iniquity.
In my faithfulness I will reward them
   and make an everlasting covenant with
      them.
⁹ Their descendants will be known among the
      nations
   and their offspring among the peoples.
All who see them will acknowledge
   that they are a people the Lord has
      blessed."

¹⁰ I delight greatly in the Lord;
   my soul rejoices in my God.
For he has clothed me with garments of
      salvation
   and arrayed me in a robe of righteousness,
as a bridegroom adorns his head like a priest,
   and as a bride adorns herself with her
      jewels.
¹¹ For as the soil makes the sprout come up
   and a garden causes seeds to grow,
so the Sovereign Lord will make
   righteousness and praise
spring up before all nations.

Zion's New Name

62 For Zion's sake I will not keep silent,
   for Jerusalem's sake I will not remain
      quiet,
till her righteousness shines out like the dawn,
   her salvation like a blazing torch.
² The nations will see your righteousness,
   and all kings your glory;
you will be called by a new name
   that the mouth of the Lord will bestow.
³ You will be a crown of splendor in the Lord's
      hand,
   a royal diadem in the hand of your God.
⁴ No longer will they call you Deserted,
   or name your land Desolate.
But you will be called Hephzibah,[b]
   and your land Beulah[c];
for the Lord will take delight in you,
   and your land will be married.

---

[a] 1 Hebrew; Septuagint *the blind*   [b] 4 *Hephzibah* means *my delight is in her*.   [c] 4 *Beulah* means *married*.

THEY WILL BE CALLED OAKS OF
RIGHTEOUSNESS, A PLANTING OF
THE LORD FOR THE DISPLAY OF
HIS SPLENDOR.

Isaiah 61:3

Oaks of Righteousness

LUCI SHAW

READ | ISAIAH 61:1–11

Isaiah 61 contains a splendid description of an oak tree, crowned with the beauty of its early spring leaves, cloaked with green praise instead of the despair of winter snow. I do want to be "an oak of righteousness, planted by the LORD to display his glory" (see Isaiah 61:3). But only after many seasons of fall, and falling leaves, and winter, frigid and bleak, will I have grown tall enough to fill that job description. The glory and beauty don't come cheap. They must be earned with perseverance and patience, through the seasons of life. And the growth, often so slow it seems barely perceptible, adds ring to annual ring from the core of the trunk outward, and inch to inch as upward growth occurs, until that maturity is gained. The scriptural counterpart is: "Add to your faith goodness; and to goodness, knowledge; and to knowledge, self-control; and to self-control," — see how incremental this growth is! — "perseverance; and to perseverance, godliness . . ." [2 Peter 1:5–6].

Once again, the persistence and perseverance of trees tells us something about our own lives. Redwood trees have an almost uncanny ability to survive the holocausts of forest fires, retaining vital green foliage in spite of having the hearts literally eaten out of them by the flames. Madrona trees, those cinnamon-red, thin-skinned trees that decorate the cliff rocks of the Pacific coast, are able to embrace with young, healthy tissue their dead or damaged branches, the new growth, smooth as a well-tanned human arm, contrasting with striated, gray deadwood, not rejecting it, but filling in the gaps and breaks and making the old wood a part of the pattern of the whole. Here are lessons for us in the human community; the old and the young need and benefit each other; age has important lessons for youth, and youth can invigorate age with its enthusiasm.

O Lord, help me to be an oak of righteousness — strong and growing steady and sure through all the stages of life. Give me patience to persevere and a beauty that radiates your love and glory. Amen.

Your next devotion is located on page 1014.

GRANDCHILD IN FOCUS • PRAYER

Relationships at Home

O Lord, I pray that you will bless the home and family of my grandchild. May the relationships she has with her parents and siblings enhance her well-being, support her self-confidence and increase her faith. May her home life reflect your love, your grace, your compassion and your peace. Guide her parents to direct her in love and truth, so she will grow into a strong and compassionate individual. Amen.

5 As a young man marries a maiden,
 so will your sons*a* marry you;
as a bridegroom rejoices over his bride,
 so will your God rejoice over you.

6 I have posted watchmen on your walls,
  O Jerusalem;
 they will never be silent day or night.
You who call on the LORD,
 give yourselves no rest,
7 and give him no rest till he establishes
  Jerusalem
 and makes her the praise of the earth.

8 The LORD has sworn by his right hand
 and by his mighty arm:
"Never again will I give your grain
 as food for your enemies,
and never again will foreigners drink the new
  wine
 for which you have toiled;
9 but those who harvest it will eat it
 and praise the LORD,
and those who gather the grapes will drink it
 in the courts of my sanctuary."

10 Pass through, pass through the gates!
 Prepare the way for the people.
Build up, build up the highway!
 Remove the stones.
Raise a banner for the nations.

11 The LORD has made proclamation
 to the ends of the earth:
"Say to the Daughter of Zion,
 'See, your Savior comes!
See, his reward is with him,
 and his recompense accompanies him.'"
12 They will be called the Holy People,
 the Redeemed of the LORD;
and you will be called Sought After,
 the City No Longer Deserted.

God's Day of Vengeance and Redemption

63 Who is this coming from Edom,
 from Bozrah, with his garments stained
  crimson?

Who is this, robed in splendor,
 striding forward in the greatness of his
  strength?

"It is I, speaking in righteousness,
 mighty to save."

2 Why are your garments red,
 like those of one treading the winepress?

3 "I have trodden the winepress alone;
 from the nations no one was with me.
I trampled them in my anger
 and trod them down in my wrath;
their blood spattered my garments,
 and I stained all my clothing.
4 For the day of vengeance was in my heart,
 and the year of my redemption has come.
5 I looked, but there was no one to help,
 I was appalled that no one gave support;
so my own arm worked salvation for me,
 and my own wrath sustained me.
6 I trampled the nations in my anger;
 in my wrath I made them drunk
 and poured their blood on the ground."

Praise and Prayer

7 I will tell of the kindnesses of the LORD,
 the deeds for which he is to be praised,
 according to all the LORD has done for
  us—
yes, the many good things he has done
 for the house of Israel,
 according to his compassion and many
  kindnesses.
8 He said, "Surely they are my people,
 sons who will not be false to me";
 and so he became their Savior.
9 In all their distress he too was distressed,
 and the angel of his presence saved them.
In his love and mercy he redeemed them;
 he lifted them up and carried them
 all the days of old.
10 Yet they rebelled
 and grieved his Holy Spirit.

a 5 Or Builder

Patriotism

Patriotism is an interesting topic of conversation to have with your grandchildren. Perhaps your grandchildren are memorizing your country's constitution or other special document in school. Talk to them about what they are learning. If they ask for your help or want to show you what they've learned, you have the perfect opportunity to start a conversation.

You may want to discuss how your family came to live in your country, what they did or stories about how they survived. Or you may want to discuss the meaning and importance of displaying the flag and have them help you put up a flag holder or flagpole. Other questions you can discuss are: What does our country's motto mean? What are the words on our currency? What do they mean?

Long-Distance Variation: Your grandkids might appreciate a letter from you detailing some of the highlights of your family's history in your country: where your family lived, the jobs family members held, etc. If your family has recently immigrated to your country, tell that story as well.

God of peace, thank you for the country I live in. I pray today for worldwide peace and look forward to the ultimate coming of your kingdom of peace. Help my grandchildren to understand the dynamics of peace and freedom, to appreciate your blessings and to respect our country. Amen.

Your next devotion is located on page 1016.

GRANDCHILD IN FOCUS · PRAYER

Friends

Dear Lord and Father, I pray for my grandchild's social life and his friends. Bring diverse friends into his life who will love and encourage him, who will bring joy and laughter to the good times and comfort and support through difficulties and disappointments. Grant him wisdom and discernment as he selects his friends; help him to avoid cliques that restrict, activities that endanger, and foolish and dangerous behaviors that harm. I ask that you fill his life with close and caring relationships. Amen.

PRAYING THE SCRIPTURES

Thankfulness

ISAIAH 63:7

May my grandchild tell of your kindnesses, O Lord, the deeds for which you are to be praised, according to all you have done for him—yes, the many good things you have done, according to your compassion and many kindnesses.

Next prayer in Thankfulness Prayer Track: Ephesians 5:20

So he turned and became their enemy
  and he himself fought against them.

[11] Then his people recalled[a] the days of old,
  the days of Moses and his people—
where is he who brought them through the sea,
  with the shepherd of his flock?
Where is he who set
  his Holy Spirit among them,
[12] who sent his glorious arm of power
  to be at Moses' right hand,
who divided the waters before them,
  to gain for himself everlasting renown,
[13] who led them through the depths?
Like a horse in open country,
  they did not stumble;
[14] like cattle that go down to the plain,
  they were given rest by the Spirit of the
    Lord.
This is how you guided your people
  to make for yourself a glorious name.

[15] Look down from heaven and see
  from your lofty throne, holy and glorious.
Where are your zeal and your might?
  Your tenderness and compassion are
    withheld from us.
[16] But you are our Father,
  though Abraham does not know us
or Israel acknowledge us;

you, O Lord, are our Father,
  our Redeemer from of old is your name.
[17] Why, O Lord, do you make us wander from
    your ways
  and harden our hearts so we do not revere
    you?
Return for the sake of your servants,
  the tribes that are your inheritance.
[18] For a little while your people possessed your
    holy place,
  but now our enemies have trampled down
    your sanctuary.
[19] We are yours from of old;
  but you have not ruled over them,
  they have not been called by your name.[b]

64 Oh, that you would rend the heavens
    and come down,
  that the mountains would tremble before
    you!
[2] As when fire sets twigs ablaze
  and causes water to boil,
come down to make your name known to
    your enemies
  and cause the nations to quake before you!
[3] For when you did awesome things that we
    did not expect,
  you came down, and the mountains
    trembled before you.
[4] Since ancient times no one has heard,
  no ear has perceived,
no eye has seen any God besides you,
  who acts on behalf of those who wait for
    him.
[5] You come to the help of those who gladly do
    right,
  who remember your ways.
But when we continued to sin against them,
  you were angry.
  How then can we be saved?
[6] All of us have become like one who is
    unclean,
  and all our righteous acts are like filthy rags;

[a] 11 Or *But may he recall*   [b] 19 Or *We are like those you have never ruled, / like those never called by your name*

Worship the Lord

I will listen to what God the LORD will say;
  he promises peace to his people, his saints—
  but let them not return to folly.
Surely his salvation is near those who fear him,
  that his glory may dwell in our land.

Love and faithfulness meet together;
  righteousness and peace kiss each other.
Faithfulness springs forth from the earth,
  and righteousness looks down from heaven.
The LORD will indeed give what is good,
  and our land will yield its harvest.
Righteousness goes before him
  and prepares the way for his steps.

Psalm 85:8—13

I praise you, Lord, for your promise of peace; always remind me that my obedience is its prerequisite. I thank you for faithfully giving me good gifts and for allowing me to live in a land of plenty. Grant me the wisdom to use your gifts to grow your kingdom and prepare for the day when you come again. Amen.

Your next devotion is located on page 1018.

GRANDCHILD IN FOCUS • PRAYER

Self-Image

O loving God, I praise you for creating my grandchild as a unique individual. Now I ask you to help her appreciate her uniqueness. Build up her self-image so she can enjoy her individuality. Help her to stand firm for who she is, where she has come from and what she believes in. Encourage her not only to have hopes and dreams but to also enjoy each day as it comes. In Jesus' name, amen.

we all shrivel up like a leaf,
and like the wind our sins sweep us away.
⁷No one calls on your name
or strives to lay hold of you;
for you have hidden your face from us
and made us waste away because of our
sins.

⁸Yet, O Lord, you are our Father.
We are the clay, you are the potter;
we are all the work of your hand.
⁹Do not be angry beyond measure, O Lord;
do not remember our sins forever.
Oh, look upon us, we pray,
for we are all your people.
¹⁰Your sacred cities have become a desert;
even Zion is a desert, Jerusalem a
desolation.
¹¹Our holy and glorious temple, where our
fathers praised you,
has been burned with fire,
and all that we treasured lies in ruins.
¹²After all this, O Lord, will you hold yourself
back?
Will you keep silent and punish us beyond
measure?

Judgment and Salvation

65 "I revealed myself to those who did not
ask for me;
I was found by those who did not seek me.
To a nation that did not call on my name,
I said, 'Here am I, here am I.'
²All day long I have held out my hands
to an obstinate people,
who walk in ways not good,
pursuing their own imaginations—
³a people who continually provoke me
to my very face,
offering sacrifices in gardens
and burning incense on altars of brick;
⁴who sit among the graves
and spend their nights keeping secret vigil;
who eat the flesh of pigs,
and whose pots hold broth of unclean
meat;

⁵who say, 'Keep away; don't come near me,
for I am too sacred for you!'
Such people are smoke in my nostrils,
a fire that keeps burning all day.

⁶"See, it stands written before me:
I will not keep silent but will pay back in
full;
I will pay it back into their laps—
⁷both your sins and the sins of your
fathers,"
says the Lord.
"Because they burned sacrifices on the
mountains
and defied me on the hills,
I will measure into their laps
the full payment for their former deeds."

⁸This is what the Lord says:

"As when juice is still found in a cluster of
grapes
and men say, 'Don't destroy it,
there is yet some good in it,'
so will I do in behalf of my servants;
I will not destroy them all.
⁹I will bring forth descendants from Jacob,
and from Judah those who will possess my
mountains;
my chosen people will inherit them,
and there will my servants live.
¹⁰Sharon will become a pasture for flocks,
and the Valley of Achor a resting place for
herds,
for my people who seek me.

¹¹"But as for you who forsake the Lord
and forget my holy mountain,
who spread a table for Fortune
and fill bowls of mixed wine for Destiny,
¹²I will destine you for the sword,
and you will all bend down for the
slaughter;
for I called but you did not answer,
I spoke but you did not listen.
You did evil in my sight
and chose what displeases me."

ALL OF US HAVE BECOME LIKE
ONE WHO IS UNCLEAN, AND ALL
OUR RIGHTEOUS ACTS ARE LIKE
FILTHY RAGS.

Isaiah 64:6

When Best Isn't Good Enough

NETA JACKSON

READ | ISAIAH 64:1–12

Before I had grandkids to spoil, I had talented nieces and nephews. So of course I wanted to see Nephew #3 (age 8) in *Oliver!* when my husband and I were visiting his ailing parents in a nursing home. I agreed to get back from the nursing home (an hour's drive) in time to cook supper for Nephews #1 and #2 and then drive them 30 minutes to the play by 7:00 P.M.

The day at the nursing home had been tiring, but all was going as planned. On the drive home, I shopped for groceries and then cooked a hot supper for the boys. At 5:15, just as I was dishing up salmon fillets, the phone rang. "The play starts at 6:00, not 7:00! You can make it if you leave now. Hurry!"

Leave now? Were they kidding? I was exhausted after a long, stressful day. Everyone needed to eat. Supper was on the table. It wasn't my fault they'd told me the wrong time. "We'll be there as soon as we can," I promised.

We ate. We piled in the car. We arrived at 6:15, missing the cute opening number, though Nephew #3 was in a couple of other scenes and musical numbers as one of the "orphans." The play was great.

But the family was deeply disappointed. I had failed to get Big Brothers there in time to see Little Brother in the opening scene, which I could have done if I'd dropped everything the moment they had called. I felt defensive. I'd done the best I could, hadn't I?

But a few days later, the reality of a spiritual truth hit home: Yes, I'd done what I thought best. But my best missed the mark. No wonder Isaiah 64:6, as worded in The Message, says, "We're all sin-infected, sin-contaminated. Our best efforts are grease-stained rags."

O God, give me the grace to acknowledge that even my best sometimes lets people down. I'm so grateful you cover my efforts with your righteousness, which never fails.

Your next devotion is located on page 1058.

GRANDCHILD IN FOCUS • PRAYER

Protection From Worldliness

O Sovereign Lord, the world surrounds my grandchild, pressing in and tempting him in so many ways. Help him set appropriate limits. Give him sound judgment to choose wisely. Guard him from temptation; protect him from physical and mental predators; lead him into paths of righteousness and light. And reassure me with your promise that you are holding him in your hands. Amen.

¹³Therefore this is what the Sovereign Lord says:

"My servants will eat,
  but you will go hungry;
my servants will drink,
  but you will go thirsty;
my servants will rejoice,
  but you will be put to shame.
¹⁴My servants will sing
  out of the joy of their hearts,
but you will cry out
  from anguish of heart
  and wail in brokenness of spirit.
¹⁵You will leave your name
  to my chosen ones as a curse;
the Sovereign Lord will put you to death,
  but to his servants he will give another
    name.
¹⁶Whoever invokes a blessing in the land
  will do so by the God of truth;
he who takes an oath in the land
  will swear by the God of truth.
For the past troubles will be forgotten
  and hidden from my eyes.

New Heavens and a New Earth

¹⁷"Behold, I will create
  new heavens and a new earth.
The former things will not be remembered,
  nor will they come to mind.
¹⁸But be glad and rejoice forever
  in what I will create,
for I will create Jerusalem to be a delight
  and its people a joy.
¹⁹I will rejoice over Jerusalem
  and take delight in my people;
the sound of weeping and of crying
  will be heard in it no more.

²⁰"Never again will there be in it
  an infant who lives but a few days,
  or an old man who does not live out his
    years;
he who dies at a hundred
  will be thought a mere youth;

he who fails to reach *a* a hundred
  will be considered accursed.
²¹They will build houses and dwell in them;
  they will plant vineyards and eat their
    fruit.
²²No longer will they build houses and others
    live in them,
  or plant and others eat.
For as the days of a tree,
  so will be the days of my people;
my chosen ones will long enjoy
  the works of their hands.
²³They will not toil in vain
  or bear children doomed to misfortune;
for they will be a people blessed by the Lord,
  they and their descendants with them.
²⁴Before they call I will answer;
  while they are still speaking I will hear.
²⁵The wolf and the lamb will feed together,
  and the lion will eat straw like the ox,
  but dust will be the serpent's food.
They will neither harm nor destroy
  on all my holy mountain,"

                              says the Lord.

TALKING POINTS

Prayer
God answers quickly.
ISAIAH 65:24

For more on prayer, go to Jeremiah 33:3.

Judgment and Hope

66 This is what the Lord says:

"Heaven is my throne,
  and the earth is my footstool.
Where is the house you will build for me?
  Where will my resting place be?

a 20 Or / the sinner who reaches

²Has not my hand made all these things,
   and so they came into being?"
                    declares the LORD.

"This is the one I esteem:
   he who is humble and contrite in spirit,
   and trembles at my word.
³But whoever sacrifices a bull
   is like one who kills a man,
and whoever offers a lamb,
   like one who breaks a dog's neck;
whoever makes a grain offering
   is like one who presents pig's blood,
and whoever burns memorial incense,
   like one who worships an idol.
They have chosen their own ways,
   and their souls delight in their
      abominations;
⁴so I also will choose harsh treatment for
      them
   and will bring upon them what they dread.
For when I called, no one answered,
   when I spoke, no one listened.
They did evil in my sight
   and chose what displeases me."

⁵Hear the word of the LORD,
   you who tremble at his word:
"Your brothers who hate you,
   and exclude you because of my name, have
      said,
'Let the LORD be glorified,
   that we may see your joy!'
   Yet they will be put to shame.
⁶Hear that uproar from the city,
   hear that noise from the temple!
It is the sound of the LORD
   repaying his enemies all they deserve.

⁷"Before she goes into labor,
   she gives birth;
before the pains come upon her,
   she delivers a son.
⁸Who has ever heard of such a thing?
   Who has ever seen such things?
Can a country be born in a day
   or a nation be brought forth in a moment?

Yet no sooner is Zion in labor
   than she gives birth to her children.
⁹Do I bring to the moment of birth
   and not give delivery?" says the LORD.
"Do I close up the womb
   when I bring to delivery?" says your God.
¹⁰"Rejoice with Jerusalem and be glad for her,
   all you who love her;
rejoice greatly with her,
   all you who mourn over her.
¹¹For you will nurse and be satisfied
   at her comforting breasts;
you will drink deeply
   and delight in her overflowing abundance."

¹²For this is what the LORD says:

"I will extend peace to her like a river,
   and the wealth of nations like a flooding
      stream;
you will nurse and be carried on her arm
   and dandled on her knees.
¹³As a mother comforts her child,
   so will I comfort you;
   and you will be comforted over Jerusalem."

PRAYING THE SCRIPTURES

Comfort
ISAIAH 66:12–13

Lord, comfort my grandchild, for this is what
you have said: "I will extend peace to her like
a river . . . As a mother comforts her child, so
will I comfort you."

Next prayer in Comfort Prayer Track: Jeremiah 31:13

¹⁴When you see this, your heart will rejoice
   and you will flourish like grass;
the hand of the LORD will be made known to
      his servants,
   but his fury will be shown to his foes.

¹⁵ See, the Lord is coming with fire,
  and his chariots are like a whirlwind;
he will bring down his anger with fury,
  and his rebuke with flames of fire.
¹⁶ For with fire and with his sword
  the Lord will execute judgment upon all
    men,
  and many will be those slain by the Lord.

¹⁷ "Those who consecrate and purify themselves to go into the gardens, following the one in the midst of ^a those who eat the flesh of pigs and rats and other abominable things — they will meet their end together," declares the Lord.

¹⁸ "And I, because of their actions and their imaginations, am about to come ^b and gather all nations and tongues, and they will come and see my glory.

¹⁹ "I will set a sign among them, and I will send some of those who survive to the nations — to Tarshish, to the Libyans ^c and Lydians (famous as archers), to Tubal and Greece, and to the distant islands that have not heard of my fame or seen my glory. They will proclaim my glory among the nations. ²⁰ And they will bring all your brothers, from all the nations, to my holy mountain in Jerusalem as an offering to the Lord — on horses, in chariots and wagons, and on mules and camels," says the Lord. "They will bring them, as the Israelites bring their grain offerings, to the temple of the Lord in ceremonially clean vessels. ²¹ And I will select some of them also to be priests and Levites," says the Lord.

²² "As the new heavens and the new earth that I make will endure before me," declares the Lord, "so will your name and descendants endure. ²³ From one New Moon to another and from one Sabbath to another, all mankind will come and bow down before me," says the Lord. ²⁴ "And they will go out and look upon the dead bodies of those who rebelled against me; their worm will not die, nor will their fire be quenched, and they will be loathsome to all mankind."

^a 17 Or *gardens behind one of your temples, and*   ^b 18 The meaning of the Hebrew for this clause is uncertain.   ^c 19 Some Septuagint manuscripts *Put* (Libyans); Hebrew *Pul*

Nothing IS TOO HARD FOR GOD

God's people were on a path to utter destruction and exile in a foreign land. While Jeremiah prophesied about the judgment, punishment and captivity of Judah, he also assured the people that God's plan for them included hope in a future of forgiveness and restoration.

God chose Jeremiah to deliver some tough words to the people of Judah, and Jeremiah took on the task with passion. Between Jeremiah's fiery warnings of judgment were his intense displays of distress and sorrow for his faltering people (see Jeremiah 4:19; 9:1; 10:19; 23:9). Though his messages were often grim and upsetting, the people needed to hear them — for the sake of their relationship with their Lord.

As a grandmother you too can have a powerful influence on the spiritual lives of people in future generations. If you lack the courage to speak up, read the story of God's calling of the prophet Jeremiah (see Jeremiah 1:4–19). Like Jeremiah did for God's people, your actions, wisdom and influence can have a major impact on the lives of your grandchildren in turning their hearts to the Lord and guiding them in following him. Situations in our lives or in the lives of those dear to us may appear to be utterly hopeless and impossible, but they aren't. Nothing is impossible for the King of creation.

VERSE *to* REMEMBER | JEREMIAH 32:17

"Ah, Sovereign LORD, you have made the heavens and the earth by your great power and outstretched arm. Nothing is too hard for you."

ABOUT JEREMIAH

WRITTEN BY:
The prophet Jeremiah

WRITTEN FOR:
The people of Judah

DATE WRITTEN:
Between 626 and about 585 B.C.

WHY WRITTEN:
To warn the people that God would punish them for their sinfulness by allowing the Babylonians to destroy their nation and take them into exile

1

The words of Jeremiah son of Hilkiah, one of the priests at Anathoth in the territory of Benjamin. ²The word of the LORD came to him in the thirteenth year of the reign of Josiah son of Amon king of Judah, ³and through the reign of Jehoiakim son of Josiah king of Judah, down to the fifth month of the eleventh year of Zedekiah son of Josiah king of Judah, when the people of Jerusalem went into exile.

The Call of Jeremiah

⁴The word of the LORD came to me, saying,

⁵"Before I formed you in the womb I knew *a* you,
  before you were born I set you apart;
  I appointed you as a prophet to the nations."

◆ TALKING POINTS ◆

Self-Esteem

God had a plan for us before we were born.

JEREMIAH 1:5

For more on self-esteem, go to Zephaniah 3:17.

⁶"Ah, Sovereign LORD," I said, "I do not know how to speak; I am only a child."

⁷But the LORD said to me, "Do not say, 'I am only a child.' You must go to everyone I send you to and say whatever I command you. ⁸Do not be afraid of them, for I am with you and will rescue you," declares the LORD.

⁹Then the LORD reached out his hand and touched my mouth and said to me, "Now, I have put my words in your mouth. ¹⁰See, today I appoint you over nations and kingdoms to uproot and tear down, to destroy and overthrow, to build and to plant."

¹¹The word of the LORD came to me: "What do you see, Jeremiah?"

"I see the branch of an almond tree," I replied.

¹²The LORD said to me, "You have seen correctly, for I am watching *b* to see that my word is fulfilled."

¹³The word of the LORD came to me again: "What do you see?"

"I see a boiling pot, tilting away from the north," I answered.

¹⁴The LORD said to me, "From the north disaster will be poured out on all who live in the land. ¹⁵I am about to summon all the peoples of the northern kingdoms," declares the LORD.

"Their kings will come and set up their thrones
  in the entrance of the gates of Jerusalem;
they will come against all her surrounding walls
  and against all the towns of Judah.
¹⁶I will pronounce my judgments on my people
  because of their wickedness in forsaking me,
in burning incense to other gods
  and in worshiping what their hands have made.

¹⁷"Get yourself ready! Stand up and say to them whatever I command you. Do not be terrified by them, or I will terrify you before them. ¹⁸Today I have made you a fortified city, an iron pillar and a bronze wall to stand against the whole land—against the kings of Judah, its officials, its priests and the people of the land. ¹⁹They will fight against you but will not overcome you, for I am with you and will rescue you," declares the LORD.

Israel Forsakes God

2

The word of the LORD came to me: ²"Go and proclaim in the hearing of Jerusalem:

a 5 Or *chose*   *b 12* The Hebrew for *watching* sounds like the Hebrew for *almond tree.*

" 'I remember the devotion of your youth,
>   how as a bride you loved me
> and followed me through the desert,
>   through a land not sown.
> ³ Israel was holy to the LORD,
>   the firstfruits of his harvest;
> all who devoured her were held guilty,
>   and disaster overtook them,' "
>   declares the LORD.

⁴ Hear the word of the LORD, O house of Jacob,
>   all you clans of the house of Israel.

⁵ This is what the LORD says:

"What fault did your fathers find in me,
>   that they strayed so far from me?
> They followed worthless idols
>   and became worthless themselves.
> ⁶ They did not ask, 'Where is the LORD,
>   who brought us up out of Egypt
> and led us through the barren wilderness,
>   through a land of deserts and rifts,
> a land of drought and darkness,ᵃ
>   a land where no one travels and no one
>   lives?'
> ⁷ I brought you into a fertile land
>   to eat its fruit and rich produce.
> But you came and defiled my land
>   and made my inheritance detestable.
> ⁸ The priests did not ask,
>   'Where is the LORD?'
> Those who deal with the law did not
>   know me;
>   the leaders rebelled against me.
> The prophets prophesied by Baal,
>   following worthless idols.

⁹ "Therefore I bring charges against you again,"
>   declares the LORD.
>   "And I will bring charges against your
>   children's children.
> ¹⁰ Cross over to the coasts of Kittimᵇ and look,
>   send to Kedarᶜ and observe closely;
>   see if there has ever been anything like this:
> ¹¹ Has a nation ever changed its gods?
>   (Yet they are not gods at all.)

But my people have exchanged theirᵈ Glory
>   for worthless idols.
> ¹² Be appalled at this, O heavens,
>   and shudder with great horror,"
>   declares the LORD.
> ¹³ "My people have committed two sins:
>   They have forsaken me,
>   the spring of living water,
>   and have dug their own cisterns,
>   broken cisterns that cannot hold water.
> ¹⁴ Is Israel a servant, a slave by birth?
>   Why then has he become plunder?
> ¹⁵ Lions have roared;
>   they have growled at him.
> They have laid waste his land;
>   his towns are burned and deserted.
> ¹⁶ Also, the men of Memphisᵉ and Tahpanhes
>   have shaved the crown of your head.ᶠ
> ¹⁷ Have you not brought this on yourselves
>   by forsaking the LORD your God
>   when he led you in the way?
> ¹⁸ Now why go to Egypt
>   to drink water from the Shihorᵍ?
> And why go to Assyria
>   to drink water from the Riverʰ?
> ¹⁹ Your wickedness will punish you;
>   your backsliding will rebuke you.
> Consider then and realize
>   how evil and bitter it is for you
> when you forsake the LORD your God
>   and have no awe of me,"
>   declares the Lord,
>   the LORD Almighty.

²⁰ "Long ago you broke off your yoke
>   and tore off your bonds;
>   you said, 'I will not serve you!'
> Indeed, on every high hill
>   and under every spreading tree
>   you lay down as a prostitute.
> ²¹ I had planted you like a choice vine
>   of sound and reliable stock.

ᵃ 6 Or *and the shadow of death*   ᵇ 10 That is, Cyprus and western
coastlands   ᶜ 10 The home of Bedouin tribes in the Syro-Arabian
desert   ᵈ 11 Masoretic Text; an ancient Hebrew scribal tradition
my   ᵉ 16 Hebrew *Noph*   ᶠ 16 Or *have cracked your skull*
ᵍ 18 That is, a branch of the Nile   ʰ 18 That is, the Euphrates

How then did you turn against me
　　into a corrupt, wild vine?
²² Although you wash yourself with soda
　　and use an abundance of soap,
　　the stain of your guilt is still before me,"
　　　　　　　declares the Sovereign LORD.
²³ "How can you say, 'I am not defiled;
　　I have not run after the Baals'?
See how you behaved in the valley;
　　consider what you have done.
You are a swift she-camel
　　running here and there,
²⁴ a wild donkey accustomed to the desert,
　　sniffing the wind in her craving—
　　in her heat who can restrain her?
Any males that pursue her need not tire
　　　　themselves;
　　at mating time they will find her.
²⁵ Do not run until your feet are bare
　　and your throat is dry.
But you said, 'It's no use!
　　I love foreign gods,
　　and I must go after them.'

²⁶ "As a thief is disgraced when he is caught,
　　so the house of Israel is disgraced—
they, their kings and their officials,
　　their priests and their prophets.
²⁷ They say to wood, 'You are my father,'
　　and to stone, 'You gave me birth.'
They have turned their backs to me
　　and not their faces;
yet when they are in trouble, they say,
　　'Come and save us!'
²⁸ Where then are the gods you made for
　　　　yourselves?
　　Let them come if they can save you
　　when you are in trouble!
For you have as many gods
　　as you have towns, O Judah.

²⁹ "Why do you bring charges against me?
　　You have all rebelled against me,"
　　　　　　　declares the LORD.
³⁰ "In vain I punished your people;
　　they did not respond to correction.

Your sword has devoured your prophets
　　like a ravening lion.

³¹ "You of this generation, consider the word
　of the LORD:

"Have I been a desert to Israel
　　or a land of great darkness?
Why do my people say, 'We are free to roam;
　　we will come to you no more'?
³² Does a maiden forget her jewelry,
　　a bride her wedding ornaments?
Yet my people have forgotten me,
　　days without number.
³³ How skilled you are at pursuing love!
　　Even the worst of women can learn from
　　　　your ways.
³⁴ On your clothes men find
　　the lifeblood of the innocent poor,
　　though you did not catch them breaking
　　　　in.
Yet in spite of all this
³⁵ 　you say, 'I am innocent;
　　he is not angry with me.'
But I will pass judgment on you
　　because you say, 'I have not sinned.'
³⁶ Why do you go about so much,
　　changing your ways?
You will be disappointed by Egypt
　　as you were by Assyria.
³⁷ You will also leave that place
　　with your hands on your head,
for the LORD has rejected those you trust;
　　you will not be helped by them.

3 　"If a man divorces his wife
　　and she leaves him and marries another
　　　　man,
should he return to her again?
　　Would not the land be completely defiled?
But you have lived as a prostitute with many
　　　　lovers—
　　would you now return to me?"
　　　　　　　declares the LORD.
² "Look up to the barren heights and see.
　　Is there any place where you have not been
　　　　ravished?

By the roadside you sat waiting for lovers,
  sat like a nomad *a* in the desert.
You have defiled the land
  with your prostitution and wickedness.
³Therefore the showers have been withheld,
  and no spring rains have fallen.
Yet you have the brazen look of a prostitute;
  you refuse to blush with shame.
⁴Have you not just called to me:
  'My Father, my friend from my youth,
⁵will you always be angry?
  Will your wrath continue forever?'
This is how you talk,
  but you do all the evil you can."

Unfaithful Israel

⁶During the reign of King Josiah, the LORD said to me, "Have you seen what faithless Israel has done? She has gone up on every high hill and under every spreading tree and has committed adultery there. ⁷I thought that after she had done all this she would return to me but she did not, and her unfaithful sister Judah saw it. ⁸I gave faithless Israel her certificate of divorce and sent her away because of all her adulteries. Yet I saw that her unfaithful sister Judah had no fear; she also went out and committed adultery. ⁹Because Israel's immorality mattered so little to her, she defiled the land and committed adultery with stone and wood. ¹⁰In spite of all this, her unfaithful sister Judah did not return to me with all her heart, but only in pretense," declares the LORD.

¹¹The LORD said to me, "Faithless Israel is more righteous than unfaithful Judah. ¹²Go, proclaim this message toward the north:

" 'Return, faithless Israel,' declares the
    LORD,
  'I will frown on you no longer,
  for I am merciful,' declares the LORD,
  'I will not be angry forever.
¹³Only acknowledge your guilt—
  you have rebelled against the LORD your
    God,

you have scattered your favors to foreign
    gods
  under every spreading tree,
  and have not obeyed me,' "

                    declares the LORD.

¹⁴"Return, faithless people," declares the LORD, "for I am your husband. I will choose you—one from a town and two from a clan—and bring you to Zion. ¹⁵Then I will give you shepherds after my own heart, who will lead you with knowledge and understanding. ¹⁶In those days, when your numbers have increased greatly in the land," declares the LORD, "men will no longer say, 'The ark of the covenant of the LORD.' It will never enter their minds or be remembered; it will not be missed, nor will another one be made. ¹⁷At that time they will call Jerusalem The Throne of the LORD, and all nations will gather in Jerusalem to honor the name of the LORD. No longer will they follow the stubbornness of their evil hearts. ¹⁸In those days the house of Judah will join the house of Israel, and together they will come from a northern land to the land I gave your forefathers as an inheritance.

¹⁹"I myself said,

" 'How gladly would I treat you like sons
    and give you a desirable land,
    the most beautiful inheritance of any
      nation.'
I thought you would call me 'Father'
    and not turn away from following me.
²⁰But like a woman unfaithful to her husband,
    so you have been unfaithful to me,
      O house of Israel,"

                    declares the LORD.

²¹A cry is heard on the barren heights,
    the weeping and pleading of the people of
      Israel,
  because they have perverted their ways
    and have forgotten the LORD their God.

²²"Return, faithless people;
    I will cure you of backsliding."

a 2 Or an Arab

"Yes, we will come to you,
  for you are the LORD our God.
²³ Surely the ⌐idolatrous⌐ commotion on the
      hills
  and mountains is a deception;
surely in the LORD our God
  is the salvation of Israel.
²⁴ From our youth shameful gods have
      consumed
  the fruits of our fathers' labor—
their flocks and herds,
  their sons and daughters.
²⁵ Let us lie down in our shame,
  and let our disgrace cover us.
We have sinned against the LORD our God,
  both we and our fathers;
from our youth till this day
  we have not obeyed the LORD our God."

4 "If you will return, O Israel,
    return to me,"

                    declares the LORD.
  "If you put your detestable idols out of my
      sight
    and no longer go astray,
² and if in a truthful, just and righteous way
    you swear, 'As surely as the LORD lives,'
  then the nations will be blessed by him
    and in him they will glory."

³ This is what the LORD says to the men of Judah and to Jerusalem:

  "Break up your unplowed ground
    and do not sow among thorns.
⁴ Circumcise yourselves to the LORD,
    circumcise your hearts,
    you men of Judah and people of Jerusalem,
  or my wrath will break out and burn like fire
    because of the evil you have done—
    burn with no one to quench it.

Disaster From the North

⁵ "Announce in Judah and proclaim in
    Jerusalem and say:
  'Sound the trumpet throughout the land!'

Cry aloud and say:
  'Gather together!
  Let us flee to the fortified cities!'
⁶ Raise the signal to go to Zion!
  Flee for safety without delay!
For I am bringing disaster from the north,
  even terrible destruction."

⁷ A lion has come out of his lair;
  a destroyer of nations has set out.
He has left his place
  to lay waste your land.
Your towns will lie in ruins
  without inhabitant.
⁸ So put on sackcloth,
  lament and wail,
for the fierce anger of the LORD
  has not turned away from us.

⁹ "In that day," declares the LORD,
  "the king and the officials will lose heart,
the priests will be horrified,
  and the prophets will be appalled."

¹⁰ Then I said, "Ah, Sovereign LORD, how completely you have deceived this people and Jerusalem by saying, 'You will have peace,' when the sword is at our throats."

¹¹ At that time this people and Jerusalem will be told, "A scorching wind from the barren heights in the desert blows toward my people, but not to winnow or cleanse; ¹² a wind too strong for that comes from me.ᵃ Now I pronounce my judgments against them."

¹³ Look! He advances like the clouds,
  his chariots come like a whirlwind,
his horses are swifter than eagles.
  Woe to us! We are ruined!
¹⁴ O Jerusalem, wash the evil from your heart
    and be saved.
  How long will you harbor wicked
    thoughts?
¹⁵ A voice is announcing from Dan,
  proclaiming disaster from the hills of
    Ephraim.

ᵃ 12 Or comes at my command

16 "Tell this to the nations,
        proclaim it to Jerusalem:
'A besieging army is coming from a distant
        land,
    raising a war cry against the cities of Judah.
17 They surround her like men guarding a field,
    because she has rebelled against me,'"
                                        declares the LORD.

18 "Your own conduct and actions
    have brought this upon you.
This is your punishment.
    How bitter it is!
    How it pierces to the heart!"

19 Oh, my anguish, my anguish!
    I writhe in pain.
Oh, the agony of my heart!
    My heart pounds within me,
    I cannot keep silent.
For I have heard the sound of the trumpet;
    I have heard the battle cry.
20 Disaster follows disaster;
    the whole land lies in ruins.
In an instant my tents are destroyed,
    my shelter in a moment.
21 How long must I see the battle standard
    and hear the sound of the trumpet?

22 "My people are fools;
    they do not know me.
They are senseless children;
    they have no understanding.
They are skilled in doing evil;
    they know not how to do good."

23 I looked at the earth,
    and it was formless and empty;
and at the heavens,
    and their light was gone.
24 I looked at the mountains,
    and they were quaking;
    all the hills were swaying.
25 I looked, and there were no people;
    every bird in the sky had flown away.
26 I looked, and the fruitful land was a desert;
    all its towns lay in ruins
    before the LORD, before his fierce anger.

27 This is what the LORD says:

"The whole land will be ruined,
    though I will not destroy it completely.
28 Therefore the earth will mourn
    and the heavens above grow dark,
because I have spoken and will not relent,
    I have decided and will not turn back."

29 At the sound of horsemen and archers
    every town takes to flight.
Some go into the thickets;
    some climb up among the rocks.
All the towns are deserted;
    no one lives in them.

30 What are you doing, O devastated one?
    Why dress yourself in scarlet
    and put on jewels of gold?
Why shade your eyes with paint?
    You adorn yourself in vain.
Your lovers despise you;
    they seek your life.

31 I hear a cry as of a woman in labor,
    a groan as of one bearing her first child—
the cry of the Daughter of Zion gasping for
        breath,
    stretching out her hands and saying,
"Alas! I am fainting;
    my life is given over to murderers."

Not One Is Upright

5 "Go up and down the streets of Jerusalem,
    look around and consider,
        search through her squares.
If you can find but one person
        who deals honestly and seeks the truth,
        I will forgive this city.
2 Although they say, 'As surely as the LORD
            lives,'
    still they are swearing falsely."

3 O LORD, do not your eyes look for truth?
    You struck them, but they felt no pain;
    you crushed them, but they refused
        correction.

They made their faces harder than stone
   and refused to repent.
⁴I thought, "These are only the poor;
   they are foolish,
for they do not know the way of the LORD,
   the requirements of their God.
⁵So I will go to the leaders
   and speak to them;
surely they know the way of the LORD,
   the requirements of their God."
But with one accord they too had broken off
   the yoke
   and torn off the bonds.
⁶Therefore a lion from the forest will attack
   them,
   a wolf from the desert will ravage them,
a leopard will lie in wait near their towns
   to tear to pieces any who venture out,
for their rebellion is great
   and their backslidings many.

⁷"Why should I forgive you?
   Your children have forsaken me
   and sworn by gods that are not gods.
I supplied all their needs,
   yet they committed adultery
   and thronged to the houses of prostitutes.
⁸They are well-fed, lusty stallions,
   each neighing for another man's wife.
⁹Should I not punish them for this?"
   declares the LORD.
"Should I not avenge myself
   on such a nation as this?

¹⁰"Go through her vineyards and ravage them,
   but do not destroy them completely.
Strip off her branches,
   for these people do not belong to the
      LORD.
¹¹The house of Israel and the house of Judah
   have been utterly unfaithful to me,"
                           declares the LORD.

¹²They have lied about the LORD;
   they said, "He will do nothing!
No harm will come to us;
   we will never see sword or famine.
¹³The prophets are but wind
   and the word is not in them;
   so let what they say be done to them."

¹⁴Therefore this is what the LORD God Almighty says:

"Because the people have spoken these words,
   I will make my words in your mouth a fire
   and these people the wood it consumes.
¹⁵O house of Israel," declares the LORD,
   "I am bringing a distant nation against
      you—
an ancient and enduring nation,
   a people whose language you do not know,
   whose speech you do not understand.
¹⁶Their quivers are like an open grave;
   all of them are mighty warriors.
¹⁷They will devour your harvests and food,
   devour your sons and daughters;
they will devour your flocks and herds,
   devour your vines and fig trees.
With the sword they will destroy
   the fortified cities in which you trust.

¹⁸"Yet even in those days," declares the LORD, "I will not destroy you completely. ¹⁹And when the people ask, 'Why has the LORD our God done all this to us?' you will tell them, 'As you have forsaken me and served foreign gods in your own land, so now you will serve foreigners in a land not your own.'

²⁰"Announce this to the house of Jacob
   and proclaim it in Judah:
²¹Hear this, you foolish and senseless people,
   who have eyes but do not see,
   who have ears but do not hear:
²²Should you not fear me?" declares the LORD.
   "Should you not tremble in my presence?
I made the sand a boundary for the sea,
   an everlasting barrier it cannot cross.
The waves may roll, but they cannot prevail;
   they may roar, but they cannot cross it.
²³But these people have stubborn and
      rebellious hearts;
   they have turned aside and gone away.

²⁴ They do not say to themselves,
  'Let us fear the LORD our God,
who gives autumn and spring rains in season,
  who assures us of the regular weeks of
    harvest.'
²⁵ Your wrongdoings have kept these away;
  your sins have deprived you of good.

²⁶ "Among my people are wicked men
  who lie in wait like men who snare birds
  and like those who set traps to catch men.
²⁷ Like cages full of birds,
  their houses are full of deceit;
they have become rich and powerful
²⁸ and have grown fat and sleek.
  Their evil deeds have no limit;
    they do not plead the case of the fatherless
      to win it,
    they do not defend the rights of the poor.
²⁹ Should I not punish them for this?"
    declares the LORD.
  "Should I not avenge myself
    on such a nation as this?

³⁰ "A horrible and shocking thing
  has happened in the land:
³¹ The prophets prophesy lies,
  the priests rule by their own authority,
and my people love it this way.
  But what will you do in the end?

Jerusalem Under Siege

6 "Flee for safety, people of Benjamin!
  Flee from Jerusalem!
Sound the trumpet in Tekoa!
  Raise the signal over Beth Hakkerem!
For disaster looms out of the north,
  even terrible destruction.
² I will destroy the Daughter of Zion,
  so beautiful and delicate.
³ Shepherds with their flocks will come against
    her;
  they will pitch their tents around her,
  each tending his own portion."

⁴ "Prepare for battle against her!
  Arise, let us attack at noon!

But, alas, the daylight is fading,
  and the shadows of evening grow long.
⁵ So arise, let us attack at night
  and destroy her fortresses!"

⁶ This is what the LORD Almighty says:

"Cut down the trees
  and build siege ramps against Jerusalem.
This city must be punished;
  it is filled with oppression.
⁷ As a well pours out its water,
  so she pours out her wickedness.
Violence and destruction resound in her;
  her sickness and wounds are ever
    before me.
⁸ Take warning, O Jerusalem,
  or I will turn away from you
and make your land desolate
  so no one can live in it."

⁹ This is what the LORD Almighty says:

"Let them glean the remnant of Israel
  as thoroughly as a vine;
pass your hand over the branches again,
  like one gathering grapes."

¹⁰ To whom can I speak and give warning?
  Who will listen to me?
Their ears are closed ᵃ
  so they cannot hear.
The word of the LORD is offensive to them;
  they find no pleasure in it.
¹¹ But I am full of the wrath of the LORD,
  and I cannot hold it in.

"Pour it out on the children in the street
  and on the young men gathered together;
both husband and wife will be caught in it,
  and the old, those weighed down with
    years.
¹² Their houses will be turned over to others,
  together with their fields and their wives,
when I stretch out my hand
  against those who live in the land,"
      declares the LORD.

ᵃ 10 Hebrew uncircumcised

¹³ "From the least to the greatest,
all are greedy for gain;
prophets and priests alike,
all practice deceit.
¹⁴ They dress the wound of my people
as though it were not serious.
'Peace, peace,' they say,
when there is no peace.
¹⁵ Are they ashamed of their loathsome conduct?
No, they have no shame at all;
they do not even know how to blush.
So they will fall among the fallen;
they will be brought down when I punish
them,"
says the LORD.

¹⁶ This is what the LORD says:

"Stand at the crossroads and look;
ask for the ancient paths,
ask where the good way is, and walk in it,
and you will find rest for your souls.
But you said, 'We will not walk in it.'

TALKING POINTS

Knowing God's Will

We're called to ask for guidance
and yield to God's will.

JEREMIAH 6:16

For more on knowing God's will, go to Jeremiah 29:11.

¹⁷ I appointed watchmen over you and said,
'Listen to the sound of the trumpet!'
But you said, 'We will not listen.'
¹⁸ Therefore hear, O nations;
observe, O witnesses,
what will happen to them.
¹⁹ Hear, O earth:
I am bringing disaster on this people,
the fruit of their schemes,

because they have not listened to my words
and have rejected my law.
²⁰ What do I care about incense from Sheba
or sweet calamus from a distant land?
Your burnt offerings are not acceptable;
your sacrifices do not please me."

²¹ Therefore this is what the LORD says:

"I will put obstacles before this people.
Fathers and sons alike will stumble over
them;
neighbors and friends will perish."

²² This is what the LORD says:

"Look, an army is coming
from the land of the north;
a great nation is being stirred up
from the ends of the earth.
²³ They are armed with bow and spear;
they are cruel and show no mercy.
They sound like the roaring sea
as they ride on their horses;
they come like men in battle formation
to attack you, O Daughter of Zion."

²⁴ We have heard reports about them,
and our hands hang limp.
Anguish has gripped us,
pain like that of a woman in labor.
²⁵ Do not go out to the fields
or walk on the roads,
for the enemy has a sword,
and there is terror on every side.
²⁶ O my people, put on sackcloth
and roll in ashes;
mourn with bitter wailing
as for an only son,
for suddenly the destroyer
will come upon us.

²⁷ "I have made you a tester of metals
and my people the ore,
that you may observe
and test their ways.
²⁸ They are all hardened rebels,
going about to slander.

They are bronze and iron;
> they all act corruptly.
29 The bellows blow fiercely
> to burn away the lead with fire,
but the refining goes on in vain;
> the wicked are not purged out.
30 They are called rejected silver,
> because the Lord has rejected them."

False Religion Worthless

7 This is the word that came to Jeremiah from the Lord: 2 "Stand at the gate of the Lord's house and there proclaim this message:

" 'Hear the word of the Lord, all you people of Judah who come through these gates to worship the Lord. 3 This is what the Lord Almighty, the God of Israel, says: Reform your ways and your actions, and I will let you live in this place. 4 Do not trust in deceptive words and say, "This is the temple of the Lord, the temple of the Lord, the temple of the Lord!" 5 If you really change your ways and your actions and deal with each other justly, 6 if you do not oppress the alien, the fatherless or the widow and do not shed innocent blood in this place, and if you do not follow other gods to your own harm, 7 then I will let you live in this place, in the land I gave your forefathers for ever and ever. 8 But look, you are trusting in deceptive words that are worthless.

9 " 'Will you steal and murder, commit adultery and perjury,[a] burn incense to Baal and follow other gods you have not known, 10 and then come and stand before me in this house, which bears my Name, and say, "We are safe"— safe to do all these detestable things? 11 Has this house, which bears my Name, become a den of robbers to you? But I have been watching! declares the Lord.

12 " 'Go now to the place in Shiloh where I first made a dwelling for my Name, and see what I did to it because of the wickedness of my people Israel. 13 While you were doing all these things, declares the Lord, I spoke to you again and again, but you did not listen; I called you, but you did not answer. 14 Therefore, what I did to Shiloh I will now do to the house that bears my Name, the temple you trust in, the place I gave to you and your fathers. 15 I will thrust you from my presence, just as I did all your brothers, the people of Ephraim.'

16 "So do not pray for this people nor offer any plea or petition for them; do not plead with me, for I will not listen to you. 17 Do you not see what they are doing in the towns of Judah and in the streets of Jerusalem? 18 The children gather wood, the fathers light the fire, and the women knead the dough and make cakes of bread for the Queen of Heaven. They pour out drink offerings to other gods to provoke me to anger. 19 But am I the one they are provoking? declares the Lord. Are they not rather harming themselves, to their own shame?

20 " 'Therefore this is what the Sovereign Lord says: My anger and my wrath will be poured out on this place, on man and beast, on the trees of the field and on the fruit of the ground, and it will burn and not be quenched.

21 " 'This is what the Lord Almighty, the God of Israel, says: Go ahead, add your burnt offerings to your other sacrifices and eat the meat yourselves! 22 For when I brought your forefathers out of Egypt and spoke to them, I did not just give them commands about burnt offerings and sacrifices, 23 but I gave them this command: Obey me, and I will be your God and you will be my people. Walk in all the ways I command you, that it may go well with you. 24 But they did not listen or pay attention; instead, they followed the stubborn inclinations of their evil hearts. They went backward and not forward. 25 From the time your forefathers left Egypt until now, day after day, again and again I sent you my servants the prophets. 26 But they did not listen to me or pay attention. They were stiff-necked and did more evil than their forefathers.'

27 "When you tell them all this, they will not listen to you; when you call to them, they will not answer. 28 Therefore say to them, 'This is the nation that has not obeyed the Lord its God or

---

a 9 Or and swear by false gods

responded to correction. Truth has perished; it has vanished from their lips. ²⁹Cut off your hair and throw it away; take up a lament on the barren heights, for the LORD has rejected and abandoned this generation that is under his wrath.

The Valley of Slaughter

³⁰" 'The people of Judah have done evil in my eyes, declares the LORD. They have set up their detestable idols in the house that bears my Name and have defiled it. ³¹They have built the high places of Topheth in the Valley of Ben Hinnom to burn their sons and daughters in the fire—something I did not command, nor did it enter my mind. ³²So beware, the days are coming, declares the LORD, when people will no longer call it Topheth or the Valley of Ben Hinnom, but the Valley of Slaughter, for they will bury the dead in Topheth until there is no more room. ³³Then the carcasses of this people will become food for the birds of the air and the beasts of the earth, and there will be no one to frighten them away. ³⁴I will bring an end to the sounds of joy and gladness and to the voices of bride and bridegroom in the towns of Judah and the streets of Jerusalem, for the land will become desolate.

8 " 'At that time, declares the LORD, the bones of the kings and officials of Judah, the bones of the priests and prophets, and the bones of the people of Jerusalem will be removed from their graves. ²They will be exposed to the sun and the moon and all the stars of the heavens, which they have loved and served and which they have followed and consulted and worshiped. They will not be gathered up or buried, but will be like refuse lying on the ground. ³Wherever I banish them, all the survivors of this evil nation will prefer death to life, declares the LORD Almighty.'

Sin and Punishment

⁴"Say to them, 'This is what the LORD says:

" 'When men fall down, do they not get up?
  When a man turns away, does he not
    return?

⁵Why then have these people turned away?
  Why does Jerusalem always turn away?
They cling to deceit;
  they refuse to return.
⁶I have listened attentively,
  but they do not say what is right.
No one repents of his wickedness,
  saying, "What have I done?"
Each pursues his own course
  like a horse charging into battle.
⁷Even the stork in the sky
  knows her appointed seasons,
and the dove, the swift and the thrush
  observe the time of their migration.
But my people do not know
  the requirements of the LORD.

⁸" 'How can you say, "We are wise,
  for we have the law of the LORD,"
when actually the lying pen of the scribes
  has handled it falsely?
⁹The wise will be put to shame;
  they will be dismayed and trapped.
Since they have rejected the word of the
    LORD,
  what kind of wisdom do they have?
¹⁰Therefore I will give their wives to other
    men
  and their fields to new owners.
From the least to the greatest,
  all are greedy for gain;
prophets and priests alike,
  all practice deceit.
¹¹They dress the wound of my people
  as though it were not serious.
"Peace, peace," they say,
  when there is no peace.
¹²Are they ashamed of their loathsome
    conduct?
  No, they have no shame at all;
  they do not even know how to blush.
So they will fall among the fallen;
  they will be brought down when they are
    punished,
    says the LORD.

13 " 'I will take away their harvest,
  declares the LORD.
 There will be no grapes on the vine.
 There will be no figs on the tree,
  and their leaves will wither.
 What I have given them
  will be taken from them.ᵃ' "

14 "Why are we sitting here?
  Gather together!
 Let us flee to the fortified cities
  and perish there!
 For the LORD our God has doomed us to
   perish
  and given us poisoned water to drink,
 because we have sinned against him.
15 We hoped for peace
  but no good has come,
 for a time of healing
  but there was only terror.
16 The snorting of the enemy's horses
  is heard from Dan;
 at the neighing of their stallions
  the whole land trembles.
 They have come to devour
  the land and everything in it,
  the city and all who live there."

17 "See, I will send venomous snakes among
   you,
  vipers that cannot be charmed,
  and they will bite you,"
  declares the LORD.

18 O my Comforterᵇ in sorrow,
  my heart is faint within me.
19 Listen to the cry of my people
  from a land far away:
 "Is the LORD not in Zion?
  Is her King no longer there?"

 "Why have they provoked me to anger with
   their images,
  with their worthless foreign idols?"

20 "The harvest is past,
  the summer has ended,
  and we are not saved."

21 Since my people are crushed, I am crushed;
  I mourn, and horror grips me.
22 Is there no balm in Gilead?
  Is there no physician there?
 Why then is there no healing
  for the wound of my people?

9 ¹ Oh, that my head were a spring of water
  and my eyes a fountain of tears!
 I would weep day and night
  for the slain of my people.
² Oh, that I had in the desert
  a lodging place for travelers,
 so that I might leave my people
  and go away from them;
 for they are all adulterers,
  a crowd of unfaithful people.

³ "They make ready their tongue
  like a bow, to shoot lies;
 it is not by truth
  that they triumphᶜ in the land.
 They go from one sin to another;
  they do not acknowledge me,"
  declares the LORD.
⁴ "Beware of your friends;
  do not trust your brothers.
 For every brother is a deceiver,ᵈ
  and every friend a slanderer.
⁵ Friend deceives friend,
  and no one speaks the truth.
 They have taught their tongues to lie;
  they weary themselves with sinning.
⁶ Youᵉ live in the midst of deception;
  in their deceit they refuse to acknowledge
   me,"
  declares the LORD.

⁷ Therefore this is what the LORD Almighty
says:

 "See, I will refine and test them,
  for what else can I do
  because of the sin of my people?

ᵃ 13 The meaning of the Hebrew for this sentence is uncertain.
ᵇ 18 The meaning of the Hebrew for this word is uncertain.
ᶜ 3 Or lies; / they are not valiant for truth   ᵈ 4 Or a deceiving Jacob
ᵉ 6 That is, Jeremiah (the Hebrew is singular)

8 Their tongue is a deadly arrow;
  it speaks with deceit.
With his mouth each speaks cordially to his
    neighbor,
  but in his heart he sets a trap for him.
9 Should I not punish them for this?"
  declares the LORD.
"Should I not avenge myself
  on such a nation as this?"

10 I will weep and wail for the mountains
  and take up a lament concerning the desert
    pastures.
They are desolate and untraveled,
  and the lowing of cattle is not heard.
The birds of the air have fled
  and the animals are gone.

11 "I will make Jerusalem a heap of ruins,
  a haunt of jackals;
and I will lay waste the towns of Judah
  so no one can live there."

12 What man is wise enough to understand this? Who has been instructed by the LORD and can explain it? Why has the land been ruined and laid waste like a desert that no one can cross? 13 The LORD said, "It is because they have forsaken my law, which I set before them; they have not obeyed me or followed my law. 14 Instead, they have followed the stubbornness of their hearts; they have followed the Baals, as their fathers taught them." 15 Therefore, this is what the LORD Almighty, the God of Israel, says: "See, I will make this people eat bitter food and drink poisoned water. 16 I will scatter them among nations that neither they nor their fathers have known, and I will pursue them with the sword until I have destroyed them."

17 This is what the LORD Almighty says:

"Consider now! Call for the wailing women
    to come;
  send for the most skillful of them.
18 Let them come quickly
  and wail over us

till our eyes overflow with tears
  and water streams from our eyelids.
19 The sound of wailing is heard from Zion:
  'How ruined we are!
  How great is our shame!
We must leave our land
  because our houses are in ruins.' "

20 Now, O women, hear the word of the LORD;
  open your ears to the words of his mouth.
Teach your daughters how to wail;
  teach one another a lament.
21 Death has climbed in through our windows
  and has entered our fortresses;
it has cut off the children from the streets
  and the young men from the public
    squares.

22 Say, "This is what the LORD declares:

" 'The dead bodies of men will lie
  like refuse on the open field,
like cut grain behind the reaper,
  with no one to gather them.' "

23 This is what the LORD says:

"Let not the wise man boast of his wisdom
  or the strong man boast of his strength
  or the rich man boast of his riches,
24 but let him who boasts boast about this:
  that he understands and knows me,
that I am the LORD, who exercises kindness,
  justice and righteousness on earth,
  for in these I delight,"

                    declares the LORD.

TALKING POINTS

Values
Boast only in the Lord.
JEREMIAH 9:23–24

For more on values, go to Matthew 22:36–40.

25 "The days are coming," declares the LORD, "when I will punish all who are circumcised only in the flesh— 26 Egypt, Judah, Edom, Ammon, Moab and all who live in the desert in distant places.[a] For all these nations are really uncircumcised, and even the whole house of Israel is uncircumcised in heart."

God and Idols

10:12–16pp — Jer 51:15–19

10 Hear what the LORD says to you, O house of Israel. 2 This is what the LORD says:

"Do not learn the ways of the nations
  or be terrified by signs in the sky,
  though the nations are terrified by them.
3 For the customs of the peoples are worthless;
  they cut a tree out of the forest,
  and a craftsman shapes it with his chisel.
4 They adorn it with silver and gold;
  they fasten it with hammer and nails
  so it will not totter.
5 Like a scarecrow in a melon patch,
  their idols cannot speak;
they must be carried
  because they cannot walk.
Do not fear them;
  they can do no harm
  nor can they do any good."

6 No one is like you, O LORD;
  you are great,
  and your name is mighty in power.
7 Who should not revere you,
  O King of the nations?
  This is your due.
Among all the wise men of the nations
  and in all their kingdoms,
  there is no one like you.
8 They are all senseless and foolish;
  they are taught by worthless wooden idols.
9 Hammered silver is brought from Tarshish
  and gold from Uphaz.
What the craftsman and goldsmith have made
  is then dressed in blue and purple—
  all made by skilled workers.

10 But the LORD is the true God;
  he is the living God, the eternal King.
When he is angry, the earth trembles;
  the nations cannot endure his wrath.

11 "Tell them this: 'These gods, who did not make the heavens and the earth, will perish from the earth and from under the heavens.'"[b]

12 But God made the earth by his power;
  he founded the world by his wisdom
  and stretched out the heavens by his
    understanding.
13 When he thunders, the waters in the heavens
    roar;
  he makes clouds rise from the ends of the
    earth.
He sends lightning with the rain
  and brings out the wind from his
    storehouses.

14 Everyone is senseless and without knowledge;
  every goldsmith is shamed by his idols.
His images are a fraud;
  they have no breath in them.
15 They are worthless, the objects of mockery;
  when their judgment comes, they will
    perish.
16 He who is the Portion of Jacob is not like
    these,
  for he is the Maker of all things,
  including Israel, the tribe of his inheritance—
    the LORD Almighty is his name.

Coming Destruction

17 Gather up your belongings to leave the land,
  you who live under siege.
18 For this is what the LORD says:
  "At this time I will hurl out
    those who live in this land;
  I will bring distress on them
    so that they may be captured."

19 Woe to me because of my injury!
  My wound is incurable!

---

[a] 26 Or *desert and who clip the hair by their foreheads*
[b] 11 The text of this verse is in Aramaic.

Yet I said to myself,
"This is my sickness, and I must endure it."
20 My tent is destroyed;
all its ropes are snapped.
My sons are gone from me and are no more;
no one is left now to pitch my tent
or to set up my shelter.
21 The shepherds are senseless
and do not inquire of the LORD;
so they do not prosper
and all their flock is scattered.
22 Listen! The report is coming—
a great commotion from the land of the north!
It will make the towns of Judah desolate,
a haunt of jackals.

Jeremiah's Prayer

23 I know, O LORD, that a man's life is not his own;
it is not for man to direct his steps.
24 Correct me, LORD, but only with justice—
not in your anger,
lest you reduce me to nothing.
25 Pour out your wrath on the nations
that do not acknowledge you,
on the peoples who do not call on your name.
For they have devoured Jacob;
they have devoured him completely
and destroyed his homeland.

The Covenant Is Broken

11 This is the word that came to Jeremiah from the LORD: 2 "Listen to the terms of this covenant and tell them to the people of Judah and to those who live in Jerusalem. 3 Tell them that this is what the LORD, the God of Israel, says: 'Cursed is the man who does not obey the terms of this covenant— 4 the terms I commanded your forefathers when I brought them out of Egypt, out of the iron-smelting furnace.' I said, 'Obey me and do everything I command you, and you will be my people, and I will be your God. 5 Then I will fulfill the oath I swore to your forefathers, to give them a land flowing with milk and honey'—the land you possess today."

I answered, "Amen, LORD."

6 The LORD said to me, "Proclaim all these words in the towns of Judah and in the streets of Jerusalem: 'Listen to the terms of this covenant and follow them. 7 From the time I brought your forefathers up from Egypt until today, I warned them again and again, saying, "Obey me." 8 But they did not listen or pay attention; instead, they followed the stubbornness of their evil hearts. So I brought on them all the curses of the covenant I had commanded them to follow but that they did not keep.'"

9 Then the LORD said to me, "There is a conspiracy among the people of Judah and those who live in Jerusalem. 10 They have returned to the sins of their forefathers, who refused to listen to my words. They have followed other gods to serve them. Both the house of Israel and the house of Judah have broken the covenant I made with their forefathers. 11 Therefore this is what the LORD says: 'I will bring on them a disaster they cannot escape. Although they cry out to me, I will not listen to them. 12 The towns of Judah and the people of Jerusalem will go and cry out to the gods to whom they burn incense, but they will not help them at all when disaster strikes. 13 You have as many gods as you have towns, O Judah; and the altars you have set up to burn incense to that shameful god Baal are as many as the streets of Jerusalem.'

14 "Do not pray for this people nor offer any plea or petition for them, because I will not listen when they call to me in the time of their distress.

15 "What is my beloved doing in my temple
as she works out her evil schemes with many?
Can consecrated meat avert ˌyour punishment˳?
When you engage in your wickedness,
then you rejoice.ᵃ"

ᵃ 15 Or Could consecrated meat avert your punishment? / Then you would rejoice

¹⁶The LORD called you a thriving olive tree
    with fruit beautiful in form.
But with the roar of a mighty storm
    he will set it on fire,
    and its branches will be broken.

¹⁷The LORD Almighty, who planted you, has decreed disaster for you, because the house of Israel and the house of Judah have done evil and provoked me to anger by burning incense to Baal.

Plot Against Jeremiah

¹⁸Because the LORD revealed their plot to me, I knew it, for at that time he showed me what they were doing. ¹⁹I had been like a gentle lamb led to the slaughter; I did not realize that they had plotted against me, saying,

"Let us destroy the tree and its fruit;
    let us cut him off from the land of the
        living,
    that his name be remembered no more."
²⁰But, O LORD Almighty, you who judge
    righteously
    and test the heart and mind,
let me see your vengeance upon them,
    for to you I have committed my cause.

²¹"Therefore this is what the LORD says about the men of Anathoth who are seeking your life and saying, 'Do not prophesy in the name of the LORD or you will die by our hands'— ²²therefore this is what the LORD Almighty says: 'I will punish them. Their young men will die by the sword, their sons and daughters by famine. ²³Not even a remnant will be left to them, because I will bring disaster on the men of Anathoth in the year of their punishment.'"

Jeremiah's Complaint

12 You are always righteous, O LORD,
    when I bring a case before you.
Yet I would speak with you about your
      justice:
Why does the way of the wicked prosper?
Why do all the faithless live at ease?

²You have planted them, and they have taken
    root;
    they grow and bear fruit.
You are always on their lips
    but far from their hearts.
³Yet you know me, O LORD;
    you see me and test my thoughts about
      you.
Drag them off like sheep to be butchered!
    Set them apart for the day of slaughter!
⁴How long will the land lie parched[a]
    and the grass in every field be withered?
Because those who live in it are wicked,
    the animals and birds have perished.
Moreover, the people are saying,
    "He will not see what happens to us."

God's Answer

⁵"If you have raced with men on foot
    and they have worn you out,
    how can you compete with horses?
If you stumble in safe country,[b]
    how will you manage in the thickets by[c]
      the Jordan?
⁶Your brothers, your own family—
    even they have betrayed you;
    they have raised a loud cry against you.
Do not trust them,
    though they speak well of you.

⁷"I will forsake my house,
    abandon my inheritance;
I will give the one I love
    into the hands of her enemies.
⁸My inheritance has become to me
    like a lion in the forest.
She roars at me;
    therefore I hate her.
⁹Has not my inheritance become to me
    like a speckled bird of prey
    that other birds of prey surround and
      attack?
Go and gather all the wild beasts;
    bring them to devour.

---

[a] 4 Or *land mourn*   [b] 5 Or *If you put your trust in a land of safety*
[c] 5 Or *the flooding of*

¹⁰Many shepherds will ruin my vineyard
  and trample down my field;
they will turn my pleasant field
  into a desolate wasteland.
¹¹It will be made a wasteland,
  parched and desolate before me;
the whole land will be laid waste
  because there is no one who cares.
¹²Over all the barren heights in the desert
  destroyers will swarm,
for the sword of the LORD will devour
  from one end of the land to the other;
  no one will be safe.
¹³They will sow wheat but reap thorns;
  they will wear themselves out but gain
      nothing.
So bear the shame of your harvest
  because of the LORD's fierce anger."

¹⁴This is what the LORD says: "As for all my wicked neighbors who seize the inheritance I gave my people Israel, I will uproot them from their lands and I will uproot the house of Judah from among them. ¹⁵But after I uproot them, I will again have compassion and will bring each of them back to his own inheritance and his own country. ¹⁶And if they learn well the ways of my people and swear by my name, saying, 'As surely as the LORD lives'—even as they once taught my people to swear by Baal—then they will be established among my people. ¹⁷But if any nation does not listen, I will completely uproot and destroy it," declares the LORD.

A Linen Belt

13 This is what the LORD said to me: "Go and buy a linen belt and put it around your waist, but do not let it touch water." ²So I bought a belt, as the LORD directed, and put it around my waist.

³Then the word of the LORD came to me a second time: ⁴"Take the belt you bought and are wearing around your waist, and go now to Perath ᵃ and hide it there in a crevice in the rocks." ⁵So I went and hid it at Perath, as the LORD told me.

⁶Many days later the LORD said to me, "Go now to Perath and get the belt I told you to hide there." ⁷So I went to Perath and dug up the belt and took it from the place where I had hidden it, but now it was ruined and completely useless.

⁸Then the word of the LORD came to me: ⁹"This is what the LORD says: 'In the same way I will ruin the pride of Judah and the great pride of Jerusalem. ¹⁰These wicked people, who refuse to listen to my words, who follow the stubbornness of their hearts and go after other gods to serve and worship them, will be like this belt—completely useless! ¹¹For as a belt is bound around a man's waist, so I bound the whole house of Israel and the whole house of Judah to me,' declares the LORD, 'to be my people for my renown and praise and honor. But they have not listened.'

Wineskins

¹²"Say to them: 'This is what the LORD, the God of Israel, says: Every wineskin should be filled with wine.' And if they say to you, 'Don't we know that every wineskin should be filled with wine?' ¹³then tell them, 'This is what the LORD says: I am going to fill with drunkenness all who live in this land, including the kings who sit on David's throne, the priests, the prophets and all those living in Jerusalem. ¹⁴I will smash them one against the other, fathers and sons alike, declares the LORD. I will allow no pity or mercy or compassion to keep me from destroying them.' "

Threat of Captivity

¹⁵Hear and pay attention,
  do not be arrogant,
  for the LORD has spoken.
¹⁶Give glory to the LORD your God
  before he brings the darkness,
before your feet stumble
  on the darkening hills.
You hope for light,
  but he will turn it to thick darkness
  and change it to deep gloom.

ᵃ 4 Or possibly *the Euphrates*; also in verses 5-7

¹⁷ But if you do not listen,
  I will weep in secret
  because of your pride;
my eyes will weep bitterly,
  overflowing with tears,
  because the LORD's flock will be taken
    captive.

¹⁸ Say to the king and to the queen mother,
  "Come down from your thrones,
for your glorious crowns
  will fall from your heads."
¹⁹ The cities in the Negev will be shut up,
  and there will be no one to open them.
All Judah will be carried into exile,
  carried completely away.

²⁰ Lift up your eyes and see
  those who are coming from the north.
Where is the flock that was entrusted to you,
  the sheep of which you boasted?
²¹ What will you say when ⌊the LORD⌋ sets over
    you
  those you cultivated as your special allies?
Will not pain grip you
  like that of a woman in labor?
²² And if you ask yourself,
  "Why has this happened to me?"—
it is because of your many sins
  that your skirts have been torn off
  and your body mistreated.
²³ Can the Ethiopian ^a change his skin
  or the leopard its spots?
Neither can you do good
  who are accustomed to doing evil.

²⁴ "I will scatter you like chaff
  driven by the desert wind.
²⁵ This is your lot,
  the portion I have decreed for you,"
        declares the LORD,
"because you have forgotten me
  and trusted in false gods.
²⁶ I will pull up your skirts over your face
  that your shame may be seen—
²⁷ your adulteries and lustful neighings,
  your shameless prostitution!

I have seen your detestable acts
  on the hills and in the fields.
Woe to you, O Jerusalem!
  How long will you be unclean?"

Drought, Famine, Sword

14 This is the word of the LORD to Jeremiah
    concerning the drought:

² "Judah mourns,
  her cities languish;
they wail for the land,
  and a cry goes up from Jerusalem.
³ The nobles send their servants for water;
  they go to the cisterns
  but find no water.
They return with their jars unfilled;
  dismayed and despairing,
  they cover their heads.
⁴ The ground is cracked
  because there is no rain in the land;
the farmers are dismayed
  and cover their heads.
⁵ Even the doe in the field
  deserts her newborn fawn
  because there is no grass.
⁶ Wild donkeys stand on the barren heights
  and pant like jackals;
their eyesight fails
  for lack of pasture."

⁷ Although our sins testify against us,
  O LORD, do something for the sake of your
    name.
For our backsliding is great;
  we have sinned against you.
⁸ O Hope of Israel,
  its Savior in times of distress,
why are you like a stranger in the land,
  like a traveler who stays only a night?
⁹ Why are you like a man taken by surprise,
  like a warrior powerless to save?
You are among us, O LORD,
  and we bear your name;
  do not forsake us!

a 23 Hebrew *Cushite* (probably a person from the upper Nile region)

¹⁰This is what the LORD says about this people:

"They greatly love to wander;
  they do not restrain their feet.
So the LORD does not accept them;
  he will now remember their wickedness
  and punish them for their sins."

¹¹Then the LORD said to me, "Do not pray for the well-being of this people. ¹²Although they fast, I will not listen to their cry; though they offer burnt offerings and grain offerings, I will not accept them. Instead, I will destroy them with the sword, famine and plague."

¹³But I said, "Ah, Sovereign LORD, the prophets keep telling them, 'You will not see the sword or suffer famine. Indeed, I will give you lasting peace in this place.'"

¹⁴Then the LORD said to me, "The prophets are prophesying lies in my name. I have not sent them or appointed them or spoken to them. They are prophesying to you false visions, divinations, idolatries ᵃ and the delusions of their own minds. ¹⁵Therefore, this is what the LORD says about the prophets who are prophesying in my name: I did not send them, yet they are saying, 'No sword or famine will touch this land.' Those same prophets will perish by sword and famine. ¹⁶And the people they are prophesying to will be thrown out into the streets of Jerusalem because of the famine and sword. There will be no one to bury them or their wives, their sons or their daughters. I will pour out on them the calamity they deserve.

¹⁷"Speak this word to them:

"'Let my eyes overflow with tears
  night and day without ceasing;
for my virgin daughter—my people—
  has suffered a grievous wound,
  a crushing blow.
¹⁸If I go into the country,
  I see those slain by the sword;
if I go into the city,
  I see the ravages of famine.
Both prophet and priest
  have gone to a land they know not.'"

¹⁹Have you rejected Judah completely?
  Do you despise Zion?
Why have you afflicted us
  so that we cannot be healed?
We hoped for peace
  but no good has come,
for a time of healing
  but there is only terror.
²⁰O LORD, we acknowledge our wickedness
  and the guilt of our fathers;
  we have indeed sinned against you.
²¹For the sake of your name do not despise us;
  do not dishonor your glorious throne.
Remember your covenant with us
  and do not break it.
²²Do any of the worthless idols of the nations
    bring rain?
  Do the skies themselves send down
    showers?
No, it is you, O LORD our God.
  Therefore our hope is in you,
  for you are the one who does all this.

15 Then the LORD said to me: "Even if Moses and Samuel were to stand before me, my heart would not go out to this people. Send them away from my presence! Let them go! ²And if they ask you, 'Where shall we go?' tell them, 'This is what the LORD says:

"'Those destined for death, to death;
  those for the sword, to the sword;
  those for starvation, to starvation;
  those for captivity, to captivity.'

³"I will send four kinds of destroyers against them," declares the LORD, "the sword to kill and the dogs to drag away and the birds of the air and the beasts of the earth to devour and destroy. ⁴I will make them abhorrent to all the kingdoms of the earth because of what Manasseh son of Hezekiah king of Judah did in Jerusalem.

⁵"Who will have pity on you, O Jerusalem?
  Who will mourn for you?
  Who will stop to ask how you are?

ᵃ 14 Or visions, worthless divinations

⁶ You have rejected me," declares the LORD.
  "You keep on backsliding.
So I will lay hands on you and destroy you;
  I can no longer show compassion.
⁷ I will winnow them with a winnowing fork
  at the city gates of the land.
I will bring bereavement and destruction on
  my people,
  for they have not changed their ways.
⁸ I will make their widows more numerous
  than the sand of the sea.
At midday I will bring a destroyer
  against the mothers of their young men;
suddenly I will bring down on them
  anguish and terror.
⁹ The mother of seven will grow faint
  and breathe her last.
Her sun will set while it is still day;
  she will be disgraced and humiliated.
I will put the survivors to the sword
  before their enemies,"
                              declares the LORD.

¹⁰ Alas, my mother, that you gave me birth,
  a man with whom the whole land strives
    and contends!
I have neither lent nor borrowed,
  yet everyone curses me.

¹¹ The LORD said,

"Surely I will deliver you for a good
    purpose;
  surely I will make your enemies plead
    with you
  in times of disaster and times of distress.

¹² "Can a man break iron —
  iron from the north — or bronze?
¹³ Your wealth and your treasures
  I will give as plunder, without charge,
because of all your sins
  throughout your country.
¹⁴ I will enslave you to your enemies
  in ᵃ a land you do not know,
for my anger will kindle a fire
  that will burn against you."

¹⁵ You understand, O LORD;
  remember me and care for me.
  Avenge me on my persecutors.
You are long-suffering — do not take me
    away;
  think of how I suffer reproach for your
    sake.
¹⁶ When your words came, I ate them;
  they were my joy and my heart's delight,
for I bear your name,
  O LORD God Almighty.
¹⁷ I never sat in the company of revelers,
  never made merry with them;
I sat alone because your hand was on me
  and you had filled me with indignation.
¹⁸ Why is my pain unending
  and my wound grievous and incurable?
Will you be to me like a deceptive brook,
  like a spring that fails?

¹⁹ Therefore this is what the LORD says:

"If you repent, I will restore you
  that you may serve me;
if you utter worthy, not worthless, words,
  you will be my spokesman.
Let this people turn to you,
  but you must not turn to them.
²⁰ I will make you a wall to this people,
  a fortified wall of bronze;
they will fight against you
  but will not overcome you,
for I am with you
  to rescue and save you,"
                              declares the LORD.
²¹ "I will save you from the hands of the wicked
  and redeem you from the grasp of the
    cruel."

Day of Disaster

16 Then the word of the LORD came to me:
²"You must not marry and have sons or
daughters in this place." ³For this is what the LORD

ᵃ 14 Some Hebrew manuscripts, Septuagint and Syriac (see also Jer.
17:4); most Hebrew manuscripts *I will cause your enemies to bring
you / into*

says about the sons and daughters born in this land and about the women who are their mothers and the men who are their fathers: ⁴"They will die of deadly diseases. They will not be mourned or buried but will be like refuse lying on the ground. They will perish by sword and famine, and their dead bodies will become food for the birds of the air and the beasts of the earth."

⁵For this is what the LORD says: "Do not enter a house where there is a funeral meal; do not go to mourn or show sympathy, because I have withdrawn my blessing, my love and my pity from this people," declares the LORD. ⁶"Both high and low will die in this land. They will not be buried or mourned, and no one will cut himself or shave his head for them. ⁷No one will offer food to comfort those who mourn for the dead—not even for a father or a mother—nor will anyone give them a drink to console them.

⁸"And do not enter a house where there is feasting and sit down to eat and drink. ⁹For this is what the LORD Almighty, the God of Israel, says: Before your eyes and in your days I will bring an end to the sounds of joy and gladness and to the voices of bride and bridegroom in this place.

¹⁰"When you tell these people all this and they ask you, 'Why has the LORD decreed such a great disaster against us? What wrong have we done? What sin have we committed against the LORD our God?' ¹¹then say to them, 'It is because your fathers forsook me,' declares the LORD, 'and followed other gods and served and worshiped them. They forsook me and did not keep my law. ¹²But you have behaved more wickedly than your fathers. See how each of you is following the stubbornness of his evil heart instead of obeying me. ¹³So I will throw you out of this land into a land neither you nor your fathers have known, and there you will serve other gods day and night, for I will show you no favor.'

¹⁴"However, the days are coming," declares the LORD, "when men will no longer say, 'As surely as the LORD lives, who brought the Israelites up out of Egypt,' ¹⁵but they will say, 'As surely as the LORD lives, who brought the Israelites up out of the land of the north and out of all the countries where he had banished them.' For I will restore them to the land I gave their forefathers.

¹⁶"But now I will send for many fishermen," declares the LORD, "and they will catch them. After that I will send for many hunters, and they will hunt them down on every mountain and hill and from the crevices of the rocks. ¹⁷My eyes are on all their ways; they are not hidden from me, nor is their sin concealed from my eyes. ¹⁸I will repay them double for their wickedness and their sin, because they have defiled my land with the lifeless forms of their vile images and have filled my inheritance with their detestable idols."

¹⁹O LORD, my strength and my fortress,
  my refuge in time of distress,
to you the nations will come
  from the ends of the earth and say,
"Our fathers possessed nothing but false
    gods,
  worthless idols that did them no good.
²⁰Do men make their own gods?
  Yes, but they are not gods!"

²¹"Therefore I will teach them—
  this time I will teach them
  my power and might.
Then they will know
  that my name is the LORD.

17

"Judah's sin is engraved with an iron
    tool,
  inscribed with a flint point,
on the tablets of their hearts
  and on the horns of their altars.
²Even their children remember
  their altars and Asherah poles ᵃ
beside the spreading trees
  and on the high hills.
³My mountain in the land
  and your ᵇ wealth and all your treasures
I will give away as plunder,
  together with your high places,
  because of sin throughout your country.

ᵃ 2 That is, symbols of the goddess Asherah   ᵇ 2,3 Or hills / ³and the mountains of the land. / Your

⁴Through your own fault you will lose
    the inheritance I gave you.
I will enslave you to your enemies
    in a land you do not know,
for you have kindled my anger,
    and it will burn forever."

⁵This is what the LORD says:

"Cursed is the one who trusts in man,
    who depends on flesh for his strength
    and whose heart turns away from the
        LORD.
⁶He will be like a bush in the wastelands;
    he will not see prosperity when it comes.
He will dwell in the parched places of the
        desert,
    in a salt land where no one lives.

⁷"But blessed is the man who trusts in the
        LORD,
    whose confidence is in him.
⁸He will be like a tree planted by the water
    that sends out its roots by the stream.
It does not fear when heat comes;
    its leaves are always green.
It has no worries in a year of drought
    and never fails to bear fruit."

⁹The heart is deceitful above all things
    and beyond cure.
    Who can understand it?

¹⁰"I the LORD search the heart
    and examine the mind,
to reward a man according to his conduct,
    according to what his deeds deserve."

¹¹Like a partridge that hatches eggs it did not
        lay
    is the man who gains riches by unjust
        means.
When his life is half gone, they will desert
        him,
    and in the end he will prove to be a fool.

¹²A glorious throne, exalted from the
        beginning,
    is the place of our sanctuary.

¹³O LORD, the hope of Israel,
    all who forsake you will be put to shame.
Those who turn away from you will be
        written in the dust
    because they have forsaken the LORD,
    the spring of living water.

¹⁴Heal me, O LORD, and I will be healed;
    save me and I will be saved,
    for you are the one I praise.

PRAYING THE SCRIPTURES

Well-Being

JEREMIAH 17:14

Heal, my grandchild, O Lord, and save her,
for you are the one we praise.

Next prayer in Well-being Prayer Track: Jeremiah 33:6,9

¹⁵They keep saying to me,
    "Where is the word of the LORD?
    Let it now be fulfilled!"
¹⁶I have not run away from being your
        shepherd;
    you know I have not desired the day of
        despair.
    What passes my lips is open before you.
¹⁷Do not be a terror to me;
    you are my refuge in the day of disaster.
¹⁸Let my persecutors be put to shame,
    but keep me from shame;
let them be terrified,
    but keep me from terror.
Bring on them the day of disaster;
    destroy them with double destruction.

Keeping the Sabbath Holy

¹⁹This is what the LORD said to me: "Go and stand at the gate of the people, through which the kings of Judah go in and out; stand also at all the other gates of Jerusalem. ²⁰Say to them, 'Hear the word of the LORD, O kings of Judah

and all people of Judah and everyone living in Jerusalem who come through these gates. ²¹This is what the LORD says: Be careful not to carry a load on the Sabbath day or bring it through the gates of Jerusalem. ²²Do not bring a load out of your houses or do any work on the Sabbath, but keep the Sabbath day holy, as I commanded your forefathers. ²³Yet they did not listen or pay attention; they were stiff-necked and would not listen or respond to discipline. ²⁴But if you are careful to obey me, declares the LORD, and bring no load through the gates of this city on the Sabbath, but keep the Sabbath day holy by not doing any work on it, ²⁵then kings who sit on David's throne will come through the gates of this city with their officials. They and their officials will come riding in chariots and on horses, accompanied by the men of Judah and those living in Jerusalem, and this city will be inhabited forever. ²⁶People will come from the towns of Judah and the villages around Jerusalem, from the territory of Benjamin and the western foothills, from the hill country and the Negev, bringing burnt offerings and sacrifices, grain offerings, incense and thank offerings to the house of the LORD. ²⁷But if you do not obey me to keep the Sabbath day holy by not carrying any load as you come through the gates of Jerusalem on the Sabbath day, then I will kindle an unquenchable fire in the gates of Jerusalem that will consume her fortresses.' "

At the Potter's House

18 This is the word that came to Jeremiah from the LORD: ²"Go down to the potter's house, and there I will give you my message." ³So I went down to the potter's house, and I saw him working at the wheel. ⁴But the pot he was shaping from the clay was marred in his hands; so the potter formed it into another pot, shaping it as seemed best to him.

⁵Then the word of the LORD came to me: ⁶"O house of Israel, can I not do with you as this potter does?" declares the LORD. "Like clay in the hand of the potter, so are you in my hand, O house of Israel. ⁷If at any time I announce that a nation

or kingdom is to be uprooted, torn down and destroyed, ⁸and if that nation I warned repents of its evil, then I will relent and not inflict on it the disaster I had planned. ⁹And if at another time I announce that a nation or kingdom is to be built up and planted, ¹⁰and if it does evil in my sight and does not obey me, then I will reconsider the good I had intended to do for it.

¹¹"Now therefore say to the people of Judah and those living in Jerusalem, 'This is what the LORD says: Look! I am preparing a disaster for you and devising a plan against you. So turn from your evil ways, each one of you, and reform your ways and your actions.' ¹²But they will reply, 'It's no use. We will continue with our own plans; each of us will follow the stubbornness of his evil heart.' "

¹³Therefore this is what the LORD says:

"Inquire among the nations:
    Who has ever heard anything like this?
A most horrible thing has been done
    by Virgin Israel.
¹⁴Does the snow of Lebanon
    ever vanish from its rocky slopes?
Do its cool waters from distant sources
    ever cease to flow? ᵃ
¹⁵Yet my people have forgotten me;
    they burn incense to worthless idols,
which made them stumble in their ways
    and in the ancient paths.
They made them walk in bypaths
    and on roads not built up.
¹⁶Their land will be laid waste,
    an object of lasting scorn;
all who pass by will be appalled
    and will shake their heads.
¹⁷Like a wind from the east,
    I will scatter them before their enemies;
I will show them my back and not my face
    in the day of their disaster."

¹⁸They said, "Come, let's make plans against Jeremiah; for the teaching of the law by the priest

---

ᵃ 14 The meaning of the Hebrew for this sentence is uncertain.

will not be lost, nor will counsel from the wise, nor the word from the prophets. So come, let's attack him with our tongues and pay no attention to anything he says."

¹⁹ Listen to me, O LORD;
hear what my accusers are saying!
²⁰ Should good be repaid with evil?
Yet they have dug a pit for me.
Remember that I stood before you
and spoke in their behalf
to turn your wrath away from them.
²¹ So give their children over to famine;
hand them over to the power of the sword.
Let their wives be made childless and
widows;
let their men be put to death,
their young men slain by the sword in
battle.
²² Let a cry be heard from their houses
when you suddenly bring invaders against
them,
for they have dug a pit to capture me
and have hidden snares for my feet.
²³ But you know, O LORD,
all their plots to kill me.
Do not forgive their crimes
or blot out their sins from your sight.
Let them be overthrown before you;
deal with them in the time of your anger.

19 This is what the LORD says: "Go and buy a clay jar from a potter. Take along some of the elders of the people and of the priests ² and go out to the Valley of Ben Hinnom, near the entrance of the Potsherd Gate. There proclaim the words I tell you, ³ and say, 'Hear the word of the LORD, O kings of Judah and people of Jerusalem. This is what the LORD Almighty, the God of Israel, says: Listen! I am going to bring a disaster on this place that will make the ears of everyone who hears of it tingle. ⁴ For they have forsaken me and made this a place of foreign gods; they have burned sacrifices in it to gods that neither they nor their fathers nor the kings of Judah

ever knew, and they have filled this place with the blood of the innocent. ⁵ They have built the high places of Baal to burn their sons in the fire as offerings to Baal—something I did not command or mention, nor did it enter my mind. ⁶ So beware, the days are coming, declares the LORD, when people will no longer call this place Topheth or the Valley of Ben Hinnom, but the Valley of Slaughter.

⁷ "'In this place I will ruin^a the plans of Judah and Jerusalem. I will make them fall by the sword before their enemies, at the hands of those who seek their lives, and I will give their carcasses as food to the birds of the air and the beasts of the earth. ⁸ I will devastate this city and make it an object of scorn; all who pass by will be appalled and will scoff because of all its wounds. ⁹ I will make them eat the flesh of their sons and daughters, and they will eat one another's flesh during the stress of the siege imposed on them by the enemies who seek their lives.'

¹⁰ "Then break the jar while those who go with you are watching, ¹¹ and say to them, 'This is what the LORD Almighty says: I will smash this nation and this city just as this potter's jar is smashed and cannot be repaired. They will bury the dead in Topheth until there is no more room. ¹² This is what I will do to this place and to those who live here, declares the LORD. I will make this city like Topheth. ¹³ The houses in Jerusalem and those of the kings of Judah will be defiled like this place, Topheth—all the houses where they burned incense on the roofs to all the starry hosts and poured out drink offerings to other gods.'"

¹⁴ Jeremiah then returned from Topheth, where the LORD had sent him to prophesy, and stood in the court of the LORD's temple and said to all the people, ¹⁵ "This is what the LORD Almighty, the God of Israel, says: 'Listen! I am going to bring on this city and the villages around it every disaster I pronounced against them, because they were stiff-necked and would not listen to my words.'"

^a 7 The Hebrew for *ruin* sounds like the Hebrew for *jar* (see verses 1 and 10).

Jeremiah and Pashhur

20 When the priest Pashhur son of Immer, the chief officer in the temple of the LORD, heard Jeremiah prophesying these things, ²he had Jeremiah the prophet beaten and put in the stocks at the Upper Gate of Benjamin at the LORD's temple. ³The next day, when Pashhur released him from the stocks, Jeremiah said to him, "The LORD's name for you is not Pashhur, but Magor-Missabib.ᵃ ⁴For this is what the LORD says: 'I will make you a terror to yourself and to all your friends; with your own eyes you will see them fall by the sword of their enemies. I will hand all Judah over to the king of Babylon, who will carry them away to Babylon or put them to the sword. ⁵I will hand over to their enemies all the wealth of this city—all its products, all its valuables and all the treasures of the kings of Judah. They will take it away as plunder and carry it off to Babylon. ⁶And you, Pashhur, and all who live in your house will go into exile to Babylon. There you will die and be buried, you and all your friends to whom you have prophesied lies.'"

Jeremiah's Complaint

⁷O LORD, you deceivedᵇ me, and I was
    deceivedᵇ;
  you overpowered me and prevailed.
  I am ridiculed all day long;
    everyone mocks me.
⁸Whenever I speak, I cry out
    proclaiming violence and destruction.
  So the word of the LORD has brought me
    insult and reproach all day long.
⁹But if I say, "I will not mention him
    or speak any more in his name,"
  his word is in my heart like a fire,
    a fire shut up in my bones.
  I am weary of holding it in;
    indeed, I cannot.
¹⁰I hear many whispering,
    "Terror on every side!
  Report him! Let's report him!"
  All my friends
    are waiting for me to slip, saying,

  "Perhaps he will be deceived;
    then we will prevail over him
    and take our revenge on him."

¹¹But the LORD is with me like a mighty
    warrior;
  so my persecutors will stumble and not
    prevail.
  They will fail and be thoroughly
    disgraced;
    their dishonor will never be forgotten.
¹²O LORD Almighty, you who examine the
    righteous
  and probe the heart and mind,
  let me see your vengeance upon them,
    for to you I have committed my cause.

¹³Sing to the LORD!
  Give praise to the LORD!
  He rescues the life of the needy
    from the hands of the wicked.

¹⁴Cursed be the day I was born!
  May the day my mother bore me not be
    blessed!
¹⁵Cursed be the man who brought my father
    the news,
  who made him very glad, saying,
    "A child is born to you—a son!"
¹⁶May that man be like the towns
    the LORD overthrew without pity.
  May he hear wailing in the morning,
    a battle cry at noon.
¹⁷For he did not kill me in the womb,
    with my mother as my grave,
    her womb enlarged forever.
¹⁸Why did I ever come out of the womb
    to see trouble and sorrow
    and to end my days in shame?

God Rejects Zedekiah's Request

21 The word came to Jeremiah from the LORD when King Zedekiah sent to him Pashhur son of Malkijah and the priest Zephaniah son of Maaseiah. They said: ²"Inquire now of

---

ᵃ 3 Magor-Missabib means terror on every side.   ᵇ 7 Or persuaded the LORD for us because Nebuchadnezzar[a] king of Babylon is attacking us. Perhaps the LORD will perform wonders for us as in times past so that he will withdraw from us."

3 But Jeremiah answered them, "Tell Zedekiah, 4 'This is what the LORD, the God of Israel, says: I am about to turn against you the weapons of war that are in your hands, which you are using to fight the king of Babylon and the Babylonians[b] who are outside the wall besieging you. And I will gather them inside this city. 5 I myself will fight against you with an outstretched hand and a mighty arm in anger and fury and great wrath. 6 I will strike down those who live in this city — both men and animals — and they will die of a terrible plague. 7 After that, declares the LORD, I will hand over Zedekiah king of Judah, his officials and the people in this city who survive the plague, sword and famine, to Nebuchadnezzar king of Babylon and to their enemies who seek their lives. He will put them to the sword; he will show them no mercy or pity or compassion.'

8 "Furthermore, tell the people, 'This is what the LORD says: See, I am setting before you the way of life and the way of death. 9 Whoever stays in this city will die by the sword, famine or plague. But whoever goes out and surrenders to the Babylonians who are besieging you will live; he will escape with his life. 10 I have determined to do this city harm and not good, declares the LORD. It will be given into the hands of the king of Babylon, and he will destroy it with fire.'

11 "Moreover, say to the royal house of Judah, 'Hear the word of the LORD; 12 O house of David, this is what the LORD says:

" 'Administer justice every morning;
    rescue from the hand of his oppressor
    the one who has been robbed,
or my wrath will break out and burn like fire
    because of the evil you have done —
    burn with no one to quench it.
13 I am against you, Jerusalem,
    you who live above this valley
    on the rocky plateau,
            declares the LORD —

you who say, "Who can come against us?
    Who can enter our refuge?"
14 I will punish you as your deeds deserve,
            declares the LORD.
I will kindle a fire in your forests
    that will consume everything around you.' "

Judgment Against Evil Kings

22 This is what the LORD says: "Go down to the palace of the king of Judah and proclaim this message there: 2 'Hear the word of the LORD, O king of Judah, you who sit on David's throne — you, your officials and your people who come through these gates. 3 This is what the LORD says: Do what is just and right. Rescue from the hand of his oppressor the one who has been robbed. Do no wrong or violence to the alien, the fatherless or the widow, and do not shed innocent blood in this place. 4 For if you are careful to carry out these commands, then kings who sit on David's throne will come through the gates of this palace, riding in chariots and on horses, accompanied by their officials and their people. 5 But if you do not obey these commands, declares the LORD, I swear by myself that this palace will become a ruin.' "

6 For this is what the LORD says about the palace of the king of Judah:

"Though you are like Gilead to me,
    like the summit of Lebanon,
I will surely make you like a desert,
    like towns not inhabited.
7 I will send destroyers against you,
    each man with his weapons,
and they will cut up your fine cedar beams
    and throw them into the fire.

8 "People from many nations will pass by this city and will ask one another, 'Why has the LORD done such a thing to this great city?' 9 And the answer will be: 'Because they have forsaken the covenant of the LORD their God and have worshiped and served other gods.' "

---

[a] 2 Hebrew *Nebuchadrezzar*, of which *Nebuchadnezzar* is a variant; here and often in Jeremiah and Ezekiel   [b] 4 Or *Chaldeans*; also in verse 9

¹⁰Do not weep for the dead ⌊king⌋ or mourn his
 loss;
  rather, weep bitterly for him who is exiled,
 because he will never return
  nor see his native land again.

¹¹For this is what the LORD says about Shallum*ᵃ*
son of Josiah, who succeeded his father as king of
Judah but has gone from this place: "He will never
return. ¹²He will die in the place where they have
led him captive; he will not see this land again."

¹³"Woe to him who builds his palace by
  unrighteousness,
 his upper rooms by injustice,
  making his countrymen work for nothing,
  not paying them for their labor.
¹⁴He says, 'I will build myself a great palace
  with spacious upper rooms.'
 So he makes large windows in it,
  panels it with cedar
  and decorates it in red.

¹⁵"Does it make you a king
  to have more and more cedar?
 Did not your father have food and drink?
  He did what was right and just,
  so all went well with him.
¹⁶He defended the cause of the poor and needy,
  and so all went well.
 Is that not what it means to know me?"
  declares the LORD.
¹⁷"But your eyes and your heart
  are set only on dishonest gain,
 on shedding innocent blood
  and on oppression and extortion."

¹⁸Therefore this is what the LORD says about Jehoiakim son of Josiah king of Judah:

 "They will not mourn for him:
  'Alas, my brother! Alas, my sister!'
 They will not mourn for him:
  'Alas, my master! Alas, his splendor!'
¹⁹He will have the burial of a donkey—
  dragged away and thrown
  outside the gates of Jerusalem."

²⁰"Go up to Lebanon and cry out,
  let your voice be heard in Bashan,
 cry out from Abarim,
  for all your allies are crushed.
²¹I warned you when you felt secure,
  but you said, 'I will not listen!'
 This has been your way from your youth;
  you have not obeyed me.
²²The wind will drive all your shepherds
  away,
  and your allies will go into exile.
 Then you will be ashamed and disgraced
  because of all your wickedness.
²³You who live in 'Lebanon,'ᵇ
  who are nestled in cedar buildings,
 how you will groan when pangs come upon
  you,
  pain like that of a woman in labor!

²⁴"As surely as I live," declares the LORD, "even
if you, Jehoiachinᶜ son of Jehoiakim king of Judah, were a signet ring on my right hand, I would
still pull you off. ²⁵I will hand you over to those
who seek your life, those you fear—to Nebuchadnezzar king of Babylon and to the Babylonians.ᵈ
²⁶I will hurl you and the mother who gave you
birth into another country, where neither of
you was born, and there you both will die. ²⁷You
will never come back to the land you long to return to."

²⁸Is this man Jehoiachin a despised, broken pot,
  an object no one wants?
 Why will he and his children be hurled out,
  cast into a land they do not know?
²⁹O land, land, land,
  hear the word of the LORD!
³⁰This is what the LORD says:
 "Record this man as if childless,
  a man who will not prosper in his lifetime,
 for none of his offspring will prosper,
  none will sit on the throne of David
  or rule anymore in Judah."

The Righteous Branch

23 "Woe to the shepherds who are destroying and scattering the sheep of my pasture!" declares the LORD. ²Therefore this is what the LORD, the God of Israel, says to the shepherds who tend my people: "Because you have scattered my flock and driven them away and have not bestowed care on them, I will bestow punishment on you for the evil you have done," declares the LORD. ³"I myself will gather the remnant of my flock out of all the countries where I have driven them and will bring them back to their pasture, where they will be fruitful and increase in number. ⁴I will place shepherds over them who will tend them, and they will no longer be afraid or terrified, nor will any be missing," declares the LORD.

⁵"The days are coming," declares the LORD,
  "when I will raise up to David *ᵃ* a righteous
    Branch,
  a King who will reign wisely
    and do what is just and right in the land.
⁶In his days Judah will be saved
    and Israel will live in safety.
  This is the name by which he will be called:
    The LORD Our Righteousness.

⁷"So then, the days are coming," declares the LORD, "when people will no longer say, 'As surely as the LORD lives, who brought the Israelites up out of Egypt,' ⁸but they will say, 'As surely as the LORD lives, who brought the descendants of Israel up out of the land of the north and out of all the countries where he had banished them.' Then they will live in their own land."

Lying Prophets

⁹Concerning the prophets:

My heart is broken within me;
    all my bones tremble.
I am like a drunken man,
    like a man overcome by wine,
because of the LORD
    and his holy words.

¹⁰The land is full of adulterers;
  because of the curse *ᵇ* the land lies
    parched *ᶜ*
  and the pastures in the desert are withered.
The ⌐prophets⌐ follow an evil course
  and use their power unjustly.

¹¹"Both prophet and priest are godless;
  even in my temple I find their wickedness,"
                declares the LORD.
¹²"Therefore their path will become slippery;
  they will be banished to darkness
    and there they will fall.
I will bring disaster on them
  in the year they are punished,"
                declares the LORD.

¹³"Among the prophets of Samaria
    I saw this repulsive thing:
  They prophesied by Baal
    and led my people Israel astray.
¹⁴And among the prophets of Jerusalem
    I have seen something horrible:
  They commit adultery and live a lie.
  They strengthen the hands of evildoers,
    so that no one turns from his wickedness.
  They are all like Sodom to me;
    the people of Jerusalem are like
      Gomorrah."

¹⁵Therefore, this is what the LORD Almighty says concerning the prophets:

"I will make them eat bitter food
    and drink poisoned water,
because from the prophets of Jerusalem
    ungodliness has spread throughout the
      land."

¹⁶This is what the LORD Almighty says:

"Do not listen to what the prophets are
    prophesying to you;
  they fill you with false hopes.
They speak visions from their own minds,
  not from the mouth of the LORD.

*ᵃ 5 Or up from David's line   ᵇ 10 Or because of these things
ᶜ 10 Or land mourns*

17 They keep saying to those who despise me,
  'The LORD says: You will have peace.'
And to all who follow the stubbornness of
    their hearts
  they say, 'No harm will come to you.'
18 But which of them has stood in the council
    of the LORD
  to see or to hear his word?
  Who has listened and heard his word?
19 See, the storm of the LORD
  will burst out in wrath,
  a whirlwind swirling down
  on the heads of the wicked.
20 The anger of the LORD will not turn back
  until he fully accomplishes
  the purposes of his heart.
In days to come
  you will understand it clearly.
21 I did not send these prophets,
  yet they have run with their message;
I did not speak to them,
  yet they have prophesied.
22 But if they had stood in my council,
  they would have proclaimed my words to
    my people
  and would have turned them from their evil
    ways
  and from their evil deeds.

23 "Am I only a God nearby,"
                          declares the LORD,
  "and not a God far away?
24 Can anyone hide in secret places
  so that I cannot see him?"
                          declares the LORD.
  "Do not I fill heaven and earth?"
                          declares the LORD.

25 "I have heard what the prophets say who
prophesy lies in my name. They say, 'I had a
dream! I had a dream!' 26 How long will this
continue in the hearts of these lying prophets,
who prophesy the delusions of their own minds?
27 They think the dreams they tell one another
will make my people forget my name, just as
their fathers forgot my name through Baal wor-

ship. 28 Let the prophet who has a dream tell his
dream, but let the one who has my word speak it
faithfully. For what has straw to do with grain?"
declares the LORD. 29 "Is not my word like fire," declares the LORD, "and like a hammer that breaks
a rock in pieces?

30 "Therefore," declares the LORD, "I am against
the prophets who steal from one another words
supposedly from me. 31 Yes," declares the LORD,
"I am against the prophets who wag their own
tongues and yet declare, 'The LORD declares.'
32 Indeed, I am against those who prophesy false
dreams," declares the LORD. "They tell them and
lead my people astray with their reckless lies, yet
I did not send or appoint them. They do not benefit these people in the least," declares the LORD.

False Oracles and False Prophets

33 "When these people, or a prophet or a priest,
ask you, 'What is the oracle a of the LORD?' say to
them, 'What oracle? b I will forsake you, declares
the LORD.' 34 If a prophet or a priest or anyone
else claims, 'This is the oracle of the LORD,' I will
punish that man and his household. 35 This is
what each of you keeps on saying to his friend
or relative: 'What is the LORD's answer?' or 'What
has the LORD spoken?' 36 But you must not mention 'the oracle of the LORD' again, because every
man's own word becomes his oracle and so you
distort the words of the living God, the LORD Almighty, our God. 37 This is what you keep saying
to a prophet: 'What is the LORD's answer to you?'
or 'What has the LORD spoken?' 38 Although you
claim, 'This is the oracle of the LORD,' this is what
the LORD says: You used the words, 'This is the oracle of the LORD,' even though I told you that you
must not claim, 'This is the oracle of the LORD.'
39 Therefore, I will surely forget you and cast you
out of my presence along with the city I gave to
you and your fathers. 40 I will bring upon you everlasting disgrace — everlasting shame that will not
be forgotten."

a 33 Or burden (see Septuagint and Vulgate)   b 33 Hebrew;
Septuagint and Vulgate 'You are the burden. (The Hebrew for oracle
and burden is the same.)

Two Baskets of Figs

24 After Jehoiachin*ᵃ* son of Jehoiakim king of Judah and the officials, the craftsmen and the artisans of Judah were carried into exile from Jerusalem to Babylon by Nebuchadnezzar king of Babylon, the Lord showed me two baskets of figs placed in front of the temple of the Lord. ² One basket had very good figs, like those that ripen early; the other basket had very poor figs, so bad they could not be eaten.

³ Then the Lord asked me, "What do you see, Jeremiah?"

"Figs," I answered. "The good ones are very good, but the poor ones are so bad they cannot be eaten."

⁴ Then the word of the Lord came to me: ⁵ "This is what the Lord, the God of Israel, says: 'Like these good figs, I regard as good the exiles from Judah, whom I sent away from this place to the land of the Babylonians.*ᵇ* ⁶ My eyes will watch over them for their good, and I will bring them back to this land. I will build them up and not tear them down; I will plant them and not uproot them. ⁷ I will give them a heart to know me, that I am the Lord. They will be my people, and I will be their God, for they will return to me with all their heart.

⁸ " 'But like the poor figs, which are so bad they cannot be eaten,' says the Lord, 'so will I deal with Zedekiah king of Judah, his officials and the survivors from Jerusalem, whether they remain in this land or live in Egypt. ⁹ I will make them abhorrent and an offense to all the kingdoms of the earth, a reproach and a byword, an object of ridicule and cursing, wherever I banish them. ¹⁰ I will send the sword, famine and plague against them until they are destroyed from the land I gave to them and their fathers.' "

Seventy Years of Captivity

25 The word came to Jeremiah concerning all the people of Judah in the fourth year of Jehoiakim son of Josiah king of Judah, which was the first year of Nebuchadnezzar king of Babylon. ² So Jeremiah the prophet said to all the people of Judah and to all those living in Jerusalem: ³ For twenty-three years—from the thirteenth year of Josiah son of Amon king of Judah until this very day—the word of the Lord has come to me and I have spoken to you again and again, but you have not listened.

⁴ And though the Lord has sent all his servants the prophets to you again and again, you have not listened or paid any attention. ⁵ They said, "Turn now, each of you, from your evil ways and your evil practices, and you can stay in the land the Lord gave to you and your fathers for ever and ever. ⁶ Do not follow other gods to serve and worship them; do not provoke me to anger with what your hands have made. Then I will not harm you."

⁷ "But you did not listen to me," declares the Lord, "and you have provoked me with what your hands have made, and you have brought harm to yourselves."

⁸ Therefore the Lord Almighty says this: "Because you have not listened to my words, ⁹ I will summon all the peoples of the north and my servant Nebuchadnezzar king of Babylon," declares the Lord, "and I will bring them against this land and its inhabitants and against all the surrounding nations. I will completely destroy*ᶜ* them and make them an object of horror and scorn, and an everlasting ruin. ¹⁰ I will banish from them the sounds of joy and gladness, the voices of bride and bridegroom, the sound of millstones and the light of the lamp. ¹¹ This whole country will become a desolate wasteland, and these nations will serve the king of Babylon seventy years.

¹² "But when the seventy years are fulfilled, I will punish the king of Babylon and his nation, the land of the Babylonians,*ᵇ* for their guilt," declares the Lord, "and will make it desolate forever. ¹³ I will bring upon that land all the things I have spoken against it, all that are written in this book and prophesied by Jeremiah against all the nations. ¹⁴ They themselves will be enslaved by

---

ᵃ 1 Hebrew *Jeconiah,* a variant of *Jehoiachin*   *ᵇ 5,12* Or *Chaldeans*   *ᶜ 9* The Hebrew term refers to the irrevocable giving over of things or persons to the Lord, often by totally destroying them.

many nations and great kings; I will repay them according to their deeds and the work of their hands."

The Cup of God's Wrath

¹⁵This is what the LORD, the God of Israel, said to me: "Take from my hand this cup filled with the wine of my wrath and make all the nations to whom I send you drink it. ¹⁶When they drink it, they will stagger and go mad because of the sword I will send among them."

¹⁷So I took the cup from the LORD's hand and made all the nations to whom he sent me drink it: ¹⁸Jerusalem and the towns of Judah, its kings and officials, to make them a ruin and an object of horror and scorn and cursing, as they are today; ¹⁹Pharaoh king of Egypt, his attendants, his officials and all his people, ²⁰and all the foreign people there; all the kings of Uz; all the kings of the Philistines (those of Ashkelon, Gaza, Ekron, and the people left at Ashdod); ²¹Edom, Moab and Ammon; ²²all the kings of Tyre and Sidon; the kings of the coastlands across the sea; ²³Dedan, Tema, Buz and all who are in distant places^a; ²⁴all the kings of Arabia and all the kings of the foreign people who live in the desert; ²⁵all the kings of Zimri, Elam and Media; ²⁶and all the kings of the north, near and far, one after the other—all the kingdoms on the face of the earth. And after all of them, the king of Sheshach^b will drink it too.

²⁷"Then tell them, 'This is what the LORD Almighty, the God of Israel, says: Drink, get drunk and vomit, and fall to rise no more because of the sword I will send among you.' ²⁸But if they refuse to take the cup from your hand and drink, tell them, 'This is what the LORD Almighty says: You must drink it! ²⁹See, I am beginning to bring disaster on the city that bears my Name, and will you indeed go unpunished? You will not go unpunished, for I am calling down a sword upon all who live on the earth, declares the LORD Almighty.'

³⁰"Now prophesy all these words against them and say to them:

" 'The LORD will roar from on high;
   he will thunder from his holy dwelling
   and roar mightily against his land.
He will shout like those who tread the
      grapes,
   shout against all who live on the earth.
³¹The tumult will resound to the ends of the
      earth,
   for the LORD will bring charges against the
      nations;
he will bring judgment on all mankind
   and put the wicked to the sword,' "
                  declares the LORD.

³²This is what the LORD Almighty says:

"Look! Disaster is spreading
   from nation to nation;
a mighty storm is rising
   from the ends of the earth."

³³At that time those slain by the LORD will be everywhere—from one end of the earth to the other. They will not be mourned or gathered up or buried, but will be like refuse lying on the ground.

³⁴Weep and wail, you shepherds;
   roll in the dust, you leaders of the flock.
For your time to be slaughtered has come;
   you will fall and be shattered like fine
      pottery.
³⁵The shepherds will have nowhere to flee,
   the leaders of the flock no place to escape.
³⁶Hear the cry of the shepherds,
   the wailing of the leaders of the flock,
   for the LORD is destroying their pasture.
³⁷The peaceful meadows will be laid waste
   because of the fierce anger of the LORD.
³⁸Like a lion he will leave his lair,
   and their land will become desolate
because of the sword^c of the oppressor
   and because of the LORD's fierce anger.

^a 23 Or *who clip the hair by their foreheads*   ^b 26 *Sheshach* is a cryptogram for Babylon.   ^c 38 Some Hebrew manuscripts and Septuagint (see also Jer. 46:16 and 50:16); most Hebrew manuscripts *anger*

Jeremiah Threatened With Death

26 Early in the reign of Jehoiakim son of Josiah king of Judah, this word came from the LORD: ²"This is what the LORD says: Stand in the courtyard of the LORD's house and speak to all the people of the towns of Judah who come to worship in the house of the LORD. Tell them everything I command you; do not omit a word. ³Perhaps they will listen and each will turn from his evil way. Then I will relent and not bring on them the disaster I was planning because of the evil they have done. ⁴Say to them, 'This is what the LORD says: If you do not listen to me and follow my law, which I have set before you, ⁵and if you do not listen to the words of my servants the prophets, whom I have sent to you again and again (though you have not listened), ⁶then I will make this house like Shiloh and this city an object of cursing among all the nations of the earth.'"

⁷The priests, the prophets and all the people heard Jeremiah speak these words in the house of the LORD. ⁸But as soon as Jeremiah finished telling all the people everything the LORD had commanded him to say, the priests, the prophets and all the people seized him and said, "You must die! ⁹Why do you prophesy in the LORD's name that this house will be like Shiloh and this city will be desolate and deserted?" And all the people crowded around Jeremiah in the house of the LORD.

¹⁰When the officials of Judah heard about these things, they went up from the royal palace to the house of the LORD and took their places at the entrance of the New Gate of the LORD's house. ¹¹Then the priests and the prophets said to the officials and all the people, "This man should be sentenced to death because he has prophesied against this city. You have heard it with your own ears!"

¹²Then Jeremiah said to all the officials and all the people: "The LORD sent me to prophesy against this house and this city all the things you have heard. ¹³Now reform your ways and your actions and obey the LORD your God. Then the LORD will relent and not bring the disaster he has pronounced against you. ¹⁴As for me, I am in your hands; do with me whatever you think is good and right. ¹⁵Be assured, however, that if you put me to death, you will bring the guilt of innocent blood on yourselves and on this city and on those who live in it, for in truth the LORD has sent me to you to speak all these words in your hearing."

¹⁶Then the officials and all the people said to the priests and the prophets, "This man should not be sentenced to death! He has spoken to us in the name of the LORD our God."

¹⁷Some of the elders of the land stepped forward and said to the entire assembly of people, ¹⁸"Micah of Moresheth prophesied in the days of Hezekiah king of Judah. He told all the people of Judah, 'This is what the LORD Almighty says:

" 'Zion will be plowed like a field,
　Jerusalem will become a heap of rubble,
　　the temple hill a mound overgrown with
　　　thickets.'ᵃ

¹⁹"Did Hezekiah king of Judah or anyone else in Judah put him to death? Did not Hezekiah fear the LORD and seek his favor? And did not the LORD relent, so that he did not bring the disaster he pronounced against them? We are about to bring a terrible disaster on ourselves!"

²⁰(Now Uriah son of Shemaiah from Kiriath Jearim was another man who prophesied in the name of the LORD; he prophesied the same things against this city and this land as Jeremiah did. ²¹When King Jehoiakim and all his officers and officials heard his words, the king sought to put him to death. But Uriah heard of it and fled in fear to Egypt. ²²King Jehoiakim, however, sent Elnathan son of Acbor to Egypt, along with some other men. ²³They brought Uriah out of Egypt and took him to King Jehoiakim, who had him struck down with a sword and his body thrown into the burial place of the common people.)

²⁴Furthermore, Ahikam son of Shaphan supported Jeremiah, and so he was not handed over to the people to be put to death.

ᵃ 18 Micah 3:12

Judah to Serve Nebuchadnezzar

27 Early in the reign of Zedekiah*ª* son of Josiah king of Judah, this word came to Jeremiah from the Lord: ²This is what the Lord said to me: "Make a yoke out of straps and crossbars and put it on your neck. ³Then send word to the kings of Edom, Moab, Ammon, Tyre and Sidon through the envoys who have come to Jerusalem to Zedekiah king of Judah. ⁴Give them a message for their masters and say, 'This is what the Lord Almighty, the God of Israel, says: "Tell this to your masters: ⁵With my great power and outstretched arm I made the earth and its people and the animals that are on it, and I give it to anyone I please. ⁶Now I will hand all your countries over to my servant Nebuchadnezzar king of Babylon; I will make even the wild animals subject to him. ⁷All nations will serve him and his son and his grandson until the time for his land comes; then many nations and great kings will subjugate him.

⁸" ' "If, however, any nation or kingdom will not serve Nebuchadnezzar king of Babylon or bow its neck under his yoke, I will punish that nation with the sword, famine and plague, declares the Lord, until I destroy it by his hand. ⁹So do not listen to your prophets, your diviners, your interpreters of dreams, your mediums or your sorcerers who tell you, 'You will not serve the king of Babylon.' ¹⁰They prophesy lies to you that will only serve to remove you far from your lands; I will banish you and you will perish. ¹¹But if any nation will bow its neck under the yoke of the king of Babylon and serve him, I will let that nation remain in its own land to till it and to live there, declares the Lord." ' "

¹²I gave the same message to Zedekiah king of Judah. I said, "Bow your neck under the yoke of the king of Babylon; serve him and his people, and you will live. ¹³Why will you and your people die by the sword, famine and plague with which the Lord has threatened any nation that will not serve the king of Babylon? ¹⁴Do not listen to the words of the prophets who say to you, 'You will not serve the king of Babylon,' for they

are prophesying lies to you. ¹⁵'I have not sent them,' declares the Lord. 'They are prophesying lies in my name. Therefore, I will banish you and you will perish, both you and the prophets who prophesy to you.' "

¹⁶Then I said to the priests and all these people, "This is what the Lord says: Do not listen to the prophets who say, 'Very soon now the articles from the Lord's house will be brought back from Babylon.' They are prophesying lies to you. ¹⁷Do not listen to them. Serve the king of Babylon, and you will live. Why should this city become a ruin? ¹⁸If they are prophets and have the word of the Lord, let them plead with the Lord Almighty that the furnishings remaining in the house of the Lord and in the palace of the king of Judah and in Jerusalem not be taken to Babylon. ¹⁹For this is what the Lord Almighty says about the pillars, the Sea, the movable stands and the other furnishings that are left in this city, ²⁰which Nebuchadnezzar king of Babylon did not take away when he carried Jehoiachin*ᵇ* son of Jehoiakim king of Judah into exile from Jerusalem to Babylon, along with all the nobles of Judah and Jerusalem— ²¹yes, this is what the Lord Almighty, the God of Israel, says about the things that are left in the house of the Lord and in the palace of the king of Judah and in Jerusalem: ²²'They will be taken to Babylon and there they will remain until the day I come for them,' declares the Lord. 'Then I will bring them back and restore them to this place.' "

The False Prophet Hananiah

28 In the fifth month of that same year, the fourth year, early in the reign of Zedekiah king of Judah, the prophet Hananiah son of Azzur, who was from Gibeon, said to me in the house of the Lord in the presence of the priests and all the people: ²"This is what the Lord Almighty, the God of Israel, says: 'I will break the yoke of the king of Babylon. ³Within two years I

ª 1 A few Hebrew manuscripts and Syriac (see also Jer. 27:3,12 and 28:1); most Hebrew manuscripts *Jehoiakim* (Most Septuagint manuscripts do not have this verse.)   *ᵇ 20* Hebrew *Jeconiah,* a variant of *Jehoiachin* will bring back to this place all the articles of the LORD's house that Nebuchadnezzar king of Babylon removed from here and took to Babylon. [4]I will also bring back to this place Jehoiachin[a] son of Jehoiakim king of Judah and all the other exiles from Judah who went to Babylon,' declares the LORD, 'for I will break the yoke of the king of Babylon.' "

[5]Then the prophet Jeremiah replied to the prophet Hananiah before the priests and all the people who were standing in the house of the LORD. [6]He said, "Amen! May the LORD do so! May the LORD fulfill the words you have prophesied by bringing the articles of the LORD's house and all the exiles back to this place from Babylon. [7]Nevertheless, listen to what I have to say in your hearing and in the hearing of all the people: [8]From early times the prophets who preceded you and me have prophesied war, disaster and plague against many countries and great kingdoms. [9]But the prophet who prophesies peace will be recognized as one truly sent by the LORD only if his prediction comes true."

[10]Then the prophet Hananiah took the yoke off the neck of the prophet Jeremiah and broke it, [11]and he said before all the people, "This is what the LORD says: 'In the same way will I break the yoke of Nebuchadnezzar king of Babylon off the neck of all the nations within two years.' " At this, the prophet Jeremiah went on his way.

[12]Shortly after the prophet Hananiah had broken the yoke off the neck of the prophet Jeremiah, the word of the LORD came to Jeremiah: [13]"Go and tell Hananiah, 'This is what the LORD says: You have broken a wooden yoke, but in its place you will get a yoke of iron. [14]This is what the LORD Almighty, the God of Israel, says: I will put an iron yoke on the necks of all these nations to make them serve Nebuchadnezzar king of Babylon, and they will serve him. I will even give him control over the wild animals.' "

[15]Then the prophet Jeremiah said to Hananiah the prophet, "Listen, Hananiah! The LORD has not sent you, yet you have persuaded this nation to trust in lies. [16]Therefore, this is what the LORD says: 'I am about to remove you from the face of the earth. This very year you are going to die, because you have preached rebellion against the LORD.' "

[17]In the seventh month of that same year, Hananiah the prophet died.

A Letter to the Exiles

29 This is the text of the letter that the prophet Jeremiah sent from Jerusalem to the surviving elders among the exiles and to the priests, the prophets and all the other people Nebuchadnezzar had carried into exile from Jerusalem to Babylon. [2](This was after King Jehoiachin[a] and the queen mother, the court officials and the leaders of Judah and Jerusalem, the craftsmen and the artisans had gone into exile from Jerusalem.) [3]He entrusted the letter to Elasah son of Shaphan and to Gemariah son of Hilkiah, whom Zedekiah king of Judah sent to King Nebuchadnezzar in Babylon. It said:

[4]This is what the LORD Almighty, the God of Israel, says to all those I carried into exile from Jerusalem to Babylon: [5]"Build houses and settle down; plant gardens and eat what they produce. [6]Marry and have sons and daughters; find wives for your sons and give your daughters in marriage, so that they too may have sons and daughters. Increase in number there; do not decrease. [7]Also, seek the peace and prosperity of the city to which I have carried you into exile. Pray to the LORD for it, because if it prospers, you too will prosper." [8]Yes, this is what the LORD Almighty, the God of Israel, says: "Do not let the prophets and diviners among you deceive you. Do not listen to the dreams you encourage them to have. [9]They are prophesying lies to you in my name. I have not sent them," declares the LORD.

[10]This is what the LORD says: "When seventy years are completed for Babylon, I will come to you and fulfill my gracious promise

---

[a] 4,2 Hebrew *Jeconiah*, a variant of *Jehoiachin*

to bring you back to this place. ¹¹For I know the plans I have for you," declares the LORD, "plans to prosper you and not to harm you, plans to give you hope and a future.

TALKING POINTS

Knowing God's Will

God has good plans for us.

JEREMIAH 29:11

For more on knowing God's will,
go to Matthew 26:36–39.

¹²Then you will call upon me and come and pray to me, and I will listen to you. ¹³You will seek me and find me when you seek me with all your heart. ¹⁴I will be found by you," declares the LORD, "and will bring you back from captivity.[a] I will gather you from all the nations and places where I have banished you," declares the LORD, "and will bring you back to the place from which I carried you into exile."

¹⁵You may say, "The LORD has raised up prophets for us in Babylon," ¹⁶but this is what the LORD says about the king who sits on David's throne and all the people who remain in this city, your countrymen who did not go with you into exile— ¹⁷yes, this is what the LORD Almighty says: "I will send the sword, famine and plague against them and I will make them like poor figs that are so bad they cannot be eaten. ¹⁸I will pursue them with the sword, famine and plague and will make them abhorrent to all the kingdoms of the earth and an object of cursing and horror, of scorn and reproach, among all the nations where I drive them. ¹⁹For they have not listened to my words," declares the LORD, "words that I sent to them again and again by my servants the prophets. And you exiles have not listened either," declares the LORD.

²⁰Therefore, hear the word of the LORD, all you exiles whom I have sent away from Jerusalem to Babylon. ²¹This is what the LORD Almighty, the God of Israel, says about Ahab son of Kolaiah and Zedekiah son of Maaseiah, who are prophesying lies to you in my name: "I will hand them over to Nebuchadnezzar king of Babylon, and he will put them to death before your very eyes. ²²Because of them, all the exiles from Judah who are in Babylon will use this curse: 'The LORD treat you like Zedekiah and Ahab, whom the king of Babylon burned in the fire.' ²³For they have done outrageous things in Israel; they have committed adultery with their neighbors' wives and in my name have spoken lies, which I did not tell them to do. I know it and am a witness to it," declares the LORD.

Message to Shemaiah

²⁴Tell Shemaiah the Nehelamite, ²⁵"This is what the LORD Almighty, the God of Israel, says: You sent letters in your own name to all the people in Jerusalem, to Zephaniah son of Maaseiah the priest, and to all the other priests. You said to Zephaniah, ²⁶'The LORD has appointed you priest in place of Jehoiada to be in charge of the house of the LORD; you should put any madman

TALKING POINTS

Encouragement

God has a good plan for our lives.

JEREMIAH 29:11–13

For more on encouragement, go to Habakkuk 3:17–19.

[a] 14 Or *will restore your fortunes*

"FOR I KNOW THE PLANS I HAVE
FOR YOU," DECLARES THE LORD,
"PLANS TO PROSPER YOU AND
NOT TO HARM YOU, PLANS TO
GIVE YOU HOPE AND A FUTURE."
Jeremiah 29:11

Mouse in a Maze

TERRI BLACKSTOCK

READ | JEREMIAH 29:1 – 14

I often think my life is much like that of a mouse in a maze. There's a plan and a path that is perfect for me, and it's not so hard to find. But I can convince myself that I have a better way — a shortcut or a more interesting route to where I'm going. Sometimes, I even think the destination I choose is better than what has been ordained for me.

I picture God standing above the maze, urging me to make the turns and twists he's planned for me, luring me this way and that, showing me open doors and nudging me past the closed ones . . . but so often I ignore him and go in my own direction. Sometimes I kick down the doors that would keep me out of trouble, and I forge headfirst into what lies behind them. Those are the times when God must weep, then let me have my way. But when I realize it and turn back, he is there waiting.

Sometimes I return to God with the consequences my choices have cost me, consequences that have made his plan for my life more difficult. But he continues to work with me, guiding me away from the dead ends, opening the doors that will lead me to what he wants me to have. Miraculously, he takes the suffering my choices caused me, the consequences that remain, and turns them into a testimony that can help others. Instead of damaged goods, I become someone he can use.

That's the grace of a Father who loved me — a poor, ignorant, rebellious, vagabond mouse — enough to send his Son to die so that I could master that maze once and for all. With my eyes on the cross, I don't have to bump into walls and turn in circles and backtrack through the corridors of my life. All I have to do is follow him. And trust.

Abundant life? You bet it is.

Father God, I thank you for the freedom you've given me to make my own choices. I cherish that freedom and desire to use it in ways that are consistent with your plan and purpose for my life. I know that your plan is designed to keep me safe from harm and bring me fulfillment and success in all I do. Continue to teach me to use my freedom in ways that are pleasing to you.

Your next devotion is located on page 1061.

GRANDCHILD IN FOCUS • PRAYER

Respect for Authority

Dear Lord, I pray that my grandchild will continually grow to respect those in authority. May she learn to be cooperative and fair in work and play. Instill in her a high regard for officials who govern our land and enforce the laws. May her relationships with parents, teachers, coaches, mentors and bosses be respectful, admirable, constructive and caring. Amen.

who acts like a prophet into the stocks and neck-irons. ²⁷So why have you not reprimanded Jeremiah from Anathoth, who poses as a prophet among you? ²⁸He has sent this message to us in Babylon: It will be a long time. Therefore build houses and settle down; plant gardens and eat what they produce.'"

²⁹Zephaniah the priest, however, read the letter to Jeremiah the prophet. ³⁰Then the word of the Lord came to Jeremiah: ³¹"Send this message to all the exiles: 'This is what the Lord says about Shemaiah the Nehelamite: Because Shemaiah has prophesied to you, even though I did not send him, and has led you to believe a lie, ³²this is what the Lord says: I will surely punish Shemaiah the Nehelamite and his descendants. He will have no one left among this people, nor will he see the good things I will do for my people, declares the Lord, because he has preached rebellion against me.'"

Restoration of Israel

30 This is the word that came to Jeremiah from the Lord: ²"This is what the Lord, the God of Israel, says: 'Write in a book all the words I have spoken to you. ³The days are coming,' declares the Lord, 'when I will bring my people Israel and Judah back from captivity ᵃ and restore them to the land I gave their forefathers to possess,' says the Lord.'"

⁴These are the words the Lord spoke concerning Israel and Judah: ⁵"This is what the Lord says:

" 'Cries of fear are heard—
    terror, not peace.
⁶ Ask and see:
    Can a man bear children?
Then why do I see every strong man
    with his hands on his stomach like a
        woman in labor,
    every face turned deathly pale?
⁷ How awful that day will be!
    None will be like it.
It will be a time of trouble for Jacob,
    but he will be saved out of it.

⁸ " 'In that day,' declares the Lord Almighty,
    'I will break the yoke off their necks
and will tear off their bonds;
    no longer will foreigners enslave them.
⁹ Instead, they will serve the Lord their God
    and David their king,
    whom I will raise up for them.

¹⁰ " 'So do not fear, O Jacob my servant;
    do not be dismayed, O Israel,'
                        declares the Lord.
'I will surely save you out of a distant place,
    your descendants from the land of their
        exile.
Jacob will again have peace and security,
    and no one will make him afraid.
¹¹ I am with you and will save you,'
    declares the Lord.
'Though I completely destroy all the nations
    among which I scatter you,
    I will not completely destroy you.
I will discipline you but only with justice;
    I will not let you go entirely unpunished.'

¹² "This is what the Lord says:

" 'Your wound is incurable,
    your injury beyond healing.
¹³ There is no one to plead your cause,
    no remedy for your sore,
    no healing for you.
¹⁴ All your allies have forgotten you;
    they care nothing for you.
I have struck you as an enemy would
    and punished you as would the cruel,
because your guilt is so great
    and your sins so many.
¹⁵ Why do you cry out over your wound,
    your pain that has no cure?
Because of your great guilt and many sins
    I have done these things to you.

¹⁶ " 'But all who devour you will be devoured;
    all your enemies will go into exile.
Those who plunder you will be plundered;
    all who make spoil of you I will despoil.

ᵃ 3 Or will restore the fortunes of my people Israel and Judah

¹⁷ But I will restore you to health
    and heal your wounds,'
                    declares the Lord,
'because you are called an outcast,
    Zion for whom no one cares.'

¹⁸ "This is what the Lord says:

" 'I will restore the fortunes of Jacob's tents
    and have compassion on his dwellings;
the city will be rebuilt on her ruins,
    and the palace will stand in its proper place.
¹⁹ From them will come songs of thanksgiving
    and the sound of rejoicing.
I will add to their numbers,
    and they will not be decreased;
I will bring them honor,
    and they will not be disdained.
²⁰ Their children will be as in days of old,
    and their community will be established
        before me;
I will punish all who oppress them.
²¹ Their leader will be one of their own;
    their ruler will arise from among them.
I will bring him near and he will come close
        to me,
    for who is he who will devote himself
to be close to me?'
                    declares the Lord.
²² " 'So you will be my people,
    and I will be your God.' "

²³ See, the storm of the Lord
    will burst out in wrath,
a driving wind swirling down
    on the heads of the wicked.
²⁴ The fierce anger of the Lord will not turn
        back
    until he fully accomplishes
    the purposes of his heart.
In days to come
    you will understand this.

31 "At that time," declares the Lord, "I will be the God of all the clans of Israel, and they will be my people."

² This is what the Lord says:

"The people who survive the sword
    will find favor in the desert;
    I will come to give rest to Israel."

³ The Lord appeared to us in the past,ᵃ saying:

"I have loved you with an everlasting love;
    I have drawn you with loving-kindness.
⁴ I will build you up again
    and you will be rebuilt, O Virgin Israel.
Again you will take up your tambourines
    and go out to dance with the joyful.
⁵ Again you will plant vineyards
    on the hills of Samaria;
the farmers will plant them
    and enjoy their fruit.
⁶ There will be a day when watchmen cry out
    on the hills of Ephraim,
'Come, let us go up to Zion,
    to the Lord our God.' "

⁷ This is what the Lord says:

"Sing with joy for Jacob;
    shout for the foremost of the nations.
Make your praises heard, and say,
    'O Lord, save your people,
    the remnant of Israel.'
⁸ See, I will bring them from the land of the
        north
    and gather them from the ends of the
        earth.
Among them will be the blind and the lame,
    expectant mothers and women in labor;
    a great throng will return.
⁹ They will come with weeping;
    they will pray as I bring them back.
I will lead them beside streams of water
    on a level path where they will not
        stumble,
because I am Israel's father,
    and Ephraim is my firstborn son.

¹⁰ "Hear the word of the Lord, O nations;
    proclaim it in distant coastlands:

ᵃ 3 Or Lord has appeared to us from afar

The Great Ocean of God's Love

CORRIE TEN BOOM

READ | JEREMIAH 31:1–14

God's love is the greatest reality, here and now—not only if we live in a beautiful house and have enough to eat, but even if the very worst happens in the life of a child of God, the best remains, namely God's love.

I experienced that love when I was imprisoned in a concentration camp during the war. Each morning they held roll call. The supervisor used that time to demonstrate her cruelty. One morning I could hardly bear to see and hear what was happening in front of me. Then a lark started to sing in the air. All the prisoners looked up. I looked up too and listened to the bird, but I looked further and saw heaven. I thought of Psalm 103:11, "For as high as the heavens are above the earth, so great is his love [for] those who fear him." I suddenly saw that the ocean of God's great love is greater than human cruelty. God sent the lark every day for three weeks to teach us to direct our eyes to Him.

God wants to conquer our largest and smallest difficulties through His love. Think of the problems in your life at this moment. Are there problems that you cannot conquer with human love? Do it from now on with God's love, God's "agape," which never falls short.

When we are on the beach, we only see a small part of the ocean. However, we know that there is much more beyond the horizon. We only see a small part of God's great love, a few jewels of His great riches, but we know that there is much more beyond the horizon. The best is yet to come, when we see Jesus face-to-face.

Thank you, God, that you have poured out your love into my heart through the Holy Spirit. Thank you, Father, that your love conquers today's problems. Hallelujah. Amen.

Your next devotion is located on page 1064.

GRANDCHILD IN FOCUS · PRAYER

Courage

O Father, builder of character and courage, may my grandchild grow strong in the light of your love. Grant him courage to stand for what is right, to guard the truth and to ensure justice in every aspect of life. May he boldly grow in grace, revere your name and proudly proclaim you as the Lord of lords and King of kings. Amen.

'He who scattered Israel will gather them
and will watch over his flock like a
shepherd.'
¹¹ For the LORD will ransom Jacob
and redeem them from the hand of those
stronger than they.
¹² They will come and shout for joy on the
heights of Zion;
they will rejoice in the bounty of the
LORD —
the grain, the new wine and the oil,
the young of the flocks and herds.
They will be like a well-watered garden,
and they will sorrow no more.
¹³ Then maidens will dance and be glad,
young men and old as well.
I will turn their mourning into gladness;
I will give them comfort and joy instead of
sorrow.

PRAYING THE SCRIPTURES

Comfort

JEREMIAH 31:13

O Lord, as you promised the Israelites long
ago, turn the mourning of my grandchild
into gladness. Exchange his sorrow, I pray,
for comfort and joy.

Next prayer in Comfort Prayer Track: John 16:20

¹⁴ I will satisfy the priests with abundance,
and my people will be filled with my
bounty,"
declares the LORD.

¹⁵ This is what the LORD says:

"A voice is heard in Ramah,
mourning and great weeping,
Rachel weeping for her children
and refusing to be comforted,
because her children are no more."

¹⁶ This is what the LORD says:

"Restrain your voice from weeping
and your eyes from tears,
for your work will be rewarded,"
declares the LORD.
"They will return from the land of the
enemy.
¹⁷ So there is hope for your future,"
declares the LORD.
"Your children will return to their own
land.

¹⁸ "I have surely heard Ephraim's moaning:
'You disciplined me like an unruly calf,
and I have been disciplined.
Restore me, and I will return,
because you are the LORD my God.
¹⁹ After I strayed,
I repented;
after I came to understand,
I beat my breast.
I was ashamed and humiliated
because I bore the disgrace of my youth.'
²⁰ Is not Ephraim my dear son,
the child in whom I delight?
Though I often speak against him,
I still remember him.
Therefore my heart yearns for him;
I have great compassion for him,"
declares the LORD.

²¹ "Set up road signs;
put up guideposts.
Take note of the highway,
the road that you take.
Return, O Virgin Israel,
return to your towns.
²² How long will you wander,
O unfaithful daughter?
The LORD will create a new thing on earth —
a woman will surround ᵃ a man."

²³ This is what the LORD Almighty, the God of
Israel, says: "When I bring them back from cap-

ᵃ 22 Or will go about seeking; or will protect

tivity,[a] the people in the land of Judah and in its towns will once again use these words: 'The LORD bless you, O righteous dwelling, O sacred mountain.' 24 People will live together in Judah and all its towns—farmers and those who move about with their flocks. 25 I will refresh the weary and satisfy the faint."

26 At this I awoke and looked around. My sleep had been pleasant to me.

27 "The days are coming," declares the LORD, "when I will plant the house of Israel and the house of Judah with the offspring of men and of animals. 28 Just as I watched over them to uproot and tear down, and to overthrow, destroy and bring disaster, so I will watch over them to build and to plant," declares the LORD. 29 "In those days people will no longer say,

'The fathers have eaten sour grapes,
    and the children's teeth are set on edge.'

30 Instead, everyone will die for his own sin; whoever eats sour grapes—his own teeth will be set on edge.

31 "The time is coming," declares the LORD,
    "when I will make a new covenant
  with the house of Israel
    and with the house of Judah.
32 It will not be like the covenant
    I made with their forefathers
  when I took them by the hand
    to lead them out of Egypt,
  because they broke my covenant,
    though I was a husband to[b] them,[c]"
                    declares the LORD.
33 "This is the covenant I will make with the
        house of Israel
    after that time," declares the LORD.
  "I will put my law in their minds
    and write it on their hearts.
  I will be their God,
    and they will be my people.
34 No longer will a man teach his neighbor,
    or a man his brother, saying, 'Know the
        LORD,'

because they will all know me,
    from the least of them to the greatest,"
                    declares the LORD.
"For I will forgive their wickedness
    and will remember their sins no more."

35 This is what the LORD says,

he who appoints the sun
    to shine by day,
who decrees the moon and stars
    to shine by night,
who stirs up the sea
    so that its waves roar—
    the LORD Almighty is his name:
36 "Only if these decrees vanish from my sight,"
        declares the LORD,
  "will the descendants of Israel ever cease
    to be a nation before me."

37 This is what the LORD says:

"Only if the heavens above can be measured
    and the foundations of the earth below be
        searched out
will I reject all the descendants of Israel
    because of all they have done,"
                    declares the LORD.

38 "The days are coming," declares the LORD, "when this city will be rebuilt for me from the Tower of Hananel to the Corner Gate. 39 The measuring line will stretch from there straight to the hill of Gareb and then turn to Goah. 40 The whole valley where dead bodies and ashes are thrown, and all the terraces out to the Kidron Valley on the east as far as the corner of the Horse Gate, will be holy to the LORD. The city will never again be uprooted or demolished."

Jeremiah Buys a Field

32 This is the word that came to Jeremiah from the LORD in the tenth year of Zedekiah king of Judah, which was the eighteenth year of Nebuchadnezzar. 2 The army of the king

---

[a] 23 Or I restore their fortunes   [b] 32 Hebrew; Septuagint and Syriac / and I turned away from   [c] 32 Or was their master

> "FOR I WILL FORGIVE
> THEIR WICKEDNESS AND
> WILL REMEMBER THEIR
> SINS NO MORE."
> *Jeremiah 31:34*

Remembering No More

DORIS WYNBEEK RIKKERS

READ | JEREMIAH 31:31 – 37

It happened again the other day. I entered the grocery store knowing I had to pick up three things. Items one and two came to me quickly, but in a "senior moment," I forgot what the third thing was. (I hate it when that happens!) I chastised myself for not making a list. But even when I write a list, I usually leave it at home, stuck with a magnet to my refrigerator door. So I gave myself some time and pushed my cart around. As I turned down the baking aisle, I remembered — flour. That's what the third thing was!

It's human to forget. But something happens and suddenly we are reminded — of a past hurt, of an injustice, of a crushing blow or of a terrible sin in our lives. We forget about a grievance of long ago, perhaps even from our childhood, but then something comes up and the memory of the hurt and pain is revived. We can forget for a while, but then we drag it out of our memory bank. Now we remember.

God, on the other hand, doesn't just forget about our indiscretions, our atrocious thoughts, our vile deeds. He remembers them *no more*. Have you thought about that? God doesn't just forget something, only to be reminded of it again when we commit the same sin. He remembers it *no more*. It never, never crosses his mind again. If we blow it for the 30th time or the 500th time, he doesn't keep count. "Oh, there she goes again" is not a phrase he utters.

Nothing will remind him of our sin. Nothing will make him search through his database of indexed sins and find ours. Instead, he forgives us and remembers it no more. Done, finished, clean slate. What a joy. What a blessing. What a loving God!

Dear loving Lord, thank you for forgiving me of all my sins. Thank you for your wonderful gift of not remembering my past sinfulness and misdeeds. Help me to understand how completely and absolutely I am forgiven through your love and grace. Amen.

Your next devotion is located on page 1082.

GRANDCHILD IN FOCUS · PRAYER

Future Spouse

Dear Lord, if it is your will, I pray my grandchild will be united in a loving and Christian marriage. Keep her sexually pure so that she will honor you with her body and mind. As she seeks a spouse who will honor and care for her, give her patience and discernment. May her choice for a life partner be your choice for her, so that she and her husband will together glorify you in a lasting love. I pray this in Jesus' name, amen.

of Babylon was then besieging Jerusalem, and Jeremiah the prophet was confined in the courtyard of the guard in the royal palace of Judah.

³Now Zedekiah king of Judah had imprisoned him there, saying, "Why do you prophesy as you do? You say, 'This is what the LORD says: I am about to hand this city over to the king of Babylon, and he will capture it. ⁴Zedekiah king of Judah will not escape out of the hands of the Babylonians*ᵃ* but will certainly be handed over to the king of Babylon, and will speak with him face to face and see him with his own eyes. ⁵He will take Zedekiah to Babylon, where he will remain until I deal with him, declares the LORD. If you fight against the Babylonians, you will not succeed.'"

⁶Jeremiah said, "The word of the LORD came to me: ⁷Hanamel son of Shallum your uncle is going to come to you and say, 'Buy my field at Anathoth, because as nearest relative it is your right and duty to buy it.'

⁸"Then, just as the LORD had said, my cousin Hanamel came to me in the courtyard of the guard and said, 'Buy my field at Anathoth in the territory of Benjamin. Since it is your right to redeem it and possess it, buy it for yourself.'

"I knew that this was the word of the LORD; ⁹so I bought the field at Anathoth from my cousin Hanamel and weighed out for him seventeen shekels*ᵇ* of silver. ¹⁰I signed and sealed the deed, had it witnessed, and weighed out the silver on the scales. ¹¹I took the deed of purchase—the sealed copy containing the terms and conditions, as well as the unsealed copy— ¹²and I gave this deed to Baruch son of Neriah, the son of Mahseiah, in the presence of my cousin Hanamel and of the witnesses who had signed the deed and of all the Jews sitting in the courtyard of the guard.

¹³"In their presence I gave Baruch these instructions: ¹⁴'This is what the LORD Almighty, the God of Israel, says: Take these documents, both the sealed and unsealed copies of the deed of purchase, and put them in a clay jar so they will last a long time. ¹⁵For this is what the LORD Almighty, the God of Israel, says: Houses, fields and vineyards will again be bought in this land.'

¹⁶"After I had given the deed of purchase to Baruch son of Neriah, I prayed to the LORD:

¹⁷"Ah, Sovereign LORD, you have made the heavens and the earth by your great power and outstretched arm. Nothing is too hard for you. ¹⁸You show love to thousands but

---

TALKING POINTS

Eating Disorders
Nothing is too hard for God.
JEREMIAH 32:17

For more on eating disorders, go to Zechariah 4:6.

---

bring the punishment for the fathers' sins into the laps of their children after them. O great and powerful God, whose name is the LORD Almighty, ¹⁹great are your purposes and mighty are your deeds. Your eyes are open to all the ways of men; you reward everyone according to his conduct and as his deeds deserve. ²⁰You performed miraculous signs and wonders in Egypt and have continued them to this day, both in Israel and among all mankind, and have gained the renown that is still yours. ²¹You brought your people Israel out of Egypt with signs and wonders, by a mighty hand and an outstretched arm and with great terror. ²²You gave them this land you had sworn to give their forefathers, a land flowing with milk and honey. ²³They came in and took possession of it, but they did not obey you or follow your law; they did not do what you commanded them to do. So you brought all this disaster upon them.

²⁴"See how the siege ramps are built up to take the city. Because of the sword, famine

---

ᵃ 4 Or Chaldeans; also in verses 5, 24, 25, 28, 29 and 43   ᵇ 9 That is, about 7 ounces (about 200 grams) and plague, the city will be handed over to the Babylonians who are attacking it. What you said has happened, as you now see. ²⁵ And though the city will be handed over to the Babylonians, you, O Sovereign LORD, say to me, 'Buy the field with silver and have the transaction witnessed.' "

²⁶ Then the word of the LORD came to Jeremiah: ²⁷ "I am the LORD, the God of all mankind. Is anything too hard for me? ²⁸ Therefore, this is what the LORD says: I am about to hand this city over to the Babylonians and to Nebuchadnezzar king of Babylon, who will capture it. ²⁹ The Babylonians who are attacking this city will come in and set it on fire; they will burn it down, along with the houses where the people provoked me to anger by burning incense on the roofs to Baal and by pouring out drink offerings to other gods.

³⁰ "The people of Israel and Judah have done nothing but evil in my sight from their youth; indeed, the people of Israel have done nothing but provoke me with what their hands have made, declares the LORD. ³¹ From the day it was built until now, this city has so aroused my anger and wrath that I must remove it from my sight. ³² The people of Israel and Judah have provoked me by all the evil they have done — they, their kings and officials, their priests and prophets, the men of Judah and the people of Jerusalem. ³³ They turned their backs to me and not their faces; though I taught them again and again, they would not listen or respond to discipline. ³⁴ They set up their abominable idols in the house that bears my Name and defiled it. ³⁵ They built high places for Baal in the Valley of Ben Hinnom to sacrifice their sons and daughters ᵃ to Molech, though I never commanded, nor did it enter my mind, that they should do such a detestable thing and so make Judah sin.

³⁶ "You are saying about this city, 'By the sword, famine and plague it will be handed over to the king of Babylon'; but this is what the LORD, the God of Israel, says: ³⁷ I will surely gather them from all the lands where I banish them in my furious anger and great wrath; I will bring them back to this place and let them live in safety. ³⁸ They will be my people, and I will be their God. ³⁹ I will give them singleness of heart and action, so that they will always fear me for their own good and the good of their children after them. ⁴⁰ I will make an everlasting covenant with them: I will never stop doing good to them, and I will inspire them to fear me, so that they will never turn away from me. ⁴¹ I will rejoice in doing them good and will assuredly plant them in this land with all my heart and soul.

⁴² "This is what the LORD says: As I have brought all this great calamity on this people, so I will give them all the prosperity I have promised them. ⁴³ Once more fields will be bought in this land of which you say, 'It is a desolate waste, without men or animals, for it has been handed over to the Babylonians.' ⁴⁴ Fields will be bought for silver, and deeds will be signed, sealed and witnessed in the territory of Benjamin, in the villages around Jerusalem, in the towns of Judah and in the towns of the hill country, of the western foothills and of the Negev, because I will restore their fortunes, ᵇ declares the LORD."

Promise of Restoration

33 While Jeremiah was still confined in the courtyard of the guard, the word of the LORD came to him a second time: ² "This is what the LORD says, he who made the earth, the LORD who formed it and established it — the LORD is his name: ³ 'Call to me and I will answer you and tell you great and unsearchable things you do not know.' ⁴ For this is what the LORD, the God of Israel, says about the houses in this city and the royal palaces of Judah that have been torn down to be used against the siege ramps and the sword ⁵ in the fight with the Babylonians ᶜ: 'They will be filled with the dead bodies of the men I will slay in my anger and wrath. I will hide my face from this city because of all its wickedness.

ᵃ 35 Or *to make their sons and daughters pass through ˌthe fireˌ*   ᵇ 44 Or *will bring them back from captivity*   ᶜ 5 Or *Chaldeans*

TALKING POINTS

Prayer

God will share great things with us.

JEREMIAH 33:3

For more on prayer, go to Matthew 7:7–11.

⁶ " 'Nevertheless, I will bring health and healing to it; I will heal my people and will let them enjoy abundant peace and security. ⁷I will bring Judah and Israel back from captivity *ᵃ* and will rebuild them as they were before. ⁸I will cleanse them from all the sin they have committed against me and will forgive all their sins of rebellion against me. ⁹Then this city will bring me renown, joy, praise and honor before all nations on earth that hear of all the good things I do for it; and they will be in awe and will tremble at the abundant prosperity and peace I provide for it.'

PRAYING THE SCRIPTURES

Well-Being

JEREMIAH 33:6,9

Dear Lord, bring health and healing to my grandchild; heal him and let him enjoy abundant peace and security. Let him respond by bringing you renown, joy, praise and honor, so that others may hear of all the good things you have done for him.

Next prayer in Well-being Prayer Track: Acts 4:30

¹⁰ "This is what the LORD says: 'You say about this place, "It is a desolate waste, without men or animals." Yet in the towns of Judah and the streets of Jerusalem that are deserted, inhabited by neither men nor animals, there will be heard once more ¹¹the sounds of joy and gladness, the voices of bride and bridegroom, and the voices of those who bring thank offerings to the house of the LORD, saying,

"Give thanks to the LORD Almighty,
    for the LORD is good;
    his love endures forever."

For I will restore the fortunes of the land as they were before,' says the LORD.

¹² "This is what the LORD Almighty says: 'In this place, desolate and without men or animals — in all its towns there will again be pastures for shepherds to rest their flocks. ¹³In the towns of the hill country, of the western foothills and of the Negev, in the territory of Benjamin, in the villages around Jerusalem and in the towns of Judah, flocks will again pass under the hand of the one who counts them,' says the LORD.

¹⁴ " 'The days are coming,' declares the LORD, 'when I will fulfill the gracious promise I made to the house of Israel and to the house of Judah.

¹⁵ " 'In those days and at that time
    I will make a righteous Branch sprout
        from David's line;
    he will do what is just and right in the
        land.
¹⁶In those days Judah will be saved
    and Jerusalem will live in safety.
This is the name by which it *ᵇ* will be called:
    The LORD Our Righteousness.'

¹⁷For this is what the LORD says: 'David will never fail to have a man to sit on the throne of the house of Israel, ¹⁸nor will the priests, who are Levites, ever fail to have a man to stand before me continually to offer burnt offerings, to burn grain offerings and to present sacrifices.' "

¹⁹The word of the LORD came to Jeremiah: ²⁰ "This is what the LORD says: 'If you can break my covenant with the day and my covenant with the night, so that day and night no longer come at their appointed time, ²¹then my covenant with David my servant — and my covenant with the

ᵃ 7 Or will restore the fortunes of Judah and Israel   ᵇ 16 Or he

Levites who are priests ministering before me—can be broken and David will no longer have a descendant to reign on his throne. ²²I will make the descendants of David my servant and the Levites who minister before me as countless as the stars of the sky and as measureless as the sand on the seashore.'"

²³The word of the LORD came to Jeremiah: ²⁴"Have you not noticed that these people are saying, 'The LORD has rejected the two kingdoms*a* he chose'? So they despise my people and no longer regard them as a nation. ²⁵This is what the LORD says: 'If I have not established my covenant with day and night and the fixed laws of heaven and earth, ²⁶then I will reject the descendants of Jacob and David my servant and will not choose one of his sons to rule over the descendants of Abraham, Isaac and Jacob. For I will restore their fortunes *b* and have compassion on them.'"

Warning to Zedekiah

34 While Nebuchadnezzar king of Babylon and all his army and all the kingdoms and peoples in the empire he ruled were fighting against Jerusalem and all its surrounding towns, this word came to Jeremiah from the LORD: ²"This is what the LORD, the God of Israel, says: Go to Zedekiah king of Judah and tell him, 'This is what the LORD says: I am about to hand this city over to the king of Babylon, and he will burn it down. ³You will not escape from his grasp but will surely be captured and handed over to him. You will see the king of Babylon with your own eyes, and he will speak with you face to face. And you will go to Babylon.

⁴" 'Yet hear the promise of the LORD, O Zedekiah king of Judah. This is what the LORD says concerning you: You will not die by the sword; ⁵you will die peacefully. As people made a funeral fire in honor of your fathers, the former kings who preceded you, so they will make a fire in your honor and lament, "Alas, O master!" I myself make this promise, declares the LORD.'"

⁶Then Jeremiah the prophet told all this to Zedekiah king of Judah, in Jerusalem, ⁷while the army of the king of Babylon was fighting against Jerusalem and the other cities of Judah that were still holding out—Lachish and Azekah. These were the only fortified cities left in Judah.

Freedom for Slaves

⁸The word came to Jeremiah from the LORD after King Zedekiah had made a covenant with all the people in Jerusalem to proclaim freedom for the slaves. ⁹Everyone was to free his Hebrew slaves, both male and female; no one was to hold a fellow Jew in bondage. ¹⁰So all the officials and people who entered into this covenant agreed that they would free their male and female slaves and no longer hold them in bondage. They agreed, and set them free. ¹¹But afterward they changed their minds and took back the slaves they had freed and enslaved them again.

¹²Then the word of the LORD came to Jeremiah: ¹³"This is what the LORD, the God of Israel, says: I made a covenant with your forefathers when I brought them out of Egypt, out of the land of slavery. I said, ¹⁴'Every seventh year each of you must free any fellow Hebrew who has sold himself to you. After he has served you six years, you must let him go free.'*c* Your fathers, however, did not listen to me or pay attention to me. ¹⁵Recently you repented and did what is right in my sight: Each of you proclaimed freedom to his countrymen. You even made a covenant before me in the house that bears my Name. ¹⁶But now you have turned around and profaned my name; each of you has taken back the male and female slaves you had set free to go where they wished. You have forced them to become your slaves again.

¹⁷"Therefore, this is what the LORD says: You have not obeyed me; you have not proclaimed freedom for your fellow countrymen. So I now proclaim 'freedom' for you, declares the LORD—'freedom' to fall by the sword, plague and famine. I will make you abhorrent to all the kingdoms of the earth. ¹⁸The men who have violated my

---

a 24 Or *families*   *b 26* Or *will bring them back from captivity*
c 14 Deut. 15:12

covenant and have not fulfilled the terms of the covenant they made before me, I will treat like the calf they cut in two and then walked between its pieces. ¹⁹The leaders of Judah and Jerusalem, the court officials, the priests and all the people of the land who walked between the pieces of the calf, ²⁰I will hand over to their enemies who seek their lives. Their dead bodies will become food for the birds of the air and the beasts of the earth.

²¹"I will hand Zedekiah king of Judah and his officials over to their enemies who seek their lives, to the army of the king of Babylon, which has withdrawn from you. ²²I am going to give the order, declares the LORD, and I will bring them back to this city. They will fight against it, take it and burn it down. And I will lay waste the towns of Judah so no one can live there."

The Recabites

35 This is the word that came to Jeremiah from the LORD during the reign of Jehoiakim son of Josiah king of Judah: ²"Go to the Recabite family and invite them to come to one of the side rooms of the house of the LORD and give them wine to drink."

³So I went to get Jaazaniah son of Jeremiah, the son of Habazziniah, and his brothers and all his sons—the whole family of the Recabites. ⁴I brought them into the house of the LORD, into the room of the sons of Hanan son of Igdaliah the man of God. It was next to the room of the officials, which was over that of Maaseiah son of Shallum the doorkeeper. ⁵Then I set bowls full of wine and some cups before the men of the Recabite family and said to them, "Drink some wine."

⁶But they replied, "We do not drink wine, because our forefather Jonadab son of Recab gave us this command: 'Neither you nor your descendants must ever drink wine. ⁷Also you must never build houses, sow seed or plant vineyards; you must never have any of these things, but must always live in tents. Then you will live a long time in the land where you are nomads.' ⁸We have obeyed everything our forefather Jonadab son of Recab commanded us. Neither we nor our wives nor our sons and daughters have ever drunk wine ⁹or built houses to live in or had vineyards, fields or crops. ¹⁰We have lived in tents and have fully obeyed everything our forefather Jonadab commanded us. ¹¹But when Nebuchadnezzar king of Babylon invaded this land, we said, 'Come, we must go to Jerusalem to escape the Babylonian*a* and Aramean armies.' So we have remained in Jerusalem."

¹²Then the word of the LORD came to Jeremiah, saying: ¹³"This is what the LORD Almighty, the God of Israel, says: Go and tell the men of Judah and the people of Jerusalem, 'Will you not learn a lesson and obey my words?' declares the LORD. ¹⁴'Jonadab son of Recab ordered his sons not to drink wine and this command has been kept. To this day they do not drink wine, because they obey their forefather's command. But I have spoken to you again and again, yet you have not obeyed me. ¹⁵Again and again I sent all my servants the prophets to you. They said, "Each of you must turn from your wicked ways and reform your actions; do not follow other gods to serve them. Then you will live in the land I have given to you and your fathers." But you have not paid attention or listened to me. ¹⁶The descendants of Jonadab son of Recab have carried out the command their forefather gave them, but these people have not obeyed me.'

¹⁷"Therefore, this is what the LORD God Almighty, the God of Israel, says: 'Listen! I am going to bring on Judah and on everyone living in Jerusalem every disaster I pronounced against them. I spoke to them, but they did not listen; I called to them, but they did not answer.'"

¹⁸Then Jeremiah said to the family of the Recabites, "This is what the LORD Almighty, the God of Israel, says: 'You have obeyed the command of your forefather Jonadab and have followed all his instructions and have done everything he ordered.' ¹⁹Therefore, this is what the LORD Almighty, the God of Israel, says: 'Jonadab son of Recab will never fail to have a man to serve me.'"

a 11 Or *Chaldean*

Jehoiakim Burns Jeremiah's Scroll

36 In the fourth year of Jehoiakim son of Josiah king of Judah, this word came to Jeremiah from the LORD: ²"Take a scroll and write on it all the words I have spoken to you concerning Israel, Judah and all the other nations from the time I began speaking to you in the reign of Josiah till now. ³Perhaps when the people of Judah hear about every disaster I plan to inflict on them, each of them will turn from his wicked way; then I will forgive their wickedness and their sin."

⁴So Jeremiah called Baruch son of Neriah, and while Jeremiah dictated all the words the LORD had spoken to him, Baruch wrote them on the scroll. ⁵Then Jeremiah told Baruch, "I am restricted; I cannot go to the LORD's temple. ⁶So you go to the house of the LORD on a day of fasting and read to the people from the scroll the words of the LORD that you wrote as I dictated. Read them to all the people of Judah who come in from their towns. ⁷Perhaps they will bring their petition before the LORD, and each will turn from his wicked ways, for the anger and wrath pronounced against this people by the LORD are great."

⁸Baruch son of Neriah did everything Jeremiah the prophet told him to do; at the LORD's temple he read the words of the LORD from the scroll. ⁹In the ninth month of the fifth year of Jehoiakim son of Josiah king of Judah, a time of fasting before the LORD was proclaimed for all the people in Jerusalem and those who had come from the towns of Judah. ¹⁰From the room of Gemariah son of Shaphan the secretary, which was in the upper courtyard at the entrance of the New Gate of the temple, Baruch read to all the people at the LORD's temple the words of Jeremiah from the scroll.

¹¹When Micaiah son of Gemariah, the son of Shaphan, heard all the words of the LORD from the scroll, ¹²he went down to the secretary's room in the royal palace, where all the officials were sitting: Elishama the secretary, Delaiah son of Shemaiah, Elnathan son of Acbor, Gemariah son of Shaphan, Zedekiah son of Hananiah, and all the other officials. ¹³After Micaiah told them everything he had heard Baruch read to the people from the scroll, ¹⁴all the officials sent Jehudi son of Nethaniah, the son of Shelemiah, the son of Cushi, to say to Baruch, "Bring the scroll from which you have read to the people and come." So Baruch son of Neriah went to them with the scroll in his hand. ¹⁵They said to him, "Sit down, please, and read it to us."

So Baruch read it to them. ¹⁶When they heard all these words, they looked at each other in fear and said to Baruch, "We must report all these words to the king." ¹⁷Then they asked Baruch, "Tell us, how did you come to write all this? Did Jeremiah dictate it?"

stories to share

JEREMIAH 36:1–32

Jehoiakim Burns Jeremiah's Scroll

LIFE LESSON: God expects us to listen to his messages.

TO TALK ABOUT

✦ What was written on Jeremiah's scroll?

✦ Why do you think King Jehoiakim burned up the scroll?

✦ How would you feel if your teacher tore up a paper you had worked hard on?

✦ Who was the king really rejecting the most, God or Jeremiah?

¹⁸"Yes," Baruch replied, "he dictated all these words to me, and I wrote them in ink on the scroll."

¹⁹Then the officials said to Baruch, "You and Jeremiah, go and hide. Don't let anyone know where you are."

²⁰After they put the scroll in the room of Elishama the secretary, they went to the king in the courtyard and reported everything to him. ²¹The king sent Jehudi to get the scroll, and Jehudi brought it from the room of Elishama the secretary and read it to the king and all the officials standing beside him. ²²It was the ninth month and the king was sitting in the winter apartment, with a fire burning in the firepot in front of him. ²³Whenever Jehudi had read three or four columns of the scroll, the king cut them off with a scribe's knife and threw them into the firepot, until the entire scroll was burned in the fire. ²⁴The king and all his attendants who heard all these words showed no fear, nor did they tear their clothes. ²⁵Even though Elnathan, Delaiah and Gemariah urged the king not to burn the scroll, he would not listen to them. ²⁶Instead, the king commanded Jerahmeel, a son of the king, Seraiah son of Azriel and Shelemiah son of Abdeel to arrest Baruch the scribe and Jeremiah the prophet. But the LORD had hidden them.

²⁷After the king burned the scroll containing the words that Baruch had written at Jeremiah's dictation, the word of the LORD came to Jeremiah: ²⁸"Take another scroll and write on it all the words that were on the first scroll, which Jehoiakim king of Judah burned up. ²⁹Also tell Jehoiakim king of Judah, 'This is what the LORD says: You burned that scroll and said, "Why did you write on it that the king of Babylon would certainly come and destroy this land and cut off both men and animals from it?" ³⁰Therefore, this is what the LORD says about Jehoiakim king of Judah: He will have no one to sit on the throne of David; his body will be thrown out and exposed to the heat by day and the frost by night. ³¹I will punish him and his children and his attendants for their wickedness; I will bring on them and those living in Jerusalem and the people of Judah every disaster I pronounced against them, because they have not listened.' "

³²So Jeremiah took another scroll and gave it to the scribe Baruch son of Neriah, and as Jeremiah dictated, Baruch wrote on it all the words of the scroll that Jehoiakim king of Judah had burned in the fire. And many similar words were added to them.

Jeremiah in Prison

37 Zedekiah son of Josiah was made king of Judah by Nebuchadnezzar king of Babylon; he reigned in place of Jehoiachin[a] son of Jehoiakim. ²Neither he nor his attendants nor the people of the land paid any attention to the words the LORD had spoken through Jeremiah the prophet.

³King Zedekiah, however, sent Jehucal son of Shelemiah with the priest Zephaniah son of Maaseiah to Jeremiah the prophet with this message: "Please pray to the LORD our God for us."

⁴Now Jeremiah was free to come and go among the people, for he had not yet been put in prison. ⁵Pharaoh's army had marched out of Egypt, and when the Babylonians[b] who were besieging Jerusalem heard the report about them, they withdrew from Jerusalem.

⁶Then the word of the LORD came to Jeremiah the prophet: ⁷"This is what the LORD, the God of Israel, says: Tell the king of Judah, who sent you to inquire of me, 'Pharaoh's army, which has marched out to support you, will go back to its own land, to Egypt. ⁸Then the Babylonians will return and attack this city; they will capture it and burn it down.'

⁹"This is what the LORD says: Do not deceive yourselves, thinking, 'The Babylonians will surely leave us.' They will not! ¹⁰Even if you were to defeat the entire Babylonian[c] army that is attacking you and only wounded men were left in their tents, they would come out and burn this city down."

---

[a] 1 Hebrew *Coniah*, a variant of *Jehoiachin*   [b] 5 Or *Chaldeans*; also in verses 8, 9, 13 and 14   [c] 10 Or *Chaldean*; also in verse 11

[11] After the Babylonian army had withdrawn from Jerusalem because of Pharaoh's army, [12] Jeremiah started to leave the city to go to the territory of Benjamin to get his share of the property among the people there. [13] But when he reached the Benjamin Gate, the captain of the guard, whose name was Irijah son of Shelemiah, the son of Hananiah, arrested him and said, "You are deserting to the Babylonians!"

[14] "That's not true!" Jeremiah said. "I am not deserting to the Babylonians." But Irijah would not listen to him; instead, he arrested Jeremiah and brought him to the officials. [15] They were angry with Jeremiah and had him beaten and imprisoned in the house of Jonathan the secretary, which they had made into a prison.

[16] Jeremiah was put into a vaulted cell in a dungeon, where he remained a long time. [17] Then King Zedekiah sent for him and had him brought to the palace, where he asked him privately, "Is there any word from the LORD?"

"Yes," Jeremiah replied, "you will be handed over to the king of Babylon."

[18] Then Jeremiah said to King Zedekiah, "What crime have I committed against you or your officials or this people, that you have put me in prison? [19] Where are your prophets who prophesied to you, 'The king of Babylon will not attack you or this land'? [20] But now, my lord the king, please listen. Let me bring my petition before you: Do not send me back to the house of Jonathan the secretary, or I will die there."

[21] King Zedekiah then gave orders for Jeremiah to be placed in the courtyard of the guard and given bread from the street of the bakers each day until all the bread in the city was gone. So Jeremiah remained in the courtyard of the guard.

Jeremiah Thrown Into a Cistern

38 Shephatiah son of Mattan, Gedaliah son of Pashhur, Jehucal[a] son of Shelemiah, and Pashhur son of Malkijah heard what Jeremiah was telling all the people when he said, [2] "This is what the LORD says: 'Whoever stays in this city will die by the sword, famine or plague, but whoever goes over to the Babylonians[b] will live. He will escape with his life; he will live.' [3] And this is what the LORD says: 'This city will certainly be handed over to the army of the king of Babylon, who will capture it.'"

[4] Then the officials said to the king, "This man should be put to death. He is discouraging the soldiers who are left in this city, as well as all the people, by the things he is saying to them. This man is not seeking the good of these people but their ruin."

[5] "He is in your hands," King Zedekiah answered. "The king can do nothing to oppose you."

[6] So they took Jeremiah and put him into the cistern of Malkijah, the king's son, which was in the courtyard of the guard. They lowered Jeremiah by ropes into the cistern; it had no water in it, only mud, and Jeremiah sank down into the mud.

[7] But Ebed-Melech, a Cushite,[c] an official[d] in the royal palace, heard that they had put Jeremiah into the cistern. While the king was sitting in the Benjamin Gate, [8] Ebed-Melech went out of the palace and said to him, [9] "My lord the king, these men have acted wickedly in all they have done to Jeremiah the prophet. They have thrown him into a cistern, where he will starve to death when there is no longer any bread in the city."

[10] Then the king commanded Ebed-Melech the Cushite, "Take thirty men from here with you and lift Jeremiah the prophet out of the cistern before he dies."

[11] So Ebed-Melech took the men with him and went to a room under the treasury in the palace. He took some old rags and worn-out clothes from there and let them down with ropes to Jeremiah in the cistern. [12] Ebed-Melech the Cushite said to Jeremiah, "Put these old rags and worn-out clothes under your arms to pad the ropes." Jeremiah did so, [13] and they pulled him up with the ropes and lifted him out of the cistern. And Jeremiah remained in the courtyard of the guard.

---

[a] 1 Hebrew *Jucal*, a variant of *Jehucal*   [b] 2 Or *Chaldeans*; also in verses 18, 19 and 23   [c] 7 Probably from the upper Nile region   [d] 7 Or *a eunuch*

JEREMIAH 38:1–28

Jeremiah Is Saved From Death

LIFE LESSON: God requires our obedience.

TO TALK ABOUT

✦ Where did the king's officials put Jeremiah?

✦ Why did King Zedekiah change his mind about Jeremiah after Ebed-Melech talked to him?

✦ Did Zedekiah listen to Jeremiah's advice to surrender? What happened to Zedekiah? To Ebed-Melech? To Jeremiah? (Hint: Read chapter 39.)

Zedekiah Questions Jeremiah Again

¹⁴Then King Zedekiah sent for Jeremiah the prophet and had him brought to the third entrance to the temple of the LORD. "I am going to ask you something," the king said to Jeremiah. "Do not hide anything from me."

¹⁵Jeremiah said to Zedekiah, "If I give you an answer, will you not kill me? Even if I did give you counsel, you would not listen to me."

¹⁶But King Zedekiah swore this oath secretly to Jeremiah: "As surely as the LORD lives, who has given us breath, I will neither kill you nor hand you over to those who are seeking your life."

¹⁷Then Jeremiah said to Zedekiah, "This is what the LORD God Almighty, the God of Israel, says: 'If you surrender to the officers of the king of Babylon, your life will be spared and this city will not be burned down; you and your family will live. ¹⁸But if you will not surrender to the officers of the king of Babylon, this city will be handed over to the Babylonians and they will burn it down; you yourself will not escape from their hands.'"

¹⁹King Zedekiah said to Jeremiah, "I am afraid of the Jews who have gone over to the Babylonians, for the Babylonians may hand me over to them and they will mistreat me."

²⁰"They will not hand you over," Jeremiah replied. "Obey the LORD by doing what I tell you. Then it will go well with you, and your life will be spared. ²¹But if you refuse to surrender, this is what the LORD has revealed to me: ²²All the women left in the palace of the king of Judah will be brought out to the officials of the king of Babylon. Those women will say to you:

" 'They misled you and overcame you—
those trusted friends of yours.
Your feet are sunk in the mud;
your friends have deserted you.'

²³"All your wives and children will be brought out to the Babylonians. You yourself will not escape from their hands but will be captured by the king of Babylon; and this city will ᵃ be burned down."

²⁴Then Zedekiah said to Jeremiah, "Do not let anyone know about this conversation, or you may die. ²⁵If the officials hear that I talked with you, and they come to you and say, 'Tell us what you said to the king and what the king said to you; do not hide it from us or we will kill you,' ²⁶then tell them, 'I was pleading with the king not to send me back to Jonathan's house to die there.'"

²⁷All the officials did come to Jeremiah and question him, and he told them everything the king had ordered him to say. So they said no more to him, for no one had heard his conversation with the king.

ᵃ 23 Or *and you will cause this city to*

²⁸And Jeremiah remained in the courtyard of the guard until the day Jerusalem was captured.

The Fall of Jerusalem

39:1–10pp — 2Ki 25:1–12; Jer 52:4–16

39 This is how Jerusalem was taken: ¹In the ninth year of Zedekiah king of Judah, in the tenth month, Nebuchadnezzar king of Babylon marched against Jerusalem with his whole army and laid siege to it. ²And on the ninth day of the fourth month of Zedekiah's eleventh year, the city wall was broken through. ³Then all the officials of the king of Babylon came and took seats in the Middle Gate: Nergal-Sharezer of Samgar, Nebo-Sarsekim ᵃ a chief officer, Nergal-Sharezer a high official and all the other officials of the king of Babylon. ⁴When Zedekiah king of Judah and all the soldiers saw them, they fled; they left the city at night by way of the king's garden, through the gate between the two walls, and headed toward the Arabah. ᵇ

⁵But the Babylonian ᶜ army pursued them and overtook Zedekiah in the plains of Jericho. They captured him and took him to Nebuchadnezzar king of Babylon at Riblah in the land of Hamath, where he pronounced sentence on him. ⁶There at Riblah the king of Babylon slaughtered the sons of Zedekiah before his eyes and also killed all the nobles of Judah. ⁷Then he put out Zedekiah's eyes and bound him with bronze shackles to take him to Babylon.

⁸The Babylonians ᵈ set fire to the royal palace and the houses of the people and broke down the walls of Jerusalem. ⁹Nebuzaradan commander of the imperial guard carried into exile to Babylon the people who remained in the city, along with those who had gone over to him, and the rest of the people. ¹⁰But Nebuzaradan the commander of the guard left behind in the land of Judah some of the poor people, who owned nothing; and at that time he gave them vineyards and fields.

¹¹Now Nebuchadnezzar king of Babylon had given these orders about Jeremiah through Nebuzaradan commander of the imperial guard: ¹²"Take him and look after him; don't harm him but do for him whatever he asks." ¹³So Nebuzaradan the commander of the guard, Nebushazban a chief officer, Nergal-Sharezer a high official and all the other officers of the king of Babylon ¹⁴sent and had Jeremiah taken out of the courtyard of the guard. They turned him over to Gedaliah son of Ahikam, the son of Shaphan, to take him back to his home. So he remained among his own people.

¹⁵While Jeremiah had been confined in the courtyard of the guard, the word of the Lord came to him: ¹⁶"Go and tell Ebed-Melech the Cushite, 'This is what the Lord Almighty, the God of Israel, says: I am about to fulfill my words against this city through disaster, not prosperity. At that time they will be fulfilled before your eyes. ¹⁷But I will rescue you on that day, declares the Lord; you will not be handed over to those you fear. ¹⁸I will save you; you will not fall by the sword but will escape with your life, because you trust in me, declares the Lord.'"

Jeremiah Freed

40 The word came to Jeremiah from the Lord after Nebuzaradan commander of the imperial guard had released him at Ramah. He had found Jeremiah bound in chains among all the captives from Jerusalem and Judah who were being carried into exile to Babylon. ²When the commander of the guard found Jeremiah, he said to him, "The Lord your God decreed this disaster for this place. ³And now the Lord has brought it about; he has done just as he said he would. All this happened because you people sinned against the Lord and did not obey him. ⁴But today I am freeing you from the chains on your wrists. Come with me to Babylon, if you like, and I will look after you; but if you do not want to, then don't come. Look, the whole country lies before you; go wherever you please." ⁵However, before Jeremiah turned to go, ᵉ Nebuzaradan added, "Go back to Gedaliah son of Ahikam, the son

of Shaphan, whom the king of Babylon has appointed over the towns of Judah, and live with him among the people, or go anywhere else you please."

Then the commander gave him provisions and a present and let him go. ⁶So Jeremiah went to Gedaliah son of Ahikam at Mizpah and stayed with him among the people who were left behind in the land.

Gedaliah Assassinated

40:7–9; 41:1–3pp — 2Ki 25:22–26

⁷When all the army officers and their men who were still in the open country heard that the king of Babylon had appointed Gedaliah son of Ahikam as governor over the land and had put him in charge of the men, women and children who were the poorest in the land and who had not been carried into exile to Babylon, ⁸they came to Gedaliah at Mizpah—Ishmael son of Nethaniah, Johanan and Jonathan the sons of Kareah, Seraiah son of Tanhumeth, the sons of Ephai the Netophathite, and Jaazaniah *ᵃ* the son of the Maacathite, and their men. ⁹Gedaliah son of Ahikam, the son of Shaphan, took an oath to reassure them and their men. "Do not be afraid to serve the Babylonians, *ᵇ*" he said. "Settle down in the land and serve the king of Babylon, and it will go well with you. ¹⁰I myself will stay at Mizpah to represent you before the Babylonians who come to us, but you are to harvest the wine, summer fruit and oil, and put them in your storage jars, and live in the towns you have taken over."

¹¹When all the Jews in Moab, Ammon, Edom and all the other countries heard that the king of Babylon had left a remnant in Judah and had appointed Gedaliah son of Ahikam, the son of Shaphan, as governor over them, ¹²they all came back to the land of Judah, to Gedaliah at Mizpah, from all the countries where they had been scattered. And they harvested an abundance of wine and summer fruit.

¹³Johanan son of Kareah and all the army officers still in the open country came to Gedaliah at Mizpah ¹⁴and said to him, "Don't you know that Baalis king of the Ammonites has sent Ishmael son of Nethaniah to take your life?" But Gedaliah son of Ahikam did not believe them.

¹⁵Then Johanan son of Kareah said privately to Gedaliah in Mizpah, "Let me go and kill Ishmael son of Nethaniah, and no one will know it. Why should he take your life and cause all the Jews who are gathered around you to be scattered and the remnant of Judah to perish?"

¹⁶But Gedaliah son of Ahikam said to Johanan son of Kareah, "Don't do such a thing! What you are saying about Ishmael is not true."

41 In the seventh month Ishmael son of Nethaniah, the son of Elishama, who was of royal blood and had been one of the king's officers, came with ten men to Gedaliah son of Ahikam at Mizpah. While they were eating together there, ²Ishmael son of Nethaniah and the ten men who were with him got up and struck down Gedaliah son of Ahikam, the son of Shaphan, with the sword, killing the one whom the king of Babylon had appointed as governor over the land. ³Ishmael also killed all the Jews who were with Gedaliah at Mizpah, as well as the Babylonian *ᶜ* soldiers who were there.

⁴The day after Gedaliah's assassination, before anyone knew about it, ⁵eighty men who had shaved off their beards, torn their clothes and cut themselves came from Shechem, Shiloh and Samaria, bringing grain offerings and incense with them to the house of the Lord. ⁶Ishmael son of Nethaniah went out from Mizpah to meet them, weeping as he went. When he met them, he said, "Come to Gedaliah son of Ahikam." ⁷When they went into the city, Ishmael son of Nethaniah and the men who were with him slaughtered them and threw them into a cistern. ⁸But ten of them said to Ishmael, "Don't kill us! We have wheat and barley, oil and honey, hidden in a field." So he let them alone and did not kill them with the others. ⁹Now the cistern where he threw all the bodies of the men he had killed along with Gedaliah was the one King Asa had made as part of

---

ᵃ 8 Hebrew Jezaniah, a variant of Jaazaniah   ᵇ 9 Or Chaldeans; also in verse 10   ᶜ 3 Or Chaldean his defense against Baasha king of Israel. Ishmael son of Nethaniah filled it with the dead.

¹⁰Ishmael made captives of all the rest of the people who were in Mizpah—the king's daughters along with all the others who were left there, over whom Nebuzaradan commander of the imperial guard had appointed Gedaliah son of Ahikam. Ishmael son of Nethaniah took them captive and set out to cross over to the Ammonites.

¹¹When Johanan son of Kareah and all the army officers who were with him heard about all the crimes Ishmael son of Nethaniah had committed, ¹²they took all their men and went to fight Ishmael son of Nethaniah. They caught up with him near the great pool in Gibeon. ¹³When all the people Ishmael had with him saw Johanan son of Kareah and the army officers who were with him, they were glad. ¹⁴All the people Ishmael had taken captive at Mizpah turned and went over to Johanan son of Kareah. ¹⁵But Ishmael son of Nethaniah and eight of his men escaped from Johanan and fled to the Ammonites.

Flight to Egypt

¹⁶Then Johanan son of Kareah and all the army officers who were with him led away all the survivors from Mizpah whom he had recovered from Ishmael son of Nethaniah after he had assassinated Gedaliah son of Ahikam: the soldiers, women, children and court officials he had brought from Gibeon. ¹⁷And they went on, stopping at Geruth Kimham near Bethlehem on their way to Egypt ¹⁸to escape the Babylonians.ᵃ They were afraid of them because Ishmael son of Nethaniah had killed Gedaliah son of Ahikam, whom the king of Babylon had appointed as governor over the land.

42 Then all the army officers, including Johanan son of Kareah and Jezaniahᵇ son of Hoshaiah, and all the people from the least to the greatest approached ²Jeremiah the prophet and said to him, "Please hear our petition and pray to the LORD your God for this entire remnant. For as you now see, though we were once many, now only a few are left. ³Pray that the LORD your

God will tell us where we should go and what we should do."

⁴"I have heard you," replied Jeremiah the prophet. "I will certainly pray to the LORD your God as you have requested; I will tell you everything the LORD says and will keep nothing back from you."

⁵Then they said to Jeremiah, "May the LORD be a true and faithful witness against us if we do not act in accordance with everything the LORD your God sends you to tell us. ⁶Whether it is favorable or unfavorable, we will obey the LORD our God, to whom we are sending you, so that it will go well with us, for we will obey the LORD our God."

⁷Ten days later the word of the LORD came to Jeremiah. ⁸So he called together Johanan son of Kareah and all the army officers who were with him and all the people from the least to the greatest. ⁹He said to them, "This is what the LORD, the God of Israel, to whom you sent me to present your petition, says: ¹⁰'If you stay in this land, I will build you up and not tear you down; I will plant you and not uproot you, for I am grieved over the disaster I have inflicted on you. ¹¹Do not be afraid of the king of Babylon, whom you now fear. Do not be afraid of him, declares the LORD, for I am with you and will save you and deliver you from his hands. ¹²I will show you compassion so that he will have compassion on you and restore you to your land.'

¹³"However, if you say, 'We will not stay in this land,' and so disobey the LORD your God, ¹⁴and if you say, 'No, we will go and live in Egypt, where we will not see war or hear the trumpet or be hungry for bread,' ¹⁵then hear the word of the LORD, O remnant of Judah. This is what the LORD Almighty, the God of Israel, says: 'If you are determined to go to Egypt and you do go to settle there, ¹⁶then the sword you fear will overtake you there, and the famine you dread will follow you into Egypt, and there you will die. ¹⁷Indeed, all who are determined to go to Egypt to settle there

---

ᵃ 18 Or Chaldeans   ᵇ 1 Hebrew; Septuagint (see also 43:2) Azariah will die by the sword, famine and plague; not one of them will survive or escape the disaster I will bring on them.' ¹⁸This is what the LORD Almighty, the God of Israel, says: 'As my anger and wrath have been poured out on those who lived in Jerusalem, so will my wrath be poured out on you when you go to Egypt. You will be an object of cursing and horror, of condemnation and reproach; you will never see this place again.'

¹⁹"O remnant of Judah, the LORD has told you, 'Do not go to Egypt.' Be sure of this: I warn you today ²⁰that you made a fatal mistake ᵃ when you sent me to the LORD your God and said, 'Pray to the LORD our God for us; tell us everything he says and we will do it.' ²¹I have told you today, but you still have not obeyed the LORD your God in all he sent me to tell you. ²²So now, be sure of this: You will die by the sword, famine and plague in the place where you want to go to settle."

43 When Jeremiah finished telling the people all the words of the LORD their God—everything the LORD had sent him to tell them— ²Azariah son of Hoshaiah and Johanan son of Kareah and all the arrogant men said to Jeremiah, "You are lying! The LORD our God has not sent you to say, 'You must not go to Egypt to settle there.' ³But Baruch son of Neriah is inciting you against us to hand us over to the Babylonians, ᵇ so they may kill us or carry us into exile to Babylon."

⁴So Johanan son of Kareah and all the army officers and all the people disobeyed the LORD's command to stay in the land of Judah. ⁵Instead, Johanan son of Kareah and all the army officers led away all the remnant of Judah who had come back to live in the land of Judah from all the nations where they had been scattered. ⁶They also led away all the men, women and children and the king's daughters whom Nebuzaradan commander of the imperial guard had left with Gedaliah son of Ahikam, the son of Shaphan, and Jeremiah the prophet and Baruch son of Neriah. ⁷So they entered Egypt in disobedience to the LORD and went as far as Tahpanhes.

⁸In Tahpanhes the word of the LORD came to Jeremiah: ⁹"While the Jews are watching, take some large stones with you and bury them in clay in the brick pavement at the entrance to Pharaoh's palace in Tahpanhes. ¹⁰Then say to them, 'This is what the LORD Almighty, the God of Israel, says: I will send for my servant Nebuchadnezzar king of Babylon, and I will set his throne over these stones I have buried here; he will spread his royal canopy above them. ¹¹He will come and attack Egypt, bringing death to those destined for death, captivity to those destined for captivity, and the sword to those destined for the sword. ¹²He ᶜ will set fire to the temples of the gods of Egypt; he will burn their temples and take their gods captive. As a shepherd wraps his garment around him, so will he wrap Egypt around himself and depart from there unscathed. ¹³There in the temple of the sun ᵈ in Egypt he will demolish the sacred pillars and will burn down the temples of the gods of Egypt.' "

Disaster Because of Idolatry

44 This word came to Jeremiah concerning all the Jews living in Lower Egypt—in Migdol, Tahpanhes and Memphis ᵉ—and in Upper Egypt ᶠ: ²"This is what the LORD Almighty, the God of Israel, says: You saw the great disaster I brought on Jerusalem and on all the towns of Judah. Today they lie deserted and in ruins ³because of the evil they have done. They provoked me to anger by burning incense and by worshiping other gods that neither they nor you nor your fathers ever knew. ⁴Again and again I sent my servants the prophets, who said, 'Do not do this detestable thing that I hate!' ⁵But they did not listen or pay attention; they did not turn from their wickedness or stop burning incense to other gods. ⁶Therefore, my fierce anger was poured out; it raged against the towns of Judah and the streets of Jerusalem and made them the desolate ruins they are today.

⁷"Now this is what the LORD God Almighty, the God of Israel, says: Why bring such great

---

ᵃ 20 Or *you erred in your hearts*   ᵇ 3 Or *Chaldeans*   ᶜ 12 Or *I*
ᵈ 13 Or *in Heliopolis*   ᵉ 1 Hebrew *Noph*   ᶠ 1 Hebrew *in Pathros*

disaster on yourselves by cutting off from Judah the men and women, the children and infants, and so leave yourselves without a remnant? ⁸Why provoke me to anger with what your hands have made, burning incense to other gods in Egypt, where you have come to live? You will destroy yourselves and make yourselves an object of cursing and reproach among all the nations on earth. ⁹Have you forgotten the wickedness committed by your fathers and by the kings and queens of Judah and the wickedness committed by you and your wives in the land of Judah and the streets of Jerusalem? ¹⁰To this day they have not humbled themselves or shown reverence, nor have they followed my law and the decrees I set before you and your fathers.

¹¹"Therefore, this is what the LORD Almighty, the God of Israel, says: I am determined to bring disaster on you and to destroy all Judah. ¹²I will take away the remnant of Judah who were determined to go to Egypt to settle there. They will all perish in Egypt; they will fall by the sword or die from famine. From the least to the greatest, they will die by sword or famine. They will become an object of cursing and horror, of condemnation and reproach. ¹³I will punish those who live in Egypt with the sword, famine and plague, as I punished Jerusalem. ¹⁴None of the remnant of Judah who have gone to live in Egypt will escape or survive to return to the land of Judah, to which they long to return and live; none will return except a few fugitives."

¹⁵Then all the men who knew that their wives were burning incense to other gods, along with all the women who were present—a large assembly—and all the people living in Lower and Upper Egypt,ᵃ said to Jeremiah, ¹⁶"We will not listen to the message you have spoken to us in the name of the LORD! ¹⁷We will certainly do everything we said we would: We will burn incense to the Queen of Heaven and will pour out drink offerings to her just as we and our fathers, our kings and our officials did in the towns of Judah and in the streets of Jerusalem. At that time we had plenty of food and were well off and suffered no harm. ¹⁸But ever since we stopped burning incense to the Queen of Heaven and pouring out drink offerings to her, we have had nothing and have been perishing by sword and famine."

¹⁹The women added, "When we burned incense to the Queen of Heaven and poured out drink offerings to her, did not our husbands know that we were making cakes like her image and pouring out drink offerings to her?"

²⁰Then Jeremiah said to all the people, both men and women, who were answering him, ²¹"Did not the LORD remember and think about the incense burned in the towns of Judah and the streets of Jerusalem by you and your fathers, your kings and your officials and the people of the land? ²²When the LORD could no longer endure your wicked actions and the detestable things you did, your land became an object of cursing and a desolate waste without inhabitants, as it is today. ²³Because you have burned incense and have sinned against the LORD and have not obeyed him or followed his law or his decrees or his stipulations, this disaster has come upon you, as you now see."

²⁴Then Jeremiah said to all the people, including the women, "Hear the word of the LORD, all you people of Judah in Egypt. ²⁵This is what the LORD Almighty, the God of Israel, says: You and your wives have shown by your actions what you promised when you said, 'We will certainly carry out the vows we made to burn incense and pour out drink offerings to the Queen of Heaven.'

"Go ahead then, do what you promised! Keep your vows! ²⁶But hear the word of the LORD, all Jews living in Egypt: 'I swear by my great name,' says the LORD, 'that no one from Judah living anywhere in Egypt will ever again invoke my name or swear, "As surely as the Sovereign LORD lives." ²⁷For I am watching over them for harm, not for good; the Jews in Egypt will perish by sword and famine until they are all destroyed. ²⁸Those who escape the sword and return to the land of Judah from Egypt will be very few. Then the whole

ᵃ 15 Hebrew *in Egypt and Pathros*

remnant of Judah who came to live in Egypt will know whose word will stand—mine or theirs.

29 " 'This will be the sign to you that I will punish you in this place,' declares the LORD, 'so that you will know that my threats of harm against you will surely stand.' 30 This is what the LORD says: 'I am going to hand Pharaoh Hophra king of Egypt over to his enemies who seek his life, just as I handed Zedekiah king of Judah over to Nebuchadnezzar king of Babylon, the enemy who was seeking his life.' "

A Message to Baruch

45 This is what Jeremiah the prophet told Baruch son of Neriah in the fourth year of Jehoiakim son of Josiah king of Judah, after Baruch had written on a scroll the words Jeremiah was then dictating: 2 "This is what the LORD, the God of Israel, says to you, Baruch: 3 You said, 'Woe to me! The LORD has added sorrow to my pain; I am worn out with groaning and find no rest.' "

4 ⌊The LORD said,⌋ "Say this to him: 'This is what the LORD says: I will overthrow what I have built and uproot what I have planted, throughout the land. 5 Should you then seek great things for yourself? Seek them not. For I will bring disaster on all people, declares the LORD, but wherever you go I will let you escape with your life.' "

A Message About Egypt

46 This is the word of the LORD that came to Jeremiah the prophet concerning the nations:

2 Concerning Egypt:

This is the message against the army of Pharaoh Neco king of Egypt, which was defeated at Carchemish on the Euphrates River by Nebuchadnezzar king of Babylon in the fourth year of Jehoiakim son of Josiah king of Judah:

3 "Prepare your shields, both large and small,
　　and march out for battle!
4 Harness the horses,
　　mount the steeds!

Take your positions
　　with helmets on!
Polish your spears,
　　put on your armor!
5 What do I see?
　　They are terrified,
they are retreating,
　　their warriors are defeated.
They flee in haste
　　without looking back,
　　and there is terror on every side,"
　　　　　　　　　declares the LORD.
6 "The swift cannot flee
　　nor the strong escape.
In the north by the River Euphrates
　　they stumble and fall.

7 "Who is this that rises like the Nile,
　　like rivers of surging waters?
8 Egypt rises like the Nile,
　　like rivers of surging waters.
She says, 'I will rise and cover the earth;
　　I will destroy cities and their people.'
9 Charge, O horses!
　　Drive furiously, O charioteers!
March on, O warriors—
　　men of Cush a and Put who carry shields,
　　men of Lydia who draw the bow.
10 But that day belongs to the Lord, the LORD
　　Almighty—
　　a day of vengeance, for vengeance on his
　　　　foes.
The sword will devour till it is satisfied,
　　till it has quenched its thirst with blood.
For the Lord, the LORD Almighty, will offer
　　sacrifice
　　in the land of the north by the River
　　　　Euphrates.

11 "Go up to Gilead and get balm,
　　O Virgin Daughter of Egypt.
But you multiply remedies in vain;
　　there is no healing for you.
12 The nations will hear of your shame;
　　your cries will fill the earth.

a 9 That is, the upper Nile region

One warrior will stumble over another;
both will fall down together."

13 This is the message the LORD spoke to Jeremiah the prophet about the coming of Nebuchadnezzar king of Babylon to attack Egypt:

14 "Announce this in Egypt, and proclaim it in
Migdol;
proclaim it also in Memphis[a] and
Tahpanhes:
'Take your positions and get ready,
for the sword devours those around you.'
15 Why will your warriors be laid low?
They cannot stand, for the LORD will push
them down.
16 They will stumble repeatedly;
they will fall over each other.
They will say, 'Get up, let us go back
to our own people and our native lands,
away from the sword of the oppressor.'
17 There they will exclaim,
'Pharaoh king of Egypt is only a loud
noise;
he has missed his opportunity.'

18 "As surely as I live," declares the King,
whose name is the LORD Almighty,
"one will come who is like Tabor among the
mountains,
like Carmel by the sea.
19 Pack your belongings for exile,
you who live in Egypt,
for Memphis will be laid waste
and lie in ruins without inhabitant.

20 "Egypt is a beautiful heifer,
but a gadfly is coming
against her from the north.
21 The mercenaries in her ranks
are like fattened calves.
They too will turn and flee together,
they will not stand their ground,
for the day of disaster is coming upon them,
the time for them to be punished.
22 Egypt will hiss like a fleeing serpent
as the enemy advances in force;

they will come against her with axes,
like men who cut down trees.
23 They will chop down her forest,"
declares the LORD,
"dense though it be.
They are more numerous than locusts,
they cannot be counted.
24 The Daughter of Egypt will be put to shame,
handed over to the people of the north."

25 The LORD Almighty, the God of Israel, says: "I am about to bring punishment on Amon god of Thebes,[b] on Pharaoh, on Egypt and her gods and her kings, and on those who rely on Pharaoh. 26 I will hand them over to those who seek their lives, to Nebuchadnezzar king of Babylon and his officers. Later, however, Egypt will be inhabited as in times past," declares the LORD.

27 "Do not fear, O Jacob my servant;
do not be dismayed, O Israel.
I will surely save you out of a distant place,
your descendants from the land of their
exile.
Jacob will again have peace and security,
and no one will make him afraid.
28 Do not fear, O Jacob my servant,
for I am with you," declares the LORD.
"Though I completely destroy all the nations
among which I scatter you,
I will not completely destroy you.
I will discipline you but only with justice;
I will not let you go entirely unpunished."

A Message About the Philistines

47 This is the word of the LORD that came to Jeremiah the prophet concerning the Philistines before Pharaoh attacked Gaza:

2 This is what the LORD says:

"See how the waters are rising in the north;
they will become an overflowing torrent.
They will overflow the land and everything
in it,
the towns and those who live in them.

---

[a] 14 Hebrew *Noph*; also in verse 19   [b] 25 Hebrew *No*

The people will cry out;
all who dwell in the land will wail
³ at the sound of the hoofs of galloping
steeds,
at the noise of enemy chariots
and the rumble of their wheels.
Fathers will not turn to help their children;
their hands will hang limp.
⁴ For the day has come
to destroy all the Philistines
and to cut off all survivors
who could help Tyre and Sidon.
The Lord is about to destroy the Philistines,
the remnant from the coasts of Caphtor.ᵃ
⁵ Gaza will shave her head in mourning;
Ashkelon will be silenced.
O remnant on the plain,
how long will you cut yourselves?

⁶ "'Ah, sword of the Lord,' ⌐you cry,⌐
'how long till you rest?
Return to your scabbard;
cease and be still.'
⁷ But how can it rest
when the Lord has commanded it,
when he has ordered it
to attack Ashkelon and the coast?"

A Message About Moab

48:29–36pp — Isa 16:6–12

48 Concerning Moab:

This is what the Lord Almighty, the God of
Israel, says:

"Woe to Nebo, for it will be ruined.
Kiriathaim will be disgraced and captured;
the strongholdᵇ will be disgraced and
shattered.
² Moab will be praised no more;
in Heshbonᶜ men will plot her downfall:
'Come, let us put an end to that nation.'
You too, O Madmen,ᵈ will be silenced;
the sword will pursue you.
³ Listen to the cries from Horonaim,
cries of great havoc and destruction.

⁴ Moab will be broken;
her little ones will cry out.ᵉ
⁵ They go up the way to Luhith,
weeping bitterly as they go;
on the road down to Horonaim
anguished cries over the destruction are
heard.
⁶ Flee! Run for your lives;
become like a bushᶠ in the desert.
⁷ Since you trust in your deeds and riches,
you too will be taken captive,
and Chemosh will go into exile,
together with his priests and officials.
⁸ The destroyer will come against every town,
and not a town will escape.
The valley will be ruined
and the plateau destroyed,
because the Lord has spoken.
⁹ Put salt on Moab,
for she will be laid wasteᵍ;
her towns will become desolate,
with no one to live in them.

¹⁰ "A curse on him who is lax in doing the
Lord's work!
A curse on him who keeps his sword from
bloodshed!

¹¹ "Moab has been at rest from youth,
like wine left on its dregs,
not poured from one jar to another—
she has not gone into exile.
So she tastes as she did,
and her aroma is unchanged.
¹² But days are coming,"
declares the Lord,
"when I will send men who pour from jars,
and they will pour her out;
they will empty her jars
and smash her jugs.
¹³ Then Moab will be ashamed of Chemosh,
as the house of Israel was ashamed
when they trusted in Bethel.

ᵃ 4 That is, Crete   ᵇ 1 Or / Misgab   ᶜ 2 The Hebrew for
Heshbon sounds like the Hebrew for plot.   ᵈ 2 The name of the
Moabite town Madmen sounds like the Hebrew for be silenced.
ᵉ 4 Hebrew; Septuagint / proclaim it to Zoar   ᶠ 6 Or like Aroer
ᵍ 9 Or Give wings to Moab, / for she will fly away

> "MOAB HAS BEEN AT REST FROM
> YOUTH, LIKE WINE LEFT ON ITS
> DREGS, NOT POURED FROM ONE JAR TO
> ANOTHER — SHE HAS NOT GONE INTO
> EXILE. SO SHE TASTES AS SHE DID, AND
> HER AROMA IS UNCHANGED."
>
> *Jeremiah 48:11*

Change Is Good

ANNE ORTLUND

READ | JEREMIAH 48:1 – 13

Grandmother,

Is your life right now in a state of change?

Are there new developments
that make you feel unsure of things, a little off balance?
I know the feeling!

Jeremiah 48:11 reads,
"Moab [one of the heathen Gentile nations] has
been at rest from youth,
like wine left on its dregs,
not poured from one jar to another —
she has not gone into exile.
So she tastes as she did,
and her aroma is unchanged."
And so Moab, in her state of complacency,
would be smashed
and poured out completely.

But God is committed to your improvement;
He's even committed to your perfection.
So he can't leave you unchanged,
"at rest from youth."
He pours you from one jar to another —
to leave behind the dregs, the imperfections.

Don't be dismayed over disruptions and change.
"Give thanks in all circumstances,
for this is God's will for you in Christ Jesus" (1 Thessalonians 5:18).

The choice is renewal or stagnation.

Let him pour you.
It's his process to make you more and more like Christ.

GRANDCHILD IN FOCUS • PRAYER

School/Career

Dear God, may learning be a joy rather than a chore for my grandchild. May exploration of new ideas bring a sense of wonder, awe and excitement. Grant him clarity of mind, the ability to concentrate on the task at hand and recollection of what has been learned. Help him to appreciate the tasks that come easily and to persevere through those that challenge. Amen.

O God, help me to be open to change, knowing that you are in control, that it is for my good and for achieving my perfection. Amen.

Your next devotion is located on page 1087.

14 "How can you say, 'We are warriors,
   men valiant in battle'?
15 Moab will be destroyed and her towns
       invaded;
   her finest young men will go down in the
       slaughter,"
   declares the King, whose name is the
       LORD Almighty.
16 "The fall of Moab is at hand;
   her calamity will come quickly.
17 Mourn for her, all who live around her,
   all who know her fame;
   say, 'How broken is the mighty scepter,
   how broken the glorious staff!'

18 "Come down from your glory
       and sit on the parched ground,
   O inhabitants of the Daughter of
       Dibon,
   for he who destroys Moab
       will come up against you
       and ruin your fortified cities.
19 Stand by the road and watch,
   you who live in Aroer.
   Ask the man fleeing and the woman
       escaping,
   ask them, 'What has happened?'
20 Moab is disgraced, for she is shattered.
   Wail and cry out!
   Announce by the Arnon
       that Moab is destroyed.
21 Judgment has come to the plateau—
   to Holon, Jahzah and Mephaath,
22   to Dibon, Nebo and Beth Diblathaim,
23   to Kiriathaim, Beth Gamul and Beth
       Meon,
24   to Kerioth and Bozrah—
   to all the towns of Moab, far and near.
25 Moab's horn *a* is cut off;
   her arm is broken,"
                      declares the LORD.

26 "Make her drunk,
   for she has defied the LORD.
   Let Moab wallow in her vomit;
   let her be an object of ridicule.

27 Was not Israel the object of your ridicule?
   Was she caught among thieves,
   that you shake your head in scorn
   whenever you speak of her?
28 Abandon your towns and dwell among the
       rocks,
   you who live in Moab.
   Be like a dove that makes its nest
       at the mouth of a cave.

29 "We have heard of Moab's pride—
   her overweening pride and conceit,
   her pride and arrogance
       and the haughtiness of her heart.
30 I know her insolence but it is futile,"
                      declares the LORD,
   "and her boasts accomplish nothing.
31 Therefore I wail over Moab,
   for all Moab I cry out,
   I moan for the men of Kir Hareseth.
32 I weep for you, as Jazer weeps,
   O vines of Sibmah.
   Your branches spread as far as the sea;
       they reached as far as the sea of Jazer.
   The destroyer has fallen
       on your ripened fruit and grapes.
33 Joy and gladness are gone
       from the orchards and fields of Moab.
   I have stopped the flow of wine from the
       presses;
   no one treads them with shouts of joy.
   Although there are shouts,
       they are not shouts of joy.

34 "The sound of their cry rises
       from Heshbon to Elealeh and Jahaz,
   from Zoar as far as Horonaim and Eglath
       Shelishiyah,
   for even the waters of Nimrim are
       dried up.
35 In Moab I will put an end
       to those who make offerings on the high
       places
   and burn incense to their gods,"
                      declares the LORD.

---

a 25 Horn here symbolizes strength.

36 "So my heart laments for Moab like a flute;
  it laments like a flute for the men of Kir
    Hareseth.
  The wealth they acquired is gone.
37 Every head is shaved
  and every beard cut off;
  every hand is slashed
  and every waist is covered with sackcloth.
38 On all the roofs in Moab
  and in the public squares
  there is nothing but mourning,
    for I have broken Moab
    like a jar that no one wants,"
                    declares the LORD.
39 "How shattered she is! How they wail!
  How Moab turns her back in shame!
  Moab has become an object of ridicule,
    an object of horror to all those around
      her."

40 This is what the LORD says:

  "Look! An eagle is swooping down,
    spreading its wings over Moab.
41 Kerioth a will be captured
  and the strongholds taken.
  In that day the hearts of Moab's warriors
    will be like the heart of a woman in labor.
42 Moab will be destroyed as a nation
  because she defied the LORD.
43 Terror and pit and snare await you,
  O people of Moab,"
                    declares the LORD.
44 "Whoever flees from the terror
    will fall into a pit,
  whoever climbs out of the pit
    will be caught in a snare;
  for I will bring upon Moab
    the year of her punishment,"
                    declares the LORD.

45 "In the shadow of Heshbon
    the fugitives stand helpless,
  for a fire has gone out from Heshbon,
    a blaze from the midst of Sihon;
  it burns the foreheads of Moab,
    the skulls of the noisy boasters.

46 Woe to you, O Moab!
  The people of Chemosh are destroyed;
  your sons are taken into exile
    and your daughters into captivity.

47 "Yet I will restore the fortunes of Moab
  in days to come,"
                    declares the LORD.

Here ends the judgment on Moab.

A Message About Ammon

49 Concerning the Ammonites:

This is what the LORD says:

"Has Israel no sons?
  Has she no heirs?
Why then has Molech b taken possession of
    Gad?
  Why do his people live in its towns?
2 But the days are coming,"
    declares the LORD,
  "when I will sound the battle cry
    against Rabbah of the Ammonites;
  it will become a mound of ruins,
    and its surrounding villages will be set on
      fire.
  Then Israel will drive out
    those who drove her out,"
                    says the LORD.
3 "Wail, O Heshbon, for Ai is destroyed!
  Cry out, O inhabitants of Rabbah!
  Put on sackcloth and mourn;
    rush here and there inside the walls,
  for Molech will go into exile,
    together with his priests and officials.
4 Why do you boast of your valleys,
    boast of your valleys so fruitful?
  O unfaithful daughter,
    you trust in your riches and say,
    'Who will attack me?'
5 I will bring terror on you
    from all those around you,"
                    declares the Lord, the LORD Almighty.

a 41 Or The cities   b 1 Or their king; Hebrew malcam; also in
verse 3

"Every one of you will be driven away,
    and no one will gather the fugitives.

6 "Yet afterward, I will restore the fortunes of
    the Ammonites,"
                        declares the Lord.

A Message About Edom

49:9–10pp — Ob 5–6
49:14–16pp — Ob 1–4

7 Concerning Edom:

This is what the Lord Almighty says:

"Is there no longer wisdom in Teman?
    Has counsel perished from the prudent?
    Has their wisdom decayed?
8 Turn and flee, hide in deep caves,
    you who live in Dedan,
for I will bring disaster on Esau
    at the time I punish him.
9 If grape pickers came to you,
    would they not leave a few grapes?
If thieves came during the night,
    would they not steal only as much as they
      wanted?
10 But I will strip Esau bare;
    I will uncover his hiding places,
so that he cannot conceal himself.
His children, relatives and neighbors will
      perish,
    and he will be no more.
11 Leave your orphans; I will protect their lives.
    Your widows too can trust in me."

12 This is what the Lord says: "If those who do not deserve to drink the cup must drink it, why should you go unpunished? You will not go unpunished, but must drink it. 13 I swear by myself," declares the Lord, "that Bozrah will become a ruin and an object of horror, of reproach and of cursing; and all its towns will be in ruins forever."

14 I have heard a message from the Lord:
    An envoy was sent to the nations to say,
"Assemble yourselves to attack it!
    Rise up for battle!"

15 "Now I will make you small among the
      nations,
    despised among men.
16 The terror you inspire
    and the pride of your heart have deceived
      you,
you who live in the clefts of the rocks,
    who occupy the heights of the hill.
Though you build your nest as high as the
      eagle's,
    from there I will bring you down,"
                    declares the Lord.
17 "Edom will become an object of horror;
    all who pass by will be appalled and will
      scoff
because of all its wounds.
18 As Sodom and Gomorrah were overthrown,
    along with their neighboring towns,"
                  says the Lord,
"so no one will live there;
    no man will dwell in it.

19 "Like a lion coming up from Jordan's thickets
    to a rich pastureland,
I will chase Edom from its land in an instant.
    Who is the chosen one I will appoint for
      this?
Who is like me and who can challenge me?
    And what shepherd can stand against me?"
20 Therefore, hear what the Lord has planned
    against Edom,
    what he has purposed against those who
      live in Teman:
The young of the flock will be dragged
      away;
    he will completely destroy their pasture
      because of them.
21 At the sound of their fall the earth will
      tremble;
    their cry will resound to the Red Sea. *a*
22 Look! An eagle will soar and swoop down,
    spreading its wings over Bozrah.
In that day the hearts of Edom's warriors
    will be like the heart of a woman in labor.

a 21 Hebrew Yam Suph; that is, Sea of Reeds

A Message About Damascus

²³ Concerning Damascus:

"Hamath and Arpad are dismayed,
for they have heard bad news.
They are disheartened,
troubled like ª the restless sea.
²⁴ Damascus has become feeble,
she has turned to flee
and panic has gripped her;
anguish and pain have seized her,
pain like that of a woman in labor.
²⁵ Why has the city of renown not been
abandoned,
the town in which I delight?
²⁶ Surely, her young men will fall in the
streets;
all her soldiers will be silenced in that
day,"
declares the LORD Almighty.
²⁷ "I will set fire to the walls of Damascus;
it will consume the fortresses of
Ben-Hadad."

A Message About Kedar and Hazor

²⁸ Concerning Kedar and the kingdoms of Hazor, which Nebuchadnezzar king of Babylon attacked:

This is what the LORD says:

"Arise, and attack Kedar
and destroy the people of the East.
²⁹ Their tents and their flocks will be taken;
their shelters will be carried off
with all their goods and camels.
Men will shout to them,
'Terror on every side!'

³⁰ "Flee quickly away!
Stay in deep caves, you who live in
Hazor,"
declares the LORD.
"Nebuchadnezzar king of Babylon has
plotted against you;
he has devised a plan against you.

³¹ "Arise and attack a nation at ease,
which lives in confidence,"
declares the LORD,
"a nation that has neither gates nor bars;
its people live alone.
³² Their camels will become plunder,
and their large herds will be booty.
I will scatter to the winds those who are in
distant places ᵇ
and will bring disaster on them from every
side,"
declares the LORD.
³³ "Hazor will become a haunt of jackals,
a desolate place forever.
No one will live there;
no man will dwell in it."

A Message About Elam

³⁴ This is the word of the LORD that came to
Jeremiah the prophet concerning Elam, early in
the reign of Zedekiah king of Judah:

³⁵ This is what the LORD Almighty says:

"See, I will break the bow of Elam,
the mainstay of their might.
³⁶ I will bring against Elam the four winds
from the four quarters of the heavens;
I will scatter them to the four winds,
and there will not be a nation
where Elam's exiles do not go.
³⁷ I will shatter Elam before their foes,
before those who seek their lives;
I will bring disaster upon them,
even my fierce anger,"
declares the LORD.
"I will pursue them with the sword
until I have made an end of them.
³⁸ I will set my throne in Elam
and destroy her king and officials,"
declares the LORD.

³⁹ "Yet I will restore the fortunes of Elam
in days to come,"
declares the LORD.

ª 23 Hebrew *on or by*   ᵇ 32 Or *who clip the hair by their foreheads*

Off to the Park

A perennial favorite for kids is a carefree trip to the park. Even a few hours at the local park with you can be special to your grandchildren. But if you want to add a bit of excitement, take your grandkids to a place they haven't been before. Scout out parks in neighboring towns. You might find an exceptional set of play equipment, or a Frisbee golf course or nature trails, ponds and streams at nearby parks that you never even realized were so nearby.

Younger kids might want to spend the whole time enjoying the new play equipment or rolling down a hill. But older grandkids will enjoy exploring new territory and hearing you point out things that you find interesting about this spot.

Pack a picnic and spend the day exploring the new surroundings. Be sure to snap some pictures as reminders of the day.

Long-Distance Variation: Suggest that your out-of-town grandchildren take pictures of their own visit to the park, including images of whatever strikes them. Share your two sets of photos. Enjoy both the variations and the similarities in your experiences and tastes.

Creator God, thank you for the beauty all around us — beauty in nature and beauty in people. Help us to be alert for the surprises of nature: from unexpected splashes of color to the smell of freshly mown grass to the variety of bird songs. Help us today to enjoy and appreciate one another's insights, abilities and laughter. Amen.

Your next devotion is located on page 1094.

GRANDCHILD IN FOCUS · PRAYER

Character

Dear Lord and Father, I ask that you fill my grandchild with your Spirit so her character reflects your goodness and love. Give her kindness and love for others. Bring joy to her life so she will be a joy to others. Grant her patience and self-control through difficult and trying times. May she show mercy and generosity to those who are less fortunate. Grant her integrity and a sense of justice, and surround her with your peace. Amen.

A Message About Babylon

51:15–19pp — Jer 10:12–16

50 This is the word the LORD spoke through Jeremiah the prophet concerning Babylon and the land of the Babylonians [a]:

² "Announce and proclaim among the nations,
  lift up a banner and proclaim it;
  keep nothing back, but say,
  'Babylon will be captured;
  Bel will be put to shame,
  Marduk filled with terror.
  Her images will be put to shame
  and her idols filled with terror.'
³ A nation from the north will attack her
  and lay waste her land.
  No one will live in it;
  both men and animals will flee away.

⁴ "In those days, at that time,"
  declares the LORD,
  "the people of Israel and the people of Judah
     together
  will go in tears to seek the LORD their God.
⁵ They will ask the way to Zion
  and turn their faces toward it.
  They will come and bind themselves to the
     LORD
  in an everlasting covenant
  that will not be forgotten.

⁶ "My people have been lost sheep;
  their shepherds have led them astray
  and caused them to roam on the
     mountains.
  They wandered over mountain and hill
  and forgot their own resting place.
⁷ Whoever found them devoured them;
  their enemies said, 'We are not guilty,
  for they sinned against the LORD, their true
     pasture,
  the LORD, the hope of their fathers.'

⁸ "Flee out of Babylon;
  leave the land of the Babylonians,
  and be like the goats that lead the flock.

⁹ For I will stir up and bring against Babylon
  an alliance of great nations from the land
     of the north.
  They will take up their positions against her,
  and from the north she will be captured.
  Their arrows will be like skilled warriors
  who do not return empty-handed.
¹⁰ So Babylonia [b] will be plundered;
  all who plunder her will have their fill,"
                               declares the LORD.

¹¹ "Because you rejoice and are glad,
  you who pillage my inheritance,
  because you frolic like a heifer threshing
     grain
  and neigh like stallions,
¹² your mother will be greatly ashamed;
  she who gave you birth will be disgraced.
  She will be the least of the nations—
  a wilderness, a dry land, a desert.
¹³ Because of the LORD's anger she will not be
     inhabited
  but will be completely desolate.
  All who pass Babylon will be horrified and
     scoff
  because of all her wounds.

¹⁴ "Take up your positions around Babylon,
  all you who draw the bow.
  Shoot at her! Spare no arrows,
  for she has sinned against the LORD.
¹⁵ Shout against her on every side!
  She surrenders, her towers fall,
  her walls are torn down.
  Since this is the vengeance of the LORD,
  take vengeance on her;
  do to her as she has done to others.
¹⁶ Cut off from Babylon the sower,
  and the reaper with his sickle at harvest.
  Because of the sword of the oppressor
  let everyone return to his own people,
  let everyone flee to his own land.

¹⁷ "Israel is a scattered flock
  that lions have chased away.

---

[a] 1 Or *Chaldeans*; also in verses 8, 25, 35 and 45   [b] 10 Or *Chaldea*

The first to devour him
    was the king of Assyria;
the last to crush his bones
    was Nebuchadnezzar king of Babylon."

18 Therefore this is what the LORD Almighty,
the God of Israel, says:

"I will punish the king of Babylon and his
    land
    as I punished the king of Assyria.
19 But I will bring Israel back to his own pasture
    and he will graze on Carmel and Bashan;
his appetite will be satisfied
    on the hills of Ephraim and Gilead.
20 In those days, at that time,"
    declares the LORD,
"search will be made for Israel's guilt,
    but there will be none,
and for the sins of Judah,
    but none will be found,
    for I will forgive the remnant I spare.

21 "Attack the land of Merathaim
    and those who live in Pekod.
Pursue, kill and completely destroy*a* them,"
        declares the LORD.
    "Do everything I have commanded you.
22 The noise of battle is in the land,
    the noise of great destruction!
23 How broken and shattered
    is the hammer of the whole earth!
How desolate is Babylon
    among the nations!
24 I set a trap for you, O Babylon,
    and you were caught before you knew it;
you were found and captured
    because you opposed the LORD.
25 The LORD has opened his arsenal
    and brought out the weapons of his wrath,
for the Sovereign LORD Almighty has work
    to do
    in the land of the Babylonians.
26 Come against her from afar.
    Break open her granaries;
    pile her up like heaps of grain.

Completely destroy her
    and leave her no remnant.
27 Kill all her young bulls;
    let them go down to the slaughter!
Woe to them! For their day has come,
    the time for them to be punished.
28 Listen to the fugitives and refugees from
      Babylon
    declaring in Zion
how the LORD our God has taken vengeance,
    vengeance for his temple.

29 "Summon archers against Babylon,
    all those who draw the bow.
Encamp all around her;
    let no one escape.
Repay her for her deeds;
    do to her as she has done.
For she has defied the LORD,
    the Holy One of Israel.
30 Therefore, her young men will fall in the
      streets;
    all her soldiers will be silenced in that day,"
                declares the LORD.
31 "See, I am against you, O arrogant one,"
    declares the Lord, the LORD Almighty,
"for your day has come,
    the time for you to be punished.
32 The arrogant one will stumble and fall
    and no one will help her up;
I will kindle a fire in her towns
    that will consume all who are around her."

33 This is what the LORD Almighty says:

"The people of Israel are oppressed,
    and the people of Judah as well.
All their captors hold them fast,
    refusing to let them go.
34 Yet their Redeemer is strong;
    the LORD Almighty is his name.
He will vigorously defend their cause
    so that he may bring rest to their land,
    but unrest to those who live in Babylon.

---

a 21 The Hebrew term refers to the irrevocable giving over of things
or persons to the LORD, often by totally destroying them; also in
verse 26.

35 "A sword against the Babylonians!"
   declares the LORD—
"against those who live in Babylon
   and against her officials and wise men!
36 A sword against her false prophets!
   They will become fools.
A sword against her warriors!
   They will be filled with terror.
37 A sword against her horses and chariots
   and all the foreigners in her ranks!
   They will become women.
A sword against her treasures!
   They will be plundered.
38 A drought on ^{a} her waters!
   They will dry up.
For it is a land of idols,
   idols that will go mad with terror.

39 "So desert creatures and hyenas will live
   there,
and there the owl will dwell.
It will never again be inhabited
   or lived in from generation to generation.
40 As God overthrew Sodom and Gomorrah
   along with their neighboring towns,"
                declares the LORD,
"so no one will live there;
   no man will dwell in it.

41 "Look! An army is coming from the north;
   a great nation and many kings
   are being stirred up from the ends of the
     earth.
42 They are armed with bows and spears;
   they are cruel and without mercy.
They sound like the roaring sea
   as they ride on their horses;
they come like men in battle formation
   to attack you, O Daughter of Babylon.
43 The king of Babylon has heard reports about
   them,
   and his hands hang limp.
Anguish has gripped him,
   pain like that of a woman in labor.
44 Like a lion coming up from Jordan's thickets
   to a rich pastureland,

I will chase Babylon from its land in an
   instant.
Who is the chosen one I will appoint for
   this?
Who is like me and who can challenge me?
   And what shepherd can stand against me?"
45 Therefore, hear what the LORD has planned
   against Babylon,
what he has purposed against the land of
   the Babylonians:
The young of the flock will be dragged away;
   he will completely destroy their pasture
   because of them.
46 At the sound of Babylon's capture the earth
   will tremble;
   its cry will resound among the nations.

51 This is what the LORD says:

"See, I will stir up the spirit of a destroyer
   against Babylon and the people of
   Leb Kamai. ^{b}
2 I will send foreigners to Babylon
   to winnow her and to devastate her land;
they will oppose her on every side
   in the day of her disaster.
3 Let not the archer string his bow,
   nor let him put on his armor.
Do not spare her young men;
   completely destroy ^{c} her army.
4 They will fall down slain in Babylon, ^{d}
   fatally wounded in her streets.
5 For Israel and Judah have not been forsaken
   by their God, the LORD Almighty,
though their land ^{e} is full of guilt
   before the Holy One of Israel.

6 "Flee from Babylon!
   Run for your lives!
   Do not be destroyed because of her sins.
It is time for the LORD's vengeance;
   he will pay her what she deserves.

^{a} 38 Or A sword against ^{b} 1 Leb Kamai is a cryptogram for
Chaldea, that is, Babylonia. ^{c} 3 The Hebrew term refers to the
irrevocable giving over of things or persons to the LORD, often by
totally destroying them. ^{d} 4 Or Chaldea ^{e} 5 Or / and the land
of the Babylonians

7 Babylon was a gold cup in the LORD's hand;
  she made the whole earth drunk.
The nations drank her wine;
  therefore they have now gone mad.
8 Babylon will suddenly fall and be broken.
  Wail over her!
Get balm for her pain;
  perhaps she can be healed.

9 " 'We would have healed Babylon,
  but she cannot be healed;
let us leave her and each go to his own land,
  for her judgment reaches to the skies,
  it rises as high as the clouds.'

10 " 'The LORD has vindicated us;
  come, let us tell in Zion
  what the LORD our God has done.'

11 "Sharpen the arrows,
  take up the shields!
The LORD has stirred up the kings of the
  Medes,
  because his purpose is to destroy
  Babylon.
The LORD will take vengeance,
  vengeance for his temple.
12 Lift up a banner against the walls of
  Babylon!
  Reinforce the guard,
station the watchmen,
  prepare an ambush!
The LORD will carry out his purpose,
  his decree against the people of Babylon.
13 You who live by many waters
  and are rich in treasures,
your end has come,
  the time for you to be cut off.
14 The LORD Almighty has sworn by himself:
  I will surely fill you with men, as with a
  swarm of locusts,
  and they will shout in triumph over you.

15 "He made the earth by his power;
  he founded the world by his wisdom
  and stretched out the heavens by his
  understanding.

16 When he thunders, the waters in the heavens
  roar;
  he makes clouds rise from the ends of the
  earth.
He sends lightning with the rain
  and brings out the wind from his
  storehouses.

17 "Every man is senseless and without
  knowledge;
  every goldsmith is shamed by his idols.
His images are a fraud;
  they have no breath in them.
18 They are worthless, the objects of mockery;
  when their judgment comes, they will
  perish.
19 He who is the Portion of Jacob is not like
  these,
  for he is the Maker of all things,
including the tribe of his inheritance—
  the LORD Almighty is his name.

20 "You are my war club,
  my weapon for battle—
with you I shatter nations,
  with you I destroy kingdoms,
21 with you I shatter horse and rider,
  with you I shatter chariot and driver,
22 with you I shatter man and woman,
  with you I shatter old man and youth,
  with you I shatter young man and
  maiden,
23 with you I shatter shepherd and flock,
  with you I shatter farmer and oxen,
  with you I shatter governors and officials.

24 "Before your eyes I will repay Babylon and
all who live in Babylonia ^a for all the wrong they
have done in Zion," declares the LORD.

25 "I am against you, O destroying mountain,
  you who destroy the whole earth,"
                          declares the LORD.
"I will stretch out my hand against you,
  roll you off the cliffs,
  and make you a burned-out mountain.

^a 24 Or Chaldea; also in verse 35

²⁶No rock will be taken from you for a
    cornerstone,
  nor any stone for a foundation,
  for you will be desolate forever,"
             declares the LORD.

²⁷"Lift up a banner in the land!
  Blow the trumpet among the nations!
Prepare the nations for battle against her;
  summon against her these kingdoms:
  Ararat, Minni and Ashkenaz.
Appoint a commander against her;
  send up horses like a swarm of locusts.
²⁸Prepare the nations for battle against her —
  the kings of the Medes,
their governors and all their officials,
  and all the countries they rule.
²⁹The land trembles and writhes,
  for the LORD's purposes against Babylon
    stand —
to lay waste the land of Babylon
  so that no one will live there.
³⁰Babylon's warriors have stopped fighting;
  they remain in their strongholds.
Their strength is exhausted;
  they have become like women.
Her dwellings are set on fire;
  the bars of her gates are broken.
³¹One courier follows another
  and messenger follows messenger
to announce to the king of Babylon
  that his entire city is captured,
³²the river crossings seized,
  the marshes set on fire,
  and the soldiers terrified."

³³This is what the LORD Almighty, the God of
Israel, says:

  "The Daughter of Babylon is like a threshing
    floor
    at the time it is trampled;
    the time to harvest her will soon come."

³⁴"Nebuchadnezzar king of Babylon has
    devoured us,
  he has thrown us into confusion,
  he has made us an empty jar.

Like a serpent he has swallowed us
  and filled his stomach with our delicacies,
  and then has spewed us out.
³⁵May the violence done to our flesh ᵃ be upon
    Babylon,"
  say the inhabitants of Zion.
"May our blood be on those who live in
    Babylonia,"
  says Jerusalem.

³⁶Therefore, this is what the LORD says:

"See, I will defend your cause
  and avenge you;
I will dry up her sea
  and make her springs dry.
³⁷Babylon will be a heap of ruins,
  a haunt of jackals,
an object of horror and scorn,
  a place where no one lives.
³⁸Her people all roar like young lions,
  they growl like lion cubs.
³⁹But while they are aroused,
  I will set out a feast for them
  and make them drunk,
so that they shout with laughter —
  then sleep forever and not awake,"
             declares the LORD.
⁴⁰"I will bring them down
  like lambs to the slaughter,
  like rams and goats.

⁴¹"How Sheshach ᵇ will be captured,
  the boast of the whole earth seized!
What a horror Babylon will be
  among the nations!
⁴²The sea will rise over Babylon;
  its roaring waves will cover her.
⁴³Her towns will be desolate,
  a dry and desert land,
a land where no one lives,
  through which no man travels.
⁴⁴I will punish Bel in Babylon
  and make him spew out what he has
    swallowed.

ᵃ 35 Or *done to us and to our children*   ᵇ 41 *Sheshach* is a
cryptogram for Babylon.

The nations will no longer stream to him.
    And the wall of Babylon will fall.

45 "Come out of her, my people!
    Run for your lives!
Run from the fierce anger of the LORD.
46 Do not lose heart or be afraid
    when rumors are heard in the land;
one rumor comes this year, another the
       next,
    rumors of violence in the land
    and of ruler against ruler.
47 For the time will surely come
    when I will punish the idols of Babylon;
her whole land will be disgraced
    and her slain will all lie fallen within her.
48 Then heaven and earth and all that is in
       them
    will shout for joy over Babylon,
for out of the north
    destroyers will attack her,"
                    declares the LORD.

49 "Babylon must fall because of Israel's slain,
    just as the slain in all the earth
    have fallen because of Babylon.
50 You who have escaped the sword,
    leave and do not linger!
Remember the LORD in a distant land,
    and think on Jerusalem."

51 "We are disgraced,
    for we have been insulted
    and shame covers our faces,
because foreigners have entered
    the holy places of the LORD's house."

52 "But days are coming," declares the LORD,
    "when I will punish her idols,
and throughout her land
    the wounded will groan.
53 Even if Babylon reaches the sky
    and fortifies her lofty stronghold,
    I will send destroyers against her,"
                    declares the LORD.

54 "The sound of a cry comes from Babylon,
    the sound of great destruction
    from the land of the Babylonians. *a*
55 The LORD will destroy Babylon;
    he will silence her noisy din.
Waves ⌐of enemies⌐ will rage like great waters;
    the roar of their voices will resound.
56 A destroyer will come against Babylon;
    her warriors will be captured,
    and their bows will be broken.
For the LORD is a God of retribution;
    he will repay in full.
57 I will make her officials and wise men drunk,
    her governors, officers and warriors as
       well;
they will sleep forever and not awake,"
    declares the King, whose name is the LORD
       Almighty.

58 This is what the LORD Almighty says:

"Babylon's thick wall will be leveled
    and her high gates set on fire;
the peoples exhaust themselves for nothing,
    the nations' labor is only fuel for the
       flames."

59 This is the message Jeremiah gave to the staff officer Seraiah son of Neriah, the son of Mahseiah, when he went to Babylon with Zedekiah king of Judah in the fourth year of his reign. 60 Jeremiah had written on a scroll about all the disasters that would come upon Babylon—all that had been recorded concerning Babylon. 61 He said to Seraiah, "When you get to Babylon, see that you read all these words aloud. 62 Then say, 'O LORD, you have said you will destroy this place, so that neither man nor animal will live in it; it will be desolate forever.' 63 When you finish reading this scroll, tie a stone to it and throw it into the Euphrates. 64 Then say, 'So will Babylon sink to rise no more because of the disaster I will bring upon her. And her people will fall.' "

The words of Jeremiah end here.

a 54 Or Chaldeans

Worship the Lord

May God be gracious to us and bless us
and make his face shine upon us,

that your ways may be known on earth,
your salvation among all nations.

Selah

May the peoples praise you, O God;
may all the peoples praise you.
May the nations be glad and sing for joy,
for you rule the peoples justly
and guide the nations of the earth.

Selah

May the peoples praise you, O God;
may all the peoples praise you.

Then the land will yield its harvest,
and God, our God, will bless us.
God will bless us,
and all the ends of the earth will
fear him.

Psalm 67

O God, you have been so gracious to me.
I see your blessings all around me. I feel
your warmth as you shine your face on me.
For all this I praise your name and sing for
joy. Amen.

Your next devotion is located on page 1103.

GRANDCHILD IN FOCUS • PRAYER

Talents

*Dear Lord, the giver of gifts, bless my
grandchild as he develops his talents. Help him
identify his talents and be proud and confident of
the gifts you have given him. Give him patience and
understanding, Lord, so he will not grow weary of
striving and searching to reach the goals you have
set for him. May each milestone bring satisfaction and a healthy desire for greater
achievement and success to bring
glory to you. Amen.*

The Fall of Jerusalem

52:1–3pp — 2Ki 24:18–20; 2Ch 36:11–16
52:4–16pp — Jer 39:1–10
52:4–21pp — 2Ki 25:1–21; 2Ch 36:17–20

52 Zedekiah was twenty-one years old when he became king, and he reigned in Jerusalem eleven years. His mother's name was Hamutal daughter of Jeremiah; she was from Libnah. ²He did evil in the eyes of the LORD, just as Jehoiakim had done. ³It was because of the LORD's anger that all this happened to Jerusalem and Judah, and in the end he thrust them from his presence.

Now Zedekiah rebelled against the king of Babylon.

⁴So in the ninth year of Zedekiah's reign, on the tenth day of the tenth month, Nebuchadnezzar king of Babylon marched against Jerusalem with his whole army. They camped outside the city and built siege works all around it. ⁵The city was kept under siege until the eleventh year of King Zedekiah.

⁶By the ninth day of the fourth month the famine in the city had become so severe that there was no food for the people to eat. ⁷Then the city wall was broken through, and the whole army fled. They left the city at night through the gate between the two walls near the king's garden, though the Babylonians*ᵃ* were surrounding the city. They fled toward the Arabah,*ᵇ* ⁸but the Babylonian*ᶜ* army pursued King Zedekiah and overtook him in the plains of Jericho. All his soldiers were separated from him and scattered, ⁹and he was captured.

He was taken to the king of Babylon at Riblah in the land of Hamath, where he pronounced sentence on him. ¹⁰There at Riblah the king of Babylon slaughtered the sons of Zedekiah before his eyes; he also killed all the officials of Judah. ¹¹Then he put out Zedekiah's eyes, bound him with bronze shackles and took him to Babylon, where he put him in prison till the day of his death.

¹²On the tenth day of the fifth month, in the nineteenth year of Nebuchadnezzar king of Babylon, Nebuzaradan commander of the imperial guard, who served the king of Babylon, came to Jerusalem. ¹³He set fire to the temple of the LORD, the royal palace and all the houses of Jerusalem. Every important building he burned down. ¹⁴The whole Babylonian army under the commander of the imperial guard broke down all the walls around Jerusalem. ¹⁵Nebuzaradan the commander of the guard carried into exile some of the poorest people and those who remained in the city, along with the rest of the craftsmen*ᵈ* and those who had gone over to the king of Babylon. ¹⁶But Nebuzaradan left behind the rest of the poorest people of the land to work the vineyards and fields.

¹⁷The Babylonians broke up the bronze pillars, the movable stands and the bronze Sea that were at the temple of the LORD and they carried all the bronze to Babylon. ¹⁸They also took away the pots, shovels, wick trimmers, sprinkling bowls, dishes and all the bronze articles used in the temple service. ¹⁹The commander of the imperial guard took away the basins, censers, sprinkling bowls, pots, lampstands, dishes and bowls used for drink offerings — all that were made of pure gold or silver.

²⁰The bronze from the two pillars, the Sea and the twelve bronze bulls under it, and the movable stands, which King Solomon had made for the temple of the LORD, was more than could be weighed. ²¹Each of the pillars was eighteen cubits high and twelve cubits in circumference*ᵉ*; each was four fingers thick, and hollow. ²²The bronze capital on top of the one pillar was five cubits*ᶠ* high and was decorated with a network and pomegranates of bronze all around. The other pillar, with its pomegranates, was similar. ²³There were ninety-six pomegranates on the sides; the total number of pomegranates above the surrounding network was a hundred.

²⁴The commander of the guard took as pris-

ᵃ 7 Or Chaldeans; also in verse 17   ᵇ 7 Or the Jordan Valley
ᶜ 8 Or Chaldean; also in verse 14   ᵈ 15 Or populace   ᵉ 21 That is, about 27 feet (about 8.1 meters) high and 18 feet (about 5.4 meters) in circumference   ᶠ 22 That is, about 7 1/2 feet (about 2.3 meters)

oners Seraiah the chief priest, Zephaniah the priest next in rank and the three doorkeepers. ²⁵Of those still in the city, he took the officer in charge of the fighting men, and seven royal advisers. He also took the secretary who was chief officer in charge of conscripting the people of the land and sixty of his men who were found in the city. ²⁶Nebuzaradan the commander took them all and brought them to the king of Babylon at Riblah. ²⁷There at Riblah, in the land of Hamath, the king had them executed.

So Judah went into captivity, away from her land. ²⁸This is the number of the people Nebuchadnezzar carried into exile:

in the seventh year, 3,023 Jews;
²⁹in Nebuchadnezzar's eighteenth year,
832 people from Jerusalem;
³⁰in his twenty-third year,
745 Jews taken into exile by Nebuzara-

dan the commander of the imperial guard.
There were 4,600 people in all.

Jehoiachin Released
52:31–34pp — 2Ki 25:27–30

³¹In the thirty-seventh year of the exile of Jehoiachin king of Judah, in the year Evil-Merodach[a] became king of Babylon, he released Jehoiachin king of Judah and freed him from prison on the twenty-fifth day of the twelfth month. ³²He spoke kindly to him and gave him a seat of honor higher than those of the other kings who were with him in Babylon. ³³So Jehoiachin put aside his prison clothes and for the rest of his life ate regularly at the king's table. ³⁴Day by day the king of Babylon gave Jehoiachin a regular allowance as long as he lived, till the day of his death.

[a] *31* Also called *Amel-Marduk*

A Good
CRY

The identity of the author of the book of Lamentations is uncertain, but tradition points to Jeremiah, who is sometimes referred to as the "weeping prophet." This book is a compilation of mournful poems about the people of Judah who had been taken into captivity in Babylon. God had warned the people that he would send invaders to conquer their city and nation as punishment for their continued rebellion and sin. Once in exile, the people wept and grieved for their losses: their nation, the holy city of Jerusalem and the once magnificent temple, which lay in ruins far, far away. Through this grief-filled book, we feel deeply the people's pain, loss and misery.

Yet, in the midst of all this despair, grief and suffering we find hope, for God's love for his people remained steadfast. He promised that someday they would be restored. More than 2,500 years later, his love continues. Because of God's unfailing compassion for us, we will never be consumed by evil or loss or grief. His faithfulness is so great that it will sustain us as we face the sorrows that occur in our lives.

VERSE *to* REMEMBER | LAMENTATIONS 3:22 – 23

Because of the LORD's great love we are not consumed, for his compassions never fail. They are new every morning; great is your faithfulness.

ABOUT LAMENTATIONS

WRITTEN BY:
Probably Jeremiah

WRITTEN FOR:
The Jewish captives
in Babylon

DATE WRITTEN:
After the Babylonians
destroyed Jerusalem
in 586 B.C.

WHY WRITTEN:
To express the sorrow of the
captives exiled in Babylon,
and to show that they fully
realized they were being
punished for their sin

1 *a* How deserted lies the city,
    once so full of people!
How like a widow is she,
    who once was great among the nations!
She who was queen among the provinces
    has now become a slave.

2 Bitterly she weeps at night,
    tears are upon her cheeks.
Among all her lovers
    there is none to comfort her.
All her friends have betrayed her;
    they have become her enemies.

3 After affliction and harsh labor,
    Judah has gone into exile.
She dwells among the nations;
    she finds no resting place.
All who pursue her have overtaken her
    in the midst of her distress.

4 The roads to Zion mourn,
    for no one comes to her appointed feasts.
All her gateways are desolate,
    her priests groan,
her maidens grieve,
    and she is in bitter anguish.

5 Her foes have become her masters;
    her enemies are at ease.
The LORD has brought her grief
    because of her many sins.
Her children have gone into exile,
    captive before the foe.

6 All the splendor has departed
    from the Daughter of Zion.
Her princes are like deer
    that find no pasture;
in weakness they have fled
    before the pursuer.

7 In the days of her affliction and wandering
    Jerusalem remembers all the treasures
    that were hers in days of old.
When her people fell into enemy hands,
    there was no one to help her.
Her enemies looked at her
    and laughed at her destruction.

8 Jerusalem has sinned greatly
    and so has become unclean.
All who honored her despise her,
    for they have seen her nakedness;
she herself groans
    and turns away.

9 Her filthiness clung to her skirts;
    she did not consider her future.
Her fall was astounding;
    there was none to comfort her.
"Look, O LORD, on my affliction,
    for the enemy has triumphed."

10 The enemy laid hands
    on all her treasures;
she saw pagan nations
    enter her sanctuary—
those you had forbidden
    to enter your assembly.

11 All her people groan
    as they search for bread;
they barter their treasures for food
    to keep themselves alive.
"Look, O LORD, and consider,
    for I am despised."

12 "Is it nothing to you, all you who pass by?
    Look around and see.
Is any suffering like my suffering
    that was inflicted on me,
that the LORD brought on me
    in the day of his fierce anger?

13 "From on high he sent fire,
    sent it down into my bones.
He spread a net for my feet
    and turned me back.
He made me desolate,
    faint all the day long.

14 "My sins have been bound into a yoke *b*;
    by his hands they were woven together.
They have come upon my neck
    and the Lord has sapped my strength.

---

a This chapter is an acrostic poem, the verses of which begin with the successive letters of the Hebrew alphabet.   *b* 14 Most Hebrew manuscripts; Septuagint *He kept watch over my sins*

He has handed me over
to those I cannot withstand.

15 "The Lord has rejected
all the warriors in my midst;
he has summoned an army against me
to*a* crush my young men.
In his winepress the Lord has trampled
the Virgin Daughter of Judah.

16 "This is why I weep
and my eyes overflow with tears.
No one is near to comfort me,
no one to restore my spirit.
My children are destitute
because the enemy has prevailed."

17 Zion stretches out her hands,
but there is no one to comfort her.
The LORD has decreed for Jacob
that his neighbors become his foes;
Jerusalem has become
an unclean thing among them.

18 "The LORD is righteous,
yet I rebelled against his command.
Listen, all you peoples;
look upon my suffering.
My young men and maidens
have gone into exile.

19 "I called to my allies
but they betrayed me.
My priests and my elders
perished in the city
while they searched for food
to keep themselves alive.

20 "See, O LORD, how distressed I am!
I am in torment within,
and in my heart I am disturbed,
for I have been most rebellious.
Outside, the sword bereaves;
inside, there is only death.

21 "People have heard my groaning,
but there is no one to comfort me.
All my enemies have heard of my distress;
they rejoice at what you have done.

May you bring the day you have announced
so they may become like me.

22 "Let all their wickedness come before you;
deal with them
as you have dealt with me
because of all my sins.
My groans are many
and my heart is faint."

2*b* How the Lord has covered the Daughter
of Zion
with the cloud of his anger*c*!
He has hurled down the splendor of Israel
from heaven to earth;
he has not remembered his footstool
in the day of his anger.

2 Without pity the Lord has swallowed up
all the dwellings of Jacob;
in his wrath he has torn down
the strongholds of the Daughter of Judah.
He has brought her kingdom and its princes
down to the ground in dishonor.

3 In fierce anger he has cut off
every horn*d* of Israel.
He has withdrawn his right hand
at the approach of the enemy.
He has burned in Jacob like a flaming fire
that consumes everything around it.

4 Like an enemy he has strung his bow;
his right hand is ready.
Like a foe he has slain
all who were pleasing to the eye;
he has poured out his wrath like fire
on the tent of the Daughter of Zion.

5 The Lord is like an enemy;
he has swallowed up Israel.
He has swallowed up all her palaces
and destroyed her strongholds.

a 15 Or *has set a time for me / when he will*   *b* This chapter is an acrostic poem, the verses of which begin with the successive letters of the Hebrew alphabet.   *c 1* Or *How the Lord in his anger / has treated the Daughter of Zion with contempt*   *d 3* Or / *all the strength;* or *every king; horn* here symbolizes strength.

He has multiplied mourning and
lamentation
for the Daughter of Judah.

⁶ He has laid waste his dwelling like a garden;
he has destroyed his place of meeting.
The LORD has made Zion forget
her appointed feasts and her Sabbaths;
in his fierce anger he has spurned
both king and priest.

⁷ The Lord has rejected his altar
and abandoned his sanctuary.
He has handed over to the enemy
the walls of her palaces;
they have raised a shout in the house of the
LORD
as on the day of an appointed feast.

⁸ The LORD determined to tear down
the wall around the Daughter of Zion.
He stretched out a measuring line
and did not withhold his hand from
destroying.
He made ramparts and walls lament;
together they wasted away.

⁹ Her gates have sunk into the ground;
their bars he has broken and destroyed.
Her king and her princes are exiled among
the nations,
the law is no more,
and her prophets no longer find
visions from the LORD.

¹⁰ The elders of the Daughter of Zion
sit on the ground in silence;
they have sprinkled dust on their heads
and put on sackcloth.
The young women of Jerusalem
have bowed their heads to the ground.

¹¹ My eyes fail from weeping,
I am in torment within,
my heart is poured out on the ground
because my people are destroyed,
because children and infants faint
in the streets of the city.

¹² They say to their mothers,
"Where is bread and wine?"
as they faint like wounded men
in the streets of the city,
as their lives ebb away
in their mothers' arms.

¹³ What can I say for you?
With what can I compare you,
O Daughter of Jerusalem?
To what can I liken you,
that I may comfort you,
O Virgin Daughter of Zion?
Your wound is as deep as the sea.
Who can heal you?

¹⁴ The visions of your prophets
were false and worthless;
they did not expose your sin
to ward off your captivity.
The oracles they gave you
were false and misleading.

¹⁵ All who pass your way
clap their hands at you;
they scoff and shake their heads
at the Daughter of Jerusalem:
"Is this the city that was called
the perfection of beauty,
the joy of the whole earth?"

¹⁶ All your enemies open their mouths
wide against you;
they scoff and gnash their teeth
and say, "We have swallowed her up.
This is the day we have waited for;
we have lived to see it."

¹⁷ The LORD has done what he planned;
he has fulfilled his word,
which he decreed long ago.
He has overthrown you without pity,
he has let the enemy gloat over you,
he has exalted the horn *ᵃ* of your foes.

¹⁸ The hearts of the people
cry out to the Lord.

ᵃ 17 Horn here symbolizes strength.

O wall of the Daughter of Zion,
   let your tears flow like a river
   day and night;
give yourself no relief,
   your eyes no rest.

¹⁹ Arise, cry out in the night,
   as the watches of the night begin;
pour out your heart like water
   in the presence of the Lord.
Lift up your hands to him
   for the lives of your children,
who faint from hunger
   at the head of every street.

²⁰ "Look, O LORD, and consider:
   Whom have you ever treated like this?
Should women eat their offspring,
   the children they have cared for?
Should priest and prophet be killed
   in the sanctuary of the Lord?

²¹ "Young and old lie together
   in the dust of the streets;
my young men and maidens
   have fallen by the sword.
You have slain them in the day of your anger;
   you have slaughtered them without pity.

²² "As you summon to a feast day,
   so you summoned against me terrors on
      every side.
In the day of the LORD's anger
   no one escaped or survived;
those I cared for and reared,
   my enemy has destroyed."

3 ^a I am the man who has seen affliction
   by the rod of his wrath.
² He has driven me away and made me walk
   in darkness rather than light;
³ indeed, he has turned his hand against me
   again and again, all day long.

⁴ He has made my skin and my flesh grow old
   and has broken my bones.
⁵ He has besieged me and surrounded me

with bitterness and hardship.
⁶ He has made me dwell in darkness
   like those long dead.

⁷ He has walled me in so I cannot escape;
   he has weighed me down with chains.
⁸ Even when I call out or cry for help,
   he shuts out my prayer.
⁹ He has barred my way with blocks of stone;
   he has made my paths crooked.

¹⁰ Like a bear lying in wait,
   like a lion in hiding,
¹¹ he dragged me from the path and mangled
      me
   and left me without help.
¹² He drew his bow
   and made me the target for his arrows.

¹³ He pierced my heart
   with arrows from his quiver.
¹⁴ I became the laughingstock of all my people;
   they mock me in song all day long.
¹⁵ He has filled me with bitter herbs
   and sated me with gall.

¹⁶ He has broken my teeth with gravel;
   he has trampled me in the dust.
¹⁷ I have been deprived of peace;
   I have forgotten what prosperity is.
¹⁸ So I say, "My splendor is gone
   and all that I had hoped from the LORD."

¹⁹ I remember my affliction and my wandering,
   the bitterness and the gall.
²⁰ I well remember them,
   and my soul is downcast within me.
²¹ Yet this I call to mind
   and therefore I have hope:

²² Because of the LORD's great love we are not
      consumed,
   for his compassions never fail.
²³ They are new every morning;
   great is your faithfulness.

^a This chapter is an acrostic poem; the verses of each stanza begin
with the successive letters of the Hebrew alphabet, and the verses
within each stanza begin with the same letter.

24 I say to myself, "The Lord is my portion;
  therefore I will wait for him."

25 The Lord is good to those whose hope is in
  him,
  to the one who seeks him;
26 it is good to wait quietly
  for the salvation of the Lord.
27 It is good for a man to bear the yoke
  while he is young.

28 Let him sit alone in silence,
  for the Lord has laid it on him.
29 Let him bury his face in the dust—
  there may yet be hope.
30 Let him offer his cheek to one who would
  strike him,
  and let him be filled with disgrace.

31 For men are not cast off
  by the Lord forever.
32 Though he brings grief, he will show
  compassion,
  so great is his unfailing love.
33 For he does not willingly bring affliction
  or grief to the children of men.

34 To crush underfoot
  all prisoners in the land,
35 to deny a man his rights
  before the Most High,
36 to deprive a man of justice—
  would not the Lord see such things?

37 Who can speak and have it happen
  if the Lord has not decreed it?
38 Is it not from the mouth of the Most High
  that both calamities and good things
  come?
39 Why should any living man complain
  when punished for his sins?

40 Let us examine our ways and test them,
  and let us return to the Lord.
41 Let us lift up our hearts and our hands
  to God in heaven, and say:
42 "We have sinned and rebelled
  and you have not forgiven.

43 "You have covered yourself with anger and
  pursued us;
  you have slain without pity.
44 You have covered yourself with a cloud
  so that no prayer can get through.
45 You have made us scum and refuse
  among the nations.

46 "All our enemies have opened their mouths
  wide against us.
47 We have suffered terror and pitfalls,
  ruin and destruction."
48 Streams of tears flow from my eyes
  because my people are destroyed.

49 My eyes will flow unceasingly,
  without relief,
50 until the Lord looks down
  from heaven and sees.
51 What I see brings grief to my soul
  because of all the women of my city.

52 Those who were my enemies without cause
  hunted me like a bird.
53 They tried to end my life in a pit
  and threw stones at me;
54 the waters closed over my head,
  and I thought I was about to be cut off.

55 I called on your name, O Lord,
  from the depths of the pit.
56 You heard my plea: "Do not close your ears
  to my cry for relief."

BECAUSE OF THE LORD'S GREAT LOVE
WE ARE NOT CONSUMED, FOR HIS
COMPASSIONS NEVER FAIL. THEY ARE
NEW EVERY MORNING; GREAT IS YOUR
FAITHFULNESS ... THE LORD IS GOOD
TO THOSE WHOSE HOPE IS IN HIM.

Lamentations 3:22 – 23, 25

Proving God's Faithfulness

RUTHANNE GARLOCK

READ | LAMENTATIONS 3:1 – 27

Throughout the book of Lamentations, the prophet Jeremiah — the likely author of the book — mourned the suffering of his people, which was caused by their rebellion against God. Yet, because of the Lord's great love and mercy, Jeremiah boldly declared, "Great is your faithfulness."

This is a statement I have affirmed countless times since my husband died suddenly and without warning early one December morning in 2003. Although I felt as if my world had collapsed, I knew, even in my grief and confusion, that God's faultless record of faithfulness had not changed.

As I cried out to him for comfort and strength, the Lord reminded me of ways he had prepared me for this crisis.

About a year earlier, the Holy Spirit had prompted me to once again make personal prayer time my top priority. John and I prayed together every day when he was not traveling, but I began getting up earlier to make sure I had a private time of prayer and Bible reading. This reinforced the spiritual foundation that has sustained me in this season of my life.

Another example: The very day before his death, John and I had signed papers to refinance our house. The lower payment and shorter term of the loan made it more feasible for me to remain in the home we built together. Every day I thank God for this blessing.

Now I'm the only grandparent left to my stepdaughters' four children, ranging in age from 15 to 30. I look for ways to help them understand how blessed they are to have had such a special grandfather. And I pray my life will continue to be an example to them of God's faithfulness.

Lord, how I thank you for your steadfast love and faithfulness! In my times of loneliness, help me to count my blessings and rejoice in your goodness and provision. Amen.

Your next devotion is located on page 1122.

GRANDCHILD IN FOCUS • PRAYER

SELECT ONE OF YOUR
GRANDCHILDREN TO FOCUS ON
IN PRAYER FOR THE NEXT 14 DAYS.

Salvation

Dear Lord, please guide my grandchild to your gift of salvation. I pray that she will come to know you, to love you and to walk close to you throughout her life. May she boldly claim Jesus as her Lord and Savior. Guide her as she makes choices that have eternal consequences. Help her to follow you each moment of her life. I pray this in Jesus' name, amen.

⁵⁷ You came near when I called you,
    and you said, "Do not fear."

⁵⁸ O Lord, you took up my case;
    you redeemed my life.
⁵⁹ You have seen, O Lᴏʀᴅ, the wrong done to
        me.
    Uphold my cause!
⁶⁰ You have seen the depth of their vengeance,
    all their plots against me.

⁶¹ O Lᴏʀᴅ, you have heard their insults,
    all their plots against me—
⁶² what my enemies whisper and mutter
    against me all day long.
⁶³ Look at them! Sitting or standing,
    they mock me in their songs.

⁶⁴ Pay them back what they deserve, O Lᴏʀᴅ,
    for what their hands have done.
⁶⁵ Put a veil over their hearts,
    and may your curse be on them!
⁶⁶ Pursue them in anger and destroy them
    from under the heavens of the Lᴏʀᴅ.

4 ᵃ How the gold has lost its luster,
    the fine gold become dull!
  The sacred gems are scattered
    at the head of every street.

² How the precious sons of Zion,
    once worth their weight in gold,
  are now considered as pots of clay,
    the work of a potter's hands!

³ Even jackals offer their breasts
    to nurse their young,
  but my people have become heartless
    like ostriches in the desert.

⁴ Because of thirst the infant's tongue
    sticks to the roof of its mouth;
  the children beg for bread,
    but no one gives it to them.

⁵ Those who once ate delicacies
    are destitute in the streets.
  Those nurtured in purple
    now lie on ash heaps.

⁶ The punishment of my people
    is greater than that of Sodom,
  which was overthrown in a moment
    without a hand turned to help her.

⁷ Their princes were brighter than snow
    and whiter than milk,
  their bodies more ruddy than rubies,
    their appearance like sapphires. ᵇ

⁸ But now they are blacker than soot;
    they are not recognized in the streets.
  Their skin has shriveled on their bones;
    it has become as dry as a stick.

⁹ Those killed by the sword are better off
    than those who die of famine;
  racked with hunger, they waste away
    for lack of food from the field.

¹⁰ With their own hands compassionate women
    have cooked their own children,
  who became their food
    when my people were destroyed.

¹¹ The Lᴏʀᴅ has given full vent to his wrath;
    he has poured out his fierce anger.
  He kindled a fire in Zion
    that consumed her foundations.

¹² The kings of the earth did not believe,
    nor did any of the world's people,
  that enemies and foes could enter
    the gates of Jerusalem.

¹³ But it happened because of the sins of her
        prophets
    and the iniquities of her priests,
  who shed within her
    the blood of the righteous.

¹⁴ Now they grope through the streets
    like men who are blind.
  They are so defiled with blood
    that no one dares to touch their garments.

¹⁵ "Go away! You are unclean!" men cry to them.
    "Away! Away! Don't touch us!"

ᵃ This chapter is an acrostic poem, the verses of which begin with the
successive letters of the Hebrew alphabet.   ᵇ 7 Or lapis lazuli

When they flee and wander about,
  people among the nations say,
  "They can stay here no longer."

¹⁶ The LORD himself has scattered them;
  he no longer watches over them.
The priests are shown no honor,
  the elders no favor.

¹⁷ Moreover, our eyes failed,
  looking in vain for help;
from our towers we watched
  for a nation that could not save us.

¹⁸ Men stalked us at every step,
  so we could not walk in our streets.
Our end was near, our days were numbered,
  for our end had come.

¹⁹ Our pursuers were swifter
  than eagles in the sky;
they chased us over the mountains
  and lay in wait for us in the desert.

²⁰ The LORD's anointed, our very life breath,
  was caught in their traps.
We thought that under his shadow
  we would live among the nations.

²¹ Rejoice and be glad, O Daughter of Edom,
  you who live in the land of Uz.
But to you also the cup will be passed;
  you will be drunk and stripped naked.

²² O Daughter of Zion, your punishment will
    end;
  he will not prolong your exile.
But, O Daughter of Edom, he will punish
    your sin
  and expose your wickedness.

5 Remember, O LORD, what has happened
    to us;
  look, and see our disgrace.
² Our inheritance has been turned over to
    aliens,
  our homes to foreigners.

³ We have become orphans and fatherless,
  our mothers like widows.
⁴ We must buy the water we drink;
  our wood can be had only at a price.
⁵ Those who pursue us are at our heels;
  we are weary and find no rest.
⁶ We submitted to Egypt and Assyria
  to get enough bread.
⁷ Our fathers sinned and are no more,
  and we bear their punishment.
⁸ Slaves rule over us,
  and there is none to free us from their
    hands.
⁹ We get our bread at the risk of our lives
  because of the sword in the desert.
¹⁰ Our skin is hot as an oven,
  feverish from hunger.
¹¹ Women have been ravished in Zion,
  and virgins in the towns of Judah.
¹² Princes have been hung up by their hands;
  elders are shown no respect.
¹³ Young men toil at the millstones;
  boys stagger under loads of wood.
¹⁴ The elders are gone from the city gate;
  the young men have stopped their music.
¹⁵ Joy is gone from our hearts;
  our dancing has turned to mourning.
¹⁶ The crown has fallen from our head.
  Woe to us, for we have sinned!
¹⁷ Because of this our hearts are faint,
  because of these things our eyes grow dim
¹⁸ for Mount Zion, which lies desolate,
  with jackals prowling over it.

¹⁹ You, O LORD, reign forever;
  your throne endures from generation to
    generation.
²⁰ Why do you always forget us?
  Why do you forsake us so long?
²¹ Restore us to yourself, O LORD, that we may
    return;
  renew our days as of old
²² unless you have utterly rejected us
  and are angry with us beyond measure.

Personal
RESPONSIBILITY

Ezekiel was among the residents of Judah who, in 597 B.C., comprised the second group to be taken from their homeland into captivity in Babylon. Using vivid physical illustrations (see, for example, Ezekiel 4:1 — 5:17), Ezekiel described to the people the final destruction of their beloved city, Jerusalem. Until the prophecy eventually came true, Ezekiel's ability to speak was limited; he could only speak when the Lord prompted him to proclaim his harsh message (see Ezekiel 3:24 – 27; 24:25 – 27). Once he received the news that Jerusalem had fallen, the ban on Ezekiel's speech was lifted (see Ezekiel 33:21 – 22). The prophet's message then became one filled with promises of God's restoration of the nation and the building of a new, glorious temple.

Although many of Ezekiel's words pertain directly to a specific time in history, they also have many realistic applications for us today. For instance, Ezekiel talked specifically about the personal responsibility we have in relation to others (see Ezekiel 21:24; 22:30). As God's watchmen, believers are called to warn others of God's approaching judgment (see Ezekiel 33:1 – 9).

Although each person is responsible for his or her own choices, as grandmothers we can rejoice in the knowledge that God will give us the words to encourage our children and grandchildren to be strong in character, to submit to God's Spirit, to turn their hearts and lives over to him, and to live responsibly for the Lord.

VERSE *to* REMEMBER | EZEKIEL 36:26 – 27

"I will give you a new heart and put a new spirit in you; I will remove from you your heart of stone and give you a heart of flesh. And I will put my Spirit in you and move you to follow my decrees and be careful to keep my laws."

ABOUT EZEKIEL

WRITTEN BY:
The prophet Ezekiel

WRITTEN FOR:
The Jewish captives in Babylon

DATE WRITTEN:
Between 593 and 571 B.C.

WHY WRITTEN:
To explain God's judgment on the wicked people still in Judah, and to reveal God's plan to restore them and give them a glorious new future

The Living Creatures and the Glory of the LORD

1 In the[a] thirtieth year, in the fourth month on the fifth day, while I was among the exiles by the Kebar River, the heavens were opened and I saw visions of God.

[2] On the fifth of the month—it was the fifth year of the exile of King Jehoiachin— [3] the word of the LORD came to Ezekiel the priest, the son of Buzi,[b] by the Kebar River in the land of the Babylonians.[c] There the hand of the LORD was upon him.

[4] I looked, and I saw a windstorm coming out of the north—an immense cloud with flashing lightning and surrounded by brilliant light. The center of the fire looked like glowing metal, [5] and in the fire was what looked like four living creatures. In appearance their form was that of a man, [6] but each of them had four faces and four wings. [7] Their legs were straight; their feet were like those of a calf and gleamed like burnished bronze. [8] Under their wings on their four sides they had the hands of a man. All four of them had faces and wings, [9] and their wings touched one another. Each one went straight ahead; they did not turn as they moved.

[10] Their faces looked like this: Each of the four had the face of a man, and on the right side each had the face of a lion, and on the left the face of an ox; each also had the face of an eagle. [11] Such were their faces. Their wings were spread out upward; each had two wings, one touching the wing of another creature on either side, and two wings covering its body. [12] Each one went straight ahead. Wherever the spirit would go, they would go, without turning as they went. [13] The appearance of the living creatures was like burning coals of fire or like torches. Fire moved back and forth among the creatures; it was bright, and lightning flashed out of it. [14] The creatures sped back and forth like flashes of lightning.

[15] As I looked at the living creatures, I saw a wheel on the ground beside each creature with its four faces. [16] This was the appearance and structure of the wheels: They sparkled like chrys-olite, and all four looked alike. Each appeared to be made like a wheel intersecting a wheel. [17] As they moved, they would go in any one of the four directions the creatures faced; the wheels did not turn about[d] as the creatures went. [18] Their rims were high and awesome, and all four rims were full of eyes all around.

[19] When the living creatures moved, the wheels beside them moved; and when the living creatures rose from the ground, the wheels also rose. [20] Wherever the spirit would go, they would go, and the wheels would rise along with them, because the spirit of the living creatures was in the wheels. [21] When the creatures moved, they also moved; when the creatures stood still, they also stood still; and when the creatures rose from the ground, the wheels rose along with them, because the spirit of the living creatures was in the wheels.

[22] Spread out above the heads of the living creatures was what looked like an expanse, sparkling like ice, and awesome. [23] Under the expanse their wings were stretched out one toward the other, and each had two wings covering its body. [24] When the creatures moved, I heard the sound of their wings, like the roar of rushing waters, like the voice of the Almighty,[e] like the tumult of an army. When they stood still, they lowered their wings.

[25] Then there came a voice from above the expanse over their heads as they stood with lowered wings. [26] Above the expanse over their heads was what looked like a throne of sapphire,[f] and high above on the throne was a figure like that of a man. [27] I saw that from what appeared to be his waist up he looked like glowing metal, as if full of fire, and that from there down he looked like fire; and brilliant light surrounded him. [28] Like the appearance of a rainbow in the clouds on a rainy day, so was the radiance around him.

This was the appearance of the likeness of the glory of the LORD. When I saw it, I fell facedown, and I heard the voice of one speaking.

[a] 1 Or *my*   [b] 3 Or *Ezekiel son of Buzi the priest*
[c] 3 Or *Chaldeans*   [d] 17 Or *aside*   [e] 24 Hebrew *Shaddai*
[f] 26 Or *lapis lazuli*

Ezekiel's Call

2 He said to me, "Son of man, stand up on your feet and I will speak to you." ²As he spoke, the Spirit came into me and raised me to my feet, and I heard him speaking to me.

³He said: "Son of man, I am sending you to the Israelites, to a rebellious nation that has rebelled against me; they and their fathers have been in revolt against me to this very day. ⁴The people to whom I am sending you are obstinate and stubborn. Say to them, 'This is what the Sovereign LORD says.' ⁵And whether they listen or fail to listen—for they are a rebellious house—they will know that a prophet has been among them. ⁶And you, son of man, do not be afraid of them or their words. Do not be afraid, though briers and thorns are all around you and you live among scorpions. Do not be afraid of what they say or terrified by them, though they are a rebellious house. ⁷You must speak my words to them, whether they listen or fail to listen, for they are rebellious. ⁸But you, son of man, listen to what I say to you. Do not rebel like that rebellious house; open your mouth and eat what I give you."

⁹Then I looked, and I saw a hand stretched out to me. In it was a scroll, ¹⁰which he unrolled before me. On both sides of it were written words of lament and mourning and woe.

3 And he said to me, "Son of man, eat what is before you, eat this scroll; then go and speak to the house of Israel." ²So I opened my mouth, and he gave me the scroll to eat.

³Then he said to me, "Son of man, eat this scroll I am giving you and fill your stomach with it." So I ate it, and it tasted as sweet as honey in my mouth.

⁴He then said to me: "Son of man, go now to the house of Israel and speak my words to them. ⁵You are not being sent to a people of obscure speech and difficult language, but to the house of Israel— ⁶not to many peoples of obscure speech and difficult language, whose words you cannot understand. Surely if I had sent you to them, they would have listened to you. ⁷But the house of Israel is not willing to listen to you be-

cause they are not willing to listen to me, for the whole house of Israel is hardened and obstinate. ⁸But I will make you as unyielding and hardened as they are. ⁹I will make your forehead like the hardest stone, harder than flint. Do not be afraid of them or terrified by them, though they are a rebellious house."

¹⁰And he said to me, "Son of man, listen carefully and take to heart all the words I speak to you. ¹¹Go now to your countrymen in exile and speak to them. Say to them, 'This is what the Sovereign LORD says,' whether they listen or fail to listen."

¹²Then the Spirit lifted me up, and I heard behind me a loud rumbling sound—May the glory of the LORD be praised in his dwelling place!—¹³the sound of the wings of the living creatures brushing against each other and the sound of the wheels beside them, a loud rumbling sound. ¹⁴The Spirit then lifted me up and took me away, and I went in bitterness and in the anger of my spirit, with the strong hand of the LORD upon me. ¹⁵I came to the exiles who lived at Tel Abib near the Kebar River. And there, where they were living, I sat among them for seven days—overwhelmed.

Warning to Israel

¹⁶At the end of seven days the word of the LORD came to me: ¹⁷"Son of man, I have made you a watchman for the house of Israel; so hear the word I speak and give them warning from me. ¹⁸When I say to a wicked man, 'You will surely die,' and you do not warn him or speak out to dissuade him from his evil ways in order to save his life, that wicked man will die for ᵃ his sin, and I will hold you accountable for his blood. ¹⁹But if you do warn the wicked man and he does not turn from his wickedness or from his evil ways, he will die for his sin; but you will have saved yourself.

²⁰"Again, when a righteous man turns from his righteousness and does evil, and I put a stumbling block before him, he will die. Since you did

---

ᵃ 18 Or in; also in verses 19 and 20

not warn him, he will die for his sin. The righteous things he did will not be remembered, and I will hold you accountable for his blood. [21] But if you do warn the righteous man not to sin and he does not sin, he will surely live because he took warning, and you will have saved yourself."

[22] The hand of the LORD was upon me there, and he said to me, "Get up and go out to the plain, and there I will speak to you." [23] So I got up and went out to the plain. And the glory of the LORD was standing there, like the glory I had seen by the Kebar River, and I fell facedown.

[24] Then the Spirit came into me and raised me to my feet. He spoke to me and said: "Go, shut yourself inside your house. [25] And you, son of man, they will tie with ropes; you will be bound so that you cannot go out among the people. [26] I will make your tongue stick to the roof of your mouth so that you will be silent and unable to rebuke them, though they are a rebellious house. [27] But when I speak to you, I will open your mouth and you shall say to them, 'This is what the Sovereign LORD says.' Whoever will listen let him listen, and whoever will refuse let him refuse; for they are a rebellious house.

Siege of Jerusalem Symbolized

4 "Now, son of man, take a clay tablet, put it in front of you and draw the city of Jerusalem on it. [2] Then lay siege to it: Erect siege works against it, build a ramp up to it, set up camps against it and put battering rams around it. [3] Then take an iron pan, place it as an iron wall between you and the city and turn your face toward it. It will be under siege, and you shall besiege it. This will be a sign to the house of Israel.

[4] "Then lie on your left side and put the sin of the house of Israel upon yourself. [a] You are to bear their sin for the number of days you lie on your side. [5] I have assigned you the same number of days as the years of their sin. So for 390 days you will bear the sin of the house of Israel.

[6] "After you have finished this, lie down again, this time on your right side, and bear the sin of the house of Judah. I have assigned you 40 days,

a day for each year. [7] Turn your face toward the siege of Jerusalem and with bared arm prophesy against her. [8] I will tie you up with ropes so that you cannot turn from one side to the other until you have finished the days of your siege.

[9] "Take wheat and barley, beans and lentils, millet and spelt; put them in a storage jar and use them to make bread for yourself. You are to eat it during the 390 days you lie on your side. [10] Weigh out twenty shekels [b] of food to eat each day and eat it at set times. [11] Also measure out a sixth of a hin [c] of water and drink it at set times. [12] Eat the food as you would a barley cake; bake it in the sight of the people, using human excrement for fuel." [13] The LORD said, "In this way the people of Israel will eat defiled food among the nations where I will drive them."

[14] Then I said, "Not so, Sovereign LORD! I have never defiled myself. From my youth until now I have never eaten anything found dead or torn by wild animals. No unclean meat has ever entered my mouth."

[15] "Very well," he said, "I will let you bake your bread over cow manure instead of human excrement."

[16] He then said to me: "Son of man, I will cut off the supply of food in Jerusalem. The people will eat rationed food in anxiety and drink rationed water in despair, [17] for food and water will be scarce. They will be appalled at the sight of each other and will waste away because of [d] their sin.

5 "Now, son of man, take a sharp sword and use it as a barber's razor to shave your head and your beard. Then take a set of scales and divide up the hair. [2] When the days of your siege come to an end, burn a third of the hair with fire inside the city. Take a third and strike it with the sword all around the city. And scatter a third to the wind. For I will pursue them with drawn sword. [3] But take a few strands of hair and tuck them away in the folds of your garment. [4] Again, take a few of these and throw them into the fire

---

[a] 4 Or *your side*   [b] 10 That is, about 8 ounces (about 0.2 kilogram)   [c] 11 That is, about 2/3 quart (about 0.6 liter)   [d] 17 Or *away in*

and burn them up. A fire will spread from there to the whole house of Israel.

⁵ "This is what the Sovereign LORD says: This is Jerusalem, which I have set in the center of the nations, with countries all around her. ⁶ Yet in her wickedness she has rebelled against my laws and decrees more than the nations and countries around her. She has rejected my laws and has not followed my decrees.

⁷ "Therefore this is what the Sovereign LORD says: You have been more unruly than the nations around you and have not followed my decrees or kept my laws. You have not even ᵃ conformed to the standards of the nations around you.

⁸ "Therefore this is what the Sovereign LORD says: I myself am against you, Jerusalem, and I will inflict punishment on you in the sight of the nations. ⁹ Because of all your detestable idols, I will do to you what I have never done before and will never do again. ¹⁰ Therefore in your midst fathers will eat their children, and children will eat their fathers. I will inflict punishment on you and will scatter all your survivors to the winds. ¹¹ Therefore as surely as I live, declares the Sovereign LORD, because you have defiled my sanctuary with all your vile images and detestable practices, I myself will withdraw my favor; I will not look on you with pity or spare you. ¹² A third of your people will die of the plague or perish by famine inside you; a third will fall by the sword outside your walls; and a third I will scatter to the winds and pursue with drawn sword.

¹³ "Then my anger will cease and my wrath against them will subside, and I will be avenged. And when I have spent my wrath upon them, they will know that I the LORD have spoken in my zeal.

¹⁴ "I will make you a ruin and a reproach among the nations around you, in the sight of all who pass by. ¹⁵ You will be a reproach and a taunt, a warning and an object of horror to the nations around you when I inflict punishment on you in anger and in wrath and with stinging rebuke. I the LORD have spoken. ¹⁶ When I shoot at you with my deadly and destructive arrows of fam-

ine, I will shoot to destroy you. I will bring more and more famine upon you and cut off your supply of food. ¹⁷ I will send famine and wild beasts against you, and they will leave you childless. Plague and bloodshed will sweep through you, and I will bring the sword against you. I the LORD have spoken."

A Prophecy Against the Mountains of Israel

6 The word of the LORD came to me: ² "Son of man, set your face against the mountains of Israel; prophesy against them ³ and say: 'O mountains of Israel, hear the word of the Sovereign LORD. This is what the Sovereign LORD says to the mountains and hills, to the ravines and valleys: I am about to bring a sword against you, and I will destroy your high places. ⁴ Your altars will be demolished and your incense altars will be smashed; and I will slay your people in front of your idols. ⁵ I will lay the dead bodies of the Israelites in front of their idols, and I will scatter your bones around your altars. ⁶ Wherever you live, the towns will be laid waste and the high places demolished, so that your altars will be laid waste and devastated, your idols smashed and ruined, your incense altars broken down, and what you have made wiped out. ⁷ Your people will fall slain among you, and you will know that I am the LORD.

⁸ "'But I will spare some, for some of you will escape the sword when you are scattered among the lands and nations. ⁹ Then in the nations where they have been carried captive, those who escape will remember me — how I have been grieved by their adulterous hearts, which have turned away from me, and by their eyes, which have lusted after their idols. They will loathe themselves for the evil they have done and for all their detestable practices. ¹⁰ And they will know that I am the LORD; I did not threaten in vain to bring this calamity on them.

¹¹ "'This is what the Sovereign LORD says:

ᵃ 7 Most Hebrew manuscripts; some Hebrew manuscripts and Syriac You have

Strike your hands together and stamp your feet and cry out "Alas!" because of all the wicked and detestable practices of the house of Israel, for they will fall by the sword, famine and plague. ¹²He that is far away will die of the plague, and he that is near will fall by the sword, and he that survives and is spared will die of famine. So will I spend my wrath upon them. ¹³And they will know that I am the LORD, when their people lie slain among their idols around their altars, on every high hill and on all the mountaintops, under every spreading tree and every leafy oak — places where they offered fragrant incense to all their idols. ¹⁴And I will stretch out my hand against them and make the land a desolate waste from the desert to Diblah *a* — wherever they live. Then they will know that I am the LORD.' "

The End Has Come

7 The word of the LORD came to me: ²"Son of man, this is what the Sovereign LORD says to the land of Israel: The end! The end has come upon the four corners of the land. ³The end is now upon you and I will unleash my anger against you. I will judge you according to your conduct and repay you for all your detestable practices. ⁴I will not look on you with pity or spare you; I will surely repay you for your conduct and the detestable practices among you. Then you will know that I am the LORD.

⁵"This is what the Sovereign LORD says: Disaster! An unheard-of *b* disaster is coming. ⁶The end has come! The end has come! It has roused itself against you. It has come! ⁷Doom has come upon you — you who dwell in the land. The time has come, the day is near; there is panic, not joy, upon the mountains. ⁸I am about to pour out my wrath on you and spend my anger against you; I will judge you according to your conduct and repay you for all your detestable practices. ⁹I will not look on you with pity or spare you; I will repay you in accordance with your conduct and the detestable practices among you. Then you will know that it is I the LORD who strikes the blow.

¹⁰"The day is here! It has come! Doom has

burst forth, the rod has budded, arrogance has blossomed! ¹¹Violence has grown into *c* a rod to punish wickedness; none of the people will be left, none of that crowd — no wealth, nothing of value. ¹²The time has come, the day has arrived. Let not the buyer rejoice nor the seller grieve, for wrath is upon the whole crowd. ¹³The seller will not recover the land he has sold as long as both of them live, for the vision concerning the whole crowd will not be reversed. Because of their sins, not one of them will preserve his life. ¹⁴Though they blow the trumpet and get everything ready, no one will go into battle, for my wrath is upon the whole crowd.

¹⁵"Outside is the sword, inside are plague and famine; those in the country will die by the sword, and those in the city will be devoured by famine and plague. ¹⁶All who survive and escape will be in the mountains, moaning like doves of the valleys, each because of his sins. ¹⁷Every hand will go limp, and every knee will become as weak as water. ¹⁸They will put on sackcloth and be clothed with terror. Their faces will be covered with shame and their heads will be shaved. ¹⁹They will throw their silver into the streets, and their gold will be an unclean thing. Their silver and gold will not be able to save them in the day of the LORD's wrath. They will not satisfy their hunger or fill their stomachs with it, for it has made them stumble into sin. ²⁰They were proud of their beautiful jewelry and used it to make their detestable idols and vile images. Therefore I will turn these into an unclean thing for them. ²¹I will hand it all over as plunder to foreigners and as loot to the wicked of the earth, and they will defile it. ²²I will turn my face away from them, and they will desecrate my treasured place; robbers will enter it and desecrate it.

²³"Prepare chains, because the land is full of bloodshed and the city is full of violence. ²⁴I will bring the most wicked of the nations to take possession of their houses; I will put an end to the

---

a 14 Most Hebrew manuscripts; a few Hebrew manuscripts *Riblah*
b 5 Most Hebrew manuscripts; some Hebrew manuscripts and Syriac *Disaster after*   *c 11* Or *The violent one has become*

pride of the mighty, and their sanctuaries will be desecrated. [25] When terror comes, they will seek peace, but there will be none. [26] Calamity upon calamity will come, and rumor upon rumor. They will try to get a vision from the prophet; the teaching of the law by the priest will be lost, as will the counsel of the elders. [27] The king will mourn, the prince will be clothed with despair, and the hands of the people of the land will tremble. I will deal with them according to their conduct, and by their own standards I will judge them. Then they will know that I am the LORD."

Idolatry in the Temple

8 In the sixth year, in the sixth month on the fifth day, while I was sitting in my house and the elders of Judah were sitting before me, the hand of the Sovereign LORD came upon me there. [2] I looked, and I saw a figure like that of a man.[a] From what appeared to be his waist down he was like fire, and from there up his appearance was as bright as glowing metal. [3] He stretched out what looked like a hand and took me by the hair of my head. The Spirit lifted me up between earth and heaven and in visions of God he took me to Jerusalem, to the entrance to the north gate of the inner court, where the idol that provokes to jealousy stood. [4] And there before me was the glory of the God of Israel, as in the vision I had seen in the plain.

[5] Then he said to me, "Son of man, look toward the north." So I looked, and in the entrance north of the gate of the altar I saw this idol of jealousy.

[6] And he said to me, "Son of man, do you see what they are doing—the utterly detestable things the house of Israel is doing here, things that will drive me far from my sanctuary? But you will see things that are even more detestable."

[7] Then he brought me to the entrance to the court. I looked, and I saw a hole in the wall. [8] He said to me, "Son of man, now dig into the wall." So I dug into the wall and saw a doorway there.

[9] And he said to me, "Go in and see the wicked and detestable things they are doing here." [10] So I went in and looked, and I saw portrayed all over the walls all kinds of crawling things and detestable animals and all the idols of the house of Israel. [11] In front of them stood seventy elders of the house of Israel, and Jaazaniah son of Shaphan was standing among them. Each had a censer in his hand, and a fragrant cloud of incense was rising.

[12] He said to me, "Son of man, have you seen what the elders of the house of Israel are doing in the darkness, each at the shrine of his own idol? They say, 'The LORD does not see us; the LORD has forsaken the land.'" [13] Again, he said, "You will see them doing things that are even more detestable."

[14] Then he brought me to the entrance to the north gate of the house of the LORD, and I saw women sitting there, mourning for Tammuz. [15] He said to me, "Do you see this, son of man? You will see things that are even more detestable than this."

[16] He then brought me into the inner court of the house of the LORD, and there at the entrance to the temple, between the portico and the altar, were about twenty-five men. With their backs toward the temple of the LORD and their faces toward the east, they were bowing down to the sun in the east.

[17] He said to me, "Have you seen this, son of man? Is it a trivial matter for the house of Judah to do the detestable things they are doing here? Must they also fill the land with violence and continually provoke me to anger? Look at them putting the branch to their nose! [18] Therefore I will deal with them in anger; I will not look on them with pity or spare them. Although they shout in my ears, I will not listen to them."

Idolaters Killed

9 Then I heard him call out in a loud voice, "Bring the guards of the city here, each with a weapon in his hand." [2] And I saw six men coming from the direction of the upper gate, which faces north, each with a deadly weapon in his hand. With them was a man clothed in linen who

---

[a] 2 Or saw a fiery figure

had a writing kit at his side. They came in and stood beside the bronze altar.

³Now the glory of the God of Israel went up from above the cherubim, where it had been, and moved to the threshold of the temple. Then the LORD called to the man clothed in linen who had the writing kit at his side ⁴and said to him, "Go throughout the city of Jerusalem and put a mark on the foreheads of those who grieve and lament over all the detestable things that are done in it."

⁵As I listened, he said to the others, "Follow him through the city and kill, without showing pity or compassion. ⁶Slaughter old men, young men and maidens, women and children, but do not touch anyone who has the mark. Begin at my sanctuary." So they began with the elders who were in front of the temple.

⁷Then he said to them, "Defile the temple and fill the courts with the slain. Go!" So they went out and began killing throughout the city. ⁸While they were killing and I was left alone, I fell face-down, crying out, "Ah, Sovereign LORD! Are you going to destroy the entire remnant of Israel in this outpouring of your wrath on Jerusalem?"

⁹He answered me, "The sin of the house of Israel and Judah is exceedingly great; the land is full of bloodshed and the city is full of injustice. They say, 'The LORD has forsaken the land; the LORD does not see.' ¹⁰So I will not look on them with pity or spare them, but I will bring down on their own heads what they have done."

¹¹Then the man in linen with the writing kit at his side brought back word, saying, "I have done as you commanded."

The Glory Departs From the Temple

10 I looked, and I saw the likeness of a throne of sapphire[a] above the expanse that was over the heads of the cherubim. ²The LORD said to the man clothed in linen, "Go in among the wheels beneath the cherubim. Fill your hands with burning coals from among the cherubim and scatter them over the city." And as I watched, he went in.

³Now the cherubim were standing on the south side of the temple when the man went in, and a cloud filled the inner court. ⁴Then the glory of the LORD rose from above the cherubim and moved to the threshold of the temple. The cloud filled the temple, and the court was full of the radiance of the glory of the LORD. ⁵The sound of the wings of the cherubim could be heard as far away as the outer court, like the voice of God Almighty[b] when he speaks.

⁶When the LORD commanded the man in linen, "Take fire from among the wheels, from among the cherubim," the man went in and stood beside a wheel. ⁷Then one of the cherubim reached out his hand to the fire that was among them. He took up some of it and put it into the hands of the man in linen, who took it and went out. ⁸(Under the wings of the cherubim could be seen what looked like the hands of a man.)

⁹I looked, and I saw beside the cherubim four wheels, one beside each of the cherubim; the wheels sparkled like chrysolite. ¹⁰As for their appearance, the four of them looked alike; each was like a wheel intersecting a wheel. ¹¹As they moved, they would go in any one of the four directions the cherubim faced; the wheels did not turn about[c] as the cherubim went. The cherubim went in whatever direction the head faced, without turning as they went. ¹²Their entire bodies, including their backs, their hands and their wings, were completely full of eyes, as were their four wheels. ¹³I heard the wheels being called "the whirling wheels." ¹⁴Each of the cherubim had four faces: One face was that of a cherub, the second the face of a man, the third the face of a lion, and the fourth the face of an eagle.

¹⁵Then the cherubim rose upward. These were the living creatures I had seen by the Kebar River. ¹⁶When the cherubim moved, the wheels beside them moved; and when the cherubim spread their wings to rise from the ground, the wheels did not leave their side. ¹⁷When the cherubim stood still, they also stood still; and when the cherubim rose, they rose with them, because the spirit of the living creatures was in them.

---

[a] 1 Or *lapis lazuli*   [b] 5 Hebrew *El-Shaddai*   [c] 11 Or *aside*

[18] Then the glory of the LORD departed from over the threshold of the temple and stopped above the cherubim. [19] While I watched, the cherubim spread their wings and rose from the ground, and as they went, the wheels went with them. They stopped at the entrance to the east gate of the LORD's house, and the glory of the God of Israel was above them.

[20] These were the living creatures I had seen beneath the God of Israel by the Kebar River, and I realized that they were cherubim. [21] Each had four faces and four wings, and under their wings was what looked like the hands of a man. [22] Their faces had the same appearance as those I had seen by the Kebar River. Each one went straight ahead.

Judgment on Israel's Leaders

11 Then the Spirit lifted me up and brought me to the gate of the house of the LORD that faces east. There at the entrance to the gate were twenty-five men, and I saw among them Jaazaniah son of Azzur and Pelatiah son of Benaiah, leaders of the people. [2] The LORD said to me, "Son of man, these are the men who are plotting evil and giving wicked advice in this city. [3] They say, 'Will it not soon be time to build houses?[a] This city is a cooking pot, and we are the meat.' [4] Therefore prophesy against them; prophesy, son of man."

[5] Then the Spirit of the LORD came upon me, and he told me to say: "This is what the LORD says: That is what you are saying, O house of Israel, but I know what is going through your mind. [6] You have killed many people in this city and filled its streets with the dead.

[7] "Therefore this is what the Sovereign LORD says: The bodies you have thrown there are the meat and this city is the pot, but I will drive you out of it. [8] You fear the sword, and the sword is what I will bring against you, declares the Sovereign LORD. [9] I will drive you out of the city and hand you over to foreigners and inflict punishment on you. [10] You will fall by the sword, and I will execute judgment on you at the borders of Israel. Then you will know that I am the LORD.

[11] This city will not be a pot for you, nor will you be the meat in it; I will execute judgment on you at the borders of Israel. [12] And you will know that I am the LORD, for you have not followed my decrees or kept my laws but have conformed to the standards of the nations around you."

[13] Now as I was prophesying, Pelatiah son of Benaiah died. Then I fell facedown and cried out in a loud voice, "Ah, Sovereign LORD! Will you completely destroy the remnant of Israel?"

[14] The word of the LORD came to me: [15] "Son of man, your brothers—your brothers who are your blood relatives[b] and the whole house of Israel—are those of whom the people of Jerusalem have said, 'They are[c] far away from the LORD; this land was given to us as our possession.'

Promised Return of Israel

[16] "Therefore say: 'This is what the Sovereign LORD says: Although I sent them far away among the nations and scattered them among the countries, yet for a little while I have been a sanctuary for them in the countries where they have gone.'

[17] "Therefore say: 'This is what the Sovereign LORD says: I will gather you from the nations and bring you back from the countries where you have been scattered, and I will give you back the land of Israel again.'

[18] "They will return to it and remove all its vile images and detestable idols. [19] I will give them an undivided heart and put a new spirit in them; I will remove from them their heart of stone and give them a heart of flesh. [20] Then they will follow my decrees and be careful to keep my laws. They will be my people, and I will be their God. [21] But as for those whose hearts are devoted to their vile images and detestable idols, I will bring down on their own heads what they have done, declares the Sovereign LORD."

[22] Then the cherubim, with the wheels beside them, spread their wings, and the glory of the God of Israel was above them. [23] The glory of the

---

[a] 3 Or *This is not the time to build houses.*   [b] 15 Or *are in exile with you* (see Septuagint and Syriac)   [c] 15 Or *those to whom the people of Jerusalem have said, 'Stay*

LORD went up from within the city and stopped above the mountain east of it. [24]The Spirit lifted me up and brought me to the exiles in Babylonia[a] in the vision given by the Spirit of God.

Then the vision I had seen went up from me, [25]and I told the exiles everything the LORD had shown me.

The Exile Symbolized

12 The word of the LORD came to me: [2]"Son of man, you are living among a rebellious people. They have eyes to see but do not see and ears to hear but do not hear, for they are a rebellious people.

[3]"Therefore, son of man, pack your belongings for exile and in the daytime, as they watch, set out and go from where you are to another place. Perhaps they will understand, though they are a rebellious house. [4]During the daytime, while they watch, bring out your belongings packed for exile. Then in the evening, while they are watching, go out like those who go into exile. [5]While they watch, dig through the wall and take your belongings out through it. [6]Put them on your shoulder as they are watching and carry them out at dusk. Cover your face so that you cannot see the land, for I have made you a sign to the house of Israel."

[7]So I did as I was commanded. During the day I brought out my things packed for exile. Then in the evening I dug through the wall with my hands. I took my belongings out at dusk, carrying them on my shoulders while they watched.

[8]In the morning the word of the LORD came to me: [9]"Son of man, did not that rebellious house of Israel ask you, 'What are you doing?'

[10]"Say to them, 'This is what the Sovereign LORD says: This oracle concerns the prince in Jerusalem and the whole house of Israel who are there.' [11]Say to them, 'I am a sign to you.'

"As I have done, so it will be done to them. They will go into exile as captives.

[12]"The prince among them will put his things on his shoulder at dusk and leave, and a hole will be dug in the wall for him to go through. He will cover his face so that he cannot see the land. [13]I will spread my net for him, and he will be caught in my snare; I will bring him to Babylonia, the land of the Chaldeans, but he will not see it, and there he will die. [14]I will scatter to the winds all those around him—his staff and all his troops—and I will pursue them with drawn sword.

[15]"They will know that I am the LORD, when I disperse them among the nations and scatter them through the countries. [16]But I will spare a few of them from the sword, famine and plague, so that in the nations where they go they may acknowledge all their detestable practices. Then they will know that I am the LORD."

[17]The word of the LORD came to me: [18]"Son of man, tremble as you eat your food, and shudder in fear as you drink your water. [19]Say to the people of the land: 'This is what the Sovereign LORD says about those living in Jerusalem and in the land of Israel: They will eat their food in anxiety and drink their water in despair, for their land will be stripped of everything in it because of the violence of all who live there. [20]The inhabited towns will be laid waste and the land will be desolate. Then you will know that I am the LORD.'"

[21]The word of the LORD came to me: [22]"Son of man, what is this proverb you have in the land of Israel: 'The days go by and every vision comes to nothing'? [23]Say to them, 'This is what the Sovereign LORD says: I am going to put an end to this proverb, and they will no longer quote it in Israel.' Say to them, 'The days are near when every vision will be fulfilled. [24]For there will be no more false visions or flattering divinations among the people of Israel. [25]But I the LORD will speak what I will, and it shall be fulfilled without delay. For in your days, you rebellious house, I will fulfill whatever I say, declares the Sovereign LORD.'"

[26]The word of the LORD came to me: [27]"Son of man, the house of Israel is saying, 'The vision he sees is for many years from now, and he prophesies about the distant future.'

[28]"Therefore say to them, 'This is what the Sovereign LORD says: None of my words will be

delayed any longer; whatever I say will be fulfilled, declares the Sovereign LORD.'"

False Prophets Condemned

13 The word of the LORD came to me: ²"Son of man, prophesy against the prophets of Israel who are now prophesying. Say to those who prophesy out of their own imagination: 'Hear the word of the LORD! ³This is what the Sovereign LORD says: Woe to the foolish[a] prophets who follow their own spirit and have seen nothing! ⁴Your prophets, O Israel, are like jackals among ruins. ⁵You have not gone up to the breaks in the wall to repair it for the house of Israel so that it will stand firm in the battle on the day of the LORD. ⁶Their visions are false and their divinations a lie. They say, "The LORD declares," when the LORD has not sent them; yet they expect their words to be fulfilled. ⁷Have you not seen false visions and uttered lying divinations when you say, "The LORD declares," though I have not spoken?

⁸"'Therefore this is what the Sovereign LORD says: Because of your false words and lying visions, I am against you, declares the Sovereign LORD. ⁹My hand will be against the prophets who see false visions and utter lying divinations. They will not belong to the council of my people or be listed in the records of the house of Israel, nor will they enter the land of Israel. Then you will know that I am the Sovereign LORD.

¹⁰"'Because they lead my people astray, saying, "Peace," when there is no peace, and because, when a flimsy wall is built, they cover it with whitewash, ¹¹therefore tell those who cover it with whitewash that it is going to fall. Rain will come in torrents, and I will send hailstones hurtling down, and violent winds will burst forth. ¹²When the wall collapses, will people not ask you, "Where is the whitewash you covered it with?"

¹³"'Therefore this is what the Sovereign LORD says: In my wrath I will unleash a violent wind, and in my anger hailstones and torrents of rain will fall with destructive fury. ¹⁴I will tear down the wall you have covered with whitewash and

will level it to the ground so that its foundation will be laid bare. When it[b] falls, you will be destroyed in it; and you will know that I am the LORD. ¹⁵So I will spend my wrath against the wall and against those who covered it with whitewash. I will say to you, "The wall is gone and so are those who whitewashed it, ¹⁶those prophets of Israel who prophesied to Jerusalem and saw visions of peace for her when there was no peace, declares the Sovereign LORD."'

¹⁷"Now, son of man, set your face against the daughters of your people who prophesy out of their own imagination. Prophesy against them ¹⁸and say, 'This is what the Sovereign LORD says: Woe to the women who sew magic charms on all their wrists and make veils of various lengths for their heads in order to ensnare people. Will you ensnare the lives of my people but preserve your own? ¹⁹You have profaned me among my people for a few handfuls of barley and scraps of bread. By lying to my people, who listen to lies, you have killed those who should not have died and have spared those who should not live.

²⁰"'Therefore this is what the Sovereign LORD says: I am against your magic charms with which you ensnare people like birds and I will tear them from your arms; I will set free the people that you ensnare like birds. ²¹I will tear off your veils and save my people from your hands, and they will no longer fall prey to your power. Then you will know that I am the LORD. ²²Because you disheartened the righteous with your lies, when I had brought them no grief, and because you encouraged the wicked not to turn from their evil ways and so save their lives, ²³therefore you will no longer see false visions or practice divination. I will save my people from your hands. And then you will know that I am the LORD.'"

Idolaters Condemned

14 Some of the elders of Israel came to me and sat down in front of me. ²Then the word of the LORD came to me: ³"Son of man, these men have set up idols in their hearts and

---

[a] 3 Or wicked   [b] 14 Or the city

put wicked stumbling blocks before their faces. Should I let them inquire of me at all? ⁴Therefore speak to them and tell them, 'This is what the Sovereign Lᴏʀᴅ says: When any Israelite sets up idols in his heart and puts a wicked stumbling block before his face and then goes to a prophet, I the Lᴏʀᴅ will answer him myself in keeping with his great idolatry. ⁵I will do this to recapture the hearts of the people of Israel, who have all deserted me for their idols.'

⁶"Therefore say to the house of Israel, 'This is what the Sovereign Lᴏʀᴅ says: Repent! Turn from your idols and renounce all your detestable practices!

⁷" 'When any Israelite or any alien living in Israel separates himself from me and sets up idols in his heart and puts a wicked stumbling block before his face and then goes to a prophet to inquire of me, I the Lᴏʀᴅ will answer him myself. ⁸I will set my face against that man and make him an example and a byword. I will cut him off from my people. Then you will know that I am the Lᴏʀᴅ.

⁹" 'And if the prophet is enticed to utter a prophecy, I the Lᴏʀᴅ have enticed that prophet, and I will stretch out my hand against him and destroy him from among my people Israel. ¹⁰They will bear their guilt—the prophet will be as guilty as the one who consults him. ¹¹Then the people of Israel will no longer stray from me, nor will they defile themselves anymore with all their sins. They will be my people, and I will be their God, declares the Sovereign Lᴏʀᴅ.' "

Judgment Inescapable

¹²The word of the Lᴏʀᴅ came to me: ¹³"Son of man, if a country sins against me by being unfaithful and I stretch out my hand against it to cut off its food supply and send famine upon it and kill its men and their animals, ¹⁴even if these three men—Noah, Daniel*a* and Job—were in it, they could save only themselves by their righteousness, declares the Sovereign Lᴏʀᴅ.

¹⁵"Or if I send wild beasts through that country and they leave it childless and it becomes des-olate so that no one can pass through it because of the beasts, ¹⁶as surely as I live, declares the Sovereign Lᴏʀᴅ, even if these three men were in it, they could not save their own sons or daughters. They alone would be saved, but the land would be desolate.

¹⁷"Or if I bring a sword against that country and say, 'Let the sword pass throughout the land,' and I kill its men and their animals, ¹⁸as surely as I live, declares the Sovereign Lᴏʀᴅ, even if these three men were in it, they could not save their own sons or daughters. They alone would be saved.

¹⁹"Or if I send a plague into that land and pour out my wrath upon it through bloodshed, killing its men and their animals, ²⁰as surely as I live, declares the Sovereign Lᴏʀᴅ, even if Noah, Daniel and Job were in it, they could save neither son nor daughter. They would save only themselves by their righteousness.

²¹"For this is what the Sovereign Lᴏʀᴅ says: How much worse will it be when I send against Jerusalem my four dreadful judgments—sword and famine and wild beasts and plague—to kill its men and their animals! ²²Yet there will be some survivors—sons and daughters who will be brought out of it. They will come to you, and when you see their conduct and their actions, you will be consoled regarding the disaster I have brought upon Jerusalem—every disaster I have brought upon it. ²³You will be consoled when you see their conduct and their actions, for you will know that I have done nothing in it without cause, declares the Sovereign Lᴏʀᴅ."

Jerusalem, A Useless Vine

15 The word of the Lᴏʀᴅ came to me: ²"Son of man, how is the wood of a vine better than that of a branch on any of the trees in the forest? ³Is wood ever taken from it to make anything useful? Do they make pegs from it to hang things on? ⁴And after it is thrown on the fire as fuel and the fire burns both ends and chars the

---

a 14 Or *Danel*; the Hebrew spelling may suggest a person other than the prophet Daniel; also in verse 20.

middle, is it then useful for anything? ⁵If it was not useful for anything when it was whole, how much less can it be made into something useful when the fire has burned it and it is charred?

⁶"Therefore this is what the Sovereign LORD says: As I have given the wood of the vine among the trees of the forest as fuel for the fire, so will I treat the people living in Jerusalem. ⁷I will set my face against them. Although they have come out of the fire, the fire will yet consume them. And when I set my face against them, you will know that I am the LORD. ⁸I will make the land desolate because they have been unfaithful, declares the Sovereign LORD."

An Allegory of Unfaithful Jerusalem

16 The word of the LORD came to me: ²"Son of man, confront Jerusalem with her detestable practices ³and say, 'This is what the Sovereign LORD says to Jerusalem: Your ancestry and birth were in the land of the Canaanites; your father was an Amorite and your mother a Hittite. ⁴On the day you were born your cord was not cut, nor were you washed with water to make you clean, nor were you rubbed with salt or wrapped in cloths. ⁵No one looked on you with pity or had compassion enough to do any of these things for you. Rather, you were thrown out into the open field, for on the day you were born you were despised.

⁶"'Then I passed by and saw you kicking about in your blood, and as you lay there in your blood I said to you, "Live!"ᵃ ⁷I made you grow like a plant of the field. You grew up and developed and became the most beautiful of jewels.ᵇ Your breasts were formed and your hair grew, you who were naked and bare.

⁸"'Later I passed by, and when I looked at you and saw that you were old enough for love, I spread the corner of my garment over you and covered your nakedness. I gave you my solemn oath and entered into a covenant with you, declares the Sovereign LORD, and you became mine.

⁹"'I bathedᶜ you with water and washed the blood from you and put ointments on you. ¹⁰I

clothed you with an embroidered dress and put leather sandals on you. I dressed you in fine linen and covered you with costly garments. ¹¹I adorned you with jewelry: I put bracelets on your arms and a necklace around your neck, ¹²and I put a ring on your nose, earrings on your ears and a beautiful crown on your head. ¹³So you were adorned with gold and silver; your clothes were of fine linen and costly fabric and embroidered cloth. Your food was fine flour, honey and olive oil. You became very beautiful and rose to be a queen. ¹⁴And your fame spread among the nations on account of your beauty, because the splendor I had given you made your beauty perfect, declares the Sovereign LORD.

¹⁵"'But you trusted in your beauty and used your fame to become a prostitute. You lavished your favors on anyone who passed by and your beauty became his.ᵈ ¹⁶You took some of your garments to make gaudy high places, where you carried on your prostitution. Such things should not happen, nor should they ever occur. ¹⁷You also took the fine jewelry I gave you, the jewelry made of my gold and silver, and you made for yourself male idols and engaged in prostitution with them. ¹⁸And you took your embroidered clothes to put on them, and you offered my oil and incense before them. ¹⁹Also the food I provided for you—the fine flour, olive oil and honey I gave you to eat—you offered as fragrant incense before them. That is what happened, declares the Sovereign LORD.

²⁰"'And you took your sons and daughters whom you bore to me and sacrificed them as food to the idols. Was your prostitution not enough? ²¹You slaughtered my children and sacrificed themᵉ to the idols. ²²In all your detestable practices and your prostitution you did not remember the days of your youth, when you were naked and bare, kicking about in your blood.

ᵃ 6 A few Hebrew manuscripts, Septuagint and Syriac; most Hebrew manuscripts *"Live!" And as you lay there in your blood I said to you, "Live!"* ᵇ 7 Or *became mature* ᶜ 9 Or *I had bathed* ᵈ 15 Most Hebrew manuscripts; one Hebrew manuscript (see some Septuagint manuscripts) *by. Such a thing should not happen* ᵉ 21 Or *and made them pass through ⸤the fire⸥*

23 " 'Woe! Woe to you, declares the Sovereign Lord. In addition to all your other wickedness, 24 you built a mound for yourself and made a lofty shrine in every public square. 25 At the head of every street you built your lofty shrines and degraded your beauty, offering your body with increasing promiscuity to anyone who passed by. 26 You engaged in prostitution with the Egyptians, your lustful neighbors, and provoked me to anger with your increasing promiscuity. 27 So I stretched out my hand against you and reduced your territory; I gave you over to the greed of your enemies, the daughters of the Philistines, who were shocked by your lewd conduct. 28 You engaged in prostitution with the Assyrians too, because you were insatiable; and even after that, you still were not satisfied. 29 Then you increased your promiscuity to include Babylonia,ᵃ a land of merchants, but even with this you were not satisfied.

30 " 'How weak-willed you are, declares the Sovereign Lord, when you do all these things, acting like a brazen prostitute! 31 When you built your mounds at the head of every street and made your lofty shrines in every public square, you were unlike a prostitute, because you scorned payment.

32 " 'You adulterous wife! You prefer strangers to your own husband! 33 Every prostitute receives a fee, but you give gifts to all your lovers, bribing them to come to you from everywhere for your illicit favors. 34 So in your prostitution you are the opposite of others; no one runs after you for your favors. You are the very opposite, for you give payment and none is given to you.

35 " 'Therefore, you prostitute, hear the word of the Lord! 36 This is what the Sovereign Lord says: Because you poured out your wealthᵇ and exposed your nakedness in your promiscuity with your lovers, and because of all your detestable idols, and because you gave them your children's blood, 37 therefore I am going to gather all your lovers, with whom you found pleasure, those you loved as well as those you hated. I will gather them against you from all around and will strip you in front of them, and they will see all your nakedness. 38 I will sentence you to the punishment of women who commit adultery and who shed blood; I will bring upon you the blood vengeance of my wrath and jealous anger. 39 Then I will hand you over to your lovers, and they will tear down your mounds and destroy your lofty shrines. They will strip you of your clothes and take your fine jewelry and leave you naked and bare. 40 They will bring a mob against you, who will stone you and hack you to pieces with their swords. 41 They will burn down your houses and inflict punishment on you in the sight of many women. I will put a stop to your prostitution, and you will no longer pay your lovers. 42 Then my wrath against you will subside and my jealous anger will turn away from you; I will be calm and no longer angry.

43 " 'Because you did not remember the days of your youth but enraged me with all these things, I will surely bring down on your head what you have done, declares the Sovereign Lord. Did you not add lewdness to all your other detestable practices?

44 " 'Everyone who quotes proverbs will quote this proverb about you: "Like mother, like daughter." 45 You are a true daughter of your mother, who despised her husband and her children; and you are a true sister of your sisters, who despised their husbands and their children. Your mother was a Hittite and your father an Amorite. 46 Your older sister was Samaria, who lived to the north of you with her daughters; and your younger sister, who lived to the south of you with her daughters, was Sodom. 47 You not only walked in their ways and copied their detestable practices, but in all your ways you soon became more depraved than they. 48 As surely as I live, declares the Sovereign Lord, your sister Sodom and her daughters never did what you and your daughters have done.

49 " 'Now this was the sin of your sister Sodom: She and her daughters were arrogant, overfed

ᵃ 29 Or Chaldea   ᵇ 36 Or lust

and unconcerned; they did not help the poor and needy. ⁵⁰They were haughty and did detestable things before me. Therefore I did away with them as you have seen. ⁵¹Samaria did not commit half the sins you did. You have done more detestable things than they, and have made your sisters seem righteous by all these things you have done. ⁵²Bear your disgrace, for you have furnished some justification for your sisters. Because your sins were more vile than theirs, they appear more righteous than you. So then, be ashamed and bear your disgrace, for you have made your sisters appear righteous.

⁵³ 'However, I will restore the fortunes of Sodom and her daughters and of Samaria and her daughters, and your fortunes along with them, ⁵⁴so that you may bear your disgrace and be ashamed of all you have done in giving them comfort. ⁵⁵And your sisters, Sodom with her daughters and Samaria with her daughters, will return to what they were before; and you and your daughters will return to what you were before. ⁵⁶You would not even mention your sister Sodom in the day of your pride, ⁵⁷before your wickedness was uncovered. Even so, you are now scorned by the daughters of Edom *a* and all her neighbors and the daughters of the Philistines — all those around you who despise you. ⁵⁸You will bear the consequences of your lewdness and your detestable practices, declares the Lord.

⁵⁹ 'This is what the Sovereign Lord says: I will deal with you as you deserve, because you have despised my oath by breaking the covenant. ⁶⁰Yet I will remember the covenant I made with you in the days of your youth, and I will establish an everlasting covenant with you. ⁶¹Then you will remember your ways and be ashamed when you receive your sisters, both those who are older than you and those who are younger. I will give them to you as daughters, but not on the basis of my covenant with you. ⁶²So I will establish my covenant with you, and you will know that I am the Lord. ⁶³Then, when I make atonement for you for all you have done, you will remember and be ashamed and never again open your mouth because of your humiliation, declares the Sovereign Lord.' "

Two Eagles and a Vine

17 The word of the Lord came to me: ²"Son of man, set forth an allegory and tell the house of Israel a parable. ³Say to them, 'This is what the Sovereign Lord says: A great eagle with powerful wings, long feathers and full plumage of varied colors came to Lebanon. Taking hold of the top of a cedar, ⁴he broke off its topmost shoot and carried it away to a land of merchants, where he planted it in a city of traders.

⁵ "'He took some of the seed of your land and put it in fertile soil. He planted it like a willow by abundant water, ⁶and it sprouted and became a low, spreading vine. Its branches turned toward him, but its roots remained under it. So it became a vine and produced branches and put out leafy boughs.

⁷ "'But there was another great eagle with powerful wings and full plumage. The vine now sent out its roots toward him from the plot where it was planted and stretched out its branches to him for water. ⁸It had been planted in good soil by abundant water so that it would produce branches, bear fruit and become a splendid vine.'

⁹"Say to them, 'This is what the Sovereign Lord says: Will it thrive? Will it not be uprooted and stripped of its fruit so that it withers? All its new growth will wither. It will not take a strong arm or many people to pull it up by the roots. ¹⁰Even if it is transplanted, will it thrive? Will it not wither completely when the east wind strikes it — wither away in the plot where it grew?' "

¹¹Then the word of the Lord came to me: ¹²"Say to this rebellious house, 'Do you not know what these things mean?' Say to them: 'The king of Babylon went to Jerusalem and carried off her king and her nobles, bringing them back with him to Babylon. ¹³Then he took a member of the royal family and made a treaty with him, putting him under oath. He also carried away the leading

---

a 57 Many Hebrew manuscripts and Syriac; most Hebrew manuscripts, Septuagint and Vulgate *Aram* men of the land, [14] so that the kingdom would be brought low, unable to rise again, surviving only by keeping his treaty. [15] But the king rebelled against him by sending his envoys to Egypt to get horses and a large army. Will he succeed? Will he who does such things escape? Will he break the treaty and yet escape?

[16] " 'As surely as I live, declares the Sovereign Lord, he shall die in Babylon, in the land of the king who put him on the throne, whose oath he despised and whose treaty he broke. [17] Pharaoh with his mighty army and great horde will be of no help to him in war, when ramps are built and siege works erected to destroy many lives. [18] He despised the oath by breaking the covenant. Because he had given his hand in pledge and yet did all these things, he shall not escape.

[19] " 'Therefore this is what the Sovereign Lord says: As surely as I live, I will bring down on his head my oath that he despised and my covenant that he broke. [20] I will spread my net for him, and he will be caught in my snare. I will bring him to Babylon and execute judgment upon him there because he was unfaithful to me. [21] All his fleeing troops will fall by the sword, and the survivors will be scattered to the winds. Then you will know that I the Lord have spoken.

[22] " 'This is what the Sovereign Lord says: I myself will take a shoot from the very top of a cedar and plant it; I will break off a tender sprig from its topmost shoots and plant it on a high and lofty mountain. [23] On the mountain heights of Israel I will plant it; it will produce branches and bear fruit and become a splendid cedar. Birds of every kind will nest in it; they will find shelter in the shade of its branches. [24] All the trees of the field will know that I the Lord bring down the tall tree and make the low tree grow tall. I dry up the green tree and make the dry tree flourish.

" 'I the Lord have spoken, and I will do it.' "

The Soul Who Sins Will Die

18 The word of the Lord came to me: [2] "What do you people mean by quoting this proverb about the land of Israel:

" 'The fathers eat sour grapes,
   and the children's teeth are set on edge'?

[3] "As surely as I live, declares the Sovereign Lord, you will no longer quote this proverb in Israel. [4] For every living soul belongs to me, the father as well as the son—both alike belong to me. The soul who sins is the one who will die.

[5] "Suppose there is a righteous man
   who does what is just and right.
[6] He does not eat at the mountain shrines
   or look to the idols of the house of Israel.
He does not defile his neighbor's wife
   or lie with a woman during her period.
[7] He does not oppress anyone,
   but returns what he took in pledge for
      a loan.
He does not commit robbery
   but gives his food to the hungry
   and provides clothing for the naked.
[8] He does not lend at usury
   or take excessive interest. [a]
He withholds his hand from doing wrong
   and judges fairly between man and man.
[9] He follows my decrees
   and faithfully keeps my laws.
That man is righteous;
   he will surely live,
                  declares the Sovereign Lord.

[10] "Suppose he has a violent son, who sheds blood or does any of these other things [b] [11] (though the father has done none of them):

"He eats at the mountain shrines.
He defiles his neighbor's wife.
[12] He oppresses the poor and needy.
He commits robbery.
He does not return what he took in pledge.
He looks to the idols.
He does detestable things.
[13] He lends at usury and takes excessive interest.

Will such a man live? He will not! Because he has done all these detestable things, he will surely be

---

[a] 8 Or *take interest;* similarly in verses 13 and 17   [b] 10 Or *things to a brother*

> "ALL THE TREES OF THE FIELD WILL KNOW
> THAT I THE LORD BRING DOWN THE TALL
> TREE AND MAKE THE LOW TREE GROW TALL.
> I DRY UP THE GREEN TREE AND MAKE THE
> DRY TREE FLOURISH. I THE LORD HAVE
> SPOKEN, AND I WILL DO IT."
>
> *Ezekiel 17:24*

Humps and Bumps

KAREN O'CONNOR

READ | EZEKIEL 17:1 – 24

We walked the trail in the Patriarch Forest in California, stopping here and there to comment on the shape or color or texture of these amazing specimens that were the only survivors in this soil for thousands of years. I could hardly put my mind around this fact. I felt a kind of reverence for each tree. I wanted to congratulate them for making it, for being steadfast, for doing what God had created them to do. They had survived this barren place yet were still standing, proof of the stuff they were made of.

Knots, humps, bumps, gnarled branches and chubby trunks abounded. These trees were not beautiful like a graceful willow or tall and slender like a stately palm, but they were elegant in their own way. The ravages of age and weather had given them a beauty impossible to describe.

Then I thought about myself, an older woman who had a few humps and bumps of my own. I had been discounting myself lately, finding fault with the changes my body reflected and with the aging process that had become more evident each year. In a flash of insight I suddenly wept. How is it that I could see beauty in the trees but not in myself? Why is getting older a good thing for a tree, but a bad thing for me? Why do I look in the mirror and bemoan the wrinkles that line my face but see in the trees a quiet dignity that has nothing to do with shape or age?

Charles and I drove back in silence, each of us wrapped in thought. What had begun as a pleasant side trip turned into a personal retreat. Bubbling conversation had given way to quiet reflection.

O Lord, how ungrateful of me to judge my worth by how I look. I know that I am so much more to you than a lump of aging clay. Thank you for the gifts of wisdom and discernment, for curiosity, for peace and for your everlasting love.

Your next devotion is located on page 1125.

GRANDCHILD IN FOCUS · PRAYER

Physical Well-Being

Almighty God, Creator of us all, I pray that you will watch over my grandchild's physical development. May he grow in strength through the stages of his life. As he grows in awareness of his body, help him to understand that each body develops uniquely, yet is within your plan and your control. Please guard his health so that his diseases are few, his injuries are minor and his infirmities are brief. Amen.

put to death and his blood will be on his own head.

[14]"But suppose this son has a son who sees all the sins his father commits, and though he sees them, he does not do such things:

[15]"He does not eat at the mountain shrines
　　or look to the idols of the house of Israel.
He does not defile his neighbor's wife.
[16]He does not oppress anyone
　　or require a pledge for a loan.
He does not commit robbery
　　but gives his food to the hungry
　　and provides clothing for the naked.
[17]He withholds his hand from sin[a]
　　and takes no usury or excessive interest.
He keeps my laws and follows my decrees.

He will not die for his father's sin; he will surely live. [18]But his father will die for his own sin, because he practiced extortion, robbed his brother and did what was wrong among his people.

[19]"Yet you ask, 'Why does the son not share the guilt of his father?' Since the son has done what is just and right and has been careful to keep all my decrees, he will surely live. [20]The soul who sins is the one who will die. The son will not share the guilt of the father, nor will the father share the guilt of the son. The righteousness of the righteous man will be credited to him, and the wickedness of the wicked will be charged against him.

[21]"But if a wicked man turns away from all the sins he has committed and keeps all my decrees and does what is just and right, he will surely live; he will not die. [22]None of the offenses he has committed will be remembered against him. Because of the righteous things he has done, he will live. [23]Do I take any pleasure in the death of the wicked? declares the Sovereign LORD. Rather, am I not pleased when they turn from their ways and live?

[24]"But if a righteous man turns from his righteousness and commits sin and does the same detestable things the wicked man does, will he live? None of the righteous things he has done will be remembered. Because of the unfaithfulness he is guilty of and because of the sins he has committed, he will die.

[25]"Yet you say, 'The way of the Lord is not just.' Hear, O house of Israel: Is my way unjust? Is it not your ways that are unjust? [26]If a righteous man turns from his righteousness and commits sin, he will die for it; because of the sin he has committed he will die. [27]But if a wicked man turns away from the wickedness he has committed and does what is just and right, he will save his life. [28]Because he considers all the offenses he has committed and turns away from them, he will surely live; he will not die. [29]Yet the house of Israel says, 'The way of the Lord is not just.' Are my ways unjust, O house of Israel? Is it not your ways that are unjust?

[30]"Therefore, O house of Israel, I will judge you, each one according to his ways, declares the Sovereign LORD. Repent! Turn away from all your offenses; then sin will not be your downfall. [31]Rid yourselves of all the offenses you have committed, and get a new heart and a new spirit. Why will you die, O house of Israel? [32]For I take no pleasure in the death of anyone, declares the Sovereign LORD. Repent and live!

A Lament for Israel's Princes

19 "Take up a lament concerning the princes of Israel [2]and say:

" 'What a lioness was your mother
　　among the lions!
She lay down among the young lions
　　and reared her cubs.
[3]She brought up one of her cubs,
　　and he became a strong lion.
He learned to tear the prey
　　and he devoured men.
[4]The nations heard about him,
　　and he was trapped in their pit.
They led him with hooks
　　to the land of Egypt.

[5]" 'When she saw her hope unfulfilled,
　　her expectation gone,

[a] 17 Septuagint (see also verse 8); Hebrew *from the poor*

she took another of her cubs
    and made him a strong lion.
⁶He prowled among the lions,
    for he was now a strong lion.
He learned to tear the prey
    and he devoured men.
⁷He broke down *ᵃ* their strongholds
    and devastated their towns.
The land and all who were in it
    were terrified by his roaring.
⁸Then the nations came against him,
    those from regions round about.
They spread their net for him,
    and he was trapped in their pit.
⁹With hooks they pulled him into a cage
    and brought him to the king of
        Babylon.
They put him in prison,
    so his roar was heard no longer
    on the mountains of Israel.

¹⁰ " 'Your mother was like a vine in your
    vineyard *ᵇ*
planted by the water;
    it was fruitful and full of branches
    because of abundant water.
¹¹Its branches were strong,
    fit for a ruler's scepter.
It towered high
    above the thick foliage,
conspicuous for its height
    and for its many branches.
¹²But it was uprooted in fury
    and thrown to the ground.
The east wind made it shrivel,
    it was stripped of its fruit;
its strong branches withered
    and fire consumed them.
¹³Now it is planted in the desert,
    in a dry and thirsty land.
¹⁴Fire spread from one of its main *ᶜ* branches
    and consumed its fruit.
No strong branch is left on it
    fit for a ruler's scepter.'

This is a lament and is to be used as a lament."

Rebellious Israel

20 In the seventh year, in the fifth month on the tenth day, some of the elders of Israel came to inquire of the LORD, and they sat down in front of me.

²Then the word of the LORD came to me: ³"Son of man, speak to the elders of Israel and say to them, 'This is what the Sovereign LORD says: Have you come to inquire of me? As surely as I live, I will not let you inquire of me, declares the Sovereign LORD.'

⁴"Will you judge them? Will you judge them, son of man? Then confront them with the detestable practices of their fathers ⁵and say to them: 'This is what the Sovereign LORD says: On the day I chose Israel, I swore with uplifted hand to the descendants of the house of Jacob and revealed myself to them in Egypt. With uplifted hand I said to them, "I am the LORD your God." ⁶On that day I swore to them that I would bring them out of Egypt into a land I had searched out for them, a land flowing with milk and honey, the most beautiful of all lands. ⁷And I said to them, "Each of you, get rid of the vile images you have set your eyes on, and do not defile yourselves with the idols of Egypt. I am the LORD your God."

⁸" 'But they rebelled against me and would not listen to me; they did not get rid of the vile images they had set their eyes on, nor did they forsake the idols of Egypt. So I said I would pour out my wrath on them and spend my anger against them in Egypt. ⁹But for the sake of my name I did what would keep it from being profaned in the eyes of the nations they lived among and in whose sight I had revealed myself to the Israelites by bringing them out of Egypt. ¹⁰Therefore I led them out of Egypt and brought them into the desert. ¹¹I gave them my decrees and made known to them my laws, for the man who obeys them will live by them. ¹²Also I gave them my Sabbaths as a sign between us, so they would know that I the LORD made them holy.

ᵃ 7 Targum (see Septuagint); Hebrew *He knew*   *ᵇ 10* Two Hebrew manuscripts; most Hebrew manuscripts *your blood*   *ᶜ 14* Or *from under its*

> "ALSO I GAVE THEM MY SABBATHS AS A SIGN BETWEEN US, SO THEY WOULD KNOW THAT I THE LORD MADE THEM HOLY."
>
> *Ezekiel 20:12*

Get Me to the Church

BOBBIE WOLGEMUTH

READ | EZEKIEL 20:1 – 12

Abby, my ten-year-old granddaughter, loves to hear stories at bedtime — and she doesn't want fairy tales. She says, "Tell me a true story, Nanny."

One night, as Abby settled into bed, I rubbed her back and began: "Once there were two little girls who lived in the neighborhood where I grew up. I'm sad to tell you that the sisters grew up in a family that didn't go to church. A nice neighbor noticed the sisters wandering around or riding their bikes on Sunday mornings week after week. The neighbor thought the girls would enjoy making new friends, so she invited them to go to church with her family.

"Attending Sunday school and church became a weekly event for the little girls. Wearing their fancy dresses every Sunday, they enjoyed hugs, Bible stories and beautiful music. They felt loved in the place where they could hear about Jesus. One Sunday morning the girls invited Jesus to live in their hearts. They felt new and happier on the inside.

"That was a long time ago. The girls are grown up now, but they still go to church, and sing the songs they learned when they were small."

Abby rolled over in bed to look at my face. "Why are you crying, Nanny?" she asked.

"Well, I'm really happy about the way the story turned out," I said with a smile. "You see, one of those little girls who long ago was invited to go to church by her neighbor — was me."

Leaving a legacy of faith may be as simple as telling your own story. Let your grandchild hear about the path that led you to Jesus.

We experience God's presence in a special way at church. Encourage your grandchildren to find him there. Is there someone you or your grandchild could invite to church this week?

Father in heaven, thank you for establishing the church as a stable, loving, serving family on earth. Help my children and grandchildren to overcome the challenges of their family's schedule and remember your gift of coming together as believers one day each week. Amen.

Your next devotion is located on page 1147.

GRANDCHILD IN FOCUS · PRAYER

Emotional Development

O God, Creator of mind and body, I pray that you will give my grandchild emotional health and strength. Where there is anger, bring peace. Where there is confusion, bring clarity and focus. Where there are dark shadows, cast a ray of hope. Fill her with the sunshine of your Spirit. Warm her with the presence of your peace. Amen.

13 " 'Yet the people of Israel rebelled against me in the desert. They did not follow my decrees but rejected my laws—although the man who obeys them will live by them—and they utterly desecrated my Sabbaths. So I said I would pour out my wrath on them and destroy them in the desert. 14 But for the sake of my name I did what would keep it from being profaned in the eyes of the nations in whose sight I had brought them out. 15 Also with uplifted hand I swore to them in the desert that I would not bring them into the land I had given them—a land flowing with milk and honey, most beautiful of all lands— 16 because they rejected my laws and did not follow my decrees and desecrated my Sabbaths. For their hearts were devoted to their idols. 17 Yet I looked on them with pity and did not destroy them or put an end to them in the desert. 18 I said to their children in the desert, "Do not follow the statutes of your fathers or keep their laws or defile yourselves with their idols. 19 I am the LORD your God; follow my decrees and be careful to keep my laws. 20 Keep my Sabbaths holy, that they may be a sign between us. Then you will know that I am the LORD your God."

21 " 'But the children rebelled against me: They did not follow my decrees, they were not careful to keep my laws—although the man who obeys them will live by them—and they desecrated my Sabbaths. So I said I would pour out my wrath on them and spend my anger against them in the desert. 22 But I withheld my hand, and for the sake of my name I did what would keep it from being profaned in the eyes of the nations in whose sight I had brought them out. 23 Also with uplifted hand I swore to them in the desert that I would disperse them among the nations and scatter them through the countries, 24 because they had not obeyed my laws but had rejected my decrees and desecrated my Sabbaths, and their eyes ˻lusted˼ after their fathers' idols. 25 I also gave them over to statutes that were not good and laws they could not live by; 26 I let them become defiled through their gifts—the sacrifice of every firstborn[a]—that I might fill them with horror so they would know that I am the LORD.'

27 "Therefore, son of man, speak to the people of Israel and say to them, 'This is what the Sovereign LORD says: In this also your fathers blasphemed me by forsaking me: 28 When I brought them into the land I had sworn to give them and they saw any high hill or any leafy tree, there they offered their sacrifices, made offerings that provoked me to anger, presented their fragrant incense and poured out their drink offerings. 29 Then I said to them: What is this high place you go to?' " (It is called Bamah[b] to this day.)

Judgment and Restoration

30 "Therefore say to the house of Israel: 'This is what the Sovereign LORD says: Will you defile yourselves the way your fathers did and lust after their vile images? 31 When you offer your gifts—the sacrifice of your sons in[c] the fire—you continue to defile yourselves with all your idols to this day. Am I to let you inquire of me, O house of Israel? As surely as I live, declares the Sovereign LORD, I will not let you inquire of me.

32 " 'You say, "We want to be like the nations, like the peoples of the world, who serve wood and stone." But what you have in mind will never happen. 33 As surely as I live, declares the Sovereign LORD, I will rule over you with a mighty hand and an outstretched arm and with outpoured wrath. 34 I will bring you from the nations and gather you from the countries where you have been scattered—with a mighty hand and an outstretched arm and with outpoured wrath. 35 I will bring you into the desert of the nations and there, face to face, I will execute judgment upon you. 36 As I judged your fathers in the desert of the land of Egypt, so I will judge you, declares the Sovereign LORD. 37 I will take note of you as you pass under my rod, and I will bring you into the bond of the covenant. 38 I will purge you of those who revolt and rebel against me. Although I will bring them out of the land where they are living, yet they will not enter the land of Israel. Then you will know that I am the LORD.

---

[a] 26 Or —making every firstborn pass through ˻the fire˼
[b] 29 Bamah means high place.   [c] 31 Or —making your sons pass through

39 " 'As for you, O house of Israel, this is what the Sovereign LORD says: Go and serve your idols, every one of you! But afterward you will surely listen to me and no longer profane my holy name with your gifts and idols. 40 For on my holy mountain, the high mountain of Israel, declares the Sovereign LORD, there in the land the entire house of Israel will serve me, and there I will accept them. There I will require your offerings and your choice gifts,*a* along with all your holy sacrifices. 41 I will accept you as fragrant incense when I bring you out from the nations and gather you from the countries where you have been scattered, and I will show myself holy among you in the sight of the nations. 42 Then you will know that I am the LORD, when I bring you into the land of Israel, the land I had sworn with uplifted hand to give to your fathers. 43 There you will remember your conduct and all the actions by which you have defiled yourselves, and you will loathe yourselves for all the evil you have done. 44 You will know that I am the LORD, when I deal with you for my name's sake and not according to your evil ways and your corrupt practices, O house of Israel, declares the Sovereign LORD.' "

Prophecy Against the South

45 The word of the LORD came to me: 46 "Son of man, set your face toward the south; preach against the south and prophesy against the forest of the southland. 47 Say to the southern forest: 'Hear the word of the LORD. This is what the Sovereign LORD says: I am about to set fire to you, and it will consume all your trees, both green and dry. The blazing flame will not be quenched, and every face from south to north will be scorched by it. 48 Everyone will see that I the LORD have kindled it; it will not be quenched.' "

49 Then I said, "Ah, Sovereign LORD! They are saying of me, 'Isn't he just telling parables?' "

Babylon, God's Sword of Judgment

21 The word of the LORD came to me: 2 "Son of man, set your face against Jerusalem and preach against the sanctuary. Prophesy against the land of Israel 3 and say to her: 'This is what the LORD says: I am against you. I will draw my sword from its scabbard and cut off from you both the righteous and the wicked. 4 Because I am going to cut off the righteous and the wicked, my sword will be unsheathed against everyone from south to north. 5 Then all people will know that I the LORD have drawn my sword from its scabbard; it will not return again.'

6 "Therefore groan, son of man! Groan before them with broken heart and bitter grief. 7 And when they ask you, 'Why are you groaning?' you shall say, 'Because of the news that is coming. Every heart will melt and every hand go limp; every spirit will become faint and every knee become as weak as water.' It is coming! It will surely take place, declares the Sovereign LORD."

8 The word of the LORD came to me: 9 "Son of man, prophesy and say, 'This is what the Lord says:

" 'A sword, a sword,
    sharpened and polished—
10 sharpened for the slaughter,
    polished to flash like lightning!

" 'Shall we rejoice in the scepter of my son Judah؟ The sword despises every such stick.

11 " 'The sword is appointed to be polished,
    to be grasped with the hand;
it is sharpened and polished,
    made ready for the hand of the slayer.
12 Cry out and wail, son of man,
    for it is against my people;
it is against all the princes of Israel.
They are thrown to the sword
    along with my people.
Therefore beat your breast.

13 " 'Testing will surely come. And what if the scepter ؛of Judah؛, which the sword despises, does not continue? declares the Sovereign LORD.'

14 "So then, son of man, prophesy
    and strike your hands together.

---

a 40 Or and the gifts of your firstfruits

Let the sword strike twice,
even three times.
It is a sword for slaughter—
a sword for great slaughter,
closing in on them from every side.
¹⁵So that hearts may melt
and the fallen be many,
I have stationed the sword for slaughter ᵃ
at all their gates.
Oh! It is made to flash like lightning,
it is grasped for slaughter.
¹⁶O sword, slash to the right,
then to the left,
wherever your blade is turned.
¹⁷I too will strike my hands together,
and my wrath will subside.
I the LORD have spoken."

¹⁸The word of the LORD came to me: ¹⁹"Son of man, mark out two roads for the sword of the king of Babylon to take, both starting from the same country. Make a signpost where the road branches off to the city. ²⁰Mark out one road for the sword to come against Rabbah of the Ammonites and another against Judah and fortified Jerusalem. ²¹For the king of Babylon will stop at the fork in the road, at the junction of the two roads, to seek an omen: He will cast lots with arrows, he will consult his idols, he will examine the liver. ²²Into his right hand will come the lot for Jerusalem, where he is to set up battering rams, to give the command to slaughter, to sound the battle cry, to set battering rams against the gates, to build a ramp and to erect siege works. ²³It will seem like a false omen to those who have sworn allegiance to him, but he will remind them of their guilt and take them captive.

²⁴"Therefore this is what the Sovereign LORD says: 'Because you people have brought to mind your guilt by your open rebellion, revealing your sins in all that you do—because you have done this, you will be taken captive.

²⁵"'O profane and wicked prince of Israel, whose day has come, whose time of punishment has reached its climax, ²⁶this is what the Sovereign LORD says: Take off the turban, remove the crown. It will not be as it was: The lowly will be exalted and the exalted will be brought low. ²⁷A ruin! A ruin! I will make it a ruin! It will not be restored until he comes to whom it rightfully belongs; to him I will give it.'

²⁸"And you, son of man, prophesy and say, 'This is what the Sovereign LORD says about the Ammonites and their insults:

"'A sword, a sword,
drawn for the slaughter,
polished to consume
and to flash like lightning!
²⁹Despite false visions concerning you
and lying divinations about you,
it will be laid on the necks
of the wicked who are to be slain,
whose day has come,
whose time of punishment has reached its
climax.
³⁰Return the sword to its scabbard.
In the place where you were created,
in the land of your ancestry,
I will judge you.
³¹I will pour out my wrath upon you
and breathe out my fiery anger against
you;
I will hand you over to brutal men,
men skilled in destruction.
³²You will be fuel for the fire,
your blood will be shed in your land,
you will be remembered no more;
for I the LORD have spoken.'"

Jerusalem's Sins

22 The word of the LORD came to me: ²"Son of man, will you judge her? Will you judge this city of bloodshed? Then confront her with all her detestable practices ³and say: 'This is what the Sovereign LORD says: O city that brings on herself doom by shedding blood in her midst and defiles herself by making idols, ⁴you have become guilty because of the blood you have shed

---

ᵃ 15 Septuagint; the meaning of the Hebrew for this word is uncertain.

and have become defiled by the idols you have made. You have brought your days to a close, and the end of your years has come. Therefore I will make you an object of scorn to the nations and a laughingstock to all the countries. [5] Those who are near and those who are far away will mock you, O infamous city, full of turmoil.

[6] " 'See how each of the princes of Israel who are in you uses his power to shed blood. [7] In you they have treated father and mother with contempt; in you they have oppressed the alien and mistreated the fatherless and the widow. [8] You have despised my holy things and desecrated my Sabbaths. [9] In you are slanderous men bent on shedding blood; in you are those who eat at the mountain shrines and commit lewd acts. [10] In you are those who dishonor their fathers' bed; in you are those who violate women during their period, when they are ceremonially unclean. [11] In you one man commits a detestable offense with his neighbor's wife, another shamefully defiles his daughter-in-law, and another violates his sister, his own father's daughter. [12] In you men accept bribes to shed blood; you take usury and excessive interest[a] and make unjust gain from your neighbors by extortion. And you have forgotten me, declares the Sovereign LORD.

[13] " 'I will surely strike my hands together at the unjust gain you have made and at the blood you have shed in your midst. [14] Will your courage endure or your hands be strong in the day I deal with you? I the LORD have spoken, and I will do it. [15] I will disperse you among the nations and scatter you through the countries; and I will put an end to your uncleanness. [16] When you have been defiled[b] in the eyes of the nations, you will know that I am the LORD.' "

[17] Then the word of the LORD came to me: [18] "Son of man, the house of Israel has become dross to me; all of them are the copper, tin, iron and lead left inside a furnace. They are but the dross of silver. [19] Therefore this is what the Sovereign LORD says: 'Because you have all become dross, I will gather you into Jerusalem. [20] As men gather silver, copper, iron, lead and tin into a furnace to melt it with a fiery blast, so will I gather you in my anger and my wrath and put you inside the city and melt you. [21] I will gather you and I will blow on you with my fiery wrath, and you will be melted inside her. [22] As silver is melted in a furnace, so you will be melted inside her, and you will know that I the LORD have poured out my wrath upon you.' "

[23] Again the word of the LORD came to me: [24] "Son of man, say to the land, 'You are a land that has had no rain or showers[c] in the day of wrath.' [25] There is a conspiracy of her princes[d] within her like a roaring lion tearing its prey; they devour people, take treasures and precious things and make many widows within her. [26] Her priests do violence to my law and profane my holy things; they do not distinguish between the holy and the common; they teach that there is no difference between the unclean and the clean; and they shut their eyes to the keeping of my Sabbaths, so that I am profaned among them. [27] Her officials within her are like wolves tearing their prey; they shed blood and kill people to make unjust gain. [28] Her prophets whitewash these deeds for them by false visions and lying divinations. They say, 'This is what the Sovereign LORD says'—when the LORD has not spoken. [29] The people of the land practice extortion and commit robbery; they oppress the poor and needy and mistreat the alien, denying them justice.

[30] "I looked for a man among them who would build up the wall and stand before me in the gap on behalf of the land so I would not have to destroy it, but I found none. [31] So I will pour out my wrath on them and consume them with my fiery anger, bringing down on their own heads all they have done, declares the Sovereign LORD."

Two Adulterous Sisters

23 The word of the LORD came to me: [2] "Son of man, there were two women, daughters of the same mother. [3] They became prostitutes in

---

[a] 12 Or *usury and interest*   [b] 16 Or *When I have allotted you your inheritance*   [c] 24 Septuagint; Hebrew *has not been cleansed or rained on*   [d] 25 Septuagint; Hebrew *prophets*

Egypt, engaging in prostitution from their youth. In that land their breasts were fondled and their virgin bosoms caressed. ⁴The older was named Oholah, and her sister was Oholibah. They were mine and gave birth to sons and daughters. Oholah is Samaria, and Oholibah is Jerusalem.

⁵"Oholah engaged in prostitution while she was still mine; and she lusted after her lovers, the Assyrians—warriors ⁶clothed in blue, governors and commanders, all of them handsome young men, and mounted horsemen. ⁷She gave herself as a prostitute to all the elite of the Assyrians and defiled herself with all the idols of everyone she lusted after. ⁸She did not give up the prostitution she began in Egypt, when during her youth men slept with her, caressed her virgin bosom and poured out their lust upon her.

⁹"Therefore I handed her over to her lovers, the Assyrians, for whom she lusted. ¹⁰They stripped her naked, took away her sons and daughters and killed her with the sword. She became a byword among women, and punishment was inflicted on her.

¹¹"Her sister Oholibah saw this, yet in her lust and prostitution she was more depraved than her sister. ¹²She too lusted after the Assyrians—governors and commanders, warriors in full dress, mounted horsemen, all handsome young men. ¹³I saw that she too defiled herself; both of them went the same way.

¹⁴"But she carried her prostitution still further. She saw men portrayed on a wall, figures of Chaldeans *a* portrayed in red, ¹⁵with belts around their waists and flowing turbans on their heads; all of them looked like Babylonian chariot officers, natives of Chaldea. *b* ¹⁶As soon as she saw them, she lusted after them and sent messengers to them in Chaldea. ¹⁷Then the Babylonians came to her, to the bed of love, and in their lust they defiled her. After she had been defiled by them, she turned away from them in disgust. ¹⁸When she carried on her prostitution openly and exposed her nakedness, I turned away from her in disgust, just as I had turned away from her sister. ¹⁹Yet she became more and more promiscuous as she recalled the days of her youth, when she was a prostitute in Egypt. ²⁰There she lusted after her lovers, whose genitals were like those of donkeys and whose emission was like that of horses. ²¹So you longed for the lewdness of your youth, when in Egypt your bosom was caressed and your young breasts fondled. *c*

²²"Therefore, Oholibah, this is what the Sovereign Lord says: I will stir up your lovers against you, those you turned away from in disgust, and I will bring them against you from every side— ²³the Babylonians and all the Chaldeans, the men of Pekod and Shoa and Koa, and all the Assyrians with them, handsome young men, all of them governors and commanders, chariot officers and men of high rank, all mounted on horses. ²⁴They will come against you with weapons, *d* chariots and wagons and with a throng of people; they will take up positions against you on every side with large and small shields and with helmets. I will turn you over to them for punishment, and they will punish you according to their standards. ²⁵I will direct my jealous anger against you, and they will deal with you in fury. They will cut off your noses and your ears, and those of you who are left will fall by the sword. They will take away your sons and daughters, and those of you who are left will be consumed by fire. ²⁶They will also strip you of your clothes and take your fine jewelry. ²⁷So I will put a stop to the lewdness and prostitution you began in Egypt. You will not look on these things with longing or remember Egypt anymore.

²⁸"For this is what the Sovereign Lord says: I am about to hand you over to those you hate, to those you turned away from in disgust. ²⁹They will deal with you in hatred and take away everything you have worked for. They will leave you naked and bare, and the shame of your prostitution will be exposed. Your lewdness and promiscuity ³⁰have brought this upon you, because you lusted after the nations and defiled yourself with their

a 14 Or *Babylonians*   *b 15* Or *Babylonia*; also in verse 16
c 21 Syriac (see also verse 3); Hebrew *caressed because of your young breasts*   *d 24* The meaning of the Hebrew for this word is uncertain.

idols. ³¹You have gone the way of your sister; so I will put her cup into your hand.

³²"This is what the Sovereign LORD says:

"You will drink your sister's cup,
    a cup large and deep;
it will bring scorn and derision,
    for it holds so much.
³³You will be filled with drunkenness and
        sorrow,
    the cup of ruin and desolation,
    the cup of your sister Samaria.
³⁴You will drink it and drain it dry;
    you will dash it to pieces
    and tear your breasts.

I have spoken, declares the Sovereign LORD.

³⁵"Therefore this is what the Sovereign LORD says: Since you have forgotten me and thrust me behind your back, you must bear the consequences of your lewdness and prostitution."

³⁶The LORD said to me: "Son of man, will you judge Oholah and Oholibah? Then confront them with their detestable practices, ³⁷for they have committed adultery and blood is on their hands. They committed adultery with their idols; they even sacrificed their children, whom they bore to me,ᵃ as food for them. ³⁸They have also done this to me: At that same time they defiled my sanctuary and desecrated my Sabbaths. ³⁹On the very day they sacrificed their children to their idols, they entered my sanctuary and desecrated it. That is what they did in my house.

⁴⁰"They even sent messengers for men who came from far away, and when they arrived you bathed yourself for them, painted your eyes and put on your jewelry. ⁴¹You sat on an elegant couch, with a table spread before it on which you had placed the incense and oil that belonged to me.

⁴²"The noise of a carefree crowd was around her; Sabeansᵇ were brought from the desert along with men from the rabble, and they put bracelets on the arms of the woman and her sister and beautiful crowns on their heads. ⁴³Then I said about the one worn out by adultery, 'Now let them use her as a prostitute, for that is all she is.' ⁴⁴And they slept with her. As men sleep with a prostitute, so they slept with those lewd women, Oholah and Oholibah. ⁴⁵But righteous men will sentence them to the punishment of women who commit adultery and shed blood, because they are adulterous and blood is on their hands.

⁴⁶"This is what the Sovereign LORD says: Bring a mob against them and give them over to terror and plunder. ⁴⁷The mob will stone them and cut them down with their swords; they will kill their sons and daughters and burn down their houses.

⁴⁸"So I will put an end to lewdness in the land, that all women may take warning and not imitate you. ⁴⁹You will suffer the penalty for your lewdness and bear the consequences of your sins of idolatry. Then you will know that I am the Sovereign LORD."

The Cooking Pot

24 In the ninth year, in the tenth month on the tenth day, the word of the LORD came to me: ²"Son of man, record this date, this very date, because the king of Babylon has laid siege to Jerusalem this very day. ³Tell this rebellious house a parable and say to them: 'This is what the Sovereign LORD says:

"'Put on the cooking pot; put it on
    and pour water into it.
⁴Put into it the pieces of meat,
    all the choice pieces—the leg and the
        shoulder.
Fill it with the best of these bones;
⁵   take the pick of the flock.
Pile wood beneath it for the bones;
    bring it to a boil
    and cook the bones in it.

⁶"'For this is what the Sovereign LORD says:

"'Woe to the city of bloodshed,
    to the pot now encrusted,
    whose deposit will not go away!

ᵃ 37 Or even made the children they bore to me pass through ⌞the fire⌟   ᵇ 42 Or drunkards

Empty it piece by piece
without casting lots for them.

7 " 'For the blood she shed is in her midst:
She poured it on the bare rock;
she did not pour it on the ground,
where the dust would cover it.
8 To stir up wrath and take revenge
I put her blood on the bare rock,
so that it would not be covered.

9 " 'Therefore this is what the Sovereign Lord says:

" 'Woe to the city of bloodshed!
I, too, will pile the wood high.
10 So heap on the wood
and kindle the fire.
Cook the meat well,
mixing in the spices;
and let the bones be charred.
11 Then set the empty pot on the coals
till it becomes hot and its copper glows
so its impurities may be melted
and its deposit burned away.
12 It has frustrated all efforts;
its heavy deposit has not been removed,
not even by fire.

13 " 'Now your impurity is lewdness. Because I tried to cleanse you but you would not be cleansed from your impurity, you will not be clean again until my wrath against you has subsided.

14 " 'I the Lord have spoken. The time has come for me to act. I will not hold back; I will not have pity, nor will I relent. You will be judged according to your conduct and your actions, declares the Sovereign Lord.' "

Ezekiel's Wife Dies

15 The word of the Lord came to me: 16 "Son of man, with one blow I am about to take away from you the delight of your eyes. Yet do not lament or weep or shed any tears. 17 Groan quietly; do not mourn for the dead. Keep your turban fastened and your sandals on your feet; do not cover the lower part of your face or eat the customary food ⌞of mourners⌟."

18 So I spoke to the people in the morning, and in the evening my wife died. The next morning I did as I had been commanded.

19 Then the people asked me, "Won't you tell us what these things have to do with us?"

20 So I said to them, "The word of the Lord came to me: 21 Say to the house of Israel, 'This is what the Sovereign Lord says: I am about to desecrate my sanctuary—the stronghold in which you take pride, the delight of your eyes, the object of your affection. The sons and daughters you left behind will fall by the sword. 22 And you will do as I have done. You will not cover the lower part of your face or eat the customary food ⌞of mourners⌟. 23 You will keep your turbans on your heads and your sandals on your feet. You will not mourn or weep but will waste away because of[a] your sins and groan among yourselves. 24 Ezekiel will be a sign to you; you will do just as he has done. When this happens, you will know that I am the Sovereign Lord.'

25 "And you, son of man, on the day I take away their stronghold, their joy and glory, the delight of their eyes, their heart's desire, and their sons and daughters as well— 26 on that day a fugitive will come to tell you the news. 27 At that time your mouth will be opened; you will speak with him and will no longer be silent. So you will be a sign to them, and they will know that I am the Lord."

A Prophecy Against Ammon

25 The word of the Lord came to me: 2 "Son of man, set your face against the Ammonites and prophesy against them. 3 Say to them, 'Hear the word of the Sovereign Lord. This is what the Sovereign Lord says: Because you said "Aha!" over my sanctuary when it was desecrated and over the land of Israel when it was laid waste and over the people of Judah when they went into exile, 4 therefore I am going to give you to

a 23 Or away in

the people of the East as a possession. They will set up their camps and pitch their tents among you; they will eat your fruit and drink your milk. [5]I will turn Rabbah into a pasture for camels and Ammon into a resting place for sheep. Then you will know that I am the LORD. [6]For this is what the Sovereign LORD says: Because you have clapped your hands and stamped your feet, rejoicing with all the malice of your heart against the land of Israel, [7]therefore I will stretch out my hand against you and give you as plunder to the nations. I will cut you off from the nations and exterminate you from the countries. I will destroy you, and you will know that I am the LORD.'"

A Prophecy Against Moab

[8]"This is what the Sovereign LORD says: 'Because Moab and Seir said, "Look, the house of Judah has become like all the other nations," [9]therefore I will expose the flank of Moab, beginning at its frontier towns—Beth Jeshimoth, Baal Meon and Kiriathaim—the glory of that land. [10]I will give Moab along with the Ammonites to the people of the East as a possession, so that the Ammonites will not be remembered among the nations; [11]and I will inflict punishment on Moab. Then they will know that I am the LORD.'"

A Prophecy Against Edom

[12]"This is what the Sovereign LORD says: 'Because Edom took revenge on the house of Judah and became very guilty by doing so, [13]therefore this is what the Sovereign LORD says: I will stretch out my hand against Edom and kill its men and their animals. I will lay it waste, and from Teman to Dedan they will fall by the sword. [14]I will take vengeance on Edom by the hand of my people Israel, and they will deal with Edom in accordance with my anger and my wrath; they will know my vengeance, declares the Sovereign LORD.'"

A Prophecy Against Philistia

[15]"This is what the Sovereign LORD says: 'Because the Philistines acted in vengeance and took revenge with malice in their hearts, and with ancient hostility sought to destroy Judah, [16]therefore this is what the Sovereign LORD says: I am about to stretch out my hand against the Philistines, and I will cut off the Kerethites and destroy those remaining along the coast. [17]I will carry out great vengeance on them and punish them in my wrath. Then they will know that I am the LORD, when I take vengeance on them.'"

A Prophecy Against Tyre

26 In the eleventh year, on the first day of the month, the word of the LORD came to me: [2]"Son of man, because Tyre has said of Jerusalem, 'Aha! The gate to the nations is broken, and its doors have swung open to me; now that she lies in ruins I will prosper,' [3]therefore this is what the Sovereign LORD says: I am against you, O Tyre, and I will bring many nations against you, like the sea casting up its waves. [4]They will destroy the walls of Tyre and pull down her towers; I will scrape away her rubble and make her a bare rock. [5]Out in the sea she will become a place to spread fishnets, for I have spoken, declares the Sovereign LORD. She will become plunder for the nations, [6]and her settlements on the mainland will be ravaged by the sword. Then they will know that I am the LORD.

[7]"For this is what the Sovereign LORD says: From the north I am going to bring against Tyre Nebuchadnezzar[a] king of Babylon, king of kings, with horses and chariots, with horsemen and a great army. [8]He will ravage your settlements on the mainland with the sword; he will set up siege works against you, build a ramp up to your walls and raise his shields against you. [9]He will direct the blows of his battering rams against your walls and demolish your towers with his weapons. [10]His horses will be so many that they will cover you with dust. Your walls will tremble at the noise of the war horses, wagons and chariots when he enters your gates as men enter a city whose walls have been broken through. [11]The hoofs of his horses will trample all your streets; he will kill

---

[a] 7 Hebrew Nebuchadrezzar, of which Nebuchadnezzar is a variant; here and often in Ezekiel and Jeremiah

your people with the sword, and your strong pillars will fall to the ground. ¹²They will plunder your wealth and loot your merchandise; they will break down your walls and demolish your fine houses and throw your stones, timber and rubble into the sea. ¹³I will put an end to your noisy songs, and the music of your harps will be heard no more. ¹⁴I will make you a bare rock, and you will become a place to spread fishnets. You will never be rebuilt, for I the LORD have spoken, declares the Sovereign LORD.

¹⁵"This is what the Sovereign LORD says to Tyre: Will not the coastlands tremble at the sound of your fall, when the wounded groan and the slaughter takes place in you? ¹⁶Then all the princes of the coast will step down from their thrones and lay aside their robes and take off their embroidered garments. Clothed with terror, they will sit on the ground, trembling every moment, appalled at you. ¹⁷Then they will take up a lament concerning you and say to you:

" 'How you are destroyed, O city of renown,
        peopled by men of the sea!
You were a power on the seas,
        you and your citizens;
you put your terror
        on all who lived there.
¹⁸Now the coastlands tremble
        on the day of your fall;
the islands in the sea
        are terrified at your collapse.'

¹⁹"This is what the Sovereign LORD says: When I make you a desolate city, like cities no longer inhabited, and when I bring the ocean depths over you and its vast waters cover you, ²⁰then I will bring you down with those who go down to the pit, to the people of long ago. I will make you dwell in the earth below, as in ancient ruins, with those who go down to the pit, and you will not return or take your place ª in the land of the living. ²¹I will bring you to a horrible end and you will be no more. You will be sought, but you will never again be found, declares the Sovereign LORD."

A Lament for Tyre

27 The word of the LORD came to me: ²"Son of man, take up a lament concerning Tyre. ³Say to Tyre, situated at the gateway to the sea, merchant of peoples on many coasts, 'This is what the Sovereign LORD says:

" 'You say, O Tyre,
        "I am perfect in beauty."
⁴Your domain was on the high seas;
        your builders brought your beauty to
            perfection.
⁵They made all your timbers
        of pine trees from Senir ᵇ;
they took a cedar from Lebanon
        to make a mast for you.
⁶Of oaks from Bashan
        they made your oars;
of cypress wood ᶜ from the coasts of Cyprus ᵈ
        they made your deck, inlaid with ivory.
⁷Fine embroidered linen from Egypt was your
            sail
        and served as your banner;
your awnings were of blue and purple
        from the coasts of Elishah.
⁸Men of Sidon and Arvad were your oarsmen;
        your skilled men, O Tyre, were aboard as
            your seamen.
⁹Veteran craftsmen of Gebal ᵉ were on board
        as shipwrights to caulk your seams.
All the ships of the sea and their sailors
        came alongside to trade for your wares.

¹⁰" 'Men of Persia, Lydia and Put
        served as soldiers in your army.
They hung their shields and helmets on your
            walls,
        bringing you splendor.
¹¹Men of Arvad and Helech
        manned your walls on every side;
men of Gammad
        were in your towers.
They hung their shields around your walls;
        they brought your beauty to perfection.

ª 20 Septuagint; Hebrew *return, and I will give glory*   ᵇ 5 That is, Hermon   ᶜ 6 Targum; the Masoretic Text has a different division of the consonants.   ᵈ 6 Hebrew *Kittim*   ᵉ 9 That is, Byblos

12 " 'Tarshish did business with you because of your great wealth of goods; they exchanged silver, iron, tin and lead for your merchandise.

13 " 'Greece, Tubal and Meshech traded with you; they exchanged slaves and articles of bronze for your wares.

14 " 'Men of Beth Togarmah exchanged work horses, war horses and mules for your merchandise.

15 " 'The men of Rhodes a traded with you, and many coastlands were your customers; they paid you with ivory tusks and ebony.

16 " 'Aram b did business with you because of your many products; they exchanged turquoise, purple fabric, embroidered work, fine linen, coral and rubies for your merchandise.

17 " 'Judah and Israel traded with you; they exchanged wheat from Minnith and confections, c honey, oil and balm for your wares.

18 " 'Damascus, because of your many products and great wealth of goods, did business with you in wine from Helbon and wool from Zahar.

19 " 'Danites and Greeks from Uzal bought your merchandise; they exchanged wrought iron, cassia and calamus for your wares.

20 " 'Dedan traded in saddle blankets with you.

21 " 'Arabia and all the princes of Kedar were your customers; they did business with you in lambs, rams and goats.

22 " 'The merchants of Sheba and Raamah traded with you; for your merchandise they exchanged the finest of all kinds of spices and precious stones, and gold.

23 " 'Haran, Canneh and Eden and merchants of Sheba, Asshur and Kilmad traded with you. 24 In your marketplace they traded with you beautiful garments, blue fabric, embroidered work and multicolored rugs with cords twisted and tightly knotted.

25 " 'The ships of Tarshish serve
   as carriers for your wares.
You are filled with heavy cargo
   in the heart of the sea.

26 Your oarsmen take you
   out to the high seas.
But the east wind will break you to pieces
   in the heart of the sea.
27 Your wealth, merchandise and wares,
   your mariners, seamen and shipwrights,
your merchants and all your soldiers,
   and everyone else on board
will sink into the heart of the sea
   on the day of your shipwreck.
28 The shorelands will quake
   when your seamen cry out.
29 All who handle the oars
   will abandon their ships;
the mariners and all the seamen
   will stand on the shore.
30 They will raise their voice
   and cry bitterly over you;
they will sprinkle dust on their heads
   and roll in ashes.
31 They will shave their heads because of you
   and will put on sackcloth.
They will weep over you with anguish of soul
   and with bitter mourning.
32 As they wail and mourn over you,
   they will take up a lament concerning you:
"Who was ever silenced like Tyre,
   surrounded by the sea?"
33 When your merchandise went out on the seas,
   you satisfied many nations;
with your great wealth and your wares
   you enriched the kings of the earth.
34 Now you are shattered by the sea
   in the depths of the waters;
your wares and all your company
   have gone down with you.
35 All who live in the coastlands
   are appalled at you;
their kings shudder with horror
   and their faces are distorted with fear.
36 The merchants among the nations hiss at you;
   you have come to a horrible end
   and will be no more.' "

---

a 15 Septuagint; Hebrew *Dedan*   b 16 Most Hebrew manuscripts; some Hebrew manuscripts and Syriac *Edom*   c 17 The meaning of the Hebrew for this word is uncertain.

A Prophecy Against the King of Tyre

28 The word of the LORD came to me: [2] "Son of man, say to the ruler of Tyre, 'This is what the Sovereign LORD says:

> " 'In the pride of your heart
>   you say, "I am a god;
> I sit on the throne of a god
>   in the heart of the seas."
> But you are a man and not a god,
>   though you think you are as wise as a god.
> [3] Are you wiser than Daniel[a]?
>   Is no secret hidden from you?
> [4] By your wisdom and understanding
>   you have gained wealth for yourself
> and amassed gold and silver
>   in your treasuries.
> [5] By your great skill in trading
>   you have increased your wealth,
> and because of your wealth
>   your heart has grown proud.

[6] " 'Therefore this is what the Sovereign LORD says:

> " 'Because you think you are wise,
>   as wise as a god,
> [7] I am going to bring foreigners against you,
>   the most ruthless of nations;
> they will draw their swords against your
>   beauty and wisdom
>   and pierce your shining splendor.
> [8] They will bring you down to the pit,
>   and you will die a violent death
>   in the heart of the seas.
> [9] Will you then say, "I am a god,"
>   in the presence of those who kill you?
> You will be but a man, not a god,
>   in the hands of those who slay you.
> [10] You will die the death of the uncircumcised
>   at the hands of foreigners.

I have spoken, declares the Sovereign LORD.' "

[11] The word of the LORD came to me: [12] "Son of man, take up a lament concerning the king of Tyre and say to him: 'This is what the Sovereign LORD says:

> " 'You were the model of perfection,
>   full of wisdom and perfect in beauty.
> [13] You were in Eden,
>   the garden of God;
> every precious stone adorned you:
>   ruby, topaz and emerald,
>   chrysolite, onyx and jasper,
>   sapphire,[b] turquoise and beryl.[c]
> Your settings and mountings[d] were made of
>   gold;
>   on the day you were created they were
>   prepared.
> [14] You were anointed as a guardian cherub,
>   for so I ordained you.
> You were on the holy mount of God;
>   you walked among the fiery stones.
> [15] You were blameless in your ways
>   from the day you were created
>   till wickedness was found in you.
> [16] Through your widespread trade
>   you were filled with violence,
>   and you sinned.
> So I drove you in disgrace from the mount of
>   God,
>   and I expelled you, O guardian cherub,
>   from among the fiery stones.
> [17] Your heart became proud
>   on account of your beauty,
> and you corrupted your wisdom
>   because of your splendor.
> So I threw you to the earth;
>   I made a spectacle of you before kings.
> [18] By your many sins and dishonest trade
>   you have desecrated your sanctuaries.
> So I made a fire come out from you,
>   and it consumed you,
> and I reduced you to ashes on the ground
>   in the sight of all who were watching.
> [19] All the nations who knew you
>   are appalled at you;
> you have come to a horrible end
>   and will be no more.' "

[a] 3 Or *Danel*; the Hebrew spelling may suggest a person other than the prophet Daniel.   [b] 13 Or *lapis lazuli*   [c] 13 The precise identification of some of these precious stones is uncertain.
[d] 13 The meaning of the Hebrew for this phrase is uncertain.

A Prophecy Against Sidon

²⁰The word of the LORD came to me: ²¹"Son of man, set your face against Sidon; prophesy against her ²²and say: 'This is what the Sovereign LORD says:

" 'I am against you, O Sidon,
and I will gain glory within you.
They will know that I am the LORD,
when I inflict punishment on her
and show myself holy within her.
²³I will send a plague upon her
and make blood flow in her streets.
The slain will fall within her,
with the sword against her on every side.
Then they will know that I am the LORD.

²⁴" 'No longer will the people of Israel have malicious neighbors who are painful briers and sharp thorns. Then they will know that I am the Sovereign LORD.

²⁵" 'This is what the Sovereign LORD says: When I gather the people of Israel from the nations where they have been scattered, I will show myself holy among them in the sight of the nations. Then they will live in their own land, which I gave to my servant Jacob. ²⁶They will live there in safety and will build houses and plant vineyards; they will live in safety when I inflict punishment on all their neighbors who maligned them. Then they will know that I am the LORD their God.' "

A Prophecy Against Egypt

29 In the tenth year, in the tenth month on the twelfth day, the word of the LORD came to me: ²"Son of man, set your face against Pharaoh king of Egypt and prophesy against him and against all Egypt. ³Speak to him and say: 'This is what the Sovereign LORD says:

" 'I am against you, Pharaoh king of Egypt,
you great monster lying among your streams.
You say, "The Nile is mine;
I made it for myself."

⁴But I will put hooks in your jaws
and make the fish of your streams stick to your scales.
I will pull you out from among your streams,
with all the fish sticking to your scales.
⁵I will leave you in the desert,
you and all the fish of your streams.
You will fall on the open field
and not be gathered or picked up.
I will give you as food
to the beasts of the earth and the birds of the air.

⁶Then all who live in Egypt will know that I am the LORD.

" 'You have been a staff of reed for the house of Israel. ⁷When they grasped you with their hands, you splintered and you tore open their shoulders; when they leaned on you, you broke and their backs were wrenched.ᵃ

⁸" 'Therefore this is what the Sovereign LORD says: I will bring a sword against you and kill your men and their animals. ⁹Egypt will become a desolate wasteland. Then they will know that I am the LORD.

" 'Because you said, "The Nile is mine; I made it," ¹⁰therefore I am against you and against your streams, and I will make the land of Egypt a ruin and a desolate waste from Migdol to Aswan, as far as the border of Cush.ᵇ ¹¹No foot of man or animal will pass through it; no one will live there for forty years. ¹²I will make the land of Egypt desolate among devastated lands, and her cities will lie desolate forty years among ruined cities. And I will disperse the Egyptians among the nations and scatter them through the countries.

¹³" 'Yet this is what the Sovereign LORD says: At the end of forty years I will gather the Egyptians from the nations where they were scattered. ¹⁴I will bring them back from captivity and return them to Upper Egypt,ᶜ the land of their ancestry. There they will be a lowly kingdom. ¹⁵It will be

---

ᵃ 7 Syriac (see also Septuagint and Vulgate); Hebrew *and you caused their backs to stand*   ᵇ 10 That is, the upper Nile region   ᶜ 14 Hebrew *to Pathros* the lowliest of kingdoms and will never again exalt itself above the other nations. I will make it so weak that it will never again rule over the nations. ¹⁶Egypt will no longer be a source of confidence for the people of Israel but will be a reminder of their sin in turning to her for help. Then they will know that I am the Sovereign Lord.'"

¹⁷In the twenty-seventh year, in the first month on the first day, the word of the Lord came to me: ¹⁸"Son of man, Nebuchadnezzar king of Babylon drove his army in a hard campaign against Tyre; every head was rubbed bare and every shoulder made raw. Yet he and his army got no reward from the campaign he led against Tyre. ¹⁹Therefore this is what the Sovereign Lord says: I am going to give Egypt to Nebuchadnezzar king of Babylon, and he will carry off its wealth. He will loot and plunder the land as pay for his army. ²⁰I have given him Egypt as a reward for his efforts because he and his army did it for me, declares the Sovereign Lord. ²¹"On that day I will make a horn^a grow for the house of Israel, and I will open your mouth among them. Then they will know that I am the Lord."

A Lament for Egypt

30 The word of the Lord came to me: ²"Son of man, prophesy and say: 'This is what the Sovereign Lord says:

" 'Wail and say,
    "Alas for that day!"
³For the day is near,
    the day of the Lord is near—
a day of clouds,
    a time of doom for the nations.
⁴A sword will come against Egypt,
    and anguish will come upon Cush.^b
When the slain fall in Egypt,
    her wealth will be carried away
    and her foundations torn down.

⁵Cush and Put, Lydia and all Arabia, Libya^c and the people of the covenant land will fall by the sword along with Egypt.

⁶" 'This is what the Lord says:

" 'The allies of Egypt will fall
    and her proud strength will fail.
From Migdol to Aswan
    they will fall by the sword within her,
            declares the Sovereign Lord.
⁷" 'They will be desolate
    among desolate lands,
and their cities will lie
    among ruined cities.
⁸Then they will know that I am the Lord,
    when I set fire to Egypt
    and all her helpers are crushed.

⁹" 'On that day messengers will go out from me in ships to frighten Cush out of her complacency. Anguish will take hold of them on the day of Egypt's doom, for it is sure to come.

¹⁰" 'This is what the Sovereign Lord says:

" 'I will put an end to the hordes of Egypt
    by the hand of Nebuchadnezzar king of
        Babylon.
¹¹He and his army—the most ruthless of
        nations—
    will be brought in to destroy the land.
They will draw their swords against Egypt
    and fill the land with the slain.
¹²I will dry up the streams of the Nile
    and sell the land to evil men;
by the hand of foreigners
    I will lay waste the land and everything in it.

I the Lord have spoken.

¹³" 'This is what the Sovereign Lord says:

" 'I will destroy the idols
    and put an end to the images in Memphis.^d
No longer will there be a prince in Egypt,
    and I will spread fear throughout the land.
¹⁴I will lay waste Upper Egypt,^e
    set fire to Zoan
    and inflict punishment on Thebes.^f

^a 21 Horn here symbolizes strength.   ^b 4 That is, the upper Nile region; also in verses 5 and 9   ^c 5 Hebrew Cub   ^d 13 Hebrew Noph; also in verse 16   ^e 14 Hebrew waste Pathros   ^f 14 Hebrew No; also in verses 15 and 16

¹⁵ I will pour out my wrath on Pelusium, *^a*
  the stronghold of Egypt,
  and cut off the hordes of Thebes.
¹⁶ I will set fire to Egypt;
  Pelusium will writhe in agony.
 Thebes will be taken by storm;
  Memphis will be in constant distress.
¹⁷ The young men of Heliopolis *^b* and
    Bubastis *^c*
  will fall by the sword,
  and the cities themselves will go into
    captivity.
¹⁸ Dark will be the day at Tahpanhes
  when I break the yoke of Egypt;
  there her proud strength will come to an
    end.
 She will be covered with clouds,
  and her villages will go into captivity.
¹⁹ So I will inflict punishment on Egypt,
  and they will know that I am the LORD.' "

²⁰ In the eleventh year, in the first month on the seventh day, the word of the LORD came to me: ²¹ "Son of man, I have broken the arm of Pharaoh king of Egypt. It has not been bound up for healing or put in a splint so as to become strong enough to hold a sword. ²² Therefore this is what the Sovereign LORD says: I am against Pharaoh king of Egypt. I will break both his arms, the good arm as well as the broken one, and make the sword fall from his hand. ²³ I will disperse the Egyptians among the nations and scatter them through the countries. ²⁴ I will strengthen the arms of the king of Babylon and put my sword in his hand, but I will break the arms of Pharaoh, and he will groan before him like a mortally wounded man. ²⁵ I will strengthen the arms of the king of Babylon, but the arms of Pharaoh will fall limp. Then they will know that I am the LORD, when I put my sword into the hand of the king of Babylon and he brandishes it against Egypt. ²⁶ I will disperse the Egyptians among the nations and scatter them through the countries. Then they will know that I am the LORD."

A Cedar in Lebanon

31 In the eleventh year, in the third month on the first day, the word of the LORD came to me: ² "Son of man, say to Pharaoh king of Egypt and to his hordes:

 " 'Who can be compared with you in majesty?
³ Consider Assyria, once a cedar in Lebanon,
  with beautiful branches overshadowing the
    forest;
  it towered on high,
   its top above the thick foliage.
⁴ The waters nourished it,
   deep springs made it grow tall;
  their streams flowed
   all around its base
  and sent their channels
   to all the trees of the field.
⁵ So it towered higher
   than all the trees of the field;
  its boughs increased
   and its branches grew long,
   spreading because of abundant waters.
⁶ All the birds of the air
   nested in its boughs,
  all the beasts of the field
   gave birth under its branches;
  all the great nations
   lived in its shade.
⁷ It was majestic in beauty,
   with its spreading boughs,
  for its roots went down
   to abundant waters.
⁸ The cedars in the garden of God
   could not rival it,
  nor could the pine trees
   equal its boughs,
  nor could the plane trees
   compare with its branches—
  no tree in the garden of God
   could match its beauty.
⁹ I made it beautiful
   with abundant branches,

---

^a 15 Hebrew *Sin;* also in verse 16   *^b 17* Hebrew *Awen* (or *On*)
^c 17 Hebrew *Pi Beseth*

the envy of all the trees of Eden
in the garden of God.

¹⁰" 'Therefore this is what the Sovereign Lord says: Because it towered on high, lifting its top above the thick foliage, and because it was proud of its height, ¹¹I handed it over to the ruler of the nations, for him to deal with according to its wickedness. I cast it aside, ¹²and the most ruthless of foreign nations cut it down and left it. Its boughs fell on the mountains and in all the valleys; its branches lay broken in all the ravines of the land. All the nations of the earth came out from under its shade and left it. ¹³All the birds of the air settled on the fallen tree, and all the beasts of the field were among its branches. ¹⁴Therefore no other trees by the waters are ever to tower proudly on high, lifting their tops above the thick foliage. No other trees so well-watered are ever to reach such a height; they are all destined for death, for the earth below, among mortal men, with those who go down to the pit.

¹⁵" 'This is what the Sovereign Lord says: On the day it was brought down to the grave[a] I covered the deep springs with mourning for it; I held back its streams, and its abundant waters were restrained. Because of it I clothed Lebanon with gloom, and all the trees of the field withered away. ¹⁶I made the nations tremble at the sound of its fall when I brought it down to the grave with those who go down to the pit. Then all the trees of Eden, the choicest and best of Lebanon, all the trees that were well-watered, were consoled in the earth below. ¹⁷Those who lived in its shade, its allies among the nations, had also gone down to the grave with it, joining those killed by the sword.

¹⁸" 'Which of the trees of Eden can be compared with you in splendor and majesty? Yet you, too, will be brought down with the trees of Eden to the earth below; you will lie among the uncircumcised, with those killed by the sword.

" 'This is Pharaoh and all his hordes, declares the Sovereign Lord.' "

A Lament for Pharaoh

32 In the twelfth year, in the twelfth month on the first day, the word of the Lord came to me: ²"Son of man, take up a lament concerning Pharaoh king of Egypt and say to him:

" 'You are like a lion among the nations;
you are like a monster in the seas
thrashing about in your streams,
churning the water with your feet
and muddying the streams.

³" 'This is what the Sovereign Lord says:

" 'With a great throng of people
I will cast my net over you,
and they will haul you up in my net.
⁴I will throw you on the land
and hurl you on the open field.
I will let all the birds of the air settle on you
and all the beasts of the earth gorge
themselves on you.
⁵I will spread your flesh on the mountains
and fill the valleys with your remains.
⁶I will drench the land with your flowing
blood
all the way to the mountains,
and the ravines will be filled with your
flesh.
⁷When I snuff you out, I will cover the
heavens
and darken their stars;
I will cover the sun with a cloud,
and the moon will not give its light.
⁸All the shining lights in the heavens
I will darken over you;
I will bring darkness over your land,
declares the Sovereign Lord.
⁹I will trouble the hearts of many peoples
when I bring about your destruction
among the nations,
among[b] lands you have not known.
¹⁰I will cause many peoples to be appalled at
you,

---

a 15 Hebrew *Sheol*; also in verses 16 and 17   b 9 Hebrew;
Septuagint *bring you into captivity among the nations, / to*

and their kings will shudder with horror
   because of you
when I brandish my sword before them.
On the day of your downfall
   each of them will tremble
   every moment for his life.

¹¹ " 'For this is what the Sovereign LORD says:

" 'The sword of the king of Babylon
   will come against you.
¹² I will cause your hordes to fall
   by the swords of mighty men—
   the most ruthless of all nations.
They will shatter the pride of Egypt,
   and all her hordes will be overthrown.
¹³ I will destroy all her cattle
   from beside abundant waters
no longer to be stirred by the foot of man
   or muddied by the hoofs of cattle.
¹⁴ Then I will let her waters settle
   and make her streams flow like oil,
      declares the Sovereign LORD.
¹⁵ When I make Egypt desolate
   and strip the land of everything in it,
when I strike down all who live there,
   then they will know that I am the LORD.'

¹⁶ "This is the lament they will chant for her. The daughters of the nations will chant it; for Egypt and all her hordes they will chant it, declares the Sovereign LORD."

¹⁷ In the twelfth year, on the fifteenth day of the month, the word of the LORD came to me: ¹⁸ "Son of man, wail for the hordes of Egypt and consign to the earth below both her and the daughters of mighty nations, with those who go down to the pit. ¹⁹ Say to them, 'Are you more favored than others? Go down and be laid among the uncircumcised.' ²⁰ They will fall among those killed by the sword. The sword is drawn; let her be dragged off with all her hordes. ²¹ From within the grave[a] the mighty leaders will say of Egypt and her allies, 'They have come down and they lie with the uncircumcised, with those killed by the sword.'

²² "Assyria is there with her whole army; she is surrounded by the graves of all her slain, all who have fallen by the sword. ²³ Their graves are in the depths of the pit and her army lies around her grave. All who had spread terror in the land of the living are slain, fallen by the sword.

²⁴ "Elam is there, with all her hordes around her grave. All of them are slain, fallen by the sword. All who had spread terror in the land of the living went down uncircumcised to the earth below. They bear their shame with those who go down to the pit. ²⁵ A bed is made for her among the slain, with all her hordes around her grave. All of them are uncircumcised, killed by the sword. Because their terror had spread in the land of the living, they bear their shame with those who go down to the pit; they are laid among the slain.

²⁶ "Meshech and Tubal are there, with all their hordes around their graves. All of them are uncircumcised, killed by the sword because they spread their terror in the land of the living. ²⁷ Do they not lie with the other uncircumcised warriors who have fallen, who went down to the grave with their weapons of war, whose swords were placed under their heads? The punishment for their sins rested on their bones, though the terror of these warriors had stalked through the land of the living.

²⁸ "You too, O Pharaoh, will be broken and will lie among the uncircumcised, with those killed by the sword.

²⁹ "Edom is there, her kings and all her princes; despite their power, they are laid with those killed by the sword. They lie with the uncircumcised, with those who go down to the pit.

³⁰ "All the princes of the north and all the Sidonians are there; they went down with the slain in disgrace despite the terror caused by their power. They lie uncircumcised with those killed by the sword and bear their shame with those who go down to the pit.

³¹ "Pharaoh—he and all his army—will see them and he will be consoled for all his hordes that were killed by the sword, declares the Sov-

---

[a] 21 Hebrew *Sheol*; also in verse 27

ereign Lord. ³²Although I had him spread terror in the land of the living, Pharaoh and all his hordes will be laid among the uncircumcised, with those killed by the sword, declares the Sovereign Lord."

Ezekiel a Watchman

33 The word of the Lord came to me: ²"Son of man, speak to your countrymen and say to them: 'When I bring the sword against a land, and the people of the land choose one of their men and make him their watchman, ³and he sees the sword coming against the land and blows the trumpet to warn the people, ⁴then if anyone hears the trumpet but does not take warning and the sword comes and takes his life, his blood will be on his own head. ⁵Since he heard the sound of the trumpet but did not take warning, his blood will be on his own head. If he had taken warning, he would have saved himself. ⁶But if the watchman sees the sword coming and does not blow the trumpet to warn the people and the sword comes and takes the life of one of them, that man will be taken away because of his sin, but I will hold the watchman accountable for his blood.'

⁷"Son of man, I have made you a watchman for the house of Israel; so hear the word I speak and give them warning from me. ⁸When I say to the wicked, 'O wicked man, you will surely die,' and you do not speak out to dissuade him from his ways, that wicked man will die for[a] his sin, and I will hold you accountable for his blood. ⁹But if you do warn the wicked man to turn from his ways and he does not do so, he will die for his sin, but you will have saved yourself.

¹⁰"Son of man, say to the house of Israel, 'This is what you are saying: "Our offenses and sins weigh us down, and we are wasting away because of[b] them. How then can we live?" ' ¹¹Say to them, 'As surely as I live, declares the Sovereign Lord, I take no pleasure in the death of the wicked, but rather that they turn from their ways and live. Turn! Turn from your evil ways! Why will you die, O house of Israel?'

¹²"Therefore, son of man, say to your countrymen, 'The righteousness of the righteous man will not save him when he disobeys, and the wickedness of the wicked man will not cause him to fall when he turns from it. The righteous man, if he sins, will not be allowed to live because of his former righteousness.' ¹³If I tell the righteous man that he will surely live, but then he trusts in his righteousness and does evil, none of the righteous things he has done will be remembered; he will die for the evil he has done. ¹⁴And if I say to the wicked man, 'You will surely die,' but he then turns away from his sin and does what is just and right— ¹⁵if he gives back what he took in pledge for a loan, returns what he has stolen, follows the decrees that give life, and does no evil, he will surely live; he will not die. ¹⁶None of the sins he has committed will be remembered against him. He has done what is just and right; he will surely live.

¹⁷"Yet your countrymen say, 'The way of the Lord is not just.' But it is their way that is not just. ¹⁸If a righteous man turns from his righteousness and does evil, he will die for it. ¹⁹And if a wicked man turns away from his wickedness and does what is just and right, he will live by doing so. ²⁰Yet, O house of Israel, you say, 'The way of the Lord is not just.' But I will judge each of you according to his own ways."

Jerusalem's Fall Explained

²¹In the twelfth year of our exile, in the tenth month on the fifth day, a man who had escaped from Jerusalem came to me and said, "The city has fallen!" ²²Now the evening before the man arrived, the hand of the Lord was upon me, and he opened my mouth before the man came to me in the morning. So my mouth was opened and I was no longer silent.

²³Then the word of the Lord came to me: ²⁴"Son of man, the people living in those ruins in the land of Israel are saying, 'Abraham was only one man, yet he possessed the land. But we are many; surely the land has been given to us

---

[a] 8 Or *in*; also in verse 9   [b] 10 Or *away in*

as our possession.' ²⁵Therefore say to them, 'This is what the Sovereign LORD says: Since you eat meat with the blood still in it and look to your idols and shed blood, should you then possess the land? ²⁶You rely on your sword, you do detestable things, and each of you defiles his neighbor's wife. Should you then possess the land?'

²⁷"Say this to them: 'This is what the Sovereign LORD says: As surely as I live, those who are left in the ruins will fall by the sword, those out in the country I will give to the wild animals to be devoured, and those in strongholds and caves will die of a plague. ²⁸I will make the land a desolate waste, and her proud strength will come to an end, and the mountains of Israel will become desolate so that no one will cross them. ²⁹Then they will know that I am the LORD, when I have made the land a desolate waste because of all the detestable things they have done.'

³⁰"As for you, son of man, your countrymen are talking together about you by the walls and at the doors of the houses, saying to each other, 'Come and hear the message that has come from the LORD.' ³¹My people come to you, as they usually do, and sit before you to listen to your words, but they do not put them into practice. With their mouths they express devotion, but their hearts are greedy for unjust gain. ³²Indeed, to them you are nothing more than one who sings love songs with a beautiful voice and plays an instrument well, for they hear your words but do not put them into practice.

³³"When all this comes true—and it surely will—then they will know that a prophet has been among them."

Shepherds and Sheep

34 The word of the LORD came to me: ²"Son of man, prophesy against the shepherds of Israel; prophesy and say to them: 'This is what the Sovereign LORD says: Woe to the shepherds of Israel who only take care of themselves! Should not shepherds take care of the flock? ³You eat the curds, clothe yourselves with the wool and slaughter the choice animals, but you do not take care of the flock. ⁴You have not strengthened the weak or healed the sick or bound up the injured. You have not brought back the strays or searched for the lost. You have ruled them harshly and brutally. ⁵So they were scattered because there was no shepherd, and when they were scattered they became food for all the wild animals. ⁶My sheep wandered over all the mountains and on every high hill. They were scattered over the whole earth, and no one searched or looked for them.

⁷ 'Therefore, you shepherds, hear the word of the LORD: ⁸As surely as I live, declares the Sovereign LORD, because my flock lacks a shepherd and so has been plundered and has become food for all the wild animals, and because my shepherds did not search for my flock but cared for themselves rather than for my flock, ⁹therefore, O shepherds, hear the word of the LORD: ¹⁰This is what the Sovereign LORD says: I am against the shepherds and will hold them accountable for my flock. I will remove them from tending the flock so that the shepherds can no longer feed themselves. I will rescue my flock from their mouths, and it will no longer be food for them.

¹¹ 'For this is what the Sovereign LORD says: I myself will search for my sheep and look after them. ¹²As a shepherd looks after his scattered flock when he is with them, so will I look after my sheep. I will rescue them from all the places where they were scattered on a day of clouds and darkness. ¹³I will bring them out from the nations and gather them from the countries, and I will bring them into their own land. I will pasture them on the mountains of Israel, in the ravines and in all the settlements in the land. ¹⁴I will tend them in a good pasture, and the mountain heights of Israel will be their grazing land. There they will lie down in good grazing land, and there they will feed in a rich pasture on the mountains of Israel. ¹⁵I myself will tend my sheep and have them lie down, declares the Sovereign LORD. ¹⁶I will search for the lost and bring back the strays. I will bind up the injured and strengthen the weak, but the sleek and the strong I will destroy. I will shepherd the flock with justice.

17 "'As for you, my flock, this is what the Sovereign LORD says: I will judge between one sheep and another, and between rams and goats. 18 Is it not enough for you to feed on the good pasture? Must you also trample the rest of your pasture with your feet? Is it not enough for you to drink clear water? Must you also muddy the rest with your feet? 19 Must my flock feed on what you have trampled and drink what you have muddied with your feet?

20 "'Therefore this is what the Sovereign LORD says to them: See, I myself will judge between the fat sheep and the lean sheep. 21 Because you shove with flank and shoulder, butting all the weak sheep with your horns until you have driven them away, 22 I will save my flock, and they will no longer be plundered. I will judge between one sheep and another. 23 I will place over them one shepherd, my servant David, and he will tend them; he will tend them and be their shepherd. 24 I the LORD will be their God, and my servant David will be prince among them. I the LORD have spoken.

25 "'I will make a covenant of peace with them and rid the land of wild beasts so that they may live in the desert and sleep in the forests in safety. 26 I will bless them and the places surrounding my hill. a I will send down showers in season; there will be showers of blessing. 27 The trees of the field will yield their fruit and the ground will yield its crops; the people will be secure in their land. They will know that I am the LORD, when I break the bars of their yoke and rescue them from the hands of those who enslaved them. 28 They will no longer be plundered by the nations, nor will wild animals devour them. They will live in safety, and no one will make them afraid. 29 I will provide for them a land renowned for its crops, and they will no longer be victims of famine in the land or bear the scorn of the nations. 30 Then they will know that I, the LORD their God, am with them and that they, the house of Israel, are my people, declares the Sovereign LORD. 31 You my sheep, the sheep of my pasture, are people, and I am your God, declares the Sovereign LORD.'"

A Prophecy Against Edom

35 The word of the LORD came to me: 2 "Son of man, set your face against Mount Seir; prophesy against it 3 and say: 'This is what the Sovereign LORD says: I am against you, Mount Seir, and I will stretch out my hand against you and make you a desolate waste. 4 I will turn your towns into ruins and you will be desolate. Then you will know that I am the LORD.

5 "'Because you harbored an ancient hostility and delivered the Israelites over to the sword at the time of their calamity, the time their punishment reached its climax, 6 therefore as surely as I live, declares the Sovereign LORD, I will give you over to bloodshed and it will pursue you. Since you did not hate bloodshed, bloodshed will pursue you. 7 I will make Mount Seir a desolate waste and cut off from it all who come and go. 8 I will fill your mountains with the slain; those killed by the sword will fall on your hills and in your valleys and in all your ravines. 9 I will make you desolate forever; your towns will not be inhabited. Then you will know that I am the LORD.

10 "'Because you have said, "These two nations and countries will be ours and we will take possession of them," even though I the LORD was there, 11 therefore as surely as I live, declares the Sovereign LORD, I will treat you in accordance with the anger and jealousy you showed in your hatred of them and I will make myself known among them when I judge you. 12 Then you will know that I the LORD have heard all the contemptible things you have said against the mountains of Israel. You said, "They have been laid waste and have been given over to us to devour." 13 You boasted against me and spoke against me without restraint, and I heard it. 14 This is what the Sovereign LORD says: While the whole earth rejoices, I will make you desolate. 15 Because you rejoiced when the inheritance of the house of Israel became desolate, that is how I will treat you. You will be desolate, O Mount Seir, you and all of Edom. Then they will know that I am the LORD.'"

a 26 Or I will make them and the places surrounding my hill a blessing

A Prophecy to the Mountains of Israel

36 "Son of man, prophesy to the mountains of Israel and say, 'O mountains of Israel, hear the word of the LORD. ²This is what the Sovereign LORD says: The enemy said of you, "Aha! The ancient heights have become our possession."' ³Therefore prophesy and say, 'This is what the Sovereign LORD says: Because they ravaged and hounded you from every side so that you became the possession of the rest of the nations and the object of people's malicious talk and slander, ⁴therefore, O mountains of Israel, hear the word of the Sovereign LORD: This is what the Sovereign LORD says to the mountains and hills, to the ravines and valleys, to the desolate ruins and the deserted towns that have been plundered and ridiculed by the rest of the nations around you— ⁵this is what the Sovereign LORD says: In my burning zeal I have spoken against the rest of the nations, and against all Edom, for with glee and with malice in their hearts they made my land their own possession so that they might plunder its pastureland.' ⁶Therefore prophesy concerning the land of Israel and say to the mountains and hills, to the ravines and valleys: 'This is what the Sovereign LORD says: I speak in my jealous wrath because you have suffered the scorn of the nations. ⁷Therefore this is what the Sovereign LORD says: I swear with uplifted hand that the nations around you will also suffer scorn.

⁸" 'But you, O mountains of Israel, will produce branches and fruit for my people Israel, for they will soon come home. ⁹I am concerned for you and will look on you with favor; you will be plowed and sown, ¹⁰and I will multiply the number of people upon you, even the whole house of Israel. The towns will be inhabited and the ruins rebuilt. ¹¹I will increase the number of men and animals upon you, and they will be fruitful and become numerous. I will settle people on you as in the past and will make you prosper more than before. Then you will know that I am the LORD. ¹²I will cause people, my people Israel, to walk upon you. They will possess you, and you will

be their inheritance; you will never again deprive them of their children.

¹³" 'This is what the Sovereign LORD says: Because people say to you, "You devour men and deprive your nation of its children," ¹⁴therefore you will no longer devour men or make your nation childless, declares the Sovereign LORD. ¹⁵No longer will I make you hear the taunts of the nations, and no longer will you suffer the scorn of the peoples or cause your nation to fall, declares the Sovereign LORD.' "

¹⁶Again the word of the LORD came to me: ¹⁷"Son of man, when the people of Israel were living in their own land, they defiled it by their conduct and their actions. Their conduct was like a woman's monthly uncleanness in my sight. ¹⁸So I poured out my wrath on them because they had shed blood in the land and because they had defiled it with their idols. ¹⁹I dispersed them among the nations, and they were scattered through the countries; I judged them according to their conduct and their actions. ²⁰And wherever they went among the nations they profaned my holy name, for it was said of them, 'These are the LORD's people, and yet they had to leave his land.' ²¹I had concern for my holy name, which the house of Israel profaned among the nations where they had gone.

²²"Therefore say to the house of Israel, 'This is what the Sovereign LORD says: It is not for your sake, O house of Israel, that I am going to do these things, but for the sake of my holy name, which you have profaned among the nations where you have gone. ²³I will show the holiness of my great name, which has been profaned among the nations, the name you have profaned among them. Then the nations will know that I am the LORD, declares the Sovereign LORD, when I show myself holy through you before their eyes.

²⁴" 'For I will take you out of the nations; I will gather you from all the countries and bring you back into your own land. ²⁵I will sprinkle clean water on you, and you will be clean; I will cleanse you from all your impurities and from all your idols. ²⁶I will give you a new heart and put a new

spirit in you; I will remove from you your heart of stone and give you a heart of flesh. ²⁷ And I will put my Spirit in you and move you to follow my decrees and be careful to keep my laws. ²⁸ You will live in the land I gave your forefathers; you will be my people, and I will be your God. ²⁹ I will save you from all your uncleanness. I will call for the grain and make it plentiful and will not bring famine upon you. ³⁰ I will increase the fruit of the trees and the crops of the field, so that you will no longer suffer disgrace among the nations because of famine. ³¹ Then you will remember your evil ways and wicked deeds, and you will loathe yourselves for your sins and detestable practices. ³² I want you to know that I am not doing this for your sake, declares the Sovereign Lord. Be ashamed and disgraced for your conduct, O house of Israel!

³³ "This is what the Sovereign Lord says: On the day I cleanse you from all your sins, I will resettle your towns, and the ruins will be rebuilt. ³⁴ The desolate land will be cultivated instead of lying desolate in the sight of all who pass through it. ³⁵ They will say, "This land that was laid waste has become like the garden of Eden; the cities that were lying in ruins, desolate and destroyed, are now fortified and inhabited." ³⁶ Then the nations around you that remain will know that I the Lord have rebuilt what was destroyed and have replanted what was desolate. I the Lord have spoken, and I will do it.'

³⁷ "This is what the Sovereign Lord says: Once again I will yield to the plea of the house of Israel and do this for them: I will make their people as numerous as sheep, ³⁸ as numerous as the flocks for offerings at Jerusalem during her appointed feasts. So will the ruined cities be filled with flocks of people. Then they will know that I am the Lord."

The Valley of Dry Bones

37 The hand of the Lord was upon me, and he brought me out by the Spirit of the Lord and set me in the middle of a valley; it was full of bones. ² He led me back and forth among them, and I saw a great many bones on the floor of the valley, bones that were very dry. ³ He asked me, "Son of man, can these bones live?"

I said, "O Sovereign Lord, you alone know."

⁴ Then he said to me, "Prophesy to these bones and say to them, 'Dry bones, hear the word of the Lord! ⁵ This is what the Sovereign Lord says to these bones: I will make breath^a enter you, and you will come to life. ⁶ I will attach tendons to you and make flesh come upon you and cover you with skin; I will put breath in you, and you

^a 5 The Hebrew for this word can also mean *wind* or *spirit* (see verses 6-14).

stories to share

EZEKIEL 37:1–14

The Valley of Dry Bones

LIFE LESSON: God remembers and keeps his promises.

TO TALK ABOUT

✦ In Ezekiel's vision, what was the valley full of?

✦ After the bones came together and were covered with skin, what was still missing?

✦ What did God mean by the "graves" he would open (verse 13)? Did God keep his promise of bringing his people back to their land?

✦ What promises has God kept for you and your family?

"I WILL GIVE YOU A NEW HEART
AND PUT A NEW SPIRIT IN YOU;
I WILL REMOVE FROM YOU YOUR
HEART OF STONE AND GIVE YOU
A HEART OF FLESH."

Ezekiel 36:26

Heart Specialist

RUTH A. DEJAGER

READ | EZEKIEL 36:16–38

God is a heart specialist. In fact, he does transplants! Here in this passage, he promises Israel a transplant that will never fail or be rejected. He assures his people that he will take their hearts of stone — their cold, hard hearts — and give them new hearts of flesh.

I can't quite imagine what my life would be like if this weren't true — if Jesus hadn't given me a new heart. I can't tell you how many times when, after or during an argument with my husband, I hear a still, small voice saying: "Relent. Forgive. Soften up." It happens, too, when I'm reading the newspaper, and I'm caught with prejudice coloring my thinking. Or I'm turning green with envy over someone's (seemingly) carefree lifestyle. Or I'm wandering on my own little myopic path away from God.

It's often a line or principle from Scripture that starts the surgery. When Jesus does heart surgery with the Word, you know it. It's that double-edged sword mentioned in the book of Hebrews: "For the word of God is living and active. Sharper than any double-edged sword, it penetrates even to dividing soul and spirit, joints and marrow; it judges the thoughts and attitudes of the heart" (Hebrews 4:12). Ouch!

The big caveat to this is that I have to sign a consent form, figuratively speaking. I have to be willing to have my heart examined and changed, like the psalmist did: "Search me, O God . . . See if there is any offensive way in me, and lead me in the way everlasting" (Psalm 139:23–24). Asking God to change our hearts is a prayer he never answers "no" to. For just in the asking we show our willingness to go back under the knife. It's a life-saving operation.

Jesus, you are the Great Physician. Only you see and know which of my attitudes and thought patterns need surgery. Only you know exactly how my heart needs renewing and softening. Thank you for the precision of the surgery you accomplish with your Word and with your holy presence.

Your next devotion is located on page 1175.

GRANDCHILD IN FOCUS • PRAYER

Spiritual Growth

Dear Lord, today I pray for my grandchild's spiritual growth. I ask that you instill in him the desire to read and memorize your Word. Give him a passion to be in conversation with you. May loving and serving you be part of his daily life. I ask that you stay close to him and lead him to be transformed to your likeness, to reflect your grace and to radiate your love. I pray this in Jesus' name, amen.

will come to life. Then you will know that I am the Lord.'"

[7] So I prophesied as I was commanded. And as I was prophesying, there was a noise, a rattling sound, and the bones came together, bone to bone. [8] I looked, and tendons and flesh appeared on them and skin covered them, but there was no breath in them.

[9] Then he said to me, "Prophesy to the breath; prophesy, son of man, and say to it, 'This is what the Sovereign Lord says: Come from the four winds, O breath, and breathe into these slain, that they may live.'" [10] So I prophesied as he commanded me, and breath entered them; they came to life and stood up on their feet—a vast army.

[11] Then he said to me: "Son of man, these bones are the whole house of Israel. They say, 'Our bones are dried up and our hope is gone; we are cut off.' [12] Therefore prophesy and say to them: 'This is what the Sovereign Lord says: O my people, I am going to open your graves and bring you up from them; I will bring you back to the land of Israel. [13] Then you, my people, will know that I am the Lord, when I open your graves and bring you up from them. [14] I will put my Spirit in you and you will live, and I will settle you in your own land. Then you will know that I the Lord have spoken, and I have done it, declares the Lord.'"

One Nation Under One King

[15] The word of the Lord came to me: [16] "Son of man, take a stick of wood and write on it, 'Belonging to Judah and the Israelites associated with him.' Then take another stick of wood, and write on it, 'Ephraim's stick, belonging to Joseph and all the house of Israel associated with him.' [17] Join them together into one stick so that they will become one in your hand.

[18] "When your countrymen ask you, 'Won't you tell us what you mean by this?' [19] say to them, 'This is what the Sovereign Lord says: I am going to take the stick of Joseph—which is in Ephraim's hand—and of the Israelite tribes associated with him, and join it to Judah's stick,

making them a single stick of wood, and they will become one in my hand.' [20] Hold before their eyes the sticks you have written on [21] and say to them, 'This is what the Sovereign Lord says: I will take the Israelites out of the nations where they have gone. I will gather them from all around and bring them back into their own land. [22] I will make them one nation in the land, on the mountains of Israel. There will be one king over all of them and they will never again be two nations or be divided into two kingdoms. [23] They will no longer defile themselves with their idols and vile images or with any of their offenses, for I will save them from all their sinful backsliding,[a] and I will cleanse them. They will be my people, and I will be their God.

[24] "'My servant David will be king over them, and they will all have one shepherd. They will follow my laws and be careful to keep my decrees. [25] They will live in the land I gave to my servant Jacob, the land where your fathers lived. They and their children and their children's children will live there forever, and David my servant will be their prince forever. [26] I will make a covenant of peace with them; it will be an everlasting covenant. I will establish them and increase their numbers, and I will put my sanctuary among them forever. [27] My dwelling place will be with them; I will be their God, and they will be my people. [28] Then the nations will know that I the Lord make Israel holy, when my sanctuary is among them forever.'"

A Prophecy Against Gog

38 The word of the Lord came to me: [2] "Son of man, set your face against Gog, of the land of Magog, the chief prince of[b] Meshech and Tubal; prophesy against him [3] and say: 'This is what the Sovereign Lord says: I am against you, O Gog, chief prince of[c] Meshech and Tubal. [4] I will turn you around, put hooks in your jaws and bring you out with your whole army—your

---

[a] 23 Many Hebrew manuscripts (see also Septuagint); most Hebrew manuscripts *all their dwelling places where they sinned* [b] 2 Or *the prince of Rosh,* [c] 3 Or *Gog, prince of Rosh,*

horses, your horsemen fully armed, and a great horde with large and small shields, all of them brandishing their swords. ⁵Persia, Cush ᵃ and Put will be with them, all with shields and helmets, ⁶also Gomer with all its troops, and Beth Togarmah from the far north with all its troops—the many nations with you.

⁷"'Get ready; be prepared, you and all the hordes gathered about you, and take command of them. ⁸After many days you will be called to arms. In future years you will invade a land that has recovered from war, whose people were gathered from many nations to the mountains of Israel, which had long been desolate. They had been brought out from the nations, and now all of them live in safety. ⁹You and all your troops and the many nations with you will go up, advancing like a storm; you will be like a cloud covering the land.

¹⁰"'This is what the Sovereign LORD says: On that day thoughts will come into your mind and you will devise an evil scheme. ¹¹You will say, "I will invade a land of unwalled villages; I will attack a peaceful and unsuspecting people—all of them living without walls and without gates and bars. ¹²I will plunder and loot and turn my hand against the resettled ruins and the people gathered from the nations, rich in livestock and goods, living at the center of the land." ¹³Sheba and Dedan and the merchants of Tarshish and all her villages ᵇ will say to you, "Have you come to plunder? Have you gathered your hordes to loot, to carry off silver and gold, to take away livestock and goods and to seize much plunder?"'

¹⁴"Therefore, son of man, prophesy and say to Gog: 'This is what the Sovereign LORD says: In that day, when my people Israel are living in safety, will you not take notice of it? ¹⁵You will come from your place in the far north, you and many nations with you, all of them riding on horses, a great horde, a mighty army. ¹⁶You will advance against my people Israel like a cloud that covers the land. In days to come, O Gog, I will bring you against my land, so that the nations may know me when I show myself holy through you before their eyes.

¹⁷"'This is what the Sovereign LORD says: Are you not the one I spoke of in former days by my servants the prophets of Israel? At that time they prophesied for years that I would bring you against them. ¹⁸This is what will happen in that day: When Gog attacks the land of Israel, my hot anger will be aroused, declares the Sovereign LORD. ¹⁹In my zeal and fiery wrath I declare that at that time there shall be a great earthquake in the land of Israel. ²⁰The fish of the sea, the birds of the air, the beasts of the field, every creature that moves along the ground, and all the people on the face of the earth will tremble at my presence. The mountains will be overturned, the cliffs will crumble and every wall will fall to the ground. ²¹I will summon a sword against Gog on all my mountains, declares the Sovereign LORD. Every man's sword will be against his brother. ²²I will execute judgment upon him with plague and bloodshed; I will pour down torrents of rain, hailstones and burning sulfur on him and on his troops and on the many nations with him. ²³And so I will show my greatness and my holiness, and I will make myself known in the sight of many nations. Then they will know that I am the LORD.'

39 "Son of man, prophesy against Gog and say: 'This is what the Sovereign LORD says: I am against you, O Gog, chief prince of ᶜ Meshech and Tubal. ²I will turn you around and drag you along. I will bring you from the far north and send you against the mountains of Israel. ³Then I will strike your bow from your left hand and make your arrows drop from your right hand. ⁴On the mountains of Israel you will fall, you and all your troops and the nations with you. I will give you as food to all kinds of carrion birds and to the wild animals. ⁵You will fall in the open field, for I have spoken, declares the Sovereign LORD. ⁶I will send fire on Magog and on those who live in safety in the coastlands, and they will know that I am the LORD.

⁷"'I will make known my holy name among my people Israel. I will no longer let my holy

---

ᵃ 5 That is, the upper Nile region ᵇ 13 Or her strong lions ᶜ 1 Or Gog, prince of Rosh, name be profaned, and the nations will know that I the LORD am the Holy One in Israel. ⁸It is coming! It will surely take place, declares the Sovereign LORD. This is the day I have spoken of.

⁹" 'Then those who live in the towns of Israel will go out and use the weapons for fuel and burn them up—the small and large shields, the bows and arrows, the war clubs and spears. For seven years they will use them for fuel. ¹⁰They will not need to gather wood from the fields or cut it from the forests, because they will use the weapons for fuel. And they will plunder those who plundered them and loot those who looted them, declares the Sovereign LORD.

¹¹" 'On that day I will give Gog a burial place in Israel, in the valley of those who travel east toward ᵃ the Sea. ᵇ It will block the way of travelers, because Gog and all his hordes will be buried there. So it will be called the Valley of Hamon Gog. ᶜ

¹²" 'For seven months the house of Israel will be burying them in order to cleanse the land. ¹³All the people of the land will bury them, and the day I am glorified will be a memorable day for them, declares the Sovereign LORD.

¹⁴" 'Men will be regularly employed to cleanse the land. Some will go throughout the land and, in addition to them, others will bury those that remain on the ground. At the end of the seven months they will begin their search. ¹⁵As they go through the land and one of them sees a human bone, he will set up a marker beside it until the gravediggers have buried it in the Valley of Hamon Gog. ¹⁶(Also a town called Hamonah ᵈ will be there.) And so they will cleanse the land.'

¹⁷"Son of man, this is what the Sovereign LORD says: Call out to every kind of bird and all the wild animals: 'Assemble and come together from all around to the sacrifice I am preparing for you, the great sacrifice on the mountains of Israel. There you will eat flesh and drink blood. ¹⁸You will eat the flesh of mighty men and drink the blood of the princes of the earth as if they were rams and lambs, goats and bulls—all of them fattened animals from Bashan. ¹⁹At the sacrifice I am preparing for you, you will eat fat till you are glutted and drink blood till you are drunk. ²⁰At my table you will eat your fill of horses and riders, mighty men and soldiers of every kind,' declares the Sovereign LORD.

²¹"I will display my glory among the nations, and all the nations will see the punishment I inflict and the hand I lay upon them. ²²From that day forward the house of Israel will know that I am the LORD their God. ²³And the nations will know that the people of Israel went into exile for their sin, because they were unfaithful to me. So I hid my face from them and handed them over to their enemies, and they all fell by the sword. ²⁴I dealt with them according to their uncleanness and their offenses, and I hid my face from them.

²⁵"Therefore this is what the Sovereign LORD says: I will now bring Jacob back from captivity ᵉ and will have compassion on all the people of Israel, and I will be zealous for my holy name. ²⁶They will forget their shame and all the unfaithfulness they showed toward me when they lived in safety in their land with no one to make them afraid. ²⁷When I have brought them back from the nations and have gathered them from the countries of their enemies, I will show myself holy through them in the sight of many nations. ²⁸Then they will know that I am the LORD their God, for though I sent them into exile among the nations, I will gather them to their own land, not leaving any behind. ²⁹I will no longer hide my face from them, for I will pour out my Spirit on the house of Israel, declares the Sovereign LORD."

The New Temple Area

40 In the twenty-fifth year of our exile, at the beginning of the year, on the tenth of the month, in the fourteenth year after the fall of the city—on that very day the hand of the LORD was upon me and he took me there. ²In visions of God he took me to the land of Israel and set me on a very high mountain, on whose south

---

ᵃ 11 Or of   ᵇ 11 That is, the Dead Sea   ᶜ 11 Hamon Gog means hordes of Gog.   ᵈ 16 Hamonah means horde.   ᵉ 25 Or now restore the fortunes of Jacob side were some buildings that looked like a city. ³He took me there, and I saw a man whose appearance was like bronze; he was standing in the gateway with a linen cord and a measuring rod in his hand. ⁴The man said to me, "Son of man, look with your eyes and hear with your ears and pay attention to everything I am going to show you, for that is why you have been brought here. Tell the house of Israel everything you see."

The East Gate to the Outer Court

⁵I saw a wall completely surrounding the temple area. The length of the measuring rod in the man's hand was six long cubits, each of which was a cubit *a* and a handbreadth. *b* He measured the wall; it was one measuring rod thick and one rod high.

⁶Then he went to the gate facing east. He climbed its steps and measured the threshold of the gate; it was one rod deep. *c* ⁷The alcoves for the guards were one rod long and one rod wide, and the projecting walls between the alcoves were five cubits thick. And the threshold of the gate next to the portico facing the temple was one rod deep.

⁸Then he measured the portico of the gateway; ⁹it *d* was eight cubits deep and its jambs were two cubits thick. The portico of the gateway faced the temple.

¹⁰Inside the east gate were three alcoves on each side; the three had the same measurements, and the faces of the projecting walls on each side had the same measurements. ¹¹Then he measured the width of the entrance to the gateway; it was ten cubits and its length was thirteen cubits. ¹²In front of each alcove was a wall one cubit high, and the alcoves were six cubits square. ¹³Then he measured the gateway from the top of the rear wall of one alcove to the top of the opposite one; the distance was twenty-five cubits from one parapet opening to the opposite one. ¹⁴He measured along the faces of the projecting walls all around the inside of the gateway—sixty cubits. The measurement was up to the portico *e* facing the courtyard. *f* ¹⁵The distance from the entrance of the gateway to the far end of its portico was fifty cubits. ¹⁶The alcoves and the projecting walls inside the gateway were surmounted by narrow parapet openings all around, as was the portico; the openings all around faced inward. The faces of the projecting walls were decorated with palm trees.

The Outer Court

¹⁷Then he brought me into the outer court. There I saw some rooms and a pavement that had been constructed all around the court; there were thirty rooms along the pavement. ¹⁸It abutted the sides of the gateways and was as wide as they were long; this was the lower pavement. ¹⁹Then he measured the distance from the inside of the lower gateway to the outside of the inner court; it was a hundred cubits on the east side as well as on the north.

The North Gate

²⁰Then he measured the length and width of the gate facing north, leading into the outer court. ²¹Its alcoves—three on each side—its projecting walls and its portico had the same measurements as those of the first gateway. It was fifty cubits long and twenty-five cubits wide. ²²Its openings, its portico and its palm tree decorations had the same measurements as those of the gate facing east. Seven steps led up to it, with its portico opposite them. ²³There was a gate to the inner court facing the north gate, just as there was on the east. He measured from one gate to the opposite one; it was a hundred cubits.

The South Gate

²⁴Then he led me to the south side and I saw a gate facing south. He measured its jambs and its portico, and they had the same measurements as

---

a 5 The common cubit was about 1 1/2 feet (about 0.5 meter).
b 5 That is, about 3 inches (about 8 centimeters)   *c 6* Septuagint;
Hebrew *deep, the first threshold, one rod deep*   *d 8,9* Many
Hebrew manuscripts, Septuagint, Vulgate and Syriac; most Hebrew
manuscripts *gateway facing the temple; it was one rod deep. ⁹Then he
measured the portico of the gateway; it*   *e 14* Septuagint; Hebrew
projecting wall   *f 14* The meaning of the Hebrew for this verse is
uncertain.

the others. ²⁵ The gateway and its portico had narrow openings all around, like the openings of the others. It was fifty cubits long and twenty-five cubits wide. ²⁶ Seven steps led up to it, with its portico opposite them; it had palm tree decorations on the faces of the projecting walls on each side. ²⁷ The inner court also had a gate facing south, and he measured from this gate to the outer gate on the south side; it was a hundred cubits.

Gates to the Inner Court

²⁸ Then he brought me into the inner court through the south gate, and he measured the south gate; it had the same measurements as the others. ²⁹ Its alcoves, its projecting walls and its portico had the same measurements as the others. The gateway and its portico had openings all around. It was fifty cubits long and twenty-five cubits wide. ³⁰ (The porticoes of the gateways around the inner court were twenty-five cubits wide and five cubits deep.) ³¹ Its portico faced the outer court; palm trees decorated its jambs, and eight steps led up to it.

³² Then he brought me to the inner court on the east side, and he measured the gateway; it had the same measurements as the others. ³³ Its alcoves, its projecting walls and its portico had the same measurements as the others. The gateway and its portico had openings all around. It was fifty cubits long and twenty-five cubits wide. ³⁴ Its portico faced the outer court; palm trees decorated the jambs on either side, and eight steps led up to it.

³⁵ Then he brought me to the north gate and measured it. It had the same measurements as the others, ³⁶ as did its alcoves, its projecting walls and its portico, and it had openings all around. It was fifty cubits long and twenty-five cubits wide. ³⁷ Its portico ᵃ faced the outer court; palm trees decorated the jambs on either side, and eight steps led up to it.

The Rooms for Preparing Sacrifices

³⁸ A room with a doorway was by the portico in each of the inner gateways, where the burnt offerings were washed. ³⁹ In the portico of the gateway were two tables on each side, on which the burnt offerings, sin offerings and guilt offerings were slaughtered. ⁴⁰ By the outside wall of the portico of the gateway, near the steps at the entrance to the north gateway were two tables, and on the other side of the steps were two tables. ⁴¹ So there were four tables on one side of the gateway and four on the other — eight tables in all — on which the sacrifices were slaughtered. ⁴² There were also four tables of dressed stone for the burnt offerings, each a cubit and a half long, a cubit and a half wide and a cubit high. On them were placed the utensils for slaughtering the burnt offerings and the other sacrifices. ⁴³ And double-pronged hooks, each a handbreadth long, were attached to the wall all around. The tables were for the flesh of the offerings.

Rooms for the Priests

⁴⁴ Outside the inner gate, within the inner court, were two rooms, one ᵇ at the side of the north gate and facing south, and another at the side of the south ᶜ gate and facing north. ⁴⁵ He said to me, "The room facing south is for the priests who have charge of the temple, ⁴⁶ and the room facing north is for the priests who have charge of the altar. These are the sons of Zadok, who are the only Levites who may draw near to the LORD to minister before him."

⁴⁷ Then he measured the court: It was square — a hundred cubits long and a hundred cubits wide. And the altar was in front of the temple.

The Temple

⁴⁸ He brought me to the portico of the temple and measured the jambs of the portico; they were five cubits wide on either side. The width of the entrance was fourteen cubits and its projecting walls were ᵈ three cubits wide on either side. ⁴⁹ The portico was twenty cubits wide, and twelve ᵉ cubits from front to back. It was reached

ᵃ 37 Septuagint (see also verses 31 and 34); Hebrew *jambs*
ᵇ 44 Septuagint; Hebrew *were rooms for singers, which were*
ᶜ 44 Septuagint; Hebrew *east*   ᵈ 48 Septuagint; Hebrew *entrance was*   ᵉ 49 Septuagint; Hebrew *eleven*

by a flight of stairs,[a] and there were pillars on each side of the jambs.

41 Then the man brought me to the outer sanctuary and measured the jambs; the width of the jambs was six cubits[b] on each side.[c] [2]The entrance was ten cubits wide, and the projecting walls on each side of it were five cubits wide. He also measured the outer sanctuary; it was forty cubits long and twenty cubits wide.

[3]Then he went into the inner sanctuary and measured the jambs of the entrance; each was two cubits wide. The entrance was six cubits wide, and the projecting walls on each side of it were seven cubits wide. [4]And he measured the length of the inner sanctuary; it was twenty cubits, and its width was twenty cubits across the end of the outer sanctuary. He said to me, "This is the Most Holy Place."

[5]Then he measured the wall of the temple; it was six cubits thick, and each side room around the temple was four cubits wide. [6]The side rooms were on three levels, one above another, thirty on each level. There were ledges all around the wall of the temple to serve as supports for the side rooms, so that the supports were not inserted into the wall of the temple. [7]The side rooms all around the temple were wider at each successive level. The structure surrounding the temple was built in ascending stages, so that the rooms widened as one went upward. A stairway went up from the lowest floor to the top floor through the middle floor.

[8]I saw that the temple had a raised base all around it, forming the foundation of the side rooms. It was the length of the rod, six long cubits. [9]The outer wall of the side rooms was five cubits thick. The open area between the side rooms of the temple [10]and the ⌊priests'⌋ rooms was twenty cubits wide all around the temple. [11]There were entrances to the side rooms from the open area, one on the north and another on the south; and the base adjoining the open area was five cubits wide all around.

[12]The building facing the temple courtyard on the west side was seventy cubits wide. The wall of the building was five cubits thick all around, and its length was ninety cubits.

[13]Then he measured the temple; it was a hundred cubits long, and the temple courtyard and the building with its walls were also a hundred cubits long. [14]The width of the temple courtyard on the east, including the front of the temple, was a hundred cubits.

[15]Then he measured the length of the building facing the courtyard at the rear of the temple, including its galleries on each side; it was a hundred cubits.

The outer sanctuary, the inner sanctuary and the portico facing the court, [16]as well as the thresholds and the narrow windows and galleries around the three of them—everything beyond and including the threshold was covered with wood. The floor, the wall up to the windows, and the windows were covered. [17]In the space above the outside of the entrance to the inner sanctuary and on the walls at regular intervals all around the inner and outer sanctuary [18]were carved cherubim and palm trees. Palm trees alternated with cherubim. Each cherub had two faces: [19]the face of a man toward the palm tree on one side and the face of a lion toward the palm tree on the other. They were carved all around the whole temple. [20]From the floor to the area above the entrance, cherubim and palm trees were carved on the wall of the outer sanctuary.

[21]The outer sanctuary had a rectangular doorframe, and the one at the front of the Most Holy Place was similar. [22]There was a wooden altar three cubits high and two cubits square[d]; its corners, its base[e] and its sides were of wood. The man said to me, "This is the table that is before the LORD." [23]Both the outer sanctuary and the Most Holy Place had double doors. [24]Each door had two leaves—two hinged leaves for each door. [25]And on the doors of the outer sanctuary were carved cherubim and palm trees like those

[a] 49 Hebrew; Septuagint *Ten steps led up to it*   [b] 1 The common cubit was about 1 1/2 feet (about 0.5 meter).   [c] 1 One Hebrew manuscript and Septuagint; most Hebrew manuscripts *side, the width of the tent*   [d] 22 Septuagint; Hebrew *long*   [e] 22 Septuagint; Hebrew *length*

LESLIE PARROTT

Dream Big

The last section of the book of Ezekiel (Ezekiel 40–48) records the prophet's grand vision of Israel's glorious future as the redeemed and perfected kingdom of God in the world. So many of us, as women, don't think much about dreaming big dreams. But I've interviewed enough women in their second half of life to know that it's never too late to get excited about dreaming a big dream.

I once talked to Sharon, who at 64 is passionate about her new dream of reading "the classics." She came across a list of the top 50 classic books in literary history, and she's decided to read one each quarter. "I'm already on my third book, and I'll have read all 50 in just 12 years!" she exclaimed. "I'll be 76 when I've read them all, and think of all I'll be learning!"

Dreams Aren't Just for the Young

A friend recently asked me if a woman in her 20s finds it easier to dream big because she has so many options and choices. "On the contrary," I replied, "if you attended one of the college courses I teach and interviewed even the most thoughtful young women with their lives before them, you'd soon see how most of them struggle to dream big dreams. Most are consumed with navigating their social life and finding time to sleep."

"Yes," my friend countered, "but don't you think a woman in her 40s and older finds the idea of dreaming at all somewhat painful? I mean, she has had to surrender some of her dreams and grieve their loss. Aren't her days of dreaming big dreams over?"

My heart ached to hear this question. A woman's days of dreaming big dreams over? Absolutely not!

Of course I didn't shout this out; instead, I answered, "In some of the courses I teach, sprinkled among the 20-year-olds, you'll find a few women in their 40s, 50s and beyond who are returning to college to realize a new dream they have for their lives."

I told her about Betty, a woman in her 50s, who always wanted to be a nurse. With her two children recently married, and living in an empty nest with her husband, she — now a grandmother — is returning to the classroom to make her dream come true. And she's loving every minute of it.

Another woman who had always been interested in the history of Europe came back to college for a second degree — 45 years after earning her first one. On the first day of class, as we introduced ourselves, she said she couldn't remember what she had majored in the first time. The students howled, but she laughed the loudest. At graduation she rewarded herself with a European trip with her young classmates.

Too late for a woman to dream? Never!

The Need to Keep Dreaming

Almost all of us in the second half of life have regrets. We have opportunities we may have passed up, doors we closed too soon or life's circumstances that were out of our control. That's life. But this doesn't mean we are forever walled off from dreaming big dreams. The eventual pain that results from not dreaming will always eclipse the pain of a dream that never comes true.

Why? Because a big dream almost always leads us to something good that we would have never experienced otherwise.

What do you aspire to?

What yearning and passion has God placed in your heart?

What do you dream about?

Dreams Change Over Time

My personal dreams these days, as opposed to my dreams from 20 years ago, have more to do with "significance" than "success." In addition to the character qualities of my sons, I care deeply about the state of marriage in our country. I think that if the divorce rate could be lowered significantly, it would be one of the single greatest social revolutions of our lifetime. So I put a lot of my energy into that dream. I dream about seeing seasoned couples mentoring younger couples. With my husband, I write about it, speak about it and work with others to do what we can to make this dream come true. I also have a dream of helping a local ministry for the needy in Seattle become the best it can be. I volunteer my time there when I can. I support it financially.

Dreams change over time and as we age. And what may seem like a "big" dream to some women will seem rather puny to others. Whatever your dreams are, you can be assured that they are a vital means to helping you discover how you are designed to make a difference.

carved on the walls, and there was a wooden over-hang on the front of the portico. ²⁶On the side-walls of the portico were narrow windows with palm trees carved on each side. The side rooms of the temple also had overhangs.

Rooms for the Priests

42 Then the man led me northward into the outer court and brought me to the rooms opposite the temple courtyard and opposite the outer wall on the north side. ²The building whose door faced north was a hundred cubits *a* long and fifty cubits wide. ³Both in the section twenty cu-bits from the inner court and in the section op-posite the pavement of the outer court, gallery faced gallery at the three levels. ⁴In front of the rooms was an inner passageway ten cubits wide and a hundred cubits *b* long. Their doors were on the north. ⁵Now the upper rooms were narrower, for the galleries took more space from them than from the rooms on the lower and middle floors of the building. ⁶The rooms on the third floor had no pillars, as the courts had; so they were smaller in floor space than those on the lower and middle floors. ⁷There was an outer wall paral-lel to the rooms and the outer court; it extended in front of the rooms for fifty cubits. ⁸While the row of rooms on the side next to the outer court was fifty cubits long, the row on the side nearest the sanctuary was a hundred cubits long. ⁹The lower rooms had an entrance on the east side as one enters them from the outer court.

¹⁰On the south side *c* along the length of the wall of the outer court, adjoining the temple courtyard and opposite the outer wall, were rooms ¹¹with a passageway in front of them. These were like the rooms on the north; they had the same length and width, with similar ex-its and dimensions. Similar to the doorways on the north ¹²were the doorways of the rooms on the south. There was a doorway at the beginning of the passageway that was parallel to the corre-sponding wall extending eastward, by which one enters the rooms.

¹³Then he said to me, "The north and south rooms facing the temple courtyard are the priests' rooms, where the priests who approach the LORD will eat the most holy offerings. There they will put the most holy offerings—the grain offerings, the sin offerings and the guilt offerings—for the place is holy. ¹⁴Once the priests enter the holy precincts, they are not to go into the outer court until they leave behind the garments in which they minister, for these are holy. They are to put on other clothes before they go near the places that are for the people."

¹⁵When he had finished measuring what was inside the temple area, he led me out by the east gate and measured the area all around: ¹⁶He mea-sured the east side with the measuring rod; it was five hundred cubits. *d* ¹⁷He measured the north side; it was five hundred cubits *e* by the measur-ing rod. ¹⁸He measured the south side; it was five hundred cubits by the measuring rod. ¹⁹Then he turned to the west side and measured; it was five hundred cubits by the measuring rod. ²⁰So he measured the area on all four sides. It had a wall around it, five hundred cubits long and five hundred cubits wide, to separate the holy from the common.

The Glory Returns to the Temple

43 Then the man brought me to the gate fac-ing east, ²and I saw the glory of the God of Israel coming from the east. His voice was like the roar of rushing waters, and the land was radi-ant with his glory. ³The vision I saw was like the vision I had seen when he *f* came to destroy the city and like the visions I had seen by the Kebar River, and I fell facedown. ⁴The glory of the LORD entered the temple through the gate facing east. ⁵Then the Spirit lifted me up and brought me into the inner court, and the glory of the LORD filled the temple.

⁶While the man was standing beside me, I heard someone speaking to me from inside the

---

a 2 The common cubit was about 1 1/2 feet (about 0.5 meter). *b 4* Septuagint and Syriac; Hebrew *and one cubit* *c 10* Septuagint; Hebrew *Eastward* *d 16* See Septuagint of verse 17; Hebrew *rods*; also in verses 18 and 19. *e 17* Septuagint; Hebrew *rods* *f 3* Some Hebrew manuscripts and Vulgate; most Hebrew manuscripts *I* temple. ⁷He said: "Son of man, this is the place of my throne and the place for the soles of my feet. This is where I will live among the Israelites forever. The house of Israel will never again defile my holy name—neither they nor their kings—by their prostitution^a and the lifeless idols^b of their kings at their high places. ⁸When they placed their threshold next to my threshold and their doorposts beside my doorposts, with only a wall between me and them, they defiled my holy name by their detestable practices. So I destroyed them in my anger. ⁹Now let them put away from me their prostitution and the lifeless idols of their kings, and I will live among them forever.

¹⁰"Son of man, describe the temple to the people of Israel, that they may be ashamed of their sins. Let them consider the plan, ¹¹and if they are ashamed of all they have done, make known to them the design of the temple—its arrangement, its exits and entrances—its whole design and all its regulations^c and laws. Write these down before them so that they may be faithful to its design and follow all its regulations.

¹²"This is the law of the temple: All the surrounding area on top of the mountain will be most holy. Such is the law of the temple.

The Altar

¹³"These are the measurements of the altar in long cubits, that cubit being a cubit^d and a handbreadth^e: Its gutter is a cubit deep and a cubit wide, with a rim of one span^f around the edge. And this is the height of the altar: ¹⁴From the gutter on the ground up to the lower ledge it is two cubits high and a cubit wide, and from the smaller ledge up to the larger ledge it is four cubits high and a cubit wide. ¹⁵The altar hearth is four cubits high, and four horns project upward from the hearth. ¹⁶The altar hearth is square, twelve cubits long and twelve cubits wide. ¹⁷The upper ledge also is square, fourteen cubits long and fourteen cubits wide, with a rim of half a cubit and a gutter of a cubit all around. The steps of the altar face east."

¹⁸Then he said to me, "Son of man, this is what the Sovereign LORD says: These will be the regulations for sacrificing burnt offerings and sprinkling blood upon the altar when it is built: ¹⁹You are to give a young bull as a sin offering to the priests, who are Levites, of the family of Zadok, who come near to minister before me, declares the Sovereign LORD. ²⁰You are to take some of its blood and put it on the four horns of the altar and on the four corners of the upper ledge and all around the rim, and so purify the altar and make atonement for it. ²¹You are to take the bull for the sin offering and burn it in the designated part of the temple area outside the sanctuary.

²²"On the second day you are to offer a male goat without defect for a sin offering, and the altar is to be purified as it was purified with the bull. ²³When you have finished purifying it, you are to offer a young bull and a ram from the flock, both without defect. ²⁴You are to offer them before the LORD, and the priests are to sprinkle salt on them and sacrifice them as a burnt offering to the LORD.

²⁵"For seven days you are to provide a male goat daily for a sin offering; you are also to provide a young bull and a ram from the flock, both without defect. ²⁶For seven days they are to make atonement for the altar and cleanse it; thus they will dedicate it. ²⁷At the end of these days, from the eighth day on, the priests are to present your burnt offerings and fellowship offerings^g on the altar. Then I will accept you, declares the Sovereign LORD."

The Prince, the Levites, the Priests

44 Then the man brought me back to the outer gate of the sanctuary, the one facing east, and it was shut. ²The LORD said to me, "This gate is to remain shut. It must not be opened; no

---

^a 7 Or *their spiritual adultery*; also in verse 9   ^b 7 Or *the corpses*; also in verse 9   ^c 11 Some Hebrew manuscripts and Septuagint; most Hebrew manuscripts *regulations and its whole design*
^d 13 The common cubit was about 1 1/2 feet (about 0.5 meter).
^e 13 That is, about 3 inches (about 8 centimeters)   ^f 13 That is, about 9 inches (about 22 centimeters)   ^g 27 Traditionally *peace offerings*

one may enter through it. It is to remain shut because the Lord, the God of Israel, has entered through it. ³The prince himself is the only one who may sit inside the gateway to eat in the presence of the Lord. He is to enter by way of the portico of the gateway and go out the same way."

⁴Then the man brought me by way of the north gate to the front of the temple. I looked and saw the glory of the Lord filling the temple of the Lord, and I fell facedown.

⁵The Lord said to me, "Son of man, look carefully, listen closely and give attention to everything I tell you concerning all the regulations regarding the temple of the Lord. Give attention to the entrance of the temple and all the exits of the sanctuary. ⁶Say to the rebellious house of Israel, 'This is what the Sovereign Lord says: Enough of your detestable practices, O house of Israel! ⁷In addition to all your other detestable practices, you brought foreigners uncircumcised in heart and flesh into my sanctuary, desecrating my temple while you offered me food, fat and blood, and you broke my covenant. ⁸Instead of carrying out your duty in regard to my holy things, you put others in charge of my sanctuary. ⁹This is what the Sovereign Lord says: No foreigner uncircumcised in heart and flesh is to enter my sanctuary, not even the foreigners who live among the Israelites.

¹⁰" 'The Levites who went far from me when Israel went astray and who wandered from me after their idols must bear the consequences of their sin. ¹¹They may serve in my sanctuary, having charge of the gates of the temple and serving in it; they may slaughter the burnt offerings and sacrifices for the people and stand before the people and serve them. ¹²But because they served them in the presence of their idols and made the house of Israel fall into sin, therefore I have sworn with uplifted hand that they must bear the consequences of their sin, declares the Sovereign Lord. ¹³They are not to come near to serve me as priests or come near any of my holy things or my most holy offerings; they must bear the shame of their detestable practices. ¹⁴Yet I will put them

in charge of the duties of the temple and all the work that is to be done in it.

¹⁵" 'But the priests, who are Levites and descendants of Zadok and who faithfully carried out the duties of my sanctuary when the Israelites went astray from me, are to come near to minister before me; they are to stand before me to offer sacrifices of fat and blood, declares the Sovereign Lord. ¹⁶They alone are to enter my sanctuary; they alone are to come near my table to minister before me and perform my service.

¹⁷" 'When they enter the gates of the inner court, they are to wear linen clothes; they must not wear any woolen garment while ministering at the gates of the inner court or inside the temple. ¹⁸They are to wear linen turbans on their heads and linen undergarments around their waists. They must not wear anything that makes them perspire. ¹⁹When they go out into the outer court where the people are, they are to take off the clothes they have been ministering in and are to leave them in the sacred rooms, and put on other clothes, so that they do not consecrate the people by means of their garments.

²⁰" 'They must not shave their heads or let their hair grow long, but they are to keep the hair of their heads trimmed. ²¹No priest is to drink wine when he enters the inner court. ²²They must not marry widows or divorced women; they may marry only virgins of Israelite descent or widows of priests. ²³They are to teach my people the difference between the holy and the common and show them how to distinguish between the unclean and the clean.

²⁴" 'In any dispute, the priests are to serve as judges and decide it according to my ordinances. They are to keep my laws and my decrees for all my appointed feasts, and they are to keep my Sabbaths holy.

²⁵" 'A priest must not defile himself by going near a dead person; however, if the dead person was his father or mother, son or daughter, brother or unmarried sister, then he may defile himself. ²⁶After he is cleansed, he must wait seven days. ²⁷On the day he goes into the inner court

of the sanctuary to minister in the sanctuary, he is to offer a sin offering for himself, declares the Sovereign LORD.

28 " 'I am to be the only inheritance the priests have. You are to give them no possession in Israel; I will be their possession. 29 They will eat the grain offerings, the sin offerings and the guilt offerings; and everything in Israel devoted ^{a} to the LORD will belong to them. 30 The best of all the firstfruits and of all your special gifts will belong to the priests. You are to give them the first portion of your ground meal so that a blessing may rest on your household. 31 The priests must not eat anything, bird or animal, found dead or torn by wild animals.

Division of the Land

45 " 'When you allot the land as an inheritance, you are to present to the LORD a portion of the land as a sacred district, 25,000 cubits long and 20,000 ^{b} cubits wide; the entire area will be holy. 2 Of this, a section 500 cubits square is to be for the sanctuary, with 50 cubits around it for open land. 3 In the sacred district, measure off a section 25,000 cubits ^{c} long and 10,000 cubits ^{d} wide. In it will be the sanctuary, the Most Holy Place. 4 It will be the sacred portion of the land for the priests, who minister in the sanctuary and who draw near to minister before the LORD. It will be a place for their houses as well as a holy place for the sanctuary. 5 An area 25,000 cubits long and 10,000 cubits wide will belong to the Levites, who serve in the temple, as their possession for towns to live in. ^{e}

6 " 'You are to give the city as its property an area 5,000 cubits wide and 25,000 cubits long, adjoining the sacred portion; it will belong to the whole house of Israel.

7 " 'The prince will have the land bordering each side of the area formed by the sacred district and the property of the city. It will extend westward from the west side and eastward from the east side, running lengthwise from the western to the eastern border parallel to one of the tribal portions. 8 This land will be his possession in Israel. And my princes will no longer oppress my people but will allow the house of Israel to possess the land according to their tribes.

9 " 'This is what the Sovereign LORD says: You have gone far enough, O princes of Israel! Give up your violence and oppression and do what is just and right. Stop dispossessing my people, declares the Sovereign LORD. 10 You are to use accurate scales, an accurate ephah ^{f} and an accurate bath. ^{g} 11 The ephah and the bath are to be the same size, the bath containing a tenth of a homer ^{h} and the ephah a tenth of a homer; the homer is to be the standard measure for both. 12 The shekel ^{i} is to consist of twenty gerahs. Twenty shekels plus twenty-five shekels plus fifteen shekels equal one mina. ^{j}

Offerings and Holy Days

13 " 'This is the special gift you are to offer: a sixth of an ephah from each homer of wheat and a sixth of an ephah from each homer of barley. 14 The prescribed portion of oil, measured by the bath, is a tenth of a bath from each cor (which consists of ten baths or one homer, for ten baths are equivalent to a homer). 15 Also one sheep is to be taken from every flock of two hundred from the well-watered pastures of Israel. These will be used for the grain offerings, burnt offerings and fellowship offerings ^{k} to make atonement for the people, declares the Sovereign LORD. 16 All the people of the land will participate in this special gift for the use of the prince in Israel. 17 It will be the duty of the prince to provide the burnt offerings, grain offerings and drink offerings at the festivals, the New Moons and the Sabbaths — at all the appointed feasts of the house of Israel. He will provide the sin offerings, grain offerings,

^{a} 29 The Hebrew term refers to the irrevocable giving over of things or persons to the LORD. ^{b} 1 Septuagint (see also verses 3 and 5 and 48:9); Hebrew 10,000 ^{c} 3 That is, about 7 miles (about 12 kilometers) ^{d} 3 That is, about 3 miles (about 5 kilometers) ^{e} 5 Septuagint; Hebrew temple; they will have as their possession 20 rooms ^{f} 10 An ephah was a dry measure. ^{g} 10 A bath was a liquid measure. ^{h} 11 A homer was a dry measure. ^{i} 12 A shekel weighed about 2/5 ounce (about 11.5 grams). ^{j} 12 That is, 60 shekels; the common mina was 50 shekels. ^{k} 15 Traditionally peace offerings; also in verse 17 burnt offerings and fellowship offerings to make atonement for the house of Israel.

18 " 'This is what the Sovereign LORD says: In the first month on the first day you are to take a young bull without defect and purify the sanctuary. 19 The priest is to take some of the blood of the sin offering and put it on the doorposts of the temple, on the four corners of the upper ledge of the altar and on the gateposts of the inner court. 20 You are to do the same on the seventh day of the month for anyone who sins unintentionally or through ignorance; so you are to make atonement for the temple.

21 " 'In the first month on the fourteenth day you are to observe the Passover, a feast lasting seven days, during which you shall eat bread made without yeast. 22 On that day the prince is to provide a bull as a sin offering for himself and for all the people of the land. 23 Every day during the seven days of the Feast he is to provide seven bulls and seven rams without defect as a burnt offering to the LORD, and a male goat for a sin offering. 24 He is to provide as a grain offering an ephah for each bull and an ephah for each ram, along with a hin ^{a} of oil for each ephah.

25 " 'During the seven days of the Feast, which begins in the seventh month on the fifteenth day, he is to make the same provision for sin offerings, burnt offerings, grain offerings and oil.

46 " 'This is what the Sovereign LORD says: The gate of the inner court facing east is to be shut on the six working days, but on the Sabbath day and on the day of the New Moon it is to be opened. 2 The prince is to enter from the outside through the portico of the gateway and stand by the gatepost. The priests are to sacrifice his burnt offering and his fellowship offerings. ^{b} He is to worship at the threshold of the gateway and then go out, but the gate will not be shut until evening. 3 On the Sabbaths and New Moons the people of the land are to worship in the presence of the LORD at the entrance to that gateway. 4 The burnt offering the prince brings to the LORD on the Sabbath day is to be six male lambs and a ram, all without defect. 5 The grain offering given with the ram is to be an ephah, ^{c} and the grain offering with the lambs is to be as much as he pleases, along with a hin ^{a} of oil for each ephah. 6 On the day of the New Moon he is to offer a young bull, six lambs and a ram, all without defect. 7 He is to provide as a grain offering one ephah with the bull, one ephah with the ram, and with the lambs as much as he wants to give, along with a hin of oil with each ephah. 8 When the prince enters, he is to go in through the portico of the gateway, and he is to come out the same way.

9 " 'When the people of the land come before the LORD at the appointed feasts, whoever enters by the north gate to worship is to go out the south gate; and whoever enters by the south gate is to go out the north gate. No one is to return through the gate by which he entered, but each is to go out the opposite gate. 10 The prince is to be among them, going in when they go in and going out when they go out.

11 " 'At the festivals and the appointed feasts, the grain offering is to be an ephah with a bull, an ephah with a ram, and with the lambs as much as one pleases, along with a hin of oil for each ephah. 12 When the prince provides a freewill offering to the LORD — whether a burnt offering or fellowship offerings — the gate facing east is to be opened for him. He shall offer his burnt offering or his fellowship offerings as he does on the Sabbath day. Then he shall go out, and after he has gone out, the gate will be shut.

13 " 'Every day you are to provide a year-old lamb without defect for a burnt offering to the LORD; morning by morning you shall provide it. 14 You are also to provide with it morning by morning a grain offering, consisting of a sixth of an ephah with a third of a hin of oil to moisten the flour. The presenting of this grain offering to the LORD is a lasting ordinance. 15 So the lamb and the grain offering and the oil shall be provided morning by morning for a regular burnt offering.

^{a} 24,5 That is, probably about 4 quarts (about 4 liters)
^{b} 2 Traditionally peace offerings; also in verse 12 ^{c} 5 That is, probably about 3/5 bushel (about 22 liters)

16 " 'This is what the Sovereign LORD says: If the prince makes a gift from his inheritance to one of his sons, it will also belong to his descendants; it is to be their property by inheritance. 17 If, however, he makes a gift from his inheritance to one of his servants, the servant may keep it until the year of freedom; then it will revert to the prince. His inheritance belongs to his sons only; it is theirs. 18 The prince must not take any of the inheritance of the people, driving them off their property. He is to give his sons their inheritance out of his own property, so that none of my people will be separated from his property.' "

19 Then the man brought me through the entrance at the side of the gate to the sacred rooms facing north, which belonged to the priests, and showed me a place at the western end. 20 He said to me, "This is the place where the priests will cook the guilt offering and the sin offering and bake the grain offering, to avoid bringing them into the outer court and consecrating the people."

21 He then brought me to the outer court and led me around to its four corners, and I saw in each corner another court. 22 In the four corners of the outer court were enclosed[a] courts, forty cubits long and thirty cubits wide; each of the courts in the four corners was the same size. 23 Around the inside of each of the four courts was a ledge of stone, with places for fire built all around under the ledge. 24 He said to me, "These are the kitchens where those who minister at the temple will cook the sacrifices of the people."

The River From the Temple

47 The man brought me back to the entrance of the temple, and I saw water coming out from under the threshold of the temple toward the east (for the temple faced east). The water was coming down from under the south side of the temple, south of the altar. 2 He then brought me out through the north gate and led me around the outside to the outer gate facing east, and the water was flowing from the south side.

3 As the man went eastward with a measuring line in his hand, he measured off a thousand cubits[b] and then led me through water that was ankle-deep. 4 He measured off another thousand cubits and led me through water that was knee-deep. He measured off another thousand and led me through water that was up to the waist. 5 He measured off another thousand, but now it was a river that I could not cross, because the water had risen and was deep enough to swim in—a river that no one could cross. 6 He asked me, "Son of man, do you see this?"

Then he led me back to the bank of the river. 7 When I arrived there, I saw a great number of trees on each side of the river. 8 He said to me, "This water flows toward the eastern region and goes down into the Arabah,[c] where it enters the Sea.[d] When it empties into the Sea,[d] the water there becomes fresh. 9 Swarms of living creatures will live wherever the river flows. There will be large numbers of fish, because this water flows there and makes the salt water fresh; so where the river flows everything will live. 10 Fishermen will stand along the shore; from En Gedi to En Eglaim there will be places for spreading nets. The fish will be of many kinds—like the fish of the Great Sea.[e] 11 But the swamps and marshes will not become fresh; they will be left for salt. 12 Fruit trees of all kinds will grow on both banks of the river. Their leaves will not wither, nor will their fruit fail. Every month they will bear, because the water from the sanctuary flows to them. Their fruit will serve for food and their leaves for healing."

The Boundaries of the Land

13 This is what the Sovereign LORD says: "These are the boundaries by which you are to divide the land for an inheritance among the twelve tribes of Israel, with two portions for Joseph. 14 You are to divide it equally among them. Because I swore with uplifted hand to give it to your forefathers, this land will become your inheritance.

---

a 22 The meaning of the Hebrew for this word is uncertain. b 3 That is, about 1,500 feet (about 450 meters) c 8 Or the Jordan Valley d 8 That is, the Dead Sea e 10 That is, the Mediterranean; also in verses 15, 19 and 20

15 "This is to be the boundary of the land:

"On the north side it will run from the Great Sea by the Hethlon road past Lebo *a* Hamath to Zedad, 16 Berothah *b* and Sibraim (which lies on the border between Damascus and Hamath), as far as Hazer Hatticon, which is on the border of Hauran. 17 The boundary will extend from the sea to Hazar Enan, *c* along the northern border of Damascus, with the border of Hamath to the north. This will be the north boundary.

18 "On the east side the boundary will run between Hauran and Damascus, along the Jordan between Gilead and the land of Israel, to the eastern sea and as far as Tamar. *d* This will be the east boundary.

19 "On the south side it will run from Tamar as far as the waters of Meribah Kadesh, then along the Wadi ˌof Egyptˌ to the Great Sea. This will be the south boundary.

20 "On the west side, the Great Sea will be the boundary to a point opposite Lebo *e* Hamath. This will be the west boundary.

21 "You are to distribute this land among yourselves according to the tribes of Israel. 22 You are to allot it as an inheritance for yourselves and for the aliens who have settled among you and who have children. You are to consider them as native-born Israelites; along with you they are to be allotted an inheritance among the tribes of Israel. 23 In whatever tribe the alien settles, there you are to give him his inheritance," declares the Sovereign LORD.

The Division of the Land

48 "These are the tribes, listed by name: At the northern frontier, Dan will have one portion; it will follow the Hethlon road to Lebo *f* Hamath; Hazar Enan and the northern border of Damascus next to Hamath will be part of its border from the east side to the west side.

2 "Asher will have one portion; it will border the territory of Dan from east to west.

3 "Naphtali will have one portion; it will border the territory of Asher from east to west.

4 "Manasseh will have one portion; it will border the territory of Naphtali from east to west.

5 "Ephraim will have one portion; it will border the territory of Manasseh from east to west.

6 "Reuben will have one portion; it will border the territory of Ephraim from east to west.

7 "Judah will have one portion; it will border the territory of Reuben from east to west.

8 "Bordering the territory of Judah from east to west will be the portion you are to present as a special gift. It will be 25,000 cubits *g* wide, and its length from east to west will equal one of the tribal portions; the sanctuary will be in the center of it.

9 "The special portion you are to offer to the LORD will be 25,000 cubits long and 10,000 cubits *h* wide. 10 This will be the sacred portion for the priests. It will be 25,000 cubits long on the north side, 10,000 cubits wide on the west side, 10,000 cubits wide on the east side and 25,000 cubits long on the south side. In the center of it will be the sanctuary of the LORD. 11 This will be for the consecrated priests, the Zadokites, who were faithful in serving me and did not go astray as the Levites did when the Israelites went astray. 12 It will be a special gift to them from the sacred portion of the land, a most holy portion, bordering the territory of the Levites.

13 "Alongside the territory of the priests, the Levites will have an allotment 25,000 cubits long and 10,000 cubits wide. Its total length will be 25,000 cubits and its width 10,000 cubits. 14 They must not sell or exchange any of it. This is the best of the land and must not pass into other hands, because it is holy to the LORD.

15 "The remaining area, 5,000 cubits wide and 25,000 cubits long, will be for the common use

---

a 15 Or *past the entrance to*   *b* 15,16 See Septuagint and Ezekiel 48:1; Hebrew *road to go into Zedad,* 16*Hamath, Berothah*   *c* 17 Hebrew *Enon,* a variant of *Enan*   *d* 18 Septuagint and Syriac; Hebrew *Israel. You will measure to the eastern sea*   *e* 20 Or *opposite the entrance to*   *f* 1 Or *to the entrance to*   *g* 8 That is, about 7 miles (about 12 kilometers)   *h* 9 That is, about 3 miles (about 5 kilometers) of the city, for houses and for pastureland. The city will be in the center of it [16]and will have these measurements: the north side 4,500 cubits, the south side 4,500 cubits, the east side 4,500 cubits, and the west side 4,500 cubits. [17]The pastureland for the city will be 250 cubits on the north, 250 cubits on the south, 250 cubits on the east, and 250 cubits on the west. [18]What remains of the area, bordering on the sacred portion and running the length of it, will be 10,000 cubits on the east side and 10,000 cubits on the west side. Its produce will supply food for the workers of the city. [19]The workers from the city who farm it will come from all the tribes of Israel. [20]The entire portion will be a square, 25,000 cubits on each side. As a special gift you will set aside the sacred portion, along with the property of the city.

[21]"What remains on both sides of the area formed by the sacred portion and the city property will belong to the prince. It will extend eastward from the 25,000 cubits of the sacred portion to the eastern border, and westward from the 25,000 cubits to the western border. Both these areas running the length of the tribal portions will belong to the prince, and the sacred portion with the temple sanctuary will be in the center of them. [22]So the property of the Levites and the property of the city will lie in the center of the area that belongs to the prince. The area belonging to the prince will lie between the border of Judah and the border of Benjamin.

[23]"As for the rest of the tribes: Benjamin will have one portion; it will extend from the east side to the west side.

[24]"Simeon will have one portion; it will border the territory of Benjamin from east to west.

[25]"Issachar will have one portion; it will border the territory of Simeon from east to west.

[26]"Zebulun will have one portion; it will border the territory of Issachar from east to west.

[27]"Gad will have one portion; it will border the territory of Zebulun from east to west.

[28]"The southern boundary of Gad will run south from Tamar to the waters of Meribah Kadesh, then along the Wadi ⌊of Egypt⌋ to the Great Sea.[a]

[29]"This is the land you are to allot as an inheritance to the tribes of Israel, and these will be their portions," declares the Sovereign LORD.

The Gates of the City

[30]"These will be the exits of the city: Beginning on the north side, which is 4,500 cubits long, [31]the gates of the city will be named after the tribes of Israel. The three gates on the north side will be the gate of Reuben, the gate of Judah and the gate of Levi.

[32]"On the east side, which is 4,500 cubits long, will be three gates: the gate of Joseph, the gate of Benjamin and the gate of Dan.

[33]"On the south side, which measures 4,500 cubits, will be three gates: the gate of Simeon, the gate of Issachar and the gate of Zebulun.

[34]"On the west side, which is 4,500 cubits long, will be three gates: the gate of Gad, the gate of Asher and the gate of Naphtali.

[35]"The distance all around will be 18,000 cubits.

"And the name of the city from that time on will be:

THE LORD IS THERE."

[a] 28 That is, the Mediterranean

Daniel

Get WISDOM

Next to Solomon (and Jesus, of course), Daniel may have been the wisest person described in the Bible. He was a young member of Judah's nobility when he was taken into captivity to Babylon in 605 B.C. His wisdom, which he openly accredited to God, gave him the ability to interpret the dreams of the mighty king Nebuchadnezzar, ruler of the Babylonian Empire. The first part of the book of Daniel contains impressive stories of God's power and presence in the lives of Daniel and his friends Shadrach, Meshach and Abednego. The second part recounts Daniel's prophecies of the future, as revealed to him through visions and dreams.

Daniel lived an exemplary life. Although he endured difficult times and faced threats of death, he remained obedient to God and to his values as God's servant. For example, upon arriving at the king's palace, Daniel refused to defile himself by eating the king's food (see Daniel 1:8). He was also willing to openly profess his faith in God and to pray to him when the king's decree banned such actions (see Daniel 6). Through the worst of trials and circumstances, Daniel remained faithful to God.

While we may never find ourselves, as Daniel did, in a den of lions, our testimony and faith before others may, in a similar way, influence those around us — especially our children and grandchildren.

VERSE *to* REMEMBER | DANIEL 12:3

"Those who are wise will shine like the brightness of the heavens, and those who lead many to righteousness, like the stars for ever and ever."

ABOUT DANIEL

WRITTEN BY:
Daniel, a Jew who became an important official in Babylon and Persia

WRITTEN FOR:
The Jewish captives in Babylon

DATE WRITTEN:
Probably about 535 B.C., near the end of Daniel's life

WHY WRITTEN:
To remind the Jewish people that God is in control

Daniel's Training in Babylon

1 In the third year of the reign of Jehoiakim king of Judah, Nebuchadnezzar king of Babylon came to Jerusalem and besieged it. ²And the Lord delivered Jehoiakim king of Judah into his hand, along with some of the articles from the temple of God. These he carried off to the temple of his god in Babylonia *a* and put in the treasure house of his god.

³Then the king ordered Ashpenaz, chief of his court officials, to bring in some of the Israelites from the royal family and the nobility— ⁴young men without any physical defect, handsome, showing aptitude for every kind of learning, well informed, quick to understand, and qualified to serve in the king's palace. He was to teach them the language and literature of the Babylonians. *b* ⁵The king assigned them a daily amount of food and wine from the king's table. They were to be trained for three years, and after that they were to enter the king's service.

⁶Among these were some from Judah: Daniel, Hananiah, Mishael and Azariah. ⁷The chief official gave them new names: to Daniel, the name Belteshazzar; to Hananiah, Shadrach; to Mishael, Meshach; and to Azariah, Abednego.

⁸But Daniel resolved not to defile himself with the royal food and wine, and he asked the chief official for permission not to defile himself this way. ⁹Now God had caused the official to show favor and sympathy to Daniel, ¹⁰but the official told Daniel, "I am afraid of my lord the king, who has assigned your *c* food and drink. Why should he see you looking worse than the other young men your age? The king would then have my head because of you."

¹¹Daniel then said to the guard whom the chief official had appointed over Daniel, Hananiah, Mishael and Azariah, ¹²"Please test your servants for ten days: Give us nothing but vegetables to eat and water to drink. ¹³Then compare our appearance with that of the young men who eat the royal food, and treat your servants in accordance with what you see." ¹⁴So he agreed to this and tested them for ten days.

¹⁵At the end of the ten days they looked healthier and better nourished than any of the young men who ate the royal food. ¹⁶So the guard took away their choice food and the wine they were to drink and gave them vegetables instead.

¹⁷To these four young men God gave knowledge and understanding of all kinds of literature and learning. And Daniel could understand visions and dreams of all kinds.

¹⁸At the end of the time set by the king to bring them in, the chief official presented them to Nebuchadnezzar. ¹⁹The king talked with them, and he found none equal to Daniel, Hananiah, Mishael and Azariah; so they entered the king's service.

a 2 Hebrew *Shinar*   *b 4* Or *Chaldeans*   *c 10* The Hebrew for *your* and *you* in this verse is plural.

stories to share

DANIEL 1:1–21

Daniel's Wise Decision

LIFE LESSON: Obedience honors God and witnesses to others.

TO TALK ABOUT

✦ Why was Daniel in Babylon, so far away from home?

✦ Why did Daniel ask permission to eat only vegetables?

✦ How did God show his power and control after Daniel and his friends were given permission not to eat the royal food?

✦ When has your obedience to God been a witness to others?

²⁰In every matter of wisdom and understanding about which the king questioned them, he found them ten times better than all the magicians and enchanters in his whole kingdom.

²¹And Daniel remained there until the first year of King Cyrus.

Nebuchadnezzar's Dream

2 In the second year of his reign, Nebuchadnezzar had dreams; his mind was troubled and he could not sleep. ²So the king summoned the magicians, enchanters, sorcerers and astrologers^a to tell him what he had dreamed. When they came in and stood before the king, ³he said to them, "I have had a dream that troubles me and I want to know what it means.^b"

⁴Then the astrologers answered the king in Aramaic,^c "O king, live forever! Tell your servants the dream, and we will interpret it."

⁵The king replied to the astrologers, "This is what I have firmly decided: If you do not tell me what my dream was and interpret it, I will have you cut into pieces and your houses turned into piles of rubble. ⁶But if you tell me the dream and explain it, you will receive from me gifts and rewards and great honor. So tell me the dream and interpret it for me."

⁷Once more they replied, "Let the king tell his servants the dream, and we will interpret it."

⁸Then the king answered, "I am certain that you are trying to gain time, because you realize that this is what I have firmly decided: ⁹If you do not tell me the dream, there is just one penalty for you. You have conspired to tell me misleading and wicked things, hoping the situation will change. So then, tell me the dream, and I will know that you can interpret it for me."

¹⁰The astrologers answered the king, "There is not a man on earth who can do what the king asks! No king, however great and mighty, has ever asked such a thing of any magician or enchanter or astrologer. ¹¹What the king asks is too difficult. No one can reveal it to the king except the gods, and they do not live among men."

¹²This made the king so angry and furious that he ordered the execution of all the wise men of Babylon. ¹³So the decree was issued to put the wise men to death, and men were sent to look for Daniel and his friends to put them to death.

¹⁴When Arioch, the commander of the king's guard, had gone out to put to death the wise men of Babylon, Daniel spoke to him with wisdom and tact. ¹⁵He asked the king's officer, "Why did the king issue such a harsh decree?" Arioch then explained the matter to Daniel. ¹⁶At this, Daniel went in to the king and asked for time, so that he might interpret the dream for him.

¹⁷Then Daniel returned to his house and explained the matter to his friends Hananiah, Mishael and Azariah. ¹⁸He urged them to plead for mercy from the God of heaven concerning this mystery, so that he and his friends might not be executed with the rest of the wise men of Babylon. ¹⁹During the night the mystery was revealed to Daniel in a vision. Then Daniel praised the God of heaven ²⁰and said:

"Praise be to the name of God for ever
   and ever;
      wisdom and power are his.
²¹He changes times and seasons;
      he sets up kings and deposes them.
   He gives wisdom to the wise
      and knowledge to the discerning.

^a 2 Or *Chaldeans*; also in verses 4, 5 and 10   ^b 3 Or *was*
^c 4 The text from here through chapter 7 is in Aramaic.

PRAYING THE SCRIPTURES

Wisdom

DANIEL 2:21

Dear God, I pray for my grandchild that she will be wise, for you give wisdom to the wise and provide knowledge to the discerning.

Next prayer in Wisdom Prayer Track: Ephesians 1:17

²²He reveals deep and hidden things;
   he knows what lies in darkness,
   and light dwells with him.
²³I thank and praise you, O God of my fathers:
   You have given me wisdom and power,
  you have made known to me what we asked
    of you,
    you have made known to us the dream of
    the king."

Daniel Interprets the Dream

²⁴Then Daniel went to Arioch, whom the king had appointed to execute the wise men of Babylon, and said to him, "Do not execute the wise men of Babylon. Take me to the king, and I will interpret his dream for him."

²⁵Arioch took Daniel to the king at once and said, "I have found a man among the exiles from Judah who can tell the king what his dream means."

²⁶The king asked Daniel (also called Belteshazzar), "Are you able to tell me what I saw in my dream and interpret it?"

²⁷Daniel replied, "No wise man, enchanter, magician or diviner can explain to the king the mystery he has asked about, ²⁸but there is a God in heaven who reveals mysteries. He has shown King Nebuchadnezzar what will happen in days to come. Your dream and the visions that passed through your mind as you lay on your bed are these:

²⁹"As you were lying there, O king, your mind turned to things to come, and the revealer of mysteries showed you what is going to happen. ³⁰As for me, this mystery has been revealed to me, not because I have greater wisdom than other living men, but so that you, O king, may know the interpretation and that you may understand what went through your mind.

³¹"You looked, O king, and there before you stood a large statue—an enormous, dazzling statue, awesome in appearance. ³²The head of the statue was made of pure gold, its chest and arms of silver, its belly and thighs of bronze, ³³its legs of iron, its feet partly of iron and partly of baked clay. ³⁴While you were watching, a rock was cut out, but not by human hands. It struck the statue on its feet of iron and clay and smashed them. ³⁵Then the iron, the clay, the bronze, the silver and the gold were broken to pieces at the same time and became like chaff on a threshing floor in the summer. The wind swept them away without leaving a trace. But the rock that struck the statue became a huge mountain and filled the whole earth.

³⁶"This was the dream, and now we will interpret it to the king. ³⁷You, O king, are the king of kings. The God of heaven has given you dominion and power and might and glory; ³⁸in your hands he has placed mankind and the beasts of the field and the birds of the air. Wherever they live, he has made you ruler over them all. You are that head of gold.

³⁹"After you, another kingdom will rise, inferior to yours. Next, a third kingdom, one of bronze, will rule over the whole earth. ⁴⁰Finally, there will be a fourth kingdom, strong as iron—for iron breaks and smashes everything—and as iron breaks things to pieces, so it will crush and break all the others. ⁴¹Just as you saw that the feet and toes were partly of baked clay and partly of iron, so this will be a divided kingdom; yet it will have some of the strength of iron in it, even as you saw iron mixed with clay. ⁴²As the toes were partly iron and partly clay, so this kingdom will be partly strong and partly brittle. ⁴³And just as you saw the iron mixed with baked clay, so the people will be a mixture and will not remain united, any more than iron mixes with clay.

⁴⁴"In the time of those kings, the God of heaven will set up a kingdom that will never be destroyed, nor will it be left to another people. It will crush all those kingdoms and bring them to an end, but it will itself endure forever. ⁴⁵This is the meaning of the vision of the rock cut out of a mountain, but not by human hands—a rock that broke the iron, the bronze, the clay, the silver and the gold to pieces.

"The great God has shown the king what will take place in the future. The dream is true and the interpretation is trustworthy."

⁴⁶Then King Nebuchadnezzar fell prostrate

before Daniel and paid him honor and ordered that an offering and incense be presented to him. ⁴⁷The king said to Daniel, "Surely your God is the God of gods and the Lord of kings and a revealer of mysteries, for you were able to reveal this mystery."

⁴⁸Then the king placed Daniel in a high position and lavished many gifts on him. He made him ruler over the entire province of Babylon and placed him in charge of all its wise men. ⁴⁹Moreover, at Daniel's request the king appointed Shadrach, Meshach and Abednego administrators over the province of Babylon, while Daniel himself remained at the royal court.

The Image of Gold and the Fiery Furnace

3 King Nebuchadnezzar made an image of gold, ninety feet high and nine feet *ᵃ* wide, and set it up on the plain of Dura in the province of Babylon. ²He then summoned the satraps, prefects, governors, advisers, treasurers, judges, magistrates and all the other provincial officials to come to the dedication of the image he had set up. ³So the satraps, prefects, governors, advisers, treasurers, judges, magistrates and all the other provincial officials assembled for the dedication of the image that King Nebuchadnezzar had set up, and they stood before it.

⁴Then the herald loudly proclaimed, "This is what you are commanded to do, O peoples, nations and men of every language: ⁵As soon as you hear the sound of the horn, flute, zither, lyre, harp, pipes and all kinds of music, you must fall down and worship the image of gold that King Nebuchadnezzar has set up. ⁶Whoever does not fall down and worship will immediately be thrown into a blazing furnace."

⁷Therefore, as soon as they heard the sound of the horn, flute, zither, lyre, harp and all kinds of music, all the peoples, nations and men of every language fell down and worshiped the image of gold that King Nebuchadnezzar had set up.

⁸At this time some astrologers *ᵇ* came forward and denounced the Jews. ⁹They said to King Nebuchadnezzar, "O king, live forever! ¹⁰You have issued a decree, O king, that everyone who hears the sound of the horn, flute, zither, lyre, harp, pipes and all kinds of music must fall down and worship the image of gold, ¹¹and that whoever does not fall down and worship will be thrown into a blazing furnace. ¹²But there are some Jews whom you have set over the affairs of the province of Babylon—Shadrach, Meshach and Abednego—who pay no attention to you, O king. They neither serve your gods nor worship the image of gold you have set up."

¹³Furious with rage, Nebuchadnezzar summoned Shadrach, Meshach and Abednego. So these men were brought before the king, ¹⁴and Nebuchadnezzar said to them, "Is it true, Shadrach, Meshach and Abednego, that you do not serve my gods or worship the image of gold I have set up? ¹⁵Now when you hear the sound of the horn, flute, zither, lyre, harp, pipes and all kinds of music, if you are ready to fall down and worship the image I made, very good. But if you do not worship it, you will be thrown immediately into a blazing furnace. Then what god will be able to rescue you from my hand?"

¹⁶Shadrach, Meshach and Abednego replied to the king, "O Nebuchadnezzar, we do not need to defend ourselves before you in this matter. ¹⁷If we are thrown into the blazing furnace, the God we serve is able to save us from it, and he will res-

TALKING POINTS

Trust

Shadrach, Meshach and Abednego trusted God even if it meant they would die in the fiery furnace.

DANIEL 3:1–30

For more on trust, go to Nahum 1:7.

ᵃ 1 Aramaic *sixty cubits high and six cubits wide* (about 27 meters high and 2.7 meters wide)   *ᵇ 8* Or *Chaldeans*

DANIEL 3:1–30

The Fiery Furnace

LIFE LESSON: God wants us to trust and obey him, no matter what.

TO TALK ABOUT

✦ What was King Nebuchadnezzar's royal decree?

✦ Why was the king so angry with Shadrach, Meshach and Abednego?

✦ Did Shadrach, Meshach and Abednego know for sure that God would save them?

✦ What would you have done if you had been one of these three young men?

cue us from your hand, O king. ¹⁸But even if he does not, we want you to know, O king, that we will not serve your gods or worship the image of gold you have set up."

¹⁹Then Nebuchadnezzar was furious with Shadrach, Meshach and Abednego, and his attitude toward them changed. He ordered the furnace heated seven times hotter than usual ²⁰and commanded some of the strongest soldiers in his army to tie up Shadrach, Meshach and Abednego and throw them into the blazing furnace. ²¹So these men, wearing their robes, trousers, turbans and other clothes, were bound and thrown into the blazing furnace. ²²The king's command was so urgent and the furnace so hot that the flames of the fire killed the soldiers who took up Sha-

drach, Meshach and Abednego, ²³and these three men, firmly tied, fell into the blazing furnace.

²⁴Then King Nebuchadnezzar leaped to his feet in amazement and asked his advisers, "Weren't there three men that we tied up and threw into the fire?"

They replied, "Certainly, O king."

²⁵He said, "Look! I see four men walking around in the fire, unbound and unharmed, and the fourth looks like a son of the gods."

²⁶Nebuchadnezzar then approached the opening of the blazing furnace and shouted, "Shadrach, Meshach and Abednego, servants of the Most High God, come out! Come here!"

So Shadrach, Meshach and Abednego came out of the fire, ²⁷and the satraps, prefects, governors and royal advisers crowded around them. They saw that the fire had not harmed their bodies, nor was a hair of their heads singed; their robes were not scorched, and there was no smell of fire on them.

²⁸Then Nebuchadnezzar said, "Praise be to the God of Shadrach, Meshach and Abednego, who has sent his angel and rescued his servants! They trusted in him and defied the king's command and were willing to give up their lives rather than serve or worship any god except their own God. ²⁹Therefore I decree that the people of any nation or language who say anything against the God of Shadrach, Meshach and Abednego be cut into pieces and their houses be turned into piles of rubble, for no other god can save in this way."

³⁰Then the king promoted Shadrach, Meshach and Abednego in the province of Babylon.

Nebuchadnezzar's Dream of a Tree

4 King Nebuchadnezzar,

To the peoples, nations and men of every language, who live in all the world:

May you prosper greatly!

²It is my pleasure to tell you about the miraculous signs and wonders that the Most High God has performed for me.

³How great are his signs,
how mighty his wonders!
His kingdom is an eternal kingdom;
his dominion endures from
generation to generation.

⁴I, Nebuchadnezzar, was at home in my palace, contented and prosperous. ⁵I had a dream that made me afraid. As I was lying in my bed, the images and visions that passed through my mind terrified me. ⁶So I commanded that all the wise men of Babylon be brought before me to interpret the dream for me. ⁷When the magicians, enchanters, astrologers^a and diviners came, I told them the dream, but they could not interpret it for me. ⁸Finally, Daniel came into my presence and I told him the dream. (He is called Belteshazzar, after the name of my god, and the spirit of the holy gods is in him.)

⁹I said, "Belteshazzar, chief of the magicians, I know that the spirit of the holy gods is in you, and no mystery is too difficult for you. Here is my dream; interpret it for me. ¹⁰These are the visions I saw while lying in my bed: I looked, and there before me stood a tree in the middle of the land. Its height was enormous. ¹¹The tree grew large and strong and its top touched the sky; it was visible to the ends of the earth. ¹²Its leaves were beautiful, its fruit abundant, and on it was food for all. Under it the beasts of the field found shelter, and the birds of the air lived in its branches; from it every creature was fed.

¹³"In the visions I saw while lying in my bed, I looked, and there before me was a messenger,^b a holy one, coming down from heaven. ¹⁴He called in a loud voice: 'Cut down the tree and trim off its branches; strip off its leaves and scatter its fruit. Let the animals flee from under it and the birds from its branches. ¹⁵But let the stump and its roots, bound with iron and bronze, remain in the ground, in the grass of the field.

" 'Let him be drenched with the dew of heaven, and let him live with the animals among the plants of the earth. ¹⁶Let his mind be changed from that of a man and let him be given the mind of an animal, till seven times^c pass by for him.

¹⁷" 'The decision is announced by messengers, the holy ones declare the verdict, so that the living may know that the Most High is sovereign over the kingdoms of men and gives them to anyone he wishes and sets over them the lowliest of men.'

¹⁸"This is the dream that I, King Nebuchadnezzar, had. Now, Belteshazzar, tell me what it means, for none of the wise men in my kingdom can interpret it for me. But you can, because the spirit of the holy gods is in you."

Daniel Interprets the Dream

¹⁹Then Daniel (also called Belteshazzar) was greatly perplexed for a time, and his thoughts terrified him. So the king said, "Belteshazzar, do not let the dream or its meaning alarm you."

Belteshazzar answered, "My lord, if only the dream applied to your enemies and its meaning to your adversaries! ²⁰The tree you saw, which grew large and strong, with its top touching the sky, visible to the whole earth, ²¹with beautiful leaves and abundant fruit, providing food for all, giving shelter to the beasts of the field, and having nesting places in its branches for the birds of the air— ²²you, O king, are that tree! You have become great and strong; your greatness has grown until it reaches the sky, and your dominion extends to distant parts of the earth.

²³"You, O king, saw a messenger, a holy one, coming down from heaven and saying, 'Cut down the tree and destroy it, but leave the stump, bound with iron and bronze, in

^a 7 Or Chaldeans   ^b 13 Or watchman; also in verses 17 and 23
^c 16 Or years; also in verses 23, 25 and 32

the grass of the field, while its roots remain in the ground. Let him be drenched with the dew of heaven; let him live like the wild animals, until seven times pass by for him.'

24 "This is the interpretation, O king, and this is the decree the Most High has issued against my lord the king: 25 You will be driven away from people and will live with the wild animals; you will eat grass like cattle and be drenched with the dew of heaven. Seven times will pass by for you until you acknowledge that the Most High is sovereign over the kingdoms of men and gives them to anyone he wishes. 26 The command to leave the stump of the tree with its roots means that your kingdom will be restored to you when you acknowledge that Heaven rules. 27 Therefore, O king, be pleased to accept my advice: Renounce your sins by doing what is right, and your wickedness by being kind to the oppressed. It may be that then your prosperity will continue."

The Dream Is Fulfilled

28 All this happened to King Nebuchadnezzar. 29 Twelve months later, as the king was walking on the roof of the royal palace of Babylon, 30 he said, "Is not this the great Babylon I have built as the royal residence, by my mighty power and for the glory of my majesty?"

31 The words were still on his lips when a voice came from heaven, "This is what is decreed for you, King Nebuchadnezzar: Your royal authority has been taken from you. 32 You will be driven away from people and will live with the wild animals; you will eat grass like cattle. Seven times will pass by for you until you acknowledge that the Most High is sovereign over the kingdoms of men and gives them to anyone he wishes."

33 Immediately what had been said about Nebuchadnezzar was fulfilled. He was driven away from people and ate grass like cattle. His body was drenched with the dew of heav-

en until his hair grew like the feathers of an eagle and his nails like the claws of a bird.

34 At the end of that time, I, Nebuchadnezzar, raised my eyes toward heaven, and my sanity was restored. Then I praised the Most High; I honored and glorified him who lives forever.

His dominion is an eternal dominion;
    his kingdom endures from generation to
        generation.
35 All the peoples of the earth
    are regarded as nothing.
He does as he pleases
    with the powers of heaven
    and the peoples of the earth.
No one can hold back his hand
    or say to him: "What have you done?"

36 At the same time that my sanity was restored, my honor and splendor were returned to me for the glory of my kingdom. My advisers and nobles sought me out, and I was restored to my throne and became even greater than before. 37 Now I, Nebuchadnezzar, praise and exalt and glorify the King of heaven, because everything he does is right and all his ways are just. And those who walk in pride he is able to humble.

The Writing on the Wall

5 King Belshazzar gave a great banquet for a thousand of his nobles and drank wine with them. 2 While Belshazzar was drinking his wine, he gave orders to bring in the gold and silver goblets that Nebuchadnezzar his father *a* had taken from the temple in Jerusalem, so that the king and his nobles, his wives and his concubines might drink from them. 3 So they brought in the gold goblets that had been taken from the temple of God in Jerusalem, and the king and his nobles, his wives and his concubines drank from them. 4 As they drank the wine, they praised the gods of gold and silver, of bronze, iron, wood and stone.

5 Suddenly the fingers of a human hand ap-

a 2 Or *ancestor;* or *predecessor;* also in verses 11, 13 and 18 peared and wrote on the plaster of the wall, near the lampstand in the royal palace. The king watched the hand as it wrote. ⁶His face turned pale and he was so frightened that his knees knocked together and his legs gave way.

⁷The king called out for the enchanters, astrologers*ᵃ* and diviners to be brought and said to these wise men of Babylon, "Whoever reads this writing and tells me what it means will be clothed in purple and have a gold chain placed around his neck, and he will be made the third highest ruler in the kingdom."

⁸Then all the king's wise men came in, but they could not read the writing or tell the king what it meant. ⁹So King Belshazzar became even more terrified and his face grew more pale. His nobles were baffled.

DANIEL 5:1–31

stories to share

The Writing on the Wall

LIFE LESSON: God punishes sinful pride.

TO TALK ABOUT

✦ What were King Belshazzar and his guests drinking from?

✦ What made the king so scared that his knees knocked together?

✦ What did the words on the wall mean? What was the king's sin?

✦ Is it ever OK to be proud? Why or why not?

¹⁰The queen,*ᵇ* hearing the voices of the king and his nobles, came into the banquet hall. "O king, live forever!" she said. "Don't be alarmed! Don't look so pale! ¹¹There is a man in your kingdom who has the spirit of the holy gods in him. In the time of your father he was found to have insight and intelligence and wisdom like that of the gods. King Nebuchadnezzar your father—your father the king, I say—appointed him chief of the magicians, enchanters, astrologers and diviners. ¹²This man Daniel, whom the king called Belteshazzar, was found to have a keen mind and knowledge and understanding, and also the ability to interpret dreams, explain riddles and solve difficult problems. Call for Daniel, and he will tell you what the writing means."

¹³So Daniel was brought before the king, and the king said to him, "Are you Daniel, one of the exiles my father the king brought from Judah? ¹⁴I have heard that the spirit of the gods is in you and that you have insight, intelligence and outstanding wisdom. ¹⁵The wise men and enchanters were brought before me to read this writing and tell me what it means, but they could not explain it. ¹⁶Now I have heard that you are able to give interpretations and to solve difficult problems. If you can read this writing and tell me what it means, you will be clothed in purple and have a gold chain placed around your neck, and you will be made the third highest ruler in the kingdom."

¹⁷Then Daniel answered the king, "You may keep your gifts for yourself and give your rewards to someone else. Nevertheless, I will read the writing for the king and tell him what it means.

¹⁸"O king, the Most High God gave your father Nebuchadnezzar sovereignty and greatness and glory and splendor. ¹⁹Because of the high position he gave him, all the peoples and nations and men of every language dreaded and feared him. Those the king wanted to put to death, he put to death; those he wanted to spare, he spared; those he wanted to promote, he promoted; and those he wanted to humble, he humbled. ²⁰But

ᵃ 7 Or Chaldeans; also in verse 11   ᵇ 10 Or queen mother

when his heart became arrogant and hardened with pride, he was deposed from his royal throne and stripped of his glory. [21] He was driven away from people and given the mind of an animal; he lived with the wild donkeys and ate grass like cattle; and his body was drenched with the dew of heaven, until he acknowledged that the Most High God is sovereign over the kingdoms of men and sets over them anyone he wishes.

[22] "But you his son,[a] O Belshazzar, have not humbled yourself, though you knew all this. [23] Instead, you have set yourself up against the Lord of heaven. You had the goblets from his temple brought to you, and you and your nobles, your wives and your concubines drank wine from them. You praised the gods of silver and gold, of bronze, iron, wood and stone, which cannot see or hear or understand. But you did not honor the God who holds in his hand your life and all your ways. [24] Therefore he sent the hand that wrote the inscription.

[25] "This is the inscription that was written:

MENE, MENE, TEKEL, PARSIN [b]

[26] "This is what these words mean:

Mene[c]: God has numbered the days of your reign and brought it to an end.

[27] *Tekel*[d]: You have been weighed on the scales and found wanting.

[28] *Peres*[e]: Your kingdom is divided and given to the Medes and Persians."

[29] Then at Belshazzar's command, Daniel was clothed in purple, a gold chain was placed around his neck, and he was proclaimed the third highest ruler in the kingdom.

[30] That very night Belshazzar, king of the Babylonians,[f] was slain, [31] and Darius the Mede took over the kingdom, at the age of sixty-two.

Daniel in the Den of Lions

6 It pleased Darius to appoint 120 satraps to rule throughout the kingdom, [2] with three administrators over them, one of whom was Daniel. The satraps were made accountable to them so that the king might not suffer loss. [3] Now Daniel so distinguished himself among the administrators and the satraps by his exceptional qualities that the king planned to set him over the whole kingdom. [4] At this, the administrators and the satraps tried to find grounds for charges against Daniel in his conduct of government affairs, but they were unable to do so. They could find no corruption in him, because he was trustworthy and neither corrupt nor negligent. [5] Finally these men said, "We will never find any basis for charges against this man Daniel unless it has something to do with the law of his God."

[6] So the administrators and the satraps went as a group to the king and said: "O King Darius, live forever! [7] The royal administrators, prefects, satraps, advisers and governors have all agreed that the king should issue an edict and enforce the decree that anyone who prays to any god or man during the next thirty days, except to you, O king, shall be thrown into the lions' den. [8] Now, O king, issue the decree and put it in writing so that it cannot be altered—in accordance with the laws of the Medes and Persians, which cannot be repealed." [9] So King Darius put the decree in writing.

[10] Now when Daniel learned that the decree had been published, he went home to his upstairs room where the windows opened toward Jerusalem. Three times a day he got down on his knees and prayed, giving thanks to his God, just as he had done before. [11] Then these men went as a group and found Daniel praying and asking God for help. [12] So they went to the king and spoke to him about his royal decree: "Did you not publish a decree that during the next thirty days anyone who prays to any god or man except to you, O king, would be thrown into the lions' den?"

---

[a] 22 Or *descendant*; or *successor*   [b] 25 Aramaic *UPARSIN* (that is, *AND PARSIN*)   [c] 26 *Mene* can mean *numbered* or *mina* (a unit of money).   [d] 27 *Tekel* can mean *weighed* or *shekel*.   [e] 28 *Peres* (the singular of *Parsin*) can mean *divided* or *Persia* or *a half mina* or *a half shekel*.   [f] 30 Or *Chaldeans*

The king answered, "The decree stands—in accordance with the laws of the Medes and Persians, which cannot be repealed."

¹³Then they said to the king, "Daniel, who is one of the exiles from Judah, pays no attention to you, O king, or to the decree you put in writing. He still prays three times a day." ¹⁴When the king heard this, he was greatly distressed; he was determined to rescue Daniel and made every effort until sundown to save him.

¹⁵Then the men went as a group to the king and said to him, "Remember, O king, that according to the law of the Medes and Persians no decree or edict that the king issues can be changed."

¹⁶So the king gave the order, and they brought Daniel and threw him into the lions' den. The king said to Daniel, "May your God, whom you serve continually, rescue you!"

¹⁷A stone was brought and placed over the mouth of the den, and the king sealed it with his own signet ring and with the rings of his nobles, so that Daniel's situation might not be changed. ¹⁸Then the king returned to his palace and spent the night without eating and without any entertainment being brought to him. And he could not sleep.

¹⁹At the first light of dawn, the king got up and hurried to the lions' den. ²⁰When he came near the den, he called to Daniel in an anguished voice, "Daniel, servant of the living God, has your God, whom you serve continually, been able to rescue you from the lions?"

²¹Daniel answered, "O king, live forever! ²²My God sent his angel, and he shut the mouths of the lions. They have not hurt me, because I was found innocent in his sight. Nor have I ever done any wrong before you, O king."

²³The king was overjoyed and gave orders to lift Daniel out of the den. And when Daniel was lifted from the den, no wound was found on him, because he had trusted in his God.

²⁴At the king's command, the men who had falsely accused Daniel were brought in and thrown into the lions' den, along with their wives and children. And before they reached the

stories to share

DANIEL 6:1–28

Daniel in the Lions' Den

LIFE LESSON: God rewards obedience and protects his own.

TO TALK ABOUT

✦ How did the royal administrators and satraps trick King Darius?

✦ Why couldn't the king protect Daniel from the lions' den?

✦ Does God sometimes allow his obedient people to be mistreated or killed?

✦ Is it still true that God rewards obedience and protects his own? Why or why not?

floor of the den, the lions overpowered them and crushed all their bones.

²⁵Then King Darius wrote to all the peoples, nations and men of every language throughout the land:

"May you prosper greatly!

²⁶"I issue a decree that in every part of my kingdom people must fear and reverence the God of Daniel.

"For he is the living God
 and he endures forever;
his kingdom will not be destroyed,
 his dominion will never end.

> NOW WHEN DANIEL LEARNED THAT THE
> DECREE HAD BEEN PUBLISHED, HE WENT
> HOME TO HIS UPSTAIRS ROOM WHERE THE
> WINDOWS OPENED TOWARD JERUSALEM.
> THREE TIMES A DAY HE GOT DOWN ON HIS
> KNEES AND PRAYED, GIVING THANKS TO
> HIS GOD, JUST AS HE HAD DONE BEFORE.
>
> *Daniel 6:10*

Pray Like Daniel

HELEN HAIDLE

READ | DANIEL 6:1 – 28

A phone call from Oma (our German grandmother) brought discouraging news: "Because of my eye problems and my knee surgery, the doctor won't let me travel anymore," she said. "I can't fly out to see you next month. In fact I can't do much of anything. Certainly can't sew or bake like I once did. I just sit around with my leg elevated, totally useless!"

The next evening Oma phoned again. "God showed me something special I can do every day—in fact, three times a day," she said cheerfully. "I can pray like Daniel—morning, noon and night. So I've made a commitment to pray for all of you three times each day."

Until the day she died five years later, Oma faithfully continued her "Daniel prayers." She knew it was her "work," an assignment from God.

Before getting out of bed each morning, she praised God, then prayed for her family and others in need. Specific prayers were said for each child and grandchild. She included her eight brothers and sisters, their children and grandchildren, praying for each one by name.

After lunch she would read her worn Bible and pray once more. At night, she prayed again.

"I'm praying down three generations," she explained. "My mother did this for her children, grandchildren and great-grandchildren. Now I'm doing the same. I hope you will too," she added. "Remember how Lois handed her faith down to Eunice and also to Timothy." (See 2 Timothy 1:5.)

Many people learned to value Oma's daily prayers. After her funeral, we all asked each other, "Who will pray for us now?"

When I left the gravesite, a new thought comforted me: Her prayers still surround us and will continue to bless us.

Thank you, dear Lord, for the privilege of intercession. You've promised to hear my prayers and answer them. Help me to never grow weary as I intercede for my family and for those in need—three times a day and three generations down. Amen.

Your next devotion is located on page 1177.

GRANDCHILD IN FOCUS • PRAYER

Relationships at Home

O Lord, I pray that you will bless the home and family of my grandchild. May the relationships she has with her parents and siblings enhance her well-being, support her self-confidence and increase her faith. May her home life reflect your love, your grace, your compassion and your peace. Guide her parents to direct her in love and truth, so she will grow into a strong and compassionate individual. Amen.

27 He rescues and he saves;
    he performs signs and wonders
      in the heavens and on the earth.
    He has rescued Daniel
      from the power of the lions."

28 So Daniel prospered during the reign of Darius and the reign of Cyrus [a] the Persian.

Daniel's Dream of Four Beasts

7 In the first year of Belshazzar king of Babylon, Daniel had a dream, and visions passed through his mind as he was lying on his bed. He wrote down the substance of his dream.

2 Daniel said: "In my vision at night I looked, and there before me were the four winds of heaven churning up the great sea. 3 Four great beasts, each different from the others, came up out of the sea.

4 "The first was like a lion, and it had the wings of an eagle. I watched until its wings were torn off and it was lifted from the ground so that it stood on two feet like a man, and the heart of a man was given to it.

5 "And there before me was a second beast, which looked like a bear. It was raised up on one of its sides, and it had three ribs in its mouth between its teeth. It was told, 'Get up and eat your fill of flesh!'

6 "After that, I looked, and there before me was another beast, one that looked like a leopard. And on its back it had four wings like those of a bird. This beast had four heads, and it was given authority to rule.

7 "After that, in my vision at night I looked, and there before me was a fourth beast — terrifying and frightening and very powerful. It had large iron teeth; it crushed and devoured its victims and trampled underfoot whatever was left. It was different from all the former beasts, and it had ten horns.

8 "While I was thinking about the horns, there before me was another horn, a little one, which came up among them; and three of the first horns were uprooted before it. This horn had eyes like the eyes of a man and a mouth that spoke boastfully.

9 "As I looked,

"thrones were set in place,
    and the Ancient of Days took his seat.
His clothing was as white as snow;
    the hair of his head was white like wool.
His throne was flaming with fire,
    and its wheels were all ablaze.
10 A river of fire was flowing,
    coming out from before him.
Thousands upon thousands attended him;
    ten thousand times ten thousand stood
      before him.
The court was seated,
    and the books were opened.

11 "Then I continued to watch because of the boastful words the horn was speaking. I kept looking until the beast was slain and its body destroyed and thrown into the blazing fire. 12 (The other beasts had been stripped of their authority, but were allowed to live for a period of time.)

13 "In my vision at night I looked, and there before me was one like a son of man, coming with the clouds of heaven. He approached the Ancient of Days and was led into his presence. 14 He was given authority, glory and sovereign power; all peoples, nations and men of every language worshiped him. His dominion is an everlasting dominion that will not pass away, and his kingdom is one that will never be destroyed.

The Interpretation of the Dream

15 "I, Daniel, was troubled in spirit, and the visions that passed through my mind disturbed me. 16 I approached one of those standing there and asked him the true meaning of all this.

"So he told me and gave me the interpretation of these things: 17 'The four great beasts are four kingdoms that will rise from the earth. 18 But the saints of the Most High will receive the kingdom and will possess it forever — yes, for ever and ever.'

---

[a] 28 Or Darius, that is, the reign of Cyrus

Yard Sale for Charity

All of us can benefit from periodically weeding out, sorting through and simplifying our "stuff." Invite your grandchildren to help in organizing and setting up a yard sale with you. Their helping hands and sturdy legs will save you from doing all the work alone. And they may have plenty of contributions from their homes as well. If their friends or your neighbors want to participate, welcome them. Arrange to have any unsold merchandise picked up by a local organization.

Talk with your grandchildren about donating the proceeds of the sale to a worthy cause. Be sure everyone agrees in advance on which particular charity you want to contribute to when the proceeds from your sale are counted up. You might feel comfortable advertising the cause, or you may prefer to keep your intended giving a matter between you and God.

Long-Distance Variation: Invite the out-of-towners to send the proceeds from their own sale to you for inclusion in the charitable offering.

O Lord, we've been blessed with so much more than we need, and yet all around us are people who lack even life's basic necessities. Fill us with the spirit of Christian charity and let this activity bring joy to our lives. Amen.

Your next devotion is located on page 1182.

GRANDCHILD IN FOCUS • PRAYER

Friends

Dear Lord and Father, I pray for my grandchild's social life and his friends. Bring diverse friends into his life who will love and encourage him, who will bring joy and laughter to the good times and comfort and support through difficulties and disappointments. Grant him wisdom and discernment as he selects his friends; help him to avoid cliques that restrict, activities that endanger, and foolish and dangerous behaviors that harm. I ask that you fill his life with close and caring relationships. Amen.

¹⁹"Then I wanted to know the true meaning of the fourth beast, which was different from all the others and most terrifying, with its iron teeth and bronze claws—the beast that crushed and devoured its victims and trampled underfoot whatever was left. ²⁰I also wanted to know about the ten horns on its head and about the other horn that came up, before which three of them fell—the horn that looked more imposing than the others and that had eyes and a mouth that spoke boastfully. ²¹As I watched, this horn was waging war against the saints and defeating them, ²²until the Ancient of Days came and pronounced judgment in favor of the saints of the Most High, and the time came when they possessed the kingdom.

²³"He gave me this explanation: 'The fourth beast is a fourth kingdom that will appear on earth. It will be different from all the other kingdoms and will devour the whole earth, trampling it down and crushing it. ²⁴The ten horns are ten kings who will come from this kingdom. After them another king will arise, different from the earlier ones; he will subdue three kings. ²⁵He will speak against the Most High and oppress his saints and try to change the set times and the laws. The saints will be handed over to him for a time, times and half a time.ᵃ

²⁶"'But the court will sit, and his power will be taken away and completely destroyed forever. ²⁷Then the sovereignty, power and greatness of the kingdoms under the whole heaven will be handed over to the saints, the people of the Most High. His kingdom will be an everlasting kingdom, and all rulers will worship and obey him.'

²⁸"This is the end of the matter. I, Daniel, was deeply troubled by my thoughts, and my face turned pale, but I kept the matter to myself."

Daniel's Vision of a Ram and a Goat

8 In the third year of King Belshazzar's reign, I, Daniel, had a vision, after the one that had already appeared to me. ²In my vision I saw myself in the citadel of Susa in the province of Elam; in the vision I was beside the Ulai Canal. ³I looked up, and there before me was a ram with two horns, standing beside the canal, and the horns were long. One of the horns was longer than the other but grew up later. ⁴I watched the ram as he charged toward the west and the north and the south. No animal could stand against him, and none could rescue from his power. He did as he pleased and became great.

⁵As I was thinking about this, suddenly a goat with a prominent horn between his eyes came from the west, crossing the whole earth without touching the ground. ⁶He came toward the two-horned ram I had seen standing beside the canal and charged at him in great rage. ⁷I saw him attack the ram furiously, striking the ram and shattering his two horns. The ram was powerless to stand against him; the goat knocked him to the ground and trampled on him, and none could rescue the ram from his power. ⁸The goat became very great, but at the height of his power his large horn was broken off, and in its place four prominent horns grew up toward the four winds of heaven.

⁹Out of one of them came another horn, which started small but grew in power to the south and to the east and toward the Beautiful Land. ¹⁰It grew until it reached the host of the heavens, and it threw some of the starry host down to the earth and trampled on them. ¹¹It set itself up to be as great as the Prince of the host; it took away the daily sacrifice from him, and the place of his sanctuary was brought low. ¹²Because of rebellion, the host ⌐of the saints⌐ᵇ and the daily sacrifice were given over to it. It prospered in everything it did, and truth was thrown to the ground.

¹³Then I heard a holy one speaking, and another holy one said to him, "How long will it take for the vision to be fulfilled—the vision concerning the daily sacrifice, the rebellion that causes desolation, and the surrender of the sanctuary and of the host that will be trampled underfoot?"

¹⁴He said to me, "It will take 2,300 evenings

ᵃ 25 Or for a year, two years and half a year   ᵇ 12 Or rebellion, the armies and mornings; then the sanctuary will be reconsecrated."

The Interpretation of the Vision

¹⁵While I, Daniel, was watching the vision and trying to understand it, there before me stood one who looked like a man. ¹⁶And I heard a man's voice from the Ulai calling, "Gabriel, tell this man the meaning of the vision."

¹⁷As he came near the place where I was standing, I was terrified and fell prostrate. "Son of man," he said to me, "understand that the vision concerns the time of the end."

¹⁸While he was speaking to me, I was in a deep sleep, with my face to the ground. Then he touched me and raised me to my feet.

¹⁹He said: "I am going to tell you what will happen later in the time of wrath, because the vision concerns the appointed time of the end.ᵃ ²⁰The two-horned ram that you saw represents the kings of Media and Persia. ²¹The shaggy goat is the king of Greece, and the large horn between his eyes is the first king. ²²The four horns that replaced the one that was broken off represent four kingdoms that will emerge from his nation but will not have the same power.

²³"In the latter part of their reign, when rebels have become completely wicked, a stern-faced king, a master of intrigue, will arise. ²⁴He will become very strong, but not by his own power. He will cause astounding devastation and will succeed in whatever he does. He will destroy the mighty men and the holy people. ²⁵He will cause deceit to prosper, and he will consider himself superior. When they feel secure, he will destroy many and take his stand against the Prince of princes. Yet he will be destroyed, but not by human power.

²⁶"The vision of the evenings and mornings that has been given you is true, but seal up the vision, for it concerns the distant future."

²⁷I, Daniel, was exhausted and lay ill for several days. Then I got up and went about the king's business. I was appalled by the vision; it was beyond understanding.

Daniel's Prayer

9 In the first year of Darius son of Xerxesᵇ (a Mede by descent), who was made ruler over the Babylonianᶜ kingdom— ²in the first year of his reign, I, Daniel, understood from the Scriptures, according to the word of the LORD given to Jeremiah the prophet, that the desolation of Jerusalem would last seventy years. ³So I turned to the Lord God and pleaded with him in prayer and petition, in fasting, and in sackcloth and ashes.

⁴I prayed to the LORD my God and confessed:

"O Lord, the great and awesome God, who keeps his covenant of love with all who love him and obey his commands, ⁵we have sinned and done wrong. We have been wicked and have rebelled; we have turned away from your commands and laws. ⁶We have not listened to your servants the prophets, who spoke in your name to our kings, our princes and our fathers, and to all the people of the land.

⁷"Lord, you are righteous, but this day we are covered with shame—the men of Judah and people of Jerusalem and all Israel, both near and far, in all the countries where you have scattered us because of our unfaithfulness to you. ⁸O LORD, we and our kings, our princes and our fathers are covered with

---

ᵃ 19 Or because the end will be at the appointed time   ᵇ 1 Hebrew Ahasuerus   ᶜ 1 Or Chaldean

TALKING POINTS

Rebellion

God forgives the rebellion of a repentant person.

DANIEL 9:4–10

For more on rebellion, go to Luke 15:11–20.

shame because we have sinned against you. [9]The Lord our God is merciful and forgiving, even though we have rebelled against him; [10]we have not obeyed the LORD our God or kept the laws he gave us through his servants the prophets. [11]All Israel has transgressed your law and turned away, refusing to obey you.

PRAYING THE SCRIPTURES

Forgiveness

DANIEL 9:9

Even though we have all rebelled against you, Lord, I praise you because you are merciful and forgiving.

Next prayer in Forgiveness Prayer Track: Micah 7:18–19

"Therefore the curses and sworn judgments written in the Law of Moses, the servant of God, have been poured out on us, because we have sinned against you. [12]You have fulfilled the words spoken against us and against our rulers by bringing upon us great disaster. Under the whole heaven nothing has ever been done like what has been done to Jerusalem. [13]Just as it is written in the Law of Moses, all this disaster has come upon us, yet we have not sought the favor of the LORD our God by turning from our sins and giving attention to your truth. [14]The LORD did not hesitate to bring the disaster upon us, for the LORD our God is righteous in everything he does; yet we have not obeyed him.

[15]"Now, O Lord our God, who brought your people out of Egypt with a mighty hand and who made for yourself a name that endures to this day, we have sinned, we have done wrong. [16]O Lord, in keeping with all your righteous acts, turn away your anger and your wrath from Jerusalem, your city, your holy hill. Our sins and the iniquities of our fathers have made Jerusalem and your people an object of scorn to all those around us.

[17]"Now, our God, hear the prayers and petitions of your servant. For your sake, O Lord, look with favor on your desolate sanctuary. [18]Give ear, O God, and hear; open your eyes and see the desolation of the city that bears your Name. We do not make requests of you because we are righteous, but because of your great mercy. [19]O Lord, listen! O Lord, forgive! O Lord, hear and act! For your sake, O my God, do not delay, because your city and your people bear your Name."

The Seventy "Sevens"

[20]While I was speaking and praying, confessing my sin and the sin of my people Israel and making my request to the LORD my God for his holy hill— [21]while I was still in prayer, Gabriel, the man I had seen in the earlier vision, came to me in swift flight about the time of the evening sacrifice. [22]He instructed me and said to me, "Daniel, I have now come to give you insight and understanding. [23]As soon as you began to pray, an answer was given, which I have come to tell you, for you are highly esteemed. Therefore, consider the message and understand the vision:

[24]"Seventy 'sevens'[a] are decreed for your people and your holy city to finish[b] transgression, to put an end to sin, to atone for wickedness, to bring in everlasting righteousness, to seal up vision and prophecy and to anoint the most holy.[c]

[25]"Know and understand this: From the issuing of the decree[d] to restore and rebuild Jerusalem until the Anointed One,[e] the ruler, comes, there will be seven 'sevens,' and sixty-two 'sevens.' It will be rebuilt with streets and a trench, but in times of trouble. [26]After the sixty-two 'sevens,'

---

[a] 24 Or *'weeks'*; also in verses 25 and 26   [b] 24 Or *restrain*
[c] 24 Or *Most Holy Place*; or *most holy One*   [d] 25 Or *word*
[e] 25 Or *an anointed one*; also in verse 26

the Anointed One will be cut off and will have nothing.[a] The people of the ruler who will come will destroy the city and the sanctuary. The end will come like a flood: War will continue until the end, and desolations have been decreed. 27He will confirm a covenant with many for one 'seven.'[b] In the middle of the 'seven'[b] he will put an end to sacrifice and offering. And on a wing ⌞of the temple⌟ he will set up an abomination that causes desolation, until the end that is decreed is poured out on him.[c]"[d]

Daniel's Vision of a Man

10 In the third year of Cyrus king of Persia, a revelation was given to Daniel (who was called Belteshazzar). Its message was true and it concerned a great war.[e] The understanding of the message came to him in a vision.

2At that time I, Daniel, mourned for three weeks. 3I ate no choice food; no meat or wine touched my lips; and I used no lotions at all until the three weeks were over.

4On the twenty-fourth day of the first month, as I was standing on the bank of the great river, the Tigris, 5I looked up and there before me was a man dressed in linen, with a belt of the finest gold around his waist. 6His body was like chrysolite, his face like lightning, his eyes like flaming torches, his arms and legs like the gleam of burnished bronze, and his voice like the sound of a multitude.

7I, Daniel, was the only one who saw the vision; the men with me did not see it, but such terror overwhelmed them that they fled and hid themselves. 8So I was left alone, gazing at this great vision; I had no strength left, my face turned deathly pale and I was helpless. 9Then I heard him speaking, and as I listened to him, I fell into a deep sleep, my face to the ground.

10A hand touched me and set me trembling on my hands and knees. 11He said, "Daniel, you who are highly esteemed, consider carefully the words I am about to speak to you, and stand up, for I have now been sent to you." And when he said this to me, I stood up trembling.

12Then he continued, "Do not be afraid, Daniel. Since the first day that you set your mind to gain understanding and to humble yourself before your God, your words were heard, and I have come in response to them. 13But the prince of the Persian kingdom resisted me twenty-one days. Then Michael, one of the chief princes, came to help me, because I was detained there with the king of Persia. 14Now I have come to explain to you what will happen to your people in the future, for the vision concerns a time yet to come."

15While he was saying this to me, I bowed with my face toward the ground and was speechless. 16Then one who looked like a man[f] touched my lips, and I opened my mouth and began to speak. I said to the one standing before me, "I am overcome with anguish because of the vision, my lord, and I am helpless. 17How can I, your servant, talk with you, my lord? My strength is gone and I can hardly breathe."

18Again the one who looked like a man touched me and gave me strength. 19"Do not be afraid, O man highly esteemed," he said. "Peace! Be strong now; be strong."

When he spoke to me, I was strengthened and said, "Speak, my lord, since you have given me strength."

20So he said, "Do you know why I have come to you? Soon I will return to fight against the prince of Persia, and when I go, the prince of Greece will come; 21but first I will tell you what is written in the Book of Truth. (No one supports me against

11 them except Michael, your prince. 1And in the first year of Darius the Mede, I took my stand to support and protect him.)

The Kings of the South and the North

2"Now then, I tell you the truth: Three more kings will appear in Persia, and then a fourth, who will be far richer than all the others. When

<hr/>

a 26 Or off and will have no one; or off, but not for himself
b 27 Or 'week'   c 27 Or it   d 27 Or And one who causes desolation will come upon the pinnacle of the abominable ⌞temple⌟, until the end that is decreed is poured out on the desolated ⌞city⌟,
e 1 Or true and burdensome   f 16 Most manuscripts of the Masoretic Text; one manuscript of the Masoretic Text, Dead Sea Scrolls and Septuagint Then something that looked like a man's hand

Worship the Lord

Come, let us sing for joy to the LORD;
    let us shout aloud to the Rock of our salvation.
Let us come before him with thanksgiving
    and extol him with music and song.

For the LORD is the great God,
    the great King above all gods.
In his hand are the depths of the earth,
    and the mountain peaks belong to him.
The sea is his, for he made it,
    and his hands formed the dry land.

Come, let us bow down in worship,
    let us kneel before the LORD our Maker;
for he is our God
    and we are the people of his
        pasture,
    the flock under his care.

Psalm 95:1 – 7a

God of glory, you are present in the darkest cave, on the mountain summit, in the deepest ocean and on the desert sand. Be present to me. I bow to worship you. I fall to my knees in wonder of you. For you are my God, the great God who claims me as one of his own children. Amen.

Your next devotion is located on page 1185.

GRANDCHILD IN FOCUS • PRAYER

Self-Image

O loving God, I praise you for creating my grandchild as a unique individual. Now I ask you to help her appreciate her uniqueness. Build up her self-image so she can enjoy her individuality. Help her to stand firm for who she is, where she has come from and what she believes in. Encourage her not only to have hopes and dreams but to also enjoy each day as it comes.
In Jesus' name, amen.

he has gained power by his wealth, he will stir up everyone against the kingdom of Greece. [3] Then a mighty king will appear, who will rule with great power and do as he pleases. [4] After he has appeared, his empire will be broken up and parceled out toward the four winds of heaven. It will not go to his descendants, nor will it have the power he exercised, because his empire will be uprooted and given to others.

[5] "The king of the South will become strong, but one of his commanders will become even stronger than he and will rule his own kingdom with great power. [6] After some years, they will become allies. The daughter of the king of the South will go to the king of the North to make an alliance, but she will not retain her power, and he and his power[a] will not last. In those days she will be handed over, together with her royal escort and her father[b] and the one who supported her.

[7] "One from her family line will arise to take her place. He will attack the forces of the king of the North and enter his fortress; he will fight against them and be victorious. [8] He will also seize their gods, their metal images and their valuable articles of silver and gold and carry them off to Egypt. For some years he will leave the king of the North alone. [9] Then the king of the North will invade the realm of the king of the South but will retreat to his own country. [10] His sons will prepare for war and assemble a great army, which will sweep on like an irresistible flood and carry the battle as far as his fortress.

[11] "Then the king of the South will march out in a rage and fight against the king of the North, who will raise a large army, but it will be defeated. [12] When the army is carried off, the king of the South will be filled with pride and will slaughter many thousands, yet he will not remain triumphant. [13] For the king of the North will muster another army, larger than the first; and after several years, he will advance with a huge army fully equipped.

[14] "In those times many will rise against the king of the South. The violent men among your own people will rebel in fulfillment of the vision, but without success. [15] Then the king of the North will come and build up siege ramps and will capture a fortified city. The forces of the South will be powerless to resist; even their best troops will not have the strength to stand. [16] The invader will do as he pleases; no one will be able to stand against him. He will establish himself in the Beautiful Land and will have the power to destroy it. [17] He will determine to come with the might of his entire kingdom and will make an alliance with the king of the South. And he will give him a daughter in marriage in order to overthrow the kingdom, but his plans[c] will not succeed or help him. [18] Then he will turn his attention to the coastlands and will take many of them, but a commander will put an end to his insolence and will turn his insolence back upon him. [19] After this, he will turn back toward the fortresses of his own country but will stumble and fall, to be seen no more.

[20] "His successor will send out a tax collector to maintain the royal splendor. In a few years, however, he will be destroyed, yet not in anger or in battle.

[21] "He will be succeeded by a contemptible person who has not been given the honor of royalty. He will invade the kingdom when its people feel secure, and he will seize it through intrigue. [22] Then an overwhelming army will be swept away before him; both it and a prince of the covenant will be destroyed. [23] After coming to an agreement with him, he will act deceitfully, and with only a few people he will rise to power. [24] When the richest provinces feel secure, he will invade them and will achieve what neither his fathers nor his forefathers did. He will distribute plunder, loot and wealth among his followers. He will plot the overthrow of fortresses—but only for a time.

[25] "With a large army he will stir up his strength and courage against the king of the South. The king of the South will wage war with a large and very powerful army, but he will not be able to

---

[a] 6 Or offspring   [b] 6 Or child (see Vulgate and Syriac)
[c] 17 Or but she

stand because of the plots devised against him. 26 Those who eat from the king's provisions will try to destroy him; his army will be swept away, and many will fall in battle. 27 The two kings, with their hearts bent on evil, will sit at the same table and lie to each other, but to no avail, because an end will still come at the appointed time. 28 The king of the North will return to his own country with great wealth, but his heart will be set against the holy covenant. He will take action against it and then return to his own country.

29 "At the appointed time he will invade the South again, but this time the outcome will be different from what it was before. 30 Ships of the western coastlands *a* will oppose him, and he will lose heart. Then he will turn back and vent his fury against the holy covenant. He will return and show favor to those who forsake the holy covenant.

31 "His armed forces will rise up to desecrate the temple fortress and will abolish the daily sacrifice. Then they will set up the abomination that causes desolation. 32 With flattery he will corrupt those who have violated the covenant, but the people who know their God will firmly resist him.

33 "Those who are wise will instruct many, though for a time they will fall by the sword or be burned or captured or plundered. 34 When they fall, they will receive a little help, and many who are not sincere will join them. 35 Some of the wise will stumble, so that they may be refined, purified and made spotless until the time of the end, for it will still come at the appointed time.

The King Who Exalts Himself

36 "The king will do as he pleases. He will exalt and magnify himself above every god and will say unheard-of things against the God of gods. He will be successful until the time of wrath is completed, for what has been determined must take place. 37 He will show no regard for the gods of his fathers or for the one desired by women, nor will he regard any god, but will exalt himself above them all. 38 Instead of them, he will honor a god of fortresses; a god unknown to his fathers he will honor with gold and silver, with precious stones and costly gifts. 39 He will attack the mightiest fortresses with the help of a foreign god and will greatly honor those who acknowledge him. He will make them rulers over many people and will distribute the land at a price. *b*

40 "At the time of the end the king of the South will engage him in battle, and the king of the North will storm out against him with chariots and cavalry and a great fleet of ships. He will invade many countries and sweep through them like a flood. 41 He will also invade the Beautiful Land. Many countries will fall, but Edom, Moab and the leaders of Ammon will be delivered from his hand. 42 He will extend his power over many countries; Egypt will not escape. 43 He will gain control of the treasures of gold and silver and all the riches of Egypt, with the Libyans and Nubians in submission. 44 But reports from the east and the north will alarm him, and he will set out in a great rage to destroy and annihilate many. 45 He will pitch his royal tents between the seas at *c* the beautiful holy mountain. Yet he will come to his end, and no one will help him.

The End Times

12 "At that time Michael, the great prince who protects your people, will arise. There will be a time of distress such as has not happened from the beginning of nations until then. But at that time your people — everyone whose name is found written in the book — will be delivered. 2 Multitudes who sleep in the dust of the earth will awake: some to everlasting life, others to shame and everlasting contempt. 3 Those who are wise *d* will shine like the brightness of the heavens, and those who lead many to righteousness, like the stars for ever and ever. 4 But you, Daniel, close up and seal the words of the scroll until the time of the end. Many will go here and there to increase knowledge."

5 Then I, Daniel, looked, and there before me stood two others, one on this bank of the river

a 30 Hebrew of Kittim   *b 39 Or land for a reward*   *c 45 Or the sea and*   *d 3 Or who impart wisdom*

"THOSE WHO ARE WISE WILL SHINE
LIKE THE BRIGHTNESS OF THE
HEAVENS, AND THOSE WHO LEAD
MANY TO RIGHTEOUSNESS, LIKE
THE STARS FOR EVER AND EVER."

Daniel 12:3

The Wise Shine

CHARLOTTE STEMPLE

READ | DANIEL 12:1–13

When I was a missionary in Vietnam, a missionary friend and I were invited by a Korean general to an important military ceremony. The only women amidst thousands of Korean, Vietnamese and American troops, we sat on the reviewing stand with the three nation's generals to watch the elaborate ceremonies.

Thoroughly mystified as to why we had been invited, we were conducted to the general's mess where we ate a sumptuous meal on crested china and gold-plated flatware.

Finally, at the end of the meal, the Korean general called for his interpreter and said to me, "I am sure you are wondering why I invited you here today!" He continued with this remarkable comment: "When I was a small boy in Korea, an American lady missionary led me to Jesus Christ, and I never had the opportunity to thank her. So wherever I go, I look up missionaries and honor them!"

There are no doubt many who have illuminated our paths through this life. As we are obedient to God's command, there will be those whose lives we may brighten. Let your light so shine!

So many people have illumined my path, Lord, that I cannot even count them. I honor them in your name, and I thank you for the blessing they have been to me. If there is someone whose life I can brighten, Lord, show me their need, and allow me to shine on them as they continue their path to you.

Your next devotion is located on page 1189.

GRANDCHILD IN FOCUS · PRAYER

Protection From Worldliness

O Sovereign Lord, the world surrounds my grandchild, pressing in and tempting him in so many ways. Help him set appropriate limits. Give him sound judgment to choose wisely. Guard him from temptation; protect him from physical and mental predators; lead him into paths of righteousness and light. And reassure me with your promise that you are holding him in your hands. Amen.

and one on the opposite bank. ⁶One of them said to the man clothed in linen, who was above the waters of the river, "How long will it be before these astonishing things are fulfilled?"

⁷The man clothed in linen, who was above the waters of the river, lifted his right hand and his left hand toward heaven, and I heard him swear by him who lives forever, saying, "It will be for a time, times and half a time.ᵃ When the power of the holy people has been finally broken, all these things will be completed."

⁸I heard, but I did not understand. So I asked, "My lord, what will the outcome of all this be?"

⁹He replied, "Go your way, Daniel, because the words are closed up and sealed until the time of the end. ¹⁰Many will be purified, made spotless and refined, but the wicked will continue to be wicked. None of the wicked will understand, but those who are wise will understand.

¹¹"From the time that the daily sacrifice is abolished and the abomination that causes desolation is set up, there will be 1,290 days. ¹²Blessed is the one who waits for and reaches the end of the 1,335 days.

¹³"As for you, go your way till the end. You will rest, and then at the end of the days you will rise to receive your allotted inheritance."

ᵃ 7 Or *a year, two years and half a year*

Staying FAITHFUL

The marital life of the prophet Hosea, who prophesied during a time of materialism and spiritual decay in the northern kingdom of Israel, is the focus for this short book that bears his name. Under God's direction, Hosea married Gomer, an adulterous woman (see Hosea 1:2). Eventually, after Gomer had either become a slave or sold herself into prostitution, Hosea purchased her freedom and brought her back home (see Hosea 3:1–3). Though her adultery was grounds for divorce, God told Hosea to offer her forgiveness.

Hosea was told to record his marital experiences because his marriage to Gomer mirrored the relationship between God and his unfaithful "wife" (Israel). Despite God's repeated calls for his people to repent and return to him, Israel remained unfaithful. The people's "spiritual adultery" brought them terrible suffering, yet God remained committed to them. He promised Israel that, like Hosea did for Gomer, he would bring them home someday to his Messianic kingdom (see Hosea 3:4–5).

Hosea may have prophesied his message many years ago, but the lessons to be learned from it are timeless. Perhaps you have a spiritually wayward child or grandchild within your family. God's message to us through Hosea is to remain faithful to them, even when they have turned away from us. As God is faithful in his love to us, so we should be faithful in our love to others, confident that God has good plans for our lives.

VERSE *to* REMEMBER | HOSEA 3:1

The LORD said to me, "Go, show your love to your wife again, though she is loved by another and is an adulteress. Love her as the LORD loves the Israelites, though they turn to other gods and love the sacred raisin cakes."

ABOUT HOSEA

WRITTEN BY:
The prophet Hosea

WRITTEN FOR:
Primarily for the people of the northern kingdom of Israel, but also for the people of Judah

DATE WRITTEN:
Though most of Hosea's ministry took place in Israel prior to its fall in 722 B.C., his prophecies were likely recorded in Judah shortly thereafter.

WHY WRITTEN:
To warn the people of Israel and Judah that their unfaithfulness to God would result in punishment unless they sought his loving forgiveness

1

The word of the Lord that came to Hosea son of Beeri during the reigns of Uzziah, Jotham, Ahaz and Hezekiah, kings of Judah, and during the reign of Jeroboam son of Jehoash[a] king of Israel:

Hosea's Wife and Children

2 When the Lord began to speak through Hosea, the Lord said to him, "Go, take to yourself an adulterous wife and children of unfaithfulness, because the land is guilty of the vilest adultery in departing from the Lord." 3 So he married Gomer daughter of Diblaim, and she conceived and bore him a son.

4 Then the Lord said to Hosea, "Call him Jezreel, because I will soon punish the house of Jehu for the massacre at Jezreel, and I will put an end to the kingdom of Israel. 5 In that day I will break Israel's bow in the Valley of Jezreel."

6 Gomer conceived again and gave birth to a daughter. Then the Lord said to Hosea, "Call her Lo-Ruhamah,[b] for I will no longer show love to the house of Israel, that I should at all forgive them. 7 Yet I will show love to the house of Judah; and I will save them — not by bow, sword or battle, or by horses and horsemen, but by the Lord their God."

8 After she had weaned Lo-Ruhamah, Gomer had another son. 9 Then the Lord said, "Call him Lo-Ammi,[c] for you are not my people, and I am not your God.

10 "Yet the Israelites will be like the sand on the seashore, which cannot be measured or counted. In the place where it was said to them, 'You are not my people,' they will be called 'sons of the living God.' 11 The people of Judah and the people of Israel will be reunited, and they will appoint one leader and will come up out of the land, for great will be the day of Jezreel.

2

"Say of your brothers, 'My people,' and of your sisters, 'My loved one.'

Israel Punished and Restored

2 "Rebuke your mother, rebuke her,
    for she is not my wife,
    and I am not her husband.

Let her remove the adulterous look from her
        face
    and the unfaithfulness from between her
        breasts.
3 Otherwise I will strip her naked
    and make her as bare as on the day she was
        born;
I will make her like a desert,
    turn her into a parched land,
    and slay her with thirst.
4 I will not show my love to her children,
    because they are the children of adultery.
5 Their mother has been unfaithful
    and has conceived them in disgrace.
She said, 'I will go after my lovers,
    who give me my food and my water,
    my wool and my linen, my oil and my
        drink.'
6 Therefore I will block her path with
        thornbushes;
    I will wall her in so that she cannot find
        her way.
7 She will chase after her lovers but not catch
        them;
    she will look for them but not find them.
Then she will say,
    'I will go back to my husband as at first,
    for then I was better off than now.'
8 She has not acknowledged that I was the one
    who gave her the grain, the new wine and
        oil,
who lavished on her the silver and gold —
    which they used for Baal.

9 "Therefore I will take away my grain when it
        ripens,
    and my new wine when it is ready.
I will take back my wool and my linen,
    intended to cover her nakedness.
10 So now I will expose her lewdness
    before the eyes of her lovers;
    no one will take her out of my hands.
11 I will stop all her celebrations:
    her yearly festivals, her New Moons,

---

a 1 Hebrew Joash, a variant of Jehoash   b 6 Lo-Ruhamah means not loved.   c 9 Lo-Ammi means not my people.

WHEN THE LORD BEGAN TO SPEAK THROUGH
HOSEA, THE LORD SAID TO HIM, "GO,
TAKE TO YOURSELF AN ADULTEROUS WIFE
AND CHILDREN OF UNFAITHFULNESS,
BECAUSE THE LAND IS GUILTY OF THE VILEST
ADULTERY IN DEPARTING FROM THE LORD."

Hosea 1:2

Loving the Extra Child

DONNA HUISJEN

READ | HOSEA 1:1 — 2:1

God instructed Hosea to do the seemingly impossible: accept and love an adulterous woman as his wife, and accept her children. The first child was Hosea's (see Hosea 1:3). Who fathered the other two is questionable (see Hosea 1:6,8).

Many of us have a similar challenge in accepting and nurturing "grandchildren" who are not related to us. We may have stepgrandchildren, foster grandchildren or adopted grandchildren.

Who are these children to us? How should we care for them? God answers this question for us. All children are God's children, and Jesus reminds us to welcome them: "Whoever welcomes one of these little children in my name welcomes me" (Mark 9:37).

I have an "additional" grandchild. My daughter's children live with her ex-husband. He also has a son, Dakota, by another relationship. Although I am fortunate to still see my grandchildren, I struggle with my feelings for Dakota. How can I love him in the same way or similarly to how I love my daughter's children?

My head may not be able to figure it all out, but my heart can overcome it. All children need love, acceptance and attention. Everyone wants to belong to a family. The psalmist reminds us that "God sets the lonely in families" (Psalm 68:6). I've learned that, like the word "neighbor" in Luke 10:25 – 37, "family" is a fluid term in God's vocabulary. As Christians we can love all our grandchildren with God's help. We have been instructed: "Since God so loved us, we also ought to love one another" (1 John 4:11).

With God's grace, I can show love. Perhaps by continually expressing actions of love to Dakota and any other "additional" grandchildren who come into my life, my heart will be unable to distinguish between them.

Creator of all, you who knits together each child in its mother's womb, help me to embrace each little one in my family with equal enthusiasm and commitment. Amen.

Your next devotion is located on page 1202.

GRANDCHILD IN FOCUS • PRAYER

Respect for Authority

Dear Lord, I pray that my grandchild will continually grow to respect those in authority. May she learn to be cooperative and fair in work and play. Instill in her a high regard for officials who govern our land and enforce the laws. May her relationships with parents, teachers, coaches, mentors and bosses be respectful, admirable, constructive and caring. Amen.

her Sabbath days—all her appointed
feasts.
¹² I will ruin her vines and her fig trees,
which she said were her pay from her
lovers;
I will make them a thicket,
and wild animals will devour them.
¹³ I will punish her for the days
she burned incense to the Baals;
she decked herself with rings and jewelry,
and went after her lovers,
but me she forgot,"
declares the LORD.

¹⁴ "Therefore I am now going to allure her;
I will lead her into the desert
and speak tenderly to her.
¹⁵ There I will give her back her vineyards,
and will make the Valley of Achor[a] a door
of hope.
There she will sing[b] as in the days of her
youth,
as in the day she came up out of Egypt.

¹⁶ "In that day," declares the LORD,
"you will call me 'my husband';
you will no longer call me 'my master.'[c]
¹⁷ I will remove the names of the Baals from her
lips;
no longer will their names be invoked.
¹⁸ In that day I will make a covenant for them
with the beasts of the field and the birds of
the air
and the creatures that move along the
ground.
Bow and sword and battle
I will abolish from the land,
so that all may lie down in safety.
¹⁹ I will betroth you to me forever;
I will betroth you in[d] righteousness and
justice,
in[e] love and compassion.
²⁰ I will betroth you in faithfulness,
and you will acknowledge the LORD.

²¹ "In that day I will respond,"
declares the LORD—

"I will respond to the skies,
and they will respond to the earth;
²² and the earth will respond to the grain,
the new wine and oil,
and they will respond to Jezreel.[f]
²³ I will plant her for myself in the land;
I will show my love to the one I called 'Not
my loved one.'[g]
I will say to those called 'Not my people,'[h]
'You are my people';
and they will say, 'You are my God.' "

Hosea's Reconciliation With His Wife

3 The LORD said to me, "Go, show your love
to your wife again, though she is loved by another and is an adulteress. Love her as the LORD
loves the Israelites, though they turn to other
gods and love the sacred raisin cakes."

² So I bought her for fifteen shekels[i] of silver
and about a homer and a lethek[j] of barley. ³ Then
I told her, "You are to live with[k] me many days;
you must not be a prostitute or be intimate with
any man, and I will live with[k] you."

⁴ For the Israelites will live many days without
king or prince, without sacrifice or sacred stones,
without ephod or idol. ⁵ Afterward the Israelites
will return and seek the LORD their God and David their king. They will come trembling to the
LORD and to his blessings in the last days.

The Charge Against Israel

4 Hear the word of the LORD, you Israelites,
because the LORD has a charge to bring
against you who live in the land:
"There is no faithfulness, no love,
no acknowledgment of God in the land.
² There is only cursing,[l] lying and murder,
stealing and adultery;
they break all bounds,
and bloodshed follows bloodshed.

---

^a 15 *Achor* means *trouble.*   ^b 15 Or *respond*   ^c 16 Hebrew *baal*
^d 19 Or *with*; also in verse 20   ^e 19 Or *with*   ^f 22 *Jezreel* means
God plants.   ^g 23 Hebrew *Lo-Ruhamah*   ^h 23 Hebrew *Lo-
Ammi*   ⁱ 2 That is, about 6 ounces (about 170 grams)   ^j 2 That
is, probably about 10 bushels (about 330 liters)   ^k 3 Or *wait for*
^l 2 That is, to pronounce a curse upon

³ Because of this the land mourns, *a*
  and all who live in it waste away;
the beasts of the field and the birds of the air
  and the fish of the sea are dying.

⁴ "But let no man bring a charge,
  let no man accuse another,
for your people are like those
  who bring charges against a priest.
⁵ You stumble day and night,
  and the prophets stumble with you.
So I will destroy your mother—
⁶   my people are destroyed from lack of
      knowledge.

"Because you have rejected knowledge,
  I also reject you as my priests;
because you have ignored the law of your
      God,
  I also will ignore your children.
⁷ The more the priests increased,
  the more they sinned against me;
they exchanged *b* their *c* Glory for
      something disgraceful.
⁸ They feed on the sins of my people
  and relish their wickedness.
⁹ And it will be: Like people, like priests.
  I will punish both of them for their ways
  and repay them for their deeds.

¹⁰ "They will eat but not have enough;
  they will engage in prostitution but not
      increase,
because they have deserted the LORD
  to give themselves ¹¹to prostitution,
to old wine and new,
  which take away the understanding ¹²of
      my people.
They consult a wooden idol
  and are answered by a stick of wood.
A spirit of prostitution leads them astray;
  they are unfaithful to their God.
¹³ They sacrifice on the mountaintops
  and burn offerings on the hills,
under oak, poplar and terebinth,
  where the shade is pleasant.

Therefore your daughters turn to
      prostitution
  and your daughters-in-law to adultery.

¹⁴ "I will not punish your daughters
  when they turn to prostitution,
nor your daughters-in-law
  when they commit adultery,
because the men themselves consort with
      harlots
  and sacrifice with shrine prostitutes—
a people without understanding will come
      to ruin!

¹⁵ "Though you commit adultery, O Israel,
  let not Judah become guilty.

"Do not go to Gilgal;
  do not go up to Beth Aven. *d*
  And do not swear, 'As surely as the LORD
      lives!'
¹⁶ The Israelites are stubborn,
  like a stubborn heifer.
How then can the LORD pasture them
  like lambs in a meadow?
¹⁷ Ephraim is joined to idols;
  leave him alone!
¹⁸ Even when their drinks are gone,
  they continue their prostitution;
  their rulers dearly love shameful ways.
¹⁹ A whirlwind will sweep them away,
  and their sacrifices will bring them
      shame.

Judgment Against Israel

5 "Hear this, you priests!
  Pay attention, you Israelites!
Listen, O royal house!
  This judgment is against you:
You have been a snare at Mizpah,
  a net spread out on Tabor.
² The rebels are deep in slaughter.
  I will discipline all of them.

---

a 3 Or *dries up*   *b* 7 Syriac and an ancient Hebrew scribal
tradition; Masoretic Text *I will exchange*   *c* 7 Masoretic Text; an
ancient Hebrew scribal tradition *my*   *d* 15 *Beth Aven* means *house
of wickedness* (a name for Bethel, which means *house of God*).

³I know all about Ephraim;
  Israel is not hidden from me.
Ephraim, you have now turned to prostitution;
  Israel is corrupt.

⁴"Their deeds do not permit them
  to return to their God.
A spirit of prostitution is in their heart;
  they do not acknowledge the LORD.
⁵Israel's arrogance testifies against them;
  the Israelites, even Ephraim, stumble in
    their sin;
  Judah also stumbles with them.
⁶When they go with their flocks and herds
  to seek the LORD,
they will not find him;
  he has withdrawn himself from them.
⁷They are unfaithful to the LORD;
  they give birth to illegitimate children.
Now their New Moon festivals
  will devour them and their fields.

⁸"Sound the trumpet in Gibeah,
  the horn in Ramah.
Raise the battle cry in Beth Aven ᵃ;
  lead on, O Benjamin.
⁹Ephraim will be laid waste
  on the day of reckoning.
Among the tribes of Israel
  I proclaim what is certain.
¹⁰Judah's leaders are like those
  who move boundary stones.
I will pour out my wrath on them
  like a flood of water.
¹¹Ephraim is oppressed,
  trampled in judgment,
  intent on pursuing idols. ᵇ
¹²I am like a moth to Ephraim,
  like rot to the people of Judah.

¹³"When Ephraim saw his sickness,
  and Judah his sores,
then Ephraim turned to Assyria,
  and sent to the great king for help.
But he is not able to cure you,
  not able to heal your sores.

¹⁴For I will be like a lion to Ephraim,
  like a great lion to Judah.
I will tear them to pieces and go away;
  I will carry them off, with no one to rescue
    them.
¹⁵Then I will go back to my place
  until they admit their guilt.
And they will seek my face;
  in their misery they will earnestly seek me."

Israel Unrepentant

6 "Come, let us return to the LORD.
  He has torn us to pieces
    but he will heal us;
  he has injured us
    but he will bind up our wounds.
²After two days he will revive us;
  on the third day he will restore us,
  that we may live in his presence.
³Let us acknowledge the LORD;
  let us press on to acknowledge him.
As surely as the sun rises,
  he will appear;
he will come to us like the winter rains,
  like the spring rains that water the earth."

⁴"What can I do with you, Ephraim?
  What can I do with you, Judah?
Your love is like the morning mist,
  like the early dew that disappears.
⁵Therefore I cut you in pieces with my
    prophets,
  I killed you with the words of my mouth;
  my judgments flashed like lightning upon
    you.
⁶For I desire mercy, not sacrifice,
  and acknowledgment of God rather than
    burnt offerings.
⁷Like Adam, ᶜ they have broken the
    covenant—
  they were unfaithful to me there.
⁸Gilead is a city of wicked men,
  stained with footprints of blood.

ᵃ 8 *Beth Aven* means *house of wickedness* (a name for Bethel, which means *house of God*).   ᵇ 11 The meaning of the Hebrew for this word is uncertain.   ᶜ 7 Or *As at Adam;* or *Like men*

9 As marauders lie in ambush for a man,
 so do bands of priests;
they murder on the road to Shechem,
 committing shameful crimes.
10 I have seen a horrible thing
 in the house of Israel.
There Ephraim is given to prostitution
 and Israel is defiled.

11 "Also for you, Judah,
 a harvest is appointed.

"Whenever I would restore the fortunes of
 my people,
7 1 whenever I would heal Israel,
 the sins of Ephraim are exposed
 and the crimes of Samaria revealed.
They practice deceit,
 thieves break into houses,
 bandits rob in the streets;
2 but they do not realize
 that I remember all their evil deeds.
Their sins engulf them;
 they are always before me.

3 "They delight the king with their wickedness,
 the princes with their lies.
4 They are all adulterers,
 burning like an oven
whose fire the baker need not stir
 from the kneading of the dough till it rises.
5 On the day of the festival of our king
 the princes become inflamed with wine,
 and he joins hands with the mockers.
6 Their hearts are like an oven;
 they approach him with intrigue.
Their passion smolders all night;
 in the morning it blazes like a flaming fire.
7 All of them are hot as an oven;
 they devour their rulers.
All their kings fall,
 and none of them calls on me.

8 "Ephraim mixes with the nations;
 Ephraim is a flat cake not turned over.
9 Foreigners sap his strength,
 but he does not realize it.

His hair is sprinkled with gray,
 but he does not notice.
10 Israel's arrogance testifies against him,
 but despite all this
he does not return to the Lord his God
 or search for him.

11 "Ephraim is like a dove,
 easily deceived and senseless—
now calling to Egypt,
 now turning to Assyria.
12 When they go, I will throw my net over them;
 I will pull them down like birds of the air.
When I hear them flocking together,
 I will catch them.
13 Woe to them,
 because they have strayed from me!
Destruction to them,
 because they have rebelled against me!
I long to redeem them
 but they speak lies against me.
14 They do not cry out to me from their hearts
 but wail upon their beds.
They gather together a for grain and new wine
 but turn away from me.
15 I trained them and strengthened them,
 but they plot evil against me.
16 They do not turn to the Most High;
 they are like a faulty bow.
Their leaders will fall by the sword
 because of their insolent words.
For this they will be ridiculed
 in the land of Egypt.

Israel to Reap the Whirlwind

8 "Put the trumpet to your lips!
 An eagle is over the house of the Lord
because the people have broken my covenant
 and rebelled against my law.
2 Israel cries out to me,
 'O our God, we acknowledge you!'
3 But Israel has rejected what is good;
 an enemy will pursue him.

a 14 Most Hebrew manuscripts; some Hebrew manuscripts and
Septuagint *They slash themselves*

⁴They set up kings without my consent;
  they choose princes without my approval.
With their silver and gold
  they make idols for themselves
  to their own destruction.
⁵Throw out your calf-idol, O Samaria!
  My anger burns against them.
How long will they be incapable of purity?
⁶ They are from Israel!
This calf—a craftsman has made it;
  it is not God.
It will be broken in pieces,
  that calf of Samaria.

⁷"They sow the wind
  and reap the whirlwind.
The stalk has no head;
  it will produce no flour.
Were it to yield grain,
  foreigners would swallow it up.
⁸Israel is swallowed up;
  now she is among the nations
  like a worthless thing.
⁹For they have gone up to Assyria
  like a wild donkey wandering alone.
Ephraim has sold herself to lovers.
¹⁰Although they have sold themselves among
    the nations,
  I will now gather them together.
They will begin to waste away
  under the oppression of the mighty king.

¹¹"Though Ephraim built many altars for sin
    offerings,
  these have become altars for sinning.
¹²I wrote for them the many things of my law,
  but they regarded them as something alien.
¹³They offer sacrifices given to me
  and they eat the meat,
  but the LORD is not pleased with them.
Now he will remember their wickedness
  and punish their sins:
  They will return to Egypt.
¹⁴Israel has forgotten his Maker
  and built palaces;
  Judah has fortified many towns.

But I will send fire upon their cities
  that will consume their fortresses."

Punishment for Israel

9 Do not rejoice, O Israel;
  do not be jubilant like the other nations.
For you have been unfaithful to your God;
  you love the wages of a prostitute
  at every threshing floor.
²Threshing floors and winepresses will not
    feed the people;
  the new wine will fail them.
³They will not remain in the LORD's land;
  Ephraim will return to Egypt
  and eat unclean ᵃ food in Assyria.
⁴They will not pour out wine offerings to the
    LORD,
  nor will their sacrifices please him.
Such sacrifices will be to them like the bread
    of mourners;
  all who eat them will be unclean.
This food will be for themselves;
  it will not come into the temple of the
    LORD.

⁵What will you do on the day of your
    appointed feasts,
  on the festival days of the LORD?
⁶Even if they escape from destruction,
  Egypt will gather them,
  and Memphis will bury them.
Their treasures of silver will be taken over by
    briers,
  and thorns will overrun their tents.
⁷The days of punishment are coming,
  the days of reckoning are at hand.
  Let Israel know this.
Because your sins are so many
  and your hostility so great,
the prophet is considered a fool,
  the inspired man a maniac.
⁸The prophet, along with my God,
  is the watchman over Ephraim, ᵇ

ᵃ 3 That is, ceremonially unclean   ᵇ 8 Or The prophet is the
watchman over Ephraim, / the people of my God

yet snares await him on all his paths,
  and hostility in the house of his God.
⁹ They have sunk deep into corruption,
  as in the days of Gibeah.
God will remember their wickedness
  and punish them for their sins.

¹⁰ "When I found Israel,
  it was like finding grapes in the desert;
when I saw your fathers,
  it was like seeing the early fruit on the fig
    tree.
But when they came to Baal Peor,
  they consecrated themselves to that
    shameful idol
  and became as vile as the thing they loved.
¹¹ Ephraim's glory will fly away like a bird—
  no birth, no pregnancy, no conception.
¹² Even if they rear children,
  I will bereave them of every one.
Woe to them
  when I turn away from them!
¹³ I have seen Ephraim, like Tyre,
  planted in a pleasant place.
But Ephraim will bring out
  their children to the slayer."

¹⁴ Give them, O Lord—
  what will you give them?
Give them wombs that miscarry
  and breasts that are dry.

¹⁵ "Because of all their wickedness in Gilgal,
  I hated them there.
Because of their sinful deeds,
  I will drive them out of my house.
I will no longer love them;
  all their leaders are rebellious.
¹⁶ Ephraim is blighted,
  their root is withered,
  they yield no fruit.
Even if they bear children,
  I will slay their cherished offspring."

¹⁷ My God will reject them
  because they have not obeyed him;
  they will be wanderers among the nations.

10 Israel was a spreading vine;
  he brought forth fruit for himself.
As his fruit increased,
  he built more altars;
as his land prospered,
  he adorned his sacred stones.
² Their heart is deceitful,
  and now they must bear their guilt.
The Lord will demolish their altars
  and destroy their sacred stones.

³ Then they will say, "We have no king
  because we did not revere the Lord.
But even if we had a king,
  what could he do for us?"
⁴ They make many promises,
  take false oaths
  and make agreements;
therefore lawsuits spring up
  like poisonous weeds in a plowed field.
⁵ The people who live in Samaria fear
  for the calf-idol of Beth Aven.ᵃ
Its people will mourn over it,
  and so will its idolatrous priests,
those who had rejoiced over its splendor,
  because it is taken from them into
    exile.
⁶ It will be carried to Assyria
  as tribute for the great king.
Ephraim will be disgraced;
  Israel will be ashamed of its wooden
    idols.ᵇ
⁷ Samaria and its king will float away
  like a twig on the surface of the waters.
⁸ The high places of wickednessᶜ will be
    destroyed—
  it is the sin of Israel.
Thorns and thistles will grow up
  and cover their altars.
Then they will say to the mountains,
  "Cover us!"
  and to the hills, "Fall on us!"

ᵃ 5 Beth Aven means house of wickedness (a name for Bethel, which
means house of God).   ᵇ 6 Or its counsel   ᶜ 8 Hebrew aven, a
reference to Beth Aven (a derogatory name for Bethel)

⁹"Since the days of Gibeah, you have sinned,
O Israel,
and there you have remained.ᵃ
Did not war overtake
the evildoers in Gibeah?
¹⁰When I please, I will punish them;
nations will be gathered against them
to put them in bonds for their double sin.
¹¹Ephraim is a trained heifer
that loves to thresh;
so I will put a yoke
on her fair neck.
I will drive Ephraim,
Judah must plow,
and Jacob must break up the ground.
¹²Sow for yourselves righteousness,
reap the fruit of unfailing love,
and break up your unplowed ground;
for it is time to seek the LORD,
until he comes
and showers righteousness on you.
¹³But you have planted wickedness,
you have reaped evil,
you have eaten the fruit of deception.
Because you have depended on your own
strength
and on your many warriors,
¹⁴the roar of battle will rise against your people,
so that all your fortresses will be
devastated—
as Shalman devastated Beth Arbel on the day
of battle,
when mothers were dashed to the ground
with their children.
¹⁵Thus will it happen to you, O Bethel,
because your wickedness is great.
When that day dawns,
the king of Israel will be completely
destroyed.

God's Love for Israel

11 "When Israel was a child, I loved him,
and out of Egypt I called my son.
²But the more Iᵇ called Israel,
the further they went from me.ᶜ

They sacrificed to the Baals
and they burned incense to images.
³It was I who taught Ephraim to walk,
taking them by the arms;
but they did not realize
it was I who healed them.
⁴I led them with cords of human kindness,
with ties of love;
I lifted the yoke from their neck
and bent down to feed them.

⁵"Will they not return to Egypt
and will not Assyria rule over them
because they refuse to repent?
⁶Swords will flash in their cities,
will destroy the bars of their gates
and put an end to their plans.
⁷My people are determined to turn
from me.
Even if they call to the Most High,
he will by no means exalt them.

⁸"How can I give you up, Ephraim?
How can I hand you over, Israel?
How can I treat you like Admah?
How can I make you like Zeboiim?
My heart is changed within me;
all my compassion is aroused.
⁹I will not carry out my fierce anger,
nor will I turn and devastate Ephraim.
For I am God, and not man—
the Holy One among you.
I will not come in wrath.ᵈ
¹⁰They will follow the LORD;
he will roar like a lion.
When he roars,
his children will come trembling from
the west.
¹¹They will come trembling
like birds from Egypt,
like doves from Assyria.
I will settle them in their homes,"
declares the LORD.

ᵃ 9 Or there a stand was taken   ᵇ 2 Some Septuagint manuscripts;
Hebrew they   ᶜ 2 Septuagint; Hebrew them   ᵈ 9 Or come
against any city

Israel's Sin

¹²Ephraim has surrounded me with lies,
  the house of Israel with deceit.
And Judah is unruly against God,
  even against the faithful Holy One.

12 ¹Ephraim feeds on the wind;
  he pursues the east wind all day
and multiplies lies and violence.
He makes a treaty with Assyria
  and sends olive oil to Egypt.
²The LORD has a charge to bring against Judah;
  he will punish Jacob[a] according to his ways
and repay him according to his deeds.
³In the womb he grasped his brother's heel;
  as a man he struggled with God.
⁴He struggled with the angel and overcame
    him;
  he wept and begged for his favor.
He found him at Bethel
  and talked with him there—
⁵the LORD God Almighty,
  the LORD is his name of renown!
⁶But you must return to your God;
  maintain love and justice,
  and wait for your God always.

⁷The merchant uses dishonest scales;
  he loves to defraud.
⁸Ephraim boasts,
  "I am very rich; I have become wealthy.
With all my wealth they will not find in me
  any iniquity or sin."

⁹"I am the LORD your God,
  ⌞who brought you⌟ out of[b] Egypt;
I will make you live in tents again,
  as in the days of your appointed feasts.
¹⁰I spoke to the prophets,
  gave them many visions
  and told parables through them."

¹¹Is Gilead wicked?
  Its people are worthless!
Do they sacrifice bulls in Gilgal?
  Their altars will be like piles of stones
  on a plowed field.

¹²Jacob fled to the country of Aram[c];
  Israel served to get a wife,
  and to pay for her he tended sheep.
¹³The LORD used a prophet to bring Israel up
    from Egypt,
  by a prophet he cared for him.
¹⁴But Ephraim has bitterly provoked him to
    anger;
  his Lord will leave upon him the guilt of
    his bloodshed
  and will repay him for his contempt.

The LORD's Anger Against Israel

13 When Ephraim spoke, men trembled;
  he was exalted in Israel.
  But he became guilty of Baal worship and
    died.
²Now they sin more and more;
  they make idols for themselves from their
    silver,
cleverly fashioned images,
  all of them the work of craftsmen.
It is said of these people,
  "They offer human sacrifice
  and kiss[d] the calf-idols."
³Therefore they will be like the morning mist,
  like the early dew that disappears,
  like chaff swirling from a threshing floor,
  like smoke escaping through a window.

⁴"But I am the LORD your God,
  ⌞who brought you⌟ out of[b] Egypt.
You shall acknowledge no God but me,
  no Savior except me.
⁵I cared for you in the desert,
  in the land of burning heat.
⁶When I fed them, they were satisfied;
  when they were satisfied, they became
    proud;
  then they forgot me.
⁷So I will come upon them like a lion,
  like a leopard I will lurk by the path.

---

[a] 2 *Jacob* means *he grasps the heel* (figuratively, *he deceives*).
[b] 9,4 Or *God / ever since you were in*   [c] 12 That is, Northwest
Mesopotamia   [d] 2 Or *"Men who sacrifice / kiss*

⁸Like a bear robbed of her cubs,
    I will attack them and rip them open.
Like a lion I will devour them;
    a wild animal will tear them apart.

⁹"You are destroyed, O Israel,
    because you are against me, against your
       helper.
¹⁰Where is your king, that he may save you?
    Where are your rulers in all your towns,
of whom you said,
    'Give me a king and princes'?
¹¹So in my anger I gave you a king,
    and in my wrath I took him away.
¹²The guilt of Ephraim is stored up,
    his sins are kept on record.
¹³Pains as of a woman in childbirth come to him,
    but he is a child without wisdom;
when the time arrives,
    he does not come to the opening of the
       womb.

¹⁴"I will ransom them from the power of the
       grave ᵃ;
    I will redeem them from death.
Where, O death, are your plagues?
    Where, O grave, ᵃ is your destruction?

"I will have no compassion,
15   even though he thrives among his brothers.
An east wind from the LORD will come,
    blowing in from the desert;
his spring will fail
    and his well dry up.
His storehouse will be plundered
    of all its treasures.
¹⁶The people of Samaria must bear their guilt,
    because they have rebelled against their
       God.
They will fall by the sword;
    their little ones will be dashed to the
       ground,
    their pregnant women ripped open."

Repentance to Bring Blessing

14 Return, O Israel, to the LORD your God.
Your sins have been your downfall!

²Take words with you
    and return to the LORD.
Say to him:
    "Forgive all our sins
and receive us graciously,
    that we may offer the fruit of our lips. ᵇ
³Assyria cannot save us;
    we will not mount war-horses.
We will never again say 'Our gods'
    to what our own hands have made,
    for in you the fatherless find compassion."

⁴"I will heal their waywardness
    and love them freely,
    for my anger has turned away from them.

ᵃ 14 Hebrew Sheol   ᵇ 2 Or offer our lips as sacrifices of bulls

stories to share

HOSEA 14:1–9

Repentance Brings Blessing

LIFE LESSON: God forgives his people when they ask for forgiveness.

TO TALK ABOUT

✦ What did Hosea ask the people to say to God?

✦ How would God respond?

✦ How do God's ways make rebellious people "stumble" (verse 9)?

✦ Why is it hard for unrepentant people to understand and accept God's authority? (Hint: Read 1 Corinthians 1:18–25.)

⁵I will be like the dew to Israel;
    he will blossom like a lily.
Like a cedar of Lebanon
    he will send down his roots;
⁶ his young shoots will grow.
His splendor will be like an olive tree,
    his fragrance like a cedar of Lebanon.
⁷Men will dwell again in his shade.
    He will flourish like the grain.
He will blossom like a vine,
    and his fame will be like the wine from
      Lebanon.

⁸O Ephraim, what more have I*ᵃ* to do with idols?
    I will answer him and care for him.
I am like a green pine tree;
    your fruitfulness comes from me."

⁹Who is wise? He will realize these things.
    Who is discerning? He will understand
      them.
The ways of the Lᴏʀᴅ are right;
    the righteous walk in them,
    but the rebellious stumble in them.

ᵃ 8 Or What more has Ephraim

Bad News,
GOOD NEWS

Plague. The very word makes people tremble. Plagues are the horror stories of Israel's history. The plague of locusts in Joel's time was so severe that successive generations talked about the army of locusts that came in waves and destroyed every bit of vegetation in the land (see Joel 1:2 – 4).

Although people today still worry about plagues, they are considered a natural phenomenon rather than a punishment from God. Joel, however, used the fear of plagues to call the people back to God in light of the coming great and dreadful "day of the LORD" (Joel 1:15; 2:1,11,31; 3:14). He assured the people that God would restore them to fullness only after they were judged and then repented of their sins (see Joel 2:12 – 14).

God's call for us to repent continues today. Out of great compassion and love for us, he calls us back to him. When we repent, he promises to restore all the blessings and peace that were lost (see Joel 2:25 – 26). What a comforting promise to those of us with children or grandchildren who have distanced themselves from God's love and his family. Joel makes it clear that someday in the future — whether immediate or distant — God's Spirit will change the direction of their lives and restore their relationships with him (see Joel 2:28 – 29).

VERSE to REMEMBER | JOEL 2:13

Rend your heart and not your garments. Return to the LORD your God, for he is gracious and compassionate, slow to anger and abounding in love, and he relents from sending calamity.

ABOUT JOEL

WRITTEN BY:
The prophet Joel

WRITTEN FOR:
The people of Judah

DATE WRITTEN:
Unknown

WHY WRITTEN:
To encourage the people of Judah to repent of their sins and return to the Lord

1

The word of the LORD that came to Joel son of Pethuel.

An Invasion of Locusts

²Hear this, you elders;
  listen, all who live in the land.
Has anything like this ever happened in your
    days
  or in the days of your forefathers?
³Tell it to your children,
  and let your children tell it to their
    children,
  and their children to the next generation.
⁴What the locust swarm has left
  the great locusts have eaten;
what the great locusts have left
  the young locusts have eaten;
what the young locusts have left
  other locusts ᵃ have eaten.

⁵Wake up, you drunkards, and weep!
  Wail, all you drinkers of wine;
wail because of the new wine,
  for it has been snatched from your lips.
⁶A nation has invaded my land,
  powerful and without number;
it has the teeth of a lion,
  the fangs of a lioness.
⁷It has laid waste my vines
  and ruined my fig trees.
It has stripped off their bark
  and thrown it away,
  leaving their branches white.

⁸Mourn like a virgin ᵇ in sackcloth
  grieving for the husband ᶜ of her youth.
⁹Grain offerings and drink offerings
  are cut off from the house of the LORD.
The priests are in mourning,
  those who minister before the LORD.
¹⁰The fields are ruined,
  the ground is dried up ᵈ;
the grain is destroyed,
  the new wine is dried up,
  the oil fails.
¹¹Despair, you farmers,
  wail, you vine growers;

grieve for the wheat and the barley,
  because the harvest of the field is
    destroyed.
¹²The vine is dried up
  and the fig tree is withered;
the pomegranate, the palm and the apple
    tree—
  all the trees of the field—are dried up.
Surely the joy of mankind
  is withered away.

A Call to Repentance

¹³Put on sackcloth, O priests, and mourn;
  wail, you who minister before the altar.
Come, spend the night in sackcloth,
  you who minister before my God;
for the grain offerings and drink offerings
  are withheld from the house of your God.
¹⁴Declare a holy fast;
  call a sacred assembly.
Summon the elders
  and all who live in the land
to the house of the LORD your God,
  and cry out to the LORD.

¹⁵Alas for that day!
  For the day of the LORD is near;
  it will come like destruction from the
    Almighty. ᵉ

¹⁶Has not the food been cut off
  before our very eyes—
joy and gladness
  from the house of our God?
¹⁷The seeds are shriveled
  beneath the clods. ᶠ
The storehouses are in ruins,
  the granaries have been broken down,
  for the grain has dried up.
¹⁸How the cattle moan!
  The herds mill about
because they have no pasture;
  even the flocks of sheep are suffering.

ᵃ 4 The precise meaning of the four Hebrew words used here for
locusts is uncertain.   ᵇ 8 Or young woman   ᶜ 8 Or betrothed
ᵈ 10 Or ground mourns   ᵉ 15 Hebrew Shaddai
ᶠ 17 The meaning of the Hebrew for this word is uncertain.

TELL IT TO YOUR CHILDREN,
AND LET YOUR CHILDREN TELL
IT TO THEIR CHILDREN, AND
THEIR CHILDREN TO THE NEXT
GENERATION.

Joel 1:3

Pass It On

CLAUDIA ARP

READ | JOEL 1:1–12

The Israelites had a long history of passing on to subsequent generations their stories of God's wonderful acts of deliverance and provision (see Exodus 10:1–2; 12:23–27; Deuteronomy 4:9; Psalm 78:1–6). But in his book, the prophet Joel exhorted the people to tell future generations about a devastating invasion of locusts. Confronted by this crisis, he called on young and old alike to repent and return to the Lord. Joel called for change and renewal in his generation — renewal that would perpetuate through future generations.

The older I get, the more I realize how important it is to pass the torch along to my children and grandchildren. After my mother died, I was sorting through her things and found a small devotional journal in which my grandmother had recorded her devotions and prayers. My mother had been given this journal and had received comfort from it for years. Now I can pass it on to my own children and grandchildren.

Why not pass on your own "story"? Think about how meaningful it might be for your great-grandchildren to someday read about your spiritual journey, your experience of God's grace and loving discipline. If you don't especially like to write, you could record history in other ways, such as by making photo albums or videotaping a message to future generations in your family. Talk about the highlights of your life and how God has walked with you through the days and years — both the mountaintops *and* the valleys. Someday it may be a legacy that your descendants will appreciate.

Dear Lord, please help me to pass on a godly heritage to my children and grandchildren. Give me opportunities to talk about you and tell my grandchildren stories of how you have worked in my life.

Your next devotion is located on page 1204.

GRANDCHILD IN FOCUS • PRAYER

Courage

O Father, builder of character and courage, may my grandchild grow strong in the light of your love. Grant him courage to stand for what is right, to guard the truth and to ensure justice in every aspect of life. May he boldly grow in grace, revere your name and proudly proclaim you as the Lord of lords and King of kings. Amen.

¹⁹ To you, O Lord, I call,
    for fire has devoured the open pastures
    and flames have burned up all the trees of
        the field.
²⁰ Even the wild animals pant for you;
    the streams of water have dried up
    and fire has devoured the open pastures.

An Army of Locusts

2 Blow the trumpet in Zion;
    sound the alarm on my holy hill.
Let all who live in the land tremble,
    for the day of the Lord is coming.
It is close at hand—
² a day of darkness and gloom,
    a day of clouds and blackness.
Like dawn spreading across the mountains
    a large and mighty army comes,
such as never was of old
    nor ever will be in ages to come.

³ Before them fire devours,
    behind them a flame blazes.
Before them the land is like the garden of
        Eden,
    behind them, a desert waste—
    nothing escapes them.
⁴ They have the appearance of horses;
    they gallop along like cavalry.
⁵ With a noise like that of chariots
    they leap over the mountaintops,
like a crackling fire consuming stubble,
    like a mighty army drawn up for battle.

⁶ At the sight of them, nations are in anguish;
    every face turns pale.
⁷ They charge like warriors;
    they scale walls like soldiers.
They all march in line,
    not swerving from their course.
⁸ They do not jostle each other;
    each marches straight ahead.
They plunge through defenses
    without breaking ranks.
⁹ They rush upon the city;
    they run along the wall.

They climb into the houses;
    like thieves they enter through the
        windows.

¹⁰ Before them the earth shakes,
    the sky trembles,
the sun and moon are darkened,
    and the stars no longer shine.
¹¹ The Lord thunders
    at the head of his army;
his forces are beyond number,
    and mighty are those who obey his
        command.
The day of the Lord is great;
    it is dreadful.
Who can endure it?

Rend Your Heart

¹² "Even now," declares the Lord,
    "return to me with all your heart,
    with fasting and weeping and mourning."

¹³ Rend your heart
    and not your garments.
Return to the Lord your God,
    for he is gracious and compassionate,
slow to anger and abounding in love,
    and he relents from sending calamity.
¹⁴ Who knows? He may turn and have pity
    and leave behind a blessing—
grain offerings and drink offerings
    for the Lord your God.

¹⁵ Blow the trumpet in Zion,
    declare a holy fast,
    call a sacred assembly.
¹⁶ Gather the people,
    consecrate the assembly;
bring together the elders,
    gather the children,
    those nursing at the breast.
Let the bridegroom leave his room
    and the bride her chamber.
¹⁷ Let the priests, who minister before the Lord,
    weep between the temple porch and the
        altar.

REND YOUR HEART AND NOT YOUR GARMENTS. RETURN TO THE LORD YOUR GOD, FOR HE IS GRACIOUS AND COMPASSIONATE, SLOW TO ANGER AND ABOUNDING IN LOVE, AND HE RELENTS FROM SENDING CALAMITY.

Joel 2:13

God Pours Out His Grace

BARBARA JOHNSON

READ | JOEL 2:1 – 17

A friend of mine looked around her home one day and noticed something: every room contained several empty containers of different sizes and shapes. My friend realized these various containers were a metaphor for herself: she was an empty vessel waiting to be filled. She was thirsty for grace. Then she considered that each pitcher in her home was equipped with a pour spout. God seemed to be telling her that he wanted her to pour out his fullness into the lives of others. She wondered how effective she had been at doing that.

Surely, God's intention is that we overflow when he fills us to the brim! And it doesn't take a monumental feat to exercise grace toward others. It can be as simple as letting someone ahead of you in line. It can be saying to a sister in Christ, "Let me be your emotional bra." Grace always remembers that it's not your job to get people to like you, it's your job to like people.

You are only a decision away from pouring out grace. Here are some of its expressions:

"You did a good job."

"I was wrong."

"What do you think?"

"Thank you."

You can even say these to yourself, and cut yourself some slack. Everyone who got where she is had to begin where she was — including you!

Too many folks go through life running from something that isn't after them. But the poet Emily Dickinson wrote, "The soul should always stand ajar." Grace is all around and within you, just like my friend's empty vessels. So stand still awhile, your soul ajar. Notice grace. Appreciate it. As it flows into your open soul, drink deeply. And then from your fullness in Christ, pour out his grace on others.

Dear God, fill me to overflow with your grace. Help me to notice it, appreciate it, receive it with joy and pass it on to others. Amen.

Your next devotion is located on page 1207.

GRANDCHILD IN FOCUS • PRAYER

Future Spouse

Dear Lord, if it is your will, I pray my grandchild will be united in a loving and Christian marriage. Keep her sexually pure so that she will honor you with her body and mind. As she seeks a spouse who will honor and care for her, give her patience and discernment. May her choice for a life partner be your choice for her, so that she and her husband will together glorify you in a lasting love. I pray this in Jesus' name, amen.

Let them say, "Spare your people, O Lord.
   Do not make your inheritance an object of
      scorn,
   a byword among the nations.
Why should they say among the peoples,
   'Where is their God?' "

The Lord's Answer

¹⁸ Then the Lord will be jealous for his land
   and take pity on his people.

¹⁹ The Lord will reply[a] to them:

"I am sending you grain, new wine and oil,
   enough to satisfy you fully;
never again will I make you
   an object of scorn to the nations.

²⁰ "I will drive the northern army far from you,
   pushing it into a parched and barren land,
with its front columns going into the eastern
      sea[b]
   and those in the rear into the western sea.[c]
And its stench will go up;
   its smell will rise."

Surely he has done great things.[d]
²¹ Be not afraid, O land;
   be glad and rejoice.
Surely the Lord has done great things.
²² Be not afraid, O wild animals,
   for the open pastures are becoming green.

PRAYING THE SCRIPTURES

Joy
JOEL 2:21,23

O Lord, you have done great things for my grandchild. Help him not to be afraid but to be glad and rejoice in you, the Lord his God, who shows faithfulness by sending rain to the earth.

Next prayer in Joy Prayer Track: Romans 15:13

The trees are bearing their fruit;
   the fig tree and the vine yield their riches.
²³ Be glad, O people of Zion,
   rejoice in the Lord your God,
for he has given you
   the autumn rains in righteousness.[e]
He sends you abundant showers,
   both autumn and spring rains, as before.
²⁴ The threshing floors will be filled with grain;
   the vats will overflow with new wine and
      oil.

²⁵ "I will repay you for the years the locusts
      have eaten —
   the great locust and the young locust,
   the other locusts and the locust swarm[f] —
my great army that I sent among you.
²⁶ You will have plenty to eat, until you are full,
   and you will praise the name of the Lord
      your God,
   who has worked wonders for you;
never again will my people be shamed.
²⁷ Then you will know that I am in Israel,
   that I am the Lord your God,
   and that there is no other;
never again will my people be shamed.

The Day of the Lord

²⁸ "And afterward,
   I will pour out my Spirit on all people.
Your sons and daughters will prophesy,
   your old men will dream dreams,
   your young men will see visions.
²⁹ Even on my servants, both men and women,
   I will pour out my Spirit in those days.
³⁰ I will show wonders in the heavens
   and on the earth,
   blood and fire and billows of smoke.
³¹ The sun will be turned to darkness
   and the moon to blood
   before the coming of the great and
      dreadful day of the Lord.

[a] 18,19 Or Lord was jealous . . . / and took pity . . . / ¹⁹The Lord replied [b] 20 That is, the Dead Sea [c] 20 That is, the Mediterranean [d] 20 Or rise. / Surely it has done great things." [e] 23 Or / the teacher for righteousness: [f] 25 The precise meaning of the four Hebrew words used here for locusts is uncertain.

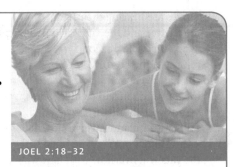

JOEL 2:18–32

A Bright Future for God's People

LIFE LESSON: God has a glorious future prepared for his people.

TO TALK ABOUT

✦ What did God promise his people?

✦ What promise did God make to the wild animals in Israel?

✦ Verses 28–32 are about the "day of the LORD." When did God first pour out his Spirit on all his people? (Hint: Read Acts 2:1–21.) Does he still do this today?

✦ Do you think some of what is described in this passage about the "day of the LORD" is still in the future?

³² And everyone who calls
    on the name of the LORD will be saved;
for on Mount Zion and in Jerusalem
    there will be deliverance,
    as the LORD has said,
among the survivors
    whom the LORD calls.

The Nations Judged

3 "In those days and at that time,
    when I restore the fortunes of Judah and
        Jerusalem,

² I will gather all nations
    and bring them down to the Valley of
        Jehoshaphat. ᵃ
There I will enter into judgment against them
    concerning my inheritance, my people
        Israel,
for they scattered my people among the
        nations
    and divided up my land.
³ They cast lots for my people
    and traded boys for prostitutes;
they sold girls for wine
    that they might drink.

⁴ "Now what have you against me, O Tyre and Sidon and all you regions of Philistia? Are you repaying me for something I have done? If you are paying me back, I will swiftly and speedily return on your own heads what you have done. ⁵ For you took my silver and my gold and carried off my finest treasures to your temples. ⁶ You sold the people of Judah and Jerusalem to the Greeks, that you might send them far from their homeland.

⁷ "See, I am going to rouse them out of the places to which you sold them, and I will return on your own heads what you have done. ⁸ I will sell your sons and daughters to the people of Judah, and they will sell them to the Sabeans, a nation far away." The LORD has spoken.

⁹ Proclaim this among the nations:
    Prepare for war!
Rouse the warriors!
    Let all the fighting men draw near and
        attack.
¹⁰ Beat your plowshares into swords
    and your pruning hooks into spears.
Let the weakling say,
    "I am strong!"
¹¹ Come quickly, all you nations from every
        side,
    and assemble there.

Bring down your warriors, O LORD!

ᵃ 2 *Jehoshaphat* means *the* LORD *judges*; also in verse 12.

AND EVERYONE WHO CALLS ON THE
NAME OF THE LORD WILL BE SAVED; FOR
ON MOUNT ZION AND IN JERUSALEM
THERE WILL BE DELIVERANCE, AS THE
LORD HAS SAID, AMONG THE SURVIVORS
WHOM THE LORD CALLS.

Joel 2:32

The Name Above All Names

JANE SCHLENVOGT

READ | JOEL 2:18 – 32

The titles designated for our Lord are indeed precious vessels deserving of places high on our list of preferred verbiage. Our God is identified with names befitting him alone. He is the only one who continually and without fail lives up to those names: the Almighty, heavenly Father, provider, all-sufficient Creator, Savior, Redeemer, Alpha and Omega, Lord above all, Comforter, I am who I am, the way, the truth, the life, the gate, living water, Lamb of God. The list goes on and on. These names serve as reminders that he who hears our prayers means everything to us, and we owe our lives to him. "And everyone who calls on the name of the LORD will be saved" (Joel 2:32).

Using God's name in our prayers is a privilege. Be careful not to store it away high on a shelf of neglected vessels for only occasional use. We can be guilty of dusting off the precious name of Jesus no more than weekly — some of us uttering the name of Jesus in our prayers only in the setting of public worship, chanting it somewhat mindlessly. Handle this name above all names with care, but make daily use of it. Let our Lord's name bring you to new heights of happiness and joy as you bring glory to it in secret sentences spoken to God in prayer.

Almighty God, when I consider all of your names, I get a glimpse of your greatness, your power, your holiness. May I never speak your names lightly, but use them in reverence, awe and joy. Amen.

Your next devotion is located on page 1212.

GRANDCHILD IN FOCUS • PRAYER

School/Career

Dear God, may learning be a joy rather than a chore for my grandchild. May exploration of new ideas bring a sense of wonder, awe and excitement. Grant him clarity of mind, the ability to concentrate on the task at hand and recollection of what has been learned. Help him to appreciate the tasks that come easily and to persevere through those that challenge. Amen.

12 "Let the nations be roused;
    let them advance into the Valley of
        Jehoshaphat,
    for there I will sit
        to judge all the nations on every side.
13 Swing the sickle,
    for the harvest is ripe.
Come, trample the grapes,
    for the winepress is full
    and the vats overflow—
so great is their wickedness!"

14 Multitudes, multitudes
    in the valley of decision!
For the day of the LORD is near
    in the valley of decision.
15 The sun and moon will be darkened,
    and the stars no longer shine.
16 The LORD will roar from Zion
    and thunder from Jerusalem;
    the earth and the sky will tremble.
But the LORD will be a refuge for his
        people,
    a stronghold for the people of Israel.

Blessings for God's People

17 "Then you will know that I, the LORD your
        God,
    dwell in Zion, my holy hill.
Jerusalem will be holy;
    never again will foreigners invade her.

18 "In that day the mountains will drip new wine,
    and the hills will flow with milk;
    all the ravines of Judah will run with water.
A fountain will flow out of the LORD's house
    and will water the valley of acacias. [a]
19 But Egypt will be desolate,
    Edom a desert waste,
because of violence done to the people of
        Judah,
    in whose land they shed innocent blood.
20 Judah will be inhabited forever
    and Jerusalem through all generations.
21 Their bloodguilt, which I have not pardoned,
    I will pardon."

        The LORD dwells in Zion!

a 18 Or Valley of Shittim

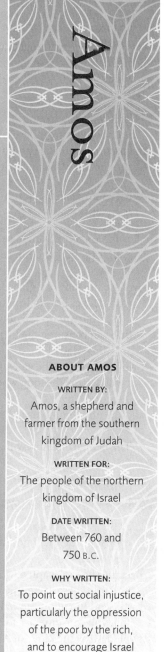

Standing UP FOR GOD

In this book Amos cries out for social justice in response to the mistreatment of the poor by the wealthy Israelites who were focusing on their own wealth and prosperity. Unfortunately, many parallels exist between ancient Israel's quest for self-seeking comfort and society's pursuits today. Many times, we too are selfishly focused on wealth and materialism.

Amos reminds us that God has a different set of priorities. God wants justice to be the driving force in society (see Amos 5:24). God detested the Israelites' oppression of the poor (see Amos 2:6–8), their complacency (see Amos 6:1), and their pride (see Amos 6:8). Therefore, judgment would come; but restoration would follow judgment (see Amos 9).

Too often our children and grandchildren fall into the trap of valuing what the world values and of desiring what the world says people deserve to have. Through our actions, our teaching and our Christian values, we as grandmothers can encourage our children and grandchildren to seek social justice and to stand up for God's standards in a self-obsessed world. Through our example and encouragement we can promote sharing instead of selfishness, giving instead of hoarding, and compassion instead of complacency.

VERSE *to* REMEMBER | AMOS 5:14

Seek good, not evil, that you may live. Then the LORD God Almighty will be with you, just as you say he is.

ABOUT AMOS

WRITTEN BY:
Amos, a shepherd and farmer from the southern kingdom of Judah

WRITTEN FOR:
The people of the northern kingdom of Israel

DATE WRITTEN:
Between 760 and 750 B.C.

WHY WRITTEN:
To point out social injustice, particularly the oppression of the poor by the rich, and to encourage Israel to stop sinning against God

1 The words of Amos, one of the shepherds of Tekoa — what he saw concerning Israel two years before the earthquake, when Uzziah was king of Judah and Jeroboam son of Jehoash *a* was king of Israel.

² He said:

"The Lᴏʀᴅ roars from Zion
 and thunders from Jerusalem;
the pastures of the shepherds dry up, *b*
 and the top of Carmel withers."

Judgment on Israel's Neighbors

³ This is what the Lᴏʀᴅ says:

"For three sins of Damascus,
 even for four, I will not turn back ⌐my wrath⌐.
Because she threshed Gilead
 with sledges having iron teeth,
⁴ I will send fire upon the house of Hazael
 that will consume the fortresses of Ben-Hadad.
⁵ I will break down the gate of Damascus;
 I will destroy the king who is in *c* the Valley of Aven *d*
and the one who holds the scepter in Beth Eden.
 The people of Aram will go into exile to Kir,"

                    says the Lᴏʀᴅ.

⁶ This is what the Lᴏʀᴅ says:

"For three sins of Gaza,
 even for four, I will not turn back ⌐my wrath⌐.
Because she took captive whole communities
 and sold them to Edom,
⁷ I will send fire upon the walls of Gaza
 that will consume her fortresses.
⁸ I will destroy the king *e* of Ashdod
 and the one who holds the scepter in Ashkelon.
I will turn my hand against Ekron,
 till the last of the Philistines is dead,"

                    says the Sovereign Lᴏʀᴅ.

⁹ This is what the Lᴏʀᴅ says:

"For three sins of Tyre,
 even for four, I will not turn back ⌐my wrath⌐.
Because she sold whole communities of captives to Edom,
 disregarding a treaty of brotherhood,
¹⁰ I will send fire upon the walls of Tyre
 that will consume her fortresses."

¹¹ This is what the Lᴏʀᴅ says:

"For three sins of Edom,
 even for four, I will not turn back ⌐my wrath⌐.
Because he pursued his brother with a sword,
 stifling all compassion, *f*
because his anger raged continually
 and his fury flamed unchecked,
¹² I will send fire upon Teman
 that will consume the fortresses of Bozrah."

¹³ This is what the Lᴏʀᴅ says:

"For three sins of Ammon,
 even for four, I will not turn back ⌐my wrath⌐.
Because he ripped open the pregnant women of Gilead
 in order to extend his borders,
¹⁴ I will set fire to the walls of Rabbah
 that will consume her fortresses
amid war cries on the day of battle,
 amid violent winds on a stormy day.
¹⁵ Her king *g* will go into exile,
 he and his officials together,"

                    says the Lᴏʀᴅ.

2 This is what the Lᴏʀᴅ says:

"For three sins of Moab,
 even for four, I will not turn back ⌐my wrath⌐.

---

a 1 Hebrew *Joash,* a variant of *Jehoash*   *b 2* Or *shepherds mourn*   *c 5* Or *the inhabitants of*   *d 5* *Aven* means *wickedness.*   *e 8* Or *inhabitants*   *f 11* Or *sword / and destroyed his allies*   *g 15* Or */ Molech;* Hebrew *malcam*

Because he burned, as if to lime,
the bones of Edom's king,
² I will send fire upon Moab
that will consume the fortresses of
Kerioth. *a*
Moab will go down in great tumult
amid war cries and the blast of the trumpet.
³ I will destroy her ruler
and kill all her officials with him,"
says the LORD.

⁴ This is what the LORD says:

"For three sins of Judah,
even for four, I will not turn back ⌐my
wrath⌐.
Because they have rejected the law of the
LORD
and have not kept his decrees,
because they have been led astray by false
gods, *b*
the gods *c* their ancestors followed,
⁵ I will send fire upon Judah
that will consume the fortresses of
Jerusalem."

Judgment on Israel

⁶ This is what the LORD says:

"For three sins of Israel,
even for four, I will not turn back ⌐my
wrath⌐.
They sell the righteous for silver,
and the needy for a pair of sandals.
⁷ They trample on the heads of the poor
as upon the dust of the ground
and deny justice to the oppressed.
Father and son use the same girl
and so profane my holy name.
⁸ They lie down beside every altar
on garments taken in pledge.
In the house of their god
they drink wine taken as fines.

⁹ "I destroyed the Amorite before them,
though he was tall as the cedars
and strong as the oaks.

I destroyed his fruit above
and his roots below.
¹⁰ "I brought you up out of Egypt,
and I led you forty years in the desert
to give you the land of the Amorites.
¹¹ I also raised up prophets from among your
sons
and Nazirites from among your young
men.
Is this not true, people of Israel?"
declares the LORD.
¹² "But you made the Nazirites drink wine
and commanded the prophets not to
prophesy.

¹³ "Now then, I will crush you
as a cart crushes when loaded with grain.
¹⁴ The swift will not escape,
the strong will not muster their strength,
and the warrior will not save his life.
¹⁵ The archer will not stand his ground,
the fleet-footed soldier will not get away,
and the horseman will not save his life.
¹⁶ Even the bravest warriors
will flee naked on that day,"
declares the LORD.

Witnesses Summoned Against Israel

3 Hear this word the LORD has spoken against
you, O people of Israel—against the whole
family I brought up out of Egypt:

² "You only have I chosen
of all the families of the earth;
therefore I will punish you
for all your sins."

³ Do two walk together
unless they have agreed to do so?
⁴ Does a lion roar in the thicket
when he has no prey?
Does he growl in his den
when he has caught nothing?
⁵ Does a bird fall into a trap on the ground
where no snare has been set?

a 2 Or of her cities   *b 4 Or by lies*   *c 4 Or lies*

Special Pet Day

Most kids have an affinity for animals, whether they have one at home or not. Whatever your grandchild's pet — a goldfish, a caterpillar in a jar, a new kitten, a bunny, guinea pig, hamster or parakeet, they feel competent in caring for their pet and closely connected to it.

If your grandchild has a pet, take some time to sit and talk about what a great pet it is. Or get to know that pet better by offering to have the pet come along on a visit with your grandchild. If you like, record on tape or in writing some stories (real or made up) of your grandkid's adventures with their pet. Share your grandchild's enthusiasm for their pet by taking them to a pet supply store. Together you can select an appropriate treat or toy.

Long-Distance Variation: Ask the kids to write a funny animal story, factual or fictional, and send it to you for family distribution and appreciation.

Creator of all, thank you for pets that bring companionship and happiness to me and my grandchildren. Bless this time together; let it be a fun time for us as we share our love for animals together. Amen.

Your next devotion is located on page 1217.

GRANDCHILD IN FOCUS • PRAYER

Character

Dear Lord and Father, I ask that you fill my grandchild with your Spirit so her character reflects your goodness and love. Give her kindness and love for others. Bring joy to her life so she will be a joy to others. Grant her patience and self-control through difficult and trying times. May she show mercy and generosity to those who are less fortunate. Grant her integrity and a sense of justice, and surround her with your peace. Amen.

Does a trap spring up from the earth
 when there is nothing to catch?
⁶When a trumpet sounds in a city,
 do not the people tremble?
When disaster comes to a city,
 has not the Lord caused it?

⁷Surely the Sovereign Lord does nothing
 without revealing his plan
 to his servants the prophets.

⁸The lion has roared—
 who will not fear?
The Sovereign Lord has spoken—
 who can but prophesy?

⁹Proclaim to the fortresses of Ashdod
 and to the fortresses of Egypt:
"Assemble yourselves on the mountains of
 Samaria;
 see the great unrest within her
 and the oppression among her people."

¹⁰"They do not know how to do right," declares
 the Lord,
 "who hoard plunder and loot in their
 fortresses."

¹¹Therefore this is what the Sovereign Lord
says:

"An enemy will overrun the land;
 he will pull down your strongholds
 and plunder your fortresses."

¹²This is what the Lord says:

"As a shepherd saves from the lion's mouth
 only two leg bones or a piece of an ear,
 so will the Israelites be saved,
those who sit in Samaria
 on the edge of their beds
 and in Damascus on their couches.ᵃ"

¹³"Hear this and testify against the house of Jacob," declares the Lord, the Lord God Almighty.

¹⁴"On the day I punish Israel for her sins,
 I will destroy the altars of Bethel;
the horns of the altar will be cut off
 and fall to the ground.

¹⁵I will tear down the winter house
 along with the summer house;
the houses adorned with ivory will be
 destroyed
 and the mansions will be demolished,"
 declares the Lord.

Israel Has Not Returned to God

4 Hear this word, you cows of Bashan on
 Mount Samaria,
 you women who oppress the poor and
 crush the needy
 and say to your husbands, "Bring us some
 drinks!"
²The Sovereign Lord has sworn by his holiness:
 "The time will surely come
when you will be taken away with hooks,
 the last of you with fishhooks.
³You will each go straight out
 through breaks in the wall,
 and you will be cast out toward Harmon,ᵇ"
 declares the Lord.

⁴"Go to Bethel and sin;
 go to Gilgal and sin yet more.
Bring your sacrifices every morning,
 your tithes every three years.ᶜ
⁵Burn leavened bread as a thank offering
 and brag about your freewill offerings—
boast about them, you Israelites,
 for this is what you love to do,"
 declares the Sovereign Lord.

⁶"I gave you empty stomachsᵈ in every city
 and lack of bread in every town,
 yet you have not returned to me,"
 declares the Lord.

⁷"I also withheld rain from you
 when the harvest was still three months
 away.
I sent rain on one town,
 but withheld it from another.
One field had rain;
 another had none and dried up.

ᵃ 12 The meaning of the Hebrew for this line is uncertain.
ᵇ 3 Masoretic Text; with a different word division of the Hebrew (see
Septuagint) out, O mountain of oppression   ᶜ 4 Or tithes on the
third day   ᵈ 6 Hebrew you cleanness of teeth

8 People staggered from town to town for
   water
   but did not get enough to drink,
   yet you have not returned to me,"
               declares the LORD.

9 "Many times I struck your gardens and
   vineyards,
   I struck them with blight and mildew.
   Locusts devoured your fig and olive trees,
   yet you have not returned to me,"
               declares the LORD.

10 "I sent plagues among you
   as I did to Egypt.
   I killed your young men with the sword,
   along with your captured horses.
   I filled your nostrils with the stench of your
   camps,
   yet you have not returned to me,"
               declares the LORD.

11 "I overthrew some of you
   as I[a] overthrew Sodom and Gomorrah.
   You were like a burning stick snatched from
   the fire,
   yet you have not returned to me,"
               declares the LORD.

12 "Therefore this is what I will do to you, Israel,
   and because I will do this to you,
   prepare to meet your God, O Israel."

13 He who forms the mountains,
   creates the wind,
   and reveals his thoughts to man,
   he who turns dawn to darkness,
   and treads the high places of the earth—
   the LORD God Almighty is his name.

A Lament and Call to Repentance

5 Hear this word, O house of Israel, this lament
   I take up concerning you:

2 "Fallen is Virgin Israel,
   never to rise again,
   deserted in her own land,
   with no one to lift her up."

3 This is what the Sovereign LORD says:

"The city that marches out a thousand strong
   for Israel
   will have only a hundred left;
the town that marches out a hundred strong
   will have only ten left."

4 This is what the LORD says to the house of
Israel:

"Seek me and live;
5   do not seek Bethel,
   do not go to Gilgal,
   do not journey to Beersheba.
   For Gilgal will surely go into exile,
   and Bethel will be reduced to nothing.[b]"
6 Seek the LORD and live,
   or he will sweep through the house of
   Joseph like a fire;
   it will devour,
   and Bethel will have no one to quench it.

7 You who turn justice into bitterness
   and cast righteousness to the ground
8 (he who made the Pleiades and Orion,
   who turns blackness into dawn
   and darkens day into night,
   who calls for the waters of the sea
   and pours them out over the face of the
   land—
   the LORD is his name—
9 he flashes destruction on the stronghold
   and brings the fortified city to ruin),
10 you hate the one who reproves in court
   and despise him who tells the truth.

11 You trample on the poor
   and force him to give you grain.
Therefore, though you have built stone
   mansions,
   you will not live in them;
   though you have planted lush vineyards,
   you will not drink their wine.
12 For I know how many are your offenses
   and how great your sins.

---

[a] 11 Hebrew God   [b] 5 Or grief; or wickedness; Hebrew aven, a
reference to Beth Aven (a derogatory name for Bethel)

You oppress the righteous and take bribes
and you deprive the poor of justice in the
courts.
13 Therefore the prudent man keeps quiet in
such times,
for the times are evil.

14 Seek good, not evil,
that you may live.
Then the LORD God Almighty will be with
you,
just as you say he is.
15 Hate evil, love good;
maintain justice in the courts.
Perhaps the LORD God Almighty will have
mercy
on the remnant of Joseph.

TALKING POINTS

Social Justice

We must pursue good and avoid evil.

AMOS 5:14–15

For more on social justice, go to Amos 5:24.

---

16 Therefore this is what the Lord, the LORD
God Almighty, says:

"There will be wailing in all the streets
and cries of anguish in every public square.
The farmers will be summoned to weep
and the mourners to wail.
17 There will be wailing in all the vineyards,
for I will pass through your midst,"
says the LORD.

The Day of the LORD

18 Woe to you who long
for the day of the LORD!
Why do you long for the day of the LORD?
That day will be darkness, not light.

19 It will be as though a man fled from a lion
only to meet a bear,
as though he entered his house
and rested his hand on the wall
only to have a snake bite him.
20 Will not the day of the LORD be darkness, not
light—
pitch-dark, without a ray of brightness?

21 "I hate, I despise your religious feasts;
I cannot stand your assemblies.
22 Even though you bring me burnt offerings
and grain offerings,
I will not accept them.
Though you bring choice fellowship
offerings, *a*
I will have no regard for them.
23 Away with the noise of your songs!
I will not listen to the music of your harps.
24 But let justice roll on like a river,
righteousness like a never-failing stream!

25 "Did you bring me sacrifices and offerings
forty years in the desert, O house of Israel?
26 You have lifted up the shrine of your king,
the pedestal of your idols,
the star of your god *b*—
which you made for yourselves.
27 Therefore I will send you into exile beyond
Damascus,"
says the LORD, whose name is God
Almighty.

*a 22 Traditionally peace offerings   b 26 Or lifted up Sakkuth your
king / and Kaiwan your idols, / your star-gods; Septuagint lifted up the
shrine of Molech / and the star of your god Rephan, / their idols*

TALKING POINTS

Social Justice

We must strive for justice in this world.

AMOS 5:24

For more on social justice, go to Zechariah 7:9–10.

Woe to the Complacent

6 Woe to you who are complacent in Zion,
  and to you who feel secure on Mount Samaria,
you notable men of the foremost nation,
  to whom the people of Israel come!
²Go to Calneh and look at it;
  go from there to great Hamath,
  and then go down to Gath in Philistia.
  Are they better off than your two kingdoms?
  Is their land larger than yours?
³You put off the evil day
  and bring near a reign of terror.
⁴You lie on beds inlaid with ivory
  and lounge on your couches.
  You dine on choice lambs
  and fattened calves.
⁵You strum away on your harps like David
  and improvise on musical instruments.
⁶You drink wine by the bowlful
  and use the finest lotions,
  but you do not grieve over the ruin of Joseph.
⁷Therefore you will be among the first to go into exile;
  your feasting and lounging will end.

The Lord Abhors the Pride of Israel

⁸The Sovereign Lord has sworn by himself—the Lord God Almighty declares:

  "I abhor the pride of Jacob
    and detest his fortresses;
  I will deliver up the city
    and everything in it."

⁹If ten men are left in one house, they too will die. ¹⁰And if a relative who is to burn the bodies comes to carry them out of the house and asks anyone still hiding there, "Is anyone with you?" and he says, "No," then he will say, "Hush! We must not mention the name of the Lord."

¹¹For the Lord has given the command,
  and he will smash the great house into pieces
  and the small house into bits.

¹²Do horses run on the rocky crags?
  Does one plow there with oxen?
  But you have turned justice into poison
    and the fruit of righteousness into bitterness—
¹³you who rejoice in the conquest of Lo Debar ᵃ
  and say, "Did we not take Karnaim ᵇ by our own strength?"

¹⁴For the Lord God Almighty declares,
  "I will stir up a nation against you,
    O house of Israel,
  that will oppress you all the way
    from Lebo ᶜ Hamath to the valley of the Arabah."

Locusts, Fire and a Plumb Line

7 This is what the Sovereign Lord showed me: He was preparing swarms of locusts after the king's share had been harvested and just as the second crop was coming up. ²When they had stripped the land clean, I cried out, "Sovereign Lord, forgive! How can Jacob survive? He is so small!"

³So the Lord relented.

"This will not happen," the Lord said.

⁴This is what the Sovereign Lord showed me: The Sovereign Lord was calling for judgment by fire; it dried up the great deep and devoured the land. ⁵Then I cried out, "Sovereign Lord, I beg you, stop! How can Jacob survive? He is so small!"

⁶So the Lord relented.

"This will not happen either," the Sovereign Lord said.

⁷This is what he showed me: The Lord was standing by a wall that had been built true to plumb, with a plumb line in his hand. ⁸And the Lord asked me, "What do you see, Amos?"

"A plumb line," I replied.

Then the Lord said, "Look, I am setting a plumb line among my people Israel; I will spare them no longer.

ᵃ 13 Lo Debar means nothing.   ᵇ 13 Karnaim means horns; horn here symbolizes strength.   ᶜ 14 Or from the entrance to

Worship the Lord

Clap your hands, all you nations;
　　shout to God with cries of joy.
How awesome is the LORD Most High,
　　the great King over all the earth!
He subdued nations under us,
　　peoples under our feet.
He chose our inheritance for us,
　　the pride of Jacob, whom he loved. 　*Selah*

God has ascended amid shouts of joy,
　　the LORD amid the sounding of
　　　　trumpets.
Sing praises to God, sing praises;
　　sing praise to our King, sing
　　　　praises.

For God is the King of all the earth;
　　sing to him a psalm of praise.
God reigns over the nations;
　　God is seated on his holy throne.
The nobles of the nations assemble
　　as the people of the God of
　　　　Abraham,
for the kings of the earth belong to God;
　　he is greatly exalted.

Psalm 47

GRANDCHILD IN FOCUS • PRAYER

Talents

Dear Lord, the giver of gifts, bless my grandchild as he develops his talents. Help him identify his talents and be proud and confident of the gifts you have given him. Give him patience and understanding, Lord, so he will not grow weary of striving and searching to reach the goals you have set for him. May each milestone bring satisfaction and a healthy desire for greater achievement and success to bring glory to you. Amen.

King of kings and Lord of lords, I praise you for your power and majesty. Although nations wage war, and evil often appears to be winning, I find comfort in the psalmist's words that you reign over the mightiest armies, the greatest nations, the most powerful human rulers. You alone are the Almighty God of the universe. For that I will praise you. Amen.

Your next devotion is located on page 1227.

9 "The high places of Isaac will be
    destroyed
  and the sanctuaries of Israel will be
    ruined;
  with my sword I will rise against the
    house of Jeroboam."

Amos and Amaziah

10 Then Amaziah the priest of Bethel sent a message to Jeroboam king of Israel: "Amos is raising a conspiracy against you in the very heart of Israel. The land cannot bear all his words. 11 For this is what Amos is saying:

  " 'Jeroboam will die by the sword,
    and Israel will surely go into exile,
    away from their native land.' "

12 Then Amaziah said to Amos, "Get out, you seer! Go back to the land of Judah. Earn your bread there and do your prophesying there. 13 Don't prophesy anymore at Bethel, because this is the king's sanctuary and the temple of the kingdom."

14 Amos answered Amaziah, "I was neither a prophet nor a prophet's son, but I was a shepherd, and I also took care of sycamore-fig trees. 15 But the LORD took me from tending the flock and said to me, 'Go, prophesy to my people Israel.' 16 Now then, hear the word of the LORD. You say,

  " 'Do not prophesy against Israel,
    and stop preaching against the house of
      Isaac.'

17 "Therefore this is what the LORD says:

  " 'Your wife will become a prostitute in the
      city,
    and your sons and daughters will fall by
      the sword.
  Your land will be measured and divided up,
    and you yourself will die in a pagan[a]
      country.
  And Israel will certainly go into exile,
    away from their native land.' "

A Basket of Ripe Fruit

8 This is what the Sovereign LORD showed me: a basket of ripe fruit. 2 "What do you see, Amos?" he asked.

"A basket of ripe fruit," I answered.

Then the LORD said to me, "The time is ripe for my people Israel; I will spare them no longer.

3 "In that day," declares the Sovereign LORD, "the songs in the temple will turn to wailing.[b] Many, many bodies—flung everywhere! Silence!"

4 Hear this, you who trample the needy
    and do away with the poor of the land,

5 saying,

  "When will the New Moon be over
    that we may sell grain,
  and the Sabbath be ended
    that we may market wheat?"—
  skimping the measure,
    boosting the price
    and cheating with dishonest scales,
6 buying the poor with silver
    and the needy for a pair of sandals,
    selling even the sweepings with the wheat.

7 The LORD has sworn by the Pride of Jacob: "I will never forget anything they have done.

8 "Will not the land tremble for this,
    and all who live in it mourn?
  The whole land will rise like the Nile;
    it will be stirred up and then sink
    like the river of Egypt.

9 "In that day," declares the Sovereign LORD,

  "I will make the sun go down at noon
    and darken the earth in broad daylight.
10 I will turn your religious feasts into
      mourning
    and all your singing into weeping.
  I will make all of you wear sackcloth
    and shave your heads.

_____
a 17 Hebrew an unclean   b 3 Or "the temple singers will wail

I will make that time like mourning for an
    only son
  and the end of it like a bitter day.

11 "The days are coming," declares the Sovereign
    Lord,
  "when I will send a famine through the
    land—
not a famine of food or a thirst for water,
  but a famine of hearing the words of the
    Lord.
12 Men will stagger from sea to sea
  and wander from north to east,
searching for the word of the Lord,
  but they will not find it.

13 "In that day

"the lovely young women and strong young
    men
  will faint because of thirst.
14 They who swear by the shame[a] of Samaria,
  or say, 'As surely as your god lives,
    O Dan,'
  or, 'As surely as the god[b] of Beersheba
    lives'—
they will fall,
  never to rise again."

Israel to Be Destroyed

9 I saw the Lord standing by the altar, and he
said:

"Strike the tops of the pillars
  so that the thresholds shake.
Bring them down on the heads of all the
    people;
  those who are left I will kill with the sword.
Not one will get away,
  none will escape.
2 Though they dig down to the depths of the
    grave,[c]
from there my hand will take them.
Though they climb up to the heavens,
  from there I will bring them down.
3 Though they hide themselves on the top of
    Carmel,

there I will hunt them down and seize
    them.
Though they hide from me at the bottom of
    the sea,
  there I will command the serpent to bite
    them.
4 Though they are driven into exile by their
    enemies,
  there I will command the sword to slay
    them.
I will fix my eyes upon them
  for evil and not for good."

5 The Lord, the Lord Almighty,
  he who touches the earth and it melts,
  and all who live in it mourn—
the whole land rises like the Nile,
  then sinks like the river of Egypt—
6 he who builds his lofty palace[d] in the heavens
  and sets its foundation[e] on the earth,
who calls for the waters of the sea
  and pours them out over the face of the
    land—
  the Lord is his name.

7 "Are not you Israelites
  the same to me as the Cushites[f]?"
               declares the Lord.
"Did I not bring Israel up from Egypt,
  the Philistines from Caphtor[g]
  and the Arameans from Kir?

8 "Surely the eyes of the Sovereign Lord
  are on the sinful kingdom.
I will destroy it
  from the face of the earth—
yet I will not totally destroy
  the house of Jacob,"
               declares the Lord.

9 "For I will give the command,
  and I will shake the house of Israel
  among all the nations

---

a 14 Or by Ashima; or by the idol   b 14 Or power   c 2 Hebrew
to Sheol   d 6 The meaning of the Hebrew for this phrase is
uncertain.   e 6 The meaning of the Hebrew for this word is
uncertain.   f 7 That is, people from the upper Nile region
g 7 That is, Crete

as grain is shaken in a sieve,
    and not a pebble will reach the ground.
10 All the sinners among my people
    will die by the sword,
all those who say,
    'Disaster will not overtake or meet us.'

Israel's Restoration

11 "In that day I will restore
    David's fallen tent.
I will repair its broken places,
    restore its ruins,
    and build it as it used to be,
12 so that they may possess the remnant of
        Edom
    and all the nations that bear my name,*"
                        declares the LORD,
                    who will do these things.

13 "The days are coming," declares the LORD,

"when the reaper will be overtaken by the
        plowman
    and the planter by the one treading grapes.
New wine will drip from the mountains
    and flow from all the hills.
14 I will bring back my exiled b people Israel;
    they will rebuild the ruined cities and live
        in them.
They will plant vineyards and drink their wine;
    they will make gardens and eat their fruit.
15 I will plant Israel in their own land,
    never again to be uprooted
    from the land I have given them,"

                        says the LORD your God.

a 12 Hebrew; Septuagint *so that the remnant of men / and all the
nations that bear my name may seek ⌐the Lord⌐*   b 14 Or *will restore
the fortunes of my*

The Downside
OF PRIDE

The book of Obadiah reinforces the proverb "Pride goes before destruction, a haughty spirit before a fall" (Proverbs 16:18). Though Obadiah's message is short, it gets straight to the point: The nation of Edom, which had been at enmity with the Israelites for centuries, was to be destroyed. Edom was a country southeast of Judah. Because the Edomites lived high on the cliffs, they thought the geography of their land would protect them from enemy invasion and destruction. Not so, as Obadiah revealed.

The Edomites were proud of their position and confident of their safety. And when Judah was invaded and conquered, they not only gloated over the fact but looted Judah in the aftermath (see Obadiah 11 – 14). What made the situation more disturbing was that the Edomites and Israelites were related. The people of Edom were descended from Esau, the twin brother of Jacob (see Obadiah 10), one of Israel's patriarchs. God had no patience with the Edomites' attitude, and, through Obadiah, God told the Edomites they would be destroyed, while the Israelites would eventually return to their land.

As we read through this short book, we see the eternal truth that position, pride, power and prestige do not exclude us or protect us from God's scrutiny. No one, no matter what kind of house they live in, is sheltered from God's judgment.

VERSE *to* REMEMBER | OBADIAH 4

"Though you soar like the eagle and make your nest among the stars, from there I will bring you down," declares the LORD.

ABOUT OBADIAH

WRITTEN BY:
The prophet Obadiah

WRITTEN FOR:
The Edomites and
the people of Judah

DATE WRITTEN:
Probably during the
Babylonian attacks on
Jerusalem, between
605 and 586 B.C.

WHY WRITTEN:
To tell God's people
that God would punish
the Edomites

Obadiah

¹The vision of Obadiah.

1–4pp — Jer 49:14–16
5–6pp — Jer 49:9–10

This is what the Sovereign LORD says about Edom—

We have heard a message from the LORD:
  An envoy was sent to the nations to say,
"Rise, and let us go against her for
      battle"—

²"See, I will make you small among the
      nations;
  you will be utterly despised.
³The pride of your heart has deceived you,
  you who live in the clefts of the rocks*ᵃ*
  and make your home on the heights,
you who say to yourself,
  'Who can bring me down to the ground?'
⁴Though you soar like the eagle
  and make your nest among the stars,
  from there I will bring you down,"
                    declares the LORD.
⁵"If thieves came to you,
  if robbers in the night—
Oh, what a disaster awaits you—
  would they not steal only as much as they
      wanted?
If grape pickers came to you,
  would they not leave a few grapes?
⁶But how Esau will be ransacked,
  his hidden treasures pillaged!
⁷All your allies will force you to the border;
  your friends will deceive and overpower
      you;
those who eat your bread will set a trap for
      you,*ᵇ*
  but you will not detect it.

⁸"In that day," declares the LORD,
  "will I not destroy the wise men of Edom,
  men of understanding in the mountains of
      Esau?
⁹Your warriors, O Teman, will be terrified,
  and everyone in Esau's mountains
  will be cut down in the slaughter.

¹⁰Because of the violence against your brother
      Jacob,
  you will be covered with shame;
  you will be destroyed forever.
¹¹On the day you stood aloof
  while strangers carried off his wealth
and foreigners entered his gates
  and cast lots for Jerusalem,
  you were like one of them.
¹²You should not look down on your brother
  in the day of his misfortune,
nor rejoice over the people of Judah
  in the day of their destruction,
nor boast so much
  in the day of their trouble.
¹³You should not march through the gates of
      my people
  in the day of their disaster,
nor look down on them in their calamity
  in the day of their disaster,
nor seize their wealth
  in the day of their disaster.
¹⁴You should not wait at the crossroads
  to cut down their fugitives,
nor hand over their survivors
  in the day of their trouble.

¹⁵"The day of the LORD is near
  for all nations.
As you have done, it will be done to you;
  your deeds will return upon your own head.
¹⁶Just as you drank on my holy hill,
  so all the nations will drink continually;
they will drink and drink
  and be as if they had never been.
¹⁷But on Mount Zion will be deliverance;
  it will be holy,
and the house of Jacob
  will possess its inheritance.
¹⁸The house of Jacob will be a fire
  and the house of Joseph a flame;
the house of Esau will be stubble,
  and they will set it on fire and consume it.

ᵃ 3 Or *of Sela*   ᵇ 7 The meaning of the Hebrew for this clause is uncertain.

There will be no survivors
  from the house of Esau."
                    The Lord has spoken.

19 People from the Negev will occupy
  the mountains of Esau,
and people from the foothills will possess
  the land of the Philistines.
They will occupy the fields of Ephraim and
  Samaria,
  and Benjamin will possess Gilead.

20 This company of Israelite exiles who are in
  Canaan
  will possess the land as far as Zarephath;
the exiles from Jerusalem who are in
  Sepharad
  will possess the towns of the Negev.
21 Deliverers will go up on *a* Mount Zion
  to govern the mountains of Esau.
  And the kingdom will be the Lord's.

a 21 Or *from*

Stop RUNNING AWAY

Children everywhere love the well-known story about the man who ran away from God, was swallowed by a giant fish, and lived to tell about it. But there's much more to Jonah's story than the three days he spent inside the fish.

Jonah was a prophet from the northern kingdom of Israel who lived during the reign of King Jeroboam II (see 2 Kings 14:25). While other prophets were prophesying the judgment of Israel and Judah, Jonah was called to the distant city of Nineveh to warn the Ninevites of God's judgment. Instead of obeying God's call, Jonah ran away. He believed the Ninevites, who were known for their cruelty, were not deserving of God's mercy. But God calls every one of us to tell *all* people about his love. Everyone is worthy of his forgiveness. He's not selective and neither should we be.

As grandmothers we are called to share the good news of salvation not only with our grandchildren, but also with everyone around us. Each life, in a sense, is our "Nineveh." And like Jonah needed God's help to fulfill his calling, we too, with God's help, can stifle the urge to run and can instead fulfill our "vow" to God by openly and willingly sharing the stories of God's Word with those around us.

VERSE *to* REMEMBER | JONAH 2:9

"But I, with a song of thanksgiving, will sacrifice to you. What I have vowed I will make good. Salvation comes from the LORD."

Jonah

ABOUT JONAH

WRITTEN BY:
The prophet Jonah

WRITTEN FOR:
The people of Israel

DATE WRITTEN:
About 760 B.C.

WHY WRITTEN:
To show that God has compassion for all people and does not punish those who repent and are truly sorry for their sins

Jonah Flees From the LORD

1 The word of the LORD came to Jonah son of Amittai: ²"Go to the great city of Nineveh and preach against it, because its wickedness has come up before me."

³But Jonah ran away from the LORD and headed for Tarshish. He went down to Joppa, where he found a ship bound for that port. After paying the fare, he went aboard and sailed for Tarshish to flee from the LORD.

⁴Then the LORD sent a great wind on the sea, and such a violent storm arose that the ship threatened to break up. ⁵All the sailors were afraid and each cried out to his own god. And they threw the cargo into the sea to lighten the ship.

But Jonah had gone below deck, where he lay down and fell into a deep sleep. ⁶The captain went to him and said, "How can you sleep? Get up and call on your god! Maybe he will take notice of us, and we will not perish."

⁷Then the sailors said to each other, "Come, let us cast lots to find out who is responsible for this calamity." They cast lots and the lot fell on Jonah.

⁸So they asked him, "Tell us, who is responsible for making all this trouble for us? What do you do? Where do you come from? What is your country? From what people are you?"

⁹He answered, "I am a Hebrew and I worship the LORD, the God of heaven, who made the sea and the land."

¹⁰This terrified them and they asked, "What have you done?" (They knew he was running away from the LORD, because he had already told them so.)

¹¹The sea was getting rougher and rougher. So they asked him, "What should we do to you to make the sea calm down for us?"

¹²"Pick me up and throw me into the sea," he replied, "and it will become calm. I know that it is my fault that this great storm has come upon you."

¹³Instead, the men did their best to row back to land. But they could not, for the sea grew

stories to share

JONAH 1:1–17

Jonah and the Great Fish

LIFE LESSON: It's impossible to run away from God.

TO TALK ABOUT

✦ What did God ask Jonah to do?

✦ Why didn't Jonah want to preach to the people in Nineveh? (Hint: Read Jonah 4:1–2.) What good did he think running away would do?

✦ Have you ever tried to run away from something? Whether or not you realized it, were you actually trying to run away from God?

even wilder than before. ¹⁴Then they cried to the LORD, "O LORD, please do not let us die for taking this man's life. Do not hold us accountable for killing an innocent man, for you, O LORD, have done as you pleased." ¹⁵Then they took Jonah and threw him overboard, and the raging sea grew calm. ¹⁶At this the men greatly feared the LORD, and they offered a sacrifice to the LORD and made vows to him.

¹⁷But the LORD provided a great fish to swallow Jonah, and Jonah was inside the fish three days and three nights.

Jonah's Prayer

2 From inside the fish Jonah prayed to the LORD his God. ²He said:

"In my distress I called to the LORD,
  and he answered me.
From the depths of the grave*ᵃ* I called for
    help,
  and you listened to my cry.

³You hurled me into the deep,
  into the very heart of the seas,
  and the currents swirled about me;
all your waves and breakers
    swept over me.
⁴I said, 'I have been banished
    from your sight;
yet I will look again
    toward your holy temple.'
⁵The engulfing waters threatened me,*ᵇ*
  the deep surrounded me;
  seaweed was wrapped around my head.
⁶To the roots of the mountains I sank down;
  the earth beneath barred me in forever.
But you brought my life up from the pit,
  O LORD my God.

⁷"When my life was ebbing away,
  I remembered you, LORD,
and my prayer rose to you,
  to your holy temple.

⁸"Those who cling to worthless idols
    forfeit the grace that could be theirs.
⁹But I, with a song of thanksgiving,
    will sacrifice to you.
What I have vowed I will make good.
  Salvation comes from the LORD."

¹⁰And the LORD commanded the fish, and it vomited Jonah onto dry land.

Jonah Goes to Nineveh

3 Then the word of the LORD came to Jonah a second time: ²"Go to the great city of Nineveh and proclaim to it the message I give you."

³Jonah obeyed the word of the LORD and went to Nineveh. Now Nineveh was a very important city—a visit required three days. ⁴On the first day, Jonah started into the city. He proclaimed: "Forty more days and Nineveh will be overturned." ⁵The Ninevites believed God. They declared a fast, and all of them, from the greatest to the least, put on sackcloth.

⁶When the news reached the king of Nineveh, he rose from his throne, took off his royal robes, covered himself with sackcloth and sat down in the dust. ⁷Then he issued a proclamation in Nineveh:

"By the decree of the king and his nobles:

  Do not let any man or beast, herd or flock, taste anything; do not let them eat or drink. ⁸But let man and beast be covered with sackcloth. Let everyone call urgently on God. Let them give up their evil ways and their violence. ⁹Who knows? God may yet relent and with compassion turn from his fierce anger so that we will not perish."

¹⁰When God saw what they did and how they turned from their evil ways, he had compassion and did not bring upon them the destruction he had threatened.

Jonah's Anger at the LORD's Compassion

4 But Jonah was greatly displeased and became angry. ²He prayed to the LORD, "O LORD, is this not what I said when I was still at home? That is why I was so quick to flee to Tarshish. I knew that you are a gracious and compassionate God, slow to anger and abounding in love, a God who relents from sending calamity. ³Now,

---

ᵃ 2 Hebrew *Sheol*   *ᵇ* 5 Or *waters were at my throat*

"WHEN MY LIFE WAS EBBING
AWAY, I REMEMBERED YOU,
LORD, AND MY PRAYER ROSE TO
YOU, TO YOUR HOLY TEMPLE."
Jonah 2:7

Remembering the Lord

BOBBIE WOLGEMUTH

READ | JONAH 2:1 – 10

One of the great things about getting older is the collection of memories that are stored in the scrapbooks of our minds — including all the places we have lived. Each home has its own story. But getting to that collection of stories has meant moving from one location to another, and that hasn't been easy. Finding a buyer before we were able to move or hunting for just the right place in an unknown city was sometimes a painful and frustrating experience.

Story times with our grandchildren often include telling them how we made it through tough circumstances and unknown times with the Lord's help. When our "location, location, location" was not what a realtor would consider ideal, God had an important lesson to teach us.

Jonah was in a bad location: stuck in the belly of the fish, surrounded by rancid seaweed. He wondered if he would ever get out of that terrible place. Have you been there? Is a member of your family there? Can you tell your kids or grandkids — from your memory book — about a God who rescues?

Look at Jonah's response when he was stuck in a terrible place in his life. He remembered the Lord.

Stories that display God's character — his past faithfulness, his promises and his pattern of working in the many years of your life — are an encouragement your kids and grandkids need to hear when they're in a desperate situation. What word from Scripture did you cling to? What hymn did you sing? What prayer did you pray when your own life was engulfed by catastrophe?

Remember the Lord. Give your family the gift only you can give: stories of God's deliverance on your behalf. And, like Jonah, you will be filled with thanksgiving and able to tell everyone that "salvation comes from the LORD" (Jonah 2:9).

O Lord, we call out to you today in our distress. You are a God who rescues and restores. We remember your past faithfulness and wait for your salvation. Amen.

Your next devotion is located on page 1233.

GRANDCHILD IN FOCUS • PRAYER

SELECT ONE OF YOUR
GRANDCHILDREN TO FOCUS ON
IN PRAYER FOR THE NEXT 14 DAYS.

Salvation

Dear Lord, please guide my grandchild to your gift of salvation. I pray that she will come to know you, to love you and to walk close to you throughout her life. May she boldly claim Jesus as her Lord and Savior. Guide her as she makes choices that have eternal consequences. Help her to follow you each moment of her life. I pray this in Jesus' name, amen.

O Lord, take away my life, for it is better for me to die than to live."

⁴But the Lord replied, "Have you any right to be angry?"

⁵Jonah went out and sat down at a place east of the city. There he made himself a shelter, sat in its shade and waited to see what would happen to the city. ⁶Then the Lord God provided a vine and made it grow up over Jonah to give shade for his head to ease his discomfort, and Jonah was very happy about the vine. ⁷But at dawn the next day God provided a worm, which chewed the vine so that it withered. ⁸When the sun rose, God provided a scorching east wind, and the sun blazed on Jonah's head so that he grew faint. He wanted to die, and said, "It would be better for me to die than to live."

⁹But God said to Jonah, "Do you have a right to be angry about the vine?"

"I do," he said. "I am angry enough to die."

¹⁰But the Lord said, "You have been concerned about this vine, though you did not tend it or make it grow. It sprang up overnight and died overnight. ¹¹But Nineveh has more than a hundred and twenty thousand people who cannot tell their right hand from their left, and many cattle as well. Should I not be concerned about that great city?"

What God WANTS FROM US

Sometimes in today's "me-centered" society, finding justice, equality and fairness can be difficult to do. It's one thing to talk about social justice in theory; it's another thing to put it into practice. Politicians debate it and want to claim the idea as their own. But long ago, even from Israel's days of wandering in the desert, God spoke about the importance of social justice (see, for example, Exodus 23:1–9). Here again in the book of Micah, it is clearly directed.

Micah, a prophet from southern Judah, prophesied during the reigns of Jotham, Ahaz and Hezekiah, kings of Judah. He predicted the fall of Samaria (the capital of the northern kingdom of Israel) and preached the need for social justice in Israel and Judah (see, for example, Micah 2:1–2; 3:8–12). He gave clear instructions about how God's people should live. While people often use prayer to ask God for what they want, Micah turned it around and asked, "What does God want from me?" The answer is simple: act justly, love mercy and walk humbly with God (see Micah 6:8).

Though social justice may be difficult to achieve, we must continue to work toward it. This lesson from Micah 6:8 is a gem that we, as grandmothers, mothers and astute women, can emulate and teach to our grandchildren and those around us.

VERSE to REMEMBER | MICAH 6:8

He has showed you, O man, what is good. And what does the LORD require of you? To act justly and to love mercy and to walk humbly with your God.

Micah

ABOUT MICAH

WRITTEN BY:
The prophet Micah

WRITTEN FOR:
The people of Judah and Israel

DATE WRITTEN:
Sometime between 750 and 686 B.C.

WHY WRITTEN:
To reveal God's concern for justice in Israel and Judah

1 The word of the LORD that came to Micah of Moresheth during the reigns of Jotham, Ahaz and Hezekiah, kings of Judah—the vision he saw concerning Samaria and Jerusalem.

² Hear, O peoples, all of you,
    listen, O earth and all who are in it,
that the Sovereign LORD may witness against
        you,
    the Lord from his holy temple.

Judgment Against Samaria and Jerusalem

³ Look! The LORD is coming from his dwelling
        place;
    he comes down and treads the high places
        of the earth.
⁴ The mountains melt beneath him
    and the valleys split apart,
like wax before the fire,
    like water rushing down a slope.
⁵ All this is because of Jacob's transgression,
    because of the sins of the house of Israel.
What is Jacob's transgression?
    Is it not Samaria?
What is Judah's high place?
    Is it not Jerusalem?

⁶ "Therefore I will make Samaria a heap of
        rubble,
    a place for planting vineyards.
I will pour her stones into the valley
    and lay bare her foundations.
⁷ All her idols will be broken to pieces;
    all her temple gifts will be burned with
        fire;
    I will destroy all her images.
Since she gathered her gifts from the wages of
        prostitutes,
    as the wages of prostitutes they will again
        be used."

Weeping and Mourning

⁸ Because of this I will weep and wail;
    I will go about barefoot and naked.
I will howl like a jackal
    and moan like an owl.

⁹ For her wound is incurable;
    it has come to Judah.
It ᵃ has reached the very gate of my people,
    even to Jerusalem itself.
¹⁰ Tell it not in Gath ᵇ;
    weep not at all. ᶜ
In Beth Ophrah ᵈ
    roll in the dust.
¹¹ Pass on in nakedness and shame,
    you who live in Shaphir. ᵉ
Those who live in Zaanan ᶠ
    will not come out.
Beth Ezel is in mourning;
    its protection is taken from you.
¹² Those who live in Maroth ᵍ writhe in pain,
    waiting for relief,
because disaster has come from the LORD,
    even to the gate of Jerusalem.
¹³ You who live in Lachish, ʰ
    harness the team to the chariot.
You were the beginning of sin
    to the Daughter of Zion,
for the transgressions of Israel
    were found in you.
¹⁴ Therefore you will give parting gifts
    to Moresheth Gath.
The town of Aczib ⁱ will prove deceptive
    to the kings of Israel.
¹⁵ I will bring a conqueror against you
    who live in Mareshah. ʲ
He who is the glory of Israel
    will come to Adullam.
¹⁶ Shave your heads in mourning
    for the children in whom you delight;
make yourselves as bald as the vulture,
    for they will go from you into exile.

Man's Plans and God's

2 Woe to those who plan iniquity,
    to those who plot evil on their beds!

ᵃ 9 Or He   ᵇ 10 Gath sounds like the Hebrew for tell.
ᶜ 10 Hebrew; Septuagint may suggest not in Acco. The Hebrew for in
Acco sounds like the Hebrew for weep.   ᵈ 10 Beth Ophrah means
house of dust.   ᵉ 11 Shaphir means pleasant.   ᶠ 11 Zaanan
sounds like the Hebrew for come out.   ᵍ 12 Maroth sounds like
the Hebrew for bitter.   ʰ 13 Lachish sounds like the Hebrew for
team.   ⁱ 14 Aczib means deception.   ʲ 15 Mareshah sounds like
the Hebrew for conqueror.

At morning's light they carry it out
   because it is in their power to do it.
² They covet fields and seize them,
   and houses, and take them.
They defraud a man of his home,
   a fellowman of his inheritance.

³ Therefore, the LORD says:

"I am planning disaster against this people,
   from which you cannot save yourselves.
You will no longer walk proudly,
   for it will be a time of calamity.
⁴ In that day men will ridicule you;
   they will taunt you with this mournful
      song:
'We are utterly ruined;
   my people's possession is divided up.
He takes it from me!
   He assigns our fields to traitors.' "

⁵ Therefore you will have no one in the
   assembly of the LORD
   to divide the land by lot.

False Prophets

⁶ "Do not prophesy," their prophets say.
   "Do not prophesy about these things;
   disgrace will not overtake us."
⁷ Should it be said, O house of Jacob:
   "Is the Spirit of the LORD angry?
   Does he do such things?"

"Do not my words do good
   to him whose ways are upright?
⁸ Lately my people have risen up
   like an enemy.
You strip off the rich robe
   from those who pass by without a care,
   like men returning from battle.
⁹ You drive the women of my people
   from their pleasant homes.
You take away my blessing
   from their children forever.
¹⁰ Get up, go away!
   For this is not your resting place,
because it is defiled,
   it is ruined, beyond all remedy.

¹¹ If a liar and deceiver comes and says,
   'I will prophesy for you plenty of wine and
      beer,'
   he would be just the prophet for this
      people!

Deliverance Promised

¹² "I will surely gather all of you, O Jacob;
   I will surely bring together the remnant of
      Israel.
I will bring them together like sheep in a pen,
   like a flock in its pasture;
   the place will throng with people.
¹³ One who breaks open the way will go up
      before them;
   they will break through the gate and go
      out.
Their king will pass through before them,
   the LORD at their head."

Leaders and Prophets Rebuked

3 Then I said,

"Listen, you leaders of Jacob,
   you rulers of the house of Israel.
Should you not know justice,
²   you who hate good and love evil;
who tear the skin from my people
   and the flesh from their bones;
³ who eat my people's flesh,
   strip off their skin
   and break their bones in pieces;
who chop them up like meat for the pan,
   like flesh for the pot?"

⁴ Then they will cry out to the LORD,
   but he will not answer them.
At that time he will hide his face from them
   because of the evil they have done.

⁵ This is what the LORD says:

"As for the prophets
   who lead my people astray,
if one feeds them,
   they proclaim 'peace';

if he does not,
they prepare to wage war against him.
⁶Therefore night will come over you, without
visions,
and darkness, without divination.
The sun will set for the prophets,
and the day will go dark for them.
⁷The seers will be ashamed
and the diviners disgraced.
They will all cover their faces
because there is no answer from God."

⁸But as for me, I am filled with power,
with the Spirit of the LORD,
and with justice and might,
to declare to Jacob his transgression,
to Israel his sin.
⁹Hear this, you leaders of the house of Jacob,
you rulers of the house of Israel,
who despise justice
and distort all that is right;
¹⁰who build Zion with bloodshed,
and Jerusalem with wickedness.
¹¹Her leaders judge for a bribe,
her priests teach for a price,
and her prophets tell fortunes for
money.
Yet they lean upon the LORD and say,
"Is not the LORD among us?
No disaster will come upon us."
¹²Therefore because of you,
Zion will be plowed like a field,
Jerusalem will become a heap of rubble,
the temple hill a mound overgrown with
thickets.

The Mountain of the LORD

4:1–3pp — Isa 2:1–4

4 In the last days

the mountain of the LORD's temple will be
established
as chief among the mountains;
it will be raised above the hills,
and peoples will stream to it.

²Many nations will come and say,

"Come, let us go up to the mountain of the
LORD,
to the house of the God of Jacob.
He will teach us his ways,
so that we may walk in his paths."
The law will go out from Zion,
the word of the LORD from Jerusalem.
³He will judge between many peoples
and will settle disputes for strong nations
far and wide.
They will beat their swords into plowshares
and their spears into pruning hooks.
Nation will not take up sword against nation,
nor will they train for war anymore.
⁴Every man will sit under his own vine
and under his own fig tree,
and no one will make them afraid,
for the LORD Almighty has spoken.
⁵All the nations may walk
in the name of their gods;
we will walk in the name of the LORD
our God for ever and ever.

The LORD's Plan

⁶"In that day," declares the LORD,

"I will gather the lame;
I will assemble the exiles
and those I have brought to grief.
⁷I will make the lame a remnant,
those driven away a strong nation.
The LORD will rule over them in Mount Zion
from that day and forever.
⁸As for you, O watchtower of the flock,
O stronghold[a] of the Daughter of Zion,
the former dominion will be restored to you;
kingship will come to the Daughter of
Jerusalem."

⁹Why do you now cry aloud—
have you no king?
Has your counselor perished,
that pain seizes you like that of a woman in
labor?

a 8 Or hill

> MANY NATIONS WILL COME AND
> SAY, "COME, LET US GO UP TO THE
> MOUNTAIN OF THE LORD, TO THE
> HOUSE OF THE GOD OF JACOB. HE
> WILL TEACH US HIS WAYS, SO THAT
> WE MAY WALK IN HIS PATHS."
> *Micah 4:2*

Mountaintop Experiences

ANNE ORTLUND

READ | MICAH 4:1–5

At a recent conference somebody said something like, "Well, we just can't stay on the mountaintop wanting to build tabernacles; we have to go back to reality again in the valley" — and frankly, it seemed to my husband, Ray, and me as if this person was really saying, "I'm afraid of possible 'mountaintop experiences.' I'm more comfortable bustling about with life as usual."

We discussed this remark later. We wondered, "What was waiting for the disciples when they came down from the mountaintop where Jesus was transfigured and got back into the valley again? What was their 'reality'?"

We know what happened next: There was a huge, crashing fall into temptation for all the disciples, and they abandoned Christ in his hour of need. And death was waiting as well: the cross.

The "valleys" of our lives can hold plenty of perils, sins and defeats. Ask God for some "mountains"! The disciples' mountaintop experience was incredible — as Jesus' deity, normally shrouded, was magnificently exposed. He "led them up a high mountain by themselves. There he was transfigured before them" (Matthew 17:1–2). Years later Peter was still talking about it: "We were eyewitnesses of his majesty" (2 Peter 1:16).

Micah lived during a time when the Israelites were far from the Lord. As a result, Micah predicted that Jerusalem and the temple would be destroyed (see Micah 3:12). This tragic event did indeed occur about a century later. Micah 4:1–5 is a wonderful salvation oracle that begins with the promise that the Lord's temple will be reestablished. This promise is a comfort for people whose lives are in the valley: there will be a mountaintop experience for them some day. God promises high points — fresh encounters with him that give us direction, focus and encouragement so that we can continue our work in the valley.

Dear Lord, "My heart says of you, 'Seek his face!' Your face, Lord, I will seek."

Your next devotion is located on page 1236.

GRANDCHILD IN FOCUS • PRAYER

Physical Well-Being

Almighty God, Creator of us all, I pray that you will watch over my grandchild's physical development. May he grow in strength through the stages of his life. As he grows in awareness of his body, help him to understand that each body develops uniquely, yet is within your plan and your control. Please guard his health so that his diseases are few, his injuries are minor and his infirmities are brief. Amen.

¹⁰ Writhe in agony, O Daughter of Zion,
  like a woman in labor,
for now you must leave the city
  to camp in the open field.
You will go to Babylon;
  there you will be rescued.
There the LORD will redeem you
  out of the hand of your enemies.

¹¹ But now many nations
  are gathered against you.
They say, "Let her be defiled,
  let our eyes gloat over Zion!"
¹² But they do not know
  the thoughts of the LORD;
they do not understand his plan,
  he who gathers them like sheaves to the
    threshing floor.

¹³ "Rise and thresh, O Daughter of Zion,
  for I will give you horns of iron;
I will give you hoofs of bronze
  and you will break to pieces many nations."

You will devote their ill-gotten gains to the
  LORD,
  their wealth to the Lord of all the earth.

A Promised Ruler From Bethlehem

5 Marshal your troops, O city of troops, [a]
  for a siege is laid against us.
They will strike Israel's ruler
  on the cheek with a rod.

² "But you, Bethlehem Ephrathah,
  though you are small among the clans [b] of
    Judah,
out of you will come for me
  one who will be ruler over Israel,
whose origins [c] are from of old,
  from ancient times. [d]"

³ Therefore Israel will be abandoned
  until the time when she who is in labor
    gives birth
and the rest of his brothers return
  to join the Israelites.

⁴ He will stand and shepherd his flock
  in the strength of the LORD,
  in the majesty of the name of the LORD his
    God.
And they will live securely, for then his
    greatness
  will reach to the ends of the earth.
⁵   And he will be their peace.

Deliverance and Destruction

When the Assyrian invades our land
  and marches through our fortresses,
we will raise against him seven shepherds,
  even eight leaders of men.
⁶ They will rule [e] the land of Assyria with the
    sword,
  the land of Nimrod with drawn sword. [f]
He will deliver us from the Assyrian
  when he invades our land
  and marches into our borders.

⁷ The remnant of Jacob will be
  in the midst of many peoples
like dew from the LORD,
  like showers on the grass,
which do not wait for man
  or linger for mankind.
⁸ The remnant of Jacob will be among the
    nations,
  in the midst of many peoples,
like a lion among the beasts of the forest,
  like a young lion among flocks of sheep,
which mauls and mangles as it goes,
  and no one can rescue.
⁹ Your hand will be lifted up in triumph over
    your enemies,
  and all your foes will be destroyed.

¹⁰ "In that day," declares the LORD,

"I will destroy your horses from among you
  and demolish your chariots.
¹¹ I will destroy the cities of your land
  and tear down all your strongholds.

---

a 1 Or *Strengthen your walls, O walled city*   *b* 2 Or *rulers*
c 2 Hebrew *goings out*   *d* 2 Or *from days of eternity*
e 6 Or *crush*   *f* 6 Or *Nimrod in its gates*

¹²I will destroy your witchcraft
    and you will no longer cast spells.
¹³I will destroy your carved images
    and your sacred stones from among you;
you will no longer bow down
    to the work of your hands.
¹⁴I will uproot from among you your Asherah
      poles[a]
    and demolish your cities.
¹⁵I will take vengeance in anger and wrath
    upon the nations that have not obeyed me."

The Lord's Case Against Israel

6 Listen to what the Lord says:

"Stand up, plead your case before the
      mountains;
    let the hills hear what you have to say.
²Hear, O mountains, the Lord's accusation;
    listen, you everlasting foundations of the
      earth.
For the Lord has a case against his people;
    he is lodging a charge against Israel.

³"My people, what have I done to you?
    How have I burdened you? Answer me.
⁴I brought you up out of Egypt
    and redeemed you from the land of
      slavery.
I sent Moses to lead you,
    also Aaron and Miriam.
⁵My people, remember
    what Balak king of Moab counseled
    and what Balaam son of Beor answered.
Remember ⌊your journey⌋ from Shittim to
      Gilgal,
    that you may know the righteous acts of
      the Lord."

⁶With what shall I come before the Lord
    and bow down before the exalted God?
Shall I come before him with burnt offerings,
    with calves a year old?
⁷Will the Lord be pleased with thousands of
      rams,
    with ten thousand rivers of oil?

Shall I offer my firstborn for my
      transgression,
    the fruit of my body for the sin of my
      soul?
⁸He has showed you, O man, what is good.
    And what does the Lord require of you?
To act justly and to love mercy
    and to walk humbly with your God.

TALKING POINTS

Responsibility

God requires us to act justly,
love mercy and walk humbly with him.

MICAH 6:8

For more on responsibility, go to Matthew 25:14–30.

Israel's Guilt and Punishment

⁹Listen! The Lord is calling to the city—
    and to fear your name is wisdom—
    "Heed the rod and the One who appointed
      it.[b]
¹⁰Am I still to forget, O wicked house,
    your ill-gotten treasures
    and the short ephah,[c] which is accursed?
¹¹Shall I acquit a man with dishonest scales,
    with a bag of false weights?
¹²Her rich men are violent;
    her people are liars
    and their tongues speak deceitfully.
¹³Therefore, I have begun to destroy you,
    to ruin you because of your sins.
¹⁴You will eat but not be satisfied;
    your stomach will still be empty.[d]
You will store up but save nothing,
    because what you save I will give to the
      sword.

[a] 14 That is, symbols of the goddess Asherah   [b] 9 The meaning of the Hebrew for this line is uncertain.   [c] 10 An ephah was a dry measure.   [d] 14 The meaning of the Hebrew for this word is uncertain.

He has showed you, O man, what is good. And what does the Lord require of you? To act justly and to love mercy and to walk humbly with your God.

Micah 6:8

Acting Justly and Loving Mercy

CLAUDIA ARP

READ | MICAH 6:1–8

Baking cookies at Grammy's house is always fun for five-year-old Morgan and three-year-old Jason. Today they are diligently sharing assignments. While Morgan cracks the eggs, Jason sifts the flour. With a sudden "poof," flour is in the air and all over the floor!

"It's your fault, Jason!" Morgan cries indignantly as Jason looks helplessly at the mess on the floor. What just a moment before was pure pleasure is now spoiled by angry accusations.

Grammy, taking a deep breath, steps in to help and kneels beside the frozen little boy. "Jason, the cleanup sponge is under the sink. While you're wiping up, I'll get the dustpan."

When Morgan's accusations persist, Grammy reminds her that she may need to collect herself on the little chair just around the corner. Jason whispers, "I'm sorry, Grammy. I made a mess."

"I'm sorry too, Jason," Grammy lovingly responds. "But sometimes accidents happen when I try new things. This is just a kitchen floor; we can clean it."

Frowning, Morgan watches from the corner of her eye as the cleanup proceeds. As Grammy and Jason get underway once again, her heart changes. Whirling around, she hugs Grammy. "I love you, Grammy! Jason, let's sift the flour again."

Our young grandchildren still have a sweet innocence that affirms justice and mercy when they see it happening around them. If only we could have a pure heart like a child, we would deeply understand Micah 6:8. When we act justly, we live out what we believe through how we treat one another. When we love mercy, we are forgiving, compassionate and tolerant. And as we walk humbly with God, we develop faithfulness. Then daily, with confidence and calmness, we can live out our commitment to each other and to God — even when we're making cookies with our grandkids.

Dear Father, please help me to live out justice, mercy and a humble walk with you in all my relationships — especially with my grandchildren. And help me to always remember that flour on the floor can easily be cleaned up.

GRANDCHILD IN FOCUS • PRAYER

Emotional Development

O God, Creator of mind and body, I pray that you will give my grandchild emotional health and strength. Where there is anger, bring peace. Where there is confusion, bring clarity and focus. Where there are dark shadows, cast a ray of hope. Fill her with the sunshine of your Spirit. Warm her with the presence of your peace. Amen.

Your next devotion is located on page 1241.

¹⁵ You will plant but not harvest;
  you will press olives but not use the oil on
    yourselves,
  you will crush grapes but not drink the
    wine.
¹⁶ You have observed the statutes of Omri
  and all the practices of Ahab's house,
  and you have followed their traditions.
  Therefore I will give you over to ruin
  and your people to derision;
  you will bear the scorn of the nations. ^{*a*}"

Israel's Misery

7 What misery is mine!
  I am like one who gathers summer fruit
    at the gleaning of the vineyard;
  there is no cluster of grapes to eat,
    none of the early figs that I crave.
² The godly have been swept from the land;
  not one upright man remains.
  All men lie in wait to shed blood;
  each hunts his brother with a net.
³ Both hands are skilled in doing evil;
  the ruler demands gifts,
  the judge accepts bribes,
  the powerful dictate what they desire—
  they all conspire together.
⁴ The best of them is like a brier,
  the most upright worse than a thorn hedge.
  The day of your watchmen has come,
  the day God visits you.
  Now is the time of their confusion.
⁵ Do not trust a neighbor;
  put no confidence in a friend.
  Even with her who lies in your embrace
  be careful of your words.
⁶ For a son dishonors his father,
  a daughter rises up against her mother,
  a daughter-in-law against her mother-in-
    law—
  a man's enemies are the members of his
    own household.

⁷ But as for me, I watch in hope for the Lord,
  I wait for God my Savior;
  my God will hear me.

Israel Will Rise

⁸ Do not gloat over me, my enemy!
  Though I have fallen, I will rise.
  Though I sit in darkness,
  the Lord will be my light.
⁹ Because I have sinned against him,
  I will bear the Lord's wrath,
  until he pleads my case
  and establishes my right.
  He will bring me out into the light;
  I will see his righteousness.
¹⁰ Then my enemy will see it
  and will be covered with shame,
  she who said to me,
  "Where is the Lord your God?"

---

^{*a*} 16 Septuagint; Hebrew *scorn due my people*   ^{*b*} 14 Or *in the middle of Carmel*

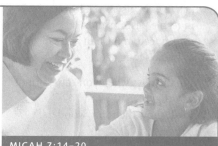

MICAH 7:14–20

Prayer and Praise

LIFE LESSON: God forgives and blesses his people when they repent.

TO TALK ABOUT

- ✦ Who is like a shepherd and who are like sheep?

- ✦ What good things does God promise in this passage?

- ✦ Why will wicked nations be ashamed when God shows his power?

- ✦ Look for the quotation marks in this passage. Who is having a conversation with whom?

stories to share

My eyes will see her downfall;
    even now she will be trampled underfoot
    like mire in the streets.

¹¹ The day for building your walls will come,
    the day for extending your boundaries.
¹² In that day people will come to you
    from Assyria and the cities of Egypt,
    even from Egypt to the Euphrates
    and from sea to sea
    and from mountain to mountain.
¹³ The earth will become desolate because of its
    inhabitants,
    as the result of their deeds.

Prayer and Praise

¹⁴ Shepherd your people with your staff,
    the flock of your inheritance,
    which lives by itself in a forest,
    in fertile pasturelands.*ᵇ*
Let them feed in Bashan and Gilead
    as in days long ago.

¹⁵ "As in the days when you came out of
    Egypt,
    I will show them my wonders."

¹⁶ Nations will see and be ashamed,
    deprived of all their power.
They will lay their hands on their mouths
    and their ears will become deaf.
¹⁷ They will lick dust like a snake,
    like creatures that crawl on the ground.
They will come trembling out of their dens;

they will turn in fear to the LORD our God
    and will be afraid of you.
¹⁸ Who is a God like you,
    who pardons sin and forgives the
        transgression
    of the remnant of his inheritance?
You do not stay angry forever
    but delight to show mercy.
¹⁹ You will again have compassion on us;
    you will tread our sins underfoot
    and hurl all our iniquities into the depths
        of the sea.
²⁰ You will be true to Jacob,
    and show mercy to Abraham,
as you pledged on oath to our fathers
    in days long ago.

PRAYING THE SCRIPTURES

Forgiveness

MICAH 7:18–19

O Lord, who is a God like you, who pardons sin and forgives transgressions? You do not stay angry forever but delight to show mercy. My grandchild can count on your compassion when he turns to you; you will tread his sins underfoot and hurl all his iniquities into the depths of the sea.

Next prayer in Forgiveness Prayer Track: Ephesians 4:32

Trusting God
THROUGH THE BAD TIMES

The book of Nahum appears to be addressed to Nineveh, the capital city of Assyria, which was the dominant world power at the time. But Nahum's message, in reality, was for the people of Judah.

The Assyrians were known for their cruel war practices, for deporting large groups of conquered peoples, and for torture and destruction. Around a century earlier, God had sent the prophet Jonah to Nineveh to warn the people of God's coming judgment. They repented at that time and averted God's judgment, but they soon returned to their cruelty, wickedness and pride. The Assyrians conquered the northern kingdom of Israel and took its citizens captive to Assyria. Now the people of Judah were facing the threat of a similar fate, and the prospect of an Assyrian invasion left the people filled with terror. In the midst of this anguish, Nahum the prophet spoke words of hope and comfort. He wanted to let them know that God, the God of all nations, was in control of not only their lives but all that happens throughout history.

Believers today can also find comfort in Nahum's words. Our world is similarly one of wars, turmoil and uncertainty. Sometimes we wonder if God is in control, if he really sees what is happening on Earth. Nahum the prophet reminds us that through all time — through the rise and fall of nations, through wars and threats of war — God's goodness and love endures. God is in control.

VERSE *to* REMEMBER | NAHUM 1:7 – 8

The LORD is good, a refuge in times of trouble. He cares for those who trust in him, but with an overwhelming flood he will make an end of ⌐Nineveh⌐; he will pursue his foes into darkness.

ABOUT NAHUM

WRITTEN BY:
The prophet Nahum

WRITTEN FOR:
The people of Judah

DATE WRITTEN:
Sometime between 663 and 612 B.C.

WHY WRITTEN:
To assure his people that God would destroy Nineveh, the capital city of Assyria, their great enemy

1

An oracle concerning Nineveh. The book of the vision of Nahum the Elkoshite.

The LORD's Anger Against Nineveh

2 The LORD is a jealous and avenging God;
  the LORD takes vengeance and is filled with
    wrath.
The LORD takes vengeance on his foes
  and maintains his wrath against his enemies.
3 The LORD is slow to anger and great in power;
  the LORD will not leave the guilty
    unpunished.
His way is in the whirlwind and the storm,
  and clouds are the dust of his feet.

TALKING POINTS

Guilt

God is patient with his repentant children but will punish the guilty.

NAHUM 1:3

For more on guilt, go to Hebrews 10:22–23.

4 He rebukes the sea and dries it up;
  he makes all the rivers run dry.
Bashan and Carmel wither
  and the blossoms of Lebanon fade.
5 The mountains quake before him
  and the hills melt away.
The earth trembles at his presence,
  the world and all who live in it.
6 Who can withstand his indignation?
  Who can endure his fierce anger?
His wrath is poured out like fire;
  the rocks are shattered before him.

7 The LORD is good,
  a refuge in times of trouble.
He cares for those who trust in him,
8   but with an overwhelming flood

TALKING POINTS

Trust

Trust God to take care of you.

NAHUM 1:7

For more on trust, go to Romans 15:13.

he will make an end of ⌊Nineveh⌋;
  he will pursue his foes into darkness.

9 Whatever they plot against the LORD
  he *a* will bring to an end;
  trouble will not come a second time.
10 They will be entangled among thorns
  and drunk from their wine;
  they will be consumed like dry stubble. *b*
11 From you, ⌊O Nineveh,⌋ has one come forth
  who plots evil against the LORD
  and counsels wickedness.

12 This is what the LORD says:

"Although they have allies and are numerous,
  they will be cut off and pass away.
Although I have afflicted you, ⌊O Judah,⌋
  I will afflict you no more.
13 Now I will break their yoke from your neck
  and tear your shackles away."

14 The LORD has given a command concerning
    you, ⌊Nineveh⌋:
  "You will have no descendants to bear your
    name.
I will destroy the carved images and cast idols
  that are in the temple of your gods.
I will prepare your grave,
  for you are vile."

15 Look, there on the mountains,
  the feet of one who brings good news,
  who proclaims peace!

a 9 Or What do you foes plot against the LORD? / He *b 10 The meaning of the Hebrew for this verse is uncertain.*

> THE LORD IS GOOD, A REFUGE
> IN TIMES OF TROUBLE. HE CARES
> FOR THOSE WHO TRUST IN HIM.
> *Nahum 1:7*

The Hand Goes Up

CHERYL BAKER

READ | NAHUM 1:1–15

As Maggie, my toddler granddaughter, was circling the backyard, she was drawn to a specific pathway. A sharp, concrete patio corner lined one side and a heavy, potted cactus bordered the other. Tomorrow, Grandpa would have to remove the cactus from the backyard, but today the solution was to follow closely in my granddaughter's footsteps. As she approached the trail, I instructed, "Hold Grandma's hand, honey. I don't want you to fall and get hurt."

Each time she circled the yard and approached the hazardous pathway, Maggie automatically raised her hand up to me. She never checked to see if I was following her closely, she just lifted her hand high over her head with confidence, knowing that I would not let her fall.

If I could only be that trusting of God! As I approach a hazardous point in my life's pathway, how I wish that I would always have the complete trust to automatically put my hand up to him. I know with confidence that he is there; however, sometimes I try to take matters into my own hands. When I choose to rely only on myself, I usually fall and get hurt.

Although most of the book of Nahum contains words of prophetic judgment directed to Nineveh, the dreaded oppressor of Judah, the book was meant for the Israelites. Through Nahum the Lord assured his people that "he cares for those who trust in him" (Nahum 1:7).

I realize that my precious granddaughter is quickly approaching her two-year birthday. With that milestone, she will slip into the "I wanna do this by myself" stage. And for a time, she will stop raising her hand up to those of us who want to protect her. As her family, it is crucial that we teach her about the love of Christ and demonstrate our reliance on God's power to keep us from falling.

Dear Lord and Father, thank you for your protection during the difficult times of my life. As my grandchildren grow up, I pray that when they approach hazardous turning points along their pathway, they will lift their hands with confidence toward you. Amen.

Your next devotion is located on page 1248.

GRANDCHILD IN FOCUS • PRAYER

Spiritual Growth

Dear Lord, today I pray for my grandchild's spiritual growth. I ask that you instill in him the desire to read and memorize your Word. Give him a passion to be in conversation with you. May loving and serving you be part of his daily life. I ask that you stay close to him and lead him to be transformed to your likeness, to reflect your grace and to radiate your love. I pray this in Jesus' name, amen.

Celebrate your festivals, O Judah,
  and fulfill your vows.
No more will the wicked invade you;
  they will be completely destroyed.

Nineveh to Fall

2 An attacker advances against you,
    ⌞Nineveh⌟.
  Guard the fortress,
  watch the road,
  brace yourselves,
  marshal all your strength!

2 The LORD will restore the splendor of Jacob
    like the splendor of Israel,
  though destroyers have laid them waste
    and have ruined their vines.

3 The shields of his soldiers are red;
    the warriors are clad in scarlet.
  The metal on the chariots flashes
    on the day they are made ready;
    the spears of pine are brandished. *a*
4 The chariots storm through the streets,
    rushing back and forth through the
      squares.
  They look like flaming torches;
    they dart about like lightning.

5 He summons his picked troops,
    yet they stumble on their way.
  They dash to the city wall;
    the protective shield is put in place.
6 The river gates are thrown open
    and the palace collapses.
7 It is decreed *b* that ⌞the city⌟
    be exiled and carried away.
  Its slave girls moan like doves
    and beat upon their breasts.
8 Nineveh is like a pool,
    and its water is draining away.
  "Stop! Stop!" they cry,
    but no one turns back.
9 Plunder the silver!
  Plunder the gold!
  The supply is endless,
    the wealth from all its treasures!

10 She is pillaged, plundered, stripped!
  Hearts melt, knees give way,
    bodies tremble, every face grows pale.
11 Where now is the lions' den,
    the place where they fed their young,
  where the lion and lioness went,
    and the cubs, with nothing to fear?
12 The lion killed enough for his cubs
    and strangled the prey for his mate,
  filling his lairs with the kill
    and his dens with the prey.

13 "I am against you,"
    declares the LORD Almighty.
  "I will burn up your chariots in smoke,
    and the sword will devour your young lions.
  I will leave you no prey on the earth.
  The voices of your messengers
    will no longer be heard."

Woe to Nineveh

3 Woe to the city of blood,
    full of lies,
  full of plunder,
    never without victims!
2 The crack of whips,
    the clatter of wheels,
  galloping horses
    and jolting chariots!
3 Charging cavalry,
    flashing swords
    and glittering spears!
  Many casualties,
    piles of dead,
  bodies without number,
    people stumbling over the corpses—
4 all because of the wanton lust of a harlot,
    alluring, the mistress of sorceries,
  who enslaved nations by her prostitution
    and peoples by her witchcraft.

5 "I am against you," declares the LORD
      Almighty.
  "I will lift your skirts over your face.

a 3 Hebrew; Septuagint and Syriac / *the horsemen rush to and fro*
b 7 The meaning of the Hebrew for this word is uncertain.

I will show the nations your nakedness
    and the kingdoms your shame.
⁶I will pelt you with filth,
    I will treat you with contempt
    and make you a spectacle.
⁷All who see you will flee from you and say,
    'Nineveh is in ruins—who will mourn for
        her?'
    Where can I find anyone to comfort you?"

⁸Are you better than Thebes,ᵃ
    situated on the Nile,
    with water around her?
The river was her defense,
    the waters her wall.
⁹Cushᵇ and Egypt were her boundless strength;
    Put and Libya were among her allies.
¹⁰Yet she was taken captive
    and went into exile.
Her infants were dashed to pieces
    at the head of every street.
Lots were cast for her nobles,
    and all her great men were put in chains.
¹¹You too will become drunk;
    you will go into hiding
    and seek refuge from the enemy.

¹²All your fortresses are like fig trees
    with their first ripe fruit;
when they are shaken,
    the figs fall into the mouth of the eater.
¹³Look at your troops—
    they are all women!
The gates of your land
    are wide open to your enemies;
    fire has consumed their bars.

¹⁴Draw water for the siege,
    strengthen your defenses!
Work the clay,
    tread the mortar,
    repair the brickwork!
¹⁵There the fire will devour you;
    the sword will cut you down
    and, like grasshoppers, consume you.
Multiply like grasshoppers,
    multiply like locusts!
¹⁶You have increased the number of your
        merchants
    till they are more than the stars of the sky,
but like locusts they strip the land
    and then fly away.
¹⁷Your guards are like locusts,
    your officials like swarms of locusts
    that settle in the walls on a cold day—
but when the sun appears they fly away,
    and no one knows where.

¹⁸O king of Assyria, your shepherdsᶜ
        slumber;
    your nobles lie down to rest.
Your people are scattered on the
        mountains
    with no one to gather them.
¹⁹Nothing can heal your wound;
    your injury is fatal.
Everyone who hears the news about you
    claps his hands at your fall,
for who has not felt
    your endless cruelty?

ᵃ 8 Hebrew *No Amon*   ᵇ 9 That is, the upper Nile region
ᶜ 18 Or *rulers*

They Won't
GET AWAY WITH IT

"Do you think they'll get away with it?" "Will that person get acquitted?" We're not always confident that justice will prevail in our society today. Sometimes it appears as though people are literally getting away with murder. We tearfully ask God, "How can you let this happen?" Or perhaps our grandchildren are asking these questions as they struggle to understand why being a Christian isn't "paying off." They wonder why non-Christians seem to have such easy lives.

The prophet Habakkuk, drawing from the problems he witnessed in and around Judah, asked similar questions of God. Habakkuk likely prophesied during the reign of the malicious King Jehoiakim, who often arrested God's prophets and even killed one of them. Sin was out of control in Judah as the Babylonian Empire gained more power and the people turned their backs on God. Habakkuk complained to God about the evil in Judah but was baffled as to why God would use the extremely wicked Babylonians to correct his own people.

The answers to all of Habakkuk's complaints and questions are here in this short book: God is in control and is judging evil actions even as they are inflicted on others. The wicked may appear to succeed, but they have no real power. Those who love and obey God will, in the end, experience the ultimate victory.

VERSE *to* REMEMBER | HABAKKUK 3:2

LORD, I have heard of your fame; I stand in awe of your deeds, O LORD. Renew them in our day, in our time make them known; in wrath remember mercy.

ABOUT HABAKKUK

WRITTEN BY:
The prophet Habakkuk

WRITTEN FOR:
The people of Judah

DATE WRITTEN:
Around 605 B.C.

WHY WRITTEN:
To show that people do not get away with being wicked but will ultimately be punished by God

1
The oracle that Habakkuk the prophet received.

Habakkuk's Complaint

[2] How long, O LORD, must I call for help,
  but you do not listen?
Or cry out to you, "Violence!"
  but you do not save?
[3] Why do you make me look at injustice?
  Why do you tolerate wrong?
Destruction and violence are before me;
  there is strife, and conflict abounds.
[4] Therefore the law is paralyzed,
  and justice never prevails.
The wicked hem in the righteous,
  so that justice is perverted.

The LORD's Answer

[5] "Look at the nations and watch—
  and be utterly amazed.
For I am going to do something in your days
  that you would not believe,
  even if you were told.
[6] I am raising up the Babylonians,[a]
  that ruthless and impetuous people,
who sweep across the whole earth
  to seize dwelling places not their own.
[7] They are a feared and dreaded people;
  they are a law to themselves
  and promote their own honor.
[8] Their horses are swifter than leopards,
  fiercer than wolves at dusk.
Their cavalry gallops headlong;
  their horsemen come from afar.
They fly like a vulture swooping to devour;
[9]   they all come bent on violence.
Their hordes[b] advance like a desert wind
  and gather prisoners like sand.
[10] They deride kings
  and scoff at rulers.
They laugh at all fortified cities;
  they build earthen ramps and capture them.
[11] Then they sweep past like the wind and go
  on—
  guilty men, whose own strength is their
  god."

Habakkuk's Second Complaint

[12] O LORD, are you not from everlasting?
  My God, my Holy One, we will not die.
O LORD, you have appointed them to execute
  judgment;
  O Rock, you have ordained them to
  punish.
[13] Your eyes are too pure to look on evil;
  you cannot tolerate wrong.
Why then do you tolerate the treacherous?
  Why are you silent while the wicked
swallow up those more righteous than
  themselves?
[14] You have made men like fish in the sea,
  like sea creatures that have no ruler.
[15] The wicked foe pulls all of them up with
  hooks,
  he catches them in his net,
he gathers them up in his dragnet;
  and so he rejoices and is glad.
[16] Therefore he sacrifices to his net
  and burns incense to his dragnet,
for by his net he lives in luxury
  and enjoys the choicest food.
[17] Is he to keep on emptying his net,
  destroying nations without mercy?

2
I will stand at my watch
  and station myself on the ramparts;
I will look to see what he will say to me,
  and what answer I am to give to this
  complaint.[c]

The LORD's Answer

[2] Then the LORD replied:

"Write down the revelation
  and make it plain on tablets
  so that a herald[d] may run with it.
[3] For the revelation awaits an appointed
  time;
  it speaks of the end
  and will not prove false.

---

[a] 6 Or Chaldeans   [b] 9 The meaning of the Hebrew for this word
is uncertain.   [c] 1 Or and what to answer when I am rebuked
[d] 2 Or so that whoever reads it

Though it linger, wait for it;
it[a] will certainly come and will not delay.

4 "See, he is puffed up;
his desires are not upright—
but the righteous will live by his faith[b] —
5 indeed, wine betrays him;
he is arrogant and never at rest.
Because he is as greedy as the grave[c]
and like death is never satisfied,
he gathers to himself all the nations
and takes captive all the peoples.

6 "Will not all of them taunt him with ridicule and scorn, saying,

" 'Woe to him who piles up stolen goods
and makes himself wealthy by extortion!
How long must this go on?'
7 Will not your debtors[d] suddenly arise?
Will they not wake up and make you
tremble?
Then you will become their victim.
8 Because you have plundered many nations,
the peoples who are left will plunder you.
For you have shed man's blood;
you have destroyed lands and cities and
everyone in them.

9 "Woe to him who builds his realm by unjust
gain
to set his nest on high,
to escape the clutches of ruin!
10 You have plotted the ruin of many peoples,
shaming your own house and forfeiting
your life.
11 The stones of the wall will cry out,
and the beams of the woodwork will
echo it.

12 "Woe to him who builds a city with bloodshed
and establishes a town by crime!
13 Has not the LORD Almighty determined
that the people's labor is only fuel for the
fire,
that the nations exhaust themselves for
nothing?

14 For the earth will be filled with the
knowledge of the glory of the LORD,
as the waters cover the sea.

15 "Woe to him who gives drink to his
neighbors,
pouring it from the wineskin till they are
drunk,
so that he can gaze on their naked bodies.
16 You will be filled with shame instead of
glory.
Now it is your turn! Drink and be
exposed[e]!
The cup from the LORD's right hand is
coming around to you,
and disgrace will cover your glory.

TALKING POINTS

Addictions
Drunkenness leads to shame.
HABAKKUK 2:15–16

For more on addictions, go to 1 Corinthians 6:9–11.

17 The violence you have done to Lebanon will
overwhelm you,
and your destruction of animals will
terrify you.
For you have shed man's blood;
you have destroyed lands and cities and
everyone in them.

18 "Of what value is an idol, since a man has
carved it?
Or an image that teaches lies?
For he who makes it trusts in his own
creation;
he makes idols that cannot speak.

---

[a] 3 Or Though he linger, wait for him; / he   [b] 4 Or faithfulness
[c] 5 Hebrew Sheol   [d] 7 Or creditors   [e] 16 Masoretic Text; Dead
Sea Scrolls, Aquila, Vulgate and Syriac (see also Septuagint) and
stagger

19 Woe to him who says to wood, 'Come
   to life!'
   Or to lifeless stone, 'Wake up!'
   Can it give guidance?
   It is covered with gold and silver;
     there is no breath in it.
20 But the LORD is in his holy temple;
     let all the earth be silent before him."

Habakkuk's Prayer

3 A prayer of Habakkuk the prophet. On *shig-
   ionoth.* *a*

2 LORD, I have heard of your fame;
   I stand in awe of your deeds, O LORD.
   Renew them in our day,
     in our time make them known;
     in wrath remember mercy.

3 God came from Teman,
     the Holy One from Mount Paran.   *Selah* *b*
   His glory covered the heavens
     and his praise filled the earth.
4 His splendor was like the sunrise;
     rays flashed from his hand,
     where his power was hidden.
5 Plague went before him;
     pestilence followed his steps.
6 He stood, and shook the earth;
     he looked, and made the nations
       tremble.
   The ancient mountains crumbled
     and the age-old hills collapsed.
     His ways are eternal.
7 I saw the tents of Cushan in distress,
     the dwellings of Midian in anguish.

8 Were you angry with the rivers, O LORD?
     Was your wrath against the streams?
   Did you rage against the sea
     when you rode with your horses
     and your victorious chariots?
9 You uncovered your bow,
     you called for many arrows.   *Selah*
   You split the earth with rivers;
10   the mountains saw you and writhed.

Torrents of water swept by;
     the deep roared
     and lifted its waves on high.
11 Sun and moon stood still in the heavens
     at the glint of your flying arrows,
     at the lightning of your flashing spear.
12 In wrath you strode through the earth
     and in anger you threshed the nations.
13 You came out to deliver your people,
     to save your anointed one.
   You crushed the leader of the land of
       wickedness,
     you stripped him from head to foot.   *Selah*
14 With his own spear you pierced his head
     when his warriors stormed out to scatter us,
   gloating as though about to devour
     the wretched who were in hiding.
15 You trampled the sea with your horses,
     churning the great waters.

16 I heard and my heart pounded,
     my lips quivered at the sound;
   decay crept into my bones,
     and my legs trembled.
   Yet I will wait patiently for the day of
       calamity
     to come on the nation invading us.
17 Though the fig tree does not bud
     and there are no grapes on the vines,

---

a 1 Probably a literary or musical term   *b 3* A word of uncertain
meaning; possibly a musical term; also in verses 9 and 13

TALKING POINTS

Joy and Happiness

Even when things go wrong,
we can find joy in our
relationship with God.

HABAKKUK 3:17–18

This is the last talking point on joy and happiness.

> THOUGH THE FIG TREE DOES NOT BUD
> AND THERE ARE NO GRAPES ON THE VINES,
> THOUGH THE OLIVE CROP FAILS AND THE
> FIELDS PRODUCE NO FOOD, THOUGH THERE
> ARE NO SHEEP IN THE PEN AND NO CATTLE
> IN THE STALLS, YET I WILL REJOICE IN THE
> LORD, I WILL BE JOYFUL IN GOD MY SAVIOR.
> *Habakkuk 3:17–18*

I Am Determined

JEAN E. SYSWERDA

READ | HABAKKUK 3:16–19

God showed the prophet Habakkuk that the powerful Babylonians were soon to destroy Judah. Yet Habakkuk concluded his book with an expression of faith—actually more than that: an expression of joy in the face of disaster—that is one of the Bible's most incredible passages. Some might find it hard to keep faith when they stub a toe. Habakkuk was determined ("I will . . . I will") to keep faith when all seemed lost. The word *determined* is key here. Like Job (see Job 13:15), Habakkuk determined beforehand not to let his faith falter in the face of pain or tragedy.

I have known some rough times in my life. Illness and house fires are not small things. Through them all, my faith remained firm, no problem. But when my youngest granddaughter died suddenly, when I held my own daughter as she cried, "My baby, my baby," my faith took a hit. How could I trust a God who would allow/permit/do/carry out (take your pick according to your theological inclination) such a horror, not just to us but to her, three months old and so innocent? How could I follow a God who ruled a world with such sorrow in it? How could I even go on at all?

And that's where determination came into play. Like Habakkuk, I had to choose to rejoice. I had to choose to trust in God even when disaster hit and despair followed. Only two choices stood before me: I could turn away from God, or I could turn toward him. As I considered those choices, I looked away and discovered complete and frightening nothingness. Then I looked toward God and decided that even if he provides no answers, even if more tragedy follows, even if the cloud never lifts from our lives, I will trust in him. I will rejoice in him. I am determined!

O Lord, what is the meaning of such suffering in life? Is there a purpose in it all? I've chosen to trust you, to believe that there is meaning and that you know what you are doing. I've decided that no matter what happens, I will rejoice in you, Lord; I will be joyful in God my Savior. Amen.

Your next devotion is located on page 1252.

GRANDCHILD IN FOCUS • PRAYER

Relationships at Home

O Lord, I pray that you will bless the home and family of my grandchild. May the relationships she has with her parents and siblings enhance her well-being, support her self-confidence and increase her faith. May her home life reflect your love, your grace, your compassion and your peace. Guide her parents to direct her in love and truth, so she will grow into a strong and compassionate individual. Amen.

though the olive crop fails
and the fields produce no food,
though there are no sheep in the pen
and no cattle in the stalls,
¹⁸ yet I will rejoice in the LORD,
I will be joyful in God my Savior.

¹⁹ The Sovereign LORD is my strength;
he makes my feet like the feet of a deer,
he enables me to go on the heights.

For the director of music. On my stringed
instruments.

TALKING POINTS

Encouragement

No matter what our circumstances,
we can rejoice in God our Savior,
who gives us his strength.

HABAKKUK 3:17–19

For more on encouragement, go to Romans 8:28.

Cheering US ON

The message delivered by Zephaniah, who prophesied during the reign of King Josiah, was similar to that of many of the other prophets: The people of Judah would suffer God's wrath because of their sinfulness. Zephaniah prophesied of a coming "day of the LORD," a time when God would judge the nations, including Judah. God's wrath would be intense: "I will sweep away everything from the face of the earth," God told the people (Zephaniah 1:2).

But like so many of the other prophets, Zephaniah also shared a wonderful message of hope for God's people: Those who seek the Lord will be restored. "Sing, O Daughter of Zion; shout aloud, O Israel! . . . The LORD has taken away your punishment, he has turned back your enemy" (Zephaniah 3:14–15).

As we read through Zephaniah's prophecy, we can rejoice along with Israel. Our God will be faithful to us, delight in us, love us and show his mercy to us. What wonderful words of assurance in the face of difficulties and troubled times.

VERSE *to* REMEMBER | ZEPHANIAH 3:17

"The LORD your God is with you, he is mighty to save. He will take great delight in you, he will quiet you with his love, he will rejoice over you with singing."

Zephaniah

ABOUT ZEPHANIAH

WRITTEN BY:
The prophet Zephaniah

WRITTEN FOR:
The people of Judah

DATE WRITTEN:
Probably during the early years of King Josiah's reign (640–609 B.C.)

WHY WRITTEN:
To warn Judah that God will judge sinful people

1

The word of the Lord that came to Zephaniah son of Cushi, the son of Gedaliah, the son of Amariah, the son of Hezekiah, during the reign of Josiah son of Amon king of Judah:

Warning of Coming Destruction

2 "I will sweep away everything
　　from the face of the earth,"
　　　　　　　　　declares the Lord.
3 "I will sweep away both men and animals;
　　I will sweep away the birds of the air
　　and the fish of the sea.
The wicked will have only heaps of rubble *a*
　　when I cut off man from the face of
　　　the earth,"
　　　　　　　　　declares the Lord.

Against Judah

4 "I will stretch out my hand against Judah
　　and against all who live in Jerusalem.
I will cut off from this place every remnant of
　　Baal,
　　the names of the pagan and the idolatrous
　　　priests—
5 those who bow down on the roofs
　　to worship the starry host,
　　those who bow down and swear by the Lord
　　and who also swear by Molech, *b*
6 those who turn back from following the
　　Lord
　　and neither seek the Lord nor inquire of
　　　him.
7 Be silent before the Sovereign Lord,
　　for the day of the Lord is near.
The Lord has prepared a sacrifice;
　　he has consecrated those he has invited.
8 On the day of the Lord's sacrifice
　　I will punish the princes
　　and the king's sons
　　and all those clad
　　in foreign clothes.
9 On that day I will punish
　　all who avoid stepping on the threshold, *c*
who fill the temple of their gods
　　with violence and deceit.

10 "On that day," declares the Lord,
　　"a cry will go up from the Fish Gate,
　　wailing from the New Quarter,
　　and a loud crash from the hills.
11 Wail, you who live in the market district *d*;
　　all your merchants will be wiped out,
　　all who trade with *e* silver will be ruined.
12 At that time I will search Jerusalem with
　　lamps
　　and punish those who are complacent,
　　who are like wine left on its dregs,
who think, 'The Lord will do nothing,
　　either good or bad.'
13 Their wealth will be plundered,
　　their houses demolished.
They will build houses
　　but not live in them;
they will plant vineyards
　　but not drink the wine.

The Great Day of the Lord

14 "The great day of the Lord is near—
　　near and coming quickly.
Listen! The cry on the day of the Lord will be
　　bitter,
　　the shouting of the warrior there.
15 That day will be a day of wrath,
　　a day of distress and anguish,
a day of trouble and ruin,
　　a day of darkness and gloom,
　　a day of clouds and blackness,
16 a day of trumpet and battle cry
　　against the fortified cities
　　and against the corner towers.
17 I will bring distress on the people
　　and they will walk like blind men,
　　because they have sinned against the Lord.
Their blood will be poured out like dust
　　and their entrails like filth.
18 Neither their silver nor their gold
　　will be able to save them
　　on the day of the Lord's wrath.

---

a 3 The meaning of the Hebrew for this line is uncertain.
b 5 Hebrew *Malcam,* that is, Milcom　　*c 9* See 1 Samuel 5:5.
d 11 Or *the Mortar*　　*e 11* Or *in*

The Pros and Cons of Affluence

There's no doubt that "money talks." But what does it say to your grandchildren?

If the kids are old enough to think abstractly, ask them to come up with lists of the advantages and disadvantages of money. Point out what Jesus said about money (see Matthew 6:19–24). Show them some Old Testament texts that refer to wealth as God's blessing (see Deuteronomy 8:18; 1 Chronicles 29:12). Then discuss how money can be a bad thing (see Ecclesiastes 5:10). You may also want to check out "Talking Points" on the topic of money to find Biblical texts to help you discuss this topic.

Once you have discussed what God says about money and how we should view it, you may want to close with this question: What action can each of us take to share our abundance with those who enjoy fewer advantages?

Long-Distance Variation: Share your observations, Scriptures passages and questions in writing or by phone. Then share with your grandchildren what you've learned and how you intend to change your own approach to God's blessings.

Dear Lord, giver of all blessings, help me never to take your blessings for granted. May this exercise develop in all of us a healthier and more generous attitude toward the wealth you have given us. Amen.

Your next devotion is located on page 1254.

GRANDCHILD IN FOCUS • PRAYER

Friends

Dear Lord and Father, I pray for my grandchild's social life and his friends. Bring diverse friends into his life who will love and encourage him, who will bring joy and laughter to the good times and comfort and support through difficulties and disappointments. Grant him wisdom and discernment as he selects his friends; help him to avoid cliques that restrict, activities that endanger, and foolish and dangerous behaviors that harm. I ask that you fill his life with close and caring relationships. Amen.

In the fire of his jealousy
    the whole world will be consumed,
for he will make a sudden end
    of all who live in the earth."

2 Gather together, gather together,
    O shameful nation,
2 before the appointed time arrives
    and that day sweeps on like chaff,
before the fierce anger of the LORD comes
        upon you,
    before the day of the LORD's wrath comes
        upon you.
3 Seek the LORD, all you humble of the land,
    you who do what he commands.
Seek righteousness, seek humility;
    perhaps you will be sheltered
    on the day of the LORD's anger.

Against Philistia

4 Gaza will be abandoned
    and Ashkelon left in ruins.
At midday Ashdod will be emptied
    and Ekron uprooted.
5 Woe to you who live by the sea,
    O Kerethite people;
the word of the LORD is against you,
    O Canaan, land of the Philistines.

"I will destroy you,
    and none will be left."

6 The land by the sea, where the Kerethites[a]
    dwell,
    will be a place for shepherds and sheep
        pens.
7 It will belong to the remnant of the house of
    Judah;
    there they will find pasture.
In the evening they will lie down
    in the houses of Ashkelon.
The LORD their God will care for them;
    he will restore their fortunes.[b]

Against Moab and Ammon

8 "I have heard the insults of Moab
    and the taunts of the Ammonites,
who insulted my people
    and made threats against their land.
9 Therefore, as surely as I live,"
    declares the LORD Almighty, the God of
        Israel,
"surely Moab will become like Sodom,
    the Ammonites like Gomorrah —
a place of weeds and salt pits,
    a wasteland forever.
The remnant of my people will plunder
    them;
    the survivors of my nation will inherit
        their land."

10 This is what they will get in return for their
    pride,
    for insulting and mocking the people of
        the LORD Almighty.
11 The LORD will be awesome to them
    when he destroys all the gods of the land.
The nations on every shore will worship him,
    every one in its own land.

Against Cush

12 "You too, O Cushites,[c]
    will be slain by my sword."

Against Assyria

13 He will stretch out his hand against the north
    and destroy Assyria,
leaving Nineveh utterly desolate
    and dry as the desert.
14 Flocks and herds will lie down there,
    creatures of every kind.
The desert owl and the screech owl
    will roost on her columns.
Their calls will echo through the windows,
    rubble will be in the doorways,
    the beams of cedar will be exposed.
15 This is the carefree city
    that lived in safety.
She said to herself,
    "I am, and there is none besides me."

---

a 6 The meaning of the Hebrew for this word is uncertain.
b 7 Or *will bring back their captives*   c 12 That is, people from the
upper Nile region

Worship the Lord

Shout with joy to God, all the earth!
  Sing the glory of his name;
  make his praise glorious!
Say to God, "How awesome are your deeds!
  So great is your power
  that your enemies cringe before you.
All the earth bows down to you;
  they sing praise to you,
  they sing praise to your name."   *Selah*

Come and listen, all you who fear God;
  let me tell you what he has done for me.
I cried out to him with my mouth;
  his praise was on my tongue.
If I had cherished sin in my heart,
  the Lord would not have listened;
but God has surely listened
  and heard my voice in prayer.
Praise be to God,
  who has not rejected my prayer
  or withheld his love from me!

Psalm 66:1−4,16−20

*Dear God, I come to you today, certain that
you will listen to my request and hear my
prayer. With praise and joy, let me tell others
of all you have done for me. Let me share your
love with all who surround me so that together we
will bring glory to your name. Amen.*

Your next devotion is located on page 1256.

GRANDCHILD IN FOCUS · PRAYER

Self-Image

*O loving God, I praise you for creating my
grandchild as a unique individual. Now I ask you
to help her appreciate her uniqueness. Build up her
self-image so she can enjoy her individuality. Help
her to stand firm for who she is, where she has
come from and what she believes in. Encourage
her not only to have hopes and dreams but
to also enjoy each day as it comes.
In Jesus' name, amen.*

What a ruin she has become,
a lair for wild beasts!
All who pass by her scoff
and shake their fists.

The Future of Jerusalem

3 Woe to the city of oppressors,
rebellious and defiled!
² She obeys no one,
she accepts no correction.
She does not trust in the Lord,
she does not draw near to her God.
³ Her officials are roaring lions,
her rulers are evening wolves,
who leave nothing for the morning.
⁴ Her prophets are arrogant;
they are treacherous men.
Her priests profane the sanctuary
and do violence to the law.
⁵ The Lord within her is righteous;
he does no wrong.
Morning by morning he dispenses his justice,
and every new day he does not fail,
yet the unrighteous know no shame.

⁶ "I have cut off nations;
their strongholds are demolished.
I have left their streets deserted,
with no one passing through.
Their cities are destroyed;
no one will be left — no one at all.
⁷ I said to the city,
'Surely you will fear me
and accept correction!'
Then her dwelling would not be cut off,
nor all my punishments come upon her.
But they were still eager
to act corruptly in all they did.
⁸ Therefore wait for me," declares the Lord,
"for the day I will stand up to testify.ᵃ
I have decided to assemble the nations,
to gather the kingdoms
and to pour out my wrath on them —
all my fierce anger.
The whole world will be consumed
by the fire of my jealous anger.

⁹ "Then will I purify the lips of the peoples,
that all of them may call on the name of
the Lord
and serve him shoulder to shoulder.
¹⁰ From beyond the rivers of Cush ᵇ
my worshipers, my scattered people,
will bring me offerings.
¹¹ On that day you will not be put to shame
for all the wrongs you have done to me,
because I will remove from this city
those who rejoice in their pride.

ᵃ 8 Septuagint and Syriac; Hebrew *will rise up to plunder*
ᵇ 10 That is, the upper Nile region

ZEPHANIAH 3:14–20

stories to share

Jerusalem's Bright Future

LIFE LESSON: God has a glorious future prepared for his people.

TO TALK ABOUT

✦ What does Zephaniah tell the people to do at the beginning of this passage?

✦ Why should they do this?

✦ What are some of the beautiful promises God makes here through his prophet?

✦ Have you ever imagined that God "rejoice[s] over you with singing" (verse 17)? How does that idea make you feel?

THE LORD YOUR GOD IS WITH
YOU, HE IS MIGHTY TO SAVE. HE
WILL TAKE GREAT DELIGHT IN
YOU, HE WILL QUIET YOU WITH
HIS LOVE, HE WILL REJOICE
OVER YOU WITH SINGING.
Zephaniah 3:17

The Kindergarten Circus

KAREN MAINS

READ | ZEPHANIAH 3:1 – 20

This is the season of my life when I attend events like the spring Kindergarten Circus for the morning class. My granddaughter, Joscelyn, was part of the elephant dance, the last act — after the tightrope walkers, the seals, the strong people, etc. Josie was dressed in what looked to be a very warm elephant outfit. She and her two partners had to sit in the front row under hot lights and wait a whole hour for their turn.

"Weren't you hot, Josie?" I asked after I had praised her for her remarkable two-step with the other elephant kindergartners. Pushing up her floppy elephant trunk, she shook her head up and down.

"I'm so sorry Papa couldn't come, but I'll tell him all about it."

"Oh, that's OK," she replied, "You were here and that's what makes it so very special to me."

Coming home, I began to consider: Isn't much of life like the Kindergarten Circus? Everyone else comes first, doing their tumbling and fake weight lifting and rigged magic acts, and we're sitting in some conspicuous place wearing a hot, uncomfortable costume, waiting for our turn to do our little two-step. Then we realize that Someone is in the audience, Someone who has come just to watch us do whatever it is we do. We scoot around in our uncomfortable costume, but now it's OK.

God has come to be with us, to cheer and applaud, to wave from the audience, to say to our hearts, "I'm so very proud of you." None of the inconveniences really matter. Nor the fact that other people have been watching their children and don't care that we are hot and the wait has been long. God is present. That, indeed, is what makes everything so very special.

O Lord, help us to remember that when life begins to seem futile, you are always watching us — watching us with the unstinting favor of a proud and delighted grandparent. Amen.

Your next devotion is located on page 1266.

GRANDCHILD IN FOCUS • PRAYER

Protection From Worldliness

O Sovereign Lord, the world surrounds my grandchild, pressing in and tempting him in so many ways. Help him set appropriate limits. Give him sound judgment to choose wisely. Guard him from temptation; protect him from physical and mental predators; lead him into paths of righteousness and light. And reassure me with your promise that you are holding him in your hands. Amen.

Never again will you be haughty
  on my holy hill.
¹²But I will leave within you
  the meek and humble,
  who trust in the name of the LORD.
¹³The remnant of Israel will do no wrong;
  they will speak no lies,
  nor will deceit be found in their
    mouths.
They will eat and lie down
  and no one will make them afraid."

¹⁴Sing, O Daughter of Zion;
  shout aloud, O Israel!
Be glad and rejoice with all your heart,
  O Daughter of Jerusalem!
¹⁵The LORD has taken away your
    punishment,
  he has turned back your enemy.
The LORD, the King of Israel, is with you;
  never again will you fear any harm.
¹⁶On that day they will say to Jerusalem,
  "Do not fear, O Zion;
  do not let your hands hang limp.
¹⁷The LORD your God is with you,
  he is mighty to save.
He will take great delight in you,
  he will quiet you with his love,
  he will rejoice over you with singing."

TALKING POINTS

Self-Esteem

God takes great delight in his people.

ZEPHANIAH 3:17

For more on self-esteem, go to Colossians 2:9–10.

---

¹⁸"The sorrows for the appointed feasts
  I will remove from you;
  they are a burden and a reproach to you. ᵃ
¹⁹At that time I will deal
  with all who oppressed you;
I will rescue the lame
  and gather those who have been scattered.
I will give them praise and honor
  in every land where they were put to shame.
²⁰At that time I will gather you;
  at that time I will bring you home.
I will give you honor and praise
  among all the peoples of the earth
when I restore your fortunes ᵇ
  before your very eyes,"

                              says the LORD.

ᵃ 18 Or "I will gather you who mourn for the appointed feasts; / your reproach is a burden to you   ᵇ 20 Or I bring back your captives

The Number-One PRIORITY

Haggai preached to the Jews who had returned to Judah after their exile in Babylon. Led by Zerubbabel and others, many Jews had returned and had begun to rebuild the temple. The people completed the foundation, but opposition from neighboring peoples and their own laziness had resulted in the temple remaining unfinished.

Haggai called the people to reprioritize their lives. They were building their own homes and businesses and focusing on themselves, rather than thinking about God and rebuilding the temple. Haggai told the people that rebuilding God's house and their relationship with him was to be their top priority (see Haggai 1:2–11). Once their enthusiasm returned and God's temple was complete, Haggai promised them hope for a bright future.

As the people of Judah discovered, it is easy to get our priorities mixed up. Our lives get busy with our many commitments to family, friends, work, personal goals and ministries. Even good things, like commitments to our church or volunteering in the community, can overwhelm us and distract us from our top priority: seeking God, his will and his ways.

VERSE to REMEMBER | HAGGAI 1:4–5

"Is it a time for you yourselves to be living in your paneled houses, while this house remains a ruin?" Now this is what the LORD Almighty says: "Give careful thought to your ways."

ABOUT HAGGAI

WRITTEN BY:
The prophet Haggai

WRITTEN FOR:
The Jews who had returned to Judah from exile

DATE WRITTEN:
520 B.C.

WHY WRITTEN:
To inform the people that they were to put God first and finish rebuilding his temple

A Call to Build the House of the LORD

1 In the second year of King Darius, on the first day of the sixth month, the word of the LORD came through the prophet Haggai to Zerubbabel son of Shealtiel, governor of Judah, and to Joshua[a] son of Jehozadak, the high priest:

²This is what the LORD Almighty says: "These people say, 'The time has not yet come for the LORD's house to be built.'"

³Then the word of the LORD came through the prophet Haggai: ⁴"Is it a time for you yourselves to be living in your paneled houses, while this house remains a ruin?"

⁵Now this is what the LORD Almighty says: "Give careful thought to your ways. ⁶You have planted much, but have harvested little. You eat, but never have enough. You drink, but never have your fill. You put on clothes, but are not warm. You earn wages, only to put them in a purse with holes in it."

⁷This is what the LORD Almighty says: "Give careful thought to your ways. ⁸Go up into the mountains and bring down timber and build the house, so that I may take pleasure in it and be honored," says the LORD. ⁹"You expected much, but see, it turned out to be little. What you brought home, I blew away. Why?" declares the LORD Almighty. "Because of my house, which remains a ruin, while each of you is busy with his own house. ¹⁰Therefore, because of you the heavens have withheld their dew and the earth its crops. ¹¹I called for a drought on the fields and the mountains, on the grain, the new wine, the oil and whatever the ground produces, on men and cattle, and on the labor of your hands."

¹²Then Zerubbabel son of Shealtiel, Joshua son of Jehozadak, the high priest, and the whole remnant of the people obeyed the voice of the LORD their God and the message of the prophet Haggai, because the LORD their God had sent him. And the people feared the LORD.

¹³Then Haggai, the LORD's messenger, gave this message of the LORD to the people: "I am with you," declares the LORD. ¹⁴So the LORD stirred up the spirit of Zerubbabel son of Shealtiel, governor of Judah, and the spirit of Joshua son of Jehozadak, the high priest, and the spirit of the whole remnant of the people. They came and began to work on the house of the LORD Almighty, their God, ¹⁵on the twenty-fourth day of the sixth month in the second year of King Darius.

The Promised Glory of the New House

2 On the twenty-first day of the seventh month, the word of the LORD came through the prophet Haggai: ²"Speak to Zerubbabel son of Shealtiel, governor of Judah, to Joshua son of Jehozadak, the high priest, and to the remnant of the people. Ask them, ³'Who of you is left who saw this house in its former glory? How does it look to you now? Does it not seem to you like nothing? ⁴But now be strong, O Zerubbabel,' declares the LORD. 'Be strong, O Joshua son of Jehozadak, the high priest. Be strong, all you people of the land,' declares the LORD, 'and work. For I am with you,' declares the LORD Almighty. ⁵'This is what I covenanted with you when you came out of Egypt. And my Spirit remains among you. Do not fear.'

⁶"This is what the LORD Almighty says: 'In a little while I will once more shake the heavens and the earth, the sea and the dry land. ⁷I will shake all nations, and the desired of all nations will come, and I will fill this house with glory,' says the LORD Almighty. ⁸'The silver is mine and the gold is mine,' declares the LORD Almighty. ⁹'The glory of this present house will be greater than the glory of the former house,' says the LORD Almighty. 'And in this place I will grant peace,' declares the LORD Almighty."

Blessings for a Defiled People

¹⁰On the twenty-fourth day of the ninth month, in the second year of Darius, the word of the LORD came to the prophet Haggai: ¹¹"This is what the LORD Almighty says: 'Ask the priests what the law says: ¹²If a person carries consecrated

---

a 1 A variant of *Jeshua*; here and elsewhere in Haggai

meat in the fold of his garment, and that fold touches some bread or stew, some wine, oil or other food, does it become consecrated?'"

The priests answered, "No."

13Then Haggai said, "If a person defiled by contact with a dead body touches one of these things, does it become defiled?"

"Yes," the priests replied, "it becomes defiled."

14Then Haggai said, "'So it is with this people and this nation in my sight,' declares the LORD. 'Whatever they do and whatever they offer there is defiled.

15"'Now give careful thought to this from this day on*—consider how things were before one stone was laid on another in the LORD's temple. 16When anyone came to a heap of twenty measures, there were only ten. When anyone went to a wine vat to draw fifty measures, there were only twenty. 17I struck all the work of your hands with blight, mildew and hail, yet you did not turn to me,' declares the LORD. 18'From this day on, from this twenty-fourth day of the ninth month, give careful thought to the day when the foundation of the LORD's temple was laid. Give careful thought: 19Is there yet any seed left in the barn? Until now, the vine and the fig tree, the pomegranate and the olive tree have not borne fruit.

"'From this day on I will bless you.'"

Zerubbabel the LORD's Signet Ring

20The word of the LORD came to Haggai a second time on the twenty-fourth day of the month: 21"Tell Zerubbabel governor of Judah that I will shake the heavens and the earth. 22I will overturn royal thrones and shatter the power of the foreign kingdoms. I will overthrow chariots and their drivers; horses and their riders will fall, each by the sword of his brother.

23"'On that day,' declares the LORD Almighty, 'I will take you, my servant Zerubbabel son of Shealtiel,' declares the LORD, 'and I will make you like my signet ring, for I have chosen you,' declares the LORD Almighty."

a 15 Or *to the days past*

God IS IN CONTROL

Like Haggai, Zechariah prophesied to the Jews who had returned from exile in Babylon. The people had come back to rebuild the temple, but once they got home, they became discouraged when the building project didn't go as smoothly as they had hoped it would. The people made a good start, but they faced opposition from neighbors and struggled with their own priorities (see the introduction to the book of Haggai).

While Haggai and Zechariah sternly challenged the people to devote themselves to the Lord in general and get back to work on the temple in particular, they also gave some much-needed words of encouragement. In fact, encouragement is the focus of the book of Zechariah. Through a series of visions, Zechariah became aware of the promising future God had in store for the nation. He prophesied of God's long-range plan: the coming of the Messiah and the Lord's reign in the final kingdom. These visions inspired the people to obey God and gave them hope for the future.

Although much of this book is full of symbolism, one theme is clear: God is in control. His power and might cannot be surpassed, and by the power of his Spirit all things are possible. This was true for the exiles in ancient Israel, and it is still true for us today.

VERSE *to* REMEMBER | ZECHARIAH 4:6

So [the angel] said to me, "This is the word of the LORD to Zerubbabel: 'Not by might nor by power, but by my Spirit,' says the LORD Almighty."

ABOUT ZECHARIAH

WRITTEN BY:
The prophet Zechariah

WRITTEN FOR:
The Jews who had returned to Judah from exile

DATE WRITTEN:
Most of the book was written in 520 B.C. or shortly thereafter; chapters 9–14 were likely written a number of years later.

WHY WRITTEN:
To encourage the people of Judah, especially to finish rebuilding the temple

A Call to Return to the LORD

1 In the eighth month of the second year of Darius, the word of the LORD came to the prophet Zechariah son of Berekiah, the son of Iddo:

² "The LORD was very angry with your forefathers. ³ Therefore tell the people: This is what the LORD Almighty says: 'Return to me,' declares the LORD Almighty, 'and I will return to you,' says the LORD Almighty. ⁴ Do not be like your forefathers, to whom the earlier prophets proclaimed: This is what the LORD Almighty says: 'Turn from your evil ways and your evil practices.' But they would not listen or pay attention to me, declares the LORD. ⁵ Where are your forefathers now? And the prophets, do they live forever? ⁶ But did not my words and my decrees, which I commanded my servants the prophets, overtake your forefathers?

"Then they repented and said, 'The LORD Almighty has done to us what our ways and practices deserve, just as he determined to do.' "

The Man Among the Myrtle Trees

⁷ On the twenty-fourth day of the eleventh month, the month of Shebat, in the second year of Darius, the word of the LORD came to the prophet Zechariah son of Berekiah, the son of Iddo.

⁸ During the night I had a vision—and there before me was a man riding a red horse! He was standing among the myrtle trees in a ravine. Behind him were red, brown and white horses.

⁹ I asked, "What are these, my lord?"

The angel who was talking with me answered, "I will show you what they are."

¹⁰ Then the man standing among the myrtle trees explained, "They are the ones the LORD has sent to go throughout the earth."

¹¹ And they reported to the angel of the LORD, who was standing among the myrtle trees, "We have gone throughout the earth and found the whole world at rest and in peace."

¹² Then the angel of the LORD said, "LORD Almighty, how long will you withhold mercy from Jerusalem and from the towns of Judah, which you have been angry with these seventy years?" ¹³ So the LORD spoke kind and comforting words to the angel who talked with me.

¹⁴ Then the angel who was speaking to me said, "Proclaim this word: This is what the LORD Almighty says: 'I am very jealous for Jerusalem and Zion, ¹⁵ but I am very angry with the nations that feel secure. I was only a little angry, but they added to the calamity.'

¹⁶ "Therefore, this is what the LORD says: 'I will return to Jerusalem with mercy, and there my house will be rebuilt. And the measuring line will be stretched out over Jerusalem,' declares the LORD Almighty.

¹⁷ "Proclaim further: This is what the LORD Almighty says: 'My towns will again overflow with prosperity, and the LORD will again comfort Zion and choose Jerusalem.' "

Four Horns and Four Craftsmen

¹⁸ Then I looked up—and there before me were four horns! ¹⁹ I asked the angel who was speaking to me, "What are these?"

He answered me, "These are the horns that scattered Judah, Israel and Jerusalem."

²⁰ Then the LORD showed me four craftsmen. ²¹ I asked, "What are these coming to do?"

He answered, "These are the horns that scattered Judah so that no one could raise his head, but the craftsmen have come to terrify them and throw down these horns of the nations who lifted up their horns against the land of Judah to scatter its people."

A Man With a Measuring Line

2 Then I looked up—and there before me was a man with a measuring line in his hand! ² I asked, "Where are you going?"

He answered me, "To measure Jerusalem, to find out how wide and how long it is."

³ Then the angel who was speaking to me left, and another angel came to meet him ⁴ and said to him: "Run, tell that young man, 'Jerusalem will be a city without walls because of the great

number of men and livestock in it. [5] And I myself will be a wall of fire around it,' declares the LORD, 'and I will be its glory within.'

[6] "Come! Come! Flee from the land of the north," declares the LORD, "for I have scattered you to the four winds of heaven," declares the LORD.

[7] "Come, O Zion! Escape, you who live in the Daughter of Babylon!" [8] For this is what the LORD Almighty says: "After he has honored me and has sent me against the nations that have plundered you — for whoever touches you touches the apple of his eye — [9] I will surely raise my hand against them so that their slaves will plunder them.[a] Then you will know that the LORD Almighty has sent me.

[10] "Shout and be glad, O Daughter of Zion. For I am coming, and I will live among you," declares the LORD. [11] "Many nations will be joined with the LORD in that day and will become my people. I will live among you and you will know that the LORD Almighty has sent me to you. [12] The LORD will inherit Judah as his portion in the holy land and will again choose Jerusalem. [13] Be still before the LORD, all mankind, because he has roused himself from his holy dwelling."

Clean Garments for the High Priest

3 Then he showed me Joshua[b] the high priest standing before the angel of the LORD, and Satan[c] standing at his right side to accuse him. [2] The LORD said to Satan, "The LORD rebuke you, Satan! The LORD, who has chosen Jerusalem, rebuke you! Is not this man a burning stick snatched from the fire?"

[3] Now Joshua was dressed in filthy clothes as he stood before the angel. [4] The angel said to those who were standing before him, "Take off his filthy clothes."

Then he said to Joshua, "See, I have taken away your sin, and I will put rich garments on you."

[5] Then I said, "Put a clean turban on his head." So they put a clean turban on his head and clothed him, while the angel of the LORD stood by.

[6] The angel of the LORD gave this charge to Joshua: [7] "This is what the LORD Almighty says: 'If you will walk in my ways and keep my requirements, then you will govern my house and have charge of my courts, and I will give you a place among these standing here.

[8] " 'Listen, O high priest Joshua and your associates seated before you, who are men symbolic of things to come: I am going to bring my servant, the Branch. [9] See, the stone I have set in front of Joshua! There are seven eyes[d] on that one stone, and I will engrave an inscription on it,' says the LORD Almighty, 'and I will remove the sin of this land in a single day.

[10] " 'In that day each of you will invite his neighbor to sit under his vine and fig tree,' declares the LORD Almighty."

The Gold Lampstand and the Two Olive Trees

4 Then the angel who talked with me returned and wakened me, as a man is wakened from his sleep. [2] He asked me, "What do you see?"

I answered, "I see a solid gold lampstand with a bowl at the top and seven lights on it, with seven channels to the lights. [3] Also there are two olive trees by it, one on the right of the bowl and the other on its left."

[4] I asked the angel who talked with me, "What are these, my lord?"

[5] He answered, "Do you not know what these are?"

"No, my lord," I replied.

[6] So he said to me, "This is the word of the LORD to Zerubbabel: 'Not by might nor by power, but by my Spirit,' says the LORD Almighty.

[7] "What[e] are you, O mighty mountain? Before Zerubbabel you will become level ground. Then he will bring out the capstone to shouts of 'God bless it! God bless it!' "

[8] Then the word of the LORD came to me: [9] "The hands of Zerubbabel have laid the foundation of

[a] 8,9 Or says after . . . eye: [9] "I . . . plunder them."   [b] 1 A variant of Jeshua; here and elsewhere in Zechariah   [c] 1 Satan means accuser.   [d] 9 Or facets   [e] 7 Or Who

Eating Disorders

God's Spirit comes to our assistance.

ZECHARIAH 4:6

This is the last talking point on eating disorders.

this temple; his hands will also complete it. Then you will know that the LORD Almighty has sent me to you.

¹⁰"Who despises the day of small things? Men will rejoice when they see the plumb line in the hand of Zerubbabel.

"(These seven are the eyes of the LORD, which range throughout the earth.)"

¹¹Then I asked the angel, "What are these two olive trees on the right and the left of the lampstand?"

¹²Again I asked him, "What are these two olive branches beside the two gold pipes that pour out golden oil?"

¹³He replied, "Do you not know what these are?"

"No, my lord," I said.

¹⁴So he said, "These are the two who are anointed to^a serve the Lord of all the earth."

The Flying Scroll

5 I looked again—and there before me was a flying scroll!

²He asked me, "What do you see?"

I answered, "I see a flying scroll, thirty feet long and fifteen feet wide.^b"

³And he said to me, "This is the curse that is going out over the whole land; for according to what it says on one side, every thief will be banished, and according to what it says on the other, everyone who swears falsely will be banished. ⁴The LORD Almighty declares, 'I will send it out, and it will enter the house of the thief and the

house of him who swears falsely by my name. It will remain in his house and destroy it, both its timbers and its stones.'"

The Woman in a Basket

⁵Then the angel who was speaking to me came forward and said to me, "Look up and see what this is that is appearing."

⁶I asked, "What is it?"

He replied, "It is a measuring basket.^c" And he added, "This is the iniquity^d of the people throughout the land."

⁷Then the cover of lead was raised, and there in the basket sat a woman! ⁸He said, "This is wickedness," and he pushed her back into the basket and pushed the lead cover down over its mouth.

⁹Then I looked up—and there before me were two women, with the wind in their wings! They had wings like those of a stork, and they lifted up the basket between heaven and earth.

¹⁰"Where are they taking the basket?" I asked the angel who was speaking to me.

¹¹He replied, "To the country of Babylonia^e to build a house for it. When it is ready, the basket will be set there in its place."

Four Chariots

6 I looked up again—and there before me were four chariots coming out from between two mountains—mountains of bronze! ²The first chariot had red horses, the second black, ³the third white, and the fourth dappled—all of them powerful. ⁴I asked the angel who was speaking to me, "What are these, my lord?"

⁵The angel answered me, "These are the four spirits^f of heaven, going out from standing in the presence of the Lord of the whole world. ⁶The one with the black horses is going toward the north country, the one with the white horses toward the west,^g and the one with the dappled horses toward the south."

⁷When the powerful horses went out, they

^a 14 Or *two who bring oil and*   ^b 2 Hebrew *twenty cubits long and ten cubits wide* (about 9 meters long and 4.5 meters wide)   ^c 6 Hebrew *an ephah; also in verses 7-11*   ^d 6 Or *appearance*   ^e 11 Hebrew *Shinar*   ^f 5 Or *winds*   ^g 6 Or *horses after them*

were straining to go throughout the earth. And he said, "Go throughout the earth!" So they went throughout the earth.

⁸Then he called to me, "Look, those going toward the north country have given my Spirit*a* rest in the land of the north."

A Crown for Joshua

⁹The word of the LORD came to me: ¹⁰"Take ⌐silver and gold⌐ from the exiles Heldai, Tobijah and Jedaiah, who have arrived from Babylon. Go the same day to the house of Josiah son of Zephaniah. ¹¹Take the silver and gold and make a crown, and set it on the head of the high priest, Joshua son of Jehozadak. ¹²Tell him this is what the LORD Almighty says: 'Here is the man whose name is the Branch, and he will branch out from his place and build the temple of the LORD. ¹³It is he who will build the temple of the LORD, and he will be clothed with majesty and will sit and rule on his throne. And he will be a priest on his throne. And there will be harmony between the two.' ¹⁴The crown will be given to Heldai,*b* Tobijah, Jedaiah and Hen*c* son of Zephaniah as a memorial in the temple of the LORD. ¹⁵Those who are far away will come and help to build the temple of the LORD, and you will know that the LORD Almighty has sent me to you. This will happen if you diligently obey the LORD your God."

Justice and Mercy, Not Fasting

7 In the fourth year of King Darius, the word of the LORD came to Zechariah on the fourth day of the ninth month, the month of Kislev. ²The people of Bethel had sent Sharezer and Regem-Melech, together with their men, to entreat the LORD ³by asking the priests of the house of the LORD Almighty and the prophets, "Should I mourn and fast in the fifth month, as I have done for so many years?"

⁴Then the word of the LORD Almighty came to me: ⁵"Ask all the people of the land and the priests, 'When you fasted and mourned in the fifth and seventh months for the past seventy years, was it really for me that you fasted? ⁶And

when you were eating and drinking, were you not just feasting for yourselves? ⁷Are these not the words the LORD proclaimed through the earlier prophets when Jerusalem and its surrounding towns were at rest and prosperous, and the Negev and the western foothills were settled?' "

⁸And the word of the LORD came again to Zechariah: ⁹"This is what the LORD Almighty says: 'Administer true justice; show mercy and compassion to one another. ¹⁰Do not oppress the widow or the fatherless, the alien or the poor. In your hearts do not think evil of each other.'

a 8 Or *spirit*   *b* 14 Syriac; Hebrew *Helem*   *c* 14 Or *and the gracious one, the*

TALKING POINTS

Social Justice
We should administer justice, especially to those who are most vulnerable.
ZECHARIAH 7:9–10

For more on social justice, go to James 2:1–9.

PRAYING THE SCRIPTURES

Guidance
ZECHARIAH 7:9–10
O Lord Almighty, I pray that my grandchild will advocate and practice true justice, showing mercy and compassion to others. Guard his steps, that he may never oppress the widow or the fatherless, the alien or the poor. Prevent his heart from even thinking evil of others.

Next prayer in Guidance Prayer Track: Ephesians 3:20

THEN THE WORD OF THE LORD ALMIGHTY
CAME TO ME: "ASK ALL THE PEOPLE OF THE
LAND AND THE PRIESTS, 'WHEN YOU FASTED
AND MOURNED IN THE FIFTH AND SEVENTH
MONTHS FOR THE PAST SEVENTY YEARS, WAS
IT REALLY FOR ME THAT YOU FASTED?' "

Zechariah 7:4 – 5

Pure Hearts

TERRI BLACKSTOCK

READ | ZECHARIAH 7:1 – 14

I've read this passage before, and it has gone right over my head. But this time, it shone in my face like a beacon illuminating my own sins. I go to God expecting a pat on the back for all the good deeds I've done, all the people I've helped, all the enemies I've forgiven, all the worship I've sacrificed my time to offer. And in response, God says: "Get real, Terri. Were you doing those things for me or for yourself? . . . I want your heart to be pure. Your good deeds amount to nothing but filthy rags if your heart isn't pure. If worshiping me is a sacrifice and your good deeds are nothing more than markings on the score sheet of your life, you still don't get it."

God isn't interested in a score sheet or a legalistic report card. He's already done all the work to save us. He sent his Son to die on the cross for all of our sins and demonstrate our inheritance in his resurrection.

So many times I've run myself ragged trying to do things that I believe are pleasing to God, only to realize sometime later that I've neglected my prayer life and my Bible study — in fact, I've left God out of it entirely. "Was it really for me you fasted?" God asked. That's an interesting question — and a painful one. God must sit quietly, watching and shaking his head, wondering when I will learn.

I'm so grateful that God doesn't wash his hands of us. Instead, he asks those probing, painful questions that remind us what is important. He never stops teaching us.

May our hearts be so pure, so full of his righteousness, so Christlike, that our good deeds burst forth as acts of worship, rather than sacrifice.

And may God never stop working on me.

Lord God, forgive me for the times I've busied myself with activities that I believed I was doing for you but that I was really doing for me. From this day forward, I want my good deeds to follow my righteous heart — a heart that listens and obeys your commandments, a heart that is pleasing to you. Amen.

Your next devotion is located on page 1269.

GRANDCHILD **IN FOCUS** · PRAYER

Respect for Authority

Dear Lord, I pray that my grandchild will continually grow to respect those in authority. May she learn to be cooperative and fair in work and play. Instill in her a high regard for officials who govern our land and enforce the laws. May her relationships with parents, teachers, coaches, mentors and bosses be respectful, admirable, constructive and caring. Amen.

¹¹"But they refused to pay attention; stubbornly they turned their backs and stopped up their ears. ¹²They made their hearts as hard as flint and would not listen to the law or to the words that the LORD Almighty had sent by his Spirit through the earlier prophets. So the LORD Almighty was very angry.

¹³"'When I called, they did not listen; so when they called, I would not listen,' says the LORD Almighty. ¹⁴'I scattered them with a whirlwind among all the nations, where they were strangers. The land was left so desolate behind them that no one could come or go. This is how they made the pleasant land desolate.'"

The LORD Promises to Bless Jerusalem

8 Again the word of the LORD Almighty came to me. ²This is what the LORD Almighty says: "I am very jealous for Zion; I am burning with jealousy for her."

³This is what the LORD says: "I will return to Zion and dwell in Jerusalem. Then Jerusalem will be called the City of Truth, and the mountain of the LORD Almighty will be called the Holy Mountain."

⁴This is what the LORD Almighty says: "Once again men and women of ripe old age will sit in the streets of Jerusalem, each with cane in hand because of his age. ⁵The city streets will be filled with boys and girls playing there."

⁶This is what the LORD Almighty says: "It may seem marvelous to the remnant of this people at that time, but will it seem marvelous to me?" declares the LORD Almighty.

⁷This is what the LORD Almighty says: "I will save my people from the countries of the east and the west. ⁸I will bring them back to live in Jerusalem; they will be my people, and I will be faithful and righteous to them as their God."

⁹This is what the LORD Almighty says: "You who now hear these words spoken by the prophets who were there when the foundation was laid for the house of the LORD Almighty, let your hands be strong so that the temple may be built. ¹⁰Before that time there were no wages

for man or beast. No one could go about his business safely because of his enemy, for I had turned every man against his neighbor. ¹¹But now I will not deal with the remnant of this people as I did in the past," declares the LORD Almighty.

¹²"The seed will grow well, the vine will yield its fruit, the ground will produce its crops, and the heavens will drop their dew. I will give all these things as an inheritance to the remnant of this people. ¹³As you have been an object of cursing among the nations, O Judah and Israel, so will I save you, and you will be a blessing. Do not be afraid, but let your hands be strong."

¹⁴This is what the LORD Almighty says: "Just as I had determined to bring disaster upon you and showed no pity when your fathers angered me," says the LORD Almighty, ¹⁵"so now I have determined to do good again to Jerusalem and Judah. Do not be afraid. ¹⁶These are the things you are to do: Speak the truth to each other, and render true and sound judgment in your courts; ¹⁷do not plot evil against your neighbor, and do not love to swear falsely. I hate all this," declares the LORD.

¹⁸Again the word of the LORD Almighty came to me. ¹⁹This is what the LORD Almighty says: "The fasts of the fourth, fifth, seventh and tenth months will become joyful and glad occasions and happy festivals for Judah. Therefore love truth and peace."

²⁰This is what the LORD Almighty says: "Many peoples and the inhabitants of many cities will yet come, ²¹and the inhabitants of one city will go to another and say, 'Let us go at once to entreat the LORD and seek the LORD Almighty. I myself am going.' ²²And many peoples and powerful nations will come to Jerusalem to seek the LORD Almighty and to entreat him."

²³This is what the LORD Almighty says: "In those days ten men from all languages and nations will take firm hold of one Jew by the hem of his robe and say, 'Let us go with you, because we have heard that God is with you.'"

Judgment on Israel's Enemies
An Oracle

9 The word of the LORD is against the land
of Hadrach
and will rest upon Damascus—
for the eyes of men and all the tribes of
Israel
are on the LORD— [a]
² and upon Hamath too, which borders on it,
and upon Tyre and Sidon, though they are
very skillful.
³ Tyre has built herself a stronghold;
she has heaped up silver like dust,
and gold like the dirt of the streets.
⁴ But the Lord will take away her possessions
and destroy her power on the sea,
and she will be consumed by fire.
⁵ Ashkelon will see it and fear;
Gaza will writhe in agony,
and Ekron too, for her hope will wither.
Gaza will lose her king
and Ashkelon will be deserted.
⁶ Foreigners will occupy Ashdod,
and I will cut off the pride of the
Philistines.
⁷ I will take the blood from their mouths,
the forbidden food from between their
teeth.
Those who are left will belong to our God
and become leaders in Judah,
and Ekron will be like the Jebusites.
⁸ But I will defend my house
against marauding forces.
Never again will an oppressor overrun my
people,
for now I am keeping watch.

The Coming of Zion's King

⁹ Rejoice greatly, O Daughter of Zion!
Shout, Daughter of Jerusalem!
See, your king [b] comes to you,
righteous and having salvation,
gentle and riding on a donkey,
on a colt, the foal of a donkey.

¹⁰ I will take away the chariots from Ephraim
and the war-horses from Jerusalem,
and the battle bow will be broken.
He will proclaim peace to the nations.
His rule will extend from sea to sea
and from the River [c] to the ends of the
earth. [d]
¹¹ As for you, because of the blood of my
covenant with you,
I will free your prisoners from the
waterless pit.
¹² Return to your fortress, O prisoners of hope;
even now I announce that I will restore
twice as much to you.
¹³ I will bend Judah as I bend my bow
and fill it with Ephraim.
I will rouse your sons, O Zion,
against your sons, O Greece,
and make you like a warrior's sword.

The LORD Will Appear

¹⁴ Then the LORD will appear over them;
his arrow will flash like lightning.
The Sovereign LORD will sound the
trumpet;
he will march in the storms of the south,
15   and the LORD Almighty will shield
them.
They will destroy
and overcome with slingstones.
They will drink and roar as with wine;
they will be full like a bowl
used for sprinkling [e] the corners of the
altar.
¹⁶ The LORD their God will save them on that
day
as the flock of his people.
They will sparkle in his land
like jewels in a crown.
¹⁷ How attractive and beautiful they will be!
Grain will make the young men thrive,
and new wine the young women.

---

[a] 1 Or *Damascus. / For the eye of the* LORD *is on all mankind, / as
well as on the tribes of Israel,*   [b] 9 Or *King*   [c] 10 That is, the
Euphrates   [d] 10 Or *the end of the land*   [e] 15 Or *bowl, / like*

THE LORD THEIR GOD WILL SAVE THEM ON
THAT DAY AS THE FLOCK OF HIS PEOPLE.
THEY WILL SPARKLE IN HIS LAND LIKE
JEWELS IN A CROWN. HOW ATTRACTIVE AND
BEAUTIFUL THEY WILL BE!

Zechariah 9:16–17

Precious Jewels

NATALIE J. BLOCK

READ | ZECHARIAH 9:9–17

Though my maternal grandmother died when I was six years old, she made a huge impression on my life during those few years. Because she lived next door to us, it was easy for my older sister and me to run over to her house to play with her or ask for a nickel so we could skip to the corner store for a popsicle.

My grandmother loved music. I remember sitting on her lap in front of her old-fashioned pump organ; I pulled the stops and "played" the keys while Grandma worked the foot pedals.

One of the songs Grandma taught me was "When He Cometh," a song written in 1856 by William Cushing:

> When He cometh, when He cometh
> To make up His jewels,
> All His jewels, precious jewels,
> His loved and His own.
>
> Like the stars of the morning,
> His bright crown adorning,
> They shall shine in their beauty,
> Bright gems for His crown.

I don't remember singing that song very often after Grandma died. But after I had my first child, the words to that song slowly came back to my mind, and it became one of the "oldies" that I sang as I rocked my baby to sleep. It brought back memories of Grandma and her love for me, and it reminded me of how special my little one and I were to God.

It's comforting to know that God sees us, our children and our grandchildren as precious jewels — gems that shine like the stars as we adorn his crown. What a glorious picture of our value, beauty and significance!

GRANDCHILD IN FOCUS • PRAYER

Courage

O Father, builder of character and courage, may my grandchild grow strong in the light of your love. Grant him courage to stand for what is right, to guard the truth and to ensure justice in every aspect of life. May he boldly grow in grace, revere your name and proudly proclaim you as the Lord of lords and King of kings. Amen.

Dear God, I'm overwhelmed by your love for me, my children and my grandchildren. Thank you that each of us is special to you. Help me to treasure my grandchildren for the precious jewels that they are, and use me to make a difference in their lives.

Your next devotion is located on page 1271.

The LORD Will Care for Judah

10 Ask the LORD for rain in the springtime;
it is the LORD who makes the storm
clouds.
He gives showers of rain to men,
and plants of the field to everyone.
²The idols speak deceit,
diviners see visions that lie;
they tell dreams that are false,
they give comfort in vain.
Therefore the people wander like sheep
oppressed for lack of a shepherd.

³"My anger burns against the shepherds,
and I will punish the leaders;
for the LORD Almighty will care
for his flock, the house of Judah,
and make them like a proud horse in
battle.
⁴From Judah will come the cornerstone,
from him the tent peg,
from him the battle bow,
from him every ruler.
⁵Together they*ᵃ* will be like mighty men
trampling the muddy streets in battle.
Because the LORD is with them,
they will fight and overthrow the
horsemen.

⁶"I will strengthen the house of Judah
and save the house of Joseph.
I will restore them
because I have compassion on them.
They will be as though
I had not rejected them,
for I am the LORD their God
and I will answer them.
⁷The Ephraimites will become like mighty
men,
and their hearts will be glad as with wine.
Their children will see it and be joyful;
their hearts will rejoice in the LORD.
⁸I will signal for them
and gather them in.
Surely I will redeem them;
they will be as numerous as before.

⁹Though I scatter them among the peoples,
yet in distant lands they will remember me.
They and their children will survive,
and they will return.
¹⁰I will bring them back from Egypt
and gather them from Assyria.
I will bring them to Gilead and Lebanon,
and there will not be room enough for
them.
¹¹They will pass through the sea of trouble;
the surging sea will be subdued
and all the depths of the Nile will dry up.
Assyria's pride will be brought down
and Egypt's scepter will pass away.

ᵃ 4,5 Or ruler, all of them together. / ⁵They

stories to share

ZECHARIAH 10:1–12

The Lord Will Care for Judah

LIFE LESSON: God takes care of his own.

TO TALK ABOUT

✦ Why would the people ask for rain in the springtime? Who brings the rain?

✦ Why was God angry at Israel's "shepherds"? Who are the shepherds today?

✦ What promises did God make in this passage?

✦ On whose strength do you rely?

> "THEY WILL PASS THROUGH THE SEA OF TROUBLE; THE SURGING SEA WILL BE SUBDUED . . . I WILL STRENGTHEN THEM IN THE LORD AND IN HIS NAME THEY WILL WALK," DECLARES THE LORD.
>
> *Zechariah 10:11–12*

Passing Through Trouble

DORIS WYNBEEK RIKKERS

READ | ZECHARIAH 10:1–12

As a mother of ten, my maternal grandmother, Johanna Wynbeek, had many wise sayings about raising children. One family favorite was, "When they're little, the troubles are little; when they're big, the troubles are big."

Everyone who has raised children will acknowledge the wisdom in those words. We've been through the little troubles of infants and young children: ear infections, potty training, fear of monsters. We know the midsize troubles of adolescents and teens: being picked on, body image, poor grades. We have suffered and agonized with our children as they graduated from trouble to trouble. We've dropped everything when they've called, counseled them through sleepless nights, assisted and encouraged them in their decision making. As our children move into adulthood, we expect them to handle their troubles on their own; and yet we are never fully free because we love and care for them.

No one is exempt from trouble; the Bible is clear on that. Jesus said, "In this world you will have trouble" (John 16:33). But the Bible also gives us good news about trouble. God has promised that although there will be trouble, we will "pass through" it (Zechariah 10:11); he will be with us no matter what — nothing will separate us from his love (see Romans 8:35–39). And God will strengthen us again when the trouble is past (Zechariah 10:12).

My grandmother experienced her share of trouble: her first-born daughter died as an infant; another daughter suffered illness and seizures; her husband died at age 48, leaving her alone to raise her children. Yet Johanna's faith remained constant; she knew the Lord would provide, and he would give her strength to face whatever troubles life presented. He was there for Johanna; he is there for us too.

Dear Lord, thank you for your presence in all the troubles that I face in life. Thank you for the promise that trouble will pass and that you will strengthen me to continue my walk with you. Amen.

Your next devotion is located on page 1279.

GRANDCHILD IN FOCUS • PRAYER

Future Spouse

Dear Lord, if it is your will, I pray my grandchild will be united in a loving and Christian marriage. Keep her sexually pure so that she will honor you with her body and mind. As she seeks a spouse who will honor and care for her, give her patience and discernment. May her choice for a life partner be your choice for her, so that she and her husband will together glorify you in a lasting love. I pray this in Jesus' name, amen.

¹²I will strengthen them in the LORD
    and in his name they will walk,"
                      declares the LORD.

11 Open your doors, O Lebanon,
    so that fire may devour your cedars!
²Wail, O pine tree, for the cedar has fallen;
    the stately trees are ruined!
Wail, oaks of Bashan;
    the dense forest has been cut down!
³Listen to the wail of the shepherds;
    their rich pastures are destroyed!
Listen to the roar of the lions;
    the lush thicket of the Jordan is ruined!

Two Shepherds

⁴This is what the LORD my God says: "Pasture the flock marked for slaughter. ⁵Their buyers slaughter them and go unpunished. Those who sell them say, 'Praise the LORD, I am rich!' Their own shepherds do not spare them. ⁶For I will no longer have pity on the people of the land," declares the LORD. "I will hand everyone over to his neighbor and his king. They will oppress the land, and I will not rescue them from their hands."

⁷So I pastured the flock marked for slaughter, particularly the oppressed of the flock. Then I took two staffs and called one Favor and the other Union, and I pastured the flock. ⁸In one month I got rid of the three shepherds.

The flock detested me, and I grew weary of them ⁹and said, "I will not be your shepherd. Let the dying die, and the perishing perish. Let those who are left eat one another's flesh."

¹⁰Then I took my staff called Favor and broke it, revoking the covenant I had made with all the nations. ¹¹It was revoked on that day, and so the afflicted of the flock who were watching me knew it was the word of the LORD.

¹²I told them, "If you think it best, give me my pay; but if not, keep it." So they paid me thirty pieces of silver.

¹³And the LORD said to me, "Throw it to the potter"—the handsome price at which they priced me! So I took the thirty pieces of silver and threw them into the house of the LORD to the potter.

¹⁴Then I broke my second staff called Union, breaking the brotherhood between Judah and Israel.

¹⁵Then the LORD said to me, "Take again the equipment of a foolish shepherd. ¹⁶For I am going to raise up a shepherd over the land who will not care for the lost, or seek the young, or heal the injured, or feed the healthy, but will eat the meat of the choice sheep, tearing off their hoofs.

¹⁷"Woe to the worthless shepherd,
    who deserts the flock!
May the sword strike his arm and his right
      eye!
    May his arm be completely withered,
    his right eye totally blinded!"

Jerusalem's Enemies to Be Destroyed
An Oracle

12 This is the word of the LORD concerning Israel. The LORD, who stretches out the heavens, who lays the foundation of the earth, and who forms the spirit of man within him, declares: ²"I am going to make Jerusalem a cup that sends all the surrounding peoples reeling. Judah will be besieged as well as Jerusalem. ³On that day, when all the nations of the earth are gathered against her, I will make Jerusalem an immovable rock for all the nations. All who try to move it will injure themselves. ⁴On that day I will strike every horse with panic and its rider with madness," declares the LORD. "I will keep a watchful eye over the house of Judah, but I will blind all the horses of the nations. ⁵Then the leaders of Judah will say in their hearts, 'The people of Jerusalem are strong, because the LORD Almighty is their God.'

⁶"On that day I will make the leaders of Judah like a firepot in a woodpile, like a flaming torch among sheaves. They will consume right and left all the surrounding peoples, but Jerusalem will remain intact in her place.

7 "The LORD will save the dwellings of Judah first, so that the honor of the house of David and of Jerusalem's inhabitants may not be greater than that of Judah. 8 On that day the LORD will shield those who live in Jerusalem, so that the feeblest among them will be like David, and the house of David will be like God, like the Angel of the LORD going before them. 9 On that day I will set out to destroy all the nations that attack Jerusalem.

Mourning for the One They Pierced

10 "And I will pour out on the house of David and the inhabitants of Jerusalem a spirit[a] of grace and supplication. They will look on[b] me, the one they have pierced, and they will mourn for him as one mourns for an only child, and grieve bitterly for him as one grieves for a firstborn son. 11 On that day the weeping in Jerusalem will be great, like the weeping of Hadad Rimmon in the plain of Megiddo. 12 The land will mourn, each clan by itself, with their wives by themselves: the clan of the house of David and their wives, the clan of the house of Nathan and their wives, 13 the clan of the house of Levi and their wives, the clan of Shimei and their wives, 14 and all the rest of the clans and their wives.

Cleansing From Sin

13 "On that day a fountain will be opened to the house of David and the inhabitants of Jerusalem, to cleanse them from sin and impurity.

2 "On that day, I will banish the names of the idols from the land, and they will be remembered no more," declares the LORD Almighty. "I will remove both the prophets and the spirit of impurity from the land. 3 And if anyone still prophesies, his father and mother, to whom he was born, will say to him, 'You must die, because you have told lies in the LORD's name.' When he prophesies, his own parents will stab him.

4 "On that day every prophet will be ashamed of his prophetic vision. He will not put on a prophet's garment of hair in order to deceive. 5 He will say, 'I am not a prophet. I am a farmer; the

land has been my livelihood since my youth.'[c] 6 If someone asks him, 'What are these wounds on your body[d]?' he will answer, 'The wounds I was given at the house of my friends.'

The Shepherd Struck, the Sheep Scattered

7 "Awake, O sword, against my shepherd,
    against the man who is close to me!"
    declares the LORD Almighty.
"Strike the shepherd,
    and the sheep will be scattered,
    and I will turn my hand against the little
        ones.
8 In the whole land," declares the LORD,
    "two-thirds will be struck down and
        perish;
    yet one-third will be left in it.
9 This third I will bring into the fire;
    I will refine them like silver
    and test them like gold.
They will call on my name
    and I will answer them;
I will say, 'They are my people,'
    and they will say, 'The LORD is our God.'"

The LORD Comes and Reigns

14 A day of the LORD is coming when your plunder will be divided among you. 2 I will gather all the nations to Jerusalem to fight against it; the city will be captured, the houses ransacked, and the women raped. Half of the city will go into exile, but the rest of the people will not be taken from the city.

3 Then the LORD will go out and fight against those nations, as he fights in the day of battle. 4 On that day his feet will stand on the Mount of Olives, east of Jerusalem, and the Mount of Olives will be split in two from east to west, forming a great valley, with half of the mountain moving north and half moving south. 5 You will flee by my mountain valley, for it will extend to Azel. You will flee as you fled from the earthquake[e]

---

[a] 10 Or the Spirit   [b] 10 Or to   [c] 5 Or farmer; a man sold me in my youth   [d] 6 Or wounds between your hands   [e] 5 Or My mountain valley will be blocked and will extend to Azel. It will be blocked as it was blocked because of the earthquake

in the days of Uzziah king of Judah. Then the Lord my God will come, and all the holy ones with him.

⁶On that day there will be no light, no cold or frost. ⁷It will be a unique day, without daytime or nighttime—a day known to the Lord. When evening comes, there will be light.

⁸On that day living water will flow out from Jerusalem, half to the eastern sea ᵃ and half to the western sea, ᵇ in summer and in winter.

⁹The Lord will be king over the whole earth. On that day there will be one Lord, and his name the only name.

¹⁰The whole land, from Geba to Rimmon, south of Jerusalem, will become like the Arabah. But Jerusalem will be raised up and remain in its place, from the Benjamin Gate to the site of the First Gate, to the Corner Gate, and from the Tower of Hananel to the royal winepresses. ¹¹It will be inhabited; never again will it be destroyed. Jerusalem will be secure.

¹²This is the plague with which the Lord will strike all the nations that fought against Jerusalem: Their flesh will rot while they are still standing on their feet, their eyes will rot in their sockets, and their tongues will rot in their mouths. ¹³On that day men will be stricken by the Lord with great panic. Each man will seize the hand of another, and they will attack each other. ¹⁴Judah too will fight at Jerusalem. The wealth of all the surrounding nations will be collected—great quantities of gold and silver and clothing. ¹⁵A similar plague will strike the horses and mules, the camels and donkeys, and all the animals in those camps.

¹⁶Then the survivors from all the nations that have attacked Jerusalem will go up year after year to worship the King, the Lord Almighty, and to celebrate the Feast of Tabernacles. ¹⁷If any of the peoples of the earth do not go up to Jerusalem to worship the King, the Lord Almighty, they will have no rain. ¹⁸If the Egyptian people do not go up and take part, they will have no rain. The Lord ᶜ will bring on them the plague he inflicts on the nations that do not go up to celebrate the Feast of Tabernacles. ¹⁹This will be the punishment of Egypt and the punishment of all the nations that do not go up to celebrate the Feast of Tabernacles.

²⁰On that day HOLY TO THE LORD will be inscribed on the bells of the horses, and the cooking pots in the Lord's house will be like the sacred bowls in front of the altar. ²¹Every pot in Jerusalem and Judah will be holy to the Lord Almighty, and all who come to sacrifice will take some of the pots and cook in them. And on that day there will no longer be a Canaanite ᵈ in the house of the Lord Almighty.

ᵃ 8 That is, the Dead Sea   ᵇ 8 That is, the Mediterranean
ᶜ 18 Or part, then the Lord   ᵈ 21 Or merchant

The Way
TO GOD'S BLESSINGS

Malachi preached to the people of Judah about a hundred years after the first Jewish exiles returned to their homeland. Many of the sins condemned by Malachi were the same as those addressed in the book of Nehemiah. And many of the reforms Nehemiah instituted to deal with these failures were subsequently ignored after Nehemiah, Judah's governor, returned to Persia.

Malachi confronted the people with their complacency and unfaithfulness: They were not worshiping God wholeheartedly. They were marrying outside the faith. They were breaking their marriage covenants through divorce. They were not honoring God with their tithes and offerings. And they weren't sure if it was worth their while to serve God. Sound familiar? Some of the things Malachi warned his people about are issues we struggle with in our communities today.

But Malachi — who was called to renew the people's relationship with the Lord — assured the people that if they returned to God and obeyed him, God would pour out his blessings on them and fill them with joy.

When we find that our relationship with God and our worship practices are growing cold, we can remember Malachi's call to the people of Judah: Return to God and worship him wholeheartedly!

VERSE *to* REMEMBER | MALACHI 4:2

"But for you who revere my name, the sun of righteousness will rise with healing in its wings. And you will go out and leap like calves released from the stall."

ABOUT MALACHI

WRITTEN BY:
The prophet Malachi

WRITTEN FOR:
The people of Judah

DATE WRITTEN:
Around 430 B.C.

WHY WRITTEN:
To confront the people with their sins and to restore their relationship with God

1 An oracle: The word of the LORD to Israel through Malachi.ᵃ

Jacob Loved, Esau Hated

²"I have loved you," says the LORD.

"But you ask, 'How have you loved us?'"

"Was not Esau Jacob's brother?" the LORD says. "Yet I have loved Jacob, ³but Esau I have hated, and I have turned his mountains into a wasteland and left his inheritance to the desert jackals."

⁴Edom may say, "Though we have been crushed, we will rebuild the ruins."

But this is what the LORD Almighty says: "They may build, but I will demolish. They will be called the Wicked Land, a people always under the wrath of the LORD. ⁵You will see it with your own eyes and say, 'Great is the LORD—even beyond the borders of Israel!'"

Blemished Sacrifices

⁶"A son honors his father, and a servant his master. If I am a father, where is the honor due me? If I am a master, where is the respect due me?" says the LORD Almighty. "It is you, O priests, who show contempt for my name.

"But you ask, 'How have we shown contempt for your name?'

⁷"You place defiled food on my altar.

"But you ask, 'How have we defiled you?'

"By saying that the LORD's table is contemptible. ⁸When you bring blind animals for sacrifice, is that not wrong? When you sacrifice crippled or diseased animals, is that not wrong? Try offering them to your governor! Would he be pleased with you? Would he accept you?" says the LORD Almighty.

⁹"Now implore God to be gracious to us. With such offerings from your hands, will he accept you?"—says the LORD Almighty.

¹⁰"Oh, that one of you would shut the temple doors, so that you would not light useless fires on my altar! I am not pleased with you," says the LORD Almighty, "and I will accept no offering from your hands. ¹¹My name will be great among the nations, from the rising to the setting of the sun. In every place incense and pure offerings will be brought to my name, because my name will be great among the nations," says the LORD Almighty.

¹²"But you profane it by saying of the Lord's table, 'It is defiled,' and of its food, 'It is contemptible.' ¹³And you say, 'What a burden!' and you sniff at it contemptuously," says the LORD Almighty.

"When you bring injured, crippled or diseased animals and offer them as sacrifices, should I accept them from your hands?" says the LORD. ¹⁴"Cursed is the cheat who has an acceptable male in his flock and vows to give it, but then sacrifices a blemished animal to the Lord. For I am a great king," says the LORD Almighty, "and my name is to be feared among the nations.

Admonition for the Priests

2 "And now this admonition is for you, O priests. ²If you do not listen, and if you do not set your heart to honor my name," says the LORD Almighty, "I will send a curse upon you, and I will curse your blessings. Yes, I have already cursed them, because you have not set your heart to honor me.

³"Because of you I will rebukeᵇ your descendantsᶜ; I will spread on your faces the offal from your festival sacrifices, and you will be carried off with it. ⁴And you will know that I have sent you this admonition so that my covenant with Levi may continue," says the LORD Almighty. ⁵"My covenant was with him, a covenant of life and peace, and I gave them to him; this called for reverence and he revered me and stood in awe of my name. ⁶True instruction was in his mouth and nothing false was found on his lips. He walked with me in peace and uprightness, and turned many from sin.

⁷"For the lips of a priest ought to preserve knowledge, and from his mouth men should seek instruction—because he is the messenger of the LORD Almighty. ⁸But you have turned from the way and by your teaching have caused many to

---

ᵃ 1 Malachi means *my messenger.*   ᵇ 3 Or *cut off* (see Septuagint)
ᶜ 3 Or *will blight your grain*

stumble; you have violated the covenant with Levi," says the LORD Almighty. [9]"So I have caused you to be despised and humiliated before all the people, because you have not followed my ways but have shown partiality in matters of the law."

Judah Unfaithful

[10]Have we not all one Father[a]? Did not one God create us? Why do we profane the covenant of our fathers by breaking faith with one another?

[11]Judah has broken faith. A detestable thing has been committed in Israel and in Jerusalem: Judah has desecrated the sanctuary the LORD loves, by marrying the daughter of a foreign god. [12]As for the man who does this, whoever he may be, may the LORD cut him off from the tents of Jacob[b]—even though he brings offerings to the LORD Almighty.

[13]Another thing you do: You flood the LORD's altar with tears. You weep and wail because he no longer pays attention to your offerings or accepts them with pleasure from your hands. [14]You ask, "Why?" It is because the LORD is acting as the witness between you and the wife of your youth, because you have broken faith with her, though she is your partner, the wife of your marriage covenant.

[15]Has not ˌthe LORDˌ made them one? In flesh and spirit they are his. And why one? Because he was seeking godly offspring.[c] So guard yourself in your spirit, and do not break faith with the wife of your youth.

[16]"I hate divorce," says the LORD God of Israel, "and I hate a man's covering himself[d] with violence as well as with his garment," says the LORD Almighty.

So guard yourself in your spirit, and do not break faith.

The Day of Judgment

[17]You have wearied the LORD with your words.

"How have we wearied him?" you ask.

By saying, "All who do evil are good in the eyes of the LORD, and he is pleased with them" or "Where is the God of justice?"

TALKING POINTS

Divorce

God hates divorce.

MALACHI 2:16

For more on divorce, go to Matthew 5:31–32.

3 "See, I will send my messenger, who will prepare the way before me. Then suddenly the Lord you are seeking will come to his temple; the messenger of the covenant, whom you desire, will come," says the LORD Almighty.

[2]But who can endure the day of his coming? Who can stand when he appears? For he will be like a refiner's fire or a launderer's soap. [3]He will sit as a refiner and purifier of silver; he will purify the Levites and refine them like gold and silver. Then the LORD will have men who will bring offerings in righteousness, [4]and the offerings of Judah and Jerusalem will be acceptable to the LORD, as in days gone by, as in former years.

[5]"So I will come near to you for judgment. I will be quick to testify against sorcerers, adulterers

[a] 10 Or father [b] 12 Or [12]May the LORD cut off from the tents of Jacob anyone who gives testimony in behalf of the man who does this [c] 15 Or [15]But the one ˌwho is our fatherˌ did not do this, not as long as life remained in him. And what was he seeking? An offspring from God [d] 16 Or his wife

TALKING POINTS

Adoption

God will judge those who oppress the fatherless.

MALACHI 3:5

For more on adoption, go to Matthew 29:13–14.

and perjurers, against those who defraud laborers of their wages, who oppress the widows and the fatherless, and deprive aliens of justice, but do not fear me," says the LORD Almighty.

Robbing God

⁶"I the LORD do not change. So you, O descendants of Jacob, are not destroyed. ⁷Ever since the time of your forefathers you have turned away from my decrees and have not kept them. Return to me, and I will return to you," says the LORD Almighty.

"But you ask, 'How are we to return?'

⁸"Will a man rob God? Yet you rob me.

"But you ask, 'How do we rob you?'

"In tithes and offerings. ⁹You are under a curse—the whole nation of you—because you are robbing me. ¹⁰Bring the whole tithe into the storehouse, that there may be food in my house. Test me in this," says the LORD Almighty, "and see if I will not throw open the floodgates of heaven and pour out so much blessing that you will not have room enough for it. ¹¹I will prevent

PRAYING THE SCRIPTURES

Blessing

MALACHI 3:10

May my grandchild have a generous and giving heart. O Lord Almighty, throw open the floodgates of heaven and pour out so much blessing on my grandchild that she will not have room enough for it.

Next prayer in Blessing Prayer Track: Philippians 4:7

pests from devouring your crops, and the vines in your fields will not cast their fruit," says the LORD Almighty. ¹²"Then all the nations will call you blessed, for yours will be a delightful land," says the LORD Almighty.

¹³"You have said harsh things against me," says the LORD.

"Yet you ask, 'What have we said against you?'

¹⁴"You have said, 'It is futile to serve God. What did we gain by carrying out his requirements and going about like mourners before the LORD Almighty? ¹⁵But now we call the arrogant blessed. Certainly the evildoers prosper, and even those who challenge God escape.'"

¹⁶Then those who feared the LORD talked with each other, and the LORD listened and heard. A scroll of remembrance was written in his presence concerning those who feared the LORD and honored his name.

¹⁷"They will be mine," says the LORD Almighty, "in the day when I make up my treasured possession.ᵃ I will spare them, just as in compassion a man spares his son who serves him. ¹⁸And you will again see the distinction between the righteous and the wicked, between those who serve God and those who do not.

The Day of the LORD

4 "Surely the day is coming; it will burn like a furnace. All the arrogant and every evildoer will be stubble, and that day that is coming will set them on fire," says the LORD Almighty. "Not a root or a branch will be left to them. ²But for you who revere my name, the sun of righteousness will rise with healing in its wings. And you will go out and leap like calves released from the stall. ³Then you will trample down the wicked; they will be ashes under the soles of your feet on the day when I do these things," says the LORD Almighty.

⁴"Remember the law of my servant Moses, the decrees and laws I gave him at Horeb for all Israel.

⁵"See, I will send you the prophet Elijah before that great and dreadful day of the LORD comes. ⁶He will turn the hearts of the fathers to their children, and the hearts of the children to their fathers; or else I will come and strike the land with a curse."

ᵃ 17 Or Almighty, "my treasured possession, in the day when I act

THEN THOSE WHO FEARED THE LORD
TALKED WITH EACH OTHER, AND THE
LORD LISTENED AND HEARD. A SCROLL
OF REMEMBRANCE WAS WRITTEN IN HIS
PRESENCE CONCERNING THOSE WHO FEARED
THE LORD AND HONORED HIS NAME.

Malachi 3:16

A Scroll of Remembrance

HELEN KOOIMAN HOSIER

READ | MALACHI 3:6–18

The connectedness bridge — the link to family history is ours to provide, but we do have to put forth the effort. The importance of the family, its roots and ties even to other countries, is kept in remembrance for future generations when we are diligent to assume the responsibility for preserving it.

Whatever you do, be sure you pass on your reminiscences, the "pages" from your life book that will be meaningful to your grandchildren. If you can't find much from your predecessors, and if you no longer have grandparents or other relatives with whom you can visit, at least make sure that your own life story becomes known to your loved ones. What do you include? The most important aspect of the heritage you pass on to your grandchildren relates to what God has done in your life, what you have learned, and what you hold dear. What are your favorite verses, passages, stories in the Bible? What are some of your favorite songs — old hymns, praise songs, anthems? When did you invite Christ into your heart?

I have found that thinking about the past and recording remembrances is therapeutic for me, and I know it will someday be especially appreciated by my family. The events of our lives and of the lives of those who preceded us make for a sort of blueprint that can endure.

Almighty God, you have given me riches of Scripture and songs and stories to pass on to my grandchildren. I ask you to bless all these things as I record them and share them, that they will bear fruit in many generations to come.

Your next devotion is located on page 1280.

GRANDCHILD IN FOCUS • PRAYER

School/Career

Dear God, may learning be a joy rather than a chore for my grandchild. May exploration of new ideas bring a sense of wonder, awe and excitement. Grant him clarity of mind, the ability to concentrate on the task at hand and recollection of what has been learned. Help him to appreciate the tasks that come easily and to persevere through those that challenge. Amen.

TOGETHER
TIME

Number-One Fan

Whether the occasion is athletic (a soccer tournament, a T-ball game or a swim meet) or of the fine-arts variety (a recital, a play or a concert), your grandchildren of all ages will be thrilled to demonstrate their skills and talents to an appreciative grandmother. Whether they win or lose, place first, fifth or last, you're sure to praise them for their efforts, form, sportsmanship or enthusiasm. Just knowing you cared enough to come and see them participate in the event will greatly encourage your grandkids and build their self-esteem.

Long-Distance Variation: Put together a scrapbook of each grandchild's achievements. Talk to the parents and have them send you newspaper clippings, photographs, copies of certificates, report cards, children's artwork or writing samples, thank-you notes, etc.—anything you might find useful in compiling a scrapbook for each child. This may be a great help to overly busy moms and dads and will be a treasured keepsake. (You may want to do this even if you live nearby.)

Dear Lord, help me to appreciate all of my grandchildren for the special people you've created them to be. Thank you for letting me enjoy the activities of my grandsons and granddaughters who live nearby. Help me to find creative ways to participate in the activities of my grandchildren who live farther away. May all that they do be to your honor and glory. Amen.

Your next devotion is located on page 1281.

GRANDCHILD IN FOCUS • PRAYER

Character

Dear Lord and Father, I ask that you fill my grandchild with your Spirit so her character reflects your goodness and love. Give her kindness and love for others. Bring joy to her life so she will be a joy to others. Grant her patience and self–control through difficult and trying times. May she show mercy and generosity to those who are less fortunate. Grant her integrity and a sense of justice, and surround her with your peace. Amen.

Worship the Lord

Sing to the LORD a new song;
>sing to the LORD, all the earth.
Sing to the LORD, praise his name;
>proclaim his salvation day after day.
Declare his glory among the nations,
>his marvelous deeds among all peoples.

For great is the LORD and most worthy of
>praise;
>he is to be feared above all gods.
For all the gods of the nations are
>idols,
>but the LORD made the heavens.
Splendor and majesty are before
>him;
>strength and glory are in his
>sanctuary.

Ascribe to the LORD, O families of
>nations,
>ascribe to the LORD glory and
>strength.
Ascribe to the LORD the glory due his name;
>bring an offering and come into his courts.
Worship the LORD in the splendor of his holiness;
>tremble before him, all the earth.

Psalm 96:1 — 9

GRANDCHILD IN FOCUS • PRAYER

Talents

Dear Lord, the giver of gifts, bless my grandchild as he develops his talents. Help him identify his talents and be proud and confident of the gifts you have given him. Give him patience and understanding, Lord, so he will not grow weary of striving and searching to reach the goals you have set for him. May each milestone bring satisfaction and a healthy desire for greater achievement and success to bring glory to you. Amen.

O God of all gods, grant me courage to declare that you are the Creator of heaven and earth, the God of all gods, the Lord of all nations. Strengthen me to put aside all the idols I have made, and clear out the clutter in my life so that I can focus on you and worship you with a pure heart. Amen.

Your next devotion is located on page 1287.

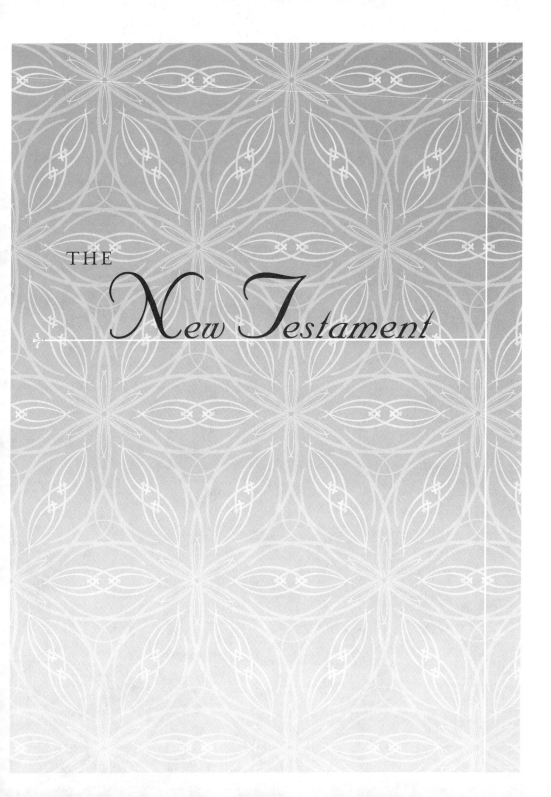

THE

New Testament

A Shining LIGHT

It was so obvious: Jesus the Messiah had come. The long-awaited king whom the prophets had promised had finally arrived. And yet so many people missed him. Matthew wrote this account of Jesus primarily for Jewish readers. Throughout his book, Matthew spotlighted Old Testament passages to connect the dots between the past and the present, showing his readers who Jesus is.

Matthew began his Gospel with a genealogy that portrays the lineage of Jesus — proving that "he's the right one." Matthew then explained how Jesus perfectly fulfilled all of "the Law" and "the Prophets" (Matthew 5:17) — the entire Old Testament. Although the other Gospel writers also quoted the Old Testament, Matthew used the Jewish Scriptures more than any of the other writers, proving to his readers that Jesus fulfilled all of the Old Testament predictions concerning the Messiah.

Like Matthew, we are called to shine the light of Jesus to an unbelieving world. As grandmothers we have a unique opportunity to influence generations of believers. But all the facts and proof texts will be meaningless unless our actions and our words convey God's love and power through the Holy Spirit. As we show Christ's compassion, forgiveness and healing to each grandchild, friend and person we encounter, we will be illuminating the way for many more as the light gets passed from one to another.

VERSE *to* REMEMBER | MATTHEW 5:16

In the same way, let your light shine before men, that they may see your good deeds and praise your Father in heaven.

Matthew

ABOUT MATTHEW

WRITTEN BY:
Matthew, one of Jesus' twelve disciples

WRITTEN FOR:
Primarily the Jewish people

DATE WRITTEN:
Sometime between A.D. 50 and 80

WHY WRITTEN:
To prove that Jesus is the Messiah who was promised in the Old Testament

The Genealogy of Jesus

1:1–17pp — Lk 3:23–38
1:3–6pp — Ru 4:18–22
1:7–11pp — 1Ch 3:10–17

1 A record of the genealogy of Jesus Christ the son of David, the son of Abraham:

² Abraham was the father of Isaac,
   Isaac the father of Jacob,
   Jacob the father of Judah and his brothers,
³ Judah the father of Perez and Zerah, whose mother was Tamar,
   Perez the father of Hezron,
   Hezron the father of Ram,
⁴ Ram the father of Amminadab,
   Amminadab the father of Nahshon,
   Nahshon the father of Salmon,
⁵ Salmon the father of Boaz, whose mother was Rahab,
   Boaz the father of Obed, whose mother was Ruth,
   Obed the father of Jesse,
⁶ and Jesse the father of King David.

David was the father of Solomon, whose mother had been Uriah's wife,
⁷ Solomon the father of Rehoboam,
   Rehoboam the father of Abijah,
   Abijah the father of Asa,
⁸ Asa the father of Jehoshaphat,
   Jehoshaphat the father of Jehoram,
   Jehoram the father of Uzziah,
⁹ Uzziah the father of Jotham,
   Jotham the father of Ahaz,
   Ahaz the father of Hezekiah,
¹⁰ Hezekiah the father of Manasseh,
   Manasseh the father of Amon,
   Amon the father of Josiah,
¹¹ and Josiah the father of Jeconiah *a* and his brothers at the time of the exile to Babylon.

¹² After the exile to Babylon:
   Jeconiah was the father of Shealtiel,
   Shealtiel the father of Zerubbabel,
¹³ Zerubbabel the father of Abiud,
   Abiud the father of Eliakim,
   Eliakim the father of Azor,
¹⁴ Azor the father of Zadok,
   Zadok the father of Akim,
   Akim the father of Eliud,
¹⁵ Eliud the father of Eleazar,
   Eleazar the father of Matthan,
   Matthan the father of Jacob,
¹⁶ and Jacob the father of Joseph, the husband of Mary, of whom was born Jesus, who is called Christ.

¹⁷ Thus there were fourteen generations in all from Abraham to David, fourteen from David to the exile to Babylon, and fourteen from the exile to the Christ. *b*

The Birth of Jesus Christ

¹⁸ This is how the birth of Jesus Christ came about: His mother Mary was pledged to be married to Joseph, but before they came together, she was found to be with child through the Holy Spirit. ¹⁹ Because Joseph her husband was a righteous man and did not want to expose her to public disgrace, he had in mind to divorce her quietly.

²⁰ But after he had considered this, an angel of the Lord appeared to him in a dream and said, "Joseph son of David, do not be afraid to take Mary home as your wife, because what is conceived in her is from the Holy Spirit. ²¹ She will give birth to a son, and you are to give him the name Jesus, *c* because he will save his people from their sins."

²² All this took place to fulfill what the Lord had said through the prophet: ²³ "The virgin will be with child and will give birth to a son, and they will call him Immanuel" *d* —which means, "God with us."

²⁴ When Joseph woke up, he did what the angel of the Lord had commanded him and took Mary home as his wife. ²⁵ But he had no union with her until she gave birth to a son. And he gave him the name Jesus.

---

a 11 That is, Jehoiachin; also in verse 12   *b 17* Or *Messiah.*
"The Christ" (Greek) and "the Messiah" (Hebrew) both mean "the Anointed One."   *c 21* *Jesus* is the Greek form of *Joshua,* which means *the LORD saves.*   *d 23* Isaiah 7:14

What Shall We Be Called?

> "THE VIRGIN WILL BE WITH CHILD AND WILL GIVE BIRTH TO A SON, AND THEY WILL CALL HIM IMMANUEL" — WHICH MEANS, "GOD WITH US."
>
> *Matthew 1:23*

CAROL KUYKENDALL

READ | MATTHEW 1:1 – 25

Soon after my husband and I received the thrilling news that we would become first-time grandparents, our family and friends began asking, "What do you want to be called?"

Wow, the question stumped us as we considered the importance and fun of this opportunity. For the first time in our lives, we got to choose our own names, ones that would identify us, not only to this grandchild, but to all the rest yet to come.

For the next several months, more seasoned grandparents gave us advice about choosing names:

Choose something simple to say, but be ready for little ones to morph it into something else. One Grandma became Mee-mo, a Grammy became Mimi, and a Grampy and Grammy became Shampy and Shammy. Some children morph the names as they grow up when Mee-mo no longer fits their level of maturity.

Take advantage of the chance to cooperate, not compete, with the other set of grandparents. Be open to choices different from their choice. After all, there are many variations of Grandma and Grandpa, including Mama and Papa, Nana or Nonna and Boppa. One grandmother simply went by Grand.

Try a totally unique name, like the grandmother who chose Gigi, the name she'd always wanted to be called as a child.

Many choose Grandmother and Grandfather in another language. For instance, Abuela or Abuelita, which means "little grandma" in Spanish.

This last suggestion is the one that finally clicked with us. We are both Dutch, and the names Oma and Opa seemed just right. Thankfully, those names are easy for small children to say, and we've happily been known as Oma and Opa for the last five years.

Lord, we know that names matter to you, and we pray they matter to our grandchildren. We also pray you will imprint our names in their precious souls for a lifetime. May we be worthy of that blessing.

Your next devotion is located on page 1292.

GRANDCHILD IN FOCUS • PRAYER

SELECT ONE OF YOUR GRANDCHILDREN TO FOCUS ON IN PRAYER FOR THE NEXT 14 DAYS.

Salvation

Dear Lord, please guide my grandchild to your gift of salvation. I pray that she will come to know you, to love you and to walk close to you throughout her life. May she boldly claim Jesus as her Lord and Savior. Guide her as she makes choices that have eternal consequences. Help her to follow you each moment of her life. I pray this in Jesus' name, amen.

The Visit of the Magi

2 After Jesus was born in Bethlehem in Judea, during the time of King Herod, Magi[a] from the east came to Jerusalem [2]and asked, "Where is the one who has been born king of the Jews? We saw his star in the east[b] and have come to worship him."

[3]When King Herod heard this he was disturbed, and all Jerusalem with him. [4]When he had called together all the people's chief priests and teachers of the law, he asked them where the Christ[c] was to be born. [5]"In Bethlehem in Judea," they replied, "for this is what the prophet has written:

[6]" 'But you, Bethlehem, in the land of Judah,
    are by no means least among the rulers of
        Judah;

for out of you will come a ruler
    who will be the shepherd of my people
        Israel.'[d]"

[7]Then Herod called the Magi secretly and found out from them the exact time the star had appeared. [8]He sent them to Bethlehem and said, "Go and make a careful search for the child. As soon as you find him, report to me, so that I too may go and worship him."

[9]After they had heard the king, they went on their way, and the star they had seen in the east[e] went ahead of them until it stopped over the place where the child was. [10]When they saw the star, they were overjoyed. [11]On coming to the house, they saw the child with his mother Mary, and they bowed down and worshiped him. Then they opened their treasures and presented him with gifts of gold and of incense and of myrrh. [12]And having been warned in a dream not to go back to Herod, they returned to their country by another route.

The Escape to Egypt

[13]When they had gone, an angel of the Lord appeared to Joseph in a dream. "Get up," he said, "take the child and his mother and escape to Egypt. Stay there until I tell you, for Herod is going to search for the child to kill him."

[14]So he got up, took the child and his mother during the night and left for Egypt, [15]where he stayed until the death of Herod. And so was fulfilled what the Lord had said through the prophet: "Out of Egypt I called my son."[f]

[16]When Herod realized that he had been outwitted by the Magi, he was furious, and he gave orders to kill all the boys in Bethlehem and its vicinity who were two years old and under, in accordance with the time he had learned from the Magi. [17]Then what was said through the prophet Jeremiah was fulfilled:

[18]"A voice is heard in Ramah,
    weeping and great mourning,

stories to share

MATTHEW 2:1–12

The Magi Visit Jesus

LIFE LESSON: Jesus, our King, is worthy of worship and praise.

TO TALK ABOUT

✦ Why did the Magi make the long trip to Jerusalem?

✦ Did King Herod really want to go and worship Jesus? How do you know?

✦ What did the Magi do when they found Jesus?

✦ How can you show Jesus that he is worthy of your worship?

[a] 1 Traditionally *Wise Men*   [b] 2 Or *star when it rose*
[c] 4 Or *Messiah*   [d] 6 Micah 5:2   [e] 9 Or *seen when it rose*
[f] 15 Hosea 11:1

Rachel weeping for her children
and refusing to be comforted,
because they are no more."[a]

The Return to Nazareth

[19]After Herod died, an angel of the Lord appeared in a dream to Joseph in Egypt [20]and said, "Get up, take the child and his mother and go to the land of Israel, for those who were trying to take the child's life are dead."

[21]So he got up, took the child and his mother and went to the land of Israel. [22]But when he heard that Archelaus was reigning in Judea in place of his father Herod, he was afraid to go there. Having been warned in a dream, he withdrew to the district of Galilee, [23]and he went and lived in a town called Nazareth. So was fulfilled what was said through the prophets: "He will be called a Nazarene."

John the Baptist Prepares the Way
3:1–12pp — Mk 1:3–8; Lk 3:2–17

3 In those days John the Baptist came, preaching in the Desert of Judea [2]and saying, "Repent, for the kingdom of heaven is near." [3]This is he who was spoken of through the prophet Isaiah:

"A voice of one calling in the desert,
'Prepare the way for the Lord,
make straight paths for him.' "[b]

[4]John's clothes were made of camel's hair, and he had a leather belt around his waist. His food was locusts and wild honey. [5]People went out to him from Jerusalem and all Judea and the whole region of the Jordan. [6]Confessing their sins, they were baptized by him in the Jordan River.

[7]But when he saw many of the Pharisees and Sadducees coming to where he was baptizing, he said to them: "You brood of vipers! Who warned you to flee from the coming wrath? [8]Produce fruit in keeping with repentance. [9]And do not think you can say to yourselves, 'We have Abraham as our father.' I tell you that out of these stones God can raise up children for Abraham.

[10]The ax is already at the root of the trees, and every tree that does not produce good fruit will be cut down and thrown into the fire.

[11]"I baptize you with[c] water for repentance. But after me will come one who is more powerful than I, whose sandals I am not fit to carry. He will baptize you with the Holy Spirit and with fire. [12]His winnowing fork is in his hand, and he will clear his threshing floor, gathering his wheat into the barn and burning up the chaff with unquenchable fire."

The Baptism of Jesus
3:13–17pp — Mk 1:9–11; Lk 3:21,22; Jn 1:31–34

[13]Then Jesus came from Galilee to the Jordan to be baptized by John. [14]But John tried to deter

---

[a] 18 Jer. 31:15   [b] 3 Isaiah 40:3   [c] 11 Or *in*

MATTHEW 3:1–17

stories to share

The Baptism of Jesus

LIFE LESSON: Jesus is the Son of God.

TO TALK ABOUT

✦ What kind of person was John the Baptist? What role did he play in God's plan?

✦ How did John compare himself to Jesus?

✦ Where was Jesus baptized?

✦ The Bible never uses the word *trinity*, yet we believe in the Father, Son and Holy Spirit. What does this story tells us about the Trinity?

him, saying, "I need to be baptized by you, and do you come to me?"

¹⁵Jesus replied, "Let it be so now; it is proper for us to do this to fulfill all righteousness." Then John consented.

¹⁶As soon as Jesus was baptized, he went up out of the water. At that moment heaven was opened, and he saw the Spirit of God descending like a dove and lighting on him. ¹⁷And a voice from heaven said, "This is my Son, whom I love; with him I am well pleased."

The Temptation of Jesus

4:1–11pp — Mk 1:12,13; Lk 4:1–13

4 Then Jesus was led by the Spirit into the desert to be tempted by the devil. ²After fasting forty days and forty nights, he was hungry. ³The tempter came to him and said, "If you are the Son of God, tell these stones to become bread."

⁴Jesus answered, "It is written: 'Man does not live on bread alone, but on every word that comes from the mouth of God.'ᵃ"

⁵Then the devil took him to the holy city and had him stand on the highest point of the temple. ⁶"If you are the Son of God," he said, "throw yourself down. For it is written:

" 'He will command his angels concerning
        you,
    and they will lift you up in their hands,
so that you will not strike your foot against
        a stone.'ᵇ"

⁷Jesus answered him, "It is also written: 'Do not put the Lord your God to the test.'ᶜ"

⁸Again, the devil took him to a very high mountain and showed him all the kingdoms of the world and their splendor. ⁹"All this I will give you," he said, "if you will bow down and worship me."

¹⁰Jesus said to him, "Away from me, Satan! For it is written: 'Worship the Lord your God, and serve him only.'ᵈ"

¹¹Then the devil left him, and angels came and attended him.

stories to share

MATTHEW 4:1–11

Jesus Is Tempted

LIFE LESSON: Like Jesus, we can say no to temptation.

TO TALK ABOUT

✦ What three things did Satan try to get Jesus to do?

✦ How did Jesus respond? What was his source for each response?

✦ When have you given in to temptation? When have you said no to it?

✦ What helps us say no to temptation?

Jesus Begins to Preach

¹²When Jesus heard that John had been put in prison, he returned to Galilee. ¹³Leaving Nazareth, he went and lived in Capernaum, which was by the lake in the area of Zebulun and Naphtali— ¹⁴to fulfill what was said through the prophet Isaiah:

¹⁵"Land of Zebulun and land of Naphtali,
    the way to the sea, along the Jordan,
    Galilee of the Gentiles—
¹⁶the people living in darkness
    have seen a great light;
on those living in the land of the shadow of
        death
    a light has dawned."ᵉ

ᵃ 4 Deut. 8:3   ᵇ 6 Psalm 91:11,12   ᶜ 7 Deut. 6:16
ᵈ 10 Deut. 6:13   ᵉ 16 Isaiah 9:1,2

[17] From that time on Jesus began to preach, "Repent, for the kingdom of heaven is near."

The Calling of the First Disciples

4:18–22pp — Mk 1:16–20; Lk 5:2–11; Jn 1:35–42

[18] As Jesus was walking beside the Sea of Galilee, he saw two brothers, Simon called Peter and his brother Andrew. They were casting a net into the lake, for they were fishermen. [19] "Come, follow me," Jesus said, "and I will make you fishers of men." [20] At once they left their nets and followed him.

[21] Going on from there, he saw two other brothers, James son of Zebedee and his brother John. They were in a boat with their father Zebedee, preparing their nets. Jesus called them, [22] and immediately they left the boat and their father and followed him.

Jesus Heals the Sick

[23] Jesus went throughout Galilee, teaching in their synagogues, preaching the good news of the kingdom, and healing every disease and sickness among the people. [24] News about him spread all over Syria, and people brought to him all who

TALKING POINTS

Illness

Jesus healed the sick.

MATTHEW 4:23–24

For more on illness, go to 3 John 2.

were ill with various diseases, those suffering severe pain, the demon-possessed, those having seizures, and the paralyzed, and he healed them. [25] Large crowds from Galilee, the Decapolis,[a] Jerusalem, Judea and the region across the Jordan followed him.

The Beatitudes

5:3–12pp — Lk 6:20–23

5 Now when he saw the crowds, he went up on a mountainside and sat down. His disciples came to him, [2] and he began to teach them, saying:

[3] "Blessed are the poor in spirit,
　for theirs is the kingdom of heaven.
[4] Blessed are those who mourn,
　for they will be comforted.
[5] Blessed are the meek,
　for they will inherit the earth.
[6] Blessed are those who hunger and thirst for
　　righteousness,
　for they will be filled.
[7] Blessed are the merciful,
　for they will be shown mercy.
[8] Blessed are the pure in heart,
　for they will see God.
[9] Blessed are the peacemakers,
　for they will be called sons of God.
[10] Blessed are those who are persecuted because
　　of righteousness,
　for theirs is the kingdom of heaven.

[11] "Blessed are you when people insult you, persecute you and falsely say all kinds of evil against you because of me. [12] Rejoice and be glad, because great is your reward in heaven, for in the same way they persecuted the prophets who were before you.

Salt and Light

[13] "You are the salt of the earth. But if the salt loses its saltiness, how can it be made salty again? It is no longer good for anything, except to be thrown out and trampled by men.

[14] "You are the light of the world. A city on a hill cannot be hidden. [15] Neither do people light a lamp and put it under a bowl. Instead they put it on its stand, and it gives light to everyone in the house. [16] In the same way, let your light shine before men, that they may see your good deeds and praise your Father in heaven.

a 25 That is, the Ten Cities

> "YOU ARE THE LIGHT OF THE
> WORLD . . . LET YOUR LIGHT
> SHINE BEFORE MEN, THAT THEY
> MAY SEE YOUR GOOD DEEDS
> AND PRAISE YOUR FATHER IN
> HEAVEN."
>
> *Matthew 5:14,16*

Let Your Light Shine

CYNTHIA HEALD

READ | MATTHEW 5:1 – 16

My grandmother was born in 1894, married at age 14, and raised 13 children. She had a third-grade education, but I have always thought her to be one of the wisest women I have ever known. She never wore makeup, but to me she was beautiful. Although we did not see each other often, I loved her deeply.

As I think about her life, I recall her welcoming embrace, her broad smile and her gravelly voice saying, "Get in this house!" Her weathered face showed the years she spent hoeing in her garden. She once said, "If a storm was coming, and I had to choose to go to a storm cellar or the pea patch, I'd choose the pea patch because it has saved my life so many times."

I remember her as soft, kind and at peace. Every time I was with her, she was always the same — loving, accepting of her circumstances and wanting to serve any and all who came into her home. She had an amazing ability to make each person feel special. I am one of 35 grandchildren, and we all agree that each of us felt that we were her favorite.

Her good deeds consisted of loving unconditionally, being a role model of what it looks like to trust God, and sharing anything she had to help others. Her faithful serving is still remembered and continues to result in praise to our Father in heaven.

A few years before her death, I was visiting with her, and she told me that her favorite song was "This Little Light of Mine." The lyrics go, "This little light of mine, I'm going let it shine." And so she did.

Father, thank you for godly grandmothers who love you and are willing to let their light shine in this dark world. As I reflect on the godly women who have shaped my life, I pray that my life, like theirs, will result in praise and glory to your name. Amen.

Your next devotion is located on page 1296.

GRANDCHILD IN FOCUS • PRAYER

Physical Well-Being

Almighty God, Creator of us all, I pray that you will watch over my grandchild's physical development. May he grow in strength through the stages of his life. As he grows in awareness of his body, help him to understand that each body develops uniquely, yet is within your plan and your control. Please guard his health so that his diseases are few, his injuries are minor and his infirmities are brief. Amen.

MATTHEW 5:1–16; 6:5–15

Jesus Teaches on a Mountain

LIFE LESSON: Jesus is our wise teacher.

TO TALK ABOUT

✦ Who are "salt" and "light"?

✦ For what did Jesus tell us to pray?

✦ How do you pray to Jesus?

✦ How do Jesus' teachings help you live a better life?

The Fulfillment of the Law

[17] "Do not think that I have come to abolish the Law or the Prophets; I have not come to abolish them but to fulfill them. [18] I tell you the truth, until heaven and earth disappear, not the smallest letter, not the least stroke of a pen, will by any means disappear from the Law until everything is accomplished. [19] Anyone who breaks one of the least of these commandments and teaches others to do the same will be called least in the kingdom of heaven, but whoever practices and teaches these commands will be called great in the kingdom of heaven. [20] For I tell you that unless your righteousness surpasses that of the Pharisees and the teachers of the law, you will certainly not enter the kingdom of heaven.

Murder

5:25,26pp — Lk 12:58,59

[21] "You have heard that it was said to the people long ago, 'Do not murder,[a] and anyone who

murders will be subject to judgment.' [22] But I tell you that anyone who is angry with his brother[b] will be subject to judgment. Again, anyone who says to his brother, 'Raca,'[c] is answerable to the Sanhedrin. But anyone who says, 'You fool!' will be in danger of the fire of hell.

[23] "Therefore, if you are offering your gift at the altar and there remember that your brother has something against you, [24] leave your gift there in front of the altar. First go and be reconciled to your brother; then come and offer your gift.

[25] "Settle matters quickly with your adversary who is taking you to court. Do it while you are still with him on the way, or he may hand you over to the judge, and the judge may hand you over to the officer, and you may be thrown into prison. [26] I tell you the truth, you will not get out until you have paid the last penny.[d]

Adultery

[27] "You have heard that it was said, 'Do not commit adultery.'[e] [28] But I tell you that anyone who looks at a woman lustfully has already committed adultery with her in his heart. [29] If your right eye causes you to sin, gouge it out and throw it away. It is better for you to lose one part of your body than for your whole body to be thrown into hell. [30] And if your right hand causes you to sin, cut it off and throw it away. It is better for you to lose one part of your body than for your whole body to go into hell.

Divorce

[31] "It has been said, 'Anyone who divorces his wife must give her a certificate of divorce.'[f] [32] But I tell you that anyone who divorces his wife, except for marital unfaithfulness, causes her to become an adulteress, and anyone who marries the divorced woman commits adultery.

Oaths

[33] "Again, you have heard that it was said to the people long ago, 'Do not break your oath, but

---

[a] 21 Exodus 20:13   [b] 22 Some manuscripts *brother without cause*
[c] 22 An Aramaic term of contempt   [d] 26 Greek *kodrantes*
[e] 27 Exodus 20:14   [f] 31 Deut. 24:1

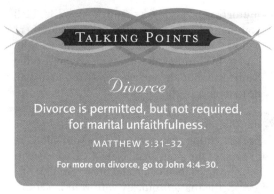

TALKING POINTS

Divorce

Divorce is permitted, but not required,
for marital unfaithfulness.

MATTHEW 5:31–32

For more on divorce, go to John 4:4–30.

keep the oaths you have made to the Lord.' [34] But I tell you, Do not swear at all: either by heaven, for it is God's throne; [35] or by the earth, for it is his footstool; or by Jerusalem, for it is the city of the Great King. [36] And do not swear by your head, for you cannot make even one hair white or black. [37] Simply let your 'Yes' be 'Yes,' and your 'No,' 'No'; anything beyond this comes from the evil one.

An Eye for an Eye

[38] "You have heard that it was said, 'Eye for eye, and tooth for tooth.'[a] [39] But I tell you, Do not resist an evil person. If someone strikes you on the right cheek, turn to him the other also. [40] And if someone wants to sue you and take your tunic, let him have your cloak as well. [41] If someone forces you to go one mile, go with him two miles. [42] Give to the one who asks you, and do not turn away from the one who wants to borrow from you.

Love for Enemies

[43] "You have heard that it was said, 'Love your neighbor[b] and hate your enemy.' [44] But I tell you: Love your enemies[c] and pray for those who persecute you, [45] that you may be sons of your Father in heaven. He causes his sun to rise on the evil and the good, and sends rain on the righteous and the unrighteous. [46] If you love those who love you, what reward will you get? Are not even the tax collectors doing that? [47] And if you greet only your brothers, what are you doing more than others? Do not even pagans do that? [48] Be perfect, therefore, as your heavenly Father is perfect.

Giving to the Needy

6 "Be careful not to do your 'acts of righteousness' before men, to be seen by them. If you do, you will have no reward from your Father in heaven.

[2] "So when you give to the needy, do not announce it with trumpets, as the hypocrites do in the synagogues and on the streets, to be honored by men. I tell you the truth, they have received their reward in full. [3] But when you give to the needy, do not let your left hand know what your right hand is doing, [4] so that your giving may be in secret. Then your Father, who sees what is done in secret, will reward you.

Prayer

6:9–13pp — Lk 11:2–4

[5] "And when you pray, do not be like the hypocrites, for they love to pray standing in the synagogues and on the street corners to be seen by men. I tell you the truth, they have received their reward in full. [6] But when you pray, go into your room, close the door and pray to your Father, who is unseen. Then your Father, who sees what is done in secret, will reward you. [7] And when you pray, do not keep on babbling like pagans, for they think they will be heard because of their many words. [8] Do not be like them, for your Father knows what you need before you ask him.

[9] "This, then, is how you should pray:

" 'Our Father in heaven,
    hallowed be your name,
[10] your kingdom come,
    your will be done
        on earth as it is in heaven.
[11] Give us today our daily bread.
[12] Forgive us our debts,
    as we also have forgiven our debtors.

[a] 38 Exodus 21:24; Lev. 24:20; Deut. 19:21   [b] 43 Lev. 19:18
[c] 44 Some late manuscripts *enemies, bless those who curse you, do good to those who hate you*

¹³And lead us not into temptation,
but deliver us from the evil one.^{*a*}

¹⁴For if you forgive men when they sin against you, your heavenly Father will also forgive you. ¹⁵But if you do not forgive men their sins, your Father will not forgive your sins.

Fasting

¹⁶"When you fast, do not look somber as the hypocrites do, for they disfigure their faces to show men they are fasting. I tell you the truth, they have received their reward in full. ¹⁷But when you fast, put oil on your head and wash your face, ¹⁸so that it will not be obvious to men that you are fasting, but only to your Father, who is unseen; and your Father, who sees what is done in secret, will reward you.

Treasures in Heaven

6:22,23pp — Lk 11:34–36

¹⁹"Do not store up for yourselves treasures on earth, where moth and rust destroy, and where thieves break in and steal. ²⁰But store up for yourselves treasures in heaven, where moth and rust do not destroy, and where thieves do not break in and steal. ²¹For where your treasure is, there your heart will be also.

²²"The eye is the lamp of the body. If your eyes are good, your whole body will be full of light. ²³But if your eyes are bad, your whole body will be full of darkness. If then the light within you is darkness, how great is that darkness!

²⁴"No one can serve two masters. Either he will hate the one and love the other, or he will be devoted to the one and despise the other. You cannot serve both God and Money.

Do Not Worry

6:25–33pp — Lk 12:22–31

²⁵"Therefore I tell you, do not worry about your life, what you will eat or drink; or about your body, what you will wear. Is not life more important than food, and the body more important than clothes? ²⁶Look at the birds of the air; they do not sow or reap or store away in barns, and yet your heavenly Father feeds them. Are you not much more valuable than they? ²⁷Who of you by worrying can add a single hour to his life^{*b*}?

²⁸"And why do you worry about clothes? See how the lilies of the field grow. They do not labor or spin. ²⁹Yet I tell you that not even Solomon in all his splendor was dressed like one of these. ³⁰If that is how God clothes the grass of the field, which is here today and tomorrow is thrown into the fire, will he not much more clothe you, O you of little faith? ³¹So do not worry, saying, 'What shall we eat?' or 'What shall we drink?' or 'What shall we wear?' ³²For the pagans run after all these things, and your heavenly Father knows that you need them. ³³But seek first his kingdom and his righteousness, and all these things will be given to you as well. ³⁴Therefore do not worry about tomorrow, for tomorrow will worry about itself. Each day has enough trouble of its own.

Judging Others

7:3–5pp — Lk 6:41,42

7 "Do not judge, or you too will be judged. ²For in the same way you judge others, you will be judged, and with the measure you use, it will be measured to you.

³"Why do you look at the speck of sawdust in your brother's eye and pay no attention to the plank in your own eye? ⁴How can you say to your

TALKING POINTS

Contentment

Keep your priorities straight.

MATTHEW 6:19–21

For more on contentment, go to Philippians 4:10–13.

---

^{*a*} 13 Or *from evil*; some late manuscripts *one, / for yours is the kingdom and the power and the glory forever. Amen.* ^{*b*} 27 Or *single cubit to his height*

> "BUT SEEK FIRST HIS KINGDOM AND HIS RIGHTEOUSNESS, AND ALL THESE THINGS WILL BE GIVEN TO YOU AS WELL."
>
> *Matthew 6:33*

Seek First His Kingdom

DEBBY KERNER RETTINO

READ | MATTHEW 6:25 – 34

"Mom, I'm pregnant." The words hung in the air — part statement, part anxious question — as my 16-year-old daughter searched my face, waiting for my reaction. I was stunned. What about all of my dreams for her: the college diploma and the brilliant career?

Then my dreams for my own life rudely pushed their way to the forefront of my thoughts. My husband and I had placed so many things on hold for the last 20 years. Shouldn't it be our turn to do the things we wanted? As we talked through the situation, I knew that my daughter's words revealed the probable course of my next 20 years, and I was exhausted just from thinking about the demands of raising a baby, a toddler, a teenager!

My daughter gave the best effort she could at being a mom, but she was too young and not equipped for all of the demands of raising a child. So, she did the best thing she knew how to do: She asked us if we would take care of our grandson. We could not say no.

Yes, there were plenty of times when I longed to sleep in rather than get a first-grader to school. Now, as he enters adolescence, battling over homework and checking on whom he is hanging out with wear me out. When I feel like I am going down for the third time with fatigue and frustration, I recall that God provides for all my needs as I seek him first. Just as he takes care of the birds and wildflowers, God gives me the stamina and stick-to-itiveness to parent my grandchild. I accept God's strength, and I rejoice as I cheer at soccer games, cuddle during bedtime stories and accept the awkward kiss of a young teenager heading to his first dance. Those are the gifts of grandmothering and the blessings of God in my life.

Father, you are all-powerful. Only through your Son, Jesus, can I have righteousness and the hope of heaven. Thank you that your kingdom is not only in the future, but it is right now, and you, my source, are able to provide everything I need. When I am weak, I trust you to give me strength. When I am discouraged, I trust you to give me joy. When I am inadequate, I trust you to be enough. Help me to turn to you first. Amen.

GRANDCHILD IN FOCUS • PRAYER

Emotional Development

O God, Creator of mind and body, I pray that you will give my grandchild emotional health and strength. Where there is anger, bring peace. Where there is confusion, bring clarity and focus. Where there are dark shadows, cast a ray of hope. Fill her with the sunshine of your Spirit. Warm her with the presence of your peace. Amen.

Your next devotion is located on page 1298.

brother, 'Let me take the speck out of your eye,' when all the time there is a plank in your own eye? [5] You hypocrite, first take the plank out of your own eye, and then you will see clearly to remove the speck from your brother's eye.

[6] "Do not give dogs what is sacred; do not throw your pearls to pigs. If you do, they may trample them under their feet, and then turn and tear you to pieces.

Ask, Seek, Knock
7:7–11pp — Lk 11:9–13

[7] "Ask and it will be given to you; seek and you will find; knock and the door will be opened to you. [8] For everyone who asks receives; he who seeks finds; and to him who knocks, the door will be opened.

[9] "Which of you, if his son asks for bread, will give him a stone? [10] Or if he asks for a fish, will give him a snake? [11] If you, then, though you are evil, know how to give good gifts to your children, how much more will your Father in heaven give good gifts to those who ask him! [12] So in everything, do to others what you would have them do to you, for this sums up the Law and the Prophets.

TALKING POINTS

Prayer

God loves to give good gifts in response to our prayers.

MATTHEW 7:7–11

For more on prayer, go to Luke 18:1–8.

The Narrow and Wide Gates

[13] "Enter through the narrow gate. For wide is the gate and broad is the road that leads to destruction, and many enter through it. [14] But small is the gate and narrow the road that leads to life, and only a few find it.

A Tree and Its Fruit

[15] "Watch out for false prophets. They come to you in sheep's clothing, but inwardly they are ferocious wolves. [16] By their fruit you will recognize them. Do people pick grapes from thornbushes, or figs from thistles? [17] Likewise every good tree bears good fruit, but a bad tree bears bad fruit. [18] A good tree cannot bear bad fruit, and a bad tree cannot bear good fruit. [19] Every tree that does not bear good fruit is cut down and thrown into the fire. [20] Thus, by their fruit you will recognize them.

[21] "Not everyone who says to me, 'Lord, Lord,' will enter the kingdom of heaven, but only he who does the will of my Father who is in heaven. [22] Many will say to me on that day, 'Lord, Lord, did we not prophesy in your name, and in your name drive out demons and perform many miracles?' [23] Then I will tell them plainly, 'I never knew you. Away from me, you evildoers!'

The Wise and Foolish Builders
7:24–27pp — Lk 6:47–49

[24] "Therefore everyone who hears these words of mine and puts them into practice is like a wise man who built his house on the rock. [25] The rain came down, the streams rose, and the winds blew and beat against that house; yet it did not fall, because it had its foundation on the rock. [26] But everyone who hears these words of mine and does not put them into practice is like a foolish man who built his house on sand. [27] The rain came down, the streams rose, and the winds blew and beat against that house, and it fell with a great crash."

[28] When Jesus had finished saying these things, the crowds were amazed at his teaching, [29] because he taught as one who had authority, and not as their teachers of the law.

The Man With Leprosy
8:2–4pp — Mk 1:40–44; Lk 5:12–14

8 When he came down from the mountainside, large crowds followed him. [2] A man

"ASK AND IT WILL BE GIVEN TO
YOU; SEEK AND YOU WILL FIND;
KNOCK AND THE DOOR WILL BE
OPENED TO YOU."

Matthew 7:7

Childlike Faith

CAROL CYMBALA

READ | MATTHEW 7:7 – 12

Just as my grandmother's faith in a prayer-answering God was passed down to me, I have seen the same grace of God in my own offspring. A great example of that is my granddaughter, Claire, who was six years old when she learned firsthand about God's faithfulness.

Claire had a Persian cat named Bella, whom she loved dearly and who had become part of the family. Imagine the pain in Claire's little heart when she discovered one day that the cat was missing. In the midst of the traffic coming in and out of the house on Christmas Eve, the front door was left open long enough for Bella to curiously wander outside. The outside world of Roslyn, New York, in the dead of winter is no place for a delicate cat like Bella, and the family's hopes of retrieving her dimmed as the days passed. Although they scoured the neighborhood and posted signs everywhere, Bella seemed to be gone forever. Claire cried daily over the loss of her precious cat.

Eight days after Bella's disappearance, my son-in-law Brian was putting his daughter to bed, and Claire had a chance to pray aloud. Suddenly she began to pour her broken heart out to God, and she pleaded for the return of her cat. Her prayer was desperate and filled with the childlike faith that God has promised to answer.

At 9 A.M. the next morning, Claire's teacher called my daughter Susan and reported that she was almost sure she had spotted Bella in her backyard. Susan and Claire rushed over, and there was Bella, safe and sound, although worn by the extreme weather and outdoor conditions. When Claire saw her cat, she started jumping and crying out, "Mommy, God really answered my prayer!" What an illustration to my granddaughter's impressionable heart and mind! God still answers prayer!

Lord, may we all come before you with childlike faith. We thank you that you are the same yesterday, today and forever and that your ear is ever open to the cries of your children. Our faith and trust are in you alone. Amen.

GRANDCHILD IN FOCUS · PRAYER

Spiritual Growth

Dear Lord, today I pray for my grandchild's spiritual growth. I ask that you instill in him the desire to read and memorize your Word. Give him a passion to be in conversation with you. May loving and serving you be part of his daily life. I ask that you stay close to him and lead him to be transformed to your likeness, to reflect your grace and to radiate your love. I pray this in Jesus' name, amen.

Your next devotion is located on page 1303.

with leprosy[a] came and knelt before him and said, "Lord, if you are willing, you can make me clean."

[3] Jesus reached out his hand and touched the man. "I am willing," he said. "Be clean!" Immediately he was cured[b] of his leprosy. [4] Then Jesus said to him, "See that you don't tell anyone. But go, show yourself to the priest and offer the gift Moses commanded, as a testimony to them."

The Faith of the Centurion
8:5–13pp — Lk 7:1–10

[5] When Jesus had entered Capernaum, a centurion came to him, asking for help. [6] "Lord," he said, "my servant lies at home paralyzed and in terrible suffering."

[7] Jesus said to him, "I will go and heal him."

[8] The centurion replied, "Lord, I do not deserve to have you come under my roof. But just say the word, and my servant will be healed. [9] For I myself am a man under authority, with soldiers under me. I tell this one, 'Go,' and he goes; and that one, 'Come,' and he comes. I say to my servant, 'Do this,' and he does it."

[10] When Jesus heard this, he was astonished and said to those following him, "I tell you the truth, I have not found anyone in Israel with such great faith. [11] I say to you that many will come from the east and the west, and will take their places at the feast with Abraham, Isaac and Jacob in the kingdom of heaven. [12] But the subjects of the kingdom will be thrown outside, into the darkness, where there will be weeping and gnashing of teeth."

[13] Then Jesus said to the centurion, "Go! It will be done just as you believed it would." And his servant was healed at that very hour.

Jesus Heals Many
8:14–16pp — Mk 1:29–34; Lk 4:38–41

[14] When Jesus came into Peter's house, he saw Peter's mother-in-law lying in bed with a fever. [15] He touched her hand and the fever left her, and she got up and began to wait on him.

[16] When evening came, many who were demon-possessed were brought to him, and he drove out the spirits with a word and healed all the sick. [17] This was to fulfill what was spoken through the prophet Isaiah:

"He took up our infirmities
    and carried our diseases."[c]

The Cost of Following Jesus
8:19–22pp — Lk 9:57–60

[18] When Jesus saw the crowd around him, he gave orders to cross to the other side of the lake. [19] Then a teacher of the law came to him and said, "Teacher, I will follow you wherever you go."

[20] Jesus replied, "Foxes have holes and birds of the air have nests, but the Son of Man has no place to lay his head."

[21] Another disciple said to him, "Lord, first let me go and bury my father."

[22] But Jesus told him, "Follow me, and let the dead bury their own dead."

Jesus Calms the Storm
8:23–27pp — Mk 4:36–41; Lk 8:22–25
8:23–27Ref — Mt 14:22–33

[23] Then he got into the boat and his disciples followed him. [24] Without warning, a furious storm came up on the lake, so that the waves swept over the boat. But Jesus was sleeping. [25] The disciples went and woke him, saying, "Lord, save us! We're going to drown!"

[26] He replied, "You of little faith, why are you so afraid?" Then he got up and rebuked the winds and the waves, and it was completely calm.

[27] The men were amazed and asked, "What kind of man is this? Even the winds and the waves obey him!"

The Healing of Two Demon-possessed Men
8:28–34pp — Mk 5:1–17; Lk 8:26–37

[28] When he arrived at the other side in the region of the Gadarenes,[d] two demon-possessed men coming from the tombs met him. They

---

[a] 2 The Greek word was used for various diseases affecting the skin—not necessarily leprosy.   [b] 3 Greek *made clean*
[c] 17 Isaiah 53:4   [d] 28 Some manuscripts *Gergesenes*; others *Gerasenes*

were so violent that no one could pass that way. [29]"What do you want with us, Son of God?" they shouted. "Have you come here to torture us before the appointed time?"

[30]Some distance from them a large herd of pigs was feeding. [31]The demons begged Jesus, "If you drive us out, send us into the herd of pigs."

[32]He said to them, "Go!" So they came out and went into the pigs, and the whole herd rushed down the steep bank into the lake and died in the water. [33]Those tending the pigs ran off, went into the town and reported all this, including what had happened to the demon-possessed men. [34]Then the whole town went out to meet Jesus. And when they saw him, they pleaded with him to leave their region.

Jesus Heals a Paralytic
9:2–8pp — Mk 2:3–12; Lk 5:18–26

9 Jesus stepped into a boat, crossed over and came to his own town. [2]Some men brought to him a paralytic, lying on a mat. When Jesus saw their faith, he said to the paralytic, "Take heart, son; your sins are forgiven."

[3]At this, some of the teachers of the law said to themselves, "This fellow is blaspheming!"

[4]Knowing their thoughts, Jesus said, "Why do you entertain evil thoughts in your hearts? [5]Which is easier: to say, 'Your sins are forgiven,' or to say, 'Get up and walk'? [6]But so that you may know that the Son of Man has authority on earth to forgive sins . . ." Then he said to the paralytic, "Get up, take your mat and go home." [7]And the man got up and went home. [8]When the crowd saw this, they were filled with awe; and they praised God, who had given such authority to men.

The Calling of Matthew
9:9–13pp — Mk 2:14–17; Lk 5:27–32

[9]As Jesus went on from there, he saw a man named Matthew sitting at the tax collector's booth. "Follow me," he told him, and Matthew got up and followed him.

[10]While Jesus was having dinner at Matthew's house, many tax collectors and "sinners" came and ate with him and his disciples. [11]When the Pharisees saw this, they asked his disciples, "Why does your teacher eat with tax collectors and 'sinners'?"

[12]On hearing this, Jesus said, "It is not the healthy who need a doctor, but the sick. [13]But go and learn what this means: 'I desire mercy, not sacrifice.'[a] For I have not come to call the righteous, but sinners."

Jesus Questioned About Fasting
9:14–17pp — Mk 2:18–22; Lk 5:33–39

[14]Then John's disciples came and asked him, "How is it that we and the Pharisees fast, but your disciples do not fast?"

[15]Jesus answered, "How can the guests of the bridegroom mourn while he is with them? The time will come when the bridegroom will be taken from them; then they will fast.

[16]"No one sews a patch of unshrunk cloth on an old garment, for the patch will pull away from the garment, making the tear worse. [17]Neither do men pour new wine into old wineskins. If they do, the skins will burst, the wine will run out and the wineskins will be ruined. No, they pour new wine into new wineskins, and both are preserved."

A Dead Girl and a Sick Woman
9:18–26pp — Mk 5:22–43; Lk 8:41–56

[18]While he was saying this, a ruler came and knelt before him and said, "My daughter has just died. But come and put your hand on her, and she will live." [19]Jesus got up and went with him, and so did his disciples.

[20]Just then a woman who had been subject to bleeding for twelve years came up behind him and touched the edge of his cloak. [21]She said to herself, "If I only touch his cloak, I will be healed."

[22]Jesus turned and saw her. "Take heart, daughter," he said, "your faith has healed you." And the woman was healed from that moment.

[23]When Jesus entered the ruler's house and saw the flute players and the noisy crowd, [24]he said, "Go away. The girl is not dead but asleep."

[a] 13 Hosea 6:6

But they laughed at him. ²⁵After the crowd had been put outside, he went in and took the girl by the hand, and she got up. ²⁶News of this spread through all that region.

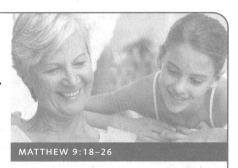

MATTHEW 9:18–26

Jesus Raises a Girl From the Dead

LIFE LESSON: Jesus has power over death.

TO TALK ABOUT

✦ How did the ruler show his strong faith in Jesus?

✦ How was Jesus interrupted on the way to the ruler's house? Did Jesus mind?

✦ When Jesus said that the girl wasn't dead but asleep, he meant that she wasn't permanently dead. How did Jesus prove his point?

✦ Does Jesus still have power over death today? In what way?

Jesus Heals the Blind and Mute

²⁷As Jesus went on from there, two blind men followed him, calling out, "Have mercy on us, Son of David!"

²⁸When he had gone indoors, the blind men came to him, and he asked them, "Do you believe that I am able to do this?"

"Yes, Lord," they replied.

²⁹Then he touched their eyes and said, "According to your faith will it be done to you"; ³⁰and their sight was restored. Jesus warned them sternly, "See that no one knows about this." ³¹But they went out and spread the news about him all over that region.

³²While they were going out, a man who was demon-possessed and could not talk was brought to Jesus. ³³And when the demon was driven out, the man who had been mute spoke. The crowd was amazed and said, "Nothing like this has ever been seen in Israel."

³⁴But the Pharisees said, "It is by the prince of demons that he drives out demons."

The Workers Are Few

³⁵Jesus went through all the towns and villages, teaching in their synagogues, preaching the good news of the kingdom and healing every disease and sickness. ³⁶When he saw the crowds, he had compassion on them, because they were harassed and helpless, like sheep without a shepherd. ³⁷Then he said to his disciples, "The harvest is plentiful but the workers are few. ³⁸Ask the Lord of the harvest, therefore, to send out workers into his harvest field."

Jesus Sends Out the Twelve

10:2–4pp — Mk 3:16–19; Lk 6:14–16; Ac 1:13
10:9–15pp — Mk 6:8–11; Lk 9:3–5; 10:4–12
10:19–22pp — Mk 13:11–13; Lk 21:12–17
10:26–33pp — Lk 12:2–9
10:34,35pp — Lk 12:51–53

10 He called his twelve disciples to him and gave them authority to drive out evil *ᵃ* spirits and to heal every disease and sickness.

²These are the names of the twelve apostles: first, Simon (who is called Peter) and his brother Andrew; James son of Zebedee, and his brother John; ³Philip and Bartholomew; Thomas and Matthew the tax collector; James son of Alphaeus, and Thaddaeus; ⁴Simon the Zealot and Judas Iscariot, who betrayed him.

⁵These twelve Jesus sent out with the following

ᵃ 1 Greek unclean

instructions: "Do not go among the Gentiles or enter any town of the Samaritans. ⁶Go rather to the lost sheep of Israel. ⁷As you go, preach this message: 'The kingdom of heaven is near.' ⁸Heal the sick, raise the dead, cleanse those who have leprosy,ᵃ drive out demons. Freely you have received, freely give. ⁹Do not take along any gold or silver or copper in your belts; ¹⁰take no bag for the journey, or extra tunic, or sandals or a staff; for the worker is worth his keep.

¹¹"Whatever town or village you enter, search for some worthy person there and stay at his house until you leave. ¹²As you enter the home, give it your greeting. ¹³If the home is deserving, let your peace rest on it; if it is not, let your peace return to you. ¹⁴If anyone will not welcome you or listen to your words, shake the dust off your feet when you leave that home or town. ¹⁵I tell you the truth, it will be more bearable for Sodom and Gomorrah on the day of judgment than for that town. ¹⁶I am sending you out like sheep among wolves. Therefore be as shrewd as snakes and as innocent as doves.

¹⁷"Be on your guard against men; they will hand you over to the local councils and flog you in their synagogues. ¹⁸On my account you will be brought before governors and kings as witnesses to them and to the Gentiles. ¹⁹But when they arrest you, do not worry about what to say or how to say it. At that time you will be given what to say, ²⁰for it will not be you speaking, but the Spirit of your Father speaking through you.

²¹"Brother will betray brother to death, and a father his child; children will rebel against their parents and have them put to death. ²²All men will hate you because of me, but he who stands firm to the end will be saved. ²³When you are persecuted in one place, flee to another. I tell you the truth, you will not finish going through the cities of Israel before the Son of Man comes.

²⁴"A student is not above his teacher, nor a servant above his master. ²⁵It is enough for the student to be like his teacher, and the servant like his master. If the head of the house has been called Beelzebub,ᵇ how much more the members of his household!

²⁶"So do not be afraid of them. There is nothing concealed that will not be disclosed, or hidden that will not be made known. ²⁷What I tell you in the dark, speak in the daylight; what is whispered in your ear, proclaim from the roofs. ²⁸Do not be afraid of those who kill the body but cannot kill the soul. Rather, be afraid of the One who can destroy both soul and body in hell. ²⁹Are not two sparrows sold for a pennyᶜ? Yet not one of them will fall to the ground apart from the will of your Father. ³⁰And even the very hairs of your head are all numbered. ³¹So don't be afraid; you are worth more than many sparrows.

TALKING POINTS

Fear

Each of us, and every aspect of our lives, is important to God.

MATTHEW 10:29–31

This is the last talking point on fear.

³²"Whoever acknowledges me before men, I will also acknowledge him before my Father in heaven. ³³But whoever disowns me before men, I will disown him before my Father in heaven.

³⁴"Do not suppose that I have come to bring peace to the earth. I did not come to bring peace, but a sword. ³⁵For I have come to turn

" 'a man against his father,
    a daughter against her mother,
  a daughter-in-law against her mother-in-law—
³⁶   a man's enemies will be the members of his own household.'ᵈ

ᵃ 8 The Greek word was used for various diseases affecting the skin — not necessarily leprosy.   ᵇ 25 Greek *Beezeboul* or *Beelzeboul*   ᶜ 29 Greek *an assarion*   ᵈ 36 Micah 7:6

> "ARE NOT TWO SPARROWS SOLD FOR A
> PENNY? YET NOT ONE OF THEM WILL FALL
> TO THE GROUND APART FROM THE WILL OF
> YOUR FATHER. AND EVEN THE VERY HAIRS
> OF YOUR HEAD ARE ALL NUMBERED. SO
> DON'T BE AFRAID; YOU ARE WORTH MORE
> THAN MANY SPARROWS."
>
> *Matthew 10:29–31*

Details

RUTH GRAHAM

READ | MATTHEW 10:1–31

God is a personal God, interested in the details of our lives. Jesus said the very hairs on our head are numbered! My grandson, Wyatt, and I have personally experienced God's caring for life's little details.

Some years ago we discovered that my grandson was very farsighted. He hated his prescription glasses with their thick lenses, so he was a bit careless in how he treated them, much to his mom's frustration.

One evening my phone rang. Wyatt was on the other end, but I could not understand what he was trying to tell me between his sobs. Finally he was able to tell me that he had lost his glasses. His mom had lost patience with him, demanding he locate his glasses NOW (they were new and expensive).

His distress was palpable over the phone. I asked the typical questions: "Where did you last have them?" "Do you remember taking them off?" He either couldn't remember or assured me that he had looked everywhere. Finally, with desperation and diminishing hope, I said, "Wyatt, let's ask Jesus to help you find your glasses."

We prayed together over the phone and asked Jesus to help Wyatt find the glasses. Wyatt hung up with a sigh. As I put the receiver down, my faith wavered. Had I set Wyatt up for disappointment? I quietly asked God to answer in a way that would build Wyatt's faith — and my own. "Lord, I do believe. Help me overcome my unbelief" (see Mark 9:24).

Wyatt later called back with a much happier tone in his voice. He had found his glasses on the bookshelf next to his bed! We prayed again, thanking God for answering our prayer and asking God to build our faith. I then thanked him for caring about the details of not only my grandson's life, but my life as well.

O God, increase my faith. May I never doubt your Word or your promise that you care about the smallest details in my life. Let me confidently come to you and place my every concern at your feet. Amen.

Your next devotion is located on page 1305.

GRANDCHILD IN FOCUS • PRAYER

Relationships at Home

O Lord, I pray that you will bless the home and family of my grandchild. May the relationships she has with her parents and siblings enhance her well-being, support her self-confidence and increase her faith. May her home life reflect your love, your grace, your compassion and your peace. Guide her parents to direct her in love and truth, so she will grow into a strong and compassionate individual. Amen.

[37]"Anyone who loves his father or mother more than me is not worthy of me; anyone who loves his son or daughter more than me is not worthy of me; [38]and anyone who does not take his cross and follow me is not worthy of me. [39]Whoever finds his life will lose it, and whoever loses his life for my sake will find it.

[40]"He who receives you receives me, and he who receives me receives the one who sent me. [41]Anyone who receives a prophet because he is a prophet will receive a prophet's reward, and anyone who receives a righteous man because he is a righteous man will receive a righteous man's reward. [42]And if anyone gives even a cup of cold water to one of these little ones because he is my disciple, I tell you the truth, he will certainly not lose his reward."

Jesus and John the Baptist
11:2–19pp — Lk 7:18–35

11 After Jesus had finished instructing his twelve disciples, he went on from there to teach and preach in the towns of Galilee.[a]

[2]When John heard in prison what Christ was doing, he sent his disciples [3]to ask him, "Are you the one who was to come, or should we expect someone else?"

[4]Jesus replied, "Go back and report to John what you hear and see: [5]The blind receive sight, the lame walk, those who have leprosy[b] are cured, the deaf hear, the dead are raised, and the good news is preached to the poor. [6]Blessed is the man who does not fall away on account of me."

[7]As John's disciples were leaving, Jesus began to speak to the crowd about John: "What did you go out into the desert to see? A reed swayed by the wind? [8]If not, what did you go out to see? A man dressed in fine clothes? No, those who wear fine clothes are in kings' palaces. [9]Then what did you go out to see? A prophet? Yes, I tell you, and more than a prophet. [10]This is the one about whom it is written:

" 'I will send my messenger ahead of you,
 who will prepare your way before you.'[c]

[11]I tell you the truth: Among those born of women there has not risen anyone greater than John the Baptist; yet he who is least in the kingdom of heaven is greater than he. [12]From the days of John the Baptist until now, the kingdom of heaven has been forcefully advancing, and forceful men lay hold of it. [13]For all the Prophets and the Law prophesied until John. [14]And if you are willing to accept it, he is the Elijah who was to come. [15]He who has ears, let him hear.

[16]"To what can I compare this generation? They are like children sitting in the marketplaces and calling out to others:

[17]" 'We played the flute for you,
  and you did not dance;
 we sang a dirge,
  and you did not mourn.'

[18]For John came neither eating nor drinking, and they say, 'He has a demon.' [19]The Son of Man came eating and drinking, and they say, 'Here is a glutton and a drunkard, a friend of tax collectors and "sinners." ' But wisdom is proved right by her actions."

Woe on Unrepentant Cities
11:21–23pp — Lk 10:13–15

[20]Then Jesus began to denounce the cities in which most of his miracles had been performed, because they did not repent. [21]"Woe to you, Korazin! Woe to you, Bethsaida! If the miracles that were performed in you had been performed in Tyre and Sidon, they would have repented long ago in sackcloth and ashes. [22]But I tell you, it will be more bearable for Tyre and Sidon on the day of judgment than for you. [23]And you, Capernaum, will you be lifted up to the skies? No, you will go down to the depths.[d] If the miracles that were performed in you had been performed in Sodom, it would have remained to this day. [24]But I tell you that it will be more bearable for Sodom on the day of judgment than for you."

---

[a] 1 Greek *in their towns*   [b] 5 The Greek word was used for various diseases affecting the skin — not necessarily leprosy.   [c] 10 Mal. 3:1   [d] 23 Greek *Hades*

FAITH IN
ACTION

"*RAK 'Em*"

This pronounceable acronym might become a catchphrase for you and your grandkids. "RAK" stands for "random act of kindness." Although your grandchildren may think this is something new, let them know it's really from the Bible (see Ephesians 4:32; 1 Thessalonians 5:15).

Explain the concept to your grandkids, then take them on a drive or walk to show them how this idea works. When an opportunity for a caring action arises, someone calls out, "RAK 'em!" The possibilities for performing kind deeds are endless: brushing snow off a parked car, giving someone directions, leaving an extra-large tip for a waitress, returning garbage cans to the house from the curb, bagging someone's groceries, carrying the groceries out to the car, etc.

"Random" will sometimes mean "anonymous," but on other occasions you'll want to offer assistance in person. Be sure they understand that, while performing good deeds will make them feel good about themselves, their motivation should be love, not pride.

Long-Distance Variation: Introduce the concept to your grandkids with a RAK of your own. Send a small, for-no-special-reason surprise. Then ask them to adopt the routine with others, reporting back to you occasionally, until the action becomes ingrained.

God of all kindness, help me to be aware of the opportunities for caring that you place in my path every day. Grant both me and my grandchildren sensitive hearts, observant eyes and loving hands. Amen.

Your next devotion is located on page 1308.

GRANDCHILD IN FOCUS • PRAYER

Friends

Dear Lord and Father, I pray for my grandchild's social life and his friends. Bring diverse friends into his life who will love and encourage him, who will bring joy and laughter to the good times and comfort and support through difficulties and disappointments. Grant him wisdom and discernment as he selects his friends; help him to avoid cliques that restrict, activities that endanger, and foolish and dangerous behaviors that harm. I ask that you fill his life with close and caring relationships. Amen.

Rest for the Weary

11:25–27pp — Lk 10:21,22

25 At that time Jesus said, "I praise you, Father, Lord of heaven and earth, because you have hidden these things from the wise and learned, and revealed them to little children. 26 Yes, Father, for this was your good pleasure.

27 "All things have been committed to me by my Father. No one knows the Son except the Father, and no one knows the Father except the Son and those to whom the Son chooses to reveal him.

28 "Come to me, all you who are weary and burdened, and I will give you rest. 29 Take my yoke upon you and learn from me, for I am gentle and humble in heart, and you will find rest for your souls. 30 For my yoke is easy and my burden is light."

Lord of the Sabbath

12:1–8pp — Mk 2:23–28; Lk 6:1–5
12:9–14pp — Mk 3:1–6; Lk 6:6–11

12 At that time Jesus went through the grainfields on the Sabbath. His disciples were hungry and began to pick some heads of grain and eat them. 2 When the Pharisees saw this, they said to him, "Look! Your disciples are doing what is unlawful on the Sabbath."

3 He answered, "Haven't you read what David did when he and his companions were hungry? 4 He entered the house of God, and he and his companions ate the consecrated bread—which was not lawful for them to do, but only for the priests. 5 Or haven't you read in the Law that on the Sabbath the priests in the temple desecrate the day and yet are innocent? 6 I tell you that one[a] greater than the temple is here. 7 If you had known what these words mean, 'I desire mercy, not sacrifice,'[b] you would not have condemned the innocent. 8 For the Son of Man is Lord of the Sabbath."

9 Going on from that place, he went into their synagogue, 10 and a man with a shriveled hand was there. Looking for a reason to accuse Jesus, they asked him, "Is it lawful to heal on the Sabbath?"

11 He said to them, "If any of you has a sheep and it falls into a pit on the Sabbath, will you not take hold of it and lift it out? 12 How much more valuable is a man than a sheep! Therefore it is lawful to do good on the Sabbath."

13 Then he said to the man, "Stretch out your hand." So he stretched it out and it was completely restored, just as sound as the other. 14 But the Pharisees went out and plotted how they might kill Jesus.

God's Chosen Servant

15 Aware of this, Jesus withdrew from that place. Many followed him, and he healed all their sick, 16 warning them not to tell who he was. 17 This was to fulfill what was spoken through the prophet Isaiah:

18 "Here is my servant whom I have chosen,
the one I love, in whom I delight;
I will put my Spirit on him,
and he will proclaim justice to the nations.
19 He will not quarrel or cry out;
no one will hear his voice in the streets.
20 A bruised reed he will not break,
and a smoldering wick he will not snuff out,
till he leads justice to victory.
21 In his name the nations will put their
hope."[c]

Jesus and Beelzebub

12:25–29pp — Mk 3:23–27; Lk 11:17–22

22 Then they brought him a demon-possessed man who was blind and mute, and Jesus healed him, so that he could both talk and see. 23 All the people were astonished and said, "Could this be the Son of David?"

24 But when the Pharisees heard this, they said, "It is only by Beelzebub,[d] the prince of demons, that this fellow drives out demons."

25 Jesus knew their thoughts and said to them, "Every kingdom divided against itself will be ruined, and every city or household divided against

---

a 6 Or something; also in verses 41 and 42   *b 7 Hosea 6:6*
c 21 Isaiah 42:1-4   *d 24 Greek Beezeboul or Beelzeboul*; also in verse 27

itself will not stand. ²⁶If Satan drives out Satan, he is divided against himself. How then can his kingdom stand? ²⁷And if I drive out demons by Beelzebub, by whom do your people drive them out? So then, they will be your judges. ²⁸But if I drive out demons by the Spirit of God, then the kingdom of God has come upon you.

²⁹"Or again, how can anyone enter a strong man's house and carry off his possessions unless he first ties up the strong man? Then he can rob his house.

³⁰"He who is not with me is against me, and he who does not gather with me scatters. ³¹And so I tell you, every sin and blasphemy will be forgiven men, but the blasphemy against the Spirit will not be forgiven. ³²Anyone who speaks a word against the Son of Man will be forgiven, but anyone who speaks against the Holy Spirit will not be forgiven, either in this age or in the age to come.

³³"Make a tree good and its fruit will be good, or make a tree bad and its fruit will be bad, for a tree is recognized by its fruit. ³⁴You brood of vipers, how can you who are evil say anything good? For out of the overflow of the heart the mouth speaks. ³⁵The good man brings good things out of the good stored up in him, and the evil man brings evil things out of the evil stored up in him. ³⁶But I tell you that men will have to give account on the day of judgment for every careless word they have spoken. ³⁷For by your words you will be acquitted, and by your words you will be condemned."

TALKING POINTS

Profanity

God holds us accountable
for careless words.

MATTHEW 12:36

For more on profanity, go to James 3:5–10.

TALKING POINTS

Accountability

We are accountable for our words.

MATTHEW 12:36–37

For more on accountability, go to Hebrews 4:13.

The Sign of Jonah
12:39–42pp — Lk 11:29–32
12:43–45pp — Lk 11:24–26

³⁸Then some of the Pharisees and teachers of the law said to him, "Teacher, we want to see a miraculous sign from you."

³⁹He answered, "A wicked and adulterous generation asks for a miraculous sign! But none will be given it except the sign of the prophet Jonah. ⁴⁰For as Jonah was three days and three nights in the belly of a huge fish, so the Son of Man will be three days and three nights in the heart of the earth. ⁴¹The men of Nineveh will stand up at the judgment with this generation and condemn it; for they repented at the preaching of Jonah, and now one^a greater than Jonah is here. ⁴²The Queen of the South will rise at the judgment with this generation and condemn it; for she came from the ends of the earth to listen to Solomon's wisdom, and now one greater than Solomon is here.

⁴³"When an evil^b spirit comes out of a man, it goes through arid places seeking rest and does not find it. ⁴⁴Then it says, 'I will return to the house I left.' When it arrives, it finds the house unoccupied, swept clean and put in order. ⁴⁵Then it goes and takes with it seven other spirits more wicked than itself, and they go in and live there. And the final condition of that man is worse than the first. That is how it will be with this wicked generation."

^a 41 Or *something*; also in verse 42   ^b 43 Greek *unclean*

Worship the Lord

How many are your works, O LORD!
    In wisdom you made them all;
    the earth is full of your creatures.
There is the sea, vast and spacious,
      teeming with creatures beyond number—
    living things both large and small.
There the ships go to and fro,
    and the leviathan, which you formed to frolic there.

These all look to you
    to give them their food at the proper
        time.
When you give it to them,
    they gather it up;
when you open your hand,
    they are satisfied with good
        things.
When you hide your face,
    they are terrified;
when you take away their breath,
    they die and return to the dust.
When you send your Spirit,
    they are created,
    and you renew the face of the
        earth.

Psalm 104:24–30

GRANDCHILD IN FOCUS • PRAYER

Self-Image

*O loving God, I praise you for creating my
grandchild as a unique individual. Now I ask you
to help her appreciate her uniqueness. Build up her
self-image so she can enjoy her individuality. Help
her to stand firm for who she is, where she has
come from and what she believes in. Encourage
her not only to have hopes and dreams but
to also enjoy each day as it comes.
In Jesus' name, amen.*

*You are incredible, Lord, for you have established a world of
ecological perfection. Grant me wisdom so that, as a steward of your
creation, I can find a balance between enjoying and conserving your gifts. I pray that my thoughts
and actions will be pleasing to you as I rejoice in your name. Amen.*

Your next devotion is located on page 1310.

Jesus' Mother and Brothers
12.46 50pp — Mk 3;31–35; Lk 8:19–21

⁴⁶While Jesus was still talking to the crowd, his mother and brothers stood outside, wanting to speak to him. ⁴⁷Someone told him, "Your mother and brothers are standing outside, wanting to speak to you."ᵃ

⁴⁸He replied to him, "Who is my mother, and who are my brothers?" ⁴⁹Pointing to his disciples, he said, "Here are my mother and my brothers. ⁵⁰For whoever does the will of my Father in heaven is my brother and sister and mother."

The Parable of the Sower
13:1–15pp — Mk 4:1–12; Lk 8:4–10
13:16,17pp — Lk 10:23,24
13:18–23pp — Mk 4:13–20; Lk 8:11–15

13 That same day Jesus went out of the house and sat by the lake. ²Such large crowds gathered around him that he got into a boat and sat in it, while all the people stood on the shore. ³Then he told them many things in parables, saying: "A farmer went out to sow his seed. ⁴As he was scattering the seed, some fell along the path, and the birds came and ate it up. ⁵Some fell on rocky places, where it did not have much soil. It sprang up quickly, because the soil was shallow. ⁶But when the sun came up, the plants were scorched, and they withered because they had no root. ⁷Other seed fell among thorns, which grew up and choked the plants. ⁸Still other seed fell on good soil, where it produced a crop—a hundred, sixty or thirty times what was sown. ⁹He who has ears, let him hear."

¹⁰The disciples came to him and asked, "Why do you speak to the people in parables?"

¹¹He replied, "The knowledge of the secrets of the kingdom of heaven has been given to you, but not to them. ¹²Whoever has will be given more, and he will have an abundance. Whoever does not have, even what he has will be taken from him. ¹³This is why I speak to them in parables:

"Though seeing, they do not see;
 though hearing, they do not hear or
  understand.

¹⁴In them is fulfilled the prophecy of Isaiah:

" 'You will be ever hearing but never
   understanding;
  you will be ever seeing but never
   perceiving.
¹⁵For this people's heart has become calloused;
  they hardly hear with their ears,
  and they have closed their eyes.
Otherwise they might see with their eyes,
  hear with their ears,
  understand with their hearts
and turn, and I would heal them.'ᵇ

¹⁶But blessed are your eyes because they see, and your ears because they hear. ¹⁷For I tell you the truth, many prophets and righteous men longed to see what you see but did not see it, and to hear what you hear but did not hear it.

¹⁸"Listen then to what the parable of the sower means: ¹⁹When anyone hears the message about the kingdom and does not understand it, the evil one comes and snatches away what was sown in his heart. This is the seed sown along the path. ²⁰The one who received the seed that fell on rocky places is the man who hears the word and at once receives it with joy. ²¹But since he has no root, he lasts only a short time. When trouble or persecution comes because of the word, he quickly falls away. ²²The one who received the seed that fell among the thorns is the man who hears the word, but the worries of this life and the deceitfulness of wealth choke it, making it unfruitful. ²³But the one who received the seed that fell on good soil is the man who hears the word and understands it. He produces a crop, yielding a hundred, sixty or thirty times what was sown."

The Parable of the Weeds

²⁴Jesus told them another parable: "The kingdom of heaven is like a man who sowed good seed in his field. ²⁵But while everyone was sleeping, his enemy came and sowed weeds among the wheat, and went away. ²⁶When the wheat sprouted and formed heads, then the weeds also appeared.

ᵃ 47 Some manuscripts do not have verse 47.   ᵇ 15 Isaiah 6:9,10

> "WHEN ANYONE HEARS THE MESSAGE ABOUT THE KINGDOM AND DOES NOT UNDERSTAND IT, THE EVIL ONE COMES AND SNATCHES AWAY WHAT WAS SOWN IN HIS HEART."
>
> *Matthew 13:19*

Give Them Corn as Well as the Husk

DEE BRESTIN

READ | MATTHEW 13:1 – 23

My four grandchildren had come to Sanibel Island to vacation with me. That meant golden days of sunshine, shelling and sandcastles. One morning while they all still slept, I sat on the porch with my mug of coffee, watching the ocean turn crimson as the sun crept over the horizon. I thought of how God had assured Job that he was, indeed, in control of life (see Job 38:1 – 15). At that moment nine-year-old Simeon appeared, rubbing sleep from his eyes. I knew what he was going to ask before he even spoke. The hotel had a video arcade that had been drawing little boys like magnets.

"Grandma, can I please have a dollar for the video arcade?"

"Come here, honey. Climb on Grandma's lap."

He climbed up and snuggled for ten seconds before asking again, "Can I have a dollar, please?"

"Memorize the first three verses of Job 38 and you may."

He hopped down, running for a Bible. In five minutes he was back, reciting the verses perfectly.

"Wonderful, Simeon! Now tell me why God said that to Job."

"You didn't tell me I had to know what it meant!" My grandson and I exchanged smiles. He knew me well enough to know there would be no dollar until he had captured the meaning. Charles Spurgeon said that if we give children stories without being sure they understand the meaning, it is like giving them the husk of the corn without the golden kernels.

Simeon climbed back on my lap, and we had a ten-minute discussion. When we were done, I asked again, "Why did God say that to Job?"

"Sometimes God asks us questions to help us trust him." I nodded.

"YES!" Simeon exclaimed, hopping down to bring me my purse.

Father, as I tell my grandchildren your amazing stories, help me to help them understand the meaning behind them. May the meaning penetrate deep into their hearts so that the evil one cannot snatch it away.

Your next devotion is located on page 1315.

GRANDCHILD IN FOCUS • PRAYER

Protection From Worldliness

O Sovereign Lord, the world surrounds my grandchild, pressing in and tempting him in so many ways. Help him set appropriate limits. Give him sound judgment to choose wisely. Guard him from temptation; protect him from physical and mental predators; lead him into paths of righteousness and light. And reassure me with your promise that you are holding him in your hands. Amen.

27 "The owner's servants came to him and said, 'Sir, didn't you sow good seed in your field? Where then did the weeds come from?'

28 " 'An enemy did this,' he replied.

"The servants asked him, 'Do you want us to go and pull them up?'

29 " 'No,' he answered, 'because while you are pulling the weeds, you may root up the wheat with them. 30 Let both grow together until the harvest. At that time I will tell the harvesters: First collect the weeds and tie them in bundles to be burned; then gather the wheat and bring it into my barn.' "

The Parables of the Mustard Seed and the Yeast

13:31,32pp — Mk 4:30–32
13:31–33pp — Lk 13:18–21

31 He told them another parable: "The kingdom of heaven is like a mustard seed, which a man took and planted in his field. 32 Though it is the smallest of all your seeds, yet when it grows, it is the largest of garden plants and becomes a tree, so that the birds of the air come and perch in its branches."

33 He told them still another parable: "The kingdom of heaven is like yeast that a woman took and mixed into a large amount *a* of flour until it worked all through the dough."

34 Jesus spoke all these things to the crowd in parables; he did not say anything to them without using a parable. 35 So was fulfilled what was spoken through the prophet:

"I will open my mouth in parables,
      I will utter things hidden since the creation
            of the world." *b*

The Parable of the Weeds Explained

36 Then he left the crowd and went into the house. His disciples came to him and said, "Explain to us the parable of the weeds in the field."

37 He answered, "The one who sowed the good seed is the Son of Man. 38 The field is the world, and the good seed stands for the sons of the kingdom. The weeds are the sons of the evil one, 39 and the enemy who sows them is the devil. The harvest is the end of the age, and the harvesters are angels.

40 "As the weeds are pulled up and burned in the fire, so it will be at the end of the age. 41 The Son of Man will send out his angels, and they will weed out of his kingdom everything that causes sin and all who do evil. 42 They will throw them into the fiery furnace, where there will be weeping and gnashing of teeth. 43 Then the righteous will shine like the sun in the kingdom of their Father. He who has ears, let him hear.

The Parables of the Hidden Treasure and the Pearl

44 "The kingdom of heaven is like treasure hidden in a field. When a man found it, he hid it again, and then in his joy went and sold all he had and bought that field.

45 "Again, the kingdom of heaven is like a merchant looking for fine pearls. 46 When he found one of great value, he went away and sold everything he had and bought it.

The Parable of the Net

47 "Once again, the kingdom of heaven is like a net that was let down into the lake and caught all kinds of fish. 48 When it was full, the fishermen pulled it up on the shore. Then they sat down and collected the good fish in baskets, but threw the bad away. 49 This is how it will be at the end of the age. The angels will come and separate the wicked from the righteous 50 and throw them into the fiery furnace, where there will be weeping and gnashing of teeth.

51 "Have you understood all these things?" Jesus asked.

"Yes," they replied.

52 He said to them, "Therefore every teacher of the law who has been instructed about the kingdom of heaven is like the owner of a house who brings out of his storeroom new treasures as well as old."

a 33 Greek *three satas* (probably about 1/2 bushel or 22 liters)
b 35 Psalm 78:2

A Prophet Without Honor
13:54–58pp — Mk 6:1–6

⁵³When Jesus had finished these parables, he moved on from there. ⁵⁴Coming to his hometown, he began teaching the people in their synagogue, and they were amazed. "Where did this man get this wisdom and these miraculous powers?" they asked. ⁵⁵"Isn't this the carpenter's son? Isn't his mother's name Mary, and aren't his brothers James, Joseph, Simon and Judas? ⁵⁶Aren't all his sisters with us? Where then did this man get all these things?" ⁵⁷And they took offense at him.

But Jesus said to them, "Only in his hometown and in his own house is a prophet without honor."

⁵⁸And he did not do many miracles there because of their lack of faith.

John the Baptist Beheaded
14:1–12pp — Mk 6:14–29

14 At that time Herod the tetrarch heard the reports about Jesus, ²and he said to his attendants, "This is John the Baptist; he has risen from the dead! That is why miraculous powers are at work in him."

³Now Herod had arrested John and bound him and put him in prison because of Herodias, his brother Philip's wife, ⁴for John had been saying to him: "It is not lawful for you to have her." ⁵Herod wanted to kill John, but he was afraid of the people, because they considered him a prophet.

⁶On Herod's birthday the daughter of Herodias danced for them and pleased Herod so much ⁷that he promised with an oath to give her whatever she asked. ⁸Prompted by her mother, she said, "Give me here on a platter the head of John the Baptist." ⁹The king was distressed, but because of his oaths and his dinner guests, he ordered that her request be granted ¹⁰and had John beheaded in the prison. ¹¹His head was brought in on a platter and given to the girl, who carried it to her mother. ¹²John's disciples came and took his body and buried it. Then they went and told Jesus.

Jesus Feeds the Five Thousand
14:13–21pp — Mk 6:32–44; Lk 9:10–17; Jn 6:1–13
14:13–21Ref — Mt 15:32–38

¹³When Jesus heard what had happened, he withdrew by boat privately to a solitary place. Hearing of this, the crowds followed him on foot from the towns. ¹⁴When Jesus landed and saw a large crowd, he had compassion on them and healed their sick.

¹⁵As evening approached, the disciples came to him and said, "This is a remote place, and it's already getting late. Send the crowds away, so they can go to the villages and buy themselves some food."

¹⁶Jesus replied, "They do not need to go away. You give them something to eat."

¹⁷"We have here only five loaves of bread and two fish," they answered.

¹⁸"Bring them here to me," he said. ¹⁹And he directed the people to sit down on the grass. Taking the five loaves and the two fish and looking up to heaven, he gave thanks and broke the loaves. Then he gave them to the disciples, and the disciples gave them to the people. ²⁰They all ate and were satisfied, and the disciples picked up twelve basketfuls of broken pieces that were left over. ²¹The number of those who ate was about five thousand men, besides women and children.

Jesus Walks on the Water
14:22–33pp — Mk 6:45–51; Jn 6:16–21
14:34–36pp — Mk 6:53–56

²²Immediately Jesus made the disciples get into the boat and go on ahead of him to the other side, while he dismissed the crowd. ²³After he had dismissed them, he went up on a mountainside by himself to pray. When evening came, he was there alone, ²⁴but the boat was already a considerable distance[a] from land, buffeted by the waves because the wind was against it.

²⁵During the fourth watch of the night Jesus went out to them, walking on the lake. ²⁶When the disciples saw him walking on the lake, they

---

ª 24 Greek *many stadia*

were terrified. "It's a ghost," they said, and cried out in fear.

²⁷But Jesus immediately said to them: "Take courage! It is I. Don't be afraid."

²⁸"Lord, if it's you," Peter replied, "tell me to come to you on the water."

²⁹"Come," he said.

Then Peter got down out of the boat, walked on the water and came toward Jesus. ³⁰But when he saw the wind, he was afraid and, beginning to sink, cried out, "Lord, save me!"

³¹Immediately Jesus reached out his hand and caught him. "You of little faith," he said, "why did you doubt?"

³²And when they climbed into the boat, the wind died down. ³³Then those who were in the boat worshiped him, saying, "Truly you are the Son of God."

³⁴When they had crossed over, they landed at Gennesaret. ³⁵And when the men of that place recognized Jesus, they sent word to all the surrounding country. People brought all their sick to him ³⁶and begged him to let the sick just touch the edge of his cloak, and all who touched him were healed.

Clean and Unclean

15:1–20pp — Mk 7:1–23

15 Then some Pharisees and teachers of the law came to Jesus from Jerusalem and asked, ²"Why do your disciples break the tradition of the elders? They don't wash their hands before they eat!"

³Jesus replied, "And why do you break the command of God for the sake of your tradition? ⁴For God said, 'Honor your father and mother'ᵃ and 'Anyone who curses his father or mother must be put to death.'ᵇ ⁵But you say that if a man says to his father or mother, 'Whatever help you might otherwise have received from me is a gift devoted to God,' ⁶he is not to 'honor his father'ᶜ with it. Thus you nullify the word of God for the sake of your tradition. ⁷You hypocrites! Isaiah was right when he prophesied about you:

⁸" 'These people honor me with their lips,
    but their hearts are far from me.
⁹They worship me in vain;
    their teachings are but rules taught by
      men.'ᵈ"

¹⁰Jesus called the crowd to him and said, "Listen and understand. ¹¹What goes into a man's mouth does not make him 'unclean,' but what comes out of his mouth, that is what makes him 'unclean.' "

¹²Then the disciples came to him and asked, "Do you know that the Pharisees were offended when they heard this?"

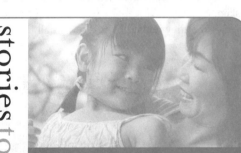

MATTHEW 14:22–36

Jesus Walks on the Water

LIFE LESSON: Faith means trusting Jesus.

TO TALK ABOUT

✦ Why wasn't Jesus in the boat with the disciples?

✦ Can you see yourself being willing to get out of the boat and walk toward Jesus?

✦ Why did Peter lose faith when he was already partway to Jesus?

✦ Do you sometimes focus more on your problems than on Jesus?

stories to share

ᵃ 4 Exodus 20:12; Deut. 5:16   ᵇ 4 Exodus 21:17; Lev. 20:9
ᶜ 6 Some manuscripts *father or his mother*   ᵈ 9 Isaiah 29:13

¹³He replied, "Every plant that my heavenly Father has not planted will be pulled up by the roots. ¹⁴Leave them; they are blind guides.[a] If a blind man leads a blind man, both will fall into a pit."

¹⁵Peter said, "Explain the parable to us."

¹⁶"Are you still so dull?" Jesus asked them. ¹⁷"Don't you see that whatever enters the mouth goes into the stomach and then out of the body? ¹⁸But the things that come out of the mouth come from the heart, and these make a man 'unclean.' ¹⁹For out of the heart come evil thoughts, murder, adultery, sexual immorality, theft, false testimony, slander. ²⁰These are what make a man 'unclean'; but eating with unwashed hands does not make him 'unclean.'"

The Faith of the Canaanite Woman

15:21–28pp — Mk 7:24–30

²¹Leaving that place, Jesus withdrew to the region of Tyre and Sidon. ²²A Canaanite woman from that vicinity came to him, crying out, "Lord, Son of David, have mercy on me! My daughter is suffering terribly from demon-possession."

²³Jesus did not answer a word. So his disciples came to him and urged him, "Send her away, for she keeps crying out after us."

²⁴He answered, "I was sent only to the lost sheep of Israel."

²⁵The woman came and knelt before him. "Lord, help me!" she said.

²⁶He replied, "It is not right to take the children's bread and toss it to their dogs."

²⁷"Yes, Lord," she said, "but even the dogs eat the crumbs that fall from their masters' table."

²⁸Then Jesus answered, "Woman, you have great faith! Your request is granted." And her daughter was healed from that very hour.

Jesus Feeds the Four Thousand

15:29–31pp — Mk 7:31–37
15:32–39pp — Mk 8:1–10
15:32–39Ref — Mt 14:13–21

²⁹Jesus left there and went along the Sea of Galilee. Then he went up on a mountainside and sat down. ³⁰Great crowds came to him, bringing the lame, the blind, the crippled, the mute and many others, and laid them at his feet; and he healed them. ³¹The people were amazed when they saw the mute speaking, the crippled made well, the lame walking and the blind seeing. And they praised the God of Israel.

³²Jesus called his disciples to him and said, "I have compassion for these people; they have already been with me three days and have nothing to eat. I do not want to send them away hungry, or they may collapse on the way."

³³His disciples answered, "Where could we get enough bread in this remote place to feed such a crowd?"

³⁴"How many loaves do you have?" Jesus asked.

"Seven," they replied, "and a few small fish."

TALKING POINTS

Disability

Jesus has compassion for the disabled; he healed those who came to him and miraculously fed the crowds.

MATTHEW 15:29–39

For more on disability, go to 2 Corinthians 12:7–10.

³⁵He told the crowd to sit down on the ground. ³⁶Then he took the seven loaves and the fish, and when he had given thanks, he broke them and gave them to the disciples, and they in turn to the people. ³⁷They all ate and were satisfied. Afterward the disciples picked up seven basketfuls of broken pieces that were left over. ³⁸The number of those who ate was four thousand, besides women and children. ³⁹After Jesus had sent the crowd away, he got into the boat and went to the vicinity of Magadan.

[a] 14 Some manuscripts *guides of the blind*

"EVERY PLANT THAT MY
HEAVENLY FATHER HAS NOT
PLANTED WILL BE PULLED UP
BY THE ROOTS."

Matthew 15:13

Pursuits With Roots

DIANE KOMP, M.D.

READ | MATTHEW 15:1–20

For many years I enjoyed the passionate pursuit of growing orchids. I built a greenhouse for my collection and was always on the lookout for new friends who shared the same obsession. There's a name for that process of visiting other orchid fanatics — to "go orchiding."

To go orchiding is to learn that not just people have generations worthy of consideration. Let me tell you how really quaint orchid fanciers are. When we go orchiding, we have been known to ooh and aah over plain green leaves of tiny seedlings that have not yet come into bloom. To an orchid nut, the unpretentious leaves hint about the future. Without reference to labels or records, a true orchid maven knows each valued plant's parentage. To imagine what is yet to be, you listen to the recitation of the generations that came before. The botanical lineage predicts shape, form and color of future flowers. If a plant is not true to its heritage, I will relegate it to a back bench when it blooms. Even its price depends on who its parents are and how faithfully its potential is realized.

Lord, baby orchid plants remind me what it means to be your offspring, even on those days when nothing beautiful is apparent in my life. Knowing who my Father is defines my potential. I have been "born from above" to display a new parentage in my life. Praise God!

Your next devotion is located on page 1319.

GRANDCHILD IN FOCUS • PRAYER

Respect for Authority

Dear Lord, I pray that my grandchild will continually grow to respect those in authority. May she learn to be cooperative and fair in work and play. Instill in her a high regard for officials who govern our land and enforce the laws. May her relationships with parents, teachers, coaches, mentors and bosses be respectful, admirable, constructive and caring. Amen.

The Demand for a Sign

16:1–12pp — Mk 8:11–21

16 The Pharisees and Sadducees came to Jesus and tested him by asking him to show them a sign from heaven.

[2] He replied,[a] "When evening comes, you say, 'It will be fair weather, for the sky is red,' [3] and in the morning, 'Today it will be stormy, for the sky is red and overcast.' You know how to interpret the appearance of the sky, but you cannot interpret the signs of the times. [4] A wicked and adulterous generation looks for a miraculous sign, but none will be given it except the sign of Jonah." Jesus then left them and went away.

The Yeast of the Pharisees and Sadducees

[5] When they went across the lake, the disciples forgot to take bread. [6] "Be careful," Jesus said to them. "Be on your guard against the yeast of the Pharisees and Sadducees."

[7] They discussed this among themselves and said, "It is because we didn't bring any bread."

[8] Aware of their discussion, Jesus asked, "You of little faith, why are you talking among yourselves about having no bread? [9] Do you still not understand? Don't you remember the five loaves for the five thousand, and how many basketfuls you gathered? [10] Or the seven loaves for the four thousand, and how many basketfuls you gathered? [11] How is it you don't understand that I was not talking to you about bread? But be on your guard against the yeast of the Pharisees and Sadducees." [12] Then they understood that he was not telling them to guard against the yeast used in bread, but against the teaching of the Pharisees and Sadducees.

Peter's Confession of Christ

16:13–16pp — Mk 8:27–29; Lk 9:18–20

[13] When Jesus came to the region of Caesarea Philippi, he asked his disciples, "Who do people say the Son of Man is?"

[14] They replied, "Some say John the Baptist; others say Elijah; and still others, Jeremiah or one of the prophets."

[15] "But what about you?" he asked. "Who do you say I am?"

[16] Simon Peter answered, "You are the Christ,[b] the Son of the living God."

[17] Jesus replied, "Blessed are you, Simon son of Jonah, for this was not revealed to you by man, but by my Father in heaven. [18] And I tell you that you are Peter,[c] and on this rock I will build my church, and the gates of Hades[d] will not overcome it.[e] [19] I will give you the keys of the kingdom of heaven; whatever you bind on earth will be[f] bound in heaven, and whatever you loose on earth will be[f] loosed in heaven." [20] Then he warned his disciples not to tell anyone that he was the Christ.

Jesus Predicts His Death

16:21–28pp — Mk 8:31–9:1; Lk 9:22–27

[21] From that time on Jesus began to explain to his disciples that he must go to Jerusalem and suffer many things at the hands of the elders, chief priests and teachers of the law, and that he must be killed and on the third day be raised to life.

[22] Peter took him aside and began to rebuke him. "Never, Lord!" he said. "This shall never happen to you!"

[23] Jesus turned and said to Peter, "Get behind me, Satan! You are a stumbling block to me; you do not have in mind the things of God, but the things of men."

[24] Then Jesus said to his disciples, "If anyone would come after me, he must deny himself and take up his cross and follow me. [25] For whoever wants to save his life[g] will lose it, but whoever loses his life for me will find it. [26] What good will it be for a man if he gains the whole world, yet forfeits his soul? Or what can a man give in exchange for his soul? [27] For the Son of Man is going to come in his Father's glory with his angels, and then he will reward each person according to what he has done. [28] I tell you the truth, some who

---

[a] 2 Some early manuscripts do not have the rest of verse 2 and all of verse 3.   [b] 16 Or *Messiah*; also in verse 20   [c] 18 *Peter* means *rock*.   [d] 18 Or *hell*   [e] 18 Or *not prove stronger than it*   [f] 19 Or *have been*   [g] 25 The Greek word means either *life* or *soul*; also in verse 26.

are standing here will not taste death before they see the Son of Man coming in his kingdom."

The Transfiguration

17:1–8pp — Lk 9:28–36
17:1–13pp — Mk 9:2–13

17 After six days Jesus took with him Peter, James and John the brother of James, and led them up a high mountain by themselves. ²There he was transfigured before them. His face shone like the sun, and his clothes became as white as the light. ³Just then there appeared before them Moses and Elijah, talking with Jesus.

⁴Peter said to Jesus, "Lord, it is good for us to be here. If you wish, I will put up three shelters—one for you, one for Moses and one for Elijah."

⁵While he was still speaking, a bright cloud enveloped them, and a voice from the cloud said, "This is my Son, whom I love; with him I am well pleased. Listen to him!"

⁶When the disciples heard this, they fell facedown to the ground, terrified. ⁷But Jesus came and touched them. "Get up," he said. "Don't be afraid." ⁸When they looked up, they saw no one except Jesus.

⁹As they were coming down the mountain, Jesus instructed them, "Don't tell anyone what you have seen, until the Son of Man has been raised from the dead."

¹⁰The disciples asked him, "Why then do the teachers of the law say that Elijah must come first?"

¹¹Jesus replied, "To be sure, Elijah comes and will restore all things. ¹²But I tell you, Elijah has already come, and they did not recognize him, but have done to him everything they wished. In the same way the Son of Man is going to suffer at their hands." ¹³Then the disciples understood that he was talking to them about John the Baptist.

The Healing of a Boy With a Demon

17:14–19pp — Mk 9:14–28; Lk 9:37–42

¹⁴When they came to the crowd, a man approached Jesus and knelt before him. ¹⁵"Lord,

have mercy on my son," he said. "He has seizures and is suffering greatly. He often falls into the fire or into the water. ¹⁶I brought him to your disciples, but they could not heal him."

¹⁷"O unbelieving and perverse generation," Jesus replied, "how long shall I stay with you? How long shall I put up with you? Bring the boy here to me." ¹⁸Jesus rebuked the demon, and it came out of the boy, and he was healed from that moment.

¹⁹Then the disciples came to Jesus in private and asked, "Why couldn't we drive it out?"

²⁰He replied, "Because you have so little faith. I tell you the truth, if you have faith as small as a mustard seed, you can say to this mountain, 'Move from here to there' and it will move. Nothing will be impossible for you. *ᵃ*"

ᵃ 20 Some manuscripts you. ²¹But this kind does not go out except by prayer and fasting.

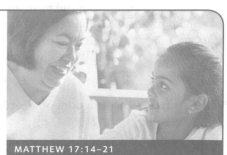

stories to share

MATTHEW 17:14–21

Jesus Heals a Boy

LIFE LESSON: With faith, nothing is impossible.

TO TALK ABOUT

✦ Why couldn't Jesus' disciples heal the boy?

✦ Why did demons always obey Jesus?

✦ What did Jesus mean when he said faith can move a mountain?

✦ What "mountains" has your faith or your family's faith moved?

²²When they came together in Galilee, he said to them, "The Son of Man is going to be betrayed into the hands of men. ²³They will kill him, and on the third day he will be raised to life." And the disciples were filled with grief.

The Temple Tax

²⁴After Jesus and his disciples arrived in Capernaum, the collectors of the two-drachma tax came to Peter and asked, "Doesn't your teacher pay the temple tax *a*?"

²⁵"Yes, he does," he replied.

When Peter came into the house, Jesus was the first to speak. "What do you think, Simon?" he asked. "From whom do the kings of the earth collect duty and taxes—from their own sons or from others?"

²⁶"From others," Peter answered.

"Then the sons are exempt," Jesus said to him. ²⁷"But so that we may not offend them, go to the lake and throw out your line. Take the first fish you catch; open its mouth and you will find a four-drachma coin. Take it and give it to them for my tax and yours."

The Greatest in the Kingdom of Heaven
18:1–5pp — Mk 9:33–37; Lk 9:46–48

18 At that time the disciples came to Jesus and asked, "Who is the greatest in the kingdom of heaven?"

²He called a little child and had him stand among them. ³And he said: "I tell you the truth, unless you change and become like little children, you will never enter the kingdom of heaven. ⁴Therefore, whoever humbles himself like this child is the greatest in the kingdom of heaven.

⁵"And whoever welcomes a little child like this in my name welcomes me. ⁶But if anyone causes one of these little ones who believe in me to sin, it would be better for him to have a large millstone hung around his neck and to be drowned in the depths of the sea.

⁷"Woe to the world because of the things that

stories to share

MATTHEW 18:1–4

The Way to Greatness

LIFE LESSON: True faith is humble faith, the kind little children have.

TO TALK ABOUT

✦ What question did the disciples ask Jesus?

✦ What did Jesus do before he answered their question?

✦ How would the disciples have to change if they wanted to enter the kingdom of heaven?

✦ What can get in the way of a grown-up's faith? Why isn't this as much of a problem for children?

cause people to sin! Such things must come, but woe to the man through whom they come! ⁸If your hand or your foot causes you to sin, cut it off and throw it away. It is better for you to enter life maimed or crippled than to have two hands or two feet and be thrown into eternal fire. ⁹And if your eye causes you to sin, gouge it out and throw it away. It is better for you to enter life with one eye than to have two eyes and be thrown into the fire of hell.

The Parable of the Lost Sheep
18:12–14pp — Lk 15:4–7

¹⁰"See that you do not look down on one of these little ones. For I tell you that their angels

a 24 Greek the two drachmas

> "I TELL YOU THE TRUTH, UNLESS YOU CHANGE AND BECOME LIKE LITTLE CHILDREN, YOU WILL NEVER ENTER THE KINGDOM OF HEAVEN."
>
> *Matthew 18:3*

Our Childlike Hearts

CAROL KUYKENDALL

READ | MATTHEW 18:1–4

My grandchildren and I have a favorite harmless spider we've watched spin a web on an outside corner of our house. We also have a favorite anthill where we spy on a zillion busy ants crawling in and out of their house holes.

We sing lots of songs, like "Twinkle, Twinkle Little Star," and we love to blow bubbles in the sunshine and watch our puppy jump up to catch them. We like to read books, play dress up, hunt for shiny rocks in the driveway and have tea parties. We've gone on flashlight walks in the dark, and we have a huge supply of crayons and blank paper, so we can draw all the pictures we see in our imaginations.

You may think that these activities are all about my two-, three- and four-year-old grandchildren, but they are also about me, because playing with my grandchildren has rekindled a passionate childlikeness that still lives in me.

Surely we're born with that childlikeness. We don't use it all up in our own childhoods because it quickly gets buried in the business of growing up. We get a second chance to experience childlikeness when we become mothers, but it often gets buried in busyness. But, aha! As grandmothers, we get a third chance to experience that childlikeness as we share the awe of God's creation and his possibilities for our lives.

No wonder that the third time is the best of all!

Lord, I think you placed a divine sense of childlikeness within us and then gave us the gift of grandchildren to rekindle that passion and draw us nearer to you in this season of our lives. Thank you.

Your next devotion is located on page 1320.

GRANDCHILD IN FOCUS • PRAYER

Courage

O Father, builder of character and courage, may my grandchild grow strong in the light of your love. Grant him courage to stand for what is right, to guard the truth and to ensure justice in every aspect of life. May he boldly grow in grace, revere your name and proudly proclaim you as the Lord of lords and King of kings. Amen.

"AND WHOEVER WELCOMES A
LITTLE CHILD LIKE THIS IN MY
NAME WELCOMES ME."

Matthew 18:5

A Moment to Shine

DOTTIE RAMBO

READ | MATTHEW 18:5 – 9

My life has not been what you would call "normal." But my grandkids have never noticed. They've always thought all grandmothers were like "GranDot." Didn't all grandmas wear beaded gowns, ride tour buses and sing on television? They seemed to think so.

Loving my grandbabies like I do, I have always enjoyed showing them off — giving them a chance to sparkle and shine. So I decided to take them along to one of my concerts. I had the perfect song for them: "Germs," a song about an invisible dog that my grandson, Israel, loved singing.

So the night came. My two grandchildren, Destiny, age five, and Israel, age three, were led on stage. As I introduced the song — telling about its place on my children's album — I failed to notice that Israel had been drawn to the glint of my guitar's tuning keys.

While I chatted away, he started turning each shiny chrome tuner. The audience laughed and shouted, but I thought they were just being lively. That is until I tried to start the song! When I hit what was supposed to be the first chord, my low E string fell off. I looked to Igs and Des, who were both giggling, I looked at the audience, who were now roaring with laughter, and I started laughing myself. There's nothing like a spontaneous moment between you, your grandkids and a few thousand people!

God's the same way. He sets you up to sparkle and shine. And if you somehow untune everything your first time out, he'll just smile and laugh because he loves you.

Heavenly Father, thank you for the times we get to spend with our grandchildren. May each moment shimmer and shine in the glow of your love. In Jesus' precious name, amen.

Your next devotion is located on page 1328.

GRANDCHILD IN FOCUS • PRAYER

Future Spouse

Dear Lord, if it is your will, I pray my grandchild will be united in a loving and Christian marriage. Keep her sexually pure so that she will honor you with her body and mind. As she seeks a spouse who will honor and care for her, give her patience and discernment. May her choice for a life partner be your choice for her, so that she and her husband will together glorify you in a lasting love. I pray this in Jesus' name, amen.

in heaven always see the face of my Father in heaven.[a]

[12]"What do you think? If a man owns a hundred sheep, and one of them wanders away, will he not leave the ninety-nine on the hills and go to look for the one that wandered off? [13]And if he finds it, I tell you the truth, he is happier about that one sheep than about the ninety-nine that did not wander off. [14]In the same way your Father in heaven is not willing that any of these little ones should be lost.

A Brother Who Sins Against You

[15]"If your brother sins against you,[b] go and show him his fault, just between the two of you. If he listens to you, you have won your brother over. [16]But if he will not listen, take one or two others along, so that 'every matter may be established by the testimony of two or three witnesses.'[c] [17]If he refuses to listen to them, tell it to the church; and if he refuses to listen even to the church, treat him as you would a pagan or a tax collector.

[18]"I tell you the truth, whatever you bind on earth will be[d] bound in heaven, and whatever you loose on earth will be[d] loosed in heaven.

[19]"Again, I tell you that if two of you on earth agree about anything you ask for, it will be done for you by my Father in heaven. [20]For where two or three come together in my name, there am I with them."

The Parable of the Unmerciful Servant

[21]Then Peter came to Jesus and asked, "Lord, how many times shall I forgive my brother when he sins against me? Up to seven times?"

[22]Jesus answered, "I tell you, not seven times, but seventy-seven times.[e]

[23]"Therefore, the kingdom of heaven is like a king who wanted to settle accounts with his servants. [24]As he began the settlement, a man who owed him ten thousand talents[f] was brought to him. [25]Since he was not able to pay, the master ordered that he and his wife and his children and all that he had be sold to repay the debt.

TALKING POINTS

Forgiveness

Continuously forgive others, even for their repeated offenses against you.

MATTHEW 18:21–22

This is the last talking point on forgiveness.

[26]"The servant fell on his knees before him. 'Be patient with me,' he begged, 'and I will pay back everything.' [27]The servant's master took pity on him, canceled the debt and let him go.

[28]"But when that servant went out, he found one of his fellow servants who owed him a hundred denarii.[g] He grabbed him and began to choke him. 'Pay back what you owe me!' he demanded.

[29]"His fellow servant fell to his knees and begged him, 'Be patient with me, and I will pay you back.'

[30]"But he refused. Instead, he went off and had the man thrown into prison until he could pay the debt. [31]When the other servants saw what had happened, they were greatly distressed and went and told their master everything that had happened.

[32]"Then the master called the servant in. 'You wicked servant,' he said, 'I canceled all that debt of yours because you begged me to. [33]Shouldn't you have had mercy on your fellow servant just as I had on you?' [34]In anger his master turned him over to the jailers to be tortured, until he should pay back all he owed.

[35]"This is how my heavenly Father will treat each of you unless you forgive your brother from your heart."

---

[a] 10 Some manuscripts *heaven.* [11]*The Son of Man came to save what was lost.*   [b] 15 Some manuscripts do not have *against you.*
[c] 16 Deut. 19:15   [d] 18 Or *have been*   [e] 22 Or *seventy times seven*
[f] 24 That is, millions of dollars   [g] 28 That is, a few dollars

Divorce

19:1–9pp — Mk 10:1–12

19 When Jesus had finished saying these things, he left Galilee and went into the region of Judea to the other side of the Jordan. ²Large crowds followed him, and he healed them there.

³Some Pharisees came to him to test him. They asked, "Is it lawful for a man to divorce his wife for any and every reason?"

⁴"Haven't you read," he replied, "that at the beginning the Creator 'made them male and female,'ᵃ ⁵and said, 'For this reason a man will leave his father and mother and be united to his wife, and the two will become one flesh'ᵇ? ⁶So they are no longer two, but one. Therefore what God has joined together, let man not separate."

⁷"Why then," they asked, "did Moses command that a man give his wife a certificate of divorce and send her away?"

⁸Jesus replied, "Moses permitted you to divorce your wives because your hearts were hard. But it was not this way from the beginning. ⁹I tell you that anyone who divorces his wife, except for marital unfaithfulness, and marries another woman commits adultery."

¹⁰The disciples said to him, "If this is the situation between a husband and wife, it is better not to marry."

¹¹Jesus replied, "Not everyone can accept this word, but only those to whom it has been given. ¹²For some are eunuchs because they were born that way; others were made that way by men; and others have renounced marriageᶜ because of the kingdom of heaven. The one who can accept this should accept it."

The Little Children and Jesus

19:13–15pp — Mk 10:13–16; Lk 18:15–17

¹³Then little children were brought to Jesus for him to place his hands on them and pray for them. But the disciples rebuked those who brought them.

¹⁴Jesus said, "Let the little children come to me, and do not hinder them, for the kingdom of heaven belongs to such as these." ¹⁵When he had placed his hands on them, he went on from there.

TALKING POINTS

Adoption

Jesus cares about children.

MATTHEW 19:13–14

This is the last talking point on adoption.

The Rich Young Man

19:16–29pp — Mk 10:17–30; Lk 18:18–30

¹⁶Now a man came up to Jesus and asked, "Teacher, what good thing must I do to get eternal life?"

¹⁷"Why do you ask me about what is good?" Jesus replied. "There is only One who is good. If you want to enter life, obey the commandments."

¹⁸"Which ones?" the man inquired.

Jesus replied, " 'Do not murder, do not commit adultery, do not steal, do not give false testimony, ¹⁹honor your father and mother,'ᵈ and 'love your neighbor as yourself.'ᵉ"

²⁰"All these I have kept," the young man said. "What do I still lack?"

²¹Jesus answered, "If you want to be perfect, go, sell your possessions and give to the poor, and you will have treasure in heaven. Then come, follow me."

²²When the young man heard this, he went away sad, because he had great wealth.

²³Then Jesus said to his disciples, "I tell you the truth, it is hard for a rich man to enter the kingdom of heaven. ²⁴Again I tell you, it is easier for a camel to go through the eye of a needle than for a rich man to enter the kingdom of God."

ᵃ 4 Gen. 1:27   ᵇ 5 Gen. 2:24   ᶜ 12 Or *have made themselves eunuchs*   ᵈ 19 Exodus 20:12-16; Deut. 5:16-20   ᵉ 19 Lev. 19:18

25 When the disciples heard this, they were greatly astonished and asked, "Who then can be saved?"

26 Jesus looked at them and said, "With man this is impossible, but with God all things are possible."

27 Peter answered him, "We have left everything to follow you! What then will there be for us?"

28 Jesus said to them, "I tell you the truth, at the renewal of all things, when the Son of Man sits on his glorious throne, you who have followed me will also sit on twelve thrones, judging the twelve tribes of Israel. 29 And everyone who has left houses or brothers or sisters or father or mother *a* or children or fields for my sake will receive a hundred times as much and will inherit eternal life. 30 But many who are first will be last, and many who are last will be first.

The Parable of the Workers in the Vineyard

20 "For the kingdom of heaven is like a landowner who went out early in the morning to hire men to work in his vineyard. 2 He agreed to pay them a denarius for the day and sent them into his vineyard.

3 "About the third hour he went out and saw others standing in the marketplace doing nothing. 4 He told them, 'You also go and work in my vineyard, and I will pay you whatever is right.' 5 So they went.

"He went out again about the sixth hour and the ninth hour and did the same thing. 6 About the eleventh hour he went out and found still others standing around. He asked them, 'Why have you been standing here all day long doing nothing?'

7 " 'Because no one has hired us,' they answered.

"He said to them, 'You also go and work in my vineyard.'

8 "When evening came, the owner of the vineyard said to his foreman, 'Call the workers and pay them their wages, beginning with the last ones hired and going on to the first.'

9 "The workers who were hired about the elev-

enth hour came and each received a denarius. 10 So when those came who were hired first, they expected to receive more. But each one of them also received a denarius. 11 When they received it, they began to grumble against the landowner. 12 'These men who were hired last worked only one hour,' they said, 'and you have made them equal to us who have borne the burden of the work and the heat of the day.'

13 "But he answered one of them, 'Friend, I am not being unfair to you. Didn't you agree to work for a denarius? 14 Take your pay and go. I want to give the man who was hired last the same as I gave you. 15 Don't I have the right to do what I want with my own money? Or are you envious because I am generous?'

16 "So the last will be first, and the first will be last."

Jesus Again Predicts His Death
20:17–19pp — Mk 10:32–34; Lk 18:31–33

17 Now as Jesus was going up to Jerusalem, he took the twelve disciples aside and said to them, 18 "We are going up to Jerusalem, and the Son of Man will be betrayed to the chief priests and the teachers of the law. They will condemn him to death 19 and will turn him over to the Gentiles to be mocked and flogged and crucified. On the third day he will be raised to life!"

A Mother's Request
20:20–28pp — Mk 10:35–45

20 Then the mother of Zebedee's sons came to Jesus with her sons and, kneeling down, asked a favor of him.

21 "What is it you want?" he asked.

She said, "Grant that one of these two sons of mine may sit at your right and the other at your left in your kingdom."

22 "You don't know what you are asking," Jesus said to them. "Can you drink the cup I am going to drink?"

"We can," they answered.

a 29 Some manuscripts mother or wife

²³Jesus said to them, "You will indeed drink from my cup, but to sit at my right or left is not for me to grant. These places belong to those for whom they have been prepared by my Father."

²⁴When the ten heard about this, they were indignant with the two brothers. ²⁵Jesus called them together and said, "You know that the rulers of the Gentiles lord it over them, and their high officials exercise authority over them. ²⁶Not so with you. Instead, whoever wants to become great among you must be your servant, ²⁷and whoever wants to be first must be your slave— ²⁸just as the Son of Man did not come to be served, but to serve, and to give his life as a ransom for many."

Two Blind Men Receive Sight

20:29–34pp — Mk 10:46–52; Lk 18:35–43

²⁹As Jesus and his disciples were leaving Jericho, a large crowd followed him. ³⁰Two blind men were sitting by the roadside, and when they heard that Jesus was going by, they shouted, "Lord, Son of David, have mercy on us!"

³¹The crowd rebuked them and told them to be quiet, but they shouted all the louder, "Lord, Son of David, have mercy on us!"

³²Jesus stopped and called them. "What do you want me to do for you?" he asked.

³³"Lord," they answered, "we want our sight."

³⁴Jesus had compassion on them and touched their eyes. Immediately they received their sight and followed him.

The Triumphal Entry

21:1–9pp — Mk 11:1–10; Lk 19:29–38
21:4–9pp — Jn 12:12–15

21 As they approached Jerusalem and came to Bethphage on the Mount of Olives, Jesus sent two disciples, ²saying to them, "Go to the village ahead of you, and at once you will find a donkey tied there, with her colt by her. Untie them and bring them to me. ³If anyone says anything to you, tell him that the Lord needs them, and he will send them right away."

⁴This took place to fulfill what was spoken through the prophet:

⁵"Say to the Daughter of Zion,
 'See, your king comes to you,
gentle and riding on a donkey,
 on a colt, the foal of a donkey.' "ᵃ

⁶The disciples went and did as Jesus had instructed them. ⁷They brought the donkey and the colt, placed their cloaks on them, and Jesus sat on them. ⁸A very large crowd spread their cloaks on the road, while others cut branches from the trees and spread them on the road. ⁹The crowds that went ahead of him and those that followed shouted,

"Hosanna ᵇ to the Son of David!"

"Blessed is he who comes in the name of
 the Lord!"ᶜ

"Hosanna ᵇ in the highest!"

¹⁰When Jesus entered Jerusalem, the whole city was stirred and asked, "Who is this?"

¹¹The crowds answered, "This is Jesus, the prophet from Nazareth in Galilee."

Jesus at the Temple

21:12–16pp — Mk 11:15–18; Lk 19:45–47

¹²Jesus entered the temple area and drove out all who were buying and selling there. He overturned the tables of the money changers and the benches of those selling doves. ¹³"It is written," he said to them, " 'My house will be called a house of prayer,'ᵈ but you are making it a 'den of robbers.'ᵉ "

¹⁴The blind and the lame came to him at the temple, and he healed them. ¹⁵But when the chief priests and the teachers of the law saw the wonderful things he did and the children shouting in the temple area, "Hosanna to the Son of David," they were indignant.

¹⁶"Do you hear what these children are saying?" they asked him.

ᵃ 5 Zech. 9:9   ᵇ 9 A Hebrew expression meaning "Save!" which became an exclamation of praise; also in verse 15   ᶜ 9 Psalm 118:26   ᵈ 13 Isaiah 56:7   ᵉ 13 Jer. 7:11

"Yes," replied Jesus, "have you never read,

" 'From the lips of children and infants
  you have ordained praise' *a*?"

[17] And he left them and went out of the city to Bethany, where he spent the night.

The Fig Tree Withers

21:18–22pp — Mk 11:12–14,20–24

[18] Early in the morning, as he was on his way back to the city, he was hungry. [19] Seeing a fig tree by the road, he went up to it but found nothing on it except leaves. Then he said to it, "May you never bear fruit again!" Immediately the tree withered.

[20] When the disciples saw this, they were amazed. "How did the fig tree wither so quickly?" they asked.

[21] Jesus replied, "I tell you the truth, if you have faith and do not doubt, not only can you do what was done to the fig tree, but also you can say to this mountain, 'Go, throw yourself into the sea,' and it will be done. [22] If you believe, you will receive whatever you ask for in prayer."

The Authority of Jesus Questioned

21:23–27pp — Mk 11:27–33; Lk 20:1–8

[23] Jesus entered the temple courts, and, while he was teaching, the chief priests and the elders of the people came to him. "By what authority are you doing these things?" they asked. "And who gave you this authority?"

[24] Jesus replied, "I will also ask you one question. If you answer me, I will tell you by what authority I am doing these things. [25] John's baptism — where did it come from? Was it from heaven, or from men?"

They discussed it among themselves and said, "If we say, 'From heaven,' he will ask, 'Then why didn't you believe him?' [26] But if we say, 'From men' — we are afraid of the people, for they all hold that John was a prophet."

[27] So they answered Jesus, "We don't know."

Then he said, "Neither will I tell you by what authority I am doing these things.

The Parable of the Two Sons

[28] "What do you think? There was a man who had two sons. He went to the first and said, 'Son, go and work today in the vineyard.'

[29] " 'I will not,' he answered, but later he changed his mind and went.

[30] "Then the father went to the other son and said the same thing. He answered, 'I will, sir,' but he did not go.

[31] "Which of the two did what his father wanted?"

"The first," they answered.

Jesus said to them, "I tell you the truth, the tax collectors and the prostitutes are entering the kingdom of God ahead of you. [32] For John came to you to show you the way of righteousness, and you did not believe him, but the tax collectors and the prostitutes did. And even after you saw this, you did not repent and believe him.

The Parable of the Tenants

21:33–46pp — Mk 12:1–12; Lk 20:9–19

[33] "Listen to another parable: There was a landowner who planted a vineyard. He put a wall around it, dug a winepress in it and built a watchtower. Then he rented the vineyard to some farmers and went away on a journey. [34] When the harvest time approached, he sent his servants to the tenants to collect his fruit.

[35] "The tenants seized his servants; they beat one, killed another, and stoned a third. [36] Then he sent other servants to them, more than the first time, and the tenants treated them the same way. [37] Last of all, he sent his son to them. 'They will respect my son,' he said.

[38] "But when the tenants saw the son, they said to each other, 'This is the heir. Come, let's kill him and take his inheritance.' [39] So they took him and threw him out of the vineyard and killed him.

[40] "Therefore, when the owner of the vineyard comes, what will he do to those tenants?"

[41] "He will bring those wretches to a wretched end," they replied, "and he will rent the vineyard

a 16 Psalm 8:2

to other tenants, who will give him his share of the crop at harvest time."

⁴²Jesus said to them, "Have you never read in the Scriptures:

" 'The stone the builders rejected
has become the capstone ᵃ;
the Lord has done this,
and it is marvelous in our eyes' ᵇ?

⁴³"Therefore I tell you that the kingdom of God will be taken away from you and given to a people who will produce its fruit. ⁴⁴He who falls on this stone will be broken to pieces, but he on whom it falls will be crushed." ᶜ

⁴⁵When the chief priests and the Pharisees heard Jesus' parables, they knew he was talking about them. ⁴⁶They looked for a way to arrest him, but they were afraid of the crowd because the people held that he was a prophet.

The Parable of the Wedding Banquet
22:2–14Ref — Lk 14:16–24

22 Jesus spoke to them again in parables, saying: ²"The kingdom of heaven is like a king who prepared a wedding banquet for his son. ³He sent his servants to those who had been invited to the banquet to tell them to come, but they refused to come.

⁴"Then he sent some more servants and said, 'Tell those who have been invited that I have prepared my dinner: My oxen and fattened cattle have been butchered, and everything is ready. Come to the wedding banquet.'

⁵"But they paid no attention and went off—one to his field, another to his business. ⁶The rest seized his servants, mistreated them and killed them. ⁷The king was enraged. He sent his army and destroyed those murderers and burned their city.

⁸"Then he said to his servants, 'The wedding banquet is ready, but those I invited did not deserve to come. ⁹Go to the street corners and invite to the banquet anyone you find.' ¹⁰So the servants went out into the streets and gathered all the people they could find, both good and bad, and the wedding hall was filled with guests.

¹¹"But when the king came in to see the guests, he noticed a man there who was not wearing wedding clothes. ¹²'Friend,' he asked, 'how did you get in here without wedding clothes?' The man was speechless.

¹³"Then the king told the attendants, 'Tie him hand and foot, and throw him outside, into the darkness, where there will be weeping and gnashing of teeth.'

¹⁴"For many are invited, but few are chosen."

Paying Taxes to Caesar
22:15–22pp — Mk 12:13–17; Lk 20:20–26

¹⁵Then the Pharisees went out and laid plans to trap him in his words. ¹⁶They sent their disciples to him along with the Herodians. "Teacher," they said, "we know you are a man of integrity and that you teach the way of God in accordance with the truth. You aren't swayed by men, because you pay no attention to who they are. ¹⁷Tell us then, what is your opinion? Is it right to pay taxes to Caesar or not?"

¹⁸But Jesus, knowing their evil intent, said, "You hypocrites, why are you trying to trap me? ¹⁹Show me the coin used for paying the tax." They brought him a denarius, ²⁰and he asked them, "Whose portrait is this? And whose inscription?"

²¹"Caesar's," they replied.

Then he said to them, "Give to Caesar what is Caesar's, and to God what is God's."

²²When they heard this, they were amazed. So they left him and went away.

Marriage at the Resurrection
22:23–33pp — Mk 12:18–27; Lk 20:27–40

²³That same day the Sadducees, who say there is no resurrection, came to him with a question. ²⁴"Teacher," they said, "Moses told us that if a man dies without having children, his brother must marry the widow and have children for him.

ᵃ 42 Or *cornerstone*   ᵇ 42 Psalm 118:22,23   ᶜ 44 Some manuscripts do not have verse 44.

25 Now there were seven brothers among us. The first one married and died, and since he had no children, he left his wife to his brother. 26 The same thing happened to the second and third brother, right on down to the seventh. 27 Finally, the woman died. 28 Now then, at the resurrection, whose wife will she be of the seven, since all of them were married to her?"

29 Jesus replied, "You are in error because you do not know the Scriptures or the power of God. 30 At the resurrection people will neither marry nor be given in marriage; they will be like the angels in heaven. 31 But about the resurrection of the dead—have you not read what God said to you, 32 'I am the God of Abraham, the God of Isaac, and the God of Jacob'*a*? He is not the God of the dead but of the living."

33 When the crowds heard this, they were astonished at his teaching.

The Greatest Commandment
22:34–40pp — Mk 12:28–31

34 Hearing that Jesus had silenced the Sadducees, the Pharisees got together. 35 One of them, an expert in the law, tested him with this question: 36 "Teacher, which is the greatest commandment in the Law?"

37 Jesus replied: " 'Love the Lord your God with all your heart and with all your soul and with all your mind.'*b* 38 This is the first and greatest commandment. 39 And the second is like it: 'Love your neighbor as yourself.'*c* 40 All the Law and the Prophets hang on these two commandments."

Whose Son Is the Christ?
22:41–46pp — Mk 12:35–37; Lk 20:41–44

41 While the Pharisees were gathered together, Jesus asked them, 42 "What do you think about the Christ*d*? Whose son is he?"

"The son of David," they replied.

43 He said to them, "How is it then that David, speaking by the Spirit, calls him 'Lord'? For he says,

44 " 'The Lord said to my Lord:
  "Sit at my right hand
  until I put your enemies
    under your feet." '*e*

45 If then David calls him 'Lord,' how can he be his son?" 46 No one could say a word in reply, and from that day on no one dared to ask him any more questions.

Seven Woes
23:1–7pp — Mk 12:38,39; Lk 20:45,46
23:37–39pp — Lk 13:34,35

23 Then Jesus said to the crowds and to his disciples: 2 "The teachers of the law and the Pharisees sit in Moses' seat. 3 So you must obey them and do everything they tell you. But do not do what they do, for they do not practice what they preach. 4 They tie up heavy loads and put them on men's shoulders, but they themselves are not willing to lift a finger to move them.

5 "Everything they do is done for men to see: They make their phylacteries*f* wide and the tassels on their garments long; 6 they love the place of honor at banquets and the most important seats in the synagogues; 7 they love to be greeted in the marketplaces and to have men call them 'Rabbi.'

8 "But you are not to be called 'Rabbi,' for you have only one Master and you are all brothers. 9 And do not call anyone on earth 'father,' for you have one Father, and he is in heaven. 10 Nor are you to be called 'teacher,' for you have one Teacher,

TALKING POINTS

Values
Love should be our highest priority.
MATTHEW 22:36–40

This is the last talking point on values.

a 32 Exodus 3:6   *b 37* Deut. 6:5   *c 39* Lev. 19:18
d 42 Or *Messiah*   *e 44* Psalm 110:1   *f 5* That is, boxes
containing Scripture verses, worn on forehead and arm

> JESUS REPLIED: " 'LOVE THE
> LORD YOUR GOD WITH ALL
> YOUR HEART AND WITH ALL
> OF YOUR SOUL AND WITH
> ALL YOUR MIND.' "
>
> *Matthew 22:37*

Crawling to Daddy

CHERYL BAKER

READ | MATTHEW 22:34–40

Our first granddaughter, Maggie, learned quickly that surprises and toys lived in a special toy box that occupied a predominant corner of our dining room. Sometimes we lifted her inside, and she would pass out toys she wanted to play with later. Our younger granddaughter, Chloe, had not shown much interest in the toy box. She was happy playing with things that her older sister brought over to her.

While babysitting for the girls one afternoon, I had one of those "grandma moments" when Chloe discovered the toy box. With a frown on her face, she cautiously crawled over to it, pulled herself up and peeked over the top. With her wide, toothless smile, she began exploring one toy before quickly moving on to the next. Maggie, caught up in the fun, climbed into the toy box and started passing toys out to Chloe. All three of us were laughing out loud as toys were strewn across the room.

As my son came through the front door to pick up the kids, he shouted, "Hi, girls. Did you have a good time at Grandma's house?" Chloe could not see her daddy, but she heard the sound of his voice. She immediately dropped the toy in her hand and fell to her hands and knees. She crawled rapidly and determinedly, going around blocks, books and miniature cars to get to her father.

As my son picked up his daughter and hugged her tightly, I was aware that I was witnessing another "grandma moment." I was watching a living, breathing example of God's love for his child and the devotion of the child to her Father. Without question or hesitation, the child went to her father, on her hands and knees, fully expecting—and receiving—his loving embrace.

Dear Lord and Father, thank you for the examples I see around me of your devotion and love echoed in the love and care we have among our family members. May I always remember to come to you without hesitation.

Your next devotion is located on page 1331.

GRANDCHILD IN FOCUS • PRAYER

School/Career

Dear God, may learning be a joy rather than a chore for my grandchild. May exploration of new ideas bring a sense of wonder, awe and excitement. Grant him clarity of mind, the ability to concentrate on the task at hand and recollection of what has been learned. Help him to appreciate the tasks that come easily and to persevere through those that challenge. Amen.

the Christ.[a] [11]The greatest among you will be your servant. [12]For whoever exalts himself will be humbled, and whoever humbles himself will be exalted.

[13]"Woe to you, teachers of the law and Pharisees, you hypocrites! You shut the kingdom of heaven in men's faces. You yourselves do not enter, nor will you let those enter who are trying to.[b]

[15]"Woe to you, teachers of the law and Pharisees, you hypocrites! You travel over land and sea to win a single convert, and when he becomes one, you make him twice as much a son of hell as you are.

[16]"Woe to you, blind guides! You say, 'If anyone swears by the temple, it means nothing; but if anyone swears by the gold of the temple, he is bound by his oath.' [17]You blind fools! Which is greater: the gold, or the temple that makes the gold sacred? [18]You also say, 'If anyone swears by the altar, it means nothing; but if anyone swears by the gift on it, he is bound by his oath.' [19]You blind men! Which is greater: the gift, or the altar that makes the gift sacred? [20]Therefore, he who swears by the altar swears by it and by everything on it. [21]And he who swears by the temple swears by it and by the one who dwells in it. [22]And he who swears by heaven swears by God's throne and by the one who sits on it.

[23]"Woe to you, teachers of the law and Pharisees, you hypocrites! You give a tenth of your spices—mint, dill and cummin. But you have neglected the more important matters of the law—justice, mercy and faithfulness. You should have practiced the latter, without neglecting the former. [24]You blind guides! You strain out a gnat but swallow a camel.

[25]"Woe to you, teachers of the law and Pharisees, you hypocrites! You clean the outside of the cup and dish, but inside they are full of greed and self-indulgence. [26]Blind Pharisee! First clean the inside of the cup and dish, and then the outside also will be clean.

[27]"Woe to you, teachers of the law and Pharisees, you hypocrites! You are like whitewashed tombs, which look beautiful on the outside but on the inside are full of dead men's bones and everything unclean. [28]In the same way, on the outside you appear to people as righteous but on the inside you are full of hypocrisy and wickedness.

[29]"Woe to you, teachers of the law and Pharisees, you hypocrites! You build tombs for the prophets and decorate the graves of the righteous. [30]And you say, 'If we had lived in the days of our forefathers, we would not have taken part with them in shedding the blood of the prophets.' [31]So you testify against yourselves that you are the descendants of those who murdered the prophets. [32]Fill up, then, the measure of the sin of your forefathers!

[33]"You snakes! You brood of vipers! How will you escape being condemned to hell? [34]Therefore I am sending you prophets and wise men and teachers. Some of them you will kill and crucify; others you will flog in your synagogues and pursue from town to town. [35]And so upon you will come all the righteous blood that has been shed on earth, from the blood of righteous Abel to the blood of Zechariah son of Berekiah, whom you murdered between the temple and the altar. [36]I tell you the truth, all this will come upon this generation.

[37]"O Jerusalem, Jerusalem, you who kill the prophets and stone those sent to you, how often I have longed to gather your children together, as a hen gathers her chicks under her wings, but you were not willing. [38]Look, your house is left to you desolate. [39]For I tell you, you will not see me again until you say, 'Blessed is he who comes in the name of the Lord.'[c]"

Signs of the End of the Age

24:1–51pp — Mk 13:1–37; Lk 21:5–36

24 Jesus left the temple and was walking away when his disciples came up to him to call his attention to its buildings. [2]"Do you see all these things?" he asked. "I tell you the truth,

---

[a] 10 Or Messiah   [b] 13 Some manuscripts to. [14]Woe to you, teachers of the law and Pharisees, you hypocrites! You devour widows' houses and for a show make lengthy prayers. Therefore you will be punished more severely.   [c] 39 Psalm 118:26

not one stone here will be left on another; every one will be thrown down."

³As Jesus was sitting on the Mount of Olives, the disciples came to him privately. "Tell us," they said, "when will this happen, and what will be the sign of your coming and of the end of the age?"

⁴Jesus answered: "Watch out that no one deceives you. ⁵For many will come in my name, claiming, 'I am the Christ,ᵃ' and will deceive many. ⁶You will hear of wars and rumors of wars, but see to it that you are not alarmed. Such things must happen, but the end is still to come. ⁷Nation will rise against nation, and kingdom against kingdom. There will be famines and earthquakes in various places. ⁸All these are the beginning of birth pains.

⁹"Then you will be handed over to be persecuted and put to death, and you will be hated by all nations because of me. ¹⁰At that time many will turn away from the faith and will betray and hate each other, ¹¹and many false prophets will appear and deceive many people. ¹²Because of the increase of wickedness, the love of most will grow cold, ¹³but he who stands firm to the end will be saved. ¹⁴And this gospel of the kingdom will be preached in the whole world as a testimony to all nations, and then the end will come.

¹⁵"So when you see standing in the holy place 'the abomination that causes desolation,'ᵇ spoken of through the prophet Daniel—let the reader understand— ¹⁶then let those who are in Judea flee to the mountains. ¹⁷Let no one on the roof of his house go down to take anything out of the house. ¹⁸Let no one in the field go back to get his cloak. ¹⁹How dreadful it will be in those days for pregnant women and nursing mothers! ²⁰Pray that your flight will not take place in winter or on the Sabbath. ²¹For then there will be great distress, unequaled from the beginning of the world until now—and never to be equaled again. ²²If those days had not been cut short, no one would survive, but for the sake of the elect those days will be shortened. ²³At that time if anyone says to you, 'Look, here is the Christ!' or, 'There he is!' do not believe it. ²⁴For false Christs and false prophets will appear and perform great signs and miracles to deceive even the elect—if that were possible. ²⁵See, I have told you ahead of time.

²⁶"So if anyone tells you, 'There he is, out in the desert,' do not go out; or, 'Here he is, in the inner rooms,' do not believe it. ²⁷For as lightning that comes from the east is visible even in the west, so will be the coming of the Son of Man. ²⁸Wherever there is a carcass, there the vultures will gather.

²⁹"Immediately after the distress of those days

" 'the sun will be darkened,
    and the moon will not give its light;
the stars will fall from the sky,
    and the heavenly bodies will be shaken.'ᶜ

³⁰"At that time the sign of the Son of Man will appear in the sky, and all the nations of the earth will mourn. They will see the Son of Man coming on the clouds of the sky, with power and great glory. ³¹And he will send his angels with a loud trumpet call, and they will gather his elect from the four winds, from one end of the heavens to the other.

³²"Now learn this lesson from the fig tree: As soon as its twigs get tender and its leaves come out, you know that summer is near. ³³Even so, when you see all these things, you know that itᵈ is near, right at the door. ³⁴I tell you the truth, this generationᵉ will certainly not pass away until all these things have happened. ³⁵Heaven and earth will pass away, but my words will never pass away.

The Day and Hour Unknown

24:37–39pp — Lk 17:26,27
24:45–51pp — Lk 12:42–46

³⁶"No one knows about that day or hour, not even the angels in heaven, nor the Son,ᶠ but only the Father. ³⁷As it was in the days of Noah, so it will be at the coming of the Son of Man. ³⁸For in the days before the flood, people were eating and drinking, marrying and giving in marriage,

---

ᵃ 5 Or *Messiah*; also in verse 23   ᵇ 15 Daniel 9:27; 11:31; 12:11
ᶜ 29 Isaiah 13:10; 34:4   ᵈ 33 Or *he*   ᵉ 34 Or *race*   ᶠ 36 Some manuscripts do not have *nor the Son*.

Buried Treasure

If you have access to a sandbox or a beach, conduct your own "archaeological dig." Here's a chance for the kids to dig for family "treasures." If you use your imagination, you're sure to find plenty of "artifacts" to catch the kids' interest. Some options: a key, a small vase, an old tool or kitchen utensil, a military medal or sports trophy. Enclose the object in plastic or a box (or both if you don't want it to get too sandy or if it is small). Try to have everyone locate something. (Be sure nothing remains buried.) Discuss the history and significance of each discovery.

Long-Distance Variation: Send or provide a large box filled with Styrofoam popcorn or confetti — along with plenty of small treasures, edible and otherwise, appropriate for either boys or girls. Ask Mom or Dad to supervise a "dig," passing the box on to the next child as soon as something is "excavated."

Thank you, Father, for the treasures of our family's past and for the opportunity to share them with my family. May this exercise help my grandchildren feel securely grounded in our family's history. Help them also to feel grounded in their faith in you. Amen.

Your next devotion is located on page 1332.

GRANDCHILD IN FOCUS • PRAYER

Character

Dear Lord and Father, I ask that you fill my grandchild with your Spirit so her character reflects your goodness and love. Give her kindness and love for others. Bring joy to her life so she will be a joy to others. Grant her patience and self-control through difficult and trying times. May she show mercy and generosity to those who are less fortunate. Grant her integrity and a sense of justice, and surround her with your peace. Amen.

Worship the Lord

Sing to the LORD a new song,
   for he has done marvelous things;
his right hand and his holy arm
   have worked salvation for him.
The LORD has made his salvation known
   and revealed his righteousness to the nations.
He has remembered his love
   and his faithfulness to the house of Israel;
all the ends of the earth have seen
   the salvation of our God.

Shout for joy to the LORD, all the earth,
   burst into jubilant song with music;
make music to the LORD with the harp,
   with the harp and the sound of
      singing,
with trumpets and the blast of the ram's
      horn—
   shout for joy before the LORD,
      the King.

Psalm 98:1–6

O Lord my King, I come before you with praises and singing. You fill the world with marvelous things. You surround me with your strength and salvation. You shower your love over all the earth. For all this I sing for joy and praise your name. Amen.

GRANDCHILD IN FOCUS • PRAYER

Talents

Dear Lord, the giver of gifts, bless my grandchild as he develops his talents. Help him identify his talents and be proud and confident of the gifts you have given him. Give him patience and understanding, Lord, so he will not grow weary of striving and searching to reach the goals you have set for him. May each milestone bring satisfaction and a healthy desire for greater achievement and success to bring glory to you. Amen.

Your next devotion is located on page 1335.

up to the day Noah entered the ark; [39] and they knew nothing about what would happen until the flood came and took them all away. That is how it will be at the coming of the Son of Man. [40] Two men will be in the field; one will be taken and the other left. [41] Two women will be grinding with a hand mill; one will be taken and the other left.

[42] "Therefore keep watch, because you do not know on what day your Lord will come. [43] But understand this: If the owner of the house had known at what time of night the thief was coming, he would have kept watch and would not have let his house be broken into. [44] So you also must be ready, because the Son of Man will come at an hour when you do not expect him.

[45] "Who then is the faithful and wise servant, whom the master has put in charge of the servants in his household to give them their food at the proper time? [46] It will be good for that servant whose master finds him doing so when he returns. [47] I tell you the truth, he will put him in charge of all his possessions. [48] But suppose that servant is wicked and says to himself, 'My master is staying away a long time,' [49] and he then begins to beat his fellow servants and to eat and drink with drunkards. [50] The master of that servant will come on a day when he does not expect him and at an hour he is not aware of. [51] He will cut him to pieces and assign him a place with the hypocrites, where there will be weeping and gnashing of teeth.

The Parable of the Ten Virgins

25 "At that time the kingdom of heaven will be like ten virgins who took their lamps and went out to meet the bridegroom. [2] Five of them were foolish and five were wise. [3] The foolish ones took their lamps but did not take any oil with them. [4] The wise, however, took oil in jars along with their lamps. [5] The bridegroom was a long time in coming, and they all became drowsy and fell asleep.

[6] "At midnight the cry rang out: 'Here's the bridegroom! Come out to meet him!'

[7] "Then all the virgins woke up and trimmed their lamps. [8] The foolish ones said to the wise, 'Give us some of your oil; our lamps are going out.'

[9] " 'No,' they replied, 'there may not be enough for both us and you. Instead, go to those who sell oil and buy some for yourselves.'

[10] "But while they were on their way to buy the oil, the bridegroom arrived. The virgins who were ready went in with him to the wedding banquet. And the door was shut.

[11] "Later the others also came. 'Sir! Sir!' they said. 'Open the door for us!'

[12] "But he replied, 'I tell you the truth, I don't know you.'

[13] "Therefore keep watch, because you do not know the day or the hour.

The Parable of the Talents
25:14–30Ref — Lk 19:12–27

[14] "Again, it will be like a man going on a journey, who called his servants and entrusted his property to them. [15] To one he gave five talents[a] of money, to another two talents, and to another one talent, each according to his ability. Then he went on his journey. [16] The man who had received the five talents went at once and put his money to work and gained five more. [17] So also, the one with the two talents gained two more. [18] But the man who had received the one talent went off, dug a hole in the ground and hid his master's money.

[19] "After a long time the master of those servants returned and settled accounts with them. [20] The man who had received the five talents brought the other five. 'Master,' he said, 'you entrusted me with five talents. See, I have gained five more.'

[21] "His master replied, 'Well done, good and faithful servant! You have been faithful with a few things; I will put you in charge of many things. Come and share your master's happiness!'

[22] "The man with the two talents also came.

---

[a] 15 A talent was worth more than a thousand dollars.

'Master,' he said, 'you entrusted me with two talents; see, I have gained two more.'

²³"His master replied, 'Well done, good and faithful servant! You have been faithful with a few things; I will put you in charge of many things. Come and share your master's happiness!'

²⁴"Then the man who had received the one talent came. 'Master,' he said, 'I knew that you are a hard man, harvesting where you have not sown and gathering where you have not scattered seed. ²⁵So I was afraid and went out and hid your talent in the ground. See, here is what belongs to you.'

²⁶"His master replied, 'You wicked, lazy servant! So you knew that I harvest where I have not sown and gather where I have not scattered seed? ²⁷Well then, you should have put my money on deposit with the bankers, so that when I returned I would have received it back with interest.

²⁸" 'Take the talent from him and give it to the one who has the ten talents. ²⁹For everyone who has will be given more, and he will have an abundance. Whoever does not have, even what he has will be taken from him. ³⁰And throw that worthless servant outside, into the darkness, where there will be weeping and gnashing of teeth.'

TALKING POINTS

Responsibility

We are responsible to God
for our use of what he gives us.

MATTHEW 25:14–30

For more on responsibility, go to Romans 13:7–8.

The Sheep and the Goats

³¹"When the Son of Man comes in his glory, and all the angels with him, he will sit on his throne in heavenly glory. ³²All the nations will be gathered before him, and he will separate the people one from another as a shepherd separates the sheep from the goats. ³³He will put the sheep on his right and the goats on his left.

³⁴"Then the King will say to those on his right, 'Come, you who are blessed by my Father; take your inheritance, the kingdom prepared for you since the creation of the world. ³⁵For I was hungry and you gave me something to eat, I was thirsty and you gave me something to drink, I was a stranger and you invited me in, ³⁶I needed clothes and you clothed me, I was sick and you looked after me, I was in prison and you came to visit me.'

³⁷"Then the righteous will answer him, 'Lord, when did we see you hungry and feed you, or thirsty and give you something to drink? ³⁸When did we see you a stranger and invite you in, or needing clothes and clothe you? ³⁹When did we see you sick or in prison and go to visit you?'

⁴⁰"The King will reply, 'I tell you the truth, whatever you did for one of the least of these brothers of mine, you did for me.'

⁴¹"Then he will say to those on his left, 'Depart from me, you who are cursed, into the eternal fire prepared for the devil and his angels. ⁴²For I was hungry and you gave me nothing to eat, I was thirsty and you gave me nothing to drink, ⁴³I was a stranger and you did not invite me in, I needed clothes and you did not clothe me, I was sick and in prison and you did not look after me.'

⁴⁴"They also will answer, 'Lord, when did we see you hungry or thirsty or a stranger or needing clothes or sick or in prison, and did not help you?'

⁴⁵"He will reply, 'I tell you the truth, whatever you did not do for one of the least of these, you did not do for me.'

⁴⁶"Then they will go away to eternal punishment, but the righteous to eternal life."

The Plot Against Jesus

26:2–5pp — Mk 14:1,2; Lk 22:1,2

26 When Jesus had finished saying all these things, he said to his disciples, ²"As you know, the Passover is two days away—and the Son of Man will be handed over to be crucified."

> "HIS MASTER REPLIED, 'WELL DONE,
> GOOD AND FAITHFUL SERVANT! YOU
> HAVE BEEN FAITHFUL WITH A FEW
> THINGS; I WILL PUT YOU IN CHARGE
> OF MANY THINGS. COME AND SHARE
> YOUR MASTER'S HAPPINESS!' "
>
> *Matthew 25:23*

Invest Your Influence

ELISA MORGAN

READ | MATTHEW 25:14–30

You are a person of influence with the power to influence others. What are you doing with your power to influence?

It's tough to fully realize the power of our influence. Some days we spend our time in hidden service — babysitting a grandchild, running errands, helping out with the daily busyness of life. During those times we may wonder about our "return on investment." Who really cares? Did anyone notice? Other moments in our days and weeks are more convincing of their significance — presenting a report, chairing a committee, praying with a gravely ill friend. During those times we know that we are needed and that what we are giving will bring results.

Matthew 25:14–30 presents the parable of the talents. In this familiar story, we read of the faithful servants who invested all they'd been given, increased their possessions and pleased their master to the point that they received more to continue investing. And we also read of the fearful servant who plunked the goods down in a hole, hoping to just hold on to them until they were once again required.

We tend to "rate" the value of what we've been given just as much as we rate what we do with it. Big, important gifts seem worthy of serious investment and therefore bring a measurable return. Small, seemingly ordinary abilities may be overlooked. In truth, God gives vital capacities to each of us. Our job is to wake up to his giftings — fully and wholly — and invest them. Our money, yes. Our faith, of course. But especially our influence over those in our lives.

Dear Master who has entrusted influence to each of us, I pray that you would reorient my perspective to see the sacred capacity that is much needed from me in your kingdom work: my influence. I freely offer it to my children and grandchildren and to those I work and serve alongside, yielding responsibility for the results of this investment to you. Amen.

Your next devotion is located on page 1344.

GRANDCHILD IN FOCUS · PRAYER

SELECT ONE OF YOUR GRANDCHILDREN TO FOCUS ON IN PRAYER FOR THE NEXT 14 DAYS.

Salvation

Dear Lord, please guide my grandchild to your gift of salvation. I pray that she will come to know you, to love you and to walk close to you throughout her life. May she boldly claim Jesus as her Lord and Savior. Guide her as she makes choices that have eternal consequences. Help her to follow you each moment of her life. I pray this in Jesus' name, amen.

³Then the chief priests and the elders of the people assembled in the palace of the high priest, whose name was Caiaphas, ⁴and they plotted to arrest Jesus in some sly way and kill him. ⁵"But not during the Feast," they said, "or there may be a riot among the people."

Jesus Anointed at Bethany

26:6–13pp — Mk 14:3–9
26:6–13Ref — Lk 7:37,38; Jn 12:1–8

⁶While Jesus was in Bethany in the home of a man known as Simon the Leper, ⁷a woman came to him with an alabaster jar of very expensive perfume, which she poured on his head as he was reclining at the table.

⁸When the disciples saw this, they were indignant. "Why this waste?" they asked. ⁹"This perfume could have been sold at a high price and the money given to the poor."

¹⁰Aware of this, Jesus said to them, "Why are you bothering this woman? She has done a beautiful thing to me. ¹¹The poor you will always have with you, but you will not always have me. ¹²When she poured this perfume on my body, she did it to prepare me for burial. ¹³I tell you the truth, wherever this gospel is preached throughout the world, what she has done will also be told, in memory of her."

Judas Agrees to Betray Jesus

26:14–16pp — Mk 14:10,11; Lk 22:3–6

¹⁴Then one of the Twelve—the one called Judas Iscariot—went to the chief priests ¹⁵and asked, "What are you willing to give me if I hand him over to you?" So they counted out for him thirty silver coins. ¹⁶From then on Judas watched for an opportunity to hand him over.

The Lord's Supper

26:17–19pp — Mk 14:12–16; Lk 22:7–13
26:20–24pp — Mk 14:17–21
26:26–29pp — Mk 14:22–25; Lk 22:17–20;
   1Co 11:23–25

¹⁷On the first day of the Feast of Unleavened Bread, the disciples came to Jesus and asked, "Where do you want us to make preparations for you to eat the Passover?"

¹⁸He replied, "Go into the city to a certain man and tell him, 'The Teacher says: My appointed time is near. I am going to celebrate the Passover with my disciples at your house.'" ¹⁹So the disciples did as Jesus had directed them and prepared the Passover.

²⁰When evening came, Jesus was reclining at the table with the Twelve. ²¹And while they were eating, he said, "I tell you the truth, one of you will betray me."

²²They were very sad and began to say to him one after the other, "Surely not I, Lord?"

²³Jesus replied, "The one who has dipped his hand into the bowl with me will betray me. ²⁴The Son of Man will go just as it is written about him. But woe to that man who betrays the Son of Man! It would be better for him if he had not been born."

²⁵Then Judas, the one who would betray him, said, "Surely not I, Rabbi?"

Jesus answered, "Yes, it is you."ᵃ

²⁶While they were eating, Jesus took bread, gave thanks and broke it, and gave it to his disciples, saying, "Take and eat; this is my body."

²⁷Then he took the cup, gave thanks and offered it to them, saying, "Drink from it, all of you. ²⁸This is my blood of theᵇ covenant, which is poured out for many for the forgiveness of sins. ²⁹I tell you, I will not drink of this fruit of the vine from now on until that day when I drink it anew with you in my Father's kingdom."

³⁰When they had sung a hymn, they went out to the Mount of Olives.

Jesus Predicts Peter's Denial

26:31–35pp — Mk 14:27–31; Lk 22:31–34

³¹Then Jesus told them, "This very night you will all fall away on account of me, for it is written:

" 'I will strike the shepherd,
   and the sheep of the flock will be
      scattered.'ᶜ

ᵃ *25* Or *"You yourself have said it"*   ᵇ *28* Some manuscripts *the new*   ᶜ *31* Zech. 13:7

³²But after I have risen, I will go ahead of you into Galilee."

³³Peter replied, "Even if all fall away on account of you, I never will."

³⁴"I tell you the truth," Jesus answered, "this very night, before the rooster crows, you will disown me three times."

³⁵But Peter declared, "Even if I have to die with you, I will never disown you." And all the other disciples said the same.

Gethsemane

26:36–46pp — Mk 14:32–42; Lk 22:40–46

³⁶Then Jesus went with his disciples to a place called Gethsemane, and he said to them, "Sit here while I go over there and pray." ³⁷He took Peter and the two sons of Zebedee along with him, and he began to be sorrowful and troubled. ³⁸Then he said to them, "My soul is overwhelmed with sorrow to the point of death. Stay here and keep watch with me."

³⁹Going a little farther, he fell with his face to the ground and prayed, "My Father, if it is possible, may this cup be taken from me. Yet not as I will, but as you will."

TALKING POINTS

Knowing God's Will

Even Jesus submitted his wishes and prayers to God's will.

MATTHEW 26:36–39

For more on knowing God's will, go to James 3:17.

⁴⁰Then he returned to his disciples and found them sleeping. "Could you men not keep watch with me for one hour?" he asked Peter. ⁴¹"Watch and pray so that you will not fall into temptation. The spirit is willing, but the body is weak."

⁴²He went away a second time and prayed, "My Father, if it is not possible for this cup to be taken away unless I drink it, may your will be done."

⁴³When he came back, he again found them sleeping, because their eyes were heavy. ⁴⁴So he left them and went away once more and prayed the third time, saying the same thing.

⁴⁵Then he returned to the disciples and said to them, "Are you still sleeping and resting? Look, the hour is near, and the Son of Man is betrayed into the hands of sinners. ⁴⁶Rise, let us go! Here comes my betrayer!"

Jesus Arrested

26:47–56pp — Mk 14:43–50; Lk 22:47–53

⁴⁷While he was still speaking, Judas, one of the Twelve, arrived. With him was a large crowd armed with swords and clubs, sent from the chief priests and the elders of the people. ⁴⁸Now the betrayer had arranged a signal with them: "The one I kiss is the man; arrest him." ⁴⁹Going at once to Jesus, Judas said, "Greetings, Rabbi!" and kissed him.

⁵⁰Jesus replied, "Friend, do what you came for."*

Then the men stepped forward, seized Jesus and arrested him. ⁵¹With that, one of Jesus' companions reached for his sword, drew it out and struck the servant of the high priest, cutting off his ear.

⁵²"Put your sword back in its place," Jesus said to him, "for all who draw the sword will die by the sword. ⁵³Do you think I cannot call on my Father, and he will at once put at my disposal more than twelve legions of angels? ⁵⁴But how then would the Scriptures be fulfilled that say it must happen in this way?"

⁵⁵At that time Jesus said to the crowd, "Am I leading a rebellion, that you have come out with swords and clubs to capture me? Every day I sat in the temple courts teaching, and you did not arrest me. ⁵⁶But this has all taken place that the writings of the prophets might be fulfilled." Then all the disciples deserted him and fled.

ª 50 Or "Friend, why have you come?"

Before the Sanhedrin

26:57–68pp — Mk 14:53–65; Jn 18:12,13,19–24

⁵⁷Those who had arrested Jesus took him to Caiaphas, the high priest, where the teachers of the law and the elders had assembled. ⁵⁸But Peter followed him at a distance, right up to the courtyard of the high priest. He entered and sat down with the guards to see the outcome.

⁵⁹The chief priests and the whole Sanhedrin were looking for false evidence against Jesus so that they could put him to death. ⁶⁰But they did not find any, though many false witnesses came forward.

Finally two came forward ⁶¹and declared, "This fellow said, 'I am able to destroy the temple of God and rebuild it in three days.'"

⁶²Then the high priest stood up and said to Jesus, "Are you not going to answer? What is this testimony that these men are bringing against you?" ⁶³But Jesus remained silent.

The high priest said to him, "I charge you under oath by the living God: Tell us if you are the Christ,ᵃ the Son of God."

⁶⁴"Yes, it is as you say," Jesus replied. "But I say to all of you: In the future you will see the Son of Man sitting at the right hand of the Mighty One and coming on the clouds of heaven."

⁶⁵Then the high priest tore his clothes and said, "He has spoken blasphemy! Why do we need any more witnesses? Look, now you have heard the blasphemy. ⁶⁶What do you think?"

"He is worthy of death," they answered.

⁶⁷Then they spit in his face and struck him with their fists. Others slapped him ⁶⁸and said, "Prophesy to us, Christ. Who hit you?"

Peter Disowns Jesus

26:69–75pp — Mk 14:66–72; Lk 22:55–62; Jn 18:16–18,25–27

⁶⁹Now Peter was sitting out in the courtyard, and a servant girl came to him. "You also were with Jesus of Galilee," she said.

⁷⁰But he denied it before them all. "I don't know what you're talking about," he said.

⁷¹Then he went out to the gateway, where another girl saw him and said to the people there, "This fellow was with Jesus of Nazareth."

⁷²He denied it again, with an oath: "I don't know the man!"

⁷³After a little while, those standing there went up to Peter and said, "Surely you are one of them, for your accent gives you away."

⁷⁴Then he began to call down curses on himself and he swore to them, "I don't know the man!"

Immediately a rooster crowed. ⁷⁵Then Peter remembered the word Jesus had spoken: "Before the rooster crows, you will disown me three times." And he went outside and wept bitterly.

Judas Hangs Himself

27 Early in the morning, all the chief priests and the elders of the people came to the decision to put Jesus to death. ²They bound him, led him away and handed him over to Pilate, the governor.

³When Judas, who had betrayed him, saw that Jesus was condemned, he was seized with remorse and returned the thirty silver coins to the chief priests and the elders. ⁴"I have sinned," he said, "for I have betrayed innocent blood."

"What is that to us?" they replied. "That's your responsibility."

⁵So Judas threw the money into the temple and left. Then he went away and hanged himself.

⁶The chief priests picked up the coins and said, "It is against the law to put this into the treasury, since it is blood money." ⁷So they decided to use the money to buy the potter's field as a burial place for foreigners. ⁸That is why it has been called the Field of Blood to this day. ⁹Then what was spoken by Jeremiah the prophet was fulfilled: "They took the thirty silver coins, the price set on him by the people of Israel, ¹⁰and they used them to buy the potter's field, as the Lord commanded me."ᵇ

ᵃ 63 Or *Messiah*; also in verse 68   ᵇ 10 See Zech. 11:12,13; Jer. 19:1-13; 32:6-9.

Jesus Before Pilate

27:11–26pp — Mk 15:2–15; Lk 23:2,3,18–25;
Jn 18:29–19:16

¹¹Meanwhile Jesus stood before the governor, and the governor asked him, "Are you the king of the Jews?"

"Yes, it is as you say," Jesus replied.

¹²When he was accused by the chief priests and the elders, he gave no answer. ¹³Then Pilate asked him, "Don't you hear the testimony they are bringing against you?" ¹⁴But Jesus made no reply, not even to a single charge—to the great amazement of the governor.

¹⁵Now it was the governor's custom at the Feast to release a prisoner chosen by the crowd. ¹⁶At that time they had a notorious prisoner, called Barabbas. ¹⁷So when the crowd had gathered, Pilate asked them, "Which one do you want me to release to you: Barabbas, or Jesus who is called Christ?" ¹⁸For he knew it was out of envy that they had handed Jesus over to him.

¹⁹While Pilate was sitting on the judge's seat, his wife sent him this message: "Don't have anything to do with that innocent man, for I have suffered a great deal today in a dream because of him."

²⁰But the chief priests and the elders persuaded the crowd to ask for Barabbas and to have Jesus executed.

²¹"Which of the two do you want me to release to you?" asked the governor.

"Barabbas," they answered.

²²"What shall I do, then, with Jesus who is called Christ?" Pilate asked.

They all answered, "Crucify him!"

²³"Why? What crime has he committed?" asked Pilate.

But they shouted all the louder, "Crucify him!"

²⁴When Pilate saw that he was getting nowhere, but that instead an uproar was starting, he took water and washed his hands in front of the crowd. "I am innocent of this man's blood," he said. "It is your responsibility!"

²⁵All the people answered, "Let his blood be on us and on our children!"

²⁶Then he released Barabbas to them. But he had Jesus flogged, and handed him over to be crucified.

The Soldiers Mock Jesus

27:27–31pp — Mk 15:16–20

²⁷Then the governor's soldiers took Jesus into the Praetorium and gathered the whole company of soldiers around him. ²⁸They stripped him and put a scarlet robe on him, ²⁹and then twisted together a crown of thorns and set it on his head. They put a staff in his right hand and knelt in front of him and mocked him. "Hail, king of the Jews!" they said. ³⁰They spit on him, and took the staff and struck him on the head again and again. ³¹After they had mocked him, they took off the robe and put his own clothes on him. Then they led him away to crucify him.

The Crucifixion

27:33–44pp — Mk 15:22–32; Lk 23:33–43;
Jn 19:17–24

³²As they were going out, they met a man from Cyrene, named Simon, and they forced him to carry the cross. ³³They came to a place called Golgotha (which means The Place of the Skull). ³⁴There they offered Jesus wine to drink, mixed with gall; but after tasting it, he refused to drink it. ³⁵When they had crucified him, they divided up his clothes by casting lots.ᵃ ³⁶And sitting down, they kept watch over him there. ³⁷Above his head they placed the written charge against him: THIS IS JESUS, THE KING OF THE JEWS. ³⁸Two robbers were crucified with him, one on his right and one on his left. ³⁹Those who passed by hurled insults at him, shaking their heads ⁴⁰and saying, "You who are going to destroy the temple and build it in three days, save yourself! Come down from the cross, if you are the Son of God!"

⁴¹In the same way the chief priests, the teachers of the law and the elders mocked him. ⁴²"He saved others," they said, "but he can't save himself! He's the King of Israel! Let him come down

---

ᵃ 35 A few late manuscripts *lots that the word spoken by the prophet might be fulfilled: "They divided my garments among themselves and cast lots for my clothing"* (Psalm 22:18) now from the cross, and we will believe in him. [43] He trusts in God. Let God rescue him now if he wants him, for he said, 'I am the Son of God.' " [44] In the same way the robbers who were crucified with him also heaped insults on him.

The Death of Jesus

27:45–56pp — Mk 15:33–41; Lk 23:44–49; Jn 19:29–30

[45] From the sixth hour until the ninth hour darkness came over all the land. [46] About the ninth hour Jesus cried out in a loud voice, *"Eloi, Eloi,[a] lama sabachthani?"* — which means, "My God, my God, why have you forsaken me?"[b] [47] When some of those standing there heard this, they said, "He's calling Elijah."

[48] Immediately one of them ran and got a sponge. He filled it with wine vinegar, put it on a stick, and offered it to Jesus to drink. [49] The rest said, "Now leave him alone. Let's see if Elijah comes to save him."

[50] And when Jesus had cried out again in a loud voice, he gave up his spirit.

[51] At that moment the curtain of the temple was torn in two from top to bottom. The earth shook and the rocks split. [52] The tombs broke open and the bodies of many holy people who had died were raised to life. [53] They came out of the tombs, and after Jesus' resurrection they went into the holy city and appeared to many people.

[54] When the centurion and those with him who were guarding Jesus saw the earthquake and all that had happened, they were terrified, and exclaimed, "Surely he was the Son[c] of God!"

[55] Many women were there, watching from a distance. They had followed Jesus from Galilee to care for his needs. [56] Among them were Mary Magdalene, Mary the mother of James and Joses, and the mother of Zebedee's sons.

The Burial of Jesus

27:57–61pp — Mk 15:42–47; Lk 23:50–56; Jn 19:38–42

[57] As evening approached, there came a rich man from Arimathea, named Joseph, who had himself become a disciple of Jesus. [58] Going to Pilate, he asked for Jesus' body, and Pilate ordered that it be given to him. [59] Joseph took the body, wrapped it in a clean linen cloth, [60] and placed it in his own new tomb that he had cut out of the rock. He rolled a big stone in front of the entrance to the tomb and went away. [61] Mary Magdalene and the other Mary were sitting there opposite the tomb.

The Guard at the Tomb

[62] The next day, the one after Preparation Day, the chief priests and the Pharisees went to Pilate. [63] "Sir," they said, "we remember that while he was still alive that deceiver said, 'After three days I will rise again.' [64] So give the order for the tomb to be made secure until the third day. Otherwise, his disciples may come and steal the body and tell the people that he has been raised from the dead. This last deception will be worse than the first."

[65] "Take a guard," Pilate answered. "Go, make the tomb as secure as you know how." [66] So they went and made the tomb secure by putting a seal on the stone and posting the guard.

The Resurrection

28:1–8pp — Mk 16:1–8; Lk 24:1–10; Jn 20:1–8

28 After the Sabbath, at dawn on the first day of the week, Mary Magdalene and the other Mary went to look at the tomb.

[2] There was a violent earthquake, for an angel of the Lord came down from heaven and, going to the tomb, rolled back the stone and sat on it. [3] His appearance was like lightning, and his clothes were white as snow. [4] The guards were so afraid of him that they shook and became like dead men.

[5] The angel said to the women, "Do not be afraid, for I know that you are looking for Jesus, who was crucified. [6] He is not here; he has risen, just as he said. Come and see the place where he lay. [7] Then go quickly and tell his disciples: 'He has risen from the dead and is going ahead of you into Galilee. There you will see him.' Now I have told you."

[a] 46 Some manuscripts Eli, Eli *[b] 46 Psalm 22:1* *[c] 54 Or a son*

⁸So the women hurried away from the tomb, afraid yet filled with joy, and ran to tell his disciples. ⁹Suddenly Jesus met them. "Greetings," he said. They came to him, clasped his feet and worshiped him. ¹⁰Then Jesus said to them, "Do not be afraid. Go and tell my brothers to go to Galilee; there they will see me."

The Guards' Report

¹¹While the women were on their way, some of the guards went into the city and reported to the chief priests everything that had happened. ¹²When the chief priests had met with the elders and devised a plan, they gave the soldiers a large sum of money, ¹³telling them, "You are to say, 'His disciples came during the night and stole him away while we were asleep.' ¹⁴If this report gets to the governor, we will satisfy him and keep you out of trouble." ¹⁵So the soldiers took the money and did as they were instructed. And this story has been widely circulated among the Jews to this very day.

The Great Commission

¹⁶Then the eleven disciples went to Galilee, to the mountain where Jesus had told them to go. ¹⁷When they saw him, they worshiped him; but some doubted. ¹⁸Then Jesus came to them and said, "All authority in heaven and on earth has been given to me. ¹⁹Therefore go and make disciples of all nations, baptizing them in *ᵃ* the name

TALKING POINTS

Sharing Your Faith

Jesus asks us to share our faith.

MATTHEW 28:18-20

For more on sharing your faith, go to Acts 1:8.

of the Father and of the Son and of the Holy Spirit, ²⁰and teaching them to obey everything I have commanded you. And surely I am with you always, to the very end of the age."

ᵃ 19 Or *into*; see Acts 8:16; 19:5; Romans 6:3; 1 Cor. 1:13; 10:2 and Gal. 3:27.

PRAYING THE SCRIPTURES

Protection

MATTHEW 28:20

Dear Jesus, according to your promise to your first disciples, I pray that you will be with my grandchild always, to the very end.

Next prayer in Protection Prayer Track:
2 Thessalonians 3:3,5

Action-Packed LIVING

We are a society that bustles with activity. Television bombards us with action-packed reality shows. TV dramas contain high-speed chases and exciting exploits. Cell phones and email force us to respond quickly to others. We're even active grandmothers, as we mentor, coach and care for our grandchildren — being actively involved in their lives while still living dynamic lives of our own.

So we should relate easily to the book of Mark. This Gospel is a fast-paced story that focuses on what Jesus did while on Earth: He healed the sick, cast out demons, called his disciples, prayed to his Father and taught the people. Mark used a Greek word that is translated "immediately," "at once," "without delay," "quickly" or "just then" 47 times, lending a sense of urgency to his account of Jesus' life. Mark devoted much of his book to Jesus' final days, highlighting the importance of Christ's sacrifice made for our salvation.

The Gospel of Mark emphasizes that God is a God of action — nothing can stop him. These are precious words of reassurance whenever we face seemingly insurmountable difficulties in our lives or in the lives of our children or grandchildren. We may see the entire set of circumstances as totally hopeless — completely impossible. But that's just our perspective. With God all things are possible.

VERSE *to* REMEMBER | MARK 10:27

Jesus looked at them and said, "With man this is impossible, but not with God; all things are possible with God."

ABOUT MARK

WRITTEN BY:
John Mark, who recorded and arranged the stories that Peter told about Jesus

WRITTEN FOR:
Gentile readers, probably in the church at Rome

DATE WRITTEN:
Sometime between A.D. 50 and 70

WHY WRITTEN:
To show people who Jesus is by telling them what he did

John the Baptist Prepares the Way
1:2–8pp — Mt 3:1–11; Lk 3:2–16

1 The beginning of the gospel about Jesus Christ, the Son of God.[a]

²It is written in Isaiah the prophet:

"I will send my messenger ahead of you,
who will prepare your way"[b]—
³"a voice of one calling in the desert,
'Prepare the way for the Lord,
make straight paths for him.'"[c]

⁴And so John came, baptizing in the desert region and preaching a baptism of repentance for the forgiveness of sins. ⁵The whole Judean countryside and all the people of Jerusalem went out to him. Confessing their sins, they were baptized by him in the Jordan River. ⁶John wore clothing made of camel's hair, with a leather belt around his waist, and he ate locusts and wild honey. ⁷And this was his message: "After me will come one more powerful than I, the thongs of whose sandals I am not worthy to stoop down and untie. ⁸I baptize you with[d] water, but he will baptize you with the Holy Spirit."

The Baptism and Temptation of Jesus
1:9–11pp — Mt 3:13–17; Lk 3:21,22
1:12,13pp — Mt 4:1–11; Lk 4:1–13

⁹At that time Jesus came from Nazareth in Galilee and was baptized by John in the Jordan. ¹⁰As Jesus was coming up out of the water, he saw heaven being torn open and the Spirit descending on him like a dove. ¹¹And a voice came from heaven: "You are my Son, whom I love; with you I am well pleased."

¹²At once the Spirit sent him out into the desert, ¹³and he was in the desert forty days, being tempted by Satan. He was with the wild animals, and angels attended him.

The Calling of the First Disciples
1:16–20pp — Mt 4:18–22; Lk 5:2–11; Jn 1:35–42

¹⁴After John was put in prison, Jesus went into Galilee, proclaiming the good news of God.

¹⁵"The time has come," he said. "The kingdom of God is near. Repent and believe the good news!"

¹⁶As Jesus walked beside the Sea of Galilee, he saw Simon and his brother Andrew casting a net into the lake, for they were fishermen. ¹⁷"Come, follow me," Jesus said, "and I will make you fishers of men." ¹⁸At once they left their nets and followed him.

¹⁹When he had gone a little farther, he saw James son of Zebedee and his brother John in a boat, preparing their nets. ²⁰Without delay he called them, and they left their father Zebedee in the boat with the hired men and followed him.

Jesus Drives Out an Evil Spirit
1:21–28pp — Lk 4:31–37

²¹They went to Capernaum, and when the Sabbath came, Jesus went into the synagogue and began to teach. ²²The people were amazed at his teaching, because he taught them as one who had authority, not as the teachers of the law. ²³Just then a man in their synagogue who was possessed by an evil[e] spirit cried out, ²⁴"What do you want with us, Jesus of Nazareth? Have you come to destroy us? I know who you are—the Holy One of God!"

²⁵"Be quiet!" said Jesus sternly. "Come out of him!" ²⁶The evil spirit shook the man violently and came out of him with a shriek.

²⁷The people were all so amazed that they asked each other, "What is this? A new teaching—and with authority! He even gives orders to evil spirits and they obey him." ²⁸News about him spread quickly over the whole region of Galilee.

Jesus Heals Many
1:29–31pp — Mt 8:14,15; Lk 4:38,39
1:32–34pp — Mt 8:16,17; Lk 4:40,41

²⁹As soon as they left the synagogue, they went with James and John to the home of Simon and Andrew. ³⁰Simon's mother-in-law was in bed with a fever, and they told Jesus about her. ³¹So he went to her, took her hand and helped her up. The fever left her and she began to wait on them.

---

[a] 1 Some manuscripts do not have *the Son of God.*   [b] 2 Mal. 3:1   [c] 3 Isaiah 40:3   [d] 8 Or *in*   [e] 23 Greek *unclean*; also in verses 26 and 27

SIMON'S MOTHER-IN-LAW WAS IN
BED WITH A FEVER, AND THEY TOLD
JESUS ABOUT HER. SO HE WENT TO
HER, TOOK HER HAND AND HELPED
HER UP. THE FEVER LEFT HER AND
SHE BEGAN TO WAIT ON THEM.

Mark 1:30 – 31

Holiness and Domesticity

PHYLLIS TICKLE

READ | MARK 1:29 – 34

I have been thinking about this reading. There are few stories in the Gospels — few private glimpses of daily life — that are dearer to my reading time than this one. The Gospel writers must have felt the same way, for three out of the four include Peter's mother-in-law in their writings, and it seems especially significant that hers should be one of the stories opening Mark's Gospel as well as our new year [of the church calendar]. Its placement at the beginning of things becomes an assertion of sorts, an assertion of the humanness of the Christ and of domesticity as integral to his incarnation.

No part of life flies so completely in the face of our human notions of holiness and saintliness and transcendence as does domesticity, with its diurnal responsibilities, financial anxieties, marital tensions and physical labor. Nothing draws us farther from meditation and more into immediacy than does the world of the home. Nothing. Yet here and throughout Jesus' biography, Holy Writ speaks frequently in domestic metaphors, and often of his domestic concerns. What, I wonder this morning, am I to infer from all this save that in engaging life prayerfully, he would have us know that we are engaging the kingdom?

Lord Jesus, your Word shows how deeply you cared about this woman with a fever and about her daily life. Thank you for caring for me as I go about my daily life, doing all the routine things running a household involves. Bless my work, Lord, that it may bless those for whom I do it.

Your next devotion is located on page 1346.

GRANDCHILD IN FOCUS • PRAYER

Physical Well-Being

Almighty God, Creator of us all, I pray that you will watch over my grandchild's physical development. May he grow in strength through the stages of his life. As he grows in awareness of his body, help him to understand that each body develops uniquely, yet is within your plan and your control. Please guard his health so that his diseases are few, his injuries are minor and his infirmities are brief. Amen.

³²That evening after sunset the people brought to Jesus all the sick and demon-possessed. ³³The whole town gathered at the door, ³⁴and Jesus healed many who had various diseases. He also drove out many demons, but he would not let the demons speak because they knew who he was.

Jesus Prays in a Solitary Place
1:35–38pp — Lk 4:42,43

³⁵Very early in the morning, while it was still dark, Jesus got up, left the house and went off to a solitary place, where he prayed. ³⁶Simon and his companions went to look for him, ³⁷and when they found him, they exclaimed: "Everyone is looking for you!"

³⁸Jesus replied, "Let us go somewhere else—to the nearby villages—so I can preach there also. That is why I have come." ³⁹So he traveled throughout Galilee, preaching in their synagogues and driving out demons.

A Man With Leprosy
1:40–44pp — Mt 8:2–4; Lk 5:12–14

⁴⁰A man with leprosy*ᵃ* came to him and begged him on his knees, "If you are willing, you can make me clean."

⁴¹Filled with compassion, Jesus reached out his hand and touched the man. "I am willing," he said. "Be clean!" ⁴²Immediately the leprosy left him and he was cured.

⁴³Jesus sent him away at once with a strong warning: ⁴⁴"See that you don't tell this to anyone. But go, show yourself to the priest and offer the sacrifices that Moses commanded for your cleansing, as a testimony to them." ⁴⁵Instead he went out and began to talk freely, spreading the news. As a result, Jesus could no longer enter a town openly but stayed outside in lonely places. Yet the people still came to him from everywhere.

Jesus Heals a Paralytic
2:3–12pp — Mt 9:2–8; Lk 5:18–26

2 A few days later, when Jesus again entered Capernaum, the people heard that he had come home. ²So many gathered that there was no room left, not even outside the door, and he preached the word to them. ³Some men came, bringing to him a paralytic, carried by four of them. ⁴Since they could not get him to Jesus because of the crowd, they made an opening in the roof above Jesus and, after digging through it, lowered the mat the paralyzed man was lying on. ⁵When Jesus saw their faith, he said to the paralytic, "Son, your sins are forgiven."

⁶Now some teachers of the law were sitting there, thinking to themselves, ⁷"Why does this fellow talk like that? He's blaspheming! Who can forgive sins but God alone?"

⁸Immediately Jesus knew in his spirit that this

ᵃ 40 The Greek word was used for various diseases affecting the skin—not necessarily leprosy.

stories to share

MARK 2:1–12

A Hole in the Roof

LIFE LESSON: Jesus has the power to forgive sins and to heal people.

TO TALK ABOUT

✦ Why did the man's friends have to lower him through the roof?

✦ What did Jesus say to the paralyzed man? Does this surprise you? Why or why not?

✦ What did Jesus want to teach the Pharisees in this situation?

✦ Which is more important to you: forgiven sins or a healthy body? Why?

> VERY EARLY IN THE MORNING,
> WHILE IT WAS STILL DARK, JESUS
> GOT UP, LEFT THE HOUSE AND
> WENT OFF TO A SOLITARY PLACE,
> WHERE HE PRAYED.
>
> *Mark 1:35*

Mimi's Quilt Pieces of Grace

BOBBIE WOLGEMUTH

READ | MARK 1:35 – 39

Mimi was a grandmother from Pennsylvania farm country who was a powerhouse of prayer. She made gorgeous quilts with hand stitches so tiny that patterned works of art burst forth from the fabric. Mimi spent her early mornings kneeling in prayer next to a small bed draped with one of her handmade quilts. With her elbows up on the edge of the quilt, she prayed for her children and grandchildren, for missionaries, for churches, for the neighbors, for world events, for just about everything that the Lord Jesus brought to her mind as she knelt beside the bed every morning.

During the day, as she canned fruit, cooked, cleaned or shopped, Mimi continued her prayer service for those who came to her mind. At age 97, Mimi died, and her family gathered her few simple belongings and set aside a quilt for each grandchild. There was one particular quilt that was the family's most prized possession. Not having one of the prettiest patterns or colors, the treasured quilt was the one with two small spots on the edge where Mimi's elbows had worn into the fabric when she knelt to pray.

One of Mimi's granddaughters now has the prayer quilt and the next generation will be told about the small woman who delighted in time on her knees before the throne of God. What will your children and grandchildren treasure when you're gone? Maybe a prayer journal in which you've written their names and a verse you prayed for each child will be the most valuable thing you leave behind. Invest in time before the Father's throne today. Rocking chairs, piano benches and quilts can become places of prayer that carry your children and grandchildren to the place of blessing. Leave behind pieces of grace for every child.

Father in heaven, thank you for the privilege of prayer. Today remind me that you are the giver of gifts that last forever. Help me to invest in eternal things that will remind my grandchildren and great-grandchildren of your love and power. I want to give them the gift of prayer. Amen.

Your next devotion is located on page 1348.

GRANDCHILD IN FOCUS • PRAYER

Emotional Development

O God, Creator of mind and body, I pray that you will give my grandchild emotional health and strength. Where there is anger, bring peace. Where there is confusion, bring clarity and focus. Where there are dark shadows, cast a ray of hope. Fill her with the sunshine of your Spirit. Warm her with the presence of your peace. Amen.

was what they were thinking in their hearts, and he said to them, "Why are you thinking these things? ⁹Which is easier: to say to the paralytic, 'Your sins are forgiven,' or to say, 'Get up, take your mat and walk'? ¹⁰But that you may know that the Son of Man has authority on earth to forgive sins . . ." He said to the paralytic, ¹¹"I tell you, get up, take your mat and go home." ¹²He got up, took his mat and walked out in full view of them all. This amazed everyone and they praised God, saying, "We have never seen anything like this!"

The Calling of Levi

2:14–17pp — Mt 9:9–13; Lk 5:27–32

¹³Once again Jesus went out beside the lake. A large crowd came to him, and he began to teach them. ¹⁴As he walked along, he saw Levi son of Alphaeus sitting at the tax collector's booth. "Follow me," Jesus told him, and Levi got up and followed him.

¹⁵While Jesus was having dinner at Levi's house, many tax collectors and "sinners" were eating with him and his disciples, for there were many who followed him. ¹⁶When the teachers of the law who were Pharisees saw him eating with the "sinners" and tax collectors, they asked his disciples: "Why does he eat with tax collectors and 'sinners'?"

¹⁷On hearing this, Jesus said to them, "It is not the healthy who need a doctor, but the sick. I have not come to call the righteous, but sinners."

Jesus Questioned About Fasting

2:18–22pp — Mt 9:14–17; Lk 5:33–38

¹⁸Now John's disciples and the Pharisees were fasting. Some people came and asked Jesus, "How is it that John's disciples and the disciples of the Pharisees are fasting, but yours are not?"

¹⁹Jesus answered, "How can the guests of the bridegroom fast while he is with them? They cannot, so long as they have him with them. ²⁰But the time will come when the bridegroom will be taken from them, and on that day they will fast.

²¹"No one sews a patch of unshrunk cloth on an old garment. If he does, the new piece will pull away from the old, making the tear worse. ²²And no one pours new wine into old wineskins. If he does, the wine will burst the skins, and both the wine and the wineskins will be ruined. No, he pours new wine into new wineskins."

Lord of the Sabbath

2:23–28pp — Mt 12:1–8; Lk 6:1–5
3:1–6pp — Mt 12:9–14; Lk 6:6–11

²³One Sabbath Jesus was going through the grainfields, and as his disciples walked along, they began to pick some heads of grain. ²⁴The Pharisees said to him, "Look, why are they doing what is unlawful on the Sabbath?"

²⁵He answered, "Have you never read what David did when he and his companions were hungry and in need? ²⁶In the days of Abiathar the high priest, he entered the house of God and ate the consecrated bread, which is lawful only for priests to eat. And he also gave some to his companions."

²⁷Then he said to them, "The Sabbath was made for man, not man for the Sabbath. ²⁸So the Son of Man is Lord even of the Sabbath."

3 Another time he went into the synagogue, and a man with a shriveled hand was there. ²Some of them were looking for a reason to accuse Jesus, so they watched him closely to see if he would heal him on the Sabbath. ³Jesus said to the man with the shriveled hand, "Stand up in front of everyone."

⁴Then Jesus asked them, "Which is lawful on the Sabbath: to do good or to do evil, to save life or to kill?" But they remained silent.

⁵He looked around at them in anger and, deeply distressed at their stubborn hearts, said to the man, "Stretch out your hand." He stretched it out, and his hand was completely restored. ⁶Then the Pharisees went out and began to plot with the Herodians how they might kill Jesus.

Crowds Follow Jesus

3:7–12pp — Mt 12:15,16; Lk 6:17–19

⁷Jesus withdrew with his disciples to the lake, and a large crowd from Galilee followed. ⁸When

WHILE JESUS WAS HAVING
DINNER AT LEVI'S HOUSE, MANY
TAX COLLECTORS AND "SINNERS"
WERE EATING WITH HIM AND
HIS DISCIPLES, FOR THERE WERE
MANY WHO FOLLOWED HIM.

Mark 2:15

The Gift of Hospitality

MARY RUTH HOWES

READ | MARK 2:13 – 17

For the years of his ministry, Jesus had no permanent home. He stayed in other people's homes and ate other people's meals. He told some would-be followers that though birds and animals had nests and lairs, he had no place to lay his head. Yet Jesus had a strong sense of home — God was his home. Even at twelve, he wanted to be in his Father's house.

But his lack of a place of his own meant that he offered the people he met a chance to show hospitality. And so we keep reading in the gospels of invitations to meals that Jesus accepted — sometimes with pleasure, sometimes with frustration.

I saw the gift of hospitality worked out in my parents' lives. In spite of never owning a physical house in their forty-seven years of marriage, they were continually opening their home — wherever or whatever it was — to others. Even in the Japanese internment camp in China during World War II, our family of four would have one or another of the single folk up to our cubicle (we shared one seventeen-by-forty-five-foot room with nine other people) to eat with us and share our "homeness." And though he lived alone for ten years after my mother died, my father still invited people over to share his homemade turkey soup on Sunday after church — often a newcomer, or one or two single people.

Lord, forgive me for feeling I must wait until my house is in perfect order before I can invite others in. Help me to remember that a home is created far more by the spirit of the people who live in it than by its physical perfection.

Your next devotion is located on page 1353.

GRANDCHILD IN FOCUS • PRAYER

Spiritual Growth

Dear Lord, today I pray for my grandchild's spiritual growth. I ask that you instill in him the desire to read and memorize your Word. Give him a passion to be in conversation with you. May loving and serving you be part of his daily life. I ask that you stay close to him and lead him to be transformed to your likeness, to reflect your grace and to radiate your love. I pray this in Jesus' name, amen.

they heard all he was doing, many people came to him from Judea, Jerusalem, Idumea, and the regions across the Jordan and around Tyre and Sidon. [9]Because of the crowd he told his disciples to have a small boat ready for him, to keep the people from crowding him. [10]For he had healed many, so that those with diseases were pushing forward to touch him. [11]Whenever the evil[a] spirits saw him, they fell down before him and cried out, "You are the Son of God." [12]But he gave them strict orders not to tell who he was.

The Appointing of the Twelve Apostles
3:16–19pp — Mt 10:2–4; Lk 6:14–16; Ac 1:13

[13]Jesus went up on a mountainside and called to him those he wanted, and they came to him. [14]He appointed twelve—designating them apostles[b]—that they might be with him and that he might send them out to preach [15]and to have authority to drive out demons. [16]These are the twelve he appointed: Simon (to whom he gave the name Peter); [17]James son of Zebedee and his brother John (to them he gave the name Boanerges, which means Sons of Thunder); [18]Andrew, Philip, Bartholomew, Matthew, Thomas, James son of Alphaeus, Thaddaeus, Simon the Zealot [19]and Judas Iscariot, who betrayed him.

Jesus and Beelzebub
3:23–27pp — Mt 12:25–29; Lk 11:17–22

[20]Then Jesus entered a house, and again a crowd gathered, so that he and his disciples were not even able to eat. [21]When his family heard about this, they went to take charge of him, for they said, "He is out of his mind."

[22]And the teachers of the law who came down from Jerusalem said, "He is possessed by Beelzebub[c]! By the prince of demons he is driving out demons."

[23]So Jesus called them and spoke to them in parables: "How can Satan drive out Satan? [24]If a kingdom is divided against itself, that kingdom cannot stand. [25]If a house is divided against itself, that house cannot stand. [26]And if Satan opposes himself and is divided, he cannot stand; his end

has come. [27]In fact, no one can enter a strong man's house and carry off his possessions unless he first ties up the strong man. Then he can rob his house. [28]I tell you the truth, all the sins and blasphemies of men will be forgiven them. [29]But whoever blasphemes against the Holy Spirit will never be forgiven; he is guilty of an eternal sin."

[30]He said this because they were saying, "He has an evil spirit."

Jesus' Mother and Brothers
3:31–35pp — Mt 12:46–50; Lk 8:19–21

[31]Then Jesus' mother and brothers arrived. Standing outside, they sent someone in to call him. [32]A crowd was sitting around him, and they told him, "Your mother and brothers are outside looking for you."

[33]"Who are my mother and my brothers?" he asked.

[34]Then he looked at those seated in a circle around him and said, "Here are my mother and my brothers! [35]Whoever does God's will is my brother and sister and mother."

The Parable of the Sower
4:1–12pp — Mt 13:1–15; Lk 8:4–10
4:13–20pp — Mt 13:18–23; Lk 8:11–15

4 Again Jesus began to teach by the lake. The crowd that gathered around him was so large that he got into a boat and sat in it out on the lake, while all the people were along the shore at the water's edge. [2]He taught them many things by parables, and in his teaching said: [3]"Listen! A farmer went out to sow his seed. [4]As he was scattering the seed, some fell along the path, and the birds came and ate it up. [5]Some fell on rocky places, where it did not have much soil. It sprang up quickly, because the soil was shallow. [6]But when the sun came up, the plants were scorched, and they withered because they had no root. [7]Other seed fell among thorns, which grew up and choked the plants, so that they did not bear grain. [8]Still other seed fell on good soil. It came

---

[a] 11 Greek *unclean;* also in verse 30   [b] 14 Some manuscripts do not have *designating them apostles.*   [c] 22 Greek *Beezeboul* or *Beelzeboul*

up, grew and produced a crop, multiplying thirty, sixty, or even a hundred times."

⁹Then Jesus said, "He who has ears to hear, let him hear."

¹⁰When he was alone, the Twelve and the others around him asked him about the parables. ¹¹He told them, "The secret of the kingdom of God has been given to you. But to those on the outside everything is said in parables ¹²so that,

" 'they may be ever seeing but never
> perceiving,
and ever hearing but never understanding;
otherwise they might turn and be forgiven!' ᵃ"

¹³Then Jesus said to them, "Don't you understand this parable? How then will you understand any parable? ¹⁴The farmer sows the word. ¹⁵Some people are like seed along the path, where the word is sown. As soon as they hear it, Satan comes and takes away the word that was sown in them. ¹⁶Others, like seed sown on rocky places, hear the word and at once receive it with joy. ¹⁷But since they have no root, they last only a short time. When trouble or persecution comes because of the word, they quickly fall away. ¹⁸Still others, like seed sown among thorns, hear the word; ¹⁹but the worries of this life, the deceitfulness of wealth and the desires for other things come in and choke the word, making it unfruitful. ²⁰Others, like seed sown on good soil, hear the word, accept it, and produce a crop—thirty, sixty or even a hundred times what was sown."

A Lamp on a Stand

²¹He said to them, "Do you bring in a lamp to put it under a bowl or a bed? Instead, don't you put it on its stand? ²²For whatever is hidden is meant to be disclosed, and whatever is concealed is meant to be brought out into the open. ²³If anyone has ears to hear, let him hear."

²⁴"Consider carefully what you hear," he continued. "With the measure you use, it will be measured to you—and even more. ²⁵Whoever has will be given more; whoever does not have, even what he has will be taken from him."

The Parable of the Growing Seed

²⁶He also said, "This is what the kingdom of God is like. A man scatters seed on the ground. ²⁷Night and day, whether he sleeps or gets up, the seed sprouts and grows, though he does not know how. ²⁸All by itself the soil produces grain—first the stalk, then the head, then the full kernel in the head. ²⁹As soon as the grain is ripe, he puts the sickle to it, because the harvest has come."

The Parable of the Mustard Seed
4:30–32pp — Mt 13:31,32; Lk 13:18,19

³⁰Again he said, "What shall we say the kingdom of God is like, or what parable shall we use to describe it? ³¹It is like a mustard seed, which is the smallest seed you plant in the ground. ³²Yet when planted, it grows and becomes the largest of all garden plants, with such big branches that the birds of the air can perch in its shade."

³³With many similar parables Jesus spoke the word to them, as much as they could understand. ³⁴He did not say anything to them without using a parable. But when he was alone with his own disciples, he explained everything.

Jesus Calms the Storm
4:35–41pp — Mt 8:18,23–27; Lk 8:22–25

³⁵That day when evening came, he said to his disciples, "Let us go over to the other side." ³⁶Leaving the crowd behind, they took him along, just as he was, in the boat. There were also other boats with him. ³⁷A furious squall came up, and the waves broke over the boat, so that it was nearly swamped. ³⁸Jesus was in the stern, sleeping on a cushion. The disciples woke him and said to him, "Teacher, don't you care if we drown?"

³⁹He got up, rebuked the wind and said to the waves, "Quiet! Be still!" Then the wind died down and it was completely calm.

⁴⁰He said to his disciples, "Why are you so afraid? Do you still have no faith?"

⁴¹They were terrified and asked each other, "Who is this? Even the wind and the waves obey him!"

ᵃ 12 Isaiah 6:9,10

MARK 4:35–41

Jesus Calms the Storm

LIFE LESSON: Jesus has power over nature.

TO TALK ABOUT

✦ Where was Jesus during the storm? What was he doing?

✦ What did the frightened disciples ask Jesus after they woke him up?

✦ After Jesus calmed the storm, why did the disciples ask each other, "Who is this?"

✦ What makes you afraid? How can Jesus help calm your fear?

The Healing of a Demon-possessed Man

5:1–17pp — Mt 8:28–34; Lk 8:26–37
5:18–20pp — Lk 8:38,39

5 They went across the lake to the region of the Gerasenes. [a] ²When Jesus got out of the boat, a man with an evil [b] spirit came from the tombs to meet him. ³This man lived in the tombs, and no one could bind him any more, not even with a chain. ⁴For he had often been chained hand and foot, but he tore the chains apart and broke the irons on his feet. No one was strong enough to subdue him. ⁵Night and day among the tombs and in the hills he would cry out and cut himself with stones.

⁶When he saw Jesus from a distance, he ran and fell on his knees in front of him. ⁷He shouted at the top of his voice, "What do you want with me, Jesus, Son of the Most High God? Swear to God that you won't torture me!" ⁸For Jesus had said to him, "Come out of this man, you evil spirit!"

⁹Then Jesus asked him, "What is your name?"

"My name is Legion," he replied, "for we are many." ¹⁰And he begged Jesus again and again not to send them out of the area.

¹¹A large herd of pigs was feeding on the nearby hillside. ¹²The demons begged Jesus, "Send us among the pigs; allow us to go into them." ¹³He gave them permission, and the evil spirits came out and went into the pigs. The herd, about two thousand in number, rushed down the steep bank into the lake and were drowned.

¹⁴Those tending the pigs ran off and reported this in the town and countryside, and the people went out to see what had happened. ¹⁵When they came to Jesus, they saw the man who had been possessed by the legion of demons, sitting there, dressed and in his right mind; and they were afraid. ¹⁶Those who had seen it told the people what had happened to the demon-possessed man—and told about the pigs as well. ¹⁷Then the people began to plead with Jesus to leave their region.

¹⁸As Jesus was getting into the boat, the man who had been demon-possessed begged to go with him. ¹⁹Jesus did not let him, but said, "Go home to your family and tell them how much the Lord has done for you, and how he has had mercy on you." ²⁰So the man went away and began to tell in the Decapolis [c] how much Jesus had done for him. And all the people were amazed.

A Dead Girl and a Sick Woman

5:22–43pp — Mt 9:18–26; Lk 8:41–56

²¹When Jesus had again crossed over by boat to the other side of the lake, a large crowd gathered around him while he was by the lake. ²²Then one of the synagogue rulers, named Jairus, came there. Seeing Jesus, he fell at his feet ²³and pleaded earnestly with him, "My little daughter is dying.

---

[a] 1 Some manuscripts *Gadarenes*; other manuscripts *Gergesenes*
[b] 2 Greek *unclean*; also in verses 8 and 13   [c] 20 That is, the Ten Cities

Please come and put your hands on her so that she will be healed and live." ²⁴So Jesus went with him.

A large crowd followed and pressed around him. ²⁵And a woman was there who had been subject to bleeding for twelve years. ²⁶She had suffered a great deal under the care of many doctors and had spent all she had, yet instead of getting better she grew worse. ²⁷When she heard about Jesus, she came up behind him in the crowd and touched his cloak, ²⁸because she thought, "If I just touch his clothes, I will be healed." ²⁹Immediately her bleeding stopped and she felt in her body that she was freed from her suffering.

³⁰At once Jesus realized that power had gone out from him. He turned around in the crowd and asked, "Who touched my clothes?"

³¹"You see the people crowding against you," his disciples answered, "and yet you can ask, 'Who touched me?'"

³²But Jesus kept looking around to see who had done it. ³³Then the woman, knowing what had happened to her, came and fell at his feet and, trembling with fear, told him the whole truth. ³⁴He said to her, "Daughter, your faith has healed you. Go in peace and be freed from your suffering."

³⁵While Jesus was still speaking, some men came from the house of Jairus, the synagogue ruler. "Your daughter is dead," they said. "Why bother the teacher any more?"

³⁶Ignoring what they said, Jesus told the synagogue ruler, "Don't be afraid; just believe."

³⁷He did not let anyone follow him except Peter, James and John the brother of James. ³⁸When they came to the home of the synagogue ruler, Jesus saw a commotion, with people crying and wailing loudly. ³⁹He went in and said to them, "Why all this commotion and wailing? The child is not dead but asleep." ⁴⁰But they laughed at him.

After he put them all out, he took the child's father and mother and the disciples who were with him, and went in where the child was. ⁴¹He took her by the hand and said to her, "Talitha koum!" (which means, "Little girl, I say to you,

get up!"). ⁴²Immediately the girl stood up and walked around (she was twelve years old). At this they were completely astonished. ⁴³He gave strict orders not to let anyone know about this, and told them to give her something to eat.

A Prophet Without Honor
6:1–6pp — Mt 13:54–58

6 Jesus left there and went to his hometown, accompanied by his disciples. ²When the Sabbath came, he began to teach in the synagogue, and many who heard him were amazed.

"Where did this man get these things?" they asked. "What's this wisdom that has been given him, that he even does miracles! ³Isn't this the carpenter? Isn't this Mary's son and the brother of James, Joseph,ᵃ Judas and Simon? Aren't his sisters here with us?" And they took offense at him.

⁴Jesus said to them, "Only in his hometown, among his relatives and in his own house is a prophet without honor." ⁵He could not do any miracles there, except lay his hands on a few sick people and heal them. ⁶And he was amazed at their lack of faith.

Jesus Sends Out the Twelve
6:7–11pp — Mt 10:1,9–14; Lk 9:1,3–5

Then Jesus went around teaching from village to village. ⁷Calling the Twelve to him, he sent them out two by two and gave them authority over evilᵇ spirits.

⁸These were his instructions: "Take nothing for the journey except a staff—no bread, no bag, no money in your belts. ⁹Wear sandals but not an extra tunic. ¹⁰Whenever you enter a house, stay there until you leave that town. ¹¹And if any place will not welcome you or listen to you, shake the dust off your feet when you leave, as a testimony against them."

¹²They went out and preached that people should repent. ¹³They drove out many demons and anointed many sick people with oil and healed them.

ᵃ 3 Greek *Joses*, a variant of *Joseph*   ᵇ 7 Greek *unclean*

> WHEN THE SABBATH CAME, HE BEGAN
> TO TEACH IN THE SYNAGOGUE, AND
> MANY WHO HEARD HIM WERE AMAZED.
> "WHERE DID THIS MAN GET THESE
> THINGS?" THEY ASKED. "WHAT'S THIS
> WISDOM THAT HAS BEEN GIVEN HIM,
> THAT HE EVEN DOES MIRACLES!"
>
> *Mark 6:2*

Unconventional

PATSY CLAIRMONT

READ | MARK 6:1 – 6

Jesus' conspicuously unconventional behavior caused others to take a second gander. I mean, this humble man made divine proclamations that caused even the clergy to huddle. Dismayed by Jesus' bizarre ways and his influence on the populace, the religious leaders plotted his demise.

Folks were abuzz when the off-putting Bethlehem man showed up in their town and healed the afflicted on the Sabbath. Jesus left people aghast and in awe as he created outlandish controversy wherever he went. He deliberately stepped across traditional lines in such miraculous and peculiar ways: turning water into wine, touching lepers, forgiving prostitutes, raising the dead, keeping company with social outcasts, and casting out demons — to name just a few of his startling choices.

Do you think the Lord's ways seem outlandish to us because just capturing a glimpse of him causes us to gasp with wonder? Because he's so much more than we can think or imagine?

Perhaps that's how Isaiah felt when he saw the Lord sitting on a throne, high and lofty. Listen in to Isaiah's response: "Woe to me! . . . I am ruined! For I am a man of unclean lips, and I live among a people of unclean lips, and my eyes have seen the King, the LORD Almighty" (Isaiah 6:5). Seeing the Lord caused Isaiah to realize his own unfit condition, for it stood in direct contrast to the Lord of hosts' holiness.

Christ came to rescue us from our smallness, our emptiness, our busyness, our loneliness and our sinfulness. He longs for us to experience radical transformation of what comes naturally. Isn't that outlandish?

Yes, the Lord makes seemingly outrageous requests of us. But when we see him as he is, we long to be different, truly transformed — even outlandish, like him.

Lord Jesus, sometimes when I see how radical you are, I am awed and amazed. Amazed at the wonderful ways you have rescued me from my empty, lonely, status-quo existence and lifted me into your presence. Amen.

Your next devotion is located on page 1355.

GRANDCHILD IN FOCUS • PRAYER

Relationships at Home

O Lord, I pray that you will bless the home and family of my grandchild. May the relationships she has with her parents and siblings enhance her well-being, support her self-confidence and increase her faith. May her home life reflect your love, your grace, your compassion and your peace. Guide her parents to direct her in love and truth, so she will grow into a strong and compassionate individual. Amen.

John the Baptist Beheaded

6:14–29pp — Mt 14:1–12
6:14–16pp — Lk 9:7–9

¹⁴King Herod heard about this, for Jesus' name had become well known. Some were saying,ᵃ "John the Baptist has been raised from the dead, and that is why miraculous powers are at work in him."

¹⁵Others said, "He is Elijah."

And still others claimed, "He is a prophet, like one of the prophets of long ago."

¹⁶But when Herod heard this, he said, "John, the man I beheaded, has been raised from the dead!"

¹⁷For Herod himself had given orders to have John arrested, and he had him bound and put in prison. He did this because of Herodias, his brother Philip's wife, whom he had married. ¹⁸For John had been saying to Herod, "It is not lawful for you to have your brother's wife." ¹⁹So Herodias nursed a grudge against John and wanted to kill him. But she was not able to, ²⁰because Herod feared John and protected him, knowing him to be a righteous and holy man. When Herod heard John, he was greatly puzzledᵇ; yet he liked to listen to him.

²¹Finally the opportune time came. On his birthday Herod gave a banquet for his high officials and military commanders and the leading men of Galilee. ²²When the daughter of Herodias came in and danced, she pleased Herod and his dinner guests.

The king said to the girl, "Ask me for anything you want, and I'll give it to you." ²³And he promised her with an oath, "Whatever you ask I will give you, up to half my kingdom."

²⁴She went out and said to her mother, "What shall I ask for?"

"The head of John the Baptist," she answered.

²⁵At once the girl hurried in to the king with the request: "I want you to give me right now the head of John the Baptist on a platter."

²⁶The king was greatly distressed, but because of his oaths and his dinner guests, he did not want to refuse her. ²⁷So he immediately sent an executioner with orders to bring John's head. The man went, beheaded John in the prison, ²⁸and brought back his head on a platter. He presented it to the girl, and she gave it to her mother. ²⁹On hearing of this, John's disciples came and took his body and laid it in a tomb.

Jesus Feeds the Five Thousand

6:32–44pp — Mt 14:13–21; Lk 9:10–17; Jn 6:5–13
6:32–44Ref — Mk 8:2–9

³⁰The apostles gathered around Jesus and reported to him all they had done and taught. ³¹Then, because so many people were coming and going that they did not even have a chance to eat, he said to them, "Come with me by yourselves to a quiet place and get some rest."

³²So they went away by themselves in a boat to a solitary place. ³³But many who saw them leaving recognized them and ran on foot from all the towns and got there ahead of them. ³⁴When Jesus landed and saw a large crowd, he had compassion on them, because they were like sheep without a shepherd. So he began teaching them many things.

³⁵By this time it was late in the day, so his disciples came to him. "This is a remote place," they said, "and it's already very late. ³⁶Send the people away so they can go to the surrounding countryside and villages and buy themselves something to eat."

³⁷But he answered, "You give them something to eat."

They said to him, "That would take eight months of a man's wagesᶜ! Are we to go and spend that much on bread and give it to them to eat?"

³⁸"How many loaves do you have?" he asked. "Go and see."

When they found out, they said, "Five—and two fish."

³⁹Then Jesus directed them to have all the people sit down in groups on the green grass. ⁴⁰So they sat down in groups of hundreds and fifties. ⁴¹Taking the five loaves and the two fish and looking up to heaven, he gave thanks and broke the

---

ᵃ 14 Some early manuscripts *He was saying*   ᵇ 20 Some early manuscripts *he did many things*   ᶜ 37 Greek *take two hundred denarii*

LET'S TALK

Dreamy Stuff

Everybody dreams. Some of us remember our dreams; some of us don't. But it's always an interesting subject to talk about. Spend time with your grandchildren discussing some of your most vivid or unusual dreams. Do any of you experience recurring dreams? What do you often dream about? Are some of your dreams scary? Funny? Happy? Sad? Do you think they have any meaning?

Numerous dreams are recounted in the Bible: Genesis 37; 41; 1 Kings 3; Daniel 2; 4; Matthew 1. Pick a favorite and share it with your grandchildren. Why do they think God used dreams in those early days to communicate truth or coming events? What might take the place of such dreams in our lives today?

Long-Distance Variation: Write down what you can remember of a dream and send it to a grandchild, asking him or her to send a similar letter back. If you can recall a dream that featured this particular grandchild, or perhaps something significant from your own childhood, you'll be sure to have a winner.

Thank you, God, for dreams and my amazing subconscious. I praise you for your concern about all of the "little" things in my life and in the lives of my grandchildren. Thank you for treasuring each of us so much that you even orchestrate our dream life. Amen.

Your next devotion is located on page 1356.

GRANDCHILD IN FOCUS • PRAYER

Friends

Dear Lord and Father, I pray for my grandchild's social life and his friends. Bring diverse friends into his life who will love and encourage him, who will bring joy and laughter to the good times and comfort and support through difficulties and disappointments. Grant him wisdom and discernment as he selects his friends; help him to avoid cliques that restrict, activities that endanger, and foolish and dangerous behaviors that harm. I ask that you fill his life with close and caring relationships. Amen.

Worship the Lord

The LORD reigns, let the earth be glad;
    let the distant shores rejoice.

Clouds and thick darkness surround him;
    righteousness and justice are the foundation of his throne.
Fire goes before him
    and consumes his foes on every side.
His lightning lights up the world;
    the earth sees and trembles.
The mountains melt like wax before the LORD,
    before the Lord of all the earth.
The heavens proclaim his righteousness,
    and all the peoples see his glory.

Psalm 97:1 – 6

I am struck by how you are so holy, Lord, and yet how you care so lovingly for the lowliest creatures. Your throne is surrounded by clouds and thick darkness, and yet you still see fit to shed light and joy on me. I rejoice in you, Lord, and praise your holy name. Amen.

Your next devotion is located on page 1359.

GRANDCHILD IN FOCUS • PRAYER

Self-Image

O loving God, I praise you for creating my grandchild as a unique individual. Now I ask you to help her appreciate her uniqueness. Build up her self-image so she can enjoy her individuality. Help her to stand firm for who she is, where she has come from and what she believes in. Encourage her not only to have hopes and dreams but to also enjoy each day as it comes. In Jesus' name, amen.

loaves. Then he gave them to his disciples to set before the people. He also divided the two fish among them all. ⁴²They all ate and were satisfied, ⁴³and the disciples picked up twelve basketfuls of broken pieces of bread and fish. ⁴⁴The number of the men who had eaten was five thousand.

Jesus Walks on the Water

6:45–51pp — Mt 14:22–32; Jn 6:15–21
6:53–56pp — Mt 14:34–36

⁴⁵Immediately Jesus made his disciples get into the boat and go on ahead of him to Bethsaida, while he dismissed the crowd. ⁴⁶After leaving them, he went up on a mountainside to pray.

⁴⁷When evening came, the boat was in the middle of the lake, and he was alone on land. ⁴⁸He saw the disciples straining at the oars, because the wind was against them. About the fourth watch of the night he went out to them, walking on the lake. He was about to pass by them, ⁴⁹but when they saw him walking on the lake, they thought he was a ghost. They cried out, ⁵⁰because they all saw him and were terrified.

Immediately he spoke to them and said, "Take courage! It is I. Don't be afraid." ⁵¹Then he climbed into the boat with them, and the wind died down. They were completely amazed, ⁵²for they had not understood about the loaves; their hearts were hardened.

⁵³When they had crossed over, they landed at Gennesaret and anchored there. ⁵⁴As soon as they got out of the boat, people recognized Jesus. ⁵⁵They ran throughout that whole region and carried the sick on mats to wherever they heard he was. ⁵⁶And wherever he went — into villages, towns or countryside — they placed the sick in the marketplaces. They begged him to let them touch even the edge of his cloak, and all who touched him were healed.

Clean and Unclean

7:1–23pp — Mt 15:1–20

7 The Pharisees and some of the teachers of the law who had come from Jerusalem gathered around Jesus and ²saw some of his disciples eating food with hands that were "unclean," that is, unwashed. ³(The Pharisees and all the Jews do not eat unless they give their hands a ceremonial washing, holding to the tradition of the elders. ⁴When they come from the marketplace they do not eat unless they wash. And they observe many other traditions, such as the washing of cups, pitchers and kettles.ᵃ)

⁵So the Pharisees and teachers of the law asked Jesus, "Why don't your disciples live according to the tradition of the elders instead of eating their food with 'unclean' hands?"

⁶He replied, "Isaiah was right when he prophesied about you hypocrites; as it is written:

" 'These people honor me with their lips,
    but their hearts are far from me.
⁷They worship me in vain;
    their teachings are but rules taught by
        men.'ᵇ

⁸You have let go of the commands of God and are holding on to the traditions of men."

⁹And he said to them: "You have a fine way of setting aside the commands of God in order toᶜ observe your own traditions! ¹⁰For Moses said, 'Honor your father and your mother,'ᵈ and, 'Anyone who curses his father or mother must be put to death.'ᵉ ¹¹But you say that if a man says to his father or mother: 'Whatever help you might otherwise have received from me is Corban' (that is, a gift devoted to God), ¹²then you no longer let him do anything for his father or mother. ¹³Thus you nullify the word of God by your tradition that you have handed down. And you do many things like that."

¹⁴Again Jesus called the crowd to him and said, "Listen to me, everyone, and understand this. ¹⁵Nothing outside a man can make him 'unclean' by going into him. Rather, it is what comes out of a man that makes him 'unclean.'ᶠ"

¹⁷After he had left the crowd and entered the

ᵃ 4 Some early manuscripts *pitchers, kettles and dining couches*   ᵇ 6,7 Isaiah 29:13   ᶜ 9 Some manuscripts *set up*   ᵈ 10 Exodus 20:12; Deut. 5:16   ᵉ 10 Exodus 21:17; Lev. 20:9   ᶠ 15 Some early manuscripts *'unclean.' ¹⁶If anyone has ears to hear, let him hear.*

house, his disciples asked him about this parable. [18]"Are you so dull?" he asked. "Don't you see that nothing that enters a man from the outside can make him 'unclean'? [19]For it doesn't go into his heart but into his stomach, and then out of his body." (In saying this, Jesus declared all foods "clean.")

[20]He went on: "What comes out of a man is what makes him 'unclean.' [21]For from within, out of men's hearts, come evil thoughts, sexual immorality, theft, murder, adultery, [22]greed, malice, deceit, lewdness, envy, slander, arrogance and folly. [23]All these evils come from inside and make a man 'unclean.'"

The Faith of a Syrophoenician Woman
7:24–30pp — Mt 15:21–28

[24]Jesus left that place and went to the vicinity of Tyre.[a] He entered a house and did not want anyone to know it; yet he could not keep his presence secret. [25]In fact, as soon as she heard about him, a woman whose little daughter was possessed by an evil[b] spirit came and fell at his feet. [26]The woman was a Greek, born in Syrian Phoenicia. She begged Jesus to drive the demon out of her daughter.

[27]"First let the children eat all they want," he told her, "for it is not right to take the children's bread and toss it to their dogs."

[28]"Yes, Lord," she replied, "but even the dogs under the table eat the children's crumbs."

[29]Then he told her, "For such a reply, you may go; the demon has left your daughter."

[30]She went home and found her child lying on the bed, and the demon gone.

The Healing of a Deaf and Mute Man
7:31–37pp — Mt 15:29–31

[31]Then Jesus left the vicinity of Tyre and went through Sidon, down to the Sea of Galilee and into the region of the Decapolis.[c] [32]There some people brought to him a man who was deaf and could hardly talk, and they begged him to place his hand on the man. [33]After he took him aside, away from the crowd, Jesus put his fingers into the man's ears. Then he spit and touched the man's tongue. [34]He looked up to heaven and with a deep sigh said to him, "*Ephphatha!*" (which means, "Be opened!"). [35]At this, the man's ears were opened, his tongue was loosened and he began to speak plainly.

[36]Jesus commanded them not to tell anyone. But the more he did so, the more they kept talking about it. [37]People were overwhelmed with amazement. "He has done everything well," they said. "He even makes the deaf hear and the mute speak."

Jesus Feeds the Four Thousand
8:1–9pp — Mt 15:32–39
8:1–9Ref — Mk 6:32–44
8:11–21pp — Mt 16:1–12

8 During those days another large crowd gathered. Since they had nothing to eat, Jesus called his disciples to him and said, [2]"I have compassion for these people; they have already been with me three days and have nothing to eat. [3]If I send them home hungry, they will collapse on the way, because some of them have come a long distance."

[4]His disciples answered, "But where in this remote place can anyone get enough bread to feed them?"

[5]"How many loaves do you have?" Jesus asked.

"Seven," they replied.

[6]He told the crowd to sit down on the ground. When he had taken the seven loaves and given thanks, he broke them and gave them to his disciples to set before the people, and they did so. [7]They had a few small fish as well; he gave thanks for them also and told the disciples to distribute them. [8]The people ate and were satisfied. Afterward the disciples picked up seven basketfuls of broken pieces that were left over. [9]About four thousand men were present. And having sent them away, [10]he got into the boat with his disciples and went to the region of Dalmanutha.

---

[a] 24 Many early manuscripts *Tyre and Sidon* [b] 25 Greek *unclean*
[c] 31 That is, the Ten Cities

> "YES, LORD," SHE REPLIED,
> "BUT EVEN THE DOGS
> UNDER THE TABLE EAT THE
> CHILDREN'S CRUMBS."
>
> Mark 7:28

Crumby Faith

ELISA MORGAN

READ | MARK 7:24–30

We messed up yesterday. We did worse the day before. We know we'll likely not make it through this day without error. It's not for lack of trying. We try. Our failures have to do with who we are: human.

There was a woman who likewise knew she was undeserving. Coming not from the chosen people of Israel but rather as a Gentile from Syrian Phoenicia, this woman approached Jesus, begging him to help her daughter, who was possessed by an evil spirit. Acknowledging that she could not fix the child herself, admitting that she didn't deserve his attention because she came from outside the faith . . . still the woman came.

But notice her request. She wanted the crumbs. The leftovers. She wanted what would have been tossed aside or eaten by dogs. She stood on a scrap of faith, believing that a scrap was enough for a miracle.

At first this request seems ridiculous. Undignified. Humiliating. Looking again, we can find resolve, desperation and great hope in the request. This woman trusted the saving power of Jesus to such an extent that she believed a crumb would suffice. And Jesus declared her puny plea to be a stunning statement of faith.

Where, like this woman, might we beg for crumbs, knowing that in receiving them comes a feast because of faith?

Dear God, I ask that you would create a feast from my small gestures of faith. Increase my belief in what I might receive from you, that I would view you without limits, as able to intercede eternally in my life. Amen.

Your next devotion is located on page 1365.

GRANDCHILD IN FOCUS • PRAYER

Protection From Worldliness

O Sovereign Lord, the world surrounds my grandchild, pressing in and tempting him in so many ways. Help him set appropriate limits. Give him sound judgment to choose wisely. Guard him from temptation; protect him from physical and mental predators; lead him into paths of righteousness and light. And reassure me with your promise that you are holding him in your hands. Amen.

[11]The Pharisees came and began to question Jesus. To test him, they asked him for a sign from heaven. [12]He sighed deeply and said, "Why does this generation ask for a miraculous sign? I tell you the truth, no sign will be given to it." [13]Then he left them, got back into the boat and crossed to the other side.

The Yeast of the Pharisees and Herod

[14]The disciples had forgotten to bring bread, except for one loaf they had with them in the boat. [15]"Be careful," Jesus warned them. "Watch out for the yeast of the Pharisees and that of Herod."

[16]They discussed this with one another and said, "It is because we have no bread."

[17]Aware of their discussion, Jesus asked them: "Why are you talking about having no bread? Do you still not see or understand? Are your hearts hardened? [18]Do you have eyes but fail to see, and ears but fail to hear? And don't you remember? [19]When I broke the five loaves for the five thousand, how many basketfuls of pieces did you pick up?"

"Twelve," they replied.

[20]"And when I broke the seven loaves for the four thousand, how many basketfuls of pieces did you pick up?"

They answered, "Seven."

[21]He said to them, "Do you still not understand?"

The Healing of a Blind Man at Bethsaida

[22]They came to Bethsaida, and some people brought a blind man and begged Jesus to touch him. [23]He took the blind man by the hand and led him outside the village. When he had spit on the man's eyes and put his hands on him, Jesus asked, "Do you see anything?"

[24]He looked up and said, "I see people; they look like trees walking around."

[25]Once more Jesus put his hands on the man's eyes. Then his eyes were opened, his sight was restored, and he saw everything clearly. [26]Jesus sent him home, saying, "Don't go into the village.[a]"

Peter's Confession of Christ

8:27–29pp — Mt 16:13–16; Lk 9:18–20

[27]Jesus and his disciples went on to the villages around Caesarea Philippi. On the way he asked them, "Who do people say I am?"

[28]They replied, "Some say John the Baptist; others say Elijah; and still others, one of the prophets."

[29]"But what about you?" he asked. "Who do you say I am?"

Peter answered, "You are the Christ.[b]"

[30]Jesus warned them not to tell anyone about him.

Jesus Predicts His Death

8:31–9:1pp — Mt 16:21–28; Lk 9:22–27

[31]He then began to teach them that the Son of Man must suffer many things and be rejected by the elders, chief priests and teachers of the law, and that he must be killed and after three days rise again. [32]He spoke plainly about this, and Peter took him aside and began to rebuke him.

[33]But when Jesus turned and looked at his disciples, he rebuked Peter. "Get behind me, Satan!" he said. "You do not have in mind the things of God, but the things of men."

[34]Then he called the crowd to him along with his disciples and said: "If anyone would come after me, he must deny himself and take up his cross and follow me. [35]For whoever wants to save his life[c] will lose it, but whoever loses his life for me and for the gospel will save it. [36]What good is it for a man to gain the whole world, yet forfeit his soul? [37]Or what can a man give in exchange for his soul? [38]If anyone is ashamed of me and my words in this adulterous and sinful generation, the Son of Man will be ashamed of him when he comes in his Father's glory with the holy angels."

9 And he said to them, "I tell you the truth, some who are standing here will not taste death before they see the kingdom of God come with power."

[a] 26 Some manuscripts *Don't go and tell anyone in the village*
[b] 29 Or *Messiah*. "The Christ" (Greek) and "the Messiah" (Hebrew) both mean "the Anointed One."   [c] 35 The Greek word means either *life* or *soul*; also in verse 36.

The Transfiguration

9:2–8pp — Lk 9:28–36
9:2–13pp — Mt 17.1–13

[2] After six days Jesus took Peter, James and John with him and led them up a high mountain, where they were all alone. There he was transfigured before them. [3] His clothes became dazzling white, whiter than anyone in the world could bleach them. [4] And there appeared before them Elijah and Moses, who were talking with Jesus.

[5] Peter said to Jesus, "Rabbi, it is good for us to be here. Let us put up three shelters — one for you, one for Moses and one for Elijah." [6] (He did not know what to say, they were so frightened.)

[7] Then a cloud appeared and enveloped them, and a voice came from the cloud: "This is my Son, whom I love. Listen to him!"

[8] Suddenly, when they looked around, they no longer saw anyone with them except Jesus.

[9] As they were coming down the mountain, Jesus gave them orders not to tell anyone what they had seen until the Son of Man had risen from the dead. [10] They kept the matter to themselves, discussing what "rising from the dead" meant.

[11] And they asked him, "Why do the teachers of the law say that Elijah must come first?"

[12] Jesus replied, "To be sure, Elijah does come first, and restores all things. Why then is it written that the Son of Man must suffer much and be rejected? [13] But I tell you, Elijah has come, and they have done to him everything they wished, just as it is written about him."

The Healing of a Boy With an Evil Spirit

9:14–28,30–32pp — Mt 17:14–19,22,23;
Lk 9:37–45

[14] When they came to the other disciples, they saw a large crowd around them and the teachers of the law arguing with them. [15] As soon as all the people saw Jesus, they were overwhelmed with wonder and ran to greet him.

[16] "What are you arguing with them about?" he asked.

[17] A man in the crowd answered, "Teacher, I brought you my son, who is possessed by a spirit that has robbed him of speech. [18] Whenever it seizes him, it throws him to the ground. He foams at the mouth, gnashes his teeth and becomes rigid. I asked your disciples to drive out the spirit, but they could not."

[19] "O unbelieving generation," Jesus replied, "how long shall I stay with you? How long shall I put up with you? Bring the boy to me."

[20] So they brought him. When the spirit saw Jesus, it immediately threw the boy into a convulsion. He fell to the ground and rolled around, foaming at the mouth.

[21] Jesus asked the boy's father, "How long has he been like this?"

"From childhood," he answered. [22] "It has often thrown him into fire or water to kill him. But if you can do anything, take pity on us and help us."

[23] " 'If you can'?" said Jesus. "Everything is possible for him who believes."

[24] Immediately the boy's father exclaimed, "I do believe; help me overcome my unbelief!"

[25] When Jesus saw that a crowd was running to the scene, he rebuked the evil[a] spirit. "You deaf and mute spirit," he said, "I command you, come out of him and never enter him again."

[26] The spirit shrieked, convulsed him violently and came out. The boy looked so much like a corpse that many said, "He's dead." [27] But Jesus took him by the hand and lifted him to his feet, and he stood up.

[28] After Jesus had gone indoors, his disciples asked him privately, "Why couldn't we drive it out?"

[29] He replied, "This kind can come out only by prayer.[b]"

[30] They left that place and passed through Galilee. Jesus did not want anyone to know where they were, [31] because he was teaching his disciples. He said to them, "The Son of Man is going to be betrayed into the hands of men. They will kill him, and after three days he will rise." [32] But they did not understand what he meant and were afraid to ask him about it.

a 25 Greek *unclean*   *b 29* Some manuscripts *prayer and fasting*

Who Is the Greatest?

9:33–37pp — Mt 18:1–5; Lk 9:46–48

³³They came to Capernaum. When he was in the house, he asked them, "What were you arguing about on the road?" ³⁴But they kept quiet because on the way they had argued about who was the greatest.

³⁵Sitting down, Jesus called the Twelve and said, "If anyone wants to be first, he must be the very last, and the servant of all."

³⁶He took a little child and had him stand among them. Taking him in his arms, he said to them, ³⁷"Whoever welcomes one of these little children in my name welcomes me; and whoever welcomes me does not welcome me but the one who sent me."

Whoever Is Not Against Us Is for Us

9:38–40pp — Lk 9:49,50

³⁸"Teacher," said John, "we saw a man driving out demons in your name and we told him to stop, because he was not one of us."

³⁹"Do not stop him," Jesus said. "No one who does a miracle in my name can in the next moment say anything bad about me, ⁴⁰for whoever is not against us is for us. ⁴¹I tell you the truth, anyone who gives you a cup of water in my name because you belong to Christ will certainly not lose his reward.

Causing to Sin

⁴²"And if anyone causes one of these little ones who believe in me to sin, it would be better for him to be thrown into the sea with a large millstone tied around his neck. ⁴³If your hand causes you to sin, cut it off. It is better for you to enter life maimed than with two hands to go into hell, where the fire never goes out. *ᵃ* ⁴⁵And if your foot causes you to sin, cut it off. It is better for you to enter life crippled than to have two feet and be thrown into hell. *ᵇ* ⁴⁷And if your eye causes you to sin, pluck it out. It is better for you to enter the kingdom of God with one eye than to have two eyes and be thrown into hell, ⁴⁸where

" 'their worm does not die,
 and the fire is not quenched.' *ᶜ*

⁴⁹Everyone will be salted with fire.

⁵⁰"Salt is good, but if it loses its saltiness, how can you make it salty again? Have salt in yourselves, and be at peace with each other."

Divorce

10:1–12pp — Mt 19:1–9

10 Jesus then left that place and went into the region of Judea and across the Jordan. Again crowds of people came to him, and as was his custom, he taught them.

²Some Pharisees came and tested him by asking, "Is it lawful for a man to divorce his wife?"

³"What did Moses command you?" he replied.

⁴They said, "Moses permitted a man to write a certificate of divorce and send her away."

⁵"It was because your hearts were hard that Moses wrote you this law," Jesus replied. ⁶"But at the beginning of creation God 'made them male and female.' *ᵈ* ⁷'For this reason a man will leave his father and mother and be united to his wife, *ᵉ* ⁸and the two will become one flesh.' *ᶠ* So they are no longer two, but one. ⁹Therefore what God has joined together, let man not separate."

¹⁰When they were in the house again, the disciples asked Jesus about this. ¹¹He answered, "Anyone who divorces his wife and marries another woman commits adultery against her. ¹²And if she divorces her husband and marries another man, she commits adultery."

The Little Children and Jesus

10:13–16pp — Mt 19:13–15; Lk 18:15–17

¹³People were bringing little children to Jesus to have him touch them, but the disciples rebuked them. ¹⁴When Jesus saw this, he was indignant. He said to them, "Let the little children come to me, and do not hinder them, for the kingdom of God belongs to such as these. ¹⁵I tell you the

---

ᵃ 43 Some manuscripts *out, ⁴⁴where / " 'their worm does not die, / and the fire is not quenched.'* *ᵇ 45* Some manuscripts *hell, ⁴⁶where / " 'their worm does not die, / and the fire is not quenched.'* *ᶜ 48* Isaiah 66:24 *ᵈ 6* Gen. 1:27 *ᵉ 7* Some early manuscripts do not have *and be united to his wife.* *ᶠ 8* Gen. 2:24

truth, anyone who will not receive the kingdom of God like a little child will never enter it." ¹⁶And he took the children in his arms, put his hands on them and blessed them.

MARK 10:13–16

Jesus and the Little Children

LIFE LESSON: Jesus wants us all to have the faith of little children.

TO TALK ABOUT

✦ What did the disciples do when people were bringing their little ones to Jesus?

✦ Was Jesus too busy for the children?

✦ What is special about the faith of a little child?

✦ How can a grown-up have childlike faith?

The Rich Young Man
10:17–31pp — Mt 19:16–30; Lk 18:18–30

¹⁷As Jesus started on his way, a man ran up to him and fell on his knees before him. "Good teacher," he asked, "what must I do to inherit eternal life?"

¹⁸"Why do you call me good?" Jesus answered. "No one is good—except God alone. ¹⁹You know the commandments: 'Do not murder, do not commit adultery, do not steal, do not give false testimony, do not defraud, honor your father and mother.'ᵃ"

²⁰"Teacher," he declared, "all these I have kept since I was a boy."

²¹Jesus looked at him and loved him. "One thing you lack," he said. "Go, sell everything you have and give to the poor, and you will have treasure in heaven. Then come, follow me."

²²At this the man's face fell. He went away sad, because he had great wealth.

²³Jesus looked around and said to his disciples, "How hard it is for the rich to enter the kingdom of God!"

²⁴The disciples were amazed at his words. But Jesus said again, "Children, how hard it is ᵇ to enter the kingdom of God! ²⁵It is easier for a camel to go through the eye of a needle than for a rich man to enter the kingdom of God."

²⁶The disciples were even more amazed, and said to each other, "Who then can be saved?"

²⁷Jesus looked at them and said, "With man this is impossible, but not with God; all things are possible with God."

²⁸Peter said to him, "We have left everything to follow you!"

²⁹"I tell you the truth," Jesus replied, "no one who has left home or brothers or sisters or mother or father or children or fields for me and the gospel ³⁰will fail to receive a hundred times as much in this present age (homes, brothers, sisters, mothers, children and fields—and with them, persecutions) and in the age to come, eternal life. ³¹But many who are first will be last, and the last first."

Jesus Again Predicts His Death
10:32–34pp — Mt 20:17–19; Lk 18:31–33

³²They were on their way up to Jerusalem, with Jesus leading the way, and the disciples were astonished, while those who followed were afraid. Again he took the Twelve aside and told them what was going to happen to him. ³³"We are going up to Jerusalem," he said, "and the Son of Man will be betrayed to the chief priests and teachers of the law. They will condemn him to death and will hand him over to the Gentiles,

---

ᵃ 19 Exodus 20:12-16; Deut. 5:16-20   ᵇ 24 Some manuscripts is for those who trust in riches

34who will mock him and spit on him, flog him and kill him. Three days later he will rise."

The Request of James and John
10:35–45pp — Mt 20:20–28

35Then James and John, the sons of Zebedee, came to him. "Teacher," they said, "we want you to do for us whatever we ask."

36"What do you want me to do for you?" he asked.

37They replied, "Let one of us sit at your right and the other at your left in your glory."

38"You don't know what you are asking," Jesus said. "Can you drink the cup I drink or be baptized with the baptism I am baptized with?"

39"We can," they answered.

Jesus said to them, "You will drink the cup I drink and be baptized with the baptism I am baptized with, 40but to sit at my right or left is not for me to grant. These places belong to those for whom they have been prepared."

41When the ten heard about this, they became indignant with James and John. 42Jesus called them together and said, "You know that those who are regarded as rulers of the Gentiles lord it over them, and their high officials exercise authority over them. 43Not so with you. Instead, whoever wants to become great among you must be your servant, 44and whoever wants to be first must be slave of all. 45For even the Son of Man did not come to be served, but to serve, and to give his life as a ransom for many."

Blind Bartimaeus Receives His Sight
10:46–52pp — Mt 20:29–34; Lk 18:35–43

46Then they came to Jericho. As Jesus and his disciples, together with a large crowd, were leaving the city, a blind man, Bartimaeus (that is, the Son of Timaeus), was sitting by the roadside begging. 47When he heard that it was Jesus of Nazareth, he began to shout, "Jesus, Son of David, have mercy on me!"

48Many rebuked him and told him to be quiet, but he shouted all the more, "Son of David, have mercy on me!"

49Jesus stopped and said, "Call him."

So they called to the blind man, "Cheer up! On your feet! He's calling you." 50Throwing his cloak aside, he jumped to his feet and came to Jesus.

51"What do you want me to do for you?" Jesus asked him.

The blind man said, "Rabbi, I want to see."

52"Go," said Jesus, "your faith has healed you." Immediately he received his sight and followed Jesus along the road.

The Triumphal Entry
11:1–10pp — Mt 21:1–9; Lk 19:29–38
11:7–10pp — Jn 12:12–15

11 As they approached Jerusalem and came to Bethphage and Bethany at the Mount of Olives, Jesus sent two of his disciples, 2saying to them, "Go to the village ahead of you, and just as you enter it, you will find a colt tied there, which no one has ever ridden. Untie it and bring it here. 3If anyone asks you, 'Why are you doing this?' tell him, 'The Lord needs it and will send it back here shortly.'"

4They went and found a colt outside in the street, tied at a doorway. As they untied it, 5some people standing there asked, "What are you doing, untying that colt?" 6They answered as Jesus had told them to, and the people let them go. 7When they brought the colt to Jesus and threw their cloaks over it, he sat on it. 8Many people spread their cloaks on the road, while others spread branches they had cut in the fields. 9Those who went ahead and those who followed shouted,

"Hosanna!ᵃ"

"Blessed is he who comes in the name of
    the Lord!"ᵇ

10"Blessed is the coming kingdom of our father
    David!"

"Hosanna in the highest!"

11Jesus entered Jerusalem and went to the temple. He looked around at everything, but since

a 9 A Hebrew expression meaning "Save!" which became an exclamation of praise; also in verse 10   b 9 Psalm 118:25,26

"NOT SO WITH YOU. INSTEAD, WHOEVER WANTS TO BECOME GREAT AMONG YOU MUST BE YOUR SERVANT, AND WHOEVER WANTS TO BE FIRST MUST BE SLAVE OF ALL."

Mark 10:43−44

Servant of All

DAWN SCOTT JONES

READ | MARK 10:35 – 45

My granddaughter Victoria was up to something. She had that mischievous look on her face — a sparkle flashed from her eyes, accentuating their vivid green color. Her lips slightly curled up with a prankish expression. Our second granddaughter, Alexia, was taking her first step, and to Victoria's chagrin, the spotlight of attention was now shining solely on her wobbling little sister. Victoria did not realize it, but I was observing her dilemma with sneaky delight, curious to see how she would handle being "stage left."

That's when she made her move. Nonchalantly, Victoria pirouetted over by Alexia. Pretending to execute a ballet move, she twirled into her and pushed her over. *Splat!* Alexia went down flat. Victoria secretly smiled.

I chuckle when I recall that moment, but it also reveals a lesson in human nature: We long to be first, to be the center of attention, to have control. We hate to admit it, but we can struggle with insecurity and jealousy and sometimes become threatened when others succeed. We find secret satisfaction when our rival fails. We yearn for significance, to accomplish something great.

But Jesus redirects our earthly rationale by teaching us that being great means serving, choosing to be second, stepping out of the limelight so someone else can shine. We are on our way to greatness in God's perspective when we roll up our sleeves and offer our gifts wherever they are needed.

When I picture greatness, it usually does not look like a little four-year-old girl helping her sister learn to walk. But in God's economy, it is.

Dear Lord Jesus, your words ring through my heart today. I want to be great for you and for your kingdom. I see that I can do that simply by serving. Let my life make a difference in this world, as I serve others for Jesus' sake. Amen.

Your next devotion is located on page 1367.

GRANDCHILD IN FOCUS • PRAYER

Respect for Authority

Dear Lord, I pray that my grandchild will continually grow to respect those in authority. May she learn to be cooperative and fair in work and play. Instill in her a high regard for officials who govern our land and enforce the laws. May her relationships with parents, teachers, coaches, mentors and bosses be respectful, admirable, constructive and caring. Amen.

stories to share

MARK 11:1–11

The Triumphal Entry

LIFE LESSON: Jesus is the Messiah.

TO TALK ABOUT

✦ What did Jesus ask his disciples to do?

✦ Were they allowed to take the colt?

✦ Did all of the cheering people believe that Jesus was the Messiah? How do you know?

✦ Do you think Jesus loves the praise of a crowd more than the praise of one heart? Why or why not?

it was already late, he went out to Bethany with the Twelve.

Jesus Clears the Temple

11:12–14pp — Mt 21:18–22
11:15–18pp — Mt 21:12–16; Lk 19:45–47; Jn 2:13–16

¹²The next day as they were leaving Bethany, Jesus was hungry. ¹³Seeing in the distance a fig tree in leaf, he went to find out if it had any fruit. When he reached it, he found nothing but leaves, because it was not the season for figs. ¹⁴Then he said to the tree, "May no one ever eat fruit from you again." And his disciples heard him say it.

¹⁵On reaching Jerusalem, Jesus entered the temple area and began driving out those who were buying and selling there. He overturned the tables of the money changers and the benches of those selling doves, ¹⁶and would not allow anyone to carry merchandise through the temple courts. ¹⁷And as he taught them, he said, "Is it not written:

" 'My house will be called
a house of prayer for all nations'[a]?

But you have made it 'a den of robbers.'[b]"

¹⁸The chief priests and the teachers of the law heard this and began looking for a way to kill him, for they feared him, because the whole crowd was amazed at his teaching.

¹⁹When evening came, they[c] went out of the city.

The Withered Fig Tree

11:20–24pp — Mt 21:19–22

²⁰In the morning, as they went along, they saw the fig tree withered from the roots. ²¹Peter remembered and said to Jesus, "Rabbi, look! The fig tree you cursed has withered!"

²²"Have[d] faith in God," Jesus answered. ²³"I tell you the truth, if anyone says to this mountain, 'Go, throw yourself into the sea,' and does not doubt in his heart but believes that what he says will happen, it will be done for him. ²⁴Therefore

TALKING POINTS

Doubt

Faith without doubt is powerful.

MARK 11:23

For more on doubt, go to John 20:24–29.

I tell you, whatever you ask for in prayer, believe that you have received it, and it will be yours. ²⁵And when you stand praying, if you hold anything against anyone, forgive him, so that your Father in heaven may forgive you your sins.[e]"

---

[a] 17 Isaiah 56:7   [b] 17 Jer. 7:11   [c] 19 Some early manuscripts he   [d] 22 Some early manuscripts If you have   [e] 25 Some manuscripts sins. ²⁶But if you do not forgive, neither will your Father who is in heaven forgive your sins.

> "THEREFORE I TELL YOU, WHATEVER
> YOU ASK FOR IN PRAYER, BELIEVE
> THAT YOU HAVE RECEIVED IT, AND IT
> WILL BE YOURS."
>
> Mark 11:24

A Tale of Two Angels

CAROL KENT

READ | MARK 11:12–25

Our son, a recent graduate of the U.S. Naval Academy, called with unexpected news: "My orders have changed. I have to be at Surface Warfare Officers' School in Newport, Rhode Island, on September 8. April and I are in love, and we want to get married next Friday."

I was stunned. My son was asking to marry a woman I had never met, a previously married woman with two children—*next Friday*. Rational thinking slowly returned. We asked Jason and his fiancée if they would wait three weeks and be married in our hometown. They agreed.

Jason and April walked through our front door with arms encircling each other's waists. April had been married at the age of 16 to a man ten years her senior, and she had been through more of the "tough stuff of life" than anyone deserves. Behind them were six-year-old Chelsea and three-year-old Hannah. Minutes later Chelsea took my hand in her two hands, looked up and said, "You're my new favorite Grammy!"

Every morning Hannah ate her cereal, singing between bites, "I love Jesus; he loves me!" The girls invaded my closet and dressed up in chiffon and long beads. They won my heart very quickly.

As the wedding day approached, I saw deep love in the eyes of my son and his bride. And I already loved my big brown-eyed granddaughters. I wasn't there for their births, but they were filling my heart with so much joy. Two little angels entered my life at an unexpected time and showered me with unconditional love and acceptance. I had a new name: Grammy! And I had a new passion: to provide godly influence to my granddaughters.

I had prayed for a godly daughter-in-law. Though the answer came in a different package than I was expecting, God *did* answer my prayer.

Father, sometimes I get upset for no reason. My thoughts are anxious and my heart is disquieted. Help me to choose prayer over worry and to experience your peace in the midst of uncertainty. As you work out your will in my life, help me to accept your good gifts in whatever packages they appear. Amen.

Your next devotion is located on page 1379.

GRANDCHILD IN FOCUS • PRAYER

Courage

O Father, builder of character and courage, may my grandchild grow strong in the light of your love. Grant him courage to stand for what is right, to guard the truth and to ensure justice in every aspect of life. May he boldly grow in grace, revere your name and proudly proclaim you as the Lord of lords and King of kings. Amen.

The Authority of Jesus Questioned
11:27–33pp — Mt 21:23–27; Lk 20:1–8

²⁷ They arrived again in Jerusalem, and while Jesus was walking in the temple courts, the chief priests, the teachers of the law and the elders came to him. ²⁸ "By what authority are you doing these things?" they asked. "And who gave you authority to do this?"

²⁹ Jesus replied, "I will ask you one question. Answer me, and I will tell you by what authority I am doing these things. ³⁰ John's baptism — was it from heaven, or from men? Tell me!"

³¹ They discussed it among themselves and said, "If we say, 'From heaven,' he will ask, 'Then why didn't you believe him?' ³² But if we say, 'From men'..." (They feared the people, for everyone held that John really was a prophet.)

³³ So they answered Jesus, "We don't know."

Jesus said, "Neither will I tell you by what authority I am doing these things."

The Parable of the Tenants
12:1–12pp — Mt 21:33–46; Lk 20:9–19

12 He then began to speak to them in parables: "A man planted a vineyard. He put a wall around it, dug a pit for the winepress and built a watchtower. Then he rented the vineyard to some farmers and went away on a journey. ² At harvest time he sent a servant to the tenants to collect from them some of the fruit of the vineyard. ³ But they seized him, beat him and sent him away empty-handed. ⁴ Then he sent another servant to them; they struck this man on the head and treated him shamefully. ⁵ He sent still another, and that one they killed. He sent many others; some of them they beat, others they killed.

⁶ "He had one left to send, a son, whom he loved. He sent him last of all, saying, 'They will respect my son.'

⁷ "But the tenants said to one another, 'This is the heir. Come, let's kill him, and the inheritance will be ours.' ⁸ So they took him and killed him, and threw him out of the vineyard.

⁹ "What then will the owner of the vineyard do? He will come and kill those tenants and give the vineyard to others. ¹⁰ Haven't you read this scripture:

"'The stone the builders rejected
    has become the capstone[a];
¹¹ the Lord has done this,
    and it is marvelous in our eyes'[b]?"

¹² Then they looked for a way to arrest him because they knew he had spoken the parable against them. But they were afraid of the crowd; so they left him and went away.

Paying Taxes to Caesar
12:13–17pp — Mt 22:15–22; Lk 20:20–26

¹³ Later they sent some of the Pharisees and Herodians to Jesus to catch him in his words. ¹⁴ They came to him and said, "Teacher, we know you are a man of integrity. You aren't swayed by men, because you pay no attention to who they are; but you teach the way of God in accordance with the truth. Is it right to pay taxes to Caesar or not? ¹⁵ Should we pay or shouldn't we?"

But Jesus knew their hypocrisy. "Why are you trying to trap me?" he asked. "Bring me a denarius and let me look at it." ¹⁶ They brought the coin, and he asked them, "Whose portrait is this? And whose inscription?"

"Caesar's," they replied.

¹⁷ Then Jesus said to them, "Give to Caesar what is Caesar's and to God what is God's."

And they were amazed at him.

Marriage at the Resurrection
12:18–27pp — Mt 22:23–33; Lk 20:27–38

¹⁸ Then the Sadducees, who say there is no resurrection, came to him with a question. ¹⁹ "Teacher," they said, "Moses wrote for us that if a man's brother dies and leaves a wife but no children, the man must marry the widow and have children for his brother. ²⁰ Now there were seven brothers. The first one married and died without leaving any children. ²¹ The second one married the widow, but he also died, leaving no child. It was the same with the third. ²² In fact, none of the seven

---

a 10 Or cornerstone   *b 11 Psalm 118:22,23*

left any children. Last of all, the woman died too. [23] At the resurrection[a] whose wife will she be, since the seven were married to her?"

[24] Jesus replied, "Are you not in error because you do not know the Scriptures or the power of God? [25] When the dead rise, they will neither marry nor be given in marriage; they will be like the angels in heaven. [26] Now about the dead rising—have you not read in the book of Moses, in the account of the bush, how God said to him, 'I am the God of Abraham, the God of Isaac, and the God of Jacob'[b]? [27] He is not the God of the dead, but of the living. You are badly mistaken!"

The Greatest Commandment

12:28–34pp — Mt 22:34–40

[28] One of the teachers of the law came and heard them debating. Noticing that Jesus had given them a good answer, he asked him, "Of all the commandments, which is the most important?"

[29] "The most important one," answered Jesus, "is this: 'Hear, O Israel, the Lord our God, the Lord is one.[c] [30] Love the Lord your God with all your heart and with all your soul and with all your mind and with all your strength.'[d] [31] The second is this: 'Love your neighbor as yourself.'[e] There is no commandment greater than these."

[32] "Well said, teacher," the man replied. "You are right in saying that God is one and there is no other but him. [33] To love him with all your heart, with all your understanding and with all your strength, and to love your neighbor as yourself is more important than all burnt offerings and sacrifices."

[34] When Jesus saw that he had answered wisely, he said to him, "You are not far from the kingdom of God." And from then on no one dared ask him any more questions.

Whose Son Is the Christ?

12:35–37pp — Mt 22:41–46; Lk 20:41–44
12:38–40pp — Mt 23:1–7; Lk 20:45–47

[35] While Jesus was teaching in the temple courts, he asked, "How is it that the teachers of the law say that the Christ[f] is the son of David?

[36] David himself, speaking by the Holy Spirit, declared:

"'The Lord said to my Lord:
"Sit at my right hand
until I put your enemies
under your feet."'[g]

[37] David himself calls him 'Lord.' How then can he be his son?"

The large crowd listened to him with delight.

[38] As he taught, Jesus said, "Watch out for the teachers of the law. They like to walk around in flowing robes and be greeted in the marketplaces, [39] and have the most important seats in the synagogues and the places of honor at banquets. [40] They devour widows' houses and for a show make lengthy prayers. Such men will be punished most severely."

The Widow's Offering

12:41–44pp — Lk 21:1–4

[41] Jesus sat down opposite the place where the offerings were put and watched the crowd putting their money into the temple treasury. Many rich people threw in large amounts. [42] But a poor widow came and put in two very small copper coins,[h] worth only a fraction of a penny.[i]

[43] Calling his disciples to him, Jesus said, "I tell you the truth, this poor widow has put more into

---

[a] 23 Some manuscripts *resurrection, when men rise from the dead,* [b] 26 Exodus 3:6 [c] 29 Or *the Lord our God is one Lord* [d] 30 Deut. 6:4,5 [e] 31 Lev. 19:18 [f] 35 Or *Messiah* [g] 36 Psalm 110:1 [h] 42 Greek *two lepta* [i] 42 Greek *kodrantes*

TALKING POINTS

Money

The definition of *generosity* can vary; it depends on a person's resources.

MARK 12:41–44

For more on money, go to Luke 12:15.

the treasury than all the others. **44**They all gave out of their wealth; but she, out of her poverty, put in everything—all she had to live on.”

Signs of the End of the Age
13:1–37pp — Mt 24:1–51; Lk 21:5–36

13 As he was leaving the temple, one of his disciples said to him, “Look, Teacher! What massive stones! What magnificent buildings!”

2“Do you see all these great buildings?” replied Jesus. “Not one stone here will be left on another; every one will be thrown down.”

3As Jesus was sitting on the Mount of Olives opposite the temple, Peter, James, John and Andrew asked him privately, **4**“Tell us, when will these things happen? And what will be the sign that they are all about to be fulfilled?”

5Jesus said to them: “Watch out that no one deceives you. **6**Many will come in my name, claiming, ‘I am he,’ and will deceive many. **7**When you hear of wars and rumors of wars, do not be alarmed. Such things must happen, but the end is still to come. **8**Nation will rise against nation, and kingdom against kingdom. There will be earthquakes in various places, and famines. These are the beginning of birth pains.

9“You must be on your guard. You will be handed over to the local councils and flogged in the synagogues. On account of me you will stand before governors and kings as witnesses to them. **10**And the gospel must first be preached to all nations. **11**Whenever you are arrested and brought to trial, do not worry beforehand about what to say. Just say whatever is given you at the time, for it is not you speaking, but the Holy Spirit.

12“Brother will betray brother to death, and a father his child. Children will rebel against their parents and have them put to death. **13**All men will hate you because of me, but he who stands firm to the end will be saved.

14“When you see ‘the abomination that causes desolation’*a* standing where it*b* does not belong—let the reader understand—then let those who are in Judea flee to the mountains. **15**Let no one on the roof of his house go down or enter the house to take anything out. **16**Let no one in the field go back to get his cloak. **17**How dreadful it will be in those days for pregnant women and nursing mothers! **18**Pray that this will not take place in winter, **19**because those will be days of distress unequaled from the beginning, when God created the world, until now—and never to be equaled again. **20**If the Lord had not cut short those days, no one would survive. But for the sake of the elect, whom he has chosen, he has shortened them. **21**At that time if anyone says to you, ‘Look, here is the Christ*c*!’ or, ‘Look, there he is!’ do not believe it. **22**For false Christs and false prophets will appear and perform signs and miracles to deceive the elect—if that were possible. **23**So be on your guard; I have told you everything ahead of time.

24“But in those days, following that distress,

“ ‘the sun will be darkened,
    and the moon will not give its light;
25the stars will fall from the sky,
    and the heavenly bodies will be shaken.’*d*

26“At that time men will see the Son of Man coming in clouds with great power and glory. **27**And he will send his angels and gather his elect from the four winds, from the ends of the earth to the ends of the heavens.

28“Now learn this lesson from the fig tree: As soon as its twigs get tender and its leaves come out, you know that summer is near. **29**Even so, when you see these things happening, you know that it is near, right at the door. **30**I tell you the truth, this generation*e* will certainly not pass away until all these things have happened. **31**Heaven and earth will pass away, but my words will never pass away.

The Day and Hour Unknown
32“No one knows about that day or hour, not even the angels in heaven, nor the Son, but only the Father. **33**Be on guard! Be alert*f*! You do not

a 14 Daniel 9:27; 11:31; 12:11   *b 14* Or *he;* also in verse 29
c 21 Or *Messiah*   *d 25* Isaiah 13:10; 34:4   *e 30* Or *race*
f 33 Some manuscripts *alert and pray*

know when that time will come. ³⁴It's like a man going away: He leaves his house and puts his servants in charge, each with his assigned task, and tells the one at the door to keep watch.

³⁵"Therefore keep watch because you do not know when the owner of the house will come back—whether in the evening, or at midnight, or when the rooster crows, or at dawn. ³⁶If he comes suddenly, do not let him find you sleeping. ³⁷What I say to you, I say to everyone: 'Watch!'"

Jesus Anointed at Bethany

14:1–11pp — Mt 26:2–16
14:1,2,10,11pp — Lk 22:1–6
14:3–8Ref — Jn 12:1–8

14 Now the Passover and the Feast of Unleavened Bread were only two days away, and the chief priests and the teachers of the law were looking for some sly way to arrest Jesus and kill him. ²"But not during the Feast," they said, "or the people may riot."

³While he was in Bethany, reclining at the table in the home of a man known as Simon the Leper, a woman came with an alabaster jar of very expensive perfume, made of pure nard. She broke the jar and poured the perfume on his head.

⁴Some of those present were saying indignantly to one another, "Why this waste of perfume? ⁵It could have been sold for more than a year's wages *ᵃ* and the money given to the poor." And they rebuked her harshly.

⁶"Leave her alone," said Jesus. "Why are you bothering her? She has done a beautiful thing to me. ⁷The poor you will always have with you, and you can help them any time you want. But you will not always have me. ⁸She did what she could. She poured perfume on my body beforehand to prepare for my burial. ⁹I tell you the truth, wherever the gospel is preached throughout the world, what she has done will also be told, in memory of her."

¹⁰Then Judas Iscariot, one of the Twelve, went to the chief priests to betray Jesus to them. ¹¹They were delighted to hear this and promised to give him money. So he watched for an opportunity to hand him over.

The Lord's Supper

14:12–26pp — Mt 26:17–30; Lk 22:7–23
14:22–25pp — 1Co 11:23–25

¹²On the first day of the Feast of Unleavened Bread, when it was customary to sacrifice the Passover lamb, Jesus' disciples asked him, "Where do you want us to go and make preparations for you to eat the Passover?"

¹³So he sent two of his disciples, telling them, "Go into the city, and a man carrying a jar of water will meet you. Follow him. ¹⁴Say to the owner of the house he enters, 'The Teacher asks: Where is my guest room, where I may eat the Passover

ᵃ 5 Greek than three hundred denarii

stories to share

MARK 14:12–26

The Last Supper

LIFE LESSON: Jesus wants us to remember his sacrifice.

TO TALK ABOUT

✦ What instructions did Jesus give to two of his disciples? What happened?

✦ What did Jesus say one of the Twelve was about to do?

✦ What did Jesus say the bread represented? What did he say the cup represented?

✦ How do we remember the last supper of Jesus today in our worship?

with my disciples?' ¹⁵He will show you a large upper room, furnished and ready. Make preparations for us there."

¹⁶The disciples left, went into the city and found things just as Jesus had told them. So they prepared the Passover.

¹⁷When evening came, Jesus arrived with the Twelve. ¹⁸While they were reclining at the table eating, he said, "I tell you the truth, one of you will betray me—one who is eating with me."

¹⁹They were saddened, and one by one they said to him, "Surely not I?"

²⁰"It is one of the Twelve," he replied, "one who dips bread into the bowl with me. ²¹The Son of Man will go just as it is written about him. But woe to that man who betrays the Son of Man! It would be better for him if he had not been born."

²²While they were eating, Jesus took bread, gave thanks and broke it, and gave it to his disciples, saying, "Take it; this is my body."

²³Then he took the cup, gave thanks and offered it to them, and they all drank from it.

²⁴"This is my blood of the ^a covenant, which is poured out for many," he said to them. ²⁵"I tell you the truth, I will not drink again of the fruit of the vine until that day when I drink it anew in the kingdom of God."

²⁶When they had sung a hymn, they went out to the Mount of Olives.

Jesus Predicts Peter's Denial
14:27–31pp — Mt 26:31–35

²⁷"You will all fall away," Jesus told them, "for it is written:

" 'I will strike the shepherd,
    and the sheep will be scattered.' ^b

²⁸But after I have risen, I will go ahead of you into Galilee."

²⁹Peter declared, "Even if all fall away, I will not."

³⁰"I tell you the truth," Jesus answered, "today—yes, tonight—before the rooster crows twice ^c you yourself will disown me three times."

³¹But Peter insisted emphatically, "Even if I have to die with you, I will never disown you." And all the others said the same.

Gethsemane
14:32–42pp — Mt 26:36–46; Lk 22:40–46

³²They went to a place called Gethsemane, and Jesus said to his disciples, "Sit here while I pray." ³³He took Peter, James and John along with him, and he began to be deeply distressed and troubled. ³⁴"My soul is overwhelmed with sorrow to the point of death," he said to them. "Stay here and keep watch."

³⁵Going a little farther, he fell to the ground and prayed that if possible the hour might pass from him. ³⁶"Abba, ^d Father," he said, "everything is possible for you. Take this cup from me. Yet not what I will, but what you will."

TALKING POINTS

Loneliness
Jesus was left all alone in the garden.
MARK 14:32–42
For more on loneliness, go to John 14:16–17.

³⁷Then he returned to his disciples and found them sleeping. "Simon," he said to Peter, "are you asleep? Could you not keep watch for one hour? ³⁸Watch and pray so that you will not fall into temptation. The spirit is willing, but the body is weak."

³⁹Once more he went away and prayed the same thing. ⁴⁰When he came back, he again found them sleeping, because their eyes were heavy. They did not know what to say to him.

⁴¹Returning the third time, he said to them, "Are you still sleeping and resting? Enough! The

^a 24 Some manuscripts the new   ^b 27 Zech. 13:7   ^c 30 Some early manuscripts do not have twice.   ^d 36 Aramaic for Father

hour has come. Look, the Son of Man is betrayed into the hands of sinners. ⁴²Rise! Let us go! Here comes my betrayer!"

Jesus Arrested

14:43–50pp — Mt 26:47–56; Lk 22:47–50; Jn 18:3–11

⁴³Just as he was speaking, Judas, one of the Twelve, appeared. With him was a crowd armed with swords and clubs, sent from the chief priests, the teachers of the law, and the elders.

⁴⁴Now the betrayer had arranged a signal with them: "The one I kiss is the man; arrest him and lead him away under guard." ⁴⁵Going at once to Jesus, Judas said, "Rabbi!" and kissed him. ⁴⁶The men seized Jesus and arrested him. ⁴⁷Then one of those standing near drew his sword and struck the servant of the high priest, cutting off his ear.

⁴⁸"Am I leading a rebellion," said Jesus, "that you have come out with swords and clubs to capture me? ⁴⁹Every day I was with you, teaching in the temple courts, and you did not arrest me. But the Scriptures must be fulfilled." ⁵⁰Then everyone deserted him and fled.

⁵¹A young man, wearing nothing but a linen garment, was following Jesus. When they seized him, ⁵²he fled naked, leaving his garment behind.

Before the Sanhedrin

14:53–65pp — Mt 26:57–68; Jn 18:12,13,19–24
14:61–63pp — Lk 22:67–71

⁵³They took Jesus to the high priest, and all the chief priests, elders and teachers of the law came together. ⁵⁴Peter followed him at a distance, right into the courtyard of the high priest. There he sat with the guards and warmed himself at the fire.

⁵⁵The chief priests and the whole Sanhedrin were looking for evidence against Jesus so that they could put him to death, but they did not find any. ⁵⁶Many testified falsely against him, but their statements did not agree.

⁵⁷Then some stood up and gave this false testimony against him: ⁵⁸"We heard him say, 'I will destroy this man-made temple and in three days will build another, not made by man.'" ⁵⁹Yet even then their testimony did not agree.

⁶⁰Then the high priest stood up before them and asked Jesus, "Are you not going to answer? What is this testimony that these men are bringing against you?" ⁶¹But Jesus remained silent and gave no answer.

Again the high priest asked him, "Are you the Christ,ᵃ the Son of the Blessed One?"

⁶²"I am," said Jesus. "And you will see the Son of Man sitting at the right hand of the Mighty One and coming on the clouds of heaven."

⁶³The high priest tore his clothes. "Why do we need any more witnesses?" he asked. ⁶⁴"You have heard the blasphemy. What do you think?"

They all condemned him as worthy of death. ⁶⁵Then some began to spit at him; they blindfolded him, struck him with their fists, and said, "Prophesy!" And the guards took him and beat him.

Peter Disowns Jesus

14:66–72pp — Mt 26:69–75; Lk 22:56–62;
Jn 18:16–18,25–27

⁶⁶While Peter was below in the courtyard, one of the servant girls of the high priest came by. ⁶⁷When she saw Peter warming himself, she looked closely at him.

"You also were with that Nazarene, Jesus," she said.

⁶⁸But he denied it. "I don't know or understand what you're talking about," he said, and went out into the entryway.ᵇ

⁶⁹When the servant girl saw him there, she said again to those standing around, "This fellow is one of them." ⁷⁰Again he denied it.

After a little while, those standing near said to Peter, "Surely you are one of them, for you are a Galilean."

⁷¹He began to call down curses on himself, and he swore to them, "I don't know this man you're talking about."

⁷²Immediately the rooster crowed the second time.ᶜ Then Peter remembered the word Jesus had spoken to him: "Before the rooster crows

---

ᵃ 61 Or *Messiah*   ᵇ 68 Some early manuscripts *entryway and the rooster crowed*   ᶜ 72 Some early manuscripts do not have *the second time.*

twice[a] you will disown me three times." And he broke down and wept.

Jesus Before Pilate

15:2–15pp — Mt 27:11–26; Lk 23:2,3,18–25; Jn 18:29–19:16

15 Very early in the morning, the chief priests, with the elders, the teachers of the law and the whole Sanhedrin, reached a decision. They bound Jesus, led him away and handed him over to Pilate.

² "Are you the king of the Jews?" asked Pilate.

"Yes, it is as you say," Jesus replied.

³ The chief priests accused him of many things. ⁴ So again Pilate asked him, "Aren't you going to answer? See how many things they are accusing you of."

⁵ But Jesus still made no reply, and Pilate was amazed.

⁶ Now it was the custom at the Feast to release a prisoner whom the people requested. ⁷ A man called Barabbas was in prison with the insurrectionists who had committed murder in the uprising. ⁸ The crowd came up and asked Pilate to do for them what he usually did.

⁹ "Do you want me to release to you the king of the Jews?" asked Pilate, ¹⁰ knowing it was out of envy that the chief priests had handed Jesus over to him. ¹¹ But the chief priests stirred up the crowd to have Pilate release Barabbas instead.

¹² "What shall I do, then, with the one you call the king of the Jews?" Pilate asked them.

¹³ "Crucify him!" they shouted.

¹⁴ "Why? What crime has he committed?" asked Pilate.

But they shouted all the louder, "Crucify him!"

¹⁵ Wanting to satisfy the crowd, Pilate released Barabbas to them. He had Jesus flogged, and handed him over to be crucified.

The Soldiers Mock Jesus

15:16–20pp — Mt 27:27–31

¹⁶ The soldiers led Jesus away into the palace (that is, the Praetorium) and called together the whole company of soldiers. ¹⁷ They put a purple robe on him, then twisted together a crown of thorns and set it on him. ¹⁸ And they began to call out to him, "Hail, king of the Jews!" ¹⁹ Again and again they struck him on the head with a staff and spit on him. Falling on their knees, they paid homage to him. ²⁰ And when they had mocked him, they took off the purple robe and put his own clothes on him. Then they led him out to crucify him.

The Crucifixion

15:22–32pp — Mt 27:33–44; Lk 23:33–43; Jn 19:17–24

²¹ A certain man from Cyrene, Simon, the father of Alexander and Rufus, was passing by on his way in from the country, and they forced him to carry the cross. ²² They brought Jesus to the place called Golgotha (which means The Place of the Skull). ²³ Then they offered him wine mixed with myrrh, but he did not take it. ²⁴ And they crucified him. Dividing up his clothes, they cast lots to see what each would get.

²⁵ It was the third hour when they crucified him. ²⁶ The written notice of the charge against him read: THE KING OF THE JEWS. ²⁷ They crucified two robbers with him, one on his right and one on his left.[b] ²⁹ Those who passed by hurled insults at him, shaking their heads and saying, "So! You who are going to destroy the temple and build it in three days, ³⁰ come down from the cross and save yourself!"

³¹ In the same way the chief priests and the teachers of the law mocked him among themselves. "He saved others," they said, "but he can't save himself! ³² Let this Christ,[c] this King of Israel, come down now from the cross, that we may see and believe." Those crucified with him also heaped insults on him.

The Death of Jesus

15:33–41pp — Mt 27:45–56; Lk 23:44–49; Jn 19:29–30

³³ At the sixth hour darkness came over the whole land until the ninth hour. ³⁴ And at the

---

[a] 72 Some early manuscripts do not have *twice*.   [b] 27 Some manuscripts *left,* ²⁸*and the scripture was fulfilled which says, "He was counted with the lawless ones"* (Isaiah 53:12)   [c] 32 Or *Messiah*

ninth hour Jesus cried out in a loud voice, *"Eloi, Eloi, lama sabachthani?"* — which means, "My God, my God, why have you forsaken me?" [a]

³⁵ When some of those standing near heard this, they said, "Listen, he's calling Elijah."

³⁶ One man ran, filled a sponge with wine vinegar, put it on a stick, and offered it to Jesus to drink. "Now leave him alone. Let's see if Elijah comes to take him down," he said.

³⁷ With a loud cry, Jesus breathed his last.

³⁸ The curtain of the temple was torn in two from top to bottom. ³⁹ And when the centurion, who stood there in front of Jesus, heard his cry

MARK 15:16–47

The Crucifixion of Jesus

LIFE LESSON: Jesus, our King, died for our sins.

TO TALK ABOUT

✦ What kinds of things did the people around the cross say to Jesus?

✦ Could Jesus have saved himself from death on the cross? If so, why didn't he?

✦ How and why did God forsake Jesus? Why did this have to happen in order for us to be saved from sin?

✦ In what ways is Jesus our King?

and [b] saw how he died, he said, "Surely this man was the Son [c] of God!"

⁴⁰ Some women were watching from a distance. Among them were Mary Magdalene, Mary the mother of James the younger and of Joses, and Salome. ⁴¹ In Galilee these women had followed him and cared for his needs. Many other women who had come up with him to Jerusalem were also there.

The Burial of Jesus

15:42–47pp — Mt 27:57–61; Lk 23:50–56; Jn 19:38–42

⁴² It was Preparation Day (that is, the day before the Sabbath). So as evening approached, ⁴³ Joseph of Arimathea, a prominent member of the Council, who was himself waiting for the kingdom of God, went boldly to Pilate and asked for Jesus' body. ⁴⁴ Pilate was surprised to hear that he was already dead. Summoning the centurion, he asked him if Jesus had already died. ⁴⁵ When he learned from the centurion that it was so, he gave the body to Joseph. ⁴⁶ So Joseph bought some linen cloth, took down the body, wrapped it in the linen, and placed it in a tomb cut out of rock. Then he rolled a stone against the entrance of the tomb. ⁴⁷ Mary Magdalene and Mary the mother of Joses saw where he was laid.

The Resurrection

16:1–8pp — Mt 28:1–8; Lk 24:1–10

16 When the Sabbath was over, Mary Magdalene, Mary the mother of James, and Salome bought spices so that they might go to anoint Jesus' body. ² Very early on the first day of the week, just after sunrise, they were on their way to the tomb ³ and they asked each other, "Who will roll the stone away from the entrance of the tomb?"

⁴ But when they looked up, they saw that the stone, which was very large, had been rolled away. ⁵ As they entered the tomb, they saw a young man dressed in a white robe sitting on the right side, and they were alarmed.

---

[a] 34 Psalm 22:1 [b] 39 Some manuscripts do not have *heard his cry and* [c] 39 Or *a son*

6 "Don't be alarmed," he said. "You are looking for Jesus the Nazarene, who was crucified. He has risen! He is not here. See the place where they laid him. 7 But go, tell his disciples and Peter, 'He is going ahead of you into Galilee. There you will see him, just as he told you.'"

8 Trembling and bewildered, the women went out and fled from the tomb. They said nothing to anyone, because they were afraid.

[The earliest manuscripts and some other ancient witnesses do not have Mark 16:9–20.]

9 When Jesus rose early on the first day of the week, he appeared first to Mary Magdalene, out of whom he had driven seven demons. 10 She went and told those who had been with him and who were mourning and weeping. 11 When they heard that Jesus was alive and that she had seen him, they did not believe it.

12 Afterward Jesus appeared in a different form to two of them while they were walking in the country. 13 These returned and reported it to the rest; but they did not believe them either.

14 Later Jesus appeared to the Eleven as they were eating; he rebuked them for their lack of faith and their stubborn refusal to believe those who had seen him after he had risen.

15 He said to them, "Go into all the world and preach the good news to all creation. 16 Whoever believes and is baptized will be saved, but whoever does not believe will be condemned. 17 And these signs will accompany those who believe: In my name they will drive out demons; they will speak in new tongues; 18 they will pick up snakes with their hands; and when they drink deadly poison, it will not hurt them at all; they will place their hands on sick people, and they will get well."

19 After the Lord Jesus had spoken to them, he was taken up into heaven and he sat at the right hand of God. 20 Then the disciples went out and preached everywhere, and the Lord worked with them and confirmed his word by the signs that accompanied it.

Christlike RELATIONSHIPS

"Tell Me the Story of Jesus." This title of a classic church school song could easily be the subtitle of the Gospel of Luke, because Luke's Gospel contains many of the best-known stories of Jesus' life: from his birth and childhood to his baptism, from the beginning of his earthly ministry to its ending, from his death to his resurrection and ascension. Luke wrote down this collection of stories for the "most excellent Theophilus" (Luke 1:3) so that he and future readers could "know the certainty of the things" they had been taught (Luke 1:4).

Luke's account focuses on Jesus' relationships with all kinds of people. To the chagrin of his disciples and the "acceptable" citizens of his day, Jesus sought out the people thought to be the least valued of society: women, children, the poor and the outcasts. He interacted with them — defending, healing and teaching. He did more than "touch base" with them; he cared deeply for them, and they knew it. He blessed them with unforgettable moments with their Savior, and they spread the news: "God has come to help his people" (Luke 7:16).

Luke's Gospel provides us with some of the most touching stories of Jesus' life. This book gives us endless examples of how we can be more Christlike in our relationships with our grandchildren, our family members and friends, and everyone we encounter.

VERSE *to* REMEMBER | LUKE 18:16

Jesus called the children to him and said, "Let the little children come to me, and do not hinder them, for the kingdom of God belongs to such as these."

ABOUT LUKE

WRITTEN BY:
Luke, a Gentile physician who traveled as a missionary with Paul

WRITTEN FOR:
Specifically for Theophilus, but also for all people

DATE WRITTEN:
Probably around A.D. 60

WHY WRITTEN:
To show that the gospel is for the whole world

Introduction

1:1–4Ref — Ac 1:1

1 Many have undertaken to draw up an account of the things that have been fulfilled *a* among us, ²just as they were handed down to us by those who from the first were eyewitnesses and servants of the word. ³Therefore, since I myself have carefully investigated everything from the beginning, it seemed good also to me to write an orderly account for you, most excellent Theophilus, ⁴so that you may know the certainty of the things you have been taught.

The Birth of John the Baptist Foretold

⁵In the time of Herod king of Judea there was a priest named Zechariah, who belonged to the priestly division of Abijah; his wife Elizabeth was also a descendant of Aaron. ⁶Both of them were upright in the sight of God, observing all the Lord's commandments and regulations blamelessly. ⁷But they had no children, because Elizabeth was barren; and they were both well along in years.

⁸Once when Zechariah's division was on duty and he was serving as priest before God, ⁹he was chosen by lot, according to the custom of the priesthood, to go into the temple of the Lord and burn incense. ¹⁰And when the time for the burning of incense came, all the assembled worshipers were praying outside.

¹¹Then an angel of the Lord appeared to him, standing at the right side of the altar of incense. ¹²When Zechariah saw him, he was startled and was gripped with fear. ¹³But the angel said to him: "Do not be afraid, Zechariah; your prayer has been heard. Your wife Elizabeth will bear you a son, and you are to give him the name John. ¹⁴He will be a joy and delight to you, and many will rejoice because of his birth, ¹⁵for he will be great in the sight of the Lord. He is never to take wine or other fermented drink, and he will be filled with the Holy Spirit even from birth. *b* ¹⁶Many of the people of Israel will he bring back to the Lord their God. ¹⁷And he will go on before the Lord, in the spirit and power of Elijah, to turn the hearts of the fathers to their children and the disobedient to the wisdom of the righteous—to make ready a people prepared for the Lord."

¹⁸Zechariah asked the angel, "How can I be sure of this? I am an old man and my wife is well along in years."

¹⁹The angel answered, "I am Gabriel. I stand in the presence of God, and I have been sent to speak to you and to tell you this good news. ²⁰And now you will be silent and not able to speak until the day this happens, because you did not believe my words, which will come true at their proper time."

²¹Meanwhile, the people were waiting for Zechariah and wondering why he stayed so long in the temple. ²²When he came out, he could not speak to them. They realized he had seen a vision in the temple, for he kept making signs to them but remained unable to speak.

²³When his time of service was completed, he returned home. ²⁴After this his wife Elizabeth became pregnant and for five months remained in seclusion. ²⁵"The Lord has done this for me," she said. "In these days he has shown his favor and taken away my disgrace among the people."

The Birth of Jesus Foretold

²⁶In the sixth month, God sent the angel Gabriel to Nazareth, a town in Galilee, ²⁷to a virgin pledged to be married to a man named Joseph, a descendant of David. The virgin's name was Mary. ²⁸The angel went to her and said, "Greetings, you who are highly favored! The Lord is with you."

²⁹Mary was greatly troubled at his words and wondered what kind of greeting this might be. ³⁰But the angel said to her, "Do not be afraid, Mary, you have found favor with God. ³¹You will be with child and give birth to a son, and you are to give him the name Jesus. ³²He will be great and will be called the Son of the Most High. The Lord God will give him the throne of his father David,

a 1 Or been surely believed   b 15 Or from his mother's womb

BUT THE ANGEL SAID TO HIM: "DO NOT BE AFRAID, ZECHARIAH; YOUR PRAYER HAS BEEN HEARD. YOUR WIFE ELIZABETH WILL BEAR YOU A SON . . . HE WILL . . . MAKE READY A PEOPLE PREPARED FOR THE LORD."

Luke 1:13,17

When Hope Fades

HELEN HAIDLE

READ | LUKE 1:5 – 22

Zechariah was "well along in years" (Luke 1:7) when he was chosen by lot to burn incense in the temple. Most likely he had never had this opportunity in the preceding years of his faithful priestly service. For most priests, it was a once-in-a-lifetime experience to burn incense in God's sanctuary while the people prayed outside.

What does this tell us about God's "timing"? Perhaps Zechariah had given up all hope of being selected to burn incense. From his response to the angel, it is certain that Zechariah never expected an angelic encounter while the smoke from the incense filled the Holy Place. Nor did he expect to hear the promise of a son to be born to him and Elizabeth in their old age.

The angel told Zechariah, "Your prayer has been heard" (Luke 1:13).

Was Zechariah still praying for a son? From his skeptical response, it seems he had quit praying for a child long ago. He had good reasons to doubt the angel's message. It seemed too late for this prayer to be answered. It was now a physical impossibility!

Yet the baby God gave these two "elders" was no ordinary child. Jesus later said, "Among those born of women there is no one greater than John" (Luke 7:28).

The older I get, the more this story renews my hope that God can and does "birth" new things — even extraordinary things — in and through older people. Zechariah and Elizabeth also remind us that nothing is impossible with God. Our faithful God can be trusted to make us fruitful as we age. God wants to use us. God wants to answer "impossible" prayers we pray. We can trust God to keep his promise: "[The righteous] will still bear fruit in old age, they will stay fresh and green" (Psalm 92:14).

Dear Lord, I'm available! Let your power and perfect timing be seen in my life. I desire to "bear fruit" and "stay fresh and green." Bless me and continue to use me all the days of my life. I trust you can and will do it! Amen. So be it.

Your next devotion is located on page 1380.

GRANDCHILD IN FOCUS • PRAYER

Future Spouse

Dear Lord, if it is your will, I pray my grandchild will be united in a loving and Christian marriage. Keep her sexually pure so that she will honor you with her body and mind. As she seeks a spouse who will honor and care for her, give her patience and discernment. May her choice for a life partner be your choice for her, so that she and her husband will together glorify you in a lasting love. I pray this in Jesus' name, amen.

1379

> "THE LORD HAS DONE THIS
> FOR ME," SHE SAID. "IN THESE
> DAYS HE HAS SHOWN HIS FAVOR
> AND TAKEN AWAY MY DISGRACE
> AMONG THE PEOPLE."
>
> Luke 1:25

Valued

MARY RUTH HOWES

READ | LUKE 1:18 – 25

Luke is the gospel of women. He tells more stories about more women than any of the other gospel writers, and he gives the names of many of them. He begins his gospel with the name of a couple — an old man and an old woman, Zechariah and Elizabeth. All her life, Elizabeth had wanted a child. Now, in her old age, her dream was coming true. Now, "The Lord has done this for me," she said. "In these days he has shown his favor and taken away my disgrace among the people."

In many parts of the world, including our own, being old, and especially an old woman, means being invisible. In her book *The Desert Blooms*, Sarah-Patton Boyle recounts the terrible pain she experienced when, after a full and rewarding life in which she was recognized as a complete person, she came to be treated as a non-entity — because people saw only her gray hair, they considered her of no value. *The Desert Blooms* also tells about her courageous journey out of resulting depression and despair.

The good news of the gospel is that as women — even gray-haired women — we are not only valued by God, but our names are also recorded in his history, and we may play a pivotal role in the working out of God's purposes.

Thank you, Father, that you count even my gray hairs, that my name is important to you, and that you continue to have a place for me.

Your next devotion is located on page 1384.

GRANDCHILD IN FOCUS • PRAYER

School/Career

Dear God, may learning be a joy rather than a chore for my grandchild. May exploration of new ideas bring a sense of wonder, awe and excitement. Grant him clarity of mind, the ability to concentrate on the task at hand and recollection of what has been learned. Help him to appreciate the tasks that come easily and to persevere through those that challenge. Amen.

LUKE 1:26–38

An Angel Visits Mary

LIFE LESSON: Nothing is impossible with God.

TO TALK ABOUT

✦ How did Mary react when the angel appeared to her?

✦ What did the angel tell her?

✦ Do you think it was hard for Mary to believe the angel?

✦ Why do you think God chose Mary to be Jesus' mom?

33 and he will reign over the house of Jacob forever; his kingdom will never end."

34 "How will this be," Mary asked the angel, "since I am a virgin?"

35 The angel answered, "The Holy Spirit will come upon you, and the power of the Most High will overshadow you. So the holy one to be born will be called*a* the Son of God. 36 Even Elizabeth your relative is going to have a child in her old age, and she who was said to be barren is in her sixth month. 37 For nothing is impossible with God."

38 "I am the Lord's servant," Mary answered. "May it be to me as you have said." Then the angel left her.

Mary Visits Elizabeth

39 At that time Mary got ready and hurried to a town in the hill country of Judea, 40 where she entered Zechariah's home and greeted Elizabeth. 41 When Elizabeth heard Mary's greeting, the baby leaped in her womb, and Elizabeth was filled with the Holy Spirit. 42 In a loud voice she exclaimed: "Blessed are you among women, and blessed is the child you will bear! 43 But why am I so favored, that the mother of my Lord should come to me? 44 As soon as the sound of your greeting reached my ears, the baby in my womb leaped for joy. 45 Blessed is she who has believed that what the Lord has said to her will be accomplished!"

Mary's Song

1:46–53pp — 1Sa 2:1–10

46 And Mary said:

"My soul glorifies the Lord
47   and my spirit rejoices in God my Savior,
48 for he has been mindful
    of the humble state of his servant.
  From now on all generations will call me
      blessed,
49   for the Mighty One has done great things
      for me —
    holy is his name.
50 His mercy extends to those who fear him,
    from generation to generation.
51 He has performed mighty deeds with his
      arm;
  he has scattered those who are proud in
      their inmost thoughts.
52 He has brought down rulers from their
      thrones
  but has lifted up the humble.
53 He has filled the hungry with good things
  but has sent the rich away empty.
54 He has helped his servant Israel,
    remembering to be merciful
55 to Abraham and his descendants forever,
    even as he said to our fathers."

56 Mary stayed with Elizabeth for about three months and then returned home.

a 35 Or So the child to be born will be called holy,

The Birth of John the Baptist

⁵⁷When it was time for Elizabeth to have her baby, she gave birth to a son. ⁵⁸Her neighbors and relatives heard that the Lord had shown her great mercy, and they shared her joy.

⁵⁹On the eighth day they came to circumcise the child, and they were going to name him after his father Zechariah, ⁶⁰but his mother spoke up and said, "No! He is to be called John."

⁶¹They said to her, "There is no one among your relatives who has that name."

⁶²Then they made signs to his father, to find out what he would like to name the child. ⁶³He asked for a writing tablet, and to everyone's astonishment he wrote, "His name is John." ⁶⁴Immediately his mouth was opened and his tongue was loosed, and he began to speak, praising God. ⁶⁵The neighbors were all filled with awe, and throughout the hill country of Judea people were talking about all these things. ⁶⁶Everyone who heard this wondered about it, asking, "What then is this child going to be?" For the Lord's hand was with him.

Zechariah's Song

⁶⁷His father Zechariah was filled with the Holy Spirit and prophesied:

⁶⁸"Praise be to the Lord, the God of Israel,
   because he has come and has redeemed
      his people.
⁶⁹He has raised up a horn ᵃ of salvation for us
   in the house of his servant David
⁷⁰(as he said through his holy prophets of
      long ago),
⁷¹salvation from our enemies
   and from the hand of all who hate us—
⁷²to show mercy to our fathers
   and to remember his holy covenant,
⁷³   the oath he swore to our father Abraham:
⁷⁴to rescue us from the hand of our enemies,
   and to enable us to serve him without
      fear
⁷⁵   in holiness and righteousness before him
      all our days.

⁷⁶And you, my child, will be called a prophet of
      the Most High;
   for you will go on before the Lord to
      prepare the way for him,
⁷⁷to give his people the knowledge of salvation
   through the forgiveness of their sins,
⁷⁸because of the tender mercy of our God,
   by which the rising sun will come to us
      from heaven
⁷⁹to shine on those living in darkness
   and in the shadow of death,
   to guide our feet into the path of peace."

⁸⁰And the child grew and became strong in spirit; and he lived in the desert until he appeared publicly to Israel.

The Birth of Jesus

2 In those days Caesar Augustus issued a decree that a census should be taken of the entire Roman world. ²(This was the first census that took place while Quirinius was governor of Syria.) ³And everyone went to his own town to register.

⁴So Joseph also went up from the town of Nazareth in Galilee to Judea, to Bethlehem the town of David, because he belonged to the house and line of David. ⁵He went there to register with Mary, who was pledged to be married to him and was expecting a child. ⁶While they were there, the time came for the baby to be born, ⁷and she gave birth to her firstborn, a son. She wrapped him in cloths and placed him in a manger, because there was no room for them in the inn.

The Shepherds and the Angels

⁸And there were shepherds living out in the fields nearby, keeping watch over their flocks at night. ⁹An angel of the Lord appeared to them, and the glory of the Lord shone around them, and they were terrified. ¹⁰But the angel said to them, "Do not be afraid. I bring you good news of great joy that will be for all the people. ¹¹Today in the town of David a Savior has been born to

---

ᵃ 69 *Horn* here symbolizes strength.

you; he is Christ[a] the Lord. [12]This will be a sign to you: You will find a baby wrapped in cloths and lying in a manger."

[13]Suddenly a great company of the heavenly host appeared with the angel, praising God and saying,

[14]"Glory to God in the highest,
and on earth peace to men on whom his favor rests."

[15]When the angels had left them and gone into heaven, the shepherds said to one another, "Let's go to Bethlehem and see this thing that has happened, which the Lord has told us about."

[16]So they hurried off and found Mary and Jo-

LUKE 2:1–20

Baby Jesus Is Born

LIFE LESSON: Jesus was born to save us.

TO TALK ABOUT

✦ What is a manger and where are they usually found? Is this the kind of place where you would expect God's Son to be born?

✦ What did the angel say to the shepherds?

✦ What did the shepherds do after they saw Jesus? How can we follow their example?

✦ Why did God send his angels to announce Jesus' birth to the shepherds?

seph, and the baby, who was lying in the manger. [17]When they had seen him, they spread the word concerning what had been told them about this child, [18]and all who heard it were amazed at what the shepherds said to them. [19]But Mary treasured up all these things and pondered them in her heart. [20]The shepherds returned, glorifying and praising God for all the things they had heard and seen, which were just as they had been told.

Jesus Presented in the Temple

[21]On the eighth day, when it was time to circumcise him, he was named Jesus, the name the angel had given him before he had been conceived.

[22]When the time of their purification according to the Law of Moses had been completed, Joseph and Mary took him to Jerusalem to present him to the Lord [23](as it is written in the Law of the Lord, "Every firstborn male is to be consecrated to the Lord"[b]), [24]and to offer a sacrifice in keeping with what is said in the Law of the Lord: "a pair of doves or two young pigeons."[c]

[25]Now there was a man in Jerusalem called Simeon, who was righteous and devout. He was waiting for the consolation of Israel, and the Holy Spirit was upon him. [26]It had been revealed to him by the Holy Spirit that he would not die before he had seen the Lord's Christ. [27]Moved by the Spirit, he went into the temple courts. When the parents brought in the child Jesus to do for him what the custom of the Law required, [28]Simeon took him in his arms and praised God, saying:

[29]"Sovereign Lord, as you have promised,
you now dismiss[d] your servant in peace.
[30]For my eyes have seen your salvation,
[31]   which you have prepared in the sight of all people,
[32]a light for revelation to the Gentiles
and for glory to your people Israel."

[a] 11 Or Messiah. "The Christ" (Greek) and "the Messiah" (Hebrew) both mean "the Anointed One"; also in verse 26.
[b] 23 Exodus 13:2,12   [c] 24 Lev. 12:8   [d] 29 Or promised, / now dismiss

Family Traditions

Every family has traditions, whether they realize it or not. Things that you take for granted may actually be a tradition that is unique to your family. Perhaps it's a favorite food that you always make at Christmas or hunting for Easter eggs even when it snows or going camping for a week in the summer. Perhaps it's an action by a family member: Grandpa always falls asleep after dinner; Uncle Dave sneezes ten times after eating spaghetti. Sometimes traditions happen without us really thinking about it. So today, take some time with your grandchildren to think about what things have become your family traditions.

You may also want to talk about what family traditions you had when you were a child — and if they are still part of your family traditions or if they have been forgotten or blended with other things. What's old and what's new in the traditions your family shares? Do you know how they got started? Ask the kids if there is something they would like to start doing that could become a new family tradition. They may have some very creative ideas.

Thank you, Lord, for the meaningful traditions we have in our family, especially the spiritual ones that remind me of you and your love. Help me to impress upon my grandchildren the importance of family traditions and the bonds they build through the generations. Amen.

Your next devotion is located on page 1389.

GRANDCHILD IN FOCUS • PRAYER

Character

Dear Lord and Father, I ask that you fill my grandchild with your Spirit so her character reflects your goodness and love. Give her kindness and love for others. Bring joy to her life so she will be a joy to others. Grant her patience and self-control through difficult and trying times. May she show mercy and generosity to those who are less fortunate. Grant her integrity and a sense of justice, and surround her with your peace. Amen.

stories to share

LUKE 2:21–40

Mary and Joseph Take Jesus to the Temple

LIFE LESSON: Jesus is the Messiah, our source of salvation.

TO TALK ABOUT

✦ Who did Mary and Joseph meet at the temple?

✦ How did these two people know who Jesus was?

✦ What did Simeon say about Jesus?

✦ How do you think Mary and Joseph felt about these prophecies?

---

³³The child's father and mother marveled at what was said about him. ³⁴Then Simeon blessed them and said to Mary, his mother: "This child is destined to cause the falling and rising of many in Israel, and to be a sign that will be spoken against, ³⁵so that the thoughts of many hearts will be revealed. And a sword will pierce your own soul too."

³⁶There was also a prophetess, Anna, the daughter of Phanuel, of the tribe of Asher. She was very old; she had lived with her husband seven years after her marriage, ³⁷and then was a widow until she was eighty-four.[a] She never left the temple but worshiped night and day, fasting and praying. ³⁸Coming up to them at that very moment, she gave thanks to God and spoke about the child to all who were looking forward to the redemption of Jerusalem.

³⁹When Joseph and Mary had done everything required by the Law of the Lord, they returned to Galilee to their own town of Nazareth. ⁴⁰And the child grew and became strong; he was filled with wisdom, and the grace of God was upon him.

The Boy Jesus at the Temple

⁴¹Every year his parents went to Jerusalem for the Feast of the Passover. ⁴²When he was twelve years old, they went up to the Feast, according to the custom. ⁴³After the Feast was over, while his parents were returning home, the boy Jesus stayed behind in Jerusalem, but they were unaware of it. ⁴⁴Thinking he was in their company, they traveled on for a day. Then they began looking for him among their relatives and friends. ⁴⁵When they did not find him, they went back to Jerusalem to look for him. ⁴⁶After three days they found him in the temple courts, sitting among the teachers, listening to them and asking them questions. ⁴⁷Everyone who heard him was amazed at his understanding and his answers. ⁴⁸When his parents saw him, they were astonished. His mother said to him, "Son, why have you treated us like this? Your father and I have been anxiously searching for you."

⁴⁹"Why were you searching for me?" he asked. "Didn't you know I had to be in my Father's house?" ⁵⁰But they did not understand what he was saying to them.

⁵¹Then he went down to Nazareth with them and was obedient to them. But his mother treasured all these things in her heart. ⁵²And Jesus grew in wisdom and stature, and in favor with God and men.

John the Baptist Prepares the Way

3:2–10pp — Mt 3:1–10; Mk 1:3–5
3:16,17pp — Mt 3:11,12; Mk 1:7,8

3 In the fifteenth year of the reign of Tiberius Caesar—when Pontius Pilate was governor of Judea, Herod tetrarch of Galilee, his brother Philip tetrarch of Iturea and Traconitis, and

---

[a] 37 Or widow for eighty-four years

stories to share

LUKE 2:41–52

Jesus Stays Behind at the Temple

LIFE LESSON: Jesus came to Earth for a heavenly purpose.

TO TALK ABOUT

✦ Why did Jesus and his parents travel to Jerusalem?

✦ How old was Jesus when this happened?

✦ How could Jesus be sinless and still stay behind at the temple? Who was he obeying?

✦ How do Jesus' words show that he realized he was God's Son?

Lysanias tetrarch of Abilene— ²during the high priesthood of Annas and Caiaphas, the word of God came to John son of Zechariah in the desert. ³He went into all the country around the Jordan, preaching a baptism of repentance for the forgiveness of sins. ⁴As is written in the book of the words of Isaiah the prophet:

> "A voice of one calling in the desert,
> 'Prepare the way for the Lord,
>   make straight paths for him.
> ⁵Every valley shall be filled in,
>   every mountain and hill made low.
> The crooked roads shall become straight,
>   the rough ways smooth.
> ⁶And all mankind will see God's salvation.' "ᵃ

⁷John said to the crowds coming out to be baptized by him, "You brood of vipers! Who warned you to flee from the coming wrath? ⁸Produce fruit in keeping with repentance. And do not begin to say to yourselves, 'We have Abraham as our father.' For I tell you that out of these stones God can raise up children for Abraham. ⁹The ax is already at the root of the trees, and every tree that does not produce good fruit will be cut down and thrown into the fire."

¹⁰"What should we do then?" the crowd asked.

¹¹John answered, "The man with two tunics should share with him who has none, and the one who has food should do the same."

¹²Tax collectors also came to be baptized. "Teacher," they asked, "what should we do?"

¹³"Don't collect any more than you are required to," he told them.

¹⁴Then some soldiers asked him, "And what should we do?"

He replied, "Don't extort money and don't accuse people falsely—be content with your pay."

¹⁵The people were waiting expectantly and were all wondering in their hearts if John might possibly be the Christ.ᵇ ¹⁶John answered them all, "I baptize you withᶜ water. But one more powerful than I will come, the thongs of whose sandals I am not worthy to untie. He will baptize you with the Holy Spirit and with fire. ¹⁷His winnowing fork is in his hand to clear his threshing floor and to gather the wheat into his barn, but he will burn up the chaff with unquenchable fire." ¹⁸And with many other words John exhorted the people and preached the good news to them.

¹⁹But when John rebuked Herod the tetrarch because of Herodias, his brother's wife, and all the other evil things he had done, ²⁰Herod added this to them all: He locked John up in prison.

The Baptism and Genealogy of Jesus

3:21,22pp — Mt 3:13–17; Mk 1:9–11
3:23–38pp — Mt 1:1–17

²¹When all the people were being baptized, Jesus was baptized too. And as he was praying,

---

ᵃ 6 Isaiah 40:3-5   ᵇ 15 Or Messiah   ᶜ 16 Or in

heaven was opened ²²and the Holy Spirit descended on him in bodily form like a dove. And a voice came from heaven: "You are my Son, whom I love; with you I am well pleased."

²³Now Jesus himself was about thirty years old when he began his ministry. He was the son, so it was thought, of Joseph,

the son of Heli, ²⁴the son of Matthat,
the son of Levi, the son of Melki,
the son of Jannai, the son of Joseph,
²⁵the son of Mattathias, the son of Amos,
the son of Nahum, the son of Esli,
the son of Naggai, ²⁶the son of Maath,
the son of Mattathias, the son of Semein,
the son of Josech, the son of Joda,
²⁷the son of Joanan, the son of Rhesa,
the son of Zerubbabel, the son of Shealtiel,
the son of Neri, ²⁸the son of Melki,
the son of Addi, the son of Cosam,
the son of Elmadam, the son of Er,
²⁹the son of Joshua, the son of Eliezer,
the son of Jorim, the son of Matthat,
the son of Levi, ³⁰the son of Simeon,
the son of Judah, the son of Joseph,
the son of Jonam, the son of Eliakim,
³¹the son of Melea, the son of Menna,
the son of Mattatha, the son of Nathan,
the son of David, ³²the son of Jesse,
the son of Obed, the son of Boaz,
the son of Salmon,ᵃ the son of Nahshon,
³³the son of Amminadab, the son of Ram,ᵇ
the son of Hezron, the son of Perez,
the son of Judah, ³⁴the son of Jacob,
the son of Isaac, the son of Abraham,
the son of Terah, the son of Nahor,
³⁵the son of Serug, the son of Reu,
the son of Peleg, the son of Eber,
the son of Shelah, ³⁶the son of Cainan,
the son of Arphaxad, the son of Shem,
the son of Noah, the son of Lamech,
³⁷the son of Methuselah, the son of Enoch,
the son of Jared, the son of Mahalalel,
the son of Kenan, ³⁸the son of Enosh,
the son of Seth, the son of Adam,
the son of God.

The Temptation of Jesus

4:1–13pp — Mt 4:1–11; Mk 1:12,13

4 Jesus, full of the Holy Spirit, returned from the Jordan and was led by the Spirit in the desert, ²where for forty days he was tempted by the devil. He ate nothing during those days, and at the end of them he was hungry.

³The devil said to him, "If you are the Son of God, tell this stone to become bread."

⁴Jesus answered, "It is written: 'Man does not live on bread alone.'ᶜ"

⁵The devil led him up to a high place and showed him in an instant all the kingdoms of the world. ⁶And he said to him, "I will give you all their authority and splendor, for it has been given to me, and I can give it to anyone I want to. ⁷So if you worship me, it will all be yours."

⁸Jesus answered, "It is written: 'Worship the Lord your God and serve him only.'ᵈ"

⁹The devil led him to Jerusalem and had him stand on the highest point of the temple. "If you are the Son of God," he said, "throw yourself down from here. ¹⁰For it is written:

" 'He will command his angels concerning you
to guard you carefully;
¹¹they will lift you up in their hands,
so that you will not strike your foot against a stone.'ᵉ"

¹²Jesus answered, "It says: 'Do not put the Lord your God to the test.'ᶠ"

¹³When the devil had finished all this tempting, he left him until an opportune time.

Jesus Rejected at Nazareth

¹⁴Jesus returned to Galilee in the power of the Spirit, and news about him spread through the whole countryside. ¹⁵He taught in their synagogues, and everyone praised him.

ᵃ 32 Some early manuscripts *Sala*   *ᵇ 33* Some manuscripts *Amminadab, the son of Admin, the son of Arni;* other manuscripts vary widely.   *ᶜ 4* Deut. 8:3   *ᵈ 8* Deut. 6:13   *ᵉ 11* Psalm 91:11,12   *ᶠ 12* Deut. 6:16

16 He went to Nazareth, where he had been brought up, and on the Sabbath day he went into the synagogue, as was his custom. And he stood up to read. 17 The scroll of the prophet Isaiah was handed to him. Unrolling it, he found the place where it is written:

18 "The Spirit of the Lord is on me,
> because he has anointed me
> to preach good news to the poor.
> He has sent me to proclaim freedom for the prisoners
> and recovery of sight for the blind,
> to release the oppressed,
19 to proclaim the year of the Lord's favor." [a]

20 Then he rolled up the scroll, gave it back to the attendant and sat down. The eyes of everyone in the synagogue were fastened on him, 21 and he began by saying to them, "Today this scripture is fulfilled in your hearing."

22 All spoke well of him and were amazed at the gracious words that came from his lips. "Isn't this Joseph's son?" they asked.

23 Jesus said to them, "Surely you will quote this proverb to me: 'Physician, heal yourself! Do here in your hometown what we have heard that you did in Capernaum.'"

24 "I tell you the truth," he continued, "no prophet is accepted in his hometown. 25 I assure you that there were many widows in Israel in Elijah's time, when the sky was shut for three and a half years and there was a severe famine throughout the land. 26 Yet Elijah was not sent to any of them, but to a widow in Zarephath in the region of Sidon. 27 And there were many in Israel with leprosy [b] in the time of Elisha the prophet, yet not one of them was cleansed—only Naaman the Syrian."

28 All the people in the synagogue were furious when they heard this. 29 They got up, drove him out of the town, and took him to the brow of the hill on which the town was built, in order to throw him down the cliff. 30 But he walked right through the crowd and went on his way.

Jesus Drives Out an Evil Spirit
4:31–37pp — Mk 1:21–28

31 Then he went down to Capernaum, a town in Galilee, and on the Sabbath began to teach the people. 32 They were amazed at his teaching, because his message had authority.

33 In the synagogue there was a man possessed by a demon, an evil [c] spirit. He cried out at the top of his voice, 34 "Ha! What do you want with us, Jesus of Nazareth? Have you come to destroy us? I know who you are—the Holy One of God!"

35 "Be quiet!" Jesus said sternly. "Come out of him!" Then the demon threw the man down before them all and came out without injuring him.

36 All the people were amazed and said to each other, "What is this teaching? With authority and power he gives orders to evil spirits and they come out!" 37 And the news about him spread throughout the surrounding area.

Jesus Heals Many
4:38–41pp — Mt 8:14–17
4:38–43pp — Mk 1:29–38

38 Jesus left the synagogue and went to the home of Simon. Now Simon's mother-in-law was suffering from a high fever, and they asked Jesus to help her. 39 So he bent over her and rebuked the fever, and it left her. She got up at once and began to wait on them.

40 When the sun was setting, the people brought to Jesus all who had various kinds of sickness, and laying his hands on each one, he healed them. 41 Moreover, demons came out of many people, shouting, "You are the Son of God!" But he rebuked them and would not allow them to speak, because they knew he was the Christ. [d]

42 At daybreak Jesus went out to a solitary place. The people were looking for him and when they came to where he was, they tried to keep him from leaving them. 43 But he said, "I

---

[a] 19 Isaiah 61:1,2   [b] 27 The Greek word was used for various diseases affecting the skin—not necessarily leprosy.   [c] 33 Greek *unclean*; also in verse 36   [d] 41 Or *Messiah*

Worship the Lord

Do you not know?
  Have you not heard?
The LORD is the everlasting God,
  the Creator of the ends of the earth.
He will not grow tired or weary,
  and his understanding no one can fathom.
He gives strength to the weary
  and increases the power of the weak.
Even youths grow tired and weary,
  and young men stumble and fall;
but those who hope in the LORD
  will renew their strength.
They will soar on wings like eagles;
  they will run and not grow weary,
  they will walk and not be faint.

Isaiah 40:28 – 31

*What a comfort I find in these words, Lord.
When I become weary in meeting each
day's demands and opportunities, remind
me of your promise to renew my strength
when I put my hope in you. Amen.*

Your next devotion is located on page 1392.

GRANDCHILD IN FOCUS • PRAYER

Talents

*Dear Lord, the giver of gifts, bless my
grandchild as he develops his talents. Help him
identify his talents and be proud and confident of
the gifts you have given him. Give him patience and
understanding, Lord, so he will not grow weary of
striving and searching to reach the goals you have
set for him. May each milestone bring satisfaction and a healthy desire for greater
achievement and success to bring
glory to you. Amen.*

must preach the good news of the kingdom of God to the other towns also, because that is why I was sent." **44**And he kept on preaching in the synagogues of Judea. *a*

The Calling of the First Disciples
5:1–11pp — Mt 4:18–22; Mk 1:16–20; Jn 1:40–42

5 One day as Jesus was standing by the Lake of Gennesaret, *b* with the people crowding around him and listening to the word of God, **2**he saw at the water's edge two boats, left there by the fishermen, who were washing their nets. **3**He got into one of the boats, the one belonging to Simon, and asked him to put out a little from shore. Then he sat down and taught the people from the boat.

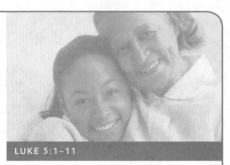

LUKE 5:1–11

Jesus Chooses His Disciples

LIFE LESSON: Jesus is worth following.

TO TALK ABOUT

✦ How did Simon Peter know that Jesus was someone special?

✦ Did Simon Peter ask Jesus to help him catch fish? Why do you think Jesus helped Peter?

✦ Do you think Simon Peter would have followed Jesus even if he didn't see a miracle?

✦ Why do you follow Jesus?

4When he had finished speaking, he said to Simon, "Put out into deep water, and let down *c* the nets for a catch."

5Simon answered, "Master, we've worked hard all night and haven't caught anything. But because you say so, I will let down the nets."

6When they had done so, they caught such a large number of fish that their nets began to break. **7**So they signaled their partners in the other boat to come and help them, and they came and filled both boats so full that they began to sink.

8When Simon Peter saw this, he fell at Jesus' knees and said, "Go away from me, Lord; I am a sinful man!" **9**For he and all his companions were astonished at the catch of fish they had taken, **10**and so were James and John, the sons of Zebedee, Simon's partners.

Then Jesus said to Simon, "Don't be afraid; from now on you will catch men." **11**So they pulled their boats up on shore, left everything and followed him.

The Man With Leprosy
5:12–14pp — Mt 8:2–4; Mk 1:40–44

12While Jesus was in one of the towns, a man came along who was covered with leprosy. *d* When he saw Jesus, he fell with his face to the ground and begged him, "Lord, if you are willing, you can make me clean."

13Jesus reached out his hand and touched the man. "I am willing," he said. "Be clean!" And immediately the leprosy left him.

14Then Jesus ordered him, "Don't tell anyone, but go, show yourself to the priest and offer the sacrifices that Moses commanded for your cleansing, as a testimony to them."

15Yet the news about him spread all the more, so that crowds of people came to hear him and to be healed of their sicknesses. **16**But Jesus often withdrew to lonely places and prayed.

a 44 Or the land of the Jews; some manuscripts Galilee *b 1 That is, Sea of Galilee* *c 4 The Greek verb is plural.* *d 12 The Greek word was used for various diseases affecting the skin—not necessarily leprosy.*

Jesus Heals a Paralytic

5:18–26pp — Mt 9:2–8; Mk 2:3–12

¹⁷One day as he was teaching, Pharisees and teachers of the law, who had come from every village of Galilee and from Judea and Jerusalem, were sitting there. And the power of the Lord was present for him to heal the sick. ¹⁸Some men came carrying a paralytic on a mat and tried to take him into the house to lay him before Jesus. ¹⁹When they could not find a way to do this because of the crowd, they went up on the roof and lowered him on his mat through the tiles into the middle of the crowd, right in front of Jesus.

²⁰When Jesus saw their faith, he said, "Friend, your sins are forgiven."

²¹The Pharisees and the teachers of the law began thinking to themselves, "Who is this fellow who speaks blasphemy? Who can forgive sins but God alone?"

²²Jesus knew what they were thinking and asked, "Why are you thinking these things in your hearts? ²³Which is easier: to say, 'Your sins are forgiven,' or to say, 'Get up and walk'? ²⁴But that you may know that the Son of Man has authority on earth to forgive sins . . ." He said to the paralyzed man, "I tell you, get up, take your mat and go home." ²⁵Immediately he stood up in front of them, took what he had been lying on and went home praising God. ²⁶Everyone was amazed and gave praise to God. They were filled with awe and said, "We have seen remarkable things today."

The Calling of Levi

5:27–32pp — Mt 9:9–13; Mk 2:14–17

²⁷After this, Jesus went out and saw a tax collector by the name of Levi sitting at his tax booth. "Follow me," Jesus said to him, ²⁸and Levi got up, left everything and followed him.

²⁹Then Levi held a great banquet for Jesus at his house, and a large crowd of tax collectors and others were eating with them. ³⁰But the Pharisees and the teachers of the law who belonged to their sect complained to his disciples, "Why do you eat and drink with tax collectors and 'sinners'?"

³¹Jesus answered them, "It is not the healthy who need a doctor, but the sick. ³²I have not come to call the righteous, but sinners to repentance."

Jesus Questioned About Fasting

5:33–39pp — Mt 9:14–17; Mk 2:18–22

³³They said to him, "John's disciples often fast and pray, and so do the disciples of the Pharisees, but yours go on eating and drinking."

³⁴Jesus answered, "Can you make the guests of the bridegroom fast while he is with them? ³⁵But the time will come when the bridegroom will be taken from them; in those days they will fast."

³⁶He told them this parable: "No one tears a patch from a new garment and sews it on an old one. If he does, he will have torn the new garment, and the patch from the new will not match the old. ³⁷And no one pours new wine into old wineskins. If he does, the new wine will burst the skins, the wine will run out and the wineskins will be ruined. ³⁸No, new wine must be poured into new wineskins. ³⁹And no one after drinking old wine wants the new, for he says, 'The old is better.'"

Lord of the Sabbath

6:1–11pp — Mt 12:1–14; Mk 2:23–3:6

6 One Sabbath Jesus was going through the grainfields, and his disciples began to pick some heads of grain, rub them in their hands and eat the kernels. ²Some of the Pharisees asked, "Why are you doing what is unlawful on the Sabbath?"

³Jesus answered them, "Have you never read what David did when he and his companions were hungry? ⁴He entered the house of God, and taking the consecrated bread, he ate what is lawful only for priests to eat. And he also gave some to his companions." ⁵Then Jesus said to them, "The Son of Man is Lord of the Sabbath."

⁶On another Sabbath he went into the synagogue and was teaching, and a man was there whose right hand was shriveled. ⁷The Pharisees

ONE DAY AS HE WAS TEACHING, PHARISEES
AND TEACHERS OF THE LAW, WHO HAD COME
FROM EVERY VILLAGE OF GALILEE AND FROM
JUDEA AND JERUSALEM, WERE SITTING THERE
. . . SOME MEN CAME CARRYING A PARALYTIC
ON A MAT AND TRIED TO TAKE HIM INTO THE
HOUSE TO LAY HIM BEFORE JESUS.

Luke 5:17–18

Sitting . . . Carrying

JONI EARECKSON TADA

READ | LUKE 5:17 – 26

Remember the story in Luke chapter 5 about the four friends who carried their paralyzed companion to see Jesus? They ripped a hole in the roof and lowered their friend down in front of the feet of the Lord. The Pharisees and teachers of the law sat there, shocked and angered that Jesus not only healed the man, but forgave his sins.

In the story, there are two groups of main characters—the Pharisees, who were sitting, and the men who came carrying. Compare the activities of the two. One group is sitting and listening; they are the critics and complainers. The other group is carrying a friend; they are the ones believing and taking action.

God requires us to do more than merely listen to Him. We are to do what He says. And when we stop criticizing and start taking action to carry the burdens of others, we always receive more from the Lord than we anticipate. Just consider the paralyzed man and his four friends. They went to Jesus hoping for a healing, but received so much more: forgiveness of sin!

If you specialize in doing what the Word says, you will always receive more than you anticipate. God will surprise you with a blessing for which you're not even seeking. Do not merely sit in the church but carry the burdens of the church.

Jesus, my teacher and healer, I don't want to be like the Pharisees, who were very good at sitting and listening; I want to be like the four friends of the paralyzed man. When I see a person in need today, inspire me to believe and take action. Help me to carry that person's burden, and in so doing, together we will glorify you.

Your next devotion is located on page 1395.

GRANDCHILD IN FOCUS · PRAYER

SELECT ONE OF YOUR
GRANDCHILDREN TO FOCUS ON
IN PRAYER FOR THE NEXT 14 DAYS.

Salvation

Dear Lord, please guide my grandchild to your gift of salvation. I pray that she will come to know you, to love you and to walk close to you throughout her life. May she boldly claim Jesus as her Lord and Savior. Guide her as she makes choices that have eternal consequences. Help her to follow you each moment of her life. I pray this in Jesus' name, amen.

and the teachers of the law were looking for a reason to accuse Jesus, so they watched him closely to see if he would heal on the Sabbath. **8**But Jesus knew what they were thinking and said to the man with the shriveled hand, "Get up and stand in front of everyone." So he got up and stood there.

9Then Jesus said to them, "I ask you, which is lawful on the Sabbath: to do good or to do evil, to save life or to destroy it?"

10He looked around at them all, and then said to the man, "Stretch out your hand." He did so, and his hand was completely restored. **11**But they were furious and began to discuss with one another what they might do to Jesus.

The Twelve Apostles

6:13–16pp — Mt 10:2–4; Mk 3:16–19; Ac 1:13

12One of those days Jesus went out to a mountainside to pray, and spent the night praying to God. **13**When morning came, he called his disciples to him and chose twelve of them, whom he also designated apostles: **14**Simon (whom he named Peter), his brother Andrew, James, John, Philip, Bartholomew, **15**Matthew, Thomas, James son of Alphaeus, Simon who was called the Zealot, **16**Judas son of James, and Judas Iscariot, who became a traitor.

Blessings and Woes

6:20–23pp — Mt 5:3–12

17He went down with them and stood on a level place. A large crowd of his disciples was there and a great number of people from all over Judea, from Jerusalem, and from the coast of Tyre and Sidon, **18**who had come to hear him and to be healed of their diseases. Those troubled by evil*ᵃ* spirits were cured, **19**and the people all tried to touch him, because power was coming from him and healing them all.

20Looking at his disciples, he said:

"Blessed are you who are poor,
  for yours is the kingdom of God.
21Blessed are you who hunger now,
  for you will be satisfied.

Blessed are you who weep now,
  for you will laugh.
22Blessed are you when men hate you,
  when they exclude you and insult you
  and reject your name as evil,
    because of the Son of Man.

23"Rejoice in that day and leap for joy, because great is your reward in heaven. For that is how their fathers treated the prophets.

24"But woe to you who are rich,
  for you have already received your
    comfort.
25Woe to you who are well fed now,
  for you will go hungry.
Woe to you who laugh now,
  for you will mourn and weep.
26Woe to you when all men speak well of you,
  for that is how their fathers treated the
    false prophets.

Love for Enemies

6:29,30pp — Mt 5:39–42

27"But I tell you who hear me: Love your enemies, do good to those who hate you, **28**bless those who curse you, pray for those who mistreat you. **29**If someone strikes you on one cheek, turn to him the other also. If someone takes your cloak, do not stop him from taking your tunic. **30**Give to everyone who asks you, and if anyone takes what belongs to you, do not demand it back. **31**Do to others as you would have them do to you.

32"If you love those who love you, what credit is that to you? Even 'sinners' love those who love them. **33**And if you do good to those who are good to you, what credit is that to you? Even 'sinners' do that. **34**And if you lend to those from whom you expect repayment, what credit is that to you? Even 'sinners' lend to 'sinners,' expecting to be repaid in full. **35**But love your enemies, do good to them, and lend to them without expecting to get anything back. Then your reward will

ᵃ 18 Greek unclean

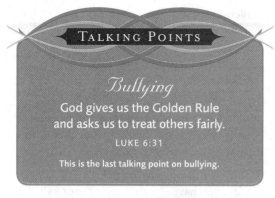

be great, and you will be sons of the Most High, because he is kind to the ungrateful and wicked. [36] Be merciful, just as your Father is merciful.

Judging Others
6:37–42pp — Mt 7:1–5

[37] "Do not judge, and you will not be judged. Do not condemn, and you will not be condemned. Forgive, and you will be forgiven. [38] Give, and it will be given to you. A good measure, pressed down, shaken together and running over, will be poured into your lap. For with the measure you use, it will be measured to you."

[39] He also told them this parable: "Can a blind man lead a blind man? Will they not both fall into a pit? [40] A student is not above his teacher, but everyone who is fully trained will be like his teacher.

[41] "Why do you look at the speck of sawdust in your brother's eye and pay no attention to the plank in your own eye? [42] How can you say to your brother, 'Brother, let me take the speck out of your eye,' when you yourself fail to see the plank in your own eye? You hypocrite, first take the plank out of your eye, and then you will see clearly to remove the speck from your brother's eye.

A Tree and Its Fruit
6:43,44pp — Mt 7:16,18,20

[43] "No good tree bears bad fruit, nor does a bad tree bear good fruit. [44] Each tree is recognized by its own fruit. People do not pick figs from thorn-bushes, or grapes from briers. [45] The good man brings good things out of the good stored up in his heart, and the evil man brings evil things out of the evil stored up in his heart. For out of the overflow of his heart his mouth speaks.

The Wise and Foolish Builders
6:47–49pp — Mt 7:24–27

[46] "Why do you call me, 'Lord, Lord,' and do not do what I say? [47] I will show you what he is like who comes to me and hears my words and puts them into practice. [48] He is like a man building a house, who dug down deep and laid the foundation on rock. When a flood came, the torrent struck that house but could not shake it, because it was well built. [49] But the one who hears my words and does not put them into practice is like a man who built a house on the ground without a foundation. The moment the torrent struck that house, it collapsed and its destruction was complete."

The Faith of the Centurion
7:1–10pp — Mt 8:5–13

7 When Jesus had finished saying all this in the hearing of the people, he entered Capernaum. [2] There a centurion's servant, whom his master valued highly, was sick and about to die. [3] The centurion heard of Jesus and sent some elders of the Jews to him, asking him to come and heal his servant. [4] When they came to Jesus, they pleaded earnestly with him, "This man deserves to have you do this, [5] because he loves our nation and has built our synagogue." [6] So Jesus went with them.

He was not far from the house when the centurion sent friends to say to him: "Lord, don't trouble yourself, for I do not deserve to have you come under my roof. [7] That is why I did not even consider myself worthy to come to you. But say the word, and my servant will be healed. [8] For I myself am a man under authority, with soldiers under me. I tell this one, 'Go,' and he goes; and that one, 'Come,' and he comes. I say to my servant, 'Do this,' and he does it."

[9] When Jesus heard this, he was amazed at him, and turning to the crowd following him, he said,

> "THE GOOD MAN BRINGS GOOD
> THINGS OUT OF THE GOOD
> STORED UP IN HIS HEART,
> AND THE EVIL MAN BRINGS
> EVIL THINGS OUT OF THE EVIL
> STORED UP IN HIS HEART."
> *Luke 6:45*

Something Stinky Beneath the Waters

KAREN MAINS

READ | LUKE 6:43–45

The big red Ace Hardware garbage pail I use to haul away garden debris that won't compost quickly had over-wintered in the new bed I have been cultivating for the last three years. When I checked it one cool morning this spring, I distinctly saw what I thought was the top of some animal submerged beneath the deep accumulation of rainwater. *Eeyoou*, I thought to myself.

I couldn't bear to face the task of emptying the garbage pail with its disgusting contents. (This is called avoidance.)

"David!" I called. "Some animal has drowned in this garbage pail. Will you take it out to the woods and empty it for me? I don't have the stomach for this." No wonder my husband hates gardening.

For many of us, something dead is stinking and moldering beneath the waters. Most of us do not want to take the dreaded look. (Avoidance again.) Self-examination is the cure for our default reaction of looking away. In self-examination, we sit still, take our Bibles and see if any Scriptures pop out, and we ask the Holy Spirit to bring anything rank and poisonous to our attention. If something becomes clear (if we glimpse the top of that head floating around), we confess the fact that we have found a dead thing stewing in its own poisonous soup, sending up putrid bubbles from the depths of our souls.

Then we ask, "What is it about me? Why have I left it to stew so long? What is wrong that I haven't been willing to face this dreadful dead thing?"

The regular task of self-reflection is a cure for avoidance, and if we are quiet, the Holy Spirit will make things perfectly plain. He may even help us empty the big red Ace Hardware garbage pail.

Please, please, God, don't let me avoid looking at any stinky things bobbing beneath the waters of my soul. Give me the courage to consider whether I bring forth good things or evil things with my life. Amen.

Your next devotion is located on page 1404.

GRANDCHILD IN FOCUS • PRAYER

Physical Well-Being

Almighty God, Creator of us all, I pray that you will watch over my grandchild's physical development. May he grow in strength through the stages of his life. As he grows in awareness of his body, help him to understand that each body develops uniquely, yet is within your plan and your control. Please guard his health so that his diseases are few, his injuries are minor and his infirmities are brief. Amen.

"I tell you, I have not found such great faith even in Israel." [10] Then the men who had been sent returned to the house and found the servant well.

Jesus Raises a Widow's Son

7:11–16Ref — 1Ki 17:17–24; 2Ki 4:32–37; Mk 5:21–24,35–43; Jn 11:1–44

[11] Soon afterward, Jesus went to a town called Nain, and his disciples and a large crowd went along with him. [12] As he approached the town gate, a dead person was being carried out—the only son of his mother, and she was a widow. And a large crowd from the town was with her. [13] When the Lord saw her, his heart went out to her and he said, "Don't cry."

[14] Then he went up and touched the coffin, and those carrying it stood still. He said, "Young man, I say to you, get up!" [15] The dead man sat up and began to talk, and Jesus gave him back to his mother.

[16] They were all filled with awe and praised God. "A great prophet has appeared among us," they said. "God has come to help his people." [17] This news about Jesus spread throughout Judea[a] and the surrounding country.

Jesus and John the Baptist

7:18–35pp — Mt 11:2–19

[18] John's disciples told him about all these things. Calling two of them, [19] he sent them to the Lord to ask, "Are you the one who was to come, or should we expect someone else?"

[20] When the men came to Jesus, they said, "John the Baptist sent us to you to ask, 'Are you the one who was to come, or should we expect someone else?' "

[21] At that very time Jesus cured many who had diseases, sicknesses and evil spirits, and gave sight to many who were blind. [22] So he replied to the messengers, "Go back and report to John what you have seen and heard: The blind receive sight, the lame walk, those who have leprosy[b] are cured, the deaf hear, the dead are raised, and the good news is preached to the poor. [23] Blessed is the man who does not fall away on account of me."

[24] After John's messengers left, Jesus began to speak to the crowd about John: "What did you go out into the desert to see? A reed swayed by the wind? [25] If not, what did you go out to see? A man dressed in fine clothes? No, those who wear expensive clothes and indulge in luxury are in palaces. [26] But what did you go out to see? A prophet? Yes, I tell you, and more than a prophet. [27] This is the one about whom it is written:

" 'I will send my messenger ahead of you,
    who will prepare your way before you.'[c]

[28] I tell you, among those born of women there is no one greater than John; yet the one who is least in the kingdom of God is greater than he."

[29] (All the people, even the tax collectors, when they heard Jesus' words, acknowledged that God's way was right, because they had been baptized by John. [30] But the Pharisees and experts in the law rejected God's purpose for themselves, because they had not been baptized by John.)

[31] "To what, then, can I compare the people of this generation? What are they like? [32] They are like children sitting in the marketplace and calling out to each other:

" 'We played the flute for you,
    and you did not dance;
we sang a dirge,
    and you did not cry.'

[33] For John the Baptist came neither eating bread nor drinking wine, and you say, 'He has a demon.' [34] The Son of Man came eating and drinking, and you say, 'Here is a glutton and a drunkard, a friend of tax collectors and "sinners." ' [35] But wisdom is proved right by all her children."

Jesus Anointed by a Sinful Woman

7:37–39Ref — Mt 26:6–13; Mk 14:3–9; Jn 12:1–8
7:41,42Ref — Mt 18:23–34

[36] Now one of the Pharisees invited Jesus to have dinner with him, so he went to the Pharisee's house and reclined at the table. [37] When a

---

[a] 17 Or the land of the Jews   [b] 22 The Greek word was used for various diseases affecting the skin—not necessarily leprosy.
[c] 27 Mal. 3:1

woman who had lived a sinful life in that town learned that Jesus was eating at the Pharisee's house, she brought an alabaster jar of perfume, ³⁸and as she stood behind him at his feet weeping, she began to wet his feet with her tears. Then she wiped them with her hair, kissed them and poured perfume on them.

³⁹When the Pharisee who had invited him saw this, he said to himself, "If this man were a prophet, he would know who is touching him and what kind of woman she is—that she is a sinner."

⁴⁰Jesus answered him, "Simon, I have something to tell you."

"Tell me, teacher," he said.

⁴¹"Two men owed money to a certain moneylender. One owed him five hundred denarii,[a] and the other fifty. ⁴²Neither of them had the money to pay him back, so he canceled the debts of both. Now which of them will love him more?"

⁴³Simon replied, "I suppose the one who had the bigger debt canceled."

"You have judged correctly," Jesus said.

⁴⁴Then he turned toward the woman and said to Simon, "Do you see this woman? I came into your house. You did not give me any water for my feet, but she wet my feet with her tears and wiped them with her hair. ⁴⁵You did not give me a kiss, but this woman, from the time I entered, has not stopped kissing my feet. ⁴⁶You did not put oil on my head, but she has poured perfume on my feet. ⁴⁷Therefore, I tell you, her many sins have been forgiven—for she loved much. But he who has been forgiven little loves little."

⁴⁸Then Jesus said to her, "Your sins are forgiven."

⁴⁹The other guests began to say among themselves, "Who is this who even forgives sins?"

⁵⁰Jesus said to the woman, "Your faith has saved you; go in peace."

The Parable of the Sower

8:4–15pp — Mt 13:2–23; Mk 4:1–20

8 After this, Jesus traveled about from one town and village to another, proclaiming the good news of the kingdom of God. The Twelve were with him, ²and also some women who had been cured of evil spirits and diseases: Mary (called Magdalene) from whom seven demons had come out; ³Joanna the wife of Cuza, the manager of Herod's household; Susanna; and many others. These women were helping to support them out of their own means.

⁴While a large crowd was gathering and people were coming to Jesus from town after town, he told this parable: ⁵"A farmer went out to sow his seed. As he was scattering the seed, some fell along the path; it was trampled on, and the birds of the air ate it up. ⁶Some fell on rock, and when it came up, the plants withered because they had no moisture. ⁷Other seed fell among thorns, which grew up with it and choked the plants. ⁸Still other seed fell on good soil. It came up and yielded a crop, a hundred times more than was sown."

When he said this, he called out, "He who has ears to hear, let him hear."

⁹His disciples asked him what this parable meant. ¹⁰He said, "The knowledge of the secrets of the kingdom of God has been given to you, but to others I speak in parables, so that,

" 'though seeing, they may not see;
   though hearing, they may not understand.'[b]

¹¹"This is the meaning of the parable: The seed is the word of God. ¹²Those along the path are the ones who hear, and then the devil comes and takes away the word from their hearts, so that they may not believe and be saved. ¹³Those on the rock are the ones who receive the word with joy when they hear it, but they have no root. They believe for a while, but in the time of testing they fall away. ¹⁴The seed that fell among thorns stands for those who hear, but as they go on their way they are choked by life's worries, riches and pleasures, and they do not mature. ¹⁵But the seed on good soil stands for those with a noble and good heart, who hear the word, retain it, and by persevering produce a crop.

---

[a] *41* A denarius was a coin worth about a day's wages.
[b] *10* Isaiah 6:9

A Lamp on a Stand

¹⁶"No one lights a lamp and hides it in a jar or puts it under a bed. Instead, he puts it on a stand, so that those who come in can see the light. ¹⁷For there is nothing hidden that will not be disclosed, and nothing concealed that will not be known or brought out into the open. ¹⁸Therefore consider carefully how you listen. Whoever has will be given more; whoever does not have, even what he thinks he has will be taken from him."

Jesus' Mother and Brothers

8:19–21pp — Mt 12:46–50; Mk 3:31–35

¹⁹Now Jesus' mother and brothers came to see him, but they were not able to get near him because of the crowd. ²⁰Someone told him, "Your mother and brothers are standing outside, wanting to see you."

²¹He replied, "My mother and brothers are those who hear God's word and put it into practice."

Jesus Calms the Storm

8:22–25pp — Mt 8:23–27; Mk 4:36–41
8:22–25Ref — Mk 6:47–52; Jn 6:16–21

²²One day Jesus said to his disciples, "Let's go over to the other side of the lake." So they got into a boat and set out. ²³As they sailed, he fell asleep. A squall came down on the lake, so that the boat was being swamped, and they were in great danger.

²⁴The disciples went and woke him, saying, "Master, Master, we're going to drown!"

He got up and rebuked the wind and the raging waters; the storm subsided, and all was calm. ²⁵"Where is your faith?" he asked his disciples.

In fear and amazement they asked one another, "Who is this? He commands even the winds and the water, and they obey him."

The Healing of a Demon-possessed Man

8:26–37pp — Mt 8:28–34
8:26–39pp — Mk 5:1–20

²⁶They sailed to the region of the Gerasenes,ᵃ which is across the lake from Galilee. ²⁷When

Jesus stepped ashore, he was met by a demon-possessed man from the town. For a long time this man had not worn clothes or lived in a house, but had lived in the tombs. ²⁸When he saw Jesus, he cried out and fell at his feet, shouting at the top of his voice, "What do you want with me, Jesus, Son of the Most High God? I beg you, don't torture me!" ²⁹For Jesus had commanded the evilᵇ spirit to come out of the man. Many times it had seized him, and though he was chained hand and foot and kept under guard, he had broken his chains and had been driven by the demon into solitary places.

³⁰Jesus asked him, "What is your name?"

"Legion," he replied, because many demons had gone into him. ³¹And they begged him repeatedly not to order them to go into the Abyss.

³²A large herd of pigs was feeding there on the hillside. The demons begged Jesus to let them go into them, and he gave them permission. ³³When the demons came out of the man, they went into the pigs, and the herd rushed down the steep bank into the lake and was drowned.

³⁴When those tending the pigs saw what had happened, they ran off and reported this in the town and countryside, ³⁵and the people went out to see what had happened. When they came to Jesus, they found the man from whom the demons had gone out, sitting at Jesus' feet, dressed and in his right mind; and they were afraid. ³⁶Those who had seen it told the people how the demon-possessed man had been cured. ³⁷Then all the people of the region of the Gerasenes asked Jesus to leave them, because they were overcome with fear. So he got into the boat and left.

³⁸The man from whom the demons had gone out begged to go with him, but Jesus sent him away, saying, ³⁹"Return home and tell how much God has done for you." So the man went away and told all over town how much Jesus had done for him.

ᵃ 26 Some manuscripts Gadarenes; other manuscripts Gergesenes; also in verse 37 ᵇ 29 Greek unclean

A Dead Girl and a Sick Woman

8:40–56pp — Mt 9:18–26; Mk 5:22–43

40 Now when Jesus returned, a crowd welcomed him, for they were all expecting him. **41** Then a man named Jairus, a ruler of the synagogue, came and fell at Jesus' feet, pleading with him to come to his house **42** because his only daughter, a girl of about twelve, was dying.

As Jesus was on his way, the crowds almost crushed him. **43** And a woman was there who had been subject to bleeding for twelve years,*a* but no one could heal her. **44** She came up behind him and touched the edge of his cloak, and immediately her bleeding stopped.

45 "Who touched me?" Jesus asked.

When they all denied it, Peter said, "Master, the people are crowding and pressing against you."

46 But Jesus said, "Someone touched me; I know that power has gone out from me."

47 Then the woman, seeing that she could not go unnoticed, came trembling and fell at his feet. In the presence of all the people, she told why she had touched him and how she had been instantly healed. **48** Then he said to her, "Daughter, your faith has healed you. Go in peace."

49 While Jesus was still speaking, someone came from the house of Jairus, the synagogue ruler. "Your daughter is dead," he said. "Don't bother the teacher any more."

50 Hearing this, Jesus said to Jairus, "Don't be afraid; just believe, and she will be healed."

51 When he arrived at the house of Jairus, he did not let anyone go in with him except Peter, John and James, and the child's father and mother. **52** Meanwhile, all the people were wailing and mourning for her. "Stop wailing," Jesus said. "She is not dead but asleep."

53 They laughed at him, knowing that she was dead. **54** But he took her by the hand and said, "My child, get up!" **55** Her spirit returned, and at once she stood up. Then Jesus told them to give her something to eat. **56** Her parents were astonished, but he ordered them not to tell anyone what had happened.

Jesus Sends Out the Twelve

9:3–5pp — Mt 10:9–15; Mk 6:8–11
9:7–9pp — Mt 14:1,2; Mk 6:14–16

9 When Jesus had called the Twelve together, he gave them power and authority to drive out all demons and to cure diseases, **2** and he sent them out to preach the kingdom of God and to heal the sick. **3** He told them: "Take nothing for the journey—no staff, no bag, no bread, no money, no extra tunic. **4** Whatever house you enter, stay there until you leave that town. **5** If people do not welcome you, shake the dust off your feet when you leave their town, as a testimony against them." **6** So they set out and went from village to village, preaching the gospel and healing people everywhere.

7 Now Herod the tetrarch heard about all that was going on. And he was perplexed, because some were saying that John had been raised from the dead, **8** others that Elijah had appeared, and still others that one of the prophets of long ago had come back to life. **9** But Herod said, "I beheaded John. Who, then, is this I hear such things about?" And he tried to see him.

Jesus Feeds the Five Thousand

9:10–17pp — Mt 14:13–21; Mk 6:32–44; Jn 6:5–13
9:13–17Ref — 2Ki 4:42–44

10 When the apostles returned, they reported to Jesus what they had done. Then he took them with him and they withdrew by themselves to a town called Bethsaida, **11** but the crowds learned about it and followed him. He welcomed them and spoke to them about the kingdom of God, and healed those who needed healing.

12 Late in the afternoon the Twelve came to him and said, "Send the crowd away so they can go to the surrounding villages and countryside and find food and lodging, because we are in a remote place here."

13 He replied, "You give them something to eat."

They answered, "We have only five loaves of

---

a 43 Many manuscripts *years, and she had spent all she had on doctors* bread and two fish—unless we go and buy food for all this crowd." ¹⁴(About five thousand men were there.)

But he said to his disciples, "Have them sit down in groups of about fifty each." ¹⁵The disciples did so, and everybody sat down. ¹⁶Taking the five loaves and the two fish and looking up to heaven, he gave thanks and broke them. Then he gave them to the disciples to set before the people. ¹⁷They all ate and were satisfied, and the disciples picked up twelve basketfuls of broken pieces that were left over.

Peter's Confession of Christ
9:18–20pp — Mt 16:13–16; Mk 8:27–29
9:22–27pp — Mt 16:21–28; Mk 8:31–9:1

¹⁸Once when Jesus was praying in private and his disciples were with him, he asked them, "Who do the crowds say I am?"

¹⁹They replied, "Some say John the Baptist; others say Elijah; and still others, that one of the prophets of long ago has come back to life."

²⁰"But what about you?" he asked. "Who do you say I am?"

Peter answered, "The Christ ᵃ of God."

²¹Jesus strictly warned them not to tell this to anyone. ²²And he said, "The Son of Man must suffer many things and be rejected by the elders, chief priests and teachers of the law, and he must be killed and on the third day be raised to life."

²³Then he said to them all: "If anyone would come after me, he must deny himself and take up his cross daily and follow me. ²⁴For whoever wants to save his life will lose it, but whoever loses his life for me will save it. ²⁵What good is it for a man to gain the whole world, and yet lose or forfeit his very self? ²⁶If anyone is ashamed of me and my words, the Son of Man will be ashamed of him when he comes in his glory and in the glory of the Father and of the holy angels. ²⁷I tell you the truth, some who are standing here will not taste death before they see the kingdom of God."

The Transfiguration
9:28–36pp — Mt 17:1–8; Mk 9:2–8

²⁸About eight days after Jesus said this, he took Peter, John and James with him and went up onto a mountain to pray. ²⁹As he was praying, the appearance of his face changed, and his clothes became as bright as a flash of lightning. ³⁰Two men, Moses and Elijah, ³¹appeared in glorious splendor, talking with Jesus. They spoke about his departure, which he was about to bring to fulfillment at Jerusalem. ³²Peter and his companions were very sleepy, but when they became fully awake, they saw his glory and the two men standing with him. ³³As the men were leaving Jesus, Peter said to him, "Master, it is good for us to be here. Let us put up three shelters—one for you, one for Moses and one for Elijah." (He did not know what he was saying.)

³⁴While he was speaking, a cloud appeared and enveloped them, and they were afraid as they entered the cloud. ³⁵A voice came from the cloud, saying, "This is my Son, whom I have chosen; listen to him." ³⁶When the voice had spoken, they found that Jesus was alone. The disciples kept this to themselves, and told no one at that time what they had seen.

The Healing of a Boy With an Evil Spirit
9:37–42,43–45pp — Mt 17:14–18,22,23;
Mk 9:14–27,30–32

³⁷The next day, when they came down from the mountain, a large crowd met him. ³⁸A man in the crowd called out, "Teacher, I beg you to look at my son, for he is my only child. ³⁹A spirit seizes him and he suddenly screams; it throws him into convulsions so that he foams at the mouth. It scarcely ever leaves him and is destroying him. ⁴⁰I begged your disciples to drive it out, but they could not."

⁴¹"O unbelieving and perverse generation," Jesus replied, "how long shall I stay with you and put up with you? Bring your son here."

ᵃ *20 Or Messiah*

⁴²Even while the boy was coming, the demon threw him to the ground in a convulsion. But Jesus rebuked the evil*ᵃ* spirit, healed the boy and gave him back to his father. ⁴³And they were all amazed at the greatness of God.

While everyone was marveling at all that Jesus did, he said to his disciples, ⁴⁴"Listen carefully to what I am about to tell you: The Son of Man is going to be betrayed into the hands of men." ⁴⁵But they did not understand what this meant. It was hidden from them, so that they did not grasp it, and they were afraid to ask him about it.

Who Will Be the Greatest?

9:46–48pp — Mt 18:1–5
9:46–50pp — Mk 9:33–40

⁴⁶An argument started among the disciples as to which of them would be the greatest. ⁴⁷Jesus, knowing their thoughts, took a little child and had him stand beside him. ⁴⁸Then he said to them, "Whoever welcomes this little child in my name welcomes me; and whoever welcomes me welcomes the one who sent me. For he who is least among you all—he is the greatest."

⁴⁹"Master," said John, "we saw a man driving out demons in your name and we tried to stop him, because he is not one of us."

⁵⁰"Do not stop him," Jesus said, "for whoever is not against you is for you."

Samaritan Opposition

⁵¹As the time approached for him to be taken up to heaven, Jesus resolutely set out for Jerusalem. ⁵²And he sent messengers on ahead, who went into a Samaritan village to get things ready for him; ⁵³but the people there did not welcome him, because he was heading for Jerusalem. ⁵⁴When the disciples James and John saw this, they asked, "Lord, do you want us to call fire down from heaven to destroy them*ᵇ*?" ⁵⁵But Jesus turned and rebuked them, ⁵⁶and*ᶜ* they went to another village.

The Cost of Following Jesus

9:57–60pp — Mt 8:19–22

⁵⁷As they were walking along the road, a man said to him, "I will follow you wherever you go."

⁵⁸Jesus replied, "Foxes have holes and birds of the air have nests, but the Son of Man has no place to lay his head."

⁵⁹He said to another man, "Follow me."

But the man replied, "Lord, first let me go and bury my father."

⁶⁰Jesus said to him, "Let the dead bury their own dead, but you go and proclaim the kingdom of God."

⁶¹Still another said, "I will follow you, Lord; but first let me go back and say good-by to my family."

⁶²Jesus replied, "No one who puts his hand to the plow and looks back is fit for service in the kingdom of God."

Jesus Sends Out the Seventy-two

10:4–12pp — Lk 9:3–5
10:13–15,21,22pp — Mt 11:21–23,25–27
10:23,24pp — Mt 13:16,17

10 After this the Lord appointed seventy-two*ᵈ* others and sent them two by two ahead of him to every town and place where he was about to go. ²He told them, "The harvest is plentiful, but the workers are few. Ask the Lord of the harvest, therefore, to send out workers into his harvest field. ³Go! I am sending you out like lambs among wolves. ⁴Do not take a purse or bag or sandals; and do not greet anyone on the road.

⁵"When you enter a house, first say, 'Peace to this house.' ⁶If a man of peace is there, your peace will rest on him; if not, it will return to you. ⁷Stay in that house, eating and drinking whatever they give you, for the worker deserves his wages. Do not move around from house to house.

ᵃ 42 Greek unclean   ᵇ 54 Some manuscripts them, even as Elijah did   ᶜ 55,56 Some manuscripts them. And he said, "You do not know what kind of spirit you are of, for the Son of Man did not come to destroy men's lives, but to save them." ⁵⁶And   ᵈ 1 Some manuscripts seventy; also in verse 17

8"When you enter a town and are welcomed, eat what is set before you. 9Heal the sick who are there and tell them, 'The kingdom of God is near you.' 10But when you enter a town and are not welcomed, go into its streets and say, 11'Even the dust of your town that sticks to our feet we wipe off against you. Yet be sure of this: The kingdom of God is near.' 12I tell you, it will be more bearable on that day for Sodom than for that town.

13"Woe to you, Korazin! Woe to you, Bethsaida! For if the miracles that were performed in you had been performed in Tyre and Sidon, they would have repented long ago, sitting in sackcloth and ashes. 14But it will be more bearable for Tyre and Sidon at the judgment than for you. 15And you, Capernaum, will you be lifted up to the skies? No, you will go down to the depths. a

16"He who listens to you listens to me; he who rejects you rejects me; but he who rejects me rejects him who sent me."

17The seventy-two returned with joy and said, "Lord, even the demons submit to us in your name."

18He replied, "I saw Satan fall like lightning from heaven. 19I have given you authority to trample on snakes and scorpions and to overcome all the power of the enemy; nothing will harm you. 20However, do not rejoice that the spirits submit to you, but rejoice that your names are written in heaven."

21At that time Jesus, full of joy through the Holy Spirit, said, "I praise you, Father, Lord of heaven and earth, because you have hidden these things from the wise and learned, and revealed them to little children. Yes, Father, for this was your good pleasure.

22"All things have been committed to me by my Father. No one knows who the Son is except the Father, and no one knows who the Father is except the Son and those to whom the Son chooses to reveal him."

23Then he turned to his disciples and said privately, "Blessed are the eyes that see what you see.

24For I tell you that many prophets and kings wanted to see what you see but did not see it, and to hear what you hear but did not hear it."

The Parable of the Good Samaritan
10:25–28pp — Mt 22:34–40; Mk 12:28–31

25On one occasion an expert in the law stood up to test Jesus. "Teacher," he asked, "what must I do to inherit eternal life?"

26"What is written in the Law?" he replied. "How do you read it?"

27He answered: " 'Love the Lord your God with all your heart and with all your soul and

a 15 Greek *Hades*

LUKE 10:25–37

stories to share

The Parable of the Good Samaritan

LIFE LESSON: Jesus wants us to show mercy to anyone in need.

TO TALK ABOUT

✦ What question prompted Jesus to tell this parable?

✦ Who passed by the injured man without helping him?

✦ Why was it significant that the man who showed mercy was a Samaritan? (Hint: Read John 4:9.)

✦ When have you had a chance to be a "good Samaritan"? Did you take the opportunity?

with all your strength and with all your mind'[a]; and, 'Love your neighbor as yourself.'[b]"

28 "You have answered correctly," Jesus replied, "Do this and you will live."

29 But he wanted to justify himself, so he asked Jesus, "And who is my neighbor?"

30 In reply Jesus said: "A man was going down from Jerusalem to Jericho, when he fell into the hands of robbers. They stripped him of his clothes, beat him and went away, leaving him half dead. 31 A priest happened to be going down the same road, and when he saw the man, he passed by on the other side. 32 So too, a Levite, when he came to the place and saw him, passed by on the other side. 33 But a Samaritan, as he traveled, came where the man was; and when he saw him, he took pity on him. 34 He went to him and bandaged his wounds, pouring on oil and wine. Then he put the man on his own donkey, took him to an inn and took care of him. 35 The next day he took out two silver coins[c] and gave them to the innkeeper. 'Look after him,' he said, 'and when I return, I will reimburse you for any extra expense you may have.'

36 "Which of these three do you think was a neighbor to the man who fell into the hands of robbers?"

37 The expert in the law replied, "The one who had mercy on him."

Jesus told him, "Go and do likewise."

At the Home of Martha and Mary

38 As Jesus and his disciples were on their way, he came to a village where a woman named Martha opened her home to him. 39 She had a sister called Mary, who sat at the Lord's feet listening to what he said. 40 But Martha was distracted by all the preparations that had to be made. She came to him and asked, "Lord, don't you care that my sister has left me to do the work by myself? Tell her to help me!"

41 "Martha, Martha," the Lord answered, "you are worried and upset about many things, 42 but only one thing is needed.[d] Mary has chosen what is better, and it will not be taken away from her."

stories to share

LUKE 10:38-42

Jesus Visits Mary and Martha

LIFE LESSON: Jesus deserves to be our first priority.

TO TALK ABOUT

✦ Why was Martha upset with Mary? What did she ask Jesus to do?

✦ Was Martha doing anything wrong? Why was Mary doing something better?

✦ How can you make Jesus your first priority?

✦ Is it still important to be helpful at home? How can you be like both Mary and Martha?

Jesus' Teaching on Prayer
11:2–4pp — Mt 6:9–13
11:9–13pp — Mt 7:7–11

11 One day Jesus was praying in a certain place. When he finished, one of his disciples said to him, "Lord, teach us to pray, just as John taught his disciples."

2 He said to them, "When you pray, say:

" 'Father,[e]
hallowed be your name,
your kingdom come.[f]

---

[a] 27 Deut. 6:5   [b] 27 Lev. 19:18   [c] 35 Greek *two denarii*
[d] 42 Some manuscripts *but few things are needed—or only one*   [e] 2 Some manuscripts *Our Father in heaven*   [f] 2 Some manuscripts *come. May your will be done on earth as it is in heaven.*

> BUT MARTHA WAS DISTRACTED BY ALL
> THE PREPARATIONS THAT HAD TO BE
> MADE. SHE CAME TO HIM AND ASKED,
> "LORD, DON'T YOU CARE THAT MY
> SISTER HAS LEFT ME TO DO THE WORK
> BY MYSELF? TELL HER TO HELP ME!"
> *Luke 10:40*

The Martha Disease

DIANE KOMP, M.D.

READ | LUKE 10:38 – 42

With the help of a cookbook from a friend from the Republic of Georgia, I engineered a multi-course international feast. It took two days to prepare the meal. My housemates would all help. Or so they said.

An hour before we were to eat, my roommate Barbara left for work and didn't get back in time to make the salad. Roland, our ministry leader, called up the stairwell to say that he was short on time and had errands to run. No one else at home asked if I needed help until just before they all appeared, and we sat down to eat. By that time, I had run up and down the narrow, winding stairs of our house three times and had taken care of everything myself. After my final trek to get the rest of the food, I found one of our housemates clearing the table I had set and replacing it with a different tablecloth and dishes. At that point, I could have killed them all.

I was not in a good mood, for I was having a "Martha" day. Here are typical symptoms of her distress:

Martha doesn't give assignments; she waits for people to volunteer.

When no one volunteers, Martha gets annoyed.

When people do volunteer, Martha says that she doesn't need help.

After dinner, I spent some "Mary" time at Jesus' feet to unload all the tension that "Martha" unnecessarily brought upon herself. If you feel the first symptoms of the Martha disease coming on, get yourself to the Great Physician.

Dear Jesus, when I begin to be Martha-like, help me to remember to serve others out of a joyful and giving spirit rather than out of a need to control. Replace my pride with humility and remind me that I don't have to do it all, that asking others to help gives them an opportunity to serve too.

Your next devotion is located on page 1407.

GRANDCHILD IN FOCUS • PRAYER

Emotional Development

O God, Creator of mind and body, I pray that you will give my grandchild emotional health and strength. Where there is anger, bring peace. Where there is confusion, bring clarity and focus. Where there are dark shadows, cast a ray of hope. Fill her with the sunshine of your Spirit. Warm her with the presence of your peace. Amen.

3 Give us each day our daily bread.
4 Forgive us our sins,
> for we also forgive everyone who sins
> against us.[a]

And lead us not into temptation.[b] ' "

5 Then he said to them, "Suppose one of you has a friend, and he goes to him at midnight and says, 'Friend, lend me three loaves of bread, 6 because a friend of mine on a journey has come to me, and I have nothing to set before him.'

7 "Then the one inside answers, 'Don't bother me. The door is already locked, and my children are with me in bed. I can't get up and give you anything.' 8 I tell you, though he will not get up and give him the bread because he is his friend, yet because of the man's boldness[c] he will get up and give him as much as he needs.

9 "So I say to you: Ask and it will be given to you; seek and you will find; knock and the door will be opened to you. 10 For everyone who asks receives; he who seeks finds; and to him who knocks, the door will be opened.

11 "Which of you fathers, if your son asks for[d] a fish, will give him a snake instead? 12 Or if he asks for an egg, will give him a scorpion? 13 If you then, though you are evil, know how to give good gifts to your children, how much more will your Father in heaven give the Holy Spirit to those who ask him!"

Jesus and Beelzebub

11:14,15,17–22,24–26pp — Mt 12:22,24–29,43–45
11:17–22pp — Mk 3:23–27

14 Jesus was driving out a demon that was mute. When the demon left, the man who had been mute spoke, and the crowd was amazed. 15 But some of them said, "By Beelzebub,[e] the prince of demons, he is driving out demons." 16 Others tested him by asking for a sign from heaven.

17 Jesus knew their thoughts and said to them: "Any kingdom divided against itself will be ruined, and a house divided against itself will fall. 18 If Satan is divided against himself, how can his kingdom stand? I say this because you claim that I drive out demons by Beelzebub. 19 Now if I drive out demons by Beelzebub, by whom do your followers drive them out? So then, they will be your judges. 20 But if I drive out demons by the finger of God, then the kingdom of God has come to you.

21 "When a strong man, fully armed, guards his own house, his possessions are safe. 22 But when someone stronger attacks and overpowers him, he takes away the armor in which the man trusted and divides up the spoils.

23 "He who is not with me is against me, and he who does not gather with me, scatters.

24 "When an evil[f] spirit comes out of a man, it goes through arid places seeking rest and does not find it. Then it says, 'I will return to the house I left.' 25 When it arrives, it finds the house swept clean and put in order. 26 Then it goes and takes seven other spirits more wicked than itself, and they go in and live there. And the final condition of that man is worse than the first."

27 As Jesus was saying these things, a woman in the crowd called out, "Blessed is the mother who gave you birth and nursed you."

28 He replied, "Blessed rather are those who hear the word of God and obey it."

The Sign of Jonah

11:29–32pp — Mt 12:39–42

29 As the crowds increased, Jesus said, "This is a wicked generation. It asks for a miraculous sign, but none will be given it except the sign of Jonah. 30 For as Jonah was a sign to the Ninevites, so also will the Son of Man be to this generation. 31 The Queen of the South will rise at the judgment with the men of this generation and condemn them; for she came from the ends of the earth to listen to Solomon's wisdom, and now one[g] greater than Solomon is here. 32 The men of Nineveh will stand up at the judgment with this generation and condemn it; for they repented at the preaching of Jonah, and now one greater than Jonah is here.

---

[a] 4 Greek *everyone who is indebted to us*   [b] 4 Some manuscripts *temptation but deliver us from the evil one*   [c] 8 Or *persistence*
[d] 11 Some manuscripts *for bread, will give him a stone; or if he asks for*   [e] 15 Greek *Beezeboul* or *Beelzeboul*; also in verses 18 and 19
[f] 24 Greek *unclean*   [g] 31 Or *something*; also in verse 32

The Lamp of the Body

11:34,35pp — Mt 6:22,23

³³"No one lights a lamp and puts it in a place where it will be hidden, or under a bowl. Instead he puts it on its stand, so that those who come in may see the light. ³⁴Your eye is the lamp of your body. When your eyes are good, your whole body also is full of light. But when they are bad, your body also is full of darkness. ³⁵See to it, then, that the light within you is not darkness. ³⁶Therefore, if your whole body is full of light, and no part of it dark, it will be completely lighted, as when the light of a lamp shines on you."

Six Woes

³⁷When Jesus had finished speaking, a Pharisee invited him to eat with him; so he went in and reclined at the table. ³⁸But the Pharisee, noticing that Jesus did not first wash before the meal, was surprised.

³⁹Then the Lord said to him, "Now then, you Pharisees clean the outside of the cup and dish, but inside you are full of greed and wickedness. ⁴⁰You foolish people! Did not the one who made the outside make the inside also? ⁴¹But give what is inside ⌊the dish⌋^a to the poor, and everything will be clean for you.

⁴²"Woe to you Pharisees, because you give God a tenth of your mint, rue and all other kinds of garden herbs, but you neglect justice and the love of God. You should have practiced the latter without leaving the former undone.

⁴³"Woe to you Pharisees, because you love the most important seats in the synagogues and greetings in the marketplaces.

⁴⁴"Woe to you, because you are like unmarked graves, which men walk over without knowing it."

⁴⁵One of the experts in the law answered him, "Teacher, when you say these things, you insult us also."

⁴⁶Jesus replied, "And you experts in the law, woe to you, because you load people down with burdens they can hardly carry, and you yourselves will not lift one finger to help them.

⁴⁷"Woe to you, because you build tombs for the prophets, and it was your forefathers who killed them. ⁴⁸So you testify that you approve of what your forefathers did; they killed the prophets, and you build their tombs. ⁴⁹Because of this, God in his wisdom said, 'I will send them prophets and apostles, some of whom they will kill and others they will persecute.' ⁵⁰Therefore this generation will be held responsible for the blood of all the prophets that has been shed since the beginning of the world, ⁵¹from the blood of Abel to the blood of Zechariah, who was killed between the altar and the sanctuary. Yes, I tell you, this generation will be held responsible for it all.

⁵²"Woe to you experts in the law, because you have taken away the key to knowledge. You yourselves have not entered, and you have hindered those who were entering."

⁵³When Jesus left there, the Pharisees and the teachers of the law began to oppose him fiercely and to besiege him with questions, ⁵⁴waiting to catch him in something he might say.

Warnings and Encouragements

12:2–9pp — Mt 10:26–33

12 Meanwhile, when a crowd of many thousands had gathered, so that they were trampling on one another, Jesus began to speak first to his disciples, saying: "Be on your guard against the yeast of the Pharisees, which is hypocrisy. ²There is nothing concealed that will not be disclosed, or hidden that will not be made known. ³What you have said in the dark will be heard in the daylight, and what you have whispered in the ear in the inner rooms will be proclaimed from the roofs.

⁴"I tell you, my friends, do not be afraid of those who kill the body and after that can do no more. ⁵But I will show you whom you should fear: Fear him who, after the killing of the body, has power to throw you into hell. Yes, I tell you, fear him. ⁶Are not five sparrows sold for two pennies^b? Yet not one of them is forgotten by God.

---

^a 41 Or *what you have*   ^b 6 Greek *two assaria*

> "NO ONE LIGHTS A LAMP AND PUTS IT IN A PLACE WHERE IT WILL BE HIDDEN, OR UNDER A BOWL. INSTEAD HE PUTS IT ON ITS STAND, SO THAT THOSE WHO COME IN MAY SEE THE LIGHT."
>
> *Luke 11:33*

Shine, Christian, Shine

THELMA WELLS

READ | LUKE 11:33 – 36

It seemed to be a calm thunderstorm and lightning show, nothing severe. But suddenly all the lights went out. It was pitch dark. My grandchildren were playing throughout the house. Darkness got their immediate attention.

They screamed, "Grammy, what happened? I can't see. Where are you? Come get me! Lights! Lights!" I tried to assure them that they were safe. I found the torch and lit the candles throughout the house. The darkness was dispelled. The kids felt safer and started laughing about how scared they had been in the dark.

It's startling when the lights go out. You search for the candles and the torch to light them. You think you're prepared with flashlights or lanterns, only to find that when the lights go out, you are scrambling to find something that can illuminate the darkness.

I thought about the blackness, the darkness, the unrest of not being able to see anything clearly because there was no light. I recalled that sinning is an event of darkness in which a life is paralyzed by the inability to see things the way God sees them. Many people feel overcome by this darkness because they have nothing to illuminate their spirits. Sin engulfs them with questions similar to those of my grandchildren: "Help, where are you?" "Help, come get me." "Where is the light? Lights, pleeease."

As Christians we need to let our lights shine with the light of Jesus to illuminate the way and help repel the darkness of sin. When we do, we will have the joy of a little child who feels safe when the lights return.

Jesus, may your light that lives in me be a beacon that is clear for people to see. I pray the same for my friends. In Jesus' name, amen.

Your next devotion is located on page 1413.

GRANDCHILD IN FOCUS • PRAYER

Spiritual Growth

Dear Lord, today I pray for my grandchild's spiritual growth. I ask that you instill in him the desire to read and memorize your Word. Give him a passion to be in conversation with you. May loving and serving you be part of his daily life. I ask that you stay close to him and lead him to be transformed to your likeness, to reflect your grace and to radiate your love. I pray this in Jesus' name, amen.

[7]Indeed, the very hairs of your head are all numbered. Don't be afraid; you are worth more than many sparrows.

[8]"I tell you, whoever acknowledges me before men, the Son of Man will also acknowledge him before the angels of God. [9]But he who disowns me before men will be disowned before the angels of God. [10]And everyone who speaks a word against the Son of Man will be forgiven, but anyone who blasphemes against the Holy Spirit will not be forgiven.

[11]"When you are brought before synagogues, rulers and authorities, do not worry about how you will defend yourselves or what you will say, [12]for the Holy Spirit will teach you at that time what you should say."

TALKING POINTS

Money
Don't be greedy.
LUKE 12:15
For more on money, go to Luke 16:13.

The Parable of the Rich Fool

[13]Someone in the crowd said to him, "Teacher, tell my brother to divide the inheritance with me."

[14]Jesus replied, "Man, who appointed me a judge or an arbiter between you?" [15]Then he said to them, "Watch out! Be on your guard against all kinds of greed; a man's life does not consist in the abundance of his possessions."

[16]And he told them this parable: "The ground of a certain rich man produced a good crop. [17]He thought to himself, 'What shall I do? I have no place to store my crops.'

[18]"Then he said, 'This is what I'll do. I will tear down my barns and build bigger ones, and there I will store all my grain and my goods. [19]And I'll

say to myself, "You have plenty of good things laid up for many years. Take life easy; eat, drink and be merry." '

[20]"But God said to him, 'You fool! This very night your life will be demanded from you. Then who will get what you have prepared for yourself?'

[21]"This is how it will be with anyone who stores up things for himself but is not rich toward God."

Do Not Worry
12:22–31pp — Mt 6:25–33

[22]Then Jesus said to his disciples: "Therefore I tell you, do not worry about your life, what you will eat; or about your body, what you will wear. [23]Life is more than food, and the body more than clothes. [24]Consider the ravens: They do not sow or reap, they have no storeroom or barn; yet God feeds them. And how much more valuable you are than birds! [25]Who of you by worrying can add a single hour to his life [a]? [26]Since you cannot do this very little thing, why do you worry about the rest?

[27]"Consider how the lilies grow. They do not labor or spin. Yet I tell you, not even Solomon in all his splendor was dressed like one of these. [28]If that is how God clothes the grass of the field, which is here today, and tomorrow is thrown into the fire, how much more will he clothe you, O you of little faith! [29]And do not set your heart on what you will eat or drink; do not worry about it. [30]For the pagan world runs after

---

[a] 25 Or *single cubit to his height*

TALKING POINTS

Anxiety
Don't let worry overtake your life.
LUKE 12:22–26
For more on anxiety, go to 1 Peter 5:7.

all such things, and your Father knows that you need them. ³¹But seek his kingdom, and these things will be given to you as well.

³²"Do not be afraid, little flock, for your Father has been pleased to give you the kingdom. ³³Sell your possessions and give to the poor. Provide purses for yourselves that will not wear out, a treasure in heaven that will not be exhausted, where no thief comes near and no moth destroys. ³⁴For where your treasure is, there your heart will be also.

Watchfulness

12:35,36pp — Mt 25:1–13; Mk 13:33–37
12:39,40,42–46pp — Mt 24:43–51

³⁵"Be dressed ready for service and keep your lamps burning, ³⁶like men waiting for their master to return from a wedding banquet, so that when he comes and knocks they can immediately open the door for him. ³⁷It will be good for those servants whose master finds them watching when he comes. I tell you the truth, he will dress himself to serve, will have them recline at the table and will come and wait on them. ³⁸It will be good for those servants whose master finds them ready, even if he comes in the second or third watch of the night. ³⁹But understand this: If the owner of the house had known at what hour the thief was coming, he would not have let his house be broken into. ⁴⁰You also must be ready, because the Son of Man will come at an hour when you do not expect him."

⁴¹Peter asked, "Lord, are you telling this parable to us, or to everyone?"

⁴²The Lord answered, "Who then is the faithful and wise manager, whom the master puts in charge of his servants to give them their food allowance at the proper time? ⁴³It will be good for that servant whom the master finds doing so when he returns. ⁴⁴I tell you the truth, he will put him in charge of all his possessions. ⁴⁵But suppose the servant says to himself, 'My master is taking a long time in coming,' and he then begins to beat the menservants and maidservants and to eat and drink and get drunk. ⁴⁶The master of that servant will come on a day when he does not expect him and at an hour he is not aware of. He will cut him to pieces and assign him a place with the unbelievers.

⁴⁷"That servant who knows his master's will and does not get ready or does not do what his master wants will be beaten with many blows. ⁴⁸But the one who does not know and does things deserving punishment will be beaten with few blows. From everyone who has been given much, much will be demanded; and from the one who has been entrusted with much, much more will be asked.

Not Peace but Division

12:51–53pp — Mt 10:34–36

⁴⁹"I have come to bring fire on the earth, and how I wish it were already kindled! ⁵⁰But I have a baptism to undergo, and how distressed I am until it is completed! ⁵¹Do you think I came to bring peace on earth? No, I tell you, but division. ⁵²From now on there will be five in one family divided against each other, three against two and two against three. ⁵³They will be divided, father against son and son against father, mother against daughter and daughter against mother, mother-in-law against daughter-in-law and daughter-in-law against mother-in-law."

Interpreting the Times

⁵⁴He said to the crowd: "When you see a cloud rising in the west, immediately you say, 'It's going to rain,' and it does. ⁵⁵And when the south wind blows, you say, 'It's going to be hot,' and it is. ⁵⁶Hypocrites! You know how to interpret the appearance of the earth and the sky. How is it that you don't know how to interpret this present time?

⁵⁷"Why don't you judge for yourselves what is right? ⁵⁸As you are going with your adversary to the magistrate, try hard to be reconciled to him on the way, or he may drag you off to the judge, and the judge turn you over to the officer, and the officer throw you into prison. ⁵⁹I tell you, you will not get out until you have paid the last penny.ᵃ"

ᵃ 59 Greek *lepton*

Repent or Perish

13 Now there were some present at that time who told Jesus about the Galileans whose blood Pilate had mixed with their sacrifices. ²Jesus answered, "Do you think that these Galileans were worse sinners than all the other Galileans because they suffered this way? ³I tell you, no! But unless you repent, you too will all perish. ⁴Or those eighteen who died when the tower in Siloam fell on them—do you think they were more guilty than all the others living in Jerusalem? ⁵I tell you, no! But unless you repent, you too will all perish."

⁶Then he told this parable: "A man had a fig tree, planted in his vineyard, and he went to look for fruit on it, but did not find any. ⁷So he said to the man who took care of the vineyard, 'For three years now I've been coming to look for fruit on this fig tree and haven't found any. Cut it down! Why should it use up the soil?'

⁸" 'Sir,' the man replied, 'leave it alone for one more year, and I'll dig around it and fertilize it. ⁹If it bears fruit next year, fine! If not, then cut it down.' "

A Crippled Woman Healed on the Sabbath

¹⁰On a Sabbath Jesus was teaching in one of the synagogues, ¹¹and a woman was there who had been crippled by a spirit for eighteen years. She was bent over and could not straighten up at all. ¹²When Jesus saw her, he called her forward and said to her, "Woman, you are set free from your infirmity." ¹³Then he put his hands on her, and immediately she straightened up and praised God.

¹⁴Indignant because Jesus had healed on the Sabbath, the synagogue ruler said to the people, "There are six days for work. So come and be healed on those days, not on the Sabbath."

¹⁵The Lord answered him, "You hypocrites! Doesn't each of you on the Sabbath untie his ox or donkey from the stall and lead it out to give it water? ¹⁶Then should not this woman, a daughter of Abraham, whom Satan has kept bound for eighteen long years, be set free on the Sabbath day from what bound her?"

¹⁷When he said this, all his opponents were humiliated, but the people were delighted with all the wonderful things he was doing.

The Parables of the Mustard Seed and the Yeast

13:18,19pp — Mk 4:30–32
13:18–21pp — Mt 13:31–33

¹⁸Then Jesus asked, "What is the kingdom of God like? What shall I compare it to? ¹⁹It is like a mustard seed, which a man took and planted in his garden. It grew and became a tree, and the birds of the air perched in its branches."

²⁰Again he asked, "What shall I compare the kingdom of God to? ²¹It is like yeast that a woman took and mixed into a large amount *a* of flour until it worked all through the dough."

The Narrow Door

²²Then Jesus went through the towns and villages, teaching as he made his way to Jerusalem. ²³Someone asked him, "Lord, are only a few people going to be saved?"

He said to them, ²⁴"Make every effort to enter through the narrow door, because many, I tell you, will try to enter and will not be able to. ²⁵Once the owner of the house gets up and closes the door, you will stand outside knocking and pleading, 'Sir, open the door for us.'

"But he will answer, 'I don't know you or where you come from.'

²⁶"Then you will say, 'We ate and drank with you, and you taught in our streets.'

²⁷"But he will reply, 'I don't know you or where you come from. Away from me, all you evildoers!'

²⁸"There will be weeping there, and gnashing of teeth, when you see Abraham, Isaac and Jacob and all the prophets in the kingdom of God, but you yourselves thrown out. ²⁹People will come from east and west and north and south, and will take their places at the feast in the kingdom of

---

a 21 Greek *three satas* (probably about 1/2 bushel or 22 liters)

God. ³⁰ Indeed there are those who are last who will be first, and first who will be last."

Jesus' Sorrow for Jerusalem

13:34,35pp — Mt 23:37–39
13:34,35Ref — Lk 19:41

³¹ At that time some Pharisees came to Jesus and said to him, "Leave this place and go somewhere else. Herod wants to kill you."

³² He replied, "Go tell that fox, 'I will drive out demons and heal people today and tomorrow, and on the third day I will reach my goal.' ³³ In any case, I must keep going today and tomorrow and the next day—for surely no prophet can die outside Jerusalem!

³⁴ "O Jerusalem, Jerusalem, you who kill the prophets and stone those sent to you, how often I have longed to gather your children together, as a hen gathers her chicks under her wings, but you were not willing! ³⁵ Look, your house is left to you desolate. I tell you, you will not see me again until you say, 'Blessed is he who comes in the name of the Lord.' *[a]*"

Jesus at a Pharisee's House

14:8–10Ref — Pr 25:6,7

14 One Sabbath, when Jesus went to eat in the house of a prominent Pharisee, he was being carefully watched. ² There in front of him was a man suffering from dropsy. ³ Jesus asked the Pharisees and experts in the law, "Is it lawful to heal on the Sabbath or not?" ⁴ But they remained silent. So taking hold of the man, he healed him and sent him away.

⁵ Then he asked them, "If one of you has a son *[b]* or an ox that falls into a well on the Sabbath day, will you not immediately pull him out?" ⁶ And they had nothing to say.

⁷ When he noticed how the guests picked the places of honor at the table, he told them this parable: ⁸ "When someone invites you to a wedding feast, do not take the place of honor, for a person more distinguished than you may have been invited. ⁹ If so, the host who invited both of you will come and say to you, 'Give this man

your seat.' Then, humiliated, you will have to take the least important place. ¹⁰ But when you are invited, take the lowest place, so that when your host comes, he will say to you, 'Friend, move up to a better place.' Then you will be honored in the presence of all your fellow guests. ¹¹ For everyone who exalts himself will be humbled, and he who humbles himself will be exalted."

¹² Then Jesus said to his host, "When you give a luncheon or dinner, do not invite your friends, your brothers or relatives, or your rich neighbors; if you do, they may invite you back and so you will be repaid. ¹³ But when you give a banquet, invite the poor, the crippled, the lame, the blind, ¹⁴ and you will be blessed. Although they cannot repay you, you will be repaid at the resurrection of the righteous."

The Parable of the Great Banquet

14:16–24Ref — Mt 22:2–14

¹⁵ When one of those at the table with him heard this, he said to Jesus, "Blessed is the man who will eat at the feast in the kingdom of God."

¹⁶ Jesus replied: "A certain man was preparing a great banquet and invited many guests. ¹⁷ At the time of the banquet he sent his servant to tell those who had been invited, 'Come, for everything is now ready.'

¹⁸ "But they all alike began to make excuses. The first said, 'I have just bought a field, and I must go and see it. Please excuse me.'

¹⁹ "Another said, 'I have just bought five yoke of oxen, and I'm on my way to try them out. Please excuse me.'

²⁰ "Still another said, 'I just got married, so I can't come.'

²¹ "The servant came back and reported this to his master. Then the owner of the house became angry and ordered his servant, 'Go out quickly into the streets and alleys of the town and bring in the poor, the crippled, the blind and the lame.'

²² " 'Sir,' the servant said, 'what you ordered has been done, but there is still room.'

---

[a] 35 Psalm 118:26   *[b] 5* Some manuscripts *donkey*

23"Then the master told his servant, 'Go out to the roads and country lanes and make them come in, so that my house will be full. 24I tell you, not one of those men who were invited will get a taste of my banquet.' "

The Cost of Being a Disciple

25Large crowds were traveling with Jesus, and turning to them he said: 26"If anyone comes to me and does not hate his father and mother, his wife and children, his brothers and sisters—yes, even his own life—he cannot be my disciple. 27And anyone who does not carry his cross and follow me cannot be my disciple.

28"Suppose one of you wants to build a tower. Will he not first sit down and estimate the cost to see if he has enough money to complete it? 29For if he lays the foundation and is not able to finish it, everyone who sees it will ridicule him, 30saying, 'This fellow began to build and was not able to finish.'

31"Or suppose a king is about to go to war against another king. Will he not first sit down and consider whether he is able with ten thousand men to oppose the one coming against him with twenty thousand? 32If he is not able, he will send a delegation while the other is still a long way off and will ask for terms of peace. 33In the same way, any of you who does not give up everything he has cannot be my disciple.

34"Salt is good, but if it loses its saltiness, how can it be made salty again? 35It is fit neither for the soil nor for the manure pile; it is thrown out.

"He who has ears to hear, let him hear."

The Parable of the Lost Sheep

15:4–7pp — Mt 18:12–14

15 Now the tax collectors and "sinners" were all gathering around to hear him. 2But the Pharisees and the teachers of the law muttered, "This man welcomes sinners and eats with them."

3Then Jesus told them this parable: 4"Suppose one of you has a hundred sheep and loses one of

them. Does he not leave the ninety-nine in the open country and go after the lost sheep until he finds it? 5And when he finds it, he joyfully puts it on his shoulders 6and goes home. Then he calls his friends and neighbors together and says, 'Rejoice with me; I have found my lost sheep.' 7I tell you that in the same way there will be more rejoicing in heaven over one sinner who repents than over ninety-nine righteous persons who do not need to repent.

The Parable of the Lost Coin

8"Or suppose a woman has ten silver coins*a* and loses one. Does she not light a lamp, sweep the house and search carefully until she finds it? 9And when she finds it, she calls her friends and neighbors together and says, 'Rejoice with me; I have found my lost coin.' 10In the same way, I tell you, there is rejoicing in the presence of the angels of God over one sinner who repents."

The Parable of the Lost Son

11Jesus continued: "There was a man who had two sons. 12The younger one said to his father, 'Father, give me my share of the estate.' So he divided his property between them.

TALKING POINTS

Rebellion

In his compassion, God embraces those who repent of their rebellion.

LUKE 15:11–20

This is the last talking point on rebellion.

13"Not long after that, the younger son got together all he had, set off for a distant country and there squandered his wealth in wild living. 14After he had spent everything, there was a severe

a 8 Greek ten drachmas, each worth about a day's wages

> "SUPPOSE ONE OF YOU HAS A HUNDRED SHEEP AND LOSES ONE OF THEM. DOES HE NOT LEAVE THE NINETY-NINE IN THE OPEN COUNTRY AND GO AFTER THE LOST SHEEP UNTIL HE FINDS IT?"
>
> Luke 15:4

Caring for Each One

KAREN KINGSBURY

READ | LUKE 15:1–7

I never really knew my grandmothers. Grandma Doris on my mom's side died months before I was born, and Grandma Rosemary on my dad's side died when I was just three. Maybe for that reason I was drawn to my husband's Grandma Polly.

Grandma Polly was a farm girl in her day, tall and strong and able to keep up with the best of the boys. She raised seven kids, and none of them even considered talking back to her or letting her down. By the time I met her, Grandma Polly was in her mid–70s, but she hadn't lost a step. Not only could she keep her great-grandchildren — my kids — in line, but her mind was as sharp as it had ever been.

In a short time I came to see Grandma Polly as the grandmother I never had, the one I always wanted when I was a young girl. Her role in my life reminded me of the picture that all of us are like sheep, wandering and confused, without a whole lot of sense until we come under the care of the Good Shepherd. Though Grandma Polly had many children and dozens of grandchildren and great-grandchildren, she made me feel like I was the only granddaughter in her life.

That's the way it is with Jesus. He'll go after the one sheep and leave for a while the 99, just to show how much he loves us. And that's the way it was with Grandma Polly. She loved me and gave me extra attention, and she helped me see her faith and love for Christ at work. She died when our oldest daughter was ten. I'm not sure she ever knew how much her kindness meant to me, but I know her presence in my life was a gift from God.

Dear Lord, help me to look for the lost and lonely in my life, especially as my children have kids of their own. A young person might not be my own child or grandchild, but help me to reach out to that one, the way you, the Good Shepherd, reach out to me. Amen.

Your next devotion is located on page 1416.

GRANDCHILD IN FOCUS • PRAYER

Relationships at Home

O Lord, I pray that you will bless the home and family of my grandchild. May the relationships she has with her parents and siblings enhance her well-being, support her self-confidence and increase her faith. May her home life reflect your love, your grace, your compassion and your peace. Guide her parents to direct her in love and truth, so she will grow into a strong and compassionate individual. Amen.

famine in that whole country, and he began to be in need. ¹⁵So he went and hired himself out to a citizen of that country, who sent him to his fields to feed pigs. ¹⁶He longed to fill his stomach with the pods that the pigs were eating, but no one gave him anything.

¹⁷"When he came to his senses, he said, 'How many of my father's hired men have food to spare, and here I am starving to death! ¹⁸I will set out and go back to my father and say to him: Father, I have sinned against heaven and against you. ¹⁹I am no longer worthy to be called your son; make me like one of your hired men.' ²⁰So he got up and went to his father.

"But while he was still a long way off, his father saw him and was filled with compassion for him; he ran to his son, threw his arms around him and kissed him.

²¹"The son said to him, 'Father, I have sinned against heaven and against you. I am no longer worthy to be called your son.ᵃ'

²²"But the father said to his servants, 'Quick! Bring the best robe and put it on him. Put a ring on his finger and sandals on his feet. ²³Bring the fattened calf and kill it. Let's have a feast and celebrate. ²⁴For this son of mine was dead and is alive again; he was lost and is found.' So they began to celebrate.

²⁵"Meanwhile, the older son was in the field. When he came near the house, he heard music and dancing. ²⁶So he called one of the servants and asked him what was going on. ²⁷'Your brother has come,' he replied, 'and your father has killed the fattened calf because he has him back safe and sound.'

²⁸"The older brother became angry and refused to go in. So his father went out and pleaded with him. ²⁹But he answered his father, 'Look! All these years I've been slaving for you and never disobeyed your orders. Yet you never gave me even a young goat so I could celebrate with my friends. ³⁰But when this son of yours who has squandered your property with prostitutes comes home, you kill the fattened calf for him!'

³¹"'My son,' the father said, 'you are always

LUKE 15:11–32

The Parable of the Lost Son

LIFE LESSON: God is a loving Father who longs for us to "come home" to him.

TO TALK ABOUT

✦ Why did the younger brother want his inheritance money from his father before his father died?

✦ Did he use the money wisely? What did he do with it?

✦ Did the older brother have a right to be angry? What was the father's message to him?

✦ What does the father's treatment of his son when he returns home tell us about how God treats us? How can you relate to the "lost son"?

with me, and everything I have is yours. ³²But we had to celebrate and be glad, because this brother of yours was dead and is alive again; he was lost and is found.' "

The Parable of the Shrewd Manager

16 Jesus told his disciples: "There was a rich man whose manager was accused of wasting his possessions. ²So he called him in and asked him, 'What is this I hear about you? Give

ᵃ 21 Some early manuscripts son. Make me like one of your hired men.

an account of your management, because you cannot be manager any longer.'

³"The manager said to himself, 'What shall I do now? My master is taking away my job. I'm not strong enough to dig, and I'm ashamed to beg— ⁴I know what I'll do so that, when I lose my job here, people will welcome me into their houses.'

⁵"So he called in each one of his master's debtors. He asked the first, 'How much do you owe my master?'

⁶" 'Eight hundred gallons ᵃ of olive oil,' he replied.

"The manager told him, 'Take your bill, sit down quickly, and make it four hundred.'

⁷"Then he asked the second, 'And how much do you owe?'

" 'A thousand bushels ᵇ of wheat,' he replied.

"He told him, 'Take your bill and make it eight hundred.'

⁸"The master commended the dishonest manager because he had acted shrewdly. For the people of this world are more shrewd in dealing with their own kind than are the people of the light. ⁹I tell you, use worldly wealth to gain friends for yourselves, so that when it is gone, you will be welcomed into eternal dwellings.

¹⁰"Whoever can be trusted with very little can also be trusted with much, and whoever is dishonest with very little will also be dishonest with much. ¹¹So if you have not been trustworthy in handling worldly wealth, who will trust you with true riches? ¹²And if you have not been trustworthy with someone else's property, who will give you property of your own?

¹³"No servant can serve two masters. Either he will hate the one and love the other, or he will be devoted to the one and despise the other. You cannot serve both God and Money."

¹⁴The Pharisees, who loved money, heard all this and were sneering at Jesus. ¹⁵He said to them, "You are the ones who justify yourselves in the eyes of men, but God knows your hearts. What is highly valued among men is detestable in God's sight.

TALKING POINTS

Money

Make God, not money, your top priority.

LUKE 16:13

For more on money, go to 1 Timothy 6:6–10.

Additional Teachings

¹⁶"The Law and the Prophets were proclaimed until John. Since that time, the good news of the kingdom of God is being preached, and everyone is forcing his way into it. ¹⁷It is easier for heaven and earth to disappear than for the least stroke of a pen to drop out of the Law.

¹⁸"Anyone who divorces his wife and marries another woman commits adultery, and the man who marries a divorced woman commits adultery.

The Rich Man and Lazarus

¹⁹"There was a rich man who was dressed in purple and fine linen and lived in luxury every day. ²⁰At his gate was laid a beggar named Lazarus, covered with sores ²¹and longing to eat what fell from the rich man's table. Even the dogs came and licked his sores.

²²"The time came when the beggar died and the angels carried him to Abraham's side. The rich man also died and was buried. ²³In hell,ᶜ where he was in torment, he looked up and saw Abraham far away, with Lazarus by his side. ²⁴So he called to him, 'Father Abraham, have pity on me and send Lazarus to dip the tip of his finger in water and cool my tongue, because I am in agony in this fire.'

²⁵"But Abraham replied, 'Son, remember that in your lifetime you received your good things, while Lazarus received bad things, but now he is

---

ᵃ 6 Greek *one hundred batous* (probably about 3 kiloliters)
ᵇ 7 Greek *one hundred korous* (probably about 35 kiloliters)
ᶜ 23 Greek *Hades*

FAITH IN ACTION

Saturday Sing-Along

You can make sharing your faith with your grandkids a lot of fun by sharing your favorite hymns and choruses. Teach them some of the old songs you sang when you were a kid or share the ones that were favorites of your parents and grandparents. Then let the kids teach you some of their favorites. These newer songs will keep you in touch and allow you to sing like a pro when these new songs are included in your worship service.

Don't worry about singing a cappella or slightly off-key. The point is to share the words and let your grandkids hear you sing from your heart. If you're not sure of all the words and all the verses, pick up a hymnal from your church library, a used bookstore or e-Bay. If you're a little on the shy side about this, practice alone first so you get used to hearing yourself; then you'll be ready to confidently sing your favorites.

O Lord, help me share my faith with my grandchildren through the words and music of my favorite hymns. Instill self-confidence in me and provide strong voices so that our praises are a sweet, sweet sound to your ears. Amen.

Your next devotion is located on page 1419.

GRANDCHILD IN FOCUS • PRAYER

Friends

Dear Lord and Father, I pray for my grandchild's social life and his friends. Bring diverse friends into his life who will love and encourage him, who will bring joy and laughter to the good times and comfort and support through difficulties and disappointments. Grant him wisdom and discernment as he selects his friends; help him to avoid cliques that restrict, activities that endanger, and foolish and dangerous behaviors that harm. I ask that you fill his life with close and caring relationships. Amen.

comforted here and you are in agony. ²⁶And besides all this, between us and you a great chasm has been fixed, so that those who want to go from here to you cannot, nor can anyone cross over from there to us.'

²⁷"He answered, 'Then I beg you, father, send Lazarus to my father's house, ²⁸for I have five brothers. Let him warn them, so that they will not also come to this place of torment.'

²⁹"Abraham replied, 'They have Moses and the Prophets; let them listen to them.'

³⁰" 'No, father Abraham,' he said, 'but if someone from the dead goes to them, they will repent.'

³¹"He said to him, 'If they do not listen to Moses and the Prophets, they will not be convinced even if someone rises from the dead.' "

Sin, Faith, Duty

17 Jesus said to his disciples: "Things that cause people to sin are bound to come, but woe to that person through whom they come. ²It would be better for him to be thrown into the sea with a millstone tied around his neck than for him to cause one of these little ones to sin. ³So watch yourselves.

"If your brother sins, rebuke him, and if he repents, forgive him. ⁴If he sins against you seven times in a day, and seven times comes back to you and says, 'I repent,' forgive him."

⁵The apostles said to the Lord, "Increase our faith!"

⁶He replied, "If you have faith as small as a mustard seed, you can say to this mulberry tree, 'Be uprooted and planted in the sea,' and it will obey you.

⁷"Suppose one of you had a servant plowing or looking after the sheep. Would he say to the servant when he comes in from the field, 'Come along now and sit down to eat'? ⁸Would he not rather say, 'Prepare my supper, get yourself ready and wait on me while I eat and drink; after that you may eat and drink'? ⁹Would he thank the servant because he did what he was told to do? ¹⁰So you also, when you have done everything you were told to do, should say, 'We are unworthy servants; we have only done our duty.' "

Ten Healed of Leprosy

¹¹Now on his way to Jerusalem, Jesus traveled along the border between Samaria and Galilee. ¹²As he was going into a village, ten men who had leprosy^a met him. They stood at a distance ¹³and called out in a loud voice, "Jesus, Master, have pity on us!"

¹⁴When he saw them, he said, "Go, show yourselves to the priests." And as they went, they were cleansed.

¹⁵One of them, when he saw he was healed, came back, praising God in a loud voice. ¹⁶He

^a 12 The Greek word was used for various diseases affecting the skin — not necessarily leprosy.

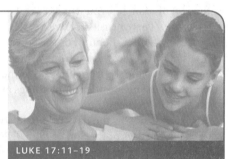

stories to share

LUKE 17:11–19

Ten Healed of Leprosy

LIFE LESSON: Jesus deserves our thanks and praise for what he has done for us.

TO TALK ABOUT

✦ Why did these ten men keep themselves at a distance from Jesus?

✦ What did Jesus tell them to do? What happened?

✦ Why is it significant that the man who thanked Jesus was a Samaritan? (Hint: Read verse 18 and John 4:9.)

✦ Why is it so easy for us to take our blessings for granted?

threw himself at Jesus' feet and thanked him — and he was a Samaritan.

¹⁷ Jesus asked, "Were not all ten cleansed? Where are the other nine? ¹⁸ Was no one found to return and give praise to God except this foreigner?" ¹⁹ Then he said to him, "Rise and go; your faith has made you well."

The Coming of the Kingdom of God
17:26,27pp — Mt 24:37–39

²⁰ Once, having been asked by the Pharisees when the kingdom of God would come, Jesus replied, "The kingdom of God does not come with your careful observation, ²¹ nor will people say, 'Here it is,' or 'There it is,' because the kingdom of God is within *a* you."

²² Then he said to his disciples, "The time is coming when you will long to see one of the days of the Son of Man, but you will not see it. ²³ Men will tell you, 'There he is!' or 'Here he is!' Do not go running off after them. ²⁴ For the Son of Man in his day *b* will be like the lightning, which flashes and lights up the sky from one end to the other. ²⁵ But first he must suffer many things and be rejected by this generation.

²⁶ "Just as it was in the days of Noah, so also will it be in the days of the Son of Man. ²⁷ People were eating, drinking, marrying and being given in marriage up to the day Noah entered the ark. Then the flood came and destroyed them all.

²⁸ "It was the same in the days of Lot. People were eating and drinking, buying and selling, planting and building. ²⁹ But the day Lot left Sodom, fire and sulfur rained down from heaven and destroyed them all.

³⁰ "It will be just like this on the day the Son of Man is revealed. ³¹ On that day no one who is on the roof of his house, with his goods inside, should go down to get them. Likewise, no one in the field should go back for anything. ³² Remember Lot's wife! ³³ Whoever tries to keep his life will lose it, and whoever loses his life will preserve it. ³⁴ I tell you, on that night two people will be in one bed; one will be taken and the other left. ³⁵ Two women will be grinding grain together; one will be taken and the other left. *c*"

³⁷ "Where, Lord?" they asked.

He replied, "Where there is a dead body, there the vultures will gather."

The Parable of the Persistent Widow

18 Then Jesus told his disciples a parable to show them that they should always pray and not give up. ² He said: "In a certain town there was a judge who neither feared God nor cared about men. ³ And there was a widow in that town who kept coming to him with the plea, 'Grant me justice against my adversary.'

⁴ "For some time he refused. But finally he said to himself, 'Even though I don't fear God or care about men, ⁵ yet because this widow keeps bothering me, I will see that she gets justice, so that she won't eventually wear me out with her coming!' "

⁶ And the Lord said, "Listen to what the unjust judge says. ⁷ And will not God bring about justice for his chosen ones, who cry out to him day and night? Will he keep putting them off? ⁸ I tell you, he will see that they get justice, and quickly. However, when the Son of Man comes, will he find faith on the earth?"

TALKING POINTS

Prayer

Jesus tells us to pray with persistence.

LUKE 18:1–8

For more on prayer, go to James 5:13–16.

The Parable of the Pharisee and the Tax Collector

⁹ To some who were confident of their own righteousness and looked down on everybody else, Jesus told this parable: ¹⁰ "Two men went up to the temple to pray, one a Pharisee and the

---

a 21 Or *among*   *b 24* Some manuscripts do not have *in his day.*
c 35 Some manuscripts *left.* ³⁶ *Two men will be in the field; one will be taken and the other left.*

Worship the Lord

Praise the LORD.

Praise, O servants of the LORD,
    praise the name of the LORD.
Let the name of the LORD be praised,
    both now and forevermore.
From the rising of the sun to the place where
    it sets,
    the name of the LORD is to be praised.

The LORD is exalted over all the nations,
    his glory above the heavens.
Who is like the LORD our God,
    the One who sits enthroned on
    high,
who stoops down to look
    on the heavens and the earth?

He raises the poor from the dust
    and lifts the needy from the ash
    heap;
he seats them with princes,
    with the princes of their people.
He settles the barren woman in her home
    as a happy mother of children.

Praise the LORD.

Psalm 113

GRANDCHILD IN FOCUS · PRAYER

Self-Image

*O loving God, I praise you for creating my
grandchild as a unique individual. Now I ask you
to help her appreciate her uniqueness. Build up her
self-image so she can enjoy her individuality. Help
her to stand firm for who she is, where she has
come from and what she believes in. Encourage
her not only to have hopes and dreams but
to also enjoy each day as it comes.
In Jesus' name, amen.*

*Dear Father, what a comfort to imagine you stooping down to clear my path or help me navigate
a rough spot. Thank you for caring enough to focus your attention on the poor and the needy.
Thank you for making me a mother, for you have indeed given me joy in my children and grandchildren. Amen.*

Your next devotion is located on page 1422.

other a tax collector. [11] The Pharisee stood up and prayed about[a] himself: 'God, I thank you that I am not like other men—robbers, evildoers, adulterers—or even like this tax collector. [12] I fast twice a week and give a tenth of all I get.'

[13] "But the tax collector stood at a distance. He would not even look up to heaven, but beat his breast and said, 'God, have mercy on me, a sinner.'

[14] "I tell you that this man, rather than the other, went home justified before God. For everyone who exalts himself will be humbled, and he who humbles himself will be exalted."

The Little Children and Jesus

18:15–17pp — Mt 19:13–15; Mk 10:13–16

[15] People were also bringing babies to Jesus to have him touch them. When the disciples saw this, they rebuked them. [16] But Jesus called the children to him and said, "Let the little children come to me, and do not hinder them, for the kingdom of God belongs to such as these. [17] I tell you the truth, anyone who will not receive the kingdom of God like a little child will never enter it."

The Rich Ruler

18:18–30pp — Mt 19:16–29; Mk 10:17–30

[18] A certain ruler asked him, "Good teacher, what must I do to inherit eternal life?"

[19] "Why do you call me good?" Jesus answered. "No one is good—except God alone. [20] You know the commandments: 'Do not commit adultery, do not murder, do not steal, do not give false testimony, honor your father and mother.'[b]"

[21] "All these I have kept since I was a boy," he said.

[22] When Jesus heard this, he said to him, "You still lack one thing. Sell everything you have and give to the poor, and you will have treasure in heaven. Then come, follow me."

[23] When he heard this, he became very sad, because he was a man of great wealth. [24] Jesus looked at him and said, "How hard it is for the rich to enter the kingdom of God! [25] Indeed, it is easier for a camel to go through the eye of a needle than for a rich man to enter the kingdom of God."

[26] Those who heard this asked, "Who then can be saved?"

[27] Jesus replied, "What is impossible with men is possible with God."

[28] Peter said to him, "We have left all we had to follow you!"

[29] "I tell you the truth," Jesus said to them, "no one who has left home or wife or brothers or parents or children for the sake of the kingdom of God [30] will fail to receive many times as much in this age and, in the age to come, eternal life."

Jesus Again Predicts His Death

18:31–33pp — Mt 20:17–19; Mk 10:32–34

[31] Jesus took the Twelve aside and told them, "We are going up to Jerusalem, and everything that is written by the prophets about the Son of Man will be fulfilled. [32] He will be handed over to the Gentiles. They will mock him, insult him, spit on him, flog him and kill him. [33] On the third day he will rise again."

[34] The disciples did not understand any of this. Its meaning was hidden from them, and they did not know what he was talking about.

A Blind Beggar Receives His Sight

18:35–43pp — Mt 20:29–34; Mk 10:46–52

[35] As Jesus approached Jericho, a blind man was sitting by the roadside begging. [36] When he heard the crowd going by, he asked what was happening. [37] They told him, "Jesus of Nazareth is passing by."

[38] He called out, "Jesus, Son of David, have mercy on me!"

[39] Those who led the way rebuked him and told him to be quiet, but he shouted all the more, "Son of David, have mercy on me!"

[40] Jesus stopped and ordered the man to be brought to him. When he came near, Jesus asked him, [41] "What do you want me to do for you?"

"Lord, I want to see," he replied.

a 11 Or to   b 20 Exodus 20:12-16; Deut. 5:16-20

[42]Jesus said to him, "Receive your sight; your faith has healed you." [43]Immediately he received his sight and followed Jesus, praising God. When all the people saw it, they also praised God.

Zacchaeus the Tax Collector

19 Jesus entered Jericho and was passing through. [2]A man was there by the name of Zacchaeus; he was a chief tax collector and was wealthy. [3]He wanted to see who Jesus was, but being a short man he could not, because of the crowd. [4]So he ran ahead and climbed a sycamore-fig tree to see him, since Jesus was coming that way.

LUKE 19:1–10

Zacchaeus the Tax Collector

LIFE LESSON: Jesus came to seek and save lost people.

TO TALK ABOUT

✦ Why did Zacchaeus climb into a tree? Do you think he expected anyone to see him there?

✦ Why did the people call Zacchaeus a sinner? Aren't we all sinners?

✦ How did Zacchaeus respond to Jesus reaching out to him?

✦ Do you think Zacchaeus would have followed Jesus if Jesus hadn't called him? Why or why not?

(side margin) stories to share

[5]When Jesus reached the spot, he looked up and said to him, "Zacchaeus, come down immediately. I must stay at your house today." [6]So he came down at once and welcomed him gladly.

[7]All the people saw this and began to mutter, "He has gone to be the guest of a 'sinner.' "

[8]But Zacchaeus stood up and said to the Lord, "Look, Lord! Here and now I give half of my possessions to the poor, and if I have cheated anybody out of anything, I will pay back four times the amount."

[9]Jesus said to him, "Today salvation has come to this house, because this man, too, is a son of Abraham. [10]For the Son of Man came to seek and to save what was lost."

The Parable of the Ten Minas

19:12–27Ref — Mt 25:14–30

[11]While they were listening to this, he went on to tell them a parable, because he was near Jerusalem and the people thought that the kingdom of God was going to appear at once. [12]He said: "A man of noble birth went to a distant country to have himself appointed king and then to return. [13]So he called ten of his servants and gave them ten minas.[a] 'Put this money to work,' he said, 'until I come back.'

[14]"But his subjects hated him and sent a delegation after him to say, 'We don't want this man to be our king.'

[15]"He was made king, however, and returned home. Then he sent for the servants to whom he had given the money, in order to find out what they had gained with it.

[16]"The first one came and said, 'Sir, your mina has earned ten more.'

[17]" 'Well done, my good servant!' his master replied. 'Because you have been trustworthy in a very small matter, take charge of ten cities.'

[18]"The second came and said, 'Sir, your mina has earned five more.'

[19]"His master answered, 'You take charge of five cities.'

---

[a] *13 A mina was about three months' wages.*

"FOR THE SON OF MAN CAME TO SEEK AND TO SAVE WHAT WAS LOST."

Luke 19:10

The Heart of the Gospel

GLADYS HUNT

READ | LUKE 19:1 – 10

How would you answer the question, What is the gospel?

Jesus used the occasion of his confrontation with a tree-climbing public official named Zacchaeus to tell us a great truth. He gave us his mission statement: "The Son of Man came to seek and to save what was lost." That short, simple sentence is a profound declaration.

First, the Son of Man came! That proclamation should give us the shivers. God came. The gospel is first and foremost the action of God. The gospel is God's story. While the people around Zacchaeus argued about Jesus eating with a sinner, they missed the point that God in the flesh, in the person of Jesus, was present.

We say it in the Nicene Creed: "God from God, Light from Light . . . of one being with the Father . . . For us and for our salvation he came down from heaven."

Second, it's a good practice to notice verbs when reading the Scripture. In this one sentence there are three: "came," "seek" and "save." Jesus is the subject. He came, he seeks and he saves. We are so hopelessly lost and alienated from God that it took this kind of action to make us right with him.

Lastly, the gospel is for lost people. We are not just unhappy or troubled, nor do we simply have a poor self-image. Our condition is more desperate than we know:
We are lost! Only God can find us. The gospel is *from* God and *about* God, and it is for those who realize they are lost.

Lord Jesus, thank you for coming. Thank you for seeking me. Thank you for saving me from my sin and from myself. Help me to make my life a song of praise to you. Amen.

Your next devotion is located on page 1432.

GRANDCHILD IN FOCUS • PRAYER

Protection From Worldliness

O Sovereign Lord, the world surrounds my grandchild, pressing in and tempting him in so many ways. Help him set appropriate limits. Give him sound judgment to choose wisely. Guard him from temptation; protect him from physical and mental predators; lead him into paths of righteousness and light. And reassure me with your promise that you are holding him in your hands. Amen.

²⁰"Then another servant came and said, 'Sir, here is your mina; I have kept it laid away in a piece of cloth. ²¹I was afraid of you, because you are a hard man. You take out what you did not put in and reap what you did not sow.'

²²"His master replied, 'I will judge you by your own words, you wicked servant! You knew, did you, that I am a hard man, taking out what I did not put in, and reaping what I did not sow? ²³Why then didn't you put my money on deposit, so that when I came back, I could have collected it with interest?'

²⁴"Then he said to those standing by, 'Take his mina away from him and give it to the one who has ten minas.'

²⁵" 'Sir,' they said, 'he already has ten!'

²⁶"He replied, 'I tell you that to everyone who has, more will be given, but as for the one who has nothing, even what he has will be taken away. ²⁷But those enemies of mine who did not want me to be king over them—bring them here and kill them in front of me.' "

The Triumphal Entry

19:29–38pp — Mt 21:1–9; Mk 11:1–10
19:35–38pp — Jn 12:12–15

²⁸After Jesus had said this, he went on ahead, going up to Jerusalem. ²⁹As he approached Bethphage and Bethany at the hill called the Mount of Olives, he sent two of his disciples, saying to them, ³⁰"Go to the village ahead of you, and as you enter it, you will find a colt tied there, which no one has ever ridden. Untie it and bring it here. ³¹If anyone asks you, 'Why are you untying it?' tell him, 'The Lord needs it.' "

³²Those who were sent ahead went and found it just as he had told them. ³³As they were untying the colt, its owners asked them, "Why are you untying the colt?"

³⁴They replied, "The Lord needs it."

³⁵They brought it to Jesus, threw their cloaks on the colt and put Jesus on it. ³⁶As he went along, people spread their cloaks on the road.

³⁷When he came near the place where the road goes down the Mount of Olives, the whole crowd of disciples began joyfully to praise God in loud voices for all the miracles they had seen:

³⁸"Blessed is the king who comes in the name of the Lord!"^a

"Peace in heaven and glory in the highest!"

³⁹Some of the Pharisees in the crowd said to Jesus, "Teacher, rebuke your disciples!"

⁴⁰"I tell you," he replied, "if they keep quiet, the stones will cry out."

⁴¹As he approached Jerusalem and saw the city, he wept over it ⁴²and said, "If you, even you, had only known on this day what would bring you peace—but now it is hidden from your eyes. ⁴³The days will come upon you when your enemies will build an embankment against you and encircle you and hem you in on every side. ⁴⁴They will dash you to the ground, you and the children within your walls. They will not leave one stone on another, because you did not recognize the time of God's coming to you."

Jesus at the Temple

19:45,46pp — Mt 21:12–16; Mk 11:15–18; Jn 2:13–16

⁴⁵Then he entered the temple area and began driving out those who were selling. ⁴⁶"It is written," he said to them, " 'My house will be a house of prayer'^b; but you have made it 'a den of robbers.'^c"

⁴⁷Every day he was teaching at the temple. But the chief priests, the teachers of the law and the leaders among the people were trying to kill him. ⁴⁸Yet they could not find any way to do it, because all the people hung on his words.

The Authority of Jesus Questioned

20:1–8pp — Mt 21:23–27; Mk 11:27–33

²⁰ One day as he was teaching the people in the temple courts and preaching the gospel, the chief priests and the teachers of the law, together with the elders, came up to him. ²"Tell us by what authority you are doing these things," they said. "Who gave you this authority?"

^a 38 Psalm 118:26   ^b 46 Isaiah 56:7   ^c 46 Jer. 7:11

³He replied, "I will also ask you a question. Tell me, ⁴John's baptism—was it from heaven, or from men?"

⁵They discussed it among themselves and said, "If we say, 'From heaven,' he will ask, 'Why didn't you believe him?' ⁶But if we say, 'From men,' all the people will stone us, because they are persuaded that John was a prophet."

⁷So they answered, "We don't know where it was from."

⁸Jesus said, "Neither will I tell you by what authority I am doing these things."

The Parable of the Tenants

20:9–19pp — Mt 21:33–46; Mk 12:1–12

⁹He went on to tell the people this parable: "A man planted a vineyard, rented it to some farmers and went away for a long time. ¹⁰At harvest time he sent a servant to the tenants so they would give him some of the fruit of the vineyard. But the tenants beat him and sent him away empty-handed. ¹¹He sent another servant, but that one also they beat and treated shamefully and sent away empty-handed. ¹²He sent still a third, and they wounded him and threw him out.

¹³"Then the owner of the vineyard said, 'What shall I do? I will send my son, whom I love; perhaps they will respect him.'

¹⁴"But when the tenants saw him, they talked the matter over. 'This is the heir,' they said. 'Let's kill him, and the inheritance will be ours.' ¹⁵So they threw him out of the vineyard and killed him.

"What then will the owner of the vineyard do to them? ¹⁶He will come and kill those tenants and give the vineyard to others."

When the people heard this, they said, "May this never be!"

¹⁷Jesus looked directly at them and asked, "Then what is the meaning of that which is written:

" 'The stone the builders rejected
has become the capstone*ᵃ* *ᵇ*?

¹⁸Everyone who falls on that stone will be broken to pieces, but he on whom it falls will be crushed."

¹⁹The teachers of the law and the chief priests looked for a way to arrest him immediately, because they knew he had spoken this parable against them. But they were afraid of the people.

Paying Taxes to Caesar

20:20–26pp — Mt 22:15–22; Mk 12:13–17

²⁰Keeping a close watch on him, they sent spies, who pretended to be honest. They hoped to catch Jesus in something he said so that they might hand him over to the power and authority of the governor. ²¹So the spies questioned him: "Teacher, we know that you speak and teach what is right, and that you do not show partiality but teach the way of God in accordance with the truth. ²²Is it right for us to pay taxes to Caesar or not?"

²³He saw through their duplicity and said to them, ²⁴"Show me a denarius. Whose portrait and inscription are on it?"

²⁵"Caesar's," they replied.

He said to them, "Then give to Caesar what is Caesar's, and to God what is God's."

²⁶They were unable to trap him in what he had said there in public. And astonished by his answer, they became silent.

The Resurrection and Marriage

20:27–40pp — Mt 22:23–33; Mk 12:18–27

²⁷Some of the Sadducees, who say there is no resurrection, came to Jesus with a question. ²⁸"Teacher," they said, "Moses wrote for us that if a man's brother dies and leaves a wife but no children, the man must marry the widow and have children for his brother. ²⁹Now there were seven brothers. The first one married a woman and died childless. ³⁰The second ³¹and then the third married her, and in the same way the seven died, leaving no children. ³²Finally, the woman died too. ³³Now then, at the resurrection whose wife will she be, since the seven were married to her?"

³⁴Jesus replied, "The people of this age marry and are given in marriage. ³⁵But those who are

ᵃ 17 Or *cornerstone*   *ᵇ 17* Psalm 118:22

considered worthy of taking part in that age and in the resurrection from the dead will neither marry nor be given in marriage, [30] and they can no longer die; for they are like the angels. They are God's children, since they are children of the resurrection. [37] But in the account of the bush, even Moses showed that the dead rise, for he calls the Lord 'the God of Abraham, and the God of Isaac, and the God of Jacob.'[a] [38] He is not the God of the dead, but of the living, for to him all are alive."

[39] Some of the teachers of the law responded, "Well said, teacher!" [40] And no one dared to ask him any more questions.

Whose Son Is the Christ?

20:41–47pp — Mt 22:41–23:7; Mk 12:35–40

[41] Then Jesus said to them, "How is it that they say the Christ[b] is the Son of David? [42] David himself declares in the Book of Psalms:

" 'The Lord said to my Lord:
  "Sit at my right hand
[43] until I make your enemies
  a footstool for your feet." '[c]

[44] David calls him 'Lord.' How then can he be his son?"

[45] While all the people were listening, Jesus said to his disciples, [46] "Beware of the teachers of the law. They like to walk around in flowing robes and love to be greeted in the marketplaces and have the most important seats in the synagogues and the places of honor at banquets. [47] They devour widows' houses and for a show make lengthy prayers. Such men will be punished most severely."

The Widow's Offering

21:1–4pp — Mk 12:41–44

21 As he looked up, Jesus saw the rich putting their gifts into the temple treasury. [2] He also saw a poor widow put in two very small copper coins.[d] [3] "I tell you the truth," he said, "this poor widow has put in more than all the others. [4] All these people gave their gifts out of

their wealth; but she out of her poverty put in all she had to live on."

Signs of the End of the Age

21:5–36pp — Mt 24; Mk 13
21:12–17pp — Mt 10:17–22

[5] Some of his disciples were remarking about how the temple was adorned with beautiful stones and with gifts dedicated to God. But Jesus said, [6] "As for what you see here, the time will come when not one stone will be left on another; every one of them will be thrown down."

[7] "Teacher," they asked, "when will these things happen? And what will be the sign that they are about to take place?"

[8] He replied: "Watch out that you are not deceived. For many will come in my name, claiming, 'I am he,' and, 'The time is near.' Do not follow them. [9] When you hear of wars and revolutions, do not be frightened. These things must happen first, but the end will not come right away."

[10] Then he said to them: "Nation will rise against nation, and kingdom against kingdom. [11] There will be great earthquakes, famines and pestilences in various places, and fearful events and great signs from heaven.

[12] "But before all this, they will lay hands on you and persecute you. They will deliver you to synagogues and prisons, and you will be brought before kings and governors, and all on account of my name. [13] This will result in your being witnesses to them. [14] But make up your mind not to worry beforehand how you will defend yourselves. [15] For I will give you words and wisdom that none of your adversaries will be able to resist or contradict. [16] You will be betrayed even by parents, brothers, relatives and friends, and they will put some of you to death. [17] All men will hate you because of me. [18] But not a hair of your head will perish. [19] By standing firm you will gain life.

[20] "When you see Jerusalem being surrounded by armies, you will know that its desolation is near. [21] Then let those who are in Judea flee to

---

[a] 37 Exodus 3:6 [b] 41 Or *Messiah* [c] 43 Psalm 110:1
[d] 2 Greek *two lepta*

the mountains, let those in the city get out, and let those in the country not enter the city. ²²For this is the time of punishment in fulfillment of all that has been written. ²³How dreadful it will be in those days for pregnant women and nursing mothers! There will be great distress in the land and wrath against this people. ²⁴They will fall by the sword and will be taken as prisoners to all the nations. Jerusalem will be trampled on by the Gentiles until the times of the Gentiles are fulfilled.

²⁵"There will be signs in the sun, moon and stars. On the earth, nations will be in anguish and perplexity at the roaring and tossing of the sea. ²⁶Men will faint from terror, apprehensive of what is coming on the world, for the heavenly bodies will be shaken. ²⁷At that time they will see the Son of Man coming in a cloud with power and great glory. ²⁸When these things begin to take place, stand up and lift up your heads, because your redemption is drawing near."

²⁹He told them this parable: "Look at the fig tree and all the trees. ³⁰When they sprout leaves, you can see for yourselves and know that summer is near. ³¹Even so, when you see these things happening, you know that the kingdom of God is near.

³²"I tell you the truth, this generation *a* will certainly not pass away until all these things have happened. ³³Heaven and earth will pass away, but my words will never pass away.

³⁴"Be careful, or your hearts will be weighed down with dissipation, drunkenness and the anxieties of life, and that day will close on you unexpectedly like a trap. ³⁵For it will come upon all those who live on the face of the whole earth. ³⁶Be always on the watch, and pray that you may be able to escape all that is about to happen, and that you may be able to stand before the Son of Man."

³⁷Each day Jesus was teaching at the temple, and each evening he went out to spend the night on the hill called the Mount of Olives, ³⁸and all the people came early in the morning to hear him at the temple.

Judas Agrees to Betray Jesus

22:1,2pp — Mt 26:2–5; Mk 14:1,2,10,11

22 Now the Feast of Unleavened Bread, called the Passover, was approaching, ²and the chief priests and the teachers of the law were looking for some way to get rid of Jesus, for they were afraid of the people. ³Then Satan entered Judas, called Iscariot, one of the Twelve. ⁴And Judas went to the chief priests and the officers of the temple guard and discussed with them how he might betray Jesus. ⁵They were delighted and agreed to give him money. ⁶He consented, and watched for an opportunity to hand Jesus over to them when no crowd was present.

The Last Supper

22:7–13pp — Mt 26:17–19; Mk 14:12–16
22:17–20pp — Mt 26:26–29; Mk 14:22–25;
*   1Co 11:23–25*
22:21–23pp — Mt 26:21–24; Mk 14:18–21;
*   Jn 13:21–30*
22:25–27pp — Mt 20:25–28; Mk 10:42–45
22:33,34pp — Mt 26:33–35; Mk 14:29–31; Jn 13:37,38

⁷Then came the day of Unleavened Bread on which the Passover lamb had to be sacrificed. ⁸Jesus sent Peter and John, saying, "Go and make preparations for us to eat the Passover."

⁹"Where do you want us to prepare for it?" they asked.

¹⁰He replied, "As you enter the city, a man carrying a jar of water will meet you. Follow him to the house that he enters, ¹¹and say to the owner of the house, 'The Teacher asks: Where is the guest room, where I may eat the Passover with my disciples?' ¹²He will show you a large upper room, all furnished. Make preparations there."

¹³They left and found things just as Jesus had told them. So they prepared the Passover.

¹⁴When the hour came, Jesus and his apostles reclined at the table. ¹⁵And he said to them, "I have eagerly desired to eat this Passover with you before I suffer. ¹⁶For I tell you, I will not eat it again until it finds fulfillment in the kingdom of God."

¹⁷After taking the cup, he gave thanks and said,

a 32 Or race

"Take this and divide it among you. ¹⁸For I tell you I will not drink again of the fruit of the vine until the kingdom of God comes."

¹⁹And he took bread, gave thanks and broke it, and gave it to them, saying, "This is my body given for you; do this in remembrance of me."

²⁰In the same way, after the supper he took the cup, saying, "This cup is the new covenant in my blood, which is poured out for you. ²¹But the hand of him who is going to betray me is with mine on the table. ²²The Son of Man will go as it has been decreed, but woe to that man who betrays him." ²³They began to question among themselves which of them it might be who would do this.

²⁴Also a dispute arose among them as to which of them was considered to be greatest. ²⁵Jesus said to them, "The kings of the Gentiles lord it over them; and those who exercise authority over them call themselves Benefactors. ²⁶But you are not to be like that. Instead, the greatest among you should be like the youngest, and the one who rules like the one who serves. ²⁷For who is greater, the one who is at the table or the one who serves? Is it not the one who is at the table? But I am among you as one who serves. ²⁸You are those who have stood by me in my trials. ²⁹And I confer on you a kingdom, just as my Father conferred one on me, ³⁰so that you may eat and drink at my table in my kingdom and sit on thrones, judging the twelve tribes of Israel.

³¹"Simon, Simon, Satan has asked to sift you *a* as wheat. ³²But I have prayed for you, Simon, that your faith may not fail. And when you have turned back, strengthen your brothers."

³³But he replied, "Lord, I am ready to go with you to prison and to death."

³⁴Jesus answered, "I tell you, Peter, before the rooster crows today, you will deny three times that you know me."

³⁵Then Jesus asked them, "When I sent you without purse, bag or sandals, did you lack anything?"

"Nothing," they answered.

³⁶He said to them, "But now if you have a purse, take it, and also a bag; and if you don't have a sword, sell your cloak and buy one. ³⁷It is written: 'And he was numbered with the transgressors' *b*; and I tell you that this must be fulfilled in me. Yes, what is written about me is reaching its fulfillment."

³⁸The disciples said, "See, Lord, here are two swords."

"That is enough," he replied.

Jesus Prays on the Mount of Olives
22:40–46pp — Mt 26:36–46; Mk 14:32–42

³⁹Jesus went out as usual to the Mount of Olives, and his disciples followed him. ⁴⁰On reaching the place, he said to them, "Pray that you will not fall into temptation." ⁴¹He withdrew about a stone's throw beyond them, knelt down and prayed, ⁴²"Father, if you are willing, take this cup from me; yet not my will, but yours be done." ⁴³An angel from heaven appeared to him and strengthened him. ⁴⁴And being in anguish, he prayed more earnestly, and his sweat was like drops of blood falling to the ground. *c*

⁴⁵When he rose from prayer and went back to the disciples, he found them asleep, exhausted from sorrow. ⁴⁶"Why are you sleeping?" he asked them. "Get up and pray so that you will not fall into temptation."

Jesus Arrested
22:47–53pp — Mt 26:47–56; Mk 14:43–50;
Jn 18:3–11

⁴⁷While he was still speaking a crowd came up, and the man who was called Judas, one of the Twelve, was leading them. He approached Jesus to kiss him, ⁴⁸but Jesus asked him, "Judas, are you betraying the Son of Man with a kiss?"

⁴⁹When Jesus' followers saw what was going to happen, they said, "Lord, should we strike with our swords?" ⁵⁰And one of them struck the servant of the high priest, cutting off his right ear.

⁵¹But Jesus answered, "No more of this!" And he touched the man's ear and healed him.

⁵²Then Jesus said to the chief priests, the officers

a 31 The Greek is plural.   *b 37* Isaiah 53:12   *c 44* Some early manuscripts do not have verses 43 and 44.

of the temple guard, and the elders, who had come for him, "Am I leading a rebellion, that you have come with swords and clubs? ⁵³Every day I was with you in the temple courts, and you did not lay a hand on me. But this is your hour—when darkness reigns."

Peter Disowns Jesus

22:55–62pp — Mt 26:69–75; Mk 14:66–72;
Jn 18:16–18, 25–27

⁵⁴Then seizing him, they led him away and took him into the house of the high priest. Peter followed at a distance. ⁵⁵But when they had kindled a fire in the middle of the courtyard and had sat down together, Peter sat down with them. ⁵⁶A servant girl saw him seated there in the firelight.

LUKE 22:47–53; 22:66—23:25

Jesus Is Arrested

LIFE LESSON: Jesus was a willing sacrifice for our sins.

TO TALK ABOUT

✦ Did Jesus fight back when he was arrested? Why did he act this way?

✦ Did Pilate want Jesus to be crucified? Why did he listen to the people?

✦ Why did the people want Jesus crucified?

✦ Knowing that Jesus died for you, how does his attitude make you feel?

She looked closely at him and said, "This man was with him."

⁵⁷But he denied it. "Woman, I don't know him," he said.

⁵⁸A little later someone else saw him and said, "You also are one of them."

"Man, I am not!" Peter replied.

⁵⁹About an hour later another asserted, "Certainly this fellow was with him, for he is a Galilean."

⁶⁰Peter replied, "Man, I don't know what you're talking about!" Just as he was speaking, the rooster crowed. ⁶¹The Lord turned and looked straight at Peter. Then Peter remembered the word the Lord had spoken to him: "Before the rooster crows today, you will disown me three times." ⁶²And he went outside and wept bitterly.

The Guards Mock Jesus

22:63–65pp — Mt 26:67,68; Mk 14:65; Jn 18:22,23

⁶³The men who were guarding Jesus began mocking and beating him. ⁶⁴They blindfolded him and demanded, "Prophesy! Who hit you?" ⁶⁵And they said many other insulting things to him.

Jesus Before Pilate and Herod

22:67–71pp — Mt 26:63–66; Mk 14:61–63;
Jn 18:19–21
23:2,3pp — Mt 27:11–14; Mk 15:2–5; Jn 18:29–37
23:18–25pp — Mt 27:15–26; Mk 15:6–15;
Jn 18:39–19:16

⁶⁶At daybreak the council of the elders of the people, both the chief priests and teachers of the law, met together, and Jesus was led before them. ⁶⁷"If you are the Christ,ᵃ" they said, "tell us."

Jesus answered, "If I tell you, you will not believe me, ⁶⁸and if I asked you, you would not answer. ⁶⁹But from now on, the Son of Man will be seated at the right hand of the mighty God."

⁷⁰They all asked, "Are you then the Son of God?"

He replied, "You are right in saying I am."

⁷¹Then they said, "Why do we need any more testimony? We have heard it from his own lips."

ᵃ 67 Or *Messiah*

23 Then the whole assembly rose and led him off to Pilate. ²And they began to accuse him, saying, "We have found this man subverting our nation. He opposes payment of taxes to Caesar and claims to be Christ,ᵃ a king."

³So Pilate asked Jesus, "Are you the king of the Jews?"

"Yes, it is as you say," Jesus replied.

⁴Then Pilate announced to the chief priests and the crowd, "I find no basis for a charge against this man."

⁵But they insisted, "He stirs up the people all over Judeaᵇ by his teaching. He started in Galilee and has come all the way here."

⁶On hearing this, Pilate asked if the man was a Galilean. ⁷When he learned that Jesus was under Herod's jurisdiction, he sent him to Herod, who was also in Jerusalem at that time.

⁸When Herod saw Jesus, he was greatly pleased, because for a long time he had been wanting to see him. From what he had heard about him, he hoped to see him perform some miracle. ⁹He plied him with many questions, but Jesus gave him no answer. ¹⁰The chief priests and the teachers of the law were standing there, vehemently accusing him. ¹¹Then Herod and his soldiers ridiculed and mocked him. Dressing him in an elegant robe, they sent him back to Pilate. ¹²That day Herod and Pilate became friends—before this they had been enemies.

¹³Pilate called together the chief priests, the rulers and the people, ¹⁴and said to them, "You brought me this man as one who was inciting the people to rebellion. I have examined him in your presence and have found no basis for your charges against him. ¹⁵Neither has Herod, for he sent him back to us; as you can see, he has done nothing to deserve death. ¹⁶Therefore, I will punish him and then release him.ᶜ"

¹⁸With one voice they cried out, "Away with this man! Release Barabbas to us!" ¹⁹(Barabbas had been thrown into prison for an insurrection in the city, and for murder.)

²⁰Wanting to release Jesus, Pilate appealed to them again. ²¹But they kept shouting, "Crucify him! Crucify him!"

²²For the third time he spoke to them: "Why? What crime has this man committed? I have found in him no grounds for the death penalty. Therefore I will have him punished and then release him."

²³But with loud shouts they insistently demanded that he be crucified, and their shouts prevailed. ²⁴So Pilate decided to grant their demand. ²⁵He released the man who had been thrown into prison for insurrection and murder, the one they asked for, and surrendered Jesus to their will.

The Crucifixion
23:33–43pp — Mt 27:33–44; Mk 15:22–32; Jn 19:17–24

²⁶As they led him away, they seized Simon from Cyrene, who was on his way in from the country, and put the cross on him and made him carry it behind Jesus. ²⁷A large number of people followed him, including women who mourned and wailed for him. ²⁸Jesus turned and said to them, "Daughters of Jerusalem, do not weep for me; weep for yourselves and for your children. ²⁹For the time will come when you will say, 'Blessed are the barren women, the wombs that never bore and the breasts that never nursed!' ³⁰Then

> " 'they will say to the mountains, "Fall on us!"
> and to the hills, "Cover us!" 'ᵈ

³¹For if men do these things when the tree is green, what will happen when it is dry?"

³²Two other men, both criminals, were also led out with him to be executed. ³³When they came to the place called the Skull, there they crucified him, along with the criminals—one on his right, the other on his left. ³⁴Jesus said, "Father, forgive them, for they do not know what they are doing."ᵉ And they divided up his clothes by casting lots.

³⁵The people stood watching, and the rulers

ᵃ *2 Or Messiah; also in verses 35 and 39*   ᵇ *5 Or over the land of the Jews*   ᶜ *16 Some manuscripts him." ¹⁷Now he was obliged to release one man to them at the Feast.*   ᵈ *30 Hosea 10:8*
ᵉ *34 Some early manuscripts do not have this sentence.*

even sneered at him. They said, "He saved others; let him save himself if he is the Christ of God, the Chosen One."

[36] The soldiers also came up and mocked him. They offered him wine vinegar [37] and said, "If you are the king of the Jews, save yourself."

[38] There was a written notice above him, which read: THIS IS THE KING OF THE JEWS.

[39] One of the criminals who hung there hurled insults at him: "Aren't you the Christ? Save yourself and us!"

[40] But the other criminal rebuked him. "Don't you fear God," he said, "since you are under the same sentence? [41] We are punished justly, for we are getting what our deeds deserve. But this man has done nothing wrong."

[42] Then he said, "Jesus, remember me when you come into your kingdom.[a]"

[43] Jesus answered him, "I tell you the truth, today you will be with me in paradise."

Jesus' Death

23:44–49pp — Mt 27:45–56; Mk 15:33–41; Jn 19:29–30

[44] It was now about the sixth hour, and darkness came over the whole land until the ninth hour, [45] for the sun stopped shining. And the curtain of the temple was torn in two. [46] Jesus called out with a loud voice, "Father, into your hands I commit my spirit." When he had said this, he breathed his last.

[47] The centurion, seeing what had happened, praised God and said, "Surely this was a righteous man." [48] When all the people who had gathered to witness this sight saw what took place, they beat their breasts and went away. [49] But all those who knew him, including the women who had followed him from Galilee, stood at a distance, watching these things.

Jesus' Burial

23:50–56pp — Mt 27:57–61; Mk 15:42–47; Jn 19:38–42

[50] Now there was a man named Joseph, a member of the Council, a good and upright man, [51] who had not consented to their decision and action. He came from the Judean town of Arimathea and he was waiting for the kingdom of God. [52] Going to Pilate, he asked for Jesus' body. [53] Then he took it down, wrapped it in linen cloth and placed it in a tomb cut in the rock, one in which no one had yet been laid. [54] It was Preparation Day, and the Sabbath was about to begin.

[55] The women who had come with Jesus from Galilee followed Joseph and saw the tomb and how his body was laid in it. [56] Then they went home and prepared spices and perfumes. But they rested on the Sabbath in obedience to the commandment.

The Resurrection

24:1–10pp — Mt 28:1–8; Mk 16:1–8; Jn 20:1–8

24 On the first day of the week, very early in the morning, the women took the spices they had prepared and went to the tomb. [2] They found the stone rolled away from the tomb, [3] but when they entered, they did not find the body of the Lord Jesus. [4] While they were wondering about this, suddenly two men in clothes that gleamed like lightning stood beside them. [5] In their fright the women bowed down with their faces to the ground, but the men said to them, "Why do you look for the living among the dead? [6] He is not here; he has risen! Remember how he told you, while he was still with you in Galilee: [7] 'The Son of Man must be delivered into the hands of sinful men, be crucified and on the third day be raised again.'" [8] Then they remembered his words.

[9] When they came back from the tomb, they told all these things to the Eleven and to all the others. [10] It was Mary Magdalene, Joanna, Mary the mother of James, and the others with them who told this to the apostles. [11] But they did not believe the women, because their words seemed to them like nonsense. [12] Peter, however, got up and ran to the tomb. Bending over, he saw the strips of linen lying by themselves, and he went away, wondering to himself what had happened.

a 42 Some manuscripts come with your kingly power

LUKE 24:1–12

The Resurrection

LIFE LESSON: Jesus is stronger than death.

TO TALK ABOUT

✦ Who went to the tomb very early on Sunday morning?

✦ Why didn't the disciples believe the women? Do you think the disciples forgot that Jesus had said he would rise in three days?

✦ Why do you think the disciples didn't expect the resurrection?

✦ Why do we sometimes doubt Jesus' power?

On the Road to Emmaus

¹³Now that same day two of them were going to a village called Emmaus, about seven miles ᵃ from Jerusalem. ¹⁴They were talking with each other about everything that had happened. ¹⁵As they talked and discussed these things with each other, Jesus himself came up and walked along with them; ¹⁶but they were kept from recognizing him.

¹⁷He asked them, "What are you discussing together as you walk along?"

They stood still, their faces downcast. ¹⁸One of them, named Cleopas, asked him, "Are you only a visitor to Jerusalem and do not know the things that have happened there in these days?"

¹⁹"What things?" he asked.

"About Jesus of Nazareth," they replied. "He was a prophet, powerful in word and deed before God and all the people. ²⁰The chief priests and our rulers handed him over to be sentenced to death, and they crucified him; ²¹but we had hoped that he was the one who was going to redeem Israel. And what is more, it is the third day since all this took place. ²²In addition, some of our women amazed us. They went to the tomb early this morning ²³but didn't find his body. They came and told us that they had seen a vision of angels, who said he was alive. ²⁴Then some of our companions went to the tomb and found it just as the women had said, but him they did not see."

²⁵He said to them, "How foolish you are, and how slow of heart to believe all that the prophets have spoken! ²⁶Did not the Christ ᵇ have to suffer these things and then enter his glory?" ²⁷And beginning with Moses and all the Prophets, he explained to them what was said in all the Scriptures concerning himself.

²⁸As they approached the village to which they were going, Jesus acted as if he were going farther. ²⁹But they urged him strongly, "Stay with us, for it is nearly evening; the day is almost over." So he went in to stay with them.

³⁰When he was at the table with them, he took bread, gave thanks, broke it and began to give it to them. ³¹Then their eyes were opened and they recognized him, and he disappeared from their sight. ³²They asked each other, "Were not our hearts burning within us while he talked with us on the road and opened the Scriptures to us?"

³³They got up and returned at once to Jerusalem. There they found the Eleven and those with them, assembled together ³⁴and saying, "It is true! The Lord has risen and has appeared to Simon." ³⁵Then the two told what had happened on the way, and how Jesus was recognized by them when he broke the bread.

ᵃ 13 Greek *sixty stadia* (about 11 kilometers)   ᵇ 26 Or *Messiah*; also in verse 46

THEN THEIR EYES WERE OPENED AND THEY
RECOGNIZED HIM, AND HE DISAPPEARED FROM
THEIR SIGHT. THEY ASKED EACH OTHER,
"WERE NOT OUR HEARTS BURNING WITHIN US
WHILE HE TALKED WITH US ON THE ROAD AND
OPENED THE SCRIPTURES TO US?"

Luke 24:31–32

Your Own Emmaus Road

ANNE ORTLUND

READ | LUKE 24:13 – 35

Grandmothers, as soon as we start thinking of our Christian experience in the past tense, we're in trouble. It's the immediacy of God's work in us that continually propels us forward and upward.

Last Sunday we heard a sermon on the "glory road," the road to Emmaus (see Luke 24:13 – 35). After the spectacular events of Easter, it was a new, different, thrilling encounter with Christ. As our preacher said, the thrust of a Christian life must always be forward. No matter how glorious the past, the dynamic Christ wants to meet you on your "now" Emmaus road. As the Good Shepherd, he "goes on ahead . . . and his sheep follow him" (John 10:4). He loves to give you "a present with a future tense."

Father Lawrence Jenco and other Christians held captive in Lebanon were determined to love their Muslim captors with Jesus' love. One of the guards was so touched by this that he smuggled Father Jenco a Bible and fashioned for him a crude little metal cross.

Eventually Jenco was released. Trussed like a turkey, he was shoved into an inner tube, driven to a remote area and dumped into a ditch. For a while he wondered if he wanted to make the effort to try to survive, but then he remembered his little metal cross. He struggled to use its sharp edges to sever his ropes; then he asked Jesus to take him home. And that unfamiliar Lebanese stretch of dirt became Father Jenco's Emmaus road.

Are you in an unfamiliar place: bewildered, hurting, unsure of your future? You need a new, present work of God in your life. Ask Jesus to encounter you and guide you from this point. And the immediacy of his new, "now" work in your life will be the start of the very renewal you seek. It will put you on a road that will lead you home.

Dear Jesus, I need a fresh Emmaus road encounter with you — an encounter that will cause me to look forward to a future bright with hope and pregnant with eternal possibilities. May each new day draw my heart toward you and bring me opportunities to share your love with others. Amen.

Your next devotion is located on page 1437.

GRANDCHILD **IN FOCUS** • PRAYER

Respect for Authority

Dear Lord, I pray that my grandchild will continually grow to respect those in authority. May she learn to be cooperative and fair in work and play. Instill in her a high regard for officials who govern our land and enforce the laws. May her relationships with parents, teachers, coaches, mentors and bosses be respectful, admirable, constructive and caring. Amen.

stories to share

LUKE 24:13-35

On the Road to Emmaus

LIFE LESSON: Jesus is with us.

TO TALK ABOUT

✦ Why didn't the two followers of Jesus recognize him at first? Who did they assume Jesus was?

✦ What did Jesus explain to them while they were walking along?

✦ How can you have a better understanding of who Jesus is?

✦ Have your problems or disappointments ever kept you from realizing that God was with you? What can you do the next time that happens?

Jesus Appears to the Disciples

³⁶ While they were still talking about this, Jesus himself stood among them and said to them, "Peace be with you."

³⁷ They were startled and frightened, thinking they saw a ghost. ³⁸ He said to them, "Why are you troubled, and why do doubts rise in your minds? ³⁹ Look at my hands and my feet. It is I myself! Touch me and see; a ghost does not have flesh and bones, as you see I have."

⁴⁰ When he had said this, he showed them his hands and feet. ⁴¹ And while they still did not believe it because of joy and amazement, he asked them, "Do you have anything here to eat?" ⁴² They gave him a piece of broiled fish, ⁴³ and he took it and ate it in their presence.

⁴⁴ He said to them, "This is what I told you while I was still with you: Everything must be fulfilled that is written about me in the Law of Moses, the Prophets and the Psalms."

⁴⁵ Then he opened their minds so they could understand the Scriptures. ⁴⁶ He told them, "This is what is written: The Christ will suffer and rise from the dead on the third day, ⁴⁷ and repentance and forgiveness of sins will be preached in his name to all nations, beginning at Jerusalem. ⁴⁸ You are witnesses of these things. ⁴⁹ I am going to send you what my Father has promised; but stay in the city until you have been clothed with power from on high."

The Ascension

⁵⁰ When he had led them out to the vicinity of Bethany, he lifted up his hands and blessed them. ⁵¹ While he was blessing them, he left them and was taken up into heaven. ⁵² Then they worshiped him and returned to Jerusalem with great joy. ⁵³ And they stayed continually at the temple, praising God.

Believing AND LOVING

In the Gospel of John, the apostle painted a portrait of a God people could see, touch and hear. It is a portrait of God Incarnate, the Word who "became flesh and made his dwelling among us . . . who came from the Father, full of grace and truth" (John 1:14). This is the God who came to save us and to teach us how to love. John painted this portrait of Jesus' life so that all people would believe and have life in Jesus (see John 20:31) — and so that, after believing, they would love as Jesus loved.

Grandmothers know the power of love — how it nurtures, how it heals scraped knees and aching hearts. Though human love has the ability to do these things, if we remain connected to "the true vine," our love will bear even greater fruit (see John 15:1 – 2). Only then will we begin to express unlimited and unconditional love. Then we will have the power to love our grandchildren through every circumstance. We will love the child who's hard to relate to or the child who has chosen to be distant from us. Christ's love is the love we need to emulate: It knows no limits, it knows no boundaries, it is not judgmental. With God's Holy Spirit filling our hearts as Jesus promised (see John 14:15 – 17), we can strive to love others with God's love.

VERSE *to* REMEMBER | JOHN 13:34

"A new command I give you: Love one another. As I have loved you, so you must love one another."

ABOUT JOHN

WRITTEN BY:
John, one of Jesus' twelve disciples

WRITTEN FOR:
Everyone who wants to understand who Jesus really is

DATE WRITTEN:
Probably around A.D. 85 – 90

WHY WRITTEN:
To show that Jesus is the Son of God and to help people believe in him

The Word Became Flesh

1 In the beginning was the Word, and the Word was with God, and the Word was God. ²He was with God in the beginning.

³Through him all things were made; without him nothing was made that has been made. ⁴In him was life, and that life was the light of men. ⁵The light shines in the darkness, but the darkness has not understood *a* it.

⁶There came a man who was sent from God; his name was John. ⁷He came as a witness to testify concerning that light, so that through him all men might believe. ⁸He himself was not the light; he came only as a witness to the light. ⁹The true light that gives light to every man was coming into the world. *b*

¹⁰He was in the world, and though the world was made through him, the world did not recognize him. ¹¹He came to that which was his own, but his own did not receive him. ¹²Yet to all who received him, to those who believed in his name, he gave the right to become children of God— ¹³children born not of natural descent, *c* nor of human decision or a husband's will, but born of God.

¹⁴The Word became flesh and made his dwelling among us. We have seen his glory, the glory of the One and Only, *d* who came from the Father, full of grace and truth.

¹⁵John testifies concerning him. He cries out, saying, "This was he of whom I said, 'He who comes after me has surpassed me because he was before me.'" ¹⁶From the fullness of his grace we have all received one blessing after another. ¹⁷For the law was given through Moses; grace and truth came through Jesus Christ. ¹⁸No one has ever seen God, but God the One and Only, *d, e* who is at the Father's side, has made him known.

John the Baptist Denies Being the Christ

¹⁹Now this was John's testimony when the Jews of Jerusalem sent priests and Levites to ask him who he was. ²⁰He did not fail to confess, but confessed freely, "I am not the Christ." *f*

²¹They asked him, "Then who are you? Are you Elijah?"

He said, "I am not."

"Are you the Prophet?"

He answered, "No."

²²Finally they said, "Who are you? Give us an answer to take back to those who sent us. What do you say about yourself?"

²³John replied in the words of Isaiah the prophet, "I am the voice of one calling in the desert, 'Make straight the way for the Lord.'" *g*

²⁴Now some Pharisees who had been sent ²⁵questioned him, "Why then do you baptize if you are not the Christ, nor Elijah, nor the Prophet?"

²⁶"I baptize with *h* water," John replied, "but among you stands one you do not know. ²⁷He is the one who comes after me, the thongs of whose sandals I am not worthy to untie."

²⁸This all happened at Bethany on the other side of the Jordan, where John was baptizing.

Jesus the Lamb of God

²⁹The next day John saw Jesus coming toward him and said, "Look, the Lamb of God, who takes away the sin of the world! ³⁰This is the one I meant when I said, 'A man who comes after me has surpassed me because he was before me.' ³¹I myself did not know him, but the reason I came baptizing with water was that he might be revealed to Israel."

³²Then John gave this testimony: "I saw the Spirit come down from heaven as a dove and remain on him. ³³I would not have known him, except that the one who sent me to baptize with water told me, 'The man on whom you see the Spirit come down and remain is he who will baptize with the Holy Spirit.' ³⁴I have seen and I testify that this is the Son of God."

Jesus' First Disciples

1:40–42pp — Mt 4:18–22; Mk 1:16–20; Lk 5:2–11

³⁵The next day John was there again with two of his disciples. ³⁶When he saw Jesus passing by, he said, "Look, the Lamb of God!"

a 5 Or *darkness, and the darkness has not overcome*   *b 9* Or *This was the true light that gives light to every man who comes into the world*   *c 13* Greek *of bloods*   *d 14,18* Or *the Only Begotten*   *e 18* Some manuscripts *but the only* (or *only begotten*) *Son*   *f 20* Or *Messiah.* "The Christ" (Greek) and "the Messiah" (Hebrew) both mean "the Anointed One"; also in verse 25.   *g 23* Isaiah 40:3   *h 26* Or *in*; also in verses 31 and 33

37 When the two disciples heard him say this, they followed Jesus. 38 Turning around, Jesus saw them following and asked, "What do you want?"

They said, "Rabbi" (which means Teacher), "where are you staying?"

39 "Come," he replied, "and you will see."

So they went and saw where he was staying, and spent that day with him. It was about the tenth hour.

40 Andrew, Simon Peter's brother, was one of the two who heard what John had said and who had followed Jesus. 41 The first thing Andrew did was to find his brother Simon and tell him, "We have found the Messiah" (that is, the Christ). 42 And he brought him to Jesus.

Jesus looked at him and said, "You are Simon son of John. You will be called Cephas" (which, when translated, is Peter*a*).

Jesus Calls Philip and Nathanael

43 The next day Jesus decided to leave for Galilee. Finding Philip, he said to him, "Follow me."

44 Philip, like Andrew and Peter, was from the town of Bethsaida. 45 Philip found Nathanael and told him, "We have found the one Moses wrote about in the Law, and about whom the prophets also wrote—Jesus of Nazareth, the son of Joseph."

46 "Nazareth! Can anything good come from there?" Nathanael asked.

"Come and see," said Philip.

47 When Jesus saw Nathanael approaching, he said of him, "Here is a true Israelite, in whom there is nothing false."

48 "How do you know me?" Nathanael asked.

Jesus answered, "I saw you while you were still under the fig tree before Philip called you."

49 Then Nathanael declared, "Rabbi, you are the Son of God; you are the King of Israel."

50 Jesus said, "You believe*b* because I told you I saw you under the fig tree. You shall see greater things than that." 51 He then added, "I tell you*c* the truth, you*c* shall see heaven open, and the angels of God ascending and descending on the Son of Man."

Jesus Changes Water to Wine

2 On the third day a wedding took place at Cana in Galilee. Jesus' mother was there, 2 and Jesus and his disciples had also been invited to the wedding. 3 When the wine was gone, Jesus' mother said to him, "They have no more wine."

4 "Dear woman, why do you involve me?" Jesus replied. "My time has not yet come."

5 His mother said to the servants, "Do whatever he tells you."

6 Nearby stood six stone water jars, the kind

a 42 Both *Cephas* (Aramaic) and *Peter* (Greek) mean *rock.*
b 50 Or *Do you believe...?*   *c* 51 The Greek is plural.

stories to share

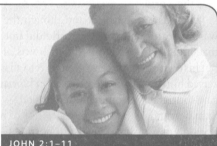

JOHN 2:1–11

Jesus Changes Water to Wine

LIFE LESSON: Jesus has power over all things.

TO TALK ABOUT

✦ What miracle did Jesus perform in this story?

✦ What did Jesus mean when he told Mary at first that his time had "not yet come" (verse 4)?

✦ What did Mary ask the servants to do?

✦ Does running out of wine seem like a big problem to you? What did Jesus prove by this first miracle?

"NAZARETH! CAN ANYTHING
GOOD COME FROM THERE?"
NATHANAEL ASKED. "COME
AND SEE," SAID PHILIP.

John 1:46

Come and See Jesus

CORRIE TEN BOOM

READ | JOHN 1:43 – 51

"Come and see," said Philip.

Have you ever said that to somebody: Come and see Jesus? Wasn't that marvelous? I believe that the most wonderful thing that can happen to a child of God is to lead someone to Jesus. You then know for sure that you have not lived in vain. He gave us all that we need for the task. The Holy Spirit, His power, supplies us with all we need to be disciples ourselves and to disciple others. We can't do it, but He can. That is why it is so very important that we are filled with the Holy Spirit. Full, right up to the very last corner of our lives. If we allow Him to live only in our study or living room, then He can't help and protect us in our kitchen or bedroom. But we can only expect to be more than conquerors everywhere and be mirrors of His love and joy if we walk hand in hand with Him through the whole house of our lives from the basement to the attic.

Would you like the Lord to speak through you today? If you don't know Him yet, then I say as Philip did: Come and see Jesus! He loves you and died for you on the cross so bring your sins to Him; and then let Him in by opening all the doors, from the basement to the attic.

Lord, work through me today with your conquering love, so that we together, you and I, can invite others to "come and see." Thank you, Lord Jesus. Hallelujah. Amen.

Your next devotion is located on page 1440.

GRANDCHILD IN FOCUS • PRAYER

Courage

O Father, builder of character and courage, may my grandchild grow strong in the light of your love. Grant him courage to stand for what is right, to guard the truth and to ensure justice in every aspect of life. May he boldly grow in grace, revere your name and proudly proclaim you as the Lord of lords and King of kings. Amen.

used by the Jews for ceremonial washing, each holding from twenty to thirty gallons. *a*

⁷Jesus said to the servants, "Fill the jars with water"; so they filled them to the brim.

⁸Then he told them, "Now draw some out and take it to the master of the banquet."

They did so, ⁹and the master of the banquet tasted the water that had been turned into wine. He did not realize where it had come from, though the servants who had drawn the water knew. Then he called the bridegroom aside ¹⁰and said, "Everyone brings out the choice wine first and then the cheaper wine after the guests have had too much to drink; but you have saved the best till now."

¹¹This, the first of his miraculous signs, Jesus performed at Cana in Galilee. He thus revealed his glory, and his disciples put their faith in him.

Jesus Clears the Temple
2:14–16pp — Mt 21:12,13; Mk 11:15–17; Lk 19:45,46

¹²After this he went down to Capernaum with his mother and brothers and his disciples. There they stayed for a few days.

¹³When it was almost time for the Jewish Passover, Jesus went up to Jerusalem. ¹⁴In the temple courts he found men selling cattle, sheep and doves, and others sitting at tables exchanging money. ¹⁵So he made a whip out of cords, and drove all from the temple area, both sheep and cattle; he scattered the coins of the money changers and overturned their tables. ¹⁶To those who sold doves he said, "Get these out of here! How dare you turn my Father's house into a market!"

¹⁷His disciples remembered that it is written: "Zeal for your house will consume me." *b*

¹⁸Then the Jews demanded of him, "What miraculous sign can you show us to prove your authority to do all this?"

¹⁹Jesus answered them, "Destroy this temple, and I will raise it again in three days."

²⁰The Jews replied, "It has taken forty-six years to build this temple, and you are going to raise it in three days?" ²¹But the temple he had spoken of

was his body. ²²After he was raised from the dead, his disciples recalled what he had said. Then they believed the Scripture and the words that Jesus had spoken.

²³Now while he was in Jerusalem at the Passover Feast, many people saw the miraculous signs he was doing and believed in his name. *c* ²⁴But Jesus would not entrust himself to them, for he knew all men. ²⁵He did not need man's testimony about man, for he knew what was in a man.

Jesus Teaches Nicodemus

3 Now there was a man of the Pharisees named Nicodemus, a member of the Jewish ruling council. ²He came to Jesus at night and said, "Rabbi, we know you are a teacher who has come from God. For no one could perform the miraculous signs you are doing if God were not with him."

³In reply Jesus declared, "I tell you the truth, no one can see the kingdom of God unless he is born again. *d*"

⁴"How can a man be born when he is old?" Nicodemus asked. "Surely he cannot enter a second time into his mother's womb to be born!"

⁵Jesus answered, "I tell you the truth, no one can enter the kingdom of God unless he is born of water and the Spirit. ⁶Flesh gives birth to flesh, but the Spirit *e* gives birth to spirit. ⁷You should not be surprised at my saying, 'You *f* must be born again.' ⁸The wind blows wherever it pleases. You hear its sound, but you cannot tell where it comes from or where it is going. So it is with everyone born of the Spirit."

⁹"How can this be?" Nicodemus asked.

¹⁰"You are Israel's teacher," said Jesus, "and do you not understand these things? ¹¹I tell you the truth, we speak of what we know, and we testify to what we have seen, but still you people do not accept our testimony. ¹²I have spoken to you of earthly things and you do not believe; how then will you believe if I speak of heavenly things?

a 6 Greek two to three metretes (probably about 75 to 115 liters) b 17 Psalm 69:9 c 23 Or and believed in him d 3 Or born from above; also in verse 7 e 6 Or but spirit f 7 The Greek is plural.

¹³No one has ever gone into heaven except the one who came from heaven — the Son of Man.ᵃ ¹⁴Just as Moses lifted up the snake in the desert, so the Son of Man must be lifted up, ¹⁵that everyone who believes in him may have eternal life.ᵇ

¹⁶"For God so loved the world that he gave his one and only Son,ᶜ that whoever believes in him shall not perish but have eternal life. ¹⁷For God did not send his Son into the world to condemn the world, but to save the world through him. ¹⁸Whoever believes in him is not condemned, but whoever does not believe stands condemned already because he has not believed in the name of God's one and only Son.ᵈ ¹⁹This is the verdict:

PRAYING THE SCRIPTURES

Salvation
JOHN 3:16

Almighty God, I pray that my grandchild will internalize this reality: You loved the world so much that you gave your one and only Son, that whoever believes in him shall not perish but have eternal life.

Next prayer in Salvation Prayer Track: John 10:28

Light has come into the world, but men loved darkness instead of light because their deeds were evil. ²⁰Everyone who does evil hates the light, and will not come into the light for fear that his deeds will be exposed. ²¹But whoever lives by the truth comes into the light, so that it may be seen plainly that what he has done has been done through God."ᵉ

John the Baptist's Testimony About Jesus

²²After this, Jesus and his disciples went out into the Judean countryside, where he spent some time with them, and baptized. ²³Now John also was baptizing at Aenon near Salim, because there was plenty of water, and people were constantly coming to be baptized. ²⁴(This was before John was put in prison.) ²⁵An argument developed between some of John's disciples and a certain Jewᶠ over the matter of ceremonial washing. ²⁶They came to John and said to him, "Rabbi, that man who was with you on the other side of the Jordan — the one you testified about — well, he is baptizing, and everyone is going to him."

²⁷To this John replied, "A man can receive only what is given him from heaven. ²⁸You yourselves can testify that I said, 'I am not the Christᵍ but

stories to share

JOHN 3:1–21

Jesus Teaches Nicodemus

LIFE LESSON: God loved the world so much that he sent Jesus.

TO TALK ABOUT

✦ Who was Nicodemus? How did most of the Pharisees feel about Jesus?

✦ Why do you think Nicodemus came to Jesus at night?

✦ What does it mean to be "born again"? Have you been born again?

✦ How does it make you feel to know that God loved the world so much that he gave us his Son Jesus (see verse 16)?

ᵃ 13 Some manuscripts *Man, who is in heaven*   ᵇ 15 Or *believes may have eternal life in him*   ᶜ 16 Or *his only begotten Son*   ᵈ 18 Or *God's only begotten Son*   ᵉ 21 Some interpreters end the quotation after verse 15.   ᶠ 25 Some manuscripts *and certain Jews*   ᵍ 28 Or *Messiah*

> "FOR GOD SO LOVED THE WORLD
> THAT HE GAVE HIS ONE AND ONLY
> SON, THAT WHOEVER BELIEVES IN
> HIM SHALL NOT PERISH BUT HAVE
> ETERNAL LIFE."
>
> *John 3:16*

Pictures in God's Wallet

PATRICIA SPRINKLE

READ | JOHN 3:1 – 21

God loves the entire world, but it is easy for us to get caught up in loving only a slice of it. Soon after Hurricane Katrina destroyed New Orleans, I was startled — and convicted — when a guest in our home prayed for "those who have nobody to pray for them."

Being a grandmother and one step removed from day-to-day parenting has some advantages. When we get tired, we can send the children home. If a visit is not convenient, we can turn it down. However, as I rejoice in the miracle of children who are part of me and yet don't need me all the time, I also find my heart and mind becoming aware of children around the world who have nobody to love them, tend to them, pray for them and advocate for them.

One Sunday, the pastor asked us to take out our wallets and look at our pictures. Then she reminded us, "Every child's picture is in God's wallet."

So many of God's children need a lap on which to rock, an advocate in the courts, a foster home, a visit in the hospital, a smile in the grocery store and to be remembered in prayer. So many parents need an older friend to whom they can turn when they need a sitter, practical advice or the ear of somebody who has already "been there, done that."

God did not merely love his Son; he loved the world. He asks us to do the same.

Lord, help me not to sink into old age as a resting place. Pierce my heart with the needs of children who are not physically mine. Help me to remember that all children are yours and that they may need me to smile at them, share with them, love them, and pray with and for them. As long as I have life and breath, let me please you by reaching out to those who need your love.

Your next devotion is located on page 1443.

GRANDCHILD IN FOCUS • PRAYER

Future Spouse

Dear Lord, if it is your will, I pray my grandchild will be united in a loving and Christian marriage. Keep her sexually pure so that she will honor you with her body and mind. As she seeks a spouse who will honor and care for her, give her patience and discernment. May her choice for a life partner be your choice for her, so that she and her husband will together glorify you in a lasting love. I pray this in Jesus' name, amen.

am sent ahead of him.' ²⁹The bride belongs to the bridegroom. The friend who attends the bridegroom waits and listens for him, and is full of joy when he hears the bridegroom's voice. That joy is mine, and it is now complete. ³⁰He must become greater; I must become less.

³¹"The one who comes from above is above all; the one who is from the earth belongs to the earth, and speaks as one from the earth. The one who comes from heaven is above all. ³²He testifies to what he has seen and heard, but no one accepts his testimony. ³³The man who has accepted it has certified that God is truthful. ³⁴For the one whom God has sent speaks the words of God, for God*ᵃ* gives the Spirit without limit. ³⁵The Father loves the Son and has placed everything in his hands. ³⁶Whoever believes in the Son has eternal life, but whoever rejects the Son will not see life, for God's wrath remains on him."*ᵇ*

Jesus Talks With a Samaritan Woman

4 The Pharisees heard that Jesus was gaining and baptizing more disciples than John, ²although in fact it was not Jesus who baptized, but his disciples. ³When the Lord learned of this, he left Judea and went back once more to Galilee.

⁴Now he had to go through Samaria. ⁵So he came to a town in Samaria called Sychar, near the plot of ground Jacob had given to his son Joseph. ⁶Jacob's well was there, and Jesus, tired as he was from the journey, sat down by the well. It was about the sixth hour.

⁷When a Samaritan woman came to draw water, Jesus said to her, "Will you give me a drink?" ⁸(His disciples had gone into the town to buy food.)

⁹The Samaritan woman said to him, "You are a Jew and I am a Samaritan woman. How can you ask me for a drink?" (For Jews do not associate with Samaritans.*ᶜ*)

¹⁰Jesus answered her, "If you knew the gift of God and who it is that asks you for a drink, you would have asked him and he would have given you living water."

¹¹"Sir," the woman said, "you have nothing to

stories to share

JOHN 4:1–42

Jesus Talks With a Samaritan Woman

LIFE LESSON: Jesus came to seek and save lost people.

TO TALK ABOUT

◆ Why were the woman and the disciples so surprised that Jesus talked to her? (Hint: See verse 9 and verse 27.)

◆ What did the woman tell people about Jesus after he spoke with her?

◆ Why do you think these Samaritans recognized Jesus as the Savior when so many Jews did not?

◆ What does it mean to worship God "in spirit and in truth" (verse 24)? Do you do that?

draw with and the well is deep. Where can you get this living water? ¹²Are you greater than our father Jacob, who gave us the well and drank from it himself, as did also his sons and his flocks and herds?"

¹³Jesus answered, "Everyone who drinks this water will be thirsty again, ¹⁴but whoever drinks the water I give him will never thirst. Indeed, the water I give him will become in him a spring of water welling up to eternal life."

ᵃ 34 Greek *he*   *ᵇ 36* Some interpreters end the quotation after verse 30.   *ᶜ 9* Or *do not use dishes Samaritans have used*

¹⁵The woman said to him, "Sir, give me this water so that I won't get thirsty and have to keep coming here to draw water."

¹⁶He told her, "Go, call your husband and come back."

¹⁷"I have no husband," she replied.

Jesus said to her, "You are right when you say you have no husband. ¹⁸The fact is, you have had five husbands, and the man you now have is not your husband. What you have just said is quite true."

¹⁹"Sir," the woman said, "I can see that you are a prophet. ²⁰Our fathers worshiped on this mountain, but you Jews claim that the place where we must worship is in Jerusalem."

²¹Jesus declared, "Believe me, woman, a time is coming when you will worship the Father neither on this mountain nor in Jerusalem. ²²You Samaritans worship what you do not know; we worship what we do know, for salvation is from the Jews. ²³Yet a time is coming and has now come when the true worshipers will worship the Father in spirit and truth, for they are the kind of worshipers the Father seeks. ²⁴God is spirit, and his worshipers must worship in spirit and in truth."

TALKING POINTS

Divorce

Jesus graciously reached out to a woman who was divorced.

JOHN 4:4–30

For more on divorce, go to 1 Corinthians 7:10–11.

²⁵The woman said, "I know that Messiah" (called Christ) "is coming. When he comes, he will explain everything to us."

²⁶Then Jesus declared, "I who speak to you am he."

The Disciples Rejoin Jesus

²⁷Just then his disciples returned and were surprised to find him talking with a woman. But no one asked, "What do you want?" or "Why are you talking with her?"

²⁸Then, leaving her water jar, the woman went back to the town and said to the people, ²⁹"Come, see a man who told me everything I ever did. Could this be the Christ ᵃ?" ³⁰They came out of the town and made their way toward him.

³¹Meanwhile his disciples urged him, "Rabbi, eat something."

³²But he said to them, "I have food to eat that you know nothing about."

³³Then his disciples said to each other, "Could someone have brought him food?"

³⁴"My food," said Jesus, "is to do the will of him who sent me and to finish his work. ³⁵Do you not say, 'Four months more and then the harvest'? I tell you, open your eyes and look at the fields! They are ripe for harvest. ³⁶Even now the reaper draws his wages, even now he harvests the crop for eternal life, so that the sower and the reaper may be glad together. ³⁷Thus the saying 'One sows and another reaps' is true. ³⁸I sent you to reap what you have not worked for. Others have done the hard work, and you have reaped the benefits of their labor."

Many Samaritans Believe

³⁹Many of the Samaritans from that town believed in him because of the woman's testimony, "He told me everything I ever did." ⁴⁰So when the Samaritans came to him, they urged him to stay with them, and he stayed two days. ⁴¹And because of his words many more became believers.

⁴²They said to the woman, "We no longer believe just because of what you said; now we have heard for ourselves, and we know that this man really is the Savior of the world."

Jesus Heals the Official's Son

⁴³After the two days he left for Galilee. ⁴⁴(Now Jesus himself had pointed out that a prophet has

ᵃ 29 Or *Messiah*

When You Don't Realize Your Thirst

SHEILA WALSH

> JESUS ANSWERED HER, "IF YOU KNEW THE GIFT OF GOD AND WHO IT IS THAT ASKS YOU FOR A DRINK, YOU WOULD HAVE ASKED HIM AND HE WOULD HAVE GIVEN YOU LIVING WATER."
>
> *John 4:10*

READ | JOHN 4:1–26

Sometimes we know we need refreshment but are too lazy in the routine of life — or too preoccupied with what we think is "important" — to stop for spiritual replenishment. Sometimes life may crowd in on us enough that we simply are not aware of our need. Think of the need for intimacy with God in terms of physical thirst. In the routine demands and distractions of the day, we can forget this most basic of all needs. I notice that on a hot day my dog, Bentley, is always returning to his water bowl for a drink. We might be playing ball, but at regular intervals he heads off for more water. Sometimes it's only in watching him that I realize how thirsty I am; I have the beginnings of a headache caused by dehydration. It's not wise to wait to change the oil when your car is running on treacle. It's not wise to wait to drink a glass of water [until] the headache is so bad you have to go and lie down in a dark room.

It is the same in our relationship with God. We can run through our days ignoring our need for him — intentionally or unintentionally — until we find ourselves dry and worn out.

If you sense you have lost touch with a thirst for God, talk to him about it. There is no glory in pretending and no shame in admitting what is true. Start with an honest confession to God that you have been distracted or negligent. Thank him for reminding you of your need — your thirst.

Lord, so often I go far too long without coming to you, the living water, to find refreshment for my soul. Sometimes it has been so long that I find myself hesitant and ashamed. But I know that your grace is great and that you welcome back your thirsty child. Thank you for your boundless goodness to me. Amen.

Your next devotion is located on page 1447.

GRANDCHILD IN FOCUS • PRAYER

School/Career

Dear God, may learning be a joy rather than a chore for my grandchild. May exploration of new ideas bring a sense of wonder, awe and excitement. Grant him clarity of mind, the ability to concentrate on the task at hand and recollection of what has been learned. Help him to appreciate the tasks that come easily and to persevere through those that challenge. Amen.

no honor in his own country.) ⁴⁵When he arrived in Galilee, the Galileans welcomed him. They had seen all that he had done in Jerusalem at the Passover Feast, for they also had been there.

⁴⁶Once more he visited Cana in Galilee, where he had turned the water into wine. And there was a certain royal official whose son lay sick at Capernaum. ⁴⁷When this man heard that Jesus had arrived in Galilee from Judea, he went to him and begged him to come and heal his son, who was close to death.

⁴⁸"Unless you people see miraculous signs and wonders," Jesus told him, "you will never believe."

⁴⁹The royal official said, "Sir, come down before my child dies."

⁵⁰Jesus replied, "You may go. Your son will live."

The man took Jesus at his word and departed. ⁵¹While he was still on the way, his servants met him with the news that his boy was living. ⁵²When he inquired as to the time when his son got better, they said to him, "The fever left him yesterday at the seventh hour."

⁵³Then the father realized that this was the exact time at which Jesus had said to him, "Your son will live." So he and all his household believed.

⁵⁴This was the second miraculous sign that Jesus performed, having come from Judea to Galilee.

The Healing at the Pool

5 Some time later, Jesus went up to Jerusalem for a feast of the Jews. ²Now there is in Jerusalem near the Sheep Gate a pool, which in Aramaic is called Bethesda ᵃ and which is surrounded by five covered colonnades. ³Here a great number of disabled people used to lie—the blind, the lame, the paralyzed. ᵇ ⁵One who was there had been an invalid for thirty-eight years. ⁶When Jesus saw him lying there and learned that he had been in this condition for a long time, he asked him, "Do you want to get well?"

⁷"Sir," the invalid replied, "I have no one to help me into the pool when the water is stirred.

While I am trying to get in, someone else goes down ahead of me."

⁸Then Jesus said to him, "Get up! Pick up your mat and walk." ⁹At once the man was cured; he picked up his mat and walked.

The day on which this took place was a Sabbath, ¹⁰and so the Jews said to the man who had been healed, "It is the Sabbath; the law forbids you to carry your mat."

¹¹But he replied, "The man who made me well said to me, 'Pick up your mat and walk.'"

¹²So they asked him, "Who is this fellow who told you to pick it up and walk?"

¹³The man who was healed had no idea who it was, for Jesus had slipped away into the crowd that was there.

¹⁴Later Jesus found him at the temple and said to him, "See, you are well again. Stop sinning or something worse may happen to you." ¹⁵The man went away and told the Jews that it was Jesus who had made him well.

Life Through the Son

¹⁶So, because Jesus was doing these things on the Sabbath, the Jews persecuted him. ¹⁷Jesus said to them, "My Father is always at his work to this very day, and I, too, am working." ¹⁸For this reason the Jews tried all the harder to kill him; not only was he breaking the Sabbath, but he was even calling God his own Father, making himself equal with God.

¹⁹Jesus gave them this answer: "I tell you the truth, the Son can do nothing by himself; he can do only what he sees his Father doing, because whatever the Father does the Son also does. ²⁰For the Father loves the Son and shows him all he does. Yes, to your amazement he will show him even greater things than these. ²¹For just as the Father raises the dead and gives them life, even so the Son gives life to whom he is pleased to give it. ²²Moreover, the Father judges no one, but has

---

ᵃ 2 Some manuscripts *Bethzatha*; other manuscripts *Bethsaida*
ᵇ 3 Some manuscripts *paralyzed—and they waited for the moving of the waters. ⁴From time to time an angel of the Lord would come down and stir up the waters. The first one into the pool after each such disturbance would be cured of whatever disease he had.*

entrusted all judgment to the Son, ²³that all may honor the Son just as they honor the Father. He who does not honor the Son does not honor the Father, who sent him.

²⁴"I tell you the truth, whoever hears my word and believes him who sent me has eternal life and will not be condemned; he has crossed over from death to life. ²⁵I tell you the truth, a time is coming and has now come when the dead will hear the voice of the Son of God and those who hear will live. ²⁶For as the Father has life in himself, so he has granted the Son to have life in himself. ²⁷And he has given him authority to judge because he is the Son of Man.

²⁸"Do not be amazed at this, for a time is coming when all who are in their graves will hear his voice ²⁹and come out—those who have done good will rise to live, and those who have done evil will rise to be condemned. ³⁰By myself I can do nothing; I judge only as I hear, and my judgment is just, for I seek not to please myself but him who sent me.

Testimonies About Jesus

³¹"If I testify about myself, my testimony is not valid. ³²There is another who testifies in my favor, and I know that his testimony about me is valid.

³³"You have sent to John and he has testified to the truth. ³⁴Not that I accept human testimony; but I mention it that you may be saved. ³⁵John was a lamp that burned and gave light, and you chose for a time to enjoy his light.

³⁶"I have testimony weightier than that of John. For the very work that the Father has given me to finish, and which I am doing, testifies that the Father has sent me. ³⁷And the Father who sent me has himself testified concerning me. You have never heard his voice nor seen his form, ³⁸nor does his word dwell in you, for you do not believe the one he sent. ³⁹You diligently study[a] the Scriptures because you think that by them you possess eternal life. These are the Scriptures that testify about me, ⁴⁰yet you refuse to come to me to have life.

⁴¹"I do not accept praise from men, ⁴²but I know you. I know that you do not have the love of God in your hearts. ⁴³I have come in my Father's name, and you do not accept me; but if someone else comes in his own name, you will accept him. ⁴⁴How can you believe if you accept praise from one another, yet make no effort to obtain the praise that comes from the only God[b]?

⁴⁵"But do not think I will accuse you before the Father. Your accuser is Moses, on whom your hopes are set. ⁴⁶If you believed Moses, you would believe me, for he wrote about me. ⁴⁷But since you do not believe what he wrote, how are you going to believe what I say?"

Jesus Feeds the Five Thousand

6:1–13pp — Mt 14:13–21; Mk 6:32–44; Lk 9:10–17

6 Some time after this, Jesus crossed to the far shore of the Sea of Galilee (that is, the Sea of Tiberias), ²and a great crowd of people followed him because they saw the miraculous signs he had performed on the sick. ³Then Jesus went up on a mountainside and sat down with his disciples. ⁴The Jewish Passover Feast was near.

⁵When Jesus looked up and saw a great crowd coming toward him, he said to Philip, "Where shall we buy bread for these people to eat?" ⁶He asked this only to test him, for he already had in mind what he was going to do.

⁷Philip answered him, "Eight months' wages[c] would not buy enough bread for each one to have a bite!"

⁸Another of his disciples, Andrew, Simon Peter's brother, spoke up, ⁹"Here is a boy with five small barley loaves and two small fish, but how far will they go among so many?"

¹⁰Jesus said, "Have the people sit down." There was plenty of grass in that place, and the men sat down, about five thousand of them. ¹¹Jesus then took the loaves, gave thanks, and distributed to those who were seated as much as they wanted. He did the same with the fish.

¹²When they had all had enough to eat, he said

---

a 39 Or *Study diligently* (the imperative)   *b* 44 Some early manuscripts *the Only One*   *c* 7 Greek *two hundred denarii*

1445

to his disciples, "Gather the pieces that are left over. Let nothing be wasted." ¹³So they gathered them and filled twelve baskets with the pieces of the five barley loaves left over by those who had eaten.

¹⁴After the people saw the miraculous sign that Jesus did, they began to say, "Surely this is the Prophet who is to come into the world." ¹⁵Jesus, knowing that they intended to come and make him king by force, withdrew again to a mountain by himself.

JOHN 6:1–15

Jesus Feeds the Five Thousand

LIFE LESSON: God wants to use whatever resources we have for his glory.

TO TALK ABOUT

✦ What did the disciple Philip say when Jesus asked him about buying bread for the crowd?

✦ If you had been the boy with the lunch, would you have offered your food? Would you have thought it was too small to be noticed?

✦ How did the boy's original amount of food compare to the leftovers?

✦ Do you ever think you're too young or have too little for God to use? What *do* you have that you could make available to God and other people?

Jesus Walks on the Water

6:16–21pp — Mt 14:22–33; Mk 6:47–51

¹⁶When evening came, his disciples went down to the lake, ¹⁷where they got into a boat and set off across the lake for Capernaum. By now it was dark, and Jesus had not yet joined them. ¹⁸A strong wind was blowing and the waters grew rough. ¹⁹When they had rowed three or three and a half miles,ᵃ they saw Jesus approaching the boat, walking on the water; and they were terrified. ²⁰But he said to them, "It is I; don't be afraid." ²¹Then they were willing to take him into the boat, and immediately the boat reached the shore where they were heading.

²²The next day the crowd that had stayed on the opposite shore of the lake realized that only one boat had been there, and that Jesus had not entered it with his disciples, but that they had gone away alone. ²³Then some boats from Tiberias landed near the place where the people had eaten the bread after the Lord had given thanks. ²⁴Once the crowd realized that neither Jesus nor his disciples were there, they got into the boats and went to Capernaum in search of Jesus.

Jesus the Bread of Life

²⁵When they found him on the other side of the lake, they asked him, "Rabbi, when did you get here?"

²⁶Jesus answered, "I tell you the truth, you are looking for me, not because you saw miraculous signs but because you ate the loaves and had your fill. ²⁷Do not work for food that spoils, but for food that endures to eternal life, which the Son of Man will give you. On him God the Father has placed his seal of approval."

²⁸Then they asked him, "What must we do to do the works God requires?"

²⁹Jesus answered, "The work of God is this: to believe in the one he has sent."

³⁰So they asked him, "What miraculous sign then will you give that we may see it and believe you? What will you do? ³¹Our forefathers ate the

---

ᵃ *19* Greek *rowed twenty-five or thirty stadia* (about 5 or 6 kilometers)

LET'S HAVE
FUN

In the Spotlight

Your grandchild will love being "in the spotlight" for an evening, a day or a weekend. Invite each of your grandchildren (one at a time) to spend time with you, giving them your undivided attention. During this time together let them select three things: (1) somewhere local they would like to go, (2) something special they would like to eat, and (3) something memorable they would like to do.

You can vary this idea by focusing the spotlight on them when they reach certain birthday "landmarks." For example, on their tenth birthday, celebrate their first double-digit birthday; on their thirteenth birthday, mark their entrance into the teen years, etc. Then be sure to continue to spotlight each grandchild in the same way as they reach that "landmark" age. Be sure you share with them how significant and special they are to you and their parents.

Older-Grandkids Variation: You may have to limit this to one of the three activities since their appetites and ideas for travel may have grown beyond that of a younger child's more simple ideas.

Long-Distance Variation: Make a plan in advance to have your grandchild come alone for a visit so you can shine the spotlight on him/her while he/she visits.

Dear Lord of light, thank you for my grandchildren and for the joy they bring into my life. May my gesture of shining a spotlight on them bring them happiness and the assurance that they are loved. Amen.

Your next devotion is located on page 1449.

GRANDCHILD IN FOCUS • PRAYER

Character

Dear Lord and Father, I ask that you fill my grandchild with your Spirit so her character reflects your goodness and love. Give her kindness and love for others. Bring joy to her life so she will be a joy to others. Grant her patience and self-control through difficult and trying times. May she show mercy and generosity to those who are less fortunate. Grant her integrity and a sense of justice, and surround her with your peace. Amen.

manna in the desert; as it is written: 'He gave them bread from heaven to eat.'^a"

³²Jesus said to them, "I tell you the truth, it is not Moses who has given you the bread from heaven, but it is my Father who gives you the true bread from heaven. ³³For the bread of God is he who comes down from heaven and gives life to the world."

³⁴"Sir," they said, "from now on give us this bread."

³⁵Then Jesus declared, "I am the bread of life. He who comes to me will never go hungry, and he who believes in me will never be thirsty. ³⁶But as I told you, you have seen me and still you do not believe. ³⁷All that the Father gives me will come to me, and whoever comes to me I will never drive away. ³⁸For I have come down from heaven not to do my will but to do the will of him who sent me. ³⁹And this is the will of him who sent me, that I shall lose none of all that he has given me, but raise them up at the last day. ⁴⁰For my Father's will is that everyone who looks to the Son and believes in him shall have eternal life, and I will raise him up at the last day."

⁴¹At this the Jews began to grumble about him because he said, "I am the bread that came down from heaven." ⁴²They said, "Is this not Jesus, the son of Joseph, whose father and mother we know? How can he now say, 'I came down from heaven'?"

⁴³"Stop grumbling among yourselves," Jesus answered. ⁴⁴"No one can come to me unless the Father who sent me draws him, and I will raise him up at the last day. ⁴⁵It is written in the Prophets: 'They will all be taught by God.'^b Everyone who listens to the Father and learns from him comes to me. ⁴⁶No one has seen the Father except the one who is from God; only he has seen the Father. ⁴⁷I tell you the truth, he who believes has everlasting life. ⁴⁸I am the bread of life. ⁴⁹Your forefathers ate the manna in the desert, yet they died. ⁵⁰But here is the bread that comes down from heaven, which a man may eat and not die. ⁵¹I am the living bread that came down from heaven. If anyone eats of this bread, he will live

forever. This bread is my flesh, which I will give for the life of the world."

⁵²Then the Jews began to argue sharply among themselves, "How can this man give us his flesh to eat?"

⁵³Jesus said to them, "I tell you the truth, unless you eat the flesh of the Son of Man and drink his blood, you have no life in you. ⁵⁴Whoever eats my flesh and drinks my blood has eternal life, and I will raise him up at the last day. ⁵⁵For my flesh is real food and my blood is real drink. ⁵⁶Whoever eats my flesh and drinks my blood remains in me, and I in him. ⁵⁷Just as the living Father sent me and I live because of the Father, so the one who feeds on me will live because of me. ⁵⁸This is the bread that came down from heaven. Your forefathers ate manna and died, but he who feeds on this bread will live forever." ⁵⁹He said this while teaching in the synagogue in Capernaum.

Many Disciples Desert Jesus

⁶⁰On hearing it, many of his disciples said, "This is a hard teaching. Who can accept it?"

⁶¹Aware that his disciples were grumbling about this, Jesus said to them, "Does this offend you? ⁶²What if you see the Son of Man ascend to where he was before! ⁶³The Spirit gives life; the flesh counts for nothing. The words I have spoken to you are spirit^c and they are life. ⁶⁴Yet there are some of you who do not believe." For Jesus had known from the beginning which of them did not believe and who would betray him. ⁶⁵He went on to say, "This is why I told you that no one can come to me unless the Father has enabled him."

⁶⁶From this time many of his disciples turned back and no longer followed him.

⁶⁷"You do not want to leave too, do you?" Jesus asked the Twelve.

⁶⁸Simon Peter answered him, "Lord, to whom shall we go? You have the words of eternal life. ⁶⁹We believe and know that you are the Holy One of God."

^a 31 Exodus 16:4; Neh. 9:15; Psalm 78:24,25   ^b 45 Isaiah 54:13   ^c 63 Or Spirit

Worship the Lord

I praise you because I am fearfully and wonderfully made;
    your works are wonderful,
    I know that full well.
My frame was not hidden from you
    when I was made in the secret place.
When I was woven together in the depths of the
      earth,
    your eyes saw my unformed body.
All the days ordained for me
    were written in your book
    before one of them came to be.

How precious to me are your
    thoughts, O God!
    How vast is the sum of them!
Were I to count them,
    they would outnumber the
    grains of sand.
When I awake,
    I am still with you.

Search me, O God, and know my heart;
    test me and know my anxious thoughts.
See if there is any offensive way in me,
    and lead me in the way everlasting.

Psalm 139:14 – 18, 23 – 24

GRANDCHILD IN FOCUS • PRAYER

Talents

Dear Lord, the giver of gifts, bless my grandchild as he develops his talents. Help him identify his talents and be proud and confident of the gifts you have given him. Give him patience and understanding, Lord, so he will not grow weary of striving and searching to reach the goals you have set for him. May each milestone bring satisfaction and a healthy desire for greater achievement and success to bring glory to you. Amen.

O Lord, from before my birth you have been my God, loving me even before I took my first breath. What a breathtaking thought that is! What a comfort to know that my life is securely in your control and that you are always with me, guiding and directing me. I praise you for creating me in the image of your wonderful self. Amen.

Your next devotion is located on page 1452.

[70] Then Jesus replied, "Have I not chosen you, the Twelve? Yet one of you is a devil!" [71] (He meant Judas, the son of Simon Iscariot, who, though one of the Twelve, was later to betray him.)

Jesus Goes to the Feast of Tabernacles

7 After this, Jesus went around in Galilee, purposely staying away from Judea because the Jews there were waiting to take his life. [2] But when the Jewish Feast of Tabernacles was near, [3] Jesus' brothers said to him, "You ought to leave here and go to Judea, so that your disciples may see the miracles you do. [4] No one who wants to become a public figure acts in secret. Since you are doing these things, show yourself to the world." [5] For even his own brothers did not believe in him.

[6] Therefore Jesus told them, "The right time for me has not yet come; for you any time is right. [7] The world cannot hate you, but it hates me because I testify that what it does is evil. [8] You go to the Feast. I am not yet [a] going up to this Feast, because for me the right time has not yet come." [9] Having said this, he stayed in Galilee.

[10] However, after his brothers had left for the Feast, he went also, not publicly, but in secret. [11] Now at the Feast the Jews were watching for him and asking, "Where is that man?"

[12] Among the crowds there was widespread whispering about him. Some said, "He is a good man."

Others replied, "No, he deceives the people." [13] But no one would say anything publicly about him for fear of the Jews.

Jesus Teaches at the Feast

[14] Not until halfway through the Feast did Jesus go up to the temple courts and begin to teach. [15] The Jews were amazed and asked, "How did this man get such learning without having studied?"

[16] Jesus answered, "My teaching is not my own. It comes from him who sent me. [17] If anyone chooses to do God's will, he will find out whether my teaching comes from God or whether I speak on my own. [18] He who speaks on his own does so to gain honor for himself, but he who works for the honor of the one who sent him is a man of truth; there is nothing false about him. [19] Has not Moses given you the law? Yet not one of you keeps the law. Why are you trying to kill me?"

[20] "You are demon-possessed," the crowd answered. "Who is trying to kill you?"

[21] Jesus said to them, "I did one miracle, and you are all astonished. [22] Yet, because Moses gave you circumcision (though actually it did not come from Moses, but from the patriarchs), you circumcise a child on the Sabbath. [23] Now if a child can be circumcised on the Sabbath so that the law of Moses may not be broken, why are you angry with me for healing the whole man on the Sabbath? [24] Stop judging by mere appearances, and make a right judgment."

Is Jesus the Christ?

[25] At that point some of the people of Jerusalem began to ask, "Isn't this the man they are trying to kill? [26] Here he is, speaking publicly, and they are not saying a word to him. Have the authorities really concluded that he is the Christ [b]? [27] But we know where this man is from; when the Christ comes, no one will know where he is from."

[28] Then Jesus, still teaching in the temple courts, cried out, "Yes, you know me, and you know where I am from. I am not here on my own, but he who sent me is true. You do not know him, [29] but I know him because I am from him and he sent me."

[30] At this they tried to seize him, but no one laid a hand on him, because his time had not yet come. [31] Still, many in the crowd put their faith in him. They said, "When the Christ comes, will he do more miraculous signs than this man?"

[32] The Pharisees heard the crowd whispering such things about him. Then the chief priests and the Pharisees sent temple guards to arrest him.

[33] Jesus said, "I am with you for only a short

---

[a] 8 Some early manuscripts do not have *yet*.   [b] 26 Or *Messiah*; also in verses 27, 31, 41 and 42

time, and then I go to the one who sent me. ³⁴You will look for me, but you will not find me; and where I am, you cannot come."

³⁵The Jews said to one another, "Where does this man intend to go that we cannot find him? Will he go where our people live scattered among the Greeks, and teach the Greeks? ³⁶What did he mean when he said, 'You will look for me, but you will not find me,' and 'Where I am, you cannot come'?"

³⁷On the last and greatest day of the Feast, Jesus stood and said in a loud voice, "If anyone is thirsty, let him come to me and drink. ³⁸Whoever believes in me, as ᵃ the Scripture has said, streams of living water will flow from within him." ³⁹By this he meant the Spirit, whom those who believed in him were later to receive. Up to that time the Spirit had not been given, since Jesus had not yet been glorified.

⁴⁰On hearing his words, some of the people said, "Surely this man is the Prophet."

⁴¹Others said, "He is the Christ."

Still others asked, "How can the Christ come from Galilee? ⁴²Does not the Scripture say that the Christ will come from David's family ᵇ and from Bethlehem, the town where David lived?" ⁴³Thus the people were divided because of Jesus. ⁴⁴Some wanted to seize him, but no one laid a hand on him.

Unbelief of the Jewish Leaders

⁴⁵Finally the temple guards went back to the chief priests and Pharisees, who asked them, "Why didn't you bring him in?"

⁴⁶"No one ever spoke the way this man does," the guards declared.

⁴⁷"You mean he has deceived you also?" the Pharisees retorted. ⁴⁸"Has any of the rulers or of the Pharisees believed in him? ⁴⁹No! But this mob that knows nothing of the law—there is a curse on them."

⁵⁰Nicodemus, who had gone to Jesus earlier and who was one of their own number, asked, ⁵¹"Does our law condemn anyone without first hearing him to find out what he is doing?"

⁵²They replied, "Are you from Galilee, too? Look into it, and you will find that a prophet ᶜ does not come out of Galilee."

———

[The earliest manuscripts and many other ancient witnesses do not have John 7:53 — 8:11.]

⁵³Then each went to his own home.

8 But Jesus went to the Mount of Olives. ²At dawn he appeared again in the temple courts, where all the people gathered around him, and he sat down to teach them. ³The teachers of the law and the Pharisees brought in a woman caught in adultery. They made her stand before the group ⁴and said to Jesus, "Teacher, this woman was caught in the act of adultery. ⁵In the Law Moses commanded us to stone such women. Now what do you say?" ⁶They were using this question as a trap, in order to have a basis for accusing him.

But Jesus bent down and started to write on the ground with his finger. ⁷When they kept on questioning him, he straightened up and said to them, "If any one of you is without sin, let him be the first to throw a stone at her." ⁸Again he stooped down and wrote on the ground.

⁹At this, those who heard began to go away one at a time, the older ones first, until only Jesus was left, with the woman still standing there. ¹⁰Jesus straightened up and asked her, "Woman, where are they? Has no one condemned you?"

¹¹"No one, sir," she said.

"Then neither do I condemn you," Jesus declared. "Go now and leave your life of sin."

———

The Validity of Jesus' Testimony

¹²When Jesus spoke again to the people, he said, "I am the light of the world. Whoever follows me will never walk in darkness, but will have the light of life."

ᵃ 37,38 Or / If anyone is thirsty, let him come to me. / And let him drink, ³⁸who believes in me. / As   ᵇ 42 Greek seed   ᶜ 52 Two early manuscripts the Prophet

WHEN THEY KEPT ON QUESTIONING
HIM, HE STRAIGHTENED UP AND
SAID TO THEM, "IF ANY ONE OF YOU
IS WITHOUT SIN, LET HIM BE THE
FIRST TO THROW A STONE AT HER."
John 8:7

Space for Grace

RUTH A. DEJAGER

READ | JOHN 7:53 — 8:11

Jesus knew how to clear a room. He was in the temple courts, with many people gathered around him, when the teachers of the law and the Pharisees brought a disheveled and likely ill-clothed woman before him. Cringing under the onslaught of accusation and shame, she was powerless and robbed of human dignity.

Jesus gave those accusatory hypocrites a quick lesson in self-examination. By stooping to write on the ground, he gave them time to cool their (self-)righteous indignation. Imagine them all slinking away one by one, his words ringing in their ears — and not only the Pharisees and teachers, but everyone who heard him. He took the attention off the woman and gave her space to breathe and to think her own thoughts about this Jesus who had defended and saved her.

We sometimes like to bring people, especially family members, to Jesus, so that he can "straighten them out." But if our prayers and our eyes are focused on people's faults and foibles, we are not allowing Jesus to deal with them in his own way. We need to give him — and them — the space to meet each other face-to-face.

It's not that we shouldn't pray for others, especially those who indulge in obvious sin. We should bring them to Jesus. But we need to view their sin in the wise and loving way Jesus did, putting the emphasis on his ability to love, forgive and redeem them in the same way he confronts us with *our* sin. If we wrap people in straitjackets of blame and judgment, there is no room for them to change or grow; we back them into a corner, where their human instinct to defend themselves keeps them prisoner. Instead we should move away and leave some space for grace, God's grace.

Lord Jesus, when I bring family members to you in prayer, remind me to have an attitude of gentleness and nonjudgment. Help me to remember that it is you who can change hearts and minds, and that your wisdom is supreme. Amen.

GRANDCHILD IN FOCUS • PRAYER

SELECT ONE OF YOUR
GRANDCHILDREN TO FOCUS ON
IN PRAYER FOR THE NEXT 14 DAYS.

Salvation

Dear Lord, please guide my grandchild to your gift of salvation. I pray that she will come to know you, to love you and to walk close to you throughout her life. May she boldly claim Jesus as her Lord and Savior. Guide her as she makes choices that have eternal consequences. Help her to follow you each moment of her life. I pray this in Jesus' name, amen.

Your next devotion is located on page 1457.

¹³The Pharisees challenged him, "Here you are, appearing as your own witness; your testimony is not valid."

¹⁴Jesus answered, "Even if I testify on my own behalf, my testimony is valid, for I know where I came from and where I am going. But you have no idea where I come from or where I am going. ¹⁵You judge by human standards; I pass judgment on no one. ¹⁶But if I do judge, my decisions are right, because I am not alone. I stand with the Father, who sent me. ¹⁷In your own Law it is written that the testimony of two men is valid. ¹⁸I am one who testifies for myself; my other witness is the Father, who sent me."

¹⁹Then they asked him, "Where is your father?"

"You do not know me or my Father," Jesus replied. "If you knew me, you would know my Father also." ²⁰He spoke these words while teaching in the temple area near the place where the offerings were put. Yet no one seized him, because his time had not yet come.

²¹Once more Jesus said to them, "I am going away, and you will look for me, and you will die in your sin. Where I go, you cannot come."

²²This made the Jews ask, "Will he kill himself? Is that why he says, 'Where I go, you cannot come'?"

²³But he continued, "You are from below; I am from above. You are of this world; I am not of this world. ²⁴I told you that you would die in your sins; if you do not believe that I am ⌐the one I claim to be¬,ᵃ you will indeed die in your sins."

²⁵"Who are you?" they asked.

"Just what I have been claiming all along," Jesus replied. ²⁶"I have much to say in judgment of you. But he who sent me is reliable, and what I have heard from him I tell the world."

²⁷They did not understand that he was telling them about his Father. ²⁸So Jesus said, "When you have lifted up the Son of Man, then you will know that I am ⌐the one I claim to be¬ and that I do nothing on my own but speak just what the Father has taught me. ²⁹The one who sent me is with me; he has not left me alone, for I always do what pleases him." ³⁰Even as he spoke, many put their faith in him.

The Children of Abraham

³¹To the Jews who had believed him, Jesus said, "If you hold to my teaching, you are really my disciples. ³²Then you will know the truth, and the truth will set you free."

³³They answered him, "We are Abraham's descendants ᵇ and have never been slaves of anyone. How can you say that we shall be set free?"

³⁴Jesus replied, "I tell you the truth, everyone who sins is a slave to sin. ³⁵Now a slave has no permanent place in the family, but a son belongs to it forever. ³⁶So if the Son sets you free, you will be free indeed. ³⁷I know you are Abraham's descendants. Yet you are ready to kill me, because you have no room for my word. ³⁸I am telling you what I have seen in the Father's presence, and you do what you have heard from your father.ᶜ"

³⁹"Abraham is our father," they answered.

"If you were Abraham's children," said Jesus, "then you would ᵈ do the things Abraham did. ⁴⁰As it is, you are determined to kill me, a man who has told you the truth that I heard from God. Abraham did not do such things. ⁴¹You are doing the things your own father does."

"We are not illegitimate children," they protested. "The only Father we have is God himself."

The Children of the Devil

⁴²Jesus said to them, "If God were your Father, you would love me, for I came from God and now am here. I have not come on my own; but he sent me. ⁴³Why is my language not clear to you? Because you are unable to hear what I say. ⁴⁴You belong to your father, the devil, and you want to carry out your father's desire. He was a murderer from the beginning, not holding to the truth, for there is no truth in him. When he lies, he speaks his native language, for he is a liar and the father of lies. ⁴⁵Yet because I tell the truth, you do not believe me! ⁴⁶Can any of you prove me guilty of sin? If I am telling the truth, why don't you

ᵃ 24 Or I am he; also in verse 28   ᵇ 33 Greek seed; also in verse 37
ᶜ 38 Or presence. Therefore do what you have heard from the Father.
ᵈ 39 Some early manuscripts "If you are Abraham's children," said Jesus, "then

believe me? [47] He who belongs to God hears what God says. The reason you do not hear is that you do not belong to God."

The Claims of Jesus About Himself

[48] The Jews answered him, "Aren't we right in saying that you are a Samaritan and demon-possessed?"

[49] "I am not possessed by a demon," said Jesus, "but I honor my Father and you dishonor me. [50] I am not seeking glory for myself; but there is one who seeks it, and he is the judge. [51] I tell you the truth, if anyone keeps my word, he will never see death."

[52] At this the Jews exclaimed, "Now we know that you are demon-possessed! Abraham died and so did the prophets, yet you say that if anyone keeps your word, he will never taste death. [53] Are you greater than our father Abraham? He died, and so did the prophets. Who do you think you are?"

[54] Jesus replied, "If I glorify myself, my glory means nothing. My Father, whom you claim as your God, is the one who glorifies me. [55] Though you do not know him, I know him. If I said I did not, I would be a liar like you, but I do know him and keep his word. [56] Your father Abraham rejoiced at the thought of seeing my day; he saw it and was glad."

[57] "You are not yet fifty years old," the Jews said to him, "and you have seen Abraham!"

[58] "I tell you the truth," Jesus answered, "before Abraham was born, I am!" [59] At this, they picked up stones to stone him, but Jesus hid himself, slipping away from the temple grounds.

Jesus Heals a Man Born Blind

9 As he went along, he saw a man blind from birth. [2] His disciples asked him, "Rabbi, who sinned, this man or his parents, that he was born blind?"

[3] "Neither this man nor his parents sinned," said Jesus, "but this happened so that the work of God might be displayed in his life. [4] As long as it is day, we must do the work of him who sent me. Night is coming, when no one can work. [5] While I am in the world, I am the light of the world."

[6] Having said this, he spit on the ground, made some mud with the saliva, and put it on the man's eyes. [7] "Go," he told him, "wash in the Pool of Siloam" (this word means Sent). So the man went and washed, and came home seeing.

[8] His neighbors and those who had formerly seen him begging asked, "Isn't this the same man who used to sit and beg?" [9] Some claimed that he was.

Others said, "No, he only looks like him."

But he himself insisted, "I am the man."

[10] "How then were your eyes opened?" they demanded.

[11] He replied, "The man they call Jesus made some mud and put it on my eyes. He told me to go to Siloam and wash. So I went and washed, and then I could see."

[12] "Where is this man?" they asked him.

"I don't know," he said.

The Pharisees Investigate the Healing

[13] They brought to the Pharisees the man who had been blind. [14] Now the day on which Jesus had made the mud and opened the man's eyes was a Sabbath. [15] Therefore the Pharisees also asked him how he had received his sight. "He put mud on my eyes," the man replied, "and I washed, and now I see."

[16] Some of the Pharisees said, "This man is not from God, for he does not keep the Sabbath."

But others asked, "How can a sinner do such miraculous signs?" So they were divided.

[17] Finally they turned again to the blind man, "What have you to say about him? It was your eyes he opened."

The man replied, "He is a prophet."

[18] The Jews still did not believe that he had been blind and had received his sight until they sent for the man's parents. [19] "Is this your son?" they asked. "Is this the one you say was born blind? How is it that now he can see?"

[20] "We know he is our son," the parents an-

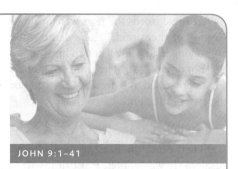

stories to share

JOHN 9:1–41

Jesus Heals a Man Born Blind

LIFE LESSON: Jesus is the light of the world.

TO TALK ABOUT

✦ What unusual method did Jesus use in healing the man born blind?

✦ This man witnessed to the Pharisees just by telling the truth. Why didn't they listen?

✦ Which is a more serious problem: physical blindness or spiritual blindness? Why?

✦ How does this story illustrate that Jesus is "the light of the world" (verse 5)?

swered, "and we know he was born blind. ²¹ But how he can see now, or who opened his eyes, we don't know. Ask him. He is of age; he will speak for himself." ²² His parents said this because they were afraid of the Jews, for already the Jews had decided that anyone who acknowledged that Jesus was the Christ ᵃ would be put out of the synagogue. ²³ That was why his parents said, "He is of age; ask him."

²⁴ A second time they summoned the man who had been blind. "Give glory to God, ᵇ" they said. "We know this man is a sinner."

²⁵ He replied, "Whether he is a sinner or not,

I don't know. One thing I do know. I was blind but now I see!"

²⁶ Then they asked him, "What did he do to you? How did he open your eyes?"

²⁷ He answered, "I have told you already and you did not listen. Why do you want to hear it again? Do you want to become his disciples, too?"

²⁸ Then they hurled insults at him and said, "You are this fellow's disciple! We are disciples of Moses! ²⁹ We know that God spoke to Moses, but as for this fellow, we don't even know where he comes from."

³⁰ The man answered, "Now that is remarkable! You don't know where he comes from, yet he opened my eyes. ³¹ We know that God does not listen to sinners. He listens to the godly man who does his will. ³² Nobody has ever heard of opening the eyes of a man born blind. ³³ If this man were not from God, he could do nothing."

³⁴ To this they replied, "You were steeped in sin at birth; how dare you lecture us!" And they threw him out.

Spiritual Blindness

³⁵ Jesus heard that they had thrown him out, and when he found him, he said, "Do you believe in the Son of Man?"

³⁶ "Who is he, sir?" the man asked. "Tell me so that I may believe in him."

³⁷ Jesus said, "You have now seen him; in fact, he is the one speaking with you."

³⁸ Then the man said, "Lord, I believe," and he worshiped him.

³⁹ Jesus said, "For judgment I have come into this world, so that the blind will see and those who see will become blind."

⁴⁰ Some Pharisees who were with him heard him say this and asked, "What? Are we blind too?"

⁴¹ Jesus said, "If you were blind, you would not be guilty of sin; but now that you claim you can see, your guilt remains."

ᵃ 22 Or *Messiah*   ᵇ 24 A solemn charge to tell the truth (see Joshua 7:19)

The Shepherd and His Flock

10 "I tell you the truth, the man who does not enter the sheep pen by the gate, but climbs in by some other way, is a thief and a robber. ²The man who enters by the gate is the shepherd of his sheep. ³The watchman opens the gate for him, and the sheep listen to his voice. He calls his own sheep by name and leads them out. ⁴When he has brought out all his own, he goes on ahead of them, and his sheep follow him because they know his voice. ⁵But they will never follow a stranger; in fact, they will run away from him because they do not recognize a stranger's voice." ⁶Jesus used this figure of speech, but they did not understand what he was telling them.

⁷Therefore Jesus said again, "I tell you the truth, I am the gate for the sheep. ⁸All who ever came before me were thieves and robbers, but the sheep did not listen to them. ⁹I am the gate; whoever enters through me will be saved.ᵃ He will come in and go out, and find pasture. ¹⁰The thief comes only to steal and kill and destroy; I have come that they may have life, and have it to the full.

¹¹"I am the good shepherd. The good shepherd lays down his life for the sheep. ¹²The hired hand is not the shepherd who owns the sheep. So when he sees the wolf coming, he abandons the sheep and runs away. Then the wolf attacks the flock and scatters it. ¹³The man runs away because he is a hired hand and cares nothing for the sheep.

¹⁴"I am the good shepherd; I know my sheep and my sheep know me— ¹⁵just as the Father knows me and I know the Father—and I lay down my life for the sheep. ¹⁶I have other sheep that are not of this sheep pen. I must bring them also. They too will listen to my voice, and there shall be one flock and one shepherd. ¹⁷The reason my Father loves me is that I lay down my life—only to take it up again. ¹⁸No one takes it from me, but I lay it down of my own accord. I have authority to lay it down and authority to take it up again. This command I received from my Father."

¹⁹At these words the Jews were again divided. ²⁰Many of them said, "He is demon-possessed and raving mad. Why listen to him?"

²¹But others said, "These are not the sayings of a man possessed by a demon. Can a demon open the eyes of the blind?"

The Unbelief of the Jews

²²Then came the Feast of Dedication ᵇ at Jerusalem. It was winter, ²³and Jesus was in the temple area walking in Solomon's Colonnade. ²⁴The Jews gathered around him, saying, "How long will you keep us in suspense? If you are the Christ,ᶜ tell us plainly."

²⁵Jesus answered, "I did tell you, but you do not believe. The miracles I do in my Father's name speak for me, ²⁶but you do not believe because you are not my sheep. ²⁷My sheep listen to my voice; I know them, and they follow me. ²⁸I give them eternal life, and they shall never perish; no one can snatch them out of my hand. ²⁹My

PRAYING THE SCRIPTURES

Salvation

JOHN 10:28

Dear Lord, help my grandchild to believe that you are the giver of eternal life. Assure him that if he believes in you, he will never perish and no one will be able to snatch him out of your hand.

Next prayer in Salvation Prayer Track: Acts 4:12

Father, who has given them to me, is greater than allᵈ; no one can snatch them out of my Father's hand. ³⁰I and the Father are one."

³¹Again the Jews picked up stones to stone him, ³²but Jesus said to them, "I have shown you

---

ᵃ 9 Or kept safe   ᵇ 22 That is, Hanukkah   ᶜ 24 Or Messiah
ᵈ 29 Many early manuscripts What my Father has given me is greater than all

"THE THIEF COMES ONLY
TO STEAL AND KILL AND
DESTROY; I HAVE COME
THAT THEY MAY HAVE LIFE,
AND HAVE IT TO THE FULL."

John 10:10

Sticky Messes

CHERYL BAKER

READ | JOHN 10:1 – 10

Playdough dotting the living room carpet, paint running down the walls, water splashing all over the bathroom counter, and food decorating the kitchen floor — these never used to elicit peals of laughter from me when I was a young mother. Now when it happens in my house, my grown children look at me with disapproval, claiming, "We didn't get to make messes like that when we were kids." Tell any other grandmother about it, however, and she "gets it." There is simply no need to explain to her why the grandchildren are allowed to eat dessert first and wipe their muddy hands on the good towels.

Reflecting over my life, I can see that I have made plenty of messes. Thankfully, God has helped me to clean up many of them. He has instructed me, supported me and loved me regardless of my choices. Through his Word, he's taught me that sometimes I need to clean up my messes immediately. Sometimes, however, I just need to wait and rely completely on him.

Our grandchildren remind us that life is fun. Jesus said that he came that his "sheep," or followers, "may have life, and have it to the full" (John 10:10). As grandmothers, we have finally learned to enjoy the moment and to cherish the love and the laughter. We find ourselves remembering the look of pure joy on our granddaughter's face while she was dancing to the music in her bare feet. So what if she knocked over the apple juice. To our surprise, we find that even scrubbing up a sticky mess can be a lot of fun!

Dear Lord and Father, thank you for sending your Son, Jesus, that we might have life — life that is full and fun. And thank you for helping me to learn that there is always time for me to clean up the messes in my life.

Your next devotion is located on page 1458.

GRANDCHILD IN FOCUS • PRAYER

Physical Well-Being

Almighty God, Creator of us all, I pray that you will watch over my grandchild's physical development. May he grow in strength through the stages of his life. As he grows in awareness of his body, help him to understand that each body develops uniquely, yet is within your plan and your control. Please guard his health so that his diseases are few, his injuries are minor and his infirmities are brief. Amen.

> "I AM THE GOOD SHEPHERD; I
> KNOW MY SHEEP AND MY SHEEP
> KNOW ME — JUST AS THE FATHER
> KNOWS ME AND I KNOW THE
> FATHER — AND I LAY DOWN MY
> LIFE FOR THE SHEEP."
> *John 10:14 – 15*

The Hired Hand

ELISA MORGAN

READ | JOHN 10:11 – 21

Hired hands can look so good. They show up at the front door at just the right moment, tool belts secured about their bellies, caps slanted backward from their foreheads in a friendly manner, pencils poised to take notes on all that needs repairing. They bring comforting promises of assured accomplishment — until the middle of the night when the rattling begins again, the window shutter bangs in the wind and the room is once again open to the elements, and the hired hand is *gone*.

In John 10:12 – 13, Jesus described the clear difference between a hired hand and a good shepherd. When things get difficult — when the wolf shows up and threatens the lives of the sheep — the hired hand takes off. He really doesn't care about the lives of the sheep like a true shepherd does; he cares only for himself. A good shepherd protects his sheep, never leaving his post, even when there is danger.

Jesus, the Good Shepherd, owns the sheep (us). He owns our errors, and he makes a way for our forgiveness. He lays down his life for the sheep. Night winds may flow through open windows, wolves may howl about the property's perimeter, but under the care of the Good Shepherd, all is well with the sheep.

Dear shepherding God, may I trust in you rather than the hired hands who come my way offering apparent security. In you alone I trust. In you alone I take refuge. In you alone I house those I love, knowing that in you alone is the security I truly desire. Amen.

Your next devotion is located on page 1462.

GRANDCHILD IN FOCUS • PRAYER

Emotional Development

O God, Creator of mind and body, I pray that you will give my grandchild emotional health and strength. Where there is anger, bring peace. Where there is confusion, bring clarity and focus. Where there are dark shadows, cast a ray of hope. Fill her with the sunshine of your Spirit. Warm her with the presence of your peace. Amen.

many great miracles from the Father. For which of these do you stone me?"

³³"We are not stoning you for any of these," replied the Jews, "but for blasphemy, because you, a mere man, claim to be God."

³⁴Jesus answered them, "Is it not written in your Law, 'I have said you are gods' *a*? ³⁵If he called them 'gods,' to whom the word of God came — and the Scripture cannot be broken — ³⁶what about the one whom the Father set apart as his very own and sent into the world? Why then do you accuse me of blasphemy because I said, 'I am God's Son'? ³⁷Do not believe me unless I do what my Father does. ³⁸But if I do it, even though you do not believe me, believe the miracles, that you may know and understand that the Father is in me, and I in the Father." ³⁹Again they tried to seize him, but he escaped their grasp.

⁴⁰Then Jesus went back across the Jordan to the place where John had been baptizing in the early days. Here he stayed ⁴¹and many people came to him. They said, "Though John never performed a miraculous sign, all that John said about this man was true." ⁴²And in that place many believed in Jesus.

The Death of Lazarus

11 Now a man named Lazarus was sick. He was from Bethany, the village of Mary and her sister Martha. ²This Mary, whose brother Lazarus now lay sick, was the same one who poured perfume on the Lord and wiped his feet with her hair. ³So the sisters sent word to Jesus, "Lord, the one you love is sick."

⁴When he heard this, Jesus said, "This sickness will not end in death. No, it is for God's glory so that God's Son may be glorified through it." ⁵Jesus loved Martha and her sister and Lazarus. ⁶Yet when he heard that Lazarus was sick, he stayed where he was two more days.

⁷Then he said to his disciples, "Let us go back to Judea."

⁸"But Rabbi," they said, "a short while ago the Jews tried to stone you, and yet you are going back there?"

⁹Jesus answered, "Are there not twelve hours of daylight? A man who walks by day will not stumble, for he sees by this world's light. ¹⁰It is when he walks by night that he stumbles, for he has no light."

¹¹After he had said this, he went on to tell them, "Our friend Lazarus has fallen asleep; but I am going there to wake him up."

¹²His disciples replied, "Lord, if he sleeps, he will get better." ¹³Jesus had been speaking of his death, but his disciples thought he meant natural sleep.

¹⁴So then he told them plainly, "Lazarus is dead, ¹⁵and for your sake I am glad I was not there, so that you may believe. But let us go to him."

¹⁶Then Thomas (called Didymus) said to the rest of the disciples, "Let us also go, that we may die with him."

Jesus Comforts the Sisters

¹⁷On his arrival, Jesus found that Lazarus had already been in the tomb for four days. ¹⁸Bethany was less than two miles *b* from Jerusalem, ¹⁹and many Jews had come to Martha and Mary to comfort them in the loss of their brother. ²⁰When Martha heard that Jesus was coming, she went out to meet him, but Mary stayed at home.

²¹"Lord," Martha said to Jesus, "if you had been here, my brother would not have died. ²²But I know that even now God will give you whatever you ask."

a 34 Psalm 82:6   *b 18* Greek *fifteen stadia* (about 3 kilometers)

TALKING POINTS

Friendship
Jesus cared about his friends.
JOHN 11:1–44
This is the last talking point on friendship.

²³ Jesus said to her, "Your brother will rise again."

²⁴ Martha answered, "I know he will rise again in the resurrection at the last day."

²⁵ Jesus said to her, "I am the resurrection and the life. He who believes in me will live, even though he dies; ²⁶ and whoever lives and believes in me will never die. Do you believe this?"

²⁷ "Yes, Lord," she told him, "I believe that you are the Christ,ᵃ the Son of God, who was to come into the world."

²⁸ And after she had said this, she went back and called her sister Mary aside. "The Teacher is here," she said, "and is asking for you." ²⁹ When Mary heard this, she got up quickly and went to him. ³⁰ Now Jesus had not yet entered the village, but was still at the place where Martha had met him. ³¹ When the Jews who had been with Mary in the house, comforting her, noticed how quickly she got up and went out, they followed her, supposing she was going to the tomb to mourn there.

³² When Mary reached the place where Jesus was and saw him, she fell at his feet and said, "Lord, if you had been here, my brother would not have died."

³³ When Jesus saw her weeping, and the Jews who had come along with her also weeping, he was deeply moved in spirit and troubled. ³⁴ "Where have you laid him?" he asked.

"Come and see, Lord," they replied.

³⁵ Jesus wept.

³⁶ Then the Jews said, "See how he loved him!"

³⁷ But some of them said, "Could not he who opened the eyes of the blind man have kept this man from dying?"

Jesus Raises Lazarus From the Dead

³⁸ Jesus, once more deeply moved, came to the tomb. It was a cave with a stone laid across the entrance. ³⁹ "Take away the stone," he said.

"But, Lord," said Martha, the sister of the dead man, "by this time there is a bad odor, for he has been there four days."

stories to share

JOHN 11:1–44

Jesus Raises Lazarus From the Dead

LIFE LESSON: Jesus has power over death.

TO TALK ABOUT

✦ Why did Mary and Martha send word for Jesus to come to Bethany?

✦ By the time Jesus got there, how long had Lazarus been dead?

✦ Why did Jesus allow Lazarus to die before his arrival in Bethany?

✦ What did Jesus mean when he said, "I am the resurrection and the life" (verse 25)?

⁴⁰ Then Jesus said, "Did I not tell you that if you believed, you would see the glory of God?"

⁴¹ So they took away the stone. Then Jesus looked up and said, "Father, I thank you that you have heard me. ⁴² I knew that you always hear me, but I said this for the benefit of the people standing here, that they may believe that you sent me."

⁴³ When he had said this, Jesus called in a loud voice, "Lazarus, come out!" ⁴⁴ The dead man came out, his hands and feet wrapped with strips of linen, and a cloth around his face.

Jesus said to them, "Take off the grave clothes and let him go."

ᵃ 27 Or Messiah

The Plot to Kill Jesus

⁴⁵Therefore many of the Jews who had come to visit Mary, and had seen what Jesus did, put their faith in him. ⁴⁶But some of them went to the Pharisees and told them what Jesus had done. ⁴⁷Then the chief priests and the Pharisees called a meeting of the Sanhedrin.

"What are we accomplishing?" they asked. "Here is this man performing many miraculous signs. ⁴⁸If we let him go on like this, everyone will believe in him, and then the Romans will come and take away both our place *a* and our nation."

⁴⁹Then one of them, named Caiaphas, who was high priest that year, spoke up, "You know nothing at all! ⁵⁰You do not realize that it is better for you that one man die for the people than that the whole nation perish."

⁵¹He did not say this on his own, but as high priest that year he prophesied that Jesus would die for the Jewish nation, ⁵²and not only for that nation but also for the scattered children of God, to bring them together and make them one. ⁵³So from that day on they plotted to take his life.

⁵⁴Therefore Jesus no longer moved about publicly among the Jews. Instead he withdrew to a region near the desert, to a village called Ephraim, where he stayed with his disciples.

⁵⁵When it was almost time for the Jewish Passover, many went up from the country to Jerusalem for their ceremonial cleansing before the Passover. ⁵⁶They kept looking for Jesus, and as they stood in the temple area they asked one another, "What do you think? Isn't he coming to the Feast at all?" ⁵⁷But the chief priests and Pharisees had given orders that if anyone found out where Jesus was, he should report it so that they might arrest him.

Jesus Anointed at Bethany

12:1–8Ref — Mt 26:6–13; Mk 14:3–9; Lk 7:37–39

12 Six days before the Passover, Jesus arrived at Bethany, where Lazarus lived, whom Jesus had raised from the dead. ²Here a dinner was given in Jesus' honor. Martha served, while Lazarus was among those reclining at the table with him. ³Then Mary took about a pint *b* of pure nard, an expensive perfume; she poured it on Jesus' feet and wiped his feet with her hair. And the house was filled with the fragrance of the perfume.

⁴But one of his disciples, Judas Iscariot, who was later to betray him, objected, ⁵"Why wasn't this perfume sold and the money given to the poor? It was worth a year's wages. *c*" ⁶He did not say this because he cared about the poor but because he was a thief; as keeper of the money bag, he used to help himself to what was put into it.

⁷"Leave her alone," Jesus replied. "It was intended that she should save this perfume for the day of my burial. ⁸You will always have the poor among you, but you will not always have me."

a 48 Or temple   b 3 Greek a litra (probably about 0.5 liter)   c 5 Greek three hundred denarii

stories to share

JOHN 12:1–8

Mary Gives Jesus a Gift

LIFE LESSON: Jesus deserves our best.

TO TALK ABOUT

◆ What gift did Mary give Jesus?

◆ Why did Judas object to the gift?

◆ What did Jesus mean when he said that Mary had done this for his burial?

◆ What gifts can you give Jesus to show your love and thankfulness for him?

THEN MARY TOOK ABOUT A PINT OF
PURE NARD, AN EXPENSIVE PERFUME;
SHE POURED IT ON JESUS' FEET AND
WIPED HIS FEET WITH HER HAIR.
AND THE HOUSE WAS FILLED WITH
THE FRAGRANCE OF THE PERFUME.

John 12:3

Looking Over the Edge

LINDA H. HOLLIES

READ | JOHN 12:1–11

The mother eagle called to her babies, "Come from the nest. It's time to fly!" They were terrified. The mother eagle called to her babies, "Come to the edge. Just look and see." Trusting her, they came. She pushed them over the edge.

And they flew!

[The season of] Lent is about hearing the call to leave the nest of our comfort zones. Lent is about leaving the edge, where we look and see the possibilities, passing up the opportunities, refusing to take risks. Lent is about hearing the persistent call to come from the nest of comfort, doing more and becoming more than we have ever imagined. For Lent is our journey forward to meet God. Lent, like all of life, is a process of progress or movement, a seeking to advance closer to the One who loves us best.

Six days before his death, Jesus needs someone, and along comes a woman named Mary. She comes and breaks open the alabaster jar filled with the embalming fragrance she more than likely purchased for her own death. The worth was equal to several years' wages. The jar alone was an object of art. Yet she breaks open the jar and walks over to pour this sweet perfume on Jesus. She anoints him as the Messiah. She becomes his ministering angel. She does the work of the high priest. She is the only disciple who is ready to fly. His approaching death pushes her out of her nest of comfortable limits.

Beloved, authentic life is moving past the traditional, the tried-and-true methods, and the *status quo*. Jesus uses Lent to call us to abundant life and to live a life of faith. Living a life of faith means not knowing the end of the story, but moving ahead into the unknown future, trusting the God of the journey.

Jesus, I ask you to give me the passion, the courage and the compassion to break out of the status quo and live abundantly in freedom and authenticity.

Your next devotion is located on page 1468.

GRANDCHILD IN FOCUS • PRAYER

Spiritual Growth

Dear Lord, today I pray for my grandchild's spiritual growth. I ask that you instill in him the desire to read and memorize your Word. Give him a passion to be in conversation with you. May loving and serving you be part of his daily life. I ask that you stay close to him and lead him to be transformed to your likeness, to reflect your grace and to radiate your love. I pray this in Jesus' name, amen.

⁹Meanwhile a large crowd of Jews found out that Jesus was there and came, not only because of him but also to see Lazarus, whom he had raised from the dead. ¹⁰So the chief priests made plans to kill Lazarus as well, ¹¹for on account of him many of the Jews were going over to Jesus and putting their faith in him.

The Triumphal Entry
12:12–15pp — Mt 21:4–9; Mk 11:7–10; Lk 19:35–38

¹²The next day the great crowd that had come for the Feast heard that Jesus was on his way to Jerusalem. ¹³They took palm branches and went out to meet him, shouting,

"Hosanna! [a]"

"Blessed is he who comes in the name of
the Lord!" [b]

"Blessed is the King of Israel!"

¹⁴Jesus found a young donkey and sat upon it, as it is written,

¹⁵"Do not be afraid, O Daughter of Zion;
see, your king is coming,
seated on a donkey's colt." [c]

¹⁶At first his disciples did not understand all this. Only after Jesus was glorified did they realize that these things had been written about him and that they had done these things to him.

¹⁷Now the crowd that was with him when he called Lazarus from the tomb and raised him from the dead continued to spread the word. ¹⁸Many people, because they had heard that he had given this miraculous sign, went out to meet him. ¹⁹So the Pharisees said to one another, "See, this is getting us nowhere. Look how the whole world has gone after him!"

Jesus Predicts His Death

²⁰Now there were some Greeks among those who went up to worship at the Feast. ²¹They came to Philip, who was from Bethsaida in Galilee, with a request. "Sir," they said, "we would like to see Jesus." ²²Philip went to tell Andrew; Andrew and Philip in turn told Jesus.

²³Jesus replied, "The hour has come for the Son of Man to be glorified. ²⁴I tell you the truth, unless a kernel of wheat falls to the ground and dies, it remains only a single seed. But if it dies, it produces many seeds. ²⁵The man who loves his life will lose it, while the man who hates his life in this world will keep it for eternal life. ²⁶Whoever serves me must follow me; and where I am, my servant also will be. My Father will honor the one who serves me.

²⁷"Now my heart is troubled, and what shall I say? 'Father, save me from this hour'? No, it was for this very reason I came to this hour. ²⁸Father, glorify your name!"

Then a voice came from heaven, "I have glorified it, and will glorify it again." ²⁹The crowd that was there and heard it said it had thundered; others said an angel had spoken to him.

³⁰Jesus said, "This voice was for your benefit, not mine. ³¹Now is the time for judgment on this world; now the prince of this world will be driven out. ³²But I, when I am lifted up from the earth, will draw all men to myself." ³³He said this to show the kind of death he was going to die.

³⁴The crowd spoke up, "We have heard from the Law that the Christ [d] will remain forever, so how can you say, 'The Son of Man must be lifted up'? Who is this 'Son of Man'?"

³⁵Then Jesus told them, "You are going to have the light just a little while longer. Walk while you have the light, before darkness overtakes you. The man who walks in the dark does not know where he is going. ³⁶Put your trust in the light while you have it, so that you may become sons of light." When he had finished speaking, Jesus left and hid himself from them.

The Jews Continue in Their Unbelief

³⁷Even after Jesus had done all these miraculous signs in their presence, they still would not

---

a 13 A Hebrew expression meaning "Save!" which became an exclamation of praise   *b 13* Psalm 118:25,26   *c 15* Zech. 9:9
d 34 Or *Messiah*

believe in him. ³⁸This was to fulfill the word of Isaiah the prophet:

"Lord, who has believed our message
and to whom has the arm of the Lord been
revealed?"ᵃ

³⁹For this reason they could not believe, because, as Isaiah says elsewhere:

⁴⁰"He has blinded their eyes
and deadened their hearts,
so they can neither see with their eyes,
nor understand with their hearts,
nor turn—and I would heal them."ᵇ

⁴¹Isaiah said this because he saw Jesus' glory and spoke about him.

⁴²Yet at the same time many even among the leaders believed in him. But because of the Pharisees they would not confess their faith for fear they would be put out of the synagogue; ⁴³for they loved praise from men more than praise from God.

⁴⁴Then Jesus cried out, "When a man believes in me, he does not believe in me only, but in the one who sent me. ⁴⁵When he looks at me, he sees the one who sent me. ⁴⁶I have come into the world as a light, so that no one who believes in me should stay in darkness.

⁴⁷"As for the person who hears my words but does not keep them, I do not judge him. For I did not come to judge the world, but to save it. ⁴⁸There is a judge for the one who rejects me and does not accept my words; that very word which I spoke will condemn him at the last day. ⁴⁹For I did not speak of my own accord, but the Father who sent me commanded me what to say and how to say it. ⁵⁰I know that his command leads to eternal life. So whatever I say is just what the Father has told me to say."

Jesus Washes His Disciples' Feet

13 It was just before the Passover Feast. Jesus knew that the time had come for him to leave this world and go to the Father. Having loved his own who were in the world, he now showed them the full extent of his love.ᶜ

---

stories to share

JOHN 13:1-17

Jesus Washes His Disciples' Feet

LIFE LESSON: Jesus wants us to serve others.

TO TALK ABOUT

✦ How did Jesus show his love for his disciples?

✦ Why do you think Jesus did something that normally only servants did?

✦ How would you have felt if you were one of the disciples and Jesus wanted to wash your feet?

✦ How can you follow Jesus' example and wash someone else's feet?

---

²The evening meal was being served, and the devil had already prompted Judas Iscariot, son of Simon, to betray Jesus. ³Jesus knew that the Father had put all things under his power, and that he had come from God and was returning to God; ⁴so he got up from the meal, took off his outer clothing, and wrapped a towel around his waist. ⁵After that, he poured water into a basin and began to wash his disciples' feet, drying them with the towel that was wrapped around him.

⁶He came to Simon Peter, who said to him, "Lord, are you going to wash my feet?"

ᵃ 38 Isaiah 53:1   ᵇ 40 Isaiah 6:10   ᶜ 1 Or he loved them to the last

7 Jesus replied, "You do not realize now what I am doing, but later you will understand."

8 "No," said Peter, "you shall never wash my feet."

Jesus answered, "Unless I wash you, you have no part with me."

9 "Then, Lord," Simon Peter replied, "not just my feet but my hands and my head as well!"

10 Jesus answered, "A person who has had a bath needs only to wash his feet; his whole body is clean. And you are clean, though not every one of you." 11 For he knew who was going to betray him, and that was why he said not every one was clean.

12 When he had finished washing their feet, he put on his clothes and returned to his place. "Do you understand what I have done for you?" he asked them. 13 "You call me 'Teacher' and 'Lord,' and rightly so, for that is what I am. 14 Now that I, your Lord and Teacher, have washed your feet, you also should wash one another's feet. 15 I have set you an example that you should do as I have done for you. 16 I tell you the truth, no servant is greater than his master, nor is a messenger greater than the one who sent him. 17 Now that you know these things, you will be blessed if you do them.

Jesus Predicts His Betrayal

18 "I am not referring to all of you; I know those I have chosen. But this is to fulfill the scripture: 'He who shares my bread has lifted up his heel against me.' *a*

19 "I am telling you now before it happens, so that when it does happen you will believe that I am He. 20 I tell you the truth, whoever accepts anyone I send accepts me; and whoever accepts me accepts the one who sent me."

21 After he had said this, Jesus was troubled in spirit and testified, "I tell you the truth, one of you is going to betray me."

22 His disciples stared at one another, at a loss to know which of them he meant. 23 One of them, the disciple whom Jesus loved, was reclining next to him. 24 Simon Peter motioned to this disciple and said, "Ask him which one he means."

25 Leaning back against Jesus, he asked him, "Lord, who is it?"

26 Jesus answered, "It is the one to whom I will give this piece of bread when I have dipped it in the dish." Then, dipping the piece of bread, he gave it to Judas Iscariot, son of Simon. 27 As soon as Judas took the bread, Satan entered into him.

"What you are about to do, do quickly," Jesus told him, 28 but no one at the meal understood why Jesus said this to him. 29 Since Judas had charge of the money, some thought Jesus was telling him to buy what was needed for the Feast, or to give something to the poor. 30 As soon as Judas had taken the bread, he went out. And it was night.

Jesus Predicts Peter's Denial

13:37,38pp — Mt 26:33–35; Mk 14:29–31; Lk 22:33,34

31 When he was gone, Jesus said, "Now is the Son of Man glorified and God is glorified in him. 32 If God is glorified in him, *b* God will glorify the Son in himself, and will glorify him at once.

33 "My children, I will be with you only a little longer. You will look for me, and just as I told the Jews, so I tell you now: Where I am going, you cannot come.

34 "A new command I give you: Love one another. As I have loved you, so you must love one another. 35 By this all men will know that you are my disciples, if you love one another."

36 Simon Peter asked him, "Lord, where are you going?"

Jesus replied, "Where I am going, you cannot follow now, but you will follow later."

37 Peter asked, "Lord, why can't I follow you now? I will lay down my life for you."

38 Then Jesus answered, "Will you really lay down your life for me? I tell you the truth, before the rooster crows, you will disown me three times!

Jesus Comforts His Disciples

14 "Do not let your hearts be troubled. Trust in God *c*; trust also in me. 2 In my Father's house are many rooms; if it were not so, I would

---

a 18 Psalm 41:9   *b 32* Many early manuscripts do not have *If God is glorified in him.*   *c 1* Or *You trust in God* may bring glory to the Father. [14] You may ask me for anything in my name, and I will do it.

Jesus Promises the Holy Spirit

[15] "If you love me, you will obey what I command. [16] And I will ask the Father, and he will give you another Counselor to be with you forever— [17] the Spirit of truth. The world cannot accept him, because it neither sees him nor knows him. But you know him, for he lives with you and will be[b] in you. [18] I will not leave you as orphans;

have told you. I am going there to prepare a place for you. [3] And if I go and prepare a place for you, I will come back and take you to be with me that you also may be where I am. [4] You know the way to the place where I am going."

Jesus the Way to the Father

[5] Thomas said to him, "Lord, we don't know where you are going, so how can we know the way?"

[6] Jesus answered, "I am the way and the truth and the life. No one comes to the Father except through me. [7] If you really knew me, you would know[a] my Father as well. From now on, you do know him and have seen him."

[8] Philip said, "Lord, show us the Father and that will be enough for us."

[9] Jesus answered: "Don't you know me, Philip, even after I have been among you such a long time? Anyone who has seen me has seen the Father. How can you say, 'Show us the Father'? [10] Don't you believe that I am in the Father, and that the Father is in me? The words I say to you are not just my own. Rather, it is the Father, living in me, who is doing his work. [11] Believe me when I say that I am in the Father and the Father is in me; or at least believe on the evidence of the miracles themselves. [12] I tell you the truth, anyone who has faith in me will do what I have been doing. He will do even greater things than these, because I am going to the Father. [13] And I will do whatever you ask in my name, so that the Son

I will come to you. [19] Before long, the world will not see me anymore, but you will see me. Because I live, you also will live. [20] On that day you will realize that I am in my Father, and you are in me, and I am in you. [21] Whoever has my commands and obeys them, he is the one who loves me. He who loves me will be loved by my Father, and I too will love him and show myself to him."

[22] Then Judas (not Judas Iscariot) said, "But, Lord, why do you intend to show yourself to us and not to the world?"

[23] Jesus replied, "If anyone loves me, he will obey my teaching. My Father will love him, and we will come to him and make our home with him. [24] He who does not love me will not obey my teaching. These words you hear are not my own; they belong to the Father who sent me.

[25] "All this I have spoken while still with you.

[a] 7 Some early manuscripts *If you really have known me, you will know*   [b] 17 Some early manuscripts *and is*

26 But the Counselor, the Holy Spirit, whom the Father will send in my name, will teach you all things and will remind you of everything I have said to you. 27 Peace I leave with you; my peace I give you. I do not give to you as the world gives. Do not let your hearts be troubled and do not be afraid.

28 "You heard me say, 'I am going away and I am coming back to you.' If you loved me, you would be glad that I am going to the Father, for the Father is greater than I. 29 I have told you now before it happens, so that when it does happen you will believe. 30 I will not speak with you much longer, for the prince of this world is coming. He has no hold on me, 31 but the world must learn that I love the Father and that I do exactly what my Father has commanded me.

"Come now; let us leave.

The Vine and the Branches

15 "I am the true vine, and my Father is the gardener. 2 He cuts off every branch in me that bears no fruit, while every branch that does bear fruit he prunes *a* so that it will be even more fruitful. 3 You are already clean because of the word I have spoken to you. 4 Remain in me, and I will remain in you. No branch can bear fruit by itself; it must remain in the vine. Neither can you bear fruit unless you remain in me.

5 "I am the vine; you are the branches. If a man remains in me and I in him, he will bear much fruit; apart from me you can do nothing. 6 If anyone does not remain in me, he is like a branch that is thrown away and withers; such branches are picked up, thrown into the fire and burned. 7 If you remain in me and my words remain in you, ask whatever you wish, and it will be given you. 8 This is to my Father's glory, that you bear much fruit, showing yourselves to be my disciples.

9 "As the Father has loved me, so have I loved you. Now remain in my love. 10 If you obey my commands, you will remain in my love, just as I have obeyed my Father's commands and re-main in his love. 11 I have told you this so that my joy may be in you and that your joy may be complete. 12 My command is this: Love each other as I have loved you. 13 Greater love has no one than this, that he lay down his life for his friends. 14 You are my friends if you do what I command. 15 I no longer call you servants, because a servant does not know his master's business. Instead, I have called you friends, for everything that I learned from my Father I have made known to you. 16 You did not choose me, but I chose you and appointed you to go and bear fruit—fruit that will last. Then the Father will give you whatever you ask in my name. 17 This is my command: Love each other.

TALKING POINTS

Love

Live in Christ's love and love others.

JOHN 15:9–17

For more on love, go to 1 Corinthians 13:1–13.

The World Hates the Disciples

18 "If the world hates you, keep in mind that it hated me first. 19 If you belonged to the world, it would love you as its own. As it is, you do not belong to the world, but I have chosen you out of the world. That is why the world hates you. 20 Remember the words I spoke to you: 'No servant is greater than his master.' *b* If they persecuted me, they will persecute you also. If they obeyed my teaching, they will obey yours also. 21 They will treat you this way because of my name, for they do not know the One who sent me. 22 If I had not come and spoken to them, they would not be guilty of sin. Now, however, they have no excuse for their sin. 23 He who hates me hates my Father as well. 24 If I had not done among them what no

a 2 The Greek for *prunes* also means *cleans.*   *b 20* John 13:16

> "As the Father has loved me, so have I loved you. Now remain in my love. If you obey my commands, you will remain in my love, just as I have obeyed my Father's commands and remain in his love."
>
> John 15:9–10

Testing Love

MARGARET FISHBACK POWERS

READ | JOHN 15:1–17

I had been diligently teaching my four-year-old grandson, Max, the importance of obeying me, so that he would always be under the umbrella of my love, as I am under God's love.

The heater was on in my office one cold and rainy winter day while Max was over for a visit. Seizing the opportunity for a teaching moment, I walked him over close to the heater. As I held his little hand in mine, I drew it close enough to the heater to show him how hot it was. Then I clearly explained to him that he should never touch it.

A few days later Max was visiting again. Suddenly I heard a yelp coming from my office. Running over to see what had happened, I discovered little Max had touched the heater in spite of my careful instructions. His finger was burned. I was very upset. "Why did you touch the heater when I told you not to? Why did you disobey me?" He shyly sighed. Then he said, "I know you love me when I obey you, Nana, but I wanted to find out if you still love me, and if God still loves me, even if I disobey."

"Isn't it much better to obey me, and remain *in* my love and *in* God's love?" I asked him.

He agreed wholeheartedly, and we both had a little cry. Needless to say, this lesson has helped him with his desire to help in the kitchen.

Dear loving Father, thank you for loving me continually — when I obey your will and even when I disobey. Help me to see how precious and secure it is to always remain in your love. Amen.

Your next devotion is located on page 1470.

GRANDCHILD IN FOCUS • PRAYER

Relationships at Home

O Lord, I pray that you will bless the home and family of my grandchild. May the relationships she has with her parents and siblings enhance her well-being, support her self-confidence and increase her faith. May her home life reflect your love, your grace, your compassion and your peace. Guide her parents to direct her in love and truth, so she will grow into a strong and compassionate individual. Amen.

one else did, they would not be guilty of sin. But now they have seen these miracles, and yet they have hated both me and my Father. [25] But this is to fulfill what is written in their Law: 'They hated me without reason.'[a]

[26] "When the Counselor comes, whom I will send to you from the Father, the Spirit of truth who goes out from the Father, he will testify about me. [27] And you also must testify, for you have been with me from the beginning.

16 "All this I have told you so that you will not go astray. [2] They will put you out of the synagogue; in fact, a time is coming when anyone who kills you will think he is offering a service to God. [3] They will do such things because they have not known the Father or me. [4] I have told you this, so that when the time comes you will remember that I warned you. I did not tell you this at first because I was with you.

The Work of the Holy Spirit

[5] "Now I am going to him who sent me, yet none of you asks me, 'Where are you going?' [6] Because I have said these things, you are filled with grief. [7] But I tell you the truth: It is for your good that I am going away. Unless I go away, the Counselor will not come to you; but if I go, I will send him to you. [8] When he comes, he will convict the world of guilt[b] in regard to sin and righteousness and judgment: [9] in regard to sin, because men do not believe in me; [10] in regard to righteousness, because I am going to the Father, where you can see me no longer; [11] and in regard to judgment, because the prince of this world now stands condemned.

[12] "I have much more to say to you, more than you can now bear. [13] But when he, the Spirit of truth, comes, he will guide you into all truth. He will not speak on his own; he will speak only what he hears, and he will tell you what is yet to come. [14] He will bring glory to me by taking from what is mine and making it known to you. [15] All that belongs to the Father is mine. That is why I said the Spirit will take from what is mine and make it known to you.

[16] "In a little while you will see me no more, and then after a little while you will see me."

The Disciples' Grief Will Turn to Joy

[17] Some of his disciples said to one another, "What does he mean by saying, 'In a little while you will see me no more, and then after a little while you will see me,' and 'Because I am going to the Father'?" [18] They kept asking, "What does he mean by 'a little while'? We don't understand what he is saying."

[19] Jesus saw that they wanted to ask him about this, so he said to them, "Are you asking one another what I meant when I said, 'In a little while you will see me no more, and then after a little while you will see me'? [20] I tell you the truth, you will weep and mourn while the world rejoices. You will grieve, but your grief will turn to joy.

PRAYING THE SCRIPTURES

Comfort

JOHN 16:20

O God, my grandchild is weeping and mourning. As your Son's resurrection turned his disciples' grief to joy, bring comfort and joy to my grandchild through your life-giving power.

Next prayer in Comfort Prayer Track: 2 Corinthians 1:3–4

[21] A woman giving birth to a child has pain because her time has come; but when her baby is born she forgets the anguish because of her joy that a child is born into the world. [22] So with you: Now is your time of grief, but I will see you again and you will rejoice, and no one will take away your joy. [23] In that day you will no longer ask me anything. I tell you the truth, my Father will give you whatever you ask in my name. [24] Until now

[a] 25 Psalms 35:19; 69:4   [b] 8 Or will expose the guilt of the world

LET'S
TALK

Life Goals and Dreams

Take some time this weekend to talk with your grandchildren about their hopes and dreams for the future.

Younger children are seldom at a loss on this subject. Ask them to expound on their plans for what they want to be when they grow up. Enjoy their responses. Then suggest that they draw pictures of themselves pursuing their aspirations. These keepsakes will elicit lots of laughs in years to come.

Elementary-aged kids and middle schoolers will probably have modified their original intentions, but their responses may still be idealistic. Ask them to expand on their goals, and encourage them to record them for future reference. Tuck away their responses for a few years and have them review them at a later date.

Older grandchildren will appreciate your interest and may use you as a sounding board to discuss options, doubts and perceived obstacles to their goals. They may appreciate your viewpoint and may ask for coaching on how to have a similar discussion with their parents. You may be just far enough removed from direct involvement to be a voice of reason and encouragement.

God of the future, there are so many options for my grandchildren's futures: careers, jobs, ministry opportunities, etc. Give them the wisdom and courage to dream and hope for the future and to actively seek your will as they mature. Amen.

Your next devotion is located on page 1471.

GRANDCHILD IN FOCUS • PRAYER

Friends

Dear Lord and Father, I pray for my grandchild's social life and his friends. Bring diverse friends into his life who will love and encourage him, who will bring joy and laughter to the good times and comfort and support through difficulties and disappointments. Grant him wisdom and discernment as he selects his friends; help him to avoid cliques that restrict, activities that endanger, and foolish and dangerous behaviors that harm. I ask that you fill his life with close and caring relationships. Amen.

Worship the Lord

Praise the LORD.

Praise the name of the LORD;
>   praise him, you servants of the LORD,
you who minister in the house of the LORD,
>   in the courts of the house of our God.

Praise the LORD, for the LORD is good;
>   sing praise to his name, for that is pleasant.
For the LORD has chosen Jacob to be his own,
>   Israel to be his treasured possession.

I know that the LORD is great,
>   that our Lord is greater than all gods.
The LORD does whatever pleases him,
>   in the heavens and on the earth,
>   in the seas and all their depths.
He makes clouds rise from the ends of
>   the earth;
>   he sends lightning with the rain
>   and brings out the wind from his
>   storehouses.

Psalm 135:1 – 7

How pleasant it is, Lord, to praise your name, for you are both good and great. Thank you that what pleases you is also your will for my well-being. Thank you for the amazing grandeur of your creation that I see in storms and in peaceful days of sunshine. Amen.

Your next devotion is located on page 1472.

GRANDCHILD IN FOCUS • PRAYER

Self-Image

O loving God, I praise you for creating my grandchild as a unique individual. Now I ask you to help her appreciate her uniqueness. Build up her self-image so she can enjoy her individuality. Help her to stand firm for who she is, where she has come from and what she believes in. Encourage her not only to have hopes and dreams but to also enjoy each day as it comes. In Jesus' name, amen.

Billy the Butler Can Do It

KAREN MAINS

> "BUT WHEN HE, THE SPIRIT OF TRUTH, COMES, HE WILL GUIDE YOU INTO ALL TRUTH. HE WILL NOT SPEAK ON HIS OWN; HE WILL SPEAK ONLY WHAT HE HEARS, AND HE WILL TELL YOU WHAT IS YET TO COME."
>
> John 16:13

READ | JOHN 16:5 – 16

"Remember," said my adult children going out the door on the way to the airport, "Billy the Butler comes to clean on Wednesday." Our mandate for their 10 days of vacation was to (1) take care of our three grandchildren and (2) decorate the new house!

After five days, I had pretty much figured out what looked best where and what needed to be repaired from the move—a pole on a column lamp, for instance, was broken at the joint. Besides those minor repairs, my husband, David, and I had to hang two oversize framed pictures, one above another, on the two-and-a-half-story wall.

On Wednesday, a van parked outside the house. The sign on the side read, "Billy (Let the Butler Do It): Cleaning, Maintenance, Window-Washing, Home Repairs, etc." By the end of the day, Billy the Butler had repaired the lamp. Then, by stringing up a ropelike contraption to steady the large frames and by stretching his long arms to pound holes for hooks, Billy the Butler managed to catch the wires on the nailed hangers. With a sigh of relief, we all concurred that by some small miracle, the two pictures, one above the other, looked even.

I have often felt that the work of the Holy Spirit is similar to that of a capable handyman. There are broken things within the household of the soul that need fixing. On our own, we do not know how to repair these damaged spaces, nor do we have the arm span or the necessary expertise to hang the pictures straight.

The household of the soul is a place with many rooms, including an attic stuffed with junk, boxes filled with historical archives we all need help understanding. As you journey inward, call on the "Holy Butler: Soul Maintenance, Repairs, Thorough Cleansing, etc."

Lord, I am broken within, full of unfixed things needing your attention. I put myself into your capable hands, believing, as Jesus taught, that you will guide me in truth. You will know how to make my crooked life straight again.

GRANDCHILD IN FOCUS • PRAYER

Protection From Worldliness

O Sovereign Lord, the world surrounds my grandchild, pressing in and tempting him in so many ways. Help him set appropriate limits. Give him sound judgment to choose wisely. Guard him from temptation; protect him from physical and mental predators; lead him into paths of righteousness and light. And reassure me with your promise that you are holding him in your hands. Amen.

Your next devotion is located on page 1475.

you have not asked for anything in my name. Ask and you will receive, and your joy will be complete.

²⁵"Though I have been speaking figuratively, a time is coming when I will no longer use this kind of language but will tell you plainly about my Father. ²⁶In that day you will ask in my name. I am not saying that I will ask the Father on your behalf. ²⁷No, the Father himself loves you because you have loved me and have believed that I came from God. ²⁸I came from the Father and entered the world; now I am leaving the world and going back to the Father."

²⁹Then Jesus' disciples said, "Now you are speaking clearly and without figures of speech. ³⁰Now we can see that you know all things and that you do not even need to have anyone ask you questions. This makes us believe that you came from God."

³¹"You believe at last!"ᵃ Jesus answered. ³²"But a time is coming, and has come, when you will be scattered, each to his own home. You will leave me all alone. Yet I am not alone, for my Father is with me.

³³"I have told you these things, so that in me you may have peace. In this world you will have trouble. But take heart! I have overcome the world."

Jesus Prays for Himself

17 After Jesus said this, he looked toward heaven and prayed:

"Father, the time has come. Glorify your Son, that your Son may glorify you. ²For you granted him authority over all people that he might give eternal life to all those you have given him. ³Now this is eternal life: that they may know you, the only true God, and Jesus Christ, whom you have sent. ⁴I have brought you glory on earth by completing the work you gave me to do. ⁵And now, Father, glorify me in your presence with the glory I had with you before the world began.

Jesus Prays for His Disciples

⁶"I have revealed youᵇ to those whom you gave me out of the world. They were yours; you gave them to me and they have obeyed your word. ⁷Now they know that everything you have given me comes from you. ⁸For I gave them the words you gave me and they accepted them. They knew with certainty that I came from you, and they believed that you sent me. ⁹I pray for them. I am not praying for the world, but for those you have given me, for they are yours. ¹⁰All I have is yours, and all you have is mine. And glory has come to me through them. ¹¹I will remain in the world no longer, but they are still in the world, and I am coming to you. Holy Father, protect them by the power of your name—the name you gave me—so that they may be one as we are one. ¹²While I was with them, I protected them and kept them safe by that name you gave me. None has been lost except the one doomed to destruction so that Scripture would be fulfilled.

¹³"I am coming to you now, but I say these things while I am still in the world, so that they may have the full measure of my joy within them. ¹⁴I have given them your word and the world has hated them, for they are not of the world any more than I am of the world. ¹⁵My prayer is not that you take them out of the world but that you protect them from the evil one. ¹⁶They are not of the world, even as I am not of it. ¹⁷Sanctifyᶜ them by the truth; your word is truth. ¹⁸As you sent me into the world, I have sent them into the world. ¹⁹For them I sanctify myself, that they too may be truly sanctified.

Jesus Prays for All Believers

²⁰"My prayer is not for them alone. I pray also for those who will believe in me

ᵃ 31 Or *"Do you now believe?"*   ᵇ 6 Greek *your name*; also in verse 26   ᶜ 17 Greek *hagiazo (set apart for sacred use* or *make holy)*; also in verse 19 through their message, [21] that all of them may be one, Father, just as you are in me and I am in you. May they also be in us so that the world may believe that you have sent me. [22] I have given them the glory that you gave me, that they may be one as we are one: [23] I in them and you in me. May they be brought to complete unity to let the world know that you sent me and have loved them even as you have loved me.

[24] "Father, I want those you have given me to be with me where I am, and to see my glory, the glory you have given me because you loved me before the creation of the world.

[25] "Righteous Father, though the world does not know you, I know you, and they know that you have sent me. [26] I have made you known to them, and will continue to make you known in order that the love you have for me may be in them and that I myself may be in them."

Jesus Arrested

18:3–11pp — Mt 26:47–56; Mk 14:43–50; Lk 22:47–53

18 When he had finished praying, Jesus left with his disciples and crossed the Kidron Valley. On the other side there was an olive grove, and he and his disciples went into it.

[2] Now Judas, who betrayed him, knew the place, because Jesus had often met there with his disciples. [3] So Judas came to the grove, guiding a detachment of soldiers and some officials from the chief priests and Pharisees. They were carrying torches, lanterns and weapons.

[4] Jesus, knowing all that was going to happen to him, went out and asked them, "Who is it you want?"

[5] "Jesus of Nazareth," they replied.

"I am he," Jesus said. (And Judas the traitor was standing there with them.) [6] When Jesus said, "I am he," they drew back and fell to the ground.

[7] Again he asked them, "Who is it you want?"

And they said, "Jesus of Nazareth."

[8] "I told you that I am he," Jesus answered. "If you are looking for me, then let these men go."

[9] This happened so that the words he had spoken would be fulfilled: "I have not lost one of those you gave me." [a]

[10] Then Simon Peter, who had a sword, drew it and struck the high priest's servant, cutting off his right ear. (The servant's name was Malchus.)

[11] Jesus commanded Peter, "Put your sword away! Shall I not drink the cup the Father has given me?"

Jesus Taken to Annas

18:12,13pp — Mt 26:57

[12] Then the detachment of soldiers with its commander and the Jewish officials arrested Jesus. They bound him [13] and brought him first to Annas, who was the father-in-law of Caiaphas, the high priest that year. [14] Caiaphas was the one who had advised the Jews that it would be good if one man died for the people.

Peter's First Denial

18:16–18pp — Mt 26:69,70; Mk 14:66–68; Lk 22:55–57

[15] Simon Peter and another disciple were following Jesus. Because this disciple was known to the high priest, he went with Jesus into the high priest's courtyard, [16] but Peter had to wait outside at the door. The other disciple, who was known to the high priest, came back, spoke to the girl on duty there and brought Peter in.

[17] "You are not one of his disciples, are you?" the girl at the door asked Peter.

He replied, "I am not."

[18] It was cold, and the servants and officials stood around a fire they had made to keep warm. Peter also was standing with them, warming himself.

The High Priest Questions Jesus

18:19–24pp — Mt 26:59–68; Mk 14:55–65; Lk 22:63–71

[19] Meanwhile, the high priest questioned Jesus about his disciples and his teaching.

[20] "I have spoken openly to the world," Jesus replied. "I always taught in synagogues or at the

a 9 John 6:39

Praying for Salvation and Spiritual Growth

QUIN SHERRER

READ | JOHN 17:1 – 26

As grandmothers there is a special place in our hearts and thoughts for our grandchildren. We can share our knowledge and faith with them and use our influence to steer them in the ways of the Lord.

But most important, we grandmas can pray for our grandchildren to receive Christ as Savior. Then we can pray that we — or someone else — will have the opportunity to share the simple gospel with them. And finally, we can pray that they in turn will be used by God to influence others.

After the funeral for her 96-year-old grandmother, Jennie and her family gathered at the old homestead to celebrate her life. They sang some of her favorite hymns. Then they listened to a cassette tape Grandma Sally had made in an effort to pass down to her descendants some of her homespun wisdom and poetry and a short account of her spiritual journey.

Jennie later told me, "I suddenly realized I am a Christian because of Grandma's prayers. She lived so far from our family that I didn't see her often, but whenever I was about to end a visit, she would say a short prayer over me. When I heard her voice on the tape, I knew for certain her prayers had followed me all my life."

Grandma Sally's example shows us that regardless of distance, our prayers can affect and reach our grandchildren. Not only can we find ways to tell them about Jesus, but we also can pray that others will encourage them in their Christian faith.

Lord, I pray that my grandchildren will come to know Jesus at an early age. Show me what to say to my grandchildren — in a letter, a phone call or a face-to-face conversation — that will encourage them to love you always and trust you with their lives. Amen.

Your next devotion is located on page 1483.

GRANDCHILD IN FOCUS • PRAYER

Respect for Authority

Dear Lord, I pray that my grandchild will continually grow to respect those in authority. May she learn to be cooperative and fair in work and play. Instill in her a high regard for officials who govern our land and enforce the laws. May her relationships with parents, teachers, coaches, mentors and bosses be respectful, admirable, constructive and caring. Amen.

temple, where all the Jews come together. I said nothing in secret. ²¹Why question me? Ask those who heard me. Surely they know what I said."

²²When Jesus said this, one of the officials nearby struck him in the face. "Is this the way you answer the high priest?" he demanded.

²³"If I said something wrong," Jesus replied, "testify as to what is wrong. But if I spoke the truth, why did you strike me?" ²⁴Then Annas sent him, still bound, to Caiaphas the high priest. *ᵃ*

Peter's Second and Third Denials

18:25–27pp — Mt 26:71–75; Mk 14:69–72; Lk 22:58–62

²⁵As Simon Peter stood warming himself, he was asked, "You are not one of his disciples, are you?"

He denied it, saying, "I am not."

²⁶One of the high priest's servants, a relative of the man whose ear Peter had cut off, challenged him, "Didn't I see you with him in the olive grove?" ²⁷Again Peter denied it, and at that moment a rooster began to crow.

Jesus Before Pilate

18:29–40pp — Mt 27:11–18,20–23; Mk 15:2–15; Lk 23:2,3,18–25

²⁸Then the Jews led Jesus from Caiaphas to the palace of the Roman governor. By now it was early morning, and to avoid ceremonial uncleanness the Jews did not enter the palace; they wanted to be able to eat the Passover. ²⁹So Pilate came out to them and asked, "What charges are you bringing against this man?"

³⁰"If he were not a criminal," they replied, "we would not have handed him over to you."

³¹Pilate said, "Take him yourselves and judge him by your own law."

"But we have no right to execute anyone," the Jews objected. ³²This happened so that the words Jesus had spoken indicating the kind of death he was going to die would be fulfilled.

³³Pilate then went back inside the palace, summoned Jesus and asked, "Are you the king of the Jews?"

³⁴"Is that your own idea," Jesus asked, "or did others talk to you about me?"

³⁵"Am I a Jew?" Pilate replied. "It was your people and your chief priests who handed you over to me. What is it you have done?"

³⁶Jesus said, "My kingdom is not of this world. If it were, my servants would fight to prevent my arrest by the Jews. But now my kingdom is from another place."

³⁷"You are a king, then!" said Pilate.

Jesus answered, "You are right in saying I am a king. In fact, for this reason I was born, and for this I came into the world, to testify to the truth. Everyone on the side of truth listens to me."

³⁸"What is truth?" Pilate asked. With this he went out again to the Jews and said, "I find no basis for a charge against him. ³⁹But it is your custom for me to release to you one prisoner at the time of the Passover. Do you want me to release 'the king of the Jews'?"

⁴⁰They shouted back, "No, not him! Give us Barabbas!" Now Barabbas had taken part in a rebellion.

Jesus Sentenced to Be Crucified

19:1–16pp — Mt 27:27–31; Mk 15:16–20

19 Then Pilate took Jesus and had him flogged. ²The soldiers twisted together a crown of thorns and put it on his head. They clothed him in a purple robe ³and went up to him again and again, saying, "Hail, king of the Jews!" And they struck him in the face.

⁴Once more Pilate came out and said to the Jews, "Look, I am bringing him out to you to let you know that I find no basis for a charge against him." ⁵When Jesus came out wearing the crown of thorns and the purple robe, Pilate said to them, "Here is the man!"

⁶As soon as the chief priests and their officials saw him, they shouted, "Crucify! Crucify!"

But Pilate answered, "You take him and crucify him. As for me, I find no basis for a charge against him."

⁷The Jews insisted, "We have a law, and according to that law he must die, because he claimed to be the Son of God."

ᵃ 24 Or (Now Annas had sent him, still bound, to Caiaphas the high priest.)

8When Pilate heard this, he was even more afraid, 9and he went back inside the palace. "Where do you come from?" he asked Jesus, but Jesus gave him no answer. 10"Do you refuse to speak to me?" Pilate said. "Don't you realize I have power either to free you or to crucify you?"

11Jesus answered, "You would have no power over me if it were not given to you from above. Therefore the one who handed me over to you is guilty of a greater sin."

12From then on, Pilate tried to set Jesus free, but the Jews kept shouting, "If you let this man go, you are no friend of Caesar. Anyone who claims to be a king opposes Caesar."

13When Pilate heard this, he brought Jesus out and sat down on the judge's seat at a place known as the Stone Pavement (which in Aramaic is Gabbatha). 14It was the day of Preparation of Passover Week, about the sixth hour.

"Here is your king," Pilate said to the Jews.

15But they shouted, "Take him away! Take him away! Crucify him!"

"Shall I crucify your king?" Pilate asked.

"We have no king but Caesar," the chief priests answered.

16Finally Pilate handed him over to them to be crucified.

The Crucifixion

19:17–24pp — Mt 27:33–44; Mk 15:22–32; Lk 23:33–43

So the soldiers took charge of Jesus. 17Carrying his own cross, he went out to the place of the Skull (which in Aramaic is called Golgotha). 18Here they crucified him, and with him two others—one on each side and Jesus in the middle.

19Pilate had a notice prepared and fastened to the cross. It read: JESUS OF NAZARETH, THE KING OF THE JEWS. 20Many of the Jews read this sign, for the place where Jesus was crucified was near the city, and the sign was written in Aramaic, Latin and Greek. 21The chief priests of the Jews protested to Pilate, "Do not write 'The King of the Jews,' but that this man claimed to be king of the Jews."

22Pilate answered, "What I have written, I have written."

23When the soldiers crucified Jesus, they took his clothes, dividing them into four shares, one for each of them, with the undergarment remaining. This garment was seamless, woven in one piece from top to bottom.

24"Let's not tear it," they said to one another. "Let's decide by lot who will get it."

This happened that the scripture might be fulfilled which said,

"They divided my garments among them
  and cast lots for my clothing."*a*

So this is what the soldiers did.

25Near the cross of Jesus stood his mother, his mother's sister, Mary the wife of Clopas, and Mary Magdalene. 26When Jesus saw his mother there, and the disciple whom he loved standing nearby, he said to his mother, "Dear woman, here is your son," 27and to the disciple, "Here is your mother." From that time on, this disciple took her into his home.

The Death of Jesus

19:29,30pp — Mt 27:48,50; Mk 15:36,37; Lk 23:36

28Later, knowing that all was now completed, and so that the Scripture would be fulfilled, Jesus said, "I am thirsty." 29A jar of wine vinegar was there, so they soaked a sponge in it, put the sponge on a stalk of the hyssop plant, and lifted it to Jesus' lips. 30When he had received the drink, Jesus said, "It is finished." With that, he bowed his head and gave up his spirit.

31Now it was the day of Preparation, and the next day was to be a special Sabbath. Because the Jews did not want the bodies left on the crosses during the Sabbath, they asked Pilate to have the legs broken and the bodies taken down. 32The soldiers therefore came and broke the legs of the first man who had been crucified with Jesus, and then those of the other. 33But when they came to Jesus and found that he was already dead, they did not break his legs. 34Instead, one of the

a 24 Psalm 22:18

soldiers pierced Jesus' side with a spear, bringing a sudden flow of blood and water. ³⁵The man who saw it has given testimony, and his testimony is true. He knows that he tells the truth, and he testifies so that you also may believe. ³⁶These things happened so that the scripture would be fulfilled: "Not one of his bones will be broken," ^a ³⁷and, as another scripture says, "They will look on the one they have pierced." ^b

The Burial of Jesus

19:38–42pp — Mt 27:57–61; Mk 15:42–47; Lk 23:50–56

³⁸Later, Joseph of Arimathea asked Pilate for the body of Jesus. Now Joseph was a disciple of Jesus, but secretly because he feared the Jews. With Pilate's permission, he came and took the body away. ³⁹He was accompanied by Nicodemus, the man who earlier had visited Jesus at night. Nicodemus brought a mixture of myrrh and aloes, about seventy-five pounds. ^c ⁴⁰Taking Jesus' body, the two of them wrapped it, with the spices, in strips of linen. This was in accordance with Jewish burial customs. ⁴¹At the place where Jesus was crucified, there was a garden, and in the garden a new tomb, in which no one had ever been laid. ⁴²Because it was the Jewish day of Preparation and since the tomb was nearby, they laid Jesus there.

The Empty Tomb

20:1–8pp — Mt 28:1–8; Mk 16:1–8; Lk 24:1–10

20 Early on the first day of the week, while it was still dark, Mary Magdalene went to the tomb and saw that the stone had been removed from the entrance. ²So she came running to Simon Peter and the other disciple, the one Jesus loved, and said, "They have taken the Lord out of the tomb, and we don't know where they have put him!"

³So Peter and the other disciple started for the tomb. ⁴Both were running, but the other disciple outran Peter and reached the tomb first. ⁵He bent over and looked in at the strips of linen lying there but did not go in. ⁶Then Simon Peter, who was behind him, arrived and went into the tomb. He saw the strips of linen lying there, ⁷as well as the burial cloth that had been around Jesus' head. The cloth was folded up by itself, separate from the linen. ⁸Finally the other disciple, who had reached the tomb first, also went inside. He saw and believed. ⁹(They still did not understand from Scripture that Jesus had to rise from the dead.)

Jesus Appears to Mary Magdalene

¹⁰Then the disciples went back to their homes, ¹¹but Mary stood outside the tomb crying. As she wept, she bent over to look into the tomb ¹²and saw two angels in white, seated where Jesus' body had been, one at the head and the other at the foot.

¹³They asked her, "Woman, why are you crying?"

"They have taken my Lord away," she said, "and I don't know where they have put him." ¹⁴At this, she turned around and saw Jesus standing there, but she did not realize that it was Jesus.

¹⁵"Woman," he said, "why are you crying? Who is it you are looking for?"

Thinking he was the gardener, she said, "Sir, if you have carried him away, tell me where you have put him, and I will get him."

¹⁶Jesus said to her, "Mary."

She turned toward him and cried out in Aramaic, "Rabboni!" (which means Teacher).

¹⁷Jesus said, "Do not hold on to me, for I have not yet returned to the Father. Go instead to my brothers and tell them, 'I am returning to my Father and your Father, to my God and your God.'"

¹⁸Mary Magdalene went to the disciples with the news: "I have seen the Lord!" And she told them that he had said these things to her.

Jesus Appears to His Disciples

¹⁹On the evening of that first day of the week, when the disciples were together, with the doors locked for fear of the Jews, Jesus came and stood among them and said, "Peace be with you!"

^a 36 Exodus 12:46; Num. 9:12; Psalm 34:20   ^b 37 Zech. 12:10
^c 39 Greek *a hundred litrai* (about 34 kilograms)

²⁰After he said this, he showed them his hands and side. The disciples were overjoyed when they saw the Lord.

²¹Again Jesus said, "Peace be with you! As the Father has sent me, I am sending you." ²²And with that he breathed on them and said, "Receive the Holy Spirit. ²³If you forgive anyone his sins, they are forgiven; if you do not forgive them, they are not forgiven."

Jesus Appears to Thomas

²⁴Now Thomas (called Didymus), one of the Twelve, was not with the disciples when Jesus came. ²⁵So the other disciples told him, "We have seen the Lord!"

But he said to them, "Unless I see the nail marks in his hands and put my finger where the nails were, and put my hand into his side, I will not believe it."

²⁶A week later his disciples were in the house again, and Thomas was with them. Though the doors were locked, Jesus came and stood among them and said, "Peace be with you!" ²⁷Then he said to Thomas, "Put your finger here; see my hands. Reach out your hand and put it into my side. Stop doubting and believe."

²⁸Thomas said to him, "My Lord and my God!"

²⁹Then Jesus told him, "Because you have seen me, you have believed; blessed are those who have not seen and yet have believed."

³⁰Jesus did many other miraculous signs in the presence of his disciples, which are not recorded in this book. ³¹But these are written that you may *ᵃ* believe that Jesus is the Christ, the Son of God, and that by believing you may have life in his name.

Jesus and the Miraculous Catch of Fish

21 Afterward Jesus appeared again to his disciples, by the Sea of Tiberias.*ᵇ* It happened this way: ²Simon Peter, Thomas (called Didymus), Nathanael from Cana in Galilee, the sons of Zebedee, and two other disciples were together. ³"I'm going out to fish," Simon Peter told them, and they said, "We'll go with you." So they went out and got into the boat, but that night they caught nothing.

⁴Early in the morning, Jesus stood on the shore, but the disciples did not realize that it was Jesus.

⁵He called out to them, "Friends, haven't you any fish?"

"No," they answered.

⁶He said, "Throw your net on the right side of the boat and you will find some." When they did, they were unable to haul the net in because of the large number of fish.

⁷Then the disciple whom Jesus loved said to Peter, "It is the Lord!" As soon as Simon Peter heard him say, "It is the Lord," he wrapped his outer garment around him (for he had taken it off) and jumped into the water. ⁸The other disciples followed in the boat, towing the net full of fish, for they were not far from shore, about a hundred yards.*ᶜ* ⁹When they landed, they saw a fire of burning coals there with fish on it, and some bread.

¹⁰Jesus said to them, "Bring some of the fish you have just caught."

¹¹Simon Peter climbed aboard and dragged the net ashore. It was full of large fish, 153, but even with so many the net was not torn. ¹²Jesus said to them, "Come and have breakfast." None of the disciples dared ask him, "Who are you?" They knew it was the Lord. ¹³Jesus came, took the bread and gave it to them, and did the same

---

TALKING POINTS

Doubt

Jesus addressed Thomas' doubts.

JOHN 20:24–29

For more on doubt, go to Jude 20–22.

ᵃ 31 Some manuscripts *may continue to*   *ᵇ 1* That is, Sea of Galilee   *ᶜ 8* Greek *about two hundred cubits* (about 90 meters) with the fish. [14] This was now the third time Jesus appeared to his disciples after he was raised from the dead.

Jesus Reinstates Peter

[15] When they had finished eating, Jesus said to Simon Peter, "Simon son of John, do you truly love me more than these?"

"Yes, Lord," he said, "you know that I love you."

Jesus said, "Feed my lambs."

[16] Again Jesus said, "Simon son of John, do you truly love me?"

He answered, "Yes, Lord, you know that I love you."

Jesus said, "Take care of my sheep."

[17] The third time he said to him, "Simon son of John, do you love me?"

Peter was hurt because Jesus asked him the third time, "Do you love me?" He said, "Lord, you know all things; you know that I love you."

Jesus said, "Feed my sheep. [18] I tell you the truth, when you were younger you dressed yourself and went where you wanted; but when you are old you will stretch out your hands, and some-one else will dress you and lead you where you do not want to go." [19] Jesus said this to indicate the kind of death by which Peter would glorify God. Then he said to him, "Follow me!"

[20] Peter turned and saw that the disciple whom Jesus loved was following them. (This was the one who had leaned back against Jesus at the supper and had said, "Lord, who is going to betray you?") [21] When Peter saw him, he asked, "Lord, what about him?"

[22] Jesus answered, "If I want him to remain alive until I return, what is that to you? You must follow me." [23] Because of this, the rumor spread among the brothers that this disciple would not die. But Jesus did not say that he would not die; he only said, "If I want him to remain alive until I return, what is that to you?"

[24] This is the disciple who testifies to these things and who wrote them down. We know that his testimony is true.

[25] Jesus did many other things as well. If every one of them were written down, I suppose that even the whole world would not have room for the books that would be written.

Actions
AND WORDS

Nothing could stop them from talking about Jesus. They had been thrown into prison because of it and had been warned repeatedly, but Peter and John boldly declared that they could not stop. They had been with Jesus; they believed in him and the power of his resurrection. Nothing and no one would stop them from talking about the Savior.

The book of Acts is filled with the great stories of the early church. Like Peter and John, most of the early believers were ordinary people, unschooled yet knowledgeable about what was most important (see Acts 4:13). Most of them hadn't been trained in the synagogue, but they were capable preachers and teachers because they taught what they were most excited about — the good news about Jesus.

As grandmothers we can relate to talking about what excites us most. Give us an opportunity, and we'll be more than happy to talk about our grandchildren. It's natural; we just cannot keep quiet about the ones who fill our lives with joy. We should be equally enthusiastic about telling others and our grandchildren about Jesus — just like the new believers in the early Christian church did. We don't need special training or years of schooling; we just need to share what Jesus has done for us.

VERSE *to* REMEMBER | ACTS 4:19 – 20

Peter and John replied, "Judge for yourselves whether it is right in God's sight to obey you rather than God. For we cannot help speaking about what we have seen and heard."

ABOUT ACTS

WRITTEN BY:
Luke, the author of the Gospel of Luke

WRITTEN FOR:
Specifically for Theophilus, but also for everyone who wants to know what happened in the early church

DATE WRITTEN:
Probably around A.D. 63

WHY WRITTEN:
To tell how the Christian faith spread to the ends of the earth

Jesus Taken Up Into Heaven

1 In my former book, Theophilus, I wrote about all that Jesus began to do and to teach ²until the day he was taken up to heaven, after giving instructions through the Holy Spirit to the apostles he had chosen. ³After his suffering, he showed himself to these men and gave many convincing proofs that he was alive. He appeared to them over a period of forty days and spoke about the kingdom of God. ⁴On one occasion, while he was eating with them, he gave them this command: "Do not leave Jerusalem, but wait for the gift my Father promised, which you have heard me speak about. ⁵For John baptized with ᵃ water, but in a few days you will be baptized with the Holy Spirit."

⁶So when they met together, they asked him, "Lord, are you at this time going to restore the kingdom to Israel?"

⁷He said to them: "It is not for you to know the times or dates the Father has set by his own authority. ⁸But you will receive power when the Holy Spirit comes on you; and you will be my witnesses in Jerusalem, and in all Judea and Samaria, and to the ends of the earth."

⁹After he said this, he was taken up before their very eyes, and a cloud hid him from their sight. ¹⁰They were looking intently up into the sky as he was going, when suddenly two men dressed in white stood beside them. ¹¹"Men of Galilee," they said, "why do you stand here looking into the sky? This same Jesus, who has been taken from you into heaven, will come back in the same way you have seen him go into heaven."

Matthias Chosen to Replace Judas

¹²Then they returned to Jerusalem from the hill called the Mount of Olives, a Sabbath day's walk ᵇ from the city. ¹³When they arrived, they went upstairs to the room where they were staying. Those present were Peter, John, James and Andrew; Philip and Thomas, Bartholomew and Matthew; James son of Alphaeus and Simon the Zealot, and Judas son of James. ¹⁴They all joined

---

stories to share

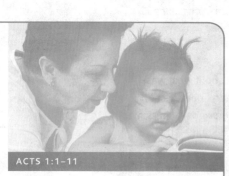

ACTS 1:1–11

Jesus Taken Up Into Heaven

LIFE LESSON: The Holy Spirit empowers us to be Christ's representatives.

TO TALK ABOUT

✦ For what "gift" (verse 4) were Jesus' disciples to wait in Jerusalem?

✦ What did Jesus say would be the result of the Holy Spirit coming on them?

✦ How can the Holy Spirit give *you* the power to be a witness for Jesus?

✦ What happened next? What did the two angels promise?

TALKING POINTS

Sharing Your Faith
The Holy Spirit gives us power to share our faith.
ACTS 1:8

For more on sharing your faith, go to Acts 8:29–35.

ᵃ 5 Or in   ᵇ 12 That is, about 3/4 mile (about 1,100 meters)

"BUT YOU WILL RECEIVE POWER WHEN THE HOLY SPIRIT COMES ON YOU; AND YOU WILL BE MY WITNESSES IN JERUSALEM, AND IN ALL JUDEA AND SAMARIA, AND TO THE ENDS OF THE EARTH."

Acts 1:8

Power to Serve

ANNE ORTLUND

READ | ACTS 1:1 – 11

If you're in a romantic mood, here's a poem I wrote to my husband, Ray, more than 60 years ago:

Sonnet for Just Us

"I want to train for mission work," you say;
"That's what I'm praying for," I answer you.
(The rows of lights down Colton Avenue
Make buttons for its coat of evening grey.)
"I hope for untried fields to conquer, Ray . . ."
And you reply, "That's just what I want,
    too . . ."
(Our talk is cool and unexcited through
The hum of leaves and crickets far away.)
But a shining thought, a trembling,
    blazing thing
Hangs over us, unspoken, shimmering.
Because of it your hand is warm on mine,
And all the world seems challenging and fine:
    "Before us lands of sin-sick millions lie;
    Oh, why not go together — you and I?"

> ## GRANDCHILD **IN FOCUS** · PRAYER
>
> ### Courage
>
> *O Father, builder of character and courage, may my grandchild grow strong in the light of your love. Grant him courage to stand for what is right, to guard the truth and to ensure justice in every aspect of life. May he boldly grow in grace, revere your name and proudly proclaim you as the Lord of lords and King of kings. Amen.*

    Twenty years and several mission board rejections later, Ray was a tired pastor asking for a fresh word from God. Sitting on a rock in the woods of Colorado, God gave him Acts 1:8.
    Over the next 30 years God sent us to minister many times over to every continent except Antarctica.
    Open your eyes, friend, to this vast, needy world! And pray with us Psalm 67:1 – 2: "May God be gracious to us and bless us and make his face shine upon us, that your ways may be known on earth, your salvation among all nations"!

Dear Lord and Savior, open my eyes to the needs of the world. Let me see how I can bring the news of salvation to others — whether they are on other continents or in my own backyard. Amen.

Your next devotion is located on page 1485.

together constantly in prayer, along with the women and Mary the mother of Jesus, and with his brothers.

[15] In those days Peter stood up among the believers[a] (a group numbering about a hundred and twenty) [16] and said, "Brothers, the Scripture had to be fulfilled which the Holy Spirit spoke long ago through the mouth of David concerning Judas, who served as guide for those who arrested Jesus— [17] he was one of our number and shared in this ministry."

[18] (With the reward he got for his wickedness, Judas bought a field; there he fell headlong, his body burst open and all his intestines spilled out. [19] Everyone in Jerusalem heard about this, so they called that field in their language Akeldama, that is, Field of Blood.)

[20] "For," said Peter, "it is written in the book of Psalms,

" 'May his place be deserted;
 let there be no one to dwell in it,'[b]

and,

" 'May another take his place of leadership.'[c]

[21] Therefore it is necessary to choose one of the men who have been with us the whole time the Lord Jesus went in and out among us, [22] beginning from John's baptism to the time when Jesus was taken up from us. For one of these must become a witness with us of his resurrection."

[23] So they proposed two men: Joseph called Barsabbas (also known as Justus) and Matthias. [24] Then they prayed, "Lord, you know everyone's heart. Show us which of these two you have chosen [25] to take over this apostolic ministry, which Judas left to go where he belongs." [26] Then they cast lots, and the lot fell to Matthias; so he was added to the eleven apostles.

The Holy Spirit Comes at Pentecost

2 When the day of Pentecost came, they were all together in one place. [2] Suddenly a sound like the blowing of a violent wind came from heaven and filled the whole house where they were sitting. [3] They saw what seemed to be tongues of fire that separated and came to rest on each of them. [4] All of them were filled with the Holy Spirit and began to speak in other tongues[d] as the Spirit enabled them.

[5] Now there were staying in Jerusalem God-fearing Jews from every nation under heaven. [6] When they heard this sound, a crowd came together in bewilderment, because each one heard them speaking in his own language. [7] Utterly amazed, they asked: "Are not all these men who are speaking Galileans? [8] Then how is it that each of us hears them in his own native language? [9] Parthians, Medes and Elamites; residents of Mesopotamia, Judea and Cappadocia, Pontus and Asia, [10] Phrygia and Pamphylia, Egypt and the parts of Libya near Cyrene; visitors from Rome [11] (both Jews and converts to Judaism); Cretans and Arabs—we hear them declaring the wonders of God in our own tongues!" [12] Amazed and perplexed, they asked one another, "What does this mean?"

[13] Some, however, made fun of them and said, "They have had too much wine.[e]"

Peter Addresses the Crowd

[14] Then Peter stood up with the Eleven, raised his voice and addressed the crowd: "Fellow Jews and all of you who live in Jerusalem, let me explain this to you; listen carefully to what I say. [15] These men are not drunk, as you suppose. It's only nine in the morning! [16] No, this is what was spoken by the prophet Joel:

[17] " 'In the last days, God says,
 I will pour out my Spirit on all people.
 Your sons and daughters will prophesy,
  your young men will see visions,
  your old men will dream dreams.
[18] Even on my servants, both men and women,
  I will pour out my Spirit in those days,
  and they will prophesy.
[19] I will show wonders in the heaven above
  and signs on the earth below,
  blood and fire and billows of smoke.

---

[a] 15 Greek *brothers*   [b] 20 Psalm 69:25   [c] 20 Psalm 109:8
[d] 4 Or *languages*; also in verse 11   [e] 13 Or *sweet wine*

WHEN THEY HEARD THIS SOUND,
A CROWD CAME TOGETHER IN
BEWILDERMENT, BECAUSE EACH
ONE HEARD THEM SPEAKING IN
HIS OWN LANGUAGE.

Acts 2:6

Babel, Pentecost, Heaven

BARBARA OWEN

READ | ACTS 2:1 – 13

I was at worship in a large chapel on a seminary campus. The bulletin noted that one of the presiding ministers was visiting from Germany. I knew that this happened occasionally; a visiting instructor would come, often bringing some of his own students.

We sang the hymns and chanted the psalm. Soon we were going to the altar for Holy Communion. We stood in a circle around the altar. "The body of Christ, given for you," said the officiant to me.

"Amen." I accepted the bread.

"Das ist der Leib Jesus Christus," said the officiant to the young man next to me.

I blinked in surprise, but the young man smiled and accepted the bread offered in German. He had sat in our pew, seemingly alone in his thoughts till now. Suddenly, by use of his native tongue, he was brought into the fold. Wondrous thoughts of our great God washed over me — of the immensity of the kingdom of God, including people of many languages.

The people in Jerusalem on the [day of] Pentecost felt some of this as they heard the gospel in their own language. The Tower of Babel experience had divided them, but the Pentecost experience made them one again, this time in Christ.

And I was one with this young man from Germany, as we had shared the body and blood of Christ in different languages. I thought about heaven, our destination, where we will all have one language again.

Jesus, in your death and resurrection and gift of the Holy Spirit you have brought us together, people of all colors and languages and nationalities. I rejoice in the community you have given me to enjoy and to love.

Your next devotion is located on page 1488.

GRANDCHILD IN FOCUS • PRAYER

Future Spouse

Dear Lord, if it is your will, I pray my grandchild will be united in a loving and Christian marriage. Keep her sexually pure so that she will honor you with her body and mind. As she seeks a spouse who will honor and care for her, give her patience and discernment. May her choice for a life partner be your choice for her, so that she and her husband will together glorify you in a lasting love. I pray this in Jesus' name, amen.

²⁰ The sun will be turned to darkness
  and the moon to blood
  before the coming of the great and
    glorious day of the Lord.
²¹ And everyone who calls
  on the name of the Lord will be saved.'ᵃ

²² "Men of Israel, listen to this: Jesus of Nazareth was a man accredited by God to you by miracles, wonders and signs, which God did among you through him, as you yourselves know. ²³ This man was handed over to you by God's set purpose and foreknowledge; and you, with the help of wicked men,ᵇ put him to death by nailing him to the cross. ²⁴ But God raised him from the dead, freeing him from the agony of death, because it was impossible for death to keep its hold on him. ²⁵ David said about him:

" 'I saw the Lord always before me.
  Because he is at my right hand,
  I will not be shaken.
²⁶ Therefore my heart is glad and my tongue
    rejoices;
  my body also will live in hope,
²⁷ because you will not abandon me to the
    grave,
  nor will you let your Holy One see decay.
²⁸ You have made known to me the paths of life;
  you will fill me with joy in your presence.'ᶜ

²⁹ "Brothers, I can tell you confidently that the patriarch David died and was buried, and his tomb is here to this day. ³⁰ But he was a prophet and knew that God had promised him on oath that he would place one of his descendants on his throne. ³¹ Seeing what was ahead, he spoke of the resurrection of the Christ,ᵈ that he was not abandoned to the grave, nor did his body see decay. ³² God has raised this Jesus to life, and we are all witnesses of the fact. ³³ Exalted to the right hand of God, he has received from the Father the promised Holy Spirit and has poured out what you now see and hear. ³⁴ For David did not ascend to heaven, and yet he said,

" 'The Lord said to my Lord:
  "Sit at my right hand

stories to share

ACTS 2:1–47

The Early Christian Church

LIFE LESSON: After Jesus left Earth, he sent his Spirit to live in the hearts of his people.

TO TALK ABOUT

✦ What happened to Jesus' followers on the day of Pentecost?

✦ What did Peter tell the people who believed his words to do?

✦ How many people joined the church on that day?

✦ How was God with his early church? How is he with his worldwide church today?

³⁵ until I make your enemies
  a footstool for your feet." 'ᵉ

³⁶ "Therefore let all Israel be assured of this: God has made this Jesus, whom you crucified, both Lord and Christ."

³⁷ When the people heard this, they were cut to the heart and said to Peter and the other apostles, "Brothers, what shall we do?"

³⁸ Peter replied, "Repent and be baptized, every one of you, in the name of Jesus Christ for the forgiveness of your sins. And you will receive the gift

ᵃ 21 Joel 2:28-32   ᵇ 23 Or of those not having the law (that is, Gentiles)   ᶜ 28 Psalm 16:8-11   ᵈ 31 Or Messiah. "The Christ" (Greek) and "the Messiah" (Hebrew) both mean "the Anointed One"; also in verse 36.   ᵉ 35 Psalm 110:1

of the Holy Spirit. ³⁹The promise is for you and your children and for all who are far off—for all whom the Lord our God will call."

⁴⁰With many other words he warned them; and he pleaded with them, "Save yourselves from this corrupt generation." ⁴¹Those who accepted his message were baptized, and about three thousand were added to their number that day.

The Fellowship of the Believers

⁴²They devoted themselves to the apostles' teaching and to the fellowship, to the breaking of bread and to prayer. ⁴³Everyone was filled with awe, and many wonders and miraculous signs were done by the apostles. ⁴⁴All the believers were together and had everything in common. ⁴⁵Selling their possessions and goods, they gave to anyone as he had need. ⁴⁶Every day they continued to meet together in the temple courts. They broke bread in their homes and ate together with glad and sincere hearts, ⁴⁷praising God and enjoying the favor of all the people. And the Lord added to their number daily those who were being saved.

Peter Heals the Crippled Beggar

3 One day Peter and John were going up to the temple at the time of prayer—at three in the afternoon. ²Now a man crippled from birth was being carried to the temple gate called Beautiful, where he was put every day to beg from those going into the temple courts. ³When he saw Peter and John about to enter, he asked them for money. ⁴Peter looked straight at him, as did John. Then Peter said, "Look at us!" ⁵So the man gave them his attention, expecting to get something from them.

⁶Then Peter said, "Silver or gold I do not have, but what I have I give you. In the name of Jesus Christ of Nazareth, walk." ⁷Taking him by the right hand, he helped him up, and instantly the man's feet and ankles became strong. ⁸He jumped to his feet and began to walk. Then he went with them into the temple courts, walking and jumping, and praising God. ⁹When all the people saw him walking and praising God, ¹⁰they recognized him as the same man who used to sit begging at the temple gate called Beautiful, and they were filled with wonder and amazement at what had happened to him.

stories to share

ACTS 3:1–10

Peter Heals the Crippled Beggar

LIFE LESSON: God sometimes chooses to cure people miraculously.

TO TALK ABOUT

✦ What did the crippled beggar ask Peter and John to give him?

✦ What did Peter give him instead?

✦ Is it all right to pray for a miraculous recovery when someone we love is sick?

✦ How are we to respond if God chooses not to heal that person?

Peter Speaks to the Onlookers

¹¹While the beggar held on to Peter and John, all the people were astonished and came running to them in the place called Solomon's Colonnade. ¹²When Peter saw this, he said to them: "Men of Israel, why does this surprise you? Why do you stare at us as if by our own power or godliness we had made this man walk? ¹³The God of Abraham, Isaac and Jacob, the God of our fathers, has glorified his servant Jesus. You handed him over to be killed, and you disowned him before Pilate,

> "YOU HAVE MADE KNOWN
> TO ME THE PATHS OF LIFE;
> YOU WILL FILL ME WITH JOY
> IN YOUR PRESENCE."
>
> Acts 2:28

Special Moments

SHEILA WALSH

READ | ACTS 2:14–41

I had one of those moments today. I was standing in the kitchen as the sun was setting behind the hills. Lights were beginning to dot the hillside, and the temperature was dropping to a comfortable place. Bentley was in the yard, lying peacefully by the flower beds, eating a bone, and I could hear Barry singing in the shower. I looked across the kitchen into the den, and my eyes rested on the navy blue stroller we have purchased for our son.

I put the kettle on to boil water for tea. As I opened the refrigerator to get the milk, I stopped to look at the photographs of family and friends that grace the door.

Suddenly I felt as if my heart was overflowing with praise to God for his goodness to me. I was surrounded by all the things that remind me of the grace and mercy of the Lord. I felt the baby kick and went to join Bentley in the evening air.

I prayed, "Lord, there are no words that could even begin to thank you for all you have done for me. I feel as if I am the richest woman on the planet. I pray for this little one moving inside of me that he will grow up to know you intimately for himself. Please help Barry and me to love him and prepare him to stand on his own with you." The next moments of silence felt holy, as if all I could do was rest in the presence of the Lord.

We look for spiritual moments in places where we think they should occur, as we gather to worship or as we kneel in prayer, but sometimes we are gifted — when it seems as if the Lord graciously allows his glory to visit our kitchen. Let us savor those moments when no one else can see us and nothing intrudes into our vision but Christ alone. Savor the moment and rest in him.

Jesus, in you I live and breathe and have my being. Thank you for the precious and unexpected moments when you visit me with your glory. Teach me to pause and savor them as I become more and more aware that you are always only a breath away.

GRANDCHILD IN FOCUS · PRAYER

School/Career

Dear God, may learning be a joy rather than a chore for my grandchild. May exploration of new ideas bring a sense of wonder, awe and excitement. Grant him clarity of mind, the ability to concentrate on the task at hand and recollection of what has been learned. Help him to appreciate the tasks that come easily and to persevere through those that challenge. Amen.

Your next devotion is located on page 1490.

though he had decided to let him go. ¹⁴You disowned the Holy and Righteous One and asked that a murderer be released to you. ¹⁵You killed the author of life, but God raised him from the dead. We are witnesses of this. ¹⁶By faith in the name of Jesus, this man whom you see and know was made strong. It is Jesus' name and the faith that comes through him that has given this complete healing to him, as you can all see.

¹⁷"Now, brothers, I know that you acted in ignorance, as did your leaders. ¹⁸But this is how God fulfilled what he had foretold through all the prophets, saying that his Christ ª would suffer. ¹⁹Repent, then, and turn to God, so that your sins may be wiped out, that times of refreshing may come from the Lord, ²⁰and that he may send the Christ, who has been appointed for you—even Jesus. ²¹He must remain in heaven until the time comes for God to restore everything, as he promised long ago through his holy prophets. ²²For Moses said, 'The Lord your God will raise up for you a prophet like me from among your own people; you must listen to everything he tells you. ²³Anyone who does not listen to him will be completely cut off from among his people.' ᵇ

²⁴"Indeed, all the prophets from Samuel on, as many as have spoken, have foretold these days. ²⁵And you are heirs of the prophets and of the covenant God made with your fathers. He said to Abraham, 'Through your offspring all peoples on earth will be blessed.' ᶜ ²⁶When God raised up his servant, he sent him first to you to bless you by turning each of you from your wicked ways."

Peter and John Before the Sanhedrin

4 The priests and the captain of the temple guard and the Sadducees came up to Peter and John while they were speaking to the people. ²They were greatly disturbed because the apostles were teaching the people and proclaiming in Jesus the resurrection of the dead. ³They seized Peter and John, and because it was evening, they put them in jail until the next day. ⁴But many who heard the message believed, and the number of men grew to about five thousand.

⁵The next day the rulers, elders and teachers of the law met in Jerusalem. ⁶Annas the high priest was there, and so were Caiaphas, John, Alexander and the other men of the high priest's family. ⁷They had Peter and John brought before them and began to question them: "By what power or what name did you do this?"

⁸Then Peter, filled with the Holy Spirit, said to them: "Rulers and elders of the people! ⁹If we are being called to account today for an act of kindness shown to a cripple and are asked how he was healed, ¹⁰then know this, you and all the people of Israel: It is by the name of Jesus Christ of Nazareth, whom you crucified but whom God raised from the dead, that this man stands before you healed. ¹¹He is

" 'the stone you builders rejected,
    which has become the capstone.' ᵈ ᵉ

¹²Salvation is found in no one else, for there is no other name under heaven given to men by which we must be saved."

PRAYING THE SCRIPTURES

Salvation

ACTS 4:12

Father, I pray that my grandchild will come to acknowledge that salvation is found only in Jesus Christ — that there is no other name by which we can and must be saved.

Next prayer in Salvation Prayer Track: Acts 20:21

¹³When they saw the courage of Peter and John and realized that they were unschooled, ordinary men, they were astonished and they took note that these men had been with Jesus. ¹⁴But since they could see the man who had been healed standing there with them, there was

---

ª 18 Or *Messiah*; also in verse 20   ᵇ 23 Deut. 18:15,18,19
ᶜ 25 Gen. 22:18; 26:4   ᵈ 11 Or *cornerstone*   ᵉ 11 Psalm 118:22

Family Art Gallery

Explain to your grandkids in advance that you'd like to display some of their best artwork in a "gallery," either at home or in a community room or other larger setting. If your older, artistically inclined grandchildren have a portfolio from which to select pieces, ask them to lend you their best works. Younger school-aged children most likely have projects at home that would display well, and the youngest ones will be proud of their latest "masterpieces." Encourage everyone to give their work a title, so you can identify each piece by title and artist's name.

You might want to surprise the children by including some of their parents' childhood or adult creations, as well as your own.

On the evening of your art show, invite the adult relatives, as well as the children, to view the gallery and enjoy refreshments.

Long-Distance Variation: Invite your grandchildren to submit their work via mail. Promise to handle it carefully and return it after the event. You may want to videotape or take pictures of the event to send to them later.

Creator God, thank you for the creativity you've instilled in each of us. Help each one in our family to appreciate their own imagination and that of others, and to delight in each other's unique gifts and talents. Amen.

Your next devotion is located on page 1493.

GRANDCHILD IN FOCUS • PRAYER

Character

Dear Lord and Father, I ask that you fill my grandchild with your Spirit so her character reflects your goodness and love. Give her kindness and love for others. Bring joy to her life so she will be a joy to others. Grant her patience and self-control through difficult and trying times. May she show mercy and generosity to those who are less fortunate. Grant her integrity and a sense of justice, and surround her with your peace. Amen.

nothing they could say. ¹⁵So they ordered them to withdraw from the Sanhedrin and then conferred together. ¹⁶"What are we going to do with these men?" they asked. "Everybody living in Jerusalem knows they have done an outstanding miracle, and we cannot deny it. ¹⁷But to stop this thing from spreading any further among the people, we must warn these men to speak no longer to anyone in this name."

¹⁸Then they called them in again and commanded them not to speak or teach at all in the name of Jesus. ¹⁹But Peter and John replied, "Judge for yourselves whether it is right in God's sight to obey you rather than God. ²⁰For we cannot help speaking about what we have seen and heard."

²¹After further threats they let them go. They could not decide how to punish them, because all the people were praising God for what had happened. ²²For the man who was miraculously healed was over forty years old.

The Believers' Prayer

²³On their release, Peter and John went back to their own people and reported all that the chief priests and elders had said to them. ²⁴When they heard this, they raised their voices together in prayer to God. "Sovereign Lord," they said, "you made the heaven and the earth and the sea, and everything in them. ²⁵You spoke by the Holy Spirit through the mouth of your servant, our father David:

" 'Why do the nations rage
    and the peoples plot in vain?
²⁶The kings of the earth take their stand
    and the rulers gather together
against the Lord
    and against his Anointed One.'ᵃᵇ

²⁷Indeed Herod and Pontius Pilate met together with the Gentiles and the peopleᶜ of Israel in this city to conspire against your holy servant Jesus, whom you anointed. ²⁸They did what your power and will had decided beforehand should happen. ²⁹Now, Lord, consider their threats and enable your servants to speak your word with great boldness. ³⁰Stretch out your hand to heal and perform miraculous signs and wonders through the name of your holy servant Jesus."

PRAYING THE SCRIPTURES

Well-Being
ACTS 4:30
O Lord, stretch out your hand, I pray, to heal my grandchild; perform a miracle on her behalf through the name of your holy servant Jesus.

Next prayer in Well-being Prayer Track: Ephesians 6:10

³¹After they prayed, the place where they were meeting was shaken. And they were all filled with the Holy Spirit and spoke the word of God boldly.

The Believers Share Their Possessions

³²All the believers were one in heart and mind. No one claimed that any of his possessions was his own, but they shared everything they had. ³³With great power the apostles continued to testify to the resurrection of the Lord Jesus, and much grace was upon them all. ³⁴There were no needy persons among them. For from time to time those who owned lands or houses sold them, brought the money from the sales ³⁵and put it at the apostles' feet, and it was distributed to anyone as he had need.

³⁶Joseph, a Levite from Cyprus, whom the apostles called Barnabas (which means Son of Encouragement), ³⁷sold a field he owned and brought the money and put it at the apostles' feet.

Ananias and Sapphira

5 Now a man named Ananias, together with his wife Sapphira, also sold a piece of property. ²With his wife's full knowledge he kept back part

ᵃ 26 That is, Christ or Messiah   ᵇ 26 Psalm 2:1,2
ᶜ 27 The Greek is plural.

of the money for himself, but brought the rest and put it at the apostles' feet.

³Then Peter said, "Ananias, how is it that Satan has so filled your heart that you have lied to the Holy Spirit and have kept for yourself some of the money you received for the land? ⁴Didn't it belong to you before it was sold? And after it was sold, wasn't the money at your disposal? What made you think of doing such a thing? You have not lied to men but to God."

⁵When Ananias heard this, he fell down and died. And great fear seized all who heard what had happened. ⁶Then the young men came forward, wrapped up his body, and carried him out and buried him.

⁷About three hours later his wife came in, not knowing what had happened. ⁸Peter asked her, "Tell me, is this the price you and Ananias got for the land?"

"Yes," she said, "that is the price."

⁹Peter said to her, "How could you agree to test the Spirit of the Lord? Look! The feet of the men who buried your husband are at the door, and they will carry you out also."

¹⁰At that moment she fell down at his feet and died. Then the young men came in and, finding her dead, carried her out and buried her beside her husband. ¹¹Great fear seized the whole church and all who heard about these events.

The Apostles Heal Many

¹²The apostles performed many miraculous signs and wonders among the people. And all the believers used to meet together in Solomon's Colonnade. ¹³No one else dared join them, even though they were highly regarded by the people. ¹⁴Nevertheless, more and more men and women believed in the Lord and were added to their number. ¹⁵As a result, people brought the sick into the streets and laid them on beds and mats so that at least Peter's shadow might fall on some of them as he passed by. ¹⁶Crowds gathered also from the towns around Jerusalem, bringing their sick and those tormented by evil[a] spirits, and all of them were healed.

The Apostles Persecuted

¹⁷Then the high priest and all his associates, who were members of the party of the Sadducees, were filled with jealousy. ¹⁸They arrested the apostles and put them in the public jail. ¹⁹But during the night an angel of the Lord opened the doors of the jail and brought them out. ²⁰"Go, stand in the temple courts," he said, "and tell the people the full message of this new life."

²¹At daybreak they entered the temple courts, as they had been told, and began to teach the people.

When the high priest and his associates arrived, they called together the Sanhedrin—the full assembly of the elders of Israel—and sent to the jail for the apostles. ²²But on arriving at the jail, the officers did not find them there. So they went back and reported, ²³"We found the jail securely locked, with the guards standing at the doors; but when we opened them, we found no one inside." ²⁴On hearing this report, the captain of the temple guard and the chief priests were puzzled, wondering what would come of this.

²⁵Then someone came and said, "Look! The men you put in jail are standing in the temple courts teaching the people." ²⁶At that, the captain went with his officers and brought the apostles. They did not use force, because they feared that the people would stone them.

²⁷Having brought the apostles, they made them appear before the Sanhedrin to be questioned by the high priest. ²⁸"We gave you strict orders not to teach in this name," he said. "Yet you have filled Jerusalem with your teaching and are determined to make us guilty of this man's blood."

²⁹Peter and the other apostles replied: "We must obey God rather than men! ³⁰The God of our fathers raised Jesus from the dead—whom you had killed by hanging him on a tree. ³¹God exalted him to his own right hand as Prince and Savior that he might give repentance and forgiveness of sins to Israel. ³²We are witnesses of these

---

[a] 16 Greek *unclean*

Worship the Lord

Praise the LORD.

Give thanks to the LORD, for he is good;
  his love endures forever.
Who can proclaim the mighty acts of the LORD
  or fully declare his praise?
Blessed are they who maintain justice,
  who constantly do what is right.
Remember me, O LORD, when you show favor to your people,
  come to my aid when you save them,
that I may enjoy the prosperity of your chosen ones,
    that I may share in the joy of your nation
    and join your inheritance in giving praise.

Praise be to the LORD, the God of Israel,
  from everlasting to everlasting.
Let all the people say, "Amen!"

Praise the LORD.

Psalm 106:1–5,48

. . . .

*O Lord, it is good to praise your name.
Let me always be ready to tell others about
who you are and all that you do. Sustain me
as I work for justice and do what is right. Let
the world come to know you in spirit and in
truth so that everyone will praise your holy name.
Amen.*

Your next devotion is located on page 1495.

GRANDCHILD IN FOCUS • PRAYER

Talents

*Dear Lord, the giver of gifts, bless my
grandchild as he develops his talents. Help him
identify his talents and be proud and confident of
the gifts you have given him. Give him patience and
understanding, Lord, so he will not grow weary of
striving and searching to reach the goals you have
set for him. May each milestone bring satisfaction and a healthy desire for greater
achievement and success to bring
glory to you. Amen.*

things, and so is the Holy Spirit, whom God has given to those who obey him."

33 When they heard this, they were furious and wanted to put them to death. 34 But a Pharisee named Gamaliel, a teacher of the law, who was honored by all the people, stood up in the Sanhedrin and ordered that the men be put outside for a little while. 35 Then he addressed them: "Men of Israel, consider carefully what you intend to do to these men. 36 Some time ago Theudas appeared, claiming to be somebody, and about four hundred men rallied to him. He was killed, all his followers were dispersed, and it all came to nothing. 37 After him, Judas the Galilean appeared in the days of the census and led a band of people in revolt. He too was killed, and all his followers were scattered. 38 Therefore, in the present case I advise you: Leave these men alone! Let them go! For if their purpose or activity is of human origin, it will fail. 39 But if it is from God, you will not be able to stop these men; you will only find yourselves fighting against God."

40 His speech persuaded them. They called the apostles in and had them flogged. Then they ordered them not to speak in the name of Jesus, and let them go.

41 The apostles left the Sanhedrin, rejoicing because they had been counted worthy of suffering disgrace for the Name. 42 Day after day, in the temple courts and from house to house, they never stopped teaching and proclaiming the good news that Jesus is the Christ.[a]

The Choosing of the Seven

6 In those days when the number of disciples was increasing, the Grecian Jews among them complained against the Hebraic Jews because their widows were being overlooked in the daily distribution of food. 2 So the Twelve gathered all the disciples together and said, "It would not be right for us to neglect the ministry of the word of God in order to wait on tables. 3 Brothers, choose seven men from among you who are known to be full of the Spirit and wisdom. We will turn this responsibility over to them 4 and

will give our attention to prayer and the ministry of the word."

5 This proposal pleased the whole group. They chose Stephen, a man full of faith and of the Holy Spirit; also Philip, Procorus, Nicanor, Timon, Parmenas, and Nicolas from Antioch, a convert to Judaism. 6 They presented these men to the apostles, who prayed and laid their hands on them.

7 So the word of God spread. The number of disciples in Jerusalem increased rapidly, and a large number of priests became obedient to the faith.

Stephen Seized

8 Now Stephen, a man full of God's grace and power, did great wonders and miraculous signs among the people. 9 Opposition arose, however, from members of the Synagogue of the Freedmen (as it was called) — Jews of Cyrene and Alexandria as well as the provinces of Cilicia and Asia. These men began to argue with Stephen, 10 but they could not stand up against his wisdom or the Spirit by whom he spoke.

11 Then they secretly persuaded some men to say, "We have heard Stephen speak words of blasphemy against Moses and against God."

12 So they stirred up the people and the elders and the teachers of the law. They seized Stephen and brought him before the Sanhedrin. 13 They produced false witnesses, who testified, "This fellow never stops speaking against this holy place and against the law. 14 For we have heard him say that this Jesus of Nazareth will destroy this place and change the customs Moses handed down to us."

15 All who were sitting in the Sanhedrin looked intently at Stephen, and they saw that his face was like the face of an angel.

Stephen's Speech to the Sanhedrin

7 Then the high priest asked him, "Are these charges true?"

2 To this he replied: "Brothers and fathers, listen to me! The God of glory appeared to our father

a 42 Or Messiah

ALL WHO WERE SITTING IN THE
SANHEDRIN LOOKED INTENTLY
AT STEPHEN, AND THEY SAW
THAT HIS FACE WAS LIKE THE
FACE OF AN ANGEL.

Acts 6:15

Face of an Angel

DAWN SCOTT JONES

READ | ACTS 6:8–15

Grandmother was beaming with radiance. Her face shone with an indescribable glow. Her skin was smooth; her hands, once bent and arthritic, were resting relaxed and easy. She was passing from this life to the next, and she was beautiful — like a bride ready to meet her groom.

It was nothing like I had expected. I thought that there would be nervousness and fear. But when I entered my grandmother's room to say farewell and to tell her that I loved her, I was instantly enveloped by immense peace. God's comfort lingered in the air like a thick cloud.

Wondering why her countenance was so peaceful, I remembered the story of Stephen's martyrdom. Even his accusers saw that his face "was like the face of an angel" (Acts 6:15). And then just before the angry mob stoned him to death, "Stephen, full of the Holy Spirit, looked up to heaven and saw the glory of God, and Jesus standing at the right hand of God" (Acts 7:55). I wondered if Stephen, before he died, looked like Grandma did now. That's when it hit me: Death for the believer is the most intimate experience one will have with God. His presence is never closer.

Psalm 116:15 declares: "Precious in the sight of the LORD is the death of his saints." We are so valuable to the Lord that he guards our life and our death with great care and compassion. His peace will never leave us. His love will not forsake us. Nothing can separate us from God — not even death.

Standing in Grandma's room that day, a song filled my heart: "In mansions of glory and endless delight, I'll ever adore Thee in heaven so bright; I'll sing with the glittering crown on my brow: If ever I loved Thee, my Jesus, 'tis now." Grandma's hand extended to the heavens in worship. An ever so slight smile appeared ... and her face was like the face of an angel.

Precious Lord, thank you for your promise to never leave me or forsake me. Help me to live in the knowledge of your ever-abiding presence and power every day. I choose to lean on you, the Love that casts out all fear, and rest in your unfailing compassion. Amen.

Your next devotion is located on page 1498.

GRANDCHILD IN FOCUS • PRAYER

SELECT ONE OF YOUR
GRANDCHILDREN TO FOCUS ON
IN PRAYER FOR THE NEXT 14 DAYS.

Salvation

Dear Lord, please guide my grandchild to your gift of salvation. I pray that she will come to know you, to love you and to walk close to you throughout her life. May she boldly claim Jesus as her Lord and Savior. Guide her as she makes choices that have eternal consequences. Help her to follow you each moment of her life. I pray this in Jesus' name, amen.

1495

Abraham while he was still in Mesopotamia, before he lived in Haran. ³'Leave your country and your people,' God said, 'and go to the land I will show you.'ª

⁴"So he left the land of the Chaldeans and settled in Haran. After the death of his father, God sent him to this land where you are now living. ⁵He gave him no inheritance here, not even a foot of ground. But God promised him that he and his descendants after him would possess the land, even though at that time Abraham had no child. ⁶God spoke to him in this way: 'Your descendants will be strangers in a country not their own, and they will be enslaved and mistreated four hundred years. ⁷But I will punish the nation they serve as slaves,' God said, 'and afterward they will come out of that country and worship me in this place.'ᵇ ⁸Then he gave Abraham the covenant of circumcision. And Abraham became the father of Isaac and circumcised him eight days after his birth. Later Isaac became the father of Jacob, and Jacob became the father of the twelve patriarchs.

⁹"Because the patriarchs were jealous of Joseph, they sold him as a slave into Egypt. But God was with him ¹⁰and rescued him from all his troubles. He gave Joseph wisdom and enabled him to gain the goodwill of Pharaoh king of Egypt; so he made him ruler over Egypt and all his palace.

¹¹"Then a famine struck all Egypt and Canaan, bringing great suffering, and our fathers could not find food. ¹²When Jacob heard that there was grain in Egypt, he sent our fathers on their first visit. ¹³On their second visit, Joseph told his brothers who he was, and Pharaoh learned about Joseph's family. ¹⁴After this, Joseph sent for his father Jacob and his whole family, seventy-five in all. ¹⁵Then Jacob went down to Egypt, where he and our fathers died. ¹⁶Their bodies were brought back to Shechem and placed in the tomb that Abraham had bought from the sons of Hamor at Shechem for a certain sum of money.

¹⁷"As the time drew near for God to fulfill his promise to Abraham, the number of our people in Egypt greatly increased. ¹⁸Then another king, who knew nothing about Joseph, became ruler of Egypt. ¹⁹He dealt treacherously with our people and oppressed our forefathers by forcing them to throw out their newborn babies so that they would die.

²⁰"At that time Moses was born, and he was no ordinary child.ᶜ For three months he was cared for in his father's house. ²¹When he was placed outside, Pharaoh's daughter took him and brought him up as her own son. ²²Moses was educated in all the wisdom of the Egyptians and was powerful in speech and action.

²³"When Moses was forty years old, he decided to visit his fellow Israelites. ²⁴He saw one of them being mistreated by an Egyptian, so he went to his defense and avenged him by killing the Egyptian. ²⁵Moses thought that his own people would realize that God was using him to rescue them, but they did not. ²⁶The next day Moses came upon two Israelites who were fighting. He tried to reconcile them by saying, 'Men, you are brothers; why do you want to hurt each other?'

²⁷"But the man who was mistreating the other pushed Moses aside and said, 'Who made you ruler and judge over us? ²⁸Do you want to kill me as you killed the Egyptian yesterday?'ᵈ ²⁹When Moses heard this, he fled to Midian, where he settled as a foreigner and had two sons.

³⁰"After forty years had passed, an angel appeared to Moses in the flames of a burning bush in the desert near Mount Sinai. ³¹When he saw this, he was amazed at the sight. As he went over to look more closely, he heard the Lord's voice: ³²'I am the God of your fathers, the God of Abraham, Isaac and Jacob.'ᵉ Moses trembled with fear and did not dare to look.

³³"Then the Lord said to him, 'Take off your sandals; the place where you are standing is holy ground. ³⁴I have indeed seen the oppression of my people in Egypt. I have heard their groaning and have come down to set them free. Now come, I will send you back to Egypt.'ᶠ

³⁵"This is the same Moses whom they had re-

ª 3 Gen. 12:1   ᵇ 7 Gen. 15:13,14   ᶜ 20 Or *was fair in the sight of God*   ᵈ 28 Exodus 2:14   ᵉ 32 Exodus 3:6   ᶠ 34 Exodus 3:5,7,8,10 jected with the words, 'Who made you ruler and judge?' He was sent to be their ruler and deliverer by God himself, through the angel who appeared to him in the bush. ³⁶He led them out of Egypt and did wonders and miraculous signs in Egypt, at the Red Sea *a* and for forty years in the desert.

³⁷"This is that Moses who told the Israelites, 'God will send you a prophet like me from your own people.' *b* ³⁸He was in the assembly in the desert, with the angel who spoke to him on Mount Sinai, and with our fathers; and he received living words to pass on to us.

³⁹"But our fathers refused to obey him. Instead, they rejected him and in their hearts turned back to Egypt. ⁴⁰They told Aaron, 'Make us gods who will go before us. As for this fellow Moses who led us out of Egypt—we don't know what has happened to him!' *c* ⁴¹That was the time they made an idol in the form of a calf. They brought sacrifices to it and held a celebration in honor of what their hands had made. ⁴²But God turned away and gave them over to the worship of the heavenly bodies. This agrees with what is written in the book of the prophets:

" 'Did you bring me sacrifices and offerings
    forty years in the desert, O house of Israel?
⁴³You have lifted up the shrine of Molech
    and the star of your god Rephan,
    the idols you made to worship.
Therefore I will send you into exile' *d* beyond
    Babylon.

⁴⁴"Our forefathers had the tabernacle of the Testimony with them in the desert. It had been made as God directed Moses, according to the pattern he had seen. ⁴⁵Having received the tabernacle, our fathers under Joshua brought it with them when they took the land from the nations God drove out before them. It remained in the land until the time of David, ⁴⁶who enjoyed God's favor and asked that he might provide a dwelling place for the God of Jacob. *e* ⁴⁷But it was Solomon who built the house for him.

⁴⁸"However, the Most High does not live in houses made by men. As the prophet says:

⁴⁹" 'Heaven is my throne,
    and the earth is my footstool.
What kind of house will you build for me?
            says the Lord.
Or where will my resting place be?
⁵⁰Has not my hand made all these things?' *f*

⁵¹"You stiff-necked people, with uncircumcised hearts and ears! You are just like your fathers: You always resist the Holy Spirit! ⁵²Was there ever a prophet your fathers did not persecute? They even killed those who predicted the coming of the Righteous One. And now you have betrayed and murdered him— ⁵³you who have received the law that was put into effect through angels but have not obeyed it."

The Stoning of Stephen

⁵⁴When they heard this, they were furious and gnashed their teeth at him. ⁵⁵But Stephen, full of the Holy Spirit, looked up to heaven and saw the glory of God, and Jesus standing at the right hand of God. ⁵⁶"Look," he said, "I see heaven open and the Son of Man standing at the right hand of God."

⁵⁷At this they covered their ears and, yelling at the top of their voices, they all rushed at him, ⁵⁸dragged him out of the city and began to stone him. Meanwhile, the witnesses laid their clothes at the feet of a young man named Saul.

⁵⁹While they were stoning him, Stephen prayed, "Lord Jesus, receive my spirit." ⁶⁰Then he fell on his knees and cried out, "Lord, do not hold this sin against them." When he had said this, he fell asleep.

8 And Saul was there, giving approval to his death.

The Church Persecuted and Scattered

On that day a great persecution broke out against the church at Jerusalem, and all except the apostles were scattered throughout Judea and Samaria. ²Godly men buried Stephen and

a 36 That is, Sea of Reeds   *b 37* Deut. 18:15   *c 40* Exodus 32:1
d 43 Amos 5:25-27   *e 46* Some early manuscripts *the house of Jacob*   *f 50* Isaiah 66:1,2

THEN HE FELL ON HIS KNEES
AND CRIED OUT, "LORD, DO NOT
HOLD THIS SIN AGAINST THEM."
WHEN HE HAD SAID THIS, HE
FELL ASLEEP.

Acts 7:60

Let It Go!

THELMA WELLS

READ | ACTS 7:54 – 60

I was the fifth generation living in the 1940s: my mother, her mother, my mother's father's mother and her mother. Three generations lived in the same back-alley apartment in Dallas, Texas. I was raised by my great-grandmother, Sarah Harrell, who cared for her mother, my Grandma Molly, in that home.

I remember Grandma Molly as clearly today as I did 60 years ago. Her smooth black skin that had no wrinkles reminded me of someone who had oiled themselves with baby oil. Her tall, stately, erect posture and the twist on the back of her head rendered her sophisticated and royal. I watched her take her hair down at night and brush her long, silky black hair until it flowed like the mane of a well-kept stallion. Everything was right about Grandma Molly but one thing: she dipped snuff.

One day I heard an awful yell. Angry words bellowed from downstairs in the flower garden. It was my great-grandmother screaming at the top of her lungs, "Mama, didn't you see me down here? You spit that snuff in the middle of my head! Don't you ever do that again! You look before you spit!" Sarah's tirade continued. Daddy Harrell had to come to Grandma Molly's rescue and exclaimed, "Sweetie, that's enough. Molly feels bad enough; she didn't see you. She would not deliberately spit on you. Now, cut that noise out!" It was quite an argument.

Have you ever been hurt by someone who loves you? Whether they intended the harm or not, cut out that noise in your mind and heart, and let it go. Be inspired by Stephen, who reacted mercifully rather than vengefully toward those who were stoning him for his beliefs and convictions.

Understanding Father, when my feelings get hurt and I feel spit upon, please give me the mind and heart to forgive and let the hurt go. In Jesus' name, amen.

Your next devotion is located on page 1512.

GRANDCHILD IN FOCUS • PRAYER

Physical Well-Being

Almighty God, Creator of us all, I pray that you will watch over my grandchild's physical development. May he grow in strength through the stages of his life. As he grows in awareness of his body, help him to understand that each body develops uniquely, yet is within your plan and your control. Please guard his health so that his diseases are few, his injuries are minor and his infirmities are brief. Amen.

mourned deeply for him. ³But Saul began to destroy the church. Going from house to house, he dragged off men and women and put them in prison.

Philip in Samaria

⁴Those who had been scattered preached the word wherever they went. ⁵Philip went down to a city in Samaria and proclaimed the Christ *a* there. ⁶When the crowds heard Philip and saw the miraculous signs he did, they all paid close attention to what he said. ⁷With shrieks, evil *b* spirits came out of many, and many paralytics and cripples were healed. ⁸So there was great joy in that city.

Simon the Sorcerer

⁹Now for some time a man named Simon had practiced sorcery in the city and amazed all the people of Samaria. He boasted that he was someone great, ¹⁰and all the people, both high and low, gave him their attention and exclaimed, "This man is the divine power known as the Great Power." ¹¹They followed him because he had amazed them for a long time with his magic. ¹²But when they believed Philip as he preached the good news of the kingdom of God and the name of Jesus Christ, they were baptized, both men and women. ¹³Simon himself believed and was baptized. And he followed Philip everywhere, astonished by the great signs and miracles he saw.

¹⁴When the apostles in Jerusalem heard that Samaria had accepted the word of God, they sent Peter and John to them. ¹⁵When they arrived, they prayed for them that they might receive the Holy Spirit, ¹⁶because the Holy Spirit had not yet come upon any of them; they had simply been baptized into *c* the name of the Lord Jesus. ¹⁷Then Peter and John placed their hands on them, and they received the Holy Spirit.

¹⁸When Simon saw that the Spirit was given at the laying on of the apostles' hands, he offered them money ¹⁹and said, "Give me also this ability so that everyone on whom I lay my hands may receive the Holy Spirit."

²⁰Peter answered: "May your money perish with you, because you thought you could buy the gift of God with money! ²¹You have no part or share in this ministry, because your heart is not right before God. ²²Repent of this wickedness and pray to the Lord. Perhaps he will forgive you for having such a thought in your heart. ²³For I see that you are full of bitterness and captive to sin."

²⁴Then Simon answered, "Pray to the Lord for me so that nothing you have said may happen to me."

²⁵When they had testified and proclaimed the word of the Lord, Peter and John returned to Jerusalem, preaching the gospel in many Samaritan villages.

Philip and the Ethiopian

²⁶Now an angel of the Lord said to Philip, "Go south to the road—the desert road—that goes down from Jerusalem to Gaza." ²⁷So he started out, and on his way he met an Ethiopian *d* eunuch, an important official in charge of all the treasury of Candace, queen of the Ethiopians. This man had gone to Jerusalem to worship, ²⁸and on his way home was sitting in his chariot reading the book of Isaiah the prophet. ²⁹The Spirit told Philip, "Go to that chariot and stay near it."

³⁰Then Philip ran up to the chariot and heard the man reading Isaiah the prophet. "Do you understand what you are reading?" Philip asked.

³¹"How can I," he said, "unless someone explains it to me?" So he invited Philip to come up and sit with him.

³²The eunuch was reading this passage of Scripture:

"He was led like a sheep to the slaughter,
    and as a lamb before the shearer is silent,
    so he did not open his mouth.
³³In his humiliation he was deprived of justice.
    Who can speak of his descendants?
    For his life was taken from the earth." *e*

---

a 5 Or *Messiah*   *b 7* Greek *unclean*   *c 16* Or *in*   *d 27* That is, from the upper Nile region   *e 33* Isaiah 53:7,8

³⁴The eunuch asked Philip, "Tell me, please, who is the prophet talking about, himself or someone else?" ³⁵Then Philip began with that very passage of Scripture and told him the good news about Jesus.

³⁶As they traveled along the road, they came to some water and the eunuch said, "Look, here is water. Why shouldn't I be baptized?"ᵃ ³⁸And he gave orders to stop the chariot. Then both Philip and the eunuch went down into the water and Philip baptized him. ³⁹When they came up out of the water, the Spirit of the Lord suddenly took Philip away, and the eunuch did not see

TALKING POINTS

Sharing Your Faith
The Holy Spirit leads us
to share our faith.

ACTS 8:29–35

For more on sharing your faith, go to Acts 22:3–8.

him again, but went on his way rejoicing. ⁴⁰Philip, however, appeared at Azotus and traveled about, preaching the gospel in all the towns until he reached Caesarea.

Saul's Conversion
9:1–19pp — Ac 22:3–16; 26:9–18

9 Meanwhile, Saul was still breathing out murderous threats against the Lord's disciples. He went to the high priest ²and asked him for letters to the synagogues in Damascus, so that if he found any there who belonged to the Way, whether men or women, he might take them as prisoners to Jerusalem. ³As he neared Damascus on his journey, suddenly a light from heaven flashed around him. ⁴He fell to the ground and heard a voice say to him, "Saul, Saul, why do you persecute me?"

⁵"Who are you, Lord?" Saul asked.

"I am Jesus, whom you are persecuting," he replied. ⁶"Now get up and go into the city, and you will be told what you must do."

⁷The men traveling with Saul stood there speechless; they heard the sound but did not see anyone. ⁸Saul got up from the ground, but when he opened his eyes he could see nothing. So they led him by the hand into Damascus. ⁹For three days he was blind, and did not eat or drink anything.

¹⁰In Damascus there was a disciple named Ananias. The Lord called to him in a vision, "Ananias!"

ACTS 8:26–40

stories to share

Philip and the Ethiopian

LIFE LESSON: Following Jesus is a great adventure.

TO TALK ABOUT

✦ What did the angel instruct Philip to do?

✦ What was the result? When the Ethiopian got home, do you think he told others what happened to him?

✦ How can the witness of one person make a difference for many?

✦ How do you know when the Holy Spirit is asking you to do something?

ᵃ 36 Some late manuscripts *baptized?" ³⁷Philip said, "If you believe with all your heart, you may." The eunuch answered, "I believe that Jesus Christ is the Son of God."*

"Yes, Lord," he answered.

[11] The Lord told him, "Go to the house of Judas on Straight Street and ask for a man from Tarsus named Saul, for he is praying. [12] In a vision he has seen a man named Ananias come and place his hands on him to restore his sight."

[13] "Lord," Ananias answered, "I have heard many reports about this man and all the harm he has done to your saints in Jerusalem. [14] And he has come here with authority from the chief priests to arrest all who call on your name."

[15] But the Lord said to Ananias, "Go! This man is my chosen instrument to carry my name before the Gentiles and their kings and before the people of Israel. [16] I will show him how much he must suffer for my name."

[17] Then Ananias went to the house and entered it. Placing his hands on Saul, he said, "Brother Saul, the Lord—Jesus, who appeared to you on the road as you were coming here—has sent me so that you may see again and be filled with the Holy Spirit." [18] Immediately, something like scales fell from Saul's eyes, and he could see again. He got up and was baptized, [19] and after taking some food, he regained his strength.

Saul in Damascus and Jerusalem

Saul spent several days with the disciples in Damascus. [20] At once he began to preach in the synagogues that Jesus is the Son of God. [21] All those who heard him were astonished and asked, "Isn't he the man who raised havoc in Jerusalem among those who call on this name? And hasn't he come here to take them as prisoners to the chief priests?" [22] Yet Saul grew more and more powerful and baffled the Jews living in Damascus by proving that Jesus is the Christ.[a]

[23] After many days had gone by, the Jews conspired to kill him, [24] but Saul learned of their plan. Day and night they kept close watch on the city gates in order to kill him. [25] But his followers took him by night and lowered him in a basket through an opening in the wall.

[26] When he came to Jerusalem, he tried to join the disciples, but they were all afraid of him, not believing that he really was a disciple. [27] But Barnabas took him and brought him to the apostles. He told them how Saul on his journey had seen the Lord and that the Lord had spoken to him, and how in Damascus he had preached fearlessly in the name of Jesus. [28] So Saul stayed with them and moved about freely in Jerusalem, speaking boldly in the name of the Lord. [29] He talked and debated with the Grecian Jews, but they tried to kill him. [30] When the brothers learned of this, they took him down to Caesarea and sent him off to Tarsus.

---

a 22 Or Messiah

stories to share

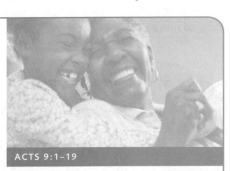

ACTS 9:1–19

Saul's Conversion

LIFE LESSON: God can use anybody to accomplish his plan, and sometimes he surprises us with his choices.

TO TALK ABOUT

✦ Why was Saul going to Damascus?

✦ What happened on the way that changed Saul (who was later known as Paul) forever?

✦ Why was Ananias so surprised at the Lord's instructions? What was the result of his obedience?

✦ What does it mean that God's ways are not always our ways (see Isaiah 55:8–9)? How does this truth apply to this story?

³¹ Then the church throughout Judea, Galilee and Samaria enjoyed a time of peace. It was strengthened; and encouraged by the Holy Spirit, it grew in numbers, living in the fear of the Lord.

Aeneas and Dorcas

³² As Peter traveled about the country, he went to visit the saints in Lydda. ³³ There he found a man named Aeneas, a paralytic who had been bedridden for eight years. ³⁴ "Aeneas," Peter said to him, "Jesus Christ heals you. Get up and take care of your mat." Immediately Aeneas got up. ³⁵ All those who lived in Lydda and Sharon saw him and turned to the Lord.

³⁶ In Joppa there was a disciple named Tabitha (which, when translated, is Dorcas ᵃ), who was always doing good and helping the poor. ³⁷ About that time she became sick and died, and her body was washed and placed in an upstairs room. ³⁸ Lydda was near Joppa; so when the disciples heard that Peter was in Lydda, they sent two men to him and urged him, "Please come at once!"

³⁹ Peter went with them, and when he arrived he was taken upstairs to the room. All the widows stood around him, crying and showing him the robes and other clothing that Dorcas had made while she was still with them.

⁴⁰ Peter sent them all out of the room; then he got down on his knees and prayed. Turning toward the dead woman, he said, "Tabitha, get up." She opened her eyes, and seeing Peter she sat up.

⁴¹ He took her by the hand and helped her to her feet. Then he called the believers and the widows and presented her to them alive. ⁴² This became known all over Joppa, and many people believed in the Lord. ⁴³ Peter stayed in Joppa for some time with a tanner named Simon.

Cornelius Calls for Peter

10 At Caesarea there was a man named Cornelius, a centurion in what was known as the Italian Regiment. ² He and all his family were devout and God-fearing; he gave generously to those in need and prayed to God regularly. ³ One day at about three in the afternoon he had a vision. He distinctly saw an angel of God, who came to him and said, "Cornelius!"

TALKING POINTS

Compassion

A man of compassion was led to become the first Gentile Christian.

ACTS 10:1–6

For more on compassion, go to 1 Peter 3:8–9.

⁴ Cornelius stared at him in fear. "What is it, Lord?" he asked.

The angel answered, "Your prayers and gifts to the poor have come up as a memorial offering before God. ⁵ Now send men to Joppa to bring back a man named Simon who is called Peter. ⁶ He is staying with Simon the tanner, whose house is by the sea."

⁷ When the angel who spoke to him had gone, Cornelius called two of his servants and a devout soldier who was one of his attendants. ⁸ He told them everything that had happened and sent them to Joppa.

TALKING POINTS

Compassion

God raised from the dead a woman who was known for her compassion.

ACTS 9:36–43

For more on compassion, go to Acts 10:1–6.

ᵃ 36 Both *Tabitha* (Aramaic) and *Dorcas* (Greek) mean *gazelle.*

Peter's Vision

10:9–32Ref — Ac 11:5–14

⁹About noon the following day as they were on their journey and approaching the city, Peter went up on the roof to pray. ¹⁰He became hungry and wanted something to eat, and while the meal was being prepared, he fell into a trance. ¹¹He saw heaven opened and something like a large sheet being let down to earth by its four corners. ¹²It contained all kinds of four-footed animals, as well as reptiles of the earth and birds of the air. ¹³Then a voice told him, "Get up, Peter. Kill and eat."

¹⁴"Surely not, Lord!" Peter replied. "I have never eaten anything impure or unclean."

¹⁵The voice spoke to him a second time, "Do not call anything impure that God has made clean."

¹⁶This happened three times, and immediately the sheet was taken back to heaven.

¹⁷While Peter was wondering about the meaning of the vision, the men sent by Cornelius found out where Simon's house was and stopped at the gate. ¹⁸They called out, asking if Simon who was known as Peter was staying there.

¹⁹While Peter was still thinking about the vision, the Spirit said to him, "Simon, three*ᵃ* men are looking for you. ²⁰So get up and go downstairs. Do not hesitate to go with them, for I have sent them."

²¹Peter went down and said to the men, "I'm the one you're looking for. Why have you come?"

²²The men replied, "We have come from Cornelius the centurion. He is a righteous and God-fearing man, who is respected by all the Jewish people. A holy angel told him to have you come to his house so that he could hear what you have to say." ²³Then Peter invited the men into the house to be his guests.

Peter at Cornelius's House

The next day Peter started out with them, and some of the brothers from Joppa went along. ²⁴The following day he arrived in Caesarea. Cor-

nelius was expecting them and had called together his relatives and close friends. ²⁵As Peter entered the house, Cornelius met him and fell at his feet in reverence. ²⁶But Peter made him get up. "Stand up," he said, "I am only a man myself."

²⁷Talking with him, Peter went inside and found a large gathering of people. ²⁸He said to them: "You are well aware that it is against our law for a Jew to associate with a Gentile or visit him. But God has shown me that I should not call any man impure or unclean. ²⁹So when I was sent for, I came without raising any objection. May I ask why you sent for me?"

³⁰Cornelius answered: "Four days ago I was in my house praying at this hour, at three in the afternoon. Suddenly a man in shining clothes stood before me ³¹and said, 'Cornelius, God has heard your prayer and remembered your gifts to the poor. ³²Send to Joppa for Simon who is called Peter. He is a guest in the home of Simon the tanner, who lives by the sea.' ³³So I sent for you immediately, and it was good of you to come. Now we are all here in the presence of God to listen to everything the Lord has commanded you to tell us."

³⁴Then Peter began to speak: "I now realize how true it is that God does not show favoritism ³⁵but accepts men from every nation who fear him and do what is right. ³⁶You know the message God sent to the people of Israel, telling the good news of peace through Jesus Christ, who is Lord of all. ³⁷You know what has happened throughout Judea, beginning in Galilee after the baptism that John preached— ³⁸how God anointed Jesus of Nazareth with the Holy Spirit and power, and how he went around doing good and healing all who were under the power of the devil, because God was with him.

³⁹"We are witnesses of everything he did in the country of the Jews and in Jerusalem. They killed him by hanging him on a tree, ⁴⁰but God raised him from the dead on the third day and caused him to be seen. ⁴¹He was not seen by all

---

ᵃ 19 One early manuscript *two*; other manuscripts do not have the number.

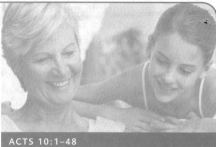

ACTS 10:1–48

Peter Sees a Vision

LIFE LESSON: God's Word is for everyone.

TO TALK ABOUT

✦ What did Peter see in his vision?

✦ Where did the angel tell Peter to go?

✦ Why wasn't Peter, as a Jew, supposed to go into Cornelius's house?

✦ God accepts all people. Can you think of someone you would like to tell about God's good news?

the people, but by witnesses whom God had already chosen—by us who ate and drank with him after he rose from the dead. ⁴²He commanded us to preach to the people and to testify that he is the one whom God appointed as judge of the living and the dead. ⁴³All the prophets testify about him that everyone who believes in him receives forgiveness of sins through his name."

⁴⁴While Peter was still speaking these words, the Holy Spirit came on all who heard the message. ⁴⁵The circumcised believers who had come with Peter were astonished that the gift of the Holy Spirit had been poured out even on the Gentiles. ⁴⁶For they heard them speaking in tongues ᵃ and praising God.

Then Peter said, ⁴⁷"Can anyone keep these people from being baptized with water? They have received the Holy Spirit just as we have." ⁴⁸So he ordered that they be baptized in the name of

Jesus Christ. Then they asked Peter to stay with them for a few days.

Peter Explains His Actions

11 The apostles and the brothers throughout Judea heard that the Gentiles also had received the word of God. ²So when Peter went up to Jerusalem, the circumcised believers criticized him ³and said, "You went into the house of uncircumcised men and ate with them."

⁴Peter began and explained everything to them precisely as it had happened: ⁵"I was in the city of Joppa praying, and in a trance I saw a vision. I saw something like a large sheet being let down from heaven by its four corners, and it came down to where I was. ⁶I looked into it and saw four-footed animals of the earth, wild beasts, reptiles, and birds of the air. ⁷Then I heard a voice telling me, 'Get up, Peter. Kill and eat.'

⁸"I replied, 'Surely not, Lord! Nothing impure or unclean has ever entered my mouth.'

⁹"The voice spoke from heaven a second time, 'Do not call anything impure that God has made clean.' ¹⁰This happened three times, and then it was all pulled up to heaven again.

¹¹"Right then three men who had been sent to me from Caesarea stopped at the house where I was staying. ¹²The Spirit told me to have no hesitation about going with them. These six brothers also went with me, and we entered the man's house. ¹³He told us how he had seen an angel appear in his house and say, 'Send to Joppa for Simon who is called Peter. ¹⁴He will bring you a message through which you and all your household will be saved.'

¹⁵"As I began to speak, the Holy Spirit came on them as he had come on us at the beginning. ¹⁶Then I remembered what the Lord had said: 'John baptized with ᵇ water, but you will be baptized with the Holy Spirit.' ¹⁷So if God gave them the same gift as he gave us, who believed in the Lord Jesus Christ, who was I to think that I could oppose God?"

ᵃ 46 Or other languages   ᵇ 16 Or in

¹⁸When they heard this, they had no further objections and praised God, saying, "So then, God has granted even the Gentiles repentance unto life."

The Church in Antioch

¹⁹Now those who had been scattered by the persecution in connection with Stephen traveled as far as Phoenicia, Cyprus and Antioch, telling the message only to Jews. ²⁰Some of them, however, men from Cyprus and Cyrene, went to Antioch and began to speak to Greeks also, telling them the good news about the Lord Jesus. ²¹The Lord's hand was with them, and a great number of people believed and turned to the Lord.

²²News of this reached the ears of the church at Jerusalem, and they sent Barnabas to Antioch. ²³When he arrived and saw the evidence of the grace of God, he was glad and encouraged them all to remain true to the Lord with all their hearts. ²⁴He was a good man, full of the Holy Spirit and faith, and a great number of people were brought to the Lord.

²⁵Then Barnabas went to Tarsus to look for Saul, ²⁶and when he found him, he brought him to Antioch. So for a whole year Barnabas and Saul met with the church and taught great numbers of people. The disciples were called Christians first at Antioch.

²⁷During this time some prophets came down from Jerusalem to Antioch. ²⁸One of them, named Agabus, stood up and through the Spirit predicted that a severe famine would spread over the entire Roman world. (This happened during the reign of Claudius.) ²⁹The disciples, each according to his ability, decided to provide help for the brothers living in Judea. ³⁰This they did, sending their gift to the elders by Barnabas and Saul.

Peter's Miraculous Escape From Prison

12 It was about this time that King Herod arrested some who belonged to the church, intending to persecute them. ²He had James, the brother of John, put to death with the sword. ³When he saw that this pleased the Jews, he proceeded to seize Peter also. This happened during the Feast of Unleavened Bread. ⁴After arresting him, he put him in prison, handing him over to be guarded by four squads of four soldiers each. Herod intended to bring him out for public trial after the Passover.

⁵So Peter was kept in prison, but the church was earnestly praying to God for him.

⁶The night before Herod was to bring him to trial, Peter was sleeping between two soldiers, bound with two chains, and sentries stood guard at the entrance. ⁷Suddenly an angel of the Lord appeared and a light shone in the cell. He struck Peter on the side and woke him up. "Quick, get up!" he said, and the chains fell off Peter's wrists.

stories to share

ACTS 12:1–17

Peter's Miraculous Escape From Prison

LIFE LESSON: Nothing can get in the way of God's purpose for his people.

TO TALK ABOUT

✦ How many soldiers were guarding Peter?

✦ How did Peter escape from prison?

✦ Why do you think God rescued Peter but doesn't always rescue other persecuted Christians?

✦ Do you think God has a specific purpose in mind for you? Why or why not?

8 Then the angel said to him, "Put on your clothes and sandals." And Peter did so. "Wrap your cloak around you and follow me," the angel told him. 9 Peter followed him out of the prison, but he had no idea that what the angel was doing was really happening; he thought he was seeing a vision. 10 They passed the first and second guards and came to the iron gate leading to the city. It opened for them by itself, and they went through it. When they had walked the length of one street, suddenly the angel left him.

11 Then Peter came to himself and said, "Now I know without a doubt that the Lord sent his angel and rescued me from Herod's clutches and from everything the Jewish people were anticipating."

12 When this had dawned on him, he went to the house of Mary the mother of John, also called Mark, where many people had gathered and were praying. 13 Peter knocked at the outer entrance, and a servant girl named Rhoda came to answer the door. 14 When she recognized Peter's voice, she was so overjoyed she ran back without opening it and exclaimed, "Peter is at the door!"

15 "You're out of your mind," they told her. When she kept insisting that it was so, they said, "It must be his angel."

16 But Peter kept on knocking, and when they opened the door and saw him, they were astonished. 17 Peter motioned with his hand for them to be quiet and described how the Lord had brought him out of prison. "Tell James and the brothers about this," he said, and then he left for another place.

18 In the morning, there was no small commotion among the soldiers as to what had become of Peter. 19 After Herod had a thorough search made for him and did not find him, he cross-examined the guards and ordered that they be executed.

Herod's Death

Then Herod went from Judea to Caesarea and stayed there a while. 20 He had been quarreling with the people of Tyre and Sidon; they now joined together and sought an audience with him. Having secured the support of Blastus, a trusted personal servant of the king, they asked for peace, because they depended on the king's country for their food supply.

21 On the appointed day Herod, wearing his royal robes, sat on his throne and delivered a public address to the people. 22 They shouted, "This is the voice of a god, not of a man." 23 Immediately, because Herod did not give praise to God, an angel of the Lord struck him down, and he was eaten by worms and died.

24 But the word of God continued to increase and spread.

25 When Barnabas and Saul had finished their mission, they returned from[a] Jerusalem, taking with them John, also called Mark.

Barnabas and Saul Sent Off

13 In the church at Antioch there were prophets and teachers: Barnabas, Simeon called Niger, Lucius of Cyrene, Manaen (who had been brought up with Herod the tetrarch) and Saul. 2 While they were worshiping the Lord and fasting, the Holy Spirit said, "Set apart for me Barnabas and Saul for the work to which I have called them." 3 So after they had fasted and prayed, they placed their hands on them and sent them off.

On Cyprus

4 The two of them, sent on their way by the Holy Spirit, went down to Seleucia and sailed from there to Cyprus. 5 When they arrived at Salamis, they proclaimed the word of God in the Jewish synagogues. John was with them as their helper.

6 They traveled through the whole island until they came to Paphos. There they met a Jewish sorcerer and false prophet named Bar-Jesus, 7 who was an attendant of the proconsul, Sergius Paulus. The proconsul, an intelligent man, sent for Barnabas and Saul because he wanted to hear the word of God. 8 But Elymas the sorcerer (for that

a 25 Some manuscripts to

is what his name means) opposed them and tried to turn the proconsul from the faith. [9] Then Saul, who was also called Paul, filled with the Holy Spirit, looked straight at Elymas and said, [10] "You are a child of the devil and an enemy of everything that is right! You are full of all kinds of deceit and trickery. Will you never stop perverting the right ways of the Lord? [11] Now the hand of the Lord is against you. You are going to be blind, and for a time you will be unable to see the light of the sun."

Immediately mist and darkness came over him, and he groped about, seeking someone to lead him by the hand. [12] When the proconsul saw what had happened, he believed, for he was amazed at the teaching about the Lord.

In Pisidian Antioch

[13] From Paphos, Paul and his companions sailed to Perga in Pamphylia, where John left them to return to Jerusalem. [14] From Perga they went on to Pisidian Antioch. On the Sabbath they entered the synagogue and sat down. [15] After the reading from the Law and the Prophets, the synagogue rulers sent word to them, saying, "Brothers, if you have a message of encouragement for the people, please speak."

[16] Standing up, Paul motioned with his hand and said: "Men of Israel and you Gentiles who worship God, listen to me! [17] The God of the people of Israel chose our fathers; he made the people prosper during their stay in Egypt, with mighty power he led them out of that country, [18] he endured their conduct[a] for about forty years in the desert, [19] he overthrew seven nations in Canaan and gave their land to his people as their inheritance. [20] All this took about 450 years.

"After this, God gave them judges until the time of Samuel the prophet. [21] Then the people asked for a king, and he gave them Saul son of Kish, of the tribe of Benjamin, who ruled forty years. [22] After removing Saul, he made David their king. He testified concerning him: 'I have found David son of Jesse a man after my own heart; he will do everything I want him to do.'

[23] "From this man's descendants God has brought to Israel the Savior Jesus, as he promised. [24] Before the coming of Jesus, John preached repentance and baptism to all the people of Israel. [25] As John was completing his work, he said: 'Who do you think I am? I am not that one. No, but he is coming after me, whose sandals I am not worthy to untie.'

[26] "Brothers, children of Abraham, and you God-fearing Gentiles, it is to us that this message of salvation has been sent. [27] The people of Jerusalem and their rulers did not recognize Jesus, yet in condemning him they fulfilled the words of the prophets that are read every Sabbath. [28] Though they found no proper ground for a death sentence, they asked Pilate to have him executed. [29] When they had carried out all that was written about him, they took him down from the tree and laid him in a tomb. [30] But God raised him from the dead, [31] and for many days he was seen by those who had traveled with him from Galilee to Jerusalem. They are now his witnesses to our people.

[32] "We tell you the good news: What God promised our fathers [33] he has fulfilled for us, their children, by raising up Jesus. As it is written in the second Psalm:

" 'You are my Son;
today I have become your Father.'[b][c]

[34] The fact that God raised him from the dead, never to decay, is stated in these words:

" 'I will give you the holy and sure blessings promised to David.'[d]

[35] So it is stated elsewhere:

" 'You will not let your Holy One see decay.'[e]

[36] "For when David had served God's purpose in his own generation, he fell asleep; he was buried with his fathers and his body decayed. [37] But the one whom God raised from the dead did not see decay.

---

[a] 18 Some manuscripts *and cared for them*   [b] 33 Or *have begotten you*   [c] 33 Psalm 2:7   [d] 34 Isaiah 55:3   [e] 35 Psalm 16:10

38 "Therefore, my brothers, I want you to know that through Jesus the forgiveness of sins is proclaimed to you. 39 Through him everyone who believes is justified from everything you could not be justified from by the law of Moses. 40 Take care that what the prophets have said does not happen to you:

41 " 'Look, you scoffers,
    wonder and perish,
for I am going to do something in your days
    that you would never believe,
    even if someone told you.' *a* "

42 As Paul and Barnabas were leaving the synagogue, the people invited them to speak further about these things on the next Sabbath. 43 When the congregation was dismissed, many of the Jews and devout converts to Judaism followed Paul and Barnabas, who talked with them and urged them to continue in the grace of God.

44 On the next Sabbath almost the whole city gathered to hear the word of the Lord. 45 When the Jews saw the crowds, they were filled with jealousy and talked abusively against what Paul was saying.

46 Then Paul and Barnabas answered them boldly: "We had to speak the word of God to you first. Since you reject it and do not consider yourselves worthy of eternal life, we now turn to the Gentiles. 47 For this is what the Lord has commanded us:

" 'I have made you *b* a light for the Gentiles,
    that you *b* may bring salvation to the ends
        of the earth.' *c* "

48 When the Gentiles heard this, they were glad and honored the word of the Lord; and all who were appointed for eternal life believed.

49 The word of the Lord spread through the whole region. 50 But the Jews incited the God-fearing women of high standing and the leading men of the city. They stirred up persecution against Paul and Barnabas, and expelled them from their region. 51 So they shook the dust from their feet in protest against them and went to Iconium.

52 And the disciples were filled with joy and with the Holy Spirit.

In Iconium

14 At Iconium Paul and Barnabas went as usual into the Jewish synagogue. There they spoke so effectively that a great number of Jews and Gentiles believed. 2 But the Jews who refused to believe stirred up the Gentiles and poisoned their minds against the brothers. 3 So Paul and Barnabas spent considerable time there, speaking boldly for the Lord, who confirmed the message of his grace by enabling them to do miraculous signs and wonders. 4 The people of the city were divided; some sided with the Jews, others with the apostles. 5 There was a plot afoot among the Gentiles and Jews, together with their leaders, to mistreat them and stone them. 6 But they found out about it and fled to the Lycaonian cities of Lystra and Derbe and to the surrounding country, 7 where they continued to preach the good news.

In Lystra and Derbe

8 In Lystra there sat a man crippled in his feet, who was lame from birth and had never walked. 9 He listened to Paul as he was speaking. Paul looked directly at him, saw that he had faith to be healed 10 and called out, "Stand up on your feet!" At that, the man jumped up and began to walk.

11 When the crowd saw what Paul had done, they shouted in the Lycaonian language, "The gods have come down to us in human form!" 12 Barnabas they called Zeus, and Paul they called Hermes because he was the chief speaker. 13 The priest of Zeus, whose temple was just outside the city, brought bulls and wreaths to the city gates because he and the crowd wanted to offer sacrifices to them.

14 But when the apostles Barnabas and Paul heard of this, they tore their clothes and rushed out into the crowd, shouting: 15 "Men, why are you doing this? We too are only men, human like you. We are bringing you good news, telling you

a 41 Hab. 1:5   *b 47* The Greek is singular.   *c 47* Isaiah 49:6

to turn from these worthless things to the living God, who made heaven and earth and sea and everything in them. ¹⁶In the past, he let all nations go their own way. ¹⁷Yet he has not left himself without testimony: He has shown kindness by giving you rain from heaven and crops in their seasons; he provides you with plenty of food and fills your hearts with joy." ¹⁸Even with these words, they had difficulty keeping the crowd from sacrificing to them.

¹⁹Then some Jews came from Antioch and Iconium and won the crowd over. They stoned Paul and dragged him outside the city, thinking he was dead. ²⁰But after the disciples had gathered around him, he got up and went back into the city. The next day he and Barnabas left for Derbe.

The Return to Antioch in Syria

²¹They preached the good news in that city and won a large number of disciples. Then they returned to Lystra, Iconium and Antioch, ²²strengthening the disciples and encouraging them to remain true to the faith. "We must go through many hardships to enter the kingdom of God," they said. ²³Paul and Barnabas appointed elders^a for them in each church and, with prayer and fasting, committed them to the Lord, in whom they had put their trust. ²⁴After going through Pisidia, they came into Pamphylia, ²⁵and when they had preached the word in Perga, they went down to Attalia.

²⁶From Attalia they sailed back to Antioch, where they had been committed to the grace of God for the work they had now completed. ²⁷On arriving there, they gathered the church together and reported all that God had done through them and how he had opened the door of faith to the Gentiles. ²⁸And they stayed there a long time with the disciples.

The Council at Jerusalem

15 Some men came down from Judea to Antioch and were teaching the brothers: "Unless you are circumcised, according to the custom taught by Moses, you cannot be saved."

²This brought Paul and Barnabas into sharp dispute and debate with them. So Paul and Barnabas were appointed, along with some other believers, to go up to Jerusalem to see the apostles and elders about this question. ³The church sent them on their way, and as they traveled through Phoenicia and Samaria, they told how the Gentiles had been converted. This news made all the brothers very glad. ⁴When they came to Jerusalem, they were welcomed by the church and the apostles and elders, to whom they reported everything God had done through them.

⁵Then some of the believers who belonged to the party of the Pharisees stood up and said, "The Gentiles must be circumcised and required to obey the law of Moses."

⁶The apostles and elders met to consider this question. ⁷After much discussion, Peter got up and addressed them: "Brothers, you know that some time ago God made a choice among you that the Gentiles might hear from my lips the message of the gospel and believe. ⁸God, who knows the heart, showed that he accepted them by giving the Holy Spirit to them, just as he did to us. ⁹He made no distinction between us and them, for he purified their hearts by faith. ¹⁰Now then, why do you try to test God by putting on the necks of the disciples a yoke that neither we nor our fathers have been able to bear? ¹¹No! We believe it is through the grace of our Lord Jesus that we are saved, just as they are."

¹²The whole assembly became silent as they listened to Barnabas and Paul telling about the miraculous signs and wonders God had done among the Gentiles through them. ¹³When they finished, James spoke up: "Brothers, listen to me. ¹⁴Simon^b has described to us how God at first showed his concern by taking from the Gentiles a people for himself. ¹⁵The words of the prophets are in agreement with this, as it is written:

¹⁶" 'After this I will return
and rebuild David's fallen tent.

---

^a 23 Or *Barnabas ordained elders*; or *Barnabas had elders elected*
^b 14 Greek *Simeon*, a variant of *Simon*; that is, Peter

Its ruins I will rebuild,
    and I will restore it,
[17] that the remnant of men may seek the Lord,
    and all the Gentiles who bear my name,
says the Lord, who does these things'[a]
[18]   that have been known for ages.[b]

[19] "It is my judgment, therefore, that we should not make it difficult for the Gentiles who are turning to God. [20] Instead we should write to them, telling them to abstain from food polluted by idols, from sexual immorality, from the meat of strangled animals and from blood. [21] For Moses has been preached in every city from the earliest times and is read in the synagogues on every Sabbath."

The Council's Letter to Gentile Believers

[22] Then the apostles and elders, with the whole church, decided to choose some of their own men and send them to Antioch with Paul and Barnabas. They chose Judas (called Barsabbas) and Silas, two men who were leaders among the brothers. [23] With them they sent the following letter:

The apostles and elders, your brothers,

To the Gentile believers in Antioch, Syria and Cilicia:

Greetings.

[24] We have heard that some went out from us without our authorization and disturbed you, troubling your minds by what they said. [25] So we all agreed to choose some men and send them to you with our dear friends Barnabas and Paul— [26] men who have risked their lives for the name of our Lord Jesus Christ. [27] Therefore we are sending Judas and Silas to confirm by word of mouth what we are writing. [28] It seemed good to the Holy Spirit and to us not to burden you with anything beyond the following requirements: [29] You are to abstain from food sacrificed to idols, from blood, from the meat of

strangled animals and from sexual immorality. You will do well to avoid these things.

Farewell.

[30] The men were sent off and went down to Antioch, where they gathered the church together and delivered the letter. [31] The people read it and were glad for its encouraging message. [32] Judas and Silas, who themselves were prophets, said much to encourage and strengthen the brothers. [33] After spending some time there, they were sent off by the brothers with the blessing of peace to return to those who had sent them.[c] [35] But Paul and Barnabas remained in Antioch, where they and many others taught and preached the word of the Lord.

Disagreement Between Paul and Barnabas

[36] Some time later Paul said to Barnabas, "Let us go back and visit the brothers in all the towns where we preached the word of the Lord and see how they are doing." [37] Barnabas wanted to take John, also called Mark, with them, [38] but Paul did not think it wise to take him, because he had deserted them in Pamphylia and had not continued with them in the work. [39] They had such a sharp disagreement that they parted company. Barnabas took Mark and sailed for Cyprus, [40] but Paul chose Silas and left, commended by the brothers to the grace of the Lord. [41] He went through Syria and Cilicia, strengthening the churches.

Timothy Joins Paul and Silas

16 He came to Derbe and then to Lystra, where a disciple named Timothy lived, whose mother was a Jewess and a believer, but whose father was a Greek. [2] The brothers at Lystra and Iconium spoke well of him. [3] Paul wanted to take him along on the journey, so he circumcised him because of the Jews who lived in that area, for they all knew that his father was a Greek. [4] As they traveled from town to town, they deliv-

---

[a] 17 Amos 9:11,12   [b] 17,18 Some manuscripts things'— / [18]known to the Lord for ages is his work   [c] 33 Some manuscripts them, [34]but Silas decided to remain there

ered the decisions reached by the apostles and elders in Jerusalem for the people to obey. ⁵So the churches were strengthened in the faith and grew daily in numbers.

Paul's Vision of the Man of Macedonia

⁶Paul and his companions traveled throughout the region of Phrygia and Galatia, having been kept by the Holy Spirit from preaching the word in the province of Asia. ⁷When they came to the border of Mysia, they tried to enter Bithynia, but the Spirit of Jesus would not allow them to. ⁸So they passed by Mysia and went down to Troas. ⁹During the night Paul had a vision of a man of Macedonia standing and begging him, "Come over to Macedonia and help us." ¹⁰After Paul had seen the vision, we got ready at once to leave for Macedonia, concluding that God had called us to preach the gospel to them.

Lydia's Conversion in Philippi

¹¹From Troas we put out to sea and sailed straight for Samothrace, and the next day on to Neapolis. ¹²From there we traveled to Philippi, a Roman colony and the leading city of that district of Macedonia. And we stayed there several days.

¹³On the Sabbath we went outside the city gate to the river, where we expected to find a place of prayer. We sat down and began to speak to the women who had gathered there. ¹⁴One of those listening was a woman named Lydia, a dealer in purple cloth from the city of Thyatira, who was a worshiper of God. The Lord opened her heart to respond to Paul's message. ¹⁵When she and the members of her household were baptized, she invited us to her home. "If you consider me a believer in the Lord," she said, "come and stay at my house." And she persuaded us.

Paul and Silas in Prison

¹⁶Once when we were going to the place of prayer, we were met by a slave girl who had a spirit by which she predicted the future. She earned a great deal of money for her owners by fortune-telling. ¹⁷This girl followed Paul and the rest of us, shouting, "These men are servants of the Most High God, who are telling you the way to be saved." ¹⁸She kept this up for many days. Finally Paul became so troubled that he turned around and said to the spirit, "In the name of Jesus Christ I command you to come out of her!" At that moment the spirit left her.

¹⁹When the owners of the slave girl realized that their hope of making money was gone, they seized Paul and Silas and dragged them into the marketplace to face the authorities. ²⁰They brought them before the magistrates and said, "These men are Jews, and are throwing our city into an uproar ²¹by advocating customs unlawful for us Romans to accept or practice."

²²The crowd joined in the attack against Paul and Silas, and the magistrates ordered them to be stripped and beaten. ²³After they had been severely flogged, they were thrown into prison, and the jailer was commanded to guard them carefully. ²⁴Upon receiving such orders, he put them in the inner cell and fastened their feet in the stocks.

²⁵About midnight Paul and Silas were praying and singing hymns to God, and the other prisoners were listening to them. ²⁶Suddenly there was such a violent earthquake that the foundations of the prison were shaken. At once all the prison doors flew open, and everybody's chains came loose. ²⁷The jailer woke up, and when he saw the prison doors open, he drew his sword and was about to kill himself because he thought the prisoners had escaped. ²⁸But Paul shouted, "Don't harm yourself! We are all here!"

²⁹The jailer called for lights, rushed in and fell trembling before Paul and Silas. ³⁰He then brought them out and asked, "Sirs, what must I do to be saved?"

³¹They replied, "Believe in the Lord Jesus, and you will be saved—you and your household." ³²Then they spoke the word of the Lord to him and to all the others in his house. ³³At that hour of the night the jailer took them and washed their wounds; then immediately he and all his family were baptized. ³⁴The jailer brought them

WEDNESDAY

WHEN SHE AND THE MEMBERS OF HER
HOUSEHOLD WERE BAPTIZED, SHE INVITED
US TO HER HOME. "IF YOU CONSIDER ME
A BELIEVER IN THE LORD," SHE SAID,
"COME AND STAY AT MY HOUSE." AND
SHE PERSUADED US.

Acts 16:15

A Family Place

THELMA WELLS

READ | ACTS 16:11 – 15

I love our home. It's a family home. It's a place where all our children and their children, with their friends, can come and be at ease. Even though I have some very nice "stuff," there's no room that's off-limits to them. The only chair they can't sit in is Papaw's green La-Z-Boy. The kids love to sit in it anyway, just to hear him say, "Git out'a my chair, little gal." He likes to sit there and hold the babies on his lap while the other kids run around the house singing, playing, dancing, creating things, teasing each other and asking Papaw if they can have juice out of the little handy refrigerator he bought so they could get their own drinks.

When I look around and see the fingerprints, crayon marks, broken toys, juice spots, pieces of paper, sticky glue, jelly stains, diapers and bottles, I think, "Boy, there's really no place like home." It's total chaos, but it's great!

It's not always chaos. Sometimes it gets downright serious when we begin to answer the children's questions or have character-building discussions. We teach them to pray, say grace, recite Bible verses and respect our country, community and other people. They learn to share and get along with others and to clean up what they mess up. As parents and grandparents we are given a charge to make our houses homes of loving and learning.

Is your house a home? Does your family feel welcome? Will people have fond memories of being there? When your children leave, will they want to come back? Will they be able to say with joy in their hearts, "There's no place like home?"

Thank you, Lord, for the gift and blessing of a home. May mine be a place of laughing, loving and learning—a place where others, especially my children and grandchildren, can always feel "at home." In Jesus' name, amen.

GRANDCHILD IN FOCUS • PRAYER

Emotional Development

O God, Creator of mind and body, I pray that you will give my grandchild emotional health and strength. Where there is anger, bring peace. Where there is confusion, bring clarity and focus. Where there are dark shadows, cast a ray of hope. Fill her with the sunshine of your Spirit. Warm her with the presence of your peace. Amen.

Your next devotion is located on page 1520.

stories to share

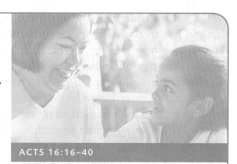

ACTS 16:16–40

Paul and Silas in Prison

LIFE LESSON: Believing in Jesus brings salvation.

TO TALK ABOUT

✦ How did the slave girl earn money for her owners? What did God do for her?

✦ What were Paul and Silas doing in prison when the earthquake came?

✦ Since jailers were held responsible for their prisoners, what did the jailer decide to do when the prison doors flew open? What happened instead?

✦ Do certain kinds of situations make people more open to the truth about Jesus? How can we as Christians be alert to such circumstances?

Roman citizens, and threw us into prison. And now do they want to get rid of us quietly? No! Let them come themselves and escort us out."

38 The officers reported this to the magistrates, and when they heard that Paul and Silas were Roman citizens, they were alarmed. **39** They came to appease them and escorted them from the prison, requesting them to leave the city. **40** After Paul and Silas came out of the prison, they went to Lydia's house, where they met with the brothers and encouraged them. Then they left.

In Thessalonica

17 When they had passed through Amphipolis and Apollonia, they came to Thessalonica, where there was a Jewish synagogue. **2** As his custom was, Paul went into the synagogue, and on three Sabbath days he reasoned with them from the Scriptures, **3** explaining and proving that the Christ[a] had to suffer and rise from the dead. "This Jesus I am proclaiming to you is the Christ,[a]" he said. **4** Some of the Jews were persuaded and joined Paul and Silas, as did a large number of God-fearing Greeks and not a few prominent women.

5 But the Jews were jealous; so they rounded up some bad characters from the marketplace, formed a mob and started a riot in the city. They rushed to Jason's house in search of Paul and Silas in order to bring them out to the crowd.[b] **6** But when they did not find them, they dragged Jason and some other brothers before the city officials, shouting: "These men who have caused trouble all over the world have now come here, **7** and Jason has welcomed them into his house. They are all defying Caesar's decrees, saying that there is another king, one called Jesus." **8** When they heard this, the crowd and the city officials were thrown into turmoil. **9** Then they made Jason and the others post bond and let them go.

In Berea

10 As soon as it was night, the brothers sent Paul and Silas away to Berea. On arriving there, they

into his house and set a meal before them; he was filled with joy because he had come to believe in God—he and his whole family.

35 When it was daylight, the magistrates sent their officers to the jailer with the order: "Release those men." **36** The jailer told Paul, "The magistrates have ordered that you and Silas be released. Now you can leave. Go in peace."

37 But Paul said to the officers: "They beat us publicly without a trial, even though we are

[a] 3 Or Messiah   [b] 5 Or the assembly of the people

went to the Jewish synagogue. ¹¹Now the Bereans were of more noble character than the Thessalonians, for they received the message with great eagerness and examined the Scriptures every day to see if what Paul said was true. ¹²Many of the Jews believed, as did also a number of prominent Greek women and many Greek men.

¹³When the Jews in Thessalonica learned that Paul was preaching the word of God at Berea, they went there too, agitating the crowds and stirring them up. ¹⁴The brothers immediately sent Paul to the coast, but Silas and Timothy stayed at Berea. ¹⁵The men who escorted Paul brought him to Athens and then left with instructions for Silas and Timothy to join him as soon as possible.

In Athens

¹⁶While Paul was waiting for them in Athens, he was greatly distressed to see that the city was full of idols. ¹⁷So he reasoned in the synagogue with the Jews and the God-fearing Greeks, as well as in the marketplace day by day with those who happened to be there. ¹⁸A group of Epicurean and Stoic philosophers began to dispute with him. Some of them asked, "What is this babbler trying to say?" Others remarked, "He seems to be advocating foreign gods." They said this because Paul was preaching the good news about Jesus and the resurrection. ¹⁹Then they took him and brought him to a meeting of the Areopagus, where they said to him, "May we know what this new teaching is that you are presenting? ²⁰You are bringing some strange ideas to our ears, and we want to know what they mean." ²¹(All the Athenians and the foreigners who lived there spent their time doing nothing but talking about and listening to the latest ideas.)

²²Paul then stood up in the meeting of the Areopagus and said: "Men of Athens! I see that in every way you are very religious. ²³For as I walked around and looked carefully at your objects of worship, I even found an altar with this inscription: TO AN UNKNOWN GOD. Now what you worship as something unknown I am going to proclaim to you.

²⁴"The God who made the world and everything in it is the Lord of heaven and earth and does not live in temples built by hands. ²⁵And he is not served by human hands, as if he needed anything, because he himself gives all men life and breath and everything else. ²⁶From one man he made every nation of men, that they should inhabit the whole earth; and he determined the times set for them and the exact places where they should live. ²⁷God did this so that men would seek him and perhaps reach out for him and find him, though he is not far from each one of us. ²⁸'For in him we live and move and have our being.' As some of your own poets have said, 'We are his offspring.'

TALKING POINTS

Finding God

God is never far away from us, whether or not we sense his presence.

ACTS 17:27

This is the last talking point on finding God.

²⁹"Therefore since we are God's offspring, we should not think that the divine being is like gold or silver or stone—an image made by man's design and skill. ³⁰In the past God overlooked such ignorance, but now he commands all people everywhere to repent. ³¹For he has set a day when he will judge the world with justice by the man he has appointed. He has given proof of this to all men by raising him from the dead."

³²When they heard about the resurrection of the dead, some of them sneered, but others said, "We want to hear you again on this subject." ³³At that, Paul left the Council. ³⁴A few men became followers of Paul and believed. Among them was Dionysius, a member of the Areopagus, also a woman named Damaris, and a number of others.

In Corinth

18 After this, Paul left Athens and went to Corinth. [2]There he met a Jew named Aquila, a native of Pontus, who had recently come from Italy with his wife Priscilla, because Claudius had ordered all the Jews to leave Rome. Paul went to see them, [3]and because he was a tentmaker as they were, he stayed and worked with them. [4]Every Sabbath he reasoned in the synagogue, trying to persuade Jews and Greeks.

[5]When Silas and Timothy came from Macedonia, Paul devoted himself exclusively to preaching, testifying to the Jews that Jesus was the Christ.[a] [6]But when the Jews opposed Paul and became abusive, he shook out his clothes in protest and said to them, "Your blood be on your own heads! I am clear of my responsibility. From now on I will go to the Gentiles."

[7]Then Paul left the synagogue and went next door to the house of Titius Justus, a worshiper of God. [8]Crispus, the synagogue ruler, and his entire household believed in the Lord; and many of the Corinthians who heard him believed and were baptized.

[9]One night the Lord spoke to Paul in a vision: "Do not be afraid; keep on speaking, do not be silent. [10]For I am with you, and no one is going to attack and harm you, because I have many people in this city." [11]So Paul stayed for a year and a half, teaching them the word of God.

[12]While Gallio was proconsul of Achaia, the Jews made a united attack on Paul and brought him into court. [13]"This man," they charged, "is persuading the people to worship God in ways contrary to the law."

[14]Just as Paul was about to speak, Gallio said to the Jews, "If you Jews were making a complaint about some misdemeanor or serious crime, it would be reasonable for me to listen to you. [15]But since it involves questions about words and names and your own law — settle the matter yourselves. I will not be a judge of such things." [16]So he had them ejected from the court. [17]Then they all turned on Sosthenes the synagogue ruler and beat him in front of the court. But Gallio showed no concern whatever.

Priscilla, Aquila and Apollos

[18]Paul stayed on in Corinth for some time. Then he left the brothers and sailed for Syria, accompanied by Priscilla and Aquila. Before he sailed, he had his hair cut off at Cenchrea because of a vow he had taken. [19]They arrived at Ephesus, where Paul left Priscilla and Aquila. He himself went into the synagogue and reasoned with the Jews. [20]When they asked him to spend more time with them, he declined. [21]But as he left, he promised, "I will come back if it is God's will." Then he set sail from Ephesus. [22]When he landed at Caesarea, he went up and greeted the church and then went down to Antioch.

[23]After spending some time in Antioch, Paul set out from there and traveled from place to place throughout the region of Galatia and Phrygia, strengthening all the disciples.

[24]Meanwhile a Jew named Apollos, a native of Alexandria, came to Ephesus. He was a learned man, with a thorough knowledge of the Scriptures. [25]He had been instructed in the way of the Lord, and he spoke with great fervor[b] and taught about Jesus accurately, though he knew only the baptism of John. [26]He began to speak boldly in the synagogue. When Priscilla and Aquila heard him, they invited him to their home and explained to him the way of God more adequately.

[27]When Apollos wanted to go to Achaia, the brothers encouraged him and wrote to the disciples there to welcome him. On arriving, he was a great help to those who by grace had believed. [28]For he vigorously refuted the Jews in public debate, proving from the Scriptures that Jesus was the Christ.

Paul in Ephesus

19 While Apollos was at Corinth, Paul took the road through the interior and arrived at Ephesus. There he found some disciples [2]and

[a] 5 Or *Messiah;* also in verse 28   [b] 25 Or *with fervor in the Spirit*

asked them, "Did you receive the Holy Spirit when[a] you believed?"

They answered, "No, we have not even heard that there is a Holy Spirit."

3 So Paul asked, "Then what baptism did you receive?"

"John's baptism," they replied.

4 Paul said, "John's baptism was a baptism of repentance. He told the people to believe in the one coming after him, that is, in Jesus." 5 On hearing this, they were baptized into[b] the name of the Lord Jesus. 6 When Paul placed his hands on them, the Holy Spirit came on them, and they spoke in tongues[c] and prophesied. 7 There were about twelve men in all.

8 Paul entered the synagogue and spoke boldly there for three months, arguing persuasively about the kingdom of God. 9 But some of them became obstinate; they refused to believe and publicly maligned the Way. So Paul left them. He took the disciples with him and had discussions daily in the lecture hall of Tyrannus. 10 This went on for two years, so that all the Jews and Greeks who lived in the province of Asia heard the word of the Lord.

11 God did extraordinary miracles through Paul, 12 so that even handkerchiefs and aprons that had touched him were taken to the sick, and their illnesses were cured and the evil spirits left them.

13 Some Jews who went around driving out evil spirits tried to invoke the name of the Lord Jesus over those who were demon-possessed. They would say, "In the name of Jesus, whom Paul preaches, I command you to come out." 14 Seven sons of Sceva, a Jewish chief priest, were doing this. 15 One day the evil spirit answered them, "Jesus I know, and I know about Paul, but who are you?" 16 Then the man who had the evil spirit jumped on them and overpowered them all. He gave them such a beating that they ran out of the house naked and bleeding.

17 When this became known to the Jews and Greeks living in Ephesus, they were all seized with fear, and the name of the Lord Jesus was held in high honor. 18 Many of those who believed now came and openly confessed their evil deeds. 19 A number who had practiced sorcery brought their scrolls together and burned them publicly. When they calculated the value of the scrolls, the total came to fifty thousand drachmas.[d] 20 In this way the word of the Lord spread widely and grew in power.

21 After all this had happened, Paul decided to go to Jerusalem, passing through Macedonia and Achaia. "After I have been there," he said, "I must visit Rome also." 22 He sent two of his helpers, Timothy and Erastus, to Macedonia, while he stayed in the province of Asia a little longer.

The Riot in Ephesus

23 About that time there arose a great disturbance about the Way. 24 A silversmith named Demetrius, who made silver shrines of Artemis, brought in no little business for the craftsmen. 25 He called them together, along with the workmen in related trades, and said: "Men, you know we receive a good income from this business. 26 And you see and hear how this fellow Paul has convinced and led astray large numbers of people here in Ephesus and in practically the whole province of Asia. He says that man-made gods are no gods at all. 27 There is danger not only that our trade will lose its good name, but also that the temple of the great goddess Artemis will be discredited, and the goddess herself, who is worshiped throughout the province of Asia and the world, will be robbed of her divine majesty."

28 When they heard this, they were furious and began shouting: "Great is Artemis of the Ephesians!" 29 Soon the whole city was in an uproar. The people seized Gaius and Aristarchus, Paul's traveling companions from Macedonia, and rushed as one man into the theater. 30 Paul wanted to appear before the crowd, but the disciples would not let him. 31 Even some of the officials of the province, friends of Paul, sent him a message begging him not to venture into the theater.

---

[a] 2 Or after   [b] 5 Or in   [c] 6 Or other languages
[d] 19 A drachma was a silver coin worth about a day's wages.

32 The assembly was in confusion: Some were shouting one thing, some another. Most of the people did not even know why they were there. 33 The Jews pushed Alexander to the front, and some of the crowd shouted instructions to him. He motioned for silence in order to make a defense before the people. 34 But when they realized he was a Jew, they all shouted in unison for about two hours: "Great is Artemis of the Ephesians!"

35 The city clerk quieted the crowd and said: "Men of Ephesus, doesn't all the world know that the city of Ephesus is the guardian of the temple of the great Artemis and of her image, which fell from heaven? 36 Therefore, since these facts are undeniable, you ought to be quiet and not do anything rash. 37 You have brought these men here, though they have neither robbed temples nor blasphemed our goddess. 38 If, then, Demetrius and his fellow craftsmen have a grievance against anybody, the courts are open and there are proconsuls. They can press charges. 39 If there is anything further you want to bring up, it must be settled in a legal assembly. 40 As it is, we are in danger of being charged with rioting because of today's events. In that case we would not be able to account for this commotion, since there is no reason for it." 41 After he had said this, he dismissed the assembly.

Through Macedonia and Greece

20 When the uproar had ended, Paul sent for the disciples and, after encouraging them, said good-by and set out for Macedonia. 2 He traveled through that area, speaking many words of encouragement to the people, and finally arrived in Greece, 3 where he stayed three months. Because the Jews made a plot against him just as he was about to sail for Syria, he decided to go back through Macedonia. 4 He was accompanied by Sopater son of Pyrrhus from Berea, Aristarchus and Secundus from Thessalonica, Gaius from Derbe, Timothy also, and Tychicus and Trophimus from the province of Asia. 5 These men went on ahead and waited for us at Troas. 6 But we sailed from Philippi after the Feast of Unleavened Bread, and five days later joined the others at Troas, where we stayed seven days.

Eutychus Raised From the Dead at Troas

7 On the first day of the week we came together to break bread. Paul spoke to the people and, because he intended to leave the next day, kept on talking until midnight. 8 There were many lamps in the upstairs room where we were meeting. 9 Seated in a window was a young man named Eutychus, who was sinking into a deep sleep as Paul talked on and on. When he was sound asleep, he fell to the ground from the third story and was picked up dead. 10 Paul went down, threw himself on the young man and put his arms around him. "Don't be alarmed," he said. "He's alive!" 11 Then he went upstairs again and broke bread and ate. After talking until daylight, he left. 12 The people took the young man home alive and were greatly comforted.

Paul's Farewell to the Ephesian Elders

13 We went on ahead to the ship and sailed for Assos, where we were going to take Paul aboard. He had made this arrangement because he was going there on foot. 14 When he met us at Assos, we took him aboard and went on to Mitylene. 15 The next day we set sail from there and arrived off Kios. The day after that we crossed over to Samos, and on the following day arrived at Miletus. 16 Paul had decided to sail past Ephesus to avoid spending time in the province of Asia, for he was in a hurry to reach Jerusalem, if possible, by the day of Pentecost.

17 From Miletus, Paul sent to Ephesus for the elders of the church. 18 When they arrived, he said to them: "You know how I lived the whole time I was with you, from the first day I came into the province of Asia. 19 I served the Lord with great humility and with tears, although I was severely tested by the plots of the Jews. 20 You know that I have not hesitated to preach anything that would be helpful to you but have taught you publicly and from house to house. 21 I have declared to both Jews and Greeks that they must turn to God in repentance and have faith in our Lord Jesus.

PRAYING THE SCRIPTURES

Salvation

ACTS 20:21

O God, help my grandchild to turn to you in repentance and put her faith in our Lord Jesus.

Next prayer in Salvation Prayer Track: Romans 3:23–24

22 "And now, compelled by the Spirit, I am going to Jerusalem, not knowing what will happen to me there. 23 I only know that in every city the Holy Spirit warns me that prison and hardships are facing me. 24 However, I consider my life worth nothing to me, if only I may finish the race and complete the task the Lord Jesus has given me—the task of testifying to the gospel of God's grace.

25 "Now I know that none of you among whom I have gone about preaching the kingdom will ever see me again. 26 Therefore, I declare to you today that I am innocent of the blood of all men. 27 For I have not hesitated to proclaim to you the whole will of God. 28 Keep watch over yourselves and all the flock of which the Holy Spirit has made you overseers. *a* Be shepherds of the church of God, *b* which he bought with his own blood. 29 I know that after I leave, savage wolves will come in among you and will not spare the flock. 30 Even from your own number men will arise and distort the truth in order to draw away disciples after them. 31 So be on your guard! Remember that for three years I never stopped warning each of you night and day with tears.

32 "Now I commit you to God and to the word of his grace, which can build you up and give you an inheritance among all those who are sanctified. 33 I have not coveted anyone's silver or gold or clothing. 34 You yourselves know that these hands of mine have supplied my own needs and the needs of my companions. 35 In everything I did, I showed you that by this kind of hard work we must help the weak, remembering the words the Lord Jesus himself said: 'It is more blessed to give than to receive.' "

36 When he had said this, he knelt down with all of them and prayed. 37 They all wept as they embraced him and kissed him. 38 What grieved them most was his statement that they would never see his face again. Then they accompanied him to the ship.

On to Jerusalem

21 After we had torn ourselves away from them, we put out to sea and sailed straight to Cos. The next day we went to Rhodes and from there to Patara. 2 We found a ship crossing over to Phoenicia, went on board and set sail. 3 After sighting Cyprus and passing to the south of it, we sailed on to Syria. We landed at Tyre, where our ship was to unload its cargo. 4 Finding the disciples there, we stayed with them seven days. Through the Spirit they urged Paul not to go on to Jerusalem. 5 But when our time was up, we left and continued on our way. All the disciples and their wives and children accompanied us out of the city, and there on the beach we knelt to pray. 6 After saying good-by to each other, we went aboard the ship, and they returned home.

7 We continued our voyage from Tyre and landed at Ptolemais, where we greeted the brothers and stayed with them for a day. 8 Leaving the next day, we reached Caesarea and stayed at the house of Philip the evangelist, one of the Seven. 9 He had four unmarried daughters who prophesied.

10 After we had been there a number of days, a prophet named Agabus came down from Judea. 11 Coming over to us, he took Paul's belt, tied his own hands and feet with it and said, "The Holy Spirit says, 'In this way the Jews of Jerusalem will bind the owner of this belt and will hand him over to the Gentiles.' "

12 When we heard this, we and the people there pleaded with Paul not to go up to Jerusalem.

a 28 Traditionally *bishops*   *b* 28 Many manuscripts *of the Lord*

¹³Then Paul answered, "Why are you weeping and breaking my heart? I am ready not only to be bound, but also to die in Jerusalem for the name of the Lord Jesus." ¹⁴When he would not be dissuaded, we gave up and said, "The Lord's will be done."

¹⁵After this, we got ready and went up to Jerusalem. ¹⁶Some of the disciples from Caesarea accompanied us and brought us to the home of Mnason, where we were to stay. He was a man from Cyprus and one of the early disciples.

Paul's Arrival at Jerusalem

¹⁷When we arrived at Jerusalem, the brothers received us warmly. ¹⁸The next day Paul and the rest of us went to see James, and all the elders were present. ¹⁹Paul greeted them and reported in detail what God had done among the Gentiles through his ministry.

²⁰When they heard this, they praised God. Then they said to Paul: "You see, brother, how many thousands of Jews have believed, and all of them are zealous for the law. ²¹They have been informed that you teach all the Jews who live among the Gentiles to turn away from Moses, telling them not to circumcise their children or live according to our customs. ²²What shall we do? They will certainly hear that you have come, ²³so do what we tell you. There are four men with us who have made a vow. ²⁴Take these men, join in their purification rites and pay their expenses, so that they can have their heads shaved. Then everybody will know there is no truth in these reports about you, but that you yourself are living in obedience to the law. ²⁵As for the Gentile believers, we have written to them our decision that they should abstain from food sacrificed to idols, from blood, from the meat of strangled animals and from sexual immorality."

²⁶The next day Paul took the men and purified himself along with them. Then he went to the temple to give notice of the date when the days of purification would end and the offering would be made for each of them.

Paul Arrested

²⁷When the seven days were nearly over, some Jews from the province of Asia saw Paul at the temple. They stirred up the whole crowd and seized him, ²⁸shouting, "Men of Israel, help us! This is the man who teaches all men everywhere against our people and our law and this place. And besides, he has brought Greeks into the temple area and defiled this holy place." ²⁹(They had previously seen Trophimus the Ephesian in the city with Paul and assumed that Paul had brought him into the temple area.)

³⁰The whole city was aroused, and the people came running from all directions. Seizing Paul, they dragged him from the temple, and immediately the gates were shut. ³¹While they were trying to kill him, news reached the commander of the Roman troops that the whole city of Jerusalem was in an uproar. ³²He at once took some officers and soldiers and ran down to the crowd. When the rioters saw the commander and his soldiers, they stopped beating Paul.

³³The commander came up and arrested him and ordered him to be bound with two chains. Then he asked who he was and what he had done. ³⁴Some in the crowd shouted one thing and some another, and since the commander could not get at the truth because of the uproar, he ordered that Paul be taken into the barracks. ³⁵When Paul reached the steps, the violence of the mob was so great he had to be carried by the soldiers. ³⁶The crowd that followed kept shouting, "Away with him!"

Paul Speaks to the Crowd
22:3–16pp — Ac 9:1–22; 26:9–18

³⁷As the soldiers were about to take Paul into the barracks, he asked the commander, "May I say something to you?"

"Do you speak Greek?" he replied. ³⁸"Aren't you the Egyptian who started a revolt and led four thousand terrorists out into the desert some time ago?"

³⁹Paul answered, "I am a Jew, from Tarsus in

"YOU WILL BE HIS WITNESS TO ALL MEN OF WHAT YOU HAVE SEEN AND HEARD."

Acts 22:15

Witnessing to Waitresses

JONI EARECKSON TADA

READ | ACTS 21:37 — 22:21

God gave my friend Jennifer a burden for waitresses. Once every two weeks, Jennifer and her Christian friends regularly meet for lunch, but before they choose a restaurant, they pray. Once it's decided where to lunch, they sit down and strike up a friendly chat with the waitress. They learn her name and ask for her suggestions from the menu.

Jennifer and her friends visit the same restaurant at least five times, asking the maître d' that they be given the same waitress. After so many luncheons, the women become friends with the waitress and invite her to church. Jennifer and her friends have been witnessing this way for years and after visiting scores of restaurants — and as many waitresses — they have seen fifteen women come to Christ.

Jennifer is only doing what's required of her from Acts 1:8, so we shouldn't think she's amazing. But what is amazing is her creativity. She and her friends not only have fun together over lunch, but they make an outreach of it. Waitresses are, in fact, their main reason for getting together.

No matter where we go or whom we meet, we can have an effective outreach for Christ in our community. No, Jennifer will never organize a group called "Eating Out for Jesus," or plan a budget or print up brochures. But she will keep on doing what comes naturally: being a witness for the Lord.

Lord Jesus, I want to be a witness for you today. I want to tell others of your love. Show me new ways to share your gospel with others and use me to make a difference in my community.

Your next devotion is located on page 1532.

GRANDCHILD IN FOCUS • PRAYER

Spiritual Growth

Dear Lord, today I pray for my grandchild's spiritual growth. I ask that you instill in him the desire to read and memorize your Word. Give him a passion to be in conversation with you. May loving and serving you be part of his daily life. I ask that you stay close to him and lead him to be transformed to your likeness, to reflect your grace and to radiate your love. I pray this in Jesus' name, amen.

Cilicia, a citizen of no ordinary city. Please let me speak to the people."

40 Having received the commander's permission, Paul stood on the steps and motioned to the crowd. When they were all silent, he said to **22** them in Aramaic*a*: **1** "Brothers and fathers, listen now to my defense."

2 When they heard him speak to them in Aramaic, they became very quiet.

Then Paul said: **3** "I am a Jew, born in Tarsus of Cilicia, but brought up in this city. Under Gamaliel I was thoroughly trained in the law of our fathers and was just as zealous for God as any of you are today. **4** I persecuted the followers of this Way to their death, arresting both men and women and throwing them into prison, **5** as also the high priest and all the Council can testify. I even obtained letters from them to their brothers in Damascus, and went there to bring these people as prisoners to Jerusalem to be punished.

6 "About noon as I came near Damascus, suddenly a bright light from heaven flashed around me. **7** I fell to the ground and heard a voice say to me, 'Saul! Saul! Why do you persecute me?'

8 " 'Who are you, Lord?' I asked.

" 'I am Jesus of Nazareth, whom you are persecuting,' he replied. **9** My companions saw the light, but they did not understand the voice of him who was speaking to me.

10 " 'What shall I do, Lord?' I asked.

" 'Get up,' the Lord said, 'and go into Damascus. There you will be told all that you have been assigned to do.' **11** My companions led me by the hand into Damascus, because the brilliance of the light had blinded me.

12 "A man named Ananias came to see me. He was a devout observer of the law and highly respected by all the Jews living there. **13** He stood beside me and said, 'Brother Saul, receive your sight!' And at that very moment I was able to see him.

14 "Then he said: 'The God of our fathers has chosen you to know his will and to see the Righteous One and to hear words from his mouth. **15** You will be his witness to all men of what you have seen and heard. **16** And now what are you waiting for? Get up, be baptized and wash your sins away, calling on his name.'

17 "When I returned to Jerusalem and was praying at the temple, I fell into a trance **18** and saw the Lord speaking. 'Quick!' he said to me. 'Leave Jerusalem immediately, because they will not accept your testimony about me.'

19 " 'Lord,' I replied, 'these men know that I went from one synagogue to another to imprison and beat those who believe in you. **20** And when the blood of your martyr *b* Stephen was shed, I stood there giving my approval and guarding the clothes of those who were killing him.'

21 "Then the Lord said to me, 'Go; I will send you far away to the Gentiles.' "

Paul the Roman Citizen

22 The crowd listened to Paul until he said this. Then they raised their voices and shouted, "Rid the earth of him! He's not fit to live!"

23 As they were shouting and throwing off their cloaks and flinging dust into the air, **24** the commander ordered Paul to be taken into the barracks. He directed that he be flogged and questioned in order to find out why the people were shouting at him like this. **25** As they stretched him out to flog him, Paul said to the centurion standing there, "Is it legal for you to flog a Roman citizen who hasn't even been found guilty?"

TALKING POINTS

Sharing Your Faith

Telling our own story is key to sharing our faith.

ACTS 22:3–8

This is the last talking point on sharing your faith.

---

a 40 Or possibly *Hebrew*; also in 22:2   *b 20* Or *witness*

1521

[26] When the centurion heard this, he went to the commander and reported it. "What are you going to do?" he asked. "This man is a Roman citizen."

[27] The commander went to Paul and asked, "Tell me, are you a Roman citizen?"

"Yes, I am," he answered.

[28] Then the commander said, "I had to pay a big price for my citizenship."

"But I was born a citizen," Paul replied.

[29] Those who were about to question him withdrew immediately. The commander himself was alarmed when he realized that he had put Paul, a Roman citizen, in chains.

Before the Sanhedrin

[30] The next day, since the commander wanted to find out exactly why Paul was being accused by the Jews, he released him and ordered the chief priests and all the Sanhedrin to assemble. Then he brought Paul and had him stand before them.

23 Paul looked straight at the Sanhedrin and said, "My brothers, I have fulfilled my duty to God in all good conscience to this day." [2] At this the high priest Ananias ordered those standing near Paul to strike him on the mouth. [3] Then Paul said to him, "God will strike you, you whitewashed wall! You sit there to judge me according to the law, yet you yourself violate the law by commanding that I be struck!"

[4] Those who were standing near Paul said, "You dare to insult God's high priest?"

[5] Paul replied, "Brothers, I did not realize that he was the high priest; for it is written: 'Do not speak evil about the ruler of your people.' [a]"

[6] Then Paul, knowing that some of them were Sadducees and the others Pharisees, called out in the Sanhedrin, "My brothers, I am a Pharisee, the son of a Pharisee. I stand on trial because of my hope in the resurrection of the dead." [7] When he said this, a dispute broke out between the Pharisees and the Sadducees, and the assembly was divided. [8] (The Sadducees say that there is no resurrection, and that there are neither angels nor spirits, but the Pharisees acknowledge them all.)

[9] There was a great uproar, and some of the teachers of the law who were Pharisees stood up and argued vigorously. "We find nothing wrong with this man," they said. "What if a spirit or an angel has spoken to him?" [10] The dispute became so violent that the commander was afraid Paul would be torn to pieces by them. He ordered the troops to go down and take him away from them by force and bring him into the barracks.

[11] The following night the Lord stood near Paul and said, "Take courage! As you have testified about me in Jerusalem, so you must also testify in Rome."

The Plot to Kill Paul

[12] The next morning the Jews formed a conspiracy and bound themselves with an oath not to eat or drink until they had killed Paul. [13] More than forty men were involved in this plot. [14] They went to the chief priests and elders and said, "We have taken a solemn oath not to eat anything until we have killed Paul. [15] Now then, you and the Sanhedrin petition the commander to bring him before you on the pretext of wanting more accurate information about his case. We are ready to kill him before he gets here."

[16] But when the son of Paul's sister heard of this plot, he went into the barracks and told Paul.

[17] Then Paul called one of the centurions and said, "Take this young man to the commander; he has something to tell him." [18] So he took him to the commander.

The centurion said, "Paul, the prisoner, sent for me and asked me to bring this young man to you because he has something to tell you."

[19] The commander took the young man by the hand, drew him aside and asked, "What is it you want to tell me?"

[20] He said: "The Jews have agreed to ask you to bring Paul before the Sanhedrin tomorrow on the pretext of wanting more accurate information about him. [21] Don't give in to them, because more than forty of them are waiting in ambush

a 5 Exodus 22:28

for him. They have taken an oath not to eat or drink until they have killed him. They are ready now, waiting for your consent to their request."

²²The commander dismissed the young man and cautioned him, "Don't tell anyone that you have reported this to me."

Paul Transferred to Caesarea

²³Then he called two of his centurions and ordered them, "Get ready a detachment of two hundred soldiers, seventy horsemen and two hundred spearmen *a* to go to Caesarea at nine tonight. ²⁴Provide mounts for Paul so that he may be taken safely to Governor Felix."

²⁵He wrote a letter as follows:

²⁶Claudius Lysias,

To His Excellency, Governor Felix:

Greetings.

²⁷This man was seized by the Jews and they were about to kill him, but I came with my troops and rescued him, for I had learned that he is a Roman citizen. ²⁸I wanted to know why they were accusing him, so I brought him to their Sanhedrin. ²⁹I found that the accusation had to do with questions about their law, but there was no charge against him that deserved death or imprisonment. ³⁰When I was informed of a plot to be carried out against the man, I sent him to you at once. I also ordered his accusers to present to you their case against him.

³¹So the soldiers, carrying out their orders, took Paul with them during the night and brought him as far as Antipatris. ³²The next day they let the cavalry go on with him, while they returned to the barracks. ³³When the cavalry arrived in Caesarea, they delivered the letter to the governor and handed Paul over to him. ³⁴The governor read the letter and asked what province he was from. Learning that he was from Cilicia, ³⁵he said, "I will hear your case when your accus-

ers get here." Then he ordered that Paul be kept under guard in Herod's palace.

The Trial Before Felix

24 Five days later the high priest Ananias went down to Caesarea with some of the elders and a lawyer named Tertullus, and they brought their charges against Paul before the governor. ²When Paul was called in, Tertullus presented his case before Felix: "We have enjoyed a long period of peace under you, and your foresight has brought about reforms in this nation. ³Everywhere and in every way, most excellent Felix, we acknowledge this with profound gratitude. ⁴But in order not to weary you further, I would request that you be kind enough to hear us briefly.

⁵"We have found this man to be a troublemaker, stirring up riots among the Jews all over the world. He is a ringleader of the Nazarene sect ⁶and even tried to desecrate the temple; so we seized him. ⁸By *b* examining him yourself you will be able to learn the truth about all these charges we are bringing against him."

⁹The Jews joined in the accusation, asserting that these things were true.

¹⁰When the governor motioned for him to speak, Paul replied: "I know that for a number of years you have been a judge over this nation; so I gladly make my defense. ¹¹You can easily verify that no more than twelve days ago I went up to Jerusalem to worship. ¹²My accusers did not find me arguing with anyone at the temple, or stirring up a crowd in the synagogues or anywhere else in the city. ¹³And they cannot prove to you the charges they are now making against me. ¹⁴However, I admit that I worship the God of our fathers as a follower of the Way, which they call a sect. I believe everything that agrees with the Law and that is written in the Prophets, ¹⁵and I have the same hope in God as these men, that

---

a 23 The meaning of the Greek for this word is uncertain.
b 6-8 Some manuscripts *him and wanted to judge him according to our law.* ⁷*But the commander, Lysias, came and with the use of much force snatched him from our hands* ⁸*and ordered his accusers to come before you. By*

there will be a resurrection of both the righteous and the wicked. ¹⁶So I strive always to keep my conscience clear before God and man.

¹⁷"After an absence of several years, I came to Jerusalem to bring my people gifts for the poor and to present offerings. ¹⁸I was ceremonially clean when they found me in the temple courts doing this. There was no crowd with me, nor was I involved in any disturbance. ¹⁹But there are some Jews from the province of Asia, who ought to be here before you and bring charges if they have anything against me. ²⁰Or these who are here should state what crime they found in me when I stood before the Sanhedrin— ²¹unless it was this one thing I shouted as I stood in their presence: 'It is concerning the resurrection of the dead that I am on trial before you today.'"

²²Then Felix, who was well acquainted with the Way, adjourned the proceedings. "When Lysias the commander comes," he said, "I will decide your case." ²³He ordered the centurion to keep Paul under guard but to give him some freedom and permit his friends to take care of his needs.

²⁴Several days later Felix came with his wife Drusilla, who was a Jewess. He sent for Paul and listened to him as he spoke about faith in Christ Jesus. ²⁵As Paul discoursed on righteousness, self-control and the judgment to come, Felix was afraid and said, "That's enough for now! You may leave. When I find it convenient, I will send for you." ²⁶At the same time he was hoping that Paul would offer him a bribe, so he sent for him frequently and talked with him.

²⁷When two years had passed, Felix was succeeded by Porcius Festus, but because Felix wanted to grant a favor to the Jews, he left Paul in prison.

The Trial Before Festus

25 Three days after arriving in the province, Festus went up from Caesarea to Jerusalem, ²where the chief priests and Jewish leaders appeared before him and presented the charges against Paul. ³They urgently requested Festus, as a favor to them, to have Paul transferred to Jerusalem, for they were preparing an ambush to kill him along the way. ⁴Festus answered, "Paul is being held at Caesarea, and I myself am going there soon. ⁵Let some of your leaders come with me and press charges against the man there, if he has done anything wrong."

⁶After spending eight or ten days with them, he went down to Caesarea, and the next day he convened the court and ordered that Paul be brought before him. ⁷When Paul appeared, the Jews who had come down from Jerusalem stood around him, bringing many serious charges against him, which they could not prove.

⁸Then Paul made his defense: "I have done nothing wrong against the law of the Jews or against the temple or against Caesar."

⁹Festus, wishing to do the Jews a favor, said to Paul, "Are you willing to go up to Jerusalem and stand trial before me there on these charges?"

¹⁰Paul answered: "I am now standing before Caesar's court, where I ought to be tried. I have not done any wrong to the Jews, as you yourself know very well. ¹¹If, however, I am guilty of doing anything deserving death, I do not refuse to die. But if the charges brought against me by these Jews are not true, no one has the right to hand me over to them. I appeal to Caesar!"

¹²After Festus had conferred with his council, he declared: "You have appealed to Caesar. To Caesar you will go!"

Festus Consults King Agrippa

¹³A few days later King Agrippa and Bernice arrived at Caesarea to pay their respects to Festus. ¹⁴Since they were spending many days there, Festus discussed Paul's case with the king. He said: "There is a man here whom Felix left as a prisoner. ¹⁵When I went to Jerusalem, the chief priests and elders of the Jews brought charges against him and asked that he be condemned.

¹⁶"I told them that it is not the Roman custom to hand over any man before he has faced his accusers and has had an opportunity to defend himself against their charges. ¹⁷When they came here with me, I did not delay the case, but convened the court the next day and ordered the man to be

brought in. [18]When his accusers got up to speak, they did not charge him with any of the crimes I had expected. [19]Instead, they had some points of dispute with him about their own religion and about a dead man named Jesus who Paul claimed was alive. [20]I was at a loss how to investigate such matters; so I asked if he would be willing to go to Jerusalem and stand trial there on these charges. [21]When Paul made his appeal to be held over for the Emperor's decision, I ordered him held until I could send him to Caesar."

[22]Then Agrippa said to Festus, "I would like to hear this man myself."

He replied, "Tomorrow you will hear him."

Paul Before Agrippa

26:12–18pp — Ac 9:3–8; 22:6–11

[23]The next day Agrippa and Bernice came with great pomp and entered the audience room with the high ranking officers and the leading men of the city. At the command of Festus, Paul was brought in. [24]Festus said: "King Agrippa, and all who are present with us, you see this man! The whole Jewish community has petitioned me about him in Jerusalem and here in Caesarea, shouting that he ought not to live any longer. [25]I found he had done nothing deserving of death, but because he made his appeal to the Emperor I decided to send him to Rome. [26]But I have nothing definite to write to His Majesty about him. Therefore I have brought him before all of you, and especially before you, King Agrippa, so that as a result of this investigation I may have something to write. [27]For I think it is unreasonable to send on a prisoner without specifying the charges against him."

26 Then Agrippa said to Paul, "You have permission to speak for yourself."

So Paul motioned with his hand and began his defense: [2]"King Agrippa, I consider myself fortunate to stand before you today as I make my defense against all the accusations of the Jews, [3]and especially so because you are well acquainted with all the Jewish customs and controversies. Therefore, I beg you to listen to me patiently.

[4]"The Jews all know the way I have lived ever since I was a child, from the beginning of my life in my own country, and also in Jerusalem. [5]They have known me for a long time and can testify, if they are willing, that according to the strictest sect of our religion, I lived as a Pharisee. [6]And now it is because of my hope in what God has promised our fathers that I am on trial today. [7]This is the promise our twelve tribes are hoping to see fulfilled as they earnestly serve God day and night. O king, it is because of this hope that the Jews are accusing me. [8]Why should any of you consider it incredible that God raises the dead?

[9]"I too was convinced that I ought to do all that was possible to oppose the name of Jesus of Nazareth. [10]And that is just what I did in Jerusalem. On the authority of the chief priests I put many of the saints in prison, and when they were put to death, I cast my vote against them. [11]Many a time I went from one synagogue to another to have them punished, and I tried to force them to blaspheme. In my obsession against them, I even went to foreign cities to persecute them.

[12]"On one of these journeys I was going to Damascus with the authority and commission of the chief priests. [13]About noon, O king, as I was on the road, I saw a light from heaven, brighter than the sun, blazing around me and my companions. [14]We all fell to the ground, and I heard a voice saying to me in Aramaic,[a] 'Saul, Saul, why do you persecute me? It is hard for you to kick against the goads.'

[15]"Then I asked, 'Who are you, Lord?'

" 'I am Jesus, whom you are persecuting,' the Lord replied. [16]'Now get up and stand on your feet. I have appeared to you to appoint you as a servant and as a witness of what you have seen of me and what I will show you. [17]I will rescue you from your own people and from the Gentiles. I am sending you to them [18]to open their eyes and turn them from darkness to light, and from the power of Satan to God, so that they may receive forgiveness of sins and a place among those who are sanctified by faith in me.'

a 14 Or Hebrew

[19] "So then, King Agrippa, I was not disobedient to the vision from heaven. [20] First to those in Damascus, then to those in Jerusalem and in all Judea, and to the Gentiles also, I preached that they should repent and turn to God and prove their repentance by their deeds. [21] That is why the Jews seized me in the temple courts and tried to kill me. [22] But I have had God's help to this very day, and so I stand here and testify to small and great alike. I am saying nothing beyond what the prophets and Moses said would happen— [23] that the Christ[a] would suffer and, as the first to rise from the dead, would proclaim light to his own people and to the Gentiles."

[24] At this point Festus interrupted Paul's defense. "You are out of your mind, Paul!" he shouted. "Your great learning is driving you insane."

[25] "I am not insane, most excellent Festus," Paul replied. "What I am saying is true and reasonable. [26] The king is familiar with these things, and I can speak freely to him. I am convinced that none of this has escaped his notice, because it was not done in a corner. [27] King Agrippa, do you believe the prophets? I know you do."

[28] Then Agrippa said to Paul, "Do you think that in such a short time you can persuade me to be a Christian?"

[29] Paul replied, "Short time or long—I pray God that not only you but all who are listening to me today may become what I am, except for these chains."

[30] The king rose, and with him the governor and Bernice and those sitting with them. [31] They left the room, and while talking with one another, they said, "This man is not doing anything that deserves death or imprisonment."

[32] Agrippa said to Festus, "This man could have been set free if he had not appealed to Caesar."

Paul Sails for Rome

27 When it was decided that we would sail for Italy, Paul and some other prisoners were handed over to a centurion named Julius, who belonged to the Imperial Regiment. [2] We boarded a ship from Adramyttium about to sail for ports along the coast of the province of Asia, and we put out to sea. Aristarchus, a Macedonian from Thessalonica, was with us.

[3] The next day we landed at Sidon; and Julius, in kindness to Paul, allowed him to go to his friends so they might provide for his needs. [4] From there we put out to sea again and passed to the lee of Cyprus because the winds were against us. [5] When we had sailed across the open sea off the coast of Cilicia and Pamphylia, we landed at Myra in Lycia. [6] There the centurion found an Alexandrian ship sailing for Italy and put us on board. [7] We made slow headway for many days and had difficulty arriving off Cnidus. When the wind did not allow us to hold our course, we sailed to the lee of Crete, opposite Salmone. [8] We moved along the coast with difficulty and came to a place called Fair Havens, near the town of Lasea.

[9] Much time had been lost, and sailing had already become dangerous because by now it was after the Fast.[b] So Paul warned them, [10] "Men, I can see that our voyage is going to be disastrous and bring great loss to ship and cargo, and to our own lives also." [11] But the centurion, instead of listening to what Paul said, followed the advice of the pilot and of the owner of the ship. [12] Since the harbor was unsuitable to winter in, the majority decided that we should sail on, hoping to reach Phoenix and winter there. This was a harbor in Crete, facing both southwest and northwest.

The Storm

[13] When a gentle south wind began to blow, they thought they had obtained what they wanted; so they weighed anchor and sailed along the shore of Crete. [14] Before very long, a wind of hurricane force, called the "northeaster," swept down from the island. [15] The ship was caught by the storm and could not head into the wind; so we gave way to it and were driven along. [16] As we passed to the lee of a small island called Cauda, we were hardly able to make the lifeboat secure. [17] When the men had hoisted it aboard, they

a 23 Or *Messiah*   *b 9* That is, the Day of Atonement (Yom Kippur)

ACTS 27:1–44

Paul's Shipwreck

LIFE LESSON: God is in control of everything that happens.

TO TALK ABOUT

✦ After the men had gone a long time without food, why was Paul able to tell them to keep up their courage?

✦ When the sailors feared the ship was going to crash into land, what did they plan to do? What did Paul tell them?

✦ What did Paul urge everyone on board to do?

✦ What are some ways in which God took control of events in this story? How can this help you when you feel like you're going through a "shipwreck" in your life?

passed ropes under the ship itself to hold it together. Fearing that they would run aground on the sandbars of Syrtis, they lowered the sea anchor and let the ship be driven along. [18] We took such a violent battering from the storm that the next day they began to throw the cargo overboard. [19] On the third day, they threw the ship's tackle overboard with their own hands. [20] When neither sun nor stars appeared for many days and the storm continued raging, we finally gave up all hope of being saved.

[21] After the men had gone a long time without food, Paul stood up before them and said: "Men, you should have taken my advice not to sail from Crete; then you would have spared yourselves this damage and loss. [22] But now I urge you to keep up your courage, because not one of you will be lost; only the ship will be destroyed. [23] Last night an angel of the God whose I am and whom I serve stood beside me [24] and said, 'Do not be afraid, Paul. You must stand trial before Caesar; and God has graciously given you the lives of all who sail with you.' [25] So keep up your courage, men, for I have faith in God that it will happen just as he told me. [26] Nevertheless, we must run aground on some island."

The Shipwreck

[27] On the fourteenth night we were still being driven across the Adriatic[a] Sea, when about midnight the sailors sensed they were approaching land. [28] They took soundings and found that the water was a hundred and twenty feet[b] deep. A short time later they took soundings again and found it was ninety feet[c] deep. [29] Fearing that we would be dashed against the rocks, they dropped four anchors from the stern and prayed for daylight. [30] In an attempt to escape from the ship, the sailors let the lifeboat down into the sea, pretending they were going to lower some anchors from the bow. [31] Then Paul said to the centurion and the soldiers, "Unless these men stay with the ship, you cannot be saved." [32] So the soldiers cut the ropes that held the lifeboat and let it fall away.

[33] Just before dawn Paul urged them all to eat. "For the last fourteen days," he said, "you have been in constant suspense and have gone without food—you haven't eaten anything. [34] Now I urge you to take some food. You need it to survive. Not one of you will lose a single hair from his head." [35] After he said this, he took some bread and gave thanks to God in front of them all. Then he broke it and began to eat. [36] They were all encouraged and ate some food themselves. [37] Altogether there

---

[a] 27 In ancient times the name referred to an area extending well south of Italy. [b] 28 Greek *twenty orguias* (about 37 meters) [c] 28 Greek *fifteen orguias* (about 27 meters)

were 276 of us on board. ³⁸When they had eaten as much as they wanted, they lightened the ship by throwing the grain into the sea.

³⁹When daylight came, they did not recognize the land, but they saw a bay with a sandy beach, where they decided to run the ship aground if they could. ⁴⁰Cutting loose the anchors, they left them in the sea and at the same time untied the ropes that held the rudders. Then they hoisted the foresail to the wind and made for the beach. ⁴¹But the ship struck a sandbar and ran aground. The bow stuck fast and would not move, and the stern was broken to pieces by the pounding of the surf.

⁴²The soldiers planned to kill the prisoners to prevent any of them from swimming away and escaping. ⁴³But the centurion wanted to spare Paul's life and kept them from carrying out their plan. He ordered those who could swim to jump overboard first and get to land. ⁴⁴The rest were to get there on planks or on pieces of the ship. In this way everyone reached land in safety.

Ashore on Malta

28 Once safely on shore, we found out that the island was called Malta. ²The islanders showed us unusual kindness. They built a fire and welcomed us all because it was raining and cold. ³Paul gathered a pile of brushwood and, as he put it on the fire, a viper, driven out by the heat, fastened itself on his hand. ⁴When the islanders saw the snake hanging from his hand, they said to each other, "This man must be a murderer; for though he escaped from the sea, Justice has not allowed him to live." ⁵But Paul shook the snake off into the fire and suffered no ill effects. ⁶The people expected him to swell up or suddenly fall dead, but after waiting a long time and seeing nothing unusual happen to him, they changed their minds and said he was a god.

⁷There was an estate nearby that belonged to Publius, the chief official of the island. He welcomed us to his home and for three days entertained us hospitably. ⁸His father was sick in bed, suffering from fever and dysentery. Paul went in to see him and, after prayer, placed his hands on

him and healed him. ⁹When this had happened, the rest of the sick on the island came and were cured. ¹⁰They honored us in many ways and when we were ready to sail, they furnished us with the supplies we needed.

Arrival at Rome

¹¹After three months we put out to sea in a ship that had wintered in the island. It was an Alexandrian ship with the figurehead of the twin gods Castor and Pollux. ¹²We put in at Syracuse and stayed there three days. ¹³From there we set sail and arrived at Rhegium. The next day the south wind came up, and on the following day we reached Puteoli. ¹⁴There we found some brothers who invited us to spend a week with them. And so we came to Rome. ¹⁵The brothers there had heard that we were coming, and they traveled as far as the Forum of Appius and the Three Taverns to meet us. At the sight of these men Paul thanked God and was encouraged. ¹⁶When we got to Rome, Paul was allowed to live by himself, with a soldier to guard him.

Paul Preaches at Rome Under Guard

¹⁷Three days later he called together the leaders of the Jews. When they had assembled, Paul said to them: "My brothers, although I have done nothing against our people or against the customs of our ancestors, I was arrested in Jerusalem and handed over to the Romans. ¹⁸They examined me and wanted to release me, because I was not guilty of any crime deserving death. ¹⁹But when the Jews objected, I was compelled to appeal to Caesar—not that I had any charge to bring against my own people. ²⁰For this reason I have asked to see you and talk with you. It is because of the hope of Israel that I am bound with this chain."

²¹They replied, "We have not received any letters from Judea concerning you, and none of the brothers who have come from there has reported or said anything bad about you. ²²But we want to hear what your views are, for we know that people everywhere are talking against this sect."

23They arranged to meet Paul on a certain day, and came in even larger numbers to the place where he was staying. From morning till evening he explained and declared to them the kingdom of God and tried to convince them about Jesus from the Law of Moses and from the Prophets. 24Some were convinced by what he said, but others would not believe. 25They disagreed among themselves and began to leave after Paul had made this final statement: "The Holy Spirit spoke the truth to your forefathers when he said through Isaiah the prophet:

26" 'Go to this people and say,
   "You will be ever hearing but never
         understanding;
      you will be ever seeing but never
         perceiving."

27For this people's heart has become calloused;
      they hardly hear with their ears,
      and they have closed their eyes.
   Otherwise they might see with their eyes,
      hear with their ears,
      understand with their hearts
   and turn, and I would heal them.' a

28"Therefore I want you to know that God's salvation has been sent to the Gentiles, and they will listen!" b

30For two whole years Paul stayed there in his own rented house and welcomed all who came to see him. 31Boldly and without hindrance he preached the kingdom of God and taught about the Lord Jesus Christ.

a 27 Isaiah 6:9,10   b 28 Some manuscripts listen!" 29After he said this, the Jews left, arguing vigorously among themselves.

It's ALL ABOUT FAITH

Grandchildren know all about faith, for they are shining examples of how it works. They have faith that if they run up to us with a big hug, we will hug them back with equal enthusiasm; they have faith that the pantry will contain their favorite treats when they visit us; they have faith that we'll laugh at their newest joke; they have faith that we'll listen to their longest story. Their faith in us is sure; it cannot be shaken. They are certain that Grandma loves them.

The book of Romans is about that kind of faith. And at the core of that faith is the truth that God reached out to us first with love and forgiveness through his Son, Jesus. We don't have to make the first move; we just need to receive what he offers us with the certainty of a child, for "God demonstrates his own love for us in this: While we were still sinners, Christ died for us" (Romans 5:8). Like our grandchildren's faith in us, we can have every confidence that we will be welcomed into our heavenly Father's presence.

We can learn a great lesson from our grandchildren. In our relationship with God, we can emulate their simple faith in our love for them, trusting that God has a deep and abiding love for us.

VERSE *to* REMEMBER | ROMANS 5:1

Therefore, since we have been justified through faith, we have peace with God through our Lord Jesus Christ.

ABOUT ROMANS

WRITTEN BY:
The apostle Paul

WRITTEN FOR:
The Christians in Rome

DATE WRITTEN:
Probably A.D. 57 from the city of Corinth

WHY WRITTEN:
To reveal how Jesus' death makes us right with God and how Jesus will help us live a life pleasing to God

1 Paul, a servant of Christ Jesus, called to be an apostle and set apart for the gospel of God— ²the gospel he promised beforehand through his prophets in the Holy Scriptures ³regarding his Son, who as to his human nature was a descendant of David, ⁴and who through the Spirit ᵃ of holiness was declared with power to be the Son of God ᵇ by his resurrection from the dead: Jesus Christ our Lord. ⁵Through him and for his name's sake, we received grace and apostleship to call people from among all the Gentiles to the obedience that comes from faith. ⁶And you also are among those who are called to belong to Jesus Christ.

⁷To all in Rome who are loved by God and called to be saints:

Grace and peace to you from God our Father and from the Lord Jesus Christ.

Paul's Longing to Visit Rome

⁸First, I thank my God through Jesus Christ for all of you, because your faith is being reported all over the world. ⁹God, whom I serve with my whole heart in preaching the gospel of his Son, is my witness how constantly I remember you ¹⁰in my prayers at all times; and I pray that now at last by God's will the way may be opened for me to come to you.

¹¹I long to see you so that I may impart to you some spiritual gift to make you strong— ¹²that is, that you and I may be mutually encouraged by each other's faith. ¹³I do not want you to be unaware, brothers, that I planned many times to come to you (but have been prevented from doing so until now) in order that I might have a harvest among you, just as I have had among the other Gentiles.

¹⁴I am obligated both to Greeks and non-Greeks, both to the wise and the foolish. ¹⁵That is why I am so eager to preach the gospel also to you who are at Rome.

¹⁶I am not ashamed of the gospel, because it is the power of God for the salvation of everyone who believes: first for the Jew, then for the Gentile. ¹⁷For in the gospel a righteousness from God is revealed, a righteousness that is by faith from first to last,ᶜ just as it is written: "The righteous will live by faith." ᵈ

God's Wrath Against Mankind

¹⁸The wrath of God is being revealed from heaven against all the godlessness and wickedness of men who suppress the truth by their wickedness, ¹⁹since what may be known about God is plain to them, because God has made it plain to them. ²⁰For since the creation of the world God's invisible qualities—his eternal power and divine nature—have been clearly seen, being understood from what has been made, so that men are without excuse.

²¹For although they knew God, they neither glorified him as God nor gave thanks to him, but their thinking became futile and their foolish hearts were darkened. ²²Although they claimed to be wise, they became fools ²³and exchanged the glory of the immortal God for images made to look like mortal man and birds and animals and reptiles.

²⁴Therefore God gave them over in the sinful desires of their hearts to sexual impurity for the degrading of their bodies with one another. ²⁵They exchanged the truth of God for a lie, and worshiped and served created things rather than the Creator—who is forever praised. Amen.

²⁶Because of this, God gave them over to shameful lusts. Even their women exchanged natural relations for unnatural ones. ²⁷In the same way the men also abandoned natural relations with women and were inflamed with lust for one another. Men committed indecent acts with other men, and received in themselves the due penalty for their perversion.

²⁸Furthermore, since they did not think it worthwhile to retain the knowledge of God, he gave them over to a depraved mind, to do what ought not to be done. ²⁹They have become filled with every kind of wickedness, evil, greed and

---

ᵃ 4 Or who as to his spirit   ᵇ 4 Or was appointed to be the Son of God with power   ᶜ 17 Or is from faith to faith   ᵈ 17 Hab. 2:4

I REMEMBER YOU IN MY
PRAYERS AT ALL TIMES.
Romans 1:9—10

Special Friendship

RUTH HARMS CALKIN

READ | ROMANS 1:1 – 17

Lord, this morning I thank You
With renewed appreciation
For the exquisite gift of friendship
And for my special friend
With her happy heart
Whose life is so intertwined with mine.

Thank You for her healthy optimism
Her enduring values
Her childlike trust in You.
Thank you for her creativity
So expansively shared.
Thank You for her direct honesty
Her radiant enthusiasm
Her refreshing freedom.
Thank you for her listening ear
Her ready response to needs.
Thank you for the way
Our thoughts walk arm-in-arm.
Thank You that together
We can be utterly ourselves without pretense —
Without fear.
Thank You that we can pray together
Laugh and cry together
Cushion defeats
And applaud victories together.

Thank You most of all, dear Lord
That through the tested years
Our friendship proves to be
Another joyful way of knowing You.

GRANDCHILD IN FOCUS • PRAYER

Relationships at Home

O Lord, I pray that you will bless the home and family of my grandchild. May the relationships she has with her parents and siblings enhance her well-being, support her self-confidence and increase her faith. May her home life reflect your love, your grace, your compassion and your peace. Guide her parents to direct her in love and truth, so she will grow into a strong and compassionate individual. Amen.

Lord, help me to remember that there are people out there who are lonely and without friends. May my heart be always open to welcome more friends into my life. Amen.

Your next devotion is located on page 1535.

depravity. They are full of envy, murder, strife, deceit and malice. They are gossips, [30]slanderers, God haters, insolent, arrogant and boastful; they invent ways of doing evil; they disobey their parents; [31]they are senseless, faithless, heartless, ruthless. [32]Although they know God's righteous decree that those who do such things deserve death, they not only continue to do these very things but also approve of those who practice them.

God's Righteous Judgment

2 You, therefore, have no excuse, you who pass judgment on someone else, for at whatever point you judge the other, you are condemning yourself, because you who pass judgment do the same things. [2]Now we know that God's judgment against those who do such things is based on truth. [3]So when you, a mere man, pass judgment on them and yet do the same things, do you think you will escape God's judgment? [4]Or do you show contempt for the riches of his kindness, tolerance and patience, not realizing that God's kindness leads you toward repentance?

[5]But because of your stubbornness and your unrepentant heart, you are storing up wrath against yourself for the day of God's wrath, when his righteous judgment will be revealed. [6]God "will give to each person according to what he has done." [a] [7]To those who by persistence in doing good seek glory, honor and immortality, he will give eternal life. [8]But for those who are self-seeking and who reject the truth and follow evil, there will be wrath and anger. [9]There will be trouble and distress for every human being who does evil: first for the Jew, then for the Gentile; [10]but glory, honor and peace for everyone who does good: first for the Jew, then for the Gentile. [11]For God does not show favoritism.

[12]All who sin apart from the law will also perish apart from the law, and all who sin under the law will be judged by the law. [13]For it is not those who hear the law who are righteous in God's sight, but it is those who obey the law who will be declared righteous. [14](Indeed, when Gentiles, who do not have the law, do by nature things required by the law, they are a law for themselves, even though they do not have the law, [15]since they show that the requirements of the law are written on their hearts, their consciences also bearing witness, and their thoughts now accusing, now even defending them.) [16]This will take place on the day when God will judge men's secrets through Jesus Christ, as my gospel declares.

The Jews and the Law

[17]Now you, if you call yourself a Jew; if you rely on the law and brag about your relationship to God; [18]if you know his will and approve of what is superior because you are instructed by the law; [19]if you are convinced that you are a guide for the blind, a light for those who are in the dark, [20]an instructor of the foolish, a teacher of infants, because you have in the law the embodiment of knowledge and truth— [21]you, then, who teach others, do you not teach yourself? You who preach against stealing, do you steal? [22]You who say that people should not commit adultery, do you commit adultery? You who abhor idols, do you rob temples? [23]You who brag about the law, do you dishonor God by breaking the law? [24]As it is written: "God's name is blasphemed among the Gentiles because of you." [b]

[25]Circumcision has value if you observe the law, but if you break the law, you have become as though you had not been circumcised. [26]If those who are not circumcised keep the law's requirements, will they not be regarded as though they were circumcised? [27]The one who is not circumcised physically and yet obeys the law will condemn you who, even though you have the [c] written code and circumcision, are a lawbreaker.

[28]A man is not a Jew if he is only one outwardly, nor is circumcision merely outward and physical. [29]No, a man is a Jew if he is one inwardly; and circumcision is circumcision of the heart, by the Spirit, not by the written code. Such a man's praise is not from men, but from God.

[a] 6 Psalm 62:12; Prov. 24:12   [b] 24 Isaiah 52:5; Ezek. 36:22
[c] 27 Or who, by means of a

God's Faithfulness

3 What advantage, then, is there in being a Jew, or what value is there in circumcision? ²Much in every way! First of all, they have been entrusted with the very words of God.

³What if some did not have faith? Will their lack of faith nullify God's faithfulness? ⁴Not at all! Let God be true, and every man a liar. As it is written:

"So that you may be proved right when you
speak
and prevail when you judge."ᵃ

⁵But if our unrighteousness brings out God's righteousness more clearly, what shall we say? That God is unjust in bringing his wrath on us? (I am using a human argument.) ⁶Certainly not! If that were so, how could God judge the world? ⁷Someone might argue, "If my falsehood enhances God's truthfulness and so increases his glory, why am I still condemned as a sinner?" ⁸Why not say—as we are being slanderously reported as saying and as some claim that we say—"Let us do evil that good may result"? Their condemnation is deserved.

No One Is Righteous

⁹What shall we conclude then? Are we any better ᵇ? Not at all! We have already made the charge that Jews and Gentiles alike are all under sin. ¹⁰As it is written:

"There is no one righteous, not even one;
¹¹ there is no one who understands,
no one who seeks God.
¹²All have turned away,
they have together become worthless;
there is no one who does good,
not even one."ᶜ
¹³"Their throats are open graves;
their tongues practice deceit."ᵈ
"The poison of vipers is on their lips."ᵉ
¹⁴ "Their mouths are full of cursing and
bitterness."ᶠ

ROMANS 3:9-31

The Only Way to Righteousness

LIFE LESSON: Salvation comes only by God's grace, through faith in Jesus Christ.

TO TALK ABOUT

✦ Can anyone be saved by keeping the Old Testament law? Why or why not?

✦ What purpose does God's law serve (see verse 20)?

✦ If keeping the law can't save us, how can we be made righteous before God?

✦ Do all people, both Jews and Gentiles, become right with God the same way? Can any of us boast about our spiritual accomplishments?

¹⁵"Their feet are swift to shed blood;
¹⁶ ruin and misery mark their ways,
¹⁷and the way of peace they do not know."ᵍ
¹⁸ "There is no fear of God before their
eyes."ʰ

¹⁹Now we know that whatever the law says, it says to those who are under the law, so that every mouth may be silenced and the whole world

ᵃ 4 Psalm 51:4 ᵇ 9 Or worse ᶜ 12 Psalms 14:1-3; 53:1-3; Eccles. 7:20 ᵈ 13 Psalm 5:9 ᵉ 13 Psalm 140:3 ᶠ 14 Psalm 10:7 ᵍ 17 Isaiah 59:7,8 ʰ 18 Psalm 36:1

FAITH IN
ACTION

Legacy Quilt

Using different colors and patterns, give each grandchild a square of fabric (about 4" x 4"). Have each grandchild write on their square their name and their favorite Bible verse (citing the book, chapter and verse is fine). Be sure to use a permanent marker or fabric marker. Then sew the squares together and bind them off for a legacy quilt or wall hanging.

You might want to add a larger square in the center on which you've written your own favorite Bible verse. Or you could use a verse such as "The eternal God is your refuge, and underneath are the everlasting arms" (Deuteronomy 33:27) or "As for me and my household, we will serve the LORD" (Joshua 24:15). Display the finished product prominently for all to see and admire.

Not a great seamstress? Find a friend or a local quilt shop to help you. If you don't have many grandchildren or the project seems overwhelming, make a pillow instead.

Older-Grandkids Variation: Have the kids help select the fabrics and cut the squares. They can also embroider their squares instead of writing on them and later help you assemble and sew the quilt. (Even the guys might enjoy this project if they are crafty.)

Thank you, Father, for the "family" legacy you've passed down to me in your written Word and in your Son. Help me to realize that my grandkids can only learn about the treasure of this inheritance from their parents and grandparents. Let this activity build unity and pride in our family. Amen.

Your next devotion is located on page 1536.

GRANDCHILD IN FOCUS • PRAYER

Friends

Dear Lord and Father, I pray for my grandchild's social life and his friends. Bring diverse friends into his life who will love and encourage him, who will bring joy and laughter to the good times and comfort and support through difficulties and disappointments. Grant him wisdom and discernment as he selects his friends; help him to avoid cliques that restrict, activities that endanger, and foolish and dangerous behaviors that harm. I ask that you fill his life with close and caring relationships. Amen.

Worship the Lord

Great are the works of the LORD;
>   they are pondered by all who delight in them.
Glorious and majestic are his deeds,
>   and his righteousness endures forever.
He has caused his wonders to be remembered;
>   the LORD is gracious and compassionate.
He provides food for those who fear him;
>   he remembers his covenant forever.
He has shown his people the power of his works,
>   giving them the lands of other nations.
The works of his hands are faithful and just;
>   all his precepts are trustworthy.
They are steadfast for ever and ever,
>   done in faithfulness and uprightness.
He provided redemption for his people;
>   he ordained his covenant
>   forever—
>   holy and awesome is his name.

Psalm 111:2 – 9

My God, I delight in your works and reflect on the wonder of your gracious deeds. You have been loving and compassionate to many generations. You have shown your people over and over again your almighty power. Thank you for all you do for us, especially for being our Redeemer. Amen.

Your next devotion is located on page 1539.

GRANDCHILD IN FOCUS • PRAYER

Self-Image

O loving God, I praise you for creating my grandchild as a unique individual. Now I ask you to help her appreciate her uniqueness. Build up her self-image so she can enjoy her individuality. Help her to stand firm for who she is, where she has come from and what she believes in. Encourage her not only to have hopes and dreams but to also enjoy each day as it comes.
In Jesus' name, amen.

held accountable to God. ²⁰Therefore no one will be declared righteous in his sight by observing the law; rather, through the law we become conscious of sin.

Righteousness Through Faith

²¹But now a righteousness from God, apart from law, has been made known, to which the Law and the Prophets testify. ²²This righteousness from God comes through faith in Jesus Christ to all who believe. There is no difference, ²³for all have sinned and fall short of the glory of God, ²⁴and are justified freely by his grace through the redemption that came by Christ Jesus. ²⁵God presented him as a sacrifice of atonement,ᵃ through faith in his blood. He did this to demonstrate his justice, because in his forbearance he had left the sins committed beforehand unpunished— ²⁶he did it to demonstrate his justice at the present time, so as to be just and the one who justifies those who have faith in Jesus.

PRAYING THE SCRIPTURES

Salvation

ROMANS 3:23–24

I pray, dear Lord, that my grandchild will come to realize that all people have sinned and fall short of your glory. Reveal to him that he can be justified freely by your grace through the redemption that came by Christ Jesus.

Next prayer in Salvation Prayer Track: Romans 8:1–2

²⁷Where, then, is boasting? It is excluded. On what principle? On that of observing the law? No, but on that of faith. ²⁸For we maintain that a man is justified by faith apart from observing the law. ²⁹Is God the God of Jews only? Is he not the God of Gentiles too? Yes, of Gentiles too, ³⁰since there is only one God, who will justify the circum-

cised by faith and the uncircumcised through that same faith. ³¹Do we, then, nullify the law by this faith? Not at all! Rather, we uphold the law.

Abraham Justified by Faith

4 What then shall we say that Abraham, our forefather, discovered in this matter? ²If, in fact, Abraham was justified by works, he had something to boast about—but not before God. ³What does the Scripture say? "Abraham believed God, and it was credited to him as righteousness."ᵇ

⁴Now when a man works, his wages are not credited to him as a gift, but as an obligation. ⁵However, to the man who does not work but trusts God who justifies the wicked, his faith is credited as righteousness. ⁶David says the same thing when he speaks of the blessedness of the man to whom God credits righteousness apart from works:

⁷"Blessed are they
   whose transgressions are forgiven,
   whose sins are covered.
⁸Blessed is the man
   whose sin the Lord will never count
      against him."ᶜ

⁹Is this blessedness only for the circumcised, or also for the uncircumcised? We have been saying that Abraham's faith was credited to him as righteousness. ¹⁰Under what circumstances was it credited? Was it after he was circumcised, or before? It was not after, but before! ¹¹And he received the sign of circumcision, a seal of the righteousness that he had by faith while he was still uncircumcised. So then, he is the father of all who believe but have not been circumcised, in order that righteousness might be credited to them. ¹²And he is also the father of the circumcised who not only are circumcised but who also walk in the footsteps of the faith that our father Abraham had before he was circumcised.

¹³It was not through law that Abraham and his

ᵃ 25 Or *as the one who would turn aside his wrath, taking away sin*
ᵇ 3 Gen. 15:6; also in verse 22   ᶜ 8 Psalm 32:1,2

offspring received the promise that he would be heir of the world, but through the righteousness that comes by faith. ¹⁴For if those who live by law are heirs, faith has no value and the promise is worthless, ¹⁵because law brings wrath. And where there is no law there is no transgression.

¹⁶Therefore, the promise comes by faith, so that it may be by grace and may be guaranteed to all Abraham's offspring—not only to those who are of the law but also to those who are of the faith of Abraham. He is the father of us all. ¹⁷As it is written: "I have made you a father of many nations."ᵃ He is our father in the sight of God, in whom he believed—the God who gives life to the dead and calls things that are not as though they were.

¹⁸Against all hope, Abraham in hope believed and so became the father of many nations, just as it had been said to him, "So shall your offspring be."ᵇ ¹⁹Without weakening in his faith, he faced the fact that his body was as good as dead—since he was about a hundred years old—and that Sarah's womb was also dead. ²⁰Yet he did not waver through unbelief regarding the promise of God, but was strengthened in his faith and gave glory to God, ²¹being fully persuaded that God had power to do what he had promised. ²²This is why "it was credited to him as righteousness." ²³The words "it was credited to him" were written not for him alone, ²⁴but also for us, to whom God will credit righteousness—for us who believe in him who raised Jesus our Lord from the dead. ²⁵He was delivered over to death for our sins and was raised to life for our justification.

Peace and Joy

5 Therefore, since we have been justified through faith, weᶜ have peace with God through our Lord Jesus Christ, ²through whom we have gained access by faith into this grace in which we now stand. And weᶜ rejoice in the hope of the glory of God. ³Not only so, but weᶜ also rejoice in our sufferings, because we know that suffering produces perseverance; ⁴perseverance, character; and character, hope. ⁵And hope does not disappoint us, because God has poured out his love into our hearts by the Holy Spirit, whom he has given us.

⁶You see, at just the right time, when we were still powerless, Christ died for the ungodly. ⁷Very rarely will anyone die for a righteous man, though for a good man someone might possibly dare to die. ⁸But God demonstrates his own love for us in this: While we were still sinners, Christ died for us.

⁹Since we have now been justified by his blood, how much more shall we be saved from God's wrath through him! ¹⁰For if, when we were God's enemies, we were reconciled to him through the death of his Son, how much more, having been reconciled, shall we be saved through his life! ¹¹Not only is this so, but we also rejoice in God through our Lord Jesus Christ, through whom we have now received reconciliation.

Death Through Adam, Life Through Christ

¹²Therefore, just as sin entered the world through one man, and death through sin, and in this way death came to all men, because all sinned— ¹³for before the law was given, sin was in the world. But sin is not taken into account when there is no law. ¹⁴Nevertheless, death reigned from the time of Adam to the time of Moses, even over those who did not sin by breaking a command, as did Adam, who was a pattern of the one to come.

¹⁵But the gift is not like the trespass. For if the many died by the trespass of the one man, how much more did God's grace and the gift that came by the grace of the one man, Jesus Christ, overflow to the many! ¹⁶Again, the gift of God is not like the result of the one man's sin: The judgment followed one sin and brought condemnation, but the gift followed many trespasses and brought justification. ¹⁷For if, by the trespass of the one man, death reigned through that one man, how much more will those who receive God's abundant provision of grace and of the

ᵃ 17 Gen. 17:5   ᵇ 18 Gen. 15:5   ᶜ 1,2,3 Or *let us*

> FOR JUST AS THROUGH THE
> DISOBEDIENCE OF THE ONE MAN
> THE MANY WERE MADE SINNERS, SO
> ALSO THROUGH THE OBEDIENCE OF
> THE ONE MAN THE MANY WILL BE
> MADE RIGHTEOUS.
> *Romans 5:19*

Two Women

MARI SEREBROV

READ | ROMANS 5:12–21

In Romans 5, Paul discusses how by one man sin entered the world and how through another man came eternal life.

Behind those men were women. One was a wife, the other a mother. Both women made their own choices.

When Eve was tempted in the garden, she thought only of herself. The forbidden fruit looked so delicious. Surely God wouldn't punish her—not for one little bite. Dismissing the consequences, Eve bit into the lush fruit.

Eve's sin wasn't complete until she shared the fruit with Adam. From the moment Adam bit into the fruit, their relationship with God, with each other and [with] their inner selves was strained.

Eve remembered her selfishness with each child she bore. As she watched her children quarrel, get angry and turn their backs on God, she felt responsible.

Centuries later, an angel appeared to a virgin, asking her to put her reputation, her future, on the line for God. Mary knew she could be shamed, put away or even stoned if she bore a child out of wedlock. But Mary wasn't thinking of herself. Dismissing the consequences, Mary paved the way for God to bridge the gap Eve had helped build.

Neither Eve nor Mary had an easy life. Eve grieved when one son murdered another. Mary sorrowed as her firstborn hung on the cross. In thinking only of herself, Eve helped condemn the world and lived a life of defeat. But in forgetting herself, Mary discovered victory and brought new promise to generations to come.

Lord, I pray for the wisdom, the courage and the piety to choose your ways and your will. Thank you for the model I have in Mary, a woman of devotion and selflessness.

Your next devotion is located on page 1542.

GRANDCHILD IN FOCUS • PRAYER

Protection From Worldliness

O Sovereign Lord, the world surrounds my grandchild, pressing in and tempting him in so many ways. Help him set appropriate limits. Give him sound judgment to choose wisely. Guard him from temptation; protect him from physical and mental predators; lead him into paths of righteousness and light. And reassure me with your promise that you are holding him in your hands. Amen.

gift of righteousness reign in life through the one man, Jesus Christ.

[18] Consequently, just as the result of one trespass was condemnation for all men, so also the result of one act of righteousness was justification that brings life for all men. [19] For just as through the disobedience of the one man the many were made sinners, so also through the obedience of the one man the many will be made righteous.

[20] The law was added so that the trespass might increase. But where sin increased, grace increased all the more, [21] so that, just as sin reigned in death, so also grace might reign through righteousness to bring eternal life through Jesus Christ our Lord.

Dead to Sin, Alive in Christ

6 What shall we say, then? Shall we go on sinning so that grace may increase? [2] By no means! We died to sin; how can we live in it any longer? [3] Or don't you know that all of us who were baptized into Christ Jesus were baptized into his death? [4] We were therefore buried with him through baptism into death in order that, just as Christ was raised from the dead through the glory of the Father, we too may live a new life.

[5] If we have been united with him like this in his death, we will certainly also be united with him in his resurrection. [6] For we know that our old self was crucified with him so that the body of sin might be done away with, [a] that we should no longer be slaves to sin— [7] because anyone who has died has been freed from sin.

[8] Now if we died with Christ, we believe that we will also live with him. [9] For we know that since Christ was raised from the dead, he cannot die again; death no longer has mastery over him. [10] The death he died, he died to sin once for all; but the life he lives, he lives to God.

[11] In the same way, count yourselves dead to sin but alive to God in Christ Jesus. [12] Therefore do not let sin reign in your mortal body so that you obey its evil desires. [13] Do not offer the parts of your body to sin, as instruments of wickedness, but rather offer yourselves to God, as those who have been brought from death to life; and offer the parts of your body to him as instruments of righteousness. [14] For sin shall not be your master, because you are not under law, but under grace.

Slaves to Righteousness

[15] What then? Shall we sin because we are not under law but under grace? By no means! [16] Don't you know that when you offer yourselves to someone to obey him as slaves, you are slaves to the one whom you obey—whether you are slaves to sin, which leads to death, or to obedience, which leads to righteousness? [17] But thanks be to God that, though you used to be slaves to sin, you wholeheartedly obeyed the form of teaching to which you were entrusted. [18] You have been set free from sin and have become slaves to righteousness.

[19] I put this in human terms because you are weak in your natural selves. Just as you used to offer the parts of your body in slavery to impurity and to ever-increasing wickedness, so now offer them in slavery to righteousness leading to holiness. [20] When you were slaves to sin, you were free from the control of righteousness. [21] What benefit did you reap at that time from the things you are now ashamed of? Those things result in death! [22] But now that you have been set free from sin and have become slaves to God, the benefit you reap leads to holiness, and the result is eternal life. [23] For the wages of sin is death, but the gift of God is eternal life in [b] Christ Jesus our Lord.

An Illustration From Marriage

7 Do you not know, brothers—for I am speaking to men who know the law—that the law has authority over a man only as long as he lives? [2] For example, by law a married woman is bound to her husband as long as he is alive, but if her husband dies, she is released from the law of marriage. [3] So then, if she marries another man while her husband is still alive, she is called an adulteress. But if her husband dies, she is released from

[a] 6 Or be rendered powerless   [b] 23 Or through

that law and is not an adulteress, even though she marries another man.

[4]So, my brothers, you also died to the law through the body of Christ, that you might belong to another, to him who was raised from the dead, in order that we might bear fruit to God. [5]For when we were controlled by the sinful nature,[a] the sinful passions aroused by the law were at work in our bodies, so that we bore fruit for death. [6]But now, by dying to what once bound us, we have been released from the law so that we serve in the new way of the Spirit, and not in the old way of the written code.

Struggling With Sin

[7]What shall we say, then? Is the law sin? Certainly not! Indeed I would not have known what sin was except through the law. For I would not have known what coveting really was if the law had not said, "Do not covet."[b] [8]But sin, seizing the opportunity afforded by the commandment, produced in me every kind of covetous desire. For apart from law, sin is dead. [9]Once I was alive apart from law; but when the commandment came, sin sprang to life and I died. [10]I found that the very commandment that was intended to bring life actually brought death. [11]For sin, seizing the opportunity afforded by the commandment, deceived me, and through the commandment put me to death. [12]So then, the law is holy, and the commandment is holy, righteous and good.

[13]Did that which is good, then, become death to me? By no means! But in order that sin might be recognized as sin, it produced death in me through what was good, so that through the commandment sin might become utterly sinful.

[14]We know that the law is spiritual; but I am unspiritual, sold as a slave to sin. [15]I do not understand what I do. For what I want to do I do not do, but what I hate I do. [16]And if I do what I do not want to do, I agree that the law is good. [17]As it is, it is no longer I myself who do it, but it is sin living in me. [18]I know that nothing good lives in me, that is, in my sinful nature.[c] For I have the desire

to do what is good, but I cannot carry it out. [19]For what I do is not the good I want to do; no, the evil I do not want to do—this I keep on doing. [20]Now if I do what I do not want to do, it is no longer I who do it, but it is sin living in me that does it.

[21]So I find this law at work: When I want to do good, evil is right there with me. [22]For in my inner being I delight in God's law; [23]but I see another law at work in the members of my body, waging war against the law of my mind and making me a prisoner of the law of sin at work within my members. [24]What a wretched man I am! Who will rescue me from this body of death? [25]Thanks be to God—through Jesus Christ our Lord!

So then, I myself in my mind am a slave to God's law, but in the sinful nature a slave to the law of sin.

Life Through the Spirit

8 Therefore, there is now no condemnation for those who are in Christ Jesus,[d] [2]because through Christ Jesus the law of the Spirit of life set me free from the law of sin and death. [3]For what the law was powerless to do in that it was weakened by the sinful nature,[e] God did by

---

[a] 5 Or *the flesh*; also in verse 25   [b] 7 Exodus 20:17; Deut. 5:21   [c] 18 Or *my flesh*   [d] 1 Some later manuscripts *Jesus, who do not live according to the sinful nature but according to the Spirit,*   [e] 3 Or *the flesh*; also in verses 4, 5, 8, 9, 12 and 13

PRAYING THE SCRIPTURES

Salvation

ROMANS 8:1–2

Dear God, help my grandchild to accept that there is now no condemnation for her if she is in Christ Jesus, because through him the law of the Spirit of life has set her free from the law of sin and death.

Next prayer in Salvation Prayer Track: Romans 10:10

I KNOW THAT NOTHING GOOD
LIVES IN ME, THAT IS, IN MY
SINFUL NATURE. FOR I HAVE THE
DESIRE TO DO WHAT IS GOOD,
BUT I CANNOT CARRY IT OUT.

Romans 7:18

Jesus Living in Me

MARILYN MEBERG

READ | ROMANS 7:7 – 25

The power to obey ... isn't that what we all need? It wasn't just the Israelites who blew it repeatedly and had to be jerk-chained back into line; it's every human being who's ever lived. We lack the power to obey. God knew his standard was humanly impossible, so he made sure we all knew that and then made a new covenant — one that provided for us a perfect person (Jesus) who, through his death on the cross, paid the price for our imperfections (sin). When I enter into that covenant relationship with Christ, I am washed with grace and welcomed as one of his people. My imperfection is forgiven and God forgets it.

Grasping all this and incorporating it consistently will always be a challenge to me, even though Scripture repeatedly tells me I can do nothing in and of myself that eliminates my bent toward disobedience. Nothing in and of myself will give me the power to obey, other than his empowerment.

If I truly believe in the terms of the new covenant, I will recognize that it is the Holy Spirit of God, living in me, who produces that behavior for which I long, but, paradoxically, sometimes fight against.

What is behind that huge relief effort is God's love, a stubborn love that will not let me go, a love so tenacious, so gracious, so unfathomable that he willingly made a new covenant with me at the highest price. That covenant is designed to assure me that in spite of poor performance, I am his and he is mine.

My guess is that we all need encouragement to relax in the grace of the new covenant.

Holy Spirit, draw me nearer. Live in me and fill me with your power and grace, so that in all that I do and say I will be obedient to your Word. Amen.

Your next devotion is located on page 1544.

GRANDCHILD IN FOCUS • PRAYER

Respect for Authority

Dear Lord, I pray that my grandchild will continually grow to respect those in authority. May she learn to be coopera-tive and fair in work and play. Instill in her a high regard for officials who govern our land and enforce the laws. May her relationships with parents, teachers, coaches, mentors and bosses be respectful, admirable, con-structive and caring. Amen.

⁹You, however, are controlled not by the sinful nature but by the Spirit, if the Spirit of God lives in you. And if anyone does not have the Spirit of Christ, he does not belong to Christ. ¹⁰But if Christ is in you, your body is dead because of sin, yet your spirit is alive because of righteousness. ¹¹And if the Spirit of him who raised Jesus from the dead is living in you, he who raised Christ from the dead will also give life to your mortal bodies through his Spirit, who lives in you.

¹²Therefore, brothers, we have an obligation—but it is not to the sinful nature, to live according to it. ¹³For if you live according to the sinful nature, you will die; but if by the Spirit you put to death the misdeeds of the body, you will live, ¹⁴because those who are led by the Spirit of God are sons of God. ¹⁵For you did not receive a spirit that makes you a slave again to fear, but you received the Spirit of sonship.ᵉ And by him we cry, "*Abba*,ᶠ Father." ¹⁶The Spirit himself testifies with our spirit that we are God's children. ¹⁷Now if we are children, then we are heirs—heirs of God and co-heirs with Christ, if indeed we share in his sufferings in order that we may also share in his glory.

Future Glory

¹⁸I consider that our present sufferings are not worth comparing with the glory that will be revealed in us. ¹⁹The creation waits in eager expectation for the sons of God to be revealed. ²⁰For the creation was subjected to frustration, not by its own choice, but by the will of the one who subjected it, in hope ²¹thatᵍ the creation itself will be liberated from its bondage to decay and brought into the glorious freedom of the children of God.

²²We know that the whole creation has been groaning as in the pains of childbirth right up to the present time. ²³Not only so, but we ourselves, who have the firstfruits of the Spirit, groan inwardly as we wait eagerly for our adoption as

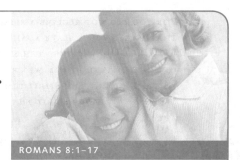
sending his own Son in the likeness of sinful man to be a sin offering.ᵃ And so he condemned sin in sinful man,ᵇ ⁴in order that the righteous requirements of the law might be fully met in us, who do not live according to the sinful nature but according to the Spirit.

⁵Those who live according to the sinful nature have their minds set on what that nature desires; but those who live in accordance with the Spirit have their minds set on what the Spirit desires. ⁶The mind of sinful manᶜ is death, but the mind controlled by the Spirit is life and peace; ⁷the sinful mindᵈ is hostile to God. It does not submit to God's law, nor can it do so. ⁸Those controlled by the sinful nature cannot please God.

ᵃ 3 Or *man, for sin*   ᵇ 3 Or *in the flesh*   ᶜ 6 Or *mind set on the flesh*   ᵈ 7 Or *The mind set on the flesh*   ᵉ 15 Or *adoption*
ᶠ 15 Aramaic for *Father*   ᵍ 20,21 Or *subjected it in hope. 21For*

FOR YOU DID NOT RECEIVE A SPIRIT THAT MAKES YOU A SLAVE AGAIN TO FEAR, BUT YOU RECEIVED THE SPIRIT OF SONSHIP. AND BY HIM WE CRY, *"Abba*, FATHER." THE SPIRIT HIMSELF TESTIFIES WITH OUR SPIRIT THAT WE ARE GOD'S CHILDREN.

Romans 8:15 – 16

Papa God

DAWN SCOTT JONES

READ | ROMANS 8:1 – 17

I had been waiting for months to hear my first grandchild speak my name. I had come close to hearing it: "Did she say ba-nana or gramma?" My ears were keenly perked, waiting to hear baby Victoria utter that word. Finally, she connected my face with my name. Victoria put her little arms out, reached for me and said, "Nama." It was, and still is today, an amazing thrill to hear all my grandchildren call me "Nama."

In the same way that we receive pure joy from hearing the ones we love speak our name, God delights in hearing us call his name. He even invites us to use his most intimate name, *Abba*.

The name *Abba* in Aramaic is the equivalent of "papa" or "dada." It denotes a close, unique and caring relationship that only a father has with his children. Using this name means we share a special relationship with God. When we use this name, he longs for us to understand who he is in our life.

When we call on *Abba*, he hears us as a daddy hears his child. Our heavenly Papa is close to us, ready to guide us, protect us, comfort us and even discipline us when we need it.

I was thrilled to hear my name, "Nama." Imagine heaven's joy when we recognize God as our *Abba* — our Papa. Imagine his delight when we lift our voice to him and say, "You are my Father and I am your child!"

"And by him we cry, '*Abba*, Father.' The Spirit himself testifies with our spirit that we are God's children" (Romans 8:15 – 16).

Papa God, your name is above all names, and I worship you. Thank you for giving me access to your throne room of grace and for allowing me to call upon your name. I bring my cares to you today, knowing that you — my Abba God — delight in hearing me, and you will answer when I call. Amen.

Your next devotion is located on page 1546.

GRANDCHILD IN FOCUS • PRAYER

Courage

O Father, builder of character and courage, may my grandchild grow strong in the light of your love. Grant him courage to stand for what is right, to guard the truth and to ensure justice in every aspect of life. May he boldly grow in grace, revere your name and proudly proclaim you as the Lord of lords and King of kings. Amen.

sons, the redemption of our bodies. ²⁴For in this hope we were saved. But hope that is seen is no hope at all. Who hopes for what he already has? ²⁵But if we hope for what we do not yet have, we wait for it patiently.

²⁶In the same way, the Spirit helps us in our weakness. We do not know what we ought to pray for, but the Spirit himself intercedes for us with groans that words cannot express. ²⁷And he who searches our hearts knows the mind of the Spirit, because the Spirit intercedes for the saints in accordance with God's will.

More Than Conquerors

²⁸And we know that in all things God works for the good of those who love him,ᵃ whoᵇ have been called according to his purpose. ²⁹For those God foreknew he also predestined to be conformed to the likeness of his Son, that he might be the firstborn among many brothers. ³⁰And those he predestined, he also called; those he called, he also justified; those he justified, he also glorified.

TALKING POINTS

Encouragement

In all circumstances God works for the good of those who love him.

ROMANS 8:28

For more on encouragement, go to 2 Thessalonians 2:16–17.

³¹What, then, shall we say in response to this? If God is for us, who can be against us? ³²He who did not spare his own Son, but gave him up for us all—how will he not also, along with him, graciously give us all things? ³³Who will bring any charge against those whom God has chosen? It is God who justifies. ³⁴Who is he that condemns? Christ Jesus, who died—more than that, who

was raised to life—is at the right hand of God and is also interceding for us. ³⁵Who shall separate us from the love of Christ? Shall trouble or hardship or persecution or famine or nakedness or danger or sword? ³⁶As it is written:

> "For your sake we face death all day long;
> we are considered as sheep to be
> slaughtered."ᶜ

³⁷No, in all these things we are more than conquerors through him who loved us. ³⁸For I am convinced that neither death nor life, neither angels nor demons,ᵈ neither the present nor the future, nor any powers, ³⁹neither height nor depth, nor anything else in all creation, will be able to separate us from the love of God that is in Christ Jesus our Lord.

God's Sovereign Choice

9 I speak the truth in Christ—I am not lying, my conscience confirms it in the Holy Spirit— ²I have great sorrow and unceasing anguish in my heart. ³For I could wish that I myself were cursed and cut off from Christ for the sake of my brothers, those of my own race, ⁴the people of Israel. Theirs is the adoption as sons; theirs the divine glory, the covenants, the receiving of the law, the temple worship and the promises. ⁵Theirs are the patriarchs, and from them is traced the human ancestry of Christ, who is God over all, forever praised!ᵉ Amen.

⁶It is not as though God's word had failed. For not all who are descended from Israel are Israel. ⁷Nor because they are his descendants are they all Abraham's children. On the contrary, "It is through Isaac that your offspring will be reckoned."ᶠ ⁸In other words, it is not the natural children who are God's children, but it is the children of the promise who are regarded as Abraham's offspring. ⁹For this was how the promise

---

ᵃ 28 Some manuscripts *And we know that all things work together for good to those who love God*   ᵇ 28 Or *works together with those who love him to bring about what is good—with those who*   ᶜ 36 Psalm 44:22   ᵈ 38 Or *nor heavenly rulers*   ᵉ 5 Or *Christ, who is over all. God be forever praised! Or Christ. God who is over all be forever praised!*   ᶠ 7 Gen. 21:12

AND WE KNOW THAT IN ALL THINGS GOD WORKS
FOR THE GOOD OF THOSE WHO LOVE HIM, WHO
HAVE BEEN CALLED ACCORDING TO HIS PURPOSE.
FOR THOSE GOD FOREKNEW HE ALSO PREDESTINED
TO BE CONFORMED TO THE LIKENESS OF HIS SON
... IF GOD IS FOR US, WHO CAN BE AGAINST US?

Romans 8:28 – 29, 31

Becoming Like Jesus

DEBBY KERNER RETTINO

READ | ROMANS 8:28 – 39

"God is for me, and it is my destiny to become like Jesus." That belongs on the dashboard of my car to remind me that God is actively working in my life in the good stuff *and* the messes I get myself into! One of the biggest problems I have is with control of my tongue. If I just said less or waited for the right moment, I could avoid a lot of trouble. The fact that I can share that weakness is proof that God is working in that area of my life, making me more like his Son.

A blessing of maturity is living long enough to see people change and grow as God works in their lives. I'm even improving with regard to keeping my mouth shut. But, with my kids and grandkids, it's hard to resist the urge to try to fix things. I keep thinking if I can fix the circumstances and get the externals right, their characters will develop properly. But God works in the circumstances to get their characters right. I confess — I am afraid of that.

As a young mother, I was afraid to dedicate my children to the Lord. I thought something terrible would happen so God could work on my character. How stupid is that? The safest place I can leave my children is in God's care. My prayer of dedication for my kids was gut-wrenching *and* liberating. I trusted that God was going to be working in their lives and that God would be for them. That didn't guarantee life would be smooth or easy, and it's still hard to keep my hands off and my mouth shut when I think I can fix things. But, God is still for me. My destiny is to become like Jesus.

Father, you know me, and you know my children and grandchildren. From before we were born you have known us. There is absolutely no-where we can go where you are not present, holding us, sustaining us and changing us to be like your Son. Help me to trust you when things are not so easy and to know that you are active and at work in my life and in the lives of my loved ones. I proclaim you as Lord. In the powerful name of Jesus, amen.

Your next devotion is located on page 1551.

GRANDCHILD IN FOCUS · PRAYER

Future Spouse

Dear Lord, if it is your will, I pray my grandchild will be united in a loving and Christian marriage. Keep her sexually pure so that she will honor you with her body and mind. As she seeks a spouse who will honor and care for her, give her patience and discernment. May her choice for a life partner be your choice for her, so that she and her husband will together glorify you in a lasting love. I pray this in Jesus' name, amen.

was stated: "At the appointed time I will return, and Sarah will have a son."[a]

[10] Not only that, but Rebekah's children had one and the same father, our father Isaac. [11] Yet, before the twins were born or had done anything good or bad—in order that God's purpose in election might stand: [12] not by works but by him who calls—she was told, "The older will serve the younger."[b] [13] Just as it is written: "Jacob I loved, but Esau I hated."[c]

[14] What then shall we say? Is God unjust? Not at all! [15] For he says to Moses,

"I will have mercy on whom I have mercy,
    and I will have compassion on whom I
        have compassion."[d]

[16] It does not, therefore, depend on man's desire or effort, but on God's mercy. [17] For the Scripture says to Pharaoh: "I raised you up for this very purpose, that I might display my power in you and that my name might be proclaimed in all the earth."[e] [18] Therefore God has mercy on whom he wants to have mercy, and he hardens whom he wants to harden.

[19] One of you will say to me: "Then why does God still blame us? For who resists his will?" [20] But who are you, O man, to talk back to God? "Shall what is formed say to him who formed it, 'Why did you make me like this?'"[f] [21] Does not the potter have the right to make out of the same lump of clay some pottery for noble purposes and some for common use?

[22] What if God, choosing to show his wrath and make his power known, bore with great patience the objects of his wrath—prepared for destruction? [23] What if he did this to make the riches of his glory known to the objects of his mercy, whom he prepared in advance for glory—[24] even us, whom he also called, not only from the Jews but also from the Gentiles? [25] As he says in Hosea:

"I will call them 'my people' who are not my
        people;
    and I will call her 'my loved one' who is
        not my loved one,"[g]

[26] and,

"It will happen that in the very place where it
        was said to them,
    'You are not my people,'
they will be called 'sons of the living God.'"[h]

[27] Isaiah cries out concerning Israel:

"Though the number of the Israelites be like
        the sand by the sea,
    only the remnant will be saved.
[28] For the Lord will carry out
    his sentence on earth with speed and
        finality."[i]

[29] It is just as Isaiah said previously:

"Unless the Lord Almighty
    had left us descendants,
we would have become like Sodom,
    we would have been like Gomorrah."[j]

Israel's Unbelief

[30] What then shall we say? That the Gentiles, who did not pursue righteousness, have obtained it, a righteousness that is by faith; [31] but Israel, who pursued a law of righteousness, has not attained it. [32] Why not? Because they pursued it not by faith but as if it were by works. They stumbled over the "stumbling stone." [33] As it is written:

"See, I lay in Zion a stone that causes men to
        stumble
    and a rock that makes them fall,
and the one who trusts in him will never be
        put to shame."[k]

[10] Brothers, my heart's desire and prayer to God for the Israelites is that they may be saved. [2] For I can testify about them that they are zealous for God, but their zeal is not based on knowledge. [3] Since they did not know the righteousness that comes from God and sought to establish their own, they did not submit to God's righteousness. [4] Christ is the end of the law so

[a] 9 Gen. 18:10,14   [b] 12 Gen. 25:23   [c] 13 Mal. 1:2,3
[d] 15 Exodus 33:19   [e] 17 Exodus 9:16   [f] 20 Isaiah 29:16; 45:9
[g] 25 Hosea 2:23   [h] 26 Hosea 1:10   [i] 28 Isaiah 10:22,23
[j] 29 Isaiah 1:9   [k] 33 Isaiah 8:14; 28:16

that there may be righteousness for everyone who believes.

⁵Moses describes in this way the righteousness that is by the law: "The man who does these things will live by them."*ᵃ* ⁶But the righteousness that is by faith says: "Do not say in your heart, 'Who will ascend into heaven?'*ᵇ*" (that is, to bring Christ down) ⁷"or 'Who will descend into the deep?'*ᶜ*" (that is, to bring Christ up from the dead). ⁸But what does it say? "The word is near you; it is in your mouth and in your heart,"*ᵈ* that is, the word of faith we are proclaiming: ⁹That if you confess with your mouth, "Jesus is Lord," and believe in your heart that God raised him from the dead, you will be saved. ¹⁰For it is with your heart that you believe and are justified, and it is with your mouth that you confess and are saved. ¹¹As the

PRAYING THE SCRIPTURES

Salvation

ROMANS 10:10

Almighty God, may my grandchild come to recognize and live out the truth that it is with his heart that he believes and is justified, and it is with his mouth that he confesses and is saved.

Next prayer in Salvation Prayer Track:
1 Corinthians 15:3–4

Scripture says, "Anyone who trusts in him will never be put to shame."*ᵉ* ¹²For there is no difference between Jew and Gentile—the same Lord is Lord of all and richly blesses all who call on him, ¹³for, "Everyone who calls on the name of the Lord will be saved."*ᶠ*

¹⁴How, then, can they call on the one they have not believed in? And how can they believe in the one of whom they have not heard? And how can they hear without someone preaching to them? ¹⁵And how can they preach unless they are sent?

As it is written, "How beautiful are the feet of those who bring good news!"*ᵍ*

¹⁶But not all the Israelites accepted the good news. For Isaiah says, "Lord, who has believed our message?"*ʰ* ¹⁷Consequently, faith comes from hearing the message, and the message is heard through the word of Christ. ¹⁸But I ask: Did they not hear? Of course they did:

"Their voice has gone out into all the earth,
	their words to the ends of the world."*ⁱ*

¹⁹Again I ask: Did Israel not understand? First, Moses says,

"I will make you envious by those who are
		not a nation;
	I will make you angry by a nation that has
		no understanding."*ʲ*

²⁰And Isaiah boldly says,

"I was found by those who did not seek me;
	I revealed myself to those who did not ask
		for me."*ᵏ*

²¹But concerning Israel he says,

"All day long I have held out my hands
	to a disobedient and obstinate people."*ˡ*

The Remnant of Israel

11 I ask then: Did God reject his people? By no means! I am an Israelite myself, a descendant of Abraham, from the tribe of Benjamin. ²God did not reject his people, whom he foreknew. Don't you know what the Scripture says in the passage about Elijah—how he appealed to God against Israel: ³"Lord, they have killed your prophets and torn down your altars; I am the only one left, and they are trying to kill me"*ᵐ*? ⁴And what was God's answer to him? "I have reserved for myself seven thousand who have not bowed the knee to Baal."*ⁿ* ⁵So too, at the present time there is a remnant chosen by grace.

ᵃ 5 Lev. 18:5	*ᵇ 6* Deut. 30:12	*ᶜ 7* Deut. 30:13
ᵈ 8 Deut. 30:14	*ᵉ 11* Isaiah 28:16	*ᶠ 13* Joel 2:32
ᵍ 15 Isaiah 52:7	*ʰ 16* Isaiah 53:1	*ⁱ 18* Psalm 19:4
ʲ 19 Deut. 32:21	*ᵏ 20* Isaiah 65:1	*ˡ 21* Isaiah 65:2
ᵐ 3 1 Kings 19:10,14	*ⁿ 4* 1 Kings 19:18

[6] And if by grace, then it is no longer by works; if it were, grace would no longer be grace. [a]

[7] What then? What Israel sought so earnestly it did not obtain, but the elect did. The others were hardened, [8] as it is written:

"God gave them a spirit of stupor,
    eyes so that they could not see
    and ears so that they could not hear,
to this very day." [b]

[9] And David says:

"May their table become a snare and a trap,
    a stumbling block and a retribution for
        them.
[10] May their eyes be darkened so they cannot see,
    and their backs be bent forever." [c]

Ingrafted Branches

[11] Again I ask: Did they stumble so as to fall beyond recovery? Not at all! Rather, because of their transgression, salvation has come to the Gentiles to make Israel envious. [12] But if their transgression means riches for the world, and their loss means riches for the Gentiles, how much greater riches will their fullness bring!

[13] I am talking to you Gentiles. Inasmuch as I am the apostle to the Gentiles, I make much of my ministry [14] in the hope that I may somehow arouse my own people to envy and save some of them. [15] For if their rejection is the reconciliation of the world, what will their acceptance be but life from the dead? [16] If the part of the dough offered as firstfruits is holy, then the whole batch is holy; if the root is holy, so are the branches.

[17] If some of the branches have been broken off, and you, though a wild olive shoot, have been grafted in among the others and now share in the nourishing sap from the olive root, [18] do not boast over those branches. If you do, consider this: You do not support the root, but the root supports you. [19] You will say then, "Branches were broken off so that I could be grafted in." [20] Granted. But they were broken off because of unbelief, and you stand by faith. Do not be arrogant, but

be afraid. [21] For if God did not spare the natural branches, he will not spare you either.

[22] Consider therefore the kindness and sternness of God: sternness to those who fell, but kindness to you, provided that you continue in his kindness. Otherwise, you also will be cut off. [23] And if they do not persist in unbelief, they will be grafted in, for God is able to graft them in again. [24] After all, if you were cut out of an olive tree that is wild by nature, and contrary to nature were grafted into a cultivated olive tree, how much more readily will these, the natural branches, be grafted into their own olive tree!

All Israel Will Be Saved

[25] I do not want you to be ignorant of this mystery, brothers, so that you may not be conceited: Israel has experienced a hardening in part until the full number of the Gentiles has come in. [26] And so all Israel will be saved, as it is written:

"The deliverer will come from Zion;
    he will turn godlessness away from Jacob.
[27] And this is [d] my covenant with them
    when I take away their sins." [e]

[28] As far as the gospel is concerned, they are enemies on your account; but as far as election is concerned, they are loved on account of the patriarchs, [29] for God's gifts and his call are irrevocable. [30] Just as you who were at one time disobedient to God have now received mercy as a result of their disobedience, [31] so they too have now become disobedient in order that they too may now [f] receive mercy as a result of God's mercy to you. [32] For God has bound all men over to disobedience so that he may have mercy on them all.

Doxology

[33] Oh, the depth of the riches of the wisdom
        and [g] knowledge of God!
    How unsearchable his judgments,
        and his paths beyond tracing out!

---

[a] 6 Some manuscripts be grace. But if by works, then it is no longer grace; if it were, work would no longer be work.   [b] 8 Deut. 29:4; Isaiah 29:10   [c] 10 Psalm 69:22,23   [d] 27 Or will be
[e] 27 Isaiah 59:20,21; 27:9; Jer. 31:33,34   [f] 31 Some manuscripts do not have now.   [g] 33 Or riches and the wisdom and the

34 "Who has known the mind of the Lord?
   Or who has been his counselor?"[a]
35 "Who has ever given to God,
   that God should repay him?"[b]
36 For from him and through him and to him
   are all things.
   To him be the glory forever! Amen.

Living Sacrifices

12 Therefore, I urge you, brothers, in view of God's mercy, to offer your bodies as living sacrifices, holy and pleasing to God—this is your spiritual[c] act of worship. ²Do not conform any longer to the pattern of this world, but be transformed by the renewing of your mind. Then you will be able to test and approve what God's will is—his good, pleasing and perfect will.

TALKING POINTS

Worldliness

Don't conform to the world;
be transformed by God.

ROMANS 12:1–2

For more on worldliness, go to James 1:27.

³For by the grace given me I say to every one of you: Do not think of yourself more highly than you ought, but rather think of yourself with sober judgment, in accordance with the measure of faith God has given you. ⁴Just as each of us has one body with many members, and these members do not all have the same function, ⁵so in Christ we who are many form one body, and each member belongs to all the others. ⁶We have different gifts, according to the grace given us. If a man's gift is prophesying, let him use it in proportion to his[d] faith. ⁷If it is serving, let him serve; if it is teaching, let him teach; ⁸if it is encouraging, let him encourage; if it is contributing to the needs of others, let him give generously; if it is leadership, let him govern diligently; if it is showing mercy, let him do it cheerfully.

Love

⁹Love must be sincere. Hate what is evil; cling to what is good. ¹⁰Be devoted to one another in brotherly love. Honor one another above yourselves. ¹¹Never be lacking in zeal, but keep your spiritual fervor, serving the Lord. ¹²Be joyful in hope, patient in affliction, faithful in prayer. ¹³Share with God's people who are in need. Practice hospitality.

¹⁴Bless those who persecute you; bless and do not curse. ¹⁵Rejoice with those who rejoice; mourn with those who mourn. ¹⁶Live in harmony with one another. Do not be proud, but be willing to associate with people of low position.[e] Do not be conceited.

¹⁷Do not repay anyone evil for evil. Be careful to do what is right in the eyes of everybody. ¹⁸If it is possible, as far as it depends on you, live at peace with everyone. ¹⁹Do not take revenge, my friends, but leave room for God's wrath, for it is written: "It is mine to avenge; I will repay,"[f] says the Lord. ²⁰On the contrary:

"If your enemy is hungry, feed him;
   if he is thirsty, give him something to drink.
In doing this, you will heap burning coals on
   his head."[g]

---

[a] 34 Isaiah 40:13   [b] 35 Job 41:11   [c] 1 Or *reasonable*
[d] 6 Or *in agreement with the*   [e] 16 Or *willing to do menial work*
[f] 19 Deut. 32:35   [g] 20 Prov. 25:21,22

TALKING POINTS

Patience

Be patient during difficult times.

ROMANS 12:12

For more on patience, go to 2 Peter 3:9.

LOVE MUST BE SINCERE. HATE WHAT IS EVIL; CLING TO WHAT IS GOOD. BE DEVOTED TO ONE ANOTHER IN BROTHERLY LOVE. HONOR ONE ANOTHER ABOVE YOURSELVES.

Romans 12:9–10

Living a Godly Life Before Your Grandchildren

JEAN E. SYSWERDA

READ | ROMANS 12:9–13

We know that Paul, the author of the book of Romans, was single during the period of his missionary journeys (see 1 Corinthians 7:8). So unless he had been married earlier, he was never a father or a grandfather. However, his advice in Romans 12:9–13 provides grandmothers everywhere with some great goals in living a godly life before their grandchildren.

Putting each one of these pieces of advice into practice will benefit our grandkids, probably in ways we can't even begin to imagine. When we love them sincerely, no fake affection allowed, we offer them a self-image of worthiness. When we hate evil and do good, we provide them a map for everyday living. When we show love to others, we teach them to live like Christ. When we honor others before ourselves, we coach them in living a selfless, rather than selfish, life. When we approach our spiritual life with fervor, we model a way to live passionately as a believer. Being joyful and patient? Those character traits go without saying. We want our grandchildren to grow up to be patient and joyful—especially when faced with adversity, which is also the proving ground for our own joy and patience.

When we're faithful in prayer, we teach our grandkids all about the wisdom of searching out God and his will for our lives and theirs. When we share with those in need, not just by plunking some money in an offering but by reaching out to neighbors and to the friends of our grandchildren, we make them aware of the needs of those around them. When we open our hearts and homes to others, we show them God's way of reaching out to those he places on our journey.

There's so much for grandchildren to learn, and often much of it is learned through their relationship with us, their grandmothers. What a blessing and a privilege is ours!

Father, I know that the life I live in front of my grandchildren speaks louder than my words. Help me to live richly and righteously before them, teaching them by my actions how you would have them live. Only in you do I have the strength to put all these things into practice. In your Son's name, amen.

Your next devotion is located on page 1553.

GRANDCHILD IN FOCUS · PRAYER

School/Career

Dear God, may learning be a joy rather than a chore for my grandchild. May exploration of new ideas bring a sense of wonder, awe and excitement. Grant him clarity of mind, the ability to concentrate on the task at hand and recollection of what has been learned. Help him to appreciate the tasks that come easily and to persevere through those that challenge. Amen.

²¹Do not be overcome by evil, but overcome evil with good.

Submission to the Authorities

13 Everyone must submit himself to the governing authorities, for there is no authority except that which God has established. The authorities that exist have been established by God. ²Consequently, he who rebels against the authority is rebelling against what God has instituted, and those who do so will bring judgment on themselves. ³For rulers hold no terror for those who do right, but for those who do wrong.

TALKING POINTS

Respect

Governing authorities have been established by God and deserve our respect.

ROMANS 13:1–7

For more on respect, go to Philippians 2:5–8.

Do you want to be free from fear of the one in authority? Then do what is right and he will commend you. ⁴For he is God's servant to do you good. But if you do wrong, be afraid, for he does not bear the sword for nothing. He is God's servant, an agent of wrath to bring punishment on the wrongdoer. ⁵Therefore, it is necessary to submit to the authorities, not only because of possible punishment but also because of conscience.

⁶This is also why you pay taxes, for the authorities are God's servants, who give their full time to governing. ⁷Give everyone what you owe him: If you owe taxes, pay taxes; if revenue, then revenue; if respect, then respect; if honor, then honor.

Love, for the Day Is Near

⁸Let no debt remain outstanding, except the continuing debt to love one another, for he who

TALKING POINTS

Responsibility

We are to pay our taxes and debts.

ROMANS 13:7–8

For more on responsibility, go to Galatians 6:7–8.

loves his fellowman has fulfilled the law. ⁹The commandments, "Do not commit adultery," "Do not murder," "Do not steal," "Do not covet,"ᵃ and whatever other commandment there may be, are summed up in this one rule: "Love your neighbor as yourself."ᵇ ¹⁰Love does no harm to its neighbor. Therefore love is the fulfillment of the law.

¹¹And do this, understanding the present time. The hour has come for you to wake up from your slumber, because our salvation is nearer now than when we first believed. ¹²The night is nearly over; the day is almost here. So let us put aside the deeds of darkness and put on the armor of light. ¹³Let us behave decently, as in the daytime, not in orgies and drunkenness, not in sexual immorality and debauchery, not in dissension and jealousy. ¹⁴Rather, clothe yourselves with the Lord Jesus Christ, and do not think about how to gratify the desires of the sinful nature.ᶜ

The Weak and the Strong

14 Accept him whose faith is weak, without passing judgment on disputable matters. ²One man's faith allows him to eat everything, but another man, whose faith is weak, eats only vegetables. ³The man who eats everything must not look down on him who does not, and the man who does not eat everything must not condemn the man who does, for God has accepted him. ⁴Who are you to judge someone else's servant? To his own master he stands or falls. And he will stand, for the Lord is able to make him stand.

ᵃ9 Exodus 20:13-15,17; Deut. 5:17-19,21   ᵇ9 Lev. 19:18
ᶜ14 Or *the flesh*

LET'S HAVE
FUN

Indoor Olympics

An evening of goofy Olympics can be fun for everyone. You can do this indoors or out, depending on the weather and the time of year.

Make sure you have a large room in which to navigate—a rec room, community room or gym. You can assign "countries" (real or imagined) for the grandkids to represent and come up with crazy "national anthems" (whatever ditties suit your collective fancy).

There's no limit to the planned activities, which may be geared toward summer, winter, "spring" or "fall" Olympics. You can try some actual Olympic events like the long jump, relay race or 50-yard dash. Or come up with your own wacky ideas: bean bag toss, candy catch and scramble, potato push race, etc. If you are able to navigate the Internet, there are a variety of websites with fun ideas for kids' games.

Long-Distance Variation: Suggest that the "foreign country" (out-of-town) grandkids duplicate your idea with wild variations, possibly in the context of a slumber party or youth group activity. Have them share pictures of their evening with you.

Dear God, thank you for creating me and my grandchildren with the ability to laugh and have fun. Let our time together be filled with the joy of being together as we participate in this activity. Let a spirit of love and friendship fill the room. Amen.

Your next devotion is located on page 1556.

GRANDCHILD **IN FOCUS** • PRAYER

Character

Dear Lord and Father, I ask that you fill my grandchild with your Spirit so her character reflects your goodness and love. Give her kindness and love for others. Bring joy to her life so she will be a joy to others. Grant her patience and self-control through difficult and trying times. May she show mercy and generosity to those who are less fortunate. Grant her integrity and a sense of justice, and surround her with your peace. Amen.

[5] One man considers one day more sacred than another; another man considers every day alike. Each one should be fully convinced in his own mind. [6] He who regards one day as special, does so to the Lord. He who eats meat, eats to the Lord, for he gives thanks to God; and he who abstains, does so to the Lord and gives thanks to God. [7] For none of us lives to himself alone and none of us dies to himself alone. [8] If we live, we live to the Lord; and if we die, we die to the Lord. So, whether we live or die, we belong to the Lord.

[9] For this very reason, Christ died and returned to life so that he might be the Lord of both the dead and the living. [10] You, then, why do you judge your brother? Or why do you look down on your brother? For we will all stand before God's judgment seat. [11] It is written:

" 'As surely as I live,' says the Lord,
'every knee will bow before me;
    every tongue will confess to God.' " [a]

[12] So then, each of us will give an account of himself to God.

TALKING POINTS

Loss/Grief

In both life and death, we belong to God.
ROMANS 14:7-9

For more on loss/grief, go to 1 Corinthians 15:51-58.

[13] Therefore let us stop passing judgment on one another. Instead, make up your mind not to put any stumbling block or obstacle in your brother's way. [14] As one who is in the Lord Jesus, I am fully convinced that no food [b] is unclean in itself. But if anyone regards something as unclean, then for him it is unclean. [15] If your brother is distressed because of what you eat, you are no longer acting in love. Do not by your eating destroy your brother for whom Christ died. [16] Do not allow what you consider good to be spoken of as evil. [17] For the kingdom of God is not a matter of eating and drinking, but of righteousness, peace and joy in the Holy Spirit, [18] because anyone who serves Christ in this way is pleasing to God and approved by men.

[19] Let us therefore make every effort to do what leads to peace and to mutual edification. [20] Do not destroy the work of God for the sake of food. All food is clean, but it is wrong for a man to eat anything that causes someone else to stumble. [21] It is better not to eat meat or drink wine or to do anything else that will cause your brother to fall.

[22] So whatever you believe about these things keep between yourself and God. Blessed is the man who does not condemn himself by what he approves. [23] But the man who has doubts is condemned if he eats, because his eating is not from faith; and everything that does not come from faith is sin.

15 We who are strong ought to bear with the failings of the weak and not to please ourselves. [2] Each of us should please his neighbor for his good, to build him up. [3] For even Christ did not please himself but, as it is written: "The insults of those who insult you have fallen on me." [c] [4] For everything that was written in the past was written to teach us, so that through endurance and the encouragement of the Scriptures we might have hope.

[5] May the God who gives endurance and encouragement give you a spirit of unity among yourselves as you follow Christ Jesus, [6] so that with one heart and mouth you may glorify the God and Father of our Lord Jesus Christ.

[7] Accept one another, then, just as Christ accepted you, in order to bring praise to God. [8] For I tell you that Christ has become a servant of the Jews [d] on behalf of God's truth, to confirm the promises made to the patriarchs [9] so that the Gentiles may glorify God for his mercy, as it is written:

---

[a] 11 Isaiah 45:23   [b] 14 Or that nothing   [c] 3 Psalm 69:9
[d] 8 Greek circumcision

"Therefore I will praise you among the
  Gentiles;
 I will sing hymns to your name."[a]

[10] Again, it says,

"Rejoice, O Gentiles, with his people."[b]

[11] And again,

"Praise the Lord, all you Gentiles,
  and sing praises to him, all you peoples."[c]

[12] And again, Isaiah says,

"The Root of Jesse will spring up,
  one who will arise to rule over the nations;
 the Gentiles will hope in him."[d]

[13] May the God of hope fill you with all joy and peace as you trust in him, so that you may overflow with hope by the power of the Holy Spirit.

PRAYING THE SCRIPTURES

Joy
ROMANS 15:13

I pray, O God of hope, that you will fill my grandchild with joy and peace as she trusts in you, so that she may overflow with hope by the power of the Holy Spirit.

Next prayer in Joy Prayer Track: Galatians 5:22–23,25

Paul the Minister to the Gentiles

[14] I myself am convinced, my brothers, that you yourselves are full of goodness, complete in knowledge and competent to instruct one another. [15] I have written you quite boldly on some points, as if to remind you of them again, because of the grace God gave me [16] to be a minister of Christ Jesus to the Gentiles with the priestly duty of proclaiming the gospel of God, so that the Gentiles might become an offering acceptable to God, sanctified by the Holy Spirit.

TALKING POINTS

Trust
Joy, peace and hope are
byproducts of trust.
ROMANS 15:13

This is the last talking point on trust.

[17] Therefore I glory in Christ Jesus in my service to God. [18] I will not venture to speak of anything except what Christ has accomplished through me in leading the Gentiles to obey God by what I have said and done— [19] by the power of signs and miracles, through the power of the Spirit. So from Jerusalem all the way around to Illyricum, I have fully proclaimed the gospel of Christ. [20] It has always been my ambition to preach the gospel where Christ was not known, so that I would not be building on someone else's foundation. [21] Rather, as it is written:

"Those who were not told about him will see,
  and those who have not heard will
  understand."[e]

[22] This is why I have often been hindered from coming to you.

Paul's Plan to Visit Rome

[23] But now that there is no more place for me to work in these regions, and since I have been longing for many years to see you, [24] I plan to do so when I go to Spain. I hope to visit you while passing through and to have you assist me on my journey there, after I have enjoyed your company for a while. [25] Now, however, I am on my way to Jerusalem in the service of the saints there. [26] For Macedonia and Achaia were pleased to make a contribution for the poor among the saints in Jerusalem. [27] They were pleased to do it, and

[a] 9 2 Samuel 22:50; Psalm 18:49   [b] 10 Deut. 32:43
[c] 11 Psalm 117:1   [d] 12 Isaiah 11:10   [e] 21 Isaiah 52:15

Worship the Lord

I delight greatly in the Lord;
  my soul rejoices in my God.
For he has clothed me with garments of salvation
  and arrayed me in a robe of righteousness,
as a bridegroom adorns his head like a priest,
  and as a bride adorns herself with her jewels.
For as the soil makes the sprout come up
  and a garden causes seeds to grow,
so the Sovereign Lord will make righteousness and praise
  spring up before all nations.

Isaiah 61:10 – 11

You, Lord, are my delight. You have wrapped your righteousness and salvation securely around me. I pray that your promise of long ago will soon be true: that your righteousness and praise will spring up before the nations and bring us peace. Amen.

Your next devotion is located on page 1560.

GRANDCHILD IN FOCUS · PRAYER

Talents

Dear Lord, the giver of gifts, bless my grandchild as he develops his talents. Help him identify his talents and be proud and confident of the gifts you have given him. Give him patience and understanding, Lord, so he will not grow weary of striving and searching to reach the goals you have set for him. May each milestone bring satisfaction and a healthy desire for greater achievement and success to bring glory to you. Amen.

indeed they owe it to them. For if the Gentiles have shared in the Jews' spiritual blessings, they owe it to the Jews to share with them their material blessings. ²⁸So after I have completed this task and have made sure that they have received this fruit, I will go to Spain and visit you on the way. ²⁹I know that when I come to you, I will come in the full measure of the blessing of Christ.

³⁰I urge you, brothers, by our Lord Jesus Christ and by the love of the Spirit, to join me in my struggle by praying to God for me. ³¹Pray that I may be rescued from the unbelievers in Judea and that my service in Jerusalem may be acceptable to the saints there, ³²so that by God's will I may come to you with joy and together with you be refreshed. ³³The God of peace be with you all. Amen.

Personal Greetings

16 I commend to you our sister Phoebe, a servant[a] of the church in Cenchrea. ²I ask you to receive her in the Lord in a way worthy of the saints and to give her any help she may need from you, for she has been a great help to many people, including me.

³Greet Priscilla[b] and Aquila, my fellow workers in Christ Jesus. ⁴They risked their lives for me. Not only I but all the churches of the Gentiles are grateful to them.

⁵Greet also the church that meets at their house.

Greet my dear friend Epenetus, who was the first convert to Christ in the province of Asia.

⁶Greet Mary, who worked very hard for you.

⁷Greet Andronicus and Junias, my relatives who have been in prison with me. They are outstanding among the apostles, and they were in Christ before I was.

⁸Greet Ampliatus, whom I love in the Lord.

⁹Greet Urbanus, our fellow worker in Christ, and my dear friend Stachys.

¹⁰Greet Apelles, tested and approved in Christ.

Greet those who belong to the household of Aristobulus.

¹¹Greet Herodion, my relative.

Greet those in the household of Narcissus who are in the Lord.

¹²Greet Tryphena and Tryphosa, those women who work hard in the Lord.

Greet my dear friend Persis, another woman who has worked very hard in the Lord.

¹³Greet Rufus, chosen in the Lord, and his mother, who has been a mother to me, too.

¹⁴Greet Asyncritus, Phlegon, Hermes, Patrobas, Hermas and the brothers with them.

¹⁵Greet Philologus, Julia, Nereus and his sister, and Olympas and all the saints with them.

¹⁶Greet one another with a holy kiss.

All the churches of Christ send greetings.

¹⁷I urge you, brothers, to watch out for those who cause divisions and put obstacles in your way that are contrary to the teaching you have learned. Keep away from them. ¹⁸For such people are not serving our Lord Christ, but their own appetites. By smooth talk and flattery they deceive the minds of naive people. ¹⁹Everyone has heard about your obedience, so I am full of joy over you; but I want you to be wise about what is good, and innocent about what is evil.

²⁰The God of peace will soon crush Satan under your feet.

The grace of our Lord Jesus be with you.

²¹Timothy, my fellow worker, sends his greetings to you, as do Lucius, Jason and Sosipater, my relatives.

²²I, Tertius, who wrote down this letter, greet you in the Lord.

²³Gaius, whose hospitality I and the whole church here enjoy, sends you his greetings.

Erastus, who is the city's director of public works, and our brother Quartus send you their greetings.[c]

²⁵Now to him who is able to establish you by my gospel and the proclamation of Jesus Christ, according to the revelation of the mystery hidden for long ages past, ²⁶but now revealed and made known through the prophetic writings by the command of the eternal God, so that all nations might believe and obey him— ²⁷to the only wise God be glory forever through Jesus Christ! Amen.

[a] 1 Or *deaconess* [b] 3 Greek *Prisca*, a variant of *Priscilla*
[c] 23 Some manuscripts *their greetings.* ²⁴*May the grace of our Lord Jesus Christ be with all of you. Amen.*

The Greatest
OF THESE IS LOVE

Grandmothers do not have to be convinced that love is the greatest. Paul didn't necessarily have a grandmother's love in mind when he wrote the well-known passage of 1 Corinthians 13, but we know just what he's talking about when we think of the love we have for our grandchildren: when we look into the eyes of a newborn grandchild; when a little one crushes our knees with a hug; when a toddler enthusiastically calls out, "Nana" (or whatever name we've been christened with); when the voice on the phone says, "I just needed to hear your voice, Grandma. How ya doin'?" At times like these, love rushes in and fills every chamber of our hearts. Yes, grandmothers know that "the greatest of these is love."

The Corinthian church, however, was much in need of Paul's teachings. They needed to learn how their lack of faith, hope and love was threatening their community. Paul's advice in this letter to the Corinthian Christians is timeless. His letter addresses lawsuits, sexual standards, marital conduct, Christian freedom, the roles of women in the church, spiritual gifts and doubt. But his statement on love hinges the themes together, and we are drawn to it when we address any issue facing us in the church or in our personal lives.

VERSE *to* REMEMBER | 1 CORINTHIANS 13:13

And now these three remain: faith, hope and love. But the greatest of these is love.

ABOUT 1 CORINTHIANS

WRITTEN BY:
The apostle Paul

WRITTEN FOR:
The Christians in Corinth

DATE WRITTEN:
About A.D. 55 from
the city of Ephesus

WHY WRITTEN:
To help the Corinthians
solve problems in
their church

1 Paul, called to be an apostle of Christ Jesus by the will of God, and our brother Sosthenes,

² To the church of God in Corinth, to those sanctified in Christ Jesus and called to be holy, together with all those everywhere who call on the name of our Lord Jesus Christ—their Lord and ours:

³ Grace and peace to you from God our Father and the Lord Jesus Christ.

Thanksgiving

⁴ I always thank God for you because of his grace given you in Christ Jesus. ⁵ For in him you have been enriched in every way—in all your speaking and in all your knowledge— ⁶ because our testimony about Christ was confirmed in you. ⁷ Therefore you do not lack any spiritual gift as you eagerly wait for our Lord Jesus Christ to be revealed. ⁸ He will keep you strong to the end, so that you will be blameless on the day of our Lord Jesus Christ. ⁹ God, who has called you into fellowship with his Son Jesus Christ our Lord, is faithful.

Divisions in the Church

¹⁰ I appeal to you, brothers, in the name of our Lord Jesus Christ, that all of you agree with one another so that there may be no divisions among you and that you may be perfectly united in mind and thought. ¹¹ My brothers, some from Chloe's household have informed me that there are quarrels among you. ¹² What I mean is this: One of you says, "I follow Paul"; another, "I follow Apollos"; another, "I follow Cephas[a]"; still another, "I follow Christ."

¹³ Is Christ divided? Was Paul crucified for you? Were you baptized into[b] the name of Paul? ¹⁴ I am thankful that I did not baptize any of you except Crispus and Gaius, ¹⁵ so no one can say that you were baptized into my name. ¹⁶ (Yes, I also baptized the household of Stephanas; beyond that, I don't remember if I baptized anyone else.) ¹⁷ For Christ did not send me to baptize, but to preach the gospel—not with words of human wisdom, lest the cross of Christ be emptied of its power.

Christ the Wisdom and Power of God

¹⁸ For the message of the cross is foolishness to those who are perishing, but to us who are being saved it is the power of God. ¹⁹ For it is written:

"I will destroy the wisdom of the wise;
　the intelligence of the intelligent I will
　　frustrate."[c]

²⁰ Where is the wise man? Where is the scholar? Where is the philosopher of this age? Has not God made foolish the wisdom of the world? ²¹ For since in the wisdom of God the world through its wisdom did not know him, God was pleased through the foolishness of what was preached to save those who believe. ²² Jews demand miraculous signs and Greeks look for wisdom, ²³ but we preach Christ crucified: a stumbling block to Jews and foolishness to Gentiles, ²⁴ but to those whom God has called, both Jews and Greeks, Christ the power of God and the wisdom of God. ²⁵ For the foolishness of God is wiser than man's wisdom, and the weakness of God is stronger than man's strength.

²⁶ Brothers, think of what you were when you were called. Not many of you were wise by human standards; not many were influential; not many were of noble birth. ²⁷ But God chose the foolish things of the world to shame the wise; God chose the weak things of the world to shame the strong. ²⁸ He chose the lowly things of this world and the despised things—and the things that are not—to nullify the things that are, ²⁹ so that no one may boast before him. ³⁰ It is because of him that you are in Christ Jesus, who has become for us wisdom from God—that is, our righteousness, holiness and redemption. ³¹ Therefore, as it is written: "Let him who boasts boast in the Lord."[d]

2 When I came to you, brothers, I did not come with eloquence or superior wisdom as I proclaimed to you the testimony about God.[e] ² For I resolved to know nothing while I was with you except Jesus Christ and him crucified.

---

[a] 12 That is, Peter　　[b] 13 Or in; also in verse 15
[c] 19 Isaiah 29:14　　[d] 31 Jer. 9:24　　[e] 1 Some manuscripts as I proclaimed to you God's mystery

> BUT GOD CHOSE THE FOOLISH THINGS OF THE
> WORLD TO SHAME THE WISE; GOD CHOSE THE WEAK
> THINGS OF THE WORLD TO SHAME THE STRONG.
> HE CHOSE THE LOWLY THINGS OF THIS WORLD AND
> THE DESPISED THINGS — AND THE THINGS THAT ARE
> NOT — TO NULLIFY THE THINGS THAT ARE, SO THAT
> NO ONE MAY BOAST BEFORE HIM.
>
> *1 Corinthians 1:27—29*

Who's in Charge?

MARILYN MEBERG

READ | 1 CORINTHIANS 1:18 – 31

Every now and then, I need to be reminded of who takes care of me and who is in charge of all of the events in my life. When I'm skipping lithely across the high wire, congratulating myself on my confidence and skill, it's easy to forget who my safety net is. Fortunately, God doesn't let me be the star of the show from start to finish. Sometimes he turns things completely upside down so that what is happening does not make sense to me at all! In fact, I lose my balance completely, and I'm forced to cling to him and rest in his peace that passes understanding.

You may find yourself in the middle of circumstances that don't make sense to you. You may be surrounded by people who would never be your choice. Possibly God is reminding you that "the battle is the Lord's" and the way he wins battles is often through people and events we'd never even think of, much less choose. Why does God do this? "So that no one [may boast before him]."

Oddly enough, that knowledge takes the pressure off of me. I can quit striving, plotting, maneuvering. I am not the star of the show; God is.

God, you know how I need to be reminded that I am not my own but belong to you. You're in charge, and that's certainly a comfort to me, for I fall down when I try to do things in my own power. Thank you for going before me in the battles of life. Amen.

Your next devotion is located on page 1569.

GRANDCHILD IN FOCUS • PRAYER

SELECT ONE OF YOUR
GRANDCHILDREN TO FOCUS ON
IN PRAYER FOR THE NEXT 14 DAYS.

Salvation

Dear Lord, please guide my grandchild to your gift of salvation. I pray that she will come to know you, to love you and to walk close to you throughout her life. May she boldly claim Jesus as her Lord and Savior. Guide her as she makes choices that have eternal consequences. Help her to follow you each moment of her life. I pray this in Jesus' name, amen.

³I came to you in weakness and fear, and with much trembling. ⁴My message and my preaching were not with wise and persuasive words, but with a demonstration of the Spirit's power, ⁵so that your faith might not rest on men's wisdom, but on God's power.

Wisdom From the Spirit

⁶We do, however, speak a message of wisdom among the mature, but not the wisdom of this age or of the rulers of this age, who are coming to nothing. ⁷No, we speak of God's secret wisdom, a wisdom that has been hidden and that God destined for our glory before time began. ⁸None of the rulers of this age understood it, for if they had, they would not have crucified the Lord of glory. ⁹However, as it is written:

> "No eye has seen,
>   no ear has heard,
> no mind has conceived
>   what God has prepared for those who love
>   him"ᵃ—

¹⁰but God has revealed it to us by his Spirit.

The Spirit searches all things, even the deep things of God. ¹¹For who among men knows the thoughts of a man except the man's spirit within him? In the same way no one knows the thoughts of God except the Spirit of God. ¹²We have not received the spirit of the world but the Spirit who is from God, that we may understand what God has freely given us. ¹³This is what we speak, not in words taught us by human wisdom but in words taught by the Spirit, expressing spiritual truths in spiritual words.ᵇ ¹⁴The man without the Spirit does not accept the things that come from the Spirit of God, for they are foolishness to him, and he cannot understand them, because they are spiritually discerned. ¹⁵The spiritual man makes judgments about all things, but he himself is not subject to any man's judgment:

> ¹⁶"For who has known the mind of the Lord
>   that he may instruct him?"ᶜ

But we have the mind of Christ.

On Divisions in the Church

3 Brothers, I could not address you as spiritual but as worldly—mere infants in Christ. ²I gave you milk, not solid food, for you were not yet ready for it. Indeed, you are still not ready. ³You are still worldly. For since there is jealousy and quarreling among you, are you not worldly? Are you not acting like mere men? ⁴For when one says, "I follow Paul," and another, "I follow Apollos," are you not mere men?

⁵What, after all, is Apollos? And what is Paul? Only servants, through whom you came to believe—as the Lord has assigned to each his task. ⁶I planted the seed, Apollos watered it, but God made it grow. ⁷So neither he who plants nor he who waters is anything, but only God, who makes things grow. ⁸The man who plants and the man who waters have one purpose, and each will be rewarded according to his own labor. ⁹For we are God's fellow workers; you are God's field, God's building.

¹⁰By the grace God has given me, I laid a foundation as an expert builder, and someone else is building on it. But each one should be careful how he builds. ¹¹For no one can lay any foundation other than the one already laid, which is Jesus Christ. ¹²If any man builds on this foundation using gold, silver, costly stones, wood, hay or straw, ¹³his work will be shown for what it is, because the Day will bring it to light. It will be revealed with fire, and the fire will test the quality of each man's work. ¹⁴If what he has built survives, he will receive his reward. ¹⁵If it is burned up, he will suffer loss; he himself will be saved, but only as one escaping through the flames.

¹⁶Don't you know that you yourselves are God's temple and that God's Spirit lives in you? ¹⁷If anyone destroys God's temple, God will destroy him; for God's temple is sacred, and you are that temple.

¹⁸Do not deceive yourselves. If any one of you thinks he is wise by the standards of this age, he should become a "fool" so that he may become

---

ᵃ 9 Isaiah 64:4   ᵇ 13 Or *Spirit, interpreting spiritual truths to spiritual men*   ᶜ 16 Isaiah 40:13

wise. [19]For the wisdom of this world is foolishness in God's sight. As it is written: "He catches the wise in their craftiness"[a]; [20]and again, "The Lord knows that the thoughts of the wise are futile."[b] [21]So then, no more boasting about men! All things are yours, [22]whether Paul or Apollos or Cephas[c] or the world or life or death or the present or the future—all are yours, [23]and you are of Christ, and Christ is of God.

Apostles of Christ

4 So then, men ought to regard us as servants of Christ and as those entrusted with the secret things of God. [2]Now it is required that those who have been given a trust must prove faithful. [3]I care very little if I am judged by you or by any human court; indeed, I do not even judge myself. [4]My conscience is clear, but that does not make me innocent. It is the Lord who judges me. [5]Therefore judge nothing before the appointed time; wait till the Lord comes. He will bring to light what is hidden in darkness and will expose the motives of men's hearts. At that time each will receive his praise from God.

[6]Now, brothers, I have applied these things to myself and Apollos for your benefit, so that you may learn from us the meaning of the saying, "Do not go beyond what is written." Then you will not take pride in one man over against another. [7]For who makes you different from anyone else? What do you have that you did not receive? And if you did receive it, why do you boast as though you did not?

[8]Already you have all you want! Already you have become rich! You have become kings—and that without us! How I wish that you really had become kings so that we might be kings with you! [9]For it seems to me that God has put us apostles on display at the end of the procession, like men condemned to die in the arena. We have been made a spectacle to the whole universe, to angels as well as to men. [10]We are fools for Christ, but you are so wise in Christ! We are weak, but you are strong! You are honored, we are dishonored! [11]To this very hour we go hungry and thirsty, we are in rags, we are brutally treated, we are homeless. [12]We work hard with our own hands. When we are cursed, we bless; when we are persecuted, we endure it; [13]when we are slandered, we answer kindly. Up to this moment we have become the scum of the earth, the refuse of the world.

[14]I am not writing this to shame you, but to warn you, as my dear children. [15]Even though you have ten thousand guardians in Christ, you do not have many fathers, for in Christ Jesus I became your father through the gospel. [16]Therefore I urge you to imitate me. [17]For this reason I am sending to you Timothy, my son whom I love, who is faithful in the Lord. He will remind you of my way of life in Christ Jesus, which agrees with what I teach everywhere in every church.

[18]Some of you have become arrogant, as if I were not coming to you. [19]But I will come to you very soon, if the Lord is willing, and then I will find out not only how these arrogant people are talking, but what power they have. [20]For the kingdom of God is not a matter of talk but of power. [21]What do you prefer? Shall I come to you with a whip, or in love and with a gentle spirit?

Expel the Immoral Brother!

5 It is actually reported that there is sexual immorality among you, and of a kind that does not occur even among pagans: A man has his father's wife. [2]And you are proud! Shouldn't you rather have been filled with grief and have put out of your fellowship the man who did this? [3]Even though I am not physically present, I am with you in spirit. And I have already passed judgment on the one who did this, just as if I were present. [4]When you are assembled in the name of our Lord Jesus and I am with you in spirit, and the power of our Lord Jesus is present, [5]hand this man over to Satan, so that the sinful nature[d] may be destroyed and his spirit saved on the day of the Lord.

[6]Your boasting is not good. Don't you know that a little yeast works through the whole batch

---

[a] 19 Job 5:13   [b] 20 Psalm 94:11   [c] 22 That is, Peter
[d] 5 Or that his body; or that the flesh

of dough? [7] Get rid of the old yeast that you may be a new batch without yeast — as you really are. For Christ, our Passover lamb, has been sacrificed. [8] Therefore let us keep the Festival, not with the old yeast, the yeast of malice and wickedness, but with bread without yeast, the bread of sincerity and truth.

[9] I have written you in my letter not to associate with sexually immoral people — [10] not at all meaning the people of this world who are immoral, or the greedy and swindlers, or idolaters. In that case you would have to leave this world. [11] But now I am writing you that you must not associate with anyone who calls himself a brother but is sexually immoral or greedy, an idolater or a slanderer, a drunkard or a swindler. With such a man do not even eat.

[12] What business is it of mine to judge those outside the church? Are you not to judge those inside? [13] God will judge those outside. "Expel the wicked man from among you." [a]

Lawsuits Among Believers

6 If any of you has a dispute with another, dare he take it before the ungodly for judgment instead of before the saints? [2] Do you not know that the saints will judge the world? And if you are to judge the world, are you not competent to judge trivial cases? [3] Do you not know that we will judge angels? How much more the things of this life! [4] Therefore, if you have disputes about such matters, appoint as judges even men of little account in the church! [b] [5] I say this to shame you. Is it possible that there is nobody among you wise enough to judge a dispute between believers? [6] But instead, one brother goes to law against another — and this in front of unbelievers!

[7] The very fact that you have lawsuits among you means you have been completely defeated already. Why not rather be wronged? Why not rather be cheated? [8] Instead, you yourselves cheat and do wrong, and you do this to your brothers.

[9] Do you not know that the wicked will not inherit the kingdom of God? Do not be deceived: Neither the sexually immoral nor idolaters nor adulterers nor male prostitutes nor homosexual offenders [10] nor thieves nor the greedy nor drunkards nor slanderers nor swindlers will inherit the kingdom of God. [11] And that is what some of you were. But you were washed, you were sanctified, you were justified in the name of the Lord Jesus Christ and by the Spirit of our God.

Sexual Immorality

[12] "Everything is permissible for me" — but not everything is beneficial. "Everything is permissible for me" — but I will not be mastered by anything. [13] "Food for the stomach and the stomach for food" — but God will destroy them both. The body is not meant for sexual immorality, but for the Lord, and the Lord for the body. [14] By his power God raised the Lord from the dead, and he will raise us also. [15] Do you not know that your bodies are members of Christ himself? Shall I then take the members of Christ and unite them with a prostitute? Never! [16] Do you not know that he who unites himself with a prostitute is one with her in body? For it is said, "The two will become one flesh." [c] [17] But he who unites himself with the Lord is one with him in spirit.

[18] Flee from sexual immorality. All other sins a man commits are outside his body, but he who sins sexually sins against his own body. [19] Do you

[a] 13 Deut. 17:7; 19:19; 21:21; 22:21,24; 24:7   [b] 4 Or *matters, do you appoint as judges men of little account in the church?*   [c] 16 Gen. 2:24

not know that your body is a temple of the Holy Spirit, who is in you, whom you have received from God? You are not your own; ²⁰you were bought at a price. Therefore honor God with your body.

TALKING POINTS

Sexuality

We are to honor God with our bodies, which are his temples.

1 CORINTHIANS 6:12–20

For more on sexuality, go to 1 Corinthians 10:13.

Marriage

7 Now for the matters you wrote about: It is good for a man not to marry.^a ²But since there is so much immorality, each man should have his own wife, and each woman her own husband. ³The husband should fulfill his marital duty to his wife, and likewise the wife to her husband. ⁴The wife's body does not belong to her alone but also to her husband. In the same way, the husband's body does not belong to him alone but also to his wife. ⁵Do not deprive each other except by mutual consent and for a time, so that you may devote yourselves to prayer. Then come together again so that Satan will not tempt you because of your lack of self-control. ⁶I say this as a concession, not as a command. ⁷I wish that all men were as I am. But each man has his own gift from God; one has this gift, another has that.

⁸Now to the unmarried and the widows I say: It is good for them to stay unmarried, as I am. ⁹But if they cannot control themselves, they should marry, for it is better to marry than to burn with passion.

¹⁰To the married I give this command (not I, but the Lord): A wife must not separate from her husband. ¹¹But if she does, she must remain

TALKING POINTS

Divorce

Divorce is not God's choice.

1 CORINTHIANS 7:10–11

For more on divorce, go to 1 Corinthians 7:12–16.

unmarried or else be reconciled to her husband. And a husband must not divorce his wife.

¹²To the rest I say this (I, not the Lord): If any brother has a wife who is not a believer and she is willing to live with him, he must not divorce her. ¹³And if a woman has a husband who is not a believer and he is willing to live with her, she must not divorce him. ¹⁴For the unbelieving husband has been sanctified through his wife, and the unbelieving wife has been sanctified through her believing husband. Otherwise your children would be unclean, but as it is, they are holy.

¹⁵But if the unbeliever leaves, let him do so. A believing man or woman is not bound in such circumstances; God has called us to live in peace. ¹⁶How do you know, wife, whether you will save your husband? Or, how do you know, husband, whether you will save your wife?

^a 1 Or "It is good for a man not to have sexual relations with a woman."

TALKING POINTS

Divorce

Having an unbelieving spouse is not a valid reason for divorce.

1 CORINTHIANS 7:12–16

This is the last talking point on divorce.

17 Nevertheless, each one should retain the place in life that the Lord assigned to him and to which God has called him. This is the rule I lay down in all the churches. 18 Was a man already circumcised when he was called? He should not become uncircumcised. Was a man uncircumcised when he was called? He should not be circumcised. 19 Circumcision is nothing and uncircumcision is nothing. Keeping God's commands is what counts. 20 Each one should remain in the situation which he was in when God called him. 21 Were you a slave when you were called? Don't let it trouble you—although if you can gain your freedom, do so. 22 For he who was a slave when he was called by the Lord is the Lord's freedman; similarly, he who was a free man when he was called is Christ's slave. 23 You were bought at a price; do not become slaves of men. 24 Brothers, each man, as responsible to God, should remain in the situation God called him to.

25 Now about virgins: I have no command from the Lord, but I give a judgment as one who by the Lord's mercy is trustworthy. 26 Because of the present crisis, I think that it is good for you to remain as you are. 27 Are you married? Do not seek a divorce. Are you unmarried? Do not look for a wife. 28 But if you do marry, you have not sinned; and if a virgin marries, she has not sinned. But those who marry will face many troubles in this life, and I want to spare you this.

29 What I mean, brothers, is that the time is short. From now on those who have wives should live as if they had none; 30 those who mourn, as if they did not; those who are happy, as if they were not; those who buy something, as if it were not theirs to keep; 31 those who use the things of the world, as if not engrossed in them. For this world in its present form is passing away.

32 I would like you to be free from concern. An unmarried man is concerned about the Lord's affairs—how he can please the Lord. 33 But a married man is concerned about the affairs of this world—how he can please his wife— 34 and his interests are divided. An unmarried woman or virgin is concerned about the Lord's affairs: Her aim is to be devoted to the Lord in both body and spirit. But a married woman is concerned about the affairs of this world—how she can please her husband. 35 I am saying this for your own good, not to restrict you, but that you may live in a right way in undivided devotion to the Lord.

36 If anyone thinks he is acting improperly toward the virgin he is engaged to, and if she is getting along in years and he feels he ought to marry, he should do as he wants. He is not sinning. They should get married. 37 But the man who has settled the matter in his own mind, who is under no compulsion but has control over his own will, and who has made up his mind not to marry the virgin—this man also does the right thing. 38 So then, he who marries the virgin does right, but he who does not marry her does even better. [a]

39 A woman is bound to her husband as long as he lives. But if her husband dies, she is free to marry anyone she wishes, but he must belong to the Lord. 40 In my judgment, she is happier if she stays as she is—and I think that I too have the Spirit of God.

Food Sacrificed to Idols

8 Now about food sacrificed to idols: We know that we all possess knowledge. [b] Knowledge puffs up, but love builds up. 2 The man who thinks he knows something does not yet know as he ought to know. 3 But the man who loves God is known by God.

4 So then, about eating food sacrificed to idols: We know that an idol is nothing at all in the world and that there is no God but one. 5 For even if there are so-called gods, whether in heaven or on earth (as indeed there are many "gods" and many "lords"), 6 yet for us there is but one God, the Father, from whom all things came and

---

a 36-38 Or 36 If anyone thinks he is not treating his daughter properly, and if she is getting along in years, and he feels she ought to marry, he should do as he wants. He is not sinning. He should let her get married. 37 But the man who has settled the matter in his own mind, who is under no compulsion but has control over his own will, and who has made up his mind to keep the virgin unmarried—this man also does the right thing. 38 So then, he who gives his virgin in marriage does right, but he who does not give her in marriage does even better.
b 1 Or "We all possess knowledge," as you say

for whom we live; and there is but one Lord, Jesus Christ, through whom all things came and through whom we live.

⁷But not everyone knows this. Some people are still so accustomed to idols that when they eat such food they think of it as having been sacrificed to an idol, and since their conscience is weak, it is defiled. ⁸But food does not bring us near to God; we are no worse if we do not eat, and no better if we do.

⁹Be careful, however, that the exercise of your freedom does not become a stumbling block to the weak. ¹⁰For if anyone with a weak conscience sees you who have this knowledge eating in an idol's temple, won't he be emboldened to eat what has been sacrificed to idols? ¹¹So this weak brother, for whom Christ died, is destroyed by your knowledge. ¹²When you sin against your brothers in this way and wound their weak conscience, you sin against Christ. ¹³Therefore, if what I eat causes my brother to fall into sin, I will never eat meat again, so that I will not cause him to fall.

The Rights of an Apostle

9 Am I not free? Am I not an apostle? Have I not seen Jesus our Lord? Are you not the result of my work in the Lord? ²Even though I may not be an apostle to others, surely I am to you! For you are the seal of my apostleship in the Lord.

³This is my defense to those who sit in judgment on me. ⁴Don't we have the right to food and drink? ⁵Don't we have the right to take a believing wife along with us, as do the other apostles and the Lord's brothers and Cephas*a*? ⁶Or is it only I and Barnabas who must work for a living?

⁷Who serves as a soldier at his own expense? Who plants a vineyard and does not eat of its grapes? Who tends a flock and does not drink of the milk? ⁸Do I say this merely from a human point of view? Doesn't the Law say the same thing? ⁹For it is written in the Law of Moses: "Do not muzzle an ox while it is treading out the grain."*b* Is it about oxen that God is concerned?

¹⁰Surely he says this for us, doesn't he? Yes, this was written for us, because when the plowman plows and the thresher threshes, they ought to do so in the hope of sharing in the harvest. ¹¹If we have sown spiritual seed among you, is it too much if we reap a material harvest from you? ¹²If others have this right of support from you, shouldn't we have it all the more?

But we did not use this right. On the contrary, we put up with anything rather than hinder the gospel of Christ. ¹³Don't you know that those who work in the temple get their food from the temple, and those who serve at the altar share in what is offered on the altar? ¹⁴In the same way, the Lord has commanded that those who preach the gospel should receive their living from the gospel.

¹⁵But I have not used any of these rights. And I am not writing this in the hope that you will do such things for me. I would rather die than have anyone deprive me of this boast. ¹⁶Yet when I preach the gospel, I cannot boast, for I am compelled to preach. Woe to me if I do not preach the gospel! ¹⁷If I preach voluntarily, I have a reward; if not voluntarily, I am simply discharging the trust committed to me. ¹⁸What then is my reward? Just this: that in preaching the gospel I may offer it free of charge, and so not make use of my rights in preaching it.

¹⁹Though I am free and belong to no man, I make myself a slave to everyone, to win as many as possible. ²⁰To the Jews I became like a Jew, to win the Jews. To those under the law I became like one under the law (though I myself am not under the law), so as to win those under the law. ²¹To those not having the law I became like one not having the law (though I am not free from God's law but am under Christ's law), so as to win those not having the law. ²²To the weak I became weak, to win the weak. I have become all things to all men so that by all possible means I might save some. ²³I do all this for the sake of the gospel, that I may share in its blessings.

a 5 That is, Peter   *b 9* Deut. 25:4

²⁴Do you not know that in a race all the runners run, but only one gets the prize? Run in such a way as to get the prize. ²⁵Everyone who competes in the games goes into strict training. They do it to get a crown that will not last; but we do it to get a crown that will last forever. ²⁶Therefore I do not run like a man running aimlessly; I do not fight like a man beating the air. ²⁷No, I beat my body and make it my slave so that after I have preached to others, I myself will not be disqualified for the prize.

Warnings From Israel's History

10 For I do not want you to be ignorant of the fact, brothers, that our forefathers were all under the cloud and that they all passed through the sea. ²They were all baptized into Moses in the cloud and in the sea. ³They all ate the same spiritual food ⁴and drank the same spiritual drink; for they drank from the spiritual rock that accompanied them, and that rock was Christ. ⁵Nevertheless, God was not pleased with most of them; their bodies were scattered over the desert.

⁶Now these things occurred as examples[a] to keep us from setting our hearts on evil things as they did. ⁷Do not be idolaters, as some of them were; as it is written: "The people sat down to eat and drink and got up to indulge in pagan revelry."[b] ⁸We should not commit sexual immorality, as some of them did—and in one day twenty-three thousand of them died. ⁹We should not test the Lord, as some of them did—and were killed by snakes. ¹⁰And do not grumble, as some of them did—and were killed by the destroying angel.

¹¹These things happened to them as examples and were written down as warnings for us, on whom the fulfillment of the ages has come. ¹²So, if you think you are standing firm, be careful that you don't fall! ¹³No temptation has seized you except what is common to man. And God is faithful; he will not let you be tempted beyond what you can bear. But when you are tempted, he will also provide a way out so that you can stand up under it.

TALKING POINTS

Peer Pressure

God will keep us strong when we are tempted by others.

1 CORINTHIANS 10:13

For more on peer pressure, go to Philippians 1:27.

Idol Feasts and the Lord's Supper

¹⁴Therefore, my dear friends, flee from idolatry. ¹⁵I speak to sensible people; judge for yourselves what I say. ¹⁶Is not the cup of thanksgiving for which we give thanks a participation in the blood of Christ? And is not the bread that we break a participation in the body of Christ? ¹⁷Because there is one loaf, we, who are many, are one body, for we all partake of the one loaf.

¹⁸Consider the people of Israel: Do not those who eat the sacrifices participate in the altar? ¹⁹Do I mean then that a sacrifice offered to an idol is anything, or that an idol is anything? ²⁰No, but the sacrifices of pagans are offered to demons, not to God, and I do not want you to be participants with demons. ²¹You cannot drink the cup of the Lord and the cup of demons too; you cannot have a part in both the Lord's table and the

---

[a] 6 Or *types*; also in verse 11   [b] 7 Exodus 32:6

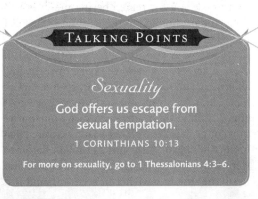

TALKING POINTS

Sexuality

God offers us escape from sexual temptation.

1 CORINTHIANS 10:13

For more on sexuality, go to 1 Thessalonians 4:3–6.

table of demons. [22]Are we trying to arouse the Lord's jealousy? Are we stronger than he?

The Believer's Freedom

[23]"Everything is permissible"—but not everything is beneficial. "Everything is permissible"—but not everything is constructive. [24]Nobody should seek his own good, but the good of others.

[25]Eat anything sold in the meat market without raising questions of conscience, [26]for, "The earth is the Lord's, and everything in it."[a]

[27]If some unbeliever invites you to a meal and you want to go, eat whatever is put before you without raising questions of conscience. [28]But if anyone says to you, "This has been offered in sacrifice," then do not eat it, both for the sake of the man who told you and for conscience' sake[b]— [29]the other man's conscience, I mean, not yours. For why should my freedom be judged by another's conscience? [30]If I take part in the meal with thankfulness, why am I denounced because of something I thank God for?

[31]So whether you eat or drink or whatever you do, do it all for the glory of God. [32]Do not cause anyone to stumble, whether Jews, Greeks or the church of God— [33]even as I try to please everybody in every way. For I am not seeking my own good but the good of many, so that they may be saved. [1]Follow my example, as I follow the example of Christ.

11

Propriety in Worship

[2]I praise you for remembering me in everything and for holding to the teachings,[c] just as I passed them on to you.

[3]Now I want you to realize that the head of every man is Christ, and the head of the woman is man, and the head of Christ is God. [4]Every man who prays or prophesies with his head covered dishonors his head. [5]And every woman who prays or prophesies with her head uncovered dishonors her head—it is just as though her head were shaved. [6]If a woman does not cover her head, she should have her hair cut off; and if it is a disgrace for a woman to have her hair cut or shaved off, she should cover her head. [7]A man ought not to cover his head,[d] since he is the image and glory of God; but the woman is the glory of man. [8]For man did not come from woman, but woman from man; [9]neither was man created for woman, but woman for man. [10]For this reason, and because of the angels, the woman ought to have a sign of authority on her head.

[11]In the Lord, however, woman is not independent of man, nor is man independent of woman. [12]For as woman came from man, so also man is born of woman. But everything comes from God. [13]Judge for yourselves: Is it proper for a woman to pray to God with her head uncovered? [14]Does not the very nature of things teach you that if a man has long hair, it is a disgrace to him, [15]but that if a woman has long hair, it is her glory? For long hair is given to her as a covering. [16]If anyone wants to be contentious about this, we have no other practice—nor do the churches of God.

The Lord's Supper

11:23–25pp — Mt 26:26–28; Mk 14:22–24; Lk 22:17–20

[17]In the following directives I have no praise for you, for your meetings do more harm than good. [18]In the first place, I hear that when you come together as a church, there are divisions among you, and to some extent I believe it. [19]No doubt there have to be differences among you to show which of you have God's approval. [20]When you come together, it is not the Lord's Supper you eat, [21]for as you eat, each of you goes ahead without waiting for anybody else. One remains hungry, another gets drunk. [22]Don't you have homes to eat and drink in? Or do you despise the church of God and humiliate those who have nothing? What shall I say to you? Shall I praise you for this? Certainly not!

---

[a] 26 Psalm 24:1   [b] 28 Some manuscripts *conscience' sake, for "the earth is the Lord's and everything in it"*   [c] 2 Or *traditions*
[d] 4-7 Or [4]*Every man who prays or prophesies with long hair dishonors his head.* [5]*And every woman who prays or prophesies with no covering of hair on her head dishonors her head—she is just like one of the "shorn women."* [6]*If a woman has no covering, let her be for now with short hair, but since it is a disgrace for a woman to have her hair shorn or shaved, she should grow it again.* [7]*A man ought not to have long hair*

SO WHETHER YOU EAT OR DRINK OR WHATEVER YOU DO, DO IT ALL FOR THE GLORY OF GOD.

1 Corinthians 10:31

Saying Grace, Singing Thanks

BOBBIE WOLGEMUTH

READ | 1 CORINTHIANS 10:23 — 11:1

Frequent visits to my grandparents' farm gave me a wonderful connection to the earth and its bounty when I was a young girl. I can still feel the warmth of the egg my grandmother pulled out from beneath her "laying hen" in the chicken house and taste the sweetness of the yellow corn steaming on my plate shortly after it was picked from the cornfield. Today we go to grocery stores, where the display of fruits and vegetables is endless and the connection to the earth and the hand of God that provided the rain and soil can be easily overlooked.

I am thankful for grandparents who openly thanked God for his bounty at every meal, no matter how sparse or grand it was. A simple "Thank you for your provisions, Lord" was automatic.

Now, one of my favorite mealtime songs when our grandchildren visit is the doxology. Joining our voices around the table to sing "Praise God from whom all blessings flow . . ." is a familiar reminder that all we have — our health, our food, our family, our every breath — is a gift from our heavenly Father's hand. As a grandmother, I want to model gratefulness for the provisions he has made for our health.

Saying grace at meals is a family ritual that binds our hearts together in appreciation for God's goodness. It is extra fun to hold hands around the table for the blessing. Let the children join to sing or say their thanks to God at mealtime.

Lord Jesus, today I am thankful for all you have provided. Help me to show my grandchildren a grateful heart so they may enter the special blessing of noticing your abundance in the small and grand gifts you bestow on us every day. Amen.

Your next devotion is located on page 1571.

GRANDCHILD IN FOCUS · PRAYER

Physical Well-Being

Almighty God, Creator of us all, I pray that you will watch over my grandchild's physical development. May he grow in strength through the stages of his life. As he grows in awareness of his body, help him to understand that each body develops uniquely, yet is within your plan and your control. Please guard his health so that his diseases are few, his injuries are minor and his infirmities are brief. Amen.

²³For I received from the Lord what I also passed on to you: The Lord Jesus, on the night he was betrayed, took bread, ²⁴and when he had given thanks, he broke it and said, "This is my body, which is for you; do this in remembrance of me." ²⁵In the same way, after supper he took the cup, saying, "This cup is the new covenant in my blood; do this, whenever you drink it, in remembrance of me." ²⁶For whenever you eat this bread and drink this cup, you proclaim the Lord's death until he comes.

²⁷Therefore, whoever eats the bread or drinks the cup of the Lord in an unworthy manner will be guilty of sinning against the body and blood of the Lord. ²⁸A man ought to examine himself before he eats of the bread and drinks of the cup. ²⁹For anyone who eats and drinks without recognizing the body of the Lord eats and drinks judgment on himself. ³⁰That is why many among you are weak and sick, and a number of you have fallen asleep. ³¹But if we judged ourselves, we would not come under judgment. ³²When we are judged by the Lord, we are being disciplined so that we will not be condemned with the world.

³³So then, my brothers, when you come together to eat, wait for each other. ³⁴If anyone is hungry, he should eat at home, so that when you meet together it may not result in judgment.

And when I come I will give further directions.

Spiritual Gifts

12 Now about spiritual gifts, brothers, I do not want you to be ignorant. ²You know that when you were pagans, somehow or other you were influenced and led astray to mute idols. ³Therefore I tell you that no one who is speaking by the Spirit of God says, "Jesus be cursed," and no one can say, "Jesus is Lord," except by the Holy Spirit.

⁴There are different kinds of gifts, but the same Spirit. ⁵There are different kinds of service, but the same Lord. ⁶There are different kinds of working, but the same God works all of them in all men.

⁷Now to each one the manifestation of the Spirit is given for the common good. ⁸To one there is given through the Spirit the message of wisdom, to another the message of knowledge by means of the same Spirit, ⁹to another faith by the same Spirit, to another gifts of healing by that one Spirit, ¹⁰to another miraculous powers, to another prophecy, to another distinguishing between spirits, to another speaking in different kinds of tongues,ᵃ and to still another the interpretation of tongues.ᵃ ¹¹All these are the work of one and the same Spirit, and he gives them to each one, just as he determines.

One Body, Many Parts

¹²The body is a unit, though it is made up of many parts; and though all its parts are many, they form one body. So it is with Christ. ¹³For we were all baptized byᵇ one Spirit into one body—whether Jews or Greeks, slave or free—and we were all given the one Spirit to drink.

¹⁴Now the body is not made up of one part but of many. ¹⁵If the foot should say, "Because I am not a hand, I do not belong to the body," it would not for that reason cease to be part of the body. ¹⁶And if the ear should say, "Because I am not an eye, I do not belong to the body," it would not for that reason cease to be part of the body. ¹⁷If the whole body were an eye, where would the sense of hearing be? If the whole body were an ear, where would the sense of smell be? ¹⁸But in fact God has arranged the parts in the body, every one of them, just as he wanted them to be. ¹⁹If they were all one part, where would the body be? ²⁰As it is, there are many parts, but one body.

²¹The eye cannot say to the hand, "I don't need you!" And the head cannot say to the feet, "I don't need you!" ²²On the contrary, those parts of the body that seem to be weaker are indispensable, ²³and the parts that we think are less honorable we treat with special honor. And the parts that are unpresentable are treated with special

ᵃ 10 Or languages; also in verse 28   ᵇ 13 Or with; or in

NOW THE BODY IS NOT MADE
UP OF ONE PART BUT OF MANY
. . . GOD HAS ARRANGED THE
PARTS IN THE BODY, EVERY ONE
OF THEM, JUST AS HE WANTED
THEM TO BE.

1 Corinthians 12:14,18

Be Who You Are

THELMA WELLS

READ | 1 CORINTHIANS 12:12–31

Honey, if you are trying to be something you know you aren't, if you are trying to do things you know you have little ability, patience, passion, commitment and tolerance for, cut it out! Be yourself! The great thing about real authority is that God gives me one thing to do, somebody else another, somebody else something else; or he may give us the same talent but have us exhibit it in different ways. Blending our authority with other people's authority creates the kind of kingdom on earth that personifies God's kingdom in heaven. The reason Lucifer was kicked out of heaven was that he tried to usurp God's authority and be something he wasn't. How very stupid when he had the fourth best position in heaven! His jealousy and rebellion cost him his position, his beauty, his ability to make angelic music and his intimacy with God. When we operate outside of our authority, we experience similar breakdowns.

But that doesn't have to happen to you. Just be who you are, what you are, how you are, the way God made you. It is his grace that creates in you the talents, inclinations, knowledge and pleasure to be yourself. Grace empowers you to perform the tasks God has given you on earth and to enjoy what he has called you to do.

Father, thank you for the gifts and talents you have given me. I confess that so often I'd rather have someone else's! Give me the discernment to recognize the tasks you have given me to do and let go of the rest. Help me to be the unique person you made me to be.

Your next devotion is located on page 1573.

GRANDCHILD IN FOCUS • PRAYER

Emotional Development

O God, Creator of mind and body, I pray that you will give my grandchild emotional health and strength. Where there is anger, bring peace. Where there is confusion, bring clarity and focus. Where there are dark shadows, cast a ray of hope. Fill her with the sunshine of your Spirit. Warm her with the presence of your peace. Amen.

modesty, ²⁴while our presentable parts need no special treatment. But God has combined the members of the body and has given greater honor to the parts that lacked it, ²⁵so that there should be no division in the body, but that its parts should have equal concern for each other. ²⁶If one part suffers, every part suffers with it; if one part is honored, every part rejoices with it.

²⁷Now you are the body of Christ, and each one of you is a part of it. ²⁸And in the church God has appointed first of all apostles, second prophets, third teachers, then workers of miracles, also those having gifts of healing, those able to help others, those with gifts of administration, and those speaking in different kinds of tongues. ²⁹Are all apostles? Are all prophets? Are all teachers? Do all work miracles? ³⁰Do all have gifts of healing? Do all speak in tongues ᵃ? Do all interpret? ³¹But eagerly desire ᵇ the greater gifts.

Love

And now I will show you the most excellent way.

13 If I speak in the tongues ᶜ of men and of angels, but have not love, I am only a resounding gong or a clanging cymbal. ²If I have the gift of prophecy and can fathom all mysteries and all knowledge, and if I have a faith that can move mountains, but have not love, I am nothing. ³If I give all I possess to the poor and surrender my body to the flames, ᵈ but have not love, I gain nothing.

⁴Love is patient, love is kind. It does not envy, it does not boast, it is not proud. ⁵It is not rude, it is not self-seeking, it is not easily angered, it keeps no record of wrongs. ⁶Love does not delight in evil but rejoices with the truth. ⁷It always protects, always trusts, always hopes, always perseveres.

⁸Love never fails. But where there are prophecies, they will cease; where there are tongues, they will be stilled; where there is knowledge, it will pass away. ⁹For we know in part and we prophesy in part, ¹⁰but when perfection comes, the imperfect disappears. ¹¹When I was a child, I talked like

stories to share

1 CORINTHIANS 13:1–13

Love Is the Greatest of All

LIFE LESSON: Love is sure proof of Christian faith.

TO TALK ABOUT

✦ What are some ways to define love?

✦ What does Paul mean when he says that "love never fails" (verse 8)?

✦ Why do you think love is greater than faith or hope?

✦ What good could a Christian do in this world without love?

a child, I thought like a child, I reasoned like a child. When I became a man, I put childish ways behind me. ¹²Now we see but a poor reflection as in a mirror; then we shall see face to face. Now

ᵃ 30 Or other languages   ᵇ 31 Or But you are eagerly desiring
ᶜ 1 Or languages   ᵈ 3 Some early manuscripts body that I may boast

TALKING POINTS

Love

Without love, we are nothing.

1 CORINTHIANS 13:1–13

For more on love, go to 1 Peter 4:8.

LOVE IS PATIENT, LOVE IS KIND.
IT DOES NOT ENVY, IT DOES NOT
BOAST, IT IS NOT PROUD. IT IS NOT
RUDE, IT IS NOT SELF-SEEKING.

1 Corinthians 13:4—5

Let Me Tell You About My Grandchildren

CYNTHIA HEALD

READ | 1 CORINTHIANS 13:1–13

For an hour and a half I listened to an acquaintance recount the sterling accomplishments of her children. She was justly proud, but her boasting devoured our lunch and left me feeling left out of the conversation and left out as a mother of high achievers. As I examined my feelings, I remembered Paul's description of the qualities of love that I needed to exercise at this time: patience, kindness and selflessness.

I also became aware of the importance of being considerate of others when I converse with them. The Scriptures are clear that if I am to be a woman who loves, I do not boast. To boast means to vaunt or extol the deeds or abilities of oneself or of another; to flaunt; to sing one's own praises. It is good and right to share stories about our families, but we cross the line of love when we become so absorbed with ourselves that we become insensitive to others.

I heard the story of a woman who had just been with her first grandchild. When this new grandmother saw a friend having lunch with a young couple in a restaurant, she rushed over to her friend and excitedly began showing pictures and sharing how cute and healthy the baby was. After she left, the couple no longer wanted to eat or talk, for they had just lost their newborn baby two weeks before. Certainly this grandmother did not know about the couple's loss, but if she had been committed to not boasting, perhaps her intrusion would not have caused such pain.

A privilege of being a grandmother is sharing how special our grandchildren are, but let us share with humility and thoughtfulness—for love does not boast.

. . . .

O Father, how easy it is to talk about "me." May I be more concerned about the interests of others than I am about my own interests. Set a guard over my lips so that boasting is restrained and replaced by love. Amen.

Your next devotion is located on page 1582.

GRANDCHILD IN FOCUS • PRAYER

Spiritual Growth

Dear Lord, today I pray for my grandchild's spiritual growth. I ask that you instill in him the desire to read and memorize your Word. Give him a passion to be in conversation with you. May loving and serving you be part of his daily life. I ask that you stay close to him and lead him to be transformed to your likeness, to reflect your grace and to radiate your love. I pray this in Jesus' name, amen.

I know in part; then I shall know fully, even as I am fully known.

[13] And now these three remain: faith, hope and love. But the greatest of these is love.

Gifts of Prophecy and Tongues

14 Follow the way of love and eagerly desire spiritual gifts, especially the gift of prophecy. [2] For anyone who speaks in a tongue[a] does not speak to men but to God. Indeed, no one understands him; he utters mysteries with his spirit.[b] [3] But everyone who prophesies speaks to men for their strengthening, encouragement and comfort. [4] He who speaks in a tongue edifies himself, but he who prophesies edifies the church. [5] I would like every one of you to speak in tongues,[c] but I would rather have you prophesy. He who prophesies is greater than one who speaks in tongues,[c] unless he interprets, so that the church may be edified.

[6] Now, brothers, if I come to you and speak in tongues, what good will I be to you, unless I bring you some revelation or knowledge or prophecy or word of instruction? [7] Even in the case of lifeless things that make sounds, such as the flute or harp, how will anyone know what tune is being played unless there is a distinction in the notes? [8] Again, if the trumpet does not sound a clear call, who will get ready for battle? [9] So it is with you. Unless you speak intelligible words with your tongue, how will anyone know what you are saying? You will just be speaking into the air. [10] Undoubtedly there are all sorts of languages in the world, yet none of them is without meaning. [11] If then I do not grasp the meaning of what someone is saying, I am a foreigner to the speaker, and he is a foreigner to me. [12] So it is with you. Since you are eager to have spiritual gifts, try to excel in gifts that build up the church.

[13] For this reason anyone who speaks in a tongue should pray that he may interpret what he says. [14] For if I pray in a tongue, my spirit prays, but my mind is unfruitful. [15] So what shall I do? I will pray with my spirit, but I will also pray with my mind; I will sing with my spirit, but I will also sing with my mind. [16] If you are praising God with your spirit, how can one who finds himself among those who do not understand[d] say "Amen" to your thanksgiving, since he does not know what you are saying? [17] You may be giving thanks well enough, but the other man is not edified.

[18] I thank God that I speak in tongues more than all of you. [19] But in the church I would rather speak five intelligible words to instruct others than ten thousand words in a tongue.

[20] Brothers, stop thinking like children. In regard to evil be infants, but in your thinking be adults. [21] In the Law it is written:

"Through men of strange tongues
  and through the lips of foreigners
I will speak to this people,
  but even then they will not listen to me,"[e]
says the Lord.

[22] Tongues, then, are a sign, not for believers but for unbelievers; prophecy, however, is for believers, not for unbelievers. [23] So if the whole church comes together and everyone speaks in tongues, and some who do not understand[f] or some unbelievers come in, will they not say that you are out of your mind? [24] But if an unbeliever or someone who does not understand[g] comes in while everybody is prophesying, he will be convinced by all that he is a sinner and will be judged by all, [25] and the secrets of his heart will be laid bare. So he will fall down and worship God, exclaiming, "God is really among you!"

Orderly Worship

[26] What then shall we say, brothers? When you come together, everyone has a hymn, or a word of instruction, a revelation, a tongue or an interpretation. All of these must be done for the strengthening of the church. [27] If anyone speaks in a tongue, two—or at the most three—should speak, one at a time, and someone must interpret.

---

[a] 2 Or another language; also in verses 4, 13, 14, 19, 26 and 27
[b] 2 Or by the Spirit   [c] 5 Or other languages; also in verses 6, 18, 22, 23 and 39   [d] 16 Or among the inquirers   [e] 21 Isaiah 28:11,12
[f] 23 Or some inquirers   [g] 24 Or or some inquirer

²⁸If there is no interpreter, the speaker should keep quiet in the church and speak to himself and God.

²⁹Two or three prophets should speak, and the others should weigh carefully what is said. ³⁰And if a revelation comes to someone who is sitting down, the first speaker should stop. ³¹For you can all prophesy in turn so that everyone may be instructed and encouraged. ³²The spirits of prophets are subject to the control of prophets. ³³For God is not a God of disorder but of peace.

As in all the congregations of the saints, ³⁴women should remain silent in the churches. They are not allowed to speak, but must be in submission, as the Law says. ³⁵If they want to inquire about something, they should ask their own husbands at home; for it is disgraceful for a woman to speak in the church.

³⁶Did the word of God originate with you? Or are you the only people it has reached? ³⁷If anybody thinks he is a prophet or spiritually gifted, let him acknowledge that what I am writing to you is the Lord's command. ³⁸If he ignores this, he himself will be ignored.[a]

³⁹Therefore, my brothers, be eager to prophesy, and do not forbid speaking in tongues. ⁴⁰But everything should be done in a fitting and orderly way.

The Resurrection of Christ

15 Now, brothers, I want to remind you of the gospel I preached to you, which you received and on which you have taken your stand. ²By this gospel you are saved, if you hold firmly to the word I preached to you. Otherwise, you have believed in vain.

³For what I received I passed on to you as of first importance[b]: that Christ died for our sins according to the Scriptures, ⁴that he was buried, that he was raised on the third day according to the Scriptures, ⁵and that he appeared to Peter,[c] and then to the Twelve. ⁶After that, he appeared to more than five hundred of the brothers at the same time, most of whom are still living, though some have fallen asleep. ⁷Then he appeared to

---

PRAYING THE SCRIPTURES

Salvation

1 CORINTHIANS 15:3–4

Dear Lord, may my grandchild acknowledge that Christ died for her sins, that he was buried, and that he was raised on the third day.

Next prayer in Salvation Prayer Track: Ephesians 2:8–10

James, then to all the apostles, ⁸and last of all he appeared to me also, as to one abnormally born.

⁹For I am the least of the apostles and do not even deserve to be called an apostle, because I persecuted the church of God. ¹⁰But by the grace of God I am what I am, and his grace to me was not without effect. No, I worked harder than all of them — yet not I, but the grace of God that was with me. ¹¹Whether, then, it was I or they, this is what we preach, and this is what you believed.

The Resurrection of the Dead

¹²But if it is preached that Christ has been raised from the dead, how can some of you say that there is no resurrection of the dead? ¹³If there is no resurrection of the dead, then not even Christ has been raised. ¹⁴And if Christ has not been raised, our preaching is useless and so is your faith. ¹⁵More than that, we are then found to be false witnesses about God, for we have testified about God that he raised Christ from the dead. But he did not raise him if in fact the dead are not raised. ¹⁶For if the dead are not raised, then Christ has not been raised either. ¹⁷And if Christ has not been raised, your faith is futile; you are still in your sins. ¹⁸Then those also who have fallen asleep in Christ are lost. ¹⁹If only for this life we have hope in Christ, we are to be pitied more than all men.

²⁰But Christ has indeed been raised from the

---

[a] 38 Some manuscripts *If he is ignorant of this, let him be ignorant*
[b] 3 Or *you at the first* [c] 5 Greek *Cephas*

dead, the firstfruits of those who have fallen asleep. [21]For since death came through a man, the resurrection of the dead comes also through a man. [22]For as in Adam all die, so in Christ all will be made alive. [23]But each in his own turn: Christ, the firstfruits; then, when he comes, those who belong to him. [24]Then the end will come, when he hands over the kingdom to God the Father after he has destroyed all dominion, authority and power. [25]For he must reign until he has put all his enemies under his feet. [26]The last enemy to be destroyed is death. [27]For he "has put everything under his feet."[a] Now when it says that "everything" has been put under him, it is clear that this does not include God himself, who put everything under Christ. [28]When he has done this, then the Son himself will be made subject to him who put everything under him, so that God may be all in all.

[29]Now if there is no resurrection, what will those do who are baptized for the dead? If the dead are not raised at all, why are people baptized for them? [30]And as for us, why do we endanger ourselves every hour? [31]I die every day—I mean that, brothers—just as surely as I glory over you in Christ Jesus our Lord. [32]If I fought wild beasts in Ephesus for merely human reasons, what have I gained? If the dead are not raised,

"Let us eat and drink,
    for tomorrow we die."[b]

[33]Do not be misled: "Bad company corrupts good character." [34]Come back to your senses as you ought, and stop sinning; for there are some who are ignorant of God—I say this to your shame.

The Resurrection Body

[35]But someone may ask, "How are the dead raised? With what kind of body will they come?" [36]How foolish! What you sow does not come to life unless it dies. [37]When you sow, you do not plant the body that will be, but just a seed, perhaps of wheat or of something else. [38]But God gives it a body as he has determined, and to each kind of seed he gives its own body. [39]All flesh is not the same: Men have one kind of flesh, animals have another, birds another and fish another. [40]There are also heavenly bodies and there are earthly bodies; but the splendor of the heavenly bodies is one kind, and the splendor of the earthly bodies is another. [41]The sun has one kind of splendor, the moon another and the stars another; and star differs from star in splendor.

[42]So will it be with the resurrection of the dead. The body that is sown is perishable, it is raised imperishable; [43]it is sown in dishonor, it is raised in glory; it is sown in weakness, it is raised in power; [44]it is sown a natural body, it is raised a spiritual body.

If there is a natural body, there is also a spiritual body. [45]So it is written: "The first man Adam became a living being"[c]; the last Adam, a life-giving spirit. [46]The spiritual did not come first, but the natural, and after that the spiritual. [47]The first man was of the dust of the earth, the second man from heaven. [48]As was the earthly man, so are those who are of the earth; and as is the man from heaven, so also are those who are of heaven. [49]And just as we have borne the likeness of the earthly man, so shall we[d] bear the likeness of the man from heaven.

[50]I declare to you, brothers, that flesh and blood cannot inherit the kingdom of God, nor does the perishable inherit the imperishable. [51]Listen, I tell you a mystery: We will not all sleep, but we will all be changed— [52]in a flash, in the twinkling of an eye, at the last trumpet. For the trumpet will sound, the dead will be raised imperishable, and we will be changed. [53]For the perishable must clothe itself with the imperishable, and the mortal with immortality. [54]When the perishable has been clothed with the imperishable, and the mortal with immortality, then the saying that is written will come true: "Death has been swallowed up in victory."[e]

[55]"Where, O death, is your victory?
    Where, O death, is your sting?"[f]

[a] 27 Psalm 8:6   [b] 32 Isaiah 22:13   [c] 45 Gen. 2:7   [d] 49 Some early manuscripts *so let us*   [e] 54 Isaiah 25:8   [f] 55 Hosea 13:14

⁵⁶The sting of death is sin, and the power of sin is the law. ⁵⁷But thanks be to God! He gives us the victory through our Lord Jesus Christ.

⁵⁸Therefore, my dear brothers, stand firm. Let nothing move you. Always give yourselves fully to the work of the Lord, because you know that your labor in the Lord is not in vain.

TALKING POINTS

Loss/Grief

Christ gives victory over death.

1 CORINTHIANS 15:51–58

This is the last talking point on loss/grief.

The Collection for God's People

16 Now about the collection for God's people: Do what I told the Galatian churches to do. ²On the first day of every week, each one of you should set aside a sum of money in keeping with his income, saving it up, so that when I come no collections will have to be made. ³Then, when I arrive, I will give letters of introduction to the men you approve and send them with your gift to Jerusalem. ⁴If it seems advisable for me to go also, they will accompany me.

Personal Requests

⁵After I go through Macedonia, I will come to you—for I will be going through Macedonia. ⁶Perhaps I will stay with you awhile, or even spend the winter, so that you can help me on my journey, wherever I go. ⁷I do not want to see you now and make only a passing visit; I hope to spend some time with you, if the Lord permits. ⁸But I will stay on at Ephesus until Pentecost, ⁹be-cause a great door for effective work has opened to me, and there are many who oppose me.

¹⁰If Timothy comes, see to it that he has nothing to fear while he is with you, for he is carrying on the work of the Lord, just as I am. ¹¹No one, then, should refuse to accept him. Send him on his way in peace so that he may return to me. I am expecting him along with the brothers.

¹²Now about our brother Apollos: I strongly urged him to go to you with the brothers. He was quite unwilling to go now, but he will go when he has the opportunity.

¹³Be on your guard; stand firm in the faith; be men of courage; be strong. ¹⁴Do everything in love.

¹⁵You know that the household of Stephanas were the first converts in Achaia, and they have devoted themselves to the service of the saints. I urge you, brothers, ¹⁶to submit to such as these and to everyone who joins in the work, and labors at it. ¹⁷I was glad when Stephanas, Fortunatus and Achaicus arrived, because they have supplied what was lacking from you. ¹⁸For they refreshed my spirit and yours also. Such men deserve recognition.

Final Greetings

¹⁹The churches in the province of Asia send you greetings. Aquila and Priscilla*ᵃ* greet you warmly in the Lord, and so does the church that meets at their house. ²⁰All the brothers here send you greetings. Greet one another with a holy kiss.

²¹I, Paul, write this greeting in my own hand.

²²If anyone does not love the Lord—a curse be on him. Come, O Lord*ᵇ*!

²³The grace of the Lord Jesus be with you.

²⁴My love to all of you in Christ Jesus. Amen.*ᶜ*

ᵃ 19 Greek *Prisca*, a variant of *Priscilla*   *ᵇ 22* In Aramaic the expression *Come, O Lord* is *Marana tha.*   *ᶜ 24* Some manuscripts do not have *Amen.*

The Source
OF COMFORT

Grandmothers are the epitome of comfort. If anyone knows how to comfort, we do. We do it with hugs and kisses, soups and stews, pies and pancakes, cupcakes and cookies. We comfort with quilts and afghans, songs and stories, trips to the zoo. When it comes to comfort, grandmothers have an overflowing supply.

The apostle Paul wrote this letter within months of writing the letter that we know as 1 Corinthians. His opening was encouraging and comforting. But the tone of his letter changed as he defended himself against the false teachers that had challenged the believers and questioned his authority. He instructed his readers and encouraged them to persevere in the truth, and he reminded them that the source of all comfort is God.

God is always willing to renew and revive us with the comfort of his loving presence, filling us up again so that we can comfort others. We can't rely on our own resources as we give out comfort to our friends, our children, our grandchildren; we will only run dry and be overwhelmed by their need. Instead we are to turn to God. He's the only One with an overflowing supply!

VERSE *to* REMEMBER | 2 CORINTHIANS 1:3 – 4

Praise be to the God and Father of our Lord Jesus Christ, the Father of compassion and the God of all comfort, who comforts us in all our troubles, so that we can comfort those in any trouble with the comfort we ourselves have received from God.

ABOUT 2 CORINTHIANS

WRITTEN BY:
The apostle Paul

WRITTEN FOR:
The Christians in Corinth

DATE WRITTEN:
About A.D. 55
from Macedonia

WHY WRITTEN:
To let the Corinthians know that Paul loved them even though they had many problems

1

Paul, an apostle of Christ Jesus by the will of God, and Timothy our brother,

To the church of God in Corinth, together with all the saints throughout Achaia:

²Grace and peace to you from God our Father and the Lord Jesus Christ.

The God of All Comfort

³Praise be to the God and Father of our Lord Jesus Christ, the Father of compassion and the God of all comfort, ⁴who comforts us in all our troubles, so that we can comfort those in any trouble with the comfort we ourselves have received from God. ⁵For just as the sufferings of Christ flow over into our lives, so also through Christ our comfort overflows. ⁶If we are distressed, it is for your comfort and salvation; if we are comforted, it is for your comfort, which produces in you patient endurance of the same sufferings we suffer. ⁷And our hope for you is firm, because we know that just as you share in our sufferings, so also you share in our comfort.

⁸We do not want you to be uninformed, brothers, about the hardships we suffered in the province of Asia. We were under great pressure, far beyond our ability to endure, so that we despaired even of life. ⁹Indeed, in our hearts we felt the sentence of death. But this happened

stories to share

2 CORINTHIANS 1:3–11

The God of All Comfort

LIFE LESSON: God's comfort in our troubles helps us to comfort other hurting people.

TO TALK ABOUT

✦ Who comforts us when bad things happen?

✦ What should we do when other people are sad?

✦ How do hard times help us learn to rely on Christ?

✦ When have you been able to comfort someone else because you had experienced a similar problem or hurt?

PRAYING THE SCRIPTURES

Comfort

2 CORINTHIANS 1:3–4

I praise you, O God and Father of our Lord Jesus Christ, the Father of compassion and the God of all comfort. Comfort my grandchild in all her troubles, so that she can comfort those in any trouble with the comfort she herself has received from you.

Next prayer in Comfort Prayer Track: Revelation 21:4–5

that we might not rely on ourselves but on God, who raises the dead. ¹⁰He has delivered us from such a deadly peril, and he will deliver us. On him we have set our hope that he will continue to deliver us, ¹¹as you help us by your prayers. Then many will give thanks on our *a* behalf for the gracious favor granted us in answer to the prayers of many.

Paul's Change of Plans

¹²Now this is our boast: Our conscience testifies that we have conducted ourselves in the

---

a 11 Many manuscripts *your*

world, and especially in our relations with you, in the holiness and sincerity that are from God. We have done so not according to worldly wisdom but according to God's grace. ¹³For we do not write you anything you cannot read or understand. And I hope that, ¹⁴as you have understood us in part, you will come to understand fully that you can boast of us just as we will boast of you in the day of the Lord Jesus.

¹⁵Because I was confident of this, I planned to visit you first so that you might benefit twice. ¹⁶I planned to visit you on my way to Macedonia and to come back to you from Macedonia, and then to have you send me on my way to Judea. ¹⁷When I planned this, did I do it lightly? Or do I make my plans in a worldly manner so that in the same breath I say, "Yes, yes" and "No, no"?

¹⁸But as surely as God is faithful, our message to you is not "Yes" and "No." ¹⁹For the Son of God, Jesus Christ, who was preached among you by me and Silas[a] and Timothy, was not "Yes" and "No," but in him it has always been "Yes." ²⁰For no matter how many promises God has made, they are "Yes" in Christ. And so through him the "Amen" is spoken by us to the glory of God. ²¹Now it is God who makes both us and you stand firm in Christ. He anointed us, ²²set his seal of ownership on us, and put his Spirit in our hearts as a deposit, guaranteeing what is to come.

²³I call God as my witness that it was in order to spare you that I did not return to Corinth. ²⁴Not that we lord it over your faith, but we work with you for your joy, because it is by faith you stand firm. ¹So I made up my mind that I would not make another painful visit to you. ²For if I grieve you, who is left to make me glad but you whom I have grieved? ³I wrote as I did so that when I came I should not be distressed by those who ought to make me rejoice. I had confidence in all of you, that you would all share my joy. ⁴For I wrote you out of great distress and anguish of heart and with many tears, not to grieve you but to let you know the depth of my love for you.

Forgiveness for the Sinner

⁵If anyone has caused grief, he has not so much grieved me as he has grieved all of you, to some extent—not to put it too severely. ⁶The punishment inflicted on him by the majority is sufficient for him. ⁷Now instead, you ought to forgive and comfort him, so that he will not be overwhelmed by excessive sorrow. ⁸I urge you, therefore, to reaffirm your love for him. ⁹The reason I wrote you was to see if you would stand the test and be obedient in everything. ¹⁰If you forgive anyone, I also forgive him. And what I have forgiven—if there was anything to forgive—I have forgiven in the sight of Christ for your sake, ¹¹in order that Satan might not outwit us. For we are not unaware of his schemes.

Ministers of the New Covenant

¹²Now when I went to Troas to preach the gospel of Christ and found that the Lord had opened a door for me, ¹³I still had no peace of mind, because I did not find my brother Titus there. So I said good-by to them and went on to Macedonia.

¹⁴But thanks be to God, who always leads us in triumphal procession in Christ and through us spreads everywhere the fragrance of the knowledge of him. ¹⁵For we are to God the aroma of Christ among those who are being saved and those who are perishing. ¹⁶To the one we are the smell of death; to the other, the fragrance of life. And who is equal to such a task? ¹⁷Unlike so many, we do not peddle the word of God for profit. On the contrary, in Christ we speak before God with sincerity, like men sent from God.

¹Are we beginning to commend ourselves again? Or do we need, like some people, letters of recommendation to you or from you? ²You yourselves are our letter, written on our hearts, known and read by everybody. ³You show that you are a letter from Christ, the result of our ministry, written not with ink but with the Spirit of the living God, not on tablets of stone but on tablets of human hearts.

---

[a] 19 Greek *Silvanus*, a variant of *Silas*

4Such confidence as this is ours through Christ before God. 5Not that we are competent in ourselves to claim anything for ourselves, but our competence comes from God. 6He has made us competent as ministers of a new covenant—not of the letter but of the Spirit; for the letter kills, but the Spirit gives life.

The Glory of the New Covenant

7Now if the ministry that brought death, which was engraved in letters on stone, came with glory, so that the Israelites could not look steadily at the face of Moses because of its glory, fading though it was, 8will not the ministry of the Spirit be even more glorious? 9If the ministry that condemns men is glorious, how much more glorious is the ministry that brings righteousness! 10For what was glorious has no glory now in comparison with the surpassing glory. 11And if what was fading away came with glory, how much greater is the glory of that which lasts!

12Therefore, since we have such a hope, we are very bold. 13We are not like Moses, who would put a veil over his face to keep the Israelites from gazing at it while the radiance was fading away. 14But their minds were made dull, for to this day the same veil remains when the old covenant is read. It has not been removed, because only in Christ is it taken away. 15Even to this day when Moses is read, a veil covers their hearts. 16But whenever anyone turns to the Lord, the veil is taken away. 17Now the Lord is the Spirit, and where the Spirit of the Lord is, there is freedom. 18And

we, who with unveiled faces all reflect a the Lord's glory, are being transformed into his likeness with ever increasing glory, which comes from the Lord, who is the Spirit.

Treasures in Jars of Clay

4 Therefore, since through God's mercy we have this ministry, we do not lose heart. 2Rather, we have renounced secret and shameful ways; we do not use deception, nor do we distort the word of God. On the contrary, by setting forth the truth plainly we commend ourselves to every man's conscience in the sight of God. 3And even if our gospel is veiled, it is veiled to those who are perishing. 4The god of this age has blinded the minds of unbelievers, so that they cannot see the light of the gospel of the glory of Christ, who is the image of God. 5For we do not preach ourselves, but Jesus Christ as Lord, and ourselves as your servants for Jesus' sake. 6For God, who said, "Let light shine out of darkness," b made his light shine in our hearts to give us the light of the knowledge of the glory of God in the face of Christ.

7But we have this treasure in jars of clay to show that this all-surpassing power is from God and not from us. 8We are hard pressed on every side, but not crushed; perplexed, but not in despair; 9persecuted, but not abandoned; struck down, but not destroyed. 10We always carry around in our body the death of Jesus, so that the life of Jesus may also be revealed in our body. 11For we who are alive are always being given over to death for Jesus' sake, so that his life may be revealed in our mortal body. 12So then, death is at work in us, but life is at work in you.

13It is written: "I believed; therefore I have spoken." c With that same spirit of faith we also believe and therefore speak, 14because we know that the one who raised the Lord Jesus from the dead will also raise us with Jesus and present us with you in his presence. 15All this is for your benefit, so that the grace that is reaching more and

a 18 Or *contemplate*   b 6 Gen. 1:3   c 13 Psalm 116:10

AND WE, WHO WITH UNVEILED FACES
ALL REFLECT THE LORD'S GLORY,
ARE BEING TRANSFORMED INTO HIS
LIKENESS WITH EVER-INCREASING
GLORY, WHICH COMES FROM THE
LORD, WHO IS THE SPIRIT.

2 Corinthians 3:18

What Do You Reflect?

CORRIE TEN BOOM

READ | 2 CORINTHIANS 3:7 – 18

A mirror doesn't have much to do. To do its job it must just hang or stand in the right direction. You and I don't have to do a great deal either. We need only to look to the Lord Jesus and He will make us like mirrors, and He does it so well! We don't need to strive and try to be a blessing but just look in the right direction. Then Jesus makes us a mirror of Himself.

We are moons, not suns. The moon only reflects the light of the sun. We need only to reflect light; then we live to His glory. In which direction are you looking? To your faith? In Hebrews 12:2 we read, "Let us fix our eyes on Jesus, the author and perfecter of our faith." Our faith is not the power but the instrument by which we can use the power of God. To your sins? Oh, turn your eyes away from your sin and look to Jesus; then you will find grace. To your concerns? If you look to Jesus, the waves in life's storm become like firm ground.

Yes, you and I must look in the right direction: away from our sins, away from our worries, and even away from our faith in Jesus, only to Jesus Himself. Who directs our gaze in the right direction? His Holy Spirit [the Lord Jesus Himself] directs our gaze and makes us mirrors of His peace and His light.

Hallelujah, what a Savior you are. In you I find solid ground on which to stand and an anchor for my soul, firm and secure. Amen.

Your next devotion is located on page 1585.

GRANDCHILD IN FOCUS • PRAYER

Relationships at Home

O Lord, I pray that you will bless the home and family of my grandchild. May the relationships she has with her parents and siblings enhance her well-being, support her self-confidence and increase her faith. May her home life reflect your love, your grace, your compassion and your peace. Guide her parents to direct her in love and truth, so she will grow into a strong and compassionate individual. Amen.

more people may cause thanksgiving to overflow to the glory of God.

[16]Therefore we do not lose heart. Though outwardly we are wasting away, yet inwardly we are being renewed day by day. [17]For our light and momentary troubles are achieving for us an eternal glory that far outweighs them all. [18]So we fix our eyes not on what is seen, but on what is unseen. For what is seen is temporary, but what is unseen is eternal.

Our Heavenly Dwelling

5 Now we know that if the earthly tent we live in is destroyed, we have a building from God, an eternal house in heaven, not built by human hands. [2]Meanwhile we groan, longing to be clothed with our heavenly dwelling, [3]because when we are clothed, we will not be found naked. [4]For while we are in this tent, we groan and are burdened, because we do not wish to be unclothed but to be clothed with our heavenly dwelling, so that what is mortal may be swallowed up by life. [5]Now it is God who has made us for this very purpose and has given us the Spirit as a deposit, guaranteeing what is to come.

[6]Therefore we are always confident and know that as long as we are at home in the body we are away from the Lord. [7]We live by faith, not by sight. [8]We are confident, I say, and would prefer to be away from the body and at home with the Lord. [9]So we make it our goal to please him, whether we are at home in the body or away from it. [10]For we must all appear before the judgment seat of Christ, that each one may receive what is due him for the things done while in the body, whether good or bad.

The Ministry of Reconciliation

[11]Since, then, we know what it is to fear the Lord, we try to persuade men. What we are is plain to God, and I hope it is also plain to your conscience. [12]We are not trying to commend ourselves to you again, but are giving you an opportunity to take pride in us, so that you can answer those who take pride in what is seen rather than in what is in the heart. [13]If we are out of our mind, it is for the sake of God; if we are in our right mind, it is for you. [14]For Christ's love compels us, because we are convinced that one died for all, and therefore all died. [15]And he died for all, that those who live should no longer live for themselves but for him who died for them and was raised again.

[16]So from now on we regard no one from a worldly point of view. Though we once regarded Christ in this way, we do so no longer. [17]Therefore, if anyone is in Christ, he is a new creation; the old has gone, the new has come! [18]All this is from God, who reconciled us to himself through Christ and gave us the ministry of reconciliation: [19]that God was reconciling the world to himself in Christ, not counting men's sins against them. And he has committed to us the message of reconciliation. [20]We are therefore Christ's ambassadors, as though God were making his appeal through us. We implore you on Christ's behalf: Be reconciled to God. [21]God made him who had no sin to be sin[a] for us, so that in him we might become the righteousness of God.

6 As God's fellow workers we urge you not to receive God's grace in vain. [2]For he says,

"In the time of my favor I heard you,
    and in the day of salvation I helped you."[b]

I tell you, now is the time of God's favor, now is the day of salvation.

Paul's Hardships

[3]We put no stumbling block in anyone's path, so that our ministry will not be discredited. [4]Rather, as servants of God we commend ourselves in every way: in great endurance; in troubles, hardships and distresses; [5]in beatings, imprisonments and riots; in hard work, sleepless nights and hunger; [6]in purity, understanding, patience and kindness; in the Holy Spirit and in sincere love; [7]in truthful speech and in the power of God; with weapons of righteousness in the right hand and

[a] 21 Or be a sin offering   [b] 2 Isaiah 49:8

in the left; [8]through glory and dishonor, bad report and good report; genuine, yet regarded as impostors; [9]known, yet regarded as unknown; dying, and yet we live on; beaten, and yet not killed; [10]sorrowful, yet always rejoicing; poor, yet making many rich; having nothing, and yet possessing everything.

[11]We have spoken freely to you, Corinthians, and opened wide our hearts to you. [12]We are not withholding our affection from you, but you are withholding yours from us. [13]As a fair exchange— I speak as to my children—open wide your hearts also.

Do Not Be Yoked With Unbelievers

[14]Do not be yoked together with unbelievers. For what do righteousness and wickedness have in common? Or what fellowship can light have with darkness? [15]What harmony is there between Christ and Belial[a]? What does a believer have in common with an unbeliever? [16]What agreement is there between the temple of God and idols? For we are the temple of the living God. As God has said: "I will live with them and walk among them, and I will be their God, and they will be my people."[b]

[17]"Therefore come out from them
  and be separate,

says the Lord.

Touch no unclean thing,
  and I will receive you."[c]

[18]"I will be a Father to you,
  and you will be my sons and daughters,
    says the Lord Almighty."[d]

7 Since we have these promises, dear friends, let us purify ourselves from everything that contaminates body and spirit, perfecting holiness out of reverence for God.

Paul's Joy

[2]Make room for us in your hearts. We have wronged no one, we have corrupted no one, we have exploited no one. [3]I do not say this to condemn you; I have said before that you have such a place in our hearts that we would live or die with you. [4]I have great confidence in you; I take great pride in you. I am greatly encouraged; in all our troubles my joy knows no bounds.

[5]For when we came into Macedonia, this body of ours had no rest, but we were harassed at every turn—conflicts on the outside, fears within. [6]But God, who comforts the downcast, comforted us by the coming of Titus, [7]and not only by his coming but also by the comfort you had given him. He told us about your longing for me, your deep sorrow, your ardent concern for me, so that my joy was greater than ever.

[8]Even if I caused you sorrow by my letter, I do not regret it. Though I did regret it—I see that my letter hurt you, but only for a little while—

[a] 15 Greek *Beliar*, a variant of *Belial*   [b] 16 Lev. 26:12; Jer. 32:38; Ezek. 37:27   [c] 17 Isaiah 52:11; Ezek. 20:34,41   [d] 18 2 Samuel 7:14; 7:8

LET'S
TALK

Do I Really Know You?

How well do you and your grandkids know each other? Why not get together and find out?

Develop a series of questions, such as, "What is your favorite color?" "What is the farthest you've traveled from home?" "Chocolate or vanilla?" Read the questions aloud and have each child answer the questions in writing, based on their knowledge of the "featured" grandchild. The featured child will answer the questions in writing without letting the other kids see the answers. Then have the grandkids read their answers, with the featured child last. The exercise will elicit some "Oh, yeah!" moments, as special memories come to mind, and the group will laugh at how close or far apart their perceptions are.

You might also prepare in advance some unfinished sentences about yourself to find out how well the grandkids know *you*. They might just be surprised at how "real" you turn out to be!

Long-Distance Variation: Prepare a series of unfinished sentences about yourself as well as about the long-distance grandchild. Send the list, mentioning that you've already finished the sentences about them to the best of your knowledge. Have the child send both lists back to you. Then compare notes in both directions.

Dear God, thank you for making each of us wonderfully unique. Bless this activity, and give us a deeper understanding and appreciation for one another. Help us to continue to honor and value each other for our similarities and our differences. Amen.

Your next devotion is located on page 1586.

GRANDCHILD IN FOCUS • PRAYER

Friends

Dear Lord and Father, I pray for my grandchild's social life and his friends. Bring diverse friends into his life who will love and encourage him, who will bring joy and laughter to the good times and comfort and support through difficulties and disappointments. Grant him wisdom and discernment as he selects his friends; help him to avoid cliques that restrict, activities that endanger, and foolish and dangerous behaviors that harm. I ask that you fill his life with close and caring relationships. Amen.

Worship the Lord

The LORD reigns, he is robed in majesty;
    the LORD is robed in majesty
    and is armed with strength.
The world is firmly established;
    it cannot be moved.
Your throne was established long ago;
    you are from all eternity.

The seas have lifted up, O LORD,
    the seas have lifted up their voice;
    the seas have lifted up their pounding waves.
Mightier than the thunder of the great waters,
    mightier than the breakers of the sea—
    the LORD on high is mighty.

Your statutes stand firm;
    holiness adorns your house
    for endless days, O LORD.

Psalm 93

O Holy Lord, you are indeed robed with majesty. All creation sings your praises. All creation reveres your might. May each person your hands have formed thank you for life and breath. May each eye look to you as Creator. May each mouth declare you are King. May that day come soon. Hallelujah! Amen.

Your next devotion is located on page 1588.

GRANDCHILD IN FOCUS • PRAYER

Self-Image

O loving God, I praise you for creating my grandchild as a unique individual. Now I ask you to help her appreciate her uniqueness. Build up her self-image so she can enjoy her individuality. Help her to stand firm for who she is, where she has come from and what she believes in. Encourage her not only to have hopes and dreams but to also enjoy each day as it comes. In Jesus' name, amen.

⁹yet now I am happy, not because you were made sorry, but because your sorrow led you to repentance. For you became sorrowful as God intended and so were not harmed in any way by us. ¹⁰Godly sorrow brings repentance that leads to salvation and leaves no regret, but worldly sorrow brings death. ¹¹See what this godly sorrow has produced in you: what earnestness, what eagerness to clear yourselves, what indignation, what alarm, what longing, what concern, what readiness to see justice done. At every point you have proved yourselves to be innocent in this matter. ¹²So even though I wrote to you, it was not on account of the one who did the wrong or of the injured party, but rather that before God you could see for yourselves how devoted to us you are. ¹³By all this we are encouraged.

In addition to our own encouragement, we were especially delighted to see how happy Titus was, because his spirit has been refreshed by all of you. ¹⁴I had boasted to him about you, and you have not embarrassed me. But just as everything we said to you was true, so our boasting about you to Titus has proved to be true as well. ¹⁵And his affection for you is all the greater when he remembers that you were all obedient, receiving him with fear and trembling. ¹⁶I am glad I can have complete confidence in you.

Generosity Encouraged

8 And now, brothers, we want you to know about the grace that God has given the Macedonian churches. ²Out of the most severe trial, their overflowing joy and their extreme poverty welled up in rich generosity. ³For I testify that they gave as much as they were able, and even beyond their ability. Entirely on their own, ⁴they urgently pleaded with us for the privilege of sharing in this service to the saints. ⁵And they did not do as we expected, but they gave themselves first to the Lord and then to us in keeping with God's will. ⁶So we urged Titus, since he had earlier made a beginning, to bring also to completion this act of grace on your part. ⁷But just as you excel in everything—in faith, in speech, in knowledge, in complete earnestness and in your love for us ᵃ—see that you also excel in this grace of giving.

⁸I am not commanding you, but I want to test the sincerity of your love by comparing it with the earnestness of others. ⁹For you know the grace of our Lord Jesus Christ, that though he was rich, yet for your sakes he became poor, so that you through his poverty might become rich.

¹⁰And here is my advice about what is best for you in this matter: Last year you were the first not only to give but also to have the desire to do so. ¹¹Now finish the work, so that your eager willingness to do it may be matched by your completion of it, according to your means. ¹²For if the willingness is there, the gift is acceptable according to what one has, not according to what he does not have.

¹³Our desire is not that others might be relieved while you are hard pressed, but that there might be equality. ¹⁴At the present time your plenty will supply what they need, so that in turn their plenty will supply what you need. Then there will be equality, ¹⁵as it is written: "He who gathered much did not have too much, and he who gathered little did not have too little." ᵇ

Titus Sent to Corinth

¹⁶I thank God, who put into the heart of Titus the same concern I have for you. ¹⁷For Titus not only welcomed our appeal, but he is coming to you with much enthusiasm and on his own initiative. ¹⁸And we are sending along with him the brother who is praised by all the churches for his service to the gospel. ¹⁹What is more, he was chosen by the churches to accompany us as we carry the offering, which we administer in order to honor the Lord himself and to show our eagerness to help. ²⁰We want to avoid any criticism of the way we administer this liberal gift. ²¹For we are taking pains to do what is right, not only in the eyes of the Lord but also in the eyes of men.

²²In addition, we are sending with them our

ᵃ 7 Some manuscripts *in our love for you*   ᵇ 15 Exodus 16:18

MONDAY

> BUT JUST AS YOU EXCEL IN EVERYTHING — IN FAITH, IN SPEECH, IN KNOWLEDGE, IN COMPLETE EARNESTNESS AND IN YOUR LOVE FOR US — SEE THAT YOU ALSO EXCEL IN THIS GRACE OF GIVING.
>
> *2 Corinthians 8:7*

A Sacrificial Gift

HELEN KOOIMAN HOSIER

READ | 2 CORINTHIANS 8:1 – 15

One of the most cherished memories of my 19 years as a Christian bookseller relates to the work-wizened, dear little elderly lady, stoop-shouldered and walking with a limp, who came into our bookstore. Opening up her well-worn purse, she found a coin purse and, turning it upside down on the counter, said, "This is what I have to spend, and I want a Bible for my grandson." She paused, wiped a tear from her eyes, and added, "He's in the service."

"Tell me about your grandson," I urged. With pride in her voice, she related how he'd enlisted in the Navy and how this would be his first Christmas away from home.

"I miss him so much," she added, taking a hanky out of her purse and using it to wipe away more tears. "He was always so good to me and made Christmas special."

I had selected several Bibles that I felt would be right for a young Navy man. "Oh, those are too expensive," she said, handling them with care.

"I don't think so," I responded "You've saved quite a bit here."

"Ohhhh, have I really? You see, I do night janitor work over at the mall . . . He is going to love this one," she brightened. "Navy blue, too — just right for a sailor. I led him to the Lord when he was just a little guy."

My prayers for her and her dearly loved seaman grandson followed her out the door and for a long time afterward. How many of these sacrificial gifts from grandparents have found their way to grandchildren? I can't help but wonder how God has blessed both the givers and the receivers.

Lord God, I ask that you inspire me to think of worthy gifts to give to my grandchildren, gifts that will help them learn and grow in wisdom, gifts that will show them my love and yours.

Your next devotion is located on page 1591.

GRANDCHILD IN FOCUS · PRAYER

Protection From Worldliness

O Sovereign Lord, the world surrounds my grandchild, pressing in and tempting him in so many ways. Help him set appropriate limits. Give him sound judgment to choose wisely. Guard him from temptation; protect him from physical and mental predators; lead him into paths of righteousness and light. And reassure me with your promise that you are holding him in your hands. Amen.

brother who has often proved to us in many ways that he is zealous, and now even more so because of his great confidence in you. ²³As for Titus, he is my partner and fellow worker among you; as for our brothers, they are representatives of the churches and an honor to Christ. ²⁴Therefore show these men the proof of your love and the reason for our pride in you, so that the churches can see it.

9 There is no need for me to write to you about this service to the saints. ²For I know your eagerness to help, and I have been boasting about it to the Macedonians, telling them that since last year you in Achaia were ready to give; and your enthusiasm has stirred most of them to action. ³But I am sending the brothers in order that our boasting about you in this matter should not prove hollow, but that you may be ready, as I said you would be. ⁴For if any Macedonians come with me and find you unprepared, we—not to say anything about you—would be ashamed of having been so confident. ⁵So I thought it necessary to urge the brothers to visit you in advance and finish the arrangements for the generous gift you had promised. Then it will be ready as a generous gift, not as one grudgingly given.

Sowing Generously

⁶Remember this: Whoever sows sparingly will also reap sparingly, and whoever sows generously will also reap generously. ⁷Each man should give what he has decided in his heart to give, not reluctantly or under compulsion, for God loves a cheerful giver. ⁸And God is able to make all grace abound to you, so that in all things at all times, having all that you need, you will abound in every good work. ⁹As it is written:

"He has scattered abroad his gifts to the poor;
  his righteousness endures forever."ᵃ

¹⁰Now he who supplies seed to the sower and bread for food will also supply and increase your store of seed and will enlarge the harvest of your righteousness. ¹¹You will be made rich in every

way so that you can be generous on every occasion, and through us your generosity will result in thanksgiving to God.

¹²This service that you perform is not only supplying the needs of God's people but is also overflowing in many expressions of thanks to God. ¹³Because of the service by which you have proved yourselves, men will praise God for the obedience that accompanies your confession of the gospel of Christ, and for your generosity in sharing with them and with everyone else. ¹⁴And in their prayers for you their hearts will go out to you, because of the surpassing grace God has given you. ¹⁵Thanks be to God for his indescribable gift!

TALKING POINTS

Thankfulness

Give thanks to God for our
salvation through Jesus.

2 CORINTHIANS 9:15

For more on thankfulness, go to 1 Thessalonians 5:18.

Paul's Defense of His Ministry

10 By the meekness and gentleness of Christ, I appeal to you—I, Paul, who am "timid" when face to face with you, but "bold" when away! ²I beg you that when I come I may not have to be as bold as I expect to be toward some people who think that we live by the standards of this world. ³For though we live in the world, we do not wage war as the world does. ⁴The weapons we fight with are not the weapons of the world. On the contrary, they have divine power to demolish strongholds. ⁵We demolish arguments and every pretension that sets itself up against the knowledge of God, and we take captive every

ᵃ 9 Psalm 112:9

thought to make it obedient to Christ. ⁶And we will be ready to punish every act of disobedience, once your obedience is complete.

⁷You are looking only on the surface of things.ᵃ If anyone is confident that he belongs to Christ, he should consider again that we belong to Christ just as much as he. ⁸For even if I boast somewhat freely about the authority the Lord gave us for building you up rather than pulling you down, I will not be ashamed of it. ⁹I do not want to seem to be trying to frighten you with my letters. ¹⁰For some say, "His letters are weighty and forceful, but in person he is unimpressive and his speaking amounts to nothing." ¹¹Such people should realize that what we are in our letters when we are absent, we will be in our actions when we are present.

¹²We do not dare to classify or compare ourselves with some who commend themselves. When they measure themselves by themselves and compare themselves with themselves, they are not wise. ¹³We, however, will not boast beyond proper limits, but will confine our boasting to the field God has assigned to us, a field that reaches even to you. ¹⁴We are not going too far in our boasting, as would be the case if we had not come to you, for we did get as far as you with the gospel of Christ. ¹⁵Neither do we go beyond our limits by boasting of work done by others.ᵇ Our hope is that, as your faith continues to grow, our area of activity among you will greatly expand, ¹⁶so that we can preach the gospel in the regions beyond you. For we do not want to boast about work already done in another man's territory. ¹⁷But, "Let him who boasts boast in the Lord."ᶜ ¹⁸For it is not the one who commends himself who is approved, but the one whom the Lord commends.

Paul and the False Apostles

11 I hope you will put up with a little of my foolishness; but you are already doing that. ²I am jealous for you with a godly jealousy. I promised you to one husband, to Christ, so that I might present you as a pure virgin to him. ³But I am afraid that just as Eve was deceived by the serpent's cunning, your minds may somehow be led astray from your sincere and pure devotion to Christ. ⁴For if someone comes to you and preaches a Jesus other than the Jesus we preached, or if you receive a different spirit from the one you received, or a different gospel from the one you accepted, you put up with it easily enough. ⁵But I do not think I am in the least inferior to those "super-apostles." ⁶I may not be a trained speaker, but I do have knowledge. We have made this perfectly clear to you in every way.

⁷Was it a sin for me to lower myself in order to elevate you by preaching the gospel of God to you free of charge? ⁸I robbed other churches by receiving support from them so as to serve you. ⁹And when I was with you and needed something, I was not a burden to anyone, for the brothers who came from Macedonia supplied what I needed. I have kept myself from being a burden to you in any way, and will continue to do so. ¹⁰As surely as the truth of Christ is in me, nobody in the regions of Achaia will stop this boasting of mine. ¹¹Why? Because I do not love you? God knows I do! ¹²And I will keep on doing what I am doing in order to cut the ground from under those who want an opportunity to be considered equal with us in the things they boast about.

¹³For such men are false apostles, deceitful workmen, masquerading as apostles of Christ. ¹⁴And no wonder, for Satan himself masquerades as an angel of light. ¹⁵It is not surprising, then, if his servants masquerade as servants of righteousness. Their end will be what their actions deserve.

Paul Boasts About His Sufferings

¹⁶I repeat: Let no one take me for a fool. But if you do, then receive me just as you would a fool, so that I may do a little boasting. ¹⁷In this self-confident boasting I am not talking as the Lord would, but as a fool. ¹⁸Since many are boasting in the way the world does, I too will boast.

ᵃ 7 Or Look at the obvious facts   ᵇ 13-15 Or ¹³We, however, will not boast about things that cannot be measured, but we will boast according to the standard of measurement that the God of measure has assigned us—a measurement that relates even to you. ¹⁴ . . . ¹⁵Neither do we boast about things that cannot be measured in regard to the work done by others.   ᶜ 17 Jer. 9:24

THE WEAPONS WE FIGHT WITH ARE NOT THE WEAPONS OF THE WORLD. ON THE CONTRARY, THEY HAVE DIVINE POWER TO DEMOLISH STRONGHOLDS. WE DEMOLISH ARGUMENTS AND EVERY PRETENSION THAT SETS ITSELF UP AGAINST THE KNOWLEDGE OF GOD, AND WE TAKE CAPTIVE EVERY THOUGHT TO MAKE IT OBEDIENT TO CHRIST.

2 Corinthians 10:4–5

The Most Powerful Weapon

DEBBY KERNER RETTINO

READ | 2 CORINTHIANS 10:1–18

The phone rings, startling me awake. It's my daughter calling, and my heart starts to pound as I pick up. The news is bad. She can't talk now, but she'll call me later with an update.

I go to prayer again. This is a battle, and I do not have a more powerful weapon. Even as I boldly go before the throne of God to intercede for my family, thoughts race across the window of my mind. The "what ifs" and the "why nots" are relentless in their attack as I play out doomsday scenarios in my imagination: they are in pain; they are helpless; the diagnosis is fatal. If I could just protect them by doing something. Why can't I be there with a body of steel to deflect the arrows that could hurt them? Oh my goodness, here come the mental vignettes in which I am the hero, saving the day with my wisdom and foresight. That is vanity par excellence!

I start over and take my thoughts captive and bring them into obedience to Christ. I picture the empty tomb of Jesus. The power of the resurrection, the proof that God wins. There is nothing I can do with my limited physical abilities, but God is able to fight for me.

The weapons we fight with are not the weapons of this world. They are spiritual weapons, with the divine power of God and the might of heaven. We cannot see the demons flee as we proclaim the name of Jesus, but we can sense the peace in our spirits as fear yields to trust. We cannot see the legions of angels fighting around us, but we can have quiet joy as the inner strongholds of our egos are demolished, and we are sure of God's ultimate victory. We can know our families are safer in God's hands than in our own.

Father God, mighty warrior, I listen for the battle cry of your Spirit. You are fearless to go into the places of my heart where I have built altars to myself. I am sorry that I have thought of myself so highly. Thank you that even though I cannot see the battle, I know that you are there fighting valiantly. I proclaim your victory in faith, in the powerful name of Jesus.

Your next devotion is located on page 1593.

GRANDCHILD IN FOCUS • PRAYER

Respect for Authority

Dear Lord, I pray that my grandchild will continually grow to respect those in authority. May she learn to be cooperative and fair in work and play. Instill in her a high regard for officials who govern our land and enforce the laws. May her relationships with parents, teachers, coaches, mentors and bosses be respectful, admirable, constructive and caring. Amen.

¹⁹You gladly put up with fools since you are so wise! ²⁰In fact, you even put up with anyone who enslaves you or exploits you or takes advantage of you or pushes himself forward or slaps you in the face. ²¹To my shame I admit that we were too weak for that!

What anyone else dares to boast about—I am speaking as a fool—I also dare to boast about. ²²Are they Hebrews? So am I. Are they Israelites? So am I. Are they Abraham's descendants? So am I. ²³Are they servants of Christ? (I am out of my mind to talk like this.) I am more. I have worked much harder, been in prison more frequently, been flogged more severely, and been exposed to death again and again. ²⁴Five times I received from the Jews the forty lashes minus one. ²⁵Three times I was beaten with rods, once I was stoned, three times I was shipwrecked, I spent a night and a day in the open sea, ²⁶I have been constantly on the move. I have been in danger from rivers, in danger from bandits, in danger from my own countrymen, in danger from Gentiles; in danger in the city, in danger in the country, in danger at sea; and in danger from false brothers. ²⁷I have labored and toiled and have often gone without sleep; I have known hunger and thirst and have often gone without food; I have been cold and naked. ²⁸Besides everything else, I face daily the pressure of my concern for all the churches. ²⁹Who is weak, and I do not feel weak? Who is led into sin, and I do not inwardly burn?

³⁰If I must boast, I will boast of the things that show my weakness. ³¹The God and Father of the Lord Jesus, who is to be praised forever, knows that I am not lying. ³²In Damascus the governor under King Aretas had the city of the Damascenes guarded in order to arrest me. ³³But I was lowered in a basket from a window in the wall and slipped through his hands.

Paul's Vision and His Thorn

12 I must go on boasting. Although there is nothing to be gained, I will go on to visions and revelations from the Lord. ²I know a man in Christ who fourteen years ago was caught up to the third heaven. Whether it was in the body or out of the body I do not know—God knows. ³And I know that this man—whether in the body or apart from the body I do not know, but God knows— ⁴was caught up to paradise. He heard inexpressible things, things that man is not permitted to tell. ⁵I will boast about a man like that, but I will not boast about myself, except about my weaknesses. ⁶Even if I should choose to boast, I would not be a fool, because I would be speaking the truth. But I refrain, so no one will think more of me than is warranted by what I do or say.

⁷To keep me from becoming conceited because of these surpassingly great revelations, there was given me a thorn in my flesh, a messenger of Satan, to torment me. ⁸Three times I pleaded with the Lord to take it away from me. ⁹But he said to me, "My grace is sufficient for you, for my power is made perfect in weakness." Therefore I will boast all the more gladly about my weaknesses, so that Christ's power may rest on me. ¹⁰That is why, for Christ's sake, I delight in weaknesses, in insults, in hardships, in persecutions, in difficulties. For when I am weak, then I am strong.

TALKING POINTS

Disability

Christ's power is perfected
in our weakness.

2 CORINTHIANS 12:7–10

This is the last talking point on disability.

Paul's Concern for the Corinthians

¹¹I have made a fool of myself, but you drove me to it. I ought to have been commended by you, for I am not in the least inferior to the "super-apostles," even though I am nothing. ¹²The things that mark an apostle—signs, wonders and

I WILL BOAST ALL THE MORE GLADLY
ABOUT MY WEAKNESSES, SO THAT
CHRIST'S POWER MAY REST ON ME. THAT
IS WHY, FOR CHRIST'S SAKE, I DELIGHT IN
WEAKNESSES, IN INSULTS, IN HARDSHIPS, IN
PERSECUTIONS, IN DIFFICULTIES. FOR WHEN
I AM WEAK, THEN I AM STRONG.

2 Corinthians 12:9–10

Honey, You're Doing So Well

KAREN MAINS

READ | 2 CORINTHIANS 12:1–10

One evening, my three grandchildren were bowed in absorbed earnestness, fitting colored beads onto a framed template. Reading nearby, I heard Josie (age 9) say to her cousin Elias (age 6), "Oh, honey, you're doing so well." How cute, I thought. She's three years older, but to her, Elias is still "honey."

Next I heard Josie say to her brother Ayden (age 5), "Good job. You really are making a wonderful picture."

We all need words of praise to keep us going, no matter what our age. I have numbers dyslexia that leaves me vulnerable to the accusation by certain family members that I am "detail ditzy." I will not bore you with descriptions of my lifetime of misadventures, but just last week, the day before flying out, I noticed that the tickets I booked to visit my son's family in Phoenix left O'Hare Airport at 9:00 P.M. (not A.M.) on February 17; this meant that I would arrive the next day, February 18, at 12:30 A.M. instead of at 12:30 P.M. on February 17.

However, what I am learning is this: My inadequacies are an opportunity for God's adequacies. That lost Friday, for example, when I was supposed to arrive in Phoenix around noon but arrived around midnight — well, I really, really needed that whole day to finish up a pile of work I didn't know I would have to finish.

When God looks at my life, he says, "Honey, you're doing so well." He knows about my brain-glitch thingy (keys left in the ignition of running parked cars, etc.), and he doesn't get frustrated, distressed, irritated or bent out of sorts with me. Instead, he says, "Let me show you what I can do with these inadequacies of yours." So, I am attempting to apply his (and my granddaughter's) salve to my own inward and frequent frustration: "Honey . . ."

Lord, it is hard to love myself, flaws and all, so help me to delight in the sometimes funny, but always intriguing, ways you use my weaknesses to bring me to the realization that I am going to always be dependent upon your strength. Amen.

Your next devotion is located on page 1594.

GRANDCHILD IN FOCUS • PRAYER

Courage

O Father, builder of character and courage, may my grandchild grow strong in the light of your love. Grant him courage to stand for what is right, to guard the truth and to ensure justice in every aspect of life. May he boldly grow in grace, revere your name and proudly proclaim you as the Lord of lords and King of kings. Amen.

EXAMINE YOURSELVES TO SEE
WHETHER YOU ARE IN THE FAITH; TEST
YOURSELVES. DO YOU NOT REALIZE THAT
CHRIST JESUS IS IN YOU — UNLESS, OF
COURSE, YOU FAIL THE TEST?

2 Corinthians 13:5

Tests Aren't Just for Kids

SUE BUCHANAN

READ | 2 CORINTHIANS 13:1 – 14

"Oh, Grandma, I sure am happy to see you," said the little boy as he jumped into the arms of his maternal grandmother.

"Now maybe Daddy will do the trick he has been promising us."

The grandmother was curious. "What trick is that?" she asked.

"Daddy told Mommy that he would climb the walls if you came to visit," the boy answered innocently.

Eeek! This might be just a cute story or an age-old joke, but it brings up a subject we might not want to deal with: What kind of image are we presenting to those we love? Is there something we don't recognize about ourselves? Might there be a cloud hanging over us? A cloud of discontent, of bickering or of self-righteousness. Perhaps we need to do a check of our conversational patterns. What about the "me, me, me's"? The "I, I, I's"? What *I* think? What *I* want? What you need to do to fit into *my* agenda?

Should we stop, right here and now, and examine our hearts, asking God to show us where we fall short?

It's time to do damage control — God's damage control — so that we don't, in fact, cause our loved ones to climb the walls!

Dear God, all the pretty platitudes that come from my mouth won't make up for my actions and the way I behave. Show me myself in your light. Amen.

Your next devotion is located on page 1600.

GRANDCHILD **IN FOCUS** • PRAYER

Future Spouse

Dear Lord, if it is your will, I pray my grandchild will be united in a loving and Christian marriage. Keep her sexually pure so that she will honor you with her body and mind. As she seeks a spouse who will honor and care for her, give her patience and discernment. May her choice for a life partner be your choice for her, so that she and her husband will together glorify you in a lasting love. I pray this in Jesus' name, amen.

miracles—were done among you with great perseverance. [13]How were you inferior to the other churches, except that I was never a burden to you? Forgive me this wrong!

[14]Now I am ready to visit you for the third time, and I will not be a burden to you, because what I want is not your possessions but you. After all, children should not have to save up for their parents, but parents for their children. [15]So I will very gladly spend for you everything I have and expend myself as well. If I love you more, will you love me less? [16]Be that as it may, I have not been a burden to you. Yet, crafty fellow that I am, I caught you by trickery! [17]Did I exploit you through any of the men I sent you? [18]I urged Titus to go to you and I sent our brother with him. Titus did not exploit you, did he? Did we not act in the same spirit and follow the same course?

[19]Have you been thinking all along that we have been defending ourselves to you? We have been speaking in the sight of God as those in Christ; and everything we do, dear friends, is for your strengthening. [20]For I am afraid that when I come I may not find you as I want you to be, and you may not find me as you want me to be. I fear that there may be quarreling, jealousy, outbursts of anger, factions, slander, gossip, arrogance and disorder. [21]I am afraid that when I come again my God will humble me before you, and I will be grieved over many who have sinned earlier and have not repented of the impurity, sexual sin and debauchery in which they have indulged.

Final Warnings

13 This will be my third visit to you. "Every matter must be established by the testimony of two or three witnesses." [a] [2]I already gave you a warning when I was with you the second time. I now repeat it while absent: On my return I will not spare those who sinned earlier or any of the others, [3]since you are demanding proof that Christ is speaking through me. He is not weak in dealing with you, but is powerful among you. [4]For to be sure, he was crucified in weakness, yet he lives by God's power. Likewise, we are weak in him, yet by God's power we will live with him to serve you.

[5]Examine yourselves to see whether you are in the faith; test yourselves. Do you not realize that Christ Jesus is in you—unless, of course, you fail the test? [6]And I trust that you will discover that we have not failed the test. [7]Now we pray to God that you will not do anything wrong. Not that people will see that we have stood the test but that you will do what is right even though we may seem to have failed. [8]For we cannot do anything against the truth, but only for the truth. [9]We are glad whenever we are weak but you are strong; and our prayer is for your perfection. [10]This is why I write these things when I am absent, that when I come I may not have to be harsh in my use of authority—the authority the Lord gave me for building you up, not for tearing you down.

Final Greetings

[11]Finally, brothers, good-by. Aim for perfection, listen to my appeal, be of one mind, live in peace. And the God of love and peace will be with you.

[12]Greet one another with a holy kiss. [13]All the saints send their greetings.

[14]May the grace of the Lord Jesus Christ, and the love of God, and the fellowship of the Holy Spirit be with you all.

[a] 1 Deut. 19:15

Living BY THE SPIRIT

When it comes to our grandchildren, legalism isn't in our vocabulary. We would much rather go with the spirit of things than the rules. Maybe we were strict enforcers of the rules when our children were small, but we've softened. We prefer to woo a child to bed with a story rather than point at the clock. We prefer to forgo the brussels sprouts they dislike and dispense cookies instead. This is the way we operate.

Legalism isn't in God's vocabulary either. Paul's letter to the believers in Galatia is about living by and through the Spirit, not the law. He wrote to rebuke them for turning away from the gospel of grace. It was by grace through faith alone that they had been saved, and Paul called them to the freedom that was theirs because they were children of God.

At the heart of Paul's letter is the teaching that Jesus' followers are to live by the Spirit. If believers live in the Spirit and are filled with the Spirit, they will bear the fruit of the Spirit: love, joy, peace, patience, kindness, goodness, faithfulness, gentleness and self-control. These beautiful characteristics are what we're cultivating as women and as grandmothers. What better way to teach our grandchildren and those around us what it means to follow Jesus?

VERSE *to* REMEMBER | GALATIANS 5:22 – 23

But the fruit of the Spirit is love, joy, peace, patience, kindness, goodness, faithfulness, gentleness and self-control. Against such things there is no law.

Galatians

ABOUT GALATIANS

WRITTEN BY:
The apostle Paul

WRITTEN FOR:
The believers in the churches in Galatia

DATE WRITTEN:
Probably sometime between A.D. 48 and 53 from Antioch or Corinth

WHY WRITTEN:
To challenge the Galatian believers to rely on Jesus rather than on trying to keep the law

1 Paul, an apostle—sent not from men nor by man, but by Jesus Christ and God the Father, who raised him from the dead— ²and all the brothers with me,

To the churches in Galatia:

³Grace and peace to you from God our Father and the Lord Jesus Christ, ⁴who gave himself for our sins to rescue us from the present evil age, according to the will of our God and Father, ⁵to whom be glory for ever and ever. Amen.

No Other Gospel

⁶I am astonished that you are so quickly deserting the one who called you by the grace of Christ and are turning to a different gospel— ⁷which is really no gospel at all. Evidently some people are throwing you into confusion and are trying to pervert the gospel of Christ. ⁸But even if we or an angel from heaven should preach a gospel other than the one we preached to you, let him be eternally condemned! ⁹As we have already said, so now I say again: If anybody is preaching to you a gospel other than what you accepted, let him be eternally condemned!

¹⁰Am I now trying to win the approval of men, or of God? Or am I trying to please men? If I were still trying to please men, I would not be a servant of Christ.

Paul Called by God

¹¹I want you to know, brothers, that the gospel I preached is not something that man made up. ¹²I did not receive it from any man, nor was I taught it; rather, I received it by revelation from Jesus Christ.

¹³For you have heard of my previous way of life in Judaism, how intensely I persecuted the church of God and tried to destroy it. ¹⁴I was advancing in Judaism beyond many Jews of my own age and was extremely zealous for the traditions of my fathers. ¹⁵But when God, who set me apart from birth[a] and called me by his grace, was pleased ¹⁶to reveal his Son in me so that I might preach him among the Gentiles, I did not

consult any man, ¹⁷nor did I go up to Jerusalem to see those who were apostles before I was, but I went immediately into Arabia and later returned to Damascus.

¹⁸Then after three years, I went up to Jerusalem to get acquainted with Peter[b] and stayed with him fifteen days. ¹⁹I saw none of the other apostles—only James, the Lord's brother. ²⁰I assure you before God that what I am writing you is no lie. ²¹Later I went to Syria and Cilicia. ²²I was personally unknown to the churches of Judea that are in Christ. ²³They only heard the report: "The man who formerly persecuted us is now preaching the faith he once tried to destroy." ²⁴And they praised God because of me.

Paul Accepted by the Apostles

2 Fourteen years later I went up again to Jerusalem, this time with Barnabas. I took Titus along also. ²I went in response to a revelation and set before them the gospel that I preach among the Gentiles. But I did this privately to those who seemed to be leaders, for fear that I was running or had run my race in vain. ³Yet not even Titus, who was with me, was compelled to be circumcised, even though he was a Greek. ⁴This matter arose because some false brothers had infiltrated our ranks to spy on the freedom we have in Christ Jesus and to make us slaves. ⁵We did not give in to them for a moment, so that the truth of the gospel might remain with you.

⁶As for those who seemed to be important— whatever they were makes no difference to me; God does not judge by external appearance— those men added nothing to my message. ⁷On the contrary, they saw that I had been entrusted with the task of preaching the gospel to the Gentiles,[c] just as Peter had been to the Jews.[d] ⁸For God, who was at work in the ministry of Peter as an apostle to the Jews, was also at work in my ministry as an apostle to the Gentiles. ⁹James, Peter[e] and John, those reputed to be pillars, gave me and Barnabas the right hand of fellowship

---

[a] 15 Or *from my mother's womb*   [b] 18 Greek *Cephas*   [c] 7 Greek *uncircumcised*   [d] 7 Greek *circumcised*; also in verses 8 and 9   [e] 9 Greek *Cephas*; also in verses 11 and 14

when they recognized the grace given to me. They agreed that we should go to the Gentiles, and they to the Jews. ¹⁰All they asked was that we should continue to remember the poor, the very thing I was eager to do.

Paul Opposes Peter

¹¹When Peter came to Antioch, I opposed him to his face, because he was clearly in the wrong. ¹²Before certain men came from James, he used to eat with the Gentiles. But when they arrived, he began to draw back and separate himself from the Gentiles because he was afraid of those who belonged to the circumcision group. ¹³The other Jews joined him in his hypocrisy, so that by their hypocrisy even Barnabas was led astray.

¹⁴When I saw that they were not acting in line with the truth of the gospel, I said to Peter in front of them all, "You are a Jew, yet you live like a Gentile and not like a Jew. How is it, then, that you force Gentiles to follow Jewish customs?

¹⁵"We who are Jews by birth and not 'Gentile sinners' ¹⁶know that a man is not justified by observing the law, but by faith in Jesus Christ. So we, too, have put our faith in Christ Jesus that we may be justified by faith in Christ and not by observing the law, because by observing the law no one will be justified.

¹⁷"If, while we seek to be justified in Christ, it becomes evident that we ourselves are sinners, does that mean that Christ promotes sin? Absolutely not! ¹⁸If I rebuild what I destroyed, I prove that I am a lawbreaker. ¹⁹For through the law I died to the law so that I might live for God. ²⁰I have been crucified with Christ and I no longer live, but Christ lives in me. The life I live in the body, I live by faith in the Son of God, who loved me and gave himself for me. ²¹I do not set aside the grace of God, for if righteousness could be gained through the law, Christ died for nothing!"ᵃ

Faith or Observance of the Law

3 You foolish Galatians! Who has bewitched you? Before your very eyes Jesus Christ was clearly portrayed as crucified. ²I would like to learn just one thing from you: Did you receive the Spirit by observing the law, or by believing what you heard? ³Are you so foolish? After beginning with the Spirit, are you now trying to attain your goal by human effort? ⁴Have you suffered so much for nothing—if it really was for nothing? ⁵Does God give you his Spirit and work miracles among you because you observe the law, or because you believe what you heard?

⁶Consider Abraham: "He believed God, and it was credited to him as righteousness."ᵇ ⁷Understand, then, that those who believe are children of Abraham. ⁸The Scripture foresaw that God would justify the Gentiles by faith, and announced the gospel in advance to Abraham: "All nations will be blessed through you."ᶜ ⁹So those who have faith are blessed along with Abraham, the man of faith.

¹⁰All who rely on observing the law are under a curse, for it is written: "Cursed is everyone who does not continue to do everything written in the Book of the Law."ᵈ ¹¹Clearly no one is justified before God by the law, because, "The righteous will live by faith."ᵉ ¹²The law is not based on faith; on the contrary, "The man who does these things will live by them."ᶠ ¹³Christ redeemed us from the curse of the law by becoming a curse for us, for it is written: "Cursed is everyone who is hung on a tree."ᵍ ¹⁴He redeemed us in order that the blessing given to Abraham might come to the Gentiles through Christ Jesus, so that by faith we might receive the promise of the Spirit.

The Law and the Promise

¹⁵Brothers, let me take an example from everyday life. Just as no one can set aside or add to a human covenant that has been duly established, so it is in this case. ¹⁶The promises were spoken to Abraham and to his seed. The Scripture does not say "and to seeds," meaning many people, but "and to your seed,"ʰ meaning one person, who is Christ. ¹⁷What I mean is this: The law, intro-

---

ᵃ 21 Some interpreters end the quotation after verse 14.
ᵇ 6 Gen. 15:6   ᶜ 8 Gen. 12:3; 18:18; 22:18   ᵈ 10 Deut. 27:26
ᵉ 11 Hab. 2:4   ᶠ 12 Lev. 18:5   ᵍ 13 Deut. 21:23
ʰ 16 Gen. 12:7; 13:15; 24:7

duced 430 years later, does not set aside the covenant previously established by God and thus do away with the promise. [18]For if the inheritance depends on the law, then it no longer depends on a promise; but God in his grace gave it to Abraham through a promise.

[19]What, then, was the purpose of the law? It was added because of transgressions until the Seed to whom the promise referred had come. The law was put into effect through angels by a mediator. [20]A mediator, however, does not represent just one party; but God is one.

[21]Is the law, therefore, opposed to the promises of God? Absolutely not! For if a law had been given that could impart life, then righteousness would certainly have come by the law. [22]But the Scripture declares that the whole world is a prisoner of sin, so that what was promised, being given through faith in Jesus Christ, might be given to those who believe.

[23]Before this faith came, we were held prisoners by the law, locked up until faith should be revealed. [24]So the law was put in charge to lead us to Christ[a] that we might be justified by faith. [25]Now that faith has come, we are no longer under the supervision of the law.

Sons of God

[26]You are all sons of God through faith in Christ Jesus, [27]for all of you who were baptized into Christ have clothed yourselves with Christ. [28]There is neither Jew nor Greek, slave nor free, male nor female, for you are all one in Christ Jesus. [29]If you belong to Christ, then you are Abraham's seed, and heirs according to the promise.

4 What I am saying is that as long as the heir is a child, he is no different from a slave, although he owns the whole estate. [2]He is subject to guardians and trustees until the time set by his father. [3]So also, when we were children, we were in slavery under the basic principles of the world. [4]But when the time had fully come, God sent his Son, born of a woman, born under law, [5]to redeem those under law, that we might receive the full rights of sons. [6]Because you are sons, God

sent the Spirit of his Son into our hearts, the Spirit who calls out, "Abba,[b] Father." [7]So you are no longer a slave, but a son; and since you are a son, God has made you also an heir.

Paul's Concern for the Galatians

[8]Formerly, when you did not know God, you were slaves to those who by nature are not gods. [9]But now that you know God—or rather are known by God—how is it that you are turning back to those weak and miserable principles? Do you wish to be enslaved by them all over again? [10]You are observing special days and months and seasons and years! [11]I fear for you, that somehow I have wasted my efforts on you.

[12]I plead with you, brothers, become like me, for I became like you. You have done me no wrong. [13]As you know, it was because of an illness that I first preached the gospel to you. [14]Even though my illness was a trial to you, you did not treat me with contempt or scorn. Instead, you welcomed me as if I were an angel of God, as if I were Christ Jesus himself. [15]What has happened to all your joy? I can testify that, if you could have done so, you would have torn out your eyes and given them to me. [16]Have I now become your enemy by telling you the truth?

[17]Those people are zealous to win you over, but for no good. What they want is to alienate you ⌊from us⌋, so that you may be zealous for them. [18]It is fine to be zealous, provided the purpose is good, and to be so always and not just when I am with you. [19]My dear children, for whom I am again in the pains of childbirth until Christ is formed in you, [20]how I wish I could be with you now and change my tone, because I am perplexed about you!

Hagar and Sarah

[21]Tell me, you who want to be under the law, are you not aware of what the law says? [22]For it is written that Abraham had two sons, one by the slave woman and the other by the free woman. [23]His son by the slave woman was born in the

a 24 Or charge until Christ came   *b 6 Aramaic for Father*

> THERE IS NEITHER JEW NOR
> GREEK, SLAVE NOR FREE, MALE
> NOR FEMALE, FOR YOU ARE
> ALL ONE IN CHRIST JESUS.
>
> *Galatians 3:28*

No Longer Outcasts

THELMA WELLS

READ | GALATIANS 3:26 — 4:7

I grew up in the segregated South in the 1940s and 1950s, when there was designated seating for "Colored" and "White" people in street cars, theaters and schools as well as water fountains marked for each race. Fascinated by the designations and always curious about the difference in those signs, I bravely determined, by disobeying the signs, that the only difference between the "Colored" water and the "White" water was the temperature. The "Colored" was hot; the "White" was cold.

My granddaddy often took me to the Majestic Theatre, where we had to sit in the balcony (called the "buzzard roost") and eat the stale candy and popcorn. I'll always remember his prediction: "Pooch (that's what he affectionately called me), one of these days you're gonna be able to walk in this theater through the front door and sit in the front row or box seats. You watch and see."

It's true. I've been through the front door and strolled down to the front row, center aisle, of that very theater. In God's time, he makes all things beautiful—no matter how ugly they may seem.

You might feel discriminated against or like an outcast in one way or the other. Jesus did. He wasn't welcome in his own hometown. He knows how you feel. He never discriminates against you—no matter who you are. He loves you and wants the best for you.

When you feel like an outcast, remember that Jesus calls you his child. You're safe with him, just like I was safe with my granddaddy. Jesus has opened the door for you to walk in and have a front-row seat in his presence. You're always welcome!

Kind Father, thank you for making all believers one in Christ Jesus. Thank you that there are no barriers between us and that all of your children are always welcome in your presence. Help me to treat others the way you treat me. In Jesus' name, amen.

Your next devotion is located on page 1602.

GRANDCHILD IN FOCUS • PRAYER

School/Career

Dear God, may learning be a joy rather than a chore for my grandchild. May exploration of new ideas bring a sense of wonder, awe and excitement. Grant him clarity of mind, the ability to concentrate on the task at hand and recollection of what has been learned. Help him to appreciate the tasks that come easily and to persevere through those that challenge. Amen.

ordinary way; but his son by the free woman was born as the result of a promise.

²⁴These things may be taken figuratively, for the women represent two covenants. One covenant is from Mount Sinai and bears children who are to be slaves: This is Hagar. ²⁵Now Hagar stands for Mount Sinai in Arabia and corresponds to the present city of Jerusalem, because she is in slavery with her children. ²⁶But the Jerusalem that is above is free, and she is our mother. ²⁷For it is written:

"Be glad, O barren woman,
    who bears no children;
break forth and cry aloud,
    you who have no labor pains;
because more are the children of the desolate
        woman
    than of her who has a husband."ᵃ

²⁸Now you, brothers, like Isaac, are children of promise. ²⁹At that time the son born in the ordinary way persecuted the son born by the power of the Spirit. It is the same now. ³⁰But what does the Scripture say? "Get rid of the slave woman and her son, for the slave woman's son will never share in the inheritance with the free woman's son."ᵇ ³¹Therefore, brothers, we are not children of the slave woman, but of the free woman.

Freedom in Christ

5 It is for freedom that Christ has set us free. Stand firm, then, and do not let yourselves be burdened again by a yoke of slavery.

²Mark my words! I, Paul, tell you that if you let yourselves be circumcised, Christ will be of no value to you at all. ³Again I declare to every man who lets himself be circumcised that he is obligated to obey the whole law. ⁴You who are trying to be justified by law have been alienated from Christ; you have fallen away from grace. ⁵But by faith we eagerly await through the Spirit the righteousness for which we hope. ⁶For in Christ Jesus neither circumcision nor uncircumcision has any value. The only thing that counts is faith expressing itself through love.

⁷You were running a good race. Who cut in on you and kept you from obeying the truth? ⁸That kind of persuasion does not come from the one who calls you. ⁹"A little yeast works through the whole batch of dough." ¹⁰I am confident in the Lord that you will take no other view. The one who is throwing you into confusion will pay the penalty, whoever he may be. ¹¹Brothers, if I am still preaching circumcision, why am I still being persecuted? In that case the offense of the cross has been abolished. ¹²As for those agitators, I wish they would go the whole way and emasculate themselves!

¹³You, my brothers, were called to be free. But do not use your freedom to indulge the sinful natureᶜ; rather, serve one another in love. ¹⁴The entire law is summed up in a single command: "Love your neighbor as yourself."ᵈ ¹⁵If you keep on biting and devouring each other, watch out or you will be destroyed by each other.

Life by the Spirit

¹⁶So I say, live by the Spirit, and you will not gratify the desires of the sinful nature. ¹⁷For the sinful nature desires what is contrary to the Spirit, and the Spirit what is contrary to the sinful nature. They are in conflict with each other, so that

---

ᵃ 27 Isaiah 54:1   ᵇ 30 Gen. 21:10   ᶜ 13 Or the flesh; also in verses 16, 17, 19 and 24   ᵈ 14 Lev. 19:18

PRAYING THE SCRIPTURES

Joy
GALATIANS 5:22–23,25

Dear Father, I ask you to fill my grandchild with the fruit of your Spirit—love, joy, peace, patience, kindness, goodness, faithfulness, gentleness and self-control—so that he may live by the Spirit and keep in step with the Spirit.

This is the last prayer in the Joy Prayer Track.

It's E-Day!

With the prevalence of email and digital photography, this method of staying in touch should work for most everyone.

Pick a certain day of each month (the first Saturday, the third Sunday, the number of the day of your birthday or whatever day is good for everyone) and declare it "E-Day." This is a date for everyone to touch base, to share their family's freshest news and to display their most up-to-date photos via the Internet. Be sure to encourage everyone to participate, especially the young adults who are off on their own.

Another option is to set up a family website where everyone can chat and contribute whenever it's convenient.

Thank you, Lord, for technology that allows us to stay in touch. Help all of us to appreciate and utilize the opportunity to share ourselves and what is happening in our lives. May our prayers for one another unite us in your love. Amen.

Your next devotion is located on page 1603.

GRANDCHILD IN FOCUS • PRAYER

Character

Dear Lord and Father, I ask that you fill my grandchild with your Spirit so her character reflects your goodness and love. Give her kindness and love for others. Bring joy to her life so she will be a joy to others. Grant her patience and self-control through difficult and trying times. May she show mercy and generosity to those who are less fortunate. Grant her integrity and a sense of justice, and surround her with your peace. Amen.

Worship the Lord

It is good to praise the LORD
    and make music to your name, O Most High,
to proclaim your love in the morning
    and your faithfulness at night,
to the music of the ten-stringed lyre
    and the melody of the harp.

For you make me glad by your deeds, O LORD;
    I sing for joy at the works of your hands.
How great are your works, O LORD,
    how profound your thoughts!

The righteous will flourish like a palm
      tree,
    they will grow like a cedar of
      Lebanon;
planted in the house of the LORD,
    they will flourish in the courts of
      our God.
They will still bear fruit in old age,
    they will stay fresh and green,
proclaiming, "The LORD is upright;
    he is my Rock, and there is no
      wickedness in him."

Psalm 92:1 – 5,12 – 15

GRANDCHILD IN FOCUS • PRAYER

Talents

Dear Lord, the giver of gifts, bless my grandchild as he develops his talents. Help him identify his talents and be proud and confident of the gifts you have given him. Give him patience and understanding, Lord, so he will not grow weary of striving and searching to reach the goals you have set for him. May each milestone bring satisfaction and a healthy desire for greater achievement and success to bring glory to you. Amen.

O God Most High, when I lift up my voice to you in song, my heart swells with love; my soul is quieted with your peace; my life is renewed. I will sing of your great love forever — in the morning, in the evening and throughout my day. For you are my God and my Redeemer, the Rock of my salvation. Amen.

Your next devotion is located on page 1605.

you do not do what you want. ¹⁸But if you are led by the Spirit, you are not under law.

¹⁹The acts of the sinful nature are obvious: sexual immorality, impurity and debauchery; ²⁰idolatry and witchcraft; hatred, discord, jealousy, fits of rage, selfish ambition, dissensions, factions ²¹and envy; drunkenness, orgies, and the like. I warn you, as I did before, that those who live like this will not inherit the kingdom of God.

²²But the fruit of the Spirit is love, joy, peace, patience, kindness, goodness, faithfulness, ²³gentleness and self-control. Against such things there is no law. ²⁴Those who belong to Christ Jesus have crucified the sinful nature with its passions and desires. ²⁵Since we live by the Spirit, let us keep in step with the Spirit. ²⁶Let us not become conceited, provoking and envying each other.

Doing Good to All

6 Brothers, if someone is caught in a sin, you who are spiritual should restore him gently. But watch yourself, or you also may be tempted. ²Carry each other's burdens, and in this way you will fulfill the law of Christ. ³If anyone thinks he is something when he is nothing, he deceives himself. ⁴Each one should test his own actions. Then he can take pride in himself, without comparing himself to somebody else, ⁵for each one should carry his own load.

⁶Anyone who receives instruction in the word must share all good things with his instructor.

⁷Do not be deceived: God cannot be mocked.

TALKING POINTS

Responsibility

We are responsible for our actions and will face consequences for them.

GALATIANS 6:7–8

For more on responsibility, go to Titus 2:6–8.

A man reaps what he sows. ⁸The one who sows to please his sinful nature, from that nature ᵃ will reap destruction; the one who sows to please the Spirit, from the Spirit will reap eternal life. ⁹Let us not become weary in doing good, for at the proper time we will reap a harvest if we do not give up. ¹⁰Therefore, as we have opportunity, let us do good to all people, especially to those who belong to the family of believers.

TALKING POINTS

Laziness

Gratification comes to those who don't give up.

GALATIANS 6:9

For more on laziness, go to Colossians 3:23–24.

Not Circumcision but a New Creation

¹¹See what large letters I use as I write to you with my own hand!

¹²Those who want to make a good impression outwardly are trying to compel you to be circumcised. The only reason they do this is to avoid being persecuted for the cross of Christ. ¹³Not even those who are circumcised obey the law, yet they want you to be circumcised that they may boast about your flesh. ¹⁴May I never boast except in the cross of our Lord Jesus Christ, through which ᵇ the world has been crucified to me, and I to the world. ¹⁵Neither circumcision nor uncircumcision means anything; what counts is a new creation. ¹⁶Peace and mercy to all who follow this rule, even to the Israel of God.

¹⁷Finally, let no one cause me trouble, for I bear on my body the marks of Jesus.

¹⁸The grace of our Lord Jesus Christ be with your spirit, brothers. Amen.

ᵃ 8 Or *his flesh, from the flesh*   ᵇ 14 Or *whom*

THE FRUIT OF THE SPIRIT IS
LOVE, JOY, PEACE, PATIENCE,
KINDNESS, GOODNESS,
FAITHFULNESS, GENTLENESS
AND SELF-CONTROL.
Galatians 5:22 – 23

Fruity Folks

ELISA MORGAN

READ | GALATIANS 5:16 – 26

We tend to think two crazy truths about the fruit of the Spirit: First, we think that the fruit of the Spirit is all about being nice, nice, nice all the time. Visions of "Church Lady" come into our thinking. (I wonder why, since she was not really all that nice.) The fruit of the Spirit is *not* about being nice. It's about being like Jesus.

Jesus was always filled with the fruit of the Spirit. But he wasn't always nice. When he told the Pharisees to stop making faith harder than God makes it, that wasn't nice. Or when he told the woman caught in adultery to stop sinning, that wasn't nice. Or when he drove the money changers out of the temple, that wasn't nice. Jesus wasn't always nice. But he was always filled with the Spirit.

Second, we think that it is all up to us to grow the fruit of the Spirit. We think that if we try hard enough, we'll evidence these qualities. This will never happen! No matter how much we strain and stretch, we cannot grow such attributes in our lives. The fruit of the Spirit is just that: God's character reproduced by his power in our lives. These traits are up to *him* to grow, not us.

The fruit of the Spirit represents the qualities we possess when we look like God.

Dear plant-growing God, please cultivate in me your character qualities. I yield to you to re-produce in me the traits that come from your nature. Let these characteristics be evidence to this world of your love so that those who are truly hungry will find a relationship with you. Amen.

Your next devotion is located on page 1608.

GRANDCHILD IN FOCUS • PRAYER

SELECT ONE OF YOUR
GRANDCHILDREN TO FOCUS ON
IN PRAYER FOR THE NEXT 14 DAYS.

Salvation

Dear Lord, please guide my grandchild to your gift of salvation. I pray that she will come to know you, to love you and to walk close to you throughout her life. May she boldly claim Jesus as her Lord and Savior. Guide her as she makes choices that have eternal consequences. Help her to follow you each moment of her life. I pray this in Jesus' name, amen.

All
IN THE FAMILY

Ephesians is all about family—the universal family of God, the local church family and our own immediate families. This book is a wonderfully warm letter from Paul to the church in Ephesus that lifts the eyes of his readers to the grand scope of God's eternal purpose. Paul's letter confirms us as God's cherished children, adopted through Christ Jesus. And because we are God's children, we inherit all the treasures of God's grace—treasures of redemption, hope and wisdom. As God's beloved, we will know how "wide and long and high and deep is the love of Christ" (Ephesians 3:18).

Ephesians teaches God's children how to live in unity, in the church and at home. Paul's timeless encouragement and wise instruction are shining gems for us not only to share with our grandchildren but to cherish in our own lives as well.

Ephesians emphasizes that our identity is in Jesus Christ. As grandmothers our desire is to nurture in our grandchildren a self-concept rooted in the reality of who they are in Christ, establishing a foundation for their entire lives. Ephesians clearly lays that groundwork. How can we use this truth to minister to our grandchildren? We can take Paul's words to heart and be authentic models of the truth taught in this vital letter.

VERSE *to* **REMEMBER** | EPHESIANS 3:14 – 15

For this reason I kneel before the Father, from whom his whole family in heaven and on earth derives its name.

ABOUT EPHESIANS

WRITTEN BY:
The apostle Paul

WRITTEN FOR:
The Christians in Ephesus

DATE WRITTEN:
About A.D. 60 from Rome, where Paul was in prison

WHY WRITTEN:
To help the believers in Ephesus to see their wonderful new identity as God's children

1

Paul, an apostle of Christ Jesus by the will of God,

To the saints in Ephesus,[a] the faithful[b] in Christ Jesus:

[2] Grace and peace to you from God our Father and the Lord Jesus Christ.

Spiritual Blessings in Christ

[3] Praise be to the God and Father of our Lord Jesus Christ, who has blessed us in the heavenly realms with every spiritual blessing in Christ. [4] For he chose us in him before the creation of the world to be holy and blameless in his sight. In love [5] he[c] predestined us to be adopted as his sons through Jesus Christ, in accordance with his pleasure and will — [6] to the praise of his glorious grace, which he has freely given us in the One he loves. [7] In him we have redemption through his blood, the forgiveness of sins, in accordance with the riches of God's grace [8] that he lavished on us with all wisdom and understanding. [9] And he[d] made known to us the mystery of his will according to his good pleasure, which he purposed in Christ, [10] to be put into effect when the times will have reached their fulfillment — to bring all things in heaven and on earth together under one head, even Christ.

[11] In him we were also chosen,[e] having been predestined according to the plan of him who works out everything in conformity with the purpose of his will, [12] in order that we, who were the first to hope in Christ, might be for the praise of his glory. [13] And you also were included in Christ when you heard the word of truth, the gospel of your salvation. Having believed, you were marked in him with a seal, the promised Holy Spirit, [14] who is a deposit guaranteeing our inheritance until the redemption of those who are God's possession — to the praise of his glory.

Thanksgiving and Prayer

[15] For this reason, ever since I heard about your faith in the Lord Jesus and your love for all the saints, [16] I have not stopped giving thanks for you, remembering you in my prayers. [17] I keep asking that the God of our Lord Jesus Christ, the glorious Father, may give you the Spirit[f] of wisdom and revelation, so that you may know him better. [18] I pray also that the eyes of your heart

PRAYING THE SCRIPTURES

Wisdom

EPHESIANS 1:17

I pray, O God and glorious Father of our Lord Jesus Christ, that you will grant my grandchild the Spirit of wisdom and revelation, so that she may know you better.

This is the last prayer in the Wisdom Prayer Track.

may be enlightened in order that you may know the hope to which he has called you, the riches of his glorious inheritance in the saints, [19] and his incomparably great power for us who believe. That power is like the working of his mighty strength, [20] which he exerted in Christ when he raised him from the dead and seated him at his right hand in the heavenly realms, [21] far above all rule and authority, power and dominion, and every title that can be given, not only in the present age but also in the one to come. [22] And God placed all things under his feet and appointed him to be head over everything for the church, [23] which is his body, the fullness of him who fills everything in every way.

Made Alive in Christ

2

As for you, you were dead in your transgressions and sins, [2] in which you used to live when you followed the ways of this world and of the ruler of the kingdom of the air, the spirit who is now at work in those who are disobedient.

---

[a] 1 Some early manuscripts do not have *in Ephesus.*   [b] 1 Or *believers who are*   [c] 4,5 Or *sight in love.* [5] *He*   [d] 8,9 Or *us. With all wisdom and understanding,* [9] *he*   [e] 11 Or *were made heirs*   [f] 17 Or *a spirit*

IN HIM WE HAVE REDEMPTION THROUGH
HIS BLOOD, THE FORGIVENESS OF SINS, IN
ACCORDANCE WITH THE RICHES OF GOD'S
GRACE THAT HE LAVISHED ON US WITH ALL
WISDOM AND UNDERSTANDING.

Ephesians 1:7—8

God Approves of Spa Day, and I, for One, Am Glad!

SUE BUCHANAN

READ | EPHESIANS 1:1 – 14

Ephesians 1:3 – 8 lists a number of spiritual blessings we have in Christ: adoption, redemption, forgiveness, being made holy and blameless in his sight, and much more. But the part that catches my eye is the phrase in verse 8, which says, " . . . that he lavished on us with all wisdom and understanding." I simply love that word *lavish*!

I've been to the spa at a five-star hotel (thanks to a friend), and I know what lavish means in earthly terms. It means putting on a velvety robe, sitting in a room profuse with a mind-clearing fragrance, soaking myself in an overflowing bath of volcanic ash, followed by a deep-cleansing steam bath and therapeutic massage. It means the undivided attention of an attendant who is there to pamper you. It means your choice of flavored water—cucumbers floating in a pitcher of water, or lemons if you'd prefer. Add to that a movie-star facial, a manicure, lotions, creams and a pedicure complete with a small daisy on my left toenail.

Lavish means extravagant, overdone, excessive, being spoiled rotten! Lavish is the ultimate spa day!

And just think! A spa day as we know it is but a microcosm compared to the lavishness of the heavenly Father.

Dear God, I get it! I understand! You don't just give us blessings beyond our wildest imaginations, you lavish them on us. You "spoil us rotten"! Thank you . . . oh, thank you!

Your next devotion is located on page 1611.

GRANDCHILD IN FOCUS • PRAYER

Physical Well-Being

Almighty God, Creator of us all, I pray that you will watch over my grandchild's physical development. May he grow in strength through the stages of his life. As he grows in awareness of his body, help him to understand that each body develops uniquely, yet is within your plan and your control. Please guard his health so that his diseases are few, his injuries are minor and his infirmities are brief. Amen.

³All of us also lived among them at one time, gratifying the cravings of our sinful nature ª and following its desires and thoughts. Like the rest, we were by nature objects of wrath. ⁴But because of his great love for us, God, who is rich in mercy, ⁵made us alive with Christ even when we were dead in transgressions—it is by grace you have been saved. ⁶And God raised us up with Christ and seated us with him in the heavenly realms in Christ Jesus, ⁷in order that in the coming ages he might show the incomparable riches of his grace, expressed in his kindness to us in Christ Jesus. ⁸For it is by grace you have been saved, through faith—and this not from yourselves, it is the gift of God— ⁹not by works, so that no one can boast. ¹⁰For we are God's workmanship, created in Christ Jesus to do good works, which God prepared in advance for us to do.

PRAYING THE SCRIPTURES

Salvation

EPHESIANS 2:8–10

Dear Lord and Father, I pray that my grandchild may acknowledge that it is by grace he has been saved, through faith—that his salvation is not from himself but is a gift from you—not based on his works, so that he cannot boast. And may he realize that you have created him to live out his salvation with a life of service.

Next prayer in Salvation Prayer Track: 1 Peter 1:8–9

One in Christ

¹¹Therefore, remember that formerly you who are Gentiles by birth and called "uncircumcised" by those who call themselves "the circumcision" (that done in the body by the hands of men)— ¹²remember that at that time you were separate from Christ, excluded from citizenship in Israel and foreigners to the covenants of the promise, without hope and without God in the world. ¹³But now in Christ Jesus you who once were far away have been brought near through the blood of Christ.

¹⁴For he himself is our peace, who has made the two one and has destroyed the barrier, the dividing wall of hostility, ¹⁵by abolishing in his flesh the law with its commandments and regulations. His purpose was to create in himself one new man out of the two, thus making peace, ¹⁶and in this one body to reconcile both of them to God through the cross, by which he put to death their hostility. ¹⁷He came and preached peace to you who were far away and peace to those who were near. ¹⁸For through him we both have access to the Father by one Spirit.

¹⁹Consequently, you are no longer foreigners and aliens, but fellow citizens with God's people and members of God's household, ²⁰built on the foundation of the apostles and prophets, with Christ Jesus himself as the chief cornerstone. ²¹In him the whole building is joined together and rises to become a holy temple in the Lord. ²²And in him you too are being built together to become a dwelling in which God lives by his Spirit.

Paul the Preacher to the Gentiles

3 For this reason I, Paul, the prisoner of Christ Jesus for the sake of you Gentiles—

²Surely you have heard about the administration of God's grace that was given to me for you, ³that is, the mystery made known to me by revelation, as I have already written briefly. ⁴In reading this, then, you will be able to understand my insight into the mystery of Christ, ⁵which was not made known to men in other generations as it has now been revealed by the Spirit to God's holy apostles and prophets. ⁶This mystery is that through the gospel the Gentiles are heirs together with Israel, members together of one body, and sharers together in the promise in Christ Jesus.

⁷I became a servant of this gospel by the gift of God's grace given me through the working of his power. ⁸Although I am less than the least of all

ª 3 Or our flesh

God's people, this grace was given me: to preach to the Gentiles the unsearchable riches of Christ, [9]and to make plain to everyone the administration of this mystery, which for ages past was kept hidden in God, who created all things. [10]His intent was that now, through the church, the manifold wisdom of God should be made known to the rulers and authorities in the heavenly realms, [11]according to his eternal purpose which he accomplished in Christ Jesus our Lord. [12]In him and through faith in him we may approach God with freedom and confidence. [13]I ask you, therefore, not to be discouraged because of my sufferings for you, which are your glory.

A Prayer for the Ephesians

[14]For this reason I kneel before the Father, [15]from whom his whole family[a] in heaven and on earth derives its name. [16]I pray that out of his glorious riches he may strengthen you with power through his Spirit in your inner being, [17]so that Christ may dwell in your hearts through faith. And I pray that you, being rooted and established in love, [18]may have power, together with all the saints, to grasp how wide and long and high and deep is the love of Christ, [19]and to know this love that surpasses knowledge—that you may be filled to the measure of all the fullness of God.

[20]Now to him who is able to do immeasurably more than all we ask or imagine, according to his

PRAYING THE SCRIPTURES

Guidance
EPHESIANS 3:20

O Father, may my grandchild come to experience and believe that you are able to do immeasurably more than she can ask or even imagine, according to your power that is at work within her.

Next prayer in Guidance Prayer Track: Hebrews 13:5

power that is at work within us, [21]to him be glory in the church and in Christ Jesus throughout all generations, for ever and ever! Amen.

Unity in the Body of Christ

4 As a prisoner for the Lord, then, I urge you to live a life worthy of the calling you have received. [2]Be completely humble and gentle; be patient, bearing with one another in love. [3]Make every effort to keep the unity of the Spirit through the bond of peace. [4]There is one body and one Spirit—just as you were called to one hope when you were called— [5]one Lord, one faith, one baptism; [6]one God and Father of all, who is over all and through all and in all.

[7]But to each one of us grace has been given as Christ apportioned it. [8]This is why it[b] says:

> "When he ascended on high,
>   he led captives in his train
>   and gave gifts to men."[c]

[9](What does "he ascended" mean except that he also descended to the lower, earthly regions[d]? [10]He who descended is the very one who ascended higher than all the heavens, in order to fill the whole universe.) [11]It was he who gave some to be apostles, some to be prophets, some to be evangelists, and some to be pastors and teachers, [12]to prepare God's people for works of service, so that the body of Christ may be built up [13]until we all reach unity in the faith and in the knowledge of the Son of God and become mature, attaining to the whole measure of the fullness of Christ.

[14]Then we will no longer be infants, tossed back and forth by the waves, and blown here and there by every wind of teaching and by the cunning and craftiness of men in their deceitful scheming. [15]Instead, speaking the truth in love, we will in all things grow up into him who is the Head, that is, Christ. [16]From him the whole body, joined and held together by every supporting ligament, grows and builds itself up in love, as each part does its work.

[a] 15 Or *whom all fatherhood*   [b] 8 Or *God*   [c] 8 Psalm 68:18
[d] 9 Or *the depths of the earth*

MAKE EVERY EFFORT TO KEEP
THE UNITY OF THE SPIRIT
THROUGH THE BOND OF PEACE.

Ephesians 4:3

Keeping the Peace

PATRICIA SPRINKLE

READ | EPHESIANS 4:1–16

As we left our son's house the day they brought their first child home from the hospital, my husband asked, "Can we trust mere parents to raise our grandson?"

As a grandmother, I'm learning how hard that can be. After all my years of parenting experience, why do they want to do things *their* way instead of asking me how to do them? Then I remember how my mother-in-law objected to putting "that poor little baby" in a car seat every trip. That was the closest she and I ever came to quarreling. I insisted because *I* was the mother. Eventually she reluctantly consented.

It is tragic when differences of opinion in a family escalate into quarrels that estrange grandparents from their adult children and precious grandchildren. That's why we grandmothers need to remember Paul's exhortation to make *every effort* to preserve unity through the bond of peace. In relating to our children who are also parents, "every effort" may include swallowing our advice—and our pride. It includes praise when our children parent better than we did. It includes searching hard for a tactful way to put forth an alternative suggestion. And when discussions get heated? I once heard: "Always apologize. If you are right, you can afford to. If you are wrong, you can't afford not to."

Staying connected to our grandchildren's lives is well worth the price.

Lord, remind me that my adult children do not need my advice as much as they need my love and support as they parent their own children. Amen.

Your next devotion is located on page 1613.

GRANDCHILD **IN FOCUS** • PRAYER

Emotional Development

O God, Creator of mind and body, I pray that you will give my grandchild emotional health and strength. Where there is anger, bring peace. Where there is confusion, bring clarity and focus. Where there are dark shadows, cast a ray of hope. Fill her with the sunshine of your Spirit. Warm her with the presence of your peace. Amen.

Living as Children of Light

[17] So I tell you this, and insist on it in the Lord, that you must no longer live as the Gentiles do, in the futility of their thinking. [18] They are darkened in their understanding and separated from the life of God because of the ignorance that is in them due to the hardening of their hearts. [19] Having lost all sensitivity, they have given themselves over to sensuality so as to indulge in every kind of impurity, with a continual lust for more.

[20] You, however, did not come to know Christ that way. [21] Surely you heard of him and were taught in him in accordance with the truth that is in Jesus. [22] You were taught, with regard to your former way of life, to put off your old self, which is being corrupted by its deceitful desires; [23] to be made new in the attitude of your minds; [24] and to put on the new self, created to be like God in true righteousness and holiness.

[25] Therefore each of you must put off falsehood and speak truthfully to his neighbor, for we are all members of one body. [26] "In your anger do not sin"[a]: Do not let the sun go down while you are still angry, [27] and do not give the devil a foothold. [28] He who has been stealing must steal no longer, but must work, doing something useful with his own hands, that he may have something to share with those in need.

[29] Do not let any unwholesome talk come out of your mouths, but only what is helpful for building others up according to their needs, that it may benefit those who listen. [30] And do not grieve the Holy Spirit of God, with whom you were sealed for the day of redemption. [31] Get rid of all bitterness, rage and anger, brawling and slander, along with every form of malice. [32] Be kind and compassionate to one another, forgiving each other, just as in Christ God forgave you.

PRAYING THE SCRIPTURES

Forgiveness
EPHESIANS 4:32

Dear Lord, may my grandchild be kind and compassionate, forgiving others, just as in Christ you have forgiven her.

Next prayer in Forgiveness Prayer Track: Colossians 3:13

5 Be imitators of God, therefore, as dearly loved children [2] and live a life of love, just as Christ loved us and gave himself up for us as a fragrant offering and sacrifice to God.

[3] But among you there must not be even a hint of sexual immorality, or of any kind of impurity, or of greed, because these are improper for God's holy people. [4] Nor should there be obscenity, foolish talk or coarse joking, which are out of place, but rather thanksgiving. [5] For of this you can be sure: No immoral, impure or greedy person—such a man is an idolater—has any inheritance in the kingdom of Christ and of God.[b] [6] Let no one deceive you with empty words, for because of such things God's wrath comes on those who are disobedient. [7] Therefore do not be partners with them.

[8] For you were once darkness, but now you are light in the Lord. Live as children of light [9] (for the fruit of the light consists in all goodness, righteousness and truth) [10] and find out what pleases the Lord. [11] Have nothing to do with the fruitless deeds of darkness, but rather expose them. [12] For it is shameful even to mention what the disobedient do in secret. [13] But everything exposed by the

TALKING POINTS

Anger
Don't let your anger escalate.
Don't prolong it.
EPHESIANS 4:26–27

This is the last talking point on anger.

[a] 26 Psalm 4:4   [b] 5 Or kingdom of the Christ and God

DO NOT LET ANY UNWHOLESOME TALK COME OUT OF YOUR MOUTHS, BUT ONLY WHAT IS HELPFUL FOR BUILDING OTHERS UP ACCORDING TO THEIR NEEDS, THAT IT MAY BENEFIT THOSE WHO LISTEN.

Ephesians 4:29

Out of the Mouths

GAYLE ROPER

READ | EPHESIANS 4:17 – 32

Four-year-old PJ and I were food shopping together, and he wasn't a very happy boy.

"Grandmom, can I have those cookies?"

"I don't think so, honey."

"Then I want a candy bar."

"Not today."

"Ice cream. You can get me ice cream."

"No ice cream. I told you that you could get one thing—which is more than I used to tell your daddy—and you already picked it out. That's it, sweetheart."

He looked at me with great dislike, folded his arms over his chest and said, "I'm going to get my mommy to beat you up."

I didn't laugh in his face, but it was a struggle to keep a straight face. He looked so disgruntled, a little eaglet with all his feathers ruffled, a strong-willed child resentful about not getting his own way.

When a little guy says something so outrageous, it's funny, but how many times do we supposedly mature adults say things just as ridiculous? "Do that again, and you're grounded for life!" "I don't care if spinach makes you throw up. Eat it."

Even worse, how often do we say things that are hurtful? "You are such a dunce!" "Man, am I glad you're not my kid. At least I can send you home to your parents."

That old platitude about sticks and stones breaking our bones but words never hurting is *so* untrue. Words can wound, and even kill the spirit. Instead, we can choose words that build up. We can season our speech with grace. We can make our grandkids feel they're the most important people in the world, at least our world, with the right words.

Father, may I speak words that are wholesome and that build up my grandchildren and all the others in my life. May I think before I speak. Amen.

Your next devotion is located on page 1621.

GRANDCHILD IN FOCUS • PRAYER

Spiritual Growth

Dear Lord, today I pray for my grandchild's spiritual growth. I ask that you instill in him the desire to read and memorize your Word. Give him a passion to be in conversation with you. May loving and serving you be part of his daily life. I ask that you stay close to him and lead him to be transformed to your likeness, to reflect your grace and to radiate your love. I pray this in Jesus' name, amen.

1613

REBECCA LUTZER

Setting
AND MAINTAINING BOUNDARIES

Grandmothering is hard work. Often there is no praise, thanks or recognition. Recently, I was babysitting for two of my grandchildren. While three-year-old Anna napped, six-year-old Samuel and I were hanging out together. Matter-of-factly he said, "Grandma, you're nothing compared to my mom. She's a Montessori teacher!" Though my ego had taken quite a hit, I remained calm. Agreeing that his mom was a very good teacher, I dialoged with him about homeschooling and what he liked to study.

It was time to regain my status. "Samuel, did you know that Grandma is a nurse?" His eyes widened, as he asked, "Are you really?" (He knows who nurses are from his checkups and a couple of visits to the ER.) Straightening up taller, I replied, "Oh, yes. I've taken care of lots of sick people and helped the doctors make them better." My position of respect was restored when he said, "Wow, Grandma! I think you're the best nurse in the world!"

In the first few years of being a grandmother, I made many demands of myself. I longed to be with those precious babies and offered—even insisted at times—to care for them to the point of exhaustion. I saw how worn out and frazzled my daughters were. They needed a break from childcare and housework. I felt driven to help them beyond my limits. This was very unwise and caused me much pain physically and emotionally.

Other factors influenced me: my daughters' real and perceived expectations; the geographical distance between us; my inability to see them more often; my empathetic nature and spiritual gift of service.

I didn't want to disappoint my daughters. Sometimes I demanded more of myself than they would ever demand of me. I failed to properly communicate with them to find out what their expectations were. On a few occasions I did feel that I was taken advantage of, but I hesitated to speak up.

How do we set and maintain boundaries with our children and grandchildren? How do we maintain balance when being involved? How do we acknowledge our physical limitations and diminished energy without feeling guilty?

Communication

Communication is key to all relationships. Clear, honest, timely communication.

Ephesians 4:29 offers some practical advice: "Do not let any unwholesome talk come out of your mouths, but only what is helpful for building others up according to their needs, that it may benefit those who listen."

If we follow God's wise words, we will find that our communications are enhanced. Misunderstandings and false expectations are eliminated. Schedules are clarified. Personal preferences are explained. Compromises are worked out. And grace will come to all who live by this teaching.

Submission

Submission brings peace to troubled relationships and prevents conflict. Ephesians 5:21 instructs us to "submit to one another out of reverence for Christ." Humble, mutual submission honors the Lord. When we compromise with our children and submit to their routines, preferences or discipline methods, our relationships can be harmonious. This enables us to refrain from making a hurtful comment. It allows us to give up our own rights in order to maintain peace.

Kindness and Forgiveness

Kindness and forgiveness cover a multitude of sins: anger, bitterness, hurt feelings, misunderstandings, unrealistic expectations. Ephesians 4:32 commands: "Be kind and compassionate to one another, forgiving each other, just as in Christ God forgave you." Here we are taught what to do when mistakes are made and feelings are hurt. We follow Christ's example of forgiveness. When we choose to obey God's Word, the Holy Spirit helps us and redeems wounded relationships.

Grandchildren Are a Treasure

From a practical standpoint, I have learned several things: to recognize and admit my physical limitations; to pace myself and not work to the point of exhaustion; to not try to make up for all the time I haven't seen my grandchildren in just one short visit; to leave plenty of time to just have fun and relax.

All of us must learn some hard lessons on our journey. Being a grandmother is a privilege and great responsibility. The joyful news is that children and grandchildren are a treasure to enjoy!

light becomes visible, [14]for it is light that makes everything visible. This is why it is said:

> "Wake up, O sleeper,
>   rise from the dead,
> and Christ will shine on you."

[15]Be very careful, then, how you live—not as unwise but as wise, [16]making the most of every opportunity, because the days are evil. [17]Therefore do not be foolish, but understand what the Lord's will is. [18]Do not get drunk on wine, which leads to debauchery. Instead, be filled with the Spirit. [19]Speak to one another with psalms, hymns and spiritual songs. Sing and make music in your heart to the Lord, [20]always giving thanks to God the Father for everything, in the name of our Lord Jesus Christ.

[21]Submit to one another out of reverence for Christ.

PRAYING THE SCRIPTURES

Thankfulness

EPHESIANS 5:20

O God, our Father, let my grandchild always give thanks to you for everything, in the name of our Lord Jesus Christ.

Next prayer in Thankfulness Prayer Track:
1 Thessalonians 2:13

Wives and Husbands

5:22–6:9pp — Col 3:18–4:1

[22]Wives, submit to your husbands as to the Lord. [23]For the husband is the head of the wife as Christ is the head of the church, his body, of which he is the Savior. [24]Now as the church submits to Christ, so also wives should submit to their husbands in everything.

[25]Husbands, love your wives, just as Christ loved the church and gave himself up for her [26]to make her holy, cleansing[a] her by the washing

with water through the word, [27]and to present her to himself as a radiant church, without stain or wrinkle or any other blemish, but holy and blameless. [28]In this same way, husbands ought to love their wives as their own bodies. He who loves his wife loves himself. [29]After all, no one ever hated his own body, but he feeds and cares for it, just as Christ does the church— [30]for we are members of his body. [31]"For this reason a man will leave his father and mother and be united to his wife, and the two will become one flesh."[b] [32]This is a profound mystery—but I am talking about Christ and the church. [33]However, each one of you also must love his wife as he loves himself, and the wife must respect her husband.

Children and Parents

6 Children, obey your parents in the Lord, for this is right. [2]"Honor your father and mother"—which is the first commandment with a promise— [3]"that it may go well with you and that you may enjoy long life on the earth."[c]

[4]Fathers, do not exasperate your children; instead, bring them up in the training and instruction of the Lord.

Slaves and Masters

[5]Slaves, obey your earthly masters with respect and fear, and with sincerity of heart, just as you would obey Christ. [6]Obey them not only to win

---

[a] 26 Or *having cleansed*   [b] 31 Gen. 2:24   [c] 3 Deut. 5:16

their favor when their eye is on you, but like slaves of Christ, doing the will of God from your heart. ⁷Serve wholeheartedly, as if you were serving the Lord, not men, ⁸because you know that the Lord will reward everyone for whatever good he does, whether he is slave or free.

⁹And masters, treat your slaves in the same way. Do not threaten them, since you know that he who is both their Master and yours is in heaven, and there is no favoritism with him.

The Armor of God

¹⁰Finally, be strong in the Lord and in his mighty power. ¹¹Put on the full armor of God so that you can take your stand against the devil's schemes. ¹²For our struggle is not against flesh and blood, but against the rulers, against the authorities, against the powers of this dark world and against the spiritual forces of evil in the heavenly realms. ¹³Therefore put on the full armor of

PRAYING THE SCRIPTURES

Well-Being

EPHESIANS 6:10

I pray, O God, that my grandchild may be strong in you and in your mighty power.

Next prayer in Well-being Prayer Track: 3 John 2

God, so that when the day of evil comes, you may be able to stand your ground, and after you have done everything, to stand. ¹⁴Stand firm then, with the belt of truth buckled around your waist, with the breastplate of righteousness in place, ¹⁵and with your feet fitted with the readiness that comes from the gospel of peace. ¹⁶In addition to all this, take up the shield of faith, with which you can extinguish all the flaming arrows of the evil one. ¹⁷Take the helmet of salvation and the sword of the Spirit, which is the word of God. ¹⁸And pray in the Spirit on all occasions with all kinds of

stories to share

EPHESIANS 6:10–20

The Armor of God

LIFE LESSON: God equips us to stand against evil.

TO TALK ABOUT

✦ What pieces of spiritual armor are we to wear in our fight against evil?

✦ Who is our real enemy?

✦ When would you need to use your spiritual armor?

✦ How can we use the "word of God" (verse 17) as an offensive weapon?

prayers and requests. With this in mind, be alert and always keep on praying for all the saints.

¹⁹Pray also for me, that whenever I open my mouth, words may be given me so that I will fearlessly make known the mystery of the gospel, ²⁰for which I am an ambassador in chains. Pray that I may declare it fearlessly, as I should.

Final Greetings

²¹Tychicus, the dear brother and faithful servant in the Lord, will tell you everything, so that you also may know how I am and what I am doing. ²²I am sending him to you for this very purpose, that you may know how we are, and that he may encourage you.

²³Peace to the brothers, and love with faith from God the Father and the Lord Jesus Christ. ²⁴Grace to all who love our Lord Jesus Christ with an undying love.

Joy IN CHRISTIAN LIVING

We and our grandchildren are constantly bombarded with messages telling us that we have the right to be happy. Our culture tells us that the perfect vacation or the latest electronic device will bring us happiness. The world tells us to look to possessions to find joy, but too often what we find instead is disappointment.

Paul wrote this short but joyous letter to the church at Philippi. Although he was in prison, unsure whether he would live or die, he wanted his readers to know that his joy was grounded in knowing Jesus Christ as his Lord and Savior. He explained that the key to his joy was modeling the humility of Christ, which is the antidote to selfishness and the secret to living a thankful, contented life.

We are privileged to help our grandchildren look beyond worldly messages and to point them toward "whatever is true, whatever is noble, whatever is right, whatever is pure, whatever is lovely, whatever is admirable" (Philippians 4:8). It's not always easy to teach our grandchildren to look to the best things in life, but as we rejoice in experiencing the daily presence of Jesus, our grandchildren will see and want to do likewise.

Live in the joy of the Lord and help your grandchildren know Christ, your reason for rejoicing.

VERSE *to* REMEMBER | PHILIPPIANS 4:4

Rejoice in the Lord always. I will say it again: Rejoice!

Philippians

ABOUT PHILIPPIANS

WRITTEN BY:
The apostle Paul

WRITTEN FOR:
The Christians in Philippi

DATE WRITTEN:
About A.D. 61 from Rome, where Paul was in prison

WHY WRITTEN:
To thank the Philippians for their love and gifts and to give them instructions on how to live Christian lives

1 Paul and Timothy, servants of Christ Jesus,

To all the saints in Christ Jesus at Philippi, together with the overseers [a] and deacons:

[2]Grace and peace to you from God our Father and the Lord Jesus Christ.

Thanksgiving and Prayer

[3]I thank my God every time I remember you. [4]In all my prayers for all of you, I always pray with joy [5]because of your partnership in the gospel from the first day until now, [6]being confident of this, that he who began a good work in you will carry it on to completion until the day of Christ Jesus.

PRAYING THE SCRIPTURES

Reassurance

PHILIPPIANS 1:6

Father God, reassure my grandchild that you will carry on to completion the good work you have begun in him.

This is the last prayer in the Reassurance Prayer Track.

[7]It is right for me to feel this way about all of you, since I have you in my heart; for whether I am in chains or defending and confirming the gospel, all of you share in God's grace with me. [8]God can testify how I long for all of you with the affection of Christ Jesus.

[9]And this is my prayer: that your love may abound more and more in knowledge and depth of insight, [10]so that you may be able to discern what is best and may be pure and blameless until the day of Christ, [11]filled with the fruit of righteousness that comes through Jesus Christ—to the glory and praise of God.

Paul's Chains Advance the Gospel

[12]Now I want you to know, brothers, that what has happened to me has really served to advance the gospel. [13]As a result, it has become clear throughout the whole palace guard [b] and to everyone else that I am in chains for Christ. [14]Because of my chains, most of the brothers in the Lord have been encouraged to speak the word of God more courageously and fearlessly.

[15]It is true that some preach Christ out of envy and rivalry, but others out of goodwill. [16]The latter do so in love, knowing that I am put here for the defense of the gospel. [17]The former preach Christ out of selfish ambition, not sincerely, supposing that they can stir up trouble for me while I am in chains. [c] [18]But what does it matter? The important thing is that in every way, whether from false motives or true, Christ is preached. And because of this I rejoice.

Yes, and I will continue to rejoice, [19]for I know that through your prayers and the help given by the Spirit of Jesus Christ, what has happened to me will turn out for my deliverance. [d] [20]I eagerly expect and hope that I will in no way be ashamed, but will have sufficient courage so that now as always Christ will be exalted in my body, whether by life or by death. [21]For to me, to live is Christ and to die is gain. [22]If I am to go on living in the body, this will mean fruitful labor for me. Yet what shall I choose? I do not know! [23]I am torn between the two: I desire to depart and be with Christ, which is better by far; [24]but it is more necessary for you that I remain in the body. [25]Convinced of this, I know that I will remain, and I will continue with all of you for your progress and joy in the faith, [26]so that through my being with you again your joy in Christ Jesus will overflow on account of me.

[27]Whatever happens, conduct yourselves in a manner worthy of the gospel of Christ. Then, whether I come and see you or only hear about you in my absence, I will know that you stand firm in one spirit, contending as one man for the faith of the gospel [28]without being frightened in any way by those who oppose you. This is a sign

[a] 1 Traditionally *bishops*   [b] 13 Or *whole palace*   [c] 16,17 Some late manuscripts have verses 16 and 17 in reverse order.   [d] 19 Or *salvation*

to them that they will be destroyed, but that you will be saved—and that by God. [29] For it has been granted to you on behalf of Christ not only to believe on him, but also to suffer for him, [30] since you are going through the same struggle you saw I had, and now hear that I still have.

Imitating Christ's Humility

2 If you have any encouragement from being united with Christ, if any comfort from his love, if any fellowship with the Spirit, if any tenderness and compassion, [2] then make my joy complete by being like-minded, having the same love, being one in spirit and purpose. [3] Do nothing out of selfish ambition or vain conceit, but in humility consider others better than yourselves. [4] Each of you should look not only to your own interests, but also to the interests of others.

[5] Your attitude should be the same as that of Christ Jesus:

[6] Who, being in very nature[a] God,
did not consider equality with God
something to be grasped,
[7] but made himself nothing,
taking the very nature[b] of a servant,
being made in human likeness.
[8] And being found in appearance as a man,
he humbled himself
and became obedient to death—
even death on a cross!
[9] Therefore God exalted him to the highest place
and gave him the name that is above every
name,
[10] that at the name of Jesus every knee should
bow,
in heaven and on earth and under the
earth,
[11] and every tongue confess that Jesus Christ
is Lord,
to the glory of God the Father.

Shining as Stars

[12] Therefore, my dear friends, as you have always obeyed—not only in my presence, but now much more in my absence—continue to work out your salvation with fear and trembling, [13] for it is God who works in you to will and to act according to his good purpose.

[14] Do everything without complaining or arguing, [15] so that you may become blameless and pure, children of God without fault in a crooked and depraved generation, in which you shine like stars in the universe [16] as you hold out[c] the word of life—in order that I may boast on the day of Christ that I did not run or labor for nothing. [17] But even if I am being poured out like a drink offering on the sacrifice and service coming from your faith, I am glad and rejoice with all of you. [18] So you too should be glad and rejoice with me.

Timothy and Epaphroditus

[19] I hope in the Lord Jesus to send Timothy to you soon, that I also may be cheered when I receive news about you. [20] I have no one else

[a] 6 Or *in the form of*   [b] 7 Or *the form*   [c] 16 Or *hold on to*

> DO EVERYTHING WITHOUT COMPLAINING OR ARGUING, SO THAT YOU MAY BECOME BLAMELESS AND PURE, CHILDREN OF GOD WITHOUT FAULT IN A CROOKED AND DEPRAVED GENERATION, IN WHICH YOU SHINE LIKE STARS IN THE UNIVERSE.
>
> *Philippians 2:14–15*

Sparkle Factor

CAROL KUYKENDALL

READ | PHILIPPIANS 2:12–18

One sunny summer Saturday, our family sat around a table on the patio of a creek-side restaurant in a small town in the Colorado Rockies. While waiting for our lunch orders, we passed 10-month-old Gabriella from lap to lap, aunt to uncle, grandfather to father, delighting in this first child of a new generation. She loved the routine, opening her arms wide and clapping her hands in sheer joy with each new lap.

I marveled at how this small grandchild served as a mood enhancer for our whole family, able to illuminate the face of each adult who interacted with her. Without even realizing it, she bonded us together with the joy of giving and receiving this new kind of love.

I saw our children do the same thing in my mother's life. They were young during the last years of her life, when she was mostly confined to her bed as she battled emphysema. She loved those times when they burst through her front door to say hi, to check the supply of candy she stashed under her bed or to crawl up beside her and read books with her. Sparkles. That's what she said her grandchildren brought into her life. Observing that kind of love helped us all through a hard place in our lives.

As I gathered Gabriella in my arms on that summer Saturday, I realized how her sparkles were contagious and how a grandchild's love enlarges our capacity to love, enhancing and enriching all the relationships within our family circle.

Soon our food came, and I offered my own silent prayer of thanks.

Lord, you want us to "shine like stars in the universe," and I'm thankful that you give us grandchildren who make your love and our love shine brighter.

Your next devotion is located on page 1622.

GRANDCHILD IN FOCUS • PRAYER

Relationships at Home

O Lord, I pray that you will bless the home and family of my grandchild. May the relationships she has with her parents and siblings enhance her well-being, support her self-confidence and increase her faith. May her home life reflect your love, your grace, your compassion and your peace. Guide her parents to direct her in love and truth, so she will grow into a strong and compassionate individual. Amen.

Baskets of Love

Ask your grandchildren if they know any people who are isolated in their homes. Be prepared with a list of shut-ins from within your family, church or neighborhood, or from among your acquaintances. Perhaps your grandchild would prefer to prepare activity baskets for children who are hospitalized or for a classmate who is ill.

Brainstorm with the kids to determine what each of you might want to include in simple love baskets for the person or people you choose.

Invite your grandchildren individually to deliver the baskets to the recipients. Then take the child to a restaurant for a sandwich or a snack, and discuss what the experience has meant to each of you and how God calls us to care for others (see Leviticus 19:9–10).

Long-Distance Variation: Over the phone discuss the idea and do all the planning. When you deliver the basket, take a picture of the recipient with the gift. Send it to your grandchild and then talk about the event together. Or let the parents know what you're doing so they can help as needed. Send the supplies, have your grandchild put the basket together and deliver it to someone special and send *you* the picture.

Father, let this simple activity teach my grandchildren the importance of compassion. Implant this trait in their hearts so they will grow in kindness. Thank you for each of these precious children. Please bless this one-on-one time together; help them to understand how our faith is revealed in our actions. Amen.

Your next devotion is located on page 1623.

GRANDCHILD IN FOCUS • PRAYER

Friends

Dear Lord and Father, I pray for my grandchild's social life and his friends. Bring diverse friends into his life who will love and encourage him, who will bring joy and laughter to the good times and comfort and support through difficulties and disappointments. Grant him wisdom and discernment as he selects his friends; help him to avoid cliques that restrict, activities that endanger, and foolish and dangerous behaviors that harm. I ask that you fill his life with close and caring relationships. Amen.

Worship the Lord

O LORD, you have searched m
and you know me.
You know when I sit and when I rise;
you perceive my thoughts from afar.
You discern my going out and my lying down;
you are familiar with all my ways.
Before a word is on my tongue
you know it completely, O LORD.

You hem me in — behind and before;
you have laid your hand upon me.
Such knowledge is too wonderful for
me,
too lofty for me to attain.

Where can I go from your Spirit?
Where can I flee from your
presence?
If I go up to the heavens, you are
there;
if I make my bed in the depths,
you are there.
If I rise on the wings of the dawn,
if I settle on the far side of the sea,
even there your hand will guide me,
your right hand will hold me fast.

Psalm 139:1 — 10

GRANDCHILD IN FOCUS • PRAYER

Self-Image

O loving God, I praise you for creating my grandchild as a unique individual. Now I ask you to help her appreciate her uniqueness. Build up her self-image so she can enjoy her individuality. Help her to stand firm for who she is, where she has come from and what she believes in. Encourage her not only to have hopes and dreams but to also enjoy each day as it comes.
In Jesus' name, amen.

Dear Lord, I am at peace knowing that you are by my side, knowing that you notice the details of my life: each word, each step, each move I make. It is both daunting to know I cannot escape from your presence and comforting to know I cannot escape from your love. Keep me close to you, Lord, and be my guide. Amen.

Your next devotion is located on page 1625.

like him, who takes a genuine interest in your welfare. ²¹For everyone looks out for his own interests, not those of Jesus Christ. ²²But you know that Timothy has proved himself, because as a son with his father he has served with me in the work of the gospel. ²³I hope, therefore, to send him as soon as I see how things go with me. ²⁴And I am confident in the Lord that I myself will come soon.

²⁵But I think it is necessary to send back to you Epaphroditus, my brother, fellow worker and fellow soldier, who is also your messenger, whom you sent to take care of my needs. ²⁶For he longs for all of you and is distressed because you heard he was ill. ²⁷Indeed he was ill, and almost died. But God had mercy on him, and not on him only but also on me, to spare me sorrow upon sorrow. ²⁸Therefore I am all the more eager to send him, so that when you see him again you may be glad and I may have less anxiety. ²⁹Welcome him in the Lord with great joy, and honor men like him, ³⁰because he almost died for the work of Christ, risking his life to make up for the help you could not give me.

No Confidence in the Flesh

3 Finally, my brothers, rejoice in the Lord! It is no trouble for me to write the same things to you again, and it is a safeguard for you.

²Watch out for those dogs, those men who do evil, those mutilators of the flesh. ³For it is we who are the circumcision, we who worship by the Spirit of God, who glory in Christ Jesus, and who put no confidence in the flesh— ⁴though I myself have reasons for such confidence.

If anyone else thinks he has reasons to put confidence in the flesh, I have more: ⁵circumcised on the eighth day, of the people of Israel, of the tribe of Benjamin, a Hebrew of Hebrews; in regard to the law, a Pharisee; ⁶as for zeal, persecuting the church; as for legalistic righteousness, faultless.

⁷But whatever was to my profit I now consider loss for the sake of Christ. ⁸What is more, I consider everything a loss compared to the surpassing greatness of knowing Christ Jesus my Lord,

for whose sake I have lost all things. I consider them rubbish, that I may gain Christ ⁹and be found in him, not having a righteousness of my own that comes from the law, but that which is through faith in Christ—the righteousness that comes from God and is by faith. ¹⁰I want to know Christ and the power of his resurrection and the fellowship of sharing in his sufferings, becoming like him in his death, ¹¹and so, somehow, to attain to the resurrection from the dead.

Pressing on Toward the Goal

¹²Not that I have already obtained all this, or have already been made perfect, but I press on to

stories to share

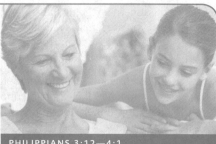

PHILIPPIANS 3:12—4:1

Pressing on Toward the Goal

LIFE LESSON: The Christian life is a journey.

TO TALK ABOUT

✦ What prize was Paul continuously striving toward?

✦ Was Paul bragging when he asked Christians to follow his example? Why or why not?

✦ If we can never become perfect in this life, why should we keep on trying?

✦ How do non-Christians see Christ at work in our world?

I DO NOT CONSIDER MYSELF YET TO HAVE
TAKEN HOLD OF IT. BUT ONE THING I DO:
FORGETTING WHAT IS BEHIND AND STRAINING
TOWARD WHAT IS AHEAD, I PRESS ON TOWARD
THE GOAL TO WIN THE PRIZE FOR WHICH GOD
HAS CALLED ME HEAVENWARD IN CHRIST JESUS.

Philippians 3:13—14

The Rearview Mirror

TERRI BLACKSTOCK

READ | PHILIPPIANS 3:12 — 4:1

I wish I were the kind of person who had lived life according to God's best plan for me, but my free will got in the way so many times, leaving me with a series of regrets that rear their ugly head with hair-trigger consistency. Though I read the words that Paul wrote in Philippians 3:13 – 14, "Forgetting what is behind and straining toward what is ahead, I press on toward the goal to win the prize for which God has called me heavenward in Christ Jesus," I find myself constantly looking in my rearview mirror, working through the thing I should have done, wondering how different things would be if I had.

I realize that God is in control of the universe. The mistakes in my past, though dramatic to me, cannot ruin God's plan beyond repair. God is sovereign, and his plans cannot be thwarted by human beings like me. He can fill in the blanks of my mistakes, teaching my children what I failed to teach, restoring what I destroyed, rebuilding what I tore down, redeeming what I sold away.

The Bible tells me to stop looking back, to press on toward the prize. God knew my mistakes before I ever made them, yet he planned to use me anyway. He didn't see me as the Great Loser, but as someone uniquely gifted with something of use to his kingdom work. Where I see myself as a disappointment, he sees me as an asset. He already knows the fruit I will bear for him, and my future is on his mind, so much more than my past.

If God can see me that way, why wouldn't I want to press on toward the goal and wave goodbye to my fragmented, imperfect past? The future is so much brighter in Christ, and I have so many sisters and brothers who need strengthening.

Heavenly Father, I'm so grateful that your power and authority are so much greater than my mistakes. As I press forward, leaving my past behind, I pray that you will strengthen me and establish the purpose for which you have called me.

Your next devotion is located on page 1627.

GRANDCHILD IN FOCUS • PRAYER

Protection From Worldliness

O Sovereign Lord, the world surrounds my grandchild, pressing in and tempting him in so many ways. Help him set appropriate limits. Give him sound judgment to choose wisely. Guard him from temptation; protect him from physical and mental predators; lead him into paths of righteousness and light. And reassure me with your promise that you are holding him in your hands. Amen.

take hold of that for which Christ Jesus took hold of me. [13] Brothers, I do not consider myself yet to have taken hold of it. But one thing I do: Forgetting what is behind and straining toward what is ahead, [14] I press on toward the goal to win the prize for which God has called me heavenward in Christ Jesus.

[15] All of us who are mature should take such a view of things. And if on some point you think differently, that too God will make clear to you. [16] Only let us live up to what we have already attained.

[17] Join with others in following my example, brothers, and take note of those who live according to the pattern we gave you. [18] For, as I have often told you before and now say again even with tears, many live as enemies of the cross of Christ. [19] Their destiny is destruction, their god is their stomach, and their glory is in their shame. Their mind is on earthly things. [20] But our citizenship is in heaven. And we eagerly await a Savior from there, the Lord Jesus Christ, [21] who, by the power that enables him to bring everything under his control, will transform our lowly bodies so that they will be like his glorious body.

4 Therefore, my brothers, you whom I love and long for, my joy and crown, that is how you should stand firm in the Lord, dear friends!

Exhortations

[2] I plead with Euodia and I plead with Syntyche to agree with each other in the Lord. [3] Yes, and I ask you, loyal yokefellow,[a] help these women who have contended at my side in the cause of the gospel, along with Clement and the rest of my fellow workers, whose names are in the book of life.

[4] Rejoice in the Lord always. I will say it again: Rejoice! [5] Let your gentleness be evident to all. The Lord is near. [6] Do not be anxious about anything, but in everything, by prayer and petition, with thanksgiving, present your requests to God. [7] And the peace of God, which transcends all understanding, will guard your hearts and your minds in Christ Jesus.

PRAYING THE SCRIPTURES

Blessing

PHILIPPIANS 4:7

Almighty God, I pray that your peace, which transcends all understanding, will guard the heart and mind of my grandchild as she lives in Christ Jesus.

Next prayer in Blessing Prayer Track:
1 Thessalonians 5:23

[8] Finally, brothers, whatever is true, whatever is noble, whatever is right, whatever is pure, whatever is lovely, whatever is admirable—if anything is excellent or praiseworthy—think about such things. [9] Whatever you have learned or received or heard from me, or seen in me—put it into practice. And the God of peace will be with you.

Thanks for Their Gifts

[10] I rejoice greatly in the Lord that at last you have renewed your concern for me. Indeed, you have been concerned, but you had no opportunity to show it. [11] I am not saying this because I am in need, for I have learned to be content whatever the circumstances. [12] I know what it is to be in need, and I know what it is to have plenty. I have learned the secret of being content in any and every situation, whether well fed or hungry,

[a] 3 Or loyal Syzygus

TALKING POINTS

Contentment
Trust in God regardless of circumstances.
PHILIPPIANS 4:10–13
This is the last talking point on contentment.

> DO NOT BE ANXIOUS ABOUT ANYTHING, BUT IN
> EVERYTHING, BY PRAYER AND PETITION, WITH
> THANKSGIVING, PRESENT YOUR REQUESTS TO GOD.
> AND THE PEACE OF GOD, WHICH TRANSCENDS ALL
> UNDERSTANDING, WILL GUARD YOUR HEARTS AND
> YOUR MINDS IN CHRIST JESUS.
> *Philippians 4:6 – 7*

Pray About Everything

RUTHANNE GARLOCK

READ | PHILIPPIANS 4:2 – 9

We've heard that some things are better "caught than taught," such as helping our children and grand-children understand the value of prayer. This was the case with my friend Paula.

After having her two three-year-old granddaughters spend the night with her, they had breakfast on the patio the next morning. As the girls sat at their little picnic table and Paula enjoyed her coffee in a lounge chair with her feet up, a bee landed on her ankle and stung her. Her first thought was to rush to the doctor's office since she's allergic to bee stings.

"See this red spot on Honey's ankle?" she said to the girls. "A bee just stung me, and in a few minutes my foot will be all sore and swollen. I'm sorry, but I'm going to have to call your mothers to come pick you up right away so I can go to the doctor."

"No, Honey, no!" Alex declared insistently as she ran over to examine the spot. "We'll pray for you, and Jesus will heal you!" The two youngsters put their hands on Paula's ankle, bowed their heads and prayed a simple prayer, asking Jesus to heal the bee sting.

"When they took their hands away, the spot was gone, and the swelling I'd expected never happened," Paula told me. "Instead, we had a fun day together. I had been telling them that Jesus hears and answers our prayers, but their simple, childlike faith truly humbled me."

Lord, help me to remember that my words and actions have an effect on my grandchildren and can influence their faith in you in days to come. May my example before them cause each one to love you and put their trust in you. Amen.

Your next devotion is located on page 1628.

GRANDCHILD IN FOCUS • PRAYER

Respect for Authority

Dear Lord, I pray that my grandchild will continually grow to respect those in authority. May she learn to be coopera-tive and fair in work and play. Instill in her a high regard for officials who govern our land and enforce the laws. May her relationships with parents, teachers, coaches, mentors and bosses be respectful, admirable, con-structive and caring. Amen.

I CAN DO EVERYTHING THROUGH
HIM WHO GIVES ME STRENGTH.
Philippians 4:13

A Life Verse

JAN KARON

READ | PHILIPPIANS 4:10 – 20

Many Christians have what they call a life verse. [It's] a single verse from the vast lexicon of the Word of God that will serve in any situation, no matter what. That's a lot to ask of one small verse. My brother Barry claims Proverbs 3:5 – 6. I take this text from the King James translation:

"Trust in the LORD with all thine heart; and lean not unto thine own understanding. In all thy ways acknowledge him, and he shall direct thy paths."

So. If we trust Him, seek His wisdom, and acknowledge Him in all our ways, look what happens, look what we're promised:

He will direct our paths.

This is very potent stuff. Indeed, I want and need Him to direct my path, for I remember what happened when I did all the directing myself. Not good.

If I had to absolutely, positively come up with a verse to live by in this tough and out-of-control age, it's one you'll find again and again in the Mitford books.

"[I can do everything through him who gives me strength]" (Philippians 4:13).

Indeed, Olivia Davenport and Father Tim have a little "family joke," if you will. They say to each other, "Philippians four-thirteen, for Pete's sake."

Don't have a verse of your own? I hope you'll find one, for Pete's sake. You'll be amazed at how often you call upon its reassurance and tonic wisdom.

Father, thank you for the rich treasures I find in your Word, for the reassurance, comfort and wisdom I discover in its pages. Amen.

Your next devotion is located on page 1635.

GRANDCHILD IN FOCUS • PRAYER

Courage

O Father, builder of character and courage, may my grandchild grow strong in the light of your love. Grant him courage to stand for what is right, to guard the truth and to ensure justice in every aspect of life. May he boldly grow in grace, revere your name and proudly proclaim you as the Lord of lords and King of kings. Amen.

whether living in plenty or in want. [13] I can do everything through him who gives me strength.

[14] Yet it was good of you to share in my troubles. [15] Moreover, as you Philippians know, in the early days of your acquaintance with the gospel, when I set out from Macedonia, not one church shared with me in the matter of giving and receiving, except you only; [16] for even when I was in Thessalonica, you sent me aid again and again when I was in need. [17] Not that I am looking for a gift, but I am looking for what may be credited to your account. [18] I have received full payment and even more; I am amply supplied, now that I have received from Epaphroditus the gifts you sent. They are a fragrant offering, an acceptable sacrifice, pleasing to God. [19] And my God will meet all your needs according to his glorious riches in Christ Jesus.

[20] To our God and Father be glory for ever and ever. Amen.

Final Greetings

[21] Greet all the saints in Christ Jesus. The brothers who are with me send greetings. [22] All the saints send you greetings, especially those who belong to Caesar's household.

[23] The grace of the Lord Jesus Christ be with your spirit. Amen. [a]

[a] 23 Some manuscripts do not have *Amen*.

Devoted
TO PRAYER

This short letter to the Colossians firmly asserts the supremacy of Christ — all that he is and all that he has done, saving and freeing God's people from the bonds of the law, sin and death.

Paul wrote this letter to dispel the false teachings that were circulating among the Colossians. So, after exalting Christ as Lord, he instructed the believers to live holy lives in freedom and gratitude, letting the "peace of Christ rule in [their] hearts" (Colossians 3:15). Paul gave his readers practical instructions on what that freedom and peace should look like: They were to set their hearts and minds on Christ and live lives of love, forgiveness and unity. And they were to devote themselves to prayer.

Prayer is the perfect banner over our lives. It is at the heart of our roles as Christian grandmothers. We should pray *with* our grandchildren, and we should pray *for* them — anytime, anywhere and under any kind of circumstance. Our fervent prayers are not dependent on proximity to our grandchildren, nor are our prayers dependent on the depth of our relationship with our grandchildren. As Paul said, we should devote ourselves to prayer, for through prayer we draw ourselves and our grandchildren closer to God.

VERSE *to* REMEMBER | COLOSSIANS 4:2

Devote yourselves to prayer, being watchful and thankful.

Colossians

ABOUT COLOSSIANS

WRITTEN BY:
The apostle Paul

WRITTEN FOR:
The Christians in Colosse

DATE WRITTEN:
About A.D. 60,
when Paul was
in prison in Rome

WHY WRITTEN:
To refute false teaching
by declaring the supremacy
of Christ and to explain
what that meant for the
Colossians' everyday lives

1 Paul, an apostle of Christ Jesus by the will of God, and Timothy our brother,

²To the holy and faithful[a] brothers in Christ at Colosse:

Grace and peace to you from God our Father.[b]

Thanksgiving and Prayer

³We always thank God, the Father of our Lord Jesus Christ, when we pray for you, ⁴because we have heard of your faith in Christ Jesus and of the love you have for all the saints— ⁵the faith and love that spring from the hope that is stored up for you in heaven and that you have already heard about in the word of truth, the gospel ⁶that has come to you. All over the world this gospel is bearing fruit and growing, just as it has been doing among you since the day you heard it and understood God's grace in all its truth. ⁷You learned it from Epaphras, our dear fellow servant, who is a faithful minister of Christ on our[c] behalf, ⁸and who also told us of your love in the Spirit.

⁹For this reason, since the day we heard about you, we have not stopped praying for you and asking God to fill you with the knowledge of his will through all spiritual wisdom and understanding. ¹⁰And we pray this in order that you may live a life worthy of the Lord and may please him in every way: bearing fruit in every good work, growing in the knowledge of God, ¹¹being strengthened with all power according to his glorious might so that you may have great endurance and patience, and joyfully ¹²giving thanks to the Father, who has qualified you[d] to share in the inheritance of the saints in the kingdom of light. ¹³For he has rescued us from the dominion of darkness and brought us into the kingdom of the Son he loves, ¹⁴in whom we have redemption,[e] the forgiveness of sins.

The Supremacy of Christ

¹⁵He is the image of the invisible God, the first-born over all creation. ¹⁶For by him all things were created: things in heaven and on earth, visible and invisible, whether thrones or powers or rulers or authorities; all things were created by him and for him. ¹⁷He is before all things, and in him all things hold together. ¹⁸And he is the head of the body, the church; he is the beginning and the firstborn from among the dead, so that in everything he might have the supremacy. ¹⁹For God was pleased to have all his fullness dwell in him, ²⁰and through him reconcile to himself all things, whether things on earth or things in heaven, by making peace through his blood, shed on the cross.

²¹Once you were alienated from God and were enemies in your minds because of[f] your evil behavior. ²²But now he has reconciled you by Christ's physical body through death to present you holy in his sight, without blemish and free from accusation— ²³if you continue in your faith, established and firm, not moved from the hope held out in the gospel. This is the gospel that you heard and that has been proclaimed to every creature under heaven, and of which I, Paul, have become a servant.

Paul's Labor for the Church

²⁴Now I rejoice in what was suffered for you, and I fill up in my flesh what is still lacking in regard to Christ's afflictions, for the sake of his body, which is the church. ²⁵I have become its servant by the commission God gave me to present to you the word of God in its fullness— ²⁶the mystery that has been kept hidden for ages and generations, but is now disclosed to the saints. ²⁷To them God has chosen to make known among the Gentiles the glorious riches of this mystery, which is Christ in you, the hope of glory.

²⁸We proclaim him, admonishing and teaching everyone with all wisdom, so that we may present everyone perfect in Christ. ²⁹To this end I labor, struggling with all his energy, which so powerfully works in me.

[a] 2 Or *believing*   [b] 2 Some manuscripts *Father and the Lord Jesus Christ*   [c] 7 Some manuscripts *your*   [d] 12 Some manuscripts *us*   [e] 14 A few late manuscripts *redemption through his blood*   [f] 21 Or *minds, as shown by*

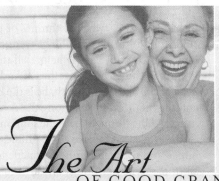

EMILIE BARNES

The Art
OF GOOD GRANDPARENTING

One of our goals as grandmothers is to bring out the very best in our grandchildren. Professionals in the business and education fields constantly look into new areas of research to find out what makes good managers and teachers. The common strand for success in both of these areas is to have a genuine caring attitude for the people you are responsible for. That is true of grandparenting too. To be effective, you must show your grandchildren that you really care for them — not just in your words but also in your actions. Children are continually asking through their music, friends, clothes and grades, "Do you really love me?" As grandparents we need to know how to express genuine caring. Here are qualities that exhibit good grandparenting:

Really Listen

Listening means turning off the radio or TV and putting down the newspaper or magazine so you can give 100 percent of your attention to your conversation. Tell the other members of the family that you are not to be disturbed unless there's a major emergency. Be like one grandparent who said, "I hear not only with my ears, but with my eyes and my guts. I don't want to miss anything, either verbally or nonverbally."

Take an Interest in Your Grandchildren as People

Be interested in them as people and not only as your grandchildren. Ask them questions: How did school go? How's Mary? How's football? How's church? How's your stomachache? Stay involved with their activities as much as you can, so you really know what is going on in their lives. Care about them.

Be Clear in Your Expectations

Let your grandchildren know of your expectations for them in whatever you are doing. Then step back and give them freedom to follow through. Each grandchild may do things differently, based upon his or her temperament. Some grandchildren do things with little flair while others do things with great flair.

Be Willing to Transmit Your Knowledge to Your Grandchildren

Take time to explain, demonstrate and answer their questions — even if their questions seem simple to you. Give your grandkids time when you're walking, when you lie down and when you get up (see Deuteronomy 6:7).

Trust Your Grandchildren to Fulfill Their Promises

Train them how to keep their word. One of my favorite mottos is "Just do what you say you are going to do." Reinforce to your grandchildren that they are to keep their word by keeping appointments, calling back when they say they will and turning in homework assignments on time. Let your grandchildren work out the details by themselves.

Be Flexible and Remain Open to Good Ideas

Admit you are wrong when the evidence shows it, and be willing to change your mind. Don't think you have all the answers. Let answers to the questions come from all members of the family.

Have a Good Sense of Humor

Humor and enthusiasm are infectious and create a friendly, productive atmosphere. Learn to laugh at yourself.

Be a Leader and Role Model in the Family

Even when there are difficulties, family members find great comfort and support when the leaders within the family are in control of themselves. That includes language, body movements, attitudes, temperament and balance. We as grandparents must exhibit the highest standards. We can't ask our children and grandchildren to go beyond a standard that we don't exhibit ourselves.

Ask God to give you the strength and endurance to be faithful in your Christian walk so that you will be an example to your grandchildren in all you do. The fruit that you bear will be seen in your children and grandchildren (see Colossians 1:10–12). Listen carefully. Love unconditionally.

2 I want you to know how much I am struggling for you and for those at Laodicea, and for all who have not met me personally. ²My purpose is that they may be encouraged in heart and united in love, so that they may have the full riches of complete understanding, in order that they may know the mystery of God, namely, Christ, ³in whom are hidden all the treasures of wisdom and knowledge. ⁴I tell you this so that no one may deceive you by fine-sounding arguments. ⁵For though I am absent from you in body, I am present with you in spirit and delight to see how orderly you are and how firm your faith in Christ is.

Freedom From Human Regulations Through Life With Christ

⁶So then, just as you received Christ Jesus as Lord, continue to live in him, ⁷rooted and built up in him, strengthened in the faith as you were taught, and overflowing with thankfulness.

⁸See to it that no one takes you captive through hollow and deceptive philosophy, which depends on human tradition and the basic principles of this world rather than on Christ.

⁹For in Christ all the fullness of the Deity lives in bodily form, ¹⁰and you have been given fullness in Christ, who is the head over every power and authority. ¹¹In him you were also circumcised, in the putting off of the sinful nature,ᵃ not with a circumcision done by the hands of men but with the circumcision done by Christ, ¹²having been buried with him in baptism and raised with him through your faith in the power of God, who raised him from the dead.

¹³When you were dead in your sins and in the uncircumcision of your sinful nature,ᵇ God made youᶜ alive with Christ. He forgave us all our sins, ¹⁴having canceled the written code, with its regulations, that was against us and that stood opposed to us; he took it away, nailing it to the cross. ¹⁵And having disarmed the powers and authorities, he made a public spectacle of them, triumphing over them by the cross.ᵈ

¹⁶Therefore do not let anyone judge you by what you eat or drink, or with regard to a religious festival, a New Moon celebration or a Sabbath day. ¹⁷These are a shadow of the things that were to come; the reality, however, is found in Christ. ¹⁸Do not let anyone who delights in false humility and the worship of angels disqualify you for the prize. Such a person goes into great detail about what he has seen, and his unspiritual mind puffs him up with idle notions. ¹⁹He has lost connection with the Head, from whom the whole body, supported and held together by its ligaments and sinews, grows as God causes it to grow.

²⁰Since you died with Christ to the basic principles of this world, why, as though you still belonged to it, do you submit to its rules: ²¹"Do not handle! Do not taste! Do not touch!"? ²²These are all destined to perish with use, because they are based on human commands and teachings. ²³Such regulations indeed have an appearance of wisdom, with their self-imposed worship, their false humility and their harsh treatment of the body, but they lack any value in restraining sensual indulgence.

Rules for Holy Living

3 Since, then, you have been raised with Christ, set your hearts on things above, where Christ is seated at the right hand of God. ²Set your minds on things above, not on earthly things. ³For you died, and your life is now hidden

TALKING POINTS

Self-Esteem

We are complete in Christ.

COLOSSIANS 2:9–10

For more on self-esteem, go to 1 John 3:1.

ᵃ 11 Or *the flesh*   ᵇ 13 Or *your flesh*   ᶜ 13 Some manuscripts *us*
ᵈ 15 Or *them in him*

> FOR IN CHRIST ALL THE
> FULLNESS OF THE DEITY LIVES
> IN BODILY FORM, AND YOU
> HAVE BEEN GIVEN FULLNESS IN
> CHRIST, WHO IS THE HEAD OVER
> EVERY POWER AND AUTHORITY.
>
> *Colossians 2:9—10*

Missing Pieces

GIGI GRAHAM TCHIVIDJIAN

READ | COLOSSIANS 2:6 – 23

He was an interesting and slightly eccentric character — an archeologist with a passion for broken china. Most of us don't have much patience with such things, and broken dishes usually get thrown out with the trash. To this man, however, they represented a challenge. In fact, he had built an entire house from all the old, discarded scraps and bric-a-brac he could find. And although it was quite a monstrosity, to his mind he had created a thing of beauty. He then sifted through the dirt around his home, collected bits and pieces of pottery and glass and patiently glued them back together.

Once, while visiting him, Mother asked if she might have a sample of his work. Delighted, he went to select one of his more "perfect" specimens. She said she would much prefer to have one that was cracked, marred — even incomplete. He looked puzzled.

"You see," she explained, "you remind me of God, who so carefully and lovingly takes the broken fragments of our lives and puts them together again. Here and there a piece may be missing — a death, a divorce, an accident, wrong choices. But God takes the pieces of our shattered lives and makes us whole and complete again."

No one is perfect. We are all marred in some way. We have all failed, made mistakes, known defeat and disappointment. Many of us have been physically or emotionally crushed.

But God looks beyond our faults and sees our needs. Tenderly, patiently, He sifts through the debris, lifts His broken creature, and brings healing and wholeness. And if a piece is still missing, His strength and love are sufficient.

His perfection meets the deep needs of our being. His completeness flows around our incompleteness, and we are complete in Him.

Jesus, lover of my soul, I ask you today to put together the broken pieces of my life, forming them into something beautiful, something that reflects your perfection and completeness. Amen.

Your next devotion is located on page 1637.

GRANDCHILD IN FOCUS · PRAYER

Future Spouse

Dear Lord, if it is your will, I pray my grandchild will be united in a loving and Christian marriage. Keep her sexually pure so that she will honor you with her body and mind. As she seeks a spouse who will honor and care for her, give her patience and discernment. May her choice for a life partner be your choice for her, so that she and her husband will together glorify you in a lasting love. I pray this in Jesus' name, amen.

COLOSSIANS 3:1–17

Rules for Holy Living

LIFE LESSON: God wants Christians to live holy lives in gratitude for salvation.

TO TALK ABOUT

✦ On what does Paul want us to set our hearts and minds?

✦ How do your thoughts affect your actions?

✦ What do you think motivates a Christian to live a holy life?

✦ What signs of holy living do you see in yourself?

with Christ in God. ⁴When Christ, who is your*ᵃ* life, appears, then you also will appear with him in glory.

⁵Put to death, therefore, whatever belongs to your earthly nature: sexual immorality, impurity, lust, evil desires and greed, which is idolatry. ⁶Because of these, the wrath of God is coming.*ᵇ* ⁷You used to walk in these ways, in the life you once lived. ⁸But now you must rid yourselves of all such things as these: anger, rage, malice, slander, and filthy language from your lips. ⁹Do not lie to each other, since you have taken off your old self with its practices ¹⁰and have put on the new self, which is being renewed in knowledge in the image of its Creator. ¹¹Here there is no Greek or Jew, circumcised or uncircumcised, barbarian, Scythian, slave or free, but Christ is all, and is in all.

¹²Therefore, as God's chosen people, holy and dearly loved, clothe yourselves with compassion, kindness, humility, gentleness and patience. ¹³Bear with each other and forgive whatever grievances you may have against one another. Forgive as the Lord forgave you. ¹⁴And over all these virtues put on love, which binds them all together in perfect unity.

¹⁵Let the peace of Christ rule in your hearts, since as members of one body you were called to peace. And be thankful. ¹⁶Let the word of Christ dwell in you richly as you teach and admonish one another with all wisdom, and as you sing psalms, hymns and spiritual songs with gratitude in your hearts to God. ¹⁷And whatever you do, whether in word or deed, do it all in the name of the Lord Jesus, giving thanks to God the Father through him.

PRAYING THE SCRIPTURES

Forgiveness
COLOSSIANS 3:13

I pray, O God, that my grandchild will be tolerant of others and forgive whatever grievances he may have against them. Help him to forgive as you, O Lord, have forgiven him.

Next prayer in Forgiveness Prayer Track: 1 John 1:9

Rules for Christian Households
3:18–4:1pp — Eph 5:22–6:9

¹⁸Wives, submit to your husbands, as is fitting in the Lord.

¹⁹Husbands, love your wives and do not be harsh with them.

²⁰Children, obey your parents in everything, for this pleases the Lord.

²¹Fathers, do not embitter your children, or they will become discouraged.

ᵃ 4 Some manuscripts our   ᵇ 6 Some early manuscripts coming on those who are disobedient

> THEREFORE, AS GOD'S CHOSEN PEOPLE, HOLY AND DEARLY LOVED, CLOTHE YOURSELVES WITH COMPASSION, KINDNESS, HUMILITY, GENTLENESS AND PATIENCE.
>
> *Colossians 3:12*

The Best-Dressed Child

NETA JACKSON

READ | COLOSSIANS 3:1 – 17

Four-year-old Liam scurried up the front porch steps. "It's me, Grandpa!" he announced to my husband, who was sitting in a wooden Adirondack chair, both eyes bandaged after eye surgery. "Daddy and I brought you a game to play!"

It wasn't the first time Liam had shown concern for the ordeal his grandpa was going through. It began with one eye operation, which kept my husband facedown for three weeks. Liam made a paper chain out of construction paper, so that Grandpa could tear one off for each day that passed. The phone rang every few days, and Liam would ask, "How are your eyes doing today, Grandpa?"

Then things began to go wrong. Another operation . . . another procedure . . . and another . . . until my husband's eye was so traumatized the doctors didn't dare try another. So they bandaged both eyes and told him to "keep still; don't move."

Not being able to see was the greatest test of all.

But now our son and grandson showed up, ready to play. "A game?" asked my husband, as he reached for the little boy and pulled him into a hug. "But I can't see right now."

"That's OK, Grandpa. It's a smelling game. And I'm going to play it with you."

He instructed his daddy to blindfold him, "just like Grandpa." Then the game was brought out: a tray of little tins with smelly items in them—garlic, a flower, vinegar, horse-radish, etc.—and grandpa with his eye patches and grandson with his blindfold tried to guess each smell.

As I watched Liam putting himself in his grandpa's place and trying to cheer him up, my own eyes got teary. I had just read the third chapter of Colossians, and realized I was seeing a truly "best-dressed" child.

God, let me be more concerned with being "clothed" with compassion and kindness than about how my hair looks or whether my outfit is dated. Children don't care what they're wearing; they just want to love and be loved.

Your next devotion is located on page 1638.

GRANDCHILD IN FOCUS • PRAYER

School/Career

Dear God, may learning be a joy rather than a chore for my grandchild. May exploration of new ideas bring a sense of wonder, awe and excitement. Grant him clarity of mind, the ability to concentrate on the task at hand and recollection of what has been learned. Help him to appreciate the tasks that come easily and to persevere through those that challenge. Amen.

1637

LET'S HAVE FUN

Games, Games, Games

Spend an afternoon or evening playing board games with your grandchildren. Pull out your old favorites or their parents' old favorites. Teach the kids how to play games that perhaps they are not familiar with. You might want to also share some stories of how you remember playing games with your friends or brothers and sisters.

Or have the kids bring their favorite game with them to your house. There are always new games on the market, and you'll have fun learning something new. A very creative grandchild might want to seize the opportunity to create their own game or a variation of their favorite, so be prepared for some very creative rules and regulations.

Older-Grandkids Variation: Find out what games intrigue your grandchildren. It may be chess or a card game, or it may be a video game. If it's a game you don't know, have them teach you the basics. You'll probably be impressed with their expertise.

Dear Lord, thank you for creative minds that can play games. Bless this activity as we share this time together learning a new skill, analyzing our moves, strategizing and just having fun. Let us not take winning or losing too seriously, but rather let us focus on being involved and being together. Amen.

Your next devotion is located on page 1639.

GRANDCHILD IN FOCUS • PRAYER

Character

Dear Lord and Father, I ask that you fill my grandchild with your Spirit so her character reflects your goodness and love. Give her kindness and love for others. Bring joy to her life so she will be a joy to others. Grant her patience and self-control through difficult and trying times. May she show mercy and generosity to those who are less fortunate. Grant her integrity and a sense of justice, and surround her with your peace. Amen.

Worship the Lord

I will extol the LORD at all times;
  his praise will always be on my lips.
My soul will boast in the LORD;
  let the afflicted hear and rejoice.
Glorify the LORD with me;
  let us exalt his name together.

I sought the LORD, and he answered me;
  he delivered me from all my fears.
Those who look to him are radiant;
  their faces are never covered with shame.
This poor man called, and the LORD heard him;
  he saved him out of all his troubles.
The angel of the LORD encamps around
      those who fear him,
  and he delivers them.

Taste and see that the LORD is good;
  blessed is the man who takes
    refuge in him.

Psalm 34:1 – 8

○ God, I praise your name, for you have
showered me with blessings too numerous
to name or count. I thank you for hearing my
cries for help, my pleas for forgiveness, my requests for solutions. Protect me from the troubles
of the world, for you are my refuge. Amen.

Your next devotion is located on page 1643.

GRANDCHILD IN FOCUS • PRAYER

Talents

*Dear Lord, the giver of gifts, bless my
grandchild as he develops his talents. Help him
identify his talents and be proud and confident of
the gifts you have given him. Give him patience and
understanding, Lord, so he will not grow weary of
striving and searching to reach the goals you have
set for him. May each milestone bring satisfaction and a healthy desire for greater
achievement and success to bring
glory to you. Amen.*

²²Slaves, obey your earthly masters in everything; and do it, not only when their eye is on you and to win their favor, but with sincerity of heart and reverence for the Lord. ²³Whatever you do, work at it with all your heart, as working for the Lord, not for men, ²⁴since you know that you will receive an inheritance from the Lord as a reward. It is the Lord Christ you are serving. ²⁵Anyone who does wrong will be repaid for his wrong, and there is no favoritism.

TALKING POINTS

Laziness

No matter what the task at hand, we need to work at it with all our heart.

COLOSSIANS 3:23–24

For more on laziness, go to Hebrews 6:10–12.

4 Masters, provide your slaves with what is right and fair, because you know that you also have a Master in heaven.

Further Instructions

²Devote yourselves to prayer, being watchful and thankful. ³And pray for us, too, that God may open a door for our message, so that we may proclaim the mystery of Christ, for which I am in chains. ⁴Pray that I may proclaim it clearly, as I should. ⁵Be wise in the way you act toward outsiders; make the most of every opportunity. ⁶Let your conversation be always full of grace, seasoned with salt, so that you may know how to answer everyone.

Final Greetings

⁷Tychicus will tell you all the news about me. He is a dear brother, a faithful minister and fellow servant in the Lord. ⁸I am sending him to you for the express purpose that you may know about our*ᵃ* circumstances and that he may encourage your hearts. ⁹He is coming with Onesimus, our faithful and dear brother, who is one of you. They will tell you everything that is happening here.

¹⁰My fellow prisoner Aristarchus sends you his greetings, as does Mark, the cousin of Barnabas. (You have received instructions about him; if he comes to you, welcome him.) ¹¹Jesus, who is called Justus, also sends greetings. These are the only Jews among my fellow workers for the kingdom of God, and they have proved a comfort to me. ¹²Epaphras, who is one of you and a servant of Christ Jesus, sends greetings. He is always wrestling in prayer for you, that you may stand firm in all the will of God, mature and fully assured. ¹³I vouch for him that he is working hard for you and for those at Laodicea and Hierapolis. ¹⁴Our dear friend Luke, the doctor, and Demas send greetings. ¹⁵Give my greetings to the brothers at Laodicea, and to Nympha and the church in her house.

¹⁶After this letter has been read to you, see that it is also read in the church of the Laodiceans and that you in turn read the letter from Laodicea.

¹⁷Tell Archippus: "See to it that you complete the work you have received in the Lord."

¹⁸I, Paul, write this greeting in my own hand. Remember my chains. Grace be with you.

ᵃ 8 Some manuscripts *that he may know about your*

Be KIND

"Try to get along." "Be nice to each other." These words are timeless . . . and Biblical! Grandmothers have been using those Bible-based expressions for years, perhaps without knowing their source. In fact, kindness is at the heart of Paul's letter to the Christians in Thessalonica.

This short letter contains the basic ingredients found in almost all of Paul's letters — encouragement, news and advice. Paul talked about life and death in Christ, giving Christians of all times hope for the present and the future. He also related news about his present circumstances. In chapter 5 he packed a lot into every word of advice, urging his readers to live in readiness for the coming of Christ and encouraging them to live righteously each day as they wait. He exhorted his readers to "live in peace with each other . . . encourage the timid . . . help the weak, [and] be patient with everyone" (1 Thessalonians 5:13 – 14).

Within every family there are misunderstandings and differences. And often grandmothers wish that "everyone could just get along." Paul's words remind us that kindness is a key ingredient in resolving conflicts within our families and communities. So the next time you instruct your family to "be kind," remember that they are words of wisdom rooted in God's Word.

VERSE *to* REMEMBER | 1 THESSALONIANS 5:15

Make sure that nobody pays back wrong for wrong, but always try to be kind to each other and to everyone else.

ABOUT 1 THESSALONIANS

WRITTEN BY:
The apostle Paul

WRITTEN FOR:
The Christians in Thessalonica

DATE WRITTEN:
About A.D. 51 from Corinth

WHY WRITTEN:
To teach the Christians in Thessalonica how to please God

1

Paul, Silas[a] and Timothy,

To the church of the Thessalonians in God the Father and the Lord Jesus Christ:

Grace and peace to you.[b]

Thanksgiving for the Thessalonians' Faith

[2] We always thank God for all of you, mentioning you in our prayers. [3] We continually remember before our God and Father your work produced by faith, your labor prompted by love, and your endurance inspired by hope in our Lord Jesus Christ.

[4] For we know, brothers loved by God, that he has chosen you, [5] because our gospel came to you not simply with words, but also with power, with the Holy Spirit and with deep conviction. You know how we lived among you for your sake. [6] You became imitators of us and of the Lord; in spite of severe suffering, you welcomed the message with the joy given by the Holy Spirit. [7] And so you became a model to all the believers in Macedonia and Achaia. [8] The Lord's message rang out from you not only in Macedonia and Achaia—your faith in God has become known everywhere. Therefore we do not need to say anything about it, [9] for they themselves report what kind of reception you gave us. They tell how you turned to God from idols to serve the living and true God, [10] and to wait for his Son from heaven, whom he raised from the dead—Jesus, who rescues us from the coming wrath.

Paul's Ministry in Thessalonica

2

You know, brothers, that our visit to you was not a failure. [2] We had previously suffered and been insulted in Philippi, as you know, but with the help of our God we dared to tell you his gospel in spite of strong opposition. [3] For the appeal we make does not spring from error or impure motives, nor are we trying to trick you. [4] On the contrary, we speak as men approved by God to be entrusted with the gospel. We are not trying to please men but God, who tests our hearts.

[5] You know we never used flattery, nor did we put on a mask to cover up greed—God is our witness. [6] We were not looking for praise from men, not from you or anyone else.

As apostles of Christ we could have been a burden to you, [7] but we were gentle among you, like a mother caring for her little children. [8] We loved you so much that we were delighted to share with you not only the gospel of God but our lives as well, because you had become so dear to us. [9] Surely you remember, brothers, our toil and hardship; we worked night and day in order not to be a burden to anyone while we preached the gospel of God to you.

[10] You are witnesses, and so is God, of how holy, righteous and blameless we were among you who believed. [11] For you know that we dealt with each of you as a father deals with his own children, [12] encouraging, comforting and urging you to live lives worthy of God, who calls you into his kingdom and glory.

[13] And we also thank God continually because, when you received the word of God, which you heard from us, you accepted it not as the word of men, but as it actually is, the word of God, which is at work in you who believe. [14] For you, brothers, became imitators of God's churches in Judea,

---

[a] 1 Greek *Silvanus*, a variant of *Silas*   [b] 1 Some early manuscripts *you from God our Father and the Lord Jesus Christ*

PRAYING THE SCRIPTURES

Thankfulness
1 THESSALONIANS 2:13

God, I thank you continually because, when my grandchild received your Word, which she heard from me, she accepted it not as my words, but as it actually is: the Word of God, which is at work in her because she believes.

Next prayer in Thankfulness Prayer Track: Revelation 7:12

YOU BECAME IMITATORS OF US AND OF THE
LORD; IN SPITE OF SEVERE SUFFERING, YOU
WELCOMED THE MESSAGE WITH THE JOY
GIVEN BY THE HOLY SPIRIT. AND SO YOU
BECAME A MODEL TO ALL THE BELIEVERS IN
MACEDONIA AND ACHAIA . . . YOUR FAITH
IN GOD HAS BECOME KNOWN EVERYWHERE.

1 Thessalonians 1:6 – 8

A Dose of Cod Liver Oil

KAREN MAINS

READ | 1 THESSALONIANS 1:1 – 10

When I was a little girl, my mother used to give me a dose of cod liver oil every morning. I can't remember specifically how Mother justified giving a small child this vile-tasting stuff. She probably said to me, "Karen Sue, it's good for you."

A nutritional health newsletter I receive informs me that polyunsaturated fish oils have always had a stellar reputation. "Three new studies showed that the omega – 3 fats in fish oil protected people from sudden death," it reports. Healthy women who ate fish at least five times a week had a 45 percent lower risk of dying of heart disease over the next 16 years than healthy women who ate fish less than once a month.

See, my mother was right: Her tablespoonful of cod liver oil *was* good for me.

All of us need a daily dose of oil — both physically and spiritually. Think about the people who provide your daily "dose" as they help you increase your spiritual hunger. They may be dead — saints whose lives and passion for God have stirred members of Christ's church through the centuries — or they may be folks you knew earlier in your life but with whom you've now lost connection.

Yet whoever they are (or were) and wherever they lived, being in their presence was like being bathed in the anointing oil of God. They turned your mind toward heavenly things. Their faith was astounding and practiced daily. Joy overflowed from them despite their circumstances. You wanted to be with them more because being with them made you want to be with God more. Maybe you're not as hungry for God as you should be because you need a dose of this holy oil.

Spend time with a holy friend. It's really good for you.

Lord, I pray that you will help me receive doses of the right kind of oil — your servants who have a passion for you — to make me spiritually healthy. Amen.

Your next devotion is located on page 1645.

GRANDCHILD IN FOCUS · PRAYER

SELECT ONE OF YOUR
GRANDCHILDREN TO FOCUS ON
IN PRAYER FOR THE NEXT 14 DAYS.

Salvation

Dear Lord, please guide my grandchild to your gift of salvation. I pray that she will come to know you, to love you and to walk close to you throughout her life. May she boldly claim Jesus as her Lord and Savior. Guide her as she makes choices that have eternal consequences. Help her to follow you each moment of her life. I pray this in Jesus' name, amen.

1643

which are in Christ Jesus: You suffered from your own countrymen the same things those churches suffered from the Jews, ¹⁵who killed the Lord Jesus and the prophets and also drove us out. They displease God and are hostile to all men ¹⁶in their effort to keep us from speaking to the Gentiles so that they may be saved. In this way they always heap up their sins to the limit. The wrath of God has come upon them at last.ᵃ

Paul's Longing to See the Thessalonians

¹⁷But, brothers, when we were torn away from you for a short time (in person, not in thought), out of our intense longing we made every effort to see you. ¹⁸For we wanted to come to you—certainly I, Paul, did, again and again—but Satan stopped us. ¹⁹For what is our hope, our joy, or the crown in which we will glory in the presence of our Lord Jesus when he comes? Is it not you? ²⁰Indeed, you are our glory and joy.

3 So when we could stand it no longer, we thought it best to be left by ourselves in Athens. ²We sent Timothy, who is our brother and God's fellow workerᵇ in spreading the gospel of Christ, to strengthen and encourage you in your faith, ³so that no one would be unsettled by these trials. You know quite well that we were destined for them. ⁴In fact, when we were with you, we kept telling you that we would be persecuted. And it turned out that way, as you well know. ⁵For this reason, when I could stand it no longer, I sent to find out about your faith. I was afraid that in some way the tempter might have tempted you and our efforts might have been useless.

Timothy's Encouraging Report

⁶But Timothy has just now come to us from you and has brought good news about your faith and love. He has told us that you always have pleasant memories of us and that you long to see us, just as we also long to see you. ⁷Therefore, brothers, in all our distress and persecution we were encouraged about you because of your faith. ⁸For now we really live, since you are standing firm in the Lord. ⁹How can we thank God enough for

you in return for all the joy we have in the presence of our God because of you? ¹⁰Night and day we pray most earnestly that we may see you again and supply what is lacking in your faith.

¹¹Now may our God and Father himself and our Lord Jesus clear the way for us to come to you. ¹²May the Lord make your love increase and overflow for each other and for everyone else, just as ours does for you. ¹³May he strengthen your hearts so that you will be blameless and holy in the presence of our God and Father when our Lord Jesus comes with all his holy ones.

Living to Please God

4 Finally, brothers, we instructed you how to live in order to please God, as in fact you are living. Now we ask you and urge you in the Lord Jesus to do this more and more. ²For you know what instructions we gave you by the authority of the Lord Jesus.

³It is God's will that you should be sanctified: that you should avoid sexual immorality; ⁴that each of you should learn to control his own bodyᶜ in a way that is holy and honorable, ⁵not in passionate lust like the heathen, who do not know God; ⁶and that in this matter no one should wrong his brother or take advantage of him. The Lord will punish men for all such sins, as we have already told you and warned you. ⁷For God did not call us to be impure, but to live a holy life. ⁸Therefore, he who rejects this instruction does

ᵃ 16 Or *them fully*   ᵇ 2 Some manuscripts *brother and fellow worker*; other manuscripts *brother and God's servant*   ᶜ 4 Or *learn to live with his own wife*; or *learn to acquire a wife*

TALKING POINTS

Sexuality

We are to control our sexual passions.

1 THESSALONIANS 4:3–6

For more on sexuality, go to Hebrews 4:14–16.

We were gentle among you, like a mother caring for her little children.

1 Thessalonians 2:7

Caring and Leading

FLORENCE LITTAUER

READ | 1 THESSALONIANS 2:1–16

As my four-year-old granddaughter and I sat on the sofa watching *Cinderella,* Lianna began to play with my hand. She stroked the back of my hand and asked, "What are these things?" "Those are wrinkles," I replied. "Wrinkles? I don't have any of those," she said, examining her own hand. She put my hand next to hers, studied them both and looked up at me. With a serious expression she stated firmly, "You are OLD!"

Before I could say anything, her mother called out, "Don't say that to Grammy. She isn't old." Lianna looked toward her mother and repeatedly loudly, "She *is* old!"

There was no point in trying to change her mind, so I agreed with her, and we went back to *Cinderella.* Later I got an idea on how to turn this child's candid observation into a positive lesson. When we go out to lunch and I let Lianna out of her car seat, she leaps out and bolts across the parking lot toward the restaurant. She always wants to be first, especially in line at McDonald's.

Before we went out the next time, I sat down with Lianna and said, "You were right when you said I was old, so I really need your help." I explained that when we grandmothers get old, we don't see well, and we need a young person to lead us and watch out for us. She warmed up to this idea immediately. On our next trip, she undid her seat belt, dropped to the curb, reached for my hand and said, "I'll take care of you." She led me across the parking lot, looking both ways for cars.

I have become her responsibility instead of her being mine, and she loves it. I'm still next to her and alert to potential problems, but *she* is in control.

Dear Lord Jesus, help me to teach responsibility to my little ones and to thank them for any maturity and caring they demonstrate. Give me a sense of balance between being overly protective and putting too much responsibility on them at an early age. As you, Jesus, care for me, may I care for my little ones and become a beacon of your love and kindness. Amen.

GRANDCHILD IN FOCUS • PRAYER

Physical Well-Being

Almighty God, Creator of us all, I pray that you will watch over my grandchild's physical development. May he grow in strength through the stages of his life. As he grows in awareness of his body, help him to understand that each body develops uniquely, yet is within your plan and your control. Please guard his health so that his diseases are few, his injuries are minor and his infirmities are brief. Amen.

Your next devotion is located on page 1647.

not reject man but God, who gives you his Holy Spirit.

⁹Now about brotherly love we do not need to write to you, for you yourselves have been taught by God to love each other. ¹⁰And in fact, you do love all the brothers throughout Macedonia. Yet we urge you, brothers, to do so more and more. ¹¹Make it your ambition to lead a quiet life, to mind your own business and to work with your hands, just as we told you, ¹²so that your daily life may win the respect of outsiders and so that you will not be dependent on anybody.

The Coming of the Lord

¹³Brothers, we do not want you to be ignorant about those who fall asleep, or to grieve like the rest of men, who have no hope. ¹⁴We believe that Jesus died and rose again and so we believe that God will bring with Jesus those who have fallen asleep in him. ¹⁵According to the Lord's own word, we tell you that we who are still alive, who are left till the coming of the Lord, will certainly not precede those who have fallen asleep. ¹⁶For the Lord himself will come down from heaven, with a loud command, with the voice of the archangel and with the trumpet call of God, and the dead in Christ will rise first. ¹⁷After that, we who are still alive and are left will be caught up together with them in the clouds to meet the Lord in the air. And so we will be with the Lord forever. ¹⁸Therefore encourage each other with these words.

5 Now, brothers, about times and dates we do not need to write to you, ²for you know very well that the day of the Lord will come like a thief in the night. ³While people are saying, "Peace and safety," destruction will come on them suddenly, as labor pains on a pregnant woman, and they will not escape.

⁴But you, brothers, are not in darkness so that this day should surprise you like a thief. ⁵You are all sons of the light and sons of the day. We do not belong to the night or to the darkness. ⁶So then, let us not be like others, who are asleep, but let us be alert and self-controlled. ⁷For those who

stories to share

1 THESSALONIANS 4:13—5:11

Jesus Is Coming Again

LIFE LESSON: Jesus will return.

TO TALK ABOUT

- What does Paul say will happen to believers who are alive when Jesus returns?

- Does God want us to know the exact day when that will happen? Why or why not?

- Why can believers face Christ's return with joy instead of fear?

- Are you looking forward to that day? Why or why not?

sleep, sleep at night, and those who get drunk, get drunk at night. ⁸But since we belong to the day, let us be self-controlled, putting on faith and love as a breastplate, and the hope of salvation as a helmet. ⁹For God did not appoint us to suffer wrath but to receive salvation through our Lord Jesus Christ. ¹⁰He died for us so that, whether we are awake or asleep, we may live together with him. ¹¹Therefore encourage one another and build each other up, just as in fact you are doing.

Final Instructions

¹²Now we ask you, brothers, to respect those who work hard among you, who are over you in the Lord and who admonish you. ¹³Hold them in

Praying Continually and With Camel Knees!

SUE BUCHANAN

READ | 1 THESSALONIANS 5:12 – 28

When my daughter Dana was first diagnosed with breast cancer, my dearest friend, Deb, ended her email to me with these words: "I have camel knees for you."

Camel knees? Camel knees? I didn't get it. I emailed back: "Whut?"

"Around the clock! 24/7! You and Dana are on my mind in prayer continually," she responded. I still didn't get the camel part.

The phone rang. Deb, of course.

"Duh!" she said. "Don't you get it?" She was laughing. "*I'm wearing out my knees!* Get it? I'm on my knees so much they've become wrinkled and gnarled! Like a camel's!"

I'd never seen a camel up close, but I got it. And Dana got it too.

All through Dana's treatment, it seemed we were being reminded about Deb's knees. It often turned a somber mood into a lighter one. And it diverted our thoughts from the c-word.

At Christmastime, Dana and I had a bright idea. We visited Target and bought a line of bath products that could easily have the labels changed. And thanks to the art program on the computer — which just happened to have a magnificent camel stowed in its archives — we were able to present Deb with her own very professional-looking line of Camel Knee products. Soaks, creams, body wash, gels and bubble bath. "Made with pure camel butter," said our modified labels.

For me, words sometimes just don't sink in, but if I can paint a visual picture, I rarely forget something. All the better if there is a camel and a tad of humor attached. Now when we want to assure each other that we are praying continually, we simply say "Camel knees!"

Dear God, help me be creative in the way I present your truths to the children and grandchildren in my charge. As I pray for those I love, give me camel knees of my own! Amen.

Your next devotion is located on page 1651.

GRANDCHILD IN FOCUS • PRAYER

Emotional Development

O God, Creator of mind and body, I pray that you will give my grandchild emotional health and strength. Where there is anger, bring peace. Where there is confusion, bring clarity and focus. Where there are dark shadows, cast a ray of hope. Fill her with the sunshine of your Spirit. Warm her with the presence of your peace. Amen.

the highest regard in love because of their work. Live in peace with each other. ¹⁴And we urge you, brothers, warn those who are idle, encourage the timid, help the weak, be patient with everyone. ¹⁵Make sure that nobody pays back wrong for wrong, but always try to be kind to each other and to everyone else.

¹⁶Be joyful always; ¹⁷pray continually; ¹⁸give thanks in all circumstances, for this is God's will for you in Christ Jesus.

²³May God himself, the God of peace, sanctify you through and through. May your whole spirit, soul and body be kept blameless at the coming of our Lord Jesus Christ. ²⁴The one who calls you is faithful and he will do it.

²⁵Brothers, pray for us. ²⁶Greet all the brothers with a holy kiss. ²⁷I charge you before the Lord to have this letter read to all the brothers.

²⁸The grace of our Lord Jesus Christ be with you.

TALKING POINTS

Thankfulness

With God's help, we can give thanks in all circumstances.

1 THESSALONIANS 5:18

For more on thankfulness, go to Hebrews 12:28.

PRAYING THE SCRIPTURES

Blessing

1 THESSALONIANS 5:23

I pray, O God, that you, the God of peace, will sanctify my grandchild through and through. May his whole spirit, soul and body be kept blameless at the coming of our Lord Jesus Christ.

Next prayer in Blessing Prayer Track:
2 Thessalonians 3:16

---

¹⁹Do not put out the Spirit's fire; ²⁰do not treat prophecies with contempt. ²¹Test everything. Hold on to the good. ²²Avoid every kind of evil.

2 Thessalonians

The Very BEST PROTECTION

Protection is fundamental to a peaceful lifestyle and to peace of mind. All of us want to know that we are safe. We also want our grandchildren to be safe and protected from people who might harm them, from kids who might taunt them on the playground, from sickness and even from things that "go bump in the night." We want to protect them from all the evils of the world and see that they are treated justly. But our power to protect them has limits. That's why we need to rely on God's presence and protection for them.

Paul assured the Thessalonians that God was their ultimate protection. The believers in Thessalonica were undergoing persecution for their faith, and Paul promised that God saw and cared about their suffering. God would in due course see justice done and reward his children for their perseverance.

This letter was a brief follow-up to the first letter Paul had written to the believers in Thessalonica. He needed to set the record straight concerning the coming of the Lord. He instructed his readers to keep working, to do good, and to be responsible while they waited in hope for Christ's coming. He reminded them that it is in God's time that Jesus will come again. Though no one knows when this will be, it will be glorious. Until then, we are to persevere.

VERSE *to* REMEMBER | 2 THESSALONIANS 3:3

The Lord is faithful, and he will strengthen and protect you from the evil one.

ABOUT 2 THESSALONIANS

WRITTEN BY:
The apostle Paul

WRITTEN FOR:
The Christians in Thessalonica

DATE WRITTEN:
About A.D. 51 or 52 from Corinth

WHY WRITTEN:
To encourage Christians to continue working hard until Christ comes again

1

Paul, Silas[a] and Timothy,

To the church of the Thessalonians in God our Father and the Lord Jesus Christ:

[2] Grace and peace to you from God the Father and the Lord Jesus Christ.

Thanksgiving and Prayer

[3] We ought always to thank God for you, brothers, and rightly so, because your faith is growing more and more, and the love every one of you has for each other is increasing. [4] Therefore, among God's churches we boast about your perseverance and faith in all the persecutions and trials you are enduring.

[5] All this is evidence that God's judgment is right, and as a result you will be counted worthy of the kingdom of God, for which you are suffering. [6] God is just: He will pay back trouble to those who trouble you [7] and give relief to you who are troubled, and to us as well. This will happen when the Lord Jesus is revealed from heaven in blazing fire with his powerful angels. [8] He will punish those who do not know God and do not obey the gospel of our Lord Jesus. [9] They will be punished with everlasting destruction and shut out from the presence of the Lord and from the majesty of his power [10] on the day he comes to be glorified in his holy people and to be marveled at among all those who have believed. This includes you, because you believed our testimony to you.

[11] With this in mind, we constantly pray for you, that our God may count you worthy of his calling, and that by his power he may fulfill every good purpose of yours and every act prompted by your faith. [12] We pray this so that the name of our Lord Jesus may be glorified in you, and you in him, according to the grace of our God and the Lord Jesus Christ.[b]

The Man of Lawlessness

2

Concerning the coming of our Lord Jesus Christ and our being gathered to him, we ask you, brothers, [2] not to become easily unsettled or alarmed by some prophecy, report or letter supposed to have come from us, saying that the day of the Lord has already come. [3] Don't let anyone deceive you in any way, for ⌊that day will not come⌋ until the rebellion occurs and the man of lawlessness[c] is revealed, the man doomed to destruction. [4] He will oppose and will exalt himself over everything that is called God or is worshiped, so that he sets himself up in God's temple, proclaiming himself to be God.

[5] Don't you remember that when I was with you I used to tell you these things? [6] And now you know what is holding him back, so that he may be revealed at the proper time. [7] For the secret power of lawlessness is already at work; but the one who now holds it back will continue to do so till he is taken out of the way. [8] And then the lawless one will be revealed, whom the Lord Jesus will overthrow with the breath of his mouth and destroy by the splendor of his coming. [9] The coming of the lawless one will be in accordance with the work of Satan displayed in all kinds of counterfeit miracles, signs and wonders, [10] and in every sort of evil that deceives those who are perishing. They perish because they refused to love the truth and so be saved. [11] For this reason God sends them a powerful delusion so that they will believe the lie [12] and so that all will be condemned who have not believed the truth but have delighted in wickedness.

Stand Firm

[13] But we ought always to thank God for you, brothers loved by the Lord, because from the beginning God chose you[d] to be saved through the sanctifying work of the Spirit and through belief in the truth. [14] He called you to this through our gospel, that you might share in the glory of our Lord Jesus Christ. [15] So then, brothers, stand firm and hold to the teachings[e] we passed on to you, whether by word of mouth or by letter.

[16] May our Lord Jesus Christ himself and God our Father, who loved us and by his grace gave us eternal encouragement and good hope,

---

[a] 1 Greek *Silvanus*, a variant of *Silas*   [b] 12 Or *God and Lord, Jesus Christ*   [c] 3 Some manuscripts *sin*   [d] 13 Some manuscripts *because God chose you as his firstfruits*   [e] 15 Or *traditions*

With this in mind, we constantly pray for you, that our God may count you worthy of his calling, and that by his power he may fulfill every good purpose of yours and every act prompted by your faith.

2 Thessalonians 1:11

The Pickle Party

CAROL KENT

READ | 2 THESSALONIANS 1:1–12

We were delighted that our hotel lived up to the description in the brochure. "Grammy," Hannah exclaimed, "there's a bathtub big enough to be a pool in your bedroom! Let's go swimming!"

The next day we donned our swimming suits and filled the tub with water. I stacked pickles on a plate, and we called our Jacuzzi outing "The Pickle Party." In between our chatter, we took turns picking dill pickles off the plate as we munched our way through the next hour.

"Hannah," I said, "what's the best part of today?"

Her response was right on: "Talking to each other about being a woman is *definitely* the best part of today."

"How do you think I can help you best, Hannah?" I asked.

"Well," she said, admiring her image in the big mirror next to the tub, "I think you can teach me how to be a good mom."

"Hannah," I said, "Grammy's been praying for your future husband."

Her eyes grew big, and she laughed. "It's too early to pray for my husband, Grammy. I'm just a kid."

I piled soapy hair on top of her head in a coiffure as I said, "It's never too early to pray about whom you're going to marry. It's one of the most important decisions of your life."

"Well, that's not going to happen for a long time," she stated emphatically, "but thanks for praying for me." Then, chomping down on her sixth dill pickle, she abruptly decided we had taken enough time for adult discussion, and it was time to play. We made a memory that day — Grammy and Hannah — as we had a pickle party while talking about growing up and the necessity of prayer.

Father, thank you for the opportunity I have to pray for my grandchildren in the area of your design for marriage and family. Help me to use every opportunity to instill your principles into our conversations, so living a life based on your Word becomes natural for my grandchildren to live. Amen.

Your next devotion is located on page 1656.

GRANDCHILD IN FOCUS • PRAYER

Spiritual Growth

Dear Lord, today I pray for my grandchild's spiritual growth. I ask that you instill in him the desire to read and memorize your Word. Give him a passion to be in conversation with you. May loving and serving you be part of his daily life. I ask that you stay close to him and lead him to be transformed to your likeness, to reflect your grace and to radiate your love. I pray this in Jesus' name, amen.

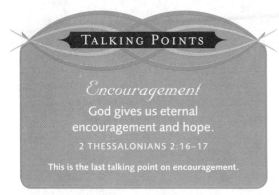

TALKING POINTS

Encouragement
God gives us eternal
encouragement and hope.
2 THESSALONIANS 2:16–17

This is the last talking point on encouragement.

[17] encourage your hearts and strengthen you in every good deed and word.

Request for Prayer

3 Finally, brothers, pray for us that the message of the Lord may spread rapidly and be honored, just as it was with you. [2] And pray that we may be delivered from wicked and evil men, for not everyone has faith. [3] But the Lord is faithful, and he will strengthen and protect you from the evil one. [4] We have confidence in the Lord that you are doing and will continue to do the things we command. [5] May the Lord direct your hearts into God's love and Christ's perseverance.

PRAYING THE SCRIPTURES

Protection
2 THESSALONIANS 3:3,5
I thank you, O Lord, that you are faithful to my grandchild. Strengthen and protect him from the evil one. Direct his heart, I pray, into your love and Christ's perseverance.

This is the last prayer in the Protection Prayer Track.

Warning Against Idleness

[6] In the name of the Lord Jesus Christ, we command you, brothers, to keep away from every brother who is idle and does not live according to the teaching[a] you received from us. [7] For you yourselves know how you ought to follow our example. We were not idle when we were with you, [8] nor did we eat anyone's food without paying for it. On the contrary, we worked night and day, laboring and toiling so that we would not be a burden to any of you. [9] We did this, not because we do not have the right to such help, but in order to make ourselves a model for you to follow. [10] For even when we were with you, we gave you this rule: "If a man will not work, he shall not eat."

[11] We hear that some among you are idle. They are not busy; they are busybodies. [12] Such people we command and urge in the Lord Jesus Christ to settle down and earn the bread they eat. [13] And as for you, brothers, never tire of doing what is right.

[14] If anyone does not obey our instruction in this letter, take special note of him. Do not associate with him, in order that he may feel ashamed. [15] Yet do not regard him as an enemy, but warn him as a brother.

Final Greetings

[16] Now may the Lord of peace himself give you peace at all times and in every way. The Lord be with all of you.

[17] I, Paul, write this greeting in my own hand, which is the distinguishing mark in all my letters. This is how I write.

[18] The grace of our Lord Jesus Christ be with you all.

[a] 6 Or *tradition*

PRAYING THE SCRIPTURES

Blessing
2 THESSALONIANS 3:16
O Lord of peace, give peace to my grandchild at all times and in every way. And be with her always.

Next prayer in Blessing Prayer Track: Hebrews 13:20

A Living EXAMPLE

Paul was a missionary, a writer and a mentor to young leaders of the church. He wrote two letters to his young protégé Timothy to encourage and instruct him in his role as a new pastor to the church in Ephesus. Paul called Timothy his "true son in the faith" (1 Timothy 1:2). Within that close bond of trust, Paul exhorted Timothy to "fight the good fight of the faith" (1 Timothy 6:12). Although Timothy was younger than many in the church he was pastoring, he was to lead by example. His life was to be a model for all the young men of the church — a pattern of faith and a pure life.

Paul's instruction to Timothy to set a good example is intended for all Christians. Our lives should be shining illustrations of what it means to live lives rooted in Christ. The next generation needs guidance and wisdom to find its way in our complex and often dissolute society. Our example of Christian love, values and virtues — as seen in our speech and actions — can give hope and promise to those with which we interact.

Like Paul, we too can be mentors to the next generation of church leaders. They need to hear our words of encouragement and praise, and our "trustworthy sayings" (see 1 Timothy 1:15; 3:1; 4:9 – 10). And if they are anything like Timothy, it's very likely that we will learn from them as well.

VERSE *to* REMEMBER | 1 TIMOTHY 4:12

Don't let anyone look down on you because you are young, but set an example for the believers in speech, in life, in love, in faith and in purity.

ABOUT 1 TIMOTHY

WRITTEN BY:
The apostle Paul

WRITTEN FOR:
Timothy, Paul's helper and friend

DATE WRITTEN:
Probably about A.D. 64 from Macedonia

WHY WRITTEN:
To give Timothy advice on how to do his important work

1 Paul, an apostle of Christ Jesus by the command of God our Savior and of Christ Jesus our hope,

[2] To Timothy my true son in the faith:

Grace, mercy and peace from God the Father and Christ Jesus our Lord.

Warning Against False Teachers of the Law

[3] As I urged you when I went into Macedonia, stay there in Ephesus so that you may command certain men not to teach false doctrines any longer [4] nor to devote themselves to myths and endless genealogies. These promote controversies rather than God's work—which is by faith. [5] The goal of this command is love, which comes from a pure heart and a good conscience and a sincere faith. [6] Some have wandered away from these and turned to meaningless talk. [7] They want to be teachers of the law, but they do not know what they are talking about or what they so confidently affirm.

[8] We know that the law is good if one uses it properly. [9] We also know that law[a] is made not for the righteous but for lawbreakers and rebels, the ungodly and sinful, the unholy and irreligious; for those who kill their fathers or mothers, for murderers, [10] for adulterers and perverts, for slave traders and liars and perjurers—and for whatever else is contrary to the sound doctrine [11] that conforms to the glorious gospel of the blessed God, which he entrusted to me.

The Lord's Grace to Paul

[12] I thank Christ Jesus our Lord, who has given me strength, that he considered me faithful, appointing me to his service. [13] Even though I was once a blasphemer and a persecutor and a violent man, I was shown mercy because I acted in ignorance and unbelief. [14] The grace of our Lord was poured out on me abundantly, along with the faith and love that are in Christ Jesus.

[15] Here is a trustworthy saying that deserves full acceptance: Christ Jesus came into the world to save sinners—of whom I am the worst. [16] But for that very reason I was shown mercy so that in me, the worst of sinners, Christ Jesus might display his unlimited patience as an example for those who would believe on him and receive eternal life. [17] Now to the King eternal, immortal, invisible, the only God, be honor and glory for ever and ever. Amen.

[18] Timothy, my son, I give you this instruction in keeping with the prophecies once made about you, so that by following them you may fight the good fight, [19] holding on to faith and a good conscience. Some have rejected these and so have shipwrecked their faith. [20] Among them are Hymenaeus and Alexander, whom I have handed over to Satan to be taught not to blaspheme.

Instructions on Worship

2 I urge, then, first of all, that requests, prayers, intercession and thanksgiving be made for everyone— [2] for kings and all those in authority, that we may live peaceful and quiet lives in all godliness and holiness. [3] This is good, and pleases God our Savior, [4] who wants all men to be saved and to come to a knowledge of the truth. [5] For there is one God and one mediator between God and men, the man Christ Jesus, [6] who gave himself as a ransom for all men—the testimony given in its proper time. [7] And for this purpose I was appointed a herald and an apostle—I am telling the truth, I am not lying—and a teacher of the true faith to the Gentiles.

[8] I want men everywhere to lift up holy hands in prayer, without anger or disputing.

[9] I also want women to dress modestly, with decency and propriety, not with braided hair or gold or pearls or expensive clothes, [10] but with good deeds, appropriate for women who profess to worship God.

[11] A woman should learn in quietness and full submission. [12] I do not permit a woman to teach or to have authority over a man; she must be silent. [13] For Adam was formed first, then Eve. [14] And Adam was not the one deceived; it was the woman who was deceived and became a sinner.

[a] 9 Or that the law

¹⁵But women [a] will be saved [b] through childbearing—if they continue in faith, love and holiness with propriety.

Overseers and Deacons

3 Here is a trustworthy saying: If anyone sets his heart on being an overseer,[c] he desires a noble task. ²Now the overseer must be above reproach, the husband of but one wife, temperate, self-controlled, respectable, hospitable, able to teach, ³not given to drunkenness, not violent but gentle, not quarrelsome, not a lover of money. ⁴He must manage his own family well and see that his children obey him with proper respect. ⁵(If anyone does not know how to manage his own family, how can he take care of God's church?) ⁶He must not be a recent convert, or he may become conceited and fall under the same judgment as the devil. ⁷He must also have a good reputation with outsiders, so that he will not fall into disgrace and into the devil's trap.

⁸Deacons, likewise, are to be men worthy of respect, sincere, not indulging in much wine, and not pursuing dishonest gain. ⁹They must keep hold of the deep truths of the faith with a clear conscience. ¹⁰They must first be tested; and then if there is nothing against them, let them serve as deacons.

¹¹In the same way, their wives [d] are to be women worthy of respect, not malicious talkers but temperate and trustworthy in everything.

¹²A deacon must be the husband of but one wife and must manage his children and his household well. ¹³Those who have served well gain an excellent standing and great assurance in their faith in Christ Jesus.

¹⁴Although I hope to come to you soon, I am writing you these instructions so that, ¹⁵if I am delayed, you will know how people ought to conduct themselves in God's household, which is the church of the living God, the pillar and foundation of the truth. ¹⁶Beyond all question, the mystery of godliness is great:

He [e] appeared in a body,[f]
was vindicated by the Spirit,
was seen by angels,
was preached among the nations,
was believed on in the world,
was taken up in glory.

Instructions to Timothy

4 The Spirit clearly says that in later times some will abandon the faith and follow deceiving spirits and things taught by demons. ²Such teachings come through hypocritical liars, whose consciences have been seared as with a hot iron. ³They forbid people to marry and order them to abstain from certain foods, which God created to be received with thanksgiving by those who believe and who know the truth. ⁴For everything God created is good, and nothing is to be rejected if it is received with thanksgiving, ⁵because it is consecrated by the word of God and prayer.

⁶If you point these things out to the brothers, you will be a good minister of Christ Jesus, brought up in the truths of the faith and of the good teaching that you have followed. ⁷Have nothing to do with godless myths and old wives' tales; rather, train yourself to be godly. ⁸For physical training is of some value, but godliness has value for all things, holding promise for both the present life and the life to come.

⁹This is a trustworthy saying that deserves full acceptance ¹⁰(and for this we labor and strive), that we have put our hope in the living God, who is the Savior of all men, and especially of those who believe.

¹¹Command and teach these things. ¹²Don't let anyone look down on you because you are young, but set an example for the believers in speech, in life, in love, in faith and in purity. ¹³Until I come, devote yourself to the public reading of Scripture, to preaching and to teaching. ¹⁴Do not neglect your gift, which was given you through a prophetic message when the body of elders laid their hands on you.

---

[a] 15 Greek *she* [b] 15 Or *restored* [c] 1 Traditionally *bishop*; also in verse 2 [d] 11 Or *way, deaconesses* [e] 16 Some manuscripts *God* [f] 16 Or *in the flesh*

FRIDAY

DO NOT NEGLECT YOUR GIFT, WHICH WAS GIVEN YOU THROUGH A PROPHETIC MESSAGE WHEN THE BODY OF ELDERS LAID THEIR HANDS ON YOU.

1 Timothy 4:14

Your Special Gift

DOTTIE RAMBO

READ | 1 TIMOTHY 4:1 – 16

The makeup of what we call family has changed, but not that much. There has always been "extended" family — those who are special additions. I've got three grandchildren like that. But don't you tell me they're not my own, oh no! I believe I have the gift of surrogate grandmothering. And I never take it for granted.

Before Destiny and Israel there was Dionne. She's my stepgrandbaby. Her freckled face could out-shine the sun. She and I would play dolls and run and frolic in the autumn leaves. Her presence in the Rambo home added more love. Now she's a talented lady with a wonderful husband and child of her own. Dyson's my first great-grandbaby!

Then after Destiny and Israel came two babies who have kept me young. Although they have their own grandmothers, Christian and Pierce live close by. They're the two bright boys of my manager, Larry. They have gotten to sing and play silly games with me while they keep on growing. Somehow in the middle of helping keep an eye on them, they entwined themselves into my heart.

That's so like God. While we're busy with our plans, he comes along and taps on our shoulder. He whispers in my ear, "If you could help out with this one . . ." And another one is grafted onto the family tree.

God, while I'm living my day-to-day life, help me to keep my ears open and my gifts at the ready for you. In the precious name of Jesus, amen.

Your next devotion is located on page 1659.

GRANDCHILD IN FOCUS • PRAYER

Relationships at Home

O Lord, I pray that you will bless the home and family of my grandchild. May the relationships she has with her parents and siblings enhance her well-being, support her self-confidence and increase her faith. May her home life reflect your love, your grace, your compassion and your peace. Guide her parents to direct her in love and truth, so she will grow into a strong and compassionate individual. Amen.

TALKING POINTS

Dating

No matter what our age,
we are to set an example for others
in speech, life, love, faith and purity.

1 TIMOTHY 4:12

For more on dating, go to 2 Timothy 2:22.

[15] Be diligent in these matters; give yourself wholly to them, so that everyone may see your progress. [16] Watch your life and doctrine closely. Persevere in them, because if you do, you will save both yourself and your hearers.

Advice About Widows, Elders and Slaves

5 Do not rebuke an older man harshly, but exhort him as if he were your father. Treat younger men as brothers, [2] older women as mothers, and younger women as sisters, with absolute purity.

[3] Give proper recognition to those widows who are really in need. [4] But if a widow has children or grandchildren, these should learn first of all to put their religion into practice by caring for their own family and so repaying their parents and grandparents, for this is pleasing to God. [5] The widow who is really in need and left all alone puts her hope in God and continues night and day to pray

TALKING POINTS

Parents

When we care for our parents,
we show our love and faith.

1 TIMOTHY 5:4

This is the last talking point on parents.

and to ask God for help. [6] But the widow who lives for pleasure is dead even while she lives. [7] Give the people these instructions, too, so that no one may be open to blame. [8] If anyone does not provide for his relatives, and especially for his immediate family, he has denied the faith and is worse than an unbeliever.

[9] No widow may be put on the list of widows unless she is over sixty, has been faithful to her husband,[a] [10] and is well known for her good deeds, such as bringing up children, showing hospitality, washing the feet of the saints, helping those in trouble and devoting herself to all kinds of good deeds.

[11] As for younger widows, do not put them on such a list. For when their sensual desires overcome their dedication to Christ, they want to marry. [12] Thus they bring judgment on themselves, because they have broken their first pledge. [13] Besides, they get into the habit of being idle and going about from house to house. And not only do they become idlers, but also gossips and busybodies, saying things they ought not to. [14] So I counsel younger widows to marry, to have children, to manage their homes and to give the enemy no opportunity for slander. [15] Some have in fact already turned away to follow Satan.

[16] If any woman who is a believer has widows in her family, she should help them and not let the church be burdened with them, so that the church can help those widows who are really in need.

[17] The elders who direct the affairs of the church well are worthy of double honor, especially those whose work is preaching and teaching. [18] For the Scripture says, "Do not muzzle the ox while it is treading out the grain,"[b] and "The worker deserves his wages."[c] [19] Do not entertain an accusation against an elder unless it is brought by two or three witnesses. [20] Those who sin are to be rebuked publicly, so that the others may take warning.

[21] I charge you, in the sight of God and Christ Jesus and the elect angels, to keep these instructions

[a] 9 Or *has had but one husband*   [b] 18 Deut. 25:4
[c] 18 Luke 10:7

without partiality, and to do nothing out of favoritism.

²²Do not be hasty in the laying on of hands, and do not share in the sins of others. Keep yourself pure.

²³Stop drinking only water, and use a little wine because of your stomach and your frequent illnesses.

²⁴The sins of some men are obvious, reaching the place of judgment ahead of them; the sins of others trail behind them. ²⁵In the same way, good deeds are obvious, and even those that are not cannot be hidden.

6 All who are under the yoke of slavery should consider their masters worthy of full respect, so that God's name and our teaching may not be slandered. ²Those who have believing masters are not to show less respect for them because they are brothers. Instead, they are to serve them even better, because those who benefit from their service are believers, and dear to them. These are the things you are to teach and urge on them.

Love of Money

³If anyone teaches false doctrines and does not agree to the sound instruction of our Lord Jesus Christ and to godly teaching, ⁴he is conceited and understands nothing. He has an unhealthy interest in controversies and quarrels about words that result in envy, strife, malicious talk, evil suspicions ⁵and constant friction between men of corrupt mind, who have been robbed of the truth and who think that godliness is a means to financial gain.

⁶But godliness with contentment is great gain. ⁷For we brought nothing into the world, and we can take nothing out of it. ⁸But if we have food and clothing, we will be content with that. ⁹People who want to get rich fall into temptation and a trap and into many foolish and harmful desires that plunge men into ruin and destruction. ¹⁰For the love of money is a root of all kinds of evil. Some people, eager for money, have wandered from the faith and pierced themselves with many griefs.

TALKING POINTS

Money

Loving money leads to evil.

1 TIMOTHY 6:6–10

This is the last talking point on money.

Paul's Charge to Timothy

¹¹But you, man of God, flee from all this, and pursue righteousness, godliness, faith, love, endurance and gentleness. ¹²Fight the good fight of the faith. Take hold of the eternal life to which you were called when you made your

stories to share

1 TIMOTHY 6:17–19

Riches That Count for Eternity

LIFE LESSON: The kinds of riches that matter are good deeds and generosity.

TO TALK ABOUT

✦ What attitude does Paul want rich people to take toward their wealth?

✦ What temptations do rich people face? (Hint: See 1 Timothy 6:6–10.)

✦ What kinds of riches really matter?

✦ What treasure have you deposited in heaven?

LET'S TALK

I Believe In...

Everybody believes in something or somebody. Get your grandkids thinking and talking about what they really believe in. Start out in neutral territory that is age appropriate. For the younger kids you might say, "I believe in the magic of fairy tales." They might say, "I believe in the tooth fairy" or "I believe that Mommy loves me." To encourage discussion, you can stop at any point and ask them why.

You could start on a different level with your older grandchildren, opening with "I believe in the sanctity of life" or "I believe in being kind to other people." Encourage them to think about what they believe in. At any time you can initiate a discussion of that topic. Their belief in God or the Bible or other religious topics might come naturally once you get into this thought pattern. Or you may have to bring it up with an "I believe" statement of your own. Either way, it is a great way to start and continue a discussion about your faith.

Dear Father in heaven, thank you for the joy of sharing with my grandchildren. Bless this exercise; help us feel comfortable talking about things on our minds and hearts. Help us to freely share all that we believe and be able to talk openly about you. Amen.

Your next devotion is located on page 1660.

GRANDCHILD IN FOCUS • PRAYER

Friends

Dear Lord and Father, I pray for my grandchild's social life and his friends. Bring diverse friends into his life who will love and encourage him, who will bring joy and laughter to the good times and comfort and support through difficulties and disappointments. Grant him wisdom and discernment as he selects his friends; help him to avoid cliques that restrict, activities that endanger, and foolish and dangerous behaviors that harm. I ask that you fill his life with close and caring relationships. Amen.

Worship the Lord

I will exalt you, O LORD,
> for you lifted me out of the depths
> and did not let my enemies gloat over me.
O LORD my God, I called to you for help
> and you healed me.
O LORD, you brought me up from the grave;
> you spared me from going down into the pit.

Sing to the LORD, you saints of his;
> praise his holy name.
For his anger lasts only a moment,
> but his favor lasts a lifetime;
weeping may remain for a night,
> but rejoicing comes in the morning.

Psalm 30:1—5

*I've experienced nights of weeping, Father
—numerous nights over the course of my
life. But refreshment and joy never fail to
take their place. Your favor heals my feelings of confusion and sorrow; your compassion has been the theme of my life.
Thank you for your faithfulness. Amen.*

Your next devotion is located on page 1664.

GRANDCHILD IN FOCUS • PRAYER

Self-Image

*O loving God, I praise you for creating my
grandchild as a unique individual. Now I ask you
to help her appreciate her uniqueness. Build up her
self-image so she can enjoy her individuality. Help
her to stand firm for who she is, where she has
come from and what she believes in. Encourage
her not only to have hopes and dreams but
to also enjoy each day as it comes.
In Jesus' name, amen.*

good confession in the presence of many witnesses. [13] In the sight of God, who gives life to everything, and of Christ Jesus, who while testifying before Pontius Pilate made the good confession, I charge you [14] to keep this command without spot or blame until the appearing of our Lord Jesus Christ, [15] which God will bring about in his own time — God, the blessed and only Ruler, the King of kings and Lord of lords, [16] who alone is immortal and who lives in unapproachable light, whom no one has seen or can see. To him be honor and might forever. Amen.

[17] Command those who are rich in this present world not to be arrogant nor to put their hope in wealth, which is so uncertain, but to put their hope in God, who richly provides us with everything for our enjoyment. [18] Command them to do good, to be rich in good deeds, and to be generous and willing to share. [19] In this way they will lay up treasure for themselves as a firm foundation for the coming age, so that they may take hold of the life that is truly life.

[20] Timothy, guard what has been entrusted to your care. Turn away from godless chatter and the opposing ideas of what is falsely called knowledge, [21] which some have professed and in so doing have wandered from the faith.

Grace be with you.

The Spirit OF POWER

Paul wrote a second letter of encouragement to the young leader Timothy. Paul felt a pressing need to teach this young man how to endure the difficult times and challenging tasks that he and the church would undoubtedly face. Paul told Timothy to be faithful, to keep on keeping on in the faith, to follow, day after day, the "pattern of sound teaching, with faith and love in Christ Jesus" (2 Timothy 1:13).

Although Paul was writing to his young friend Timothy, we too can benefit from his words of encouragement. We may become weary in our struggle to be faithful day after day and year after year. We may be afraid that we are not worthy or qualified to handle the new tasks God asks of us. Have you heard someone protest, "Oh, not me. I can't do that"? It's not humility holding that person back, it's timidity.

Following Jesus is not for the fainthearted, yet Paul reminds us that the Holy Spirit living in us is powerful, loving and self-disciplined. With God's Spirit we can step out in faith and tackle new challenges as they present themselves. We can move forward in confidence, knowing that God will equip us with the right stuff to get the task done.

VERSE to REMEMBER | 2 TIMOTHY 1:7

God did not give us a spirit of timidity, but a spirit of power, of love and of self-discipline.

ABOUT 2 TIMOTHY

WRITTEN BY:
The apostle Paul

WRITTEN FOR:
Timothy, Paul's young helper

DATE WRITTEN:
About A.D. 67

WHY WRITTEN:
To express concern for Timothy and the churches before his life ended

1 Paul, an apostle of Christ Jesus by the will of God, according to the promise of life that is in Christ Jesus,

2 To Timothy, my dear son:

Grace, mercy and peace from God the Father and Christ Jesus our Lord.

Encouragement to Be Faithful

3 I thank God, whom I serve, as my forefathers did, with a clear conscience, as night and day I constantly remember you in my prayers. 4 Recalling your tears, I long to see you, so that I may be filled with joy. 5 I have been reminded of your sincere faith, which first lived in your grandmother Lois and in your mother Eunice and, I am per-suaded, now lives in you also. 6 For this reason I remind you to fan into flame the gift of God, which is in you through the laying on of my hands. 7 For God did not give us a spirit of timidity, but a spirit of power, of love and of self-discipline.

8 So do not be ashamed to testify about our Lord, or ashamed of me his prisoner. But join with me in suffering for the gospel, by the power of God, 9 who has saved us and called us to a holy life — not because of anything we have done but because of his own purpose and grace. This grace was given us in Christ Jesus before the beginning of time, 10 but it has now been revealed through the appearing of our Savior, Christ Jesus, who has destroyed death and has brought life and immortality to light through the gospel. 11 And of this gospel I was appointed a herald and an apostle and a teacher. 12 That is why I am suffering as I am. Yet I am not ashamed, because I know whom I have believed, and am convinced that he is able to guard what I have entrusted to him for that day.

13 What you heard from me, keep as the pattern of sound teaching, with faith and love in Christ Jesus. 14 Guard the good deposit that was entrusted to you — guard it with the help of the Holy Spirit who lives in us.

15 You know that everyone in the province of Asia has deserted me, including Phygelus and Hermogenes.

16 May the Lord show mercy to the household of Onesiphorus, because he often refreshed me and was not ashamed of my chains. 17 On the contrary, when he was in Rome, he searched hard for me until he found me. 18 May the Lord grant that he will find mercy from the Lord on that day! You know very well in how many ways he helped me in Ephesus.

2 You then, my son, be strong in the grace that is in Christ Jesus. 2 And the things you have heard me say in the presence of many witnesses entrust to reliable men who will also be qualified to teach others. 3 Endure hardship with us like a good soldier of Christ Jesus. 4 No one serving as a soldier gets involved in civilian affairs — he

stories to share

2 TIMOTHY 1:1–7

Fan Into Flame the Gift of God

LIFE LESSON: God gives us good gifts to do his work.

TO TALK ABOUT

✦ Who taught Timothy to have faith in God?

✦ What did Paul want Timothy to do?

✦ How can we "fan into flame" the gifts God has given us?

✦ What special gifts has God given you? Do you sometimes feel too timid to use them?

I HAVE BEEN REMINDED OF YOUR
SINCERE FAITH, WHICH FIRST
LIVED IN YOUR GRANDMOTHER
LOIS AND IN YOUR MOTHER
EUNICE AND, I AM PERSUADED,
NOW LIVES IN YOU ALSO.

2 Timothy 1:5

Godly Grandmothers

ROBIN LEE HATCHER

READ | 2 TIMOTHY 1:1 – 18

My dad died when I was an infant, and my widowed grandmother came to live with us so my mom could work. I have lots of memories of Grandma — she was a wonderful storyteller and could entertain children and adults alike for hours. But the predominant memory I have of Grandma is of her sitting in the chair near the fireplace, her big, black and very worn Bible open on her lap. She read it, she knew it and she lived it.

I was too young to realize the importance of Grandma's example to me — she passed away when I was 12 — but as an adult, I've looked back often in thanksgiving for the witness of her faith as well as the witness of my mother's faith.

Now it's my turn to be an example to my grandchildren. I want them to see me living my faith daily, to see my hunger for God's Word, his touch and his voice. I pray that, years from now when they look back and think of me, they will remember the relationship I had with God and be thankful for it. I pray that the legacy of my grandmother's faith will be passed from generation to generation until Christ returns.

Abba, Father, help me to be a godly example to those I love, especially to those in my family. Thank you for the blessing of children and grandchildren. May each one of them and their entire households come to believe in the Lord Jesus. To you, God, be the glory. Amen.

Your next devotion is located on page 1669.

GRANDCHILD IN FOCUS • PRAYER

Protection From Worldliness

O Sovereign Lord, the world surrounds my grandchild, pressing in and tempting him in so many ways. Help him set appropriate limits. Give him sound judgment to choose wisely. Guard him from temptation; protect him from physical and mental predators; lead him into paths of righteousness and light. And reassure me with your promise that you are holding him in your hands. Amen.

wants to please his commanding officer. ⁵Similarly, if anyone competes as an athlete, he does not receive the victor's crown unless he competes according to the rules. ⁶The hardworking farmer should be the first to receive a share of the crops. ⁷Reflect on what I am saying, for the Lord will give you insight into all this.

⁸Remember Jesus Christ, raised from the dead, descended from David. This is my gospel, ⁹for which I am suffering even to the point of being chained like a criminal. But God's word is not chained. ¹⁰Therefore I endure everything for the sake of the elect, that they too may obtain the salvation that is in Christ Jesus, with eternal glory.

¹¹Here is a trustworthy saying:

If we died with him,
    we will also live with him;
¹²if we endure,
    we will also reign with him.
If we disown him,
    he will also disown us;
¹³if we are faithless,
    he will remain faithful,
    for he cannot disown himself.

A Workman Approved by God

¹⁴Keep reminding them of these things. Warn them before God against quarreling about words; it is of no value, and only ruins those who listen. ¹⁵Do your best to present yourself to God as one approved, a workman who does not need to be ashamed and who correctly handles the word of truth. ¹⁶Avoid godless chatter, because those who indulge in it will become more and more ungodly. ¹⁷Their teaching will spread like gangrene. Among them are Hymenaeus and Philetus, ¹⁸who have wandered away from the truth. They say that the resurrection has already taken place, and they destroy the faith of some. ¹⁹Nevertheless, God's solid foundation stands firm, sealed with this inscription: "The Lord knows those who are his,"ᵃ and, "Everyone who confesses the name of the Lord must turn away from wickedness."

²⁰In a large house there are articles not only of gold and silver, but also of wood and clay; some are for noble purposes and some for ignoble. ²¹If a man cleanses himself from the latter, he will be an instrument for noble purposes, made holy, useful to the Master and prepared to do any good work.

²²Flee the evil desires of youth, and pursue righteousness, faith, love and peace, along with those who call on the Lord out of a pure heart. ²³Don't have anything to do with foolish and stupid arguments, because you know they produce quarrels. ²⁴And the Lord's servant must not quarrel; instead, he must be kind to everyone, able to teach, not resentful. ²⁵Those who oppose him he must gently instruct, in the hope that God will grant them repentance leading them to a knowledge of the truth, ²⁶and that they will come to their senses and escape from the trap of the devil, who has taken them captive to do his will.

TALKING POINTS

Dating

Avoid evil desires;
pursue godliness and purity.

2 TIMOTHY 2:22

This is the last talking point on dating.

Godlessness in the Last Days

3 But mark this: There will be terrible times in the last days. ²People will be lovers of themselves, lovers of money, boastful, proud, abusive, disobedient to their parents, ungrateful, unholy, ³without love, unforgiving, slanderous, without self-control, brutal, not lovers of the good, ⁴treacherous, rash, conceited, lovers of pleasure rather than lovers of God— ⁵having a form of godliness but denying its power. Have nothing to do with them.

⁶They are the kind who worm their way into

ᵃ 19 Num. 16:5 (see Septuagint)

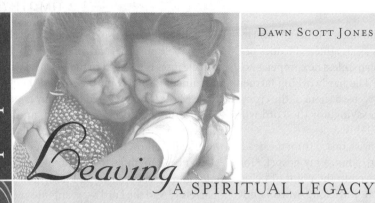

DAWN SCOTT JONES

Leaving A SPIRITUAL LEGACY

A legacy is a gift or inheritance that lives on after we are gone. As grandmothers, God gives us the opportunity to leave something that will endure long after we depart to our heavenly home: a spiritual inheritance.

My grandparents left a legacy for me—not one of natural currency, but one more valuable than earthly riches. I received an inheritance of spiritual wealth that has shaped my life. Now that I am a grandmother, I want to bequeath a spiritual inheritance through my influence that will enrich my grandchildren's lives and strengthen the foundations they will build upon.

By being intentional in the following areas, we grandmothers can be assured that our influence will make a difference and that our lives and love will have a lasting impact.

Impart the Story

As a child, I heard stories—lots of stories! I did not realize it then, but I was in the process of receiving a legacy. Quietly threaded throughout my grandparents' stories was the testimony of God's greatness. I heard about his magnificent miracles. I heard about God's great love and his faithfulness. I was becoming the benefactor of a spiritual heritage through the power of their story—hidden lessons from their past—teaching me the ways, works and Word of God.

We can do the same thing in casual ways. While shopping, doing yard work or washing dishes, we can tell stories of God's faithfulness in our lives. We will bond with our grandkids and impart God's Word at the same time.

Imprint Their Hearts

Another aspect of giving our grandchildren a legacy is imprinting their hearts with memories. An imprint is something that leaves its mark—an impression made firmly on the mind or heart. Our grandchildren will remember their time with us, so let's make the most of it.

Strategically transform common, even painful, events into powerful, pleasant memories by modeling godly character and a positive attitude. Those positive memories — godly marks indelibly imprinted on their young hearts — will be an anchor to truth in adulthood.

Enhance Their Outlook

In today's turbulent culture, it is important for children to have security and stability. Creating meaningful traditions — regular and unique customs between us and our grandchildren — will provide a beautiful backdrop of stability, enhancing their outlook and appreciation for life. Whether decorating a Christmas tree, sending cards on birthdays or taking them on a summer vacation, our consistency sends a message that says, "You are loved, valued and special."

Impact Their Life

To *impact* means to influence or affect someone to the point of moving them from one place to another. Our spiritual influence can move our grandchildren into a deeper relationship with God. Praying over your grandchildren is one way to impact them. It is moving to hear your name on the lips of your grandparents as they speak to God for you. I have fond memories of hearing my grandmother intercede for me. There were many lost and lonely days when my only hope in life was that Grandma was praying for me. The impact of this thought kept me pressing on!

Empower Their Future

No one can give encouragement like a grandma! When we speak words of support and unconditional love to our grandchildren, we bolster their self-esteem and empower them toward maturity. My favorite job as a grandmother is to whisper words of affirmation to my granddaughters. I tell them how smart and talented they are and what a bright future I see for them. Their faces light up, soaking in every word like a thirsty sponge.

Leaving a spiritual legacy for your grandchildren is the greatest inheritance you can pass down. By telling your story, building laughable memories, creating special traditions, influencing a deeper walk with Christ and speaking words of affirmation, you can be assured that your grandchildren will receive an inheritance that will never fade.

"I have been reminded of your sincere faith, which first lived in your grandmother Lois and in your mother Eunice and, I am persuaded, now lives in you also" (2 Timothy 1:5).

homes and gain control over weak-willed women, who are loaded down with sins and are swayed by all kinds of evil desires, [7] always learning but never able to acknowledge the truth. [8] Just as Jannes and Jambres opposed Moses, so also these men oppose the truth — men of depraved minds, who, as far as the faith is concerned, are rejected. [9] But they will not get very far because, as in the case of those men, their folly will be clear to everyone.

Paul's Charge to Timothy

[10] You, however, know all about my teaching, my way of life, my purpose, faith, patience, love, endurance, [11] persecutions, sufferings — what kinds of things happened to me in Antioch, Iconium and Lystra, the persecutions I endured. Yet the Lord rescued me from all of them. [12] In fact, everyone who wants to live a godly life in Christ Jesus will be persecuted, [13] while evil men and impostors will go from bad to worse, deceiving and being deceived. [14] But as for you, continue in what you have learned and have become convinced of, because you know those from whom you learned it, [15] and how from infancy you have known the holy Scriptures, which are able to make you wise for salvation through faith in Christ Jesus. [16] All Scripture is God-breathed and is useful for teaching, rebuking, correcting and training in righteousness, [17] so that the man of God may be thoroughly equipped for every good work.

4 In the presence of God and of Christ Jesus, who will judge the living and the dead, and in view of his appearing and his kingdom, I give you this charge: [2] Preach the Word; be prepared in season and out of season; correct, rebuke and encourage — with great patience and careful instruction. [3] For the time will come when men will not put up with sound doctrine. Instead, to suit their own desires, they will gather around them a great number of teachers to say what their itching ears want to hear. [4] They will turn their ears away from the truth and turn aside to myths. [5] But you, keep your head in all situations, endure hardship, do the work of an evangelist, discharge all the duties of your ministry.

[6] For I am already being poured out like a drink offering, and the time has come for my departure. [7] I have fought the good fight, I have finished the race, I have kept the faith. [8] Now there is in store for me the crown of righteousness, which the Lord, the righteous Judge, will award to me on that day — and not only to me, but also to all who have longed for his appearing.

Personal Remarks

[9] Do your best to come to me quickly, [10] for Demas, because he loved this world, has deserted me and has gone to Thessalonica. Crescens has gone to Galatia, and Titus to Dalmatia. [11] Only Luke is with me. Get Mark and bring him with you, because he is helpful to me in my ministry. [12] I sent Tychicus to Ephesus. [13] When you come, bring the cloak that I left with Carpus at Troas, and my scrolls, especially the parchments.

[14] Alexander the metalworker did me a great deal of harm. The Lord will repay him for what he has done. [15] You too should be on your guard against him, because he strongly opposed our message.

[16] At my first defense, no one came to my support, but everyone deserted me. May it not be held against them. [17] But the Lord stood at my side and gave me strength, so that through me the message might be fully proclaimed and all the Gentiles might hear it. And I was delivered from the lion's mouth. [18] The Lord will rescue me from every evil attack and will bring me safely to his heavenly kingdom. To him be glory for ever and ever. Amen.

Final Greetings

[19] Greet Priscilla [a] and Aquila and the household of Onesiphorus. [20] Erastus stayed in Corinth, and I left Trophimus sick in Miletus. [21] Do your best to get here before winter. Eubulus greets you, and so do Pudens, Linus, Claudia and all the brothers.

[22] The Lord be with your spirit. Grace be with you.

[a] 19 Greek *Prisca*, a variant of *Priscilla*

THE LORD BE WITH YOUR SPIRIT.
GRACE BE WITH YOU.

2 Timothy 4:22

Postcards

BARBARA OWEN

READ | 2 TIMOTHY 4:19 – 22

I love to send postcards when traveling. And here I was in Europe for the first time, debating over a rack of wonderful postcards. Carefully I chose ten of the fifty varieties, making a mental note of to whom each card would go.

But later, in my hotel room, with the cards spread on the bed, I debated. Perhaps Russell would enjoy the picture of the old fort better than the river picture. My roommate Shirley bought all one kind of postcard so she wouldn't have this problem. But I needed variety. I'd asked friends and relatives at home to save the cards for me. These pictures would then supplement my snapshots.

At last I decided, addressing each card before writing a message. There were so many things to tell. The first cards got filled with thoughts of the trip. But by cards eight, nine and ten, a few lines, written large, seemed to do.

I think of another correspondent — Saint Paul. He was a great letter writer. If he sent anything as short as a postcard, we don't have it recorded that way. But the rather personal closings of his letters show the same warmth of feeling that we feel for our friends and relatives. Often he [sent] greetings to several people, and then he may [have mentioned] several people with him who [wanted] to be remembered to his readers: "Greet Priscilla and Aquila and the household of Onesiphorus . . . The Lord be with your spirit. Grace be with you" (2 Timothy 4:19,22).

I fan through my cards again.

O God, go with my correspondence. May it bring blessings to my friends and family. May I keep those who are far from me in my thoughts and prayers. Guard and keep us till we meet again, for Jesus' sake.

Your next devotion is located on page 1673.

GRANDCHILD IN FOCUS • PRAYER

Respect for Authority

Dear Lord, I pray that my grandchild will continually grow to respect those in authority. May she learn to be cooperative and fair in work and play. Instill in her a high regard for officials who govern our land and enforce the laws. May her relationships with parents, teachers, coaches, mentors and bosses be respectful, admirable, constructive and caring. Amen.

Living EXAMPLES

Although Paul had entrusted the church on the island of Crete to young Titus, he still wanted to write him a letter of encouragement and include advice on leadership. Paul listed all the things Titus was to teach the various groups, and when he came to the young, Paul said that the best way to lead was by example (see Titus 2:6–8). Titus was to do what was "good," so that no one could rebuke him or the church for lack of integrity. There is no better way for church leaders, parents or grandmothers to teach than to let their lives be examples of how they want the next generation to conduct themselves.

We've all heard the irrational statement "Do as I say, not as I do." No child ever fell for that one. "Actions speak louder than words" is a saying that more accurately reflects reality. Actions drown out the finely crafted speeches of even the most highly esteemed leaders. And to our grandchildren, actions are everything. All the words we can ever say to them are empty if we do not exhibit integrity—that is, if our words and actions do not convey the same message. It is through words that are backed up by doing "what is good" that we "preach" the word of God.

VERSE *to* REMEMBER | TITUS 2:7–8

In everything set them an example by doing what is good. In your teaching show integrity, seriousness and soundness of speech that cannot be condemned, so that those who oppose you may be ashamed because they have nothing bad to say about us.

ABOUT TITUS

WRITTEN BY:
The apostle Paul

WRITTEN FOR:
Titus, Paul's friend and helper

DATE WRITTEN:
Probably about A.D. 64 from Macedonia

WHY WRITTEN:
To show Titus how to be a good teacher and leader

1 Paul, a servant of God and an apostle of Jesus Christ for the faith of God's elect and the knowledge of the truth that leads to godliness— [2]a faith and knowledge resting on the hope of eternal life, which God, who does not lie, promised before the beginning of time, [3]and at his appointed season he brought his word to light through the preaching entrusted to me by the command of God our Savior,

[4]To Titus, my true son in our common faith:

Grace and peace from God the Father and Christ Jesus our Savior.

Titus's Task on Crete

1:6–8Ref — 1Ti 3:2–4

[5]The reason I left you in Crete was that you might straighten out what was left unfinished and appoint[a] elders in every town, as I directed you. [6]An elder must be blameless, the husband of but one wife, a man whose children believe and are not open to the charge of being wild and disobedient. [7]Since an overseer[b] is entrusted with God's work, he must be blameless—not overbearing, not quick-tempered, not given to drunkenness, not violent, not pursuing dishonest gain. [8]Rather he must be hospitable, one who loves what is good, who is self-controlled, upright, holy and disciplined. [9]He must hold firmly to the trustworthy message as it has been taught, so that he can encourage others by sound doctrine and refute those who oppose it.

[10]For there are many rebellious people, mere talkers and deceivers, especially those of the circumcision group. [11]They must be silenced, because they are ruining whole households by teaching things they ought not to teach—and that for the sake of dishonest gain. [12]Even one of their own prophets has said, "Cretans are always liars, evil brutes, lazy gluttons." [13]This testimony is true. Therefore, rebuke them sharply, so that they will be sound in the faith [14]and will pay no attention to Jewish myths or to the commands of those who reject the truth. [15]To the pure, all things are pure, but to those who are corrupt-

ed and do not believe, nothing is pure. In fact, both their minds and consciences are corrupted. [16]They claim to know God, but by their actions they deny him. They are detestable, disobedient and unfit for doing anything good.

What Must Be Taught to Various Groups

2 You must teach what is in accord with sound doctrine. [2]Teach the older men to be temperate, worthy of respect, self-controlled, and sound in faith, in love and in endurance.

[3]Likewise, teach the older women to be reverent in the way they live, not to be slanderers or addicted to much wine, but to teach what is good. [4]Then they can train the younger women to love their husbands and children, [5]to be self-controlled and pure, to be busy at home, to be kind, and to be subject to their husbands, so that no one will malign the word of God.

[6]Similarly, encourage the young men to be self-controlled. [7]In everything set them an example by doing what is good. In your teaching show integrity, seriousness [8]and soundness of speech that cannot be condemned, so that those who oppose you may be ashamed because they have nothing bad to say about us.

TALKING POINTS

Responsibility

We are to be good role models.

TITUS 2:6–8

This is the last talking point on responsibility.

[9]Teach slaves to be subject to their masters in everything, to try to please them, not to talk back to them, [10]and not to steal from them, but to show that they can be fully trusted, so that in every way

they will make the teaching about God our Savior attractive.

[11] For the grace of God that brings salvation has appeared to all men. [12] It teaches us to say "No" to ungodliness and worldly passions, and to live self-controlled, upright and godly lives in this present age, [13] while we wait for the blessed hope—the glorious appearing of our great God and Savior, Jesus Christ, [14] who gave himself for us to redeem us from all wickedness and to purify for himself a people that are his very own, eager to do what is good.

[15] These, then, are the things you should teach. Encourage and rebuke with all authority. Do not let anyone despise you.

Doing What Is Good

3 Remind the people to be subject to rulers and authorities, to be obedient, to be ready to do whatever is good, [2] to slander no one, to be peaceable and considerate, and to show true humility toward all men.

TALKING POINTS

Respect

Be subject to those in authority.

TITUS 3:1–2

This is the last talking point on respect.

[3] At one time we too were foolish, disobedient, deceived and enslaved by all kinds of passions and pleasures. We lived in malice and envy, being hated and hating one another. [4] But when the kindness and love of God our Savior appeared, [5] he saved us, not because of righteous things we had done, but because of his mercy. He saved us through the washing of rebirth and renewal by the Holy Spirit, [6] whom he poured out on us generously through Jesus Christ our Savior, [7] so that,

stories to share

TITUS 3:1–8

Do What Is Good

LIFE LESSON: God wants Christians to live godly lives.

TO TALK ABOUT

✦ Why did God save us?

✦ How did he save us?

✦ What are some good qualities Paul urges Christians to demonstrate in their lives?

✦ Are you a Christian? If so, how are you different from people who aren't Christians?

having been justified by his grace, we might become heirs having the hope of eternal life. [8] This is a trustworthy saying. And I want you to stress these things, so that those who have trusted in God may be careful to devote themselves to doing what is good. These things are excellent and profitable for everyone.

[9] But avoid foolish controversies and genealogies and arguments and quarrels about the law, because these are unprofitable and useless. [10] Warn a divisive person once, and then warn him a second time. After that, have nothing to do with him. [11] You may be sure that such a man is warped and sinful; he is self-condemned.

Final Remarks

[12] As soon as I send Artemas or Tychicus to you, do your best to come to me at Nicopolis,

HE SAVED US, NOT BECAUSE
OF RIGHTEOUS THINGS WE HAD
DONE, BUT BECAUSE OF HIS
MERCY. HE SAVED US THROUGH
THE WASHING OF REBIRTH AND
RENEWAL BY THE HOLY SPIRIT.
— *Titus 3:5*

Thirsty

JOY MORGAN DAVIS

READ | TITUS 3:1 – 8

Yesterday the August air
Lay cumbersome and close,
Smothering the ground
And all that grew. . .
The fields wasted away,
The flowers wilted. . .
And like the flowers
I am frail.
I felt my faith
Would wilt
In the slow, silent fever
Of adversity and fear.

And then last night
As we lay sleeping,
The dew drops fell
Like furtive rain
From heaven's reservoir. . .
The flowers lifted,
The fields revived
Revisited by God's grace.

Spirit of the living God,
Fall fresh on me.

Your next devotion is located on page 1681.

GRANDCHILD IN FOCUS • PRAYER

Courage

O Father, builder of character and courage, may my
grandchild grow strong in the light of your love. Grant him
courage to stand for what is right, to guard the truth and to
ensure justice in every aspect of life. May he boldly grow
in grace, revere your name and proudly proclaim you
as the Lord of lords and King of kings. Amen.

because I have decided to winter there. [13] Do everything you can to help Zenas the lawyer and Apollos on their way and see that they have everything they need. [14] Our people must learn to devote themselves to doing what is good, in order that they may provide for daily necessities and not live unproductive lives.

[15] Everyone with me sends you greetings. Greet those who love us in the faith.

Grace be with you all.

Share
YOUR FAITH

Don't you love it when you get real mail — an invitation, a note from a friend, a card for a special occasion? The art of letter writing has almost been forgotten. And yet this short letter from Paul to his friend Philemon has been preserved through history. In this letter Paul asked Philemon to welcome back his slave Onesimus. He endorsed Onesimus to Philemon as a brand-new Christian, saying in effect, "Take him back. He's different now. He's become a brother in Christ."

Let this brief letter inspire you to write a letter of endorsement about your grandchild to his parents — or just write a letter to your grandchild. You may want to record the feelings you experienced at your grandchild's birth or at some major milestone in his life. You may want to commend him for an accomplishment or for his talents and personality. Or better yet, tell your faith story in a handwritten letter so that your grandchild will know how God has molded your life. No matter what age or stage your grandchild is in, a letter in your handwriting will mark a place in his history and be cherished for years to come.

VERSE *to* REMEMBER | PHILEMON 6

I pray that you may be active in sharing your faith, so that you will have a full understanding of every good thing we have in Christ.

ABOUT PHILEMON

WRITTEN BY:
The apostle Paul

WRITTEN FOR:
Philemon, Paul's
Christian friend

DATE WRITTEN:
About A.D. 60, while
Paul was in prison
in Rome

WHY WRITTEN:
To ask Philemon to
welcome back his runaway
slave Onesimus, who had
become a Christian

¹Paul, a prisoner of Christ Jesus, and Timothy our brother,

To Philemon our dear friend and fellow worker, ²to Apphia our sister, to Archippus our fellow soldier and to the church that meets in your home:

³Grace to you and peace from God our Father and the Lord Jesus Christ.

Thanksgiving and Prayer

⁴I always thank my God as I remember you in my prayers, ⁵because I hear about your faith in the Lord Jesus and your love for all the saints. ⁶I pray that you may be active in sharing your faith, so that you will have a full understanding of every good thing we have in Christ. ⁷Your love has given me great joy and encouragement, because you, brother, have refreshed the hearts of the saints.

Paul's Plea for Onesimus

⁸Therefore, although in Christ I could be bold and order you to do what you ought to do, ⁹yet I appeal to you on the basis of love. I then, as Paul—an old man and now also a prisoner of Christ Jesus— ¹⁰I appeal to you for my son Onesimus,ᵃ who became my son while I was in chains. ¹¹Formerly he was useless to you, but now he has become useful both to you and to me.

¹²I am sending him—who is my very heart— back to you. ¹³I would have liked to keep him with me so that he could take your place in helping me while I am in chains for the gospel. ¹⁴But I did not want to do anything without your consent, so that any favor you do will be spontaneous and not forced. ¹⁵Perhaps the reason he was separated from you for a little while was that you might have him back for good— ¹⁶no longer as a slave, but better than a slave, as a dear brother. He is very dear to me but even dearer to you, both as a man and as a brother in the Lord.

¹⁷So if you consider me a partner, welcome him as you would welcome me. ¹⁸If he has done you any wrong or owes you anything, charge it to me. ¹⁹I, Paul, am writing this with my own hand. I will pay it back—not to mention that you owe me your very self. ²⁰I do wish, brother, that I may have some benefit from you in the Lord; refresh my heart in Christ. ²¹Confident of your obedience, I write to you, knowing that you will do even more than I ask.

²²And one thing more: Prepare a guest room for me, because I hope to be restored to you in answer to your prayers.

²³Epaphras, my fellow prisoner in Christ Jesus, sends you greetings. ²⁴And so do Mark, Aristarchus, Demas and Luke, my fellow workers.

²⁵The grace of the Lord Jesus Christ be with your spirit.

ᵃ 10 *Onesimus* means *useful.*

Faithful LEGACY

The book of Hebrews was written to Jewish Christians. This fact becomes quite obvious as we read through the many references to the Old Testament: the Sabbath rest, the tabernacle, the law, the high priests, the shadowy Melchizedek and a steady supply of Old Testament quotations. It can be quite a mystery for those who are unfamiliar with these Old Testament concepts. But the writer of this letter to the Hebrews wanted to make it clear to these Jewish converts who were being tempted to give up their new faith and revert back to Judaism that Jesus Christ is supreme, that his sacrifice on the cross is an all-sufficient means of grace for God's people, and that the new covenant in Christ is far superior to their old law-based religion.

After defining Jesus as the supreme mediator of God's grace, the author encouraged his readers to follow Jesus even in the face of uncertainty, doubt and persecution. It takes faith to persevere in such circumstances, and the well-known eleventh chapter of Hebrews details the lives of many of the Bible's main characters as they lived their lives in faith.

Reading through this book, we realize that it is by faith that we, and all the believers who have come before us for millennia, are saved. As the author of Hebrews calls the roll of those saved by faith, we realize how important it is that we tell their stories to our grandchildren so that they too can be listed in the roll call of those saved by faith.

VERSE *to* REMEMBER | HEBREWS 11:1

Now faith is being sure of what we hope for and certain of what we do not see.

ABOUT HEBREWS

WRITTEN BY:
Unknown

WRITTEN FOR:
Jewish Christians

DATE WRITTEN:
Probably sometime before the destruction of the temple in Jerusalem (A.D. 70)

WHY WRITTEN:
To show how the new covenant in Christ is superior to the old covenant of the Jewish religious system

The Son Superior to Angels

1 In the past God spoke to our forefathers through the prophets at many times and in various ways, [2] but in these last days he has spoken to us by his Son, whom he appointed heir of all things, and through whom he made the universe. [3] The Son is the radiance of God's glory and the exact representation of his being, sustaining all things by his powerful word. After he had provided purification for sins, he sat down at the right hand of the Majesty in heaven. [4] So he became as much superior to the angels as the name he has inherited is superior to theirs.

[5] For to which of the angels did God ever say,

"You are my Son;
    today I have become your Father" [a][b]?

Or again,

"I will be his Father,
    and he will be my Son" [c]?

[6] And again, when God brings his firstborn into the world, he says,

"Let all God's angels worship him." [d]

[7] In speaking of the angels he says,

"He makes his angels winds,
    his servants flames of fire." [e]

[8] But about the Son he says,

"Your throne, O God, will last for ever and
        ever,
    and righteousness will be the scepter of
        your kingdom.
[9] You have loved righteousness and hated
        wickedness;
    therefore God, your God, has set you above
        your companions
    by anointing you with the oil of joy." [f]

[10] He also says,

"In the beginning, O Lord, you laid the
        foundations of the earth,
    and the heavens are the work of your
        hands.
[11] They will perish, but you remain;
    they will all wear out like a garment.
[12] You will roll them up like a robe;
    like a garment they will be changed.
But you remain the same,
    and your years will never end." [g]

[13] To which of the angels did God ever say,

"Sit at my right hand
until I make your enemies
    a footstool for your feet" [h]?

[14] Are not all angels ministering spirits sent to serve those who will inherit salvation?

Warning to Pay Attention

2 We must pay more careful attention, therefore, to what we have heard, so that we do not drift away. [2] For if the message spoken by angels was binding, and every violation and disobedience received its just punishment, [3] how shall we escape if we ignore such a great salvation? This salvation, which was first announced by the Lord, was confirmed to us by those who heard him. [4] God also testified to it by signs, wonders and various miracles, and gifts of the Holy Spirit distributed according to his will.

Jesus Made Like His Brothers

[5] It is not to angels that he has subjected the world to come, about which we are speaking. [6] But there is a place where someone has testified:

"What is man that you are mindful of him,
    the son of man that you care for him?
[7] You made him a little [i] lower than the angels;
    you crowned him with glory and honor
[8]   and put everything under his feet." [j]

In putting everything under him, God left nothing that is not subject to him. Yet at present we do not see everything subject to him. [9] But we see Jesus, who was made a little lower than the

---

[a] 5 Or *have begotten you*   [b] 5 Psalm 2:7   [c] 5 2 Samuel 7:14;
1 Chron. 17:13   [d] 6 Deut. 32:43 (see Dead Sea Scrolls
and Septuagint)   [e] 7 Psalm 104:4   [f] 9 Psalm 45:6,7
[g] 12 Psalm 102:25-27   [h] 13 Psalm 110:1   [i] 7 Or *him for a
little while*; also in verse 9   [j] 8 Psalm 8:4-6

angels, now crowned with glory and honor because he suffered death, so that by the grace of God he might taste death for everyone.

[10] In bringing many sons to glory, it was fitting that God, for whom and through whom everything exists, should make the author of their salvation perfect through suffering. [11] Both the one who makes men holy and those who are made holy are of the same family. So Jesus is not ashamed to call them brothers. [12] He says,

> "I will declare your name to my brothers;
> in the presence of the congregation
> I will sing your praises." [a]

[13] And again,

> "I will put my trust in him." [b]

And again he says,

> "Here am I, and the children God has
> given me." [c]

[14] Since the children have flesh and blood, he too shared in their humanity so that by his death he might destroy him who holds the power of death—that is, the devil— [15] and free those who all their lives were held in slavery by their fear of death. [16] For surely it is not angels he helps, but Abraham's descendants. [17] For this reason he had to be made like his brothers in every way, in order that he might become a merciful and faithful high priest in service to God, and that he might make atonement for [d] the sins of the people. [18] Because he himself suffered when he was tempted, he is able to help those who are being tempted.

Jesus Greater Than Moses

3 Therefore, holy brothers, who share in the heavenly calling, fix your thoughts on Jesus, the apostle and high priest whom we confess. [2] He was faithful to the one who appointed him, just as Moses was faithful in all God's house. [3] Jesus has been found worthy of greater honor than Moses, just as the builder of a house has greater honor than the house itself. [4] For every house is built by someone, but God is the builder of everything. [5] Moses was faithful as a servant in all God's house, testifying to what would be said in the future. [6] But Christ is faithful as a son over God's house. And we are his house, if we hold on to our courage and the hope of which we boast.

Warning Against Unbelief

[7] So, as the Holy Spirit says:

> "Today, if you hear his voice,
> [8] do not harden your hearts
> as you did in the rebellion,
> during the time of testing in the desert,
> [9] where your fathers tested and tried me
> and for forty years saw what I did.
> [10] That is why I was angry with that
> generation,
> and I said, 'Their hearts are always going
> astray,
> and they have not known my ways.'
> [11] So I declared on oath in my anger,
> 'They shall never enter my rest.' " [e]

[12] See to it, brothers, that none of you has a sinful, unbelieving heart that turns away from the living God. [13] But encourage one another daily, as long as it is called Today, so that none of you may be hardened by sin's deceitfulness. [14] We have come to share in Christ if we hold firmly till the end the confidence we had at first. [15] As has just been said:

> "Today, if you hear his voice,
> do not harden your hearts
> as you did in the rebellion." [f]

[16] Who were they who heard and rebelled? Were they not all those Moses led out of Egypt? [17] And with whom was he angry for forty years? Was it not with those who sinned, whose bodies fell in the desert? [18] And to whom did God swear that they would never enter his rest if not to those who disobeyed [g]? [19] So we see that they were not able to enter, because of their unbelief.

---

[a] 12 Psalm 22:22   [b] 13 Isaiah 8:17   [c] 13 Isaiah 8:18
[d] 17 Or *and that he might turn aside God's wrath, taking away*
[e] 11 Psalm 95:7-11   [f] 15 Psalm 95:7,8   [g] 18 Or *disbelieved*

A Sabbath-Rest for the People of God

4 Therefore, since the promise of entering his rest still stands, let us be careful that none of you be found to have fallen short of it. [2] For we also have had the gospel preached to us, just as they did; but the message they heard was of no value to them, because those who heard did not combine it with faith.[a] [3] Now we who have believed enter that rest, just as God has said,

> "So I declared on oath in my anger,
> 'They shall never enter my rest.' "[b]

And yet his work has been finished since the creation of the world. [4] For somewhere he has spoken about the seventh day in these words: "And on the seventh day God rested from all his work."[c] [5] And again in the passage above he says, "They shall never enter my rest."

[6] It still remains that some will enter that rest, and those who formerly had the gospel preached to them did not go in, because of their disobedience. [7] Therefore God again set a certain day, calling it Today, when a long time later he spoke through David, as was said before:

> "Today, if you hear his voice,
> do not harden your hearts."[d]

[8] For if Joshua had given them rest, God would not have spoken later about another day. [9] There remains, then, a Sabbath-rest for the people of God; [10] for anyone who enters God's rest also rests from his own work, just as God did from his. [11] Let us, therefore, make every effort to enter that rest, so that no one will fall by following their example of disobedience.

[12] For the word of God is living and active. Sharper than any double-edged sword, it penetrates even to dividing soul and spirit, joints and marrow; it judges the thoughts and attitudes of the heart. [13] Nothing in all creation is hidden from God's sight. Everything is uncovered and laid bare before the eyes of him to whom we must give account.

TALKING POINTS

Accountability

God sees everything.

HEBREWS 4:13

For more on accountability, go to 1 Peter 4:5.

Jesus the Great High Priest

[14] Therefore, since we have a great high priest who has gone through the heavens,[e] Jesus the Son of God, let us hold firmly to the faith we profess. [15] For we do not have a high priest who is unable to sympathize with our weaknesses, but we have one who has been tempted in every way, just as we are—yet was without sin. [16] Let us then approach the throne of grace with confidence, so that we may receive mercy and find grace to help us in our time of need.

TALKING POINTS

Sexuality

Jesus empathizes with our struggles and will help us overcome temptation.

HEBREWS 4:14–16

This is the last talking point on sexuality.

5 Every high priest is selected from among men and is appointed to represent them in matters related to God, to offer gifts and sacrifices for sins. [2] He is able to deal gently with those who are ignorant and are going astray, since he himself is subject to weakness. [3] This is why he

---

[a] 2 Many manuscripts *because they did not share in the faith of those who obeyed*   [b] 3 Psalm 95:11; also in verse 5   [c] 4 Gen. 2:2
[d] 7 Psalm 95:7,8   [e] 14 Or *gone into heaven*

NOTHING IN ALL CREATION IS
HIDDEN FROM GOD'S SIGHT.
EVERYTHING IS UNCOVERED AND
LAID BARE BEFORE THE EYES OF HIM
TO WHOM WE MUST GIVE ACCOUNT.

Hebrews 4:13

The Resurrector of Dreams

SUSAN LENZKES

READ | HEBREWS 4:12 – 16

The Lord has a way of looking into the very heart of things, especially the human heart. And there's no use trying to hide what's there.

One day I came to his Word with a nameless ache tucked away inside, troubling me, as it had been for several days. I read Luke's account of Jesus entering the town of Nain, where he came upon a heartbroken widow following the coffin of her only son.

As I pondered what this story could possibly have to do with me, the Lord looked into my heart and said, "Something has died in you, Susan. What is this thing you're mourning and carrying in a coffin?"

I was startled, for I hadn't known that a funeral was going on inside me. But he reached out and touched the coffin that I was indeed laboring beneath, and I finally stood still and looked. An important dream was being taken for burial — a dream the Lord knew I needed to have alive.

Very quietly, from within the depths of me, I heard Jesus whisper, "Do you suppose that if I can resurrect people, I can resurrect dreams too?"

I read the story again and saw the compassion, the power and the truth. When our last hope is being taken for burial, Jesus sees, wipes away the tears of sorrow and speaks life into our emptiness.

Praise God! You are the Lord of the resurrection! The Lord of hope! In choosing you as Savior and Lord, I have chosen abundant, eternal life. And it starts in this world.

Your next devotion is located on page 1687.

GRANDCHILD IN FOCUS • PRAYER

Future Spouse

Dear Lord, if it is your will, I pray my grandchild will be united in a loving and Christian marriage. Keep her sexually pure so that she will honor you with her body and mind. As she seeks a spouse who will honor and care for her, give her patience and discernment. May her choice for a life partner be your choice for her, so that she and her husband will together glorify you in a lasting love. I pray this in Jesus' name, amen.

has to offer sacrifices for his own sins, as well as for the sins of the people.

⁴No one takes this honor upon himself; he must be called by God, just as Aaron was. ⁵So Christ also did not take upon himself the glory of becoming a high priest. But God said to him,

"You are my Son;
today I have become your Father." ᵃ" ᵇ

⁶And he says in another place,

"You are a priest forever,
in the order of Melchizedek." ᶜ

⁷During the days of Jesus' life on earth, he offered up prayers and petitions with loud cries and tears to the one who could save him from death, and he was heard because of his reverent submission. ⁸Although he was a son, he learned obedience from what he suffered ⁹and, once made perfect, he became the source of eternal salvation for all who obey him ¹⁰and was designated by God to be high priest in the order of Melchizedek.

Warning Against Falling Away

6:4–6Ref — Heb 10:26–31

¹¹We have much to say about this, but it is hard to explain because you are slow to learn. ¹²In fact, though by this time you ought to be teachers, you need someone to teach you the elementary truths of God's word all over again. You need milk, not solid food! ¹³Anyone who lives on milk, being still an infant, is not acquainted with the teaching about righteousness. ¹⁴But solid food is for the mature, who by constant use have trained themselves to distinguish good from evil.

6 Therefore let us leave the elementary teachings about Christ and go on to maturity, not laying again the foundation of repentance from acts that lead to death, ᵈ and of faith in God, ²instruction about baptisms, the laying on of hands, the resurrection of the dead, and eternal judgment. ³And God permitting, we will do so.

⁴It is impossible for those who have once been enlightened, who have tasted the heavenly gift,

who have shared in the Holy Spirit, ⁵who have tasted the goodness of the word of God and the powers of the coming age, ⁶if they fall away, to be brought back to repentance, because ᵉ to their loss they are crucifying the Son of God all over again and subjecting him to public disgrace.

⁷Land that drinks in the rain often falling on it and that produces a crop useful to those for whom it is farmed receives the blessing of God. ⁸But land that produces thorns and thistles is worthless and is in danger of being cursed. In the end it will be burned.

⁹Even though we speak like this, dear friends, we are confident of better things in your case—things that accompany salvation. ¹⁰God is not unjust; he will not forget your work and the love you have shown him as you have helped his people and continue to help them. ¹¹We want each of you to show this same diligence to the very end, in order to make your hope sure. ¹²We do not want you to become lazy, but to imitate those who through faith and patience inherit what has been promised.

TALKING POINTS

Laziness

Don't be lazy; demonstrate your love for God by helping his people.

HEBREWS 6:10–12

This is the last talking point on laziness.

The Certainty of God's Promise

¹³When God made his promise to Abraham, since there was no one greater for him to swear by, he swore by himself, ¹⁴saying, "I will surely bless you and give you many descendants." ᶠ ¹⁵And so

ᵃ 5 Or *have begotten you*   ᵇ 5 Psalm 2:7   ᶜ 6 Psalm 110:4
ᵈ 1 Or *from useless rituals*   ᵉ 6 Or *repentance while*
ᶠ 14 Gen. 22:17

after waiting patiently, Abraham received what was promised.

¹⁶Men swear by someone greater than themselves, and the oath confirms what is said and puts an end to all argument. ¹⁷Because God wanted to make the unchanging nature of his purpose very clear to the heirs of what was promised, he confirmed it with an oath. ¹⁸God did this so that, by two unchangeable things in which it is impossible for God to lie, we who have fled to take hold of the hope offered to us may be greatly encouraged. ¹⁹We have this hope as an anchor for the soul, firm and secure. It enters the inner sanctuary behind the curtain, ²⁰where Jesus, who went before us, has entered on our behalf. He has become a high priest forever, in the order of Melchizedek.

Melchizedek the Priest

7 This Melchizedek was king of Salem and priest of God Most High. He met Abraham returning from the defeat of the kings and blessed him, ²and Abraham gave him a tenth of everything. First, his name means "king of righteousness"; then also, "king of Salem" means "king of peace." ³Without father or mother, without genealogy, without beginning of days or end of life, like the Son of God he remains a priest forever.

⁴Just think how great he was: Even the patriarch Abraham gave him a tenth of the plunder! ⁵Now the law requires the descendants of Levi who become priests to collect a tenth from the people—that is, their brothers—even though their brothers are descended from Abraham. ⁶This man, however, did not trace his descent from Levi, yet he collected a tenth from Abraham and blessed him who had the promises. ⁷And without doubt the lesser person is blessed by the greater. ⁸In the one case, the tenth is collected by men who die; but in the other case, by him who is declared to be living. ⁹One might even say that Levi, who collects the tenth, paid the tenth through Abraham, ¹⁰because when Melchizedek met Abraham, Levi was still in the body of his ancestor.

Jesus Like Melchizedek

¹¹If perfection could have been attained through the Levitical priesthood (for on the basis of it the law was given to the people), why was there still need for another priest to come—one in the order of Melchizedek, not in the order of Aaron? ¹²For when there is a change of the priesthood, there must also be a change of the law. ¹³He of whom these things are said belonged to a different tribe, and no one from that tribe has ever served at the altar. ¹⁴For it is clear that our Lord descended from Judah, and in regard to that tribe Moses said nothing about priests. ¹⁵And what we have said is even more clear if another priest like Melchizedek appears, ¹⁶one who has become a priest not on the basis of a regulation as to his ancestry but on the basis of the power of an indestructible life. ¹⁷For it is declared:

"You are a priest forever,
in the order of Melchizedek." ᵃ

¹⁸The former regulation is set aside because it was weak and useless ¹⁹(for the law made nothing perfect), and a better hope is introduced, by which we draw near to God.

²⁰And it was not without an oath! Others became priests without any oath, ²¹but he became a priest with an oath when God said to him:

"The Lord has sworn
and will not change his mind:
'You are a priest forever.' " ᵃ

²²Because of this oath, Jesus has become the guarantee of a better covenant.

²³Now there have been many of those priests, since death prevented them from continuing in office; ²⁴but because Jesus lives forever, he has a permanent priesthood. ²⁵Therefore he is able to save completely ᵇ those who come to God through him, because he always lives to intercede for them.

²⁶Such a high priest meets our need—one who is holy, blameless, pure, set apart from sinners,

ᵃ 17 Psalm 110:4   ᵇ 25 Or forever

exalted above the heavens. ²⁷Unlike the other high priests, he does not need to offer sacrifices day after day, first for his own sins, and then for the sins of the people. He sacrificed for their sins once for all when he offered himself. ²⁸For the law appoints as high priests men who are weak; but the oath, which came after the law, appointed the Son, who has been made perfect forever.

The High Priest of a New Covenant

8 The point of what we are saying is this: We do have such a high priest, who sat down at the right hand of the throne of the Majesty in heaven, ²and who serves in the sanctuary, the true tabernacle set up by the Lord, not by man.

³Every high priest is appointed to offer both gifts and sacrifices, and so it was necessary for this one also to have something to offer. ⁴If he were on earth, he would not be a priest, for there are already men who offer the gifts prescribed by the law. ⁵They serve at a sanctuary that is a copy and shadow of what is in heaven. This is why Moses was warned when he was about to build the tabernacle: "See to it that you make everything according to the pattern shown you on the mountain."ᵃ ⁶But the ministry Jesus has received is as superior to theirs as the covenant of which he is mediator is superior to the old one, and it is founded on better promises.

⁷For if there had been nothing wrong with that first covenant, no place would have been sought for another. ⁸But God found fault with the people and saidᵇ:

"The time is coming, declares the Lord,
    when I will make a new covenant
with the house of Israel
    and with the house of Judah.
⁹It will not be like the covenant
    I made with their forefathers
when I took them by the hand
    to lead them out of Egypt,
because they did not remain faithful to my
    covenant,
and I turned away from them,
                        declares the Lord.

¹⁰This is the covenant I will make with the
    house of Israel
    after that time, declares the Lord.
I will put my laws in their minds
    and write them on their hearts.
I will be their God,
    and they will be my people.
¹¹No longer will a man teach his neighbor,
    or a man his brother, saying, 'Know
        the Lord,'
because they will all know me,
    from the least of them to the greatest.
¹²For I will forgive their wickedness
    and will remember their sins no
        more."ᶜ

¹³By calling this covenant "new," he has made the first one obsolete; and what is obsolete and aging will soon disappear.

Worship in the Earthly Tabernacle

9 Now the first covenant had regulations for worship and also an earthly sanctuary. ²A tabernacle was set up. In its first room were the lampstand, the table and the consecrated bread; this was called the Holy Place. ³Behind the second curtain was a room called the Most Holy Place, ⁴which had the golden altar of incense and the gold-covered ark of the covenant. This ark contained the gold jar of manna, Aaron's staff that had budded, and the stone tablets of the covenant. ⁵Above the ark were the cherubim of the Glory, overshadowing the atonement cover.ᵈ But we cannot discuss these things in detail now.

⁶When everything had been arranged like this, the priests entered regularly into the outer room to carry on their ministry. ⁷But only the high priest entered the inner room, and that only once a year, and never without blood, which he offered for himself and for the sins the people had committed in ignorance. ⁸The Holy Spirit was showing by this that the way into the Most Holy Place had not yet been disclosed as long as the first tab-

---

ᵃ 5 Exodus 25:40   ᵇ 8 Some manuscripts may be translated *fault and said to the people.*   ᶜ 12 Jer. 31:31-34   ᵈ 5 Traditionally *the mercy seat* ernacle was still standing. ⁹This is an illustration for the present time, indicating that the gifts and sacrifices being offered were not able to clear the conscience of the worshiper. ¹⁰They are only a matter of food and drink and various ceremonial washings — external regulations applying until the time of the new order.

The Blood of Christ

¹¹When Christ came as high priest of the good things that are already here,ᵃ he went through the greater and more perfect tabernacle that is not man-made, that is to say, not a part of this creation. ¹²He did not enter by means of the blood of goats and calves; but he entered the Most Holy Place once for all by his own blood, having obtained eternal redemption. ¹³The blood of goats and bulls and the ashes of a heifer sprinkled on those who are ceremonially unclean sanctify them so that they are outwardly clean. ¹⁴How much more, then, will the blood of Christ, who through the eternal Spirit offered himself unblemished to God, cleanse our consciences from acts that lead to death,ᵇ so that we may serve the living God!

¹⁵For this reason Christ is the mediator of a new covenant, that those who are called may receive the promised eternal inheritance — now that he has died as a ransom to set them free from the sins committed under the first covenant.

¹⁶In the case of a will,ᶜ it is necessary to prove the death of the one who made it, ¹⁷because a will is in force only when somebody has died; it never takes effect while the one who made it is living. ¹⁸This is why even the first covenant was not put into effect without blood. ¹⁹When Moses had proclaimed every commandment of the law to all the people, he took the blood of calves, together with water, scarlet wool and branches of hyssop, and sprinkled the scroll and all the people. ²⁰He said, "This is the blood of the covenant, which God has commanded you to keep."ᵈ ²¹In the same way, he sprinkled with the blood both the tabernacle and everything used in its ceremonies. ²²In fact, the law requires that nearly every-

thing be cleansed with blood, and without the shedding of blood there is no forgiveness.

²³It was necessary, then, for the copies of the heavenly things to be purified with these sacrifices, but the heavenly things themselves with better sacrifices than these. ²⁴For Christ did not enter a man-made sanctuary that was only a copy of the true one; he entered heaven itself, now to appear for us in God's presence. ²⁵Nor did he enter heaven to offer himself again and again, the way the high priest enters the Most Holy Place every year with blood that is not his own. ²⁶Then Christ would have had to suffer many times since the creation of the world. But now he has appeared once for all at the end of the ages to do away with sin by the sacrifice of himself. ²⁷Just as man is destined to die once, and after that to face judgment, ²⁸so Christ was sacrificed once to take away the sins of many people; and he will appear a second time, not to bear sin, but to bring salvation to those who are waiting for him.

Christ's Sacrifice Once for All

10 The law is only a shadow of the good things that are coming — not the realities themselves. For this reason it can never, by the same sacrifices repeated endlessly year after year, make perfect those who draw near to worship. ²If it could, would they not have stopped being offered? For the worshipers would have been cleansed once for all, and would no longer have felt guilty for their sins. ³But those sacrifices are an annual reminder of sins, ⁴because it is impossible for the blood of bulls and goats to take away sins.

⁵Therefore, when Christ came into the world, he said:

"Sacrifice and offering you did not desire,
　but a body you prepared for me;
⁶with burnt offerings and sin offerings
　you were not pleased.

ᵃ 11 Some early manuscripts *are to come* 　 ᵇ 14 Or *from useless rituals* 　 ᶜ 16 Same Greek word as *covenant*; also in verse 17 　 ᵈ 20 Exodus 24:8

⁷Then I said, 'Here I am—it is written about
me in the scroll—
I have come to do your will, O God.' "ᵃ

⁸First he said, "Sacrifices and offerings, burnt offerings and sin offerings you did not desire, nor
were you pleased with them" (although the law
required them to be made). ⁹Then he said, "Here
I am, I have come to do your will." He sets aside
the first to establish the second. ¹⁰And by that
will, we have been made holy through the sacrifice of the body of Jesus Christ once for all.

¹¹Day after day every priest stands and performs his religious duties; again and again he
offers the same sacrifices, which can never take
away sins. ¹²But when this priest had offered for
all time one sacrifice for sins, he sat down at the
right hand of God. ¹³Since that time he waits for
his enemies to be made his footstool, ¹⁴because
by one sacrifice he has made perfect forever those
who are being made holy.

¹⁵The Holy Spirit also testifies to us about this.
First he says:

¹⁶"This is the covenant I will make with them
after that time, says the Lord.
I will put my laws in their hearts,
and I will write them on their minds."ᵇ

¹⁷Then he adds:

"Their sins and lawless acts
I will remember no more."ᶜ

¹⁸And where these have been forgiven, there is no
longer any sacrifice for sin.

A Call to Persevere

¹⁹Therefore, brothers, since we have confidence to enter the Most Holy Place by the blood
of Jesus, ²⁰by a new and living way opened for us
through the curtain, that is, his body, ²¹and since
we have a great priest over the house of God, ²²let
us draw near to God with a sincere heart in full
assurance of faith, having our hearts sprinkled
to cleanse us from a guilty conscience and having our bodies washed with pure water. ²³Let us

TALKING POINTS

Guilt

God takes away our guilt.

HEBREWS 10:22–23

This is the last talking point on guilt.

hold unswervingly to the hope we profess, for he
who promised is faithful. ²⁴And let us consider
how we may spur one another on toward love
and good deeds. ²⁵Let us not give up meeting together, as some are in the habit of doing, but let
us encourage one another—and all the more as
you see the Day approaching.

²⁶If we deliberately keep on sinning after we
have received the knowledge of the truth, no sacrifice for sins is left, ²⁷but only a fearful expectation of judgment and of raging fire that will
consume the enemies of God. ²⁸Anyone who rejected the law of Moses died without mercy on
the testimony of two or three witnesses. ²⁹How
much more severely do you think a man deserves
to be punished who has trampled the Son of God
under foot, who has treated as an unholy thing
the blood of the covenant that sanctified him,
and who has insulted the Spirit of grace? ³⁰For
we know him who said, "It is mine to avenge; I
will repay,"ᵈ and again, "The Lord will judge his
people."ᵉ ³¹It is a dreadful thing to fall into the
hands of the living God.

³²Remember those earlier days after you had
received the light, when you stood your ground
in a great contest in the face of suffering. ³³Some-
times you were publicly exposed to insult and
persecution; at other times you stood side by
side with those who were so treated. ³⁴You sym-
pathized with those in prison and joyfully accepted the confiscation of your property, because you

ᵃ 7 Psalm 40:6-8 (see Septuagint)   ᵇ 16 Jer. 31:33
ᶜ 17 Jer. 31:34   ᵈ 30 Deut. 32:35   ᵉ 30 Deut. 32:36; Psalm 135:14

LET US HOLD UNSWERVINGLY TO
THE HOPE WE PROFESS, FOR HE
WHO PROMISED IS FAITHFUL.
Hebrews 10:23

Violets or Zinnias?

MARJORIE PARKER

READ | HEBREWS 10:19 – 25

Roses around the door can brighten any home, whether it be a cottage or a mansion. Someone who lives within has added a touch of beauty to a sometimes sad and sordid world. Jesus was a lover of beauty in nature, for He spoke of how the lilies grew; of fields white unto the harvest; of birds of the air. Indeed He is the Creator of all things beautiful.

The petals of a rose are soft to the touch, but they must be handled carefully or they will bruise. Azaleas with their delicate colors are beautiful to see, but they will produce only if soil and sunshine are exactly to their liking. Gladiolus will stand straight and tall, but if you bend them, they will break. We admire the velvet of the violets, but they must be constantly encouraged. The morning-glory will bloom brightly in the morning but wilts in the heat of the day.

There are hardy varieties of flowers, however, that are the delight of the amateur gardener, for they do not need any special attention. The common zinnia and the vivid petunia seem willing to go on blooming day after day without having someone fuss over and pamper them. They keep on producing without expecting any special care.

There are all kinds of flowers and there are all kinds of Christians. What kind are you — a violet or a zinnia?

Jesus, whether I am a zinnia or a violet or a lovely rose, you are the source of my comfort, my strength, my life. Fill me with your living water so that I may bloom regardless of the hot sun or harsh winds that blow through my life. Keep me rooted in your love so that my colors will last and reflect you to all who come into my garden. Help me to hold unswervingly to the hope I have in you. You, and your promises, are faithful!

Your next devotion is located on page 1689.

GRANDCHILD **IN FOCUS** • PRAYER

School/Career

Dear God, may learning be a joy rather than a chore for my grandchild. May exploration of new ideas bring a sense of wonder, awe and excitement. Grant him clarity of mind, the ability to concentrate on the task at hand and recollection of what has been learned. Help him to appreciate the tasks that come easily and to persevere through those that challenge. Amen.

knew that you yourselves had better and lasting possessions.

³⁵So do not throw away your confidence; it will be richly rewarded. ³⁶You need to persevere so that when you have done the will of God, you will receive what he has promised. ³⁷For in just a very little while,

> "He who is coming will come and will not
>   delay.
> ³⁸ But my righteous one *ᵃ* will live by faith.
> And if he shrinks back,
>   I will not be pleased with him." *ᵇ*

³⁹But we are not of those who shrink back and are destroyed, but of those who believe and are saved.

By Faith

11 Now faith is being sure of what we hope for and certain of what we do not see. ²This is what the ancients were commended for.

³By faith we understand that the universe was formed at God's command, so that what is seen was not made out of what was visible.

⁴By faith Abel offered God a better sacrifice than Cain did. By faith he was commended as a righteous man, when God spoke well of his offerings. And by faith he still speaks, even though he is dead.

⁵By faith Enoch was taken from this life, so that he did not experience death; he could not be found, because God had taken him away. For before he was taken, he was commended as one who pleased God. ⁶And without faith it is impossible to please God, because anyone who comes to him must believe that he exists and that he rewards those who earnestly seek him.

⁷By faith Noah, when warned about things not yet seen, in holy fear built an ark to save his family. By his faith he condemned the world and became heir of the righteousness that comes by faith.

⁸By faith Abraham, when called to go to a place he would later receive as his inheritance, obeyed and went, even though he did not know where he was going. ⁹By faith he made his home in the promised land like a stranger in a foreign country; he lived in tents, as did Isaac and Jacob, who were heirs with him of the same promise. ¹⁰For he was looking forward to the city with foundations, whose architect and builder is God.

¹¹By faith Abraham, even though he was past age—and Sarah herself was barren—was enabled to become a father because he *ᶜ* considered him faithful who had made the promise. ¹²And

ᵃ 38 One early manuscript *But the righteous*   *ᵇ 38* Hab. 2:3,4
ᶜ 11 Or *By faith even Sarah, who was past age, was enabled to bear children because she*

stories to share

HEBREWS 11:1–40

What Is Faith?

LIFE LESSON: Faith is being sure of what we hope for and certain of what we can't yet see.

TO TALK ABOUT

✦ Does this chapter remind you of any favorite Bible stories? If so, which ones?

✦ Is it possible to please God without faith? Why or why not?

✦ The Biblical characters in this chapter didn't receive their reward during their lifetimes. How hard is it to believe in something in the distant future?

✦ When will we receive the reward of our faith?

A Special-Days Calendar

Every family has a string of birthdays, anniversaries and other special occasions to keep track of throughout the year. Turn this record-keeping task into a fun project by making an official family "special days" calendar with your grandchildren. On your calendar, besides the usual boxes for each day of the month, include a space for a photo or a seasonally appropriate picture (drawn by one of your grandchildren). Fill in the boxes, letting your grandkids add symbols and small pictures where appropriate. You can also add stickers or color in the numbers. Get as creative as your grandchildren's attention span and time will allow. Or create a special calendar together on the computer, using a simple publishing program.

Duplicate your calendar at a copy center, punch holes and add a ribbon hanger, and — voilà! — you have a timeless reminder for each family member, the perfect Christmas gift for loved ones near and far.

If you want to get a little fancier, select family photographs that are appropriate for each month. The copy center can duplicate the calendar in color and bind it with a spiral binding.

Long-Distance Variation: Ask your grandkids to contribute pictures and any special dates.

* * *

Thank you, Father, for all of the special dates that punctuate our family calendar year after year. I praise and thank you for all the people and memorable events our family has to cherish. Amen.

Your next devotion is located on page 1690.

GRANDCHILD IN FOCUS • PRAYER

Character

Dear Lord and Father, I ask that you fill my grandchild with your Spirit so her character reflects your goodness and love. Give her kindness and love for others. Bring joy to her life so she will be a joy to others. Grant her patience and self-control through difficult and trying times. May she show mercy and generosity to those who are less fortunate. Grant her integrity and a sense of justice, and surround her with your peace. Amen.

Worship the Lord

"Praise be to the name of God for ever and ever;
    wisdom and power are his.
He changes times and seasons;
    he sets up kings and deposes them.
He gives wisdom to the wise
    and knowledge to the discerning.
He reveals deep and hidden things;
    he knows what lies in darkness,
    and light dwells with him.
I thank and praise you, O God of my fathers:
    You have given me wisdom and power,
you have made known to me what we asked
        of you,
    you have made know to us the dream
        of the king."

Daniel 2:20 – 23

O God of my fathers, you are all wise and all powerful, in control of the rulers and nations of the earth. This knowledge comforts me when news of strife and injustice continue year after year. Let your wisdom and power shine through the darkness and give me hope of a new heaven and a new earth. Amen.

Your next devotion is located on page 1693.

GRANDCHILD IN FOCUS • PRAYER

Talents

Dear Lord, the giver of gifts, bless my grandchild as he develops his talents. Help him identify his talents and be proud and confident of the gifts you have given him. Give him patience and understanding, Lord, so he will not grow weary of striving and searching to reach the goals you have set for him. May each milestone bring satisfaction and a healthy desire for greater achievement and success to bring glory to you. Amen.

so from this one man, and he as good as dead, came descendants as numerous as the stars in the sky and as countless as the sand on the seashore.

¹³All these people were still living by faith when they died. They did not receive the things promised; they only saw them and welcomed them from a distance. And they admitted that they were aliens and strangers on earth. ¹⁴People who say such things show that they are looking for a country of their own. ¹⁵If they had been thinking of the country they had left, they would have had opportunity to return. ¹⁶Instead, they were longing for a better country—a heavenly one. Therefore God is not ashamed to be called their God, for he has prepared a city for them.

¹⁷By faith Abraham, when God tested him, offered Isaac as a sacrifice. He who had received the promises was about to sacrifice his one and only son, ¹⁸even though God had said to him, "It is through Isaac that your offspring[a] will be reckoned."[b] ¹⁹Abraham reasoned that God could raise the dead, and figuratively speaking, he did receive Isaac back from death.

²⁰By faith Isaac blessed Jacob and Esau in regard to their future.

²¹By faith Jacob, when he was dying, blessed each of Joseph's sons, and worshiped as he leaned on the top of his staff.

²²By faith Joseph, when his end was near, spoke about the exodus of the Israelites from Egypt and gave instructions about his bones.

²³By faith Moses' parents hid him for three months after he was born, because they saw he was no ordinary child, and they were not afraid of the king's edict.

²⁴By faith Moses, when he had grown up, refused to be known as the son of Pharaoh's daughter. ²⁵He chose to be mistreated along with the people of God rather than to enjoy the pleasures of sin for a short time. ²⁶He regarded disgrace for the sake of Christ as of greater value than the treasures of Egypt, because he was looking ahead to his reward. ²⁷By faith he left Egypt, not fearing the king's anger; he persevered because he saw him who is invisible. ²⁸By faith he kept the

Passover and the sprinkling of blood, so that the destroyer of the firstborn would not touch the firstborn of Israel.

²⁹By faith the people passed through the Red Sea[c] as on dry land; but when the Egyptians tried to do so, they were drowned.

³⁰By faith the walls of Jericho fell, after the people had marched around them for seven days.

³¹By faith the prostitute Rahab, because she welcomed the spies, was not killed with those who were disobedient.[d]

³²And what more shall I say? I do not have time to tell about Gideon, Barak, Samson, Jephthah, David, Samuel and the prophets, ³³who through faith conquered kingdoms, administered justice, and gained what was promised; who shut the mouths of lions, ³⁴quenched the fury of the flames, and escaped the edge of the sword; whose weakness was turned to strength; and who became powerful in battle and routed foreign armies. ³⁵Women received back their dead, raised to life again. Others were tortured and refused to be released, so that they might gain a better resurrection. ³⁶Some faced jeers and flogging, while still others were chained and put in prison. ³⁷They were stoned[e]; they were sawed in two; they were put to death by the sword. They went about in sheepskins and goatskins, destitute, persecuted and mistreated— ³⁸the world was not worthy of them. They wandered in deserts and mountains, and in caves and holes in the ground.

³⁹These were all commended for their faith, yet none of them received what had been promised. ⁴⁰God had planned something better for us so that only together with us would they be made perfect.

God Disciplines His Sons

12 Therefore, since we are surrounded by such a great cloud of witnesses, let us throw off everything that hinders and the sin that so easily entangles, and let us run with

---

[a] 18 Greek seed   [b] 18 Gen. 21:12   [c] 29 That is, Sea of Reeds
[d] 31 Or unbelieving   [e] 37 Some early manuscripts stoned; they were put to the test;

perseverance the race marked out for us. [2]Let us fix our eyes on Jesus, the author and perfecter of our faith, who for the joy set before him endured the cross, scorning its shame, and sat down at the right hand of the throne of God. [3]Consider him who endured such opposition from sinful men, so that you will not grow weary and lose heart.

[4]In your struggle against sin, you have not yet resisted to the point of shedding your blood. [5]And you have forgotten that word of encouragement that addresses you as sons:

"My son, do not make light of the Lord's
    discipline,
  and do not lose heart when he rebukes you,
[6]because the Lord disciplines those he loves,
  and he punishes everyone he accepts as
    a son."[a]

[7]Endure hardship as discipline; God is treating you as sons. For what son is not disciplined by his father? [8]If you are not disciplined (and everyone undergoes discipline), then you are illegitimate children and not true sons. [9]Moreover, we have all had human fathers who disciplined us and we respected them for it. How much more should we submit to the Father of our spirits and live! [10]Our fathers disciplined us for a little while as they thought best; but God disciplines us for our good, that we may share in his holiness. [11]No discipline seems pleasant at the time, but painful. Later on, however, it produces a harvest of righteousness and peace for those who have been trained by it.

[12]Therefore, strengthen your feeble arms and weak knees. [13]"Make level paths for your feet,"[b] so that the lame may not be disabled, but rather healed.

Warning Against Refusing God

[14]Make every effort to live in peace with all men and to be holy; without holiness no one will see the Lord. [15]See to it that no one misses the grace of God and that no bitter root grows up to cause trouble and defile many. [16]See that no one is sexually immoral, or is godless like Esau, who

TALKING POINTS

Bitterness

Don't allow bitterness to grow and cause trouble for yourself and others.

HEBREWS 12:15

This is the last talking point on bitterness.

for a single meal sold his inheritance rights as the oldest son. [17]Afterward, as you know, when he wanted to inherit this blessing, he was rejected. He could bring about no change of mind, though he sought the blessing with tears.

[18]You have not come to a mountain that can be touched and that is burning with fire; to darkness, gloom and storm; [19]to a trumpet blast or to such a voice speaking words that those who heard it begged that no further word be spoken to them, [20]because they could not bear what was commanded: "If even an animal touches the mountain, it must be stoned."[c] [21]The sight was so terrifying that Moses said, "I am trembling with fear."[d]

[22]But you have come to Mount Zion, to the heavenly Jerusalem, the city of the living God. You have come to thousands upon thousands of angels in joyful assembly, [23]to the church of the firstborn, whose names are written in heaven. You have come to God, the judge of all men, to the spirits of righteous men made perfect, [24]to Jesus the mediator of a new covenant, and to the sprinkled blood that speaks a better word than the blood of Abel.

[25]See to it that you do not refuse him who speaks. If they did not escape when they refused him who warned them on earth, how much less will we, if we turn away from him who warns us from heaven? [26]At that time his voice shook the earth, but now he has promised, "Once more I will

[a]6 Prov. 3:11,12   [b]13 Prov. 4:26   [c]20 Exodus 19:12,13
[d]21 Deut. 9:19

WE HAVE ALL HAD HUMAN FATHERS WHO DISCIPLINED US AND WE RESPECTED THEM FOR IT. HOW MUCH MORE SHOULD WE SUBMIT TO THE FATHER OF OUR SPIRITS AND LIVE!

Hebrews 12:9

Complete Surrender

CORRIE TEN BOOM

READ | HEBREWS 12:1–13

The Lord expects complete surrender from us. The potter can't shape clay that is not completely in his hands. Complete surrender means making our life available to God. God wants our lives in His hands, like a potter shapes the clay. If we reject God's desire as too extreme, then we are just "interested," like the window-shopper who doesn't want to pay the price. Our interest soon passes away.

What exactly is surrender? We know that we may not compromise. In her book *A Table Full of Gifts*, Annie van Essen-Bosch writes of how we can only really receive God's gifts if we bring our sins and problems to the Lord. Then there is room for what God wants to give us. If pride, resentment, hard-heartedness, and all our burdens are brought to the Lord, indeed our whole life, then He can richly give that life back to us. Then we are no longer owners, but stewards. We can feel so rich and joyful if we give Him, the Creator, the ownership of our life.

I saw such a good example of surrender in my father. He sometimes said, "My name is on my watchmaker's shop but actually God's name should be on it. Because I am a watchmaker by the grace of God." He knew what surrender meant, and how we can be stewards.

Lord, will you prepare us for your return? I submit myself completely to you, so that you, who began a good work in me, may carry it on to completion until the day of Christ Jesus. Hallelujah. Amen.

Your next devotion is located on page 1695.

GRANDCHILD IN FOCUS · PRAYER

SELECT ONE OF YOUR GRANDCHILDREN TO FOCUS ON IN PRAYER FOR THE NEXT 14 DAYS.

Salvation

Dear Lord, please guide my grandchild to your gift of salvation. I pray that she will come to know you, to love you and to walk close to you throughout her life. May she boldly claim Jesus as her Lord and Savior. Guide her as she makes choices that have eternal consequences. Help her to follow you each moment of her life. I pray this in Jesus' name, amen.

shake not only the earth but also the heavens."[a] [27] The words "once more" indicate the removing of what can be shaken — that is, created things — so that what cannot be shaken may remain.

[28] Therefore, since we are receiving a kingdom that cannot be shaken, let us be thankful, and so worship God acceptably with reverence and awe, [29] for our "God is a consuming fire."[b]

TALKING POINTS

Thankfulness
Be thankful for the gift of God's kingdom.

HEBREWS 12:28

This is the last talking point on thankfulness.

Concluding Exhortations

13 Keep on loving each other as brothers. [2] Do not forget to entertain strangers, for by so doing some people have entertained angels without knowing it. [3] Remember those in prison as if you were their fellow prisoners, and those who are mistreated as if you yourselves were suffering.

[4] Marriage should be honored by all, and the marriage bed kept pure, for God will judge the adulterer and all the sexually immoral. [5] Keep your lives free from the love of money and be content with what you have, because God has said,

"Never will I leave you;
  never will I forsake you."[c]

[6] So we say with confidence,

"The Lord is my helper; I will not be afraid.
  What can man do to me?"[d]

[7] Remember your leaders, who spoke the word of God to you. Consider the outcome of their way of life and imitate their faith. [8] Jesus Christ is the same yesterday and today and forever.

PRAYING THE SCRIPTURES

Guidance
HEBREWS 13:5

Dear God, help my grandchild to keep his life free from the love of money and to be content with what he has, remembering that you have promised never to leave or forsake him.

This is the last prayer in the Guidance Prayer Track.

[9] Do not be carried away by all kinds of strange teachings. It is good for our hearts to be strengthened by grace, not by ceremonial foods, which are of no value to those who eat them. [10] We have an altar from which those who minister at the tabernacle have no right to eat.

[11] The high priest carries the blood of animals into the Most Holy Place as a sin offering, but the bodies are burned outside the camp. [12] And so Jesus also suffered outside the city gate to make the people holy through his own blood. [13] Let us, then, go to him outside the camp, bearing the disgrace he bore. [14] For here we do not have an enduring city, but we are looking for the city that is to come.

[15] Through Jesus, therefore, let us continually offer to God a sacrifice of praise — the fruit of lips that confess his name. [16] And do not forget to do good and to share with others, for with such sacrifices God is pleased.

[17] Obey your leaders and submit to their authority. They keep watch over you as men who must give an account. Obey them so that their work will be a joy, not a burden, for that would be of no advantage to you.

[18] Pray for us. We are sure that we have a clear conscience and desire to live honorably in every way. [19] I particularly urge you to pray so that I may be restored to you soon.

[a] 26 Haggai 2:6 [b] 29 Deut. 4:24 [c] 5 Deut. 31:6
[d] 6 Psalm 118:6,7

KEEP YOUR LIVES FREE FROM
THE LOVE OF MONEY AND BE
CONTENT WITH WHAT YOU HAVE,
BECAUSE GOD HAS SAID, "NEVER
WILL I LEAVE YOU; NEVER WILL I
FORSAKE YOU."

Hebrews 13:5

Relatively Speaking

DONNA HUISJEN

READ | HEBREWS 13:1–25

Last fall an advertisement appeared on a double billboard close to my home. One side pictured a young girl wrinkling her nose in protest against the cottage cheese and Jell-O "pink stuff" on her family's overly abundant Thanksgiving table. The adjoining billboard featured a little girl walking along a windswept sidewalk, hand clasped in that of an adult. I remember precisely what was being endorsed: a local homeless shelter. The faces on both sides of the billboard were unhappy, but one was dirty and pinched rather than peeved.

The girl at the Thanksgiving table suddenly came to symbolize for me the "enemy" that is too often us. She became the unwitting representative of all in our culture that is selfish, pampered, demanding and complacent. Satisfaction, the comparison reminded me, is truly relative.

My home may be modest, but it's sound, and my neighborhood is stable. My table is anything but lavish — but God has always been present, providing daily bread, fulfilling all my basic needs.

As a single mom my situation has been far from ideal, but I'm thankful for the heavenly guardian who's always at my side. I know I can ask God at any time with childlike trust to pick me up, knowing he will readily comply. In the words of one of my favorite verses, "The one the LORD loves rests between his shoulders" (Deuteronomy 33:12). Because I am a child of God, I confidently rest in knowing I am "the one." I am content knowing that he will never leave me; he will never forsake me.

My provider, impress upon my heart the secret of relativity. Help me, as I rest securely between your shoulders, to remember my priorities and to revel in your goodness and reliability, appreciating what you've given me rather than grousing over what I may picture myself as lacking. Amen.

Your next devotion is located on page 1699.

GRANDCHILD IN FOCUS • PRAYER

Physical Well-Being

Almighty God, Creator of us all, I pray that you will watch over my grandchild's physical development. May he grow in strength through the stages of his life. As he grows in awareness of his body, help him to understand that each body develops uniquely, yet is within your plan and your control. Please guard his health so that his diseases are few, his injuries are minor and his infirmities are brief. Amen.

²⁰May the God of peace, who through the blood of the eternal covenant brought back from the dead our Lord Jesus, that great Shepherd of the sheep, ²¹equip you with everything good for doing his will, and may he work in us what is pleasing to him, through Jesus Christ, to whom be glory for ever and ever. Amen.

²²Brothers, I urge you to bear with my word of exhortation, for I have written you only a short letter.

²³I want you to know that our brother Timothy has been released. If he arrives soon, I will come with him to see you.

²⁴Greet all your leaders and all God's people. Those from Italy send you their greetings.

²⁵Grace be with you all.

PRAYING THE SCRIPTURES

Blessing

HEBREWS 13:20

I pray, O God, that you, the God of peace, who through the blood of the eternal covenant brought back from the dead our Lord Jesus, that great Shepherd of the sheep, will equip my grandchild with everything good for doing your will, and that you will work in him what is pleasing to you. Amen.

Next prayer in Blessing Prayer Track: Jude 2

Faith IN ACTION

James, the brother of Jesus, wrote this letter to "the twelve tribes scattered among the nations" (James 1:1). It isn't clear if this reference is to Christians in general or to Jewish believers specifically. Perhaps James, a leader of the early church in Jerusalem, wrote this letter to those who were scattered by persecution (see Acts 8:1; 11:19). His message, however, is clear: Christianity is more than head knowledge of Bible stories, creeds or Scripture references. Faith is more than claiming salvation, for if faith is not accompanied by action, it is not faith. Our belief in Jesus must move from our heads and hearts into our daily lives.

And what does that look like? One who has true faith, James declared, watches his or her tongue, perseveres in trials, shows mercy to the poor and helpless, is humble, is patient in suffering and obeys the Word of God.

There are so many rich lessons to learn in the book of James and so many behaviors to model for our children and grandchildren. But the real issue is the condition of our hearts. It's about our motives. It's about wisdom and what we have learned about being "peace-loving, considerate, submissive, full of mercy and good fruit, impartial and sincere" (James 3:17). And ultimately, it's about drawing near to God (see James 4:8). If we do these things, our grandchildren will see that our faith is more than words — it's Jesus *alive* in us.

VERSE *to* REMEMBER | JAMES 1:22

Do not merely listen to the word, and so deceive yourselves. Do what it says.

ABOUT JAMES

WRITTEN BY:
James, the brother
of Jesus

WRITTEN FOR:
Jewish believers scattered
by persecution, but also for
Christians in general

DATE WRITTEN:
Probably about A.D. 49

WHY WRITTEN:
To show Christians how to
live out their faith

1

James, a servant of God and of the Lord Jesus Christ,

To the twelve tribes scattered among the nations:

Greetings.

Trials and Temptations

²Consider it pure joy, my brothers, whenever you face trials of many kinds, ³because you know that the testing of your faith develops perseverance. ⁴Perseverance must finish its work so that you may be mature and complete, not lacking anything. ⁵If any of you lacks wisdom, he should ask God, who gives generously to all without finding fault, and it will be given to him. ⁶But when he asks, he must believe and not doubt, because he who doubts is like a wave of the sea, blown and tossed by the wind. ⁷That man should not think he will receive anything from the Lord; ⁸he is a double-minded man, unstable in all he does.

⁹The brother in humble circumstances ought to take pride in his high position. ¹⁰But the one who is rich should take pride in his low position, because he will pass away like a wild flower. ¹¹For the sun rises with scorching heat and withers the plant; its blossom falls and its beauty is destroyed. In the same way, the rich man will fade away even while he goes about his business.

¹²Blessed is the man who perseveres under trial, because when he has stood the test, he will receive the crown of life that God has promised to those who love him.

¹³When tempted, no one should say, "God is tempting me." For God cannot be tempted by evil, nor does he tempt anyone; ¹⁴but each one is tempted when, by his own evil desire, he is dragged away and enticed. ¹⁵Then, after desire has conceived, it gives birth to sin; and sin, when it is full-grown, gives birth to death.

¹⁶Don't be deceived, my dear brothers. ¹⁷Every good and perfect gift is from above, coming down from the Father of the heavenly lights, who does not change like shifting shadows. ¹⁸He chose to give us birth through the word of truth, that we might be a kind of firstfruits of all he created.

Listening and Doing

¹⁹My dear brothers, take note of this: Everyone should be quick to listen, slow to speak and slow to become angry, ²⁰for man's anger does not bring about the righteous life that God desires. ²¹Therefore, get rid of all moral filth and the evil that is so prevalent and humbly accept the word planted in you, which can save you.

²²Do not merely listen to the word, and so deceive yourselves. Do what it says. ²³Anyone who listens to the word but does not do what it says is like a man who looks at his face in a mirror ²⁴and, after looking at himself, goes away and immediately forgets what he looks like. ²⁵But the man who looks intently into the perfect law that gives freedom, and continues to do this, not forgetting what he has heard, but doing it—he will be blessed in what he does.

²⁶If anyone considers himself religious and yet does not keep a tight rein on his tongue, he deceives himself and his religion is worthless. ²⁷Religion that God our Father accepts as pure and faultless is this: to look after orphans and widows in their distress and to keep oneself from being polluted by the world.

TALKING POINTS

Worldliness
Avoid getting polluted by the world.
JAMES 1:27

For more on worldliness, go to 1 John 2:15–17.

Favoritism Forbidden

2

My brothers, as believers in our glorious Lord Jesus Christ, don't show favoritism. ²Suppose a man comes into your meeting wearing a gold ring and fine clothes, and a poor man in shabby clothes also comes in. ³If you show special attention to the man wearing fine clothes and say,

CONSIDER IT PURE JOY, MY BROTHERS, WHENEVER YOU FACE TRIALS OF MANY KINDS, BECAUSE YOU KNOW THAT THE TESTING OF YOUR FAITH DEVELOPS PERSEVERANCE. PERSEVERANCE MUST FINISH ITS WORK SO THAT YOU MAY BE MATURE AND COMPLETE, NOT LACKING ANYTHING.

James 1:2 – 4

Patient Perseverance

EMILIE BARNES

READ | JAMES 1:1 – 18

A few years ago our family went to Lake Tahoe to ski. As we walked on the icy slopes of this beautiful resort, we were surrounded by the best — the best cars, skis, clothes and beauty. We couldn't believe our eyes. We had never seen so much sizzle in one place. So I said to myself, "No way am I going to compete with them." After being coaxed into a group ski lesson, I found that members of the "sizzle group" were also in my class, and they couldn't ski any better than I could!

So much of life is painted with speed, flash and sizzle that we can be so intimidated that we don't even want to enter the fray, let alone persevere. But Scripture teaches that perseverance is enduring with patience. In the Bible, perseverance describes those Christians who remain steadfast in the face of opposition, attack and discouragement. When we persevere with patience, we exhibit our ability to stay faithful with calmness and without complaint.

Commitment and discipline are not words "the world" is comfortable with. People living in the new millennium want everything to feel good — but perseverance doesn't always feel good. It sometimes demands pain and denial of self. That's why trusting and having faith in God's guidance is so important.

Scripture is clear. It teaches we are to persevere: in prayer (see Ephesians 6:18), in obedience (see Revelation 14:12) and in self-control (see 2 Peter 1:5 – 7).

Scripture promises us certain blessings if we endure: final deliverance (see Matthew 24:13), the reward of faith (see Hebrews 11:6) and an eternal inheritance (see Revelation 21:7).

As we live out our lives and persevere daily through trials and against temptations, we are rewarded by the Lord with the fruit of his Spirit for all eternity: "love, joy, peace, patience, kindness, goodness, faithfulness, gentleness and self-control" (Galatians 5:22 – 23).

Father God, in life's difficulties, help me to look to you to see what you are trying to teach me. I so want to be a good student in life and to persevere to the end. Let me not become distracted along the way. Amen.

Your next devotion is located on page 1702.

GRANDCHILD IN FOCUS • PRAYER

Emotional Development

O God, Creator of mind and body, I pray that you will give my grandchild emotional health and strength. Where there is anger, bring peace. Where there is confusion, bring clarity and focus. Where there are dark shadows, cast a ray of hope. Fill her with the sunshine of your Spirit. Warm her with the presence of your peace. Amen.

"Here's a good seat for you," but say to the poor man, "You stand there" or "Sit on the floor by my feet," [4]have you not discriminated among yourselves and become judges with evil thoughts?

TALKING POINTS

Social Justice

We should not show favoritism.

JAMES 2:1–9

This is the last talking point on social justice.

[5]Listen, my dear brothers: Has not God chosen those who are poor in the eyes of the world to be rich in faith and to inherit the kingdom he promised those who love him? [6]But you have insulted the poor. Is it not the rich who are exploiting you? Are they not the ones who are dragging you into court? [7]Are they not the ones who are slandering the noble name of him to whom you belong?

[8]If you really keep the royal law found in Scripture, "Love your neighbor as yourself,"[a] you are doing right. [9]But if you show favoritism, you sin and are convicted by the law as lawbreakers. [10]For whoever keeps the whole law and yet stumbles at just one point is guilty of breaking all of it. [11]For he who said, "Do not commit adultery,"[b] also said, "Do not murder."[c] If you do not commit adultery but do commit murder, you have become a lawbreaker.

[12]Speak and act as those who are going to be judged by the law that gives freedom, [13]because judgment without mercy will be shown to anyone who has not been merciful. Mercy triumphs over judgment!

Faith and Deeds

[14]What good is it, my brothers, if a man claims to have faith but has no deeds? Can such faith save him? [15]Suppose a brother or sister is without clothes and daily food. [16]If one of you says to him, "Go, I wish you well; keep warm and well fed," but does nothing about his physical needs, what good is it? [17]In the same way, faith by itself, if it is not accompanied by action, is dead.

[18]But someone will say, "You have faith; I have deeds."

Show me your faith without deeds, and I will show you my faith by what I do. [19]You believe that there is one God. Good! Even the demons believe that—and shudder.

[20]You foolish man, do you want evidence that faith without deeds is useless[d]? [21]Was not our ancestor Abraham considered righteous for what

[a] *8* Lev. 19:18   [b] *11* Exodus 20:14; Deut. 5:18
[c] *11* Exodus 20:13; Deut. 5:17   [d] *20* Some early manuscripts *dead*

stories to share

JAMES 2:14–26

Faith and Deeds

LIFE LESSON: Salvation comes by faith alone, but good deeds show we have faith.

TO TALK ABOUT

✦ How does James describe faith without deeds?

✦ Is it possible to do good deeds without having faith?

✦ Is it possible to have faith without doing good deeds?

✦ If salvation comes by faith alone, why do we do good deeds?

he did when he offered his son Isaac on the altar? [22] You see that his faith and his actions were working together, and his faith was made complete by what he did. [23] And the scripture was fulfilled that says, "Abraham believed God, and it was credited to him as righteousness,"[a] and he was called God's friend. [24] You see that a person is justified by what he does and not by faith alone.

[25] In the same way, was not even Rahab the prostitute considered righteous for what she did when she gave lodging to the spies and sent them off in a different direction? [26] As the body without the spirit is dead, so faith without deeds is dead.

Taming the Tongue

3 Not many of you should presume to be teachers, my brothers, because you know that we who teach will be judged more strictly. [2] We all stumble in many ways. If anyone is never at fault in what he says, he is a perfect man, able to keep his whole body in check.

[3] When we put bits into the mouths of horses to make them obey us, we can turn the whole animal. [4] Or take ships as an example. Although they are so large and are driven by strong winds, they are steered by a very small rudder wherever the pilot wants to go. [5] Likewise the tongue is a small part of the body, but it makes great boasts. Consider what a great forest is set on fire by a small spark. [6] The tongue also is a fire, a world of evil among the parts of the body. It corrupts the whole person, sets the whole course of his life on fire, and is itself set on fire by hell.

[7] All kinds of animals, birds, reptiles and creatures of the sea are being tamed and have been tamed by man, [8] but no man can tame the tongue. It is a restless evil, full of deadly poison.

[9] With the tongue we praise our Lord and Father, and with it we curse men, who have been made in God's likeness. [10] Out of the same mouth come praise and cursing. My brothers, this should not be. [11] Can both fresh water and salt[b] water flow from the same spring? [12] My brothers, can a fig tree bear olives, or a grapevine bear figs? Neither can a salt spring produce fresh water.

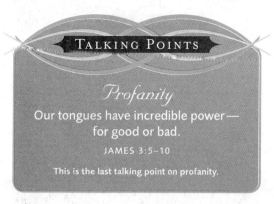

TALKING POINTS

Profanity

Our tongues have incredible power—
for good or bad.

JAMES 3:5–10

This is the last talking point on profanity.

Two Kinds of Wisdom

[13] Who is wise and understanding among you? Let him show it by his good life, by deeds done in the humility that comes from wisdom. [14] But if you harbor bitter envy and selfish ambition in your hearts, do not boast about it or deny the truth. [15] Such "wisdom" does not come down from heaven but is earthly, unspiritual, of the devil. [16] For where you have envy and selfish ambition, there you find disorder and every evil practice.

[17] But the wisdom that comes from heaven is first of all pure; then peace-loving, considerate, submissive, full of mercy and good fruit, impartial and sincere. [18] Peacemakers who sow in peace raise a harvest of righteousness.

TALKING POINTS

Knowing God's Will

Read this checklist of heavenly wisdom.

JAMES 3:17

This is the last talking point on knowing God's will.

Submit Yourselves to God

4 What causes fights and quarrels among you? Don't they come from your desires that battle

[a] 23 Gen. 15:6   [b] 11 Greek *bitter* (see also verse 14)

INSTEAD, YOU OUGHT TO SAY, "IF IT IS THE LORD'S WILL, WE WILL LIVE AND DO THIS OR THAT."

James 4:15

God at the Controls

JANE SCHLENVOGT

READ | JAMES 4:1–17

I love to travel. Some of my most peaceful days with Christ have been spent on the road. Travel clears the mind of daily clutter. (Of which many would say I have plenty!) And it provides new horizons and perspectives on life. I love getting behind the wheel of a car and being in control for a dozen hours a day.

Though the activities vary, control is important to all of us. When life gets out of control, we remember what we should have prayed: "Your will be done."

Let go. Women have this mothering instinct, which in more general terms means that we crave to be more or less in control. Somehow we have come to believe that any half-organized day revolves around us and our ability to keep everything going with some semblance of order.

Give it up, ladies. Let go. Give God control. (He'll be in charge whether you render control to him or not.) Put your feet up on the hassock of your mind. He will not disappoint you. He will energize you with the deep massage of his Word for your spiritual aching and provide aromatic emollients for your emotional stress. You'll be ever so energized, rising to the occasion on the assignments and expectations that God has outlined just for you. In the "letting go" comes the confidence that God provides for every need.

Dear Savior, so often I've tried to control my life, where I go and what I do, and it hasn't gotten me anywhere at all. Give me the will and courage to let go of the controls and trust you to steer me where you want me to go. Help me to rest in you. Amen.

Your next devotion is located on page 1704.

GRANDCHILD IN FOCUS • PRAYER

Spiritual Growth

Dear Lord, today I pray for my grandchild's spiritual growth. I ask that you instill in him the desire to read and memorize your Word. Give him a passion to be in conversation with you. May loving and serving you be part of his daily life. I ask that you stay close to him and lead him to be transformed to your likeness, to reflect your grace and to radiate your love. I pray this in Jesus' name, amen.

within you? ²You want something but don't get it. You kill and covet, but you cannot have what you want. You quarrel and fight. You do not have, because you do not ask God. ³When you ask, you do not receive, because you ask with wrong motives, that you may spend what you get on your pleasures.

⁴You adulterous people, don't you know that friendship with the world is hatred toward God? Anyone who chooses to be a friend of the world becomes an enemy of God. ⁵Or do you think Scripture says without reason that the spirit he caused to live in us envies intensely?ᵃ ⁶But he gives us more grace. That is why Scripture says:

> "God opposes the proud
> but gives grace to the humble."ᵇ

⁷Submit yourselves, then, to God. Resist the devil, and he will flee from you. ⁸Come near to God and he will come near to you. Wash your hands, you sinners, and purify your hearts, you double-minded. ⁹Grieve, mourn and wail. Change your laughter to mourning and your joy to gloom. ¹⁰Humble yourselves before the Lord, and he will lift you up.

¹¹Brothers, do not slander one another. Anyone who speaks against his brother or judges him speaks against the law and judges it. When you judge the law, you are not keeping it, but sitting in judgment on it. ¹²There is only one Lawgiver and Judge, the one who is able to save and destroy. But you — who are you to judge your neighbor?

Boasting About Tomorrow

¹³Now listen, you who say, "Today or tomorrow we will go to this or that city, spend a year there, carry on business and make money." ¹⁴Why, you do not even know what will happen tomorrow. What is your life? You are a mist that appears for a little while and then vanishes. ¹⁵Instead, you ought to say, "If it is the Lord's will, we will live and do this or that." ¹⁶As it is, you boast and brag. All such boasting is evil. ¹⁷Anyone, then, who knows the good he ought to do and doesn't do it, sins.

TALKING POINTS

Prayer

We should pray in faith.

JAMES 5:13–16

This is the last talking point on prayer.

Warning to Rich Oppressors

5 Now listen, you rich people, weep and wail because of the misery that is coming upon you. ²Your wealth has rotted, and moths have eaten your clothes. ³Your gold and silver are corroded. Their corrosion will testify against you and eat your flesh like fire. You have hoarded wealth in the last days. ⁴Look! The wages you failed to pay the workmen who mowed your fields are crying out against you. The cries of the harvesters have reached the ears of the Lord Almighty. ⁵You have lived on earth in luxury and self-indulgence. You have fattened yourselves in the day of slaughter.ᶜ ⁶You have condemned and murdered innocent men, who were not opposing you.

Patience in Suffering

⁷Be patient, then, brothers, until the Lord's coming. See how the farmer waits for the land to yield its valuable crop and how patient he is for the autumn and spring rains. ⁸You too, be patient and stand firm, because the Lord's coming is near. ⁹Don't grumble against each other, brothers, or you will be judged. The Judge is standing at the door!

¹⁰Brothers, as an example of patience in the face of suffering, take the prophets who spoke in the name of the Lord. ¹¹As you know, we consider blessed those who have persevered. You have

---

ᵃ 5 Or that God jealously longs for the spirit that he made to live in us; or that the Spirit he caused to live in us longs jealously
ᵇ 6 Prov. 3:34   ᶜ 5 Or yourselves as in a day of feasting

Grandma's Prayers

DAWN SCOTT JONES

READ | JAMES 5:13 – 20

My eyes slowly fluttered open. The soft, rhythmic sound of Grandma's voice echoed through the early morning, awakening my senses. It was summer vacation in Elkhart, Indiana, and all of us in Grandma and Grandpa's country farmhouse were still sleeping — everyone but Grandma, that is. She was in the kitchen enjoying a private conversation. "Who is she talking to?" my little girl curiosity wondered. I listened intently, but Grandma's sweet tone was the only voice I could hear. Whoever this mystery person was, she knew him well, for she was sharing her deepest secrets with this patient listener and finding great joy and strength in their time together.

I soon discovered that Grandma was a prayer warrior. It was her practice to rise early in the morning and engage God in conversation. She did not speak with the eloquence of a skilled orator; rather, her dialogue was simple, honest and determined. She opened up her heart and poured its contents at the feet of Jesus. Grandma's prayers were powerful. She pursued God, and things happened.

God's Word says here in James 5:16 that the prayers of the righteous — those living in *right standing* with God — get effective, powerful results. That Scripture virtually means that the prayers of one whose life is right before God are a mighty force to be reckoned with! The secret of success in prayer is not in our choice of vocabulary but in our relationship with Christ. When our prayers and petitions flow out of a pure heart, we should expect to see mountains move, situations change and lives transform. Grandma was a force to be reckoned with. We can be too!

Precious Lord, thank you for the privilege of talking to you personally and for the promise that you will hear and answer my prayers. Today I bring you all the concerns and requests of my heart. I trust you to meet every need according to your plan and purpose. Amen.

Your next devotion is located on page 1709.

GRANDCHILD IN FOCUS • PRAYER

Relationships at Home

O Lord, I pray that you will bless the home and family of my grandchild. May the relationships she has with her parents and siblings enhance her well-being, support her self-confidence and increase her faith. May her home life reflect your love, your grace, your compassion and your peace. Guide her parents to direct her in love and truth, so she will grow into a strong and compassionate individual. Amen.

heard of Job's perseverance and have seen what the Lord finally brought about. The Lord is full of compassion and mercy.

¹²Above all, my brothers, do not swear—not by heaven or by earth or by anything else. Let your "Yes" be yes, and your "No," no, or you will be condemned.

The Prayer of Faith

¹³Is any one of you in trouble? He should pray. Is anyone happy? Let him sing songs of praise. ¹⁴Is any one of you sick? He should call the elders of the church to pray over him and anoint him with oil in the name of the Lord. ¹⁵And the prayer offered in faith will make the sick person well; the Lord will raise him up. If he has sinned, he will be forgiven. ¹⁶Therefore confess your sins to each other and pray for each other so that you may be healed. The prayer of a righteous man is powerful and effective.

¹⁷Elijah was a man just like us. He prayed earnestly that it would not rain, and it did not rain on the land for three and a half years. ¹⁸Again he prayed, and the heavens gave rain, and the earth produced its crops.

¹⁹My brothers, if one of you should wander from the truth and someone should bring him back, ²⁰remember this: Whoever turns a sinner from the error of his way will save him from death and cover over a multitude of sins.

Using YOUR GIFTS

The apostle Peter's first letter to the Christians who were scattered by persecution highlights how they were to live in spite of the suffering they were enduring. Peter reminded them that they were God's chosen people, a royal priesthood, a holy nation, blessed with new life and hope in Christ Jesus; *therefore*, they were to live holy lives. They were to be self-controlled, submit to authority, refrain from retaliation, pray, love each other deeply, practice hospitality, and use whatever gifts they had been given in service to others.

Each of us has different gifts, abilities, interests and talents. When it comes to being grandmothers, we also have unique gifts. You might not fit the stereotype of a grandma: Perhaps you don't "do" cookies or diapers. Maybe you don't know the difference between a glue stick and a Popsicle stick. Or you may think "warm and fuzzy" only applies to slippers. But it may be that you ski, have a knack for finding great books to read or know how to fix a car. No matter what your gifts, faithfully use them in God's service. One of the best ways to do this is to nurture and love your grandchildren in your own unique and wonderful way.

VERSE *to* REMEMBER | 1 PETER 4:10

Each one should use whatever gift he has received to serve others, faithfully administering God's grace in its various forms.

ABOUT 1 PETER

WRITTEN BY:
The apostle Peter

WRITTEN FOR:
Specifically for Christians scattered throughout Asia Minor, but also for Christians everywhere

DATE WRITTEN:
Probably about A.D. 62–64 from Rome

WHY WRITTEN:
To encourage Christians to live holy lives in spite of suffering

1 Peter, an apostle of Jesus Christ,

To God's elect, strangers in the world, scattered throughout Pontus, Galatia, Cappadocia, Asia and Bithynia, [2] who have been chosen according to the foreknowledge of God the Father, through the sanctifying work of the Spirit, for obedience to Jesus Christ and sprinkling by his blood:

Grace and peace be yours in abundance.

Praise to God for a Living Hope

[3] Praise be to the God and Father of our Lord Jesus Christ! In his great mercy he has given us new birth into a living hope through the resurrection of Jesus Christ from the dead, [4] and into an inheritance that can never perish, spoil or fade—kept in heaven for you, [5] who through faith are shielded by God's power until the coming of the salvation that is ready to be revealed in the last time. [6] In this you greatly rejoice, though now for a little while you may have had to suffer grief in all kinds of trials. [7] These have come so that your faith—of greater worth than gold, which perishes even though refined by fire—may be proved genuine and may result in praise, glory and honor when Jesus Christ is revealed. [8] Though you have not seen him, you love him;

PRAYING THE SCRIPTURES

Salvation

1 PETER 1:8–9

I pray, dear Jesus, that although my grandchild has not seen you, she will love you; and even though she does not see you now, she will believe in you and be filled with an inexpressible and glorious joy, as she receives the goal of her faith, the salvation of her soul.

This is the last prayer in the Salvation Prayer Track.

and even though you do not see him now, you believe in him and are filled with an inexpressible and glorious joy, [9] for you are receiving the goal of your faith, the salvation of your souls.

[10] Concerning this salvation, the prophets, who spoke of the grace that was to come to you, searched intently and with the greatest care, [11] trying to find out the time and circumstances to which the Spirit of Christ in them was pointing when he predicted the sufferings of Christ and the glories that would follow. [12] It was revealed to them that they were not serving themselves but you, when they spoke of the things that have now been told you by those who have preached the gospel to you by the Holy Spirit sent from heaven. Even angels long to look into these things.

Be Holy

[13] Therefore, prepare your minds for action; be self-controlled; set your hope fully on the grace to be given you when Jesus Christ is revealed. [14] As obedient children, do not conform to the evil desires you had when you lived in ignorance. [15] But just as he who called you is holy, so be holy in all you do; [16] for it is written: "Be holy, because I am holy."[a]

[17] Since you call on a Father who judges each man's work impartially, live your lives as strangers here in reverent fear. [18] For you know that it was not with perishable things such as silver or gold that you were redeemed from the empty way of life handed down to you from your forefathers, [19] but with the precious blood of Christ, a lamb without blemish or defect. [20] He was chosen before the creation of the world, but was revealed in these last times for your sake. [21] Through him you believe in God, who raised him from the dead and glorified him, and so your faith and hope are in God.

[22] Now that you have purified yourselves by obeying the truth so that you have sincere love for your brothers, love one another deeply, from the heart.[b] [23] For you have been born again, not

[a] 16 Lev. 11:44,45; 19:2   [b] 22 Some early manuscripts *from a pure heart*

of perishable seed, but of imperishable, through the living and enduring word of God. ²⁴For,

"All men are like grass,
    and all their glory is like the flowers of the field;
the grass withers and the flowers fall,
²⁵   but the word of the Lord stands forever."ᵃ

And this is the word that was preached to you.

2 Therefore, rid yourselves of all malice and all deceit, hypocrisy, envy, and slander of every kind. ²Like newborn babies, crave pure spiritual milk, so that by it you may grow up in your salvation, ³now that you have tasted that the Lord is good.

The Living Stone and a Chosen People

⁴As you come to him, the living Stone—rejected by men but chosen by God and precious to him— ⁵you also, like living stones, are being built into a spiritual house to be a holy priesthood, offering spiritual sacrifices acceptable to God through Jesus Christ. ⁶For in Scripture it says:

"See, I lay a stone in Zion,
    a chosen and precious cornerstone,
and the one who trusts in him
    will never be put to shame."ᵇ

⁷Now to you who believe, this stone is precious. But to those who do not believe,

"The stone the builders rejected
    has become the capstone,ᶜ"ᵈ

⁸and,

"A stone that causes men to stumble
    and a rock that makes them fall."ᵉ

They stumble because they disobey the message—which is also what they were destined for.

⁹But you are a chosen people, a royal priesthood, a holy nation, a people belonging to God, that you may declare the praises of him who called you out of darkness into his wonderful light. ¹⁰Once you were not a people, but now you are the people of God; once you had not received mercy, but now you have received mercy.

¹¹Dear friends, I urge you, as aliens and strangers in the world, to abstain from sinful desires, which war against your soul. ¹²Live such good lives among the pagans that, though they accuse you of doing wrong, they may see your good deeds and glorify God on the day he visits us.

Submission to Rulers and Masters

¹³Submit yourselves for the Lord's sake to every authority instituted among men: whether to the king, as the supreme authority, ¹⁴or to governors, who are sent by him to punish those who do wrong and to commend those who do right. ¹⁵For it is God's will that by doing good you should silence the ignorant talk of foolish men. ¹⁶Live as free men, but do not use your freedom as a cover-up for evil; live as servants of God. ¹⁷Show proper respect to everyone: Love the brotherhood of believers, fear God, honor the king.

¹⁸Slaves, submit yourselves to your masters with all respect, not only to those who are good and considerate, but also to those who are harsh. ¹⁹For it is commendable if a man bears up under the pain of unjust suffering because he is conscious of God. ²⁰But how is it to your credit if you receive a beating for doing wrong and endure it? But if you suffer for doing good and you endure it, this is commendable before God. ²¹To this you were called, because Christ suffered for you, leaving you an example, that you should follow in his steps.

²²"He committed no sin,
    and no deceit was found in his mouth."ᶠ

²³When they hurled their insults at him, he did not retaliate; when he suffered, he made no threats. Instead, he entrusted himself to him who judges justly. ²⁴He himself bore our sins in his body on the tree, so that we might die to sins and live for righteousness; by his wounds you have been healed. ²⁵For you were like sheep going astray, but now you have returned to the Shepherd and Overseer of your souls.

ᵃ 25 Isaiah 40:6-8   ᵇ 6 Isaiah 28:16   ᶜ 7 Or *cornerstone*
ᵈ 7 Psalm 118:22   ᵉ 8 Isaiah 8:14   ᶠ 22 Isaiah 53:9

FAITH IN
ACTION

My Spiritual Favorite Things

In advance of getting together, prepare and duplicate for each grandchild a list of your "favorite spiritual things." You could include: a hymn or worship song, a recording artist or CD, a Scripture verse or passage, a devotional book, a spiritual event, a Christian who has influenced you, answers to prayer or significant dates of your spiritual life.

When you get together, share some of your favorites and tell the kids a story or two related to that item. Then give each child a large sheet of cardboard or paper, along with whatever supplies you have on hand, and have them prepare a similar list in pictures and words. Younger children may focus on their favorite things; but encourage them to include a few spiritual favorites: a Bible story, Bible verse or song. Let the kids share their list with their mom and dad. They're sure to be treasured, especially in conjunction with your gift.

Holy Father, what could be more important than the treasures I have in you and your Word? Help me to point my grandchildren toward the things that truly matter, both now and for all eternity. Amen.

Your next devotion is located on page 1710.

GRANDCHILD IN FOCUS • PRAYER

Friends

Dear Lord and Father, I pray for my grandchild's social life and his friends. Bring diverse friends into his life who will love and encourage him, who will bring joy and laughter to the good times and comfort and support through difficulties and disappointments. Grant him wisdom and discernment as he selects his friends; help him to avoid cliques that restrict, activities that endanger, and foolish and dangerous behaviors that harm. I ask that you fill his life with close and caring relationships. Amen.

Worship the Lord

Praise the LORD.

Sing to the LORD a new song,
    his praise in the assembly of the saints.

Let Israel rejoice in their Maker;
    let the people of Zion be glad in their King.
Let them praise his name with dancing
    and make music to him with tambourine and harp.
For the LORD takes delight in his people;
    he crowns the humble with salvation.
Let the saints rejoice in this honor
    and sing for joy on their beds.

May the praise of God be in their mouths.

Psalm 149:1 — 6a

I can hardly comprehend that you take such delight in me, Father. How wonderful that you have crowned me with your salvation. Liberate my soul today to dance before you with irrepressible joy. Let me sing praises to you till the close of the day and as I lie down to sleep tonight. Amen.

Your next devotion is located on page 1712.

GRANDCHILD IN FOCUS • PRAYER

Self-Image

O loving God, I praise you for creating my grandchild as a unique individual. Now I ask you to help her appreciate her uniqueness. Build up her self-image so she can enjoy her individuality. Help her to stand firm for who she is, where she has come from and what she believes in. Encourage her not only to have hopes and dreams but to also enjoy each day as it comes.
In Jesus' name, amen.

Wives and Husbands

3 Wives, in the same way be submissive to your husbands so that, if any of them do not believe the word, they may be won over without words by the behavior of their wives, ²when they see the purity and reverence of your lives. ³Your beauty should not come from outward adornment, such as braided hair and the wearing of gold jewelry and fine clothes. ⁴Instead, it should be that of your inner self, the unfading beauty of a gentle and quiet spirit, which is of great worth in God's sight. ⁵For this is the way the holy women of the past who put their hope in God used to make themselves beautiful. They were submissive to their own husbands, ⁶like Sarah, who obeyed Abraham and called him her master. You are her daughters if you do what is right and do not give way to fear.

⁷Husbands, in the same way be considerate as you live with your wives, and treat them with respect as the weaker partner and as heirs with you of the gracious gift of life, so that nothing will hinder your prayers.

Suffering for Doing Good

⁸Finally, all of you, live in harmony with one another; be sympathetic, love as brothers, be compassionate and humble. ⁹Do not repay evil with evil or insult with insult, but with blessing, because to this you were called so that you may inherit a blessing. ¹⁰For,

"Whoever would love life
and see good days

must keep his tongue from evil
and his lips from deceitful speech.
¹¹He must turn from evil and do good;
he must seek peace and pursue it.
¹²For the eyes of the Lord are on the righteous
and his ears are attentive to their prayer,
but the face of the Lord is against those who
do evil."ᵃ

¹³Who is going to harm you if you are eager to do good? ¹⁴But even if you should suffer for what is right, you are blessed. "Do not fear what they fearᵇ; do not be frightened."ᶜ ¹⁵But in your hearts set apart Christ as Lord. Always be prepared to give an answer to everyone who asks you to give the reason for the hope that you have. But do this with gentleness and respect, ¹⁶keeping a clear conscience, so that those who speak maliciously against your good behavior in Christ may be ashamed of their slander. ¹⁷It is better, if it is God's will, to suffer for doing good than for doing evil. ¹⁸For Christ died for sins once for all, the righteous for the unrighteous, to bring you to God. He was put to death in the body but made alive by the Spirit, ¹⁹through whomᵈ also he went and preached to the spirits in prison ²⁰who disobeyed long ago when God waited patiently in the days of Noah while the ark was being built. In it only a few people, eight in all, were saved through water, ²¹and this water symbolizes baptism that now saves you also—not the removal of dirt from the body but the pledgeᵉ of a good conscience toward God. It saves you by the resurrection of Jesus Christ, ²²who has gone into heaven and is at God's right hand—with angels, authorities and powers in submission to him.

Living for God

4 Therefore, since Christ suffered in his body, arm yourselves also with the same attitude, because he who has suffered in his body is done with sin. ²As a result, he does not live the rest of his earthly life for evil human desires, but rather

ᵃ 12 Psalm 34:12-16   ᵇ 14 Or *not fear their threats*
ᶜ 14 Isaiah 8:12   ᵈ 18,19 Or *alive in the spirit,* ¹⁹*through which*
ᵉ 21 Or *response*

YOUR BEAUTY SHOULD NOT COME FROM OUTWARD ADORNMENT, SUCH AS BRAIDED HAIR AND THE WEARING OF GOLD JEWELRY AND FINE CLOTHES. INSTEAD, IT SHOULD BE THAT OF YOUR INNER SELF, THE UNFADING BEAUTY OF A GENTLE AND QUIET SPIRIT, WHICH IS OF GREAT WORTH IN GOD'S SIGHT.

1 Peter 3:3–4

Precious

KAREN O'CONNOR

READ | 1 PETER 3:1–7

Dear God:

It was agonizing to watch Mom decline and then to receive word that she had died in her sleep. But that alone was an answer to prayer. I had asked You for months to please take her peacefully as she lay sleeping.

It was difficult to imagine her time here on Earth coming to an end. I kept thinking of her as the young, vibrant mother I remember from my youth. She was my Girl Scouts leader, schoolroom mom and seamstress extraordinaire. And she could bake apple slices to die for! My mouth waters just thinking about them.

But I will never taste them again — at least not from her hand. I miss her and the times we shared — whether over the stove, over a good book, over a cup of tea or over a good conversation. She's with You now. Lucky You, Lord! (I hope You don't mind my saying so!) I know You are taking good care of her.

She was a senior with flair, with pizzazz, with dazzle, with class.

I hope I'm like her at least a little bit as I grow older and as I, like her, notice more and more of those senior moments that we both used to laugh about.

Lord, I'm grateful for my mother, who was/is beautiful on the outside and within. But if my mother was not like the mother described here, I pray that I can appreciate the women in my life who have influenced me with their support and godly example. I pray that I will continue to seek out mentors to strengthen my faith. And I pray that I will in turn mentor my children, grandchildren and others.

Your next devotion is located on page 1714.

GRANDCHILD IN FOCUS • PRAYER

Protection From Worldliness

O Sovereign Lord, the world surrounds my grandchild, pressing in and tempting him in so many ways. Help him set appropriate limits. Give him sound judgment to choose wisely. Guard him from temptation; protect him from physical and mental predators; lead him into paths of righteousness and light. And reassure me with your promise that you are holding him in your hands. Amen.

for the will of God. ³For you have spent enough time in the past doing what pagans choose to do—living in debauchery, lust, drunkenness, orgies, carousing and detestable idolatry. ⁴They think it strange that you do not plunge with them into the same flood of dissipation, and they heap abuse on you. ⁵But they will have to give account to him who is ready to judge the living and the dead. ⁶For this is the reason the gospel

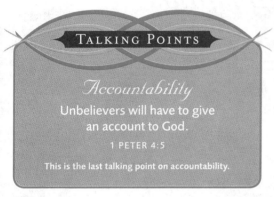

was preached even to those who are now dead, so that they might be judged according to men in regard to the body, but live according to God in regard to the spirit.

⁷The end of all things is near. Therefore be clear minded and self-controlled so that you can pray. ⁸Above all, love each other deeply, because love covers over a multitude of sins. ⁹Offer hospitality to one another without grumbling. ¹⁰Each one should use whatever gift he has received to serve others, faithfully administering God's grace

in its various forms. ¹¹If anyone speaks, he should do it as one speaking the very words of God. If anyone serves, he should do it with the strength God provides, so that in all things God may be praised through Jesus Christ. To him be the glory and the power for ever and ever. Amen.

Suffering for Being a Christian

¹²Dear friends, do not be surprised at the painful trial you are suffering, as though something strange were happening to you. ¹³But rejoice that you participate in the sufferings of Christ, so that you may be overjoyed when his glory is revealed. ¹⁴If you are insulted because of the name of Christ, you are blessed, for the Spirit of glory and of God rests on you. ¹⁵If you suffer, it should not be as a murderer or thief or any other kind of criminal, or even as a meddler. ¹⁶However, if you suffer as a Christian, do not be ashamed, but praise God that you bear that name. ¹⁷For it is time for judgment to begin with the family of God; and if it begins with us, what will the outcome be for those who do not obey the gospel of God? ¹⁸And,

> "If it is hard for the righteous to be saved,
>   what will become of the ungodly and the
>   sinner?"ᵃ

¹⁹So then, those who suffer according to God's will should commit themselves to their faithful Creator and continue to do good.

To Elders and Young Men

5 To the elders among you, I appeal as a fellow elder, a witness of Christ's sufferings and one who also will share in the glory to be revealed: ²Be shepherds of God's flock that is under your care, serving as overseers—not because you must, but because you are willing, as God wants you to be; not greedy for money, but eager to serve; ³not lording it over those entrusted to you, but being examples to the flock. ⁴And when the Chief Shepherd appears, you will receive the crown of glory that will never fade away.

ᵃ *18* Prov. 11:31

ABOVE ALL, LOVE EACH OTHER
DEEPLY, BECAUSE LOVE COVERS
OVER A MULTITUDE OF SINS.

1 Peter 4:8

A Symbol for Christmas

GAYLE ROPER

READ | 1 PETER 4:7–11

"I'm the smallest kid in my class," ten-year-old Ashley wailed. "I'm the slowest, the dumbest, the skinniest and the ugliest!"

I looked at my beautiful granddaughter. "You're like a butterfly, sweetheart. You might not feel so great now, but you're going to grow into something lovely and graceful."

Shortly after that conversation I saw a colorful enameled butterfly and got it for Ashley. I hoped it would remind her that she was going to break out of her chrysalis some day soon.

At Christmas I saw another butterfly made to be a tree decoration, and a tradition was born. We chose symbols for our four other grandchildren and gave the kids their tree decorations at the family Thanksgiving meal so they could enjoy them for the whole holiday season. In recent years we have added a verse that we ask each child to read before opening the ornaments.

Ashley gets butterflies and 2 Corinthians 5:17: "Therefore, if anyone is in Christ, he is a new creation; the old has gone, the new has come!"

Brianne gets hearts and 1 Peter 4:8: "Above all, love each other deeply, because love covers over a multitude of sins."

Abbie gets stars and Philippians 2:15–16: "You [will] shine like stars in the universe as you hold out the word of life."

Devan gets angels and Psalm 91:11: "For he will command his angels concerning you to guard you in all your ways."

PJ gets snowmen and 1 Timothy 6:11: "But you, man of God, flee from all this, and pursue righteousness, godliness, faith, love, endurance and gentleness."

On some future day, the kids can hang their ornaments in their own homes and hopefully carry on the tradition for another generation.

Lord, give me creative ideas for instilling your Word in my grandchildren's hearts and minds in a way that becomes evident in their lives. Amen.

GRANDCHILD IN FOCUS · PRAYER

Respect for Authority

Dear Lord, I pray that my grandchild will continually grow to respect those in authority. May she learn to be cooperative and fair in work and play. Instill in her a high regard for officials who govern our land and enforce the laws. May her relationships with parents, teachers, coaches, mentors and bosses be respectful, admirable, constructive and caring. Amen.

Your next devotion is located on page 1715.

AND THE GOD OF ALL GRACE, WHO CALLED
YOU TO HIS ETERNAL GLORY IN CHRIST,
AFTER YOU HAVE SUFFERED A LITTLE WHILE,
WILL HIMSELF RESTORE YOU AND MAKE YOU
STRONG, FIRM AND STEADFAST.

1 Peter 5:10

Strong, Firm and Steadfast

GLADYS HUNT

READ | 1 PETER 5:1 – 11

"After you have suffered a little while," Peter wrote to Christian believers who were truly suffering for their faith. Rather than be surprised by suffering, they were to expect it. He put it in perspective by reminding them that "Christ suffered for you, leaving you an example, that you should follow in his steps" (1 Peter 2:21).

Unlike millions around the world who regularly experience suffering for their faith, we in the West know little of suffering. We don't like suffering; we have pills to avoid it. Yet there is a kind of suffering that can't be medicated; it is the suffering of the heart. All human beings know about this.

Notice, however, that Peter's comment on suffering is only a clause. It is not the primary subject in the verse above. We often let suffering become the subject. Peter makes *God* the subject. What is there about God that should change our suffering?

First, Peter calls him "the God of all grace." Grace — God's favor toward me — is not what I deserve. And not just a little grace is sprinkled on my life, but *all* grace — grace enough to cover my disappointments, my pain, my despair.

Second, in his grace God has called me "to his eternal glory in Christ." Consider what this means! As a believer I am placed in Christ. When God looks at me, he sees Jesus. Because of my relationship with him, I have an eternal glory that begins here on Earth and goes on into the future.

Third, because God has no lesser purpose than to make me like Jesus, he is beginning that work in my life right now. He is getting me ready for heaven, using all the pieces in my life, including my pain. He purposes to "restore [me] and make [me] strong, firm and steadfast."

The next time I complain, remind me that the God of all grace is meeting my needs day by day. He is developing my spiritual muscles to make me steadfast.

O God of all grace, help me to be strong, firm and steadfast. Amen.

Your next devotion is located on page 1719.

GRANDCHILD IN FOCUS • PRAYER

Courage

O Father, builder of character and courage, may my grandchild grow strong in the light of your love. Grant him courage to stand for what is right, to guard the truth and to ensure justice in every aspect of life. May he boldly grow in grace, revere your name and proudly proclaim you as the Lord of lords and King of kings. Amen.

⁵Young men, in the same way be submissive to those who are older. All of you, clothe yourselves with humility toward one another, because,

"God opposes the proud
    but gives grace to the humble."ᵃ

⁶Humble yourselves, therefore, under God's mighty hand, that he may lift you up in due time. ⁷Cast all your anxiety on him because he cares for you.

TALKING POINTS

Anxiety
Leave your anxieties with God.
1 PETER 5:7

This is the last talking point on anxiety.

⁸Be self-controlled and alert. Your enemy the devil prowls around like a roaring lion looking for someone to devour. ⁹Resist him, standing firm in the faith, because you know that your brothers throughout the world are undergoing the same kind of sufferings.

¹⁰And the God of all grace, who called you to his eternal glory in Christ, after you have suffered a little while, will himself restore you and make you strong, firm and steadfast. ¹¹To him be the power for ever and ever. Amen.

Final Greetings

¹²With the help of Silas,ᵇ whom I regard as a faithful brother, I have written to you briefly, encouraging you and testifying that this is the true grace of God. Stand fast in it.

¹³She who is in Babylon, chosen together with you, sends you her greetings, and so does my son Mark. ¹⁴Greet one another with a kiss of love.

Peace to all of you who are in Christ.

ᵃ 5 Prov. 3:34   ᵇ 12 Greek *Silvanus*, a variant of *Silas*

God IS PATIENT

"Hurry up, Lord. I need an answer. I need to know now." We are an impatient lot when it comes to most things. We want to know how our grandchildren will turn out. We want assurance *now* that they will grow in the faith and come to love Jesus. Perhaps their faith isn't growing at the pace we'd like. Perhaps they seem to have their priorities all wrong, or they are going through a period of doubt and uncertainty. But our timing is not God's timing. And he has all the time he needs to draw people to himself. He is patient.

That is one of the themes of Peter's second letter to the persecuted Christians scattered throughout Asia Minor (see 1 Peter 1:1 with 2 Peter 3:1). In his second letter Peter wrote concerning the "day of the Lord" (2 Peter 3:10), when there will be a reckoning of good and evil. He assured his readers that all things will be made right in God's good time. He declared that their task was to live holy and godly lives as they looked forward to that day. That is our task as well as we look forward to the day of salvation for our grandchildren, forward to "a new heaven and new earth" (2 Peter 3:13), forward to the day when all God's promises will be fulfilled. God has control of the future. He desires repentance for everyone. So be patient. God is.

VERSE *to* REMEMBER | 2 PETER 3:9

The Lord is not slow in keeping his promise, as some understand slowness. He is patient with you, not wanting anyone to perish, but everyone to come to repentance.

ABOUT 2 PETER

WRITTEN BY:
The apostle Peter

WRITTEN FOR:
Specifically for those scattered throughout Asia Minor, but also for Christians everywhere

DATE WRITTEN:
Near the end of Peter's life, probably between A.D. 65 and 68, from Rome

WHY WRITTEN:
To warn Christians against false teachers and to encourage watchfulness in light of the Lord's return

1 Simon Peter, a servant and apostle of Jesus Christ,

To those who through the righteousness of our God and Savior Jesus Christ have received a faith as precious as ours:

²Grace and peace be yours in abundance through the knowledge of God and of Jesus our Lord.

Making One's Calling and Election Sure

³His divine power has given us everything we need for life and godliness through our knowledge of him who called us by his own glory and goodness. ⁴Through these he has given us his very great and precious promises, so that through them you may participate in the divine nature and escape the corruption in the world caused by evil desires.

⁵For this very reason, make every effort to add to your faith goodness; and to goodness, knowledge; ⁶and to knowledge, self-control; and to self-control, perseverance; and to perseverance, godliness; ⁷and to godliness, brotherly kindness; and to brotherly kindness, love. ⁸For if you possess these qualities in increasing measure, they will keep you from being ineffective and unproductive in your knowledge of our Lord Jesus Christ. ⁹But if anyone does not have them, he is nearsighted and blind, and has forgotten that he has been cleansed from his past sins.

¹⁰Therefore, my brothers, be all the more eager to make your calling and election sure. For if you do these things, you will never fall, ¹¹and you will receive a rich welcome into the eternal kingdom of our Lord and Savior Jesus Christ.

Prophecy of Scripture

¹²So I will always remind you of these things, even though you know them and are firmly established in the truth you now have. ¹³I think it is right to refresh your memory as long as I live in the tent of this body, ¹⁴because I know that I will soon put it aside, as our Lord Jesus Christ has made clear to me. ¹⁵And I will make every effort to see that after my departure you will always be able to remember these things.

¹⁶We did not follow cleverly invented stories when we told you about the power and coming of our Lord Jesus Christ, but we were eyewitnesses of his majesty. ¹⁷For he received honor and glory from God the Father when the voice came to him from the Majestic Glory, saying, "This is my Son, whom I love; with him I am well pleased."[a] ¹⁸We ourselves heard this voice that came from heaven when we were with him on the sacred mountain.

¹⁹And we have the word of the prophets made more certain, and you will do well to pay attention to it, as to a light shining in a dark place, until the day dawns and the morning star rises

stories to share

2 PETER 1:1–9

Living Godly Lives

LIFE LESSON: God calls us to live godly lives.

TO TALK ABOUT

✦ Besides faith, what qualities does Peter want Christians to develop in their lives?

✦ What are the dangers if Christians don't develop these qualities?

✦ Why do you think God encourages us to live godly lives?

✦ How do you see God helping you to live a godly life?

a 17 Matt. 17:5; Mark 9:7; Luke 9:35

His divine power has given us everything we need for life and godliness through our knowledge of him who called us by his own glory and goodness.

2 Peter 1:3

God's Arms Hold Us

BARBARA JOHNSON

READ | 2 PETER 1:1–11

Most of us were taught rules as children: rules at the dining table, rules for play, rules for friendship, and so on. We started out believing life would be fair to us if we followed the rules. So we try to do well, to be "good." Then we, or someone we love, falls through the cracks. We experience some of life's exceptions, and we don't like it one bit. When things go wrong, we wonder, *Why? What about the rules?* And we exclaim, "This just isn't fair!"

It isn't fair, but then, God never said life would be fair. Life on this earth doesn't always play out according to rigid rules. Remember, God has been creating exceptions to the rules since time began. I, for one, am glad he doesn't treat me according to "the rules." Where would I be if I got what my sin really deserves?

We all need a way to survive our losses, to live with life's exceptions, to celebrate our joys in spite of our sorrows. We do that by grace, by remembering that God is never taken by surprise. His exceptions were built in before the dawn of time. So when you or the people you love fall through the cracks, you are going to fall right into his arms of grace. Hang in there! And learn to glory in the fact that God's grace in exceptions makes life fun as well as functional.

....

O God, my God, how it encourages me to know that your loving arms are always held out to me, to my children and to my grandchildren. When life's exceptions break the rules we thought we knew, guide us instead to the knowledge of your glory and goodness.

Your next devotion is located on page 1721.

GRANDCHILD IN FOCUS • PRAYER

Future Spouse

Dear Lord, if it is your will, I pray my grandchild will be united in a loving and Christian marriage. Keep her sexually pure so that she will honor you with her body and mind. As she seeks a spouse who will honor and care for her, give her patience and discernment. May her choice for a life partner be your choice for her, so that she and her husband will together glorify you in a lasting love. I pray this in Jesus' name, amen.

in your hearts. [20]Above all, you must understand that no prophecy of Scripture came about by the prophet's own interpretation. [21]For prophecy never had its origin in the will of man, but men spoke from God as they were carried along by the Holy Spirit.

False Teachers and Their Destruction

2 But there were also false prophets among the people, just as there will be false teachers among you. They will secretly introduce destructive heresies, even denying the sovereign Lord who bought them—bringing swift destruction on themselves. [2]Many will follow their shameful ways and will bring the way of truth into disrepute. [3]In their greed these teachers will exploit you with stories they have made up. Their condemnation has long been hanging over them, and their destruction has not been sleeping.

[4]For if God did not spare angels when they sinned, but sent them to hell,[a] putting them into gloomy dungeons[b] to be held for judgment; [5]if he did not spare the ancient world when he brought the flood on its ungodly people, but protected Noah, a preacher of righteousness, and seven others; [6]if he condemned the cities of Sodom and Gomorrah by burning them to ashes, and made them an example of what is going to happen to the ungodly; [7]and if he rescued Lot, a righteous man, who was distressed by the filthy lives of lawless men [8](for that righteous man, living among them day after day, was tormented in his righteous soul by the lawless deeds he saw and heard)— [9]if this is so, then the Lord knows how to rescue godly men from trials and to hold the unrighteous for the day of judgment, while continuing their punishment.[c] [10]This is especially true of those who follow the corrupt desire of the sinful nature[d] and despise authority.

Bold and arrogant, these men are not afraid to slander celestial beings; [11]yet even angels, although they are stronger and more powerful, do not bring slanderous accusations against such beings in the presence of the Lord. [12]But these men blaspheme in matters they do not understand.

They are like brute beasts, creatures of instinct, born only to be caught and destroyed, and like beasts they too will perish.

[13]They will be paid back with harm for the harm they have done. Their idea of pleasure is to carouse in broad daylight. They are blots and blemishes, reveling in their pleasures while they feast with you.[e] [14]With eyes full of adultery, they never stop sinning; they seduce the unstable; they are experts in greed—an accursed brood! [15]They have left the straight way and wandered off to follow the way of Balaam son of Beor, who loved the wages of wickedness. [16]But he was rebuked for his wrongdoing by a donkey—a beast without speech—who spoke with a man's voice and restrained the prophet's madness.

[17]These men are springs without water and mists driven by a storm. Blackest darkness is reserved for them. [18]For they mouth empty, boastful words and, by appealing to the lustful desires of sinful human nature, they entice people who are just escaping from those who live in error. [19]They promise them freedom, while they themselves are slaves of depravity—for a man is a slave to whatever has mastered him. [20]If they have escaped the corruption of the world by knowing our Lord and Savior Jesus Christ and are again entangled in it and overcome, they are worse off at the end than they were at the beginning. [21]It would have been better for them not to have known the way of righteousness, than to have known it and then to turn their backs on the sacred command that was passed on to them. [22]Of them the proverbs are true: "A dog returns to its vomit,"[f] and, "A sow that is washed goes back to her wallowing in the mud."

The Day of the Lord

3 Dear friends, this is now my second letter to you. I have written both of them as reminders to stimulate you to wholesome thinking. [2]I want you to recall the words spoken in the past

[a] 4 Greek *Tartarus*   [b] 4 Some manuscripts *into chains of darkness*
[c] 9 Or *unrighteous for punishment until the day of judgment*
[d] 10 Or *the flesh*   [e] 13 Some manuscripts *in their love feasts*
[f] 22 Prov. 26:11

> BUT IN KEEPING WITH HIS PROMISE WE ARE LOOKING FORWARD TO A NEW HEAVEN AND A NEW EARTH, THE HOME OF RIGHTEOUSNESS. SO THEN, DEAR FRIENDS, SINCE YOU ARE LOOKING FORWARD TO THIS, MAKE EVERY EFFORT TO BE FOUND SPOTLESS, BLAMELESS AND AT PEACE WITH HIM.
>
> *2 Peter 3:13–14*

Between the Light and Dark

SUSAN LENZKES

READ | 2 PETER 3:1–18

Life is sweet. It offers sunrises, fat baby fists, darting hummingbirds, commitments, outstretched arms, spring breezes, pussies, giggles, surprise parties, strawberries, voices in harmony, dimples, sheets on a clothes line, curls on little girls, compliments, fresh-baked bread, red wagons, great oak trees, whiskered men. Love letters, pink parasols, marching bands, harvest time, feather pillows, waterfalls, boys on bikes, praise songs, full moons, cozy fires, communion, reunion, daisies, helping hands, pounding surf, butterflies, and white clouds mounded in blue skies.

Life is sharp. It pierces with good-byes, fevered brows, screams, empty beds, tornadoes and earthquakes, prejudice, poison ivy, traffic jams, tear-stained cheeks, ignorance, failure, war, drought, explosions, greed, lies, criticism, head-on collisions, rust and rot, hands that slap or steal, despair, divorce, rape, depression, broken bones, broken promises, broken dreams, broken hearts, broken lives, and dark clouds mounded in gray skies.

How can we enjoy the sweetness of this life without being pricked by its jagged thorns? How can we feel at home in a world blighted by sin yet blessed with the redeeming grace and presence of God?

God's children are not at home here; but we are here, nonetheless. And we discover that it's impossible to enjoy this world's sunshine without enduring its clouds and storms. There is no way to withdraw from only one part of life. Resistance to pain inevitably numbs us to joy.

Lord, help me accept the reality that this world of clashing darkness and light is where I am required to live and mature. Some day all things will be made new in your Son, Jesus Christ. But for now my job is to stand firm and grow where I am planted by using all the sunshine and rain that comes my way. As I look forward to a new heaven and a new earth, I strive to be found spotless, blameless and at peace with you.

Your next devotion is located on page 1722.

GRANDCHILD IN FOCUS • PRAYER

School/Career

Dear God, may learning be a joy rather than a chore for my grandchild. May exploration of new ideas bring a sense of wonder, awe and excitement. Grant him clarity of mind, the ability to concentrate on the task at hand and recollection of what has been learned. Help him to appreciate the tasks that come easily and to persevere through those that challenge. Amen.

All Grown Up

Many children love to act grown up and to be treated like grown-ups. Spend a little time planning a special grown-up event for your grandchildren. Adjust the event and amount of time to their interest. For the youngest group you may want to keep it to a simple "tea party" one afternoon, with cookies and milk served in cups. But have them dress up and make the event special.

For those a bit older, you could have a grown-up dinner party and serve dinner in your dining room, complete with linen napkins, china, etc. Encourage them to dress up, and they will feel privileged and special. This would also be a great opportunity to teach some basic manners as well.

Your oldest grandchildren may enjoy a dinner party at your home that includes their friends. Plan ahead for topics to discuss at the table. Keep it all very special. Or if your budget allows and you prefer, take your grandchildren to a nice restaurant to celebrate the fact that they are becoming adults.

O Lord, thank you for my grandchildren, who are so special to me. Help them know how much I care about them through my actions and words. Let our time of playing grown-up be a special time for all of us. Amen.

Your next devotion is located on page 1723.

GRANDCHILD IN FOCUS • PRAYER

Character

Dear Lord and Father, I ask that you fill my grandchild with your Spirit so her character reflects your goodness and love. Give her kindness and love for others. Bring joy to her life so she will be a joy to others. Grant her patience and self-control through difficult and trying times. May she show mercy and generosity to those who are less fortunate. Grant her integrity and a sense of justice, and surround her with your peace. Amen.

Worship the Lord

Many, O Lord my God,
   are the wonders you have done.
The things you planned for us
   no one can recount to you;
were I to speak and tell of them,
   they would be too many to declare.

Sacrifice and offering you did not desire,
   but my ears you have pierced;
burnt offerings and sin offerings
   you did not require.
Then I said, "Here I am, I have come —
   it is written about me in the scroll.
I desire to do your will, O my God;
   your law is within my heart."

Psalm 40:5 – 8

O my God, you have directed my life, and
I have learned that all things will work for
my good. You have filled my life to overflowing with good things in which I delight. In gratitude, I want to do your will.
Let me hear your voice and follow willingly:
"Here I am; use me." Amen.

Your next devotion is located on page 1727.

GRANDCHILD IN FOCUS • PRAYER

Talents

*Dear Lord, the giver of gifts, bless my
grandchild as he develops his talents. Help him
identify his talents and be proud and confident of
the gifts you have given him. Give him patience and
understanding, Lord, so he will not grow weary of
striving and searching to reach the goals you have
set for him. May each milestone bring satisfaction and a healthy desire for greater
achievement and success to bring
glory to you. Amen.*

by the holy prophets and the command given by our Lord and Savior through your apostles.

³First of all, you must understand that in the last days scoffers will come, scoffing and following their own evil desires. ⁴They will say, "Where is this 'coming' he promised? Ever since our fathers died, everything goes on as it has since the beginning of creation." ⁵But they deliberately forget that long ago by God's word the heavens existed and the earth was formed out of water and by water. ⁶By these waters also the world of that time was deluged and destroyed. ⁷By the same word the present heavens and earth are reserved for fire, being kept for the day of judgment and destruction of ungodly men.

⁸But do not forget this one thing, dear friends: With the Lord a day is like a thousand years, and a thousand years are like a day. ⁹The Lord is not slow in keeping his promise, as some understand slowness. He is patient with you, not wanting anyone to perish, but everyone to come to repentance.

¹⁰But the day of the Lord will come like a thief. The heavens will disappear with a roar; the elements will be destroyed by fire, and the earth and everything in it will be laid bare.ᵃ

¹¹Since everything will be destroyed in this way, what kind of people ought you to be? You ought to live holy and godly lives ¹²as you look forward to the day of God and speed its coming.ᵇ That day will bring about the destruction of the heavens by fire, and the elements will melt in the heat. ¹³But in keeping with his promise we are looking forward to a new heaven and a new earth, the home of righteousness.

¹⁴So then, dear friends, since you are looking forward to this, make every effort to be found spotless, blameless and at peace with him. ¹⁵Bear in mind that our Lord's patience means salvation, just as our dear brother Paul also wrote you with the wisdom that God gave him. ¹⁶He writes the same way in all his letters, speaking in them of these matters. His letters contain some things that are hard to understand, which ignorant and unstable people distort, as they do the other Scriptures, to their own destruction.

¹⁷Therefore, dear friends, since you already know this, be on your guard so that you may not be carried away by the error of lawless men and fall from your secure position. ¹⁸But grow in the grace and knowledge of our Lord and Savior Jesus Christ. To him be glory both now and forever! Amen.

TALKING POINTS

Patience

God is patient with us.

2 PETER 3:9

This is the last talking point on patience.

ᵃ 10 Some manuscripts *be burned up*   ᵇ 12 Or *as you wait eagerly for the day of God to come*

1 John

Making
GOD'S LOVE COMPLETE

The book of 1 John, a passionate letter from the apostle John, was written as a loving father would write to correct his children: "My dear children . . ." (see, for example 1 John 2:1). Because he cared about them, John wanted to see his children in the faith follow his teaching. He wrote to remind them that Jesus is the Son of God, fully human and fully divine. This letter was a rebuke, but it was a rebuke framed in love. Today John still invites us into fellowship with him because he belongs to the family who claims God as Father. John reminds us that Jesus Christ, God's Son, is the supreme expression of the Father's love.

First John asserts one of the elemental teachings of Scripture: "Whoever lives in love lives in God, and God in him" (1 John 4:16). And we can make God's love "complete" (see 1 John 2:5; 4:12,17) by obeying his Word, by walking in the light and by loving God's children because we love the same Father.

This is an absolutely perfect command for a grandmother. Let God fill you up with his love. Walk in his light. Obey his Word. Then love your grandchildren as God has loved you. And invite your grandchildren to join God's family. Make God's love complete.

VERSE *to* REMEMBER | 1 JOHN 4:12

No one has ever seen God; but if we love one another, God lives in us and his love is made complete in us.

ABOUT 1 JOHN

WRITTEN BY:
The apostle John

WRITTEN FOR:
Specifically for Christians in and around Ephesus, but also for Christians everywhere

DATE WRITTEN:
Probably about A.D. 90 from Ephesus

WHY WRITTEN:
To show Christians how to live close to God and how to love other people

The Word of Life

1 That which was from the beginning, which we have heard, which we have seen with our eyes, which we have looked at and our hands have touched—this we proclaim concerning the Word of life. [2] The life appeared; we have seen it and testify to it, and we proclaim to you the eternal life, which was with the Father and has appeared to us. [3] We proclaim to you what we have seen and heard, so that you also may have fellowship with us. And our fellowship is with the Father and with his Son, Jesus Christ. [4] We write this to make our[a] joy complete.

Walking in the Light

[5] This is the message we have heard from him and declare to you: God is light; in him there is no darkness at all. [6] If we claim to have fellowship with him yet walk in the darkness, we lie and do not live by the truth. [7] But if we walk in the light, as he is in the light, we have fellowship with one another, and the blood of Jesus, his Son, purifies us from all[b] sin.

[8] If we claim to be without sin, we deceive ourselves and the truth is not in us. [9] If we confess our sins, he is faithful and just and will forgive us our sins and purify us from all unrighteousness. [10] If we claim we have not sinned, we make him out to be a liar and his word has no place in our lives.

PRAYING THE SCRIPTURES

Forgiveness

1 JOHN 1:9

Dear Lord, guide my grandchild in the realization that if she confesses her sins, you will be faithful and just and will forgive her sins and purify her from all unrighteousness.

This is the last prayer in the Forgiveness Prayer Track.

TALKING POINTS

Faithfulness

If we confess our sins, God is faithful to forgive our sins and purify us.

1 JOHN 1:9

This is the last talking point on faithfulness.

---

2 My dear children, I write this to you so that you will not sin. But if anybody does sin, we have one who speaks to the Father in our defense—Jesus Christ, the Righteous One. [2] He is the atoning sacrifice for our sins, and not only for ours but also for[c] the sins of the whole world.

[3] We know that we have come to know him if we obey his commands. [4] The man who says, "I know him," but does not do what he commands is a liar, and the truth is not in him. [5] But if anyone obeys his word, God's love[d] is truly made complete in him. This is how we know we are in him: [6] Whoever claims to live in him must walk as Jesus did.

[7] Dear friends, I am not writing you a new command but an old one, which you have had since the beginning. This old command is the message you have heard. [8] Yet I am writing you a new command; its truth is seen in him and you, because the darkness is passing and the true light is already shining.

[9] Anyone who claims to be in the light but hates his brother is still in the darkness. [10] Whoever loves his brother lives in the light, and there is nothing in him[e] to make him stumble. [11] But whoever hates his brother is in the darkness and walks around in the darkness; he does not know where he is going, because the darkness has blinded him.

[a] 4 Some manuscripts *your*   [b] 7 Or *every*   [c] 2 Or *He is the one who turns aside God's wrath, taking away our sins, and not only ours but also*   [d] 5 Or *word, love for God*   [e] 10 Or *it*

BUT IF WE WALK IN THE LIGHT, AS HE IS IN THE LIGHT, WE HAVE FELLOWSHIP WITH ONE ANOTHER, AND THE BLOOD OF JESUS, HIS SON, PURIFIES US FROM ALL SIN.

1 John 1:7

The Light People

PATRICIA SPRINKLE

READ | 1 JOHN 1:5 — 2:14

Do you know any "light people"? Light people spread light wherever they go. Some radiate joy when they enter a room, and draw us into that joy. Some stand up for truth when truth comes hard, and set an example we can follow. Some explain or clarify things that have been difficult to understand. Some have a gentle spirit that penetrates grief, depression or anxiety and offers compassion and encouragement.

Light people can be very different from one another, but they have two things in common: They all know that Christ brings life and light to the world, and they aren't hung up on their own sins and shortcomings. Instead, they accept God's forgiveness and get on with spreading light in the world God loves. Another thing about light people: their light — the light of Christ — is contagious across generations.

My father's mother was a light person. She raised nine children on a farm in days when keeping house meant hours of time-consuming work. What her sons remember, though, is that Grandmother always had time to leave her dishpan to join a child in looking at a sunset, or she would abandon the week's washing to help chase a butterfly.

Grandmother died before I was born, but she passed her sense of joy and wonder down to my dad. He passed it to me. Every time I take a child's hand to stand in awe before a hummingbird or enjoy together the miracle of a new flower, I feel very close to her, and I know I am passing on the light.

Lord, the One who came to bring light and life to this often dark earth, I want to be a light person. Help me not to just curse the darkness but to walk in the light. And help me to spread your light to the upcoming generations. Amen.

Your next devotion is located on page 1731.

GRANDCHILD IN FOCUS • PRAYER

SELECT ONE OF YOUR GRANDCHILDREN TO FOCUS ON IN PRAYER FOR THE NEXT 14 DAYS.

Salvation

Dear Lord, please guide my grandchild to your gift of salvation. I pray that she will come to know you, to love you and to walk close to you throughout her life. May she boldly claim Jesus as her Lord and Savior. Guide her as she makes choices that have eternal consequences. Help her to follow you each moment of her life. I pray this in Jesus' name, amen.

^{12}I write to you, dear children,
    because your sins have been forgiven on
       account of his name.
^{13}I write to you, fathers,
    because you have known him who is from
       the beginning.
 I write to you, young men,
    because you have overcome the evil one.
 I write to you, dear children,
    because you have known the Father.
^{14}I write to you, fathers,
    because you have known him who is from
       the beginning.
 I write to you, young men,
    because you are strong,
    and the word of God lives in you,
    and you have overcome the evil one.

Do Not Love the World

^{15}Do not love the world or anything in the world. If anyone loves the world, the love of the Father is not in him. ^{16}For everything in the world—the cravings of sinful man, the lust of his eyes and the boasting of what he has and does—comes not from the Father but from the world. ^{17}The world and its desires pass away, but the man who does the will of God lives forever.

TALKING POINTS

Worldliness

Don't love the transitory
things of the world.
1 JOHN 2:15–17

This is the last talking point on worldliness.

Warning Against Antichrists

^{18}Dear children, this is the last hour; and as you have heard that the antichrist is coming, even now many antichrists have come. This is how we know it is the last hour. ^{19}They went out from us, but they did not really belong to us. For if they had belonged to us, they would have remained with us; but their going showed that none of them belonged to us.

^{20}But you have an anointing from the Holy One, and all of you know the truth.^{a} ^{21}I do not write to you because you do not know the truth, but because you do know it and because no lie comes from the truth. ^{22}Who is the liar? It is the man who denies that Jesus is the Christ. Such a man is the antichrist—he denies the Father and the Son. ^{23}No one who denies the Son has the Father; whoever acknowledges the Son has the Father also.

^{24}See that what you have heard from the beginning remains in you. If it does, you also will remain in the Son and in the Father. ^{25}And this is what he promised us—even eternal life.

^{26}I am writing these things to you about those who are trying to lead you astray. ^{27}As for you, the anointing you received from him remains in you, and you do not need anyone to teach you. But as his anointing teaches you about all things and as that anointing is real, not counterfeit—just as it has taught you, remain in him.

Children of God

^{28}And now, dear children, continue in him, so that when he appears we may be confident and unashamed before him at his coming.

^{29}If you know that he is righteous, you know that everyone who does what is right has been born of him.

3 How great is the love the Father has lavished on us, that we should be called children of God! And that is what we are! The reason the world does not know us is that it did not know him. ^{2}Dear friends, now we are children of God, and what we will be has not yet been made known. But we know that when he appears,^{b} we shall be like him, for we shall see him as he is. ^{3}Everyone who has this hope in him purifies himself, just as he is pure.

---

^{a} 20 Some manuscripts *and you know all things* ^{b} 2 Or *when it is made known*

TALKING POINTS

Self-Esteem

We are children of God.

1 JOHN 3:1

This is the last talking point on self-esteem.

⁴Everyone who sins breaks the law; in fact, sin is lawlessness. ⁵But you know that he appeared so that he might take away our sins. And in him is no sin. ⁶No one who lives in him keeps on sinning. No one who continues to sin has either seen him or known him.

⁷Dear children, do not let anyone lead you astray. He who does what is right is righteous, just as he is righteous. ⁸He who does what is sinful is of the devil, because the devil has been sinning from the beginning. The reason the Son of God appeared was to destroy the devil's work. ⁹No one who is born of God will continue to sin, because God's seed remains in him; he cannot go on sinning, because he has been born of God. ¹⁰This is how we know who the children of God are and who the children of the devil are: Anyone who does not do what is right is not a child of God; nor is anyone who does not love his brother.

Love One Another

¹¹This is the message you heard from the beginning: We should love one another. ¹²Do not be like Cain, who belonged to the evil one and murdered his brother. And why did he murder him? Because his own actions were evil and his brother's were righteous. ¹³Do not be surprised, my brothers, if the world hates you. ¹⁴We know that we have passed from death to life, because we love our brothers. Anyone who does not love remains in death. ¹⁵Anyone who hates his brother is a murderer, and you know that no murderer has eternal life in him.

¹⁶This is how we know what love is: Jesus Christ laid down his life for us. And we ought to lay down our lives for our brothers. ¹⁷If anyone has material possessions and sees his brother in need but has no pity on him, how can the love of God be in him? ¹⁸Dear children, let us not love with words or tongue but with actions and in truth. ¹⁹This then is how we know that we belong to the truth, and how we set our hearts at rest in his presence ²⁰whenever our hearts condemn us. For God is greater than our hearts, and he knows everything.

²¹Dear friends, if our hearts do not condemn us, we have confidence before God ²²and receive from him anything we ask, because we obey his commands and do what pleases him. ²³And this is his command: to believe in the name of his Son, Jesus Christ, and to love one another as he commanded us. ²⁴Those who obey his commands live in him, and he in them. And this is

stories to share

1 JOHN 3:16–24; 4:7–21

Love One Another

LIFE LESSON: God is love.

TO TALK ABOUT

✦ How do you know what love is?

✦ How have you experienced God's love?

✦ What does it mean to you that God lives in you and that you live in God?

✦ How can you show love to others?

how we know that he lives in us: We know it by the Spirit he gave us.

Test the Spirits

4 Dear friends, do not believe every spirit, but test the spirits to see whether they are from God, because many false prophets have gone out into the world. ²This is how you can recognize the Spirit of God: Every spirit that acknowledges that Jesus Christ has come in the flesh is from God, ³but every spirit that does not acknowledge Jesus is not from God. This is the spirit of the antichrist, which you have heard is coming and even now is already in the world.

⁴You, dear children, are from God and have overcome them, because the one who is in you is greater than the one who is in the world. ⁵They are from the world and therefore speak from the viewpoint of the world, and the world listens to them. ⁶We are from God, and whoever knows God listens to us; but whoever is not from God does not listen to us. This is how we recognize the Spirit*a* of truth and the spirit of falsehood.

God's Love and Ours

⁷Dear friends, let us love one another, for love comes from God. Everyone who loves has been born of God and knows God. ⁸Whoever does not love does not know God, because God is love. ⁹This is how God showed his love among us: He sent his one and only Son*b* into the world that we might live through him. ¹⁰This is love: not that we loved God, but that he loved us and sent his Son as an atoning sacrifice for*c* our sins. ¹¹Dear friends, since God so loved us, we also ought to love one another. ¹²No one has ever seen God; but if we love one another, God lives in us and his love is made complete in us.

¹³We know that we live in him and he in us, because he has given us of his Spirit. ¹⁴And we have seen and testify that the Father has sent his Son to be the Savior of the world. ¹⁵If anyone acknowledges that Jesus is the Son of God, God lives in him and he in God. ¹⁶And so we know and rely on the love God has for us.

God is love. Whoever lives in love lives in God, and God in him. ¹⁷In this way, love is made complete among us so that we will have confidence on the day of judgment, because in this world we are like him. ¹⁸There is no fear in love. But perfect love drives out fear, because fear has to do with punishment. The one who fears is not made perfect in love.

¹⁹We love because he first loved us. ²⁰If anyone says, "I love God," yet hates his brother, he is a liar. For anyone who does not love his brother, whom he has seen, cannot love God, whom he has not seen. ²¹And he has given us this command: Whoever loves God must also love his brother.

Faith in the Son of God

5 Everyone who believes that Jesus is the Christ is born of God, and everyone who loves the father loves his child as well. ²This is how we know that we love the children of God: by loving God and carrying out his commands. ³This is love for God: to obey his commands. And his commands are not burdensome, ⁴for everyone born of God overcomes the world. This is the victory that has overcome the world, even our faith. ⁵Who is it that overcomes the world? Only he who believes that Jesus is the Son of God.

⁶This is the one who came by water and blood — Jesus Christ. He did not come by water only, but by water and blood. And it is the Spirit who testifies, because the Spirit is the truth. ⁷For there are three that testify: ⁸the*d* Spirit, the water and the blood; and the three are in agreement. ⁹We accept man's testimony, but God's testimony is greater because it is the testimony of God, which he has given about his Son. ¹⁰Anyone who believes in the Son of God has this testimony in his heart. Anyone who does not believe God has made him out to be a liar, because he has not believed the testimony God has given about his Son. ¹¹And this is the testimony: God has given

---

a 6 Or *spirit*   *b* 9 Or *his only begotten Son*   *c* 10 Or *as the one who would turn aside his wrath, taking away*   *d* 7,8 Late manuscripts of the Vulgate *testify in heaven: the Father, the Word and the Holy Spirit, and these three are one. ⁸And there are three that testify on earth: the* (not found in any Greek manuscript before the fourteenth century)

The Comfort of Grandma's Lap

DEBBY KERNER RETTINO

READ | 1 JOHN 4:7 – 21

"Grandma, you are so comfortable," my grandson sighed, as he snuggled on my lap and rested his head on the soft underside of my upper arm. "Why is that?" I asked. "Because you are so squishy," he answered. I like his perspective. The image in the mirror tells me I could stand to lose more than a few pounds. But my grandson complained when I shed enough pudge that he could feel bones beneath my comfy cushioning.

My grandkids know they are safe and loved when they are sitting on Grandma's lap. In turn, my grandchildren show me they love me by making me drawings, buying me oversized costume jewelry at school fairs, and giving me baby-wet kisses. I repay the compliments by keeping the drawings where everybody can admire them, by proudly wearing the oversized costume jewelry to work, and by relishing grandbaby slobber. Our family is composed of a variety of religious and non-religious persuasions, and I might be the best example of the love of Christ my grandkids will know.

When I admire my granddaughter's poetry or wonder at the ability of my young grandson to make stop-frame animation, they know I am their cheerleader. In my eyes, my granddaughter's poetry is the most beautiful in the world, and surely my grandson has a future in video technology! They cannot see God, but they can see me, and they can feel the unconditional love I have for them. This love comes from God. So I don't measure up to a magazine model's ideal. I am the perfect size to be a welcoming, squishy, living gospel and a comfy place for my grandchildren to relax, knowing they are loved.

Give me spiritual eyes to see, Lord. Help me to know that I am your hands and feet and lap. I pray this in the powerful name of Jesus. Amen.

Your next devotion is located on page 1732.

GRANDCHILD IN FOCUS • PRAYER

Physical Well-Being

Almighty God, Creator of us all, I pray that you will watch over my grandchild's physical development. May he grow in strength through the stages of his life. As he grows in awareness of his body, help him to understand that each body develops uniquely, yet is within your plan and your control. Please guard his health so that his diseases are few, his injuries are minor and his infirmities are brief. Amen.

THIS IS THE CONFIDENCE WE HAVE IN APPROACHING GOD: THAT IF WE ASK ANYTHING ACCORDING TO HIS WILL, HE HEARS US. AND IF WE KNOW THAT HE HEARS US — WHATEVER WE ASK — WE KNOW THAT WE HAVE WHAT WE ASKED OF HIM.

1 John 5:14 – 15

The Power of Grandparents' Prayers

RUTHANNE GARLOCK

READ | 1 JOHN 5:13 – 21

Jo was a frightened 15-year-old victim of date rape when her mom took her to a home for unwed mothers where the babies were given up for adoption. Before giving birth, Jo signed papers agreeing not to see the baby after giving birth. But neither she nor her parents ever forgot the experience. Every day the grandparents prayed that their firstborn grandson would come to know Jesus as Lord and Savior.

Jo later married and had three other children, while the birth of her first child remained a family secret. Jo's children grew to adulthood, and her parents died without seeing any fruit from their years of prayer.

One day Jo felt compelled to share her secret with one of her daughters, who searched the Internet for clues about her half brother. Among hundreds of listings she found one that aligned with all the facts Jo had given her.

A barrage of email exchanges followed. Then Michael wrote: "I am the only one in my adopted family who is a Christian." Shortly thereafter Jo met her 42-year-old son and heard his story of God's faithfulness.

Throughout most of his life Michael knew nothing about the Bible and rarely went to church. But after his younger sister died when he was 17, he wandered into a Christian bookshop, hoping to find a book with answers to his questions about life. He purchased *Good News for Modern Man* and began reading the New Testament in a contemporary version. A few weeks later, after Michael knelt by his bed and invited Jesus into his life, everything changed.

"I enjoy a wonderful relationship with my son and daughter-in-law, and the five grandchildren I never knew I had," Jo reports. "I rejoice in God's answer to my parents' faithful prayers over the years."

Thank you, Lord, that despite painful circumstances in my family, I can trust you to hear and answer prayer in amazing ways. Help me to remain faithful in prayer. Amen.

Your next devotion is located on page 1736.

GRANDCHILD IN FOCUS • PRAYER

Emotional Development

O God, Creator of mind and body, I pray that you will give my grandchild emotional health and strength. Where there is anger, bring peace. Where there is confusion, bring clarity and focus. Where there are dark shadows, cast a ray of hope. Fill her with the sunshine of your Spirit. Warm her with the presence of your peace. Amen.

us eternal life, and this life is in his Son. ¹²He who has the Son has life; he who does not have the Son of God does not have life.

Concluding Remarks

¹³I write these things to you who believe in the name of the Son of God so that you may know that you have eternal life. ¹⁴This is the confidence we have in approaching God: that if we ask anything according to his will, he hears us. ¹⁵And if we know that he hears us—whatever we ask—we know that we have what we asked of him.

¹⁶If anyone sees his brother commit a sin that does not lead to death, he should pray and God will give him life. I refer to those whose sin does not lead to death. There is a sin that leads to death. I am not saying that he should pray about that. ¹⁷All wrongdoing is sin, and there is sin that does not lead to death.

¹⁸We know that anyone born of God does not continue to sin; the one who was born of God keeps him safe, and the evil one cannot harm him. ¹⁹We know that we are children of God, and that the whole world is under the control of the evil one. ²⁰We know also that the Son of God has come and has given us understanding, so that we may know him who is true. And we are in him who is true—even in his Son Jesus Christ. He is the true God and eternal life.

²¹Dear children, keep yourselves from idols.

Watch OUT!

When we sense that our grandchildren are in danger, we want to shout, "Watch out!" We want to warn them, but we primarily want to protect them from the evils of the world that threaten to attack their peace and security. So much in our culture is based on appearances rather than content, and sometimes what is untrue is shaded, stretched and packaged in a way that makes it look true.

In this short letter, John warned his readers to watch out for false teachings that may deceive them and lead them away from the truth. In John's time there were many teachers who worked to spread their own version of the gospel. John addressed his letter to "the chosen lady and her children, whom I love in the truth." He wanted to reassure them that they were walking the straight line of truth, believing that Jesus is indeed the Son of God.

Are we as grandmothers like "the chosen lady"? Do we guard the truth? Are we discerning enough to see what teachings are true and what teachings have been shaded and packaged to *appear* true? How can we warn our grandchildren about false teachers and help them walk in truth, obedience and love?

VERSE *to* REMEMBER | 2 JOHN 6

And this is love: that we walk in obedience to his commands. As you have heard from the beginning, his command is that you walk in love.

ABOUT 2 JOHN

WRITTEN BY:
The apostle John

WRITTEN FOR:
"The chosen lady and her children" — either a local church or an influential family in John's life

DATE WRITTEN:
Probably about A.D. 90 from Ephesus

WHY WRITTEN:
To emphasize that following Christ includes practicing love and living in the truth; and to warn against false teachers

[1] The elder,

To the chosen lady and her children, whom I love in the truth—and not I only, but also all who know the truth— [2] because of the truth, which lives in us and will be with us forever:

[3] Grace, mercy and peace from God the Father and from Jesus Christ, the Father's Son, will be with us in truth and love.

[4] It has given me great joy to find some of your children walking in the truth, just as the Father commanded us. [5] And now, dear lady, I am not writing you a new command but one we have had from the beginning. I ask that we love one another. [6] And this is love: that we walk in obedience to his commands. As you have heard from the beginning, his command is that you walk in love.

[7] Many deceivers, who do not acknowledge Jesus Christ as coming in the flesh, have gone out into the world. Any such person is the deceiver and the antichrist. [8] Watch out that you do not lose what you have worked for, but that you may be rewarded fully. [9] Anyone who runs ahead and does not continue in the teaching of Christ does not have God; whoever continues in the teaching has both the Father and the Son. [10] If anyone comes to you and does not bring this teaching, do not take him into your house or welcome him. [11] Anyone who welcomes him shares in his wicked work.

[12] I have much to write to you, but I do not want to use paper and ink. Instead, I hope to visit you and talk with you face to face, so that our joy may be complete.

[13] The children of your chosen sister send their greetings.

AND NOW, DEAR LADY, I AM NOT
WRITING YOU A NEW COMMAND
BUT ONE WE HAVE HAD FROM
THE BEGINNING. I ASK THAT WE
LOVE ONE ANOTHER.

2 John 5

A Model of Christ's Love

KAREN KINGSBURY

READ | 2 JOHN 1 – 13

It is not an easy thing to love the way Jesus loved. His love was marked by sacrifice and suffering, a love that gave without limits. And this is the type of love he calls us to have for each other (see John 13:34 – 35). As I came to have a stronger relationship with Jesus, I began to consider this love — this giving, selfless love, and I realized it was being demonstrated in my life from my very own mother. Always, my mom's activities were geared around showing love for me and my four siblings, and for our dad — who has struggled with health issues for decades. My mom worked tirelessly to help our family: She cooked for us, cleaned for us and worked behind the scenes so that our family would be happy and whole.

But not until I had kids of my own did I really understand my mother's unconditional love. I realized then that my siblings and I had at times acted in ways that must have disappointed her. Yet I never felt her love waiver — not for me or my siblings, not ever. And so I've looked to her way of loving as an example of how I should, in turn, love my children.

The best part is this: Now I get the privilege of watching my mother love my kids the same way she has always loved me and my siblings. She is supportive of her grandkids if they are failing in math or struggling with health or are in the limelight finding great success. I am grateful that God gave me a mother who not only raised me right, but who also modeled the sort of love I, in turn, need to show my children and grandchildren. It's a love that Christ taught us — a love that he commanded we show one another.

Dear Lord, help me to look to those around me who have portrayed your love so clearly. Thank you for godly mothers, who are examples to all of us. And thank you for being the first one to show us what love really means. In Jesus' name, amen.

Your next devotion is located on page 1739.

GRANDCHILD IN FOCUS • PRAYER

Spiritual Growth

Dear Lord, today I pray for my grandchild's spiritual growth. I ask that you instill in him the desire to read and memorize your Word. Give him a passion to be in conversation with you. May loving and serving you be part of his daily life. I ask that you stay close to him and lead him to be transformed to your likeness, to reflect your grace and to radiate your love. I pray this in Jesus' name, amen.

The Greatest
OF JOYS

There is nothing that makes a grandmother happier than to know that her grandchildren are doing well — that they are healthy and happy and headed for a bright future, that they are developing their gifts and maturing in wisdom. And what a joy it is to hear them acknowledge that Jesus is their Lord and Savior! Some may commit to the faith while very young; others may take much longer to make their commitment. But making such a commitment is our hope and prayer for all of them.

With this in mind, we can understand John's joy as he wrote this letter of praise to Gaius, who was "walking in the truth" (3 John 4). John commended him for being hospitable and kind to the traveling preachers and evangelists whom John had commissioned. Those actions were in stark contrast with the domineering and controlling attitude of Diotrephes, who, it seems, was gossiping maliciously about John, putting people out of the church and disobeying the command to love.

John expressed a pride and joy in Gaius that we'd all like to express in our grandchildren.

VERSE *to* **REMEMBER** | 3 JOHN 4

I have no greater joy than to hear that my children are walking in the truth.

ABOUT 3 JOHN

WRITTEN BY:
The apostle John

WRITTEN FOR:
Gaius, John's
Christian friend

DATE WRITTEN:
Probably about A.D. 90
from Ephesus

WHY WRITTEN:
To commend Gaius for
his hospitality and to
encourage him in his
Christian life

¹The elder,

To my dear friend Gaius, whom I love in the truth.

²Dear friend, I pray that you may enjoy good health and that all may go well with you, even as your soul is getting along well. ³It gave me great joy to have some brothers come and tell about your faithfulness to the truth and how you continue to walk in the truth. ⁴I have no greater joy than to hear that my children are walking in the truth.

TALKING POINTS

Illness

Pray a blessing of good health.

3 JOHN 2

This is the last talking point on illness.

⁵Dear friend, you are faithful in what you are doing for the brothers, even though they are strangers to you. ⁶They have told the church about your love. You will do well to send them on their way in a manner worthy of God. ⁷It was for the sake of the Name that they went out, receiving no help from the pagans. ⁸We ought therefore to show hospitality to such men so that we may work together for the truth.

PRAYING THE SCRIPTURES

Well-Being

3 JOHN 2

Dear God, I pray that my grandchild may enjoy good health and that all may go well with him in both body and soul.

This is the last prayer in the Well-being Prayer Track.

⁹I wrote to the church, but Diotrephes, who loves to be first, will have nothing to do with us. ¹⁰So if I come, I will call attention to what he is doing, gossiping maliciously about us. Not satisfied with that, he refuses to welcome the brothers. He also stops those who want to do so and puts them out of the church.

¹¹Dear friend, do not imitate what is evil but what is good. Anyone who does what is good is from God. Anyone who does what is evil has not seen God. ¹²Demetrius is well spoken of by everyone—and even by the truth itself. We also speak well of him, and you know that our testimony is true.

¹³I have much to write you, but I do not want to do so with pen and ink. ¹⁴I hope to see you soon, and we will talk face to face.

Peace to you. The friends here send their greetings. Greet the friends there by name.

I HAVE NO GREATER JOY THAN
TO HEAR THAT MY CHILDREN
ARE WALKING IN THE TRUTH.

3 John 4

Grandma to the Rescue!

CAROL KENT

READ | 3 JOHN 1 – 14

When he was little, our son, Jason, spent a few days with his grandparents. One morning Grandpa helped prepare breakfast. Opening a jar of canned prunes, he filled three bowls with the wrinkled fruit and covered them with the juice. Soon the three of them joined hands and Grandpa asked the blessing. Grandma had prepared eggs, sausage and toast. And there sat the prunes—lots of prunes.

Jason finished his breakfast but hadn't touched the prunes. Grandpa observed his reluctance to eat the squishy fruit and announced, "Jason, if you want to keep your 'plumbing' working properly, you'll have to eat your prunes, son."

Jason had always been an obedient child, but the smell of prunes made his stomach rumble. Amid gags and gulps, he finally managed to swallow all of the prunes.

Grandpa spoke, "Jason, the juice is just as good for you as the prunes, so why don't you empty that bowl, son?"

Jason gazed up at his grandma with desperation. Suddenly, Grandma said, "Clyde (that was Grandpa), I forgot to get the chicken out of the freezer in time to thaw for tonight's supper. Would you go downstairs and take care of that?"

While Grandpa headed to the basement, Grandma picked up Jason's prune juice and dumped it down the drain. Moving fast, she placed the bowl back on the table.

Grandpa returned, chicken in hand. Peering at Jason's empty bowl, he asked, "Now that wasn't so bad after all, was it?"

Jason's eyes locked with Grandma's, and they shared a moment of relief and humor before admitting what really had happened. It was a day that bonded Jason and Grandma—and they spent many future visits talking about Biblical truths while weaving joyful memories into their precious times together.

Father, my earnest desire is to pass truth on to the next generation. Help me to remember that children learn best when they have a healthy balance of laughter and joy. Amen.

Your next devotion is located on page 1742.

GRANDCHILD IN FOCUS • PRAYER

Relationships at Home

O Lord, I pray that you will bless the home and family of my grandchild. May the relationships she has with her parents and siblings enhance her well-being, support her self-confidence and increase her faith. May her home life reflect your love, your grace, your compassion and your peace. Guide her parents to direct her in love and truth, so she will grow into a strong and compassionate individual. Amen.

Words
OF WARNING

Without frightening our grandchildren, we want to warn them about people who might do them bodily harm, about those who would be a bad influence, and about activities that might steal them away from Christian values and ruin their lives. Like Jude, we want to shout, "Warning, danger ahead! Be careful. Don't listen to those people. Follow the truth as we have taught you."

Jude wrote this brief letter in order to warn his readers against false teachers who would destroy their faith and the church. In verses 12–13 he described these deceivers by using several word pictures, such as "autumn trees, without fruit and uprooted—twice dead." These metaphors paint a dark picture indeed.

Jude closed his short letter with encouraging words to build his readers up in their faith. Verse 20 is a wonderful command for Jude's readers as well as for us today. And like Jude's readers, we can be assured that God our Savior is "able to keep [us] from falling and to present [us] before his glorious presence without fault and with great joy" (Jude 24). It is with that sure knowledge and with steadfast prayer that we, like fruitful trees, will stay rooted so that we can protect ourselves, our children and our grandchildren.

VERSE *to* REMEMBER | JUDE 20

But you, dear friends, build yourselves up in your most holy faith and pray in the Holy Spirit.

ABOUT JUDE

WRITTEN BY:
Jude, the brother
of Jesus and James

WRITTEN FOR:
An unspecified
Christian audience

DATE WRITTEN:
Probably around A.D. 65

WHY WRITTEN:
To warn Christians
about false teachers

¹Jude, a servant of Jesus Christ and a brother of James,

To those who have been called, who are loved by God the Father and kept by*a* Jesus Christ:

²Mercy, peace and love be yours in abundance.

PRAYING THE SCRIPTURES

Blessing

JUDE 2

O God, may your mercy, peace and love be with my grandchild in abundance.

This is the last prayer in the Blessing Prayer Track.

The Sin and Doom of Godless Men

³Dear friends, although I was very eager to write to you about the salvation we share, I felt I had to write and urge you to contend for the faith that was once for all entrusted to the saints. ⁴For certain men whose condemnation was written about*b* long ago have secretly slipped in among you. They are godless men, who change the grace of our God into a license for immorality and deny Jesus Christ our only Sovereign and Lord.

⁵Though you already know all this, I want to remind you that the Lord*c* delivered his people out of Egypt, but later destroyed those who did not believe. ⁶And the angels who did not keep their positions of authority but abandoned their own home—these he has kept in darkness, bound with everlasting chains for judgment on the great Day. ⁷In a similar way, Sodom and Gomorrah and the surrounding towns gave themselves up to sexual immorality and perversion. They serve as an example of those who suffer the punishment of eternal fire.

⁸In the very same way, these dreamers pollute their own bodies, reject authority and slander celestial beings. ⁹But even the archangel Michael, when he was disputing with the devil about the body of Moses, did not dare to bring a slanderous accusation against him, but said, "The Lord rebuke you!" ¹⁰Yet these men speak abusively against whatever they do not understand; and what things they do understand by instinct, like unreasoning animals—these are the very things that destroy them.

¹¹Woe to them! They have taken the way of Cain; they have rushed for profit into Balaam's error; they have been destroyed in Korah's rebellion. ¹²These men are blemishes at your love feasts, eating with you without the slightest qualm—shepherds who feed only themselves. They are clouds without rain, blown along by the wind; autumn trees, without fruit and uprooted—twice dead. ¹³They are wild waves of the sea, foaming up their shame; wandering stars, for whom blackest darkness has been reserved forever.

¹⁴Enoch, the seventh from Adam, prophesied about these men: "See, the Lord is coming with thousands upon thousands of his holy ones ¹⁵to judge everyone, and to convict all the ungodly of all the ungodly acts they have done in the ungodly way, and of all the harsh words ungodly sinners have spoken against him." ¹⁶These men are grumblers and faultfinders; they follow their own evil desires; they boast about themselves and flatter others for their own advantage.

A Call to Persevere

¹⁷But, dear friends, remember what the apostles of our Lord Jesus Christ foretold. ¹⁸They said to you, "In the last times there will be scoffers who will follow their own ungodly desires." ¹⁹These are the men who divide you, who follow mere natural instincts and do not have the Spirit.

²⁰But you, dear friends, build yourselves up in your most holy faith and pray in the Holy Spirit. ²¹Keep yourselves in God's love as you wait for the mercy of our Lord Jesus Christ to bring you to eternal life.

²²Be merciful to those who doubt; ²³snatch

Remember When . . .

Take a trip together down Memory Lane this Saturday, going only as far back as each individual grandchild can remember. If smaller ones don't recall specific situations or weren't yet on the scene, they'll probably love hearing the stories about when they were little.

Recall a family situation or event by starting your story with "Remember when . . ." Try to think of things that involved as many of the kids as possible. Go around in a circle, allowing each child to recall a scenario. For added fun, encourage them to think of a situation that comes to mind when you say a certain word. Words like *funny*, *scary*, *cold*, *sad*, *dangerous*, *exciting*, *painful*, *brave*, *awesome* or whatever will trigger memories of a certain situation. Allow ample time for responses and feedback, for laughter and tears, and for additional comments and memories. The kids will go home feeling connected and emotionally validated.

Long-Distance Variation: Enjoy a similar exercise at a family reunion, involving all ages. Your own kids will enjoy this tremendously, and your grandkids will come to appreciate their parents' generation in a new way.

God of families, thank you for the numerous experiences we've shared. Help us through this activity to savor the memories and cement our lifelong bond as family. Amen.

Your next devotion is located on page 1743.

GRANDCHILD IN FOCUS • PRAYER

Friends

Dear Lord and Father, I pray for my grandchild's social life and his friends. Bring diverse friends into his life who will love and encourage him, who will bring joy and laughter to the good times and comfort and support through difficulties and disappointments. Grant him wisdom and discernment as he selects his friends; help him to avoid cliques that restrict, activities that endanger, and foolish and dangerous behaviors that harm. I ask that you fill his life with close and caring relationships. Amen.

Worship the Lord

O God, you are my God,
  earnestly I seek you;
my soul thirsts for you,
  my body longs for you,
in a dry and wary land
  where there is no water.

I have seen you in the sanctuary
  and beheld your power and your glory.
Because your love is better then life,
  my lips will glorify you.
I will praise you as long as I live,
  and in your name I will lift up my hands.
My soul will be satisfied as with the richest
    of foods;
  with singing lips my mouth will
    praise you.

Psalm 63:1 – 5

O God, sometimes I yearn to be with you, to know you better, to follow your every command. Make those feelings a permanent longing in my life. I want to put knowing and serving you at the top of my priority list, so my soul will be satisfied and my life will be rich with your love. Amen.

Your next devotion is located on page 1744.

GRANDCHILD IN FOCUS • PRAYER

Self-Image

O loving God, I praise you for creating my grandchild as a unique individual. Now I ask you to help her appreciate her uniqueness. Build up her self-image so she can enjoy her individuality. Help her to stand firm for who she is, where she has come from and what she believes in. Encourage her not only to have hopes and dreams but to also enjoy each day as it comes.
In Jesus' name, amen.

> TO HIM WHO IS ABLE TO KEEP YOU FROM
> FALLING AND TO PRESENT YOU BEFORE HIS
> GLORIOUS PRESENCE WITHOUT FAULT AND WITH
> GREAT JOY — TO THE ONLY GOD OUR SAVIOR
> BE GLORY, MAJESTY, POWER AND AUTHORITY,
> THROUGH JESUS CHRIST OUR LORD, BEFORE ALL
> AGES, NOW AND FOREVERMORE! AMEN.
>
> *Jude 24 – 25*

Keep Us From Falling

BOBBIE WOLGEMUTH

READ | JUDE 1 – 25

Sitting on folding chairs in the retreat lodge, our extended family was gathered for prayer requests and worship at the Dourte family reunion. A favorite elderly aunt who was well into her 90s lifted her voice. Surrounded by her grandchildren and great-grandchildren, Aunt Ruth said, "Pray that I don't fall." At her age, Ruth acknowledged how fragile she was and knew that slipping could mean a broken hip or serious injury.

One of the cousins began to pray aloud for Aunt Ruth and then for the rest of those in the room: "Lord, please keep *all of us* from falling."

Jude, Jesus' half brother, understood the dangers of falling. He was living at a time when moral perversion was rampant and false teaching rendered Christianity vulnerable to intense spiritual warfare. The Savior's followers were routinely persecuted for their faith. Jude was speaking hope to believers then *and* now. He assures us that the power of the omnipotent God will sustain the humble believer. God's grace is available to keep us and our children from falling into the temptations of an ungodly culture that surrounds all of us.

Ask each member of your family how you can pray for them. Tell them that your request for yourself — and for each of them — is that we don't "fall." Follow the Lord Jesus. Walk in obedience and trust. Hold on to him. Pray for one another. God alone can keep each one of us from falling.

Lord Jesus, thank you for the promise of your power to keep me and my family from stumbling into sin. Thank you for your grace and forgiveness. We want to obey and trust and hold on to you. Amen.

Your next devotion is located on page 1750.

GRANDCHILD IN FOCUS • PRAYER

Protection From Worldliness

O Sovereign Lord, the world surrounds my grandchild, pressing in and tempting him in so many ways. Help him set appropriate limits. Give him sound judgment to choose wisely. Guard him from temptation; protect him from physical and mental predators; lead him into paths of righteousness and light. And reassure me with your promise that you are holding him in your hands. Amen.

others from the fire and save them; to others show mercy, mixed with fear—hating even the clothing stained by corrupted flesh.

Doxology

[24]To him who is able to keep you from falling and to present you before his glorious presence without fault and with great joy— [25]to the only God our Savior be glory, majesty, power and authority, through Jesus Christ our Lord, before all ages, now and forevermore! Amen.

TALKING POINTS

Doubt

We are called to be empathetic toward those who doubt.

JUDE 20–22

This is the last talking point on doubt.

Revelation

A Bright
AND GLORIOUS FUTURE

For some of us, Revelation can seem a bit spooky. The book's visions seem obscure and daunting. Too weird, too odd. But take another look. Written by the aging apostle John, exiled on the island of Patmos, the book shows God's people a vision of a future bright with hope, a time when God will make all things new. John described a wonderful future when there will be a new heaven and a new earth, a time when there will be no crying, no sorrow, no pain, no death. And best of all, God will live with us (see Revelation 21:1–5).

The book of Revelation contains visions of the second coming of Christ. As we study its pages, it reveals to us a picture of Jesus that not only cautions us but also gives us comfort and blessing. "Do not be afraid. I am the First and the Last. I am the Living One; I was dead, and behold I am alive for ever and ever!" (Revelation 1:17).

There is nothing to fear in this vision of the future, for we know the One who holds that future. If your grandchildren express fear of the future, remind them that the future holds promises of life with God. Show them that God is waiting to bring us to a bright and glorious tomorrow.

VERSE *to* REMEMBER | REVELATION 21:3

And I heard a loud voice from the throne saying, "Now the dwelling of God is with men, and he will live with them. They will be his people, and God himself will be with them and be their God."

ABOUT REVELATION

WRITTEN BY:
The apostle John

WRITTEN FOR:
Specifically for Christians in seven churches in the Roman province of Asia (in modern Turkey), but also for Christians everywhere

DATE WRITTEN:
About A.D. 95 from Patmos

WHY WRITTEN:
To warn and encourage persecuted Christians in light of God's sovereignty and Christ's return

Prologue

1 The revelation of Jesus Christ, which God gave him to show his servants what must soon take place. He made it known by sending his angel to his servant John, ²who testifies to everything he saw—that is, the word of God and the testimony of Jesus Christ. ³Blessed is the one who reads the words of this prophecy, and blessed are those who hear it and take to heart what is written in it, because the time is near.

Greetings and Doxology

⁴John,

To the seven churches in the province of Asia:

Grace and peace to you from him who is, and who was, and who is to come, and from the seven spirits *a* before his throne, ⁵and from Jesus Christ, who is the faithful witness, the firstborn from the dead, and the ruler of the kings of the earth.

To him who loves us and has freed us from our sins by his blood, ⁶and has made us to be a kingdom and priests to serve his God and Father—to him be glory and power for ever and ever! Amen.

⁷Look, he is coming with the clouds,
　　and every eye will see him,
even those who pierced him;
　　and all the peoples of the earth will mourn
　　　　because of him.
　　　　　　So shall it be! Amen.

⁸"I am the Alpha and the Omega," says the Lord God, "who is, and who was, and who is to come, the Almighty."

One Like a Son of Man

⁹I, John, your brother and companion in the suffering and kingdom and patient endurance that are ours in Jesus, was on the island of Patmos because of the word of God and the testimony of Jesus. ¹⁰On the Lord's Day I was in the Spirit, and I heard behind me a loud voice like a trumpet, ¹¹which said: "Write on a scroll what you see and send it to the seven churches: to Ephesus, Smyrna, Pergamum, Thyatira, Sardis, Philadelphia and Laodicea."

¹²I turned around to see the voice that was speaking to me. And when I turned I saw seven golden lampstands, ¹³and among the lampstands was someone "like a son of man," *b* dressed in a robe reaching down to his feet and with a golden sash around his chest. ¹⁴His head and hair were white like wool, as white as snow, and his eyes were like blazing fire. ¹⁵His feet were like bronze glowing in a furnace, and his voice was like the sound of rushing waters. ¹⁶In his right hand he held seven stars, and out of his mouth came a sharp double-edged sword. His face was like the sun shining in all its brilliance.

¹⁷When I saw him, I fell at his feet as though dead. Then he placed his right hand on me and said: "Do not be afraid. I am the First and the Last. ¹⁸I am the Living One; I was dead, and behold I am alive for ever and ever! And I hold the keys of death and Hades.

¹⁹"Write, therefore, what you have seen, what is now and what will take place later. ²⁰The mystery of the seven stars that you saw in my right hand and of the seven golden lampstands is this: The seven stars are the angels *c* of the seven churches, and the seven lampstands are the seven churches.

To the Church in Ephesus

2 "To the angel *d* of the church in Ephesus write:

These are the words of him who holds the seven stars in his right hand and walks among the seven golden lampstands: ²I know your deeds, your hard work and your perseverance. I know that you cannot tolerate wicked men, that you have tested those who claim to be apostles but are not, and have found them false. ³You have persevered and have endured hardships for my name, and have not grown weary.

---

a 4 Or the sevenfold Spirit　　*b 13 Daniel 7:13*　　*c 20 Or messengers*　　*d 1 Or messenger; also in verses 8, 12 and 18*

[4]Yet I hold this against you: You have forsaken your first love. [5]Remember the height from which you have fallen! Repent and do the things you did at first. If you do not repent, I will come to you and remove your lampstand from its place. [6]But you have this in your favor: You hate the practices of the Nicolaitans, which I also hate.

[7]He who has an ear, let him hear what the Spirit says to the churches. To him who overcomes, I will give the right to eat from the tree of life, which is in the paradise of God.

To the Church in Smyrna

[8]"To the angel of the church in Smyrna write:

These are the words of him who is the First and the Last, who died and came to life again. [9]I know your afflictions and your poverty—yet you are rich! I know the slander of those who say they are Jews and are not, but are a synagogue of Satan. [10]Do not be afraid of what you are about to suffer. I tell you, the devil will put some of you in prison to test you, and you will suffer persecution for ten days. Be faithful, even to the point of death, and I will give you the crown of life.

[11]He who has an ear, let him hear what the Spirit says to the churches. He who overcomes will not be hurt at all by the second death.

To the Church in Pergamum

[12]"To the angel of the church in Pergamum write:

These are the words of him who has the sharp, double-edged sword. [13]I know where you live—where Satan has his throne. Yet you remain true to my name. You did not renounce your faith in me, even in the days of Antipas, my faithful witness, who was put to death in your city—where Satan lives.

[14]Nevertheless, I have a few things against you: You have people there who hold to the teaching of Balaam, who taught Balak to entice the Israelites to sin by eating food sacrificed to idols and by committing sexual immorality. [15]Likewise you also have those who hold to the teaching of the Nicolaitans. [16]Repent therefore! Otherwise, I will soon come to you and will fight against them with the sword of my mouth.

[17]He who has an ear, let him hear what the Spirit says to the churches. To him who overcomes, I will give some of the hidden manna. I will also give him a white stone with a new name written on it, known only to him who receives it.

To the Church in Thyatira

[18]"To the angel of the church in Thyatira write:

These are the words of the Son of God, whose eyes are like blazing fire and whose feet are like burnished bronze. [19]I know your deeds, your love and faith, your service and perseverance, and that you are now doing more than you did at first.

[20]Nevertheless, I have this against you: You tolerate that woman Jezebel, who calls herself a prophetess. By her teaching she misleads my servants into sexual immorality and the eating of food sacrificed to idols. [21]I have given her time to repent of her immorality, but she is unwilling. [22]So I will cast her on a bed of suffering, and I will make those who commit adultery with her suffer intensely, unless they repent of her ways. [23]I will strike her children dead. Then all the churches will know that I am he who searches hearts and minds, and I will repay each of you according to your deeds. [24]Now I say to the rest of you in Thyatira, to you who do not hold to her teaching and have not learned Satan's so-called deep secrets (I will not impose any other burden on you): [25]Only hold on to what you have until I come.

[26]To him who overcomes and does my will to the end, I will give authority over the nations—

27 'He will rule them with an iron scepter;
   he will dash them to pieces like
      pottery' [a] —

just as I have received authority from my Father. 28 I will also give him the morning star. 29 He who has an ear, let him hear what the Spirit says to the churches.

To the Church in Sardis

3 "To the angel [b] of the church in Sardis write:

These are the words of him who holds the seven spirits [c] of God and the seven stars. I know your deeds; you have a reputation of being alive, but you are dead. 2 Wake up! Strengthen what remains and is about to die, for I have not found your deeds complete in the sight of my God. 3 Remember, therefore, what you have received and heard; obey it, and repent. But if you do not wake up, I will come like a thief, and you will not know at what time I will come to you.

4 Yet you have a few people in Sardis who have not soiled their clothes. They will walk with me, dressed in white, for they are worthy. 5 He who overcomes will, like them, be dressed in white. I will never blot out his name from the book of life, but will acknowledge his name before my Father and his angels. 6 He who has an ear, let him hear what the Spirit says to the churches.

To the Church in Philadelphia

7 "To the angel of the church in Philadelphia write:

These are the words of him who is holy and true, who holds the key of David. What he opens no one can shut, and what he shuts no one can open. 8 I know your deeds. See, I have placed before you an open door that no one can shut. I know that you have little strength, yet you have kept my word and have not denied my name. 9 I will make those who are of the synagogue of Satan, who claim to be Jews though they are not, but are liars—I will make them come and fall down at your feet and acknowledge that I have loved you. 10 Since you have kept my command to endure patiently, I will also keep you from the hour of trial that is going to come upon the whole world to test those who live on the earth.

11 I am coming soon. Hold on to what you have, so that no one will take your crown. 12 Him who overcomes I will make a pillar in the temple of my God. Never again will he leave it. I will write on him the name of my God and the name of the city of my God, the new Jerusalem, which is coming down out of heaven from my God; and I will also write on him my new name. 13 He who has an ear, let him hear what the Spirit says to the churches.

To the Church in Laodicea

14 "To the angel of the church in Laodicea write:

These are the words of the Amen, the faithful and true witness, the ruler of God's creation. 15 I know your deeds, that you are neither cold nor hot. I wish you were either one or the other! 16 So, because you are lukewarm—neither hot nor cold—I am about to spit you out of my mouth. 17 You say, 'I am rich; I have acquired wealth and do not need a thing.' But you do not realize that you are wretched, pitiful, poor, blind and naked. 18 I counsel you to buy from me gold refined in the fire, so you can become rich; and white clothes to wear, so you can cover your shameful nakedness; and salve to put on your eyes, so you can see.

19 Those whom I love I rebuke and discipline. So be earnest, and repent. 20 Here I am! I stand at the door and knock. If anyone hears my voice and opens the door, I will come in and eat with him, and he with me.

---

[a] 27 Psalm 2:9   [b] 1 Or messenger; also in verses 7 and 14
[c] 1 Or the sevenfold Spirit

Knocking at the Door

MARGARET FISHBACK POWERS

READ | REVELATION 3:14–22

At ten years of age, I meticulously memorized a number of special Bible chapters for a contest at my Sunday school. At the end of the year, I was excited to be rewarded with the gift of a beautiful silver tinplate picture of Jesus standing and knocking at the door. It was always on my bedroom wall while I was growing up, and I treasure it even today.

With pleasure I enjoy sharing with my grandchildren the significance of Jesus standing and knocking at our heart's door. He wants to be invited in to forgive our sin and be our forever friend in fun and fellowship. Jesus will not push the door open, however, just as my grandchildren would never push the door to my bedroom open. Instead they continually and patiently knock until I open the door and answer them. Jesus does the same. He keeps knocking, but he wants our hearts today!

My grandkids love to play a game on Saturday mornings by knocking gently on my door. They knock with a certain musical rhythm to see if I can guess which one of them it is. I laugh and make up various guesses, like Tinker Bell, the tooth fairy, etc., even though I know each of their voices.

Jesus is knocking at our heart's door, asking us to open our lives to him. He knows our voice and is waiting for us to respond. Children everywhere have faith to understand this illustration of love. They are always thrilled to receive one of my tiny pictures of Jesus at the door as a gift that I hand out when I am traveling.

Jesus is knocking. Open the door of your heart and welcome him in.

O Jesus, our forever friend, I pray for your children, those of all ages and of all places. Open their ears that they will hear your knock and your voice calling them. Open their hearts that they will welcome you into their lives. Amen.

Your next devotion is located on page 1755.

GRANDCHILD IN FOCUS • PRAYER

Respect for Authority

Dear Lord, I pray that my grandchild will continually grow to respect those in authority. May she learn to be cooperative and fair in work and play. Instill in her a high regard for officials who govern our land and enforce the laws. May her relationships with parents, teachers, coaches, mentors and bosses be respectful, admirable, constructive and caring. Amen.

²¹To him who overcomes, I will give the right to sit with me on my throne, just as I overcame and sat down with my Father on his throne. ²²He who has an ear, let him hear what the Spirit says to the churches."

The Throne in Heaven

4 After this I looked, and there before me was a door standing open in heaven. And the voice I had first heard speaking to me like a trumpet said, "Come up here, and I will show you what must take place after this." ²At once I was in the Spirit, and there before me was a throne in heaven with someone sitting on it. ³And the one who sat there had the appearance of jasper and carnelian. A rainbow, resembling an emerald, encircled the throne. ⁴Surrounding the throne were twenty-four other thrones, and seated on them were twenty-four elders. They were dressed in white and had crowns of gold on their heads. ⁵From the throne came flashes of lightning, rumblings and peals of thunder. Before the throne, seven lamps were blazing. These are the seven spirits[a] of God. ⁶Also before the throne there was what looked like a sea of glass, clear as crystal.

In the center, around the throne, were four living creatures, and they were covered with eyes, in front and in back. ⁷The first living creature was like a lion, the second was like an ox, the third had a face like a man, the fourth was like a flying eagle. ⁸Each of the four living creatures had six wings and was covered with eyes all around, even under his wings. Day and night they never stop saying:

> "Holy, holy, holy
> is the Lord God Almighty,
> who was, and is, and is to come."

⁹Whenever the living creatures give glory, honor and thanks to him who sits on the throne and who lives for ever and ever, ¹⁰the twenty-four elders fall down before him who sits on the throne, and worship him who lives for ever and ever. They lay their crowns before the throne and say:

> ¹¹"You are worthy, our Lord and God,
> to receive glory and honor and power,
> for you created all things,
> and by your will they were created
> and have their being."

The Scroll and the Lamb

5 Then I saw in the right hand of him who sat on the throne a scroll with writing on both sides and sealed with seven seals. ²And I saw a mighty angel proclaiming in a loud voice, "Who is worthy to break the seals and open the scroll?" ³But no one in heaven or on earth or under the earth could open the scroll or even look inside it. ⁴I wept and wept because no one was found who was worthy to open the scroll or look inside. ⁵Then one of the elders said to me, "Do not weep! See, the Lion of the tribe of Judah, the Root of David, has triumphed. He is able to open the scroll and its seven seals."

⁶Then I saw a Lamb, looking as if it had been slain, standing in the center of the throne, encircled by the four living creatures and the elders. He had seven horns and seven eyes, which are the seven spirits[a] of God sent out into all the earth. ⁷He came and took the scroll from the right hand of him who sat on the throne. ⁸And when he had taken it, the four living creatures and the twenty-four elders fell down before the Lamb. Each one had a harp and they were holding golden bowls full of incense, which are the prayers of the saints. ⁹And they sang a new song:

> "You are worthy to take the scroll
> and to open its seals,
> because you were slain,
> and with your blood you purchased men
> for God
> from every tribe and language and people
> and nation.
> ¹⁰You have made them to be a kingdom and
> priests to serve our God,
> and they will reign on the earth."

a 5,6 Or the sevenfold Spirit

REVELATION 5:1–14

The Scroll and the Lamb

LIFE LESSON: Only Jesus, the perfect (divine) human being, can save sinners.

TO TALK ABOUT

◆ Who was the Lamb who was worthy to open the scroll?

◆ Why did the Lamb have to be slain (killed)?

◆ Why did the Lamb have to be both human and divine (God) to pay for human sin?

◆ How do Jesus' death and resurrection reflect the two sides of God's nature: his justice and his mercy?

¹¹Then I looked and heard the voice of many angels, numbering thousands upon thousands, and ten thousand times ten thousand. They encircled the throne and the living creatures and the elders. ¹²In a loud voice they sang:

"Worthy is the Lamb, who was slain,
to receive power and wealth and wisdom and
    strength
and honor and glory and praise!"

¹³Then I heard every creature in heaven and on earth and under the earth and on the sea, and all that is in them, singing:

"To him who sits on the throne and to the
    Lamb
be praise and honor and glory and power,
    for ever and ever!"

¹⁴The four living creatures said, "Amen," and the elders fell down and worshiped.

The Seals

6 I watched as the Lamb opened the first of the seven seals. Then I heard one of the four living creatures say in a voice like thunder, "Come!" ²I looked, and there before me was a white horse! Its rider held a bow, and he was given a crown, and he rode out as a conqueror bent on conquest.

³When the Lamb opened the second seal, I heard the second living creature say, "Come!" ⁴Then another horse came out, a fiery red one. Its rider was given power to take peace from the earth and to make men slay each other. To him was given a large sword.

⁵When the Lamb opened the third seal, I heard the third living creature say, "Come!" I looked, and there before me was a black horse! Its rider was holding a pair of scales in his hand. ⁶Then I heard what sounded like a voice among the four living creatures, saying, "A quart*ᵃ* of wheat for a day's wages,*ᵇ* and three quarts of barley for a day's wages,*ᵇ* and do not damage the oil and the wine!"

⁷When the Lamb opened the fourth seal, I heard the voice of the fourth living creature say, "Come!" ⁸I looked, and there before me was a pale horse! Its rider was named Death, and Hades was following close behind him. They were given power over a fourth of the earth to kill by sword, famine and plague, and by the wild beasts of the earth.

⁹When he opened the fifth seal, I saw under the altar the souls of those who had been slain because of the word of God and the testimony they had maintained. ¹⁰They called out in a loud voice, "How long, Sovereign Lord, holy and true,

ᵃ 6 Greek a choinix (probably about a liter)   ᵇ 6 Greek a denarius until you judge the inhabitants of the earth and avenge our blood?" ¹¹Then each of them was given a white robe, and they were told to wait a little longer, until the number of their fellow servants and brothers who were to be killed as they had been was completed.

¹²I watched as he opened the sixth seal. There was a great earthquake. The sun turned black like sackcloth made of goat hair, the whole moon turned blood red, ¹³and the stars in the sky fell to earth, as late figs drop from a fig tree when shaken by a strong wind. ¹⁴The sky receded like a scroll, rolling up, and every mountain and island was removed from its place.

¹⁵Then the kings of the earth, the princes, the generals, the rich, the mighty, and every slave and every free man hid in caves and among the rocks of the mountains. ¹⁶They called to the mountains and the rocks, "Fall on us and hide us from the face of him who sits on the throne and from the wrath of the Lamb! ¹⁷For the great day of their wrath has come, and who can stand?"

144,000 Sealed

7 After this I saw four angels standing at the four corners of the earth, holding back the four winds of the earth to prevent any wind from blowing on the land or on the sea or on any tree. ²Then I saw another angel coming up from the east, having the seal of the living God. He called out in a loud voice to the four angels who had been given power to harm the land and the sea: ³"Do not harm the land or the sea or the trees until we put a seal on the foreheads of the servants of our God." ⁴Then I heard the number of those who were sealed: 144,000 from all the tribes of Israel.

⁵From the tribe of Judah 12,000 were sealed,
from the tribe of Reuben 12,000,
from the tribe of Gad 12,000,
⁶from the tribe of Asher 12,000,
from the tribe of Naphtali 12,000,
from the tribe of Manasseh 12,000,

⁷from the tribe of Simeon 12,000,
from the tribe of Levi 12,000,
from the tribe of Issachar 12,000,
⁸from the tribe of Zebulun 12,000,
from the tribe of Joseph 12,000,
from the tribe of Benjamin 12,000.

The Great Multitude in White Robes

⁹After this I looked and there before me was a great multitude that no one could count, from every nation, tribe, people and language, standing before the throne and in front of the Lamb. They were wearing white robes and were holding palm branches in their hands. ¹⁰And they cried out in a loud voice:

> "Salvation belongs to our God,
> who sits on the throne,
> and to the Lamb."

¹¹All the angels were standing around the throne and around the elders and the four living creatures. They fell down on their faces before the throne and worshiped God, ¹²saying:

> "Amen!
> Praise and glory
> and wisdom and thanks and honor
> and power and strength
> be to our God for ever and ever.
> Amen!"

¹³Then one of the elders asked me, "These in white robes—who are they, and where did they come from?"

TALKING POINTS

Praise

Praise belongs to God forever.

REVELATION 7:11–12

This is the last talking point on praise.

PRAYING THE SCRIPTURES

Thankfulness

REVELATION 7:12

Dear Lord, I pray that my grandchild will worship you passionately, proclaiming, "Amen! Praise and glory and wisdom and thanks and honor and power and strength be to our God for ever and ever. Amen!"

This is the last prayer in the Thankfulness Prayer Track.

¹⁴I answered, "Sir, you know."

And he said, "These are they who have come out of the great tribulation; they have washed their robes and made them white in the blood of the Lamb. ¹⁵Therefore,

"they are before the throne of God
    and serve him day and night in his temple;
and he who sits on the throne will spread his
    tent over them.
¹⁶Never again will they hunger;
    never again will they thirst.
The sun will not beat upon them,
    nor any scorching heat.
¹⁷For the Lamb at the center of the throne will
    be their shepherd;
    he will lead them to springs of living water.
And God will wipe away every tear from their
    eyes."

The Seventh Seal and the Golden Censer

8 When he opened the seventh seal, there was silence in heaven for about half an hour.

²And I saw the seven angels who stand before God, and to them were given seven trumpets.

³Another angel, who had a golden censer, came and stood at the altar. He was given much incense to offer, with the prayers of all the saints, on the golden altar before the throne. ⁴The smoke of the incense, together with the prayers of the saints, went up before God from the angel's hand. ⁵Then the angel took the censer, filled it with fire from the altar, and hurled it on the earth; and there came peals of thunder, rumblings, flashes of lightning and an earthquake.

The Trumpets

⁶Then the seven angels who had the seven trumpets prepared to sound them.

⁷The first angel sounded his trumpet, and there came hail and fire mixed with blood, and it was hurled down upon the earth. A third of the earth was burned up, a third of the trees were burned up, and all the green grass was burned up.

⁸The second angel sounded his trumpet, and something like a huge mountain, all ablaze, was thrown into the sea. A third of the sea turned into blood, ⁹a third of the living creatures in the sea died, and a third of the ships were destroyed.

¹⁰The third angel sounded his trumpet, and a great star, blazing like a torch, fell from the sky on a third of the rivers and on the springs of water— ¹¹the name of the star is Wormwood.ᵃ A third of the waters turned bitter, and many people died from the waters that had become bitter.

¹²The fourth angel sounded his trumpet, and a third of the sun was struck, a third of the moon, and a third of the stars, so that a third of them turned dark. A third of the day was without light, and also a third of the night.

¹³As I watched, I heard an eagle that was flying in midair call out in a loud voice: "Woe! Woe! Woe to the inhabitants of the earth, because of the trumpet blasts about to be sounded by the other three angels!"

9 The fifth angel sounded his trumpet, and I saw a star that had fallen from the sky to the earth. The star was given the key to the shaft of the Abyss. ²When he opened the Abyss, smoke rose from it like the smoke from a gigantic furnace. The sun and sky were darkened by the smoke from the Abyss. ³And out of the smoke locusts came down upon the earth and were given power like that of scorpions of the earth. ⁴They were told not to harm the grass of the earth or

ᵃ 11 That is, Bitterness

THE SMOKE OF THE INCENSE, TOGETHER WITH THE PRAYERS OF THE SAINTS, WENT UP BEFORE GOD FROM THE ANGEL'S HAND.

Revelation 8:4

A Pleasing Sacrifice to God

HELEN HAIDLE

READ | REVELATION 8:1–5

What a sight the apostle John saw in heaven: Seven angels held trumpets. An angel with a golden censer burned incense on a golden altar. Then the prayers of God's people were offered up together with the incense, the swirls of smoke ascending to God's throne in heaven.

This image of sweet-smelling incense swirling around the throne of God reminds us how much God delights in our prayer-offerings.

Grandma Ella prayed ten years for her son and grandson after they stopped attending church. One day, while in prayer, God gave her a vision of both men weeping. At first she felt alarmed. Then the vision widened, allowing her to see her son and grandson on their knees in front of Jesus.

The vision encouraged Ella to praise God even though she did not witness its fulfillment. Years later, before she died, she reminded me of the vision and said, "I *know* it will happen, sooner or later."

It's never easy to pray. It always involves a sacrifice of time and energy on our part. But consider the needs of our own children and grandchildren. Think of neighborhood families and the children all around us. If we don't offer up prayers for them, who will?

God is able to do more than we could ever ask or imagine (see Ephesians 3:20)! So we can shift our focus from our problems to God as we offer our prayers. We can give thanks that God will work out every situation and circumstance.

God's Word promises that, because we are in Christ, every prayer is heard and accepted and eventually answered — even if it isn't answered exactly the way we would like it to be.

Let the incense of our prayers ascend to God's throne right now. We can be sure our petitions and praises give God great pleasure.

Dear Lord, I trust that your wide-open arms will receive my prayer-offerings. Help me to continually offer up a sacrifice of praise as I worship you, my Lord and God. I thank you ahead of time for every answer. Amen.

Your next devotion is located on page 1760.

GRANDCHILD **IN FOCUS** • PRAYER

Courage

O Father, builder of character and courage, may my grandchild grow strong in the light of your love. Grant him courage to stand for what is right, to guard the truth and to ensure justice in every aspect of life. May he boldly grow in grace, revere your name and proudly proclaim you as the Lord of lords and King of kings. Amen.

any plant or tree, but only those people who did not have the seal of God on their foreheads. [5]They were not given power to kill them, but only to torture them for five months. And the agony they suffered was like that of the sting of a scorpion when it strikes a man. [6]During those days men will seek death, but will not find it; they will long to die, but death will elude them.

[7]The locusts looked like horses prepared for battle. On their heads they wore something like crowns of gold, and their faces resembled human faces. [8]Their hair was like women's hair, and their teeth were like lions' teeth. [9]They had breastplates like breastplates of iron, and the sound of their wings was like the thundering of many horses and chariots rushing into battle. [10]They had tails and stings like scorpions, and in their tails they had power to torment people for five months. [11]They had as king over them the angel of the Abyss, whose name in Hebrew is Abaddon, and in Greek, Apollyon. [a]

[12]The first woe is past; two other woes are yet to come.

[13]The sixth angel sounded his trumpet, and I heard a voice coming from the horns [b] of the golden altar that is before God. [14]It said to the sixth angel who had the trumpet, "Release the four angels who are bound at the great river Euphrates." [15]And the four angels who had been kept ready for this very hour and day and month and year were released to kill a third of mankind. [16]The number of the mounted troops was two hundred million. I heard their number.

[17]The horses and riders I saw in my vision looked like this: Their breastplates were fiery red, dark blue, and yellow as sulfur. The heads of the horses resembled the heads of lions, and out of their mouths came fire, smoke and sulfur. [18]A third of mankind was killed by the three plagues of fire, smoke and sulfur that came out of their mouths. [19]The power of the horses was in their mouths and in their tails; for their tails were like snakes, having heads with which they inflict injury.

[20]The rest of mankind that were not killed by these plagues still did not repent of the work of their hands; they did not stop worshiping demons, and idols of gold, silver, bronze, stone and wood—idols that cannot see or hear or walk. [21]Nor did they repent of their murders, their magic arts, their sexual immorality or their thefts.

The Angel and the Little Scroll

10 Then I saw another mighty angel coming down from heaven. He was robed in a cloud, with a rainbow above his head; his face was like the sun, and his legs were like fiery pillars. [2]He was holding a little scroll, which lay open in his hand. He planted his right foot on the sea and his left foot on the land, [3]and he gave a loud shout like the roar of a lion. When he shouted, the voices of the seven thunders spoke. [4]And when the seven thunders spoke, I was about to write; but I heard a voice from heaven say, "Seal up what the seven thunders have said and do not write it down."

[5]Then the angel I had seen standing on the sea and on the land raised his right hand to heaven. [6]And he swore by him who lives for ever and ever, who created the heavens and all that is in them, the earth and all that is in it, and the sea and all that is in it, and said, "There will be no more delay! [7]But in the days when the seventh angel is about to sound his trumpet, the mystery of God will be accomplished, just as he announced to his servants the prophets."

[8]Then the voice that I had heard from heaven spoke to me once more: "Go, take the scroll that lies open in the hand of the angel who is standing on the sea and on the land."

[9]So I went to the angel and asked him to give me the little scroll. He said to me, "Take it and eat it. It will turn your stomach sour, but in your mouth it will be as sweet as honey." [10]I took the little scroll from the angel's hand and ate it. It tasted as sweet as honey in my mouth, but when I had eaten it, my stomach turned sour. [11]Then I was told, "You must prophesy again about many peoples, nations, languages and kings."

[a] 11 Abaddon and Apollyon mean Destroyer.   [b] 13 That is, projections

The Two Witnesses

11 I was given a reed like a measuring rod and was told, "Go and measure the temple of God and the altar, and count the worshipers there. ²But exclude the outer court; do not measure it, because it has been given to the Gentiles. They will trample on the holy city for 42 months. ³And I will give power to my two witnesses, and they will prophesy for 1,260 days, clothed in sackcloth." ⁴These are the two olive trees and the two lampstands that stand before the Lord of the earth. ⁵If anyone tries to harm them, fire comes from their mouths and devours their enemies. This is how anyone who wants to harm them must die. ⁶These men have power to shut up the sky so that it will not rain during the time they are prophesying; and they have power to turn the waters into blood and to strike the earth with every kind of plague as often as they want.

⁷Now when they have finished their testimony, the beast that comes up from the Abyss will attack them, and overpower and kill them. ⁸Their bodies will lie in the street of the great city, which is figuratively called Sodom and Egypt, where also their Lord was crucified. ⁹For three and a half days men from every people, tribe, language and nation will gaze on their bodies and refuse them burial. ¹⁰The inhabitants of the earth will gloat over them and will celebrate by sending each other gifts, because these two prophets had tormented those who live on the earth.

¹¹But after the three and a half days a breath of life from God entered them, and they stood on their feet, and terror struck those who saw them. ¹²Then they heard a loud voice from heaven saying to them, "Come up here." And they went up to heaven in a cloud, while their enemies looked on.

¹³At that very hour there was a severe earthquake and a tenth of the city collapsed. Seven thousand people were killed in the earthquake, and the survivors were terrified and gave glory to the God of heaven.

¹⁴The second woe has passed; the third woe is coming soon.

The Seventh Trumpet

¹⁵The seventh angel sounded his trumpet, and there were loud voices in heaven, which said:

"The kingdom of the world has become
  the kingdom of our Lord and of his Christ,
and he will reign for ever and ever."

¹⁶And the twenty-four elders, who were seated on their thrones before God, fell on their faces and worshiped God, ¹⁷saying:

"We give thanks to you, Lord God Almighty,
  the One who is and who was,
because you have taken your great power
  and have begun to reign.
¹⁸The nations were angry;
  and your wrath has come.
The time has come for judging the dead,
  and for rewarding your servants the prophets
and your saints and those who reverence your name,
  both small and great—
and for destroying those who destroy the earth."

¹⁹Then God's temple in heaven was opened, and within his temple was seen the ark of his covenant. And there came flashes of lightning, rumblings, peals of thunder, an earthquake and a great hailstorm.

The Woman and the Dragon

12 A great and wondrous sign appeared in heaven: a woman clothed with the sun, with the moon under her feet and a crown of twelve stars on her head. ²She was pregnant and cried out in pain as she was about to give birth. ³Then another sign appeared in heaven: an enormous red dragon with seven heads and ten horns and seven crowns on his heads. ⁴His tail swept a third of the stars out of the sky and flung them to the earth. The dragon stood in front of the woman who was about to give birth, so that he might devour her child the moment it was born. ⁵She

gave birth to a son, a male child, who will rule all the nations with an iron scepter. And her child was snatched up to God and to his throne. ⁶The woman fled into the desert to a place prepared for her by God, where she might be taken care of for 1,260 days.

⁷And there was war in heaven. Michael and his angels fought against the dragon, and the dragon and his angels fought back. ⁸But he was not strong enough, and they lost their place in heaven. ⁹The great dragon was hurled down—that ancient serpent called the devil, or Satan, who leads the whole world astray. He was hurled to the earth, and his angels with him.

¹⁰Then I heard a loud voice in heaven say:

"Now have come the salvation and the power
    and the kingdom of our God,
  and the authority of his Christ.
For the accuser of our brothers,
  who accuses them before our God day and
    night,
  has been hurled down.
¹¹They overcame him
  by the blood of the Lamb
  and by the word of their testimony;
they did not love their lives so much
  as to shrink from death.
¹²Therefore rejoice, you heavens
  and you who dwell in them!
But woe to the earth and the sea,
  because the devil has gone down to you!
He is filled with fury,
  because he knows that his time is short."

¹³When the dragon saw that he had been hurled to the earth, he pursued the woman who had given birth to the male child. ¹⁴The woman was given the two wings of a great eagle, so that she might fly to the place prepared for her in the desert, where she would be taken care of for a time, times and half a time, out of the serpent's reach. ¹⁵Then from his mouth the serpent spewed water like a river, to overtake the woman and sweep her away with the torrent. ¹⁶But the earth helped the woman by opening its mouth and swallowing the river that the dragon had spewed out of his mouth. ¹⁷Then the dragon was enraged at the woman and went off to make war against the rest of her offspring—those who obey God's commandments and hold to the testimony of

13 Jesus. ¹And the dragon ᵃ stood on the shore of the sea.

The Beast out of the Sea

And I saw a beast coming out of the sea. He had ten horns and seven heads, with ten crowns on his horns, and on each head a blasphemous name. ²The beast I saw resembled a leopard, but had feet like those of a bear and a mouth like that of a lion. The dragon gave the beast his power and his throne and great authority. ³One of the heads of the beast seemed to have had a fatal wound, but the fatal wound had been healed. The whole world was astonished and followed the beast. ⁴Men worshiped the dragon because he had given authority to the beast, and they also worshiped the beast and asked, "Who is like the beast? Who can make war against him?"

⁵The beast was given a mouth to utter proud words and blasphemies and to exercise his authority for forty-two months. ⁶He opened his mouth to blaspheme God, and to slander his name and his dwelling place and those who live in heaven. ⁷He was given power to make war against the saints and to conquer them. And he was given authority over every tribe, people, language and nation. ⁸All inhabitants of the earth will worship the beast—all whose names have not been written in the book of life belonging to the Lamb that was slain from the creation of the world. ᵇ

⁹He who has an ear, let him hear.

¹⁰If anyone is to go into captivity,
  into captivity he will go.
If anyone is to be killed ᶜ with the sword,
  with the sword he will be killed.

This calls for patient endurance and faithfulness on the part of the saints.

ᵃ 1 Some late manuscripts And I   ᵇ 8 Or written from the creation of the world in the book of life belonging to the Lamb that was slain   ᶜ 10 Some manuscripts anyone kills

The Beast out of the Earth

[11] Then I saw another beast, coming out of the earth. He had two horns like a lamb, but he spoke like a dragon. [12] He exercised all the authority of the first beast on his behalf, and made the earth and its inhabitants worship the first beast, whose fatal wound had been healed. [13] And he performed great and miraculous signs, even causing fire to come down from heaven to earth in full view of men. [14] Because of the signs he was given power to do on behalf of the first beast, he deceived the inhabitants of the earth. He ordered them to set up an image in honor of the beast who was wounded by the sword and yet lived. [15] He was given power to give breath to the image of the first beast, so that it could speak and cause all who refused to worship the image to be killed. [16] He also forced everyone, small and great, rich and poor, free and slave, to receive a mark on his right hand or on his forehead, [17] so that no one could buy or sell unless he had the mark, which is the name of the beast or the number of his name.

[18] This calls for wisdom. If anyone has insight, let him calculate the number of the beast, for it is man's number. His number is 666.

The Lamb and the 144,000

14 Then I looked, and there before me was the Lamb, standing on Mount Zion, and with him 144,000 who had his name and his Father's name written on their foreheads. [2] And I heard a sound from heaven like the roar of rushing waters and like a loud peal of thunder. The sound I heard was like that of harpists playing their harps. [3] And they sang a new song before the throne and before the four living creatures and the elders. No one could learn the song except the 144,000 who had been redeemed from the earth. [4] These are those who did not defile themselves with women, for they kept themselves pure. They follow the Lamb wherever he goes. They were purchased from among men and offered as firstfruits to God and the Lamb. [5] No lie was found in their mouths; they are blameless.

The Three Angels

[6] Then I saw another angel flying in midair, and he had the eternal gospel to proclaim to those who live on the earth — to every nation, tribe, language and people. [7] He said in a loud voice, "Fear God and give him glory, because the hour of his judgment has come. Worship him who made the heavens, the earth, the sea and the springs of water."

[8] A second angel followed and said, "Fallen! Fallen is Babylon the Great, which made all the nations drink the maddening wine of her adulteries."

[9] A third angel followed them and said in a loud voice: "If anyone worships the beast and his image and receives his mark on the forehead or on the hand, [10] he, too, will drink of the wine of God's fury, which has been poured full strength into the cup of his wrath. He will be tormented with burning sulfur in the presence of the holy angels and of the Lamb. [11] And the smoke of their torment rises for ever and ever. There is no rest day or night for those who worship the beast and his image, or for anyone who receives the mark of his name." [12] This calls for patient endurance on the part of the saints who obey God's commandments and remain faithful to Jesus.

[13] Then I heard a voice from heaven say, "Write: Blessed are the dead who die in the Lord from now on."

"Yes," says the Spirit, "they will rest from their labor, for their deeds will follow them."

The Harvest of the Earth

[14] I looked, and there before me was a white cloud, and seated on the cloud was one "like a son of man"[a] with a crown of gold on his head and a sharp sickle in his hand. [15] Then another angel came out of the temple and called in a loud voice to him who was sitting on the cloud, "Take your sickle and reap, because the time to reap has come, for the harvest of the earth is ripe." [16] So he who was seated on the cloud swung his sickle over the earth, and the earth was harvested.

a 14 Daniel 7:13

THEN I HEARD A VOICE FROM HEAVEN SAY, "WRITE: BLESSED ARE THE DEAD WHO DIE IN THE LORD FROM NOW ON." "YES," SAYS THE SPIRIT, "THEY WILL REST FROM THEIR LABOR, FOR THEIR DEEDS WILL FOLLOW THEM."

Revelation 14:13

Their Deeds Will Follow Them

DORIS WYNBEEK RIKKERS

READ | REVELATION 14:6–13

"Their deeds will follow them." Now there's something to think about. The thought can be comforting or a bit disconcerting, depending on what we've been up to in life. But if we take those words in the context of the rest of the sentence — "they will rest from their labor" — it certainly appears that the deeds are the reason for resting.

Many of our grandmothers have blessedly died in the Lord and are resting from their labor. Their acts of kindness, the labors of their hands, have gone with them. Many of their acts have long been forgotten by the next generation, but now they are blessed by God for all the things they did in his name and for his glory.

A variety of contributors to this Bible have written devotions describing the deeds of their grandmothers. They remember their songs of faith, their prayers, their lives dedicated to Christ, and their constant love for God. One wrote of her grandmother's passion for reading, another remembered her grandmother kneeling in prayer, another recalled how her grandmother made each one of her 35 grandchildren feel like her favorite.

Those of us who have received a heritage of faith from our grandmothers are blessed by their memories; many of us have testified of the faith our grandmothers passed down to us. Because of our grandmothers, we can attest to God's goodness and faithfulness through all generations.

Those of us who have not been blessed with a warm memory of our grandmothers can still resonate with the idea of being a grandmother who has faith in God and love for children and grandchildren. As we strive to pass on that heritage of faith in God, we can imagine the type of grandmother we want to be: one who will say, "My deeds follow me, and I am blessed!"

Dear Lord and Father, I thank you for those grandmothers of the past who shared your love and faithfulness with their grandchildren through songs, words and deeds. Give me the wisdom and faith in you to be that kind of grandmother as well.

Your next devotion is located on page 1765.

GRANDCHILD IN FOCUS • PRAYER

Future Spouse

Dear Lord, if it is your will, I pray my grandchild will be united in a loving and Christian marriage. Keep her sexually pure so that she will honor you with her body and mind. As she seeks a spouse who will honor and care for her, give her patience and discernment. May her choice for a life partner be your choice for her, so that she and her husband will together glorify you in a lasting love. I pray this in Jesus' name, amen.

¹⁷Another angel came out of the temple in heaven, and he too had a sharp sickle. ¹⁸Still another angel, who had charge of the fire, came from the altar and called in a loud voice to him who had the sharp sickle, "Take your sharp sickle and gather the clusters of grapes from the earth's vine, because its grapes are ripe." ¹⁹The angel swung his sickle on the earth, gathered its grapes and threw them into the great winepress of God's wrath. ²⁰They were trampled in the winepress outside the city, and blood flowed out of the press, rising as high as the horses' bridles for a distance of 1,600 stadia.ᵃ

Seven Angels With Seven Plagues

15 I saw in heaven another great and marvelous sign: seven angels with the seven last plagues—last, because with them God's wrath is completed. ²And I saw what looked like a sea of glass mixed with fire and, standing beside the sea, those who had been victorious over the beast and his image and over the number of his name. They held harps given them by God ³and sang the song of Moses the servant of God and the song of the Lamb:

"Great and marvelous are your deeds,
 Lord God Almighty.
Just and true are your ways,
 King of the ages.
⁴Who will not fear you, O Lord,
 and bring glory to your name?
For you alone are holy.
All nations will come
 and worship before you,
for your righteous acts have been revealed."

⁵After this I looked and in heaven the temple, that is, the tabernacle of the Testimony, was opened. ⁶Out of the temple came the seven angels with the seven plagues. They were dressed in clean, shining linen and wore golden sashes around their chests. ⁷Then one of the four living creatures gave to the seven angels seven golden bowls filled with the wrath of God, who lives for ever and ever. ⁸And the temple was filled with smoke from the glory of God and from his power, and no one could enter the temple until the seven plagues of the seven angels were completed.

The Seven Bowls of God's Wrath

16 Then I heard a loud voice from the temple saying to the seven angels, "Go, pour out the seven bowls of God's wrath on the earth."

²The first angel went and poured out his bowl on the land, and ugly and painful sores broke out on the people who had the mark of the beast and worshiped his image.

³The second angel poured out his bowl on the sea, and it turned into blood like that of a dead man, and every living thing in the sea died.

⁴The third angel poured out his bowl on the rivers and springs of water, and they became blood. ⁵Then I heard the angel in charge of the waters say:

"You are just in these judgments,
 you who are and who were, the Holy One,
 because you have so judged;
⁶for they have shed the blood of your saints
  and prophets,
 and you have given them blood to drink as
  they deserve."

⁷And I heard the altar respond:

"Yes, Lord God Almighty,
 true and just are your judgments."

⁸The fourth angel poured out his bowl on the sun, and the sun was given power to scorch people with fire. ⁹They were seared by the intense heat and they cursed the name of God, who had control over these plagues, but they refused to repent and glorify him.

¹⁰The fifth angel poured out his bowl on the throne of the beast, and his kingdom was plunged into darkness. Men gnawed their tongues in agony ¹¹and cursed the God of heaven because of their pains and their sores, but they refused to repent of what they had done.

ᵃ 20 That is, about 180 miles (about 300 kilometers)

¹²The sixth angel poured out his bowl on the great river Euphrates, and its water was dried up to prepare the way for the kings from the East. ¹³Then I saw three evil^a spirits that looked like frogs; they came out of the mouth of the dragon, out of the mouth of the beast and out of the mouth of the false prophet. ¹⁴They are spirits of demons performing miraculous signs, and they go out to the kings of the whole world, to gather them for the battle on the great day of God Almighty.

¹⁵"Behold, I come like a thief! Blessed is he who stays awake and keeps his clothes with him, so that he may not go naked and be shamefully exposed."

¹⁶Then they gathered the kings together to the place that in Hebrew is called Armageddon.

¹⁷The seventh angel poured out his bowl into the air, and out of the temple came a loud voice from the throne, saying, "It is done!" ¹⁸Then there came flashes of lightning, rumblings, peals of thunder and a severe earthquake. No earthquake like it has ever occurred since man has been on earth, so tremendous was the quake. ¹⁹The great city split into three parts, and the cities of the nations collapsed. God remembered Babylon the Great and gave her the cup filled with the wine of the fury of his wrath. ²⁰Every island fled away and the mountains could not be found. ²¹From the sky huge hailstones of about a hundred pounds each fell upon men. And they cursed God on account of the plague of hail, because the plague was so terrible.

The Woman on the Beast

17 One of the seven angels who had the seven bowls came and said to me, "Come, I will show you the punishment of the great prostitute, who sits on many waters. ²With her the kings of the earth committed adultery and the inhabitants of the earth were intoxicated with the wine of her adulteries."

³Then the angel carried me away in the Spirit into a desert. There I saw a woman sitting on a scarlet beast that was covered with blasphemous names and had seven heads and ten horns. ⁴The woman was dressed in purple and scarlet, and was glittering with gold, precious stones and pearls. She held a golden cup in her hand, filled with abominable things and the filth of her adulteries. ⁵This title was written on her forehead:

MYSTERY
BABYLON THE GREAT
THE MOTHER OF PROSTITUTES
AND OF THE ABOMINATIONS OF THE EARTH.

⁶I saw that the woman was drunk with the blood of the saints, the blood of those who bore testimony to Jesus.

When I saw her, I was greatly astonished. ⁷Then the angel said to me: "Why are you astonished? I will explain to you the mystery of the woman and of the beast she rides, which has the seven heads and ten horns. ⁸The beast, which you saw, once was, now is not, and will come up out of the Abyss and go to his destruction. The inhabitants of the earth whose names have not been written in the book of life from the creation of the world will be astonished when they see the beast, because he once was, now is not, and yet will come.

⁹"This calls for a mind with wisdom. The seven heads are seven hills on which the woman sits. ¹⁰They are also seven kings. Five have fallen, one is, the other has not yet come; but when he does come, he must remain for a little while. ¹¹The beast who once was, and now is not, is an eighth king. He belongs to the seven and is going to his destruction.

¹²"The ten horns you saw are ten kings who have not yet received a kingdom, but who for one hour will receive authority as kings along with the beast. ¹³They have one purpose and will give their power and authority to the beast. ¹⁴They will make war against the Lamb, but the Lamb will overcome them because he is Lord of lords and King of kings—and with him will be his called, chosen and faithful followers."

^a 13 Greek unclean

[15] Then the angel said to me, "The waters you saw, where the prostitute sits, are peoples, multitudes, nations and languages. [16] The beast and the ten horns you saw will hate the prostitute. They will bring her to ruin and leave her naked; they will eat her flesh and burn her with fire. [17] For God has put it into their hearts to accomplish his purpose by agreeing to give the beast their power to rule, until God's words are fulfilled. [18] The woman you saw is the great city that rules over the kings of the earth."

The Fall of Babylon

18 After this I saw another angel coming down from heaven. He had great authority, and the earth was illuminated by his splendor. [2] With a mighty voice he shouted:

"Fallen! Fallen is Babylon the Great!
  She has become a home for demons
and a haunt for every evil[a] spirit,
  a haunt for every unclean and detestable
    bird.
[3] For all the nations have drunk
  the maddening wine of her adulteries.
The kings of the earth committed adultery
    with her,
  and the merchants of the earth grew rich
    from her excessive luxuries."

[4] Then I heard another voice from heaven say:

"Come out of her, my people,
  so that you will not share in her sins,
  so that you will not receive any of her
    plagues;
[5] for her sins are piled up to heaven,
  and God has remembered her crimes.
[6] Give back to her as she has given;
  pay her back double for what she has done.
  Mix her a double portion from her own
    cup.
[7] Give her as much torture and grief
  as the glory and luxury she gave herself.
In her heart she boasts,
  'I sit as queen; I am not a widow,
  and I will never mourn.'

[8] Therefore in one day her plagues will
    overtake her:
  death, mourning and famine.
She will be consumed by fire,
  for mighty is the Lord God who judges her.

[9] "When the kings of the earth who committed adultery with her and shared her luxury see the smoke of her burning, they will weep and mourn over her. [10] Terrified at her torment, they will stand far off and cry:

" 'Woe! Woe, O great city,
  O Babylon, city of power!
In one hour your doom has come!'

[11] "The merchants of the earth will weep and mourn over her because no one buys their cargoes any more— [12] cargoes of gold, silver, precious stones and pearls; fine linen, purple, silk and scarlet cloth; every sort of citron wood, and articles of every kind made of ivory, costly wood, bronze, iron and marble; [13] cargoes of cinnamon and spice, of incense, myrrh and frankincense, of wine and olive oil, of fine flour and wheat; cattle and sheep; horses and carriages; and bodies and souls of men.

[14] "They will say, 'The fruit you longed for is gone from you. All your riches and splendor have vanished, never to be recovered.' [15] The merchants who sold these things and gained their wealth from her will stand far off, terrified at her torment. They will weep and mourn [16] and cry out:

" 'Woe! Woe, O great city,
  dressed in fine linen, purple and scarlet,
    and glittering with gold, precious stones
      and pearls!
[17] In one hour such great wealth has been
    brought to ruin!'

"Every sea captain, and all who travel by ship, the sailors, and all who earn their living from the sea, will stand far off. [18] When they see the smoke of her burning, they will exclaim, 'Was there ever a city like this great city?' [19] They will throw dust

---

[a] 2 Greek *unclean*

on their heads, and with weeping and mourning
cry out:

> " 'Woe! Woe, O great city,
>> where all who had ships on the sea
>> became rich through her wealth!
> In one hour she has been brought to ruin!
> 20 Rejoice over her, O heaven!
>> Rejoice, saints and apostles and prophets!
> God has judged her for the way she treated
>> you.' "

21 Then a mighty angel picked up a boulder the
size of a large millstone and threw it into the sea,
and said:

> "With such violence
>> the great city of Babylon will be thrown
>> down,
>> never to be found again.
> 22 The music of harpists and musicians, flute
>> players and trumpeters,
>> will never be heard in you again.
> No workman of any trade
>> will ever be found in you again.
> The sound of a millstone
>> will never be heard in you again.
> 23 The light of a lamp
>> will never shine in you again.
> The voice of bridegroom and bride
>> will never be heard in you again.
> Your merchants were the world's great men.
>> By your magic spell all the nations were led
>> astray.
> 24 In her was found the blood of prophets and
>> of the saints,
>> and of all who have been killed on the
>> earth."

Hallelujah!

19 After this I heard what sounded like the
roar of a great multitude in heaven shouting:

> "Hallelujah!
> Salvation and glory and power belong to our
>> God,
> 2   for true and just are his judgments.

He has condemned the great prostitute
>> who corrupted the earth by her
>> adulteries.
> He has avenged on her the blood of his
>> servants."

3 And again they shouted:

> "Hallelujah!
> The smoke from her goes up for ever
>> and ever."

4 The twenty-four elders and the four living
creatures fell down and worshiped God, who was
seated on the throne. And they cried:

> "Amen, Hallelujah!"

5 Then a voice came from the throne, saying:

> "Praise our God,
>> all you his servants,
> you who fear him,
>> both small and great!"

6 Then I heard what sounded like a great multitude, like the roar of rushing waters and like loud
peals of thunder, shouting:

> "Hallelujah!
>> For our Lord God Almighty reigns.
> 7 Let us rejoice and be glad
>> and give him glory!
> For the wedding of the Lamb has come,
>> and his bride has made herself ready.
> 8 Fine linen, bright and clean,
>> was given her to wear."

(Fine linen stands for the righteous acts of the
saints.)

9 Then the angel said to me, "Write: 'Blessed
are those who are invited to the wedding supper
of the Lamb!' " And he added, "These are the true
words of God."

10 At this I fell at his feet to worship him. But
he said to me, "Do not do it! I am a fellow servant with you and with your brothers who hold
to the testimony of Jesus. Worship God! For the
testimony of Jesus is the spirit of prophecy."

THEN THE ANGEL SAID TO ME, "WRITE: 'BLESSED ARE THOSE WHO ARE INVITED TO THE WEDDING SUPPER OF THE LAMB!'" AND HE ADDED, "THESE ARE THE TRUE WORDS OF GOD."

Revelation 19:9

Foretaste

JOY MORGAN DAVIS

READ | REVELATION 19:1–10

This morning
As sunlight streamed
Through stained glass
Windows, a beautiful
Black woman, radiant in a
Rich crimson robe,
Sang from her soul. . .
"I'm gonna' eat at
God's great welcome table
One of these days!"

I know, Lord, that I'll
Be there too,
At Your heavenly
Banquet for believers,
But I'm so spiritually
Hungry. . .
I need nourishment
Now!
Could I please have
An appetizer,
Just a foretaste
Of things to come. . .

So I can wait
Till it's time
For the feast?

GRANDCHILD IN FOCUS • PRAYER

School/Career

Dear God, may learning be a joy rather than a chore for my grandchild. May exploration of new ideas bring a sense of wonder, awe and excitement. Grant him clarity of mind, the ability to concentrate on the task at hand and recollection of what has been learned. Help him to appreciate the tasks that come easily and to persevere through those that challenge. Amen.

Lord, I long to be seated at the wedding supper of the Lamb. What a glorious day that will be! Until that time, strengthen me and nourish me with your Spirit and your Word. Amen.

Your next devotion is located on page 1767.

The Rider on the White Horse

¹¹ I saw heaven standing open and there before me was a white horse, whose rider is called Faithful and True. With justice he judges and makes war. ¹² His eyes are like blazing fire, and on his head are many crowns. He has a name written on him that no one knows but he himself. ¹³ He is dressed in a robe dipped in blood, and his name is the Word of God. ¹⁴ The armies of heaven were following him, riding on white horses and dressed in fine linen, white and clean. ¹⁵ Out of his mouth comes a sharp sword with which to strike down the nations. "He will rule them with an iron scepter."^a He treads the winepress of the fury of the wrath of God Almighty. ¹⁶ On his robe and on his thigh he has this name written:

KING OF KINGS AND LORD OF LORDS.

¹⁷ And I saw an angel standing in the sun, who cried in a loud voice to all the birds flying in midair, "Come, gather together for the great supper of God, ¹⁸ so that you may eat the flesh of kings, generals, and mighty men, of horses and their riders, and the flesh of all people, free and slave, small and great."

¹⁹ Then I saw the beast and the kings of the earth and their armies gathered together to make war against the rider on the horse and his army. ²⁰ But the beast was captured, and with him the false prophet who had performed the miraculous signs on his behalf. With these signs he had deluded those who had received the mark of the beast and worshiped his image. The two of them were thrown alive into the fiery lake of burning sulfur. ²¹ The rest of them were killed with the sword that came out of the mouth of the rider on the horse, and all the birds gorged themselves on their flesh.

The Thousand Years

20 And I saw an angel coming down out of heaven, having the key to the Abyss and holding in his hand a great chain. ² He seized the dragon, that ancient serpent, who is the devil, or Satan, and bound him for a thousand years.

³ He threw him into the Abyss, and locked and sealed it over him, to keep him from deceiving the nations anymore until the thousand years were ended. After that, he must be set free for a short time.

⁴ I saw thrones on which were seated those who had been given authority to judge. And I saw the souls of those who had been beheaded because of their testimony for Jesus and because of the word of God. They had not worshiped the beast or his image and had not received his mark on their foreheads or their hands. They came to life and reigned with Christ a thousand years. ⁵ (The rest of the dead did not come to life until the thousand years were ended.) This is the first resurrection. ⁶ Blessed and holy are those who have part in the first resurrection. The second death has no power over them, but they will be priests of God and of Christ and will reign with him for a thousand years.

Satan's Doom

⁷ When the thousand years are over, Satan will be released from his prison ⁸ and will go out to deceive the nations in the four corners of the earth — Gog and Magog — to gather them for battle. In number they are like the sand on the seashore. ⁹ They marched across the breadth of the earth and surrounded the camp of God's people, the city he loves. But fire came down from heaven and devoured them. ¹⁰ And the devil, who deceived them, was thrown into the lake of burning sulfur, where the beast and the false prophet had been thrown. They will be tormented day and night for ever and ever.

The Dead Are Judged

¹¹ Then I saw a great white throne and him who was seated on it. Earth and sky fled from his presence, and there was no place for them. ¹² And I saw the dead, great and small, standing before the throne, and books were opened. Another book was opened, which is the book of life. The dead were judged according to what

^a 15 Psalm 2:9

Interview a Family Member

Plan a get-together at which pairs of family members "present" one another to the group based on interviews they've conducted in advance. Suggest that the questions touch on memorable or humorous events, spiritual themes, special abilities and achievements, likes and dislikes, hopes and dreams, etc.

Make sure to set the date early enough to allow time for out-of-town family members to send in their interviews, and have someone read these as well, "introducing" the individuals in their absence.

A fun follow-up might be to have someone type up the handwritten interview responses and distribute the collective "data" in a document labeled "Meet Our Family" (or some other creative title).

If one of your older grandchildren is into video production, this would be an excellent project for him/her to take on for the family.

Younger-Grandkids Variation: Have a parent ask the child simple questions. (Be sure to jot down the responses if you're planning on creating a document.)

Thank you, Lord, for placing each of us in our family. May this activity assure each family member that they belong and are valued and appreciated. I pray that each of my grandchildren will also choose to join your forever family and come to know you as their Savior. Amen.

Your next devotion is located on page 1770.

GRANDCHILD IN FOCUS • PRAYER

Character

Dear Lord and Father, I ask that you fill my grandchild with your Spirit so her character reflects your goodness and love. Give her kindness and love for others. Bring joy to her life so she will be a joy to others. Grant her patience and self-control through difficult and trying times. May she show mercy and generosity to those who are less fortunate. Grant her integrity and a sense of justice, and surround her with your peace. Amen.

they had done as recorded in the books. ¹³The sea gave up the dead that were in it, and death and Hades gave up the dead that were in them, and each person was judged according to what he had done. ¹⁴Then death and Hades were thrown into the lake of fire. The lake of fire is the second death. ¹⁵If anyone's name was not found written in the book of life, he was thrown into the lake of fire.

The New Jerusalem

21 Then I saw a new heaven and a new earth, for the first heaven and the first earth had passed away, and there was no longer any sea. ²I saw the Holy City, the new Jerusalem, coming down out of heaven from God, prepared as a bride beautifully dressed for her husband. ³And I heard a loud voice from the throne saying, "Now the dwelling of God is with men, and he will live with them. They will be his people, and God himself will be with them and be their God. ⁴He will wipe every tear from their eyes. There will be no more death or mourning or crying or pain, for the old order of things has passed away."

⁵He who was seated on the throne said, "I am making everything new!" Then he said, "Write this down, for these words are trustworthy and true."

PRAYING THE SCRIPTURES

Comfort

REVELATION 21:4–5

Almighty God, may my grandchild find hope and peace in knowing that someday you will wipe every tear from his eyes. There will be no more death or mourning or crying or pain, for the old order of things will have passed away and you will have made everything new.

This is the last prayer in the Comfort Prayer Track.

⁶He said to me: "It is done. I am the Alpha and the Omega, the Beginning and the End. To him who is thirsty I will give to drink without cost from the spring of the water of life. ⁷He who overcomes will inherit all this, and I will be his God and he will be my son. ⁸But the cowardly, the unbelieving, the vile, the murderers, the sexually immoral, those who practice magic arts, the idolaters and all liars—their place will be in the fiery lake of burning sulfur. This is the second death."

⁹One of the seven angels who had the seven bowls full of the seven last plagues came and said to me, "Come, I will show you the bride, the wife of the Lamb." ¹⁰And he carried me away in the Spirit to a mountain great and high, and showed me the Holy City, Jerusalem, coming down out of heaven from God. ¹¹It shone with the glory of God, and its brilliance was like that of a very precious jewel, like a jasper, clear as crystal. ¹²It had a great, high wall with twelve gates, and with twelve angels at the gates. On the gates were written the names of the twelve tribes of Israel. ¹³There were three gates on the east, three on the north, three on the south and three on the west. ¹⁴The wall of the city had twelve foundations, and on them were the names of the twelve apostles of the Lamb.

¹⁵The angel who talked with me had a measuring rod of gold to measure the city, its gates and its walls. ¹⁶The city was laid out like a square, as long as it was wide. He measured the city with the rod and found it to be 12,000 stadia ᵃ in length, and as wide and high as it is long. ¹⁷He measured its wall and it was 144 cubits ᵇ thick, ᶜ by man's measurement, which the angel was using. ¹⁸The wall was made of jasper, and the city of pure gold, as pure as glass. ¹⁹The foundations of the city walls were decorated with every kind of precious stone. The first foundation was jasper, the second sapphire, the third chalcedony, the fourth emerald, ²⁰the fifth sardonyx, the sixth carnelian, the seventh chrysolite, the eighth beryl, the ninth topaz, the tenth chrysoprase, the eleventh jacinth, and the twelfth

ᵃ *16* That is, about 1,400 miles (about 2,200 kilometers)
ᵇ *17* That is, about 200 feet (about 65 meters)   ᶜ *17* Or *high*

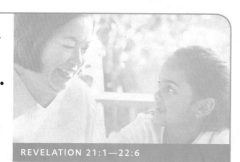

REVELATION 21:1—22:6

The New Jerusalem

LIFE LESSON: Eternity with God will be beautiful, joyful and perfect.

TO TALK ABOUT

- What are some of the wonderful descriptions here of heaven?

- What is required for entrance into heaven? (Hint: See Revelation 21:27.)

- Do you think we'll remember our old lives when we're in heaven? If so, what will keep us from being sad?

- How will it make a difference for us to fully understand God's eternal purpose and plan?

amethyst.[a] 21 The twelve gates were twelve pearls, each gate made of a single pearl. The great street of the city was of pure gold, like transparent glass.

22 I did not see a temple in the city, because the Lord God Almighty and the Lamb are its temple. 23 The city does not need the sun or the moon to shine on it, for the glory of God gives it light, and the Lamb is its lamp. 24 The nations will walk by its light, and the kings of the earth will bring their splendor into it. 25 On no day will its gates ever be shut, for there will be no night there. 26 The glory and honor of the nations will be brought into it. 27 Nothing impure will ever enter it, nor will

anyone who does what is shameful or deceitful, but only those whose names are written in the Lamb's book of life.

The River of Life

22 Then the angel showed me the river of the water of life, as clear as crystal, flowing from the throne of God and of the Lamb 2 down the middle of the great street of the city. On each side of the river stood the tree of life, bearing twelve crops of fruit, yielding its fruit every month. And the leaves of the tree are for the healing of the nations. 3 No longer will there be any curse. The throne of God and of the Lamb will be in the city, and his servants will serve him. 4 They will see his face, and his name will be on their foreheads. 5 There will be no more night. They will not need the light of a lamp or the light of the sun, for the Lord God will give them light. And they will reign for ever and ever.

6 The angel said to me, "These words are trustworthy and true. The Lord, the God of the spirits of the prophets, sent his angel to show his servants the things that must soon take place."

Jesus Is Coming

7 "Behold, I am coming soon! Blessed is he who keeps the words of the prophecy in this book."

8 I, John, am the one who heard and saw these things. And when I had heard and seen them, I fell down to worship at the feet of the angel who had been showing them to me. 9 But he said to me, "Do not do it! I am a fellow servant with you and with your brothers the prophets and of all who keep the words of this book. Worship God!"

10 Then he told me, "Do not seal up the words of the prophecy of this book, because the time is near. 11 Let him who does wrong continue to do wrong; let him who is vile continue to be vile; let him who does right continue to do right; and let him who is holy continue to be holy."

12 "Behold, I am coming soon! My reward is with me, and I will give to everyone according to what

a 20 The precise identification of some of these precious stones is uncertain.

Worship the Lord

By the word of the LORD were the heavens made,
    their starry host by the breath of his mouth.
He gathers the waters of the sea into jars;
    he puts the deep into storehouses.
Let all the earth fear the LORD;
    let all the people of the world revere him.
For he spoke, and it came to be;
    he commanded, and it stood firm.
The LORD foils the plans of the nations;
    he thwarts the purposes of the peoples.
But the plans of the LORD stand firm forever,
    the purposes of his heart through all
        generations.

Psalm 33:6 – 11

Thank you for the permanence of your plans, Lord, and the unchanging purpose of your heart. I pray that you watch over those who will follow me for generations to come, drawing them to yourself. Amen.

GRANDCHILD IN FOCUS • PRAYER

Talents

Dear Lord, the giver of gifts, bless my grandchild as he develops his talents. Help him identify his talents and be proud and confident of the gifts you have given him. Give him patience and understanding, Lord, so he will not grow weary of striving and searching to reach the goals you have set for him. May each milestone bring satisfaction and a healthy desire for greater achievement and success to bring glory to you. Amen.

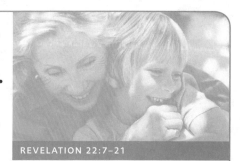

stories to share

REVELATION 22:7–21

Jesus Is Coming

LIFE LESSON: Jesus is coming back soon, and the whole world is invited to come to him in the meantime.

TO TALK ABOUT

✦ Why didn't the angel want John to worship him? Who should we worship instead?

✦ Jesus said he is coming "soon" (verse 20). How does it make a difference that God's timing is different from ours?

✦ Who sent the angel who gave John his heavenly vision?

✦ Who is the bride who joins the Spirit in saying "Come!"? What is the invitation, and who is it for?

he has done. [13] I am the Alpha and the Omega, the First and the Last, the Beginning and the End.

[14] "Blessed are those who wash their robes, that they may have the right to the tree of life and may go through the gates into the city. [15] Outside are the dogs, those who practice magic arts, the sexually immoral, the murderers, the idolaters and everyone who loves and practices falsehood.

[16] "I, Jesus, have sent my angel to give you[a] this testimony for the churches. I am the Root and the Offspring of David, and the bright Morning Star."

[17] The Spirit and the bride say, "Come!" And let him who hears say, "Come!" Whoever is thirsty, let him come; and whoever wishes, let him take the free gift of the water of life.

[18] I warn everyone who hears the words of the prophecy of this book: If anyone adds anything to them, God will add to him the plagues described in this book. [19] And if anyone takes words away from this book of prophecy, God will take away from him his share in the tree of life and in the holy city, which are described in this book.

[20] He who testifies to these things says, "Yes, I am coming soon."

Amen. Come, Lord Jesus.

[21] The grace of the Lord Jesus be with God's people. Amen.

[a] 16 The Greek is plural.

Contents

Acknowledgments

Page 86 [Ex 1]
Adapted from *Mother Goose Meets a Woman Called Wisdom* by Linda H. Hollies. Copyright © 2000 by Pilgrim Press, The United Church Press. Published by United Church Press, Cleveland, OH 44115.

Page 194 [Nu 9]
Taken from *Meditation Moments* by Millie Stamm. Copyright © 1976 by Zondervan, Grand Rapids, MI. Used by permission of Zondervan.

Page 201 [Nu 14]
Taken from *Water My Soul: Cultivating the Interior Life* by Luci Shaw. Copyright © 1998 by Luci Shaw. Published by Zondervan, Grand Rapids, MI. Used by permission of Luci Shaw.

Page 210 [Nu 21]
Taken from *Could You Hurry Up the Dawn, Lord?: Poems, Prayers, and Lively Conversations with a Loving God.* Copyright © 1994 by Joy Morgan Davis. Published by Joyful Noise Publications, 2108 Kessler Ct., Dallas, TX 75208. Used by permission.

Page 258 [Dt 16]
Taken from *Lord, You Love to Say Yes* by Ruth Harms Calkin. Copyright © 1976 by Ruth Harms Calkin. Published by Living Books, a trademark of Tyndale House Publisher, Inc., Wheaton, IL.

Page 275 [Dt 31]
Taken from *Extravagant Grace* by Barbara E. Johnson; Patsy Clairmont; Luci Swindoll; Sheila Walsh; Marilyn Meberg; Thelma Wells. Copyright © 2000 by Women of Faith, Inc. Published by Zondervan, Grand Rapids, MI. Used by permission of Zondervan.

Page 280 [Dt 33]
Taken from *Meditation Moments* by Millie Stamm. Copyright © 1976 by Zondervan, Grand Rapids, Michigan. Used by permission of Zondervan.

Page 347 [Ru 1]
Adapted from *Mother Goose Meets a Woman Called Wisdom* by Linda H. Hollies. Copyright © 2000 by Pilgrim Press, The United Church Press. Published by United Church Press, Cleveland, OH 44115.

Page 391 [1Sa 20]
Taken from *Gifts for Your Soul* by Sheila Walsh. Copyright © 1997 by Sheila Walsh. Published by Zondervan, Grand Rapids, Michigan. Used by permission of Zondervan.

Page 437 [2Sa 22]
Taken from *Weather of the Heart: Glimpses of God in Sunlight and Storm* by Gigi Graham Tchividjian. Copyright © 1991 by Gigi Graham Tchividjian. Published by WaterBrook Multnomah Press, Colorado Springs, CO 80921. Used by permission of WaterBrook

Multnomah Publishing Group, a division of Random House, Inc.

Page 440 [2Sa 24]

Taken from *365 Meditations for Women*. Copyright © 1989 by Abingdon Press. Published by Abingdon Press, Nashville, TN. Used by permission of Gloria Gaither.

Page 459 [1Ki 8]

Taken from *365 Meditations for Women*. Copyright © 1989 by Abingdon Press. Published by Abingdon Press, Nashville, TN. Used by permission of Barbara Owen.

Page 461 [1Ki 8]

Taken from *Help Lord! I'm Having a Senior Moment — Again! Laughing Through the Realities of Growing Older* by Karen O'Connor. Copyright © 2005 by Karen O'Connor. Published by Regal Books from Gospel Light, Ventura, CA.

Page 528 [1Ch 3]

Taken from *Breakfast for the Heart: Meditations to Nourish Your Soul* by Diane M. Komp, M.D. Copyright © 1996 by Diane M. Komp. Published by Zondervan, Grand Rapids, MI. Used by permission of Diane M. Komp.

Page 541 [1Ch 9]

Taken from *When Life Takes What Matters: Devotions to Comfort You Through Crisis & Change* by Susan Lenzkes. Copyright © 1993 by Susan Lenzkes. Published by Discovery House Publishers, Grand Rapids, MI 49501. Used by permission of Discovery House Publishers. All rights reserved.

Page 549 [1Ch 16]

Taken from *Diamonds in the Dust* by Joni Eareckson Tada. Copyright © 1993 by Joni Eareckson Tada. Published by Zondervan, Grand Rapids, MI. Used by permission of Zondervan.

Page 575 [2Ch 9]

Taken from *Second Cup of Coffee: Proverbs for Today's Woman* by Jean Shaw. Copyright © 1981 by Zondervan. A Daybreak Book: Published by Zondervan, Grand Rapids, MI. Used by permission of Zondervan.

Page 641 [Ne 12]

Taken from *Extravagant Grace* by Barbara E. Johnson; Patsy Clairmont; Luci Swindoll; Sheila Walsh; Marilyn Meberg; Thelma Wells. Copyright © 2000 by Women of Faith, Inc. Published by Zondervan, Grand Rapids, Michigan. Used by permission of Zondervan.

Page 649 [Est 4]

Adapted from *Squeeze the Moment* by Karen O'Connor. Copyright © 2005 by Karen O'Connor. Published by Regal Books from Gospel Light, Ventura, CA.

Page 654 [Est 7]

Taken from *Extravagant Grace* by Barbara E. Johnson; Patsy Clairmont; Luci Swindoll; Sheila Walsh; Marilyn Meberg; Thelma Wells. Copyright © 2000 by Women of Faith, Inc. Published by Zondervan, Grand Rapids, Michigan. Used by permission of Zondervan.

Page 664 [Job 2]

Taken from *365 Meditations for Women*. Copyright © 1989 by Abingdon Press. Published by Abingdon Press, Nashville, TN. Used by permission of Mari Serebrov.

Page 692 [Job 35]

Taken from *Be Still and Know* by Millie Stamm. Copyright © 1978 by Millie Stamm. Published by Daybreak Books, a division of Zondervan, Grand Rapids, MI. Used by permission of Zondervan.

Page 701 [Job 42]

Taken from *Extravagant Grace* by Barbara E. Johnson; Patsy Clairmont; Luci Swindoll;

Sheila Walsh; Marilyn Meberg; Thelma Wells. Copyright © 2000 by Women of Faith, Inc. Published by Zondervan, Grand Rapids, Michigan. Used by permission of Zondervan.

Page 815 [Ps 119]
Taken from *Weather of the Heart: Glimpses of God in Sunlight and Storm* by Gigi Graham Tchividjian. Copyright © 1991 by Gigi Graham Tchividjian. Published by WaterBrook Multnomah Press, Colorado Springs, CO 80921. Used by permission of WaterBrook Multnomah Publishing Group, a division of Random House, Inc.

Page 838 [Ps 145]
Taken from *The Mitford Bedside Companion* by Jan Karon. Copyright © 2006 by Jan Karon. Published by the Penguin Group (USA), Inc., New York, New York 10014. Used by permission of Viking Penguin, a division of Penguin Group (USA), Inc.

Page 867 [Pr 16]
Taken from *Diamonds in the Dust* by Joni Eareckson Tada. Copyright © 1993 by Joni Eareckson Tada. Published by Zondervan, Grand Rapids, MI. Used by permission of Zondervan.

Page 890 [Pr 30]
Taken from *Lord, You Love to Say Yes* by Ruth Harms Calkin. Copyright © 1976 by Ruth Harms Calkin. Published by Living Books, a trademark of Tyndale House Publisher, Inc., Wheaton, IL.

Page 901 [Ecc 3]
Taken from *Could You Hurry Up the Dawn, Lord?: Poems, Prayers, and Lively Conversations with a Loving God.* Copyright © 1994 by Joy Morgan Davis. Published by Joyful Noise Publications, 2108 Kessler Ct., Dallas, TX 75208. Used by permission.

Page 909 [Ecc 10]
Taken from *Second Cup of Coffee: Proverbs for Today's Woman* by Jean Shaw. Copyright © 1981 by Zondervan. A Daybreak Book: Published by Zondervan, Grand Rapids, MI. Used by permission of Zondervan.

Page 916 [SS 4]
Taken from *Extravagant Grace* by Barbara E. Johnson, Patsy Clairmont, Luci Swindoll, Sheila Walsh, Marilyn Meberg, Thelma Wells, pages 154–155. Copyright © 2000 by Women of Faith, Inc. Published by Zondervan, Grand Rapids, Michigan. Used by permission of Zondervan.

Page 954 [Isa 26]
Taken from *365 Meditations for Women.* Copyright © 1989 by Abingdon Press. Published by Abingdon Press, Nashville, TN. Used by permission of Martha Hickman.

Page 960 [Isa 30]
Taken from *Be Still and Know* by Millie Stamm. Copyright © 1978 by Millie Stamm. Published by Daybreak Books, a division of Zondervan, Grand Rapids, MI. Used by permission of Zondervan.

Page 969 [Isa 35]
Taken from *No Rain No Gain: Devotions to Guide You Through the Storms of Life* by Susan Lenzkes. Copyright © 1995 by Susan Lenzkes. Published by Discovery House Publishers, Grand Rapids, MI 49501. Used by permission of Discovery House Publishers. All rights reserved.

Page 996 [Isa 49]
Adapted from *Soul Restoration: Hope for the Weary* by Terri Blackstock. Copyright © 2005 by Terri Blackstock. Published by Inspiro, the gift group of Zondervan, Grand Rapids, Michigan 49530. Used by permission of Zondervan.

Page 999 [Isa 51]
Taken from *365 Meditations for Women*. Copyright © 1989 by Abingdon Press. Published by Abingdon Press, Nashville, TN. Used by permission of Gloria Gaither.

Page 1012 [Isa 61]
Taken from *Water My Soul: Cultivating the Interior Life* by Luci Shaw. Copyright © 1998 by Luci Shaw. Published by Zondervan, Grand Rapids, Michigan. Used by permission of Luci Shaw.

Page 1058 [Jer 29]
Adapted from *Soul Restoration: Hope for the Weary* by Terri Blackstock. Copyright © 2005 by Terri Blackstock. Published by Inspiro, the gift group of Zondervan, Grand Rapids, Michigan 49530. Used by permission of Zondervan.

Page 1061 [Jer 31]
Taken from *Messages of God's Abundance* by Corrie ten Boom. Copyright © 2002 by Stichting Trans World Radio voor Nederland en België. Published by Zondervan, Grand Rapids, MI 49530. Used by permission of Zondervan.

Page 1122 [Eze 17]
Adapted from *Squeeze the Moment* by Karen O'Connor. Copyright © 2005 by Karen O'Connor. Published by Regal Books from Gospel Light, Ventura, CA.

Page 1185 [Da 12]
Taken from *Women in God's Presence*, compiled by Delores Taylor. Copyright © 1988 by Christian Publications, Camp Hill, PA. Used by permission of Christian Publications.

Page 1204 [Joel 2]
Taken from *Extravagant Grace* by Barbara E. Johnson, Patsy Clairmont, Luci Swindoll, Sheila Walsh, Marilyn Meberg, Thelma Wells. Copyright © 2000 by Women of Faith, Inc. Published by Zondervan, Grand Rapids, Michigan. Used by permission of Zondervan.

Page 1207 [Joel 2]
Adapted from *The Gift of Prayer* by Jane Schlenvogt. Copyright © 2003 by Northwestern Publishing House. Published by Northwestern Publishing House, Milwaukee, WI.

Page 1266 [Zec 7]
Adapted from *Soul Restoration: Hope for the Weary* by Terri Blackstock. Copyright © 2005 by Terri Blackstock. Published by Inspiro, the gift group of Zondervan, Grand Rapids, Michigan 49530. Used by permission of Zondervan.

Page 1279 [Mal 3]
Taken from *Living the Lois Legacy: Passing on Last Faith to Your Grandchildren*, A Focus on the Family Book, published by Tyndale House Publishers, Inc., Wheaton, IL, 2002. Used by permission of Helen Kooiman Hosier.

Page 1315 [Mt 15]
Taken from *Breakfast for the Heart: Meditations to Nourish Your Soul* by Diane M. Komp, M.D. Copyright © 1996 by Diane M. Komp. Published by Zondervan, Grand Rapids, MI. Used by permission of Diane M. Komp.

Page 1344 [Mk 1]
Taken from *365 Meditations for Women*. Copyright © 1989 by Abingdon Press. Published by Abingdon Press, Nashville, TN. Used by permission of Phyllis Tickle.

Page 1348 [Mk 2]
Taken from *365 Meditations for Women*. Copyright © 1989 by Abingdon Press. Published by Abingdon Press, Nashville, TN. Used by permission of Mary Ruth Howes.

Page 1353 [Mk 6]
Taken from *Boundless Love* by Barbara E. Johnson, Patsy Clairmont, Luci Swindoll,

Sheila Walsh, Marilyn Meberg, Thelma Wells. Copyright © 2000 by Women of Faith, Inc. Published by Zondervan, Grand Rapids, MI. Used by permission of Zondervan.

Page 1380 [Lk 1]
Taken from *365 Meditations for Women*. Copyright © 1989 by Abingdon Press. Published by Abingdon Press, Nashville, TN. Used by permission of Mary Ruth Howes.

Page 1392 [Lk 5]
Taken from *Diamonds in the Dust* by Joni Eareckson Tada. Copyright © 1993 by Joni Eareckson Tada. Published by Zondervan, Grand Rapids, MI. Used by permission of Zondervan.

Page 1404 [Lk 10]
Taken from *Breakfast for the Heart: Meditations to Nourish Your Soul* by Diane M. Komp, M.D. Copyright © 1996 by Diane M. Komp. Published by Zondervan, Grand Rapids, MI. Used by permission of Diane M. Komp.

Page 1437 [Jn 1]
Taken from *Messages of God's Abundance* by Corrie ten Boom. Copyright © 2002 by Stichting Trans World Radio voor Nederland en België. Published by Zondervan, Grand Rapids, MI 49530. Used by permission of Zondervan.

Page 1443 [Jn 4]
Taken from *Gifts for Your Soul* by Sheila Walsh. Copyright © 1997 by Sheila Walsh. Published by Zondervan, Grand Rapids, MI. Used by permission of Zondervan.

Page 1462 [Jn 12]
Adapted from *Mother Goose Meets a Woman Called Wisdom* by Linda H. Hollies. Copyright © 2000 by Pilgrim Press, The United Church Press. Published by United Church Press, Cleveland, OH 44115.

Page1485 [Ac 2]
Taken from *365 Meditations for Women*. Copyright © 1989 by Abingdon Press. Published by Abingdon Press, Nashville, TN. Used by permission of Barbara Owen.

Page 1488 [Ac 2]
Taken from *Gifts for Your Soul* by Sheila Walsh. Copyright © 1997 by Sheila Walsh. Published by Zondervan, Grand Rapids, MI. Used by permission of Zondervan.

Page 1520 [Ac 22]
Taken from *Diamonds in the Dust* by Joni Eareckson Tada. Copyright © 1993 by Joni Eareckson Tada. Published by Zondervan, Grand Rapids, MI. Used by permission of Zondervan.

Page 1532 [Ro 1]
Taken from *Lord, You Love to Say Yes* by Ruth Harms Calkin. Copyright © 1976 by Ruth Harms Calkin. Published by Living Books, a trademark of Tyndale House Publisher, Inc., Wheaton, IL. Used by permission of Ruth Harms Calkin.

Page 1539 [Ro 5]
Taken from *365 Meditations for Women*. Copyright © 1989 by Abingdon Press. Published by Abingdon Press, Nashville, TN. Used by permission of Mari Serebrov.

Page 1542 [Ro 7]
Taken from *Boundless Love* by Barbara E. Johnson, Patsy Clairmont, Luci Swindoll, Sheila Walsh, Marilyn Meberg, Thelma Wells. Copyright © 2000 by Women of Faith, Inc. Published by Zondervan, Grand Rapids, MI. Used by permission of Zondervan.

Page 1560 [1Co 1]
Taken from *Outrageous Joy* by Barbara E. Johnson, Patsy Clairmont, Luci Swindoll, Sheila Walsh, Marilyn Meberg, Thelma Wells.

Copyright © 1999 by Women of Faith, Inc. Published by Zondervan, Grand Rapids, MI. Used by permission of Zondervan.

Page 1571 [1Co 12]

Taken from *Extravagant Grace* by Barbara E. Johnson, Patsy Clairmont, Luci Swindoll, Sheila Walsh, Marilyn Meberg, Thelma Wells. Copyright © 2000 by Women of Faith, Inc. Published by Zondervan, Grand Rapids, Michigan. Used by permission of Zondervan.

Page 1582 [2Co 3]

Taken from *Messages of God's Abundance* by Corrie ten Boom. Copyright © 2002 by Stichting Trans World Radio voor Nederland en België. Published by Zondervan, Grand Rapids, MI 49530. Used by permission of Zondervan.

Page 1588 [2Co 8]

Taken from *Living the Lois Legacy: Passing on Last Faith to Your Grandchildren*. A Focus on the Family Book, published by Tyndale House Publishers, Inc., Wheaton, IL, 2002. Used by permission of Helen Kooiman Hosier

Page 1625 [Php 3]

Adapted from *Soul Restoration: Hope for the Weary* by Terri Blackstock. Copyright © 2005 by Terri Blackstock. Published by Inspiro, the gift group of Zondervan, Grand Rapids, Michigan 49530. Used by permission of Zondervan.

Page 1628 [Php 4]

Taken from *The Mitford Bedside Companion* by Jan Karon. Copyright © 2006 by Jan Karon. Published by the Penguin Group (USA), Inc., New York, New York 10014. Used by permission of Viking Penguin, a division of Penguin Group (USA), Inc.

Page 1635 [Col 2]

Taken from *Weather of the Heart: Glimpses of God in Sunlight and Storm* by Gigi Graham Tchividjian. Copyright © 1991 by Gigi Graham Tchividjian. Published by WaterBrook Multnomah Press, Colorado Springs, CO 80921. Used by permission of WaterBrook Multnomah Publishing Group, a division of Random House, Inc.

Page 1669 [2Ti 4]

Taken from *365 Meditations for Women*. Copyright © 1989 by Abingdon Press. Published by Abingdon Press, Nashville, TN. Used by permission of Barbara Owen.

Page 1673 [Tit 3]

Taken from *Could You Hurry Up the Dawn, Lord?: Poems, Prayers, and Lively Conversations with a Loving God*. Copyright © 1994 by Joy Morgan Davis. Published by Joyful Noise Publications, 2108 Kessler Ct., Dallas, TX 75208. Used by permission.

Page 1681 [Heb 4]

Taken from *When Life Takes What Matters: Devotions to Comfort You Through Crisis & Change* by Susan Lenzkes. Copyright © 1993 by Susan Lenzkes. Published by Discovery House Publishers, Grand Rapids, MI 49501. Used by permission of Discovery House Publishers. All rights reserved.

Page 1687 [Heb 10]

Taken from *Bread from My Oven* by Marjorie Parker. Copyright © 1972 by Moody Publishers. Published by Moody Press, Chicago, IL. Used by permission of Moody Press.

Page 1693 [Heb 12]

Taken from *Messages of God's Abundance* by Corrie ten Boom. Copyright © 2002 by Stichting Trans World Radio voor Nederland en België. Published by Zondervan, Grand Rapids, MI 49530. Used by permission of Zondervan.

Page 1702 [Jas 4]

Adapted from *The Gift of Prayer* by Jane

Schlenvogt Copyright © 2003 by Northwestern Publishing House. Published by Northwestern Publishing House, Milwaukee, WI.

Page 1712 [1Pe 3]

Taken from *Help Lord! I'm Having a Senior Moment — Again! Laughing Through the Realities of Growing Older* by Karen O'Connor. Copyright © 2005 by Karen O'Connor. Published by Regal Books from Gospel Light, Ventura, CA.

Page 1719 [2Pe 1]

Taken from *Extravagant Grace* by Barbara E. Johnson, Patsy Clairmont, Luci Swindoll, Sheila Walsh, Marilyn Meberg, Thelma Wells. Copyright © 2000 by Women of Faith, Inc. Published by Zondervan, Grand Rapids, Michigan. Used by permission of Zondervan.

Page 1721 [2Pe 3]

Taken from *No Rain No Gain: Devotions to Guide You Through the Storms of Life* by Susan Lenzkes. Copyright © 1995 by Susan Lenzkes. Published by Discovery House Publishers, Grand Rapids, MI 49501. Used by permission of Discovery House Publishers. All rights reserved.

Page 1765 [Rev 19]

Taken from *Could You Hurry Up the Dawn, Lord?: Poems, Prayers, and Lively Conversations with a Loving God.* Copyright © 1994 by Joy Morgan Davis. Published by Joyful Noise Publications, 2108 Kessler Ct., Dallas, TX 75208. Used by permission.

Contributor Biographies

Claudia Arp is a marriage and family educator, speaker and coauthor (with husband David) of more than 30 books, including the Gold Medallion Award–winning, *The Second Half of Marriage*, the *10 Great Dates* series and the *10 Great Dates* DVD-based marriage education program. She lives in Northern Virginia with her husband, David, and has three sons and eight grandchildren. Their website is *www.marriagealive.com*. *Devotions by this author can be found on pages 6, 35, 446, 786, 822, 1202 and 1236. An article by this author can be found on page 420.*

Cheryl Baker and her husband, John, are cofounders of a Christ-based recovery program, Celebrate Recovery, at Saddleback Church in California. For 16 years Celebrate Recovery has helped people deal with alcoholism and drug abuse along with other issues such as sexual addiction, child abuse, codependency and sexual abuse. Before retiring, Cheryl worked as a director of a preschool for 20 years. She has a daughter, Laura, a son, Johnny, who is married to Jeni, and two granddaughters, Maggie and Chloe. *Devotions by this author can be found on pages 1241, 1328 and 1457.*

Emilie Barnes teaches women creative ways to get organized through her bestselling books and her highly successful ministry, More Hours in My Day. She is a popular speaker, sharing her difficult, faith-building experience with cancer. Emilie and her husband, Bob, live in Newport Beach, California, where they enjoy spending time with their two grown children and five grandchildren. *Devotions by this author can be found on pages 743, 808, 848 and 1699. An article by this author can be found on page 174.*

Terri Blackstock began writing for the Christian market a decade ago. She has more than 30 Christian titles, many of which have been number one bestsellers. Her most recent bestsellers include *Last Light*, *Night Light* and *True Light*, the first three books in her Restoration Series. Terri has appeared on national television programs such as *The 700 Club* and *Home Life*, and has been a guest on numerous radio programs across the country. *Devotions by this author can be found on pages 996, 1058, 1266 and 1625.*

Natalie J. Block is a freelance writer and editor. She is the author of *Entering God's Presence*, a Bible study on prayer, as well as the 52 "Enjoying God" Bible studies in the *NIV Women of Faith Study Bible*. She has two adult daughters and lives with her husband, Greg, in Belmont, Michigan. *Devotions by this author can be found on pages 587 and 1269.*

Dee Brestin is known for her Bible study guides, her classic book, *The Friendships of Women*, and *Falling in Love with Jesus*, a video curriculum coauthored with Kathy Troccoli. Dee's 59-year-old husband, Steve, recently lost his battle with colon cancer. Dee is so thankful for the love they shared, and for their five children and four grandchildren who are walking with the Lord. Dee's website is *www.deebrestin. com*. *Devotions by this author can be found on pages 349 and 1310.*

Sue Buchanan is an author, speaker and cheerleader. Her award-winning children's books include *The Song of God's Love* series and *Mud Pie Annie*. Sue's good humor and optimism delight and encourage everyone who knows her. *Devotions by this author can be found on pages 243, 841, 1594, 1608 and 1647. An article by this author can be found on page 16.*

Ruth Harms Calkin is the author of many books of poetry, including *Lord, Could You Hurry a Little?*, *Lord, I Keep Running Back to You* and *Lord, You Love to Say Yes*. She is a gifted poet who makes her home in Clairmont, California. *Devotions by this author can be found on pages 258, 890 and 1532.*

Speaker and author **Patsy Clairmont** travels the world with Women of Faith telling more than 350,000 people annually about the God who set her free. Patsy's command of God's Word, quick wit and fast-paced humor keep audiences and readers bouncing between laughter and tears, helping them find grace, freedom and a sense of humor in the valleys of life. Patsy and her husband, Les, live in Michigan and Texas. *Devotions by this author can be found on pages 654 and 1353.*

Lori Copeland is the author of more than 90 titles, including both historical and contemporary fiction, including her newest release, *Simple Gifts*. With more than 3 million copies of her books in print, she has developed a loyal following among her rapidly growing fan base in the inspirational market. In 2000 Lori was inducted into the Missouri Writers Hall of Fame. She lives in the beautiful Ozarks with her husband, Lance, their three children and five grandchildren. *Devotions by this author can be found on pages 3, 823, 871, 981 and 994.*

Carol Cymbala directs the 275-member, four-time Grammy Award–winning Brooklyn Tabernacle Choir. She and her husband, Jim, lead the *Fresh Wind, Fresh Fire* seminars, which share the unique ministry of The Brooklyn Tabernacle with pastors and choir directors across the country. They have three children and five grandchildren, and live and minister in the New York City metro area. *Devotions by this author can be found on pages 874 and 1298.*

Joy Morgan Davis is an actress, popular public speaker and author of seven books, including *Pressed Petals*, *Gold and Silver for the Soul* and *I'm Ready for My Rainbow, Lord*. Joy lives in Texas with her husband, Jewell. They have two children and four charming grandchildren — three girls and a boy. *Devotions by this author can be found on pages 210, 901, 1673 and 1765.*

Ruth A. DeJager is a freelance editor and writer living with her husband, Rick, in Marne, Michigan. A former Zondervan editor, Ruth managed the *Women's Devotional Bible 2*, the *Spiritual Formation Bible* and the *Encouragement Bible*, among others. She is the author of the Bible study *Making Praise a Priority* and has contributed devotional and prayer material to a number of other titles. She is a quilt and fiber artist who has shown pieces locally and in the Sacred Threads exhibit in Ohio. *Devotions by this author can be found on pages 70, 128, 427, 595, 928, 1147 and 1452.*

Ruthanne Garlock, an author and Bible teacher living near San Antonio, Texas, has co-authored, with Quin Sherrer, 18 books on prayer and related subjects, including their bestseller, *A Woman's Guide to Spiritual Warfare*. They also cowrote *Grandma, I Need Your Prayers*. Since her husband's death in 2003, Ruthanne is the sole remaining grandparent of her four grandchildren: Amanda, Rachel, Lydia and Joel. *Devotions by this author can be found on pages 24, 771, 1103, 1627 and 1732.*

Elizabeth George is an author, teacher and speaker whose ministry is dedicated to teaching the Bible to women in a way that changes their lives. Her radio program, *A Woman After God's Own Heart*, is heard daily nationwide. Fourteen of her books have achieved bestseller status. Elizabeth and her husband, Jim, have two married daughters and seven grandchildren, and live and write on the beautiful Olympic Peninsula in Washington. *A devotion by this author can be found on page 354.*

Ruth Graham is an experienced conference speaker and Bible teacher known for her honesty and authenticity as she shares her sometimes painful journey of faith. She is the author of *In Every Pew Sits a Broken Heart*, *A Legacy of Love*, *A Legacy of Faith* and the coauthor of *I'm Pregnant . . . Now What?* She has three children and four grandchildren and lives in Virginia. *Devotions by this author can be found on pages 734 and 1303. Articles by this author can be found on pages 116 and 1002.*

A resident of Portland, Oregon, **Helen Haidle** is an award-winning author of more than 30 children's books, including *What Would Jesus Do?*, *What Did Jesus Promise?* and *Cookies and Milk Devotions with Grandma*. She and her husband, David, greatly enjoy spending time with their grandchildren. *Devotions by this author can be found on pages 79, 188, 371, 1175, 1379 and 1755.*

Robin Lee Hatcher is the author of more than 50 novels. She's a recipient of the Christy Award for Excellence in Christian Fiction, the RITA Award for Best Inspirational Romance and RWA's Lifetime Achievement Award. Robin lives in Idaho, not too far from her two lovely daughters and six beautiful grandchildren. *A devotion by this author can be found on page 1664.*

Cynthia Heald and her husband, Jack, serve on the staff of The Navigators in Tucson, Arizona.

They have four children and eight grandchildren. Cynthia is an author and speaker whose books include the *Becoming a Woman of . . .* Bible study series, *A Woman's Journey to the Heart of God* and *Maybe God Is Right After All*. She enjoys spending time with her family, reading, taking bubble baths and eating out. *Devotions by this author can be found on pages 1292 and 1573. An article by this author can be found on page 250.*

Martha Whitmore Hickman has written books for children and adults. She has also taught creative writing classes and has worked with children in a variety of settings. *A devotion by this author can be found on page 954.*

The **Reverend Dr. Linda H. Hollies** is a noted author, teacher and preacher who brings stories to life with an interpretive voice. She is the author of *Pilgrim Prayers for Grandmothers Raising Grandchildren* and *On Their Way to Wonderful: A Journey with Naomi and Ruth*. *Devotions by this author can be found on pages 86, 347 and 1462.*

For many years **Helen Kooiman Hosier** co-owned Christian bookstores in Bellflower and Buena Park, California, and served as an active member in the Christian Booksellers' Association. She has been writing for 46 years and has written and/or coauthored 63 books. Her bestselling book was *Cameos: Women Fashioned by God*, and most recently she wrote *100 Christian Women Who Changed the 20th Century*. *Devotions by this author can be found on pages 1279 and 1588.*

Mary Ruth Howes has been a writer and editor in the field of religious publishing for many years. She grew up in China, the daughter of missionary parents. She lives in Jersey City, New Jersey. *Devotions by this author can be found on pages 1348 and 1380.*

Donna Huisjen is an author and editor. Her books include *Every Single Day: Devotional Moments for the Solo Mom* and *My Tall Book of Psalms*. She is a single, adoptive mother of three grown daughters and is a grandmother of four. *Devotions by this author can be found on pages 1189 and 1695. An article by this author can be found on page 60.*

Gladys Hunt, a grandmother and author of 30 books and numerous articles and Bible study guides, is perhaps best known for the classics *Honey for a Child's Heart, Honey for a Teen's Heart* and *Honey for a Woman's Heart*. She and her husband, Keith, have ministered to university students in InterVarsity Christian Fellowship and coauthored two books, *For Christ and the University* and *We Need Each Other: The Miracle of Relationships*. *Devotions by this author can be found on pages 58, 383, 625, 695, 1422 and 1715. An article by this author can be found on page 90.*

Neta Jackson and her husband, Dave, are an award-winning writing team best known for the Trailblazer books — a 40-book series of historical fiction for young people. Neta is also the author of the popular novel *The Yada Yada Prayer Group* and its sequels. These novels were inspired by a real women's Bible study and prayer group that, as Neta says, "God has used to turn my life upside down and rightside up." Neta and Dave are the parents of three grown children, including a Cambodian foster daughter, all with families of their own. (For more information, go to *www.daveneta.com.*) *Devotions by this author can be found on pages 709, 731, 992, 1018 and 1637.*

Barbara Johnson's bestselling books include *Plant a Geranium in Your Cranium, Living Somewhere Between Estrogen and Death* and *Stick a Geranium in Your Hat and Be Happy*. Barbara delivered her comforting, humor-filled message of love across the country at Women of Faith conferences for six years before illness forced her to leave the tour and continue her ministry of encouragement from home. Lovingly known as "The Geranium Lady," Barbara and husband, Bill, founded the nonprofit Spatula Ministries, an organization tailored to help parents in crisis. Barbara died of cancer in 2007 at the age of 79. *Devotions by this author can be found on pages 275, 701, 916, 1204 and 1719.*

Dawn Scott Jones of Grand Rapids, Michigan, is an ordained minister active in pastoral and teaching ministry. An author, Bible teacher, recording artist and conference speaker, Dawn is also involved in prison ministry, inner city outreach and TV and radio broadcasts. Married 27 years, Dawn and her husband, Terry, have three children, a son-in-law and three beautiful granddaughters. *Devotions by this author can be found on pages 214, 705, 1365, 1495, 1544 and 1704. An article by this author can be found on page 1666.*

Jan Karon is the author of the popular The Mitford Years Series. After a successful 40-year career, she left advertising to write books, and moved to Blowing Rock, North Carolina, a tiny town of 1,800 perched 5,000 feet above sea level in the Blue Ridge Mountains. Blowing Rock is the inspiration for Mitford, home of the beloved Father Tim and his neighbors and friends. Jan has a daughter, Candace Freeland, who is a photojournalist and musician. *Devotions by this author can be found on pages 838 and 1628.*

Carol Kent is the bestselling author of *When I Lay My Isaac Down* and *A New Kind of Normal*. She is also the president of Speak Up Speaker Services, a Christian speakers' agency. Carol is an international speaker and is frequently featured at Women of Faith and Time Out for Women events. She says, "Life is much more fulfilling with grandchildren." Her website address is *www.carolkent.org. Devotions by this author can be found on pages 357, 1367, 1651 and 1739.*

Karen Kingsbury is one of America's favorite inspirational novelists with more than 5 million books in print. Her Life-Changing Fiction™ has produced multiple bestsellers, including *Even Now*, *One Tuesday Morning*, *Beyond Tuesday Morning* and the popular Redemption Series. An award-winning author and newly published songwriter, Karen lives in Washington State with her husband, Don, and their six children, three of whom were adopted from Haiti. *Devotions by this author can be found on pages 29, 100, 722, 1413 and 1736.*

Diane Komp, M.D., is professor emeritus of pediatrics at Yale School of Medicine, New Haven, Connecticut. She has written several books, including *Images of Grace: A Window to Heaven*, *Why Me? A Doctor Looks at the Book of Job*, *Hope Springs from Mended Places*, *The Healer's Heart*, and *A Child Shall Lead Them*. *Devotions by this author can be found on pages 528, 1315 and 1404.*

Carol Kuykendall is an author and speaker who works with MOPS International. She has authored and coauthored nine books. She also writes for *Daily Guideposts*. She and her husband, Lynn, live in Boulder, Colorado, where they are Oma and Opa to three granddaughters, and are looking forward to that number growing. *Devotions by this author can be found on pages 288, 978, 1287, 1319 and 1621.*

Susan Lenzkes is a writer, speaker and Bible study leader who lives in San Diego, California. She has written *Crossing the Bridge Between You and Me*, *Everybody's Breaking Pieces Off of Me*, *When Life Takes What Matters* and *No Rain, No Gain*. *Devotions by this author can be found on pages 541, 969, 1681 and 1721.*

A legend in her own time, **Florence Littauer** has changed the world of Christian speaking through her company CLASS, which is a full-service agency for speakers and authors. Her teaching on Biblical truths, relationship issues and life skills has been touching hearts and inspiring people at women's events, church conferences and business conventions for more than 30 years. She wrote her first book in 1978 and has written at least one each year since, a total of 40. Florence is the mother of two daughters and one son and is the grandmother of five. *Devotions by this author can be found on pages 879 and 1645.*

Rebecca Lutzer serves on the board of Moody Church in Chicago, Illinois, where her husband, Edwin, is senior pastor. She and Edwin have co-authored the books *Jesus, Lover of a Woman's Soul* and *The DaVinci Deception Experience*. She has three married children and six grandchildren. *Devotions by this author can be found on pages 662 and 883. An article by this author can be found on page 1616.*

Karen Mains directs the ministry Hungry Souls, which seeks to assist those who are hungry for more of God. She and her husband of four decades, David, have reached that point where they are grateful for just one more day to joyfully serve God together — of all their accomplishments, this is the one of which they are most proud. The Mains also are delighted with their six grandchildren and, at the time of the printing of this Bible, one more on the way! *Devotions by this author can be found on pages 752, 784, 811, 1256, 1395, 1472, 1593 and 1643.*

Never one to avoid the hard questions of life, **Marilyn Meberg** shares the wisdom she's gained from two master's degrees, a private counseling practice and the many joys and sorrows of a life well lived. In addition to speaking each year to 350,000 women at the Women of Faith conferences, Marilyn is also the author of several books. This year she joined forces with long-time friend Luci Swindoll to write *Free Inside and Out*. Marilyn lives in Texas; she has two children and two grandchildren. *Devotions by this author can be found on pages 1542 and 1560.*

Since 1989, **Elisa Morgan** has been the CEO of MOPS International (*www.mops.org*). She also serves as publisher of "FullFill," a leadership resource for women (*www.fullfill.org*). With a bachelor's degree in psychology and a master of divinity, Elisa has authored many books, including the *Mom's Devotional Bible*. Elisa and her husband, Evan, have been married for almost 30 years. They have two adult children, Eva and Ethan. Elisa's grandson, Marcus, affectionately refers to her as "Yia Yia"! *Devotions by this author can be found on pages 764, 1335, 1359, 1458 and 1605.*

Fern Nichols is the president and founder of Moms In Touch International (MITI), a prayer ministry that impacts children and schools worldwide by gathering mothers to pray. As a grandmother of six, she firmly believes that grandparents can play a vital role in the lives of their grandchildren through prayer. She meets weekly with other grandmas to pray, and says, "One of my greatest joys is hearing another grandmother say my grandchild's name in prayer." *Devotions by this author can be found on pages 242, 794, 827 and 834.*

Karen O'Connor is an award-winning author of more than 50 books for adults and young people, including fiction and nonfiction on a variety of topics from stepparenting to grandparenting, from developing a heart of thanksgiving to growing older with grace and gratitude. Her specialty is inspiration laced with gentle humor. Karen is currently on the teaching staff of the Long Ridge Writers Group in Connecticut and a mentor for the Jerry B. Jenkins Christian Writers Guild. She is also a regular guest presenter at a variety of writing conferences. *Devotions by this author can be found on pages 461, 649, 1122 and 1712.*

Anne Ortlund is the author of more than a dozen books, including *Children Are Wet Cement* and *Building a Great Marriage*. She is a speaker at conferences all over the world through Re-

newal Ministries. She has two daughters and two sons, all grown. Devotions by this author can be found on pages 21, 796, 931, 1082, 1233, 1432 and 1483.

Barbara Owen has written books for children and adults, as well as numerous magazine stories and articles. As both a writer and a writing teacher, she is a frequent lecturer at schools, libraries and writer's conferences. Barbara lives with her husband in Annapolis, Maryland. *Devotions by this author can be found on pages 459, 1485 and 1669.*

Marjorie Parker was the wife of Monroe Parker, President of Pillsbury Baptist Bible College in Owatonna, Minnesota. She was the mother of two children. *A devotion by this author can be found on page 1687.*

Leslie Parrott, Ed.D., a marriage and family therapist, is cofounder (with her husband Les) of *www.realrelationships.com* and the author of *You Matter More Than You Think. Articles by this author can be found on pages 886 and 1154.*

Bestselling author and internationally acclaimed speaker **Rebecca Manley Pippert** is the founder of Salt Shaker Ministries. Becky is the author of several books, including *Out of the Salt Shaker*, which was named by *Christianity Today* as one of the books that has most influenced Christian thought in the past 50 years. Becky is married and has two college-age children. She lives in Louisville, Kentucky. *Devotions by this author can be found on pages 359, 361, 388, 397, 404. An article by this author can be found on page 384.*

Margaret Fishback Powers is a poet and author, and has been a teacher of public education and music education for more than 40 years. In 1966 she and her husband, Paul, created the Little People's Ministry Association with the motto, "Unless we reach their hearts today, they will break our hearts tomorrow." Her goal is to change the world and bring focus to the needs of children. Her life has been touched in various ways by her four grandchildren, and she treasures each one individually. "Nana" desires to always learn new and special things from experiences with her grandchildren. *Devotions by this author can be found on pages 935, 976, 1468 and 1750.*

Grammy award-winning performer/songwriter **Dottie Rambo** is anchored in family. Her family includes her grandchildren, Israel and Destiny Rambo-McGuire; her stepgranddaughter, Dionne Dismuke (and great-grandchild Dyson); plus two boys, Christian and Pierce Ferguson, who have adopted her as "GranDot." She makes Nashville, Tennessee, her home. *Devotions by this author can be found on pages 238, 379, 862, 968, 1320 and 1656.*

Debby Kerner Rettino and her husband of more than 30 years, Ernie Rettino, are the creators and producers of the Psalty albums and DVDs. A Grammy-nominated musician, author and speaker, Debby is the director of Worship Leadership at Saddleback Church in California and has two daughters and four grandchildren. *Devotions by this author can be found on pages 42, 107, 1296, 1546, 1591 and 1731.*

Doris Wynbeek Rikkers is a writer, editor and product developer who has been in Christian publishing, focusing on Bible development, for 30 years. Her bestselling children's books include *Little Jesus, Little Me* and *God Loves Me Bible*. She lives in western Michigan with her husband, Bill, and two sons. *Devotions by this author can be found on pages 134, 158, 320, 335, 492, 629, 1064, 1271 and 1760. Articles by this author can be found on pages 508 and 524.*

Gayle Roper is an inspirational speaker and an award-winning author who writes contemporary mysteries with wit and romance. She has writ-

ten many books, including *Allah's Fire, Winter Winds, Autumn Dreams* and *See No Evil*. She has five wonderful grandchildren, *Devotions by this author can be found on pages 284, 769, 1613 and 1714.*

Jane Schlenvogt is a teacher who inspires and advises, making examples of real-life experiences. When she is not engaged in teaching—her first love—she enjoys traveling, spending time with her friends and indulging in her hobby of baking muffins. *Devotions by this author can be found on pages 1207 and 1702.*

The author of several books, **Mari Serebrov** has written for numerous publications and has taught journalism at public and private universities. She values the Christian legacy her grandmothers gave her and is passing it on to her grandchildren. She and her husband, Job, have two children and two grandchildren. *Devotions by this author can be found on pages 664 and 1539.*

Jean Shaw is a freelance writer and charter member of the Claywood Garden Club. Her books include *Second Cup of Coffee* and *Devotions for Gardeners*. A devotion by this author can be found on page 909.

Luci Shaw is an accomplished poet, essayist and teacher. She is the Writer in Residence at Regent College in Vancouver, Canada, and poetry editor of Radix Magazine. She has published a number of books, and her writings, both prose and poetry, have been included in many anthologies. Luci is a frequent speaker at scholarly and writer's conferences, conducts workshops and retreats, and regularly gives poetry readings of her works. She was cofounder, with her husband, of Harold Shaw Publishers and was vice president of the firm until his death in 1986 when she became president. Luci Shaw is the mother of five and grandmother of five. *Devotions by this author can be found on pages 201, 575 and 1012.*

Quin Sherrer, an award-winning author, has written or coauthored 27 books, including *Grandma, I Need Your Prayers* and *Lord, I Need to Pray With Power*. In addition to speaking at conferences, she has appeared on more than 300 radio and television programs. Quin earned her journalism degree from Florida State University. She is the happy grandmother of six. *Devotions by this author can be found on pages 774, 851, 857 and 1475. An article by this author can be found on page 940.*

Dorothy E. Sickal was a minister, speaker and writer. She coauthored with her granddaughters, Amy and Suzanne Gaither, and her daughter, Gloria Gaither, *Hands Across the Seasons*. *Devotions by this author can be found on pages 440 and 999.*

Jan Silvious believes that women do best when they are free to be who God created them to be. She is the author of several books, including *The 5-Minute Devotional*, *Foolproofing Your Life* and *Look at It This Way*. Jan and her husband, Charlie, live in Chattanooga, Tennessee, not far from their three grown sons, two wonderful daughters-in-law and five grandchildren. *Devotions by this author can be found on pages 77, 82, 245, 832 and 899.*

Patricia Sprinkle has a master's degree in religious studies, has authored 30 books for the Christian and general markets and is a former annual contributor to *Daily Guideposts*. She and her husband have two sons, one daughter-in law and two grandsons. When not writing, Patricia likes to read, swim, work with children and plants, and do nothing. *Devotions by this author can be found on pages 19, 741, 1440, 1611 and 1727.*

Millie Stamm, national executive prayer secretary of Stonecroft Ministries and a popular speaker, writes her inspirational devotions out of the needs of the women she works with in her ministry. She has written *He Is Real, Be Still and Know, Beside Still Waters* and *Meditation Moments*. *Devotions by this author can be found on pages 194, 280, 692 and 960.*

Charlotte Stemple, with her husband, the Rev. Woodford (Woody) Stemple Jr., is on the staff of the Christian and Missionary Alliance. *A devotion by this author can be found on page 1185.*

Leslie Strobel, who lives in Southern California, is a wife to Lee, a mom to Alison and Kyle, a mother-in-law to Daniel and Kelli, daughter to Helen and a very proud grandmother to Abigail (and hopefully others someday). When she's not playing with Abby, she's happiest when she's with one of the above or with friends. *An article by this author can be found on page 818.*

Jean E. Syswerda is an author and a former editor and associate publisher at Zondervan. Jean coauthored the bestselling book *Women of the Bible* and the *Read With Me Bible*, and she is also the general editor of the *NIV Women of Faith Study Bible*. Jean's most recent book, *The Women's Devotional Guide to the Bible*, was released in the fall of 2006. Jean and her husband, John, have three grown children and seven grandchildren. Both of them enjoy gardening, camping, traveling and spending time with their grandchildren. *Devotions by this author can be found on pages 315, 757, 788, 1248 and 1551. An article by this author can be found on page 674.*

Joni Eareckson Tada is the founder and president of JAF (Joni and Friends) Ministries, an organization that accelerates Christian outreach in the disability community. Through JAF Ministries, Joni has strived to pass on encouragement to other people with disabilities and their families worldwide. Joni and her husband, Ken, make their home in California. *Devotions by this author can be found on pages 549, 867, 1392 and 1520.*

Gigi Graham Tchividjian is a renowned author, lecturer and counselor. She has written five books, including the award-winning *Weather of the Heart*. Gigi is married to clinical psychologist, Stephen Tchividjian. *Devotions by this author can be found on pages 437, 815 and 1635.*

Corrie ten Boom and her family helped hide Jews in their home in the Netherlands during the Nazi occupation. Corrie shared these experiences in her bestselling book *The Hiding Place*. After the war and until her death in 1983, Corrie traveled and spoke extensively about the need for a close walk with God as a means to finding daily strength and contentment. *Devotions by this author can be found on pages 1061, 1437, 1582 and 1693.*

Phyllis Ten Elshof is editor of books and Bibles for the Resources Department of Christianity Today International in Carol Stream, Illinois. She also spent time as a magazine editor and feature reporter for a newspaper in Jackson, Mississippi. Phyllis is a survivor of breast cancer, non-Hodgkin's lymphoma and acute leukemia and is the author of *What Cancer Cannot Do*. She and her husband, Paul, have two children and four grandchildren. *An article by this author can be found on page 656.*

Phyllis Tickle, founding editor of the Religion Department of *Publishers Weekly*, the international journal of the book industry, is an authority on religion in America and a much sought after lecturer on the subject. In addition to lectures and numerous essays, articles and interviews, Phyllis is the author of more than two dozen religion and spirituality books, most notably the *Divine Hours* series of manuals for observing fixed-hour prayer. She is also the mother of seven children and, with her physician-husband, makes her home on a small farm in rural West Tennessee. Visit her website at *www.phyllistickle.com*. *A devotion by this author can be found on page 1344.*

Sheila Walsh is an author, speaker, worship leader, television talk show host and Bible teacher. In addition to serving as a featured speaker with Women of Faith, she is also the author of the bestselling memoir *Honestly* and the Gold Medallion Award – nominated book *The Heartache No One Sees*. Sheila's newest book, *God Has A Dream For Your Life*, released in 2007. *Gigi, God's Little Princess*, Sheila's new line of books and videos for little girls, won the National Retailer's Choice Award in 2006. Sheila is currently working on completing a master's degree in theology. She lives in Dallas, Texas, with her husband, Barry, and son, Christian. *Devotions by this author can be found on pages 391, 641, 1443 and 1488.*

Thelma Wells is a popular author, speaker and businesswoman. As an African-American woman, Thelma was instrumental in bringing racial diversity to the Women of Faith conferences. She has had her own television show, been an assistant vice president of a bank and an inspirational public speaker/business consultant. Thelma and her husband, George, live in Texas, where they enjoy spending time with their children and grandchildren. *Devotions by this author can be found on pages 1407, 1498, 1512, 1571 and 1600.*

Bobbie Wolgemuth is the author or coauthor of several books, including *With Love from Mom*, *Hymns for a Kid's Heart* and the four-book series *Great Hymns of Our Faith*. Bobbie and her husband, Robert, have two married daughters and five grandchildren and live in central Florida. *Devotions by this author can be found on pages 136, 324, 489, 616, 711, 903, 1125, 1227, 1346, 1569 and 1744.*

Topical and Feature Index

*Indicates that this topic and the first entry of a linked chain belonging to this topic are located in the Bible text as *Talking Points*

Abba

Mk 14:36	Jesus used this name to address his Father
Ro 8:15	We cry this name
Gal 4:6	The Spirit calls out this name

Abel

See Cain and Abel

Abortion

Ex 21:22 – 25	Law regarding death of the unborn
Ps 51:5	Sinful nature present at conception
Ps 139:13 – 16	God forms a child in the womb
Isa 46:3	God cares for the unborn
Isa 49:1	God calls us before birth
Jer 1:5	God knows us from conception
Mt 1:18	A fetus is called a child
Gal 1:15	God sets us apart from birth
	Devotions, 86

Abraham

Ge 17:16	God promised him a son by Sarah
Ge 21:1 – 7	Isaac, son of Abraham and Sarah, born
Ro 4:3,10 – 22	Abraham justified by faith
Heb 6:13 – 15	God's promise fulfilled
Heb 11:8 – 12, 17 – 19	Abraham's faith
	Stories to Share, 20, 36

Absalom

2Sa 15:1 – 12	Rebelled against his father, David
2Sa 18:9 – 14	Hung by his hair in a tree; killed by Joab

Acceptance

Mt 7:1 – 2	Do not judge
Lk 6:31	The Golden Rule
Ac 10:34 – 35	God accepts people of all nations
Ro 15:7	Accept one another, as Christ accepted you
Gal 3:28	We are one in Christ
Eph 5:21	Submit to one another
1Pe 4:8	Love one another
	Devotions, 82, 221, 335, 379, 801, 883, 1189, 1367, 1452, 1600
	Perspectives, 420
	Stories to Share, 1441, 1504

Accountability*

2Ch 6:30*	God knows our hearts
Ecc 3:15	God will judge the past
Mt 12:36 – 37	We are accountable for our words
Ro 14:12	We will give an account to God
Heb 4:13	God sees everything
Heb 13:17	Leaders will give an account to God
1Pe 4:5	Unbelievers will give an account to God
	Devotions, 427, 649

Addictions*

Ge 9:20 – 21*	Alcohol loosens morals
Hab 2:15 – 16	Drunkenness leads to shame
Mk 10:27	All things are possible with God
Ro 8:1 – 17	Live to please the Spirit, not the sinful nature
Ro 13:13 – 14	Behave decently
1Co 6:9 – 11	There is grace for sex addicts who turn to God

Ambition (cont.)

Mt 16:26 – 27	Rewards for work done
Ro 15:20	Paul's ambition to preach
Heb 6:10 – 11	Be diligent and persevere in work
	Devotions, 701, 1470

Angels

Ps 34:7; 91:11	Protect God's people
Da 6:22	Protected Daniel from the lions
Mt 2:13	Warned Joseph
Mt 28:2	Do God's will
Mt 28:3 – 4	Appearance produces human fear
Lk 1:26 – 38	Bring messages from God
Ac 27:23 – 24	Guide God's people
Col 1:16	Created by God
Col 2:18	Not to be worshiped
2Th 1:7	Will return with Christ
Heb 1:14	Are spirits sent to serve God's people
	Devotions, 1639
	Stories to Share, 1381

Anger*

Nu 20:1 – 13*	Moses responded in anger and disobeyed God
Ps 4:4	Examine your heart when you are angry
Pr 14:16 – 17	When angry, proceed slowly; respond, don't react
Pr 29:11	Wise persons control their anger
Pr 29:22	Anger leads to dissension and sin
Eph 4:26 – 27	Don't let anger escalate or continue
Col 3:8	Rid yourself of anger
Jas 1:19 – 20	Listen more; talk less; be slow to become angry
	Stories to Share, 9

Animals

Ge 1:20 – 25	God created them
Ge 1:26	Man is to rule over them
Ge 2:19 – 20	Adam named them
Nu 22:21 – 38	The talking donkey
1Sa 17:34 – 37	David killed a lion and bear
Isa 11:6 – 9	Will live and lie down together in peace
	Devotions, 1212

See also Snakes

Anxiety*

Ex 33:14*	God's presence brings peace and rest
Ps 73:26	God gives strength to the weak
Ps 94:18 – 19	God will support and console us
Ecc 11:10	Banish anxiety from your heart
Isa 45:5 – 7	God alone is sovereign; everything is under his control
Mt 6:28 – 34	Don't worry about tomorrow; God knows our needs
Lk 12:22 – 26	Don't let worry overtake your life
Php 4:6 – 7	Don't be anxious; prayer brings peace
1Pe 5:7	Bring your anxieties to God
	Devotions, 104, 377, 401, 437, 641, 960, 1449

See also Worry

Appearance

1Sa 16:7	God looks at the heart
Gal 6:2	"God does not judge by external appearance"
	Devotions, 379, 383, 978, 1122, 1637, 1699, 1712, 1731
	Perspectives, 384

Ark, Noah's

Ge 6:13 – 16	God's instructions for building the ark

Ark of the Covenant

Ex 30:6	Symbolized God's presence
Ex 37:1 – 9	Its construction
Nu 7:89	Moses heard God's voice speaking from above it
2Sa 6:1 – 11	Symbolized God's holiness and power (Uzzah)
Heb 9:4	Items it held
	Stories to Share, 547

Asking for Help

Ex 18:17 – 18, 21 – 24	Moses advised to get help from others
Jer 33:3	Call on God for guidance
Jnh 2:2	Call on God for help

Asking for Help (cont.)

Lk 11:9–10	Ask and you will receive
Gal 6:2	Carry each other's burdens
Heb 4:16	God will graciously help us
	Devotions, 1404

Attitude

Mic 7:7	Attitude of hope
Mk 10:43–45	Attitude of a servant
Ro 12:1–2	Attitude that pleases God
1Co 16:13–14	Attitude of courage and love
Php 2:5–8	Imitate Christ's attitude of humility
Php 4:4	Attitude of rejoicing
Php 4:5	Attitude of gentleness
1Pe 4:1–2	Imitate Christ's attitude in suffering
1Pe 5:5–6	Attitude of humility; God opposes the proud
	Devotions, 641, 654, 788, 1147, 1392, 1404, 1457, 1594
	Stories to Share, 209

Babel

See Tower of Babel

Baptism

Mt 28:19	In the name of the Father, Son, Holy Spirit
Mk 16:16	Faith is essential
Jn 1:29–34	Of Jesus
Ac 2:38	Repentance required
Ac 8:36–38	With water
Ac 11:16	With the Holy Spirit
Ac 16:31–34	Of the jailer and his family
Eph 4:5	One baptism
	Stories to Share, 1289

Bible Study

Job 34:4	Learn and discern truth
Ps 19:7–11	God's law is perfect
Ps 119:97	Love for God's law
Ps 119:99–105	God's Word is a lamp
Ps 119:130	God's Word gives light
Pr 30:5	Every word of God is flawless
Lk 11:28	Blessed are those who hear and obey God's Word
Col 2:2–3	Know the mystery of God: Christ

2Ti 3:14–15	Knowing the Scriptures will make you wise
Heb 4:12	God's Word is living and active
	Devotions, application with, 242, 243, 317, 1310; commitment to, 21; memorization and, 815, 1628; play acting and, 779; value of, 461, 796, 848, 890, 963
	Stories to Share, 1615

Bitterness*

1Sa 30	Causes sinful desires
Job 3:20–26*	A sinful human attribute to be overcome
Ps 71:20	God can restore us from it
Pr 14:10	Each heart knows its own
Ro 3:9–14	A sign of unrighteousness and need for Christ
Ro 12:17–21	Don't take revenge; God will judge and avenge
Eph 4:31–32	Replace with kindness, compassion and forgiveness
Heb 12:15	A bitter root grows up to cause trouble
	Devotions, 354

Blended Family*

Ge 21:8–11*	Struggles in a blended family
Ge 37; 50:15–21	Don't hold grudges; forgive and reconcile
Jos 24:14–15	Choose to serve God
Est 2:5–7	Esther raised by her cousin Mordecai
Ps 68:6	God sets the lonely in families
Ps 133	Unity in the family brings blessing
Ro 12:4–5	In Christ we are one body
Ro 12:18	Do all you can to live at peace with everyone
Ro 15:5–6	Unity glorifies God
1Co 1:10	Be united in mind and thought
1Co 12:14–20	Many parts make up the whole
Eph 4:1–6	Humility, gentleness, love and patience bring unity
Eph 6:1–4	General rules for all families
1Ti 5:8	Provide for those in your family

Commitment (cont.)

Ro 12:11	Never lack zeal
Gal 6:9	Do not grow weary of doing good
Eph 6:7–8	Serve wholeheartedly
Php 3:14	Press on toward the goal
	Devotions, 347, 1699

Communication

Ps 19:14	May our words be pleasing to God
Ps 37:30	Speak what is wise and just
Pr 16:24	Pleasant words are sweet
Pr 17:27; 21:23	Guard your words; choose them carefully
Pr 22:11	Speak graciously
Pr 25:11	Aptly spoken words are golden
Ecc 9:17	Quiet words of the wise are to be heeded
Ecc 10:12	Words of a wise man are gracious
Eph 4:15	Speak the truth in love
Col 4:6	Conversations full of grace
	Devotions, 1573, 1602, 1613
	Perspectives, 420, 1614, 1632

Compassion*

Ps 103:8–18*	God is compassionate and gracious
Isa 54:7–10	God has great compassion for us
La 3:22	God's compassions never fail
Mt 25:31–40	What we do for others, we do for Jesus
Lk 10:25–37	Parable of the Good Samaritan
Ac 9:36–43	A compassionate woman raised from the dead
Ac 10:1–6	A compassionate man the first recorded Gentile Christian
Eph 4:32	Imitate God; be kind and compassionate to others
Col 3:12	Be clothed with compassion
Jas 5:11	God is full of compassion and mercy
1Pe 3:8–9	Be compassionate and humble
	Devotions, God's for us, 318, 536, 966, 1419, 1536, 1660; ours for others, 598, 801, 842, 1236, 1392, 1622, 1637
	Stories to Share, 1402

Confession

Ps 32:5	Acknowledge our sin to God
Jas 5:15	Confess your sins to each other
1Jn 1:9	Confession brings God's forgiveness
	Devotions, 595, 625, 879, 1395

Confidence

Ps 27:13	In God's goodness
Pr 3:26	God is our confidence
Isa 32:17	A by-product of righteousness
Ro 8:38–39	In God's love
Php 4:13	We can do everything through Christ
Heb 4:16	Approach God's throne with confidence
Heb 10:35	Will be rewarded
Heb 13:6	In God's help; don't be afraid
1Jn 5:14	To ask anything of God

Conflict

Pr 13:10	Pride breeds quarrels
Pr 15:1	Confront wrath with a gentle answer
Pr 17:14	Drop an issue before it turns into a dispute
Pr 20:3	It is honorable to avoid strife
Ecc 7:9	Do not be quickly provoked
Ro 12:21	Overcome evil with good
Ro 15:5–6	Promote unity
1Co 1:10	Avoid divisions; be united in mind and thought
	Devotions, 629, 1611
	Perspectives, 420

See also Unity

Conscience

2Sa 24:10	David was conscience-stricken
Ro 2:14–15	Everyone has a conscience
2Co 1:12	Good conduct promotes a good conscience
1Ti 1:5	Love comes from a good conscience
1Ti 1:18–19	Hold on to a good conscience
1Ti 3:9	Keep a clear conscience
Heb 10:19–22	Christ cleanses our guilty conscience

Consequences

Dt 6:18	Reward for doing what is right
Dt 30:15–18	Choices have consequences
Ps 18:24	Reward for righteousness
Pr 11:21	Judgment is certain
Ro 2:9	Trouble and distress for doing evil

Devotions, 361, 1058
Stories to Share, 8, 9, 15, 208

Contentment*

Ps 63:3–5*	Comes from recognizing God's love
Pr 15:13–17	Brings perspective to life
Pr 19:23	Comes from fear of the Lord
Pr 30:8–9	Comes from moderation
Mt 6:19–21	Set proper priorities
Php 4:10–13	Secret to contentment is trusting in God
1Ti 6:6–10	Love of money causes discontent and trouble

Devotions, 1695, 1715

Courage

Jos 1:9	"Be strong and courageous"
Ps 27:1,13–14	The Lord is my strength
Ps 118:6	"The LORD is with me; I will not be afraid"
Pr 3:24–26	The Lord is our confidence
Ro 8:35–39	Nothing can separate us from God's love
2Ti 1:7	God has given us a spirit of power

Devotions, 86
Stories to Share, 198, 381, 624, 648

Covenant

Ge 9:9–11	God's covenant with Noah
Ge 17:3–16	God's covenant with Abraham
1Ch 16:15	God remembers his covenant forever
Ps 105:8	God remembers his covenant forever
Lk 22:20	Blood as a symbol of the covenant
Heb 8:8	Promise of a new covenant

Devotions, 29, 1542

Creation

Ge 1–2	Two accounts of the creation of the universe
Ps 8	The glory of creation
Ps 148	Praises God, the Creator
Jer 51:15–16	Created by the power of God
Ro 8:19–22	Creation one day liberated from curse of sin

Devotions, caring for, 754, 1308; displays God's power, 603, 755, 966, 1182, 1356, 1449, 1471, 1586, 1770; enjoying, 1087, 1212, 1687; praises God, 454, 921

Perspectives, 1002
Stories to Share, 2, 4
See also Ecology; Environment

Creativity

Devotions, 128, 136, 862, 1520, 1647, 1714

Crucifixion

Mt 27:22	The crowd yells, "Crucify"
Mt 27:32–44	Jesus' crucifixion
1Co 1:23	"We preach Christ crucified"
Gal 2:20	"I have been crucified with Christ"

Daniel

Da 2:31–45	Interpreted the king's dream of a statute
Da 4:19–27	Interpreted the king's dream of a tree
Da 5:17–31	Interpreted the writing on the wall
Da 6	In the den of lions
Da 7	His dream of four beasts
Da 8	His vision of a ram and a goat

Stories to Share, 1165, 1174

Dating*

Job 31:1*	Commit to control your thought life
Pr 1:8–9	Seek parents' advice
Pr 6:20–23	Follow parents' advice; seek their counsel
Pr 6:24–25	Warning against adultery
Ecc 12:1	"Remember your Creator in the days of your youth"

Ezekiel (cont.)

Eze 10:1–22	His description of the cherubim
Eze 37:1–14	The valley of dry bones
	Stories to Share, 1146

Faith

Mt 17:20	Can move mountains
Mt 21:22	If we believe, we will receive
Mk 9:23	Everything is possible with faith
Ro 1:17	"The righteous will live by faith"
Ro 10:9,17	If you confess and believe, you will be saved
2Co 5:7	"Live by faith, not by sight"
Heb 11:1,6	Definition of faith
Heb 11:2–40	Heroes of faith
1Pe 1:8–9	Goal of faith
2Pe 1:5–8	Characteristics to add to your faith

Devotions, 24, 383, 695, 757, 901, 1303, 1359, 1462, 1627
Stories to Share, and miracles, 286, 490, 1169, 1390; childlike, 1318, 1363; for the "impossible," 30, 1317; God rewards, 488; requires action, 20, 1700; when afraid, 1313; to obey, 36, 325, 490, 1169; what it is, 1688

See also Sharing Your Faith

Faithfulness*

Dt 7:9*	God is faithful to countless generations of those who love and obey him
2Sa 22:21–27	God is faithful to those who are faithful to him
Ps 57:3,9–10	God's faithfulness "reaches to the skies"
Ps 91:1–4	God's faithfulness will protect us
Ps 100	God's faithfulness is never-ending
La 3:19–24	"Great is [God's] faithfulness"
Gal 5:22–25	Our ability to be faithful comes from the Holy Spirit
1Jn 1:9	God is faithful to forgive us when we repent

Devotions, experience of God's, 901, 1103; God's eternal, 27, 228, 352; God's in time of need, 214; God's through generations, 245, 549, 728; God's to his promises, 869; ours to God, 437, 1687; paired with love, 1016
Stories to Share, 12, 504, 792

Falling Away

Ro 8:35–39	Know that nothing can separate us from God
1Co 10:13	God will supply a way out of temptation
2Ti 3:14–17	Continue in sound teaching; read God's Word
Heb 3:1–14	Associate with other believers
Heb 5:11 — 6:12	Remain diligent and grow in faith
2Pe 1:5–10	Grow in Christian character
2Pe 3:17	Caution against false teaching
Jude 20–21,24	Keep in God's love

Devotions, 1744

Family

Jos 24:15	Choose to serve God as a family
Ps 128	A blessing on family
Ps 133:1	Live in unity
Pr 31:10–31	A wife of noble character praised
Ro 12:10	Be devoted to one another; honor others
Gal 6:10	Do good to all, especially to God's family
Eph 5:21	"Submit to one another"
Eph 5:31	Establishment of family
Eph 6:2–3	Honor father and mother
Col 3:12–14	Proper behavior of God's children
1Pe 4:8	"Love covers over a multitude of sins"

Devotions, activities, 1689; bonding of, 725, 1328, 1535, 1602, 1621, 1742; commitment to, 349; history of, 451, 868, 1014, 1331, 1767; of God, 221; traditions, 1384
Perspectives, 16, 524

See also Heritage

Favoritism

Ge 25:28; 27:5 – 17	Leads to deception
Ge 29:30 – 35	Leads to unhealthy competition
Ge 37:3 – 5, 18 – 28	Leads to hate and sinful actions
Job 34:18 – 19	God shows no partiality; he created all persons equal
Mt 5:43	God provides sun and rain for benefit of all
Ac 10:34 – 35	"God does not show favoritism" (racial)
Ro 10:12 – 13	No favoritism in salvation (ethnic)
1Co 4:6 – 8	Leads to division
Eph 6:9	There is no favoritism with God (economic)
Col 3:25	No favoritism (fair judgment for sin)
1Ti 5:21	"Do nothing out of favoritism" Devotions, 58

Fear*

Jos 1:9*	God is always with us
Ps 27:1,14	Be strong, take heart and wait for the Lord
Ps 46	"God is our refuge and strength"
Ps 56	Trust in God; he is stronger than any adversary
Isa 50:10	Rely on, and trust in, God
Mt 10:29 – 31	We are important to God
Jn 14:27	God gives peace to overcome fear
Ac 18:9 – 10	Do not be afraid to speak about God Devotions, 104, 214, 245, 377, 383, 401, 698, 825, 978, 1639 Perspectives, 384 Stories to Share, 198, 1351

See also Courage

Finances

See Money

Finding God*

1Ki 19:1 – 13*	God in the gentle whisper
1Ch 28:9	If we earnestly seek God, we will find him
2Ch 15:1 – 4	If we seek God in our distress, he will be found
Ps 139:7 – 10	God is everywhere
Isa 55:6 – 7	"Seek the Lord while he may be found"
Ac 17:27	God is never far from us
Jas 4:8	"Come near to God and he will come near to you"
1Jn 4:12	God lives in us Devotions, 848, 1743

Flood

Ge 6 – 8	The great flood
Mt 24:38 – 39	People didn't know the great flood was coming
2Pe 2:5	Great flood came as punishment for sin

Forgiveness*

2Ch 7:13 – 14*	God longs to forgive and heal
Ps 130:3 – 4	God doesn't keep a record of our sins
Pr 19:11	Overlook an offense
Pr 24:17	Don't gloat over others' failures
Da 9:15 – 19	Daniel's cry for corporate forgiveness
Mt 6:12 – 15	If we don't forgive others, God won't forgive us
Mt 18:21 – 22	Continually forgive others, even for repeated offenses
Mk 11:25	God forgives us if we forgive others
Eph 4:32	Forgive others as Christ forgave you
Col 3:13	Forgive the grievances of others, as God forgave you Devotions, 70, 459, 1064, 1498, 1639, 1660, 1727 Perspectives, 1614 Praying the Scriptures, 746 Stories to Share, 81, 209, 1198, 1237, 1345, 1414

Friendship*

Ru 1*	Friends stick together
1Sa 18:1 – 4	David and Jonathan's friendship

Friendship (cont.)

1Sa 20	Friends love each other and stick up for each other
Pr 17:17	"A friend loves at all times"
Pr 27:9	True friends offer sincere advice
Ecc 4:9 – 12	"Two are better than one"
Lk 10:38 – 42	Jesus visits his friends
Jn 11:1 – 44	Jesus cared about his friends
Jn 15:15	Christ calls us his friends
	Devotions, 391, 649, 801, 842, 899, 1532, 1643
	Perspectives, 886
	Stories to Share, 346, 386

Frustration

Ps 34:19	God will deliver us from all our troubles
Ps 55:22	God will sustain us
Ps 138:7 – 8	God will fulfill his purposes for us
Isa 41:10	Do not be dismayed
Isa 55:8 – 9	Our thoughts and ways are not like God's
Jer 33:3	Call to God and he will answer
Ro 8:28	God works for the good of those who love him
1Co 10:13	God will provide a way
Heb 12:1 – 3	Do not grow weary

Future

Pr 23:18	Surely a future hope
Ecc 8:7	No one knows the future
Jer 29:11	God has plans for your future
Ro 8:28	God works for the good of those who love him
Ro 8:38	Nothing can separate us from God's love
1Co 3:18 – 23	The future is ours in Christ
	Devotions, 275, 446, 701, 764, 1625, 1470
	Perspectives, 1154
	Stories to Share, 67, 1255, 1688, 1769

Generosity

See Giving

Giants

Nu 13:31 – 33	The Nephilim
Dt 3:11	Giant's bed
1Sa 17:4 – 6	Goliath
2Sa 21:15 – 22	Descendants of Rapha; six-fingered giant
	Perspectives, 384

Gideon

Jdg 6:36 – 40	Test of the fleece
Jdg 7	Defeated the Midianites
Heb 11:32	A hero of faith
	Stories to Share, 325, 326

Giving

Ex 25:2	Give what your heart prompts you to give
Ex 35:5	Give willingly
Ezr 2:69	Give according to your ability
Mal 3:10	Tithing brings blessing
Mt 6:1 – 4	Giving rewarded
2Co 8:2 – 3	Giving generously even in poverty
2Co 9:6	Sow generously and you will reap generously
2Co 9:7	"God loves a cheerful giver"
	Devotions, 374, 440, 575, 1177, 1252, 1588
	Perspectives, 90
	Stories to Share, 1446, 1461

See also Talents

God's Compassion

See Compassion

God's Control

Dt 10:17	"God is God of gods"
Ps 24:1	Everything belongs to God
Ps 47	Kings and nations are under his control
Isa 45:5 – 7	God alone is sovereign; everything is under his control
Da 7:14	God's sovereign power
Jn 19:11	God puts authorities in power

God's Control (cont.)

Php 3:20 – 21   Everything is under his control
Devotions, 357, 1217, 1449, 1471, 1560, 1625, 1690, 1702
Stories to Share, 67, 95

See also Miracles

God's Faithfulness

See Faithfulness

God's Holiness

Lev 11:44   God says he is holy
1Sa 2:2   God is unique in his holiness
Ps 99   Worship God for he is holy
Ps 111:9   His name is holy
Isa 6:3   The angels call him holy
Rev 4:8   Day and night the living creatures proclaim him holy
Devotions, 268, 1356, 1536, 1586
Stories to Share, 112, 164, 547

God's Love

Ps 13:5 – 6   Is unfailing
Ps 57:9 – 10   Is great, reaching to the heavens
Ps 89:1 – 2   Stands firm forever
Jn 3:16   "For God so loved the world . . ."
Ro 5:5,8   God's demonstration of his love
Eph 3:16 – 19   Christ's love surpasses knowledge
1Jn 3:1   The extent of God's love
1Jn 4:16   We can rely on God's love for us
Devotions, compared to a parent's, 1328; endures forever, 377, 549; for all he has made, 869, 832, 1440; for us, 107, 318, 832, 871, 981, 1468, 1542; is unfailing, 805, 1061; proclaimed, 1603
Stories to Share, 1439

God's Omnipresence

See God's Presence

Gods, Other

Ex 20:1 – 6   The command not to worship them
Jer 10:1 – 15   Description of worthless idols
1Jn 5:21   "Keep yourselves from idols"

Devotions, 1281
Perspectives, 116

God's Plan

Ps 33:10 – 11   God's plans stand firm forever
Isa 25:1   God planned things long ago
Isa 46:11   God will do what he has planned
Jer 29:11   God has a plan for us
Eph 1:11   Everything works according to God's plan
Php 2:13   God works in us according to his good purpose
Devotions, 371, 701, 874, 992, 1058, 1625, 1470, 1723, 1770
Stories to Share, 65, 85, 95, 285, 337, 900, 1505

God's Power

2Ch 20:6   Power and might are in his hand
Ps 66:7   "He rules forever by his power"
Ps 147:5   He is mighty in power
Ro 4:21   He has the power to do what he has promised
2Co 12:9   Is made perfect in our weakness
Php 3:21   Everything is under his control
1Pe 1:5   We are shielded by his power
2Pe 1:3   Gives us everything we need
Devotions, over all people, 166, 1217, 1770; over nature, 454, 755, 1356, 1586, 1770; seen in his mighty deeds, 846, 1254, 1536, 1723; to help his people, 74, 728, 996, 1296, 1419, 1536, 1690, 1744
Stories to Share, 15, 30, 105, 326, 474

God's Presence

Dt 31:6   God will never leave us
Ps 22:10 – 11   God has been with us since birth
Ps 139:7 – 10   God is everywhere
Zep 3:17   God is with us and delights in us
Ac 17:27   God is not far from each one of us
Jas 4:8   Come near to God and he will come near to you

Guilt (cont.)

Isa 1:18	God cleanses us so we are "white as snow"
Isa 43:25	God forgives and forgets
Mic 7:18–19	God hurls our iniquities into the depths of the sea
Na 1:3	God is patient but will punish the guilty
Heb 10:22–23	God cleanses us from a guilty conscience
	Devotions, 70, 397, 427, 996, 1018, 1064

Hagar and Ishmael

Ge 16	Story of
Gal 4:21–31	Hagar a symbol of the old covenant (slavery to the law)

Healing

Isa 53:5	"By [Christ's] wounds we are healed"
Jer 17:14	"Heal me, O LORD, and I will be healed"
Mt 4:24	Jesus healed various diseases
Mt 8:16	Jesus "healed all the sick"
Mt 9:22	Faith plays a role
Mt 14:36	All who touched Jesus were healed
	Devotions, 1344, 1627, 1635, 1660
	Stories to Share, 1345, 1417, 1455, 1487

Healthy Living

1Sa 25:6	A blessing for good health
Pr 14:30	"A heart at peace gives life to the body"
Pr 15:30	"Good news gives health to the bones"
1Ti 4:7–8	Train yourself to be spiritually healthy
Tit 2:12	Live a self-controlled life
	Devotions, 158, 398, 1553

Heaven

Lk 12:33–34	Lasting treasure in heaven
Lk 23:43	"Today you will be with me in paradise"
Jn 14:2–3	"In my Father's house are many rooms"
2Co 4:17	Eternal glory far outweighs earthly trials
2Co 5:1	"An eternal house in heaven"
2Pe 3:13	Looking forward to a new heaven
Rev 7:9	Great multitude before the throne
Rev 21:1–4	New heaven and new earth
	Devotions, 825, 892, 903, 968, 1765
	Stories to Share, 1769

Heritage

Devotions, cultural, 221; family heirlooms, 461, 1331, 1535; family history, 320, 451, 528, 868, 1014, 1202, 1279, 1742; family traditions, 1384; of faith, 29, 35, 741, 1315
Perspectives, 16, 524

See also Family

Holidays

Devotions, 722, 1714
Perspectives, 656

Holiness

Dt 10:12	What God asks of us
1Ch 28:9	Serve God wholeheartedly
Ro 12:1	Offer our bodies as living sacrifices
Eph 4:22–24	Put off "old self" and put on "new self"
1Th 3:13	Be blameless and holy
1Th 4:7	Live a holy life
Heb 12:14	Be holy
1Pe 2:9	A chosen people, royal priesthood, holy nation, people belonging to God
	Devotions, 1018, 1437, 1472
	Stories to Share, 1636

See also God's Holiness

Holy Spirit

Ge 1:2	Involved in creation
Lk 1:32,35	Is God

Illness (cont.)

3Jn 2 — Pray a blessing of good health
Devotions, 978, 1344, 1647, 1622, 1660

Impossible

Mt 17:21 — Nothing impossible for those with faith
Mt 19:26 — Salvation impossible for man
Lk 1:37 — Nothing impossible for God
Ac 2:24 — Impossible for death to hold Christ
Heb 6:18 — Impossible for God to lie
Heb 11:6 — Impossible to please God without faith
Devotions, 383, 1379

Influence

Pr 3:27 — Use your influence for good
Devotions, 771, 1335

Integrity

2Ki 12:15 — Honesty promotes trust
1Ch 29:17 — Is pleasing to God
Ps 7:8 — God judges us according to our integrity
Ps 15 — Defined
Ps 25:21 — Protects
Ps 41:11 – 12 — God upholds us in our integrity
Pr 10:9 — Those with integrity walk secure
Pr 11:3 — Guides us
Tit 2:7 – 8 — In teaching
Stories to Share, 47

See also Character

Isaiah

Isa 6 — The calling of
Stories to Share, 932, 1001

Jacob

Ge 25:29 – 34 — Used deception to get Esau's birthright
Ge 27 — Used deception to get Esau's blessing
Ge 28:10 – 22 — Dreamed of a ladder reaching to heaven

Ge 32:22 – 32 — Wrestled with God
Stories to Share, 40, 44, 46, 47

Jealousy

Ge 30:1 — Rachel was jealous of her sister
Ge 37:11 — Joseph's brothers were jealous of him
Pr 27:4 — Is powerful
Ac 5:17 – 18 — High priest was jealous of apostles
Ac 13:45 — Jews were jealous of Paul
Ro 13:13 — Get rid of it
1Co 3:3 – 4 — Leads to quarreling
Gal 5:20 — An act of the sinful nature
Devotions, 1365
Stories to Share, 9, 59

Jeremiah

Jer 1:4 – 19 — Called by God
Jer 20:1 – 3 — Put in stocks
Jer 38:1 – 13 — Thrown into a cistern
Jer 43:1 – 7 — Taken to Egypt
Stories to Share, 1073

Jericho

Dt 34:3 — Called "City of the Palms"
Jos 6:1 – 23 — Walls fell
Stories to Share, 285, 290

Jerusalem

2Sa 5:6 – 7 — Conquered by David; called City of David
2Ki 25:1 – 21 — Fell to Nebuchadnezzar
Lk 13:34 – 35 — Jesus' sorrow for

Jesus

Mt 28:18 – 20 — Sent out his disciples
Mt 28:20 — Is with us always
Jn 5:18 — Equal with God
Jn 10:30 — One with the Father
Jn 14:1 — We must trust in him
Ac 1:11 — Will return
Php 2:10 — Every knee will bow before him
Devotions, 1353

Miracles of Jesus

Mt 4:23–24	Jesus healed "every disease and sickness"
Jn 21:25	Not all are recorded in the Bible
	Devotions, 1353, 1359
	Stories to Share, 1436, 1446, 1455, 1460

Money*

Dt 8:17–18*	God gives the ability to make money
1Ch 29:12–14	God is the source of wealth
Ps 50:8–12	Everything belongs to God
Pr 3:9	Honor God with your wealth
Ecc 5:10	Doesn't satisfy
Ecc 5:19	Enjoying wealth is a gift from God
Mk 10:17–25	Wealth can hinder our spiritual life
Mk 12:41–44	Definition of *generosity* varies based on resources
Lk 12:15	Don't be greedy
Lk 16:13	"You cannot serve both God and Money"
Col 3:5	Greed is idolatry
1Ti 6:6–10	Loving money leads to evil
1Ti 6:17	Put your hope in God, not wealth
1Pe 5:2–4	Don't be greedy
	Devotions, 1252
	Stories to Share, 1658

Moses

Ex 33:11	Spoke to God face-to-face, like a friend
Ex 33:12–23	Saw God's glory (God's "back")
Nu 12:3	A very humble man
Dt 32:48–52	Not allowed to enter the promised land
	Stories to Share, 88, 108, 130, 208

Music

See Songs

Name

Ex 20:7	Do not misuse God's name
Pr 22:1	Importance of a good name
Isa 42:8	God declared his name
Isa 43:1	God calls us by name
Isa 45:3	God summons us by name
Php 2:9–10	At the name of Jesus
	Devotions, 992, 1207, 1287, 1544

Nature

See Creation; Ecology

Nehemiah

Ne 6:15	Rebuilt Jerusalem's walls in 52 days
	Stories to Share, 624

Nicodemus

Jn 3:1–8	You must be "born again"
Jn 19:38–42	Buried Jesus after the crucifixion
	Stories to Share, 1439

Noah

Ge 6:9–22	Built the ark
Ge 9:1–17	God's covenant with
Heb 11:7	Saved through faith
1Pe 3:20	"Saved through water"
	Stories to Share, 11, 12

Obedience

Dt 10:12–13	God's command to obey
Ps 103:17–18	God loves those who obey his precepts
Ps 119:101	Keep your feet from the evil path
Jer 7:23	God's command to obey
Jn 14:21	If we love God, we will obey
Ac 5:29	"Obey God rather than men"
Jas 1:22–24	Listen and do
1Jn 5:2–3	To love God is to obey his commands
2Jn 6	Walk in obedience
	Devotions, 158, 318, 1468, 1723
	Stories to Share, God deserves our, 112; God rewards, 176, 290, 490, 1073, 1169; is a witness to others, 1165; may be difficult, 11, 36, 88, 932; to God first, 1386

Other Gods

See Gods, Other

Parables

Ps 78:1 – 2	Used for teaching
Mk 4:2,33 – 34	Used by Jesus in his teaching
	Stories to Share, 1402, 1414

Parents*

Ge 46 – 47	Jacob's sons cared for him
Ex 20:12*	Honor parents
Lev 19:3	Respect parents
Pr 1:8 – 9	Heed the instruction and teaching of parents
Pr 6:20 – 23	Parental advice leads us on the right path
Mt 10:21	Children will rebel against parents
Eph 6:1 – 3	Obeying and honoring parents brings blessing
Eph 6:4	Do not exasperate your children
Col 3:20	Honoring our parents pleases God
1Ti 5:4	Care for parents and grandparents
	Devotions, 1736

Passover

Ex 12	First Passover
Lk 2:41	Jesus' parents observed Passover
Lk 22	Jesus observed Passover
Jn 1:29,36	Jesus is the "Lamb of God"
Rev 5:6 – 12	Honor and glory to the Lamb (Christ)

Patience*

Ps 40:1*	Wait patiently for God
Pr 14:29	To be patient is to be wise
Pr 16:32	Is better than might
Ecc 7:8	"Patience is better than pride"
Ro 8:25	Wait patiently with hope
Ro 12:12	Be "patient in affliction"
1Ti 1:16	Jesus has "unlimited patience" for us
Jas 1:2 – 4	Leads to maturity
2Pe 3:9	God is patient with us
	Devotions, 531, 651, 734, 1012

Patriotism

	Devotions, 1014

Paul

Ac 8:1 – 3	Persecuted the church
Ac 9:1 – 19	His conversion
Gal 1:13 – 14	Tried to destroy the church
	Stories to Share, 1501, 1513, 1527

Peace

Ps 4:8	Sleep in peace
Ps 29:11	God blesses people with peace
Ps 37:11	Meek will enjoy peace
Pr 14:30	"A heart at peace gives life to the body"
Isa 26:3	Trust in God brings perfect peace
Jn 14:27	"Peace I leave with you"
Ro 2:9 – 10	A reward for doing good
Gal 5:22	Fruit of the Spirit is peace
Php 4:7	A blessing of peace
	Devotions, 280, 743, 771, 1016, 1495, 1623

Peer Pressure*

Ps 1:1 – 2*	Don't hang out with wicked people
Pr 4:14 – 15	Don't follow evil people
Pr 22:24 – 25	Choose friends carefully
Pr 28:10	Leading others astray brings trouble
Isa 51:7 – 8	Be strong in the face of criticism
1Co 10:13	No temptation is too strong to resist
2Co 6:14	Use caution when befriending unbelievers
Gal 6:1	Be careful in how you counsel others
Php 1:27	Behave in a manner worthy of Christ
Col 3:23 – 24	Do everything for the Lord
Jas 1:12	Reward for persevering
1Jn 4:4	The Spirit in us is greater than evil
	Devotions, 801

Perseverance

Ro 5:3 – 4	"Suffering produces perseverance; perseverance, character"
Heb 12:1	Run the race with perseverance
Jas 1:3 – 4	Testing develops perseverance; perseverance produces maturity
Jas 5:11	Those who persevere are blessed

Perseverance (cont.)

2Pe 1:5 – 8	To be added to faith
Jude 17 – 23	A call to persevere
	Devotions, 629, 976, 1012, 1248, 1699

Perspective

1Sa 16:7	The Lord looks at the heart
Ecc 7:14	Good and bad times come to all
2Co 4:18	Fix our eyes on the unseen
Php 2:2 – 5	"Consider others better than yourselves"
Col 3:23 – 24	Do everything as for the Lord
Heb 12:1 – 2	Fix our eyes on Jesus
	Devotions, 42, 134, 275, 335, 752, 978, 1367, 1594, 1731
	Perspectives, 174, 420, 674

See also Priorities

Peter

Mt 16:18 – 19	Confession of Jesus as the Christ
Mt 26:69 – 75	Denied Jesus three times
Jn 21:15 – 19	Expressed love for, and reinstated by, Jesus
	Stories to Share, 1313, 1487, 1504. 1505

Praise*

2Sa 22:47 – 50	Sing praise to God
1Ch 16:7 – 13*	Praise and thank God for all he has done
Job 1:13 – 22	Praise God even in times of calamity
Ps 34:1	Praise God at all times
Ps 100	God is worthy of our praise and worship
Ps 103	Praise the Lord
Ps 150	"Let everything . . . praise the LORD"
Lk 2:13,20	Angels and shepherds praised God
Heb 13:15	Offer "a sacrifice of praise"
Rev 7:11 – 12	Praise belongs to God forever
Rev 19:6 – 8	The great multitude in heaven praises God
	Devotions, for answered prayer, 1254, 1639; for/by creation, 454, 603, 709, 921, 1449; for deliverance, 1660; for God's

faithfulness, 228, 869, 966, 1603; for God's holiness, 268; for God's love, 1493; for God's power, 755, 846, 897, 1217, 1419, 1471, 1690; for salvation, 1332, 1556; in celebration, 258; in dance, 841; in song, 541, 711, 1416; in worship, 27, 166, 731, 1281, 1710, 1743

Stories to Share, 710, 792, 843, 1366

Prayer*

2Ch 7:11 – 15	If we pray, then God will hear
Ne 4:6 – 9*	Prayer and action work together
Pr 15:29	God hears the prayer of the righteous
Isa 65:24	Someday God will answer before we even call to him
Jer 33:3	God answers prayer and shares great things with us
Mt 6:5 – 13	How to pray
Mt 7:7 – 11	God loves to give good gifts in response to prayer
Mk 11:24	Ask in prayer, believe, receive
Lk 18:1 – 8	Pray with persistence
Ro 8:26	Holy Spirit helps us pray
1Th 5:17	Pray continually
Heb 4:16	Pray with confidence
Jas 5:13 – 16	Prayers offered in faith are powerful and effective
1Pe 3:12	God is attentive to our prayers
	Devotions, answered, 536, 834, 848, 1298, 1303, 1475, 1627, 1639, 1660, 1732; as a calling, 371, 625, 867, 1175; at mealtime, 1569; for grandchildren, 79; God's timing and, 1103, 1379; heard by God, 1254; in Jesus' name, 1207; intimacy with God in, 796, 808, 954; is powerful, 976, 1591, 1704; legacy of, 794, 1346, 1651; modeling, 850; perseverance in, 1647; pleases God, 838, 1755

Protection (cont.)

401, 536, 966, 897; spiritual,
1591
Praying the Scriptures, 435
Stories to Share, 500, 720, 1174,
1505, 1527, 1615

See also Safety

Provision

Ps 68:10	God provides for the poor
Ps 121:7–8	God watches over us
Isa 46:4	God will sustain us
Mt 6:8	God knows our needs
Ac 14:17	God provides food
1Co 10:13	God provides a way out of temptation
1Ti 6:17	God provides everything for our enjoyment
2Ti 4:18	God will rescue
Jas 1:17	Every gift is from above
2Pe 1:3	God's power gives us everything we need

Devotions, 24, 210, 966, 1103,
1271, 1308, 1419, 1471, 1536,
1695
Stories to Share, 108, 110, 366,
720, 1270

Queen

1Ki 10:1–13	Queen of Sheba visits Solomon
Est 1	Queen Vashti deposed
Est 2:1–18	Esther made queen

Devotions, 575, 654

Quietness

See Meditation

Quiet Time

See Bible Study; Meditation; Prayer

Raising Grandchildren

Devotions, 1296

Reassurance

Devotions, 104, 377, 616
Praying the Scriptures, 283

Rebellion*

2Sa 15–18*	Led to Absalom's death and family heartache
Jer 32:26–35	God punishes those who rebel against him
Da 9:4–10	God forgives the rebellion of a repentant person
Hos 14:9	The rebellious stumble
Lk 15:11–20	God embraces those who repent of rebellion
Ro 13:1–2	God requires us to submit to authority
Col 3:20	Children should obey their parents

Devotions, 361

Reconciliation

Mt 5:23–24	End personal conflicts before worshiping God
Mt 18:15–16	Reconciling with those who sin against you
Ac 15:1–31	Conflicts resolved in the church
1Co 1:10	No divisions in the church
2Co 5:20	Be reconciled to God
Col 3:13	Forgive as God forgave you
1Jn 4:20–21	Love God, love your brother

Red Sea

Ex 13:17 —14:31	Israelites pass through; Pharaoh's army killed

Stories to Share, 105

Regret

Devotions, 1625, 1635

Relationship With God

Devotions, 652, 1693
See also Bible Study; God's Presence; Prayer

Relationships

Ecc 4:9–12	Two are better than one
Mt 20:26–28	Have a servant attitude
Ro 13:7–8	Give what you owe
1Co 1:10	Be united in mind
2Co 6:14–17	Do not be "yoked together" with unbelievers

Role Model (cont.)

238; of faith, 315, 771, 1551, 1664; of marriage, 6, 446; of prayer, 850, 1627; of sharing, 1292; of social justice, 625; of unconditional love, 1736
Perspectives, 508, 1002, 1666

Ruth

Ru 4:13 – 22	An ancestor of David
Mt 1:5	An ancestor of Jesus
	Stories to Share, 346

Safety

Ps 4:8	We dwell in safety
Ps 12:7	God will keep us safe
Ps 16:1	Request for safety
Pr 1:32 – 33	Live in safety by listening to wisdom
Pr 28:18	The blameless are kept safe
1Jn 5:18	Jesus protects us from the evil one
	Devotions, 104, 401, 996, 1407, 1449, 1458, 1623, 1660

See also Protection

Salvation

Ps 27:1	"The LORD is my light and my salvation"
Lk 2:28 – 32	Simeon's song
Jn 10:28	Assurance of
Ac 4:12	Found only in Christ
Ro 10:9	Confess and believe and you will be saved
2Co 7:10	Repentance leads to salvation
Eph 2:8 – 9	By grace through faith
Php 2:12	"Work out your salvation"
	Devotions, 781, 871, 989, 1422, 1437, 1475, 1483, 1542, 1750
	Praying the Scriptures, 239
	Stories to Share, 1001, 1375, 1428, 1439, 1501, 1534

Samaritan

Lk 10:25 – 37	The parable of the Good Samaritan
Jn 4:1 – 26, 39 – 42	The Samaritan woman at the well

Samson

Jdg 13 – 16	His life and death
Heb 11:32	Called a man of faith
	Devotions, 335
	Stories to Share, 337

Samuel

1Sa 1	His birth and dedication to God
Heb 11:32	Called a man of faith
	Devotions, 359, 361
	Stories to Share, 362, 380

Sarah

Ge 17:15	Name changed from Sarai to Sarah
Ge 17:16 – 22	God promised her a son
Ge 18:10 – 15	Sarah laughed at promise of a son
	Stories to Share, 30

Saul/Paul

See Paul

Saul, King

1Sa 9 – 10	Anointed king by Samuel
1Sa 15	Rejected as king by God
1Sa 28	Visited witch of Endor
1Sa 31	Took his own life
	Perspectives, 384
	Stories to Share, 366

Second Coming

Mt 24	Signs of the end of the age
Jn 14:1 – 4	Jesus' promise to come back
1Co 15:12 – 28, 51 – 52	The resurrection of the dead
1Th 4:13 — 5:11	The Lord's coming
	Stories to Share, 1646, 1771

Security

See Protection; Safety

Self – Esteem*

Ge 1:26 – 27*	We were created in God's image
Ps 139:13 – 18	God formed us and values us
Jer 1:5	God has a plan for us
Zep 3:17	God takes great delight in us

Self–Esteem (cont.)

Eph 1:3–14	We were created for God's pleasure and praise
Col 2:9–10	We are complete in Christ
1Jn 3:1	We are children of God
	Devotions, 317, 832, 992, 1269, 1280, 1571, 1447
	Stories to Share, 4

Self-Image

See Identity; Self-Esteem

Separation (Distance)

Devotions, 827, 1475, 1669
Perspectives, 60

Serving

Dt 13:4	Serve and obey the Lord
Jos 22:5	Serve God wholeheartedly
Jos 24:15	Choose whom you will serve
Mt 4:10	Serve God only
Mt 23:11	The greatest will serve
Mk 10:43–44	Whoever wants to be first must be a slave
Lk 22:26–27	Jesus is "one who serves"
Jn 13:14–17	Serve one another
1Co 9:19–22	Become a "slave to everyone" for the gospel
Gal 5:13	"Serve one another in love"
1Pe 4:11	Serve with God's strength
	Devotions, 440, 722, 989, 1266, 1292, 1305, 1365, 1392, 1404, 1622
	Stories to Share, 1464

Sexuality*

Ge 1:28; 2:24	God created us as sexual beings
SS 2:3–7*	God designed sex to be part of marriage
Mt 5:27–28	Adultery of the heart and mind
1Co 6:12–20	Our bodies are God's temples
1Co 10:13	God offers escape from sexual temptation
1Th 4:3–6	Control sexual passions

Heb 4:14–16	Jesus understands our struggles and will help us
1Pe 2:11–12	Desires are at war with our souls

Sharing Your Faith*

Dt 6:4–9	Pass faith on to your children
Da 3:16–18	Declaration of faith by Daniel's friends
Mt 5:14–16	Our good deeds are a light to the world
Mt 28:18–20*	Jesus asks us to share our faith
Ac 1:8	The Holy Spirit gives us power to share our faith
Ac 8:29–35	The Holy Spirit leads us into faith-sharing situations
Ac 18:9–10	Don't be afraid to share your faith
Ac 22:3–8	Tell your own story of faith
1Co 9:22–23	Be relevant
1Co 10:31–33	Our actions should lead others to, not away from, Christ
2Co 5:17–20	Our relationship with God is a witness to others
Eph 6:19–20	Pray for boldness
Php 2:14–16	Our lives should "shine like stars in the universe"
1Pe 2:12	Our deeds are a witness to others
1Pe 3:13–16	Always be ready to give a reason for your hope
	Devotions, activities for, 697, 771, 963, 1416, 1535, 1659, 1709; by inviting to church, 1125; courage in, 805, 1281, 1437; in a relevant way, 379; in everyday life, 1520, 1727; missionary stories, 1185, 1483; simply, 492
	Perspectives, 508, 818, 1002
	Stories to Share, 463, 1500, 1504, 1513

Shepherd

Ps 23	"The LORD is my shepherd"
Isa 40:11	God tends us like a shepherd tends his flock
Lk 2:8–20	Heard of Jesus' birth from angels
Jn 10:1–18	Jesus is the Good Shepherd

Spiritual Life

Mt 7:24 – 27	The wise and foolish builders
Jn 15:4 – 5,7 – 8	Remain in Christ; vine and branches
Gal 5:22 – 25	Fruit of the Spirit
Eph 4:14 – 15	Mature in Christ
Php 3:13 – 14	"Press on toward the goal"
2Ti 2:15	Present yourself as one approved
Tit 2:11 – 12	Say no to worldly passions; be self-controlled
1Pe 2:2 – 3	"Grow up in your salvation"
2Pe 1:6 – 8	Characteristics to add to your faith
	Devotions, 969, 1058, 1233, 1443, 1605, 1643

Stars/Constellations

Ge 1:16	Made by God
Ge 22:17	Abraham's descendants as numerous as
2Ki 21:3	The ungodly worship the stars
Job 38:31 – 32	Constellations named
Ps 148:3	Must praise God
Isa 40:26	God calls each by name
Mt 2:2,9	Star of Bethlehem

Stewardship

Dt 8:18	God gives ability to produce wealth
1Ch 29:12	Wealth comes from God
1Ch 29:14	Everything comes from God
Mt 25:14 – 30	Parable of the talents
Lk 6:38	"Give, and it will be given to you"
1Ti 6:17 – 19	Put hope in God not wealth
	Devotions, 1693

Strength

Ne 8:10	"The joy of the LORD is your strength"
Ps 29:11	God gives strength
Ps 46:1 – 3	God is our refuge and strength
Pr 24:5	Knowledge increases strength
Isa 12:2	"The LORD . . . is my strength and my song"
Isa 40:29 – 31	"Run and not grow weary"
Isa 41:10	God promises to give strength
Hab 3:19	The Lord is my strength
2Co 12:9	God's "power is made perfect in weakness"

Eph 6:10	"Be strong in the Lord"
Php 4:13	"I can do everything through him who gives me strength"
	Devotions, 214, 347, 383, 404, 629, 757, 815, 1389

Stress

See Anxiety; Worry

Struggle

Ex 14:14	"The LORD will fight for you"
2Co 10:4	Use divine power
2Ti 4:7 – 8	"I have fought the good fight"
Heb 12:2 – 3	"Fix our eyes on Jesus"
Heb 12:7 – 11	Endure hardship
Jas 1:2 – 3	Joy when facing trials
1Pe 4:12 – 16	Rejoice in suffering
	Devotions, 404
	Perspectives, 384, 420

Suffering

Job 36:15	God speaks to us in our affliction
Ac 3:18	Christ suffered
1Pe 1:6 – 7	Suffering proves genuine faith
1Pe 4:16	Rejoice if you suffer as a Christian
Rev 2:10	Do not be afraid of persecution
	Devotions, 1715, 1721

See also Problems, Struggle, Trials

Talents

Ex 31:3 – 5	God gives skills and ability
Ecc 2:26	God gives wisdom and knowledge
Mt 25:14 – 30	Parable of the talents
Ro 12:6 – 8	Different gifts given by God
1Co 7:7	Each has his own gift from God
1Co 12:4 – 11	Different gifts, same Spirit
1Ti 4:14	Do not neglect your gift
Jas 1:17	"Every good and perfect gift is from above"
1Pe 4:10	Use your gift to serve others
	Devotions, 128, 136, 437, 862, 994, 1280, 1335, 1490, 1535, 1571
	Perspectives, 90
	Stories to Share, 1663

See also Giving; Money

Temple

1Ki 6	Solomon's
Ezr 3:10–12; 6:15	Zerubbabel's
Lk 21:5–6	Herod's
	Devotions, 459, 595
	Stories to Share, 573, 610

Temptation

Mt 4:1–11	Jesus tempted by Satan
Mt 6:13	"Lead us not into temptation"
Mt 26:41	Prayer helps us resist temptation
1Co 10:13	No temptation is too strong to resist
1Ti 6:9	Desire for riches leads to temptation
	Devotions, 361, 931
	Stories to Share, 1290

Ten Commandments

Ex 20	List of
Ex 31:18	Tablets "inscribed by the finger of God"
Ex 32:15–16,19	Moses broke tablets in anger
Ex 34:1,27	Second set of tablets made

Ten Plagues

Ex 7:14 — 12:30	Described

Thankfulness*

2Ch 5:13	Give thanks to the Lord
Job 1:21–22	God gives and takes away
Ps 136:1*	For God's goodness
Ps 147:7–9	For the wonders of nature
1Co 15:57	For God's victory over death
2Co 9:15	For God's "indescribable gift" of salvation
Col 2:6–7	Overflow with thankfulness
Col 3:15–17	Have gratitude in your hearts
Col 4:2	Be thankful
1Th 5:18	In all circumstances
1Ti 4:4	Receive everything with thanksgiving
Heb 12:28	For God's kingdom
	Devotions, 26, 210, 352, 641, 711, 869, 1182, 1488, 1493, 1569
	Praying the Scriptures, 760
	Stories to Share, 792, 1417, 1461

Tower of Babel

Ge 11:1–9	Story of
	Stories to Share, 15

Traditions

	Devotions, 722, 774, 1569, 1714

See also Holidays

Trials

1Th 3:3	We are destined for trials
2Th 1:4	Our response to trials may inspire others
Jas 1:2–3	Trials test faith and produce perseverance
1Pe 1:6–7	Trials are temporary; they prove genuine faith
2Pe 2:9	God rescues the godly from trials
	Devotions, 664, 692, 757, 897, 976 1248, 1699

Trouble

See Problems; Struggle; Trials

Trust*

Ps 37:3–6*	Trusting God reaps great rewards
Ps 143:8	God blesses those who trust him
Pr 3:5–6	"Trust in the LORD with all your heart"
Isa 12:2	Trusting God leads to confidence
Isa 26:3–4	Trusting God brings peace
Da 3	Daniel's friends trusted God in the fiery furnace
Na 1:7	God cares for those who trust in him
Mt 14:22–32	Peter trusted God until his circumstances overwhelmed him
Ro 15:13	Trusting God brings joy, peace and hope
	Devotions, God alone, 228, 897, 1458; God during trials, 201, 388; God when afraid, 850; God when grieving, 662, 935; God when we question, 695; God while we wait, 976; God with our children, 42, 1546; God to

Trust (cont.)

protect, 1241; God to provide, 1695

Perspectives, 384, 674

Stories to Share, 36, 105, 110, 326, 412, 733

Truth

Ps 40:11	God's truth protects us
Pr 16:13	People who speak the truth are valued by others
Isa 45:19	God speaks the truth
Zec 8:16	Speak the truth to each other
Lk 20:21	Jesus taught the truth
Jn 3:21	Live by the truth
Jn 8:32	The truth sets us free
Jn 14:6	Jesus is the truth
Jn 16:13	The Holy Spirit, the Spirit of truth, guides us into all truth
Jn 17:17	God's word is truth
Ro 1:18	The wicked suppress the truth

Devotions, 999, 1472

Unity

Ps 133	Unity in the family brings blessing
Ro 12:4–5	In Christ we are one body
Ro 12:18	Do all you can to live at peace with everyone
Ro 15:5–6	Unity glorifies God
1Co 1:10	Be united in mind and thought
1Co 12:14–20	Many parts make up the whole
Eph 4:1–6	Humility, gentleness, love and patience bring unity

Devotions, 221

Values*

1Sa 16:1–7*	God values our character, not our appearance
1Ki 2:2–3	Value God's Word and his ways
2Ch 31:20–21	Value service and obedience to God
Pr 4:7	Value wisdom and understanding
Jer 9:23–24	Boast only in the Lord
Mt 6:31–33	Put God's kingdom and his righteousness first
Mt 22:36–40	Love should be our highest priority

1Co 15:58	Our work for God is not in vain
Php 4:8	Think about what is good
1Ti 4:8	Godliness has great value

Devotions, 221, 697, 999, 1651

Stories to Share, 40

Victory

1Co 15:54	Death swallowed up in victory
1Co 15:57	Thanks be to God for victory over death
Col 2:15	Jesus' victory over evil powers at the cross
2Ti 4:7–8	"I have fought the good fight"

Waiting

Nu 9:8	Wait to hear from the Lord before acting
Jdg 6:18	God waited from Gideon to bring his offering
Ps 5:3	Wait in expectation for God to answer prayer
Ps 27:14	"Wait for the LORD"
Ps 33:20	Wait in hope
Ps 37:7	Wait patiently
Ps 130:5–6	Wait and hope
Pr 20:22	Wait for God to deliver you; God will avenge
Isa 64:4	God acts on our behalf if we wait for him

Devotions, 194, 734, 935, 976

See also Patience

Water

Jer 2:13	God is the "spring of living water"
Eze 36:25	A symbol of cleansing from sin
Jn 4:10	Jesus is the source of "living water"
Jn 7:38–39	A symbol of the Holy Spirit
Ac 8:36–38	Used in baptism
Rev 7:17	The Lamb will lead us to "springs of living water"
Rev 22:1–2	A symbol of heavenly peace

Wealth

See Money

Weariness

2Sa 17:2	The weary are susceptible to attack
Ps 119:28	God's Word supplies strength to those weary from sorrow
Isa 40:28–31	God gives strength to the weary
Jer 31:25	God refreshes the weary
Mt 11:28	"Come to me, all you who are weary"
Gal 6:9	Do not become weary in doing good
Heb 12:1–3	Look to Jesus as the example, so you don't grow weary

Devotions, 541, 1296, 1389, 1672

Well – Being

Ps 6:2	A cry for healing
Ps 46:1	God is our refuge and strength
Pr 3:7–8	Recipe for health
Isa 6:10	Turn to God and be healed
Jer 17:14	A request for healing
Jer 33:6	God's promise of healing
Ac 4:30	A request for healing
Eph 6:10	Be strong in the Lord
3Jn 2	A prayer for good health

Devotions, 158, 398
Praying the Scriptures, 707

Wisdom

Ps 111:10	Fearing God is the beginning of wisdom
Pr 4:5–7	Get wisdom; it is supreme
Pr 13:20	Become wise by walking with the wise
Pr 24:14	"Wisdom is sweet to your soul"
Ecc 2:26	God gives wisdom to those who please him
Ecc 7:11–12	Is good and beneficial
Da 2:20–21	Belongs to God
Da 12:3	Those who are wise shine like the heavens
Eph 1:17	Spirit of wisdom comes from God
Jas 1:5	Ask God for wisdom
Jas 3:17	Characteristics of wisdom from heaven

Devotions, 357, 999, 1470, 1690
Praying the Scriptures, 450
Stories to Share, 448, 850

Wise Men

See Magi

Witchcraft

See Magic/Witchcraft

Witnessing

See Sharing Your Faith

Women

Ge 1:27	Created in God's image
Ge 2:18–24	Created as a companion to man
Pr 31	The wife of noble character
Mt 28:1–10	First witnesses of Jesus' resurrection
Lk 8:1–3	Financially supported Jesus and his ministry
Lk 10:38–42	Jesus affirmed Mary, a woman eager to learn
Ac 1:14	Prayed in group meetings
Ac 9:36–41	Tabitha (Dorcas) brought back to life by Peter
Ac 18:26	Priscilla taught Apollos
Ro 16:1–2	Phoebe was a worker in the church
1Co 14:33–35	Were to be silent in the early churches
Gal 3:28	In Christ there is neither male nor female
Gal 4:4–5	Salvation came through a woman
Php 4:2–3	Should be unified and work together in ministry
1Ti 2:11–12	Role in church

Devotions, 86, 320, 397, 664, 1380, 1539
Perspectives, 886
Stories to Share, leaders, 319, 463, 646, 648; mothers, 30, 893, 1381; of prayer, 356; made by God, 4; of faith, 30, 285, 473, 1381, 1403, 1441, 1461; of deception, 337; of loyalty, 346; of courage, 285, 648, 1381, 1441; of character, 893, 1381; of service, 1403, 1461

Wonders

See Miracles

The Grandmother's Bible

EXECUTIVE EDITOR:	Doris Rikkers
DEVELOPMENT EDITOR:	Jeannette Taylor
PROJECT MANAGEMENT AND EDITORIAL:	Shari Vanden Berg
EDITORIAL ASSISTANCE:	Amy Ballor Natalie Block Ruth DeJager Judy Schafer Michael Vander Klipp
THEOLOGICAL REVIEW:	Andrew Sloan, M.Div., Oral Roberts University
PRODUCTION MANAGEMENT:	Phil Herich
ART DIRECTION AND COVER DIRECTION:	Jamie DeBruyn
INTERIOR DESIGN:	Gayle Raymer
PROOFREADING:	Peachtree Editorial and Proofreading Service, Peachtree, GA
INTERIOR TYPESETTING:	Nancy Wilson

Personal Memories

Personal Memories

Personal Memories